PIGGUL (Lit., 'abhorred'); flesh of the sacrifice which the officiating priest has formed the intention of eating at an improper time. V. Lev. VII, 18.

RESH GALUTHA. Head of the Exile, the title of the official head of Babylonian and Persian Jewry.

SANHEDRIN (συνέδριον); the council of state and supreme tribunal of the Jewish people during the century or more preceding the fall of the Second Temple. It consisted of seventy-one members, and was presided over by the High Priest. A minor court (for judicial purposes only) consisting of twenty-three members was known as the 'Small Sanhedrin'.

SHEBUTH (Lit., 'cessation'); an act forbidden by the Rabbis to be performed on the Sabbath.

SHECHINAH (Lit., 'abiding [of God]' 'Divine presence'); the spirit of the Omnipresent as manifested on earth.

SHECHITAH. Ritual slaughter, without which an animal is not fit for food.

SHEḲEL. Coin or weight, equal to two *denarii* or ten *ma'ah* (q.v.). The sacred *sheḳel* was worth twenty *ma'ah* or *gerah* (cf. Ex. XXX, 13), twice the value of the common *sheḳel*.

SHEMA' (Lit., 'hear'); the biblical verse, '*Hear, o Israel*' etc. (Deut. VI, 4); also the three sections (Deut. VI, 5-9; Deut. XI, 13-20; and Num. XV, 37-41) which are recited after this verse in the morning and evening prayers.

SHEREẒ. Unclean reptile (including rodents).

SHOFAR (Lit., 'ram's horn'); a horn used as a trumpet for military and religious purposes, particularly in the service of the New Year and at the conclusion of the Day of Atonement.

SUKKAH. 'Booth'; esp. the festive booth for Tabernacles (Lev. XXIII, 34ff), the roof of which must be made of something that grows from the ground such as reeds, branches or leaves of a prescribed size, quantity and quality.

TALMID ḤAKAM (Lit., 'disciple of the wise'); scholar, student of the Torah.

TAMID. The continual or daily burnt-offering, sacrificed every morning and evening.

ṬEBEL. Produce, already at the stage of liability to the Levitical and priestly dues (v. *terumah*), before these have been separated.

ṬEBILLAH. The act of taking a ritual bath in a *miḳweh*, q.v.

ṬEBUL YOM (Lit., 'bathed during the day'); a person who has bathed to cleanse himself at the end of the period of his defilement, but who must wait until sunset to regain his ritual purity (Lev. XXII, 7).

TEFILLIN. Phylacteries; small cases containing passages from the Scripture and affixed to the forehead and arm during the recital of morning prayers, in accordance with Deut. VI, 8.

TEḤUM. The boundary beyond which one must not walk on the Sabbath, which is two thousand cubits without the town limits; this can be extended by another two thousand cubits by means of an *'erub*, q.v.

TERUMAH. 'That which is lifted or separated'; the heave-offering given from the yields of the yearly harvests, from certain sacrifices, and from the *shekels* collected in a special chamber in the Temple (*terumath ha-lishkah*). *Terumah gedolah* (great offering): the first levy on the produce of the year given to the priest, (v. Num. XVIII, 8ff). Its quantity varied according to the generosity of the owner, who could give one-fortieth, one-fiftieth, or one-sixtieth of his harvest. *Terumath ma'aser* (heave-offering of the tithe): the heave-offering given to the priest by the Levite from the tithes he receives, (v. Num. XVIII, 25ff).

TORAH (Lit., 'teaching', 'learning', 'instruction'); (*a*) the Pentateuch (Written Law); (*b*) the Mishnah (Oral Law); (*c*) the whole body of Jewish religious literature.

ṬREFA or ṬEREFA (Lit., 'torn'); (*a*) an animal torn by a wild beast; (*b*) any animal suffering from a serious organic disease, whose meat is forbidden even if it has been ritually slaughtered.

YEBAMAH. A brother's childless widow. V. Deut. XXV, 5-10.

ZAB (fem. ZABAH). The biblical term for a person who has experienced seminal emission (Lev. XV, 2).

PRINTED IN THE NETHERLANDS
BY JOH. ENSCHEDÉ EN ZONEN, HAARLEM

AGGADAH (Lit., 'tale', 'lesson'); the name given to those sections of Rabbinic literature which contain homiletic expositions of the Bible, stories, legends, folk-lore, anecdotes or maxims. Opposed to *halachah*, q.v.

'AM HA AREẒ pl. *'amme ha-areẓ*, (lit., 'people of the land', 'country people'); the name given in Rabbinic literature to (*a*) a person who through ignorance was careless in the observance of the laws of Levitical purity and of those relating to the priestly and Levitical gifts. In this sense opposed to *ḥaber*, q.v.; (*b*) an illiterate or uncultured man, as opposed to *talmid ḥakam*, q.v.

AMORA. 'Speaker', 'interpreter'; originally denoted the interpreter who attended upon the public preacher or lecturer for the purpose of expounding at length and in popular style the heads of the discourse given to him by the latter. Subsequently (pl. Amoraim) the name given to the Rabbinic authorities responsible for the Gemara, as opposed to the Mishnah or Baraitha (v. Tanna).

ANINUTH. The state of being an *onen*, q.v.

ASHERAH. The biblical name given to a tree or pole which was the object of idolatrous worship.

BA'AL ḲERI. One unclean through nocturnal pollution.

BARAITHA (Lit., 'outside'); a teaching or a tradition of the Tannaim that has been excluded from the Mishnah and incorporated in a later collection compiled by R. Ḥiyya and R. Oshaiah, generally introduced by 'Our Rabbis taught', or, 'It has been taught'.

BATH ḲOL (Lit., 'daughter of a voice'); (*a*) a reverberating sound; (*b*) a voice descending from heaven (cf. Dan. IV, 28) to offer guidance in human affairs, and regarded as a lower grade of prophecy.

BETH DIN (Lit., 'house of law or judgment'); a gathering of three or more learned men acting as a Jewish court of law.

BETH HAMIDRASH. House of study; the college or academy where the study of the Torah was carried on under the guidance of a Rabbinical authority.

DEMAI (Lit., 'dubious', 'suspicious'); produce concerning which there is a doubt as to whether the rules relating to the priestly and Levitical dues and ritual cleanness and uncleanness were strictly observed. Any produce bought from an *'am ha-areẓ* (q.v.), unless the contrary is known, is treated as *demai;* and *terumah gedolah* and *terumah* (q.v.) of the tithe must be separated from it.

DENAR. *Denarius,* a silver or gold coin, the former being worth one twenty-fourth (according to others one twenty-fifth) of the latter.

EMURIM (Lit., 'the consecrated parts'); the parts of a sacrifice which were to be burnt on the altar.

'ERUB (Lit., 'mixture'); a quantity of food, enough for two meals, placed (*a*) 2000 cubits from the town boundary, so as to extend the Sabbath limit by that distance; (*b*) in a room or in a court-yard to enable all the residents to carry to and fro in the court-yard on Sabbath.

ERUSIN (Lit., 'betrothal'); a formal betrothal, which cannot be annulled without a bill of divorce.

GEZERAH SHAWAH (Lit., 'equal cut'); the application to one subject of a rule already known to apply to another, on the strength of a common expression used in connection with both in the Scriptures.

HABDALAH (Lit., 'separation'); the blessing (usually made over wine) by which the Sabbath or any other Holy-day is ushered out.

ḤABER. 'Fellow', 'associate', opp. to *'am ha-areẓ* (q.v.); one scrupulous in the observance of the law, particularly in relation to ritual cleanness and the separation of the priestly and Levitical dues.

ḤADASH ('new'); the new cereal crops, which may not be eaten before the waving of the 'sheaf' (*'omer*); v. Lev. XXIII, 10-14.

HAFTARAH (Lit., 'leave-taking'); a section from the Prophetical books recited after the reading from the Pentateuch on Sabbaths and Holy-days.

HALACHAH (Lit., 'step', 'guidance'), (*a*) the final decision of the Rabbis, whether based on tradition or argument, on disputed rules of conduct; (*b*) those sections of Rabbinic literature which deal with legal questions, as opposed to the *Aggadah*.

ḤALIẒAH (Lit., 'drawing off'); the ceremony of taking off the shoe of the brother of a husband who has died childless. (V. Deut. XXV, 5-9).

ḤALLAH. The portion of the dough which belongs to the priest (v. Num. XV, 20f); in the Diaspora this is not given to the priest but burnt.

ḤALUẒAH. A woman who has performed *ḥaliẓah* (q.v.).

ḤANUKKAH. The Festival of Dedication (frequently designated the Feast of Lights); a minor eight days' festival, from the twenty-fifth of Kislev to the second or third of Tebeth, in commemoration of the rededication of the Temple in 165 B.C.E. after its desecration by Antiochus Epiphanes.

ḤAROSETH. A mixture of apples, nuts and wine, so made as to resemble mortar, into which the bitter herbs are dipped on the first two nights of Passover.

HAZA'AH. The sprinkling of the blood of sacrifices, and of the water of purification, upon the unclean.

HEFḲER. Property which has no owner: a renunciation of ownership in favour of all and sundry. When used in reference to a court of law, it denotes an act of transfer of property from one person to another, in virtue of the power of the court to declare property ownerless, after which it can assign it to another.

HEḲDESH. Any object consecrated to the Sanctuary.

HEḲḲESH. Analogy, proving that the law in respect of one thing applies also to another, either because both have some feature in common or there is a Biblical intimation to the effect.

ḤULLIN (Lit., 'profane'); ordinary unhallowed food, as opposed to *terumah*, q.v.; unconsecrated animals, as opposed to *heḳdesh*, q.v.

KARETH. 'Cutting off'; divine punishment for a number of sins for which no human penalty is specified. Sudden death is described as '*kareth* of days', premature death at sixty as '*kareth* of years'.

KIL'AYIM (Lit., 'junction of diverse kinds'); the prohibition either (*a*) of seeds or plants for sowing; (*b*) of animals for propagation; and (*c*) of material containing wool and linen for wearing (v. Lev. XIX, 19; Deut. XXII, 9ff).

KUTAḤ. A preserve or relish made of bread-crusts and sour milk.

LULAB. The palm-branch used in the ceremony of the Feast of Tabernacles (v. Lev. XXIII, 40).

MA'AH. The smallest current silver coin, weighing sixteen barleycorns, equal in value to two *dupondia*, a sixth of the silver *denar* or *zuz*.

MAẒẒAH. Unleavened bread (in the form of fairly thin wafers) eaten during Passover.

MEZUZAH (Lit., 'doorpost'); a small case containing certain passages from the Scripture affixed to the post of a door (v. Deut. VI, 9).

MIḲWEH (Lit., 'a gathering [of water]'); a ritual bath containing not less than forty *se'ahs* of water.

MIN pl. *minim*, (lit., 'kind', 'species'); (*a*) a heretic, esp. (*b*) a member of the sect of the early Jewish Christians.

MINḤAH. The afternoon service, about two and a half hours before nightfall.

MISHNAH (rt. SHaNaH, 'to learn', 'to repeat'); (*a*) the collection of the statements, discussions and Biblical interpretations of the Tannaim in the form edited by R. Judah the Patriarch c. 200; (*b*) similar minor collections by previous editors; (*c*) a single clause or paragraph the author of which was a Tanna.

MUḲẒEH (Lit., 'set aside'); that which may not be used or handled on the Sabbath or Festivals, though its use does not constitute actual labour.

NEBELAH (pl. *nebeloth*); an animal slaughtered in any manner other than that prescribed by Jewish ritual law; the least deviation therefrom, e.g., if the knife has the slightest notch, renders the animal *nebelah*.

NIDDAH. A woman in the period of her menstruation.

NOTHAR ('left over'); portions of sacrifices left over after the prescribed time within which they must be eaten.

'OMER (Lit., 'sheaf'); the sheaf of barley offered on the sixteenth of Nisan, before which the new cereals of that year were forbidden for use (v. Lev. XXIII, 10).

ONEN. A mourner while his dead relative is awaiting burial; opposite to *abel*, a mourner from the time of burial for a period of seven or thirty days.

'ORLAH ('uncircumcised'); applied to newly-planted trees for a period of three years during which their fruits must not be eaten (v. Lev. XIX, 23ff).

PARASANG. A Persian mile, about 4000 yards.

PE'AH ('corner'); the corner of a field that is being reaped, which must be left for the poor (v. Lev. XIX, 9ff).

PERUṬAH. The smallest copper coin, equal to one-eighth of an *issar* or one-sixteenth of a *dupondium*.

ABBREVIATIONS

Ab.	Aboth.
Alfasi	R. Isaac b. Jacob Alfasi (1013-1103).
Aruch	Talmudic Dictionary by R. Nathan b. Jeḥiel of Rome (d. 1106).
Asheri	R. Asher b. Jeḥiel (1250-1327).
A.Z.	'Abodah Zarah.
b.	ben, bar: son of.
B.B.	Baba Bathra.
BaḤ.	Bayith Ḥadash, Glosses by R. Joel b. Samuel Sirkes (1561-1640).
Bek.	Bekoroth.
Ber.	Berakoth.
Beẓ.	Beẓah.
B.Ḳ.	Baba Ḳamma.
B.M.	Baba Meẓi'a.
Cur. ed(d).	Current edition(s).
D.S.	*Diḳduḳe Soferim*, by R. Rabbinowicz.
'Ed.	'Eduyyoth.
E.J.	*Encyclopaedia Judaica.*
Et.St.	*Etymologische Studien*, Joseph Perles 1835-1894.
E.V.	English Version.
Giṭ.	Giṭṭin.
G.K.	Gesenius-Kautzsch, Hebrew Grammar.
Glos.	Glossary.
Golds.	Translation of the Babylonian Talmud in German by L. Goldschmidt.
Graetz	Graetz, H., *Geschichte der Juden* (4th ed.).
Ḥag.	Ḥagigah.
Ḥananel	R. Ḥananel b. Ḥushiel of Kairwan (about 990-1050).
Hor.	Horayoth.
Ḥul.	Ḥullin.
J.E.	*Jewish Encyclopedia.*
JQR.	*Jewish Quarterly Review.*
J.T.	Jerusalem Talmud.
Jast.	M. Jastrow's Dictionary of the Targumim, the Talmud Bible and Yerushalmi, and the Midrashic Literature.
Keth.	Kethuboth.
Ḳid.	Ḳiddushin.
Kil.	Kil'ayim.
Maharsha	R. Samuel Eliezer Halevi Edels (1555-1631).
Maim.	Moses Maimonides (1135-1204).
Mak.	Makkoth.
Meg.	Megillah.
Men.	Menaḥoth.
MGWJ.	*Monatsschrift für Geschichte und Wissenschaft des Judentums.*
Mid.	Middoth.
M.Ḳ.	Mo'ed Ḳaṭan.
MS.M.	Munich Codex of the Talmud.
Ned.	Nedarim.
Nid.	Niddah.
Obermeyer	Obermeyer J., *Die Landschaft Babylonien.*
P.B.	*The authorised Daily Prayer Book*, S. Singer.
R.	Rab, Rabban, Rabbenu, Rabbi.
Rashal	Notes and Glosses on the Talmud by R. Solomon Luria (d. 1573).
Rashi	Commentary of R. Isaac Yiẓḥaḳi (d. 1105).
REJ.	*Revue des Etudes Juives.*
R.H.	Rosh Hashanah.
R.V.	Revised version of the Bible.
Sanh.	Sanhedrin.
Shab.	Shabbath.
Shebu.	Shebu'oth.
Sheḳ.	Sheḳalim.
Sof.	Soferim
Sonc. ed.	English Translation of the Babylonian Talmud. Soncino Press, London.
Soṭ.	Soṭah.
Strashun.	Annotations by Samuel Strashun (1794—1872) in the Wilna editions of the Talmud.
Suk.	Sukkah.
Ta'an.	Ta'anith.
T.A.	*Talmudische Archäologie*, by S. Krauss.
T.J.	Talmud Jerusalemi.
Tosaf.	Tosafoth.
Tosef.	Tosefta.
Wilna Gaon	Notes by Elijah of Wilna (1720-1797) in the Wilna editions of the Talmud.
Yeb.	Yebamoth.
Zeb.	Zebaḥim.

TRANSLITERATION OF HEBREW LETTERS

א (in middle of word)	= '
ב	= b
ו	= w
ח	= ḥ
ט	= ṭ
כ	= k
ע	= '
פ	= f
צ	= ẓ
ק	= ḳ
ת	= th

Full particulars regarding the method and scope of the translation are given in the Editor's Introduction in the first Shabbath volume (Mo'ed, Vol. I).

להם הטומאה וכיוצא בהן מטמאי טומאת מגע אבל לא לטמאים שטומאה יוצאה מגופן ואם אכלו פטורין ואפילו אכלו טמאי מת מהאימורין שלו פטורין. *בד"א שהפסח נאכל בטומאה כשנטמאו הציבור קודם זריקת הדם אבל אם נטמאו לאחר זריקת הדם לא יאכל· שחטוהו בטהרה ונטמאו רוב הציבור קודם זריקה זורק את הדם והפסח לא יאכל. היו כלי שרת טמאים בשרץ וכיוצא בו אע"פ שמטמאין את הבשר לא יעשוהו אלא הטהורים ויאכל אע"פ שהוא טמא שמוטב שיאכל בטומאת בשר שהיא בלאו ולא יאכלוהו טמאי הגוף שהם בכרת: מה בין פסח ראשון לשני הראשון אסור בחמץ בבל יראה ובל ימצא ואינו נשחט על חמץ [*וצריך ביקור ד' ימים] ואין מוציאין ממנו חוץ לחבורה וטעון הלל באכילתו ומביאין עמו חגיגה ואפשר שיבא בטומאה אם נטמא רוב הקהל טומאת מת אבל פסח שני חמץ ומצה עמו בבית *[ואין נשחט בג' כתות ואין צריך ביקור] ואינו טעון הלל באכילתו

ומוציאין אותו חוץ לחבורתו *ואין מביאין עמו חגיגה ואינו בא בטומאה ושניהם דוחין את השבת וטעונין הלל בעשייתן ונאכלין צלי בבית אחד על מצה ומרור ואין מותירין מהן ואין שוברין בהן את העצם: נשים שנדחו לשני בין מפני טומאה ודרך רחוקה בין משאר אונס ושגגה הרי פסח שני להן רשות לפיכך אינן שוחטין עליהן בפני עצמן בשבת בפסח שני. *האונן שמת לו מת אחר חצות בי"ד שכבר נתחייב בק"פ שוחטין עליו וטובל ואוכל שאנינות לילה מדרבנן וכן *מת לו מת בי"ג ונקבר בי"ד אבל מת לו מת קודם חצות ידחה לשני ואם שחטו וזרקו עליו טובל ואוכל לערב. גר שנתגייר בין פסח ראשון לשני וכן קטן שהגדיל בין ב' פסחים חייבין בפסח שני ואם שחטו עליו בראשון פטור. הזאה אינה דוחה שבת כגון (*זב) שהגיע ז' שלו בי"ד בשבת אין מזין עליו ואפילו חל הי"ג בשבת אין מזין עליו בי"ג אלא למחרת בי"ד ואין שוחטין עליו אלא ידחה לשני:

whose uncleanness was suspended, and the like, of those contaminated by contact, but not by unclean ones from whose body contamination emanates. If they ate of it, however, they are exempt. Even if those contaminated by a corpse ate from the sacrificial parts, they are exempt. When is this true that the Passover sacrifice may be eaten in an unclean state? When the majority of the congregation became contaminated prior to the sprinkling of the blood, but if they became contaminated after the sprinkling of the blood, it may not be eaten. If they slaughtered it in a clean state, and the majority of the congregation became contaminated prior to the sprinkling of the blood, the blood must be sprinkled, but the Passover sacrifice may not be eaten. If the ministerial vessels were unclean because of a dead reptile or the like, although they convey contamination to the flesh, only clean people may perform the Passover sacrifice, and it is eaten although it is unclean, for it is preferable that it be eaten when the flesh is unclean, which is prohibited by a negative precept, rather than allow those whose bodies are unclean to eat, an act punishable by *kareth.*

What is the difference between the first Passover sacrifice and the second one? The first one bears with it a prohibition of leaven, that it may neither be seen nor found, and it may not be slaughtered while leaven is still found in the possession of one of those engaged in its sacrifice, [and it requires examination four days,] and we may not carry it out of the group, and it requires the recitation of Hallel while it is being eaten, and we bring it with a *ḥagigah,* and it may possibly be brought in an unclean state if the majority of the congregation became contaminated through a corpse, but as for the second Passover sacrifice, there may be leaven and *matzah* with him in the house [and it is not slaughtered in three groups, and it does not require examination, and it does not require the recitation of Hallel while it is being eaten, and we may carry it out of its group, and we do not bring with it a *ḥagigah,* and it is not brought in an unclean state, and both of them supersede the Sabbath and require Hallel during the sacrificial service, and they must be eaten roasted, in one house, together with unleavened bread and bitter herbs, and we may not leave over of them, and we may not break any of their bones.

Women who were suspended to the second one, either because of contamination or a journey afar off, or because of any other unavoidable accident or inadvertency—the performance of the second Passover is optional for them. Therefore, we may not slaughter a Passover sacrifice for them alone on the second Passover. An *onen,* whose close kin died in the afternoon on the fourteenth day, who was already obligated to bring a Passover sacrifice—we may slaughter for him, and he immerses himself and eats, for *aninuth* of the night (following) is a Rabbinical enactment, and likewise, if his kin died on the thirteenth and was buried on the fourteenth, but if the kin died before noon, he is suspended to the second Passover sacrifice. But if they slaughtered and sprinkled the blood for him, he must immerse himself, and he may eat in the evening. became a proselyte between the first Passover and the second, and likewise, a minor who reached his majority between the first and the second, are obligated to bring a second Passover sacrifice, and if they slaughtered for him on the first Passover, he is exempt.

The sprinkling of the purification water does not supersede the Sabbath, e.g. if the seventh day of purification fell on the fourteenth which was a Sabbath, we may not sprinkle the purification water on him, and even if the thirteenth fell on the Sabbath, we may not sprinkle it on him on the thirteenth, but on the morrow, on the fourteenth, and we may not slaughter the Passover sacrifice for him, but he is suspended to the second Passover.

לערב אין שוחטין עליו ונדחה לשני בד"א שנטמא בטומאת מת שהנזיר מגלח עליהן אבל בטומאת מת שאין הנזיר מגלח עליהן שוחטין עליו בז' שלו אחר הזאה וטבילה . מי שעשה פסח בחזקת שהוא טהור ואח"כ נודע לו שהיה טמא בטומאת התהום פטור מפסח שני אבל נודע לו שנטמא בטומאת ודאי חייב בפסח שני . בד"א בטהור אבל טמא כגון *טמא מת שנטמא בטומאת התהום בששי שלו אע"פ שנודע לו אחר שעשה הפסח חייב בפסח שני שחזקת הטמא טמא עד שנטהר ספק טומאת התהום טהור לפסח : בטומאת מת בין ודאי בין ספקו יחידים שהן מיעוט הצבור נדחין ולא צבור אפילו הם מחצה קהל אין נדחין שאם היה בפסח ראשון רוב הקהל או הכהנים או כלי השרת טמאים בטומאת מת עושין הפסח הטמאים עם הטהורים בטומאה אפילו היה ברוב הטמאים רק א' [עודף] · היו מחצה על מחצה כולן עושין בראשון והטהורים עושין לעצמן בטהרה וטמאים לעצמן בטומאה. היו הנשים משלימין לרוב טהורים הטהורים עושין הראשון והטמאין אינן עושין לא הראשון ולא השני . היו רוב הקהל טמאים בשאר טומאות ומיעוטן טמאי מת אותן טמאי מת אינן עושין לא בראשון לפי שהן מיעוט וגם שני אינן עושין לפי שאין היחידים עושין בשני אלא בזמן שרוב הקהל עשו הראשון · וכן אם היו רוב הקהל טמאי מתים ומיעוטן בשאר טומאות הטמאי מתים עושין בראשון והמיעוטין אינן עושין לא בראשון לפי שאין טומאה דוחה בראשון אלא טומאת מת לבד ובשני אינן עושין לפי שאין עושין בפסח שני אלא אם נעשה הראשון בטהרה · היו שליש הקהל טהורים ושליש טמאי מתים ושליש טמאים בשאר טומאות הטמאי מתים אינן עושין לא בראשון שהרי הן מיעוטין לגבי טהורים עם הטמאים משאר טומאות ובשני אינן עושין שהרי מיעוט עשו בראשון . כיצד משערין הפסח לידע אם רוב הקהל טמאים או טהורים אין משערין בכל האוכלין שאפשר שיהיו עשרים נמנים על פסח א' ומשלחין אותו לשחוט ביד א' אלא משערין בכל הנכנסין לעזרה . ועד שהן מבחוץ קודם שתכנס כת הראשונה משערין אותן . פסח שהקריבוהו בטומאה נאכל בטומאה שמתחלתו לא בא אלא לאכילה . ואינו נאכל אלא לטמאי מת שנדחית

Passover sacrifice for him, and he is suspended until the second one. When is this true? If he contracted ritual contamination for which a *nazir* must shave off his hair, but for those ritual contaminations emanating from a corpse, for which a *nazir* need not shave off his hair, we slaughter the Passover sacrifice on the seventh day of his purification after sprinkling the purification water on him and after his immersion.

One who offered up a Passover sacrifice with the assumption that he was ritually pure, and later discovered that he was ritually unclean by dint of contamination of the deep, is exempt from a second Passover sacrifice. But, if he discovered that he had contracted definite contamination, he is required to bring a second Passover sacrifice. When is this true? If he had already become purified. But, if he was unclean, e.g. one who contracted ritual contamination who became unclean by dint of the contamination of the deep on the sixth day of his purification, although he discovered it after he had offered up the Passover sacrifice, he is required to bring a second Passover sacrifice, for one who is unclean is deemed unclean until he is purified. One who has doubtfully come in contact with the contamination of the deep is deemed clean in regard to the observance of the Passover sacrifice.

As for the ritual contamination of a corpse, either certain or doubtful, individuals who constitute the minority of the nation, are suspended, but not the nation; even if they are one half of the nation, the nation is not suspended, for if, at the time of the first Passover, the majority of the nation was unclean, or the priests, or the ministerial vessels are unclean because of the ritual contamination of a corpse, the unclean and the clean offer up the Passover sacrifice together in an unclean state even if the majority of the unclean people consisted of only one more than the clean. If they were half and half, they all perform it on the first Passover, and the clean ones perform it separately in a clean state, and the unclean ones perform it separately in an unclean state. If women created the majority of the clean ones, the clean ones perform the first one, and the unclean ones perform neither the first nor the second. If the majority of the nation were unclean because of other types of contamination, and their minority were unclean because of a corpse, those contaminated by a corpse can perform neither the first one, since they are the minority, nor can they perform the second one, since individuals do not perform the second one unless the majority of the congregation performed the first one. Likewise, if the majority of the congregation were unclean because of a corpse and their minority with other types of uncleanness, those unclean because of a corpse perform the first one, and the minority perform it neither on the first, since uncleanness is not suspended for the performance of the first Passover sacrifice except uncleanness emanating from a corpse, and on the second Passover, they may not perform it, since they do not perform the second Passover sacrifice unless the first one was performed in a state of purity. If a third of the congregation was pure, a third unclean because of a corpse, and a third unclean because of other types of contamination, those unclean because of a corpse perform neither the first Passover sacrifice, since they are a minority vis-a-vis the clean ones and those unclean because of other types of contamination, nor do they perform the second Passover sacrifice, since (only) a minority has already performed the first Passover sacrifice. How do we compute the Passover sacrifice to determine whether the majority of the congregation is unclean or clean? We do not count all the eaters, for it is possible that twenty people will be counted on one Passover sacrifice, and they send one person to slaughter it, but we count all those who enter the forecourt, and while they are still outside, before the first group enters, we count them.

The second Passover sacrifice may not be eaten except by those unclean because of a corpse

פסקי הלכות פסח שני בקצרה

דף צט.

כתיב בתורה איש איש כי יהיה טמא לנפש או בדרך רחוקה לכם או לדורותיכם ועשה פסח לה׳ בחדש השני בארבעה עשר יום בין הערבים יעשו אותו וגו׳ ככל חקת הפסח יעשו אותו. ושנינו שאף כל אונס במשמע שאם נאנס או שגג בראשון יעשה בשני אלא שטמא ודרך רחוקה פטורין מן הכרת אפילו הזיד בשני ושאר אונסין בראשון אם הזיד בשני חייב כרת · אבל הזיד בראשון בלא שום אונס ושגגה אפילו נאנס בשני חייב כרת: איזהו דרך רחוקה מי שהיה בינו ובין ירושלים יום י״ד עם עליית השמש ט״ו מיל או יותר היה פחות מזה ולא הגיע לירושלים מפני שעכבוהו בהמות או שהיה בירושלים והיה חולה ברגליו ולא הגיע לעזרה עד שעבר זמן הקרבה הרי זה אנוס ואינו בדרך רחוקה. היה חבוש ביד ישראל חוץ לחומת ירושלים והבטיחוהו לצאת לערב שוחטין עליו אבל נחבש ביד נכרים אין שוחטין עליו עד שיצא ואם שחטו עליו ויצא הרי זה אוכל. שחטו עליו ולא יצא וכן האונן והחולה והזקן שיכולין לאכול ששחטו עליהן ואחר שנזרק הדם נטמאו במת ואינן יכולין לאכול פטורין מפסח שני [וכן כל מי שהיה ראוי בשעת·שחיטה וזריקה ונדחה אחר כך פטור מפסח שני]. טמא שיכול להטהר בפסח ראשון ולא טבל וישב בטומאתו וכן הערל שלא מל בראשון הרי זה הזיד בראשון: ואיזהו טמא שנדחה לפסח שני כגון זבים וזבות נדות ויולדות ובועלי נדות אבל הנוגע בנבלה ושרץ וכיוצא בהם ביום י״ד הרי זה טובל ושוחטין עליו אחר שיטבול ואוכל לערב. וזב שראה ב׳ ראיות וטבל בשביעי שוחטין עליו ואוכל לערב וכן שומרת יום כנגד יום ואם ראו אחר זריקת הדם פטורין מפסח שני ואין שוחטין על הנדה בשביעי שלה: טמא מת שחל ז׳ שלו בע״פ אף על פי שהוזה עליו וטבל וראוי לאכול קדשים

HALACHIC DECISIONS REGARDING THE SECOND PASSOVER SACRIFICE IN BRIEF

It is written in the Torah, "(Num. ix. 10ff.) If any man of you or of your generations shall be unclean by reason of a dead body, or be in a journey afar off, yet he shall keep the Passover unto the Lord. In the second month on the fourteenth day at dusk they shall keep it etc. according to all the statute of the Passover they shall keep it." We learned that any unpreventable interference is included in this ruling, that if one was prevented by an accident or if he inadvertently neglected to observe the first Passover, he must perform the second one. The distinction is, however, that if one is unclean or in a journey afar off, he is exempt from *kareth* even if he wilfully neglects the second Passover sacrifice, but if other accidents prevented him from observing the first, if he wilfully neglected the second one, he is liable to *kareth*. If, however, he wilfully neglected the first Passover sacrifice without any accident or inadvertence, even if he was unavoidably prevented from observing the second one, he is liable to *kareth*.

What is deemed a journey afar off? If one was fifteen *mil* or more from Jerusalem, on the fourteenth day at sunrise. If he was nearer than that, but he did not reach Jerusalem because animals prevented him, or if he was in Jerusalem, but suffered foot ailments, and did not reach the forecourt until after the time of the sacrifice, he is regarded as being unavoidably prevented, but he is not regarded as having been in a journey afar off. If he was imprisoned by Jews outside the wall of Jerusalem, and they promised to release him in the evening, we may slaughter the Passover sacrifice for him, but if he was imprisoned by gentiles, we may not slaughter the Passover sacrifice for him until he is released. If they did slaughter it for him, however, and he was, in fact, released, he may eat of it. If they slaughtered it for him and he was not released, and likewise, an *onen,* (one whose close kin died on that day), or a sick person, or an old man, who can eat the prescribed amount, for whom they slaughtered the Passover sacrifice, and after they sprinkled the blood, they (i.e. the *onen)* became contaminated through a corpse, and they (i.e. the old and the sick) cannot eat thereof, they are exempt from bringing a second Passover sacrifice. [And likewise, anyone who was fit during the slaughtering and the sprinkling and was suspended afterwards, is exempt from the second Passover sacrifice.] An unclean person who can purify himself to bring the first Passover sacrifice, but did not immerse himself and consequently remained unclean, and likewise, an uncircumcised man who did not circumcise himself for the first Passover sacrifice, are deemed as having wilfully neglected the first Passover sacrifice.

Now which is the unclean one who is suspended until the second Passover sacrifice? For instance, a man or a woman who experienced a flux, menstruating women, or men who were intimate with a menstruant. But, one who touched a carcass, a dead reptile, or the like on the fourteenth day, must immerse himself, and we may slaughter for him after he immerses. He may then eat it in the evening. If a *zab,* a man who experienced a flux, experienced two issues and immersed himself on the seventh day, we may slaughter for him, and he eats in the evening. Likewise, a woman who must wait a day corresponding to a day in which she experienced a flux. But if they experienced a flux after the sprinkling of the blood, they are exempt from bringing a second Passover sacrifice. We may not slaughter for a menstruant on the seventh day of her flux. One unclean through a corpse, whose seventh day fell on the eve of Passover, although the purification water was sprinkled on him, and he immersed himself, and he is fit to eat of hallowed foods in the evening, we may not slaughter the

יקריב כולו שלמים ומעות פסח שנותר יקריב ג"כ שלמים ופסח שלא בזמנו יקריב שלמים. מחוסרי כפורים שחל יום הבאת קרבנותיהן בי"ד שוחטין עליהן ומקריבין קרבנותיהן בי"ד בין קודם שחיטת הפסח בין אחר שחיטתו ואוכלין פסחיהן לערב ואין שוחטין עליהן עד שימסרו קרבנותיהן ביד ב"ד שמא יפשעו: מצורע שחל שמיני שלו בי"ד וראה

קרי בו ביום הרי זה טובל ונכנס לעזרת נשים. ישראל ערל שמל בע"פ שוחטין עליו אחר שמל אבל גר שמל וטבל בי"ד אין שוחטין עליו: מי שבא בבית הפרס ה"ז מנפח והולך ואם לא מצא עצם ולא נטמא שוחט ואוכל פסחו וכן בית הפרס שנידוש טהור לעושה פסח:

them must be offered up as peace-offerings, and the money set aside for a Passover sacrifice that was left over, must also be sacrificed as a peace-offering. A Passover sacrifice not in the time of Passover, must also be sacrificed as a peace-offering. Those wanting the ceremony of atonement for full restoration to cleanness, whose day for bringing their sacrifices fell on the fourteenth day (of Nissan)—we slaughter for them and they offer up their sacrifices on the fourteenth, either prior to the slaughtering of the Passover sacrifice or after its slaughtering, and they eat their Passover sacrifice in the evening, but we may not slaughter the Passover sacrifice for them until they deliver their purification sacrifices into the hands of the court, lest they neglect to bring them. A leper, whose eighth day (of recovery) fell on the fourteenth, and he experienced a seminal emission on that day, may immerse himself and enter the women's court. If an uncircumcised Jew was circumcised on the eve of Passover, we may slaughter a Passover sacrifice for him after his circumcision, but if a proselyte was circumcised on the eve of the Passover, we may not slaughter the Passover sacrifice for him.

One who came upon a *beth hap'ras,* an area declared unclean because of crushed bones carried over from a ploughed grave, may blow as he goes, and if he did not find a bone, and he did not become contaminated, he may slaughter and eat his Passover sacrifice. Similarly, a *beth hap'ras* that was trampled is deemed clean for those who wish to offer up the Passover sacrifice.

זמן שלא נשחט עדיין יכולין למנות עליו ולמשוך ידיהן ממנו ואף כולן יכולין למשוך ממנו רק שישאר א' מהם ואין נמנין על שני פסחים כאחד וכשנמנה על שנים יאכל מן הנשחט ראשון . ואין צולין שני פסחים כאחד . אין עושין חבורה נשים ועבדים קטנים ועבדים אבל עושין חבורה כל אחד לעצמן ולכתחילה אין עושין חבורה כולה קטנים או חולים זקנים ואוננים וגרים . שחטו לכשרים ולפסולים כשר אבל זרק הדם לכשרים ולפסולים פסול שהזריקה חמורה שהוא עיקר הקרבן אפי' חישב בשעת שחיטה ע"מ לזרוק לכשרים ולפסולים פסול אבל חישב לזרוק שלא לאוכליו כשר שאין מחשבת אוכלין בזריקה . שוחט אדם בשביל אחרים שהן ברשותו כגון בנו ובתו הקטנים ועבדו ושפחתו הכנענים אפי' שלא מדעתן ומי שאינו ברשותו שוחט עליו מדעתו ממין שצוה לו ואם שינה פסול ובנו ובתו הגדולים ועבדו ושפחתו העברים ואשתו כ"ז שלא מיחו הוי מדעתן . ואין שוחטין על חצי עבד וחצי בן חורין : זמן אכילת הפסח מן התורה כל הלילה ומדרבנן עד חצות ומה שנותר עד הבוקר באש תשרף : טעון הלל בשעת אכילתו. אסור לשבר עצם מפסח טהור שיש עליו כזית בשר או שיש בו מוח אפי' לאחר זמן אכילתו אפי' מפסח שנפסל ובלבד שהיתה לו שעת הכושר בשחיטה וזריקה . לפיכך שורפין עצמות הפסח בכלל הנותר שלא יבוא לידי תקלה . וכל הנאכל בשור הגדול אחר שנתבשל הוא שמותר לאכול כנגדו מן הגדי הרך אחר צלייתו : *כשמקריבין הפסח בחול ובטהרה ובחבורה גדולה שהאוכלים מרובים מקריבין חגיגה עמו כדי שיהא הפסח נאכל על השובע ואוכל מחגיגה תחלה ומברך בא"י אמ"ה אקב"ו על אכילת הזבח ובאחרונה אוכל מגוף הפסח כדי שיהא הפסח גמר שביעה ומברך בא"י אמ"ה אקב"ו על אכילת הפסח ואוכל אפי' כזית מבשר הפסח ואינו טועם אחריו כלום. והחגיגה נאכלת כשאר שלמים . ובשר חגיגה שעלה עם הפסח על השלחן זמן אכילתו כפסח עצמו. מי שאבד פסחו ומצאו אחר שהפריש פסח אחר יקריב איזו שירצה והשני יקריב שלמים . פסח שנתערב בשלמים

marrow of the thigh-bone, and as long as it was not yet slaughtered, they can be counted on it and withdraw from it. Even all of them may withdraw from it, as long as one remains. One may not be counted on two Passover sacrifices at once, and when he is counted on two, he must eat from the one slaughtered first. We may not roast two Passover sacrifices at once. We may not make a group of woment and slaves or children of slaves, but they may make a group of any of them alone. From the outset, we may not make a group completely of children, sick people, old people, *onanim,* or proselytes. If he slaughtered it for those qualified and those unqualified, it is acceptable. But if he sprinkled the blood for those qualified and those unqualified, it is unacceptable, for sprinkling the blood is more stringent, for that is the main part of the sacrifice. Even if he intended at the time of slaughtering to sprinkle the blood for both qualified and disqualified ones, it is unacceptable, but if he intended to sprinkle the blood for those who do not eat of the sacrifice, it is acceptable, for there is no intention of eaters in the sprinkling. A person may slaughter for others who are in his domain, e.g. his minor son and daughter, and his gentile manslave and woman slave, even without their knowledge, but for those who are not in his domain, he may slaughter with their knowledge, of the species that they ordered him. And if he deviated, it is unacceptable. As for his adult sons and daughters, his Hebrew slave and maidservant, and his wife, as long as they did not protest, it is regarded that he is following their wishes. We may not slaughter for one who is half slave and half freeman.

The time for eating the Passover sacrifice is, according to the Torah, the entire night, but, according to the Rabbis, it is only until midnight, and what is left over until morning, must be burnt in fire. The Passover sacrifice requires the recitation of Hallel while eating it. It is prohibited to break a bone of a ritually clean Passover sacrifice if an olive-sized amount of meat is on it or if there is marrow in it. This applies even after the time allotted for eating it and even if the Passover sacrifice became unacceptable, provided it had a time of acceptance at the time of slaughtering and sprinkling the blood. Therefore, we burn the bones of the Passover sacrifice along with the *nothar,* lest one come to a pitfall. Any part edible in a large bull after being cooked, the corresponding part may be eaten in a tender kid after its being roasted.

When we offer up the Passover sacrifice on weekdays in ritual purity and with a large company, i.e. with many eaters, we offer up a *ḥagigah* (a festival sacrifice) with it, in order that the Passover sacrifice be eaten while sated, and he eats from the *hagigah* first and recites the blessing, ‘Blessed art Thou, O Lord our God, King of the universe, Who hallowed us with His commandments and commanded us concerning the eating of the sacrifice.’ And at the end, he eats of the Passover sacrifice itself in order that the Passover sacrifice be the completion of his satiety, and he recites the blessing, ‘Blessed art Thou, O Lord our God, King of the universe, Who hallowed us with His commandments and commanded us concerning the eating of the Passover sacrifice.’ And he must eat at least an olive-sized amount of the flesh of the Passover sacrifice and may not taste anything afterwards. And the *ḥagigah* is eaten as other peace-offerings, and the flesh of the *ḥagigah* that was brought upon the table with the Passover sacrifice must be eaten in the time allotted for the Passover sacrifice. If someone lost his Passover sacrifice and found it after he had set aside another Passover sacrifice, he may sacrifice either one he wishes, and the second one must be offered up as a peace-offering. If a Passover offering became mingled with a peace-offering, all of

ומבושל אפילו לאחר צלייתו ומותר לסוך אותו בשעת צלייתו או לטבל בשעת אכילתו במי פירות חוץ ממים: **ואחר** שצלאו אוכלו לערב וחותך הבשר ואוכל וחותך העצמות מן הפרק ומפרקן אם רצה וכשיגיע לגיד הנשה מוציאו ומניחו עם שאר הגידין והעצמות והקרומות שיוצאין בשעת אכילה. ולא יאכל ממנו כזית צלי מבעו"י. וכל האוכל מן הפסח אינו אוכל אלא בחבורה אחת ואין מוציאין ממנו מן החבורה שיאכל בה (אבל ב' חבורות יכולין לאכול פסח א' בב' מקומות) (כ"פ הב"מ) ובשר הפסח שהוציאו בעקירה והנחה חוץ לחבורתו מן האגף ולחוץ נאסר באכילה. הפסח אינו נאכל אלא בהיקף מחיצה וב' חבורות שאוכלין בבית א' צריכין כל חבורה לעשות היקף מחיצה לעצמן ואלו הופכין פניהם לכאן ואלו לכאן שלא יראו מעורבין וכלה מותרת להחזיר פניה ושמש א' שמשמש לשניהם והתחיל לאכול ואוכלו בפיו כשהולך לשמש לחבורה אחרת קופץ פיו ומחזיר פניו עד שמגיע אצל חבורתו נפרצה המחיצה אינן אוכלין וכן אם נעשה מחיצה בין חבורה א' אינן אוכלין עד שתסתלק: בתחלת הסעודה שנכנסו רק ב' מהחבורה צריכין להמתין על השאר אבל ג' שנכנסו בזמן הסעודה אין צריכין להמתין: נטמא מקצת האברים שורף את הטמאים ואוכל הטהורים. נטמא שלם או רובו שורפין אותו לפני הבירה כדי לביישן שלא נזהרו בו ונשרף מעצי המערכה ואם רצו הבעלים לשורפו בקש ובקנים משל עצמן שורפין. ונטמא מיעוטו והנותר שורפין בחצרותיהן מעצי עצמן. נטמאו הבעלים מקצתן אע"פ שהתחילו כבר לאכול ונטמאו זכו הטהורים בחלקם של טמאים אבל התחילו כולן לאכול ונטמאו מקצתן חלק הטמאים ישרף וה"ה אם מתו. אין הפסח נשחט ונזרק ונאכל אלא למנויו ולנמולים ולטהורים ולשם פסח. המאכיל פסח ראשון או שני למומר או גר תושב ולנכרי אף על פי שנימול מכין אותו מכת מרדות וישראל ערל שאכל פסח חייב מלקות: מילת בניו ועבדיו וטבילת שפחותיו של גדול מעכבתו מלשחט ולאכול הפסח ולא עבדיו ושפחותיו של קטן מעכבים את הקטן. לכתחלה לא ישחוט על יחיד ואם שחט צריך שיהיה ראוי לאכול את כולו וכן אין שוחטין אלא על מי שראוי לאכול כזית ממנו משעת שחיטה עד שעת זריקה. הרבה נמנין על פסח א' עד שיהא כזית לכל א' ונמנין על מוח שבראש אבל לא על הגידין הרכין שסופן להקשות ולא על מוח שבקולית. וכל

after its roasting. We may anoint it during its roasting or dip it while eating it, in fruit juices, but not in water.

And after he has roasted it, he eats it in the evening and cuts the meat and eats it, and he cuts the bones from the joint and separates them if he so desires. And when he reaches the hip sinew, he removes it and places it with the other sinews, bones, and membranes that come out during the eating. And he may not eat an olive-sized amount of it roasted during the day. And whoever eats of the Passover sacrifice may not eat except in one group, and we may not take it out of the group to eat of it. (But two groups may eat of one Passover sacrifice in two places.) And the flesh of the Passover sacrifice that was taken out by picking it up and setting it down outside its group from the threshhold and outside, is prohibited to be eaten. The Passover sacrifice may not be eaten unless surrounded by a partition, and if two groups eat in one house, each group must make a separate partition, and these turn their faces this way, and these the other way, lest they mingle. And a bride may turn her face away. And one waiter who serves them both and commenced eating, and his food is in his mouth, when he goes to wait on another group, he must close his mouth and turn away his face until he reaches his group. If the partition was breached, they may not eat. And similarly, if a partition was made within one group, they may not eat until it is removed. From the beginning of the meal, when only two of the group have entered, they must wait for the rest, but if three entered at the time of the meal, they need not wait.

If part of the limbs of the Passover sacrifice became contaminated, he must burn the contaminated parts, and he may eat the pure ones. If it became completely contaminated, or if the majority of it became contaminated, they must burn it before the Temple in order for them to be embarrassed, since they were not careful with it, and it is burnt with the wood of the arrangement on the altar, but if the owners wanted to burn it with their own straw or reeds, they may do so. If a small part of it became contaminated, or if it became *nothar,* it is burnt in their own courts with their own wood. If some of the owners became contaminated, although they already commenced to eat and they became contaminated, the pure ones are awarded the share of the contaminated ones, but if all of them commenced to eat, and some of them became contaminated, the share of the contaminated ones must be burnt, and the same rule applies if they died. The Passover sacrifice may neither be slaughtered, its blood sprinkled, or eaten except by those counted on it and for circumcised people and for pure people and for the purpose of a Passover Sacrifice. Whoever feeds an apostate the flesh of a first Passover sacrifice, or a second Passover sacrifice, or a stranger dwelling in Eretz Israel, who renounces idolatry, or a gentile, although circumcised, he is flogged with disciplinary flogging. An uncircumcised who ate of the Passover sacrifice is liable to flogging.

The failure to perform circumcision on his sons, his slaves, and the failure to immerse his maidservants, prevents one who has reached his religious majority from slaughtering or eating the Passover sacrifice. But the slaves or maidservants of a minor do not prevent him. From the onset, one should not slaughter a Passover sacrifice for one person, but if he did so slaughter it, that person must be able to eat it up completely. And likewise, we may not slaughter except for one who is able to eat an olive-sized amount from the time of slaughtering until the time of sprinkling the blood. Many may be counted on one Passover sacrifice, as long as there is an olive-sized amount for each one, and they may be counted on the brain in his head, but not on the soft sinews that will ultimately become hardened, and not on the

כתיפו ועל כתף חבירו ותולה ומפשיטו . ומפשיטין את כולו וקורעו וממחה את קרביו עד שמסיר מהן הצואה והפרש ומוציא האימורין והם החלב שעל הקרב ויותרת הכבד וב' כליות והחלב שעליהן והאליה לעומת הכלה ונותנם בכלי שרת ומולחן ומקטירן הכהן ע"ג מזבח כל פסח בפני עצמו . ואסור להביא האימורין לידי נותר. נטמא הבשר ונודע לו קודם זריקה אע"פ שאימורין טהורין לא יזרוק הדם ואם זרק לא הורצה ואם נודע לו אחר הזריקה הורצה. נטמאו האימורין והבשר קיים זורק הדם והבשר נאכל לערב. נטמאו הבעלים כל החבורה אחר שנשחט לא יזרוק ואם זרק לא הורצה וחייבין בפסח שני : כל שפסולו בגופו ישרף מיד. בדם או בבעלים תעובר צורתו ואח"כ ישרף (מיד) . שלמו מלהקריב פותחין דלתות העזרה ויוצאת כת ראשונה ונכנסה כת שניה יצאת שניה נכנסה שלישית כמעשה ראשונה כך מעשה שניה ושלישית . שלמה כת ג' ויצאת רוחצים העזרה אפילו בשבת. חל י"ד בשבת מעשהו כמעשהו בחול לפי שקבוע לו זמן וא"א לעשותו קודם השבת אבל מה שהיה אפשר לעשות קודם השבת כגון הבאתו מחוץ לתחום והתיכת יבלתו בכלי אם היבלת לח וכדומה אסור או מה שאפשר לעשות אחר השבת כגון הדחת קרביו וצלייתו וכדומה[ה] אינו דוחה שבת. שכח ולא הביא הסכין בע"ש אם לא הקדישו עדיין יניחנו בין קרני הכבש או בצמרו ומכישו עד שמביאו לעזרה ומקדישו שם הואיל וקבוע לו זמן . ובשבת לבד רשאין להקטיר האימורין כל הלילה לפי שחלבי שבת קרבין בי"ט : שלמו מלהקריב בחול בעל הזבח נוטל פסחו עם העור ומביאו לביתו בירושלים ובשבת לא היו רשאין להוליך פסחיהן לבתיהן אלא כת א' יוצאין בפסחיהן ויושבין בהר הבית וכת ב' יושבת בחיל וכת ג' עומדין במקומן בעזרה ושוהים הכל עד מ"ש:

ואחר שבא לביתו *צלאו וכיצד צלאו נוטל אותו כלו שלא יחסר אבר ממנו ותוחבו מתוך פיו עד בית נקובתו בשפוד של עץ רמון ותולהו לתוך התנור שלא יגע בחרסית התנור והאש למטה וכרעיו ובני מעיו חוצה לו ואין צולין אותו בתנור שגרוף האש או ע"ג כלי אבן או כלי מתכת לפי שצריך להיות צלי אש ולא ע"י ד"א ואם היה הכלי מנוקב שנוגע בו האור צולין עליו . ואסור לאוכלו חי אפילו חצי צלי

there and placed it on his shoulder and on his friend's shoulder, and he would suspend it and flay it. They would flay it completely, tear it, and squeeze its innards until he would remove the excrement from them, and he would remove the sacrificial parts, viz. the fat that is on the innards, the lobe of the liver, the two kidneys and the fat that is upon them, and the fat tail opposite the kidneys and place them in a ministerial vessel and salt them, and the priest would offer them up on the altar, each Passover sacrifice separately. And it is forbidden to cause the sacrificial parts to become *nothar*. If the flesh became contaminated, and it became known prior to the sprinkling, although the sacrificial parts are pure, he may not sprinkle the blood. And if he did sprinkle it, it is unacceptable. If it became known to him after the sprinkling of the blood, however, it is acceptable. If the sacrificial parts became contaminated, and the flesh still remains, he must sprinkle the blood, and the flesh may be eaten in the evening. If the owners became contaminated, i.e. the entire group, after it was slaughtered, one may not sprinkle the blood, and if he did sprinkle, it is not acceptable, and they are required to bring a second Passover sacrifice.

Any Passover sacrifice that became disqualified because of itself, must be burnt immediately, but if the disqualification is due to the blood or the owners, it must become disfigured and afterwards burnt. When they finished offering up the Passover sacrifice, they would open the portals of the forecourt, the first group would leave, and the second group would enter. When the second one would leave, the third one would enter. As the procedure of the first one, so was the procedure of the second and third ones. When the third group was finished and left, they would wash the forecourt even on the Sabbath. If the fourteenth day fell on the Sabbath, its performance was like that on weekdays, since it has a set time, and it is impossible to perform it before the Sabbath, but whatever was possible to do prior to the Sabbath, e.g. bringing it from outside the Sabbath limits and removing its wart, if the wart is moist, or the like, is forbidden, or whatever is possible to do after the Sabbath, e.g. the rinsing of its innards and roasting it and the like, does not supersede the Sabbath, with the exception of offering up the sacrificial parts, for a precept in its proper time is desired. If he forgot to bring the knife before the Sabbath, if he had not yet sanctified the lamb, he should place it between the horns of the lamb or in its wool and strike it until it would bring it to the forecourt, and there he should sanctify it, since it has a set time. And on the Sabbath alone, they may offer up the sacrificial parts all night since the fats of the Sabbath may be offered up on a festival. When they finished offering up the sacrifice on a weekday, the owner of the sacrifice takes his Passover sacrifice with the hide and brings it to his house in Jerusalem. On the Sabbath, however, they were not permitted to bring their Passover sacrifices to their homes, but the first group would go out with their Passover sacrifices and would sit on the Temple Mount, the second group in the *Hel* (a place within the fortification of the Temple), and the third group would stand in their place in the forecourt, and all would wait until the departure of the Sabbath.

And after he would come home, he would roast it, and how would he roast it? He would take it completely, so that no limb thereof would be missing, and he would thrust a spit of pomegranate wood from its mouth through its anus and suspend it into an oven, so that it not touch the clay of the oven, with the fire below it and its legs and its intestines outside it, and we may not roast it in an oven from which the fire has been swept out or atop a stone vessel or a metal vessel, since it must be roasted in fire, not through any thing else. But if the vessel was perforated, so that the fire penetrates it, we may roast upon it. We may not eat it raw, or even half roasted, or boiled

סדר והלכות קרבן פסח ראשון בקצרה

דף נז:

מצות עשה לשחוט קרבן פסח בי"ד בניסן אחר חצות בכ"מ בעזרה. ואיש ואשה חייבין במצוה זו* . ובא מן הכבשים או מן העזים זכר בן שנה . ומי שביטלה במזיד והוא טהור ובדרך רחוקה לא היה חייב כרת* : ולא יהיה כזית חמץ בבית שום א' מהמתעסקים ואם היה חמץ ברשות אחד מהם לוקה והפסח כשר* . לכתחילה צריך לשחוט אותו אחר התמיד של בין הערבי' והקטרת והטבת נרות*[א] ובחול נשחט התמיד בז' ומחצה ונקרב בח' ומחצה[ב] ובשבת נשחט בו' ומחצה ונקרב בז' ומחצה והפסח אחריו* . הפטורין מקרבן ראייה פטורין מפסח* (תוס' פסחים דף ג':) ומצוה לכתחילה לחלק כל העם שעשו הפסחים לג' כתות בעזרה וכל כת לא פחות מל' בני אדם. נכנסה כת ראשונה עד שנתמלאה העזרה ונועלין הדלתות ושוחטין ואם נמצא בעל מום או טריפה שוחטין אחר אפי' בשבת אפי' מאה עד שיכשיר א' או עד שתחשך וידחה לפסח שני שהרי אנוס הוא[ג]. ויהא א' ממרס בדמו שלא יקרוש עד שיזרוק [ד] דם התמיד . והלוים קראו את ההלל בשיר כל זמן שחיטה והקרבה ואם גמרו ההלל ועדיין לא שלמו הכת מלהקריב שונים ואם שנו ולא שלמו מלהקריב משלשין ומעולם לא שלשו . ועל כל קריאה וקריאה תוקעין ג' תקיעות בחצוצרות תקיעה תרועה תקיעה [ועל כל פסח היו ט' תקיעות ומנין הקריאה והתקיעה מפורש בסוכה נד. ובתוס' ד"ה שייר] והכהנים עומדים שורות שורות ובידיהם מזרקי כסף ומזרקי זהב שורה שכולה כסף כסף ושורה שכולה זהב זהב ולא היו מעורבין משום נוי . ולא היו למזרק שוליים כדי שלא יניחום ויקרוש הדם . שחט השוחט וקיבל הכהן ונותנו לחבירו וחבירו לחבירו עד שיגיע הדם אצל הכהן הקרוב למזבח ושופכו שפיכה אחת כנגד היסוד. חזר וקיבל מזרק א' מלא ואח"כ החזיר הריקן . ואח"כ תולין הבעלים הפסח במסמרות של ברזל שהיו קבועין בכתלים ובעמודין ומי שלא מצא מקום לתלות לקח ממקלות דקים וחלקים שהיו שם והניחו על

PROCEDURE AND LAWS OF THE FIRST PASSOVER SACRIFICE IN BRIEF

It is a mandatory precept to slaughter the Passover sacrifice on the fourteenth day of Nissan after midday anywhere in the Temple forecourt. Both men and women are obligated to perform this precept. This sacrifice comes either from sheep or goats; it must be a male in the first year. One who wilfully neglected this precept when he was ritually pure and not in a journey afar off, is liable to *kareth.* There may not be an olive-sized amount of leaven in the possession of any of those engaged in its performance. If one did have leaven in his possession, he is liable to flogging, but the sacrifice is acceptable.

From the onset, it should be slaughtered after the daily afternoon offering, the burning of the incense, and the preparation of the candles either on the Sabbath or on weekdays. On weekdays, the daily sacrifice is slaughtered a half-hour after the seventh hour and offered up a half-hour after the eighth hour. On the eve of the Sabbath, the daily sacrifice is slaughtered a half-hour after the sixth hour and offered up a half-hour after the seventh hour, and the Passover sacrifice after it. Those who are exempt from the appearance sacrifice are also exempt from the Passover sacrifice. It is preferable to divide all those performing the Passover sacrifices into three groups in the forecourt, none fewer than thirty people. The first group enters until the forecourt is filled up, then they lock the doors and slaughter. If one animal is found to be blemished or *trefah,* another is slaughtered, even on the Sabbath, even one hundred, until one is qualified or it becomes dark, and its owner is then suspended until the second Passover, since his failure to perform the sacrifice was unavoidable. If he slaughtered it prior to the daily sacrifice, it is acceptable. And someone should stir its blood until the blood of the daily sacrifice has been sprinkled. If, however, its blood was sprinkled prior to the blood of the daily sacrifice, it is acceptable.

The Levites would read the Hallel as a song all during the slaughtering and the offering up, and if they completed the Hallel while the group had not yet completed sacrificing, they would repeat it, and if they repeated it and they had still not completed the sacrificing, they would say it a third time, but they never really recited it a third time. And for each reading, they would blow three blasts with the trumpets: *tekiah* (a straight blast), *teruah* (a stacatto note), *tekiah.* [And for every Passover sacrifice there were nine blasts. The number of recitations and the trumpet blasts is delineated in *Sukkah* 54a and in Tos. s.v. *Shiyer.*] And the priests would stand in rows with silver basins in their hands and with golden basins. A row that was completely silver was silver, and a row that was completely gold was gold, and for beauty's sake they were not mingled. And the basin did not have a base lest they set down and the blood congeal. The slaughterer would slaughter and the priest would receive the blood and give it to his neighbor and his neighbor, in turn, to his neighbor, until the blood would reach the priest who was nearest to the altar, who would spill it out all at once opposite the foundation. He would then receive another full basin and return the empty one. Then the owners would suspend the Passover sacrifice with iron nails that were fastened to the walls and on the pillars. And whoever did not find a place to suspend his sacrifice, took one of the thin smooth sticks that were

חידושי הגאון מוה״ר ר׳ משה פיינשטיין שליט״א

דף פ״ג. אמר רנב״י הב״ע שמצאן חלוצין עצמות הפסח דיש בהן משום שבירת העצם לבתר שניהוו נותר הוא דחלצינהו והוו להו שמוש נותר ובעו שרפה. ולכאורה תמוה דהא אף לבתר דניהוו נותר דלית בהו איסור שבירה ג״כ לא היה לו לחלצינהו דהא בעי לשורפן משום שמוש נותר ובזה שחלצינהו הרי יכשלו מזה אינשי שלא ידעו שהן עצמות הפסח. ונראה שמחמת זה פרש״י בתירוצא דר׳ זביד בד״ה עצמות קדשים דהוא ספק דלכאורה קשה מ״ט הוא ספק הא מאחר שאיכא לאו דשבירת עצם ודאי לא עבר על הלאו והיו בודאי שמוש נותר, כמו דתלינן בעצמות קדשים שהוא ודאי דחלצינהו קודם שנפסלו כדי שלא לעבור בלא תותירו כמו כן נימא בפסח שהוא ודאי דחלצינהו אח״כ שלא היה עובר על שבירת העצם והוא עוד כ״ש דהוא לחומרא, אלא הוא דהא אף אם לאחר שנעשו נותר שליכא הלאו נמי היה אסור לו לחולצם מטעם שבעו שרפה והי״ל לשורפם יחד עם המוח כדי שלא יבואו לידי תקלה, לכן אנו מסתפקים שמא גם עבר על הלאו דשבירת עצם והוי ספק. וסובר ר״נ דספק שמוש נותר נמי בעי שרפה ור׳ זביד סובר דספק שמוש נותר לא בעי שרפה. וטעם מחלקותם הוא אם שמוש נותר הוא מדאורייתא או מדרבנן דר״נ סובר שהוא מדאורייתא ספקו לחומרא ור׳ זביד סובר דהוא מדרבנן וספקו לקולא ולכן מוקים שמצאן צבורין צבורין והעליונים חלוצים דבעצמות הפסח דיש בהן משום שבירת עצם צריך בדיקה ולא אמרינן דכשם שעבר על לאו או על חשש תקלה בעליונים עבר נמי בתחתונים דכי אם עבר פעם אחת יעבור עוד פעמים, ואף אם הוא ספק הא הוא על המוח דמדאורייתא בעי שרפה, אבל בקדשים תלינן שודאי חלצינהו כמו העליונים דלא יעבור על לא תותירו רק שאם לא בדק כלל אף עליונים הרי אפשר לומר דניתותרו באונס אבל כשהעליונים בדוקים והם חלוצים תלינן שודאי גם התחתונים חלוצים, והוא פירוש נכון לדעת רש״י.

83a. — SAID R. NAḤMAN B. ISAAC: THE CIRCUMSTANCES HERE ARE E.G., IF HE FOUND THEM [THE BONES] SCOOPED OUT: . . . [BUT IN THE CASE OF] THE BONES OF THE PASSOVER-OFFERING WHICH ARE SUBJECT TO THE PROHIBITION OF BREAKING A BONE, WE ASSUME THAT THEY WERE SCOOPED OUT AFTER THEY BECAME *nothar*; HENCE THEY HAD SERVED *nothar* AND REQUIRE TO BE BURNT.

At a first glance, this is astonishing, for even after they became *nothar* and have no prohibition of breaking bones, he should not have scooped them out since he is required to burn them because they served *nothar,* and now that he scooped them out, people will "stumble" over them, for they will not know that they are bones of a Passover-offering.

It appears to me that, for this reason, Rashi states in his comment on R. Zebid's interpretation, s.v. [In the case of] bones of [other] sacrifices, that there is a doubt [whether he scooped out the bones of the Passover-offering before it became *nothar* or after it became *nothar*]. At a first glance, it is difficult to understand why there is a doubt; since there is a Torah prohibition against breaking the bones of the Passover-offering, he surely did not infract the negative precept [by breaking the bones before they became *nothar*] and they surely served *nothar,* just as we rely in [the case of] the bones of other sacrifices that he scooped them out before they became disqualified, in order not to infract the negative precept of *'You shall not leave over.'* Let us say the same thing in regards to the Passover-offering, that he surely scooped them out afterwards, since he would not infract the prohibition of breaking a bone, and this is a fortiori, since it is more stringent. We must, therefore, say that even after they became *nothar,* when there is no negative precept [of breaking a bone], it is still prohibited to scoop out the bones since they require burning, and he should have burned them together with the marrow lest they come to a pitfall. We are, therefore, in doubt that perhaps he infracted the negative precept of breaking a bone, as well, resulting in a doubtful case [of bones that have served *nothar*]. R. Naḥman holds that [in] a doubtful case of bones that have served *nothar,* they require burning, whereas R. Zebid holds that [in] a doubtful case of bones that have served *nothar,* they do not require burning. The rationale of their dispute is whether the prohibition of bones that have served *nothar* is Biblical or rabbinical. R. Naḥman holds that it is Biblical; therefore, a doubtful case must be dealt with stringently, whereas R. Zebid holds that it is rabbinical, and its doubtful case is dealt with leniently. He, therefore, qualifies the Baraitha as referring to the case in which he found them piled up in heaps, and the upper ones were scooped out. Hence, the bones of the Passover-offering, regarding which there is a negative injunction against breaking bones, must be examined, and we do not say that, just as he infracted a negative injunction of the prohibition of making a pitfall by scooping out the upper ones, he infracted a prohibition with the lower ones, as well, for, if he infracted one prohibition, must he infract another? And, even if it is a doubt, the marrow, which is under a Biblical prohibition, requires burning. Concerning the bones of other sacrifices, however, we assume that he surely scooped them out, just as he did the upper ones, for he would not infract the negative injunction of leaving over the flesh of a sacrifice. If he did not examine them, however, it is possible that they were left over by accident, but, since the upper ones were examined and found to be scooped out, we assume that surely the lower ones, too, are scooped out. This is a correct explanation of Rashi's view of the Gemara.

חידושי הגאון מוה״ר ר׳ משה פיינשטיין שליט״א

פסחים

דף כ״ד. בתוד״ה ואם אינו ענין לאכילה, לא א״ש דהיכי מצי לאוקמא באיסור אכילה דהא כתיב באש תשרף. ונראה דיש לומר דמאחר דאינו יכול ליתן ענין כל מש״כ כאן לשאר איסורין דהא נתמעט שאין כל איסורין בשרפה, ואם היינו צריכין למילף גם אכילה לא היינו ילפינן גם הנאה דמהיכי תיתי נחדש גם הנאה, בשלמא אם היה אפשר ליתן ענין גם לשרפה צריך ליתן גם לשרפה כמו שכתוב דהא תיבה זו נותן ענין למקום אחר, אבל מאחר שא״א ליתן ענין למקום אחר כמו שכתוב דנתמעט מקרא משרפה, מעתה היה שייך ליתן רק לאכילה אם היה צריך לזה ולכן הוצרך שלאכילה אינו ענין דבגופייהו כתיב ולכן נותנין ענין להנאה.

בתוד״ה פרט, ולפי הך דהכא צ״ל שהברייתא לצדדין קתני ואת החלב באור דאי בחמה חי הוא ופטור. ולכאורה תמוה הא גם בלא סוגיא זו א״א לומר דבהמחה חלב בחמה חייב דהא מפורש בברייתא בחולין דף ק״כ בנבלת עוף טהור המחהו בחמה טהור ואמר בגמרא מטעם דבחמה איסרוחי מיסרח, ובנזיר דף נ׳ מסיק הגמרא דהו״ל עפר היינו דאף לכלב אינו ראוי כדאיתא ברש״י ותוס׳ שם, ולאיסור הא אף אם נפסל רק מאדם כדהיה סובר המקשן בנזיר נמי היה פטור דהלכה כר״ש דנו״ט לפגם מותר, וא״כ אף בלא הא דא״ר אבוה א״ר יוחנן שהיינו אומרים דחייב על חלב חי היה זה רק בחלב הראוי לאדם כשיבשלוהו שהיה חייב אף באכלו חי, אבל בחלב שאינו ראוי לאדם היה ודאי פטור שלכן היה פטור בחלב שנמחה בחמה, וא״כ למה כתבו ולפי הך דהכא צריך לומר דהחלב המחה באור ולא בחמה דהא א״א כלל לומר בדרך אחר וצע״ג.

Novellae of HaGaon Rabbi Moshe Feinstein

Pesaḥim

24a — Tosafoth s.v. and if it is irrelevant in respect to eating. This does not follow correctly, for how can we explain it in reference to eating, since the verse states: *'It shall be burnt with fire'?*

It appears to me that we can explain the passage as follows: we cannot explain everything mentioned in the verse [viz. burning] as applying to other prohibitions, since other prohibitions are excluded from burning. Now, if we required this verse to prohibit eating these various foods, we could not derive therefrom a prohibition of benefit, for, how can we derive two laws from one verse? Were it possible to apply it also to burning, we would have to apply the law of burning to everything, just as it is written, since this word is to be applied somewhere else, but, since it is impossible to apply the matter to another place as it is written, since Scripture excludes other prohibitions from burning, it would be possible to explain it only in regard to eating were it necessary. Therefore, the Talmud states that for eating it is unnecessary, for the prohibition is written in each case. Therefore, we apply it to the matter of benefit.

24b — Tosafoth s.v. It is to exclude [this, viz.] that if he ate raw *ḥeleb*. [What the Talmud states in *Hakomez Rabbah* (*Menaḥoth* 21a): If blood is boiled, one does not transgress by [eating] it, as Abaye asks from what was taught in a Baraitha: If one made blood thick and ate it or melted *ḥeleb* and swallowed it, he is liable. The Talmud replies: Here is the case that he thickened it with fire, and here is the case that he thickened it in the sun.] Now, according to what the Talmud states here, we must say that the Baraitha lists the two cases in two different ways, viz.: If he thickened blood in the sun or *ḥeleb* with fire, for, if he did it with the sun, it is raw, and he is exempt.

At a first glance, this is astonishing, for, even without this passage, it would be impossible to say that if one melted *ḥeleb* in the sun, that he should be liable, for it is explicitly stated in a Baraitha in *Ḥullin* 120, concerning the carcass of a clean fowl: If one melted it in the sun, it is ritually clean. The Talmud gives the reason that in the sun it becomes putrid. In *Nazir* 50, the Talmud concludes that it is dust; i.e., it is not even fit for dogs, as Rashi and Tosafoth state there, and concerning prohibition, even if it becomes unfit for human consumption, as the questioner in Nazir thought, he would be exempt, since the halachah is in accordance with R. Simeon that something that gives a defective taste is permissible. Consequently, even without the statement of R. Abbahu in the name of R. Joḥanan, i.e., if we would say that one is liable for eating raw *ḥeleb,* that would be true only of raw *ḥeleb* that, when cooked, would become fit for human consumption, but *ḥeleb* that is unfit for human consumption certainly bears no liability. Therefore, he would be exempt for eating *ḥeleb* that was melted in the sun. If so, why did Tosafoth write that according to the passage here, we must say that the *ḥeleb* mentioned in the Baraitha was melted with fire and not in the sun? It is, in any case, impossible to explain the Baraitha in any other way. This question requires much deliberation.

[121b] R. Simlai was present at a Redemption of the First-
a born.[1] He was asked: It is obvious that for the redemption of the firstborn it is the father who must recite the blessing, 'who hast sanctified us with Thy commandments and hast given us command concerning the redemption of the firstborn.' But as for the blessing, 'Blessed . . . who hast kept us alive and preserved us and enabled us to reach this season,' does the priest[2] recite it or the child's father? Does the priest recite the blessing, since the benefit redounds to him; or does the child's father recite it, since it is he who carries out a religious duty?[3] He could not answer it, so he went and asked it at the schoolhouse, and he was told: The child's father recites both blessings. And the law is that the child's father recites both blessings.[4]

a (1) V. Ex. XIII, 13; Num. XVIII, 16. (2) Who receives the five shekels of redemption. (3) The religious duty is primarily his, since any priest could receive the redemption money. (4) Rashbam: this story is quoted here because the Mishnah too treats of two blessings.

קטז א מיי' פי"א מהל' ביכורים הלכה ה סמג עשין קמד טור ש"ע י"ד סי' שה סעי' י:

רבי שמלאי איקלע לפדיון הבן בעו מיניה פשיטא על פדיון הבן אשר קדשנו במצותיו וצונו על פדיון הבן אבי הבן מברך ברוך שהחיינו וקיימנו והגיענו לזמן הזה כהן מברך או אבי הבן מברך כהן מברך דקמטי הנאה לידיה או אבי הבן מברך דקא עביד מצוה לא הוה בידיה אתא שאיל ביה מדרשא אמרו ליה *אבי הבן מברך שתים והילכתא אבי הבן מברך שתים:

[עיין תוספות בכורות מט. ד"ה לאתויי]

הדרן עלך ערבי פסחים וסליקא לך מסכת פסחים

רשב"ם

רבי שמלאי איקלע כו'. משום דאיירי מתניתין בשני מיני ברכות באדם אחד ומעשה אחד התלוי זה בזה כגון פסח וזבח שחגיגה באה עם הפסח משום הכי נקט נמי להאי עובדא דאבי הבן מברך שתים:

רבינו חננאל

רבי שמלאי איקלע לפדיון הבן אמרו ליה על פדיון הבן פשיטא לן דודאי אבי הבן מברך אלא שהחיינו מאן מברך הכהן מברך או אבי הבן מברך ופשטוה מבי מדרשא אבי הבן מברך שתים על פדיון הבן ושהחיינו:

הדרן עלך ערבי פסחים וסליקא לך מסכת פסחים

סליקא מסכתא ברחמי שמיא וסימנהא נהור"א דכל שעת"א עב"ר לאת"ר תדיר"א איל"ן איכדי"ן איתת"א דאיסתאב"ת ברמש"א

אחר השלמת המסכת יאמר זה

ויועיל לשכחה בעזרת השם יתברך

[פירוש הגון על זה תמצא בספר החיים שחיבר אחי הגאון מהר"ל מפראג בספר זכיות ח"א ס"ג]

*הדרן עלך מסכת פסחים והדרך עלן דעתן עלך מסכת פסחים ודעתך עלן לא נתנשי מינך מסכת פסחים ולא תתנשי מינן לא בעלמא הדין ולא בעלמא דאתי:

יאמר כן שלשה פעמים ואחר כך יאמר

[כסיומא וסוף תשובת הרמ"א ז"ל וכן בסוף יש"ש בב"ק כתוב רמזים על הזכרת שמות סלון]:

יהי רצון מלפניך יי אלהינו ואלהי אבותינו שתהא תורתך אומנותינו בעולם הזה ותהא עמנו לעולם הבא *חנינא בר פפא רמי בר פפא נחמן בר פפא אחאי בר פפא אבא מרי בר פפא רפרם בר פפא רכיש בר פפא סורחב בר פפא אדא בר פפא דרו בר פפא:

הערב נא יי אלהינו את דברי תורתך בפינו ובפיפיות עמך בית ישראל ונהיה כולנו אנחנו וצאצאינו וצאצאי עמך בית ישראל כולנו יודעי שמך ולומדי תורתך: מאויבי תחכמני מצותיך כי לעולם היא לי: יהי לבי תמים בחקיך למען לא אבוש: לעולם לא אשכח פקודיך כי בם חייתני: ברוך אתה יי למדני חקיך: אמן אמן סלה ועד:

מודים אנחנו לפניך ה' אלהינו ואלהי אבותינו ששמת חלקנו מיושבי בית המדרש ולא שמת חלקנו מיושבי קרנות שאנו משכימים והם משכימים אנו משכימים לדברי תורה והם משכימים לדברים בטלים אנו עמלים והם עמלים אנו עמלים ומקבלים שכר והם עמלים ואינן מקבלים שכר אנו רצים והם רצים אנו רצים לחיי העולם הבא והם רצים לבאר שחת שנאמר ואתה אלהים תורידם לבאר שחת אנשי דמים ומרמה לא יחצו ימיהם ואני אבטח בך:

יהי רצון לפניך יי אלהי כשם שעזרתני לסיים מסכת פסחים כן תעזרני להתחיל מסכתות וספרים אחרים ולסיימם ללמוד וללמד לשמור ולעשות ולקיים את כל דברי תלמוד תורתך באהבה וזכות כל התנאים ואמוראים ותלמידי חכמים יעמוד לי ולזרעי שלא תמוש התורה מפי ומפי זרעי וזרע זרעי עד עולם ותתקיים בי בהתהלכך תנחה אותך בשכבך תשמור עליך והקיצות היא תשיחך כי בי ירבו ימיך ויוסיפו לך שנות חיים: אורך ימים בימינה בשמאלה עושר וכבוד: יי עוז לעמו יתן יי יברך את עמו בשלום:

יתגדל ויתקדש שמיה רבא בעלמא דהוא עתיד לאתחדתא ולאחיא מתיא ולאסקא לחיי עלמא ולמבני קרתא דירושלם ולשכלל היכליה בגוה ולמעקר פולחנא נוכראה מארעא ולאתבא פולחנא דשמיא לאתריה וימליך קודשא בריך הוא במלכותיה ויקריה בחייכון וביומיכון ובחיי דכל בית ישראל בעגלא ובזמן קריב ואמרו אמן: יהא שמיה רבא וכו' יתברך וכו' על ישראל וכו' יהא שלמא וכו':

חד תני אפיגול וחד תני אנותר מאן דתני אפיגול משום חשדי כהונה מאן דתני אנותר משום עצלי כהונה חד אמר כזית וחד אמר כביצה מאן דאמר כזית *כאיסורו ומאן דאמר כביצה כטומאתו: **מתני'** *בירך ברכת הפסח פטר את של זבח בירך את של זבח לא פטר את של פסח דברי רבי ישמעאל רבי עקיבא אומר [*] לא זו פוטרת זו ולא זו פוטרת זו: **גמ'** כשתמצא לומר לדברי רבי ישמעאל זריקה בכלל שפיכה ולא שפיכה בכלל זריקה לדברי רבי עקיבא *לא שפיכה בכלל זריקה ולא זריקה בכלל שפיכה:

רבי

חד תני אפיגול וחד תני אנותר. חד מפרש טעמא דמתניתין מאי טעמא מטמא פיגול את הידים וחד מפרש טעמא דנותר מאי טעמא נותר מטמא את הידים: משום חשדי כהונה. גזרו עליו טומאה שלא יפגלוהו ברצון להפסיד את הבעלים ועוד דשלמים הן ואין לכהן בהן אלא חזה ושוק וישחטם במזיד לשם חטאת כדי לאוכלן כולם ומשום הכי גזרו טומאה: משום עצלי כהונה. שלא יתעצלו באכילתן: חד אמר כזית. מהן מטמא את הידים וח"א בכביצה: **מתני'** ברכת הפסח. על אכילת פסחים על של זבח חגיגת ארבעה עשר ומברכין על אכילת שלמים: **גמ'** שירי דם בזריקה מרחוק דלא איכפת ליה אם טפלים שיריים על היסוד או לא שירי דם הפסח בשפיכה בנחת כדי שיפלו על היסוד: לא שפיכה בכלל זריקה. כלומר שאם נותן פסח בזריקה ושלמים בשפיכה לא עשה כלום וכיון דאין דומין זה לזה במתן דמים אין ברכת האחד פוטרת האחר: הכי גרסינן במתניתין בירך על הזבח לא פטר את הפסח על הפסח פטר את של זבח דברי ר' ישמעאל והכא גרסינן לדברי ר' ישמעאל זריקה בכלל שפיכה ולא שפיכה בכלל זריקה ופירוש אם נתן פסח בזריקה לא עשה כלום אבל אם נתן שלמים בשפיכה יצא לפיכך ברכת הפסח פוטרת את של שלמים שבשלמים בכלל פסח במתן דמים ושל שלמים אינה פוטרת את של פסח לפי שאין פסח במתן דמו בכלל שלמים:

הדרן עלך ערבי פסחים וסליקא לה מסכת פסחים

רשב"ם

חד תני אפיגול וחד תני אנותר. חד מפרש טעמא דמתניתין מ"ט פיגול מטמא את הידים וחד מפרש טעמא דמתניתין מאי טעמא נותר מטמא את הידים: משום חשדי כהונה. גזרו חכמים טומאה לא יפגלוהו ברצון להפסיד את הבעלים ויאמרו שוגגין היינו ורבינו פירש עוד טעם אחר לפי שלמים הם ואין לכהן בהן אלא חזה ושוק וישחטם במזיד לשם חטאת כדי לאוכלן כולן ולא נהירא דאין פיגול אלא בשוחט על מנת לאכול ממנו חוץ לזמנו והשוחט שלמים לשם חטאת אין כאן פיגול אלא שלא עלו לבעלים לשם חובה: משום עצלי כהונה. שלא יתעצלו באכילה וה"ה לישראל: חד אמר כזית. מהן מטמא את הידים וחד אמר כביצה ובהא לחוד הוא דפליגי: כאיסורו. איסור אכילתו בכזית: כטומאתו. טומאת אוכלין בכביצה לטמא אחרים: **מתני'** ברכת הפסח וברכת הזבח מפרש בתוספתא (זבחים) איזה ברכת הפסח בא"י אמ"ה אשר קדשנו במצותיו וצונו לאכול הפסח אי זו היא ברכת הזבח בא"י אמ"ה אשר קדשנו במצותיו וצונו לאכול הזבח והאי זבח היינו חגיגת י"ד הבאה עם הפסח אי נמי נדרים ונדבות שהקריב ערב הפסח ואוכלן בלילי הפסח: פלוגתא דרבי ישמעאל ור' עקיבא מפרשינן טעמא בגמ': הכי גרסינן בירך על הזבח לא פטר את הפסח בירך על הפסח פטר את הזבח דברי ר' ישמעאל: **גמ'** ה"ג לכשת"ל לדברי ר"י זריקה בכלל שפיכה ולא שפיכה בכלל זריקה במס' זבחים בפ' בית שמאי (דף לז:) שמעינן ליה לר' ישמעאל דאמר דפסח בשפיכה ולא בזריקה דתניא ר' ישמעאל אומר מתוך שנאמר אך בכור שור וגו' למדנו לבכור שטעון מתן דמים והימורין לגבי מזבח מעשר ופסח מנין תלמוד לומר ודם זבחיך ישפך דאלו לשאר קרבנות לא צריך דבכולהו כתיב זריקה והשתא דקאמר רבי ישמעאל דפסח בשפיכה ושמעית ליה במתניתין דאמר בברכת הפסח הוא נפטר מברכת הזבח ואינו נפטר מסל פסח בברכת הזבח אמור מעתה הניתנין בזריקה כגון שאר זבחים שניתנו בשפיכה כפסח יצא כדתניא בהדיא בפרק בית שמאי (שם) מנין לניתנין בזריקה שנתנן בשפיכה יצא תלמוד לומר ודם זבחיך ישפך אבל הניתנין בשפיכה כגון פסח שנתנן בזריקה כשלמים וכל שאר זבחים לא יצא דומיא דברכת פסח והזבח דקאמר נמי ר' ישמעאל במתניתין כי האי גוונא: ולדברי ר' עקיבא כו'. כדאמרינן נמי במת' גבי ברכת הפסח והזבח שאין זו פוטרת את זו ור"ע נמי סבר דפסח (נמי) בשפיכה דלא אשכחן תנא דאמר בזריקה אלא לר' יוסי הגלילי בפרק תמיד נשחט (לעיל סד:) דנפקא ליה מאת דמם תזרוק על המזבח דבכור את דמו לא נאמר אלא דמם לימד על בכור מעשר ופסח שטעונין זריקה והיא זריקה דפסח מתנה אחת היא כנגד היסוד מרחוק ולא כזריקת שאר קרבנות שהן שתי מתנות שהן ארבע ומקראי מפיק להו במסכת זבחים בפרק איזהו מקומן (דף נז:) מדכתיב סביב בעולה סביב בחטאת סביב באשם דשלש כתובין הבאין כאחד אין מלמדין זריקה מרחוק ושתי מתנות שהן ארבע ופסח מתנה אחת מרחוק כדפרישית שפיכה מקרוב עומד על היסוד ושופך שם בכולהו קרבנות כתיב זריקה לבר מחטאת שמתנותיהן באצבע על הקרנות כדכתיבי קראי:

רבי

כשתמצא לומר לדברי ר' ישמעאל זריקה בכלל שפיכה ולא שפיכה בכלל זריקה לדברי ר' עקיבא כו'. אם כן מוכח מכאן דלר' ישמעאל הניתנין בזריקה שנתנן בשפיכה יצא וכן מוכיח נמי כאן דס"ל דפסח בשפיכה הוא והכי נמי מוכח בפסחים בפרק האשה (דף פט:) דפריך דאלו פסח בשפיכה ושלמים בזריקה ומשני מאי נפקא מינה והתניא מנין לניתנין בזריקה שנתנן בשפיכה שיצא כו' אלמא אית ליה תרתי פסח בשפיכה וזריקה בכלל שפיכה דזריקה עומד מרחוק וזורק את הדם ליסוד ושפיכה עומד על היסוד ושופך וקשה דבזבחים פרק בית שמאי (דף לז:) משמע מאן דלית ליה פסח בשפיכה לא מצי סבר נזרקין שנתנן בשפיכה יצא וכן איפכא מאן דאית ליה נזרקין שנתנן בשפיכה יצא לית ליה פסח בשפיכה דקאמר ודם זבחיך ישפך והא מיבעי ליה לכדתניא מנין לניתנין בזריקה שנתנן בשפיכה יצא ת"ל ודם זבחיך ישפך ומשני סבר לה כרבי עקיבא דאמר לא זריקה בכלל שפיכה וכו' פי' והתניא דרשה מנין לניתנין כו' לר' ישמעאל היא ופריך והאי מיבעיא ליה לכדתניא ר' ישמעאל אומר מתוך שנאמר אך בכור שור או בכור כשב וגו' את דמם תזרוק למדנו לבכור שטעון מתן דמים למזבח מעשר ופסח מנין ת"ל ודם זבחיך ישפך ומשני סבר לה כר"ג דאמר פסח נמי בזריקה והדר פריך ליה [ור' ישמעאל] האי קרא מפיק ליה הכי ומפיק ליה הכי וקאמר תרי תנאי אליבא דר' ישמעאל אלמא ההוא תנא דר' ישמעאל דלעיל דנזרקין שנתנן בשפיכה יצא ויליף מדם זבחיך ישפך לית ליה להאי תנא דרבי ישמעאל דיליף מההוא קרא פסח בשפיכה וי"ל דודאי ר' ישמעאל אית ליה תרתי וניתנין בזריקה שנתנן בשפיכה יצא נפיק ליה מסברא דמה לי זריקה מרחוק ומה לי שפיכה בקרוב קרא כי אתא [לפסח] בשפיכה הוא דאתא והאי דלא משני ליה הכי כדפריך ליה ור' ישמעאל האי קרא היכי מפיק ליה הכי וכו' משום דדרשה של רבי יוסי הגלילי פשוט ליה טפי והתם פי' הקונט' ור' ישמעאל האי קרא דודם זבחיך ישפך מפיק ליה להכי לניתנין בזריקה שנתנן בשפיכה יצא וע"כ ההיא דניתנין לא אתיא כרבי עקיבא דלא אתיא אמאי קאמר רבי עקיבא אין ברכת פסח פוטרת של זבח והלא שלמים בכלל פסח והכל בשפיכה מההיא דניתנין ולי נמי הוה ס"ל לרבי עקיבא פסח בזריקה כרבי יוסי הגלילי כל שכן דשניהם פוטרין זה את זה ולהכי קדריש ליה [תו] לההוא קרא לפסח בשפיכה ומשני תרי תנאי וכו' והאי תנא דר' ישמעאל דיליף מודם זבחיך ישפך פסח בשפיכה לית ליה פסח פוטר את הזבח והא לא פליג רבי ישמעאל אדרבי עקיבא דהא כיון דדריש מיניה פסח בשפיכה הו לית ליה למילף מיניה דניתנין בזריקה שנתנן בשפיכה יצא והאי תנא דר' ישמעאל דיליף מיניה דניתנין בזריקה שנתנן בשפיכה יצא לית ליה פסח בשפיכה אלא בזריקה כשלמים מיהו הא סברא דידיה דפליג אדרבי עקיבא דפסח עיקר וזבח טפל ע"כ פסח פוטר את הזבח ולא ברכת זבח את הפסח ובפסחים דירושלמי אמר האי טעמא ע"כ וקשה דלעיל הוכחנו מההוא דפסחים דאית להו תרווייהו ודכתבינן לעיל ורשב"ם פירש הכי כשתמצא לומר לדברי ר' ישמעאל זריקה בכלל כו' מתוך דבריו למדנו דקאמר בירך על הפסח וכו' א"כ ס"ל דפסח בזריקה ומעתה אייתר ליה ודם זבחיך ישפך לומר דזריקה בכלל שפיכה וכל הנזרקין אם נתנן בשפיכה יצא *ול"ג ושפיכה בכלל זריקה דהא אין שום קרבן דמתנתו לכתחלה בשפיכה וקשה ההיא דפ' האשה ור' חיים כהן פי' כשתמצא לומר לדברי ר' ישמעאל זריקה בכלל שפיכה ושפיכה בכלל זריקה כך היא גירסא בספרים ישנים כלומר כל הקרבנות בזריקה ובשפיכה ואין להקפיד וברכת פסחים על עיקר לפטור את הטפל ולא הטפל את העיקר [וקשה] והלא אית ליה נמי דפסחים מתנתו בשפיכה דוקא אם כן אין זה זריקה: (וע"ע תוס' זבחים לז: ד"ה הרי תנאי וכו')

הדרן עלך ערבי פסחים וסליקא לה מסכת פסחים

רבינו חננאל

הא דתנן מטמאין את הידים רב הונא ורב חסדא חד מתני טומאה אפגול וחד מתני אנותר חד מתני כזית כאיסורו וחד מתני כביצה כטומאתו: **ברך** ברכת הפסח פטר את של זבח וכו' תאנא איזו היא ברכת הזבח אומר אקב"ו לאכול הזבח וקי"ל הפסח דמו בשפיכה כדתנן כהן הקרוב אצל המזבח זורקה זריקה אחת כנגד היסוד והזבח כגון השלמים וכיוצא בהן דמן בזריקה ואמרינן כשתמצא לומר לדברי רבי ישמעאל דאמר ברכת הפסח פוטרת של זבח ואינו צריך לברך על הזבח ברכה בפני עצמה אבל ברכת הזבח אינה פוטרת של פסח הרי זריקה בכלל שפיכה כלומר הטעון זריקה אם תורקהו בשפיכה יצא אבל אין שפיכה בכלל זריקה הטעון שפיכה ואם יורקהו לא יצא אלא טעון שפיכה לדברי ר' עקיבא דאמר לא זו פוטרת זו ולא זו פוטרת זו לא שפיכה בכלל זריקה ולא זריקה בכלל שפיכה:

קטו א [מיי' פ"ח מהל' חמץ ומצה דין ז]:

[לעיל מט.] [ברכות מט:] [זבחים לז.]

[שם]

[פסחים פ"י]

ול"ג ולא שפיכה בכלל רש"א

רש"א

[At least] as much as an egg. [121a] One taught in reference to *piggul*, while the other taught in reference to *nothar*. He who taught in reference to *piggul* [gave the reason as being] on account of the suspected priests. While he who taught in reference to *nothar* [gave the reason as being] on account of the lazy priests. One said: As much as an olive [defiles]; while the other said: [At least] as much as an egg. He who maintained, as much as an olive, [accepts the standard] as its prohibition; while he who rules, as much as an egg, [holds that the standard is the same] as its uncleanness.[2]

MISHNAH. IF HE RECITED THE BLESSING FOR THE PASSOVER-OFFERING, HE THEREBY EXEMPTS THE [FESTIVAL] SACRIFICE; [BUT] IF HE RECITED THE BLESSING FOR THE SACRIFICE, HE DOES NOT EXEMPT THE PASSOVER-OFFERING: THIS IS THE VIEW OF R. ISHMAEL. R. AKIBA SAID: THE FORMER DOES NOT EXEMPT THE LATTER, NOR DOES THE LATTER EXEMPT THE FORMER.[3]

GEMARA. When you examine the matter, [you must conclude] that in R. Ishmael's opinion sprinkling [*zeriḳah*] is included in pouring [*shefikah*], but pouring is not included in sprinkling. Whereas in R. Akiba's opinion pouring is not included in sprinkling, nor is sprinkling included in pouring.[4]

(2) V. *supra* 85*b* for notes on the whole passage. (3) The 'sacrifice' referred to is the *ḥagigah* of the fourteenth (v. *supra* 69*b*). An appropriate blessing was recited before each. (4) Rashbam: both R. Ishmael and R. Akiba hold that the blood of the Passover-offering must be poured out, i.e., the priest must stand quite close to the altar and gently pour the blood on to its base. But the blood of the *ḥagigah* requires sprinkling, i.e., from a distance and with some force. Now R. Ishmael holds that if the blood of the *ḥagigah* is poured out instead of sprinkled, the obligation of sprinkling has nevertheless been discharged. Consequently, the blessing for the Passover-offering includes that of the *ḥagigah*, since in both the blood may be poured on to the base of the altar. But if the blood of the Passover-offering is sprinkled, the obligation has not been discharged: consequently the blessing for the *ḥagigah*, whose blood is normally sprinkled, does not exempt the Passover-offering. By the same reasoning we infer that in R. Akiba's view neither includes the other.

THEY MUST NOT EAT.[2] [120b] R. JOSE SAID: IF THEY FELL INTO A LIGHT SLEEP, THEY MAY EAT; IF THEY FELL FAST ASLEEP, THEY MUST NOT EAT.[3] THE PASSOVER-OFFERING DEFILES ONE'S HANDS AFTER MIDNIGHT;[4] PIGGUL AND NOTHAR DEFILE ONE'S HANDS.

GEMARA. R. JOSE SAID: IF THEY FELL INTO A LIGHT SLEEP, THEY MAY EAT; IF THEY FELL FAST ASLEEP, THEY MUST NOT EAT. What condition is meant by 'A LIGHT SLEEP'?—Said R. Ashi: A sleep which is not sleep, a wakefulness which is not wakefulness. E.g., if he answers when called, cannot make a reasoned statement, yet recollects when reminded. Abaye was sitting [at the Passover meal] before Rabbah. Seeing him dozing he remarked to him, 'You, sir, are sleeping.'[5] 'I was merely dozing,' replied he, 'and we have learnt: 'IF THEY FELL INTO A LIGHT SLEEP, THEY MAY EAT; IF THEY FELL FAST ASLEEP, THEY MUST NOT EAT.'

THE PASSOVER-OFFERING DEFILES ONE'S HANDS AFTER MIDNIGHT etc. This proves that from midnight it is *nothar*. Which Tanna [holds thus]?—Said R. Joseph, It is R. Eleazar b. 'Azariah.
a For it was taught: *And they shall eat the flesh in that night:*[1] R. Eleazar b. 'Azariah said: '*In that night*' is stated here, while elsewhere it is stated, *For I will go through the land of Egypt in that night:*[2] just as there it means midnight, so here too [they may eat the Passover-offering] until midnight.[3] Said R. Akiba to him: Yet surely it is already stated, [*and ye shall eat it*] *in haste*,[4] [implying] until the time of haste.[5] If so, what is taught by '*in* [*that*] *night*?' You might think that it can be eaten like [other] sacrifices, [viz.,] by day: therefore it is stated, '*in* [*that*] *night*': it is eaten by night, but it may not be eaten by day. Now how does R. Akiba employ '*that* [night]'? He utilizes it as excluding a second night. For I might argue, Since the Passover-offering is a sacrifice of lesser sanctity,[6] and the peace-offering is a sacrifice of lesser sanctity, then just as the peace-offering is to be eaten two days and one night, so in the case of the Passover-offering, I will substitute nights for days,[7] and it may be eaten two nights and one day. Therefore the Divine Law wrote '*that* [*night*]'. And R. Eleazar b. 'Azariah?[8]—He can answer you: That is deduced from, *and ye shall let nothing of it remain until the morning*.[9] And R. Akiba?[10]—He can answer you: Had not the Divine Law written '*that* [*night*]', I would have said, what does '*morning*' mean? the *second* morning. Then what of R. Eleazar b. 'Azariah?—He can answer you: Wherever '*morning*' is written, it means the first morning.[11]

Raba said: If a man eats unleavened bread after midnight nowadays, according to R. Eleazar b. 'Azariah he does not discharge his duty.[12] That is obvious, [for] since it is assimilated to the Passover-offering, it is like the Passover-offering?—You might say, surely the Writ[13] excluded it from the analogy;[14] hence he informs
b us that when the Writ restores it, it restores it to its original state.[1]

PIGGUL AND NOTHAR DEFILE ONE'S HANDS. R. Huna and R. Ḥisda—one maintains: It is on account of suspected priests; while the other said: It is on account of the lazy priests. One maintained: As much as an olive [defiles]; while the other said:

(2) In the latter case they have all ceased to think about the Paschal lamb; when they awake it is as though they would eat in two different places, sleep breaking the continuity of action and place, and thus it is forbidden. (3) This distinction refers to the first clause, when only some of them fell asleep. (4) Because it is then *nothar*, q.v. Glos. (5) This happened while he was eating the unleavened bread at the end of the meal, and Abaye meant that he might not continue now.

a (1) Ex. XII, 8. (2) Ibid. 12. (3) After which it is *nothar*. (4) Ibid. 11. (5) I.e., when they had to make haste to leave Egypt, which was in the morning. (6) V. 24a, n. a2. (7) This is necessary, since its main eating is at night. (8) How does he refute this argument? (9) Ex. XII, 10. (10) Does he not admit this? (11) Cf. *supra* 71a and *b*. (12) Since he holds that the Passover-offering may not be eaten after midnight, while as stated *supra* 120a unleavened bread is assimilated to the Passover-offering. (13) I.e., the verse '*at even ye shall eat unleavened bread*'. (14) In that unleavened bread is declared obligatory nowadays despite the absence of the paschal lamb, v. *supra* 120a.

b (1) V. *supra* 120a. I.e., once the Writ teaches that unleavened bread nowadays is obligatory, notwithstanding the analogy, it becomes assimilated to the paschal-offering in respect of the *hours* during which the obligation can be discharged.

ר' יוסי אומר *נתנמנמו יאכלו נרדמו לא יאכלו הפסח אחר חצות מטמא את הידים *הפגול והנותר מטמאין את הידים: **גמ'** ר' יוסי אומר נתנמנמו יאכלו נרדמו לא יאכלו *ה"ד נתנמנם אמר רב אשי *נים ולא נים תיר ולא תיר כגון דקרי ליה ועני ולא ידע לאהדורי סברא וכי מדכרו ליה מדכר אביי הוה יתיב קמיה דרבה חזא דקא מנמנם א"ל מינם קא נאים מר א"ל מינומי קא מנמנם ותנן נתנמנמו יאכלו נרדמו לא יאכלו: הפסח אחר חצות מטמא את הידים וכו': אלמא מחצות ה"ל נותר מאן תנא אמר רב יוסף *ר"א בן עזריה הוא *דתניא °ואכלו את הבשר בלילה הזה ר"א בן עזריה אומר נאמר כאן בלילה הזה ונאמר להלן °ועברתי בארץ מצרים בלילה הזה מה להלן עד חצות אף כאן עד חצות אמר לו ר"ע *והלא (א) נאמר חפזון עד שעת חפזון אם כן מה ת"ל בלילה יכול יהא נאכל כקדשים ביום ת"ל בלילה *בלילה הוא נאכל ואינו נאכל ביום ור"ע האי הזה מאי עביד ליה מיבעי ליה למעוטי לילה אחר הוא דאתא ס"ד אמינא הואיל ופסח קדשים קלים ושלמים קדשים קלים מה שלמים נאכלים לשני ימים ולילה אחד אף פסח אוקים לילות במקום ימים ויהא נאכל לשני לילות ויום אחד כתב רחמנא הזה ור"א בן עזריה אמר לך °מלא תותירו עד בקר נפקא הא ור"ע אמר לך אי לא כתב רחמנא הזה הוה אמינא מאי בקר *בקר שני ור"א אמר לך כל היכא דכתב בקר בקר ראשון הוא אמר רבא *אכל מצה בזמן הזה אחר חצות לר"א בן עזריה לא יצא ידי חובתו פשיטא דכיון דאיתקש לפסח כפסח דמי מהו דתימא הא אפקיה קרא מהיקישא קמשמע לן דכי אהדריה קרא למילתא קמייתא אהדריה: הפיגול והנותר מטמא את הידים וכו': *רב הונא ורב חסדא חד אמר משום חשדי כהונה וחד אמר משום עצלי כהונה חד אמר כזית וחד אמר [ד]כביצה
חד

תורה אור: שמות יב | שם | שם

מלא תותירו עד בקר נפקא. אע"ג דדרשינן מיניה (לעיל דף פג:) ליתן לו בקר שני לשריפתו דנפקא לן מהתם דאין שורפין קדשים בי"ט אית מאן דמפיק ליה בפ"ב דשבת (דף כד:) ובמכילתין *מדוכתא אחרינא: **אמר** רבא אכל מצה בזמן הזה כו'. יש מפרשים דכך הלכה דהא סתם מתני' כוותיה ואין זה ראיה דהא פרק ב' דמגילה (דף כ:) אשכחן סתמא אחרינא דלא כוותיה דתנן זה הכלל כל דבר שמצותו בלילה כשר כל הלילה לאתויי אכילת פסחים ודלא כר"א בן עזריה *דאמר אכילת פסחים עד חצות היינו ודאי מדאורייתא ובתר הכי פסול למיכל אבל הא דאמרינן הקטר חלבים ואימורים עד חצות כדאמרינן בריש ברכות (דף ב.) לא הוי אלא מדרבנן אפילו לרבנן משום הכי אם עיכב להקטיר עד חצות לא נפסל בכך דהא מן התורה היו כשירים עד הבקר וחכמים לא עשו סייג לדבר להביאו לבית הפסול קודם הזמן ובפ' המזבח מקדש (זבחים פו:) נמי מוכח הכי דקתני עושה (פיגול) [עיכול] מדרבנן והוא דבפרק איזהו מקומן (שם נז:) דקאמ' דמתני' דהפסח אינו נאכל אלא עד חצות ר"א בן עזריה היא ופריך ממאי דאורייתא דלמא מדרבנן ור"ע היא ומשני א"כ מאי אלא פירוש אי הוה מדרבנן לא ה"ל למיתני אלא דהא לעיל גבי תודה וחטאת תנא עד חצות ולא תנא אלא דאפילו אירע דעבר על דברי חכמים ולא אכל קודם חצות לא נפסל ואוכלו לאחר חצות כדמשמע פ"ק דברכות (דף ט.) גבי ק"ש בההוא מעשה דבאו בניו של ר"ג מבית המשתה ומ"מ היכא סייג דעבר על דברי חכמים אם לא אכל קודם חצות וה"נ התם א"כ מאי אלא ותו כי הגך מה הגך דאורייתא כלומר מה הכא דאינו נאכל אלא למנויו ולאו היינו דאורייתא' אף הכך נמי דעד חצות דאורייתא ורבי אלעזר בן עזריה היא: [עי' תוס' זבחים נז: ד"ה והב"א ותוס' מגילה כא. ד"ה לאתויי] כשתמלא

רשב"ם

עד שעת חפזון. שנבהלו לצאת והיינו עד הבקר: ויום אחד. ט"ז המפסיק בין הלילות דלא ליהוי נותר עד ט"ז: הא אפקיה קרא מהיקישא. דפסח דכתיב (שמות יב) [בערב תאכלו מצות] [ששת ימים כו'] ולהקישו בהיקשא דעל מצות ומרורים יאכלוהו (במדבר ט): קמ"ל דכי אהדריה קרא· (שבעת ימים תאכל מצות) [בערב כו'] (שמות יב) למילתיה קמייתא אהדריה לעמוד במקום הפסח ולאכול עד חצות: חד

רבי יוסי אומר נתנמנמו יאכלו. הרישא קאי דקאמר ת"ק ישנו מקצתן יאכלו ואתא למימר ה"מ אם נתנמנמו אבל אם נרדמו אפילו מקצתן לא יאכלו לכשיעורו הכי מוכח בגמרא והכי הילכתא דהא רבה קאי כוותיה כדאמר בגמרא: הפסח אחר חצות מטמא את הידים· דה"ל נותר מחצות ואילך ורבנן גזרו על הנותר לטמא את הידים כדמפרש טעמא בגמרא: **גמ'** לההדורי סברא. במילתא דצריכא סברא כגון ששואלין אותו היכן הנחת כלי זה וכי מדכרו ליה הנחתו במקום פלוני מידכר ואומר הן או לאו: הוה מנמנם. רבה לאחר שהתחיל לאכול מצת חובה באחרונה: נתנמנמו יאכלו. תנן אבל אם הוא ישן אפילו הוא לבדו שוב לא היה אוכל דס"ל כרבי יוסי דאמר נרדמו אפילו מקצתן לא יאכלו: אלמא מחצות הוא דה"ל נותר. והא כתיב (שמות יב) לא תותירו ממנו עד בקר אלמא עד בקר לא הוי נותר: ר"א בן עזריה היא. דנפקא ליה מקרא דאכילת פסח עד חצות ומחצות הוי נותר והאי דכתיב לא תותירו ממנו עד בקר לשריפה אתא דעד בקר לאו בר שריפה הוא כדתניא בפ"ק דברכות (דף ט.) ר"א בן עזריה אומר בערב אתה זובח וכבא השמש אתה אוכל מועד לאתך ממצרים אתה שורף אבל כר"ע דפליג עליה לא מיתוקמא דלדידיה לא ה"ל נותר עד הבקר ולא מטמא ידים אלא מבוקר ואילך ואף על גב דלדידיה נמי אכילת פסחים עד חצות כדין לכל הנאכלין ליום ולילה רבנן הוא דעבדי הרחקה יתירא להרחיק את האדם מן העבירה כדתנן בפ"ק דברכות (דף ג.) שמא יאכל ממנו לאחר שעלה עמוד השחר ויתחייב כרת ומוטב שיבואו קדשים לבית הפסול למעט זמן אכילתו שלא לאכול אחר חצות משיאכל עד בקר ויבא לידי כרת: שעת חפזון. שנחפזו לצאת והיינו עמוד השחר כדכתיב (שמות יב) לא תצאו איש מפתח ביתו עד בקר ור"א בן עזריה סבר חפזון דמצרים בשעת מכת בכורות שעל ידיה נחפזו למהר לשלחם מן הארץ הכי מפ' בברכות (דף ט·): יכול יהא נאכל כשאר קדשים. ביום שחיטתו כדרך תודה שאף היא זמן אכילתה יום אחד והוכל כל יום שחיטתה והלילה עד הבוקר מן התורה דכתיב (ויקרא ז) ביום קרבנו יאכל לא יניח ממנו עד בקר: שלמים נאכלין לשני ימים ולילה אחד. שבינתים דכתיב (שם יט) ביום זבחכם יאכל וממחרת אף פסח נמי הואיל ואינו נאכל אלא בלילה נוקים שני לילות במקום שני ימים של שלמים ויהא נאכל לשני לילות ויום אחד לא שיאכלנו ביום אלא שיהא שהות זמן שלא יפסל באכילה בשביל המתנת היום ויאכלנו בליל השני קמ"ל כן פירש רבינו במסכת ברכות (שם) ולי נראה שאף ביום שבינתים יאכל דהא בלילה הזה לא בא למעט אלא יום שחיטתו שלפני לילה הראשון של פסח אבל מכאן ואילך יאכלנו עד עמוד השחר של ליל שני קמ"ל: מהו דתימא אפקיה. רחמנא לחובת מצה בלילה הראשון מהיקישא דאקשיה רחמנא כפסח בהאי קרא דעל מצות ומרורים יאכלוהו ואפקיה רחמנא בהאי קרא ששת ימים תאכל (עליו) מצות וביום השביעי מה שביעי רשות אף ששת ימים רשות ולילה הראשון נמי במשמע אלמא אפקיה רחמנא מהיקישא דעל מצות ומרורים לחובת מצה לילה הראשון ואוקמיה ארשות: קמ"ל. דכי אהדריה קרא לחובת מצה בלילה הראשון בזמן הזה דכתיב בערב תאכלו מצות דהכי נפקא לן לעיל למילתא קמייתא אהדריה לאכילה עד חצות כבזמן דאיכא פסח: חד אמר משום חשדי כהונה. לקמן מפרש דהנותר קאי ולא פליגי אלא חד מפרש טעמא דפיגול וחד מפרש טעמא דנותר: לקמן מפרש דאפיגול קאי: וחד אמר משום עצלי כהונה.
חד

קיא א מיי' שם טוש"ע שם:

[לעיל פג:]

קיב ב מיי' פ"ה מהל' שאר אבות הטומאו' הלכה ג:

קיג ג טוש"ע א"ח סי' תעז סעיף א:

קיד ד מיי' פ"ח מהל' שאר אבות הטומאו' הלכה ג:

[שם כח.] תענית דף יב· מגילה דף יח: יבמות דף נד: נדה דף סג.

[לעיל דף מז: ודף פה.]

[עי' תוספות תענית יב: ותוס' נדה סג. ד"ה נים]

מגילה דף כא. ברכות דף ט. זבחים דף נז:

מכילתא דר"י פרשה כא

[לעיל ע:]

[עי' תוס' לעיל עח: ד"ה כל]

לעיל דף פה:

רבינו חננאל

היכי דמי נתנמנמו אמר רב אשי נים ולא נים תיר ולא תיר כגון דקרי ליה ועני ולא ידע לאהדורי סברא וכי מדכרי ליה מדכר. אביי הוה יתיב קמיה דרבא חזייה דהוה קא מנמנם אמר ליה מינם קא ניים מר אמר ליה מתנמנומי קא מנמנם ונתנמנמו יאכלו תנן: **הפסח** אחר חצות מטמא את הידים אלמא חצות הוה ליה נותר מאן תנא אמר רב יוסף ר' אלעזר בן עזריה הוא דתניא ואכלו את הבשר בלילה הזה כתיב הכא בלילה הזה וכתיב התם ועברתי בארץ מצרים בלילה הזה מה להלן עד חצות שנא' כחצות הלילה אף כאן נמי עד חצות: **אמר** רבא לא (יאכל) [אכל] מצה בזמן הזה אלא לאחר חצות לר' אלעזר בן עזריה לא יצא ידי אכילת מצה פשיטא כיון דאתקיש לפסח שנא' על מצות ומרורים יאכלוהו כפסח דמי מהו דתימא אפקה קרא מהקישא דפסח שנאמר בערב תאכלו מצות קמ"ל דכי אהדריה קרא למלתיה קמייתא כלומר לדוכתיה אהדריה עד חצות כפסח ואע"ג דר' עקיבא פליג עליה כותיה קיימא לן דסתם מתני' כותיה: **הפיגול** והנותר מטמאין את הידים רב הונא ורב חסדא חד אמר משום חשדי כהונה שלא יגע בו הכהן למלטלו ויחשדו אותו הכהנים כי לאכלו מטלטלו לפיכך גזרו בו טומאה שלא יגע בו כלל וחד אמר משום עצלי כהונה כלומר גזרו עליו טומאה מפני שנתעצלו הכהנים באכילתו ובא לידי נותר:

הגהות הב"ח

(א) גמ' אמר לו ר"ע והלא כבר נאמר בחפזון:

עין משפט נר מצוה

קז א מיי' פ"ו מהלכות מצה הלכה א סמג עשין מ:

קח ב מיי' פ"ז מהל' מצה הלכה יד:

קט ג מיי' פ"ו מהלכות מצה הל' א סמג שם טוש"ע א"ח סי' תעה סעיף ז:

קי ד מיי' פ"ח מהל' מצה הלכה יד ופ"ח מהל' קרבן פסח הל' יד סמג עשין רכו טוש"ע א"ח סי' תעח סעיף ב:

בראשונה לא לא מיבעיא קאמר לא מיבעיא בראשונה דקאכיל לתיאבון אבל באחרונה דילמא אתי למיכל אכילה גסה אימא לא קמ"ל מר זוטרא מתני הכי אמר רב יוסף אמר רב יהודה אמר שמואל מפטירין אחר המצה אפיקומן נימא מסייע ליה אין מפטירין אחר הפסח אפיקומן אחר הפסח דלא אבל אחר מצה מפטירין לא מיבעיא קאמר לא מיבעיא אחר מצה דלא נפיש טעמיה אבל לאחר פסח אימא לא קמ"ל מיתיבי הסופגנין והדובשנין והאיסקריטין אדם ממלא כריסו מהן ובלבד שיאכל (אכילת) כזית מצה באחרונה באחרונה אין בראשונה לא לא מיבעיא קאמר לא מיבעיא בראשונה דקאכיל לתיאבון אבל באחרונה דאתי למיכלה אכילה גסה אימא לא קמ"ל: אמר רבא *מצה בזמן הזה דאורייתא ומרור דרבנן ומאי שנא מרור דכתיב על מצות ומרורים (א) בזמן דאיכא פסח יש מרור ובזמן דליכא פסח ליכא מרור מצה נמי הא כתיב על מצות ומרורים (ב) מצה מיהדר הדר ביה קרא בערב תאכלו (ג) מצות *ורב אחא בר יעקב אמר אחד זה ואחד זה דרבנן אלא הכתיב בערב תאכלו מצות ההיא *מיבעי ליה לטמא ושהיה בדרך רחוקה דס"ד אמינא כיון דפסח לא אכלי מצה ומרור נמי לא ניכול קמ"ל ורבא אמר לך טמא ושהיה בדרך רחוקה לא צריך קרא דלא גרעי מערל ובן נכר דתניא כל ערל לא יאכל בו *בו אינו אוכל אבל אוכל במצה ומרור ואידך *כתיב בהאי וכתיב בהאי *צריכי תניא כוותיה דרבא ששת ימים תאכל מצות וביום השביעי עצרת לה' אלהיך *מה שביעי רשות אף ששת רשות מאי טעמא הוי דבר שהיה בכלל ויצא מן הכלל ללמד לא ללמד על עצמו יצא אלא ללמד על הכלל כולו יצא יכול אף לילה הראשון רשות תלמוד לומר על מצות ומרורים יאכלוהו אין לי אלא בזמן שבית המקדש קיים בזמן שאין בית המקדש קיים מנין ת"ל בערב תאכלו מצות הכתוב קבעו חובה: **מתני'** ישנו מקצתן יאכלו כולן לא יאכלו ר'

בראשונה לא. דאין אדם רשאי לאכול כלום אחר מצת חובה: מה שביעי רשות. דכתיב וביום השביעי עצרת דלא כתיב תאכלו מצות שהרי הוציאו מן הכלל אף ששת ימים רשות שאם רוצה יכול לאכול בשר בלא לחם או להתענות: **מתני'** כולם לא (ד) יאכלו. אם התחילו לאכול פסחים וישנו ועדיין לא אכלו כל פסחם לא יאכלו דנראין כאוכלי פסחם בשתי *חבורות או בזמן הזה שאין פסח אם ישנו כולם: **גמ'** עד

רשב"ם

בראשונה לא. דאין אדם רשאי לאכול כלום אחר מצת חובה: מצה בזמן הזה דאורייתא. לילה הראשון חובה: ההיא מבעי ליה לטמא ושהיה בדרך רחוקה. ובזמן שביהמ"ק קיים: כתיב בהאי וכתיב בהאי וצריכא. דטמא ושהיה בדרך רחוקה לא יליף מערל ובן נכר דהא אית ליה תשלומין לפסח שני הלכך לא יאכל מצה בראשון עד שיעשה פסח שני ויקיים על מצות ומרורים יאכלוהו אבל ערל ובן נכר דין הוא שיאכלו מצה בראשון דהא לא אכלי בשני ואי לא כתב רחמנא בערב תאכלו מצות הוה מוקמי לה בערל ובן נכר משום דלית ליה תשלומין אבל טמא ודרך רחוקה דאית להו תשלומין לא ליחייבו בראשון הלכך כתב רחמנא טמא ושהיה בדרך רחוקה: שביעי רשות. דכתיב וביום השביעי עצרת ולא כתיב תאכל מצות שהרי הוציאו מן הכלל: אף ששת ימים רשות. שאם רצה לאכול בשר בלא לחם או להתענות הרשות בידו: הוי דבר שהיה בכלל. דכתיב שבעת ימים תאכל מצות ויצא מן הכלל בהאי קרא דששת ימים כתיב ללמד שהיא רשות ולא ללמד על עצמו בלבד יצא אלא ללמד על הכלל כולו דהיינו ז' ימים דו אחת מי"ג מדות שהתורה נדרשת בהן מהכא שמעינן דמצה בזמן הזה דאורייתא ומרור דרבנן דהא תניא כוותיה דרבא וקיימא לן נמי כר' יוחנן דאמר דאין אוכלין אחר מצת חובה שבאחרונה כלום שלא ליבטל טעם מצה מפיה אבל שתיית יין לא מבטלה דשתיה לא מבטלא אכילה מיניה: **מתני'** ישנו כולן לא יאכלו. אם התחילו לאכול פסחן וישנו לא יאכלו דנראה כאוכל פסחו בב' מקומות דמאחר שישנו הסיחו דעתן לאכול עוד וחשיב ליה תנא כאכילת שני מקומות וחומרא בעלמא הוא וליכא לפרושי משום דדמי לאכילת שתי חבורות משום דאם כן קשיא סתמא אסתמא דהא בכילד צולין (לעיל דף פו.) סתם לן כר' יהודה דפסח נאכל בשתי חבורות אבל אין האוכל אוכל בשני מקומות הלכך טעמא דמתני' משום אכילת שני מקומות והוא הדין נמי במצה בזמן הזה לאחר שהתחיל לאכול מצת חובה באחרונה וישן הפסק אכילה היא ושוב לא יאכל משום דעבידא זכר לפסח בזמן שבית המקדש קיים וכן מוכיח בגמרא דאפילו בזמן הזה מיירי תנא וליכא לפרושי טעמו משום דאין מפטירין אחר מצה אפיקומן דאם כן תקשי לאידך לישנא דאמרינן מפטירין אמאי לא אותביניה מיניה לעיל: רבי

באחרונה אין בראשונה לא. פי' בראשונה בלא אחרונה לא כגון דלית ליה אלא כזית מצה ותו לא דטוב לאוכלו על השובע ולהיות טעם מצה בפיו אבל ודאי אי אית ליה מצה לכל סעודתו טוב לו לאכול מצה בתחלה לתיאבון ולברך עליה ואח"כ בגמר סעודתו יאכל כזית מצה ויהיה טעם מצה בפיו ועיקר מצוה על הראשונה שהיא באה לתיאבון וגם יהא לבסוף טעם מצה בפיו באותו כזית אחרון ואפילו אם עיקר מצוה באחרונה אין זה תימה אם אנו מברכין על הראשונה כדי לפטור המצה של אחרונה שהרי אין לברך על האחרונה משום שלאחר שמילא כריסו הוא אבל יכול הוא לברך על הראשונה ותיפטר האחרונה שהיא עיקר המצוה כדפרישית לעיל* לרב חסדא גבי תרי טיבולי דמרור וכן צ"ל להלל שהיה כורך מצה ופסח בסוף הסעודה והכי הוי אכיל מצה דאורייתא אם כן בתחלת סעודה היה מברך על המצה ואוכל דמועלת אותה ברכה לברכת מצה עם הפסח שבסוף ומיהו להאי פירוש' דלעיל דלרב חסדא בעי לחזור על שאר ירקות לטיבול ראשון כדי שיברך על המרור בטיבול שני א"כ ה"נ יחזור כמו כן על הסופגנין לאכול בתחלה כדי שיברך על אכילת מצה לבסוף מיהו לפי' אחר שגם לרב חסדא אין צריך לחזור על שאר ירקות אלא מברך על המרור בטיבול ראשון ובאותה ברכה יצא בטיבול שני ה"נ יברך על מצה דמתחלה ויצא בשל מצות מצה שלבסוף: **מפטירין** אחר מצה אפיקומן. וא"ת אחר הפסח מאי טעמא אין מפטירין הא נפיש טעמיה טפי ממצה יש לומר כדמפרש בירושלמי דמשום הכי נאכל על השובע שלא יבא לידי שבירת עצם וכתיב (שמות יב) ועצם לא תשברו בו ומש"ה אין אוכלין שום דבר וא"ת הא במנחה נמי אמרי' בתמורה (דף כג.) ובמנחות (דף כא:) דנאכלת על השובע וליכא למימר האי טעמא י"ל דהתם ה"ט שלא יצא משלחן רבו רעב אבל במצה לא שייך האי טעמא דלאו משלחן רבו הויא כולי האי וחגיגה הבאה עם הפסח אע"ג דאיכא למ"ד* דאית בה משום שבירת עצם ואפ"ה אינה נאכלת על השובע היינו משום דפסח° בן שנתו הוא ורכיך וחיישינן לשבירת עצם אבל חגיגה לא ומאן דאמר אין מפטירין אחר מצה ופסח אם כן לא ס"ל כטעם הירושלמי אלא סבר דבעינן שיהא טעם מצה ופסח בפיו: **כל** בן נכר לא יאכל בו בו אינו אוכל. אין לפרש בו אינו חייב לאכול דהא ודאי חייב לאכול דהא חייב בכל המצות אלא שאינו רוצה ונראה לפרש דמיירי בישראל מומר בשעת שחיטה וחזר ועשה תשובה וקאמר אף על גב דישראל מעליא הוא כיון שלא נמנה עליו בשעת שחיטה שוב אינו אוכל בו אבל אוכל הוא במצה ובמרור וערל היינו שמתו אחיו מחמת מילה וחייב בכל המצות ומקיים כולן אלא שאינו בפסח ובפרק מי שהיה טמא (לעיל דף צו.) גרס תרוייהו כל ערל לא יאכל בו כל בן נכר לא יאכל בו למה לי ומשני צריכי דאי אתמר ערל משום דמאיס כו' לכאורה משמע דאיצטריך גופיה דקרא ולא נהירא דלמה לי צריכותא אפילו דמו להדדי לגמרי וכי מזהירין מן הדין פשיטא דתרוייהו צריכי למכתב אלא אדיוקא דקראי קאי דדייקינן בו הוא דאינו אוכל אבל אוכל הוא במצה ובמרור קיימא הך צריכותא והכי מיפרשא התם צריכא דאי אשמעינן כלומר תרוייהו צריכי לדיוקא דקרא אבל אוכל הוא במצה ובמרור דאי אשמעינן ערל משום דלבו לשמים אבל בן נכר אימא לא ואי אשמעינן בן נכר משום דלא מאיס אבל ערל אימא לא ואף על גב דגמרא לא קאמר הכי ליכא למיחש שלא בא להשמיענו אלא שחלוקים זה מזה והוי כאילו צריכי לגופייהו ודכוותה אשכחן בפ"ק דב"ק (דף ג.) גבי ושלח דמשמע שן ומשמע רגל כו': (שייך לעיל) **רב** אחא בר יעקב אמר אחד זה ואחד זה מדרבנן. ל"ע בההיא סוגיא דפרק כל שעה (לעיל דף כח:) דמשמע בין לר' יהודה בין לר"ש סבירא להו דאי דאורייתא *מר נפקא לן מעליו מדכתיב שבעת ימים תאכל עליו מצות דעליו של פסח הוא חייב לאכול מצות ומר נפקא לן מבערב תאכלו מצות כדרבא וצ"ל דההיא פלוגתא אליבא דרבא ולא כרב אחא בר יעקב ומ"מ תימה דרבי יהודה מצריך קרא לטמא ושהיה בדרך רחוקה וערל ובן נכר כסברת רב אחא בר יעקב דלית הילכתא כוותיה והא קיימא לן *כרבי יהודה לגבי רבי שמעון: מלה

רבינו חננאל

באחרונה ש"מ אין מפטירין אחר מצה אפיקומן ודחי' דלמא לעולם מפטירין וה"ק בראשונה דלתאבון קא אכיל(זה) לה למצה ודאי נפיק אלא אפי' באחרונה דאיכא למימר דלמא אתא למיכל למצה אכילה גסה קמ"ל: **מר** זוטרא מתני להא דשמואל מפטירין אחר מצה אפיקומן לימא מתני' מסייע ליה אין מפטירין אחר הפסח אפיקומן כו': **אמר** רבה מצה בזמן הזה דאורייתא מרור מדרבנן מאי שנא מרור דכתיב על מצות ומרורים יאכלוהו בזמן דאיכא פסח איכא מרור והאידנא דליכא פסח אמרור נמי לא איחייב אי הכי אמצה נמי דהא על מצות ומרורים כתיב מרור דומיא דמצה ופרקי' לא מצה הדר אהדרה קרא בערב תאכלו מצות הכתוב קבעו חובה אע"ג דליכא פסח רב אחא בר יעקב אמר אחד מצה ואחד מרור בזמן הזה דרבנן. תניא כותיה דרבא ששת ימים תאכל מצות וביום השביעי עצרת מה שביעי רשות אף ששי נמי רשות מאי טעמא שביעי הוה ליה דבר שהיה בכלל ויצא מן הכלל שנאמר ששת ימים תאכל מצות וביום השביעי ללמד לא ללמד על עצמו יצא אלא ללמד על הכלל כל ויצא שאכילה (פסח) [מצה] באלו הימים רשות יכול אף לילה הראשון רשות ת"ל על מצות ומרורים אין לי אלא בזמן שבית המקדש קיים אין בית המקדש קיים מנין ת"ל בערב תאכלו מצות הכתוב קבעו חובה וקיימא לן כרבה במצה דאורייתא ומרור בזמן הזה דרבנן: **מתני'** ישנו מקצתן יאכלו כלן לא יאכלו נתנמנמו יאכלו

הגהות הב"ח

(א) גמרא ומרורים יאכלוהו בזמן דאיכא: (ב) שם ומרורים יאכלוהו מצה מיהדר: (ג) שם הדר ביה קרא בערב תאכלו: נ"ב ע"ש בתוס' פ"ק דקידושין דף לז ע"ב ד"ה מושב ובזה בזמן משמע דגרסינן הכא קרא דבכל מושבותיכם תאכלו מצות וע"ש וכן הקשו תוס' לעיל דף כח ע"ב: (ד) רש"י ד"ה כולם לא וכו' אם ישנו כולם אחר שני כוסות הראשונים שלאחר הסידור לכוסות האחרונים הפסק סעודה הוא לא יאכלו הס"ד:

גליון הש"ס

תוס' ד"ה מפטירין וכו' דפסח בן שנתו הוא ורכיך. עי' תשובות מהר"ח או"ז סימן כ"ב:

at the end. [This implies], only at the end, [120a] but not at the beginning![8]—[No:] He proceeds to a climax. [If he eats it] at the beginning it goes without saying [that his duty is discharged], since he eats it with an appetite; but at the end, [where] he may come to eat it as mere gorging, I might say that he does not [do his duty]. Hence he [the Tanna] informs us [otherwise].

Mar Zuṭra recited it thus: R. Joseph said in Rab Judah's name in Samuel's name: One may conclude after the unleavened bread [by saying] 'Now to the entertainment.' Shall we say that this supports him: ONE MAY NOT CONCLUDE AFTER THE PASCHAL MEAL [BY SAYING], 'NOW TO THE ENTERTAINMENT'; hence one may not conclude thus [only] after the Paschal lamb, yet one may conclude thus after the unleavened bread?—[No:]—he proceeds to a climax. After the unleavened bread it need not be stated, seeing that its taste is not substantial; but I would say [that it is] not so after the Paschal lamb; hence [the Tanna] informs us [otherwise]. An objection is raised: [As for] sponge-cakes, honey-cakes, and *iskeriṭin*, a man may fill his stomach therewith, providing that he eats as much as an olive of unleavened bread at the end. Thus it is only at the end, but not at the beginning?—He proceeds to a climax: at the beginning, when he eats with an appetite, it is unnecessary [to teach it]; but at the end, where he may merely gorge, I might say [that it is] not [permitted]; hence [the Tanna] informs us [that it is].

Raba said: [The eating of] unleavened bread nowadays is a Scriptural obligation, whereas [that of] bitter herbs is Rabbinical. Yet wherein do bitter herbs differ? Because it is written, *they shall*
a *eat it* [the Passover-offering] *with unleavened bread and bitter herbs,*[1] [which implies], when [the law of] the Passover-offering is in force, [that of] bitter herbs is in force, and when the Passover-offering is not in force, bitter herbs are not required either! Then in the case of unleavened bread too, surely it is written, *'they shall eat it with unleavened bread and bitter herbs'?*—Scripture indeed repeated [the precept] in the case of unleavened bread: *at even ye shall eat unleavened bread.*[2] But R. Aḥa b. Jacob maintained: Both the one and the other are [only] Rabbinical. But surely it is written, *'at even ye shall eat unleavened bread'?*—That is required in respect of
b an unclean person and one who was on a journey afar off.[1] For you might argue: Since they cannot eat of the Passover-offering, they need not eat unleavened bread or bitter herbs either; hence [the verse] informs us [otherwise]. And Raba?[2]—He can answer you: In respect of an unclean person and one who was on a journey afar off a verse is not required, for they are no worse than an uncircumcised person and an alien.[3] For it was taught: *No uncircumcised person shall eat thereof:*[4] *'thereof'* he may not eat, but he must eat unleavened bread and bitter herbs. And the other?[5]—It is written in the case of the one [the uncircumcised etc.] and it is written in the case of the other [the unclean etc.], and they are both necessary.[6]

It was taught in accordance with Raba: *Six days thou shalt eat unleavened bread, and on the seventh day shall be a solemn assembly to the Lord thy God:*[7] just as [on] the seventh day [the eating of unleavened bread] is voluntary,[8] so [on] the six days it is voluntary. What is the reason?[9] Because it is something which was included in the general law and then excluded from the general law, in order to illumine [other cases], [which means that] it was excluded not in order to throw light upon itself, but in order to throw light upon the entire general law.[10] You might think that on the first night too it is [merely] voluntary; therefore it is stated, *'they shall eat it with unleavened bread and bitter herbs.'* I know this only when the Temple is in existence; whence do we know it when the Temple is not in existence? From the verse, *'at even ye shall eat unleavened bread'*: thus the Writ made it a permanent obligation.

c *MISHNAH.* IF SOME OF THEM[1] FELL ASLEEP, THEY MAY EAT [WHEN THEY AWAKE]; IF ALL OF THEM FELL ASLEEP

(8) And the presumed reason is because nothing may be eaten after the last unleavened bread.

a (1) Num. IX, 11. (2) Ex. XII, 18. BaḤ (on the basis of Tosaf. in Ḳid. 37b) suggests that the following verse should be quoted instead: *in all your habitations shall ye eat unleavened bread* (ibid. 20).

b (1) But who will be fit by the evening. (2) Does he not admit this? and if he does, on what grounds does he differentiate between unleavened bread and bitter herbs? (3) I.e., one who does not observe Jewish law; v. *supra*, 28b, n. b5. (4) Ex. XII. 48. (5) R. Aḥa b. Jacob: how does he answer this? (6) An unclean person etc. cannot be deduced from an 'alien,' for since the former will observe the second Passover a month hence, I would argue that he can *then* discharge his obligation of eating unleavened bread and bitter herbs too. But an 'alien' will not have that opportunity, and therefore he is naturally bound to eat the unleavened bread and the bitter herbs now. By the same reasoning, if there were only one verse, I would apply it to the latter, but not to the former. (7) Deut. XVI, 8. (8) But not obligatory. (9) Why do I interpret it thus, seemingly in contradiction to the literal meaning? (10) This is a principle of exegesis. Now the general rule is stated: *seven days shall ye eat unleavened bread* (Ex. XII, 15); when the seventh is excluded by the verse, *'six days'* etc., this throws light not on the seventh alone, but upon the whole period, teaching that the eating of unleavened bread therein is voluntary.

c (1) *Sc.* of a company at a Passover meal.

We learned elsewhere: Where it is the practice [119b] to repeat,[13] he must repeat; to recite it once only,[14] he must recite them once only; to pronounce a blessing after it [*sc.* the *Hallel*], he must pronounce a blessing upon it: it all depends on local custom. Abaye observed: This was taught only [about a blessing] after it, but a blessing before it is obligatory, for Rab Judah said in Samuel's name: A blessing must be recited for all religious duties before ['*ober*] they are performed. How is it implied that '*ober* connotes priority?—Said R. Naḥman b. Isaac: Because it is written, *Then Ahimaaz ran by the way of the Plain, and overran* [wa-ya'abor, i.e., ran
a before] *the Cushite*.[1] Abaye said: [It follows] from this: *And he himself passed over* ['abar] *before them*.[2] Others quote the following: *And their king is passed on* [wa-ya'abor] *before them, and the Lord at the head of them*.[3]

It was taught: Rabbi repeated [certain] verses of it[4] [*sc. Hallel*]; R. Eleazar b. Perata added passages[5] to it. What did he add? Said Abaye: He added [passages] for repetition from '*I will give thanks to thee*' and onwards.

R. 'Awira lectured, sometimes stating it in R. Ammi's, sometimes in R. Assi's name: What is meant by, *And the child grew, and was weaned* [wa-yiggamel]?[6] The Holy One, blessed be He, will make a great banquet for the righteous on the day He manifests [*yigmol*] His love to the seed of Isaac.[7] After they have eaten and drunk, the cup of Grace[8] will be offered to our father Abraham, that he should recite Grace, but he will answer them, 'I cannot say Grace, because Ishmael issued from me.' Then Isaac will be asked, 'Take it and say Grace.' 'I cannot say Grace,' he will reply, 'because Esau issued from me.' Then Jacob will be asked: 'Take it and say Grace.' 'I cannot say Grace,' he will reply, 'because I married two sisters during [both] their lifetimes, whereas the Torah was destined to forbid them to me.' Then Moses will be asked, 'Take it and say Grace.' 'I cannot say Grace, because I was not privileged to enter Eretz Yisrael either in life or in death.' Then Joshua will be asked: 'Take it and say Grace.' 'I cannot say Grace,' he will reply, 'because I was not privileged to have a son,' for it is written, *Joshua the son of Nun;*[9] *Nun his son, Joshua his son*.[10] Then David will be asked: 'Take it and say Grace.' 'I will say Grace, and it is fitting for me to say Grace,' he will reply, as it is said, *I will lift up the cup of salvation, and call upon the name of the Lord*.[11]

MISHNAH. ONE MAY NOT CONCLUDE AFTER THE PASCHAL MEAL [BY SAYING], 'NOW TO THE ENTERTAINMENT!
b [APIKOMAN].'[1]

GEMARA. What does APIKOMAN mean? Said Rab: That they must not remove from one company to another.[2] Samuel said: E.g., mushrooms for myself and pigeons for Abba.[3] R. Ḥanina b. Shila and R. Joḥanan said: E.g., dates, parched ears of corn, and nuts. It was taught as R. Joḥanan: You must not conclude after the Paschal meal with e.g., dates, parched ears, and nuts.

Rab Judah said: One may not conclude after the [last] unleavened bread [is eaten][4] by saying, 'Now to the entertainment!' We learned: YOU MAY NOT CONCLUDE AFTER THE PASCHAL MEAL [BY SAYING], 'NOW TO THE ENTERTAINMENT!' Thus it is forbidden only after the Paschal meal, but you may conclude [thus] after the unleavened bread?—He proceeds to a climax:[5] After the unleavened bread it need not be stated, since its taste is not substantial;[6] but [I might think] that there is no objection after the Paschal lamb, whose taste is substantial and cannot [easily] be wiped out. Hence he [the Tanna] informs us [otherwise].

Shall we say that this supports him: [As for] sponge cakes, honey-cakes and *iskeriṭin*,[7] a man may fill his stomach with them, providing that he eats as much as an olive of unleavened bread

(13) Certain verses at the end of *Hallel*, viz., Ps. CXVIII, 21-29. Every verse of the rest of the Psalm is repeated in the text, either actually or by parallelism, and therefore these four verses are repeated when they are recited. (14) Lit., 'to (say it) straight off.'

a (1) II Sam. XVIII, 23. (2) Gen. XXXIII, 3. (3) Mic. II, 13. (4) [Rashi (Suk. 39a): 'from "We beseech thee, O Lord, etc." onwards.'] (5) [I.e., to those repeated by Rabbi (Rashi loc. cit.)]. (6) Gen. XXI, 8: the verse continues: *And Abraham made a great feast on the day that Isaac was weaned*. (7) I.e., when Israel is vindicated and his glories restored. (8) The cup of wine over which Grace after meals is recited. (9) Num. XIV, 38 *et passim*. (10) I Chron. VII, 27. This occurs in the genealogical lists, and since it is not carried beyond Joshua, we must assume that he was not blessed with a son. (11) Ps. CXVI, 13.

b (1) ἐπικώμιον. (2) V. *supra* 86a for notes. (3) I.e., Rab. Rab and Samuel used to eat pigeons and mushrooms respectively after the meal, as dessert, and Samuel says that this must not be done after the Paschal meal. Thus his interpretation (and R. Joḥanan's which follows) is stricter than Rab's. For Rab only forbids further eating elsewhere, whereas Samuel forbids it in the same place. (4) I.e., nowadays at the end of the meal in memory of the Paschal lamb. (5) Lit., 'he says, "it is unnecessary".' (6) He must finish the meal with the taste of the Paschal lamb and the unleavened bread predominant in his mouth. Now the taste of the latter is not substantial and enduring, and therefore it is superfluous to teach that nothing may be eaten after it. (7) V. *supra* 37a. These are regarded as 'rich *mazzah*' and therefore the duty of eating *mazzah*, which must be 'bread of affliction (poverty)' cannot be discharged with them.

קה א מיי' פ"ג מהל' הטובה הלכה יא טוש"ע א"ח סימן תכב סעיף ג:

קו ב ג מיי' פ"ח מהל' חמץ ומצה הלכה ט סמג עשין מא טוש"ע א"ח סי' תעח סעיף א:

*לכפול יכפול לפשוט יפשוט לברך אחריו יברך הכל כמנהג המדינה אמר אביי *לא שנו אלא לאחריו אבל לפניו [מצוה] לברך *דא"ר יהודה אמר שמואל כל המצות מברך עליהן עובר לעשייתן *מאי משמע דהאי עובר לישנא דאקדומי הוא א"ר נחמן בר יצחק דכתיב °וירץ אחימעץ דרך הככר ויעבור את הכושי אביי אמר מהכא °והוא עבר לפניהם איכא דאמרי מהכא °ויעבור מלכם לפניהם וה' בראשם תניא *רבי כופל בה דברים רבי אלעזר בן פרטא מוסיף בה דברים מאי מוסיף אמר אביי מוסיף לכפול מאודך למטה דרש רב עוירא זימנין א"ל משמיה דרב* וזימנין א"ל משמיה דרב (אשי) מאי דכתיב °ויגדל הילד ויגמל עתיד הקב"ה לעשות סעודה לצדיקים ביום שיגמל חסדו לזרעו של יצחק לאחר שאוכלין ושותין נותנין לו לאברהם אבינו כוס של ברכה לברך ואומר להן איני מברך שיצא ממני ישמעאל אומר לו ליצחק טול וברך אומר להן איני מברך שיצא ממני עשו אומר לו ליעקב טול וברך אומר להם איני מברך שנשאתי שתי אחיות בחייהן שעתידה תורה לאוסרן עלי אומר לו למשה טול וברך אומר להם איני מברך שלא זכיתי ליכנס לארץ ישראל לא בחיי ולא במותי אומר לו ליהושע טול וברך אומר להן איני מברך שלא זכיתי לבן דכתיב יהושע בן נון °נון בנו יהושע בנו אומר לו לדוד טול וברך אומר להן אני אברך ולי נאה לברך שנאמר °כוס ישועות אשא ובשם ה' אקרא: **מתני'** *אין מפטירין אחר הפסח אפיקומן: **גמ'** מאי אפיקומן אמר רב שלא יעקרו מחבורה לחבורה ושמואל אמר כגון *אורדילאי לי וגווליא לאבא ורב חנינא בר שילא ורבי יוחנן (אמר) כגון תמרים קליות ואגוזים תניא כוותיה דרבי יוחנן אין מפטירין אחר הפסח כגון תמרים קליות ואגוזים אמר רב יהודה אמר שמואל *אין מפטירין אחר מצה אפיקומן תנן אין מפטירין אחר הפסח הוא דלא אבל לאחר מצה מפטירין לא מיבעיא קאמר לא מיבעיא אחר מצה דלא נפיש טעמיה אבל לאחר הפסח דנפיש טעמיה ולא מצי עבוריה לית לן בה קמשמע לן נימא מסייע ליה *הסופגנין והדובשנין והאיסקריטין אדם ממלא כריסו מהן ובלבד שיאכל כזית מצה באחרונה אין בראשונה

אבל לפניו מצוה לברך. לפי מה שפירש לעיל דהפסוקים לא הוו הפסק וברכה האחרונה היא חתימת הראשונה לא יתכן כאן דאיך יברך לפניו ולא יחתום אחריו מהר"י: **אמר** רב שלא יעקרו מחבורה לחבורה. רב מוקי למתניתין כדר' יהודה דסבר דאין הפסח נאכל בשני מקומות והכי אוקימנא שמעתא פרק כילד צולין (לעיל ד' פו:) שתי חבורות שהיו אוכלות בבית אחד אלו הופכין פניהם ואוכלין ואלו הופכין פניהם ואוכלין והשמש באמצע פירוש משום היכרא וכשהשמש עומד למזוג קופץ את פיו עד שמגיע אצל חבורתו ומוקי לה בגמרא כרבי יהודה והיינו דוקא בפסח אבל מצה לא אשכחן בשום דוכתא דליתסר בשתי מקומות ואי משום דהתקש לפסח נהא על כרחיך לא איתקש דאי לא תימא הכי ליפרך ממתני' לרב דאין מפטירין אחר הפסח אפיקומן הא אחר מצה מפטירין ולא מצי לשנויי כדמשני לשמואל דלגבי שני מקומות לא הוי רבותא פסח טפי ממצה אלא ודאי רב לא איירי אלא בפסח והא דקאמרינן לקמן אביי הוה יתיב קמיה דרבה והוה קא מנמנם פי' הקונטרס לקמן אע"ג דלא הוי בזמן הפסח הא איתקש מצה לפסח ולא נהירא ובירושלמי מפרש לה גבי תענית דאמרינן פ"ק דתענית ישן אסור לאכול ולא שם אלא ישן ממש אבל מתנמנם לא ורבה הוה מתנמנם ובעי למיסר בתר הכי וקמייתי ראיה מפסח דכי היכי דפסח לא חשיב נמנום בעלמא כשינה מעליא לענין שני מקומות ה"נ לא חשיב נמנום לענין תענית דלמחר לאיתסורי באכילה בתר הכי: באחרונה

לכפול. כל ההלל: כופל דברים. מעט היה כופל כגון מברוך הבא ולמטה: נון בנו וגו'. ממשפחת אפרים בן יוסף חשיב ואזיל עד יהושע ולא משכח ברא ליהושע: **מתני'** מפטירין. לשון *הנפטר מחבירו כשנפטרין מן הסעודה מביאין מיני המתיקה: **גמ'** אורדילאי לי. כגון אני שרגיל לאכול כמהין ופטריות לאחר סעודתי: וגוזליא לאבא. לרב שהיה רגיל לאכול גוזלים לאחר סעודתו ולשון אפיקומן הוציאו והביאו מיני מתיקה: אין מפטירין אחר מצה אפיקומן. שצריך לאכול מצה בגמר הסעודה זכר למצה הנאכלת עם הפסח וזו היא מצה הבלועה שאנו אוכלין באחרונה לשם חובת מצה אותה שלאחר אכילה ועל כרחינו אנו מברכין על אכילת מצה בראשונה (אע"פ שאינה) באה לשם חובה כדאמר רב חסדא לעיל (דף קטו:) גבי מרור דלאחר שמילא כריסו הימנו היאך חוזר ומברך עליו הכי נמי גבי מצה הלכך(א) תרווייהו מברך ברישא והדר אכיל מצה באחרונה בלא ברכה אבל לא מרור דלאו חובה הוא: בראשונה

רשב"ם

לכפול. את ההלל: כופל בה דברים. מעט היה כופל מברוך הבא ולמטה: מאודך ולמטה ולי נראה משום כבוד ישי ושמואל ודוד ואחיו שאמרוהו מאודך ולמטה כדאמרן לעיל כופלין אותו ויש לשונות אחרות ולא נהירא: ולא במותי. שנקבר מול בית פעור ולא זכו עצמותיו ליכנס בארץ כעצמות יוסף שנקברו בארץ כדכתיב (יהושע כד) ואת עצמות יוסף קברו בשכם והיינו דכתיב (דברים ד) כי אנכי מת בארץ הזאת בהולה לארץ אינני עובר את הירדן אפילו לאחר מיתה לא יעברו עצמותי את הירדן: נון בנו יהושע בנו. ממשפחת אפרים חשיב בדברי הימים עד יהושע ולא משכח קרא ברא ליהושע: **מתני'** מפטירין. לשון הנפטר מחבירו כלומר כשנפטרין מן הסעודה אין מסיימין אותה באפיקומן ובגמרא מפרש: **גמ'** אמר רב שלא יעקרו מחבורה לחבורה. אחר שאכלו הפסח בחבורה לא ילכו בחבורה אחרת לאכול לא פת ולא שום דבר גזירה דילמא אתי למיכל את הפסח בשני מקומות והכן תנן סתמא כר"י בכילד צולין (לעיל דף פו:) דפסח נאכל בשתי חבורות ואין האוכל אוכל הפסח בשני מקומות והך מילתא דרב אוקמיה התם בשעת אכילה אבל לאחר אכילה יכול ליעקר לומר הלל בחבורה אחרת ולא קפיד אלא לאכול בב' מקומות אבל לאכול דברים אחרים במקומן הראשון שרי רב ובלבד שלא יעקור לאוכלן עם חבורה אחרת והיינו דפליג עליה שמואל ורבי יוחנן ואמרי כל דבר אסור לאכול אפילו בחבורתו ראשונה וליכא לפרושי שלא יעקרו מחבורה לחבורה דלאחר שאכלו קצת מן הפסח לא יאכלו ממנו בחבורה אחרת דהא סתם לן תנא בכילד צולין (שם) וכשהשמש עומד למזוג קופץ את פיו עד שמגיע אצל חבורתו ותרי כתמי למה ולרב הכי משמע ליה אפיקו מנייכו הוציאו כליכם מכאן ונלך ונאכל במקום אחר: כגון אורדילאי לי וגוזליא לאבא. לרב דשמואל הוה רגיל לאכול בקינוח סעודה כמהין ופטריות ורב רגיל לאכול אחר סעודתו גוזלות ולשון אפיקומן הוציאו והביאו מיני מתיקה ואתא שמואל למימר דלא מיבעיא שלא יעקור מחבורתו לחבורה אחרת אלא אפילו בחבורתו אסור לאכול כלום אחר הפסח שלא יאבד ממנו טעם הפסח ולפי שדינו ליאכל בסוף על השבע וכן כל קרבנות כדכתיב (במדבר יח) למשחה לגדולה כדרך שהמלכים *אוכלין: אבא. כך שמו של רב אלא בכבוד קורין אותו רב בבבל הכי כמו שקורין לרבי יהודה הנשיא בארץ ישראל רבינו וכן מוכיח בשחיטת חולין (דף קלז:) דאמרי' מאן ריש סידרא בבבל אבא אריכא וברב מיירי שהיה רב ארוך בדורו כדאמרינן במסכת נדה (דף כד:) ורבי יוחנן כשמואל סבירא ליה אלא שהיה רגיל באלו בקינוח סעודה: אין מפטירין אחר המצה אפיקומן. שצריך לאכול מצה בגמר סעודתו זכר למצה הנאכלת עם הפסח בכריכה וזו היא מצה הבלועה שאנו אוכלין באחרונה לשם חובה ועל כרחינו אנו מברכין על אכילת מצה בראשונה אע"פ שאינה לשם חובה כדאמר רב חסדא לעיל *גבי מרור דלאחר שמילא כריסו ממנו היאך חוזר ומברך עליו הלכך מברך אתרווייהו ברישא והדר אכיל מצה באחרונה ואחר אותה מצה אין נפטרין ממנה באכילת דבר אחר שלא לשכח טעמה ובמצה בזמן הזה מיירי דליכא פסח בהדה דאי בזמן דאיכא פסח הא בהדיא תנן אין מפטירין אחר הפסח אפיקומן והיינו אחר פסח ומצה הנאכלת עמו: אחר הפסח הוא דלא· אכיל בזמן דאיכא פסח דאין אוכלין אפיקומן אחר הפסח והמצה שעמו: אחר מצה. בלא פסח מפטירין: סופגנין. רקיקין העשויין כספוג מתוך שעיסתן רכה אין תורת לחם עליהן והכן בעינן לחם דכתיב (דברים טז) לחם עוני: דובשנין. מטוגנין בשמן ודבש ואיט לחם עוני אלא לחם עשיר: בראשונה

הגהות הב"ח

(א) רשב"ם ד"ה אין מפטירין וכו' הלכך תרווייהו כו':

רבינו חננאל

לכפול יכפול לפשוט יפשוט לברך אחריו יברך · תניא ר' כופל בה דברים מאי היא מוסיף לכפול מאודך ולמטה: ענין שגומל הקב"ה חסד לזרע יצחק אחר שאוכלין ושותין אומר [לו] לאברהם טול ברך אומר איני מברך שיצא ממני ישמעאל וכו' עד נותנין לדוד ואומר אני אברך ולי נאה לברך שנא' כוס ישועות אשא וגו': אין מפטירין אחר הפסח אפיקומן מאי אפיקומן רב אמר שלא יעקרו מחבורה זו ויאכלו פסח בחבורה אחרת ושמואל אמר שלא יאכלו אחר הפסח אפילו באותה חבורה כגון קליות ואגוזים וכיוצא בהם וכל שכן בשר וכיוצא בו שמפיגין מתוך פיהם ומפכחין טעמו של פסח · תניא כותיה דרבי יוחנן אין מפטירין אחר הפסח אפיקומן כגון קליות ואגוזין: אמר רב יוסף אמר רב יהודה אמר שמואל אין מפטירין אחר מצה אפיקומן ואקשי' עליה והא אנן לא תנן אלא אין מפטירין אחר הפסח הא אחר מצה מפטירין ופרקי' לא מיבעיא קאמר לא מיבעיא מצה דלא נפיש טעמה ואתי טעמא דהני לפכוחי דכצה אלא פסח דנפיש טעמיה ולא אתו הני מפכחי טעמיה איצא מפטירין אחר הפסח קמ"ל דאין מפטירין · נימא מסייע ליה הסופגנין והדובשנין והאסקריטין אדם ממלא כריסו מהם ובלבד שיאכל כזית מצה באחרונה דייקי' מינה מדקתני באחרונה

זה המכיר מקום חבירו בישיבה. שיודע לומר זה מקום מיושב לפלוני וזה של פלוני דהואיל ומכיר הוא מקום כולם רגיל הוא לישב שם תמיד: סתרי תורה. מעשה מרכבה ומעשה בראשית: למנצח. מדלא כתיב לנצח משמע שנותן כח לבריות לנצחו: מפני מדת הדין. שמקטרגת ואומרת לא תקבלם והוא מקבלם בסתר: לולי משה בחירו. אלמא משתבח ביה קרא במשה וקרי ליה בחירו משום דהשיב חמתו מהשחית אלמא שמח הוא בכך: כמצודה זו. שפורסים לעופות לצוד ואין בה דגן ואין עוף נפנה אליה: מלחמתו של זרח במצרים גמרא אבל מלחמת זרח באסא קראי: ושיגרו להדרימון.

תורה אור

זה המכיר מקום חבירו בישיבה איכא דאמרי אמר ר"א זה המקבל פני חבירו בישיבה מאי למכסה עתיק (יומין) זה המכסה דברים שכיסה עתיק יומין ומאי נינהו סתרי תורה ואיכא דאמרי זה המגלה דברים שכיסה עתיק יומין מאי נינהו טעמי תורה אמר רב כהנא משום רבי ישמעאל ברבי יוסי מאי דכתיב °למנצח מזמור לדוד זמרו למי שנוצחין אותו ושמח בא וראה שלא כמדת הקב"ה מדת בשר ודם בשר ודם מנצחין אותו ועצב אבל הקב"ה נוצחין אותו ושמח שנאמר °ויאמר להשמידם לולי משה בחירו עמד בפרץ לפניו אמר רב כהנא *משום רבי ישמעאל בר' יוסי אמר ר"ש בן לקיש משום רבי יהודה נשיאה מאי דכתיב °וידי אדם מתחת כנפיהם ידו כתיב זה ידו של הקדוש ברוך הוא שפרוסה תחת כנפי החיות כדי לקבל בעלי תשובה *מיד מדת הדין אמר רב יהודה אמר שמואל כל כסף וזהב שבעולם יוסף ליקטו והביאו למצרים שנאמר °וילקט יוסף את כל הכסף הנמצא אין לי אלא שבארץ מצרים ושבארץ כנען בשאר ארצות מנין תלמוד לומר °וכל הארץ באו מצרימה וכשעלו ישראל ממצרים העלוהו עמהן שנאמר °וינצלו את מצרים *רב אסי אמר עשאוה כמצודה זו שאין בה דגן רבי שמעון *אמר כמצולה שאין בה דגים והיה מונח עד רחבעם בא שישק מלך מצרים ונטלו מרחבעם *שנאמר °ויהי בשנה החמישית למלך רחבעם עלה שישק מלך מצרים [על ירושלים] ויקח את אוצרות בית ה' ואת אוצרות בית המלך בא זרח מלך כוש ונטלו משישק בא אסא ונטלוהו מזרח מלך כוש ושיגרו *להדרימון בן טברימון באו בני עמון ונטלום *מהדרימון בן טברימון בא יהושפט ונטלו מבני עמון והיה מונח עד אחז בא סנחריב ונטלו מאחז בא חזקיה ונטלו מסנחריב והיה מונח עד צדקיה באו כשדיים ונטלוהו מצדקיה באו פרסיים ונטלוהו מכשדיים באו יוונים ונטלוהו מפרסיים באו רומיים ונטלוהו מיד יוונים ועדיין מונח ברומי: *אמר רבי חמא (*בר) חנינא שלש מטמוניות הטמין יוסף במצרים אחת נתגלה לקרח ואחת נתגלה לאנטונינוס בן אסוירוס ואחת גנוזה לצדיקים לעתיד לבא °עושר שמור לבעליו לרעתו אמר רבי שמעון בן לקיש זו עשרו של קרח (*שנאמר) °ואת כל היקום אשר ברגליהם א"ר אלעזר זה ממונו של אדם שמעמידו על רגליו *א"ר לוי משאוי שלש מאות פרדות לבנות היו מפתחות בית גנזיו של קרח וכולהו אקלידי וקליפי דגלדא: (דיא"ש אדי"ש כשד"ך מאוד"ך סימן) א"ר שמואל בר נחמני א"ר יונתן °אודך כי עניתני אמר דוד אבן מאסו הבונים היתה לראש פנה אמר ישי מאת ה' היתה זאת אמרו אחיו זה היום עשה ה' אמר שמואל אנא ה' הושיעה נא אמרו אחיו אנא ה' הצליחה נא אמר דוד ברוך הבא בשם ה' אמר ישי ברכנוכם מבית ה' אמר שמואל אל ה' ויאר לנו אמרו כולן אסרו חג בעבותים אמר שמואל אלי אתה ואודך אמר דוד אלהי ארוממך אמרו כולן: *תנן התם מקום שנהגו לכפול

כמצודה שאין בה דגן. דרך צידי עופות להטיל דגן במצודה ודריש וינצלו ויצולו כי למ"ד מתחלפת בדל"ת במקומות הרבה: אבל

מלך ארם לעזור לו על בעשא מלך ישראל וקראי ניהו ומלחמת יהושפט בעמונים קראי ודרך הראשונים להביא גנזיהם עמהם במלחמתם כדי שימשך לבם אחר ממונם ולא יברחו: שמעמידו על רגליו. שמשמח לבו: אקלידי. מפתחות: וקולפי. פותחות שקורין בלעז שרדור"א: דגלדי. של מרצופים של עור שעושים על סוסים וחמורים וגמלים: אבן מאסו הבונים. כלומר דוד שמימיו רועה צאן היה ונעשה ראש ונפלאת בעיניהו לשון רבים אמרו אחיו: זה היום עשה ה'. שמואל היה מתנבא עליהם שסופן לגיל ולשמוח שיושעם מיד אויביהם: הושיעה נא אמרו אחיו. כלומר על ידי דוד ודוד אמר הצליחה נא שיצליח במלכותו: ברכנוכם אמר שמואל. שיברך כולם כלומר מברכין אנו אתכם: לנו. לשון רבים: אסרו חג בעבותים. הביאו זבחים ושלמים הרבה לשמוח לכפול

רשב"ם

זה המכיר מקום חבירו בישיבה. שיודע לומר זה מקום פלוני וזה מקום פלוני דהואיל ומכיר מקום חבירו רגיל הוא לישב תמיד שם: עתיק יומין. זה הקדוש ברוך הוא דכתיב (דניאל ז) ועתיק יומין יתיב: סתרי התורה. מעשה המרכבה ומעשה בראשית ופירושו של פסוק כדכתיב (שמות ג) זה שמי לעלם והמכסה היינו שאינו מוסר אותם לכל אדם אלא למי שלבו דואג כדאמרינן בפרק אין דורשין (חגיגה דף יג.) זה המגלה דברים שכיסן עתיק יומין והכי משמע למכסה סתרי תורה שהיו מכוסין מתחלה ועתיק יומיא גילן ונתן רשות לגלותן ומי שמגלה אותן זוכה למה שאמור בפסוק זה: למנצח. לשון מפעיל מדלא כתיב לנוצח משמע שנותן גילוי לבריותיו שינצחוהו: לולי משה בחירו. אלמא קרי ליה בחירו משום דעומד בפרץ לפניו ומדמשבח ביה משמע שמח הוא בכך: מפני מדת הדין. שמקטרגת ואומרת לא תקבלם והוא מקבלם בסתר: גבי מצודה גרסינן דגן שדרך ליתן דגן במצודה שפורסין לפני העופות כשאין בה דגן אין עוף נפנה אליה גבי מצולה דהיינו מים גרסינן דגים: וינצלו. דרשינן לשון מצודה: מלחמתו של זרח במצרים גמרא אבל מלחמתו של זרח באסא קראי בד"ה (ב יד): ושיגרו להדרימון. מלך ארם שיעזור לו על בעשא מלך ישראל וקראי ניהו (שם ג טז): באו בני עמון ונטלוהו כו' · גמרא מלחמת יהושפט בעמונים קראי ודרך הראשונים להביא גנזיהם עמם במלחמתם כדי שימשך לבם אחר ממונם ולא יברחו וכשהן מנוצחין הנוצחין נוטלים ממונן: מלחמת סנחריב באחז קראי חזקיהו נטלו מסנחריב כשבא המלאך והכה המחנה: כשדיים תפשו את צדקיהו. פרסיים קבלו המלכות מכשדים דכתיב (דניאל ה) פריסת מלכותך ויהיבת למדי ופרס ויוונים קיבלו המלכות מפרסיים מפורש בספר יוסיפון וגם רומיים שקיבלו המלכות מיוונים מפורש שם ובפ"ק דע"ז (דף ה:): זה עשרו של קרח. שעל ידי רוב ממונו נתגאה ונטרד מן העולם: משוי שלש מאות · לאו דוקא וכן כל שלש מאות שבש"ס: אקלידי. מפתחות: וקולפי. פותחות: דגלדי. מרצופין של עור ולפ"כ היה משוי שלש מאות פרדות: אבן מאסו הבונים. זה דוד שהיה צעיר באחיו ורועה: נפלאת בעינינו. לשון רבים אמרו אחיו: זה היום עשה ה'. שמואל היה מתנבא עליהם שסופן לגיל ולשמוח בו שיושעם מאויביהם: הצליחה נא אמר דוד. שיצליח במלכותו: אסרו חג בעבותים. הביאו זבחים ושלמים הרבה לשמוח ומתן דמן למזבח: לכפול

רבינו חננאל

לפני ה' זה המקבל פני חבירו בישיבה: וידי אדם מתחת כנפיהם ידו כתיב ידו של הקב"ה שהיא פשוטה לקבל שבים מפני מדת הדין כל אלו דברים פשוטין הן: ענין כל כסף שבעולם לקטו יוסף והביאו לפרעה כשעלו ישראל ממצרים נטלוהו שעשו מצרים כמצולה שאין בה דגן איכא דאמרי כמצודה: בא שישק נטלו מרחבעם בא זרח נטלו משישק וכו' · ואת כל היקום אשר ברגליהם זו עשרו של אדם שמעמידו על רגליו א"ר לוי משאוי שלש מאות פרדות היו מפתחות גנזיו של קרח וכלהו אקלידי קלפי דגילדאי: אמר רבי יונתן אודך כי עניתני אמר דוד אבן מאסו הבונים אמר ישי מאת ה' היתה זאת אמרו אחיו זה היום עשה ה' אמר שמואל: תנן התם מקום שנהגו לכפול

[משום רבי ישמעאל בר' יוסי ורבנן אמרי]

[בן לקיש כצ"ל וכן איתא בברכות ט: וכ"א בילקוט]

[ת"ע מהדרימון]

[ת"ע בר']

[בסנהדרין ליתא תיבת שנאמר]

—Said R. Eleazar: [119a] They who recognize their colleagues' place in the academy. Others state, R. Eleazar said: They who welcome their colleagues in the academy.[2] What does *'and for stately clothing'* [li-mekasseh 'athiḳ][3] mean? That refers to him who *'conceals'* [mekasseh] the things which the Ancient [*'athiḳ*] of days[4] concealed. And what is that? The secrets of the Torah.[5] Others explain: That refers to him who reveals the things which the Ancient of days concealed [*kissah*]. And what is it? The reasons of the Torah.[6]

R. Kahana said on the authority of R. Ishmael b. R. Jose: What is meant by, *'For the leader* [la-menaẓẓeaḥ]: *a Psalm of David?*[7] Sing praises to Him who rejoices when they conquer Him.[8] Come and see how the character of the Holy One, blessed be He, is not like that of mortal man. The character of mortal man is such that when he is conquered he is unhappy, but when the Holy One is conquered He rejoices, for it is said, *Therefore He said that He would destroy them, had not Moses His chosen stood before Him in the breach,* [*to turn back His wrath*].[9]

R. Kahana said on the authority of R. Ishmael son of R. Jose, and our Rabbis said in the name of R. Judah Nisi'ah:[10] What is implied by the verse, *And they had the hands of a man under their wings?*[11] *Yado* [his hand] is written:[12] this refers to the Hand of the Holy One, blessed be He, which is spread out under the wings of the *Ḥayyoth,*[13] in order to accept penitents [and shield them] from[14] the Attribute of Justice.[15]

Rab Judah said in Samuel's name: All the gold and silver in the world Joseph gathered in and brought to Egypt, for it is said, *And Joseph gathered up all the money that was found* [*in the land of Egypt,*
a *and in the land of Canaan*].[1] Now I know it only about that of Egypt and Canaan; whence do we know it about that of other countries? Because it is stated, *And all the countries came unto Egypt* [*to Joseph to buy corn*].[2] And when the Israelites migrated from Egypt they carried it away with them, for it is said, *and they despoiled the Egyptians.*[3] R. Assi said: They made it like a trap in which there is no corn;[4] R. Simeon b. Laḳish said: Like a pond without fish.[5] Thus it [the treasure] lay until Rehoboam, when Shishak king of Egypt came and seized it from Rehoboam, for it is said, *And it came to pass in the fifth year of king Rehoboam, that Shishak king of Egypt came up against Jerusalem; and he took away the treasures of the house of the Lord, and the treasures of the king's house.*[6] Then Zerah, king of Ethiopia, came and seized it from Shishak; then Assa came and seized it from Zerah king of Ethiopia and sent it to Hadrimon the son of Tabrimon. The Ammonites came and seized it from Hadrimon the son of Tabrimon. Jehoshaphat came and seized it from the Ammonites, and it remained so until Ahaz, when Sennacherib came and took it from Ahaz. Then Hezekiah came and took it from Sennacherib, and it remained thus until Zedekiah, when the Babylonians [Chaldeans] came and seized it from Zedekiah. The Persians came and took it from the Chaldeans; the Greeks came and took it from the Persians; the Romans came and took it from the Greeks, and it is still lying in Rome.

R. Ḥama son of R. Ḥanina said: Three treasures did Joseph hide in Egypt: one was revealed to Korah; one to Antoninus the son of Severus;[7] and the third is stored up for the righteous for the future time.

Riches kept by the owner thereof to his hurt:[8] R. Simeon b. Laḳish said: This refers to Korah's wealth. *And all the substance that was*
b *at their feet:*[1] R. Eleazar said: This refers to a man's wealth, which puts him on his feet. R. Levi said: The keys of Korah's treasure-house were a load for three hundred white mules,[2] though all the keys and locks were of leather.[3]

(Mnemonic: *DiYASh, ADYiSh, KaShDeK, me-Odeka*)[4] R. Samuel b. Naḥmani said in R. Jonathan's name: *I will give thanks unto Thee, for Thou hast answered me*[5] was said by David; *The stone which the builders rejected is become the chief corner-stone;*[6] by Yishai [Jesse]; *This is the Lord's doing,*[7] by his brothers; *This is the day which the Lord hath made*[8] by Samuel. *We beseech Thee, O Lord, save now!*[9] was said by his brothers: *We beseech Thee, O Lord, make us now to prosper!* by David; *Blessed be he that cometh in the name of the Lord,*[10] by Jesse; *We bless you out of the house of the Lord,*[10] by Samuel; *The Lord is God, and hath given us light,*[11] by all of them; *Order the festival procession with boughs,* by Samuel; *Thou art my God, and I will give thanks unto Thee,*[12] by David; *Thou art my God, I will exalt Thee,* by all of them.

(2) I.e., who treat them in a friendly fashion. Maharsha: who are among the earliest, so that they can greet their colleagues who arrive later. (3) This completes the verse. (4) God; v. Dan. VII, 13. (5) Esoteric teaching, which was to be confined to the few. (6) It is meritorious to investigate the reasons of Scriptural laws. (7) This is the superscription of a number of psalms; *menaẓẓeaḥ* is derived from *naẓẓeaḥ*, to be victorious. (8) I.e., prevail upon Him to rescind intended punishment. *La-menaẓẓeaḥ* is now understood in a causative sense: to Him who makes men victorious. (9) Ps. CVI, 23. (10) The Prince. I.e., R. Judah II,—The text is as emended in the margin. (11) Ezek. I, 8. (12) Instead of *yede*, the hands of. (13) Lit., 'living creatures'—the angels that bore the Divine Chariot, as described in Ezek. I. (14) Var. lec.: on account of. (15) Justice, Mercy, etc., are often hypostasized.

a (1) Gen. XLVII, 14. (2) Ibid. XLI, 57. (3) Ex. XII, 36. (4) To attract the birds. Bird-traps were set with corn. [*Aliter:* Like a fortress without corn (provisions). Var. lec.: like a net without fish.] (5) Var. lec. (v. *D.S.*): like husks without grain. (6) I Kings XIV, 25f. (7) On his identity v. Sanh., 91a, n. 7. (8) Eccl. V, 12.

b (1) Deut. XI, 6. (2) This of course is not to be taken literally. (3) Instead of metal, so as to be light in weight, yet they were such a load. (4) *D* = David; *Y* = *Yishay* (Jesse); *A* = *Eḥaw* (his brothers); *Sh* = *Shemuel* (Samuel); *K* = *kulan* (all of them); *me-Odeka* = on the passage commencing *Odeka, 'I will give thanks unto Thee'*. (5) Ps. CXVIII, 21. (6) Ibid. 22. (7) Ibid. 23. (8) Ibid. 24. (9) Ibid. 25. (10) Ibid. 26. (11) Ibid. 27. (12) Ibid. 28.

go down and cool it within [118b] and heat it without,[3] and will thus perform a double miracle.[4] Said the Holy One, blessed be He, to him, 'Go down.' It was then that Gabriel commenced [with praise] and said, '*And the truth of the Lord endureth for ever.*'

R. Nathan said: It was the fish in the sea who said, '*and the truth of the Lord endureth for ever,*' this being in accordance with R. Huna. For R. Huna said: The Israelites of that generation [*sc.* of the Egyptian exodus] were men of little faith, and as Rabbah b. Mari expounded: What is taught by the verse, *But they were rebellious at the sea, even at the Red Sea?*[5] This teaches that in that moment the Israelites were rebellious and said: Just as we ascend at one side [of the sea] so do the Egyptians ascend from another. Whereupon the Holy One, blessed be He, ordered the Prince of the Sea,[6] 'Spue them forth on to the dry land.' Said he to Him, 'Sovereign of the Universe! Does a master make a gift to his servant and then take it back from him!' 'I will give you one and a half times their number,' He replied. 'Sovereign of the Universe,' he pleaded, 'can a servant claim [a debt] from his Master!' 'Let the brook of Kishon be surety for Me,' He answered. Straightway he spued them forth on to the dry land, and Israel came and saw them, as
a it is said, *and Israel saw the Egyptians dead on the sea-shore.*[1]

What is [this allusion to] 'one and a half times their number'? For in the case of Pharaoh it is written, [*and he took*] *six hundred chosen chariots,*[2] whereas in the case of Sisera it is written, [*And Sisera gathered . . .*] *nine hundred chariots of iron.*[3] When Sisera came [to fight Israel] he advanced against them with iron staves. Thereupon the Holy One, blessed be He, brought forth the stars out of their orbits against them, as it is written, *The stars in their courses fought against Sisera.*[4] As soon as the stars of heaven descended upon them they heated those iron staves; so they went down to cool them and to refresh themselves in the brook of Kishon. Said the Holy One, blessed be He, to the brook of Kishon, 'Go and deliver your pledge.' Straightway the brook of Kishon swept them out and cast them into the sea, as it is said, *The brook Kishon swept them away, that ancient brook.*[5] What does '*that ancient brook*' mean? The brook that became a surety in ancient times. In that hour the fish in the sea opened [their mouths] and exclaimed, '*and the truth of the Lord endureth for ever.*'

R. Simeon b. Laḳish said, What means '*Who maketh the barren woman* ['aḳereth] *to dwell in her house*'?[6] The congregation of Israel said before the Holy One, blessed be He, 'Sovereign of the Universe! Thy sons have made me like a weasel that dwells in the vaults ['*iḳare*][7] of houses.'[8]

Raba lectured, What means, *I love that the Lord should hear* [*my*
b *voice and my supplications*]?[1] The congregation of Israel said: Sovereign of the Universe! When am I loved by Thee? When Thou hearest the voice of my supplications. *I was brought low* [dallothi], *and He saved me.*[2] The congregation of Israel spoke before the Holy One, blessed be He, Sovereign of the Universe! Though I am poor [*dallah*] in religious deeds, yet I am Thine, and it is fitting that I should be saved.

R. Kahana said: When R. Ishmael son of R. Jose fell sick, Rabbi sent to him: Tell us two or three things which you have said to us in your father's name. He sent back to him, Thus did my father say: What is meant by the verse, *O praise the Lord, all ye nations:*[3] What business have the nations of the world here?[4] This is its meaning: '*O praise the Lord, all ye nations*' for the mighty and wondrous deeds which He wrought for them; all the more we, since '*His mercy is great toward us.*' Furthermore [he sent word to him]: Egypt is destined to bring a gift to the Messiah. He will think not to accept it from them, but the Holy One, blessed be He, will instruct him, 'Accept it from them: they furnished hospitality to My children in Egypt.' Immediately, '*Nobles shall come out of Egypt* [*bringing gifts*].[5] Then Ethiopia shall argue with herself: If those [the Egyptians] who enslaved them are thus [treated], how much the more we, who did not enslave them! At that the Holy One, blessed be He, shall bid him: 'Accept it from them.' Straightway, '*Ethiopia shall hasten to stretch out her hands unto God.*'[6] Then shall the wicked Roman State argue with herself: If those who are not their brethren are thus [accepted], how much the more we, their brethren.[7] But the Holy One, blessed be He, will say to Gabriel: *Rebuke the wild beast of the reeds* [ḳaneh]; *the multitude of* ['adath] *the bulls:*[8] rebuke the wild beast [Rome] and take thee possession [*ḳeneh*] of the congregation ['*edah*].[9] Another interpretation: *rebuke the wild beast of the reeds,* i.e., that dwells among the reeds, as it is written, *The boar out of the wood doth ravage*
c *it, that which moveth in the field feedeth on it.*[1] R. Ḥiyya b. Abba interpreted it in R. Joḥanan's name: Rebuke the wild beast all of whose actions may be recorded with the same pen.[2] '*The multitude of the bulls* [abbirim], *with the calves of the people*':[3] that means that they slaughtered the valiant [*abbirim*] like calves which have no owners.[4] '*Everyone opening his hand with the desire of money*':[5] they stretch out their hand to accept the money, but do not carry out its owners' wishes. '*He hath scattered the people that delight in approaches*': what caused Israel to be scattered among the nations? The approaches [to the nations] which they desired.[6]

He also sent to him: There are three hundred and sixty five thoroughfares in the great city of Rome, and in each there were three hundred and sixty five palaces; and in each palace there were three hundred and sixty five storeys,[7] and each storey contained sufficient to provide the whole world with food.[8] R. Simeon b. Rabbi asked Rabbi—others say, R. Ishmael son of R. Jose asked Rabbi—For whom are all these [other storeys]?—For you, your companions and acquaintances, as it is said, *And her gain and her hire shall be holiness to the Lord; it shall not be stored nor treasured; for her gain shall be for them that dwell before the Lord.*[9] What does '*it shall not be stored*' mean?—R. Joseph learned: '*It shall not be stored*' refers to a storehouse [granary]; '*nor treasured,*' to a
d treasure house.[1] What means '*for them that dwell before the Lord*'?

(3) To burn those who threw them into it; cf. Dan. III, 22. (4) Lit. 'a miracle within a miracle.' (5) Ps. CVI, 7. (6) According to ancient beliefs the sea, like the elements in general, were in charge of particular angels.

a (1) Ex. XIV, 30. (2) Ibid. 7. (3) Judg. IV, 13. (4) Ibid. V, 20. (5) Ibid. 21. (6) Ps. CXIII, 9. (7) Lit., 'roots' 'foundations' hence 'vaults'. (8) The congregation of Israel is personified here as a woman, as often, and she complains that through the sins of her less worthy children she is ashamed of the daylight but must hide like the weasels in the dark vaults of houses.

b (1) Ps. CXVI, 1. (2) Ibid. 6. (3) Ibid. CXVII, 1. (4) Why should *they* praise God because '*His mercy is great toward us*' (ibid. 2)? (5) Ps. LXVIII, 32. (6) Ibid. (7) Rome was always identified with Edom, the state built by Esau's descendants; v. Gen. XXXV, 1. (8) Ps. LXVIII, 31. (9) I.e., Israel.

c (1) Ps. LXXX, 14. *Ḳaneh* is now interpreted as the cane reeds of the forest, the boar (or, swine) being Rome. This interpretation is probably connected with the legend that when Solomon married Pharaoh's daughter an angel planted a large reed in the sea whereon Rome was built (Midrash Rabbah on Cant. 1, 6). (2) *Ḳaneh* is now connected with the same word meaning feather, quill.—All their activities are of the same nature—evil to Israel. (3) Ps. LXVIII, 31. (4) To protect them. (5) Reading *mithrapes* as *mattir pas*—the letters are almost the same—opening the hand, and connecting *raẓe* with *raẓon*, desire; the money that is given to ensure the fulfilment of one's wishes. E.V.: *Every one submitting himself with pieces of silver.* (6) Maharsha retains the natural translation 'war': had they submitted to Nebuchadnezzar and Titus at the first and second Temples respectively, instead of desiring war, they would not have gone into exile. (7) מעלה means a stairway, and is probably to be understood as in the text. (8) Maharsha: The number three hundred and sixty five is symbolic, because the Gentiles depend on the solar year of three hundred and sixty five days. (9) Isa. XXIII, 18.

d (1) I.e., of gold and silver.

ואקדיה מבחוץ. לשרוף את הזורקים אותן לתוך האור דכתיב (דניאל ג) גובריא אילך די הסיקו לשדרך מישך ועבד נגו קטיל הימון שביבא דנורא: ואמת ה' לעולם. שקיים לי דברו ושמר לי הבטחתו שהבטיחני להציל מבני בניו של אברהם: שנתן לו רבו מתנה. פרנסה לדגים: ה"ג כיון דנחיתו כוכבי שמיא עלייהו נחיתו לאקורי נפשייהו בנחל קישון: ואמת ה' לעולם. שקיים לנו מתנותינו מחיל פרעה להתפרנס ממנו: שמוני בניך. מרוב הטלטם בגלות: כחולדה זו שדרה בעיקרי בתים. והיינו עקרת הבית: אומות העולם מאי עבידתייהו. לשבוחי משום דגבר עלינו חסדו הא עלן לשבוחי: אגבורות ונפלאות. דחזיתו שעשה לי: וקנה. עדת ישראל בין הקנים ביער: חזיר מיער. זה אדום שכתוב בה (שם ז) אכלה ומדקה ושארא ברגלה רפסה וזה דרכו של חזיר: שכל מעשיה נכתבים בקולמוס אחד. כלו' פה אחד להם להרע: מתרפס. מתיר פס פושט יד: ברצי. כלומר מתנים עם ישראל לעשות רצונם בשוחד שהם מקבלים ואין מקיימין דבריהם:

זה

רשב"ם

ואקדיה מבחוץ. לשרוף את הזורקין אותן לתוך האור כדכתיב גובריא אילך די הסיקו לשדרך וגו' עד קטיל הימון שביבא דנורא: פלוט אותן ליבשה. וניתנו לקבורה שם בזכות שאמרו (שמות יד) כי ה' נלחם להם במצרים והיינו דכתיב (שם טו) נטית ימינך תבלעמו ארץ שנשבע הקב"ה לארץ שלא תענש על קבורתן: שנותן לו רבו מתנה. פרנסה לדגים: כיון דנחיתו כוכבי שמיא עלייהו. נחיתו לאקורי נפשייהו בנחל קישון: *פתחו דגים. שבים: נחל קישון גרפם. לים כדכתיב (קהלת א) כל הנחלים הולכים אל הים: ואמת ה' לעולם. שקיים לנו מתנותינו מחיל פרעה להתפרנס ממנו: אמרה כנסת ישראל. הזקנים והחשובים שבהן אמרו על שאינם חשובים כל כך כדמשמע אם הבנים שהאם צועקת על הבנים ששמוה עקרת הבית: שמוני בניך. מרוב הטלטם בגלות: כחולדה זו הדרה בעיקרי בתים. והיינו עקרת הבית: אני אהובה לפניך. אהבתי משמע כמו אהבתני כלומר אהבת אותי: לי נאה להושיע. יותר מכל האומות שהרי ישראל ייחדוך: כשחלה רבי ישמעאל ברבי יוסי שלח לו כו'. בהרבה מקומות בש"ס מצינו ששלח לו רבי לרבי ישמעאל ברבי יוסי בחליו כן והדברים שהשיב לו כאן לא השיב לו פעם אחרת ושמא חלאים הרבה חלה רבי ישמעאל ובכל פעם ופעם שלח לו רבי והוא משיב לו אי נמי כולן השיבן בפעם אחת ובש"ס סידרן במסכתות כל אחת על מקומה: אומות העולם מאי עבידתייהו. לשבוחי משום דעלינו גבר חסדו הא עלן לשבוחיה: אגבורות ונפלאות. דחזינן שעשה בעולם וכל שכן אנו כי גבר עלינו חסדו יותר מכל אומה ולשון: יאתיו חשמנים. דורונות למלך המשיח

מן שמים נלחמו הכוכבי' ממסילותם. במקומן היו עומדים ורא[ש]ן מגיע עד לארץ וכן פירש"י בנימוקי מקרא ותימה למ"ד בפ' מי שהיה (לעיל דף נד:) כל העולם כולו תחת כוכב א' עומד האיך ירדו הכוכבים הלא מאחד נתמלא העולם וי"ל דלא איירי אלא בכוכבים של גלגל שהן מזלות קבועים אבל שאר כוכבים קטנים הם*:

כמעודה

ואקדיה מבחוץ ואעשה *נס בתוך נס אמר לו הקב"ה רד באותה שעה פתח גבריאל ואמר ואמת ה' לעולם ר' נתן אומר ואמת ה' לעולם דגים שבים אמרוהו כדרב הונא דאמר רב הונא ישראל שבאותו הדור מקטני אמנה היו *וכדדרש רבה בר מרי מאי דכתיב °וימרו על ים בים סוף מלמד שהמרו ישראל באותה שעה ואמרו כשם שאנו עולין מצד אחד כך מצריים עולים מצד אחר אמר לו הקב"ה לשר של ים פלוט אותן ליבשה אמר לפניו רבש"ע כלום יש עבד שנותן לו רבו מתנה וחוזר ונוטל ממנו אמר לו אתן לך אחד ומחצה שבהן אמר לו רבש"ע יש עבד שתובע את רבו אמר לו נחל קישון יהא לי ערב מיד פלט אותן ליבשה ובאו ישראל וראו אותן שנאמר °וירא ישראל את מצרים מת על שפת הים מאי אחד ומחצה שבהן דאילו בפרעה כתיב °שש מאות רכב בחור ואילו בסיסרא כתיב °תשע מאות רכב ברזל כי אתא סיסרא [אתא עלייהו בדקרי דפרזלא הוציא הקב"ה עליהם כוכבים ממסילותם דכתיב] °מן שמים נלחמו הכוכבים כיון דנחיתו כוכבי שמים עלייהו אקדירו הני דקרי דפרזלא נחיתו לאקרורי למיסחי נפשייהו בנחל קישון אמר לו הקב"ה לנחל קישון לך והשלם ערבונך מיד גרפם נחל קישון והשליכן לים שנאמר °נחל קישון גרפם נחל קדומים מאי נחל קדומים נחל שנעשה ערב מקדם באותה שעה פתחו דגים של ים ואמרו ואמת ה' לעולם אמר רבי שמעון בן לקיש מאי דכתיב °מושיבי עקרת הבית אמרה כנסת ישראל לפני הקב"ה רבש"ע שמוני בניך* כחולדה זו הדרה בעיקרי בתים: דרש רבא *מאי דכתיב °אהבתי כי ישמע ה' אמרה כנסת ישראל רבש"ע אימת אני אהובה לפניך בזמן שתשמע קול תחנוני דלותי ולי יהושיע אמרה כנסת ישראל לפני הקב"ה רבש"ע אע"פ שדלה אני במצות לך אני ולי נאה להושיע אמר רב כהנא כשחלה רבי ישמעאל בר' יוסי שלח לו ר' אמור לנו שנים ושלשה דברים שאמרת לנו משום אביך שלח לו כך אמר אבא מאי דכתיב °הללו את ה' כל גוים אומות העולם מאי עבידתייהו ה"ק הללו את ה' כל גוים אגבורות ונפלאות דעביד בהדייהו כל שכן אנו דגבר עלינו חסדו (אמר לו) ועוד *(חדא) עתידה מצרים שתביא דורון למשיח כסבור אינו מקבל מהם אמר לו הקב"ה למשיח קבל מהם אכסניא עשו לבניי במצרים מיד °יאתיו חשמנים מני מצרים נשאה כוש ק"ו בעצמה ומה הללו שנשתעבדו בהן כך אני שלא נשתעבדתי בהן לא כ"ש אמר לו הקב"ה קבל מהם מיד °כוש תריץ ידיו לאלהים נשאה מלכות [רומי] הרשעה ק"ו בעצמה ומה הללו שאין אחיהן כך אנו שאנו אחיהן לא כ"ש אמר לו הקדוש ברוך הוא לגבריאל °גער חית קנה גער חיה וקנה לך עדה דבר אחר געור חית קנה שדרה בין הקנים דכתיב °יכרסמנה חזיר מיער וזיז שדי ירענה *אמר רבי חייא בר אבא אמר רבי יוחנן געור בחיה שכל מעשיה נכתבין בקולמוס אחד °עדת אבירים בעגלי עמים ששחטו אבירים כעגלים שאין להם בעלים °מתרפס ברצי כסף שפושטין יד לקבל ממון ואין עושין רצון בעלים °*פיזר עמים קרבות יחפצון מי גרם להם לישראל שיתפזרו לבין אומות העולם קריבות שהיו חפצין בהן ועוד שלח לו ג' מאות וששים וחמשה שווקים בכרך גדול של רומי וכל אחד ואחד היו בו שלש מאות וששים וחמשה בירניות וכל בירנית ובירנית היו בו שלש מאות וששים וחמשה מעלות וכל מעלה ומעלה היו בו כדי לזון את כל העולם כולו אמר רבי *(ישמעאל) לרבי ואמרי לה *(לר' ישמעאל בר יוסי) הני למן לך ולחברך ולחברותך שנאמר °סחרה ואתננה קודש לה' לא יאצר ולא יחסן כי ליושבים לפני ה' יהיה וגו' מאי לא יאצר תני רב יוסף לא יאצר זה בית אוצר ולא יחסן זה בית גניזה מאי כי ליושבים לפני ה' אר"א

זה

לירושלים כדכתיב לעיל מיניה מהיכלך על ירושלים לך יובילו מלכים שי: געור חיה. אומה הרשעה: וקנה לך עדה. ישראל ואית דמפרשי מצרים וכוש דכתיב אבירים ולא נהירא דסתם עדה ישראל: קנה. דריש לשון קנים: בין הקנים. ביער דחזיר ביער זו אדום שכתוב בה אכלה ומדקה ושארא ברגלה רפסה זה דרכו של חזיר: נכתבין בקולמוס אחד. כלומר כולן פה אחד להרע לישראל אם בא ישראל לדין לפניהם כולן מחייבין אותו מדכתיב קנה ולא כתיב קנים משמע קולמוס אחד: בעגלי עמים. עגלים של כל העולם הפקר שאין לה בעלים: מתרפס. מתיר פס פושט יד: ברצי. כלומר מהנין עם ישראל לעשות רצונם בשוחד שהן מקבלין ואין מקיימין דבריהן: בירניות. מגדלים: לחברותך. לחברי חבירך: בית אוצרותיהן. של תירוש דגן ויצהר: ולא יחסן. לשון חוסן זה בית גנזיהן של כסף וזהב הגנוזין וטמונים בחוזק ובחוסן:

זה

רבינו חננאל

לכבשן האש ועניין חנניה מישאל ועזריה שהפילן נבוכדנצר לכבשן האש ועניין וימרו על ים בים סוף ישראל שבאותו הדור קטני אמנה היו אמרו כשם שאנו עולין מצד זה כך המצרים עולו מן הצד האחר וכו': **אמרה** כנסת ישראל אע"פ שדלה אני מן המצות לי נאה להושיע אהבתי כי ישמע ה' הללו את ה' כל גוים וכל שכן אנו דגבר עלינו חסדו ועניין יאתיו חשמנים מני מצרים למלך המשיח לא יאצר ולא יחסן כי ליושבים

ה"ג רביעי גומר עליו את ההלל ואומר עליו הלל הגדול: שהקדוש ברוך הוא יושב ברומו של עולם כו' · דכתיב הודו לאל השמים נותן לחם לכל בשר והיינו דבר גדול: עשיר בשורו. מפסידו ממון [ומכפר] על גופו: קשין נקביו של אדם. כשהוא עצור כיום המיתה:

מאי ברכת השיר רב יהודה אמר יהללוך. וקמ"ל דאפילו במקום שלא נהגו לברך אחריו בלילי פסח צריך לברך דאי נהגו פשיטא א"נ דאפילו במקום שנהגו ה"א דוקא בימים אבל בלילה אין צריך לברך קא משמע לן: **רבי** יוחנן אמר נשמת כל חי. נראה ה"פ אף נשמת כל חי אחר יהללוך דאי לא תימא הכי אנן כמאן עבדינן וקורא נשמת כל חי ברכת השיר לפי שבשבתות אומרים אותו אחר פסוקי דזמרה ורבינו חיים כהן לא היה חותם ביהללוך כי אם בנשמת לבדו משום דלישנא דברכת השיר משמע חדא ברכה: **מהודו** עד על נהרות בבל. וכן אנו עושים ורגנו לדיקים בה' אינו מן המזמור:

קג א ב ג מיי' פ"ח מהל' חו"מ הל' י' וסמג שם טוש"ע או"ח סימן תפ ·
קד ד מיי' פ"ו מהל' יו"ט הלכה יז:

רשב"ם

יהללוך. (*נשמת כל חי) וגומרין בו בא"י מלך מהולל בתשבחות וזו היא ברכת השיר דמתניתין כלומר ברכת השבח: ור' יוחנן אמר נשמת כל חי אף נשמת דהיינו ברכת השיר דמתני' דאילו יהללוך אנו אומרים בכל יום שאומרים בו את ההלל ומאי שנא ליל פסח דנקט אם לא להוסיף עוד ברכה אחרת והיינו דאמר הלכה כרבי יוחנן בתרוייהו וקבעוהו לאחר הלל הגדול שצריך לאומרן כדלקמן דהשתא איכא ברכה בכל חדא וחדא והכי הויא מילתא שפיר כך נראה בעיני: ה"ג ת"ר רביעי גומר עליו את ההלל ואומר עליו הלל הגדול: ה' רועי. על שם המזון שאכלו צריך לומר: שהקדוש ברוך הוא יושב ברומו של עולם כו'. דכתיב ביה נותן לחם לכל בשר והיינו דבר גדול: בטובתו. בטובה שהשפיע לו והכי משמע כי טוב כי לעולם חסדו חסד הוא עושה לעולם בכי טוב כלומר בטוב שנתן לו: עשיר בשורו עני בשיו. מפסידו ממון ומכפר על גופו: בעצבון. תרי משמע: כקריעת ים סוף. כלומר נס גדול עושה לו הקדוש ברוך הוא למי שנותן לו מזונות כאשר עשה לישראל שקרע להם ים סוף ונפקא מיניה למבעי רחמי: קשין נקביו של אדם · כשהוא עצור: צועה. לשון עצור וחגור כמו צועה ברב כחו (ישעיה סג): כל המבזה את המועדות. שעושה מלאכה בחולו של מועד דכתיב את חג המצות תשמור ונפקא לן במסכת חגיגה (דף יח·) איסור מלאכה בחולו של מועד: המקבל לשון הרע. שמקבלו ומאמינו על חבירו אע"ג דלקבוליה לא מיבעי ליה למיחש ליה מיבעי כדמפרש במסכת נדה (דף סא·): וקרי ביה לא תשיא. נראה בעיני דלא גרסינן ליה דכולהו משתמעי מלא תשא שכשמספר או מעיד הרי נושא בפיו שמע שוא: וכי מאחר דאיכא הלל הגדול · שמשובח יותר כמו שפירש רבי יוחנן למעלה משום דכתיב ביה נותן לחם לכל בשר אנן מאי טעמא אמרינן האי הלילא על כל פרק ופרק ועל כל צרה שלא תבא על הציבור כשנגאלין: חמשה דברים. דמיירי נמי בגאולה: ההרים רקדו כאילים. בשעת מתן תורה דכתיב (תהלים סח) למה תרצדון הרים וגו': גבריאל אמרו. כשניצולו חנניה מישאל ועזריה והוא היה שם דכתיב (דניאל ג) ורויה די רביעאה דמי לבר אלהין לפי שהקדוש ברוך הוא הבטיחו על כך כשנשלך אברהם באור כשדים וכשקיים לו אמר ואמת ה' לעולם שקיים הבטחתו: בשעה שהפיל נמרוד. שעל שם כן *נקרא אמרפל על שם שאמר והפיל את אברהם בכבשן ואקדיח

תורה אור

מאי ברכת השיר רב יהודה אמר *יהללוך ה' אלהינו ורבי יוחנן אמר בנשמת כל חי ת"ר רביעי גומר עליו את ההלל ואומר הלל הגדול דברי ר"ט וי"א °ה' רועי לא אחסר מהיכן הלל הגדול רבי יהודה אומר ג°מהודו עד °נהרות בבל ורבי יוחנן אומר משיר המעלות עד נהרות בבל רב אחא בר יעקב אמר °מכי יעקב בחר לו יה עד נהרות בבל ולמה נקרא שמו הלל הגדול א"ר יוחנן מפני שהקב"ה יושב ברומו של עולם ומחלק מזונות לכל בריה א"ר יהושע בן לוי הני עשרים וששה הודו כנגד מי כנגד כ"ו דורות שברא הקב"ה בעולמו ולא נתן להם תורה וזן אותם בחסדו *אמר רב חסדא מאי דכתיב °הודו לה' כי טוב הודו לה' שגובה חובתו של אדם בטובתו עשיר בשורו ועני בשיו יתום בביצתו אלמנה בתרנגולתה א"ר יוחנן קשין מזונותיו של אדם כפליים כיולדה דאילו ביולדה כתי' °בעצב ובמזונות כתי' °בעצבון* (א"ר) יוחנן קשין מזונותיו של אדם יותר מן הגאולה דאילו בגאולה כתיב °המלאך הגואל אותי מכל רע מלאך בעלמא ואילו במזונות כתיב °האלהים הרועה אותי א"ר יהושע בן לוי *בשעה שאמר הקב"ה לאדם °וקוץ ודרדר תצמיח לך זלגו עיניו דמעות אמר לפניו רבש"ע אני וחמורי נאכל באבוס אחד כיון שאמר לו °בזעת אפך תאכל לחם נתקררה דעתו אמר ר"ש בן לקיש אשרינו *אם עמדנו בראשונה ועדיין לא פלטינן מינה דקא אכלינן עיסבי דדברא אמר רב שיזבי משמיה דרבי אלעזר בן עזריה קשין מזונותיו של אדם כקריעת ים סוף דכתיב °נותן לחם לכל בשר וסמיך ליה לגוזר ים סוף לגזרים אמר ר"א בן עזריה *קשין נקביו של אדם כיום המיתה וכקריעת ים סוף שנאמר °מהר צועה להפתח וכתיב בתרי' רוגע הים ויהמו גליו *ואמר רב ששת משום ר"א בן עזריה °כל המבזה את המועדות כאילו עובד ע"ז שנאמר °אלהי מסכה לא תעשה לך וכתיב בתריה את חג המצות תשמור ואמר רב ששת משום ר"א בן עזריה כל המספר לשון הרע וכל המקבל לשון הרע וכל המעיד עדות שקר בחבירו ראוי להשליכו לכלבים שנאמר °לכלב תשליכון אותו וכתיב בתריה °לא תשא שמע שוא וקרי ביה לא תשיא וכי מאחר דאיכא הלל הגדול אנן מ"ט אמרינן האי משום שיש בו ה' דברים הללו יציאת מצרים וקריעת ים סוף ומתן תורה ותחיית המתים וחבלו של משיח יציאת מצרים דכתי' °בצאת ישראל ממצרים וקריעת ים סוף דכתיב °הים ראה וינוס מתן תורה דכתי' °ההרים רקדו כאילים תחיית המתים דכתיב °אתהלך לפני ה' חבלו של משיח דכתיב °לא לנו ה' לא לנו וא"ר יוחנן לא לנו ה' לא לנו זו שעבוד מלכיות איכא דאמרי אמר רבי יוחנן לא לנו ה' לא לנו זו מלחמת גוג ומגוג רב נחמן בר יצחק אמר מפני שיש בו °מילוט נפשות של צדיקים מגיהנם שנא' °אנה ה' מלטה נפשי חזקיה אמר מפני שיש בו ירידתן של צדיקים לכבשן האש ועלייתן ממנו ירידתן דכתיב לא לנו ה' לא לנו °אמר חנניה כי לשמך תן כבוד אמר מישאל על חסדך ועל אמיתך אמר עזריה למה יאמרו הגוים אמרו כולן עלייתן מכבשן האש דכתיב °הללו את ה' כל גוים אמר חנניה שבחוהו כל האומים אמר מישאל כי גבר עלינו חסדו אמר עזריה ואמת ה' לעולם הללויה אמרו כולן ויש אומרים ואמת ה' לעולם גבריאל אמרו בשעה שהפיל נמרוד הרשע את אברהם אבינו לתוך כבשן האש אמר גבריאל לפני הקדוש ברוך הוא רבש"ע ארד ואצנן ואציל את הצדיק מכבשן האש אמר לו הקב"ה אני יחיד בעולמי והוא יחיד בעולמו נאה ליחיד להציל את היחיד ולפי שהקב"ה *אינו מקפח שכר כל בריה אמר תזכה ותציל שלשה מבני בניו דרש ר"ש השילוני בשעה שהפיל נבוכדנצר הרשע *חנניה מישאל ועזריה לתוך כבשן האש עמד °יורקמו שר הברד לפני הקב"ה אמר לפניו רבש"ע ארד ואצנן את הכבשן ואציל לצדיקים הללו מכבשן האש אמר לו גבריאל אין גבורתו של הקב"ה בכך שאתה *שר ברד והכל יודעין שהמים מכבין את האש אלא אני שר של אש ארד ואקרר מבפנים ואקדיח

[עי' בעין יעקב ובילקוט ישעיה סימן כ"א]

עין כסף משנה סימן תפ · שם קלו · ס"א ואמר ר' יהושע בן לוי · [נ"ל ואמר] · [עיין אדר"נ פס"א] · ס"א שלא עמדנו בראשונה אמר אביי ועדיין · מכות כג · [מיר כג: ג"ק לח: הוריות י:] · נ"ל את חנניה · שר של ברד · [עירובין נג·]

גליון הש"ס

גמרא אמר חנניה כי לשמך · עי' ירושלמי פ"ח דשבת הל' ו ובנ"פ שם · שם יורקמו · עי' בכבודי ע' דיש חנניה · פורש"י ושמ"ע:

הגהות מהר"ב רנשבורג

[א] גמ' מהר צועה להפתח · ב"ב חסר סיפא דקרא ולא ימות ועי' מהרש"א בח"א:

רבינו חננאל

מאי ברכת השיר ר' יהודה אומר יהללוך ר' יוחנן אומר נשמת כל חי: ת"ר (חמישי) [רביעי] אומר עליו הלל הגדול דברי ר"ט וי"א ה' רועי לא אחסר מהיכן הוא אומר הלל הגדול רב אמר מהודו עד על נהרות בבל רבי יוחנן אומר משיר המעלות עד על נהרות בבל רב אחא בר יעקב אמר מכי יעקב בחר לו יה ועד על נהרות בבל: למה נקרא הלל הגדול אמר רבי יוחנן מפני שהקב"ה יושב ברומו של עולם ומחלק מזון לכל בריה: אמר רבי יהושע בן לוי כ"ו הודו כנגד כ"ו דור שלא היתה להם תורה וזנם הקב"ה בחסדו · מאי דכתיב הודו לה' כי טוב הודו למי שגובה חובו של אדם בטובתו פי' מכל אדם כפי השג ידו עשיר בשורו עני בשיו אלמנה בתרנגולתה יתום בביצתו: א"ר יוחנן קשין מזונותיו של אדם כפלים כיולדה [דאילו] ביולדה כתיב בעצב תלדי בנים ובמזונות כתיב בעצבון תאכלנה · ר' אלעזר אומר כקריעת ים סוף שנאמר לגוזר ים סוף לגזרים וסמיך ליה נותן לחם לכל בשר · רבי לוי אמר יתר מן הגאולה שנאמר המלאך הגואל אותי מכל רע על ידי מלאך ובמזונות כתיב האלהים הרועה אותי · רבי אלעזר בן עזריה אומר כקריעת ים סוף שנאמר מהר צועה להפתח וכתיב בתריה רוגע הים ויהמו גליו ה' צבאות שמו רבי חמא ברבי חנינא אמר כיום המיתה שנאמר לא ימות לשחת ולא יחסר לחמו: אמר רב ששת קשין נקביו של אדם כקריעת ים סוף שנאמר מהר צועה להפתח וכתיב בתריה רוגע הים וגו' אמר רב ששת המבזה את המועדות כאלו עובד ע"ז שנא' אלהי מסכה וגו' וכתיב בתריה את חג המצות תשמור ועוד אמר [רב ששת משום ראב"ע] המספר לה"ר והמקבלו והמעיד עדות שקר ראוי להשליכו לכלבים שנא' לא תשא שמע שוא וסמיך ליה לכלב תשליכון אותו ואקשי' וכי מאחר דאיכא הלל הגדול מאי טעמא שבקי' ליה וקרינן להאי ופריק ר' יוחנן מפני שיש בו ה' דברים יציאת מצרים שנא' בצאת ישראל ממצרים קריעת ים סוף שנאמר הים ראה וינוס מתן תורה שנאמר ההרים רקדו כאילים תחיית המתים שנאמר אתהלך לפני ה' בארצות החיים חבלו של משיח שנאמר לא לנו ה' לא לנו · רב נחמן אמר מפני שיש בו מלוט הצדיקים מגיהנם שנאמר אנה ה' מלטה נפשי: ענין אברהם אבינו שהפילו נמרוד לכבשן

Continuation of translation from previous page as indicated by ◁

'Azariah: He who despises the Festivals[9] is as though he engaged in idolatry, for it is said, *Thou shalt make thee no molten gods,*[10] which is followed by, *The feast of unleavened bread shalt thou keep.*[11]

R. Shesheth also said on the authority of R. Eleazar b. 'Azariah: Whoever relates slander, and whoever accepts slander, and whoever gives false testimony against his neighbour, deserve to be cast to dogs, for it is said, *ye shall cast to the dogs,*[12] which is followed
c by, *Thou shalt not take up a false report,*[1] which may be read *tashshi.*[2]

Now since there is the great *Hallel*, why do we recite this one?[3] Because it includes [a mention of] the following five things: The exodus from Egypt, the dividing of the Red Sea, the giving of the Torah [Revelation], the resurrection of the dead, and the pangs of Messiah.[4] The exodus from Egypt, as it is written, *When Israel came forth out of Egypt;*[5] the dividing of the Red Sea: *The sea saw it, and fled;*[6] the giving of the Torah: *The mountains skipped like rams;*[7] resurrection of the dead: *I shall walk before the Lord* [*in the land of the living*];[8] the pangs of Messiah: *Not unto us, O Lord, not unto us.*[9]

R. Joḥanan also said: '*Not unto us, O Lord, not unto us*' refers to the servitude to [foreign] powers. Others state, R. Joḥanan said: '*Not unto us, O Lord, not unto us*' refers to the war of Gog and Magog.[10] R. Naḥman b. Isaac said: [*Hallel* is recited] because it contains [an allusion to] the deliverance of the souls of the righteous from the Gehenna, as it is said, *I beseech Thee, O Lord, deliver my soul.*[11] Hezekiah said: Because it alludes to the descent of the righteous[12] into the fiery furnace and their ascent from it. 'Their descent,' for it is written, *Not unto us, O Lord, not unto us:* [this] Hananiah said; '*But unto Thy name give glory*' was said by Mishael; *For Thy mercy, and for Thy truth's sake*, by Azariah; *Wherefore should the nations say?*[13] by all of them. 'Their ascent from the fiery furnace,' for it is written, *O praise the Lord, all ye nations;*[14] [this] Hananiah said; *Laud Him, all ye peoples*, was said by Mishael; *For His mercy is great toward us,*[15] by Azariah; '*And the truth of the Lord endureth for ever,*' by all of them. Others maintain [that] it was Gabriel who said, '*And the truth of the Lord endureth for ever.*' [For] when the wicked Nimrod cast our father Abraham into the fiery furnace, Gabriel said to the Holy One, blessed be He: 'Sovereign of the Universe! Let me go down, cool [it], and deliver that righteous man from the fiery furnace.' Said the Holy One, blessed be He, to him: 'I am unique in My world, and he is unique in his world: it is fitting for Him who is unique to deliver him who is unique.' But because the Holy One, blessed be He, does not withhold the [merited] reward of any creature, he said to him, 'Thou shalt be
d priviliged to deliver three of his descendants.'[1]

R. Simeon the Shilonite lectured: When the wicked Nebuchadnezzar cast Hananiah, Mishael, and Azariah into the fiery furnace, Yurkami, Prince of hail,[2] rose before the Holy One, blessed be He, and said to Him: 'Sovereign of the Universe! Let me go down and cool the furnace and save these righteous men from the fiery furnace.' Said Gabriel to him, 'The might of the Holy One, blessed be He, is not thus [manifested], for thou art the Prince of hail, and all know that water extinguishes fire. But I, the Prince of fire, will

(9) The Intermediate Days of the Festival. doing unnecessary work thereon (Rashi). (10) Ex. XXXIV, 17. (11) Ibid. 18. (12) Ex. XXII, 30.
c (1) Ex. XXIII, 1. (2) [תַּשִּׂיא from rt. meaning 'to entice', 'induce', 'mislead', hence attempting to influence the judge to one side by bearing false testimony against another person, v. Sanh., 7*b*, n. 10]. Rashbam deletes this phrase, holding that the whole follows from the verse as it stands. (3) Viz., Ps. CXIII-CXVIII. (4) I.e., the suffering which must precede his coming. (5) Ibid. CXIV, 1. (6) Ibid. 3. (7) Ibid. 4; cf. Judg. V, 4f. (8) Ps. CXVI, 9. (9) Ibid. CXV, 1. This is now interpreted as a prayer to be spared the great distress of that time; cf. Sanh. 97*a*. (10) V. Ezek. XXXVIII and Sanh., 94*a*, n. 7. (11) Ps. CXVI, 4. (12) Hananiah, Mishael and Azariah. (13) Ps. CXV, 2. (14) Ps. CXVII, 1. (15) Ibid. 2.
d (1) And when that promise was fulfilled, Gabriel said '*and the truth*' etc. (2) The presiding genius over hail-storms.

קג א ב ג מיי' פ"ח מהל' חו"מ הל' י' וסמג שם טוש"ע או"ח סימן תפ:

קד ד מיי' פ"ו מהל' יום טוב הלכה יז:

ה"ג רביעי גומר עליו את ההלל ואומר עליו הלל הגדול: שהקדוש ברוך הוא יושב ברומו של עולם כו'. דכתיב הודו לאל השמים נותן לחם לכל בשר והייתו דבר גדול: עשיר בשורו. מפסידו ממון [ומכפר] על גופו: קשין נקביו של אדם. כשהוא עצור כיום המיתה:

רשב"ם

יהללוך. (*נשמת כל חי) וגומרין בו בא"י מלך מהולל בתשבחות וזו היא ברכת השיר דמתניתין כלומר ברכת השבח: ור' יוחנן אמר נשמת כל חי אף נשמת דהיינו ברכת השיר דמתני' דאילו יהללוך אנו אומרים בכל יום שאומרים בו את ההלל ומאי שנא ליל פסח דנקט אם לא להוסיף עוד ברכה אחרת והיינו דאמר הלכה כרבי יוחנן בתרוייהו וקבעוהו לאחר הלל הגדול שצריך לאומרו כדלקמן דהשתא איכא ברכה בכל חדא וחדא והכי הויא מילתא שפיר כך נראה בעיני: ה"ג ת"ר רביעי גומר עליו את ההלל ואומר עליו הלל הגדול: ה' רועי. על שם המזון שאכלו צריך לומר: שהקדוש ברוך הוא יושב ברומו של עולם כו'. דכתיב ביה נותן לחם לכל בשר והייתו דבר גדול: בטובתו. בטובה שהשפיע לו והכי משמע כי טוב לעולם חסדו חסד הוא עושה לעולם בכי טוב כלומר בטוב שנתן לו: עשיר בשורו עני בשיו. מפסידו ממון ומכפר על גופו: בעצבון. תרי משמע: כקריעת ים סוף. כלומר נס גדול עושה לו הקדוש ברוך הוא למי שנותן לו מזונות כאשר עשה לישראל שקרע להם ים סוף ונפקא מיניה למבעי רחמי: קשין נקביו של אדם. כשהוא עצור: לועה. לשון עצור וחגור כמו לועה ברב טוחו (ישעיה סג): כל המבזה את המועדות. שעושה מלאכה בחולו של מועד דכתיב את חג המצות תשמור ונפקא לן במסכת חגיגה (דף יח.) איסור מלאכה בחולו של מועד: המקבל לשון הרע. שמקבלו ומאמינו על חבירו אע"ג דלקבוליה לא מיבעי ליה למיחש ליה מיבעי כדמפרש במסכת נדה (דף סא.): וקרי ביה לא תשיא. נראה בעיני דלא גרסינן ליה דכולהו משתמע מלא תשא שכשמספר או מעיד הרי נושא בפיו שמע שוא: וכי מאחר דאיכא הלל הגדול. שמשובח יותר כמו שפירש רבי יוחנן למעלה משום דכתיב ביה נותן לחם לכל בשר אנן מאי טעמא אמרינן האי הלילא על כל פרק ופרק ועל כל צרה שלא תבא על הציבור לכשנגאלין: חמשה דברים. דמיירי נמי בגאולה: ההרים רקדו כאילים. בשעת מתן תורה דכתיב (תהלים סח) למה תרצדון הרים וגו': גבריאל אמרו. כשניצולו חנניה מישאל ועזריה והוא היה שם דכתיב (דניאל ג) ורויה די רביעאה דמי לבר אלהין לפי שהקדוש ברוך הוא הבטיחו על כך כשנשלך אברהם באור כשדים וכשקיים לו אמר ואמת ה' לעולם שקיים הבטחתו: בשעה שהפיל נמרוד. שעל שם כן *נקרא אמרפל על שם שאמר והפיל את אברהם בכבשן: ואקדיח

תורה אור

מאי ברכת השיר רב יהודה אמר יהללוך ה' אלהינו ורבי יוחנן אמר נשמת כל חי ת"ר רביעי גומר עליו את ההלל ואומר הלל הגדול דברי ר"ט וי"א ה' רועי לא אחסר מהיכן הלל הגדול רבי יהודה אומר מהודו עד נהרות בבל ורבי יוחנן אומר משיר המעלות עד נהרות בבל רב אחא בר יעקב אמר מכי יעקב בחר לו יה עד נהרות בבל ולמה נקרא שמו הלל הגדול א"ר יוחנן מפני שהקב"ה יושב ברומו של עולם ומחלק מזונות לכל בריה א"ר יהושע בן לוי הני עשרים וששה הודו כנגד מי כנגד כ"ו דורות שברא הקב"ה בעולמו ולא נתן להם תורה וזן אותם בחסדו *אמר רב חסדא מאי דכתיב הודו לה' כי טוב הודו לה' שגובה חובתו של אדם בטובתו עשיר בשורו ועני בשיו יתום בביצתו אלמנה בתרנגולתה א"ר יוחנן קשין מזונותיו של אדם כפליים כיולדה דאילו ביולדה כתי' בעצב ובמזונות כתי' בעצבון (א"ר) יוחנן קשין מזונותיו של אדם יותר מן הגאולה דאילו בגאולה כתיב המלאך הגואל אותי מכל רע מלאך בעלמא ואילו במזונות כתיב האלהים הרועה אותי א"ר יהושע בן לוי בשעה שאמר הקב"ה לאדם וקוץ ודרדר תצמיח לך זלגו עיניו דמעות אמר לפניו רבש"ע אני וחמורי נאכל באבוס אחד כיון שאמר לו בזעת אפך תאכל לחם נתקררה דעתו אמר ר"ש בן לקיש אשרינו *אם עמדנו בראשונה ועדיין לא פלטינן מינה דקא אכלינן עיסבי דדברא אמר רב שיזבי משמיה דרבי אלעזר בן עזריה קשין מזונותיו של אדם כקריעת ים סוף דכתיב נותן לחם לכל בשר וסמיך ליה לגוזר ים סוף לגזרים אמר ר"א בן עזריה *קשין נקביו של אדם כיום המיתה וכקריעת ים סוף שנאמר מהר צועה להפתח וכתיב בתריה רוגע הים ויהמו גליו *ואמר רב ששת משום ר"א בן עזריה כל המבזה את המועדות כאילו עובד ע"ז שנאמר אלהי מסכה לא תעשה לך וכתיב בתריה את חג המצות תשמור ואמר רב ששת משום ר"א בן עזריה כל המספר לשון הרע וכל המקבל לשון הרע וכל המעיד עדות שקר בחבירו ראוי להשליכו לכלבים שנאמר לכלב תשליכון אותו וכתיב בתריה לא תשא שמע שוא וקרי ביה לא תשיא וכי מאחר דאיכא הלל הגדול אנן מ"ט אמרינן האי משום שיש בו ה' דברים הללו יציאת מצרים וקריעת ים סוף ומתן תורה ותחיית המתים וחבלו של משיח יציאת מצרים דכתי' בצאת ישראל ממצרים וקריעת ים סוף דכתיב הים ראה וינוס מתן תורה דכתי' ההרים רקדו כאילים תחיית המתים דכתיב אתהלך לפני ה' חבלו של משיח דכתיב לא לנו ה' לא לנו וא"ר יוחנן לא לנו ה' לא לנו זו שעבוד מלכיות איכא דאמרי אמר רבי יוחנן לא לנו ה' לא לנו זו מלחמת גוג ומגוג רב נחמן בר יצחק אמר מפני שיש בו מילוט נפשות של צדיקים מגיהנם שנא' אנה ה' מלטה נפשי חזקיה אמר מפני שיש בו ירידתן של צדיקים לכבשן האש ועלייתן ממנו ירידתן דכתיב לא לנו ה' לא לנו אמר חנניה כי לשמך תן כבוד אמר מישאל על חסדך ועל אמיתך אמר עזריה למה יאמרו הגוים אמרו כולן עלייתן מכבשן האש דכתיב הללו את ה' כל גוים אמר חנניה שבחוהו כל האומים אמר מישאל כי גבר עלינו חסדו אמר עזריה ואמת ה' לעולם הללויה אמרו כולן ויש אומרים ואמת ה' לעולם גבריאל אמרו בשעה שהפיל נמרוד הרשע את אברהם אבינו לתוך כבשן האש אמר גבריאל לפני הקדוש ברוך הוא רבש"ע ארד ואצנן ואציל את הצדיק מכבשן האש אמר לו הקב"ה אני יחיד בעולמי והוא יחיד בעולמו נאה ליחיד להציל את היחיד ולפי שהקב"ה *אינו מקפח שכר כל בריה אמר תזכה ותציל שלשה מבני בניו דרש ר"ש השילוני בשעה שהפיל נבוכדנצר הרשע *חנניה מישאל ועזריה לתוך כבשן האש עמד יורקמו שר הברד לפני הקב"ה אמר לפניו רבש"ע ארד ואצנן את הכבשן ואציל לצדיקים הללו מכבשן האש אמר לו גבריאל אין גבורתו של הקב"ה בכך שאתה *שר ברד והכל יודעין שהמים מכבין את האש אלא אני שר של אש ארד ואקרר מבפנים ואקדיח

תוספות

מאי ברכת השיר רב יהודה אמר יהללוך. וקמ"ל דאפילו במקום שלא נהגו לברך אחריו בלילי פסח צריך לברך דאי נהגו פשיטא א"נ דאפילו במקום שנהגו ה"א דוקא בימים אבל בלילה אינו צריך לברך קא משמע לן: רבי יוחנן אמר נשמת כל חי. נראה ה"פ אף נשמת כל חי אחר יהללוך דאי לא תימא הכי אנן כמאן עבדינן וקורא נשמת כל חי ברכת השיר לפי שבשבתות אומרים אותו אחר פסוקי דזמרה ורבינו חיים כהן לא היה חותם ביהללוך כי אם בנשמת לבדו משום דלישנא דברכת השיר משמע חדא ברכה: מהודו עד על נהרות בבל. וכן אנו עושים ורגנו לדיקים בה' אינו מן המזמור: מן

[ע' בעין יעקב ובילקוט ישעיה סימן נ"א]

רבינו חננאל

מאי ברכת השיר ר' יהודה אומר יהללוך ר' יוחנן אומר נשמת כל חי: ת"ר (חמישי) [רביעי] אומר עליו הלל הגדול דברי ר"ט וי"א ה' רועי לא אחסר מהיכן הוא אומר הלל הגדול רב אמר מהודו עד על נהרות בבל רבי יוחנן אומר משיר המעלות עד על נהרות בבל רב אחא בר יעקב אמר מכי יעקב בחר לו יה ועד על נהרות בבל: למה נקרא הלל הגדול אמר רבי יוחנן מפני שהקב"ה יושב ברומו של עולם ומחלק מזון לכל בריה: אמר רבי יהושע בן לוי כ"ו הודו כנגד כ"ו דור שלא היתה להם תורה וזנם הקב"ה בחסדו · מאי דכתיב הודו לה' כי טוב הודו למי שגובה חובו של אדם בטובתו פי' מכל אדם כפי השג ידו עשיר בשורו עני בשיו אלמנה בתרנגולתה יתום בביצתו: א"ר יוחנן קשין מזונותיו של אדם כפלים כיולדה [דאילו] ביולדה כתיב בעצב תלדי בנים ובמזונות כתיב בעצבון תאכלנה · ר' אלעזר אומר כקריעת ים סוף שנאמר לגוזר ים סוף לגזרים וסמיך ליה נותן לחם לכל בשר · רבי לוי אמר יתר מן הגאולה שנאמר המלאך הגואל אותי מכל רע על ידי מלאך ובמזונות

כתיב האלהים הרועה אותי · רבי אלעזר בן עזריה אומר כקריעת ים סוף שנאמר מהר צועה להפתח וכתיב בתריה רוגע הים ויהמו גליו ה' צבאות שמו רבי חמא ברבי חנינא אמר כיום המיתה שנאמר לא ימות לשחת ולא יחסר לחמו: אמר רב ששת קשין נקביו של אדם כקריעת ים סוף שנאמר מהר צועה להפתח וכתיב בתריה רוגע הים וגו' אמר רב ששת המבזה את המועדות כאלו עובד ע"ז שנא' אלהי מסכה וגו' וכתיב בתריה את חג המצות תשמור ועוד אמר [רב ששת משום ראב"ע] המספר לה"ר והמקבלו והמעיד עדות שקר ראוי להשליכו לכלבים שנא' לא תשא שמע שוא וסמיך ליה לכלב תשליכון אותו ואקשי' וכי מאחר דאיכא הלל הגדול מאי טעמא שבקי' ליה וקרינן להאי ופריק ר' יוחנן מפני שיש בו ה' דברים יציאת מצרים שנא' בצאת ישראל ממצרים קריעת ים סוף שנאמר הים ראה וינוס מתן תורה שנאמר ההרים רקדו כאילים תחיית המתים שנאמר אתהלך לפני ה' בארצות החיים חבלו של משיח שנאמר לא לנו ה' לא לנו · רב נחמן אמר מפני שיש בו מלוט הצדיקים מגיהנם שנאמר אנה ה' מלטה נפשי : ענין אברהם אבינו שהפילו נמרוד לכבשן

[ברכות נ"ט] ס"א ואמר ר' יהושע בן לוי · [צ"ל ואמר] · [עיין אדר"נ ספ"ה] · ס"א שלא עמדנו בראשונה אמר אביי ועדיין · מכות כג: · צ"ל את חנניה · שר של ברד · [עירובין נג:]

גליון הש"ס

גמרא אמר חנניה כי לשמך תן כבוד

הגהות מהר"ב רנשבורג

[א] גמ' מהר צועה להפתח

AND RECITES THE GRACE OF SONG. [118a] What is 'THE GRACE OF SONG'? Rab Judah said: 'They shall praise Thee, O Lord our God'; while R. Johanan said: 'The breath of all living [etc.]'[8]

Our Rabbis taught: At the fourth he concludes the *Hallel* and recites the great *Hallel*: this is the view of R. Ṭarfon. Others say: '*The Lord is my shepherd; I shall not want*.'[9] What comprises the great *Hallel*? Rab[10] Judah said: From '*O give thanks*' until '*the rivers*
a *of Babylon*.'[1] While R. Joḥanan said: From '*A song of ascents*' until '*the rivers of Babylon*.'[2] R. Aḥa b. Jacob said: From '*for the Lord hath chosen Jacob unto himself*'[3] until '*the rivers of Babylon*.' And why is it called the great *Hallel*?—Said R. Joḥanan: Because the Holy One, blessed be He, sits in the heights of the universe and distributes food to all creatures.[4]

R. Joshua b. Levi said: To what do these twenty-six [verses of] '*Give thanks*'[5] correspond? To the twenty-six generations which the Holy One, blessed be He, created in His world; though He did not give them the Torah, He sustained them by His love.[6]

R. Ḥisda said:[7] What is meant by the verse, *O give thanks unto the Lord, for He is good*?[8] Give thanks unto the Lord who exacts man's debts by means of His goodness:[9] the wealthy man through his ox and the poor man through his sheep,[10] the fatherless through his egg and the widow through her fowl.

R. Joḥanan said: Man's sustenance involves twice as much suffering as [that of] a woman in childbirth. For of a woman in childbirth it is written, *in pain* [be-'eẓeb—*thou shalt bring forth children*],[11] whereas of sustenance it is written, *in toil* [be-'iẓẓabon—*shalt thou eat*].[12] R. Joḥanan also said: Man's sustenance is more difficult [to come by] than the redemption, for of redemption it is written, *the* angel *who hath redeemed me from all evil*,[13] thus a mere angel [sufficed], whereas of sustenance it is written, *the* God *who hath fed* [*shepherded*] *me*.[14]

R. Joshua b. Levi said: When the Holy One, blessed be He,
b said to Adam, '*Thorns also and thistles shall it bring forth to thee*,'[1] tears flowed from his eyes, and he pleaded before Him, 'Sovereign of the Universe! Shall I and my ass eat out of the same crib!' But as soon as He said to him, '*In the sweat of thy face shalt thou eat bread*,'[2] his mind was set at rest. R. Simeon b. Laḳish said: Happy are we that we did not remain subject to the first! Abaye observed: Yet we have still not [altogether] escaped from it, for we eat herbs of the field.[3]

R. Shizbi said in the name of R. Eleazar b. 'Azariah: A man's sustenance is as difficult [to provide] as the dividing of the Red Sea, for it is written, *Who giveth food to all flesh*,[4] and near it, *To Him who divided the Red Sea in sunder*.[5]

R. Eleazar b. 'Azariah said: A man's excretory organs [when blocked up] are as painful as the day of death and [as difficult to overcome][6] as the dividing of the Red Sea, for it is said, *The prisoner hasteneth to be loosed; [and he shall not go down dying into the pit, neither shall his bread fail]*;[7] and that is followed by [*For I am the Lord thy God*,] *who stirreth up the sea, that the waves thereof roar*.[8]

Again, R. Shesheth said on the authority of R. Eleazar b.

(8) V. *P.B.* p. 125. (9) Ps. XXIII, 1. (10) Text as read by Asheri.
a (1) I.e., Ps. CXXXVII. (2) Ps. CXX-CXXXIV all bear the superscription '*A song of ascents*.' Hence he probably means Ps. CXX-CXXXVI. (3) Ps. CXXXV, 4. (4) The subject matter of Ps. CXXXVI, 25-26. Which is a great thing indeed, and for that He is praised by the reciting of the great *Hallel*. (5) Ps. CXXXVI contains twenty-six verses, each of which expresses gratitude to God. (6) There were twenty-six generations from Adam until Moses. These, lacking the Torah, could not be sustained through their own merit but only through God's love. (7) Var. lec.: R. Joshua b. Levi also said. (8) Ps. CXXXVI, 1. (9) I.e., from what He has granted to man. (10) When people must suffer loss in expiation of wrong, the loss is regulated according to their means. (11) Gen. III, 16. (12) Ibid. 17 '*Iẓẓabon* is more emphatic than '*eẓeb* (both belong to the same root), and therefore denotes greater suffering. (13) Gen. XLVIII, 16. (14) Ibid. 15.
b (1) Gen. III, 18. (2) Ibid. 19. (3) Wild herbs. The translation is that of the amended text given in the margin. [Cur. edd.: 'Happy were we had we remained subject to the first,' that is, and thus been spared the sweat of the brow in search for a livelihood. Thereupon Abaye observes—we still retain part of this advantage in that there are wild herbs which provide food without toil.] (4) Ps. CXXXVI, 25. (5) Ibid. 13. (6) The Heb. קשה has both meanings. (7) Isa. LI, 14. (8) Ibid. 15. This is understood as an allusion to the dividing of the Red Sea.

◁ *For the continuation of the English translation of this page see overleaf.*

not unto us.'[3] [117b] Surely then they differ in this: he who says, until '*as a joyous mother of children*', holds that [the following] 'Hallelujah' [*praise ye the Lord*] is the beginning of the [next] psalm; while he who says until, '*when Israel came forth out of Egypt*', holds that 'Hallelujah' is the *end* of the [previous] psalm![4]—R. Ḥisda reconciles it with his view. All agree that 'Hallelujah' is the end of the psalm. Hence the statement, until '*when Israel came forth out of Egypt*' is well; while the statement, until '*as a joyous mother of children*' is meant inclusively. Then let him say, 'up to "Hallelujah"'? And should you answer, because we would not know which 'Hallelujah,' then let him say, 'up to the "Hallelujah" of "*as a joyous mother of children*"'? This is a difficulty. Rabbah b. R. Huna reconciles it with his view. All agree that 'Hallelujah' is the beginning of the psalm. Hence the statement, until '*as a joyous mother of children*' is well. While he who says, until '*when Israel came forth*' does not mean it inclusively. Then let him say, 'until "Hallelujah"'? And should you answer, because we would not know which 'Hallelujah' is meant, then let him say, 'until the Hallelujah of "*when Israel came forth*"'? This is a difficulty.

AND HE CONCLUDES WITH [A FORMULA OF] REDEMPTION. Raba said: [The ending of the benediction following] the reciting
a of the *shema*'[1] and *Hallel* is 'who redeemed Israel';[2] that of prayer[3] is 'the redeemer of Israel'.[4] What is the reason? Because it is a petition.[5] R. Zera said: [The formula] in *ḳiddush* is 'who did sanctify us with His commandments and did command us'; that of prayer is 'sanctify us with Thy commandments.' What is the reason? Because it is supplication. R. Aḥa b. Jacob said: And he must refer to the Egyptian exodus in the *ḳiddush* of the day. [For] here it is written, *that thou mayest remember the day* [*when thou camest forth out of the land of Egypt*],[6] while there it is written, *Remember the Sabbath day, to hallow it* [by reciting *ḳiddush*].[7]

Rabbah b. Shila said: [The formula] in Prayer is 'who causest the horn of salvation to spring forth,'[8] while that of the *haftarah*[9] is 'the shield of David.' *And I will make thee a great man, like unto the name of the great ones* [*that are in the earth*].[10] R. Joseph taught: that alludes to the fact that we say 'the shield of David.'[11]

R. Simeon b. Laḳish said: *And I will make thee a great nation:*[12] that means that we say, 'the God of Abraham'; *and I will bless thee*—that we say, 'the God of Isaac'; *and make thy name great*,—that we say, 'the God of Jacob.' You might think that we conclude with [a reference to] all of them: therefore it is said, *and be* thou *a blessing*: with thee do we conclude, but we do not conclude with all of them.

Raba said: I found the elders of Pumbeditha[13] sitting and stating:
b On the Sabbath, both in Prayer[1] and in *ḳiddush* [we conclude the benediction with] 'who sanctifiest the Sabbath.' On a festival, both in Prayer and in *ḳiddush* [we conclude with] 'who sanctifiest Israel and the [festive] seasons.' Said I to them, On the contrary, [the formula] of Prayer both on the Sabbath and on a festival is 'who sanctifiest Israel.' In the *ḳiddush* of the Sabbath [the formula is] 'who sanctifiest the Sabbath'; on a festival, 'who sanctifiest Israel and the seasons.' Now I will state my reason and your reason. Your reason is: the Sabbath is permanently fixed, hence both in Prayer and in *ḳiddush* 'who sanctifiest the Sabbath' [is said].[2] On festivals, which are fixed by Israel, for they intercalate the months[3] and fix [the beginnings of] the years,[4] 'who sanctifiest Israel and the seasons' [is said].[5] My reason: Prayer, which is [carried on] in public, [requires] 'who sanctifiest Israel';[6] as for *ḳiddush*, which is [recited] privately [at home], on the Sabbath [the formula is] 'who sanctifiest the Sabbath,' while on festivals it is 'who sanctifiest Israel and the seasons.'[7] That [argument] however is incorrect: is not prayer [recited] privately [too], and is not *ḳiddush* recited publicly?—Raba, however, holds: Follow the main [practice].[8]

'Ulla b. Rab visited Raba. He recited [*ḳiddush*] in accordance with the elders of Pumbeditha, and he said nothing to him [in protest]. This proves that Raba retracted. R. Nathan the father of R. Huna the son of R. Nathan[9] visited R. Papa. He recited it in accordance with the elders of Pumbeditha, whereupon R. Papa praised him. Rabina said: I visited Meremar at Sura, when
c the reader[1] went down [to the reading desk][2] and recited it as the elders of Pumbeditha. Everybody made to silence him, but he said to them, 'Leave him alone: the law is as the elders of Pumbeditha.' Then they did not silence him.[3]

MISHNAH. THEY FILLED THE THIRD CUP FOR HIM. HE THEN RECITES GRACE AFTER MEALS. OVER THE FOURTH [CUP] HE CONCLUDES THE HALLEL, AND RECITES THE GRACE OF SONG.[4] BETWEEN THESE CUPS[5] HE MAY DRINK IF HE WISHES; BETWEEN THE THIRD AND THE FOURTH HE MAY NOT DRINK.

GEMARA. R. Ḥanan said to Raba: This proves that Grace after meals requires a cup [of wine]. Said he to him: Our Rabbis instituted four cups as symbolizing freedom:[6] let us perform a religious act with each.[7]

OVER THE FOURTH [CUP] HE CONCLUDES THE HALLEL,

(3) Ibid. CXV, 1. In each case whereas the Mishnah quotes the *ending* of the chapters according to our edd., the Baraitha quotes the *beginning* of the following chapters. (4) This of course is on the view of Beth Shammai. The differences in the view of Beth Hillel are then stated for the sake of parallelism (Rashbam).

a (1) This is followed by one benediction in the morning and two in the evening, before the 'Prayer,' i.e., the Eighteen Benedictions. (2) In the past tense. (3) The *'Amidah* on weekdays. It consists of the Eighteen Benedictions, the fifth of which is a prayer for redemption. (4) In the present tense. (5) For the future. Hence the past tense would be inappropriate. (6) Deut. XVI, 3. (7) Ex. XX, 8. '*Remember*' in the second verse, i.e., the reciting of *ḳiddush* (and the Sabbath is an example of *all* holy days, including Festivals), must include the '*remember*' of the first verse, viz., the Egyptian exodus. (8) That is the ending of the fifteenth benediction. (9) V. Glos. It is followed by four benedictions. The reference here is to the third, whose subject-matter is the same as the fifteenth benediction mentioned in the preceding note. (10) II Sam. VII, 9. (11) It is a great honour to David that God is designated 'the shield of David' in the conclusion of a benediction. (12) Ex. XII, 2. (13) Rab Judah and R. 'Ena, v. Sanh. 17b.

b (1) The *'Amidah* on Sabbath and Festivals consists of seven benedictions. (2) Because its sanctification depends entirely on God. (3) The Jewish month consists of either 29 or 30 days, the length of each month being fixed by the Jewish authorities. (4) Thereby fixing the dates of festivals too. (5) Thus Israel must be mentioned, because through Israel the festivals are sanctified. (6) I.e., a reference to the whole community. (7) The emphasis being on the sacred nature of the *day*. 'Israel' must be mentioned in the latter case because the sanctification of the seasons is dependent thereon (*supra*). (8) Prayer is essentially intended for the community, notwithstanding that private prayer too is possible. Again, *ḳiddush* is chiefly intended for the home ('in the place of the meal'), though it is also recited in the synagogue on account of the wayfarers. (9) 'The son of R. Nathan' should probably be deleted.

c (1) Lit., 'the deputy of the congregation.' In the Talmud this is the name of the reader who leads the congregation in prayer; the modern title '*ḥazzan*' dates from the post-Talmudic period. (2) In Talmudic times this was on a lower level than the rest of the synagogue building, in accordance with Ps. CXXX, 1: *out of the* depths *have I called Thee, O Lord*. (3) Omitted in MS.M. Var. lec. add: And the law is as the elders of Pumbeditha. (4) The phrase is explained in the Gemara. (5) Viz., first, second and third. (6) This is omitted in Rashbam. (7) Hence Grace is recited over the third. But on other occasions a cup may not be required for Grace after meals.

מאי לאו בהא קמיפלגי למ"ד עד אם הבנים
שמחה סבר הללויה ריש פירקא ומאן דאמר
עד בצאת ישראל סבר הללויה סוף פירקא
רב חסדא מתרץ לטעמיה דכולי עלמא סברי
הללויה סוף פירקא מ"ד עד בצאת ישראל
שפיר ומאן דאמר עד אם הבנים שמחה *עד
ועד בכלל ונימא עד הללויה וכי תימא דלא
ידעינן הי הללויה ונימא הללויה של אם
הבנים שמחה קשיא רבה בר רב הונא מתרץ
לטעמיה דכולי עלמא הללויה ריש פירקא
מאן דאמר עד אם הבנים שמחה שפיר ומאן
דאמר עד בצאת ישראל סבר עד ולא עד
בכלל ונימא עד הללויה וכי תימא דלא
ידעינן הי הללויה ונימא עד הללויה שבצאת
ישראל קשיא: וחותם בגאולה: אמר רבא
ק"ש והלל גאל ישראל דצלותא גואל ישראל
מ"ט דרחמי נינהו אמר רבי זירא דקידושא
אשר קדשנו במצותיו [א] וצונו דצלותא קדשנו
במצותיך מ"ט דרחמי נינהו אמר רב אחא
בר יעקב וצריך שיזכיר יציאת מצרים בקידוש
היום כתיב הכא °למען תזכור את יום וכתיב
התם °זכור את יום השבת לקדשו אמר רבה בר שילא דצלותא מצמיח קרן
ישועה דאפטרתא מגן דוד °ועשיתי לך שם גדול כשם הגדולים תני רב יוסף
זהו שאומרים מגן דוד א"ר שמעון בן לקיש °ואעשך לגוי גדול זהו שאומרים
אלהי אברהם ואברכך זהו שאומרים אלהי יצחק ואגדלה שמך זהו שאומרים
אלהי יעקב יכול יהו חותמין בכולן ת"ל והיה ברכה בך חותמין ואין חותמין
בכולן אמר רבא אשכחתינא לסבי דפומבדיתא דיתבי וקאמרי *בשבתא בין
בצלותא בין בקידושא מקדש השבת ביומא טבא בין בצלותא ובין בקידושא
מקדש ישראל והזמנים ואמינא להו אנא אדרבה דצלותא בין בשבתא בין
ביומא טבא מקדש ישראל בקידושא דשבתא מקדש השבת ביומא טבא
מקדש ישראל והזמנים ואנא אמינא טעמא דידי וטעמא דידכו טעמא דידכו
שבת דקביעא וקיימא בין בצלותא ובין בקידושא מקדש השבת יומא טבא
דישראל הוא דקבעי ליה דקמעברי ירחי וקבעי לשני מקדש ישראל והזמנים
טעמא דידי צלותא דברבים איתא מקדש ישראל קידוש דביחיד איתא
בשבת מקדש השבת ביום טוב מקדש ישראל והזמנים ולא היא צלותא
ביחיד מי ליתיה וקידושא ברבים מי ליתיה ורבא סבר זיל בתר עיקר עולא
בר רב נחית קמיה דרבא אמר כסבי דפומבדיתא ולא א"ל ולא מידי אלמא
הדר ביה רבא רב נתן אבוה דרב הונא *בריה דרב נתן נחית קמיה דרב
פפא אמר כסבי דפומבדיתא ושבחיה רב פפא אמר רבינא אנא איקלע לסורא
קמיה דמרימר ונחית קמיה שלוחא דציבורא ואמר כסבי דפומבדיתא והוו
משתקי ליה כולי עלמא אמר להו שבקוהו הילכתא כסבי דפומבדיתא
ולא הוו משתקו ליה: **מתני'** מזגו לו כוס שלישי מברך על מזונו
רביעי גומר עליו את הלל ואומר עליו ברכת השיר *בין הכוסות הללו אם
רוצה לשתות ישתה בין שלישי לרביעי לא ישתה: **גמ'** א"ל רב חנן לרבא
ש"מ *ברכת המזון טעונה כוס א"ל ארבע כסי תיקנו רבנן דרך חירות כל חד
וחד נעביד ביה מצוה: רביעי גומר עליו את ההלל ואומר עליו ברכת השיר:
מאי

למען תזכור את יום צאתך מארץ מצרים. לכך קבעו זכר ליציאת מצרים ושמעתי מהר"ם שיש במדרש לפי שבמצרים עבדו בהם בישראל בפרך ופרך בא"ת ב"ש וג"ל שהם מלאכות ארבעים חסר אחת וכשנגאלו ממצרים הזהירם על השבת לשבות מהם ל"ט מלאכות: **רביעי** אומר עליו הלל הגדול. רביעי גרסי' ולא גרסינן חמישי ולה"ר יוסף טוב עלם שכתב בסדרו* קימא לשתות מים יכנס אם חולה הוא או איסטניס ואי בעי משתיה חמרא משום אונס לומר בחמישי הלל הגדול ישתנס תימה כיון שאוסר לשתות איך תיקנו כוס חמישי הא ארבע כוסות תיקנו ולא חמישי וכן מה שאוסר לשתות אפי' מים הא לא מבטלי טעם מצה דאפילו אחר הפסח לא אסר לקמן רק מיני מיכלא אבל מיני משקיא אפילו יין לא מצינן לאסור והא דאמר בין שלישי לרביעי לא ישתה מפרש בירושלמי שלא ישתכר ושלא יוכל לומר הלל וכן פסק רבי' שמואל לקמן* דכל שתיה מותרת ואפי' לפי המפרשים בין שלישי לרביעי לא ישתה שלא יבטל טעם מצה מ"מ במים לא מיירי אלא ביין דומיא דבין ראשון לשני ישתה דמיירי ביין כי היכי דניגררייה לליבה כדאמרי' לעיל [דף קח.] ומיהו רוב עמא דבר לשתות וגם רב אלפס התיר מים ולא אסר רק יין: מאי

קסבר עד ועד בכלל. ואי אמינא עד בצאת דאף בצאת סברי עלמא דאף בצאת בכלל משום הכי אמר עד אם הבנים שמחה והו לה: [עד ולא עד בכלל.] ואי הוה אמינא עד אם הבנים הוה משמע עד אם הבנים ולא אם הבנים בכלל: ה"ג כתיב הכא למען תזכור את יום צאתך וגו' וכתיב התם זכור את יום השבת לקדשו: כשם הגדולים. כאברהם יצחק ויעקב: דברבים איתא. משום כבוד רבים אומר מקדש ישראל: ה"ג

רשב"ם

מאי לאו בהא קמיפלגי. דהנך תנאי אליבא דב"ש בהללויה פליגי אי סוף פירקא הוא אי ריש פירקא הוא הלכך האי נקט מילתיה בהך לישנא והאי מילתיה באידך לישנא אבל אליבא דבית הלל דליכא הללויה עד חלמיש למעינו מים לא פליגי כו' אלא איידי דמיפלגי מילתיה דב"ש משום הללויה אי ריש פירקא הוא אי לא מיחלפי נמי מילתייהו דבית הלל למינקט האי מילתיה סוף פירקא והאידך ריש פירקא כי היכי דלאמרי אליבא דב"ש: מ"ד עד בצאת סבר עד ולא עד בכלל. ואי הוה אמר עד אם הבנים הוה משמע ולא אם הבנים שמחה בכלל: ומ"ד עד אם הבנים קסבר עד ועד בכלל. ואי הוה אמר *בצאת הוה משמע דאף בצאת בכלל ופלוגתייהו דבית הלל איכא לפרושי נמי בהכי: ונימא עד הללויה. למ"ד עד ולא עד בכלל: קרית שמע. ברכת גאולה שאחר ק"ש: והלל. של ערבי פסחים שחותם גאל ישראל כר"ט דמתניתין שמספר ומשבח על גאולת ישראל שעברה: דצלותא גואל ישראל. שאנו מתפללין על העתיד: דקידושא וקדשנו. הודאה היא על שעבר דצלותא קדשנו. לפי שאנו אומרים אותה בתפלה ראוי לאומרה בלשון בקשה: צריך שיזכיר יציאת מצרים בקידוש היום. בין בכוס בין בתפלה של שבת בגזירה שוה דפסח ובשאר מועדים במה מצינו מפסח: ה"ג כתיב הכא למען תזכור את יום צאתך וכתיב התם זכור את יום השבת: דאפטרתא. במסכת סופרים (*פרק יג) תניא להו לברכות ההפטרה ומפרש למגן דוד הוא אומר ובצלותא צריך לומר טפי מצמיח קרן ישועה משום דרחמי נינהו ואנו מבקשין שיצמיח קרן ישועה לישראל ורבינו שלמה היה אומר משום הכי לא שייך למימר בתפלה מגן דוד שכבר אמרנו מגן אברהם ותרי חתימות כהדדי לא שייך בתפלה: כשם הגדולים אשר בארץ. נתן הנביא אמר לדוד כן מפי הקב"ה שכשם שחותמים במגן אברהם חותמין במגן דוד הגדולים אברהם יצחק ויעקב ואע"ג דבשלשתן לא חתמינן היינו לפי שאין חותמין בשתים כדכתיב והיה ברכה מיהו שלשתן נזכרין בברכת אבות אבל דוד שהוא יחיד בברכה הקבועה לו במי יחתומו אם לא במגן דוד: סבי דפומבדיתא. רב יהודה ורב עינא בסוף פרק ראשון דסנהדרין (דף יז:): בשבתא. בשבת דעלמא שאינו י"ט: יומא טבא. בלא שבתא דאילו בשבת ויום טוב חתים תרווייהו מקדש השבת וישראל והזמנים כדמפרש במסכת ביצה (דף יז): שבתא דקביעא וקיימא. מששת ימי בראשית ואינה תלויה בקביעת החודש: דברבים איתא. משום כבוד רבים אומר מקדש ישראל: קידוש ברבים מי ליתא. בבית הכנסת ובסעודת חתן: **מתני'** ברכת השיר. בגמרא מפרש: בין הכוסות הללו. בין שנים הראשונים לשנים האחרונים אם רצה לשתות ישתה: בין ג' לד' לא ישתה. מפרש בגמרא ירושלמי למה לא ישתה כדי שלא ישתכר דתו לא מצי למימר הלל ופריך התם והלא כבר משוכר הוא ששתה כבר הרבה בסעודתו ומשני יין שבתוך המזון אינו משכר שלאחר המזון משכר וה"ה נמי דיין שלפני המזון אינו משכר ואם רצה לשתות בין ראשון לשני ישתה דהא לא ממעט הנא אלא בין ג' לד': **גמ'** ש"מ ברכת המזון טעונה כוס. דהא במסכת ברכות לא מתני' בהדיא דטעונה כוס הלא מדיוקא קמעינן ליה דאמר בריש פירקא (דף קה:) שמעת מינה מהא מתני' תמני ש"מ ברכת המזון טעונה כוס ולימא נמי דממתני' קמעינן ליה: ה"ג ארבע כוסות תקינו להו רבנן כל חד וחד נעביד ביה מצוה. כלומר ראוי שיעשה בו מצוה אבל בשאר ימות השנה לא בעי כוס שאף כאן אין הכוס בא בשביל ברכת המזון:

יהללוך

תורה אור
שמות כ

[ברכות כו: וש"נ]
נ"ל עד בצאת
[*מהלכה ט והילך]
[לעיל קח.]
[לעיל קה:]

הגהות הגר"א
[א] גמרא קידושא אשר קדשנו במצותיו דצלותא כו':

צח א מיי' פ"ב מהלכות תפלה הל' ה' ופכ"ט מהלכות שבת הלכה ג והלכה יט סמג עשין יט כט טוא"ח סימן רסח וטוש"ע א"ח סימן תפז סעיף א:

[לשבת הגדול סמוך לסוף פיוט קוד' תסל סדור פסח]

צט ב מיי' פ"ז ופ"ח מהלכות מצה הלכה י סמג עשין מא טוש"ע א"ח סימן תעט:
ק ג מיי' וסמג שם טוש"ע א"ח סי' תפ:
קא ד מיי' פ"ז שם וסמג שם טוש"ע א"ח סימן תעג סעיף ג:
קב ה מיי' וסמג שם טוש"ע א"ח סי' תעט:

[קכ. בסוף הסוגיא]

[עי' לעיל מג: מ"ש שם עה"ג]

ס"א והילכתא כסבי דפומבדיתא

רבינו חננאל

והחתם בגאולה אמרי ק"ש והלל וחותמין גאל ישראל צלותא גואל ישראל מאי טעמא רחמי נינהו אמ' רבי זירא ברכה דקידוש אק"ב אבל של תפלה קדשנו במצותיך מאי טעמא דתפלה רחמי נינהו וצריך שיזכיר יציאת מצרים (בלילות) [בקידוש היום] כתיב הבא זכור את יום השבת לקדשו וכתיב התם למען תזכור את יום צאתך וגו'. אמר רבה בר זירא בצלותא חותמין מצמיח קרן ישועה בהפטרה מגן דוד שנאמר ועשיתי לך שם גדול כשם הגדולים אשר בארץ. תאני רב יוסף שחותמין בהפטרה מגן דוד כדרך שחותמין בתפלה מגן אברהם. אמר ריש לקיש ואעשך לגוי גדול זה שאומר אלהי אברהם ואברכך זהו שאומרים אלהי יצחק ואגדלה שמך זה שאומרים אלהי יעקב יכול יהו חותמין בכלן ת"ל והיה ברכה אין חותמין אלא בך בלבד. אמר רבא אשכחתינהו לסבי דפומבדיתא דהוו אמרו בשבתא בין בקידושא בין בצלותא ביום טוב בין בצלותא בין בקידושא מקדש ישראל והזמנים ואמינא להו אנא ואסיקנא כסבי דפומבדיתא מדאמר רבינא אנא אקלעי לסורא לגבי מרימר ונחית שליח צבור לקמיה ואמר כסבי דפומבדיתא והוו כולי עלמא משתקי ליה ואמר להו מרימר שבקוה דהלכתא כסבי דפומבדיתא: כוס שלישי ברך על מזונו אמר לו רבינא לרבא ש"מ ברכה טעונה כוס אמר ליה ארבע כוסות דתקון רבנן דרך חירות כל חד וחד נעביד ביה מצוה. רביעי גומר עליו את ההלל ואומר עליו ברכת השיר
מאי

א"ר חסדא א"ר יוחנן הללויה וכסיה וידידיה אחת הן רב אמר כסיה ומרחביה אחת הן *רבה אמר מרחביה בלבד איבעיא להו מרחב יה לרב חסדא מאי תיקו איבעיא להו ידידיה לרב מאי ת"ש דאמר רב ידידיה נחלק לשנים לפיכך ידיד חול יה קודש איבעיא להו הללויה לרב מאי ת"ש דאמר רב חזינא תילי דבי חביבא דכתיב בהו הללו בחד גיסא ויה בחד גיסא ופליגא דריב"ל דאמר ריב"ל מאי הללויה הללוהו בהלולים הרבה ופליגא דידיה אדידיה דאמר ריב"ל בעשרה מאמרות של שבח נאמר ספר תהלים בניצוח בנגון במשכיל במזמור בשיר באשרי בתהלה בתפלה בהודאה בהללויה גדול מכולן הללויה שכולל שם ושבח בבת אחת אמר רב יהודה אמר שמואל שיר שבתורה משה וישראל אמרוהו בשעה שעלו מן הים והלל זה מי אמרו נביאים שביניהן תקנו להן לישראל שיהו אומרין אותו על כל פרק ופרק ועל כל צרה וצרה שלא תבא עליהן ולכשנגאלין אומרים אותו על גאולתן תניא היה ר"מ אומר כל תושבחות האמורות בספר תהלים כלן דוד אמרן שנאמר °כלו תפלות דוד בן ישי אל תיקרי כלו אלא כל אלו הלל זה מי אמרו רבי יוסי אומר אלעזר בני אומר משה וישראל אמרוהו בשעה שעלו מן הים וחלוקין עליו חביריו לומר שדוד אמרו ונראין דבריו מדבריהן *אפשר ישראל שחטו את פסחיהן ונטלו לולביהן ולא אמרו שירה ד"א פסלו של מיכה עומד בבכי וישראל אומרים את ההלל: ת"ר כל שירות ותושבחות שאמר דוד בספר תהלים ר"א אומר כנגד עצמו אמרן רבי יהושע אומר כנגד ציבור אמרן וחכ"א יש מהן כנגד ציבור ויש מהן כנגד עצמו האמורות בלשון יחיד כנגד עצמו האמורות בלשון רבים כנגד ציבור ניצוח וניגון לעתיד לבא משכיל על ידי תורגמן לדוד מזמור מלמד ששרתה עליו שכינה ואחר כך אמר שירה מזמור לדוד מלמד שאמר שירה ואחר כך שרתה עליו שכינה *ללמדך שאין השכינה שורה לא מתוך עצלות ולא מתוך עצבות ולא מתוך שחוק ולא מתוך קלות ראש ולא מתוך דברים בטלים אלא מתוך דבר שמחה של מצוה שנאמר °ועתה קחו לי מנגן והיה כנגן המנגן ותהי עליו יד ה' אמר רב יהודה אמר רב וכן לדבר הלכה אמר רב נחמן וכן לחלום טוב איני *והאמר רב גידל אמר רב כל ת"ח היושב לפני רבו ואין שפתותיו נוטפות מר תכוינה שנאמר °שפתותיו שושנים נוטפות מור עובר *אל תקרי מור עובר אלא מר עובר אל תקרי שושנים אלא ששונים לא קשיא הא ברבה הא בתלמידא ואי בעית אימא הא והא ברבה ולא קשיא הא מקמי דפתח והא לבתר דפתח כי הא דרבה מקמי דפתח להו לרבנן אמר מילתא דבדיחותא ובדחו רבנן ולבסוף יתיב באימתא ופתח בשמעתא ת"ר הלל זה מי אמרו ר"א אומר משה וישראל אמרוהו בשעה שעמדו על הים הם אמרו °לא לנו ה' לא לנו משיבה רוח הקודש ואמרה להן °למעני למעני אעשה רבי יהודה אומר יהושע וישראל אמרוהו בשעה שעמדו עליהן מלכי כנען הם אמרו לא לנו ומשיבה וכו' רבי אלעזר המודעי אומר דבורה וברק אמרוהו בשעה שעמד עליהם סיסרא הם אמרו לא לנו ורוח הקודש משיבה ואומרת להם למעני למעני אעשה ר' אלעזר בן עזריה אומר חזקיה וסייעתו אמרוהו בשעה שעמד עליהם סנחריב הם אמרו לא לנו ומשיבה וכו' רבי עקיבא אומר חנניה מישאל ועזריה אמרוהו בשעה שעמד עליהם נבוכדנצר הרשע הם אמרו לא לנו ומשיבה וכו' רבי יוסי הגלילי אומר מרדכי ואסתר אמרוהו בשעה שעמד עליהם המן הרשע הם אמרו לא לנו ומשיבה וכו' וחכמים אומרים נביאים שביניהן תיקנו להם לישראל שיהו אומרים אותו על כל פרק ופרק ועל כל צרה וצרה שלא תבא עליהם לישראל ולכשנגאלין אומרים אותו על גאולתן: אמר רב חסדא הללויה סוף פירקא רבה בר רב הונא אמר הללויה ריש פירקא אמר רב חסדא חזינא להו לתילי דבי רב חנין בר רב דכתיב בהו הללויה באמצע פירקא אלמא מספקא ליה אמר רב חנין בר רבא הכל מודים °בתהלת ה' ידבר פי ויברך כל בשר שם קדשו לעולם ועד (הללויה) הללויה דבתריה ריש פירקא °רשע יראה וכעס שניו יחרק ונמס תאות רשעים תאבד הללויה דבתריה ריש פירקא °ושעומדים בבית ה' הללויה דבתריה ריש פירקא קראי מוסיפין אף את אלו °מנחל בדרך ישתה על כן ירים ראש הללויה דבתריה ריש פירקא °ראשית חכמה יראת ה' שכל טוב לכל עושיהם הללויה דבתריה ריש פירקא נימא כתנאי *עד היכן הוא אומר בית שמאי אומרים עד °אם הבנים שמחה ובית הלל אומרים עד °חלמיש למעינו מים ותניא אידך עד היכן הוא אומר בית שמאי אומרים עד °בצאת ישראל ממצרים ובית הלל אומרים עד °לא לנו ה' לא לנו

מאי

רש"י

אחת היא. כלומר תיבה אחת היא ואין התיבה נחלקת לשנים: הללו בהך גיסא. בסוף שיטה ויה בתחלת שיטה האחרת: שיר שבתורה. אז ישיר משה: ועל כל צרה שלא תבא עליהם. לישנא מעליא הוא דנקט כלומר שאם חס ושלום תבוא צרה עליהן ויושעו ממנה אומרים אותו על גאולתן כגון חנוכה: כל תפלות. כל מזמורים הפותחים בתפלה כגון תפלה לעני כי יעטוף (תהלים קב): אפשר ישראל שוחטין את פסחיהן. מיציאת מצרים ועד דוד ולא אמרו עליו הלל: ד"א פסלו של מיכה עומד. בימי דוד בבכי באותו מקום וישראל אומרים הלל שכתוב בו כמוהם יהיו עושיהם וגו' אלא ודאי על הים נאמר תחלה ושוב לא פסק: ניצוח וניגון לעתיד לבא. כל מקום שנאמר למנצח בנגינות מלעתיד הוא מדבר: ע"י מתורגמן. הוא אומר ואחר מפרש: יהושע וכל ישראל אמרוהו. כלומר אף יהושע וכל ישראל אמרוהו: הללויה. כולהו דבספר תהלים: קראי מוסיפין. בעלי מקרא מוסיפין אף אלו:

רשב"ם קסבר

לדוד מזמור. משמע תחלה היה לדוד רוח הקודש ואח"כ מזמור: מזמור לדוד. משמע מתוך המזמור באה שכינה לדוד: ללמד מכאן כו'. מכאן אתה למד וגם מפסוק אחר מוכיח שנאמר ועתה קחו לי מנגן וגו': שמחה של מצוה. כי הך דקחו לי מנגן שהיה מתכוין שתשרה עליו שכינה: וכן לחלום. אם הולך לישן מתוך שמחה רואה חלום טוב: הא ברבה. צריך ללמוד מתוך דבר שמחה: שעמדו על הים. לאחר שעברו כדכתיב (תהלים קיד) הים ראה וינוס והתפללו לא לנו פן יעבור פרעה ויחזו אחריהם: יהושע וכל ישראל אמרוהו. כלומר אף ישראל ויהושע אמרוהו וכן פירש רבינו ולא נהירא לי שאם כן בכולן אתה צריך לפרש כן ואם כן מאי בינייהו ובין חכמים שאומרים נביאים שביניהן אמרוהו וכו' ואתי למימר דכל הני דאמרן לעיל אמרוהו על צרתן שהרי תקנוהו נביאים לכך אלא כל אחד מן התנאים הכי קים ליה מרביה: הללויה ריש פירקא. כולהו הנך דספר תהלים שאין בו כי אם אחת לבדו בין פרק לפרק אבל מקום שיש שני פעמים הללויה בין פרק לפרק לא פליגי רב חסדא ורבה בר רב הונא דחד מלעיל וחד מלרע: קראי מוסיפין. בעלי מקרא מוסיפין אף אלו:

מאי

תוספות

ה"ג שעומדים בבית ה' בחצרות בית אלהינו הללויה דבתריה ריש פירקא. ולא גרסינן העומדים בבית ה' בלילות דאם כן ה"ל למינקט יברכך ה' מציון שזהו פסוק למעלה מהללויה ולא ה"ל למינקט שלשה פסוקים למעלה לכך נראה דגרסינן כדפרישית ולפי זה אנו צריכין לומר בו הללויה הללו את שם ה' הללו עבדי ה' שעומדים בבית ה' וגו' שלמעלה מזה אינו תחלת המזמור דלא יתכן שיהיה המזמור שני פסוקים °ועוד דאמרי' *במדרש קמ"ז מזמורים יש בספר תהלים כנגד שנות יעקב אלא הוא סופו של שיר המעלות הנה ברכו וגו' ואתי שפיר דקאמרינן לקמן רב אחא בר יעקב דמתחיל הלל הגדול מכי יעקב בחר לו יה דהוי תחלת המזמור דבע"א לא יתכן שיהיה מתחיל הלל מאמצע המזמור:

למען

[א"ה בספר מב"ס, מכאן. (?)]

רבינו חננאל

ענין דהללויה כסיה ידידיה דבור אחד הוא. ת"ש ידידיה נחלק לשנים לפיכך ידיד חול יה קדש: אמר ר"י בן לוי בעשרה דברים נאמר ספר תהלים בנצוח בנגון במשכיל במזמור בשיר באשרי בתפלה בתהלה בהודאה בהלל גדול שבכלן הללויה שכולל שם ושבח בבת אחת: ת"ר שיר שבתורה משה וישראל אמרוה בשעה שעמדו על הים הלל זה הללויה הללו עבדי ה' נביאים תקנוהו שיהו אומרין על כל פרק ועל כל צרה שנגאלין ממנה וכו' ר"מ אומר כל שירות שבתילים דוד אמרן כו' עד וכי פסל מיכה עומד בבכי וישראל אומרין שירה ופשוטה היא: תניא כל שיר האמור בתלים בלשון יחיד דוד אמרו בפני עצמו וכל האמור בלשון רבים כנגד צבור אמרו וכל האמור בנצוח בניגון לעתיד לבוא ור"ל האמור במשכיל על ידי תורגמן אמרו וכל האמור לדוד מזמור שרתה שכינה עליו ואחר כך מזמור וכל האמור מזמור לדוד אמר שירה ואח"כ שרתה עליו שכינה ללמדך שאין השכינה שורה לא מתוך עצבות וכו' עד אלא מתוך שמחה שנא' ועתה קחו לי מנגן וכו' וכן להלכה וכן לחלום טוב ואסיקנא כי הא דרבא מקמי דלפתח בשמעתא הוה אמר מילתא דבדיחותא קמי רבנן לבדוחי לביהו והדר הוה יתיב באימתא ופתח בשמעתא וכל שכן תלמיד דלא ליתיב אלא באימתא: ת"ר רבי אליעזר אומר הלל זה משה וישראל אמרוהו בשעה שעמד עליהם פרעה אמרו הן לא לנו משיבה רוח הקדש למעני למעני אעשה ר' יהושע אומר יהושע וישראל אמרוהו וכו' ר' אלעזר המודעי אומר דבורה וברק אמרוהו כו' ר' אלעזר בן עזריה אומר חנניה מישאל ועזריה אמרוהו כו' ר' יוסי הגלילי אומר מרדכי ואסתר אמרוהו והכמים אומרים נביאים שביניהם תקנוהו שיהו אומרין אותו על כל פרק ופרק ועל כל צרה וצרה שתבוא עליהן ולכשנגאלין אומרין אותו על גאולתן: מתני' עד היכן אומר ב"ה אומר עד חלמיש למעינו מים והלכה כב"א

עין משפט נר מצוה

צו א מיי' פ"ז מהלכות יסודי התורה הל' ד:
צז ב מיי' פ"ח מהלכות מגלה הל' ה סמג עשין מא טור א"ח סי' תעג:

תורה אור

תהלים עב · מ"ב ג · שיר ה · תהלים קטו ישעיה מח · תהלים קמה · תהלים קיב · שם קלה · שם קי · שם קיא · [לעיל קטז:] · שם קיג · שם קיד · שם קיד · שם קטו

מסורת הש"ס

[גירסת רש"ל ותוי"ט פ"ד מ"ה דמסכת סוכה רבא ע"ש] · לעיל דף קה: · שבת ל: ע"ש (ברכות דף לא.) · שבת ל: · שבת דף פח: [ודף ל:]

גליון הש"ס

תוס' ד"ה שעומדים וכו' ועוד דאמרינן במדרש. וכ"ה במס' סופרים פי"ח הלכה א' ובירושלמי פט"ו דשבת:

Continuation of translation from previous page as indicated by ◁

But that is not so, for R. Giddal said in Rab's name: If a scholar sits before his teacher and his lips do not drip anxiety,[4] they shall be burnt, for it is said, *His lips are as lilies* [shoshanim], *dropping with flowing myrrh* [mor 'ober]:[5] read not *shoshanim* but *sheshonim* [that study]; read not *mor 'ober* but *mar 'ober* [dropping anxiety]?—There is no difficulty: one applies to the teacher, the other to the disciple. Alternatively, both refer to the teacher, yet there is no difficulty: the one holds good before he commences; the other, after he commences. Even as Rabbah used to say something humorous to his scholars before he commenced [his discourse], in order to amuse them;[6] after that he sat in awe and commenced the lecture.

Our Rabbis taught: Who uttered this *Hallel?* R. Eleazar said: Moses and Israel uttered it when they stood by the [Red] Sea. They exclaimed, *'Not unto us, not unto us,'*[7] and the Holy Spirit responded, *'For Mine own sake, for Mine own sake, will I do it.'*[8] R. Judah said: Joshua and Israel uttered it when the kings of Canaan attacked them. They exclaimed, *'Not unto us* [etc.]' and the Holy Spirit responded etc. R. Eleazar the Modiite said: Deborah and Barak uttered it when Sisera attacked them. They exclaimed, *'Not unto us* [etc.],' and the Holy Spirit responded, *'For Mine own sake, for Mine own sake, will I do it.'* R. Eleazar b. 'Azariah said: Hezekiah and his companions uttered it when Sennacherib attacked them. They exclaimed, *'Not unto us* [etc.]' and the Holy Spirit responded etc. R. Akiba said: Hananiah, Mishael and Azariah uttered it when the wicked Nebuchadnezzar rose against them. They exclaimed, *'Not unto us* etc.,' and the Holy Spirit responded etc. R. Jose the Galilean said: Mordecai and Esther uttered it when the wicked Haman rose against them. They supplicated, *'Not unto us* etc.', and the Holy Spirit responded etc. But the Sages maintain: The prophets among them enacted that the Israelites should recite it at every epoch and at every trouble—may it not come to them!—and when they are redeemed, they recite it [in thankfulness] for their delivery.

R. Ḥisda said: *Hallelujah* marks the end of a chapter; Rabbah b. R. Huna said: *Hallelujah* marks the beginning of a
d chapter.[1] R. Ḥisda observed: I saw that in the copies of the Psalms used in the college of R. Ḥanin b. Rab, *'Hallelujah'* was written in the *middle* of the chapter,[2] which proves that he was in doubt.

R. Ḥanin b. Raba said: All agree that in the case of, *'My mouth shall speak the praise of the Lord, and let all flesh bless His holy name for ever and ever,'*[3] 'Hallelujah' which follows it is the beginning of the [next] psalm. In *the wicked shall see, and be vexed; he shall gnash with his teeth, and melt away, the desire of the wicked shall perish:*[4] the 'Hallelujah' which follows it commences the [next] psalm. Again, in the passage, *'that stand in the house of the Lord in the night seasons,*[5] the following 'Hallelujah' commences the [next] psalm.[6] Bible scholars[7] add the following: *He will drink of the brook by the way, therefore will he lift up the head:*[8] Hallelujah which follows it is the beginning of the next psalm. *The fear of the Lord is the beginning of wisdom; a good understanding have all they that do thereafter;*
e *His praise endureth for ever.*[1] 'Hallelujah' which follows it is the beginning of the [next] psalm.

Shall we say that this is dependent on Tannaim? [For we learned:] HOW FAR DOES HE RECITE IT? BETH SHAMMAI MAINTAIN: UNTIL 'AS A JOYOUS MOTHER OF CHILDREN,' WHILE BETH HILLEL SAY: UNTIL 'THE FLINT INTO A FOUNTAIN OF WATERS.' But another [Baraitha] taught: How far does he recite it? Beth Shammai maintain: Until *'when Israel came forth out of Egypt,'*[2] while Beth Hillel say: Until, *'Not unto us, O Lord,*

(4) Lit., 'bitterness'. To show due reverence. (5) Cant. V, 13. (6) Lit., 'and the scholars rejoiced'. (7) Ps. CXV, 1. (8) Isa. XLVIII, 11.

d (1) Where a single *'Hallelujah'* separates two psalms (e.g., Ps. CXXXIV and CXXXV), R. Ḥisda maintains that it ends the first, while Rabbah b. R. Huna places it at the beginning of the second. (2) I.e., the two were run into one with *'Hallelujah'* in the middle. (3) Ps. CXLV, 21. (4) Ps. CXII, 10. (5) Ibid. CXXXIV, 1. (6) This is somewhat difficult, as 'Hallelujah' does not immediately follow. Possibly the phrase is quoted loosely to indicate which psalm is meant, viz., CXXXIV, 'Hallelujah,' then commencing the next. Tosaf. however quotes *'Ye that stand in the house of the Lord, in the courts of the house of our God'*. In our edd. this is Ps. CXXXV, 2, and does not end the psalm; but according to Tosaf. it does, while v. 3, which begins with 'Hallelujah,' (E.V. *Praise ye the Lord*) is the beginning of another psalm. (7) Presumably scholars who specialized in the study of the Bible. (8) Ps. CX, 7.

e (1) Ps. CXI, 10. (2) Ibid. CXIV, 1.

צו א מיי' פ"ז מהלכות יסודי התורה הל' ד:
צז ב מיי' פ"ח מהלכות מגלה הל' ה סמג עשין מא טור א"ח סי' תעג:

אחת היא. כלומר תיבה אחת היא ואין התיבה נחלקת לשנים: הללו בהך גיסא. בסוף שיטה ויה בתחלת שיטה האחרת: שיר שבתורה. אז ישיר משה: ועל כל צרה שלא תבא עליהם. לישנא מעליא הוא דנקט כלומר שאם חס ושלום תבוא צרה עליהן ויושעו ממנה אומרים אותו על גאולתן כגון חנוכה: כל תפלות. כל מזמורים הפותחים בתפלה כגון תפלה לעני כי יעטוף (תהלים קב): אפשר ישראל שוחטין את פסחיהן. מיציאת מצרים ועד דוד ולא אמרו עליו הלל: ד"א פסלו של מיכה עומד. בימי דוד בבכי במקום וישראל אומרים הלל שכתוב בו כמותם יהיו עושיהם וגו' אלא ודאי על הים נאמר תחלה ושוב לא פסק: ניצוח וניגון לעתיד לבא. כל מקום שנאמר למנצח בנגינות מלעתיד הוא מדבר: ע"י מתורגמן. הוא לומר ואחר מפרש: יהושע וכל ישראל אמרוהו. כלומר אף יהושע וכל ישראל אמרוהו: הללויה. כולהו דבספר תהלים: קראי מוסיפין. בעלי מקרא מוסיפין אף אלו:

תורה אור

א"ר חסדא א"ר יוחנן הללויה וכסיה וידידיה אחת הן רב אמר כסיה ומרחביה אחת הן *רבה אמר מרחביה בלבד איבעיא להו מרחב יה לרב חסדא מאי תיקו איבעיא להו ידידיה לרב מאי ת"ש דאמר רב ידידיה נחלק לשנים לפיכך ידיד חול יה קודש איבעיא להו הללויה לרב מאי ת"ש דאמר רב חזינא תילי דבי חביבא דכתיב בהו הללו בחד גיסא ויה בחד גיסא ופליגא דריב"ל דאמר ריב"ל מאי הללויה הללוהו בהלולים הרבה ופליגא דידיה אדידיה דאמר ריב"ל בעשרה מאמרות של שבח נאמר ספר תהלים בניצוח בנגון במשכיל במזמור בשיר באשרי בתהלה בתפלה בהודאה בהללויה גדול מכולן הללויה שכולל שם ושבח בבת אחת אמר רב יהודה אמר שמואל שיר שבתורה משה וישראל אמרוהו בשעה שעלו מן הים והלל זה מי אמרו נביאים שביניהן תקנו להן לישראל שיהו אומרין אותו על כל פרק ופרק ועל כל צרה וצרה שלא תבא עליהן ולכשנגאלין אומרים אותו על גאולתן תניא היה ר"מ אומר כל תושבחות האמורות בספר תהלים כלן דוד אמרן שנאמר (תהלים עב) °כלו תפלות דוד בן ישי אל תיקרי כלו אלא כל אלו הלל זה מי אמרו רבי יוסי אומר אלעזר בני אומר משה וישראל אמרוהו בשעה שעלו מן הים וחלוקין עליו חביריו לומר שדוד אמרו ונראין דבריו מדבריהן *אפשר ישראל שחטו את פסחיהן ונטלו לולביהן ולא אמרו שירה ד"א פסלו של מיכה עומד בבכי וישראל אומרים את ההלל: ת"ר כל שירות ותושבחות שאמר דוד בספר תהלים ר"א אומר כנגד עצמו אמרן רבי יהושע אומר כנגד ציבור אמרן וחכ"א יש מהן כנגד ציבור ויש מהן כנגד עצמו האמורות בלשון יחיד כנגד עצמו האמורות בלשון רבים כנגד ציבור ניצוח וניגון לעתיד לבא משכיל על ידי תורגמן לדוד מזמור מלמד ששרתה עליו שכינה ואחר כך אמר שירה מזמור לדוד מלמד שאמר שירה ואחר כך שרתה עליו שכינה *ללמדך שאין השכינה שורה לא מתוך עצלות ולא מתוך עצבות ולא מתוך שחוק ולא מתוך קלות ראש ולא מתוך דברים בטלים אלא מתוך דבר שמחה של מצוה שנאמר (מ"ב ג) °ועתה קחו לי מנגן והיה כנגן המנגן ותהי עליו יד ה' אמר רב יהודה אמר רב וכן לדבר הלכה אמר רב נחמן וכן לחלום טוב איני *והאמר רב גידל אמר רב כל ת"ח היושב לפני רבו ואין שפתותיו נוטפות מר תכוינה שנאמר (שיר ה') °שפתותיו שושנים נוטפות מור עובר *אל תקרי שושנים אלא ששונים אל תקרי מור עובר אלא מר עבר לא קשיא הא ברבה הא בתלמידא ואי בעית אימא הא והא ברבה ולא קשיא הא מקמי דפתח והא לבתר דפתח כי הא דרבה מקמי דפתח להו לרבנן אמר מילתא דבדיחותא ובדחו רבנן ולבסוף יתיב באימתא ופתח בשמעתא ת"ר הלל זה מי אמרו ר"א אומר משה וישראל אמרוהו בשעה שעמדו על הים הם אמרו (תהלים קטו) °לא לנו ה' לא לנו משיבה רוח הקודש ואמרה להן (ישעיה מח) °למעני למעני אעשה רבי יהודה אומר יהושע וישראל אמרוהו בשעה שעמדו עליהן מלכי כנען הם אמרו לא לנו ומשיבה וכו' רבי אלעזר המודעי אומר דבורה וברק אמרוהו בשעה שעמד עליהם סיסרא הם אמרו לא לנו ורוח הקודש משיבה ואומרת להם למעני למעני אעשה ר' אלעזר בן עזריה אומר חזקיה וסייעתו אמרוהו בשעה שעמד עליהם סנחריב הם אמרו לא לנו ומשיבה וכו' רבי עקיבא אומר חנניה מישאל ועזריה אמרוהו בשעה שעמד עליהם נבוכדנצר הרשע הם אמרו לא לנו ומשיבה וכו' רבי יוסי הגלילי אומר מרדכי ואסתר אמרוהו בשעה שעמד עליהם המן הרשע הם אמרו לא לנו ומשיבה וכו' וחכמים אומרים נביאים שביניהן תיקנו להם לישראל שיהו אומרים אותו על כל פרק ופרק ועל כל צרה וצרה שלא תבא עליהם לישראל ולכשנגאלין אומרים אותו על גאולתן: אמר רב חסדא הללויה סוף פירקא רבה בר רב הונא אמר הללויה ריש פירקא אמר רב חסדא חזינא להו לתילי דבי רב חנין בר רב דכתיב בהו הללויה באמצע פירקא אלמא מספקא ליה אמר רב חנין בר רבא הכל מודים (תהלים קמה) °בתהלת ה' ידבר פי ויברך כל בשר שם קדשו לעולם ועד (הללויה) הללויה דבתריה ריש פירקא (שם קי) °רשע יראה וכעס שניו יחרק ונמס תאות רשעים תאבד הללויה דבתריה ריש פירקא °ושעומדים בבית ה' הללויה דבתריה ריש פירקא קראי מוסיפין אף את אלו °מנחל בדרך ישתה על כן ירים ראש הללויה דבתריה ריש פירקא °ראשית חכמה יראת ה' שכל טוב לכל עושיהם הללויה דבתריה ריש פירקא נימא כתנאי *עד היכן הוא אומר בית שמאי אומרים עד (שם קיג) °אם הבנים שמחה ובית הלל אומרים עד (שם קיד) °חלמיש למעינו מים ותניא אידך עד היכן הוא אומר בית שמאי אומרים עד °בצאת ישראל ממצרים ובית הלל אומרים עד °לא לנו ה' לא לנו

מאי

ה"ג שעומדים בבית ה' בחצרות בית אלהינו הללויה דבתריה ריש פירקא. ולא גרסינן העומדים בבית ה' בלילות דאם כן ה"ל למינקט יברכך ה' מציון שזהו פסוק למעלה מהללויה ולא ה"ל למינקט שלשה פסוקים למעלה לכך נראה דגרסינן כדפרישית ולפי זה אנו צריכין לומר בו הללויה הללו את שם ה' הללו עבדי ה' שעומדים בבית ה' וגו' שלמעלה מזה אינו תחלת המזמור דלא יתכן שיהיה המזמור שני פסוקים *ועוד דאמרי' *במדרש קמ"ז מזמורים יש בספר תהלים כנגד שנות יעקב אלא הוא סופו של שיר המעלות הנה ברכו וגו' ואתי שפיר דקאמרינן לקמן רב אחא בר יעקב דמתחיל הלל הגדול מכי יעקב בחר לו יה דהוי תחלת המזמור דבע"א לא יתכן שהיה מתחיל הלל מאמצע המזמור:

למען

רשב"ם

קסבר לדוד מזמור. משמע תחלה היה לדוד רוח הקודש ואח"כ מזמור: מזמור לדוד. משמע מתוך המזמור באה שכינה לדוד: ללמד מכאן כו'. מכאן אתה למד וגם מפסוק אחר מוכיח שנאמר ועתה קחו לי מנגן וגו': שמחה של מצוה. כי הך דקחו לי מנגן שהיה מתכוין שתשרה עליו שכינה: וכן לחלום. אם הולך לישן מתוך שמחה רואה חלום טוב: הא ברבה. צריך ללמוד מתוך דבר שמחה: שעמדו על הים. לאחר שעברו כדכתיב (תהלים קיד) הים ראה וינוס והתפללו לא לנו פן יעבור פרעה וחילו אחריהם: יהושע וכל ישראל אמרוהו. כלומר אף ישראל ויהושע אמרוהו וכן פירש רבינו ולא נהירא לי שאם כן בכולן אתה צריך לפרש כן ואם כן מאי בינייהו ובין חכמים שאומרים נביאים שביניהן אמרוהו וכו' ואתי למימר דכל הני דאמרן לעיל אמרוהו על צרתן שהרי תקנוהו נביאים לכך אלא כל אחד מן התנאים הכי קים ליה מרביה: הללויה ריש פירקא. כולהו הנך דספר תהלים שאין בו כי אם אחת לבדו בין פרק לפרק אבל מקום שיש שני פעמים הללויה בין פרק לפרק לא פליגי רב חסדא ורבה בר רב הונא דחד מלעיל וחד מלרע: קראי מוסיפין. בעלי מקרא מוסיפין אף אלו:

מאי

רבינו חננאל

ענין דהללויה כסיה ידידיה דבור אחד היא. ת"ש ידידיה נחלק לשנים לפיכך ידיד חול יה קודש: אמר ר"י בן לוי בעשרה דברים נאמר ספר תהלים בנצוח בנגון במשכיל במזמור בשיר באשרי בתפלה בתהלה בהודאה בהלל גדול שבכלן הללויה שכולל שם ושבח בבת אחת: ת"ר שיר שבתורה משה וישראל אמרוה בשעה שעמדו על הים הלל זה הללויה הללו עבדי ה' נביאים תקנוהו שיהו אומרין על כל פרק ועל כל צרה שנגאלין ממנה וכו' ר"מ אומר כל שירות שבתילים דוד אמרן כו' עד וכי פסל מיכה עומד בבכי וישראל אומרין שירה ופשוטה היא: תניא כל שיר האמור בתלים בלשון יחיד דוד אמרו בפני עצמו וכל האמור בלשון רבים כנגד צבור אמרו וכל האמור בנצוח בניגון לעתיד לבוא ור"ל האמור במשכיל על ידי תורגמן אמרו וכל האמור לדוד מזמור שרתה שכינה עליו ואחר כך מזמור וכל האמור מזמור לדוד אמר שירה ואח"כ שרתה עליו שכינה ללמדך שאין השכינה שורה לא מתוך עצבות וכו' עד אלא מתוך שמחה שנא' ועתה קחו לי מנגן וכו' וכן להלכה וכן לחלום טוב ואסיקנא כי הא דרבא מקמי דלפתח בשמעתא הוה אמר מילתא דבדירותא קמי רבנן לבדוחי ליבהו והדר הוה יתיב באימתא ופתח בשמעתא וכל שכן תלמיד דלא ליתיב אלא באימתא: ת"ר רבי אליעזר אומר הלל זה משה וישראל אמרוהו בשעה שעמד עליהם פרעה אמרו הן לא לנו משיבה רוח הקודש למעני למעני אעשה ר' יהושע אומר יהושע וישראל אמרוהו וכו' ר' אלעזר המודעי אומר דבורה וברק אמרוהו כו' ר' אלעזר בן עזריה אומר חנניה מישאל ועזריה אמרוהו כו' ר' יוסי הגלילי אומר מרדכי ואסתר אמרוהו והחכמים אומרים נביאים שביניהם תקנוהו שיהו אומרין אותו על כל פרק ופרק ועל כל צרה וצרה שתבוא עליהן ולכשנגאלין אומרין אותו על גאולתן: מתני' עד היכן ב"ה אומר עד חלמיש למעינו מים והלכה כב"א

תהלים קיג | שם קלה | שם קיז | [לעיל קטז:] | שם קיד | שם קטו

לעיל דף לה:
שבת ד' ל: ע"ש (ברכות דף לא)
שבת ל:
שבת דף פח: [ודף ל:]
תהלים קטו ישעיה מח

גליון הש"ס

תוס' ד"ה שעומדים וכו' ועוד דאמרינן במדרש. וכ"ה במס' סופרים פט"ז הלכה י"א ובירושל' פט"ו דשבת:

תהלים קמה | שם קי | שם קיג | שם קיד

THEREFORE IT IS OUR DUTY. [117a] R. Ḥisda said in R.
a Joḥanan's name: *Hallelujah, Kesjah*[1] and *Jedidjah*[2] are single words.[3] Rab said: *Kesjah* and *merḥabjah*[4] are single words. Rabbah[5] said: *Merḥabjah* alone [is a single word]. The scholars asked: What about *merḥab Jah* in R. Ḥisda's view?[6] The question stands. The scholars asked: What about Jedidjah in Rab's view?—Come and hear: Jedidjah is divisible into two, therefore Jedid is non-sacred while Jah [the Lord] is sacred.[7] The scholars asked: What about Hallelujah in Rab's view? Come and hear, for Rab said: I saw [a copy of] the Psalms in my friend's college,[8] wherein '*Hallelu*' was written on one line and '*Jah*' on the following.[9] Now he disagrees with R. Joshua b. Levi, for R. Joshua b. Levi said: What is the meaning of 'Hallelujah'? Praise him with many praises.[10] Further, he [R. Joshua b. Levi] is self-contradictory. For R. Joshua b. Levi said: The Book of Psalms was uttered with ten synonyms of praise, viz.: *nizzuaḥ* [victory], *niggun* [melody], *maskil*,[11] *mizmor* [psalm], *shir* [song], *ashre* [happy], *tehillah* [praise], *tefillah* [prayer], *hodayah* [thanksgiving] [and] *hallelujah*. The greatest of all is '*hallelujah*,' because it embraces the [Divine] Name and praise simultaneously.[12]

Rab Judah said in Samuel's name: The Song in the Torah[13] was uttered by Moses and Israel when they ascended from the [Red] Sea. And who recited this *Hallel?*[14] The prophets among them ordained that Israel should recite it at every important epoch and at every misfortune—may it not come upon them!—and when they are redeemed they recite it [in gratitude] for their redemption.

It was taught, R. Meir used to say: All the praises which are stated in the Book of Psalms, David uttered all of them, for it is
b said, *The prayers of David the son of Jesse are ended* [kallu]:[1] read not *kallu* but *kol ellu* [all these].[2] Who recited this *Hallel?* R. Jose said: My son Eleazar maintains [that] Moses and Israel said it when they ascended from the [Red] Sea, but his colleagues disagree with him, averring that David said it. But his view is preferable to theirs: Is it possible that Israel slaughtered their Passover-offerings or took their palm-branches without uttering song![3] Another argument: Micah's image[4] stands at Beki[5] and Israel recites the *Hallel!*[6]

Our Rabbis taught: As for all the songs and praises to which David gave utterance in the Book of Psalms, R. Eliezer said: He spoke them in reference to himself; R. Joshua said: He spoke them with reference to the [Jewish] community; while the Sages maintain: Some of them refer to the community, while others refer to himself. [Thus:] those which are couched in the singular bear upon himself, while those which are couched in the plural allude to the community. *Nizzuaḥ* and *niggun*[7] [introduce psalms] relating to the future; *maskil* [indicates that it was spoken] through a *meturgeman* [interpreter]; [the superscription] '*To David, a Psalm*' intimates that the *Shechinah* rested upon him and then he uttered [that] song; '*a Psalm of David*' intimates that he [first] uttered [that particular] psalm and then the *Shechinah* rested upon him. This teaches you that the *Shechinah* rests [upon man] neither in indolence nor in gloom nor in frivolity nor in levity, nor in vain pursuits,[8] but only in rejoicing connected with a religious act, for it is said, '*But now bring me a minstrel.*' *And it came to pass, when*
c *the minstrel played, that the hand of the Lord came upon him.*[1] Rab Judah said in Rab's name: And it is likewise so in a matter of *halachah*.[2] R. Naḥman said: And it is likewise so for a good dream.[3]

a (1) In Ex. XVII, 16: *The hand upon kesjah* (E.V.: *the throne of the Lord*). (2) II Sam. XII, 25: *and he called his name Jedidjah* (E.V. *Jedidiah*). (3) Though Jah means the 'Lord,' it combines to form a single word. (4) Ps. CXVIII, 5: He answered me *ba-merḥabjah* (E.V.: *with great enlargement*); lit., 'with the Lord's enlargement.' (5) Rashal reads: Raba: (6) Is it one word or two? (7) This would affect e.g., the manner of its writing. If 'Jedid' is written incorrectly, it can be erased and re-written. But Jah, being sacred (i.e., God's name), must not be erased and would have to be cut out entirely, together with its parchment. (8) I.e., at the college of R. Ḥiyya. (9) Thus he evidently regards it as two words. (10) Since he interprets the whole word thus, he evidently regards it as one. (11) V. e.g., superscriptions to Ps. XLII, XLIV, and XLV; perhaps lit., 'a psalm giving instruction.' (12) Thus he interprets 'Jah' separately. (13) 'Torah' bears here its narrower connotation of Pentateuch. The 'Song' referred to is that contained in Ex. XV. (14) Ps. CXIII-CXVIII. [MS.M. (gloss) inserts: Moses and Israel recited it].

b (1) Ps. LXXII, 20. (2) The verse thus reads: *All these are the prayers* etc. (3) Until the time of David—surely not. (4) V. Judg. XVII. (5) [Probably a variant of Bochin, v. Judg. II, 1]. (6) Rashbam: Hallel, which contains a sweeping condemnation of idolatry (v. Ps. CXV, 5-8), could not have been composed in the days of David while Micah's idolatrous image was still in existence; hence it must have been composed at the Red Sea. (7) V. *supra*. (8) Lit., 'idle words' or chatter.

c (1) II Kings III, 15. Maharsha in Shab. 30a observes that the verse is quoted to show that the *Shechinah* does not rest on a man who is plunged in gloom, Elisha requiring the minstrel to dissipate the gloom occasioned by Jehoram's visit. (2) Serious study should be preceded by light-hearted conversation. (3) Going to sleep in good spirits promotes happy dreams.

◁ *For the continuation of the English translation of this page see overleaf.*

NOT MAKE MENTION OF[2] [116b] THESE THREE THINGS ON PASSOVER DOES NOT DISCHARGE HIS DUTY, AND THESE ARE THEY: THE PASSOVER-OFFERING, UNLEAVENED BREAD, AND BITTER HERBS. THE PASSOVER-OFFERING IS [SACRIFICED] BECAUSE THE OMNIPRESENT PASSED OVER THE HOUSES OF OUR FATHERS IN EGYPT, AS IT IS SAID, THEN YE SHALL SAY: IT IS THE SACRIFICE OF THE LORD'S PASSOVER, FOR THAT HE PASSED OVER etc.[3] THE UNLEAVENED BREAD IS [EATEN] BECAUSE OUR FATHERS WERE REDEEMED FROM EGYPT, AS IT IS SAID, AND THEY BAKED UNLEAVENED CAKES OF THE DOUGH WHICH THEY BROUGHT FORTH OUT OF EGYPT etc.[4] THE BITTER HERB IS [EATEN] BECAUSE THE EGYPTIANS EMBITTERED THE LIVES OF OUR FATHERS IN EGYPT, AS IT IS SAID, AND THEY MADE THEIR LIVES BITTER etc.[5] IN EVERY GENERATION A MAN IS BOUND TO REGARD HIMSELF AS THOUGH HE PERSONALLY HAD GONE FORTH FROM EGYPT, BECAUSE IT IS SAID, AND THOU SHALT TELL THY SON IN THAT DAY, SAYING: IT IS BECAUSE OF THAT WHICH THE LORD DID FOR ME WHEN I CAME FORTH OUT OF EGYPT.[6] THEREFORE IT IS OUR DUTY TO THANK, PRAISE, LAUD, GLORIFY, EXALT, HONOUR, BLESS, EXTOL, AND ADORE HIM WHO WROUGHT ALL THESE MIRACLES FOR OUR FATHERS AND OURSELVES; HE BROUGHT US FORTH FROM BONDAGE INTO FREEDOM, FROM SORROW INTO JOY, FROM MOURNING INTO FESTIVITY, FROM DARKNESS INTO GREAT LIGHT, AND FROM SERVITUDE INTO REDEMPTION. THEREFORE LET US
a SAY BEFORE HIM, HALLELUJAH![1] HOW FAR DOES ONE RECITE IT? BETH SHAMMAI MAINTAIN: UNTIL 'AS A JOYOUS MOTHER OF CHILDREN,'[2] WHILE BETH HILLEL SAY: UNTIL 'THE FLINT INTO A FOUNTAIN OF WATERS,'[3] AND HE CONCLUDES WITH [A FORMULA OF] REDEMPTION. R. ṬARFON USED TO SAY 'WHO REDEEMED US AND REDEEMED OUR FATHERS FROM EGYPT,' BUT HE DID NOT CONCLUDE [WITH A BLESSING].[4] R. AKIBA SAID: 'SO MAY THE LORD OUR GOD AND THE GOD OF OUR FATHERS SUFFER US TO REACH OTHER SEASONS AND FESTIVALS WHICH COME TOWARDS US FOR PEACE, REJOICING IN THE REBUILDING OF THY CITY AND GLAD IN THY SERVICE, AND THERE WE WILL PARTAKE OF THE SACRIFICES AND THE PASSOVER-OFFERINGS'[5] etc. AS FAR AS 'BLESSED ART THOU, O LORD, WHO HAST REDEEMED ISRAEL.'

GEMARA. Raba said: He must say 'and us did he bring forth from there.'

Raba said: He must lift up the unleavened bread, and he must lift up the bitter herb,[6] but he need not lift up the meat;[7] moreover, it would appear as though he ate sacrifices without [the Temple].[8]

R. Aḥa b. Jacob said: A blind person is exempt from reciting
b the *Haggadah*. [For] here it is written, *It is because of that* [zeh],[1] while elsewhere it is written, *This our son* [zeh]:[2] just as there the blind are excluded,[3] so here too the blind are excluded. But that is not so, for Meremar said: I asked the scholars of the School of R. Joseph, Who recites the *Aggadah*[4] at R. Joseph's? And they told me, R. Joseph; Who recites the *Aggadah* at R. Shesheth's? And they told me, R. Shesheth.[5]—These Rabbis held that unleavened bread nowadays is a Rabbinical obligation.[6] Hence it follows that R. Aḥa b. Jacob holds that unleavened bread nowadays is a Scriptural obligation?[7] But surely it was R. Aha b. Jacob himself who said: [The obligation of eating] unleavened bread nowadays is Rabbinical!—He holds, Whatever our Rabbis enacted, they enacted it similar to the Scriptural law.[8] But according to R. Shesheth and R. Joseph too, surely it is certain that whatever our Rabbis enacted, they enacted similar to a Scriptural law?—How compare![9] As for there, it is well: since it should have been written, 'He is our son,' whereas it is written, '*This our son*,'[10] you may infer that it comes to exclude blind persons. But here, if not '*for the sake of this*' what should be written? Hence it comes [to intimate], 'for the sake of the unleavened bread and bitter herbs.'[11]

(2) Perhaps better: 'explain,' as R. Gamaliel's main point is that their purpose must be explained; v. Kaplan, *Redaction of the Talmud*, p. 203. (3) Ex. XII, 27. (4) Ibid. 39. (5) Ex. I, 14. (6) Ibid. XIII, 8.

a (1) 'Praise ye the Lord,' with which Hallel commences. (2) Ps. CXIII, 9. (3) Ibid. CXIV, 8. (4) *Ḥatham* is the technical term meaning to round off a liturgical passage with a blessing formula, 'Blessed art Thou, O Lord.' (5) So the text as emended, 'sacrifices' referring to the *ḥagigah* of the fourteenth, which was eaten before the Passover-offering (v. *supra* 70a); hence it is mentioned before too. (6) When saying, 'This unleavened bread' . . . 'this bitter herb.' (7) Which is set in memory of the Passover-offering; v. R. Joseph's dictum *supra* 114b. (8) If he lifted up the meat as he said 'This Passover-offering,' it would look as if he had actually consecrated it as a sacrifice, which is forbidden, since sacrifices may not be offered without the Temple (Raba refers to post-Temple times). Hence he must *not* lift up the meat.

b (1) Lit., 'this'. (2) Deut. XXI, 20. (3) For '*this our son*' implies that his parents see and point at him. (4) *Haggadah*. (5) R. Joseph and R. Shesheth were both blind. (6) *Sc.* that unleavened bread must be eaten on the first night of Passover (the interdict of leavened bread of course is Biblical).—Hence the reciting of the *Haggadah* is likewise Rabbinical, and therefore unaffected by R. Aḥa b. Jacob's deduction. (7) For he states his law generally, and therefore meant it for post-Temple times too. (8) On which it is based. Hence since the blind were exempt from reciting the *Haggadah* when it was a Scriptural obligation, they are still exempt now that it is only Rabbinical. (9) They reject the law entirely, together with the analogy on which it is based. (10) V. Sanh., 71b, nn. 2 and 3. (11) I.e., it does not intimate that he who recites must see it, but simply means: it is for this reason that I eat unleavened bread and bitter herbs viz., because of what the Lord did for me etc.

עין משפט
נר מצוה

צג א מיי׳ פ"ז מהל׳ חמץ ומצה הלכה ו:
צד ב ג מיי׳ שם פ"ח הלכה ה:
צה ד מיי׳ שם הל׳ ד וסמג עשין מא טוש"ע א"ח סי׳ תעג סעיף ו:

וחותם בגאולה. ת"ק לא פי׳ כיצד ופליגי במילתיה ר"ט ור"ע ר׳ טרפון אינו חותם בברוך שלא היה מאריך בדברי בקשה ולא היה אומר אלא הודאה ור"ע סבר דחותם בה בברוך לפי שמאריך בדברי בקשה ואומר כן ה׳ אלהינו יגיענו כו׳ וקי"ל (עירובין דף מו:) הלכה כר׳ עקיבא מחבירו וכן מלינו בסנהדרין (דף כח.) גבי לא ירבה לו נשים ובריש חזקת הבתים (ב"ב דף כח.) דפליגי תנאי במילתיה דתנא קמא*:

ה"ג **ונאמר** לפניו שירה חדשה (א) וכן נודה לך שיר חדש על גאולתנו*. דהכי תניא במכילתא כל השירות לשון נקבה חוץ משירה דלעתיד דלשון זכר כלומר שהנקבה יש לה צער לידה אף כל הנסים יש אחריהם צער חוץ מלעתיד שאין אחריה צער וכן יסד הפייט* בזולת אי פתרוס שירות אלה לשון נקבה מיוסדים כי תשועתם כיולדה וגו׳ תוקף שיר אחרון כזכרים לא יולדים שירו לה׳ שיר חדש כו׳ וגרסינן שם מן הזבחים ומן הפסחים שחגיגת ארבעה עשר נאכלת קודם לפסח לפי שהפסח נאכל על השובע:

[וע"ע תוספות לעיל סג. ד"ה ר"ש]

[הגליה ד׳ קמב: קמג. האריך בביאור דברי תוס׳ הללו]

[שביעי ואחרון ש"ס]

רבינו חננאל

אמר רבא מצה צריך להגביה כשאומר מצה זו שאנו אוכלין וכו׳ וכן מרור צריך להגביה אבל בשר אינו צריך להגביהו מפני שנראה כמקדיש בשר ואוכל קדשים בחוץ אמר רב אחא בר יעקב סומא פטור לומר הגדה כו׳ ואסיקנא כשר הוא לומר הגדה דמצה בזמן הזה דרבנן ואקשי׳ מכלל דרב אחא בר יעקב סבר מצה בזמן הזה דאורייתא והא איהו דאמר בסוף פירקי׳ מצה בזמן הזה דרבנן ופרקי׳ קסבר רבנן כעין דאורי׳ תקון. מאי בעבור זה בעבור מצ׳ ומרו׳ דהוא׳

[סנהדרין ע"ח:]

[לסומא כל"ל]

הגהות הב"ח

(א) תוס׳ ד"ה ה"ג ונאמר לפניו שירה חדשה וכסוף נרסינן ונודה לך:

גליון הש"ס

גמ׳ קסברי רבנן מלה בזה"ז דרבנן עי׳ מגילה יט ע"ב תוס׳ ד"ה ורבי:

שלשה דברים אלו בפסח לא יצא ידי חובתו ואלו הן פסח מצה ומרור פסח על שום שפסח המקום על בתי אבותינו במצרים [שנאמר °ואמרתם זבח פסח הוא לה׳ אשר פסח וגו׳] מצה על שום שנגאלו אבותינו ממצרים [שנאמר °ויאפו את הבצק אשר הוציאו ממצרים וגו׳] מרור על שום שמררו המצריים את חיי אבותינו במצרים שנאמר [°וימררו את חייהם וגו׳] *בכל דור ודור חייב אדם לראות את עצמו כאילו הוא יצא ממצרים שנאמר °והגדת לבנך ביום ההוא לאמר בעבור זה עשה ה׳ לי בצאתי ממצרים °לפיכך אנחנו חייבים להודות להלל לשבח לפאר לרומם להדר לברך לעלה ולקלס *למי שעשה לאבותינו ולנו את כל הנסים האלו הוציאנו מעבדות לחרות מיגון לשמחה ומאבל ליום טוב ומאפלה לאור גדול ומשעבוד לגאולה ונאמר לפניו הללויה *עד היכן הוא אומר בש"א עד אם הבנים שמחה ובה"א °עד חלמיש למעינו מים וחותם בגאולה ר"ט אומר אשר גאלנו וגאל את אבותינו ממצרים ולא היה חותם רבי עקיבא אומר כן ה׳ אלהינו ואלהי אבותינו יגיענו למועדים ולרגלים אחרים הבאים לקראתנו לשלום שמחים בבנין עירך וששים בעבודתך ונאכל שם (מן הפסחים ומן הזבחים) כו׳ עד בא"י גאל ישראל: **גמ׳** אמר רבא צריך שיאמר ואותנו הוציא משם אמר רבא °מצה צריך להגביה ומרור צריך להגביה בשר א"צ להגביה ולא עוד אלא שנראה כאוכל קדשים בחוץ אמר רב אחא בר יעקב סומא פטור מלומר הגדה כתיב הכא בעבור זה וכתיב התם *°בננו זה מה להלן פרט *לסומא אף כאן פרט *לסומין איני והאמר מרימר שאלתינהו לרבנן דבי רב יוסף מאן דאמר אגדתא בי רב יוסף מ"ד אגדתא בי רב ששת אמרו רב יוסף רב ששת °קסברי רבנן מצה בזמן הזה דרבנן מכלל דרב אחא בר יעקב סבר *מצה בזמן הזה דאורייתא והא *רב אחא בר יעקב הוא דאמר מצה בזמן הזה דרבנן קסבר כל דתקון רבנן כעין דאורייתא תיקון לרב ששת ולרב יוסף נמי הא ודאי כל דתקון רבנן *כעין דאורייתא תיקון הכי השתא בשלמא התם מדהוה ליה למיכתב *בננו הוא וכתיב בננו זה ש"מ פרט לסומין הוא דאתא אבל הכא אי לאו בעבור זה מאי לכתוב אלא בעבור מצה ומרור הוא דאתא: לפיכך אנחנו חייבין:

שמות יב / שם / שם / שם א / שמות יג / דברים כא / תהלים קיד

רשב"ם

גמ׳ צריך להגביה. כשהוא אומר מצה זו שאנו אוכלין: בשר אין מגביה. כשהוא אומר פסח שהיו אבותינו (במצרים) אוכלים לא יגביה הבשר שהוא זכר לפסח: ה"ג בשר אינו צריך להגביה ולא עוד אלא שנראה כמקדיש כו׳: אין צריך להגביה. דהא לא מצי למימר פסח זה: רב יוסף ורב ששת מאורי עיינים היו: הא הוא דאמר. בסופא דהאי פירקא (דף קכ.) אחד זה ואחד זה דרבנן:

מתני׳ שלשה דברים הללו. (שלא פירש) [שפירש] טעמן*: **גמ׳** צריך שיאמר. פסוק זה ואותנו הוציא משם שצריך להראות את עצמו כאילו יצא משם שאף אותנו גאל הקב"ה: צריך להגביה. כשאומר מצה זו שאנו אוכלין מרור זה שאנו אוכלין כדי להראותן למסובים ותחבב מצוה בעיניהן וכן בתשובת הגאונים דהא דאמר צריך להגביה היינו במצ׳ זו דאגדת׳: בשר. של *מיני תבשילין אין צריך להגביה כשהן אומרים פסח שהיו אבותינו אוכלין ולא יגביה הבשר שהוא זכר לפסח: ה"ג בשר אין צריך להגביה ולא עוד אלא שנראה כמקדיש בהמתו · אין צריך להגביה דהא לא מצי למימר פסח זה ולא עוד אלא אם היה מגביהו נראה כמי שמקדיש בהמתו מחיים לפסח: פרט לסומין. מדכתיב זה משמע שיכירוהו בראיית העין: רב ששת ורב יוסף מאורי עינים הוו: קסברי רבנן. רב ששת ורב יוסף: רב אחא בר יעקב הוא דאמר. בסופא דהאי פירקא (דף קכ.) אחד זה ואחד זה מדרבנן: כעין דאורייתא תקון. וכשם שבזמן שבית המקדש קיים פטור השתא נמי פטור ואינו מוציא אחרים ידי חובתן: בעבור מצה ומרור הוא דאתא. לכך אני אוכל מצה ומרור זכר למה שעשו לי בצאתי ממצרים ורב ששת ורב יוסף גזירה שוה לא גמרי: **מתני׳** וחותם בגאולה. מסיים את ההגדה בברכת גאולה והשתא לא מפרש היאך מברכין אותה ולקמן פליגי בה רבי טרפון ורבי עקיבא בההיא ברכה דלרבי טרפון פותח בברוך ואינו חותם בברוך מידי דהוה אברכת פירות וברכת המצות דכולה הודאה היא ולר׳ עקיבא חותם בה נמי בברוך לפי שמוסיף בה דברי ריצוי ובקשה: כן יגיענו וגו׳. והיינו דעבדינן כר"ע מחבירו ות"ק דקאמר וחותם בגאולה אינו תנא שלישי דא"כ אמאי עבדינן כר"ע הואיל ורבנן פליגי עליה הא אין הלכה כר"ע מחבירו והא דקאמר ת"ק וחותם בגאולה ד"ה היא ולא בא למעט מילתייהו דר"ט ור"ע אלא לאשמעינן שמסיימין בברכת גאולה דלא תימא אין מברכין כלל בסיום הגדה כי אם ברכת היין לבד על הכוס השני וראיה לדבר במסכת כתובות בפרק אע"פ (דף נז:) דאיכא נמי פלוגתייהו דר׳ טרפון ור"ע כה"ג דפליגי בסתם משנה דתנן הגיע זמן ולא נישאו אוכלת משלו ואוכלת בתרומה ר׳ טרפון אומר נותנין לה הכל תרומה ר"ע אומר מחצה חולין ומחצה תרומה וכי היכי דפליגי התם ר"ט ור"ע בפירושא דאוכלת בתרומה ולאו תלתא תנאי הוו הכי נמי פליגי תרווייהו הכא בפירושא וחותם בגאולה ולאו תלתא תנאי הוו שהתנא סתם דבריו בין הכא בין בכתובות והדר מפרש לה בפלוגתא דר"ט ור"ע וחותם דתנא קמא סיום בעלמא ואינו חותם דר"ט חתימת סוף ברכה היא: *הללויה· תיבה אחת היא כמו הילול כגון תחתיה[א] הגזרה והבניה (יחזקאל מא) וכמו כן כסיה: ידידיה· ויקרא שמו ידידיה (ש"ב יב) נתן הנביא קרא כן לשלמה: מרחביה. כמו מרחב: אחת. כלומר תיבה אחת היא ואין התיבה נחלקת לשנים: לרב מאי. מפליג פליג או אוסופי מוסיף אבל רבה פשיטא דפליג מדקאמר בלבד: חביבי. דודי ר׳ חייא: הללו בהך גיסא. בסוף שיטה ויה בתחלת שיטה אחרת: בהלולים הרבה. בהללויה הרבה וכולהו הללויה דריש ליה הכי אלמא תיבה אחת היא: בתהלה. תהלה לדוד: בתפלה. תפלה לעני כי יעטוף תפלה למשה: בהודאה. הודו לה׳ כי טוב: שיר שבתורה. אז ישיר משה: משה וישראל כו׳. כלומר באותו פסיקא לן דמשה וישראל באותה שעה שעלו מן הים תיקנוהו ולא היה מקודם לכן אבל הלל דראשי חדשים וימים טובים מי תיקנו: על כל פרק ופרק ועל כל רגל ורגל ועל כל צרה שלא תבא עליהן. לישנא מעליא נקט כלומר שאם ח"ו תהא צרה עליהן ויושעו ממנה אומר אותה על גאולתה כגון חנוכה: דוד אמרן. על המאורעות שאירעו: כל אלו. תפלות: הלל זה. בספר תהלים שאנו אומרים על כל פרק ופרק: משה וישראל אמרוהו. דכתיב ביה בצאת ישראל ממצרים הים ראה וינוס ואח"כ קבעו דוד בספרו: אפשר ישראל שוחטין את פסחיהן. מיציאת מצרים ועד דוד ולא אמרו עליו הלל: ד"א פסלו של מיכה עומד בבכי. באותו מקום דבימי דוד היה דכתיב ביה עד גלות כל הארץ (שופטים יח) וישראל אומרים הלל שכתוב בו כמוהם יהיו עושיהם בתמיה אלא ודאי על הים נאמר תחלה ושוב לא פסק כך שמעתי. ול"ג בבכי כיעי הוא לגנאי כלומר עומד בשמחה: וישראל *אמרו לפניו ל"ג ואי גרס ליה מפרשינן ליה כמו בפני הבית בעודו קיים: כנגד ציבור. כנסת ישראל שנתנבא על גלותן והתפלל עליהן: ניצוח וניגון לעתיד לבא. כל מקום שנאמר ניצוח למנצח בנגינות לעתיד לבא הוא מדבר ולא ידענא היכי משמע אלא הכי הוה קים להו: ע"י תורגמן. הוא אומר ואחר משמיע לרבים והיינו משכיל נותן לתורגמן:

לדוד

מסורת הש"ס

[הגהות כי בגמרא של הרבנים הי׳ המשנה נחלקת לשתים]

[ברכות ג.]

לקמן קיח.

[מוהרבינו הפסחים כל"ל וכ"א במשנה שבמשניות ונכרי׳ ורא"ש והרמב"ם]

[לסומין כל"ל]

[לעיל קטו.]

[לקמן קכ.]

[לעיל ז: וש"נ]

[סנהדרין עח:]

מכאן עיין לדף שאחר זה

פ"א עמוד

הגהות מהר"ב רנשבורג

[א] רשב"ם ד"ה הללויה וכו׳ תחתיה וכו׳ כ"כ בתחתיה הוא ביחזקאל מ"א וה"ל לכתוב תחת כ"ד ה׳ וכו׳ שם הגזרה והבניה הוא ביחזקאל מ"א כגזיר והבנין לפרש"י ורד"ק שם אלא שדרך הכתוב לכתוב לכתוב ה׳ באותיות ה׳ וכה"ג בגלויה הדבה:

אף כאן בפרוסה. לברך על אכילת מצה ושתי שלימות מייתי משום ברכת המוציא דלא גרע משאר ימים טובים שצריך לבצוע על שתי ככרות שלימות ובולע מאחת מהשלימות: אף כאן הוא מסיק ואשתו אופה. כדי שלא תחמיץ: משום קפא. שרף החזרת קשה ויש בו ארס: קפא דחסא חמא. מי שאכל חזרת ואלה בשביל הקפא יאכל כנון וירפא: קפא דחמא כרתי. מי שאכל כנון וקשה לו יאכל כרתי: חמימי · ישתה מים חמין: קפא דכולהו חמימי. ארס של כל ירקות חמין רפואה להן: זכר לתפוח. שהיו יולדות בניהן שם בלא עצב שלא יכירו בהן מצריים דכתיב תחת התפוח עוררתיך (שיר ח): לסמוכיה. להטיל ולכתוש בו הרבה כדי שיהיה עב וצריך לקהוייה להטיל בו תפוחים ויין ומילתא דאית בו קיוהא: צריך לקהוייה. זכר לתפוח וצריך לסמוכיה זכר לטיט: תבלין. ירקות שמטילין בחרוסת זכר לתבן וחרוסת שכותשים בו הדק זכר לטיט: תגרי חרך. חנוונים היושבים אצל חנותיהם ומוכרין כמו מציץ מן החרכים (שם ב): מתני' וכאן הבן שואל אביו. כאן במזיגת כוס שני הבן שואל את אביו מה נשתנה עכשיו שמוזגין כוס שני קודם אכילה:

גמרא

"אף כאן בפרוסה דבר אחר מה דרכו של עני הוא מסיק ואשתו אופה אף כאן נמי הוא מסיק ואשתו אופה: אע"פ שאין חרוסת מצוה: ואי לא מצוה משום מאי מייתי לה א"ר אמי משום קפא אמר רב אסי קפא דחסא חמא קפא דחמא כרתי [קפא דכרתי חמימי] קפא דכולהו חמימי אדהכי והכי נימא הכי קפא קפא דכירנא לך ולשב בנתיך ולתמני כלתך: רבי אלעזר בר' צדוק אומר מצוה וכו': מאי מצוה רבי לוי אומר זכר לתפוח ור' יוחנן אומר זכר לטיט אמר אביי הלכך צריך לקהוייה וצריך לסמוכיה לקהוייה זכר לתפוח וצריך לסמוכיה זכר לטיט תניא כוותיה דרבי יוחנן תבלין זכר לתבן חרוסת זכר לטיט אמר רבי אלעזר בר' צדוק כך היו אומרים תגרי *חרך שבירושלים בואו וטלו לכם תבלין למצוה: **מתני'** מזגו לו כוס שני וכאן הבן שואל אביו ואם אין דעת בבן אביו מלמדו מה נשתנה הלילה הזה מכל הלילות שבכל הלילות אנו אוכלין חמץ ומצה הלילה הזה כולו מצה שבכל הלילות אנו אוכלין שאר ירקות הלילה הזה מרור שבכל הלילות אנו אוכלין בשר צלי שלוק ומבושל *הלילה הזה כולו צלי שבכל הלילות (אין) אנו (*חייבים לטבל אפילו) פעם אחת הלילה הזה שתי פעמים ולפי דעתו של בן אביו מלמדו מתחיל בגנות ומסיים בשבח ודורש °מארמי אובד אבי עד שיגמור כל הפרשה כולה: **גמ'** ת"ר חכם בנו שואלו ואם אינו חכם אשתו שואלתו ואם לאו הוא שואל לעצמו ואפילו שני תלמידי חכמים שיודעין בהלכות הפסח שואלין זה לזה: מה נשתנה הלילה הזה מכל הלילות שבכל הלילות אנו מטבילין פעם אחת הלילה הזה שתי פעמים: מתקיף לה רבא אטו כל יומא לא סגיא דלא מטבלא חדא זימנא אלא אמר רבא הכי קתני שבכל הלילות אין אנו חייבין לטבל אפילו פעם אחת הלילה הזה שתי פעמים מתקיף לה רב ספרא חיובא לדרדקי אלא אמר רב ספרא הכי קתני אין אנו מטבילין אפילו פעם אחת הלילה הזה שתי פעמים: מתחיל בגנות ומסיים בשבח: מאי בגנות רב אמר מתחלה עובדי עבודת גלולים היו אבותינו [ושמואל] אמר עבדים היינו אמר ליה רב נחמן לדרו עבדיה עבדא דמפיק ליה מריה לחירות ויהיב ליה כספא ודהבא מאי בעי למימר ליה אמר ליה בעי לאודויי ולשבוחי א"ל [א] פטרתן מלומר מה נשתנה פתח ואמר עבדים היינו: **מתני'** רבן גמליאל היה אומר *כל שלא אמר שלשה

[גירסת הערוך חרך] [לעיל ע.] [מטבילין ועי' תוס' וכמשנה שבמשניות וכן בפסיקתא בגמ' דכמון] דברים כו [נ"ל וחרוסת] [נ"א מי]

רשב"ם

אף כאן בפרוסה. לברך על אכילת מצה ושתי שלימות מייתינן משום המוציא דלא גרע משאר ימים טובים שצריך לבצוע על שתי ככרות ובולע מאחת מהשלימות: דרכו של עני הוא מסיק ואשתו אופה · ונותנו מיד לתנור כשנגמר היסקו שירא שמא יצטנן התנור קודם שיזדמן עוסקין שניהם זה בהיסק התנור וזו בעיסה אף כאן הוא מסיק ואשתו אופה כדי שלא תחמיץ: משום קפא · שרף החזרת קשה הוא והרי הוא כארס: קפא דחסא. מי שאכל חזרת ואלה בשביל הקפא יאכל כנון וירפא: קפא דחמא כרתי · מי שאכל כנון וקשה לו יאכל כרתי כרישים: חמימי. ישתה מים חמין: קפא דכולהו חמימי. ארס של כל הירקות מים חמין רפואה להם: זכר לתפוח. במסכת סוטה (דף יא:) שהיו יולדות שם בניהם בלא עצב שלא יכירו בהן מצריים דכתיב תחת התפוח עוררתיך (שיר ח): לסמוכיה. לכתוש בו ירקות הרבה כדי שיהא עבה: וצריך לקהוייה. להטיל בו תפוחין דאית ביה קיוהא זכר לתפוח וצריך לסמוכיה זכר לטיט: תבלין. בשמים שמטילין בחרוסת זכר לתבן (*וחרס) שכותשין בו הדק זכר לטיט: תגרי חרך. כמו מציץ מן החרכים (שם ב) חנוונים היושבים אצל חנויותיהן ומוכרין: **מתני'** וכאן הבן שואל את אביו. כאן במזיגת כוס שני הבן שואל את אביו אם הוא חכם מה נשתנה עכשיו שמוזגין כוס שני קודם אכילה ורבינו קבל מרבו ר' יעקב בן יקר וכן הבן שואל כמו כן בנות צלפחד (במדבר כז) כלומר דין הוא שיהא שואל במזיגת כוס שני מה נשתנה: מטבילין פעם אחת. טיבול ירקות בתוך הסעודה ובגמרא פריך לה: שתי פעמים · טיבול ראשון דשאר ירקות וטיבול שני דמרור: הלילה הזה כולו צלי. בזמן שבית המקדש קיים היה שואל כן: ולפי דעתו של בן אביו מלמדו. אם מבין הרבה יפרש הכל: מתחיל בגנות. מפרש בגמרא: **גמ'** אטו כל יומי לא סגיא דלא מטבלינן. דקתני שבכל הלילות (אין) אנו מטבילין פעם אחת הא שבכל הלילות אנו אוכלין שאר ירקות ליכא למיפרך הכי דהתם ה"ק בכל הלילות אין אנו מחזרין אחר מרור: חיובא לדרדקי. בתמיה הא משום היכרא דתינוקות כדי שישאלו קעבדינן: אלא אמר רב ספרא כו'. מהכא שמעינן דהכי אית לן למימר שבכל הלילות אין אנו מטבילין [אפילו] פעם אחת והאומר אין אנו חייבין לטבל שיבוש הוא בידו: פתח ואמר. לאחר שאלת הבן התחיל לומר עבדים היינו וגומר הגדה בשבח והודאה כלומר כן עשה לנו הקב"ה שהיינו עבדים והוציאנו משם: שלשה

תוספות

מה דרכו של עני בפרוסה. נראה דגם המוציא צריך לברך על הפרוסה וכן משמע בפ' כיצד מברכין (ברכות דף לט:) דקאמר הכל מודים לענין פסח שמניח פרוסה בתוך השלימות ובוצע פי' אפילו למ"ד מברך על השלימה ופוטר את הפתיתין מודה לענין פסח דאינו מברך על השלימה אלא על הפרוסה משום מה דרכו של עני כו' ומניחה בתוך השלימה כדי שיהא נראה שבלע על השלימה ומשמע דלענין המוציא קמיירי וקאמר בתר הכי *א"ר חייא בר אבא בשבת חייב לבצוע על שני ככרות שנאמר לקטו לחם משנה ועיקר מילתיה דר' חייא בר אבא בפרק כל כתבי (שבת ד' קיז:) אלא להכי מייתי התם אחר פסח לומר שצריך שם מצה שלישית משום לחם משנה וחייב לבצוע על שתי ככרות בין בשבת בין בי"ט דאי לאו הכי למה הביא שם מילתיה דר' חייא וכן פסק רב אלפס דצריך לבצוע על שתי ככרות ביום טוב והטעם לפי שהיה לחם משנה יורד בערבי ימים טובים וקשה שאנו מתפללים באתה קדשת וברכתו מכל הימים וקדשתו מכל הזמנים ואמר (במכילתא פרש' בשלח) במן ברכו במן קדשו משמע בי"ט היה מן יורד *וכן היה נוהג ה"ר מנחם מיוני וה"ר יום טוב שהיו מברכין הכל על הפרוסה אך ר"י היה מברך המוציא על השלימה והדר על אכילת מצה על הפרוסה ובוצע משתיהן יחד וכן עמא דבר ולכך עושין על השלישית כריכה כדי לקיים מצוה בשלשתן:

צריך לסמוכיה וצריך לקהוייה. ובירושלמי אמר אית דעבדי זכר לדם ומשום הכי קרי ליה טיבולו במשקה וכן עמא דבר לסמוכי ובשעת אכילה מקלשין אותו ביין וחומץ ובתשובת הגאונים מפרש לעשות חרוסת בפירות שנדמה לכנסת ישראל בשיר השירים (ח) תחת התפוח עוררתיך כפלח הרמון התאנה חנטה אמרתי אעלה בתמר אגוז אל גנת אגוז ושקדים על שם ששקד הקב"ה על הקץ: **תגרי** חרך שבירושלים. משמע דהלכה כר' אלעזר בר' צדוק וגם בספרים כתב ר' יוסי ונימוקו עמו וכן עשה ה"ר יוסף בסדרו חרוסת זכר לטיט:

הלילה הזה מרור. הא דלא אמר כולו מרור משום דאכלינן שאר ירקות בטיבול ראשון: **כולו** צלי. רב חסדא מוקי לה באלו דברים (לעיל דף ע·) כבן תימא דאמר חגיגה הבאה עם הפסח אינה נאכלת אלא צלי ואע"ג דקאמר התם ואמר רב חסדא ובפרקין ליתיה דרך הגמרא כן:

*ואמרתם זבח פסח הוא. פי' באמירה שצריך לומר פסח זה שאנו אוכלין ואיתקש מצה ומרור לפסח וצ"ל כמי מצה זו מרו' זה: *לפיכך אנחנו כו'. י"א שבע הודאות ולא יותר כנגד ז' רקיעים: וחותם

[דברים כו] [ג"ז שם]

עין משפט נר מצוה

פז א מיי' פ"ח מהל' מצה הל' ו סמג עשין מא טוש"ע א"ח סי' תעה סעיף א וסי' תעג סעי' ו:

פח ב טוש"ע א"ח סי' תס סעיף ג:

פט ג ד מיי' פ"ז מהל' מצה הל' יא סמג עשין מא טוש"ע א"ח סי' תעג סעיף ה בהג"ה:

[בברכות שם ובשבת קיז: איתא רבי אבא]

צ ה ו מיי' פ"ז ופ"ח מהל' מצה הלכה ב סמג שם טוש"ע שם ס"ז:

צא ז שם סעי' ז בהג"ה:

צב ח מיי' פ"ז שם הל' ה ופ"ח הל' ·

[וע"ע תוספות עירובין לח: ד"ה ואין ותוספות ביצה ג: ד"ה והי"]

רבינו חננאל

אוכלין כו' ד"א לחם עוני מה דרכו של עני הוא מסיק ואשתו אופה וכו' אע"פ שאין חרוסת מצוה ואמאי מייתי ליה משום קפא כדפירשנו למעלה. ר' אליעזר בר' צדוק החרוסת מצוה והביא ראיה לדבריו שכך היו תגרי ירושלים אומרים קחו לכם תבלין [למצוה] מכלל שחרוסת מצוה מאי מצוה ר' לוי אמ' זכר לתפוח שנאמר (שיר ח ה) תחת התפוח עוררתיך וגו' ר' יוחנן אומר זכר לטיט אמר אביי הלכך צריך לקיוהא זכר לתפוח וצריך לסמוכיה וזכר לטיט. תגרי חרך שבירושלים היו אומרין בואו וקחו לכם תבלין למצוה כגון קנמון וכיוצא בו זכר לתבן שבטיט: מתני' מזגו לו כוס שני וכאן הבן שואל וכו' ת"ר אם היה הבן חכם הבן שואל את אביו ואם לאו אשתו שואלתו ואפי' שני תלמידי חכמים הבקיאין בהלכות הפסח שואלין זה את זה מה נשתנה וכו' ואסיק אמר רבא שבכל הלילות אין אנו מטבילין אפי' פעם אחת הלילה הזה שתי פעמים מתחיל בגנות מאי היא אמר רבא מתחלה עובדי כוכבים היו אבותינו רב יוסף אמר עבדים היינו לפרעה והאידנא עבדינן כתרוייהו:

הגהות מהר"ב רנשבורג

[א] גמ' אמר ליה פטרתן מלומר מה נשתנה · נ"ב עיין לעיל דף קטו ע"ב בתוספות ד"ה כדי שיכיר וכו' ובפר"ח סי' תע"ג ס"ק ז' ודו"ק:

as a beggar generally has a piece, [116a] so here too a piece [is taken].[3] Another interpretation: just as a poor man fires [the oven] and his wife bakes,[4] so here too, he heats and she bakes.[5]

THOUGH ḤAROSETH IS NOT A RELIGIOUS REQUIREMENT. Then if it is not a religious requirement, on what account does he bring it?—Said R. Ammi: On account of the *ḳappa*.[6] R. Assi said: The *ḳappa* of lettuce [is counteracted by] radishes; the *ḳappa* of radishes, [by] leeks; the *ḳappa* of leeks, [by] hot water; the *ḳappa* of all these, [by] hot water. And in the meanwhile[7] let him say thus: '*Ḳappa, ḳappa*, I remember you and your seven daughters and your eight daughters-in-law.'

R. ELEAZAR SON OF R. ZADOK SAID: IT IS A RELIGIOUS REQUIREMENT. Why is it a religious requirement? R. Levi said: In memory of the apple-tree;[8] R. Johanan said: In memory of the clay.[9] Abaye observed: Therefore one must make it acrid and thicken it: make it acrid, in memory of the apple-tree; and thicken it, in memory of the clay. It was taught in accordance with R. Johanan: The condiments[10] are in memory of the straw;[11] [and] the *ḥaroseth* [itself] is a reminder of the clay. R. Eleazar son of R. Zadok said: Thus did the grocers[12] of Jerusalem cry, 'Come and buy ingredients for your religious requirements.'

MISHNAH. THEY FILLED A SECOND CUP FOR HIM. AT
a THIS STAGE[1] THE SON QUESTIONS HIS FATHER;[2] IF THE SON IS UNINTELLIGENT, HIS FATHER INSTRUCTS HIM [TO ASK]: 'WHY IS THIS NIGHT DIFFERENT FROM ALL [OTHER] NIGHTS. FOR ON ALL [OTHER] NIGHTS WE EAT LEAVENED AND UNLEAVENED BREAD, WHEREAS ON THIS NIGHT [WE EAT] ONLY UNLEAVENED BREAD; ON ALL OTHER NIGHTS WE EAT ALL KINDS OF HERBS, ON THIS NIGHT BITTER HERBS; ON ALL OTHER NIGHTS WE EAT MEAT ROAST, STEWED OR BOILED, ON THIS NIGHT, ROAST ONLY.[3] ON ALL OTHER NIGHTS WE DIP[4] ONCE, BUT ON THIS NIGHT WE DIP TWICE.' AND ACCORDING TO THE SON'S INTELLIGENCE HIS FATHER INSTRUCTS HIM.[5] HE COMMENCES WITH SHAME AND CONCLUDES WITH PRAISE; AND EXPOUNDS FROM 'A WANDERING ARAMEAN WAS MY FATHER'[6] UNTIL HE COMPLETES THE WHOLE SECTION.

GEMARA. Our Rabbis taught: If his son is intelligent he asks him, while if he is not intelligent his wife asks him; but if not,[7] he asks himself. And even two scholars who know the laws of Passover ask one another.

WHY IS THIS NIGHT DIFFERENT FROM ALL OTHER NIGHTS? FOR ON ALL OTHER NIGHTS WE DIP ONCE, WHILE ON THIS NIGHT WE DIP TWICE. To this Raba demurred: Is then dipping once indispensable all other days? Rather, said Raba, It was thus taught: For on all other nights we are not obliged to dip even once, whereas on this night, twice. To this R. Safra demurred: A statutory obligation on account of children![8] Rather, said R. Safra, He teaches thus: We do not dip even once, whereas this night [we dip] twice.

HE COMMENCES WITH SHAME AND CONCLUDES WITH PRAISE. What is 'WITH SHAME'? Rab said: 'Aforetime our fathers
b were idolaters'; while Samuel said: 'We were slaves.'[1] R. Naḥman asked his slave Daru: 'When a master liberates his slave and gives him gold and silver, what should he say to him?' 'He should thank and praise him,' replied he. 'You have excused us from saying "Why [is this night] different?"' observed he. [Thereupon] he commenced by reciting, 'We were slaves.'

MISHNAH. R. GAMALIEL USED TO SAY: WHOEVER DOES

(3) The blessing for the unleavened bread must be said over a piece of *mazzah* only, not over a whole one, to emphasize Israel's poverty in Egypt. (Hence three *mazzoth* are required, two because every festival and the Sabbath require two loaves, and a third which is broken, so that the blessing may be recited over the piece.) (4) Without delay, as they cannot afford more fuel should the oven cool. (5) Even wealthy people must bake the unleavened bread without unnecessary delay, lest it turn leaven. (6) V. *supra* 115*b*. (7) While waiting for the cure to take effect—or perhaps, until he takes these. (8) Under which the Israelitish women in Egypt gave birth to their children; v. Soṭ. 11*b*. (9) With which they made bricks. (10) Which are mixed in the *ḥaroseth*. (11) Just as the straw was kneaded into the clay. (12) Lit., 'parched-grain merchants'—such would sell spices etc. too. Rashi and Rashbam: vendors who sat behind latticed windows.

a (1) Lit., 'and here'. (2) Why all this unusual procedure? (3) I.e., in Temple times, v. *supra* 70*a*. (4) So the text as emended, and it is thus quoted in the Gemara; v. O.Ḥ. 473, 7 and ט״ז § 9 a.l. (5) The answer must be intelligible to the child. (6) Deut. XXVI, 5. (7) If he has no wife. (8) 'Obliged' (*ḥayyabin*) connotes a religious precept, whereas as stated *supra* 114*b* the first dipping is merely to stimulate the children's wonder.

b (1) The modern liturgy combines both, commencing however with the latter.

from this that the lettuce [115b] must be plunged right into the *ḥaroseth*[4] to counteract the *ḳappa*.[5] For if you should think that it need not be sunk into it, why is the washing of the hands required?[6] Surely he does not touch [the *ḥaroseth*]?[7] Yet perhaps I may maintain that in truth it need not be sunk [into the *ḥaroseth*], the *ḳappa* dying from its smell; yet why is washing of the hands required? *In case* he plunges it in.

R. Papa also said: A man must not keep the bitter herbs [an appreciable time] in the *ḥaroseth*, because the sweetness of its ingredients [*sc.* the *ḥaroseth*] may neutralize its bitterness, whereas the taste of bitter herbs is essential, but it is then absent.

R. Ḥisda brought[8] Rabbana 'Uḳba[9] and he lectured: If he washed his hands at the first dipping, he must wash his hands at the second dipping [too]. The Rabbis discussed this before R. Papa: This was stated in general,[10] for if you should think that it was stated here [in connection with Passover], why must he wash his hands twice? Surely he has [already] washed his hands
a once?[1] Said R. Papa to them: On the contrary, it was stated here, for if you should think that it was stated in general, why two dippings?[2] What then? It was stated here? Then why must he wash his hands twice: surely he has [already] washed his hands once? —I will tell you: since he is to recite the *Haggadah*[3] and *Hallel*,[4] he may let his thoughts wander[5] and touch [something unclean].

Raba said: If he swallows unleavened bread, he discharges his duty;[6] if he swallows bitter herbs, he does not discharge his duty.[7] If he swallows unleavened bread and bitter herbs [together], he discharges his duty of unleavened bread, [but] not his duty of bitter herbs. If he wraps them in bast and swallows them, he does not discharge his duty of unleavened bread either.

R. Simi b. Ashi said: Unleavened bread [must be set] before each person [of the company], bitter herbs before each person, and *ḥaroseth* before each person, but we remove the table[8] only from before him who recites the *Haggadah*. R. Huna said: All these too [are set only] before him who recites the *Haggadah*.[9] And the law is as R. Huna.

Why do we remove the table?—The School of R. Jannai said: So that the children may perceive [the unusual proceeding] and enquire [its reasons]. Abaye was sitting before Rabbah, [when] he saw the tray taken up from before him. Said he to them: We have not yet eaten, and they have [already] come [and] removed the tray from before us! Said Rabbah to him: You have exempted us from reciting, 'Why [is this night] different?'[10]

Samuel said: *Bread of* ['oni][11] [means] bread over which we
b recite ['*onin*] many words.[1] It was taught likewise: '*Bread of* ['oni]' means bread over which we recite ['*onin*] many words. Another interpretation: '*Bread of* ['oni]': '*ani* [poverty] is written:[2] just

(4) Which is a liquid. (5) A poisonous substance in the *ḥazereth*. (6) For the first dipping, v. *infra*. (7) With his hand, if the lettuce is only dipped lightly in it. (8) ארבריה. (9) 'Rabbana' is a Babylonian title, probably the equivalent of the Palestinian '*Rabban*,' lit., 'our teacher,' which is a peculiar title of honour, higher than 'Rabbi.' (10) When a man eats vegetables at other times of the year. Since the eating of vegetables then is not statutory, each time he eats them (after dipping) even at the same meal counts as a separate act, for when he ate the first time he did not intend eating them again; hence he must wash his hands at each.

a (1) Knowing that he would eat vegetables a second time; hence once should suffice. (2) The vegetable having been dipped once into vinegar, it need not be dipped again. (3) The narrative of the exodus, which is an essential part of the ritual. (4) 'Praise,' i.e., Ps. CXIII-CXVIII. (5) I.e., not think about keeping his hands clean. (6) Of eating unleavened bread, though he has not chewed it. (7) Because he has not tasted its bitterness, which is essential. Rashi reads: if he swallows bitter herbs, he has discharged his duty—because even then he cannot altogether avoid tasting its bitterness. (8) V. 100*b*, n. a7. (9) Since the meal has not yet commenced it is sufficient to place the food before one. (10) V. Mishnah *infra* 116*a*. By your observation you have in fact asked that question. (11) E.V. '*affliction*'. Deut. XVI, 3.

b (1) V. *supra* 36*a*, n. a10. (2) Defective, though it is read plene, denoting 'reciting'.

*צריך לשקועיה בחרוסת משום קפא דאי ס"ד לא צריך לשקועיה נטילת ידים למה לי הא לא נגע ודילמא לעולם אימא לך לא צריך לשקועיה וקפא מריחא מיית אלא למה לי נטילת ידים דילמא משקעו ליה ואמר רב פפא לא נישהי איניש מרור בחרוסת דילמא אגב חלייה דתבלין מבטיל ליה למרוריה ובעינן טעם מרור וליכא אדבריה רב חסדא לרבנא עוקבא ודרש נטל ידיו בטיבול ראשון נוטל ידיו בטיבול שני אמרוה רבנן קמיה דרב פפא הא בעלמא איתמר דאי סלקא דעתך הכא איתמר למה לי נטילת ידים תרי זימני הא משא ליה ידיה חדא זימנא אמר להו רב פפא אדרבה הכא איתמר דאי ס"ד בעלמא איתמר למה לי תרי טיבולי אלא מאי הכא איתמר נטילת ידים תרי זימני למה לי הא משא ליה ידיה חדא זימנא אמרי כיון דבעי למימר אגדתא והלילא דילמא אסוחי אסחיה לדעתיה ונגע אמר רבא בלע מצה יצא בלע מרור לא יצא בלע מצה ומרור ידי מצה יצא ידי מרור לא יצא כרכן בסיב ובלען אף ידי מצה נמי לא יצא אמר רב שימי בר אשי מצה לפני כל אחד ואחד מרור לפני כל אחד ואחד וחרוסת לפני כל אחד ואחד ואין עוקרין את השלחן אלא לפני מי שאומר הגדה רב הונא אומר כולהו נמי לפני מי שאומר הגדה והלכתא כרב הונא למה עוקרין את השולחן אמרי דבי ר' ינאי כדי שיכירו תינוקות וישאלו אביי הוה יתיב קמיה דרבה חזא דקא מדלי תבא מקמיה אמר להו עדיין לא קא אכלינן אתו קא מעקרי תבא מיקמן אמר ליה רבה פטרתן מלומר מה נשתנה: *אמר שמואל לחם עוני (כתיב) לחם שעונין עליו דברים תניא נמי הכי לחם עוני לחם שעונין עליו דברים הרבה דבר אחר לחם עוני עני כתיב מה עני שדרכו בפרוסה אף

תורה אור — דברים טז

לעיל דף קט.

צריך לשקועיה בחרוסת משום קפא. ארס שבחזרת שהסרף שבחזרת יש בו ארס כדרך הבללים: הא לא נגע. ידו במשקה: הא בעלמא איתמר. בשאר טיבולין שאינן קבע צריך שיטול ידיו לטיבול דכשנטל ידיו לראשון לא היה יודע שסוף שני לבוא: דאי ס"ד הכא. גבי מרור איתמר אמאי הא משי ליה חדא זמנא בטיבול ראשון: אסחיה לדעתיה ונגע· בבשרו: בלע מצה. ולא לעסה יצא: בלע מרור (לא) יצא.[אי] אפשר שלא טעם בו טעם מרור: בלע מצה ומרור. יחד ולא אכל עדיין לא מזה ולא מזה יצא ידי מצה שאינה צריכה טעם אבל ידי מרור לא יצא הואיל ולא לעסו ואוכל מצה עמו אין לו שום טעם: כרכן. שניהם יחד בסיב הדקל לא יצא שהרי לא היה ממש בפיו לא זה ולא זה: ואין עוקרין את השלחן. א"נ להגביה קערה כשמתחיל הגדה אלא מלפני הגדול שבהן שעושה הסדר ואומר ההגדה: אף

רשב"ם

צריך לשקועיה בחרוסת משום קפא. ארס שחזרת יש בו ארס כדרך הבללים והלכך צריך נט"י לטיבול ראשון כדלקמן שהרי נוגע במשקין כשמשקע את החזרת בחרוסת ור"ח פירש קפא תולעת דתניא בתרומות התולעים שבעיקרי אילנות ואת הקפא שבירק יבחושין שבחומץ ושביין מותרין סיכנס במסננת אסורין דכיון דפריש ממקום רביתיה הוי ליה כשרץ השורץ על הארץ כדאמר בשילהי אלו טריפות (חולין דף סז:) ועיקר: הא לא נגע. ידו במשקה: אגב חולייה. שנותנין בו תפוחין כדמוכח לקמן זכר לתפוח: לטיבול ראשון. של שאר ירקי: לטיבול שני. חזרת: הא בעלמא איתמר. בשאר טיבולין שבשאר ימות השנה שאינן קבע וכשנטל ידיו לראשון לא היה יודע שסוף שני לבוא והסיח דעתו: דאי ס"ד הכא. גבי מרור איתמר אמאי הא משא ליה ידיה חדא זמנא בטיבול ראשון: אסחיה לדעתיה. ונגע בשום דבר טינוף: בלע מצה. ולא לעסה יצא שהרי קיים בערב תאכלו מצות (שמות יב) שהרי אכילה היא לו ומיהו לכתחלה טעם מצה בעינן: בלע מרור לא יצא. דבעינן טעם מרור וליכא דמשום הכי קפיד רחמנא למרר את פיו של אוכל זכר לוימררו את חייהם (שם א) כך מצאתי כתוב בכל הספרים ובפי' ר"ח ורבינו פי' בלע מרור יצא א"א שלא יהא בו טעם מרור בלע מצה ומרור יחד ולא אכל עדיין לא מזה ולא מזה ידי מצה יצא ידי מרור לא יצא הואיל ולא לעסו ואכל מצה עמו אין לו שום טעם ולפי הכתוב בספרים צריך לפרש בלע מצה ומרור ידי מצה מיהו יצא דלא תימא אף ידי מצה לא יצא דאיכא תרתי לריעותא שלא טעם טעם מצה וגם לא נגע בגרונו שהמרור חוצץ בינתים: כרכן. שניהן יחד בסיב הגדל סביב הדקל לא יצא שהרי לא היה ממש בפיו לא זה ולא זה וכזורק אבן לחמת דמי: מצה לפני כל אחד ואחד. מנהג שלהן היה להסב על המטות והיה שלחן לפני כל אחד ואחד הלכך צריך מצה ומרור לפני כל אחד ואחד על שולחנו אבל לדידן אין צריך כי אם לפני מי שעושה הסדר והוא יחלק לכל אחד מצה ומרור: ואין עוקר את השלחן. שמצוה היא לעקור את השלחן כדלקמן כי היכי דליהוי הכירא לתינוקות וה"מ לדידהו דהוי להו שלחן קטן לפני מי שאומר הגדה לבדו וכן לכל אחד אבל אנו מסלקין את הקערה שבה מצה ומרור ושני תבשילין לסוף השלחן ודי לנו בכך ויש שנוהגין להגביה את הקערה על הכף ומוציאין הבשר מן הקערה ולאו מלתא היא דהא דאמר לקמן בשר אין צריך להגביה ה"מ בשעה שאומר הגדה פסח שהיו אבותינו כו' וכיון דלא מצי למימר פסח זה אם היה מגביהו לתבשיל שהיה בידו נראה כמקדיש בהמתו מחיים אבל כשמגביה הקערה כדי שיכיר תינוק וישאל היאך נראה כמקדיש קדשים לפיכך אין צריך להוציא ממנה התבשיל וגם הגבהתה חנם ואין כאן היכר לתינוק אבל עוקרין הקערה לגמרי ויניחנה בקרן זוית כאילו כבר אכלו כדי שיכיר התינוק וישאל דדמי לעקירת שלחן: פטרתן מלומר מה נשתנה. דתניא לקמן חכם בנו שואלו ואם לאו שואל הוא לעצמו מה נשתנה וכיון ששאלו לנו מה נשתנה אין אנו צריכין לומר מה נשתנה אלא להשיב על דבריו (של בנו) לפי שנשתעבדנו במצרים אנו עושין כל הדברים הללו: אף

אבל במרור נוגע בב' ידיו וקאמר הסיבו מביאין להם מים אע"פ שכל אחד כבר נטל ידו אחת חוזר ונוטל ב' ידיו אע"ג דאמרינן (ידים פ"ב מ"א) נטל ידו אחת משטיפה אחת טהורה צריך ליטול שתיהן ולפי שנטילה ראשונה לא היתה לשם קדושה לכך סבר המקשה דבהך נטילה ליכא למיגזר שמא יגע ולפי זה נראה דאין לברך על אותה נטילה כיון דליכא הכא מצוה לשמוע דברי ר"א בן ערך (חולין דף קו.) וכ"ש אנן שאין אנו נזהרין מלטמאות עצמנו ומלהטביל אוכלין טמאין ואין אנו צריכין לאותה נטילה והמברך הרי זה מברך ברכה לבטלה ובכל סדרים כתיב שצריך על הנטילה לברך ואין נראה כדפרישית: **קפא**. פי' ר"ח תולעת כדתניא התולעת שבעיקרי זיתים ושבעיקרי גפנים והקפא שבירק והיבחושין שביין וחומץ הרי אלו מותרים וא"ת תיקשי מינה לשמואל דאמר בסוף אלו טריפות (חולין דף סז:) קישות שהתליע באביה אסור משום שרץ השורץ על הארץ ומיהו שמואל סבר כאידך ברייתא דמייתי התם ומיהו ק"ק דמ"מ אמאי לא מייתי הך ברייתא התם ועוד שמואל היכי אכיל מרור בפסח וכי תימא דבדיק להו הלא שלא יהא שם קפא א"כ אמאי צריך חרוסת כיון דליכא קפא ושמא ברוב ירקות אין בהם קפא וסמיך שמואל ארובא ומשום סכנה דקפא חיישינן למיעוטא ולריך חרוסת: **צריך** שיטול בטיבול שני. לאו דוקא נקט בטיבול שני דהא עביד ליה בתר המוציא דבעי נטילת ידים אלא אגב טיבול ראשון נקט טיבול שני והנטילה נמי גם לגורך טיבול בזה: **אסוחי** מסח דעתיה ונגע. תימה מה צריך להאי טעמא תיפוק ליה דנטילה ראשונה לא היתה לשם קדושה אלא שלא יטמא את המשקין וי"ל דס"ד דכיון שנטל יועיל אפילו לגהמא דחולין לא בעי כוונה לכך צריך להאי טעמא: **ידי** מצה יצא ידי מרור לא יצא. וא"ת כיון שאין במרור זה מצוה מדרבנן ליבטיל מרור להאי מצה דבהדיה וי"ל דלא שייך ביטול אלא כשלועסן יחד דהא מבטל טעם אחד את חבירו אבל כשהם שלמים אפילו יהיה יותר מחבירו לא מבטל ליה: **מצה** לפני כל אחד ואחד מרור כו'. נראה דטעמא כדי שיטעום תיכף לברכה מיד כיון שזאת הברכה היא לשם חובה אבל בשאר ימות השנה דאין הברכה חובה אין צריך לטעום תיכף לברכה מיד: **למה** עוקרין את השלחן. דוקא שלהן שהן קטנים אבל שלנו שהן גדולים איכא טורח גדול בעקירתו נהגו לסלק הקערה לצד אחד דליהוי כעקירת שלחן ומה שנוהגין לסלק שני תבשילין בשעת הגבהה כדי שלא יהא נראה כמקדיש קדשים בחוץ וכן יסד ה"ר יוסף בסדרו מושך מהקערה שני תבשילין ומגביה קערה ולימא הא לחמא עניא כו' ולא יתכן דהא דאמר בשר אינו צריך להגביה היינו בשעה שאומר פסח זה דלאו ודאי נראה כאוכל קדשים: **כדי** שיכיר התינוק וישאל. כלומר ומתוך כך יבא לישאל בשאר דברים אבל במה ששאל למה אנו עוקרין השלחן לא יפטר ממה נשתנה והיא דאביי לא פי' הגמ' אלא תחלת שאילתו: מה

רבינו חננאל

נטילת ידים צריך לשקועיה משום קפא כדי שתמות הקפא שבאותו הירקמן ההומץ שבחרוס' פי' קפא תולעת דתניא [בתוספתא] דתרומות האוכל תולעים שבעקרי אילנות ואת הקפא שבירק חייב יבחושין שבחומץ ושביין *מותרין סננן במסננת אסורין דאי לא משקע ליה למה ליה נטילת ידים: **אדבריה** רב חסדא לרבנא עוקבא ודרש הנוטל ידיו בטבול ראשון צריך שיטול ידיו בטבול שני ואמרי' למה לי נטילת ידים שני' הא משא ידיה חדא זימנא ופרקי' כיון דמפסיק בינייהו ואמר אגדתא והלילא דלמא מסח דעתיה ונגע במידי דמטנף הלכך צריך נטילת ידים שניה: **אמר** רבא בלע מצה יצא בלע מרור לא יצא בלע מצה ומרור ידי מצה יצא ידי מרור לא יצא כרכן בסיב ובלען אף ידי מצה לא יצא. אמר רב שימי בר אשי מצה ומרור וחרוסת בפני כל אחד ואחד ואין עוקרין השלחן אלא לפני מי שאומר הגדה רב כהנא אמר כלהו לפני מי שאומר הגדה ולמה עוקרין השלחן כדי שישאלו התינוקות כי הא דאביי הוה יתיב קמי רבא חזי דמגבה פתורא אמר אכתי לא אכילנן כו': **גרסי'** בפ' כיצד מברכין על הפירות אמר רב פפא הכל מודים [בפסח] שמניח פרוסה בתוך שלימה ובוצע מ"ט לחם עוני כתיב וקיי"ל מפני שהוא יום טוב צריך לבצוע על שתי ככרות כשבת דכתיב ביה לקטו לחם משנה הלכך בפסח מניח פרוסה בתוך שלימה ובוצע ומסתברא אפרוסה ויש אומרים אשלימה: **תניא** לחם עוני לחם שעונין עליו דברים · פי' אומר עליו הגדה מצה זו שאנו

פב א ב ג מיי' פ"ח מהל' מלה הל' ו יח סמג עשין מא טוש"ע א"ח סי' תעה סעיף א:
פג ד [מיי' פרק ו מהל' מלה דין ב] טוש"ע שם סעיף ג:
פד ה מיי' שם פ"ח הלכה א וסמג שם טוש"ע א"ח סי' תעג סעיף ד:
פה ו מיי' שם פ"ז הל' ג טוש"ע שם סעיף ו:
פו ז ח שם סעיף ז:

*) בתוספתא שם שלפנינו הגי' אסורין אך הגר"א ז"ל הגיה מותרין וגי' רבינו מסייע ליה ודברי הגר"א ז"ל ביו"ד סי' פ"ד סק"ח תמוה לפי זה וצ"ע:

עט א מיי' פ"ח מהל' מצה הלכה יב סמג עשין מא טוש"ע א"ח סי' תעה סעיף ב:

פ ב מיי' שם הלכה ו טוש"ע שם סעיף א:

פא ג מיי' שם הלכה א ופ"ו מהל' ברכות הלכה א סמג שם ועשין כז טוש"ע א"ח סי' תעג סעיף ו וסי' קנח סעי' ד [רב אלפס ברכות פ"ח דף מה. וברא"ש פ' כל הבשר סי' יו"ד]:

מתקיף לה רב חסדא לאחר שמילא כריסו ממנו חוזר ומברך עליה אלא אמר רב חסדא מעיקרא מברך עליה בורא פרי האדמה ועל אכילת מרור ואכיל ולבסוף אכיל אכילת חסא בלא ברכה בסוריא עבדי כרב הונא ורב ששת בריה דרב יהושע עביד כרב חסדא *והלכתא כוותיה דרב חסדא רב אחא בריה דרבא מהדר אשאר ירקות לאפוקי נפשיה מפלוגתא אמר רבינא אמר לי רב משרשיא בריה דרב נתן הכי אמר הלל *משמיה דגמרא לא ניכרוך איניש מצה ומרור בהדי הדדי וניכול משום דסבירא לן *מצה בזמן הזה דאורייתא ומרור דרבנן ואתי מרור דרבנן ומבטיל ליה למצה דאורייתא ואפילו למ"ד מצות אין מבטלות זו את זו ה"מ דאורייתא בדאורייתא או דרבנן בדרבנן אבל דאורייתא ודרבנן אתי דרבנן ומבטיל ליה לדאורייתא מאן תנא *דשמעת לי' מצות אין מבטלות זו את זו הלל היא *דתניא אמרו עליו על הלל שהיה כורכן בבת אחת ואוכלן שנאמר °על מצות ומרורים יאכלוהו אמר [א] רבי יוחנן חולקין עליו חביריו על הלל דתניא יכול יהא כורכן בבת אחת ואוכלן כדרך שהלל אוכלן תלמוד לומר [ב] על מצות ומרורים יאכלוהו אפילו זה בפני עצמו וזה בפני עצמו מתקיף לה רב אשי אי הכי מאי אפילו אלא אמר רב אשי האי תנא הכי קתני יכול לא יצא בהו ידי חובתו אא"כ כורכן בבת אחת ואוכלן כדרך שהלל אוכלן תלמוד לומר על מצות ומרורים יאכלוהו אפילו זה בפני עצמו וזה בפני עצמו השתא דלא איתמר הלכתא לא כהלל ולא כרבנן גמברך על אכילת מצה ואכיל והדר מברך על אכילת מרור ואכיל והדר אכיל מצה וחסא בהדי הדדי בלא ברכה זכר למקדש כהלל אמר רבי אלעזר אמר רב אושעיא דכל שטיבולו במשקה צריך נטילת ידים אמר רב פפא שמע מינה האי חסא צריך

במדבר ט

[יבמות מו. יע"ש בפרש"י קידושין נג. ע"ש בפרש"י] [לקמן קטו: קכ.] [זבחים עט.] שם

ולבסוף אכיל. בלא ברכה משום דבעינן תרי טבולין: ומבטל ליה. לטעם מצה דאורייתא: שהיה כורכן בבת אחת. פסח מצה ומרור: זכר למקדש כהלל. זכר למה שהיה עושה הלל בזמן שבהמ"ק קיים שהיו אוכלים פסחים: צריך נטילת ידים. משום המשקין שהידים שניות וכל הפוסל בתרומה מטמא משקין וכו' צריך

תורה אור

רשב"ם

ולבסוף אכיל. בלא ברכה משום דבעי' תרי טבולי: מצה בזמן הזה דאורייתא ומרור דרבנן. וטעמא מפרש בשילהי פירקין (דף קכ.): אפילו למ"ד כו'. דכיון דכי הדדי נינהו כולהו קום מצות נינהו ולא מבטלי אהדדי: ומבטל לה. לטעם מצה דאורייתא: כורכן בבת אחת. (מצה) פסח מצה ומרור כורכן בכרך אחד כמו כורכו בגמי (עירובין דף קג:): יאכלוהו. כל אחד בפני עצמו מדלא כתיב יאכלו (אותו) ולא יאכלו את הבשר: מתקיף לה רב אשי כו'. ומיהו חולקין עליו חביריו כרבי יוחנן אבל מהכא לא שמעינן: והשתא דלא איתמר הלכתא לא כהלל ולא כרבנן. דהא רבנן דברייתא מודו להלל דכריכה נמי שפיר דמי אבל ר' יוחנן קאמר דפליגי עליה דרבנן לגמרי לית להו כריכה כלל: מברך. המצה לחודה כו': זכר למקדש כהלל. כמו שהיה עושה הלל בזמן שבית המקדש קיים שהיו אוכלים פסחים: כל שטיבולו במשקין. כגון ירק בחומץ צריך נטילת ידים משום משקה שהידים שניות וכל הפוסל את התרומה מטמא משקים להיות תחלה: צריך

גליון הש"ס

תוס' ד"ה מתקיף לה ר"ח וכו' ומועלת הברכה שבירך בטיבול ראשון. עי' לקמן קב ע"א תוס' ד"ה נאמרים: שם ד"ה והדר אכיל וכו' ולא שייך כאן חבילות. עי' ברכות לט ע"ב תוס' ד"ה בצל מדים:

תוספות

מתקיף לה רב חסדא לאחר שמילא כריסו כו'. רב חסדא נמי נראה דסבר כר"ל דבעי כוונה אע"פ שסבר דאין כון לברך בטיבול שני כיון שכבר מילא כריסו דאי סבר דאין צריכות כוונה ה"ל למימר בהדיא דנפיק בטיבול ראשון ואם יברך בטיבול שני הויא ברכה לבטלה ולא צריך לרב חסדא להדורי אשאר ירקי ומברך לרב חסדא בטיבול ראשון על אכילת מרור אע"ג דעיקר מצות מרור לא נפיק אלא בטיבול שני אחר מצה *ומועלת הברכה שבירך בטיבול ראשון לטיבול שני מאחר שאכל ממנו מעט בטיבול ראשון מידי דהוה אברכת שופר דמברך אתקיעות דישיבה ומועלת ברכה לתקיעות שבעמידה שהם עיקר ועושים על סדר ברכות והשתא כל אלו אמוראי סברי דבעי כוונה וסתמא דמסדר הש"ס סבר הכי מדאיצטריך לפסוק כרב חסדא ואי אין צריכות כוונה פשיטא דלא יברך בטיבול שני דאפילו לא בירך בטיבול ראשון נפק ביה ואי יברך בטיבול שני הויא ברכה לבטלה ולית הלכתא כוותיה דאבוה דשמואל דאית ליה בפרק ראוהו ב"ד (ר"ה דף כח:) אין צריכות כוונה דקאמר בכפאו ואכל מצה יצא ומוקי לה בכפאוהו פרסיים והתם לא מייתי מאכלו בלא מתכוין משום דלגבי אכילה לא בעינן כוונה כולי האי כמו בתפלה ותקיעה ומש"ה נמי לא מייתי הכא ברייתות דהתם דבעו כוונה דגבי תפלה ותקיעה בעי כוונה טפי כדפרישית:

והדר אכיל הסא בלא ברכה. ונראה דאין צריך לברך בפה"א אע"ג דהגדה הוי הפסק כדפרישית לעיל ולא מיפטר בברכה של טיבול ראשון מ"מ ברכת המוציא פוטרתן דהוה להו דברים הבאים בתוך הסעודה מחמת הסעודה שהרי ירקות גוררין הלב וקרי ליה נמי למרור פרפרת הפת וכן אמר בכילד מברכין (ברכות ד' מב.) בירך על הפת פטר את הפרפרת פרפר' היינו דברים הממשיכים האכילה כגון דגים קטנים ותמרים וירקות והיו רגילים לאוכלם בתוך הסעודה בין מאכל למאכל ולכך פטר את הפרפרת לפי שבא לצורך שעל ידי כך אוכל יותר ואין לומר דפרפרת היינו דבר שבא ללפת בו את הפת דהא הוי בכלל הא דקתני התם דמברך על העיקר ופוטר את הטפילה וקאמר נמי רבי חייא פת פוטרת כל מיני מאכל ורב פפא נמי פסיק התם הלכתא דברים הבאים תוך הסעודה מחמת הסעודה והיינו הפרפרת כדפי' אין טעונין ברכה לא לפניהם ולא לאחריהם שלא מחמת הסעודה תוך הסעודה כגון תאנים וענבים שאינן באין להמשיך המאכל ולא ללפת אלא לתענוג צריכין ברכה לפניהם ולא לאחריהם אחר הסעודה אפילו פרפרת טעונין ברכה בין לפניהם בין לאחריהם וה"ר יוסף טוב עלם כתב בסדרו למה שאנו ירקות באין תחלה לפטור חזרת מברכה ראויה לה וליתא דהא משום היכרא באין °ולא שייך כאן חבילות אלא בתרי מילי ועוד דרב חסדא מברך שתיקן אחזרת ועוד דמשמע דלא פטר ליה פת ושמא אינו מחשיבו פרפרת הפת כיון שאינו אוכל ממנו אלא כזית: אתי מרור דרבנן ומבטל למצה דאורייתא. וכל שכן דאי לא הוי מרור אפי' מדרבנן דמבטל להמצה כדמשמע לקמן והא דשרי בהקומץ (מנחות דף כג:) מצה מתובלת לא אתו בשמים ומבטלו למצה דאין מן הבשמים כי אם דבר מועט *ודלא כאותן שאסרו מצה מתובלת בשם רש"י אף בימים אחרונים משום דמחמעי לה: אלא אמר רב אשי. אין נראה כפירוש הקונטרס דמשבש רב אשי מילתיה דרבי יוחנן שהרי טוב להגיה הברייתא אפילו לחסר כמו שאנו מגיהין כמה ברייתות מלשבש דברי ר' יוחנן אלא רב אשי מתקיף אבני ישיבה דמפרשי דחולקין רבנן ואסרי לכרוך דא"כ מאי אפילו אלא רבנן סברי דבכל ענין מצותו בין ע"י כריכה בין כל אחד לבדו ופליגי אהלל דמצריך לכרוך ונקטי רבנן אפילו משום הלל וא"ת מנא לן דסבר הלל דאין מבטלות דילמא שאני הכא דגלי קרא ועוד הא לרבנן נמי אין מבטלות דהא אם כרכן נמי יצא וי"ל מדסבר דלכתחלה יש לו לכרוך ובדיעבד נפיק כי לא כריך אם כן בעלמא אין מבטלות א"כ איצטריך קרא הכא להתיר כריכה ולומר דהכא לא מבטלי והלכך לרבנן דמוקי קרא בדיעבד שמעינן דבעלמא מבטלות ושאני הכא דגלי קרא: א מברך המצה ואכיל ומברך אמרור כו'. אם היה כורך שניהם יחד תחלה הוה אתי מרור דרבנן ומבטל למצה ואם היה אוכל מצה בלא מרור תחלה כשהיה כורכן אחר כך אתי מצה דרשות ומבטל מרור דרבנן ומיהו אי הוה קיימא לן כהלל הוה עבדינן הכי מצה לחודא והדר מצה ומרור בכריכה כיון שצריך לעשות מדרבנן מצות כריכה כהלל הוה דרבנן ודרבנן: כל שטיבולו במשקה צריך נטילה. פי' בקונ' אע"ג דקי"ל (חולין דף קו.) הנוטל ידיו לפירות ה"ז מגסי הרוח כיון דאיכא משקין וקיי"ל (פ"ה פ"ח משנה ז) כל הפוסל את התרומה מטמא משקין להיות תחלה הוה להו הנך פירות כמו כהמא וצריך ליטול כמו בנהמא ואין נראה לפרש כן דאם כן כי פריך למה לי נטילת ידים הא לא נגע ומאי נפקא מיניה אפילו אי לא נגע כיון דסוף סוף אכיל משקה המטובל לא גרע מאוכל מחמת מאכיל דבעי נטילת ידים *ועוד וכי לא ידע המקשה דאיכא למיחש דילמא נגע כדאמר רב פפא ונראה דנטילה דהכא לא משום קדושה ונקיות כמו בנהמא אלא משום שלא יטמא המשקין להיות תחלה ויהא אסור לשתותן ולפסול את גופו כדתנן בפ"ב דחולין (דף לג.) השוחט ולא יצא מהן דם כו' הא יצא מהן דם אין נאכלין בידים מסואבות ואמר נמי בסדר הסיבה (*ברכות דף מג.) הביאו להן יין כל אחד נוטל ידו אחת פי' שלא יטמא היין ויפסול גופו והתם סגי ביד אחת הכל

[ועי' תוספות זבחים עט. ד"ה אלא ותוספות מנחות כג: ד"ה אלא למ"ד]

[חולין קו:]

[עי' מ"ש תוס' שם ד"ה כל אחד כו' ותוס' ת"ג יח: ד"ה הטמא]

רבינו חננאל

ואסיקנא רב חסדא אמר מברך אחזרת מעיקרא בורא פרי האדמה ועל אכילת מרור ובסוף אוכל חזרת בלא ברכה והלכתא כרב חסדא. רב אחא מהדר אשאר ירקי לאפוקי נפשיה מפלוגתא: אמר רבא לא ניכול איניש מצה ומרו' בהדי' הדדי דסביר' לן (מצה) [דמרור] בזמן הזה דרבנן ואתי מרור דרבנן ומבטל מצה דאורייתא ואפי' למאן דאמר מצות אין מבטלות זו את זו ה"מ דאורייתא ודאורייתא כגון מצה ומרור בזמן שבית המקדש קיים דתרווייהו מדאורייתא אבל בזמן הזה דמרור דרבנן הוא לא. מאן תנא דאמר מצות אין מבטלות זו את זו הלל דתניא אמרו עליו על הלל שהיה כורך המרור על המצה ואוכלו בבת אחת כו' אמר ר' יוחנן חלוקין עליו חבריו על הלל דתניא יכול לא יהא אדם יוצא ידי חובתו בפסח אלא אם כן כורכן בבת אחת מצה ומרור ואוכל כדרך שהלל אוכלן ת"ל על מצות ומרורים יאכלוהו [אפי'] זה בפני עצמו וזה בפני עצמו השתא דלא אתמר הלכתא לא כרבנן ולא כהלל מברך אמצה לחודיה ואכיל ומברך אמרור לחודיה ואכיל והדר כריך ליה למרור אמצה ואכיל להו בבת אחת בלא ברכה זכר למקדש כהלל: אמר ר' אושעיא כל שטיבולו במשקין צריך נטילת ידים אמר רב פפא ש"מ מדקתני מרור צריך

הגהות מהר"ב רנ"י בורג

[א] בגמ' אמר ר' יוחנן חולקין עליו חביריו על הלל. נ"ב עיין ביאור סוגיין ולשון רשב"ם ותוספות בשו"ת שער אפרים סי' כ"א כ"ג כ"ד ובשו"ת בית יעקב סי' ס"א באורך מאד וכמדומה שכולם שמו אחר הדלת לשון הרז"ה והרמב"ן בספר מלחמות בסוגיין יעוי"ה: [ב] שם תלמוד לומר על מצות ומרורים יאכלוהו. נמחקו תיבות על מצות ומרורים ונ"ב [מצות על מרורים] כצ"ל לפרשב"ם בד"ה יאכלוהו והבן ודו"ק:

the eating of bitter herbs' and eats. [115a] To this R. Ḥisda demurred: After filling his stomach with it he returns and recites a blessing over it!—Rather, said R. Ḥisda: On the first occasion he recites over it, 'Who createst the fruit of the ground,' and, 'concerning the eating of bitter herbs,' and eats, while subsequently he eats the lettuce without a blessing. In Syria they acted in accordance with R. Huna, while R. Shesheth the son of R. Joshua acted according to R. Ḥisda. And the law is in accordance with R. Ḥisda. R. Aḥa the son of Raba used
a to go in search of other vegetables, so as to avoid controversy.[1]

Rabina said, R. Mesharsheya son of R. Nathan told me: Thus did Hillel[2] say on the authority of tradition:[3] A man must not make a sandwich of *mazzah* and bitter herbs together and eat them, because we hold that *mazzah* nowadays[4] is a Biblical obligation, whereas bitter herbs are a Rabbinical requirement, and thus the bitter herbs, which are Rabbinical, will come and nullify the *mazzah*, which is Biblical. And even on the view that precepts cannot nullify each other, that applies only to a Biblical [precept] with a Biblical [precept], or a Rabbinical [precept] with a Rabbinical [precept], but in the case of a Scriptural and a Rabbinical [precept], the Rabbinical [one] comes and nullifies the Scriptural [one]. Which Tanna do you know [to hold] that precepts do not nullify each other?—It is Hillel.[5] For it was taught, It was related of Hillel that he used to wrap them together,[6] for it is said, *they shall eat it with unleavened bread and bitter herbs.*[7] R. Joḥanan observed: Hillel's colleagues disagreed with him. For it was taught: You might think that he should wrap them together and eat them, in the manner that Hillel ate it, therefore it is stated, *they shall eat it with unleavened bread and bitter herbs,* [intimating] even each separately.[8] To this R. Ashi demurred: If so, what is [the meaning of] 'even'?[9] Rather, said R. Ashi, this Tanna teaches thus: You might think that he does not discharge his duty unless he wraps them together and eats them, in the manner of Hillel, therefore it is stated, *they shall eat it with unleavened bread and bitter herbs,* [intimating] even each separately. Now that the law was not stated either as Hillel or as the Rabbis,[10] one recites the blessing, '[Who hast commanded us] concerning the eating of unleavened bread' and eats; then he recites the blessing, 'concerning the eating of bitter herbs,' and eats; and then he eats unleavened bread and lettuce together without a blessing, in memory of
b the Temple, as Hillel [did].[1]

R. Eleazar said in R. Oshaia's name: Whatever is dipped in a liquid[2] requires the washing of the hands.[3] Said R. Papa: Infer

a (1) Lit., 'to exclude himself from a controversy'. (2) The reference is to R. Hillel, the fourth century Babylonian amora, and not to Hillel, the great Nasi who flourished in the first century B.C.E. (3) I.e., it came to him anonymously; Kaplan, *Redaction of the Talmud*, p. 227. (4) I.e., after the destruction of the Temple and the cessation of sacrifices. (5) Hillel I. (6) Place the paschal meat of bitter herbs between *mazzah*. (7) Num. IX, 11. (8) This is deduced from the sing. '*it*.' (9) 'Even' shows that they may certainly be eaten together. (10) Though the aforementioned Tanna does not disagree with Hillel, as R. Ashi has shown, it was nevertheless held that some Rabbis did disagree.

b (1) Thus he acts on both views, by eating them first separately and then together. (2) Vegetables, which are dipped into vinegar. (3) Unwashed hands are unclean in the second degree and therefore disqualify *terumah* (v. Mishnah *supra* 14a and note a.l.), and whatever disqualifies *terumah* defiles liquids in the first degree (*supra* 14b). Therefore the hands must be washed.

GEMARA. [114*b*] Resh Lakish said: This[11] proves that precepts require intention, [for] since he does not eat it[12] at the stage when bitter herbs are compulsory, he eats it with [the blessing,] 'Who createst the fruit of the ground,' and perhaps he did not intend [to fulfil the obligation of] bitter herbs; therefore he must dip it again with the express purpose of [eating] bitter herbs. For if you should think [that] precepts do not require intention,
a why two dippings: surely he has [already] dipped it once?[1] But whence [does this follow]? Perhaps after all precepts do not require intention, and as to what you argue, why two dippings, [the answer is,] that there may be a distinction for [the sake of] the children.[2] And should you say, if so, we should be informed about other vegetables:[3] If we were informed about other vegetables I would say: Only where other vegetables [are eaten first] do we require two dippings, but lettuce alone[4] does not require two dippings:[5] hence he informs us that even lettuce [alone] requires two dippings, so that there may be a distinction [shown] therewith for the children. Moreover, it was taught: If he ate them [the bitter herbs] while *demai*,[6] he has discharged [his duty]; if he ate them without intention, he has discharged [his duty]; if he ate them in half quantities,[7] he has discharged [his duty], providing that he does not wait between one eating and the next more than is required for the eating of half [a loaf]?[8]—It is [dependent on] Tannaim. For it was taught, R. Jose said: Though he has [already] dipped the lettuce [*ḥazereth*], it is a religious requirement to bring lettuce and *ḥaroseth* and two dishes before him.[9] Yet still, whence [does this follow]: perhaps R. Jose holds [that] precepts do not require intention, and the reason that we require two dippings is that there may be a distinction [shown]
b for the children?—If so, what is the 'religious requirement?'[1]

What are the two dishes?—Said R. Huna: Beet and rice.[2] Raba used to be particular for[3] beet and rice, since it had [thus] issued from the mouth of R. Huna. R. Ashi said: From R. Huna you may infer that none pay heed to the following [ruling] of R. Joḥanan b. Nuri. For it was taught, R. Joḥanan b. Nuri said: Rice is a species of corn and *kareth* is incurred for [eating it in] its leavened state and a man discharges his duty with it on Passover.[4] Hezekiah said: Even a fish and the egg on it.[5] R. Joseph said: Two kinds of meat are necessary, one in memory of the Passover-offering and the second in memory of the *ḥagigah*.[6] Rabina said: Even a bone and [its] broth.

It is obvious that where other vegetables are present, he recites[7] the blessing, 'who createst the fruit of the ground' over the other vegetables and eats, and then[8] recites the blessing, '[Who hast commanded us] concerning the eating of bitter herbs,' and eats.[9] But what if he has lettuce only? Said R. Huna: First he recites a blessing over the bitter herbs, 'Who createst the fruit of the ground,' and eats, and then [later] he recites over it 'concerning

(11) The fact that he dips lettuce twice. (12) The first lettuce.

a (1) The first lettuce is eaten before it is obligatory (v. n. 8 in Mishnah); hence the ordinary blessing for vegetables is recited, not 'who hast commanded us concerning the eating of bitter herbs,' though later it will be eaten as an obligation. Thus he did not discharge his duty of eating bitter herbs with the first lettuce, because that was not his intention, which proves that one does not discharge one's duty unless it is expressly done with that intention. (2) V. 114*a*, n. b8. (3) The Mishnah should state that a vegetable is dipped into water and eaten. Why specify *ḥazereth* (lettuce), which is one of the vegetables which may be eaten as bitter herbs (v. *supra* 39*a*)? (4) I.e., where lettuce alone is eaten. (5) For once he has eaten it he has done his duty in respect of bitter herbs. (6) V. Glos. (7) I.e., as much as half an olive the first time and the same the second time, as much as an olive being the minimum quantity which must be eaten. (8) V. *supra* 44*a*, n. a9. — This distinctly contradicts Resh Lakish. (9) And Resh Lakish maintains that R. Jose's reason is because precepts require intention.

b (1) *Mizwah* implies that it is an essential obligation. (2) Even these constitute two dishes, and of course two kinds of meat all the more (Rashbam and Tosaf.). (3) Lit., 'go in search of.' (4) *Tabshil* denotes a *boiled* dish: hence if it were a species of corn, boiling would make it leaven. (5) I.e., the egg with which it is smeared before it is prepared. Though it becomes all one, yet it counts as two dishes. (6) V. Mishnah *supra* 69*b*. (7) At the first dipping. (8) At the second dipping. (9) Each blessing being over a *different* vegetable.

אמר ר"ל זאת אומרת *מצות צריכות כוונה כיון דלא בעידן חיובא דמרור הוא דאכיל ליה בבורא פה"א הוא דאכיל ליה ודילמא לא איכוון למרור הלכך בעי למהדר לאטבולי לשם מרור דאי סלקא דעתך מצוה לא בעיא כוונה למה לך תרי טיבולי והא טביל ליה חדא זימנא ממאי דילמא לעולם *מצות אין צריכות כוונה ודקאמרת תרי טיבולי למה לי כי היכי דליהוי היכירא לתינוקות וכי תימא א"כ לישמעינן שאר ירקות אי אשמעינן שאר ירקות הוה אמינא היכא דאיכא שאר ירקות הוא דבעינן תרי טיבולי אבל חזרת לחודא לא בעי תרי טיבולי קמשמע לן דאפי' חזרת בעינן תרי טיבולי כי היכי דליהוי ביה היכירא לתינוקות ועוד תניא אכלן דמאי יצא אכלן בלא מתכוין יצא אכלן לחצאין יצא ובלבד שלא ישהא בין אכילה לחבירתה יותר מכדי אכילת פרס תנאי היא דתניא רבי יוסי אומר אע"פ שטיבל בחזרת מצוה להביא לפניו חזרת וחרוסת ושני תבשילין ואכתי ממאי דילמא קסבר רבי יוסי מצות אין צריכות כוונה והאי דבעינן תרי טיבולי כי היכי דתיהוי היכירא לתינוקות א"כ מאי מצוה מאי שני תבשילין אמר רב הונא סילקא וארוזא רבא הוה מיהדר אסילקא וארוזא הואיל ונפיק מפומיה דרב הונא אמר רב אשי שמע מינה (א) דרב הונא לית דחייש להא דרבי יוחנן בן נורי דתניא רבי יוחנן בן נורי אומר *אורז מין דגן הוא וחייבין על חימוצו כרת ואדם יוצא בו ידי חובתו בפסח חזקיה אמר אפי' דג וביצה שעליו רב יוסף אמר צריך שני מיני בשר אחד זכר לפסח וא' זכר לחגיגה רבינא אמר אפילו גרמא ובישולא פשיטא היכא דאיכא שאר ירקות מברך אשאר ירקות בורא פרי האדמה ואכיל והדר מברך על אכילת מרור ואכיל היכא דליכא אלא חסא מאי אמר רב הונא מברך מעיקרא אמרור ב"פ האדמה ואכיל ולבסוף מברך עליה על אכילת מרור ואכיל מתקיף

זאת אומרת מצות לריכות כונה. משום הכי בעי תרי טיבולי שמא לא נתכוון לשם מרור הואיל ובירך בורא פרי האדמה כשאר ירקות דעלמא: דילמא הא קמשמע לן דבעינן תרי טיבולי. משום תינוקות שישאלו ועבדינן היכירא טובא: אכלן חצאין. חצי זית בפעם ראשונה וחצי זית בפעם שניה ובמרור קא איירי: תנאי היא. דהאי תנא לית ליה לריכות כונה ורבי יוסי אית ליה לריכות כונה: ש"מ. מדקאמר רב הונא דמבשלין אורז בפסח ולא חייש לחימוץ לית דחש לה לדרבי יוחנן: אפילו דג וביצה שעליו. שהיו רגילין להטיח את הדג בבילים: ואחד זכר. לחגיגת ארבעה עשר: גרמא ובישולא. חתיכת בשר ומרק: פשיטא היכא דאיכא שאר ירקי. מברך מעיקרא אירקי בורא פרי האדמה דאסור ליהנות מן העולם בלא ברכה וכיון דיש לו שאר ירקות הכי שפיר טפי שיברך בפה"א על הירקות תחלה דהיינו ברכה הראויה להם ויפטור את המרור הבא אחריו מברכת בפה"א ואח"כ יברך על החזרת על אכילת מרור: ולבסוף

רשב"ם

זאת אומרת מצות לריכות כונה. משום הכי בעי תרי טיבולי שמא לא נתכוון בראשון לשם מרור הואיל ובירך עליו בפה"א כשאר ירקות דעלמא שהרי אין עדיין אכילת מצות מרור לברך עליו על אכילת מרור עד לאחר המצה: דילמא הא קמ"ל. דבעינן תרי טיבולי משום תינוקות שישאלו ועבדי היכירא טובא ומיהו ממרור קמא יצא ידי חובתו ומהדר ר"ל אי"ב דמשום היכירא דתינוקות לחוד נקט תרי טיבולי ולאו לאשמועינן מצות לריכות כוונה לאשמועינן שאר ירקות בטיבול ראשון ומרור בטיבול שני דאיכא נמי היכר לתינוקות אבל במרור לחודיה לא בעינן תרי טיבולי דכולי האי לא עבדינן משום היכירא דתינוקות להקדים אכילת מרור קודם זמנו: ועוד תניא. בהדיא דמצות אין לריכות כוונה ותיובתא דריש לקיש: אכלן דמאי יצא. דאי בעי מפקר לנכסיה והוי עני וחזי ליה השתא נמי חזי ליה: אכלן חצאין. חצי זית בפעם ראשון וחצי זית בפעם שני ובמרור מיירי: תנאי היא. דהאי תנא לית ליה מצות לריכות כוונה ורבי יוסי אית ליה: אע"ג שטיבל בחזרת. טיבול קמא היכא דליכא שאר ירקות: מצוה להביא כו'. כלומר מצוה להביא מן התורה דהאכתי לא קיים מצות אכילת מרור הואיל ולא נתכוון דמצות לריכות כוונה: אי הכי מאי מצוה להביא כו'. מביאין הוה ליה למיתני: סילקא. תרדין ורבותא היא וכל שכן שני מיני בשר: הואיל ונפק מפומיה דרב הונא. בשביל חיבתו להראות הלכה כמותו: ש"מ. מדקאמר רב הונא שמבשלין אורז בפסח ולא חייש לחימוץ לית דחש לדר' יוחנן בן נורי: אפי' דג וביצה שעליו. שהיו רגילין להטיח את הדג בבילים והיינו רבותא דאע"ג דדמי לתבשיל אחד חשיב שני תבשילין: ואחד זכר. לחגיגת ארבעה עשר הבאה עם הפסח: שני מיני בשר. אלו כנגד הפסח ומבושל כנגד חגיגה כך פירש רבינו חננאל מרומי: גרמא ובשולא. חתיכת בשר ומרק שנתבשלה בו: פשיטא היכא דאיכא שאר ירקות. מברך מעיקרא בטיבול ראשון אשאר ירקות בורא פרי האדמה דאסור ליהנות מן העולם הזה בלא ברכה דכיון שיש לו שאר ירקות הכי שפיר טפי שיברך בפה"א תחלה דהיינו ברכה הראויה להן ויפטור את המרור מברכת פרי האדמה ואחר כך יברך על החזרת על אכילת מרור: ולבסוף

זאת אומרת מצות לריכות כוונה. ר"ש לקיש סבר דמתני' סתמא קתני ומיירי אפי' יכול למצוא שאר ירקות אין לו לטרוח אחר שאר ירקות אלא עושה שני טיבולין במרור והיינו משום דמצות לריכות כוונה וכיון דלא בעידן כו' ובבורא פרי האדמה הוא דאכיל ליה כלומר שלא בירך על אכילת מרור ודילמא לא איכוון ודילמא לאו דוקא כלומר ודאי לא איכוון למרור דאין מצוה אלא עד טיבול שני אחר מצה הלכך בעי למהדר ואטבולי פי' ולברך על אכילת מרור ולא נקט וברוכי משום דרב חסדא אית ליה בשמעתין דמברך על אכילת מרור בטיבול ראשון והא דקאמר ובבורא פרי האדמה אכיל ליה היינו כלומר שאינו אוכל לשם אכילת מרור אלא אכלו לצאת בבורא פרי האדמה דאי סלקא דעתך לא בעי כוונה אם כן יצא חובת מרור בטיבול ראשון אע"ג דאכלו לפני מצה וכתיב על מצות ומרורים לא הויא עיכובא אמאי צריך תרי טיבולי במרור הוה ליה לאהדורי אשאר ירקות משום היכירא בטיבול ראשון ואחר מצה בטיבול שני יאכל מרור והגמרא דאי דלעולם אין לריכות כוונה ומהדרינן אשאר ירקי משום היכירא וכדי לאכול מרור אחר המצה ומתניתין קמ"ל היכא דליכא שאר ירקי דאפי' במרור בעינן תרי טיבולי כדי לאכול מרור כמצוותו ומשום היכירא ולא אמרי' שלא יאכל מרור עד לבסוף ולא נחוש להיכירא:

אכלן דמאי יצא. אבל ודאי לא יצא אע"ג דמעשר ירק דרבנן כדאמרינן גבי מצה בכל שעה (לעיל דף לה:) אבל לא בטבל ומוקי לה בטבל טבול מדרבנן ואיתקש מרור למצה ובדמאי יצא נמי במצה משום דאי בעי מפקיר נכסיה וחזי ליה וטעמא דהחמירו בודאי דרבנן דטבל דאורייתא מפיק התם (לעיל דף לה:) מלא תאכל עליו חמץ יצא זה שאיסורו משום בל תאכל טבל ואיתקש מצה לחמץ:

אכלן בלא מתכוין יצא. קשיא לריש לקיש ואע"ג דריש לקיש דייק ממתניתין ע"כ מתניתין לא איירי בכל ענין אלא בדליכא שאר ירקות וקא משני תנאי היא וכיון דאיכא תנא דסבר כריש לקיש דייק שפיר ריש לקיש ממתניתין דלריכות כוונה כי מסתמא איירי בכל ענין אפי' איכא שאר ירקות:

סילקא וארוזא. וכ"ש שני מיני בשר:

לית דחש לה לדר' יוחנן בן נורי. וטעמא דאיכא לידי חימוץ אלא לידי סרחון בפ' כל שעה (לעיל דף לה.):

שני מיני בשר. פירוש ר"ח אלו זכר לפסח ומבושל זכר לחגיגה ולא נהירא דקיימא לן כבן תימא (לעיל דף ע.) דאין חגיגה נאכלת אלא צלי דמתניתין* אתיא כוותיה לכך נראה דתרוייהו מבושלין וכן משמע לשון תבשילין:

אחד זכר לפסח ואחד לחגיגה. כשחל י"ד להיות בשבת אין צריך רק בישול אחד °דחגיגת י"ד אינה דוחה את השבת ומיהו אומר ר"י דמ"מ אין לחלק דדמי לחובה אם היינו מניחים מלעשות שני תבשילין וגם יש לחוש שמא לא יעשו בשאר פסחים ואין שום חשש אם אנו עושין אע"ג דלא צריך דליכא למיחש שמא יבנה בית המקדש ויאמרו אשתקד עשינו זכר לחגיגה בשבת והשתא נמי נקריבה בשבת דהקרבה מסורה לזריזין וכשיבנה משה ואהרן יהא עמנו וליכא למיטעי אך הבא להניח מלעשות שני תבשילין אין מזהירין אותו:

אמר רב הונא מברך כו'. רב הונא סבר כריש לקיש דבעי כוונה ואפי' אית ליה שאר ירקות עביד במרור שני טיבולי: מתקיף

*) נ"ל אחד לצלי זכר לפסח ואחד מבושל זכר לחגיגה כנ"ל וכ"כ הרשב"ם והתוס' מחמו כאן

רבינו חננאל

אמר ר"ל זאת אומרת מצות צריכות כונה דכיון דהאי חזרת לאו בעידן חיובא דמרור אכיל ליה בבורא פרי האדמה אכליליה לפיכך בעי טבול אחרינא דלא אכוון בקמייתא ואקשי' ודלמא מצות אין צריכות כונה ואמאי מטבלינן תרי זימני כי היכי דתהוי הכירא לתינוקות וישאלו אמאי מטבלינן תרויזימני ואסיקנא אפי' במרור לחודיה בעינן תרי טבולי כי היכא דלהוי היכרא לתינוקות ולאו משמע דמצות צריכות כונה: **וע"ד** תניא אכלן דמאי או אכלן בלא כונה או חצאין יצא ובלבד שלא ישהה באכילת הצאין בין אכילה לאכילה יותר מכדי אכילת פרס הנה תניא בהדיא דלא בעו כונה ופרקי' תנאי היא דתניא ר' יוסי אומר אע"פ שטבל בחזרת מצוה להביא לפניו מצה וחזרת וחרוסת ושני תבשילין לאו מכלל דר' יוסי סבר מצות צריכות כונה ודחי' ודלמא ר' יוסי נמי צריך תרי טבולי כי היכי דלהוי הכירא לתינוקות ואמרי' אם כן אמאי קתני מצוה אלא משום דסבר מצות צריכות כונה: **מאי** שני תבשילין אמר רב חתא אפי' סלקא וארוזא אמר רב אשי ש"מ מדקאמר אורז מבושל דלית הלכתא כר' יוחנן בן נורי דאמר אורז מין דגן הוא. חזקיה אמר אפי' דג וביצה רב יוסף אמר שני מיני בשר אחד זכר *) לצלי ואחד זכר לחגיגה מבושל ורבינא אמר אפי' גרמא ובישולא הן שני תבשילין. אסיקנא היכא דאיכא שאר ירקי מברך אשאר ירקי בורא פרי האדמה ואכיל וכי מטי לאכילת מרור מברך על אכילת מרור ואכיל ליה היכא דלית ליה אלא חזרת בלבד היכי עביד

גליון הש"ס

תוס' ד"ה אחד זכר לפסח וכו' דחגיגת י"ד אינה דוחה את השבת. ע"ל נט ע"ב תוס' ד"ה בי"ד שהל וכדף ע ע"ב תוספות ד"ה מ"ע:

[ברכות יג. עירובין צה:]

[עירובין צו. ר"ה כח:]

הגהות הב"ח

(א) גמ' שמע מינה מדרב הונא דלית דחייש:

ברכות דף לו לעיל דף לה.

[לקמן קטו. ע' תוספות שם ד"ה כולן]

רבי יצחק בן אחא דשמעתתא הוא רבי יצחק בן פנחס דאגדתא (א) וסימניך* (שמעו נא אחי ורעיי) אמר רבה בר בר חנה א"ר יוחנן משמיה דר' יהודה בר' אילעי אכול בצל ושב בצל ולא תיכול אווזין ותרנגולין ויהא לבך רודף עליך פחות ממיכלך וממשתיך ותוסיף על דירתך כי אתא עולא אמר מתלא מתלין במערבא דאכיל אליתא משי בעליתא דאכיל קקולי *אקיקלי דמתא שכיב:

מתני' מזגו לו כוס ראשון ב"ש אומרים מברך על היום ואחר כך מברך על היין וב"ה אומרים *מברך על היין ואחר כך מברך על היום: גמ' *ת"ר דברים שבין ב"ש וב"ה בסעודה ב"ש אומרים מברך על היום ואח"כ מברך על היין מפני שהיום גורם ליין שיבא וכבר קידש היום ועדיין יין לא בא וב"ה אומרים *מברך על היין ואח"כ מברך על היום מפני שהיין גורם לקידוש שתאמר *דבר אחר ברכת היין תדירה וברכת היום אינה תדירה תדיר ושאינו תדיר תדיר קודם והילכתא כדברי ב"ה מאי ד"א וכ"ת התם תרתי והכא חדא הכא נמי תרתי נינהו תדיר ושאינו תדיר תדיר קודם והלכה כדברי ב"ה פשיטא דהא נפיק בת קול איבעית אימא קודם בת קול ואי בעית אימא לאחר בת קול *ורבי יהושע היא דאמר אין משגיחין בבת קול: מתני' הביאו לפניו *מטבל בחזרת עד שמגיע לפרפרת הפת *הביאו לפניו מצה וחזרת וחרוסת* ושני תבשילין אע"פ שאין חרוסת מצוה ר"א (*בן) צדוק אומר מצוה *ובמקדש היו מביאין לפניו גופו של פסח: גמ' אמר

ס"א ירקות וחזרת

רש"י

רבי יצחק ב"ר אחא דשמעתתא. רבי יצחק סתם האמור בהגדתא ר' יצחק בן פנחס הוא: שמעו נא אחיי. דשמעתתא בן אחא: ולבך רודף עליך. מתאוה לאכול כל שעה שהורגלת: קקולי. ירקות: אקיקלי דמתא. על אשפות העיר מקום שאר בני העיר יושבין הוא יושב ואין תובעין לו כלום: מתני' מברך על היין. וה"ה למקדש על הפת: גמ' שהיין גורם לקידוש שיאמר. שאם אין לו יין או פת אינו מקדש: מתני' הביאו לפניו. ירקות: מטבל בחזרת. זהו לשון הגמרא כדתניא לעיל (דף קז:) השמש מטבל בבני מעים לפי שכל מאכלים ע"י טיבול: מטבל בחזרת. כלומר אם אין שם ירק אחר מטבל החזרת בחרוסת ואוכל: עד שמגיע לפרפרת הפת. קודם שיגיע לאותה חזרת שהוא אוכל אחר המצה שהוא מברך עליה על אכילת מרור וטיבול ראשון כדי שיכיר תינוק וישאל לפי שאין רגילין בני אדם לאכול ירק קודם סעודה: הביאו לפניו. אחר אותו טיבול: מצה מרור וחרוסת ושני תבשילין ואף על פי שאין החרוסת מצוה · ולקמיה פריך הואיל ולאו מצוה אמאי מייתי לה: גמ' זאת

תוספות

*ואין מיסב בסעודת מצוה. היינו סעודת מילה דאמר במדרש דניאל למדינה של ניגהם וסעודת נישואין בת ת"ח ובת כהן לכהן ודוקא שיש שם בני אדם מהוגנין כדאמרינן בזה בורר (סנהדרין דף כג.) נקיי הדעת שבירושלים לא היו מסובין בסעודה אלא כן יודעין מי מיסב עמהם:

*צריך לנהוג בו כבוד. בשלא למד ממנו דבלמד ממנו אמרינן (אבות פ"ו) בדוד (עשאו) [קראו] רבו אלופו אע"פ שלא למד אלא שני דברים מאחיתופל:

דאמר אין משגיחים בבת קול. וא"ת מאי שנא דקי"ל כבת קול דב"ה ולא קי"ל *כב"ק דרבי אליעזר וי"ל דהכא ב"ה הוו רובא אלא דב"ש מחדדי טפי אבל התם דב"ק היה כנגד רבים לא קי"ל הכי ובת קול לא יצתה אלא לכבודו כדקאמרינן התם מן השמים יוכיחו וא"ת א"כ היכי קאמר רבי יהושע היא הא רבי יהושע קאי אבת קול דר"א וי"ל מדקאמר אין משגיחין בב"ק משום דלא (מן השמים) היא משמע דבכל דוכתא לית לן למיזל בתר בת קול:

הביאו לפניו. פי' רשב"ם ירקות ואין נראה מדלא קתני בהדיא הביאו לפניו חזרת כדקתני בסמוך הביאו לפניו מצה ונראה כפי' ר"ח הביאו לפניו שלחן שהרי אין מביאין השלחן עד אחר קידוש ועל השלחן מונח החזרת:

מטבל בחזרת. כלומר אוכל החזרת בטיבול כמו השמש מטבל בבני מעים וכן מטבל בירקות ובקרא כמו משתעי הכי כי תקרעי בפוך עיניך (ירמיה ד) שמנחת הפוך בעינים ופי' רשב"ם דהאי טיבול לאו בחרוסת דהא אכתי לא בא כדקתני סיפא הביאו לפניו מצה וחזרת וחרוסת ואין זה ראיה דהא קתני הכא חזרת ותניא נמי בסיפא ועוד דחזרת צריך להטביל בחרוסת משום קפא. ומיהו היכא שהטיבול ראשון הוי בשאר ירקות אין צריך לטבול בחרוסת אלא או בחומץ או במים ומלח כמו שהיה נוהג ר"ת דהא אמר בגמרא דחרוסת משום קפא וליכא קפא אלא במרור וכ"ש לר"א בר צדוק דקאמר מצוה זכר לטיט דלא שייך אלא במרור לזכר דוימררו את חייהם בחומר (שמות א) ועוד דלא שייך מצוה שטיבול ראשון אינו אלא להיכרא ודלא כה"ר יוסף שעשה בסדרו ויטבול בחרוסת וכן רבינו שלמה בסידרו וה"ר שמעיה:

עד שמגיע לפרפרת הפת. פרפרת קרי המרור שאוכל אחר המצה ופרפרת כלומר ממשכת המאכל כמו פרפראות לחכמה (אבות פ"ג מי"ח) שהירקות ממשיכות הלב למאכל ומדקרי למרור פרפרת הפת רמז במשנה דמצה קודמת למרור כדאמר בגמרא:

הביאו לפניו מצה. לפי שעקרו השלחן לפני מי שאומר הגדה ועושה הסדר קתני הביאו לפניו מצה ועקירת שלחן היא כדי שישאל הבן ואביו עונה לו עדיין יביאו שלחן לעשות טיבול שני והבן ישאל למה אנו מטבילין שתי פעמים ומיד כשעוקרין מחזירין לפניו והמצה והמרור עליו שהרי צריך לומר בהגדה מצה זו מרור זה וכדאמר (לעיל לו· ולקמן דף קטו:) לחם עוני שעונין עליו דברים הרבה:

אע"פ שאין חרוסת מצוה. ואם תאמר אמאי לא אתי חרוסת דרשות ומבטל חזרת דמצוה [א] וי"ל דכיון דכל עיקר מרור לא ניתקן רק בטיבול בחרוסת משום קפא לא מקרי ביטול בכך:

רשב"ם

רבי יצחק ב"ר אחא דשמעתתא. מילתא באפי נפשה היא כל רבי יצחק סתם הנזכר בשמעתתא הוא רבי יצחק ב"ר אחא הוא רבי יצחק סתם בהגדתא הוא רבי יצחק בן פנחס: שמעו נא אחיי. דשמעתתא בן אחא: אכול בצל. אכול בצל או ירקות ותשב בצל ביתך ולא תצטרך למכור ביתך: ולבך רודף עליך. ומתאוה לאכול כל שעה שהורגלת: דאכיל אליתא. אליה כלומר בשר שמן תמיד: טשי בעליתא. כשבאין לתובעו הקפותיו הוא נסתר שאין בידו מה לפרוע: קקולי. ירקות: אקיקלי דמתא. על אשפות (הנהר) [העיר] מקום שאר בני העיר יושבין הוא יושב ואין תובעין לו כלום: מתני' על היין. והוא הדין למקדש על הפת וטעמא מפרש בגמרא: גמ' דברים שבין בית שמאי וב"ה בסעודה. הכא לא חשיב אלא חדא מפלוגתייהו אבל במס' ברכות (דף נא:) היכא טובא: גורם ליין שיבא. קודם סעודה: וכבר קידש היום. טעם אחר נותן לדבריו דמשקיבלו עליו מיציאת הכוכבים קידש היום ועדיין לא בא יין לשלחן וכשם שקודם לכניסה כך קודם לברכה: שהיין גורם לקידוש שתיאמר. שאם אין לו יין או פת אינו מקדש והמקדש על הפת כמקדש על היין וברכת הפת קודם: תדיר קודם. במס' זבחים *נפקא לן מהאי קרא דכתיב במוספין מלבד עולת הבוקר אשר לעולת התמיד מלבד משמע לאחר שהקרבת התמיד תקריב המוספין וקא דרשינן אשר לעולת התמיד קרא יתירא הוא אתא למילף דבשביל שהוא תדיר הקדימו הכתוב ומכאן אתה דן לכל התדירין: דהא נפקא ב"ק. במסכת עירובין בפ"ק*: ור' יהושע היא. בב"מ בפרק הזהב* גבי תנור שחתכו חוליות עמד ר' יהושע ואמר אין *(משתמשין) בב"ק והלכך לדידיה הוצרך לומר בזו הילכתא כב"ה שבשאר מחלוקת דב"ש וב"ה שלא הוקבע בפירוש הלכה כב"ה ס"ל שהרוצה לעשות כדברי ב"ש עושה וכדברי ב"ה עושה כדתניא באלו טריפות (דף מד·) ומוקמינן לה אליבא דר' יהושע: מתני' הביאו לפניו. הירקות אחר שבירך על היין: מטבל בחזרת. זהו לשון הגמרא כדתניא לעיל (דף קז:) השמש מטבל בבני מעיים לפי שכל מאכלים על ידי טיבול והאי טיבול לאו בחרוסת הוא כדקתני לקמן הביאו לפניו מצה וחזרת וחרוסת מכלל דעדיין לא הביאו והך חזרת לאו דוקא אלא אם (כן) אין שם ירק אחר מטבל בחזרת ואוכל: עד שמגיע לפרפרת הפת. קודם שיגיע לאותה חזרת שהוא אוכל אחר מצה שהוא מברך על אכילת מרור כדכתיב על מצות ומרורים (במדבר ט) בתחלה מצה ואח"כ מרור וטיבול ראשון זה כדי שיכיר תינוק וישאל לפי שאין בני אדם רגילין לאכול ירק קודם סעודה: מביאו לפניו. אחר אותו טיבול: מצה וחזרת וב' תבשילין אע"פ שאין חרוסת מצוה. ובגמרא פריך הואיל ולאו מצוה למה מייתי לה: שני תבשילין. בגמרא מפרש כנגד מי: גמ' זאת

עין משפט נר מצוה

עד א מיי' פ"ח מהלכות מלה הלכה א סמג עשין מא טוש"ע א"ח סי' תעג סעיף א:

עה ב מיי' פכ"ט מהל' שבת הלכה י סמג עשין כט טוש"ע א"ח סי' רעא סעיף י:

עו ג מיי' פ"ח מהל' מלה הלכה א סמג עשין מא טוש"ע א"ח סי' תעג סעיף ד:

עז ד מיי' פ"ז מהל' מלה הלכה יא:

עח ה מיי' פ"ח מהל' מלה הלכה א:

[מאשפות ירים אביון (תהלים קיג) מתרגמינן מקיקלתא מרים חשוכא כן פרש"י בע"ז כח ד"ה ניקרא וכ"כ רש"י כ"ק כא. ד"ה אקיקלתא]

רבינו חננאל

רבי יצחק בר אחא וסימנך שמעוני אחי ועמי *) הנזכר בן אחא הוא בעל השמועה: מאן דאכל אליתא משי בעליתא · כלומר מי שמנהגו לקנות בשר שומן באשראי ואוכל מתחבא בעליות שלא יבוא הקצב ויאמר לו איני מניחך עד שתתן לי דמי הבשר אבל מי שמנהגו לאכול ירקות שדה יושב על השוק שבאשפה ואינו חושש שאין מי שנושה בו: מתני' מזגו לו כוס ראשון ב"ש אומ' מברך על היום וכו' וב"ה אומ' מברך על היין ואחר כך מברך על היום: ת"ר דברים שבין ב"ש וב"ה בסעודה ב"ה אומר מברך על היין ואחר כך מברך על היום שהיין גורם לקדושה שתאמר ד"א ברכת היין תדירה וברכת היום אינה תדירה תדיר ושאינו תדיר תדיר קודם והלכתא כב"ה והאסקנא דר' יהושע היא דאמר אין משגיחין בבת קול הוא דאמר הכא הלכה כב"ה: הביאו לפניו מטבל בחזרת. פי' הביאו לפניו השלחן מטבל החזרת בחרוסת ומברך בורא פרי האדמה ומפסיק עד שמגיע לפרפרת הפת והיא עת אכילת המצה הביאו לפניו מצה חזרת וחרוסת:

מסורת הש"ס

[נ"ל שמעוני אחי ועמי]

ברכות דף נא: סוכה דף נו. [תוספתא דברכות פ"ה]

ב"ה שם כסוכה וזבחים דף צא.

ברכות דף נב. עירובין דף ז. יבמות דף יד. ב"מ דף נט: חולין דף מד.

[נ"ל ברבי]

הגהות הב"ח

(א) גמרא דאגדתא הוא וסימנך:

[דף פט.]

[דף יג:] [דף נט:]

[נ"ל משגיחין]

הגהות מהר"ב רנשבורג

[א] תוס' ד"ה אע"פ שאין חרוסת מצוה וכו' וי"ל דכיון דכל עיקר מרור וכו'. נ"ב עיין מהר"מ כרכי המס על תירוצם שאינו מספיק לרהב"ל דס"ל חרוסת מצוה זכר לטיט' ולפע"ד נראה כרור דכוונת התוס' בזה ג"כ כהר"ן דכיון דטיבול בעל זה הוא ואינו אכילה אינו מבטל וכמ"ש התוס' נמי במנחות דף כ"ב ע"ב ד"ה מכאן וכו' וא"כ אף לרהב"ל א"ש באופן בזירוז התוס' והר"ן בזה שפה אחת ודברים אחדים הם והנלענ"ד כתבתי ודוק ועיין רדב"ז חלק ג' דפוס פיורדא סי' תקמ"ד שכתב מעין דברי אלה:

*) נראה דצ"ל ר' יצחק הנזכר בשמעת' בן אחא הוא בעל השמועה:

b. Ḥaḳla, and with R. Isaac b. Ila'a.[7] [114a] R. Isaac b. Aḥa mentioned in legal discussions is the same as R. Isaac b. Phineas mentioned in homilies, and the token is *'Hear me* [shema'uni], *my brethren* [aḥay], *and my people.'*[8]

Rabbah b. Bar Ḥanah said in R. Joḥanan's name in the name of R. Judah b. R. Il'ai: Eat onions [*bazel*] and dwell in the pro-
a tection [*bezel*] [of your house],[1] and do not eat geese and fowls lest your heart pursue you;[2] reduce your food and drink and increase [expenditure] on your house. When 'Ulla came, he said: In the West [Palestine] a proverb is current: He who eats the fat tail [*allitha*] must hide in the loft [*'alitha*],[3] but he who eats cress [*kaḳule*] may lie by the dunghill [*kiḳle*][4] of the town.[5]

MISHNAH. THEY FILLED[6] THE FIRST CUP FOR HIM; BETH SHAMMAI MAINTAIN: HE RECITES A BLESSING FOR THE DAY [FIRST],[7] AND THEN RECITES A BLESSING OVER THE WINE; WHILE BETH HILLEL RULE: HE RECITES A BLESSING OVER THE WINE [FIRST], AND THEN RECITES A BLESSING FOR THE DAY.

GEMARA. Our Rabbis taught: [These are] the matters which are disputed by Beth Shammai and Beth Hillel in respect to the meal: Beth Shammai maintain: He recites a blessing for the day [first] and then recites a blessing over the wine, because the day is responsible for the presence of the wine;[8] moreover, the day has already become sanctified while the wine has not yet come.[9] But Beth Hillel maintain: He recites a blessing over the wine and then recites a blessing for the day, because the wine enables the *kiddush* to be recited.[10] Another reason: the blessing for wine is constant, while the blessing for the day is not constant,[11] [and of] that which is constant and that which is not constant, that
b which is constant comes first. Now the law[1] is as the ruling of Beth Hillel. Why state [another reason]?[2]—[This:] for should you argue: there we have two [reasons], whereas here there is [only] one,[3] [I answer that] here also there are two, [for of] that which is constant and that which is not constant, that which is constant comes first. 'Now the law is as the ruling of Beth Hillel': that is obvious, since there issued a *Bath Ḳol?*[4]—If you wish I can answer that this was before the *Bath Ḳol*. Alternatively, it was after the *Bath Ḳol*, and this is [in accordance with] R. Joshua who maintained: We disregard a *Bath Ḳol.*[5]

MISHNAH. THEY THEN[6] SET [IT] BEFORE HIM.[7] HE DIPS THE LETTUCE[8] BEFORE YET HE HAS REACHED THE AFTER-COURSE OF THE BREAD.[9] THEY SET BEFORE HIM MAẒẒAH, LETTUCE [ḤAZERETH], AND ḤAROSETH[10] AND TWO DISHES, THOUGH THE ḤAROSETH IS NOT COMPULSORY. R. ELEAZAR SON OF R. ZADOK SAID: IT IS COMPULSORY. AND IN THE TEMPLE THEY USED TO BRING THE BODY OF THE PASSOVER-OFFERING BEFORE HIM.

(7) In the edd. there follows *'hu* R. Isaac b. Aḥa': the same is R. Isaac b. Aḥa; BaḤ however deletes *hu*, in which case another person is now referred to. (8) I Chron. XXVIII, 2. Thus in legal discussions (*shema'ta*, connected with *shema'uni*) his name appears as b. Aḥa (connected with *aḥay*).

a (1) Do not spend overmuch on food, then you will be able to afford your house. (2) Do not cultivate a greedy appetite so that you are always wanting to eat. (3) He who squanders his money on costly dishes must hide from his creditors. (4) [*Aliter:* 'place of assembly' from Grk. κύκλος, a circle]. (5) Afraid of none—not being in debt. (6) Lit., 'mixed.' (7) I.e., the blessing on the sanctity of the Festival. (8) If it were not a festival no wine would be required. (9) The festival automatically commences with the appearance of the stars, even if no wine has yet been brought to the table. Thus it is first in time, and therefore first in respect to a blessing too. (10) Without wine or bread *kiddush* cannot be said. Bread is the equivalent of wine in this respect, and the blessing for bread precedes the blessing for the day. (11) Whenever wine is drunk a blessing over it is required, whereas the blessing of sanctification is confined to festivals.

b (1) [MS.M.: the *halachah*]. (2) Is not the first sufficient? (3) Beth Shammai give two reasons for their view, whereas only one supports Beth Hillel's. (4) Proclaiming the law always to be as Beth Hillel; v. 'Er. 13*b*. (5) V. B.M. 59*b*. (6) After having recited the *kiddush* over the wine. (7) Rashi and Rashbam: vegetables. R. Ḥan.: the table with the food, which was brought after *kiddush*. (8) Tosaf.: into water or vinegar, and eats it. This is to stimulate the child's wonder, as it is unusual to commence the meal thus. (9) Viz., the bitter herbs, which are eaten after the unleavened bread. Bertinoro reads: before he has reached the breaking (i.e., the distribution) of the bread. (10) V. Glos.

R. Safra was a bachelor living in a large town. [113b] Now a tanna recited [R. Joḥanan's dictum] before Raba and R. Safra, [whereupon] R. Safra's face lit up. Said Raba to him: It does not mean such as you, but such as R. Ḥanina and R. Oshaia, who were cobblers in Eretz Yisrael and dwelt in a street of harlots and made shoes for harlots and went in to them:[1] they [the harlots] looked at them, but they [these scholars] would not lift their eyes to look at them, and their [the harlots'] oath was 'by the life of the holy Rabbis of Eretz Yisrael.'[2]

Three the Holy One, blessed be He, loves: he who does not display temper, he who does not become intoxicated, and he who does not insist on his [full] rights.[3]

Three the Holy One, blessed be He, hates: he who speaks one thing with his mouth and another thing in his heart; and he who possesses evidence concerning his neighbour and does not testify for him; and he who sees something indecent in his neighbour and testifies against him alone.[4] As it once happened that Tobias sinned and Zigud alone came and testified against him before R. Papa, [whereupon] he had Zigud punished. 'Tobias sinned and Zigud is punished!' exclaimed he. 'Even so,' said he to him, 'for it is written, *one witness shall not rise up against a man*,[5] whereas you have testified against him alone: you merely bring him into ill repute.'[6] R. Samuel son of R. Isaac said in Rab's name: Yet he may hate him,[7] for it is said, *If thou see the ass of thine enemy lying under its burden*.[8] Now which enemy [is meant]: Shall we say, a Gentile enemy,—but it was taught: The enemy of whom they spoke is an Israelite enemy, not a Gentile enemy? Hence it obviously means an Israelite enemy. But is it permitted to hate him? Surely it is written, *Thou shalt not hate thy brother in thy heart?*[9] Again if there are witnesses that he had committed wrong, then *all* indeed hate him! why particularly this person? Hence it must surely apply to such a case where he had seen something indecent in him. R. Naḥman b. Isaac said: It is a duty to hate him, as it is said, *The fear of the Lord is to hate evil*.[10] R. Aḥa son of Raba asked R. Ashi: What about telling his teacher, that he should hate him?—Said he to him: If he knows that his teacher regards him as trustworthy as two [witnesses], he should tell him; but if not, he must not tell him.

Our Rabbis taught: There are three whose life is not life; the [over-] compassionate, the hot-tempered, and the [too] fastidious; whereon R. Joseph observed: And all these [qualities] are found in me.

Our Rabbis taught: Three hate one another, viz.: dogs, fowls, and Parsee priests;[1] some say, harlots too; some say, scholars in Babylonia too.

Our Rabbis taught: Three love each other, viz.: proselytes, slaves, and ravens. Four are too impossible for words:[2] a poor man who is arrogant, the wealthy man who flatters,[3] a lecherous old man, and a leader who lords it over the community without cause. Some say: Also he who divorces his wife a first and a second time and takes her back. And the first Tanna?[4]—It may be that her *kethubah*[5] is large,[6] or else he has children from her and cannot divorce her.[7]

Five things did Canaan charge his sons: Love one another, love robbery, love lewdness, hate your masters and do not speak the truth. Six things were said of a horse: it loves promiscuity, it loves battle, it has a proud spirit, it despises sleep, eats much and excretes little. Some say: It also seeks to slay its master in battle. Seven are banned[8] by Heaven; these are they: A Jew who has no wife; he who has a wife but no children;[9] and he who has children but does not bring them up to the study of the Torah; and he who has no phylacteries on his head and on his arm, no fringes on his garment and no *mezuzah* on his door, and he who denies his feet shoes. And some say: Also he who never sits in a company assembled for a religious purpose.[10]

Rabbah b. Bar Ḥanah said in the name of R. Samuel b. Martha in Rab's name on the authority of R. Jose of Huẓal: How do we know that you must not consult astrologers?[1] Because it is said: *Thou shalt be whole-hearted with the Lord thy God*.[2] And how do we know that one who knows that his neighbour is greater than himself even in one thing must show him honour? Because it is said, *Because a surpassing [superior] spirit was in him, and the king thought to set him over the whole realm*.[3] And she [a woman] who sits over clean blood is forbidden intercourse;[4] for how long? Said Rab: An *'onah*.[5]

A Tanna taught: Joseph of Huẓal is identical with Joseph the Babylonian, with Issi b. Gur Aryeh, with Issi b. Judah, with Issi b. Gamaliel and with Issi b. Mahallalel, and what was his [real] name? Issi b. 'Akabia.[6] R. Isaac b. Ṭabla is identical with R. Isaac

a (1) To deliver the shoes. (2) Thus by their chastity in face of great temptation they sanctified the Divine Name. (3) In the sense that he does not retaliate. (4) Being the only person who has seen it. (5) Deut. XIX, 15. (6) Since no action can follow your unsupported testimony. (7) As an evildoer—hate is morally wrong otherwise. (8) Ex. XXIII, 5. (9) Lev. XIX, 17. (10) Prov. VIII, 13.

b (1) והחברין Guebers, [*Aliter*: 'partners' v. Strashun]. (2) Lit., 'the mind does not tolerate them'. (3) I.e., who denies his true feelings. (4) Why does he not include the last? (5) Marriage settlement, which she can claim from him on divorce. (6) So that he must take her back, as he cannot pay it. (7) I.e., he cannot remain constant to the divorce. (8) Var. lec.: as banned. (9) By his own volition. (10) E.g., at a circumcision feast.

c (1) Lit., 'Chaldeans,' who were well versed in astrological arts. (2) Deut. XVIII, 13. (3) Dan. VI, 4. (4) This is based on the Scriptural law that for a period of thirty-three or sixty-six days beginning respectively on the eighth or the fifteenth day after childbirth a woman's blood is clean (v. Lev. XII, 1-5), i.e., it does not defile her and cohabitation is permitted. When this period is ended, she is designated 'a woman sitting over clean blood,' and cohabitation is forbidden, lest she have a blood discharge and think that just as her blood did not defile before, it does not defile her now either. (5) Lit., 'a period'—Rashi: one night.—Thus the law applies to the forty-first or the eighty-first night only. (6) [Issi (a variant of Joseph) was the son of 'Akabia b. Mahallalel, the story of whose excommunication is told in 'Ed. V, 6, 7; and it was in order to be spared the tragic memories associated with the name of 'Akabia that Issi did not describe himself as the son of 'Akabia; v. Derenbourg, *Essai* p. 484].

שראה בו דבר ערוה · ואם תאמר דאמרו מציאות (ב"מ דף לב: ושם) המריבן אוהב לפרוק ושונא לטעון מצוה בשונא כדי לכוף את יצרו והשתא מה כפיית יצר שייך כיון דמצוה לשנאתו וי"ל כיון שהוא שונאו גם חבירו שונא אותו דכתיב (משלי כז) כמים הפנים לפנים כן לב האדם לאדם ובאין מתוך כך לידי שנאה גמורה ושייך כפיית יצר :

***ואין** לו בנים · נראה דוקא על ידי פשיעתו שאינו מתעסק בפרי' ורביה דומיא דאחריני ומי שאין לו תפילין בראשו ובזרועו וציצית בבגדו מיירי בשיש לו ואינו מניחן אי נמי אפי' אין לו °יש לחזר ולהביא עצמו לידי חיוב כדאשכחן (סוטה דף יד·) במשה שהיה תאב ליכנס לארץ ישראל כדי לקיים מצות שבה והא דאמרי' (שבת דף מט·) תפילין צריכין גוף נקי כאלישע היינו כדמפרש שלא יפיח בהן ולא יישן בהן ובשעת ק"ש כדי לקבל עליו מלכות שמים שלימה בקל יכול ליזהר :

שלשה חייהן אינם חיים הרתחנין כו' · תימה דבפרק המביא (ביצה דף לב·) תניא ג' חייהן אינם חיים המצפה לשלחן חבירו ומי שאשתו מושלת עליו ומי שייסורין מושלין בגופו ואמאי לא מני לכולהו הכא ויש לומר דהכא לא מיירי אלא בהנך דהוו תולדת האדם משום דלעיל נמי איירי דדמי להנך שלשה הקב"ה אוהבן מי שאינו כועס :

תני תנא · להך מתניתא שלשה מכריז הקב"ה עליהן לשבח בכל יום : מותר לשנוא אותו · הרואה דבר ערוה בחבירו יחידי אע"פ שאינו רשאי להעיד מותר לשנאתו : אין הדעת סובלתן · אפילו הן עצמן מתחרטין לאחר זמן ונבזין הן בפני עצמן : בכלדיים · *בעלי אוב : היושבת על דם · אף על פי שפסק המעין שלא ראתה : עונה · יום ולילה צריכין להמתין :

רשב"ם

תני תנא · להך מתני' שלשה הקב"ה מכריז עליהן לשבח:ומומתייהו·שבועה שלהן : חטא · בעבירה : שם רע הוא דקא מפקת עילויה· מאחר שאין אתה נאמן.בעדות לא יתקבל עדותך אין לך עליך מצוה להעיד הרי אתה עובר על לאו דלא תלך רכיל (ויקרא יט) : דכתיב לא יקום עד אחד וגו' · כלומר המקרא מעיד שאי אתה נאמן בעדות זו : מותר לשנאתו · הרואה יחידי דבר ערוה בחבירו אע"פ שאינו רשאי להעיד לו מותר לשנאתו שהרי הוא יודע בודאי שהוא רשע : מאי שונא · כלומר מי הוא שונא שאמר הכתוב : ה"ג אי נימא שונא ישראל · כלומר שהוא שונא ישראל מי שרי למיסגייה ומסתמא לאו ברשיעי איירי קרא : הרחמנין · יותר מדאי והני שלשה מילי דבר התדיר בהן כל שעה וכיון דהוא מקפיד עליהן אין חייו חיים שאין לו מנוחה: אין הדעת סובלתן·של בריות: המתגאה על הציבור בחנם · נוהג עליהם שררה ואינו עומד עליהן בשעת דוחקן : צוה כנען את בניו · כלומר מנהגן כן הוא כאילו צוה עליהן אביהן ונפקא מינה שצריך אדם ליזהר מהן : בחבורת מצוה · כגון משתה של ברית מילה או בת כהן לכהן : כלדיים · בעלי אוב לפי פירש רבינו ולא נהירא דקרא כתיב בהדיא אל תפנו אל האובות ואלו שמעתי חוזים בכוכבים *וכן עיקר : תמים תהיה · להיות בוטח בו בכל קורות ותולדות הבאות לך : היושבת על דם טהור · אשה שלנו ימי טוהר שלה והגיע ליל ארבעים ואחד לזכר או ליל שמונים ואחד לנקבה שאם תראה עכשיו תהא נדה אסורה לשמש ואע"פ שלא ראתה דהואיל ולמודה היא עד עכשיו להיות משמשת עם ראייתה גזירה שמא תראה ותשמש : עונה · יום ולילה כך פירש רבינו ולא נהירא אלא לילה אחד דהיינו ליל ארבעים ואחד כדמפרש רבה (נדה דף סג:) אזהרה לבני ישראל שיפרשו מנשותיהן סמוך לווסתן וכמה עונה ומפרש או יום או לילה :

תורה אור

תני תנא קמיה דרבא ורב ספרא *צהבו פניו דרב ספרא אמר לו רבא לאו כגון מר אלא כגון רב חנינא ורב אושעיא דהוו אושכפי בארעא דישראל והוו יתבי בשוקא דזונות ועבדי להו מסאני לזונות ועיילי להו *אינהו מסתכלי בהו ואינהו לא מדלן עינייהו לאיסתכולי בהו ומומתייהו הכי בחייהן רבנן קדישי דבארעא דישראל : שלשה הקדוש ברוך הוא אוהבן מי שאינו כועס ומי שאינו משתכר ומי שאינו מעמיד *על מדותיו שלשה הקדוש ברוך הוא שונאן °המדבר א' בפה ואחד בלב והיודע עדות בחבירו ואינו מעיד לו *והרואה דבר ערוה בחבירו ומעיד בו יחידי כי הא דטוביה חטא ואתא זיגוד לחודיה ואסהיד ביה קמיה דרב פפא נגדיה לזיגוד א"ל *טוביה חטא וזיגוד מינגד אמר ליה אין דכתיב °לא יקום עד אחד באיש ואת לחודך אסהדת ביה שם רע בעלמא קא מפקת ביה אמר רבי שמואל בר רב יצחק אמר רב מותר לשנאתו שנאמר °כי תראה חמור שנאך רובץ תחת משאו מאי שונא אילימא שונא נכרי והא *תניא שונא שאמרו שונא ישראל ולא שונא נכרי אלא פשיטא שונא ישראל ומי שריא למסניה והכתיב °לא תשנא את אחיך בלבבך אלא דאיכא סהדי דעביד איסורא כולי עלמא נמי מיסני סני ליה מאי שנא האי אלא לאו °כי האי גוונא דחזיא ביה איהו דבר ערוה רב נחמן בר יצחק אמר °מצוה לשנאתו שנאמר °יראת ה' (שונאי) רע אמר רב אחא בריה דרבא לרב אשי מהו למימרא ליה לרביה למשנייה אמר ליה אי ידע דמהימן לרביה כבי תרי לימא ליה ואי לא לא לימא ליה תנו רבנן *שלשה חייהן אינם חיים הרחמנין והרתחנין ואניני הדעת ואמר רב יוסף כולהו איתנהו בי תנו רבנן שלשה שונאין זה את זה אלו הן הכלבים והתרנגולין *והחברין וי"א אף הזונות וי"א אף תלמידי חכמים שבבבל ת"ר שלשה אוהבין זה את זה אלו הן הגרים ועבדים ועורבין ארבעה אין הדעת סובלתן אלו הן דל גאה ועשיר מכחש וזקן מנאף ופרנס מתגאה על הציבור בחנם ויש אומרים אף המגרש את אשתו פעם ראשונה ושניה ומחזירה ותנא קמא זימנא *דכתובתה מרובה אי נמי יש לו בנים הימנה *ולא מצי מגרש לה חמשה דברים צוה כנען את בניו אהבו זה את זה ואהבו את הגזל ואהבו את הזמה ושנאו את אדוניכם ואל תדברו אמת ששה דברים נאמרים בסוס אוהב את הזנות ואוהב את המלחמה ורוחו גסה ומואס את השינה ואוכל הרבה ומוציא קמעה* וי"א אף מבקש להרוג בעליו במלחמה שבעה *מנודין לשמים אלו הן יהודי שאין לו אשה ושיש לו אשה ואין לו בנים* ומי שיש לו בנים ואין מגדלן לתלמוד תורה ומי שאין לו תפילין בראשו ותפילין בזרועו וציצית בבגדו ומזוזה בפתחו והמונע מנעלים מרגליו וי"א °אף *מי שאין מיסב בחבורה של מצוה אמר רבה בר בר חנה אמר רבי שמואל בר מרתא אמר רב משום רבי יוסי איש הוצל מניין °שאין שואלין בכלדיים שנאמר °תמים תהיה עם ה' אלהיך ומניין היודע בחבירו שהוא גדול ממנו אפילו בדבר אחד שחייב לנהוג בו כבוד שנאמר °כל קבל די רוח יתירא ביה [ומלכא *עשית להקמותיה על כל מלכותא] והיושבת על דם טהור אסורה לשמש עד כמה אמר רב עונה *תנא הוא יוסף איש הוצל הוא יוסף הבבלי (א) הוא איסי בן גור אריה הוא איסי בן יהודה הוא איסי בן גמליאל הוא איסי בן מהללאל ומה שמו איסי בן עקביה שמו הוא רבי יצחק בן טבלא הוא רבי יצחק בן חקלא הוא רבי יצחק בן אלעא (ב) הוא רבי

עין משפט נר מצוה

סט א מיי' פי"ג מהל' רוצח הלכה י"ד סמג לאוין רג טוש"ע חו"מ סימן כח סעיף א [עי' בהגה' מיי' פ"ד מהלכות עדות הל' א] :

[פי' במח עי' פירש"י במנחו' יח. סח: חולין ז:]

[שייך לאחר ד"ה שלשה]

ע ב מיי' פ"ו מהלכות דעות הלכה ה ופי"ג מהלכות רוצח הלכה יד טוש"ע חו"מ סימן ערב סעיף יא :

עא ג ד מיי' שם סמג עשין פא טור שו"ע שם :

עב ה טוש"ע יו"ד סי' רסה סעיף יב בהג"ה:

עג ו מיי' פי"א מהלכות ע"ז הלכה טז סמג לאוין כז טוש"ע יו"ד סימן קעט סעיף א :

מכות יח.

רבינו חננאל

שלשה הקב"ה שונאן המדבר אחת בפה ואחת בלב והיודע עדות לחברו ואינו מעיד לו והרואה דבר ערוה יחידי ומעיד לו כי הא דטוביה חטא אתיא זיגוד ואסהיד עליה ונתחייב מלקות כו'. שלשה חייהם אינן חיים הרחמנין והרתחנין ואניני הדעת אמר רב יוסף כולהו איתנהו בי. ארבעה אין הדעת סובלתן דל גאה ועשיר מכחש וזקן מנאף פרנס המתגאה על הצבור בחנם ויש אומרים אף המגרש את אשתו פעם ראשונה ומחזירה.חמשה דברים צוה כנען את בניו אהבו זה את זה אהבו הגזל והזמה ושנאו אדוניכם ואל תדברו אמת:ת"ר שמונה*) הן כמנודין לשמים מי שאין לו אשה ומי שיש לו אשה ואין לו בנים ואינו נושא אשה אחרת ומי שיש לו בן ואינו מגדלו לתלמוד תורה ומי שאינו לובש תפילין ומי שאין לו ציצית בטליתו ומי שאין לו מזוזה בביתו והמהלך יחף ויש אומרי' אף מי שאינו יושב בחבורת מצוה כגון קידוש וכיוצא בו. מניין שאין שואלים לכלדיים שנאמר תמים תהיה עם ה' אלהיך. מנין ליודע בחברו שגדול ממנו אפי' בדבר אחד שצריך לנהוג בו כבוד שנאמר כל קבל די רוח יתירא ביה. והיושבת על דם טהור. פי' צריך להמנע בתשלו' ימי טהרה מלשמש מטתו שכל דם שרואה אחרי מלאת שלשה ושלשים יום לזכר ששה וששים יום לנקבה דם נדה הוא כך צריך להתרחק ממנה וכמה רבא אמר עונה וכמה היא עונה או יום או לילה: **הוא** יוסף איש הוצל וכו' יצחק בר אחא דשמעתא יצחק חקלא יצחק בן אלעזר יצחק בן טבלא יצחק נפחא אלו כולן בעלי אגדות ומתנייתא ונזכר שמם פעם כך ופעם כך אבל כשמדברין מפיו שמועה מזכירין שמו ר'

*) אולי חסיב תפילין בתרתי .

מסורת הש"ס

[עי' תוס' שבת קנו: ד"ה כלדאי כו' שהביאו על פי' רשב"י דהכא]

[נ"ל אינהו]

[ונ"ל רש"י מגילה כח. לא עמדתי על מדותי לשלם ג"ול על מי שציערני גם בקדושין עא. פירש"י ולא עומד על מדותיו לנטור איבה]

מכות יח.

הגהות הב"ח

(א) גמ' יוסף איש הוצל (הוא יוסף הבבלי) תא"מ ונ"ב עי' תוס' יומא דף כ"ב ע"ב : (ב) שם ר' יצחק בן אלעזר ר' יצחק בן אלעא ר' יצחק כצ"ל ותיבת הוא נמחק :

[נ"ל שנאת]

[ביצה לב: ע"ש]

[עפרש"י שבת יא. ד"ה חבר וכן פירש רבינו שבת קיט ע"א קנו ע"ב וביבמות סג ע"ב]

[עירובין מא:]

[פי' דלא מצי קאי בגירושין מהרש"א]

ס"א ומהלך על צדי דרכים

ס"א כמעדרין

ס"א ואינו מגרשה

[עי' תוס' לקמן ריש קיד.]

[פי' המלך פי' הושב בלבו]

יומא כב:[וע"ש בתוספות ד"ה הוא וכנדה לוי ד"ה איסי]

גליון הש"ס גמ' המדבר אחד בפה וכו'. עיין בגה מציעא דף מט ע"א : תוס' ד"ה ואין לו בנים כו' יש לחזר. עי' מנחות דף מא ע"א :

גזייתא נינהו דשמטי סוסיא ואתו דברי לדהו *(וא"ל) רב לרב אסי לא תדור במתא דלא צניף בה סוסיא ולא נבח בה כלבא ואל תדור בעיר *דריש מתא אסיא ולא תנסיב תרתי אי נסבת תרתי נסיב תלת א"ל רב לרב כהנא הפוך בנבילתא ולא תיפוך במילי **פשוט נבילתא בשוקא ושקיל אגרא ולא תימא כהנא אנא וגברא רבא אנא וסניא בי מלתא סלקת לאיגרא שירותך בהדך מאה קרי במתא בזוזא תותי כנפיך ניהוו א"ל רב לחייא בריה לא תשתי סמא ולא תשוור ניגרא ולא תעקר ככא ולא תקנא בחיויא ולא תקנא בארמאה תנו רבנן ג' אין מתקנאין בהן ואלו הן נכרי קטן ונחש קטן ותלמיד קטן מ"ט דמלכותיהו אחורי אודנייהו קאי א"ל רב לאיבו בריה טרחי בך בשמעתא ולא מסתייע מילתא תא אגמרך מילי דעלמא אדחלא אברעיך זבינך זבין כל מילי זבין ותחרט בר מחמרא דזבין ולא תחרט שרי כיסך פתח שקיך קבא מארעא ולא כורא מאיגרא תמרא בחלוזך לבית סודנא רהיט ועד כמה אמר רבא עד תלתא סאה אמר רב פפא אי לא דרמאי שברא לא איעתרי א"ד אמר רב חסדא אי לא דרמאי שברא לא איעתרי מאי סודנא אמר רב חסדא סוד נאה וגמילות חסדים אמר רב פפא כל אגב גביא בעי כל אשראי ספק אתי ספק לא אתי ודאתי מעות רעות נינהו ג' דברים א"ר יוחנן משום אנשי ירושלים כשאתה יוצא למלחמה אל תצא בראשונה אלא תצא באחרונה כדי שתכנס בראשונה *ועשה שבתך חול ואל תצטרך לבריות *והוי משתדל עם מי שהשעה משחקת לו *(א"ר) שלשה דברים א"ר יהושע בן לוי משום אנשי ירושלים אל תרבה *בגנות משום מעשה שהיה בתך בגרה שחרר עבדך ותן לה *והוי זהיר באשתך מחתנה הראשון מ"ט רב חסדא אמר משום ערוה רב כהנא אמר משום ממון(א) הא והא איתנהו אמר רבי יוחנן שלשה מנוחלי העוה"ב אלו הן הדר בא"י והמגדל בניו לתלמוד תורה והמבדיל על היין במוצאי שבתות מאי היא דמשייר מקידושא לאבדלתא א"ר יוחנן שלשה מכריז עליהן הקב"ה בכל יום על רווק הדר בכרך ואינו חוטא ועל עני המחזיר אבידה לבעליה ועל עשיר המעשר פירותיו בצינעה רב ספרא רווק הדר בכרך הוה
תני

תוספות

ולא תימא כהנא אנא · פירשתי בהלו עוברין (לעיל דף מט:*) [ד"ה אמר]

אמר רב פפא אי לאו דרמאי שיכרא לא איעתרי · ובשילהי אלו עוברין (שם) קאמר רב פפא אי לאו דנסיבי כהנתא לא איעתרי י"ל דהא והא גרמא ליה:

עשה שבתך חול ולא תצטרך לבריות · והא דאמרינן בפ"ב דביצה (דף טז:) דהוצאת שבתות וימים טובים אם פוחת פוחתין לו היינו בשלו אם יש לו:

דמשייר מקודשא לאבדלתא · שמונע שתייתו בשביל הבדלה ותימה דהא דוקא *קידוש לילה קודם לכיבוד יום אבל הבדלה אינה קודמת *ומפרש מורי הר"י דקידוש יום קרי כיבוד יום והכי איתא בירושלמי פרק שלשה שאכלו רבי יוסי בשם רבי יעקב ב"ר אחא איזהו כיבוד יום בפה"ג:
סרחה

רשב"ם

גזייתא · כשמהלכים במבואות שבילי כרמים וסוסיהן משתמטין מהן ובורחין ביישוב אתו ודברי להו: שרלאה אסיא · רופא ואמרי לה ת"ח ותרוייהו חד טעמא: סוסיא · משום דהוה נטירותא בקרתא מאויבים ומגנבים: ולא תינסב תרי · נשים שמא תתיעצנה עליך רעה: נסיב תלת · שאם תתיעצנה השלישית מגלה לך: פשוט נבילתא · הפשט עורה: סלקת לאיגרא שירותך בהדך · כשתלך לדרך אפי' קרובה לא ומזונותיך עמך: מאה קרי בזוזא תותי כנפיך להוו · אפילו המזונות בזול אעפ"כ הוליכם עמך: לא תשתי סמא · לא תלמוד לשתות סמים מפני שתקבע להון אותם ויהא לבך שולך ותפזר מעות · ל"א לא תהא רגיל לשתות סממנים כדאמר (לעיל מב:) (*כולהו שקייני) דמעלי להאי וקשה להאי: לא תשוור ניגרא · פסיעה גסה שנוטלת מאור עיניים*: ולא תעקר ככא · שן ממש משום חולי: דמלכותייהו אחורי אודנייהו קיימי · כלומר עתידין לגדל ותגדל אימתן וינקמו ממך: אדחלא על כרעך זביך זבין · בעוד שהחול על רגליך כשבאת מן הדרך מכור מה שהבאת כדי שתחזור ותקנה ותביא: שרי כיסך ופתח שקך · כלומר תקבל תחלה המעות ותנס בכיסך ואח"כ פתח השק ותן התבואה ללוקחים: קבא מארעא ולא כורא מאיגרא · כלומר טוב שילך למקום קרוב ולהשתכר מעט מלהשתכר הרבה במדינת הים: תמרי בחלוזך לבי סודנא רהוט · אם יש לך תמרים באותו כלי שנותנים בו תמרים רוץ מיד לבית עושה שכר לעשות מהן שכר שאם תמתין תאכלם בין כך ובין כך ותפסיד: מאי סודנא · למה נקרא שם השכר סודנא: סוד נאה · עלה טובה שהרי מתעשרין הימנה: וגמילות חסדים · יכול לתת מתנה לעניים ולעשות צדקה וחסד: כל אגב גביא בעיא · כל דבר שצריך לכתוב שטר עליו כגון מלוה ואמנה בעייא גביא כלומר עדיין עומד הוא לגבות ויש לו טורח בו: מעות רעות · דפרע להו נהלייהו זוזא זוזא: לא באחרונה · שאם תנוס תכנס לביתך בראשונה: אל תרבה בגנות · כלומר אל תהא רגיל לעשות בית בפרהסיא במקום מגולה: משום מעשה שהיה · בדוד ובת שבע: משום ממון · שמבזבזת לו ממונך: רווק · פנוי:
תני

רשב"ם

גזייתא · כשהולכין במבואות שבילי כרמים וסוסיהן משתמטין ובורחין ביישוב: דרישא אסיא · רופא *מפני שטרוד ברפואותיו ואינו עוסק בצרכי ציבור: ולא תדור במתא דלא צניף בה סוסיא · כלומר שאין בה סוס משום דהוי נטירותא דקרתא מגנבי לרדוף אחריהן ולתופסן: ולא תנסוב תרתי נשי · שלא תתיעצנה עליך רעה: נסיב תלת · שאם תתיעצנה השתים השלישית מגלה לך: פשוט נבילתא בשוקא · פשוט עורה בשכר: סלקת לאיגרא שירותך בידך · כשתלא לדרך אפי' במקום קרוב מזונותיך עמך: מאה קרי בזוזא תותי כנפיך להוי · אפילו המזונות בזול יהיו עמך: לא תשתי סמא · אל תשתה סמים מפני שנקבע להם ווסת ויהא לבך שולך ותפסיד מעות ואפילו לרפואה לא תישתי אם אפשר לרפואה אחרת: לא תשוור ניגרא · פסיעה גסה נוטלת מאור העינים ואית דמפרשי ניגרא אמת המים ורגילין בני אדם לקפוץ מעבר זה לעבר זה לקצר דרכן: לא תעקר ככא · שן ממש ומשום חולי שסופו תרפא: דמלכותייהו אחורי אודנייהו קיימין · כלומר עתידין ליגדל ותגדל אימתן ויכקמו ממך: אדחלא אכרעך זביך זבין · בעוד החול על רגליך כשבאת מן הדרך מכור מה שהבאת כדי שתחזור מהרה ותקנה ותביא ותמכרנו: זבין ותיחרט · כלומר אם יוקיר יכול אתה להתחרט על שמהרת למכור: בר מחמרא · שמא אילו לא מכרו היה מחמיץ: שרי כיסך ופתח שקיך · קבל המעות תחלה ותנס בתוך כיסך ואח"כ פתח השק ותנס ללוקח: קבא מארעא ולא כורא מאיגרא · מוטב שילך למקום קרוב להשתכר דבר מועט מלהשתכר הרבה במקום רחוק: תמרי בחלוזך לבי סודנא רהוט · אם יש תמרים באותו כלי שנותנין בו תמרים מהר לעשות מהם שכר שאם תמתין תאכלם ובין כך ובין כך תפסיד: מאי סודנא · למה נקרא עושה שכר סודנא: סוד נאה · עלה טובה היא שהרי מתעשרין הימנה: וגמילות חסדים · יכול לתת הימנה לעניים לעשות מהן לדקה וחסד שהרי אין בה קרן גדול: כל אגב גבייא בעיא · כל דבר שצריך לכתוב שטר עליו כגון מלוה ואמנה גביא בעי כלומר עדיין הוא צריך לגבות ויש בו טורח: מעות רעות · דפרע ליה ניהליה זוזא זוזא: כדי שתכנס בראשונה · אם תנוס: אל תרבה בגנות · כלומר אל תהי רגיל לעשות דבריך בפרהסיא במקום מגולה: משום מעשה שהיה · דדוד ובת שבע דכתיב (ש"ב יא) וירא (והנה) אשה רוחצת מעל הגג: משום ממון · שמבזבזת לו ממונך: דמשייר מקידושא · שיש לו מעט יין ומונע שתייתו בשביל הבדלה: רווק · פנוי:
תני

רבינו חננאל

רב לרב כהנא הפוך נבלה ולא תהפוך במילי נפוש נבלה ושקול אגרא ולא תימא אנא גברא רבא וזילא בי מילתא. סלקת לאיגרא שירותיך בהדך. כלומר כבר סעודתך תהיה עמך. קרי בזוזא במתא ונזדמן לך קרא בשדה אל תזלזל בו אלא הביאהו בידך. אמר ליה רב לחייא בריה לא תשתה סמא דמתגרצ נופך בהאי ולא תשדי באיגרא כי המעלות מכחישות הגוף ואל תעקר ככא מפני העין פי' ככא המכתש והוא אל צרם בלשון ישמעאל וכדכתיב (קהלת י"ב ג') ובטלו הטוחנות כי מיעטו כלומר אם יכאב לך אל תעקרהו שמא תכחש עיניך ואל תקני בחויא ולא בארמאה שמא יפגעו בך ולא תשוור נינרא: אמר ליה רב לאיבו בריה טרחי בך בשמעתא ולא אסתייעא מילתא תא אגמרך מילי דעלמא אדחלא דאורחא פי' בעודנו אבק הדרך על רגליך קודם שתרחצם זבינך זבון כל מילי זבין ואיחרט וכו': שלשה דברים צוה ר' יהושע אל תרבה בגנות משום מעשה שהיה מעשה דדוד שעלה על הגג וראה בת שבע ושלח ולקחה ובתך בגרה שחרר עבדך ותן לה הוי זהיר באשתך מחתנה ראשון או בעברה או בממון: א"ר יצחק שלשה מנוחלי העוה"ב הדר בארץ ישראל והמגדל בנו לתלמוד תורה והמשייר יין מן הקידוש כדי להבדיל עליו. שלשה הקב"ה מכריז עליהן על רווק הדר בכרך כגון ר' הושיעא ור' חנינא דהוו יתבי בשוק של זונות ולא מדלי עינייהו וסתכלו בהו וכד אשתבעי אפרי הכי בחיי רבנן קדישי ארעא ועל העשיר המעשר פירותיו בצנעה ועל עני המחזיר אבידה לבעלה. רב ספרא רווק הדר בכרך הוה כו'. שלשה הקב"ה אוהבן מי שאינו כועס ומי שאינו משתכר ומי שאינו עומד על מדותיו.
שלשה

עין משפט נר מצוה

סח א מיי' פ"י מהלכות מתנות עניים הלכה יח טור שו"ע יו"ד סימן רנה סעיף א:

[ד"ה אמר] [לעיל קה:] [עיין מהרש"א בחידושי הלכות] [לעיל קיב.] [ליתא בע"י]

מסורת הש"ס

[נ"ל א"ל] ב"ב קי. ע"ש כל מילי [ברכות מג:] לעיל קיב. שבת קיח. ע"ש ס"א בגנות [עי' בפירוש רשב"ם ב"ב נה: ד"ה כי תמוה ועי' תוס' שם נא.] [וכב"ב קי. מפ' ר"ת בע"א ע"ש כתו' ד"ה ולא]

הגהות הב"ח

(א) גמ' משום ממון והא:

גליון הש"ס

גמ' דריש מתא אסיא. עי' תוס' ב"ב דף קי. ד"ה ולא תימא:

Those are [113a] the narrow paths [which they frequent], whence their horses bolt and come [into civilized places] bringing them along.

Rab said to R. Assi: Do not dwell in a town in which no horses neigh or dogs bark.[2] And do not dwell in a town where the leader of the community is a physician.[3] And do not marry two [women],[4] [but] if you do marry two, marry a third.[5]

Rab said to R. Kahana: Deal in carcases, but do not deal in words;[6] flay carcases in the market place and earn wages and do not say, 'I am a priest and a great man and it is beneath my dignity.'[7] [Even] if you [merely] ascend the roof, [take] victuals with you.[8] [Even] if a hundred pumpkins cost but a *zuz* in town, let them be under your skirts.[9]

a Rab said to his son Ḥiyya: Do not take drugs[1] and do not leap in great jumps;[2] do not have a tooth extracted,[3] and do not provoke serpents and do not provoke a Syrian woman.

Our Rabbis taught: Three must not be provoked, viz.: an insignificant Gentile,[4] a little snake, and a humble pupil. What is the reason? Because their kingdom stands behind their ears.[5]

Rab said to his son Aibu: I have laboured over your studies but without success, [so] come and I will teach you worldly wisdom. Sell your wares while the sand is still on your feet.[6] Everything you may sell and regret,[7] except wine, which you can sell without regrets.[8] Untie your purse and [then] open your sacks.[9] Better a *ḳab* from the ground than a *kor* from the roof.[10] When the dates are in your bag run to the brewery [*beth sudna*].[11] And to what extent?—Said Raba: Up to three *se'ahs*. R. Papa said: If I were not a beer manufacturer I would not have become wealthy. Others say, R. Ḥisda said: If I were not a beer manufacturer, I would not have become wealthy. What is [the meaning of] *sudna?*[12] Said R. Ḥisda: A pleasant secret [*sod na'eh*] and the exercise of charity.[13]

R. Papa said: Every bill[14] requires collecting;[15] in every credit sale it is doubtful whether it [payment] will be forthcoming or
b not, and when it is forthcoming it may be bad money.[1]

Three things did R. Joḥanan say in the name of the men of Jerusalem: when you go out to battle, do not go out among the first but among the last, so that you may return among the first; and treat your Sabbath like a weekday rather than be dependent on your fellow-beings, and strive to be on good terms with him upon whom the hour smiles.

Three things did R. Joshua b. Levi say in the name of the men of Jerusalem. Do not practise immodesty[2] on account of the incident which occurred;[3] if your daughter has attained puberty, free your slave and give [him] to her;[4] and beware of your wife with her first son-in-law. What is the reason?—R. Ḥisda said: On account of immorality: R. Kahana said: On account of money.[5] And [in fact] both are correct.

R. Joḥanan said: Three are of those who will inherit the world to come, viz.: he who dwells in Eretz Yisrael; and he who brings up his sons to the study of the Torah; and he who recites *habdalah* over wine at the termination of the Sabbath. Who is that? He who leaves over [wine] from *ḳiddush* for *habdalah*.[6]

R. Joḥanan said: Concerning three does the Holy One, blessed be He, make proclamation every day:[7] a bachelor who lives in a large town without sinning, a poor man who returns lost property to its owner, and a wealthy man who tithes his produce in secret.[8]

(2) These guard the town: the dogs raise the alarm and the marauders are pursued on horseback. (3) There seems to be no adequate reason for this. Possibly a doctor would be too busy to give proper attention to communal matters. R. Tam in B.B. 110a s.v. לא תימא reads אסי instead of אסיא, i.e., do not dwell in a town whose head is (R.) Assi—a playful warning against the cares of office, which leave but little time for study. (4) Lest they devise plots against you. (5) She will reveal their designs. (6) Gossip or quibbling. (7) The greatest man is not degraded by honest work. (8) Do not undertake the least journey without provisions. (9) Keep them in stock and do not wait to buy until you actually need them.

a (1) Even as a medicine, as they are habit forming. (2) Or: do not jump over a brook—the strain affects the eyesight. (3) When you have toothache—it will eventually cease in any case. [R. Hananel refers it to a molar tooth, the extraction of which according to popular belief affects the eyesight. Preuss, *Biblisch—talmudische Medizin*, p. 330, quotes Celsus: *majore periculo in superioribus dentibus fit (extractio), quia potest tempora oculosque concutere*]. (4) Lit., 'a little Gentile'. (5) They will grow up and take revenge. The particular expression may have been occasioned by Diocletian's rise to be Emperor of Rome though born of slaves—according to the Rabbis he was a swineherd originally. When Emperor he tried to avenge insults offered to him in his lowly position. (6) Immediately you return from buying, sell. (7) If the price advances—you might have received more. (8) Had you waited it might have turned to vinegar. (9) Pocket the money for a purchase before delivering it. (10) Rather earn little near home than much far away. (11) To brew beer of them—otherwise you may eat them. (12) That it is employed to denote a brewery. (13) It is a pleasant secret—it is profitable and affords the means of charity. (14) Lit., 'everything on account (of which a bill or bond must be indited).' (15) Do not be certain of the money until you have actually collected it.

b (1) If payment is made in small instalments the money may be frittered away. (2) Do not frequent places where immodest sights are to be seen. Var. lec.: do not frequent roofs. (3) Viz., David's sin with Bath Sheba. (4) Marry her at the earliest possible moment. (5) She is likely to spend your money on him. (6) He has only a little wine and specially reserves for *habdalah* that which remains over from *ḳiddush*. (7) As having earned His special approval. (8) I.e., without ostentation.

[it refers] even to a widow, for [112*b*] not all fingers[4] are alike). Enjoying the produce without interest[5] is a good deed and profitable investment.[6] A religious deed which leaves the body pure is marrying a woman when one [already] has children.

Four things did our holy Teacher[7] command his children: Do not dwell in Shekanzib,[8] because [its inhabitants] are scoffers and will corrupt you to disbelief. And do not sit upon the bed of a Syrian woman. Some say, [that means:] do not lie down to sleep without reading the *shema'*; while others explain: do not marry a proselyte. But others explain 'Syrian' literally, [the reason
a being] on account of what happened to R. Papa.[1] And do not seek to evade toll tax, lest they discover you and deprive you of all that you possess. And do not stand in front of an ox when he comes up from the meadow, because Satan dances between his horns.[2] Said R. Samuel: this refers to a black ox and in the month of Nisan.[3] R. Oshaia recited: One must remove a distance of fifty cubits from an ox that is a *tam*[4] [and] as far as the eye can see from an ox that is a *mu'ad*. A Tanna taught in R. Meir's name: [Even] when the ox's head is in the feeding-bag, climb up to the roof and throw away the ladder from under you.

Rab said: The cry for an ox[5] is *'hen, hen'*; for a lion, *'zeh zeh'*; for a camel, *'da da'*; a ship's cry is *'helani hayya hela we-hiluk hulia.'*[6]

Abaye said: Skin, a fish, a cup, hot water, eggs, and the vermin in linen are all injurious to 'something else'.[7] Skin: [that means] he who sleeps on a tanner's hide.[8] A fish: [viz.,] *shibuṭa*[9] during Nisan. A cup: the residue of fish hash. Hot water: pouring extremely hot water over oneself.[10] Eggs: [i.e.,] he who treads on [their] shells. Vermin in linen: if one launders his garment and does not wait eight days before putting it on, the vermin[11] are produced and harmful for 'something else'.

R. Papa said: A man should not enter a house in which there is a cat, without shoes. What is the reason? Because the cat may kill a snake and eat it; now the snake has little bones, and if a bone sticks into his foot it will not come out, and will endanger him. Others say: A man should not enter a house where there is no cat, in the dark.[12] What is the reason? Lest a snake wind itself about him without his knowing, and he come to danger.

Three things did R. Ishmael son of R. Jose charge Rabbi:
b (Mnemonic: *MaḲaSH*).[1] Do not inflict a blemish upon yourself. (What does that mean? Do not engage in a lawsuit with three, for one will be your opponent and the other two witnesses [against you].) And do not feign interest in[2] a purchase when you have no money.[3] When your wife has performed *ṭebillah*, do not be intimate with her the first night. Said Rab: That refers to a *niddah* by Scriptural law,[4] [for] since there is the presumption of an open well,[5] she may continue with gonorrhoeic discharge.[6]

Three things did R. Jose son of R. Judah charge Rabbi. Do not go out alone at night, and do not stand naked in front of a lamp, and do not enter a new bath-house, lest it [the floor] split.[7] How long [is it regarded as new]?—Said R. Joshua b. Levi: For twelve months. 'And do not stand naked in front of a lamp,' for it was taught: He who stands naked in front of a lamp will be an epileptic, and he who cohabits by the light of a lamp will have epileptic children.

Our Rabbis taught: If one cohabits in a bed where an infant is sleeping, that infant [will be] an epileptic. Now that was said only if he is less than one year old; but if he is a year old, it does not matter. Again, this was said only if he is sleeping at [their] feet; but if he is sleeping at [their] head, it does not matter. Again, this was said only if he does not lay his hand upon him; but if he lays his hand upon him, it does not matter.

'And do not go out alone at night', for it was taught: One should not go out alone at night, i.e., on the nights of neither Wednesday nor Sabbaths, because Igrath the daughter of Mahalath,[8] she and 180,000 destroying angels go forth, and each has permission to wreak destruction independently. Originally they were about all day. On one occasion she met R. Ḥanina b. Dosa [and] said to him, 'Had they not made an announcement concerning you in Heaven, "Take heed of Ḥanina and his learning," I would have put you in danger.' 'If I am of account in Heaven,' replied he, 'I order you never to pass through settled regions.' 'I beg you,' she pleaded, 'leave me a little room.' So he left her the nights of Sabbaths and the nights of Wednesdays. On another occasion she met Abaye. Said she to him, 'Had they not made an announce-
c ment about you in Heaven, "Take heed of Naḥmani[1] and his learning," I would have put you in danger.' 'If I am of account in Heaven,' replied he, 'I order you never to pass through settled regions.' But we see that she does pass through?—I will tell you:

(4) Euphemism: The wife thinks always of her first husband. (5) Lit., 'hire.' (6) Lit., 'a large body'. The passage is a difficult one, particularly with the reading of the ed. לא, but it would seem to refer to lending money on a field and receiving some of its produce in part repayment. But as its value is probaly calculated at less than market price, this is a profitable investment, yet at the same time there is no actual interest. Such a transaction is permitted (B.M. 67*b*). 'Ar. and MS.M. read: ולו, and Jast. accordingly translates: An act of charity and at the same time a good investment is the act of him who helps to produce fruits, while he has the reward (e.g., one who loans money to a husbandman on security, allowing payment in small instalments). (7) I.e., R. Judah ha-Nasi. (8) A town in Babylonia, on the east side of the Tigris; v. Obermeyer, *Landschaft*, pp. 190f. It is there (p. 191, n. 4) pointed out, however, that R. Judah, a Palestinian, would have had no occasion to warn his children against living in a town in Babylonia, nor could he have known the character of its inhabitants well enough to justify this warning; hence it is conjectured that 'Raba' should be read here instead.

a (1) V. Ber. 8*b*. (2) Rashbam: the ox is mad, as explained *infra*. (3) The first month—about April. (4) The technical name of an ox that has not yet gored three times. When it has, it is called *mu'ad*. (5) With which to chase it away or to urge it to work. (6) Perhaps the ancient equivalent of 'yo heave ho'. [MS.M. reads simply: *'hayya, hayya'*]. (7) Leprosy. (8) Rashi and Rashbam. I.e., before it is completely dressed. (9) Probably mullet (Jast.). (10) At a bath. (11) Which it may still contain. (12) MS.M.: Without shoes.

b (1) V. 68*b*, n. a8. *M* = *Mum* (blemish); *Ḳ* = *meḲah* (a purchase); *SH* = *iSHteka* (your wife). (2) Lit., 'stand over.' (3) V. B.M. 58*b* and notes a.l in Sonc. ed. (4) By which a woman performs *ṭebillah* seven days after the *beginning* of menstruation, even if menstruation lasted all the seven days. Subsequently, however, it was enacted that she must wait seven days from the *end* of menstruation. Rab observes that R. Ishmael's charge held good only when the more lenient Scriptural law was practised. (5) I.e., her blood-flow has continued almost until *ṭebillah*. (6) During intimacy. (7) Through the heat. (8) The queen of demons.

c (1) Abaye was so called because he was brought up in the house of Rabbah b. Naḥman.

*שאין כל אצבעות שוות מצוה וגוף גדול אוכל פירות ולא שכר מצוה וגוף טהור נושא אשה ולו בנים ארבעה דברים צוה רבינו הקדוש את בניו אל תדור בשכנציב משום דליצני הוו ומשכו לך בליצנותא *ואל תשב על מטת ארמית איכא דאמרי דלא תיגני בלא קרית שמע ואיכא דאמרי דלא תינסב גיורתא ואיכא דאמרי ארמאית ממש ומשום מעשה דרב פפא ואל תבריח עצמך מן המכס דילמא משכחו לך ושקלי מנך כל דאית לך ואל תעמוד בפני השור בשעה שעולה מן האגם מפני שהשטן מרקד בין קרניו אמר רבי שמואל בשור שחור וביומי ניסן *תני רב אושעיא מרחיקין משור תם חמשים אמה משור מועד כמלא עיניו תנא משמיה דרבי מאיר ריש תורא בדיקולא סק לאיגרא ושדי דרגא מתותך אמר רב ניזהא דתורא הן הן ניזהא דאריה זה זה ניזהא דגמלא דא דא ניזהא דארבא הילני הייא הילא והילוק הוליא אמר אביי עור דג וכוס חמין וביצים וכנים לבנים כולן קשין לדבר אחר עור מאן דגני אמשכא דצלא דג שיבוטא ביומי ניסן כוס שיורי כסא דהרסנא חמין חמימי דחמימי משדרו עילויה ביצים מאן דמדרך אקליפים כינים לבנים מאן דמחוור לבושיה ולא נטיר ליה תמניא יומי והדר לבוש לה בריין הנך כינים וקשין לדבר אחר אמר רב פפא ביתא דאית ביה שונרא לא ניעול בה איניש בלא מסני מאי טעמא משום דשונרא קטיל לחיויא ואכיל ליה ואית ביה חיויא גרמי קטיני ואי יתיב לה גרמא דחיויא אכרעיה לא נפיק ואסתכן ליה איכא דאמרי ביתא דלית ביה שונרא לא ניעול ביה איניש *בהכרא מאי טעמא דילמא מיכריך ביה חויא ולא ידע ומסתכן ג' דברים צוה ר' ישמעאל בר' יוסי את רבי (מק"ש סימן) אל תעש מום בעצמך מאי היא לא תיהוי לך דינא בהדי תלתא דחד הוי בעל דינך ותרי סהדי *ואל תעמוד על המקח בשעה שאין לך דמים אשתך טבלה אל תזקק לה לילה הראשונה אמר רב ובנדה דאורייתא הואיל והוחזק מעין פתוח דילמא משכה זיבה שלשה דברים צוה רבי יוסי בר' יהודה את רבי אל תצא יחידי בלילה ואל תעמוד בפני הנר ערום ואל תכנס למרחץ חדש שמא תפחת עד כמה אריב"ל עד י"ב חדש ואל תעמוד בפני הנר ערום דתניא *העומד בפני הנר ערום הוי נכפה **והמשמש מטתו לאור הנר הויין לו בנים נכפין ת"ר המשמש מטתו על מטה שתינוק ישן עליה אותו תינוק נכפה ולא אמרן אלא דלא הוי בר שתא אבל בר שתא לית לן בה ולא אמרן אלא דגני להדי כרעיה אבל גני להדי רישיה לית לן בה ולא אמרן אלא דלא מנח ידיה עילויה אבל מנח ידיה עילויה לית לן בה *אל תצא יחידי בלילה דתניא לא יצא יחידי בלילה לא בלילי רביעיות ולא בלילי שבתות מפני שאגרת בת מחלת היא ושמונה עשרה רבוא של מלאכי חבלה יוצאין וכל אחד ואחד יש לו רשות לחבל בפני עצמו מעיקרא הוו שכיחי כולי יומא זמנא חדא פגעה ברבי חנינא בן דוסא אמרה ליה אי לאו דמכרזן עלך ברקיע הזהרו בחנינא ובתורתו סכנתיך אמר לה אי חשיבנא ברקיע גוזר אני עליך שלא תעבורי ביישוב לעולם אמרה ליה במטותא מינך שבק לי רווחא פורתא שבק לה לילי שבתות ולילי רביעיות ותו חדא זמנא פגעה ביה באביי אמרה ליה אי לאו דמכרזי עלך ברקיע הזהרו בנחמני ובתורתו הוה סכנתיך א"ל אי חשיבנא ברקיע גוזרני עלייכי שלא תעבורי ביישוב לעולם הא קא חזינן דעברה אמרי הני

גזייתא

רשב"ם

שאין כל האצבעות שוות. אבל תשמיש ומתוך שאין תשמישו של זה נוח לה כשל ראשון תשנא אותו: מלוה וגוף גדול. מלוה וגם תשתכר בה: אוכל פירות ולא שכר. הלוה מעות לחבירך על קרקע לאכול פירות בנכייתא בזול [שתנכה] לו דבר מועט מן הדמים כמשכנתא דסורא (ב"מ דף סז:) והיינו ריוח גדול וגם מלוה היא שיש לו ללוה שכר ריוח שצריך למעות לסחורה: דלא תיגני בלא ק"ש. שזהו מנהג דארמאין: וא"ד. על מטה ארמית ממש משום מעשה דרב פפא שהיתה ארמית אחת חייבת לו מעות ונכנס בביתה לגבות הימנה חנקה את בנה ונתנתו על המטה וכשנכנס רב פפא אמרה לו שב על המטה עד שאביא מעותיך וכן עשה כשבאתה אמרה לו המתה את בני וברח לו מן המדינה: לא תינסב גיורתא. משום דאמרינן גיורא עד עשרה דרי לא תבזי ארמאה באפיה (סנהדרין צד.): מפני שהשטן מרקד. לאו דווקא אלא משוגע כדמפרש לקמן: וביומי ניסן. שהצמחים עולין וגם לבו ונוגח: ריש תורא בדיקולא. רבותא היא אפילו כשראש השור בתוך הסל שהוא אוכל בו וטרוד באכילתו: שדי דרגא. פן יעלה אחריך: ניזהא דתורא. לחש על השור שלא יגחנו כך פירש רבינו ונראה בעיני שאינו לחש אלא גערה שגוער בו בלשון הזה להבריחו מעליו או כדי שיעשה מלאכה וכן כולן: ניזהא. גערה: ניזהא דארבא. כדי למושכה בחבל ולהוליכה לנהר: אמר אביי עור ודג כו'. לקמן מפרש להו ואזיל: משכא דצלא. הישן על העור קודם שתגמר עבודתו צלא הוא עבדן כדאמרי' בב"ב (דף ה.) ארבעה לצלא וארבעה לצללא: חמימי שדא עליה. אם רגיל לשפוך מים חמין יותר מדאי על בשרו: מאן דמחוור לבושיה. ולבוש להו מקמי שמנה יומי דאכתי לא מטו שמנה יומי שכיבסן הנהו כינים הדרי ואיכא בהו חיותא וקשין לדבר אחר לרעת: בהכרא. בחושך: דחד הוי בעל דיקך. ותרי לסהדו עלך ויחלקו בין שלשתן ומתוך שנאה שנחלקת עמהן יעשו עליך קנוניא זו לתבוע ממך: אל תעמוד על המקח. לסחור והמוכר ישראל הוא ואין לך דמים לקנות המקח ונמצא מפסידו שגם שלא יקחנו אחר מאחר שאתה מהפך בו: בנדה דאורייתא. קודם שהחמירו על עצמן לישב שבעה נקיים ואפילו רואות כל שבעה טובלות בליל שמונה ומשמשות ואל תזקק באותו הלילה הואיל והיום ראתה והוחזק מעין פתוח דילמא שפעה זיבה בשעת תשמיש: שמא תפחת. ותחתיה חלל מלא מים: בנחמני. אביי ואפי' שגידלו רבה בר נחמני קרוי כן:

גזייתא

שאין כל האצבעות שוות. אבל תשמיש שלא יהא תשמיש זה טוב לה כראשון ותזלזל בו: מלוה וגוף גדול. אם תרצה לעשות מלוה וגם תשתכר בה שיגדל ממונך: אוכל פירות ולא שכר. הלוה חבירך מעות על הקרקע לאכול פירות בנכייתא בזול שתנכה לו דבר מועט מן הדמים והיינו ריוח גדול וגם מלוה היא שיש ללוה שכר ריוח שצריך למעות ולסחורה: דלא תיגני בלא ק"ש. שזה מנהג הארמאין: איכא דאמרי אל תשב במטה ארמית ממש משום מעשה דרב פפא שהיתה ארמית אחת חייבת לו מעות ונכנס מדי יום יום בביתה לגבות הימנה יום אחד חנקה את בנה ונתנתו על המטה וכשנכנס רב פפא אמרה לו שב עד שאביא מעותיך וכן עשה כשבאתה אמרה המתה את בני וברח מן המדינה: וביומי ניסן. שהצמחים עולין וגם לבו בהן ונוגח: בדיקולא. בטרסקל שהוא אוכל בו: ניזהא (א) דתורא. *לחש על השור שלא יגחנו: אמשכא דצלא. הישן על עור בבית העבדנין קודם שתגמר מלאכתו: חמימי דחמימי דשדא עילויה. אם רגיל לשפוך עליו מים חמים יותר מדאי על בשרו: מאן דמחוור לבושי'. ולביש להו מקמי ח' יומי דאכתי לא מטי ח' יומי דאשלחינהו הנהו כינים הדרי ואכתי איכא בהו חיותא ואכלי ליה וקשין לדבר אחר: בהדי תלתא. דהוה חד בעל דיקך ותרי ליהוי סהדך: ובנדה דאורייתא. קודם שהחמירו על עצמן לישב ז' נקיים וטובלת ביום שפסק המעין אל תזקק באותו לילה הואיל והיום ראתה והוחזק מעין פתוח דילמא שפעה זיבה: שמא תפחת. ותחתיה חלל מלא מים:

גזייתא

עין משפט נר מצוה

סו א מיי' פכ"א מהלכות אסורי ביאה הלכה י סמג לאוין קכו טוש"ע או"ח סי' רמ סעיף יא וטוש"ע אה"ע סימן כה סעיף ה:

סז ב טוש"ע או"ח סי' רמ סעיף טז:

ברכות נג.

[בתמיד לב. איתא בהברא ופי' המפרש כחושך וכ"ה בערוך ערך הכר ע"ש ועי' הוריות יב. ובכריתות ה: ובפירוש רש"י שם]

מס' ד"א פי"א וגם איתא דמו בראשו

מסורת הש"ס

[נדה סו.]

ברכות ח: [וע"ש כמה שנויים בין המעשה שהובא שם ובין מה שהביא רש"י ורשב"ם]

[ועי' רש"י סנהדרין מה: ד"ה מנוולתא וכו' משמע כפי' שכתב הרשב"ם הכא לשון גערה]

[ב"מ נח: ע"ש]

מס' כלה פרק י. וגם איתא הרי זה משנה

[ברכות מג: חולין קה.]

הגהות הב"ח

(א) רש"י ד"ה ניזהא כו' ל"ב ולשון ניזהא הוא המדבר בקושי ובחוזק והכרסם דכך הוא הלחש לתחרים פי' פסוק עיין רש"י בפ' היו בודקין דף מ"א ע"ב:

רבינו חננאל

מצוה וגוף גדול אוכל פירות ולו שכר. פלוני מלוה את חברו ועושה מצוה ומשתלם ממנו מן השכר מצוה והגוף נקי נושא אשה ולו בנים: ארבעה דברים צוה רבינו את בנו אל תדור בשכנציב דליצני נינהו דילמא משכו לך ואל תשב במטת ארמית משום מעשה דרב פפא שהיה נושה בארמאי ממון ובא לביתו לפרעו והיה לאותו ארמאי בן ומת והיה מוטל על המטה כיון שנכנס רב פפא אמר ליה שב על המטה כיון שישב על המטה צעק כי אתה הרגת את בני כו' איכא דאמרי אל תשב אל תישן בלא ק"ש איכא דאמרי לא תנסב גיורת ואל תבריח עצמך מן המכס דאי משכחי ליה בידך שקלי לכוליה עסקך ואל תעמוד בפני השור וכו' נזהא דתורא וכו': שלשה דברים צוה ר' ישמעאל בר' יוסי את רב אל תעש מום בעצמך מאי היא לא יהוי לך דינא בהדי תלתא דחד הוי בעל דין ותרי מיניהו סהדי ואל תעמוד על המקח בשעה שאין לך דמים שמגמצאת פחתת המקח בעיני בעליו אשתך טבלה אל תזדקק לה לילה הראשונה אמר רבא בנדה דאורייתא שטובלת בתשלום שבעת ימים לראייתה הואיל והוחזק מעין פתוח אבל בטובלת שבעה נקיים לא וכן עוד צוה ר' יוסי בר' יהודה אל תצא יחידי בלילה ואל תעמוד בפני הנר ערום ואל תכנס במרחץ חדשה שמא תפחת העומד בפני הנר ערום נכפה והמשמש מטתו לאור הנר הויין לו בנים נכפים: ת"ר המשמש מטתו ותינוק קטן בה נכפה. אגרת בת מחלת שנראת לר' חנינא ולאביי פשוטה היא: אמר ליה

דמסוכר. מקיז דם מן הכתפיים לשון סיכורי: ידא אאוסיא. שרגיל להניח ידו אצל נחיריו על שפתיו: דרגא לפחדא. דרך הוא להביא לו פחד רוח רעה: לול שפן אניגרון אנירדפי. לחש הוא: בי בליעי ושמיני. הנה סביבותי אנשים כחושים ושמנים ותניחוני: ונימא ליה. לחיכא מיא: הוי עז. התחזק במצוה יותר משיכולת בידך: אל תשב בגובהה של עיר ותשנה. מקום שבני העיר עוברים ושבין שמא כשהן עוברים ושבין *יבטלוך ויפסיקוך ממשנתך: ואל תדור בעיר שראשיה תלמידי חכמים. דטרוד בגרסיה ולא במילי דציבורא: לא למיזבן מיניה ולא לזבוני ליה. דאיידי דעדיף מזליה נגח וזכי ליה להאי: אמר ליה ר"ש בן יוחי ומי בסכנה. והלא העגל בסכנה ומה לך בכך: אם בקשת ליחנק. לומר דבר שיהיה נשמע לבריות ויקבלו ממך: היתלה באילן גדול. אמור בשם אדם גדול: בחדתא. כשהתינוק למד בחדש כשהוא מתחיל ללמוד: שאין

תורה אור

**דמסוכר ולא משי ידיה מפחיד שבעה יומי דשקיל מזייה ולא משי ידיה מפחיד תלתא יומי דשקיל טופריה ולא משי ידיה מפחיד חד יומא ולא ידע מאי קא מפחיד ידא אאוסיא דרגא לפחדא *ידא אפותא דרגא לשינתא תנא אוכלין ומשקין תחת המטה [*] אפילו מחופין בכלי ברזל *רוח רעה שורה עליהן ת"ר לא ישתה אדם מים לא בלילי רביעיות ולא בלילי שבתות ואם שתה דמו בראשו מפני סכנה מאי סכנה רוח רעה ואם צחי מאי תקנתיה (*נימא) שבעה קולות שאמר דוד על המים והדר נישתי שנאמר °קול ה' על המים אל הכבוד הרעים ה' על מים רבים קול ה' בכח קול ה' בהדר קול ה' שובר ארזים וישבר ה' את ארזי הלבנון קול ה' חוצב להבות אש קול ה' יחיל מדבר יחיל ה' מדבר קדש קול ה' יחולל אילות ויחשוף יערות ובהיכלו כולו אומר כבוד ואי לא (*נימא) הכי לול שפן אניגרון אנירדפין בין כוכבי יתיבנא בין בליעי שמיני אזילנא ואי לא אי איכא איניש בהדיה ניתעריה ולימא ליה פלניא בר פלנתא צחינא מיא והדר נישתי ואי לא מקרקש נכתמא אחצבא והדר נישתי ואי לא נישדי בה מידי והדר נישתי *ת"ר לא ישתה אדם מים לא מן הנהרות ולא מן האגמים בלילה ואם שתה דמו בראשו מפני הסכנה מאי סכנה סכנת שברירי ואי צחי מאי תקנתיה אי איכא איניש בהדיה לימא ליה פלניא בר פלנתא צחינא מיא ואי לא (*נימא) איהו לנפשיה פלניא אמרה לי אימי איזדהר משברירי שברירי בריריו רירי ירי רי צחינא מיא בכסי חורי: ואפילו מן התמחוי וכו': פשיטא לא נצרכא אלא אפילו לר"ע דאמר *עשה שבתך חול ואל תצטרך לבריות הכא משום פרסומי ניסא (*מודי) תנא דבי אליהו אע"פ שאמר ר"ע עשה שבתך חול ואל תצטרך לבריות אבל עושה הוא דבר מועט בתוך ביתו מאי ניהו (א) אמר רב פפא כסא דהרסנא *כדתנן *ר' יהודה בן תימא אומר הוי עז כנמר וקל כנשר רץ כצבי וגבור כארי לעשות רצון אביך שבשמים ת"ר שבעה דברים צוה ר"ע את רבי יהושע בנו בני אל תשב בגובהה של עיר ותשנה ואל תדור בעיר שראשיה תלמידי חכמים ואל תכנס לביתך *פתאום כ"ש לבית חבירך ואל תמנע מנעלים מרגליך *השכם ואכול בקיץ מפני החמה ובחורף מפני הצינה ועשה שבתך חול ואל תצטרך לבריות *והוי משתדל עם אדם שהשעה משחקת לו אמר רב פפא לא למיזבן מיניה ולא לזבוני ליה אלא למעבד אשותפות בהדיה והשתא *דאמר רב שמואל בר יצחק מאי דכתיב °מעשה ידיו ברכת כל הנוטל פרוטה מאיוב מתברך אפילו למיזבן מיניה ולזבוני ליה שפיר דמי חמשה דברים צוה ר"ע את רבי שמעון בן יוחי כשהיה חבוש בבית האסורין אמר לו רבי למדני תורה אמר איני מלמדך אמר לו אם אין אתה מלמדני אני אומר ליוחי אבא ומוסרך למלכות אמר לו בני יותר ממה שהעגל רוצה לינק פרה רוצה להניק אמר לו ומי בסכנה והלא עגל בסכנה אמר לו *אם בקשת ליחנק היתלה באילן גדול וכשאתה מלמד את בנך למדהו בספר מוגה מאי היא אמר רבא ואיתימא רב משרשיא בחדתא *שבשתא כיון דעל על לא תבשל בקדירה שבישל בה חבירך מאי ניהו גרושה בחיי בעלה דאמר מר גרוש שנשא גרושה ארבע דעות במטה ואי בעית אימא אפילו באלמנה לפי שאין

תהלים כט | איוב א | [ב"ק צב.]

תוספות

צוה רבי עקיבא את רבי יהושע בנו. פירש רשב"ם דהוא ר' יהושע בן קרחה דר"ע קרח היה כדאמרינן [בבכורות] (דף נח.) שהיה בן עזאי אומר כל חכמי ישראל דומין לפני כקליפת השום חוץ מן הקרח הזה ואין נראה שיהיה הגמרא קורא אותו בן קרחה דרך גנאי שהרי נענשו הנערים שקראו לאלישע עלה קרח (מלכים ב ב) ובן עזאי קראו כן דרך *בדיחותא:

שבשתא דעל על. תימה דרבא גופא איתא ליה בלא יחפור (ב"ב דף כא.) שבשתא ממילא נפקא ויש לומר דהייט כשלומד קמי דגרים ולא דייק שיכול להבין מעצמו כשיגדל אבל כאן דאיירי בספר שאינו מוגה סומך על ספרו ואינו יוצא מידי טעותו: ולא

רשב"ם

דמסוכר. מקיז דם מן הכתפיים: ידא אאוסיא. שרגיל להניח ידו על שפתו אצל נחיריו: דרגא לפחדא. סולם ודרך הוא לעלות עליו פחד רוח רעה: אפותא. מצח: בלילי רביעיות. בלא נר: לול שפן אניגרון. לחש הוא: בי בליעי ושמיני. הנה סביבותי אנשים כחושים ושמינים בחרו וקחו לכם והניחוני: שברירי. סנורים (בראשית יט) מתרגמינן כן: לימא ליה לחיכא מיא בכסי חורי. ממוכה על כוסות של חרס: הוי עז כנמר. התחזק במצות יותר משהיכולת בידך: ר' יהושע בן קרחה. הוא בן ר"ע שרבי עקיבא קרח היה כדאמרי' במסכת [בכורות] (דף נח.) כל חכמי ישראל דומין לפני כקליפת השום חוץ מן הקרח הזה: אל תשב בגובהה של עיר ותשנה. מקום שבני העיר עוברין ושבין ויבטלוך ויפסיקוך ממשנתך: ואל תדור בעיר שראשיה ת"ח. דטריד בגירסא ולא טריד במילי דציבורא: ולא תכנס בביתך פתאום. אלא השמע את קולך להם קודם בואך דילמא עבדי מילתא דלגיעותא [בויקרא רבה] (פכ"א) ר' יוחנן כי הוה עייל לביתא מגעגע משום שנאמר ונשמע קולו בבואו אל הקודש: ואל תמנע מנעלים מרגליך. שגנאי הדבר לתלמיד חכם שילך יחף כדאמרינן התם (שבת דף קכט.) ימכור אדם כל מה שיש לו ויקח מנעלים לרגליו: השכם ואכול כו'. מקראי נפקא לן בבבא קמא (דף נב:) לא ירעבו ולא יצמאו ולא יכם שרב ושמש אי נמי מדכתיב וברך את לחמך ואת מימיך והדר והסירותי מחלה מקרבך: לא למיזבן מיניה ולא לזבוני ליה. דאיידי דהעדיף מזליה נגח וזכי ליה להאי: כשהיה חבוש בבית האסורין. כדאיתא בברכות (דף סא:): איני מלמדך. שלפי שהיה עסוק בתורה נתפש כדאמרינן בברכות (שם): אמר לו רבי שמעון בן יוחי ומי בסכנה. והלא עגל בסכנה ומה לך בכך: ואם בקשת ליחנק היתלה באילן גדול. לומר דבר שישמע לבריות ויקבלו ממך ומשום דנקט ליחנק *דחניקה נקט היתלה באילן למוד בפני רב ואמור שמועותיו משמו: בחדתא. כשהתחיל מתחיל ללמוד מחדש: ארבע דיעות. בשעת תשמיש זה לבו לאשתו ראשונה וזאת לבעלה הראשון ותניא לא ישמש אדם עם אשתו ויתן עיניו באשה אחרת ויהיו בניו קרובין לממזרין הנקראין בני גרושת הלב במסכת נדרים (דף כ:) שאין

עין משפט נר מצוה

סד א טוש"ע או"ח סי' ד סעיף יט:
סד [א] טוש"ע יו"ד סי' קטז סעיף ס ועיין רמב"ם פי"ב מה' רוצח ושמירת נפש הל"ה [וכרב אלפס פ"ב דע"ז דף שם. וברא"ש שם סס' יג ול"ע]:
סה ב מיי' פ"ל מהלכות שבת הלכה ז ופ"י מהלכות מתנות עניים הלכה יח סמג עשין ג' טוש"ע או"ח סימן רמב טוש"ע יו"ד סימן רנה סעיף א:

[וע"ע תוס' שבת קג. ותוספות ב"ב קי. ד"ה ומטו ותוס' בכורות נח.]

מסורת הש"ס

[דמסוכר גי' כשמוך ערך סכר] | [דרך בני אדם כשיש ידו על פדחתו. ערוך ערך פג] | [לימא] | [לימא] | פי' יב: ע"ש [וכתוס' שם] | [לימא] | [לקמן קיג. שבת קיח.] | עי' כבי' בטוא"ח סימן רמ"ב דלא גרים ליה | [נדה טז: מס' ד"א פ"ס] | [לקמן קיג.] | [כ"ב טו:] | [מודה] | אבות פ"ה מ"כ | ב"ק לב: ב"מ קז:

הגהות הב"ח

(א) גמ' מאי ניהו אמר רב פפא:

פי' אם רצית לשאול בדבר איסור כלומר שאתה צריך לדון דין חמור כד"ג שאל לחכ' גדול ועשה כהוראתו. ערוך ערך חנק] ס"א משום דנקט ליחנק דהיתלה באילן נקט ליחנק דחניקה. מ"מ:

רבינו חננאל

לתלתין יומין דמסכר פי' מקיז דם ולא משי ידיה מפחד שבעה יומין שקל מזייה ולא משי ידיה מפחד לתלתין יומין שקל טופריה ולא משי ידיה מפחד יום אחד דמשי רישיה ולא משי כרעיה מפחד יום אחד ולא ידע ממה מפחד ידא אפנא דירכא לפחדא ידא אפגא דירכא לשינתא. אוכלין ומשקין תחת המטה ואפי' מחופין בכלי ברזל רוח רעה שורה עליהן: ת"ר לא ישתה אדם בלילי רביעיות ובלילי שבתות במחשך ואי צחי למיא לימא שבעה קולות קול ה' על המים וכו' וישתה לא ישתה אדם מן הנהרות בלילה כו': ואפי' מן התמחוי. ואסיקנא אפילו לר' עקיבא דאמר עשה שבתך חול ואל תצטרך לבריות הכא משום ניסא מתיר שיקח אפילו מן התמחוי: תנא רבי אליהו אע"פ שאמר ר' עקיבא עשה שבתך חול ואל תצטרך לבריות עושה אדם דבר מועט בתוך ביתו כגון כסא דהרסנא כדתנן הוה עז כנמר קל כנשר ורץ כצבי וגבור כארי לעשות רצון אביך שבשמים: ששה דברים צוה ר' עקיבא לר' יהושע בנו אל תשב בגובהה של עיר ותשנה ואל תדור בעיר שראשיה תלמידי חכמים ואל תכנס לבית פתאום ואל תמנע מנעלים מרגליך השכם ואכול בין בקיץ בין בחורף. עשה שבתך חול ואל תצטרך לבריות פי' אל תאמר חייב אני לענג השבת אם אין ידך משגת אלא עשה שבתך במאכל ובמשקה ובמלבוש [כמו יום החול] ואל תצטרך לבריות ותשתדל עם שהשעה משחקת לו להשתתף עמו ואפילו למזבן ולזבוני מיניה: חמשה דברים צוה ר' עקיבא את ר' שמעון בן יוחאי אם בקשת ליחנק התלה באילן גדול פי' אם רצית לשאול בדבר איסור שאל חכם גדול יעשה כהוראתו וכשתבקש ללמד לבנך למדהו בספר מוגה דשבשתא דעל על כלומר אם יקרא בנך בטעות הטעות שנכנס בלבו כבר נכנס מי יסירהו מלבו ואל תבשל בקדרה שבשל בה הברך בין גרושה בין אלמנה:

גליון הש"ס

גמ' רוח רעה שורה עליהן. עי' תורת חיים שבועות דף ט ע"ב ד"ה ריב"ל: רש"י ד"ה אל תשב. יבטלוך ויפסיקו לך. עי' בסדר הדורות בסדר תנאים אות י דף קיח ע"ב:

[112a] He who lets blood without washing his hands will be afraid seven days. He who trims his hair and does not wash his hands will be afraid three days. He who pares his nails and does not wash his hands will be afraid one day without knowing what affrights him.

[Putting] one's hand to one's nostrils is a step to fear; [putting] one's hand to one's forehead is a step to sleep.

It was taught: If food and drink [are kept] under the bed, even if they are covered in iron vessels, an evil spirit rests upon them.

Our Rabbis taught: A man must not drink water either on the nights of the fourth days [Wednesdays] or on the nights of
a Sabbath,[1] and if he does drink, his blood is on his own head, because of the danger. What is the danger? An evil spirit. Yet if he is thirsty what is his remedy? Let him recite the seven 'voices' which David uttered over the water and then drink, as it is said: *The voice of the Lord is upon the waters; the God of glory thundereth, even the Lord upon many waters. The voice of the Lord is powerful; the voice of the Lord is full of majesty. The voice of the Lord breaketh the cedars; yea, the Lord breaketh in pieces the cedars of the Lebanon . . . The voice of the Lord heweth out flames of fire. The voice of the Lord shaketh the wilderness; the Lord shaketh the wilderness of Kadesh. The voice of the Lord maketh the hinds to calve, and strippeth the forests bare; and in His temple all say: 'Glory.'*[2] But if [he does] not [say this], let him say thus: '*Lul shafan anigron anirdafin*,[3] I dwell among the stars, I walk among lean and fat people.' But if [he does] not [say this], if there is a man with him, he should rouse him and say to him, 'So-and-so the son of So-and-so, I am thirsty for water,' and then he can drink. But if not, he knocks the lid against the pitcher, and then he can drink. But if not, let him throw something into it and then drink.

Our Rabbis taught: A man should not drink water from rivers or pools at night, and if he drinks, his blood is on his own head, because of the danger. What is the danger? The danger of blindness.[4] But if he is thirsty, what is his remedy? If a man is with him he should say to him, 'So-and-so the son of So-and-so, I am thirsty for water.' But if not, let him say to himself, 'O So-and-so,[5] my mother told me, "Beware of shabrire": Shabrire, berire, rire, ire re,[6] I am thirsty for water in a white glass.'

AND EVEN [IF HE RECEIVES RELIEF] FROM THE CHARITY PLATE ETC. That is obvious?—It is necessary only even according
b to R. Akiba who said: Treat your Sabbath like a weekday[1] rather than be dependent on man; yet here, in order to advertise the miracle, he agrees.[2]

Tanna debe Eliyahu [taught]:[3] Though R. Akiba said, 'Treat your Sabbath like a weekday rather than be dependent on men,' yet one must prepare something trifling at home.[4] What is it? Said R. Papa: Fish hash. As we learned, R. Judah b. Tema said: Be strong as the leopard and swift as the eagle, fleet as the deer and valiant as a lion to do the will of thy Father in heaven.[5]

Our Rabbis taught: Seven things did R. Akiba charge his son R. Joshua: My son, do not sit and study at the highest point of the town;[6] do not dwell in a town whose leaders are scholars;[7] do not enter your own house suddenly, and all the more your neighbour's house; and do not withhold shoes from your feet.[8] Arise early and eat, in summer on account of the sun [i.e., heat] and in winter on account of the cold; treat your Sabbath like a weekday rather than be dependent on man, and strive to be on good terms with the man upon whom the hour smiles. R. Papa observed: [That does] not [mean] to buy from or to sell to him, but to enter into partnership with him. But now that R. Samuel b. Isaac said: What is meant by the verse, *Thou hast blessed the work of his hands?*[9] Whoever took a farthing [*perutah*] from Job was blessed; even to buy from and to sell to him is advisable.

Five things did R. Akiba charge R. Simeon b. Yoḥai when he was immured in prison.[10] He [the latter] said to him, 'Master, teach me Torah.' 'I will not teach you,' he replied.[11] 'If thou wilt not teach me,' said he, 'I will tell my father Yoḥai and he will deliver thee to the state.' 'My son,' answered he, 'more than the calf wishes to suck does the cow desire to suckle.' Said he to him,
c 'Yet who is in danger: surely the calf is in danger!'[1] Said he to him: 'If you wish to be strangled, be hanged on a large tree,[2] and when you teach your son, teach him from a corrected scroll.' (What is that? Said Raba,—others state, R. Mesharsheya: A new one, for once an error has entered, it remains.)[3] 'Do not cook in a pot in which your neighbour has cooked.' (What does that mean? [Do not marry] a divorced woman during her husband's lifetime. For a Master said: When a divorced man marries a divorced woman, there are four minds in the bed. Alternatively,

a (1) Rashbam: without a light. (2) Ps. XXIX, 3-5, 7-9. (3) This is an incantation. (4) Shabrire, v. Giṭ., 69a, n. 4. (5) Addressing himself thus. (6) [An incantation against the demon of blindness resembling an Abracadabra amulet, in which each succeeding line is reduced by one letter].

b (1) In the matter of food and drink. (2) That he must take from charity. (3) V. 94a, n. c1. (4) In honour of the Sabbath. (5) Thus even the poorest must make an effort to honour the Sabbath. (6) Many pass there, and they will disturb your studies. (7) Intent on their studies, they neglect the affairs of the town! (8) Cf. Shab. 129a. (9) Job I, 10. (10) R. Akiba was kept in prison several years and then martyred for defying Hadrian's edict against practising and teaching Judaism, Ber. 61b; v. *J.E.* 1, 305[1]. (11) He did not wish to endanger him.

c (1) He pleaded to be allowed to take the risk. (2) If you must depend on an authority, see that he is a great one. (3) An error learned in childhood is difficult to dispel.

[111*b*] If one eases oneself on the stump of a palm-tree, the demon Palga[2] will seize him, and if one leans one's head on the stump of a palm-tree, the demon Zerada[3] will seize him. He who steps over a palm-tree, if it had been cut down, he will be cut down [killed]; if it had been uprooted, he will be uprooted and die. But that is only if he does not place his foot upon it; but if he places his foot upon it, it does not matter.

There are five shades:[4] the shade of a single palm-tree, the shade of a kanda-tree,[5] the shade of a caper-tree, [and] the shade of sorb bushes.[6] Some say: Also the shade of a ship and the shade of a willow. This is the general rule: Whatever has many branches, its shade is harmful, and whatever has hard prickles [or, wood], its shade is harmful, except the service-tree, whose shade is not harmful although its wood is hard, because Shida [the demon] said to her son, 'Fly from the service-tree, because it is that which killed your father'; and, it also killed him. R. Ashi said: I saw R. Kahana avoid all shades.

[The demons] of caper-trees are [called] *Ruḥe* [spirits]: those of sorb-bushes are [called] *Shide* [demons]: those which haunt roofs are [called] *Rishpe* [fiery-bolts]. In respect of what does it
a matter? In respect of amulets.[1] [The demon] of caper-trees is a creature without eyes. What does it matter? In respect of fleeing from it.[2] A scholar was once about to ease himself among the caper-trees, when he heard it advancing upon him, so he fled from it. When he had gone, it embraced a palm-tree,[3] whereupon the palm-tree cried out[4] and it [the demon] burst.

[The demons] of sorb-bushes are [called] *Shide*. A sorb-bush which is near a town has not less than sixty *Shide* [demons] [haunting it]. How does this matter? In respect of writing an amulet. A certain town-officer went and stood by a sorb-bush near a town, whereupon he was set upon by sixty demons and his life was in danger. He then went to a scholar who did not know that it was a sorb-bush haunted by sixty demons, and so he wrote a one-demon amulet for it. Then he heard how they suspended a *ḥinga*[5] on it [the tree][6] and sing thus: 'The man's turban is like a scholar's, [yet] we have examined the man [and find] that he does not know "Blessed art Thou".'[7] Then a certain scholar came who knew that it was a sorb-bush of sixty demons and wrote a sixty-demon amulet for it. Then he heard them saying, 'Clear away your vessels from here.'

Ḳeṭeb Meriri:[8] there are two *Ḳeṭebs*, one before noon and one after noon; the one before noon is called Ḳeṭeb Meriri, and looks like a ladle turning in the jug of *ḳamka*.[9] That of the afternoon is called Ḳeṭeb Yashud Ẓaharaim [*'Destruction that wasteth at noonday'*];[10] it looks like a goat's horn, and wings compass it about.

Abaye was walking along, with R. Papa on his right and R. Huna son of R. Joshua on his left. Seeing a *Ḳeṭeb Meriri* approaching him on the left, he transferred R. Papa to his left and R. Huna son of R. Joshua to his right. Said R. Papa to him: 'Wherein am I different that you were not afraid on my behalf?' 'The time is
b in your favour,' replied he.[1]

From the first of Tammuz[2] until the sixteenth they are certainly to be found; henceforth it is doubtful whether they are about or not, and they are found in the shadow of *ḥazube*[3] which have not grown a cubit, and in the morning and evening shadows when these are less than a cubit [in length], but mainly in the shadow of a privy.

R. Joseph said: The following three things cause defective eyesight: combing one's head [when it is] dry, drinking the drip-drop [of wine], and putting on shoes while the feet are still damp.

[Eatables] suspended in a house lead[4] to poverty, as people say, 'He who suspends a basket [of food] puts his food in suspense.' Yet this relates only to bread, but it does not matter about meat and fish, [since] that is the usual way [of keeping them]. Bran[5] in a house leads to poverty. Crumbs in a house lead to poverty: the demons rest upon them on the nights of Sabbaths and on the nights of the fourth days.

The genius appointed over sustenance is called *Neḳi'ah* [Cleanliness]; the genius appointed over poverty is called *Nabal* [Folly or Filth]. Dirt on the spout of a pitcher leads to poverty. He who drinks water out of a plate is liable to a cataract. He who eats cress without [first] washing his hands will suffer fear thirty days.

(2) Jast. conjectures paralysis. [*Aruch*: 'headache on one side of the head', megrim, connecting it with rt. meaning 'to divide']. (3) Perhaps vertigo; Rashi: megrim. (4) Involving danger on account of the demons that inhabit them. (5) MS.M.: *kinura*, the name of a shrubby tree, Christ's-thorn or lote (Jast.). (6) [Var. lec.: add as fifth 'the shade of the willow-tree].

a (1) Charms to counteract them, in which their names are written. (2) As it is sightless it cannot follow. (3) In error. Rashi and Rashbam read נפקא ארקלא, it tripped over a palm-tree. (4) [Or, withered v. *supra* 110*b*, n. a5.] (5) A musical instrument. (6) Jast. Perhaps: they danced in chorus about it. (7) He does not know which benediction to recite when he puts it on—they ridiculed his pretensions to scholarship. (8) 'Bitter destruction' (v. Deut. XXXII, 24). Regarded here as the name of a demon. (9) A kind of sauce made of milk and bread-crumbs.—The translation follows the reading of Rashi and Rashbam, which differs from cur. edd. (10) Ps. XCI, 6.

b (1) You have been blessed with good fortune, so the demon will not harm you. (2) The fourth month of the Jewish year, roughly corresponding to July. (3) A species of shrub. (4) Lit., 'are harmful.' (5) So Rashbam.

האי מאן דמפני אגירדא דדיקלא אחדא ליה לדידיה רוח פלגא והאי מאן דמצלי רישיה אגירדא דדיקלא אחדא ליה רוח צרדא האי מאן דפסעי אדיקלא אי מיקטל קטיל אי איעקר מיעקר ומיית (א) הנ"מ דלא מנח כרעיה עילויה אבל מנח כרעיה עילויה לית לן בה *חמשה טולי הוי טולא דדיקלא יחידא טולא *דכנדא טולא דפרחא טולא דורדתא [א] איכא דאמרי אף טולא דארבא וטולא דערבתא כללא דמילתא כל דנפיש ענפיה קשי טוליה וכל דקשי סיליה קשי טולי' לבר מכרו משא אע"ג דקשי סילויה לא קשי טוליה דאמרה לה שידא לברה פירחי נפשיך מכרו משא דאיהו הוא דקטיל לאבוך וקטיל לדידיה אמר רב אשי חזינא לרב כהנא דפריש מכולהו טולי בי פרחי רוחי דבי זרדתא שידא דבי איגרי רישפי למאי נפקא מינה לקמיעא דבי פרחי בריה שאין לה עינים למאי נפקא מינה לגזוזי לה זימנא חדא הוה אזיל צורבא מרבנן לאפגויי לבי פרחי שמע דקא אתא עילויה וגזי לה כי אזלא חבקיה לדיקלא צווח דיקלא ופקעה היא [ב] פרחא דבי זרדתא שידי הא זרדתא דסמיכה למתא לא פחתא משיתין שידי למאי נפקא מינה למיכתב לה קמיעא *ההוא בר קשא דמתא דאזיל וקאי גבי זרדתא דהוה סמיך למתא עלו ביה שיתין שידי ואיסתכן אתא להוא מרבנן דלא ידע דזרדתא דשיתין שידי היא כתב לה קמיע לחדא שידא שמע דתלו חינגא בגוויה וקא משרו הכי סודריה דמר כי צורבא מרבנן בדיקנא ביה במר דלא ידע ברוך אתא ההוא מרבנן דידע דזרדתא שיתין שידי הוה כתב לה קמיעא דשיתין שידי שמע דקא אמרו פנו מניכו מהבא קטב מרירי תרי קטבי הוו חד מקמי טיהרא וחד מבתר טיהרא דמקמי טיהרא קטב מרירי שמו ומיחזי בי כדא דכמכא והדר ביה בחשא דבתר טיהרא °קטב ישוד צהרים שמו ומיחזי בי קרנא דעיזא והדר ביה בנפיא תהלים צא אביי הוה שקיל ואזיל ורב פפא מימיניה ורב הונא בריה דרב יהושע משמאליה חזייה להההוא קטב מרירי דקא אתי לאפיה דשמאליה אהדרא לרב פפא לשמאליה ולרב הונא בריה דרב יהושע לימיניה אמר ליה רב פפא אנא מאי שנא דלא חשש לי אמר ליה את שעתא קיימת לך מחד בתמוז עד שיתסר ביה ודאי שביחי מכאן ואילך ספק שביחי ספק לא שביחי ומשתכחי בטולי דחצבא דלא חצב גרמידא ובטולי דצפרא ופניא דלא הוי גרמידא ועיקר בטולי דבית הכסא אמר רב יוסף הני תלת מילי יהיב ארבונא לנהורא (ב) מן דסריק רישיה יבש ומן דשתי טיף טיף ומן דסיים מסני אדמייתניה כרעא תלאי בביתא קשי לעניותא כדאמרי אינשי תלא סילתא תלא מזוניה ולא אמרן אלא ריפתא אבל בישרא וכוורי לית לן בה אורחיה היא פארי בביתא קשי לעניותא *נשורא בביתא קשי לעניותא בלילי שבתות ובלילי רביעית שרו מזיקין עילויה איסרא דמזוני נקיד שמיה איסרא דעניותא נבל שמיה אפומא דחצבא קשי לעניותא מאן דשתי מיא בצעי קשי לברוקתי דאכיל תחלי ולא משי ידיה מפחיד תלתין יומין

דמסוכר

האי מאן דמפני אגרדא (ג) דדיקלא : אי מיקטל קטיל . אם נקצץ האילן נהרג האיש ואם נעקר האילן האיש מת : ה"ג הני מילי היכא דלא מנח כרעיה עילויה כו' : (ד) האי מאן דמפני אגירדא דדיקלא אחדא ליה רוח פלגא : פלגדי"ן בלע"ז : צרדא . כאב חצי הראש : חמשה טולי הוו . שרוח רעה שורה תחתיהם : טולא דכנדא . שם האילן : טולא דפרחא . כלף קרפי"ף בלע"ז : זרדתא . שונדכיי"ר : טולא דארבא . ספינה : טולא דערבתא . כל אילן ערבה : דקשה סילויה . עלו : דבי פרחי רוחי . כך הוא שמם : דבי זרדתא . שדים שמן : דבי איגרי . המלויין בגגות רשפי שמם : ונפקא מינה . לכתוב קמיעא בשם אילן כגון אם הוזק תחת בי פרחא יכתוב לו קמיעא בשם רוחי : למאי נפקא מינה לגזויי לה . לברוח מפניה לפי שאין לה עינים ואינה רודפתו : גזייה . ברח מפניה : כי אזלא נפקא אדיקלא . כשהלכה אחריו נתקלה ונפלה על עיקר אילן : ה"ג פקעה היא וצווח דיקלא . יבש הדקל : בר קשא . שומר העיר : ה"ג סודרא דמר דומה כי צורבא מרבנן : בדקנה למר לא ידע ליה למימר ברוך . שאינו יודע לברך על הסודר *ברוך עוטר ישראל: בחשא . כף הקדירה : והדר בכדא דכמכא . מתגלגל בתוך כד של כותח: ומשתכח בטולא דהלבא . חלב שתיחס יהושע בו לישראל את הארץ* : דלא חלב גרמידא . שלא גדל אמה: ארבונא . עיורון : אדמתנא כרעיה . בעוד שרגליו לחים ממי הרחיצה : תליא בביתא . התולה פתו באויר בתוך סל אחד : תלא לסילתיה . לסלו ופת בתוכו : נשורא . פירורין : איסרא דמזוני . מלאך הממונה לזמן מזונות : נקוד שמיה . לשון נקידו כמו מנקד אצירו לפיכך אינו רוצה שיהו פרורים נשלכים לידרס ברגל : איסרא דעניותא נבל שמיה . (ה) ושמא נכנס לבית שהוא רואה שאין נוהגים מנהג נקיות בפת : לברוקתי . כליון עינים : מפחד . ואינו יודע למה : דמסוכר

תורה אור

ואזיל רב פפא מימיניה . מלדד אילדודי הוה דאמר בפרק הממונה (יומא דף לז.) המהלך לימין רבו הרי זה בור :

תליא בביתא קשי לעניותא . מכאן קשה לרש"י דפירש בפרק קמא דחגיגה (דף ה.) היינו דאמרי אינשי זוזי לתליתא שכיחא למגלא לא שכיח ופי' לתליתא לקנות פת לצורך היום שתולין בסל ואין דרך לתלותו בסל דהא אמרינן הכא דקשי לעניותא ור"ת מפרש שם לתליתא כשדוחקין אותו לפרוע מוצא לווין אבל לקנות תבואה לאכול אינו מוצא לווין : לוה

רשב"ם

דמפני אגירדא דדיקלא . דקל קצוץ : רוח פלגא . מורשי"ן בלע"ז : צרדא . כאב חצי הראש : אי מקטל קטיל . אם נקצץ האילן נהרג האיש ואם נעקר האילן האיש מת : ה"ג הני מילי היכא דלא מנח כרעיה עילויה : חמשה טולי הוו . שהרוח רעה שורה תחתיהן : טולא כנדא . שם אילן : טולא דפרחא . ללף: זרדתא . שונבי"ר: טולא דארבא . ספינה: טולא דערבתא . כל אילן ערבה : טופיה . ענפיו : סילויה . עלו : דבי פרחי רוחי . אותן שדים דבי פרחי שמן רוחי ולקמן מפרש למאי נפקא מינה : דבי זרדתא שידי . שמן : דבי איגרי . המלויין בגגות רשפי שמן : למיכתב קמיעא . בשם אלו כגון אם הוזק תחת בי פרחי יכתוב לו קמיעא בשם רוחי : למאי נפקא מינה לגזויי מינה . לברוח מפניה לפי שאין לה עינים ואינה רודפתו : גזייה . ברח מפניה : כי אזלא נפקא אדקלא . כשהלכה אחריו נתקלה ונפלה על עיקר אילן : הכי גרסינן פקע היא וצווח דקלא . יבש הדקל : בר קשא . שוטר העיר : דקא תלו ביה חינגא בגוויה . דאילן : הכי גרסינן סודריה דמר כצורבא מרבנן בדיקנא ליה למר ולא ידע למימר ברוך . שאינו יודע לברך על הסודר *ברוך עוטר ישראל בתפארה : בחשא בקדרא והדר בכדא דכמכא . מתגלגל בתוך כד של כותח : ואהדריה לרב הונא מימיניה ולרב פפא משמאליה : מאי שנא . כי אינך חושש בי אם אזוק : שעתא קיימא לך . עשיר אתה ויש לך מזל טוב ולא תיזוק : ומשתכחא בטולא דהלובא . חלב עשב שתיחס בו יהושע את הארץ לישראל* : דלא חלב גרמידא . שלא גדל אמה : ארבונא . עיורון : ושתי טיף טיף . יין המטפטף מן החבית : אדמיתנא כרעיה . בעוד שרגליו לחים במי הרחיצה : תלאי בביתיה . התולה פתו באויר בתוך סל אחד : תלא סילתיה . סל ופת בתוכו : פארי . מורסן : נשורא . פירורין של פת : נקיד שמיה . לשון נקיות לפיכך אינו רוצה שיהו פירורין נשלכין לידרס ברגל : איסרא דעניותא נבל שמיה . לשון לכלוך (ו) ושמא נכנס בבית שהוא רואה שאין נוהגין מנהג נקיון בפת : בלעא . בקערה : לברוקתי . בליון עינים : מפחיד . ואינו יודע למה : דמסוכר

רבינו חננאל

הני תלת מילי יהבי ארבונא בנהורא מאן דסריק יבש ומאן דשתי טיף טיף ומאן דסאים מסאניה כי רטיבתא כרעיה תלא לחמא קשי לעניותא דאכיל תחלי ולא משי ידיה מפחד

הגהות הב"ח

(א) גמ' ומיית והנ"מ דלא : (ב) שם מאן דסריק וכו' ומאן דשתי וכו' ומאן דסיים מסני אדמתונא כרעא : (ג) רש"י ד"ה האי מאן וכו' דדיקלא דקל (קלוף) [קצוץ] הס"ד : (ד) ד"ה האי מאן וד"ה צרדא צ"ל קודם ד"ה אי מיקטל : (ה) ד"ה איסרא דעניותא נבל שמיה נכנס לבית שר ואה כצ"ל ותיבת ושמא נמחק : (ו) רשב"ם ד"ה איסרא וכו' לכלוך ואינו נכנס בבית וכו' מנהג בזיון בפת :

הגהות הגר"א

[א] גמ' טולא דורדתא טולא דערבתא א"ד אף טולא דארבא כללא כו' כצ"ל (וכזה מיושב מ"ש בהגהות הגרי"ב . וע"ע נ"א במנורת המאור) : [ב] שם פרחא . נמחק :

מסורת הש"ס

[לכאורה צ"ל ארבעה]
[גי' הערוך דכינרא ועי' רשב"ם ב"ב מח: ד"ה סלי לפפי]
[ברכות ס:]
כ"ב ט.
[שבת קי. וע"ש פרש"י ב"ב קי: וע"א רשב"ם]
[חולין קה:]
[ברכות ס:]
כ"ב ט.

תורה אור

חוץ מן המים ור' יוחנן אמר אפילו מים אמר רב פפא לא אמרן אלא חמימי לגו קרירי וקרירי לגו חמימי אבל חמימי לגו חמימי וקרירי לגו קרירי לא אמר ריש לקיש ארבעה דברים העושה אותן דמו *בראשו ומתחייב בנפשו אלו הן הנפנה בין דקל לכותל והעובר בין שני דקלים והשותה מים שאולין והעובר על מים שפוכין ואפילו שפכתו אשתו בפניו הנפנה בין דקל לכותל לא אמרן אלא דלית ליה ארבע אמות אבל אית ליה ארבע אמות לית לן בה וכי לית ליה ארבע אמות לא אמרן אלא דליכא דירכא אחרינא אבל איכא דירכא אחרינא לית לן בה והעובר בין שני דקלים לא אמרן אלא דלא פסקינהו רשות הרבים אבל פסקינהו רשות הרבים לית לן בה השותה מים שאולין לא אמרן אלא דשיילינהו קטן אבל גדול לית לן בה ואפילו שיילינהו קטן נמי לא אמרן אלא בשדה דלא שכיחי אבל בעיר דשכיחי לית לן בה ואפילו בשדה נמי לא אמרן אלא מיא אבל חמרא ושיכרא לית לן בה והעובר על מים שפוכין לא אמרן אלא דלא אפסקינהו בעפרא ולא תף בהו רוקא אבל אפסקינהו (א) או תף בהו רוקא לית לן בה ולא אמרן אלא דלא עבר עלייהו שימשא ולא עבר עלייהו שיתין ניגרי *אבל עבר עלייהו שימשא ועבר עלייהו שיתין ניגרי לית לן בה ולא אמרן אלא דלא רכיב חמרא ולא סיים מסני אבל רכיב חמרא וסיים מסני לית לן בה וה"מ היכא דליכא למיחש לכשפים אבל היכא דאיכא למיחש לכשפים אע"ג דאיכא כל הני חיישינן (*וההוא) (ב) גברא דרכיב חמרא וסיים מסני וגמוד מסאניה וצוו כרעיה ת"ר שלשה אין ממצעין ולא מתמצעין ואלו הן הכלב והדקל והאשה וי"א אף החזיר וי"א אף הנחש ואי ממצעין מאי תקנתיה אמר רב פפא נפתח באל ונפסיק באל א"נ נפתח בלא ונפסיק בלא הני בי תרי דמצעא להו אשה נדה אם תחלת נדתה היא הורגת א' מהן אם סוף נדתה היא מריבה עושה ביניהן מאי תקנתיה נפתח באל ונפסיק באל הני תרי נשי דיתבן בפרשת דרכים חדא בהאי גיסא דשבילא וחדא באידך גיסא ומכוונן אפייהו להדדי ודאי בכשפים עסיקן מאי תקנתיה אי איכא דירכא אחרינא ליזיל בה ואי ליכא דירכא אחרינא אי איכא איניש אחרינא בהדיה נינקטו לידייהו בהדי הדדי ונחלפו ואי ליכא איניש אחרינא נימא הכי אגרת אזלת אסיא בלוסיא מתקטלא בחיק קבל האי מאן *דפגע באיתתא בעידנא דסלקא מטבילת מצוה אי איהו קדים ומשמש אחדא ליה לדידיה רוח זנונים אי איהי קדמה ומשמשה אחדא לה לדידה רוח זנונים מאי תקנתיה *לימא הכי °שופך בוז על נדיבים ויתעם בתוהו לא דרך א"ר יצחק מאי דכתיב °גם כי אלך בגיא צלמות לא אירא רע כי אתה עמדי זה הישן בצל דקל יחידי ובצל לבנה ובצל דקל יחידי לא אמרן אלא דלא נפיל טולא דחבריה עילויה אבל נפל טולא דחבריה עילויה לית לן בה אלא הא דתניא הישן בצל דקל יחידי בחצר והישן בצל לבנה דמו בראשו היכי דמי אי לימא דלא נפל טולא דחבריה עילויה אפילו בשדה נמי אלא לאו שמע מינה בחצר אף על גב דנפיל טולא דחבריה עילויה שמע מינה ובצילה של לבנה לא אמרן אלא במערבה אבל במדינחתא לית לן בה

האי

תהלים קז | שם כג

חוץ ממים. מזוגים כגון קרירי בחמימי וחמימי בקרירי דמיא לא מזיגה הוא ואם היה שותה בתחלה יין אין אלו מצטרפות לו : ולא אמרן. (ג) מים מזוגין אין מצטרפין ליין מזוג : ארבעה דברים. כולן משום רוח רעה : אלא דלא הוי ד' אמות. דלא שביק רווחא [לשידא] לעבור בין דקל לכותל משום הכי מזיק ליה : אלא דליכא דירכא אחרינא. שאהא שידא יכולה להלך בו דעכשיו זה בא בגבולה והפסיד דרכה ולהכי מזיק ליה : ולא אמרן. דרוח רעה שורה על המים אלא בעיר המקום צר הן שולטין ושורה עליהן. לישנא אחרינא דשרי עלייהו אלא בשדה דלא שכיחי מיא דמסרה נפשה לאזוקא: דלא אפסקינהו בעפרא. שלא פיזר עליהן עפר : גמוד מסאני. נתכווצו המנעלין : וצוו כרעיה. ויבשו רגליו: אין ממצעין. לא יעברו בין שני אנשים : ואין מתמצעין. לא יעבור איש אחד בין ב' כלבים בין שתי נשים בין שתי דקלים : נפתח באל ונסיים באל. אל מוציאם ממצרים (במדבר כג) כי לא נחש ביעקב וגו' עד מה פעל אל: נפתח בלא ונסיים בלא. לא איש אל עד לא יקימנו (שם): הורגת אחד מהן. שמזיקתן במה שעברה ביניהן : אגרא אזלת אוסייא בלוסייא. אותן שדים שאתם מתעסקות בהן:מתקטלי בחיק קבל. כבר הן הרוגים בחילים:חיק קבל. אר"ק בליסטר"א כמו ומחי קבלו יתן [בחומותיך] (בחרבותיו) (יחזקאל כו) מפי המורה [א] הגמ' ומקרא אשר שמע מפי רבו : דקל יחידי. שאין דקל אחר סמוך לו אבל כשיש דקל אחר מסתלקת השידא לדקל האחר ואינה מזיקתו:בחצר. שהמקום צר ואין לה דרך לנטות ימין ושמאל ושורה עליו ומזיקתו:

האי

נפתח באל. פי' רשב"ם אל מוציאם ממצרים ונפתח בלא לא איש אל ויכזב ואע"ג *דאסור להתרפאות בדברי תורה להגן שרי והא דאמרי' בפ' במה אשה (שבת דף סז:) לאישתא למירתא לישקול סכינא וכו' ולימא ויאמר משה אסורה נא ואראה וגו' משום סכנה שרי ור"ח פי' נפתח באל לימא הכי אל אלהים ה' הצילנו מכל רע ומכל נזק אשר בידך כח וגבורה כי אתה אל ונפתח בלא לא תטשני אלהי ולא תעזבני שמרני כאישון בת עין טרם אקרא תענני ואל תאמר לא :

אם תחלת נדה היא הורגת. יש מפרש אם עושה להן כישוף :

ואזיל

רשב"ם

חוץ. מקרירי בחמימי וחמימי בקרירי דהא לא מזיגה היא דמין במין ניהו מה לי קרירי ומה לי חמימי מ"מ מין א' הוא ושם א' הוא ואם שתה בתחל' יין מזוג אין אלו מצטרפות לו : אמר רב פפא לא אמרן כו'. אדר' יוחנן קאי דאמר אפילו מים ובא רב פפא לפרש לא אמרן דמצטרפין אלא קרירי בחמימי וחמימי בקרירי דההיא חשיב ר' יוחנן מזוג אבל חמימי לגו חמימי וקרירי לגו קרירי דלכולי עלמא לא מיקרי מזוג ולא מצטרפי : ארבעה דברים כו'. משום רוח רעה ולקמן מפרש להו חדא חדא: אלא דלא הוי ארבע אמות. דלא שבק רווחא לשידא לעבור בין דקל לכותל משום הכי מזיק ליה : אלא דליכא דירכא אחרינא. שאהא שידא יכולה להלך בו דעכשיו בא זה בגבולה והפסידה את דרכה ולהכי מזיק ליה : אבל פסקינהו. דשכיחי רבים לית ליה רשות להזיק את הרבים : ולא אמרן. דשורה על המים אלא בשדה דלא שכיחי מיא ומסרה נפשה לשתות : דלא אפסקינהו בעפרא. שלא פיזר עליהן עפר : גמוד מסאני. נתכווצו המנעלים : וצוו כרעיה. יבשו רגליו : לא ממצעין. לא יעברו בין אנשים : ולא מתמצעין. ולא יעבור איש אחד בין שני כלבים בין שתי נשים בין שני דקלים : נפתח באל ונסיים באל. אל מוציאם ממצרים וגו' כי לא נחש ביעקב וגו' עד מה פעל אל : נפתח בלא ומסיים בלא. לא איש אל ויכזב וגו' עד ולא יקימנה : הורגת אחד מהן. שמזיקתן במה שעברה ביניהן : אגרת אזלא אוסיא בלוסיא. אותן שדים שאתן עוסקות בהן בכשפים : מתקטלין בחיק קבל. כבר הרוגים הן בחצים כמו ומחי קבלו כך שמע רבינו מרבו ורבו מפי רבינו גרשום זצ"ל : אגרת. היא אגרת בת מחלת שם שידה : דקל יחידי. שאין דקל אחר סמוך לו : בצלה של לבנה. אי נמי ההולך בלילה כשהלבנה זורחת והוא הולך בצל הכתלים שדרך השדים להלוך בלילה ובזמן שהלבנה זורחת מתיראין לילך במקום האור והולכין במקום הצל : טולא דחבריה. אם יש דקל אחר סמוך לו מסתלקת השידה לדקל אחר ואינו מזיקתו : בחצר. שהמקום צר שאין לה דרך לנטות ימין ושמאל ושורה עליו ומזיקתו : ובצלה של לבנה לא אמרן אלא במערבה. הייט בסוף החודש שהלבנה זורחת במזרח ואם שוכב אצל כותל לצד המערב הוי הצל במערב : אבל במדינחא. הייט תחלת החדש שהלבנה זורחת במערב ועושה צל במזרח כגון ששוכב אצל כותל מצד המזרח :

דמפני

רבינו חננאל

אמר ר' יוחנן כל חמרא מצטרף ואפי' מים ור"פ חמימי לגו קרירי או קרירי לגו חמימי : ארבעה דברים העושה אותן דמו בראשו הנפנה בין דקל לכותל והעובר בין ב' דקלים והעובר על מים שפוכין ואפי' שפכתן בתו והשותה מים שאולין ולא אמרן אלא דשיילינהו קטן בדברא [אבל שיילינהו גדול] או קטן במתא או חמרא ושכרא לית לן בה. תרי דפסקינהו נדה אם תחלת נדת היא הורגת אחד מהן ואם סוף נדה היא עושה מריבה בינידם מאי תקנתיה נפתח באל ונסים באל [וי"א נפתח בלא ונסיים בלא] יש מי שאומר יפתח פסוק באל ויסיים באל כגון (במדבר כ"ג כ"ג) אל מוציאם ממצרים עד מה פעל אל [ונפתח בלא כגון לא איש אל וגו'] ויש מי שאומר דלא אלא יפתח אל ה' הצילני מכל רע ומכל נזק וחלי ובידך כח וגבורה כי אתה אל וכן יפתח ויאמר לא תטשני אלהי ולא תעזבני שמרני כאישון בת עין מלא שאלתי ותן לי בקשותי טרם אקראך תענני ואל תאמר לא : מאן דפגע בנדה כי סלקא מטבילת מצוה אי איהו קדים ומשמש אחד ליה רוח זנונים אי איהי קדמה ומשמשה אחרא לדידה רוח זנונים מאי תקנתיה נימא הכי שופך בוז על נדיבים וגו'

הגהות הב"ח

(א) גמ' אבל אפסקינהו בעפרא או תף : (ב) שם דההוא גברא דרכיב : (ג) רש"י ד"ה ולא אמרן דמים מזוגין מצטרפין כצ"ל ותיבת אין נמחק :

הגה"ת מהר"ב רנשבורג

[א] כל מקום שמזכיר רש"י המורה הוא רבו של רש"י כן מוכח בלשון רש"י בד"ה חיק קבל וכו' ובלשון הרשב"ם שם בד"ה מתקטלין וכו' ומשם נלמוד נמי דרבו דרבו של רש"י היה רבינו גרשום :

[פי' בפרש"י נדה יז. ד"ה דמו]

עי' לקמן קיג.

[צ"ל ההוא]

[עי' תוס' ב"מ סד. ד"ה יחיב ואשערי מבילה]

[עי' ש"ך י"ד סוף סי' קלח]

גליון הש"ס

תוס' ד"ה נפתח כו'. ואף על גב דאסור להתרפאות בד"ת. שבועות טו ע"ב :

[111a] except water;[9] while R. Joḥanan maintained: Even water. R. Papa said: This was said only of hot [water] mixed with cold or cold mixed with hot; but not [if it is] hot mixed with hot or
a cold with cold.[1]

Resh Lakish said: There are four actions for which he who does them has his blood on his own head and forfeits his life,[2] viz.: easing oneself between a palm tree and the wall; passing between two palm trees; drinking borrowed water, and passing over spilt water, even if his wife poured it out in his presence. 'Easing oneself between a palm tree and the wall': this was said only if there is not four cubits,[3] but if he leaves four cubits it does not matter. And even if he does not leave four cubits [space], it was said only where there is no other path;[4] but if there is another path, it does not matter.

'Passing between two palm-trees.' This was said only where a public thoroughfare does not cross between them; but if a public thoroughfare crosses between them, it does not matter.

'Drinking borrowed water.' That was said only if a child borrowed it; but [if] an adult, it does not matter. And even if a child borrowed it, this was said only in respect to the countryside, where it is not found [in abundance]; but in the town, where it is found in abundance, it does not matter. And even in respect to the countryside, this was said only of water, but there is no objection against [borrowed] wine and beer.

'And passing over spilt water.' This was said only if he did not interpose dust[5] or spit into it; but if he interposed dust or spit into it, it does not matter. Again, this was said only if the sun had not passed over it nor did he walk sixty steps over it; but if the sun had passed over it and he walked sixty steps over it, it does not matter. Again, this was said only if he was not riding an ass and was not wearing shoes; but if he was riding an ass and was wearing shoes, it does not matter. Yet that is only where there is nought to fear of witchcraft; but where there is aught to fear of witchcraft, even if there are all these [safeguards], we still fear, as in the case of a certain man who rode on an ass and was wearing his shoes; his shoes shrank, and his feet withered.

Our Rabbis taught: There are three who must not pass between [two men], nor may [others] pass between them, viz.: a dog, a palm tree, and a woman. Some say: a swine too; some say, a snake too. And if they pass between, what is the remedy?—Said R. Papa: Let them commence [a verse] with *el* [God] and end with
b *el.*[1] Others say: Let them commence [a Scriptural passage] with *lo* [not] and finish with *lo.*[2] If a menstruant woman passes between two [men], if it is at the beginning of her menses she will slay one of them,[3] and if it is at the end of her menses she will cause strife between them. What is the remedy? Let them commence [a verse] with *el* and end with *el.* When two women sit at a cross-road, one on one side of the road, and one on the other side of the road, facing each other, they are certainly engaged in witchcraft. What is the remedy? If there is another road [available], let one go through it. While if there is no other road, [then] if another man is with him, let them clasp hands and pass through; while if there is no other man, let him say thus: 'Igrath Izlath, Asya, Belusia[4] have been slain with arrows.'[5]

When one meets a woman coming up from her statutory *ṭebillah,*[6] if [subsequently] *he* is the first to have intercourse, a spirit of immorality will infect him; while if *she* is the first to have intercourse, a spirit of immorality will infect her. What is the remedy? Let him say thus: '*He poureth contempt upon princes, and causeth them to wander in the waste, where there is no way.*'[7]

R. Isaac said: What is meant by the verse, *Yea, though I walk through the valley of the shadow of death, I will fear no evil, for Thou art with me?*[8] This refers to him who sleeps in the shadow of a single palm-tree or in the shadow of the moon. Now in respect to the shadow of a single palm-tree, this holds good only where the shadow of the neighbouring [tree] does not fall upon it; but if the shadow of the neighbouring tree falls upon it, it does not matter. Then when it was taught: He who sleeps in the shadow of a single palm-tree in a courtyard and he who sleeps in the shadow of the moon, has his blood on his own head, how is it meant? Shall we say that the shadow of the neighbouring tree does not fall upon it,—then even in a field too [it is dangerous]? Hence you may surely infer from this that in a courtyard [there is danger] even if the shadow of the neighbouring tree fall on it. This proves it. And in respect to the shadow of the moon too,
c this holds good only when [it falls] in the west,[1] but when it is in the east it does not matter.

(9) Cold water mixed with hot water is not regarded as a mixed drink and does not combine with other mixed drinks.

a (1) R. Joḥanan too admits that this is not a mixture, and it does not combine with other mixed drinks. (2) I.e., whatever happens, he has only himself to blame. (3) Between them: this leaves no room for the evil spirits to pass comfortably and so they injure him. (4) For the demon to pass through. (5) I.e., he did not scatter dust upon the water before passing over it.

b (1) Rashbam: Num. XXIII, 22f, which commence and finish with *el* in Heb. (2) Ibid. 19. (3) I.e., cause perjury to one of them (Rashbam). (4) The demons by whose aid you seek to work witchcraft. (5) The text is obscure. (6) After her period of menstruation. (7) Ps. CVII, 40. (8) Ps. XXIII, 4.

c (1) I.e., at the end of the month, when the moon is in the east and casts its shadow in the west.

the wind carry off your crumbs,[6] [110b] your spices be scattered, the wind carry off the new saffron which ye are holding, ye sorceresses; as long as He showed grace to me and to you, I had not come among [you]; now that I have come among you, your grace and my grace have cooled.'[7]

In the West [Palestine] they were not particular about 'pairs.' R. Dimi of Nehardea was particular even about the marks on a [wine-] barrel:[8] it once happened that a barrel burst.[9] This is the position in general: when one is particular, they [the demons] are particular about him,[10] while when one is not particular,[11] they are not particular about him. Nevertheless one should take heed.

a When R. Dimi came,[1] he said: Two eggs, two nuts, two cucumbers and something else—[these are] *halachah* from Moses at Sinai;[2] but the Rabbis were doubtful what this something else was, and so the Rabbis forbid all 'pairs' on account of the 'something else.' And as to what we have said, Ten, eight, six and four are not subject to 'pairs,' that was said only in respect to the harmful spirits [*mazziḳin*], but where witchcraft is concerned we fear even many.[3] As [it once happened in] the case of a certain man who divorced his wife, [whereupon] she went and married a shopkeeper. Every day he [her first husband] used to go and drink wine, [and though] she exercised her witchcraft against him, she could avail nought, because he was heedful of 'pairs.' One day he drank to excess and did not know how much he drank; until sixteen [cups] he was clear-headed and on his guard; after that he was not clear-headed and took no care, [and] she turned him out at an even [number of drinks]. As he was going along an Arab met him and observed to him: A corpse is walking here![4] He went and clasped a palm tree; the palm tree cried out[5] and he burst.

R. 'Awira said: Plates and loaves are not subject to even numbers. This is the general rule: That which is completed by man is not subject to even numbers; [but in the case of] that which is completed by Heaven, such as various kinds of eatables, we fear [even numbers]. A shop is not subject to even numbers.[6] If a man changes his mind,[7] it is not subject to even numbers. A guest is not subject to even numbers.[8] A woman is not subject to even numbers; but if she is an important woman, we take heed.

R. Ḥinena son of R. Joshua said: Asparagus [-wine] combines [with other liquors] for good, but does not combine
b for harm.[1]

Rabina said in Raba's name: [A doubt concerning] even numbers [is resolved] stringently;[2] others state: [A doubt concerning] even numbers [is resolved] leniently.[3]

R. Joseph said: Two [cups] of wine and one of beer do not combine; two of beer and one of wine combine, and your token [is this]: 'This is the general principle: Whatever is joined thereto of a material more stringent than itself is unclean; of a material more lenient than itself, is clean.'[4]

R. Naḥman said in Rab's name: Two [cups] before the meal[5] and one during the meal combine; one before the meal and two during the meal do not combine. R. Mesharsheya demurred: Do we then desire to effect a remedy for the meal: we desire to effect a remedy for the person, and surely the person stands remedied![6] Yet all agree that two during the meal and one after the meal do not combine, in accordance with the story of Rabbah b. Naḥmani.[7]

Rab Judah said in Samuel's name: All mixed drinks combine,[8]

(6) Likewise used in the practice of witchcraft. Rashbam holds that this is an allusion to Ezek. XIII, 18f, q.v. (7) I have not taken sufficient care of myself. (8) Indicating the quantities sold. He took care that there should not be an even number of these. (9) When an even number of marks had been made on it. (10) They are more anxious to injure him. (11) Takes no great pains to save himself from demons.

a (1) From Palestine to Babylonia. (2) It is a tradition dating back from Moses that even numbers of these and of another unnamed commodity are harmful. (3) A large multiple of two, such as six, eight, etc. (4) He recognized that he was doomed. (5) Probably, made a rustling noise. [Var. lec., 'withered']. (6) I.e., if one drinks in two shops. Others: if one drinks an even number of glasses in one shop, for these are harmful at home only. The incident related above, however, took place in a tavern. (7) He drank one glass, not intending to drink more; then decided to drink another. (8) He does not know how much will be offered him, therefore at each he is regarded as having decided afresh.

b (1) Cf. 109b, n. a5. (2) If a man does not know whether he has drunk an even number or not, he should drink another. This turns an even number into odd, not an odd into even, because in the latter case this glass represents a fresh decision (cf. n. a8), and does not combine with the others. (3) Thus showing that he is not particular about it and thereby removing the hostility of the demons (cf. *supra*). (4) Materials, to become unclean, must be of a certain minimum size, which varies according to the value of the material: the greater the value, the more stringent it is, i.e., the smaller its minimum. If the material is less than the minimum and a piece of another material is joined to it, making it up to the minimum, the rule is as stated. Thus here too, wine, being more valuable than beer, combines with it; beer being less valuable than wine, it is disregarded. (5) Lit., 'tray.' (6) Since he has drunk three. (7) V. B.M. 86a. (8) If a man drinks mixed (i.e., diluted) wine and then any other mixed drink (so Rashbam), they combine.

איבדור תבלונייכי פרחא זיקא למוריקא חדתא דנקטיתו נשים כשפניות ארחנני ותננבי לא אתיתי לגו השתא דאתיתי לגו קרחנני ותננבי במערבא לא קפדי אזוגי רב דימי מנהרדעא קפיד אפילו ארושמא דחביתא הוה עובדא ופקע חביתא כללא דמילתא כל דקפיד קפדי בהדיה ודלא קפיד לא קפדי בהדיה ומיהו *למיחש מיבעי כי אתא רב דימי אמר שתי ביצים ושתי אגוזין שתי קישואין ודבר אחר הלכה למשה מסיני ומסתפקא להו לרבנן מאי ניהו דבר אחר וגזור רבנן בכולהו זוגי משום דבר אחר והא דאמרן עשרה תמניא שיתא ארבעה אין בהן משום זוגי לא אמרן אלא לענין מזיקין אבל לענין כשפים אפילו טובא נמי חיישינן כי הא דההוא גברא דגרשה לדביתהו (אזיל) אינסבה לחנואה כל יומא הוה אזיל ושתי חמרא הוה קא עבדא ליה כשפים ולא קא מהניא לה ביה משום דהוה מזדהר בנפשיה בזוגא יומא חד אשתי טובא ולא הוה ידע כמה שתי עד שיתסר הוה צייל ואיזדהר בנפשיה מכאן ואילך לא הוה צייל ולא איזדהר בנפשיה אפיקתיה בזוגא כי הוה אזיל גם ביה ההוא טייעא א"ל גברא קטילא הוא דאזיל הכא אזיל חבקיה לדיקלא *צווח דיקלא ופקע הוא אמר רב עוירא קערות וכברות אין בהם משום זוגות כללא דמילתא כל שגמרו בידי אדם אין בהן משום זוגות גמרו בידי שמים במילי מיני דמיכל חיישינן חנות אין בהן משום זוגות נמלך אין בהן משום זוגות אורח אין בו משום זוגות אשה אין בה משום זוגות ואי אשה חשובה חיישינן אמר רב חיננא בריה דרבי יהושע איספרגוס מצטרף לטובה ואין מצטרף לרעה אמר רבינא משמיה דרבא זוגי לחומרא ואמרי ליה זוגי לקולא אמר רב יוסף תרי דחמרא וחד דשיכרא לא מצטרף תרי דשיכרא וחד דחמרא מצטרף וסימניך *זה הכלל כל המחובר לו מן החמור ממנו טמא מן הקל ממנו טהור אמר רב נחמן אמר רב תרי קמא תבא וחד אתבא מצטרפי חד מקמי תבא ותרי אתבא לא מצטרפין מתקיף לה רב משרשיא אטו אנן לתקוני תבא קא בעינן לתקוני גברא בעינן וגברא קא מיתקן וקאי (אלא א"ר משרשיא) דכולי עלמא תרי אתבא וחד לבתר תבא לא מצטרפי כי ההיא מעשה דרבה בר נחמני אמר רב יהודה אמר שמואל כל המזוג מצטרף

חוץ

רשב"ם

איבדור תבלונייכי. יהו מפוזרין תבלין שלכם: פרחיה זיקא למוריקא חדתא דנקטיתו. ישא הרוח אותו בושם חדש שאתן אוחזות בידכן לכסף בו: ארחנני ותננבי לא אתיתי לגו. כל זמן שחסו עלי מן השמים ואני חסתי על עצמי ואתן חסתן עלי לא באתי ביניכם: השתא דאתית לגו קרחנני ותננבי. השתא שבאתי ביניכם יודע אני שנתקררו עלי רחמיכם וגם רחמי נתקררו שלא חסתי על עצמי. *ל"א גרסי' תרי חמימי בדיקולי בזייא לוחה רותחת בסלים קרועין יהא לפומייכו נשי חרשייתא אותן תרי יהא מזונות לפיכם כשפניות. בתשובות הגאונים: קפיד ארושמא דחביתא. כשמוכרים יין חוקקין פגימות בחבית למספר האיפות וקפיד עלייהו שלא יאלו בזוגות: כל דקפיד. יותר מדאי קפדי בהדיה השדים להזיקו ודלא קפיד כ"כ לא קפדי בהדיה להזיקו: ומיהו למיחש מיבעי אפילו מאן דלא קפיד דלא קפדינן בהדיה דאי קימא דלא קפדי בהדיה כלל א"כ זוגות למה נזכרו בגמרא כך היה להם לחכמים לומר לא יזהר אדם בזוגות דלא לקפדו בהדיה: וד"א. עדיין יש פרי אחד שמקפידין בזוגותיו הלכה למשה מסיני דמזיק: והא דאמרת לעיל עשרה אין בהן משום זוגות. ה"מ היכא דליכא נשים כשפניות: גם ביה. פגע בו ל"א הבין בו שהיה מכוון: אזיל חבקיה לדקלא. מתוך חולי ודאגה נסמך עליו: ה"ג צווח דיקלא ופקע בו הדקל יבש מכח הכשפים: קערות. אם אכל שתי קערות תבשיל: גמרו בידי שמים. חיישינן דההוא דבר אחר דגזרו בשבילו כל זוגות גמרו בידי שמים הוי פירות וכל דדמי ליה: חנות אין בה משום זוגות. אם שתה בשתי חנויות לא אמרי' כשני כוסות דמי לשון אחר ועיקר חנות השותה בו זוגות לא קפדי מזיקין עליה דלאו קביעותא היא והואי עובדא דלעיל דההוא גברא דשתה בחנות כשפים שאני שעשתה לו גרושתו: אורח אין בו משום זוגות. דאינו יודע אם ישקוהו עוד הלכך אכל כסא הוי ליה כנמלך: אשה. שאינה חשובה כאורח דמיא דאינה קבועה לשתות: איספרגוס. בלשון פרסי קורין לכרוב אספרגוס וזהו ששנינו* הנודר מן הכרוב אסור באספרגוס ומשקין הוא שעושין מכרוב ומיין ורגילין היו לשתותו בכל בוקר לרפואה קודם אכילה והלכך מצטרף לטובה ולא לרעה דמידי דרפואה הוא: לטובה. אם שתה שנים ושתה זה שלישי מצטרף לאפוקי מזוגות: לרעה. אם שתה א' וזה שני לא יצטרף לראשון: זוגי לחומרא. אם אינו יודע אם שתה זוגות אם לאו ישתה ואם שתה זוגות הואיל ודעתו לגרפן מצטרפין לטובה ואם לא שתה זוגות נמלך ואינו מצטרף לרעה: ואמרי לה זוגי לקולא. שלא ישתה דכיון דשתי גלי אדעתיה דקפיד אזוגות ואי מעיקרא לא בזוגות הוה קאי והשתא שתי מצטרפי להו בהדי הדדי הלכך לא ישתה דאפילו אי בזוגות הוה קאי דילמא כיון דלא קפיד לא קפדי בהדיה: כל המחובר לו. גבי טומאות קאי דתנן מפץ חמש על חמש מחללת ששה על ששה וה"ק אם יש מחללת חמשה ואינו מקבל טומאה וטפח ממפץ מחובר לו הואיל וחמור ממנו מצטרף לו ומקבל טומאה אבל אם יש מפץ ארבע וטפח מחללת מחובר לו הואיל וקל ממנו אין מצטרף לו הכא נמי הואיל ושתי תרי שיכרא והדר שתי חד חמרא מצטרף להם הואיל וחשוב יותר: ה"ג אמר רב נחמן תרי מקמי תכא וחד אתכא מצטרפין. חד מקמי תכא ותרי אתכא לא מצטרפי הואיל ושתי אתכא זוגות לא מהני ליה צירוף: ודכ"ע. אפי' לרב משרשיא תרי אתכא וחד בתר תכא לא מצטרפי משום מעשה דרבה בר נחמני דאצרכינהו לאהדורי תכא קמיה [דף פו.] בב"מ בהשוכר את הפועלים* דאי חד דבתר תכא מצטרף לתרי דתכא לשקינהו כוס שלישי בתר תכא בלא אהדורי תכא: כל המזוג. אם שתה יין מזוג ואח"כ שתה משקה מזוג אחר המזוג מצטרף בין לרעה בין לטובה דכיון דתרווייהו מזוגין ניהו כמין אחד חשיבי ומצטרפי:

חוץ

[ל"א מכאן עד סוף הדבור ליתא בכת"י]

איבדור תבלונייכי. יהו מפוזרים תבלין שלכם: פרחיה זיקא למוריקא חדתא דנקטיתו. ישא הרוח אותו כרכום חדש שאתן אוחזות בידכן לכסף בו: ארחנני ותננבי לא (א) אתי לגו. כל זמן שחסו עלי מן השמים ואני חסתי על עצמי ואתם חסתם על ביאתי לא באתי ביניכם: והשתא דאתיתי לגו קרחנני ותננבי. הואיל ובאתי ביניכם יודע אני שנתקררו רחמיכן מעלי וגם רחמי נתקררו שלא חסתי על עצמי: קפיד ארושמא דחביתא. כשמוכרין יין חוקקין פגימות הרבה בחבית למספר האיפות וקפיד עלייהו רב דימי שלא יניחום בזוגות ויאלו: וד"א. יש פרי אחד שמקפידין בזוגותיו: והא דאמרן לעיל עשרה תמניא כו' אין בהן משום זוגות. ה"מ היכא דליכא נשים כשפניות: גם ביה. פגע בו: ה"ג פקע הוא וצווח דקלא. יבש הדקל מכח כשפים: קערות. אם אכלה שתי קערות: חנות אין בה משום זוגות. אם שתה בשתי חנויות לא אמרינן כשתי כוסות דמי לשון אחר חנות השותה בה זוגות לא קפדי מזיקין עלה דלאו קביעותא היא והואה עובדא דלעיל כשפים שאני: איספרגוס. משקין לשתות קודם אכילתו בבוקר: זוגי לחומרא. אם אינו יודע אם שתה זוגות אם לאו ישתה דאם שתה זוגות הואיל ודעתו לגרפן מצטרפין לטובה ואם לא שתה זוגות נמלך הוא ואין מצטרפות לרעה: ואמרי לה זוגי לקולא. שלא ישתה דכיון דשתי גלי דעתיה דקפיד אזוגות ואי מעיקרא לאו בזוגות קאי והשתא שתי הוה מצטרפי להו וקפדי להו בהדיה: כל המחובר לו. גבי טומאות קאי דתנן (כלים פכ"ז מ"ב) מפץ חמשה על חמשה מחללת ששה על ששה והכי קאמר אם יש מחללת ששה על ששה ואינו מקבל טומאה וטפח מפץ מחובר לו הואיל והחמור הימנו מצטרף לו ומקבל טומאה אבל אם מפץ ארבעה וטפח מחללת מחובר לו הואיל וקל הוא ממנו אין מצטרף לו: ה"ג אמר רב נחמן תרי מקמי תכא וחדא אתכא מצטרפי חד מקמי תכא ותרי אתכא לא מצטרפי. הואיל ושתי אתכא זוגות לא מהני ליה צירוף: ודכ"ע. אפילו רב משרשיא תרי אתכא וחד בתר תכא לא מצטרפי: משום מעשה דרבה בר נחמני. דאצרכינהו לאהדורי תכא קמיה בב"מ בהשוכר את הפועלים (דף פו.): כל המזוג. אם שתה יין מזוג ואח"כ שתה משקה אחר המזון מצטרף בין לטובה בין לרעה:

חוץ

רבינו חננאל

ואסק' כל דקפיד קפדי בהדיה. שני ביצים שני אגוזים שני קשואים ודבר אחר הלכה למשה מסיני ומזו רבנן על (ד"א) [כולהו זוגי] משום ד"א שלא נתפרש. ההוא דגרשה לדביתהו ואזלא ואנסבא להנואה שהוא רגיל בעלה קדמאה למשתי גביה ואשקייה זוגות כו'. קערות וכוסות אין בהן משום זוגות זה הכלל כל שגמרו בידי שמים חיישינן כגון פירות וביצים גמרו בידי אדם לא חיישינן אמר רב יוסף תרי דשכרא וחד דחמרא (לא) מצטרף [תרי דחמרי וחד דשכרא לא מצטרף] וסימנך כדתנן כל המחובר לו (הרי הוא כמוהו) [מן החמור ממנו כמו] היין טמא (קל) [מן הקל] ממנו כמו השכר טהור כולי עלמא תרי אתכא וחד בתר תכא לא מצטרף משום מעשה דרבה בר נחמני ופי' [ר'] בפרק השוכר:

[גירסת הערוך צווח ופקע ועי' לעיל ע. בגמ' ובפירש"י שם ד"ה לאו וכו' וע"ש לקמן קיא. ועו כרש"י ובתוס' והרמב"ם שם]

[נדרים נה:]

[מס' סה.]

[נ"ל אולה]

יש כאן עירוב לשון בגירסת המשנה שבכלים רש"י והבא"ש דשם משנה ב' איתא כעור ה' על ה' והמפץ ו' על ו' וכתב שהכילו רש"י סוכה טו. ד"ה תע"ש וצ"ע

כלים פכ"ז מ"ב

הגהות הב"ח

(א) רש"י ד"ה ארחנני ותננבי לא אתיתי לגו:

מלוה באנפי נפשה היא. ואין מצטרפין זה לזה: אמאי נמלך הוא. ואין מצטרפין לזוגות: הכי קאמר לא יאכל תרי ויעשה צרכיו אפילו פעם אחת או אם שתה לא ישמש: דילמא חליש. מחמת תשמיש איידי דבזוגות קאי מיתרע: שלא ראה פני השוק. בין כוס לכוס: ולא אמרן. דמרעי ליה זוגות אלא לצאת לדרך אחר הזוגות אבל לעמוד בביתו לית לן בה: מני כשורי. כששותה כוס זה מסתכל בקורה זו וכשהוא שותה שני מסתכל באחרת ולפי חשבון הקורות מזדהר בזוגות: כי הוה שתי חד כסא מנקטא תרי כסי. דהוו להו תלתא: אדם חשוב שאני. דמסרי שדים נפשייהו לאזוקי: עשרה כוסות דבית האבל. מפרש טעמא בכתובות בפ"ק (דף ח:): שלום. תיבה שביעית לישא ה' פניו אליך וגו': לטובה מצטרף (א). אם שתה שבעה וחזר ושתה את השמיני אין שמיני מצטרף עמהן: אפקינהו לרבנן בארבעה. פעמים הרבה כשהיו נפטרים ממנו היה משקן ויש פעמים שלא היה משקן אלא ד' פעמים ונפטרין: דאותבן בפרקא הוה. שהיה רגיל להקשות בשעת הדרשה: לא אתקרי מזיק. ולא חיישינן לזוגות: בתרי. כסי קטלינא ליה משום זוגות: איקרי ונפיק. בזוגות מאי תקנתיה: זקפא. אגודל: ואי שמע קלא. ואפילו קול אדם או אשה דאמר ארבעה נימא איהו חמשה: רישתינהי דנשים כשפניות. השולטות עליהם אמרה לי דבר זה: חרי חמימי בדיקולי בזייא. צואה חמה בסלים נקובים וקרועים לפומייכו: נשי חרשייתא. יזדמנו לפיכם נשים כשפניות: קרח קרחייכי. יהי רצון שימרטו אותן שערות שלכם שאתן מכשפות בהן: פרח פרחייכי. ישא הרוח אותן פירורי לחם שאתן מכשפות בהן: איבדור

מצוה באפי נפשה הוא לא יעשה צרכיו תרי אמאי נמלך הוא אמר אביי הכי קאמר לא יאכל תרי *וישתה תרי ולא יעשה צרכיו אפילו פעם אחת דילמא חליש ומיתרע ת"ר שותה כפלים דמו בראשו אמר רב יהודה אימתי בזמן שלא ראה פני השוק אבל ראה פני השוק הרשות בידו אמר רב אשי חזינא ליה לרב חנניא בר ביבי דאכל כסא הוה נפיק וחזי אפי שוקא ולא אמרן אלא לצאת לדרך אבל בביתו לא אמר ר' זירא ולישן כלצאת לדרך דמי אמר רב פפא ולצאת לבית הכסא כלצאת לדרך דמי ובביתו לא והא רבא מני כשורי ואביי כי שתי חד כסא מנקיט ליה אימיה תרי כסי בתרי ידיה ורב נחמן בר יצחק כי הוה שתי תרי כסי מנקיט ליה שמעיה חד כסא חד כסא מנקיט ליה תרי כסי בתרי ידיה *אדם חשוב שאני אמר עולא עשרה כוסות אין בהם משום זוגות עולא לטעמיה דאמר עולא ואמרי לה במתניתא תנא *עשרה כוסות תיקנו חכמים בבית האבל ואי ס"ד עשרה כוסות יש בהן משום זוגות היכי קיימי רבנן ותקנו מילתא דאתי לידי סכנה אבל תמניא יש בהן משום זוגות רב חסדא ורבה בר רב הונא דאמרי תרוייהו שלום לטובה מצטרף לרעה לא מצטרף אבל שיתא יש בהן משום זוגות רבה ורב יוסף דאמרי תרוייהו ויחנך לטובה מצטרף לרעה לא מצטרף אבל ארבעה יש בהן משום זוגות אביי ורבא דאמרי תרוייהו וישמרך לטובה מצטרף לרעה לא מצטרף ואזדא רבא לטעמיה דרבא אפקינהו לרבנן בארבעה כוסות אע"ג דאיתזק רבא בר ליואי לא חש לה למילתא דאמר ההוא משום דאותבן בפירקא הוה אמר רב יוסף אמר לי יוסף שידא אשמדאי מלכא דשידי ממונה הוא אכולהו זוגי ומלכא לא איקרי מזיק איכא דאמרי לה להאי גיסא אדרבה מלכא [רתחנא הוא] מאי דבעי עביד *שהמלך פורץ גדר לעשות לו דרך ואין מוחין בידו אמר רב פפא אמר לי יוסף שידא בתרי קטלינן בארבעה לא קטלינן בארבעה מזקינן בתרי בין בשוגג בין במזיד בארבעה במזיד אין בשוגג לא ואי אישתלי ואיקרי ונפק מאי תקנתיה לינקוט זקפא דידיה דימיניה בידא דשמאליה וזקפא דשמאליה בידא דימיניה ונימא הכי אתון ואנא הא תלתא ואי שמיע ליה דאמר אתון ואנא הא ארבעה נימא ליה אתון ואנא הא חמשה ואי שמיע ליה דאמר אתון ואנא הא שיתא נימא ליה אתון ואנא הא שבעה הוה עובדא עד מאה וחד ופקע שידא אמר אמימר אמרה לי רישתינהי דנשים כשפניות האי מאן דפגע בהו בנשים כשפניות נימא הכי חרי חמימי בדיקולא בזייא לפומייכו נשי דחרשייא קרח קרחייכי פרח פרחייכי איבדור

עשרה אין בהם משום זוגות. ולית ליה דרבא דאמר לעיל כוס של ברכה אין מצטרף לרעה דבאותן עשרה כוסות איכא ברכת המזון: ומלכא לא מקרי מזיק. והא דתניא לא יאכל תרי היינו משום כשפים ורשב"ם פירש דפעמים מזיק: (שייך לקמן דף קיא ע"א) האי מאן דפגע באיתתא כו'. והא דאמר כמי שמתו (ברכות דף כ:) ר' יוחנן הוה קאזיל ויתיב אשערי טבילה כי היכי דילדן זרעא כוותיה הכא דפגע בעת שעולה מן המים ור' יוחנן אשערי טבילה יתיב אי נמי כמי רבי יוחנן היה אומר שופך בוז על וגו': נפתח

רבינו חננאל

נשוארו ג' כוסות. רבינא אמר כל הדא והדא מצות בפני עצמה היא ואינן מצטרפין זה עם זה. השותה [שני] כוסות דמו בראשו ואם ראה פני השוק *או ישן או יצא לבית הכסא אינו חושש. עשרה (זוגות) כוסות אין בהן משום זוגות מדתקינהו רבנן בבית האבל. וישמרך שהוא סוף ג' תיבות ויחנך שהוא סוף חמשה שלום שהוא תיבה שביעית הני כולהו לא מצטרפי לרעה כלומר כוס הה' אינו מצטרף עם הד' ולא הז' עם הו' ולא הו' עם הה'. רבה בר ליואי דאיתזק משום דאותביה לרבא בפרקא. אמר יוסף שידא אתרי קטלינן בין בשוגג בין במזיד ד' במזיד מזיקין.

*) נראה דצ"ל לרבינו ג' אחרת כגמרא דאם ישן או יוצא לבית הכסא אינו חושש משום זוגות וצ"ע:

הגהות הב"ח

(א) רש"י ד"ה לטובה מצטרף לרעה לא מצטרף אם שתה כו':

פי' ויעשה צרכיו ולא ישתה תרי ויעשה צרכיו

[ברכות יט. וש"נ]

[כתובות ח:]

[סנהדרין כ: ב"ק ס: יבמות עו:]

רשב"ם

מצוה באנפי נפשיה היא. ואין מצטרפין זה לזה: נמלך הוא. דתשמיש ראשון גמרה ביאתו ובטל תאותו: הכי קאמר לא יאכל תרי. ויעשה צרכיו אפי' פעם אחת כלומר אדם שאכל זוגות יזהר בעצמו שלא ישמש מטתו אחרי כן עד זמן מרובה דילמא חליש מחמת תשמיש ואיידי דבזוגות קאי מיתרע מזליה: כפלים. כמו זוגות: דמו בראשו. עון מיתתו על ראשו מוטל שהוא ממית עצמו: בזמן שלא ראה פני השוק. בין כוס לכוס: ולא אמרן. דמרעי ליה זוגות אלא לצאת לדרך אבל לעמוד בביתו לית לן בה: מני כשורי. כששותה כוס זה מסתכל בקורה זו וכששותה שני מסתכל באחרת ולפי חשבון הקורות יזהר בזוגות ובכל פעם ופעם עושה כן אע"פ שאינו יוצא לדרך: אביי כי הוה שתי חד כסא מנקטא ליה אימיה תרי כסי. דהוי להו תלתא ולכך מזמנים אותם ביחד שלא יבוא הדבר לידי שכחה ויעמוד בזוגות: אביי עיברתו אמו מת אביו ילדתו אמו מתה אמו והא דאמר אביי אמרה לי אם ההיא מרבינתיה הואי בקדושין (ד' לא:): אדם חשוב שאני. דמסרי שדים נפשייהו לאזוקי: עשרה כוסות אין בהן משום זוגות. וכל שכן טפי: עשרה כוסות תיקנו בבית האבל. בפרק קמא דכתובות מפרש טעמא: שלום. תיבה שביעית היא דכתיב ישא ה' וגו' לטובה מצטרף אם שתה ששה ושתה השביעי מצטרף לבטל זוגות: אבל לא לרעה. שאם ישתה כוס שמיני אחריו אין שמיני מצטרף על השביעי להזיק וסברא הוא כיון שבירכן בשלום שהוא תיבה שביעית אין שום היזק בעולם: רבה ורב יוסף. כמו שהיו הדורות זו אחר זו היו מקילין בזוגות והולכין ופוחתין: רבא אפקינהו בארבעה. פעמים הרבה כשהיו נפטרין ממנו היה משקן ופעמים שלא היה משקן אלא ארבעה כוסות ונפטרין ואף על גב דתניא *רבה לעיל כוס של ברכה כו' אלמא סבירא ליה דארבע יש בהן משום זוגות אי לאו משום כוס של ברכה איכא לתרולי דנהי דארבע להזיק ליכא למיחש לכשפים מיהא איכא למיחש כדלקמן והלכך איצטריך רבא לתרולי לעיל הכי דלית להו לרבנן לתקוני מילתא דאתי בה לידי סכנה ואפילו סכנת כשפים: דאותבן בפירקא. שהקשה לי בשעת הדרשה וביישני ברבים שדרכו היה להקשות לו ברבים: לא איקרי מזיק. אין רגיל בכך דגנאי הוא לו ולא חיישינן לזוגות דמילתא דלא שכיחא היא ומיהו זימנין דניזוק והרוצה להחמיר ולעשות כטירותא יתירתא עביד: בתרי כסי קטלינן ליה. משום זוגות: איקרי ונפק. בזוגות מהו תקנתיה: זקפא. גודל: אי שמע. ואפילו קול אדם או קול אשה דאמר ד' נימא איהו חמשה שלא יעמוד בזוגות: עד מאה וחד. שהיה שד מונה זוגות והוא היה מוסיף אחת שלא לעמוד בזוגות: פקע שידא. מרוב צער: רישתינהי דנשים כשפניות. גבירתן של נשים כשפניות השולטת עליהן ומלמדתן אמרה לי דבר זה: חרי חמימי בדיקולי בזייא. צואה חמה בסלים קרועין ונקובין: לפומייכו חרשייתא. לפיכם נשים כשפניות: קרח קרחייכו. יהי רצון שימרטו אותן שערות שלכם שאתם מכשפין בהן: פרח פרחייכו. הרוח ישא אותם פירורי לחם שאתם מכשפות בו ונראה לי דהאי דכתיב בנשים כשפניות ביחזקאל (יג) הנני אל כסתותיכנה אשר אתנה מצודדות שם את הנפשות לפורחות אחד מכלי אומנות של כשוף: איבדור

[צ"ל רבא]

bolizing liberty: each one [110a] is a separate obligation.[6]

'He must not perform his requirements twice.' Why? Has he not [newly] decided?[7]—Said Abaye, This is what he [the Tanna] means: He must not eat in pairs and drink in pairs and he must not perform his needs even once [after eating or drinking in pairs], lest he be weakened[8] and be affected.[9]

Our Rabbis taught: He who drinks in pairs, his blood is upon his own head. Said Rab Judah: When is that? If he had not seen the street;[10] but if he has seen the street, he is at liberty [to drink a second cup]. R. Ashi said: I saw that R. Ḥanania b. Bibi used to go out and see the street at each cup. Now we have said [this][11] only [if he intends] to set out on a journey [after drinking]; but [if he intends to stay] at home, it is not [harmful]. R. Zera observed: And going to sleep is like setting out on a journey. R. Papa said: And going to the privy is like setting out on a journey. Now [if he intends to stay] at home it is not [dangerous]? Yet surely Raba counted the beams,[12] while when Abaye had drunk one cup, his mother would offer him *two* cups in her two hands;[13] again, when R. Naḥman b. Isaac had drunk two cups, his attendant would offer him one cup; [if he had drunk] one cup, he would offer him
a two cups in his two hands?[1]—An important person is different.[2]

'Ulla said: Ten cups are not subject to [the danger of] pairs. 'Ulla is consistent with his view, for 'Ulla said, while others maintain, It was taught in a Baraitha: The Sages instituted ten cups in a mourner's house. Now if you should think that ten cups are subject to [the danger of] pairs, how could our Rabbis arise and enact a regulation whereby one is led into danger! But eight are subject to 'pairs.' R. Ḥisda and Rabbah son of R. Huna both maintained: *'Shalom'* [peace] combines [with others] for good, but does not combine for evil;[3] but six is subject to 'pairs'. Rabbah and R. Joseph both maintained: *Wiyḥuneka* ['and be gracious unto thee'] combines [with others] for good, but does not combine for evil;[4] but four is subject to 'pairs.' Abaye and Raba both maintained: *We-yishmereka* ['and keep thee'] combines [with others] for good, but does not combine for evil.[5] Now Raba is consistent with his view, for Raba allowed the Rabbis to depart [from his house] after four cups, [and] though Raba b. Liwai[6] came to harm, he paid no heed to the matter, saying, 'That was [his punishment] because he raises difficulties at the public session.'[7]

R. Joseph said: The demon Joseph told me [that] Ashmedai the king of the demons is appointed over all 'pairs,'[8] and a king is not designated a harmful spirit.[9] Others explain it in the opposite sense: On the contrary, a king is quick-tempered [and] does whatever he wishes, for a king can break through a wall to make
b a pathway for himself and none may stay him.[1]

R. Papa said, Joseph the demon told me: For two we kill; for four we do not kill, [but] for four we harm [the drinker]. For two [we hurt] whether [they are drunk] unwittingly or deliberately; for four, only if it is deliberate, but not if it is unwitting. And if a man forgot himself and happened to go out,[2] what is his remedy? Let him take his right-hand thumb in his left hand and his left-hand thumb in his right hand and say thus: 'Ye [two thumbs] and I, surely that is three!'[3] But if he hears one saying, 'Ye and I, surely that is four!' let him retort to him, 'Ye and I are surely five!' And if he hears one saying, 'Ye and I are six,' let him retort to him, 'Ye and I are seven.'[4] This once happened until a hundred and one, and the demon burst [with mortification].

Amemar said: The chief of the sorceresses told me: He who meets sorceresses should say thus: 'Hot dung in perforated baskets for your mouths, o ye witches! may your heads become bald,[5]

(6) Hence they do not combine. (7) The second is occasioned by a new desire, and does not combine with the first. (8) Through intimacy. (9) Since eating or drinking in pairs has already made him more susceptible to hurt than he would otherwise have been. (10) I.e., if he does not go out between the drinks. (11) That pairs is harmful. (12) At each cup he mentally counted one beam, to ensure not drinking in pairs. (13) Likewise that he should not drink in pairs.

a (1) Though in all these cases they were remaining at home. (2) The demons are at greater pains to hurt him; hence he is endangered even when staying at home. (3) *'Shalom'* (peace) is the seventh word (in Heb.) of the verse *The Lord lift up His countenance upon thee, and give thee peace* (Num. VI, 26). Hence the seventh cup combines with others for good etc. as on 109*b*, n. a5. (4) *Wiyḥuneka* is the fifth Hebrew word of the verse, *The Lord make His face to shine upon thee, and be gracious unto thee* (ibid. 25). (5) This is the third word of the verse, *The Lord bless thee, and keep thee* (ibid. 24). (6) Or, the Levite. (7) He would raise difficulties in the course of my public lectures, thereby putting me to shame. (8) Those who drink in pairs are at his mercy. (9) It is beneath his dignity to cause hurt. Hence there is generally no danger in pairs (though occasionally he may disregard his dignity—Rashbam).

b (1) Hence the danger is all the greater. (2) After drinking 'pairs.' (3) Thus breaking the spell of pairs. (4) And so on. (5) Lit., 'bald be your baldness'—they practised witchcraft with their hair.

[109b] A square cubit by three cubits' depth, and the Sages estimated the standard of the water of a *miḳweh* at forty *se'ahs*.[7]

R. Ashi said: Rabin b. Ḥinena told me, The Table in the Sanctuary was jointed.[8] For if you should think that it was [permanently] fastened, how could one immerse a cubit in a cubit?[9] What difficulty is this! Perhaps it was immersed in the sea which Solomon made. For R. Ḥiyya taught: The sea which Solomon made held one hundred and fifty clean [i.e., regulation-sized] *miḳwoth*.

AND THEY SHOULD GIVE HIM NOT LESS THAN FOUR [CUPS]. How could our Rabbis enact something whereby one is led into danger: surely it was taught: A man must not eat in pairs, nor
a drink in pairs,[1] nor cleanse [himself] twice nor perform his requirements[2] twice?—Said R. Naḥman: Scripture saith, [*It is*] *a night of guarding* [*unto the Lord*]:[3] [i.e.,] it is a night that is guarded for all time[4] from harmful spirits. Raba said: The cup of Grace [after meals] combines [with the others] for good, but does not combine for evil.[5] Rabina said: Our Rabbis instituted four cups as sym-

(7) 1 *se'ah* = 6 *ḳabs*; 1 *ḳab* = 4 *logs*; 1 *log* = 4 *rebi'ith*; 1 cubit = 6 handbreadths; 1 handbreadth = 4 fingerbreadths. On this basis R. Ḥisda arrives at his estimate. [Thus: 1 *se'ah* = 96 *rebi'ith*; 40 *se'ahs* = 96×40 = 3840 *rebi'ith*. Hence cubic capacity of *miḳweh* is 3840 × 10·8 = 41472 fingerbreadths which is the equivalent of cubic capacity of 3 cubic cubits, 1 cubic cubit being equal to 24^3 (= 13824 fingerbreadths), and 3 cubic cubits being equal to 3 × 13824 = 41472]. (8) And the joints could be taken apart. (9) The Table was a cubit square, while a *miḳweh*, as stated here, was likewise a cubit square; hence it would be impossible to immerse the Table in the *miḳweh* if it became unclean and needed a ritual bath.

a (1) I.e., he must not eat or drink two or a multiple of two of anything, a malignant potency being ascribed to twos. (2) A euphemism for intimacy. (3) Ex. XII, 42. (4) Lit., 'that is guarded and comes on.' (5) The third cup, which is drunk in connection with Grace after meals, combines with others to break the spell of evil which might be caused by drinking the first two, but is not counted in the four for harm.

סג א טור א"ח סימן תפו וש"ע סימן תפא סעי' ב בהגה"ה

אמה על אמה ברום שלש אמות ושיערו חכמים שיעור מי מקוה ארבעים סאה אמר רב אשי אמר לי רבין בר חיננא שולחן של מקדש של פרקים הוה דאי ס"ד הדוקי הוה מיהדק אמתא באמתא היכי מטבליה מאי קושיא דילמא בים שעשה שלמה הוה מטביל ליה *דתני ר' חייא ים שעשה שלמה מחזיק מאה וחמשים מקוה טהרה: ולא יפחתו לו מארבעה: היכי מתקני רבנן מידי דאתי בה לידי סכנה והתניא לא יאכל אדם תרי ולא ישתה תרי ולא יקנח תרי ולא יעשה צרכיו תרי אמר רב נחמן אמר קרא *°ליל שמורים *ליל המשומר ובא מן המזיקין רבא אמר כוס של ברכה מצטרף לטובה ואינו מצטרף לרעה רבינא אמר ארבעה כסי תקינו רבנן דרך חירות כל חד וחד מצוה

תורה אור: שמות יב

עירובין יח: | [ר"ס יא:]

תוספות

הנשאר בגובה שהוא אחד מכ"ד ישאר שיעור הירושלמי יתר בדבר מועט ולחומרא לא דק ועוד מפרש דבירושלמי איירי בעגולות שיוכל לרבע אצבעים על אצבעים מתוכם דהוי תילתא טפי כדאמר ריבועא מגו עיגולא פלגא פירוש פלגא של ריבוע הפנימי וכשתסיר שליש מגובה שהם י"ג חומשין וחצי ישארו ט' חומשין שהם אצבעים חסר חומש והתם נקט חסר שתות נקט כפי הירושלמי והירושלמי לא דק לחומרא והא דיסד הפייט (שם) לריבוע כוס ישועות לא שהוא מרובע אלא קאמר שאותו רביעית מוכן לד' כוסות של פסח שניתקנו כנגד גאולה וישועה: **אמה** על אמה. אדם מחזיק עם בגדיו אמה באמה כדאמרי' בעירובין* מקומו של אדם אמה ובשמעתא דכוכין (ב"ב דף קא.) משמע דכוך מחזיק אמה עם דופני הארון אלמא גוף האדם אין מחזיק אמה ובמקוה דבעינן אמה כדי שיכנס בריוח עם זרועותיו דאין נדבקין לגופו*: **ברום** שלש אמות. ואע"ג דקומת אדם שלש אמות בלא הראש ולכך מצריך בכוכין ארבע אמות בשביל הראש ועובי הדפין במקוה סגי בשלש אמות דכשטובל עולין המים למעלה ומיירי כשהכלי גבוה משלש אמות דאם לא כן כשיכנס יפלו המים למטה ויחסר השיעור ובתרגום (בני פ"ע) דמגילה דהשיב שלש אמות לכל א' קטועי ראש היו*: **אמתא** באמתא היכי יתיב. *וא"ת אפילו אי אמתא באמתא יתיב תיקשי ליה היאך יכול להטביל השלחן אמתים ארכו ואמה רחבו ואמה וחצי קומתו במקוה דהוי אמה על אמה וי"ל שעם הרגלים היתה קומתו אמה וחצי והרגלים לא היו מחוברין עם השלחן וכן פירש רש"י בפרשת תרומה: **בים** שעשה שלמה. ובירושלמי פריך והלא שאובין הן ואע"ג דכלי שמחזיק מ' סאה בלח שהן כורים ביבש אינו מקבל טומאה דאין מיטלטל מלא וריקן לענין שאיבה כלי הוא כדאמר בי"ח דבר (שבת דף יז:) גבי המניח כלים תחת הצינור כו' ועוד ים שעשה שלמה היה של נחושת ומקבל טומאה אע"ג דאין מיטלטל מלא וריקן דדוקא כלי עץ איתקש לשק ומשני תיפתר בשהיו רגלי השוורים שהיה עומד עליו נקובים כמוציא רמון והיו מחוברין למעיין בתחתיהן והא דנקט כמוציא רמון היינו לבטל השוורים מתורת כלי שלא יקבל טומאה אבל להכשיר המים בכונס סגי כשפופרת הנוד כדתנן בפ"ו דמקואות (משנה ה) ומטבילין בשידה תיבה ומגדל שהן נקובין כשפופרת הנוד ומורי הר"ר יחיאל פי' דצריך כאן כמוציא רמון לפי שהשוורים מפסיקין בין הים למעיין והוה ליה כצורך מקום אבל כלי כיון דמרחקי טובא וצריך שיבואו שם מים בשפע והביא ראיה מתוספתא: **ארבעה** כוסות. ירושלמי תמן תנינן *אין מבשלין יין של תרומה מפני שממעטו ר' יהודה מתיר מפני שמשביחו א"ר יוחנן מיחלפא שיטתיה דרבי יהודה פי' דקתני תורמין יין שלא מבושל על המבושל אבל לא מן המבושל על שאינו מבושל ולכך מחליף ותני אין מבשלין יין של תרומה מפני שממעטו דברי רבי יהודה וחכמים מתירין מפני שמשביחו ורבי לאלעזר פליג עליה התם ולא מחליף והלכה כרבי יוחנן וכרבנן ואם כן יוצאין ארבע כוסות במבושל ומקדשין עליו ומברכין עליו בפה"ג: **רבא** אמר כוס של ברכה אין מצטרף לרעה. אע"ג דרבא גופיה קאמר לקמן ויממרך לרעה לא מצטרף וד' אין בהם משום זוגות תירץ רשב"ם דהיינו דוקא ממזיקין אבל לכשפים איכא למיחש:

[דף מח.] עי' סוכה ז:

[וע"ע תוספות יומא לא. סד"ה אמה]

[וע"ע תוספות שבת לב: ד"ה אשתכח ובעירובין מח: ד"ה גופו וחגיגה יא: ד"ה ברום וביומא לא. ד"ה אמה ובב"ב ק: ד"ה והכוכין]

רשב"ם

אמה על אמה ברום שלש אמות. מחזיקין ארבעים סאה חלקהו תחלה כולו ברומו שלש אמות יש בהן שמונה עשר טפחים חלקם לי"ו חלקים ותמצא לכל חלק וחלק טפח וחצי אצבע ומחזיק אחד מי"ו במ' סאה כמה הן ב' סאין וחצי סאה טפח וחצי אצבע כמה חומשי אצבעות הן עשרים ושנים וחצי חומש(א) הטפח כ' חומשים חצי אצבע ב' חומשין וחצי חלוק כ"ב חומשים וחצי לחמשה חלקים תמצא בכל חלק ד' חומשין וחצי חלוק ב' סאין וחצי סאה לחמשה חלקים תמצא בכל חלק חצי סאה נמצא דארבע חומשין וחצי חומש מחזיק חצי סאה ועוד ד' חומשין וחצי חומש מחזיק חצי סאה [ועוד ד' חומשין וחצי חומש מחזיק חצי סאה] נמצא כל אמה על אמה ברום י"ג חומשין וחצי חומש מחזיק סאה וחצי סאה חשוב סאה וחצי סאה ללוגין תמצא ל"ו לוגין כיצד סאה וחצי סאה תשעה קבין ששה קבים לסאה והקב ד' לוגין הרי ל"ו לוגין בכלי אמה על אמה ברום י"ג חומשים וחצי חומש חלוק הכלי באורך ורוחב לטפחים תמצא האמה על אמה ל"ו טפחים בטפח על טפח שהאמה ו' טפחים וכשתחלקנו לאורכו ברצועות שהן רחבות טפח תמצא בו ו' רצועות כל אחת ואחת רחבה טפח וארכה ששה חלוק כל רצועה לארכה לשש תמצא בשש רצועות ל"ו טפחים בטפח על טפח ומחזיק ל"ו לוגין נמצא כלי שהוא טפח על טפח ברום י"ג חומשים וחצי חומש מחזיק לוג וטפח ארבע אצבעות חלוק ארבע אצבעות על ד' אצבעות שתי וערב לד' נמצא כל רביעית אצבעים על אצבעים נמצא כל אצבעים על אצבעים ברום י"ג חומשים וחצי חומש מחזיק רביעית הלוג חשוב י"ג חומשים וחצי ותמצא בהן אצבעים וחצי אצבע וחומש אצבע: של פרקים הוה. שיכולין לפרוק רחבו לשנים: דאי סלקא דעתך הדוקי מיהדק. שאין יכולין לפרוק רחבו: היכי מצי מטבלי ליה. הואיל ורחבו אמה כבכלי שהוא אמה על אמה: תרי. זוגות: ולא יעשה אדם צרכיו. תשמיש: כוס של ברכת המזון. שהוא (רביעי) לרעה אין מצטרף. אבל בעלמא מצטרף כגון אם שתה שני כוסות והוא שלישי ולרעה אין מצטרף כגון אם שתה שלש והוא רביעי מליה

[שלישי כצ"ל]

רשב"ם

דהיינו אמה על אמה ברום שלש אמות. צריך שיהא הכלי מלא מים שיטבול בו האדם ושיערו חכמים דהיינו ארבעים סאה ומינה ילפינן לרביעית של תורה כיצד חלקהו מתחלה כולו לרומו של מקוה שלש אמות דהיינו שמונה עשר טפחים וחלקם לששה עשר חלקים ותמצא בכל חלק וחלק טפח וחצי אצבע גובה ברוחב אמה על אמה ומחזיק אחד מששה עשר בארבעים סאה דהיינו שני סאין וחצי סאה טפח וחצי אצבע כמה חומשי אצבעות הן עשרים ושנים וחצי חומש מד' אצבעות עשרים חומשין ומחצי אצבע ב' חומשין וחצי חלקם להי כ"ב חומשין וחצי לחמשה חלקים ותמצא בכל חלק וחלק ארבעה חומשין וחצי השלך מהן שני חלקים שהן תשעה חומשין ועכב בידך שלשה חלקים שהן שלשה עשר חומשין וחצי של רום הכלי דהיינו רום הכלי שני אצבעים וחצי אצבע וחומש אצבע וכאשר מיעטת רום הכלי שני חלקים מחמשה ונשארו שלשה חלקים כן תמעיט את המשקין שנשארו בידיו מארבעים סאה שני סאין וחצי דהיינו חמשה חצאין השלך השני חלקים ועכב השלשה חלקים שהן סאה וחצי נמצא כלי של אמה מרובע ברום (ג) [א]אצבע וחצי אצבע וחומש אצבע מחזיק סאה וחצי חלקהו לרחבו אמה על אמה יש בו ששה ושלשים חתיכות של טפח על טפח והסאה וחצי יש להם שלשים וששה לוגין נמצא כלי של טפח על טפח ברום אצבעים וחצי אצבע וחומש אצבע מחזיק לוג דהיינו ארבע רביעיות חלקהו לרוחבו שתי וערב ותמצא בו ארבע פעמים אצבעים על אצבעים כנגד ארבע רביעיות נמצא כלי של אצבעים על אצבעים ברום אצבעים וחצי אצבע וחומש אצבע מחזיק רביעית דהיינו ביצה ומחצה לשון קצר שמעתי מרבי יעקב בר יקר רבו זצ"ל איפה שלש סאין סאה ששה קבין קב ארבע לוגין לוג ששה ביצים דהיינו ארבע רביעיות פירושא דקבלה לא גרסינן כלל עד אמר רב אשי ופירוש הוא מהלכות גדולות של רב יהודאי אמה על אמה יש בה שלשים וששה טפחים בטפח על טפח שהאמה ו' טפחים וכשתחלקנו לאורכו ברצועות שהן רחבות [טפח] תמצא בו ו' [רצועות] כל אחת ואחת רחבה טפח וארכה ו' טפחים ואח"כ חלק כל רצועה לארכה לששה תמצא בה ששה פעמים טפח על טפח וכן לששה רצועות הרי ל"ו טפחים: שולחן של מקדש. שולחן של זהב שעשה משה וכתיב ביה (שמות כה) אמתים ארכו ואמה רחבו ואמה וחצי קומתו: של פרקים הוה. שיכולין לפרק רוחבו לשנים וכן רגלי השלחן אינן מחוברין יפה ויכולין לפרקן: דאי ס"ד הדוקי מיהדק. שאין יכולין לפרק רחבו: היכי מצי מטביל ליה. הואיל ורחבו אמה בכלי שהוא אמה על אמה דמקוה היה שם בעזרה כדאי' בסדר יומא (ד' לא.) א"נ באמת המים שבעזרה שבה מטבילין כלי שרת שנטמאו והיתה רחבה אמה ועל שם כך נקראת אמה כדתנן (יומא דף נה:) אלו ואלו מתערבין באמה ולשון ראשון לשון רבינו יעקב מדאמר רב אשי למלתיה גבי מקוה: השלחן מקבל טומאה כדאמרינן בחומר בקודש (חגיגה ד' כו:) דאמר ר"ל מאי דכתיב השלחן הטהור מכלל שהוא טמא: מחזיק מאה וחמשים מקוה טהרה. במס' עירובין מפרש מנא לן: מי מתקני. ארבע כוסות שהן זוגות דאתי בהו לידי סכנה דאפילו למ"ד לקמן דארבעה אין בו משום זוגות אלא בתרי לענין כשפים מיהא חיישינן לקמן בשמעתין: תרי. זוגות וה"ה לארבעה: צרכיו. תשמיש: רבא אמר כוס של בהמ"ז. שהוא שלישי לרעה אינו מצטרף להשלים זוגות לסכנה אם שותה רביעי אחריו וכי האי גוונא אמרי' לקמן ויממרך לרעה אינו מצטרף:

רבינו חננאל

בהן וכמה הן אמה על אמה ברום שלש שיערו חכמי' מי מקוה ארבעים סאה פי' רביעית של תורה ביצה ומחצה כי הלוג הוא ששה ביצים רביעית היא ביצה ומחצה ותנן לוג וחצי לוג ורביעית אלמא רביעית רביע לוג הוא הין הוא שנים עשר לוג שנאמר שמן משחת קדש יהיה זה לי זה בגימט' י"ב (הוא) נמצא שיעור ההין י"ב לוג והן מ"ח רביעיות שהן ע"ב ביצים ושיעור הקב ארבעת לוגין שהן ט"ז רביעיות כדתנן הלל אומר מלא הין מים שאובין פוסלין את המקוה וכמה שיעור ההין שנים עשר לוג ב"ש אומר תשעת קבין שהן ל"ו לוג אלמא קב ארבעת לוגין היא שיעור הסאה ששת קבין שהן שני הינין שהן כ"ד לוג שהן צ"ו רביעיות שהן קמ"ד ביצים איפה שלשת סאין שהן י"ח קבין שהן (ד') [וי"ו] הינין שהן (ר"צ) [ע"ב] לוגין שהן רפ"ח רביעיות שהן תל"ב ביצים שיעור חלה (מעשירית) [הוא עשירית] האיפה (ועוטר) *זה הוא מ"ג ביצים וחומש ביצה וכן שיעור חלת מצה בפסח: רביעית של תורה אצבעים על אצבעים ברום אצבעים וחצי אצבע [וחומש אצבע] ובגידל שהן בתבריתא י"א אצבעות חסר חומש אצבע באצבע רוחב ובאצבע רום מי מקוה אמה על אמה ברום שלש שיעורם הכמים ארבעים סאה וכל סאה ששת קבין וכל קב ארבע לוגין וכל לוג ארבע רביעיות נמצא שיעור המקוה תתק"ם לוג ג' אלפים תת"מ רביעיות והאמה ו' טפחים וכל טפח ד' אצבעות בגודל כשתחלוק מ' סאה לג' אמות נמצא בכל אמה על אמה ברום [אמה] י"ג סאין ושליש סאה ונמצא באמה על אמה ברום טפח שהוא ששות אמה סאתים וחמשת לוגין ושליש לוג נמצא על זה החשבון באמה על אמה ברום אצבע שהוא רובע טפח י"ב לוג ושליש ונמצאו באמה על אמה ברום (אצבע) [אמה] י"ג אלף (ותתכ"ד) [ותתכ"ד] אצבע נמצאו (בד') [בג'] אמות אחד ומ' אלף אצבע ותע"ב אצבעות באצבע [אורך ובאצבע] רוחב ורום אצבע וכשתחשוב מ' סאה שיעור המקוה בכל סאה צ"ו רביעיות כמו שבארנוהו למעלה נמצאו ג' אלפים תת"מ רביעיות שיעור המקוה עוד חשוב כ"ד אורך בי"ב רוחב וקב ושני שלישי קב בו' רוחב קב חסר שתות שהוא ג' רביעיות הקב ושליש (כ"ג) [בג'] רוחב רביע הקב ושני שלישי רביע שהן עשר ביצים ברוחב אצבע שלש ביצים ושליש ביצה עד כאן מדת הרוחב מכאן ואילך מדת האורך י"ב אצבע אורך באצבע רוחב וברום אצבע ביצה ושני שלישי ביצה נמצאו ביצה ושני שלישיה [שהן] עשרה שתותי ביצה (נשאר) [מחזיק] י"ב אצבעות אורך ברום אצבע ורוחב אצבע כשתחלוק אלו י"ב אצבעות לי' שתותיהן מגיע לכל שתות אצבע וחומש אצבע הוצא מהן אצבע וחומש לשתות הא' נשתיירו י"א אצבעות חסר חומש אצבע לט' שתותיהן שהן ביצה ומחצה שהיא רביעית של תורה עוד דרך אחרת כשתחלוק קמ"א אלף אצבע ותע"ב אצבעות לג' אלפים ותת"מ רביעיות [יגיע] י"א אצבעות פחות חומש לכל רביעית נמצאים בכל רביע י"א אצבע חסר חומש אצבע: **תאני** ר"ח ים שעשה שלמה מחזיק ק"נ מקוה טהרה' כבר פרשנוהו בעירובין במקומו פי' מבואר: **לא** יפחתו לו כו' אפשר מתקני רבנן מילתא דאית בה סכנה והתניא לא יאכל תרי ולא ישתה תרי ולא יעשה צרכיו תרי ופרקי' ליל שמורים המשומר מכל היזק רבא אמר כוס של ברכה מצטרף לטובה ולא לרעה וכשתסיר כוס של ברכה נשתיירו

* נראה דצ"ל כמו העומר והוא מ"ג ביצים

הגהות הב"ח

(א) רש"י ד"ה אמה וכו' וחצי חומש כ' הטפח כו': (ב) רשב"ם ד"ה דהיינו אמה וכו' נמצא כלי של אמה מרובע ברום אצבעים וחצי:

גליון הש"ס

תוס' ד"ה וא"ת אפילו אי אמתא. עיין בספר ברית שלום על התורה פ' תרומה בפסוק ועשית שלחן:

הגהות מהר"ב רנשבורג

[א] רשב"ם ד"ה דהיינו וכו' ברום אצבע. נ"ל אצבעים:

תורה אור

קליות ואגוזין בערב פסח כדי שלא ישנו וישאלו אמרו עליו על רבי *עקיבא שהיה מחלק קליות ואגוזין לתינוקות בערב פסח כדי שלא ישנו וישאלו תניא רבי אליעזר אומר *חוטפין (א)מצות בלילי פסחים בשביל תינוקות *שלא ישנו (ב)תניא *אמרו עליו על ר' עקיבא מימיו לא אמר הגיע עת לעמוד בבהמ"ד *חוץ מערבי פסחים *וערב יום הכפורים בע"פ בשביל תינוקות כדי שלא ישנו וערב יוה"כ כדי שיאכילו את בניהם ת"ר *חייב אדם לשמח בניו ובני ביתו ברגל שנא' *ושמחת בחגך (דברים טז) במה משמחם ביין רבי יהודה אומר אנשים בראוי להם ונשים בראוי להן אנשים בראוי להם ביין ונשים במאי תני רב יוסף בבבל בבגדי צבעונין בארץ ישראל בבגדי פשתן מגוהצין תניא רבי יהודה בן בתירא אומר בזמן שבית המקדש קיים אין שמחה אלא בבשר שנאמר °וזבחת שלמים ואכלת (דברים כז) שם ושמחת לפני ה' אלהיך ועכשיו שאין בית המקדש קיים *אין שמחה אלא ביין שנאמר °ויין ישמח לבב אנוש (תהלים קד) אמר רבי יצחק *קסתא דמוריסא דהוה בציפורי היא הות כמין לוגא דמקדשא ובה משערין רביעית של פסח אמר רבי יוחנן תמנייתא קדמייתא דהוה בטבריא הות יתירה על דא ריבעא ובה משערין רביעית של פסח א"ר חסדא רביעית של תורה אצבעים על אצבעים ברום אצבעים וחצי אצבע וחומש אצבע *כדתניא °ורחץ (ויקרא טו) במים את כל בשרו *שלא יהא דבר חוצץ בין בשרו למים *במים במי מקוה את כל בשרו מים שבכל גופו עולה בהן וכמה הן אמה

ס"א ר' טרפון | ס"א כדי שישאלו | [תוספתא יומא פ"ד] | ושמחת אתה וביתך במה משמחם רש"א | [גי' הערוך קיסטא] | ס"א בכרברבתא עירובין ד: יד: יומא לא. חגיגה יא. סוכה ו:

קליות. קלי מחטים יבשים: חוטפין מצה. מגביהין את הקערה בשביל תינוקות שישאלו ואית דמפרש חוטפין מצה אוכלין מהר וזה הלשון עיקר מדמייתי הא דר"ע בהדה: חוץ מערבי פסחים. כדי שישנו התינוקות, ביום ולא בלילה בשעת הגדה: קסתא דמוריסא. מדה שמוכרין בה את המוריים: תמנתא קדמיתא. מדה שהיתה בה בכבר בטבריא: הות יתירה. על תמנתא דהשתא רביעית: ובה משערין רביעית לפסח. שהיו ממלאין אותה ומערין אותה לתוך אותה של עכשיו עד שהיא מליאה ומים הנשארים בתמנתא הן הן רביעית: ברום אצבעים. וכרום חצי אצבע וכרום חומש אצבע: בכרברבתא. בגודל שיש בטפח ארבע אצבעות מהן: אמה

רשב"ם

קליות. קלי מחטים יבשים דחדש אסור עדיין בלילה הראשון של פסח ומקומות יש בספרד שמייבשין חטים יבשים במחבת על גבי האור ואוכלין אותם עם אגוזים בקיטת סעודה מפי רבינו שמואל החסיד וגם במשנה מצינו קליות מחטים יבשים וטויה במסכת תרומות (פ"ה משנה ג) אגב גררא דתנן סאה תרומה טהורה שנפלה לפחות ממאה חולין טמאין תירוס ותיפרך רבי אליעזר אומר תעלה [א] ותאכל נקודים או קליות או תלוש במי פירות: חוטפין מצה. מגביהין את הקערה בשביל תינוקות שישאלו ואית דמפרשי חוטפין מצה אוכלין מהר שני לשונות הללו פירש רבינו ויש גורסין מצות מגביהין את הקערה שיש בה מצה ומרור וב' תבשילין ולי נראה חוטפין מסלקין את הלחם מיד התינוקות שלא יהו ישנים מתוך מאכל הרבה כדרך התינוק אחר אכילתו ושוב לא ישאלו אבל עכשיו כשחוטפים מהן לא ישנו וישאלו כלומר לא ישנו שלא אכלו כדי שבען וישאלו כשיראו השינויים שאנו עושין היכירא לתינוקות כדלקמן וכן מוכח לשון התוספתא דתניא רבי אליעזר אומר חוטפין מצה לתינוק כדי שלא יישן רבי יהודה אומר משמו אפילו לא אכל אלא חזרת אחת ולא טיבל אלא פרפרת אחת חוטפין מצה לתינוק כדי שלא יישן כלומר גוזלין ורבינו פי' שכן עיקר אותו הלשון שפירשתי חוטפין ממהרין לאכול מדקתני הא דר"ע בתרה ואיכא למימר דאגב גררא דקאמר כדי שלא יישן קא מייתי נמי להא עובדא דר' עקיבא דחייש שלא ישנו ותרי מילי נינהו רבי אליעזר איירי לחטוף מן התינוקות אחר שאכלו מעט כדי שלא יישנו ור"ע איירי שצריך למהר לעשות הסדר טרם יישנו: חוץ מערבי פסחים. כדי שייטנו את התינוקות ביום ולא בלילה בשעת הגדה א"נ כשמעכבין עד הלילה לאחר שהחשיך ישנים התינוקות: אנשים בראוי להם ביין. גמ' קאמר לה: קסתא דמוריסא. מדה שמוכרין בה המוריים: ובה משערין רביעית של פסח. שממלאין אותה ומחלקין אותה לארבע כוסות לרבע רביעיות: תמניתא. מדה והיינו תומן ועוכלא דמסכת סוטה (דף ו:): הות יתירה על דא. תמניתא: ובה משערין רביעית של פסח. שהיו ממלאין אותה ומערין לתוך אותה של עכשיו עד שהיא מלאה ומים הנשארים בתומניתא היא רביעית: רביעית [רביעית] של תורה. כגון רביעית יין של נזיר הלכה למשה מסיני (סוכה דף ו') ורביעית דם הבאה משני מתים דנפקא לן מקרא (נזיר דף לח:) וכגון רביעית שמן לרקיקי נזיר דהיכא דיליף לה מקראי במנחות (דף פט) ומדת חלל הכלי בריבוע הוי אצבעים אורך על אצבעים רוחב ברום אצבעים וחצי אצבע וחומש אצבע ומנא לן מקוה: כדתניא ורחץ במים את כל בשרו במי מקוה· מים המיוחדים שנקוו מתחלה מעצמן מדלא כתב במים למעוטי שאובין דחזיל השתא ומייתי וטבל: כל בשרו. מדלא כתב בשרו משמע שכל גופו עולה בהן שאינו נראה אלא סולו מכוסה בהן: דהיינו

תוספות

חוץ מערבי פסחים. ה"ג רביט שמואל ולא נהירא דאטו לא יוכלו ליטן בלא אביהם וטעם שני שפירש שמא יעכבו עד שיחשך הרבה אם כן לא היו צריכין לעמוד ביום כי אם בלילה לכך נראה דגרים לילי פסחים והיו רגילין בבית המדרש לילי י"ט כדאמרינן (ביצה דף כא:) מעשה בשמעון התימני שלא בא בלילי י"ט לבית המדרש למחר מלאו רבי יהודה בן בבא: שנאמר ושמחת אתה וביתך. תימה דהאי קרא גבי מעשר שני כתיב בפ' ראה ולא מייתי קרא דכתיב בפ' ראה גבי רגל ושמחת אתה ובנך ובתך וי"ל דיליף ממעשר דכתיב ביתו בהדיא: בא"י בכלי פשתן המגוהצין. אבל בבבל לא היו בקיאים לגהץ כדאמר (תענית כט:) גיהוץ שלנו ככיבוס שלהם: במה משמחו ביין. היינו בזמן הזה אבל בזמן בית המקדש אין שמחה אלא בבשר: וזבחת שלמים ואכלת שם ושמחת. תימה דהאי קרא בהר עיבל כתיב ולא מייתי קרא דושמחת בחגך דדרשינן מיניה בחגיגה (דף ח) לרבות כל מיני שמחות לשמחה מכאן אמרו ישראל יוצאין ידי חובתן בנדרים ונדבות וי"ל משום דהכא בהדיא כתיב וזבחת שלמים ושמחת: תמניתא. פי' רשב"ם דהיינו תומן ועוכלא ולא נהירא דבהמוכר את הספינה (ב"ב דף צ.) חשיב לוג ורביעית הלוג תומן ועוכלא וכל מדה ומדה פוחתת והולכת וכאן משמע שהיא יותר מרביעית: רביעית של תורה אצבעים. מכאן קשה על פירוש רבותיו של רבינו שלמה שפי' דרביעית בכל מקום היינו רובע הקב כי לפי זה החשבון הוא רביעית הלוג פר"ת רום המקוה ע"ב אצבעות השלך רביעית ישאר כ"ד קח מכל עשרים אחד יעלה אצבעים וחצי אצבע וחומש וכן תקח ברוחב אחד מי"ב וכן באורך הרי אצבעים על אצבעים ברום אצבעים וחצי אצבע וחומש אצבע וכן תעשה במים ויעלה רביעית (ב) רביעית הגמלא השלך החולה ומן הנותרים קח אחד מעשרים ופעמים יוסר חלק שנים עשר או תקח אחד מכ"ד והם ג' אצבעות חלק על חומשין והשלך העשירית ישארו שלשה עשר חומשין והם ב' אצבעים וחצי וחומש אצבע או קח רביעית והם י"ח אצבעים והשלך הרביעי ישארו י"ג אצבעות וחצי וטול החמישית (ג) מהר"י. קחה רובע וככה תשלך וחלק החמישי קח ולך או השלך עשירית המים ישארו ל"ו יעלה ב' סאין לכל טפח ולג' אצבעות סאה וחצי השלך מג' אצבעות העשירית כאשר השלכנו מן המים(ד). ולפי תלמוד שלנו החשבון מכוון אבל על גירסת ירושלמי דקאמר אצבעים על אצבעים ברום אצבע ומחצה ושליש אצבע וכן עשה הפייט ועל גובה חסר שתות מאצבעים והכל א' קשה כי לפי שיעור המקוה אינו מכוון וי"ל דבירושלמי איירי באצבעות צפוריית והכא במדבריית והאצבעים וחצי וחומש הם י"ג שתותים וחומש שתות באו לירושלים נכנס הכל בי"ג שתותים וחצי באו לצפורי נכנס הכל בי"א שתותים ורביע שתות שהם אצבעים חסר שתות ונשאר רביע שתות בתלמוד שלנו יתר וכמו כן צריך למעט מרובע כי בתלמוד שלנו מיירי במרובעות וירושל' בעגולות כמו שיסד *הפייט הכוס סובב אצבעים על אצבעים סובב משמע עגול ואצבעים על אצבעים עגולות עולה לאצבעים על [אצבע] וחצי דמרובע יתר על העיגול רביע ואצבעים על אצבעים מרובעות מחזיקות יותר מכוסות באצבעות על אצבעים עגולות לפיריות ויש בעגולות יותר ד'שתותי שתות שהוא אחד מתשעה הסר ממנו רביע שתות הנשאר

(פיוט גשם)

עין משפט נר מצוה

נט א ב מיי' פ"ז מהל' מצה הלכה ג סמג עשין מא טוש"ע א"ח סי' תעב סעיף א:

ס ג מיי' פ"ו מהל' י"ט הל' יז סמג לאוין עה טוש"ע א"ח סימן תקכ"ט ס"ב:

סא ד מיי' פי"א מהל' איסורי ביאה הלכה טז ופ"א מהל' מקוואות הל' יב סמג לאוין קיא ועשין רמח טור ש"ע י"ד סי' קצח ס"א:

סוכה כתי' ע"ש דניתא רבי עקיבא

סב ה מיי' פי"א מהל' א"ב שם ופ"ד מהל' מקוואות הלכה א סמג שם טוש"ע י"ד סי' רא סעיף א:

רבינו חננאל

מחלק לתינוקות קליות ואגוזים כדי שישאלו וכן היה רבי טרפון עושה: תניא רבי אליעזר הגדול אומר חוטפין מצה בלילי הפסח בשביל התינוקות שלא ישנו וישאלו אמרו על רבי עקיבא מימיו לא אמר הגיע זמן לעמוד מבית המדרש אלא לילי הפסח בשביל התינוקות שלא ישנו וערב יוה"כ כדי להאכיל בניו ובני ביתו: ת"ר חייב אדם לשמח ביתו ברגל רבי יהודה אומר שמחת אנשים ביין ושמחת הנשים בבבל בבגדי צבעונין ושבארץ ישראל בבגדי פשתן מגוהצין בזמן שבית המקדש קיים אין שמחה אלא בבשר ועכשיו אין שמחה אלא ביין שנאמר ויין ישמח לבב אנוש: א"ר חסדא רביעית של תורה אצבעים על אצבעים ברום [אצבעים] וחצי אצבע [וחומש אצבע] ובגודל כדתניא ורחץ במים את כל בשרו במים מי מקוה את כל בשרו מים שכל בשרו עולה

גליון הש"ס

גמרא אין שמחה אלא ביין. עי' ב"י א"ח סימן תקכ"ט ובש"ס פ"ב דביצה:

הגהות הב"ח

(א) גמרא חוטפין מצה בלילי פסחים בשביל תינוקות (שלא ישנו) תא"מ · וכ"כ לפי' קמא דרש"י לא גרסינן ליה: (ב) תוס' ד"ה רביעית וכו' וכן תעשה במים ויעלה רביעית הלוג כיצד רביעית הגמלא השלך החולה ומן הנותרים קח אחד מעשרים ופעמים יוסר נ"ב פי' א' מעשרים שהוא סאה ומחצה ואח"כ יוסר שתי פעמים חלק י"ב כיצד מסאה ומחצה ג' לוגין שהוא חלק י"ב מל"ו לוג ואח"כ חלק י"ב מג' לוגין היא רביעית הלוג: (ג) בא"ד וטול החמישית וכן תעשה במים קח הרובע וככה תשלך כצ"ל ותיבת מהר"י נמחק: (ד) בא"ד כאשר השלכנו מן המים מהר"י ולפי תלמוד שלנו:

הגהות מהר"ב רנשבורג

[א] רשב"ם ד"ה קליות וכו' ר"א אומר תעלה וכו' נ"ב יש כאן גמגום. ועיין בלשון הרשב"ם כי לשון הזה לא נמצא שם בכל המשניות באותו הפרק וצ"ע להגיהו גם יפלא קצת ראית הרשב"ם משם וזה י"ל בדוחק:

is wine to children? But we distribute to them [109a] parched ears of corn and nuts on the eve of Passover, so that they should not fall asleep, and ask [the 'questions'].[8] It was related of R. Akiba that he used to distribute parched ears and nuts to children on the eve of Passover, so that they might not fall asleep but ask [the 'questions'].

a It was taught, R. Eliezer said: The *mazzoth* are eaten hastily[1] on the night of Passover, on account of the children, so that they should not fall asleep.[2] It was taught: It was related of R. Akiba[3] [that] never did he say in the Beth Hamidrash, 'It is time to rise [cease study]', except on the eve of Passover and the eve of the Day of Atonement. On the eve of Passover, because of the children, so that they might not fall asleep. On the eve of the Day of Atonement, in order that they should give food to their children.

Our Rabbis taught: A man is in duty bound to make his children and his household rejoice on a Festival, for it is said, *And thou shalt rejoice in thy feast, [thou and thy son, and thy daughter, etc.]*[4] Wherewith does he make them rejoice? With wine. R. Judah said: Men with what is suitable for them, and women with what is suitable for them. 'Men with what is suitable for them': with wine. And women with what? R. Joseph recited: In Babylonia, with coloured garments; in Eretz Yisrael, with ironed linen garments.

It was taught, R. Judah b. Bathyra said: When the Temple was in existence there could be no rejoicing save with meat, as it is said, *And thou shalt sacrifice peace-offerings, and shalt eat there; and thou shalt rejoice before the Lord thy God.*[5] But now that the Temple is no longer in existence, there is no rejoicing save with wine, as it is said, *and wine that maketh glad the heart of man.*[6]

b R. Isaac said: The *xestes*[1] for *muries* in Sepphoris was about equal to the Temple *log*, and thereby we gauge the *rebi'ith* of [wine for] Passover.[2] R. Johanan said: The ancient *tomanta* which was in Tiberias exceeded this by a quarter, and thereby we gauge the *rebi'ith* of [wine for] Passover. R. Ḥisda said: The *rebi'ith* of the Torah[3] is [the cubic content of a vessel] two fingerbreadths square by two and seven-tenths[4] fingerbreadths in depth.[5] As it was taught: *Then he shall bathe all his flesh in water:*[6] [this intimates] that nothing must interpose between his flesh and the water; *'in water'* [means] in the water of a *mikweh; 'all his flesh'* [implies sufficient] water for his whole body to be covered therein. And how much is that?

(8) V. *infra* 116a Mishnah.

a (1) Others: the plate containing the *mazzoth* is lifted, to draw the attention of the children to the unusual fare; others, the *mazzoth* are taken away from the children before they have eaten their fill, as a heavy meal conduces to sleep. (2) Var. lec.: so that they should ask 'questions'. This agrees with the first alternative translation in the preceding note. R. Ḥan. reads both: so that they should not fall asleep but ask. (3) In Suk. 28a this is attributed to R. Johanan b. Zakkai. (4) Deut. XVI, 14. Presumably the proof lies in the bracketed passage, which is absent in the text. Possibly too he reads: *we-simmakta* (*pi'el*) and thou shalt cause to rejoice' instead of *we-samakta* 'and thou shalt rejoice. Tosaf.'s reading, however, and Maharsha emends text accordingly, is: *and thou shalt rejoice, thou and thy household* (ib. XIV 26). This refers to the eating of the second tithe in Jerusalem, and its teaching is applied here to Festivals. (5) Deut. XXVII, 7. (6) Ps. CIV, 15.

b (1) A measure kept as a standard; it was somewhat less than a pint. (2) Required for the four cups. (3) In respect to several Biblical laws a *rebi'ith* is specified by the Rabbis. (4) Lit., 'two and a half and a fifth.' (5) Hence the volume of a *rebi'ith* is $2 \times 2 \times 2{\cdot}7 = 10{\cdot}8$ cubic fingerbreadths. (6) Lev. XV, 16.

four cups, [108b] because they too were included in that miracle.[6]

Rab Judah said in Samuel's name: These four cups must contain sufficient for the mixing of a generous cup.[7] If he drank them raw [undiluted], he has discharged [his duty].[8] If he drank them [all] at once,[9] he has discharged [his duty]. If he gave his sons
a and household to drink of them,[1] he has discharged [his duty].

'If he drank them raw [undiluted], he has discharged [his duty].' Raba observed: He has discharged [his duty] of wine, but he has not discharged [his duty] of [symbolizing his] freedom.[2] If he drank them [all] at once, Rab said:[3] He has discharged [his duty of drinking] wine,[4] [but] he has not discharged [his duty of] four cups.[5] 'If he gave his sons and household to drink of them, he has discharged [his duty]': Said R. Naḥman b. Isaac: Providing that he [himself] drank the greater part of [each] cup.

An objection is raised: These four cups must contain the standard of a *rebi'ith*, whether neat or diluted, whether new [wine] or old; R. Judah said: It must possess the taste and the appearance of wine. Thus it is incidentally taught, 'the standard of a *rebi'ith*,' whereas you say, 'a generous cup'?—I will answer you: Both are the same standard, [for] what does he mean by 'sufficient for the mixing of a generous cup'? For each one separately [of the four cups], which is a *rebi'ith* for all of them together.[6]

'R. Judah said: It must possess the taste and appearance of wine.' Said Raba, What is R. Judah's reason? Because it is written, *Look not thou upon the wine when it is red.*[7]

Our Rabbis taught: All are bound to [drink] the four cups, men, women, and children. Said R. Judah: Of what benefit then

(6) Of liberation; v. Soṭ. 11b, where it is stated that the Israelites were redeemed as a reward to the righteous women of that generation. (7) Their wine was too strong to be drunk neat. 'A generous cup' is one of sufficient quantity for Grace, viz., a *rebi'ith* (quarter of a *log*), and Rab Judah said that each of these four cups must contain enough undiluted wine to make up to a *rebi'ith* of diluted wine.—The usual mixture was one part wine to three parts water. (8) Providing that he drank a *rebi'ith* on each occasion (Rashbam). (9) Without following the order prescribed *infra* 114a and 116a-b.

a (1) Possibly separate cups were not set for each member of the household, as is done nowadays; v. *supra* 99b Tosaf. s.v. לא יפחתו לו מארבע כוסות (2) I.e., he has discharged his duty in a poor way, since drinking undiluted wine is hardly drinking at all.—This does not refer to wine nowadays, which is not so strong and does not require dilution. (3) Alfasi and Asheri omit: Rab said. (4) V. *infra* 109: a man must rejoice on a Festival by drinking wine; this duty he has now discharged. (5) But all count as one cup, and another three are necessary. (6) I.e., a *rebi'ith* of the raw wine, which when diluted will make four *rebi'ith* of drinkable wine, a *rebi'ith* for each cup. (7) Prov. XXIII, 31. Thus it does not merit the name wine unless it has its appearance too.

עין משפט
נר מצוה

נה א ב מיי' פ"ז מהל' מלה הלכה ט סמג עשין מ"א [טור או"ח סימן תעב]:

נו ג ד מיי' וסמג שם טוש"ע או"ח סי' תעב סעיף ח

[שבת כג: מגילה ד. ערכין ג.]

נז ה שם סעיף טו :

נח ו מיי' שם הלכה ג' טוש"ע שם סעיף טז:

[ועיין תוספות מגילה ד: ד"ה שאף הן]

ערך עשר

[ועי' תוספות ברכות נ: ד"ה מודים וכו']

*שאף הן היו באותו הנס *א"ר יהודה אמר שמואל ארבעה כוסות הללו צריך שיהא בהן כדי מזיגת כוס יפה שתאן חי יצא שתאן בבת אחת יצא השקה מהן לבניו ולבני ביתו יצא שתאן חי יצא אמר רבא *ידי יין יצא ידי חירות לא יצא שתאן בבת אחת *רב אמר ידי יין יצא ידי ארבעה כוסות לא יצא השקה מהן לבניו ולבני ביתו יצא אמר רב נחמן בר יצחק והוא דאשתי רובא דכסא מיתיבי ד' כוסות הללו צריך שיהא בהן כדי רביעית אחד חי ואחד מזוג אחד חדש ואחד ישן רבי יהודה אומר צריך שיהא בו טעם ומראה יין קתני מיהת כדי רביעית ואת אמרת כוס יפה אמרי אידי ואידי חד שיעורא הוא מאי כדי מזיגת כוס יפה דקאמר לכל חד וחד דהוי להו כולהו רביעית רבי יהודה אומר צריך שיהא בו טעם ומראה אמר רבא מאי טעמא דרבי יהודה דכתיב °אל תרא יין כי יתאדם (משלי כג) ת"ר הכל חייבין בארבעה כוסות הללו אחד אנשים ואחד נשים ואחד תינוקות א"ר יהודה וכי מה תועלת יש לתינוקות ביין אלא מחלקין להן קליות

תוספות

שאף הן היו באותו הנס . ואי לאו האי טעמא לא היו חייבות משום דנשים פטורות ממצות עשה שהזמן גרמא אף ע"ג דלארבעה כוסות דרבנן כעין דאורייתא תיקון : היו באותו הנס . פי' רשב"ם שעל ידם נגאלו וכן במגילה ע"י אסתר ובחנוכה ע"י יהודית וקשה דאף משמע שאינן עיקר ועוד דבירושלמי גרים שאף הן היו באותו ספק משמע באותה סכנה דלהשמיד להרוג ולאבד והא דאמרינן דפטורות מסוכה אע"ג דאף הן היו באותו הנס כי בסוכות הושבתי התם בעשה דאורייתא אבל בארבעה כוסות דרבנן תיקנו גם לנשים כיון שהיו באותו הנס* : שתאן חי יצא · משמע דלכתחלה בעי מזיגה וכן בפ' שלשה שאכלו (ברכות ד' נ:) אמרינן הכל מודים בכוס של ברכה שאין מברכין עליו עד שיתן לתוכו מים וקשה דבפ' שלשה שאכלו (שם נא·) אמר י' דברים נאמרו בכוס של ברכה וצריך חי ורש"י פי' שם דהא דקאמרינן דצריך חי היינו שיתנוהו חי בכוס ברכת המזון לאפוקי שלא ימזגנו בכוס זה וישפוך בכוס אחר ויברך ור"ת פי' דחי דהתם היינו מזיג ולא מזיג כדאמר בבן סורר (סנהדרין ד' ע·) אינו נעשה בן סורר עד שישתה יין חי ומוקי לה במזיג ולא מזיג והא דמשמע בהמוציא יין (שבת ד' עו:) שמוזגו כראוי דקאמרינן כדי שימזגנו ויעמוד על רביעית היינו בברכת הארץ דאמר בפרק שלשה שאכלו (ברכות ד' נא·) ומוסיף בברכת הארץ ואומר ר"ת דמוסיף מים ולא כפרש"י דמוסיף יין וכן מפרש בערוך* וכן נראה מפרש"י מפרשי דחי קאי אכוס שיהא שלם ולא שבור כדאמרי' בפ' בתרא דמכות (ד' טז:) ריסק תשע נמלים ואי' חיה והיינו שלם דאפילו מת נמי חשיב בריה כדאמרינן בסוף גיד הנשה (חולין ד' קב:) גבי לפור טמאה בין בחייה בין במיתתה בכל שהו ואמרינן נמי (ב"ק ד' נד·) שבירתן זו היא מיתתן ואתי שפיר דכולהו עשרה דברים אכוס קיימי ונראה דדוקא בייעות שלהם שהיו חזקים לריך מזיגה אבל בשלנו לא* : בבת אחת . נראה כפירוש רשב"ם שבתאן רלופין ולא כפירש"י שעירה ארבעתן לתוך כוס אחד דשתאן משמע הרבה כוסות: ידי יין יצא . פי' ידי שמחת יו"ט דס"ד הואיל ותיקנו ד' כוסות לא נפיק מידי שמחת יו"ט אלא אם כן יצא ידי ארבעה כוסות : אחד חדש ואחד ישן . פירש שפירש רשב"ם דישן עדיף הוא עיקר כדאמרינן (מגילה ד' טז:) ולאביו שלח כזאת וגו' יין ישן שרוח זקנים נוחה הימנו ואמרינן (ב"ב ד' צח:) כל מילי עתיקא מעלו והא דנקט שאינו פשוט קודם פירשנו לעיל בכולן (ד' קה:) גבי אחד עלם כו' : רובא דכסא . היינו כמלא לוגמיו כדפרי' לעיל ומיהו לכתחילה צריך לשתות רביעית : ואת אמרת כדי מזיגת כוס יפה . לית ספרים דגרסי מאי כדי מזיג' כוס יפה לכל אחד ואחד ולפי זה ס"ד דמקשה דמזיגת כוס יפה דקאמר שמואל בין כולם קאמר דהיינו רובע רביעית הלוג וברייתא קתני רביעית הלוג יין חי בין כולן רובע רביעית לכל אחד ואחד והא דקתני אחד מזוג לא שדי ברביעית מזוג אלא כלומר אחד יכול לשתותו מזוג אבל מ"מ ברייתא לא איירי אלא בחי דסגי רביעית לכל ד' אך קשה איך היה סבור המקשה דסגי לכולהו במזיגת כוס יפה והא איכא בהני ארבעה כוסות כוס של ברכה שהוא כוס יפה ורשב"ם נמי הקשה הכא בריית' סתמא קתני לכך נראה כספרים דגרסי אידי ואידי חד שיעורא הוא דכדי מזיגת כוס יפה וזהו רובע רביעית הלוג יין חי לכל אחד כדי שיהא רביעית עם המזיגה וה"ל מיירי ברייתא דמצרכה רביעית עם המזיגה ומתחילה היה סבור דמצרכינן יין חי הרביעית עם המזיגה לכל אחד ואחד ומזוג אמתניה קאי ולא ארביעית דברייתא אבל לבתר דשני קאי שפיר ארביעית והך סוגיא כרב נחמן וכרבא דריש המוציא (שבת ד' עו:) דסברי כוס של ברכה לריך שיהא בו רובע רביעית הלוג יין חי כדי שימזגנו ויעמוד על רביעית הלוג ושיעור הוצאת יין תנן התם דהוי כמזיגת הכוס יפה דהיינו רובע רביעית וע"י מזיגה יעמוד על רביעית כשיעור כל המשקין דקתני סיפא ושאר כל המשקין ברביעית דאביי פריך עלה התם חדא דתנן ובמזוג שני חלקי מים ועוד מים בכד ומלטרפין ונראה לפרש דלאביי לריך רביעית בלימה להוצאת שבת וכן משמע התם בההיא שמעתא דקאמר אביי עד כאן לא קאמר רבי נתן הכא דכוית בעי רביעית כו' ופרש"י דהתם לא נהירא כמו שמפורש שם וסבר דכוס של ברכה בעי רביעית יין בין חי בין מזוג אבל מים בכד לא מצטרפים :

אל תרא יין כי יתאדם. הכא מייתי האי קרא לחשיבות יין אדום ובהמוכר פירות(ב"ב ד' צז·)פי' רשב"ם התם דמייתי לה לגריעותא ושם מפורש:

רש"י

תורה אור

שאף הן היו באותו הנס . כדאמרינן (סוטה דף יא:) בשכר נשים לדקניות שבאותו הדור נגאלו וכן גבי מקרא מגילה נמי אמרינן הכי דמשום דע"י אסתר נגאלו וכן גבי נר חנוכה במסכת שבת (ד' כג:) : [כדי מזיגת כוס יפה . שיעורא/רובע] רביעית כדי שימזגנו ויעמוד על רביעית לוג דחמרא דלא דרי על חד תלת מיא לאו חמרא הוא וקא סלקא דעתך דבין כולם קאמר שמואל דליהוי רובע רביעית יין : שתאן חי . שלא מזגו במים: בבת אחת. עירה ארבעתן לתוך כוס אחד: ידי יין יצא. ששתה ד' כוסות : ידי חירות לא יצא . כלומר אין זו מצוה שלימה : כדי רביעית . בין כולן קשיא לשמואל דאמר רובע רביעית דהיינו כוס יפה : ה"ג מאי כוס יפה דקאמר שמואל לכל חד וחד דהוו להו כולהו רביעית : אל תרא יין כי יתאדם . אלמא יין מראה בעי :

קליות

רשב"ם

שאף הן היו באותו הנס. דאמר במס' סוטה (ד' יא:) בשכר נשים לדקניות שהיו באותו הדור נגאלו וכן גבי מקרא מגילה אמר הכי משום דעל ידי אסתר הוה וכן גבי חנוכה במס' שבת (ד' כג·) לשון מורינו הלוי : אמר ר"י אמר שמואל ד' כוסות הללו לריך שיהא בהן · בכל אחד כדי שיהא בהן מזיגת כוס יפה של ברכה שיעורו רובע רביעית לוג כדי שימזגנו ויעמוד על רביעית לוג דכל חמרא דלא דרי על חד תלת מיא לאו חמרא הוא הכי מפרשינן לה במס' שבת בהמוציא יין (ד' עז·) והשתא קס"ד דמזיגת כוס יפה ורובע רביעית לאו חד שיעורא הוא כוס יפה כוס של בהמ"ז משום דעשרה דברים נאמרו בכוס של ברכה כו' כדאי' במס' ברכות (ד' נא·) : שתאן חי . שלא מזגן במים יצא וכגון שיש בו רביעית לוג דבבציר מרביעית לאו כלום הוא דכי היכי דמזוג בעינן רביעית בין הכל ה"נ חי בעינן רביעית : בבת אחת . עירה ארבעתן בתוך כוס אחד כך פירש רבינו שלמה ולא נהירא דאפי' שותה הרבה בכלי אחד לא חשיב אלא כוס אחד דהאי רביעית אינו אלא למעוטי פחות מרביעית אבל טפי מרביעית בכוס אחד חשוב כוס אחד וכ"ל דהכי פירושו בבת אחת שלא על סדר משנתינו אלא שתאן רלופין : השקה מהן . מכל כוס וכוס שלא שתה כולו כדמפרש לקמן : ידי יין יצא . ששתה ארבעה כוסות: ידי חירות לא יצא. כלומר אין זו מצוה שלימה שאין חשיבות אלא ביין מזוג והני מילי בייעות שלהן דדרו על חד תלת מיא אבל ייעות שלנו לא בעי מזיגה : ידי יין יצא . משום שמחת י"ט כדתניא לקמן (דף קט·) ושמחת בחגך במה משמחו ביין : אבל ידי ארבעה כוסות לא יצא. וכולן חשובין כוס ראשון ולא יותר וצריך להביא עוד שלשה כוסות על הסדר : צריך שיהא בהן כדי רביעית . כלומר בכל אחד ואחד כדי רביעית לוג : אחד חי . צריך רביעית דבציר מרביעית לא חשיבא שתייה כדנפקא לן מכל משקה אשר ישתה (ויקרא יא) : ואחד מזוג . שהיה בו רובע רביעית יין ושלשה רבעין מים דהאי בין כולהו רביעית : ואחד ישן . שאין בו טעם יין כל כך שנעשה חלש אי נמי חדש אין בו טעם יין : צריך שיהא בו טעם יין . למעוטי חדש וישן: ומראה· שיהא אדום : קתני מיהת כדי רביעית . לכל אחד ואחד ואת אמרת כדי מזיגת כוס יפה לכל אחד ואחד וס"ד דשני שיעורים הן מדלא קאמר שמואל כדי רביעית כלשון הברייתא : הכי גרסינן כמו שכתוב בספרים אידי ואידי חד שיעורא כדי מזיגת כוס יפה הייט רביעית תירוצא היא לומר שלשון שמואל ולשון הברייתא אחד הן וכדי מזיגת כוס יפה דקאמר שמואל היינו רובע רביעית יין כדי שימזגנו ויעמוד על רביעית כדאמר בהמוציא יין (שבת ד' עו:) כך נראית שיטה בעיני ועיקר ורבינו (א)פי' שכך מקשה הגמ' דקס"ד דשמואל קאמר רביעית בין כולן וברייתא קאמר לכל אחד ואחד ותירץ הגמ' דשמואל נמי קאמר לכל אחד ואחד וקשיא לי והלא ברייתא סתמא קתני צריך שיהא בהן ואיכא לפרושי נמי דבין כולן קאמר : אל תרא יין . אל תתמוד להיות רגיל בו כי יתאדם מכלל דיין נמי מראה בעי וטעמא נמי בעי כדמוזהר עליה שלא להשתכר בו : ואחד התינוקות . שגם הם נגאלו : וכי מה תועלת יש לתינוקות . הלא פטורין מן המצות :

קליות

מסורת הש"ס

מיר נא:

[גרי' ורשב"ם ליתא תיבות רב אמר]

הגהות הב"ח

(א) רשב"ם ד"ה ה"ג וכו' ורבינו שלמה פי' שכך מקשה וכו' קאמר רובע רביעית בין כולן :

רבינו חננאל

נשים שאף הן היו באותו הנס וארבעה כוסו' הללו צריך שיהא בהן כדי מזיגת כוס יפה וקיי"ל דכוס יפה הוא כוס של ברכה והוא רביעית: שתאן חי אמר רבא ידי יין יצא ידי חירות לא יצא שתאן בבת אחת אמר רבא ידי יין יצא ידי ארבעה כוסו' לא יצא · השקה מהן בניו ובני ביתו יצא והוא דשתה רובא דכסא · מיתיבי ארבעה כוסות הללו צריך שיהא בהן כדי רביעית אחד חי ואחד מזוג אחד חדש ואחד ישן ופרקי' כוס יפה הוא רביעית תרויהו חדא שיעורא: ר' יהודה אומר צריך שיהא בהן מראה יין כדכתיב אל תרא יין כי יתאדם: ת"ר ארבעה כוס' הללו צריך שיהא בהן כדי רביעית אחד אנשים ואחד נשים ואחד התינוקות ר' יהודה היה

תוך

*בין הכוסות הללו אם רצה לשתות ישתה בין שלישי לרביעי לא ישתה ואי אמרת מסעד סעיד אמאי ישתה הא קא אכיל למצה אכילה גסה אלא שמע מינה מגרר גריר רב ששת הוה יתיב בתעניתא כל מעלי יומא דפסחא נימא קא סבר רב ששת סמוך למנחה גדולה תנן ומשום פסחא הוא דילמא מימשך ואתי לאימנועי מלמעבד פיסחא הוא וסבר לה כי הא *דאמר רבי אושעיא אמר ר"א מכשיר היה בן בתירא בפסח ששחטו שחרית בארבעה עשר לשמו ומצפרא זמן פסחא הוא דכולי יומא חזי לפסחא דסבר °בין הערבים בין ערב דאתמול לערב דהאידנא אמרי לא *שאני רב ששת דאיסתנים הוה דאי טעים בצפרא מידי לאורת' לא הוה מהני ליה מיכלא: ואפילו עני שבישראל לא יאכל עד שיסב: איתמר [ג]מצה צריך הסיבה מרור אין צריך הסיבה יין איתמר משמיה דרב נחמן צריך הסיבה ואיתמר משמיה דרב נחמן אין צריך הסיבה ולא פליגי הא בתרתי כסי קמאי הא בתרתי כסי בתראי °אמרי לה להאי גיסא ואמרי לה להאי גיסא אמרי לה להאי גיסא תרי כסי קמאי בעו הסיבה דהשתא הוא דקא מתחלא לה חירות תרי כסי בתראי לא בעו הסיבה מאי דהוה הוה ואמרי לה להאי גיסא אדרבה תרי כסי בתראי בעו הסיבה ההיא שעתא דקא הויא חירות תרי כסי קמאי לא בעו הסיבה דאכתי עבדים היינו קאמר השתא דאיתמר הכי ואיתמר הכי °אידי ואידי בעו הסיבה [ד]פרקדן לא שמיה הסיבה הסיבת ימין לא שמה הסיבה ולא עוד אלא שמא יקדים קנה לוושט ויבא לידי סכנה [ה]אשה אצל בעלה לא בעיא הסיבה ואם אשה חשובה היא צריכה הסיבה [ו]בן אצל אביו בעי הסיבה איבעיא להו תלמיד אצל רבו מאי ת"ש (אמר) אביי כי הוינן בי מר זגינן אבירכי דהדדי כי אתינן לבי רב יוסף אמר לן [ז]לא צריכתו *מורא רבך כמורא שמים ואפילו תלמיד אצל רבו כי תניא ההיא מיסב בשוליא דנגרי איבעיא להו שמש מאי תא שמע דאמר ריב"ל השמש שאכל כזית מצה כשהוא מיסב יצא [ח]מיסב אין לא מיסב לא שמע מינה בעי הסיבה שמע מינה ואמר ר' יהושע בן לוי [ט]נשים חיבות בארבעה כוסות הללו שאף

בין הכוסות הללו. בין הראשון לשני: נימא קא סבר רב ששת סמוך למנחה גדולה תנן ומשום פסח. וקסבר כרבי יהודה בן בתירא דאמר כולי יומא זמן שחיטה הוא ומאי בין הערבים ערב דאתמול דהיינו משעלה עמוד השחר לערב דהאידנא משום הכי מתענה כולי יומא ואע"פ שלא היה פסח בימיו הואיל ומיתסרא בכך: לא רב ששת איסתנים. מעונג היה ואי הוה טעים מצפרא לא מצי למיטעם מצה לתיאבון לאורתא: עד שיסב. הסיבה על צד שמאל: מצה צריכה הסיבה. כבני חורין שהוא זכר לגאולה: מרור אין צריך הסיבה. שהוא זכר לעבדות: שמא יקדים. אפרקדן קאי שמתוך שגואו שוחה לאחוריו שיפוי כובע הוושט את פי הקנה נפתח ומתקפל למעלה והקנה פושט למעלה והמאכל נכנס לתוכו ונחנק: הוה זגינן אבירכי דהדדי. נשענין כל אחד על ברכי חבירו: בשוליא דנגרי. תלמידו של נגר המלמדו אומנות: ארבע כוסות. שלשה כנגד ג' כוסות שנאמרו בפסוק זה וכוס פרעה בידי וגומר ורביעי ברכת המזון: שאף

רשב"ם

בין הכוסות הללו. בין הראשון לשני בין השני לשלישי ומשום דחמרא מגרר גריר ליה הוא כדמפרש ואזיל: בין שלישי לרביעי לא ישתה. שלישי דברכת המזון דכיון דלא חיישינן עוד לגרירי ליבא לא שרינן ליה דנראה כמוסיף על ארבעה כוסות ובגמרת ירושלמי גמלא למה כדי שלא ישתכר דתו לא חזי למיגמר הלילא ופריך התם הלא כבר משוכר הוא שהרי שתה הרבה בסעודתו ומשני יין שבתוך המזון לא משכר שלאחר המזון משכר: נימא קסבר רב ששת סמוך למנחה גדולה תנן ומשום פסח. וקסבר לה בשחיטת פסח כר' יהודה בן בתירא דאמר כוליה יומא זמן שחיטה הוא ומאי בין הערבים דכתיב בפסח בין ערב דהאידנא לערב דאתמול משכלה ערב דאתמול דהיינו משיעלה עמוד השחר לערב דהאידנא משום הכי מתענה כוליה יומא והע"פ שלא היה פסח בימיו הואיל ואיתסר איתסר: ואי טעם מידי בצפרא. לא מצי למיכל מצה לתיאבון לאורתא: עד שיסב. הסיבה של צד שמאל: מצה צריכה הסיבה. כשאוכל מצה של מצוה לילה הראשון כבני חורין שהוא זכר לגאולה: מרור אין צריך הסיבה. שהוא זכר לעבדות: דההיא שעתא משתעי בחירות. ובגאולה שהוא אומר הגדה השתא שמעינן מינה דארבעה כוסות צריך הסיבה מרור אין צריך הסיבה: פרקדן. פניו (א) כלפי מעלה ושוכב על אחוריו: הסיבת ימין לאו שמה הסיבה. שהרי בימינו הוא צריך לאכול: שמא יקדים. אפרקדן קאי שמתוך שגואו שוחה לאחוריו שפוי כובע הסותם את פי הקנה נפתח ומתקפל למעלה וקנה פושט למעלה והמאכל נכנס לתוכו ונחנק כך פירש רבינו שלמה וקשיא לי אמאי לא סמכיה להאי ולא אהסיבת ימין ורבותי פירשו שמא יקדים קנה לושט דושט הוי על (דרך) [צד] ימין ונפתח הכובע שעל פי הקנה מאיליו כשהוא מטה כלפי ימין ואם יכנס בו המאכל הרי סכנה שאין אוכלין ומשקין נכנסין אלא דרך הושט ולכך נראה בעיני דלהסיבת ימין קאי מדסמכיה לדידיה: אשה אינה צריכה הסיבה. מפני אימת בעלה וכפופה לו ומפרש בשאילתות דרב אחאי *לאו דרכייהו דנשי למיזגא: בן אצל אביו צריך הסיבה. דלא הוי כפוף כל כך: בי מר. רבה: הוה זגינן אבירכי דהדדי · כל אחד נשען על ברכי חבירו: כי אתינן לבי רב יוסף. דרבה מלך מקמי דרב יוסף: כמורא שמים. דכתיב (דברים ו) את ה' אלהיך תירא לרבות תלמידי חכמים (לעיל דף כב:) השוה מורא רבו למורא שמים: בשוליא דנגרי. תלמידו של נגר שמלמדו אומנות: שמש שאכל כזית מצה. לא גרסינן באחרונה: שאף

תוספות

אלא אי אמרת מסעד סעיד. והא דאמרינן בפ' כיצד מברכין (ברכות דף לה:) דחמרא סעיד ומשמח מפרש התם דטובא גריר פורתא סעיד: רב ששת הוה יתיב בתעניתא. לאו דוקא אלא שומר עצמו מלאכול אי נמי היה מקבל עליו ממש תענית כדי שיהא נזכר ונזהר מלאכול והבכורות נהגו להתענות ערב פסח דקתני במסכת סופרים (פרק כא הלכה ג) שאין מתענין בניסן אלא הבכורות בערב הפסח: נימא קא סבר רב ששת משום פסח. ואע"ג דהשתא ליכא פסח מכל מקום האיסור שהיה בזמן הבית לא בטל ואע"ג דרבי יהודה בן בתירא לא מכשר אלא בדיעבד אבל לכתחלה אסור משום לא תשחט על חמץ * לא תשחט הפסח ועדיין חמץ קיים עד ו' שעות ולא אשכחן תנא דפליג מכל מקום כיון דדיעבד כשר סבירא ליה להחמיר שלא לאכול מן הבקר: מאי דהוה הוה. שכבר אמרו גאולה לפני הסעודה ואף על גב דמצה צריכה הסיבה ולא אמר מאי דהוה הוה שאני מצה שהיא עיקר סעודה יותר מיין ועוד ביין היסב כבר בשני כוסות הראשונים ועוד שכתובה בתורה זכר לחירות שלא הספיק בצקם להחמיץ עד שנגאלו ואע"ג דהויא לחם עוני יש לאוכלה דרך חירות ומה שצריך הסיבה במצה היינו כשמברכין על אכילת מצה ובאפיקומן: כולהו נמי צריכי הסיבה. וכל ד' כוסות צריכים הסיבה בשעת שתיה וצ"ע אם שכח ולא היסב אם יחזור וישתה וכן אם בכוס שלישי לא היסב אם יכול לחזור ולשתות בהסיבה אף על גב דבין שלישי לרביעי לא ישתה: פרקדן. פניו למעלה ולא כמפרש פניו למטה דאין דרך לאכול בענין זה וכן משמע בהמוכר את הספינה (ב"ב עד.) במתי מדבר דגנו אפרקיד ואזיל פרשא תותי כרעיה כדנקיט רומחא בידיה*: בפני רבו אין צריך הסיבה. נראה דאביו והוא רבו נמי אין צריך דלא גרע מרבו אחר מיהו סתם אב מלמד לבנו תורה כדאמרינן בפ"ק דקידושין (דף לא.) שהבן ירא מאביו יותר מאמו מפני שמלמדו תורה ואפי' הכי קאמר בפני אביו צריך הסיבה: שאף

[וע"ע תוס' ב"ב עד. ד"ה וגנו ותוס' נדה יד: ד"ה אפרקיד]

עין משפט נר מצוה

מז א מיי' פ"ז מהל' מצה הלכה (ג) [יב] טוש"ע א"ח סי' תעב ס"ג וסי' תעא ס"א בהג"ה:

מח ב מיי' פ"ז שם הלכה ח סמג עשין מא טור ש"ע א"ח סי' תעב ס"א:

מט ג מיי' שם סמג שם טוש"ע א"ח סימן תעב ס"ב וסי' תעט וסי' תפ:

נ ד מיי' וסמג שם טוש"ע א"ח סימן תעב ס"ג:

נא ה מיי' שם טוש"ע שם סעיף ד:

[כדאיתא לעיל ה:]

נב ו ז מיי' שם טור ש"ע שם ס"ה:

נג ח מיי' שם טוש"ע שם סעיף ו:

נד ט מיי' שם הלכה ז טור ש"ע שם סעיף יד:

רבינו חננאל

רב ששת הוה יתיב בתעניתא במעלי דפסחא ומסקנא משום דהוה אסתנים ואי הוה טעים מידי לא הוה מצי למיכל באורתא: אפילו עני שבישראל לא יאכל עד שיסב איתמר מצה בעיא הסיבה מרור לא בעי הסיבה יין איתמר דבעי הסיבה ואיתמר דלא בעי הסיבת ואסיקנא ארבעה כסי כולהו בעו הסיבה: פרקדן פירוש רובץ לאחוריו ויש אומרים על פניו: הסיבת ימין לא שמה הסיבה ולא עוד אלא שמא יקדים קנה לושט ויבוא לידי סכנה ואינה הסיבה אלא בשמאל · אשה חשובה בעיא הסיבה וזולתה לא · בן בפני אביו בעי הסיבה תלמיד בפני רבו לא בעי הסיבה מורא רבך כמורא שמים: אמר ר"י בן לוי נשים חייבות בארבעה כוסות כאנשים

מסורת הש"ס

לקמן קיז:

זבחים יא: [שם איתא א"ר אלעזר א"ר אושעיא וכצ"ל]

שמו' יב

ס"א כולהו נמי בעו

[נ"ל דאמר]

אבות פ"ד מי"ב

הגהות הב"ח

(א) רשב"ם ד"ה פרקדן פניו וכטנו כלפי:

גליון הש"ס

גמרא אמרי לה להאי גיסא. שבת קח ע"א ב"ב מב ע"ב: שם אידי ואידי בעו הסיבה. עיין בשו' הרלב"ח סי' ע"ט:

[פרשת לז סי' עו]

we learned: [108a] Between these cups,[7] if he wishes to drink [more] he may drink; between the third and the fourth he must not drink.[8] Now if you say that it [wine] satisfies, why may he drink? Surely he will merely gorge on the unleavened bread! Hence this proves that it sharpens the appetite.

R. Shesheth used to fast[9] the whole of the eve of Passover. Shall we say that R. Shesheth holds [that] we learned, CLOSE TO the great MINḤAH, the reason being on account of the Passover [sacrifice], lest he prolong [the meal] and refrain from performing the Passover [-offering]; and he [also] holds as R. Oshaia, who said: 'The son of Bathyra used to declare valid the Passover
a [-offering] which one slaughtered in its own name[1] on the morning of the fourteenth'; and from the morning it is the time for the Passover, for the whole day is the time for the Passover, as he holds, [*and the whole assembly . . . shall kill it*] *between the evenings*[2] [means any time] between yesterday evening and this evening?[3] —I will tell you: [that is] not [so]. R. Shesheth was different, for he was delicate, and if he ate anything in the morning his food would not benefit him in the evening.[4]

EVEN THE POOREST MAN IN ISRAEL MUST NOT EAT UNTIL HE RECLINES. It was stated: [For the eating of] the unleavened bread reclining is necessary; for the bitter herbs reclining is not necessary.[5] [As for the drinking of] the wine,—it was stated in R. Naḥman's name [that] reclining is necessary, and it was stated in R. Naḥman's name that reclining is not necessary. Yet they do not disagree: one [ruling] refers to the first two cups, and the other ruling refers to the last two cups. Some explain it in one direction, others explain it in the other direction. [Thus:] some explain it in one direction: for the first two cups reclining is necessary, because it is at this point that freedom commences; for the last two cups reclining is unnecessary, [because] what has been has been.[6] Others explain it in the contrary direction: on the contrary, the last two cups necessitate reclining, [because] it is precisely then that there is freedom; the first two cups do not necessitate reclining, [because] he is still reciting 'we were slaves.'[7] Now that it was stated thus and it was stated thus, both [the first and the last ones][8] necessitate reclining.

Lying on the back is not reclining; reclining on the right side
b is not reclining.[1] Moreover, he may put [his food] into the windpipe before the gullet,[2] and thus endanger himself.

A woman in her husband's [house] need not recline,[3] but if she is a woman of importance she must recline.[4] A son in his father's [house] must recline.[5] The scholars asked: What about a disciple in his teacher's presence?—Come and hear, for Abaye said: When we were at the Master's [Rabbah b. Naḥman's] house, we used to recline on each other's knees. When we came to R. Joseph's house he remarked to us, 'You do not need it: the fear of your teacher is as the fear of Heaven.'

An objection is raised: A man must recline with all [people], and even a disciple in his master's presence?—That was taught of a craftsman's apprentice.

The scholars asked: What about an attendant?—Come and hear, for R. Joshua b. Levi said: An attendant who ate as much as an olive of unleavened bread while reclining has discharged [his duty]. Thus, only while reclining, but not if he was not reclining. This proves that he must recline. This proves it.

R. Joshua b. Levi also said: Women are subject to [the law of] these

(7) The first and second, and the second and third. (8) The third cup is drunk in connection with Grace after meals. Having dined already, he has no need to drink for his appetite, and if he now drinks more he will appear to be adding to the statutory number (four) of cups. T.J. states that drink after the meal (apart from the two which are still to be drunk to make up the four) intoxicates and makes the person unfit to recite the *hallel*. (9) Lit., 'sit in a fast'.

a (1) I.e., as a Passover, and not as a different sacrifice. (2) Ex. XII, 6 (E.V. *at dusk*). (3) I.e., the evenings commencing the fourteenth and the fifteenth. The night must be omitted, since offerings cannot be sacrificed at night.—Though of course sacrifices had altogether ceased by the time of R. Shesheth, yet if on this view one had to fast when the Temple stood, it would still be necessary, because the interdict had never formally been rescinded. (4) I.e., he would have no appetite in the evening. (5) The former symbolizes freedom; the latter, bondage. Bitter herbs may *not* be eaten while reclining. (6) The last two cups come after the meal, by which time the whole narrative of Israel's liberation has been completed. Hence there is no need then to emphasize the theme of freedom. (7) V. *infra* 116a. (8) Var. lec.: all.

b (1) Since he must eat with his right hand. (2) If he eats lying on his back it may go down the wrong way. (3) Because she stands under his authority. (4) Isserles (O.Ḥ. 472, 4 Gloss) chivalrously remarks that all women nowadays are of high worth. (5) He does not sense his father's authority so strongly.

to prolong [the meal] [107b] and refrain from performing the Passover [-offering]; or perhaps we learned CLOSE TO the lesser MINḤAH, the reason being on account of the unleavened bread, lest he merely gorge himself with the unleavened bread?[3] Said Rabina, Come and hear: Even King Agrippa[4] who was accustomed to eat at nine hours, might not eat on that day until nightfall. Now it is well if you say that we learned, CLOSE TO the lesser MINḤAH, hence it is that which is noteworthy about Agrippa;[5] but if you say [that] we learned, CLOSE TO the great MINḤAH, what is there noteworthy about Agrippa, seeing that the interdict has [already] fallen upon him from before?[6] What then? We learned, CLOSE TO the lesser MINḤAH? Yet after all what is there remarkable about Agrippa: surely the time of the interdict has come![7]—You might say: Nine hours to Agrippa is like four hours[8] to us;[9] hence he informs us [otherwise].

a R. Jose[1] said: But he may make a meal[2] with various sweetmeats.[3] R. Isaac would make a meal with vegetables. It was taught likewise: The attendant may make a meal with the inwards,[4] and he may [also] offer them to the guests. And though there is no proof of this, yet there is a hint thereof, for it is said, *Break up for you a fallow ground, and sow not among thorns.*[5]

Raba used to drink wine the whole of Passover eve, so as to whet his appetite[6] to eat more unleavened bread in the evening. Raba said: How do I know that wine whets the appetite? Because

(3) Lit., 'a gross eating,' having eaten his fill beforehand. (4) A king of the Hasmonean dynasty, who followed Rabbinical teaching. (5) I.e., though he did not eat earlier, and at nine hours the interdict has not yet commenced (for it commences just before nine and a half hours), he might nevertheless not start then, as he would probably prolong it. (6) Surely we would not think him exempt from the interdict merely because he had not yet eaten. (7) Before he finishes his meal. For even R. Jose, who maintains that a man need not interrupt the meal once he has commenced (*supra* 99b), admits that he must not commence a meal knowing that he will prolong it beyond the forbidden period. (8) I.e., about ten a.m. (9) Since the latter hour is the general mealtime, while Agrippa did not breakfast until three p.m.

a (1) Alfasi reads: Assi. (2) Lit., 'dip.' (3) Fruit or meat, without bread: these were generally dipped into a relish.—The time meant is from *minḥah* and onwards. (4) Of an animal which he is preparing for the Festival meals. (5) Jer. IV, 3. Rashi: i.e., do not work without profit; so if a man is engaged on preparing food and is forbidden to eat thereof it causes him mental suffering. [Rashi did not seem to read: 'And he may offer them to the guests'. Rashbam and Tosaf. explain the reference to a relish prepared for whetting the appetite and the verse is quoted in illustration that the stomach must be prepared to receive food as the ground for seeds]. (6) Lit., 'draw his heart'.

ואתי לאימנועי מלמיעבד פסחא או דילמא סמוך למנחה קטנה תנן ומשום מצה דילמא אתי למיכלה למצה אבילה גסה אמר רבינא ת"ש אפילו אגריפס המלך שהוא רגיל לאכול בתשע שעות אותו היום לא יאכל עד שתחשך אי אמרת בשלמא סמוך למנחה קטנה תנן היינו רבותיה דאגריפס אלא אי אמרת סמוך למנחה גדולה תנן מאי רבותיה דאגריפס חל איסור עליה מעיקרא (א) אלא *סמוך למנחה קטנה תנן סוף סוף מאי רבותיה דאגריפס הא מטיא ליה זמן איסורא מהו דתימא תשע שעות לאגריפס כארבע שעות (ב) דידן דמי קמ"ל אמר רבי (*יוסי) אבל מטביל הוא במיני תרגימא ר' יצחק מטביל בירקי תניא נמי הכי *השמש מטביל בבני מעיין ונותנן לפני האורחים ואע"פ שאין ראיה לדבר זכר לדבר שנאמר °נירו לכם ניר ואל תזרעו אל קוצים *רבא הוה שתי חמרא כולי מעלי יומא דפיסחא כי היכי דניגרריה לליביה דניכול מצה טפי לאורתא אמר רבא מנא אמינא לה דחמרא מיגרר גריר דתנן בין

תורה אור: ירמיה ד

או דילמא סמוך למנחה קטנה. בתשע שעות כשהוא מאוחר בפרק תמיד (לעיל דף נח.): ומשום מצה. שיכנס לה כשהוא תאוה: אגריפס המלך. לא היה אוכל עד תשע שעות: אי אמרת בשלמא סמוך למנחה קטנה היינו רבותיה דאע"ג דעדיין לא אכל וזמן איסוריה אכתי לא מטא בשעה תשיעית עד לאחר תשע אפ"ה לא יאכל משום דמשיך ליה עד זמן איסורא יתענה ולא יאכל: אלא אי אמרת. ממנחה גדולה ואילך אסור מאי רבותיה דאגריפס והא כבר חל זמן איסוריה משש שעות ואילך וצריכא למימר דאסור בתמיה דאטו משום דלא אכל בעי למיעבד איסורא וכשרי למיכל מתחלת תשע: אבל. יכול אדם לטבול ולאכול מיני תרגימא פירות והאי דנקט מטביל לפי שמאכלם על ידי טיבול: בירקי. היה אוכל ירק מן המנחה ולמעלה לפי שאין משביע: בבני מעים. הואיל ועסוק בסעודה יכול הוא לאכול בבני מעים מה שדרך השמש לאכול רשאי הוא לעשות כן מן המנחה ולמעלה דהואיל והוא עסוק בהן מגער ליה אי לא אכיל ואי אכיל לא משבעו ליה: נירו לכם ניר. כשאתם טורחים תטרחו בדבר שאתם יכולין ליהנות ממנו ושמש זה שעוסק בסעודה ובית המטבחים אם אינו נהנה מגער ליה: בין

רשב"ם

או דילמא סמוך למנחה קטנה. והיינו בגמר ט' שעות דמתשע שעות ומחלה הוי זמן דהקרבת תמיד של כל השנה כשהוא מאוחר דהשתא משום אימנועי מפסח ליכא דערב הפסח היה התמיד קרב בשמונה ומחלה והפסח אחריו מיד לפיכך אם בא לאכול סמוך למנחה קטנה דהיינו בגמר תשעה וכבר נשחט הפסח ואין כאן לחוש אלא משום מצה שלא יאכלנה אכילה גסה והכי נמי דמשום פסח איכא למיחש לאכילה גסה דאע"ג דהוא נאכל על השובע אכילה גסה מיהא איכא אכילה וקדשים מזיק הוא דחשבינן ליה ביבמות (דף מ.) אלא משום דלגבי לחם הויא אכילה גסה באכילה מועטת נקט מצה אי נמי רבותא קאמר והכי קאמר או דילמא סמוך למנחה קטנה ואפילו בזמן דליכא פסח דליכא למיחש לעשייתו ולא לאכילתו משום אכילת מצה מיהא איכא דלא ליהוי אכילה גסה חיישינן: אגריפס המלך. מלך כשר היה *ממלכי חשמונאי ולא היה אוכל עד שעה ט': רבותיה דאגריפס. כלומר היינו רבותא דקתני בברייתא אפי' אגריפס דאע"ג דעדיין לא אכל וזמן איסורא לא מטא אכתי בשעה תשיעית עד לאחר תשעה אפילו הכי לא יאכל משום דמשיך ליה עד זמן איסור ויתענה ולא יאכל: אלא אי אמרת. ממנחה גדולה ולמעלה אסור מאי אפילו אגריפס הא מטא כבר זמן איסוריה משש שעות ומחלה ואילך וצריכא למימר דאסור בתמיה דאטו משום דלא אכל בעי למיעבד איסורא: כדבעינן למימר לקמן לא גרס ליה: סוף סוף מאי רבותיה דאגריפס הא מטא ליה עידן איסוריה. קודם שיגמור סעודתו דאפילו רבי יוסי דפליג בהפסקת ערב הפסח בריש פירקא ואמר שלא להפסיק מאחר שהתחיל לאכול בהיתר הכא מודי דאסור דמעיקרא לדעת כן היה אוכל בתשע שעות שגמר סעודתו בתוך זמן איסוריה ומתחיל לאכול אחר זמן איסורו דמי ואסיר: מהו דתימא ט' דאגריפס כארבע שעות לדידן דמי. דכיון דלמוד לאכול בתשע שעות כארבע שעות לדידן דמי ויאכל גם הוא מצה לתיאבון גם הוא כמותינו שאוכלין בד' שעות ביום והלכך הואיל ואכתי לא מטא זמן איסורא ניסרי לאכול בתחלת ט' אע"פ שתמשך סעודתו לאחר ט' קמ"ל דאסור לאכול אבל אי הוה תנינן סמוך למנחה גדולה ליכא רבותא כלל ולא הוה שייך למיתני אפי' דכיון דטעמא משום דילמא אתו לאימנועי מפסח ולא משום אכילה גסה מצה ליכא למימר הכי מהו דתימא ט' לאגריפס כד' לדידן דמי הלכך שמעינן מינה דמנחה קטנה תנן: מטבל ואוכל. מן המנחה ולמעלה: תרגימא. פירות ובשר בלא לחם והא דנקט מטבל שכל מאכלם ע"י טיבול: בירקא. היה אוכל ירק מן המנחה ולמעלה לפי שאינו משביע ונראה בעיני דמגרר ליבא למיכל ואכל מצה לתיאבון יותר ולפיכך היה אוכל [ירק] ולא היה טוב. כן כי אם ערב הפסח כדי להמשיך ולאכול בלילה כדאמרי' במס' שבת בפ' חולין (דף קמ:) אמר רב חסדא בר בי רב לא ליכול ירקא משום דמגררי ליבא כו' וכדאמר נמי בסמוך רבא הוי שתי חמרא במעלי יומא דפסחא כי היכי דנגריר לליביה ודברים הללו כגון מיני תרגימא וירקות ממשיכין את הלב כדמוכח נמי בברכות (ד' לה:) שהיו רגילין לאכול פרפרת קודם אכילת הפת לגרר את הלב כדתנן בירך על הפת פטר את הפרפרת על הפרפרת לא פטר את הפת אלמא דפרפרת קודם לפת: תניא נמי הכי. דאוכלין מיני תרגימא ערב הפסח כדי להמשיך את הלב: השמש מטבל בבני מעים. כלומר בבני מעים של בהמות הנשחטות לסעודת יו"ט וגם נותן מהם לפני האורחין המצויין יחד על הפסח כדי שיאכלו מצה ופסח לתיאבון ובערב הפסח קאי בתוספתא דפסחים ואפי' מן המנחה ולמעלה דלעיל מינה תניא ע"פ סמוך למנחה לא יאכל כו': ואע"פ שאין ראיה לדבר זכר לדבר. דאכילה מושכת אכילה זכר לדבר יש קצת דכתיב נירו לכם ניר ראה לנו הנביא דוגמא שחורשין את הקרקע כדי לקבל את הזריעה ואם אינה חרושה אינה מקבלת הזריעה אף אדם האוכל דברים שאין משביעין את האדם פותחים בני מעים ומרחיבין אותן ויקבל המאכל של סעודה אחרי כן לתיאבון כך נראה בעיני שיטה זו ועיקרה ורבינו שלמה זקני פירשה כן בני מעיים הואיל ועסוק בסעודה יכול הוא לאכול בני מעיים מה שדרך השמש לאכול רשאי הוא לעשות כן מן המנחה ולמעלה דהואיל ועסוק בהן מגערי ליה אי לא אכיל ואי אכיל לא משבעי ליה: נירו לכם ניר. כשאתם טורחים תטרחו שתוכלו ליהנות ממנו ושמש זה שעסוק בסעודה או בבית המטבחים אם אינו נהנה מגער ליה ולא נהירא עוד יש לשון אחר ואין בו ממש: בין

ואתי לאימנועי מפסח. ואפילו אחר שיעשה פסח אסור כדי שלא ימהר לאכול ויעשה פסח שלא כראוי: דילמא אתי למיכל אכילה גסה. ואינה אכילה כדאמרינן בפרק בתרא דיומא (דף פ:) האוכל אכילה גסה ביום הכפורים פטור וקשה דאמרי' בנזיר (דף כג.) גבי פסח זה שאכלו אכילה גסה ופושעים יכשלו בם ופריך רשע קרית ליה נהי דלא עביד מצוה מן המובחר פסח מיהא קא עביד ואומר ר"ת דתרי גווני אכילה גסה אחת שנפשו קצה מלאכול ועל אותה פטור ביוה"כ ויש אכילה גסה שאינו מתאוה לאכול אך יש בה טעם והא דפסח נאכל על השבע היינו שמתאוה לאכול קצת ועוד י"ל דאין לו לקרותו רשע כיון שקיים מצות פסח אע"פ שלא קיים מצות אכילה דאכילת פסחים לא מעכבא *ומה שפירש רשב"ם דנקט מצה משום דשייכא אפילו בזמן הזה דליכא פסח לא נהירא דאפילו הוי טעמא משום פסח אסור בזמן הזה כדמוכח בסמוך גבי רב ששת דהוה יתיב כולי יומא בתעניתא ופירוש *אחר עיקר שפי' דנקט מצה דבאכילה מועטת הוי אכילה גסה: אפי' אגריפס המלך. פי' רשב"ם מלך כשר ומבני חשמונאי היה ולא דק דבסוטה (דף מא.) אמרי' כשהגיע למקרב אחיך תשים עליך מלך זלגו עיניו דמעות: שהיה רגיל לאכול בתשע שעות. °י"מ לפי שדרך מלכים לעמוד בג' שעות והיה מתנהג כתלמיד חכם לאכול בשעה ששית *אחרי קומו ואין נראה דא"כ הוה ליה למימר ט' שעות לאגריפס כשש שעות לת"ח: מיני תרגימא. פי' רשב"ם פירות ובשר בלא לחם ולא נהירא דאמרינן בתוספתא דכילד מברכין הביאו לפניו מיני תרגימא מברך בורא מיני מזונות ואין מברכין בורא מיני מזונות אלא על חמשת המינים ומיהו בפרק בתרא דיומא (דף עט:*) איכא חד שינויא דמשני ואיבעית אימא מאי מיני תרגימא פרי: נירו לכם ניר. פי' רשב"ם דעל ידי החרישה מקבלת הזריעה ה"נ ע"י אכילת תרגימא יאכל מצה מיהו חרישה וזריעה תרי מילי נינהו ולא דמי לשתי אכילות ונראה שזה הפסוק משל הוא כענין זה דכתיב (ירמיה ד) אם תשוב ישראל נאם ה' אלי תשוב אם תסיר שקוציך וגו' פי' לאחר שתסירו שקוצים אז תשובו אלי וכל זמן שהשקוצים עמכם ונתייאשתם ממני לא תוכלו לשוב כי כה אמר ה' נירו לכם ניר ואל תזרעו אל קוצים כל זמן שהקוצים בתוכה אינה מועלת זריעתה כלום וה"נ מייתי זכר לדבר כשאכל קצת לבו נמשך יותר אבל כשלא אכל כלל ונתייאש אין לבו נמשך אחר אכילה והוי כזורע אבן לחמתו: אלא

*) [אולי דצ"ל כלומר היה אוכל זה מן המנחה ולמעלה אבל לא היה מטבל במיני תרגימא]

עין משפט נר מצוה

מו א ב ג מיי' פ"ו מהל' מצה הלכה יב סמג עשין מ טוש"ע א"ח סי' תעא ס"א:

[וע"ע תוס' נזיר כג. ד"ה פסח ותוס' יבמות מ. ד"ה אכילה ותוס' ב"ק דף קי. ד"ה אכילה]

נ"א ופירוש א'

[כדאיתא לעיל יב:]

[ע"ש בגמ' ובתוס' שם ד"ה מיני ותוס' סוכה דף כז. ד"ה במיני]

רבינו חננאל

אוקימנא סמוך למנחה קטנה מדתניא אפילו אגריפס המלך שרגיל לאכול בתשע לא יאכל עד שתחשך אמר רב יוסף אבל מטבל הוא במיני תרגימא. פי' רב האי תרגימא כענין של מיני מתיקה דתנינן בתוספתא דברכות הביאו לפניו מיני תרגימא מברך עליהן בורא מיני [מזונו']: רבי צדוק מטבל בירקי כלומר *) היה אוכל זה מיני תרגימא וזה היה אוכל מן המנחה ולמעלה תניא נמי הכי השמש טובל בבני מעים ונותן לפני האורחים רבא הוה שתי חמרא טובא במעלי דפסחא אמר כי היכי דנגרריה ללביה ונכפין [ונאכל] למצה וכו':

מסורת הש"ס

[ברב אלפס איתא ר' אסי]

[תוספתא פ"י]

ברכות דף לה:

[ס"א ממלכי אורדוס]

הגהות הב"ח

(א) גמ' אלא מאי סמוך למנחה קטנה תנן סוף: (ב) שם כארבע שעות לדידן דמי:

גליון הש"ס

תוס' ד"ה שהיה כו' י"מ. עי' תענית כט ע"ב רש"י ד"ה שכן מליס:

אמר רבא הילכתא טעם מקדש *וטעם מבדיל ומי שלא קידש בערב שבת מקדש והולך כל היום כולו עד מוצאי שבת *מי שלא הבדיל במוצאי שבת מבדיל והולך כל השבת כולו *אמימר פתח לה להא שמעתא דרבא בהאי לישנא אמר רבא הילכתא טעם מקדש טעם מבדיל מי שלא קידש בע"ש מקדש והולך כל היום כולו מי שלא הבדיל במוצ"ש מבדיל והולך כל היום כולו אמרי ליה *מר ינוקא ומר קשישא בריה דרב חסדא לרב אשי זימנא חדא איקלע *אמימר לאתרין ולא הוה לן חמרא אייתינא ליה שיכרא ולא אבדיל ובת טוות למחר טרחנא ואייתינא ליה חמרא ואבדיל וטעים מידי לשנה תו איקלע לאתרין לא הוה לן חמרא אייתינא שיכרא אמר אי הכי *חמר מדינה הוא אבדיל וטעים מידי שמע מינה תלת ש"מ *המבדיל בתפלה צריך שיבדיל על הכוס ושמע מינה אסור לו לאדם *שיאכל קודם שיבדיל ושמע מינה מי שלא הבדיל במוצ"ש מבדיל והולך כל השבת כולו בעא מיניה (א) רב הונא מרב חסדא מהו לקדושי אשיכרא אמר השתא ומה פירזומא ותאיני ואסני דבעאי מיניה מרב ורב מר' חייא ורבי חייא מרבי ולא פשט ליה שיכרא מיבעיא סבור מינה קדושי הוא דלא מקדשינן עילויה אבל אבדולי מבדלינן אמר להו רב חסדא הכי אמר רב כשם שאין מקדשין עליו כך אין מבדילין עליו איתמר נמי אמר רב תחליפא בר אבימי אמר שמואל כשם שאין מקדשין עליו כך אין מבדילין עליו לוי שדר ליה לר' שיכרא בר תליסר מגני טעמיה הוה בסים טובא אמר כגון זה ראוי לקדש עליו ולומר עליו כל שירות ותושבחות שבעולם בליליא צעריה אמר *מיסרן ומפייס אמר רב יוסף אדור ברבים דלא אישתי שיכרא אמר רבא אישתי מי זוריון ולא אישתי שיכרא ואמר רבא תיהוי שקיותיה שיכרא מאן דמקדש אשיכרא רב אשכחיה רב הונא דקדיש אשיכרא אמר ליה שרי אבא למיקני איסתירי משיכרא ת"ר אין מקדשין אלא על היין ואין מברכין אלא על היין אטו מי לא מברכין עליהו שהכל נהיה בדברו אמר אביי הכי קאמר אין אומרים הבא כוס של ברכה לברך אלא על היין ת"ר אין מקדשין על השכר משום ר' אלעזר בר רבי שמעון אמרו מקדשין ממעמת יין כל שהוא ר' יוסי בר יהודה אומר מלא לוגמא אמר רב הונא אמר רב וכן תני רב גידל דמן נרש *המקדש וטעם מלא לוגמא יצא ואם לאו לא יצא אמר רב נחמן בר יצחק אנא תנינא לה לא גידול בר מנשיא ולא גידול בר מניומי אלא גידול סתמא למאי נפקא מינה למירמא דידי' אדידיה: סמוך למנחה: איבעיא להו סמוך למנחה גדולה תנן או דילמא סמוך למנחה קטנה תנן סמוך למנחה גדולה תנן ומשום פסח דילמא אתי למימשך ואתי

ס"א מרימר

כל השבת. כדאמרן לעיל עד יום רביעי: פירזומא. שכר שעורים בלשון לעז ברוי"ש: ותאיני. שכר תאנים: ואסני. שכר תותים: שיכרא. שכר תמרים: בר תליסר מגני. שנתנו מים על התמרים ואחר שזבו נתן על תמרים אחרים וכן הביא תמרים עד י"ג פעמים: מייסרן ומפייס. מלערין (ג) ובשעת שתיה מפייסין הן כלומר טובים הן וראוי לומר עליהן קידוש והבדלה: אדור ברבים. נדר שאין לו הפרה: מי זוריון. מי משרת הפשתן: שרי ליה אבא. התחלת לעשות שכר ולהשתכר בו (ג) מערב לכך הוא יפה בעיניך ומקדש אתה עליו: כוס של ברכה. ברהמ"ז: מטעמת יין בכל שהוא. אותה טעימה שאמרו המברך צריך שיטעום (ד) בכל שהוא: מנחה גדולה. (*משבע) שעות ומחצה ולמעלה זמן הקרבת תמיד כשאתה בא להקדימו: ומשום פסח. שמא ישב בסעודה וימנע ויפשע מעשות פסח:

או

רשב"ם

כל השבת כולה. כדאמרן לעיל עד יום רביעי ואפי' קי"ל כרבא דאמר טעם מקדש ואם שכח ולא קידש מקדש למחר כל היום כולו וכן טעם מבדיל ואם לא הבדיל מבדיל והולך עד יום רביעי: ובת טוות. לן מעונה שלא אכל וקרא הוא בדניאל (ו): חמר מדינה. אין יין אחר בעיר הזאת כי אם שכר הלכך מבדילין בו וכן הלכה אבל מים לא איקרו חמר מדינה ואין מבדילין על המים אפילו היכא דליכא שכר ויין: שמעת מינה תלת. ג' דברים בסידרי הבדלה ואף על גב דשמעינן מינה דמבדילין על חמר מדינה אע"פ שאינו יין לא חשיב דלא איירי אלא בסדר הבדלה אי נמי מילתא דפשיטא הוא דכיון דאין יין אחר בעיר טוב לו שיבדיל על השכר משלא יבדיל כלל: מהו לקדושי אשכרא. במקום שאין יין: פירזומא. שכר שעורין: ותאיני. שכר תאנים: ואסני. שעושין שכר מפרי סנה כגון תותין והללו השובין יותר מכתם שכר שלהם שהיה של תמרים: אבל אבדולי מבדלינן. אליבא דרב: תליסר מגני. שנתן המים על התמרים ואח"כ נותנן על תמרים אחרים וכן הביא אחרים עד שלש עשרה פעמים ומגני נראה שהוא לשון אשר מגן צריך בידך (בראשית יד) ומתרגמינן ומסר והוא לשון מסר כך השיכרא היה כותש ג"כ ומשבר התמרים חדשים שלש עשרה פעמים: צעריה. שלשול דתמרים משלשלין כדאמרי' בכתובות (דף י:): מיסרן ומפייס. בתמיה וכי מי שמצער ראוי הוא לפייס ולרצות להקב"ה ולומר עליו קידוש: אדור ברבים. נדר שאין לו הפרה: מי זוריון. מי משרת פשתן: תיהוי שקיותיה שיכרא. עני יהיה שלא יוכל לקנות יין מדה כנגד מדה: מקדש אשיכרא. ואע"פ שהיה יין בעירו וטעמו משום דחביב ליה כדאמר לעיל זימנין דחביבא ליה ריפתא מקדש אריפתא: שרי ליה אבא. התחיל לעשות שכר ולהשתכר בו ויפה בעיניך ומקדש אתה עליו: ואין מברכין. ברכת המזון כדמפרש לקמן: כוס של ברכה. ברכת המזון: ה"מ דלא קבע עליה אבל קבע עליה לית לן בה לא גרסינן כלל: מטעמת יין כל שהוא. אותה טעימה שאמרו המברך צריך שיטעום אותה טעימה די בכל שהוא: וטעם מלא לוגמא יצא ואם לאו לא יצא. והכי הילכתא והוא שלא טעם אחד מכל המסובין אבל טעם אחד מהם יצאו כולן ידי חובתן ואע"פ שלא טעמו: אמר רב נחמן בר יצחק אנא תנינא לה. להאי מתניתא משמיה דרב גידל (דמנרש) אבל איני מזכיר מי הוא שמא גידול בר מנשיא או גידול דמן נרש: מנחה גדולה. משש שעות ומחצה ולמעלה דהיינו זמן עשיית תמיד הערב כשאתה בא להקדימו כגון בערב הפסח שחל להיות בערב שבת שנשחט בשש ומחצה והפסח אחריו כדאמרינן בתמיד נשחט (לעיל דף נח.): ומשום פסח. שמא ישב בסעודה ויפשע מעשות פסח:

או

אמר רבא הילכתא טעם מקדש. וכן הלכה: **אמימר** מתני לה כו'. בסוף מילתיה גרסינן מבדיל והולך כל היום כולו דאי לאו הכי הייינו לישנא קמא והלכה כלישנא קמא דמבדיל עד רביעי בשבת כדאמר רבי חייא לעיל ובתשעה באב שחל להיות במוצ"ש נמי רגילין להבדיל אחר התענית וכן בסדר דרב עמרם:

ושמע מינה מבדיל כל השבת כולה. לא שמעינן מינה אלא כל היום אלא נקט הכי משום דהלכה כן:

אדור ברבים כו'. דקסבר דברבים אין לו הפרה ואין הלכה כן אלא דוקא על דעת רבים אין לו הפרה ובמקום אחר מפורש (גיטין דף לו.):

אם טעם מלא לוגמא יצא. וכדמפרש ביומא (דף פ.) כל שאילו מסלקו לצד אחד יראה כמלא לוגמיו והוי פחות מרביעית כדאמרינן התם אבל מלא לוגמיו אמרינן התם דהוי יותר מרביעית ונראה שהוא רוב רביעית דאמרינן לקמן והוא דשתה רובא דכסא ודוקא לאדם בינוני אבל לעוג מלך הבשן בעי טפי כדאמרינן התם*:

סמוך למנחה. תימה אמאי קרי ליה מנחה דאי משום דמנחה היתה קריבה בין הערבים הלא גם בשחר קריבה מנחת חביתין ומנחת תמיד וי"ל בשחר יש שם אחר תפלת שחרית ועוד דאמרינן בפרק קמא דברכות (דף ו:) הוי זהיר בתפלת מנחה שאף אליהו לא נענה אלא בתפלת מנחה ושמא בשעת הקרבת מנחה נענה ולכך קרי ליה תפלת מנחה שאז היה שעת רצון*:

ואתי

עין משפט נר מצוה

מד א מיי' פ"ו מהל' ברכות [עי' בהג' מיי' בס ס"ק ס] ופכ"ט מהל' שבת הלכה יז סמג עשין כט טוש"ע א"ח סי' קפב ס"ב וסי' ערב ס"ט וסי' רצו ס"ב:

מה ב מיי' פכ"ט מהל' שבת הלכה ז טוש"ע א"ח סי' קל סעיף ג וסי' רעא סעיף יג:

[עי' תוס' ב"ב ז: ד"ה מר ינוקא]

ס"א רבין

[ועי' תוס' ערובין עט: ד"ה אם ותוס' יומא דף פ. ד"ה הכי ותוס' שבת דף טו: ד"ה ויעמוד]

[ובאבודרהם דף מא ע"ד דפוס פראג כתב בזה"ל ונקראת זאת התפלה מנחה מפני שבשעה עשירית מן היום שנברא בו אדם הראשון חטא וזהו שכתוב לרוח היום ומתרגמינן למנח יומא עכ"ל]

מסורת הש"ס

[לעיל קה קו:]

[לעיל קו.]

[משש שעו' כ"א בפי' הרשב"ם]

[לעיל קה: וש"נ]

[עי' תוס' שבת ט: ד"ה לימא וכו' גרסת הכא לטעום כלום]

[פי' מסיר הדעת כמו המסית שבא בדבריו רכים והוא מתוק ומפתה בני אדם לשתותו ואח"כ מצער ערוך ערך מפס מוסרן גרס ומפיס]

הגהות הב"ח

(א) גמ' בעי מיניה רב חסדא מרב הונא מהו: (ב) רש"י ד"ה מייסרן ומפייס מלערין כצ"ל: (ג) שם ד"ה שרי וכו' ולהשתכר בו לכך והוכח מערב נמחק: (ד) שם ד"ה מטעמת וכו' שיטעום די בכל שהוא:

רבינו חננאל

אמר רבה הלכתא טעם מקדש טעם מבדיל ומי שלא קדש בערב שבת מקדש והולך כל היום ומי שלא הבדיל במוצאי שבת מבדיל כל היום כמרימר דמתני להא שמעתא דרבא ליומיה. פי' ובת טות לן אותה הלילה בלא אכילה. פי' חמר מדינה יין ששותין בני המדינה כולה והוא יינם ואין להם זולתו: **שכרא** בתתליסר מגאני פי' שכר מסונן בשלש עשרה מסננות כלומר הורק מכלי אל כלי: **מיסרן** ומפיס פי' מסיר הדעת כמו המסית שבא בדבריו רכין והוא מתוק ומפתה בני אדם לשתותו ואחר מצערו מלשון המפים מירפא בשבת: **רבה** בר בר חנה מקדש אשכרא. גרסינן במס' נזיר בתחלתו הריני נזיר מן הדרצנים כו' ור' שמעון נמי הכתיב מיין ושכר יזיר ההוא מבעי ליה לאסור יין מצוה כיין הרשות יין מצוה [מאי היא] קידושא ואבדלתא הרי הוא מושבע ועומד עליהן מהר סיני אלא כי הא דאמר רבא שבועה שאשתה וחזר ואמר הריני נזיר אתיא נזירות חלה אשבועה ורבנן הכתיב מבל ההוא לאסור יין מצוה כיין הרשות*: ירושלמי בשבועות פ"ג (הלכה ד) שבועה שלא איכל מצה בלילי הפסח לוקה ואוכל מצה בפסח שבועה שלא אשב בצל אסיר לישב בצל סוכה שבועה שלא אשב בצל סוכה לוקה וישב בצל סוכה. כתוב בספרי דבי רב מיין ושכר יזיר לעשות יין מצוה כיין רשות: ת"ר אין אומרין הבא כוס לברך אלא על היין ואוקימנא לא אמרן אלא דלא קביע סעודתיה עליה אבל קבע לית לן בה. ת"ר אין מקדשין על השכר משום ר"ש אמרו מקדשין ומטעימת יין כל שהוא ר' יוסי אומר מלא לוגמיו וכן תאני גידול המקדש וטעם מלא לוגמיו יצא ואם לאו לא יצא: **מתני'** סמוך למנחה כו' אוקימנא

*) [לפנינו שם בנזיר (ד' ד') הגי' ורבנן נמי הא מיבעי ליה להסור יין מצוה כיין רשות א"כ לימא קרא מיין מאי ושכר ש"מ הרתי ע"כ וגי' רבינו אינו מובן וצ"ע]

does recite *habdalah*. [107a] Raba said: The law is: He who has tasted [food] recites *ḳiddush*, and he who has tasted [food] recites *habdalah*. Again, he who did not recite *ḳiddush* on the eve of the Sabbath proceeds to recite *ḳiddush* any time during the Sabbath, until the termination of the Sabbath. He who did not recite *habdalah* at the termination of the Sabbath proceeds to recite *habdalah* any time during the week.[6] Amemar commenced this ruling of Raba in the following version: The law is: He who has tasted [food] recites *ḳiddush*, he who has tasted [food] recites *habdalah;* he who did not recite *ḳiddush* on the eve of the Sabbath proceeds to recite *ḳiddush* at any time of the day. He who did not recite *habdalah* proceeds to recite *habdalah* the whole day.[7]

a Mar Yanuḳa and Mar Ḳashisha the sons of R. Ḥisda[1] said to R. Ashi: Amemar once visited our town: lacking wine, we brought him beer [for *habdalah*], but he would not recite *habdalah* [over it], '*and passed the night fasting*.'[2] The next day we took trouble to procure wine for him, whereupon he recited *habdalah* and ate something. The following year he again visited our town, [and] we offered him beer. Said he, 'If so, it is the wine of the country';[3] [so] he recited *habdalah* and ate a little. This proves three things; [i] [Even] he who recites *habdalah* in the Prayer must recite *habdalah* over a cup [of wine];[4] [ii] a man must not eat until he has recited *habdalah;* and [iii] he who did not recite *habdalah* at the termination of the Sabbath proceeds to recite *habdalah* any time during the week.

R. Ḥisda asked R. Huna:[5] Is it permitted to recite *ḳiddush* over beer? Said he to him, Seeing that I asked Rab, and Rab asked R. Ḥiyya, and R. Ḥiyya asked Rabbi about *pirzuma*,[6] fig[-beverage], and *asne*,[7] and he could not resolve it for him, can there be a question about [barley] beer! Now it was understood from him: *Ḳiddush* indeed may not be recited over it, yet we can recite *habdalah* over it. Said R. Ḥisda to them, Thus did Rab say: Just as you may not recite *ḳiddush* over it, so may you not recite *habdalah* over it. It was stated too, R. Taḥlifa b. Abdimi said in Samuel's name: Just as you may not recite *ḳiddush* over it, so may you not recite *habdalah* over it.

b Levi sent to Rabbi beer strained thirteenfold.[1] On tasting it he found it well-flavoured. Said he: 'Over such as this it is fitting to recite *ḳiddush* and to utter all the psalms and praises in the world.' At night it caused him pains. Said he: 'Seeing that it chastises us, shall it propitiate!'[2]

R. Joseph said: I will vow in the presence of a multitude[3] not to drink beer. Raba said: I would drink flaxwater,[4] yet I would not drink beer. Raba also said: His drink shall be but beer who recites *ḳiddush* over beer.[5] Rab found R. Huna[6] reciting *ḳiddush* over beer. Said he to him: 'Abba[7] has begun to acquire *istiri*[8] with beer.'[9]

Our Rabbis taught: You recite *ḳiddush* over wine only, and you say a blessing over wine only. Do we then not recite the blessing, 'by whose word all things exist' over beer and water? —Said Abaye, This is what he means: You do not say, 'Bring a cup of blessing to say Grace [after meals],' over aught except wine.

Our Rabbis taught: You do not recite *ḳiddush* over beer. On the authority of R. Eleazar son of R. Simeon they said: You can recite *ḳiddush* [over it]. The tasting of wine [demands] but a small quantity.[10] R. Jose b. Judah said: [At least] a mouthful. R. Huna said in Rab's name, and thus did R. Gidal of Naresh[11] learn: He who recites *ḳiddush* and drinks a mouthful [of the wine] has discharged [his duty]; if not, he has not discharged [his duty]. R. Naḥman b. Isaac said: I recite this [name] neither [as] Gidal b. Menassia nor Gidal b. Manyomi, but simply Gidal. What difference does that make?—In respect of opposing [one statement] of
c his to [another statement] of his.[1]

CLOSE TO MINḤAH. The scholars asked: Did we learn, CLOSE TO the great MINḤAH, or perhaps we learned, CLOSE TO the lesser MINḤAH?[2] Did we learn, CLOSE TO the great MINḤAH, the reason being on account of the Passover-offering, lest he come

(6) V. *supra* 106a. (7) Viz., Sunday, but not the whole week.

a (1) Yanuḳa means youth; Ḳashisha, old age. Some accordingly translate: the younger and the elder sons of R. Ḥisda respectively. Others however translate: The son born to R. Ḥisda in his youth and the son born in his old age, i.e., the elder and the younger sons of R. Ḥisda respectively. Rashi in Keth. 89*b* s.v. מר and Tosaf. in B.B. 7*b* s.v. מר. (2) Dan. VI, 19. He would not eat without reciting *habdalah*. (3) Beer is evidently the popular drink and occupies the same place here that wine generally occupies elsewhere. (4) V. *supra* 105*b*, n. a4. (5) Text as emended (BaḤ). (6) Jast. A beer brewed from figs, in that case it must differ from תאיני, which is also a beverage made from figs, while ordinary beer is from barley. Rashi however regards *pirzuma* as barley beer, while ordinary beer is made from dates. (7) Jast.: a drink made of shrubbery fruit(?)—All these are superior to the ordinary barley beer about which R. Ḥisda asked.

b (1) R. Ḥan.: repeatedly strained for clarity—thirteen merely indicates many. Rashbam: beer made by pouring water on dates, then pouring the same water with its date infusion over other dates, this operation being repeated many times. (2) Rashbam: i.e., it causes pain—is it fit to propitiate God therewith, i.e., to recite *ḳiddush* over it—surely not! Others: first it entices (by its pleasant flavour) and then it causes pain. (3) A vow made in the presence of a multitude cannot be annulled, v. Giṭ. 36*a*. (4) I.e., water in which flax is steeped. (5) If he grudges the money for wine, there will come a time when he can afford only beer for his general drinking. (6) Var. lec., Rabbah b. Bar Ḥanah. (7) Lit., 'father'—a title of respect. (8) Coins. (9) I.e., you have begun trading with beer, so it has become sufficiently valuable in your eyes to recite *ḳiddush* over it. (10) He who says a blessing over wine must taste some of it (*supra* 105*b* bottom); the smallest quantity suffices. (11) Identical with Nahras or Nahr-sar, on the canal of the same name, on the east bank of the Euphrates; Obermeyer, p. 307.

c (1) If a statement by one of these two is found to contradict the present one, there is no difficulty, as he is not identical with either. Or perhaps: he may be identical with one of them, so that a contrary statement by the other does not prove a self-contradiction. (2) The time for the great *minḥah* is six and a half hours (i.e., half an hour after midday) and onwards. This is the earliest hour for the sacrificing of the evening *tamid* (v. *supra* 58*a*). The lesser *minḥah* is two and a half hours before nightfall.

R. Beruna said in Rab's name: [106*b*] He who washes his hands [before eating][7] must not recite *ḳiddush*.[8] Said R. Isaac b. Samuel b. Martha to them: Rab has not yet died[9] and we have [already] forgotten his rulings! I stood many times before Rab: sometimes he preferred bread [and] recited *ḳiddush* over bread; at others he
a preferred wine [and] recited *ḳiddush* over wine.[1]

R. Huna said in Rab's name: Once he has tasted [food] he must not recite *ḳiddush*.[2] R. Ḥana b. Ḥinena asked R. Huna: May he who has tasted [food] recite *habdalah?*[3] I maintain, replied he, [that] he who has tasted [food] recites *habdalah*. But R. Assi said: He who has tasted [food] may not recite *habdalah*.

R. Jeremiah b. Abba visited R. Assi. He forgot himself and ate something. [Then] they gave him a cup [of wine] and he recited *habdalah*. Said his [R. Assi's] wife to him [R. Assi]: But you[4] do not act thus? Leave him, replied he; he holds as his teacher.[5]

R. Joseph said in Samuel's name: He who has tasted [food] may not recite *ḳiddush;* he who has tasted [food] may not recite *habdalah*. But Rabbah said in R. Naḥman's name in Samuel's name: He who has tasted [food] does recite *ḳiddush;* and he who has tasted [food]

(7) The hands must be washed before partaking of a meal at which bread is eaten, and there must be no interruption between the washing and the eating of some bread. (8) Before breaking bread—*ḳiddush*, of course, comes first—, as it constitutes an interruption. But he must listen to another reciting the *ḳiddush;* this does not constitute an interruption, and he discharges his own duty thereby. If he does recite *ḳiddush*, he must wash again before eating. (9) Lit., 'Rab's soul has not yet gone to rest.'—Or perhaps: Rab has only just died.
a (1) Rashi and Rashbam: If he was very hungry he would wash and recite *ḳiddush* over the bread and immediately eat it. This proves that the reciting of *ḳiddush* is not an interruption and does not necessitate washing again. R. Tam: sometimes he preferred bread (being very hungry) and recited *ḳiddush* (over wine) with the intention of eating bread immediately after it (על can bear this meaning); hence he must have washed *before ḳiddush*, and as we see, another washing is unnecessary. (2) In the evening, but must wait for the morrow. (3) That evening—*sc.* at the termination of the Sabbath—, or must he too wait for the morrow. (4) Lit., 'the Master.' (5) *Sc.* Rab, in whose name R. Huna gave his ruling.

עין משפט נר מצוה

מא א ב מיי׳ פכ״ט מהלכות שבת הלכה ט סמ״ג עשין כט טוש״ע א״ח סי׳ רעא סעיף יב:

מב ג מיי׳ שם הלכה ה וסמג שם טור ש״ע א״ח שם סי׳:

מג ד מיי׳ וסמג שם טוש״ע א״ח סי׳ רעג ס״ס:

רבינו חננאל

ברונא אמר רב נטל ידיו לא יקדש ואסיקנא רב איקלע דהביבא עליה ריפתא מקדש אריפתא איפוך דחביבא עליה חמרא מקדש אחמרא:

גמרא

*הנוטל ידיו לא יקדש (א) אמר להו רב יצחק בר שמואל בר מרתא אבתי לא נח נפשיה דרב שבהנינהו לשמעתתיה זמנין סגיאין הוה קאימנא קמיה דרב [ב]זימנין דחביבא עליה ריפתא מקדש אריפתא זמנין דחביבא ליה חמרא מקדש אחמרא אמר רב הונא אמר רב טעם אינו מקדש בעא מיניה רב חנא בר חיננא מרב הונא טעם מהו שיבדיל א״ל אני אומר *טעם מבדיל ורב אסי אמר טעם אינו מבדיל רב ירמיה בר אבא איקלע לבי רב אסי אישתלי וטעים מידי הבו ליה כסא ואבדיל אמרה ליה דביתהו והא מר לא עביד הכי אמר לה שבקיה כרביה סבירא ליה אמר רב יוסף אמר שמואל טעם אינו מקדש טעם אינו מבדיל ורבה אמר רב נחמן אמר שמואל [ג]טעם מקדש [ד]וטעם מבדיל אמר

רשב״ם

נטל ידיו לא יקדש. דקידושא מפסיק בין נטילה לאכילה והוי כהיסח הדעת ובעי נטילה אחריתי בתר קידושא: דחביבא ליה ריפתא. שהיה רעב מקדש אריפתא אלמא לא בעי נטילה אחריתי אלא מעיקרא משי ואכיל כהמא דקידושא: דחביבא ליה חמרא. שהיה צמא: טעם. אם אכל שוב אינו מקדש כל הלילה: אישתלי. רב ירמיה: אמרה ליה דביתהו. דרב אסי לרב אסי: והא מר לא עביד הכי. דאמר רב אסי טעם אינו מבדיל: כרביה. כרב דרב הונא משמיה דרב הוה אמר שמעתתיה: כל

נטל ידיו לא יקדש. אלא אחר יקדש והוא יצא ידי חובתו בשמיעה ושתיה דאין כאן היסח הדעת מאחר שהוא עצמו אינו מברך אבל הוא עצמו לא יקדש אם נטל ידיו כדי שיאכל על סמך נטילה דלפני קידוש דקידוש מפסיק בין נטילה לאכילה והוי כהיסח הדעת ובעי נטילה אחריתי בתר קידושא דתכף לנטילת ידים סעודה ובשביל קידוש לא בעי נטילה דהנוטל ידיו לפירות ה״ז מגסי הרוח והא קמ״ל דנטילה שלפני קידוש אינה עולה לו לפיכך יקדש תחלה ואח״כ נוטל ידיו וכ״ש דהנוטל ידיו לא יבדיל דהא אפילו קידוש דבמקום סעודה הוא ואיכא למימר דליכא היסח הדעת אפ״ה אין יכול לסמוך על נטילה דלפני קידוש והא דקאמר נטל לא יקדש ולא אמר מקדש וחוזר ונוטל ידיו היינו משום דלא בעינן נטילת ידים תרי זימני דחדא מינייהו ברכה לבטלה הלכך לא יקדש הוא אבל חבירו יקדש לו: דחביבא ליה ריפתא. שהיה רעב מקדש אריפתא אלמא לא בעי נטילה אחריתי אלא מעיקרא משי ידיה ואכיל כהמא דקידוש אלמא קידוש שלאחר נטילה לא חשיב היסח הדעת וכן הילכתא דמי שנטל ידיו קודם קידוש א״צ לחזור וליטלן אחר קידוש ולא אפליגו רבנן בין מקדש אריפתא למקדש אחמרא מדלא קא מהדר ליה לרב יצחק בר שמואל מידי ומיהו לכתחלה מוזגין ואח״כ נוטלין לידים כב״ה במסכת ברכות (דף נא:) ומדרב שמעינן שמקדשין על הפת ואומר ויכולו ומברך המוציא ואינו אוכל גם לא יפרוס עד שיקדש אחרי כן ודוקא קידוש אבל הבדלה אינה אלא על הכוס של יין כדאמרינן (שם דף לג.) העשירו קבעוה על הכוס ומי שאין לו כוס יין במקום שרגילין לשתות יין אל יבדיל על הפת ודי לו בהבדלת תפלה בסידור רב עמרם: טעם. אם אכל לא יקדש כל הלילה אלא למחר קודם סעודה: אני אומר טעם מבדיל. ואע״ג דלגבי קידוש אמינא טעם אינו מקדש בהבדלה אין להחמיר כל כך: אשתלי. רב ירמיה: אמרה ליה דביתהו. דרב אסי: והא מר לא עביד הכי. דאמר רב אסי טעם אינו מבדיל: א״ל. רב אסי: שבקיה כרביה ס״ל. דס״ל כרב ורב הונא משמיה דרב היה אומר וכך פרש״י: כל

תוספות

הנוטל ידיו לא יקדש. פירש רשב״ם וכסדר דרב עמרם משום היסח הדעת וקשה דהא רב גופיה קאמר בפ׳ כל הבשר (חולין דף קז:) נוטל אדם ידיו שחרית ומתנה עליהם כל היום ו״ל דתנאי לא מהני אלא היכא דלא שכיחי מיא כגון שאין לו מים בסמוך או יש לו וצריך לדברים אחרים אבל היכא דשכיחי מיא ויש לו בסמוך לא יועיל תנאי כדמשמע התם דקאמר אמר להו רבא להנהו בני פקתא דערבות כגון אתון דלא שכיחי לכו מיא משו ידייכו מצפרא ואתנו עלייהו כולי יומא איכא דאמרי בשעת הדחק ופליגא דרב ואיכא דאמרי אף שלא בשעת הדחק והיינו דרב משמע דרב כמי איירי בלא שכיחי מיא כדקאמר כגון אתון דלא שכיחי לכו מיא וקאמר והיינו דרב וה״ר אלחנן מפרש (ב) נטל לא יקדש משום דמיחזי כנוטל ידיו לפירות דהרי זה מגסי הרוח: **זימנין** סגיאין הוה קאימנא קמיה דרב כו׳. השתא מסיק דקידוש לא הוי היסח הדעת וא״ת דבפרק אלו דברים (ברכות דף נא:) אמרי ב״ה מוזגין את הכוס ואח״כ נוטלין לידים ומפרש טעמא *משום דתכף לנטילת ידים סעודה וכי מוזגת הכוס הוי טפי היסח הדעת מקידוש וי״ל דשאני מזיגה שהיא בחמין וצריך דקדוק שלא יחמו ושלא יותר והוי טפי היסח [הדעת] מקידוש ור״ת פירש דהתם איירי בחול ויש לחוש שמא יטול קודם מזיגה שיעסוק בשאר דברים ולא יאכל לאלתר ולאו אדעתיה אבל בשבת אין לחוש שיפליג לדבר אחר שהשלחן ערוך ויאכל מיד: **מקדש** אריפתא. פירש רשב״ם שהיה מקדש על הפת במקום יין ואם כן היה נוטל תחלה ולא הוי קידוש הפסק וקשה לר״ת דקידוש על הפת ודאי לא הוי הפסק שהקידוש הוא לצורך המוציא והוי כמו גביל לתורי* דלא הוי הפסק בין ברכה לאכילה וכ״ש דלענין נטילה לא הוי הפסק אבל במקדש על היין שהוא קודם המוציא יהיה הפסק בין נטילה לאכילה ומיהו יש ליישב פירושו דפעמים היה דעתו לקדש אריפתא והיה נוטל ואח״כ לפעמים היה נמלך והוה מקדש אחמרא והיה סומך על אותה נטילה ואין להקשות לרשב״ם דהא משמע לקמן דאין מבדילין על הפת מדאמרינן בת טוות וא״כ כל שכן דאין מקדשין על הפת דקידוש חמור מהבדלה כדאמרינן לעיל (דף קה:) קובעת לקידוש ולא להבדלה ולקמן אמרינן סבור מינה קידושי הוא דלא מקדשינן הא אבדולי מבדלינן דהיכא קשיא דאיכא טעמא דכיון שמצוה לסעוד סעודת שבת שייך קידוש על הפת אבל הבדלה אין ענינה אלל פת אלא דוקא על היין דשייך בכל דבר הודאה ושירה מ״מ נראה לר״ת דאין מקדשין על הפת כלל והכא ה״פ הנוטל ידיו לא יקדש משום דס״ל לרב יש קידוש שלא במקום סעודה וחיישינן שמא יפליג וילך לחוץ א״ל רב יצחק כו׳ זימנין דחביבא ליה ריפתא ומקדש אריפתא כלומר הוה מקדש אחמרא על דעת לאכול מיד ריפתא והיה נוטל מיד ידיו קודם קידוש ולא דמי למזיגת הכוס כדפרישית לעיל וזימנין דחביבא ליה חמרא הוה מקדש אחמרא שלא במקום ריפתא דהיינו סעודה דסבירא ליה דיש קידוש שלא במקום סעודה ומאן דסבר אין קידוש אלא במקום סעודה כ״ש דנוטל ידיו ומקדש דלא הוי היסח (ג) ובירושלמי דברכות גבי פלוגתא דב״ש וב״ה מברך על היום ואחר כך מברך על היין משמע כפר״ת דאין מקדשין על הפת דא״ר זעירא מדברי שניהם נלמד מבדילין בלא יין ואין מקדשין בלא יין אמר רבי יוסי ב״ר בון נהיגין תמן מקום שאין יין שליח צבור יורד לפני התיבה ואומר ברכה אחת מעין שבע וחותם במקדש ישראל ויום השבת משמע שאין מקדשין על הפת וכ״ע אם מקדשין על השכר היכא דהוי חמר מדינה כמו שמבדילין וכולה שמעתין דאסרה לקדושי אשיכרא איכא לאוקמי בשאינו חמר מדינה ותדע מדקאמר רב כשם שאין מקדשין כך אין מבדילין ובחמר מדינה פשיטא דמבדילין ולקמן נמי דקאמר אין מקדשין בלא יין וכן ההיא דירושלמי שהבאתי איכא לאוקמא דלא אתי למעוטי אלא כשאינו חמר מדינה ואי מקדשין על השכר היכא דהוי חמר מדינה אתי שפיר ביום טוב שאחר השבת שיעשו יקנה״ז על השכר אבל אי אין מקדשין על השכר ולרשב״ם שאומר לקדש על הפת תימה איך יעשו אי יקנה״ז על הפת ואי על השכר ומיהו בסדר דרב עמרם יש אע״ג דאין מבדילין על הפת ביו״ט שחל במוצאי שבת מבדילין כיון דקידוש עיקר כדפסקינן יקנה״ז ומקדשין על הפת נעשה הבדלה טפילה לה ומבדיל על הפת עם הקידוש וכוס ברכת המזון נראה דמברכין על השכר היכא דהוי חמר מדינה דהא אפילו הבדלה דטעונה כוס לכולי עלמא מבדילין כל שכן ברכת המזון דאיכא ברייתא בלא דברים (ברכות נב.) שסוברת דאינה טעונה כוס ועוד דאמרינן בשמעתין אין אומרים הבא כוס של ברכה פירוש לברך ברכת המזון אלא על היין והני מילי דלא קבע סעודתיה עילויה אבל קבע סעודתיה עילויה לית לן בה משמע דאם קבע סעודתו עליו שמברכין עליו ברכת המזון וכל שכן אם הוא חמר מדינה מיהו רשב״ם מוחקו מן הספרים. מסקנא דמילתא מבדילין על השכר אם הוא חמר מדינה ולא על הפת ולר״ת אין מקדשין כמו על הפת אך יש להסתפק אם מקדשין על השכר: **טעם** אינו מקדש. פי׳ עד למחר קודם אכילה ואם תאמר למאי דפי׳ לעיל אף ידי יין יצאו כששתה בבית הכנסת א״כ איך יקדש שוב בביתו וי״ל דלא מיקרי טעם כיון שלא טעמו אלא מכוס של ברכה: **אישתלי** וטעים מידי. מה שמקשי׳ השתא בהמתן של לדיקים אין הקב״ה מביא תקלה י״ל דהכא שהמאכל מותר אלא שהשעה אסורה אין שייך להקשות ובמקום אחר מפורש (גיטין ז.*): **שבקיה** כרביה ס״ל. פי׳ בקונטרס רב דרב הונא משמיה דרב הוה אמר שמעתתיה ותימה דרב אסי נמי תלמידו של רב והלשון משמע כרביה ולא רביה אלא נראה כרביה כרב הונא [כדאמר] בפ״ב דקדושין (דף מו.) דרב ירמיה תלמידו של רב הונא דקאמר כראין דברי תלמיד ואע״ג דרב ירמיה בר אבא תלמיד חבר דרב הוה בפ׳ תפלת השחר (ברכות כז:) דקאמר ליה מי בדלת ולא קאמר ליה מר בברכות גרסינן ברוב ספרים רב ירמיה ובקדושין רבי *ירמיה: אמר

הגהות הב״ח

(א) גמ׳ הנוטל ידיו לא יקדש וכן אמר רב הונא אמר רב נטל ידיו לא יקדש אמר להו ר׳ יצחק: (ב) תוס׳ ד״ה הנוטל וכו׳ והרב אלחנן מפרש הנוטל ידיו לא יקדש: (ג) ד״ה מקדש וכו׳ דלא הוי היסח הדעת ובירושלמי:

מסורת הש״ס

[לעיל קה: לקמן קז.]

[שם נב:]

[ברכות מ.]

[כד״ה השתא ושבת יב: ד״ה ר׳ נתן]

[בדפוס שלפנינו איתא בברכות דף כז: בכל הסוגיא רבי ירמיה אבל בקדושין מה: איתא רב ירמיה]

ושמע מינה אומר ב' קדושות על כוס אחד וש"מ ב"ש היא ואליבא דרבי יהודה רב אשי אמר טעמו פגמו וכוס של ברכה צריך שיעור חדא מילתא היא וה"ק מ"ט טעמו פגמו משום דכוס של ברכה צריך שיעור רבי יעקב בר אידי קפיד אחצבא פגימא רב אידי בר שישא קפיד אכסא פגימא מר בר רב אשי קפיד *אפילו אחביתא פגימתא ת"ר °זכור את יום השבת לקדשו זוכרהו על היין אין לי אלא ביום בלילה מנין ת"ל זכור את יום השבת לקדשו בלילה מנין אדרבה עיקר קדושא בלילה הוא קדיש דכי קדיש תחלת יומא בעי לקידושי ותו בלילה מנין ת"ל זכור את יום תנא מיהדר אלילה וקא נסיב ליה קרא דיממא ה"ק °זכור את יום השבת לקדשו זוכרהו על היין בכניסתו אין לי אלא בלילה ביום מנין ת"ל זכור את יום השבת °ביום מאי מברך אמר רב יהודה בפה"ג רב אשי איקלע למחוזא אמרו ליה ליקדיש לן מר קידושא רבה הבו ליה סבר מאי ניהו קידושא רבה אמר מכדי כל הברכות כולן בפה"ג אמרי ברישא אמר בפה"ג ואגיד ביה חזייה להההוא סבא דגחין ושתי קרי אנפשיה °החכם עיניו בראשו *אמרי בני רבי חייא מי שלא הבדיל *במוצ"ש מבדיל והולך בכל השבת כולו ועד כמה א"ר זירא °עד רביעי בשבת כי הא *דיתיב רבי זירא קמיה דרב אסי ואמרי לה רב אסי קמיה דרבי יוחנן ויתיב וקאמר °לענין גיטין חדא בשבתא תרי ותלתא בתר שבתא ארבע וחמשא ומעלי יומא קמי שבתא א"ר יעקב בר אידי °אבל לא על האור אמר רב ברונא אמר רב הנוטל

תורה אור: שמות כ | קהלת ב

[ואליבא דרבי יהודה. דאמר מאור ואח"כ בשמים: משום דכוס של ברכה טעון שיעור. אבל אי הוה ביה טפי מכשיעור טעמו לא פגמו]: קפיד. קידוש והבדלה וברכת המזון אבל אם בא לשתות משום כוס פגום מברך עליו ברכת היין: לקדשו. משמע משעה שמתקדש היום: אין לי אלא ביום. לקמן פריך אדרבה עיקר קדושא בלילה הוא דבכניסתו היא קדושתו: קידושא רבה. בורא פרי הגפן ולהכי קרי ליה קידושא רבה דלכולהו קידושי אמרי לה: ואגיד ביה. האריך בו: עד רביעי בשבת. אבל מרביעי ולהלן גבי שבת הבא מתחשב: לענין גיטין. אמר לה ה"ז גיטך על מנת שתתני לי מאתים זוז אחר השבת או שאמר קודם השבת תתני לי: אבל לא על האור. אם לא בירך בורא מאורי האש במוצאי שבת שוב אינו מברך: נטל

רשב"ם

ושמע מינה אומרים ב' קדושות על כוס אחד. היכא דלית ליה אלא כוס אחד כי הכא אע"ג דאמר לעיל (דף קב:) אין אומרים ב' קדושות על כוס אחד היכא דלית ליה שאני כדמפרשינן לעיל: ושמעת מינה ב"ש היא ואליבא דרבי יהודה. דאמר לעיל מאור ואח"כ בשמים דאילו לב"ה ברישא בשמים ואח"כ מאור והא ליכא למימר ר"מ ואליבא דב"ה כדאמר לעיל וב"ה אומרים נר ובשמים מזון והבדלה ועני רבא זו דברי ר"מ הוא דה"ג פרכינן בברכות פרק אלו דברים (דף נב:) ומשני לא ס"ד מדקתני ומשלשלן לאחר המזון מכאן שמעת ליה דלית ליה הלי סברא דמזון ברישא כרבי יהודה כדאמר לעיל רבי יהודה אומר לא נחלקו ב"ש וב"ה על המזון שבתחלה ועל הבדלה שבסוף כו' אלמא רבי יהודה היא ואליבא דב"ש דאילו לר"מ מי מנא לה משלשלן לאחר המזון דלדידיה מאור ברישא בין לב"ש בין לב"ה ולא מזון כדאמר לעיל זו דברי ר"מ: משום דכוס של ברכה צריך שיעור. אבל אי הוה טפי מכשיעור וטעמו לא פגמו: קפיד אכסא פגימא. קידוש והבדלה ולבהמ"ז ולכל ברכות שתקנו לסדרן על היין שלא יברך על כוס פגום אבל אם רוצה לשתות יין צריך לברך בורא פרי הגפן שאסור ליהנות מן העולם הזה בלא ברכה ומיהו אם אין לו אלא יין פגום מקדש עליו דקפיד לכתחלה משמע: אפילו אחביתא. חביות קטנות אבל אם חבית של עץ גדולה אין להקפיד: ה"ג ת"ר זכור את יום השבת זוכרהו על היין אין לי אלא ביום בלילה מנין ת"ל זכור את יום השבת בלילה מנין אדרבה עיקר קדושא בלילה הוא דכי קדיש (א) יומא בעיא לקדושי ותו בלילה מנין תלמוד לומר זכור את יום השבת תנא מהדר אלילה ונסיב לה קרא ליממא הכי קאמר זכור את יום השבת לקדשו זוכרהו על היין בכניסתו אין לי אלא בלילה כו': לקדשו. משמע בשעה שמתקדש היום: אין לי אלא ביום. ולקמן פריך אדרבה עיקר קדושא בלילה הוא (ב) קדושתו: הכי קאמר כו'. אע"ג דלאין לפרש לשון השנוי בברייתא בענין זה אלא ע"י שלנו מסרסין אותה למפרע אפ"ה לא שייך למימר חסורי מיחסרא שהרי אין חסר ממנה כלום אלא ששנויה למפרע דבמקום שהיה לו לומר אין לי אלא בלילה ביום מנין טעה התנא בשמועתו ושנה אין לי אלא ביום בלילה מנין הלכך לא שייך למימר חסורי מיחסרא: ביום מאי מברך. דאי אמרת קידוש מרישא והגיה* שבת ויום טוב אין בהן קדושה על הכוס: אמר רב יהודה בפה"ג. אלמא כסא דחמרא וברוכי ומשתי משום כבוד שבת לחלק בין מדת שבת למדת חול שהוא ענין שיר שאין אומרים שירה אלא על היין והכי מפרש בשאילתות דרב אחאי בפרשת וישמע יתרו*: קידושא רבה. בורא פרי הגפן. וקרי ליה קידושא רבה דלכולהו קידושי קאמרי ליה: ואגיד ביה. האריך בו לדעת אם יסרהב אחד מהם לשתות ובכך יבין דבורא פרי הגפן רגילין לומר והוא לא שאם לא כן היה אומר (ג) לו [לקדש] קידוש גדול של לילה כמנהגן: עד רביעי בשבת. ולא עד בכלל אבל מרביעי ואילך גבי שבת הבאה מתחשב: לענין גיטין. אם אמר לה הרי זה גיטך על מנת שתתני לי ר' זוז אחר השבת או על מנת שתתנם לי קודם השבת: אבל לא על האור. אם לא בירך הגר בורא מאורי האש במוצ"ש שוב אינו מברך כך נ"ל טעם הדבר כדתניא במקום שנהגו (דף נד:) אין מברכין בו אלא בליל מוצ"ש הואיל ותחלת ברייתו הוא: נטל

תוספות

ושמע מינה אומר שתי קדושות על כוס אחד. ובשאין לו כדאמר לעיל (ד' קב:): משום דכוס של ברכה צריך שיעור. רב אשי לא פליג אאמוראי דבסמוך ואית ליה שפיר טעמו פגמו אלא דמהא ליכא למישמע מינה קאמר: קפיד אכסא פגימא. פירש רשב"ם דקפיד לכתחלה דוקא ואם אין לו אלא פגום יקדש עליו ותימה א"כ איך התירו לאכול קודם הבדלה משום קפידא דפגימה מיהו ראוי רשב"ם לסמוך עליו בשעת הדחק: זוכרהו על היין. דזכירה כתיב על היין זכרו כיין לבנון (הושע יד) נזכירה דודיך מיין (שיר א) והאי זכירה היינו קידוש דויכולו לא מליגו על הכוס אלא בתפלה כדאמר בשבת (ד' קיט:) ולא ניתקן על הכוס אלא להוציא בניו ובני ביתו ומה שרגילין לומר ויכולו אחר התפלה בקול רם היינו משום י"ט שחל להיות בשבת שמתפללין אתה בחרתנו ואין אומר ויכולו בתפלה ותקנו נמי לומר בכל שבתות שלא לחלק בין שבת לשבת ונראה דקידוש על היין אסמכתא היא והא דאמר במי שמתו (ברכות ד' כ:) נשים חייבות בקידוש היום דבר תורה היינו דוקא קידוש היום אבל על היין לא הויא אלא מדרבנן כדמשמע בריש נזיר (ד' ג:) דקאמר מיין ושכר יזיר לאסור יין מצוה כיין הרשות ופריך מאי ניהו קידושא והבדלה מושבע ועומד מהר סיני הוא דאיצטריך קרא למיסר אלא כי הא דאמר רבא שבועה שאשתה וחזר ואמר הריני נזיר איצטריך קרא דנזירות חל עליו אף על פי שמושבע ועומד הוא ועוד מצינו למימר דקידוש על היין דבר תורה אבל הא דאמר המברך צריך שיטעום זהו מדרבנן: הוה גחין ושתי. וא"ת דבפרק שלשה שאכלו (ברכות ד' מז.) אמרינן אין המסובין רשאין לטעום עד שיטעום המברך וי"ל דהיינו דוקא בהמוציא שצריך לאכול כדאמרי' בפרק ראוהו ב"ד (ר"ה ד' כט:) לא יפרוס אדם פרוסה לאורחין אא"כ אוכל עמהן הלכך צריך להמתין עד שיטעום המברך אבל קידוש שאין חובה לשתות להמברך א"צ להמתין ומיהו בירושלמי דברכות א"ר אבא בשם רב מסובין אסורין לטעום עד שיטעום המברך ר' יהושע בן לוי אומר שותין אע"פ שלא שתה ולא פליגי מה דא"ר אבהו כשהיו כולן זקוקין לכוס אחד מה דאמר ר' יהושע כשיש לכל אחד כוסו בידו ומשמע נמי אם אין כוסו בידו אפי' שפך מכוס ברכה לכוסות אחרים אין להם לטעום עד שיטעום המברך אבל כשיש לכל אחד כוס א"צ להמתין ולכך הוה גחין ושתי ומכאן יש להוכיח שא"צ לשפוך מכוס של ברכה לשאר כוסות ומיהו היכא דפגימי צריך לשפוך ממנו לשאר כוסות כדי שישתו כולם מכוס שאינו פגום אע"ג דשתיה לא מעכבא כדאמרינן בפרק בכל מערבין (עירובין דף מ:) וגם בהמוציא יש להוכיח מירושלמי אם יש לכל אחד ככרו א"צ להמתין ואוכל כל אחד משלו והא דאמר טול ברוך (ברכות דף מ.) ואמרינן נמי (שם דף מו.) בעל הבית בוצע כדי שיבלע בעין יפה דמשמע שאין אוכלין אלא מה שמחלק להם מיירי בשאין ככר לפני כל אחד א"נ בשבת וכגון שאין להם לחם משנה דאז צריכין לאכול מבליעתו*: הנוטל

עין משפט נר מצוה

לה א מיי' פכ"ט מהל' שבת הלכה ט טוש"ע א"ח סי' קפב סעיף ג:

לו ב מיי' שם הלכה א סמג עשין כט [טור א"ח סי' רעא]:

לז ג מיי' שם הלכה י וסמג שם טור ש"ע א"ח סי' רפט סעיף א:

לח ד מיי' שם הל' ד סמג שם טור ש"ע א"ח סי' רצט ס"ו:

לט ה מיי' פ"ט מהל' גירושין הלכה כג סמג עשין נ טוש"ע אה"ע סי' קמד ס"ו:

מ ו מיי' פכ"ט מהלכות שבת הלכה ד סמג עשין כט טוש"ע א"ח סי' רצט סעיף ו:

רבינו חננאל

לו לברך עד שיטעום וש"מ טעמו פגמו לברכה וש"מ טעם מבדיל מדקתני ומשלשלן כלן בברכת המזון ומברך בכוס אחד והבדלה ש"מ אומר שתי קדושות בכוס אחד וש"מ מקדים המאור לבשמים ב"ש היא דאי ב"ה בשמים ואח"כ מאור אמרי: ר' יעקב בר אידי קפיד אכסא פגימה רב ששת קפיד אפי' מחצבא פגימה לא הוה מברך. מר בר רב אשי קפיד אפילו מחביתא פגימה: ת"ר זכור את יום השבת לקדשו זכרהו על היין בכניסתו אין לי אלא ביום בלילה מנין ת"ל זכור ומסקנא ביום מאי ואמרי' בורא פרי הגפן והוא קידושא רבה: אמרי בני רבי חייא מי שלא הבדיל במוצאי שבת מבדיל והולך כל השבת ועד כמה עד רביעי בשבת דאמר ר' זירא בענין גיטין יום ראשון ויום שני ויום שלישי בתר שבתא יום רביעי ויום חמישי ויום ששי קמי שבתא. אמר ר' יעקב בר אידי אבל בשארי ימי השבוע המבדיל אינו מברך על האור וכן תאני שלא: ואמר רב

[לעיל קה.] [לקמן קז.]

גיטין דף עז.

הגהות הב"ח

(א) רשב"ם ד"ה ה"ג כו' דכי קדיש תחלת יומא: (ב) ד"ה אין לי אלא ביום וכו' בלילה היא דבכניסתו היא קדושתו: (ג) ד"ה ואגיד וכו' אומר להם קידוש גדול:

[לעיל קה.]

[סימן נד.]

[וע"ע תוס' ברכות דף מו. ד"ה אין]

tasted [food] he recites *habdalah*;[8] [106a] [vii] you may recite two sanctities over the same cup;[9] and [viii] this is [the ruling of] Beth Shammai as interpreted by R. Judah.[10] R. Ashi said: [The deductions that] if he tastes it he renders it defective, and that the
a cup of Grace requires a [minimum] standard, are the same thing,[1] and this is what he says: What is the reason that once he tastes of it he renders it defective? Because the cup of Grace requires a [minimum] standard. R. Jacob b. Idi objected to a defective pitcher. R. Idi b. Shisha objected to a defective cup. Mar b. R. Ashi objected even to a defective barrel.[2]

Our Rabbis taught: *Remember the sabbath day, to keep it holy*:[3] remember it over wine.[4] I know it only of the day; whence do we know it of the night?[5] Because it is stated, '*remember the sabbath day, to keep it holy*.' [You ask], 'whence do we know it of the night?' —on the contrary, the principal *kiddush* is recited at night, for when he sanctifies, he must sanctify [from] the beginning of the day. Moreover, [you say,] 'whence do we know it of the night? Because it is stated, "*remember the sabbath day, to keep it holy*"'—the Tanna seeks [proof] for the night, while he adduces a verse relating to the day[time]?—This is what he means: '*Remember the sabbath day, to keep it holy*': remember it over the wine at its commencement.[6] I know it only of the night: whence do we know it of the day? Because it is said, '*Remember the sabbath* day, *to keep it holy*.'

What blessing does he recite by day?[7]—Said Rab Judah: '... who createst the fruit of the vine.'[8] R. Ashi visited Maḥuza.[9] Said they [the Maḥuzaeans] to him, 'Let the Master recite the Great *kiddush* for us.' They gave him [the cup of wine]. Now he pondered, What is the Great *kiddush*? Let us see, he reasoned, for all blessings [of *kiddush*] we first say '... who createst the fruit
b of the vine.'[1] [So] he recited '... who createst the fruit of the vine,' and tarried over it,[2] [and then] he saw an old man bend [his head] and drink. Thereupon he applied to himself [the verse], *The wise man, his eyes are in his head*.[3]

The sons of R. Ḥiyya said: He who did not recite *habdalah* at the termination of the Sabbath proceeds to recite *habdalah* anytime during the week. And until when?—Said R. Zera: Until the fourth day of the week.[4] Even as R. Zera sat before R. Assi—others state, R. Assi sat before R. Joḥanan—and he sat and stated: In respect to divorces, the first day of the week, the second, and the third [are defined as] after the Sabbath; the fourth, the fifth, and the eve of the [Sabbath] day [rank as] before the Sabbath.[5] R. Jacob b. Idi said: But [he does] not [recite a blessing] over the light.[6]

(8) There is a contrary view *infra* 106*b*, q.v. Here we see that when there is insufficient wine, he has his meal and then recites *habdalah*. (9) *Habdalah* and Grace are two separate sanctities, i.e., religious duties. (10) That the blessing for light precedes that of spices, for Beth Hillel reverse it (*supra* 103*a*). It cannot be the ruling of Beth Hillel as interpreted by R. Meir, for on that view the blessing for light *precedes* Grace, whereas this Baraitha states that all the blessings are recited *after* Grace.

a (1) I.e., tasting it renders it unfit only when less than the minimum quantity is thereby left; otherwise it would remain fit. (2) A small barrel is meant. If *kiddush* or *habdalah* was recited over wine contained in one of these, they insisted that it should be full. (3) Ex. XX, 8. (4) *Kiddush*, whereby the Sabbath is 'remembered,' must be recited over wine. (5) That *kiddush* must be recited Friday evening over wine. (6) '*To keep it holy*' implies that it is to be 'remembered,' i.e., sanctified, by *kiddush*, when the holiness of the day commences, which is in the evening. (7) It is stated *supra* 105*a* that *kiddush* ('sanctification') is not recited by day. (8) I.e., no special benediction apart from the usual one recited over wine. (9) V. 5*b*, n. c5.

b (1) Hence it would be fitting for that to be called the Great *kiddush*, since it is recited on every occasion. (2) He paused before drinking it in order to see whether this was deemed sufficient for the *kiddush* by day. (3) Eccl. II, 14. (4) Exclusive. From the fourth day onward the days are counted with the *following* Sabbath, and it would be inappropriate to recite *habdalah* then for the preceding Sabbath. (5) E.g., if a man divorces his wife on condition that she performs a certain action after a particular Sabbath, it must be done not later than the third day following; if he stipulates, before the Sabbath, Wednesday, Thursday, or Friday are meant. (6) When he recites *habdalah* later in the week. Rashbam: the reason is presumably because the blessing for light can be recited only at the termination of the Sabbath (v. *supra* 54*a*), since it was then created for the first time.

he recites [105b] the *kiddush* of the day over it,[4] because the *kiddush* of the day takes precedence over the honour of the day. Now if this is correct,[5] let him leave it until the morrow and do both with it?[6]—A religious duty is [more] precious [when performed] at the proper time.

Yet do we say, A religious duty is [more] precious [when performed] at the proper time?[7] Surely it was taught: He who enters his house on the termination of the Sabbath recites blessings over the wine, the light and the spices, and then he recites *habdalah* over the cup [of wine]. But if he has one cup only, he leaves it until after the meal and recites them all together after it.[8] Thus we do not say, A religious duty is [more] precious at the proper time?—Said he to him, 'I am neither a self-pretended scholar[9] nor a visionary [i.e., story-teller] nor unique [in this ruling],
a but I am a teacher and systematizer of traditions,[1] and they rule thus in the Beth Hamidrash as I do; we draw a distinction between ushering the day in and ushering the day out: as for ushering the day in, the more we advance it the better, as we thereby show our love for it; but as for ushering the day out, we delay it, so that it may not be [appear] a burden upon us.[2]

You may infer eight things from this Baraitha: [i] He who recites *habdalah* during the Prayer[3] must [also] recite *habdalah* over the cup [of wine];[4] [ii] Grace [after meals] requires a cup [of wine]; [iii] the cup [of wine] for Grace demands a [minimum] standard;[5] [iv] he who says a blessing [over anything] must partake thereof;[6] [v] if he tastes it he renders it defective;[7] [vi] even when one has

(4) I.e., *kiddush* on Friday evenings, which marks the sanctification of the whole day. But he must not leave it for drinking during the meal. (5) Viz., R. Naḥman's ruling. (6) *Kiddush*, and pay honour to the day by drinking some of it during the meal. (7) Even in such a case, where by postponing it an additional purpose is served. (8) V. *supra* 102b notes. (9) I have not said this on my own authority.

a (1) The translation follows Jast. V. however, Kaplan, *Redaction of the Babylonian Talmud*, pp. 253-255, where this passage is discussed. He inclines to translate thus: I am not a *hakima* (a special class of scholar who discussed difficult halachic matter) nor a Hozean (i.e., a citizen of Be Hozae; these were notorious for their ignorance—v. *supra* 50bf—and so Hozean may have meant, an ignoramus) nor an individual, but a director of the courses of Gemara and Sidra. (2) Hence *kiddush* is said as early as possible, and it may not be deferred for the morrow. But we willingly delay the *habdalah*. (3) The *'Amidah* or the Eighteen Benedictions, which constitute the Prayer *par excellence*; a *habdalah* formula is inserted in the fourth benediction. (4) For 'he who enters his house' implies that he has been away from home, presumably at the synagogue, where he would already have recited *habdalah* in the *'Amidah* of the evening service. (5) Viz., a quarter of a *log* (*rebi'ith*). Otherwise, he could use half for *habdalah* and half for Grace. (6) Either he or one of the listeners. For otherwise he could recite *habdalah* over the cup of wine and leave it untouched for Grace. (7) It is now assumed that he had more than one *rebi'ith*, but not two. Hence he could perform *habdalah*, drink the excess, and leave a *rebi'ith* for Grace. Since this is not done, it follows that merely by drinking a little of the whole cup it becomes unfit for Grace.

קידוש היום מפני שקידוש היום קודם לכבוד יום (וכבוד לילה) ואם איתא לישבקיה עד למחר וליעביד ביה תרתי א"ל *חביבה מצוה בשעתה ומי אמרינן חביבה מצוה בשעתה והא *תניא הנכנס לביתו במוצאי שבת מברך על היין ועל המאור ועל הבשמים ואחר כך אומר הבדלה על הכוס *ואם אין לו אלא כוס אחד מניחו עד לאחר המזון ומשלשלן כולן לאחריו ולא אמרינן חביבה מצוה בשעתה א"ל אנא לא חכימא' אנא ולא חוזאה אנא ולא יחידא' אנא אלא גמרנא וסדרנא אנא וכן מורין בבי מדרשא כוותי *שאני לן בין עיולי יומא לאפוקי יומא עיולי יומא כל כמה דמקדמינן ליה עדיף ומחבבינן ליה אפוקי יומא מאחרינן ליה כי היכי דלא ליהוי עלן כטונא שמע מינה מיהא מתני' תמני ש"מ *המבדיל בתפלה צריך שיבדיל על הכוס וש"מ *ברכה טעונה כוס וש"מ *כוס של ברכה צריך שיעור וש"מ *המברך צריך שיטעו' וש"מ *טעמו פגמו וש"מ *טעם מבדיל

ושמע

תוספות

שמע מינה תמני. תימה דהוה מצי למימר תשע שמע מינה שמותר לאכול קודם הבדלה כשאין לו אלא כוס אחד ולפירוש רבינו ניסים (ג) דמיירי כשהתחיל לאכול מבעוד יום ניחא אך קשה על פירושו כדפי' לעיל: **שמע** מינה המבדיל בתפלה צריך שיבדיל על הכוס. וא"ת בפרק אין עומדין (ברכות דף לג:) דאמר ליה רבינא לרבא הלכתא מאי א"ל כקידושא מה קידושא בתפלה ועל הכוס אף הבדלה אמאי לא פשיט ליה מברייתא דהכא וי"ל משום דאיכא ברייתא התם שסוברת שא"ל להבדיל בשניהם דקתני המבדיל בזו ובזו יעוחו לו ברכות על ראשו *והכא דמשמע ליה דודאי הבדיל בתפלה אף על גב דאיכא דלא מבדלי מדאמר המבדיל בזה ובזה כו' משום דרוב בני אדם מבדילים בתפלה: **שמע** מינה ברכה טעונה כוס. קצת משמע דאפילו ביחיד טעונה כוס דהנכנס משמע שהוא יחידי וכן משמע לקמן (דף קיז:) דתנן שלישי אומר עליו ברכת המזון וקאמר בגמ' שמע מינה בהמ"ז טעונה כוס וארבעה כוסות תיקנו אפילו ביחידי מיהו יש לדחות משום דבהמ"ז טעונה כוס בג' תיקנו בפסח אפילו ביחיד כוס לברכת המזון דאי בשום פעם אינה צריכה מה ענין כוס בבהמ"ז היה להם לתקן שיר לכוס שלישי והעולם אין נוהגין לברך בהמ"ז על הכוס אלא בג' ורבינו שלמה בן רבינו מאיר אומר להטעין כוס אפילו ביחיד וכן מוכח במדרש שוחר טוב על קרא דשני רשעים שברת ועוד מוכיח מורי הר"ר יחיאל דטעונה כוס אפילו ביחיד דאי אינה טעונה כוס למה מניחו אחר המזון יבדיל לפני המזון ויאכל כל אחד בעצמו ואז לא תהא טעונה כוס וא"ת לר"ג דאמר בכילד מברכין (ברכות דף מד.) דכל ז' מינין טעונין ג' ברכות דהיינו בהמ"ז ואם יצטרך כוס גם אותו כוס יצטרך כוס אחר א"כ לא יפטר לעולם וי"ל דלא תקנו כוס אלא אחר סעודת לחם ולה"ג שאין לברך על הגפן אחר בהמ"ז אתי נמי *שפיר ונראה דכן הלכה דבהמ"ז טעונה כוס ובאלו דברים (שם דף נב.) דאיכא ברייתא דסברה אינה טעונה מוקי לה התם כתנאי אליבא דב"ש: **וש"מ** כוס של ברכה צריך שיעור. פי' מדאינו מחלקו לב' כוסות ותימה דהא מדקתני אין אלא כוס א' משמע דאין לו כלי אחר דהכי אמרי' בברכות באלו דברים (ג"ז שם) דקאמר התם וסברי ב"ש בהמ"ז טעונה כוס והתנן בא להם יין אחר המזון ואין לו אלא כוס אחד מברך על היין ואח"כ מברך על המזון מאי לאו דמברך עליה ושתי ליה מיד לא דמברך ומנח ליה ולא שתי ומניחו לבהמ"ז והאמר מר המברך צריך שיטעום דטעים ליה בידיה שיניח מעט מן היין בידו וישתה ולא יפגום ומיירי שאין שם רביעית בלמצום משמע מדמוקי לה בטעים ליה בידיה ולא קאמר שיניח היתר מרביעית בכלי אחר משום דקתני אין לו אלא כוס אחד היינו אין לו אלא כלי אחד וי"ל דהתם כיון דמיירי דאיכא טפי מרביעית א"כ אין לו אלא כוס אחד היינו על כרחך כלי אחד דאי לענין דליכא שני רביעית קאמר הלא א"ל שיעור לברך על היין לשתות דאפילו אמשהו מברך שלא יהנה בלא ברכה והרי יכול לברך ולשתות העודף על הרביעית ורביעית הנשאר יניח לברכת המזון אלא אין לו אלא כלי אחד קאמר אבל הכא אין לו אלא כוס אחד אין נראה דכלי אחד קאמר דהא הנכנס לביתו קתני שלא התחיל לאכול ואי אפשר שלא ימצא כלי אחר דמסתמא לא מיירי בגברא ערטילאי הלכך ע"כ לענין דאין לו שני שיעורין קאמר ובברכות דמיירי בא להם יין על השלחן אפשר שאין לו על השלחן אלא כלי אחד: **ש"מ** טעם מבדיל. ולא ימתין עד למחר קודם אכילה: **שמע** מינה טעמו פגמו. נראה דס"ד דאיכא טפי מרביעית ומשום דליכא שתי רביעיות קרי ליה כוס אחד והשתא מוכח שפיר דטעמו פגמו אף על גב דכוס של ברכה צריך שיעור דנהי דצריך שיעור יטעום מלא לוגמיו יותר על הרביעית והרביעית יניח לבהמ"ז ורב אשי דחי דמיירי דליכא שיעור טעימה יותר מרביעית דאם טעמו חסר שיעורו ומיהו קשה היכי מוכח טעמו פגמו מדלא טעם העודף אכתי מיקשי ליה אמאי לא טעים ליה בידיה או בכלי אחר כדאמר באלו דברים וי"ל בכוס חובה כגון הבדלה ובהמ"ז וקידוש צריך לשתות מכוס שיש בו רביעית הלכך לא אפשר למיטעם בידיה או בכלי אחר אבל בברכות דלא מיירי בכוס חובה אפשר לתקן ע"י דטעים ליה בידיה:

ושמע

רשב"ם

ולא אמרינן חביבה מצוה בשעתה. דלא מבדיל מקמי סעודתא דהוי שעת הבדלה: לא חכימא אנא. דלא אמינא ליה אלא מדעתאי להא דחביבה מצוה בשעתה: ולא חוזאה אנא. מגיד: ולא אמינא ליה משמיה דגברא יחידאה: אלא גמרנא אנא. כך שמעתי בישיבה: וסדרנא אנא. מסדר שמועות לפני רבותי תמיד: עיולי יומא. מחבבינא ליה ועבדינן קידוש מאורתא כי היכי דלנקטיה עילוי היא: לאפוקי יומא. כגון אבדלתא: מאחרינן ליה. היכא דאין לו אלא כוס אחד עד לאחר המזון: שמע מינה המבדיל בתפלה כו'. דקתני הנכנס לביתו במוצאי שבת מבדיל אף על גב דסתם בני אדם מבדילין בתפלה: וש"מ ברכה טעונה כוס. ברכת המזון: ושמע מינה. (ברכת המזון) [כוס] (א) של ברכ' צריך שיעור דאי לא צריך שיעור ליחלקי' לתרי: ושמע מינה צריך המברך שיטעום: דאי לא טעים ליה ליברך עליה תרי זימני: ושמע מינה טעמו פגמו. כבר מברכת המזון

קידוש היום. קידוש הלילה שמקדשין את היום על הכוס בלילה קודם לכבוד יום שלא ישתה אותו באמצע סעודה אלא יקדש בו בלילה קודם אכילה: וליעביד ביה תרתי. קידוש היום והוי נמי כבוד היום קצת אע"פ שאינה בתוך הסעודה: חביבה מצוה בשעתה. כדאמר באלו דברים (לעיל דף סח:) שהרי הקטר חלבים ואברים כשרים כל הלילה ואין ממתינין להם בשבת עד שתחשך שנא' (במדבר כח) עולת שבת בשבתו הלכך יקדש בו בלילה ולא ימתין בו עד מחר: ומי אמרינן. גבי ברכה חביבה מצוה בשעתה: ומשלשלן כולן לאחריו. לאחר ברכת המזון יין נר בשמים והבדלה כב"ש אליבא דר' יהודה והכי מפרשי' לקמיה ולא אמר חביבה מצוה בשעתה דלא מבדיל מקמי מזון דהוי' שעת הבדלה: לא חכימא אנא. לא אמינא לה מדעתאי להא דחביבה מצוה בשעתה: ולא חוזאה אנא. מגיד: ולא אמינא לה משמיה דגברא יחידאה: אלא גמרנא אנא. כך שמעתי בישיבה: וסדרנא אנא. מסדר שמועותי לפני רבותי כך מפרש רבינו שלמה ובתלמידי רבינו יצחק כתב ה"ג לא חכימא אנא ולא גמרנא אנא אלא מסדרנא אנא וה"ל פי' הדבר כן לא חכימא אנא לומר מה שאמרתי מעצמי מקדש והולך כל היום כולו וגם לא לצרך חביבה מצוה בשעתה ולא גמרנא אנא לא למדתי דבר זה מרבותי בסדר קידוש אלא סדרנא אנא כל סדרי ברכות קידוש והבדלה נתתי לב בהן לברר את כולן לא נתישבתי עד שעמדתי על עיקרן ועל סדרן להורות לעולם כן: עיולי יומא. מחבבינן ליה ועבדינן קידושא מאורתא כי היכי דלינקטיה עילוי הייא דחביבה מצוה בשעתה וזריזין מקדימין למצוה: לאפוקי יומא. כגון הבדלה מאחרינן ליה היכא דאשכחן שום עילה לאחוריה כגון היכא דאין לו אלא כוס אחד דמאחרינן ליה עד לאחר המזון: שמע מינה המבדיל בתפלה כו'. דקתני הנכנס לביתו במוצאי שבת מבדיל ואע"ג דסתם בני אדם מבדילין בתפלה: ש"מ ברכה טעונה כוס. ברכת המזון: וש"מ כוס של ברכה צריך שיעור. רביעית לוג דאי לא קימא הכי דצריך שיעור ליחלקיה לתרי: וש"מ המברך צריך שיטעום. או הוא או אחד מן השומעים ובשתיית אחד מהן יצאו כולן כדאמר בעירובין בפרק בכל מערבין (דף מ:) דאמר התם ליברך עליה וליניחיה ומשני המברך צריך שיטעום וליתביה ליינוקא לית הלכתא כרב אחא בר יעקב דאמר למיסרך וביום הכפורים קאי וש"מ המברך צריך שיטעום לכתחלה ואם לא טעם כי אם אחד מהן יצאו כולן ידי חובתן אבל אין מברכין על הכוס אם לא ישתה א' מהן ואפילו בשתיית תינוק שפיר דמי ומברייתא זו שמעינן דצריך שיטעום דאי לא טעים ליה ליברך עליה תרי זימני הבדלה בשעתה בלא שתיה וברכת המזון בסעודה וישתה: וש"מ טעמו פגמו. לברכת המזון מדלא מבדיל ברישא קודם אכילה ושותה ומשייר המותר לברכת המזון: וש"מ טעם מבדיל. אף על פי שאכל מבדיל ולא ימתין עד מחר קודם אכילה דאיכלה לקמן דאמר לקמן (דף קו:) טעם אינו מבדיל הכא לא גרסי' טעם אינו מקדש

ושמע

עין משפט נר מצוה

כח א מיי' פכ"ט מהל' שבת הלכה יג טוש"ע א"ח סי' רצט סעיף ד:
כט ב מיי' שם הלכה ו סמג עשין כט [טוש"ע א"ח סי' רצד ס"א]:
ל ג מיי' פ"ז מהלכות ברכות* הל' טו סמג עשין כז טוש"ע א"ח סי' קפב ס"א*:
לא ד מיי' שם הלכה יד ופכ"ט מהל' שבת הלכה ז טוש"ע א"ח סי' רעה סעיף יא:
[ומסקנא דהש"ס אם הבדיל בזו ולא הבדיל בזו יעמו לו ברכות על ראשו]
לב ה מיי' שם הלכה טו ופכ"ט מהל' שבת הל"ז טוש"ע א"ח סי' קפ ס"ד וסי' רעא סעיף יד:
לג ו מיי' פכ"ט מהל' שבת הלכ' טז טוש"ע א"ח סי' קפב סי"ג:
לד ז מיי' שם הלכה ס סמג עשין כט טוש"ע א"ח סי' רעג ס"ה:

[לקמן קיז:] [ברכות נג.] [וע"ע תוס' ברכות נז. ד"ה נתן]

רבינו חננאל

איתו מקדש ביום לפיכך לא פסיקא ליה דלא תאני ליה: ת"ש כבוד יום וכבוד לילה כבוד יום קודם ואם איתא דמקדש ביום ונשבקיה עד למחר וליעבד ביה תרתי קידוש וכבוד יום ופרקי' חביבה מצוה בשעתה כלומר כיון שהלילה קודם לקידושה מן היום אין מעבירין מצות הקידוש מן הלילה עד למחר: איני והתניא הנכנס לביתו במוצאי שבת מברך על היין ועל המאור ועל הבשמים ואומר הבדלה ואם אין לו אלא כוס אחד מניחו לאחר המזון ומשלשלן לאחריו הנה מאחרת ההבדלה לאחר המזון ולא אמרי' חביבה מצוה בשעתה ופרקי' שאני עיולי יומא מאפוקי יומא עיולי יומא מחבבינן ליה ולא מאחרינן ליה אפוקי יומא דהיא חלא בהבדלה מאחרינן ליה ואסקינן ש"מ מיהא מתניתא תמני וסימ' תלתי כסי ותלתא טעמי ושתי קדושות מדקתני מבדיל על הכוס ש"מ שהמבדיל בתפלה צריך שיבדיל על הכוס ומדקתני מניחו לאחר המזון ש"מ ברכת המזון טעונה כוס ומדלא מבדיל במקצתו ש"מ כוס של ברכה צריך שיעור כדי רביעית ואין לו אלא שיעור אחד ומדלא קתני מבדיל ומניחו לאחר המזון ומברך עוד עליו ש"מ דאסור

מסורת הש"ס

[לעיל קה: וש"נ] [לעיל דף קב. וש"נ] [ברכות נב.] שם נג. [שבת קנ: לקמן קז.] [ברכות נב.] [לקמן קז:]

הגהות הב"ח

(א) רשב"ם ד"ה ושמע מינה כוס של ברכה בהמ"ז צריך שיעור כצ"ל: (ג) תוס' ד"ה שמע מינה וכו' ולפירוש רבינו ניסים. נ"ב לעיל דף ק"ב ע"ב בד"ה מניחו:

גליון הש"ס

גמ' וש"מ ברכה טעונה כוס. עי' ס"ל מ"ד דמאי וכו"ש שם:

קשיא לעולא · שפתח בברוך ולא חתם : הודאה היא · ואין בה הפסק דבר אחר לא הפסק תחנה ולא הפסק רילוי הלכך בפתיחתן סגי ולא דמו לברכת קידוש שצריך לספר בשבח שבת וברכת יוצר אור שיש בה הפסק תחנה כגון ברחמיך הרבים וברכת אבות יש בה רצוי לפיכך צריך לפתוח ולסיים בשבחו של מקום: הוו יתבי בסעודתא· בערב שבת והאריכו בה עד שחשיכה: ונפסיק · בעקירת השלחן : ונקבעה · לסעודתינו: לשבתא · לשם שבת : לא צריכיתו · להפסיק בעקירת שלחן כדי להבדיל בין סעודת חול לסעודת שבת : שבת היא קבעתה . מעצמה היא חשובה סעודת שבת ונבדלת מסעודת חול ודי לכם בפריסת מפה וקידוש : כשם שקובעת למעשר · אפילו אכילת ערא' דשבת חשובה קבע למעשר במסכת ביצה (ד' לה:) : כך קובעת לקידוש · שאסור לטעום עד שיקדש אלמא משחשיכה היא חשובה סעודת שבת מאליה (א) : כך · יציאתה קובעת להבדלה שאם יושבים על השלחן וחשיכה במוצאי שבת אסורין לאכול עד שיבדילו : והני מילי · דלהבדלה איהי קובעת לאפסוקי סעודתא אבל אתחולי לא מתחלינן משחשיכה עד שיבדילו : הני מילי · דאין מפסיקין לאכילה אבל לשתיה לאו דבר חשוב הוא ומפסקי : ולא אמרן · דלא מתחלי אלא בחמרא ושיכרא אבל מיא לית לן בה : הזכרה בברכת המזון · של שבת רצה והחליצנו וביום טוב יעלה ויבא: כבוד יום וכבוד לילה · אם (ב) לו יין הרבה לסעודה אחת או מיני מגדים יניחם עד היום : ולא

קשיא לעולא אמר לך עולא הא נמי כברכת המצות דמיא ברכת המצות מאי טעמא משום דהודאה היא הא נמי הודאה היא רב חנניא בר שלמיא ותלמידי דרב הוו יתבי בסעודתא וקאי עלייהו רב המנונא סבא אמרו ליה זיל חזי אי מקדיש יומא נפסיק וניקבעיה לשבתא אמר להו לא צריכיתו *שבתא קבעה נפשה דאמר רב כשם שהשבת קובעת למעשר כך שבת קובעת לקידוש סבור מינה כי היכי דקבעה לקידוש כך קבעה להבדלה אמר להו רב עמרם הכי אמר רב לקידוש קובעת ולא להבדלה קובעת והני מילי לענין מיפסק דלא מפסקינן אבל אתחולי לא מתחלינן ומיפסק נמי לא אמרן אלא באכילה אבל בשתיה לא ושתיה נמי לא אמרן אלא בחמרא ושיכרא אבל מיא לית לן בה ופליגא דרב הונא דרב הונא חזייה להוא גברא דשתה מיא קודם הבדלה אמר ליה לא מיסתפי מר מאסכרה דתנא משמיה דרבי עקיבא כל הטועם כלום קודם שיבדיל מיתתו באסכרה דבי רב אשי לא קפדי אמיא בעא מיניה רבינא מרב נחמן בר יצחק מי שלא קידש בערב שבת מהו שיקדש והולך כל היום כולו א"ל מדאמרי *בני רבי חייא מי שלא הבדיל במוצאי שבת מבדיל והולך כל השבת כולו הכא נמי מי שלא קידש בערב שבת מקדש והולך כל היום כולו איתיביה *לילי שבת ולילי יום טוב יש בהן קדושה על הכוס ויש בהן הזכרה בברכת המזון שבת ויום טוב אין בהם קדושה על הכוס ויש בהן הזכרה בברכת המזון ואי סלקא דעתך מי שלא קידש בערב שבת מקדש והולך כל היום כולו שבת ויום טוב נמי משכחת להו דיש בהן קדושה על הכוס דאי לא קידש מאורתא מקדש למחר אמר ליה *דאי לא קתני איתיביה* [תוספתא דברכות פ"ג] כבוד יום וכבוד לילה כבוד יום קודם ואם אין לו אלא כוס אחד אומר עליו

קידוש

קשיא לעולא · לפירוש הקונטרס דפירש לעיל דלא אמר אלא המבדיל בין קודש לחול ותו לא קשה מאי ס"ד דמקשה הא פשיטא דלברכת הפירות דמיא דאין לך קצרה יותר מזו ועוד לימא דסבר עולא כר' יהודה הגשיא דמשמע נמי דלא הוי חתים ונראה דעולא אמר נמי כל שאר הבדלות ואישתיק בלא חתימה וס"ד דמקשה כיון דארוכה היא קצת הוה ליה למיחתם בברוך מידי דהוה אקידוש שחותמין בה אע"ג דהודאה היא כיון שיש בה אריכות קצת ומשני דדמיא שפיר לברכת פירות וכן משמע דרב יהודה לא היה שואל אלא לידע אם יחתום או כרב או כשמואל :

כך קובעת לקידוש · שאסור לאכול בלא קידוש אפילו התחיל לאכול מבעוד יום וה"נ קובעת למעשר אפי' התחיל לאכול עראי מבעוד יום כדאמרינן בסוף המביא כדי יין (ביצה ד' לה.) היה אוכל באשכול וחשכה לו שבת רבי אליעזר אומר יגמור רבי יהושע אומר לא יגמור : והנ"מ דאכלו ושתו מעיקרא · משמע שהיו אוכלים בשבת סמוך לחשיכה ותימה שלא נהגו לאכול בין מנחה למעריב וגם ר"ת כעס על רבינו משולם שהנהיג לאכול בין מנחה למעריב דאמר במדרש השותה מים בשבת בין השמשות גוזל את קרוביו המתים וכתב שפעם אחת אירע מעשה בלותיר ובא לידי סכנה ובקושי התירו ערב יום הכפורים לאכול אחר וידוי משום שכרות וגם תשעה באב שחל להיות בשבת ונדחה התירו בקושי ויש לדחות דמיירי הכא שהתחילו בהיתר ובאמצע סעודה התפללו מנחה והיכא דהתחילו בהיתר מותר להשלים : אבל לשתיה מפסיקין · פירוש שתיה בלא סעודה דאין בה קביעות ולכך מפסיקין : לא קפדי אמיא· ובריית' דכל הטועם מיתתו באסכרה לא מוקמי אמיא ומיתתו באסכרה מדה כנגד מדה הוא משביע גרונו יחנק ואסכרה במקום חנק כדאמרינן (כתובות ד' ל:) מי שנתחייב חנק או טובע בנהר או מת בסרונכי והיינו אסכרה :

שמע

רשב"ם

קשיא לעולא · שפתח בברוך ולא חתם בברוך : הא נמי הודאה היא · ואין בה הפסק דבר אחר לא הפסק תחנה ולא הפסק רצוי הלכך בפתיחתן סגי ולא דמי לברכת קידוש שצריך לספר בשבח שבת וברכת יוצר אור שיש בה הפסק תחנה כגון ברחמיך הרבים וברכת אבות יש בה דברי רצוי וצריך לפתוח ולסיים בשבחו של מקום : הוו יתבי בסעודתא · ערב שבת והאריכו בה עד שחשיכה : ונפסיק · בעקירת
שלחן : וניקבעיה · לסעודתיט : בשבתא · לשם שבת : לא צריכיתו · להפסיק בעקירת שלחן כדי להבדיל בין סעודת חול לסעודת שבת : דשבת היא קבעה נפשה · לסעודתה דמאחר שהיא אוסרת עלינו לאכול מעתה בלא קידוש אין לך הפסק גדול מזה ומעצמה סעודת שבת חשיבא נבדלת מסעודת חול ודי לכם בפריסת מפה וקידוש : כשם שקובעת למעשר · פירוש אכילת עראי דשבת חשבי אותה קבע למעשר במסכת ביצה (דף לד:) משום דהוי עונג אפי' סעודה כל שהוא דידה קבע הוא ואין אוכלין בשבת אפילו עראי מתבואה [א] שלא נגמרה מלאכתה למעשר אלא אם כן עישר מערב שבת : קובעת לקידוש · שאסור לטעום עד שיקדש אלמא משחשיכה היא חשובה אכילת שבת מאליה : כך קובעת להבדלה · כך יציאתה קובעת להבדלה שאם יושבין על השלחן וחשיכה במוצאי שבת אסור לאכול עד שיבדילו ואע"פ שלא הפסיקו סעודתן (ג) פורס מפה ומבדיל שיציאת שבת אוסרתן באכילה וקובעתן להבדלה : הבדלה אינה קובעת · דכיון שהתחיל בסעודת שבת מבעוד יום זהו כבוד שבת שיהא גומר סעודתו אף לאחר שהחשיך ולאחר שגמר סעודתו יבדיל : והני מילי · דהבדלה אינה קובעת לאפסוקי סעודתא אבל לאתחולי לא מתחלינן : והני מילי · דלא מפסקי לאכילה אבל לשתיה לאו דבר חשוב הוא ומפסיק ומבדיל : ולא אמרן · אתחולי לא אלא חמרא ושיכרא אבל מיא לית לן בה : לא קפדי אמיא · קמי הבדלה אבל קמי קידושא קפדי משום כבוד שבת והכי הלכתא ושמעינן נמי שאם היו סועדים בשבת והחשיך גומרין כל סעודתן ומזמנין ואחר כך מבדילין : מבדיל והולך כל השבת כולו · עד רביעי בשבת כדלקמן : הזכרה בברכת המזון · רצה והחליצנו וביום טוב יעלה ויבא : שבת ויום טוב · הימים ולא הלילות : אין בהן קדושה על הכוס · כי אם בורא פרי הגפן לבד : דאי לא קתני · דתנא לא בא להורות לנו דין אדם הפושע או שאירע לו מקרה ולא קיים דברי חכמים : כבוד יום וכבוד לילה · אם אין לו יין הרבה לסעודה או מיני מגדים יניחם עד היום :

קידוש

[לקמן קז.] [תוספתא ברכות פ"ג] [יבמות י. מנחות נב:]

כד א מיי' פכ"ט מהל' שבת הלכה יב סמג עשין כט טוש"ע א"ח סי' רעא סי"ד :

כה ב מיי' שם וסמג שם טוש"ע א"ח סי' רצט ס"א :

כו ג מיי' שם הלכה ד וסמג שם טור ש"ע א"ח סי' רעא ס"ח :

כז ד מיי' שם טור ש"ע סעיף ג :

רבינו חננאל

קשיא לעולא דאמר הבדלה אינה חשובה בכל אלו ופריק ברכת הבדלה נמי כברכת המצות דמיא. רב חיננא בר שלמיא תלמידי דרב הוו יתבי בסעודתא והוה קאי עלייהו רב המנונא סבא אמרי ליה חזי אי נגה יומא נפסוק ונקבעה לשבתא אמר להו לא צריכיתו שבת היא קבעה נפשה דהכי אמר רב כשם שהשבת קובעת המוקצה לענין המעשר פי' העת שהיא ספק חשכה ספק לא חשכה אין מעשרין את הודאי וכל מה שהגיעה אותה עונה ולא עישר הרי נקבע מוקצה כל השבת ותנן בתרומות פ"ו היה אוכל באשכול ונכנס מן הגנה לחצר ר' אליעזר אומר יגמור ר' יהושע אומר לא יגמור חשכה לילי שבת רבי אליעזר אומר יגמור כלומר יאכל האשכול כולו ר' יהושע אומר לא יגמור פי' שכיון שנכנסה השבת נקבע למעשר דאמרי' דעתו של אדם לענג השבת בכל מידי דבר אכילה וזה האשכול כאלו דעתיה עלוית ואסתלק מתורת עראי ונעשה קבע לפיכך אסור לאכול ממנו עד שיעשר ואע"פ שלא קבעו האדם השבת מעצמה נקבעת בחשיכת ערב שמש ונאסרו הפירות כי נקבעו למעשר ונעשו מוקצה כענין הזה כיון שחשכה נקבעה לקידוש ואע"פ שלא קדשוה בני אדם בפיהם מעצמה נתקדשה ואין אנו צריכין לחקור הגיע עת הקידוש מן הגגות ומראשי הדקלים ואתינן למימר כשם שמפסיקין לקידוש דשבת קבעת נפשה כך מפסיקין להבדלה ואסקה רב עמרם הכי אמר רב לקידוש קובעת להבדלה אינה קובעת ולא אמרן אלא לאפסוקי דלא מפסיק ומסלק השלחן בעת דספק חשכה וספק לא חשכה אבל לאתחולי קבעה ולא מתחיל בסעודה בשבת עם חשכה עד דנפיק יומא ומבדיל ומפסיק נמי דאמרן דלא מיחייב לאפסוקי סעודתייהו ולסלק השלחן הני מילי אם היא סעודת אכילה אבל אם היא משתה מפסיק ולא אמרן במשתה [היין] מפסיק אלא משתיית יין ושכר אבל משתיית מים לית לן בה ואפי' לאתחולי. דאע"ג דרב הונא חזייה להוא גברא דהוה שתי מיא מקמי הבדלה אמר לא מסתפית מאסכרה דתנא משמיה דרבי עקיבא כל הטועם קודם שיבדיל מיתתו באסכרה ולא היא דהא דרבנן דבי רב אשי לא הוו קפדי אמיא : בעא מיניה רבינא מרב נחמן בר יצחק מי שלא קידש [בע"ש] מהו שיקדש כל היום אמר ליה מדאמרי בני ר' חייא מי שלא הבדיל במוצאי שבת מבדיל והולך כל השבת כולו הכא נמי מי שלא קידש בערב שבת מקדש והולך כל היום כולו ואותבינן עליה מהא לילי שבת ויום טוב יש בהן קדושה על הכוס והזכרה בברכת המזון פי' שצריך אלהינו ואלהי אבותינו יעלה ויבוא ימים אין בהן קדושה על הכוס ויש בהן הזכרה בברכת המזון ואם איתא דמי שלא קידש בערב שבת מקדש ביום השבת גם אתה מוצא ביום השבת קדושה על הכוס כלומר לא פירש בזו הברייתא אלא דברים קבועין ועומדין אבל זה שאינו מצוי הקידוש ביום השבת אלא אם לא קדש בערב שבת

אינו

הגהות הב"ח

(א) רשב"ם ד"ה כך קובעת לקידוש וכו' מאליה הס"ד ואח"כ מ"ה כך קובעת להבדלה וכו' : (ב) ד"ה כך קובעת (כך) יציאתה : (ג) רשב"ם ד"ה כך קובעת וכו' סעודתן (פורס מפה) תא"מ ונ"ב פ"ס טוב ע"ל מה שכתבתי :

גליון הש"ס

ברשב"ם ד"ה כשם שקובעת וכו' שלא נגמרה מלאכתה. עי' ביצה דף לד ע"ב ודף לה ע"א : שם למשנה לאכולה דצריך להיות שנגמרה מלאכתו וצ"ע. שו"ר בהלכו מ"ו הגאון מו"ה ליב פיסלם נרו ד"ל דברי רשב"ם

הגהות מהר"ב רנשבורג

[א] ברשב"ם ד"ה כשם שקובעת למעשר וכו' מתבואה שלא נגמרה מלאכתה למעשר וכו'. נ"ב תימה לי דזהו נגד מסקנא דר' יוחנן בביצה דף לה ע"א דמשיק דאינו קובע אלא בדבר שנגמרה מלאכתו ואולי ... פ"ג מהלכות מעשר הלכה כ"ג בלשון הרמב"ם יעוש"ה ודפח"ח :

a [105*a*] Now this raises a difficulty according to 'Ulla?[1]—'Ulla can answer you: This too is like a blessing for precepts. [For] what is the reason in the case of a blessing over precepts?[2] Because it is [mere] praise;[3] this too is praise.[4].

R. Ḥanania b. Shelemia and the disciples of Rab were sitting at a meal, and R. Hamnuna Saba[5] was waiting on them. Said they to him, 'Go and see if the day has become holy,[6] in which case we will interrupt [the meal][7] and appoint it for the Sabbath.'[8] 'You do not need it,' he replied; 'the Sabbath itself makes it an appointed [meal].[9] For Rab said: Just as the Sabbath makes [it an] appointed [meal] in respect of tithe,[10] so does the Sabbath make [it an] appointed [meal] in respect of *ḳiddush*.'[11] Now they understood from him: just as it makes [it an] appointed [meal] in respect of *ḳiddush*, so does it make [it an] appointed [meal] in
b respect of *habdalah*.[1] Said R. Amram to them, Thus did Rab say: It makes [it an] appointed [meal] in respect of *ḳiddush*, but it does not make [it an] appointed [meal] in respect of *habdalah*.[2] But that is only in respect of interrupting [the meal], viz., that we do not interrupt [it]; we may not however commence [one].[3] And even about interrupting we said this with respect to eating only, but not with respect to drinking.[4] And with respect to drinking too we said this only of wine and beer: but as for water, it does not matter.[5]

Now he differs from R. Huna. For R. Huna saw a certain man drinking water before *habdalah*, [whereupon] he observed to him, Are you not afraid of choking?[6] For it was taught in R. Akiba's name: He who tastes anything before reciting *habdalah* shall die through choking.[7] The Rabbis of R. Ashi's academy were not particular about water.

Rabina asked R. Naḥman b. Isaac: He who did not recite *ḳiddush* on the eve of the Sabbath,[8] can he proceed to recite *ḳiddush* at any time of the day?[9]—Said he to him: Since the sons of R. Ḥiyya said, He who did not recite *habdalah* at the termination of the Sabbath can proceed to recite *habdalah* the whole week, [it follows that] here too, he who did not recite *ḳiddush* on the eve of the Sabbath can proceed to recite *ḳiddush* at any time of the day. He raised an objection to him: On the nights of the Sabbath and on the nights of a Festival there is sanctification [*ḳiddush*] over the cup [of wine] and a reference [to the Sabbath or Festival]
c in the Grace after meals.[1] On the Sabbath and a Festival[2] there is no sanctification over a cup [of wine], but there is a reference in the Grace after meals. Now if you should think that he who did not recite *ḳiddush* on the eve of the Sabbath can proceed to recite *ḳiddush* the whole day, then on the Sabbath and Festival [during the day] too there may be sanctification over the cup, for if he did not recite *ḳiddush* in the evening, he recites *ḳiddush* on the morrow?—Said he to him: He [the Tanna] does not teach a case of 'if'.

He raised an objection to him: [If a man must choose between] the honour of the day and the honour of the night,[3] the honour of the day takes precedence; and if he has only one cup [of wine],

a (1) Why did he not conclude *habdalah* with 'Blessed' etc.? (2) That we do not conclude with 'blessed'. (3) It contains nothing else, and is consequently short. (4) To God, for having made a distinction between holy and profane, and it does not treat of any other subject. (5) The aged, or the Elder. (6) I.e., if the Sabbath has commenced. (7) By removing the tables; v. *supra* 100*a*, n. b7. (8) By removing the table and then bringing it back the meal would be specially appointed as being on account of the Sabbath. (Three meals must be eaten on the Sabbath, and probably they wished to signify that this, though started before, should count as one.) (9) Since you must pause to recite *ḳiddush*, that itself gives it the character of an appointed meal for the Sabbath. (10) A man may make a light meal, but not a full ('appointed') meal of untithed produce before it is completely ready and subject to tithe. (Produce is not subject to tithe until it has been harvested, threshed and carried in through the front of the house, v. B.M., 87*b*-88*a*.) But the Sabbath confers upon every meal, even if light, the character of a full, appointed meal, so that untithed produce is then forbidden. (11) Nothing whatsoever may be eaten before *ḳiddush*; thus we see that the Sabbath automatically makes it a Sabbath meal.

b (1) One must not eat at the conclusion of the Sabbath before *habdalah*. They understood that if a man commences during the day, the conclusion of the Sabbath automatically renders what follows an appointed meal, which is forbidden before *habdalah*, hence *habdalah* must be recited in the middle of the meal. (2) For having commenced the meal on the Sabbath, he honours the Sabbath by concluding it without interruption, even if it continues beyond nightfall. (3) Even a light meal, before *habdalah*. (4) Drinking must be interrupted for *habdalah*. (5) Drinking water is of such slight consequence that it is permitted before *habdalah*. Drinking wine and beer, however, occupies an intermediate position: it is sufficiently unimportant to be interrupted for *habdalah*, but too important to start after nightfall before *habdalah*. (6) This was a rebuke. (7) Through being unable to catch his breath. (8) I.e., at the very commencement of the Sabbath, immediately after nightfall. Perhaps the phrase, 'eve of the Sabbath' indicates that the *ḳiddush* was slightly advanced, so as to avert the possibility of commencing the Sabbath too late; cf. O.H. 271, 1 and מגן אברהם a.l. (9) *Sc.* the Sabbath.

c (1) Special passages are inserted. (2) I.e., during the daytime. (3) The Sabbath is honoured by indulging in more drink and special dainties; here he lacks sufficient for additions at all meals, and must choose between them.

'Ulla visited Pumbeditha. Said Rab Judah to R. Isaac his son, 'Go and offer him a basket of fruit, and observe how he recites
a *habdalah*.'[1] He did not go, [however, but] sent Abaye. When Abaye returned, he [R. Isaac] asked him, 'What did he say [in the *habdalah*]?' 'Blessed is He who maketh a distinction between holy and profane,' replied he, 'and nothing else.' When he came before his father he asked him, 'How did he recite it?' 'I did not go myself,' replied he, '[but] I sent Abaye, and he told me [that he recited] "... who makest a distinction between holy and profane".' Said he to him, 'Your pride and your haughtiness are the cause that you are unable to state the law from his own mouth.'

An objection is raised: In all blessings you commence with 'blessed [art Thou']' and conclude with 'blessed [art Thou],' except in the blessings over precepts,[2] the blessings over fruits,[3] a blessing immediately preceding[4] another, and the last blessing of the reading of the *Shema'*;[5] in some of these you commence with 'Blessed' but do not conclude with 'Blessed', while in others you conclude with 'Blessed' but do not commence with 'Blessed'; and [in the blessing] 'Who is good and doeth good [unto all]'[6] you commence with 'Blessed' but do not conclude with 'Blessed'.[7]

a (1) Make this an excuse for staying with him, so that you observe him reciting *habdalah*. (2) A blessing is recited before the fulfilment of every precept. (3) I.e., which are recited before eating or drinking; 'fruits' is employed generically and includes such items as bread, water, vegetables etc. (4) Lit., 'near to'. (5) The morning *Shema'* (v. Glos.) is preceded by two long benedictions and followed by one; the evening *Shema'* is followed by two. (6) This is the last of the four blessings which constitute Grace after Meals; v. Singer's Prayer Book pp. 378-384 for the whole, and p. 381 for the blessing under discussion. (7) The blessings for precepts and fruits are generally short, and therefore 'Blessed' is not repeated at the conclusion. Blessings immediately preceding others: e.g., those of the *'Amidah* (the 'Eighteen Benedictions'). As each ends with the formula, 'Blessed art Thou, O Lord, who' etc., the following does not commence with 'Blessed'. Similarly, the blessing immediately preceding the *Shema'* concludes with 'Blessed' etc., and the *Shema'* together with the blessing which follows it is regarded as one long blessing; hence that too does not commence with 'Blessed'. (That benediction itself ends with 'Blessed art Thou', etc.; hence the fourth one recited in the evening—v. n. a5—which follows immediately after, likewise does not commence with 'blessed'.) The fourth blessing of Grace after meals, though immediately following a conclusion containing the formula, 'Blessed art Thou, O Lord', etc., commences with 'Blessed', notwithstanding the above general rule, because it was instituted in memory of the Jews slain at Bethar in 135 C.E. which marked the disastrous end of the Bar Cochba revolt; hence it was regarded as quite distinct and apart from the rest. It is indeed a lengthy benediction, but as much of it consists of synonyms for God it would be unfitting to repeat 'Blessed art Thou' in the conclusion.

עין משפט
נר מצוה

כג א מיי' פ"א מהל' ברכות הלכה ה ופי"א הלכה א סמג עשין כז :

וליח הלכתא כוותיה עולא איקלע לפומבדיתא אמר ליה רב יהודה לרב יצחק ברי' זיל אמטי ליה כלכלה דפירי וחזי היכי אבדיל לא אזל שדר ליה לאביי כי אתא אביי א"ל היכי אמר א"ל ברוך המבדיל בין קודש לחול אמר ותו לא אתא לקמיה דאבוה א"ל היכי אמר אמר ליה אנא לא אזלי אנא שדריתיה לאביי ואמר לי המבדיל בין קודש לחול א"ל רברבנותיה דמר וסררותיה דמר גרמא ליה למר דלא תימא שמעתיה מפומיה מיתיבי* "כל הברכות כולן פותח בברוך וחותם בהן בברוך חוץ מברכת מצות וברכת הפירות וברכה הסמוכה לחבירתה וברכה אחרונה שבקרית שמע שיש מהן פותח (בהן) בברוך ואין חותם בברוך ויש מהן שחותם בברוך ואין פותח בברוך והטוב והמטיב פותח בברוך ואינו חותם בברוך
קשיא

המבדיל בין קודש לחול. ותו לא אמר בה שאר הבדלות ולא חתם בה : היא גרמא ליה למר . שלא הלכת אתה בעלמך : וברכת המלות . כגון להתעטף בליית ועל נטילת לולב : וברכה הסמוכה לחברתה כגון אותם של שמונה עשרה : וברכה אחרונה שבקרית שמע. אע"פ שאין ברכה אחרת למעלה הימנה שהתחיל בה בברוך : יש מהן . מאלו שהזכרנו שפותח בהן בברוך ואינו חותם בברוך כגון ברכת פירות ומלות : ויש מהן שחותם ואינו פותח · כגון ברכה הסמוכה לחבירתה שהרי פוטרתה ראשונה שנפתחה בברוך : הטוב והמטיב . אף על גב דסמוכה לחבירתה שהרי התחיל בברכת המזון בברוך משום דברכה באנפי נפשה איתקן משום הרוגי ביתר וכולה הודאה כברכת הפירות ומלות :
קשיא

רשב"ם

וליח הלכתא כוותיה אלא כרב יהודה ומדהתם במולאי שבת ליום טוב חתמינן בין קדש לקדש הכא במולאי שבת לחול חתמינן בין קדש לחול כך נראה בעיני דאי לא תימא הכי שמואל דאמר כמאן ואנן היכי קיימינן כוותיה כדלקמן : וליח הלכתא כותיה . כר' יהושע בן חנניה לפי שאין חותמין בשתים בפרק שלשה שאכלו (ברכות דף מט.) אלא כשמואל דהא לייטי עלה דרב : זיל אמטי ליה . לעולא ובעלילה זו תראה היאך מבדיל : המבדיל בין קדש לחול . הוא דאמר ותו לא : א"ל . רב יהודה לרב יצחק בריה : סררותיה דמר . כעס עליו על שלא הלך הוא בעלמו : דלא תימר שמעתיה *מפומיה . דרב יצחק אלא מפומיה דאביי ואמרינן (יבמות דף צז.) כל תלמיד חכם שאומרים דבר שמועה מפיו שפתותיו דובבות בקבר : ברכת המלות . כגון להתעטף בליית ועל נטילת לולב וטעמו של דבר לפי שאין בהן ריבוי דברים : וברכה הסמוכה לחבירתה . כגון חותם של שמונה עשרה ברכות : וברכה אחרונה שבקריאת שמע . אע"פ שאין ברכה אחרת למעלה הימנה שהתחיל בה בברוך שהרי הפסיק קרית שמע אעפ"כ אינו מתחיל בה בברוך וחשבינן לה ברכה הסמוכה לחבירתה לאותה שלפני ק"ש שהרי מחובר אמת ויציב על סופו של ק"ש וכדאמרינן בברכות (דף יד:) שצריך לסמוך אמת ויציב אחר אני ה' אלהיכם כדכתיב וה' אלהים אמת הלכך כחדא ברכתא אריכתא דמיא: יש · מאלו שהזכרנו שפותח בהן בברוך ואינו חותם כגון ברכת פירות ומלות : יש מהן . שחותמין ואינו פותח כגון ברכה הסמוכה לחבירתה שהרי פוטרתה הראשונה שנפתחה בברוך : וברכת הטוב והמטיב . דברכת המזון אע"ג דסמוכה לחבירתה שהרי התחיל בברכת המזון אף על פי כן פותח בה בברוך משום דברכה באנפי נפשה איתקן משום הרוגי ביתר שניתנו לקבורה הטוב שלא הסריחו והמטיב שנתנו לקבורה אבל אנו מאריכין בה קלת כדי לומר בה שלש מלכיות כדמפרש בפ' שלשה שאכלו (שם דף מט.) הלכך כולה חדא הודאה היא כברכת הפירות וכברכת המלות ולא בעיא חתימה :
קשיא

וליח הלכתא כוותיה. וטעמא לפי שאין חותמין בשתים וברייתא סברה (כר')[כמאן] דאמר בפ' ג' שאכלו (ברכות ד' מט.) חותמין בשתים ופי' רשב"ם דהלכה כשמואל דחתים בין קודש לחול מדחתמינן במולאי שבת לי"ט בין קודש לקודש ספ"ק דחולין (דף כו:) ש"מ במולאי שבת דחול חותמין בין קודש לחול :

כל הברכות פותח בברוך וחותם בברוך . ותימה ברכה דאלהי נשמה אמאי לא פותחת בברוך דהא מעיקרא לא הוות סמוכה לחבירתה כדאמרינן בברכות (דף ס:) כי מתער אומר אלהי נשמה וכן קשה מאתה הוא עד שלא נברא העולם ותפלת הדרך שחותם ואינו פותח בברוך וי"ל לפי שאינן ברכות אלא שבח ותפלה בעלמא וברכה שאחר מגילה נראה דחתמינן בא"י האל הנפרע לעמו ישראל מכל צריהם האל המושיע שהיא ארוכה ולא דמיא לברכת פירות ומלות שהן קצרות וכן יש בירושלמי דמגילה ובגמרא דידן (דף כא:) בספרים ישנים דחותם בה בברוך האל הנפרע כו' וברכה דבורא נפשות רבות חותם בירושלמי בא"י חי העולמים : חוץ מברכה הסמוכה לחבירתה . פירוש לפי שאת' בראשונה אין צריך לפתוח השניה בברוך וברכה שלאחר ההפטרה דצור כל העולמים עד שכל דבריו אמת וצדק ויש הפסק במחזורים ומתחיל נאמן אתה הוא ואין שם ברכה לא בחתימת הראשונה ולא בפתיחת השניה ונראה דכולה ברכה אחת היא דכולה משתעיא בנאמנות ובאמיתות המקום ומה שיש הפסק במחזורים לפי שהיו רגילים כל הציבור להפסיק שם ולומר שבח כדאמר במסכת סופרים (פרק יג הלכה י) וכן משמע התם דברכה אחת היא דקאמר דמפטיר מברך ז' ברכות כנגד ז' קרואים פי' בקריאת התורה בתחלה וסוף ואחת לפני ההפטרה וד' אחריה הרי ז' ושבע ברכות של נישואין שהכל ברא לכבודו ויוצר האדם ואשר יצר את האדם כו' שפותחין בברוך פירש רש"י בכתובות (דף ח.) דשהכל ברא לכבודו נתקנה לאסיפת העם והיה ראוי לאומרה משעת אסיפה והיא ברכה בפני עצמה וכן יוצר האדם לא היתה צריכה שהרי יאמר אשר יצר אחריה אלא להזכיר שתי יצירות תיקנוה והקדימוה לאשר יצר והרי היא כמו לעצמה ואשר ברא שפותחת בברוך לפי שאומר אותה לבדה כשאין פנים חדשות ור"ת אומר דשהכל ברא לכבודו ויוצר האדם לכך פותח בברוך בלא חתימה שהם קצרות כמו ברכת פירות ומצות ופתיחתן זו היא חתימתן ובאשר יצר את האדם צריך לפתוח בברוך שאם לא היה פותח היה נראה הכל ברכה אחת וברכת לעסוק בדברי תורה והערב נא אומר שהיא ברכה אחת כיון שאין פותח והערב נא בברוך והבדלה נמי שפותחת בברוך אע"פ שסמוכה לברכת מאור משום שלא תראה ברכה אחת ומיהו בירושלמי פריך והרי הבדלה ומשני רבי הוה מפזרן . וא"ת יהללוך שאחר הלל ויראו עינינו וישתבח למה אין פותח בהן בברוך וי"ל דיהללוך הויא סמוכה לברכה דלקרוא את ההלל ויראו עינינו להשכיבנו וישתבח לברוך שאמר ולא הוו הפסוקים הפסק כמו ברכה אחרונה שבקריאת שמע דלא הוי קריאת שמע הפסק ואם כן נראה שאין להפסיק בין ברוך שאמר לישתבח ומיהו קשה מיהללוך דליל פסח דאין מברכין לקרוא את ההלל לכך נראה דברכה שאחר פסוקים אין צריך פתיחה שבלא פתיחה ניכרת התחלה ובירושלמי (דברכות פ"א) פריך והרי גאולה פי' אשר גאלנו דסמוכה לברכה דקריאת הלל ומשני שנייא היא הלל אם שמע בבהכ"נ יצא פירוש שהיו קורין הלל בלילי פסח בבית הכנסת כדאיתא במס' סופרים (פ"כ הלכה ט') התיב ר' אלעזר בר ר' יוסי והרי סופה פירש רבינו שמואל בר ר' שמעי' סופה סוף ברכה דאשר גאלנו שחותם בברוך והיא כולה הודאה ומשני שתים הן אחת להבא ואחת לשעבר פירוש שתי גאולות אשר גאלנו גאולה דלשעבר וגאולה להבא שמחים בבנין עירך ולכך חותם בברוך דאין כולה הודאה דיש בה הפסק ותפלה שיגאל אותנו ופריך מהבדלה כדפרישית לעיל ופריך והרי נברך פי' ברוך הוא שאכלנו משלו כו' דהויא ברכה בפני עצמה כדאמרינן בפ' ג' שאכלו (ברכות ד' מו:) ומתחיל ברכת הזן בברוך אע"פ שסמוכה לנברך ומשני שנייא היא שאם היו שנים אוכלים אין אומר נברך ופריך והרי הזן פי' שאומר אחריו נודך ואין פותח בברוך אע"פ שפעמים אינה סמוכה לברכת הזן כשרצו השנים לזמן והשלישי מפסיק לרב ששת עד הזן צריך לשמוע והלכה כרב ששת באיסורי וכשיגמור סעודתו קאמר התם בסוף שמעתא דרבנן אמרי יחזור למקום שפסק קשיא ועוד פריך והרי הטוב והמטיב פי' בברכת המזון דסמוכה לחברתה ופותחת בברוך שנייא ביבנה תיקנוה ופריך והרי קידוש פירוש דסמוכה לבורא פרי הגפן ופותחין בברוך שנייא היא שאם היה אוכל מבעוד יום עד שיקדש היום אינו מברך בורא פרי הגפן ופריך והרי סופה של קידוש שחותמת בברוך וסלקא דעתך דכולה הודאה היא והויא כברכת פירות ומצות א"ר יונה טופס ברכה כך היא דאמר ר' יודן מטבע קצר פותח בברוך ואינו חותם בברוך מטבע ארוך פותח בברוך וחותם בברוך פי' וקידוש הוא מטבע ארוך ויש הפסק שאומר כי הוא יום. תחלה למקראי קודש ולכך חותם בברוך : **הטוב** והמטיב פותח ואינו חותם בברוך . וא"ת והלא ארוכה היא ועוד דר"ת פי' שצריך לומר ג' גמולות ג' הטבות כמו ג' מלכיות דאמר בברכות (ד' מט.) צריכה ג' מלכיות לבד מדידיה וי"ל שאין זה אריכות אלא שמזכיר שם שמים בהרבה לשונות מלכנו יוצרנו קדושנו קדוש יעקב רוענו כו' ואין ראוי לחתום בברוך:
קשיא

רבינו חננאל

עולא איקלע לפומבדיתא ואבדיל בין קדש לחול בלבד ולא אמר ברכה בתחלה וברכה בסוף אלא אמר בא"י המבדיל בין קדש לחול בלבד אותבי' עליה כל הברכות כלן פותח בהן בברוך וחותם בהן בברוך חוץ מברכת המצות וברכת הפירות וברכה הסמוכה לחברתה וברכת אחרונה שבק"ש שיש בהם פותח בברוך ואינו חותם בברוך ויש מהן חותם בברוך ואינו פותח בברוך הטוב ומטיב פותח בה בברוך

מסורת הש"ם

ברכות דף מו.

פי' שלא יאמרו שמעתתא מסומך וגי' ס"י מסומים דרבנן

מסורת הש"ס

עין משפט נר מצוה

כב א מיי' פכ"ט מהל' שבת הל' ג טור א"ח סי' רצט:

רבינו חננאל

והא מר ארבעה הוא דאמר וליתנהו לא תלת ולא שבע ואמר להו תלת קאמינא אבל בין יום השביעי לששת ימי המעשה מעין חתימתה היא דאמר שמואל כל הברכות צריך לומר מעין חתימתן סמוך לחתימתן וקיי"ל כותיה. פומבדיתאי אמרי מעין פתיחתן סמוך לחתימתן איכא בינייהו יום טוב שחל להיות אחר שבת דחתימתן בין קדש לקדש מאן דאמר מעין חתימתן סמוך לחתימתן צריך לומר בין קדושת שבת לקדושת יום טוב הבדלת מאן דאמר מעין פתיחתן סמוך לחתימתן לא צריך: אמר רבי יוחנן בנן של קדושים אומרים הבדלה אחת ומאי איתן ר' מנחם בר סימאי ואמאי קרי להו בנן של קדושים דלא אסתכל מימיו בצורתא דזוזא: נהגו העם לומר שלש הבדלות חנניה אומרה אחת ולית הלכתא כותיה: המבדיל צריך שיאמר מעין הבדלות שבתורה

תורה אור

והא מר לא תלתא אמר ולא שבע אמר א"ל איברא בין יום השביעי לששת ימי המעשה מעין חתימה היא ואמר רב יהודה אמר שמואל המבדיל צריך שיאמר מעין חתימה סמוך לחתימתו ופומבדיתאי אמרי מעין פתיחתן (א) סמוך לחתימתן מאי בינייהו איכא בינייהו יום טוב שחל להיות אחר השבת דחתמינן בין קודש לקודש מ"ד מעין פתיחתן סמוך לחתימתן לא בעי למימר בין קדושת שבת לקדושת יום טוב הבדלת ומאן דאמר מעין חתימתן סמוך לחתימתן בעי למימר בין קדושת שבת לקדושת יום טוב הבדלת גופא אמר רבי אלעזר אמר רבי אושעיא הפוחת לא יפחות משלש והמוסיף לא יוסיף על שבע מיתיבי *אומר הבדלות במוצאי שבתות ובמוצאי ימים טובים ובמוצאי יום הכפורים ובמוצאי שבת ליום טוב ובמוצאי יום טוב לחולו של מועד אבל לא במוצאי יום טוב לשבת הרגיל אומר הרבה ושאינו רגיל אומר אחת תנאי היא דא"ר יוחנן בנן של קדושים אומר אחת ונהגו העם לומר שלש *מאן ניהו בנן של קדושים רבי מנחם בר סימאי *ואמאי קרו ליה בנן של קדושים דלא איסתכל בצורתא דזוזא שלח ליה רב שמואל בר אידי חנניא אחי אומר אחת ולית הלכתא כוותיה אמר רבי יהושע בן לוי המבדיל צריך שיאמר מעין הבדלות האמורות בתורה מיתיבי סדר הבדלות היאך אומר המבדיל בין קודש לחול בין אור לחושך בין ישראל לעמים ובין יום השביעי לששת ימי המעשה בין טמא לטהור בין הים לחרבה בין מים העליונים למים התחתונים בין כהנים ללוים וישראלים וחותם בסדר בראשית ואחרים אומרים ביוצר בראשית רבי יוסי ברבי יהודה אומר חותם מקדש ישראל ואם איתא הא בין הים לחרבה לא כתיבא ביה הבדלה סמי מכאן בין הים לחרבה אי הכי בין יום השביעי לששת ימי המעשה נמי מעין חתימה הוא בצר חדא וליכא שבע אמרי כהנים לוים וישראלים תרי מילי נינהו בין לוים לישראלים דכתיב °בעת ההיא הבדיל ה' את שבט הלוי בין הכהנים ללוים דכתיב °בני עמרם אהרן ומשה ויבדל אהרן להקדישו קדש קדשים מחתם מאי חתים רב אמר מקדש ישראל ושמואל אמר *המבדיל בין קודש לחול לייט עלה אביי ואיתימא רב יוסף אהא דרב תנא משמיה דרבי יהושע בן חנניא כל החותם מקדש ישראל והמבדיל בין קודש לחול מאריכין לו ימיו ושנותיו

ולית

דברי' י

דה"א כג

תוספות

ומר לא תלת אמר ולא שבע אמר. ומסתמא או ג' או ז' תיקנו כנגד שום דבר שלא לפחות או להוסיף כדאמר בהתכלת (מנחות דף לט.) לא יפחות מז' כנגד ז' רקיעים והמוסיף לא יוסיף על י"ג כנגד ז' רקיעים וששה אוירים: **מאי** בינייהו. דרוב הברכות הפתיחה והחתימה מעין אחד:

בעי למימר בין קדושת שבת לקדושת יום טוב הבדלת. שאל ר' אפרים את ר"ת למה נהגו העולם להוסיף ולומר ואת יום השביעי מששת ימי המעשה קדשת הבדלת וקדשת את עמך ישראל בקדושתך דאין זה לא מעין פתיחה ולא מעין חתימה והשיב לו ר"ת משום חיבת היום האריכו כדי לומר פעם אחת מעין ז' הבדלות. בין קודש לחול אחד. בין אור לחשך ב'. בין ישראל לעמים ג'. בין יום השביעי לששת ימי המעשה ד'. בין קדושת שבת לקדושת י"ט הבדלת. פירוש שבי"ט שרי מידי דאוכל נפש. ואת יום השביעי מששת ימי המעשה קדשת הייטו חולו של מועד דשרי דבר האבוד ובשבת אסור. זה חלוק שבת מי"ט והיא הבדלה אחת הרי ה'. הבדלת וקדשת את עמך ישראל בקדושתך שתי הבדלות בין כהנים לוים וישראלים ז' והוי מעין חתימה דבין קדש לקדש:

מיתיבי אומרים הבדלות כו'. הוה מצי לאתויי מרבי יהודה הנשיא דלעיל אלא דניחא ליה למיפרך מברייתא:

דלא מסתכל בצורתא דזוזא. ארבי מנחם קאי דאמר במועד קטן בפרק בתרא (דף כה:) כי קא ניחא נפשיה דר' מנחם בר רבי סימאי איכסו כל צלמניא והוו למישללייא פירוש חלקים בלא צורה ותולה קדושתו באביו שגם אביו היה קדוש*: **בין** יום השביעי לששת ימי המעשה מעין חתימה היא. ה"נ הוה מצי למיפרך הא לא כתיבא והא דלא קתני לה לבסוף פירש רשב"ם דשנאה אחר ג' הבדלות דכשאינו אומר רק ג' הבדלות הויא סמוך לחתימה ואם תאמר לר' יוסי ברבי יהודה ולרב דחתמי מקדש ישראל היכי הויא מעין חתימה אדרבה כהנים ולוים וישראלים הוי טפי מעין חתימה ויש לומר דבין יום השביעי לששת ימי המעשה הוי שפיר מעין החתימה שקדשנו הקב"ה במצותיו ונתן לנו את השבת אבל כהנים לוים וישראלים לא הזכיר ישראל אלא להקל שקלים בקדושתן מכהנים ולוים ולא הוי מעין חתימה:

[ופי' תוספות ע"ז ב. ד"ה כ"ג]

רשב"ם

והא מר לא שלש אמר. (ב) [כולן] ארבע: מעין חתימה. ולא ממנינא הוא: ה"ג י"ט שחל להיות אחר השבת. דבעי למחתם המבדיל בין קודש לקודש: ה"ג מ"ד מעין חתימתן סמוך לחתימתן בעי למימר בין קדושת שבת לקדושת יום טוב כו': האמורות בתורה. כמו הנך דלקמן: סדר הבדלות. היינו שבע הבדלות ואף על גב דאיכא תמני בין [יום] השביעי לא קא חשיב דמעין חתימה: וחותם בסדר בראשית. ברוך סודר בראשית וכולהו הנך כתיבי ולהבדיל בין הקודש ובין החול ובין הטמא ובין הטהור (ויקרא י) ויבדל אלהים בין האור ובין החשך (בראשית א) ויבדל בין המים (שם): ובין כהנים ללוים כו'. מפרש להו לקמן אבל הבדלה דשבת לא כתיב' דמעין חתימה קא חשיב ליה לקמן ולאו ממנינא: מעין חתימה היא. דקאמר וחותם בסדר בראשית והויא ליה בין יום השביעי לששת ימי המעשה מעין חתימה ובלאו להו משבע: המבדיל

והא מר לא שלש אמר ולא שבע אמר. דארבעה אמר ומה ראית אם לתפוש את המועט דייך בג' ואם לרבות באת היה לך לומר כל שבע: איברא. באמת: מעין החתימ'. ולאו ממניינא הוא: חתימה. סוף הברכה חותם בברוך: פתיחתן. התחלתן: ומאי בינייהו. דהא ברכת הבדלה מעין פתיחתן ומעין חתימתן איכא וכן רוב ברכות: יום טוב שחל להיות אחר השבת. דבעי למיחתם בין קודש לקודש: הכי גרסי' מאן דאמר מעין חתימתן סמוך לחתימתן בעי למימר בין קדושת שבת לקדושת יום טוב הבדלת והכי עבדינן לאפוקי נפשין מפלוגתא: אבל לא במוצאי יום טוב לשבת. דאפרכוס יוצא והמלך נכנס אין דרך ללוות האפרכוס שהכל נמשכין אחר המלך: הרגיל. שבקי בהן: אומר אחת. קשיא לר' אלעזר דאמר לא יפחות משלש: הכי גרסינן תנאי היא דאמר רבי יוחנן בנן של קדושים כו'. והיינו תנאי בנן של קדושים שהוא תנא: ונהגו העם. תנאים שהיו בימיו נחלקו עליו ועושין העם על פיהן הרי תנא אחר: ר' מנחם בר רבי סימאי. ואמרינן במסכת ע"ג פרק ר' ישמעאל (דף נ) אמאי קרי ליה בנן של קדושים משום דלא אסתכל בצורתא דזוזא: ולית הלכתא כוותיה. גמרא קאמר ליה: האמורות בתורה. כגון הנך דלקמן: סדר הבדלות. היינו שבע הבדלות אע"ג דאיכא שמונה בין יום השביעי לששת ימי המעשה לא חשיב דמעין חתימה היא: וחותם בסדר בראשית. ברוך סודר בראשית שבמוצאי שבת התחיל הקב"ה לסדר מעשה בראשית וכולהו הנך כתיבי ולהבדיל בין הקדש ובין החול ובין הטמא ובין הטהור ויבדל אלהים בין האור ובין החשך ויבדל בין המים וגומר ואבדיל אתכם מן העמים (ויקרא כ) אבל הבדלה דשבת לא כתיבא דמעין חתימה חשיבא לקמן ולאו ממנינא הוא והאי דלא חשיב לה לבסוף משום דלגבי שלש קתני לה דהכי לא עביד אלא שלש הבדלות קאמר לה סמוך לחתימה: בין הים לחרבה. לקמן מסמי לה מברייתא: בין כהנים ולוים וישראלים. גרסינן ולקמן מפרש ליה: מקדש ישראל. מכל עולמו שלא קידש אלא ישראל ולפי פירוש זה שייכא חתימה זו במוצאי שבת: מעין חתימה היא. דקאמרת וחותם בסדר בראשית והויא לה בין יום השביעי לששת ימי המעשה מעין חתימה ובלאו הכי משבעה: רב אמר מקדש ישראל. כר' יוסי בר' יהודה: ושמואל אמר המבדיל בין קדש לחול. שמואל לא סבירא ליה ככל הנך תנאי דלעיל אלא כרבנן סבירא ליה דתנן בסוף פרק קמא דחולין (דף כו:) גבי יום טוב שחל להיות במוצאי שבת כיצד מבדילין בין קדש *לחול כו' ואמרינן בגמרא היכא אמר לה להך ברכה בין קדש לקדש אמר רב יהודה בחתימתה רב ששת בריה דרב אידי אמר בפתיחתה

ולית

[תוספתא דברכות פ"ה]

ע"ז דף נ.

[לפני הרשב"ם לא היה הגירסא הך ואמאי וכו' עד דזוזא]

[לקדש כ"ג]

הגהות הב"ח

(א) גמ' אמרי מעין פתיחתו סמוך לחתימתו כצ"ל וכן בכל העמוד: (ב) רשב"ם ד"ה והא מר לא שלש אמר כו' דארבע היכא בס"ד ותיבת כולן נמחק:

Said he to him: [104a] 'But you said neither three nor seven?'[5] —'It is true,' answered he, '"between the seventh day and the six working days" is of the nature of the conclusion,[6] and Rab Judah said in Samuel's name: He who recites *habdalah* must say [something] in the nature of the conclusion near to its conclusion.' While the Pumbeditheans maintain: [He must say something] in the nature of the commencement just before its conclusion. Wherein do they differ?[7]—They differ in respect of a Festival which falls after the Sabbath [i.e., Sunday], when we conclude
a with '[Who makest a distinction] between holy and holy.'[1] On the view that something in the nature of the commencement [must be repeated] immediately before the conclusion, it will be unnecessary to say, 'Thou didst make a distinction between the sanctity of the Sabbath and the sanctity of the Festival';[2] but on the view that [a formula] in the nature of the conclusion [must be said] immediately before the conclusion, it is necessary to say, 'Thou didst make a distinction between the sanctity of the Sabbath and the sanctity of the Festival.'

The [above] text [stated]: 'R. Eleazar said in R. Oshaia's name: He who would recite but few [distinctions] must recite not less than three; while he who would add must not add beyond seven.' An objection is raised: *Habdalah* is recited at the conclusion of the Sabbath, at the conclusion of Festivals, at the conclusion of the Day of Atonement, at the conclusion of the Sabbath [giving place] to a Festival, and at the conclusion of a Festival [giving place] to the Intermediary Days,[3] but not at the conclusion of a Festival [leading] to the Sabbath.[4] He who is well-versed recites many [points of distinction], while he who is not well-versed recites one?—It is [dependent on] Tannaim. For R. Joḥanan said: The son of holy men recited one, but the people are accustomed to recite three.[5] Who is the son of holy men?—R. Menaḥem b. Simai; and why did they call him the son of holy men? Because he did not look at the effigy of a coin.[6] R. Samuel b. Idi sent [word] to him:[7] 'My brother Ḥanania recites one.' But the law does not agree with him.

R. Joshua b. Levi said: He who recites *habdalah* must recite [formulas] in the nature of the distinctions mentioned in the
b Torah.[1] An objection is raised: What is the order of the distinctions [recited in the *habdalah*]? He recites, 'Who makest a distinction between holy and profane, between light and darkness, between Israel and the nations, between the seventh day and the six working days, between unclean and clean, between the sea and dry land, between the upper waters and the nether waters, between Priests, Levites and Israelites'; and he concludes with the order of Creation.[2] Others say, with 'He who formed the Creation.' R. Jose b. R. Judah said: He concludes, 'Who sanctifiest Israel.' Now if this is correct, surely no distinction is mentioned [in the Torah] between the sea and the dry land?[3]—Delete 'between the sea and the dry land' from this. If so, [you must] also [delete] 'between the seventh day and the six working days'?[4] —That corresponds to the conclusion.[5] Then there is one less, so there are not seven?[6]—I will tell you: [who made a distinction between] Priests, Levites and Israelites is two formulas. Between Levites and Israelites [is one], as it is written, *At that time the Lord made distinct the tribe of Levi.*[7] Between Priests and Levites [is another], as it is written, *The sons of Amram: Aaron and Moses; and Aaron was made distinct that he should be sanctified as most holy.*[8]

How does he conclude it?—Rab said: 'Who sanctifiest Israel.' While Samuel said: 'Who makest a distinction between holy and non-holy,' Abaye,—others state, R. Joseph—denounced[9] this [ruling] of Rab. It was taught in the name of R. Joshua b. Ḥanania: When one concludes, 'Who sanctifiest Israel and makest a distinction between holy and non-holy,' his days and years are prolonged. [104b] But the law is not as he.[10]

(5) But four.
(6) *Habdalah* ends with, 'Blessed art thou, O Lord, who makest a division between holy and non-holy'. This phrase, 'between the seventh day' etc. is similar in meaning, and forms a natural bridge to the conclusion, as it were; hence it is not counted.—All benedictions commence with the formula, 'Blessed art thou, O Lord, our God, King of the Universe'; if lengthy, they conclude with the formula, 'Blessed art thou, O Lord, who 'etc. It is this latter formula which is referred to as the conclusion. (7) Seeing that in most blessings the opening and the conclusion are similar in subject. *Habdalah* itself commences with 'He who maketh a distinction between holy and non-holy', while the passage preceding the conclusion is likewise 'who makest a division between the seventh day (i.e., holy) and the six working days (non-holy)'.

a (1) Since both are holy, save that the holiness of the Sabbath is greater. (2) Since the opening phrase is 'Who makest a distinction between holy and non-holy'. (3) V. 5a, note a4.—Most of these phrases are in the plural in the original. (4) Thus *habdalah* is recited only to mark the passing of a day of higher sanctity than that which follows, but not the reverse. (5) This 'son of holy men' was a Tanna, while the common practice was likewise based on the ruling of a Tanna. Thus we have a controversy of Tannaim. (6) V. A.Z. 50a. 'Son' is probably used attributively, R. Menaḥem himself being holy (v. M.Ḳ. 25b on the effect of his death); nevertheless this mode of expression is employed because his father too was holy.—Tosaf. (7) [It is not clear to whom this refers.]

b (1) As explained anon. (2) I.e., 'Blessed art thou, O Lord, who settest the Creation in order'. (3) I.e., no phrase with the express term 'distinction'. (4) For no phrase states that God made a 'distinction' between the seventh day etc. (5) And is therefore not counted. (6) Whereas the purpose of this Baraitha is to enumerate the seven formulas of distinction referred to above. (7) Deut. X, 8. (8) I Chron. XXIII, 13. (9) Lit., 'cursed'. (10) A double ending is not employed, and the law is as Samuel.

disciples of Rab, were sitting at a meal, [103*b*] [and] R. Yeba Saba[1] waited on them. Said they to him, 'Give us [wine] and we will say Grace.' Subsequently[2] they said, 'Give us [wine] and we will drink.'[3] Said he to them, 'Thus did Rab say: Once you have said, "Give us [wine] and we will say Grace," it is forbidden to you to drink.[4] What is the reason? Because you let it pass out of your minds.'[5]

Amemar and Mar Zuṭra and R. Ashi were sitting at a meal and R. Aḥa the son of Raba waited on them. Amemar recited a separate blessing for each cup; Mar Zuṭra recited a blessing over the first cup and over the last cup;[6] [but] R. Ashi recited a blessing over the first cup and no more. Said R. Aḥa b. Raba to them: In accordance with whom are we to act?—Amemar replied: I made a [fresh] decision [each time].[7] Mar Zuṭra replied: I acted in accordance with Rab's disciples. But R. Ashi maintained: The law is not as Rab's disciples, for surely when a Festival falls after the Sabbath, Rab ruled: [The order is] *YaḲNaH*.[8] But that is not so: there[9] he had detached his mind from drinking;[10] [whereas] here he had not detached his mind from drinking.

When he came to perform *habdalah*,[11] his attendant arose and kindled a torch at a lamp.[1] Said he to him, 'Why take all this trouble? Surely the lamp is standing before us!'[2] 'My servant has acted of his own accord,' replied he. 'Had he not heard it thus from you,'[3] he retorted, 'he would not have done it.' Said he to him: 'Do you then not hold, [To employ] a torch for *habdalah* is the best way of performing the precept?'

Then he commenced [*habdalah*] and recited: 'He who makes a distinction between holy and non-holy, between light and darkness, between Israel and the nations, between the seventh day and the six working days.' Said he to him: 'Why do you need all this? Surely Rab Judah said in Rab's name: "He who makes a distinction between holy and non-holy," was the formula of *habdalah* as recited by R. Judah ha-Nasi?' 'I hold with the following,' answered he. 'For R. Eleazar said in R. Oshaia's name: He who would recite but few [distinctions] must recite not less than three; while he who would add, must not add beyond seven.'[4]

a (1) The elder; or, aged. (2) Before reciting Grace. (3) They changed their mind and did not wish to recite Grace yet. (4) Until after Grace. (5) This proves that Grace constitutes an interruption, and so the blessing over the wine must be repeated after Grace; and Raba acted in accordance with this ruling. (6) I.e., after Grace, as Raba did. (7) After each cup I intended drinking no more. Hence when I did drink another it was a new act of drinking, and so I repeated the blessing each time. Consequently my action does not involve a general ruling. (8) V. *supra* 102*b*, n. a10. Thus the benediction for wine is not recited twice, one on account of *ḳiddush* and again on account of *habdalah*. Hence the same applies to two cups in general. (9) Where Rab ruled that once they had declared their intention of saying Grace they might not drink again without a fresh blessing. (10) His decision to say Grace proved that. (11) This is a continuation of the passage narrating R. Jacob b. Aḥa's visit to Raba, which had been parenthetically interrupted by the somewhat similar story about Amemar and his companions. The meal in question took place toward the end of the Sabbath, and at the termination of the Sabbath Raba performed *habdalah*.

b (1) For the blessing over light. (2) Then let the blessing for light be said over the lamp itself. (3) 'The Master'. (4) I.e., not less than three points of distinction and not more than seven must be recited in the *habdalah*.

יח א מיי' פ"ד מהל' ברכות הלכה ח סמג עשין כז טוש"ע או"ח סי' קעד סעיף ח [וכרב"פ סי' לה] ב [וכהי' הדס סי' ה]:

יט ב מיי' שם פ"ד הל' יב (ופ"ז הל' טו) סמג שם טוש"ע או"ח סי' קעד סעיף ו וסי' קפ סעיף ב [רב אלפס ורא"ש כאן ובברכות פ"ו דף לג וברא"ש סי' לג]:

כ ג מיי' פכ"ט מהלכות שבת הלכה כו סמג עשין כט טוש"ע או"ח סי' רצ"ח סעיף ג:

כא ד מיי' שם הל' ג טור או"ח סימן רצט:

קאי עלייהו רב ייבא סבא א"ל הב לן וניבריך לסוף אמרו ליה הב לן ונישתי אמר להו הכי אמר רב "כיון דאמריתו הב לן וניבריך איתסרא לכו למישתי מאי טעמא דאסחיתו דעתייכו אמימר ומר זוטרא ורב אשי הוו יתבי בסעודה וקאי עלייהו רב אחא בריה דרבא אמימר בריך על כל כסא וכסא ומר זוטרא "בריך אכסא קמא ואכסא בתרא רב אשי בריך אכסא קמא ותו לא בריך אמר להו רב אחא בר רבא אנן כמאן נעביד אמימר אמר (א) נמלך אנא מר זוטרא אמר אנא דעבדי כתלמידי דרב ורב אשי אמר לית הילכתא כתלמידי דרב דהא יו"ט שחל להיות אחר השבת ואמר רב יקנ"ה ולא היא התם עקר דעתיה ממשתיא הכא לא עקר דעתיה ממשתיא כי מטא לאבדולי קם שמעיה ואדליק אבוקה משרגא א"ל למה לך כולי האי הא מנחא שרגא א"ל שמעא מדעתיה דנפשיה קא עביד א"ל אי לא שמיע ליה מיניה דמר לא הוה עביד א"ל לא סבר ליה מר *"אבוקה להבדלה מצוה מן המובחר פתח ואמר "המבדיל בין קודש לחול בין אור לחשך בין ישראל לעמים בין יום השביעי לששת ימי המעשה א"ל למה לך כולי האי והאמר רב יהודה אמר רב המבדיל בין קידש לחול זו היא הבדלתו של רבי יהודה הנשיא א"ל אנא כהא סבירא לי דאמר ר"א אמר רבי אושעיא הפוחת לא יפחות מג' והמוסיף לא יוסיף על ז' אמר ליה והא

רש"י

קאי עלייהו. משמש עליהו: הב (ג) וניבריך. ברכת המזון והדר אמליכו ואמרו הב בריטא ונישתי: כיון דאמריתו הב (ג) וניבריך. ברכת המזון אסחיתו דעתייכו משתיה ואסור למישתי עד לאחר ברכת המזון אלמא ברכת המזון אסוחי דעתא הוא וצריך לחזור ולברך: ואמר רב יקנ"ה. ולא בעי לברוכי ברכת היין תרי זימני חדא אקידוש וחדא אהבדלה וה"ה לתרי כסי קידוש היום וברכת המזון: כי מטא. רבא לאבדולי במוצאי שבת ולעיל קאי אלא אגב גררא אייתינהו להנך תרתי עובדי ועובדא דאבוקה בשבת הוה: קא מתלי נורא בשרגא. מדליק אבוקה בנר: א"ל. רב יעקב בר אבא למה ליה למר כולי האי הא איכא שרגא: אדעתיה דנפשיה. כלומר מעצמו אסר לא לויתיו: על שבע. מפרש להו לקמיה: והא

תוספות

דברים הרגילים לבא אחר הסעודה כגון תאנים וענבים אפי' באים בתוך הסעודה לריכין ברכה לפניהם ולאחריהם אין נראה פירוש זה כלמפרש שם ועוד דלא דמי לתאנים וענבים דיין חשיב בא מחמת הסעודה ולא לריך לברך אחריו לכולי עלמא ואע"ג דאמר התם שאלו את בן זומא מפני מה אמרו דברים הבאין מחמת הסעודה בתוך הסעוד' אין טעון ברכה לא לפניהם ולא לאחריהם מפני שפת פוטרתן אי הכי יין (ד) נפטריה פת פירוש ואמאי תנן הביאו להם יין תוך המזון כל אחד מברך לעצמו ומשני שאני יין הואיל וקובע ברכה לעצמו התם לא מיירי אלא בברכה שלפניו אבל לענין ברכה שלאחריו לא אשכחן דחשיב ואין מנהג לברך אחר היין בתוך הסעודה ואפילו יין דלאחר הסעודה נראה שאין לריך לברך אחריו דלעולם חשוב מחמת הסעודה והא דקאמר דברים הבאים אחר הסעודה לריכין ברכה לפניהם ולאחריהם היינו חוץ מיין ומיהו אנו אין אנו מסלקין ידינו מפת עד ברכת המזון והכל קרוי תוך הסעודה ואין שום דבר טעון ברכה אחריו דברכת המזון פוטר ובימי החכמים היו מסיחין מן הפת בעקירת שלחן קודם ברכת המזון ואז היו רגילין לשתות יין ולאכול פירות:

כיון דאמר הב וניבריך איתסר למישתי. וא"ת בפ' ג' שאכלו (ברכו' דמ"ה.) גבי ינאי מלכא כו' דקאמר מאן יהיב לן גברא דמברך לן דהוי הב וניבריך היכי נצטרף תו עמהן ר"ש בן שטח הא אמרי' לעיל בההוא פרקין (דף מז.) דרב ושמואל הוו יתבי בסעודתא על ואתא רב שימי בר חייא הוה קמסרהב ואכיל אמרו ליה מאי דעתך לאצטרופי בהדן אנן אכלינן אלמא כיון דגמרו מלאכול תו לא מצטרפי וי"ל בלאו הכי אמרי' התם הוא דעבד לגרמיה שהוציאם אע"פ שלא אכל כזית דגן:

בריך אכל כסא וכסא. אחריו לא היה מברך דברכת המזון פוטרת והא דשינוי מקום לריך לברך היינו דוקא לפניו ולא לאחריו כדפיר' לעיל: **רב** אשי בריך אכסא קמא ותו לא בריך. אע"ג דברכת המזון טעונה כוס לא היה מברך ובירושלמי נמי קאמר דאם התחיל לסעוד בע"ש מבעוד יום אין לריך בקידוש לברך בפה"ג משמע דכל דבר מלוה הטעון כוס א"ל לברך בפה"ג היכא דלא הוי הפסק וא"ת א"כ אמאי מברכין בכוס שני שאחר הגדה בפה"ג אפילו תהא הגדה טעונה כוס אין לריך לברך דלא הוי הפסק כדאמר הכא וי"ל דהגדה והלילא נמי הוי הפסק ואע"ג דבין ראשון לשני אם רלה לשתות ישתה מכיון דהתחיל אשר גאלנו אסור לשתות והוי כמו ברכת המזון דמסקינן הכא דלריך לברך ומ"מ חשיב קידוש במקום סעודה דלענין זה לא חשיבא הגדה הפסק ולמאי דפרישית דהויא הגדה הפסק לריך לברך אחר ירקות בורא נפשות וגם נראה לברך אחר כל ארבע כוסות על הגפן חוץ מכוס שני הסמוך לסעודה וגם אחר ב' כוסות של אירוסין ונשואין נראה דלריך לברך אחר כל אחד על הגפן:

וקאמר רב יקנ"ה. פי' בקונטרס דדייק מדלא מלריך לברך תרי זימני בפה"ג חד אקידוש וחד אהבדלה אלמא לא הוי קידוש הפסק והוא הדין נמי ברכת המזון וקשה דאיך יברך פעמים בפה"ג על כוס א' וזה לא מלינו ונראה דדייק מדלא תיקנו יין לבסוף ש"מ דלא הוי הפסק הוא הדין נמי ברכת המזון: **ולא** היא ט'. והכי מסקינן דמברכין אכסא דברכתא וקשה דאמרינן בכיסוי הדם (חולין דף פז.) דכוס של ברכה אתה שותה לו מ' זהובים אתה נוטל והשתא האיכא נ' זהובים בשביל ברכת בורא פרי הגפן וי"ל דהתם לא נקט נ' משום רב אשי דלא בריך אכסא דברכתא ועוד פעמים מברכין ברכת המזון בלא כוס:

ומר

רשב"ם

קאי עלייהו. משמש עליהן והוא עומד עליהם (בראשית יח) מתרגמינן והוא משמש: אסור לכו למישתי. אלמא ברכת המזון אסוחי דעתא הוא וצריך לחזור ולברך לאחר ברכת המזון והכי נהיגינן ואע"ג דשמעי' מהכא דברכת המזון אפסוקי סעודתא הוא לא בעי ברוכי על היין לאחריו מיקמי דנבריך ברכת המזון לפי שברכת המזון פוטרתו דהשתא אחת מעין שלש סגי להו כ"ש שלש ברכות עצמן ובהלכות גדולות נמי כתב דלא בעי לברוכי ברכת היין לאחריו עד לאחר ברכת המזון: הוו יתבי בסעודתא. דחול: על כל כסא וכסא. על כל פעם שהיה שותה בתוך המזון: ואכסא דבתרא. ברכת המזון סבירא ליה כרבא דבריך נמי לעיל אכסא קמא ואכסא דברכתא: נמלך אני. בכוס שני נמלכתי לשתות שכבר הוי לי היסח הדעת משמשתיתי כוס ראשון וכן כל פעם ופעם ששתיתי נמלכתי: כתלמידי דרב. כי ההוא עובדא דלעיל דיליף רבא מיניה דמיבעי לברוכי אכסא דברכתא אע"פ שכבר בירך איין שבתוך המזון: לית הלכתא כתלמידי דרב. כלומר כעובדא דתלמידי דרב לעיל דברכת המזון לאו אסוחי דעתא הוא ואע"ג דאמר הב וניבריך שרי למישתי ואפילו הכי לית הילכתא כרב אשי דקמו להו רבא ומר זוטרא בחד שיטתא וצריך לחזור ולברך על היין של ברכת המזון בפה"ג כמנהג שלנו וכיון דאמר הב וניבריך אסור למישתי עד לאחר ברכת המזון ועוד מדקא מייתי רב אשי סייעתא ממילתיה דרב להקשות על תלמידי דרב להכחישן מדברי רב רבן וקא מהדר גמרא ולא היא מכלל דלית הילכתא כרב אשי: ואמר רב יקנ"ה. ולא בעי לברוכי ברכת בפה"ג תרי זימני חד אקידוש וחד אהבדלה והוא הדין לתרי כסי דקידוש היום וברכת המזון וקשיא לרב ייבא סבא דאמר להו הכי אמר רב הב וניבריך אסור לכו למישתי דא"כ קשיא דרב אדרב: הכא. גבי יקנ"ה לא עקר דעתיה ממישתיא שעדיין לא שתה וכל דעתו לשתות וכ"ל דלא גרסי' כולהו חדא ברכתא אריכתא נינהו שריבוי לשון שלא לצורך הוא שכבר פירש טעמו יפה משום דלא עקר דעתו ממישתיא שעדיין לא שתה וכל דעתו לשתות: כי מטא רבא לאבדולי. לעיל קאי אהא דרב יעקב בר אבא איקלע לבי רבא וההוא עובדא בסעודת שבת אוקימנא לעיל משום הא מילתא דהכא דמשמע למוצאי שבת אתחיל רבא לברך ברכת הבדלה ואגב גררא אייתי להא עובדא דאמימר ומר זוטרא אית ליה דרבא ורב אשי לית ליה וליכא לפרושי אההוא עובדא קמא דרב הונא בר יהודה איקלע לבי רבא אייתי לקמייהו כסא דאבדלתא ובריך מאור ובשמים דלא שייך למימר כי מטא לאבדולי קם שמעיה וכו' והרי כבר אמרנו שהיה מבדיל ובירך כבר אבשמים ואמאור ועוד הא דרב יעקב בר אבא המאי מפסיק בינתים: קם שמעיה. דרבא אדליק אבוקה בשרגא: א"ל. רבי יעקב בר אבא לרבא לאחר שהבדיל למה ליה למר דעביד כולי האי הא איכא שרגא: ודעתיה דנפשיה. מעצמו אסר לא לויתיו והא דקאמר ליה רבא לא גרסי' דהא רבא עצמו הוא דקא מהדר לרב יעקב בר אבא: ה"ג המבדיל בין קודש לחול בין אור לחושך זו היא הבדלתו כו'. ולא היה אומר יותר: על שבע. מפרשינן לקמיה:

והא

רבינו חננאל

בסעודתא והוה קאי עלייהו רב ייבא סבא אמרו ליה שקול כסא הב וניבריך [הדר] אמרו ליה הב לן ונשתי אמר להו הכי אמר רב כיון דאמריתו הב וניבריך איתסר לכו למשתי. אמימר ומר זוטרא ורב אשי הוו יתבי בסעודתא קאי עלייהו רב אחא בריה דרבא אמימר בריך אכל כוס וכוס דהוה שתי מר זוטרא בריך בורא פרי הגפן אכסא קמא ואכסא דברכתא רב אשי בריך אכוס ראשון בלבד אמר להו רב אחא אנן כמאן נעביד אמימר אמר אנא נמלך אנא כלומר כיון שאני שותה הכוס אני מסיים בדעתי שלא לשתות כוס אחר וכבר פסק השתיה ונאסרתי לשתות וכשמצטירין אותי אחר כך לשתות כאלו אני מתחיל לפיכך אני צריך לברך בתחלה מר זוטרא אמר אנא עבדי כתלמידי דרב כיון דאמרי הב ונבריך איתסרו למשתי רב אשי אמר לית הילכתא כתלמידי דרב דלאו הברכה מפסקת וכל שכן אם אומר הב ונבריך דהא יום טוב אחר שבת ואמר רב יקנ"ה פי' כיון שברך בפה"ג בתחלה אע"פ שהפסיק וברך קידוש ונר וגם הבדיל שותה בלא ברכת היין פעם אחרת ש"מ כי הברכה אינה מפסקת והא תלמידי [דרב] אינה ודחי' לאו דרב אשי ואשרי' ולא היא בברכת המזון שהוא כוס אחר ולאחר הכוס שברך עליו בורא פרי הגפן ונעקר דעתיה משתי' וצריך ברכה אחרת אבל יקנ"ה שהן כולן בכוס אחר לא עקר דעתיה משתיה וכלהו כברכה א' אריכתא דמו וקיימא לן כדמר זוטרא: כי מטא לאבדולי קם שמעיה ואדליק אבוקה משרגא אמר להו האמר ר' יוחנן אבוקה להבדלה מצוה מן המובחר פתח ואמר המבדיל בין קדש לחול ובין אור לחשך ובין ישראל לעמים ובין יום השביעי לששת ימי המעשה ואקשינן הא דעבד [הכי] כו' אלעזר [עביד] דאמר הפוחת לא יפחות מג' והמוסיף לא יוסיף על ז' ואקשינן

הגהות הב"ח

(א) גמ' אמימר אמר אנא נמלך אנא: (ג) רש"י ד"ה הב לן וניבריך וכו' ואמרו הב לן בריטא: (ג) ד"ה כיון דאמריתו הב לן וניבריך: (ד) תוס' ד"ה אלא וכו' אי הכי יין נמי ניפטריה:

לעיל ת.

הכי גרסינן שאמר משום רבי יהושע בן חנניה נהי"ק: ה"ג משל דרבי יהושע כו': והלכתא כרבא. דקדושא והדר אבדלתא דכי מבדיל ברישא מיחזי עליה קדושת שבת כמשאוי: נר ומזון בשמים והבדלה. היכא דאין לו אלא כוס א': על המזון שהוא בתחלה. כיון דגמר סעודתו בההוא איחייב ברישא ואין מעבירים על המצות: אכסא קמא. כשמתחיל לשתות (ג) על המזון שבתחלה: והדר בריך. בפה"ג אכסא דברכת המזון כמו שאנו עושין בכל סעודה וסעודה ובשאר סעודות עסקינן דלאו במוצאי שבת: לא הוי ידעיתו אי משקו לכו (ג) בתר כסא קמא אי לא ומשום הכי בעיתו למיהדר וברוכי: קאי

ורבה אמר יהנ"ק ולוי אמר קנ"ה ורבנן אמרי קינ"ה מר בריה דרבנא אמר נקי"ה מרתא אמר משמיה דר' יהושע נהי"ק שלח ליה אבוה דשמואל לרבי ילמדנו רבינו סדר הבדלות היאך שלח ליה כך אמר רבי ישמעאל בר רבי יוסי שאמר משום אביו שאמר משום רבי יהושע בן חנניה נהי"ק אמר ר' חנינא משל דר' יהושע בן חנניה למלך שיוצא ואפרכוס נכנס מלווין את המלך ואח"כ יוצאים לקראת אפרכוס מאי הוי עלה אביי אמר יקונ"ה ורבא אמר יקנה"ז *והילכתא כרבא *רב הונא בר יהודה איקלע לבי רבא אייתו לקמייהו מאור ובשמים בריך רבא אבשמים ברישא והדר אמאור א"ל והא בין ב"ש ובין בית הילל מאור ברישא והדר אבשמים ומאי היא דתנן *בית שמאי אומרים נר ומזון בשמים והבדלה ובית הילל אומרים נר ובשמים ומזון והבדלה עני רבא בתריה ואמר זו דברי ר' מאיר אבל *ר' יהודה אומר לא נחלקו בית שמאי ובית הילל על המזון שהוא בתחלה ועל הבדלה שהיא בסוף על מה נחלקו על המאור ועל הבשמים ב"ש אומרים מאור ואח"כ בשמים ובית הילל אומרים בשמים ואח"כ מאור ואמר רבי יוחנן נהגו העם כבית הילל ואליבא דר' יהודה: רב יעקב בר אבא איקלע לבי רבא חזיה דבריך בורא פרי הגפן אכסא קמא והדר בריך אכסא דברכתא ואישתי א"ל למה לך כולי האי הא בריך לן מר חדא זימנא אמר ליה כי הוינן בי ריש גלותא הכי עבדינן אמר ליה תינח בי ריש גלותא דהכי עביד (א) דספק מייתי לן ספק לא מייתי לן הכא הא מנח כסא קמן ודעתן עילויה אמר ליה אנא עבדי כתלמידי דרב *דרב ברונא ורב חננאל תלמידי דרב הוו יתבי בסעודתא קאי

רשב"ם

ורבה אמר יהנ"ק. סבירא ליה כרב דמשוי מאור בין קידוש להבדלה שאין נכון בעיניו של רבה לסמוך הבדלה לקידוש שזה מכחיש כחו של זה הקידוש עושהו קודש (ד) והבדלה עושהו קודש קל וסבירא ליה כשמואל דהבדלה קודם לקידוש ומיהו יין ברישא כולן דתדיר קודם והכי נמי בברכות ירושלמי יו"ט שחל להיות במוצ"ש רבי יוחנן אמר יקנ"ה ר' חנינא אמר ינה"ק ולוי אמר יהנ"ק מסתברא דלוי דאמר מעין שניהן ונראה לי דהכא גרסינן [נמי] ולוי אמר יהנ"ק רבה אמר קנ"ה שכן דרך האמוראין רב ולוי ושמואל חברים הם ורבה אחריהן: קנ"ה. סבירא ליה דקידוש קודם להבדלה כרב (ה) ולמה אינו רוצה לומר יין ברישא לפי שא"כ אינו נראה שמבדיל על היין הואיל ומרחיק הבדלה מעל ברכת היין והרי עיקר הבדלה לא תיקנו אלא על היין אבל קידוש אפילו על הפת יכול לקדש כדלקמן (ד' קו:) הלכך קידוש ברישא והדר מאור לפי שאנו רוצין לסמוך יין להבדלה והבדלה על כרחך לבסוף תהיה כשאר כל מוצאי שבתות והאי דלא מקדים יין מקמי מאור כשאר מוצאי שבתות שאם כן היה נראה על הקידוש ולא על הבדלה אבל במוצ"ש דעלמא דליכא קידוש מקדמי ליה: קינ"ה. סבירא ליה כרב דקידוש קודם להבדלה ורוצה נמי לסמוך יין להבדלה טפי מקידוש הלכך קידוש ברישא והדר כל סדר הבדלה של סדר כל מוצאי שבת דהוי יין מאור והבדלה אי נמי רוצין להבדיל בין קידוש להבדלה בכל היכולת: נקי"ה. קידוש קודם להבדלה כרב ויין נמי רוצה לסמוך להבדלה כמו שפירשתי הלכך נקי"ה בעינן ומאור משוי ברישא מקמי קידוש דהא כל מוצאי שבת קודם להבדלה לפי שנהגה בו תחלה ה"נ קודם לקידוש שהרי נהגה בו תחלה והרי אי אפשר לאומרו בין יין להבדלה כדין שאר מוצאי שבת שהיין קודם לו בשביל שתדיר דא"כ יש כאן הפסק בין יין להבדלה: ה"ג שאמר [משום] רבי יהושע בן חנניה נהי"ק. וטעמא כדמפרש לקמן דהבדלה קודם לקידוש והלכך נר תחלה לפי שרוצה ליתן יין סמוך להבדלה ולקידוש ששניהן נתקנו על היין אבל מאור אומרו בלא יין אם אין לו כוס: ה"ג משל דר' יהושע בן חנניה כו'. אביי ורבא סבירא להו כרב דאמר יקנ"ה ובזמן הוא דפליגי אביי סבירא ליה יקזנ"ה מאחר שמתחיל לקדש יגמור כל הקידוש ויאמר זמן שאם אין כאן קידוש אין כאן זמן אבל הבדלה אינה גורמת לומר זמן ורבא ס"ל מה מצינו בכ"מ זמן לבסוף הכא נמי זמן לבסוף וטעמו של דבר *דזמן אומרו אפילו בשוק ועיקרו אינו על הכוס הלכך אומר לבסוף: והלכתא כרבא. דאמר יקנה"ז דקידושא והדר הבדלה וכי (ו) מבדיל ברישא מיחזי דהוי עליה קדושת שבת כמשוי: רב הונא בר יהודה איקלע לבי רבא. במוצאי שבת של חול: בריך אבשמים ברישא. כמנהג שלנו: א"ל. רב הונא לרבא לאחר שגמר הבדלה והא בין ב"ש כו' ולא פליגי לא גרסינן: נר ומזון בשמים והבדלה. היכא דאין לו אלא כוס אחד: זו דברי ר"מ. דהכי הוו תני לפלוגתייהו דב"ש וב"ה דסתם מתני' ר"מ: על המזון שהוא בתחלה. דכיון דגמר סעודתו בההוא מחייב ברישא ואין מעבירין על המצות ואמר רבי יוחנן נהגו כו': רב יעקב בר אבא איקלע לבי רבא. שבת הוה כדאמרינן לקמיה כי מטא לאבדולי כו' אלמא דמעיקרא סעודת שבת ביום היו אוכלין: אכסא דברכתא. ברכת המזון בירך עליו לבסוף בפה"ג כמו שאנו עושין: לא הוי ידעיתו אי משקו לכו תו בתר כסא קמא אי לא וכי ברכיתו אקמא לא הוה דעתייכו אכסא אחרינא והוה ליה כל חד כתחלת סעודתו ומשום הכי בעיתו למיהדר וברוכי: קאי

תוספות

רבה אמר יהג"ק ולוי אמר קני"ה. רשב"ם מהפך הגירסא משום דרב ושמואל ולוי חברים היו ואין צריך להפך משום זה דגמ' נקט כל אותם שאומרים יין תחלה יקנ"ה ינה"ק יהנ"ק ואח"כ אותם שאומרים קידוש ברישא קנ"ה קינ"ה ואח"כ נר תחלה נקי"ה ניה"ק ומיהו בירושל' משמע כפירוש רשב"ם: קני"ה. פירש רשב"ם דרוצה לסמוך יין להבדלה משום דמקדשין על הפת ואין מבדילין על הפת ולפי מה שפירש ר"ת לקמן (ד' קו: בד"ה מקדש) דאין מקדשין על הפת יש לפרש שאם הי' מרחיק יין מן הבדלה יאמרו שאינו בא אלא בשביל קידוש שהוא לכבוד יו"ט: והלכתא כרבא. משום [איכך] אמוראין אצטריך לפסוק כרבא ולא משום אביי דקיי"ל (*ב"ק ד' עג.) בכולי גמרא כרבא לגבי אביי בר מיע"ל קג"ם: ואמר רבי יוחנן נהגו העם כבית הלל. והשתא חולק רבי יוחנן אסתם משנה ואיכא למימר שבלשון יחיד היה שונה אותה והיה שונה בה דברי רבי מאיר בהדיא והאי נהגו לא הוי כהאי נהגו דבפרק בתרא דתענית (ד' כו:) דמפרש דאורויי לא מורינן ואי עבדי לא מחינן בידיהן*: בריך אכסא קמא. של קידוש ואכסא דברכתא של בהמ"ז והא דתנן בכיצד מברכין (ברכות דף מג.) בירך על היין שלפני המזון פטר יין שלאחר המזון היינו לאחר הסעודה וקודם ברכת המזון שהיו רגילי' לשתות יין אחר הסעודה קודם ברכת המזון: לא הוי ידעיתו אי משקו. פרשב"ם כי ברכיתו אכסא קמא לא ידעיתו אי יהבו לכו כסא אחרינא והוה כל חד כתחלת סעודה ולפירושו משמע שהיו מברכין נמי תוך הסעודה וקשה דהא משמע שהיו עושים בי ריש גלותא כרבא דבריך אכסא קמא ואכסא דברכתא ולא על כל כסא וזהו דוחק לומר שלא היו שותים בבי ריש גלותא יין באמצע הסעודה לכך נראה לפרש שלא היו מברכין תוך הסעודה כי היו יודעים שיתנו להם יין כל צרכן אבל בבהמ"ז לא היה כוס כי אם למברך והיו מסתפקים אם יגיע להם לשתות ממנו: אנא דעבדי כתלמידי דרב. פירש רשב"ם אף על גב דשמעינן מהכא דברכת המזון אפסוקי סעודתא הוא מכל מקום לא בעי לברוכי אחר יין שבסעודה מקמי דליבריך ברכת המזון לפי שברכת המזון פוטרתו דהשתא בברכה אחת מעין שלש סגי כל שכן בשלש ברכות והכי איתא בה"ג ומיהו אין זה ק"ו דהא פסקינן בברכות (דף מא:) דברים הבאים שלא מחמת הסעודה אחר הסעודה פי' וקודם ברכת המזון טעונין ברכה לפניהם ולאחריהם וכן תאנים וענבים בתוך הסעודה לרב ששת ולא מיפטרו בג' ברכות דבהמ"ז ורש"י פירש בתשובה דצריך לברך אחריו כמו תאנים וענבים לרב ששת ואין נראה דהא מסקינן התם אמר רב פפא הלכתא דברים הבאים שלא מחמת הסעודה בתוך הסעודה טעונין ברכה לפניהם ולא לאחריהם לאחר הסעודה טעונין בין לפניהם בין לאחריהם והיינו דלא כרב ששת ואע"ג דרש"י פירש התם לאחר הסעודה כלומר דברים

מסורת הש"ס

ברכות נב: | שם נג: | [ברכות נב: תוספתא ברכו' פ"ה] | חולין קו. | [עירובין מ:]

עין משפט נר מצוה

טז א מיי' פכ"ט מהל' שבת הלכה כג סמג עשין כט טוש"ע או"ח סימן תעג סעיף א:

יז ב מיי' שם הלכ' יג וכד וסמג שם טוש"ע או"ח סי' רצו סעיף א ג:

[קדושין נב.]

[ועי' תוס' ברכות נב: ד"ה נהגו ותוס' ר"ה טו: ד"ה וכו']

רבינו חננאל

אמר רב יהודה לא נחלקו ב"ש וב"ה על המזון שהוא בתחלה ועל הבדלה שהיא בסוף שלא נחלקו אלא על המאור ועל הבשמים שב"ש אומרים מאור ואחר כך בשמים וב"ה אומרים בשמים ואחר כך מאור. אמר ר' יוחנן נהגו העם כב"ה אליבא דר' יהודה דבשמים ואח"כ מאור: רב ברונא ורב חננאל תלמידי דרב הוו יתבי

הגהות הב"ח

(א) גמרא דהכי עבדינן דספק מייתי: (ב) רשב"ם ד"ה אכסא כשמתחיל לשתות הסד והשאר נמחק: (ג) ד"ה לא הוו ידעיתו אי משקו לכו תו בתר כסא קמא אי לא וכי ברכיתו אקמא לא הוה דעתייכו אכסא אחרינא וה"ל כל כוס כתחלת סעודה ומשום הכי בעיתו למיהדר וברוכי: (ד) רשב"ם ד"ה ורבה אמר וכו' הקידוש ועושהו קודש חמור והבדלה: (ה) ד"ה קני"ה וכו' ולמה אינו רוצה וכו' ומרחיק הבדלה מברכת היין כצ"ל ותיבת ולמה נמחק ותיבת על נמחק: (ו) ד"ה והלכתא וכו' דכי מבדיל:

order is] *YaNHaḲ;*[11] [103*a*] Rabbah said: *YaHNaḲ;*[12] Levi said:
a *ḲaNYaH;*[1] the Rabbis said: *ḲiYNaH;*[2] Mar the son of Rabina said: *NaḲYaH;*[3] Martha said in R. Joshua's name: *NiYHaḲ.*[4]

Samuel's father sent to Rabbi: Let our Master teach us what is the order of *habdaloth.*[5] He sent [back] to him: Thus did R. Ishmael b. R. Jose say, speaking in the name of his father who said it on the authority of R. Joshua b. Ḥananiah: [The order is] *NaHiYḲ.*[6] R. Ḥanina said: R. Joshua b. Ḥananiah's [ruling] may be compared to a king who departs [from a place] and a governor who enters: [first] you escort the king [out], and then you go forth to greet the governor.[7]

What is our decision thereon?—Abaye said: [The order is]
b *YaḲaZNaH;*[1] while Raba maintained: *YaḲNeHaZ.*[2] And the law is as Raba.

R. Huna b. Judah visited Raba's home. Light and spices were brought before them, [whereupon] Raba recited a blessing over the spices first and then one over the light. Said he to him: But both Beth Shammai and Beth Hillel [agree that] light comes first and then spices? And to what is this [allusion]?—For we learned: Beth Shammai maintain: Light and Grace [after meals], spices and *habdalah;*[3] while Beth Hillel rule: Light and spices, Grace and *habdalah!*[4] Thereat Raba answered: These are the words of R. Meir; but R. Judah said: Beth Shammai and Beth Hillel did not differ about Grace, [agreeing] that it comes at the beginning, and about *habdalah*, that it comes at the end. About what do they differ? About light and spices. Beth Shammai maintain: Light [first] and then spices; while Beth Hillel rule: Spices [first] and then light; and R. Joḥanan said [thereon]: The people act in accordance with Beth Hillel as interpreted by R. Judah.

R. Jacob b. Abba visited Raba's home. He saw him recite the blessings 'who createst the fruit of the vine' over the first cup, and then he recited a blessing over the cup of Grace[5] and drank it. Said he to him: 'Why do you need all this? Surely, sir, you have [already] recited a blessing for us once?' 'When we were at the *Resh Galutha's*[6] we did thus,' replied he. 'It is well that we did this at the *Resh Galutha's*,' said he, 'because there was a doubt whether they would bring us [more wine] or they would not bring us [more].[7] But here, surely the [second] cup stands before us and we have it in mind?' 'I acted in accordance with Rab's disciples,' he replied. For R. Beruna and R. Ḥananel,

(11) Samuel gives precedence to *habdalah* over *ḳiddush;* the reason is stated *infra* 103*a* in the illustration on the ruling of R. Joshua b. Ḥananiah. (12) He agrees with Rab that *Ner* (light) interposes between *ḳiddush* and *habdalah*, because it is illogical to recite them consecutively, since they are mutually contradictory, as it were, *ḳiddush* declaring that the day is sacred, whereas *habdalah* declares that it is not as sacred as the Sabbath. He also agrees with Samuel that *habdalah* comes before *ḳiddush*, and he places wine (*Yayin*) at the head of all, for the reason stated on 102*b*, n. a10.

a (1) He too puts *ḳiddush* before *habdalah*, but holds that if wine is put at the beginning, the interval between it and *habdalah* will be so great that it may appear that the *habdalah* is not being recited over wine, which is essential. But *ḳiddush* need not be in immediate proximity to the wine, since it may be recited over bread too. For that reason too *Ner* (light) precedes the wine, so that the latter may be nearer to *habdalah* than to *ḳiddush*.—Rashbam transposes these last two views, mainly on the basis of J.T. (2) They too place *ḳiddush* before *habdalah*. Hence we commence with *ḳiddush*, and then recite *habdalah* in its usual order, which is *Yayin* (wine), *Ner* (light) and *habdalah*. (3) He too places *ḳiddush* before *habdalah*, and also holds that wine must come near *habdalah*. But just as *Ner* generally precedes *habdalah*, because he enjoys the light first, so must it precede *ḳiddush*. Again, it cannot be recited between wine and *habdalah*, so that the wine should precede it, in accordance with the usual practice, because that would cause an interruption between the wine and the *habdalah*. (4) He places *habdalah* before *ḳiddush* for the reason stated anon. He then puts wine before *habdalah*, for since that is immediately followed by *ḳiddush*, the wine is accounted for both, which is as it should be. For both *ḳiddush* and *habdalah* should be recited over wine in the first place, though the former is permitted over bread where wine is not available. Again, he puts wine *before habdalah* and *ḳiddush* instead of between them, since wine generally precedes. Furthermore, since *Ner* generally precedes *habdalah*, for the reason stated in the last note, it must now come at the very beginning. (5) The pl. of *habdalah* employed generically. (6) V. preceding note. He however places wine between *habdalah* and *ḳiddush*, so that it should really be near to both. (7) The Sabbath, whose sanctity is greater, is the king; the Festival is the governor. Hence we first bid farewell to the Sabbath with *habdalah*, and then welcome the Festival with *ḳiddush*.

b (1) *Yayin* (wine), *Ḳiddush*, *Zeman* (season), *Ner* (light) and *Habdalah*. (2) *Yayin*, *Ḳiddush*, *Ner*, *Habdalah*, and *Zeman*. (3) This order is followed at the conclusion of the Sabbath if there is sufficient for one cup only. (4) V. Ber. 51*b*. (5) He recited Grace after meals over a second cup, and after Grace he recited the blessing for wine over it.—This is the present practice. (6) V. Glos. (7) Hence when we recited a blessing over the first cup we did not think of a second, which therefore constituted a fresh act of drinking, and so the blessing had to be repeated.

He goes on eating until nightfall.[4] [102*b*] When they finish [their meal], he recites the Grace after meals over the first cup and the sanctity of the day over the second. Yet why so: let us recite both over one cup?[5]—Said R. Huna in R. Shesheth's name: One may not recite two sanctities over the same cup.[6] What is the reason? Said R. Naḥman b. Isaac: Because you may not perform religious duties in wholesale fashion.[7] Yet [may you] not? Surely it was taught: He who enters his house at the termination of the Sabbath, recites blessings over the wine, the light and the spices,[8]
a and then recites *habdalah* over the cup [of wine].[1] But if he has one cup only, he leaves it until after the meal[2] and he recites them all together after it?[3]—Where he has not [enough,] it is different. But on the Festival which falls after the Sabbath, though he has [wine],[4] yet Rab said: [The order is] *YaḲNaH*.[5]—I will tell you: Since he [Rab] did not include 'the season' [*zeman*],[6] it follows that we are discussing the seventh day of Passover,[7] by which time he has consumed all that he had and has no more. But on the first day of the Festival he has [wine], yet Abaye said: [The order is] *YaḲZaNaH;* while Raba said: [The order is] *YaḲNeHaZ?*[8]—But *habdalah* and *ḳiddush* constitute one observance],[9] [whereas] the Grace after meals and *ḳiddush* are two [distinct observances].

[To turn to] the [main] text: When a Festival falls after the Sabbath, Rab said: [The order is] *YaḲNaH;*[10] Samuel said: [The

(4) He need not interrupt his meal but may continue until the end. (5) The difficulty is on R. Jose's view only. But on R. Judah's, since the meal must be interrupted and the table removed, it is natural that two separate cups should be required for *ḳiddush* and Grace. (6) Grace is here designated a 'sanctity': i.e., Grace and *ḳiddush* are two distinct religious duties, and therefore they require separate cups. (7) Lit., 'bundles'. I.e., each requires separate attention. (8) As is done at the termination of the Sabbath. *Ḳiddush* and *habdalah* are both recited over wine; a blessing is pronounced over light because it is then that light was created, v. *supra* 54*a*; spices are inhaled on the termination of the Sabbath to compensate for the loss of the superior ('additional') soul with which man is endowed on the Sabbath, Rashbam and Tosaf. a.l. and in Beẓ. 33*b*.

a (1) *Habdalah*, being longer, is left to the last. (2) Or perhaps, 'until after grace', מזון being elliptical for ברכת המזון. (3) Lit., 'he chains them together after it'. Thus two religious acts are combined. (4) This is assumed to refer to the first evening of Passover, when, as stated *supra* 99*b*, even the poorest man was provided with four cups of wine. (5) This is a mnemonic: *Y* = *Yayin* (wine); *Ḳ* = *Ḳiddush*; *N* = *Ner* (light, i.e., a blessing over light); and *H* = *Habdalah*. Thus *ḳiddush* and *habdalah* are both recited over the same cup. (6) The benediction 'who hast kept us alive and preserved us and enabled us to reach this season'. This is recited on the first night (in the Diaspora on the first two nights) of every Festival, as well as on certain other occasions. (7) *Ḳiddush* must be recited then too, as it follows the Intermediate Days, which are only semi-sacred; v. 5*a*, n. a4; again, if it follows the Sabbath, *habdalah* also is recited. (8) V. n. a6. *Z* = *zeman* ('season'). (9) Both being recited on account of the sanctity of the Festival, to which reference is made even in the *habdalah*. (10) Wine is first, in accordance with Beth Hillel's view in Ber. 51*b* that since wine is more constant it takes precedence. *Ḳiddush* precedes *habdalah* because it is regarded as more important; also, if he recited *habdalah* first, it might appear that the Sabbath were a burden to him, which he desired to end at the earliest possible moment. After *ḳiddush* the order is *NH* ('light' and *habdalah*), this being the usual order at the conclusion of the Sabbath.

עין משפט
נר מצוה

ט א מיי' פכ"ט מהלכות שבת הלכה יג סמג עשין כט טור שו"ע אורח חיים סימן רעא סעיף ו:

*גמרו כוס ראשון מברך עליו ברכת המזון והשני אומר עליו קדושת היום אמאי ונימרינהו לתרוייהו אחדא כסא אמר רב הונא אמר רב ששת אין אומרים שתי קדושות על כוס אחד מאי טעמא אמר רב נחמן בר יצחק *לפי שאין עושין מצות חבילות חבילות ולא והא תניא *הנכנס לביתו במוצאי שבת מברך על היין ועל המאור ועל הבשמים ואחר כך אומר הבדלה על הכוס ואם אין לו אלא כוס אחד מניחו לאחר המזון ומשלשלן כולן לאחריו אין לו שאני והא יו"ט שחל להיות אחר השבת דאית ליה ואמר רב יקנ"ה אמרי מדלא אמר זמן מכלל דבשביעי של פסח עסקינן דכל מאי דהוה ליה אכיל ליה ולית לי' והא יו"ט ראשון דאית ליה ואמר אביי יקזנ"ה ורבא אמר יקנה"ז אלא הבדלה וקידוש חדא מילתא היא ברכת המזון וקידוש תרי מילי נינהו: גופא יום טוב שחל להיות אחר השבת רב אמר יקנ"ה ושמואל אמר ינה"ק ורבה

ה"ג **ראשון** אומר עליו ברכת המזון · להפסיק והשני אומר עליו קידוש היום סמוך לסעודת שבת ולגירסא זו אתי שפיר הא דמשמע לעיל (ד' ק: ושם) דמפסיק לר' יהודה בעקירת שלחן קודם קידוש לפי שהיו רגילין לעקור שלחן לפני ברכת המזון אבל ספרים דגר' ראשון אומר עליו קידוש היום וטעמא שאינו יכול לטעום מכוס ברהמ"ז בלא קידוש קשה מנא ליה לעיל דמפסיקין לרבי יהודה בעקירת שלחן קודם קידוש · והא דקתני בתוספת' דברכות אורחין שהיו מסובין אצל בעל הבית וקדש עליהן היום עקרו עם חשיכה לבית המדרש חזרו ומזגו להם את הכוס אומר עליו קידוש דברי רבי יהודה וברכת המזון לא מזכיר כלל היינו משום דמתחלה עשו ברהמ"ז קודם יציאתם לעשות הפסק בין סעודת חול לסעודת שבת ולכך נמי עשו עקירה לבית המדרש: **ונימרינהו** לתרווייהו אחד כסא · לר' יוסי פריך כיון דתרווייהו אסעודת שבת קאתו כדפרישית לעיל (ד' ק·*) דהך סעודה עולה לו לסעודת שבת הוה ליה למימר תרווייהו אחד כסא אבל לר' יהודה לא פריך כיון דברכת המזון אסעודת חול וקידוש על סעודה הבאה אין לומר שניהם על כוס אחד: **שאין** אומרי' שתי קדושות על כוס אחד · ויש נוהגין בחופה מטעם זה שלא לומר שבע ברכות על כוס ברכת המזון אלא מביאין כוס אחר ואין מברכין על השני בפה"ג כיון שכבר בירך על כוס ברכת המזון כי אין נכון לברך פעמים אך רבינו משולם היה אומר הכל על כוס אחד דלא דמי לברכת המזון וקידוש דתרי מילי נינהו כדאמרי' בסמוך אבל הכא חדא מלתא היא דברכת המזון גורם לברכת נישואין וברכת אירוסין ונישואין נהגו לומר על שתי כוסות וטעמא דרגילים זה בלא זה כדאמר בכתובות (ד' ז:) מברכין ברכת האירוסין בבית אירוסין וברכת חתנים בבית חתנים ועוד דנהגו לקרות כתובה בינתים והוי הפסק ולכך צריך ב' כוסות: **מיתיבי** הנכנס לביתו כו'. הוה מצי למיפרך ממתני' דאלו דברים (ברכות ד' נא:) דמייתי בסמוך ב"ש אומר נר ומזון ובשמים והבדלה כו' אלא פריך מברייתא משום דבעי לשנויי אין לו שאני דקתני בברייתא אין לו אלא כוס אחד כו' ודרך הש"ס להקשות ממקום שמועה לתרץ בפשיטות: **מניחו** לאחר המזון · הקשה ה"ר נסים היאך יכול קודם הבדלה הא אמרי' לקמן אסור לאדם שיטעום כלום קודם שיבדיל ואמימר נמי בת טוות כדאמר לקמן (ד' קז·) ותירץ דהכא מיירי כשאכל מבעו"י עד שחשיכה לו ואע"ג דמפסיקין להבדלה לשמואל(ב) ול"ש לר' יהודה דמאמר טפי והך ברייתא מוקי לה בסמוך(ג) כב"ש ולאליבא דרבי יהודה הא דקאמר מניחו לאחר המזון לא שמותר לאכול אלא כלומר כשיפסיק סעודתו בברהמ"ז אז יבדיל וקשה דלשון הנכנס לביתו משמע שלא התחיל לאכול מבעו"י ועוד הקשה מורי ה"ר יחיאל דלקמן (ד' קה:) אמרי' על הך ברייתא ש"מ טעם מבדיל ולפירוש רבינו נסים דמיירי באכל מבעוד יום אין הוכיח כלום אלא י"ל דודאי בחנם אין לו לאכול קודם הבדלה אבל כשאין לו אלא כוס אחד מותר לאכול קודם הבדלה כדי לעשות על הכוס ברכת המזון: **דאית** ליה ואמר רב יקנ"ה. פי' בקונטרס דס"ד דביו"ט ראשון של פסח מיירי דאית ליה כוסות טובא כדתנן (לעיל ד' צט:) לא יפחתו לו מד' כוסות וקשה דהא כל ד' כוסות צריכי כל חד למילתיה ועוד דבסמוך דפריך מיקנה"ז לימא דבשמיני של חג מיירי דאיכא זמן ואכיל ושתה כל מה דהוה ליה ועוד דאכיל כל מה דהוה ליה לשון אכילה לא היה לו להזכיר אכוסות לכך נראה לפרש דביום טוב ראשון מסתמא אדם מכין הרבה ובשמיני של חג נמי שהוא רגל בפני עצמו רגילין להכין הרבה כדתנן (חולין ד' פג·) ד' פרקים בשנה צריך הטבח להודיע אמה מכרתי לשחוט וחשיב יו"ט האחרון של חג: **רב** אמר יקנ"ה · ומה שאין מזכיר בשמים פירש רשב"ם דטעם בשמים משום איבוד נשמה יתירה וביום טוב נמי איכא נשמה יתירה · וקשה דאם כן במוצאי יום טוב אמאי לא תקינו בשמים לכך נראה דביום טוב ליכא נשמה יתירה והכא אין מזכיר בשמים משום דשמחת יום טוב ואכילה ושתיה מועיל כמו בשמים ויש מעמים לא נכונים וזה הטעם נכון ועיקר*: **יקנ"ה**. יין ברישא וא"ת אמאי לא תקינו נמי בברכת המזון יין ברישא כמו בכל מקום וליכא למימר דפטר ליה יין שבתוך הסעודה דכיון דלאמר הב ונבריך איתסר למישתי ויש לומר דברכת המזון בא לשם גמר סעודה ומפסיק לכל מה שלפניו כדאמר לקמן (ד' קג:) דברכת המזון עקר דעתיה ממשתיא וצריך לברך אכסא דברכתא אף על גב דבירך אכסא קמא והשתא הכוס בידו ודעתו לשתות אח"כ אפילו הכי הוה הפסק לכך תיקנו לברך אין אחר ברכת המזון שאם יברך קודם יצטרך לברך שנית:

[כד"ה ר"י אומר]

[וכ"כ תוס' ב"ה נג: ד"ה כי טוין]

גמרו · סעודתן : (א) אומר עליו כו' · ר' יוסי קאמר לה: משלשלן · עד לאחר המזון אלמא אמרי' שתי ברכות על כוס אחד הבדלה וברהמ"ז : ואמר רב יקנ"ה · כדמפרש בשביעי עסקינן ובשביעי ליכא זמן ומכל מקום שמעינן מינה קידוש והבדלה על כוס אחד : ומשנינן מדלא קאמר זמן · בשביעי של פסח עסקי' דשמא עני הוא ואין לו אלא כוס א' : והא יום ראשון דאית ליה · דאפי' עני שבישראל לא יפחתו לו מד' כוסות : קידוש והבדלה חדא מלתא היא · דתרווייהו משום קדושת יו"ט נינהו וההבדלה עצמו הוא מזכיר קדוש' יו"ט דהמבדיל בין קדש לקדש קא מברך : ה"ג

רשב"ם

גמרו · סעודתן : כוס ראשון אומר עליו ברכת המזון כו' · ר' יוסי קאמר לה ורבותא הוא שאינו צריך לקדש מיד אלא יגמור סעודתו ויברך ברכת המזון ואח"כ יקדש ומיהו אם פרס מפה וקידש מודה רבי יוסי דכל שכן דשפיר טפי דאי לא תימא הכי אלא דוקא קאמר רבי יוסי ראשון מברך עליו ברהמ"ז אם כן שמואל דאמר כמאן (לעיל דף ק·) : ולימרינהו תרווייהו אחד כסא קידוש היום וברכת המזון ולרבי יוסי קא פריך דאילו לרבי יהודה כיון דמפסיקין וצריך עקירת שלחן צריך שני כוסות : שני קדושות · ברכת המזון קורא קדושה כקידוש היום כלומר שתי מלות: חבילות חבילות · דמיחזי עליה כמשוי : מברך על היין · תחלה לפי שהוא תדיר ותדיר קודם : על המאור ועל הבשמים · כב"ש מוקמינן לה במסכת ברכות בפרק אלו דברים (ד' נב.) דאמר מאור ברישא ואחר כך בשמים והבדלה לבסוף לפי שאלו הראשונות קצרות וברכת הבדלה ארוכה לפיכך אומרה לבסוף: משלשלן · לשון שלשלת שמחברם יחד עם ברכת המזון אלמא אמרינן שתי ברכות על כוס אחד הבדלה וברכת המזון: [אין לו שאני] דלית ליה יין לשני כוסות והכא בדאית ליה עסקינן : אחר השבת · מוצאי השבת : דאית ליה וקאמר רב יקנ"ה · קס"ד ביו"ט הראשון של פסח שחל להיות אחר השבת עסקינן דאית ליה כוסות הרבה דתנן לעיל (ד' צט:) אפילו עני שבישראל לא יפחתו לו מארבע כוסות ואמר רב יקנ"ה אלמא קידוש והבדלה על כוס אחד מאי אמר : ומשני מדלא אמר רב יקנה"ז אלמא בשביעי של פסח עסקינן · דשמא עני הוא ואין לו אלא כוס אחד וטעמיה דרב לקמיה אפרשנו במקומו וכן דרבא ודאביי : והא יו"ט ראשון דאית ליה · דאפי' עני שבישראל לא יפחתו לו מארבע כוסות : קידושא והבדלה חדא מילתא היא · תרוייהו משום קדושת ימים טובים נינהו וההבדלה עצמה הוא מזכיר קדושת יו"ט המבדיל בין קדש לקדש קא מברך: גופא יו"ט שחל להיות אחר השבת · צריך להבדיל ולקדש ומשמע שאם לא היה יום טוב לא היו חולקין האמוראין הללו אלא כולי עלמא מודו יין מאור והבדלה והשתא דאיכא קדושת היום פליגי ולפיכך צריך ליתן טעם לכל דבריהם ולומר שהקידוש גורם לשנות את הסדר מכמות שרגיל: רב אמר יקנ"ה · ס"ל קדושת היום עדיפא מהבדלה אי נמי דכי מבדיל ברישא מיחזי דהוי עליה קדושת היום כמשוי ולפיכך יין קודם לקידוש כבית הלל (ברכות דף נא:) דתדיר ושאינו תדיר תדיר קודם ואחר הקידוש נר והבדלה כשאר מוצאי שבתות שהנר קודם להבדלה: ושמואל אמר ינה"ק · שמואל סבירא ליה הבדלה קודם לקידוש דמפרש טעמא לקמיה משל דרבי יהושע בן חנניה למה הדבר דומה למלך שיצא ואפרכוס נכנס מלוין את המלך השבת להבדיל ואח"כ יוצאין לקראת אפרכוס לקראת יו"ט לקדשו ועל מלתיה דשמואל אמר לה בהדיא בברכות בירושלמי באלו דברים רבי חנינא אמר ינה"ק ואתי רבי חנינא כשמואל דא"ר חנינא בשם שמואל משל למלך יוצא ושלטון נכנס מלוין את המלך ואח"כ מכניסין את השלטון הלכך יין תחלה ואח"כ מאור ואח"כ הבדלה דכיון דהבדלה קודם לקידוש יעשה כל סדר הבדלה כדין מוצאי שבתות דעלמא ואח"כ יקדש ומה שאין נותנין האמוראין סימן לבשמים לפי שאין מברכין על הבשמים ביו"ט שהרי גם ביו"ט יש לנו נשמה יתירה כשבת: ורבה

רבה

רבינו חננאל

גמרו כוס ראשון אומר עליו בהמ"ז והשני מקדש עליו ואמרינן ונמרינהו כלהו בחד כסא ודחי' לפי שאין אומרים שתי קדושות על כוס אחד מאי טעמא לפי שאין עושין מצות חבילות חבילות ולא והתניא הנכנס לביתו במוצאי שבת מברך על היין ועל המאור ועל הבשמים ואח"כ אומר הבדלה ואם אין לו אלא כוס אחד מניחו לאחר המזון ומשלשלן כולן אחריו הנה אומר שתי קדושות על כוס אחד ושני' לית ליה שני והא יו"ט דאית ליה אחר שבת ואמר רב יקנ"ה ודחי' מדלא אמר רב זמן ש"מ דהאי יום טוב אחר שבת דקתני רב יקנ"ה בשביעי של פסח עסקי' דלית ליה יין דכל דהוה ליה שתיה והא יו"ט [ראשון] דאית ליה ואמר אביי (יקנ"ה) [יקזנ"ה] ורבא אמר יקנה"ז ופריק כי קאמרי' שתי קדושות אבל קידושא ואבדלתא חדא קידושא היא כלומר וברכת המזון והקידוש של יום שתי קרושות הן ומאי שנא ופירוש קידוש היום והבדלה תרוייהו קודם אכילה הן קידוש וברכת המזון הקידוש קודם אכילה וברכת המזון אחר הסעודה לפיכך שתי קדושות הן ואסיקנא יום טוב שחל להיות אחר השבת הלכתא כרבא דאמר יקנה"ז:

מסורת הש"ס

[ברכות מט. סוטה ח.]
לקמן קה:
ברכות נב.
[תוספתא דברכות פ"ה]

הגהות הב"ח

(א) רשב"ם ד"ה גמרו סעודתן כוס ראשון אומר עליו כצ"ל והד"א: (ב) תוס' ד"ה מניחו וכו' כשמואל. נ"ב לעיל בדף ק סוף ע"א: (ג) בא"ד מוקי לה בסמוך נ"ב בתחלת דף ק"ו:

מאן תנא· להך ברייתא דקתני אע"ג דדברים הטעונין ברכה לאחריהן צריך לברך רבי יהודה היא: חברים שהיו מסובין ועקרו כו'· ולא גרסינן לשתות יין: ומקשינן אלא טעמא דבדברים הטעונין ברכה לאחריהם· משום הכי פליגי רבנן עליה דר' יהודה· הא בדברים שאין טעונין ברכה לאחריהן אפילו רבנן מודו דצריך לברך פעם אחרת בתחלה: לימא תיהוי תיובתא דרבי יוחנן· דאמר לעיל שינוי מקום אין צריך לברך ולא מפליג בין דברים הטעונין לדברים שאין טעונין: לאו אותביניה חדא זימנא· לעיל: ה"ג תניא כוותיה דרב חסדא חברים שהיו מסובין לשתות יין כו'· והיינו כרב חסדא דאמר דברים שטעונין ברכה לאחריהן (א) אין צריך לברך והא בהדיא מסייעא לרב חסדא מדקתני יין אבל בההיא דלעיל לא תנא יין בהדי'· ואומר עליו קידוש היום· באמצע סעודתו: ושני מיד אומר עליו ברהמ"ז ומפסיק כדאמר ר' יהודה לעיל ומיהו הואיל והגיע עונת קידוש צריך לקדש תחלה לא גרסינן ראשון אומר עליו ברכת המזון שני אומר עליו קדושת היום:

גמרו

[עירובין נ.]

רשב"ם

מאן תנא עקירות· מאן תנא להך ברייתא דקתני אע"ג דדברים הטעונין ברכה לאחריהן במקומן צריך לברך רבי יהודה היא: ה"ג חברים שהיו מסובין ועקרו רגליהם כו'· ולא גרסי' לשתות יין: א"ר יהודה במה דברים אמורים כו'· מכלל דרבנן פליגי עליה ברישא דאע"ג דלא הניחו שם מקצת חברים אין צריך לברך כרב חסדא דא"ר יוחנן בעירובין בפרק חלון (דף צב·) כל מקום שאמר ר' יהודה במה לחלוק אימתי לפרש דברי חכמים בא: ומקשינן אלא טעמא דבדברים הטעונין ברכה לאחריהן· משום הכי פליגי רבנן עליה דרבי יהודה הא בדברים שאין טעונין אפי' רבנן מודו דצריך לברך פעם אחרת בתחלה: לימא תיהוי תיובתא דרבי יוחנן·דאמר לעיל שינוי מקום אין צריך לברך ולא מפליג בין דברים הטעונין לדברים שאין טעונין: לאו אותביניה חדא זימנא· לעיל: לימא תיהוי תיובתא נמי מהא· שאם יבא אדם ויברך להך קמייתא או ישבש אותה על ידי ברייתות אחרות נתביה מהך: להודיעך כחו דר' יהודה כו'· כשהן יוצאין טעונין ברכה למפרע כו' אבל בשאר דברים לא היה יכול לומר (ב) טעונין ברכה למפרע כו' דהא אין צריכין ברכה לאחריהן במקומן וליכא לאקשויי אדרבה לישמעינן דברים שאין צריכין ברכה לאחריהן במקומן להודיעך כחן דרבנן דמקילין כל כך שאפי' (הס) [עליה] אין צריכין לברך ומשום דכח היתרא עדיף אין לומר כך דאין כחן כח ותיובות אם אין מצריכין לברך דסברא הוא דכיון שלא היה היסח

מאן תנא עקירות רבי יהודה דתניא חברים שהיו מסובין ועקרו רגליהם לילך לבית הכנסת או לבית המדרש כשהן יוצאין אין טעונין ברכה למפרע וכשהן חוזרין אין טעונין ברכה לכתחלה אמר רבי יהודה במה דברים אמורים בזמן שהניחו שם מקצת חברים אבל לא הניחו שם מקצת חברים כשהן יוצאין טעונין ברכה למפרע וכשהן חוזרין טעונין ברכה לכתחלה אלא טעמא דבדברים הטעונין ברכה לאחריהן במקומן דכשהן יוצאין אין טעונין ברכה למפרע וכשהן חוזרין אין טעונין ברכה לכתחלה אבל דברים שאין טעונין ברכה לאחריהן במקומן אפילו לרבנן כשהן יוצאין טעונין ברכה למפרע וכשהן חוזרין טעונין ברכה לכתחילה לימא תיהוי תיובתא דר' יוחנן *ולאו מי אותביניה חדא זימנא נימא מהא נמי תיהוי תיובתא °אמר לך ר' יוחנן הוא הדין דאפילו דברים שאין טעונין ברכה לאחריהם במקומן נמי אין צריכין לברך והא דקתני עקרו רגליהן להודיעך כחו דר' יהודה דאפילו דברים שטעונין ברכה לאחריהן במקומן טעמא דהניחו מקצת חברים אבל לא הניחו מקצת חברים כשהן יוצאין טעונין ברכה למפרע וכשהן חוזרין טעונין ברכה לכתחלה תניא כוותיה דרב חסדא חברים שהיו מסובין לשתות יין ועקרו רגליהן וחזרו אין צריכין לברך תנו רבנן בני חבורה שהיו מסובין וקדש עליהן היום מביאין לו כוס של יין ואומר עליו קדושת היום ושני אומר עליו ברכת המזון דברי רבי יהודה ר' יוסי אומר אוכל והולך עד שתחשך

גמרו

לברך הייט לפניו ולא למפרע וכן פירש רשב"ס ור"ח לקמן (ד' קג:) איתסר לכו למישתי עד דבריכתו בפה"ג ואע"פ שלא היה יודע אם רוצים לשתות בלא ברכה מ"מ היה מורה להם שלא ישתו בלא ברכה וכן נראה עיקר דהא בפ' כל הבשר (חולין דף קז·) אמר השמש מברך על כל פרוסה ופרוסה לפי שמסיח דעתו ולא משמע שילטרך בכל פעם לברך ברכת המזון ועוד דלקמן גבי חד בריך אכסא קמא ואכסא דברכתא בפה"ג ומייתי ראיה מהב וניבריך דאסור למישתי עד שיברך ואי בפה"ג מייתי שפיר אבל אי אסור למישתי עד שיברך ברהמ"ז מנא ליה דאחר ברכת המזון ילטרך לברך בפה"ג אף על פי שיש לדחות דמוכח שפיר דאי אחר ברהמ"ז אין מברך בפה"ג דלא הוי הפסק בהב וניבריך אמאי אתסר למישתי אבל לא משמע הכי מדלא פי' עד דבריכיתו ברכת המזון ובפה"ג וסברא הוא כיון דהב וניבריך הוי הפסק כאילו כבר בירכו סגי בברכת בפה"ג כמו אחר ברהמ"ז והא דתניא בתוספתא דברכות בעל הבית שהיה מיסב ואוכל קראו חבירו לדבר עמו אין לריך לברך כו' הפליג לריך ברכה למפרע וכשהוא חוזר לריך ברכה לכתחלה לאו כשחוזר טעון ברכה למפרע אלא כשרולה לאכול ומיירי שקראו להפליג ומברך שמא ישהה כדפרי' ותדע דאמר בפ"ג דיומא (ד' ל·) דיבר עם חבירו והפליג טעון נטילת ידים ומשמע דה"ה ברכת המוליא אבל ברהמ"ז לא קאמר דלריך ומיירי שלא ידע מתחלה שיפליג ואין הלכה כאותן ברייתות אלא אפילו ברכה לכתחלה לא לריך דקי"ל כרב חסדא דאמר לקיבעי' קמא הדר והנהו ברייתות וההיא דתוספתא אתו כרבי יהודה:

ועקרו רגליהם לילך לבהכ"נ כו'· מכאן משמע שאם שכח להתפלל ונזכר באמצע סעוד' והתפלל שא"צ ברכה אפי' לכתחל' ומה שהביא ה"ר יוס טוב ראיה מפרק כיסוי הדם (חולין ד' פז·) דאמר מישתא וברוכי בהדי הדדי לא אפשר שצריך לברך ברהמ"ז וליטול ידיו אינה ראיה דדוקא גבי ברהמ"ז אמרינן הכי דהוי הפסק וגמר סעודה אבל תפלה אע"ג דמיכל וצלויי בהדי הדדי לא אפשר אין בכך כלום: **תניא** כוותיה דרב חסדא· פי' רשב"ס הא דלא מייתי כרב חסדא מרבנן דר' יהודה משום דבההיא לא קתני בהדיא יין וזה פי' לפי שיטתו דגרסי' הכא יין וי"ל משום הכי לא מייתי סייעתא מינה משום דאיכא דאמרי בסנהדרין (ד' כה·) דבמה נמי לפרש ואע"ג דחזרו מייתי ראיה לרב חסדא דטעמא דשינוי מקום דצריך לברך משום שעמידתו ממקומו היא גמר אכילתו וה"ה נמי חזרו:

ה"ג

הדעת בינתיה למה יחזור ויברך אבל כח דר' יהודה עדיף טפי שמחמיר שתי חומרות על דברי חכמים דלא מיבעי דברים שאין צריכין ברכה לאחריהן במקומן שחייב (לאחריהם) לברך אע"פ שחביריו פוטרין אלא אפילו דברים הצריכין ברכה לאחריהן במקומן נמי דחייב לברך הכא כח דאיסורא עדיף: ה"ג תניא כוותיה דרב חסדא *חברים שהיו מסובין לשתות יין כו' והיינו כרב חסדא דאמר דברים שטעונין ברכה לאחריהן במקומן א"צ לברך והא בהדיא מסייעא לרב חסדא מדקתני יין אבל בההוא דלעיל לא תנא יין בהדיא מיהו משמעינן מדמעמתין שינוי יין אין צריך לברך ברכת היין אבל מברך הטוב והמטיב שינוי מקום בשבעת המינין שטעונין ברכה לאחריהן במקומן מעין שלש כגון אוכל בבית זה וחזר ואכל בבית אחר קודם שבירך אחריהן או שאכל בבית זה והלך לשוק וחזר וגמר סעודתו בבית אחר בכל אלו אין צריך לחזור ולברך תחלה דלקיבעיה קמא הדר דהא תניא כוותיה דר"ח אבל שאר פירות ומשקין שאין טעונין מבשבעת המינין שאין צריכין ברכה לאחריהן במקומן ואכל בבית זה וחזר ואכל בבית אחר צריך לברך תחילה אבל מפינה לפינה בבית אחד אין צריך לברך כדתניא במתניתא דבי רב הונא ומשום דקבעי למיתני ועקרו רגליהן כדי לילך לבית המדרש להכי נקט חברים תלמידי חכמים: ה"ג תנו רבנן בני חבורה שהיו מסובין וקידש עליהן היום מביאין לו כוס של יין ואומר עליו קדושת היום והשני מיד אומר עליו ברכת המזון ומפסיק באמצע סעודתו כדאמר ר' יהודה לעיל ומיהו הואיל והגיע שעת קידוש צריך לקדש תחלה. לשון אחר גרסינן ראשון אומר עליו ברכת המזון שני אומר עליו קידוש היום ובתוספתא דברכות מוכח כלשון ראשון: ר' יוסי אומר אוכלין והולכין· עד שתגמר סעודתן אי נמי אוכלין ואוכלין משתחשך ור' יוסי לטעמיה דלדידיה אין מפסיקין כלל:

רבינו חננאל

מאן תנא עקירה שצריך [להניח] שם זקן או חולה ר' יהודה היא דתניא חברים שהיו מסובין עקרו רגליהם לילך לבית הכנסת או לבית המדרש כשיוצאין אין טעונין ברכה למפרע וכשחוזרין אין טעונין ברכה לכתחלה. א"ר יהודה בר"א כשהניח שם זקן או חולה וכו' וכיון דסלקא לדרב חסדא בקשיא אע"ג דטוקמי' לה כר' יהודה שניא הוא ולא סמכינן עלה אלא עבדינן כרב ששת דמחמיר ושפי עדיף והכן ר' יוחנן כיון דאיתותב גדוה וקיימא לן דשנוי מקום צריך לברך וכן הלכה: תניא חברים שהיו מסובין לשתות יין ועקרו רגליהן וחזרו אין צריכין לברך. ת"ר בני חבורה שהיו מסובין וקדש עליהם היום מביאין לו כוס ראשון ומקדש שני מברך עליו ברכת המזון דברי ר' יהודה ר' יוסי אומר אוכלין עד שתחשך

הגהות הב"ח

(א) רשב"ם ד"ה ה"ג וכו' אחריכן במקומן אין לריך: (ב) רשב"ם ד"ה להודיעך וכו' לא היה יכול לומר כשהן יוצאין טעונין וכו' שאפילו הכי אין לריכין:

גליון הש"ס

גמ' א"ל ר"י הה"ד וכו'. ק"ל דאם כן גם מהתם ליכא תיובתא די"ל לומר דהברייתא דשנוי מקום לריך לברך אתיא כר"י ואיהו סבר כת"ק: רשב"ם ד"ה ה"ג פ"כ דר"ח ובתוס' ד"ה ת"כ דר"ח. קשה לי למאי הוצרכו הא כפשוטו ניחא דלא מייתי ראיה מברייתא דלעיל די"ל דנקט עקרו לרבותא דר"י וכדדחי' לעיל אליבא דר' יוחנן לזה מייתי סייעתא מהך ברייתא דלא קתני פלוגתא א"כ מדנקט עקרו מוכח דדוקא בטעונה ברכה במקומה:

[102*a*] Which Tanna [rules thus on precipitate] rising? R. Judah. For it was taught: If companions were reclining, and they [precipitately] arose to go to the synagogue or to the Beth Hamidrash, when they go out they do not need a blessing beforehand, and when they return they do not need a blessing at the beginning. Said R. Judah: When is that said? When they left some of their companions behind. But if they did not leave some of their companions behind, when they go out they need a blessing beforehand, and when they return they need a blessing at the beginning.

Then [make an opposite deduction]: it is only because they are things which need a blessing in the same place that when they go out they do not need a blessing beforehand and when they return they do not need a blessing at the beginning. But for things which do not need a blessing in the same place, even on the view of the Rabbis, when they go out they need a blessing beforehand and when they return they need a blessing at the beginning: shall we say that this is a refutation of R. Joḥanan['s
a ruling]?[1]—But have we not [already] refuted him once? Shall we [then] say that from this too there is a refutation?—[No:] R. Joḥanan can answer you: The same law holds good that even for things which do not require a blessing after them in the same place it is unnecessary to recite a blessing [afresh], but as to why he teaches, 'They [precipitately] arose,' that is to inform you the extent[2] of R. Judah['s view], [viz.,] that even for things which require a blessing after them in the same place, it is only because they left some companions behind [that these additional blessings are not recited]; but if they did not leave some companions behind, when they go out they need a blessing beforehand, and when they return they need a blessing at the beginning.

It was taught in accordance with R. Ḥisda: If companions were reclining to drink wine and they arose [departed] and returned,
b they need not recite a blessing [anew].[1]

Our Rabbis taught: If members of a company were reclining when the day became holy upon them,[2] a cup of wine is brought to one of them and he recites over it the sanctity of the day [i.e., *ḳiddush*], and a second [cup is brought] over which he recites the Grace after meals:[3] these are the words of R. Judah. R. Jose said:

a (1) V. *supra* 101*b* top that for a change of place no fresh blessing is required under any circumstances. (2) Lit., 'strength'.

b (1) V. *supra* 101*b*, n. a3. According to Rashbam the proof is obvious. On the view of Tosaf. 'to drink wine' must be deleted, the reference being to bread or the five species of grain. (2) I.e., the sun set ushering in the Sabbath or Festival. (3) Immediately, without waiting to finish the meal. Nevertheless, since the Sabbath has commenced, he must first recite the *ḳiddush* and then Grace. Hence if he wishes to eat more after Grace, he must begin a new meal.

name: Both for a change of wine [101b] and for a change of place, he need not recite the benediction [again].[7]

An objection is raised: [For] a change of place, he must recite the benediction [again]; for a change of wine, he need not recite the benediction [again]?—This refutation of R. Joḥanan is [indeed] a refutation.

R. Idi b. Abin sat before R. Ḥisda, while R. Ḥisda sat and said in R. Huna's name: As to what you said, [for] a change of place he must recite the benediction [again], they taught this only [of a change] from one house to another, but not from one place to another place.[8] Said R. Idi b. Abin to him: We have learnt it thus in the Baraitha of the School of R. Henak—others state, in the School of Bar Henak—in accordance with your ruling.

a Does then R. Huna teach us a Baraitha?[1]—R. Huna had not heard the Baraitha.[2]

Furthermore, R. Ḥisda sat and said in his own name: As to what you said: For a change of place he must recite the benediction [again], we said this only of things which do not require a benediction after them in the same place;[3] but for the things which demand a blessing after them in the same place, he need not recite the benediction [again]. What is the reason? He [mentally] returns to the first appointed place.[4] But R. Shesheth maintained: Both for the one and the other he must recite the benediction [again].

An objection is raised: If the members of a company were reclining to drink, and they [precipitately] arose[5] to go out to welcome a bridegroom or a bride, when they go out, they do not need [to recite] a benediction beforehand;[6] when they return, they do not need [to recite] a benediction at the beginning.[7] When is that? If they left an old man or an invalid there;[8] but if they did not leave an old man or an invalid there, when they go out they need [to recite] a benediction beforehand, [and] when they return they need a benediction at the beginning. Now since he teaches, 'they [precipitately] arose,' it follows that we are treating of things which require a blessing after them in the same place,[9] and it is only because they left an old man or an invalid there that when they go out they do not need a benediction beforehand, and when they return they do not need a benediction at the beginning. But if they did not leave an old man or an invalid there, when they go out they need a blessing beforehand and when they return they need a blessing at the beginning: this is a difficulty according to R. Ḥisda?—Said R. Naḥman b. Isaac:

(7) If a man recites a blessing for wine and drinks, and then more wine is brought from a different barrel, even if the second is of a different quality, he does not repeat the blessing; similarly, if he recites a blessing over food or drink and then continues his meal elsewhere. Hence the same applies here.—Where a man need not recite a blessing, he may not recite, as a blessing must not be recited where there is no obligation. (8) In the same house, e.g., from one room to another.

a (1) Surely it is superfluous! (2) Rashbam deletes both the question and the answer, as it is quite usual for an amora to state what is taught in the Baraitha. (3) Where they are eaten. Rashbam: *sc.* water or fruit. After everything else, however, (i.e., wine, the seven species enumerated in Deut. VIII, 8, bread, and the five species of grain enumerated in the Mishnah *supra* 35*a*) a blessing in the nature of grace must be recited where it is consumed. Tosaf.: after everything except bread and perhaps also the five species of grain a blessing need not be recited where they are eaten. (4) Since these things must be followed by a blessing in the place where they are consumed, even when he changes his place he keeps the first in mind, so that his eating in both places should be as one act of eating, the subsequent blessing being for what he ate in both. Consequently, he does not recite a blessing *before* eating in the second place either. (5) Lit., 'detached their feet'. (6) I.e., the blessing after wine, since it is their intention to return. (7) When they drink afresh. (8) Which assures that their departure is only an interruption. (9) 'They detached their feet' implies that they hurried, on account of the bridegroom or bride, but otherwise they would have remained there, in order to recite the benediction before leaving.—According to Tosaf. (*supra* n. a3) to drink must be omitted from the Baraitha, since in their view no beverage, not even wine, is subject to this rule.

עין משפט נר מצוה

יב א ב מיי' פ"ד מהל' ברכות הלכה ג וה' סמג עשין כז טוש"ע א"ח סימן קעח סעיף א:

יג ג מיי' שם הלכה ד טוש"ע שם סעיף ב:

ואחד שינוי מקום א"צ לברך מיתיבי *שינוי מקום צריך לברך שינוי יין אין צריך לברך תיובתא דרבי יוחנן תיובתא יתיב רב אידי בר אבין קמיה דרב חסדא ויתיב רב חסדא וקאמר משמיה דרב הונא ²הא דאמרת שינוי מקום צריך לברך לא שנו אלא *מבית לבית אבל ממקום למקום לא א"ל רב אידי בר אבין הכי תנינא לי' במתניתא דבי רב הינק ואמרי ליה במתניתא דבי בר הינק כוותיך ואלא רב הונא *מתניתא קמ"ל רב הונא *מתניתא לא שמיע ליה ותו יתיב רב חסדא וקאמר משמיה דנפשיה הא דאמרת שינוי מקום צריך לברך לא אמרן אלא בדברים שאין טעונין ברכה לאחריהן במקומן אבל דברים הטעונין ברכה לאחריהן במקומן אין צריך לברך מאי טעמא לקיבעא קמא הדר ורב ששת אמר אחד זה ואחד זה צריך לברך מיתיבי ³בני חבורה שהיו מסובין לשתות ועקרו רגליהן לצאת לקראת חתן או לקראת כלה כשהן יוצאין אין טעונין ברכה למפרע כשהן חוזרין אין טעונין ברכה לכתחלה בד"א שהניחו שם זקן או חולה אבל לא הניחו שם לא זקן ולא חולה כשהן יוצאין טעונין ברכה למפרע כשהן חוזרין טעונין ברכה לכתחלה מדקתני עקרו רגליהן מכלל דבדברים הטעונין ברכה לאחריהן במקומן עסקינן וטעמא דהניחו שם זקן או חולה הוא דכשהן יוצאין אין טעונין ברכה למפרע וכשהן חוזרין אין טעונין ברכה לכתחלה אבל לא הניחו שם זקן או חולה כשהן יוצאין טעונין ברכה למפרע וכשהן חוזרין טעונין ברכה לכתחלה קשיא לרב חסדא אמר רב נחמן בר יצחק מאן

א"ל לברך. שניה על היין: ממקום למקום. מבית לעליה: בדברים שאין טעונים ברכה לאחריהם (א). כגון מים או פירות שאין טעונים ברכה חשובה בפני עצמן כגון (שבעת המינים) דודאי כיון דעמד והלך למקום אחר עמידתו זו היא גמר סעודתו והך סעודה אחריתי היא וצריך לברך בתחלה: אבל דברים הטעונים ברכה לאחריהם במקומן. כלומר ברכה חשובה בפני עצמן כגון שבעת המינין הואיל ולא בירך אחריהן ועמד לילך למקום אחר לסעוד על (ב) קביעות הראשון הלך לברך אחריהם ברכה אחת על שתיהן ולפניהם נמי אין צריך לחזור ולברך: לקיבעיה קמא הדר. כלומר על דעת סעודה הראשונה הוא אוכל עכשיו לסיים סעודתו: אחד זה ואחד זה. בין שטעונין ברכה לאחריהן במקומן בין שאינן צריכין: כשהן יוצאין אין טעונין ברכה למפרע. כלומר לברך ברכה של אחריהן הואיל ועתידין לחזור: ה"ג בד"א כו'. ולא גרס בהא רבי יהודה: מדקתני עקרו מכלל דבדברים הטעונין כו'. דעקירות (ג) משמע משום מהירות חתן וכלה הן נעקרין אבל אם לא כן עדיין היו צריכין לעמוד ולברך ברכה שלאחריהם:

רשב"ם

ואחד שינוי מקום. לכל דבר האכל אם אכל ממנו במקום זה וחוזר ואוכל במקום אחר א"ל לברך שניה וכגון שלא היה לו היסח הדעת בינתים: שינוי מקום צריך לברך. כרב ושמואל דאמרי ידי יין לא יצאו ותיובתא דרבי יוחנן: ה"ג במתני' דבי רב הינק כוותיך ותו יתיב רב חסדא וקאמר משמיה דנפשיה ולא גרסי' מתני' אתא לאשמועי' ושיבוש גמור היא שכן הוא שיטת הגמרא להשמיענו האמורא דבר המפורש בברייתא דזימנין שאין הכל בקיאין בברייתא וגם האמורא עצמו זימנין דלא ידע לה להיא ברייתא עד דמייתי ליה סייעתא מיני' ולפי שראו דיתיב רב חסדא וקאמר משמיה דנפשיה וטעו לומר מכלל שחזר בו ממה שאמר למעלה משמיה דרב הונא והגיהו בספרים קושיא זו ואינה אלא שני דברים אמר רב חסדא בההיא ברייתא חדא משמיה דרב הונא וחדא משמיה דנפשיה: בדברים שאין טעונין ברכה לאחריהן במקומן. כגון מים או פירות שאינן טעונין ברכה חשובה בפני עצמם אלא בורא נפשות רבות הלכך א"ל לברך במקומן אחריהן דודאי כיון דעמד והלך במקום אחר עמידתו זו היא גמר סעודתו והך סעודה אחריתי היא וצריך לברך בתחלה: אבל דברים הטעונין ברכה לאחריהן במקומן. כלומר ברכה חשובה בפני עצמן (והלכך) צריכין במקומן כגון שבעת המינין דאית בהו ברכה אחת מעין שלש הואיל ולא בירך אחריהן והלך במקום אחר לסעוד על דעת קביעות הראשונה הלך לברך ברכה אחת על שתיהן ולפניהן נמי א"ל לחזור ולברך מהכא שמעינן דהא דתנן (ברכות דף נא:) מי שאכל ושכח ולא בירך ב"ש אומרים כו' ושמעינן מינה דלכתחלה צריך לברך במקומו בשבעת המינין מיירי דאיכא כעין ברכת המזון ברכה אריכתא וחשיבותא מעין שלש: לקיבעיה קמא הדר. כלומר על דעת סעודה הראשונה הוא אוכל עכשיו לסיים סעודתו וא"ת אמאי אותיבניה לרבי יוחנן מהך ברייתא תיובתא הא איכא לתרוצי ברייתא כרב חסדא בשאינן טעונין ברכה לאחריהן במקומן ומילתיה דרבי יוחנן בשטעונין והלכך אין צריך לברך ליכא לתרוצי הכי דרבי יוחנן סתמא קאמר שינוי מקום אינו צריך לברך בכל דבר האכל קאמר מדלא פירש שהאמורא יש לו לפרש דבריו יותר מן הברייתא ועוד יודעין היו האמוראין שהשיבו מההיא ברייתא לרבי יוחנן דבכל מקום קאמר רבי יוחנן שינוי מקום אינו צריך לברך אבל הברייתא שקדמה להם הרבה יש להם לפרש כן וכן: אחד זה ואחד זה. בין שטעונין ברכה לאחריהן במקומן בין שאינן טעונין שאינן משבעת המינין: שהיו מסובין לשתות ועקרו רגליהן כו'. גרסינן ולא גרסי' יין: כשהן יוצאין אין טעונין ברכה (ד) לאחריהן למפרע. כלומר לברך ברכה שלאחריהם הואיל ועתידין לחזור: ה"ג בד"א כו'. ולא גרסי' בהא רבי יהודה: מדקתני עקרו מכלל דבדברים הטעונין כו'. דעקירות משמע דמשום מהירות חתן וכלה הן נעקרין אבל אם לא כן עדיין היו צריכין לעמוד ולברך ברכה שלאחריהן: קשיא לרב חסדא. דאילו לרב חסדא אפילו לא חזרו למקומן אלא גמרו סעודתן במקום אחר אין צריך לברך תחלה הואיל ועדיין לא בירך אחריהן והכא מוכח דאפילו חזרו למקומן הראשון צריך לברך תחלה:

אלא בדברים שאין טעונין ברכה לאחריהם במקומן. פירש רשב"ם כגון מים ופירות שאין צריכין אחריהם ברכה חשובה מעין שלש ומה"ט א"ל לברך במקומן הלכך עמידתו זו היא גמר סעודתו והך סעודה אחריתי היא וצריך לברך בתחלה אבל דברים הטעונין ברכה לאחריהם במקומן כגון יין וכל ז' מינין לקיבעא קמא הדר והא דתנן ברכות (דף נא.) מי שאכל ושכח ולא בירך לכתחלה צריך לברך במקומו בכל ז' מינים מיירי ובברייתא דמייתי בסמוך לא גרסינן לשתות יין מדמדקדק הגמ' דאיירי בדברים הטעונים ברכה לאחריהם במקומן מדקתני עקרו ולא דייק מדקתני יין שהוא מז' מינין אבל בברייתא דתניא כוותיה דרב חסדא גרסי' יין ומיהו קשה דאי הוה יין בכלל דברים הטעונין ברכה לאחריהן במקומן א"כ אמאי איתותב ר' יוחנן לעיל דרבי יוחנן איירי ביין דאמאי דקאמר ר' יוחנן אף ידי יין נמי יצאו קאמר ואזדא ר' יוחנן לטעמיה דאמר שינוי מקום א"ל לברך וברייתא איירי בדברים שאין טעונים ברכה לאחריהם במקומן ועוד דא"כ פליג רב חסדא ארב ושמואל דאמרי לעיל ידי יין לא יצאו ולכאורה משמע דלא פליג אלא עם רב ששת עוד קשה דאמר בירושלמי ס"פ כילד מברכין היה אוכל במזרחה של תאנה ובא לו במערבה צריך לברך אלמא בז' מינין נמי שינוי מקום צריך לברך ודוחק לומר דאתיא כרב ששת שאין הלכה כמותו לכך נראה דיין וכל ז' מינין לא הוו בכלל דברים הטעונין ברכה לאחריהם במקומן אלא פת וכל מיני פת שמברכין עליו המוציא או שמא כל מיני מזונות שיש בהם מה' מינין הוו בכלל דברים הטעונין ברכה לאחריהן במקומן ולהאי פי' נמי לא גרסינן בברייתא דבסמוך לשתות יין ולא בדתניא כוותיה דרב חסדא דבפת או בה' מינין מיירי מדקתני עקרו וכן הלכה בכל דבר חוץ מפת ומיני מזונות שהם מחמשת מינין א"ל ברכה לאחריהם במקומן ושינוי מקום צריך לברך בהם ושינוי מקום היינו אפי' בחד בית כמו מאיגרא לארעא או מחדר לבית אבל מפינה לפינה לא ולכל הפירושים אם הלך באמצע סעודה למקום אחר יכול לשתות יין או מים בלא ברכה דכיון שהוא בתוך הסעודה לקיבעיה קמא הדר: כשהן יוצאין טעונין ברכה למפרע כו'. משמע היכא דאיכא היסח הדעת לא סגי שיברך ברכת המוציא אלא צריך שיברך ברכת המזון וא"כ הא דאמר לקמן (דף קג:) כיון דאמר הב וניבריך איתסר לכו למישתי היינו עד שיברך ברהמ"ז וכן משמע בכילד מברכין (ברכות דף מב) דקאמר רבה ורבי זירא הוו אכלי סליקו תכא מקמייהו אייתי להו ריסתנא רבה אכל ורבי זירא לא אכל א"ל לא סבר לה מר סילק אסור מלאכול א"ל אנא אתכא דריש גלותא סמיכנא והשתא אם לא היה צריך לברך בהמ"ז למה לא אכל ויש לדחות דאותו מאכל היה מעורב בו לחם והיה לו טורח ליטול ידיו ולברך המוציא והא דקאמר הכא טעונין ברכה למפרע היינו משום שמא ישהו מלחזור עד שירעבו ואז לא יוכלו לברך ברהמ"ז כדאמר באלו דברים (שם דף נא:) ומיהו אם יצאו ולא בירכו למפרע כשיחזרו לא יברכו רק ברכת המוציא ותדע דאם לעולם טעונין ברכה למפרע אמאי אילטריך לאשמעינן כשהן חוזרין דמברכין ברכה לכתחלה פשיטא כיון דלעולם מברכין למפרע והא דאמר במעתין שינוי מקום צריך לברך

לברך

רבינו חננאל

ואחד שינוי מקום אין צריך לברך ואיתותב ר' יוחנן ונדחה. אמרי משמיה דרב הונא הא דאמר שינוי מקום צריך לברך לא אמרו אלא מבית לבית אבל מפנה לפנה לא ואסיקנא דאף תנינא לה במתניתא דבי בר הינק ומתניתא' וכי רב הונא מתניתא אתא לאשמעינן אלא כי הא דרב חסדא דאמר שינוי מקום צריך לברך ברכה אחרת לא אמרן אלא בדברים שאין טעונין ברכה ראשונה והיא ברכה הזמון לאחריהן במקומן [אבל דברים הטעונים ברכה לאחריהן במקומן] אם הלך למקום אחר ועמד שם וערא אין צריך לברך שם מאי טעמא לקבעיה הדר ורב ששת אמר זה ואחד זה צריך לברך ברכה במקום שהלך ואחר כך ישעום שם ואותבי' על רב חסדא מהא דתניא עקרו רגליהם לצאת לקראת חתן וכלה כשיוצאין אין [טעונין] ברכה למפרע על מה שאכלו וכשחוזרין אין טעונין ברכה לכתחלה בד"א בזמן שהניחו שם זקן או חולה ודעתן לחזור אליהם אבל אם לא הניחו שם אדם כלל כשיוצאין טעונין ברכת המזון למפרע וכשחוזרין טעונין ברכת המוציא לכתחלה ודייקי' מדקתני עקרו מכלל דבדברים שהן מין דגן וטעונין ברכה לאחריהן במקומן עסקינן דאפילו ב"ה דאמרו מברך באיזה מקום שנזכר לא אמרו אלא מי שהחזיק בדרך שחזרתו למקום שאכל היא סכנה אבל אם לא החזיק בדרכו וכ"ש מי שאינו עומד בדרך שאפי' ב"ה מודו דאינו מברך אלא במקו' שאכל וטעמא דהניחו שם זקן או חולה אבל לא הניחו שם זקן או חולה צריך לברך ואע"ג דהדר לקבעיה קשיא לרב חסדא ופריק רב נחמן בר יצחק

מסורת הש"ס

[ברכ' שבאלפס ליתא]

ברכות נב.

לא שנו אלא מבית לבית אבל מפינה לפינה לא כצ"ל רש"א

[ר"ס ת. כתובות יז.]

הגהות הב"ח

(א) רשב"ם ד"ה בדברים וכו' לאחריהן במקומן כגון מים: (ב) ד"ה אבל וכו' לסעוד על דעת קביעות: (ג) ד"ה מדקתני וכו' דעקירה משמע וכו' ולברך תחלה ברכה שלאחריהם: (ד) רשב"ם ד"ה כשהן יוצאין אין טעונין ברכה למפרע כצ"ל ותיבת לאחריהן נמחק:

אף ידי קידוש לא יצאו אלא לרב למה ליה לקדושי בביתיה כדי להוציא בניו ובני ביתו ושמואל למה לי לקדושי בבי כנישתא "לאפוקי אורחים ידי חובתן דאכלו ושתו וגנו בבי כנישתא ואזדא שמואל לטעמיה דאמר שמואל "אין קידוש אלא במקום סעודה סבור מינה הני מילי מבית לבית אבל ממקום למקום בחד ביתא לא אמר להו רב ענן בר תחליפא זימנין סגיאין הוה קאימנא קמיה דשמואל ונחית מאיגרא לארעא והדר מקדש ואף רב הונא סבר אין קידוש אלא במקום סעודה דרב הונא קדיש "ואיתעקרא ליה שרגא ועיילי ליה למניה לבי גנניה דרבה בריה דהוה שרגא וקדיש וטעים מידי אלמא קסבר אין קידוש אלא במקום סעודה ואף רבה סבר אין קידוש אלא במקום סעודה דאמר אביי כי הוינא בי מר כי הוה מקדש אמר לן טעימו מידי דילמא אראזליתו לאושפיזא מתעקרא לכו שרגא ולא מקדש לכו בבית אכילה ובקידושא דהכא לא נפקיתו דאין קידוש אלא במקום סעודה איני *והאמר אביי כל מילי דמר הוה עביד כרב לבר מהני תלת דעביד כשמואל "מתירין מבגד לבגד "ומדליקין מנר לנר והלכה כר"ש בגרירה דתניא *ר"ש אומר "גורר אדם מטה כסא וספסל בשבת ובלבד שלא יתכוין לעשות חריץ כחומרי דרב הוה עביד כקולי דרב לא הוה עביד ור' יוחנן אמר אף ידי יין נמי יצאו ואזדא ר' יוחנן לטעמיה דא"ר חנין בר אביי א"ר פרת אמר ר' יוחנן אחד שינוי יין ואחד

קידוש אלא במקום סעודה · ואם קידש ולא סעד לא יצא ידי קידוש: ממקום למקום. מבית לעליה לא צריך לחזור ולקדש אם קידש שבת בבית והלך לאכול בעליה: דילמא מיתעקרא לכו שרגא. ולא תאכלו ואפי' אתם הולכים לישן בלא אכילה בקידושא דהכא לא נפקיתו ידי קידוש (היום) דאין קידוש כו': כל מילי דמר. רבה: כחומרי דרב הוה עביד. בר מהני תלת דעביד לקולא כשמואל: כקולי דרב. כגון קידוש לא עביד: ה"ג ורבי יוחנן אמר אף ידי יין נמי יצאו: אחד שינוי יין · שהביאו לו יין מחבית אחרת: אין

פ"ש מ"ז

רשב"ם

אף ידי קידוש לא יצאו. כדפרשינן טעמיה לקמיה אין קידוש אלא במקום סעודה דכתיב (ישעיה נח) וקראת לשבת עונג במקום שאתה קורא לשבת כלומר קרייה דקידוש שם תהא עונג ומדרש הוא אי נמי סברא היא מדאיקבע קידוש על היין כדתניא לקמן (דף קו.) זוכרהו על היין מסתמא על היין שבשעת סעודה הוקבע דחשיב: אין קידוש אלא במקום סעודה. ואם קידש ולא סעד באותו מקום לא יצא ידי קידוש: ה"מ. דאין קידוש אלא במקום סעודה אלא מבית לבית אבל ממקום למקום מבית לעליה א"צ לחזור ולקדש: איתעקרא ליה שרגא · נפל הנר וכבה קודם שאכל: לבי גננא דרבה בריה. בית חופת בנו שהיו שם נרות דולקין בבית המשתה: מר. רבה: כי הוה מקדש. ואנו רוצין הייט ליפטר משם ולילך לביתנו: דילמא מיתעקרא לכו שרגא · ולא תאכלו ואפי' אתם הולכין לישן בלא אכילה בקידוש דהכא לא נפקיתו ידי קידוש כו': כל מילי דמר. רבה: מתירין מבגד לבגד. מתירין ציצית של טלית זו ונותנין אותם לטלית אחרת: מדליקין. מנר חנוכה לנר אחרת של חנוכה וא"צ להדליק בנר אחרת שאינה של חנוכה: והלכה כר"ש בגרירה · גורר אדם מטה כסא וספסל כו' דדבר שאין מתכוין מותר והני ג' מילי פלוגתא דרב ושמואל בבמה מדליקין (שבת דף כב:) וכולהו עביד רבה כשמואל דמיקל והכא אמאי עביד כשמואל להצריך קידוש במקום סעודה הואיל ובכל מילי עביד כרב בר מהני תלת ומשני כחומרי דרב עביד בר מהני תלת דעביד כשמואל לקולא (א) וכגון קידוש דקולי דרב לא עביד ואע"ג דהניא (עירובין דף ו:) העושה כחומרי ב"ש כקוליהון וכחומריהון כו' הא קי"ל ה"מ היכא דסתרן אהדדי כגון כמה חסרון בשדרה כו' ואמר שמואל וכן לטריפה דחומרא דהתם קולא הוא הכא וקולא דהתם חומרא הוא הכא ומהכא שמעינן דהלכתא כשמואל דאין קידוש אלא במקום סעודה והמקדש לאחרים חוץ מביתו נראה בעיני שאין צריך לסעוד שם שאפילו לא סעד שם יצאו בני אותו הבית דלדידהו הוי מקום סעודה: ה"ג ורבי יוחנן אמר אף ידי יין נמי יצאו. שאין צריך לחזור ולברך על היין שבתוך הסעודה שהרי לא הסיח דעתו ביציאתו מבהכ"נ שע"י יין דעתו לאכול ולשתות בביתו: אחד שינוי יין · שהביאו לו יין מחבית אחרת ויש לו טעם משונה או גרוע או משובח אין צריך לברך שנית על היין אבל הטוב והמטיב מיהא מברך אם משובח מן הראשון כדאמרי' בהרואה (ברכות דף נט:) אמר רב יוסף אמר רבי יוחנן אע"פ שאמרו שינוי יין אין צריך לברך אבל אומר הטוב והמטיב ושינוי יין היינו מחבית אחרת כדאמרינן בברכות ירושלמי בפרק כילד על כל חבית וחבית שהיה פותח היה מברך עליה ומה היה מברך ואמר רבי יצחק בשם רבי אומר ברוך הטוב והמטיב:

ואחד

תוספות

אף ידי קידוש לא יצאו. דאין קידוש אלא במקום סעודה משום דכתיב וקראת לשבת עונג · כלומר במקום קריאת קידוש שם תהא עונג:

ולשמואל למה לי לקדושי בבי כנישתא. לרב צריך לקדושי בבי כנישתא להוציא כל אותם שאין להם בני בית שלא ילמדנו לקדש בביתם:

דאכלו ושתו וגנו בבי כנישתא. וא"ת והא אמרי' בפ' בני העיר (מגילה דף כח.) בתי כנסיות אין אוכלין בהן ואין שותין בהן אע"ג לאכילה ושתיה של מצוה מותר כדאמרי' בירושלמי שהיו אוכלים שם בקידוש החדש וגם עכשיו נוהגין לשתות כוס הבדלה וברית מילה מ"מ שאינה של מצוה ושינה אסור ואפי' בשל בבל אין אוכלין בהן דקאמר התם* רבינא ורב אדא בר אהבה שלא היו רוצים ליכנס בבית הכנסת מפני הגשמים אי לאו משום דשמעתתא בעיא צלותא והא דקאמר התם בתי כנסיות של בבל על תנאי עשויין הייט לאחר שיחרבו שאין נוהגין בהן קדושה וי"ל דלאו דוקא בבי כנישתא אלא חדרים שהיו סמוכין לבית הכנסת קרי בי כנישתא ומשם היו שומעים הקידוש ולפי מה שפירשתי דממקום למקום בחד בית כשדעתו לאכול במקום אחר יש קידוש כו' אתי שפיר:

אבל ממקום למקום בחד ביתא. פי' מחדר לבית או מבית לעליה כמו מאיגרא לארעא אבל מפינה לפינה יש קידוש כי היכי דלא חשוב שינוי מקום בסמוך ולקמן גבי שינוי מקום דקאמר לא שנו אלא מבית לבית ומיהו שני מקומות בחד בית קרי ליה מבית לבית ומיהו י"ס דגרסי' הכא מפינה לפינה כו':

טעימו מידי. נראה דהייט טעימת לחם כדאמרינן בפ"ג דשבועות (דף כב:) כדאמרי אינשי ניטעום מידי ואזלי ואכלי ושתו ואם מוטעל מיני תרגימא להשלים ג' סעודות שבת כמו בסוכה הייט דוקא בסעודה שלישית אבל לא בסעודת ערבית ושחרית שהם עיקר כבוד שבת:

ובקידושא דהכא לא נפקיתו. ומה שלא היה מקפיד על סעודת שבת שלא לאכול בלא נר כדפי' בקונטרס הייט משום שיכולו לעשות למחר שלש סעודות או שמא יוכלו לאכול במקום שיש שם נר ואין יין:

מתירין מבגד לבגד. ואע"ג דשמואל אית ליה בפ' התכלת (מנחות דף מא:) כלי קופסא חייבין בציצית מודה אם אין ציצית לכל בגדיו שיתיר ציצית מבגד שמלבישו ליתן בבגד שרוצה ללבוש ותהא המצוה עליו:

והלכה כר"ש בגרירה. קשה תיפוק ליה משום דרבי יוחנן סבר כר"ש דפריך בכמה דוכתי (שבת דף פא:) והא א"ר יוחנן הלכה כסתם משנה ותנן נזיר חופף ומפספס כו' אלמא ס"ל דדבר שאין מתכוין מותר וי"ל שמא רבי יוחנן לא סבר לה כוותיה בגרירה לפי שקרוב לעשות חריץ ודמי לפסיק רישיה:

ורבי יוחנן אמר אף ידי יין יצאו. ומיירי ששתו בבית הכנסת אע"ג דלענין קידוש יצאו בשמיעה כדפי' לעיל (ג) לענין יין לא פטר אא"כ שתה דהוי הפסק כדאמרי' בפ' כילד מברכין (ברכות דף מ.) גבי המטבל שאם הפסיק שצריך לחזור ולברך:

שינוי יין א"צ לברך. מיהו הטוב והמטיב צריך לברך כדאמרינן בהרואה (שם דף נט:) ופי' רשב"ם דווקא היכא דמשובח מן הראשון וכן בהלכות גדולות וכן משמע בירושלמי דסוף כילד מברכין דקאמר אבא בר רב הונא אמר יין חדש וישן אין צריך לברך שינוי יין אין צריך לברך שינוי מקום צריך לברך הסיח הדעת כמו שהוא שינוי מקום משמע שרוצה לומר דיין חדש וישן צריך לברך לפי שהישן טוב מן החדש אבל שינוי יין סתם אין צריך לברך כיון שאין ידוע שהשני משובח מיהו עובדא דבתר הכי פליג עליה דקאמר דעל כל חבית וחבית מברך מה היה מברך ואמר רבי יצחק בשם רבי ברוך הטוב והמטיב משמע בכל ענין אפילו מטובה לגרועה מיהו יש לדחות שהיה מברך לפי שלא היה מכירו אבל אם ידוע שהשני גרוע לא ונראה דאפילו השני גרוע מברך דעל ריבוי ייטות הוא מברך ובלבד שלא יהיה האחרון רע יותר מדאי שאין יכולין לשתותו אלא מדוחק וצריך לברך הטוב והמטיב בין בשעת סעודה בין שלא בשעת סעודה ויחיד אין צריך לברך אי ליכא אחריני בהדיה כדמוכח בהרואה (שם) ודוקא ביין מברכין לפי שזיבלו כרמיהן בדמיהן של ישראל והטוב שלא הסריחו והמטיב שניתנו לקבורה: [ועיין תוספות ברכות נט: ד"ה הטוב]

אלא

עין משפט נר מצוה

ז א מיי' פכ"ט מהלכות שבת הלכה ח סמג עשין כט טור שו"ע או"ח סימן רסט:

ח ב מיי' וסמג שם טוש"ע או"ח סימן רעג סעיף א:

ט ג שם סעיף (ב) [ז]:

י ד מיי' פ"א מהלכות ציצית הלכה יג סמג עשין כו טור שו"ע או"ח סימן טו סעיף א:

יא ה מיי' פ"ד מהלכות חנוכה הלכה ט סמג עשין ה טור שו"ע או"ח סימן תרעד סעיף א:

יב ו מיי' פ"א מהלכות שבת הלכה ה סמג לאוין סה טוש"ע או"ח סימן שלז סעיף א:

[דף כח:]

רבינו חננאל

אפי' ידי קידוש לא יצאו אלא צריך לקדש בביתו ולברך נמי בורא פרי הגפן ורב מאחר שיצא ידי חובתו בבית הכנסת למה ליה למהדר קדושה בביתו ואמרינן להוציא בני ביתו ושמואל מאחר שאין אדם יוצא בקדוש בית הכנסת למה ליה לקדושי בבהכ"נ ואמרי' לאפוקי אורחין דאכלי בכנישתא וקיימא לן בהא כשמואל דאין קידוש אלא במקום סעודה: סבור מינה הני מילי מבית לבית אבל מפינה לפינה בחד ביתא לא ואסיקנא דשמואל אפי' מארעא לאיגרא הוה הדר מקדש ואף רב הונא סבר אין קידוש אלא במקום סעודה דרב הונא קדיש בעא למיכל אתעקר שרגא ועיילי' למאני' לבי גנניה דרבה בריה וקדיש ואכיל ואף רבה סבר אין קידוש אלא במקום סעודה דאמר (רב הונא) [אביי] כי הוינן בי מר הוה מקדש והוה אמר לן טעמו מידי הכא. דילמא אדאזליתו לאושפיזיכו אתעקרו לכו שרגא ובקידושא דהכא לא נפקיתו דאין קידוש אלא במקום סעודה: איני והאמר אביי כל מילי דמר דהוא רבה בר נחמני רביה עביד כרב בר מהני תלת דעביד כשמואל מתירין הציצית מבגד לבגד ותולין אותו לבגד אחר ומדליקין מנר לנר של חנוכה והלכה כר' שמעון בגרירה דתניא גורר אדם מטה כסא וספסל ובלבד שלא יתכוין לעשות חריץ ואיך עביד בהא כשמואל ואסיקנא כחומריה דרב עביד כותיה כקולי לא עביד והכא מיקל הוא: א"ר יוחנן א' שינוי יין

מסורת הש"ס

שבת כב. מ. מנחות מא:

[שם ושבת כט: מו: ביצה כג: תוספתא דביצה פ"ב]

הגהות הב"ח

(א) רשב"ם ד"ה והלכה כר"ש וכו' כשמואל לקולא כקולי דרב כגון קידוש לא עבוד ואע"ג דתניא העושה כב"ש כו"ל ותיבת כחומרא נמחק: (ג) תוס' ד"ה ורבי יוחנן וכו' כדפרישית לעיל. נ"ב בתוס' בד"ה לא יפחתו:

maintained: [101*a*] They have not done their duty in respect of *kiddush* either.

Then according to Rab, why must he [the Reader] recite *kiddush* at home?—In order to acquit his children and his household [of their duty]. And [according to] Samuel, why must he recite
a *kiddush* in the synagogue?[1]—In order to acquit travellers of their obligation, for they eat, drink, and sleep in the synagogue.[2] Now Samuel is consistent with his view, for Samuel said: *Kiddush* is [valid] only where the meal is eaten. From this it was understood [by the disciples] that only [to adjourn] from one house to another [is forbidden],[3] but [to adjourn] from one place to another in the same house is not [forbidden]. Said R. 'Anan b. Taḥlifa to them: On many occasions I was standing before Samuel, when he descended from the roof to the ground and then recited [again] *kiddush*.[4]

Now R. Huna too holds that *kiddush* is [valid] only where the meal is eaten. For [on one occasion] R. Huna recited *kiddush* and [then] his lamp was upset, whereupon he carried his utensils into the marriage chamber [*baldachin*] of his son Rabbah, where a lamp was [burning], recited *kiddush* [again], and then ate something, which proves that he holds: *kiddush* is [valid] only where the meal is eaten.

Now Rabbah too holds: *Kiddush* is [valid] only where the meal is eaten. For Abaye said: When I was at the Master's [*sc*. Rabbah's] house,[5] and he recited *kiddush*, he would say to us: 'Eat a little [here], lest by the time you reach your lodgings your lamps become upset, and you do not recite *kiddush* in the house where you eat, while you will not have discharged [your duty] with the *kiddush* of this place, because *kiddush* is [valid] only where the meal is eaten'. But that is not so, for surely Abaye said: In all matters the Master [*sc*. Rabbah] acted in accordance with Rab, except these three, where he did as Samuel: [viz.,] one may light from lamp
b to lamp;[1] one can detach [the fringes] from one garment for [insertion in] another garment;[2] and the *halachah* is as R. Simeon in respect to dragging. For it was taught, R. Simeon said: A man may drag a bed, seat, or bench,[3] providing that he does not intend to make a rut![4]—He acted upon Rab's stringent rulings,[5] but he did not act upon Rab's lenient rulings.

But R. Joḥanan maintained: They have done their duty in respect of wine too.[6] Now R. Joḥanan is consistent with his view, for R. Ḥanin b. Abaye said in the name of R. Pedath in R. Joḥanan's

a (1) Seeing that one's duty is not fulfilled thereby in any case. (2) Not actually in the synagogue, but in adjoining rooms (Tosaf. on the basis of Meg. 28*a*). Hence the synagogue is like home to them. (3) After *kiddush*, since the meal must be eaten in the same place. (4) V. R. Ḥananel. Proving that you must not adjourn from one place to another even in the same house. (5) Abaye was an orphan, and brought up in Rabbah's house.

b (1) One may kindle one Ḥanukkah lamp from another. (2) V. Num. XV, 38. (3) Over an earthen floor on the Sabbath or Festival. (4) Though the dragging will possibly make one.—Why then does he rule as Samuel in respect to *kiddush*? (5) That was the general rule stated by Abaye, the three exceptions all being leniencies, where he acted as Samuel. (6) This refers back to 100*b* bottom. Having heard the benediction for wine in the synagogue, they do not repeat the benediction at home, for in R. Joḥanan's view their departure from the synagogue does not break the continuity, as they are regarded as having had their mind set upon the meal and the wine from when they heard *kiddush*.

ḳiddush, [100b] so must one interrupt it for *habdalah*.[11] Now what does 'one must interrupt' mean: surely by removing the table?[12] —No: by [spreading] a cloth.

a Rabbah b. R. Huna visited the *Resh Galutha*.[1] When a tray [with food] was placed before him, he spread a cloth and sanctified [the day].[2] It was taught likewise: And they both agree that[3] one must not bring the table[4] unless one has recited *ḳiddush*;[5] but if it was brought, a cloth is spread [over it][6] and *ḳiddush* is recited.[7]

One [Baraitha] taught: Both[8] agree that one must not commence;[9] while another taught: And both agree that one may commence. As to what was taught, 'and both agree that one must not commence,' it is well: that holds good on the eve of Passover.[10] But as to the statement, 'And both agree that one may commence,' when [is that]? If we say, on the eve of the Sabbath,—but surely they differ?—There is no difficulty: here it means before nine [hours]; there, after nine [hours].[11]

As for people who have sanctified [the day] in the synagogue,[12] Rab said: They have not done their duty in respect of wine,[13] but they have done their duty in respect of *ḳiddush*.[14] But Samuel

(11) V. Glos. (12) Thus the mere spreading of a cloth is insufficient.

a (1) Exilarch, the official head of Babylonian Jewry. (2) It was at the beginning of the meal, the Sabbath having commenced. (3) Rashbam is inclined to delete this phrase. If retained, it refers to R. Judah and R. Jose (Tosaf. and one alternative in Rashbam): though they differ as to whether the meal must be interrupted, they agree where it has not yet begun. (4) Small tables were set for each person separately; these were brought in for the meal and removed when it was finished. (5) So that the table is then brought in honour of the Sabbath. Nevertheless it was laid before the Sabbath. (6) Cf. 100a, n. 9a. (7) This expedient is adopted nowadays that large tables are used, as it would be too troublesome to bring them in after *ḳiddush*. (8) R. Judah and R. Jose, who disagree in respect of commencing a meal on the eve of the Sabbath just before *minḥah* and also in respect of interrupting a meal at nightfall, if it was begun well before *minḥah*. (9) A meal from *minḥah* and onwards. (10) As R. Huna *supra* 99b. (11) There is no controversy in respect to the former. (12) I.e., who have listened to the *ḳiddush* recited by the Reader. (13) If they wish to drink wine at home, they must recite the benediction for wine. Even if they drank wine in the synagogue, over which a benediction had been recited, that does not exempt them at home, for the change of place breaks the continuity and renders this drinking a new act. (14) And as far as they are concerned they need not repeat the *ḳiddush* at home.

רבינו חננאל

רבה בר רב הונא איקלע לבית ריש גלותא פרס וקדש וכן הלכתא: תאני חדא ושוין שמתחילין ומוקמינן לה קודם תשע שעות. אותם בני אדם שקדשו בבית הכנסת אמר רב ידי קדוש יצאו ידי יין לא יצאו ושמואל אמר

[פרשת יתרו סימן כד]

[עי' תוספות ביצה ב: ד"ה וכיון]

[בכורות מט:]

גמרא

כך מפסיקין להבדלה מאי מפסיקין לאו לעקירת שולחן לא למפה רבה בר רב הונא איקלע לבי ריש גלותא אייתו תכא קמיה פרס מפה וקידש תניא נמי הכי (ושוין) שאין מביאין את השולחן אלא אם כן קידש ואם הביא פורס מפה ומקדש תני חדא שוין שאין מתחילין ותניא אידך שוין שמתחילין בשלמא הא דתניא שוין שאין מתחילין משכחת לה בערב הפסח אלא הא דתניא שוין שמתחילין אימת אי נימא בערב שבת הא מיפלג פליגי לא קשיא כאן קודם תשעה כאן לאחר תשעה אותם בני אדם שקידשו בבית הכנסת אמר רב ידי יין לא יצאו ידי קידוש יצאו ושמואל אמר

אף

רש"י

כך מפסיקין להבדלה. אם היו מסובין בשבת עד הלילה מפסיקין אכילתן ומבדילין: אין מביאין את השולחן. לאכול משקדש היום אא"כ קידש: ואם הביא. קודם לכן אי נמי אין מביאין את השולחן בערב הפסח אפילו מבעוד יום אא"כ קידש כדאמרן דאפי' רבי יוסי מודה בערב הפסח: (א) איקלע לבי ריש גלותא. והיו מסובין על השולחן בערב שבת וקידש עליהן היום ופרס מפה וקידש: ידי יין לא יצאו. שאם יש להם יין לשתות בביתם חייבין לברך בורא פרי הגפן שאינם פטורין בברכת הכוס (*על שתיית) יין בלא ברכה מאחר שעקרו ממקומן: אין

קידוש

רשב"ם

כך מפסיקין להבדלה. אם היו מסובין בשבת עד הלילה מפסיקין אכילתן ומבדילין: מאי לאו עקירת שולחן. ומדקאמר כשם שמפסיקין מכלל דלא סגי במפה: ה"ג רבה בר בר חנה איקלע לבי ריש גלותא אייתו תכא לקמיה פרס מפה וקידש תניא נמי הכי. ולא גרסי' ושוין אלא ה"ג אין מביאין כו' והכי פירושה רבה בר בר חנה איקלע לבי ריש גלותא ולא היו אוכלין קודם חשיכה ולאחר שיצאו מבית הכנסת החשיך אייתו תכא לקמיה הביאו את הפת על השולחן כמו שאנו עושין קודם קידוש פרס מפה על הלחם ואח"כ קידש לפי שסברלוטו לא היו מביאין את הלחם על השולחן עד לאחר קידוש כדתניא לקמיה לפיכך פרס מפה על הלחם והיינו כעין סילוק שולחן וכמי שאינו דומה ונראה לדבר שכן עושין דקתני מתני' (לקמן דף קיד.) מזגו לו כוס ראשון ואח"כ הביאו לפניו ירקות וחזרת מטבל בחזרת מכלל דעד השתא לא אייתי וטעמא כדפרים בשאילתות דרב אחאי גאון בפרשת וישמע יתרו וכתוב בהו הכי וקרובי תכא מקמי דליקדים לקדושא דשבתא לא מקרבינן מ"ט כי היכי דתיתי סעודה ליקרא דשבתא והיכי דקריבו לא מסלקינן ליה אלא פורס עליו מפה ומקדש דתניא ושוין שאין מביאין את השולחן אא"כ קידש ואם הביא פורס עליו מפה ומקדש והיכא דאתחיל סעודתא מדאגהר במעלי שבתא וקדיש עליה יומא פורס מפה ומקדש ומטעם זה נהגו לפרוס מפה ללחם עד לאחר קידוש בשבתות ויו"ט. ויש מפרשין איקלע לבי ריש גלותא והיו מסובין על השלחן בע"ש וקדיש יומא ופריס מפה וקדיש ולא נהירא לי דהא ברייתא דלקמיה דמסייעין ליה מיניה לא מפרשא בהפסקה אלא בתחלת אכילת לילי שבת: ושוין. לא ידענא אהיכא קאי והיכא למימר ושוין רבי יוסי ור' יהודה דפליגי בהפסקה הכא מודי ר' יוסי דלכתחלה מיהא אין מביאין קודם קידוש אע"פ שלא אכלו עד לאחר קידוש ואית דמפרשי ושוין ב"ש וב"ה דפליגי באלו דברים (ברכות ד' נא:) דאמרי ב"ש נוטלין לידים ואח"כ מוזגין את הכוס לקידוש וב"ה אומרים איפכא אפ"ה היכא דנטל ידיו מודין ב"ש דאין מביאין את השולחן עם האוכלין אלא א"כ קידש וכדפרישית טעמא לעיל ונראה בעיני דאיידי דאמרינן לקמיה תנא חדא שוין שאין מתחילין כו' שיבשו למעלה הספרים וכתבו נמי ושוין שאין מביאין כו' וטעות הוא בידם ולא גרסי' ליה: תני חדא שוין. ר' יהודה ורבי יוסי דפליגי לעיל בין באכילת ערב שבת מן המנחה ולמעלה בין בהפסקה: שאין מתחילין. לאכול מן המנחה ולמעלה: משכחת לה בערב הפסח. כדקאמרת דאפי' רבי יוסי מודי בערב הפסח: כאן קודם תשעה. שוין שמתחילין לאכול ומשהתחילו בהיתר אוכלין עד שתחשך אפילו לרבי יהודה: כאן לאחר ט'. הוא דפליגי דלרבי יהודה אין מתחילין כדתניא לעיל בהדיא לא יאכל אדם בערבי שבתות ובערבי ימים טובים מט' שעות ולמעלה כו' רבי יוסי אומר כו': שקידשו בבהכ"נ. הוא קידוש שמקדש שליח ציבור בלילי שבתות וימים טובים בבהכ"נ: ידי קידוש יצאו. אע"פ שלא שתו דקי"ל דהמקדש צריך שיטעום אם לא טעם אלא א' מהם יצאו כולן ידי חובתן כדמוכח בעירובין בשילהי בכל מערבין (ד' מ:) ומיהו לכתחלה צריך שיטעמו כולן ולא צריכין תו לאקדושי בביתן דלא בעי רב קידוש במקום סעודה הלכך אע"ג דלא אכלי בבית הכנסת נפקי: ידי יין לא יצאו. שאם יש להם יין בביתם לשתות חייבין לברך בפה"ג שאינן פטורין בברכת הכוס של שתיית יין ששתו בבהכ"נ מאחר שעקרו ממקומן דה"ל היסח הדעת וצריך לברך אבל המקדש בביתו על שולחנו בשבת א"צ לברך על היין שבתוך הסעודה שהרי פוטרו יין שלפני הסעודה כדתנן בכילד מברכין (ברכות ד' מב.) בירך על היין שלפני המזון פטר את היין שלאחר המזון ומוקי לה בגמרא בשבתות ובימים טובים הואיל ואדם קובע סעודתו על היין:

אף

תוספות

כך מפסיקין להבדלה. רב אית ליה לקמן *דלהבדלה אינה קובעת ואם התחילו אין מפסיקין להבדלה בהבדלה פליג אשמואל: [קיד.]

לאו לעקירת שלחן. הייט ברכת המזון כדפרישית לעיל שהיו רגילין לסלק שהיו להם שולחנות קטנים שכל אחד אוכל על שולחנו והיו מסלקין מלפני כולם ולא מלפני המברך ואנו שאנו אוכלים בשלחן אחד אין נכון לסלק:

איקלע פירס מפה וקידש. בהתחלת סעודה איירי כדפי' רשב"ם: ושוין. הכי גרסינן ושוין קאי ארבי יהודה ורבי יוסי כדפירש רשב"ם: שאין מביאין את השלחן אא"כ קידש. והא דאמר בכל כתבי (שבת דף קיט:) מלא שלחן ערוך מלאך טוב אומר כו' לא קשה דערוך הוא במקום אחר אך אין מביאין אותו למקום סעודה עד אחר קידוש ועכשיו שלחנות שלנו שהם גדולים יותר מדאי וקשה להביאם אחר קידוש שלא להפסיק כל כך בין קידוש לסעודה אנו רגילין לפרוס מפה ולקדש והטעם מפורש בשאילתות *כי היכי דתיתי סעודתא ביקרא דשבתא ויש מפרש זכר למן שלא היה יורד בשבתות *וי"ט והיה טל מלמעלה ומלמטה והמן *בינתים: [ועי' תוס' ביצה ב: ד"ה וכיון]

ידי קידוש יצאו. אף על פי שלא שתו רק שיטעום המברך או אפילו אחד מהם כדמוכח בסוף בכל מערבין (עירובין דף מ:) ולכתחלה צריך שיטעמו כולם ונראה הלכה כשמואל דאמר אין קידוש אלא במקום סעודה ואע"ג דבעלמא *הלכה כרב באיסורי וגם ר' יוחנן סבר לקמן כרב הכא הלכה כשמואל דרב הונא ורבה ואביי כולהו סברי בסמוך אין קידוש אלא במקום סעודה וכן פסק במגילת סתרים והמקדש דעתו לאכול במקום אחר יכול להוציא את האוכלים שם דלדידהו הוי מקום סעודה וכן משמע דמסתמא אחד מבני העיר היה מקדש בבהכ"נ ומוציא האורחים והיכא דליכא אורחים סמוך לבהכ"נ אין לקדש דהויא ברכה לבטלה דקי"ל כשמואל ואין לומר במקדש כאן על דעת שרוצה לאכול במקום אחר מודה שמואל דיש קידוש והא דפליגי בסתמא ולשמואל למה לי לקדושי בבי כנישתא ומיהו ממקום למקום בבית אחד כגון מאיגרא לארעא נראה דמודה שמואל אם קידש באיגרא כדי לאכול בארעא דחשיב קידוש במקום סעודה וכן מוכח בירושלמי דקאמר רבי יעקב בשם שמואל קידש בבית זה ונמלך לאכול בבית אחר צריך לקדש ר' אחא בשם ר' אושעיא אמר רב מי שסוכתו עריבה עליו מקדש ליל י"ט האחרון בביתו ועולה ואוכל בסוכתו א"ר בון ולא פליגי מאי דאמר רב בשלא היה בדעתו לאכול בבית שקידש ומאי דאמר שמואל בשהיה בדעתו לאכול בבית שקידש והא דקאמר ולא פליגי היינו ממקום למקום בחד בית ולאו דוקא נקט בירושלמי קידש בבית זה ונמלך לאכול בבית אחר ויתיישב שלא יחלוק הירושלמי עם הש"ס שלנו. כתב בשם רב נטרונאי גאון בתשובות מקדשין בבית הכנסת וטוהן לתוך עיניו לרפואה כדאמר (ברכות ד' מג:) פסיעה גסה נוטלת אחד מת"ק מאור עיניו ואימת מהדרא ליה בקידושא דבי שימשי ומיהו בתב"ו רבינו אלחנן כתב דהאי רפואה מאי למיעבד בקידוש שבביתו: ידי יין לא יצאו. וחייבין לברך בביתם בפה"ג משום שינוי מקום אבל משמע אם קידש בביתו על שולחנו שוב א"צ לברך על היין תוך הסעודה ואע"ג דסבר יש קידוש שלא במקום סעודה ולא שייך קידוש לסעודה א"כ אם הבדיל על שולחנו פטור מלברך על היין שבתוך הסעודה ואע"ג דיש הבדלה שלא במקום סעודה לכ"ע והכא יש לדחות דהיכא למימר דלא פטר אא"כ רוצה לשתות לפני המזון אבל תוך המזון לא פטר אך יש להביא ראיה מכילד מברכין (שם ד' מב.) דתנן בירך על היין שלפני המזון פוטר את היין שלאחר המזון פי' שהיו רגילין לשתות אחר הסעודה לפני ברהמ"ז משמע דכ"ש שפוטר היין שבתוך המזון שלא בא אלא לשרות אכילה שבמעיו ואפילו למאן דאמר התם בגמרא יין שבתוך המזון לא פטר יין שלאחר המזון הייט משום דאין יין שבא לשרות פוטר את היין הבא לשתות אבל יין שלפני המזון שבא לשתות עדיף טפי כ"ע מודו דפוטר את היין שבתוך המזון ועוד אם צריך לברך בתוך המזון מאי קאמר יין שלפני המזון פוטר את שלאחר המזון תיפוק ליה דפטרו יין שבתוך המזון למ"ד התם דפוטר ודוחק לומר בשלא שתו יין תוך הסעודה ואע"ג דהתם מוקי לה בשבתות וי"ט ובשעת הקזת דם שאדם קובע סעודתו על היין ה"ה בחול נמי אם דעתו לשתות יין בתוך הסעודה אלא נקט שבתות וי"ט דאז רגילות לקבוע סעודתו על היין ותדע דבי"ט אם נמלך ואין בדעתו לשתות יין לא פטר משמע דהכל תלוי בדעתו הלכך אם בירך על היין לפני המזון ודעתו לשתות בתוך המזון א"צ לברך אחריו על הגפן ולא תוך המזון בפה"ג אבל אם נמלך אינו פוטר וגם צריך לברך אחריו ברכה מעין שלש:

אף

הגהות הב"ח

(א) רש"י ד"ה איקלע נ"ל קודם ד"ה אין מביאין ונ"כ עיין במרדכי:

נ"ל לשתות

משבשתא היא · והכי איבעי ליה למיתני מט' שעות ומחלה ולמעלה ואילך וקא תנא קמיה·להך מתניתא הכי מט' שעות ולמעלה אלמא מתרצתא היא : אלא מחוורתא כרב הונא · ומן המנחה דקתני מתניתא קמייתא סמוך למנחה קאמר : הלכה מכלל דפליגי להפסקה · הא דא"ר ירמיה הלכ' כר' יהודה בערב הפסח דמשמע דפליג נמי רבי יוסי בערב הפסח להפסקה הוא דפליג דאם התחיל לאכול אף בערב הפסח אינו מפסיק אבל להתחיל מודה ר' יוסי דאסור ומתניתין בהתחלה לרבי יוסי אילטריך דקמשמע לן דמודה רבי יוסי בערב הפסח דאין מתחילין : דתניא · דבהפסקה נמי פליגי : אין הלכה כרבי יהודה · דאמר מפסיקין דמשמע עקירת שולחן : ולא כרבי יוסי · דאמר אין מפסיקין כלל : אלא פורס מפה · על השולחן ומקדש היום וחוזר ואוכל :

כך

תורה אור

דילמא משבשתא היא א"ל מרימר ואיתימא רב יימר אנא איקלעי לפירקיה דרב פנחס בריה דרב אמי וקם תנא ותני קמיה וקיבלה מיניה אי הכי קשיא אלא מחוורתא כדרב הונא ולרב הונא מי ניחא והאמר רבי ירמיה א"ר יוחנן ואיתימא א"ר אבהו א"ר יוסי בר רבי חנינא הלכה כר' יהודה בערב הפסח והלכה כר' יוסי בע"ש הלכה כר' יהודה בערב הפסח *מכלל דפליג רבי יוסי בתרוייהו לא הלכה מכלל דפליגי בהפסקה דתניא *מפסיקין לשבתות דברי רבי יהודה רבי יוסי אומר אין מפסיקין ומעשה ברשב"ג [ורבי יהודה] ורבי יוסי שהיו מסובין בעכו וקדש עליהם היום א"ל רשב"ג לרבי יוסי ברבי רצונך נפסיק וניחוש לדברי יהודה חבירנו אמר לו בכל יום ויום אתה מחבב דבריי לפני רבי יהודה ועכשיו אתה מחבב דברי רבי יהודה בפני °הגם לכבוש את המלכה עמי בבית א"ל א"ב לא נפסיק שמא יראו התלמידים ויקבעו הלכה לדורות אמרו לא זזו משם עד שקבעו הלכה כר' יוסי: אמר רב יהודה אמר שמואל אין הלכה לא כר' יהודה ולא כר' יוסי אלא *פורס מפה ומקדש איני והא אמר רב תחליפא בר אבדימי אמר שמואל כשם שמפסיקין לקידוש

כך

[שבת ק: וש"נ]

אסתר ז

[תוספתא דברכות פ"ה]

רשב"ם

דילמא משבשתא היא·דה"ל למיתני מט' שעות ומחלה ולמעלה א"נ מן המנחה ולמעלה כדתניא בההיא קמייתא:אמר מרימר · לאו משבשתא היא : אלא קשיא · הך ברייתא בתרייתא דקתני מט' ולמעלה אלמא סמוך למנחה נמי קאסר רבי יהודה בערבי שבתות ויו"ט וליכא לאוקומי השתא מתניתין כרבי יהודה דמאי שנא ערבי פסחים דנקט בהו סמוך למנחה טפי משבתות ויו"ט: אלא מחוורתא כרב הונא·דלרבי יוסי אילטריך ומן המנחה דקתני הך ברייתא סמוך למנחה קאמר : מכלל דפליג רבי יוסי בתרווייהו· אפי' בערב הפסח והיכי מוקי למתני' כר' יוסי : מכלל דפליגי להפסקה · הא דא"ר ירמיה הלכה כרבי יהודה בערב הפסח דמשמע דפליג נמי רבי יוסי בע"פ להפסקה הוא דפליג דאי התחיל לאכול אף בע"פ אינו מפסיק אבל להתחיל מודי ר' יוסי דאסור ומתני' בהתחלה ולר' יוסי אילטריך דקמ"ל דמודי ר' יוסי בערב הפסח דאין מתחילין:דתניא·דבהפסקה נמי פליגי:מפסיקין לשבתות·אם התחיל סעודתו בהיתר קודם המנחה והיה אוכל והולך עד שתחשך (א) אפי' לר' יהודה מפסיק סעודתו מיד כשיחשיך ומקדש היום : וקדש עליהן · שהחשיך : ה"ג בתוספתא דברכות אמר לו רבן גמליאל*לר' יוסי בר' רצונך שנפסיק וניחוש לדברי יהודה חבירנו אמר לו בכל יום אתה מחבב דבריי לפני יהודה ועכשיו אתה מחבב דברי יהודה בפני הגם לכבוש את המלכה עמי בבית אמר לו א"כ לא נפסיק שמא יראו כו' : ברבי · כך קרא רשב"ג לר' יוסי בר חלפתא כלומר גדול הדור:הגם לכבוש·כלומ' בפני אתה מבייש:אמר לו רשב"ג א"כ לא נפסיק כו'·שמעינן מהכא דבערבי פסחים אסור לאכול מסוף ט' שעות ולמעלה כדתנן מתני' אבל בערבי שבתות וי"ט מותר לאכול מן המנחה ולמעלה דהא סתם לן תנא דמתני' כרבי יוסי מדנקט ערבי פסחים מכלל דבשאר ע"ש וי"ט שרי וקי"ל נמי (עירובין ד' מו:) הלכה כר' יוסי מחבירו דר' יוסי אפי' להתחיל ולאכול אחר ט' שרי כדהוא לקמן בשמעתין דאמר אלא הא דתניא הא דתנן אימת בע"ש הא פליג ר' יהודה ומיהו לענין הפסקה אין הלכה כר' יוסי אלא כר' יהודה שאם התחיל לאכול קודם ט' ונמשך אכילתו עד שחשיכה צריך לעקור את השולחן מיד כשיחשיך ולהחזירו לשם פסח ובשבתות וי"ט לא יפסיק אלא פורס מפה ומקדש ואח"כ גומר סעודתו:לא כר' יהודה·דאמר מפסיקין דמשמע עקירת שולחן : ולא כר' יוסי · דאמר א"צ להפסיק כלל אלא יגמור סעודתו אפי' משחשיכה ויברכו בהמ"ז ואח"כ מביא לו כוס שני לקידוש היום כדתניא לקמן בשמעתין אלא פורס מפה על המאכל כדין כל שבתות השנה שהביאו לחם על השולחן קודם קידוש כדתני' לקמן א"כ משום סילוק פתורא ואח"כ אומר קידוש היום על הכוס וחוזר ואוכל וגומר סעודתו ונראה בעיני דס"ל לשמואל דהלכה כרבי יוסי כדקתני בברייתא שקבעו הלכה כמותו אלא שבא להחמיר על עצמו קצת שלא יגמור סעודתו ויקדש אח"כ אלא יקדש תחלה ואח"כ יגמור סעודתו דלגלי'ה שמואל דאמר' כמאן דהא בריית' דקתני פורס מפה ומקדש לא קאי אהפסקת אכיל' כלל אלא בבא לשבת לכתחלה מיירי:

כך

דילמא משבשתא היא·וברייתא קמייתא דקתני מן המנחה ולמעלה היא עיקר משום דלדידיה אתיא מתני' כשולי עלמא : **והאמר** ר' ירמיה א"ר יוחנן ואיתימא רבי אבהו א"ר יוסי בר בר' חנינא ולא גרס רבי יוחנן א"ר אבהו דרבי אבהו תלמידיה דר' יוחנן הוה: **מכלל** דפליגי בהפסקה כדתניא· לא גרס דתניא דהא בברייתא לא פליגי בהפסקה דפסח אלא כדתניא גרס ומייתי כי היכי דפליגי בהפסקה דשבת הכי קים ליה דפליגי נמי בהפסקה דפסח ומורי רבינו יחיאל אמר דגרס דתניא °ודייק מדקאמר ר' יוסי אין מפסיקין והיינו אפילו בערב הפסח דאין מתחילין דבע"ש שרי רבי יוסי אפי' להתחיל עוד נראה דקאמר לקמן (ד' קב.) בני חבורה שהיו מסובין וקדש כו' וקתני פלוגתא דר' יהודה ורבי יוסי והתם סתמא קתני וקידש בין שבת בין פסח : **מפסיקין** לשבתות· פי' בעקירת שולחן כדמוכח בסמוך והיינו שמברך ברכת המזון כדתניא לקמן (שם:) ראשון אומר עליו ברכת המזון והיו רגילין לסלק השולחן לפני ברכת המזון כדאמר בפרק [כילד מברכין] (ברכות דף מב:) סילק אסור מלאכול ולכך קאמר בסמוך דבעי לר' יהודה עקירת שולחן ולספרים דגרסי לקמן ראשון אומר עליו קידוש היום ושני ברכת המזון היו עוקרין את השולחן לפני קידוש כדי להפסיק אלא שהקידוש עושה קודם לפי שאסור לשתות כוס של ברכת המזון בלא קידוש דע"כ עקירת שולחן איכו בין קידוש לברכת המזון מדקאמר פורס מפה ומקדש ופריסת המפה היא במקום עקירת שולחן לרבי יהודה : **רבי** יוסי אומר אין מפסיקין · וגומר כל הסעודה ומברך ברכת המזון ואח"כ מקדש כדמוכח בברייתא דלקמן (דף קב:) משמע דאין צריך לעשות סעודה לשם שבת דאי צריך מה לו להמתין יפסיק מיד וא"ת ואיך יעשו קידוש בלא סעודה הלא אין קידוש אלא במקום סעודה וי"ל דחשיב קידוש במקום סעודה כיון שמיד אחר הסעודה עושה קידוש ואותה סעודה עולה לו לסעודת שבת כדמוכח בתוספתא דקתני במילתיה דרבי יוסי ומזכיר של שבת בברכת המזון ומיהו קשה לר' יוסי איך יעשו ד' כוסות כיון שלא יקדשו אלא אחר ברכת המזון ולא יעשו סעודה אחרת וי"ל דיעשו ד' כוסות שלא כסדר הרגילין לעשות כוס ברכת המזון תחלה ואחריו כוס של קידוש וירקות ואחריו כוס שלישי למה נשתנה ואחריו מרור ועל כוס רביעי הלל : **אין** מפסיקין · בהתחילו בהיתר איירי דבהתחילו באיסור מודה ר' יוסי דמפסיקין ולרבי יהודה נמי דמפסיקין היינו כשכבר קידש היום כדמוכח בעובדא דמייתי דקתני וקידש עליהן היום אבל הגיע שעת מנחה אין מפסיקין והלכה כרבי יוסי ובערבי שבתות וי"ט אפי' להתחיל שרי כר' יוסי דרבי יהודה ור' יוסי הלכה כר' יוסי כדמוכח בעירובין (דף מו:) ובערבי פסחים אסור להתחיל ואם התחיל אפי' בהיתר מפסיקין בברכת המזון דבהא פסקינן כר' יהודה ומורי רבינו יחיאל אומר מדפסיק כר' יוסי בהפסקה בההוא עובדא מכלל דלכתחלה לא קי"ל כוותיה ועוד כתב בה"ג דבע"ש אין להתחיל לאכול מן המנחה ולמעלה דאפי' ר' יוסי לא קאמר אלא דלא יפסיק אבל לאתחולי לא וע"כ ה"פ דלא קי"ל כרבי יוסי אלא להפסקה אבל לא להתחיל : **שהיו** מסובין והתחילו בהיתר שהרי רבי יהודה היה שם· ה"ג בתוספתא אמר לו א"כ לא, נפסיק וה"פ א"כ כיון שמחית לא נפסיק שמא יראו התלמידים : **אלא** פורס מפה ומקדש·פי' רשב"ם דאית ליה לשמואל דהלכה כר' יוסי אלא שבא להחמיר על דבריו שלא לגמור סעודה קודם קידוש דאי לא תימא הכי שמואל דאמר כמאן דברייתא דקתני פורס מפה ומקדש לא מיירי בהפסקת אכילה אלא בבא להתחיל לאכול ובחנם דחק דשמואל סבר כחכמים דהכי איתא בירושלמי רב יהודה בשם שמואל זו דברי ר' יהודה ור' יוסי אבל חכמים אומרים פורס מפה ומקדש וצריך לדקדק כמאן הלכה דאע"ג דאמר ר' יוחנן לעיל הלכה כר' יוסי ובמי שהוליאוהו (שם ד' מז:) משמע דהלכה כר' יוחנן לגבי שמואל איכא חד לישנא דלא א"ר יוחנן ורב נמי כבר לקמן (ד' קה:) כשמואל וקאמר שבת קבעה נפשה ואע"ג דבשל סופרים הלך אחר המיקל הייט דוקא בשוין כדאמר בפ"ק דמסכת ע"ג (ד' ז.):

כך

ו א מיי' פכ"ט מהלכות שבת הלכה יב סמג עשין כט טוש"ע או"ח סימן רעא סעיף ד :

רבינו חננאל

ואוקמי' רב הונא למתני' כר' יוסי ובערב הפסח משום חובה דמצה אסור למיכל מן המנחה ולמעלה ומודה ליה לר' יהודה בערב הפסח והא דאמר ר' יוחנן הלכה כר' יהודה בערב הפסח והלכה כר' יוסי בערבי שבתות ובערבי ימים טובים אוקימנהלהפסקה דתניא מפסיקין לשבת ועוקרין את השלחן ומקדשין ומברכין ברכת המזון דברי ר' יהודה ר' יוסי אומר אין מפסיקין אלא גומרין סעודתן ומברכין ברכת המזון ואחר כך מקדשין ומעשה בר"ג ור' יוסי ור' יהודה שהיו מסובין בעכו וכו' עד לא זזו משם עד שקבעו הלכה כר' יוסי: אמר רב יהודה אמר שמואל אין הלכה לא כר' יהודה ולא כר' יוסי אלא פורס מפה ומקדש תניא נמי הכי ושוין שאין מביאין השלחן אא"כ קדש ואם הביא פורס מפה ומקדש:

גליון הש"ס

תום' ד"ה מכלל. ודייק מדאמרינן אין מפסיקין וכו' דבע"ש שרי ר"י אפי' להתחיל. קשה לי הא ר"י אמר דאין מפסיקין אפי' אחר שתחשך דלהתחיל אסור קודם קידוש דמ"מ אין מפסיקין וצ"ע :

הגהות הב"ח

(א) רשב"ם ד"ה מפסיקין וכו' עד שתחשך לר' יהודה כצ"ל ותיבת אפילו נמחק:

* נ"ל: ר' שמעון בן גמליאל, רמ"פ

*Should read: Rabban Simeon b. Gamaliel (R.M.F.)

this is authentic? [100a] Perhaps it is a corrupted version.[3] Said Meremar to him—others state, R. Yemar; I visited the session of R. Phineas the son of R. Ammi, and a tanna arose and recited it[4] before him and he accepted it [as correct]. If so, there is a difficulty? Hence it is clearly [to be explained] as R. Huna.[5]

Yet is it satisfactory according to R. Huna? Surely R. Jeremiah said in R. Joḥanan's name—others state, R. Abbahu said in the name of R. Jose b. R. Ḥanina—: The *halachah* is as R. Judah in respect to the eve of Passover, and the *halachah* is as R. Jose in respect to the eve of the Sabbath. 'The *halachah* is as R. Judah in respect to the eve of Passover,' whence it follows that R. Jose disagrees on both?[6]—No: 'The *halachah* [etc.]' proves that they disagree in respect to interruption. For it was taught: One must interrupt [the meal] for the Sabbath:[7] this is R. Judah's ruling. R. Jose said: One need not interrupt [the meal].[1] And it once happened that R. Simeon b. Gamaliel, R. Judah and R. Jose were dining[2] at Acco, when the day became holy upon them.[3] Said R. Simeon b. Gamaliel to R. Jose: 'Berabbi,[4] is it your wish that we interrupt [our meal] and pay heed to the words of our colleague Judah?' Said he to him: 'Every [other] day you prefer my words to those of R. Judah, whereas now you prefer R. Judah's words in my very presence—"*will he even force the queen before me in my house*"?'[5] 'If so,' he rejoined, 'we will not interrupt [the meal], lest the disciples see it and establish the *halachah* [thus] for all time.'[6] It was related: They did not stir thence until they had established the *halachah* as R. Jose.

Rab Judah said in Samuel's name: The *halachah* is neither as R. Judah[7] nor as R. Jose,[8] but one must spread a cloth[9] and sanctify [the day].[10] But that is not so, for R. Taḥlifa b. Abdimi said in Samuel's name: Just as one must interrupt [the meal] for

(3) This Baraitha contradicts the previous one, and there is nothing to show that this is more correct, particularly as the latter agrees with the Mishnah as explained above. (4) The *second* Baraitha: from nine hours. (5) Hence 'from *minḥah*' in the first Baraitha means just before *minḥah*, and thus the Mishnah and both Baraithas are in agreement. (6) Whereas in R. Huna's view R. Jose agrees in respect of Passover eve. (7) The Heb. is in the plural: Sabbaths. I.e., if one started eating before the Sabbath, he must interrupt the meal when the Sabbath commences, remove the table and recite grace (the table was generally removed before grace, v. Ber. 42a), then recite *ḳiddush*, the prayer of sanctification, and proceed as with a new meal. According to a version *infra* 100b, the table was removed before *ḳiddush*, which then preceded grace (Tosaf.).

(1) But he completes the meal, recites grace, and then *ḳiddush*. Now when R. Jeremiah states that the *halachah* is as R. Judah in respect to Passover eve, whence it follows that R. Jose disagrees there too, this disagreement is likewise in reference to interrupting the meal, R. Jose maintaining that even on the eve of Passover he need not interrupt it once he has commenced (i.e., if he commenced at the permitted time—Rashbam and Tosaf). But he admits that a man must not commence a meal in the first place shortly before *minḥah*, and that is the meaning of the Mishnah too. (2) Lit., 'reclining'. (3) I.e., the Sabbath or Festival commenced. (4) A title of honour, v. Naz., 19a, n. 1. (5) Esth. VII, 8; i.e., will you shame me in my own presence? (6) Lit., 'for generations'. (7) Who maintains that one must interrupt the meal, which implies that the table must be removed. (8) Who ruled that no interruption whatsoever is required. (9) Which hides the table so that it is not there, as it were. (10) By reciting *ḳiddush*.

CHAPTER X

a *MISHNAH.* [99b] ON THE EVE OF PASSOVER[1] CLOSE TO MINḤAH[2] A MAN MUST NOT EAT UNTIL NIGHTFALL. EVEN THE POOREST MAN IN ISRAEL MUST NOT EAT [ON THE NIGHT OF PASSOVER] UNTIL HE RECLINES;[3] AND THEY[4] SHOULD GIVE HIM NOT LESS THAN FOUR CUPS [OF WINE],[5] AND EVEN [IF HE RECEIVES RELIEF] FROM THE CHARITY PLATE.[6]

GEMARA. Why particularly THE EVE OF PASSOVER? Even the eves of Sabbaths and Festivals too [are subject to this law]? For it was taught: A man must not eat on the eves of Sabbaths and Festivals from *minḥah* and onward, so that he may enter [i.e., commence] the Sabbath with an appetite [for food]: [these are] the words of R. Judah. R. Jose said: He may go on eating until nightfall!—Said R. Huna: This [our Mishnah] is necessary only on the view of R. Jose, who said: He may go on eating until nightfall: that is only on the eves of Sabbaths and [other] Festivals; but with respect to the eve of Passover he agrees [with R. Judah],
b because of the duty of [eating] unleavened bread.[1] R. Papa said: You may even say [that it must be taught on] R. Judah['s view too]: there, on the eve of Sabbaths and Festivals, it is forbidden only from *minḥah* and after, but close to *minḥah* it is permitted; whereas on the eve of Passover it is forbidden even close to *minḥah* too. Now is it permitted just before *minḥah* on the eve of the Sabbath and Festivals? Surely it was taught: A man must not eat on the eve of the Sabbath or Festivals from nine hours[2] and onwards, in order that he may enter the Sabbath with an appetite: [these are] the words of R. Judah. R. Jose said: He may go on eating until nightfall?—Said Mar Zuṭra: Who is to tell us that

a (1) Lit., 'on the eve of Passovers'. Tosaf. suggests that this may mean either on the eve when Passover-offerings are sacrificed, or on the eve of the first and second Passovers. But there is a variant reading, ON THE EVES OF PASSOVERS, the whole being in the plural; its meaning will then be on the eve of (every) Passover, as translated in the text, Heb. often using the plural in this way. (2) V. Glos.; i.e., from just before *minḥah*. (3) As a sign of freedom, this being the practice in ancient days. (4) Rashbam and Tosaf.: the charity overseers. (5) Which every Jew must drink on the night of Passover. These correspond to the four expressions of redemption employed in Ex. VI, 6f: *I will* bring *you out from under the burdens of the Egyptians, and I will* deliver *you from their bondage, and I will* redeem *you with an outstretched arm, and with great judgments; and I will* take *you to me for a people* (commentaries and Jerusalemi). (6) *Tamḥuy*, daily distributed food collected from contributors, soup kitchen (Jast.). This was available only to the poorest of the poor, for he who had enough even for two meals only might not receive from the *tamḥuy* (Pe'ah VIII, 7); even such must drink four cups of wine on the night of Passover.

b (1) For since the eating of unleavened bread on the first night of Passover is compulsory (v. Ex. XII, 18), it is unfitting that it should be eaten when one is already satisfied. (2) I.e., about three p.m., whereas *minḥah* time was nine and a half hours, about half past three p.m., two and a half hours before nightfall.

ערב פסחים *סמוך למנחה לא יאכל אדם עד שתחשך ואפילו עני שבישראל לא יאכל עד שיסב ולא יפחתו לו מארבע כוסות של יין ואפילו מן התמחוי: גמ' מאי איריא ערבי פסחים אפי' ערבי שבתות וימים טובים נמי דתניא לא יאכל אדם בערבי שבתות וימים טובים מן המנחה ולמעלה כדי שיכנס לשבת כשהוא תאוה דברי רבי יהודה רבי יוסי אומר אוכל והולך עד שתחשך אמר רב הונא לא צריכא אלא לר' יוסי דאמר אוכל והולך עד שתחשך הני מילי בערבי שבתות וימים טובים אבל בערב הפסח משום חיובא דמצה מודה רב פפא אמר אפילו תימא רבי יהודה התם בערבי שבתות וימים טובים מן המנחה ולמעלה הוא דאסור סמוך למנחה שרי אבל בערב הפסח אפילו סמוך למנחה נמי אסור ובערב שבת סמוך למנחה שרי והתניא לא יאכל אדם בערב שבת וימים טובים מתשע שעות ולמעלה כדי שיכנס לשבת כשהוא תאוה דברי רבי יהודה רבי יוסי אומר אוכל והולך עד שתחשך אמר מר זוטרא *מאן לימא לן דמתרצתא היא דילמא

ערב פסחים סמוך למנחה. קודם למנחה מעט: לא יאכל. כדי שיאכל מצה של מצוה לתיאבון משום הידור מצוה: ואפילו עני שבישראל לא יאכל. בלילי פסחים עד שיסב כדרך בני חורין (א) זכר לחירות במטה ועל השלחן: ארבע כוסות. כנגד ארבעה לשוני גאולה האמורים בגלות מצרים והוצאתי אתכם והצלתי אתכם וגאלתי אתכם ולקחתי אתכם בפרשת וארא: ואפי'. מתפרנס מתמחוי של צדקה דהיינו עני שבעניים דתנן במסכת פאה (פ"ח מ"ז) מי שיש לו מזון ב' סעודות לא יטול מן התמחוי: גמ' כשהוא תאוה. ולא תהא סעודת שבת על השובע: לא צריכא. דקתני ערב פסחים לא יאכל עד שתחשך אלא לרבי יוסי דאמר הולך ואוכל עד שתחשך: אפילו תימא. מתני' נמי רבי יהודה היא ובדין הוא דליתני ערבי פסחים לרבויי סמוך למנחה: מתשע שעות. היינו סמוך למנחה: משבשתא

פירוש רבינו שמואל תלמיד רש"י ז"ל

ערבי פסחים סמוך למנחה. מנחה קטנה קודם למנחה מעט חצי שעה בתחלת שעה עשירית דתנן (לעיל דף נח.) תמיד נשחט בשמנה ומחצה וקרב בתשעה ומחצה כמנחת מנחה קטנה בט' ומחצה וסמוך ליה היינו חצי שעה קודם בסוף שעה תשיעית ותחלת שעה עשירית: לא יאכל אדם כו'. כדי שיאכל מצה של מצוה לתיאבון משום הידור מצוה: ואפילו עני שבישראל לא יאכל. *בערבי פסחים עד שיסב כדרך בני חורין במטה ועל השלחן זכר לחירות: ולא יפחתו לו. גבאי צדקה המפרנסין את העניים כדתנן (פאה פ"ח מ"ז) אין פוחתין לעני העובר ממקום כו' אלמא לישנא דלא יפחתו אגבאי צדקה קאי והוא הדין נמי אם לא יתנו לו שצריך שיחזר בכל כחו אחריו אלא אורחא דמילתא נקט שרגילין ליתן לו ארבע כוסות וסדרן מפורש לפנינו ומצינו בב"ר (פ' פח) רב הונא בשם רבי אבא אמר כנגד ארבע לשוני גאולה האמורין בגלות מצרים והוצאתי והצלתי וגאלתי ולקחתי והצלתי בפ' וארא: ואפילו. הוא מתפרנס מתמחוי של צדקה דהיינו עני שבעניים דתנן במסכת פאה מי שיש לו מזון שתי סעודות לא יטול מן התמחוי אפילו הכי אם לא נתנו לו גבאי צדקה ימכור את מלבושו או ילוה או ישכיר את עצמו בשביל יין לארבע כוסות: גמ' אפילו ערבי שבתות כו'. אליבא דרבי יהודה כדי שיהא קידוש וסעודת שבת חביב עליו: משום חיובא דמצה. שלא תהא נאכלת על השובע וחיובא דמצה לילה הראשון חובה דכתיב (שמות יב) בערב תאכלו מצות: הכי גרסינן אפילו תימא רבי יהודה התם מן המנחה ולמעלה כו'. במילתיה דר' יהודה קתני מן המנחה ולמעלה ובמתניתין תנן סמוך למנחה: מתשע שעות ולמעלה. היינו חצי שעה סמוך למנחה: דילמא

(תוספות אחרים מערבי פסחים נמצאים בספר רב מרדכי)

ערב פסחים לא גרסינן ערבי ניחא ולי גרסינן ערב ה"ק ערב שחוטין בו (ב) פסחים א"נ ערב פסח ראשון ושני: לא יאכל אדם. פירוש אפילו התפלל ומשום מצה כדאמרינן בגמ' דבלא התפלל תפלת מנחה אפילו בשאר ימות השנה אסור כדתנן בפ"ק דשבת (ד' ט:) ול"ת ומה לא יאכל אי מצה אפילו קודם נמי אסור כדאמרינן בירושלמי כל האוכל מצה בערב הפסח כאילו בועל ארוסתו בבית חמיו ולאו במיני תרגימא הא אמר בגמרא (ד' קז:) אבל מטבל הוא במיני תרגימא וי"ל דאיירי במצה עשירה דלא אסר בירושלמי אלא במצה הראויה לצאת בה חובתו והאוכלה קודם זמנה אבל מצה עשירה שריא וכן היה נוהג ר"ת:

סמוך למנחה לא יאכל. ואם תאמר והא אמר בכל שעה (לעיל ד' מ.) בליקות של נכרים ממלא אדם כריסו מהם ובלבד שיאכל כזית מצה באחרונה והכא אסר לאכול אפי' מבעוד יום וי"ל דבאותה הסעודה אדם נזהר ואינו אוכל כל שובעו כדי שיאכל מצה לתיאבון אבל מבעוד יום אין אדם נזהר ואוכל כל שובעו וסבר שעד הלילה יתאוה ואדרבה יהיה שבע יותר כי יתברך המאכל במעיו והא דדייק רבא לקמן (ד' קז:) דחמרא גריר דאי אמרת מיסעד סעיד בין הכוסות הללו אמאי ישתה אף על גב דבאותה סעודה נזהר מלאכול שובעו (ג) אבל בשתיה אי אפשר להזהר א"נ מבין ראשון לשני דאיכא אגדתא והלל דייק דדמי לסעודה אחרת: עד שתחשך. מקשי' אמאי איצטריך עד שתחשך פשיטא ועוד דבגמרא גבי שבתות וימים טובים לא קתני ליה ואומר הר"י מקורבי"ל דגבי מצה דווקא בעינן עד שתחשך כדתניא בתוספתא* [פ"ב] הפסח ומצה ומרור מצותן משתחשך וטעמא משום דכתיב (שמות יב) ואכלו את הבשר בלילה הזה ומצה ומרור איתקשו לפסח אבל סעודת שבת וימים טובים מצי אכיל להו מבעוד יום כדאמר בפרק תפלת השחר (ברכות דף כז:) מתפלל אדם של שבת בערב שבת ואומר קידוש היום מבעוד יום ואומר מהר' יחיאל דכי פריך בגמרא מאי איריא ערבי פסחים כו' לא מצי לשנויי דנקט ערבי פסחים משום דבעי למיתני עד שתחשך דכבר אשמעינן באיזהו מקומן (זבחים ד' נו:) דקתני הפסח אינו נאכל אלא בלילה והכא אגב אורחיה תנייה בקוצר ורבינו יהודה תירץ אפילו אי בעינן גבי שבתות וימים טובים עד שתחשך הכא איצטריך למיתני דאתא לאשמועינן דאע"ג דשחיטת פסחים מבעוד יום אינו נאכל מבעוד יום כשאר קדשים וכן יש בירושלמי בריש פירקין תני ערב שבת מן המנחה ולמעלה לא יטעום כלום עד שתחשך: ואפילו עני שבישראל לא יאכל עד שיסב. דסלקא דעתך דהסיבת עני לא חשיבא הסיבה דאין לו על מה להסב ואין זה דרך חירות ויש מפרשים דאדלעיל קאי עד שתחשך ואפילו עני שבישראל פירוש אפי' עני שלא אכל כמה ימים לא יאכל עד שתחשך: לא יפחתו לו. פי' רשב"ם גבאי צדקה וגרס (ד) לא יפחתו וכן נראה מדלא קתני לא יפחות ל' יחיד וליכא למימר דיפחתו אד' כוסות קאי דאם כן הוה ליה למיתני ארבע כוסות בלא מ"ם והא דקאמר מן התמחוי לא ימנע מלקבל כדי לקיים ארבע כוסות. וארבע כוסות פירש רשב"ם כנגד ארבעה לשוני גאולה וכן יש בירושלמי: לא יפחתו לו מארבע כוסות. מתוך הלשון משמע קצת שאין נותנין לבניו ולבני ביתו כי אם לעצמו והוא מוציא את כולם בשלו וסברא הוא דמאי שנא ארבע כוסות מקידוש דכל השנה שאחד מוציא את כולם ומיהו גם בקידוש שמא היה לכל אחד כוס כדמשמע לקמן (דף קו.) גבי חזיה לההוא סבא דגחין ושתי אבל בפרק בכל מערבין (עירובין דף מ:) גבי זמן משמע קצת שלא היה לכל אחד כוסו ועוד דאמר בגמרא (לקמן דף קח:) השקה מהן לבניו ולבני ביתו יצא והוא דשתה רובא דכסא משמע דהם יצאו בשמיעה דהא בעינן רובא דכסא ועוד דמשמע דלכתחלה אין רגילות להשקותם מיהו יש לדחות בשיש להם כוס לעצמם אי נמי בבניו ובני ביתו קטנים מיירי שלא הגיעו לחינוך *ואין אשתו בכלל ומיהו בגמרא משמע שצריך כל אחד ארבע כוסות דקתני (שם) הכל חייבין בארבע כוסות אחד נשים ואחד תינוקות אמר רבי יהודה מה תועלת לתינוקות ביין משמע דלתנא קמא צריך כוס אף לתינוקות ויש לדחות דחייבין לשמוע ברכת ארבע כוסות קאמר ומשום חינוך ונראה להחמיר ולהצריך ארבע כוסות לכל אחד והמחמיר צריך ליזהר שלא יהא כוסם פגום דאמר בגמרא (לקמן ד' קה:) טעמו פגמו: מאי איריא ערבי פסחים. ואם תאמר אמאי לא משני דתנא בפסח קאי כדמשני בפרק כל שעה (לעיל ד' לז:) גבי פת עבה ויש לומר משום דבפסח קאי אין לו להניח ערבי שבתות דתדירי בכל שבוע אי נמי הכא דאיכא למיטעי ולמימר דדוקא נקט ערב פסח משום חיובא דמצה לא הוה ליה למיתני ערב פסח וכן בריש מקום שנהגו (לעיל ד' נ:) איכא למיטעי דדוקא בערב הפסח אסור לעשות מלאכה משום קרבן*: מן המנחה ולמעלה. השתא סלקא דעתא דלאו דוקא אלא הוא הדין סמוך למנחה: דילמא

עין משפט נר מצוה

א א מיי' פ"ו מהל' מצה הלכה יב סמג עשין מה טוש"ע א"ח סי' תעא סעיף א:

ב ב מיי' שם טור ש"ע א"ח סימן תעב סעיף א:

ג ג מיי' פ"ו מהל' מצה הלכה ח סמג עשין מא טוש"ע א"ח סימן תעב סעיף ב בהג"ה:

ד ד מיי' שם הלכה ז טוש"ע א"ח שם סעיף יג:

ה ה מיי' שם פ"ו הלכה יב ופ"ל מהלכות שבת הל' ד ופ"ז מהל' י"ט הל' טו סמג עשין כט ולאוין עה טוש"ע א"ח סי' רמט סעיף ב* וסי' תקכט ס"א בהג"ה*:

רבינו חננאל

ערב פסחים סמוך למנחה לא יאכל אדם עד שתחשך וכו' ואמרי' מאי איריא ערב פסחים אפי' ערבי שבתות וערבי ימים טובים דתניא לא יאכל אדם בערבי שבתות ובערבי ימים טובים מן המנחה ולמעלה כדי שיכנס לשבת כשהוא תאב דברי רבי יהודה רבי יוסי אומר אוכל והולך עד שתחשך ועוד תניא לא יאכל אדם מתשע שעות ולמעלה בערבי שבתות ובערבי ימים טובים דברי רבי יהודה ר' יוסי אומר אוכל והולך עד שתחשך ושקלינן וטרינן

הגהות הב"ח

(א) רש"י ד"ה ואפילו עני וכו' בני חורין במטה ועל השלחן זכר לחירות כס"ד: (ב) תוס' ד"ה ערב וכו' ס"ק ערב שחוטין בו פרכס פסחים: (ג) ד"ה סמוך וכו' מלאכול שובעו בשתיה כצ"ל ותיבת אבל נמחק: (ד) ד"ה לא יפחתו פי' רשב"ם וכו' וגרס. נ"ב פי' השתא דרישא קאי על עצמו שלא יאכל עד שתחשך ועד שיסב והסיפא קאי אגבאי צדקה לא גרסינן ולא יפחתו אלא לא בלא וי"ו:

מסורת הש"ס

[עי' תוספות לקמן קי: ד"ה סמוך]

[שבת קכה:]

ז"ל בלילי פסחים

[ע' תוס' לעיל נז: ד"ה תנא]

גליון הש"ס

תוס' ד"ה לא יפחתו וכו' ואין אשתו בכלל. עיין ברכות כד: תד"ה וסבירא:

*מכאן אמרו חכמים יפה שתיקה לחכמים קל וחומר לטפשים שנאמר °אויל מחריש חכם יחשב: שנים שנתערבו פסחיהם וכו': לימא מתניתין דלא כר' יהודה דתניא *ואם ימעט הבית מהיות משה *מלמד שמתמעטין והולכין ובלבד שיהא אחד מבני חבורה קיים דברי רבי יהודה רבי יוסי אומר ובלבד שלא יניחו את הפסח כמות שהוא א"ר יוחנן אפילו תימא רבי יהודה כיון דאמר רבי יהודה *אין שוחטין את הפסח על היחיד מעיקרא לאמטויי אחרינא בהדיה קאי וכאחד מבני חבורה דמי א"ר אשי מתניתין נמי דייקא דקתני וכן חמש חבורות של חמשה חמשה של עשרה עשרה חמשה אין אבל של חמשה וארבעה לא לאו משום דלא פייש חד מבני חבורה גביה שמע מינה:

משלי יז · שמות יב

מכאן אמרו. מפני דבר כזה אמרו יפה שתיקה כו' שאלו אמר ואמרו השני אין לו תקנה לא אמר ולא אמרו שניהן ראויין זה אוכל משלו כו': לימא מתני'. דקתני שנים שנתערבו פסחיהן כו' דלא כר' יהודה. דבעי שיהא א' מבני חבורה הראשונה קיים עליו דהא ודאי אותן שנים שהביאו מן השוק אינן חשובין מבני חבורה הואיל ולא היו בשעת לקיחתן ועל כרחיך רבי יהודה אבני שעת לקיחתו קפיד דלא ממעטין בתר הכי דגבי מאי איכא בין דידיה לרבי יוסי ומגלה שאם הוחלפו בשעת שחיטה על ידי השגאי והמשכה אין אחד מן הראשונים קיים עליו ויושא דקתני דבעינן שהוחלפו מכל חבורה לכל הפסח טעמא משום דבעי אתמויי ומימר אם שלך הוא הפסח הזה ידינו משוכות משלנו ונמנינו על שלך ואם לאו דהיכא חד מבעליו התם מאן קא ממני עליה והיאך יכולין לומר ונמנינו על זה בלא רשות בעליו: (א) ואם ימעט. משמע אם רצו מתמעטין ומשכין ובלבד שיהא אחד מבני החבורה קיים דאם ימעט משמע שיש שיור: כמות שהוא. בלא בעלים ואם

פסי' ד"ל ונמח פ"ו · [תוספ' פ"ט] · [לעיל נא.]

הגהות הב"ח (א) רש"י ד"ה דלא כרבי יהודה וכו' רשות בעליו סס"ד ואח"כ מ"ה מלמד שמתמעטין ואם ימעט:

רצו כולן לימשך ימנו עליו אחרים מתחלה אבל לבני חבורה ראשונה לא קפיד קרא: כיון דאמר ר' יהודה. בפרקין דלעיל (דף נא.) מעיקרא לאמטויי אחרינא עליה קאי ואפילו אין שם תערובת הלכך זה הבא מן השוק ונמנה עליו בכל מקום שהוא הוי ליה אחד מבני חבורה ראשונה: מתני' נמי דייקא. דר' יהודה היא: חמשה וארבעה לא. חמש חבורות שיש בהן אחת של ארבעה אנשים ואין בה כדי ליתן חלק אחד לכל פסח ופסח לא שרי מתני': מ"מ לאו משום דלא פש אחד מבני חבורה גביה. שאם נתחלפו פסחן של אלו לאותה חבורה שנתחדשה אחרי כן שיש ארבעה מארבע חבורות ומאותה של ארבעה לא הי' בה דלרבי יוסי טעמא משום דצריך אחד מבעליו שימנה בו את האחרון אבל לחבורה ראשונה דשעת לקיחה לא קפיד אפילו איכא בהו חבורה של ד' נמי איכא תקנתא שימשו מן השוק אחד עמהן בכל מקום שהוא פסחו ונמנו עליו חמשה אנשים כדי לחלק אחד לכל פסח ופסח אלא שמעת מינה אבני חבורה קפיד:

הדרן עלך מי שהיה טמא

הדרן עלך מי שהיה טמא וסליקא לה פסח שני

פסקי הלכות פסח שני בקצרה*

כתיב בתורה איש איש כי יהיה טמא לנפש או בדרך רחוקה לכם או לדורותיכם ועשה פסח לה' בחדש השני בארבעה עשר יום בין הערבים יעשו אותו וגו' ככל חקת הפסח יעשו אותו. ושנינו שאף כל אונס במשמע שאם נאנס או שגג בראשון יעשה בשני אלא שטמא ודרך רחוקה פטורין מן הכרת אפילו הזיד בשני ושאר אונסין בראשון אם הזיד בשני חייב כרת · אבל הזיד בראשון בלא שום אונס ושגגה אפילו נאנס בשני חייב כרת: איזהו דרך רחוקה מי שהיה ביני ובין ירושלים יום ט"ו מיל או יותר היה פחות מזה ולא הגיע לירושלים מפני שעכבוהו בהמות או שהיה בירושלים והיה חולה ברגליו ולא הגיע לעזרה עד שעבר זמן הקרבה הרי זה אנוס ואינו בדרך רחוקה. היה חבוש ביד ישראל חוץ לחומת ירושלים והבטיחוהו לצאת לערב שוחטין עליו אבל נחבש ביד נכרים אין שוחטין עליו עד שיצא ואם שחטו עליו ויצא הרי זה אוכל. שחטו עליו ולא יצא וכן האונן והחולה והזקן שיכולין לאכול ששחטו עליהן ואחר שנזרק הדם נטמאו במת ואינן יכולין לאכול פטורין מפסח שני [וכן כל מי שהיה ראוי בשעת שחיטה וזריקה ונדחה אחר כך פטור מפסח שני]. טמא שיכול להטהר בפסח ראשון ולא טבל וישב בטומאתו וכן הערל שלא מל בראשון הרי זה הזיד בראשון: ואיזהו טמא שנדחה לפסח שני כגון זבים וזבות נדות ויולדות ובועלי נדות אבל הנוגע בנבלה ושרץ וכיוצא בהם ביום י"ד הרי זה טובל ושוחטין עליו אחר שיטבול ואוכל לערב. וזב שראה ב' ראיות וטבל בשביעי שוחטין עליו ואוכל לערב וכן שומרת יום כנגד יום ואם ראו אחר זריקת הדם פטורין מפסח שני ואין שוחטין על הזבה בשביעי שלה: טמא מת שחל ז' שלו בע"פ אף על פי שהוזה עליו וטבל וראוי לאכול קדשים לערב אין שוחטין עליו ונדחה לשני בד"א שנטמא בטומאת מת שהנזיר מגלח עליהן אבל בטומאת מת שאין הנזיר מגלח עליהן שוחטין עליו בז' שלו אחר הזאה וטבילה. מי שעשה פסח בחזקת שהוא טהור ואח"כ נודע לו שהיה טמא בטומאת התהום פטור מפסח שני אבל נודע לו שנטמא בטומאת ודאי חייב בפסח שני. בד"א בטהור אבל טמא כגון *טמא מת שנטמא בטומאת התהום בשביעי שלו אע"פ שנודע לו אחר שעשה הפסח חייב בפסח שני שחזקת הטמא טמא עד שנטהר ספק טומאת התהום טהור לפסח: בטומאת מת בין ודאי בין ספקו יחידים שהן מיעוט הצבור נדחין ולא לצבור אפילו הם מחצה קהל אין נדחין שאם היה בפסח ראשון רוב הקהל או הכהנים או כלי השרת טמאים בטומאת מת עושין הפסח הטמאים עם הטהורים בטומאה אפילו היה ברוב הטמאים רק א' [עודף] · היו מחצה על מחצה כולן עושין בראשון והטהורים עושין לעצמן בטהרה וטמאים לעצמן בטומאה. היו הנשים משלימין לרוב טהורים הטהורים עושין הראשון והטמאים אינן עושין לא הראשון ולא השני. היו רוב הקהל טמאים בשאר טומאות ומיעוטן טמאי מת אותן טמאי מת אינן עושין לא בראשון לפי שהן מיעוט וגם שני אינן עושין לפי שאין היחידים עושין

בשני אלא בזמן שרוב הקהל עשו הראשון · וכן אם היו רוב הקהל טמאי מתים ומיעוטן בשאר טומאות הטמאי מתים עושין בראשון והמיעוטין אינן עושין לא בראשון לפי שאין טומאה דוחה בראשון אלא טומאת מת לבד ובשני אינן עושין לפי שאין עושין בפסח שני אלא אם נעשה הראשון בטהרה · היו שליש הקהל טהורים ושליש טמאי מתים ושליש טמאים בשאר טומאות הטמאי מתים אינן עושין לא בראשון שהרי הן מיעוטין לגבי טהורים עם הטמאים משאר טומאות ובשני אינן עושין שהרי מיעוט עשו בראשון. כיצד משערין הפסח לידע אם רוב הקהל טמאים או טהורים אין משערין בכל האוכלין שאפשר שיהיו עשרים נמנים על פסח א' ומשלחין אותו לשחוט ביד א' אלא משערין בכל הנכנסין לעזרה. ועד שהן מבחוץ קודם שתכנס כת הראשונה משערין אותן. פסח שהקריבוהו בטומאה נאכל בטומאה שמתחלתו לא בא אלא לאכילה. ואינו נאכל אלא לטמאי מת שנדחית להם הטומאה ולכיוצא בהן מטמאי טומאת מגע אבל לא לטמאים שטומאה יוצאה מגופן ואם אכלו פטורין ואפילו אכלו טמאי מת מהאימורין שלו פטורין. *בד"א שהפסח נאכל בטומאה כשנטמאו הציבור קודם זריקת הדם אבל אם נטמאו לאחר זריקת הדם לא יאכל· שחטוהו בטהרה ונטמאו רוב הציבור קודם זריקה זורק את הדם והפסח לא יאכל. היו כלי שרת טמאים בשרץ וכיוצא בו אע"פ שמטמאין את הבשר לא יעשוהו אלא הטהורים ויאכל אע"פ שהוא טמא שמוטב שיאכל בטומאת בשר שהיא בלאו ולא יאכלוהו טמאי הגוף שהם בכרת: מה בין פסח ראשון לשני הראשון אסור בחמץ בבל יראה ובל ימצא ואינו נשחט על חמץ [*וצריך ביקור ד' ימים] ואין מוציאין ממנו חוץ לחבורה וטעון הלל באכילתו ומביאין עמו חגיגה ואפשר שיבא בטומאה אם נטמא רוב הקהל טומאת מת אבל פסח שני חמץ ומצה עמו בבית *[ואין נשחט בג' כתות ואין צריך ביקור] ואינו טעון הלל באכילתו ומוציאין אותו חוץ לחבורתו *ואין מביאין עמו חגיגה ואינו בא בטומאה ושניהם דוחין את השבת וטעונין הלל בעשייתן ונאכלין צלי בבית אחד על מצה ומרור ואין מותירין מהן ואין שוברין בהן את העצם: נשים שנדחו לשני בין מפני טומאה ודרך רחוקה בין משאר אונס ושגגה הרי פסח שני להן רשות לפיכך אינן שוחטין עליהן בפני עצמן בשבת בפסח שני. *האונן שמת לו מת אחר חצות בי"ד שכבר נתחייב בק"פ שוחטין עליו וטובל ואוכל שאנינות לילה מדרבנן וכן *מת לו מת בי"ג ונקבר בי"ד אבל מת לו מת קודם חצות ידחה לשני ואם שחטו וזרקו עליו טובל ואוכל לערב. גר שנתגייר בין פסח ראשון לשני וכן קטן שהגדיל בין ב' פסחים חייבין בפסח שני ואם שחטו עליו בראשון פטור. הזאה אינה דוחה שבת כגון (*זב) שהגיע ז' שלו בי"ד בשבת אין מזין עליו ואפילו חל הי"ג בשבת אין מזין עליו בי"ג אלא למחרת בי"ד ואין שוחטין עליו אלא ידחה לשני:

(שאר עניני סדר וחובת ליל ט"ו מבואר הכל בש"ע א"ח)

בעזרת האל יתברך נשלם סדר פסח ראשון ושני

עי' כסף משנה פ"ו מהל' ק"פ כד"ה · סיים לדעת רש"י ואין כן דעת התוספות והרמב"ם ז"ל · תוספתא פ"ט · שם · מ"ר סד · נ"ל טמא מת

מכאן אמרו יפה שתיקה לחכמים ק"ו לטפשים וכתיב גם אויל מחריש חכם יחשב אטם שפתיו נבון: שתי חבורות שנתערבו פסחיהם אלו מושכין להם אחד וכו'. פי' בני חבורה זו מושכין לו כבש אחד ובני חבורה האחרת מושכין להם הכבש האחר אחד מבני חבורה זו בא ונמנה עם בני חבורה האחרת ואחד מבני חבורה האחרת בא לו ונמנה עם בני חבורה זו וכקדם אומרי' אם זה הפסח שלנו הוא ידינו משוכות משלך ונמניתה על שלנו ואם זה הפסח הוא שהיה לחבורתך ויש לך חלק בכללם הרי הוא לך וידיך משוכות משלנו תמנינו על שלך ולמה צריכין אנו לכך מפני שאנו צריכין להיות מי שנמנה עיקר על אותו הפסח מתחלה יהיה מנוי גם עכשיו עיקר וימנה אחרים עמו· וכך עושין בני חבור' האחרת כאשר פירשנו מעשה האחרת כך מעשה השנית· וכן חמש חבורות של חמשה חמשה ושל עשרה עשרה נמשכין להם אחד מכל וכך הן אומרין ופשוטה היא: שנים שנתערבו פסחיהן זה מושך לו כבש אחד וזה מושך לו כבש אחד זה מכנה עמו על פסחו אחד מן השוק וזה מכנה עמו על פסחו אחד מן השוק נמצא בכל פסח שנים שנים זה ראשון שהפריש אותו הכבש שנתערב לפסחו מניח אותו הכבש שמשך לעצמו לזה שהביאו מן השוק ומכנה עמו עליו והולך אצל שמשך אותו הכבש השני וגם הוא עושה כמעשה חברו וכן הן אומרין אם שלי הפסח הזה ידיך משוכות מאותו שנמנית שלך ונמנית על שלי ואם שלך הוא ידי משוכות משלי ונמנית על שלך וכן עושה השני נמצא אותו שהביאו מן השוק הם עקרים על הזבח והעיקרים שהיו מקודם נמנין עמהם ויתכן שכל אחד מהם יוצא בעיקר פסחו של חבירו בכלל אלו שהביאו מן השוק ולפיכך אמרנו לימא מתני' דלא כרבי יהודה דתניא ואם ימעט הבית מהיות משה מלמד שמתמעטין והולכין ובלבד שיהיה אחד מבני חבורה קיים דברי ר' יהודה ר' יוסי אומר ובלבד שלא יניח הפסח כמות שהוא כלומר לא בא הכתוב אלא ללמד שלא יניחו הפסח כמות שהוא ומשני א"ר יוחנן אפילו תימא רבי יהודה היא מתני' כיון דאמר רבי יהודה אין שוחטין את הפסח על היחיד מעיקרא לאמטויי אחרינא בהדיה קאי וכאלו האי דאתי עכשיו ונמנה בהדיה על פסחו כתחלה בהדיה הוא כאלו נמנה על הראשון ותרוייהו עיקרא נינהו הלכך כבני החבורה דמי: אמר רב אשי מתני' נמי דיקא דצריך להשאר אחד מבני חבורה מדקתני וכן חמש חבורות של חמשה חמשה ולא קתני וכן חמש חבורות של (ארבעה) [חמשה]

ארבעה אלא תני חמשה חמשה שהלכו ארבעה מהן בכל חבורה אחד מהן וישאר אחד מהן בחבורה שלו ויביאו אצלו מכל חבורה אחת נמצאו בכל חבורה חמשה ואילו היו חמש חבורות ארבעה וחבורה אחת ארבעה נמצאת חבורה שיש בה ארבעה הולך אחד מהן בכל חבורה הולכו הארבעה בארבע חבורות ולא נשאר בחבורתן אחד אלא (הן הן) הארבעה שבאו ונתקבצו בה אחד מכל חבורה ש"מ מדלא קתני ארבעה אלא חמשה חמשה צריך שישאר אחד מבני חבורתו קיים שם ש"מ: הדרן עלך מי שהיה טמא

*FOR THE TRANSLATION OF THIS SECTION, SEE END OF VOLUME

sponsible for each other.[5] [99a] Hence the Sages said: Silence is better for the wise, and how much more so for fools, as it is said, *Even a fool, when he holdeth his peace, is counted wise.*[6]

IF THE PASCHAL SACRIFICES BELONGING TO TWO [SINGLE PERSONS] BECOME MIXED UP etc. Shall we say that our Mishnah does not agree with R. Judah? For it was taught: *And if the household be too little for a lamb:*[7] this teaches that they may go on decreasing [their numbers],[8] providing, however, that one of them
a remains:[1] this is R. Judah's view. R. Jose said: Providing that they do not leave the Paschal sacrifice as it is![2]—Said R. Joḥanan: You may even say [that it agrees with] R. Judah. Since R. Judah said, One may not slaughter the Passover-offering for a single person, then from the outset he stood to register another with himself, and he [the newly-registered person] is accounted as one of the [original] members of the company. R. Ashi said: Our Mishnah too proves this, for it teaches, SIMILARLY, IF THERE ARE FIVE COMPANIES CONSISTING OF FIVE MEMBERS EACH; thus, only of five [each], but not [if some consist] of five and [others of] four; is not [the reason] because one of the [original] members of the company does not remain with it?[3] This proves it.

(5) Thus in the first case one animal must be destroyed, whatever happens, while in the second both are eaten. (6) Prov. XVII, 28. (7) Ex. XII, 4. (8) V. *supra* 89a, n. c3.

a (1) For '*if it be too few*' implies that someone at least is registered for it. (2) Without owners. Now R. Judah must mean that one of the persons who *originally* registered for it, when the animal was first set aside for a Passover-offering, must remain registered for it, while in R. Jose's opinion it is sufficient that *someone* remains, even if he is not of those who originally registered for it. For if R. Judah's view is not as stated, it does not differ in any way from R. Jose's. But in the Mishnah, when A, the only original owner of one of the sacrifices, declares, 'If this animal is not mine, I withdraw from the other and register for this', the other is left without anyone who first registered for it, since A is the only original owner. (3) If it consisted of less than five, and one joins each other's company. For if it were unnecessary for an original member to remain, the Mishnah could teach that whatever the number of original members, each company increases itself to five and then does as stated.

GEMARA. [98b] But he brings sacrifices to the place of unfitness?[5]—R. Simeon is consistent with his view, for he maintains: One may bring sacrifices to the place of unfitness.[6] For we learned: If a guilt-offering was mixed up with a peace-offering,—R. Simeon said: They must be slaughtered at the north [side of the altar][7] and eaten in accordance with [the laws of] the more stringent of them.[8] Said they to him: One may not bring sacrifices to the place of unfitness.[9]

Now according to the Rabbis, what do we do?[10]—Said Raba: We wait until they receive a blemish. Then he brings a choice
a animal and declares: 'Wherever the Passover-offering may be,[1] let it[s sanctity] be transferred to this one,'[2] and he eats them in accordance with the laws of a blemished firstling.[3]

MISHNAH. IF A COMPANY LOST THEIR PASCHAL SACRIFICE AND INSTRUCTED ONE [OF THEIR NUMBER], 'GO AND SEEK IT, AND SLAUGHTER IT ON OUR BEHALF'; AND HE WENT, FOUND, AND SLAUGHTERED IT, WHILE THEY [ALSO] TOOK AN ANIMAL AND SLAUGHTERED [IT]: IF HIS WAS SLAUGHTERED FIRST, HE EATS OF HIS AND THEY EAT WITH HIM.[4] WHILE IF THEIRS WAS FIRST SLAUGHTERED, THEY EAT OF THEIRS,[5] WHILE HE EATS OF HIS.[6] BUT IF IT IS UNKNOWN WHICH OF THEM WAS FIRST SLAUGHTERED, OR IF THEY KILLED BOTH OF THEM AT THE SAME TIME, HE EATS OF HIS, BUT THEY MAY NOT EAT WITH HIM;[7] WHILE THEIRS GOES FORTH TO THE PLACE OF BURNING,[8] AND THEY ARE EXEMPT FROM KEEPING THE SECOND PASSOVER.[9]

IF HE SAID TO THEM, 'IF I DELAY, GO FORTH AND SLAUGHTER ON MY BEHALF,'[10] [AND] THEN HE WENT AND FOUND AND SLAUGHTERED [IT], WHILE THEY TOOK [ANOTHER] AND SLAUGHTERED [IT], IF THEIRS WAS SLAUGHTERED FIRST,
b THEY EAT OF THEIRS WHILE HE EATS WITH THEM.[1] WHILE IF HIS WAS SLAUGHTERED FIRST, HE EATS OF HIS[2] AND THEY EAT OF THEIRS.[3] BUT IF IT IS UNKNOWN WHICH OF THEM WAS SLAUGHTERED FIRST, OR IF THEY SLAUGHTERED BOTH OF THEM AT THE SAME TIME, THEY EAT OF THEIRS, BUT HE MAY NOT EAT WITH THEM, WHILE HIS OWN GOES FORTH TO THE PLACE OF BURNING, AND HE IS EXEMPT FROM KEEPING THE SECOND PASSOVER.[4]

IF HE INSTRUCTED THEM, AND THEY INSTRUCTED HIM,[5] THEY MUST ALL EAT OF THE FIRST [TO BE SLAUGHTERED],[6] AND IF IT IS UNKNOWN WHICH OF THEM WAS SLAUGHTERED FIRST, BOTH GO FORTH TO THE PLACE OF BURNING.[7]

IF HE DID NOT INSTRUCT THEM AND THEY DID NOT INSTRUCT HIM,[8] THEY ARE NOT RESPONSIBLE FOR EACH OTHER.[9]

IF THE PASCHAL SACRIFICES OF TWO COMPANIES BECOME MIXED UP, THESE TAKE POSSESSION OF ONE [ANIMAL] AND THOSE TAKE POSSESSION OF ONE. ONE MEMBER OF THESE JOINS THOSE, AND ONE MEMBER OF THOSE JOINS THESE, AND THEY DECLARE THUS:[10] 'IF THIS PASCHAL SACRIFICE IS OURS, YOUR HANDS ARE WITHDRAWN FROM YOUR OWN AND YOU ARE REGISTERED FOR OURS; WHILE IF THIS PASCHAL SACRIFICE IS YOURS,[11] OUR HANDS ARE WITHDRAWN FROM OURS AND WE ARE REGISTERED FOR YOURS.[12] SIMILARLY, IF THERE ARE FIVE COMPANIES CONSISTING OF FIVE MEMBERS EACH OR OF TEN EACH, THEY DRAW ONE FROM EACH COMPANY TO THEMSELVES AND MAKE THE FOREGOING DECLA-
c RATION.[1]

IF THE PASCHAL SACRIFICES BELONGING TO TWO [SINGLE INDIVIDUALS] BECOME MIXED UP, EACH TAKES POSSESSION OF ONE [ANIMAL]; THIS ONE REGISTERS A STRANGER[2] WITH HIMSELF AND THAT ONE REGISTERS A STRANGER WITH HIMSELF.[3] THE FORMER GOES OVER TO THE LATTER SACRIFICE AND THE LATTER GOES OVER TO THE FORMER SACRIFICE, AND THEY [I.E., EACH OWNER] DECLARE THUS: 'IF THIS PASCHAL SACRIFICE IS MINE, YOUR HANDS ARE WITHDRAWN FROM YOUR OWN AND YOU ARE REGISTERED FOR MINE; WHILE IF THIS PASCHAL SACRIFICE IS YOURS, MY HANDS ARE WITHDRAWN FROM MINE AND I AM REGISTERED FOR YOURS.'[4]

GEMARA. Our Rabbis taught: If he instructed them and they instructed him, they must [all] eat of the first. If he did not instruct them and they did not instruct him, they are not re-

(5) This difficulty arises on R. Simeon's ruling. A firstling may be eaten two days and the night in between, whereas the Passover-offering may be eaten only on the first night. Thus if it is not eaten by morning he must burn it as *nothar* (v. Glos.), whereas it is actually still fit. (6) In such a case, rather than let them graze until they receive a blemish, which is the only alternative. (7) The side prescribed for the slaughtering of a guilt-offering. Peace-offerings could be slaughtered on any side of the Temple Court. (8) I.e., as guilt-offerings, viz., during one day and a night only, within the Temple precincts, and by male priests.—A peace-offering is eaten two days and one night, anywhere in Jerusalem, and by Israelites as well as priests. (9) But they must be left to graze until blemished. (10) When a Passover-offering is mixed up with a firstling.—When it is mixed up with a burnt-offering or guilt-offering, or when a peace-offering is mixed up with a guilt-offering, the expedient stated in the Mishnah is possible. But a firstling, even when blemished, cannot be redeemed in the sense that it becomes *ḥullin*, but must be eaten by a priest with its blemish; while on the other hand when a Passover-offering receives a blemish, it must be redeemed and may not be eaten otherwise.

a (1) I.e., whichever of these two animals is the Passover. (2) Thus whichever is the Passover-offering is redeemed. (3) These are: it may not be slaughtered or sold in the ordinary abattoir, nor weighed with the ordinary weights. These restrictions do not apply to a redeemed Passover-offering, and would not apply here if he knew which it was. (4) By instructing him to slaughter it on their behalf they become registered for his and cannot register for another after the first was slaughtered. Hence their own is unfit and must be burnt. (5) By slaughtering their own first they *ipso facto* cancelled their registration for the original, which is permissible, v. *supra* 89a. (6) But not of theirs, since he had not registered with them. (7) Lest their own was slaughtered first, whereby they had cancelled their registration for his. (8) For his may have been killed first; v. n. a4. (9) Because they were certainly registered for one animal at the first Passover, while the eating is not indispensable. (10) But they did not instruct him to slaughter the lost animal on their behalf.

b (1) While his own must be burnt, for according to his instructions he was now registered for theirs; hence his is unfit, having none registered for it. (2) Cf. *supra*, n. a5. (3) For they were not registered for his, since they had not instructed him to slaughter it on their behalf. (4) Cf. *supra* n. a9. (5) He instructed them to slaughter on his behalf if he delayed, and they instructed him to slaughter on their behalf if he found the lost animal. (6) For which they are all automatically registered now. (7) Each must thus go forth lest it was slaughtered last and had none registered for it. (8) To slaughter on each other's behalf. (9) Each party eats of its own, whatever the order of their slaughtering. (10) Each company declares thus to the newcomer. (11) I.e., it belongs to your first company. (12) One of each company must join the other, for otherwise each company would have to withdraw *en masse* from their own, if it had been taken by the second, thus leaving it momentarily entirely without owners, and this is forbidden.

c (1) Each company consists of four new members and one original member. The latter (or all the original members, where each company consisted of more than five) makes the foregoing declaration to each new member in turn. (2) Lit., 'a man from the street'. (3) Thus there are now two registered persons for each sacrifice. (4) The general reasoning is the same as in the previous cases.

לז א מיי' פ"ו מהל' פסולי המוקדשין הלכה טו:

לז ב מיי' שם והל' יג ופ"ד מהל' ק"פ הלכה ח:

לח ג מיי' פ"ג מהל' ק"פ הלכה ד:

לט ד מיי' שם הלכה ה:

מ ה ו מיי' שם הל' ו:

מא ז ח מיי' שם הל' ז:

מב ט מיי' שם הלכה ח:

והא קא מייתי קדשים לבית הפסול רבי שמעון לטעמיה דאמר מביאין קדשים לבית הפסול *דתנן אשם שנתערב בשלמים רבי שמעון אומר ישחטו בצפון ויאכלו כחומר שבהן אמרו לו *אין מביאין קדשים לבית הפסול ורבנן היכי עבדינן אמר רבא [ב]נמתין לו עד שיוממו ויביא בהמה שמינה ולימא כל היכא דאיתיה לפסח תחול עליה דהאי ואכיל להו בתורת בכור בעל מום:

מתני' *[ג]חבורה שאבד פסחה ואמרו לאחד צא ובקש ושחוט עלינו והלך ומצא ושחט והם לקחו ושחטו אם שלו נשחט ראשון הוא אוכל משלו והם אוכלין עמו משלו ואם שלהן נשחט ראשון הם אוכלין משלהן והוא אוכל משלו ואם אינו ידוע איזה מהן נשחט ראשון או ששחטו שניהם כאחד הוא אוכל משלו והם אינם אוכלין עמו ושלהן יצא לבית השריפה ופטורין מלעשות פסח שני [ד]אמר להן אם אחרתי צאו ושחטו עלי הלך ומצא ושחט והן לקחו ושחטו אם שלהן נשחט ראשון הן אוכלין משלהן והוא אוכל עמהן ואם שלו נשחט ראשון הוא אוכל משלו והן אוכלין משלהם ואם אינו ידוע איזה מהן נשחט ראשון או ששחטו שניהם כאחד הן אוכלין משלהן והוא אינו אוכל עמהן ושלו יצא לבית השריפה ופטור מלעשות פסח שני [ה]אמר להן ואמרו לו אוכלין כולן מן הראשון ואם אין ידוע איזה מהן נשחט ראשון שניהם יוצאין לבית השריפה [ו]לא אמר להן ולא אמרו לו אין אחראין זה לזה [ז]שתי חבורות שנתערבו פסחיהן אלו מושכין להן אחד ואלו מושכין להן אחד אחד מאלו בא לו אצל אלו ואחד מאלו בא לו אצל אלו וכך הם אומרים אם שלנו הוא הפסח הזה ידיך משוכות משלך ונמנית על שלנו ואם שלך הוא הפסח הזה ידינו משוכות משלנו ונמנינו על שלך וכן [ח]חמש חבורות של חמשה חמשה ושל עשרה עשרה מושכין להן אחד מכל חבורה וחבורה וכן הם אומרים [ט]שנים שנתערבו פסחיהן זה מושך לו אחד וזה מושך לו אחד זה ממנה עמו אחד מן השוק וזה ממנה עמו אחד מן השוק זה בא אצל זה וזה בא אצל זה וכך הם אומרים אם שלי הוא פסח זה ידיך משוכות משלך ונמנית על שלי ואם שלך הוא פסח זה ידי משוכות משלי ונמניתי על שלך:

ופטורין מלעשות פסח שני. לא דמי להא דאמר לעיל [א] (פח:) שכח לפני זריקה חייבין לעשות פסח שני:

הדרן עלך מי שהיה

גמ' תנו רבנן *אמר להן ואמרו לו אוכל מן הראשון [י]לא אמר להן ולא אמרו לו אינן אחראין זה לזה

מכאן

והא קא מייתי קדשים לבית הפסול. לר"ש קא פריך דממעט בזמן אכילת הבשר ושורפו לנותר עד בקר שלא כדין משום ספק פסח והל"ל ירעו שדין הבכור לשני ימים ולילה אחד: מביאין קדשים לבית הפסול. למעט בזמן אכילתן מוטב מלנתקן לרעייה: ישחטו בצפון. כחומר אשם ולא כשלמים בכל מקום ויאכלו כחומר שבהן כתורת האשם לזכרי כהונה ליום ולילה לפנים מן הקלעים: לבית הפסול. שממעט בזמן אכילת השלמים אלא ירעו: ורבנן. דאמרי אין מביאין היכי עבדינן לפסח שנתערב בבכורות בשלמא גבי אשם שנתערב בשלמים או פסח שנתערב בעולה ואשם איכא למימר ירעו וימכרו ויביא בדמיהן אותן קרבנות כדאמרן לעיל אבל בכור נאמר בו לא תפדה ואין לו פדיון ואינו תופס את דמיו ואינו יוצא מקדושתו לחול על המעות אלא נאכל במומו לכהן ופסח בר פדיון הוא ואינו נאכל בלא פדיון: ממתין עד שיוממו ויביא בהמה שמינה. ביפה שבהן: ונימא כל היכא דאיתיה לפסח תיחול · קדושתיה אהנך מעות ומייתי בהנך מעות שלמים כדין מותר הפסח: ואכיל להו. לכל התערובת: בתורת בכור בעל מום. ואיזו היא תורתו אין נשחט באטליז ואין נמכר באטליז ואין נשקל בליטרא ואם היה מכיר בפסח שנפדה היה שוחטו ומוכרו באטליז אם ירצה: מתני' לא ובקש. את האבוד ושחוט עלינו: אם שלו נשחט ראשון. הואיל והם אמרו לו שחוט עלינו על שלו הם נמנין ושוב אין יכולין להימנות על שלהן ושלהן ישרף דפסח בלא בעלים הוא ואוכלין כולן משלו: ואם שלהן נשחט ראשון הוא אוכל משלו · שהרי לא נמנה על שלהן והם אוכלין משלהן שהרי חזרו בהן מן האבוד ומשכו ידיהן ממנו: והן אינן אוכלין עמו. שמא שלהן נשחט ראשון ונמשכו מזה: ושלהן יצא לבית השריפה. שמא שלו נשחט ראשון ואין נמנים על השני: ופטורין מפסח שני. דממה נפשך בראשון נימנו ואכילה לא מעכבא: אמר להם אם איחרתי שחטו עלי · יחיד שהלך לבקשו ואמר לבני חבורה אם איחרתי שחטו עלי והמנוני עמכם והן לא אמרו שחוט עלינו: הוא אוכל עמהן. ושלו ישרף דכיון שהמנוהו על שלהן הרי נמשך מן הראשון וחזר בו משליחותו: ושלו יצא לבית השריפה. שמא שלהן נשחט ראשון ונמשך משלו שהרי עשאן שלוחין: ופטור מפסח שני. ממה נפשך בראשון יצא: אמר להם. שחטו עלי אם איחרתי ואמרו לו בקש ושחוט עלינו יאכלו כולן מן הראשון דהם שלוחיו והוא שלוחם: ואם אין ידוע איזהו נשחט ראשון. ישרפו שניהם ופטורין מפסח שני: אינן אחראין זה לזה. אין אחריות וטענה זה על זה ואין זה וזה חוששין איזו נשחט ראשון אלא הן אוכלים משלהם והוא אוכל משלו: אלו מושכין להם אחד · מן הפסחים ואלו מושכין אחד: אחד. מבני חבורה זו בא לו אצל חבורה ז

ואחד

ואחד מזו בא לו אצל זו: וכן הם אומרים. לאותו יחיד הבא אצלן: אם שלנו הוא פסח זה. שמשכנו אליו ויפה בררנו את שלנו משוך ידיך משלך והימנה עמנו על שלנו ואם שלך הוא פסח זה הרי אתה עליו וידינו משוכות משלנו ויהא לבני חבורה האחרת ונמנינו על זה שלך נמצא אם החליפו הרי זה הומשכו כל חבורה וחבורה משלהן ונמנו על אותו שבררו וכן בני חבורה השניה אומרים ליחיד הבא אצלן ועל כרחינו צריך אחד מאלו לבוא אצל אלו ולימנות עמהן ולא אמרינן ימשכו אלו משלהן בכל מקום שהוא ואלו משלהן ויחזרו וימנו אלו על האחד ואלו על האחד משום דאמרינן בברייתא בגמ' בין לרבי יהודה בין לר' יוסי אסור לימשך כל בני חבורה מן הפסח להניחו בלא בעלים ועכשיו כשהאחד מבני החבורה זו בא אצל החבורה האחרת ממה נפשך אין כאן פסח בלא בעלים אם יפה בררו הרי כל חבורתו עליו חוץ מן האחד שפירש מהן ומשך ידו ואם הם החליפו הרי הלך אחד מהם עם חבורה האחרת וכשמשכו הנותרים את ידיהן ממנו נשאר הוא עליו: וכן חמש חבורות של חמש חמש. בני אדם שנתערבו פסחיהם כל חבורה וחבורה מושכים להם א' מן הפסחים וחמש אנשים שבכל חבורה וחבורה מתחלקין לחמשה פסחים שאם החליפו לא יהא כאן פסח שלא יהא אחד מבעליו הראשונים עליו: וכן הם אומרים. כשנעשו עתה חבורות חדשים אומרים הארבעה לאחד אם שלך הוא פסח זה ידי ארבעתינו משוכין מארבעה פסחינו בכל מקום שהן ונימנינו עמך וכך הן חוזרין ואומרים לשני וכן הארבעה לכל א' שבחבורה וכן כל חבורה וחבורה: שנתערבו פסחיהן. ראובן ושמעון שנתערבו פסחיהן ראובן מושך לו אחד ושמעון מושך לו אחד ראובן הולך וממנה עמו את לוי מן השוק ואומר כל מקום שהוא פסח שלי הרי אתה נמנה עליו שמעון ממנה עמו את יהודה מן השוק דעכשיו יהו שנים על כל אחד כל מקום שהוא: זה בא אצל זה. ראובן בא לו אצל פסח שמשך לו שמעון ושמעון בא לו אצל פסח שמשך לו ראובן וכן אומר ראובן ליהודה הנשאר על פסח שבירר לו שמעון אם שלך הוא פסח זה שיפה בירר לו שמעון תחלה הרי ידי משוכות משלי והריני נמנה עמך על זה ואם שלי הוא פסח זה שלא כיוונו לברר תחלה יפה ואין זה פסח שנימנית עליו עם שמעון הרי ידיך משוכות משלך והמנה על זה ולכך הוצרך כל אחד להמנות אחד מן השוק שאם באו להתנות כשהן יחידין ולומר אם שלי הוא פסח זה ושלך הרי יפה בררנו ואם לאו הריני מושך משלי ונמנה על שלך נמצא כשהוא נמשך משלו הרי הוא מניח פסחו כמות שהוא כלומר בלא בעלים שעדיין לא נמנה אחר עליו ואפי' לר' יוסי *לית ליה והא ליכא למימר שימנה כל א' על של חבירו קודם שימשך משלו דהנמנה על שני פסחים אין זה מנין: גמ'

מכאן

זבחים עט.

קדושין מא:

[תוספתא פ"ט]

[לקמן צט.]

רבינו חננאל

יאכלו ואקשי' והא קא מייתי קדשים לבית הפסול שדין הבכור להאכל שני ימים ולילה אחד כדתנן בפ' איזהו מקומן של זבחים והפסח אינו נאכל אלא בלילה ומותר הפסח נמי אינו נאכל אלא ליום ולילה כמו שאמרנו בפרק שקודם זה וכיון שאתה אוכל הבכור בקדושת פסח אתה גורם לו להפסל הנותר בבקר כדין הפסח והוא כשר עדיין עד יום ג' והוי וכי מביאין קדשים כי האי גוונא לבית הפסול דתנן בזבחים פ"ח אשם שנתערב בשלמים רבי שמעון אומר שניהם ישחטו בצפון ויאכל כחמור שבהן אמר לו אין מביאין קדשים לבית הפסול אלא לרבנן היכי לעביד אמר רבא ממתין להם עד שיומםו ומביא בהמה שמינה ואומר כל היכי דאיתיה לפסח תחול קדושתיה עליה דהאי ואכיל להו לכך בתורת בכור: מתני' חבורה שאבדה פסחה ואמרו לאחד צא ובקש עלינו כו' ת"ר אמר להם ואמרו לו אוכלין מן הראשון לא אמר להם ולא אמרו לו אין אחראין זה לזה

הגהות מהר"ב רנשבורג

[א] תוס' ד"ה ופטורין וכו' דלא דמי להא דאמר לעיל וכו'. ע"כ עי' מהרש"א ולח"מ פ"ג מהלכות ק"פ הלכה ד' והגל"ת לא ראהו:

*המפריש פסחו ומת לא יביאנו בנו אחריו לשם פסח אלא לשם שלמים: **גמ'** אמר רב הונא בריה דרב יהושע שמע מינה תלת *שמע מינה בעלי חיים נדחין וש"מ דחוי מעיקרא הוי דחוי ושמע מינה יש דחוי בדמים: המפריש פסחו וכו': ת"ר *המפריש את פסחו ומת אם בנו ממונה עמו יביאנו לשום פסח אין בנו ממונה עמו יביאנו לשום שלמים לששה עשר ל"ו אין לט"ו לא קא סבר *נדרים ונדבות אין קריבין בי"ט דמית האב אימת אילימא דמית קודם חצות בנו ממונה עמו יביאנו לשום פסח הא חלה אנינות עילויה מעיקרא אלא דמית אחר חצות אין בנו ממונה עמו יביאנו לשום שלמים הא קבעתיה חצות אמר (*רבא) לעולם דמית קודם חצות ומאי יביאנו לשום פסח לשום פסח שני אביי אמר לצדדין קתני מת אחר חצות בנו ממונה עמו יביאנו לשום פסח מת קודם חצות אין בנו ממונה עמו יביאנו לשום שלמים רב שרביא אמר לעולם דמית לאחר חצות וכגון שהיה אביו גוסס בחצות רב אשי אמר *לעולם דמית לאחר חצות ור"ש היא דאמר *אין בעלי חיים נדחין רבינא אמר כגון שהפרישו אחר חצות ומתו בעלים אחר חצות וקא סבר חצות קבע: **מתני'** *הפסח שנתערב בזבחים כולן ירעו עד שיסתאבו וימכרו ויביא בדמי היפה שבהן ממין זה ובדמי היפה שבהן ממין זה *[ויפסיד] המותר מביתו נתערב בבכורות ר"ש אומר אם חבורות כהנים יאכלו: **גמ'** והא

[תוספתא פ"ט]

רש"י

המפריש פסחו ומת. לקמיה מפרש אימת מית: לא יביאנו בנו אחריו לשם פסח · דהוה ליה פסח שמתו בעליו ואין כאן מנוין: **גמ'** שמע מינה בעלי חיים נדחין. בהמה שנדחית בחיים דחויה דיחוי גמור שאף לכשנראית למה שהיתה ראויה אינה קריבה אלא רועה דהא דתנן תרעה ולא קרבה שלמים היא גופה שזו היא ראייתה כמתחלה שכל מותר פסח קרב שלמים ודלא כר"ש דאמר בעלי חיים אין נדחין בפ' שני שעירי (יומא דף סד:) דגמרי' מבעל מום שנדחה ולכשעבר מומו נראה ומרישא נמי שמעינן לה אלא משום דמהא שמעינן תלת נקט לה הכא: ושמע מינה דחוי מעיקרא הוי דחוי. דהא נקבה או זכר בן שתי שנים מתחלתו לא נראה למה שהוקדש וקאמר ירעה ולא יקרב שלמים הוא ואיכא למאן דאמר במסכת סוכה (דף לג:) דאין דחוי אלא הנראה ונדחה: ושמע מינה יש דחוי בדמים · כדפרישית בכמה מקומות בגמ' מליצו לשון זה גבי הא דאמר רבי יוחנן בהמה של שני שותפין הקדיש חציה וחזר ולקח חציה קדושה ואינה קריבה שמע מינה תלת כו' כי הכא ובמסכת קדושין (דף ז:) ובזבחים (דף יב:) ולמדתי פירושה ממסכת כריתות (דף כז:) דגרס התם בלשון זה ש"מ קדושת דמים נדחה כלומר שמע מינה אפילו דבר שלא קדש תחלה להקרבת גופו אלא לדמיו כגון הקדיש חציה וחציה השני חולין דחוי לקרב לגופו בתחלת הקדישו אינו קרב עוד לעולם דהואיל ונדחה ידחה ולא תימא אין דחוי בקדשים אלא הקדיש לגופו ונדחה מהקריב אבל קדושת דמים לא אלימא למימר ביה תורת דחוי ולי אתיא לה שעת הכשר הקרבה כגון הכא דחזר ולקח חציה תקרב והכא נמי הכי פרישנא לה יש דחוי בדמים כגון נקיבה לפסח לא חזיא גופה לפסח אלא כי אקדשה לדמים אקדשה ואיידי דדחויה דלא חזיא לאקרובי גופה לדבר שהוקדשה לה אמרינן תדחה לעולם אפילו לאחר הפסח דכל מותר הפסח הוי שלמים ונקיבה לשלמים מחזא חזיא דקתני מתני' דמיה שלמים אבל גופה לא אלמא אלימא קדושת דמים לומר בה תורת דחוי ולא אשכחן דפליגי תנאי בהא מילתא מיהו טובא אשמעינן תשובת רבינו ע"כ ותמיהא לי אמאי גרע ממותר הפסח שרלוי *לפסח כדאמרינן בהאשה (לעיל דף פט:) וגמרו וכייתי במותר: בנו ממנה עמו. אם היה בנו ממנה עמו ועדיין יש לו בעלים: אי נימא דמית קודם חצות. וכו ביום הא חל אנינות עליה ברישא ותו לא חיילא עליה חובת דפסח להביאו בפני עצמן כדתנן (לעיל דף צא.) וכולן אין שוחטין עליהן בפני עצמן ומתני' קתני יביאנו דמשמע הוא עצמו: אלא דמת אחר חצות. דכיון דחיילא עליה דין פסח ברישא שוחט לעצמו ולא חיישינן שמא יביאוהו לבית הפסול דמוזהר זהיר משום חובת פסח דחייל עליה מעיקרא אבל כי חיילא אנינות ברישא לא זהיר ובמת יום או יומים קודם לא מצי לאוקמא אלא סתמא דמילתא בו ביום היו מפרישין פסחיהן: הא קבעתו חצות. לפסח ואידחי משלמים דהא תנן (לעיל דף צו:) הפסח העומד בחצות ולא הקריבו ירעה: לשם פסח שני. אם לא עשה את הראשון מפני אנינותו: לצדדין קתני. מת אחר חצות דחיילא עליה זמן חובת דפסח ברישא ובנו ממנה עמו ונשארו לו בעלים יביאנו לשם פסח אין בנו ממנה עמו לא מיירי בה מידי וממתני' שמעינן ירעה דהא קבעתי' חצות: מת קודם חצות ואין בנו ממנה עמו יביאנו לשם שלמים. דלא קבעתיה חצות ואם בנו ממנה עמו לא איצטריך לאורויי בה מידי דודאי מיקרב לפסח שני ואשמעינן מינה דהיכא דחל עליה חובת דפסח ברישא שוחטין עליו: ל"א הא חל עליה אנינות ברישא· ותו לא חיילא עליה חובת דפסח והא דתנן (לעיל דף צא:) שוחטין על האונן ה"מ היכא דחיילא חובת פסח עליה ברישא והדר חל עליה אנינות: שהיה אביו גוסס בחצות · ומת לאחר חצות בנו ממנה עמו יביאנו לשם פסח דהא חל עליה חובת דפסח ברישא אין בנו ממנה עמו יביאנו לשם שלמים דכיון דבחצות היה גוסס ורוב גוססין למיתה לא קבעתיה חצות: לעולם דמית אחר חצות. ודקשיא לך היאך יקרב שלמים הא קבעתיה חצות ואידחי ר' שמעון היא דאמר בסדר יומא בפ' ב' שעירי (דף סד:) בעלי חיים אין נדחין אלא מחמת מום או אתנן ומחיר שאינן ראויין אבל למה שהוא ראוי יקרב והאי חזי לשלמים: ה"ג רבינא אמר כגון שהפרישו אחר חצות ומתו בעליו אחר חצות. בנו ממנה עמו יביאנו לשם פסח דחובת דפסח חיילא ברישא אין בנו ממנה עמו יביאנו לשלמים דכיון דבחצות עדיין לא הופרש אין כאן קבע לדחות וקסבר תנא דידן חצות קבע ולא כל שאר זמן שחיטה: **מתני'** הפסח שנתערב בזבחים. שלשה טלאים א' של פסח וא' של עולה וא' של אשם ונתערב הפסח ביניהן כולם ירעו עד שיסתאבו וימכרו ויביא בדמי היפה שבהן עולה דשמא היפה עולה היה ובדמי היפה שבהן אשם שמא היפה אשם היה ובדמי היפה שבהן פסח אם קודם הפסח [נסתאבו] ואם לאחר הפסח נסתאבו יביאנו שלמים דשמא היפה פסח היה ואותו מותר שהוא צריך להוסיף על השנים עד שיגיעו לדמי היפה שבהן יפסיד מביתו משלו וא"ת הרי הוא מחליף שמביא שלמים בדמי האשם או בדמי העולה והרי קדושת הבהמה חלתה על מעות דמיה ואין משנין מקדושה לקדושה כשבא לחללן להבהמות כך הוא עושה אם יפה שבהן שוה סלע מביא ג' סלעים מביתו ונוטל הסלע האחת ואומר כל מקום שהיא העולה הרי מחוללת על הסלע זו ויביא ממנו עולה ונוטל סלע השנית ואומר כל מקום שהוא האשם הרי הוא מחולל על סלע זו ומביא בו אשם וכן לשלמים: נתערב בבכורות. שמתן דמן ומתן דם הפסח שוה ואין טעונין תנופת חזה ושוק ולא סמיכה ונסכים: ר"ש אומר. אם כל החבורה כולה כהנים היו יאכלו את כולם בו בלילה ויקרב פסח לשם פסח כל מקום שהוא והבכורות לשם בכור בכל מקום שהן: **גמ'** והא

תוספות

שמע מינה דחוי מעיקרו הוי דחוי . תימה לר"י דבפרק לולב הגזול (סוכה דף לג:) מסיק גבי לולב דדחוי מעיקרו לא הוי דחוי ויש לחלק בין דחוי מעיקרו דגבי מצות לדחוי מעיקרו דהקרבה ועוד דשאני התם דמעיקרא אפשר למעוטי בתקנתא ולא דחי דחוי גמור הוא וא"ת מאי קמ"ל ר' יוחנן בפ"ק דקדושין (דף ז:) גבי בהמה של שני שותפים לכל הנהו תלת מילי דמדקדק ממילתיה שמעינן ממתני' דהכא וי"ל דלהכי אשמעינן דעושה תמורה ותמורתה כיוצא בה אע"ג דאינה קריבה כלל והא דלא קאמר התם וש"מ דעושה תמורה כיוצא בה לא חשיב אלא מילי דדחייה וא"ת וניליף ממחוסר זמן דדחוי מעיקרא הוא ולא הוי דחוי וי"ל שאני מחוסר זמן דלא איתחזי מעולם [א] לשום קרבן וזמן קבוע לו להיות ראוי ליום השמיני הלכך לא שייך למילף מיניה בעלמא: **ושמע** מינה יש דחוי בדמים. פרש"י בתשובתו דאפילו דבר שלא קדש מתחלה קדושת הגוף אלא לקדושת דמים דחוי הוי מלקרב לבסוף ולא תימא אין דחוי אלא בדבר הקדוש קדושת הגוף ונדחה מהקרבה אבל קדושת דמים לא אלימא למידחי ותימה לר"י הא כל דחוי מעיקרו הוא דחוי בדמים ואם כן כיון דאמר דדחוי מעיקרו הוי דחוי שמעינן נמי דיש דחוי בדמים ואור"י דמסקנא ליה דחוי מעיקרו בקדוש קדושת הגוף כגון ששחט וקיבל הדם בכלי שיש בו מים דראשון ראשון דחוי הוא הלכך אפילו לבסוף רבה הדם ויש בו מראית דם הוי דחוי והכי איצטריך נמי לאשמעינן דאפי' בדמים יש דחוי ובפ"ק דקדושין (דף ז:) מפורש כל הצורך: **הא** חייל עליה אנינות . אף על גב דקיימא ביה לפי אכלו בלילה מכל מקום אינו יכול לשלח קרבנותיו כדאמרינן *(זבחים דף נט:) שלמים בזמן שהוא שלם: ופטורין

עין משפט נר מצוה

לד א ב ג מיי' פ"ד מהל' ק"פ הל' ה ו

לה ד מיי' שם הל' ח:

רבינו חננאל

ש"מ מדקתני ירעה עד שיסתאב וימכר ויפלו דמיו לנדבה (כיון שאינן) קרבים שלמים ש"מ בעלי חיים נדחין ודחוי מעיקרא כי (היא) נקבה או זכר בן ב' שנים שאינן ראוין מעיקרא לשם פסח לא תימא כיון שאינן (שלמים) לשם פסח מעיקרא כי אקדשינהו לשלמים אקדשינהו אלא נדחו ומדלא קתני ויביא בדמיו שלמים אלא יפלו דמיו לנדבה ש"מ דיש דחוי בדמים: **המפריש** פסחו ומת וכו' ת"ר המפריש פסחו ומת אם בנו ממנה עמו יביאנו לשם פסח [אין בנו ממנה עמו יביאנו לשם שלמים] לששה עשר ואוקמה רבא בשמת קודם חצות וחל עליה אנינות דאורייתא והוא נדחה לפסח שני והא דתנן אונן טובל ואוכל פסחו לערב באנינות דרבנן אבל באנינות דאורי' לא ורב שרבי' אמר כגון שהיה אביו גוסס בחצות ומת אחר חצות בנו ממנה עמו יביאנו לשם פסח דהא לא חל עליה אנינות אין בנו ממנה עמו יביאנו לשם שלמים דכיון דבחצות גוסס היה לא הוה חזי למעבד פסח ולא קבעתיה חצות · רב אשי אמר לעולם דמת אחר חצות ולא חל עליה אנינות דהא משעת הפסח כיום טוב חשוב שאומר בו הלל לפיכך לא חל עליה אנינות אין בנו ממנה עמו יביאנו לשם שלמים מאי אמרת קבעתיה חצות רבי שמעון הוא דאמר בעלי חיים אין נדחין ומשום הכי מקריב לה שלמים · רבינא אמר כגון שהפרישו אחר חצות ומתו בעלים אחר חצות וקסבר לא קבעה: **מתני'** הפסח שנתערב בזבחים ירעו עד שיסתאבו וימכרו ויביא בדמי היפה שבהן ממין זה כו' עד שנתערב בבכורות רבי שמעון אומר אם חבורת כהנים

הגהות מהר"ב רנשבורג

[א] תוד"ה שמע מינה דיחוי מעיקרו כו' וי"ל דשאני מחוסר זמן דלא אתחזי מעולם וכו'· נ"ב עיין יומא סד ע"א בתוס' ד"ה התם וכו' ובתוספות ישנים שם בד"ה מי דמי וכו' ובד"ה דיליף ודו"ק:

מסורת הש"ס

יומא סד: קדושין ז: זבחים יב: כריתות כז: ודף כתי תמורה כו: [זבחים נט:]

[בנה קדי' ביצה יט: סנהדרין לו:]

[נ"ל רבה ע' שבת עב: מ"ש שם]

לעיל צו:

כנ"י ויפריש

[מ"ק טו:]

כ"א לשלמים ופי' במהרש"א

FICE, ON A PEACE-OFFERING.[3] [98a] IF A MAN SEPARATES HIS PASSOVER-OFFERING AND DIES, HIS SON AFTER HIM MUST NOT BRING IT AS A PASSOVER-OFFERING[4] BUT AS A PEACE-OFFERING.

GEMARA. R. Huna son of R. Joshua said, This proves three things: [i] Live animals may be [permanently] rejected;[5] [ii] that which is rejected [even] *ab initio* is rejected;[6] and [iii] rejection is applicable to monetary sanctity.[7]

IF A MAN SEPARATES HIS PASSOVER-OFFERING etc. Our Rabbis taught: If a man separates his Passover-offering and dies, —if his son is registered with him, he must bring it as a Passover-offering; [if] his son is not registered with him, he must bring it as a peace-offering on the sixteenth [of Nisan].[8] Only on the sixteenth, but not on the fifteenth: he holds, Vows and voluntary offerings[9] may not be offered on a Festival.

Now when did the father die? Shall we say that he died before midday, [then how is it stated], 'if his son is registered with him he must bring it as a peace-offering'?—But surely *aninuth* [be-
a reavement] has previously fallen upon him![1] Again, if he died after midday, '[if] his son is not registered with him, he must bring it as a peace-offering'?—But midday has stamped it?[2]—Said Rabbah: In truth it is meant where he died before midday, and what does 'he must bring it as a Passover-offering' mean? He must bring it for the second Passover.[3] Abaye said, It is taught disjunctively: If he died after midday, [and] his son is registered with him, he must bring it for the sake of a Passover. If he died before midday, [and] his son is not registered with him, he must bring it as a peace-offering. R. Sherabia said: In truth it means where he died after midday, the case being e.g., where his father was in a dying condition at midday.[4] R. Ashi said: In truth it means that he died after midday,[5] this being in accordance with R. Simeon, who maintained: Live animals cannot be [permanently] rejected.[6] Rabina said: [It means] e.g., where he set it aside after midday and its owner died after midday, and he holds: [only] midday establishes it.[7]

MISHNAH. IF A PASSOVER-OFFERING BECAME MIXED UP WITH OTHER SACRIFICES, ALL MUST BE LEFT TO GRAZE UNTIL THEY BECOME UNFIT [THROUGH A BLEMISH], THEN BE SOLD, AND FOR THE PRICE OF THE BEST ONE MUST PURCHASE [AN ANIMAL] OF EACH DENOMINATION, AND MAKE
b UP[1] THE EXCESS FROM ONE'S PRIVATE PURSE.[2] IF IT BECAME MIXED UP WITH FIRSTLINGS,[3]—R. SIMEON SAID: IF [THE PASSOVER-OFFERING BELONGED TO] A COMPANY OF PRIESTS, THEY EAT [ALL ON THAT NIGHT].[4]

(3) In the separate edition of the Mishnah 'On a peace-offering' is omitted, while Tosaf. in Zeb. 9b s.v. חד gives the reading as, 'and he brings a peace-offering with its money'.—By separating it for a Passover-offering he has stamped it as such, and since it is unfit, it is regarded as a rejected sacrifice, which cannot be offered itself but must be redeemed and the money expended on a sacrifice. Cf. Mishnah on *96b* and n. 6a a.l. (4) As now there are none registered for it. (5) As here: the animal being rejected from its original purpose, viz., a Passover-offering, it remains ineligible even for a peace-offering, for which it is fit, but must graze. There is an opposing view in Yoma *63b*, and quoted *infra*, that only a dead animal can be rejected permanently. (6) This animal was not eligible for its purpose from the very outset. There is an opposing view in Suk. 33b that an animal can be permanently rejected only if it was originally eligible. (7) Since this animal is unfit for a Passover-offering, it was sanctified from the very outset only for its value, viz., that its redemption money should be expended on a sacrifice. Nevertheless it becomes permanently ineligible for the altar. (8) I.e., on the first of the Intermediate Days. (9) V. *58a*, n. b3.

a (1) Before the obligation of the Passover, which commences at midday. It is stated *supra 91a* that the Passover must not be sacrificed on behalf of an *onen* (v. Glos.) by himself, whereas the present passage implies that he brings it *himself*, even when he is not registered with others. (2) As a Passover, and since it cannot be sacrificed as such it remains rejected and cannot be offered *itself*, as *supra 96b* ff. (3) If he did not keep the first through his bereavement. (4) Hence if his son was registered with him, he must bring it as a Passover, since that obligation preceded his bereavement. But if his son was not registered with him, he must bring it as a peace-offering, for since his father was already in a dying condition, midday did not establish it as a Passover-offering. (5) But was not necessarily dying at midday. (6) Save when they become actually unfit, e.g., if they receive a blemish or are given as a harlot's hire (v. Deut. XXIII, 19). (7) But not the rest of the time allotted for its slaughtering. Hence it has not been established and therefore it cannot be rejected. Consequently, if his son was not registered with him, he must bring it as a peace-offering.

b (1) Lit., 'lose'. (2) Lit., 'house'. Thus: if three lambs of unequal value, one dedicated for a Passover-offering, another for a guilt-offering, and the third for a burnt-offering, became mixed up, they must all be sold. Since the best may have been any of the three sacrifices, he must buy an animal for each sacrifice at the cost of the best; naturally he will need more than they realized, and he must make that up himself.—Instead of 'he must lose' there is a variant: 'and he must set aside'. (3) Which are offered in the same way as Passover-offerings, viz., the blood of both is sprinkled in the same way, and neither require the waving of the breast and shoulder, nor laying of the hands, nor libations. (4) Stipulating at the time of slaughtering: 'Whichever is the Passover-offering, we sacrifice it as such, and whichever is the firstling, we offer it as such'.

should be left to graze? [97b]—In accordance with R. Oshaia. For R. Oshaia said: If he set apart two sin-offerings as security,[4] he is atoned for by one of them, while the second must be left to graze. Yet surely a Passover-offering in such a case is brought as a peace-offering?[5]—Rather, Samuel holds as R. Simeon, who maintained: The five sin-offerings are left to die.[6] But surely R. Simeon does not hold at all that [any sin-offering] must be left to graze?[7]—Samuel too stated one rule [only]: Whatever must be left to perish in the case of a sin-offering must be left to graze
a in the case of a Passover-offering. Then what does he inform us?[1] —[His purpose is] to rebut R. Johanan, who said: No Passover is brought as a peace-offering except if it is found after the slaughtering, but not [if it is found] before the slaughtering, which proves that [in his opinion] the *slaughtering* stamps [it as a rejected animal]; hence he [Samuel] informs us that *midday* stamps [it].

Another version: Whereas in the case of the Passover, where it is lost and found after midday [but] before the slaughtering [of the second], it is brought as a peace-offering?[2]—Samuel agrees with Rabbah, who maintained: The slaughtering stamps [it].[3] But surely, since R. Johanan said thereon: 'No Passover-offering is brought as a peace-offering save when it is found after the slaughtering, but not [if it is found] before the slaughtering,' which proves that [in *his* opinion] the *slaughtering* stamps [it], it follows that Samuel holds [that] *midday* stamps it?—Rather Samuel agrees with Rabbi, who ruled: A lost [sacrifice] goes forth to perish. But all lost [sacrifices] are left to perish, in Rabbi's opinion, whereas in the case of the Passover-offering, where it is lost before midday and found before midday it must be left to graze?—He holds that [if it is found] before midday it is not [regarded as] lost, and he also holds: Midday stamps [it].

MISHNAH. IF A MAN SETS ASIDE A FEMALE OR A TWO-YEAR OLD MALE FOR HIS PASSOVER-OFFERING,[4] IT MUST
b BE LEFT TO GRAZE UNTIL IT BECOMES UNFIT,[1] THEN BE SOLD, AND ITS MONEY IS SPENT[2] ON A VOLUNTARY SACRI-

(4) Each as security for the other, in case the other is lost. (5) For this is definitely a case where one is a 'remainder', not a rejected sacrifice. (6) V. *supra* 97a. These die in all cases, this holding good of iv whether it was refound before atonement was made with the second or after. Similarly, if two are set aside as a security for each other, the unsacrificed one must die. (7) How then can Samuel say, 'whatever must be left to graze in the case of a sin-offering'?

a (1) Since all sin-offerings must be left to die, it follows that Samuel teaches that all lost Passover-offerings are brought as peace-offerings. But this is already taught in the Mishnah, viz., IF THE PASSOVER-OFFERING IS FOUND AFTER THE SLAUGHTERING, IT IS BROUGHT AS A PEACE-OFFERING; this is explained *supra* as meaning after the *time* for slaughtering, i.e., after midday, which proves that if it is still lost at midday it is brought as a peace-offering. (2) This is another version of the difficulty raised *supra* 97a: 'But surely an animal which was lost at the time of separating another, in the view of the Rabbis goes to pasture, whereas in the case etc. (continuing as in the text). (3) V. *supra* 96b. Hence if found before the second is slaughtered it goes to pasture. (4) Both are ineligible; v. Ex. XII, 5. 'A two-year old' means in its second year.

b (1) Through a blemish. (2) Lit., 'falls'.

כדרבי אושעיא *דא"ר אושעיא *הפריש שתי חטאות לאחריות מתכפר באחת מהן ושניה תרעה והא אילו בפסח כי האי גוונא קרב שלמים אלא שמואל כר' שמעון סבירא ליה דאמר *חמש חטאות מתות והא רועה לרבי שמעון לית ליה כלל שמואל נמי חדא קאמר כל שבחטאת מתה בפסח קרב שלמים ומאי קמ"ל לאפוקי מדר' יוחנן דאמר אין הפסח קרב שלמים אלא שנמצא אחר שחיטה אבל קודם שחיטה לא אלמא שחיטה קבע קמ"ל חצות קבע לישנא אחרינא ואילו בפסח היכא דאבד ונמצא אחר חצות קודם שחיטה יקרב שלמים שמואל כרבה ס"ל דאמר שחיטה קבע והא מדקאמר רבי יוחנן עלה אין הפסח קרב שלמים אלא שנמצא אחר שחיטה אבל קודם שחיטה לא אלמא שחיטה קבע מכלל דשמואל סבר חצות קבע אלא שמואל כרבי סבירא ליה דאמר אבודה למיתה אזלא והא כל אבודין לר' מתין ואילו בפסח היכא דאבד קודם חצות ונמצא קודם חצות רועה קסבר קודם חצות לאו אבוד הוא וקסבר חצות קבע : **מתני'** [ג]המפריש נקבה לפסחו או זכר בן שתי שנים ירעה עד שיסתאב וימכר ויפלו דמיו לנדבה *לשלמים

המפריש

לאחריות · שאם תאבד האחת יביא חבירתה והכא איכא לאקשויי הא לאו אבודה היא אלא דקא מותיב ליה קושיא אחריתי : ה"ג והא אלו בפסח כי האי גוונא קרב שלמים · דהיינו מותר הפסח גמור שהרי לכך הופרש ואין כאן דחוי : אלא · לא תיבעי רועה בחטאת היכא משכחת לה דשמואל כר"ש ס"ל דאמר במסכת תמורה חמש חטאות מתות הנזכרות למיתה מתות הן בכל ענינים שאתה מוצא וחטא' שכיפרו בעליה מתה בכל שהיא בין שנמצאת קודם כפרה בין שנמצאת לאחר כפרה בין שהפרישה לאחריות מתה הנותרת: והא רועה לר' שמעון לית ליה·ומאי היא דקאמר שמואל כל שבחטאת רועה : שמואל נמי חדא קאמר כל שבחטאת מתה · דהיינו כיפרו בעליה מ"מ בפסח קרב שלמים ותו לא אמר מידי ועל כרחין כיון דכל אבודין בפסח קריבין שלמים ושמואל חדא קאמר מוקמי' לה כר"ש דאי כר' או כרבנן דאית להו רועה בחטאת מאי סימנא קא נקיט שמואל למימר חדא כל שבחטאת מתה בפסח קרב שלמים הלא אף הרועה בחטאת קריבה שלמים בפסח אבל השתא דס"ל כר"ש הוי סימן שלם דאין לך אבוד בחטאת שאינו מת ואין לך אבוד בפסח שאינו קרב : ומאי קא משמע לן · שמואל כיון דכל אבודין בחטאת מתין ואתא שמואל למימר כל אבודין בפסח קריבין שלמים מתניתין היא הפסח שנמצא אחר שחיטה ומתרצינן לה לעיל אחר זמן שחיטה יקרב אלמא קסבר האבוד בחצות יקרב : לאפוקי מדרבי יוחנן · דפליג עליה ואמר אין הפסח קרב שלמים אלא שנמצא אחר שחיטה : אבל נמצא קודם שחיטה · ואע"ג דאבוד היה בחצות רועה דשחיטת השניה קבעה ליה לקמא בדחוי : קא משמע לן · שמואל דאמר כל שבחטאת מתה וכר' שמעון דאמר אבודה בשעת הפרשה מתה ואשמעינן שמואל אבוד בשעת הפרשה ובחצות שהוא נקרא אבוד אפי' נמצא קודם שחיטה קרב שלמים דחצות הוא דקבעיה בדחוי והשתא אע"ג דאוקימנא לשמואל חדא קאמר ליכא לאוקומא כל שבחטאת מתה אמתו לה בעליה דהא כל מתו בעליה מתות ואלו פסח מתו בעליו אחר חצות רועה וקבעתיה חצות וליכא למימר דסביר' ליה שמואל חצות לא קבעה דהא ר' יוחנן בר פלוגתיה הא סברא אית ליה הלכך על כרחיך באבודין מוקמינן ליה ועוד דר' יוחנן בר פלוגתיה לאבודין פליג דקאמר נמצא : הכי גרסינן לישנא אחרינא ואלו בפסח היכא דאבד ונמצא אחר חצות קודם שחיטה קרב שלמים · ולעיל קא מיהדר והרי אבודה בשעת הפרשה לרבנן וכו' · ואלו בפסח האבוד בחצות והפריש אחר תחתיו ונמצא זה אחר חצות קרב שלמים כר' זירא ואע"ג דאבוד היה בשעת הפרשה : ומשני בלישנא אחרינא שמואל כרבה סבירא ליה דאמר קודם שחיטה שניט שהנמצא קודם שחיטה רועה בפסח כרבנן בחטאת : ופרכינן והא מדאמר ר' יוחנן עלה אין הפסח קרב שלמים אלא שנמצא אחר שחיטה · מכלל דשמואל אמר אפילו נמצא קודם שחיטה קרב שלמים דלאו שחיטה קבעה אלא חצות קבעה וזה כיון דבחצות אבוד היה קרב שלמים אלמא לשמואל אבוד בשעת הפרשה אע"פ שהיה בשעת כפרה קרב שלמים : אלא שמואל כר' סבירא ליה · כדלעיל עד קא משמע לן חצות קבע : **מתני'** או זכר בן שתי שנים·דלאו ראוי לפסח: ירעה עד שיסתאב ויביא בדמיו שלמים · דקבעתיה הפרשה אע"פ שמעיקרו דחוי הוא הרי הוא כקבוע שנדחה שאין עצמו קרב שלמים אלא דמיו :

המפריש

כדרבי אושעיא דאמר הפריש שתי חטאות לאחריות כו' · מה שפרש"י דהוה מצי לאקשויי והא לא אבוד הוא אלא דאקשי' קושיא אחריתי לא נהירא דאין זה סוגיית הגמרא דאמאי דפריך שמואל רועה באבודה היכי משכחת לה לא משני מידי במאי דקאמר כדר' אושעיא ונראה לר"י דרבי אושעיא דקאמר השניה תרעה בכל ענין קאמר ואפי' אבדה אחר כך דלא דמיא לשאר אבודין דמתין לרבי דשאר אבודין תחלת הפרשתן להקרבה וכשאבדו נדחו מהקרבה ובדין הוא שימותו אבל מפריש ב' חטאות לאחריות דתחלת הפרשתן לדחוי כמו שרועה בלא אבדה הכי נמי באבדה אי נמי איכא למימר דאפילו לא אבדה חשיב כאבדה הואיל וכשמפרישה לא חזיא להקרבה חשיב לה אבודה ולא דמיא לאבודת לילה דהתם לא נדחת בשעה הראוי' להקרבה והוי כאילו כל שעה ראוי' להקרבה אבל הכא איכא חדא ודאי דלא קרבה :

הפריש שתי חטאות לאחריות · קשה לריב"א היכי דמי אי דאמר הרי זו חטאת וזו ולאמר הרי זו חטאת אין קדושה חל על השניה דאין אדם מביא שתי חטאות על חטא אחד ואי דאמר הרי אלו בהמות חטאות האמר רבה במי שהוציאוהו (ערכין דף כ:) כל שאינו בזה אחר זה אפי' בבת אחת אינו ואפי' אחת מהן לא קדשה וע"כ אית לן למימר כגון שאמר אחת מהן תהא חטאת והאחרת לאחריות וקשה לן בשלא נתכפר החטאת אחת אמאי שני' תרע' והא לא הוקדשה אלא לאחריות החטאת דהיינו אם תאבד אבל אם לא נתכפר לא נתקדשה ונראה לר"י דכל כי האי גוונא גמירי לה דרועה :

אלא שמואל כר' שמעון סביר' ליה · פרש"י דאי כרבי מאי סימנא דנקיט שמואל הלא אף הרועה בחטאת בפסח קריבה שלמים ולא נהירא לר"י דמאי קאמר הא באבודה לא משכחת לרבי דרועה דבהפריש שתי חטאות לאחריות פירש רש"י גופיה דלאו אבוד הוא ומיהו לפירוש ר"י דפירש דר' אושעיא מיירי אפי' באבודה אתי שפיר ונראה לר"י דכר' שמעון נמי לא מתוקם אלא באבודין דאם לא כן תיקשי דנהאבד קודם חצות ונמצא קודם חצות בפסח רועה ואבודת לילה דלאו אבודה (היא) בפסח קודם חצות מתה לרבי שמעון ואע"ג דלרבי שמעון אית ליה לקמן (ד' צח.) בעלי חיים אינן נדחין וסבירא ליה בפסח [דמים] אחר חצות קרב שלמים אע"פ שנדחה שמואל לא קסבר לה בהא כר' שמעון ורשב"ם מפרש דהא דשנינן כי קאמר שמואל באבודין בדחויין לא אמר שניא דחיקא הוא והשתא דמשני סבר לה כרבי שמעון מתרץ מילתיה דשמואל כמשמעות הראשון דמיירי בין באבודין בין בדחויין והשתא לא מצי שמואל סבר כרבי דאם כן קשיא חטאת שעברה שנתה והפריש שתי חטאות לאחריות דלרבי לאו למיתה אזלי ובפסח קריבה שלמים הלכך מוקי לה כרבי שמעון דאמר בכל חמש חטאות דלמיתה אזלי בכל ענין ואילו בפסח קרבי שלמים ואע"ג דנאבד ונמצא קודם חצות בפסח רועה ואבודה דהא קתני לה בהדיא במתני' מיהו חד לא דאבד קרב שלמים כגון נמצא אחר חצות וה"ק בכל ענין שבחטאת מתה איכא לד דבפסח קרב שלמים וקא משמע לן לאפוקי מדרבי יוחנן דבע"א לא הוה קמשמע לן מידי דבטנינים אחרים מיתנו או במשנה או בברייתא דקרב שלמים ואין ר"י יודע מנא ליה לגמרא דלר' שמעון חמש חטאות מתות בכל ענין ויש לדקדק מדקתני בפרק שני דתמורה (דף טו:) רבי שמעון אומר חמש חטאות מתות ולד חטאת ותמורת חטאת כו' ולא מפליג כדמפליג בריש ולד חטאת (תמורה דף כא:) במתני' באבדה בין כיפרו הבעלים לא כיפרו ואיהו לא מפליג לא בהא ולא באחריני משמע דבכל ענין קאמר :

המפריש נקבה לפסחו כו' ויביא בדמיה שלמים · אומר ר"ת דהא דקתני ויביא בדמיה שלמים היינו בשבשחיירה אחר הפסח כמו שלה בבא דלעיל אבל קודם הפסח יביא בדמיה פסח וכן מחלק בהדיא בברייתא בתמורה באלו קדשים (דף יט:) :

ויביא בדמיה שלמים · אבל היא עצמה אינה קריבה שלמים דיש דחוי בדמים כדאמר בגמרא שמתחלה לא הוקדשה ליקרב היא עצמה ואי"ת ימכרנה כמות שהיא בלא מום כיון שמעולם לא נתקדשה קדושת הגוף ואומר ר"י דלא מיבעיא מקדיש נקבה לפסחו דפסח קרב שלמים אחר הפסח והיא ראויה לשלמים אם תחלה הוקדשה לכך אלא אפי' מקדיש נקבה לאשמו אמר באלו קדשים (שם:) תרעה עד שתסתאב ותמכר ויביא אשם ואפילו רבי שמעון דאמר התם תימכר שלא במום מאי מודה הכא כדפרישית :

שמע

לב א מיי' פ"ד מהל' פסולי מוקדשין הלכה ה :

לג ב מיי' פ"ד מהל' ק"פ הלכה ד :

רבינו חננאל

אבודה אני [והאמרי' התם] אי הכי רועה לר' היכי משכחת לה ואמרי' רבי אושעיא דאמר בתמורה פ"ד המפריש שתי חטאות לאחריות מתכפר באחת מהן שניה רועה ואלו בפסח כי האי גונא קרב שלמים הדר' שמואל כר' שמעון סבירא ליה דאמר הא נמי כיון שנתכפרו הבעלים מתה דתניא ר' שמעון אומר אף שכפרו בעליו ושעברה שנתה יהו מתות ותנן נמי ר' שמעון אומר חמש חטאות מתות אי הכי הא דתני שמואל כל שבחטאת רועה בפסח נמי רועה הא ר' שמעון לית ליה רועה כלל (אלא לשלם שמואל כר' סבירא ליה ובאבודין אמר אבל בדחויין לא אמר ופסח שאבד ונמצא קודם חצות לאו אבוד הוא כדרבא דאמר אבידת לילה לא שמה אבידה אלא רועה לרבי היכי משכחת לה) ושני' אלא לשמואל לא אמרי' כל שבחטאת רועה בפסח נמי רועה אלא חדא קאמר כל שבחטאת מתה בפסח קרב שלמים ומאי אתא לאשמעי' לאפוקי מדר' יוחנן דאמר אין לך פסח שקרב שלמים אלא שנמצא אחר שחיטה אלמא שחיטה קבעה מכלל דשמואל סבר חצות קבע זו דקדוקה של שמועה זו ועניניה כולן פשוטין : **מתני'** המפריש נקבה לפסחו כו'.

יומא דף סה. תמורה דף כב. [ע"ש כד.] מנחות פ.

תמורה דף טו. [סוכה ו:]

[במשנה שבמשניות ליתי' תיבת לשלמים ועי' תוי"ט ודע דגם תוס' בזבחים ט: ד"ה חד הפסיק הגירסא ויביא בדמיו שלמים וכן במנחות פג: ד"ס פר]

יכול אף לפני הפסח כן תלמוד לומר הוא הוא קרב ואין תמורת הפסח קריבה היכי דמי אילימא שנמצא קודם שחיטה והמיר בו קודם שחיטה פשיטא למה לי קרא אלא לאו שנמצא קודם שחיטה והמיר בו אחר שחיטה תיובתא (א) דרבא תיובתא אמר שמואל כל שבחטאת מתה בפסח קרב שלמים וכל שבחטאת רועה בפסח נמי רועה ורבי יוחנן אמר אין הפסח קרב שלמים אלא שנמצא אחר שחיטה אבל קודם שחיטה לא מתקיף לה רב יוסף וכללא הוא והרי חטאת שעברה שנתה דלרעיה אזלא *דא"ר שמעון בן לקיש חטאת שעברה שנתה רואין אותה כאילו היא עומדת בבית הקברות ורועה ואילו בפסח כי האי גוונא קרב שלמים *דתניא כשב לרבות את הפסח לאליה כשהוא אומר אם כשב לרבות *את הפסח שעברה שנתו ושלמים הבאין מחמת פסח לכל מצות שלמים שטעונים סמיכה ונסכים ותנופת חזה ושוק כשהוא אומר אם עז הפסיק הענין לימד על העז שאין טעון אליה א"ל כי קאמר שמואל באבודין בדחויין לא אמר ואבוד מי משכחת לה והרי אבודה בשעת הפרשה לרבנן דלרעיה אזלא *דתנן הפריש חטאתו ואבדה והפריש אחרת תחתיה ונמצאת הראשונה והרי שתיהן עומדות אחת מהן תקרב ושניה תמות דברי רבי וחכמים אומרים [ג] אין חטאת מתה אלא שנמצאת לאחר שנתכפרו בעלים הא קודם שנתכפרו בעלים רועה ואילו בפסח היכא דאבד ונמצא אחר חצות קודם שחיטה קרב שלמים שמואל כר' סבירא ליה דאמר אבודה למיתה אזלא והא כל אבודה לרבי מתה ואילו בפסח היכא דאבד קודם חצות ונמצא קודם חצות רועה קודם חצות לאו אבוד הוא כדרבא *דאמר רבא [ג] אבידת לילה לאו שמה אבידה אלא רועה לרבי היכי משכחת לה כדרבי

אילימא שנמצא קודם שחיטה והמיר בו קודם שחיטה פשיטא למה לי קרא · ואע"ג דקתני ליה במתני' לאשמעינן דאיכא תמורה דלא קרבה מ"מ לא איצטריך להכי: **פשיטא** · השתא לא שייך לשנויי דקרא אסמכתא בעלמא כדשני לעיל, דאם כן קרא למאי אתא:

אלא לאו שנמצא קודם שחיטה · תימה לגיסא קמא מאי מקשה אביי לרבה מהך ברייתא והלא סיפא מסייעתא לו בהדיא כדמסיק השתא והו תימה לומר שלא ידע אביי סיפא דברייתא דמקשי מינה*:

אמר שמואל כל שבחטאת מתה כו' · שמואל כרבי זירא סבר דאמר חצות קבע מדא"ר יוחנן אין הפסח קרב שלמים אלא שנמצא אחר שחיטה והכי [דייק] לקמן:

וכללא הוא והרי כו' · תימה דפריך אסיפא דמילתיה דכל שבחטאת רועה ואריפא נמי איכא למיפרך דהא תמורת חטאת [או] שמתו בעליה דלמיתה אזלא ואלו בפסח אמרי' במתני' דתמורת הפסח רועה אם המיר קודם חצות דקבעיה חצות וכן מתו בעליו אמר לקמן דאי מת קודם חצות דקבעיה חצות:

רואין אותה כאילו היא בבית הקברות · נקט הכי משום דדחיית בית הקברות לאו דחיה היא וכמו כן עברה שנתה לא חשיב דחוי כמו מתו או נתכפרו בעליה:

ורועה · פירש רש"י ויפלו דמיה לקיץ המזבח ממדרשו של יהוידע ואין נראה לריב"א דלא נאמר מדרש יהוידע אלא בהפריש מעות לחטאתו או לאשמו ונשתייר מהם או אבדו והפריש אחרים ואחר כך נמצאו דמה שנשתייר יפלו לנדבה אבל בכי האי גוונא שלא נתכפרו עדיין בעלים אמרינן תימכר ויביא אחרת בדמיה והביא ר"י ראיה לדבריו דתנן בפרק ולד חטאת (תמורה דף כב:) ושאבדה אם משכיפרו כו' ואם עד שלא כפרו בעליה תרעה עד שתסתאב ותמכר ויביא אחרת בדמיה והשתא בדחויה גמורה כמו אבדה דמודי ריש לקיש לאחר כפרה דמתה קתני עד שלא כיפרו יביא בדמיה אחרת בעברה שנתה דלאו דחוי גמור הוא דאף לאחר שכיפרו בעליה אינה מתה לא כל שכן שאם נסתאבה קודם כפרה דיביא אחרת בדמיה:

קודם חצות לאו אבוד הוא · פירוש ובכי האי גוונא לא איירי שמואל דהא שכינן כי קאמר שמואל באבודין קאמר:

אלא רועה לרבי היכי משכחת לה · דליכא למימר כגון שנאבדה בלילה דאבידת לילה לאו שמה אבידה ושמואל באבודין איירי כדס"ד:

(שני) יכול אף לפני הפסח כן · תמורת הפסח שנמצא לפני פסח תהא קריבה שלמים: תלמוד לומר הוא · פסח הוא הפסח כשר קרב ואין תמורתו קריבה לאו תמורת הפסח דקרב קא ממעט אלא הכי קאמר יש תמורת פסח שאינה קריבה: פשיטא · דלא קרבה דהא הוקבעה ונדחה בפסח ואע"ג דלעיל אמר מתני' הא קא משמע לן דאיכא תמורת פסח דלא קרבה קרא מיהא לא איצטריך לאשמעינן הכי: ה"ג אמר שמואל כל שבחטאת מתה כו' ור' יוחנן אמר אין הפסח קרב שלמים אלא שנמצא אחר שחיטה אבל קודם שחיטה לא · כל שבחטאת מתה חמש חטאות מתות הלכה למשה מסיני טכנן לכיפה והן ולד חטאת ותמורת חטאת וחטאת שמתו בעליה וחטאת שנתכפרו בעליה על ידי אחרת שאבדה זאת ואחר כך נמצאת ושעברה שנתה ונקט שמואל גבי פסח סימנא ביה ואמר כל שבחטאת מתה אי מיתרמי הכי בפסח קרב שלמים וקא סלקא דעתך דלכולהו מתות דחטאת דאשכחנן גבי פסח קרב שלמים דהיינו תמורת פסח ופסח שמתו בעליו ושכיפרו בעליו ושעברה שנתו קריבין שלמים: וכל שבחטאת רועה · לקמן מפרש מאי היא ומיתה ורעיה לאו קולא וחומרא איכא בהדא מאידך והאי דנקט גבי מיתה דחטאת בפסח קרב וגבי רעיה דחטאת בפסח רעיה לאו טעמא קא יהיב ביה דמשום דהכא מתה הכא קרב אלא סימנא בעלמא הוא: וכללא הוא · דכל שבחטאת רועה בפסח רועה: דריש לקיש · במס' תמורה בפרק ולד חטאת (דף כב:) והתם מותיב לה ממתניתין דהתם דקתני ושעברה שנתה כו' ומתרץ לה דהכי קתני שעברה שנתה ואבדה [או אבדה] ונמצאת בעלת מום: כאילו עומדת בבית הקברות · כל מקום שהיא רואין כאילו היא בבית הקברות שאין כהן נכנס שם לשוחטה ורועה עד שתסתאב ותימכר ויפלו דמיה נדבה לשופרות שכתוב עליהן נדבה ומקיילים בה את המזבח זה מדרשו של יהוידע הכהן במסכת תמורה (דף כג:*) שכל מותר חטאת ואשם לקיץ המזבח חוץ מחטאות מתות שהן הלכה למשה מסיני: כשב לרבו' כו'.קתני מיהת פסח שעברה שנתו קרב: ה"ג כי קאמר שמואל באבודין בדחוין לא אמר ובאבודין מי משכחת לה כו'·כי אמר שמואל כל שבחטאת מתה לאו אכולהו קאי אלא אכיפרו בעליה לחודא שהיא על ידי איבוד ואמתו בעליה לא קאי דלא משכחת ביה רועה אלא אכיפרו בעליה לחוד קא משכחת ליה לרועה כדלקמן וגבי פסח נמי אכיפרו בעליו קאי וכללא הוא דכל פסח שכיפרו בעליו *באחר רועה אם כיוצא בו בחטאת רועה וקרב שלמים אם כיוצא בו בחטאת מתה אבל אם חטאת דחויה כגון עברה שנתה שעומדת בפניו והרי היא דחויה מהקריב לא אמר: והרי אבודה בשעת הפרשה · חטאת שאבדה עד שהפריש אחרת תחתיה ונמצאת קודם הקרבת השניה לרבנן דפליגי עליה דרבי במס' תמורה (דף כ:) ואמרי דלרעיה אזלא דתנן המפריש חטאתו כו': אין חטאת מתה · משום כיפרו בעליה אלא האבודה בשעת כפרה ונמצאת אחר שנתכפרו הבעלים הא נמצאת קודם כפרה כיון דאמרי רבנן לא מתה הויא לה מותר חטאת ורועה ודמיה לשופרות: ואילו בפסח · כי האי גוונא אבד בשעת הפרשה ונמצא קודם שחיטה אחר חצות: קרב שלמים · כר' זירא דאמר קודם חצות ואחר חצות שניהו אלמא פסח שהיה לפניו בשעת כפרה ובלבד שיהא אבוד בחצות קרב שלמים: שמואל כר' סבירא ליה · ורועה בחטאת דקאמר שמואל לקמיה מפרש והוא הדין דמצי לתרוצי שמואל כרבנן סבירא ליה דאמר קודם שחיטה שניהו ובפסח נמי אבוד בשעת הפרשה רועה ולקמן מפרש לה בלישנא אחרינא הכי: נמצא קודם חצות · אפי' לר' זירא רועה דקבעתיה חצות: קודם חצות · שהיא שעה שאינה ראויה לו להקרבה: לאו אבוד הוא · ואפי' הפריש אחר תחתיו קודם שנמצא לאו (מיתה) אבוד חשיב ליה: דאמר רבא · גבי חטאת אבידת לילה והפריש אחרת תחתיה בלילה ונמצאת (תחתיה) לאור הבוקר אפי' לר' לאו למיתה אזלא אלא לרעיה הואיל ולילה לאו שעת הקרבה היא: אלא רועה לרבי · באבודין היכי משכחת לה דתיקום כל שבחטאת רועה דשמואל: לאחריות

לעיל צו:] יומא דף סו. תמורה דף כב. מנחות דף פב. זבחים דף ט: תמורה דף כב: [מנחות ס.] תמורה שם.

הגהות הב"ח (א) גמ' תיובתא דרבה תיובתא:

באחרת רועה אם כיוצא בו בחטאת רועה. אבל אם חטאת כצ"ל רש"ל

כה א מיי' פ"ד מהל' ק"פ הלכה ו:
ל ב מיי' פ"ד מהל' פסולי מוקדשין הלכה ח:
לא ג שם הלכה ט:

[וכן תמהו עוד בכ"ק ד"ה לאו וכחולין עד. ד"ה ולאו וכנדה לד: ד"ה אילימא ויש מקום לעיין בתוס' מ"ק ה. ד"ה לאחוי כ"מ נד: סד"ס לעניין ובעיין י. ד"ס והתניא]

רבינו חננאל

יכול אף לפני הפסח כן ת"ל וכו' ואסיקנא אלא לאו שנמצא קודם שחיטה והמיר בו קודם שחיטה קא מטעם לה תנא דלא קרבה (מיהא כלומר הנמצא) [מיהא שטעינן דהנמצא] אחר שחיטת הפסח הוא דקרב שלמים וכן תמורתו אבל הנמצא קודם שחיטה אינו קרב לא הוא ולא תמורתו תיובתא דרבה: אמר שמואל כל שבחטאת מתה בפסח קרב שלמים·כל שבחטאת רועה בפסח נמי רועה ואתקיף עליה רב יוסף הרי חטאת שעברה שנתה דלרעיה אזלא דאמר ר"ל בתמורה פ"ד חטאת שעברה שנתה רואין כאלו עומדת בבית הקברות ורועה ואלו פסח שעברה שנתו קרב שלמים דתניא כשב לרבות פסח לאליה כשהוא אומר אם כשב לרבות פסח שעברה שנתו ושלמים הבאים וכו' ושני' כי קאמר שמואל כל שבחטאת רועה בפסח נמי רועה באבודין ונמצאו אבל בדחוין כגון שעברה שנתם ונדחו לא אמר שמואל: ובאבודין מי משכחת להא דשמואל והא אבודה בשעת הפרשת אחרת דלרבנן אע"פ שנמצאה הראשונה לרעיה אזלא דתנן בתמורה פ"ד המפריש חטאתו ואבדה והפריש אחרת תחתיה ונמצאת הראשונה והרי שתיהן עומדות תמימות וכו' ודייקי' מינה נמצא' אחר שנתכפרו בעלים מתה מכלל שאם נמצאת קודם שנתכפרו בעלים רועה ואלו בפסח היכא דאבד ונמצא אחר[חצות] (הפסח)קודם שחיט' קרב שלמים ושני' שמואל כרבא סבירא לי'*)דא"ל בשמעתא דקמי הא שחיטה קבעה והא מדאמר ר' יוחנן עלה אין לך פסח שקרב שלמים אלא שנמצא אחר שחיטה מכלל דשחיטה קבעה מכלל דשמואל סבר חצות קבעה ולא שחיטה ודחי' שמואל כרבי ס"ל דאמר אבודה בשעת הפרשה מתה והרי כ' אבודה לרבי מתה דקתני

כמסקנא' במסכת תמורה ושני' מתה דברי רבי ואלו פסח שאבד ונמצא קודם חצות רועה ודחי' אבודה ונמצאת קודם חצות לאו אבודה היא כדרבא דאמר בתמורה בתחלת פ"ד אמר רבא אבדת לילה לא שמה אבודה

*) נראה דגי' אחרת הי' לרבינו בגמ' והי' גורס שתי הלשונות דאיתא כאן ולהלן עמוד ב' הכל בלשון א' ועי'.

offering. [97*a*] You might think that it is also thus before Passover,[2] therefore it is stated, '*it*':[3] '*it*' is offered [as a peace-offering], but the substitute of a Passover-offering is not offered [as such].[4] How is it meant? If we say that it was found before slaughtering and he substituted [another] for it before slaughtering, then it is obvious![5] Why do I require a verse? Hence it must surely apply to where it was found before the slaughtering, while he substituted [another] for it after the slaughtering. Thus the refutation of Raba is indeed a refutation.[6]

Samuel said: Whatever must be left to perish in the case of a sin-offering, is brought as a peace-offering in the case of a Passover,[7]
a and whatever must be left to graze in the case of a sin-offering,[1] must also be left to graze in the case of a Passover. While R. Joḥanan said: No Passover is brought as a peace-offering save that which is found after the slaughtering, but not [if it is found] before the slaughtering. To this R. Joseph demurred: Now is this a general rule? Surely there is the sin-offering more than a year old, which goes forth to pasture,[2] for R. Simeon b. Laḳish said: A sin-offering more than a year old, we regard as though it stood in a cemetery,[3] and it must be left to graze; whereas a Passover in such a case is brought as a peace-offering, for it was taught: '[*If he bring*] *a lamb* [etc.]': this is to include the Passover-offering, in respect of its fat tail. When it is stated, '*If* [*he bring*] *a lamb*,' this is to include [an animal] more than a year old [dedicated for] a Passover and a peace-offering which comes in virtue of a Passover-offering in respect of all the regulations of a peace-offering,[4] [viz.,] that they require laying [of the hands], libations, and the waving of the breast and shoulder. Again, when it [Scripture] states, '*and if* [*his offering be*] *a goat*', it breaks across the subject and teaches of a goat that it does not require [the burning of its] fat tail [on the altar]![5]—Said he to him, Samuel spoke only of lost [sacrifices],[6] but he did not say it of rejected [animals]. Yet is [this principle] possible [in the case of] a lost [sacrifice]? Surely an [animal which was] lost at the time of separating [another],[7] in the view of the Rabbis goes to pasture [until it receives a blemish], for we learned: If he set apart [an animal as] his sin-offering and it was lost, and he [then] set apart another in its stead, and [then] the first was found again, and behold! both stand [before us], [any] one of them may be sacrificed, while the other must die: this is Rabbi's ruling. But the Sages maintain: No sin-offering must die except one found after its owner has
b been atoned for.[1] Hence [if found again] before its owner was atoned for, it must graze. Whereas in the case of a Passover-offering, if it was lost and found again after midday [but] before the slaughtering [of the second], it is brought as a peace-offering? —Samuel agrees with Rabbi, who maintained: A lost animal goes forth to perish. But every lost [sin-offering], according to Rabbi, is left to die, whereas in the case of a Passover-offering, if it was lost before midday and found again before midday it must be left to graze?—[If found] before midday it is not [regarded as lost],[2] in accordance with Raba. For Raba said: A loss at night is not designated a loss.[3]

Then according to Rabbi, how is it possible that [a sin-offering]

(2) That the substitute of a Passover which is found before Passover is offered as a peace-offering. (3) He seems to translate, If it (*hu*) is a lamb (which) he brings etc., and treats the '*it*' as a limitation. (4) This does not mean that where the Passover itself is offered as a peace-offering its substitute is not, but that there is a substitute of the Passover which is not offered as a peace-offering. (5) That it cannot be offered itself, having been rejected, as explained in n. a 6 on the Mishnah. (6) Here we cannot answer that the verse is a mere support, as above, for in that case what is the purpose of the verse? (7) There are five cases of the former: (i) the offspring of a sin-offering; (ii) the substitute of a sin-offering; (iii) a sin-offering whose owner died; (iv) a sin-offering which was lost, and refound after its owner had made atonement with another; and (v) a sin-offering more than a year old. All these must be allowed to perish. It is now assumed that all these, in the case of a Passover (the first of course is excluded, the Passover being a male), are brought as a peace-offering.

a (1) Until it receives a blemish, when it can be redeemed.—It is discussed anon which these are. (2) Until it receives a blemish. (3) Thus inaccessible to the priest for sacrifice—i.e., it cannot be sacrificed. (4) This is the point of the objection. (5) V. *supra* 96*b* for notes. (6) I.e., *supra* (iv). (7) If a sin-offering was lost and another consecrated, and then the first was found again before the second was sacrificed, so that the first was a lost animal only when the second was set apart, but not when it was sacrificed.

b (1) By another offering. (2) Even if another had been separated in its place. (3) If a sin-offering was lost at night, and another was separated in its stead, and the first was found by the morning, even on Rabbi's view it is not regarded as having been lost, since it could not have been sacrificed at night in any case, and therefore it goes forth to pasture. By the same reasoning, if the lost Passover-offering is found before midday, it is not regarded as having been lost, since it could not have been sacrificed before midday.

Continuation of translation from previous page as indicated by ◁

They learned this only if it was found after the slaughtering and he substituted [another] for it after the slaughtering. But if it was found before the slaughtering while he substituted [another] for it after the slaughtering, its substitute derives from the power of rejected sanctity, and it cannot be offered.[5]

Abaye raised an objection against him: *If [he bring] a lamb [for his offering* etc.]:[6] for what purpose is *'if [he bring] a lamb'* stated? To include the substitute of a Passover-offering after Passover, [teaching] that it is offered as a peace-offering. How is it meant? If we say that it was found after the slaughtering and he sub-
c stituted [another] for it after the slaughtering, then it is obvious:[1] why do I require a verse? Hence it must surely apply where it was found before slaughtering and he substituted [another] for it after slaughtering?[2]—No: in truth it applies where it was found after slaughtering and he substituted [another] for it after slaughtering, while the verse is a mere support.[3]

Then for what [purpose] does the verse come?[4]—For what was taught: '*[If he bring] a lamb* [etc.]': this is to include the Passover-offering, in respect of its fat tail.[5] When it is stated, '*If [he bring] a lamb,*' this is to include [an animal] more than a year old [dedicated for] a Passover-offering[6] and a peace-offering which comes in virtue of a Passover-offering[7], in respect of all the regulations of the peace-offering, [viz.,] that they require laying [of the hands],[8] libations, and the waving of the breast and shoulder. Again, when it states, *and if [his offering be] a goat,*[9] it breaks across the subject [and] teaches of a goat that it does not require [the burning of the] fat tail [on the altar].[10]

Others recite it [Raba's dictum] in reference to the first clause: THE PASSOVER-OFFERING WHICH WAS FOUND BEFORE THE SLAUGHTERING OF THE PASSOVER-OFFERING MUST GRAZE UNTIL IT BECOMES UNFIT, BE SOLD, AND ONE BRINGS A PEACE-OFFERING FOR ITS MONEY, AND THE SAME APPLIES TO ITS SUBSTITUTE. Said Raba, They learned [this] only where it was found before the slaughtering and he substituted [another] for it before the slaughtering. But if it was found before the slaughtering and he substituted [another] for it after the slaughtering, it is offered as a peace-offering. What is the reason? The slaughtering [of the Passover-offering] stamps [with its sanctity] only something that is eligible therefor, [but] it does not stamp [with
d its sanctity] that which is not eligible therefor.[1]

Abaye raised an objection against him: '*If [he bring] a lamb* [etc.]': what is its purpose? To include the substitute of a Passover-offering after Passover, [teaching] that it is offered as a peace-

(5) I.e., since the original is rejected, as explained in n. a6 on the Mishnah, the substitute is in the same position. (6) Lev. III, 7. This refers to a peace-offering, and it is superfluous. For v. 6 states, *and if his offering . . . be of the flock,* while v. 12 states, *and if his offering be a goat:* since '*flock*' only comprises goats and lambs, v. 6 must refer to lambs, which renders v. 7 unnecessary. Hence it must be written for a particular exegesis.

c (1) Since it follows from the general principle of substitution, as explained in nn. 1a and 6a on the Mishnah. (2) And we are then informed that although the original itself cannot be offered, its substitute is offered! (3) But not the actual source of the law, which follows indeed from general principles. (4) Since it is superfluous, as explained *supra,* n. b6. (5) The fat tail of all other sacrifices is explicitly stated to be part of the *emurim* which are burnt on the altar (v. Lev. III, 9; VII, 3). The burning of the *emurim* is not mentioned at all in connection with the Passover, however, but deduced from elsewhere (v. *supra* 64*b*); consequently a verse is required to teach that the fat tail too is included. (6) Hence unfit for its purpose (v. Ex. XII, 5). (7) E.g., the substitute for a Passover-offering, or where the owner of a Passover-offering registered for a different animal, so that the first is a Passover remainder; both are sacrificed as peace-offerings. (8) V. Lev. III, 2. (9) Ibid. 12. (10) '*And if*' is regarded as a disjunctive, teaching that the provisions that apply to a lamb do not apply to a goat, unless expressly stated. The fat tail is mentioned in connection with the former (v. 9) but not the latter.

d (1) I.e., if the animal is dedicated for a Passover-offering, the act or time of slaughtering the second animal stamps it with that sanctity, and since it was not offered then, it was rejected and must graze. But the act of slaughtering cannot stamp an animal with that sanctity, that it should be regarded as rejected, if it was not fit for a Passover-offering at the time, and in the latter case this substitute was indeed unfit, since at that time it was as yet unconsecrated. Consequently now that it is consecrated, it is offered *itself* as a peace-offering.

עין משפט
נר מצוה

כו א ב ג מיי' פ"ד מהל' ק"פ הלכה ו:
כז ד שם הלכה ז:
כח ה מיי' פ"ו מהל' מעשה הקרבנות הלכה יא:

אלא אחמץ מכלל דפסח מצרים לילה אחד ותו לא *והתניא רבי יוסי הגלילי אומר מנין לפסח מצרים שאין חימוצו נוהג אלא יום אחד ת"ל °לא יאכל חמץ וסמיך ליה היום אתם יוצאים אלא ה"ק לילה אחד והוא הדין לפסח דורות וחימוצו כל היום ופסח דורות נוהג כל שבעה: **מתני'** *א"ר יהושע שמעתי שתמורת פסח קריבה ותמורת פסח אינה קריבה ואין לי לפרש א"ר עקיבא אני אפרש *הפסח שנמצא קודם שחיטת הפסח ירעה עד שיסתאב וימכר ויביא בדמיו שלמים וכן תמורתו אחר שחיטת הפסח קרב שלמים וכן תמורתו: **גמ'** ולימא פסח קרב ופסח אינו קרב הא קמ"ל דאיכא תמורת הפסח דלא קרבה איתמר רבה אמר ב קודם שחיטה ולאחר שחיטה שנינו רבי זירא אמר קודם חצות ולאחר חצות שנינו ולרבי זירא הא קתני קודם שחיטת הפסח אימא קודם זמן שחיטת הפסח כתנאי הפסח שנמצא קודם שחיטה ירעה לאחר שחיטה יקרב ר"א אומר קודם חצות ירעה לאחר חצות יקרב: אחר שחיטת הפסח יביא שלמים וכו': אמר רבא (א) ג לא שנו אלא שנמצא אחר שחיטה והמיר בו אחר שחיטה אבל נמצא קודם שחיטה והמיר בו אחר שחיטה תמורתו מכח קדושה דחויה קא אתא ולא קרבה איתיביה אביי °אם כשב מה ת"ל אם כשב לרבות תמורת הפסח אחר הפסח שקרבה שלמים היכי דמי אילימא שנמצא אחר שחיט' והמיר בו אחר שחיטה פשיטא למה לי קרא אלא לאו שנמצא קודם שחיטה והמיר בו אחר שחיטה לא לעולם שנמצא אחר שחיטה והמיר בו אחר שחיטה וקרא אסמכתא בעלמא אלא קרא למאי אתא (ב) *כדתניא כשב ד לרבות את הפסח לאליה כשהוא אומר אם כשב לרבות פסח שעברה שנתו ושלמים הבאין מחמת פסח לכל מצות שלמים שטעון סמיכה ונסכים ותנופת חזה ושוק וכשהוא אומר ואם עז הפסיק הענין ה לימד על העז שאין טעונה אליה איכא דמתני לה ארישא הפסח שנמצא קודם שחיטת הפסח ירעה עד שיסתאב וימכר ויביא בדמיו שלמים וכן תמורתו אמר רבא לא שנו אלא שנמצא קודם שחיטה והמיר בו קודם שחיטה אבל נמצא קודם שחיטה והמיר בו אחר שחיטה תמורתו קריבה שלמים מאי טעמא כי קבעה שחיטה מידי דחזי ליה מידי דלא חזי ליה לא קבעה איתיביה אביי אם כשב מה תלמוד לומר לרבות תמורת הפסח אחר הפסח שקריבה שלמים יכול

תורה אור: שמות יג · ויקרא ג

רש"י

ואלא אחמץ · דאיסור חימוצו נוהג כל שבעה מכלל דלילה אחד דקתני מתני' בפסח מצרים אחמץ קאי וה"ק ואין חימוצו נוהג אלא לילה אחד ופסח דורות נוהג כל שבעה: יום א' · משמע כל היום: לא יאכל חמץ היום · וסמיך ליה היום אתם יוצאים: אלא · הכי משמע ונאכל בחפזון בלילה אחד וה"ה דפסח דורות נמי לילה אחד ופסח מצרים חימוצו נוהג כל היום ופסח דורות כל שבעה: **מתני'** שמעתי · מרבותי: שתמורת הפסח קריבה · שלמים אחר הפסח: ותמורת הפסח אינה קריבה · ויש תמורת פסח שאינה קריבה היא עצמה שלמים אלא רועה עד שיסתאב במום ותמכר ויביא בדמיה שלמים דמותר הפסח קרב שלמים: ואין לי לפרש · שכחתי על איזה שמעתי תקרב ועל איזה שמעתי תרעה: הפסח · שאבד והפריש אחר תחתיו ונמצא הראשון קודם שחיטת השני דהיה עומד לפניו בשעת שחיטה הרי קבעתו שעת שחיטה בשם פסח וזה שלא הקריבו דחהו בידים לא יקרב עוד הוא עצמו שלמים דאין זה מותר הפסח אלא פסח [דחוי]: וכן תמורתו · אם המיר הוא בו בהמת חולין אחרי כן הרי הוא כמוהו אין קרב הוא עצמו שלמים אלא דמיו ואם לאחר שחיטת השני נמצא הרי לא קבעתו שעת שחיטה בשם פסח ולא נדחה בידים ויביא שלמים ויקרב הוא עצמו שלמים וה"ה דמצי למיתני רבי יהושע אומר פסח קרב ופסח אינו קרב ובגמרא פריך לה: **גמ'** דאיכא תמורת הפסח דלא קרבה · ולא אמרינן מתחלה שלמים היא ואפילו המיר קודם שחיטה לא קבעתה זמן השחיטה בשם פסח ואין בה דחוי אלא אף היא נקבעת בפסח ונדחת: קודם שחיטה ואחר שחיטה · דוקא שנינו במשנתנו ולא שנינו בה זמן שחיטה דהיינו חצות ואשמעינן דאפילו היה אבוד בשעת חצות אם נמצא קודם שחיטת השני הוא נקבע ונדחה הואיל ונדחה להקריבו לפסח: קודם חצות שנינו · שעת חצות היא הקובעתו בפסח אם נמצא קודם חצות קבעתיה חצות שהרי נראה וכי לא אקרביה דחייה אבל נמצא אחר חצות אפי' נמצא קודם שחיטה אין כאן קביעות ולא דחוי: קודם שחיטה · של שני: קודם חצות · ונתכפר באחר ירעה: אחר חצות · ונתכפר באחר: יקרב זה שלמים · ואע"פ שבשעת שחיטת השני הרי הוא עומד בפניו: לא שנו · דתמורה קרבה אלא שנמצא אחר שחיטה שאפי' הפסח לא נדחה אבל נמצא קודם שחיטה שהוא עצמו נדחה אע"פ שתמורתו לא נדחית בידים אינה קריבה שהרי מכח קדושה דחויה באה: אם כשב · הוא מקריב גבי שלמים כתיב אם יתירא הוא דמצי למיכתב כשב הוא מקריב א"נ כשב קדריש דהא כתיב לעיל מיניה אם מן הצאן קרבנו ובפרשה תחתונה אמור ואם עז קרבנו מכלל דעד השתא בכשב איירי דאין לך עוד בצאן אלא כשב: למה לי קרא · הא מותר הפסח הוא ונפקא לן מוזבחת פסח דמותר הפסח *אחר חצות קרב שלמים כדאמרן באלו דברים (לעיל דף ע:) ותמורתו כ"ש דקריבה דלא עדיפא מיניה: והמיר בו אחר שחיטה · ואשמעינן דאע"ג דאיהו לא קרב תמורתו קריבה הואיל ולא הוקדשה קודם שחיטה: כשב · קרא יתירא כדפרישית מדכתיב בתריה ואם עז מכלל דעד השתא בכשב איירי: לאליה · דבכל קרבנות כשב אליה כתיבא עם האימורין בשלמים חלבו האליה (ויקרא ג) ובאשם כתיב (שם ז) את כל חלבו יקריב ממנו את האליה וגו' וחטאת כאשם אבל פסח אימורין גופייהו לא כתיבי בהדיא אלא כדנפקא לן (לעיל דף סד:) מאת דמם תזרוק ואת חלבם תקטיר הלכך אלייתו צריכה להתרבות בקרבנות שבשור לא הוזכרה אליה באימוריו: ושלמים הבאין מחמת פסח · מותר פסח כגון תמורתו ופסח שנתכפרו בעליו באחר כך שמעתי: לכל מצות · מצות שלמים עליהן לשון אחר הבאין מחמת פסח חגיגת ארבעה עשר וזו שמעתי [וכך קבל רבי]: ואם · הפסק הוא להפסיק בין כשב לעז שבכשב נתפרשה אליה כדכתיב האליה תמימה לעומת העלה ממקום שהכליות יועצות ובא הכתוב והפסיק ולמד על העז שאינה טעונה אליה להקריב אליה שלה למזבח יש מפרשין עז אין לו אליה וטעות הוא בידם שהרי ממקום שהכליות יועצות היא ניטלית ועוד מה לימד הכתוב הואיל ואין לו: איכא דמתני · להאי לא שנו דרבה: לא שנו · שאף תמורתו דחויה אלא שנמצא קודם שחיטה והמיר בו קודם שחיטה דחינהו לתרווייהו הני שהיו ראוין ועומדים לפסח ונקבעו: אבל המיר בו אחר שחיטה · אע"פ שהפסח רועה התמורה קריבה שהרי לא נדחית: מידי דלא חזי ליה · שעדיין לא הוקדש: יכול

תוספות

קודם שחיטת הפסח ירעה · וטעמא דדחייה בידים כדפירש רש"י ואפי' רב דאמר אין בעלי חיים נדחין ופליג אר' יוחנן בפ' שני שעירי (יומא דף סד:) היינו דוקא כגון דלא דחייה בידים כגון כשמתו בעלים או שמשכו ידיהם וא"ת והא משמע דפליג בפ"ק דקדושין (דף ז:) דא"ר יוחנן בהמה של ב' שותפין הקדיש חציה וחזר ולקחה והקדיש חציה קדושה ואינה קריבה משום דנדחית בתחלה כשהקדיש חציה ודייק עלה ש"מ בעלי חיים נדחין משמע דרב פליג וי"ל כיון דרכך הקדש דחי לה לא מיקרי כל כך דחוי בידים ובתוספתא [פ"ט] פליגי רבי יוסי ורבנן איזה מהן יקריב לכתחלה ומייתי לה בפ' שני שעירי (יומא דף סד:):

קמ"ל דאיכא תמורת הפסח דלא קרבה · דקבע לה חצות או שחיטה דס"ד דלא קבע הואיל ובאיסור הוקדשה ואין דעתו עליה לשוחטה לשם פסח קמ"ל דאפילו הכי קבע לה ור"י מפרש דס"ד הואיל ואינה קריבה לעולם לשם פסח מתחלתה שלמים היא קמ"ל ומתוך פרש"י דפי' אלא אף היא נקבעת בפסח ונדחה משמע שסובר שלפי האמת ראויה לפסח:

ושלמים הבאין מחמת הפסח · לפי אותו לשון דפירש בקונטרס דהכך שלמים היינו חגיגת י"ד אין לחוש מה *(שפירש) באלו דברים (דף ע"א: ד"ה לימד) דשלמים הבאים מחמת פסח בפרק כל הפסולים (זבחים דף לו:) היינו מותר פסח דהא כדאיתא והא כדאיתא: **ואם** עז הפסיק הענין · פירש ריב"א מדלא כלל אותו בהדי כבש אלא הפסיק הענין וכתבו לבדו ולא שינה בו כלום אלא דלא כתיב ביה אליה להכי כתביה למעוטי מתורת אליה: אילימא

רבינו חננאל

לדון ממנו גזירה שוה: **ופסח** דורות נוהג כל ז' אוקמ' הכי פסח מצרים נוהג לילה א' וכן מצתו והוא הדין לפסח דורות וחמוץ מצרים אינו נוהג אלא יום אחד שנאמר לא יאכל חמץ היום אתם יוצאים וחמוץ פסח דורות נוהג כל ז' שנאמר שבעת ימים שאור לא ימצא בבתיכם: **מתני'** א"ר יהושע שמעתי שתמורת הפסח קריבה ותמורת הפסח אינה קריבה ואין לי לפרש אמר ר' עקיבא אני אפרש הפסח שנמצא קודם שחיטה וכו' והאי דקאמר רבי יהושע תמורת הפסח ולא שנא פסח אתא לאשמעי' דאיכא תמורת פסח דלא קרבה שלמים: **איתמר** רבה אמר זה שפירש רבי עקיבא במשנתנו מי שאבד פסחו והפריש אחר אם זה הפסח האבוד נמצא קודם [שחיטת]הפסח שהפריש ירעה עד שיסתאב וכו' ואם אחר שחיטה נמצא יקרב הפסח שנמצא עכשיו שלמים כי בשעה שנמצא כבר נתכפרו בעלים ונסתלק שם פסח מעליו וכן התמורתו. ר' זירא אמר משנתנו בשנמצא קודם חצות והאי דקתני קודם שחיטה קודם זמן שחיטה הוא ועלתה כתנאי: **אחר** הפסח יביא שלמים וכן תמורתו אמר רבה לא שנו יביא שלמים וכן תמורתו אלא בפסח שנמצא אחר שחיטת הפסח שהפריש כיון שאבד זה דהתחם של זה לשלמים קאי כבר יצאו הבעלים בפסח ששחטו אבל אם נמצא קודם שחיטה והמיר בו אחר שחיטה תמורתו מכח קדושה דחויה קא אתיא דהפסח עצמו שנמצא קודם שחיטה נדחה מן הקרבה הוא בעצמו ולרעיה קאי והבא מכחו כח קדושה דחויה [הוא] לפיכך לא קרבה שלמים שלא מצינו הטפל עדיף מן העיקר ואותיב עליה אביי אם כשב מה ת"ל אם כשב לרבות תמורת הפסח ופריק ליה לעולם כשנמצא אחר שחיטה והמיר בו אחר שחיטה והאי קרא תמורתו שלמים והאי דאמרת הני שלמים מעלי ניתנה ולא בעי קרא אין הכי נמי וקרא אסמכתא בעלמא הוא. איכא דמתני להא דרבה ארישא הפסח שנמצא קודם שחיטת הפסח ירעה וכו' וכן תמורתו תרעה אמר רבה לא שנו אלא שנמצא קודם שחיטה והמיר בו קודם (תמורה)(שחיטה) דהאי תמורה מכח קדושה דחויה אתיא הלכך לא קרבה אבל נמצא קודם שחיטה והמיר בו קודם שחיטה תמורה זו קרבה שלמים מאי טעמא כי קבעה שחיטה קדושה בפסח שנמצא מידי דחזי להקרבה מידי דלא חזי להקרבה לא קבעה ומותיב עליה אביי מה ת"ל אם כבש לרבות הפסח שקרב שלמים יכול

מסורת הש"ס

לעיל ד' כח.
זבחים דף לז.
זבחים דף ט. מנחות דף פג: [לקמן לו.]
נ"ל אחר הפסח
[ס"א

הגהות הב"ח

(א) גמ' אמר רבא לא שנו:
(ב) שם למאי אתא לכדתניא כשב:

[days]? [96b]—Rather [it must refer] to leaven. Hence it follows that at the Passover of Egypt [leaven was forbidden] one night and no more; but surely it was taught, R. Jose the Galilean said: How do we know that at the Passover of Egypt the [prohibition of] leaven was in force one day only? Because it is said, *There shall no leavened bread be eaten,*[6] and in proximity [thereto] is written, *This day ye go forth!*[7]—Rather this is its meaning: [The Passover-offering is kept] one night, and the same law applies to the annual Passover-offering; while [the prohibition of] leaven [was in force] the whole day, whereas at the Passover-offering of [subsequent] generations [the interdict of leaven] holds good for the entire seven [days].

MISHNAH. R. JOSHUA SAID: I HAVE HEARD [FROM MY TEACHERS] THAT THE SUBSTITUTE OF A PASSOVER-OFFER-
a ING[1] IS OFFERED,[2] AND THAT THE SUBSTITUTE OF A PASSOVER-OFFERING IS NOT OFFERED,[3] AND I CANNOT EXPLAIN IT.[4] SAID R. AKIBA, I WILL EXPLAIN IT: THE PASSOVER-OFFERING WHICH WAS FOUND BEFORE THE SLAUGHTERING OF THE PASSOVER-OFFERING MUST BE LEFT TO GRAZE UNTIL IT BECOMES UNFIT,[5] BE SOLD, AND ONE BRINGS A PEACE-OFFERING FOR ITS MONEY; AND THE SAME APPLIES TO ITS SUBSTITUTE. [IF FOUND] AFTER THE SLAUGHTERING OF THE PASSOVER, IT IS OFFERED AS A PEACE-OFFERING, AND ITS SUBSTITUTE LIKEWISE.[6]

GEMARA. But let him say, The Passover-offering is offered, and the Passover-offering is not offered?[7]—He informs us this, [viz.,] that there is a substitute of a Passover-offering which is not offered [as a peace-offering].[8]

It was stated: Rabbah said: We learned, Before slaughtering
b and after slaughtering;[1] R. Zera maintained: We learned, Before midday and after midday.[2] But according to R. Zera, surely he teaches, BEFORE THE SLAUGHTERING OF THE PASSOVER-OFFERING?—Say: BEFORE THE TIME OF THE SLAUGHTERING OF THE PASSOVER-OFFERING.[3]

This is dependent on Tannaim: The Passover which is found before slaughtering must graze [etc.]; [if found] after slaughtering, it is offered. R. Eleazar said: [If found] before midday it must graze [etc.]; after midday, it is offered.

[IF IT IS FOUND] AFTER THE SLAUGHTERING OF THE PASSOVER, HE BRINGS IT AS A PEACE-OFFERING etc. Raba[4] said:

(6) Ibid. XIII, 3. (7) Ibid. 4; v. *supra* 28b, n. a9. Thus it was prohibited the whole day, not during the night only.

a (1) When an animal is dedicated for a sacrifice, another must not be declared as a substitute for it; if it is, both animals are holy, the holiness of the second being of the same nature as that of the first. But the substitute of a Passover-offering cannot be offered as such, but must be kept until after the Festival. Normally if a Passover-offering is not sacrificed at the proper time, e.g., if it was lost, it is subsequently sacrificed as a peace-offering. (2) As a peace-offering, after Passover. (3) As a peace-offering, but must graze until it becomes blemished, whereupon it is redeemed. (4) When it is offered and when it is not. (5) Through a blemish. (6) The animal originally dedicated for the Passover was lost, and another was dedicated in its stead. Now if it was found again before the second was slaughtered or before the time of slaughtering the Passover in general (the exact meaning is disputed in the Gemara), the fact that it was present at the time of slaughtering stamps it as a Passover, and by not slaughtering it, one has rejected it, as it were, with his own hands. Consequently, it can no longer be offered itself, but must be sold, etc. If after finding it he substituted another animal for it, that too is governed by the same law, as stated in n. a1. But if it was found *after* the second was killed, the time of the slaughtering has not stamped it with the name of a Passover-offering, nor has it been rejected therefrom. Consequently, it is brought itself after the Festival as a peace-offering. (7) Why does R. Joshua speak about the *substitute* of a Passover: surely he could say the same about the Passover itself? (8) For I might otherwise think that since the substitute cannot be sacrificed as a Passover-offering, it is as though he dedicated it in the first place for a peace-offering, and therefore must itself be offered as such in all cases, irrespective of what happens to the original. Hence he informs us that where the original cannot be offered, the substitute too cannot be offered.

b (1) I.e., if it was found before or after the second was actually slaughtered. (2) The time for slaughtering the Passover is from midday until evening. R. Zera maintains that if it is still unfound by midday, it can no longer be stamped as a Passover-offering even if it is found before the second is actually slaughtered, and therefore is subsequently sacrificed *itself* as a peace-offering. (3) This does not emend the Mishnah but rather explains it. (4) Var. lec. Rabbah.

◁ *For the continuation of the English translation of this page see overleaf.*

אלא אחמץ מכלל דפסח מצרים לילה אחד ותו לא *והתניא רבי יוסי הגלילי אומר מנין לפסח מצרים שאין חימוצו נוהג אלא יום אחד ת"ל °לא יאכל חמץ וסמיך ליה היום אתם יוצאים אלא ה"ק לילה אחד והוא הדין לפסח דורות וחימוצו כל היום ופסח דורות נוהג כל שבעה: **מתני'** *א"ר יהושע שמעתי שתמורת פסח קריבה ותמורת פסח אינה קריבה ואין לי לפרש א"ר עקיבא אני אפרש *הפסח שנמצא קודם שחיטת הפסח ירעה עד שיסתאב וימכר ויביא בדמיו שלמים וכן תמורתו אחר שחיטת הפסח קרב שלמים וכן תמורתו: **גמ'** ולימא פסח קרב ופסח אינו קרב הא קמ"ל דאיכא תמורת הפסח דלא קרבה איתמר רבה אמר *קודם שחיטה ולאחר שחיטה שנינו רבי זירא אמר קודם חצות ולאחר חצות שנינו ולרבי זירא הא קתני קודם שחיטת הפסח אימא קודם זמן שחיטת הפסח כתנאי הפסח שנמצא קודם שחיטה ירעה לאחר שחיטה יקרב ר"א אומר קודם חצות ירעה לאחר חצות יקרב: אחר שחיטת הפסח יביא שלמים וכו': אמר רבא (א) לא שנו אלא שנמצא אחר שחיטה והמיר בו אחר שחיטה אבל נמצא קודם שחיטה והמיר בו אחר שחיטה תמורתו מכח קדושה דחויה קא אתא ולא קרבה איתביה אביי °אם כשב מה ת"ל אם כשב לרבות תמורת הפסח אחר הפסח שקרבה שלמים היכי דמי אילימא שנמצא אחר שחיט' והמיר בו אחר שחיטה פשיטא למה לי קרא אלא לאו שנמצא קודם שחיטה והמיר בו אחר שחיטה לא לעולם שנמצא אחר שחיטה והמיר בו אחר שחיטה וקרא אסמכתא בעלמא אלא קרא למאי אתא (ב) *כדתניא כשב לרבות את הפסח לאליה כשהוא אומר אם כשב לרבות פסח שעברה שנתו ושלמים הבאין מחמת פסח לכל מצות שלמים שטעון סמיכה ונסכים ותנופת חזה ושוק וכשהוא אומר ואם עז הפסיק הענין °לימד על העז שאין טעונה אליה איכא דמתני לה ארישא הפסח שנמצא קודם שחיטת הפסח ירעה עד שיסתאב וימכר ויביא בדמיו שלמים וכן תמורתו אמר רבא לא שנו אלא שנמצא קודם שחיטה והמיר בו קודם שחיטה אבל נמצא קודם שחיטה והמיר בו אחר שחיטה תמורתו קריבה שלמים מאי טעמא כי קבעה שחיטה מידי דחזי ליה מידי דלא חזי ליה לא קבעה איתיביה אביי אם כשב מה תלמוד לומר לרבות תמורת הפסח אחר הפסח שקריבה שלמים
יכול

שמות יג · ויקרא ג

רש"י

ולא אחמץ · דאיסור חימוצו נוהג כל שבעה מכלל דלילה אחד דקתני מתני' בפסח מצרים אחמץ קאי וה"ק ואין חימוצו נוהג אלא לילה אחד ופסח דורות נוהג כל שבעה: יום א' · משמע כל היום: לא יאכל חמץ היום · וסמיך ליה היום אתם יוצאים: אלא · הכי משמע ונאכל בחפזון בלילה אחד וה"ה דפסח דורות נמי לילה אחד ופסח מצרים חימוצו נוהג כל היום ופסח דורות כל שבעה: **מתני'** שמעתי · מרבותי: שתמורת הפסח קריבה · שלמים אחר הפסח: ותמורת הפסח אינה קריבה · ויש תמורת פסח שאינה קריבה היא עצמה שלמים אלא רועה עד שיסתאב במום ותמכר ויביא בדמיה שלמים דמותר הפסח קרב שלמים: ואין לי לפרש · שכחתי על איזה שמעתי תקרב ועל איזה שמעתי תרעה: הפסח · שאבד והפריש אחר תחתיו ונמצא הראשון קודם שחיטת השני דהיה עומד לפניו בשעת שחיטה הרי קבעתו שעת שחיטה בשם פסח וזה שלא הקריבו דחהו בידים לא יקרב עוד הוא עצמו שלמים דאין זה מותר הפסח אלא פסח [דחוי]: וכן תמורתו · אם המיר הוא בו בהמת חולין אחרי כן הרי הוא כמוהו אין קרב הוא עצמו שלמים אלא דמיו ואם לאחר שחיטת השני נמצא הרי לא קבעתו שעת שחיטה בשם פסח ולא נדחה בידים ויביא שלמים ויקרב הוא עצמו שלמים וה"ה דמצי למיתני רבי יהושע אומר פסח קרב ופסח אינו קרב ובגמרא פריך לה: **גמ'** דאיכא תמורת הפסח דלא קרבה · ולא אמרינן מתחלה שלמים היא ואפילו המיר קודם שחיטה לא קבעתה זמן השחיטה בשם פסח ואין בה דחוי אלא אף היא נקבעת בפסח ונדחת: קודם שחיטה ואחר שחיטה · דוקא שנינו במשנתנו ולא שנינו בה זמן שחיטה דהיינו חצות ואשמעינן דאפילו היה אבוד בשעת חצות אם נמצא קודם שחיטת השני הוא נקבע ונדחה הואיל ונדחה להקריבו לפסח: קודם חצות שנינו · שעת חצות היא הקובעתו בפסח אם נמצא קודם חצות קבעתיה חצות שהרי נראה וכי לא אקרביה דחייה אבל נמצא אחר חצות אפי' נמצא קודם שחיטה אין כאן קביעות ולא דחוי: קודם שחיטה · של שני: קודם חצות · ונתכפר באחר ירעה: אחר חצות · ונתכפר באחר: יקרב זה שלמים · ואע"פ שבשעת שחיטת השני הרי הוא עומד בפניו: לא שנו · דתמורה קרבה אלא שנמצא אחר שחיטה שאפי' הפסח לא נדחה אבל נמצא קודם שחיטה שהוא עצמו נדחה אע"פ שתמורתו לא נדחית בידים אינה קריבה שהרי מכח קדושה דחויה באה: אם כשב · הוא מקריב גבי שלמים כתיב אם יתירא הוא דמצי למיכתב כשב הוא מקריב א"נ כשב קדרים דהא כתיב לעיל מיניה אם מן הצאן קרבנו ובפרשה תחתונה אמור ואם עז קרבנו מכלל דעד השתא בכשב איירי דאין לך עוד בצאן אלא כשב: למה לי קרא · הא מותר הפסח הוא ונפקא לן מזבחת פסח דמותר הפסח *אחר חצות קרב שלמים כדאמרן באלו דברים (לעיל דף ע:) ותמורתו כ"ש דקריבה דלא עדיפא מיניה: והמיר בו אחר שחיטה · ואשמעינן דאע"ג דאיהו לא קרב תמורתו קריבה הואיל ולא הוקדשה קודם שחיטה: כשב · קרא יתירא כדפרישית מדכתיב בתריה ואם עז מכלל דעד השתא בכשב איירי: לאליה · דבכל קרבנות כשב אליה כתיבא עם האימורין בשלמים חלבו האליה (ויקרא ג) ובאשם כתיב (שם ז) את כל חלבו יריס ממנו את האליה וגו' וחטאת כאשם אבל פסח אימורין גופייהו לא כתיבי בהדיא אלא כדנפקא לן (לעיל דף סד:) מאת דמם תזרוק ואת חלבם תקטיר הלכך אלייתו צריכה להתרבות בקרבנות שבשור לא הוזכרה אליה באימוריו: ושלמים הבאין מחמת פסח · מותר פסח כגון תמורתו ופסח שנתכפרו בעליו באחר כך שמעתי: לכל מצות · מצות שלמים גרסינן שיהא דין כל חומר שלמים עליהן לשון אחר הבאין מחמת פסח חגיגת ארבעה עשר וזו שמעתי [וכך קבל רבי]: ואם · הפסק הוא להפסיק בין כשב לעז שבכשב נתפרשה אליה כדכתיב האליה תמימה לעומת העצה ממקום שהכליות יועצות ובא הכתוב והפסיק ולמד על העז שאינה טעונה אליה להקריב אליה שלה למזבח יש מפרשין עז אין לו אליה וטעות הוא בידם שהרי ממקום שהכליות יועצות היא ניטלית ועוד מה לימד הכתוב הואיל ואין לו: איכא דמתני · להאי לא שנו דרבה: לא שנו · שאף תמורתו דחויה אלא שנמצא קודם שחיטה והמיר בו קודם שחיטה דכי שחטיה דחינהו לתרוייהו הני שהיו ראוין ועומדים לפסח וקבעו: אבל המיר בו אחר שחיטה · אע"פ שהפסח רועה התמורה קריבה שהרי לא נדחית: מידי דלא חזי ליה · שעדיין לא הוקדש:
יכול

תוספות

קודם שחיטת הפסח ירעה · וטעמא דדחייה בידים כדפירש רש"י ואפי' רב דאמר אין בעלי חיים נדחין ופליג אר' יוחנן בפ' שני שעירי (יומא דף סד·) הייט דוקא כגון דלא דחייה בידים כגון נטמאו בעלים או שמשכו ידיהם וא"ת והא משמע דפליג בפ"ק דקדושין (דף ז·) דא"ר יוחנן בהמה של ב' שותפין הקדיש חציה וחזר ולקחה והקדיש חציה קדושה ואינה קריבה משום דנדחת בתחלה כשהקדיש חציה ודייק עלה ש"מ בעלי חיים נדחין משמע דרב פליג וי"ל כיון דדרך הקדש דחי לה לא מיקרי כל כך דחוי בידים ובתוספתא [פ"ט] פליגי רבי יוסי ורבנן איזה מהן יקריב לכתחלה ומייתי לה בפ' שני שעירי (יומא דף סד·):

קמ"ל דאיכא תמורת הפסח דלא קרבה · דקבע לה חצות או שחיטה דס"ד דלא קבע הואיל ובאיסור הוקדשה ואין דעתו עליה לשוחטה לשם פסח קמ"ל דאפילו הכי קבע לה ור"י מפרש דס"ד הואיל ואינה קריבה לעולם לשם פסח מתחלתה שלמים היא קמ"ל ומתוך פרש"י דפי' אלא אף היא נקבעת בפסח ונדחה משמע שסובר שלפי האמת ראויה לפסח:

ושלמים הבאין מחמת הפסח · לפי אותו לשון דפירש בקונטרס דהנך שלמים היינו חגיגת י"ד אין לחוש מה (*שפירש) באלו דברים (דף ע"א: ד"ה לימד) דשלמים הבאים מחמת פסח בפרק כל הפסולים (זבחים דף לו·) היינו מותר פסח דהא כדאיתא והא כדאיתא: **ואם** עז הפסיק הענין · פירש ריב"א מדלא כלל אותו בהדי כבש אלא הפסיק הענין וכתבו לבדו ולא שינה בו כלום אלא דלא כתיב ביה אליה להכי כתביה למעוטי מתורת אליה:
אילימא

רבינו חננאל

לדון ממנו גזירה שוה: **ופסח** דורות נוהג כל ז' אקמ' הכי פסח מצרים נוהג לילה א' וכן מצתו והוא הדין לפסח דורות וחמוץ מצרים אינו נוהג אלא יום אחד שנאמר לא יאכל חמץ היום אתם יוצאים וחמוץ פסח דורות נוהג כל ז' שנאמר שבעת ימים שאור לא ימצא בבתיכם: **מתני'** א"ר יהושע שמעתי שתמורת הפסח קריבה ותמורת הפסח אינה קריבה ואין לי לפרש אמר ר' עקיבא אני אפרש הפסח שנמצא קודם שחיטה וכו' והאי דקאמר רבי יהושע תמורת הפסח ולא שנא פסח אתא לאשמועי' דאיכא תמורת פסח דלא קרבה שלמים: **איתמר** רבה אמר זה שפירש רבי עקיבא במשנתנו מי שאבד פסחו והפריש אחר אם זה הפסח האבוד נמצא קודם [שחיטת]הפסח שהפריש ירעה עד שיסתאב וכו' ואם אחר שחיטה נמצא יקרב הפסח שנמצא עכשיו שלמים כי בשעה שנמצא כבר נתכפרו בעלים ונסתלק שם פסח מעליו וכן תמורתו. ר' זירא אמר משנתנו בשנמצא קודם חצות והאי דקתני קודם שחיטה קודם זמן שחיטה הוא ותלתה כתנאי: **אחר** הפסח יביא שלמים וכן תמורתו אמר רבה לא שנו יביא שלמים וכן תמורתו אלא בפסח שנמצא אחר שחיטת הפסח שהפריש כיון שאבד זה דסתמו של זה לשלמים קאי שכבר יצאו הבעלים בפסח ששחטו אבל אם נמצא קודם שחיטה והמיר בו אחר שחיטה תמורתו מכח קדושה דחויה קא אתיא דפסח עצמו שנמצא קודם שחיטה נדחה מלהקרב הוא בעצמו ולרעיה קאי והבא מכחו כח קדושה דחויה [הוא] לפיכך לא קרבה שלמים שלא מצינו הטפל עדיף מן העיקר ואותיב עליה אביי אם כשב מה ת"ל אם כשב לרבות תמורת הפסח וכו' ושני ליה לעולם כשנמצא אחר שחיטה והמיר בו אחר שחיטה והאדקרבה תמורתו שלמים והאי דאמרת הני שלמים מעלי ניגהו ולא בעי קרא אין הכי נמי וקרא אסמכתא בעלמא הוא. איכא דמתני להא דרבה ארישא הפסח שנמצא קודם שחיטת הפסח ירעה וכו' וכן תמורתו אמר רבה לא שנו אלא שנמצא קודם שחיטה והמיר בו אחר (תמורה)[שחיטה] דהאי תמור' מכח קדושה דחויה אתיא הלכך לא קרבה אבל נמצא קודם שחיטה והמיר בו קודם שחיטה תמורה זו קרבה שלמים מאי טעמא כי קבעה שחיטה קדושה בפסח שנמצא מידי דחזי להקרבה מידי דלא חזי להקרבה לא קבעה ומותיב עליה אביי מה ת"ל אם כבש לרבות הפסח שקרב שלמים יכול

עין משפט נר מצוה

כו א ב ג מיי' פ"ד מהל' ק"פ הלכה ו:
כז ד שם הלכה ז:
כח ה מיי' פ"א מהל' מעשה קרבנות הלכה יא:

מסורת הש"ס

לעיל ד' כח:
זבחים דף ט:
זבחים דף ט. מנחות דף פג: [לקמן צו.]
צ"ל אחר הפסח
[ס"א]

הגהות הב"ח

(א) גמ' אמר רבה לא שנו: (ב) שם למאי אתא לכדתניא כשב:

מהו · מי מחייבי משום אוכלי קדשים בטומאה אי לא: אישתרי נמי טומאה אימורין · דלא מחייב בהו משום טומאה ואע"ג דאסורי משום זרות וכל זר לא יאכל קדש (ויקרא כב): מכדי · אוכל אימורין בטומאה מהיכא אתרבי לחובה: מטומאת בשר · דכתיב גבי אוכל בשר בטומאה הגוף אשר לה' לרבות את האימורין והנפש אשר תאכל בשר מזבח השלמים אשר לה': היכא אקטרינהו · שלא הוזכר בו מזבח: שויסקי (א) · בשר צלי בשפוד: ג' מזבחות · להזאת הדם אבל להקטרת אימורין לא היה שם מזבח: מתני' מקחו מבעשור · אומר זה לשם פסח דכתיב בעשור לחדש הזה וגו' (שמות יב): וטעון הזאה באגודת אזוב · גרסי': לילה אחד · מפרש בגמרא:

מהו מדאישתרי טומאת בשר אישתרי נמי טומאת אימורין או דילמא מאי דאישתרי אישתרי מאי דלא אישתרי לא אישתרי אמר רבא מכדי טומאת אימורין מהיכא איתרבי מטומאת בשר דכתיב °אשר לה' *לרבות את האימורין כל היכא דאיתיה לטומאת בשר איתיה לטומאת אימורין *כל היכא דליתיה לטומאת בשר ליתיה לטומאת אימורין בעי רבי זירא אימורי פסח מצרים היכא אקטרינהו א"ל אביי ומאן לימא לן דלא שויסקי עבוד ועוד הא תנא רב יוסף ג' מזבחות היו שם על המשקוף ועל שתי המזוזות ותו מידי אחרינא לא הוה:

מתני' °מה בין פסח מצרים לפסח דורות פסח מצרים מקחו מבעשור וטעון הזאה באגודת אזוב ועל המשקוף ועל שתי המזוזות ונאכל בחפזון בלילה אחד ופסח דורות נוהג כל שבעה:

גמ' מנא לן דכתיב °דברו אל כל עדת ישראל לאמר בעשור לחדש הזה ויקחו זה מקחו מבעשור ואין פסח דורות מקחו מבעשור אלא מעתה °והיה לכם למשמרת עד ארבעה עשר יום לחדש הזה הכי נמי זה טעון ביקור ד' ימים קודם שחיטה ואין אחר טעון ביקור *והתניא בן בג בג אומר מניין °לתמיד שטעון ביקור ד' ימים קודם שחיטה שנא' °תשמרו להקריב לי במועדו ולהלן הוא אומר והיה לכם למשמרת עד ארבעה עשר מה להלן טעון ביקור ד' ימים קודם שחיטה אף כאן טעון ביקור ד' ימים קודם שחיטה שאני התם דכתיב תשמרו ופסח דורות נמי הכתיב °ועבדת את העבודה הזאת בחדש הזה *שיהו כל עבודות חדש זה כזה אלא ההוא הזה למעוטי פסח שני דכוותיה אלא מעתה דכתיב °ואכלו את הבשר בלילה הזה ה"נ דזה נאכל בלילה ואין אחר נאכל בלילה אמר קרא ועבדת את העבודה אלא הזה למה לי *לכדר' אלעזר בן עזריה ור"ע אלא מעתה דכתיב °וכל ערל לא יאכל בו ה"נ דבו אינו אוכל אבל אוכל בפסח דורות אמר קרא °ועבדת אלא בו למה לי *בו אינו אוכל אבל הוא אוכל במצה ומרור אלא מעתה °(*וכל) בן נכר לא יאכל בו ה"נ דבו אינו אוכל אבל אוכל הוא פסח לדורות אמר °קרא ועבדת אלא בו למה לי *בו המרת דת פוסלת ואין המרת דת פוסלת בתרומה *ואיצטריך למיכתב ערל ואיצטריך למכתב בן נכר *דאי כתב רחמנא ערל משום דמאיס אבל בן נכר לא מאיס אימא לא צריכא ואי אשמעינן בן נכר משום דאין לבו לשמים אבל ערל דלבו לשמים אימא לא צריכא אלא מעתה °תושב ושכיר לא יאכל בו הכי נמי דבו הוא אינו אוכל אבל אוכל הוא בפסח דורות אמר קרא ועבדת אלא בו למה לי בו המרת דת פוסלת ואין המרת דת פוסלת בתרומה אלא מעתה °ומלתה אותו אז יאכל בו ה"נ דבו אינו אוכל אבל אוכל בפסח דורות אמר קרא ועבדת אלא בו ל"ל *בו מילת זכריו ועבדיו מעכבת ואין מילת זכריו ועבדיו מעכבת בתרומה אלא מעתה דכתיב °ועצם לא ישברו בו ה"נ דבו אינו שובר אבל שובר בפסח דורות אמר קרא ועבדת אלא בו למה לי *בו בכשר ולא בפסול אלא מעתה דכתיב °אל תאכלו ממנו נא ממנו אי אתה אוכל אבל אתה אוכל נא בפסח דורות אמר קרא ועבדת אלא ממנו למה לי *לכדרבה א"ר יצחק: ונאכל בחפזון וכו': מנא לן דאמר קרא °ואכלתם אותו בחפזון אותו נאכל בחפזון ואין אחר נאכל בחפזון: ופסח דורות נוהג כל שבעה וכו': אמאי קאי אי לימא אפסח *פסח כל שבעה מי איכא

אלא

רש"י

גמ' למשמרת · ביקור שלא יהא בו מום מבקרין אותו כל ארבעה וכתיב הזה ה"נ דממעטי [פסח דורות וכו'] שאר קרבנות: מה להלן כו' וכי היכי דלדורות בתמיד בעי ביקור ה"ה ודאי לפסח דורות: ופסח דורות נמי כו' · בכיוצא: שיהו כל עבודות של חדש הזה כזה · כל פסחי דורות הוקשו זה לזה ומיהו לענין מקחו מבעשור אמעיט מהזה והאי הזה דגבי ביקור דריש ליה למלתא אחריתא כדמפרש ואזיל: אלא הזה · דגבי ביקור למה לי: למעוטי פסח שני · מביקור ארבעה ימים: דכוותיה · דהוי יום אחד כמו פסח מצרים וכי קא ממעט דכוותיה ממעט והזה דגבי מקחו מבעשור על כרחך למעוטי פסח דורות אתא דאילו למעוטי שני לא איצטריך דהא אימעיט מהאי הזה דגבי ביקור ומימעיט מביקור ארבעה ימים וממקח מבעשור דתרוייהו משמעטי מההוא קרא דלמשמרת משמע ביקור ומקח ואידך הזה ממעט פסח דורות ממקח בעשור אבל מביקור ארבעה ימים לא ממעט ליה אם לא הפרישו מבעשור יבקר שנים ושלשה טלאים מבעשור ובשעת שחיטה יקח א' מהן: לכדר' אליעזר בן עזריה ורבי עקיבא. בפ"ק דברכות נאמר כאן בלילה הזה ונאמר להלן ועברתי בארץ מצרים בלילה הזה כו': ערל · שמתו אחיו מחמת מילה: בן נכר · שנתנכרו מעשיו לאביו שבשמים נראה בעיני דלא גרסינן גבי הדדי כל ערל וגו' כל בן נכר וגו' הכי נמי כו' אלא הכי גרסי' כל ערל לא יאכל בו הכי כו' אמר קרא ועבדת אלא בו למה לי בו המרת דת פוסלת ואין המרת דת פוסלת בתרומה ואיצטריך למיכתב ערל כו' ולא גרסי' אלא מעתה תושב ושכיר כו' דהא תושב ושכיר טולי' קרא יתירא הוא דתושב ושכיר אוכל בפסח דתושב זה קנוי כסף קנין עולם ונרצע ושכיר זה עבד עברי הקנוי קנין שנים ותרוייהו ישראל מעליא נינהו ואכלי בפסח כדאמרינן ביבמות בהערל (דף ע·) וקרא יתירא הוא ומופנה לגזירה שוה נאמר תושב ושכיר בפסח ונאמר תושב ושכיר בתרומה כדמפרש ליה התם ואיידי דכתביה כתב בו דידיה וללשון הספרים לא ידענא מאי שינויא דקא משני בו המרת דת פוסלת מאי שייך המרת דת גבי תושב ושכיר הא ישראל מעליא נינהו ועוד הא דרשה מבו דגבי בן נכר דרשינן לה בהערל (שם:) ומלתה אותו אז הבעלים יאכל בו ואי לא מל את עבדו לא יאכל איהו דמילת זכריו ועבדיו מעכבת בפסח אם יש לו בן העומד למול או עבד אינו אוכל פסח עד שימול אותם דכתיב המול לו כל זכר ואז יקרב לעשותו: כדרבה א"ר יצחק · בפ' הערל (דף עד·) נאמר ממנו בפסח ונאמר ממנו במעשר מה להלן ערל אסור במעשר אף כאן ערל אסור בפסח: *בחפזון · במהירות:

ואלא

תוספות

למעוטי פסח שני דכוותיה · דפסח דורות מרבינן מועבדת דליכא למימר דהזה דמקחו מבעשור נמי בא למעט פסח שני דאין מקחו מבעשור ולא נמעט פסח דורות דהא לפסח שני לא איצטריך כיון דלא בעי ביקור לא בעי נמי שיהא מקחו מבעשור:

אבל אתה שובר בפסח דורות אמר קרא ועבדת · תימה לריב"א אמאי איצטריך להכי ועבדת הא כיון דכתיב בפסח שני ועצם לא ישברו בו כל שכן בראשון:

אותו בחפזון ואין אחר בחפזון · קשה לריב"א אמאי לא פריך ולימא אותו בחפזון ואין פסח שני נאכל בחפזון אבל פסח דורות הכי נמי נאכל בחפזון מועבדת: (סייך לעמוד ב):

נאכל בחפזון לילה אחד וה"ה לפסח דורות · ואם תאמר א"כ אמאי תנייה כלל במתניתין כיון דשוים בזה ויש לומר דתנייה אגב דבעי למיתני וחמוצו כל היום ופסח דורות נוהג כל שבעה:

רבינו חננאל

מדאשתרי טומאת בשר אשתרי נמי טומאת החלבים או לא ופשט רבא טומאת אימורין מטומאת בשר איתרבו שנאמר אשר לה' לרבות האימורין וכיון דליתה לטומאת בשר ליתה לטומאת אימורין: בעי ר' זירא אימורי פסח מצרים היכא אקטרינהו אמר ליה ומאן לימא לן דלא שויסקי עבדינהו כלומר צלו אותם מיני מאכל ואכלום ועוד הא תאני רב יוסף שלש מזבחות היו שם אחד המשקוף ושתים בתי המזוזות שנתנו עליהם מן הדם ומזבח להקרבה לא הוה שם הלא משמע שאכלום: מה בין פסח מצרים לפסח דורות פסח מצרים מקחו מבעשור וכו' מנא לן דכתיב ויקחו להם זה מקחו מבעשור ולא לדורות מבעשור ואקשי' אי הכי כל מה דכתיב ביה הזה אמרי' לזה ולא לדורות והא כתיב ביה לכם למשמרת עד ארבעה עשר יום וכו' ותניא מנין לתמיד שטעון ביקור ארבעה ימים קודם שחיטה שנאמר תשמרו להקריב לי ונאמר בפסח מצרים והיה לכם למשמרת עד ארבעה עשר יום מה להלן ארבעה ימים קודם שחיטה אף כאן בתמיד טעון ביקור שמא יש בו מום ארבעה ימים קודם שחיטה ושני' שאני תמיד דכתיב ביה תשמרו מלמד שצריך שימור אקשי' תוב ופסח דורות אמאי אינו טעון ביקור ארבעה ימים והכתיב ועבדת את העבודה הזאת בחדש הזה שיהו כל עבודות של החדש הזה כזה ושני' אלא למעוטי מביקור ד' ימים קודם שחיטה לפסח שני הוא דממעט דכיון דהוא נמי פסח כותיה הוה מרבינן ליה קמ"ל אלא מעתה ואכלו את הבשר בלילה הזה הכי נמי דפסח מצרים נאכל בלילה הזה ולא פסח דורות ושני' שאני אכילת פסחים בלילה דאתרבי מועבדת שיהו כל עבודות של חדש הזה כזה אי הכי דאכילת בשר נוהג בזה כאשר נוהג בזה למה לי דכתב רחמנא הזה ושני' לא בא הזה אלא לכדר' אלעזר בן עזריה דיליף הזה הזה מועברתי בארץ מצרים וכתיב ביה כחצות הלילה אני יוצא וגו' מה להלן הזה דכתיב עד חצות אף הזה דכתיב באכילת פסחים עד חצות ופירושו בסוף מסכתא זו אקשי' תוב אלא מעתה כל ערל לא יאכל בו וכל בן נכר לא יאכל בו דכתיב בפסח מצרים נדחו מפסח מצרים וכשרין הן בפסח דורות ושני' שאני התם דכתיב ועבדת כדאמרן ומרבינן בפסח דורות מועבדת אכילת הבשר בלילה הזה ודחית ערל ובן נכר ותושב ושכיר פי' גר תושב ושכיר ולא גר צדק(הפסולות) ועיכוב אכילתו בפסח עד שימול עצמו וזכריו ועבדיו ושבירת עצם בו ואכילת נא ממנו אלו כולם נתרבו מועבדת את העבודה הזאת בחדש הזה שיהו כל עבודות של חדש הזה כזה פי' בפסח דורות וכיון דאתרבי בפסח דורות כפסח מצרים ממנו ממנו דכתיב בפסח מצרים דמשמע למעט למה לי ושני' הני ממנו ממנו בעינן להו כדדרשינהו רבא משמיה דר' יצחק ביבמות פ' הערל דאמרי' מנין לערל שאסור במעשר אמר רבא אמר ר' יצחק תלתא ממנו כתיבי בפסח חד לגופיה וחד מופנה לדון ממנה גזירה שוה וחד ליתן עשה אחר לא תעשה ושלשה ממנו כתיבי במעשר חד לגופיה וחד שאסור לסוך שמן של מעשר שני שנטמא כו' וחד מופנה לדון

עין משפט נר מצוה

יט א מיי' פ"ט מהל' ק"פ הלכה ח:
כ ב מיי' פ"י מהל' ק"פ הלכה ח:
כא ג מיי' פ"א מהל' תמידין הלכה ט:
כב ד מיי' פ"ט מהל' ק"פ הלכה ח:
כג ה שם הלכה ו:
כד ו מיי' פ"ט מהל' ק"פ הלכה ט:
כה ז מיי' פ"ה מהל' תרומות הל' י' ויב:

מסורת הש"ס

פ"א [לעיל כד: זבחים לו: כריתות כג:]
[מגילה ספנים ס"ח] ערכין דף יג: [מנחות מט:]
[מכות פב:]
ברכות דף ט. וש"נ
[לעיל כח: לקמן קכ. יבמות עא.]
יבמות עא:
שם עא.
[יבמות ד' עב:]
[לעיל ע. וש"נ]
[נ"ש ביבמות עא. ודף עד. ע"ש]
[לעיל לא:]
דיבור זה שייך [לעיל במשנה]
[ע"ל כו:]
יבמות עא. זבחים כב: [עי' זבחים כג: וכתוס' לקמן קכ ד"ה כל בן וביבמות עא. תוספות ד"ה כן]

הגהות הב"ח

(א) רש"י ד"ה שויסקי. ר"ל נקודין בן דף פ"ג:

Continuation of translation from previous page as indicated by ◁

is required] for [the exegesis] of R. Eleazar b. 'Azariah and R. Akiba [respectively].[9]

But if so, when it is written, *But no uncircumcised person shall eat thereof,*[10] does that too [teach] that he may not eat *'thereof,'* yet he may eat of the Passover-offering of [subsequent] generations?—[No, for] Scripture saith, *'Then thou shalt keep [this service* etc.].' Then what is the purpose of *'thereof'?—Thereof* he must not eat, but he eats unleavened bread and the bitter herbs. But if so, when it is written, *There shall no alien eat thereof,*[11] is it the case there too that he must not eat *thereof*, yet he eats of the Passover-offering of [subsequent] generations?—Scripture saith, *'Then thou shalt keep* [etc.].' Then what is the purpose of *'thereof'?*—In that case only [*'thereof'*] does apostasy disqualify, but apostasy does not disqualify in the case of *terumah*. Now it is necessary that an uncircumcised person should be stated, and it is necessary that an alien should be stated. For if the Divine Law stated an uncircumcised person, [I would say that he is disqualified] because he is repulsive, but an alien is not repulsive, [so] I would say [that he is] not [excluded] from the Passover-offering]; hence [an alien] is necessary. And if we were informed about an alien, [I would argue that he is disqualified] because his heart is not toward Heaven, but [as for] an uncircumcised person, whose heart is
c toward Heaven,[1] I would say [that he is] not [excluded]. Thus both are necessary.

But if so, [when it is written,] *A sojourner* [toshab] *and a hired servant* [sakir] *shall not eat thereof,*[2] does that too [intimate] that he must not eat *thereof*, but he does eat of the annual Passover?—Scripture saith, *'Then thou shalt keep* [etc.]'. Then what is the purpose of *'thereof'?*—Only in this case does apostasy disqualify, but apostasy does not disqualify from *terumah*.[3]

But if so, [when it is written, *But every man's servant that is bought for money,*] *when thou hast circumcised him, then shall he eat thereof,*[4] —does that too [intimate] that he must not eat *thereof*, but he does eat of the annual Passover?—Scripture saith, *'Then thou shalt keep* [etc.]'. Then what is the purpose of *'thereof'* [bo]? Only in this case [*bo*] is the circumcision of his males and his slaves indispensable,[5] but the circumcision of his males and his slaves is not indispensable in the case of *terumah*.

d But if so, when it is written, *Neither shall ye break a bone thereof,*[1] does that too [intimate] that he may not break [a bone] *thereof*, but he may break [a bone] of the annual Passover?—Scripture saith, *'Then thou shalt keep* [etc.]'. Then what is the purpose of *'thereof'? 'Thereof'* [indicates] of a fit [sacrifice], but not of an unfit [one].[2]

But if so, when it is written, *Eat not of it half-roast,*[3] [does that too intimate,] of *it* you may not eat [half-roast], but you may eat half-roast of the annual Passover-offering?—Scripture saith, *'Then thou shalt keep* etc.' Then what is the purpose of *'of it'?*—For the teaching of Rabbah in R. Isaac's name.[4]

AND WAS EATEN IN HASTE etc. How do we know it?—Because Scripture saith, *and ye shall eat it in haste:*[5] *'it'* was eaten in haste, but no other was eaten in haste.

AND THE ANNUAL PASSOVER-OFFERING IS KEPT THE WHOLE SEVEN [DAYS] etc. To what does this refer? If we say, to the Passover-offering,—is there then a Passover-offering all the seven

(9) According to the former, to teach that it may be eaten until midnight only; according to the latter, to show that it may not be eaten two nights; v. Ber. 9*a*. (10) Ibid. XII, 48. (11) Ibid. 43. By *'alien'* is understood not a non-Jew but a Jewish apostate, whose actions have alienated him from God.

c (1) For this is understood to refer to one whose brothers died through circumcision, so that he fears the operation, but would otherwise have it performed. (2) Ex. XII, 45. (3) This seems quite unintelligible; Rashi deletes the whole passage on other grounds, observing that the answer is in any case pointless. Tosaf. in Yeb. 71*a* s.v. בו defends the present reading. (4) Ibid. 44. (5) The master may not partake of the Passover-offering until the males of his household are circumcised.

d (1) Ex. XII, 46. (2) V. *supra* 70*a* and 83*a*. (3) Ibid. 9. (4) Viz., that an uncircumcised person may not eat of tithe; v. Yeb. 74*a*. (5) Ibid. 11.

מהו · מי מחייבי משום אוכלי קדשים בטומאה אי לא: אישתרי נמי טומאת אימורין · דלא מיחייב בהו משום טומאה ואע"ג דאסירי משום זרות וכל זר לא יאכל קדש (ויקרא כב): מכדי · אוכל אימורין בטומאה מהיכא אתרבי לחיובא: מטומאת בשר · דכתיב גבי אוכל בשר בטומאת הגוף אשר לה' לרבות את האימורין והנפש אשר תאכל בשר מזבח השלמים אשר לה': היכא אקטרינהו · שלא הוזכר בו מזבח: שויסקי (א) · בשר צלי בשפוד: ג' מזבחות · להזאת הדם אבל להקטרת אימורין לא היה שם מזבח: מתני' מקחו מבעשור · אומר זה לשם פסח דכתיב בעשור לחדש הזה וגו' (שמות יב): וטעון הזאה באגודת אזוב גרסי': לילה אחד · מפרש בגמרא: גמ' למשמרת · ביקור שלא יהא בו מום מבקרין אותו כל ארבעה וכתיב הזה ה"ל דממעטי [פסח דורות וכו'] שאר קרבנות: מה להלן כו' · וכי היכי דלדורות בתמיד בעי ביקור ה"ה ולאו לפסח דורות: ופסח דורות נמי כו' · בכיוצא: שיהו כל עבודות של חדש הזה כזה · כל פסחי דורות הוקשו זה לזה ומיהו לענין מקחו מבעשור לממעיט מההוא והאי הזה דגבי ביקור דריש ליה למלתא אחריתא כדמפרש ואזיל: אלא הזה · דגבי ביקור למה לי: למעוטי פסח שני · מביקור ארבעה ימים: דכוותיה · דהוי יום אחד כמו פסח מצרים וכי קא ממעט דכוותיה ממעט והזה דגבי מקחו מבעשור על כרחיך למעוטי פסח דורות אתא דאילו למעוטי שני לא איצטריך דהא אימעיט מהאי הזה דגבי ביקור ומימעיט מביקור ארבעה ימים וממקח עשור דתרוייהו משתמעי מההוא קרא דלמשמרת משמע ביקור ומקח ואידך הזה ממעט פסח דורות ממקח בעשור אבל מביקור ארבעה ימים לא ממעט ליה אם לא הפרישו מבעשור יבקר שנים ושלשה טלאים מבעשור ובשעת שחיטה יקח א' מהן: לכדר' אליעזר בן עזריה ורבי עקיבא. בפ"ק דברכות נאמר כאן בלילה הזה ונאמר להלן ועברתי בארץ מצרים בלילה הזה כו': ערל · שמתו אחיו מחמת מילה: בן נכר · שנתנכרו מעשיו לאביו שבשמים נראה בעיני דלא גרסינן גבי הדדי כל ערל וגו' כל בן נכר וגו' הכי נמי כו' אלא הכי גרסי' כל ערל לא יאכל בו הכי כו' אמר קרא ועבדת אלא בו למה לי בו המרת דת פוסלת ואין המרת דת פוסלת בתרומה ואיצטריך למיכתב ערל כו' ולא גרסי' אלא מעתה תושב ושכיר כו' דהא תושב ושכיר טולי' קרא יתירא הוא דתושב ושכיר אוכל בפסח דתושב זה קנוי קנין כסף קנין עולם ונרצע ושכיר זה עבד עברי הקנוי קנין שנים ותרוייהו ישראל מעליא נינהו ואכלי בפסח כדאמרינן ביבמות בהערל (דף ע:) וקרא יתירא הוא ומופנה לגזירה שוה נאמר תושב ושכיר בפסח ונאמר תושב ושכיר בתרומה כדמפרש ליה התם ואיידי דכתביה כתב בו דידיה וללשון הספרים לא ידענא מאי שינויא דקא משני בו המרת דת פוסלת מאי שייך המרת דת גבי תושב ושכיר הא ישראל מעליא נינהו ועוד הא דרשה מבו דגבי בן נכר דרשינן לה בהערל (שם:) ומלתה אותו אז הבעלים יאכל בו ואי לא מל את עבדו לא יאכל איהו דמילת זכריו ועבדיו מעכבת בפסח אם יש לו בן העומד למול או עבד אינו אוכל פסח עד שימול אותם דכתיב המול לו כל זכר ואז יקרב לעשותו: כדרבה א"ר יצחק · בפ' הערל (דף עד·) נאמר ממנו בפסח ונאמר ממנו במעשר מה להלן ערל אסור בפסח אף כאן ערל אסור במעשר: *בחפזון · במהירות:

ואלא

מהו מדאישתרי טומאת בשר אישתרי נמי טומאת אימורין או דילמא מאי דאישתרי אישתרי מאי דלא אישתרי לא אישתרי אמר רבא מכדי טומאת אימורין מהיכא איתרבי מטומאת בשר דכתיב °אשר לה' *לרבות את האימורין כל היכא דאיתיה לטומאת בשר איתיה לטומאת אימורין °כל היכא דליתיה לטומאת בשר ליתיה לטומאת אימורין בעי רבי זירא אימורי פסח מצרים היכא אקטרינהו א"ל אביי ומאן לימא לן דלא שויסקי עבוד ועוד הא תנא רב יוסף ג' מזבחות היו שם על המשקוף ועל שתי המזוזות ותו מידי אחרינא לא הוה:

מתני' °מה בין פסח מצרים לפסח דורות פסח מצרים מקחו מבעשור וטעון הזאה באגודת אזוב ועל המשקוף ועל שתי המזוזות ונאכל בחפזון בלילה אחד ופסח דורות נוהג כל שבעה:

גמ' מנא לן דכתיב °דברו אל כל עדת ישראל לאמר בעשור לחדש הזה ויקחו זה מקחו מבעשור ואין פסח דורות מקחו מבעשור ואלא מעתה °והיה לכם למשמרת עד ארבעה עשר יום לחדש הזה הכי נמי זה טעון ביקור ד' ימים קודם שחיטה ואין אחר טעון ביקור *והתניא בן בג בג אומר מניין °לתמיד שטעון ביקור ד' ימים קודם שחיטה שנא' °תשמרו להקריב לי במועדו ולהלן הוא אומר והיה לכם למשמרת עד ארבעה עשר מה להלן טעון ביקור ד' ימים קודם שחיטה אף כאן טעון ביקור ד' ימים קודם שחיטה שאני התם דכתיב תשמרו ופסח דורות נמי הכתיב °ועבדת את העבודה הזאת בחדש הזה *שיהו כל עבודות חדש זה כזה אלא ההוא הזה למעוטי פסח שני דכוותיה אלא מעתה דכתיב °ואכלו את הבשר בלילה הזה ה"נ דזה נאכל בלילה ואין אחר נאכל בלילה אמר קרא ועבדת את העבודה אלא הזה למה לי *לכדר' אלעזר בן עזריה ור"ע אלא מעתה דכתיב °וכל ערל לא יאכל בו ה"נ דבו אינו אוכל אבל אוכל בפסח דורות אמר קרא °ועבדת אלא בו למה לי *בו אינו אוכל אבל אוכל הוא במצה ומרור אלא מעתה °(*וכל) בן נכר לא יאכל בו ה"נ דבו אינו אוכל אבל אוכל הוא פסח לדורות אמר °קרא ועבדת אלא בו למה לי *בו המרת דת פוסלת ואין המרת דת פוסלת בתרומה *ואיצטריך למיכתב ערל ואיצטריך למכתב בן נכר *דאי כתב רחמנא ערל משום דמאיס אבל בן נכר לא מאיס אימא לא צריכא ואי אשמעינן בן נכר משום דאין לבו לשמים אבל ערל דלבו לשמים אימא לא צריכא אלא מעתה °תושב ושכיר לא יאכל בו הכי נמי דבו הוא אינו אוכל אבל אוכל הוא בפסח דורות אמר קרא ועבדת אלא בו למה לי בו המרת דת פוסלת ואין המרת דת פוסלת בתרומה אלא מעתה °ומלתה אותו אז יאכל בו ה"נ דבו אינו אוכל אבל אוכל בפסח דורות אמר קרא ועבדת אלא בו ל"ל *בו מילת זכריו ועבדיו מעכבת ואין מילת זכריו ועבדיו מעכבת בתרומה אלא מעתה דכתיב °ועצם לא ישברו בו ה"נ דבו אינו שובר אבל שובר בפסח דורות אמר קרא ועבדת אלא בו למה לי *בו בכשר ולא בפסול אלא מעתה דכתיב °אל תאכלו ממנו נא ממנו אי אתה אוכל אבל אתה אוכל נא בפסח דורות אמר קרא ועבדת אלא ממנו למה לי *לכדרבה א"ר יצחק: ונאכל בחפזון וכו': מנא לן דאמר קרא °ואכלתם אותו בחפזון אותו נאכל בחפזון ואין אחר נאכל בחפזון: ופסח דורות נוהג כל שבעה וכו': אמאי קאי אי לימא אפסח *פסח כל שבעה מי איכא

אלא

תוספות

למעוטי פסח שני דכוותיה · דפסח דורות מרבינן מועבדת דליכא למימר דהזה דמקחו מבעשור נמי בא למעט פסח שני דאין מקחו מבעשור ולא נמעט פסח דורות דהא לפסח שני לא איצטריך כיון דלא בעי ביקור לא בעי נמי שיהא מקחו מבעשור:

אבל אתה שובר בפסח דורות אמר קרא ועבדת · תימה לריב"א אמאי איצטריך להכי ועבדת הא כיון דכתיב בפסח שני ועצם לא ישברו בו כל שכן בראשון:

אותו בחפזון ואין אחר בחפזון · קשה לריב"א אמאי לא פריך ואימא אותו בחפזון ואין פסח שני נאכל בחפזון אבל פסח דורות הכי נמי נאכל בחפזון מועבדת: (שייך לעמוד ב)

נאכל בחפזון לילה אחד וה"ה לפסח דורות · ואם תאמר א"כ אמאי תנייה כלל במתניתין כיון דשוים בזה ויש לומר דתנייה אגב דבעי למיתני וחמוצו כל היום ופסח דורות נוהג כל שבעה:

עין משפט נר מצוה

יט א מיי' פ"ו מהל' ק"פ הלכה ח:
כ ב מיי' פי"ו מהלכות ק"פ הלכה טו:
כא ג מיי' פ"א מהל' תמידין הלכה ט:
כב ד מיי' פ"ט מהל' ק"פ הלכה ח:
כג ה שם הלכה ז:
כד ו מיי' פ"ט מהל' ק"פ הלכה ט:
כה ז מיי' פ"ז מהל' תרומות הל' י ויב:

מסורת הש"ס

[לעיל כד: זבחים לו:] [פירוש כב:]
[מגילת תענית פ"א] ערכין דף יג: [מנחות מט:]
[מנחות סב:]
ברכות דף ט. וש"נ
[לעיל כח: לקמן קכ. יבמות עא.]
יבמות עא:
שם עא.
[יבמות ד' עג:]
[לעיל ע. וש"נ]
[נ"ש ביבמות עא. ודף עד. פ"ש]
[לעיל נא:]
דיבור זה שייך [לעיל במשנה]

[נ"ל כל]

יבמות עא. זבחים כב: [עי' זבחים כב: ובתוס' לקמן קכ ד"ה כל בן וביבמות עא. תוספות ד"ה בו]

הגהות הב"ח

(א) רש"י ד"ה שויסקי. נ"ב בקדושין דף נ ע"ב:

רבינו חננאל

מדאשתרי טומאת בשר אשתרי נמי טומאת החלבים או לא ופשט רבא טומאת אימורין מטומאת בשר איתרבו שנאמר אשר לה' לרבות האימורין וכיון דליתא לטומאת בשר ליתא לטומאת אימורין: בעי ר' זירא אימורי פסח מצרים היכא אקטרינהו אמר ליה ומאן לימא לן דלא שויסקי עבדינהו כלומר צלו אותם מיני מאכל ואכלום ועוד הא תאני רב יוסף שלש מזבחות היו שם אחד המשקוף ושתים בתי המזוזות שנתנו עליהם מן הדם ומזבח להקרבה לא הוה שם הלא משמע שאכלום: מה בין פסח מצרים לפסח דורות פסח מצרים מקחו מבעשור וכו' מנא לן דכתיב ויקחו להם זה מקחו מבעשור ולא לדורות מבעשור ואקשי' אי הכי כל מה דכתיב ביה הזה אמרי' לזה ולא לדורות והא כתיב ביה לכם למשמרת עד ארבעה עשר יום וכו' ותניא מנין לתמיד שטעון ביקור ארבעה ימים קודם שחיטה שנאמר תשמרו להקריב לי ונאמר בפסח מצרים והיה לכם למשמרת עד ארבעה עשר יום מה להלן ארבעה ימים קודם שחיטה אף כאן בתמיד טעון ביקור שמא יש בו מום ארבעה ימים קודם שחיטה ושני' שאני תמיד דכתיב ביה תשמרו מלמד שצריך שימור אקשי' תוב ופסח דורות אמאי אינו טעון ביקור ארבעה ימים והכתיב ועבדת את העבודה הזאת בחדש הזה שיהו כל עבודות של החדש הזה כזה ושני' אלא למעוטי מביקור ד' ימים קודם שחיטה לפסח שני הוא דממעט דכיון דהוא נמי פסח כותיה הוה מרבינן ליה קמ"ל אלא מעתה ואכלו את הבשר בלילה הזה הכי נמי דפסח מצרים נאכל בלילה הזה ולא פסח דורות ושני' שאני אכילת פסחים בלילה דאתרבי מועבדת שיהיו כל עבודות של חדש הזה כזה אי הכי דאכילת בשר נוהג בזה כאשר נוהג בזה למה לי דכתב רחמנא הזה ושני' לא בא הזה אלא לכדר' אלעזר בן עזריה דיליף הזה הזה מועברתי בארץ מצרים וכתיב ביה כחצות הלילה אני יוצא וגו' מה להלן הזה דכתיב עד חצות אף הזה דכתיב באכילת פסחים עד חצות ופירושו בסוף מסכתא זו אקשי' תוב אלא מעתה כל ערל לא יאכל בו וכל בן נכר לא יאכל בו דכתיב בפסח מצרים נדחו מפסח מצרים וכשרין הן בפסח דורות ושני' שאני התם דכתיב ועבדת כדאמרן ומרבינן בפסח דורות מועבדת אכילת הבשר בלילה הזה ודחית ערל ובן נכר ותושב ושכיר פי' גר תושב ושכיר ולא גר צדק (הפסולות) ועיכוב אכילתו בפסח עד שימול עצמו וזכריו ועבדיו ושבירת עצם בו ואכילת נא ממנו אלו כולם נתרבו מועבדת את העבודה הזאת בחדש הזה שיהו כל עבודות של חדש הזה כזה פי' בפסח דורות וכיון דאתרבי פסח דורות כפסח מצרים ממנו ממנו דכתיב בפסח מצרים דמשמע למעט למה לי ושני' הני ממנו ממנו בעינן להו כדרשינהו רבא משמיה דר' יצחק ביבמות פ' הערל דאמרי' מנין לערל שאסור במעשר אמר רבא אמר ר' יצחק תלתא ממנו כתיבי בפסח חד לגופיה וחד לניתן עשה אחר לא תעשה ושלשה ממנו כתיבי במעשר חד לגופיה וחד שאוכל שמן של מעשר שני שנטמא כו' וחד מופנה לדון ממנה גזירה שוה וחד לסך שמן של מעשר שני שנטמא כו' וחד מופנה לדון

offering which came in uncleanness?[6] [96a] [Do we say,] since the uncleanness of the flesh was permitted, the uncleanness of the *emurim* too was permitted;[7] or perhaps, what was permitted was permitted, and what was not permitted was not permitted?—Said Raba, Consider: whence is the uncleanness of *emurim* included?[8] From the uncleanness of the flesh, for it is written, *That pertain unto the Lord*,[9] which includes *emurim*: [hence] wherever the uncleanness of the flesh is interdicted, the uncleanness of the *emurim* is interdicted: while wherever [the interdict of] the uncleanness of the flesh is absent, [the interdict of] the uncleanness of the *emurim* is absent.

R. Zera asked: Where did they burn the *emurim* of the Passover-offering of Egypt?[10]—Said Abaye, And who is to tell us that it was not prepared roast?[11] Moreover, surely R. Joseph learned: Three altars were there [for the sprinkling of the blood] viz., the
a lintel and the two doorposts.[1] Further, was there nothing else?[2]

MISHNAH. WHAT IS THE DIFFERENCE BETWEEN THE PASSOVER-OFFERING OF EGYPT AND THE PASSOVER-OFFERING OF [SUBSEQUENT] GENERATIONS?[3] THE PASSOVER-OFFERING IN EGYPT WAS TAKEN ON THE TENTH [OF NISAN],[4] [ITS BLOOD] REQUIRED SPRINKLING WITH A BUNCH OF HYSSOP ON THE LINTEL AND ON THE TWO DOOR-POSTS, AND IT WAS EATEN IN HASTE ON ONE NIGHT; WHEREAS THE PASSOVER-OFFERING OF [SUBSEQUENT] GENERATIONS IS KEPT THE WHOLE SEVEN [DAYS].[5]

GEMARA. Whence do we know it?—Because it is written, *Speak ye unto all the congregation of Israel, saying: In the tenth day of this month they shall take [to them every man a lamb]*:[6] the taking of this one was on the tenth, whereas the taking of the Passover-offering of [subsequent] generations is not on the tenth. If so, [when it is written,] *And ye shall keep it* [mishmereth] *until the fourteenth day of this month*,[7] does that too [intimate], this requires a four days' examination before slaughtering,[8] but no other requires examination? Surely it was taught, The son of Bag Bag[9] said: How do we know that the *tamid*[10] requires a four days' examination before slaughtering? Because it is said, *Ye shall observe* [tishmeru] *to offer unto Me in its due season*,[11] while elsewhere it is said, *And ye shall keep it* [mishmereth] *until the fourteenth* [etc.]:[12] just as there it requires a four days' examination before slaughtering, so here too it requires a four days' examination before slaughtering?—There it is different, because *tishmeru* ['ye
b shall observe'] is written.[1] And thus [in connection with] the annual Passover-offering it is indeed written, *Then thou shalt keep this service in this month*,[2] [which intimates] that all the services of this month [in subsequent generations] should be like this.[3] Hence that [word] '*this*'[4] is to exclude the second Passover, which is like itself.[5]

But [again] if so, when it is written, *And they shall eat the flesh in this night*,[6] does that too [teach] that *this* is eaten at night, but another is not eaten at night?[7]—Scripture saith, *Then thou shalt keep this service* [etc.].[8] Then what is the purpose of 'this'?—[It

(6) The *emurim* were burnt on the altar, and were therefore forbidden. (7) So that liability on eating is not incurred on the grounds of their uncleanness, although there still remains the liability for the eating of *emurim* which are reserved for the altar. (8) Whence do we learn that for eating *emurim* in an unclean state liability is incurred?—Actually only the uncleanness of the flesh is explicitly mentioned. (9) Lev. VII, 20 (10) No mention is made of an altar there. (11) And eaten.

a (1) I.e., there were three places for the sprinkling of the blood, corresponding to the altar in the Temple. But there was no altar for the burning of the *emurim*. (2) In which the Passover-offering in Egypt differed from those offered in the Temple. Surely there were many points of difference (v. next Mishnah): why then assume that in this respect they were alike? (3) I.e., the annual Passover. (4) Its owner had to take it four days beforehand, declaring, 'This is for the Passover-offering'. (5) This is explained in the Gemara. (6) Ex. XII, 3. (7) Ibid. 6. (8) It was taken on the tenth and examined every day until the fourteenth for a blemish. (9) V. Aboth, chapter V, n. 7. (10) V. Glos. (11) Num. XXVIII, 2. (12) *Tishmeru* and *mishmereth* have the same root.

b (1) Hence the animal must be examined daily for four days before it is sacrificed, and the same applies to the annual Passover-offering, though the latter is not actually declared to be taken for that purpose. (2) Ex. XIII, 5. (3) I.e., all the regulations of the Egyptian Passover hold good for the annual Passover too, and this includes the four days' examination. The special 'taking' however has been excluded by the exegesis above. (4) In the verse, '*and ye shall keep it until the fourteenth day of this month*'. (5) Just as the Egyptian Passover was only one day, so is the annual second Passover of one day's duration only, and it is logical that '*this*' should exclude another Passover which is similar to itself. Hence it teaches that the animal sacrificed at the *second* Passover does not require a four days' examination. (6) Ex. XII, 8. (7) Surely not!—the annual Passover-offering was of course eaten at night. (8) Ex. XIII, 5.

◁ *For the continuation of the English translation of this page see overleaf.*

'they shall not break a bone thereof? [95b]—*Eat not of it half-roast.*[4] By its particularization what does it exclude? *Thou shalt not offer the blood of My sacrifice with leavened bread.*[5] May I [not] reverse it?—[The inclusion of] a precept pertaining to itself is preferable.

THE FIRST REQUIRES [THE RECITING OF] HALLEL WHEN IT IS EATEN etc. Whence do we know it?—Said R. Joḥanan on the authority of R. Simeon b. Jehozadak: Scripture saith, *Ye shall have a song as in the night when a feast is hallowed:*[6] the night that is hallowed for a feast [Festival] requires [the reciting of] *Hallel* ['Song'], while the night which is not hallowed for a feast does not require [the reciting of] *Hallel.*

BUT BOTH REQUIRE [THE RECITING OF] HALLEL WHEN THEY ARE SACRIFICED etc. What is the reason?—I can either say, [Scripture] excludes the night, but not the day; or alternatively, is it possible that Israel sacrifice their Passover-offerings or take their palm-branches[7] without reciting *Hallel!*

AND THEY ARE EATEN ROAST etc. Only the Sabbath [do they override], but not uncleanness:[8] our Mishnah does not agree with R. Judah, for it was taught: It [the second Passover] overrides the Sabbath, but it does not override uncleanness; R. Judah maintained: It overrides uncleanness too. What is the reason of the first Tanna?—Seeing that I have suspended him [from the first Passover] on account of uncleanness, shall he after all keep
a it in uncleanness?[1] And R. Judah?[2]—The Torah sought [means] for him to keep it in cleanness; yet if he was not privileged [thus], he must keep it in uncleanness.

Our Rabbis taught: The first Passover overrides the Sabbath, [and] the second Passover overrides the Sabbath; the first Passover overrides uncleanness, [and] the second Passover overrides uncleanness; the first Passover requires the spending of the night [in Jerusalem], [and] the second Passover requires the spending of the night [in Jerusalem]. '[The second Passover] overrides uncleanness'. With whom [does this agree]?—With R. Judah. But according to R. Judah, does it require the spending of the night [in Jerusalem]? Surely it was taught, R. Judah said: How do we know that the second Passover does not require the spending of the night [in Jerusalem]? Because it is said, *and thou shalt turn in the morning, and go unto thy tents;*[3] and it is written, *six days thou shalt eat unleavened bread:*[4] that which is eaten six [days] requires the spending of the night [in Jerusalem], but that which is not eaten six [days] does not require the spending of the night [in Jerusalem]?[5]—There is [a controversy of] two Tannaim as to R. Judah's opinion.

MISHNAH. [WITH REGARD TO] THE PASSOVER-OFFERING WHICH COMES IN UNCLEANNESS, ZABIN AND ZABOTH, MENSTRUANT WOMEN AND WOMEN AFTER CONFINEMENT MUST NOT EAT THEREOF, YET IF THEY DID EAT THEY ARE
b EXEMPT FROM KARETH;[1] BUT R. ELIEZER EXEMPTS [THEM] EVEN [OF THE KARETH NORMALLY INCURRED] FOR ENTERING THE SANCTUARY.

GEMARA. Our Rabbis taught: If *zabin* and *zaboth*, menstruant women and women after confinement ate of the Passover-offering which was sacrificed in uncleanness, you might think that they are culpable, therefore it is stated, *Every one that is clean may eat flesh* [of sacrifices]. *But the soul that eateth of the flesh of the sacrifice of peace-offerings, that pertain unto the Lord, having his uncleanness upon him, that soul shall be cut off:*[2] with regard to that which is eaten by clean persons, you are culpable on its account on the score of uncleanness, but as to that which is not eaten by clean persons, you are not culpable on its account on the score of uncleanness.[3] R. Eliezer said: If *zabin* and lepers[4] forced their way through and entered the Temple Court at a Passover-offering which came in uncleanness, you might think that they are culpable; therefore it is stated, [*command the children of Israel,*] *that they send out of the camp every leper, and everyone that hath an issue* [zab], *and whosoever is unclean by the dead:*[5] when those who are unclean by the dead are sent out, *zabin* and lepers are sent out; when those who are unclean by the dead are not sent out, *zabin* and lepers are not sent out.

R. Joseph asked: What if persons unclean through the dead forced their way in and entered the Temple [*hekal*][6] at a Passover-offering which came in uncleanness? [Do we say,] since the uncleanness of the Temple Court was permitted, the uncleanness
c of the Temple [*hekal*] too was permitted;[1] or perhaps, what was permitted was permitted, while what was not permitted was not permitted?—Said Raba: Scripture saith, *'that they send out of the camp,'* [implying] even from part of the camp.[2] Others maintain. Raba said: Scripture saith, *without* [mi-ḥuẓ] *the camp shall ye send them:*[3] only where[4] *'without the camp shall ye send them,'* is applicable, is *'that they send out of the camp'* applicable.[5]

R. Joseph asked: What if persons unclean by the dead forced their way through [to the altar] and ate the *emurim* of a Passover-

(4) Ex. XII, 9. (5) Ex. XXXIV, 25. (6) Isa. XXX, 29. (7) On the Feast of Tabernacles, v. Lev. XXIII, 40. (8) If the majority of those who should keep the second Passover are unclean, the sacrifice is not brought.

a (1) Surely not. (2) How does he rebut this argument? (3) Deut. XVI, 7. '*Thy tents*' is understood to refer to tents pitched without Jerusalem; but it cannot mean home, firstly because one might not travel on a Festival, and secondly because the pilgrimage burnt-offering was yet to be offered. The phrase '*in the morning*' teaches that the night was to be spent in Jerusalem, even after the Passover sacrifice was consumed. (4) Ibid. 8. (5) I.e., only the Passover-offering which necessitates the eating of unleavened bread six days (actually seven; v. *infra* 120a), and prohibits leaven necessitates the spending of the night in Jerusalem; the first Passover alone fulfils this condition, but not the second.—Thus R. Judah is self-contradictory.

b (1) The usual penalty for eating sacred flesh in a state of personal uncleanness. But if they actually entered the Temple too, they are liable to *kareth* on that account. (2) Lev. VII, 19f. (3) Hence when the Passover-offering comes in uncleanness, though *zabin* etc. may not eat of it, they nevertheless do not incur *kareth*. (4) So the text as emended and *supra* 67b. (5) Num. V, 2. (6) The hall containing the golden altar; the Temple proper, as opposed to the Temple Court. Even priests might enter it only when necessary; here entry was unnecessary, since the offering was sacrificed in the Temple Court.

c (1) I.e., no penalty is incurred on account of uncleanness. (2) Even when they are not sent out of the entire camp, as here, they are sent out of the part where their presence is not necessary; hence if they enter it they incur *kareth*. (3) Num. V, 3; '*mi-ḥuẓ*' implies right outside the whole of it. (4) Lit., 'read in his case'. (5) Hence, since he is not sent out of the whole camp, he is not liable.

מאי קא מרבה °אל תאכלו ממנו נא בפרטיה מאי קא ממעטי °לא תשחט על חמץ דם זבחי איפוך אנא מצוה דגופיה עדיף: הראשון טעון הלל באכילתו וכו': מנא הני מילי א"ר יוחנן משום ר' שמעון בן יהוצדק אמר קרא °השיר יהיה לכם כליל התקדש חג לילה המקודש לחג טעון הלל לילה שאין מקודש לחג אין טעון הלל: זה וזה טעונין הלל בעשייתן כו': מ"ט איבעית אימא לילה קא ממעט יום לא קא ממעט ואיבעית אימא *אפשר ישראל שוחטין את פסחיהן ונוטלין את לולביהן ואין אומרים הלל: ונאכלין צלי וכו': שבת אין טומאה לא מתני' דלא כרבי יהודה *דתניא *דוחה את השבת ואין דוחה את הטומאה ר' יהודה אומר אף דוחה את הטומאה מ"ט דת"ק מפני טומאה דחיתיו יחזור ויעשה בטומאה ורבי יהודה התורה חזרה עליו לעשותו בטהרה לא זכה יעשה בטומאה ת"ר פסח ראשון דוחה את השבת פסח שני דוחה את השבת פסח ראשון דוחה את הטומאה פסח שני דוחה את הטומאה פסח ראשון טעון לינה פסח שני טעון לינה *דוחה את הטומאה כמאן כר' יהודה ולרבי יהודה טעון לינה והא *תניא ר' יהודה אומר מניין לפסח שני שאין טעון לינה שנאמר °ופנית בבקר והלכת לאהליך וכתיב °ששת ימים תאכל מצות הנאכל לששה טעון לינה שאין נאכל לששה אין טעון לינה תרי תנאי ואליבא דרבי יהודה: **מתני'** *הפסח שבא בטומאה לא יאכלו ממנו זבין וזבות נדות ויולדות ואם אכלו פטורין מכרת ור' אליעזר פוטר אף על ביאת מקדש: **גמ'** ת"ר זבין וזבות נדות ויולדות שאכלו בפסח שבא בטומאה יכול יהו חייבין תלמוד לומר °כל טהור יאכל בשר °והנפש אשר תאכל בשר מזבח השלמים אשר לה' וטומאתו עליו ונכרתה *נאכל לטהורים חייבים עליו משום טמא ושאינו נאכל לטהורין אין חייבין עליו משום טמא *רבי אליעזר אומר יכול דחקו *זבין ונכנסו לעזרה בפסח הבא בטומאה יכול יהו חייבין תלמוד לומר °וישלחו מן המחנה כל צרוע וכל זב וכל טמא לנפש בזמן שטמאי מתים משתלחין זבין ומצורעין משתלחין אין טמאי מתים משתלחין אין זבין ומצורעין משתלחין בעי רב יוסף דחקו טמאי מתים ונכנסו להיכל בפסח הבא בטומאה מהו מדאישתרי טומאת עזרה אישתרי נמי טומאת היכל או דילמא מאי דאישתרי אישתרי מאי דלא אישתרי לא אישתרי אמר רבא אמר קרא °וישלחו מן המחנה אפילו מקצת מחנה *איכא דאמרי אמר רבא אמר קרא וישלחו מן המחנה אל מחוץ למחנה תשלחום כל היכא דקרינן ביה אל מחוץ למחנה תשלחום קרינן ביה וישלחו מן המחנה בעי רב יוסף דחקו טמאי מתים ואכלו אימורי פסח הבא בטומאה מהו

תורה אור: שמות יב; ישעי' ל; שם; דברים טז; שם; ויקרא ז; שם; במדבר ה; שם

פסח שני אין טעון לינה. תימה לרשב"א אמאי איצטריך הא לא מרבינן מכלל חקת הפסח מצוה שאינה על גופו: **טעון** לינה. פי' יום א' וילך יום שני וקשה דבלולב וערבה (סוכה דף מז:) משמע דטעון לינה כל ז' דקאמר כסס שבטעת ימי החג טעונין קרבן שיר וברכה ולינה מאי ברכה לאו זמן לא ברכת המזון ותפלה ה"נ מסתברא דאי ס"ד זמן זמן כל ז' מי איכא משמע דקרבן ולינה ניחא ליה שיהיו כל שבעה וי"ל דהוה מצי למימר ולטעמיך לינה כל ז' מי איכא וכמו שמסיק לזמן דאי לא בריך יומא קמא זמן יברך שאר ימים ה"נ נפרש גבי לינה אם לא לן יום ראשון ילין שאר ימים ולעולם אין טעון לינה רק יום א' ופ' דם חטאת (זבחים דף צז:) *כמי דקאמר ר' טרפון ואם בישל בו בתחלת הרגל יבשל בו כל הרגל ומפרש בגמרא אמר רבי יצחק דאמר קרא ופנית בבקר עשאן הכתוב כולן בקר א' היינו דאגידי כולן זה בזה כמו בקר א' שאם לא לן אתמול ילין היום והדר ופנית בבקר וע"כ כן הוא דאי לינה כל ז' א"כ מאי קאמר שמיני רגל בפני עצמו לגבי לינה הלא כל שאר ימים שלפניו נמי טעונין לינה אלא ודאי יום ראשון ושמיני טעונין לינה ולא יותר וכן משמע בספרי בפרשת כל הבכור והלכת לאהליך מלמד שטעונין לינה פי' כל ג' רגלים מנין לרבות עופות ומנחות יין ולבונה ועצים ת"ל ופנית בבקר כל פנות שאתה פונה לא יהא אלא מבקר ואילך ר' יהודה אומר יכול יהא [פסח קטן טעון לינה ת"ל ועשית פסח כו'] וחכמים אומרים הרי הם כעלים וכלבונה שטעונים לינה משמע שאינו טעון לינה אלא אותו] לילה בלבד שאחר הבאת קרבנו ומרבי ליה כמו לינה דרגלים אלמא יום אחד הוא ותו לא ולא"ת דהכא ממעט פסח [קטן] מלינה ומי גרע ממביא קרבנו בימות החול דטעון לינה יום א' ושמא כיון דתשלומין דראשון הוא לא בעי לינה אפילו יום אחד ולא"ת דתנן (סוכה דף מב.) ההלל והשמחה שמונה א"כ ע"כ יצטרך לינה כל ז' משום שלמי שמחה דהוקא בשבת אמרינן באלו דברים (לעיל דף עא.) משמחו בכסות נקיה ויין ישן וי"ל ישמח באותן שכשחטו אתמול או בשלמי חגיגו: **כל** היכא דקרינא ביה אל מחוץ למחנה כו'. וא"ת כיון דאין חילוק בין היכל לעזרה למאי הלכתא איכתיב מן המחנה דמשמע מקצת מחנה וי"ל דעשה מיהא איכא בהיכל טפי מבעזרה דלא אישתרי מהיקשא אלא כרת: למעוטי

מאי קא מרבי אל תאכלו ממנו נא. דחייב בפסח שני: לא תשחט על חמץ. דמותר לשוחטו על חמץ כדתנן מלה וחמץ עמו בבית אע"ג דכבר מיעט ליה מהשבתת שאור ומבל ירלה הוא אמינא הכי מילי שלא בשעת שחיטה אבל בשעת שחיטה לא להכי איצטריך למעוטי מלא תשחט: השיר יהיה לכם. ביום שתגאלו מן הגלות: כליל התקדש חג. כמו שאתם נוהגים לשורר בליל התקדש חג ואין לך לילי חג להטעין שירה חוץ מלילי פסחים על אכילתו: לילה המקודש לחג. כגון פסח ראשון: שאין מקודש לחג. כגון ליל אכילת פסח שני שאינו י"ט: לילה. דפסח שני מיעט אבל יום שהוא זמן עשייתו לא מיעט והרי הוא כפסח ראשון שטעון הלל בשעת שחיטתו כדאמרן בתמיד נשחט (לעיל דף סד.) ולקמן (דף קיז.) אמרינן נביאים שביניהן תקנו להם שיהו אומרים על כל פרק ופרק ועל כל דבר חידוש: אפשר כו'. דכיון דדבר מצוה הוא טעון הלל: נוטלין את לולביהן. אגררא נסבה דברייתא היא הכי בפרק בתרא (שם): ללי (א). דאיתרבי מכלליה דמצות ומרורים: דוחה את השבת. דבשני כתיב ביה במועדו למ"ד *קרבן ה' לא הקריב במועדו בשני (לעיל דף צג:): יחזור ויעשה בטומאה. בתמיה אלא מוטב ידחה לגמרי: טעון לינה. לילה הראשון ילין בירושלים מיכן ואילך רשאי לדור חוץ לחומה בתוך התחום והייט לאהליך לאהל שחוץ לחומה ולא לביתו ממש דהא י"ט דכריסהוא ועוד דקא בעי לאיתויי עולת ראייה: הנאכל לששה. שאוכלין עליו מצות ששה ימים ולישנא דקרא נקט וקרא לדרשה אתא ללמד על ימות הפסח שהן רשות באכילת מצה חוץ מלילה הראשון בפרק בתרא (דף קכ.): טעון לינה. לילה אחד בתוך העיר: **מתני'** לא יאכלו ממנו זבין. דגבי טמא לנפש כתיב איש איש נדחה ואין ליבור נידחין אבל גבי זיבה אף ליבור נדחין בפרק אלו דברים (לעיל דף סז.): ואם אכלו פטורין מכרת. דאוכל קדשים בטומאה כדיליף בברייתא בגמרא אבל מביאת מקדש לא פטרינהו רחמנא: ורבי אליעזר פוטר. אף מכרת דביאת מקדש וטעמא יליף בגמרא: **גמ'** וישלחו מן המחנה כו'. ות"ק לא דריש להכי דכולא איצטריך כדאמרינן באלו דברים (שם) לחלקם למחנותיהם: ונכנסו להיכל. מקום שלא הותרו שם דאין שם צרכי פסח (ב) ואלו כהנים אסורין ליכנס לשם אלא לצורך משום דכתיב אל יבא בכל עת וזה שנכנס בטומאה יכול יתחייב על ביאת מקדש בטומאה: אפילו מקצת מחנה. אע"פ שאין משתלחין מכל מחנה שכינה שהרי מותרין בעזרה טמאי מתים בפסח הבא בטומאה משתלחין מיהא ממקצתו מן ההיכל: איכא דאמרי כו'. ורבא לקולא פשט דאין חייבין על ביאת מקדש דהיכל: אל מחוץ למחנה תשלחום. היינו היכל כדסמיך ליה אשר אני שוכן בתוכם: וישלחו מן המחנה. עזרה כך קבל רבי וכ"ל דאיפכא גרסי' לה כל היכא דקרינא אל מחוץ למחנה שצריך להוציאם לגמרי אף מן העזרה קרינא ביה מן המחנה היכל וכל היכא דלא קרינא ביה אל מחוץ לא קרינא ביה וישלחו מקצת מחנה: אימורי פסח. כגון כליות ויותרת הכבד:

מהו

עין משפט נר מצוה

טז א מיי' פ"ו מהל' ק"פ הלכה ו':

יז ב מיי' פ"ג מהל' ביאת מקדש הלכה יב ופ"ו מהל' ק"פ הל' ח:

יח ג מיי' פ"ד מהל' ביאת מקדש הל' יג:

מסורת הש"ס: [ערכין י:]; [לקמן קיז.]; יומא דף כט.; [ועי' תוספות יומא נא. ד"ה דוחה]; ס"א אמר מר; סוכה דף מז:; לעיל דף סו: כריתות דף יד: בכורות דף לג:; [מנחות כה: ע"ש]; לעיל דף סז: [מנחות כה:]; [זבחים דף צז:]

הגהות הב"ח

(א) רש"י ד"ה ללי דאיתרבי מכללא כו' כצ"ל:

(ב) שם ד"ה ונכנסו וכו' צרכי פסח ואפילו כהנים:

רבינו חננאל

דהא לאו שאין בו מעשה אין לוקין עליו וזה לאו שאין בו מעשה ואע"ג דדמי ליה ממעט ליה דהאי לא יראה לך שאור לית ליה בגופיה דפסח מכלליה דעצם לא תשברו בו דהוא לאו שחייבין בו מלקות ריבה אל תאכלו ממנו נא דהוא לאו שחייבין מלקות כיוצא בו בגופיה דפסח וממעט לא תשחט על חמץ דאע"ג דהוא לאו שחייבין עליו מלקות ליתיה כעין הפרט דהא ליתיה בחוביה בגופיה דפסח ובהני כולהו כללי ופרטי דדרשי' אמרינן ואפוך אנא ופרקי' מסתברא הני מצוה דבגופיה והני ליתנהו בגופיה כדפרשי' להו כל חדא וחדא: לישנא אחרינא ת"ר ככל חקת הפסח יעשו אותו יכול כשם שהראשון כו' אמרי' בכלליה דכתיב ככל חקת הפסח מאי מרבה מצוה שבגופו ותניא צליתו באש בפרטו ממעט השבתת שאור בכלליה דלא ישאירו ממנו קא מרבי לא תוציא מן הבית מן הבשר חוצה דדמי ליה דהאי מיפסל בנותר והאי מיפסל ביוצא בפרטים ממעט לא יראה ולא ימצא דדמי ליה דלא ישאירו ממנו לא לקי דהוה ליה לאו שניתק לעשה לא יראה ולא ימצא נמי לא לקי דהוה ליה לאו שאין בו מעשה בכלליה ועצם לא תשברו בו מרבה אל תאכלו ממנו נא דדמי ליה בפרטיה קא ממעט לא תשחט על חמץ ובכלהו אמרי' איפוך אנא ושני' מצוה דגופיה עדיף: הראשון טעון הלל באכילתו דכתיב השיר יהיה לכם כליל התקדש חג וכו' אלא ליל שאינו מקודש לחג זה ואין טעון הלל: ת"ר פסח ראשון ושני דוחין את השבת ואת הטומאה וטעונין לינה ואמרי' בשלמא פסח שני דוחה את הטומאה כר' יהודה אלא טעון לינה כמאן כר' יהודה והתניא ר' יהודה אומר ומנין לפסח שני שאין טעון לינה כו' ושני' תרי תנאים ואליבא דרבי יהודה חד תנא תני משמיה טעון לינה וחד תנא תני משמיה אין טעון לינה: **מתני'** הפסח שבא בטומאה לא יאכלו ממנו זבין וזבות נדות ויולדות ואם אכלו פטורין וכו' אוקימנא לר' יהושע דתאני פסח הבא שאכלו ממנו זבין וזבות נדות ויולדות יכול יהו חייבין ת"ל כל טהור יאכל בשר והנפש אשר תאכל בשר נאכלין לטהורין חייבין עליו משום טומאה וכו'. בעי רב יוסף דחקו טמאי מתים ונכנסו להיכל בפסח הבא בטומאה מהו מדאשתרי טומאת עזרה אשתרי נמי טומאת היכל כו' ופשיט רבא בלישנא קמא דלא אשתרי ובלישנא בתרא משמע דאשתרי: **בעי** רב יוסף דחקו טמאי מתים ונגעו באימורי פסח והן חלבי פסח הבא בטומאה מהו מדאשתרי

יג א מיי׳ פ״י מהל׳ ק״פ הלכה טו :
יד ב מיי׳ פ״ה מהלכות ק״פ הלכה ג :
טו ג ד מיי׳ פ״י מהל׳ ק״פ הלכה טו :

מתני׳ *מה בין פסח הראשון לשני הראשון אסור בבל יראה ובל ימצא והשני חמץ ומצה עמו בבית הראשון טעון הלל באכילתו והשני אינו טעון הלל באכילתו זה וזה טעון* הלל בעשייתן ונאכלין צלי על מצה ומרורים ודוחין את השבת: גמ׳ ת״ר ככל חוקת הפסח יעשו אותו במצוה שבגופו הכתוב מדבר מצוה שעל גופו מנין ת״ל על מצות ומרורים יאכלוהו יכול אפילו מצות שלא על גופו ת״ל ועצם לא ישברו בו מה שבירת העצם מיוחד מצוה שבגופו אף כל מצוה שבגופו איסי בן יהודה אומר יעשו אותו במצות שבגופו הכתוב מדבר אמר מר יכול אף מצוה שלא על גופו הא אמרת במצוה שבגופו הכתוב מדבר ה״ק השתא דאמרת על מצות ומרורים יאכלוהו אלמא יעשו אותו לאו דוקא הוא אימא הוה ליה כפרט וכלל ונעשה כלל מוסיף על הפרט ואפילו כל מילי נמי קמ״ל איסי בן יהודה האי עצם מאי עביד ליה מיבעי ליה *לאחד עצם שיש בו מוח ואחד עצם שאין בו מוח ורבנן האי יעשו אותו מאי עבדי ליה מיבעי ליה *שאין שוחטין את הפסח על היחיד כדכמה דאפשר לאהדורי מהדרינן ת״ר ככל חוקת הפסח יעשו אותו יכול כשם שהראשון אסור בבל יראה ובל ימצא כך שני אסור בבל יראה ובל ימצא ת״ל על מצות ומרורים יאכלוהו ואין לי אלא מצות עשה מצות ל״ת מנין ת״ל לא ישאירו ממנו עד בקר ואין לי אלא מצות ל״ת שניתק לעשה מצות ל״ת גמור מנין ת״ל ועצם לא ישברו בו מה הפרט מפורש מ״ע ול״ת שניתק לעשה ול״ת גמור אף כל מ״ע ול״ת שניתק לעשה ול״ת גמור בכלליה דמצות ומרורים מאי קא מרבי צלי אש בפרטיה מאי ממעיט ליה השבתת שאור איפוך אנא מצוה דגופיה עדיף בכלליה דלא ישאירו ממנו עד בקר מאי קא מרבה ליה לא תוציא ממנו (דדמי ליה דהאי מיפסל בנותר והאי מיפסל ביוצא) בפרטיה מאי קא ממעט ליה לא יראה ולא ימצא (דדמי ליה דהאי אינו לוקה דהוה לאו שניתק לעשה והאי אינו לוקה דהוה ליה לאו שניתק לעשה) איפוך אנא מצוה דגופיה עדיף בכלליה דעצם לא ישברו בו מאי

מתני׳ מלה וחמץ יש לו בבית. בגמ׳ יליף לה לטעמא דכולה מתניתין: גמ׳ (א) ככל חוקת הפסח וגו׳. בפסח שני כתיב: אותו. משמע גופו: במצות שבגופו הכתוב מדבר. לא ריבה את השני לדין ראשון אלא במצות שבגופו כגון סדר עבודותיו ואכילת צלי אבל לא למצות שאינן בגופו כגון השבתת שאור: מצות שעל גופו מנין. כגון מצה ומרור שהן דברים אחרים ואין חובה לו: יכול אף מצות שלא על גופו. כגון השבתת שאור ולקמיה פריך מנא תיתי והאמרת אותו משמע מצות שבגופו: מה שבירת העצם מיוחדת. לקמן יליף לה בפרט וכלל דפרטי כתיבי ברישא והדר כלל על מצות ומרורים יאכלוהו וכן לא ישאירו ממנו עד בקר ועצם לא ישברו בו פרטי הן ככל חוקת הפסח יעשו אותו כלל ולקמיה מפרש לה: איסי בן יהודה אומר. אינו צריך לא ישברו לכך אלא ללימוד אחר כדלקמן דאותו מצות שבגופו משמע: הא אמרת אותו במצות שבגופו גרסי׳: ה״ק. השתא דכתיב מצות ומרורים ואיתרבי מצוה שאינה גופו אלמא אותו לאו דוקא: והוה ליה פרט וכלל. דפרטי כתיבי ברישא: ואימא נעשה כלל מוסיף על הפרט. ואיתרבי כל מילי אפילו השבתת שאור שאינה על גופו: קמ״ל. ועצם לא ישברו דלא תדרוש כלל מוסיף על הפרט לרבויי כל מילי אפי׳ השבתת שאור דאם כן כל הני פרטי למה לי אלא להכי כתבינהו לכולהו למידרש תוספתא דכללא אכל חד וחד ומרבי דומיא דפרטי ותו לא וכולהו פרטי הוו דגופו ודעל גופו והיינו דקאמר תנא דפרטי ועצם לא ישברו ממעט מצות שלא על גופו כגון לא תשחט על חמץ כדלקמן ולקמן בברייתא מפרשי מאי מרבי כללא לכל חד וחד ומאי ממעט פרטא: מאי עביד ליה. מככל חוקת הפסח נפקא ליה דהא לדידיה אותו דוקא וממעט שלא על גופו וממילא מתרבה שבירת עצם דהא מצוה שבגופו היא ותמיהא לי אמאי לא בעי נמי לא ישאירו לאיסי מאי עביד ליה דהא מצוה שבגופו היא: מיבעי ליה לאחד עצם כו׳ דהכי דרשינן בכילד צולין (לעיל דף פה.) כשהוא אומר ועצם לא ישברו בפסח שני שאין ת״ל הוי א׳ עצם כו׳: ורבנן. דאמרי אותו לאו דוקא למאי איכתב: שאין שוחטין. פסח שני על היחיד שנדחה לו להכי כתב יעשו לשון רבים דכמה דאפשר לאהדורי אתר טמא חבירו להמנותו עמו מהדרינן כגון לטמא אחד בשרץ ואיידי דכתיב יעשו כתיב אותו דאע״ג דכתיב ברישא יעשו אותו אי לא כתביה זימנא אחריתי הוה אמינא אורחיה דקרא הוא: ת״ל על מצות ומרורים וגו׳. והדר כתיב כללא עליה לרבויי דומיא דידיה וכל מילי לא אמרינן דנירבי דא״כ כל הני פרטי למה לי ופרטא ממעט דכוותיה כדמפרש לקמן דכללא דכל חוקת הפסח מהדרינן אכולהו פרטא לרבויי בכל פרטא דומיא דידיה ולמעוטי מפרט׳ נמי דומיא דידיה ומחד מפרטיה ממעטינן בל יראה ובל ימצא לקמן ובברייתא רמוזי מרמזא ואזלא כללי מאי מרבו ופרטי מאי ממעטי ודכוותיה מרבו וממעטי: ואין לי. שיהא כלל מוסיף אלא על הפרט של עשה מצות ומרורים דכוותיה לגי אם שהוא מ״ע ופרט נמי ממעט דכוותיה השבתת שאור: ל״ת מנין. שירבה הכלל וכן הפרט ימעט ל״ת ת״ל לא ישאירו ממנו עד בקר וכתיב כללא לאהדורי עליה לרבויי דכוותיה לאו הניתק לעשה ולמעט בפרטיה לא יראה ולא ימצא דלאו שניתק לעשה ניהו כדמפרש במסקנא: ואין לי אלא כו׳ ל״ת גמורה מנין. שירבה [הכלל] וימעט פרט ת״ל לא ישברו וכתב כללא לאהדורי עליה לרבויי דכוותיה בכללא ולמעוטי דכוותיה בפרטא כדלקמן: בפרטיה מאי קא ממעט. דכל פרטא משמע מיעוטא דכוותיה דהכי משמע האי ולא מידי אחרינא השבתת שאור דהויא נמי כמצות עשה: ל״ת דמותיר לאו הניתק לעשה הוא דכתיב גבי ראשון והנותר ממנו וגו׳: לא תוציא. לאו הניתק לעשה הוא דכתיב בבית אחד יאכל לא תוציא וגו׳ ומשמע לא תוציא לאוכלו אלא בבית אחד יאכל בעמוד והחזר קאי אם הוציאו ולית ליה להאי תנא הא דתני בכילד צולין (שם*) האוכלו הרי זה בל״ת דובשר בשדה טרפה (שמות כב) אלא מותר להחזירו ולאוכלו: ולא יראה. ואם נראה תשביתהו לעולם הוא בעמוד והשבת כל ימות המועד: בכלליה דעצם לא ישברו בו. דמרבי לא תעשה גמור: מאי

מה בין ראשון לשני. בתוספ׳ (פרק ח) קתני נמי הראשון נשחט בג׳ כיתות ואין השני נשחט בג׳ כיתות והכא תנא ושייר דשייר נמי ביקור ד׳ ימים דליתיה בשני כדאמר בגמ׳ (דף צו.) ותוספתא דלא קתני ביקור דלא קחשיב אלא הנך שנוהגין בפסח לבדו וביקור נוהג נמי בתמיד:

ואיסי בן יהודה עצם לא ישברו בו מאי עביד ליה. תימה לאיסי לא ישאירו ממנו עד בקר מאי עביד ליה דהא לדידיה לא צריך למעוטי בל יראה דמאותו מפיק מצוה שלא על גופו:

מיבעי ליה שאין שוחטין את הפסח על היחיד. קשה לרשב״א דתיפוק ליה מככל חקת הפסח ולראשון נפקא לן בפרק האשה (לעיל דף צא.) דאין שוחטין אותו על היחיד מלא תוכל לזבוח את הפסח באחד וי״ל דלית ליה להאי דרשה ובפסח ראשון נפקא ליה משום דלא גר״ס מפסח שני:

בכלליה דמצות ומרורים מאי קמרבי צלי אש. משמע משום מצות ומרורים דקאי כללא עליה מרבינן צלי אש ותימה כיון דפרט וכלל הוא בלא מצות ומרורים מרבינן צלי אש וכל מילי אפילו השבתת שאור ומפרטי ממעטי מכלל חד וחד חדא מילתא כדאמר בריש מרובה (ב״ק דף סג:) דמסיק על כל דבר פשע כלל ריבויא וכל הני פרטי למה לי חד למעוטי עבדים כו׳ ויש לומר דודאי בלא מצות ומרורים ידעינן צלי אש *מכללא ומצות ומרורים לא אתא אלא למעוטי השבתת שאור ולא נקט האי לישנא בכלליה דמצות ומרורים מאי קמרבי צלי אש אלא משום דבעי למיפרך ולימא איפוך אנא:

לא תוציא מן הבית. פי׳ בקונט׳ דלאו הניתק לעשה הוא דכתיב בבית אחד יאכל לא תוציא משמע לא תוציא לאוכלו בבית אחר אלא בבית אחד יאכל בעמוד והחזר קאי אם הוציאו וקשה לר״י היכי חשבינן ליה לאו הניתק לעשה והא לאו שקדמו עשה הוא ולא חשיב לאו הניתק לעשה כדאמרינן בפרק בתרא דמכות (דף טו:):

בפרטיה קא ממעט בל יראה. כאן משמע כמו שפירש ר״י בכל שעה (לעיל כט:*) דלא יראה הוי ניתק לעשה:

רבינו חננאל

למה נקוד על ה״א לא מפני שרחוקה ודאי אלא אפי׳ מאסקופת העזרה ולחוץ: מתני׳ מה בין הראשון לשני הראשון אסור בבל יראה ובל ימצא והשני חמץ ומצה עמו בבית: ת״ר ככל חקת הפסח יעשו אותו במצוה שבגופו כגון צלייתו מצוה שעל גופו ואינה בגופו עצמו מנין ת״ל על מצות ומרורים יאכלוהו יכול אף מצוה שנוהגת בפסח ואינה לא בגופו ולא על גופו של פסח כגון השבתת שאור ת״ל ועצם לא תשברו בו מה שבירת עצם כו׳ ואקשי׳ אמאי צריך קרא למיעוטי (מצוה) [שאור] שלא על גופו כגון השבתת שאור והא כתי׳ ככל חקת הפסח יעשו אותו ואוקים׳ במצוה שבגופו הכתוב מדבר כגון צלייתו מכלל שבמצוה אחרת אינה נוהגת בו ושני׳ הכי קא״ר השתא דאתא על מצות ומרורים יאכלוהו ורבי אפי׳ מצוה שעל גופו אלמא האי דפשטנא ככל חקת הפסח במצוה שבגופו לאו דוקא הוא הואיל ואפקיה קרא אימא אפי׳ מצוה שלא על גופו תהא נוהגת בו קמ״ל ועצם לא תשברו בו מצוה שעל גופו אין מצוה שלא על גופו כגון השבתת שאור וחמץ וכיוצא בהן לא: ואיסי בן יהודה האי ועצם לא תשברו בו מבעי ליה׳ שאין שוברין בו כל עצם בין יש בו מוח בין אין בו מוח ות״ק סבר לה כר׳ דאמר מבעוד יום אין בו משום שבירת עצם הלכך כיון דאפשר ליה למתבריה מבעוד יום ולאפוקיה למוחיה ולמכליה בלילא לא אתו עשה דאפשר לקיומיה כי האי גונא ודחי לא תעשה הלכך לא אתא ועצם לא תשברו בו אלא למעוטי מצוה שלא על גופו ותיפוק לי האי סברא מיעשו אותו הדוא כא ללמד דוקא רבים מכאן שאין שוחטין את הפסח על היחיד מבעי׳ ליה דוקא יעשו רבים אבל יחיד לא מכאן שאין שוחטין את הפסח על היחיד: ת״ר ככל חקת הפסח יעשו אותו יכול כשם שהראשון כו׳. פי׳ מצאנו דפסח שני שכתב בין הערבים יעשו אותו זהו כלל פרט על מצות ומרורים יאכלוהו ועוד כתיב לא ישאירו ממנו עד בקר וכתיב עוד ועצם לא ישברו בו חזר וכלל ככל חקת הפסח יעשו אותו נמצא כלל כו׳ פרט וכלל ואנו דורשים בכל אחד ואחד כלל ופרט וכלל אי אתה דן אלא כעין הפרט הלכך בין הערבים יעשו אותו כלל על מצות ומרורים יאכלוהו פרט ככל חקת הפסח יעשו אותו חזר וכלל עכשיו באין לדון כעין הפרט מה הפרט מפורש על מצות יאכלוהו דהיא עשה אף אני ארבה דחייב לאכלו צלי דהוא עשה נרידתא וממעט השבתת שאור דאע״ג דהיא עשה נרידתא אינו על גופו מכלליה דלא ישאירו דהוא לא שניתק לעשה שנאמר והנותר ממנו עד בקר באש תשרופו ריבה לא תוציא מן הבית מן הבשר חוצה שהוא כעין הפרט שזה נפסל בנותר וזה נפסל ביוצא וממעט בל יראה לך שאור דדמי ליה דהא

[עי׳ תוס׳ יומא כט סד״ה אלא]
[לעיל פה.]
[לעיל נא. וש״נ]
[ועי׳ רש״י דכתוס ד״ה כ״ז בל״ת]

הגהות הב״ח
(א) רש״י ד״ה מלה וכו׳ דכולה מתניתין הס״ד ואח״כ מ״ה ככל וכו׳ לני דלאתרבי מכלליה דמצות ומרורי׳ הס״ד:

MISHNAH. [95*a*] WHAT IS THE DIFFERENCE BETWEEN THE FIRST PASSOVER AND THE SECOND? THE FIRST IS SUBJECT TO THE PROHIBITION OF [LEAVEN] SHALL NOT BE SEEN AND [LEAVEN] SHALL NOT BE FOUND;[4] WHILE AT THE SECOND [A MAN MAY HAVE] LEAVENED AND UNLEAVENED BREAD IN THE HOUSE WITH HIM. THE FIRST REQUIRES [THE RECITING OF] HALLEL WHEN IT [THE PASCHAL LAMB] IS EATEN, WHILE THE SECOND DOES NOT REQUIRE HALLEL WHEN IT IS EATEN. BUT BOTH REQUIRE [THE RECITING OF] HALLEL WHEN THEY ARE SACRIFICED, AND THEY ARE EATEN ROAST WITH UNLEAVENED BREAD AND BITTER HERBS, AND THEY OVERRIDE THE SABBATH.

GEMARA. Our Rabbis taught: *According to all the statute of the Passover they shall keep it:*[5] the Writ refers to the ordinance[s] pertaining to itself.[6] How do we know the ordinance[s] indirectly connected with itself?[1] Because it is said, *they shall eat it with unleavened bread and bitter herbs.*[2] You might think that regulations which are not even indirectly connected with itself [are included too]; therefore it is stated, *nor shall they break a bone thereof:*[3] just as the breaking of a bone stands out as an ordinance pertaining to itself, so is every ordinance pertaining to itself [included].[4] Issi b. Judah said: *'they shall keep it'* [implies that] the Writ treats of regulations pertaining to itself.[5]

The Master said: 'You might think that regulations which are not even indirectly connected with itself [are included too]'. But surely you have said that the Writ refers to ordinance[s] pertaining to itself?—This is what he means: now that you have quoted, *'they shall eat it with unleavened bread and bitter herbs,* which proves that *'they shall keep it'*[6] is not exact, then say that it is like a particularization and a general proposition, whereby the general proposition is accounted as adding to the particularization, so that even all regulations [are included]:[7] hence he informs us [that it is not so].

Now Issi b. Judah, how does he utilize this [law concerning a] bone?—He requires it for [teaching that] both a bone which contains marrow and a bone which does not contain marrow [are meant].[8] And the Rabbis: how do they utilize this [verse] *'they shall keep it'?*—They require it to teach that one may not kill the Passover-offering on behalf of a single person, so that as far as it is possible to procure [another unclean person] we do so.[9]

Our Rabbis taught: *'According to all the statute of the Passover they shall keep it':* you might think, just as the first is subject to the prohibition of [leaven] *'shall not be seen'* and *'shall not be found',* so is the second subject to the prohibition of [leaven] *shall not be seen* and *shall not be found:* therefore it is stated, *they shall eat it with unleavened bread and bitter herbs.*[1] Again, I know it only of positive precepts;[2] how do we know it of negative precepts? Because it is stated, *They shall leave none of it unto the morning.*[3] Also, I know it only of a negative precept modified to a positive precept;[4] how do we know it of an absolute negative precept? Because it is stated, *'and they shall not break a bone thereof':* [hence] just as the particularization is explicitly stated as a positive precept, and a negative precept modified to a positive precept, and an absolute negative precept, so every positive precept, and a negative precept modified to a positive precept, and complete negative precept [are included].[5] What is included in the general proposition as applied to *'[they shall eat it] with unleavened bread and bitter herbs'?*—Roast with fire.[6] What does it exclude in its particularization?[7]—The putting away of leaven. May I [not] reverse it?—[The inclusion of] a precept pertaining to itself is preferable. What is included in the general proposition as bearing on *'they shall leave none of it unto the morning'?*—*Thou shalt not carry forth aught [of the flesh abroad out of the house]*,[8] (which is similar thereto, since the one is disqualified through being *nothar,*[1] while the other is disqualified through going out [of its permitted boundary]).[2] What does it exclude by its particularization?—[Leaven] *'shall not be seen* and *'shall not be found,'* (which is similar thereto, for the one does not involve flagellation, since it is a negative precept modified to a positive precept, while the other does not involve flagellation, since it is a negative precept modified to a positive precept.)[3] May I [not] reverse it?—[The inclusion of] a precept pertaining to itself is preferable.

What is included in the general proposition as bearing on

(4) Ex. XII, 19; Deut. XVI, 4. (5) Num. IX, 12 with reference to the second Passover. (6) E.g., how the sacrifice shall be prepared, that it is to be eaten roast etc.; but regulations not directly pertaining to itself, e.g., the removing of leaven, are not included.

a (1) E.g., that it is to be eaten with unleavened bread and bitter herbs. (2) Num. IX, 11. (3) Ibid. 12. (4) But not others. (5) So that *'nor shall they break a bone thereof'* is unnecessary for that purpose. (6) *'It'* might imply that only the regulations directly bearing on the sacrifice itself are meant, and therefore exclude the eating of unleavened bread and bitter herbs. (7) This is a general principle of exegesis that if a law is first stated in a particular instance and then in a general form, the former does not limit the latter but on the contrary the latter generalizes the former, so that all instances are included. Here a particular instance of similarity between the first Passover and the second is stated in v. 11 while in v. 12 a general law is stated that the two are alike in all respects. (8) *Supra* 85*a*. (9) Even if we have to defile a person at the first Passover, so that there may be at least two at the second; v. *supra* 91*a*.

b (1) V. *supra*. They are alike only in respect of the regulations pertaining to or connected with itself, just like the particular case which is stated. (2) *'They shall eat it'* etc. is a positive precept, and therefore teaches that all the positive precepts applicable to the first Passover are also binding upon the second, e.g., the precept to eat it roast. (3) Num. IX, 12; hence the deduction stated in the preceding note applies to negative precepts too. (4) A prohibition which if violated must be repaired by a positive act. Thus *'and ye shall let nothing of it remain until the morning'* (Ex. XII, 10) is followed by *'but that which remaineth of it until the morning ye shall burn with fire'*. Technically such an injunction is less stringent than an ordinary negative precept and does not involve flagellation. (5) Hence the general proposition, *'according to all the statute'* etc., is applied separately to each of these three particular laws, teaching that all laws which partake of their nature are included. (6) V. n. b2. (7) For just as the general proposition includes laws unstated, so the particularization teaches that some laws are excluded, as otherwise the former alone would suffice. (8) Ex. XII, 46.

c (1) V. Glos. (2) Var. lec. omits the bracketed passage. (3) If flesh of the Passover sacrifice is left over, it must be burnt, while if leaven is not completely removed before Passover, so that it is 'seen' or 'found', it must be destroyed whenever discovered. Hence both of these negative precepts are modified to positive precepts, and he who violates them is not flagellated.—Var. lec. omits the bracketed passage.

wicked man, son of a wicked man, [94b] descendant of the wicked Nimrod, who incited the whole world to rebel [*himrid*][9] against a Me during his reign![1] How many are the years of man? Seventy years; and if by reason of strength, eighty years, for it is said, *The days of our years are threescore years and ten, or even by reason of strength fourscore years.*[2] Now from earth to heaven is a five hundred years' journey, the thickness of heaven is a five hundred years' journey, and between the first heaven and the next lies a five hundred years' journey, and similarly between each heaven,[3]— '*Yet thou shalt be brought down to the nether-world, to the uttermost parts of the pit*'.[4] This is [indeed] a refutation.

Our Rabbis taught: The Sages of Israel maintain: The *Galgal*[5] is stationary [fixed], while the *mazzaloth*[6] revolve; while the Sages of the nations of the world maintain: The *Galgal* revolves and the *mazzaloth* are stationary.[7] Rabbi observed: This disproves their view [viz.,] we never find the Wain in the south or Scorpio in the north.[8] To this R. Aha b. Jacob demurred: Perhaps it is like the pivot[9] of a millstone,[10] or like the door socket?

The Sages of Israel maintain: The sun travels beneath the sky by day and above the sky at night; while the Sages of the nations of the world maintain: It travels beneath the sky by day and below the earth at night. Said Rabbi: And their view is preferable to ours, for the wells are cold by day but warm at night.[11]

It was taught, R. Nathan said: In summer the sun travels in the heights of the heaven,[12] therefore the whole world is hot while the wells [springs] are cold; in winter the sun travels at the lower b ends of the sky,[1] therefore the whole world is cold while the wells are hot.

Our Rabbis taught: The sun travels over four courses: [during] Nisan,[2] Iyar and Sivan, it travels over the mountains, in order to melt the snows; [in] Tammuz, Ab and Elul, over the inhabited world, to ripen the fruits; [in] Tishri, Marheshwan and Kislev, over seas, to dry up the rivers; in Tebeth, Shebat and Adar, through the wilderness, so as not to dry up the seeds [in the ground].

R. ELIEZER SAID: FROM THE THRESHOLD etc. Even though he can enter, and we do not say to him, 'Arise and enter'? But it surely was taught: An uncircumcised Jew who did not circumcise himself is punished by *kareth:* this is the opinion of R. Eliezer?—Said Abaye: '*A journey afar off*' [is stated] in respect of a clean person, but '*a journey afar off*' is not [stated] in respect of an unclean person.[3] Raba said: It is [a controversy of] Tannaim. For it was taught, R. Eliezer said: Distance of place is stated in connection with the Passover, and distance of place is stated in connection with tithe:[4] just as there [it means] without [the boundaries of] its eating,[5] so here too it means outside [the place of] its eating.[6] R. Jose son of R. Judah said on R. Eliezer's authority: [It means] outside [the place] where it is sacrificed.[7] With whom does the following dictum of R. Isaac son of R. Joseph agree, [viz.:] In respect of those who are unclean, decide by the majority who c are standing in the Temple Court.[1] With whom [does it agree]? With R. Jose son of R. Judah, as he stated [the law] on R. Eliezer's authority.[2]

SAID R. JOSE TO HIM, THEREFORE etc. It was taught, R. Jose the Galilean said: [By] '*a journey afar off*' I may understand a distance of two or three days: but when it is said, *and is not in a journey*, it teaches that from the threshold of the Temple Court and without is designated a journey.[3]

(9) This is a play on the name Nimrod, deriving it from *marad*, to rebel.

a (1) According to Talmudic tradition Nimrod instigated the building of the tower of Babel to storm heaven. (2) Ps. XC, 10. (3) According to the ancient tradition there were seven heavens. (4) Isa. XIV, 15. [In Hag. 13a the distance is further extended and according to the calculation given there amounts to a total of 4,096,000 years' journey, which at the rate of eighty rabbinic *mils* in 24 hours (v. *supra*) amounts to 119,603,200,000 say—120,000 million *mils*, which shows that the Rabbis had a fair idea of stellar distance. Cf. Feldman, W. M., *Rabbinical Mathematics*, p. 213.] (5) ['Wheel sphere' probably the celestial sphere, v. n. a7.] (6) Here fixed stars. (7) [This will probably represent the Ptolemaic view according to which the stars are fixed on the surface of the celestial sphere which moves round the earth carrying the stars with it, v. op. cit. p. 71.] (8) But if the *Galgal* revolves, the *mazzaloth* too would change their position. The view of the Jewish Sages is difficult to explain. (9) Rashi. '*Aruch*: the socket. (10) Which remains fixed in its place. (11) [On this passage v. op. cit. p. 72.] (12) Above the earth.

b (1) Not above the earth but at its side. (2) The first month of the Jewish civil year, commencing some time in March. The remaining eleven months are enumerated in order. (3) V. *supra* 93b. Similarly, a man must make himself fit for the Passover, and otherwise he incurs *kareth*. But it is not his duty to bring himself within the area of obligation. Tosaf. points out an obvious difficulty: if he is uncircumcised or unclean and standing without the Temple Court, as he must be in that case, he must make himself fit and keep the Passover on penalty of *kareth;* whereas if he is already circumcised or clean and standing without he is exempt! Tosaf explains it with the principle laid down by R. Zera, v. Yeb. 104b. (4) Deut. XIV, 24 q.v. (5) The second tithe must be eaten in Jerusalem. *Anywhere* outside Jerusalem is regarded as a distant place and the law of redemption applies. (6) When Scripture states that if a man is on a journey afar off he is exempt, it means if he is anywhere outside Jerusalem, in the whole of which the Passover-offering was eaten. Hence if he is merely outside the Temple Court but in Jerusalem he is not exempt. (7) Viz., the Temple Court. Thus we have a controversy of Tannaim as to R. Eliezer's view.

c (1) When the majority of those in the Temple Court are unclean, the Passover is sacrificed in uncleanness (*supra* 79a). But those who are not in the Temple Court are disregarded entirely, as they are on a '*journey afar off*'. (2) For according to the first Tanna a majority of all in Jerusalem would be required. (3) Since 'afar off' is not mentioned here.

יא א מיי' פ"ה מהל' ק"פ הלכה ד:
יב ב מיי' פ"ה מהלכות ק"פ הלכה ו:

בן בנו של נמרוד הרשע *שהמריד את כל העולם כולו עליו במלכותו כמה שנותיו של אדם שבעים שנה ואם בגבורות שמונים שנה שנאמר °ימי שנותינו בהם שבעים שנה ואם בגבורות שמונים שנה מן הארץ עד לרקיע מהלך חמש מאות שנה ועוביו של רקיע מהלך ה' מאות שנה ובין (כל) רקיע לרקיע מהלך ה' מאות שנה וכן בין כל רקיע ורקיע °אך אל שאול תורד אל ירכתי בור תיובתא ת"ר חכמי ישראל אומרים גלגל קבוע ומזלות חוזרין וחכמי אומות העולם אומרים גלגל חוזר ומזלות קבועין א"ר תשובה לדבריהם מעולם לא מצינו *עגלה בדרום ועקרב בצפון מתקיף לה רב אחא בר יעקב ודילמא *כבוצינא דריחיא א"נ כצינורא דדשא חכמי ישראל אומרים ביום חמה מהלכת למטה מן הרקיע ובלילה למעלה מן הרקיע וחכמי אומות העולם אומרים ביום חמה מהלכת למטה מן הרקיע ובלילה למטה מן הקרקע א"ר °ונראין דבריהן מדברינו שביום מעינות צוננין ובלילה רותחין תניא ר' נתן אומר בימות החמה חמה מהלכת בגובה של רקיע לפיכך כל העולם כולו רותח ומעינות צוננין בימות הגשמים חמה מהלכת בשיפולי רקיע לפיכך כל העולם כולו צונן ומעינות רותחין תנו רבנן בארבעה שבילין חמה מהלכת ניסן אייר וסיון מהלכת בהרים כדי לפשר את השלגין תמוז אב ואלול מהלכת בישוב כדי לבשל את הפירות תשרי מרחשון וכסליו מהלכת *בימים כדי ליבש את הנהרות טבת שבט ואדר מהלכת במדבר שלא ליבש את הזרעים: ורבי אליעזר אומר מאסקופת כו': ואע"ג דמצי עייל ולא אמרינן ליה קום עייל *והתניא °יהודי ערל שלא מל ענוש כרת דברי רבי אליעזר אמר אביי *דרך רחוקה לטהור ואין דרך רחוקה לטמא רבא אמר תנאי היא דתניא רבי *אליעזר אומר נאמר ריחוק מקום בפסח ונאמר ריחוק מקום במעשר מה להלן חוץ לאכילתו אף כאן חוץ לאכילתו רבי יוסי בר רבי יהודה אומר משום רבי אליעזר חוץ לעשייתו כמאן אזלא הא דאמר רבי יצחק בר רב יוסף °בטמאים הלך אחר רוב העומדין בעזרה כמאן כרבי יוסי בר רבי יהודה שאמר משום רבי אליעזר: אמר לו רבי יוסי לפיכך וכו': תניא *רבי יוסי הגלילי אומר דרך (א) שומע אני מהלך שנים או שלשה ימים כשהוא אומר °ובדרך לא היה מגיד שמאסקופת העזרה ולחוץ קרוי דרך:
מתני'

תהלים צ | ישעיה יד | במדבר ט | [עירובין נג.] | ס"א ואורכו | [ערוך ערך ריחייא] | [בתוס' בכורות נה: ד"ה אין וכו' העתיקו בהלעז הכוכב בדף ט. באויר] | [לעיל סט.] | [לעיל נג:] | [תוספתא פ"ח] | [תוספתא פ"ח כגירסת רש"י דהכא ד"ה ה"ג בתוספתא כו']

רש"י

בן בנו של נמרוד · לאו דוקא בן בנו אלא כלומר מזרע נמרוד: שהמריד · שהיה עצה לאנשי דור הפלגה לבנות מגדל להלחם בגבהת השמים שהוא היה מלך בבבל כדכתיב (בראשית י) ותהי ראשית ממלכתו בבל: וכן בין רקיע לרקיע · לאורכו של עולם כמדת גובהו כדכתיב אשר ברא אלהים אדם על הארץ ולמקצה השמים וגו' במסכת חגיגה (דף יב:) דרים ליה הכי אלמא עולם מהלך חמש מאות שנה לא וחשוב עשר פרסאות ליום נמצא עולה לכמה אלפים ותיובתא דרבא: גלגל. כמין אופן ברקיע שהמזלות נתונים בו גלגל קבוע ואינו מגלגל אלא כעין אופן עגלה המונח בקרקע אבל המזלות מהלכים סביב הילוך מועט ואין מקיפין את הגלגל אלא כל מזל משמש את החמה כד ממקומו ומוליכו עד חבירו וחוזר למקומו לפיכך אין עגלה נראית בדרום ולא עקרב בצפון שהרי אין מקיפין אלא מהלכין הילוך מועט וחוזרין: לא מצינו עגלה בדרום ועקרב בצפון. ואי ס"ד גלגל חוזר ומזלות קבועין נמצא גלגל מוליך ומגלגל המזלות לכל ד' הרוחות (ב) כשם שהוא מגלגל והיינו כמין אופן ונתון ברקיע חציו למטה מן (ג) הרקיע וחציו למעלה מן הרקיע וכשעולה צדו זה שוקע צדו אחר לפי דברי חכמי אומות העולם שאומרים גלגל חוזר ולפי דברי חכמי ישראל שאומרים גלגל קבוע אין לפרש שוקע ועולה אלא במזלות: דילמא כי בוצינא דריחיא · כברזל התחוב בנקב רחב שברחים שהכוכב עומד במקומו והברזל חוזר ואם באת לגלגל הכוכב מתגלגל סביב הברזל והברזל עומד במקומו: אי נמי כי ציורא דדשא · שהדלת סובבת בחור המפתן העליון והמפתן במקומו עומד ואם באת לגלגל המשקוף הוא מתגלגל סביב הציר והדלת עומד במקומו וכך הגלגל מתגלגל בפני עצמו ומוליך החמה והמזלות קבועים בגלגל אחר בתוכו ואותו הגלגל אינו זז ממקומו אלא גלגל חיצון מוליך חמה על פני כל המזלות אי נמי גלגל חמה מבפנים וגלגל המזלות מבחוץ: למטה מן הרקיע · זורחת על הארץ כאשר אנו רואין ובלילה למעלה מן הרקיע זורחת ואינה נראית למטה: ה"ג וחכמי או"ה אומרים ביום למטה מן הרקיע ובלילה למטה מן הקרקע: מעינות צוננין · אין לך מים נובעין שאינו צונן ביום יותר מבלילה ואע"פ שמי נהרות חמין הן ביום בחום הקיץ הוא זה מפני שרחקו ממקום נביעתן ונתחממו בחום העולם אבל תכף נביעתן הן צונן ביום לפי שהחמה גבוהה מהן: ובלילה מעינות רותחין · שהחמה מחממתן תחת הקרקע תדע שבעלות השחר אתה רואה עשן על הנהרות: בשפולו של רקיע · סמוך לקרקע בשולי הכיפה: לפיכך כל העולם צונן · שאינה מהלכת אלא בצדי העולם: ומעינות רותחים · דהיינו אצל המים מצדי העולם שהמעינות באות מהם: בארבע שבילין · מהלכת גבורתה של חמה: ולא אמרינן ליה קום עייל · ואי לא עיילת מיחייבת כרת: ענוש כרת · משום פסח אלמא אמרינן ליה קום מהול: דרך רחוקה · פטרה את הטהור והרי הוא בדרך רחוקה דחוץ לעזרה דרך רחוק מיקרי דילפינן מריחוק מקום דמעשר מה להלן חוץ למקום הכשירו אף כאן חוץ למקום הכשירו והכשירו דפסח בעזרה היא הלכך לא אמרינן ליה קום עייל אבל אין דרך רחוקה בטמא דלאו משום טעמא דריחוק איפטר טמא אלא משום דלא מצי אכיל לאורתא והכי נמי אין דרך רחוקה לערל והאי דנקט טמא משום דלעיל (דף צג:) אמרו להאי שינויא גבי טמא וכיון דערל מצי לתקוני נפשיה מיחייב דלא פטריה רחמנא לטמא אלא משום דלא מצי למיכל באורתא והאי מצי למיכל והכי נמי ערל: נאמר ריחוק מקום בפסח · או בדרך רחוקה לכם (במדבר ט) ריחוק מקום במעשר כי ירחק ממך המקום (דברים יד) חוץ לחומת ירושלים אפילו פסיעה אחת דכתיב כי לא תוכל שאתו ואין שאת אלא אכילה במס' מכות (דף יט:): חוץ לאכילתו · חומת ירושלים אבל חוץ לעשייתו דהיינו חומת עזרה לא דאמרינן קום עול: חוץ לעשייתו · דגמרינן מריחוק דמעשר הכי מה להלן חוץ להכשירו והכשירו דפסח בעזרה אלמא איכא תנאי דפליגי בדר' אליעזר ותנא דערל שלא מל פליג ואמר דלא פטר רבי אליעזר אלא בעומד חוץ למודיעים דלא מצינו למימר ליה קום עול: הלך אחר רוב העומדים בעזרה · אם רובן טמאין אע"פ שבחוץ ישראל טהורין הרבה יעשה בטומאה דדרך רחוקה היא לאותן העומדין מבחוץ ואינן חשובין בעושי פסח ובתר הני [שבעזרה] אזלינן: ה"ג בתוספתא ר' יוסי הגלילי אומר דרך רחוקה שומע אני מהלך שנים ושלשה ימים כשהוא אומר ובדרך לא היה מגיד שמאסקופת עזרה ולחוץ קרוי דרך ובספרים היא משובשת:

תוספות

מעולם לא מצינו עגלה בדרום ועקרב בצפון · נ"ל דעגלה לאו היינו מזל שור כדפי' בקו' ועקרב נמי לאו עקרב די"ב מזלות דבפ"ק דר"ה השנה (דף יא:) קאמר די"ב מזלות לעולם ששה למטה מן הארץ וששה למעלה וכשהאחד עולה שכנגדו שוקע והכא אמר שאינן זזים ממקומן ושניהם לעולם למעלה אלא אחרים הם:

ואין דרך רחוקה לטמא · קצת תימה כשהוא עומד חוץ לעזר' והוא ערל או טמא חייב בפסח ואם ימול ויטהר יפטר מיהו דוגמת זה מצינו כל הראוי לבילה אין בילה מעכבת בו (מנחות קג:):

מה להלן חוץ לאכילתו · לא היה לרש"י להזכיר כאן ואין שאת אלא אכילה דלא צריכא לכך אלא במעשר שני בירושלים שנטמא:

אף כאן חוץ לאכילתו · ובסיפרי מסיים ואיזה מקום אכילתו מפתח ירושלים ולפנים (ד) ולא מייתי תנאי אלא כלומר כיון דאשכחן תנאי דפליגי אליבא דר' אליעזר בשיעור דרך רחוקה ה"נ ההוא דקתני ערל שלא מל ענוש כרת סבר דלר' אליעזר דרך רחוקה מן המודיעים ולחוץ דהשתא לא מצי עייל:

בטומאה הלך אחר העומדים בעזרה · פי' בעשיית פסח בטומאה הלך אחר טהורים העומדים בעזרה דאותם שבחוץ הם בדרך רחוקה:

שומע אני · רש"י לא גרס אפילו ב' וג' פרסאות והדין עמו דמשום הכי לא הוי דרך רחוקה כיון שיכול לבוא בשעת שחיטה או בשעת אכילה לכך נראה לגרוס כדאיתא בתוספתא:

הגהות הב"ח

(א) גמ' דרך רחוקה שומע אני: (ב) רש"י ד"ה לא מצינו וכו' לארבע הרוחות כ"ב פי' אף מדרום לצפון ומצפון לדרום: (ג) בא"ד כמין אופן ונתון ברקיע חציו למטה מן הרקיע וחציו למעלה מן הרקיע וכשעולה לדו זה: (ד) תוס' ד"ה אף כאן כו' ירושלים ולפנים הוא לא מייתי תנאי:

גליון הש"ס

גמ' ונראין דבריהן. עי' כתובות יג ... ד"ה ... על המעוברת ... בתפלה ובוקע חלוני רקיע עכ"ל: שם בטמאים הלך אחר הרוב עיין לעיל פ' ע"א תוס' ד"ה מצאתי וצ"ע:

רבינו חננאל

כו' אלו כולן עלו להו בתיובתא תדחו דבריו: ת"ר חכמי ישראל אומרים גלגל קבוע ומזלות חוזרין וחכמי אומות העולם אומרים גלגל חוזר ומזלות קבועין אמר רבי תשובה לדבריהם אם היו המזלות קבועין והגלגל הוא החוזר הייט רואין פעמים עגלה בדרום ועקרב בצפון מדלא חזינן הכי ש"מ הגלגל קבוע והמזלות חוזרין ואתקיף עלה רב אחא בר [רב] יעקב ודלמא כי סדנא דרחיא פי' כמו הסדן הזה אע"פ שסובב הגלגל הקבוע בו עולה ויורד שני קצות הסדן במקומן נראין לעולם אין הדרומין נראה בצפון ולא הצפוני בדרום אי נמי כצנורא והדבר אחד: ת"ר חכמי ישראל אומרים חמה מהלכת ביום למטה מן הרקיע ובלילה למעלה מן הרקיע כמו שפרשו ר' יהודה ורבה וחכמי אומות העולם אומרין חמה מהלכת ביום למעלה מן הארץ ובלילה למטה מן הארץ ואמר רבי נראין דבריהם מדברינו ומפורשת עוד בבראשית רבה. כיצד חמה ולבנה שוקעין ר' יהודה בר אילעאי אומר מאחורי כיפה [למעלה] רבנן אמרי מאחורי כיפה ולמטה ר' שמעון בן יוחאי אומר אין אנו יודעין*) באויר אם שפין הן ברקיע ואם מהלכין הן כדרכן: תניא ר' יוחנן אומר בימות החמה חמה מהלכת בגובהה של רקיע לפיכך כל העולם רותח ומעינות צוננין בימות הגשמים חמה מהלכת בשפולי הרקיע לפיכך העולם כולו צונן ומעינות רותחין: ת"ר בארבעה שבילין חמה מהלכת ניסן אייר סיון בהרים כדי לפשר השלגין תמוז אב ואלול בישוב כדי לבשל הפירות כו': ר' אליעזר אומר מאסקופת העזרה ולחוץ ואקשי' ולא אמרי' ליה עול ועביד פסח והתניא ערל שלא מל ועשה פסח חייב כרת דברי ר' אליעזר אלמא אמרי' ליה קום מהול ועביד פסחא ושני' ערל כטמא ובטהרה תלנהו רחמנא והני יכלו לטהר ולעשות פסח פשעו ולא טהרו ולא עשו חייבין אבל הטהור בדרך תלי רחמנא והוא היה בדרך ריחוק מקום כמעשר שנאמר (דברים יד כד) וכי ירחק ממך המקום וגו' חוץ לאכילתו: אמר ר' יוסי למה

*) אין אנו יודעים הם פוגמים כמה בהוור כנ"ל וכ"ה בב"ר פ"ו ע"ש:

לרב יהודה לא קשיא טמא שרץ רחמנא דחייה דכתיב °איש איש כי יהיה טמא לנפש *מי לא עסקינן שחל שביעי שלו להיות בערב הפסח ואפילו הכי אמר רחמנא לידחי: תנו רבנן היה עומד חוץ למודיעים ויכול ליכנס בסוסים ובפרדים יכול יהא חייב ת"ל °ובדרך לא היה והלה היה בדרך היה *עומד לפנים מן המודיעים ואין יכול ליכנס מפני גמלים וקרונות המעכבות אותו יכול לא יהא חייב ת"ל ובדרך לא היה והרי לא היה בדרך: אמר רבא שיתא אלפי פרסי הוי עלמא וסומכא דרקיעא אלפא פרסי חדא גמרא וחדא סברא סברא סבר לה כי הא *דאמר רבה בר בר חנה א"ר יוחנן כמה מהלך אדם בינוני ביום י' פרסאות מעלות השחר ועד הנץ החמה ה' מילין משקיעת החמה עד צאת הכוכבים חמשה מילין נמצא עוביו של רקיע אחד משישה ביום מיתיבי רבי יהודה אומר עוביו של רקיע אחד מעשרה ביום תדע כמה מהלך אדם בינוני ביום עשר פרסאות ומעלות השחר עד הנץ החמה ארבעת מילין משקיעת החמה ועד צאת הכוכבים ארבעת מילין נמצאת עוביו של רקיע אחד מעשרה ביום תיובתא דרבא תיובתא דעולא תיובתא לימא תיהוי תיובתא דר' יוחנן אמר לך אנא בימנא הוא דאמרי ורבנן הוא דקא טעו דקא חשבן דקדמא וחשוכא לימא תיהוי תיובתא דרבי חנינא לא *ויאיצו שאני ת"ש *מצרים ה' ארבע מאות פרסה על ארבע מאות פרסה ומצרים אחד משישים בכוש וכוש אחד משישים בעולם ועולם אחד משישים בגן וגן אחד משישים בעדן ועדן אחד משישים בגיהנם נמצא כל העולם כולו ככיסוי קדירה לגיהנם תיובתא תא שמע דתנא דבי אליהו רבי נתן אומר (א) *כל הישוב כולו תחת כוכב אחד יושב תדע שהרי אדם נותן עינו בכוכב אחד הולך למזרח עומד כנגדו לארבע רוחות העולם עומד כנגדו מכלל דכל הישוב כולו תחת כוכב אחד יושב תיובתא ת"ש *עגלה בצפון ועקרב בדרום וכל הישוב כולו אינו יושב אלא בין עגלה לעקרב וכל הישוב כולו אינו הוה אלא שעה אחת ביום שאין חמה נכנסת לישוב אלא שעה אחת ביום תדע שבחמש חמה במזרח ובשבע חמה במערב חצי שש וחצי שבע חמה עומדת בראש כל אדם תיובתא ת"ש דאמר *ר' יוחנן בן זכאי מה תשובה השיבתו בת קול לאותו רשע בשעה שאמר °אעלה על במתי עב אדמה לעליון יצתה בת קול ואמרה לו רשע בן רשע בן

בן

במדבר ט — שם — בראשית יט — ישעיה יד

רש"י

ולרב יהודה לא קשיא · דקסבר טמא לנפש בטמא כתיב ואפילו שביעי שלו במשמע כדלקמיה באידך פירקין (דף צ:) דסבר לה כמאן דאמר טמאי מת מזה היו שחל שביעי שלהן בערב הפסח: בסוסים ובפרדים · במרוצה: יכול יהא חייב · כרת אם לא הגיע לעזרה בשעת שחיטה: והלה היה · דחוץ למודיעין דרך רחוקה הוא: מפני גמלים וקרונות · והוא היה מבחוץ בניו ובני ביתו *עליהן: חייב · שאין זה אונס שיש לו להשכים ולילך יחידי ולשחוט: שיתא אלפי פרסי הוה עלמא · היקף שהחמה סובבת בתוך החלל ממזרח למערב: וסומכא דרקיעא · עוביו של רקיע: חדא גמרא · שיתא אלפי פרסי דעלמא גמר' הוה מרביה והא דאלפא פרסי סומכא דרקיעא הוא סבר לה מדעתי' מהאי דשית אלפי פרסי דגמרא: עוביו של רקיע אחד משישה ביום · מהלכה ועד שקיעתה שהרי אדם מהלך שלשים מילין מהלכה ועד שקיעתה ובתוך מהלך שלשים מילין לאדם היא מהלכת את כל העולם שהוא ששת אלפים פרסי וכדי מהלך חמשה מילין הוי אחד משישה בשלשים מילין אלמא סומכא דרקיעא אלפא פרסי שבכל מהלך חמשה מיל לאדם החמה מהלכת אלף פרסאות וי"מ שיתא אלפי פרסי היינו לאורך או לרוחב ולא נהירא לן כלל שהרי אין החמה מהלכת לאורכו של עולם אלא מקיפתו: ת"ש ר"י אומר כו' אחד מי' ביום · ר"י קא חשיב לכוליה יומא מעלות השחר ועד צאת הכוכבים מיהו בהא מותבינן לרבה דקתני הכא מעלות השחר ועד הנץ החמה ארבעה מילין דהיינו עובי הרקיע וכן משקיעתה ועד צאת הכוכבים ארבע' מילין פשו להו ל"ב מילין מהנץ החמה ועד שקיעה ותיובתא דרבא ודעולא דאמרי שלשים מילין: לימא תיהוי תיובתיה דר"י · כלומר לימא דהא דאמרי' לעיל בדרבה בר בר חנה מעלות השחר ועד הנץ החמה חמשה מילין כולה רבה בר בר חנה אמר לה ומשמיה דר' יוחנן ותיהוי הך נמי תיובתיה: כי אמינא אנא בימא אמרי · אני כללתי של כל היום מעלות היום עד צאת הכוכבים עשרה פרסאות ולא פירשתי כמה קודם הנץ החמה ואחר שקיעתה ורבנן עולא ורבה שפירשו הדבר טעו בקדמא וחשוכא שרוב בני אדם מהלכין חמשה מילין קודם הנץ החמה ע"י שמשכימין קודם עלות השחר וכן אחר שקיעתה על ידי שמחשכין ליכנס אחר צאת הכוכבים: תיובתיה דרבי חנינא · דאמר מסדום ועד צוער חמשה מילין והתם בהדיא מפרש קרא מעלות השחר עד הנץ החמה דכתיב (בראשית יט) וכמו השחר עלה וגו' וכתיב (שם) השמש יצא על הארץ: וכוש הוי אחד משישים בעולם · אלמא עולם טפי משיתא אלפי פרסי: כיסוי קדירה · דבר מועט: כל הישוב כולו · של בני אדם: תחת כוכב אחד עומד · וכמה כוכבים יש ברקיע לאין מספר וכיון דכוכב אחד מחזיק את כל הישוב ורואין אנו שהישוב יותר מאלף פרסה הרי כמה כוכבים שברקיע ישוב אחד לכל כוכב בימים ובנהרות ומדברות ואילו אין ברקיע אלא ששה כוכבים הרי כאן ששת אלפים פרסי לעלמא וכ"ש שיש כוכבים יותר מו' אלפים כוכב לכל פרסה: הולך למזרח · לסוף העולם לקץ שנים הרבה יראה אל אותו מקום שהיה רואהו כשהיה עומד במערב ואילו לא היה מחזיק כל הישוב כשהוא עומד במערב ורואהו על ראשו כשהוא למזרח לא היה רואהו על ראשו אלא מן הצד באלכסון כפי מה שעבר ונמשך מתחתיו: עגלה · אותן כוכבים העשוים כעגלה והוא מזל שור: בין עגלה לעקרב · ולא שמחזיק כל אויר שביניהם שהרי כמה כוכבים יש ביניהם וכל אחד כדי ישוב אלא ישוב בין שניהם עומד שהרי כל אדם רואה בצפונו עגלה ובדרומו עקרב: ובכל הישוב · אינה מהלכת החמה אלא שעה אחת ביום חצי שש וחצי שבע חמה עומדת בראש כל אדם רואה החמה על ראשו והיינו אותה שעה שהחמה מהלכת ברקיע נגד היישוב: תיובתא · דרבא דקתני דמדברות וימים ונהרות מחזיקות אחד עשר שיעורי ישוב וקא חזינן דישוב גדול מאד ונמצא עולה עולם לכמה אלפים תיובתא דרבא: לאותו רשע · נבוכדנצר:

בן

תוספות

לרב יהודה לא קשיא טמא שרץ רחמנא דחייה · וא"ת האהיל וסבר רב יהודה אין שוחטין וטמא דקרא הייט טמא שרץ אמאי לא יליף דרך רחוקה מטומאה דהיכא דלא יכול ליכנס בשעת שחיטה לא ישחטו עליו כי היכי דאין שוחטין על טמא שרץ דהא ר"ע מדמי להו לעיל (ג:) אהדדי וי"ל דסבר רב יהודה כיון דיכול ליכנס בשעת אכילה שוחטין עליו דלא דמי לטמא שרץ דהא טהור הוא ואינו חסר כלום אלא ביאה בעלמא ור' עקיבא מדמי דרך רחוקה שאינו יכול ליכנס בשעת אכילה לטמא ומייתי שפיר ראיה בהא דלא אמרי' כרבי אליעזר דאמר מאיסקופת עזרה ולחוץ ומסבר' אית לן למימר כל שאינו יכול ליכנס בשעת אכילה דהאהיל וטהור הוא אין לו לדחותו אם יכול ליכנס בשעת אכילה:

רבי יהודה אומר משקיעת החמה עד צאת הכוכבים ארבעה מילין · קשה לר"ת דבסוף במה מדליקין (שבת דף לד:) אמר איזהו בין השמשות משתשקע החמה כל זמן שפני מזרח מאדימין דברי ר"י ומסקי' התם דבין השמשות דר"י תלתא ריבעי מיל והכא קאמר ר"י גופיה ארבעה מילין וי"ל דהכא קאמר מתחלת שקיעה דהייט משעה שמתחלת החמה ליכנס בעובי הרקיע עד הלילה הוי ד' מילין והתם קאמר מסוף שקיעה*:

כל הישוב כולו תחת כוכב אחד עומד · הך פליגא אהא דאמר בעלמא כל העולם כולו שליש ימים שליש מדברות שליש ישוב דא"כ לא היה להיות ברקיע אלא שלשה כוכבים ואפילו אם נאמר דאין יש מקומות בכלל שליש ימים וקיימי כל הכוכבים כנגד יש מקומות מ"מ פליג אדאמרי' לקמן מן הארץ עד לרקיע ה' מאות שנה ובמס' תמיד (דף לב.) משמע דממזרח למערב כמו מן השמים לארץ ואי כל הישוב תחת כוכב א' עומד א"א אורך העולם כמה אלפים שנה שהרי אין מספר לכוכבים וגם חשבון של ה' מאות שנה פליג אחשבון דכוס אחד מס' בעולם:

עין משפט נר מצוה

י א מיי' פ"ה מהלכות ק"פ הלכה ט:

[וע"ע תוס' שבת לה. ד"ה תרי תילתי ותוס' מנחות כ: ד"ה נפסלו ותוס' זבחים ט. ד"ה מנין]

מסורת הש"ס

פ"ח ממו [לעיל ג.] — [לעיל צג:] — [תענית דף י.] — [פי' תוספות דלקמן קיח: ד"ה מן שמים] — עירובין ד' ט. — [חגיגה יג.]

הגהות הב"ח

(א) גמ' כל הישוב כולו. נ"ב עיין בס' ע"ס כדף קי"ח במ"ש התוס' בד"ה מן שמים: (ב) תוס' ד"ה לר' יהודה וכו' מדמי להו לעיל. נ"ב ר"ל דף צג וע"ש בתוספות:

רבינו חננאל

ושני' רחמנא תלה לפטור בדרך רחוקה והנה הוא בדרך אבל הטמא לא תלאו הכתוב ברחיקת מקום אבל בטומאה וטהרה ובשעת אכילה טמא שרץ שכבר טבל טהור הוא כי הנה בא שמשו. ופרישנא דמעלות השחר עד הנץ החמה חמשה מילין מדכתיב וכמו השחר עלה ויאיצו וגו' וכתיב השמש יצא על הארץ וגו' ואמר ר' חנינא אני ראיתי אותו מקום והוי מסדום לצוער חמשה מילין: ירושלמי מאילת השחר עד שיעלה עמוד השחר ארבעה מילין שנאמר וכמו השחר עלה מדהוה ליה למכתב כמו השחר עלה וכתב וכמו מלה דדמיא לחברתה: ת"ר היה חוץ למודיעית ויכול ליכנס בסוסים ובפרדים ולא נכנס יכול יהא חייב ת"ל ובדרך לא היה והלא היה בדרך כיוצא בו היה לפנים למודיעית ואין יכול ליכנס מפני הגמלים והקרונות שמעכבות אותו יכול יהא פטור ת"ל ובדרך לא היה וזה לא היה בדרך רחוקה: אמר רבה שיתא אלפי פרסי הוי עלמא וסומכא דרקיע אלפא פרסי הא אמר רבה שיתא אלפי פרסי הוי עלמא גמרא. ודייק מדברי ר' יוחנן דאמר כמה מהלך אדם ביום עשרה פרסאות אמר רבה בדעתו מהם חמשה מילין מעלות השחר עד הנץ החמה ומהן חמשה מילין משתשקע החמה עד צאת הכוכבים נמצא מהלך החמה ביום כולו מן המזרח למערב שלשים פרסאות נמצאת עוביו של רקיע אחד משישה ביום ופי' רבי' שמואל בברייתא שלו כי הרקיע עשוי ככובא הגלגל קבוע והמזלות הוזרין ותניא כדבעינן למימר קמן כי החמה מהלכת בלילה למעלה מן הרקיע מן המערב למזרח וכשמגעת לחלון שוורחת ממנו או לאלתר עולה עמוד השחר והחמה מהלכת בעביו של רקיע וכשתגיע לסוף עביו של רקיע לצד הנראה לבני אדם מיד מנצת על הארץ ומהלכת ביום כולו ממזרח למערב וכן בשקיעות מהלכת בעביו של רקיע וכשתצא מעיביו הרקיע כלו מיד הכוכבים נראין כיון שראה רבה כי מהלך החמה ביום כלו מן המזרח למערב לדברי ר' יוחנן עשר פרסאות ובכללם מה שמהלכת החמה בעביו של רקיע בבקר ובערב נמצא עביו של רקיע כפי הלוכו מקצה הרקיע ועד קצהו שלשים פרסה ובעביו של רקיע חמשה מילין שהן כפי מדת מהלך החמה מהנץ החמה עד ביאתה חלק משישה חלקים כי השלשים כשתחלקם שתותם חמשה והוא מהלך החמה בעובי הרקיע וכיון שהיה בידו גמרא כי העולם כולו ששת אלפים פרסאות אמר ש"מ עביו של רקיע שמהלכת בו החמה מעלות השחר ועד שתנץ החמה אלפא פרסי שהוא שתות מהלכו של עולם וכן בערב משתשקע החמה עד צאת הכוכבים ואע"פ שהחוזים בכוכבים שבזמן הזה מדברים דברים המכחישין לא משגיחינן להו אלא אנו מזהרים דברי רבותינו כתקנם ולא לחוש לדברי זולתם ואותבי' עליה מהא דתניא עביה של רקיע ארבעה מיל דתניא ר' יהודה אומר כמה מהלך אדם בינוני ביום עשר פרסאות מעלות השחר עד הנץ החמה ארבעת מילין שהן פרסה וכמותה משתשקע החמה ועד צאת הכוכבים כו' נמצאת הא מתניתא תיובתא לעולא דאמר מהלך החמה ביום מן המזרח למערב שלשים מיל ומתני' דא' שמונה פרסאות שהן שנים ושלשים מיל ותיובתא דרבה בתרתי חדא כדעולא דהא תרווייהו סדתן שוה במהלך החמה ביום שלשים מיל ותיובתא אחריתי דרבה דאמר עביו של רקיע כשיעור מהלך אדם חמשה מילין ומתני' אמרה פרסה שהיא ארבעה מילין ואתין למימר לימא תהוי הא מתניתא תיובתא נמי לר' יוחנן ומשני' לא לר' יוחנן לא הויא תיובתא דהוא לא אמר אלא כמה מהלך אדם בינוני ביום עשר פרסאות זה שאמר ר' יוחנן בלבד באו רבה ועולא ואמרו מדעתם חמשה מילין מעלות השחר עד הנץ החמה וחמשה מילין משתשקע החמה עד צאת הכוכבים הם שטעו שחשבו מאלו עשר פרסאות שאמר ר' יוחנן שמהלך אדם ביום חמשה מילין בשחר וחמשה מילין בערב ונמצאת הליכת החמה ממזרח למערב שלשים מיל ור' יוחנן לא הזכיר מהלך החמה בעביו הרקיע כמה הוא יש לומר שכך אמר ר' יוחנן בעובי הרקיע כמו הברייתא שאמרה מפרסה עשר פרסאות שנמצאת עובי הרקיע אחד מעשרה ביום ולר' חנינא נמי לא הויא היא תיובתא דיכול למימר ודאי מהלך אדם בינוני מעלות השחר עד הנץ החמה ארבעה מילין כמו שאמרה הברייתא ולוט הלך בריצה חמשה מילין: ת"ש מצרים הויא ארבע מאות פרסה על ארבע מאות פרסה כו' ת"ש כל הישוב כלו תחת כוכב אחד יושב וכו' ת"ש אמר ר' יוחנן בן זכאי מה תשובה השיבתו בת קול לאותו רשע

כו'

a is not [stated] in reference to an unclean person.[1] [94a] On Rab Judah's view there is no difficulty: When one is unclean through a reptile, the Divine Law relegated him [to the second Passover], for it is written, *'If any man shall be unclean by reason of a dead body'*: does this not refer [even] to one whose seventh day falls on the eve of Passover, yet even so the Divine Law said: Let him be relegated [to the second].[2]

Our Rabbis taught: If he was standing beyond Modi'im and is able to enter by horses and mules, you might think that he is culpable. Therefore it is stated: *'and is* not *in a journey,'*[3] whereas this man was in a journey.[4] If he was standing on the hither side of Modi'im, but could not enter on account of the camels and waggons which held him up,[5] you might think that he is not culpable. Therefore it is stated, *'and is not in a journey,'* and lo, he was not in a journey.[6]

Raba said: The world is six thousand *parasangs*,[7] and the thickness of the heaven [*raḳia'*] is one thousand *parasangs*; the first one [of these statements] is a tradition, while the other is [based on] reason. [Thus:] he agrees with Rabbah b. Bar Ḥanah's dictum in R. Joḥanan's name: What is an average man's journey in a day? Ten *parasangs*: from daybreak until the first sparklings of the rising sun five *mils*, and from sunset until the stars appear five *mils*: hence

b the thickness of the heaven is one sixth of the day['s journey].[1]

An objection is raised: Rab Judah said: The thickness of the sky is one tenth of the day's journey. The proof is this: what is an [average] man's journey in a day? Ten *parasangs*, and from daybreak until the rising sun four *mils*, [and] from sunset until the stars appear four *mils*: hence the thickness of the sky is one tenth of the day['s journey].[2] This is a refutation of Raba, and a refutation of 'Ulla! It is a refutation.[3] Shall we say that this is [also] a refutation of R. Joḥanan?—He can answer you: I spoke only of [an average man's journey] in a [complete] day, and it was the Rabbis[4] who erred by calculating [the distance for] pre-dawn and after nightfall.[5] Shall we say that this is a refutation of R. Ḥanina?[6]—No: *'and* [*the angels*] *hastened'*[7] is different.[8]

Come and hear: Egypt was four hundred *parasangs* square. Now Egypt is one sixtieth of Ethiopia [Cush], Ethiopia one sixtieth of the world, the world one sixtieth of the Garden, the Garden one sixtieth of Eden, Eden one sixtieth of the Gehenna: thus the whole world is like a pot lid [in relation] to Gehenna. This is [indeed] a refutation.[9]

c Come and hear: Tanna debe Eliyahu[1] [taught]: R. Nathan said: The whole of the inhabited world is situate under one star. The proof is that a man looks at a star, [and] when he goes eastward it is opposite, [and when he goes] to the four corners of the world it is opposite him. This proves that the whole of the inhabited world is situate under one star. This is indeed a refutation.[2]

Come and hear: The Wain ['Waggon'][3] is in the north and Scorpio is in the south, the whole of the inhabited world lies between the Wain and Scorpio, and the whole of the inhabited world represents but one hour of the day,[4] for the sun enters [the space above] the inhabited world only for one hour in the day.[5] The proof is that at the fifth [hour] the sun is in the east while at the seventh the sun is in the west: [during] half of the sixth and half of the seventh the sun stands overhead all people.[6] This is [indeed] a refutation.

Come and hear: For R. Joḥanan b. Zakkai said: What answer did the *Bath Ḳol*[7] give that wicked man [Nebuccadnezzar] when he asserted, *'I will ascend above the heights of the clouds; I will be like the Most High'*?[8] A *Bath Ḳol* came forth and rebuked him: 'Thou

a (1) V. Num. IX, 13: *But the man that is clean, and is not in a journey, and forbeareth to keep* (lit., 'do') *the Passover* etc. From this we see, (i) that the exemption for a man who is in a *'journey afar off'* applies to a clean person, and (ii) that a *'journey* (*afar off*)' is determined by his inability to do the Passover, i.e., to slaughter it. Hence if he is so far away that he cannot reach the Temple Court in time for the slaughtering, he is in a journey afar off. But an unclean person is exempt because of his uncleanness, which prevents his eating, but not his sacrificing, since that can be done by another acting on his behalf. Moreover, since Scripture specifies one who is *'unclean by reason of a dead body'* and does not state one who is unclean through a reptile, it follows that this exemption applies only to such as the former, who are unclean for a long period (seven days) and cannot be fit in the evening, but not to such as the latter, who can be fit to eat in the evening. (2) V. *supra* 90*b* and notes a.l. (3) Ibid. (4) As defined in the Mishnah. (5) He too being on one, and the road was blocked. (6) He should have completed it on foot. (7) Rashi: in diameter from east to west.

b (1) The periods from daybreak until the rising sun is in the heavens, and again from sunset until the stars appear, were regarded as the time during which the sun was passing through the sky, which was conceived as a solid vault stretched out above the earth. Hence it follows from Rabbah's dictum that since five *mils* can be walked in each of these two periods, while thirty *mils* can be walked during the day excluding these periods (ten *parasangs* = forty *mils*), the thickness of the sky is one sixth of the world's diameter. (2) The one tenth is of the inclusive figure, i.e., four in forty, whereas one sixth mentioned before was exclusive: six in thirty. But in any case they disagree. (3) Both (for 'Ulla v. *supra* 93*b*) hold that five *mils* can be walked from daybreak until the sun is in the heavens, which certainly cannot be reconciled with the present statement. (4) I.e., 'Ulla and Raba. (5) He had merely stated that an average man can walk ten *parasangs* in a day, but Raba and 'Ulla had erred by adding that one travels five *mils* in the period stated; though most people do indeed walk five *mils* by the time the sun is in the heavens, that is because they generally start a little *before* dawn; similarly in the evening they continue their journey a little after nightfall. (6) *Supra* 93*b*. (7) Gen. XIX, 15. (8) They would naturally cover a greater distance. (9) For according to the present calculation the surface area of the world is 576,000,000 sq. *parasangs* (thus: 400 × 400 × 60 × 60) whereas according to Raba, even if the 6000 is squared, we have only 36,000,000 sq. *parasangs*.

c (1) This is a Midrash consisting of two parts, 'Seder Eliyahu Rabbah' and 'Seder Eliyahu Zuta'. According to the Talmud Keṭh. 106*a* the Prophet Elijah recited this Midrash to R. 'Anan, a Babylonian Amora of the third century. Scholars are agreed that the work in its present form received its final redaction in the tenth century C.E., though they are not agreed as to where it was written. V. Bacher, *Monatsschrift*, XXIII, 267f; *idem* in *R.E.J.* XX, 144-146; Friedmann, Introduction to his edition of *Seder Eliyahu*; v. Keth., 106*a*, n. 2. (2) And since there are countless stars in the sky, it follows that the sky is immeasurably greater than the earth, not, as Raba says, only one sixth. (3) The Great Bear. (4) The sun in travelling through the sky takes one hour only to travel across the actual breadth of the world. (5) As explained in the previous note. (6) Wherever they are; thus it is during this hour only that the sun is actually above the world. This too proves that the sky is infinitely larger than the earth. (7) V. Glos. (8) Isa. XIV, 14.

means *kareth?* [93*b*] He holds that *megaddef* is one who curses[5] the [Divine] Name,[6] while of him who curses the [Divine] Name it is written, [*Whosoever curseth his God*] *shall bear his sin*,[7] and [the meaning of] this *'his sin'* is learnt from *'his sin'* there: just as there [it means] *kareth*; so here too, [it means] *kareth*.

Again, R. Nathan holds: *And forbeareth to keep the Passover, that soul shall be cut off*,' for this *ki* denotes 'because'[8] and this is what the Divine Law saith, *Because he brought not the offering of the Lord* at the first. How does he employ this [phrase] *'that man shall bear his sin'?*[9]—He holds that *megaddef* is not one who curses the [Divine] Name,[10] and so [the meaning of] this *'his sin'* [written] there is learnt from *'his sin'* [written] here; just as [it means] *kareth* here,[11] so there too [it means] *kareth*.

While R. Hanania b. 'Akabia holds [that we translate thus]:
a *'and forbeareth to keep the Passover, that soul shall be cut off'*;[1] if [also] *he brought not the offering of the Lord in its appointed season*, [viz.,] at the second. And how does he employ this *'shall bear his sin'?* —As we have stated.[2]

Therefore if [he neglected] deliberately both [Passovers], all agree that he is culpable. If [he neglected] both unwittingly, all agree that he is not culpable. If [he neglected] the first deliberately but the second unwittingly: according to Rabbi and R. Nathan he is culpable; according to R. Hanania b. 'Akabia, he is not culpable. If [he neglected] the first unwittingly but the second deliberately: according to Rabbi he is culpable; according to R. Nathan and R. Hanania b. 'Akabia he is not culpable.

MISHNAH. WHAT IS 'A JOURNEY AFAR OFF'? FROM MODI'IM[3] AND BEYOND, AND THE SAME DISTANCE ON ALL SIDES [OF JERUSALEM]: THIS IS R. AKIBA'S OPINION. R. ELIEZER SAID: FROM THE THRESHOLD OF THE TEMPLE COURT AND WITHOUT. SAID R. JOSE TO HIM: FOR THAT REASON THE HEH IS POINTED[4] IN ORDER TO TEACH: NOT BECAUSE IT IS REALLY AFAR OFF, BUT [WHEN ONE IS] FROM THE THRESHOLD OF THE TEMPLE COURT AND WITHOUT [HE IS REGARDED AS BEING 'AFAR OFF'].

GEMARA. 'Ulla said: From Modi'im to Jerusalem is fifteen *mils*.[5] He holds as Rabbah b. Bar Hanah said in R. Johanan's name: what is an [average] man's journey in a day?[6] Ten *parasangs*: five *mils* from daybreak until the first sparklings of the rising sun, [and] five *mils* from sunset until the stars appear. This leaves thirty: fifteen from the morning until midday, and fifteen from midday until evening [i.e., sunset]. 'Ulla is consistent with his view, for 'Ulla said: What is *'a journey afar off'?* Any place whence
b a man is unable to enter [Jerusalem] at the time of slaughtering.[1]

The Master said: 'Five *mils* from daybreak until the first sparklings of the rising sun.' Whence do we know it?—Because it is written, *And when the morning arose* [i.e., at daybreak], *then the angels hastened Lot, saying* etc.;[2] and it is written, *The sun was risen upon the earth when Lot came unto Zoar;*[3] while R. Hanina said: I myself saw that place and it is five *mils* [from Sodom].

The [above] text [stated]: "Ulla said, what is *"a journey afar off"?* Any place whence a man is unable to enter [Jerusalem] at the time of slaughtering.' But Rab Judah maintained: Any place whence one is unable to enter [Jerusalem] at the time of eating. Rabbah said to 'Ulla: On your view there is a difficulty, and on Rab Judah's view there is a difficulty. On your view there is a difficulty, for you say, 'Any place whence a man is unable to enter at the time of slaughtering': yet surely a man unclean through a reptile is unable to enter[4] at the time of slaughtering, yet you say, One slaughters and sprinkles on behalf of a person unclean through a reptile? On Rab Judah's view there is a difficulty, for he says, 'Any place whence one is unable to enter at the time of eating': but surely he who is unclean through a reptile is able to enter at the time of eating, yet he says, One may not slaughter and sprinkle on behalf of a man unclean through a reptile?[5] Said he to him: Neither on my view nor on Rab Judah's view is there a difficulty. On my view there is no difficulty: *'A journey afar off'* [is stated] in reference to a clean person, but *'a journey afar off'*

(5) Lit., 'blesses', a euphemism for 'curses'. (6) V. Num. XV, 30; *he blasphemeth* (Heb. *megaddef*, R.V.: reproacheth) *the Lord; and that soul shall be cut off* (i.e., *kareth*). The meaning of *megaddef* is disputed in Ker. 7*b*. (7) Lev. XXIV, 15. From Num. XV, 30 we know that he incurs *kareth*, and therefore that must be the meaning in this verse. (8) R. Nathan renders *'ki'* as *'because'*. (9) According to Rabbi it is necessary, as it refers to the punishment for the neglect of the *second*. But since R. Nathan relates it to the first, it is superfluous, having been already stated. (10) But one who takes part in an idolatrous service, e.g., by singing hymns in a heathen Temple, v. Ker. 7*b*. Consequently, Num. XV, 30 cannot be identified with Lev. XXIV, 15 (v. notes *supra*), and so there is nothing to indicate the meaning of *'shall bear his sin'* in the latter verse, which refers to blasphemy. (11) As explicitly stated in the first half of the verse.

a (1) Translating *ki* like Rabbi, except that he connects it with the preceding part of the verse. (2) In connection with R. Nathan. (3) Generally known as Modim, a town famous in Jewish history as the residence of Mattathias and his sons, where the Maccabean revolt against Antiochus flared up; it was some fifteen miles N.W. of Jerusalem. (4) The Heb. for *'a journey afar off'* (Num. IX, 10) is דרך רחוקה the ה (*heh*) being traditionally written with a dot, thus הּ. Such a point was regarded as a weakening or limitation, as though the word were not really written. (5) A *mil* = two thousand cubits, a quarter of a *parasang*. (6) From daybreak to nightfall, when the day and night are of equal length, i.e., from six a.m. to six p.m.

b (1) I.e., so far, that if a man started walking at midday, which is the earliest time for sacrificing the Passover-offering, he could not reach it by sunset, which is the latest. Taking this statement in conjunction with the preceding calculation, we see that Modim must be fifteen *mils* from Jerusalem. (2) Gen. XIX, 15. (3) Ibid. 23. (4) *Sc.* the Temple. (5) For this controversy v. *supra* 90*b*.

עין משפט נר מצוה

ח א ב ג מיי' פ"ה מהל' ק"פ הלכה ב:
[זבחים ..]
ט ד ה מיי' שם הל' ח:

קסבר *מגדף היינו מברך השם וכתיב
במברך את השם °ונשא חטאו וגמר האי
חטאו דהכא מחטאו דהתם מה להלן כרת
אף כאן נמי כרת ור' נתן סבר °וחדל
לעשות הפסח ונכרתה דהאי כי *לשון דהא
הוא וה"ק רחמנא דהא קרבן ה' לא הקריב
במועדו בראשון האי חטאו ישא מאי עביד
ליה קסבר מגדף לאו היינו מברך את השם
וגמר האי חטאו דהתם מהאי חטאו דהכא
מה הכא כרת אף התם כרת ור' חנניא בן
עקביא סבר וחדל לעשות הפסח ונכרתה
אי קרבן ה' לא הקריב במועדו בשני והאי
חטאו ישא מאי עביד ליה כדאמרן הלכך
*הזיד בזה ובזה דברי הכל חייב שגג בזה
ובזה דברי הכל פטור הזיד בראשון ושגג
בשני לרבי ולר' נתן ימחייבי לרבי חנניא
בן עקביא פטור שגג בראשון והזיד בשני
לרבי חייב לר' נתן ולר' חנניא בן עקביא
פטור: **מתני׳** *איזו היא דרך רחוקה מן
המודיעים ולחוץ וכמדתה לכל רוח דברי
רבי עקיבא ר"א אומר מאיסקופת העזרה
ולחוץ אמר ליה רבי יוסי לפיכך נקוד על °ה' לומר לא מפני שרחוק ודאי
אלא מאיסקופת העזרה ולחוץ: **גמ׳** אמר עולא *מן המודיעים לירושלים
חמשה עשר מילין הויא סבר לה כי הא דאמר *רבה בר בר חנה אמר רבי
יוחנן כמה מהלך אדם ביום עשרה פרסאות מעלות השחר ועד הנץ החמה
חמשת מילין משקיעת החמה ועד צאת הכוכבים חמשת מילין פשו להו
תלתין חמיסר מצפרא לפלגא דיומא וחמיסר מפלגא דיומא לאורתא עולא
לטעמיה דאמר עולא אי זה הוא דרך רחוקה כל שאין יכול ליכנס בשעת
שחיטה אמר מר מעלות השחר עד הנץ החמה חמשת מילין מנא לן דכתיב
°וכמו השחר עלה ויאיצו המלאכים וגו' וכתיב °השמש יצא על הארץ
ולוט בא צוערה ואמר רבי חנינא לדידי חזי לי ההוא אתרא והויא חמשה
מילין גופא אמר עולא איזה הוא דרך רחוקה כל שאין יכול ליכנס
בשעת שחיטה ורב יהודה אמר כל שאין יכול ליכנס בשעת אכילה
אמר ליה רבה לעולא לדידך קשיא ולרב יהודה קשיא °לדידך קשיא
דאמרת כל שאין יכול ליכנס בשעת שחיטה והא טמא שרץ דאין יכול
ליכנס בשעת שחיטה וקאמרת שוחטין וזורקין על טמא שרץ ולרב יהודה קשיא
דאמר כל שאין יכול ליכנס בשעת אכילה והא טמא שרץ דיכול ליכנס בשעת
אכילה וקאמר *אין שוחטין וזורקין על טמא שרץ אמר ליה לא לדידי קשיא
ולא לרב יהודה קשיא לדידי ל"ק *דרך רחוקה לטהור °ואין דרך רחוקה לטמא
לרב

רש"י

קסבר מגדף. דכתיב ביה כרת היינו מברך את השם וכיון דיש כרת במברך את השם יליף האי מיניה נשיאות חטא נשיאות חטא לגזירה שוה: ורבי נתן. מוקי ליה להאי כי בלשון דהא וקאי אדלעיל מיניה למיתב טעמא למילתיה ונכרת בראשון משום דהא קרבן ה' לא הקריב במועדו בראשון: לאו היינו מברך את השם. אלא מזמר ומשורר לע"ז דאיכא דסבירא ליה הכי בכריתות (דף ז:) ולית לן כרת במברך אי לאו מהכא גמירי לה: ורבי חנניא. נמי דריש האי כי לשון אי כו' אלא קסבר לאו מילתא אחריתי היא אלא כרת דקמא תלה ביה ונכרת במזיד דראשון אם קרבן ה' לא יקריב בשני: כדאמרן. לאגמורי כרת למברך: דברי הכל חייב. חד כרת: לר' ור' נתן חייב. דלא סבירא להו דשני תקנתא דראשון: שגג בראשון והזיד בשני לר' חייב. דאית ליה כרת בשני באנפי נפשיה: לר' נתן ור' חנניא פטור. דהא לא כתיב כרת אלא אראשון והרי שגג בו: **מתני'** מודיעים. שם העיר: נקוד על ה'. שברחוקה וכל ניקוד למעט הדבר בא דמשמע סמיוה להא תיבה מהכא: **גמ'** חמשה עשר מילין. מדקרי ליה תנא דידן דרך רחוקה לגבי פסח וסבירא ליה לעולא דרך רחוקה כל שאינו יכול ליכנס בשעת שחיטה כל שעת שחיטה מהלך ואינו מגיע ושעת שחיטה מחצות היום ואילך דבין הערבים כתיב ביה כתמיד ותמיד אע"פ שנשחט בשש ומחצה זמנו °מן התורה מתחלת שבע ואילך שמתחלת החמה להתעקם כלפי מערב קצת ומשחרי כותלי דהכי אמרינן ביומא בפ' שלישי (דף כח:) לנותיה דאברהם מכי משחרי כותלי והיינו מחצות היום והלכך אפרכינן עלה מהא דתנן תמיד נשחט בשש ומחצה ומשני שאני כותלי בית המקדש דלא מכווני רחבם מתחתיהן ולא משחרי בעיקום פורתא עד חצי שבע ומיהו זמן שחיטה מתחלת שבע ואילך ונמשך עד שתשקע החמה ומשתשקע החמה לא דדם נפסל בשקיעת החמה באיזהו מקומן (זבחים דף נו.) ומחצות ועד שקיעת החמה מהלך חמשה עשר מילין כי הא דר' יוחנן: סבר לה. עולא: כמה מהלך אדם. בינוני וביום בינוני דתקופת ניסן ותשרי שהימים והלילות שוין: עשרה פרסאות. ארבעים מילין: מעלות השחר עד הנץ החמה חמשה מיל. כך שהיית החמה לצאת בעוביו של רקיע וכנגדה שוהה בשקיעתה ליכנס דהיינו משקיעתה ועד צאת הכוכבים: פשו תלתין. מהלכה ועד שקיעתה: לאורתא. לשקיעת החמה דשוב אין זמן שחיטה דדם קדשים נפסל בשקיעת החמה כדאמרינן באיזהו מקומן בשחיטת קדשים: בשעת אכילה. כל שעת אכילה שרחוק מחצות היום כל כך שאינו יכול ליכנס כל הלילה אכילת הפסח כל הלילה ורבנן עבוד *הרחקה ואמור עד חצות לר"ע ולר"א לאורייתא עד חצות בפרק בתרא (דף קכ:) ובברכות בפ"ק (דף ט:): ולרב יהודה קשיא. דאמר כל שאינו יכול ליכנס בשעת אכילה הוא דפטור הא איחזי למיכל לאורתא חייב: והא טמא שרץ כו'. ופלוגתייהו בפ' האשה (לעיל דף צ:): לדידי לא קשיא. דאף על גב דדרך רחוקה פטורה להאי דחזי לאורתא ומחייבינא ליה גבי טמא שרץ היינו טעמא דבדרך רחוקה פטורה רחמנא לטהור והיינו דרך רחוקה שאין יכול ליכנס בשעת שחיטה דגבי עשייה כתיב ואף על גב דיכול ליכנס בשעת אכילה פטריה רחמנא אבל לטמא לא תלה רחמנא פטורא דידיה בדרך רחוקה אלא בטומאה וטעמא דטומאה משום אכילה היא ולאו משום עשיה דהא יכול לשלח קרבנותיו ועוד מדכתב טמא נפש ולא כתב בעל קרי או טמא שרץ שמעינן מיניה לא פטרי אלא בטומאה דאריכתא דלא חזי לאורתא: ולרב

תוספות

עולא לטעמיה. תימה מנא ליה לעולא דלא הוי שעת שחיטה מתחילת שקיעה דדם נפסל בשקיעת החמה דריש *ליה מביום הקריבו את זבחו והא קיימא לן בפ' שני דמגילה (דף כ:) דעד צאת הכוכבים יממא הוא: **רב** יהודה אמר כל שאינו יכול ליכנס בשעת אכילה. תימה דלרב יהודה מן המודיעים לא יכול ליכנס בחצי היום וכל הלילה ולעולא בשעת שחיטה דניחזי אנן ויש לומר דאיסתפוס דרכים כדאמרינן בר"ה (דף כג:) ועוד דאליבא דר"ע קיימי' דאית ליה* תחומין דאורייתא ולרב יהודה יכול ליכנס מן המודיעים עד סמוך לתחום בתחלת הלילה וליכא בינייהו השתא כולי האי וכן משמע בירושלמי: **וקאמרת** שוחטין וזורקין על טמא שרץ. לאלומיה פירכי' הוא דקאמר הכי ואפי' סבר אין שוחטין הוה מצי למיפרך מטבול יום דלכולי עלמא שוחטין וזורקין עליו אע"פ שאינו יכול ליכנס בשעת שחיטה: **דרך** רחוקה לטהור כו'. דתלייה בעשיה דכתיב ובדרך לא היה וחדל לעשות כו' ואע"ג דבההוא קרא גופיה כתיב טומאה והאיש אשר הוא טהור אזלינן בתר אכילה מדחייב טמא שרץ דכתיב טמא נפש ולא כתיב טמא שרץ:
לרב

רבינו חננאל

רב"נ חטאו ישא מחטאו ישא מן המברך את השם דברי ר' יהודה ור' נתן סבר וחדל וגו' הלכך הזיד בזה ובזה דברי הכל חייב שגג בזה ובזה דברי הכל פטור הזיד בראשון ושגג בשני לרבי ולרבי נתן דמחייבי בראשון חייב כרת לר' חנניא בן עקביא דסבר שניתקנתא דראשון הוא כיון דשגג בשני פטור הוא שגג בראשון והזיד בשני לר' חייב לר' נתן דסבר שני תשלומין דראשון הוא וכל הזקק לראשון וזקק לשני כיון ששגג בראשון פטור וכל שכן לר' חנניא בן עקביא דסבר שני תקנתא דראשון הוא: מתני' איזו היא דרך רחוקה מן המודיעים ולחוץ וכמדתה לכל רוח כו'. פי' שיהיה שם בחצי היום אמר עולא מן המודיעים לירושלים חמשה עשר מיל סבר לה כר' יוחנן דאמר עשר פרסאות מהלך אדם בינוני ביום חמשה מילין מעלות השחר ועד הנץ החמה וחמשה מילין משקיעת החמה ועד צאת הכוכבים פשו שלשים מיל חמשה עשר מצפרא לפלגיה דיומא וחמשה עשר מפלגיה דיומא עד לאורתא וקי"ל כל מצות התמיד מכי ינטו צללי ערב והפסח אחריו השתא אימת קא מחייב האי גברא למעבד פסח בחצות כיון דאיבעי מטייל לא מתעייל ליה עד דאיכא טמא שמא פטור כי אתר בביאת השמש שאינו שוחט כלל: עולא לטעמיה דאמר איזו היא דרך רחוקה כל שאינו יכול ליכנס בשעת שחיטה ואקשי' עליה והא טמא שרץ דטביל דכיון דערבא שמשו יכול ליכנס ולאכול ואת אמרת לעולא אין שוחטין וזורקין על טמא שרץ ושני' שאני טמא שרץ דרחמנא תליה בנפש שהוא כטמא נפש שהוא מפני שבעיני שלו להיות בערב הפסח וכתיב ולא יכלו לעשות הפסח ביום ההוא ביום ההוא לא יכלו הא למחר יכולין ואפ' הכי אמר רחמנא ידחו ואקשי' תוב לעולא אינו דכל מי שאינו יכול ליכנס בשעת שחיטה אין שוחטין עליו והא טמא שרץ שאינו יכול ליכנס בעזרה בשעת שחיטה ואמרת אתה שוחטין וזורקין על טמא שרץ

מסורת הש"ס

[כריתות ז:]
[ר"ה כ. תענית ט. גיטין ל. שבועות מט:]
[לקמן צד.]
[לעיל פט: וש"נ] [לקמן צד:]
[עיין רש"א]

תורה אור

ויקרא כד — במדבר ט — בראשית יט

גליון הש"ס

גמ' לדידך קשיא. כעין זה עירובין דף מט ע"ב. יומא דף מו ע"א. ב"ב דף קכד ע"ב: שם ואין דרך רחוקה לטמא. עי' לעיל פ. ע"א תוס' ד"ה מלמד: רש"י ד"ה חמשה עשר. מה"ת מתחלת שבעה. עיין לעיל נח ע"א רש"י ד"ה אלא:

מה טמא שספק בידו לעשות ואינו עושה אף דרך רחוקה נמי שספק בידו לעשות ואינו עושה ורב נחמן אמר לך ר' עקיבא *לטעמי' דקסבר *אין שוחטין וזורקין על טמא שרץ ואנא סבירא *ליה כמ"ד שוחטין וזורקין על טמא שרץ ת"ר *אלו שעושין את השני הזבין והזבות המצורעין והמצורעות [ונדות] ובועלי נדות והיולדות השוגגין והאנוסין והמזידין וטמא ושהיה בדרך רחוקה א"כ למה נאמר טמא למה נאמר דאי בעי למיעבד בראשון לא שבקינן ליה אלא א"כ למה נאמר בדרך רחוקה לפוטרו מן הכרת וכמ"ד הורצה אשה בשני מי מחייבא והא *תניא יכול לא יהו עושין את השני אלא טמא נפש ושהיה בדרך רחוקה זבין ומצורעין ובועלי נדות מנין ת"ל איש איש לא קשיא הא *ר' יוסי הא ר"י ור"ש ת"ר *חייב כרת על הראשון וחייב כרת על השני דברי רבי רבי נתן אומר חייב כרת על הראשון ופטור על השני ר"ח בן עקביא אומר אף [על] הראשון אינו חייב כרת אא"כ לא עשה את השני ואזדו לטעמייהו דתניא גר שנתגייר בין שני פסחים וכן קטן שהגדיל בין שני פסחים חייב לעשות פסח שני דברי רבי רבי נתן אומר כל שזקוק לראשון זקוק לשני כל שאין זקוק לראשון אין זקוק לשני במאי קמיפלגי רבי סבר שני *רגל בפני עצמו הוא רבי נתן סבר שני תשלומין דראשון הוא תקוני לראשון לא מתקין ליה ורבי חנניא בן עקביא סבר שני תקנתא דראשון הוא ושלשתן מקרא אחד דרשו והאיש אשר הוא טהור ובדרך לא היה רבי סבר וחדל לעשות הפסח ונכרתה דלא עבד בראשון אי נמי קרבן ה' לא הקריב במועדו בשני וממאי (דהא) חטאו ישא כרת הוא

קסבר

רש"י

מה טמא שיש ספק בידו לעשות. אי לאו דהדחייה רחמנא דהא קמן קאי: ואינו עושה. דקא סבר ליה רחמנא לעשות: אף דרך רחוקה שספק בידו לעשות. שהיה לו שלוחים לשלח וקאמר רחמנא דלאו עושה דמדחה דחייה: ר"ע סבר אין שוחטין וזורקין על טמא שרץ. ואע"ג דחזי לאורתא והאי ספק דקאמר ה"ק מה טמא שספק בידו לעשות דחזי למיכל לאורתא ואפילו הכי אין שוחטין וזורקין עליו ואנן ס"ל שוחטין וזורקין הלכך האי נמי דיכול ליכנס בשעת אכילה שוחטין וזורקין עליו: ובועלי נדות. שכל אלו טמאה הזובה: וטמאה. לנפש: וא"כ דאף אלו עושים את השני: למה נאמר טמא. בתמיה: אלא למה נאמר דרך רחוקה. אי משום דאי בעי למיעבד לא תעביד הא בדרך רחוקה הוא וא"ת שלא ישלח פסחו וכדרב ששת האי תנא לית ליה אלא כרב נחמן סבירא ליה דאמר הורצה דאי כרב ששת אילטריך דרך רחוקה למימר דאי בעי לא ליעביד: מי מחייבא. דקתני נדות ויולדות: יכול לא יהו כו'. ולא קתני זבות ויולדות: הא רבי יוסי. דאמר בפירקין דלעיל (דף פח:) נשים בשני שוחטין עליהן בפני עצמן: הא ר"י ור"ש. דאמרי רשות: חייב כרת על הראשון וחייב כרת על השני. חיוב כרת יש על זה ועל זה ובחד גברא לא משכחת לה דתרי קטלי בחד גברא ליכא ואם לענין דאם שגג בשניהן יתחייב שתי חטאות ליכא למימר הכי דכרת דפסח אין חייבין על שגגתו חטאת דתנן בכריתות (דף ב:) הפסח והמילה מצות עשה הוא ואין חטאת בהן אלא על שגגת כרת של לאו דכתיב (ויקרא ד) אשר לא תעשינה אלא נפקא מינה דאם שגג בא' מהן והזיד בחבירו חייב אי נמי לגר שנתגייר בין שני פסחים: ופטור על השני. ואם שגג בראשון והזיד בשני פטור: אף על הראשון. אם הזיד אינו חייב כרת עד שיזיד אף בשני אבל אם עשה את השני או שגג בו פטור לגמרי דשני תשלומים דראשון ותקנתא דראשון הוא ומזיד שלו הוא גמרו של כרת דראשון הלכך באיזה מהן שגג פטור: ואזדו לטעמייהו. רבי ורבי נתן: שהגדיל. למחר בו שערות: חייבין לעשות את השני: דקסבר רגל בפני עצמו הוא ואית ליה חיובא באנפי נפשיה ואפי' למאן דלא איחזי בראשון: תשלומין דראשון. ומאן דלא איחזי בראשון לא מיחייב בשני ומיהו תקוני לראשון לא מתקן ליה אם הזיד בראשון מכרת ולא מתקן ליה הלכך חייב כרת על הראשון ואפילו עשה את השני ופטור על השני אם שגג בראשון והזיד בשני דהא לית ליה חיובא באנפי נפשיה ובראשון הרי שגג: תקנתא דראשון. מכרת דיליה דאפילו הזיד בראשון השני פוטרו מן הכרת: אי נמי קרבן ה' לא הקריב וגו'. דכי משמש בארבע לשונות וזה בלשון אי דרשינן ליה ולא קאי אדלעיל מיניה לפרושי טעמא למילתא קמייתא כמו לשון דהא אלא מילתא אחריתי היא כמו כי יקרא (דברים כב) כי תכלה לעשר (שם כו) כי תפגע (שמות כג):

קסבר

תוספות

ה"ג בכל הספרים וכן גרסינן בספרי (פר' בהעלותך) מה טמא שאין ספק בידו ט' ומייתי התם פלוגתא דר"א ור"ע ומייתי ר"ע ראיה לדבריו מה טמא שאין ספק בידו לעשות מפני טומאה אף דרך רחוקה שאין ספק בידו לעשות שרחוק כ"כ שאין יכול לבא בשעת שחיטה לעולא או בשעת אכילה לרב יהודה ומייתי לה רב ששת מדקאמר ואינו עושה משמע דלא הורצה דלכל מילי יליף דרך רחוקה מטמאה ומשני רב נחמן דר"ע סבר אין שוחטין וזורקין ולכך יליף דרך רחוקה מטמאה דמרווייהו חזו בשעת אכילה ולא חזו בשעת שחיטה ולדידיה נמי אם זרק לא הורצה אבל אנא סבירא לי שוחטין וזורקין והשתא ליכא למילף דלא הורצה בדרך רחוקה כמו בטמאה מה דשאני טמאה מה דלא חזי בשעת אכילה ורב ששת סבר נמי שוחטין וזורקין דאין סברא שיחלוקו בזה אלא דסברי דר"ע גמר מטמאה מת אע"ג דלא דמי ליה כ"כ ונראה לר"י דלאו מהיקשא יליף דרך רחוקה מטמאה אלא במה מציע דאי מהיקשא מאי קא משני רב נחמן דסבר שוחטין מ"מ ניגמר מיניה דאין משיבין על ההיקש וק"ק לר"י דאי לאו היקשא הוא איכא טובא למיפרך: רבי עקיבא סבר אין שוחטין וזורקין. תימה מנא ליה דהא לעיל (דף כ:) אמר דמ"ד אין שוחטין סבר לה כרבי יצחק דאמר טמאי מתים היו שחל כו' וקדריש ביום ההוא אין יכולים לעשות הא למחר יכולים ואילו ר"ע בפרק הישן (סוכה ד' כה:) לית ליה דרבי יצחק: דאי בעי למיעבד לא שבקינן ליה. תימה הואיל וסבירא ליה להאי תנא שוחטין על טמא שרץ מדקאמר לפוטרו מהיכרת משמע מכרת פטור אבל אם זרק הורצה ומ"ד הורצה אסיקנא לעיל (דף פא:) דסבר שוחטין וזורקין אם כן טמא דקרא שאינו יכול לאכול בלילה והיכי קאמר התלמודא דלהכי כתביה דאי בעי למיעבד לא שבקינן ליה פשיטא דלא שבקינן ליה כיון דלא חזי למיכל א] ומלפי אכלו נפקא דטמא נמי נפק' לן מהתם כדאמר בפ"ב דזבחים (דף כג.) וי"ל דודאי קרא לא איצטריך להכי אלא פריך משום דקתני למה נאמר טמא לפוטרו מהיכרת דמשמע מכרת פטור אבל אי בעי למיעבד מלי עביד הלכך פריך הא אי בעי למיעבד לא שבקינן ליה והשתא טמא לא איצטריך למיכתב אלא לאשמעינן דאיש נדחה ואין ציבור נדחין ונראה לר"י דממתניתין דקתני שאלו פטורין מהיכרת ליכא למידק כרב נחמן מדקתני פטורין מכלל דאם זרק הורצה דה"ה אם זרק לא הורצה ואיידי דקתני סיפא חייבין תנא רישא פטורין ואתי שפיר דלעיל מייתי ראיה ממתניתין לרב ששת: אלא למה נאמר דרך רחוקה כו'. קשה לרב יהודה דאמר לקמן איזהו דרך רחוקה כל שאין יכול ליכנס בשעת אכילה דרך רחוקה דכתב רחמנא למה לי פשיטא דפטור דהא לא חזי לאכילה ואי משום דיכול ליכנס בסוסים ובפרדים א"כ לקמן דקתני היה חוץ למודיעים ויכול ליכנס בסוסים ובפרדים יכול יהא חייב ת"ל ובדרך לא היה ואמאי איצטריך ההוא קרא הא לא איצטריך למיכתב כלל דרך רחוקה אלא משום היכא דיכול ליכנס בסוסים ובפרדים ואין לומר דס"ד דחייב כרת על מה שהרחיק עצמו דאם כן מאי פריך למה נאמר טמא דאי בעי למיעבד לא שבקינן ליה הא שפיר קאמר דנאמר לפוטרו מכרת דס"ד דליחייב על מה שטימא עצמו ונראה לרשב"א דטמא ודרך רחוקה איצטריך למיכתב דלא נימא כיון דלא חזי בראשון לא ליעבד בשני וסבר כרבי נתן דשני תשלומין דראשון הוא: לא קשיא הא ר' יוסי. תימה דמוקי הך ברייתא דסבר שוחטין וזורקין על טמא שרץ כר' יוסי ובפ' כילד צולין (לעיל דף פא:) גבי טומאת התהום מסיק דקסבר ר' יוסי אין שוחטין וזורקין כו' וי"ל דהכא לא מוקי לה כר' יוסי אלא במאי דסבר דנשים בשני חובה:

עולא

עין משפט נר מצוה

ד א מיי' פ"ו מהל' ק"פ הלכה א:
ה ב מיי' שם פ"ה הלכה א ב:
ו ג מיי' שם:
ז ד מיי' שם הלכה ז:

כן לגעמים צריך מוכן ועי' בתוס' כאן ד"ה ר"ע ובקונטרס האחרון כזה:

[תוספתא פ"ח]

מסורת הש"ס

לעיל דף: וש"נ | [סבירא לי כצ"ל] | לעיל דף סו. | [לעיל נא:] | [תוספתא פ"ח] | [חגיגה ד' ט:] | [נ"ל דהאי]

במדבר ט | שם | שם | שם

רבינו חננאל

ונאמר דרך רחוקה כו' ודחה רב נחמן ר' עקיבא סבר אין שוחטין וזורקין על טמא שרץ ודרך רחוקה כטומאת שרץ דמי ואנא סבירא לי כמאן דאמר שוחטין וזורקין על טמא שרץ ודרך רחוקה כטמא שרץ דמי מה טמא שרץ אם שחטו עליו הורצה אף מי שהיה בדרך רחוקה אם זרק הורצה: ת"ר אלו שעושין את השני זבין וזבות מצורעין ובועלי נדות והיולדות והשוגגין והאנוסין והמזידין וטמא ומי שהיה בדרך רחוקה אם כן למה נאמר בדרך רחוקה הרי אנוס הוא וכבר שנה האנוסין ואמרי' לפטרו מן הכרת אליבא דמאן דאמר הורצה דאי אליבא דמאן דאמר לא הורצה סוף סוף למה לי למתנייה דאי בעי למעבד לא שבקינן ליה הייט הני אלא ש"מ היינו אליבא דמאן דאמר הורצה אלמא בר מעבד הוא ואפ"ה פטריה רחמנא מכרת ואקשי' מדקתני והזבות מכלל שהנשים חייבות בשני וכי אשה בשני חייבת והתניא יכול לא יהו עושין את השני אלא טמא נפש כו' ת"ל איש איש ולא אשה ושנינן הא דתניא שהנשים עושות את השני ר' יהודה ור' יוסי היא והא דתניא איש ולא אשה רבי שמעון כדאמרן בפ' של מעלה: ת"ר טהור שלא עשה פסח חייב כרת על הראשון וחייב כרת על השני דברי רבי מאי טעמא שני רגל בפני עצמו הוא ר' נתן אומר חייב כרת על הראשון ופטור על השני קסבר שני תשלומין דראשון הוא תקוני לראשון לא מתקן' הנניא בן עקביא אומר אף על הראשון אינו חייב אלא אם לא עשה את השני כלומר כיון שלא עשה הראשון נסתלקה חובת הראשון ונתחייב בשני ולעולם אינו חייב אלא על השני קסבר שני תקנתא דראשון הוא ואזדו לטעמיה דתניא גר שנתגייר בין שני פסחים וכן קטן שהגדיל בין שני פסחים חייבין לעשות פסח שני דברי רבי ר' נתן אומר כל הזקוק לראשון זקוק לשני וכל מי שאינו זקוק לראשון אינו זקוק לשני ושלשתן מקרא אחד דרשו והאיש אשר הוא טהור ובדרך לא היה וחדל לעשות הפסח בראשון ונכרת אי נמי קרבן ה' לא הקריב במועדו בשני חטאו ישא והוא כרת

דנסר

הגהות מהר"ב רנשבורג

א] תוס' ד"ה דאי בעי למיעבד כו' ומלפי אכלו נפקא כו'. נ"ב ע' לעיל ס"ע ע"א תוס' ד"ה שוחטין וזורקין וכו':

[93a] just as an unclean [person] is one who has the means of keeping it,[8] yet must not keep it, so [a man *'in*] *a journey afar off'* means one who has the means of keeping it,[9] yet he must not keep it.[10] And R. Naḥman?— He can answer you: R. Akiba is consistent with his view, for he holds: One must not slaughter and sprinkle on behalf of a person unclean through a reptile;[11] whereas I agree with the view that one slaughters and sprinkles on behalf of a
a person unclean through a reptile.[1]

Our Rabbis taught: The following keep the second [Passover]: *zabin* and *zaboth*,[2] male lepers and female lepers, *niddoth*[3] and those who had intercourse with *niddoth*, and women after confinement, those who [do not observe the first Passover] inadvertently, and those who are forcibly prevented, and those who [neglect it] deliberately, and he who is unclean, and he who was in *'a journey afar off'*. If so, why is an unclean person mentioned? [You ask] 'why is he mentioned'? [Surely to teach] that if he wishes to keep it at the first we do not permit him? Rather [the question is] why is [a person] on a journey afar off mentioned? —To exempt him from *kareth*, this being in accordance with the view that it is accepted.[4]

Is then a woman obliged [to keep] the second [Passover],[5] but surely it was taught: You might think that only a person unclean through the dead and one who was in *'a journey afar off'* keep the second [Passover],—whence do we know [that] *zabin* and lepers and those who had intercourse with *niddoth* [must
b keep it]? From the verse, *If any man* [etc.]?[1]—There is no difficulty: one is according to R. Jose; the other, according to R. Judah and R. Simeon.[2]

Our Rabbis taught: One incurs *kareth* on account of the first [Passover], and one incurs *kareth* on account of the second:[3] this is Rabbi's view. R. Nathan said: One incurs *kareth* on account of the first, but does not incur it on account of the second.[4] R. Ḥanania b. 'Akabia said: One does not incur *kareth* even on account of the first, unless he [deliberately] does not keep the second.

Now they are consistent with their views. For it was taught: A proselyte who became converted between the two Passovers, and similarly a minor who attained his majority between the two Passovers,[5] are bound to keep the second Passover:[6] that is Rabbi's view. R. Nathan said: Whoever is subject to the first is subject to the second, and whoever is not subject to the first is not subject to the second. Wherein do they differ?—Rabbi holds: The second is a separate Festival. R. Nathan holds: The second is a compensation for the first,[7] [but] it does not make amends for the first.[8] While R. Ḥanania b. 'Akabia holds: The second makes amends for the first.

Now the three deduce [their views] from the same verse: *But*
c *the man that is clean, and is not in a journey.*[1] Rabbi holds: *And forbeareth to keep the Passover, that soul shall be cut off*[2]—because he did not keep [it] at the first; *or* alternatively [if] *he brought not the offering of the Lord in its appointed season*[3] [i.e.,] at the second. And how do you know that that [phrase], *'that man shall bear his sin,'*[4]

(8) He is *physically* able to keep it. (9) E.g., one could sacrifice on his behalf and he could reach Jerusalem in time. (10) But *must* postpone it; hence if he does have it sacrificed on his behalf, it is not accepted. (11) Though he will be fit to eat in the evening, because at the time of sacrificing he is not fit. The present case is similar.

a (1) The translation and explanation follows cur. edd. Tosaf. records a different reading, which is supported by the Sifre (*Be-ha'alotheka*): Just as an unclean person is one who cannot possibly keep it, on account of his uncleanness, and he must not keep it, so a person in *'a journey afar off'* means one who cannot possibly reach Jerusalem in time (according to 'Ulla, for the sacrificing; according to Rab Judah, for the eating), and he too must not keep it. R. Shesheth deduces that 'he must not keep it' means that even if it is sacrificed on his behalf it is not accepted, since it is completely analogous to the case of an unclean person. R. Naḥman answers that because R. Akiba holds that you may not slaughter and sprinkle on behalf of a person unclean through a reptile, therefore he learns the case of *'a journey afar off'* from that of uncleanness, since the former two are alike in that both are unfit at the time of slaughtering and fit and able at the time of eating. Hence it is true that in R. Akiba's opinion the sacrifice is not accepted' if offered, but R. Naḥman holds that you do slaughter and sprinkle for a person unclean through a reptile. Tosaf. adds that R. Shesheth too holds thus, but that in his view R. Akiba learns it from a person unclean through the dead, though the cases are not really alike then. (2) Plural of *zab* and *zabah* respectively, q.v. Glos. (3) Pl. of *niddah*, q.v. Glos. (4) *Supra* 92*b*. For if he held that it is not accepted, then this case must be stated for that very teaching. (5) So that female lepers, menstruants and women after childbirth are included.

b (1) Num. IX, 10. Heb. איש איש, the repetition denoting extension. Thus nothing is said about women. (2) V. *supra* 91*b*. R. Jose holds that even at the second Passover a company consisting entirely of women may be formed; hence in his view the second Passover is binding upon women. Whereas R. Judah and R. Simeon hold that it is voluntary only. (3) Deliberate neglect to keep either when there is the obligation involves *kareth*. Of course, no man can actually incur *kareth* twice, but the point is that if a man sinned unwittingly in respect of one but deliberately in respect of the other he incurs *kareth*. Similarly, where a proselyte becomes converted between the two Passovers and deliberately neglects the second. (4) Hence if he inadvertently neglected the first, he does not incur *kareth* even if he *deliberately* neglects the second. (5) Thus both were exempt from the first Passover, but are in a condition to keep the second. (6) He regards it as a separate obligation entirely, even for those who were not subject to the law at all at the first, as in the present instances. (7) Hence only he who was subject to the law at the first can keep the second. (8) Hence if a person *deliberately* neglects the first he incurs *kareth* even if he keeps the second. On the other hand, if he neglects the first unwittingly, he is not liable to *kareth* even if he deliberately neglects the second, since the second is not an independent obligation apart from the first.

c (1) Num. IX, 13. (2) Ibid. (3) Ibid. *Because* (Heb. ki) *he brought not the offering* etc. *Ki* is variously translated according to the context, v. R.H. 3*a*. Rabbi renders it *'if'*. (4) Ibid.

Hillel both agree [92b] that we examine [a *beth ha-peras*] for the sake of those who would keep the Passover,[3] but we do not examine [it] for those who would eat *terumah*.[4] How is it examined? Said Rab Judah in Samuel's name: He sifts the *beth ha-peras* as he proceeds.[5] R. Judah b. Abaye[6] said in Rab's name: A *beth ha-peras* which was [thoroughly] trodden down is clean.[7]

CHAPTER IX

MISHNAH. HE WHO WAS UNCLEAN OR IN A 'JOURNEY
a AFAR OFF'[1] AND DID NOT KEEP THE FIRST [PASSOVER] MUST KEEP THE SECOND. IF HE UNWITTINGLY ERRED OR WAS ACCIDENTALLY PREVENTED AND DID NOT KEEP THE FIRST, HE MUST KEEP THE SECOND. IF SO, WHY IS AN UNCLEAN PERSON AND ONE WHO WAS IN 'A JOURNEY AFAR OFF' SPECIFIED? [TO TEACH] THAT THESE[2] ARE NOT LIABLE TO KARETH, WHEREAS THOSE ARE LIABLE TO KARETH.[3]

GEMARA. It was stated: If he was in *'a journey afar off'*[4] and they slaughtered [the Passover-offering] and sprinkled [its blood] on his behalf,—R. Naḥman said: It is accepted;[5] R. Shesheth said: It is not accepted. R. Naḥman said, It is accepted: The Divine Law indeed had compassion on him,[6] but if he kept [the first], a blessing come upon him![7] While R. Shesheth said, It is not accepted: The Divine Law did in fact suspend him, like an unclean person.[8]

R. Naḥman said, Whence do I know it? Because we learned, HE WHO WAS UNCLEAN OR IN 'A JOURNEY AFAR OFF' AND DID NOT KEEP THE FIRST [PASSOVER] MUST KEEP THE SECOND; whence it follows that if he wished, he could keep it. And R. Shesheth?[9]—He can answer you: If so, the second clause which teaches, IF HE UNWITTINGLY ERRED OR WAS ACCIDENTALLY PREVENTED AND DID NOT KEEP THE FIRST, HE MUST KEEP THE SECOND: [will you argue that] since he [the Tanna] states, AND DID NOT KEEP, it follows that had he desired he could have kept it? But surely he had unwittingly erred or been accidentally prevented! Hence [you must answer that] he teaches of deliberate
b neglect together with these;[1] so here too [in the first clause] he teaches about an *onen* together with these.[2] R. Ashi said: Our Mishnah too implies this,[3] for it is taught, THESE ARE NOT LIABLE TO KARETH, WHILE THOSE ARE LIABLE TO KARETH: Now to what [does this refer]? Shall we say, to one who errs unwittingly or is accidentally prevented? are then he who errs unwittingly and he who is accidentally prevented subject to *kareth!*[4] Hence it must surely [refer] to a deliberate offender and an *onen*. And R. Naḥman?[5]—He can answer you: In truth it refers to a deliberate offender alone,[6] and logically he should have taught, *he* is liable [in the singular]; but the reason that he teaches, THEY ARE LIABLE is that because the first clause teaches THEY ARE NOT LIABLE, the second clause teaches THEY ARE LIABLE.

R. Shesheth said: Whence do I know it? Because it was taught, R. Akiba said: *'Unclean'* is stated and *'in a journey afar off'*[7] is stated:

(3) If there is no other way to reach Jerusalem in time to sacrifice the Passover-offering save by crossing a *beth ha-peras*, the field is examined and they pass through it. (4) If a priest wishes to go somewhere to eat *terumah* and his way lies across a *beth ha-peras*, he cannot examine it but must take a circuitous course, even if this delays him a day or more.—One who passes over the *beth ha-peras* becomes unclean, and may not partake either of the Passover-offering or of *terumah*. (5) He takes up the earth *en route* and sifts it, to see if any small bones are hidden there, and if there are none he is clean, cf. note d7. (6) Var. lec.: Ammi. (7) As it is assumed that every bone which may be there has been reduced to less than the size of a wheat, which is the minimum standard for conveying uncleanness 'through contact' or treading upon it. Therefore if a man sees this he may cross it to sacrifice the Passover-offering, but not to eat *terumah*. Now the uncleanness of a *beth ha-peras* is only Rabbinical, and as we see here this law was waived somewhat in favour of the Passover-offering.

a (1) V. Num. IX, 10 f. (2) Enumerated in this Mishnah—all the four. (3) This is explained in the Gemara. (4) He can reach Jerusalem by nightfall in time to eat the offering, but not by day when the offering is sacrificed. (5) The sacrifice is valid, and he does not keep the second Passover. (6) By giving him the opportunity of a second Passover. (7) I.e., all the better. (8) So that he is not permitted to keep the first. (9) How does he rebut this?

b (1) I.e., though it is not specifically stated, yet the words 'AND DID NOT KEEP' can only apply to such, and he is therefore to be understood as included in the Mishnah. (2) I.e., the Mishnah is to be read in the first clause as including *onen* (v. R. Ḥananel). He could have kept the First Passover had he desired, v. *supra* 90b, and it is to this that the words 'AND DID NOT KEEP' refer. (3) That the first clause includes also *onen*. (4) Surely not. (5) Does he not admit this argument? (6) For the first clause does not treat of an *onen*, and consequently R. Naḥman's deduction holds good. (7) Num. IX, 10.

שבודקין לעושי פסח ואין בודקין לאוכלי תרומה מאי בודקין (לעושי פסח) *אמר רב יהודה אמר שמואל *מנפח בית הפרס והולך *רב יהודה בר *אביי משמיה דרב יהודה אמר בית הפרס שנידש טהור:

הדרן עלך האשה

מי שהיה טמא או בדרך רחוקה ולא עשה את הראשון יעשה את השני שגג או נאנס ולא עשה את הראשון יעשה את השני א"כ למה נאמר טמא או שהי' בדרך רחוקה שאלו פטורין מהכרת ואלו חייבין בהכרת: **גמ'** איתמר היה בדרך רחוקה ושחטו וזרקו עליו רב נחמן אמר הורצה רב ששת אמר לא הורצה רב נחמן אמר הורצה מיחש הוא דחס רחמנא עליו ואי עביד תבא עליו ברכה ורב ששת אמר לא הורצה מידחא דחייה רחמנא כטמא אמר ר"נ מנא אמינא לה דתנן מי שהיה טמא או בדרך רחוקה ולא עשה את הראשון יעשה את השני מכלל דאי בעי עבד ורב ששת אמר לך אי הכי סיפא דקתני שגג או נאנס ולא עשה את הראשון יעשה את השני מדקתני ולא עשה מכלל דאי בעי עבד והרי שגג והרי נאנס אלא מזיד קתני בהדייהו ה"נ אונן קתני בהדייהו אמר רב אשי מתניתין נמי דיקא דקתני אלו פטורין מהכרת ואלו חייבין בהכרת אהייא אילימא אשוגג ונאנס שוגג ונאנס בני כרת נינהו אלא לאו אמזיד ואונן ורב נחמן אמר לך לעולם אמזיד לחודיה ובדין הוא דאיבעי ליה למיתנא חייב והאי דקתני חייבין איידי דתנא רישא פטורין תנא סיפא חייבין אמר רב ששת מנא אמינא לה דתניא *ר"ע אומר נאמר °טמא ונאמר °בדרך רחוקה מה

רש"י

שבודקין · מהלכין בבית הפרס ע"י בדיקה לעשות פסח אם אין לו דרך אחרת: ואין בודקין לאוכלי תרומה · אלא ימתין ויקיף או יוסו עד שמגיע אל תרומתו ואוכלה: ה"ג מאי בודקין · הילך יבדוק: מנפח בית הפרס · הוא שדה שנחרש בה קבר כדתנן (אהלות פי"ז מ"א) החורש בית הקבר הרי זה עושה בית הפרס מלא מענה מאה אמה וגזור רבנן שמא כיתתה מחרישה את העצמות ופיזרתן באורך המענה ויש כאן עצם כשעורה ויעבור ויסיטנו ועצם כשעורה מטמאה במגע ובמשא דהיינו היסט הלכך מנפחו בפיו ואם יש עצם גדול יראנו ועצם כשעורה נדחה בנפיחתו ואהל אין מטמאו דהא אין טומאת אהל בעצמות אלא רוב בנין ורוב מנין: שנידש · ברגל טהור שדריסת הרגלים העבירתן והבא לעשות פסחו יבדוק אם נידש ויעבור אבל לאכילת תרומה לא סמכי' עלה שיכול להמתין ובית הפרס מדבריהם ולא העמידום במקום כרת דפסח:

הדרן עלך האשה

מי שהיה טמא: א"כ למה נאמר טמא · בגמ' פריך הא אילטריך דאי בעי למיעבד בראשון לא מצי עביד אלא אדרך רחוקה קאי דאנוס הוי (א) דלא מצי עביד וה"ע אמרינן בגמרא ואי בעי למיעבד ע"י שלוחו עביד כמ"ד בגמרא הורצה והלכך הואיל ושאר אונסין אידחו לשני אונס דדרך רחוקה ל"ל דאידכר רחמנא טפי מאונס אחרינא הא דרך רחוקה אנוס הוא שאינו יכול ליכנס כל שעת שחיטה כדאמרינן בגמ' ולאשמעינן דאי בעי למיעבד לא מצי עביד לא מצינן למימר דהא ודאי מצי עביד כמ"ד הורצה: שאלו פטורין מן ההכרת · טמא ודרך רחוקה ושגג ונאנס ואלו חייבין מפרש בגמרא: **גמ'** שחטו וזרקו עליו · ולערב יבא ומ"מ בדרך רחוקה הוא שאין יכול ליכנס בשעת שחיטה דהיינו כל שש שעות עד שקיעת החמה: הורצה · ופטור מן השני: כטמא · ולא עשה דקתני ולא עשה מכלל דאי בעי מצי עביד · ולטמא ליכא לאוקמא ועל כרחיך אדרך רחוקה קא מהדר: *וליטעמיך סיפא גבי שגג ונאנס דתנא תו זימנא אחריתי ולא עשה אהי מוקמת לה הלא שגג ולא ידע שהיום פסח הרי שגג ונאנס ומאי אי בעי איכא למימר הכא אלא מאי אית לך למימר בלא עשה דסיפא מזיד קתני בהדייהו ועלה קאי ולא עשה דאי בעי הוה עביד: ה"ג · גבי לא עשה דרישא אונן קתני בהדייהו ועלה קאי ולא עשה דאי בעי עביד כדאמרי' בפ' האשה (דף צא:) האונן והמפקח הגל כו' שוחטין עליהן: מתני' נמי דיקא · דמזיד ואונן קתני בה דאהייא · קתני חייבין בהכרת: ור"ע · דאמר לא תנן אונן ברישא ולא עשה אדרך רחוקה קאי אמר לך סיפא ודאי מזיד מחסרא בה ועלה קאי ולא עשה דסיפא וחייבין בהכרת נמי עליה קאי והא דתני חייבין לשון רבים פי' אידי דתנא פטורין תנא נמי חייבין (אמר המגיה בקצת פי' רש"י זה אינו) ותימה לי אמאי לא אמר ר"נ הנא אמינא לה דקתני א"כ למה נאמר דרך רחוקה שאלו פטורין כו' מדקאמר למה נאמר ש"מ דאי בעי למיעבד עביד כר"נ דאי כרב ששת אילטריך דאי בעי למיעבד דלא ליעבד (עד כאן) מה

תוספות

בודקין לעושי פסח · וא"ת דמשמע הכא דדוקא לעושי פסח התירו ע"י בדיקה משום דלא העמידו דבריהם במקום כרת ובפ' בכל מערבין (עירובין ד' כו:) תנן מערבין לכהן בבית הפרס ומפרש בגמרא *משום דמצי אזיל כדרב יהודה ואומר ר"י דהאי דקאמר הכא במקום כרת דוקא הייתו משום דאיכא נמי כרת בעשיית פסח בטומאה והייתו דקאמר בסוף חגיגה (דף כה:) לעושי פסח לא העמידו דבריהם במקום כרת לאוכלי תרומה העמידו דבריהם במקום מיתה פירוש לענין פסח טיהרוהו אע"ג דאיכא כרת באכילתו בטומאה לענין תרומה העמידו דבריהם ולא טיהרוהו אע"ג דליכא אלא מיתה לאוכלה בטומאה אבל בטומאת כהן דליכא אלא לאו שרי ליכנס בבית הפרס לצורך עירוב ויש דבר כגון ללמוד תורה ולישא אשה דשרי אפי' בלא נפוח כדאמרי' במי שהוציאוהו (עירובין דף מז.) ובע"א (דף יג.) משום דעדיפי משאר מצות*:

מאי בודקין · קשה לר"ת מאי קבעי הלא הבדיקה מפורשת בסוף אהלות באותה משנה עצמה דקתני ומודים ב"ש וב"ה שבודקין לעושי פסח ואין בודקין לאוכלי תרומ' ולנזיר ב"ש אומרים בודקין וב"ה אומרים אין בודקין כיצד הוא עושה מביא את העפר שהוא יכול להסיטו ונותן לתוך כברה שנקביה דקים כו' ואומר ר"י דבדיקה דמתני' בשכבר עבר ורב יהודה ורב חייא באין לפרש שיוכל לבא ולעבור וה"ק מאי בודקין אם רצה לעבור: [עי' תוספות בכורות כט. ד"ה היכי אזיל כו' וע"ע תוס' כתובות כה: ד"ה מנפח]:

הדרן עלך האשה

מי שהיה טמא: **אלו** פטורין מהכרת · נראה לר"י דמתני' קסבר שוחטין וזורקין על טמא שרץ והשתא איירי מתניתין בטמא מת בששי דלא חזי לאכילה לאורתא דאי קסבר אין שוחטין אם כן טמא דמתני' אף בטמא שרץ או דטמא מת בשביעי שלו א"כ אמאי פטור מהכרת כיון דיכול לטבול דהתניא בפ' אלו דברים (לעיל דף סט.) יכול לא יהא ענוש כרת אלא טהור ושלא היה בדרך רחוקה ערל וטמא שרץ ושאר טמאים מנין ת"ל והאיש ומשמע דליכא מאן דפליג עלה מדפריך מינה לרבה דקאמר דר"א פוטר מכרת וא"ת תיקשי מתני' לרב דאמר לעיל (דף נג:) אין שוחטין וזורקין על טמא שרץ וי"ל דכמה תנאי אשכחן דסברי כרב דאין שוחטין והא דפריך ליה לעיל ממתניתין דזב שראה שתי ראיות הייתו משום דרב עלה קאי ומוקי לה בשטבל:

ורב נחמן אמר הורצה · רב נחמן מצי סבר כרב יהודה דאמר לקמן *דרך רחוקה כל שאין יכול ליכנס בשעת אכילה ואפ"ה הורצה דהכי דאינו יכול הילוך ביעוני כיון דיכול לבא בסוסים ובפרדים בר אכילה הוא ולא דמי לחולה וערל וטמא:

הבא נמי אונן קתני בהדייהו · וא"ת מה בין אונן למזיד (ושוגג) דאם הוא מזיד הייתו מזיד (ואם הוא שוגג) הייתו שוגג וי"ל דלתנא תרי גווני מזיד חד שהניח בחנם ואונן שנתעצל אגב מרריה ומיירי במת לו מת אחר חצות אבל קודם חצות אינו בהכרת כדמוכח בסוף פירקין *וכן איתא בהדיא בפ' טבול יום (זבחים דף ק.) ולעיל הוי מצי למיחשב נמי אונן בהדי הנהו דהעמידו דבריהם במקום כרת קודם חצות ה"ג

עין משפט נר מצוה

נר א מיי' פ"ו מהלכות ק"פ הלכה ח:

[עם דף נ:]

א ב מיי' פ"ה מהלכות ק"פ הלכה א:
ב ג שם הלכה ב:
ג ד שם הלכה ג:

[ברכות יט: ע"ש על הגליון]

[ועיין תוס' בכורות כט. ד"ה היכי אזיל]

רבינו חננאל

ואמר רבי יוחנן דבר תורה אפי' עשה אין בו דכתיב ועמוד יהושפט וגו' בית הפרס דתנן חשין בית שמאי וב"ה שבודקין לעושי פסח ואין בודקין לאוכלי תרומה [מאי] בודקין (מפסח) [מנפח] אם אין שם עצם הרי הוא טהור ורב יהודה אמר בודקין (כלומר) אם הלכו בו בני אדם ופחר דק"ל כל עצם שהוא כשעורה [שנידש] ברגל [טהור] וכל שכן גדול ממנו: מאי שנא הני מ"שהני" פי' ערל וטמא [ואיזול] ערלה איסורא דאורייתא היא וכן הזאה נמי אי מעבר לה דרך רשות הרבי' את ילידי חלול שב' דהוא איסורא דאורייתא וכן אזיל נמי אי מבואו ליה דרך רשות הרבים איסורא דאורייתא היא העמידו דבריהם במקום כרת אבל אונן ומצורע ובית הפרס דלא אתו לידי איסורא דאורייתא לא העמידו דבריהם במקום כרת:

הדרן עלך האשה

מי שהיה טמא או בדרך רחוקה כו'. איתמר היה בדרך רחוקה ושחטו וזרקו עליו רב נחמן אמר הורצה מיחש הוא דחס רחמנא עליו ואי עביד תבא לו ברכה רב ששת אמר לא הורצה רחמנא דחייה כטמא דייק רב נחמן מי שהיה טמא או בדרך רחוקה ולא עשה את הראשון יעשה השני מכלל דאי בעי עביד ורב ששת אמר אי הכי סיפא דקתני שגג או נאנס ולא עשה הראשון יעשה השני וכי אלו יכולין לעשות הראשון והרי (שגגו) [שגג] או נאנס אלא בהדייהו והכי קתני שגג או נאנס או אפי' הזיד שהיה יכול לעשות הראשון ולא עשה יעשה השני רישא נמי מי שהיה טמא או בדרך רחוקה או אונן קתני ודייק רב אשי להא סברא מדקתני אלו חייבין בכרת מכלל דבמזיד ואונן קתני בסיפא דהא חייבין כרת קתני אבל ברישא איך נאמר אתו תני בהדייהו והא פטורין קתני אלא לעולם מזיד בלבד הוא דקתני בסיפא ואגב רישא פטורין תנא סיפא חייבין: **אמר** רב ששת מנא אמינא לה דתניא ר' עקיבא אומר נאמר טמא ונאמר

מסורת הש"ס

ברכות דף יט: עירובין דף נ: מ"ק דף ה: חגיגה דף כה: כתובות דף כח: בכורות דף כט. נדה דף מ.

[תוספתא פ"ח]

נ"א אי סבי

תורה אור

במדבר ט · שם

הגהות הב"ח

(א) רש"י ד"ה מי שהיה וכו' דלא מצי עביד ואי בעי למיעבד כצ"ל ותיבת וה"ע אמרינן בגמרא נמחק:

*והמלקט לו עצמות טובל ואוכל בקדשים גר *שנתגייר בע"פ ב"ש אומרים טובל ואוכל את פסחו לערב וב"ה אומרים הפורש מן הערלה כפורש מן הקבר: **גמ'** מ"ט קא סבר *אנינות דלילה דרבנן וגבי פסח לא העמידו דבריהם במקום כרת גבי קדשים העמידו דבריהם במקום עשה: השומע על מתו וכו': מלקט עצמות הא בעי הזאת שלישי ושביעי אימא שליקטו לו עצמות: גר שנתגייר וכו': אמר רבה בר בר חנה א"ר יוחנן מחלוקת בערל נכרי דב"ה סברי גזירה שמא יטמא לשנה הבאה ויאמר אישתקד מי לא טבלתי ואכלתי עכשיו נמי אטבול ואוכל ולא ידע דאשתקד נכרי הוה ולא מקבל טומאה עכשיו ישראל ומקבל טומאה וב"ש סברי לא גזרינן *אבל ערל ישראל דברי הכל טובל ואוכל את פסחו לערב ולא גזרינן ערל ישראל משום ערל נכרי תניא נמי הכי אמר *ר"ש בן אלעזר לא נחלקו ב"ש וב"ה על ערל ישראל שטובל ואוכל את פסחו לערב על מה נחלקו על ערל נכרי שב"ש אומרים טובל ואוכל את פסחו לערב וב"ה אומרים הפורש מן הערלה כפורש מן הקבר: אמר רבא *ערל הזאה ואיזמל העמידו דבריהן במקום כרת אונן ומצורע ובית הפרס לא העמידו דבריהן במקום כרת ערל הא דאמרן הזאה *דאמר מר הזאה שבות ואינו דוחה את השבת איזמל *דתניא כשם שאין מביאין אותו דרך רשות הרבים כך אין מביאין אותו דרך גגות ודרך חצרות ודרך קרפיפות אונן הא דאמרן מצורע מאי היא *דתניא מצורע שחל שמיני שלו בערב הפסח וראה קרי בו ביום טובל ואוכל אמרו חכמים אע"פ שטבול יום אינו נכנס נכנס זה מוטב יבא עשה שיש בו כרת וידחה עשה שאין בו כרת *וא"ר יוחנן דבר תורה אפילו עשה אין בו שנאמר ויעמד יהושפט בקהל יהודה וירושלים בבית ה' לפני החצר החדשה מאי חצר החדשה שחדשו בו דבר ואמרו טבול יום לא יכנס במחנה לויה בית הפרס *דתנן ושוין ב"ש וב"ה שבודקין

רש"י

וכן מי שליקטו לו עצמות · אביו ואמו אמרי' במועד קטן (דף ח.) מתאבל עליהן כל היום כולו ולערב אין מתאבל עליהן: טובל ואוכל בקדשים · לערב דאפילו יום גופיה מדרבנן הוא הלכך בלילה ליכא אנינות: כפורש מן הקבר · וצריך הזאה שלישי ושביעי: **גמ'** לא העמידו דבריהם · לאוסרו באכילת פסחו מפני תורה איר אנינות דדבריהם דהא פסח כרת הוא אבל אכילת קדשים עשה בעלמא הוא ואכלו אותם אשר כפר בהם (שמות כט): מלקט · משמע הוא עצמו ליקטן: מחלוקת בערל נכרי · שאינו מקבל טומאה בנכריותו דב"ה סברי גזירה שמא יטמא במת לשנה הבאה עם"פ ויאמר אשתקד לא טהרתי מכל טומאה עד יום ע"פ שנתגיירתי וטבלתי ואכלתי והשתא נמי אטבול ואיכול ולא ידע דאשתקד נכרי הוה ולא קיבל טומאה בנכריותו אבל עכשיו הוא טמא הלכך כשמתגייר ממתין שבעה שאין לך טומאה שעברה עליו שלא טהר ממנה ואע"ג דמשום זיבה בעי שמנה משום כפרה כיון דאי אפשר דלייתי כפרה דהא לא קבל טומאה בנכריותו אי אמרת גזור לא מייתי לעולם פסח וכולי האי לא גזרו: אבל ערל ישראל · שאם יש לו עכשיו טומאה הוא נזהר בה שאף בערלותו מקבל טומאה כשאר בני אדם ליכא למיגזר ביה משום שנה הבאה: ערל הזאה ואיזמל · סימני הלכות הם: הא דאמרן · דחזי לאורותא ומשום גזירה דשנה הבאה דחיוה ב"ה: ואינה דוחה שבת · בפ' אלו דברים ולא עביד פסח ושבות דרבנן הוא: אין מביאין אותו · האיזמל למילה: דרך חצרות · אף על גב דרשויות דרבנן נינהו וידחה פסחו שאם יש לו זכר למול מעכבו דתניא מילת זכריו ועבדיו מעכבין את הפסח וליכא למימר משום כרת דערל זכר אשר לא ימול וגו' דמילה דדחיא שבת בזמנה וקטן נמי לאו בר כרת הוא: אונן · אנינות לילה מדרבנן דאמרן לעיל אוכל פסחו לערב: מצורע · שטבל והעריב שמשו בשביעי נכנס בשמיני למחנה לויה לשער נקנור שלא נתקדש בקדושת עזרה כדכתיב במצורע (ויקרא יד) והעמיד הכהן המטהר את האיש המיטהר ואותם לפני ה' וגו' ובעזרה עצמה לא היה נכנס אלא מכניס ידיו לבוהנות לפי שאין מחוסר כפורים נכנס לה כדאמרי' [במכות] (דף ה:) טמא יהיה לרבות טבול יום עוד טומאתו בו לרבות מחוסר כפורים שאם נכנסו למקדש חייבין כרת: וראה קרי בו ביום · ונדחה ממחנה לויה כדאמרי' באלו דברים (דף סז:) דבעל קרי משתלח חוץ לשתי מחנות וטובל לקרוייו דלצרעתו טבל מאתמול אף על פי שטבול יום אחר דקרי איתו נכנס דכתיב (דברים כג) כי יהיה בך איש וגו' וכבא השמש יבא אל תוך המחנה זה נכנס להר הבית להכניס ידיו לבוהנות כדי שיאכל פסחו לערב: יבא עשה. דפסח שיש בו כרת וידחה עשה דטבול יום בהר הבית שאין בו כרת אלא בעזרה ואי משום דמכניס ידיו לעזרה הא אמרינן בשחיטת קדשים בפ"ג (דף לג:) איכא למ"ד ביאה במקצת לאו שמה ביאה ואיכא למ"ד הואיל והותרה לו אותה ביאה מקצת לצרעתו אע"פ שענוש כרת משום מחוסר כפורים והתירו הכתוב דכתיב לפני ה' הותרה לו אף לקרוייו: וא"ר יוחנן · עשה שאין בו כרת דקאמר תנא דברייתא לאו דוקא דאפילו עשה אין בו בטבול יום במחנה לויה אלא דרבנן הוא וקרא דכבא השמש במחנה שכינה קאמר: חצר החדשה · הר הבית וקרי לה חדשה מפני חידוש שחידשו והוסיפו על קדושתו בו ביום ואמרו טבול יום לא יכנס לה והכי גמיר ר' יוחנן מרביה דדבר זה חידוש וגבי פסח לא העמידו דבריהם להיכור (דמצורע) [דבעל קרי] מלבוא אלא התירוהו ליכנס ולטהר שלא ידחה מפסח:

שבודקין

תוספות

גבי פסח לא העמידו דבריהם במקום כרת · הא דלא קאמר משום דפסח מלוה עוברת משום דיש קדשים דמלותן נמי עוברת כגון תודה דאין נאכלת אלא ליום ולילה: **אבל** ערל ישראל ד"ה טובל · *תימה לריב"א דלא מלינו בשום מקום טבילה בישראל ערל אפילו מדרבנן: **ואמר** רבי יוחנן דבר תורה אפילו עשה אין בו · ר' יוחנן לא פליג אברייתא דלאו תנא הוא כדמוכח בפ"ק דכתובות (דף ח·) גבי אין אבלים מן המנין דלא משני אר' יוחנן רבי יוחנן תנא הוא ופליג כדמשני ארב אלא פרושי מפרש לה וכן מוכח דגבי יולדת שהיא טבולת יום ארוך כתיב (ויקרא יב) ואל המקדש לא תבוא משמע הא למחנה לויה תבא: **טבול** יום לא יכנס במחנה לויה · לא בכל המחנה אלא מעזרת נשים ולפנים כדתנן במסכת כלים (פ"א משנה ר) עזרת נשים מקודש הימנו שאין טבול יום נכנס לשם אבל בהר הבית היה נכנס וקרי חצר לעזרת נשים כדתנן פ"ב דמדות עזרת נשים היתה אורך קל"ה וארבעה לשכות היו בארבעה מקצועותיה של מ' אמה ולא היו מקורות וכן הם עתידות להיות כדכתיב ויוליאני אל החצר החיצונה וגו' וא"ת מנא ליה דגזרו על טבול יום דילמא על טמא מת גזרו שהיה מותר בכל מחנה לויה וי"ל דטמא מת אפי' בחיל גזרו שלא יכנס כדתנן במסכת כלים (שם) החיל מקודש הימנה שאין נכרים וטמאי מתים נכנסין לשם והא דנקט בברייתא וראה קרי בו ביום ולא נקט טבול יום דשאר טמאים רבותא נקט לא מיבעיא שאר טמאים דמדאורייתא מותרים ליכנס אלא אפילו בעל קרי דמשתלח מדאורייתא חוץ לשתי מחנות אפ"ה טבול יום שלו לא גזרו ביה רבנן ואם תאמר דבפרק נוטל (סוטה דף כ:) פריך אהא דקתני התם הוציאוה הוציאוה שלא תטמא את העזרה והתניא טמא מת מותר ליכנס במחנה לויה ואפילו מת עצמו כו' ומאי פריך כיון דמדרבנן אסור ליכנס וי"ל דמשמע ליה מדאורייתא מדקאמר הוציאוה הוציאוה תרי זמני שהיו ממהרין כל כך א"כ לא גזרו אלא שלא יכנס לפנים אבל אם נטמאה בפנים לא גזרו עליו לצאת והא דאמרי' בהנשרפין (סנהד' דף פב:) כהן ששימש בטומאה מוציאין אותו חוץ לעזרה ופוצעין את מוחו בגיזרין לאו דוקא חוץ לעזרה אלא הוא הדין חוץ לחיל:

בודקין

[עדיות פ"ה מ"ב]
[כריתות ט. וש"נ]
[תוספתא פ"ז ושם אי' ר"א ב"ר צדוק]
לעיל דף סה:
שבת דף קל:
יבמות דף ז: זבחים דף לב:
יבמות דף ז: הוריות דף ה: זבחים לב: ע"ש
חגיגה דף כה: אהלות פי"ח מ"ד

עין משפט נר מצוה

מט א מיי' פ"ג מהל' ביאת המקדש הל' י [ופ"ו מה' ק"פ הל' ט]:

[ע' בתוי"ט ישוב הגון] נ ב ג מיי' פ"ו מהל' ק"פ הלכה ז:

נא ד מיי' שם הלכה ו:

נב ה מיי' פ"ב מהל' מילה הלכה ו סמג עשין כח טוש"ע א"ח סי' שלא סעיף ו וטוש"ע י"ד סימן רסו סעיף ב' [רב אלפס שבת פי"ט דף מז: ובהרא"ש שם סימן ה']:

נג ו מיי' פ"ו מהלכות ק"פ הלכה ס:

[הא דלא חשיב חתיכת יבלתו וכה"ג עי' תוס' זבחים ע. ד"ה מנין ותוס' מנחות כ: ד"ה נפסל]

רבינו חננאל

קסבר אנינות לילה מדרבנן סתם לן תנא כר' שמעון דגרסי' בסוף שחיטת קדשים מאן תנא אנינות לילה מדרבנן ר' שמעון דתניא אנינות לילה דבר תורה דברי ר"י רבי שמעון אומר דרבנן שהרי אמרו אונן טובל ואוכל פסחו לערב ובא רב מרי להעמיד דברי ר' שמעון ביום מיתה אנינות לילה דאורייתא וביום קבורה אנינות לילה מדרבנן וכן אמר מר מת לו מת בארבעה עשר וקברו בארבעה עשר יום מיתה תופס לילו מדאורייתא מת לו מת בשלשה עשר וקברו בארבעה עשר לא תפיס לילו ועלתה בקשיא. ורבנן לא העמידו דבריהם בפסח שהוא במקום כרת שנא' (במדבר ט יג) וחדל לעשות הפסח ונכרתה אבל אכילת קדשים שהיא עשה העמידו דבריהם ואמרו האונן אע"פ שאנינות לילה מדרבנן אינו טובל ואוכל לערב קדשים אבל מי שלקטו לו עצמות טובל ואוכל אפילו בקדשים לערב דתניא יום שמועה כיום קבורה למצות שבעה ושלשים ולאכילת פסחים כיום ליקוט עצמות ואחד זה ואחד זה טובל ואוכל בקדשים לערב ואנינות לא פסק ליה יום טוב אלא למצות שבעה: **מתני'** גר שנתגייר ערב הפסח כו' אמר רבה בר בר חנה אמר ר' יוחנן מחלוקת בערל נכרי דב"ה סברי שמא יטמא הגר לשנה הבאה ואמר אשתקד לא טבלתי ואכלתי בערב הפסח עכשיו נמי כיון שטבלתי טהור אני כבר ואוכל והוא לא ידע דאשתקד עכו"ם הי' ולא היה מקבל טומאה השתא ישראל [הוא] ומקבל טומאה ואין הטבילה עלתה לו היום לטהר אותו בערב כטמא מת ביום שביעי שלו וב"ש לא גזרי אבל ערל ישראל דברי הכל טובל ואוכל פסחו לערב ולא גזור' על ישראל משום ערל עכו"ם. תניא נמי הכי: **אמר** רבא ערל הזאה ואיזמל אלו שלשה דברים מדאורייתא ראוין הן ורבנן הוא דגזרו בהו ואפי' במקום כרת העמידו דבריהם ערל הא דאמרן כי זה הגר ראוי הוא שיטבול ויאכל בפסח לערב דלא עדיף מישראל שאם היה ערל ישראל שמתו אחיו מחמת מילה וגדל זה בערלה ועכשיו טל עצמו בערב הפסח טובל ואוכל בערב הפסח וב"ה גזרו על הגר כמו שאמרנו למעלה ואמרי' הפורש מן הערלה כפורש מן הקבר· הזאה. שהיא שבות ואמרו חכמים אם חל י"ד להיות בשבת אינה דוחה ואין מזין על טמא מת שחל שביעי שלו בי"ד אלא (מתירין) [מת נרע] לבלתי עשות הפסח. ואיזמל אין מביאין את האיזמל בשבת כדי למול זכריו דקיימא לן מילת זכריו מעכבין אותו מלאכול הפסח שנאמר והאיש אשר הוא טהור וגו' אין מביאין האיזמל אפי' במקום שאיסורו מדרבנן דתניא כשם שאין מביאין אותו דרך רשות הרבים כך אין מביאין אותו דרך גגות דרך חצרות דרך קרפיפות' ובפ' האשה שהלך בעלה למדינת הים וכו' זו השמועה בלשון הזה אמר רבא בעאי לאותיביה ערל הזאה ואיזמל וסדין בציצית וכבשי עצרת וכיון דשנית שב ואל תעשה לאו מעיקר מילתא הוא וכו' אבל באלו שלשה דברים מדרבנן לא העמידו דבריהם במקום כרת והן אונן ומצורע ובית הפרס אונן הא דאמרן דאנינות לילה מדרבנן ובטלו דבריהם ואמרו טובל ואוכל פסחו לערב מצורע דתניא מצורע שחל שביעי [שלו] להיות בערב הפסח וראה קרי בו ביום וטובל ואוכל אמרו חכמים אע"פ שאין טבול יום אחר נכנס זה נכנס מוטב יבוא עשה שיש בו כרת וידחה עשה שאין בו כרת ואמר

a ABOUT HIS DEAD [FOR THE FIRST TIME],[1] [92a] AND ONE WHO COLLECTS THE BONES [OF HIS PARENTS],[2] PERFORM ṬEBILLAH AND EAT SACRED FLESH.[3] IF A PROSELYTE WAS CONVERTED ON THE EVE OF PASSOVER,—BETH SHAMMAI MAINTAIN: HE PERFORMS ṬEBILLAH AND EATS HIS PASSOVER-OFFERING IN THE EVENING; WHILE BETH HILLEL RULE: ONE WHO SEPARATES HIMSELF FROM [THE STATE OF] UNCIRCUMCISION IS LIKE ONE WHO SEPARATED HIMSELF FROM A GRAVE.[4]

GEMARA. What is the reason?—He holds: [The law of] *aninuth* at night is Rabbinical [only], and where the Passover-offering is concerned they did not insist on their law, since it involves[5] *kareth*;[6] but in respect to sacrifices [in general] they insisted on their law, seeing that [only] an affirmative precept is involved.[7]

ONE WHO HEARS ABOUT HIS DEAD etc. ONE WHO COLLECTS BONES?—But he requires sprinkling on the third and the seventh [days]?[8]—Say: One for whom [his parent's] bones were collected.[9]

A PROSELYTE WHO WAS CONVERTED etc. Rabbah b. Bar Ḥanah said in R. Joḥanan's name: The controversy is in respect of an uncircumcised heathen, where Beth Hillel hold: [He is forbidden to eat in the evening] as a preventive measure lest he become defiled the following year [by the dead] and he argues, 'Did I not perform *ṭebillah* last year and eat [of the Passover-offering]? So now too I will perform *ṭebillah* and eat.' But he will not understand that the previous year he was a heathen and not susceptible to uncleanness, whereas now he is an Israelite and susceptible to uncleanness. While Beth Shammai hold: We do not enact a preventive measure. But with regard to an uncircum-
b cised Israelite[1] all agree that he performs *ṭebillah* and eats his Passover-offering in the evening, and we do not preventively forbid an uncircumcised Israelite on account of an uncircumcised heathen.[2] It was taught likewise, R. Simeon b. Eleazar said: Beth Shammai and Beth Hillel did not differ about an uncircumcised Israelite, [both agreeing] that he performs *ṭebillah* and eats his Passover-offering in the evening. About what do they differ? About an uncircumcised heathen, where Beth Shammai rule: He performs *ṭebillah* and eats his Passover-offering in the evening; while Beth Hillel maintain: He who separates himself from uncircumcision is as though he separated from a grave.

Raba said: [In the case of] an uncircumcised person, sprinkling, and a knife, they [the Sages] insisted on their enactments [even] where *kareth* is involved;[3] [in the case of] an *onen*, a leper and *beth ha-peras*,[4] they did not insist on their enactments where *kareth* is involved. 'An uncircumcised person,' as stated.[5] 'Sprinkling,' for a Master said: Sprinkling is [forbidden as] a *shebuth*, yet it does not override the Sabbath.[6] 'A knife,' as it was taught: Just as one may not bring it [*sc.* a knife for circumcision] through the street, so may one not bring it by the way of roofs, court-yards,
c or enclosures.[1]

'An *onen*,' as we have stated.[2] What is this [law of] 'a leper'? For it was taught: A leper whose eighth day fell on the eve of Passover[3] and who had a nocturnal discharge [*ḳeri*] on that day,[4] performs *ṭebillah*[5] and eats [the Passover-offering in the evening].[6] [For] the Sages said: Though a *ṭebul yom*[7] may not enter [the Levitical Camp], this one does enter:[8] it is preferable that an affirmative precept which involves *kareth*[9] should come and override an affirmative precept which does not involve *kareth*.[10] Now R. Joḥanan said: By the law of Torah[11] there is not even an affirmative precept in connection therewith, for it is said, *And Jehoshaphat stood in the congregation of Judah and Jerusalem, in the house of the*
d *Lord, before the new court*.[1] What does '*the new court*' mean? That they innovated a law there and ruled: A *ṭebul yom* must not enter the Levitical Camp.[2]

'*Beth ha-peras*': for we learned: Now Beth Shammai and Beth

a (1) On the day when a man is informed of the death of a near relative, e.g., his father, he is an *onen* by Rabbinical law, even if death took place earlier. (2) He too is a mourner on that day by Rabbinical law. (3) In the evening. This applies to all sacrifices, for since even during the day he is an *onen* by Rabbinical law only, the Rabbis did not extend his *aninuth* (v. Glos.) to the evening. (4) He must be besprinkled with the water of purification on the third and seventh days after the circumcision; hence he is not yet fit in the evening. (5) Lit., 'in the place of'. (6) Since the neglect of the Passover-offering involves *kareth*, they waived their law. (7) It is an affirmative precept to eat of one's own sacrifice (Ex. XXIX, 33), but the violation of this law does not involve *kareth*. (8) The Mishnah was understood literally as meaning that he himself gathered them; but these defile just like a corpse, and he is unclean for seven days, and must be besprinkled on the third and the seventh days (Num. XIX, 19). (9) By others: he himself is nevertheless regarded as an *onen* on that day.

b (1) Who was circumcised on the eve of Passover. (2) I.e., through fear that if the former is permitted it may be thought that the latter is permitted too. (3) I.e., though thereby a Scriptural command, failure to observe which involves *kareth*, is disregarded. (4) *Peras* is half the length of a hundred-cubit furrow, hence fifty cubits; *beth ha-peras* is the technical designation for a field a square *peras* in area, declared unclean on account of crushed bones carried over it from a ploughed grave (Jast.). Its uncleanness is Rabbinical only. (5) *Supra*: Beth Hillel forbid him to eat of the Passover-offering as a preventive measure, which is only a Rabbinical enactment. (6) V. *supra* 65*b*. Thus on account of a *shebuth*, which is a Rabbinical prohibition, the unclean person may not participate in the Passover-offering.

c (1) *Ḳarpif*, pl. *ḳarpifoth*, is an enclosure not more than two *se'ahs* in area (this is slightly over seventy cubits square). If the eighth day of birth, when a child must be circumcised (v. Lev. XII, 3), falls on the Sabbath, the knife must be brought the previous day. If it was forgotten, however, it must not be brought on the Sabbath, even by way of roofs, etc., carrying on which is forbidden by Rabbinical law only, and circumcision must be postponed, notwithstanding that failure to circumcise involves *kareth* (Gen. XVII, 14).—Actually no *kareth* would be incurred in the present case, since it would be done another day, but Raba means that to the precept of circumcision there is attached the penalty of *kareth*. (2) V. Mishnah and 91*b* and n. c4. (3) When a leper was healed from his leprosy he waited seven days, performing *ṭebillah* on the seventh, and brought his sacrifices on the eighth (v. Lev. XIV, 9f). When he brought these he was still not permitted to enter the Temple Court ('the camp of the *Shechinah*) but stood at the east gate ('the gate of Nicanor'), whose sanctity was lower (it was regarded as 'the Levitical camp'), while the priest, standing inside the Temple Court, applied the blood and the oil to the thumbs and the great toes of the leper (ibid. 14f). (4) Before he had offered his sacrifices. A *ba'al ḳeri* (v. Glos.) might not enter even the Levitical Camp (v. *supra* 67*b*). (5) Again. Though he had performed *ṭebillah* the previous day, that was on his leprosy, whereas now he performs it on account of his discharge. (6) Thus after the *ṭebillah* he would bring his sacrifices for leprosy. (7) V. Glos. (8) For his purification rites; v. n. c3. (9) *Sc.* the Passover-offering. (10) *Sc.* that a *ṭebul yom* must not enter the Levitical Camp. That is derived in Naz. 45*a* from, '*he shall be unclean; his uncleanness is yet upon him*' (Num. XIX, 13); since that is an *affirmative* statement, the injunction likewise counts as an affirmative precept. Its violation does not involve *kareth*. (11) The Pentateuch.

d (1) II Chron. XX, 5. (2) Since this was an innovation, it is only Rabbinical, and as seen *supra* it was waived for the sake of the Passover-offering. V. Yeb., 7*b* notes.

a of obscenity; minors and slaves, on account of [91b] licentiousness.[1]

[To turn to] the [main] text: [As to] a woman, at the First [Passover] one slaughters for her separately, while at the second one makes her an addition to others: this is the view of R. Judah. R. Jose said: [As to] a woman, at the Second [Passover] one slaughters for her separately, and at the First it goes without saying. R. Simeon said: [As to] a woman, at the First one makes her an addition to others; at the second one may not slaughter for her at all. Wherein do they differ?—R. Judah holds: *according to the number of the souls*[2] [implies] even women.[3] And should you say, if so, even at the Second too? It is [therefore] written, *that* man *shall bear his sin:*[4] only a man, but not a woman. Yet should you argue: if so, she may not even be [made] an addition at the Second, [therefore is written,] *according to all the statute of the [first] passover*[5], which is effective in respect of [her being made] a mere addition.

And R. Jose? What is his reason!—Because in connection with the First [Passover] it is written, *'according to the number of souls,'* [implying] even a woman. Again, in connection with the Second Passover it is written, *that soul shall be cut off from his people,*[6] *'soul'* [implying] even women. While what does *'that* man *shall bear his sin'* exclude? It excludes a minor from *kareth*.

While R. Simeon [argues]: In connection with the First [Passover] *'a man'* is written:[7] only a man but not a woman. Yet should you say, If so, [she may] not even [be made] an addition: [therefore is written] *'according to the number of souls'*, which is effective in respect of [her being] an addition. But should you say, then even at the Second too,—[therefore] the Divine Law excluded [her] from the second, for it is written, *'that* man *shall bear his sin'*: [implying] only a man, but not a woman. Now from what is she excluded? If from an obligation,[8] [this cannot be maintained]: seeing that there is no [obligation] at the first, is there a question of the second! Hence [she is surely excluded] from [participation even as] an addition.

Now, what is [this] *'man'* which R. Simeon quotes? If we say, *they shall take to them every man a lamb, according to their fathers'*
b *houses* etc.[1] Surely that is required for [the teaching] of R. Isaac, who deduced: only a *'man'* can acquire [on behalf of others], but a minor cannot acquire [on behalf of others]![2] Rather [it is derived] from *'a man, according to his eating'*.[3] But since R. Jose agrees with R. Simeon,[4] R. Simeon too must agree with R. Jose,[5] and he needs that [verse to teach] that one slaughters the Passover-offering for a single person?[6]—He can answer you: If so,[7] let the Divine Law write *'according to his eating'*,[8] why [state] *'a man'?* Hence you infer two [laws] from it.

With whom does the following dictum of R. Eleazar agree,[9] [viz.]: '[The observance of the Passover-offering by] a woman at the First [Passover] is obligatory, while at the Second it is voluntary, and it overrides the Sabbath.' If voluntary, why does it override the Sabbath? Rather say: 'at the Second it is voluntary, while at the First it is obligatory and overrides the Sabbath.' With whom [does it agree]? With R. Judah.

R. Jacob said in R. Johanan's name: A company must not be formed [consisting] entirely of proselytes, lest they be [too particular about it and bring it to disqualification.[10]

Our Rabbis taught: The Passover-offering and unleavened bread and bitter herbs are obligatory on the first [night], but
c voluntary from then onwards.[1] R. Simeon said: In the case of men [it is] obligatory; in the case of women, voluntary. To what does this refer? Shall we say, to the Passover-offering—is there then a Passover-offering the whole seven days![2] Hence [it must refer] to unleavened bread and bitter herbs. Then consider the sequel: R. Simeon said: In the case of men [it is] obligatory; in the case of women, voluntary. Does then R. Simeon not agree with R. Eleazar's dictum: Women are bound to eat unleavened bread by Scriptural law, for it is said, *Thou shalt eat no leavened bread with it; seven days shalt thou eat unleavened bread therewith:*[3] whoever is subject to, *'thou shalt eat no leavened bread,'* is subject to [the law], 'arise, eat unleavened bread'; and these women, since they are subject to, *'thou shalt eat no leavened bread,'* are also subject to [the law], 'arise, eat unleavened bread?'—Rather say: The Passover-offering, unleavened bread, and bitter herbs are obligatory on the first [night]; from then onwards [the latter two] are voluntary. R. Simeon said: As for the Passover-offering, in the case of men it is obligatory, in the case of women it is voluntary.

MISHNAH. AN ONEN PERFORMS ṬEBILLAH AND EATS HIS PASSOVER-OFFERING IN THE EVENING, BUT [HE MAY] NOT [PARTAKE] OF [OTHER] SACRIFICES.[4] ONE WHO HEARS

a (1) Pederasty; cf. Weiss, *Dor*, II, 21 on the rifeness of pederasty among the Romans.—Heathen slaves are meant here. (2) Ex. XII, 4. (3) Since *men* are not specified. (4) Num. IX, 13; this refers to the Second Passover. (5) Ibid. 12. (6) Ibid. 13. (7) The Gemara discusses below which verse is meant. (8) I.e., the verse teaches that she need not keep the Second Passover.

b (1) Ex. XII, 3. (2) He deduces it from the present verse. For this person took the lamb not on his behalf alone but on behalf of *'their fathers' houses'*, who thereby gained the right to participate therein, and Scripture specifies that a *man* is required for this, not a minor. Hence a minor cannot be vested with the powers of an agent. (3) Ibid. 4. (4) That the Passover-offering may not be sacrificed at a private *bamah*, and that this is deduced from, *thou mayest not sacrifice the Passover-offering at one of the gates*, as stated *supra*. (5) That the Passover-offering may be slaughtered for a single person. (6) For if R. Simeon does not accept this view, then he should employ the verse, *'thou mayest not sacrifice the passover-offering for one'* as teaching that it may *not* be slaughtered for a single person, as R. Judah does *supra* 91a, in which case his ruling on the private *bamah* is without foundation. (7) That the verse is intended for R. Jose's teaching only. (8) Which would show that the matter depends entirely on his powers of eating. (9) Lit., 'as who does it go.' (10) In their ignorance of the law they may object to points which really do not matter, and thus disqualify it without cause.

c (1) I.e., for the rest of Passover. (2) That is surely not permitted even voluntarily. (3) Deut. XVI, 3. (4) An *onen* may not eat the flesh of sacrifices (v. Lev. X, 19f). By Scriptural law a man is an *onen* on the day of death only, but not at night; the Rabbis, however, extended these restrictions to the night too. Since, however, the Passover-offering is a Scriptural obligation, they waived their prohibition in respect of the night, and hence he may eat thereof. He is not unclean, but requires *ṭebillah* to emphasize that until the evening sacred flesh was forbidden to him, whereas now it is permitted. In respect of other sacrifices the Rabbinical law stands, and he may not partake of them.

עין משפט נר מצוה

מה א מיי' פ"ב מהלכות ק"פ הלכה ד:

מו ב מיי' פ"ב מהלכות שלוחין הלכה ג:

מז ג מיי' פ"ה מהלכות קרבן פסח הלכה ח ופ"ו הלכה ג:

מח ד מיי' שם פ"ב הלכה ד:

מט ה מיי' פ"ו מהלכות מצה הלכה א סמג עשין כו טור שו"ע או"ח סימן תעב סעיף ז:

נ ו מיי' פ"ו מהלכות קרבן פסח הלכה ט ופ"ב מהלכות ביאת מקדש הלכה י [רב אלפס ברכות פ"ב די"ב. וברא"ש שם סי' טו ושבת פ"א ז: וברא"ש שם סימן לח]:

גמרא

פריצותא גופא *אשה בראשון שוחטין עליה בפני עצמה ובשני עושין אותה טפילה לאחרים *דברי ר' יהודה ר' יוסי אומר *אשה בשני שוחטין עליה בפני עצמה ואין צ"ל בראשון ר"ש אומר אשה בראשון עושין אותה טפילה לאחרים בשני אין שוחטין עליה כל עיקר במאי קמיפלגי רבי יהודה סבר °במכסת נפשות ואפילו נשים (שמות יב) וכי תימא א"ה אפילו בשני נמי כתיב °חטאו (במדבר ט) ישא האיש ההוא איש אין אשה לא וכי תימא אי הכי אפילו טפילה נמי בשני לא אהני ככל חקת הפסח לטפילה בעלמא ורבי יוסי מ"ט דכתיב בראשון במכסת נפשות ואפילו אשה וכתיב בפסח שני °ונכרתה (שם) הנפש ההיא מישראל נפש ואפילו נשים ואלא חטאו ישא האיש ההוא למעוטי מאי למעוטי קטן מכרת ור"ש כתיב בראשון איש איש אין אשה לא וכי תימא אי הכי אפילו טפילה נמי לא אהני ליה במכסת נפשות לטפילה וכ"ת אפילו בשני נמי מיעט רחמנא בשני דכתיב חטאו ישא האיש איש אין אשה לא ממאי קממעיט ליה אי מחיוב השתא בראשון לא בשני מיבעיא אלא לאו מטפילה ומאי איש דקאמר ר"ש אי נימא °ויקחו (שמות יב) להם איש שה לבית אבות וגו' ההוא מיבעי ליה לכדרבי יצחק *דאמר ב׳איש זוכה ואין קטן זוכה ואלא °מאיש (שם) לפי אכלו הא מדר' יוסי סבר לה כר' שמעון רבי שמעון נמי סבר לה כר' יוסי וההוא מיבעי ליה דשוחטין את הפסח על היחיד אמר לך אם כן נכתוב רחמנא לפי אכלו מאי איש שמעת מינה תרתי כמאן אזלא הא דאמר רבי אלעזר *אשה בראשון חובה ובשני רשות ודוחה את השבת אי רשות אמאי דוחה את השבת אלא אימא ג׳בשני רשות ובראשון חובה ודוחה את השבת כמאן כרבי יהודה א"ר יעקב א"ר יוחנן ד׳אין עושין חבורה שכולה גרים שמא ידקדקו בו ויביאוהו לידי פסול: ת"ר *ה׳פסח ומצה ומרור בראשון חובה מכאן ואילך רשות ר' שמעון אומר באנשים חובה ובנשים רשות אהייא קאי אילימא אפסח *פסח כל שבעה מי איכא ואלא אמצה ומרור אימא סיפא ר"ש אומר באנשים חובה ובנשים רשות (א) לית ליה לרבי שמעון הא *דאמר רבי אלעזר נשים חייבות באכילת מצה דבר תורה שנאמר °לא (דברים טז) תאכל עליו חמץ שבעת ימים תאכל עליו מצות כל שישנו בבל תאכל חמץ ישנו בקום אכול מצה והני נשים הואיל וישנן בבל תאכל חמץ ישנן בקום אכול מצה אלא אימא פסח מצה ומרור בראשון חובה מכאן ואילך רשות ר' שמעון אומר פסח באנשים חובה בנשים רשות:

מתני' *ו׳אונן טובל ואוכל את פסחו לערב אבל לא בקדשים השומע על מתו והמלקט

רש"י

עבדים וקטנים משום פריצותא · דמשכב זכור: אין שוחטין עליה כל עיקר · ואפי' טפילה דלא שייכא ביה מידי ולא אכלה ביה הוה פסח נאכל שלא למנויו וה"ה לעבדים דאין אוכלין בו וכי אכלי עבדים ונשים בראשון שהן רשות בו אבל בשני לא דאפי' מרבות אימעוט כדלקמן: במכסת נפשות · מדלא כתב אנשים אפי' אשה במשמע: כתיב בשני חטאו ישא האיש ההוא · והאי משמע ליה קרא והאיש אשר הוא טהור ובדרך לא היה וחדל לעשות הפסח ראשון ונכרתה כי קרבן ה' כו' כי לשון שימוש אי כשקרבן ה' לא הקריב במועדו בשני חטאו ישא *והכי דריש בפרק מי שהיה טמא (לקמן צג.) אליבא דר"ש א"נ קרבן ה' לא הקריב במועדו בשני חטאו ישא: וכתיב בשני ונכרתה הנפש ההיא · דלת"ק דראשון קאי מיהו כי קרבן ה' אשני קאי וכדמפרשינן וגמרינן בה כרת לקמן (שם) האי חטאו ישא מוקשא חטאו למברך את השם דכתיב ביה את ה' הוא מגדף ונכרת וגו' והוי כמאן דכתיב נפש בגופיה: ואלא האיש · דגבי פסח מאי עביד ליה ליכתוב חטאו ישא ותו לא: כתיב בראשון איש · לקמן בעי מאי איש כתיב בראשון: איש זוכה · לאחרים בלקיחתו אם לקח מקח לצורך אחרים או קיבל מתנה לשם אחרים כדכתיב ויקחו איש שה לבית אבות ואין קטן זוכה דאין קטן נעשה שליח: אלא מאיש לפי אכלו · דריש ליה למעוטי אשה: והא מדר' יוסי סבר לה כר"ש · דאין שוחטין פסח בבמת יחיד מלא תוכל לזבוח: ר"ש נמי סבר לה כר' יוסי · דיליף מאיש לפי אכלו שוחטין פסח על היחיד דאי לא ס"ל כוותיה ממאי דהאי באחד לדרשה דידיה אתא הא טפי משמע שפיר כר"ש דאין שוחטין על היחיד: לפי אכלו · בלאו איש נמי נפקא לן מלשון יחיד דשוחטין פסח על היחיד ואיש דרשינן ליה למעוטי אשה: רשות ודוחה את השבת · בתמיה: ידקדקו בו · משום שאינן בני תורה יחמירו עליו לדקדק ויפסילוהו על חנם: הכי גרסינן תנו רבנן פסח מצה ומרור בראשון חובה כו' · בראשון לילה הראשון: אהייא קאי · מכאן ואילך רשות דתנא קמא אי נימא אפסח פסח כל שבעה מי איכא: ואלא אמצה ומרור · ועלה מהדר ר"ש אף בראשון דקאמרת חובה באנשים הוא דהויא אבל בנשים רשות: לית ליה לר"ש · והא ליכא למימר דליהדר אמרור לחודיה דסתמא מצה ומרור בהדי הדדי כתיב על מצות ומרורים וכשם שנשים באכילת מצה חובה הכי נמי במרור: הואיל וישנן בבל תאכל חמץ · דהשוה הכתוב אשה לאיש לכל עונשין שבתורה דכתיב (במדבר ה) איש או אשה כי יעשו מכל חטאת האדם וגו': אלא · הכי קאמר פסח מצה ומרור בראשון חובה מכאן ואילך רשות וקאי האי מכאן ואילך אמצה ומרור ור"ש פליג אפסח דקאמרת בראשון חובה באנשים הוא דהוה חובה אבל בנשים רשות ורבי שמעון לטעמיה: **מתני'** אונן טובל ואוכל את פסחו לערב · ואף על פי שעדיין לא נקבר דאין אנינות מן התורה אלא ביום שנאמר (ויקרא י) הן היום הקריבו ואני אונן ואכלתי חטאת היום יום אסור לילה מותר וטבילה בעי וזו אחת מאחת עשרה מעלות לחומר בקודש (חגיגה דף כא:) האונן והמחוסר כפורים צריכין טבילה לקודש מתוך שנאסרו עד עכשיו בקדשים אצרכינהו רבנן טבילה ואף על פי שמחוסר כפורים טבל אתמול אבל לא יאכל אונן לערב בשאר קדשים דאסור אנינות לילה מדרבנן וגבי פסח לא העמידו דבריהן במקום כרת: השומע על מתו · יום שמועה הוי אונן דרבנן: וכן

תוספות

וכתיב בשני ונכרתה הנפש ההיא אפי' אשה · ולא נפקא לרבי יוסי אשה מכלל חקת הפסח דמהתם מפיק ר"י טפילה דאי לאו הנפש ההיא ככל חקת הפסח לא הוה מוקמינן אלא לטפילה כר' יהודה ואיש למעוטי חובה הלכך גלי הנפש ההיא דלא ממעטינן אשה מאיש:

איש ולא קטן · תימה אמאי איצטריך דהיכן מצינו שחייב קטן במצות וי"ל דאיצטריך לקטן שהגדיל בין שני פסחים דס"ד דחייב לעשות פסח שני קמ"ל דשני תשלומין דראשון הוא ובפרק מי שהיה טמא (לקמן דף צג:) משמע דנפקא לן מקרא אחרינא ובפ' ד' מיתות (סנהדרין דף כד:) נמי קשה אמאי איצטריך איש פרט לקטן בבא על אשת איש ועל אשת אביו ועל הזכור ועל הבהמה:

אי נימא מאיש שה הא מיבעי ליה לכדר' יצחק כו' · תימה לר"י דבריש פ"ב דקדושין (דף מב:) משמע דמילתיה דרבי יצחק מאיש לפי אכלו נפקא ואומר ר"י דהתם משום דמאיש שה מפיק לשליחות דלא מצי מפיק שליחות מאיש לפי אכלו לכך נפקא דרבי יצחק מאיש לפי אכלו אבל תלמודא דהכא נפקא ליה שליחות מדרבי יהושע בן קרחה ולכך מוקי איש שה לכדרבי יצחק דמשמע דמיירי בזכיה טפי מאיש לפי אכלו:

איש זוכה ואין קטן זוכה · תימה אמאי איצטריך קרא והא קי"ל דאין שליחות לקטן ובפ' קמא דבבא מציעא (דף יב:) מוכח דזוכה מטעם שליחות וכי תימא מהכא קיי"ל דאין לו שליחות אכתי קשה אמאי איצטריך למעט דאינו זוכה הא אפילו לעצמו אין לו זכיה במציאתו אלא מפני דרכי שלום כדאמרינן בהניזקין (גיטין דף נט:) ויש לומר דדוקא מציאה אבל מתנה דדעת אחרת מקנה אותו עדיף כדמסיק בשנים אוחזין (ב"מ דף יב:) וכן בפרק התקבל (גיטין דף סד:) קאמרינן צרור וזורקו אגוז ונוטלו זוכה לעצמו אפי' לגבי קנין דאורייתא:

רבי שמעון נמי סבר לה כרבי יוסי · תימה דילמא סבר לה כרבי יהודה ותרתי שמעת מינה כדאמרינן לעיל לרבי יהודה:

שמא ידקדקו בו ויביאוהו לידי פסול · תימה דבעי למימר דגרים מדקדקים ביותר ודמי להא דאמרינן (חולין דף ד.) כל מצוה שהחזיקו בה *גרים וכותים הרבה מדקדקים בה יותר מישראל ובירושל' גרים אמר רבי יעקב בר יצחק בשם רבי יוסי אין עושין חבורות של גרים שמתוך שהן מקולקלים אין מדקדקין ויביאוהו לידי פסול ובכל דוכתא נמי חזינן דגרים לא דייקי במצות כישראלים והכא קאמר דגרים מדקדקים יותר: גבי

מסורת הש"ס

[תוספתא פ"ח ומכר סנהדרין דף יב:] [ומכר לקמן צג.]

בשני חטאו ישא ולא קאי אדלעיל וכפי' אמרינן בפ' מי שהיה טמא אליבא דר' כל"ל ר"מ והדיבור שאחר זה צריך להתחיל וכתיב בפסח שני.

קדושין מא.

[לעיל סט: סנהדרין יב:]

[תוספתא פ"ב]

[לקמן צו.]

לעיל מג:

זבחים צט:

[עי' ברכות מז: קדושין ע. גיטין י. חולין ד. איתא כל מצוה שהחזיקו בה כותים הרבה מדקדקי' כו' אבל מענין גרים כהך מילתא נעלם ממני מקומו]

הגהות הב"ח

(א) גמרא ובנשים רשות וכי לית לר"ש הא:

רבינו חננאל

גופא אשה בראשון שוחטין עליה בפני עצמה ובשני עושין אותה טפלה לאחרים מאי טעמא כתי' בראשון במכסת נפשות ואפילו נפש אשה משמע וכתיב בשני חטאו ישא האיש ההוא איש ולא אשה וכי תימא אי הכי אפי' טפלה נמי לא תעשה אותה בשני ת"ל ככל חקת הפסח אהני האיש למעוטה בשני מחובה אהני ככל חקת הפסח לרבויי לטפלה בעלמא ור' יוסי אומר לטעמא דאמר שוחטין את הפסח ביחיד וכתיב בראשון במכסת נפשות ובשני כתיב ונכרתה הנפש ההיא כל נפש במשמע ואפילו אשה ר' שמעון אומר בראשון עושין אותה טפלה לאחרים ובשני אין שוחטין עליה כל עיקר מאי טעמא בראשון כתיב איש לפי אכלו ובשני כתיב חטאו ישא האיש ההוא איש ולא אשה ודייקי' השתא בראשון פטור בשני מבעיא אלא מכלל שבראשון טפלה ואפילו טפלה שבראשון מיעטה בשני. וקמו להו ר' יוסי ור' שמעון בשיטתא חדא דשוחטין את הפסח על היחיד: אמר ר' יעקב אמר ר' יוחנן אין עושין חבורה שכולה גרים שמא לא ידקדקו בו ויבאוהו לידי פסול: ותרצינן להא מתניתא הכי תנו רבנן פסח מצה ומרור בלילה הראשון חובה מצה מכאן ואילך רשות ר' שמעון אומר פסח באנשים חובה (מכאן ואילך רשות) (בנשים רשות): אונן טובל ואוכל פסחו לערב אבל לא בקדשים קסבר

והמפקח את הגל וכן מי שהבטיחוהו להוציאו מבית האסורים והחולה והזקן שהן יכולין לאכול כזית שוחטין עליהן על כולם אין שוחטין עליהן בפני עצמן שמא יביאו את הפסח לידי פסול לפיכך אם אירע בהן פסול פטורין מלעשות פסח שני חוץ מן המפקח בגל שהוא טמא מתחלתו:

גמ' אמר רבה בר הונא א"ר יוחנן לא שנו אלא בית האסורין דעכו"ם אבל בית האסורין דישראל שוחטין עליו בפני עצמו כיון דאבטחוהו מפיק ליה דכתיב שארית ישראל לא יעשו עולה ולא ידברו כזב אמר רב חסדא הא דאמרת בית האסורין דעכו"ם(א) לא אמרן אלא חוץ לחומת בית פאגי אבל לפנים מחומת בית פאגי שוחטין עליו בפני עצמו מ"ט אפשר דאמטו ליה ואכיל ליה: לפיכך אם אירע וכו': אמר רבה בר בר חנה אמר ר' יוחנן לא שנו אלא גל עגול אבל גל ארוך פטור מלעשות פסח שני אימא טהור היה בשעת שחיטה תניא נמי הכי ר"ש בנו של רבי יוחנן בן ברוקה אומר מפקח בגל עתים פטור עתים חייב כיצד גל עגול ונמצא טומאה תחתיו חייב גל ארוך ונמצאת טומאה תחתיו פטור אימא טהור היה בשעת שחיטה:

מתני' אין שוחטין את הפסח על היחיד דברי רבי יהודה ורבי יוסי מתיר ואפילו חבורה של מאה שאינן יכולין לאכול כזית אין שוחטין עליהן ואין עושין חבורת נשים ועבדים וקטנים:

גמ' ת"ר מנין שאין שוחטין את הפסח על היחיד ת"ל לא תוכל לזבוח את הפסח באחד דברי ר' יהודה ורבי יוסי אומר יחיד ויכול לאכלו שוחטין עליו עשרה ואין יכולין לאכלו אין שוחטין עליהן ורבי יוסי האי באחד מאי עביד ליה מיבעי ליה לכדר"ש דתניא ר"ש אומר מניין לזובח את פסחו בבמת יחיד בשעת איסור הבמות שהוא בלא תעשה ת"ל לא תוכל לזבוח את הפסח באחד שעריך יכול אף בשעת היתר הבמות כן ת"ל באחד שעריך לא אמרו אלא בשעה שכל ישראל נכנסין בשער אחד ור' יהודה האי מנא ליה תרתי שמעת מינה ולר' יוסי ממאי דלהכי דקאמר ר"ש דילמא כדקאמר ר' יהודה הוא דאתא אמר לך לא סלקא דעתך דהא כתיב איש לפי אכלו רמי ליה רב עוקבא בר חיננא מפרישנא לרבא מי א"ר יהודה אין שוחטין את הפסח על היחיד ורמינהו אשה בראשון שוחטין עליה בפני עצמה ובשני עושין אותה טפילה לאחרים דברי ר' יהודה א"ל לא תימא בפני עצמה אלא אימא בפני עצמן אמר ליה מי עבדינן חבורה שכולה נשים והתנן אין עושין חבורת נשים ועבדים וקטנים מאי לאו נשים לחודייהו ועבדים לחודייהו וקטנים לחודייהו אמר ליה לא נשים ועבדים וקטנים נשים ועבדים משום תפלות קטנים ועבדים משום פריצותא

רש"י

והמפקח את הגל · מעל אדם ואין ידוע אם ימלאנו חי או מת · שוחטין עליו · דמכל מקום עודנו בחזקת טהרה ואנן נמי לאורחא חזי כדאמרינן בגמרא דלאכילה ליכא מדאורייתא אלא לאיטות יום כדכתיב (ויקרא י) הן היום הקריבו יום אסור לילה מותר בשחיטת קדשים* וגבי פסח לא העמידו דבריהם במקום כרת: שוחטין עליהן · בחבורת אחרים: שמא יביאוהו לידי פסול · שמא ימות אונן למתו ומפקח גל ימלאנו מת ונמלא שהאהיל על הטומאה והחבוש שמא לא יצא וחולה וזקן שמא יכבד חליו ולא יוכל לאכול כזית: לפיכך · הואיל ובשעת שחיטה ראויין היו ונזרק הדם עליהן אם אירע בהן פסול כמו שפירשתי פטורין מלעשות פסח שני: חוץ מן המפקח את הגל · ונמצא המת תחתיו שחייב לעשות פסח שני: שהוא טמא מתחלתו · קודם שחיטה שהרי האהיל על הטומאה משעה שהתחיל לפקח ובגמרא מוקי לה בגל עגול שמתחלה האהיל את כולו: גמ' לא שנו · דאין שוחטין על החבוש בפני עצמו: בית האסורין של ישראל · כגון לכופו להוציא אשה פסולה או לשלם ממון אי נמי כדקתני (כתובות דף לג:) אם יקום והתהלך בחוץ כו' וכי תעלה על דעתך זה מהלך בשוק וזה נהרג אלא מלמד שחובשין אותו עד שנראה מה תהא עליו: בית פאגי · מקום חיצון בירושלים: דמטיילי ליה · מן הפסח בתוך בית האסורין לאכול דהא לפנים מירושלים הוא: ל"ש · דמפקח גל חייב לעשות פסח שני אלא גל עגול דמתחלתו האהיל עליו אבל גל ארוך שמא בשעת שחיטה עדיין לא האהיל כנגד הטומאה וכיון דספק יצא ספק לא יצא פטור משום דלא אפשר כדאמרן לעיל (דף פח:) גבי חמשה שנתערבו עורות פסחיהן: מתני' על היחיד · טעמא יליף בגמרא: ואפילו חבורה של מאה · רבי יוסי קאמר לה כלומר לא תליא מילתא דפסח אלא באכילה יחיד ויכול לאכול כזית שוחטין עליו מאה ואין יכולין לאכול כזית בין כולם אין שוחטין עליהן: ואין עושין חבורת נשים ועבדים וקטנים · טעמא מפרש בגמרא: גמ' לא תוכל לזבוח את הפסח באחד שעריך · ודריש באחד באלפיה נפשיה על היחיד: ואין יכולים לאכלו · כזית ממנו: מנין לזובח פסחו בבמת יחיד: במה קטנה שהיא בלא תעשה להכי נקט במת יחיד ולא במת צבור דבמת צבור בשעת איסור ליכא דשעת איסור הבמות לאחר שנבנה משכן שילה ומשחרב היה להם היתר עד שנבנה בית עולמים ומשנבנה חזרו לאיסורם ושוב לא היה להם היתר: שהיא בלא תעשה · אבל כרת דשחוטי חוץ ליכא ובשחיטת קדשים בפרק בתרא (זבחים דף קיד:) מוקי לה בקודם חצות דמחוסר זמן הוא להתקבל בפנים דכתיב אשר ישחט מחוץ למחנה ואל פתח אהל מועד לא הביאו הראוי לבא אל פתח אהל מועד חייב עליו ושאינו ראוי לבא לאהל מועד אינו חייב עליו ויליף מהכא דמחוסר זמן בחוץ אע"פ שאינו בכרת בלא תעשה מיהא הוי הואיל וראוי לבא לאחר זמן: יכול אף בשעת היתר הבמות כן · יהא בלא תעשה זה דהא לא הותרה במת יחיד אלא לדבר הנידר ונידב והוי האי נגבי בשעת איסור: ת"ל כו' · דהאי לאו דהכא לא משתעי אלא בשעת איסור הבמות והכי משמעינן ליה לקרא לא תוכל לזבוח את הפסח בבמת יחיד בזמן שכל ישראל נכנסין בשער אחד כו' כי אם אל המקום אשר יבחר שם תזבחנו: ופרכינן לר' יוסי ממאי דקרא לכדרבי שמעון כו' · ולאו פירכא כולי האי דאיכא למימר מר דריש ליה הכי ומר דריש ליה הכי אלא טעמא דר' יוסי מהדר לפרושי: לא ס"ד · דלאסור פסח על היחיד אתא דכתיב איש לפי אכלו תכוסו על איש אחד השחטו ובלבד שיהא ראוי לאכילה: מפרישנא · שם מקום: אשה בראשון · חובה ובשני רשות ולקמיה יליף טעמייהו: טפילה · חיבור: קתני מיהת בפני עצמה · לשון יחיד: הנ"ז נשים ועבדים וקטנים: תפלות · עבירה: עבדים

תוספות

שהיה טמא מתחלתו · תימה לר"י מפקח הגל נמי נימא חי הוה כשהתחיל לפקח וי"ל דכיון דמלאו מת אית לן למימר שמתחלתו היה מת שכל הטומאות כשעת מציאתן*: לא שנו אלא בבית האסורין של עכו"ם · בירושלמי מוקי לה כרבי יוסי בר בון בשם רבי יוחנן כשהבטיחוהו ישראל אבל הבטיחוהו עכו"ם אין שוחטין עליו אפי' עם אחרים(ב) אשר פיהם דבר שוא והיינו איפכא משמעתין: עשרה ואין יכולין לאכלו אין שוחטין עליהן · בהא מודה אפילו ר' יהודה דבעינן שלא יביאוהו לידי פסול: האי באחד מאי עביד ליה · הוה מצי למימר דאיצטריך לכדאמרינן בכילד צולין (לעיל דף עח.) שאין היחיד מכריע: והתנן אין עושין חבורת נשים · מעיקרא דקתני בפני עצמה לא קשיא ליה אלא השתא דקאמר אימא בפני עצמן משום דמשמע ליה דלא אסרה מתניתין חבורת נשים אלא כשיש נשים הרבה שסומכות זו על זו ואין זהירין לשמור הפסח ומביאות אותו לידי פסול אבל יחידה שוחטין עליה:

וכתיב

עין משפט נר מצוה

לט א מיי' פ"ו מהלכות ק"פ הלכה י:

[עירובין, לה: נדה ד.]

מ ב ג מיי' שם פ"ה הלכה ט:

מא ד שם פ"ו הלכה י:

מב ה מיי' שם פ"ב הלכה ב ג:

מג ו שם הלכה ד:

מד ז מיי' שם פ"א הלכה ג:

[בזבחים קיד: וכן בתוספתא זבחים פי"ג ליתא]

מסורת הש"ס

[זבחים קו:]

קדושין מב. [לקמן לה. לג. יומא נח.]

[עי' תוס' לקמן לה. ד"ה מיכני]

זבחים קיד:

[סוכה נה:]

הגהות הב"ח

(א) גמ' בית האסורין דעכו"ם לא אמרן: (ב) תוס' ד"ה לא שנו וכו' אחרים דכתיב אשר פיהם:

רבינו חננאל

והמפקח בגל וכן מי שהבטיחוהו להוציאו מבית האסורין כו' אוקמא ר' יוחנן בבית האסורין של עכו"ם ואף על גב דאבטחוהו לאפוקיה אין שוחטין עליו דעבידי דמשקרי שנאמר (תהלים קמד ח) אשר פיהם דבר שוא תנו' אבל בית אסורין של ישראל כיון שהבטיחוהו להוציאו לא משקרי שנאמר שארית ישראל לא יעשו עולה ולא ידברו כזב הלכך שוחטין עליו: אמר רב חסדא וזה האסור בבית אסורין של גוים ששנינו אין שוחטין עליו בבית האסורין שהוא חוץ לחומת בית פאגי פי' מקום חוץ לחומות ירושלים שאין אוכלין שם קדשים קלים אבל אם הוא זה בבית האסורין לפנים מבית פאגי שוחטין עליו דאפשר דמעיילינן ליה פסחא תמם ואכיל ליה ואלו ששנינו במשנתנו כגון האונן ומי שהבטיחוהו להוציא מבית האסורין והחולה והזקן שיכולין לאכול כזית אין שוחטין עליהם בפני עצמן שלא יביאו הפסח לידי פסו' כלומר אפשר שלא יאכלוהו כי אינם יכולין ויפסל בנותר אבל נפסלו בגל שבודאי האהיל על המת והוא טמא מתחלה והני מילי בגל עגול אבל גל ארוך אימור טהור היה אני אומר נזרק הדם עד שלא הגיע לטומאה: תניא נמי הכי ר' ישמעאל בר' יוחנן אומר מפקח בגל עתים חייב עתים פטור כיצד גל עגול כו': אין שוחטין את הפסח על היחיד כו' תנו רבנן מנין שאין שוחטין את הפסח על היחיד שנאמר לא תוכל לזבוח את הפסח באחד שעריך דברי ר' יהודה ר' יוסי אומר יחיד ויכול לאכלו שוחטין עליו עשרה ואין יכולין וכו' ורמינן אהא דר' יהודה הא דתניא אשה בראשון שוחטין עליה בפני עצמה בשני עושין אותה טפילה לאחרים דברי ר' יהודה ומשני' תריץ ואימא הכי נשים בראשון שוחטין עליהן בפני עצמן אקשי' וכי עושין חבורה כולה נשים והתנן אין עושין חבורת נשים ועבדים וקטנים ושני' לעולם עושין חבורה כולה נשים ומשנתנו נשים ועבדים יחדו משום תפלות והוא דבר עבירה כדגרסינן רוצה אשה בקב ותפלות ולא עבדים וקטנים משום פריצותא:

נפה

a *MISHNAH*. [AS TO] AN ONEN,[1] [91a] AND ONE WHO IS REMOVING A HEAP [OF DEBRIS],[2] AND LIKEWISE ONE WHO HAS RECEIVED A PROMISE TO BE RELEASED FROM PRISON, AND AN INVALID, AND AN AGED PERSON WHO CAN EAT AS MUCH AS AN OLIVE, ONE SLAUGHTERS ON THEIR BEHALF.[3] [YET IN THE CASE OF] ALL THESE, ONE MAY NOT SLAUGHTER FOR THEM ALONE, LEST THEY BRING THE PASSOVER-OFFERING TO DISQUALIFICATION.[4] THEREFORE IF A DISQUALIFICATION OCCURS TO THEM, THEY ARE EXEMPT FROM KEEPING THE SECOND PASSOVER,[5] EXCEPT ONE WHO WAS REMOVING DEBRIS, BECAUSE HE WAS UNCLEAN FROM THE BEGINNING.[6]

GEMARA. Rabbah son of R. Huna said in R. Joḥanan's name: They learned this only of a heathen prison; but [if he is incarcerated in] an Israelite prison, one slaughters for him separately; since he was promised, he will [definitely] be released, as it is written, *The remnant of Israel shall not do iniquity, nor speak lies*.[7] R. Ḥisda observed: As to what you say, [If he is in] a heathen prison [one may] not [kill on his behalf alone]; that was said only [when the prison is] without the walls of Beth Pagi;[8] but [if it is] within the walls of Beth Pagi,[9] one slaughters on his behalf alone. What is the reason? It is possible to convey it [the flesh] to him and he will eat it.

THEREFORE IF A DISQUALIFICATION OCCURS etc. Rabbah b. Bar Ḥanah said in R. Joḥanan's name: They learned [this] only
b of a round heap;[1] but [if it was] a long heap, he is exempt from keeping the Second Passover, [for] perhaps he was clean at the time of the *shechitah*.[2] It was also taught likewise: R. Simeon the son of R. Joḥanan b. Beroḳah said: One who is removing a heap [of debris] is sometimes exempt [from the Second Passover] and sometimes liable. How so? [If it was] a round heap and uncleanness [a corpse] was found underneath it, he is liable; a long heap, and uncleanness was found underneath it, he is exempt, [for] I assume [that] he was clean at the time of *shechitah*.

MISHNAH. ONE MAY NOT SLAUGHTER THE PASSOVER-OFFERING FOR A SINGLE PERSON: THIS IS R. JUDAH'S VIEW; BUT R. JOSE PERMITS IT. AND EVEN A COMPANY OF A HUNDRED WHO CANNOT EAT AS MUCH AS AN OLIVE [JOINTLY], ONE MAY NOT KILL FOR THEM. AND ONE MAY NOT FORM A COMPANY OF WOMEN AND SLAVES AND MINORS.

GEMARA. Our Rabbis taught: How do we know that one may not slaughter the Passover-offering for a single person? Because it is said, *Thou mayest not sacrifice the passover-offering for one*:[3] this is R. Judah's opinion. But R. Jose maintained: A single person and he is able to eat it, one may slaughter on his behalf; ten who are unable to eat it, one must not slaughter on their behalf. Now R. Jose, how does he employ this '*for one*'?—He requires it for R. Simeon's [deduction]. For it was taught, R. Simeon said: How do we know that one who sacrifices his Passover-offering at a private *bamah*[4] at the time when *bamoth* were prohibited violates a negative command? Because it is said, '*Thou mayest not sacrifice the passover-offering within one of thy gates*'. You
c might think that it is also thus when *bamoth* were permitted:[1] therefore it is stated, '*within one of thy gates*': They ruled [that he violates a negative injunction] only when all Israel enter through one gate.[2] And how does R. Judah know this?—You may infer two things from it.[3]

Now according to R. Jose, whence [does he know] that its purpose is for what R. Simeon said: perhaps it comes for what was stated by R. Judah?—He can tell you: you cannot think so, for surely it is written, *according to every man's eating*.[4]

R. 'Uḳba b. Ḥinena of Parishna[5] pointed out a contradiction to Raba: Did then R. Judah say: One may not kill the Paschal lamb for a single person? But the following contradicts it: [As to] a woman; at the First [Passover] one may slaughter for her separately, but at the second one makes her an addition to others: this is the view of R. Judah.—Said he to him, Do not say, 'for her separately,' but 'for them separately.'[6] Yet may we form a company consisting entirely of women? Surely we learned, ONE MAY NOT FORM A COMPANY OF WOMEN AND SLAVES AND MINORS. Does that not mean women separately and slaves separately and minors separately?—No, he replied, [it means] women and slaves and minors [together]. Women and slaves, on account

a (1) V. Glos. Here it refers to one who became an *onen* after midday, so that the obligation of the Passover-offering was already incumbent upon him. But if he became an *onen* before midday, this obligation does not fall on him at all, as stated *infra* 98a (Tosaf). (2) Which had fallen upon a person, and it is unknown whether he is alive or dead. (3) All these *may* be fit in the evening, including an *onen*. (4) The *onen* may defile himself through the corpse; he who is removing the debris may find the person underneath it dead, in which case he himself is unclean; the prisoner may not be freed; while the invalid and aged person may grow weaker. Therefore they must be registered with others. (5) Since they were actually fit when the animal was slaughtered. (6) If he finds the person underneath dead, he himself was defiled through overshadowing the dead, and thus he was unclean when the animal was sacrificed. (7) Zeph. III, 13. (8) V. 63*b*, n. a1. (9) Hence in Jerusalem, where the Passover-offering is eaten.

b (1) I.e., one just about covering the person, so that the rescuer must have been directly over the corpse from the very beginning. (2) He may not have been actually over the corpse then. (3) Deut. XVI, 5 (E.V. *within one* [*of thy gates*]). (4) 'High place'. Before the Tabernacle was erected in Shiloh, and between its destruction and the building of the Temple, sacrifices were offered at *bamoth* (pl. of *bamah*), both private and public. During the existence of the Tabernacle at Shiloh, and since the Temple was built, even after it was destroyed, *bamoth* were forbidden.

c (1) For even then private *bamoth* were permitted only for votive sacrifices but not for obligatory offerings like the Passover, which were sacrificed at the public *bamoth*. (2) I.e., when there is a central sanctuary; but when *bamoth* were permitted there was no central sanctuary. The verse is understood thus: *Thou mayest not sacrifice the Passover-offering* at a private *bamah* when all Israel enter through *one of thy gates*. (3) Presumably by interpreting '*one*' separately and '*one of the gates*' separately. (4) Ex. XII, 4. Thus the matter depends solely on ability to eat. (5) V. *supra* 76a, n. b6. (6) This is not an emendation, but an explanation: 'for her separately' means that women need not necessarily join a company of men.

Continuation of translation from previous page as indicated by ◁

if you say that [the clause, 'IF A ZAB] HAS SUFFERED TWO ATTACKS, [ONE SLAUGHTERS ON HIS BEHALF] ON HIS SEVENTH DAY,' means where he has not performed *ṭebillah*, what is the purpose of [teaching about] one who has had three attacks? Seeing that you say that one slaughters and sprinkles on behalf of one who had two discharges, and is in his seventh day, but has not performed *ṭebillah*, so that he is quite unclean; then how much the more does one slaughter and sprinkle for one who had three attacks, and is in his eighth day, and has performed *ṭebillah* on the seventh, so that his uncleanness is of a lighter nature! Hence it surely follows that [the law] that we slaughter on behalf of one who has had two attacks and is in [his] seventh [day] refers to the case where he has performed *ṭebillah!*—No. In truth I may tell you that he has not performed *ṭebillah*, and [yet] it is necessary. I might argue: Only on the seventh day [do we slaughter for him], since [it lies] in his own hand to make himself fit; but on the eighth day, when it is not in his power to offer the sacrifice, I might say, the priests may neglect him. Hence we are informed [that it is] as R. Shemaiah [stated].[2]

AND AS TO A ZABAH, ONE SLAUGHTERS etc. A tanna recited before R. Adda b. Ahabah: And as to a *zabah*,[3] one slaughters on her behalf on her seventh day. Said he to him: Is then a *zabah* on her seventh day fit?[4] Even on the view that one slaughters and sprinkles for a person unclean through a reptile, that is only for a person unclean through a reptile, who is fit in the evening. But this one is not fit until the morrow when she brings her atone-
c ment. Say [instead], 'on the eighth.' Then it is obvious?[1]—You might say, since she lacks atonement, [one must] not slaughter [on her behalf]; hence he informs us [that it is] as R. Shemaiah [stated].

Rabina said: He [the Tanna] recited before him [about] a *niddah*,[2] [thus]: And as to a *niddah*, one slaughters for her on the seventh [day]. Said he to him: Is then a *niddah* fit on the seventh [day]? Even on the view that one slaughters and sprinkles for a person unclean through a reptile [that is] because he is fit in the evening. But a *niddah* performs *ṭebillah* in the evening of [i.e., following] the seventh day: [hence] she is not fit for eating [the Passover-offering] until the [evening after the] eighth, by when she has had the setting of the sun.[3] But say, 'on the eighth.' That is obvious: seeing that one slaughters and sprinkles for a *zabah* on the eighth day, though as yet she lacks atonement, need it be taught that one slaughters and sprinkles on behalf of a *niddah*, who does not lack atonement?[4]—He finds it necessary [to teach about] a *niddah*, [and] informs us this: only on the eighth, but not on the seventh, even as it was taught: All who are liable to *ṭebillah*,[5] their *ṭebillah* takes place by day;[6] a *niddah* and a woman in confinement, their *ṭebillah* takes place at night.[7] For it was taught: You might think that she [a *niddah*] performs *ṭebillah* by day;[8] therefore it is stated, *she shall be in her impurity seven days:*[9] let her be in her impurity *full* seven days.[10] And a woman in confinement is assimilated to *niddah*.[11]

(2) *Supra*. (3) Who had three discharges. (4) To partake of the sacrifice in the evening.

c (1) Though the same is stated in the Mishnah, it might be included there for the sake of parallelism, though unnecessary in itself. But here it is taught as an independent statement. (2) V. Glos. (3) She must not eat of sacrifices until the setting of the sun *after* her *ṭebillah*. Since she performs *ṭebillah* in the evening, when the sun has already set, she must wait until the following evening. (4) She does not require a sacrifice. (5) E.g., a *zab* and a *zabah*, a leper, and one defiled through a corpse (Shab. 121*a*). (6) The seventh day from their defilement. (7) The evening following the last day of their uncleanness. In this respect a *niddah* is more stringent than a *zabah*, who performs *ṭebillah* on the seventh *day*, and does not wait for the evening. (8) *Sc.* the seventh, like a *zabah*. (9) Lev. XV, 19. (10) But if she performs *ṭebillah* on the seventh day itself, the period is diminished. (11) For it is written, *as in the days of the impurity of* (niddath, const. of niddah) *her sickness shall she* (*sc.* a woman in confinement) *be unclean* (Lev. XII, 3).

**ואין שוחטין וזורקין על טמא שרץ ועולא אמר אף שוחטין וזורקין על טמא שרץ לרב מאי שנא טבול יום דחזי לאורתא טמא שרץ נמי חזי לאורתא מחוסר טבילה טבול יום נמי מחוסר הערב שמש *שמשא ממילא ערבא מחוסר כפורים נמי הא מחוסר כפרה שקינו בידו טמא שרץ נמי הרי מקוה לפניו דילמא פשע אי הכי מחוסר כפורים נמי דילמא פשע ג כגון דמסרינהו לב"ד וכדרב שמעיה *דאמר חזקה אין ב"ד של כהנים עומדין משם עד שיכלו מעות שבשופרות ולרב מדאורייתא מיחזא חזי ורבנן הוא דגזרו ביה (א) אלמה אמר רב *מטמאין אחד מהן בשרץ אלא לרב מדאורייתא נמי לא חזי דכתיב °איש איש כי יהיה טמא לנפש *מי [במדבר ט] לא עסקינן שחל שביעי שלו להיות בערב הפסח דהיינו טומאת שרץ ואמר רחמנא נידחי וכי תימא ממאי דהכי סבר לה כרבי יצחק *דאמר טמאי מת מצוה היו שחל שביעי שלהן להיות בערב הפסח שנאמר °ולא יכלו לעשות הפסח ביום ההוא ביום ההוא הוא דאינן יכולין לעשות אבל למחר יכולין לעשות ואמר רחמנא נדחו תנן זב שראה שתי ראיות שוחטין עליו בשביעי מאי לאו דלא טביל ושמע מינה שוחטין וזורקין על טמא שרץ לא דטביל אי טביל מאי קמ"ל הא קמ"ל דאע"ג דמחוסר הערב השמש קמ"ל דשמשא ממילא ערבא הכי נמי מסתברא מדקתני סיפא ראה שלש ראיות שוחטין עליו בשמיני אי אמרת בשלמא זב שראה שתי ראיות שוחטין עליו בשביעי דטביל איצטריך סד"א ראה שתי ראיות בשביעי הוא דלא מחוסר מעשה אבל ראה שלש בשמיני דמחוסר מעשה מחוסר כפרה לא קמ"ל דאע"ג דמחוסר כפרה שוחטין וזורקין עילויה אלא אי אמרת ראה שתי ראיות בשביעי דלא טביל ראה שלש בשמיני למה לי השתא יש לומר ראה שתי ראיות בשביעי דלא טביל דטמא מעליא הוא שחטינן וזרקינן עילויה ראה שלש בשמיני דטביל ליה בשביעי דקלישא טומאה לא כ"ש דשחטינן וזרקינן עילויה אלא לאו ש"מ ראה שתי ראיות בשביעי דשחטינן עילויה דטביל לא לעולם אימא לך דלא טביל ואיצטריך ס"ד אמינא בשביעי הוא דבידו לתקן אבל בשמיני דאין בידו להקריב קרבן אימא פשעי ביה כהנים קמ"ל כדרב שמעיה:

והזבה שוחטין וכו': תני תנא קמיה דרב אדא בר אהבה והזבה שוחטין עליה בשביעי שלה אמר ליה זבה בשביעי שלה מי חזיא אפילו למאן דאמר שוחטין וזורקין על טמא שרץ הנ"מ טמא שרץ דחזי לאורתא הא עד למחר דמיתיא כפרה לא חזיא אימא בשמיני פשיטא מהו דתימא כיון דמחסרא כפרה לא קמ"ל כדרב שמעיה רבינא אמר נדה תנא קמיה והנדה שוחטין עליה בשביעי א"ל נדה בשביעי מי חזיא אפי' למאן דאמר שוחטין וזורקין על טמא שרץ דחזי לאורתא (ב) נדה לאורתא דשביעי הוא דטבלה עד שמיני דעבדה הערב שמש לא חזיא *אלא אימא בשמיני פשיטא השתא ומה זבה דמיחסרא כפרה שוחטין וזורקין עליה בשמיני נדה דלא מיחסרא כפרה צריכה למימר דשחטינן וזרקינן עלה איצטריכא ליה הא קא משמע לן בשמיני אין בשביעי לא *כדתניא ד כל חייבי טבילות טבילתן ביום נדה ויולדת טבילתן בלילה דתניא יכול תהא טובלת מבעוד יום תלמוד לומר °שבעת ימים תהיה בנדתה תהא בנדתה כל שבעה ויולדת איתקש לנדה: **מתני'** האונן והמפקח

ואין שוחטין וזורקין על טמא שרץ · ואע"פ שבידו לטבול היום וטעמא מפרש לקמיה : פשע · ולא טביל : משם · מן העזרה : שבשופרות · שופר היה שם שכתוב עליו קינין *ואשה שיש עליה לידה וכן כל מחוסרי כפרה מטילין מעות ונותנין לתוכו ודמי הקינין קצובין היו ואוכלים בקדש לערב וסומכין על חזקת בית דין של כהנים שאין עומדין משם עד שיכלו כל מעות אותו שופר כדי שלא*) יאכלו מחוסרי כפרה בקדשים : מחוסרי כפרה · זב וזבה ומצורעת ויולדת: ופרכינן ורב דאמר. טמא פשע אלמא מדאורייתא מיחזא חזי טמא שרץ לשחוט עליו ומשום דילמא פשע גזרו ביה רבנן : והאמר רב · בכילד צולין היו ישראל מחצה טהורין ומחצה טמאין מטמאים אחד מהן בשרץ להכריע רוב ציבור לטומאה ואי מדאורייתא חזי היאך הוא מכריעם לטומאה דהיינו טמא שרץ דחזי למטבל : וממאי דהכי · דילמא מדכתיב טמא לנפש ולא כתיב טמא שרץ שמע מינה טמא מת שאינו ראוי לערב קאמר : סבר לה כרבי יצחק דאמר · בספרי אותן אנשים שבפסח מדבר שהיו טמאין לנפש אדם טמאי מת מצוה היו שחל שביעי כו' : מאי לאו דלא טביל · וקשיא לרב: הא קא משמע לן דאף על גב דמחוסר הערב שמש דשימשא ממילא ערבא· ולא הוי כמחוסר מעשה : הכי נמי מסתברא · דאטבול קאי מדאצטריך למיתנא סיפא דשוחטין על מחוסר כפורים אי אמרת בשלמא רישא לא אשמעי' [אלא] טבול יום איצטריך למיתנא סיפא לאשמעי' דשוחטין על מחוסר כפורים ס"ד אמינא האי מחוסר מעשה חשיב ליה קא משמע לן דשרי ובמסרו לב"ד של כהנים כדאמרן : אלא אי אמרת כו' יש בידו לתקן · לטבול אבל מחוסר כפרה אין בידו לתקן אלא ביד כהן : זבה טבילתה ביום שביעי · דכתיב (ויקרא טו) וספרה לה שבעת ימים ואחר תטהר אחר מעשה תטהר כיון דסיימה לה ספירה תטהר ובתחלת היום עבדה לה ספירה אבל נדה דאורייתא שאינה סופרת נקיים אלא שבעה עם ימי ראייתה אינה טובלת עד לאחר שקיעת החמה של שביעי והערב שמש בדידה לא הוי עד למחר : בשביעי לא · משום דלא חזיא לאורתא משום הערב שמש : תהיה · יתירה דריש : ויולדת איתקש לנדה · דכתיב (שם יב) כימי נדת דותה תטמא: **מתני'** האונן · שמתו מוטל לפניו כדאמרי' בשחיטת קדשים בפרק טבול יום (זבחים דף ק:) איזהו אונן כל זמן שלא נקבר : והמפקח

מחוסר טבילה · ואף על גב דמחוסר כפרה נמי צריך טבילה כדתנן בפ' חומר בקודש (חגיגה דף כה·) האונן ומחוסר כפורים צריכין טבילה לקודש היינו אלא מדרבנן כדמוכח התם ועוד דההיא טבילה לא בעי הערב שמש ולא שייך התם דילמא פשע :

עד שיכלו כל המעות שבשופר · הקשה ריב"א הא אי אפשר שלא יהא מעורב בכל קן וקן ממעות שתי נשים ואפי' למאן דאמר יש ברירה כי האי גוונא לא שייך למימר דלכן סהדי שנתערבו ואי הוה אמרינן שמכל מעות שבשופר קונה קינין יחד מאדם א' הוה אתי שפיר אבל לישנא דעד שיכלו לא משמע הכי ונראה לר"י דכל אחת היתה צוררת מעותיה ונותנת בשופר: **מי** לא עסקינן שחל שביעי שלו להיות בערב הפסח · ואם תאמר ואפילו טבל נמי לא ישחטו עליו מהאי טעמא וי"ל כי יהיה טמא כתיב והאי קלישא טומאתיה :

שחל שביעי שלו · אבל ששי שלו ליכא למימר מדכתיב ולא יכלו לעשות הפסח ביום ההוא הא למחר היו יכולים לעשות ולשחוט הן עצמן בלא שליחות מדלא כתיב ולא יכלו לאכול אי נמי דייק מביום ההוא דמיותר ואי ששי הוא לישתוק מיניה ואם תאמר למה אמר להם לדחות לפסח שני יטבלו בו ביום וישחטו עליהם ויש לומר דשמא כן עשו ובשעה ששאלו לא טבלו עדיין ואמר להו משה אם לא תטבלו היום תדחו לפסח שני :

בשמיני פשיטא · אמתניתין דקתני זב שוחטים עליו בשמיני ליכא למיפרך פשיטא דמצי למימר דקתני לה אגב רישא דזב שראה שתי ראיות ושומרת יום כנגד יום שוחטין עליה ולא חיישינן שמא תראה ותסתור : **האונן** . כגון שמת לו מת אחר חצות שכבר חל עליו חיוב פסח אבל קודם חצות חל עליו אנינות כדאמר במי שהיה טמא (לקמן דף צח·) : שהיה

לג א מיי' פ"ד מהלכות ביאת מקדש הלכה יב ופ"ו מהלכות ק"פ הלכה א סמג שם :
לד ב שם הלכה ד :
לה ג שם הלכה ג :
לו ד שם הלכה ג :
לז ה מיי' פ"א מהלכות מקואות הלכה ו ופרק ג מהלכות שגגות עבור הלכה ג ופ"ד מהל' איסורי ביאה הלכה ו סמג עשין רמג טוש"ע או"ח סימן תקנד סעיף א* וסימן תרי"ג סעיף יא* וטוש"ע יו"ד סימן קצ"ז סעיף ג וסימן רפא סעיף ה* [רב אלפס שבועות פ"ב דף רלב וברא"ש הלכות מקואות סימן לו] :
לח ו מיי' פ"ו מהלכות ק"פ הלכה ט :

רבינו חננאל

שוחטין וזורקין על טבול יום דאע"ג דמחוס' ערב שמש שמשא ממילא ערבא ועל מחוסר כפרה בשמסר קינו לב"ד של כהנים ואין שוחטין וזורקין על טמא שרץ חיישינן אף על פי שמקוה לפניו דילמא פשע ולא טבל דייקי' מינה מדקאמר דילמא פשע מכלל דמדאורייתא חזו ומשום דילמא פשע אמר רב אין שוחטין וזורקין על טמא שרץ אלמ' אמר רב מטמאין אחד מהן בשרץ ועושין הפסח בטומאה והא טמא שרץ מדאוריי' טהור מעליא הוא אלא לרב טמא שרץ מדאוריי' נמי לא חזי מאי טעמא גמר לה מטמא שחל שביעי שלו להיות בערב הפסח דאע"ג דבערב ראוי הוא כיון דהשתא לא חזי נדחה מהאי קרא דכתיב ולא יכלו לעשו' הפסח ביום ההוא ביום ההוא אינן יכולין לעשו' הפסח אבל למחר יכולין לעשות ונדחו לפסח שני כן נמי טמא שרץ ואקשי' עליה מדתנן זב שראה שתי ראיות שוחטין עליו בשביעי הנה זב בשביעי שלו כטמא שרץ הוא וקתני שוחטין עליו מאי לאו דלא טבל וקשיא לרב ומשני לא דטבל והא קמ"ל דאף על גב דמחוסר ערב שמש שמשא ממילא ערבא . דיקא נמי דקתני סיפא ראה שלש וכו' : **עולא** אמר שוחטין וזורקין אף על טמא שרץ כו': **הזבה** שוחטין עליה בשמיני והוא שמסרה קרבנה לב"ד מהו דתימא דילמ' פשעו כהנים ולא קרבו להו קמ"ל כדרב שמעי' דאמר חזקה אין ב"ד של כהנים עומדין משם עד שיכלו כל מעות שבשופר . רבינא אמר התנא נדה תנא קמיה שוחטין עליה בשביעי אמר ליה רב אדא בר אהבה אפי' למאן דאמר שוחטין וזורקין על טמא שרץ משום דחזי לאורתא אבל נדה דטבלה ליל שמיני עד דעריב עלה שמשא דיום שמיני לא חזיא אלא אימא נדה שוחטין עליה בשמיני שלה והא קמ"ל דבשמיני אין בשביעי לא כדתניא כל חייבי טבילות טבילתן ביום נדה ויולדת טבילתן בלילה . ותניא מנין לנדה שאינה טובלת ביום שביעי שלה שנאמר שבעת ימים תהיה בנדתה [תהא בנדתה] כל שבעה : **מתני'** האונן והמפקח

שקלים פ"ו מ"ה
לעיל סט. פח. לקמן צב. זבחים כב:
[נזיר סד:]
עירובין לב.
לעיל פ.
[לקמן צב.]
סוכה כה:
שבת קכא. יומא ו. פה. ע"ש
ויקרא טו

הגהות הב"ח
(א) גמ' ורבנן הוא דגזרו ביה והא אמר רב: (ב) שם דחזי לאורתא אבל נדה לאורתא דשביעי:

גליון הש"ס
גמ' ואין שוחטין וזורקין על טמא שרץ. עי' לעיל צ ע"ב תוס' ד"ה אלו פסולים:

[90b] but one may not slaughter and sprinkle for a person unclean through a reptile.[6] But 'Ulla maintained: One slaughters and sprinkles for a person unclean through a reptile. According to Rab, wherein does a *ṭebul yom* differ? Because he is fit in the evening. But one unclean through a reptile too is fit in the evening?—He lacks *ṭebillah*. Then a *ṭebul yom* too lacks the setting of the sun?[7] The sun goes down of its own accord.[8] Then one who lacks atonement too, surely lacks forgiveness?[9]—It means where his pair [of birds] are in his hand.[10] Then a person unclean through a reptile too, surely the *miḳweh*[11] stands before him?—He may neglect it. If so, he who lacks sacrifice too, perhaps he will neglect [to sacrifice]?—It means e.g., that he had delivered them [his birds] to the Beth din, this being in accordance with R. Shemaiah, who said: It is a presumption that the Beth din of Priests[12] do not rise from there[13] until the money in the horn-shaped receptacles is finished.[14]

a Now according to Rab, by Scriptural law he[1] is indeed fit, and it was the Rabbis who preventively forbade him;[2] why then did Rab say: We defile one of them with a reptile?[3]—Rather [say] according to Rab he is not fit by Biblical law either, for it is written, *If any man be unclean by reason of a dead body:*[4] does this not hold good [even] when his seventh day falls on the eve of Passover,[5] which case is [tantamount to] uncleanness through a reptile,[6] yet the Divine Law said, Let him be relegated [to the second Passover]? [But] how do you know that it is so?[7]—He holds as R. Isaac, who said: They[8] were unclean through an unattended corpse[9] whose seventh day fell on the eve of Passover, for it is said, *and they could not keep the Passover* on that day:[10] thus only on that day could they not keep it, but on the morrow they could keep it,[11] yet the Divine Law said, Let them be put off.[12]

We learned: IF A ZAB HAS SUFFERED TWO ATTACKS, ONE SLAUGHTERS ON HIS BEHALF ON HIS SEVENTH [DAY]; does that not mean where he had not performed *ṭebillah*, which proves [that] one slaughters and sprinkles for a person unclean through a reptile?[13]—No; it means where he has performed *ṭebillah*. If he has performed *ṭebillah*, what does it [the Mishnah] inform us?—If it informs us this, that though he lacks the setting of the sun, the sun sets automatically.[14] Reason too supports this [interpretation], since the second clause teaches: IF HE HAS HAD THREE ATTACKS, ONE SLAUGHTERS ON HIS BEHALF ON HIS EIGHTH [DAY]. Now it is well if you agree that [the clause] 'IF A ZAB HAS SUFFERED TWO ATTACKS, ONE SLAUGHTERS ON HIS BEHALF ON HIS SEVENTH [DAY]' means where he has performed *ṭebillah*: then [the second clause] is necessary. You might argue: Only when he has had two attacks [do we slaughter for him] on his seventh [day], because he does not lack a positive act; but [in the case of] 'one who has had three attacks, on his eighth
b day,' where an action is wanting [in that] he lacks forgiveness,[1] it is not so. Therefore [the Mishnah] informs us that though he lacks forgiveness, we slaughter and sprinkle on his behalf. But

(6) Though he can perform *ṭebillah* and be fit in the evening. (7) I.e., he too is not fit when the sacrifice is actually slaughtered. (8) No action *by himself* is wanting. (9) I.e., he is yet to bring his sacrifice, and thus he is on a par with a person unclean through a reptile, who is to perform *ṭebillah*. (10) For sacrificing, so we need not fear that he may omit to do so and the Passover-offering will have needlessly been slaughtered for him. (11) Ritual bath. (12) A special court in the Temple which dealt with priestly and sacrificial matters. (13) I.e., do not leave the Temple Court. (14) The monies for the bird-offerings were placed daily in horn-shaped receptacles, and the priestly Beth din saw to it that these were expended on the day they were received. Hence there was no fear of neglect.

a (1) The person unclean through a reptile. (2) This must be assumed, since he gives the reason because we fear that he may neglect his *ṭebillah*. (3) V. *supra* 80a; but an unclean majority means such as are unfit to partake of the Passover-offering in the evening by *Biblical* law. (4) Num. IX, 10. (5) Since Scripture does not particularize, it must include all cases. (6) Since both can be clean in the evening. (7) Since Scripture mentions a dead body, it may refer only to such uncleanness that is *not* the same as that acquired from a reptile, viz., before the seventh day. (8) The men who came to enquire of Moses and Aaron, Num. IX, 6. (9) Lit., 'a corpse of a precept'—i.e., the corpse of a person whose relatives are unknown; its burial is obligatory upon the first person who finds it. (10) Ibid. (11) This is possible only if the morrow was their eighth day. (12) Though they can make themselves fit for the evening. (13) For they are exactly alike. (14) As above.

b (1) His sacrifice is yet to be offered.

◁ *For the continuation of the English translation of this page see overleaf.*

עין משפט נר מצוה

לג א מיי' פ"ד מהלכות ביאת מקדש הלכה יב ופ"ו מהלכות ק"פ הלכה א סמג שם:
לד ב שם הלכה ד:
לה ג שם הלכה ב:
לו ד שם הלכה ג:
לז ה מיי' פ"ה מהלכות מקוואות הלכה ו ופרק ג מהלכות שביתת עשור הלכה ג ופ"ד מהל' איסורי ביאה הלכה ו סמג עשין רמג טוש"ע א"ח סימן תקנד סעיף ח' וסימן תרי"ג סעיף י"א וטוש"ע יו"ד סימן קצ"ז סעיף ג וסימן קפח סעיף ה' [רב אלפס שבועות פ"ב דף רלב וברא"ש הלכות מקוואות סימן לו]:
לח ו מיי' פ"ו מהלכות ק"פ הלכה ט:

מחוסר טבילה · ואף על גב דמחוסר כפרה נמי צריך טבילה כדתנן בפ' חומר בקודש (חגיגה דף כה:) האונן ומחוסר כפורים צריכין טבילה לקודש אינו אלא מדרבנן כדמוכח התם ועוד דההיא טבילה לא בעי הערב שמש ולא שייך התם דילמא פשע:

עד שיכלו כל המעות שבשופר · הקשה ריב"א הא אי אפשר שלא יהא מעורב בכל קן וקן ממעות שתי כנים ואפי' למאן דאמר יש ברירה כי האי גוונא לא שייך למימר דלכן שהדי שנתערבו ואי הוה אמרינן שכל מעות שבשופר קונה קינין יחד מאדם א' הוה אתי שפיר אבל ליכא דעד שיכלו לא משמע הכי ונראה לר"י דכל אחת היתה צורכת מעותיה וטותנת בשופר: **מי** לא עסקינן שחל שביעי שלו להיות בערב הפסח · ואם תאמר ואפילו טבל נמי לא ישחטו עליו מהאי טעמא וי"ל כי יהיה טמא כתיב והאי קלישא טומאתיה:

שחל שביעי שלו · אבל ששי שלו ליכא למימר מדכתיב ולא יכלו לעשות הפסח ביום ההוא הא למחר היו יכולים לעשות ולשחוט הן עצמן בלא שליחות מדלא כתיב ולא יכלו לאכול אי נמי דייק מביום ההוא דמיותר ואי ששי הוא ליטתוק מיניה ואם תאמר למה אמר להם לדחות לפסח שני יטבלו בו ביום וישחטו עליהם וים לומר דשמא כן עשו ובשעה ששאלו לא טבלו עדיין ואמר להו משה אם לא תטבלו היום תדחו לפסח שני:

בשמיני פשיטא · אמתניתין דקתני זב שוחטים עליו בשמיני ליכא למיפרך פשיטא דמצי למימר דקתני לה אגב רישא דזב שראה שתי ראיות ושומרת יום כנגד יום שוחטין עליה ולא חיישינן שמא תראה ותסתור: **האונן** · כגון שמת לו מת אחר חצות שכבר חל עליו חיוב פסח אבל קודם חצות חל עליו אנינות כדאמר במי שהיה טמא (לקמן דף צח:) מי שהיה

ואין שוחטין וזורקין על טמא שרץ · ואע"פ שבידו לטבול היום וטעמא מפרש לקמיה: פשע · ולא טביל: משם · מן העזרה: שבשופרות · שופר היה שם שכתוב עליו קינין *ואשה שיש עליה לידה וכן כל מחוסרי כפרה מביאין מעות ונותנין לתוכו ודמי הקינין קצובין היו ואוכלים בקדש לערב וסומכין על הזקת בית דין של כהנים שאין עומדין משם עד שיכלו כל מעות אותו שופר כדי שלא*) יאכלו מחוסרי כפרה בקדשים: מחוסרי כפרה · זב וזבה ומצורעת ויולדת: ופרכינן ורב דאמר. טמא פשע אלמא מדאורייתא מיחזא חזי טמא שרץ לשחוט עליו ומשום דילמא פשע גזרו ביה רבנן: והאמר רב · בכילד צולין היו ישראל מחצה טהורין ומחצה טמאין מטמאים אחד מהן בשרץ להכריע רוב ציבור לטומאה ואי מדאורייתא חזי היאך הוא מכריעם לטומאה דהייט טמא שרץ דחזי למטבל: וממאי דהכי · דילמא מדכתיב טמא לנפש ולא כתיב טמא שרץ שמע מינה טמא מת שאינו ראוי לערב קאמר: סבר לה כרבי יצחק דאמר · בספרי אותן אנשים שבפסח מדבר שהיו טמאין לנפש אדם טמאי מת מצוה היו שחל שביעי כו': מאי לאו דלא טביל · וקשיא לרב: הא קא משמע לן דאף על גב דמחוסר הערב שמש דשימשא ממילא ערבא· ולא הוי כמחוסר מעשה: הכי נמי מסתברא · דאטבול קאי מדאצטריך למיתנא סיפא דשוחטין על מחוסר כפורים אי אמרת בשלמא רישא לא אשמעי' [אלא] טבול יום איצטריך למיתנא סיפא לאשמעי' דשוחטין על מחוסר כפורים ס"ד אמינא האי מחוסר מעשה חשיב ליה קא משמע לן דשרי וכמסרו לב"ד של כהנים כדאמרן: אלא אי אמרת כו' יש בידו לתקן · לטבול אבל מחוסר כפרה אין בידו לתקן אלא ביד כהן: זבה טבילתה ביום שביעי · דכתיב (ויקרא טו) וספרה לה שבעת ימים ואחר תטהר אחר מעשה תטהר כיון דסיימה לה ספירה תטהר ובתחלת היום עבדה לה ספירה אבל נדה דאורייתא שאינה סופרת נקיים אלא שבעה עם ימי ראייתה אינה טובלת עד לאחר שקיעת החמה של שביעי והערב שמש בדידה לא הוי עד למחר: בשביעי לא · משום דלא חזיא לאורתא משום הערב שמש: תהיה · יתירה דריש: ויולדת איתקש לנדה · דכתיב (שם יב) כימי נדת דותה תטמא: **מתני'** האונן · שמתו מוטל לפניו כדאמרי' בשחיטת קדשים בפרק טבול יום (זבחים דף ק:) איזהו אונן כל זמן שלא נקבר: והמפקח

ואין שוחטין וזורקין על טמא שרץ ועולא אמר אף שוחטין וזורקין על טמא שרץ לרב מאי שנא טבול יום דחזי לאורתא טמא שרץ נמי חזי לאורתא מחוסר טבילה טבול יום נמי מחוסר הערב שמש *שמשא ממילא ערבא מחוסר כפורים נמי הא מחוסר כפרה שקינו בידו טמא שרץ נמי הרי מקוה לפניו דילמא פשע אי הכי מחוסר כפורים נמי דילמא פשע [ב]כגון דמסרינהו לב"ד וכדרב שמעיה *דאמר חזקה אין ב"ד של כהנים עומדין משם עד שיכלו מעות שבשופרות ולרב מדאורייתא מיחזא חזי ורבנן הוא דגזרו ביה (א) אלמה אמר רב *מטמאין אחד מהן בשרץ אלא לרב מדאורייתא נמי לא חזי דכתיב °איש איש כי יהיה טמא לנפש *מי לא עסקינן שחל שביעי שלו להיות בערב הפסח דהיינו טומאת שרץ ואמר רחמנא נידחי וכי תימא ממאי דהכי סבר לה כרבי יצחק *דאמר טמאי מת מצוה היו שחל שביעי שלהן להיות בערב הפסח שנאמר °ולא יכלו לעשות הפסח ביום ההוא ביום ההוא הוא דאינן יכולין לעשות אבל למחר יכולין לעשות ואמר רחמנא נדחו תנן זב שראה שתי ראיות שוחטין עליו בשביעי מאי לאו דלא טביל ושמע מינה שוחטין וזורקין על טמא שרץ לא דטביל אי טביל מאי קמ"ל הא קמ"ל דאע"ג דמחוסר הערב השמש קמ"ל דשמשא ממילא ערבא הכי נמי מסתברא מדקתני סיפא ראה שלש ראיות שוחטין עליו בשמיני אי אמרת בשלמא זב שראה שתי ראיות שוחטין עליו בשביעי דטביל איצטריך ס"ד ראה שתי ראיות בשביעי הוא דלא מחוסר מעשה אבל ראה שלש בשמיני דמחוסר מעשה מחוסר כפרה לא קמ"ל דאע"ג דמחוסר כפרה שוחטין וזורקין עילויה אלא אי אמרת ראה שתי ראיות בשביעי דלא טביל ראה שלש בשמיני למה לי השתא יש לומר ראה שתי ראיות בשביעי דלא טביל דטמא מעליא הוא שחטינן וזרקינן עילויה ראה שלש בשמיני דטביל ליה בשביעי דקלישא טומאה לא כ"ש דשחטינן וזרקינן עילויה אלא לאו ש"מ ראה שתי ראיות בשביעי דשחטינן עילויה דטביל לא לעולם אימא לך דלא טביל ואיצטריך ס"ד אמינא בשביעי הוא דבידו לתקן אבל בשמיני דאין בידו להקריב קרבן אימא פשעי ביה כהנים קמ"ל כדרב שמעיה: והזבה שוחטין וכו': תני תנא קמיה דרב אדא בר אהבה והזבה שוחטין עליה בשביעי שלה אמר ליה זבה בשביעי שלה מי חזיא אפילו למאן דאמר שוחטין וזורקין על טמא שרץ הנ"מ טמא שרץ דחזי לאורתא הא עד למחר דמתיא כפרה לא חזיא אימא בשמיני פשיטא מהו דתימא כיון דמחסרא כפרה לא קמ"ל כדרב שמעיה רבינא אמר נדה תנא קמיה והנדה שוחטין עליה בשביעי א"ל נדה בשביעי מי חזיא אפי' למאן דאמר שוחטין וזורקין על טמא שרץ דחזי לאורתא (ג) נדה לאורתא דשביעי הוא דטבלה עד שמיני דעבדה הערב שמש לא חזיא [ד]אלא אימא בשמיני פשיטא השתא ומה זבה דמיחסרא כפרה שוחטין וזורקין עליה בשמיני נדה דלא מיחסרא כפרה צריכה למימר דשחטינן וזרקינן עלה נדה איצטריכא ליה הא קא משמע לן בשמיני אין בשביעי לא *כדתניא [ה]כל חייבי טבילות טבילתן ביום נדה ויולדת טבילתן בלילה דתניא יכול תהא טובלת מבעוד יום תלמוד לומר °שבעת ימים תהיה בנדתה תהא בנדתה כל שבעה ויולדת איתקש לנדה: **מתני'** [ו]האונן והמפקח

תורה אור: במדבר ט · ויקרא טו

רבינו חננאל

שוחטין וזורקין על טבול יום דאע"ג דמחוסר ערב שמש שמשא ממילא ערבא ועל מחוסר כפרה דשמסר קינו לב"ד של כהנים ואין שוחטין וזורקין על טמא שרץ חיישינן אף על פי שמקוה לפניו דילמא פשע ולא טבל דייקי' מינה מדקאמר דילמא פשע מכלל דמדאורייתא חזו ומשום דילמא פשע אמר רב אין שוחטין וזורקין על טמא שרץ אלמא אמר רב מטמאין אחד מהן בשרץ ועושין הפסח בטומאה והא טמא שרץ דאורייתא טהור מעליא הוא אלא לרב טמא שרץ דאורייתא נמי לא חזי מאי טעמא גמר לה מטמא שחל שביעי שלו להיות בערב הפסח דאע"ג דראוי הוא כיון דהשתא לא חזי נדחה מהאי קרא דכתיב ולא יכלו לעשות הפסח ביום ההוא אבל למחר יכולין לעשות ונדחו לפסח שני ואקשי' לרב מדתנן זב שראה שתי ראיות שוחטין עליו בשביעי הנה זב בשביעי שלו כטמא שרץ הוא וקתני שוחטין עליו מאי לאו דלא טבל ושני לא דטבל והא קמ"ל אע"ג דמחוסר ערב שמש שמשא ממילא ערבא. דיקא נמי דקתני סיפא ראה שלש וכו': עולא אמר שוחטין וזורקין על טמא שרץ וכו': הזבה שוחטין עליה בשמיני והא שמסרה קרבנה לב"ד מהו דתימא דילמא פשעו כהנים ולא קרבו להו קמ"ל כדרב שמעיה דאמר חזקה אין ב"ד של כהנים עומדין משם עד שיכלו כל מעות שבשופר. רבינא אמר התנא נדה תנא קמיה שוחטין עליה בשביעי אמר ליה רב אדא בר אהבה דאמר שוחטין וזורקין על טמא שרץ משום דחזי לאורתא אבל נדה דטבלה ליל שמיני עד דעריב עלה שמשא דיום שמיני לא חזיא אימא נדה שוחטין עליה בשמיני שלה והא קמ"ל דבשמיני אין בשביעי לא כדתניא כל חייבי טבילות טבילתן ביום נדה ויולדת טבילתן בלילה. ותניא מנין לנדה שאינה טובלת ביום שביעי שלה שנאמר שבעת ימים תהיה בנדתה [תהא בנדתה] כל שבעה: מתני' האונן והמפקח

מסורת הש"ס

שקלים פ"ו מ"ה
לעיל סט. פח. לקמן צב. זבחים כב:
[נזיר סד:]
עירובין לב.
לעיל פ.
[לקמן לד.]
סוכה כה:
שבת קכא. יומא ו. פס. ע"ש

הגהות הב"ח

(א) גמ' ורבנן הוא דגזרו ביה והא אמר רב: (ג) שם דחזי לאורתא אבל נדה לאורתא דשביעי:

גליון הש"ס

גמ' ואין שוחטין וזורקין על טמא שרץ. עי' לעיל צ ע"ב תוס' ד"ה אלו פסולים:

מסורת הש"ס

אמר אביי אי לאו דאוקמה ר' אושעיא · להא דתנן לקמן דאתנן חל על המוקדשים בממנה לזונה על פסחו באתננה ואע"ג דאין אדם אוסר דבר שאינו שלו הכא אמרינן דאתנן חל עליו : ורבי היא · דאית ליה פסח ממון בעלים הוא דאמר לקמן אף מכדי מקח שאם ימעטו לו מעות לבעל הפסח ליקח חלוק וטלית ממנה אחרים עמו על פסחו ונוטל מהן מעות ועושה צרכיו אלמא שלו הוא ויכול לאוסרו אי לאו דאוקמא רבי אושעיא במסכת תמורה להההיא כדפרישית אנא הייתי מוקי לה ההיא דאתנן בקדשים קלים שנתן לה שלמים באתננה וי"ש בידו לאוסרן ורבי יוסי הגלילי היא דאמר בפרק קמא דב"ק (דף יב:) קדשים קלים ממון בעלים הם והאי מתניתא דלעיל דקתני מעות חולין הוה מוקמינא כרבי והוה אמינא דהא דשרי רבי לעשות צרכיו במעות לאו משום דפסח אית ביה שיור בקדושתו ליתפס קדושת המעות בחולין שבו אלא משום דזה שמפריש המעות שייר בקדושתו לתפס מתחת חולין לבעל הפסח והא ליכא לאוקמי כרבי יוסי דהא קתני בשלמים לא עשה כלום וההיא דאתנן כו' ובפסח לא הייתי מוקי לה דלא הוה סלקא דעתאי דפסח לרבי ממון בעלים הוא שיהא בידו לאוסרו : דלא משייר איניש בקדושת הגוף דבהמה וטעמא דרבי דאמר אף מכדי מקח משום דבמעות משייר איניש לתפס *מתחת חולין בחזקת חולין ומעיקרא אדעתא דהכי אפרישינהו ומשום הכי חולין הם דזה שהפריש לפסחו ואחר כך הימנה אחרים עמו מתנה בעלמא הוא דיהיב להו והנך יהבו ליה ממעות חולין מתנה והממנה זונה מתנה הוא שאין בידו לאוסרו ואין אתנן חל עליו : והשתא דאוקמא ר' אושעיא להההיא בממנה זונה על פסחו (א) · אלמא קא סבר ר' אושעיא פסח גופיה לר' ממון בעלים ושמעינן מינה דלאפי' בפסח משייר איניש כל שכן מעות וכ"ש דמצינן לאוקמא להך דקתני מעות שבידו חולין כרבי דהא פסח חולין הוא ויכול למוכרו ומעות של אותן אחרים חולין הוא וליכא לאקשויי היאך הקדש חל על הקדש לצאת לחולין : הרי אלו מותרין · כדיליף לקמן : עופות · תורים ובני יונה שאינן מוקדשין : שהמום פוסל בהם · אף משהוקדשו אין אתנן חל עליהם כדיליף לקמן : עופות · חולין שמום אין פוסל בהן מלהקדישם דלא נאמר תמות וזכרות בעופות אינו דין כו' : קל וחומר למוקדשין מעתה · שיחול אתנן עליהן : אלא טעמא כו' · פירכא הוא : ואם ימעט הבית וגו' · אם יהיו מעות מועטין לבעל הפסח מהיות משה שאין לו במה לקנות לצורכי הפסח ולקח הוא ושכנו הקרוב אל ביתו יקח מעות משכנו וימננו על פסחו ויקח מן המעות מה שהוא צריך לפסח : מכדי אכילה · אם יחסר לו מעות שאין לו במה ליקח צורכי אכילת הפסח כגון עצים לצלותו רשאי הוא למוכרו : ולא מכדי מקח · שאם אין לו מעות לסחורה אינו רשאי למכור פסחו לכך : כו"ע לא פליגי · דיכול להימנות אחרים ליקח במעות עצים : החייהו לשה · עשה צורכי הפסח מן המעות : ולאביי דאמר · לעיל אליבא דרבי בפסח לא משייר איניש הא קתני שעל מנת כו' אלמא פסח גופיה ממון בעלים הוא : אימא מעות פסחיהן · זה שנתמנה עמו לפסחו ונתן לו מעותיו חולין היו ונתן לו במתנה ומשום הכי יכול ליקח בהן טלית ונותן לו חלק של פסחו במתנה ומעותיו חולין הן שעל מנת כן הקדישן שאם רצה ליתנם במתנה יתנם : מתני' זב שראה שתי ראיות · שטומאתו טומאת שבעה ואינו טעון קרבן : שוחטין עליו בשביעי · ואע"פ שלא העריב שמשו דהא חזי למיכל לאורתא : ראה שלש · דלא חזי למיכל עד דמייתי כפרה : שוחטין עליו · אם חל שמיני שלו בערב הפסח ואפילו לא הביא כפרתו ומביאה לאחר מיכן דמחוסר כפורים דחי עשה דהשלמה כדאמרן בתמיד נשחט (דף נט:) : שומרת יום כנגד יום · הרואה יום אחד בתוך אחד עשר ימים שבין נדה לנדה דבעיא לספור יום המחרת שוחטין עליה ביום ספירה דכיון שספרה מקצת היום מותרת לטבול ואף על פי שמחוסרת הערב שמש שוחטין עליה : והזבה · שראתה שלשה רצופים בתוך אחד עשר יום וצריכה לספור שבעה נקיים ולהביא קרבן שוחטין עליה בשמיני ותביא כפרתה קודם שתחשך ותאכל : גמ' ואין

[ב"ק יב: ושי"נ] · ס"א נ"ג · ס"א נ"ג · [ס"א מתנה תנא] · תמורה ל: ע"ש · [שם] · [שם]

תורה אור

אמר אביי אי לאו דאוקמיה רבי אושעיא להההיא בממנה זונה על פסחו ורבי היא הוה מוקמינא לה להההיא בקדשים קלים ואליבא דרבי יוסי הגלילי דאמר *קדשים קלים ממון בעלים הוא אבל בפסח לא משייר איניש במעות ודאי משייר איניש דמעיקרא כי מפריש להו אדעתא דהכי מפריש להו והא רבי היא ומשום הכי מעות שבידו חולין (דבפסח לא משייר איניש) ובמעות ודאי משייר איניש וההיא דקא מוקי לה רבי אושעיא כרבי לא מוקמינא ליה אנא כרבי דבפסח לא משייר איניש (ובמעות משייר איניש דמעיקרא כי מפריש להו אדעתא דהכי מפריש להו) והא ליכא לאוקמי כרבי יוסי דהא תני בה והמוכר עולתו ושלמיו לא עשה ולא כלום והשתא דאוקמיה רבי אושעיא להההיא בממנה זונה על פסחו ורבי היא ש"מ דסבירא לי' אפילו בפסחו משייר איניש מאי היא דרבי אושעיא דתנן *נתן לה מוקדשין באתננה הרי אלו מותרין עופות דחולין הרי אלו אסורין שהיה בדין ומה אם מוקדשים שהמום פוסל בהן אין אתנן ומחיר חל עליהן עופות שאין המום פוסל בהן אינו דין שאין אתנן ומחיר חל עליהן ת"ל °לכל נדר לרבות את העופות *ק"ו למוקדשין מעתה מה עופות שאין המום פוסל בהן אתנן ומחיר חל עליהן מוקדשין שהמום פוסל בהן אינו דין שאתנן ומחיר חל עליהן ת"ל לכל נדר פרט לנדור אלא טעמא דכתב רחמנא נדר הא לאו הכי הוה אמינא מוקדשים חל איסור אתנן עליהן והא אין אדם אוסר דבר שאינו שלו א"ר אושעיא בממנה זונה על פסחו ורבי היא מאי רבי דתניא *°אם ימעט הבית מהיות משה החייהו משה מכדי אכילה ולא מכדי מקח רבי אומר אף מכדי מקח שאם אין לו ממנה אחר עמו על פסחו ועל חגיגתו ומעות שבידו חולין שעל מנת כן הקדישו ישראל את פסחיהן רבה ורבי זירא חד אמר בעצים לצלייתו כולי עלמא לא פליגי דכיון דתקנתא דפסח הוא כגופא דפסח דמי כי פליגי במצה ומרור רבנן סברי הא אכילה אחריתי היא ורבי סבר כיון דהכשירו דפסח הוא כגופא דפסח דמי וחד אמר במצה ומרור נמי בכולי עלמא לא פליגי דכתיב °על מצות ומרורים יאכלוהו דכיון דמכשירין דפסח נינהו כפסח דמי כי פליגי ליקח בו חלוק בו טלית רבנן סברי מהיות משה אמר רחמנא החייהו לשה ורבי סבר החייה עצמך משה ולאביי דאמר אי לאו דאוקמה רבי אושעיא להההיא בממנה זונה על פסחו ורבי היא הוי מוקמינן לה בקדשים קלים ואליבא דר"י הגלילי דאמר קדשים [קלים] ממון בעלים הוא אבל בפסח לא משייר איניש הא קתני בהדיא שעל מנת כן הקדישו ישראל את פסחיהן אימא שעל מנת כן הקדישו ישראל מעות פסחיהן : **מתני'** גזב שראה שתי ראיות שוחטין עליו בשביעי ראה שלש שוחטין עליו בשמיני שלו שומרת יום כנגד יום שוחטין עליה בשני שלה ראתה שני ימים שוחטין עליה בשלישי והזבה שוחטין עליה בשמיני : **גמ'** אמר רב יהודה אמר רב דשוחטין וזורקין על טבול יום המחוסר כפורים ואין

דברים כג · שמות יב · שם

כי פליגי במצה ומרור · להאי לישנא צריך לומר דהך דאתנן אתיא כרבי יוסי הגלילי דאמר קדשים קלים ממון בעלים הוא להכי איצטריך לכל נדר אבל כרבי לא מתוקמא כיון דסבר להאי לישנא דפסח לא משייר אלא במצה ומרור לחודיה ומיהו ההיא דלעיל דקתני מעות שבידו חולין הייטו חולין לענין מצה ומרור דכרבי יוסי הגלילי לא מיתוקמא דקתני לא עשה ולא כלום :

החייה עצמך משה · תימה כיון דמקרא נפיק מה צריך לטעמא שעל מנת כן הקדישו ישראל פסחיהם ויש לומר דקא משמע לן קרא דדעתו לכך :

עין משפט
נר מצוה

כח א מיי' פ"ד מהלכות איסורי מזבח הלכה יד טו סמג לאוין שמ :
כט ב מיי' פ"ד מהלכות ק"פ הלכה יא :
ל ג מיי' פ"ו מהלכות ק"פ הלכה ג סמג עשין רכד :
לא ד מיי' שם הלכה א סמג שם :
לב ה שם הלכה ד :

רבינו חננאל

שבידו חולין. אמר אביי אי לאו דאוקמיה ר' יאשיה להא דתנן בתמורה פ"ו נתן לה מוקדשין באתננה הרי אלו מותרין ובעופות אסורין כו' ומעטינן להו למוקדשין למיחל עלייהו איסור אתנן ומחיר [כלב] מדכתיב לא תביא אתנן זונה ומחיר כלב בית ה' אלהיך לכל נדר ודרשינן לכל נדר פרט לנדור כלומר כל דבר הנדור ומוקדש אין אתנן ומחיר חל עליהן אמאי בעינן קרא למעוטי המוקדשין תיפוק ליה דכיון דאוקדשנהו לאו דידיה אינון וקיימא לן אין אדם אוסר דבר שאינו שלו ואוקמא ר' אושעיא להא מתני' בממנה לזונה על פסחו ואליבא דר' דאמר המקדיש פסחו משייר ביה בפסחו ואם ימנה אחר עמו ויקח מעות ממנו אותן המעות חולין הן ולות הצריכה המשנה לומר אע"פ שממנה הזונה על פסחו ויש לו רשות לא נפסל הפסח ההוא ואיצטריך קרא למעוטי דהא דידי' [הוא] ומעטינן ליה לכל נדר פרט לנדור והפסח הזה כבר נדור ומופרש לשם פסח הוא : והיכן שנה ר' שמשייר אדם בפסחו דתניא ואם ימעט הבית מהיות משה מכדי אכילה ולא מכדי מקח ר' אומר אף מכדי מקח שאם אין לו ממנה אחרים עמו ומעות שבידו חולין דתקנתא דפסח הוא שעל מנת כן הקדישו ישראל את פסחיהן ואמר אביי אנא הא מתני' היינא מוקים לה בקדשים קלים ואליבא דר' יוסי הגלילי דאמר ממון בעלים הם כיון דאינון ממתיה איצטריך קרא לכל נדר פרט לנדור למעוטי הני קדשים קלים דלא חל איסור אתנן [ומחיר] עליהו והברייתא דקתני ומעות שבידו חולין לא הייתי מעמידה לרבי אלא הייתי [אומר] דבפסח לא משייר איניש אבל במעות ודאי משייר איניש דכי מפריש אדעתא דהכי מפריש להו שמשים בדעתו וכי לא יהיו דמי הכבש אלא אלו לא פחות ולא יותר יתכן שיהיו יתר ואוסיף או פחות וישאר לי *והשתא דאוקמי ר' אושעיא להההיא כר' אנא נמי אוקימנא לה להא מתניתא לרבי ולא משייר איניש בפסח אבל במעות משייר איניש *לפיכך תני מעות שבידו חולין והא ברייתא כר' יוסי הגלילי לא מצית מוקמת לה דקתני והמוכר עולתו ושלמיו לא עשה [כלום] : והא ברייתא דקתני ואם ימעט הבית חולקת רבנן ורבי חלקו רבה ור' זירא עלה חד אמר למנות עמו אחר בפסח וליטול ממנו מעות לקנות בהם עצים לצלותו דברי הכל מותר דכי גופיה דפסח הוא כי פליגי לקנות מן המעות מצה ומרור כו' וחד אמר מצה ומרור דברי הכל מותר כי פליגי לקנות מן המעות חלוק אי טלית רבנן סברי מהיות משה החייהו לשה ור' קסבר מי כתיב מהיות שה משה כתיב החייה עצמך מן השה. ירושלמי ר' אושעיא תנאי ב"ד הוא שיהא זה מפריש חולין מאליהן ואקשינן על אביי דאמר אפילו לרבי בפסח לא משייר איניש והא קתני בהדיא על מנת [כן] הקדישו ישראל את פסחיהן ושני' אימא שעל מנת [כן] הקדישו ישראל מעות פסחיהן : מתני' זב שראה שתי ראיות שוחטין עליו כו' אמר רב יהודה אמר רב שוחטין

הגהות הב"ח
(א) רש"י ד"ה והשתא וכו' על פסחו וכו' אלמא :

*) מלה לפי הענין כי אחר וישאר לו נ"ל הדבור לפיכך תני מעות כו' והדבור והשתא דאוקמי כו' נ"ל אחר סוף הדבור ונחלפו השורות בכ"י ובדפוס :

d (1) V. *supra* 81*a*, n. a3. In both these cases they are fit to eat the Passover-offering in the evening; hence we kill it on their behalf. (2) V. *supra* 81*a*, n. c5. (3) Who had three discharges. (4) V. Glos. (5) V. 18*b*, n. b1; 59*a*, n. b4.

Said Abaye: Had not R. Oshaia related that [Mishnah][10] to a case where he registers a harlot for his Passover-offering,[11] and in accordance with Rabbi,[12] I would have related it to sacrifices of a lesser sanctity[1] and in accordance with R. Jose the Galilean who maintained: Sacrifices of lesser sanctity are their owner's property. But [on Rabbi's view] a man does not leave anything over [unconsecrated] in the Passover-offering, yet he certainly does leave over in the case of money, because when he set it aside [for a Passover-offering] in the first place, he did so with this intention.[2] While this [the present Baraitha][3] is [the view of] Rabbi,[4] and for that reason the money he holds is *ḥullin*, as a man certainly leaves over [something] of money [unconsecrated]. Again, what R. Oshaia explains as the view of Rabbi, I do not explain as [the view of] Rabbi, for a man does not leave over anything [unconsecrated] of the Passover-offering.[5] But this [present Baraitha] cannot be established as agreeing with R. Jose, since it is taught therein, 'and he who sells his burnt-offering and his peace-offering has effected nothing.'[6] Now however that R. Oshaia related that [Mishnah] to the case of a man who registers a harlot in his Passover-offering, and in accordance with Rabbi, it follows that he[7] holds that a man leaves [something unconsecrated] even in his Passover-offering [itself].[8]

What is [this statement] of R. Oshaia [which is alluded to]? —For we learned: If he gave her [a harlot] consecrated animals b as her hire, they are permitted [for the altar];[1] [if he gave her] birds of *ḥullin*, they are forbidden.[2] Though [the reverse] would have been logical: if with consecrated animals, which a blemish disqualifies, yet [the interdict of] 'hire' or 'price'[3] does not fall upon them;[4] then with birds, which a blemish does not disqualify, is it not logical that [the interdict of] 'hire' and 'price' does not fall upon them? Therefore it is stated, *'for any vow,'* which includes birds. [But] now you might argue *a minori* in respect of consecrated animals: if with birds, though a blemish does not disqualify them, yet 'hire' and 'price' fall upon them, then with consecrated animals, which a blemish disqualifies, is it not logical that 'hire' and 'price' fall upon them? Therefore it is stated, *'for any vow* [neder]', which excludes that which is [already] vowed [*nadur*].[5] Now the reason is because the Divine Law wrote *'vow'*; but otherwise I would say: The interdict of *'hire'* falls upon consecrated animals: but surely a man cannot prohibit that which is not his?—Said R. Oshaia: It refers to the case of a man registering a harlot for his Passover-offering, this being according to Rabbi.

What is [this allusion to] Rabbi?—For it was taught, *And if the household be too little from being for a lamb:*[6] sustain him with [the proceeds of] the lamb in his food requirements, but not in his requirements of [general] purchases. Rabbi said: In his requirements of [general] purchases too, so that if he has nought [wherewith to purchase], he may register another in his Passover-offering and his *ḥagigah*,[7] while the money he receives is *ḥullin*, for on this condition did the Israelites consecrate their Passover-offerings.

Rabbah and R. Zera [disagree]. One maintains: None differ about fuel for roasting it, for since this makes the Passover- c offering fit [to be eaten], it is as the Passover-offering itself.[1] Their controversy is only about unleavened bread and bitter herbs: the Rabbis hold: This is a different eating;[2] while Rabbi holds: Since it is a requisite of the Passover-offering,[3] it is as the Passover-offering itself. The other maintains: None disagree about unleavened bread and bitter herbs either, for it is written, [*They shall eat the flesh . . .*] *and unleavened bread; with bitter herbs they shall eat it;*[4] hence since they are a requisite of the Passover-offering they are as the Passover-offering. Their controversy is only about buying a shirt therewith [or] buying a cloak therewith. The Rabbis hold: The Divine Law saith, *from being for a lamb* [mi-heyoth miseh]: devote it [*haḥayehu*] to the lamb;[5] while Rabbi holds: Sustain [*haḥayeh*] thyself with [the proceeds of] the lamb.

But according to Abaye, who said: 'Had not R. Oshaia related that [Mishnah] to a case where he registers a harlot in his Passover-offering, and in accordance with Rabbi, I would have related it to sacrifices of lesser sanctity, and in accordance with R. Jose the Galilean who maintained, Sacrifices of lesser sanctity are their owner's property; but [on Rabbi's view] a man does not leave anything over [unconsecrated] in the Passover-offering';—surely it is explicitly stated, 'for on this condition did the Israelites consecrate their Passover-offerings'?[6]—Say: 'for on this condition did the Israelites consecrate the *money* for their Passover-offerings.'[7]

MISHNAH. IF A ZAB HAS SUFFERED TWO ATTACKS [OF DISCHARGE], ONE SLAUGHTERS [THE PASSOVER-OFFERING] ON HIS BEHALF ON HIS SEVENTH [DAY]; IF HE HAS HAD THREE ATTACKS, ONE SLAUGHTERS ON HIS BEHALF ON HIS EIGHTH d [DAY].[1] IF A WOMAN WATCHES DAY BY DAY,[2] ONE SLAUGHTERS ON HER BEHALF ON HER SECOND DAY; IF SHE SAW [A DISCHARGE] ON TWO DAYS, ONE SLAUGHTERS ON HER BEHALF ON THE THIRD [DAY]. AND AS TO A ZABAH,[3] ONE SLAUGHTERS ON HER BEHALF ON THE EIGHTH [DAY].

GEMARA. Rab Judah said in Rab's name: One slaughters and sprinkles on behalf of a *ṭebul yom*[4] and one who lacks atonement,[5]

(10) V. *infra* in reference to a man who gave a sanctified animal to a harlot, where it is implied that but for a certain verse this would disqualify the animal from being offered as a sacrifice (v. Deut. XXIII, 19). Though a man cannot render forbidden that which does not belong to him, we say here that he would do so, though since it is sanctified it is really not his. (11) In return for the 'hire' which he owes her. (12) Rabbi rules *infra* that if a man needs money e.g., for clothes, he may register other people with him for his Passover-offering and spend the money so acquired on clothes. Thus he holds that an animal sanctified for a Passover-offering is entirely his private property; consequently he could also render it forbidden (but for the verse) by making it a harlot's hire.

a (1) V. *supra* 24a, n. a2. Thus he gave the harlot an animal consecrated for a peace-offering. (2) I.e., when Rabbi permits the owner to spend the money on clothes etc., it is not because he holds that when a man consecrates an *animal* for a Passover-offering he leaves part of it unconsecrated, as it were, so that if a man gives him consecrated money for a share in the sacrifice the sanctity of the money is transferred to that unconsecrated portion of the animal, while the money itself thereby becomes *ḥullin* and can be expended on anything. The reason is on the contrary that when a man consecrates *money* for the Passover-offering he leaves that money partly unconsecrated, as it were, in the sense that it automatically reverts to *ḥullin* when he gives it in payment for a share in a sacrifice, and in fact, the money is technically to be regarded as a gift, not as payment at all; Hence the vendor can use it as he pleases. (3) Introduced by 'our Rabbis taught'. (4) As explained in the preceding note. (5) Hence on Rabbi's view if he registers a harlot it does not prohibit it, since nothing at all of the animal is his in that sense. (6) Whereas on R. Jose's view that sacrifices of lesser sanctity are the owner's personal property, the sale of the peace-offering is valid. (7) Viz., Rabbi, in R. Oshaia's view. (8) Not only in the money set aside for the Passover-offering.

b (1) Since they were consecrated before he gave them to her, he cannot make them forbidden. (2) To be offered henceforth as a sacrifice. (3) V. Deut. XXIII, 19: *Thou shalt not bring the hire of a harlot, or the price of a dog, into the house of the Lord thy God for any vow* etc. (4) To make them forbidden. (5) The hire of a harlot cannot be vowed as a sacrifice; but a consecrated animal has already been vowed. (6) Ex. XII, 4, lit. translation. (7) Of the fourteenth.

c (1) Hence one may certainly sell a share in the sacrifice for this purpose. (2) Hence he cannot buy it with the proceeds of the sacrifice. (3) Which must be eaten with unleavened bread and bitter herbs. (4) Ex. XII, 8. The verse actually quoted, which is slightly different, is Num. IX, 11, but the Talmud probably means the verse stated here. (5) Lit., 'make it live for the lamb'—i.e., the money realized from the lamb must be expended on what is needed for the lamb, e.g., the unleavened bread and bitter herbs which accompany it. (6) This definitely implies a reservation in the sacrifice itself. (7) This is not an emendation but an interpretation.

MISHNAH. [89b] IF A MAN REGISTERS ANOTHER WITH HIM [TO SHARE] IN HIS PORTION,[6] THE MEMBERS OF THE a COMPANY[1] ARE AT LIBERTY TO GIVE HIM HIS [PORTION],[2] AND HE EATS HIS AND THEY EAT THEIRS.[3]

GEMARA. The scholars asked: Can the members of a company, one of whom is quick-handed,[4] say to him, 'Take your portion and go!' Do we rule that he can say to them, 'Surely you have accepted [me]'; or perhaps they can answer him, 'We accepted you for the purpose of the sacrifice,[5] but we did not accept you with the view that you should eat more than we'?—Come and hear: IF A MAN REGISTERS ANOTHER WITH HIM, THE MEMBERS OF THE COMPANY ARE AT LIBERTY TO GIVE HIM HIS [PORTION], AND HE EATS HIS AND THEY EAT THEIRS. What is the reason? Is it not because it is as though one of them were quick-handed:[6] and if you should think that one who is quick-handed can say to them, 'You have accepted me,'[7] then let this one be as though he is quick-handed?—I will tell you: That is not so, [for] characters differ, for even if both of them together eat [only] as much as one member of the company, they can say to him that they are not willing to have a stranger with them.

Come and hear: If the attendant ate as much as an olive at the side of the oven, if he is wise he eats his fill of it; but if the members of the company wish to do him a favour, they come and sit at his side and eat: this is R. Judah's opinion.[8] Thus, only if they wish, but not if they do not wish. Yet why so? Let him say to them, 'Surely you have accepted [me.]'[9]—There it is different, because they can say to him, 'We accepted you with the intention of troubling you to attend on us; [but] we did not accept you that we should take the trouble of attending to you.'

Come and hear: Members of a company, one of whom is quick-handed, are at liberty to say [to him], 'Take your portion and go.' And not only that, but even when five arrange for a meal in b common,[1] they are at liberty to say to him, 'Take your portion and go.' This proves it.

What does 'and not only that' mean?[2]—He proceeds to a climax.[3] In the case of Passover-offerings it goes without saying, for they can say to him, 'We accepted you for the purpose of the sacrifice.' But even in the case of a meal in common, which is mere companionship, they are at liberty to say to him, 'Take your portion and go.'

Others state: That is no problem to us,[4] but this is our question: Are the members of a company permitted to divide,[5] or are they not permitted to divide?[6]—Come and hear: Members of a company, one of whom was quick-handed, are at liberty to say to him, 'Take your portion and go.' Thus, only if he is quick-handed, but not if he is not quick-handed. This proves it.[7]

R. Papa and R. Huna the son of R. Joshua joined their bread together. But by the time R. Huna the son of R. Joshua ate one [piece], R. Papa ate four. Said he to him, 'Divide with me.' 'You have accepted [me as a partner],' he retorted. [Thereupon] he raised all these objections[8] to him, and he answered him as we have answered them. He then refuted him by [the teaching regarding] 'the members of a company [etc.]'. Said he to him, There the reason is because they can say to him, 'We accepted you for the purpose of the sacrifice.' He refuted him by [the teaching regarding] 'a meal in common [etc.]', so he divided with him. Then he went and joined bread with Rabina. By the time R. Huna the son of R. Joshua ate one [piece], Rabina ate eight. Said he: A hundred Papas rather than one Rabina!

Our Rabbis taught: If a man registers others with him for his c Passover-offering and his *hagigah*,[1] the money he holds[2] is *hullin*. And he who sells his burnt-offering and his peace-offering[3] has effected nothing,[4] and the money, however much it is,[5] is utilized[6] for a freewill-offering. But since he has not effected anything, why should it be utilized for a freewill-offering?[7] Said Raba: As a penalty.[8] And what does 'however much it is' mean?—Even if they [the animals] were only worth four [*zuz*] and he paid five, the Rabbis penalized him even in respect of that additional [*zuz*].

'Ulla—others state, R. Oshaia—said: Perhaps our Babylonian colleagues know the reason for this ruling. [Consider:] one set aside a lamb for his Passover-offering, and another set aside money for his Passover-offering: how can sanctification fall upon sanctification, that he teaches, 'the money he holds is *hullin*'?[9]—[90a]—

(6) Without the knowledge of the other members of the company.
a (1) Who disapprove of the new companion. (2) Bidding him to go and eat it elsewhere with the new companion of his choice. (3) This Tanna holds that one Paschal lamb may be eaten by two separate companies. (4) To seize food —i.e., he is a glutton and eats more than his due share. Lit., 'who has fine hands'—a euphemism. (5) We calculated that so many are required for this lamb. (6) Presumably the two will eat more than the ordinary share of one. (7) Enabling me to eat as much as I like. (8) V. *supra* 86a for notes. (9) As one of your company, and since I cannot go to you, you must come to me.
b (1) Each contributing an equal share. (2) In which way is the second ruling more noteworthy than the first? (3) Lit., 'he states, "it is unnecessary"'. (4) That the quick-handed companion may be told to take his portion and go. (5) Each to take his share. (6) But must all eat together. (7) They must eat together. (8) From the teaching cited above.
c (1) Here the Festive peace-offering which was brought on the fourteenth likewise and eaten before the Passover-offering. This was eaten by the same who had registered for the Passover-offering. (2) Which he received from those whom he registered. (3) I.e., animals which he consecrated for that purpose. (4) The sacrifice must be offered on behalf of the first owner. (5) Even if it exceeds the animal's worth. (6) Lit., 'falls'. (7) His action being null, the money remains *hullin*. (8) He should not have bought another man's sacrifice. (9) Money consecrated for a sacrifice can revert to *hullin* only if an animal of *hullin* is bought therewith, whereby the animal receives the sanctity of the money, which in turn loses it and becomes *hullin*. Here, however, the money was consecrated and given for an animal (or part of it, which is the same) which was *already* consecrated for a Passover-offering: how then can additional sanctity fall upon the animal, in the sense that the sanctity of the money is transferred thereto, leaving the money *hullin*?—It cannot be answered that this refers to unconsecrated money, for in that case it is obvious.

מתני׳ *הממנה עמו אחר בחלקו רשאין בני חבורה ליתן לו את שלו והוא אוכל משלו והן אוכלין משלהן: **גמ׳** איבעיא להו בני חבורה שהיו ידיו של אחד מהן יפות מהו שיאמרו לו טול חלקך וצא מי אמרינן מצי אמר להו הא קבילתון או דילמא מצו למימר ליה כי קבלינן לתיקוני זביחה ארעתא דאכלת טפי מינן לא קבלינך ת״ש הממנה אחרים עמו על חלקו רשאין [בני חבורה] ליתן לו את שלו והוא אוכל את שלו והן אוכלין את שלהן מאי טעמא לאו משום דהוי ליה כידים של אחד מהן יפות ואי סלקא דעתך ידיו יפות מצי אמר להו קבילתון ניהוי האי כידיו יפות אמרי לא דעות שאני דאע״ג תרווייהו כחד מבני חבורה הוא דאכלי מצי אמרי לי׳ דלא ניחא לן אינש נוכרא גבן ת״ש *השמש שאכל כזית בשר בצד התנור אם היה פקח ממלא כריסו ממנו אם רצו בני חבורה לעשות טובה עמו באין ויושבין בצדו ואוכלין דברי רבי יהודה רצו אין לא רצו לא ואמאי נימא להו הא קבילתון שאני התם דאמרי ליה כי קבלינך אדעתא דנטרחך קמן למטרח לן לדידך לא קבלינך ת״ש *בני חבורה שהיה ידיו של אחד מהן יפות רשאין לומר טול חלקך וצא ולא עוד אלא אפילו חמשה ועשו סיבולת רשאין לומר לו טול חלקך וצא שמע מינה מאי ולא עוד לא מיבעיא קאמר לא מיבעיא פסח דמצי אמרי ליה כי קבלינך לתקוני זביחה אלא אפילו סיבולת נמי דצוותא בעלמא הוא רשאין לומר לו טול חלקך וצא ואיכא דאמרי הא לא איבעיא לן אלא הכי הוא דאיבעיא לן בני חבורה רשאין לחלק או אינן רשאין לחלק ת״ש בני חבורה שהיו ידיו של אחד מהן יפות רשאין לומר לו טול חלקך וצא ידיו יפות אין ידיו יפות לא שמע מינה רב פפא ורב הונא בריה דרב יהושע עריבו ריפתא בהדי הדדי אדאכיל רב הונא בריה דרב יהושע חדא אכיל רב פפא ארבע א״ל פלוג לי אמר ליה קבילתון איתיביה כל הני תיובתא ושני כדשנינן איתיביה בני חבורה א״ל התם דאמרי לי׳ כי קבלינך לתיקוני זביחה איתיביה סיבולת פלג ליה אזל עריב בהדי רבינא אדאכיל רב הונא בריה דרב יהושע חדא אכיל רבינא תמניא אמר מאה פפי ולא חדא רבינא ת״ר *הממנה אחרי׳ עמו על פסחו ועל חגיגתו מעות שבידו חולין *והמוכר עולתו ושלמיו לא עשה ולא כלום ומעות כל שהן יפלו לנדבה וכי מאחר דלא עשה ולא כלום מעות אמאי יפלו לנדבה אמר רבא קנסא ומאי כל שהן אע״ג דלא הוו אלא ארבעה ויהבו ליה חמשה אפילו בההיא יתירא נמי קנסוהו רבנן אמר עולא ואיתימא ר׳ אושעיא *אפשר ידעי חברין בבלאי טעמא דהאי מלתא זה הפריש טלה לפסחו וזה הפריש מעות לפסחו היאך הקדש חל על הקדש דקתני מעות שבידו חולין

אמר

רש״י

מתני׳ הממנה אחרים עמו על פסחו • א׳ מבני חבורה שהמנה אחרים עמו על חלקו בלא דעת חבורה: רשאין • לומר לו טול חלקך ולא תאכל אתה וחבורתך את חלקך דאית ליה להאי תנא *פסח נאכל בב׳ חבורות: **גמ׳** ידיו יפות • לישנא מעליא ממהר לאכול הרבה: קבילתון • קבלתוני עליכם לאכול בכל כחי בדמים הללו: לתקוני זביחה • שלא יהא נותר ושיעבד למאכל שאר בני אדם: לאו משום דהוה ליה כו׳ • שיהו עמו אוכלין: דעות שאני • אין בני חבורה מרוצין להיות כל אלו הדעות בחבורתם שמא יעכבו עליהם הסעודה ולא משום אכילה יתירתא אלא אפילו לא אכלי כולהו אלא כחד גברא מלו מעכבי עליה: ממלא כריסו ממנו • כדאמרי׳ בכילד צולין (לעיל דף פו׳) שאין האוכל אוכל בשתי מקומות: לא רצו לא • אלמא משום טירחא הדרי ביה הכא נמי משום פסידא הדרי ביה: לאטרחינן לדידך לא קבלינך • אבל ידיו יפות מדלא בדקו אחריו ש״מ בכל מאכלו קיבלו עליהן: סיבולת • תערובת סעודה של כל ימות השנה: מאי ולא עוד • מאי אולמיה הא מהא: לתקוני זביחה • כמדת איש אחד: דלצוותא • וליכא למימר משום צוותא קבליה עליה בכל מאכלו: רשאין ליחלק • לחלק פסח ביניהן לכל א׳ חלק המגיעו: או אין רשאין לחלק • אלא אוכלין כאחד ונותנין המנות לפניהם כשאר סעודות: ש״מ • אין רשאין ליחלק: כל הני תיובתא • הממנה אחרים והשמש: איתיביה בני חבורה • מרישיה דקתני טול חלקך ושני ליה בההיא משום דלתקוני זביחה קבליה וכמדת איש אחד אבל אנא צוותא קבילת עלך וניחא עלך צוותי לקבולי עלך בכל סעודתי: ועל חגיגתו • חגיגת י״ד שאף היא באה לכל המנויין: מעות שבידו • שלקח מן הנמנין הללו: חולין • כדמפרש טעמא לקמיה שאף על פי שהנמנה כבר הקדיש מעותיו לכך והממנה כבר הקדיש פסחו מתחללין המעות על הפסח וטעמא מפרש: המוכר עולתו • להתכפר בה אחר לא עשה כלום ואין העולה קריבה אלא לשם בעלים הראשונים: ומעות כל שהן • כל מה שקיבל מן העולה והשלמים ואפילו יותר על כדי דמיהן יפלו המעות לנדבת ציבור לשופרות שהיו במקדש שהיו מקריבין מהן עולות לקיץ המזבח ולקמיה פריך מאחר דלא עשה ולא כלום אמאי יפלו דמיהן לנדבה: אמר רבא קנסא • קנסו רבנן לקונה דלא ליקני זימנא אחריתי עולה ושלמים דאחר ואיהו הוא דאפסיד אנפשיה דלא הוה ליה למיקני כפרת אחרים וכי האי גוונא נמי אמרי אינשי *לאו עכברא גנב אלא חורא גנב כלומר המוכר לא פשע אלא הקונה הלכך מעותיו נדבה: אף על גב דשויא ארבעה ויהבו ליה ה׳ • לא אמר אישתכח דמתנה בעלמא הוא דיהיב ליה ולא ליקנסיה: אפשר ידעין כו׳ • והלואי שיהו יודעין טעם זה ויודיעו. היאך • מעות הקדש חל על טלה הקדש אחר ליצאת הקדש של מעות לחולין מי הוציאן למעות *(של חולין) אילו היה נותנן בבהמת חולין היתה נתפסת בקדושת המעות והן יצאו לחולין אבל עכשיו מה נתפס תחתיהם שיצאו הם לחולין והא ליכא למימר במעות שלא הוקדשו עסקינן דאם כן מאי למימרא:

אמר

תוספות

דעות שאני • אע״ג דלא אכלי כולהו אלא כחד תימה לר״י מה צריך לשנויי הכי נימא ליה דשאני הכא דלא שייך למימר הא קבילתון ולא דמי כלל לידיו של א׳ מהן יפות וי״ל דאיצטריך לשנויי הכי דלא נידוק [איפכא דוקא] ממנה אחרים דלא מצי למימר הא קבילתון [הא ידיו יפות דמצי למימר קבילתון] אין רשאין ליתן חלקו ומעיקרא דהוה בעי למיפשט דהוי כידיו של א׳ מהן יפות ה״מ למפרך אדרבה איפכא מסתברא לכך משני דלא מצי למיפשט מידי: **בני** חבורה רשאין לחלק או לא • וא״ת אמאי לא פשיט ממתני׳ דדוקא אם הממנה האחרים עמו רשאין ליתן חלקו וי״ל דאיכא למידחי דבלא ממנה נמי רשאין ליחלק והא דנקט ממנה משום דבכל ענין מיירי אפי׳ התנו שלא ליחלק ואם ממנה רשאין ליחלק אבל בבריתא לא מצי למידחי דפשיטא דאם התנו שלא ליחלק אפי׳ א׳ מהם ידיו יפות אין רשאין ליתן חלקו דמסתמא על דעת כן התנו דאם אין אחד מהן ידיו יפות אין דרך ליחלק בלא תנאי:

מעות כל שהן יפלו לנדבה • ק״ק לר״י דרישא מיירי כשהקדיש מעות לשם פסח כדמוכח בסמוך וסיפא מיירי במעות חולין דאי הקדישן לשלמים איך יפלו מעות שלמים לנדבת ציבור ויקריבו מהן עולות לקיץ המזבח:

ומאחר דלא עשה ולא כלום אמאי יפלו לנדבה • פירוש אי אמרת בשלמא דעשייתו מועלת אתי שפיר דקנסינן ליה שלא ירגיל לעשות כן פעם אחרת אבל כיון דלא עשה ולא כלום אמאי קנסינן ליה כיון שאין ממש בעשייתו ומשני דמ״מ קנסינן ליה:

וזה הפריש מעות לפסחו כו׳ • דאי במעות חולין מאי קמ״ל פשיטא שהן חולין דלית לן למיקנסיה כמו בסיפא כיון דשרי למנות אחרים על פסחו וא״ת אפילו אי הוו מעות חולין מעיקרא מכל מקום איך יכול למנות אחרים אחר שהקדישו כיון דסבר דאפילו במעות לא משייר וכ״ש בפסח דלא משייר מדקשיא ליה אין הקדש חל על הקדש וי״ל דלאע״ג דלא משייר ביה מידי על דעת כן מקדישו שילאו כל אשר ימנה עליו דקרא כתיב (שמות יב) ולקח הוא ושכנו וכתיב ביה (שם) תכוסו משמע דבכל ענין אפילו הקדישו כבר משום דדעת האדם כן:

כי

עין משפט נר מצוה

כג א ב מיי׳ פ״ב מהל׳ ק״פ הלכה טו :

כד ג מיי׳ שם טוש״ע חו״מ סי׳ קטו סעיף י בהגה״ה

רש״ל

כה ד מיי׳ פ״ב מהלכות ק״פ הלכה טו :

כו ה מיי׳ פ״ד מהלכות קרבן פסח הלכה י :

כז ו מיי׳ פ״ו מהלכות מעילה הלכה ח :

רבינו חננאל

מתני׳ הממנה אחרים על חלקו רשאין ליתן להם את חלקו כו׳. פי׳ שלשה שנתחברו וקנו פסח ואמר אחד מהן לאחרים תנו לי מעות ובאו ואכלו עמי בחלקו רשאין בני חבורה לומר (לו) [ל]שלישי ולהוציאו מחבורתם ואוקימ׳ משום דאמרי ליה לא ניחא ליה דליתיב איניש נכראה גבן ואף על גב דאכלי כולהו כחד: **איבעיא** להו בני חבורה שהיו ידי אחד מהן יפות. כלומר אוכל הרבה מהו שיאמרו לו טול לחלקך וצא ופשטנא מהא דתניא בני חבורה שהיו ידי אחד מהן יפות רשאין לומר לו טול חלקך וצא ולא עוד אלא אפי׳ חמשה ועשו סיבולת רשאין לומר לו טול חלקך וצא ש״מ. מאי ולא עוד לא מבעיא קאמר לא מבעיא פסח דאמר ליה לתקוני זבחא קבלנך אלא אפילו סיבולת נמי דלצוותא בעלמא רשאין לומר לו טול חלקך וצא. איכא דאמרי הא לא איבעי להו דמצי אמרי ליה לתקוני זבחא קבלנך למיכל יתר מינך לא קבלנך כי איבעיא לן הא רשאין בני חבורה לחלק או לא ופשטנא מיהא בני חבורה שהיו ידי אחד מהן יפות רשאין לומר לו טול חלקך וצא [ידיו יפות אין שאין ידיו יפות לא ש״מ ואסיקנא אפילו סיבולת דלצוותא בעלמא רשאין לומר לו טול חלקך וצא]. ומעשה דרב הונא בהדי רב פפא ובהדי רבינא פשוט הוא: **ת״ר** הממנה אחרים עמו על פסחו ועל חגיגתו מעות שבידו חולין והמוכר עולתו ושלמיו לא עשה כלום ומעות כל שהוא יפלו לנדבה ופשטה רבא למה יפלו לנדבה קנסא מאי כל שהן יפלו לנדבה דאע״ג דשוה ארבעה ויהבו ליה חמשה כולהו חמשה יפלו לנדבה ואפילו בההוא יתירא קנסיה רבנן וכיון ששמע רבא להא אמר עולא אפשר ידעין חברין בבלאי טעמא דהא מתניתא זה הפריש טלה לפסחו וזה הקדיש מעו׳ לפסחו האיך הקדש מתחלל על הקדש מעות

[לעיל פו.]
לעיל פו.
[תוספתא פ״ז]
[תוספתא שם]
[עי׳ קדושין נו. גיטין מה. ערכין ל.]
[גיטין מה. זבחים לג. חולין מא.]
נ״ל לחולין

משום דאיכא חזה ושוק דכהנים הוא דאכלי ליה וניתי כל חד וחד כהן בהדיה האי כהן היכי דמי אי דעביד פסח דילמא האי פסח הוא ונמצא פסח נאכל שלא למנויו ואי דלא עביד פסח דילמא שלמים הוא ולא עביד פסח וניתי כל (א) חמשה °חד כהן דלא עבד פסח ונימני עילויה הני חמשה פסחים דממה נפשך איכא חד דלא עביד פסח וקא נפקי ביה אלא משום דקא ממעיט באכילת שלמים דאילו פסח ליום ולילה ואילו שלמים לשני ימים ולילה אחד °וניתי מותר הפסח ונימא אי דידי בעל מום האי דאייתי השתא ניהוי פסח אי דידי תם הוא ניהוי האי דאייתי השתא שלמים *דמותר הפסח *נאכל ליום ולילה אחד *וכי מפרישין תחלה למותרות ונטרחו ונייתי מותר הפסח אלא משום סמיכה *דאילו פסח לא בעי סמיכה ואילו מותר בעי סמיכה הא תינח קרבן אנשים קרבן נשים מאי איכא למימר אלא משום מתנות *דאילו פסח מתנה אחת ואילו שלמים שתים שהן ד' מאי נפקא מינה והא *תנן °כל הניתנין על מזבח החיצון שנתנן במתן אחת כפר אלא משום דאילו °פסח בשפיכה ואילו שלמים בזריקה מאי נפקא מינה והא *תניא °כל הניתנין בזריקה שנתנן בשפיכה יצא אימר דקא אמרינן °דאי עבד לכתחלה נמי:

מתני' *האומר לבניו הריני שוחט את הפסח על מי שיעלה מכם ראשון לירושלים כיון שהכניס הראשון ראשו ורובו זכה בחלקו ומזכה את אחיו עמו: **גמ'** ש"מ *יש ברירה א"ר יוחנן *כדי לזרזן במצות קאמר דיקא נמי דקתני ומזכה אחיו עמו אי אמרת בשלמא דאמנינהו מעיקרא שפיר אלא אי אמרת דלא אמנינהו מעיקרא לבתר דשחיט מי קא מתמנו והא תנן נמנין ומושכין ידיהן ממנו עד שישחט ש"מ תניא נמי הכי *מעשה וקדמו בנות לבנים ונמצא בנות זריזות ובנים שפלים: **מתני'** °לעולם נמנין עליו עד שיהיה בו כזית לכל אחד ואחד *נמנין ומושכין את ידיהן ממנו עד שישחט רבי שמעון אומר עד שיזרק את הדם: **גמ'** מאי קמ"ל הא קמ"ל דאע"ג דאימני עליו חבורה זו חוזרת ונמנין עליו חבורה אחרת: נמנין ומושכין את ידיהן עד שישחט וכו': אמר אביי מחלוקת לימשך דרבנן סברי °מהיות משה מחיותיה דשה ור"ש סבר *מהווייתיה דשה אבל לימנות דברי הכל עד שישחט דאמר קרא °במכסת נפשות והדר תכוסו תניא נמי הכי נמנין ומושכין את ידיהן ממנו עד שישחט רבי שמעון אומר נמנין *עד שישחט ומושכין עד שיזרק הדם:

מתני'

תורה אור

[כל הנוסחאות נמצא בגמ' לעיל] [עי' תוספות לעיל מה: ד"ה לימד] [שמות יב] [במדבר ט] [עיין ערוך ערך חי]

רש"י

משום דאיכא חזה ושוק · דשלמים שצריך ליתן לכהן וא"א לתת דהא כל חד וחד שמא האי הוי פסח ונמצא מאכילו לכהן שלא נמנה עליו: **וניתי כל חד וחד** · מינייהו חד כהן ונימניה אפסחו: ה"ג וניתי כולהו חמשה חד כהן דלא עבד פסח ונמניה בהדי כל חד וחד · דממה נפשך איכא חד דקא נפיק ביה ויאכל חזה ושוק של כולם: **דקא ממעט באכילה דשלמים** · בזמן אכילתו שאוכל את כולם ליום ולילה ושורף את הנותר ואם שלמים הוא עדיין אינו נותר ונמצא שורף קדשים כשרים: **וניתי במותר הפסח** · מתחלתו יתנה עליו אם שלי תם היה זה יהיה מותר הפסח שהוא קרב שלמים והוא כפסח שנאכל ליום ולילה [א] והכי תניא בתוספתא *דזבחים בפ' *(הפסח שנתערב) ומשני אין מפרישין קרבן מתחלה לשם (ג) נותר שהילך יכול להיות מותר הפסח והרי שם פסח לא חל עליו מעולם שהרי זה כבר יצא: **ונטרחו ונייתי במותר הפסח** · יבקשו אנשים שנותרו להם פסח חי או מעות פסח ויקחו מהן בהמות ויתנה כל אחד על שלו אם שלי בעל מום היה הרי זה פסח ואם לאו הרי הוא כמות שהוא נותר הפסח לשלמים ונאכל ליום ולילה: **בעי סמיכה** · וא"א לסמוך על זה שמא פסח הוא וקא עביד עבודה בקדשים: **קרבן נשים** · לא בעי סמיכה: **פסח בשפיכה** · בנחת מן המזרק לקיר המזבח כנגד היסוד דנפקא לן מתן דם דפסח מודם זבחיך ישפך במסכת זבחים בפ' ב"ש (דף לז:) ובשלמים כתיבא זריקה שזורק למרחוק מן המזרק למזבח ואין מתן אצבע אלא בחטאת דכתיב בה באצבעו אבל בכל שאר קרבנות וזרקו כתיב וזורק כנגד הקרן עד שהדם ניתן לקיר מערבי וקיר דרומי: **לכתחלה נמי** · בתמיה:

מתני' על מי שיעלה · משמע שאינו ממנה עליו אלא הראשון: **ומזכה את אחיו עמו** · בגמרא מפרש היכי מתמני ומתרץ דאמנינהו אבוהון מעיקרא וכדי לזרזן קאמר שיזדרזו כל אחד להיות ראשון ויהיה הוא לאחיו שיזכו על ידו וכך הודיעם: **גמ' ש"מ יש ברירה** · קס"ד דלא אימנו אלא חד: **כדי לזרזן** · וכולן אימנו עליו בין ראשון בין אחרון: **תניא נמי הכי** · דמשום זריזות נקט: **מתני' נמנין** · הרוצה לימנות **ומושכין** · הרוצה לימשך: **עד שישחט** · אבל משנשחט אין נמנין עליו ואין מושכין הימנו אפי' לר"ש דפליג ואמר עד שיזרק הא מוקים דלימשך הוא דפליג אבל בלימנות מודה: **גמ'** דאף על גב דנמנין עליו חבורה [ז חוזרין ונמנין עליו חבורה] אחרת · כל חבורה שלימה נימנו על פסח אחד ומשכו כולן ידיהן הימנו ולא כרבי יהודה דאמר לקמן בפ' מי שהיה טמא (דף נט:) ובלבד שיהא א' מבני חבורה ראשונה קיים עליו: **מחלוקת לימשך** · בהויא קאמר ר"ש עד שיזרק: **אם ימעט הבית** · אם באו לימעט ולימשך מהיות משה בעוד היותו לשה יתמעטו: **מחיותיה** · בעודו בחיים: **מהווייתיה** · קודם גמר עבודותיו:

תוספות

האי כהן היכי דמי אי דעבד פסח כו' · וא"ת וניתי כהן קטן ויש לומר דגדיפא מינה פריך: **וניתי** מותר פסח · לא כפי' הקונטרס שיקדיש לשם מותר אם שלו היה תם דבזה לא היה טועה הגמרא אלא כרב"ג לר"י שיקדיש לפסח ואם בעל מום שלו יצא בזה ואם לאו יהא מותר פסח ופריך דלא הוי מותר פסח אלא היכא שהופרש לגמרי לפסח וניתותר:

ונטרחו ונייתי מותר פסח · וא"ת ואיך יכשר מותר זה לפסח הא לקמן בפרק מי שהיה טמא (דף נט·) פליגי רבי יוסי ורבי יהודה אי בעינן אחד מבני חבורה ראשונה אבל כ"ע מודו דאם נשאר שעה אחת בלא בעלים דלא חזי תו לפסח וי"ל הכא כשהפרישו ב' פסחים לאחריות וניתותר לו א' דאינו נפסל משום שהניחוהו יחידי וא"ת אכתי למאן דלא בעי עקירה שלמים לשם פסח קשיא ועוד איך ימכרהו האמר לקמן המוכר עולתו ושלמיו לא עשה כלום וי"ל כיון דאיכא איניש דצריך ליה לכ"ע בעי עקירה כדאמרי' בתמיד נשחט (לעיל דף סד·) כגון שהיו בעלים טמאי מתים ואי מותר פסח במעות איירי כדפירש בקונטרס אתי שפיר: **דאילו** פסח ליום ולילה · קשה לר"י דתנן פ"ק דברכות (ד' ב·) כל הנאכלין ליום אחד מצותן עד שיעלה עמוד השחר וקאמר בגמרא (שם דף ט·) ואילו אכילת פסחים לא קתני ורמינהו ק"ש והלל כו' ואכילת פסחים מצותן עד שיעלה עמוד השחר ומאי קא פריך והא הכא משמע דשייך למיתני גבי פסח יום ולילה וא"כ הוי בכלל הנאכלין ליום ולילה דקתני התם וי"ל דהתם הוה ליה למיתני בהדיא אם איתא דנאכל עד עמוד השחר לאפוקי ממשנה דאיזהו מקומן (זבחים דף נו:) דקתני אינו נאכל אלא עד חצות והיינו מדאורייתא דומיא דאחריני וכיון דלא קתני ליה בהדיא ש"מ דסבר דאינו נאכל אלא עד חצות כמשנ' איזהו מקומן: **ואילן** פסח לא בעי סמיכה · סבירא ליה סמיכה בכל כחו בעינן דאי לא בעינן אלא כל דהו לא הוי עבודה בקדשים [ב] ובאין דורשין (חגיגה דף טז:) פלוגתא °דתנאי היא: **הני** מילי דיעבד · וה"ה דאכולהו אמרי' הכי אסמיכה ואמתנות ואנותר ותימה וכי בשביל דשמא יהיה נותר או משום סמיכה דלא מעכבא או לא יעשו מתנות כהלכתן יכנס לידי ספק כרת וי"ל דטוב שידחה ספק כרת בשב ואל תעשה ממה שיעשו רוכס שלא כהוגן כי כבר רוכס עשו פסח: **אלא** אי אמרת דלא אמניכהו כו' · תימה דבפ' אין בין המודר (נדרים דף לו·) מסיק רבי זירא אליבא דרבי יוחנן מהך משנה דשה לבית אבות לאו דאורייתא דאי דאורייתא אבישרא קאי ומזכה להון והכא מוקי לה רבי יוחנן בדאמניכהו מעיקרא וי"ל דהכא ה"פ אי אמרת בשלמא דחשוב כאילו אמניכהו מעיקרא דאין לריכין מינוי והיינו טעמא דשה לבית אבות לאו דאורייתא שפיר אלא אי אמרת אינו חשוב כאמניכהו מעיקרא אלא לריכין מינוי דשה לבית אבות דאורייתא אמאי מזכה אחיו עמו דפשיטא שלא המנה טלם קודם שחיטה מדקאמר הריני שוחט על מי שיעלה מכם ראשון:

דעות

עין משפט נר מצוה

טז א מיי' פ"ב מהלכות מעשה קרבנות הלכ' ... ו סמג עשין קפב:

יז ב שם פ"ה הלכה ז:

יח ג מיי' פ"ג מהלכות פסולי המוקדשין הלכה א וסמ"ג הלכה ...

יט ד מיי' פ"א מהלכות קרבן פסח הלכה ו ופ"ג הלכה ט ופ"ה מהלכות מעשה הקרבנות הלכה יז:

כ ה מיי' פ"ב מהלכות פסולי מוקדשין הל' כב:

כא ו מיי' פ"ג מהלכות ק"פ הלכה ט:

כב ז מיי' פ"ג מהלכות ק"פ הלכה יד:

רבינו חננאל

איפשרו להו בזריקה ניתי כולהו פסח אחד נמצא פסח נאכל שלא למנויו וניתי כל חד וחד פסח וניתי וכו' וניתנו במותר פסח פי' יפריש מעות ויאמר אלו מותר בפסח זה יקח כבש ויתנה ונימא אי דידי בעל מום נהוי האי פסח ואי דידי תם הוא להוי האי מותר פסח דמותר נאכל ליום ולילה כפסח ואמרינן וכי מפרישין תחלה למותר כלומר אפשר להיות העיקר הוא עצמו המופרש מותר לא יקרא מותר אלא אם הקדימו עיקר. ואמרינן ונטרח וניתי מותר הפסח פי' יבקש עד שימצא אדם שהפריש מעות לפסחו וקנה כבש ונשתיירו אצלו מן המעות דמי כבש אחד והוא מותר הפסח יקח המעות מאצל אותו האיש ויקנה בהן כבש ויתנה ויאמר אם שלי היה בעל מום זה פסח שלי ואם שלי כשר היה זה הכבש יהיה שלמים וכן לכל חד וחד והדר' אמאי לא עבדו הכי משום סמיכה דמותר הפסח אינו טעון סמיכה ואלו שלמים טעונין סמיכה התינח קרבן אנשים כו' ואסיקנא אימור דאמרי' ופטורין מלעשות פסח שני דאיעבד לכתחלה נמי מהדרי ואי משכחי' ואפשר להו לאיעבד עבדו ואי לא משכחי כלל פטירי: מתני' האומר לבניו הריני שוחט הפסח על מי שיעלה מכם ראשון לירושלים כו' ש"מ יש ברירה כדאמרי' לעיל. אמר ר' יוחנן מתניתין בששחט עליהם כלם וכי לא אמר להם כך אלא כדי לזרזן במצות ודיקא מתני' כותיה דקתני ומזכה את אחיו עמו. פי' נמנין ומושכין את ידיהן ממנו עד שישחט ר"ש אומר עד שיזרוק הדם ואוקי' מחלוקת לימשך דר"ק סבר מהיות משה מחיותיה דשה כלומר כיון שנשחט נעתק שם שה מעליו ור"ש סבר מהוייתיה דשה מדבר שהוא חי ואיזה זה הדם שהוא הנפש. תניא נמי הכי נמנין ומושכין ידיהם ממנו עד שישחט ר"ש אומר עד שיזרוק ונמשכין עד שיזרוק הדם:

מתני'

מסורת הש"ס

ס"א שצ"ל בתוספתא דפסחים

[תוספתא זבחים פ"ח] מנחות פא.

סנהדרין ד. זבחים לז.

זבחים לז.

גיטין כה. נדרים לו.

[לעיל ס. פח.]

[גיטין כה.]

[גיטין סה. נדרים לו.]

לעיל ס: יומא מט: גיטין כה.

[כצ"ל ערך חי גרס מחיותיה דשה הוא מדבר שהוא חי והוא הדם כי הדם הוא הנפש ערוך]

הגהות הב"ח

(א) גמ' וניתי כולהו חמשה חד כהן: (ג) רש"י ד"ה וניתי כו' מתחלה לשם מותר שהילך.

גליון הש"ס

גמ' חד כהן. עי' לעיל דף עח ע"א תוס' ד"ה ... שם וניתי מותר הפסח. עי' לקמן ... תוס' ד"ה ... עי' בשער המלך פ"ד מה' ...

הגהות מהר"ב רנשבורג

[א] רש"י וניתי במותר הפסח וכו' והכי תניא בתוספתא דזבחים. נ"ב עיין שער המלך פ"ו מהלכות קרבן פסח ...

[ב] תוס' ד"ה ואילן פסח וכו' ובאין דורשין פלוגתא דתנאי היא. נ"ב עיין ביאור כוונתם בזה בספר שער המלך פ"ג מהלכות מעשה הקרבנות הלכה י"ג ועיין כ"מ לעיל דף כ ע"א בתוס' ד"ה דלא וכו':

[89a] because there is the breast and the shoulder [of the peace-offering], which is eaten by priests [only].[4] Then let each one bring a priest with him?[5]—What is the position of this priest? If he has [already] sacrificed a Passover-offering, then perhaps this [too] is a Passover-offering, with the result that the Passover-offering is eaten by those who have not registered for it. While if he has not observed the Passover,[6] perhaps this is a peace-offering, and so he will not observe the Passover? Then let all the five [jointly] bring one priest who had not kept the Passover and register him for these five Passover-offerings, for on any hypothesis[7] there is one [sacrifice] with which he will discharge [his duty]![8]—Rather [the reason is] because he reduces [the time allowed for] the eating of the peace-offering, for the Passover-
a offering [is eaten] a day and a night,[1] whereas a peace-offering [is eaten] two days and one night.[2] Then let them bring a Passover-'remainder'[3] and declare, 'If mine was blemished, let this which I bring now be a Passover-offering; while if mine was unblemished, let this which I bring now be a peace-offering,' for a Passover-'remainder' is eaten one day and one night [only]?[4]—May we then set aside [animals] in the first instance to be remainders![5] Then let us take the trouble to bring a Passover-remainder?[6]—Rather [the reason is] because of the laying [of hands]; for whereas the Passover-offering does not require laying [of the hands], a remainder requires laying [of the hands].[7] That is well of a mens' sacrifice, [but] what can be said of a women's sacrifice?[8]—Rather it is on account of the [blood] applications: for whereas the Passover-offering [requires] one application, the peace-offering [requires] two, which are four.[9] [But] what does that matter? Surely we learned: All [blood] which is sprinkled on the outer altar,[10] if he [the priest] applied them with one sprinkling, he has made atonement?[11]—Rather [the reason is] because whereas [the blood
b of] the Passover-offering must be poured out [gently],[1] [that of] the peace-offerings requires dashing [against the altar].[2] But what does that matter? Surely it was taught: All [blood] which is applied by dashing [against the altar], if he [the priest] applied [it] by pouring it out, he has discharged [his duty]?[3]—Granted that we say [thus] where he has done so; [do we say thus] at the very outset too?[4]

MISHNAH. IF A MAN SAYS TO HIS CHILDREN, 'BEHOLD, I SLAUGHTER THE PASSOVER-OFFERING ON BEHALF OF WHICHEVER OF YOU GOES UP FIRST TO JERUSALEM,' AS SOON AS THE FIRST HAS INSERTED HIS HEAD AND THE GREATER PART OF HIS BODY [IN JERUSALEM] HE HAS ACQUIRED HIS PORTION, AND HE ACQUIRES IT ON BEHALF OF HIS BRETHREN WITH HIM.

GEMARA. This proves that selection is retrospective?[5]—Said R. Joḥanan: He [their father] said this in order to encourage them in [the performance of] precepts.[6] This may be proved too, for he [the Tanna] teaches: AND HE ACQUIRES IT ON BEHALF OF HIS BRETHREN WITH HIM; now it is well if you say that he had registered them beforehand, then it is correct. But if you say that he had not registered them beforehand, can they be registered *after* he has slaughtered it? Surely we learned: They may register and withdraw their hands from it *until* it is killed![7] This proves it. It was taught likewise: It once happened that the daughters outstripped the sons, and so it was seen that the daughters were zealous while the sons were indolent.

MISHNAH. ONE MAY ALWAYS REGISTER FOR IT AS LONG AS THERE IS AS MUCH AS AN OLIVE THEREIN FOR EACH ONE [REGISTERED]. THEY MAY REGISTER AND WITHDRAW THEIR HANDS FROM IT UNTIL IT IS SLAUGHTERED; R. SIMEON SAID: UNTIL THE BLOOD IS SPRINKLED.

GEMARA. What does he inform us?—He informs us this, viz., though this company had registered for it, it can retract
c [entirely] and a different company register for it.[1]

THEY MAY REGISTER AND WITHDRAW THEIR HANDS FROM IT UNTIL IT IS KILLED etc. Abaye said: The controversy is in respect of withdrawing, for the Rabbis hold: [*And if the household be too little*] *for being* [mi-heyoth] *for a lamb*[2] [implies] in the lifetime [*mi-ḥayuth*] of the lamb;[3] while R. Simeon holds [that it implies] during the existence [*mi-hawayuth*] of the lamb.[4] But in respect of registering all agree [that this can be done only] until it is killed, because the Writ saith, *according to the number of* [be-miksath] *the souls,* and then, *ye shall make your count* [takosu].[5] It was taught likewise: They may register and withdraw their hands from it until it is slaughtered. R. Simeon said: They may register until it is slaughtered and withdraw until the blood is sprinkled.

(4) And since it may be a Passover sacrifice and no priests are registered for this, they cannot eat it. (5) I.e., let a priest register for each sacrifice. (6) Having been unclean or on a distant journey at the First Passover. (7) Lit., 'whatever you will'. (8) This is Rashi's text. Cur. edd. read: there is one who has not kept the Passover and so they will discharge etc., i.e., by this device we ensure that all shall have discharged their duty.—The priest then would partake of the breast and shoulders of each sacrifice.

a (1) And what is left over after that must be burnt as *nothar*. (2) Since each sacrifice may be a Passover-offering, we can only permit the shorter period, whereas actually it may be a peace-offering. (3) [The text is not clear. R. Ḥananel reads, let him bring (an offering) and make a stipulation for (it to become if necessary) a Passover-'remainder'.] (4) If an animal is consecrated as a Passover-offering but not sacrificed as such, it is a Passover-'remainder', which is then brought as a peace-offering but eaten only during the shorter period. Hence here, let each consecrate the animal for a Passover-offering. If his animal was blemished, he discharges his duty with this one. But if his animal was unblemished, this is automatically a Passover-'remainder', since it cannot be sacrificed for its own purpose (Tosaf.; Rashi explains slightly differently.) (5) Surely not. (6) I.e., let us find an animal which was actually left over from the first Passover. (7) V. Lev. III, 2. (8) This does not reqnire laying of the hands. (9) The blood was applied to the north-east and the south-west corners of the altar, thus making it appear that the *four* corners were besprinkled; v. Zeb. 53*b*. (10) This includes the blood of the peace-offering. (11) I.e., the sacrifice is valid, though in the first place two applications are required.

b (1) From the basin on to the wall of the altar near the base. (2) Vigorously, from a distance. (3) The sacrifice is valid. (4) Surely we may not arrange at the very outset that the blood should be gently poured out where it really requires to be dashed against the altar. Hence there is no possibility of observing the Second Passover. (5) V. *supra* 87*a*. It is now assumed that only one was registered. (6) But actually he had registered all of them beforehand. (7) But not after.

c (1) This disagrees with R. Judah, who maintains *infra* 99*a* that one member at least of the original company must remain. (2) Ex. XII, 4. (3) The verse is understood to refer to withdrawal, it being translated: And if the household has become too little etc., because some of its members have withdrawn. The present interpretation of *mi-heyoth* teaches that this withdrawal is possible only while the animal is still alive. (4) I.e., as long as it still exists for its sacrificial rites to be performed, which is until the blood is sprinkled. (5) Ibid. '*Be-miksath*' and '*takosu*' are connected with a root meaning to slaughter, while at the same time retaining their connotation of numbering, i.e., registering. Hence registration is permitted only until it is slaughtered; cf. *supra* 61*a*.

a have [thus] safeguarded his master,[1] but you have not safeguarded him! He is unable to marry a [Canaanitish] bondmaid, because he is already half free; he is unable to marry a free woman, because he is still half slave. Shall he be made as nought,[2]—but surely the world was not created for aught but procreation, as it is said, *He created it not a waste, He formed it to be inhabited.*[3] Hence in the public interest we compel his master, and he makes him a free man, and he indites a bond for half his value.[4] Then Beth Hillel reverted to rule as Beth Shammai.[5]

MISHNAH. IF A MAN SAYS TO HIS SLAVE, 'GO FORTH AND SLAUGHTER THE PASSOVER-OFFERING ON MY BEHALF': IF HE SLAUGHTERED A KID, HE EATS [THEREOF], IF HE SLAUGHTERED A LAMB, HE EATS [THEREOF]. IF HE SLAUGHTERED A KID AND A LAMB, HE MUST EAT OF THE FIRST.[6] IF HE FORGOT WHAT HIS MASTER TOLD HIM, HOW SHALL HE ACT? HE SLAUGHTERS A LAMB AND A KID AND DECLARES, 'IF MY MASTER TOLD ME [TO SLAUGHTER] A KID, THE KID IS HIS [FOR HIS PASSOVER OFFERING] AND THE LAMB IS MINE; WHILE IF MY MASTER TOLD ME [TO SLAUGHTER] A LAMB, THE LAMB IS HIS AND THE KID IS MINE.' IF HIS MASTER [ALSO] FORGOT WHAT HE TOLD HIM, BOTH GO FORTH TO THE PLACE OF BURNING,[7] YET THEY ARE EXEMPT FROM SACRIFICING THE SECOND PASSOVER.[8]

GEMARA. It is obvious that if he slaughtered a kid, he [the
b master] may eat [thereof] even though he is accustomed to lamb;[1] if he slaughtered a lamb, he may eat [thereof] even though he is accustomed to a kid. But how is it stated, IF HE SLAUGHTERED A KID AND A LAMB, HE MUST EAT OF THE FIRST; surely it was taught, One cannot register for two Passover-offerings simultaneously?[2]—Our Mishnah refers to a king and a queen.[3] And it was taught even so: One may not register for two Passover-offerings simultaneously. Yet it once happened that the king and queen instructed their servants, 'Go forth and slaughter the Passover-offering on our behalf,' but they went and killed two Passover-offerings for them. [Then] they went and asked the king [which he desired and] he answered them, 'Go and ask the queen.' [When] they went and asked the queen she said to them, 'Go and ask R. Gamaliel.' They went and asked R. Gamaliel who said to them: The king and queen, who have no particular desires,[4] must eat of the first; but we [in a similar case] might not eat either of the first or of the second. On another occasion a lizard was found in the [Temple] abattoir,[5] and they wished to declare the entire repast unclean. They went and asked the king, who answered them, 'Go and ask the queen.' When they went to ask the queen she said to them, 'Go and ask R. Gamaliel.' [So] they went and asked him. Said he to them, 'Was the abattoir hot or cold?'[6] 'It was hot,' replied they. 'Then go and pour a glass of cold water over it,' he told them. They went and poured a glass of cold water over it, and it moved,[7] whereupon R. Gamaliel declared the entire repast clean. Thus the king was dependent on the queen and the queen was dependent on R. Gamaliel: hence the whole repast was dependent on R. Gamaliel.[8]

IF HE FORGOT WHAT HIS MASTER HAD TOLD HIM etc. 'MINE'?
c Whatever a slave owns his master owns![1]—Said Abaye: He repairs to a shepherd with whom his master generally has dealings,[2] who is therefore pleased to make things right for his master, and he gives him possession of one of them on condition that his master shall have no rights therein.[3]

IF HIS MASTER FORGOT WHAT HE HAD TOLD HIM etc. Abaye said: They learned this only where he forgot *after* the sprinkling, so that when the blood was sprinkled it was fit for eating. But if he [the master] forgot *before* the sprinkling, so that when the blood was sprinkled it was not fit for eating, they are bound to observe the Second Passover.

Others recite this in reference to the [following] Baraitha: If the hides of five [companies'] Passover-offerings became mixed up with each other, and a wart[4] was found on one of them, they all[5] go out to the place of burning, and they [their owners] are exempt from observing the Second Passover. Said Abaye: This was taught only where they were mixed up *after* the sprinkling, so that at least when the blood was sprinkled it was fit for eating; but if they were mixed up *before* the sprinkling, they are bound to observe the Second Passover.

He who recites [this] in reference to our Mishnah, [holds that] all the more [does it apply] to the Baraitha.[6] But he who recites it in reference to the Baraitha [holds] that [it does] not [apply] to our Mishnah: since [the sacrifices themselves] are valid, for if he reminds himself [of what the Master had told him], it would be fit for eating, it is [indeed] revealed[7] before Heaven.

The Master said: 'And [their owners] are exempt from observing the Second Passover.' But one has [definitely] not discharged
d [his duty]?[1]—[The reason is] because it is impossible [to do otherwise]. What should be done? Should each bring a [second] Passover-offering,—then they bring *ḥullin* to the Temple Court, since four of them have [already] sacrificed.[2] If all of them bring one Passover-offering, the result is that the Passover-offering is eaten by those who have not registered for it.[3] How so? Let each of them bring his Passover-offering and stipulate and declare: 'If mine was blemished, let this one which I am bringing now be a Passover-offering; while if mine was unblemished, let this one which I am bringing now be a peace-offering'?—That is impossible,

a (1) Lit., 'repaired his master',—so that he should not suffer loss. (2) Do neither and end in futility. (3) Isa. XLV, 18. (4) Which becomes an ordinary debt to his former master. (5) After having ruled in actual practice on their own view for some time (v. Halevi, *Doroth*, I, 3, p. 576), they adopted Beth Shammai's ruling. Now the law is always as Beth Hillel. Before they retracted, he could not eat of his own, because the half in him that is free is sharply differentiated from the half that is not. But when they retracted they would regard him as entirely free, even before he is actually so, since we compel his master to free him; hence he could eat of his own. (6) While the second is burnt. (7) Because they do not know which belongs to whom, and a Paschal offering may be eaten only by those registered for it. (8) For both the killing and the sprinkling of the blood were valid acts.

b (1) And that is really what the Mishnah informs us. (2) To eat subsequently whichever one chooses, because selection is not retrospective (v. *supra*, 87*a*, n. a6). Thus the same applies here. (3) Being surfeited with luxury they do not care what they eat, and generally leave it to their servants. Hence the question of retrospective validity does not arise. (4) Lit., 'their mind is light'. (5) A dead lizard (*halṭa'ah*) defiles. (6) I.e., was it found in hot water or in cold? (7) They now saw that it was alive. (8) [Derenbourg (*Essai* p. 211) identifies the King and Queen in these two stories with Agrippa I and his wife Kypros; Büchler (*Synedrion* p. 129 n. 1) with Agrippa II and his sister Berenice. On either view it is to R. Gamaliel I that reference is here made.]

c (1) How then can the slave stipulate that one of these should be his? (2) Lit., 'where his master is accustomed'. (3) Since this is in the master's own interests. (4) This is a blemish which disqualifies an animal as a sacrifice. (5) I.e., the Paschal-offerings. (6) For in the Mishnah the sacrifices themselves are both definitely fit, but that we do not know who registered for them, and yet if the doubt arose before the sprinkling they are bound to observe the Second Passover. How much the more then in the Baraitha, where the fitness of the sacrifices themselves is in question! (7) Hence even if the doubt arose *before* the sprinkling, they are exempt from observing the Second Passover.

d (1) *Sc.* the one whose offering was blemished. (2) A Passover-offering can only be brought when there is an actual obligation, and if a man not under this obligation consecrates an animal as such, the consecration is invalid and the animal remains *ḥullin* (q.v. Glos.), which may not be brought into the Temple Court for slaughtering. Here four have actually discharged their duty already, though we do not know who they are, so that four of the animals must remain unconsecrated. (3) Because the registration of those whose duty has been done is of no account.

כופין את רבו · בחליה שפחה אין כופין את רבה אלא היכא דנהגו בה מנהג הפקר *היינו משום דכשישחררה שמא לא תקיים כיון דלא מיחייבה וא"ת אמאי כופין וכי אומר לו אדם חטא בשביל שיזכה חבירו והמשחרר עבדו עובר בעשה וי"ל מצוה רבה שאני דלא תהו בראה לשבת יצרה כדמשני (ברכות דף מז:) גבי ר"א ששיחרר עבדו *מצוה דרבים שאני: **והתניא** אין נמנין על שני פסחים כאחד · פירש בקונטרס דברייתא סברה דאין ברירה ולא מצי לשנויי דמתניתין קסבר דיש ברירה דאם כן הוה ליה למיתני מאיזה שירצה יאכל וא"ת ואמאי לא משני דברייתא קתני על ב' פסחים כא' והסתודלו לא יאכל משניהם אבל מתניתין כשהמנוהו זה אחר זה דלדעתו על הראשון וי"ל דמתני' קאמר ראשון לשחיטה אע"פ שהמנה עליו לבסוף: **במלך** ומלכה · שיש להם רוב מעדנים ולא קפדי אם גדי ואם טלה אם שמן אם כחוש: **על** מנת שאין לרבו רשות בו · ולמאן דאמר בפ"ק דקדושין (דף כג:) דקני רביה עד שיתן על מנת שילא בו לחירות ה"נ יפרש שיתן לו שילא בו חובת פסח: **קמי** שמיא גליא · פירוש ולא פסיל כל כך הואיל ואינו בגוף הקרבן:

תקנתם את רבו ואת עצמו לא תקנתם לישא שפחה אינו יכול שכבר חציו בן חורין לישא בת חורין אינו יכול שעדיין חציו עבד יבטל והלא לא נברא העולם אלא לפריה ורביה שנאמר °לא תוהו בראה (אלא) לשבת יצרה [ישעיה מה] *אלא מפני תיקון העולם כופין את רבו ועושה אותו בן חורין וכותב שטר על חצי דמיו וחזרו בית הילל להורות כבית שמאי:

מתני' [ב]האומר לעבדו צא ושחוט עלי את הפסח שחט גדי יאכל שחט טלה יאכל שחט גדי וטלה יאכל מן הראשון [ג]שכח מה אמר לו רבו כיצד יעשה ישחט טלה וגדי ויאמר אם גדי אמר לי רבי גדי שלו וטלה שלי ואם טלה אמר לי רבי הטלה שלו וגדי שלי שכח רבו מה אמר לו שניהן יצאו לבית השריפה ופטורין מלעשות פסח שני:

גמ' פשיטא שחט גדי יאכל אע"ג דרגיל בטלה שחט טלה יאכל אף על גב דרגיל בגדי (א) שחט גדי וטלה יאכל מן הראשון והא תניא אין נמנין על שני פסחים כאחד מתניתין במלך ומלכה *והתניא אין נמנין על שני פסחים כאחד ומעשה במלך ומלכה שאמרו לעבדיהם צאו ושחטו עלינו את הפסח ויצאו ושחטו עליהן שני פסחים באו ושאלו את המלך אמר להם לכו ושאלו את המלכה באו ושאלו את המלכה *מן המלכה אמרה להם לכו ושאלו את ר"ג באו ושאלו את ר"ג אמר להם [ד]מלכה ומלך דדעתן קלה עליהן יאכלו מן הראשון אנן [ה]לא נאכל לא מן הראשון ולא מן השני ושוב פעם אחת נמצאת הלטאה בבית המטבחים ובקשו לטמא כל הסעודה כולה באו ושאלו את המלך אמר להם לכו ושאלו את המלכה באו ושאלו את המלכה אמרה להם לכו ושאלו את רבן גמליאל באו ושאלו אותו אמר להם בית המטבחים רותח או צונן אמרו לו רותח אמר להם לכו והטילו עליה כוס של צונן הלכו והטילו עליה כוס של צונן וריחשה וטהר ר"ג כל הסעודה כולה נמצא מלך תלוי במלכה ונמצאת מלכה תלויה בר"ג נמצאת כל הסעודה תלויה בר"ג: שכח מה שאמר לו רבו וכו': שלי *מה שקנה עבד קנה רבו אמר אביי [ו]הולך אצל רועה הרגיל רבו אצלו דניחא ליה בתקנתא דרביה ומקני ליה חד מינייהו על מנת שאין לרבו רשות בו: שכח רבו מה שאמר לו וכו': אמר אביי [ז]לא שנו אלא ששכח אחר זריקה דבעידנא דאיזריק דם הוה חזי לאביל' אבל שכח לפני זריקה דכי איזריק דם לא הוה חזי לאבילה חייבין לעשות פסח שני איכא דמתני לה אאברייתא [ח]חמשה שנתערבו עורות פסחיהן זה בזה ונמצאת יבלת באחד מהן כולן יוצאין לבית השריפה ופטורין מלעשות פסח שני אמר אביי [ט]לא שנו אלא שנתערבו לאחר זריקה דבעידנא דאיזריק דם מיהא הוה חזי לאבילה אבל נתערבו לפני זריקה חייבין לעשות פסח שני מאן דמתני אמתני' כ"ש אברייתא מאן דמתני אברייתא אבל אמתניתין לא כיון דכשירין נינהו דאי אידכר הוי חזי לאבילה קמי שמיא גליא אמר מר ופטורין מלעשות פסח שני והא איכא חד דלא נפיק משום דלא איפשר היכי ליעביד ליתי כל חד וחד פסח קא מייתי חולין לעזרה דארבעה מינייהו עבדי להו ליתי כולהו חד פסח נמצא פסח נאכל שלא למנויו האי מאי ניתי כל חד מינייהו פסחו וניתני ונימא אי דידי בעל מום האי דאייתי השתא ניהוי פסח ואי דידי תם האי דאייתי השתא נידהוי שלמים לא אפשר משום

תקנתם את רבו · שאינו מפסיד כלום מן הראוי לו : ואת עצמו לא תקנתם · מה תהא עליו : לישא שפחה אינו יכול · דלד חירות אסור בה דכתיב (דברים כג) לא יהיה קדש : לא יסב איתתא אמה : **מתני'** שחט גדי יאכל · רבו ממנו ואע"ג דרגיל בטלה דכיון דלא פריש ליה עליה סמך : יאכל מן הראשון · והשני ישרף : שכח מה אמר לו רבו · שפירש לו גדי או טלה וזה שכח · וטלה שלי · ובגמרא פריך מה שקנה עבד קנה רבו ומנא ליה לדידיה : שכח רבו מה אמר לו · וזה כבר שחט השנים : שניהם יצאו לבית השריפה · דלא ידיע הי דהאי והי דהאי ואין פסח נאכל אלא למנויו · ופטורין מפסח שני דשחיטה וזריקה מעלייתא היא חדא להאי וחדא להאי וקמי שמיא גליא : **גמ'** והתניא אין נמנין על שני פסחים כאחד · לאכול בשעת אכילה מאי זה שירצה דאין ברירה וכי בעי למיכל דילמא בשעת שחיטה לא הוה דעתיה עליה הלכך לא אכיל וזה שהמנה את רבו על שני פסחים ורבו סמך עליו היאך יאכל מן הראשון : במלך ומלכה · שתלויין על עבדיהן ואין מקפידין על סעודתן אם גדיים אם טלאים הלכך אין כאן דין ברירה דתרווייהו ניחא ליה לפיכך יאכל מן הראשון דכיון דליכא קפידא יצא בראשון ידי חובתו ואידך בכדי נשחט: ה"ג והתניא אין נמנין על שני פסחים כאחד ומעשה במלך ומלכה כו' : שני פסחים · גדי וטלה: לכו ושאלו את המלכה · בקיאה וחכמה היתה : שדעתן קלה · כדאמרן שאין מקפידין אם גדי אם טלה : אנו לא נאכל · אם היה אחד ממנו שנשחטו עליו גדי וטלה לא יאכל לא מן הראשון ולא מן השני דכיון דקפיד לא ידיע בהי ניחא ליה : הלטאה · אחד משמנה שרצים המטמאין במגען וביקשו לטמא שהיו סבורין שמתה : בית המטבחים רותח או צונן · כלומר נמצאת ברותחין או בצונן : וריחשה · ופירכסה וגבי טומאה במותס כתיב : בתקנתא דרביה (א)· שאין לו תקנה אחרת דהא לא מצי למימר גדי שלי וטלה שלמים ואם טלה אמר לי רבי טלה שלי וגדי שלמים כדמפרש לקמן (שממעט באכילתו דקא אכיל לתרווייהו באותו הלילה משום ספק פסח וחד מינייהו שלמים הוא) : לא שנו · דנפטרו מפסח שני אלא ששכח רבו לאחר זריקת שני הדמים מה אמר לו אבל בשעת זריקה עדיין הוא זכור והיה אפשר לברר איזה של רב ואיזה של עבד דכי איזדריק דם לשם אכילה איזדריק דהא ידיעי מטייו דידיה : [חייבין · דכי איזדריק לא לאכילת בשר איזדריק דהא לא ידיעי מטייו דידיה] : יבלת · מום לפסול : באחד מהם · באחד העורות ואין ידוע מאיזה פסח היה עור זה ואותו הפסח פסול הוא : ופטורין מפסח שני · ולקמן פריך והא איכא חד דלא נפק : אמר אביי לא שנו · דפטורין : הוי חזי · ארבעה הכשירין לאכילה הלכך הארבעה יאלו והחמישי פטור משום דלא ידיע מנו דלייתי ולא אפשר לאיתויי חולין לעזרה כדלקמיה : חייבין · כולן שאין כאן כשר שלא נזרק הדם לאכילת בשר : מאן דמתני · להא לא שנו דאביי אמתניתין שאע"פ ששניהן כשירין אלא שאין מטויו ניכרין קאמר דאם היה הספק בשעת זריקה חייבין בפסח שני כ"ש אברייתא דספק פסול מום יש בכולן ולא נראית זריקה שלהן קמי שמיא גליא · איזה בעלים של כל אחד והדם ניתן לזריקה שהרי אין כאן פסול קרבן ואע"פ שאסור לאוכלו : ה"ג אמר מר פטורין מלעשות פסח שני כו' · ואברייתא קאי : קא מייתי חולין לעזרה · הארבעה שכבר יצאו : שלא למנויו · שאלו שכבר יצאו אין מניס כלום : משום

עין משפט נר מצוה: [כדאיתא גיטין לח.] [ועי' תוס' שבת ד. ד"ה וכי ותוס' עירובין לב: ד"ה ולא ותוס' חגיגה ב: ד"ה כופין וגיטין מא: ד"ה כל וב"ב יג. ד"ה כופין ועי' תוס' לעיל נט. ד"ה אתי] · י א מיי' פ"ו מהלכות עבדים הלכה ז : יא ב מיי' פ"ג מהלכות ק"פ הלכה א : יב ג שם הלכה ב : יג ד ה שם הלכה א : יד ו שם הלכה ג : טו ח ט שם הלכה ט :

מסורת הש"ס: [כתובות] · כ"א את · [קדושין כג:] · ר"מ מ"ו · ס"א

הגהות הב"ח (א) גמ' דרגיל בגדי אלא שחט גדי וטלה :

הגהות מהר"ב רנשבורג [א] רש"י ד"ה בתקנתא דרביה וכו' כ"ב פי' ש"ס ח"ל סי' קכ"ח.

רבינו חננאל

מתני' האומר לעבדו צא ושחוט עלי את הפסח כו' שחט גדי וטלה יאכל מן הראשון. ואקשי' והתניא אין נמנין על שני פסחים כאחד ומשני אביי מתני' במלך ומלכה וכדתניא אין נמנין על שני פסחים כא' ומעשה במלך ומלכה שאמרו לעבדיהם צאו ושחטו עלינו את הפסח ויצאו ושחטו עליהם שני פסחים באו ושאלו המלך כו' אמר רשב"ג המלך והמלכה יאכלו את הראשון ואנו לא נאכל לא את הראשון ולא את השני נמצאת משנתנו שנויה במלך ומלכה וברייתא בשאר כל אדם וכן בהלטאה שנמצאת בבית המטבחים רותח ואמר רשב"ג הטילו עליה כוס של צונן והטילו עליה כלומר עדיין בחיים הוא וטהר רשב"ג כל המטבחי' נמצא המלך [תלוי במלכה] והמלכה תלויה ברשב"ג נמצא הכל תלוי ברשב"ג: **שכח** מה אמר לו רבו כיצד יעשה ישחוט גדי וטלה ואמרינן מנא ליה לעבד מה שקנה עבד קנה רבו . אמר אביי הולך אצל רועה הרגיל אצלו דניחא ליה בתקנתא דרביה ומקנה ליה על מנת שאין לרבו רשות בו . שכח רבו מה אמר לו שניהם יצאו לבית השרפה ופטור מלעשות פסח שני אוקמה אביי למתני' כשהיה יודע אם גדי אם טלה ועכשיו שכח לאחר זריקה דבעידנא דאזריק דם פסח ראוי לאכילה היה ונפטר בזריקה ואכילת פסח לא מעכבא אבל אם שכח לפני זריקה חייבין לעשות פסח שני : **איכא** דמתני להא דאביי אברייתא חמשה שנתערבו פסחיהן ונמצא יבלת באחד מהן כולן יצאו לבית השרפה ופטורין מלעשות פסח שני . אמר אביי לא שנו א"א שנתערבו לאחר זריקה כו' מאן דמתני לה אמתני' כי לפני זריקה חייבין כל שכן אברייתא כי חייבין שאחד מהן פסול מאן דמתני לה אברייתא אבל אמתני' כו' וקשי' אברייתא ופטורין כולן אם נתערבו לאחר זריקה דאמרינן איפטרו להו בזריקה והא איכא חד שהיה פסח בעל מום ולא יצא ושני' משום דלא אפשר היכי נעביד ניתי כל חד פסח קא מייתו ארבעה מינייהו חולין לעזרה דהא אי אפשר

תמרים ויעסקו בתורה *עולא איקלע לפומבדיתא קריבו ליה טירינא דתמרי אמר להו כמה כי הני בזוזא אמרו ליה תלת בזוזא אמר מלא צנא דדובשא בזוזא ובבלאי לא עסקי באורייתא בליליא צערוהו אמר מלא צנא סמא דמותא בזוזא בבבל ובבלאי עסקי באורייתא ואמר ר' אלעזר מאי דכתיב °והלכו עמים רבים ואמרו לכו ונעלה אל הר ה' אל בית אלהי יעקב וגו' אלהי יעקב ולא אלהי אברהם ויצחק אלא לא כאברהם שכתוב בו הר שנאמר °אשר יאמר היום בהר ה' יראה ולא *כיצחק שכתוב בו שדה שנאמר °ויצא יצחק לשוח בשדה אלא כיעקב שקראו בית שנאמר °ויקרא את שם המקום ההוא בית אל א"ר יוחנן גדול קבוץ גליות כיום שנבראו בו שמים וארץ שנאמר °ונקבצו בני יהודה ובני ישראל יחדו ושמו להם ראש אחד ועלו מן הארץ כי גדול יום יזרעאל וכתיב °ויהי ערב ויהי בוקר יום אחד: יתום ששחטו עליו אפוטרופסין וכו': שמעת מינה *יש ברירה א"ר זירא °שה לבית מ"מ ת"ר שה לבית *מלמד שאדם מביא ושוחט על ידי בנו ובתו הקטנים ועל ידי עבדו ושפחתו הכנענים בין מדעתן בין שלא מדעתן אבל אינו שוחט על ידי בנו ובתו הגדולים ועל יד עבדו ושפחתו העברים ועל יד אשתו אלא מדעתן תניא אידך *לא ישחוט אדם לא על ידי בנו ובתו הגדולים ולא על ידי עבדו ושפחתו העברים ועל יד אשתו אלא מדעתן אבל שוחט הוא על ידי בנו ובתו הקטנים ועל ידי עבדו ושפחתו הכנענים בין מדעתן ובין שלא מדעתן °וכולן ששחטו ושחט רבן עליהן יוצאין בשל רבן ואין יוצאין בשל עצמן חוץ מן האשה שיכולה למחות מאי שנא אשה אמר רבא אשה וכל דדמי לה הא גופא קשיא אמרת חוץ מן האשה שיכולה למחות טעמא דמחי הא לא מחי נפקא בשל בעלה והא קתני רישא ולא על ידי אשתו אלא מדעתן הא סתמא לא נפקא °מאי אלא מדעתן לאו דאמרי אין אלא בסתמא לאפוקי היכא דאמור לא והא כולם ששחטו ושחט רבן עליהן יוצאין בשל רבן דבסתמא וקתני חוץ מן האשה מפני שיכולה למחות אמר רבא °כיון ששחטו אין לך מיחוי גדול מזה: עבד של שני שותפין וכו': רמי ליה רב עינא סבא לר"נ תנן עבד של שני שותפין לא יאכל משל שניהן והתניא רצה מזה אוכל רצה מזה אוכל א"ל *עינא סבא ואמרי לה *פתיא אוכמא מיני ומינך תסתיים שמעתתא °מתניתין בדקפדי אהדדי ברייתא דלא קפדי אהדדי: מי שחציו עבד וחציו בן חורין לא יאכל משל רבו וכו': משל רבו הוא דלא יאכל אבל משל עצמו יאכל והא תניא לא יאכל לא משלו ולא משל רבו לא קשיא כאן כמשנה ראשונה כאן במשנה אחרונה דתנן *מי שחציו עבד וחציו בן חורין עובד את רבו יום אחד ואת עצמו יום אחד דברי בית הלל בית שמאי אומרים

תקנתם

רש"י

תמרים · יש בבבל הרבה: טירינא · סל: כמה כי הני בזוזא · כמה מלאו בזוז אחד: הר המוריה · ושדה דיצחק ובית אל דיעקב כולם בהר הבית התפללו: שקראו בית · מקום מיושב: יום יזרעאל · יום כינוסן מתרגמינן וקרי ליה יום כיצירת בראשית: יש ברירה · שהבורר שבזה נתרצה בשעת שחיטה אלו הודיעוהו: שה לבית · איש בעל הבית יקחנו לכל בני ביתו ואין צריך דעתן: על ידי · בשביל שבנו ובתו הקטנים עליו והלכך הלכך בין מדעתן דהיינו בסתמא כדמוקי לקמן בין שלא מדעתן דאמרי לא אין יכולין למחות וכן עבדו ושפחתו הכנענים על כרחם ימשכו אחריו דסמוכין עליו אבל שפחתו העבריה אף על גב דלא משכחת לה אלא בקטנה דהא יוצאה בסימנין כיון דאין עליו לחנכה יכולה למחות: ה"ג תניא אידך לא ישחוט אדם לא על ידי בנו ובתו הגדולים ולא על ידי עבדו ושפחתו העברים ולא על ידי אשתו אלא מדעתן אבל שוחט הוא כו' חוץ מן האשה שיוצאת בשל עצמה מפני שמחאתה מחאה דקיי"ל (*גיטין דף עז:) יכולה אשה שתאמר לבעלה איני כזונית מעלך ואיני עושה לצרכך: ה"ג מאי שנא אשה · כלומר מאי שנא איהי מעבדו ושפחתו העברים ובנו ובתו הגדולים: ומשני אמר רבא אשה וכל דדמי לה · דהיינו כל הני: שיכולים למחות · משמע שמחאה שלהם מחאה אלמא טעמא דמחאי הא סתמא יוצאה בשל בעלה: ה"ג לאפוקי היכא דאמור לא · אין אנו רוצין דהיינו מחאה: בדקפדי אהדדי · שני הבעלים ואין רוצין ליהנות זה מזה הלכך אפילו נתרצה האחד שיאכל העבד משלו אין חבירו רוצה שיהנה חלקו משל חבירו: כמשנה ראשונה · קודם שחזרו ב"ה לא יאכל משל עצמו מפני שאין חלק עבדו' נמשך אחר דעתו: כמשנה אחרונה · הואיל וכופין לשחררו הרי הוא כבן חורין ואוכל משל עצמו:

תקנתם

תוספות

שמעת מינה יש ברירה · הכא לא שייך מאי רוצה בשעת שחיטה דבשלמא לעיל אשמעינן דאי לא בירר בשעת שחיטה אינה אוכלת כלל אע"ג דס"ד דבתר בעלה גרירא טפי אבל הכא אם רוצה בשעת שחיטה מאי קמ"ל: שה לבית מ"מ · פי' משום דשה לבית לאו דאורייתא והכי אית ליה לר"ז גופיה בפרק אין בין המודר (נדרים דף לו·) ואם תאמר והיאך מאכיל פסח שלא למנויו נהי דקטן אוכל נבילות אין ב"ד מצווין להפרישו לספות לו בידים אסור כדאמר בפ' חרש (יבמות דף קיד·) ואור"י דהתם ילפינן מלא תאכלום ולא אסור אלא דומיא דשרצים ונבילות אבל כה"ג דאיכא חנוך מצוה שרי: על ידי בנו ובתו הקטנים · בפ"ק דב"מ (דף יב:) גבי מציאה איכא למאן דאמר דלא קטן קטן ממש אלא גדול וסמוך על שלחן אביו זהו קטן הכא ע"כ קטן ממש מדאמרי' בין מדעתו בין שלא מדעתו ושלא מדעתו אמרינן בסמוך היינו דאמרי לא וגדולים פשיטא דיש בידם למחות אפי' סמוכין על שלחן אביהן: וכולן ששחטו כו'. קמ"ל אפי' סתמא כיון דשחטו אין לך מיחוי גדול מזה כדאמרינן בסמוך: מתניתין בדקפדי אהדדי · אין לפ' דקפדי שאין כל אחד רוצה להנות את חבירו ולכך אפילו חלקו לא יאכל דאי אפשר שלא יהנה גם חלק חבירו א"כ כל אחד ששוחט עליו וכי השוחט הוא סבור שיהנה חלקו משלו ולא יהנה חלק חבירו דמסתמא איירי כששחט עליו רבו דומיא דרישא יתום ששחטו עליו כו' ועוד דמי שחציו עבד אמאי לא יאכל משל עצמו אף למשנה ראשונה דדעתו ודאי להנות אף חלק רבו כדי לצאת ידי חובה לכך נראה כפי' הקונטרס דקפדי שכל אחד אינו רוצה שיהנה חלקו משל חבירו ושוחט אף על חלק חבירו וסבור שחבירו אינו מקפיד אם יאכל חלקו משלו ולכך חציו עבד לא יאכל למשנה ראשונה אף משל עצמו: *לישא שפחה אינו יכול · ואם תאמר וליתי עשה דפרו ורבו (בראשית ט) וידחה לאו דלא יהיה קדש (דברים כג) וי"ל משום דידה ליכא עשה דאפשר לה בעבד ועוד דבתחלת ביאה מיעקר לאו ולא מיקיים עשה אלא בהוצאת זרע וא"ת וימכור עצמו בעבד עברי ויהיה מותר בשפחה וי"ל בזמן שאין היובל נוהג דאז נמי אינו נוהג עבד עברי *ועוד אומר ר"י דאסור למכור עצמו בעבד עברי כדאמרי' בפ"ק דקדושין (דף כב:) וא"ת ישא חציה שפחה וחציה בת חורין וי"ל דאתי צד עבדות ומשתמש בצד חירות ואם תאמר וישא ממזרת דממזר מותר בשפחה דבפרק האומר (שם דף סט·) אמר רבי טרפון יכולים ממזרים ליטהר כיצד ממזר נושא שפחה ומותר כמי בצד חירות דחרורי וממזירי מותרים לבא זה בזה וי"ל אי חציו עבד קודשין תופסין אתי צד עבדות ומשתמש בצד אשת איש ואי לא תפסי אם כן בעילתו בעילת זנות ובהשולח (גיטין מג·) מספקא ליה אי תפסי אי לא ועוד אור"ת דאין (א) תקנה להרבות ממזרין ואם תאמר וישא נתינה דחרורי ונתיני מותרים לבא זה בזה וי"ל דאף על גב דממזר מותר בשפחה נתין אפשר דאסור בה דקדש ועומד הוא הממזר שנולד מאיסור דלא תפסי קדושין ולכך מותר בלאו דלא יהיה קדש והא דאמרינן ביש מותרות (יבמות דף פה:) דממזרת ונתינה מרגלא ליה (ג) לפי שיכול להכשיר זרעו שישא בנו שפחה ואף על גב דנתין אסור בשפחה האי גברא לא אכפת ליה באיסור דהא קא נסיב נתינה:

כופין

עין משפט נר מצוה

ה א מיי' פ"ב מהלכות ק"פ הלכה ח:
ו ב שם הלכה ט:
ז ג שם הלכה ח:
ח ד שם הלכה י:
ט ה שם הלכה יב:

רבינו חננאל

אמר ר' אלעזר מאי דכתיב והלכו עמים רבים ואמרו לכו ונעלה אל הר ה' ואל בית אלהי יעקב ויורנו מדרכיו ונלכה בארחותיו כי מציון תצא תורה וגו': מתני' יתום ששחטו עליו אפוטרופין יאכל ממקום שרוצה ש"מ יש ברירה אמר ר' זירא שה לבית מכל מקום בין מדעתו בין בעל כרחו תניא נמי הכי שה לבית מלמד שאדם שוחט על ידי בנו ובתו הקטנים ועל [ידי] עבדו ושפחתו הכנענים בין מדעתן בין שלא מדעתן: וכלן ששחטו ושחט רבן עליהן יוצאין בשל רבן חוץ מן האשה ואוקימ' חוץ מן האשה וכל דכוותה שיכולין למחות והאשה כיון ששחטה לעצמה אע"פ שלא מיחת בפירוש שחיטתה לעצמה אין לך מיחוי גדול מזה: עבד של שני שותפין אם אלו השותפין קפדי אהדדי שלא ישמש לזה יותר מזה וכן במזונות קפדי שלא יאכילנו אלא כדי חלקו בלבד לא יאכל משל שניהם ומתני' דקפדי אהדדי ברייתא דקתני יאכל ממי שהוא רוצה בשותפין דלא קפדי אהדדי: מי שחציו עבד וחציו בן חורין במשנה ראשונה דתני עובד את רבו יום אחד ואת עצמו יום אחד לא יאכל לא משלו ולא משל רבו אבל במשנה אחרונה דתני כופין את רבו ועושין אותו בן חורין כו' [יאכל] משל עצמו כי כבן חורין הוא:

סייך לע"ב

מסורת הש"ס

תענית ט:
[עי' תוספות ברכות לד: ד"ה חציף וכו']
[כתובות נח:]
[לעיל פז. לקמן פט.]
[תוספתא פ"ז]
[מגילה יד:]
[כדאיתא קדושין כב.]
חגיגה ב: גיטין מא. ב"ב יג. ערכין ב: עדיות פ"א מי"ג

הגהות הב"ח

(א) תוס' ד"ה לישא וכו' ועוד אור"ת דאין זו תקנה: (ב) בא"ד מרגלא ליה לישראל לפי שיכול:

order that they might eat [88a] dates[3] and occupy themselves with the Torah.

'Ulla visited Pumbeditha. On being offered a basket [*ṭirama*] of dates, he asked them, How many such [are obtainable] for a *zuz*? 'Three for a *zuz*', they told him. 'A basketful [*ẓanna*][4] of honey for a *zuz*', exclaimed he, 'yet the Babylonians do not engage in [the study of] the Torah!'[5] At night they [the dates] upset him. 'A basketful of deadly poison cost a *zuz* in Babylonia,' exclaimed he, 'yet the Babylonians study the Torah!'[6]

R. Eleazar also said, What is meant by the verse, *And many people shall go and say: 'Come ye, and let us go up to the mountain of the Lord, To the house of the God of Jacob'*,[7] the God of *Jacob*, but not the God of Abraham and Isaac? But [the meaning is this: we will] not [be] like Abraham, in connection with whom '*mountain*' is written, as it is said, *As it is said to this day, 'In the* mountain *where the Lord is seen.'*[8] Nor like Isaac, in connection with whom '*field*' is written, as it is said, '*And Isaac went out to meditate in the* field *at eventide.*'[9] But [let us be] like Jacob, who called Him 'home', as it is said, '*And he called the name of that place Beth-el* [God is a home].[10]

R. Joḥanan said: The reunion of the Exiles is as important as the day when heaven and earth were created, for it is said, *And the children of Judah and the children of Israel shall be gathered together, and they shall appoint themselves one head, and shall go up out of the*
a *land; for great shall be the* day *of Jezreel;*[1] and it is written, *And there was evening and there was morning, one* day.[2]

AN ORPHAN ON WHOSE BEHALF HIS GUARDIANS SLAUGHTERED etc. You may infer from this that selection is retrospective?[3] —Said R. Zera: [No:] *a lamb according to their father's houses*[4] [implies] in all cases.[5]

Our Rabbis taught: *A lamb for a household:*[6] this teaches that a man can bring [a lamb] and slaughter [it] on behalf of his son and daughter, if minors, and on behalf of his Canaanitish [non-Jewish] slave and bondmaid, whether with their consent or without their consent. But he cannot slaughter [it] on behalf of his son and daughter, if adults, or on behalf of his Hebrew slaves and bondmaids, or on behalf of his wife, save with their consent.

Another [Baraitha] taught: A man must not slaughter [the Passover-offering] on behalf of an adult, his son and daughter, and on behalf of his Hebrew slave and bondmaid, and on behalf of his wife, save with their consent. But he may slaughter [it] on behalf of his son and daughter, if minors, and on behalf of his Canaanitish slave and bondmaid, whether with their consent or without their consent. And all of these, if they [themselves] slaughtered and their master [also] slaughtered on their behalf, can discharge [their duty] with their master's, but they cannot discharge [their duty] with their own, except a woman,[7] because she is able to protest.[8] How is a woman different?[9]—Said Raba, [It means] a woman and those who are like her.[10]

This is self-contradictory. You say, 'Except a woman, because she is able to protest.' [Thus] the reason is because she protested, but if she did not protest, she can discharge [her duty] with her husband's. Yet surely the first clause teaches: 'Nor on behalf of his wife [etc.] save with their consent': hence if nothing is said, she cannot discharge [her obligation thus]?—What does 'save with their consent' mean? Not that they said 'yes,' but when they said nothing, which excludes [the case] where they said 'no.' But surely 'and all of these, if they [themselves] killed and their master killed on their behalf, can discharge [their duty] with their master's, but they cannot discharge [their duty] with their own' means where nothing is said, yet it teaches, 'except a woman, because she can protest'?—Said Raba: Since they [themselves] slaughtered, you can have no greater protest than this.

b A SLAVE BELONGING TO TWO PARTNERS etc. R. 'Ena Saba[1] pointed out a contradiction to R. Naḥman: We learned: A SLAVE BELONGING TO TWO PARTNERS MAY NOT EAT OF EITHER'; yet it was taught: If he wishes, he can eat of this one's [and] if he wishes, he can eat of that one's? Said he to him, 'Ena Saba![2]—others say, You black pot![3] Between you and me the law will be clearly defined:[4] our Mishnah [holds good] where they are particular with each other;[5] the Baraitha [was taught] when they are not particular with each other.

HE WHO IS HALF SLAVE AND HALF FREE MUST NOT EAT OF HIS MASTER'S. It is only of his master's that he must not eat, yet he may eat of his own? But it was taught: He may not eat, either of his own or of his master's!—There is no difficulty: one is according to the earlier Mishnah, while the other is according to the later Mishnah. For we learned: He who is half slave and half free works one day for his master and one day for himself: this is the view of Beth Hillel. Beth Shammai say: [88b] You

(3) Which grow abundantly in Babylonia. (4) [The text appears to be in slight disorder. Read with MS.M.: For how much are such obtainable?—They replied, For a *zuz*. A *ẓanna* denotes a large basket with a capacity of three *ṭirama*, cf. Ta'an. 9b.] (5) With the cost of living so low, surely they have plenty of time to study. (6) Suffering makes one charitable-minded. (7) Isa. II, 3. (8) Gen. XXII, 14. (9) Ibid. XXIV, 63. (10) Ibid. XXVIII, 19. Visits to the mountain and the field are only made at certain times, but a home is permanent. Thus this teaches that man must live permanently in God.

a (1) Hos. II, 2. (2) Gen. I, 4. (3) V. *supra* 87a. (4) Ex. XII, 3. (5) I.e., the head of the house does not require the consent of the members of the household. For that reason the orphan may now eat whichever he desires and there is no question of retrospective validity. (6) Ibid. (7) She discharges her duty with her own. (8) A married woman can renounce her right to her husband's support and refuse to work for him as she is normally obliged to do. (9) I.e., an adult son and daughter and Hebrew slaves can also protest! (10) I.e., his adult son and daughter and his Hebrew slaves.

b (1) 'The old man'. (2) Probably as a pun on his name—scholarly eye! (3) He was of unattractive appearance (Jast.), perhaps swarthy. Rashi in A.Z. 16b softens this by explaining that he was either begrimed through toil (many Rabbis in Talmudic days being workmen) or that in his preoccupation with his studies he had neglected the appearance of his garments. (4) As a result of your question and my answer the exact conditions of the law will emerge. Jast. translates: this tradition will be named from myself and from thee. (5) Not to benefit from one another; hence the half of the slave which belongs to one, as it were, may not eat of the other's offering.

Continuation of translation from previous page as indicated by ◁

of Uzziah, Jotham, Ahaz, and Hezekiah, kings of Judah, and in the days of Jeroboam the son of Joash king of Israel.[7] And whence do we know that he did not heed slander? Because it is written, *Then Amaziah the priest of Beth-el sent to Jeroboam king of Israel, saying, Amos hath conspired against thee* [etc.];[8] and it is written, *For thus Amos saith: Jeroboam shall die by the sword* [etc.].[9] Said he [Jeroboam]: 'Heaven forfend that that righteous man should have said thus! Yet if he did say, what can I do to him! The *Shechinah* told it to him.'

R. Eleazar said: Even when the Holy One, blessed be He, is
c angry,[1] He remembers compassion, for it is said, *for I will no more have compassion upon the house of Israel.*[2] R. Jose son of R. Ḥanina said [i.e., deduced] it from this: *that I should in any wise pardon them.*[3]

R. Eleazar also said: The Holy One, blessed be He, did not exile Israel among the nations save in order that proselytes might join them, for it is said: *And I will sow her unto Me in the land:*[4] surely a man sows a *se'ah* in order to harvest many *kor!* While R. Johanan deduced it from this: *And I will have compassion upon her that hath not obtained compassion.*[5]

R. Joḥanan said on the authority of R. Simeon b. Yoḥai: What is meant by the verse, *Slander not a servant unto his master, lest he curse thee, and thou be found guilty?*[6] And it is written, *A generation that curse their father, and do not bless their mother:*[7] because they curse their father and do not bless their mother, therefore do not slander?[8] But [it means:] even if they [the slaves] are a generation that curse their father and do not bless their mother, yet do not slander [etc.]. Whence do we know it? From Hosea.[9]

R. Oshaia said: What is meant by the verse, *Even the righteous acts of His Ruler in Israel?*[10] The Holy One, blessed be He, showed righteousness [mercy] unto Israel by scattering them among the nations. And this is what a certain sectarian[11] said to R. Ḥanina, 'We are better than you. Of you it is written, *For Joab and all Israel remained there six months, until he had cut off every male in Edom;*[12] whereas you have been with us many years, yet we have not done anything to you!' Said he to him, 'If you agree, a disciple will debate it with you.' [Thereupon] R. Oshaia debated it with him, [and] he said to him,' [The reason is] because you do not know
d how to act. If you would destroy all, they are not among you.[1] [Should you destroy] those who are among you, then you will be called a murderous kingdom!' Said he to him, 'By the Capitol of Rome![2] with this [care] we lie down and with this [care] we get up.'[3]

R. Ḥiyya taught: What is meant by the verse, *God understandeth the way thereof, and He knoweth the place thereof?*[4] The Holy One, blessed be He, knoweth that Israel are unable to endure[5] the cruel decrees of Edom,[6] therefore He exiled them to Babylonia. R. Eleazar also said: The Holy One, blessed be He, exiled Israel to Babylonia only because it is as deep as *she'ol,* for it is said, *I shall ransom them from the power of the nether-world* [she'ol]; *I shall redeem them from death.*[7] R. Ḥanina said: Because their language is akin to the language of the Torah. R. Joḥanan said: Because He sent them back to their mother's house.[8] It may be compared to a man who becomes angry with his wife: Whither does he send her? To her mother's house. And that corresponds to [the dictum] of R. Alexandri, who said: Three returned to their original home,[9] viz., Israel, Egypt's wealth, and the writing of the Tables. Israel, as we have said. Egypt's wealth, as it is written, *And it came to pass in the fifth year of King Rehoboam, that Shishak king of Egypt came up against Jerusalem; and he took away the treasures of the house of the Lord.*[10] The writing of the Tables, for it is written,
e *and I broke them before your eyes.*[1] It was taught: The Tables were broken, yet the Letters flew up.[2] 'Ulla said: [Their exile] was in

(7) Hos. I, 1. (8) Amos. VII, 10. (9) Ibid. 11.

c (1) Lit., 'at the time of his anger'. (2) Hos. I, 6. 'Compassion' is thus mentioned even in connection with retribution. (3) Ibid. (4) Hos. II, 25. (5) Ibid. R. Joḥanan makes this refer to the Gentiles, who in God's compassion will be given the opportunity, through Israel's exile, of coming under the wings of the *Shechinah*. According to Rashi, R. Joḥanan deduces it from the concluding part of the verse, '*And I will say to them that are not My people; thou art My people*'.—This passage shows these two Rabbis in favour of proselytes. For the general attitude of the Rabbis towards proselytization v. *J.E.* art. Proselyte. (6) Prov. XXX, 10. (7) Ibid. 11. (8) What connection is there between the two verses? (9) Who was rebuked for slandering Israel to God, though they had indeed sinned. (10) Judg. V, 11. (11) *Min*, v. Glos. (12) I Kings XI, 16.

d (1) Many live among other nations. (2) Jast. Or perhaps: by the Roman eagle! (3) How to destroy you without incurring odium.—The boast in the first place was obviously fallacious, as the verse he quoted refers definitely to a state of war, which he compared with a state of peace.—V. Herford, *Christianity in the Talmud*, pp. 247ff for a discussion of this story. (4) Job. XXVIII, 23. (5) Lit., 'receive', 'accept.' (6) I.e., Rome, for which Edom was the general disguise; v. Sanh., 12*a*, n. 8. (7) Hos. XIII, 14. I.e., its very depth compels a speedy redemption. (8) Abraham having come to Palestine from Ur of the Chaldees. (9) Lit., '(the place of) their planting'. (10) I Kings XIV, 25f. The Israelites took much Egyptian wealth with them at the Exodus: v. Ex. XII, 35f.

e (1) Deut. IX, 17: 'before your eyes' implies that they saw something wonderful happen, as explained in the text. (2) Back to God.—Though physical matter may be destroyed, the spirit (symbolized by the letters) is indestructible, but waits until mankind is ready to receive it.

דבלים דבה רעה בת דבה רעה ושמואל
אמר שמתוקה בפי הכל כדבלה ורבי יוחנן
אמר שהכל דשין בה כדבלה דבר אחר גומר
אמר *רבי יהודה שבקשו לגמר ממונן של [נ"ל רב יהודה]
ישראל בימיה רבי יוחנן אמר בזזו וגמרו
שנאמר °כי אבדם מלך ארם וישימם כעפר (מלכים ב יג)
לדוש °ותהר ותלד לו בן ויאמר ה' אליו קרא (הושע א)
שמו יזרעאל כי עוד מעט ופקדתי את דמי
יזרעאל על בית יהוא והשבתי ממלכות בית ישראל ותהר עוד ותלד בת ויאמר
לו קרא שמה לא רוחמה כי לא אוסיף עוד ארחם את בית ישראל כי נשא אשא
להם ותהר ותלד בן ויאמר (ה' אליו) קרא שמו לא עמי כי אתם לא עמי ואנכי
לא אהיה לכם לאחר שנולדו [לו] שני בנים ובת אחת אמר לו הקב"ה להושע
לא היה לך ללמוד ממשה רבך שכיון שדברתי עמו פירש מן האשה אף
אתה בדול עצמך ממנה אמר לו רבש"ע יש לי בנים ממנה ואין אני יכול
להוציאה ולא לגרשה א"ל הקב"ה ומה אתה שאשתך זונה ובניך [בני] זנונים
ואין אתה יודע אם שלך הן אם של אחרים הן כך ישראל שהן בני בני
בחוני בני אברהם יצחק ויעקב אחד *מארבעה קנינין שקניתי בעולמי תורה (אבות פ"ו מכילתא פרשה בא ספרי פ' האזינו)
קנין אחד דכתיב °ה' קנני ראשית דרכו שמים וארץ קנין אחד דכתיב (משלי ח)
°קונה שמים וארץ בית המקדש קנין אחד דכתיב °הר זה קנתה ימינו (תהלים עח) (בראשית יד)
ישראל קנין אחד דכתיב °עם זו קנית ואתה אמרת העבירם באומה אחרת (שמות טו)
כיון שידע שחטא עמד לבקש רחמים על עצמו אמר לו הקב"ה עד שאתה
מבקש רחמים על עצמך בקש רחמים על ישראל שגזרתי עליהם שלש
גזירות בעבורך עמד ובקש רחמים ובטל גזירה והתחיל לברכן שנאמר
°והיה מספר בני ישראל כחול הים וגו' והיה במקום אשר יאמר להם (הושע ב)
לא עמי אתם יאמר להם בני אל חי ונקבצו בני יהודה ובני ישראל יחדו
וגו' °וזרעתיה לי בארץ ורחמתי את לא רוחמה ואמרתי ללא עמי עמי (שם)
אתה אמר רבי יוחנן אוי לה לרבנות שמקברת את בעליה שאין לך כל נביא
ונביא שלא קיפח ארבעה מלכים בימיו שנאמר °חזון ישעיהו בן אמוץ אשר (ישעיה א)
חזה על יהודה וירושלים וגו' אמר ר' יוחנן מפני מה זכה ירבעם בן יואש מלך
ישראל להמנות עם מלכי יהודה מפני שלא קבל לשון הרע על עמוס
מנלן דאימני דכתיב °דבר ה' אשר היה אל הושע בן בארי בימי עוזיה יותם (הושע א)
אחז יחזקיה מלכי יהודה ובימי ירבעם בן יואש מלך ישראל ומנלן דלא קיבל
לשון הרע דכתיב °וישלח אמציה כהן בית אל אל ירבעם מלך ישראל לאמר קשר עליך וגו' וכתיב כי כה (עמוס ז)
אמר עמוס בחרב ימות ירבעם וגו' אמר חס ושלום אמר אותו צדיק כך ואם אמר מה אעשה לו שכינה אמרה
לו אמר ר"א אפילו בשעת כעסו של הקב"ה זוכר את הרחמים שנאמר °כי לא אוסיף עוד ארחם את בית ישראל (הושע א)
ר' יוסי בר ר' חנינא אמר מהכא כי נשא אשא להם ואמר ר"א לא הגלה הקדוש ברוך הוא את ישראל לבין
האומות אלא כדי שיתוספו עליהם גרים שנאמר °וזרעתיה לי בארץ כלום אדם זורע סאה אלא להכניס כמה (שם ב)
כורין ור' יוחנן אמר מהכא °ורחמתי את לא רוחמה אמר רבי יוחנן משום ר' שמעון בן יוחי מאי דכתיב °אל (שם) (משלי ל)
תלשן עבד אל אדוניו פן יקללך ואשמת וכתיב °דור אביו יקלל ואת אמו לא יברך משום דאביו יקלל ואת (שם)
אמו לא יברך אל תלשן אלא אפילו דור שאביו יקלל ואת אמו לא יברך אל תלשן עבד אל אדוניו מנלן מהושע
א"ר אושעיא מאי דכתיב °צדקת פרזונו בישראל צדקה עשה הקב"ה בישראל שפזרן לבין האומות והיינו (שופטים ה)
דא"ל ההוא מינא לר' חנינא אנן מעלינן מינייכו כתיב בכו °כי ששת חדשים ישב שם וגו' ואלו אנן איתינכו (מ"א יא)
גבן כמה שני ולא קא עבדינן לכו מידי אמר לו רצונך יטפל לך תלמיד א' נטפל ליה ר' אושעיא א"ל משום
דלא ידעיתו היכי תעבדו תכלינן כולהו ליתנהו גבייכו מאי דאיכא גבייכו קרי לכו מלכותא קטיעתא
אמר ליה גפא דרומאי בהא נחתינן ובהא סלקינן: *תני רבי חייא מאי דכתיב °אלהים הבין דרכה והוא (איוב כח) [גיטין יז.]
ידע את מקומה יודע הקדוש ברוך הוא את ישראל שאינן יכולין לקבל גזירות אכזריות אדום
לפיכך הגלה אותם לבבל ואמר רבי אלעזר לא הגלה הקדוש ברוך הוא את ישראל לבבל אלא
מפני שעמוקה כשאול שנאמר °מיד שאול אפדם ממות אגאלם רבי חנינא אמר מפני שקרוב לשונם (הושע יג)
ללשון תורה רבי יוחנן אמר מפני ששיגרן לבית אמן משל לאדם שכעס על אשתו להיכן משגרה לבית אמה
והיינו דרבי אלכסנדרי דאמר שלשה חזרו למטעתן אלו הן ישראל כסף מצרים וכתב לוחות ישראל הא
דאמרן כסף מצרים דכתיב °ויהי בשנה החמישית למלך רחבעם עלה שישק מלך מצרים על ירושלים (מ"א יד)
וגו' כתב הלוחות דכתיב °ואשברם לעיניכם תנא לוחות נשברו ואותיות פורחות עולא אמר כדי שיאכלו (דברים ט)
תמרים

דבלים . שתי דיבות דומה בת דומה: כי אבדם מלך ארם וישימם כעפר לדוש: ותהר ותלד בן ויאמר ה' אליו קרא שמו יזרעאל . שעתיד אני לזורעם ולזרותם בגולה: ארבעה קנינין גרסינן ובית המקדש אחד מינייהו . קנינין חשובין בעיניו לקרותם קנין לו כאדם שטורח לקנות דבר החביב לו: שלש גזירות . יזרעאל דהיינו גולה ולא עמי ולא רוחמה: יאמר להם וגו' ונקבצו וגו' בטלה גזירת הגלות ורחמתי בטלה גזירת לא רוחמה ואמרתי ללא עמי עמי אתה בטלה גזירת לא עמי: קיפח. קבר האריך ימים מהם על ידי שמתגשאים ברבנות הם מתים: זכה לימנות . כדיליף לקמיה: בימי עוזיה יותם . סיפיה דקרא ובימי ירבעם בן יואש מלך ישראל: כהן בית אל. כומר לעכו"ם: זוכר את הרחמים גרסינן: כי לא אוסיף עוד ארחם . אע"ג דפורענותא הוא אידכורי הוא מידכר שם רחמים: אכי נשא אשא להם . לשון סליחה ואתמוהי מתמה ומיהו סליחה קא מידכר וסיפיה דקרא דלעיל הוא: רבי יוחנן אמר מהכא ורחמתי וגו' ואמרתי ללא עמי עמי אתה · אותם שלא היו מעמי ידבקו בהם ויהיו לי לעם: אפילו דור . רשעים שאביהן יקללו אל תלשינם: מהושע . שנתפס על שהלשין את ישראל ואף על פי שחטאו: צדקה עשה שפיזרן . שלא היו יכולין לכלותם יחד: יטפל לך תלמיד א' · להשיבך תשובה: גפא דרומאי · נשבע בע"ז: בהא נחתינן ובהא סלקינן · במחשבה זו אנן עסוקים תמיד: הגלה אותן לבבל · שאין כשדים אכזרים כשאר אומות: שעמוקה כשאול. ויפדם משם מהר כמו שהבטיחם מיד שאול אפדם: שקרוב לשונם ללשון תורה . ולא תשתכח תורה מהן מהר: לבית אמן . אברהם מאור כשדים יצא: כסף מצרים . שבזזו ישראל בצאתם ממצרים כדכתיב (שמות יב) וינצלו את מצרים ובימי רחבעם עלה שישק מלך מצרים ונטל את כל האוצרות: לעיניכם . כלומר דבר פלא ראיתם שם שהעין שונה להסתכל בו:
תמרים

תורה אור

יזרעאל. על שם העתיד שיזרעו בגולה: **והגלה** אותם לבבל . והא דאמר בגיטין (דף יז. ושם) רחמנא בטולך או בטולא דבר עשו אלמא בני עשו מעלו טפי היינו לבתר דאתו חברי לבבל:
שמעת

ישראל אחד משלשה קנינין וכו' . א"ר יוחנן אוי לה לרבנות שמקברת בעליה שאין לך נביא בישראל שלא קפח ארבעה מלכים בימיו מפני מה זכה ירבעם להמנות עם מלכי בית דוד מפני שלא קבל לשון הרע על עמוס שנאמר וישלח כהן בית אל אל ירבעם בן (נבט) [יואש] מלך ישראל וגו' אפילו דור אביו שיקלל [ואת אמו] לא יברך אל תלשן אותו מהושע כו' צדקות פרזונו צדקה עשה הקב"ה לישראל שפזרן לבין האומות · מיד שאול אפדם זו בבל שהיא עמוקה משאול . שלשה חזרו למטעתן ישראל כסף מצרים וכתב הלוחות :

[*gomerim*][11] on her; *'the daughter of* [87*b*] *Diblaim'*: [a woman of] ill fame [*dibbah*] and the daughter of [a woman of] ill fame [*dibbah*].[12] Samuel said: [It means] that she was as sweet in everyone's mouth as a cake of figs [*debelah*]. While R. Joḥanan interpreted: [It means] a that all trod upon her[1] like a cake of figs [is trodden]. Another interpretation: *'Gomer'*: Rab Judah said: They desired to destroy [*le-gammer*] the wealth of Israel in her days. R. Joḥanan said: They did indeed despoil [their wealth], for it is said, *For the king of Aram* [Syria] *destroyed them and made them like the dust in threshing.*[2]

And she conceived, and bore him a son. And the Lord said unto him: 'Call his name Jezreel; for yet a little while, and I will visit the blood of Jezreel upon the house of Jehu, and will cause to cease the kingdom of the house of Israel. And it shall come to pass at that day, that I will break the bow of Israel in the valley of Jezreel.' And she conceived again, and bore a daughter. And He said unto him: 'Call her name Lo-ruhamah [that hath not obtained compassion]; *for I will no more have compassion upon the house of Israel, that I should in any wise pardon them . . . And she conceived, and bore a son. And He said: 'Call his name Lo-ammi* [not my people]; *for ye are not My people, and I will not be yours.'*[3] After two sons and one daughter were born to him, the Holy One, blessed be He, said to Hosea: 'Shouldst thou have not learned from thy teacher Moses, for as soon as I spoke with him he parted from his wife; so do thou too part from her.' 'Sovereign of the Universe!' pleaded he: 'I have children by her, and I can neither expel her nor divorce her.' Said the Holy One, blessed be He, to him: 'Then if thou, whose wife is a harlot and thy children are the children of harlotry, and thou knowest not whether they are thine or they belong to others, yet [thou] art so; then Israel who are My children, the children of My tried ones, the children of Abraham, Isaac and Jacob; one of the four possessions which I have acquired in this world—(The Torah is one possession, for it is written, *The Lord acquired me as the beginning of His way.*[4] Heaven and earth is one possession, as it is written, [*God Most High*] *Who possesses heaven and earth.*[5] The Temple is one possession, for it is written, *This mountain* [*sc.* the Temple Mount], *which His right hand had acquired.*[6] Israel is one possession, for it is written, *This* b *people that Thou hast gotten.*)[1] Yet thou sayest, Exchange them for a different people!' As soon as he perceived that he had sinned, he arose to supplicate mercy for himself. Said the Holy One, blessed be He, to him: 'Instead of supplicating mercy for thyself, supplicate mercy for Israel, against whom I have decreed three decrees because of thee'.[2] [Thereupon] he arose and begged for mercy, and He annulled the decree[s]. Then He began to bless them, as it is said: *Yet the number of the children of Israel shall be as the sand of the sea . . . and it shall come to pass that, instead of that which was said unto them: 'Ye are not My people', it shall be said unto them: 'Ye are the children of the living God.' And the children of Judah and the children of Israel shall be gathered together . . . And I will sow her unto Me in the land; and I will have compassion upon her that hath not obtained compassion; and I will say to them that were not My people: 'Thou art My people.'*[3]

R. Joḥanan said: Woe to lordship which buries [slays] its possessor, for there is not a single prophet who did not outlive[4] four kings, as it is said, *The vision of Isaiah the son of Amoz, which he saw concerning Judah and Jerusalem, in the days of Uzziah, Jotham, Ahaz, and Hezekiah, kings of Judah.*[5]

R. Joḥanan said: How did Jeroboam the son of Joash king of Israel merit to be counted together with the kings of Judah? Because he did not heed[6] slander against Amos. Whence do we know that he was counted [with them]? Because it is written, *The word of the Lord that came unto Hosea the son of Beeri, in the days*

(11) Lit., 'to complete'. (12) He interprets *diblaim* as a dual form of *dibbah*, ill fame.

a (1) A euphemism for sexual indulgence. (2) II Kings XIII, 7. (3) Hos. I, 3-6; 8-9. (4) Prov. VIII, 22. (5) Gen. XIV, 19. (6) Ps. LXXVIII, 54.

b (1) Ex. XV, 16. V. Ab. VI, 10. (2) Jezreel, which symbolizes exile (Jezreel = *zera'*, to sow), indicating that God would sow (scatter) Israel among the nations; Lo-ammi (not my people) and Lo-Ruhamah (without compassion). (3) Hos. II, 1f, 25. (4) Lit., 'cut down in his days'. (5) Isa. I, 1. (6) Lit., 'receive', 'accept'.

◁ *For the continuation of the English translation of this page see overleaf.*

דבלים. שתי דיבות דומה בת דומה: כי אבדם מלך ארם וישימם כעפר לדוש: ותהר ותלד בן ויאמר ה' אליו קרא שמו יזרעאל. שעתיד אני לזורעם ולזרותם בגולה: ארבעה קנינין גרסינן ובית המקדש אחד מינייהו. קנינין חשובין בעיניו לקרותם קנין לו כאדם שטורח לקנות דבר החביב לו: שלש גזירות. יזרעאל דהייט גולה ולא עמי ולא רוחמה: יאמר להם וגו' ונקבצו וגו' בטלה גזירת הגלות ורחמתי בטלה גזירת לא רוחמה ואמרתי ללא עמי עמי אתה בטלה גזירת לא עמי: קיפח. קבר האריך ימים מהם תורה אור על ידי שמתנשאים ברבנות הם מתים: זכה לימנות. כדיליף לקמיה: בימי עוזיהו יותם. סיפיה דקרא ובימי ירבעם בן יואש מלך ישראל: כהן בית אל. טומר לעכו"ם: זוכר את הרחמים גרסינן: כי לא אוסיף עוד ארחם. אע"ג דפורענותא הוא אידכורי הוא מידכר שם רחמים: כי נשא אשא להם. לשון סליחה ואתמוהי מתמה ומיהו סליחה קא מידכר וסיפיה דקרא דלעיל הוא: רבי יוחנן אמר מהכא ורחמתי וגו' ואמרתי ללא עמי עמי אתה· אותם שלא היו מעמי ידבקו בהם ויהיו לי לעם: אפילו דור. רשעים שאביהן יקללו אל תלשינם: מהושע. שנתפס על שהלשין את ישראל ואף על פי שחטאו: צדקה עשה שפיזרן. שלא היו יכולין לכלותם יחד: יטפל לך תלמיד א'· להשיבך תשובה: נפא דרומאי· נשבע בע"ז: בהא נחתינן ובהא סלקינן· במחשבה זו אנן עסוקים תמיד: הגלה אותן לבבל· שאין כשדים אכזרים כשאר אומות: שעמוקה כשאול. ויפדם משם מהר כמו שהבטיחם מיד שאול אפדם: שקרוב לשונם ללשון תורה. ולא תשתכח תורה מהן מהר: לבית אמן. אברהם מאור כשדים יצא: כסף מצרים. שבזזו ישראל בצאתם ממצרים כדכתיב (שמות יב) וינצלו את מצרים ובימי רחבעם עלה שישק מלך מצרים ונטל את כל האוצרות: לעיניכם. כלומר דבר פלא ראיתם שם שהעין פונה להסתכל בו:

יזרעאל. על שם העתיד שיזרעו בגולה:

והגלה אותם לבבל. והא דאמר בגיטין (דף יז: ושם) רחמנא בטולך או בטולא או דבר עשו אלמא בני עשו מטעו טפי היינו לבתר דאתו חברי לבבל

דבלים דבה רעה בת דבה רעה ושמואל
אמר שמתוקה בפי הכל כדבלה ורבי יוחנן
אמר שהכל דשין בה כדבלה דבר אחר גומר
אמר *רבי יהודה שבקשו לגמר ממונן של
ישראל בימיה רבי יוחנן אמר בזוז וגמרו
(מלכים ב יג) שנאמר °כי אבדם מלך ארם וישימם כעפר
(הושע א) לדוש °ותהר ותלד לו בן ויאמר ה' אליו קרא
שמו יזרעאל כי עוד מעט ופקדתי את דמי
יזרעאל על בית יהוא והשבתי ממלכות בית ישראל ותהר עוד ותלד בת ויאמר
לו קרא שמה לא רוחמה כי לא אוסיף עוד ארחם את בית ישראל כי נשא אשא
להם ותהר ותלד בן ויאמר (ה' אליו) קרא שמו לא עמי כי אתם לא עמי ואנכי
לא אהיה לכם לאחר שנולדו [לו] שני בנים ובת אחת אמר לו הקב"ה להושע
לא היה לך ללמוד ממשה רבך שכיון שדברתי עמו פירש מן האשה אף
אתה בדול עצמך ממנה אמר לו רבש"ע יש לי בנים ממנה ואין אני יכול
להוציאה ולא לגרשה א"ל הקב"ה ומה אתה שאשתך זונה ובניך [בני] זנונים
ואין אתה יודע אם שלך הן אם של אחרים הן כך ישראל שהן בני בני
בחוני בני אברהם יצחק ויעקב אחד *מארבעה קנינין שקניתי בעולמי תורה
(משלי ח) קנין אחד דכתיב °ה' קנני ראשית דרכו שמים וארץ קנין אחד דכתיב
(בראשית יד) (תהלים עח) °קונה שמים וארץ בית המקדש קנין אחד דכתיב °הר זה קנתה ימינו
(שמות טו) ישראל קנין אחד דכתיב °עם זו קנית ואתה אמרת העבירם באומה אחרת
כיון שידע שחטא עמד לבקש רחמים על עצמו אמר לו הקב"ה עד שאתה
מבקש רחמים על עצמך בקש רחמים על ישראל שגזרתי עליהם שלש
גזירות בעבורך עמד ובקש רחמים ובטל גזירה והתחיל לברכן שנאמר
(הושע ב) °והיה מספר בני ישראל כחול הים וגו' והיה במקום אשר יאמר להם
לא עמי אתם יאמר להם בני אל חי ונקבצו בני יהודה ובני ישראל יחדו
(שם) וגו' °וזרעתיה לי בארץ ורחמתי את לא רוחמה ואמרתי ללא עמי עמי
אתה אמר רבי יוחנן אוי לה לרבנות שמקברת את בעליה שאין לך כל נביא
(ישעיה א) ונביא שלא קיפח ארבעה מלכים בימיו שנאמר °חזון ישעיהו בן אמוץ אשר
חזה על יהודה וירושלים וגו' אמר ר' יוחנן מפני מה זכה ירבעם בן יואש מלך
ישראל להמנות עם מלכי יהודה מפני שלא קבל לשון הרע על עמוס
(הושע א) מנלן דאימני דכתיב °דבר ה' אשר היה אל הושע בן בארי בימי עוזיה יותם
אחז יחזקיה מלכי יהודה ובימי ירבעם בן יואש מלך ישראל ומנלן דלא קיבל
(עמוס ז) לשון הרע דכתיב °וישלח אמציה כהן בית אל אל ירבעם מלך ישראל לאמר קשר עליך וגו' וכתיב כי כה
אמר עמוס בחרב ימות ירבעם וגו' אמר חס ושלום אמר אותו צדיק כך ואם אמר מה אעשה לו שכינה אמרה
(הושע א) לו אמר ר"א אפילו בשעת כעסו של הקב"ה זוכר את הרחמים שנאמר °כי לא אוסיף עוד ארחם את בית ישראל
ר' יוסי בר ר' חנינא אמר מהכא כי נשא אשא להם ואמר ר"א לא הגלה הקדוש ברוך הוא את ישראל לבין
(שם ב) האומות אלא כדי שיתוספו עליהם גרים שנאמר °וזרעתיה לי בארץ כלום אדם זורע סאה אלא להכנים כמה
(שם) (משלי ל) כורין ור' יוחנן אמר מהכא °ורחמתי את לא רוחמה אמר רבי יוחנן משום ר' שמעון בן יוחי מאי דכתיב °אל
(שם) תלשן עבד אל אדוניו פן יקללך ואשמת וכתיב °דור אביו יקלל ואת אמו לא יברך משום דאביו יקלל ואת
אמו לא יברך אל תלשן אלא אפילו דור שאביו יקלל ואת אמו לא יברך אל תלשן עבד אל אדוניו מנלן מהושע
(שופטים ה) א"ר אושעיא מאי דכתיב °צדקת פרזונו בישראל צדקה עשה הקב"ה בישראל שפזרן לבין האומות והיינו
(מ"א יא) דא"ל ההוא מינא לר' חנינא אנן מעלינן מינייכו כתיב בכו °כי ששת חדשים ישב שם וגו' ואלו אנן איתינכו
גבן כמה שני ולא קא עבדינן לכו מידי אמר לו רצונך יטפל לך תלמיד א' נטפל ליה ר' אושעיא א"ל משום
דלא ידעיתו היכי תעבדו תכלינן כולהו ליתנהו גבייכו מאי דאיכא גבייכו קרי לכו מלכותא קטיעתא
(איוב כח) אמר ליה גפא דרומאי בהא נחתינן ובהא סלקינן: *תני רבי חייא מאי דכתיב °אלהים הבין דרכה והוא [גיטין יז:]
ידע את מקומה יודע הקדוש ברוך הוא את ישראל שאינן יכולין לקבל גזירות אכזריות אדום
לפיכך הגלה אותם לבבל ואמר רבי אלעזר לא הגלה הקדוש ברוך הוא את ישראל לבבל אלא
(הושע יג) מפני שעמוקה כשאול שנאמר °מיד שאול אפדם ממות אגאלם רבי חנינא אמר מפני שקרוב לשונם
ללשון תורה רבי יוחנן אמר מפני ששיגרן לבית אמן משל לאדם שכעס על אשתו להיכן משגרה לבית אמה
והיינו דרבי אלכסנדרי דאמר שלשה חזרו למטעתן אלו הן ישראל כסף מצרים וכתב לוחות ישראל הא
(מ"א יד) דאמרן כסף מצרים דכתיב °ויהי בשנה החמישית למלך רחבעם עלה שישק מלך מצרים על ירושלים
(דברים ט) וגו' כתב הלוחות דכתיב °ואשברם לעיניכם תנא לוחות נשברו ואותיות פורחות עולא אמר כדי שיאכלו
תמרים

[ג"י רב יהודה]

אבות פ"ו מכילתא פרשה בא ספרי פר' [illegible]

יזראל אחד משלשה קנינין וכו'. א"ר יוחנן אוי לה לרבנות שמקברת בעליה שאין לך נביא בישראל שלא קפח ארבעה מלכים בימיו מפני מה זכה ירבעם להמנות עם מלכי בית דוד מפני שלא קבל לשון הרע על עמוס שנאמר וישלח כהן בית אל אל ירבעם בן (נבט) [יואש] מלך ישראל וגו' אפילו דוד אביו שיקלל [ואת אמו] לא יברך אל תלשן אותו מהרשע כו' צדקות פרזונו צדקה עשה הקב"ה לישראל שפזרן לבין האומות· מיד שאול אפדם זו בבל שהיא עמוקה כשאול. שלשה חזרו למטעתן ישראל כסף מצרים וכתב הלוחות:

מסורת הש"ס

עין משפט נר מצוה

א א מיי' פ"ב מהל' ק"פ הלכה יא:
ב ב שם הלכה יב:
ג ג שם הלכה יג:
ד ד ה שם הלכה יא:

האשה *בזמן שהיא בבית בעלה שחט עליה בעלה ושחט עליה אביה תאכל משל בעלה הלכה רגל ראשון לעשות בבית אביה שחט עליה אביה ושחט עליה בעלה תאכל במקום שהיא רוצה יתום ששחטו עליו אפוטרופסין יאכל במקום שהוא רוצה עבד של שני שותפין לא יאכל משל שניהן מי שחציו עבד וחציו בן חורין לא יאכל משל רבו:

גמ' שמעת מינה *יש ברירה מאי רוצה בשעת שחיטה ורמינהו האשה רגל הראשון אוכלת משל אביה מכאן ואילך רוצה אוכלת משל אביה רוצה משל בעלה לא קשיא כאן ברדופה לילך כאן בשאינה רדופה דכתיב אז הייתי בעיניו כמוצאת שלום *וא"ר יוחנן ככלה שנמצאת שלימה בבית חמיה ורדופה לילך להגיד שבחה בבית אביה *כדכתיב והיה ביום ההוא נאם ה' תקראי אישי ולא תקראי לי עוד בעלי אמר רבי יוחנן ככלה בבית חמיה ולא ככלה בבית אביה אחות לנו קטנה ושדים אין לה *א"ר יוחנן זו עילם שזכתה ללמוד ולא זכתה ללמד אני חומה ושדי כמגדלות *אמר רבי יוחנן אני חומה זו תורה ושדי כמגדלות אלו תלמידי חכמים *ורבא אמר אני חומה זו כנסת ישראל ושדי כמגדלות אלו בתי כנסיות ובתי מדרשות אמר רב זוטרא בר טוביה אמר רב מאי דכתיב אשר בנינו כנטיעים מגודלים בנעוריהם בנותינו כזויות מחוטבות תבנית היכל אשר בנינו כנטיעים אלו בחורי ישראל שלא טעמו טעם חטא בנותינו כזויות אלו בתולות ישראל שאוגדות פתחיהן לבעליהן וכן הוא אומר ומלאו כמזרק כזויות מזבח איבעית אימא מהכא מזוינו מלאים מפיקים מזן אל זן מחוטבות תבנית היכל אלו ואלו מעלה עליהן הכתוב כאילו נבנה היכל בימיהן. דבר ה' אשר היה אל הושע וגו' בימי עוזיהו יותם אחז יחזקיה *מלך יהודה בפרק אחד נתנבאו ד' נביאים וגדול שבכולן הושע שנאמר תחלת דבר ה' בהושע *וכי בהושע דבר תחלה והלא ממשה עד הושע כמה נביאים א"ר יוחנן תחלה לארבעה נביאים שנתנבאו באותו הפרק ואלו הן הושע ישעיה עמוס ומיכה אמר לו הקדוש ברוך הוא להושע בניך חטאו והיה לו לומר בניך הם בני חנוניך הם בני אברהם יצחק ויעקב גלגל רחמיך עליהן לא דיו שלא אמר כך אלא אמר לפניו רבש"ע כל העולם שלך הוא העבירם באומה אחרת אמר הקב"ה מה אעשה לזקן זה אומר לו לך וקח אשה זונה והוליד לך בנים זנונים ואחר כך אומר לו שלחה מעל פניך אם הוא יכול לשלוח אף אני אשלח את ישראל שנא' ויאמר ה' אל הושע לך קח לך אשת זנונים וילדי זנונים וכתיב וילך ויקח את גומר בת דבלים גומר אמר רב שהכל גומרים בה בת דבלים

האשה. תאכל משל בעלה. דמסתמא דעתה לימנות על של בעלה כל זמן שלא פירשה שיהא דעתה בשל אביה: רגל הראשון. כך דרך הנשואות ללכת לבית אביהן רגל הראשון שאחר הנשואין: תאכל ממקום שהיא רוצה. ובגמרא מוקי לה כשאינה רדופה לילך עד הנה לבית אביה תמיד הלכך מספקא לן בהי ניחא לה אלא אם כן פירשה: אפוטרופסין. שהיו לו שנים והמנוהו זה על פסחו וזה על פסחו: לא יאכל משל שניהן. לא מפסחו של זה ולא משל זה ואפילו המנהו האחד על פסחו מי נתן רשות לחלק האחר לימנות על זה ואין לו תקנה אלא א"כ רצו שניהן שימנה עם האחד: לא יאכל משל רבו. דמסתמא לא היה דעת רבו להימנות חלק החירות על פסחו: **גמ'** שמעת מינה יש ברירה. קס"ד ממקום שהיא רוצה בשעת אכילה קאמר ואמרינן הוברר דשחיטה וזריקה דהאי פסח שפיר איזדריק עלה דהאי אתתא: בשעת שחיטה. ששאלנו את פיה בשעת שחיטה ואמרה בזה אני רוצה: אוכלת משל אביה. מן הסתם: מתניתין בשאינה רדופה. לילך תמיד לבית אביה דבית בעלה חביב לה הלכך כל שאר הרגלים ודאי שייכא בתריה ורגל ראשון ספק וברייתא ברדופה הלכך רגל הראשון ודאי בתר אביה מכאן ואילך ספק: כמוצאת שלום. נתחבבתי עליו ונמצאתי שלימה לו: להגיד שבחה. היאך מקובלת היא בבית חמיה: ושדים. להניק אחרים: אין לה. שאין הנאה ממנה: זו עילם. שהיה בה דניאל שנאמר (דניאל ח) ואני (דניאל הייתי) בשושן* אשר בעילם המדינה וזכה ללמוד ולא רבן תורה בישראל אבל בבל גידלה עזרא הסופר דכתיב (עזרא ז) (הוא) הכין לבבו לדרוש (בתורת) [את תורת] ה' [ולעשות] וללמד בישראל חק ומשפט: ושדי אלו ת"ח. המניקין אחרים כשדיים הללו: כמגדלות. שמגינין על הדור: כנטיעים. נטיעות יונקות שלא נתקלקלו עדיין ולא אירע בהן שבר: שאוגדות פתחיהן לבעליהן. סותמות פתחיהן עד שמזדקקות לבעליהן ואינן נבעלות לאחרים לשון אחר שמגידות פתחיהן של נדה לבעליהן לפרוש מהן ואע"פ שתאוותן רבה: וכן הוא אומר ומלאו כמזרק כזויות מזבח. מה זויות דהתם כתיב בהו ומלאו הכא נמי בנותינו כזויות על ידי שמתמלאות תאוה ואין נזקקות אלא עד שיבואו בעליהן: כאילו נבנה היכל בימיהן. דהכי משמע מחוטבות בבנין היכל תבנית לשון בנין: בימי עוזיהו כו'. משום דאיירי בכנסת ישראל בלשון אשה הנשאת לבעל כדאמרן כמוצאת שלום נקט נמי להא דהושע דכתיב ביה *תקראי אישי כדדריש לקמיה: ארבעה נביאים. לקמיה מפרש להו וכולהו כתב בהו בימי עוזיהו יותם אחז יחזקיה שכולן התחילו להינבא בימי עוזיהו וקיפחו חיי ארבעה מלכים: לא דיו שלא אמר כן. אתה למד ממה שאמר לו הקדוש ברוך הוא קח לך אשת זנונים ולא אמר כן לנביא אחר: (מצאתי כאן הגה"ה מלשון רבינו ארבעה נביאים כולהו כתיב בהו בימי עוזיהו בר ממיכה דכתיב ביה יותם אחז יחזקיהו ובעמוס לא כתיב אלא עוזיהו ומיהו מיכה בימיו נתנבא אלא שכבר נתנגע ויותם בנו שופט על הארץ לפיכך לא נקרא על שמו אבל שלשה היו קודם שנצטרע בעמוס נאמר שנתים לפני הרעש וישעיה ביום הרעש דכתיב (ישעיה ו) וינועו אמות הספים שרעשו עליונים לשורפו ותחתונים לבולעו כמשפט קרח ועדתו שערערו על הכהונה ואותו היום נתנגע והושע קודם לכולן): הכי גרסינן אומר לו קח לך אשת זנונים ואח"כ אומר לו שלחה: וילדי זנונים. שתלד לך בנים זנונים ספק שלך ספק של אחרים: גומרין בה. ביאתם ותאוות לבם: דבלים

האשה. מאי רוצה בשעת שחיטה. ודווקא ביררה בשעת שחיטה אבל לא ביררה אינה אוכלת לא משל זה ולא משל זה אבל ברישא אפילו סתמא אוכלת משל בעלה: **כאן** ברדופה כאן בשאינה רדופה. אור"ת דכל נשים רדופות הן להגיד בבית אביהן כשנמצאו שלימות בבית חמיהן והשתא מוקי מתני' בשאינה רדופה כגון שברגל הראשון שאחר חופה לא הלכה לבית אביה ומיירי מתני' ברגל שני לחופתה והוא ראשון להליכה שברגל שלפניו לא הלכה הלכך כיון שאינה רדופה ספק הוא דשמא גם בזה לא תלך וצריכה לברר אי נמי מתניתין מיירי ברגל ראשון לחופתה ואינה רדופה לפי שמיירי שכבר קודם הרגל הגידה שבחה בבית אביה ולכך הוי ספק אף ברגל ראשון ורישא דקתני תאכל משל בעלה ברגל שני להליכתה שכבר היתה בבית אביה ברגל שלפניו ובברייתא ברדופה ברגל הראשון לחופתה ולהליכתה דודאי דעתה בשל אביה דהיא רדופה להגיד שבחה שנמצאת שלימה ומכאן ואילך דקתני היינו ברגל שני ועדיין לא הגידה שבחה דאז הוא ספק והלכה דקתני במתניתין לאו דוקא דאי דוקא כבר גילתה דעתה שרוצה בשל אביה א"כ אפילו הלכה כל זמן שלא ביררה ספק הוא אבל הלכה לעשות לא גרס ואי גרס צ"ל דלעשות לאו דווקא והשתא אתי שפיר הא דגרס דכתיב אז הייתי בעיניו כמוצאת שלום וגו' וגרס נמי וא"ר יוחנן דמייתי ראיה דסתם כלה רדופה להגיד שבחה:

כזויות מזבח. מה להלן דם אף כאן דם נדות:

בימי עוזיהו. נתנבאו ד' נביאים אע"ג דבמיכה לא כתיב ביה עוזיהו אלא בימי יותם אחז יחזקיהו מ"מ כיון דכתיב קרא סתם י"ל שבתחלת מלכות יותם נתנבא ואז היה עדיין עוזיהו חי אלא שנתנגע ומלך יותם בנו תחתיו בימיו:

אמר לו הקב"ה להושע. ממה שאמר לו לקחת אשת זנונים דריש שמסתמא כך אמר לו וכך השיבו: ירושלמי

רבינו חננאל

האשה שהיא בבית בעלה שחט עליה אביה שחט עליה בעלה כו' כיון ששנינו תאכל במקום שהיא רוצה דייקי' מינה דיש ברירה וכאלו נתברר כי מעת שחיטת הפסח בזה נמנית ושני' מאי ממקום שהיא רוצה בשעת שחיטה ורמינן עלה האשה רגל ראשון משל אביה ואם תאמר ממקום שרוצה בשעת שחיטה מה לי אביה מה לי בעלה ושני' הא מתניתא ברדופה וכרבי יוחנן דאמר מאי דכתיב אז הייתי בעיניו כמוצאת שלום כמה שנמצאת שלימה בבית חמיה ורדופה לילך להגיד שבחה בבית אביה בודאי בשל אביה רוצה אבל מכאן ואילך ממי שהיא רוצה בשעת שחיטה: **אחות** לנו קטנה אמר רבי יוחנן זו עילם שזכתה ללמוד ולא [זכתה] ללמד. בימי עוזיה מלך יהודה נתנבאו ד' נביאים הושע ישעיה עמוס ומיכה גדול שבכולן הושע שנאמר תחלת דבר ה' בהושע תחלה לארבעה נביאים באותו הפ' כו':

לקמן פט.
כתובות פח: ע"ש
קדושין מט: סנהדרין כד: ב"ב ז:
[ב"ב ח:]
שם יד:
[תקראי אישי דריש נמי למילתי' דהושע כצ"ל רש"ל]
[נ"ל מלכי]

CHAPTER VIII

MISHNAH. [87a] A WOMAN, WHEN SHE IS IN HER HUSBAND'S HOME, AND HER HUSBAND SLAUGHTERED ON HER BEHALF AND HER FATHER SLAUGHTERED ON HER BEHALF, MUST EAT OF HER HUSBAND'S. IF SHE WENT TO SPEND THE FIRST
a FESTIVAL IN HER FATHER'S HOME,[1] AND HER FATHER SLAUGHTERED ON HER BEHALF AND HER HUSBAND SLAUGHTERED ON HER BEHALF, SHE MAY EAT WHEREVER SHE PLEASES. AN ORPHAN ON WHOSE BEHALF HIS GUARDIANS SLAUGHTERED[2] MAY EAT WHEREVER HE PLEASES. A SLAVE OF TWO PARTNERS MAY NOT EAT OF EITHER.[3] HE WHO IS HALF SLAVE AND HALF FREE[4] MUST NOT EAT OF HIS MASTER'S.[5]

GEMARA. [Hence] you may infer from this that selection is retrospective?[6]—[No:] what does 'SHE PLEASES' mean? At the time of the slaughtering.[7]

Now the following contradicts this: A woman, on the first Festival, eats of her father's; thereafter, if she desires she eats of
b her father's, [while] if she desires she eats of her husband's?[1]—There is no difficulty: there it means when she is eager to go [to her father's home];[2] here [in our Mishnah] it means when she is not eager to go. For it is written, *Then was I in his eyes as one that found peace* [shalom],[3] which R. Joḥanan interpreted: Like a bride who was found perfect [*shelemah*] in her father-in-law's home and is eager to go and recount her merits in her father's house, as it is written,[4] *And it shall be at that day, saith the Lord, that thou shalt call Me My husband* [Ishi], *and thou shalt call Me no more My Master* [Ba'ali]:[5] R. Joḥanan said: [That means] like a bride in her father-in-law's house, and not like a bride in her father's house.[6]

We have a little sister, and she hath no breasts:[7] R. Joḥanan said: This alludes to Elam, who was privileged to study but not to teach.[8]

I am a wall, and my breasts like the towers thereof.[9] R. Joḥanan said: *'I am a wall'* alludes to the Torah; *'and my breasts like the towers thereof,'* to scholars. While Raba interpreted: *'I am a wall'* symbolizes the community of Israel; *'and my breasts like the towers thereof'* symbolizes the synagogues and the houses of study.

R. Zuṭra b. Ṭobiah said in Rab's name: What is meant by the verse, *We whose sons are as plants grown up in their youth; whose daughters are as corner-pillars carved after the fashion of the Temple?*[10] *'We whose sons are as plants'* alludes to the young men of Israel who have not experienced the taste of sin. *'Whose daughters are as corner-*
c *pillars,'* to the virgins of Israel who reserve themselves[1] for their husbands; and thus it is said, *And they shall be filled like the basins, like the corners of the altar.*[2] Alternatively, [a parallel is drawn] from the following, *Whose garners are full, affording all manner of store.*[3] *'Carved after the fashion of the Temple:'*[4] both the one and the other, the Writ ascribes [praise] to them as though the Temple were built in their days.

The word of the Lord that came unto Hosea the son of Beeri, in the days of Uzziah, Jotham, Ahaz, and Hezekiah, kings of Judah:[5] Four prophets prophesied in one age, and the greatest of all of them was Hosea. For it is said, *The Lord spoke at first with Hosea:*[6] did He then speak first with Hosea; were there not many prophets from Moses until Hosea? Said R. Joḥanan: He was the first of four prophets who prophesied in that age, and these are they: Hosea, Isaiah, Amos and Micah. The Holy One, blessed be He, said to Hosea, 'Thy children have sinned,' to which he should have replied, 'They are Thy children, they are the children of Thy favoured ones, they are the children of Abraham, Isaac, and Jacob; extend[7] Thy mercy to them.' Not enough that he did not say thus, but he said to Him: 'Sovereign of the Universe! The whole world is Thine; exchange them for a different nation.' Said the Holy One, blessed be He, 'What shall I do with this old man? I will order him: "Go and marry[8] a harlot and beget thee children of harlotry"; and then I will order him: "Send her away from thy presence." If he will be able to send [her] away, so will I too send Israel away.' For it is said, *And the Lord said unto Hosea: 'Go, take unto thee a wife of harlotry and children of harlotry';*[9] and it is written, *So he went and took Gomer the daughter of Diblaim.*[10] *'Gomer':* Rab said, [That intimates] that all satisfied their lust

a (1) It was the custom for a woman to spend the first Festival after her marriage in her father's house. (2) He had more than one guardian, and each killed a Passover-offering with him as one of its eaters. (3) Even if one specifically registered him in his company, since half of the slave belongs to another man. Hence he may eat only if both agree that he should be registered with one.—A slave in a Jewish house has the status of a semi-Jew, and if circumcised he ate of the Paschal offering (v. Ex. XII, 44). (4) E.g. he had belonged to two masters, and one had manumitted him. (5) As we assume that his master did not count in the free half. (6) Lit., 'there is *bererah*'. *Bererah* is a technical term denoting that a choice or selection made now has retrospective validity in a legal sense. For it is assumed that the Mishnah means that the woman may eat of whichever offering she desires *now*, though she had not yet made her choice when it was killed and its blood was sprinkled. But the Passover-offering may be eaten only by those who had registered for it and on whose behalf it was killed. Hence when we say that her *present* choice permits her to eat thereof, it proves that this choice is retrospectively valid, as though she had declared it before the offering was killed. Actually there is a controversy (B.Ḳ. 51*b*; Beẓ. 38*a*; Giṭ. 25*a*) in this matter. (7) It was then that she had declared her choice.

b (1) Whereas the Misnah states that at the *first* Festival she makes her choice. (2) Then she eats of her father's even if she had not expressed her desire previously, as it is taken for granted. Cf. Keth. 71*b*, and notes. (3) Cant. VIII, 10. (4) Var. lec.: it is written, this introducing a new passage. (5) Hos. II, 18. (6) I.e., like a bride who has already gone over to her husband completely, and is more intimate with him (viz., after *nissu'in*, the completion of marriage), and not like a bride in her father's house, which is after *erusin* (betrothal) only (Rashal). (7) Cant. VIII, 8. (8) V. Sanh., 24*a*, n. 5. (9) Ibid. 10. (10) Ps. CXLIV, 12 On *hekal* v. *infra* 95*b*, n. b6. E.V.: *a palace*.

c (1) Lit., 'seal their openings'. (2) Zech. IX, 15. (3) Ps. CXLIV, 13. (4) Ibid. 12. (5) Hos. I, 1. (6) Ibid. 2. lit. translation. E.V.: *When the Lord* etc. (7) Lit., 'roll'. (8) Lit., 'take'. (9) Ibid. (10) Ibid. 3.

this teaches that the eater may eat in two places.[5] [86b] You might think that it may be eaten in two companies. Therefore it is stated, '*In one house shall it be eaten.*'[6] Wherein do they differ? R. Judah holds: The traditional [non-vocalized] text is authoritative; while R. Simeon holds: The text as read [as vocalized] is authoritative.[7]

If they were sitting [in one company], and a partition was spread between them,[8]—on the view that [one] Paschal lamb may be eaten in two companies, they may eat [thus]; [but] on the view that [one] Paschal lamb may not be eaten in two companies, they may not eat [thus]. If they were sitting[9], when the partition was removed from between them:[10] on the view that the eater may eat in two places, they may [go on] eating [thus]; but on the view that the eater may not eat in two places, they may not [go on] eating. R. Kahana sat [and] stated this as a definite ruling. Said R. Ashi to R. Kahana: You should [rather] ask it as a question: Does the removing of a partition or the setting up of a partition transform it into two places or two companies [respectively] or not? The question stands over.

THE BRIDE TURNS HER FACE AWAY etc. What is the reason? —Said R. Ḥiyya b. Abba in R. Joḥanan's name: Because she is
a modest.[1]

R. Huna the son of R. Nathan visited the home of R. Naḥman b. Isaac. They asked him, 'What is your name?' 'Rab Huna,' replied he.[2] 'Would you, Sir, sit down on the couch,' said they, and he sat down. Then they offered him a goblet, which he accepted at the first [invitation][3] but he drank it in two times, without turning his face away. They asked him, 'What is the reason that you called yourself *Rab* Huna?' [He replied:] 'That is my name.'[4] 'What is the reason that when they told you to sit on the couch you did sit?'[5] Said he to them: 'Whatever your host tells you, do.'[6] 'What is the reason that when a goblet was offered you you accepted it at the first invitation?' Said he to them: 'One must show reluctance to a small man, but one must not show reluctance to a great man.' 'Why did you drink it in two times?' —Said he to them: 'Because it was taught: He who drinks his goblet in once is a gourmand; in two times, shows good breeding; in three times, is of the arrogant.' 'Why did you not turn your face away?'[7]—'We learned, A BRIDE TURNS HER FACE AWAY,' replied he.[8]

R. Ishmael son of R. Jose visited the home of R. Simeon b. R. Jose b. Lakunia. They offered him a goblet, which he accepted at the first invitation and drank in one draught. Said they to him: 'Do you not agree that he who drinks his goblet in one draught is greedy'? Said he to them: 'This was not said when your goblet is small, your wine sweet, and my stomach broad'.[9]

R. Huna said: The members of a company enter three at a time,
b and depart even singly.[1] Rabbah observed: But that is only if they enter at the time when people generally enter,[2] and providing that the attendant had taken notice of them.[3] Rabina said: And they must make their [full] payment;[4] and the last must pay extra.[5] But the law does not agree with him.

(5) '*They shall eat*' referring to each individual separately, who is thus permitted to eat in '*the houses*'. (6) Each Paschal lamb must be eaten in one company, but the person is not bound to retain the same position in the company all the time. (7) V. n. d1; also Sanh., 4*a*, n. 4. (8) Thus transforming them into two companies. (9) In two rooms. (10) Thus making them into one company; furthermore, a new area is added to each, and this renders the whole as another place.

a (1) And as a bride she is naturally the cynosure of all eyes. (2) Mentioning his title of Rabbi. (3) Lit., 'in one time'—he did not wait to be pressed a second time. (4) Lit., 'I am the master of the name'. Rashi: I have been called *Rab* Huna even as a child. Thus *Rab* in his case was a proper name, not only a title. [R. Ḥananel: an ordained Rabbi and known by this designation.] (5) The couch was reserved for distinguished visitors, others sitting on ordinary stools. His immediate compliance therefore savoured of arrogance. (6) Var. lec.: except 'depart'. The text reads better without this addition, but if it is retained it was probably meant humorously—a guest should not outstay his welcome until he is told to go! (7) Which would have been more mannerly in their opinion. (8) But not others. (9) R. Ishmael was very stout, v. 84*a*.

b (1) Rashi: This does not refer particularly to the Passover-offering. The members of a company should enter for meals three at a time in order to facilitate the work of the waiter, but may depart even singly though the waiter has still to attend on the rest. R. Ḥan.: When a company registers for a Passover-offering and three of them (but not less) enter the house at the normal time for eating, they can eat without waiting for the rest. But if they had already assembled and then left for some purpose, even if only one is left he can eat alone and need not wait for their return. (2) I.e., not earlier, in which case they must wait for the rest. (3) According to Rashi: They notified the waiter of their intention to depart singly. R. Ḥananel: The waiter had been sent to find them and failed. MS.M. too reads: the attendant had searched for them. (4) [To the waiter for the extra trouble incurred. R. Ḥananel: the one who eats the Paschal lamb on his own, if he ate more than his share, v. *Aruch* s.v. דייל.] (5) To the waiter for the extra trouble incurred. [R. Ḥananel omits this clause.]

ומר סבר יש אם למקרא . וא"ת והא שמעינן ליה לרבי שמעון בפ"ק דקדושין (דף יח:) דאית ליה יש אם למקרא ולמסורת דדריש בבגדו בה כבוגדו בה דאין אדם מוכר את בתו לשפחות אחר אישות ולא *לאישות אחר שפחות י"ל דהתם לא כתרי אהדדי ויכול לדרוש שניהם אבל הכא דליכא למידרש אלא חד דריש מקרא וכן בפ"ק דסנהדרין (דף ד·) והא דאמר לעיל (דף פה·) המוליא בשר פסח מחבורה לחבורה הרי הוא בלא תעשה אתי אפילו למאן דאמר פסח נאכל בשתי חבורות דאחר שנחלק ולקחו כל חבורה חלקה אסור להוליא חלק חבורה זו לחבורה אחרת :

*__הכלה__ הופכת פניה · אילטריך לאשמעינן דלא חשבינן כשתי מקומות אע"פ שאכלה מקלת סעודה בלא הפיכת פניה אי נמי קמ"ל דחייבת להפוך פניה כדאמר בגמרא כלה תנן :

אין מסרבין לגדול . אמאי דיתיב אפוריא לא שייך למימר משום דאין מסרבין דישיבת פוריא דבר גסות ושררה הוא ולא היה לו לישב אי לאו משום כל מה שיאמר בעל הבית עשה:(א)**נכנסין** בג' כו' . פירש ר"ח חבורה שנמנו על הפסח ובאו מקלת מהן בעת שדרך בני אדם לאכול ושגרו הדיילא פי' שמש לחפש אחריהם ולא מלאן אם נתקבצו רק שלשה אוכלין את הפסח ואין עליהן להמתין עד שיבואו כולם אבל פחות משלשה לא אבל אם היו מקובצים יחד ויצאו ונתאחרו והדר בהו דיילא ולא מלאן אפילו לא נשאר רק אחד מהם אין לריך להמתין כיון שהיו שם ויצאו :

אמר רבינא ונותן דמים · האוכל פסח ולית הלכתא כוותיה והנ"מ דעל בעידנא דעיילי אינשי והדר בהו דיילא :

הדרן עלך כיצד צולין

יכול יהא. עיקרו של פסח נאכל בשתי חבורות: ת"ל בבית אחד יאכל · וקסבר יש אם למקרא יאכל הפסח קאי ולא אגברי כלומר עיקר תחלת אכילתו תהא בחבורה אחת ולא יתחלק לשתי חבורות אבל גברא אי בעי קאי מהכא ואזיל ואכיל הכא דלא קפיד רחמנא אלא אעיקר תחלת אכילה מדקרינן יאכל הפסח ולא יאכל אגברא ואני שמעתי חילוף ר' יהודה סבר יש אם למקרא בבית אחד ולא בשני מקומות ור"ש סבר יש אם למסורת שמסר אונקלוס הגר בחבורה חדא יתאכל אבל אשני מקומות לא קפיד וקשה לי לאומרו דלא שמעתי מסורת כזה מעולם ועוד דקיימא לן דר' שמעון יש אם למקרא ס"ל בשמעתא קמייתא דסנהדרין* ועוד לישנא דברייתא דייקא כוותי דגבי חבורות נקט פסח נאכל ולא נקט שתי חבורות אוכלין אותו וגבי מקומות נקט האוכל אוכל ולא נקט פסח נאכל הלכך כי דרשינן בבית אחד יאכל במקרא אפסח משמע למעוטי חבורות וכי דרשינן יאכל אגברי משמע למעוטי מקומות : ונפרסה מחילה ביניהן גרסינן . היו יושבין חבורה אחת ואוכלין פסח אחד ונפרסה מחילה ביניהן ועשאום שני חבורות לדברי האומר פסח נאכל בשתי חבורות גומרין אכילתן ואע"ג דמאן דאית ליה פסח נאכל בשתי חבורות אוסר לאדם לאכול בשני מקומות הכא לא נעשה לכל חבורה וחבורה מקומם כמקום אחר שהרי אינו רואה אויר שלא ראה עד עכשיו ואין כאן מקום חדש : היו יושבין . ב' חבורות בשני בתים ואכלו שם פסחיהם ונסתלקה המחילה יש כאן אויר חדש ונעשה לכל חבורה כמקום אחר והוי ליה כאוכלים במקום הראשון ובשני הלכך לדברי האומר אין האוכל אוכל בשני מקומות אין אוכלים : פשיט ליה מפשט . אומרה לשמועה זו פשוטה ומפורשת כמו שאמרנו שעשיית מחילה עושה אותן שתי חבורות וסילוק מחילה עושה אותן שני מקומות ולא מספקא ליה בה מידי : מ"ט . למה לה להפוך פניה ומאי אורחה בהכי : מפני שהיא בושה . לאכול לעיני האנשים על ידי שמסתכלין בה : יתיב . ומטה מקום הסב חשובין היא והקטנים יושבין על גבי ספסלין ונוהג עלמו בחשיבות: קבליה בחד זימנא . ולא סריב עד שיפלרו בו : ושתייה בתרי זימני . הפסיק בו : ולא אהדר אפיה . לצד אחר אלא שתה לעיניהן : בעל השם אנא . מקטנותי כך קוראין לי רב הונא : מ"ט כי אמרי לך תיב אפוריא איתיבת . ולא ישבת על גבי קרקע ולא על גבי ספסל ולהכי בעו ליה שלא היה מנהגם כך ותמיהא להו : כל מה שיאמר לך בעל הבית עשה . מתניתא היא במסכת דרך ארץ (בפרק בן עזאי) (ד"א רבה פ"ה) : מסרבין לקטן . מלקבל דבריו עד שיפליר בו : ואין מסרבין לגדול . שכן במלאכים שאמרו לאברהם כן תעשה (בראשית יח) ולא סירבו בו וללוט אמרו כי ברחוב נלין עד ויפלר בם מאד (שם יט) : כלה הופכת פניה תנן . ואין דרך האיש להפוך פניו : רבי ישמעאל בר רבי יוסי כריסו רחבה הואי כדאמרינן בהשוכר את הפועלים (ב"מ דף פד·) : בני חבורה . לאו בפסח קאי : בני חבורה . שמש המשמש בסעודתן נכנסין בשלשה להסב ואם בא יחיד או שנים והסבו אין על השמש לשמש עלייהו : ויולאין באחד אחד . כל מי שסיים אכילתו קודם אם בא ללאת ילא ואע"פ שקשה לשמש לשרת היחידים הנשארין : והוא דעיילי בעידנא דעיילי אינשי . שאין האחרון מאריך יותר משעת סעודת האחרים וגם בכניסתן לא יאחרו להסב כדי לאחר השמש עד זמן גמר שעת סעודה : והוא דרגש בהו דיילא . שהודיעו לשמש שזה דרכן ללאת אחד אחד לפי שטורח הוא לו לשמש היחידים : וצריך האחרון להוסיף דמים . לשמש :

יכול יהא נאכל בשתי חבורות ת"ל בבית אחד יאכל במאי קמיפלגי רבי יהודה סבר יש אם למסורת ור' שמעון סבר *יש אם למקרא היו יושבין ונפרסה מחיצה ביניהם לדברי האומר פסח נאכל בשתי חבורות אוכלין לדברי האומר אין הפסח נאכל בשתי חבורות אין אוכלין היו יושבין ונסתלקה מחיצה ביניהן לדברי האומר האוכל אוכל בשני מקומות אוכלין לדברי האומר אין האוכל אוכל בשני מקומות אין אוכלין יתיב רב כהנא קא פשיט ליה מפשט א"ל רב אשי לרב כהנא ותיבעי לך איבעיא סילוק מחיצה ועשיית מחיצה מי הוי כב' מקומות וכב' חבורות דמי או לא *תיקו : הכלה הופכת את פניה וכו' : מ"ט א"ר חייא בר אבא א"ר יוחנן מפני שהיא בושה רב הונא בריה דרב נתן איקלע לבי רב נחמן בר יצחק אמרו ליה מה שמך אמר להו רב הונא אמרו ניתיב מר אפוריא יתיב יהבו ליה כסא קבליה בחד זימנא ושתייה בתרי זימני *ולא אהדר אפיה אמרו ליה מ"ט קרית לך רב הונא אמר להו בעל השם אני מ"ט כי אמרו לך ניתיב אפוריא יתבת אמר להו כל מה שיאמר לך בעל הבית עשה (**חוץ מצא) מאי טעמא כי יהבי לך כסא קבלת בחד זימנא אמר להו מסרבין לקטן ואין מסרבין לגדול מ"ט אשתיתיה בתרי זימני אמר להו *דתניא השותה כוסו בבת אחת הרי זה גרגרן שנים דרך ארץ שלשה מגסי הרוח מאי טעמא לא אהדרת אפך אמר להו כלה הופכת פניה תנן *ר' ישמעאל ברבי יוסי איקלע לבי רבי שמעון בן לקוניא יהבו ליה כסא קבליה בחד זימנא ושתייה בחד זימנא אמרי ליה לא סבר לה מר השותה כוסו בבת אחת הרי זה גרגרן אמר להו לא אמרי בכוסך קטן ויינך מתוק וכריסי רחבה אמר רב הונא *בני חבורה נכנסין בשלשה ויוצאין אפילו באחד אמר רבה והוא דעייל בעידנא דרגילי למיעל והוא דרגש בהו דיילא אמר רבינא ונותנין שכר דמים וצריך האחרון להוסיף דמים ולית הלכתא כוותיה :

הדרן עלך כיצד צולין

רבינו חננאל

אוכלו בשני מקומות מכאן שהפסח נאכל בשני בתים יכול יהא נאכל בשתי חבורות ת"ל בבית אחד יאכל במאי פליגי רבי יהודה סבר יש אם למסורת יאכל כתיב בבית אחד יש רשות לאוכל לאכלו ולאוכל קא מזהיר רחמנא שלא יאכל אותו אלא במקום אחד בלבד ולא בשני מקומות ורבי שמעון סבר יש אם למקרא יאכל קוראים על הפסח קא מזהיר רחמנא להאכל בחבורה אחת ולא בשתי חבורות אבל חבורה אחת בשני מקומות רשאין וקיימא לן כרבי יהודה דתנן סתמא כותיה: **נפרצה** מחיצה ביניהם ונתפרדו חצים לחד וחצים לחד נעשו כשתי חבורות בפסח אחד וכן אם היו שתי חבורות כל אחת בפסח שלה נסתלקה מחיצה מביניהם ונתערבו כאלו באו אלו לתוך אלו ואלו לתוך אלו ופשוטות הן :

הכלה הופכת את פניה ואוכלת · פי' מפני שהיא בושה לאכול · רב הונא כדאיקלע לבי רב נחמן בר יצחק אמרו ליה מה שמך אמר להו רב הונא פי' נסתכת בישיבה להקרות רב ובזה השם אני ידוע לפיכך **אמר** בעל השם אנא כלומר סמוך בישיבה אני וכו' ענינא מסרבין לקטן ואין מסרבין לגדול כל מה שאומר לך בעל הבית עשה והשותה כוסו בבת אחת הרי זה גרגרן אלו כולם דברים פשוטין הן : **אמר** רב הונא בני חבורה נכנסין אפילו בשלשה ויוצאין אפי' באחד כו' · פי' בני חבורה שנמנו על הפסח ובאו מקצת מהן בעת שדרך בני אדם להכנס ולאכול הפסח ושגרו הדיאלא פי' דיאלא כגון השמש שהוא השמש שלהן וחפש אחריהם אחרי הנשארים מבני חבורה ולא מצאם אפי' [אם] לא נתקבצו מכל בני החבורה ובאו אלא שלשה בלבד אוכלין את הפסח ההוא ואין עליהן להמתין להם עד שיבואו כיון שנתאחרו לבוא מדרך בני אדם כולם אבל פחות משלשה לא יאכלו אלא ימתינו עד שיבואו שאר בני החבורה זה דין הנכנסין אבל אם היו מקובצין כולן וראו מקצתן למקצתן ויצאו ונתאחרו יתר מן השיעור שאמרנו והדר בא דיאלא ולא מצאם אפילו לא ישאר מכל בני חבורה אלא אחד כגון שהיו שם כולם וראו זה את זה ויצאו אוכלו אפילו האחד הנשאר ואינם יכולין לומר לו למה לא המתנת אותנו ואמר רבינא ונותן דמים האוכל הפסח ולית הלכתא כותיה והני מילי דעל בעידנא דעיילי אינשי כרבה והדר בהו דיאלא : הדרן עלך כיצד צולין

[נ"א ולא לשפחות אחר שפחות ר"מ]

קיח א מיי' שם הל' ה:

קיט ב טוש"ע א"ח סי' קע ס"ג :

קכ ג ד שם סעיף ח :

[שייך לע"א במשנה]

קכא ה ו מיי' פ"ט מהל' ק"פ הל' ו:

סנהדרין ד' [סוכה ו: קדושין יח: וש"נ]

[דף ד׳]

[עיין תוספות בכורות מד: ד"ה ואין]

[מס' ד"א פ"ו ושם איתא כשהוא כשרות]

[שם] ביצה כה:

[בערוך ערך דייל מבאר פי' סוגיא זו באריכות ע"ש]

הגהות הב"ח

(א) תוספות ד"ה נכנסין וד"ס אמר כד"א :

גליון הש"ס

גמרא רבי ישמעאל ברבי יוסי. בירושלמי ספ"ג דמעשרו' איתא ר"א בר"ש :

מאי לאו דאכלי ליה בגגין. אלמא גגי ירושלים נתקדשו: אין מפטירין. כשהגיע זמנו להפטר מן הסעודה דהיינו אחר הפסח שהוא נאכל באחרונה על השבע שכן חובת כל הקרבנות כדקיימא לן (חולין דף קלב:) למשחה לגדולה כדרך שהמלכים אוכלין אין נפטרין על ידי אפיקומן: ואמר רב. אפיקומן לשון הוציאו כליכם מכאן ונלך ונאכל עוד בחבורה אחרת: שלא בשעת אכילה. קריאת ההלל לאחר אכילה: פעם אחת בשנה. ביוה"כ לקטורת ולהזיית בין הבדים: בשבוע. בשמיטה: מה היא צריכה. שמא תבקע החומה וצריכה תיקון אלמא עליות נתקדשו: שאני היכל. דכתיב ביה ועליותיו וכתיב הכל בכתב מיד ה' עלי השכיל אלמא קדוש: בקודש. בעזרה: ופתוחות לחול. שאין להם פתח לעזרה אלא להר הבית: תוכן חול. כקדושת הר הבית ולא כעזרה דבתר פתיחה אזיל: בשגגותיהן שוין לקרקע עזרה. שהלשכות בנויות מחילות תחת הקרקע הלכך גגים דידהו הוו להו כי ארעא: כי אמרה רבי יוחנן. להא דמחילות לא נתקדשו בפתוחות להר הבית דגבי שילוח בעל קרי המשתלח חוץ להר הבית אמרה בהלו דברים(א) דקאמר מחילות לא נתקדשו ובעל קרי משתלח חוץ לשתי מחנות ומותר ליכנס במחילות דהר הבית: כי תניא ההיא. דתוכן קודש בפתוחות לעזרה להכי נקט פתוחות דבתר פתיחתן אזלינן: והתניא מחילות שתחת היכל חול. וקא סלקא דעתך בפתוחות לעזרה קאמר ומשנינן בפתוחות לחול שמחילות מהלכות מתחת אחת עשרה אמה שאחורי בית הכפורת עד שנפתחות להר הבית מחוץ לעזרה: ת"ש וגגו קודש. גגו של היכל וסיפא דהא דרבי יהודה היא והכא לא מצי לשנויי כדלעיל מהיכל ניתיב איניש דהא גגו לא כתיב בקרא: גגין הללו. שבעזרה ולשכותיה: אין אוכלין שם קדשי קדשים. הנאכלין בעזרה ואין שוחטין שם קדשים קלים הנשחטין בכל מקום בעזרה: לאותן שתי אמות. להכי קדשי גגין לשימוש נתינת כלי קודש הצריכין לבנין אבל לא הצריכין למזבח כדאשכחן שאותן שתי אמות מקלות של מדה היו נתונות בגובה השער שהוא בגגין ובעליות: דתנן שתי אמות. קני מדה היו בשושן הבירה והוא בית הבנוי על גובה השער כדתנן במסכת מדות (פ"א מ"ג) שער המזרחי ועליו שושן הבירה צורה מצויירת ומפרשינן במנחות כדי שידעו מהיכן באו ולהכי הוא דקדשי גגין לכל דדמין לשתי אמות דלא הוי צורך המזבח אבל למילתא אחריתי לא קדשו: של משה. ששה טפחים: ולמה היו אחת גדולה ואחת קטנה. תיסגי להו בשל משה: שיהו אומנין. שנשכרו לבנות כך וכך אמות נוטלין למדת הקטנה של משה ומחזירין הבנין לגזברין למדה האחת מאלו הגדולות כדי שיוותרו משלהן להקדש ולא בצמצום שמא יהנו מן ההקדש בחנם ויבואו לידי מעילה: ותרתי. גדולות למה לי תיסגי בשל משה ובחדא מהנך: חדא לדהבא וכספא. בזו שאין יתירה על של משה אלא חצי אצבע היו לאומנות זהב וכסף כמין טבלאות ושולחנות שהן אומנות כבידה ובזו שיתירה עליהן אצבע היו מחזירין בנין אבנים ומוסיפין על תגאן אצבע לכל אמה: עובי החומה. אלמא ראש החומה נתקדש דדמו לגגין ועליות: בר שורא. חומה קטנה לפנים מן החומה גדולה והיא נמוכה ושוה לקרקע גובה העזרה שקרקע העזרה הולך וגבוה ועולה במעלות: מתני' שתי חבורות שהיו אוכלות. פסח אחד בבית אחד: אלו הופכין פניהם אילך. אינן צריכין להסב אלו כנגד אלו להיות נראין כחבורה אחת אלא רשאין להפוך פניהם אלו אילך ואלו אילך ואפילו נראין כשתי חבורות לא איכפת לן כדיליף בגמרא שהפסח נאכל אף בשתי בתים לשתי חבורות: והמיחם. שמחממין בו חמין שמוזגין בו היין רשאין לתת באמצע כדי שיהא נוח לשמש המשמש לשתיהן למזוג משם לכאן ולכאן ואין צריכין לעשות משאר מנהג כל השנה ואף על פי שמפסיק בין החבורות לא איכפת לן וכשהשמש משמש לשתיהן עומד מחבורה אחת שהתחיל לאכול עמה מן הפסח למזוג לחבורה האחרת: קופץ את פיו ומחזיר את פניו. לגד חבורתו שלא יחשדוהו שאוכל עם חבורה האחרת דסבירא ליה לתנא דידן הפסח נאכל בשתי חבורות אבל אדם אחד אינו אוכל בשני מקומות ממש ולהכי מוקי בבית אחד יאכל שאין אדם אחד אוכל בשני בתים ושתי חבורות ההופכות פניהן כשתי בתים דמו: והכלה. שהיא בושה רשאה להפוך פניה לצד אחר ולאכול כדאמרן פסח נאכל בשתי חבורות: גמ' על הבתים אשר יאכלו אותו. משמע שני בני אדם אוכלין פסח אחד בשתי בתים דכתיב יאכלו שנים אותו חד פסח בתים שנים: יכול יהא. אדם אחד אוכל בשני מקומות כגון בשני חדרים או בשתי חבורות ההופכות פניהם ת"ל בבית אחד יאכל ור' יהודה סבר יש אם למסורת כדלקמן יאכל כתיב משמע אדם אחד אוכלו בבית א' ולא בשני בתים אבל גבי אוכלים הרבה כתיב בתים הרבה: השמש. שהיה טלהו ושכח והכניס כזית לתוך פיו והוא היה נמנה עליו: אם פיקח הוא ממלא כריסו ממנו. דאם יעמוד משם שוב לא יאכל: מלמד שהאוכל אוכל בשני מקומות. ויאכלו דכתיב בקרא אכל חד וחד מאוכלין קאי: יכול

לא נצרכה אלא לאותן שתי אמות. לא בעי למימר דאותן שתי אמות היו מונחות בגגו של היכל דהא שער מזרחי שעליו (ב) שושן הבירה צורה אחת משערי העזרה היה אלא ה"ק כמו שאותו שער מזרחי היה מקודש להניח שם כלי קודש כמו כן גגו של היכל קודש דקאמר היינו להניח שם כלי קודש ולא שיהיו כלי קודש צריכין מקום מקודש כדמוכח בכמה דוכתי אלא הך קדושה אית להו להניחם שם: ומר

מאי לאו דאכלי באיגרא ואמרי באיגרא לא דאכלי בארעא ואמרי באיגרא איני *והתנן אין מפטירין אחר הפסח אפיקומן ואמר רב שלא יעקרו מחבורה לחבורה לא קשיא כאן בשעת אכילה כאן שלא בשעת אכילה ת"ש *אבא שאול אומר עליית בית קדשי הקדשים חמורה מבית קדשי הקדשים שבית קדשי הקדשים כהן גדול נכנס לו פעם אחת בשנה ועליית בית קדשי הקדשים אין נכנסין לה אלא *פעם אחת בשבוע ואמרי לה פעמים בשבוע ואמרי לה פעם אחת ביובל לידע מה היא צריכה אמר רב יוסף *מהיכל ניקום וניתיב איניש °שאני היכל דכתיב °ויתן דוד לשלמה בנו את תבנית האולם ואת בתיו ואת גנזכיו ועליותיו וחדריו הפנימים ובית הכפורת וכתיב °הכל בכתב מיד ה' עלי השכיל ת"ש *הלשכות הבנויות בקדש ופתוחות לחול תוכן חול וגגותיהן קודש תרגמא רב חסדא בשגגותיהן שוין לקרקע עזרה אי הכי אימא סיפא בנויות בחול ופתוחות לקודש תוכן קודש וגגותיהן חול ואי ס"ד בשגגותיהן שוין לקרקע עזרה הויא לה מחילות *וא"ר יוחנן מחילות לא נתקדשו כי קאמר רבי יוחנן בפתוחות להר הבית כי תניא ההיא בפתוחות לעזרה *והתני' ר"י אומר מחילות מתחת ההיכל חול כי תניא ההיא שפתוחות לחול ת"ש *וגגו קודש ותסברא והא קתני *גגין הללו אין אוכלין שם קדשי קדשים ואין שוחטין שם קדשים קלים ואלא קשיא גגו קדש אמר רב חמא בר גוריא לאותן ב' אמות *דתנן ב' אמות היה בשושן הבירה אחת על קרן מזרחית צפונית ואחת על קרן מזרחית דרומית זו שעל קרן מזרחית צפונית היתה יתירה על של משה חצי אצבע וזו שעל קרן מזרחית דרומית היתה יתירה עליה חצי אצבע נמצאת יתירה על של משה אצבע ולמה היו אחת גדולה ואחת קטנה *שיהו האומנין נוטלין בקטנה ומחזירין בגדולה כדי שלא יבואו לידי מעילה ותרתי למה לי אחת לכספא ודהבא ואחת לבנינא תנן החלונות ועובי החומה כלפנים בשלמא החלונות משכחת לה דרשויה לקרקע עזרה אלא עובי החומה היכי משכחת לה משכחת לה בבר שורא דכתיב °ויאבל חיל וחומה ואמר רבי אחא ואיתימא רבי חנינא שורא ובר שורא: **מתני'** *שתי חבורות שהיו אוכלין בבית אחד אלו הופכין את פניהם הילך ואוכלין ואלו הופכין את פניהם הילך ואוכלין *והמיחם באמצע כשהשמש עומד למזוג קופץ את פיו ומחזיר את פניו עד שמגיע אצל חבורתו ואוכל והכלה הופכת את פניה ואוכלת: **גמ'** מתני' מני רבי יהודה היא *דתניא °על הבתים אשר יאכלו אותו בהם °מלמד שהפסח נאכל בשתי חבורות יכול יהא האוכל אוכל בשתי מקומות תלמוד לומר °בבית אחד יאכל מכאן *אמרו השמש שאכל כזית בצד התנור אי פקח הוא ממלא כריסו ממנו ואם רצו בני חבורה לעשות עמו טובה באין ויושבין בצדו דברי רבי יהודה רבי שמעון אומר על הבתים אשר יאכלו אותו בהם מלמד שהאוכל אוכל בשתי מקומות יכול

עין משפט נר מצוה

קט א מיי' פ"ו מהל' בית הבחירה הלכה כג:

קי ב מיי' פ"ו מהל' בית הבחירה הל' ז:

קיא ג שם הלכה ט:

קיב ד שם הלכה ט:

קיג ה מיי' פ"ח מהל' מעילה הלכה ה:

קיד ו מיי' פ"ט מהל' בית הבחירה הל' ג:

קטו ז מיי' פ"ט מהל' ק"פ הלכה ג:

קטז ח שם הלכה ד:

קיז ט שם הלכה א:

רבינו חננאל

מאי לאו דאכלין הפסח בגג ושם קראו את ההלל דאלמא הגג נתקדש דאין לנו רשות לאכול את הפסח אלא במקום קדוש ושני' כגון שאכלו הפסח בארץ ועלו בגג לקרות את ההלל · והא דתנן אין מפטירין אחר הפסח אפיקומן פי' שלא יעברו מחבורה לחבורה התם בשעת אכילה אבל בקריאת ההלל שרי: ת"ש מהא דתנן בתחלת כלים אבא שאול אומר עליו' בית קדשי הקדשי' חמורה מבית קדשי הקדשים כו' הרי העליות נתקדשו ודחי רב יוסף וכי מהיכל ניתיב איניש כלומר שאני היכל דרחמנא גזר הכי שנא' ויתן דוד לשלמה בנו את תבנית האולם וגו' וכתי' הכל בכתב מיד ה' עלי השכיל: ת"ש מהא דתנן במעשר שני פ"ג הלשכות הבנויות בקדש ופתוחות לחול תוכן חול וגגותיהן קדש הנה הגגות נתקדשו ושני רב חסדא הגגות הללו שוין לקרקע עזרה וכקרקע הן חשובין אי הכי אימא סיפא בנויות בחול ופתוחות בקדש תוכן קדש וגגותיהן חול ואי ס"ד בשוין גגות הללו לקרקע עזרה הויא להו מחילות ואמר רבי יוחנן מחילות לא נתקדשו אמאי תנן תוכן קדש כי אמר ר' יוחנן בפתוחות להר הבית כי תניא ההיא בפתוחות לעזרה והתניא ר' יהודה אומר מחילות שתחת ההיכל חול ושני' בפתוחות לחול: ת"ש וגגו של היכל קדש ומתמהי' ותסברא גגין מי קדשי והא קתני סיפא גגין הללו אין אוכלין שם קדשי קדשי' ואין שוחטין שם קדשי' קלים ואלא קשיא וגגו של היכל קדש ושני' באותן שתי אמות כלומר הא דתניא גגו של היכל קדש באותן ב' אמות כדתנן במסכת כלים פט"ז שתי אמות היו בשושן הבירה אחת על קרן מזרחית צפונית ואחת על קרן מזרחית דרומית · יש מי שאומר מדת ב' אמות של כסף או של זהב כגון שרבים היו עשויות ומונחות באותו מקום ובהן היו משערין ונותנין לאומנין ולוקחין · ויש אומרים מקום היה בנוי בבית המקדש צורת שושן הבירה ועשו בה בנין אמה אחת כמדת משה רבינו שעשה בה כל כלי הקדש ותוספת חצי אצבע בקרן מזרחית דרומית בנין אמה ואחרת יתירה עליה בקרן מזרחית דרומית ומפורש במנחות פרק שתי הלחם בשלשה אחת אחת כיון שהביא משנה זו נראה ופרקה פירש ענין שושן הבירה הנזכר בה תנן התם במדות פ"א (מ"ג) שער המזרחי ועליו שושן הבירה צורה מאי טעמא רב יצחק בר אבדימי ורב חסדא חד אמר כדי שידעו מהיכן באו כלומר בשעבודכם גליתם לבבל ועתה משם עליתם וכל זמן שרואין אותה הצורה זוכרין הגלות והדורות הבאין מספרין לבניהם וחד אמר כדי שתהא אימת מלכות עליהן כלומר אע"פ שאנו כאן תחת מלכות פרס אנו רבי ינאי אמר לעולם תהא אימת מלכות עליך שנא' וירדו כל עבדיך אלה אלי וגו' ולא כתיב וירדת אתה ר' יוחנן אמר מהכא ויד ה' היתה אל אליהו וישנס מתניו · ועלה לתרופה חזקיה אמר להתיר פה אלמים בר קפרא אמר להתיר פה עקרות לקבל הריון ואמרינן עלה ושתי אמות למה חד לדהבא וכספא וחדא לבנינא כלומר כשנותנין לאומנין כותל לבנות דבר קצוב כך וכך אמה בכך וכך דמים נותנין אמה באמה הקטנה והן בונין באמה הגדולה כדי שלא יהנו מן ההקדש יותר מכדי מלאכתן ויבואו לידי מעילה וכן בכלי זהב כגון השלחן והמנורה וכיוצא בהן וההצוצרות וכיוצא בהן · פי' חומה שוה בקרקע עזרה כגון בר שורא והוא החל שעושין החל נמוך והחומה שורין מטנה גבוהה וזה נקרא חל וזו נקראת חומה: מתני' שתי חבורות שהיו אוכלות בבית אחד אלו הופכין את פניהם ואכלין וכו' · פירוש משנתנו פסח אחד וחלקוהו ואכלין אותו בשתי חבורות אוקימנא לרבי יהודה דתני בבית אחד יאכל ולא בשני בתים וכתיב קרא אחרינא אשר יאכלו אותו בהם מכאן שהפסח נאכל בשתי חבורות רבי שמעון אומר על הבתים אשר יאכלו אותו בהם מלמד שהאוכל אוכל

מסורת הש"ס

[סוטה מו:]

לקמן קיט:

תוספתא פ"א דכלים

[פי' תוספות שבועות יז: ד"ה ושמא ונזכר כצ"ל]

מעשר שני פ"ג מ"ח זבחים נו. יומא כה.

לעיל סז:

תמיד כז:

תוספתא דכלים פרק א

*שם

[שבועות יז:]

מנחות צח. בכורות לט: כלים פי"ז [מ"ט]

מכילתא פ' בא

לקמן פט:

הגהות הב"ח

(א) רש"י ד"ה כי אמרה וכו' בהלו דברים נ"ב סוף דף ס"ז וע"ש:

(ב) תוס' ד"ה לא נצרכה וכו' דהא שער מזרחי שעליו שושן הבירה צורה אחת משערי כצ"ל:

גליון הש"ס

גמרא שאני היכל. עיין שבועות יז ע"ב תוד"ה ושמא:

[to eat],[9] yet the Hallel[10] split the roofs![11] [86a] Does that not mean that they ate on the roof and recited [the Hallel] on the roof?—No: they ate on the ground and recited [it] on the roof. Yet that is not so, for surely we learned: You must not conclude after the Paschal meal [by saying] 'To the aftermeal entertainment!'[12] and Rab said: [That means] that they must not remove from one company to another?[13]—There is no difficulty: there it is at the time of eating;[1] here it is not at the time of eating.[2]

Come and hear: Abba Saul said: The upper chamber of the Holy of Holies was more stringent than the Holy of Holies, for the High Priest entered the Holy of Holies once a year, whereas the upper chamber of the Holy of Holies was entered only once a septennate—others say, twice a septennate—others say, once in a Jubilee— to see what it required?[3]—Said R. Joseph: Shall a man stand up and raise an objection from the *Hekal!*[4] The *Hekal* is different, because it is written, *Then David gave to Solomon his son the pattern of the porch* [of the Temple], *and of the houses thereof,*
c *and of the treasuries thereof, and of the upper rooms thereof, and of the inner chambers thereof, and of the place of the ark-cover;*[5] and it is written, *All this* [*do I give thee*] *in writing, as the Lord hath made me wise by His hand upon me.*[6]

Come and hear: [With regard to] the chambers built in the sacred area[7] and opening into the non-sacred area,[8] their inside is non-sacred,[9] while their roofs are sacred?—R. Ḥisda explained this [as meaning] where their roofs were level with the ground of the Temple Court.[10] If so, consider the second clause: [As to] those built in the non-sacred [area] and opening into the sacred [area], their inside is sacred, while their roofs are non-sacred. Now if you think that it means where their roofs are level with the ground of the Temple Court, then they are cellars, whereas R. Joḥanan said: The cellars were not sanctified?—R. Joḥanan said this only in respect of those opening into the Temple Mount; [whereas] that was taught in respect of those opening into the Temple Court. But it was taught, R. Judah said: The cellars under the *Hekal* were non-sacred?[1]—That was taught where they opened into the non-sacred [area].

Come and hear: And its roof is sacred?[2]—Now is that logical: surely he teaches: As for these roofs, you may not eat there sacrifices of the greater sanctity, nor kill there sacrifices of the lesser sanctity.[3] But in that case 'its roof is holy' presents a difficulty?—Said R. Ḥama b. Guria: [That was taught] in respect of those two cubits. For we learned: There were two cubits [measures] in Shushan the Castle,[4] one on the north-east corner and one on the south-east corner. That on the north-east corner exceeded [the cubit] of Moses[5] by half a fingerbreadth, while that on the south-east corner exceeded it [*sc.* the first cubit] by half a fingerbreadth, so that it exceeded [the cubit] of Moses by a fingerbreadth. And why was one large and one small?[6] So that the workers might receive [contracts] by the small [measure] and deliver [the work] by the large one, to avoid liability to a trespass-offering.[7] And why two? One was for [work in] gold and silver,[8] while the other was for building.[9]

We learned: THE WINDOWS AND THE THICKNESS OF THE WALL ARE AS THE INSIDE. As for the windows, it is well, this being possible where they were level with the ground of the Temple Court; but how is the thickness of the wall conceivable?[1]—It is possible in the case of the minor wall,[2] as it is written, *But he hath made the rampart and the wall to mourn,*[3] which R. Aḥa—others say, R. Ḥanina—interpreted: the wall proper and the minor wall.

MISHNAH. IF TWO COMPANIES ARE EATING IN ONE ROOM,[4] THESE MAY TURN THEIR FACES IN ONE DIRECTION AND THOSE MAY TURN THEIR FACES IN ANOTHER DIRECTION,[5] WITH THE BOILER[6] IN THE MIDDLE.[7] WHEN THE WAITER[8] RISES TO MIX [THE WINE], HE MUST SHUT HIS MOUTH AND TURN HIS FACE AWAY [FROM THE OTHER COMPANY] UNTIL HE REACHES HIS OWN COMPANY.[9] BUT A BRIDE[10] MAY TURN HER FACE AWAY AND EAT.

GEMARA. Who is [the author of] our Mishnah?—It is R. Judah. For it was taught: *Upon the houses wherein they shall eat it:*[11] this teaches that a Paschal lamb may be eaten in two companies. You might think that the eater may eat in two places,[12] therefore
d it is stated, *In one house shall he eat it.*[1] Whence it was said: If the waiter[2] ate as much as an olive at the side of the oven, if he is wise he eats his fill[3] of it; but if the members of the company wish to do him a favour, they come and sit at his side:[4] this is R. Judah's opinion. R. Simeon said: '*Upon the houses wherein they shall eat it:*'

(9) Very large companies registered for each sacrifice, so that each person could not receive more than that. (10) V. 64*a*, n. c2. (11) It was sung with such gusto. (12) It was customary among ancient nations to conclude a banquet with bouts of drinking, revelry and music. The sanctity of the Paschal meal precluded this, as it would turn an occasion of solemnity and reverential gratitude to God into one of light-hearted frivolity. (13) For the purpose mentioned in the preceding note. Thus the whole service must be carried out in the same place.

(1) Then a change of place is forbidden. (2) The *hallel* was recited after the meal was concluded; praise to God is then permissible anywhere. (3) E.g., repairs. Thus the upper chambers *were* sanctified. (4) The *Holy*, the hall containing the golden altar etc., contrad. to the Holy of Holies (Jast.). In the present passage, however, R. Joseph appears to use the word more elastically, making it embrace the Holy of Holies too. (5) I Chron. XXVIII, 11. (6) Ibid. 19. '*The Lord hath made me wise*' is understood to mean that he was Divinely inspired to sanctify all those mentioned in the forgoing, which include the '*upper room*'. (7) I.e., the Temple Court. (8) *Sc.* the Temple Mount; i.e., they had no doors opening into the Temple Court. (9) They lack the sanctity of the Temple Court, though they possess that of the Temple Mount, for their status is determined by their openings. (10) The chambers referred to being cellars.

(1) This is now assumed to refer even to those opening into the Temple Court. (2) *Sc.* the roof of the *Hekal*, this being the conclusion of R. Judah's statement. R. Joseph's answer that the *Hekal* was different on account of the explicit verse is inapplicable here, for the roofs are not mentioned in that verse. (3) V. *supra* 24*a*, n. b2. Thus it is definitely stated that they did not enjoy the sanctity of the Temple Court. (4) A chamber built above the eastern gate of the Temple, so called because the picture of the castle of Shushan, the capital of the Persian empire, was sculptured upon it. (5) I.e., the standard cubit. (6) Why not simply the standard cubit of Moses? (7) E.g., they contracted to build a certain length in terms of the standard cubit; nevertheless they completed their contract according to the length of the larger measure. The purpose was to preclude the possibility of benefiting from the Sanctuary over and above their exact due, which would involve them in trespass. (8) This being more difficult, they added only half a fingerbreadth to the standard measure. (9) Where a whole fingerbreadth was added.—Now the roofs were sanctified only in so far that these measuring rods and similar utensils or vessels which were not used in the actual service of the altar might be kept in them. But they were not sanctified in respect of anything else.

c (1) For by the thickness of the wall must be meant the top, which is the same as the upper chambers and the roofs, while the top of the city wall was certainly not on a level with the Temple Mount. (2) A smaller wall on the inside of the larger wall; the top of the former was level with the greatest height of the ground of the Temple Court, which itself reached several different heights in gradient. (3) Lam. II, 8. (4) Of the same Paschal offering. (5) They are not bound all to face each other, though they were originally one company for this offering. (6) In which water was heated for diluting the wine. (7) Though this seems further to emphasize their separateness. (8) Who is waiting on both parties. He too had registered for this offering—a Jewish waiter, of course is meant. (9) Lest he be suspected of eating with the other company too. This Tanna holds that one Paschal lamb may be eaten in two companies, but one person may not eat in two places. (10) Who in her modesty does not wish to face the company. (11) Ex. XII, 7. (12) Of the same offering. E.g., either in two separate rooms or even in one room containing two companies, which makes it like two rooms.

d (1) Ex. XII, 46. The vocalization is יֵאָכֵל (passive E.V.: *shall it be eaten*), but it may also be read יֹאכַל, and R. Judah holds that the traditional consonantal form of the word determines its meaning regardless of vocalization. (2) Engaged in roasting the offering. (3) Lit., 'fills his stomach'. (4) And eat there, but he may not go and eat with them, as he would thereby be eating in two places.

from one company to another company, how do we know [that he violates a negative injunction]?—Because it was taught: *Thou shalt not carry forth aught of the flesh abroad out of the house:*[4] I only know [that it must not be taken] from one house to another house; whence do we know [that it must not be taken] from one company to another company?[5] Because it is stated, *'abroad'*, [meaning] outside [the place of] its consumption.

R. Ammi said: He who carries out flesh of the Passover-offering from one company to another company is not culpable unless he deposits [it there]: 'carrying out' is written in connection with it as [in connection with] the Sabbath;[6] [hence] just as [in the case of] the Sabbath, [he is not culpable] unless he removes and deposits,[7] so here too [he is not culpable] unless he removes it [from one company] and deposits it [with the second]. R. Abba b. Mammel raised an objection: If they were carrying them on staves, the front bearers having gone outside the walls of the Temple Court while the rear ones had not [yet] gone out, those in front defile [their] garments while those behind do not defile their
a garments.[1] But it has not come to rest?[2] He raised the objection and he himself answered it: It refers to [carcases] which are trailed [along the ground].[3]

MISHNAH. IF PART OF A LIMB WENT OUTSIDE, HE CUTS [THE FLESH] AS FAR AS THE BONE AND PARES IT UNTIL HE REACHES THE JOINT AND CUTS IT AWAY. BUT IN THE CASE OF [OTHER] SACRIFICES HE CUTS IT OFF WITH A CHOPPER, BECAUSE THEY ARE NOT SUBJECT TO THE [PROHIBITION OF] BREAKING A BONE. FROM THE DOOR-STOP AND WITHIN RANKS AS WITHIN [THE CITY];[4] FROM THE DOOR-STOP AND WITHOUT IS AS OUTSIDE [THE CITY]. THE WINDOWS[5] AND THE THICKNESS OF THE WALL ARE AS THE INSIDE.

GEMARA. Rab Judah said in Rab's name: And it is likewise in respect of prayer.[6] He differs from R. Joshua b. Levi. For R. Joshua b. Levi said: Even an iron partition cannot interpose between Israel and their Father in Heaven.[7]

Now this is self-contradictory. You say, FROM THE DOOR-STOP AND WITHIN RANKS AS WITHIN [THE CITY]; hence the [area of] the door-stop itself is as the outside. Then consider the sequel: FROM THE DOOR-STOP AND WITHOUT IS AS OUTSIDE [THE CITY]; hence the door-stop itself is as the inside?—There
b is no difficulty: one refers to the gates of the Temple Court;[1] the other, to the gates of Jerusalem.[2] For R. Samuel b. R. Isaac said: Why were the gates of Jerusalem not sanctified?[3] Because lepers shelter under them in summer[4] from the sun and in winter[5] from the rain. R. Samuel son of R. Isaac also said: Why was the gate of Nicanor[6] not sanctified? Because lepers stand there and insert the thumbs of their hands [into the Court].[7]

THE WINDOWS AND THE THICKNESS OF THE WALL etc. Rab said: The roofs and the upper chambers were not sanctified.[8] But that is not so, for Rab said on the authority of R. Ḥiyya: There was [only] as much as an olive of the Passover-offering

(4) Ex. XII, 46. (5) Even in the same house. (6) *Sc.* in Ex. XVI, 29: *let no man go out of his place on the seventh day* (Tosaf. s.v. הוצאה). (7) Lit., 'he uproots and lays at rest'. Removing it from private and depositing it in public ground or the reverse; v. Shab. 2*a*.

a (1) This refers to the bullocks which were burnt outside the three camps (v. 67*b*, n. b2); Jerusalem itself is the third camp but the bearers defiled their garments as soon as they left the first camp, viz., the Temple Court. This is deduced in Yoma 68*a* from Lev. XVI, 27: *and the bullocks of the sin-offering . . . shall be carried forth without the camp*. (2) It was not put down, yet it defiles, though 'carrying out' is written there. (3) Which constitutes depositing. (4) The door-frame in the thick city walls of Jerusalem was of considerable breadth—sufficient for the Passover-offering to be eaten there. The Mishnah states that everywhere on the inside of this door-frame is as inside the city, while that on the outside is as the outside of the city. The Gemara discusses the status of the door-frame space itself. (5) In the city walls; these too occupied a considerable breadth. (6) Certain portions of the service are recited only when there is a quorum of ten men (called *minyan*). A man standing in the inside of the door-stop is counted with those inside the room, but not he who is standing outside the door-stop. (7) Hence even if he stands outside the door-stop, he is counted with the others.

b (1) There the space of the door-stop itself is as the inside. (2) There it is as the outside. (3) I.e., the space occupied by the thickness of the gates. (4) Lit., 'the sun'. (5) Lit., 'the rain'. (6) The east gate of the Temple Court. (7) V. Lev. XIV, 17 and Yeb. 7*b*. (8) The roofs of the houses of Jerusalem are not sanctified, in the sense that sacrifices which are eaten anywhere in Jerusalem may not be eaten on them. Similarly, the sacrifices which had to be eaten within the Temple precincts might not be eaten on its roof or in its upper chambers.

*מחבורה לחבורה מנין דתניא °לא תוציא מן הבית מן הבשר חוצה אין לי אלא מבית לבית מחבורה לחבורה מנין ת"ל חוצה חוץ לאכילתו א"ר אמי בהמוציא בשר פסח מחבורה לחבורה אינו חייב עד שיניח הוצאה כתיב ביה כשבת מה שבת עד דעבד עקירה והנחה אף ה"נ עד דעבד עקירה והנחה מתיב רבי אבא בר ממל *גהיו סובלים אותן במוטות הראשונים יצאו חוץ לחומת העזרה והאחרונים לא יצאו הראשונים מטמאין בגדים והאחרונים אין מטמאין בגדים והא לא נח הוא מותיב לה והוא מפרק לה בנגררין:

מתני' דאבר שיצא מקצתו חותך עד שמגיע לעצם וקולף עד שמגיע לפרק וחותך ובמוקדשין קוצץ בקופיץ שאין בו משום שבירת העצם מן האגף ולפנים כלפנים המן האגף ולחוץ כלחוץ *החלונות ועובי החומה כלפנים: **גמ'** אמר רב יהודה אמר רב וכן לתפלה ופליגא דריב"ל *דא"ר יהושע בן לוי ואפילו מחיצה של ברזל אינה מפסקת בין ישראל לאביהם שבשמים הא גופא קשיא אמרת מן האגף ולפנים כלפנים הא אגף עצמו כלחוץ אימא סיפא מן האגף ולחוץ כלחוץ הא אגף עצמו כלפנים לא קשיא כאן בשערי עזרה כאן בשערי ירושלים דאמר רבי שמואל בר רב יצחק מפני מה לא נתקדשו שערי ירושלים מפני שמצורעין מגינין תחתיהן בחמה מפני החמה ובגשמים מפני הגשמים ואמר רבי שמואל בר רב יצחק מפני מה לא נתקדשה שער נקנור *מפני ישמצורעין עומדין שם ומכניסין בהונות ידם: החלונות ועובי החומה וכו': אמר רב °°גגין ועליות לא נתקדשו איני והאמר רב משום רבי חייא כזיתא פסחא והלילא פקע איגרא מאי

תורה אור: שמות יב

רש"י

מחבורה לחבורה מנא לן. חבורה של שני פסחים בבית אחד: חוצה. קרא יתירא הוא למילף חוץ לחבורת אכילתו: תן חוצה לא גרסינן תן: עד שיניח. במקום חבורה האחרת: דעבד ליה עקירה והנחה. כשבת דבעינן עקירה והנחה דעד שיניח לא עמרה מלאכה וגבי שבת וכל חיובי חטאת כתיב בעשותה בעושה את כולה ולא בעושה מקצתה (שבת דף גג:) והאי נמי אע"ג דלאו בר חטאת הוא הוצאה כי התם בעינן: היו סובלין אותם במוטות. פרים הנשרפי' כגון פר ושעיר יוה"כ ופר העלם דבר ופר כהן משיח הנשרפין חוץ לג' מחנות וילפינן בסדר יומא בפ' שני שעירי (דף סח.) להלן בשאר פרים הנשרפין אתה נותן להם ג' מחנות וכאן ביום הכפורים אתה נותן להם מחנה אחת בתמיה דכתיב יוציא אל מחוץ למחנה *ושרף וגו' אלא לומר לך כיון שיצאו חוץ למחנה אחת מטמא בגדים דהא כתיב והשורף אותה יכבס בגדיו אלמא כשיוצאין מן העזרה מטמא בגדים שעליהם מיד ואע"ג דלא נח והכא הוצאה כתיבא דכתיב והוציא את הפר וגו': בנגררין. על גבי קרקע דאיכא הנחה: **מתני'** חותך עד שמגיע לעצם. כדפרישית לעיל: ובמוקדשים. בשאר קדשים שיצא מהן מקצת אבר: קוצץ. את היוצא בקופיץ: מן האגף ולפנים כלפנים. אגף קרי כל מקום הגפת הדלת שהוא חופף ונוקש שם כשסוגרו דהיינו משפת הפנימית של עובי הפתח עד מקום הנקישה שקורין רב"ן: מן האגף ולפנים. דהיינו תוך העיר ממש כלפנים ואוכלין שם קדשים קלים: מן האגף ולחוץ כלחוץ. דהיינו מקום הנקישה ואגף עצמו לא ידעי' השתא אי כלפנים אי כלחוץ ובגמרא מפרש לי': החלונות. שבחומת ירושלים ועובי ראש החומה בגובה כלפנים ואע"ג דבעובי השערים לא אמרן הכי התם כדמפרש טעמא בגמרא מפני המצורעים: **גמ'** וכן לתפלה. העומד מן האגף ולפנים מצטרף לעשרה והעומד חוץ לפסח אין מצטרף: אינה מפסקת. שאין הפסק לפני המקום שהכל גלוי וידוע לפניו ואין סתימה לפניו: אגף עצמו. עובי השער מן הנקישה ולפנים: שערי ירושלים. אגף עצמו כלחוץ שלא נתקדש עוביין: שערי עזרה. נתקדש עוביין בקדושת עזרה חוץ משער ניקנור מפני המצורע שעומד שם בעודו מחוסר כפורים ומכניס משם בהונותיו לעזרה מצורע משתלח חוץ לשלש מחנות כדאמרינן באלו דברים (לעיל סז.): מפני מה לא נתקדשה שער ניקנור. בקדושת עזרה והוא שער המזרחית של עזרה: עומדין שם. ביום שמונה לימי ספרו לאחר שנתרפא וגלח וטבל והעריב שמשו בשביעי ועודנו מחוסר כפורים ותניא בהקומץ (מנחות כז.) מחוסר כפורים שנכנס לעזרה ענשו כרת ונפקא לן מטוד טומאתו בו ומכניס ידיו משם לעזרה לתת עליהן מדם האשם שאילו מוליאו לחוץ היה נפסל ביוצא וביאה במקצת לאו שמה ביאה לענשו על כך אי נמי שמה ביאה וגזירת הכתוב היא והעמיד הכהן המטהר את האיש המיטהר לפני ה' וגו' (ויקרא יד): גגין ועליות לא נתקדשו. בין גגי ירושלים בקדושת ירושלים לקדשים קלים בין גגי לשכות העזרה בקדושת עזרה לקדושת קדשי קדשים: כזיתא פסחא. חבורות גדולות היו נמנין עד שלא היה הפסח מגיע לכל אחד כי אם כזית מן הפסח: והלילא פקע איגרא. לקול המולת ההמון מהלל דומין כאילו הגגין מתבקעים שהיו אומרים ההלל על הפסח כדתנן לקמן (דף צה.) הראשון טעון הלל על אכילתו: מאי

תוספות

הוצאה כתיב ביה כשבת. פי' אל יצא איש ממקומו והיינו אל יוציא דהא תחומים דרבנן ואפילו למ"ד תחומין דאורייתא היינו מדשני ולא כתב אל יוציא אבל לדידיה נמי קרא בהוצאה מיירי כדמשמע סוף פ"ק דעירובין (דף יז:) דתני רבי חייא לוקין על תחומין דבר תורה פי' מאל יצא ופריך לאו שניתן לאזהרת מיתת ב"ד הוא משמע דלהוצאה נמי אתא ולא"ת דבריש הזורק (שבת צו:) דריש הוצאה מויכלא העם מהביא ואומר ר"י דאיצטריך חד להוצאה דעני וחד להוצאה דבעל הבית ומשום דהוצאה מלאכה גרועה היא איצטריך למיכתב בתרוייהו ולהכי חשיב להו נמי בריש מסכת שבת (דף ב:) בתרתי לפי שכתובות בשני מקראות ומסיק אבות מאי ניהו יציאות יציאות תרתי הויין*:

בנגררין. אומר ר"י דלאו דוקא נגררין אלא שיהיו תוך ג' לקרקע דאפי' לרבנן *דר"ע דלית להו קלוטה כמו שהונחה דמיא בזורק במעביר תוך ג' מודו דהכי אמרינן בהמוציא יין (שם דף פ:) אמר רבא הוציא חצי גרוגרת והניחה וחזר והוציא חצי אחרת דרך עליה חייב ופריך והא אמר רבא תוך שלשה לרבנן צריך הנחה על גבי משהו ומשני לא קשיא כאן בזורק כאן במעביר ולאו דוקא נקט התם דרך עליה דהוא הדין שלא דרך עליה אלא תוך ג' אלא נקט דרך עליה דהשתא לא צריך שיהא תוך ג' רק שיהא תוך ג' דגרוגרת מיחייב ואם תאמר היכי ראשונים מטמאת הא בשבת לא הויא הוצאה כענין זה הוציא ולאגד הפר ביד האחרונים שבפנים כדמוכח בהמצניע (שם דף צב.) וי"ל דהכא מיירי שכל הפר חוץ לחומת העזרה ואפילו למאן דאמר התם אגד כלי שמיה אגד הנ"מ כלי שיש לו תוך דאינו חייב אם הוציא מקצתו שע"י מה שבפנים יכול להביאו מבפנים אבל ע"י משיכת המוט לא היו יכולים האחרונים להביאו אצלו:

וכן לתפלה. פי' בקונטרס לענין צירוף ואין נראה דבאלו נאמרין (סוטה דף לח:) משמע סוגיא דגמרא דהלכה כר' יהושע בן לוי דקאמר אפי' מחיצה של ברזל אינה מפסקת ובפרק כל גגות (עירובין צב:) משמע סתמא דגמרא דמחיצה מפסקת לצירוף דקאמר ט' בקטנה ואחד בגדולה אין מצטרפין ולענין שופר ומגילה נמי לא מלית לפרש דתנן בהדיא בפ' ראוהו ב"ד (ר"ה דף כז:) ושם היה עובר אחורי בית הכנסת או שהיה ביתו סמוך לבית הכנסת ושמע קול שופר או מגילה אם כוון לבו יצא ונראה לר"י דהכא מיירי לענין לענות יחיד קדושה ויהא שמיה רבא מברך דאין מחיצה מפסקת לריב"ל ולרב יהודה מפסקת כיון דהוי דבר שצריך עשרה וכי היכי דלא מצטרף לא נפיק ידי חובה אבל שופר לא בעי עשרה:

לא נתקדשה שער ניקנור. וא"ת אם כן בשערי עזרה גופה ליפלוג כאן בשאר שערים כאן בשער ניקנור וי"ל דמתניתין בפסח קאי שאינו נפסל אלא חוץ לחומת ירושלים:

החלונות ועובי החומה כלפנים. בפ"ב דשבועות (דף טו:) פליגי כיצד מהלכים שתי תודות שהיו מקדשין בהם חד אמר זו כנגד זו וחד אמר זו אחר זו משמע התם דמבפנים היו מהלכין דפריך בשלמא למאן דאמר זו אחר זו אמטו להכי פנימית נאכלת שבכר קדשה ראשונה אלא למאן דאמר כו' ואי מבחוץ היו מהלכין היכי קאמר דקדשה ראשונה לחומה והא דקאמר התם למאן דאמר זו כנגד זו פנימית הך דמקרבה לחומה אע"ג דמבפנים היו מהלכים קרי לה פנימית שהיא לצד חוץ ירושלים מפני שהיתה בין ב"ד ובין החומה אי נמי דמקרבה לחומת עזרות קאמר והא דקתני הכא שנתקדשה עובי החומה הקידוש היה תלוי בדעת ב"ד קדשה שפיר עובי החומה והלונות אי נמי למאן דמסקינן בגמרא עובי החומה בבר שורא אתי שפיר דלשם ודאי יכולים לילך ולקדש: לא

עין משפט נר מצוה

קא א ב מיי' פ"ט מהל' ק"פ הל' א:
קב ג מיי' פי"ה מהלכות פרה אדומה הל' ה:
קג ד מיי' פ"ט מהל' ק"פ הלכה ג:
קד ה מיי' שם הל' א:
קה ו מיי' פ"ח מהל' תפלה הלכה ו סמג עשין יט טוש"ע א"ח סי' נה סעיף יג:
קו ז מיי' (פ"ט) [פו] מהל' נשיאות כפים הל' א טוש"ע (סעיף ו) סימן קכ"ח סעיף כד:
קז ח מיי' פ"ד מהל' מחוסרי כפרה הלכה ג:
קח ט מיי' פ"ו מהל' בית הבחירה הלכה ז:

[וע"ע תוס' שבת ב. ד"ה פשט]

[שבת ד.]

רבינו חננאל

ביוצא כזית האיל והאוכלו בלא תעשה לא אפשר בפחות מכזית אמאי פהור ומותר ואסיקנא אלא יוצא דפסח דברי הכל לא גאו בו טומאה דבני חבורה זריזין הן כי קא מבעיא לן יוצא דקדשים ועלתה בתיקו:
תניא לא תוציא מן הבית אין לי אלא מבית לבית מחבורה לחבורה מנין ת"ל מן הבשר חוצה לאכילתו ואינו חייב עד שיעשה עקירה והנחה ומותבינן עלה מהא דתנן בשוחטות קדשים פי"א פרים הנשרפין ושעירים הנשרפין היו סוענין אותן במוטות ראשונים יצאו לחומת עזרה אחרונים לא יצאו ראשונים מטמאין בגדים אחרונים אין מטמאין בגדים עד שיצאו והא לא נח ואוקימנא בנגררים על הארץ ואינן (נעשהן) מגביהן מן הקרקע אלא נמשכין (מן) [על] הארץ דהיינו הנחתם: פי' אבר שיצא מקצתו כו' מן האגף ולפנים כלפנים מן האגף ולחוץ כלחוץ אמר רב יהודה אמר רב וכן לתפלה העומד בכנסת מן האגף ולפנים הרי הוא בכלל ברכה מן האגף ולחוץ כלחוץ ופליגא דר' יהושע בן לוי דאמר ר' יהושע בן לוי אפי' מחיצה של ברזל אינה מפסקת בין ישראל לאביהם שבשמים ואקשי' הא גופה קשיא אמרת מן האגף ולפנים כלפנים האגף עצמו חוץ אימא סיפא מן האגף ולחוץ כו' ואוקימנא בשערי ירושלים אגף עצמו כלחוץ כי לא נתקדשו מפני שמצורעין מגינין תחתיהן בחמה מפני החמה כו' וכן שערי נקנור לא נתקדשו מפני שמצורעין עומדין שם ומכניסין ידיהם לבהונות כדי שיזו עליהם אבל שערי עזרה אגף עצמו כלפנים: החלונות ועובי החומה כלפנים: אמר רב גגין ועליות של ירושלים לא נתקדשו ואקשי' עליה והא איהו דאמר משום רבי חייא פסח כזיתא והלילא פקע איגרא מאי

מסורת הש"ס

זבחים קד:
ב"ג ושרפו
[זבחים מו.]
סוטה לח:
[פי' תוספות יבמות ז: ד"ה זה נכנס כו']

גליון הש"ס

גמרא גגין ועליות. עי' מכות יב ע"א תד"ה אין, ובמהרש"א שם ובמשנה למלך פ"ו מהל' שגגות:

תורה אור

לא הכי קאמר *אחד עצם שיש עליו כזית בשר מבחוץ ואחד עצם שאין עליו כזית בשר מבחוץ ויש עליו כזית בשר מבפנים במקום שבירה *והתניא °ועצם לא תשברו בו אחד עצם שיש בו מוח ואחד עצם שאין בו מוח ומה אני מקיים °ואכלו את הבשר בלילה הזה בבשר שעל גבי העצם או אינו אלא בבשר שבתוך העצם ומה אני מקיים ועצם לא תשברו בו בעצם שאין בו מוח אבל בעצם שיש בו מוח שובר ואוכל ואל תתמה שהרי יבא עשה וידחה ל"ת כשהוא אומר °ועצם לא ישברו בו בפסח שני שאין ת"ל שהרי כבר נאמר °ככל חקת הפסח יעשו אותו הוי אומר *אחד עצם שיש בו מוח ואחד עצם שאין בו מוח מיתיבי אבר שיצא מקצתו חותך עד מקום שמגיע לעצם וקולף עד שמגיע לפרק וחותך ואי אמרת אבר שאין עליו כזית בשר במקום זה ויש (א) במקום אחר אין בו משום שבירת העצם למה לי דקולף עד שמגיע לפרק וחותך נקלוף ביה פורתא ונתבריה אביי אמר משום פקע רבינא אמר בקולית *תנן התם [ג] הפיגול והנותר (והטמא) מטמאין את הידים *רב הונא ורב חסדא חד אמר מפני *חשדי כהונה וחד אמר מפני עצלי כהונה מר מתני אפיגול ומר מתני אנותר מאן דמתני אפיגול משום חשדי כהונה ומאן דמתני אנותר משום עצלי כהונה מר מתני כזית ומר מתני כביצה מאן דמתני כזית כאיסורו ומאן דמתני כביצה כטומאתו איבעיא להו יוצא גזרו רבנן טומאה או לא מי אמרינן נותר דגזרו טומאה דאתי לאיעצולי ביה אבל יוצא אפוקי בידים לא מפקי ליה בידים לא גזרו ביה רבנן טומאה או דילמא לא שנא ת"ש אבר שיצא מקצתו חותך עד שמגיע לעצם וקולף עד שמגיע לפרק וחותך וא"א גזרו ביה רבנן טומאה כי חתיך ליה מאי הוי הא קמטמא ליה טומאת סתרים היא וטומאת סתרים לא מטמיא ולרבינא דאמר *חיבורי אוכלין לאו חיבור הוא וכמאן דמפרתי דמי מאי איכא למימר הא קנגע בהדדי וקא מטמא אלא למאן דמתני כזית דלית ביה כזית ומאן דמתני כביצה דלית ביה כביצה ת"ש המוציא בשר פסח מחבורה לחבורה אע"פ שהוא בלא תעשה טהור מאי לאו °טהור ואסור דיוצא מחבורה לחבורה כיוצא חוץ למחיצתו דמי ומפסיל ואפי' הכי קתני טהור אלמא לא גזרו רבנן טומאה לא טהור ומותר דיוצא מחבורה לחבורה לאו כיוצא חוץ למחיצתו דמי ולא מפסיל והא קא תני סיפא האוכלו הרי זה בל"ת בשלמא למאן דאמר כביצה דאית ביה כזית ולית ביה כביצה אלא למאן דאמר כזית מאי איכא למימר אלא ביוצא בפסח לא מיבעיא לן דלא גזרו רבנן טומאה מאי טעמא *בני חבורה זריזין הן ומוזהר זהירי ביה אלא כי קמיבעיא לן ביוצא בקדשים מאי תיקו ומוציא בשר פסח מחבורה

שמות יב · שם · במדבר ט · שם

לא הכי קאמר כו'. לעולם אכילה במקום שבירה בעינן ואחד עצם שאין עליו כזית בשר דקאמר הכי קאמר אין עליו בשר מבחוץ ויש בתוכו מוח מבפנים ובמקום שבירה ואשמעינן דאכילת מוח אכילה היא: והתניא. בניחותא דאסור לשבר עצם שבתוכו מוח ולא אמרינן ליתו עשה דואכלו את הבשר וידחה את לא תעשה דשבירה: ומה אני מקיים ואכלו את הבשר בבשר שעל העצם. אבל מוח לא דליכא לאוקמה במוח נמי ועל ידי גחלת דלא מצריך ליה קרא מילתא דאתי בה לידי תקלה דילמא פקע: שאין תלמוד לומר. שלא הוצרך ללמד איסור שבירה: אבר שיצא מקצתו. וצריך לחתוך את היוצא: חותך. את הבשר סביב אינקרבי"ל: עד שמגיע לעצם וקולף. הבשר שלא יצא: עד שמגיע לפרק. שמתחברין שם שני עצמות: וחותך. את הפרק ומשליך את העצם שיצא מקצתו ואוכל בשר הנקלף: נקלוף בה פורתא. במקום שבירה סביב: משום פקע. שמא יפקע וישבר תחת הבשר כשיכה על מקום הקלוף: בקולית. רדונדי"ל של היד דיש בו מוח מתוכו לא מהניא ליה קליפה: מטמאין את הידים. מדרבנן: חד אמר משום חשדי כהונה. שחשודין לפגל קרבן משום איבה גזרו על הפיגול שיטמא את הידים כדי שיהא זה צריך להטביל ידיו קודם שיגע בקודש ויטריחוהו: וחד אמר משום עצלי כהונה. המתעצלים באכילת קדשים גזרו טומאה על הנותר כדי להטריחו עליהם: מר מתני. טעמא דידי' חשדי אפיגול ומר מתני טעמא דידיה עצלי אנותר: מר מתני. בין פיגול בין נותר בכזית גזור רבנן ליטמאו: כאיסורו. כשיעור איסור אכילתו שהוא חייב עליו בכזית: כטומאתו. כשיעור טומאת אוכלים דאורייתא בכביצה: הא קא מיטמי. פנימי מחמת מגעו של יוצא המחובר לו: ומשני טומאת בית הסתרים היא. כל מגע חיבור בית הסתרים היא שאין מקום מגעו נראה וטומאת בית הסתרים נפקא לן במסכת נדה דלא מיטמיא מוידיו לא שטף במים בפ' יוצא דופן (דף מג:) דבעינן נגיעה בידים שהן בגלוי: ולרבינא דאמר. בפרק בהמה המקשה (דף עג:) לגבי מגע חיבור דאוכלים כמאן דמפרתי דמו ולא הוי חיבור ולא מגע בית הסתרים מיקרי: דלית ביה כזית. בלותו קצת: שיצא מחבורה לחבורה. לקמיה מפרש לא תעשה דיליה: מאי לאו טהור. מלטמא: ואסור. לאכול כשאר יוצא חוץ למחיצה דמחילת פסח מקום אכילתו היא ואפילו הכי קתני טהור: לא טהור ומותר. דלא פסול יוצא אית ביה אבל יוצא חוץ למחיצה לעולם אימא לך דמטמא: הרי זה בלא תעשה. כדאמר °בפרק כל שעה (לעיל כד.) לא יאכל כי קדש הם כל שבקדש פסול בא הכתוב ליתן לא תעשה על אכילתו אלמא יוצא חשיב ליה ואפי' הכי קתני טהור: בשלמא למאן. דמתני אפיגול ונותר כביצה מצי לתרוצי דגזור טומאה נמי איוצא והאי דקתני טהור בדליכא כביצה: מאי איכא למימר · מדקתני האוכלו בלא תעשה מכלל דאיכא כזית: זריזין הן. שהם רבים ומזרזים זה את זה מלהוציא ולא איצטריך לאחמורי עלייהו שלא יבואו לידי יציאה: מחבורה

אחד עצם שיש בו מוח ואחד עצם שאין בו מוח · הכא מזכיר שאינו פשוט קודם וכן בפ' החולץ (יבמות מא·) כל הנשים לא ינשאו עד ג' חדשים אחד בתולות ואחד אלמנות כו' תנא נמי ברישא בתולות שאינו פשוט והיכא דאיכא פלוגתא או קאי אקרא דרך להזכיר פשוט קודם כההיא דראש השנה (דף כט:) דתנן אמר רבי אלעזר לא התקין רבן יוחנן בן זכאי שיהו תוקעין אלא ביבנה אמרו לו אחד יבנה כו' כלומר כמו שפשוט לך שתוקעים ביבנה כך כל מקום שיש ב"ד וכן בבבא קמא (דף נ:) אחד בור אחד שיח ומערה דקאי אקרא דכתיב בור וכן בסוטה (דף מג:) אחד הבונה ואחד הלוקח כו' וכן בפ"ק דסוכה (דף ב:) גבי א' גדולה וא' קטנה כו'* : כשהוא אומר ועצם לא ישברו בו בפסח שני כו'. בפ' דם חטאת בזבחים (דף צז:) יליף מהכא דלאו עשה דוחה ל"ת בקדשים מדכתב רחמנא גבי פסח ועצם לא תשברו בו וקשה היכי יליף מינה ואמאי נמי צריך קרא הכא הא בעידנא דמיעקר לאו לא מקיים עשה *ועוד קשה לרשב"א דהכא אפשר לקיים שניהם על ידי גומרתא דהשורף בעצמות אין בו משום שבירת עצם וקיימא לן *דהיכא דיכול לקיים שניהם לא אתי עשה ודחי ל"ת ותירץ רבינו חיים לרשב"א (ב) דלרבה שפירש לעיל בגומרתא דאסור משום הפסד קדשי' אתי שפיר: משום חשדי כהונה. וא"ת כמו כן לא יחושו לעשות בטומאה וי"ל דאף לרשעים חמירא להו טומאה כדאמרינן ביומא (דף כג·) ללמדך שחמורה עליהן טהרת כלים יותר משפיכות דמים* : טומאת בית הסתרים היא. וא"ת התינח לר' יוסי אלא לר' מאיר דפליג עליה ומייתי לה בפ' בהמה המקשה (חולין עג:) דאית ליה דמטמא מאי איכא למימר וי"ל דקיימא לן כר' יוסי לגבי ר' מאיר: ולרבינא דאמר חיבורי אוכלין כמאן דמפרתי כו'. וא"ת בלא רבינא כיון דס"ד דאיכא שיעור לטמויי במה שיצא לחוץ הוה מצי לאקשויי דמסקינן בפרק בהמה המקשה (שם) דמודה ר' יוסי בשלש על שלש הבאות מבגד גדול דבשעת פרישתו מאביו מקבל טומאה מאביו וה"נ הכא וי"ל דאיכא לאוקומה בניתזות בכל כחן וכן משני בפ' אמרו לו (כריתות טו:) גבי אבר המדולדל באדם טהור מיהו הכא כיון שאינו חותך העצם אלא חותך סביבו' העצם אינו יכול להתיז בכל כחו ובירושלמי מוקי בחותך ומשליך במעט מעט : דבני חבורה זריזין הן כי קמיבעיא לן יוצא דקדשים. וא"ת דבפ' המוצא תפילין (עירובין קג·) משמע איפכא דקאמר כהנים זריזין הן אמרינן בני חבורה זריזין הן לא אמרינן ותירץ ר"י דלא דמי דגבי בני חבור' שייך למיגזר טפי שמא יתחה מלגבי כהנים דהא מילתא לא שייכא לפסח כלל אבל במידי דשייך לפסח כגון יוצא זריזין בני החבורה יותר מכהנים : הוצאה

צח א מיי' פ"י מהל' ק"פ הלכה ג:
צט [ב] מיי' פ"ח מהלכות אבות הטומאה הלכה ג]:
צט ב מיי' פ"ט מהל' ק"פ הלכה ב:
ק ג מיי' פ"ח מהל' אבות הטומאה הל' ט:

[ועיין תוס' לקמן קח: ד"ה אחד ובשבת כ: ד"ה אחד ובסוכה כ. ד"ה אחת וקדושין יג. ד"ה כשם ובכתובות כ: ד"ה אחד וזבחים לב: ד"ה אי הכי ובמנחות סג: ד"ה ר"י]

[לקמן נט.]

[ועיין בספר פסקי תוס' זבחים פ' דם חטאת סעיף סט]

[שבת קלג.]

רבינו חננאל

ריש לקיש הכי קתני אחד עצם שיש עליו כזית בשר במקום זה מבחוץ ואחד עצם שאין עליו כזית בשר מבחוץ ויש בו כזית מוח מבפנים יש בו משום שבירת עצם. והתניא הכי ועצם לא תשברו בו אחד עצם שיש בו מוח במקום שבירה ואחד עצם שאין בו מוח ומה אני מקיים ואכלו את הבשר וגו' ואסיקנא הרי אחד עצם שיש בו מוח ואחד עצם שאין בו מוח חייב ומותבינן תוב לריש לקיש אבר שיצא מקצתו פי' חוץ לירושלים ונפסל חותך בבשר עד שמגיע לעצם ומפריש בין הבשר שיצא ובין הבשר שנשאר באבר שלא יצא וקולף כלומר מפריש הבשר הכשר שלא יצא מפשיטו מן העצם עד שמגיע לפרק וחותך נמצא הבשר המופשט תלוי בפסח הבשר שיצא מחובר על העצם ושורף הבשר שיצא והעצם עמו ושאר הבשר שהפשיט מן העצם כשר לאכילה ולדברי ריש לקיש למה אמרה המשנה שצריך קליפה עד הפרק הלא הוא שבירת העצם שלא במקום בשר אינו חייב יקלוף מן הבשר מעט ולא ישאיר באותו מקום בשר וישבר העצם ומשני אביי חיישינן משום פקע כלומר כששובר העצם אינו מתפרק עמו נסירת אלא נסדק חיישי' שמא יעלה הסדק במקום לפיכך חותך בפרק רבינא אמר בקולית: אבר שיצא מקצתו כו' תנן התם בסוף מס' זו הפגול והנותר והטמא מטמאין את הידים אפגול אמרינן מ"ט גזרו בו רבנן טומאה משום חשדי כהונה שלא יחשדו כי לאכלו נגע בו הלכך גזרו בו טומאה שלא יבוא ליגע בו כלל וחד מתני אנותר מפני שנתעצלו בו והניחוהו להיות נותר חד מתני כזית מטמא הידים באיסור אכילתו מה איסור אכילתו בכזית אף איסור נגיעתו בכזית וחד אמר כביצה כטומאת אוכלין: איבעיא להו בשר היוצא חוץ למחיצתו ונפסל גזרו בו טומאה או לא ואתינן למפשט לה ממתני' דתנן אבר שיצא מקצתו חותך כו' ואי אמרת גזרו בו אע"פ שחתכו מן הבשר הנשאר באבר מבפנים נטמא מן הבשר שיצא ושנינן נגיעת הבשר בבשר במקום החתיכה היא ומקום החתיכה קודם חתיכתה מקום סתירה הוא וקי"ל זו היא טומאת סתרים ולא מטמאה וכבר פירשנוהו בפ' בהמה המקשה לולד ולשם רבינא מפריק אפילו תימא רבנן חיבורי אוכלין כמאן דמפרקי דמי וקא נגעו אהדדי כלומר כיון דלחתיכה קאי כחתוך דמי ואינה טומאת בית הסתרים אלא טומאה גלויה היא וכאלו חתיכה אחת נגעת בחברתה ושני' הא דתנן אבר שיצא חותך בבשר ובפ"ש ומה שבפנים כשר בזמן שאין בשר היוצא כזית דלא נחתא ליה טומאה כלל: ת"ש בשר פסח היוצא מחבורה לחבורה אע"פ שהוא בלא תעשה טהור מאי לאו יוצא מחבורה לחבורה טהור ומותר היא ולאו כתיב ביה לא תוציא מן הבית מן הבשר חוצה כלאו דשבירת עצם מה שבירת העצם לא פסול ליה אף יציאתו לא פסול ליה ואקשי' אי הכי טהור ומותר הוא אימא סיפא והאוכלו הרי זה בלא תעשה דתניא בתורת כהנים והבשר אשר יגע בכל טמא לא יאכל בכל לרבות היוצא והבשר כל טהור יאכל בשר לרבות בשר הפנימי שהוא מותר כמאן אמרו אבר שיצא מקצתו כו' בשלמא למאן [דאמר] ביוצא כביצה מוקי לה בדלית ליה כביצה אלא כזית הלכך עובר משום אוכל חוץ למחיצתו ואין עובר משום יוצא דהא לית ביה כביצה אלא למאן דבעי ביוצא

[זבחים לג:]

הגהות הב"ח

(א) גמרא ויש עליו כזית בשר במקום אחר אין בו: (ב) תוס' ד"ה כשהוא וכו' דלרבה שפירש לעיל. נ"ב פי' האי סוגיא ס"ל האי טעמא משום הפסד קדשים אבל לא כרבא דקאמר דילמא אכיל טרפא אלא וס"ל דאיכא דאי הפסד קדשים:

[לעיל סו:] לקמן קכ: [שם]

[פי' שלא יחשדו הנוגע בו כי לאכלו נגע בו הלכך גזרו בו טומאה כו' ערוך ערך חשד ע"ש ישוב ופשט נחמד ולפ"ז יתישב קושית תוספות בד"ה משום חשדי כהונה]

[חולין עג: עג.]

גליון הש"ס

רש"י ד"ה הרי זה בל"ת כדאמר בפ"ש. עיין לקמן דף צה ע"א ברש"י ד"ה לא תוציא: תום' ד"ה משום חשדי כהונה י"ל דאף לרשעים. עיין סנהדרין מח ע"א תד"ה מאמשין:

of flesh upon it elsewhere?—Said he to him, [85a] No: it means this: Both a bone which has as much as an olive of flesh on the outside, and a bone which has not as much as an olive of flesh on it on the outside, but contains as much as an olive of flesh [marrow] inside, [yet still] at the point of breaking. And it was taught [even so]: *'Neither shall ye break a bone thereof'*: [this refers to] both a bone which contains marrow and a bone which does not contain marrow, while to what do I apply,[3] *and they shall eat the flesh in that night?*[4] To the meat *on* the bone. Yet perhaps it is not so, but [it applies] to the meat [marrow] inside the bone [too], while to what do I apply, *'neither shall ye break a bone thereof'?* To a bone which does not contain marrow; but in the case of a bone which contains marrow he breaks [it] and eats [the marrow]; and do not wonder thereat, for the affirmative command comes and overrides the negative command![5] When, [however,] *'they shall not break a bone thereof*[6] is stated in connection with the second Passover, which need not have been taught, seeing that it has already been said, *according to all the statute of the Passover they shall keep it,*[1] deduce from this [that it means] both a bone which contains marrow and a bone which does not contain marrow.

An objection is raised: [With regard to] a limb part of which went outside,[2] he cuts [the flesh] as far as the bone, and pares it until he reaches the joint and then cuts it off.[3] Now if you say [that] a limb upon which there is not as much as an olive at this point but there is as much as an olive on it elsewhere is not subject to the [prohibition of] breaking a bone, why does he pare it until he reaches the joint and [then] cut it off? Let us scrape a little away and break it?—Abaye said: [This cannot be done] because of a [possible] split.[4] Rabina said: This refers to the thigh bone.[5]

We learned elsewhere: *Piggul* and *nothar*[6] defile the hands.[7] R. Huna and R. Ḥisda,—one maintained: It was on account of the suspects of the priesthood;[8] while the other maintained: It was on account of the lazy priests.[9] One recited [the reason] in reference to *piggul*, while the other recited it in reference to *nothar*. He who recited it in reference to *piggul* [gave the reason as being] on account of the suspects of the priesthood. While he who recited it in reference to *nothar* [stated that it was] on account of the lazy priests. One recited: As much as an olive;[10] while the other recited: As much as an egg. He who recited, as much as an olive [took the same standard] as its prohibition,[11] while he who recites, as much as an olive, [takes the same standard] as

b its uncleanness.[1]

The scholars asked: Did the Rabbis enact uncleanness in respect of what goes outside[2] or not? Do we say, they imposed uncleanness on *nothar* because they [the priests] might come to be lazy about it; but [concerning] that which goes outside, they will [certainly] not carry it out with [their own] hands, [and so] the Rabbis did not decree uncleanness in connection therewith. Or perhaps there is no difference?—Come and hear: If part of a limb went outside, he cuts [the flesh] as far as the bone and pares it until he reaches the joint and then cuts it off. Now if you say that the Rabbis imposed uncleanness upon it, what if he does cut? Surely it defiles it?[3]—It is concealed uncleanness,[4] and concealed uncleanness does not defile. But according to Rabina who maintained: The connection of foodstuffs is not a real connection, and they are as though separated,[5] what can be said: surely they[6] touch each other and it [the inner portion] is defiled?—Hence according to him who recited, as much as an olive, [we must say here] that it[7] did not contain as much as an olive; while according to him who recited, as much as an egg, [we must say] that it did not contain as much as an egg.

Come and hear: If a man carries out flesh of a Passover-offering from one company to another,[8] though he [has violated] a negative injunction, it [the flesh] is clean. Now does that not mean that it is clean yet forbidden, because that which goes out from one company to another company is like that which goes outside its boundary[9] and is disqualified [for eating], yet even so it teaches [that] it is clean, which proves that the Rabbis did not decree uncleanness!—No: it is clean and permitted, because that which goes out from company to company is not like that which goes outside its boundary, and it is not disqualified. But surely the second clause teaches: He who eats it is subject to a negative injunction? As for him who says, as much as an egg, it is well:
c [this may refer to] where it contains as much as an olive[1] but not as much as an egg. But according to him who says as much as an olive, what can be said?—Rather [say thus]: We do not ask in respect of what goes out in the case of a Passover-offering, for the Rabbis [certainly] did not decree uncleanness [there]. What is the reason? The members of a company[2] are most scrupulous, and so are very careful with it.[3] But we do ask in respect of what goes out in the case of sacrifices [in general]: what [is the law]? The question stands over.

Now he who carries out flesh of the Passover-offering [85b]

(3) Lit., 'and how do I fulfil?' (4) Ex. XII, 8. (5) V. *supra* 83b, n. b1. (6) Num. IX, 12.
(1) Num. IX, 12. (2) V. *supra* 84b, n. b2. (3) While the flesh which he cut off (i.e., which had not gone outside) is eaten. (4) When he hits the bone to break it, it may split elsewhere, not just where it was scraped. (5) Which contains marrow; hence scraping the flesh off is of no avail. (6) V. Glos. (7) By Rabbinic law; v. *infra* 120b. (8) Who were suspected of maliciously making the sacrifice *piggul* to hurt its owner, who would have to bring another; therefore the priest who handles it was declared unclean, since defilement was regarded as very serious even by the wicked (Rashi, and Tosaf. quoting Yoma 23a). Another interpretation: so that he who touched it should not be suspected of intending to eat it, as it would be known that he could not do this in his unclean state. (9) Who were too indolent to consume the flesh within the permitted period and allowed it to become *nothar*. (10) Of these defiled the hands.
(11) That quantity involves punishment if it is eaten.
b (1) As much as an egg is the smallest quantity which defiles by Biblical law. Hence when the Rabbis enacted that this defiles the hands, they adopted the same standard. (2) Its appointed boundaries. (3) The inner portion of the flesh is defiled by contact with the part which went outside. (4) This is a technical term: the actual point of contact is not visible in the same way that the contact of two *separate* pieces of flesh is visible. (5) Since foodstuffs are intended to be cut up. In his view the law of concealed uncleanness is only applicable where the object is not intended to be cut, e.g., a piece of cloth, v. Ḥul. 72b. (6) The two parts. (7) The portion which went outside. (8) Cf. Mishnah *infra* 86a. (9) Within which it must be eaten. Viz., the walls of Jerusalem.
c (1) Which involves punishment. (2) Who have registered for one paschal sacrifice. (3) Hence there is no need for a preventive measure.

[the verse refers to] a fit [sacrifice], [84b] this however is unfit;[7] but on the view that whatever is fit for eating [is subject to this law], [surely] this too is fit for eating.[8]

R. Joseph said: In such a case all agree that it is not subject to the [prohibition of] breaking a bone, for Rabbi comes to be a [more] lenient[1] and this is surely unfit. But[2] they differ where it enjoyed a period of fitness and then became unfit:[3] on the view that [the verse refers to] a fit [sacrifice], this [indeed] was fit; but on the view that [only what is] fit for eating [is meant], surely it is not fit for eating now.

Abaye said: In such a case all hold that it is not subject to the [prohibition of] breaking a bone. What is the reason? [Because] at all events it is unfit now. But they differ in respect of breaking a bone during the daytime.[4] On the view that [the verse refers to] a fit [sacrifice], this [indeed] is fit; but on the view that [only what is] fit for eating [is subject to this law], at present[5] it is not fit for eating.

An objection is raised: 'Rabbi said: One may register for the marrow in the head, but one may not register for the marrow in the thigh-bone'. Why [may one register for] the marrow in the head? Because one is able to scrape it and extract it. Now if you think that the breaking of the bone by daylight is permitted, then the thigh-bone too, let us break it during the day, extract the marrow, and register for it?—Abaye can answer you: Yet even according to your view,[6] let us still take a glowing coal *after* nightfall, place it upon it, burn it and extract the marrow and register for it? For surely it was taught: But he who *burns* the bones or cuts the *sinews* does not violate [the prohibition of] breaking a bone? Then what can you say?[7] Abaye said: Because it may split.[8] Raba said: [This is impossible] on account of the loss of sacred food, which he may destroy with [his own] hands, as the fire may destroy some of the marrow. [Hence] during the daytime too [it may not be broken], as a preventive measure on b account of after nightfall.[1]

R. Papa said: In such a case all hold that it is subject to the [prohibition of] breaking a bone. What is the reason? [Because] in the evening it is fit for eating. But they differ in respect of a limb part of which went out:[2] on the view that [the verse refers to] a fit [sacrifice], this [indeed] is fit;[3] while on the view that [only what is] fit for eating [is subject to this law], this, however, is not fit for eating, as was taught: R. Ishmael the son of R. Joḥanan b. Berokah said: A limb part of which went outside, and which he broke, is not subject to the [prohibition of] breaking a bone.

R. Shesheth the son of R. Idi said: In such a case all agree that it is not subject to the [prohibition of] breaking a bone, for this limb is surely unfit. But they differ in respect of breaking a bone of a half-roast [offering].[4] On the view that [the verse refers to] a fit [sacrifice], this is fit;[5] while on the view that [only what is] fit for eating [is subject to this law], now [however] it is not fit for eating.

R. Naḥman b. Isaac said: In such a case all agree that it is subject to the [prohibition of] breaking a bone. What is the reason? Because it is surely fit for eating, as he can roast it [completely] and eat it. But they differ in respect of [the breaking of the bone of] the fat tail. On the view that [the verse refers to] a fit [sacrifice], this is indeed fit, but on the view that [only what is] fit for eating [is subject to this law], this [however] is not fit for eating, for c the fat tail is offered to the Most High.[1]

R. Ashi said: In such a case it is certainly not subject to the [prohibition of] breaking a bone, for it is certainly unfit for eating at all. But they differ in respect of [breaking the bone of] a limb upon which there is less than an olive of flesh.[2] On the view that [the verse refers to] a fit [sacrifice], this indeed is fit; but on the view that [only what is] fit for eating [is subject to this law], we require the *standard* of eating, which is absent.

Rabina said: In such a case it is not subject to the [prohibition of] breaking a bone, because we require the *standard* of eating. But they differ in respect of a limb upon which there is less than an olive of flesh at *this* point,[3] but which contains as much as an olive of flesh elsewhere. On the view that [the verse refers to] a fit [sacrifice], this indeed is fit. But on the view that [only what is] fit for eating [is subject to this law], we require the standard of eating at the point where it is broken, which is absent.

It was taught as four of these.[4] For it was taught, Rabbi said: '*In one house shall it be eaten . . . neither shall ye break a bone thereof*': he is culpable on account of that which is fit, but he is not culpable on account of that which is not fit. [Thus:] If it had a period of fitness but became unfit by the time of eating, it is not subject to the [prohibition of] breaking a bone. If it contains the standard of eating,[5] it is subject to the [prohibition of] breaking a bone; if it does not contain the standard of eating, it is not subject to the [prohibition of] breaking a bone. That which is intended for the altar[6] is not subject to the [prohibition of] breaking a bone. [Only] at the time of eating is it subject to the [prohibition of] breaking a bone; when not at the time of eating[7] it is not subject to the [prohibition of] breaking a bone.

It was stated: If a limb does not contain as much as an olive d of flesh at *this* point,[1] but does contain as much as an olive of flesh elsewhere,—R. Joḥanan maintained: It is subject to the [prohibition of] breaking a bone; R. Simeon b. Laḳish said: It is not subject to the [prohibition of] breaking a bone. R. Joḥanan raised an objection against Resh Laḳish: '*Neither shall ye break a bone thereof*': both a bone upon which there is as much as an olive of flesh and a bone upon which there is not as much as an olive of flesh. Now what does 'there is not as much as an olive of flesh upon it' mean? Shall we say that there is not as much as an olive of flesh upon it at all, then why is it subject to the [prohibition of] breaking a bone?[2] Hence surely this is what it means: Both a bone upon which there is as much as an olive of flesh at this [very] point and a bone upon which there is not as much as an olive of flesh at this point, but there is as much as an olive

(7) Normally such is unfit, for uncleanness is merely overridden in favour of a community, but not permitted, v. *supra* 77a, n. b2; hence it is not subject to the prohibition of breaking a bone. (8) Since a Passover offered in uncleanness may be eaten in uncleanness, v. *supra* 76b.

a (1) Some versions omit this (BaḤ). (2) [Var. lec. omit 'In such a case . . . But'.] (3) E.g., the paschal sacrifice became unclean after the sprinkling of the blood. (4) Of the fourteenth, before the Festival commences on the evening of the fifteenth. (5) I.e., when he actually breaks it. (6) *Sc.* that this is forbidden. (7) Why one may not register for the marrow. (8) The fire may not burn it through but cause it to crack and split, and this is the same as breaking it.

b (1) The point of the 'too' ('during the daytime *too*') is this: just as it must not be burnt at night by Rabbinical law only, lest something else happen, so he must not break it during the day by Rabbinical law only, also because he may do something else instead, viz., break it at night. (2) Without the walls of Jerusalem. The offering had to be eaten in Jerusalem; whatever went outside became unfit. Here as only part of a limb had gone out, this part should be cut off, but this entails cutting across the bone in the limb. (3) *Sc.* the part which remained inside, and when he breaks the bone he naturally touches on that part. Consequently it is forbidden; for the remedy v. Mishnah *infra* 85b. (4) Which is itself forbidden, v. Ex. XII, 9: *Eat not of it half-roast* (so translated *supra* 41a). (5) The sacrifice itself is fit, though it may not be eaten because it was not properly prepared.

c (1) I.e., it is burnt on the altar together with the *emurim* (v. Glos.). (2) That is the least quantity which constitutes eating (3) Where he actually breaks the bone. (4) [R. Joseph, R. Naḥman b. Isaac, Abaye and Rabina (or R. Ashi). V. n. c5. Var. lec., however, omits the passage.] (5) [Either at the point where it is broken, as required by Rabina, or on the limb itself, as required by R. Ashi.] (6) I.e., the bone of the fat tail. (7) I.e., before nightfall.

d (1) At the point of breaking. (2) For R. Joḥanan and Resh Laḳish both agree that it must contain as much as an olive of flesh before it is subject to the prohibition.

צ א מיי' פ"י מהל' ק"פ הלכה א:

[דף פג.]

צא ב מיי' שם הל' ו:

צב ג מיי' שם הל' י':

צג ד מיי' שם הל' ה:

צד ה מיי' שם הל' א:

צה ו ז מיי' שם הל' ו:

צו ח מיי' שם הל' ז:

צז ט י כ מיי' שם הלכה ג:

היתה לו שעת הכושר ונפסל איכא בינייהו מאן דאמר כשר הא כשר הוא · לא משום דדריש בו בכשר ולא בפסול משמע ליה הכי דהא ר' שמעון מפרש לעיל *מילתיה דת"ק דקתני נמי בו בכשר ולא בפסול וקאמר אחד זה ואחד זה אין בו משום שבירת עצם אלא דרב יוסף לא מצי למישכח מידי דאיכא בינייהו אלא היתה לו שעת הכושר ונפסל: **אבר** שיצא מקצתו איכא בינייהו מאן דאמר כשר כשר · תימה אמאי חשיב ליה כשר טפי מבר אכילה הא מה שאינו ראוי לאכילה לאו כשר הוא:

ה"ג היתה לו שעת הכושר ונפסל אין בו משום שבירת העצם · ול"ג יש בו דלאו גר' תיקשי לרב יוסף ולא משכחינן כארבעה מינייהו ואית דגרס לעיל במילתיה דרב יוסף למ"ד כשר לאו כשר הוא למ"ד יאכל בר אכילה הוא ולפי זה מיתוקמא גירסת הספרים דגר' יש בו ואין נראה דבכולה שמעתין טפי נפיק (ה)מאכילה מדנפיק מתורת כשרות כי ההיא דאבר שילא מקלתו דכשר קרי ליה ולא בר אכילה הוא:

איתמר אבר שאין עליו כזית בשר במקום זה כו' · נראה לר"י ולריב"א דאליבא דרבי קמיפלגי דקתני בברייתא סתמא יש בו שיעור אכילה יש בו משום שבירת העצם ובפלוגתא דרבינא ורב אשי קמיפלגי אבל לרבנן לכ"ע יש בו משום שבירת עצם והא דמסיק אילימא דאין עליו כזית בשר כלל אמאי יש בו משום שבירת עצם אע"ג דמצי לאוקומ' כרבנן הוא"ל ואליבא דרבי קמיפלגי וסבירא להו כרבי מוקמי למתני' כוותיה:

האי פסול הוא · שנעשה בפסול דטומאה דחזיה היא בציבור אלא שכאן גזירת הכתוב לפוטרן בו: האי בר אכילה הוא · כדתנן (לעיל דף עו:) הפסח שבא בטומאה נאכל בטומאה: הא כשר · שנעשו עבודותיו בהכשר: מבעוד יום · שאינו שעת אכילה: נמנין על מוח שבראש · אפילו לא נמנה אלא על המוח יצא: ואין נימנין על מוח הקולית · מפני שאסור לשוברה ולהוציאו אבל מוח הראש יכול להוציא ולגוררו בקיסם דרך האף: ניתי גומרתא · גחלת ונכתי עליה עד שינקב ויוציא מוחו: אלא מאי אית לך למימר · אמאי אין נמנין ויוציאו בגחלת: אביי אמר משום פקע · שמא מחמת הגחלת יפקע במקום אחר ואין זו שריפה אלא שבירה: ורבא אמר משום הפסד קדשים · שמפסיד המוח ושורפו בידים ומוטב שיפסל מאליו הכא נמי לענין שבירה מבעוד יום אע"ג דמדאורייתא שרי רבנן גזור אטו משחשיכה: אבר שילא מקלתו · חוץ לחומת ירושלים וצריך לחתוך את היוצא איכא בינייהו: האי נמי כשר · שהרי הפנימי כשר והרי הוא שוברו ועובר משום לא תשברו בו אלא חותך עד שמגיע לעצם וקולף עד שמגיע לפרק וחותך כדתנן במתניתין (לקמן דף פה:): האי לאו בר אכילה הוא · במקום שבירה אינו ראוי לאכילה אבל אבר שילא כולו דהיינו היתה לו שעת הכושר ונפסל דכ"ע אין בו משום שבירה דהשתא מיהא פסול הוא: אליית השה קריבה עם האימורין מה שאין כן בשור ועז כדכתיב (ויקרא ג) חלבו האליה תמימה: רבינא אמר · אי ליכא כזית בשר דכולי עלמא אין בו משום שבירה אלא באין בו כזית במקום שבירה ויש בו כזית במקום אחר איכא בינייהו: ואינו חייב על הפסול · והשתא מפרש ואזיל הי פסול קא ממעט היתה לו שעת הכושר ונפסל אין בו משום שבירת העצם · גרסינן ורבי אומר גרסינן ברישא והיינו כרב יוסף למעוטי אליה כדרב נחמן בר יצחק שלא בשעת אכילה מבעוד יום כדאביי דאמר מבעוד יום אתא רבי למעוטי שיעור אכילה במקום שבירה כרבינא אי נמי למעוטי אין עליה כזית כרב אשי: אין בו משום שבירת העצם · דבעינן שיעור אכילה במקום שבירה: אמאי יש בו משום שבירת עצם · בין לר' יוחנן בין לריש לקיש כזית בעינן במקום זה · במקום שבירה: לא

האי *פסול למ"ד ראוי לאכילה האי נמי ראוי לאכילה הוא רב יוסף אמר ^כי האי גוונא דכולי עלמא אין בו משום שבירת העצם (א) דר' לאקולי קא אתי והאי הא פסול הוא אלא היתה לו שעת הכושר ונפסל איכא בינייהו למ"ד כשר ^הא כשר הוא למ"ד ראוי לאכילה הא השתא לאו ראוי לאכילה הוא אביי אמר (ב) כ"ע כל כי האי גוונא אין בו משום שבירת העצם מאי טעמא השתא מידת הא פסול הוא אלא שבירת העצם מבעוד יום איכא בינייהו למ"ד כשר הא כשר הוא למ"ד ראוי לאכילה השתא לאו בר אכילה הוא מיתיבי רבי אומר ^נמנין על מוח שבראש ואין נמנין על מוח שבקולית על מוח שבראש מ"מ הואיל ויכול לגוררו ולהוציאו ואי ס"ד שבירת העצם מבעוד יום שפיר דמי קולית נמי נתבריה מבעוד יום ונפקוה למוח דידיה ונמנו עליה אמר לך אביי ולטעמיך משחשיכה נמי נייתי גומרתא וניחות עליה ונקלה ונפקה למוח דידיה ונימני עליה דהא *תניא אבל (ג) ^השורף בעצמות והמחתך בגידין אין בו משום שבירת העצם אלא מאי אית לך למימר אביי אמר משום פקע רבא אמר משום הפסד קדשים דקא מפסיד ליה בידים דילמא אביל נורא ממוח דידיה מבעוד יום נמי גזירה מבעוד יום אטו משחשיכה רב פפא אמר ^כל כי האי גונא כ"ע יש בו משום שבירת העצם מאי טעמא לאורתא מיחזי לאכילה אלא באבר שיצא מקצתו קמיפלגי מ"ד כשר (ד) ^הא כשר הוא ומ"ד ראוי לאכילה האי לאו בר אכילה הוא כדתניא* ר' ישמעאל בנו של ר' יוחנן בן ברוקה אומר אבר שיצא מקצתו ושברו אין בו משום שבירת העצם רב ששת בריה דרב אידי אמר כל כה"ג דכולי עלמא אין בו משום שבירת העצם דהאי אבר הא פסול הוא אלא שבירת העצם בנא איכא בינייהו מ"ד כשר הא כשר הוא ומ"ד ראוי לאכילה השתא אינו ראוי לאכילה רב נחמן בר יצחק אמר ^כל כי האי גוונא יש בו משום שבירת העצם מאי טעמא דהא חזי לאכילה דמטוי ליה ואכיל ליה אלא שבירת האליה איכא בינייהו למ"ד כשר הא כשר הוא למ"ד ראוי לאכילה האי אינו ראוי לאכילה *דאליה לגבוה סלקא רב אשי אמר ^כל כי האי גוונא ודאי אין בו משום שבירת העצם דהא ודאי אינו ראוי לאכילה כלל אלא אבר שאין עליו כזית בשר איכא בינייהו למ"ד כשר הא כשר הוא למ"ד ראוי לאכילה בעינן שיעור אכילה וליכא רבינא אמר ^כל כי האי גוונא לית ביה משום שבירת העצם דבעינן שיעור אכילה אלא אבר שאין עליו כזית בשר במקום זה ויש עליו כזית בשר במקום אחר איכא בינייהו למ"ד כשר הא כשר הוא למ"ד ראוי לאכילה בעינן שיעור אכילה במקום שבירה והא ליכא תניא כארבעה מינייהו דתניא ר' אומר ^בבית אחד יאכל ^ועצם לא תשברו בו על הכשר הוא חייב ואינו חייב על הפסול היתה לו שעת הכושר ונפסל בשעת אכילה אין בו משום שבירת עצם יש בו שיעור אכילה יש בו משום שבירת עצם אין בו שיעור אכילה אין בו משום שבירת עצם הראוי למזבח אין בו משום שבירת העצם בשעת אכילה יש בו משום שבירת עצם שלא בשעת אכילה אין בו משום שבירת עצם איתמר אבר שאין עליו כזית בשר במקום זה ויש עליו כזית בשר במקום אחר רבי יוחנן אמר ^יש בו משום שבירת העצם רבי שמעון בן לקיש אמר אין בו משום שבירת עצם איתיביה רבי יוחנן לרבי שמעון בן לקיש ועצם לא תשברו בו אחד עצם שיש עליו כזית בשר ואחד עצם שאין עליו כזית בשר מאי אין עליו כזית בשר אילימא דאין עליו כזית בשר כלל ^אמאי יש בו משום שבירת העצם אלא לאו הכי קאמר אחד עצם שיש עליו כזית בשר במקום זה ואחד שאין עליו כזית בשר במקום זה ויש עליו כזית בשר במקום אחר (*קשיא לרבי שמעון בן לקיש) א"ל
לא

[פסול וראוי כצ"ל]

חולין דף יח: [תוספתא פ"ו]

[תוספתא פ"ו]

[לעיל נב.]

שמות יב

[חמש תיבות הללו נראין מיותר]

רבינו חננאל

עצם ואמרינן מכדי תרוייהו אמרי דלא לקי מאי בינייהו וחלקו בזה ר' ירמיה אמר פסח הבא בטומאה איכא בינייהו ורב יוסף אמר היתה לו שעת הכושר ונפסל איכא בינייהו ורבנכולן פשוטין הן ואסיקנא תנא כי ארבעה מינייהו ר' אומר בבית אחד יאכל ועצם לא תשברו בו על הכשר חייב ולא על הפסול היתה לו שעת הכושר ונפסלה יש בו משום שבירת העצם: **תניא** השורף בעצמות והמחתך בגידים אין בו משום שבירת העצם: **איתמר** עצם שאין עליו כזית בשר במקום זה ויש עליו כזית בשר במקום אחר ר' יוחנן אמר יש בו משום שבירת העצם ריש לקיש אמר אין בו משום שבירת העצם איתיביה ר' יוחנן לר' שמעון בן לקיש ועצם לא תשברו בו אחד עצם שיש עליו כזית בשר במקום זה [ואחד שאין עליו כזית בשר במקום זה] ויש עליו כזית בשר במקום אחר חייב ומשני

הגהות הב"ח

(א) גמ' שבירת העצם (דר' לאקולי קא אתי) הא"מ ונ"ב ס"א ל"ג ליה: (ב) שם אביי אמר כל כי האי גוונא כ"ע אין בו כצ"ל: (ג) שם אבל השורף בעצמות. נ"ב עיין בחולין דף יא המחתך בגידין והשורף בעצמות עכ"ל: (ד) שם מ"ד כשר האי נמי כשר הוא: (ה) תוס' ד"ה ה"ג ומי' טפי נפיק מתורת אכילה:

ולא מילה שלא בזמנה הבאה מק"ו רב אשי אמר °שבתון דיו"ט עשה הוא ואין עשה דוחה לא תעשה ועשה: **מתני׳** כל הנאכל בשור הגדול יאכל בגדי הרך וראשי כנפים והסחוסים: **גמ׳** רבה רמי תנן כל הנאכל בשור הגדול יאכל בגדי הרך ושאינו נאכל לא אימא סיפא ראשי כנפים והסחוסים והא הני לא מתאכלי בשור הגדול אלא תנאי היא והכי קתני כל הנאכל בשור הגדול יאכל בגדי הרך ושאינו נאכל לא וי"א אף ראשי כנפים והסחוסים רבא אמר מה הן קתני והכי קתני *כל הנאכל בשור הגדול בשלקא יאכל בגדי הרך בצלי ומה הן ראשי כנפים והסחוס׳ תניא כוותיה דרבא כל הנאכל בשור הגדול בשלקא יאכל בגדי הרך בצלי ומה הן ראשי כנפים והסחוסים וגידין הרכין נידונין כבשר *איתמר גידין שסופן להקשות רבי יוחנן אמר נמנין עליהן בפסח ריש לקיש אמר אין נמנין עליהן בפסח ר' יוחנן אמר נמנין עליהן בתר השתא אזלינן ריש לקיש אמר אין נמנין עליהן בתר בסוף אזלינן איתיביה ריש לקיש לר' יוחנן כל הנאכל בשור הגדול יאכל בגדי הרך ומה הן ראשי כנפים והסחוסים הני אין אבל גידין שסופן להקשות לא א"ל תנא הני וה"ה להנך הני מ"ט דהא מתאכלי בשור הגדול בשלקא הנך נמי מתאכלי בשור הגדול בשלקא א"ל ר' ירמיה לרבי אבין כי אזלת לקמיה דר' אבהו רמי ליה מי אמר רבי יוחנן גידין שסופן להקש' נמנין עליהן בפסח אלמא בתר השתא אזלינן והא *בעא מיניה ריש לקיש מרבי יוחנן עור הראש של עגל הרך מהו שיטמא ואמר לו אין מטמא אלמא בתר בסוף אזלינן א"ל *דרמא לך הא לא חש לקמחיה הא הדר ביה רבי יוחנן לגבי דריש לקיש וא"ל *אל תקניטני שבלשון יחיד אני שונה אותה: **מתני׳** *השובר את העצם בפסח הטהור הרי זה לוקה ארבעים *אבל המותיר בטהור והשובר בטמא אינו לוקה את הארבעים: **גמ׳** בשלמא מותיר בטהור *דתניא °לא תותירו ממנו עד בקר והנותר ממנו עד בקר וגו' בא הכתוב ליתן עשה אחר לא תעשה לומר שאין לוקה דברי רבי יהודה רבי יעקב אומר לא מן השם הוא זה אלא משום דהוה ליה לאו שאין בו מעשה ואין לוקין עליו אלא שבר בטמא מנלן דאמר קרא °ועצם לא תשברו בו *בו בכשר ולא בפסול ת"ר ועצם לא תשברו בו בו בכשר ולא בפסול ר' אומר °בבית אחד יאכל ועצם לא תשברו בו כל הראוי לאכילה יש בו משום שבירת עצם ושאין ראוי לאכילה אין בו משום שבירת עצם מאי בינייהו א"ר ירמיה פסח הבא בטומאה איכא בינייהו למ"ד כשר
האי

ויקרא כג · שמות יב · שם · שם

רש"י

ולא מילה שלא בזמנה · דלא ממעט קרא אתיא בק"ו לדחות ומה לרצח שדוחה את העבודה ועבודה דוחה את השבת מילה אף שלא בזמנה דוחה אותה אפילו במקום בהרת יקוץ בהרתו שבת שנדחת מפני עבודה אינו דין שתהא מילה דוחה ואתא קרא ומיעטה דכיון דשלא בזמנה היא כגון גר שנתגייר וקטן שנולדו אביו ועבר זמנה כשהיה למחר וגבי שריפת פסול קדשים נמי כמילה שלא בזמנה דאפשר לשהייה דמי: שבתון דיום טוב עשה הוא · דמשמע שבות והוה ליה יו"ט עשה ולא תעשה: **מתני׳** כל הנאכל בשור הגדול כו' · שכבר הוקשה כל מה שעתיד להקשות בו: יאכל בגדי הרך · ראוי לאכילה בפסח בן שמנה ימים אבל מה שאין נאכל בשור הגדול אין נמנין עליו בפסח אע"פ שעכשיו רך הוא עתיד להקשות בסופו: וראשי כנפים והסחוסים שקורין טינרו"ס שבראש גף הכתף אספלו"ן והסחוסין שאר הסחוס שבו כגון תנוך האוזן והסחוסי החזה והצלעות הקטנות שבסוף השדרה: **גמ׳** וי"א אף ראשי כנפים והסחוסין · הואיל ובשור הגדול נמי מתאכלי בשליקה בישול יותר: מה הן קתני · והכי קאמר כל הנאכל בשור הגדול בשליקה יאכל בגדי הרך צלי ומה הן ראשי כנפים והסחוסין: גידים שסופן להקשות · גידי צואר ובגדי ועלה הן רכים אבל אם היה מזקין סופן להיות קשים: ר' יוחנן אומר כו' · וגידים הרכין דקתני בהך ברייתא נידונין כבשר לר' יוחנן משמע לי' דרכין השתא ולריש לקיש משמע ליה בשאר גידים דרכין לעולם: הני אין · דס"ד מדפרים מה הן דוקא קאמר: הני מ"ט · פירושא הוא ומסקנא דקושיא: עגל הרך · מפרש בהעור והרוטב כל זמן שיונק ועור ראשו רך מולגין אותו ונאכל עמו: מהו שיטמא · טומאת אוכלין בתר השתא אזלינן ומטמא או בתר בסוף אזלינן ואינו מטמא: לא חש לקמחיה · למה שהוא טוחן אם סולת אם פסולת: הא הדר ביה ר' יוחנן · מהא דגידין שסופן להקשות כדאמר בשילהי בהמה המקשה (חולין עז:) ופשטינן לה מהא דהעור והרוטב דכי פשיט ליה רבי יוחנן עלה דהכיא אין מטמא ואותביה ריש לקיש ממתני' דהעור והרוטב דקתני אלו שעורותיהם כבשרן עור הראש של עגל הרך אלמא דבתר השתא אזלינן וא"ל רבי יוחנן אל תקניטני באותה משנה שבלשון יחיד אני שונה אותה אלמא מעיקרא הוה סמיך ר' יוחנן עליה ופליג בגידין שסופן להקשות ואידכר דיחידאה היא והדר ביה: **מתני׳** אבל המותיר בטהור · אפילו בטהור והשובר בטמא אינו לוקה (א) המותיר משום לא תותירו ולא שובר בטמא משום לא תשברו וטעמא מפרש בגמרא: **גמ׳** בא הכתוב כו' · כל לאו שניתק לעשה אין לוקין עליו דמשמע זו היא תקנתו אם תעבור על הלאו עשה זאת והיגלל ועוד דלא דמי ללאו דחסימ' שהמלקו' כסמוך לו:
האי

תוספות

ולא מילה שלא בזמנה דאתיא בק"ו · פירש בקונ' ומה לרצח שדוחה את העבודה ועבודה דוחה את השבת וקשה דרבא לית ליה האי ק"ו בפ' ר' אליעזר דמילה (שבת קלב:) דקסבר דהא דלרצח דוחה עבודה לא משום חומרא דלרצח אלא משום דגברא דלא חזי ור"ח פי' ק"ו ומה אוכל נפש שלא נכרתו עליו י"ג בריתות דוחה י"ט כו' ויש להשיב מה לאוכל נפש שכן מצוה עוברת שלמחר לא יהיה מצוה עליה ואומר ר"י דאיכא למיעבד ק"ו מנדרים ונדבות דדחו י"ט אע"פ שלא נכרתו עליהן י"ג בריתות וסבר רבא דקריבין בי"ט וליכא למיפרך מה לנדרים ונדבות שכן צורך גבוה כדפריך בפ' ר' אליעזר דמילה (שם דף קלא.) מה לעומר ושתי הלחם כו' דלאו חובה נינהו ואפילו חטאות ואשמות לא מיקרו צורך גבוה כיון דאי לאו דחטא לא בעו לאיתוייהו ונראה דרבא אית ליה הא דרב אשי די"ט עשה ולא תעשה ולהכי איצטריך ק"ו דאי לאו ק"ו לא הוה צריך למיסר וכן משמע בפ"ק דביצה (דף ח:) דפריך גבי אפר כירה מוכן לודאי כו' סוף סוף י"ט עשה הוא ואין עשה דוחה לא תעשה ועשה אלא אמר רבא כו' משמע דרבא אית ליה די"ט עשה הוא והשתא לבדו לא איצטריך לשריפת קדשים אלא על מילה דאיכא ק"ו אמר רבא פרק *(אם לא הביא)(דף קלג.) וגמרא מייתי לה הכא אשריפת קדשים דממילה ממעטי ורב אשי לא קאי למיפלג ארבא אלא מילתא דנפשיה קאמר ואקדשים קאי ואפילו אמילה כדמשמע באם לא הביא דלית ליה קל וחומר: **גידין** שסופן להקשות. פי' בקו' גידי צואר ואין נראה לריב"א דהא משמע דהשתא הם רכים כבשר לגמרי ואפי' ר"ל לא פסיל להו אלא משום בסוף ולעיל קאמר אלא פשיטא בגידי צואר משמע שהם רגילין להיות נותר ואין ראוין ליאכל כמו עצמות אלא נראה דהיינו גידי שדרה וגידים הרכים דקתני בברייתא איירי בגידי בשר דלכ"ע הוו כבשר: **הואיל** ומתאכלי בשור הגדול בשלקא · והשתא לא אזיל רבי יוחנן בתר השתא אלא בדבר הנאכל בשור הגדול בשלקא וא"ת ור"ל מאי פריך ליה לר' יוחנן אדרבה תיקשי לדידיה דמוכח בברייתא דבדבר הנאכל בשור הגדול בשלקא אזלינן בתר השתא ויש לומר דסבר ר"ל דראשי כנפים והסחוסין יש עליהם שם בשר יותר מבגידים ופריך לרבי יוחנן מדלא נקט בברייתא גידים דהוי רבותא טפי ור' יוחנן משני דאין רבותא כלל מה שאין בהן טעם בשר כל כך דהא אם היו רכים לעולם לא היה פוסלן הילכך כיון דמתאכלי בשלקא נימנין עליהן כמו ראשי כנפים והסחוסים ורשב"א מפרש טעמא דריש לקיש דגידים לא דמו לראשי כנפים והסחוסים דגידים סופן להקשות בגדי עצמו אבל ראשי כנפים והסחוסים אין סופם להקשות בגדי לעולם אלא בשור הגדול דוקא ולא שייך למיזל בהו בתר בסוף כיון דבגדי ועלה הם רכים לעולם: **הא** הדר ביה ר' יוחנן · פירוש מהך דמתניתין כדמוכח בפרק בהמה המקשה (חולין עז.) וקשה לר"י לר"ל דאותביה לר' יוחנן מההיא שעורותיהן כבשרן תיקשי לנפשיה דקסבר גבי פסח בתר בסוף אזלינן והתם אזיל בתר השתא וי"ל שאני שבעור ראש של עגל הרך יש לו טעם בשר הרבה מגידין וריב"א אומר דבירושלמי פריך דר"ל אדר"ל ומשני טעמא דר"ל מקרא ואכלו את הבשר (שמות יב) ולא גידין ובעור הראש של עגל הרך אזיל בתר דהשתא והכא הוי גזירת הכתוב:
היתה

עין משפט נר מצוה

פו א מיי' פ"י מהל' ק"פ הלכה ט :
פז ב מיי' שם הל' י :
פח ג מיי' שם הלכה א:
פט ד מיי' שם והל' יא:

רבינו חננאל

מהאי קרא הוא לבדו יעשה לכם הוא ולא מכשירין לבדו ולא מילה שלא בזמנו דאתיא בקל וחומר ומה אכל נפש שאע"פ שהוא באוהרת שכשהיא אינה מצוה דוחה יום טוב מילה שאע"פ שהיא שלא בזמנה מצוה היא שנכרתו עליה [י"ג] בריתות וחייב כרת אם לא ימול אינו דין שידחה יום טוב ת"ל לבדו ולא מילה שלא בזמנה ואם מילה שהיא מצוה והמבטלה לגמרי ענוש כרת ולא עוד אלא שהיא מצוה שנכרתו עליה שלש עשרה בריתות (אינה עשה) אינו דוחה יום טוב כל שכן של נותר שלא ידחה יום טוב שאפילו בטלו לגמרי אינו ענוש כרת: **רב** אשי מפיק ליה מהאי דכתיב בי"ט שבתון ולא תיעשה מלאכה נמצא בי"ט עשה שבתון ולא תעשה כמשמעו ואין עשה דוחה את לא תעשה ועשה: **מתני׳** כל הנאכל בשור הגדול יאכל בגדי הרך ראשי הכנפים והסחוסים כו' וכי כל מי שאינו נאכל בשור אינו נאכל בגדי הרך והרי ראשי כנפים והסחוסים שאינן נאכלין בשור הגדול שהן כעצמות ובגדי הרך נאכלין ופריק רבא ואמר הכי קאמר כל הנאכל בשור הגדול שלוק יאכל צלי בגדי הרך ומה הן ראשי כנפים והסחוסין תניא כותיה דרבא כל הנאכל בשור הגדול בשלקא כו' עד וגידין הרכין כבשר: **איתמר** גידין שסופן להקשות ר' יוחנן אמר נמנין עליהן בפסח דבתר השתא אזלינן והשתא רכין הן וכבשר הן וריש לקיש פליג עליה ומותיב עליה ממתני' ושני ליה הכי תנא תני ראשי כנפים והסחוסין הואיל ומתכלי בשור הגדול בשלקא והוא הדין לגידים [שסופן] להקשות דהני נמי מיתכלי בשור הגדול בשלקא: **רמי** ליה רבנן קמיה דר' אבהו מי אמר ר' יוחנן גידין הרכין שסופן להקשות נמנין עליהן בפסח אלמא כיון דמתכלי השתא בתר השתא אזלינן וכי בשר נינהו והא בעיא ר"ל מר"י עור הראש של עגל הרך מהו שיטמא ואמר ליה אינו מטמא דאלמא בתר בסוף אזלינן אמר ליה ר' אבהו דרמא הא לא חש לקמחיה כלומר אכילתו להפסד הולכת שאינו מתעסק בתורה כראוי לה (בפ') [הא] הדר ר' יוחנן ואמר לריש לקיש בעידנא דאקשי' עליה והתנן אלו שעורותיהן כבשרן ואחד מהן עור הראש של עגל הרך אמר לו ר' יוחנן משנה זו דברי [יחיד] הן דברי אלעזר בן יהודה איש אבלים [משום רבי] מר' יוחנן (וכגליון יעקב) הם ומפורש בפ' העור

ירושב כי אמר לו רבי יוחנן אל תקניטני בלשון יחיד אני שונה אותה: **מתני׳** אבל המותיר בטהור כו'. בשלמא מות"ר בטהור אינו לוקה דתניא לא תותירו ממנו עד בקר והנותר וגו' ובא הכתוב כו' לרבי יהודה כדאית ליה ולר' יעקב כדאית ליה אלא שובר העצם בטמא מנא לן דלא לקי ופשטינן לה כהא דת"ר ועצם לא תשברו בו בכשר ולא בפסול ר' אומר בבית אחד יאכל ועצם לא תשברו בו כל הראוי לאכילה יש בו שבירת
עצם

מסורת הש"ס

תורה אור
חולין דף עז:
חולין דף קכב:
[יומא מ. סוכה נד. ע"ש פרש"י יבמות מג:] חולין שם: [נה: קלד.] לעיל דף סג. שבועות ג. [מכות יג.]
סנהדרין דף סג. שבועות דף ג: מכות יג: ד: ודף טז: חולין דף פג: ודף קמא. תמורה דף ד:
[לעיל ע. וש"נ]

הגהות הב"ח

(א) רש"י ד"ה אבל המותיר וכו' אינו לוקה לא המותיר :

but not circumcision out of its proper time, which might [otherwise] be inferred *a fortiori*.[7] R. Ashi said: [*On the seventh day is a Sabbath of*] *solemn rest* [Shabbathon],[8] [written] in connection with Festivals, is an affirmative precept,[9] and one affirmative precept cannot override a negative precept and an affirmative precept [combined].

MISHNAH. EVERYTHING WHICH CAN BE EATEN OF A
a FULL-GROWN OX MAY BE EATEN OF A TENDER GOAT,[1] AND ALSO THE TOPS OF THE FORELEGS AND THE GRISTLES.[2]

GEMARA. Rabbah pointed out a contradiction. We learned: EVERYTHING WHICH CAN BE EATEN OF A FULL-GROWN OX MAY BE EATEN OF A TENDER GOAT; hence that which cannot be eaten [of the former] may not [be eaten of the latter]. Then consider the sequel: [AND ALSO] THE TOPS OF THE FORELEGS AND THE GRISTLES: yet surely these cannot be eaten in the case of a full-grown ox?—Rather it is [dependent on] Tannaim, and it is taught thus: EVERYTHING WHICH CAN BE EATEN OF A FULL-GROWN OX MAY BE EATEN OF A TENDER GOAT, while that which cannot be eaten [of the former] may not be eaten [of the latter]: but some maintain, also THE TOPS OF THE FORELEGS AND THE GRISTLES. Raba said: This [the second] is a defining clause,[3] and it teaches thus: EVERYTHING WHICH CAN BE EATEN OF A FULL-GROWN OX after [much] boiling MAY BE EATEN OF A TENDER GOAT when roasted, and what is it? THE TOPS OF THE FORELEGS AND THE GRISTLES.

It was taught in accordance with Raba: Everything which can be eaten of a full-grown ox after [much] boiling may be eaten of a tender goat when roasted, and what is it? The tops of the forelegs and the gristles, and the soft sinews are treated[4] as flesh.

It was stated: [With regard to] sinews which would ultimately harden,[5]—R. Joḥanan said: One may register for them in the Passover-offering; Resh Laḳish maintained: One may not register for them in the Passover-offering. R. Joḥanan said, One may register for them in the Passover-offering, [because] we decide by the present. Resh Laḳish maintained. One may not register for them in the Passover-offering, [because] we decide by its
b ultimate [condition].[1] Resh Laḳish raised an objection against R. Joḥanan: Everything which can be eaten of a full-grown ox may be eaten of a tender goat, and what is it? The tops of the forelegs and the gristles; [thus] only these,[2] but not sinews which would ultimately harden!—Said he to him: He teaches those, and the same applies to these. [Thus] why are those [permitted]? Because they can be eaten in the case of a full-grown ox after [much] boiling; [so] these too can be eaten of a full-grown ox after [much] boiling.

R. Jeremiah said to R. Abin: When you go before R. Abbahu, point out a contradiction to him. Did then R. Joḥanan say, '[With regard to] sinews which would ultimately harden, one may register for them in the Passover-offering', which shows that we decide by the present? Surely Resh Laḳish asked R. Joḥanan: 'Can the skin of the head of a tender [sucking] goat be defiled'?[3] And he answered him: 'It cannot be defiled', which proves that we decide by the future?—Said he to him: he who pointed out this contradiction to you was not particular about his flour.[4] Surely R. Joḥanan retracted in favour of Resh Laḳish['s view], and he said to him: Do not provoke me, for I learn it as the opinion of an individual.[5]

MISHNAH. HE WHO BREAKS A BONE OF A CLEAN PASSOVER-OFFERING RECEIVES FORTY [LASHES]. BUT HE WHO LEAVES OVER [FLESH] OF A CLEAN [OFFERING] OR BREAKS [A BONE] OF AN UNCLEAN [ONE] IS NOT FLAGELLATED WITH FORTY [LASHES].

GEMARA. As for leaving over [flesh] of a clean [offering], it is well. For it was taught: *And ye shall let nothing of it remain until the morning; and that which remaineth of it until the morning ye shall*
c *burn with fire.*[1] Scripture desires to state an affirmative command after a negative command, thus teaching that one is not flagellated for it; this is R. Judah's view.[2] R. Jacob said: This is not the real reason,[3] but because it is a negative injunction involving no action,[4] for which one is not flagellated. But how do we know [that] he who breaks [a bone] of an unclean [offering is not flagellated]?—Because Scripture states, *Neither shall ye break a bone thereof:*[5] '*thereof*' [implies] of a fit sacrifice but not of an unfit one.

Our Rabbis taught: '*Neither shall ye break a bone thereof*': '*thereof*' implies of a fit sacrifice but not of an unfit one. Rabbi said: *In one house shall it be eaten . . . neither shall ye break a bone thereof:*[5] [this intimates,] whatever is fit for eating is subject to the [prohibition of] breaking a bone, while whatever is not fit for eating is not subject to the [prohibition of] breaking a bone. Wherein do they differ? Said R. Jeremiah: They differ in respect of a Passover-offering which came in a state of uncleanness:[6] on the view that

(7) An infant is circumcised even on the Sabbath, if it is the eighth day after birth (Lev. XII, 3), but not otherwise. This is deduced from '*alone*', which is a limitation. But for this, one could infer *a fortiori* that it is permissible (v. Shab. 132*b*). Thus we see that an act which need not be done on a particular day may not be done on the Sabbath or on Festivals, and the same applies to unfit sacred food. (8) Lev. XXIII, 3. (9) For it intimates: rest thereon, so that work on a festival involves the transgression of both affirmative and negative precepts.

a (1) But not those portions of a full-grown ox which are too hard to be eaten (the reference, of course, is to the Passover-offering), though in the case of a young goat these are soft and edible. (2) E.g., the cartilage of the ears, the gristly portion of the breast, and the small ribs at the end of the spine. (3) Lit., 'he teaches what they are'. (4) Lit., 'judged'. (5) The sinews of the neck of a young goat fit for a Passover-offering are soft, but when it grows older they harden and are unfit for food.

b (1) Thus R. Joḥanan interprets the 'soft sinews' of the foregoing Baraitha as meaning those which are soft *now*, even if they ultimately harden; while in the view of Resh Laḳish it means only those which remain permanently soft. (2) Which even in the case of a full-grown ox can be eaten after protracted boiling. (3) At present it is edible, but not when the goat grows older. Can it be defiled as food, since it can now be eaten, or not, since it will ultimately harden. (4) Whether he milled sound wheat or the refuse! I.e., he was careless about his data. (5) This refers to the Mishnah in Ḥul. 122*a* which states that the skin of the head of a tender goat is as its flesh, i.e., can be defiled as an eatable, which proves that we decide by the present and thus contradicts R. Joḥanan's answer to Resh Laḳish. He, however, countered by stating that he regarded it as an individual's ruling only. Hence when he rules in the present discussion that we decide by the present, it must be on the assumption that that Mishnah represents the opinion of the majority, an assumption, however, which he evidently abandoned.

c (1) Ex. XII, 10. (2) This is a general principle, for when an affirmative precept follows a negative one, it is implied that if the latter is violated, the remedy lies in the former. (3) Lit., 'this is not of the same denomination'. (4) It is violated by remaining passive, not by committing a positive act. (5) Ibid. 46. (6) I.e., when the majority of the community were unclean; v. Mishnah *supra* 79*a*.

R. Zebid said: The circumstances here are e.g., [83b] that he found them piled up in heaps and some of them were scooped out:[6] [in the case of] bones of [other] sacrifices which are not subject to the prohibition of breaking a bone, [I assume] that they have all been scooped out and [the marrow] eaten; hence they do not require burning. But in the case of bones of the Passover-offering, which are subject to the prohibition of breaking a bone, [I say] perhaps it is these [only] which were scooped out, while the others[7] were not scooped out; hence they require burning.

Rab Judah said in Rab's name: All sinews are flesh, except the sinews of the neck. We learned: THE BONES, THE SINEWS, AND THE NOTHAR ARE TO BE BURNT ON THE SIXTEENTH. How are these sinews meant? If they are sinews of flesh, let us eat them!
a While if they remained over,[1] then they are [indeed] *nothar?*[2] Hence it is obvious [that] the sinews of the neck [are meant]. Now it is well if you say that they are flesh:[3] therefore they require burning. But if you say that they are not flesh, why do they require burning?—Said R. Ḥisda: This [teaching] arises only in respect of the thigh sinew, and in accordance with R. Judah. For it was taught, R. Judah said: [The prohibition of the thigh sinew] is operative only in respect of one, and reason determines, that of the right [thigh].[4] Then in that case conclude that R. Judah is in doubt,[5] for if he is really certain, let us eat that which is permitted, and throw away that which is forbidden. Why then do they [both] need burning?—Said R. Iḳa b. Ḥinena: [This law was stated] where e.g., they were [originally] distinguished but subsequently mixed up.[6]

R. Ashi said: It is necessary [to teach it] only in respect of the fat of the sinew of the thigh. For it was taught: Its fat is permitted, but the Israelites are holy and treat it as forbidden.[7]

Rabina said: It refers to the outer [sinew of the thigh], and is in accordance with Rab Judah's dictum in Samuel's name. For Rab Judah said in Samuel's name: The inner one which is near the bone is forbidden, and a person is liable on its account [to flagellation]; the outer which is near the flesh is forbidden, but a person is not liable on its account.[8]

IF THE SIXTEENTH FELL etc. Yet why so? Let the affirmative
b command come and override the negative command?[1]—Said Hezekiah, and the School of Hezekiah taught likewise: *And ye shall let nothing of it remain until the morning; but that which remaineth of it until the morning ye shall burn with fire:* now [the second] *'until the morning'* need not be stated, What then is the teaching of *'until the morning'?* [Scripture comes] to appoint a second morning for its burning.[2] Abaye said: Scripture saith, *The burnt-offering of the Sabbath* [shall be burnt] *on its Sabbath:*[3] but the burnt-offering of weekdays is not [to be burnt] on the Sabbath, nor is the burnt-offering of weekdays [to be burnt] on Festivals.[4] Raba said: Scripture saith, [*no manner of work shall be done in them—sc.* Festivals—, *save that which every man must eat,*] *that only may be done by you:*[5] *'that'* but not its preparatory requisites:[6] *'only,'* [84a]

(6) He only examined those on top and found them thus. (7) Which he did not examine.

a (1) Accidentally or through negligence. (2) Why state it separately? (3) In spite of their woodenness. (4) V. Gen. XXXII, 33. Thus actually one of the thigh sinews is permitted, though we do not know which; this one therefore is really *nothar* and must be burnt. (5) Which is forbidden and which is permitted. (6) R. Judah may be certain that the prohibition applies to the right thigh only, but these sinews referred to in our Mishnah, though distinguished when drawn out, are now mixed up and we do not know which is the right and which is the left, and hence both require burning. (7) Since therefore according to Scriptural law it can be eaten, it is *nothar* and must be burnt. On the other hand, since in actual practice it could not be eaten, the Tanna cannot include it in the term *nothar*, which generally implies flesh which could have been eaten, and must mention it separately. (8) It is forbidden by Rabbinical law only. The reasoning in the preceding note applies here too.

b (1) It is a general principle that if an affirmative command and a negative command are in conflict, the former overrides the latter. Here we have an affirmative command to burn the *nothar*, Ex. XII, 10, and a negative command forbidding work on a festival, ibid. 16. (2) Translating: but that which remaineth of it, (ye shall wait) *until the* (following) *morning* (*sc.* that of the sixteenth) (and) *burn* (it) *with fire*. (3) Num. XXVIII, 10; this is the literal translation. (4) E.g., the animal sacrificed before the Sabbath or Festival must not be burnt the following evening. Hence sacrifices and sacred food in general, if unfit, must not be burnt on Festivals, *a fortiori*. (5) Ex. XII, 16. (6) E.g., you may roast meat, but may not sharpen a spit for impaling the meat on it.

עין משפט נר מצוה

מסורת הש"ס

שמצאן צבורין צבורין ומהן חלוצין עצמות קדשים דאין בהן משום שבירת העצם לכולהו הוה חליץ להו ואכיל להו ולא בעי שריפה עצמות הפסח דיש בהן משום שבירת העצם דילמא הני דחלצינהו ולהנך לא חלצינהו ובעי שריפה א"ר יהודה אמר רב כל הגידין בשר חוץ מגידי צואר תנן העצמות והגידים והנותר ישרפו בט"ז הני גידין היכי דמי אילימא גידי בשר ניכלינהו ואי דאיתותר היינו נותר אלא פשיטא גידי צואר א"א בשלמא בשר נינהו אמטו להכי בעי שריפה אלא אי אמרת לאו בשר נינהו למה להו שריפה א"ר חסדא לא נצרכא אלא לגיד הנשה ואליבא דרבי יהודה *דתניא ר' יהודה אומר אינו נוהג אלא באחת והדעת מכרעת של ימין ואלא תפשוט דספוקי מספקא ליה לר' יהודה דאי מיפשט פשיטא ליה ההיא דהיתירא ניכליה ודאיסורא נישדייה למה ליה שריפה א"ר איקא בר חיננא כגון שהוכרו ולבסוף נתערבו רב אשי אמר לא נצרכא אלא לשמנו דגיד הנשה *דתניא *שמנו מותר וישראל קדושים הם ונוהגין בו איסור רבינא אמר בחיצון וכדר"י אמר שמואל *דאמר רב יהודה אמר שמואל ב' גידין הן פנימי הסמוך לעצם אסור וחייבין עליו חיצון הסמוך לבשר אסור ואין חייבין עליו: חל ט"ז וכו': ואמאי ניתי עשה וידחי לא תעשה *אמר חזקיה וכן תני דבי חזקיה אמר קרא °לא תותירו ממנו עד בוקר והנותר ממנו עד בוקר באש תשרופו שאין ת"ל עד בוקר מה ת"ל עד בקר ליתן לו בקר שני לשריפתו אביי אמר אמר קרא °עולת שבת בשבתו *ולא עולת חול בשבת ולא עולת חול ביום טוב רבא אמר אמר קרא °הוא לבדו יעשה לכם הוא ולא מכשיריו לבדו ולא

אי אמרת בשלמא בשר נינהו כו' · ואין להקשות אי בשר נינהו ליכלינהו דלאו בשר גמור הוא שיהא טעמם כטעם בשר מיהו לענין שריפה בעי למימר דליהוו בשר: **לא** נצרכא אלא לשומנו · קשה דבריש גיד הנשה (חולין פט.) פריך וסבר תנא דידן אין בגידין בנותן טעם והא תנן ירך שנתבשל בה גיד הנשה אם יש בה בנותן טעם אסור והשתא דילמא הא דקתני אם יש בה בנותן טעם משום שומנו דגיד הנשה קאמר דהכא קרי ליה גיד ושם פירשתי:

ליתן בקר שני לשריפתו · וא"ת אי אסור לשורפו בליל מוצאי י"ט עד הבקר היכי מוכח *דאין שריפת קדשים דוחה י"ט הא על כרחיך גזירת הכתוב היא דהא אפי' בלילה שהוא חול אסור לשורפו וי"ל דכיון דאסור לשורפו בבקר ראשון ילפינן שפיר דאין שריפת קדשים דוחה י"ט והא דאסור לשורפו בליל מוצאי י"ט אין תימה שכן מצינו בשלמים שאין נאכלים לאור שלישי ואפ"ה אין נשרפין עד היום כדאמרי' בריש מכילתין (דף ג:): **ולא** עולת חול בשבת כו'. משמע הכא דאיברי חול אין קריבין בשבת ולא בי"ט וקשה דבסוף פרק טרף בקלפי (יומא מו:) אמר אברי חול שנתותרו עושה להן מערכה בפני עצמן וסודרן אפילו בשבת ואפי' לרב הונא דפליג התם היינו דאינו עושה מערכה בפני עצמן אבל דברי הכל סודרן על המערכה גדולה כן צריך לפרש שם וכן בסוף פ"ק דשבת (דף כ:) דריש בכל מושבותיכם אי אתה מבעיר למשרי אברים ופדרים הוא דאתא והיינו איברי חול שנתותרו דאברי תמיד של שבת נפקא מעל עולת התמיד בריש אלו דברים (לעיל סו:) ודוקא אברי עולת חול ממעט הכא ותירץ ר"ת וריב"א דהתם דוקא במשלה בהן האור מיירי דנעשו כבר לחמו של מזבח שמתוך שהן לחמו של מזבח הרי הן כקרבן היום ודחו מבמועדו אפי' בשבת ולישנא דהסיק נמי התם דוקא בפסולין אי משלה בהן האור אין אי לא לא לאו למעוטי כשירין אתא אלא ה"ק דלא איצטריך כשירין לאשמעי' במשלה בהן האור ומיהו אף בכשירין לא שריא אלא במשלה בהן האור וריב"א מסופק בשאר קרבנות דלאו תמיד ומשלה בהן האור אי נעשו לחמו של מזבח למישרינהו בשבת דדילמא דוקא בתמיד מהני האי טעמא דשם תמיד דוחה שבת וא"ת דביומא (דף מו·) דריש לה מבמועדו ובפ"ק דשבת (דף כ·) דריש מבכל מושבותיכם וי"ל דקרא דבכל מושבותיכם גלי על במועדו דאיירי אפילו באיברים ופדרים של חול והא דלא נקט ביומא קרא דבכל מושבותיכם דהוי"א עיקר דרשה משום דניחא ליה למינקט דרשה דמועדו דשייכא אף גבי טומאה ובכל הקרבנות: ולא

שמצאן צבורין צבורין · ובדק עליונים ומצאן חלוצין: עצמות קדשים · לא בעו למיבדק תחתונים אבל עצמות פסח בעו למיבדק כולהו ובהא פליג רב זביד אדרב נחמן דאי מצאן חלוצין לא חמיר שימוש נותר טולי האי להצריכו שריפה מספק ולומר בתר איסורייהו חלצינהו: כל הגידין בשר · הרי הן כבשר ונמנין עליהן בפסח ויוצא ידי חובתו: חוץ מגידי צואר · שהוא ח"ל הרחב וקשה ועץ בעלמא הוא: הני גידין · דקאמר עיקרן ותחלתן לשריפה היכי דמי: ואי דאייתור · ע"י שנתעצלו באכילתן הייט נותר: אלא פשיטא בגידי צואר · קאמר ומשום שאין נאכלין מחמת קשיין מני להו בהדי עצמות וקאמר דעיקרן לשריפה דמסתמא לא אכיל להו: אי אמרת בשלמא בשר נינהו · ואי אכיל להו נפיק בהו אמטו להכי בעי שריפה כו': לא נצרכא אלא לגיד הנשה כו' · לעולם גידי צואר לאו בשר נינהו ושאר גידים בשר גמור וראוי לאכילה ומתני' דמשמע דיש גידים שהן בשר ליטען שריפה וסתמן אין נאכלין דקאמר ישרפו בט"ז בגיד הנשה שהוא רך וכשר לאכילה: לר' יהודה · דאמר אין נוהג אלא באחת ולא ידעינן בהי מינייהו הילכך מתחלה עומד אותו של היתר לשריפה משום דלא ידע ליה דליכליה: ופרכינן תיפשוט מיהא דמספקא ליה לרבי יהודה בהי נהיג דהא מילתא איבעיא לן בפ' גיד הנשה (חולין צ:) דקתני ר' יהודה אומר אין נוהג אלא באחת והדעת מכרעת של ימין ואיבעיא לן מיפשט ליה לרבי יהודה דשל ימין ומאי דעת דקא אמר דעת תורה כדמפרש התם הירך המיומנת שבירך או דילמא ספוקי מספקא ליה ומאי דעת דעת נוטה כלומר מסתברא הכי תיפשוט ממתני' מדקא אמר תחלתו לשריפה ודאי מספק' ליה הילכך שריפה בעו תרווייהו דאכל חד וחד אמר האי דהיתירא הוה והרי הוא נותר ומתחלתו לא היה יכול לאוכלו שמא זהו של איסור דאי פשיטא ליה אמאי תחלתו לשריפה דהיתירא ניכליה דאיסורא נשדייה: לעולם פשיטא ליה דשל ימין . ומתני' דלא מצי אכיל ליה ומצריך ליה שריפה כשנתערבו לאחר מכאן . בשהוכרו לאו דוקא דודאי מתחלתו הוכרו דאין לך אדם שאינו מכיר בין לד ימין לצד שמאל: רב אשי אמר · מתני' בשומנו של גיד קאמר דמותר מן התורה ונהגו איסור בו הלכך תחלתו לשריפה דכיון דמן התורה מותר חל איסור נותר עליו ובכלל נותר לא חשיב ליה דהאי על כרחו מתחלתו לכך עומד ואיצטריך למיתנייה באנפי נפשיה ולאשמעינן דאסור לאוכלו: שני גידין הן · בירך: פנימי הסמוך לעצם · זה גיד הגדול המתוח על פני כל אורך הירך ופנימי קרי ליה שהוא בצד פנימי של ירך לצד הרואה את הירך השנית: וסמוך לעצם · עצם הקולית התחוב בבוקא דאטמא וגם יוצא מבוקא דאטמא ונמתח אצל אותו עצם על פני כל אורך הירך שאסור: וחייבין עליו · מלקות: חיצון · זה גיד קצר הניתן בסוף השופי לרחבו וחיצון קרי ליה על שם שהוא מוטל לצד חיצון של ירך לצד הרואה את האויר הסמוך לבשר שמובלע בבשר: אסור · מדרבנן: ואין חייבין עליו · כדמפרש טעמא התם אשר על כף הירך ההוא דפשיט בכוליה ירך והייט פנימי אבל חיצון לא ובההוא דקאמר תנא דידן דתחלתו אינו נאכל משום איסור דרבנן וטעון שריפה דחייל עליה שם נותר דחזי מדאורייתא: ניתי עשה · דבאש תשרפו: וידחי לא תעשה · דמלאכת י"ט: שאין ת"ל עד בוקר · בתרא דהא כבר כתיב קמא: ולא עולת חול בי"ט · אלמא אפילו הקטר עולה אינו דוחה י"ט וכ"ש שריפת פסול שלה ופסח קרבן של חול הוא דזריקת דמו בארבעה עשר ואין יכול להקטירו בלילה והא דכתיב לא ילין לבקר דמשמע הא כל הלילה ילין הא אוקימנא בארבעה עשר שחל להיות בשבת בפ' תמיד נשחט (דף נט:): הוא ולא מכשיריו · היכולין ליעשות מבעוד יום: ולא

תורה אור

שמות יב · במדבר כח · שמות יב

חולין דף צ: · חולין דף צא. · שם ודף צב: · שבת דף כד: ודף קלג. תמורה דף ד: ע"ש · [לעיל נט: ע"ש]

פה א ב מיי' פ"ח מהל' מאכלות אסורות הלכה א [טוש"ע יו"ד סי' סה סעיף ח'] :

[בשבת כד:]

רבינו חננאל

שמצאן צבורין צבורין מהן חלוצין ומהן אין חלוצין עצמות קדשים שאין בהן שבירת עצם אמרי' מדהנך חלוצין הנך נמי חלוצין בעצמות פסח דאיכא שבירת עצם בעו בדיקה: **אמר** רב יהודה אמר רב כל הגידין כשרין חוץ מגידי צואר ואקשי' עלה ממתני' דקתני הגידים ישרפו הני גידים מאי עבדתייהו אי בשר הן אמאי ישרפו נכלינהו ואי נותר הן נותר אלא ודאי גידי צואר הן ולא יכול לאכלן וטעונין שריפה ואי אמרת לאו בשר הן נשדינהו ושני' גיד הנשה הוא ואליבא דר' יהודה דאמר אינו נוהג אלא בירך אחת ולא תימא (אלא ודאי) מספקא ליה אלא אפי' תימא פשיטא ליה דשל ימין אסורין וכגון שהוכרו ולבסוף נתערבו דהא לא אפשר למכלינהו הלכך טעונין שרפה: **רב** אשי אמר גידין דקתני במתני' שמנו של גיד הנשה הוא דנהגו בו ישראל קדושים איסור רבינא אמר גיד החיצון הוא ששנינו במשנתנו שאין חייבין עליו דגרסי' בפ' גיד הנשה אמר שמואל שני גידין הם פנימי סמוך לעצם אסור וחייבין עליו היצון סמוך לבשר אסור ואין חייבין עליו: **חל** ששה עשר להיות בשבת כו' אקשי' ניתי עשה שנא' (שמות י"ב ז') והנותר ממנו עד בקר באש תשרפו עשה דשריפת נותר לידחי לא תעשה כל מלאכה דיום טוב ושני חזקיה מה ת"ל עד בקר ליתן בקר שני לשריפתו אביי אמר בפי' רבתה תורה לדחות עולות ארבעה עשר מלהשרף ביום [טוב] דכתיב עולת שבת בשבתו דייקי' מינה דאין מקריבין אלא עולת שבת בשבת בלבד אבל אברי עולות חול בשבת או ביום טוב לא ואע"ג דמצותן להקריבן וכל שכן דלא שרפינן הפסולין. רבא מפיק ליה

רבה מוסיף אף ר"י הגלילי *דתניא ריה"ג אומר כל הענין כולו אינו מדבר אלא בפרים הנשרפים ובשעירי' הנשרפין לשרוף פסולידהן אבית הבירה וליתן לא תעשה על אכילתן אמרו לו חטאת שנכנס דמה לפני ולפנים מנין אמר להן °הן לא הובא את דמה אל הקדש פנימה מכלל דאי נפיק איהי א"נ עייל דמה בשריפה ורבי יוחנן סבר דם ובשר חדא מילתא היא בעלים מלתא אחריתי היא: **מתני'** *העצמות והגידין והנותר ישרפו בששה עשר חל ט"ז להיות בשבת ישרפו בי"ז לפי שאינן דוחין לא את השבת ולא את י"ט: **גמ'** אמר רב מרי בר אבוה א"ר יצחק *עצמות קדשים ששימשו נותר מטמאין את הידים הואיל ונעשה בסיס לדבר האסור נימא מסייע ליה *העצמות והגידים והנותר ישרפו בט"ז הני עצמות ה"ד אילימא דלית בהו מוח למה להו בשריפה נשדינהו אלא פשיטא דאית בהו מוח אי אמרת בשלמא שימוש נותר מילתא היא אמטו להכי בעי שריפה אלא אי אמרת שימוש נותר לאו מילתא היא למה להו שריפה נתברינהו ונחלצה למוח דידהו ונשרפיה ונשדינהו לדידהו אלא לאו שמע מינה שימוש נותר מילתא היא אמרי לא לעולם אימא לך שימוש נותר לאו מילתא היא וקסבר בו בכשר ואפי' בפסול אפי' בפסול ס"ד והא *תנן אבל המותיר בטהור והשובר בטמא אינו סופג את הארבעים לא קשיא כאן שהיתה לו שעת הכושר כאן שלא היתה לו שעת הכושר ומאן תנא דשני ליה בין שהיתה לו שעת הכושר ללא היתה לו שעת הכושר רבי יעקב היא דתניא °ועצם לא תשברו בו *בו בכשר ולא בפסול רבי יעקב אומר *היתה לו שעת הכושר ונפסל יש בו משום שבירת העצם לא היתה לו שעת הכושר אין בו משום שבירת העצם ר"ש אומר אחד זה ואחד זה אין בו משום שבירת העצם מיתיבי *כל עצמות הקדשים אין טעונין שריפה חוץ מעצמות הפסח מפני התקלה הני עצמות היכי דמי אילימא דלית בהו מוח למה להו שריפה אלא פשיטא דאית בהו מוח ואי סלקא דעתך שימוש נותר מילתא היא עצמות קדשים אמאי אין טעונין שריפה אמר רב נחמן בר יצחק הכא במאי עסקינן כגון שמצאן חלוצין עצמות קדשים דאין בהן משום שבירת העצם קמי דנהוו נותר חלצינהו ולא הוו שימוש נותר ולא בעו שריפה עצמות הפסח דיש בהן משום שבירת העצם (א) לבתר דנהוו נותר הוא דחלצינהו והוו להו שימוש נותר ובעו שריפה רב זביד אמר הכא במאי עסקינן כגון שמצאן

כל הענין כולו · כל פרשה זו וכל חטאת אשר יובא מדמה (ויקרא ו) דמוקי לה רבנן במסכת זבחים (דף פב:) בחטאות החיצונה שהכניס דמה לפנים והוא פסול שלה וקאמר רחמנא שישרף פליג ריה"ג ומוקי בחטאות הפנימיות כגון פר העלם דבר של ציבור אשר יובא מדמה כמצותה אל אהל מועד לא תאכל: באש תשרף (ובבשרה) לא אצטריך קרא דהא כתיב בגופיה (ויקרא ד) ושרף אותו על עצים וגו' אלא שאם נפסלה ביוצא ובטומאה בא הכתוב ללמדך שתשרפנה בבית הבירה ולא חוץ לג' מחנות כמצותו: וליתן לא תעשה על אכילתו: אמרו לו חטאת החיצונה שהכניס דמה לפנים מנין לך · שהיא פסולה: אמר להן · מדאמר ליה משה לאהרן הן לא הובא הא הובא בת שריפה היא ושפיר עביד דשרפוה לאלתר ומדיליף ריה"ג קדשי דורות מחטאת דאהרן אלמא ס"ל נמי דאם הובא דמה לדורות בעיא שריפה לאלתר כי חטאת דאהרן ואף על גב דפסול הדם הוא דהוי כפסולו מחמת דבר אחר וקס"ד דה"ה נמי ס"ל בפסול בעלים דלא בעי עיבור צורה אבל רבנן דלא גמירי מיניה סברי דורות משעה לא ילפינן ובההיא הוא דקאמר להו משה דאם הביאו דמה לפנים בעיא שריפה אבל לדורות בעי קרא אחרינא וגבי עיבור צורה נמי לא ילפינן מינה: ור' יוחנן · דלא חשיב ליה לריה"ג בהדייהו אמר לך נהי דשמעת ליה בפסול דם דלא בעו עיבור צורה בפסול בעלים מי שמעת ליה דקאי כרבי יוחנן בן ברוקה: דם ובשר חדא מילתא היא. והוה ליה פסולו בגופו כאילו נטמא בשר עצמו: **מתני'** העצמות. שלא יכול לשוברן מפני שנאסרה בו שבירת העצם ונותר בהן מוח והרי הוא נותר וטעון שריפה: וכן גידין · ובגמרא פריך ניכלינהו: והנותר · בשר פסח שנתעצלו באכילתו וניתותר: בששה עשר · שהוא חולו של מועד ואע"פ שנפסל בבוקר ראשון אין רשאי לשורפו בי"ט כדמפרש בגמר': **גמ'** ששימשו נותר · שנותר בהן מוח חוץ לזמנו ושימשוהו העצמות הללו: מטמאין את הידים · כנותר עצמו שגזרו חכמים שיטמא את הידים בפ' בתרא (דף קכ:) ולקמן בפירקין (דף פה·) מייתי לה בגמ': בסיס · (ב) כנו כדמתרגמי' בסיסיה (שמות ל) מקום מושבו: הני עצמות היכי דמי · דקאמר עיקרן ותחלתן בשריפה: נשדינהו · ישליכם דלא הצריך הכתוב שריפה אלא בראוי לאכילה וניתותר כדכתיב (שם יב) לא תותירו ממנו עד בקר ואם תותירו תשרפו: דאית בהו מוח · ומתחלתן לשריפה עומדים שאסור לשוברן וע"כ נעשין נותר הילכך חשיב להו באנפי נפשייהו ולא הוו בכלל והנותר דמתני': אמטו להכי בעו שריפה · אף העצמות כמוח עצמו: אלא אי לאו מילתא היא. הרי מכיון שניתותרו ונפסלו אין בהן משום איסור שבירה דאמרינן לקמן ועצם לא תשברו בו בכשר ולא בפסול: ניתברינהו · וניפקליה למוח ונישרפיה ולא יפסיד עצים וטורח לשרוף העצמות: קסבר · האי תנא בו דכתיב גבי שבירה לאו למעוטי פסול אתא אלא אורחיה דקרא הוא וכשר ואף פסול במשמע: המותיר בטהור · וכל שכן בטמא: אין סופג · לקמן בפירקין מפרש טעמא: היתה לו שעת הכושר · כגון נותר יש בו שבירת העצם: לא היתה לו שעת הכושר · כגון נטמא לפני זריקה אין בו משום שבירת עצם: ומאן ניהו תנא · דמתני' דשאני ליה בהכי לגבי שבירת העצם: כל עצמות · נותר מן הקדשים אין טעונין שריפה אלא שוברם ומוציא את המוח ושורפו ומשליך את העצמות: חוץ מעצמות הפסח. שאין יכול לשוברן מפני תקלת עצם לא תשברו בו לפיכך נשרפים על ידי מוח שבהן: למה להו שריפה · לעצמות הפסח: שמצאן חלוצין · כולה מתני' מיוקמא במוצא עצמות חלוצין כלומר שבורין ונחלץ מוח מהן: עצמות קדשים · דמותר לשוברן אמרי' כתמא דמילתא לא אתא מוח דידהו לידי נותר ומקמיה איסורייהו דניתו לידי נותר חלצינהו ואין כאן שימוש נותר: לבתר הכי · דאיפסיל חלצינהו דהו לית ביה איסור שבירה כר"ש ויש כאן שימוש נותר: שמצאן

ורבה מוסיף אף ריה"ג · וא"ת היכי נימא דריה"ג ור' יוחנן בן ברוקה אמרו דבר אחד והא פסולה דחטאת שנכנס דמה לפנים היינו לפני זריקה ור' יוחנן בן ברוקה אחר זריקה איירי ואליבא דר' יוחנן מסיק מדקא מוסיף עלי' וי"ל דרבה לא מפליג בין קודם זריקה בין לאחר זריקה כי היכי דלא מפליג ר' יוחנן דקאמר אף אחר זריקה מחלוקת:

אמר להן הן לא הובא את דמה · פירש בקונטרס דרבנן לא בעו למילף מחטאת דאהרן דלא גמרי' דורות משעה ומה שפירש כן לא משום דחטאת דאהרן היה לשעה דהא שעיר של ר"ח היה כדפירש בקונ' וכן איתא בזבחים בפרק טבול יום (דף קא:) אלא דקסברי רבנן הוראת שעה היתה כדאמר לעיל וקשה לרשב"א דלעיל שייך הוראת שעה כדפי' דקסבר מפני טומאה נשרפה דהוי פסולו בגופו ומסברא ישרף מיד אבל הכא בחטאת שנכנס דמה לפנים דהוי פסולו בדם ומסבר' בעי עיבור צורה לא שייך הוראת שעה היתה ונראה לר"י דרבנן לא בעו למילף מחטאת אהרן משום דמליט למימר דמשה לא הודה להן *על השריפה דשפיר עבוד אלא במה שלא אכלוה אבל על השריפה לא הודה להן דאפי' היה כן שלא כדין שרפוה בלא עיבור צורה וקשה דלעיל יליף מחטאת אהרן שריפה ביוצא וקאי אמתני' דסבר' דשאינו פסולו בגופו בעי עיבור צורה והיינו כרבנן דר' יוסי ואינהו לא בעו למילף הכא מחטאת אהרן:

בו בכשר ואפי' בפסול · ולא תיקשי ויוציא המוח ע"י גומרתא דליכא שבירת עצם דאיכא למיחש שמא יפקע כדאמרי' לקמן (ג) אי נמי ע"י גומרתא טריחא מילתא למיעבד:

רבי שמעון אומר אחד זה ואחד זה אין בו משום שבירת העצם. וא"ת ר"ש היינו ת"ק ונראה לר"י דר' יעקב ור"ש פליגי אליבא דת"ק כי ההיא דלא ירבה לו נשים דפרק כהן גדול (סנהדרין כא·) *והיא דחזקתן שלש שנים דחזקת הבתים (ב"ב כח:):

אימור לבתר איסורא חלצינהו · ומפני התקלה דקתני בברייתא היינו דמשום שבירת עצם לא חלצינהו קודם איסורא ולהכי ישרפו דשימשו נותר:

אי

זבחים דף פב:

[ויקרא י]

תמורה דף ה.

[חולין קכה.]

[עי' תוס' חולין קכה. ד"ה אי הכי וכו']

לקמן דף פד. מכות דף יז. שבועות דף ג:

שמות יב

[לעיל ע. וש"נ]

[תוספתא פ"ו]

הגהות הב"ח

(א) גמ' שבירת העצם אימור לבתר דניהוו: (ב) רש"י ד"ה בסיס כנו כדמתרגמינן כנו בסיסיה: (ג) תוס' ד"ה בו וכו' כי לקמן דף פ"ד ע"ב:

פא א מיי' פי"ט מה' פסולי מוקדשין הלכה ט:

פב ב מיי' פי"א מהלכות אבות הטומאה הל' ד:

פג ג מיי' פ"י מהלכות ק"פ הלכה ו:

פד ד מיי' פי"ט מהל' פסולי מוקדשין הלכה ט ופ"י מהלכות ק"פ הלכה ג:

שלא הודה להן אלא דשפיר עבוד דלא אכלוה פי' ת"מ

[ועי' בתוס' לקמן קטז: ד"ה ותוס' עירובין מח. ד"ה רבי יהודה במ"ק כד. ד"ה עצרת ובזבחים פג. ד"ה המזבח]

רבינו חננאל

ורבה מוסיף אף רבי יוסי הגלילי סבר פסולו בבעלים ישרף מיד דתניא ר' יוסי הגלילי אומר כל זה הענין דכתיב וכל חטאת אשר יובא מדמה אל אהל מועד וגו' אינו מדבר אלא בפרים הנשרפים כו' אמרו לו אם זה הענין כולו בפרים ושעירים הנשרפין הוא חטאת הנעשת בחוץ שנכנס דמה לפנים מנין שהיא פסולה ותשרף אמר להם הן לא הובא את דמה לפנים ולא היא יוצאה חוץ לקלעים אלא פנימה היתה אכול תאכלו אותה ש"מ מכלל שאם נכנס דמה לפנים או יוצאה היא חוץ לקלעים פסולה ונשרפה מיד כמעשה חטאת אהרן ור' יוחנן אמר לך פסילות דם כפסילות בשר הוא ופסולו בגופו קרינא ביה ופסילות שניא. **העצמות** והגידים והנותר ישרפו בששה עשר חל ששה עשר להיות בשבת ישרפו בשבעה עשר שאין דוחין לא שבת ולא יום טוב ולא תימא חל ממש דאם כן חל פסח להיות בבד"ו אלא אלו חל דין הוא שישרפו למחר וכך הוא מפורש בתלמוד ארץ ישראל במסכת מגילה: **אמר** מרי בר אבוה עצמות קדשים ששימשו נותר כלומר היה עליהם בשר ונעשה נותר ונפסל מטמאין הידים הואיל ונעשו בסיס לדבר האסור וסייעניה ממתני' דקתני העצמות ישרפו מכלל דאיתי בהו מוח למה להו שריפה אלא לעולם דאית בהו מוח ואי שמוש נותר לאו מילתא היא נתברינה תחלצה למוח ונשרפה ונשדינהו לעצמות אלא ש"מ שמוש נותר מלתא היא ודחי' לעולם אימא לך אי במתני' שמוש נותר לאו מלתא היא ותנא דמתני' סבר אלו הפסול אין בו שבירת עצם לפיכך תני ישרפו מפני המוח שבהן: **איני** והתנן המותיר בטהור והשובר בטמא אינו לוקה ארבעים ודחינן הא דתנן אינו לוקה מכלל דלית בה שבירת עצם בפסול מעיקרא דלא הוה ליה שעת הכושר ומתני' דקתני ישרפו ואוקימנא משום שבירת העצם דשהיתה לו שעת הכושר ונפסל ור' יעקב היא ומותבי' למארי כל עצמות קדשים אין טעונין שרפה חוץ מעצמות הפסח מפני תקלה הני עצמות ודאי בדאית להו מוח דאי לית בהו מוח אפי' עצמות פסח לא בעי שרפה אלא ודאי אית בהו מוח ואי שמוש נותר מלתא עצמות קדשים אמאי אין טעונין שרפה ומשני' כגון שנמצאו חלוצים כלומר נחלץ מוחם עצמות קדשים דלית בהו משום שבירת עצם איסור קמי איסורייהו חלצינהו ולא שמשו נותר לפיכך לא בעי שריפה עצמות פסח דאית ביה משום שבירת עצם היישינן דלמא בתר איסורייהו חלצינהו הלכך בעי שריפה: **רב** זביד אמר כגון שמצאן

Yet when it was burnt; it was burnt immediately.[3] [83a] Rabbah added: R. Jose the Galilean too. For it was taught, R. Jose the Galilean said: The whole passage speaks only of the bullocks which were burnt and the he-goats which were burnt, and its purpose is to teach that when they are disqualified, they must be burnt before the Temple, and to impose a negative injunction against eating them.[4] Said they to him: A sin-offering whose blood entered the innermost [sanctuary], whence do we know [that it is disqualified]? Said he to them, [From the verse] *Behold, the*
a *blood of it was not brought into the sanctuary within*,[1] whence it follows that if it [the sacrifice] went outside or if its blood entered within, it requires burning.[2] But R. Joḥanan[3] holds: The blood and the flesh are one thing;[4] [while the defilement of] the owners is a different thing.[5]

MISHNAH. THE BONES,[6] AND THE SINEWS, AND THE NOTHAR OF THE PASCHAL LAMB ARE TO BE BURNT ON THE SIXTEENTH.[7] IF THE SIXTEENTH FALLS ON THE SABBATH, THEY ARE TO BE BURNT ON THE SEVENTEENTH, BECAUSE THEY[8] DO NOT OVERRIDE EITHER THE SABBATH OR THE FESTIVAL.

GEMARA. R. Mari b. Abbuha said in R. Isaac's name: Bones of sacrifices which served *nothar*[9] defile the hands,[10] since they became a stand for a forbidden article.[11] Shall we say that this supports him: THE BONES, AND THE SINEWS, AND THE NOTHAR ARE TO BE BURNT ON THE SIXTEENTH. How are these bones meant? If we say that they contain no marrow, why
b burn them? Let us throw them away![1] Hence it is obvious that they contain marrow. Now, it is well if you agree that the serving of *nothar* is a [substantial] fact:[2] then it is right that they require burning.[3] But if you say [that] the serving of *nothar* is not a [substantial] fact, why do they need burning? Let us break them, scoop out their marrow and burn it, and throw them [the bones] away.[4] Hence this surely proves that the serving of *nothar* is a [substantial] fact!—I will tell you. It is not so: in truth I may argue that the serving of *nothar* is not a [substantial] fact, but he[5] holds: [*neither shall ye break a bone*] *thereof*[6] [means] of a fit [bone], and even of an unfit [one]. [You say] 'Even of an unfit [one]'—can you think so! Surely we learned: But he who leaves anything over [even] of clean [flesh], or he who breaks [a bone] of an unclean [Passover-offering], does not receive forty [lashes]?[7] —There is no difficulty: here it means where it enjoyed a period of fitness;[8] there it means where it never enjoyed a period of fitness.[9] And which Tanna admits a distinction between where it enjoyed a period of fitness and where it did not enjoy a period of fitness?—It is R. Jacob. For it was taught: '*Neither shall ye break a bone thereof*': '*thereof*' implies of a fit one, but not of an unfit one. R. Jacob said: If it enjoyed a period of fitness and became unfit, it is subject to the prohibition of breaking a bone; if it did not enjoy a period of fitness, it is not subject to the prohibition of breaking a bone. R. Simeon said: Both the one and the other are not subject to the prohibition of breaking a bone.

c An objection is raised: No bones of sacrifices require burning,[1] except the bones of the Passover-offering,[2] on account of the stumbling-block.[3] How are these bones meant? If we say that they contain no marrow, why do they need burning? Hence it is obvious that they contain marrow. Now if you should think [that] the serving of *nothar* is something substantial, why do the bones of [other] sacrifices not require burning?—Said R. Naḥman b. Isaac: The circumstances here are e.g., if he found them [the bones] scooped out:[4] [in the case of] the bones of [other] sacrifices which are not subject to the prohibition of breaking a bone, [we assume that] they were scooped out before it[5] [the marrow] became *nothar*, hence they did not serve *nothar* and do not require burning. [But in the case of] the bones of the Passover-offering which are subject to the prohibition of breaking a bone, we assume that they were scooped out after they became *nothar*; hence they had served *nothar* and require to be burnt.

(3) Hence since R. Joḥanan identifies R. Joḥanan b. Berokah's view with that of R. Nehemiah, this must be the former's opinion also, and thus they differ in our Mishnah where the owners are defiled after the sprinkling too. (4) This refers to Lev. VI, 23: *And no sin-offering, whereof any of the blood is brought into the tent of meeting to make atonement in the holy place, shall be eaten; it shall be burnt with fire.* The Rabbis relate this to a sin-offering which is sacrificed in the *outer* court, whose blood was carried into the inner court, thereby disqualifying it. But R. Jose the Galilean relates it to a sin-offering which is sacrificed in the *inner* court, e.g., the bullock brought when the entire congregation sins in ignorance (v. Lev. IV, 13 f.). Hence he interprets the verse thus: *And no sin-offering whereof any of the blood is* rightly *brought into the tent of meeting* etc., *shall be eaten*. Now this is superfluous in respect of a valid sacrifice, since it is explicitly stated in IV, 21: *and he shall carry forth the bullock without the camp, and burn it*. Hence the verse must mean that if it became unfit through going outside its legitimate boundary or through defilement, it must be burnt in front of the Birah, and not be carried '*without the camp*', i.e., beyond the Temple Mount. Further, this prohibits the eating of its flesh by a *negative* injunction, violation of which involves flagellation (Lev. IV, 21 merely contains an *affirmative* precept whose disregard is not punished by flagellation).

a (1) Lev. X, 18. (2) Now, since R. Jose the Galilean learns sacrifices for all time from Aaron's sin-offering, he evidently holds that for all time if the blood is brought within, it requires *immediate* burning without awaiting disfigurement, though the disqualification of the blood is like a disqualification through something else. Rabbah assumes that the same law viz., that it must be burnt without awaiting disfigurement, applies to the owner's defilement, though it is a disqualification through something else. Hence R. Jose the Galilean and R. Joḥanan b. Berokah say the same thing. (3) Who does not include R. Jose the Galilean. (4) Hence when the blood goes without its precincts, it is a disqualification in the sacrifice itself. (5) I.e., it is a disqualification through something else, and therefore one cannot be deduced from the other. (6) Of the paschal lamb. They may not be broken (Ex. XII, 46), and therefore their marrow becomes *nothar* (v. Glos.) and must be burnt (ibid. 10). (7) Not on the fifteenth, which is a festival day, but on the sixteenth, which is the first of the Intermediate days (*ḥol ha-mo'ed*); v. 5a, n. a4. (8) I.e., the burning of them. (9) I.e., the marrow was left in them after the time permitted for the eating of the sacrifice, and thus became *nothar*, for which the bones served as a container. (10) Just as *nothar* itself, v. *infra* 85a, 120b. (11) *Sc.* the marrow.

b (1) *Nothar*, which must be burnt, is applicable only to what can be eaten in the first place, viz., the flesh and the marrow. (2) I.e., of sufficient importance to be treated as *nothar* itself. (3) I.e., the bones themselves too. (4) For as stated anon, only a fit bone may not be broken; here, once the marrow is *nothar*, the bone ceases to be fit. (5) The Tanna of our Mishnah. (6) Ex. XII, 46. (7) Flagellation, the penalty for violating a negative injunction. V. *infra* 84a. Since he is not so punished, the prohibition evidently does not apply. (8) E.g., if a bone is rendered unfit on account of *nothar*, it was fit before it became *nothar*. Then the prohibition remains even when it becomes unfit. (9) E.g., if the bone was defiled before the sprinkling of the blood. Then it was never fit, and the prohibition does not apply to it.

c (1) Though the marrow in them, if uneaten, is *nothar*. The bones are broken, while the marrow is scooped out and burnt. (2) Where the bones themselves are burnt. (3) One might otherwise be led to violate the prohibition of breaking bones. (4) I.e., the bones were already broken and their marrow removed. (5) The plural in the text probably refers to the separate marrows distributed among the bones.

taught: If its blood was kept overnight,[7] [82b] if its blood was poured out, or if the blood passed outside the Temple enclosures, —where it is an established law that it requires burning,[8] whence do we learn it?—We deduce it from R. Simeon['s teaching]. For it was taught, R. Simeon said: *In the holy place . . . it shall be burnt with fire:*[9] this teaches of the sin-offering that is burnt in the holy place [sanctuary]. Now, I only know this alone: how do we know it of the unfit of the [other] Most Holy sacrifices and the *emurim* of the lesser Holy sacrifices? Therefore it is stated, *'in the holy place . . . it shall be burnt with fire.'*[10] We have [thus] found it of the Most Holy sacrifices; whence do we know it of the lesser Holy
a sacrifices?[1] Rather [that] wherever there is a disqualification in the sacred [sacrifices][2] burning is required, no matter whether it is the Most Holy sacrifices or the lesser Holy sacrifices;—this is known by tradition.[3] And as for Aaron's sin-offering, that is because the incident that happened, happened thus.[4]

Now, according to the tanna of the School of Rabbah b. Abbuhah who said, Even *piggul* requires disfigurement,[5] whence do we know it—[because] he learns the meaning of 'iniquity' from *nothar:*[6] yet let us learn the meaning of iniquity from Aaron's sacrifice?[7]—He can answer you: [A sacrifice such as] Aaron's sin-offering too in such a case[8] would require disfigurement in [future] generations;[9] but there it was a special dispensation.[10]

Now that we say, [that] 'wherever there is a disqualification in the sacred [sacrifices] burning is required, no matter whether it is the most sacred sacrifices or the lesser sacrifices,—this is known by tradition,' what is the purpose of *'in the holy place . . . it shall be burnt with fire'?*—That is required [to teach] that its burning [must be] in the holy place.[11] What is the purpose of, *'and the flesh that toucheth any unclean thing shall not be eaten; it shall be burnt with fire'?*—That is required for its own sake.[12] You might say, All disqualifications of the sacred [sacrifices mean] e.g., if its blood was kept overnight, if its blood was spilled, if its blood went outside, or if it was slaughtered by night: these require
b burning because they do not apply to *ḥullin.*[1] But if it became unclean, which disqualifies in the case of *ḥullin* too, I would say, since it has been treated as profane [non-holy], it does not require burning, and burial should suffice for it. Hence we are informed [that it is not so].

IF ITS OWNERS WERE DEFILED OR THEY DIED, IT MUST BECOME DISFIGURED etc. R. Joseph said: The controversy is where the owners were defiled *after* the sprinkling, so that the flesh had become fit for eating. But if the owners were defiled *before* the sprinkling, so that the flesh had not become fit for eating, all agree that it must be burnt immediately. An objection is raised: This is the general rule: Wherever its disqualification is in itself, it must be burnt immediately; [if it is] in the blood or in its owner, [their flesh] must become disfigured and [then] it goes out to the place of burning?[2] Now [the disqualification through] the owners is taught as analogous to [that of] the blood: just as [that of] the blood is *before* sprinkling, so was [the defilement of] the owners before sprinkling?—Rather if stated, it was thus stated: The controversy is where the owners were defiled before the sprinkling, so that the flesh is not fit for eating, whereby it is as though its disqualification were in itself; but if the owners were defiled after the sprinkling, so that the flesh had become fit for eating, all agree that its disqualification is through something else [extraneous] and it requires disfigurement.

But R. Joḥanan maintained: The controversy holds good [even if the owners were defiled] after sprinkling too. Now R. Joḥanan is consistent with his view. For R. Joḥanan said: R. Joḥanan b. Beroḳah and R. Nehemiah said the same thing. R. Joḥanan b. Beroḳah, this which we have stated. What is [the allusion to] R. Nehemiah?—For it was taught, R. Nehemiah said: This [Aaron's sin-offering] was burnt on account of bereavement, there-
c fore it is stated, [*and there have befallen me such things*] *as these.*[1] Now surely bereavement is as [a disqualification] after sprinkling.[2]

(7) I.e., the blood of the sacrifice had not yet been sprinkled by sunset. (8) In all these cases the blood is unfit for sprinkling and in turn the flesh cannot be eaten, and it must be burnt. (9) Lev. VI, 23. (10) V. *supra* 24a and notes a.l.
a (1) The verse quoted refers only to the *emurim* of the most Holy sacrifices. (2) Or, whatever its disqualification (that arises) in the sanctuary. (3) It is not intimated in the Bible. (4) The Bible does not record this story in order to teach, as stated above, but simply because it happened so. (5) Though the disqualification is certainly in itself; v. *supra* 34b. (6) 'Iniquity' is written in connection with *piggul* and *nothar. Piggul: and the soul that eateth of it shall bear his iniquity* (Lev. VII, 18); *nothar: but every one that eateth of it shall bear his iniquity* (ibid. XIX, 8,—this verse is applied to *nothar* in Ker. 5a). Now *nothar* is naturally disfigured, having been kept too long, and the employment of '*iniquity*' in both cases teaches that *piggul* too requires disfigurement, (7) Lev. X, 17: *and he hath given it to you to bear the iniquity of the congregation.* Hence just as it was burnt there on the *same* day, before it could become disfigured, so should *piggul* be. (8) Whatever the cause of its disqualification. On this there are two views: (i) it had been defiled; (ii) it could not be eaten because Aaron and his sons were bereaved that day by the death of Nadab and Abihu. (9) I.e., if a sin-offering becomes thus disqualified it normally requires disfigurement. (10) Lit., 'the ruling of the hour'. (11) In the Temple Court. (12) I.e., to teach that uncleanness too is a sacred disqualification in this respect.
b (1) V. Glos. *Ḥullin* remains unaffected by these. Thus in spite of these disqualifications the sacrifice has not been subjected to an indignity, as it were, which would disqualify even in the case of *ḥullin.* (2) V. *supra* 34b for notes.
c (1) Lev. X, 19; *'as these'* directly refers to his bereavement. (2) For even if Nadab and Abihu died before the sprinkling, this would not be invalid, the sin-offering being dissimilar to the Passover-offering in this respect. For the latter stands primarily to be eaten, and therefore if the owners are defiled before the sprinkling, the sprinkling is invalid, while if they are defiled *after* the sprinkling the sprinkling is valid. The purpose of the sin-offering, however, is atonement, so that even if the priests are defiled (here, bereaved) before the sprinkling and cannot eat, the sprinkling is valid. Hence this bereavement, even if it occurred *before* the blood was sprinkled, is the same as when the owners of the Passover-offering are defiled *after* the sprinkling.

גי' רש"א ומסברא

עט א מיי' פי"ט מהל' פסולי מוקדשין הלכה א:
פ ב ג מיי' פ"ד מהל' ק"פ הלכה ג:

נראה דדבור אחר הוא ומלת הואיל הוא התחלת דבור

נשפך דמה יצא דמה חוץ לקלעים דקיימא לן בשריפה מנלן נפקא לן מדר"ש דתניא* ר"ש אומר °בקדש באש תשרף ללמד על חטאת ששריפתה בקודש אין לי אלא זו בלבד שאר פסולי קדשי קדשים ואימורי קדשים קלים מנין ת"ל (וכל) בקדש באש תשרף אשכחן קדשי קדשים קדשים קלים מנלן אלא *כל פסולו בקדש בשריפה לא שנא קדשים קלים ולא שנא קדשי קדשים גמרא גמירי לה וחטאת דאהרן *משום מעשה שהיה כך היה ולתנא דבי רבה בר אבוה *דאמר אפילו פיגול טעון עיבור צורה מנא לן יליף עון עון מנותר ונילף עון עון מחטאת דאהרן אמר לך חטאת דאהרן כי האי גוונא נמי עיבור צורה לדורות בעיא והתם הוראת שעה היתה השתא דאמרינן כל פסולי דקדש בשריפה לא שנא קדשי קדשים ולא שנא קדשים קלים גמרא גמירי לה בקדש באש תשרף למה לי ההוא מבעי ליה ששריפתה בקדש °והבשר אשר יגע בכל טמא לא יאכל באש ישרף למה לי ההוא איצטריך לגופיה סד"א כל פסולי דקד"ש כגון לן דמה ונשפך דמה ויצא דמה ונשחטה בלילה דבשריפה דליתנהו בחולין אבל נטמא דבחולין נמי מפסיל אימא הואיל ואיתעביד ביה עובדין דחול אימא לא תיבעי שריפה ותיסגי ליה בקבורה קמ"ל: נטמאו הבעלים או שמתו תעובר צורתן וכו': אמר רב יוסף מחלוקת שנטמאו בעלים אחר זריקה דאיתחזי בשר לאכילה אבל נטמאו בעלים לפני זריקה דלא איתחזי בשר לאכילה דברי הכל ישרף מיד מיתיבי *זה הכלל כל שפסולו בגופו ישרף מיד בדם ובבעלים תעובר צורתו ויצא לבית השריפה קתני בעלים דומיא דדם מה דם לפני זריקה אף בעלים לפני זריקה אלא אי איתמר הכי איתמר מחלוקת שנטמאו בעלים לפני זריקה דלא איתחזי בשר לאכילה דהוה ליה כפסולו בגופו אבל נטמאו בעלים לאחר זריקה דאיתחזי בשר לאכילה דברי הכל פסולו מחמת דבר אחר ובעיא עיבור צורה ורבי יוחנן אמר אף לאחר זריקה נמי מחלוקת ואזדא ר' יוחנן לטעמיה דאמר רבי יוחנן ר"י בן ברוקה ור' נחמיה אמרו דבר אחד ר' יוחנן בן ברוקה הא דאמרן ר' נחמיה מאי היא *דתניא ר' נחמיה אומר מפני אנינות נשרפה זו לכך נאמר °כאלה והא אנינות כלאחר זריקה הויא וכי אשתרוף לאלתר (*נשתרוף) רבה

ונגמר עון עון מחטאת דאהרן. תימה לרשב"א ה"ל לשתוק מעון דפיגול *וממילא נימא דישרף מיד וי"ל דבלאו הכי איצטריך למיכתב עון בפיגול דבפרק שני דזבחים (דף כח:) יליף בפיגול כרת עון עון מנותר: **אבל** נטמא דאיתיה בחולין כו'. תימה לרשב"א ניליף כולהו מטמא ואמאי צריך הלכתא ואומר ר"י דה"א מה שטמא בחולין הוי חומרא *הואיל ומעשה חול אתעביד ביה וא"ת ונילף קל וחומר מתרומה דבעי שריפה וי"ל דאיכא למיפרך מה לתרומה שאסורה לזרים תאמר בקדשים קלים דשרי. רשב"א: **לאחר** זריקה מחלוקת. פירוש אף לאחר זריקה דאי דוקא בדם ובבעלים מאן קתני לה: **רבי** יוחנן בן ברוקה ורבי נחמיה אמרו דבר אחד. וא"ת דילמא לעולם רבי נחמיה כרבנן ס"ל דבעו עיבור צורה וחטאת אהרן שנשרף מיד מפני אנינות הוראת שעה היתה דעדיין לא פירש להם עיבור צורה כדפירש בקונטרס ואומר רשב"א דלפי מה שפירש ר"י דסברא דפסול בעלים בעי עיבור צורה אתי שפיר דהכא לא שייך הוראת שעה היתה דאנינות הוי פסול בעלים ומסברא בעי עיבור צורה ולעיל דקאמר הוראת שעה היתה קסבר דמפני טומאה נשרפה: ורבה

נשפך דמה. דאין כאן זריקה ולא הותר הבשר: וכן יצא דמה. דמהאי פנימה דלעיל נמי נפקא דמפסיל אף הדם ביציאה: דקיימא לן דכל הני בשריפה. בכל הגמרא אנו מוצאין בכל פסולי קדשים יצאו לבית השריפה ומנלן מקרא: בקדש. בעזרה: פסולי שאר קדשים. שמחילתן בכשרותן בעזרה דכתיב בהן (ויקרא ו) בחצר אהל מועד ואימורי קדשים קלים שנפסלו דבכשרותן היתה חומת העזרה מחילתה דהא הקטרה בעזרה מנין שאף כשנפסלו תהא שם שריפתן ולהכי נקט אימורים דאי ניטמא בשרן של קדשים קלים דהלכל בכל העיר שריפתן נמי בכל העיר כדתנן *שורפין אותו בחצרותיהן או על גגותיהן: קדשים קלים. דבעי שריפה כלל בשאר פסולין חוץ מטומאה מנלן ומטומאה ליכא למילף דשאני טומאה דפסלה אף בתרומה ומעשר: הלכתא גמירי לה. וחטאת דאהרן לא איצטריכא לפרושי בה שריפה בתנינותה ובאיליתה אלא מעשה שהיה הוא דאישתעי ולקמן פריך והבשר אשר יגע בכל טמא למה לי: אפי' פיגול. שפסולו בגופו טעון עיבור צורה והא דתנא דרבה בר אבוה לא איתפרש מהיכא: מנא ליה. דבעי עיבור צורה פשיטא לן דטעמא משום דגמר עון עון מנותר כתיב בפיגול (שם ז) והנפש האוכלת ממנו עונה תשא וכתיב בנותר (שם יט) ואוכליו עונו ישא והאי קרא בנותר מוקמינן ליה בכריתות (דף ה.) בגזרה שוה כתיב כי את קודש ה' חילל וכתיב ושרפת את הנותר באש לא יאכל כי קודש הוא וגמר פיגול מנותר מה נותר כבר עובר צורתו אף פיגול צריך שתעובר צורתו ולהגמר מנותר ליגמרי' מחטאת דאהרן שנשרפה בו ביום דכתיב ביה נמי עון ואותה נתן לכם לשאת את עון העדה ומשה הודה להם דכתיב וייטב בעיניו: כי האי גוונא. בין למאן דאמר בזבחים מפני אנינות נשרפה בין למאן דאמר מפני טומאה נשרפה לדורות בעיא עיבור צורה והוראת שעה היתה ששרפוה לבו ביום: ששריפתן בקדש. שצריך לשורפן בעזרה: (א) מעשה חול. שלא נזהרו ונטמאה נתחללה והוזלה בקדושתה: ותיסגי לה בקבורה. לגנוזה מן העין שלא יאכלוה כלבים: מחלוקת. דקאמר תנא קמא פסולו מחמת דבר אחר הוא ובעי עיבור צורה כגון שנטמאו הבעלים אחר זריקת הדם דנעשו כל עבודות הדם בהכשר: אבל נטמאו קודם זריקה. דרחמנא דחייה לפסח שני כמאלת זריקה שלא בבעלים וה"ל פסולו בגופו דזריקה פסולה היא וישרף מיד בי"ד: בדם. כגון נטמא הדם או נשפך לארץ: מחלוקת לפני זריקה. התם פליג ר' יוחנן בן ברוקה דחשיב ליה פסולו בגופו ותנא קמא סבר מ"מ לא בא פסול זה אלא מחמת דבר אחר ורבי יוחנן אמר אף לאחר זריקה נמי מחלוקת: מפני אנינות נשרפה. חטאת דאהרן שהיו אוננין ואסורין לאכול בקדשים דכתיב (דברים כו) לא אכלתי באוני ממנו ואתו קדשים בקל וחומר ממעשר: לכך נאמר כאלה. ותקראנה אותי כאלה שאני אונן והיאך הייתי אוכל קדשים למשה נצטוה לאמר להם קחו את המנחה הנותרת מאשי ה' ואכלוה באנינות והיה סבור שאף החטאת תאכל באנינות כמנחה ואמר לו אהרן שמא לא שמעת אלא במנחה זו שהיא קדשי שעה ליום שמיני של מלואים נצטוית אותה מנחה ואף אני מודה לך בשעיר נחשון ושעיר של יום דכתיב (ויקרא ט) ואל בני ישראל תדבר לאמר קחו שעיר עזים לחטאת שהם קדשי שעה חובה ליום ואכילתן [מותר] לאונן אבל חטאת זו שעיר ר"ח הוא וקדשי דורות הן ואסורין לאונן ור' יהודה פליג עלה התם ואמר מפני טומאה נשרפה שנטמאת באונס והאי כאלה דריש ליה אמאי דקאמר משה לאהרן שמא מתוך לערך פשעת בה ונטמאת וקאמר ליה אהרן למשה כך אני בעיניך שאני מבזה קדשי קדשים אלמלי קראוני כאלה וכאלה לא הייתי מבזה אותן: הכי גרסינן והא אנינות כלאחר זריקה היא. שאפי' מתו נדב ואביהוא לפני זריקה אין הזריקה נפסלת בכך דחטאת לא דמיא לפסח דעיקרו לאכילה דאילו חטאת לא חיישינן לאוכלין דידה דלכפרה אתיא ואכל ישראל שהיו רחוין ואם מפני שהקריבוה באנינות ונפסלה דאונן שעבד חילל לא הדיוטים הקריבוה כי אם אהרן עצמו וקיימא לן (יומא דף יג:) כהן גדול מקריב אונן ואינו אוכל והכי אמרינן בזבחים (דף קא.) ודרשינן הן היום הקריבו דקאמר ליה משה לאהרן דילמא באנינות אקריבתיה ופסלתיה ועל כן שרפתם אותה א"ל אהרן הן היום וכי הם היום הקריבו דפסל בהו אנינות אני הקרבתי דלא פסלא בי אנינות ושריפה מיד הואי בלא עיבור צורה ומדקאמר ר' יוחנן דר' נחמיה ור' יוחנן בן ברוקה אמרו דבר אחד אלמא ס"ל דפלוגתא דמתניתין אף כשנטמאו לאחר זריקה דעבודות דם נעשו בהכשר ואפילו הכי ישרף מיד מפני שאין מי שיאכלנו כי חטאת דאהרן לא היה לה פסול אחר אלא שלא היו לה אוכלין. וספרים כתב בהן והא אנינות לאחר זריקה הואי וקשיא לי מנלן הא הלא לא נתפרשו בפרשה אלא עבודות של קרבנות שמיני אבל קרבנות של ר"ח לא נתפרשו בה ועוד מדקא מהדר ליה אהרן וכי הן הקריבו והלא אני הקרבתי מכלל דקודם זריקה הואי אנינות: *ורבה מוסיף אף רבי יוסי. נמי סבירא ליה כר' יוחנן בן ברוקה דפסול בעלים לא בעי עיבור צורה: כל

רבינו חננאל

או נשפך או יצא דמה חוץ לקלעים דקיימא לן בשרפה מנא לן ואתינן לאפוקה מדר' שמעון דתני בקדש באש תשרף דכתיב בחטאת לרבות כל פסולי קדשי קדשים ואימורי קדשים קלים שהן בשרפה פסולי קדשים קלים עצמן מנין ולא אשכחן ראיה מן התורה ואסיקנא אלא כל פסול קדש בשרפה הלכתא גמירי לה וחטאת דאהרן מעשה שהיה את' לאשמעינן: ורבה בר אבוה דתני אפילו פגול טעון צורה כלומר אינו נשרף מיד אלא עד שתעובר צורתו אמר לך אפי' כעין חטאת לדורות צורה בעיו וחטאת דאהרן הוראת שעה היתה ולא שיהיה דבר זה נוהג לדורות: אמר רב חסדא מחלוקת ת"ק ור' יוחנן בן ברוקה בשנטמאו הבעלים או שמתו שזה אומר תעובר צורתו וזה אומר ישרף מיד בשמתו או נטמאו הבעלים לאחר זריקה דאיתחזי בשר לאכילה אבל לפני זריקה דלא איתחזי בשר לאכילה דברי הכל ישרף מיד איתבינן עלה וחזר ואמר אלא הכי איתמר אמר רב חסדא מחלוקת שנטמאו או שמתו לפני זריקה דלא איתחזי בשר לאכילה כלל דהוי ליה(כי)פסולו בגופו אבל לאחר זריקה דברי הכל בעי צורה ור' יוחנן אמר לאחר זריקה נמי מחלוקת כי היכי דלא תקשה לך הא תיובתא דאותבינן על רב חסדא ולא אשכח לה פירוקא: ואזדא ר' יוחנן לטעמיה דאמר ר' יוחנן ר' נחמיה ור' יוחנן בן ברוקה אמרו דבר אחד דאפי' פסול הזבחים בבעלים ישרף מיד ר' יוחנן בן ברוקה הא דמתני' ר' נחמיה דתניא ר' נחמיה אומר מפני אנינות נשרפה לכך נאמר כאלה ואנינות לאחר זריקה הואי ישרפה מיד הואי

תורה אור: ויקרא ו; שם ז; שם י

מסורת הש"ס: לעיל דף כד. | [לעיל פא:] | [ערכין סה: וש"נ] | לעיל דף לד: [ע"ש: מנחות כ:] | לעיל לד: ע"ג [תוספתא פ"ג] | זבחים דף קא. | [נ"ל אשתרוף]

הגהות הב"ח
(א) רש"י ד"ה ששריפתן וכו' בעזרה הס"ד ואח"כ מ"ה שעבדו דחול מעשה חול:

שייך לדף פ"ג

חוזר ושורפו לפני הבירה מעצי המערכה אמר רב חמא בר עוקבא לא קשיא כאן *באכסנאי כאן בבעל הבית רב פפא אמר הא והא באכסנאי כאן שהחזיק בדרך כאן שלא החזיק בדרך רב זביד אמר לעולם כדאמר מעיקרא כאן באכסנאי כאן בבעל הבית ואף ע"ג דלא החזיק בדרך אכסנאי כיון דלית ליה עשאוהו כציקנין דתנן הציקנין שורפין אותו לפני הבירה בשביל ליהנות מעצי המערכה ת"ר *באו לשורפו בחצרותיהן ומעצי המערכה אין שומעין להן לפני הבירה ומעצי עצמן אין שומעין להן בשלמא מעצי המערכה בחצרותיהן אין שומעין להן 'דילמא פיישן מינייהו ואתו בהו לידי תקלה אלא לפני הבירה מעצי עצמן מ"ט לא רב יוסף אמר *שלא לבייש את מי שאין לו רבא אמר 'מפני החשד מאי בינייהו איכא בינייהו 'דאיכא קני וחריותא דלא חזו למערכה *תנן התם 'ראש המעמד היה מעמיד את הטמאין על שער המזרח מ"ט אמר רב יוסף כדי לביישן רבא אמר 'מפני החשד מאי בינייהו איכא בינייהו מפנקי אי נמי דקא גדיל שישורא:

מתני' 'הפסח שיצא או שנטמא ישרף מיד נטמאו הבעלים או שמתו תעובר צורתו וישרף בששה עשר ר' יוחנן בן ברוקה אומר אף זה ישרף מיד לפי שאין לו אוכלין:

גמ' בשלמא נטמא כתיב °והבשר אשר יגע בכל טמא לא יאכל באש ישרף אלא יוצא מנלן דכתיב °הן לא הובא את דמה אל הקדש פנימה *אמר לו משה לאהרן מדוע לא אכלתם את החטאת שמא נכנס דמה לפני ולפנים אמר לו לאו אמר לו שמא חוץ למחיצתה יצתה אמר לו לאו בקודש היתה אמר לו אי בקודש היתה והלא הובא את דמה אל הקדש פנימה מדוע לא אכלתם אותה מכלל דאי נפקא אי נמי עייל דמה לפנים בת שריפה היא בשלמא נטמא גלי רחמנא בקדשים קלים *כ"ש בקדשי קדשים אלא יוצא אשכחן קדשי הקדשים קדשים קלים מנלן ותו הא דתניא לן דמה נשפך

חוזר ושורפו כו'. אלמא מיעוטו שנפסל מעצי המערכה נמי שרפינן: כאן באכסנאי. שאין לו עצים שורפו מעצי המערכה ומתני' בבעל הבית: שהחזיק בדרך. לא הטריחוהו לחזור על עצים דקתני וכן מי שילא אלמא בהחזיק בדרך עסקינן: רב זביד. כרב חמא מוקים לה ולהדרב פפא פליג ויהיב טעמא למילתיה דרב חמא דכיון דלית ליה עצים הם עשאוהו כציקנין והחזיק בדרך דקתני מתני' לאשמועינן חזרה נקט לה ולא משום עצים דהוא הדין בלא החזיק: באו לשורפו כו'. כדמפרש טעמא: לידי תקלה. ליהנות מהן הנאה אחרת והנאה זו אין בו מעילה דהנאה ב"ד הוא ועל מנת כן מקדישין אותו: משום חשד. שלאחר שריפתן מחזירין מותר העצים לתוך ביתן והרואה חושדן בגונבי עצי המערכה והכינן מהן: קני וחריות'. קנים וחריות של דקל הכל יודעים שאינם מעצי המערכה לפי שקלים הם ונשרפין מהר ואין אש המערכה מתקיימ' בהן ומשום חשד ליכא אבל משום בושת איכא: תנן התם. במסכת תמיד: ראש המעמד. הממונה על כך מעמיד את הטמאים של בית אב בכל בקר בשער המזרחי כניסת כל אדם להר הבית: כדי לביישן. שלא נזהרו מלטמא והרי העבודה של מחר היתה מוטלת עליהן והיה להן ליזהר: משום חשד. שלא יחשדום שמפני מלאכתן הן נמנעין מלבוא לעבוד עבודה (א) ומעמידין שם כדי שיראו אותם בני אדם ויודעין שמחמת טומאה הם חדילין ואידי דאיירי לעיל בהך פלוגתא דמפני החשד נקט לה להא: מפנקי. הכל יודעין שבטלים הן מן המלאכה ואין מניחין עבודה מפני מלאכתן הלכך משום חשד ליכא ואין צריך להעמידם שם ולמאן דאמר כדי לביישן צריך: אי נמי דקגדיל שישורא. מפשילי חבלים שהיא אומנות קלה ושכרה מעט ואין בני אדם חשודין שיחדלו מלבוא לעבודה מפני ביטול מלאכה זו: **מתני'** הפסח שנטמא או שילא ישרף מיד. בארבעה עשר ואין צריך להשהותו עד הבוקר של ששה עשר שתעובר צורתו דהיינו לילה אחד ומיהו בי"ט לא מצי שריף ליה כדיליף לקמן (דף פג:) דאין שורפין קדשים בי"ט: נטמאו הבעלים או שמתו. דאין פסולו בגופו אלא מחמת דבר אחר שאין לו אוכלין: **גמ'** בשלמא נטמא. טעון שריפה: דכתיב והבשר וגו'. וגבי קדשים קלים כתיב: שמא נכנס דמה. אל הקודש לכפר בהיכל ונפסלה כדכתיב (ויקרא ו) וכל חטאת אשר יובא מדמה וגו' א"כ הוא יפה עשיתם ששרפתם: שמא חוץ למחיצתה. חוץ לעזרה יצאת ומקרא יתירא דרשי לה דלא איצטריך פנימה אלא הכי בעא מינייהו ברישא שמא יצאתה ולא היתה פנימה ואם כן הוא יפה עשיתם ששרפתם (ב) פנימה היתה ולא יצאת הא למדת שאם יצאת היה לו לשורפה: נטמא. והבשר אשר יגע וגו' גבי שלמים כתיב וכ"ש קדשי קדשים דחמירי: אלא יוצא. בחטאת אשכחן וקדשים קלים מנלן דמצריך ליה תנא דמתניתין שריפה ליוצא דפסח: לן דמה. של בהמת קרבן דאמרינן בזבחים (דף נו:) מנין לדם שנפסל בשקיעת החמה שנא' ביום הקריבו את זבחו ביום שאתה זובח אתה מקריב כו':

רב זביד אמר לעולם כדאמר מעיקרא. פי' בקונטרס דרב זביד לא פליג אדרב חמא בר עוקבא ולאו אלא מפרש טעמו וקשה לר"י דלא מצינו בשום מקום שיאמר לעולם כו' כדי לפרש ונראה לו דרב חמא בר עוקבא ורב פפא לא פליגי דרב חמא בר עוקבא מוקי כאן באכסנאי כאן בבעה"ב ולאו דוקא בהחזיק בדרך אבל בלא החזיק אפי' אכסנאי הוי כבעה"ב אלא דלא איירי בה ורב פפא מוקי אידי ואידי באכסנאי ולא פליג אדרב חמא בר עוקבא ורב זביד פליג אתרווייהו וקסבר אכסנאי שלא החזיק עשאוהו כציקנין א"נ רב פפא ורב זביד פליגי אליבא דרב חמא בר עוקבא רב פפא סבר דרב חמא בר עוקבא איירי בהחזיק אבל בלא החזיק הוי אכסנאי כבעל הבית ורב זביד סבר דאכסנאי אפי' לא החזיק עשאוהו כציקנין ודוקא נקט רב חמא בר עוקבא בעל הבית: **היה** מעמיד את הטמאים בשער המזרח. אפילו בטומאת קריין מיירי ונראה לר"י דהאי שער המזרח היינו שער עזרת נשים ואע"ג דאמר בפ"ק דיבמות (דף ז:) ובכמה דוכתי דטבול יום אינו נכנס במחנה לויה לאו בכל מחנה לויה קאמר אלא מעזרת נשים ולפנים דהכי מוכח במסכת כלים (פ"א מ"ח) דקתני התם עזרת נשים מקודשת ממנה שאין טבולי יום נכנסין לשם: **בשלמא** נטמא דכתיב והבשר. אין לפרש דאמיד דקתני במתניתין קאי דכיון דכתיב בקרא ישרף אית לן למימר דהיינו מיד בלא עיבור צורה דאי בעיבור לישתוק קרא מיניה ואנא ידענא דישרף דהוה ליה נותר מדאמר לקמן ורבה מוסיף אף ר"י הגלילי דתניא כו' אבל לרבנן דילפי מכל חטאת אשר יובא מדמה וגו' בעי עיבור צורה אע"ג דכתיב (ג) ישרף אלמא מישרף לא משמע מיד מיהו יש לדחות דההוא ישרף מוקמינן לשריפה' בקודש ואינו מיותר אך יש להביא ראיה מדקאמר בסמוך לן דמה נשפך דמה או שילא חוץ לקלעים מנלן והתם לא בעי בע"צ מנלן שהם מיד בשריפה דהתנן בדם ובבעלים תעובר צורתו אלא מנלן בשריפה קאמר ושריפה דמיד מסברא נפקא לן ולא מקרא וא"ת ואמאי צריך קרא בפסול הדם דכיון דצריך עיבור צורה פשיטא דישרף משום נותר ואור"י דאיצטריך דלא ליעבד ליה קבורה קודם שיהיה נותר אי נמי הוה אמינא אפי' כשיהיה נותר לא ישרף דנותר שהיה ראוי לאכילה קודם שנתותר דוקא ישרף כדמשמע לא תותירו אלא תאכלוהו אבל קשה דהיכי יליף יוצא בשריפה מחטאת דאהרן דהא ע"כ לא הודה להן משה על השריפה דחטאת שנכנס דמה לפנים דפסולו בדם בעי עיבור צורה והם שרפוה מיד אלא ה"ק להו הא אם הובא יפה עשו שלא אכלוהו דהכי כתיב רישיה דקרא מדוע לא אכלתם ומיהו נראה לרשב"א דמצי למימר דאמיד בעי מנא לן וכולה שמעתין מסקא אליבא דר' יוחנן דסבירא ליה לקמן דפסול הדם הוי פסולו בגופו דחשיב דם ובשר חדא מילתא ובפסול בעלים דוקא קתני מתניתין דבעי עיבור צורה ושפיר מייתי השתא מחטאת דאהרן דמשה הודה להן אם נכנס דמה לפנים שפיר עבוד דשרפוה ולן דמה נמי קבעי מנלן דמיד אך קשה על זה כיון דמסברא לא הוה אמרינן דישרף מיד אלא בעיבור צורה אי לאו דמסיק דהלכתא גמירי לה מאי קאמר ולרבה בר אבוה דאפי' פיגול בעי עיבור צורה מנלן לימא דלא גמירי הלכתא ומה צריך גזירה שוה אלא ודאי דפסולו בגופו ישרף מיד סברא הוא ובדם ובבעלים דבעי עיבור צורה נמי סברא:

בקדש היתה. רש"י פירש דדריש מפנימה וכן ר"ח ולר"י נראה דדריש מאכל תאכלו אותה בקודש ובתורת כהנים דריש מבמקום הקדש*: **בשלמא** נטמא גלי רחמנא בקדשים קלים והוא הדין בקדשי קדשים. וא"ת והא בהדיא בהאי קרא כתיבי קדשי קדשים ומאי קאמר והוא הדין כדדרשינן בכל שעה (לעיל כד:) והבשר לרבות עצים ולבונה ויש לומר דהאי לאו הוא הדין הוא אלא מילתא דאתא לרבות קדשים קלים דלא בעו הכשר ולא קדשי קדשים:

רבינו חננאל

והנותר שורפין אותו בחצרותיהן כו' איני ששורפין אותו בחצרותיהן והתנן בסוף פרק ואלו עוברין בפסח על בשר הקדש שיצא ונפסל חוזר ושורפו לפני הבירה ושנינן לא קשיא הא באכסנאי שאין לו חצר משנתנו בבעל הבית וארמנאי זה אע"פ שלא החזיק בדרך עשאוהו כציקנין ששורפין אותו לפני הבירה בשביל ליהנות מעצי המערכה: ת"ר באו לשרפו בחצרותיהן מעצי המערכה אין שומעין להם חיישי' דלמא פיישי מינייהו ושדליק תחת תבשילו ואתי ביה לידי תקלה מעצי עצמן לפני הבירה אין שומעין להם שלא לבייש מי שאין לו אי נמי שמא ישארו לו ויקחם ויחשדוהו הרואים כי עצי הקדש לקח ואם הם קני וחריותא כגון קוצים וחריות שאין ראוין למערכה כדתנן בתמיד באלו היו רגילין במורביות של תאנה ושל אגוז ושל עץ שמן מנעין איתו שלא לבייש את מי שאין לו: תנן התם בתמיד בסוף פ"ה ראש המעמד היה מעמיד את הטמאים בשערי מזרח רב יוסף אמר כדי לביישן רבא אמר מפני החשד שלא יחשדום כי לעבוד עבודה נכנסו והם טמאים: מתני' הפסח שנטמא או שיצא ישרף מיד כו'. יוצא מנא לן דכתיב הן לא הובא את דמה אל הקדש מכלל שאם נכנס דמה לקדש בת שרפה היא כדכתיב (ויקרא ו) וכל חטאת אשר יובא מדמה אל אהל מועד לכפר בקדש לא תאכל באש תשרף פנימה כלומר פנימה היתה ולא יצאת חוץ למחיצת הקדש אכול תאכלו אותו מכלל שאלו יצאת טוב עשיתם ששרפתם אותה ש"מ בשר היוצא חוץ למחיצתו בן שרפה הוא בשלמא נטמא גלי רחמנא בשלמים שהם קדשים קלים והבשר אשר יגע בכל טמא לא יאכל באש ישרף והוא הדין לקדשי קדשים אלא יוצא אשכחן בחטאת שהיא קדשי קדשים כי היא בשרפה קדשים קלים מנא לן ותוב לן

עין משפט נר מצוה

עה א מיי' פ"ט מהל' פסולי מוקדשין הלכה יח:

עו ב ג ד מיי' פ"ד מהל' ק"פ הלכ' ג:

עז ה מיי' פ"ד מהל' תמידין הלכה ה:

עח ו מיי' פ"ד מהלכות קרבן פסח הלכה ג ופרק יט מהלכות פסולי מוקדשין הלכה ג:

מסורת הש"ס

[תוספתא פ"ג]

[תענית כו. לה. פסחים כד.]

תמיד דף כו.

זבחים דף קא.

[ועי' תוס' זבחים פב: ד"ה כיון]

הגהות הב"ח

(א) רש"י ד"ה משום חשד וכו' ומעמידים שם: (ב) שם ד"ה שמא חוץ וכו' ששרפתם אלא פנימה היתה: (ג) תוס' ד"ה בשלמא וכו' אע"ג דכתיב ישרף אלמא משרף לא משמע וכו' דפסול הפסח:

passed Scopus he burns it where he is; but if not, [82a] he returns and burns it in front of the Temple with the wood of the [altar] pile?[6]—Said R. Ḥama b. 'Uḳba, There is no difficulty: one refers to a lodger;[7] the other [our Mishnah] refers to a householder. R. Papa said, Both refer to a lodger: there he had repaired to the road;[8] here he had not repaired to the road. R. Zebid said: In truth it is as was first stated, [viz.,] there it refers to a lodger, while here it refers to a householder, and even where he had not taken to the road; [in the case of] a lodger, since he has not [wood of his own] he was regarded as a miser, for we learned: MISERS BURN IT IN FRONT OF THE TEMPLE IN ORDER TO BENEFIT FROM THE WOOD OF THE [ALTAR] PILE.

Our Rabbis taught: If they come [desire] to burn it in their own court-yards and with the wood of the [altar] pile, we do not heed [permit] them; in front of the Temple and with their own wood, we do not heed them. As for not heeding them [when they wish to burn it] with the wood of the pile in their own court-yards, that is well, [the reason being] lest some of it [the wood]
a be left over and they come to a stumbling-block through it.[1] But what is the reason that [they may] not [burn it] in front of the Temple with their own wood?—Said R. Joseph: So as not to shame him who has none [of his own]. Raba said: On account of suspicion.[2] Wherein do they differ?—They differ where he brought cane reeds and dried branches, which are not fit for the pile.[3]

We learned elsewhere: The head of the *ma'amad*[4] used to place the unclean[5] by the East Gate.[6] What is the reason? Said R. Joseph: In order to put them to shame.[7] Raba said: Because of suspicion.[8] Wherein do they differ?—They differ in respect of delicate persons or ropemakers.[9]

MISHNAH. A PASSOVER-OFFERING WHICH PASSED OUT[10] OR WAS DEFILED MUST BE BURNT IMMEDIATELY.[11] IF ITS OWNERS WERE DEFILED OR THEY DIED,[12] IT MUST BECOME DISFIGURED[13] AND BE BURNT ON THE SIXTEENTH. R. JOḤANAN B. BEROḲAH SAID: THIS TOO MUST BE BURNT IMMEDIATELY, BECAUSE THERE ARE NONE TO EAT IT.

GEMARA. As for uncleanness, it is well, because it is written, *And the flesh that toucheth any unclean thing shall not be eaten; it shall*
b *be burnt with fire*.[1] But how do we know it of what goes out?—Because it is written, *Behold, the blood of it was not brought into the sanctuary within*.[2] Moses said to Aaron: 'Why did ye not eat the sin-offering? Perhaps its blood entered the innermost [sanctuary]'?[3] 'No,' he answered him. 'Perhaps it passed without its barrier'?[4] he asked. 'No,' replied he, 'it was in the sanctuary.' Said he to him, 'If it was in the sanctuary, and "*behold, the blood of it was not brought into the sanctuary within*," wherefore have ye not eaten it?' Whence it follows that if it passed out, or if its blood entered within, it requires burning.

As for when it is defiled, it is well: the Divine Law revealed it in the case of lesser Holy sacrifices, and all the more[5] in the case of Most Holy sacrifices.[6] But as to what goes out; we have found [that it is disqualified in the case of] superior sacrifices; whence do we know [it of] inferior sacrifices? Moreover, as to what was

(6) V. Mishnah *supra* 49a for notes.—This shows that even a small portion is burnt thus. (7) Who has no home of his own and lacks the facilities for burning it at home. (8) Therefore it is too much trouble to return home, and so he burns it in front of the Temple.

a (1) They may use it for other purposes, which is forbidden. (2) He will take away any wood that is left over, but the onlooker will think that it is wood of the altar pile and so suspect him of theft. (3) Raba's reason is not applicable here, and therefore it is permitted; whereas R. Joseph's reason still holds good, hence it is forbidden. (4) Post, a division of popular representatives deputed to accompany the daily services in the Temple with prayers, and also a corresponding division in the country town, answering to the divisions (v. *supra* 57a, n. a3) of priests and Levites.—Jast. (5) Of the priestly division that should have officiated that day in the Temple. (6) That all who entered might see them. (7) For not having taken care to be clean. (8) Lest they be suspected of neglecting the Temple service for their private affairs. (9) Who receive little pay; no priest will neglect the Temple service for this. Raba's reason does not apply here, whereas R. Joseph's reason does. (10) Beyond its proper boundaries. (11) On the fourteenth. (12) So there is none to eat it. (13) V. *supra* 34a, n. b7.

b (1) Lev. VII, 19. (2) Ibid. X, 18; the previous verses relate how Moses was angry with Eleazar and Ithamar for having the sin-offering burnt instead of eating it. (3) I.e., the Holy of Holies—in that case you had rightly burnt it; v. ibid. VI, 23. (4) I.e., outside the Temple court. (5) Var. lec.: the same law applies. (6) V. *supra* 24a, n. a2. The verse quoted in connection with defilement refers to a peace-offering.

to him,[2] [81*b*] is it not logical that the 'uncleanness of the deep' was permitted to him?—I will tell you: can we then argue *a fortiori* from a traditional law: surely it was taught, R. Eliezer said to him: Akiba! That a bone [of a corpse] the size of a barley grain defiles[3] is a traditional law, whereas [that] a quarter [*log*] of blood [of a corpse defiles] is [deduced by you] *a fortiori*,[4] and we do not deduce *a fortiori* from a traditional law!—Rather said Raba: We learn [the scope of] *'its appointed time'* from the Passover-offering.[5]

And where is [the law about] the 'uncleanness of the deep' itself written?[6]—Said R. Eleazar: Scripture saith, *And if any man die beside him* ['alaw],[7] [which means] when it is quite clear beside him.[8] We have thus found [it in the case of] a nazirite; how do we know [it in the case of] one who sacrifices a Passover-offering?—Said R. Johanan: Because Scripture saith, [*If any man shall be unclean by reason of a dead body or*] *in a distant road unto you:*[9] [that means] when it is quite clear unto you. R. Simeon b. Lakish said, It is as the road: just as the road is manifest, so must the [cause of] defilement be manifest too.

An objection is raised: What is the 'uncleanness of the deep'? Wherever not [even] a person at the end of the world had been a cognizant thereof.[1] If a person at the end of the world had been cognizant thereof, it is not the 'uncleanness of the deep.' [But] according to R. Eleazar who interpreted, when it is quite clear beside him, then [it is 'uncleanness of the deep'] unless *he himself* [the nazirite] knows of it.[2] According to R. Johanan who interpreted *'unto you'* [as meaning] when it is quite clear unto you, then [at least] two should know thereof.[3] According to R. Simeon b. Lakish who said, It is as a road, then all should know of it? —Rather the 'uncleanness of the deep' is known as a traditional law, while the verse[s] are a mere support.[4]

Mar son of R. Ashi said: They learned this[5] only where it became known to him[6] *after* the sprinkling, so that when the blood was sprinkled it was rightly sprinkled; but if it was known to him *before* the sprinkling, it does not propitiate. An objection is raised: If a man finds a corpse lying across the width of a path,[7] in respect of *terumah* he is unclean;[8] in respect of [the laws of] a nazirite or one who sacrifices the Passover-offering, he is clean; and all [statements of] unclean and clean refer to the future.[9]—Rather if stated, it was thus stated: Mar son of R. Ashi said: Do not say that only if it became known to him after sprinkling does it propitiate, whereas if it became known to him before sprinkling, it does not propitiate; for even if it became known to him before sprinkling it [still] propitiates.

[To revert to] the main text: If a man finds a corpse lying across the width of a path, in respect of *terumah* he is unclean; in respect of [the laws of] a nazirite or one who sacrifices a Passover-offering, b he is clean. When is that said? If he has no room to pass by,[1] but if he has room to pass by, he is clean even in respect of *terumah*. When is that said? If he finds it whole. But if it was broken or dismembered, he is clean, as he might have passed between the pieces. But [if it lay] in a grave, even if broken and dismembered, he is unclean, because the grave unites it.[2] When is this said? If he was walking on foot. But if he was laden [with a burden] or riding, he is unclean; because he who walks on foot can avoid touching it or overshadowing it,[3] but when he is laden or riding, he cannot but touch [it] or overshadow it.[4] When is this said?[5] In the case of 'uncleanness of the deep'; but in the case of known uncleanness, he is unclean. And what is 'uncleanness of the deep'? Wherever not [even] one at the end of the world had been cognizant thereof. But if one [even] at the world's end was cognizant thereof, it is not 'uncleanness of the deep.' If he found it hidden in straw, earth, or pebbles, it is 'uncleanness of the deep'.[6] [If he found it] in water, in darkness, or in the clefts of rocks, it is not 'uncleanness of the deep.'[7] And they did not state [the law of] 'uncleanness of the deep' in respect of aught save a corpse alone.

MISHNAH. IF IT [THE PASCHAL LAMB] BECAME UNCLEAN, [EITHER] WHOLLY OR THE GREATER PART THEREOF, WE c BURN IT IN FRONT OF THE BIRAH[1] WITH THE WOOD OF THE PILE.[2] IF THE LESSER PART THEREOF BECAME UNCLEAN, ALSO NOTHAR,[3] THEY [THE PEOPLE] BURN IT IN THEIR COURT-YARDS OR ON THEIR ROOFS WITH THEIR OWN WOOD. MISERS BURN IT IN FRONT OF THE BIRAH, IN ORDER TO BENEFIT FROM THE WOOD OF THE PILE.

GEMARA. What is the reason?[4]—Said R. Jose b. Ḥanina: In order to put them to shame.[5]

IF THE LESSER PART THEREOF BECAME UNCLEAN etc. But the following contradicts it: Similarly, he who went out of Jerusalem and recollected that he had holy flesh with him, if he has

(2) In the case of the continual-offering, where none are clean. (3) A nazirite, if he touches or carries it, and he must commence again (v. Num. VI, 9-12). (4) R. Akiba deduced *a fortiori* from the former that if a nazirite is under the same covering as a quarter *log* of blood taken from a corpse he is defiled, just as in the first case; v. Naz. 57*a*. (5) *Mo'ado* (its appointed time) is written in connection with both the continual-offering and the Passover-offering (v. Num. XXVIII, 2; IX, 2). Hence just as the headplate propitiates for the 'uncleanness of the deep' in the latter case, so in the former too. (6) That the headplate propitiates in the case of a nazirite and one who sacrifices his Passover-offerings. At this stage it is as yet unknown that it is not intimated in Scripture at all but is a traditional law. (7) Num. VI, 9. (8) I.e., he becomes unclean only if the existence of the corpse is *'beside him'*, clear and known to him. But in the 'uncleanness of the deep' it was unknown hitherto. (9) Ibid. IX, 10, lit. translation.

a (1) Until after the nazirite or the Israelite sacrificing his Passover-offering was defiled by it. In that case the headplate propitiates. (2) Since the verse refers to him. (3) *'Unto you'*, Heb. *lakem*, is in the plural, hence must refer to two at least. (4) But not really the source of the law. (5) *Sc.* that the headplate propitiates for 'uncleanness of the deep' in the two cases stated. (6) The owner of the sacrifice, that he had been thus defiled. (7) Where he had passed, and he must either have actually touched or passed over it. (8) He may not eat *terumah*. (9) Thus though it is now known to him before the blood is sprinkled, the headplate propitiates, for this too was a case of 'uncleanness of the deep', since as far as is known none was aware of the corpse before.

b (1) V. *supra*, n. a7. (2) And the whole length of the grave is unclean and defiles. (3) יאהיל < אֹהֶל means to form a tent, and is the technical term for overshadowing a corpse without touching it. (4) Because the burden or the action of the riding makes him sway from side to side. (5) That a nazirite etc. is clean. (6) These completely cover a corpse and make him quite invisible; hence its presence would not be known. (7) Because one might have seen it previously.

c (1) V. *supra* 49*a*. (2) The wood specially arranged for the altar for the burning of the burnt-offerings etc. (3) That which remained over from a clean Passover sacrifice, v. Ex. XII, 10. (4) That it is burnt before the Temple, publicly. (5) For their carelessness in permitting it to become defiled.

עין משפט נר מצוה

עא א מיי' פ"ג מהל' נזירות הלכה יח:

עא ב מיי' פ"ד מהלכ' ביאת מקדש הל' ו:

עב ג מיי' פ"ו מהל' קרבן פסח הלכה יא ופי"א מהל' אבות הטומאה הלכה ג:

עג ד מיי' פ"ו מהלכות נזירות הלכה יט:

עד ה מיי' פ"ד מהל' קרבן פסח הלכה ג ופי"ט מהל' פסולי מוקדשין הלכה כ:

מסורת הש"ס

אינו דין שהותרה לו טומאת התהום אמרי ומי דיינינן ק"ו מהלכה והתניא *אמר לו רבי אליעזר עקיבא עצם כשעורה הלכה רביעית דם ק"ו ואין דנין ק"ו מהלכה אלא אמר רבא יליף מועדו מועדו מפסח וטומאת התהום גופא היכא כתיבא *אמר ר"א אמר קרא °וכי ימות מת עליו במחוורת עליו אשכחן נזיר עושה פסח מנלן א"ר יוחנן אמר קרא °בדרך רחוקה לכם במחוורת לכם רשב"ל אמר כדרך מה דרך בגלוי אף טומאה נמי בגלוי מיתיבי* *אי זהו טומאת התהום כל שלא הכיר בה אחד בסוף העולם הכיר בה אחד בסוף העולם אין זה טומאת התהום לר"א דאמר במחוורת עליו עד דידע הוא לר' יוחנן דאמר לכם במחוורת לכם עד דידעי בה תרין לרשב"ל דאמר כדרך עד דידעי כולי עלמא אלא טומאת התהום הלכתא גמירי לה וקרא אסמכתא בעלמא אמר מר בר רב אשי לא שנו אלא שנודע לו לאחר זריקה דכי אזדריק דם שפיר איזדריק אבל נודע לו לפני זריקה לא מרצה מיתיבי *המוצא מת מושכב לרחבו של דרך לתרומה טמא לנזיר ועושה פסח טהור וכל טמא וטהור להבא הוא אלא אי אתמר הכי איתמר אמר מר בר רב אשי לא תימא נודע לו לאחר זריקה הוא דמרצה אבל נודע לו לפני זריקה לא מרצה אלא *אפילו נודע לו לפני זריקה מרצה: גופא *המוצא מת מושכב לרחבו של דרך לתרומה טמא לנזיר ועושה פסח טהור בד"א שאין לו מקום לעבור אבל יש לו מקום לעבור אף לתרומה טהור בד"א שמצאו שלם אבל משובר ומפורק טהור שמא בין הפרקים עבר ובקבר אפילו משובר ומפורק טמא מפני שהקבר מצרפו בד"א במהלך ברגליו אבל טעון או רכוב טמא לפי שמהלך ברגליו אפשר שלא יגע ולא יאהל אבל טעון או רכוב אי אפשר שלא יגע ולא יאהל בד"א בטומאת התהום אבל בטומאה ידועה טמא ואי זה היא טומאת התהום כל שלא הכיר בה אחד בסוף העולם אבל הכיר בה אחד בסוף העולם אין זה טומאת התהום *מצאו טמון בתבן בעפר ובצרורות הרי זה טומאת התהום במים באפילה בנקיקי הסלעים אין זה טומאת התהום ולא אמרו *טומאת התהום אלא למת בלבד: **מתני'** *נטמא שלם או רובו שורפין אותו לפני הבירה מעצי המערכה נטמא מיעוטו והנותר שורפין אותו בחצרותיהן או על גגותיהן מעצי עצמן הציקנין שורפין אותו לפני הבירה בשביל ליהנות מעצי המערכה: **גמ'** מ"ט א"ר יוסי בר חנינא כדי לביישן: נטמא מיעוטו וכו'· ורמינהו *וכן מי שיצא מירושלים ונזכר שיש בידו בשר קדש אם עבר צופים שורפו במקומו ואם לאו

חוזר

תורה אור

במדבר ט

רש"י

אינו דין שהותרה לו טומאת התהום. היתר גמור ואפילו איכא טוארין: מהלכה. כגון קבר טומאת התהום הלכה למשה מסיני בנזיר ועושה פסח: ומי דיינינן קל וחומר מהלכה. והא טומאת התהום לא משום ספיקא מטמאין לה דנימא גלוי מילתא למפרע בעלמא היא השתא אפילו בודאי נטמאו נמי אלא בשעה שנטמא היתה טומאת התהום שלא הכיר בה אדם מעולם מטהרין ליה כדלקמן: דר"א ור"ע במסכת נזיר דאמרינן התם רביעית דם אין הנזיר מגלח על מגעה ועל משאה וקאמר רבי עקיבא ק"ו ומה עצם כשעורה שאין מטמא (את כל) אדם באהל הנזיר מגלח על מגעה ועל משאה רביעית דם שמטמאה (את כל) אדם באהל אינו דין שהנזיר מגלח על מגעה ועל משאה אמר לו ר"א לר"ע עצם כשעורה שהנזיר מגלח על מגעה ומשאה הלכה למשה מסיני ואין כתוב בתורה ורביעית דם אתה בא ללמוד ממנה בק"ו ואין דנין ק"ו מהלכה אלא מדבר הכתוב בתורה: וטומאת התהום. שהותרה בנזיר ועושה פסח היכא כתיבא והך בעיא איבעיא בי מדרשא מקמי הא בעיא דרב יוסף ובשני דרב יוסף כבר איפשיטא הך מסקנא דלקמן דטומאת התהום גמרא גמירי לה משום הכי פרכינן לעיל ומי דיינינן ק"ו מהלכה: במחוורת עליו. שתהא ברורה לו: לכם. טמא לנפש או בדרך רחוקה לכם והאי לכם קאי נמי אטמא: כי דרך. טמא לנפש דומיא דדרך רחוקה הוא: אי זהו טומאת התהום. שהותרה לנזיר ועושה פסח: לא שנו. דאין מרצה על טומאת התהום בנזיר ועושה פסח: מושכב לרחבו של דרך. והוא עבר שם וא"א שלא נגע שם או הסיט או האהיל: לתרומה. לאכול בתרומה: טמא. דלא הותרה בו טומאת התהום ואילו לאורכו של דרך אפי' טומאת התהום אין כאן: שאין לו מקום לעבור. שמחזיק וממלא את כל רוחב הדרך אף על גב דטומאת ודאי היא כיון דהיא שעתא דעבר עליה טומאת התהום הואי שלא היה שום אדם יודעו שם ואף לזה לא נודע עד שנשחטו קרבנותיו הלכה למשה מסיני היא שזורקין עליו את הדמים: אבל יש לו מקום לעבור אף לתרומה טהור· דהוי ליה ספק טומאה ברשות הרבים וספיקו טהור: בד"א. דכי ממלא את כל הדרך טמא: שהקבר מצרפו· שכל הקבר מטמא באהל ואפילו ריקן שבו דכתיב (במדבר יט) או בקבר: בד"א. [א] דמשובר ומפורק טהור: טעון. משוי על כרחו הולך נע ונד לכאן ולכאן ומאהיל על צדדיו: בד"א. דנזיר ועושה פסח טהור: אבל בטומאה הידועה. שידעו שאדם נקבר שם: טמון בעפר בתבן ובצרורות. טומאה מכוסה מכל אדם היא זו שמא גל אבנים או עפר או תבן נפל עליו ולא הכירו בו בני אדם מעולם אבל מים ואפילה ונקיקי הסלעים אין זו הטומאה מכוסה ונעלמה שהמציץ יכול לראות ולא גמירי הלכתא אלא בטומאה שהיא בתהום המכוסה מן הכל: ולא אמרו. דהותרה טומאת התהום אלא במת בלבד: **מתני'** נטמא שלם או רובו שורפין אותו לפני הבירה. כל המקדש כולו קרוי בירה ובגמרא מפרש טעמא: נטמא מיעוטו. וכן נותר של פסח טהור: הציקנין. עצרנין כלומר שהן צרי עין: שורפין אותו. את מעט שנטמא ואת הנותר: **גמ'** וכן מי שיצא. בפרק אלו עוברין: שיש בידו בשר קדש. והרי הוא פסול ביוצא: צופים. מקום שיכול לראות משם הבירה ומשם והלאה אין יכול לראותו: שורפו במקומו. לא הטריחוהו לחזור ולשורפו בירושלים הואיל וכבר נתרחק הרבה ואף על גב דקיימא לן בפרק כל שעה (דף כד.) דבמקום אכילת קדשים שם שריפתן מבקדש באש תשרף:

חוזר

תוספות

לריש לקיש דאמר כדרך עד דידעי בה כ"ע. קשה לריב"א דבנזיר בסופו (דף סג:) איתא הך מסקנא ולא מייתי התם מילתיה דר' יוחנן ולא פריך נמי אלא לר"א וקאמר בשלמא למ"ד כדרך שפיר והיא מסוגיות החלוקות: **וטמא** וטהור לכתחלה הוא. ודוקא לפני זריקה אבל לפני שחיטה לא כמו שהביא בקונטרס במתני' מתוספתא: **אלא** לפני זריקה נמי מרצה. ע"כ לפני זריקה שום דם דאם נזרק אפילו אחד מן הדמים ונטמא תנן בפרק ג' מינים (נזיר דף נז:) *יביא שאר קרבנות ויטהר אפילו בטומאה ידועה אינו סותר נזירותו וריצוי דטומאת התהום דסולה שמעתין היינו שאינו סותר נזירותו כדפי' לעיל אי בנזיר כי ימות מת עליו כו' וקשה לר"י דבפר' בתרא דנזיר (דף סג:) תנן אם עד שלא גילח נודע לו אפילו טומאת התהום סותר ומוקי ליה ר' יוחנן בגמ' כר"א דאמר תגלחת מעכבת וא"כ נודע לו לפני זריקה נמי כיון דמעכבת אמאי אינו סותר ותירץ ר"י דהכא כיון שנשחט יש לו להשלים ומרצה ציץ על טומאת התהום ואינו סותר כאילו לאחר זריקה נטמא ולא דמי לקודם גילוח ואע"ג דגילוח הוה אחר זריקה כדתנן בג' מינים (שם דף מה:) גילח על זבח ונמצא פסול תגלחתו פסולה ואי גילוח הוא לפני זריקה יביא זבח אחר לרבנן לית להו דתגלחת לא מעכבא ולכך מרצה הכא לפני זריקה: **המוצא** מת מושכב כו'. בפ' בתרא דנזיר (דף סה:) דייק על ההיא משנה דהתם המוצא פרט למצוי מת פרט להרוג מושכב פרט ליושב וקשה לריב"א דהכא ביושב אתי שפיר טפי מבמושכב דבמושכב לא הוי כולי האי טומאת התהום אם קברוהו שם וי"ל דמושכב נקט בשביל תרומה שהוא תופס כל רוחב הדרך ואי אפשר שלא יאהיל או יסיט אבל יושב לא דאיכא למימר שמא לא האהיל כנגדו: **ובקבר** אפי' כו'. וא"ת היכי שייכא טומאת התהום בקבר והלא נודע כשקברוהו שם ואיכא למימר כגון שנפל בקבר ומת והא דפי' בקונטרס שהקבר מצרפו משום דכתיב או בקבר אין נראה לר"י דשמא קרא איירי בקבר מכוסה ומשום הכי נמי הקבר מצרפו משום אהל שהכיסוי מביא את הטומאה עליו: **מצאו** טמון בתבן כו'. משום דלפי מה שמצאוהו עכשיו לא היה ראוי להכיר לאחד בסוף העולם אבל במים ראוי להכיר: **נטמא** רובו שורפין אותו לפני הבירה מעצי כו'. נראה הטעם משום דלב בית דין מתנה עליהם לפי שהזקיקוהו לשורפו לפני הבירה כדי לביישו לא הטריחוהו להביא עצים משלו ויכול להנות משל הקדש וכן בציקנין התנו (א)כמו כן ולא לכל דמתוך ציקנותן היו נמנעין מלשורפו ואתי לידי עבירה ודוקא בציקנין או באכסנאי כדאמרי' בגמרא דעשאוהו כציקנין אבל אדם אחר לא ואפילו למאן דלית ליה בפ"ק דשבועות (יא:) לב ב"ד מתנה עליהן ה"מ בקרבנות דקדישי קדושת הגוף אבל בקדושת דמים כולי עלמא מודו:

רב

רבינו חננאל

עושין אותו בטומאה אינו דין שהותרה לצבור טומאת התהום וכהן המרצה בתמיד קרבן צבור הוא וכן הוא מפורש בתלמוד ארץ ישראל ואקשי' ומי דיינינן קל וחומר מהלכה טומאת התהום ליחיד הלכה היא וקרבן ציבור קל וחומר והתניא אמר לו רבי עקיבא עקיבא עצם כשעורה הלכה ורביעית דם קל וחומר ואין דנין קל וחומר מהלכה וזו דר' עקיבא עיקרה בנזיר פ' כהן גדול ונזיר וקל וחומר דרבא מפורש בירושלמי אלא אמר רבא גמר במועדו במועדו בנזירה שוה מפסח: היכא כתיבא טומאת התהום בנזיר אמר רבי אליעזר שנאמר וכי ימות מת עליו וגו' במחוורת עליו כלומר ידיעה ברורה · בפסח ר' יוחנן אמר שנאמר טמא לנפש או בדרך רחוקה לכם לכם במחוורת לכם ריש לקיש אומר או בדרך רחוקה מה דרך בגלוי אף כל טומאה גלויה ואותבינן עלייהו איזו היא טומאת התהום כל שלא הכיר בה אחד בסוף העולם הכיר בה אחד בסוף העולם אין זו טומאת התהום קשיא לר' אליעזר דאמר וכי ימות מת עליו במחוורת עליו הוא שחייב עליה וכל מה שאינה מחוורת עליו אע"פ שאחרים יודעין אותו הרי היא טומאת התהום ולרבי יוחנן דמפיק לה מלכם תרי הא ידע בה אחד טומאת התהום קריינא ביה ולריש לקיש דמפיק לה מדרך כל שאינו גלוי לכל אדם כדרך הרי היא טומאת התהום האי מתני' דקתני אפילו ידע בה אחד בסוף העולם אין זו טומאת התהום קשיא לכלן ותרצוה ואוקימ' אלא בטומאת התהום הלכתא גמירא לה וקרא אסמכתא בעלמא: אמר מר בר רב אשי אפילו אם נודע לו שנטמא לפני זריקה הציץ מרצה המוצא מת מושכב לרחבו של דרך לתרומה טמא לנזיר ועושה פסח טהור בד"א כשאין לו מקום לעבור אבל יש לו מקום לעבור אף לתרומה טהור שאני אומר ממקום הטהור עבר בד"א שמצאו שלם אבל משובר ומפורק טהור אומר בין שקיי עבר ובקבר אפילו משובר ומפורק טמא שהקבר מצרפו בד"א במהלך ברגליו כו' מצאו טמון בתבן בעפר ובצרורות הרי זו טומאת התהום במים ובאפלה ובנקיקי הסלעים אין זו טומאת התהום ולא אמרו טומאת התהום אלא במת בלבד לאפוקי הרוג

שבת קלב: ע"ש

נזיר נז:

נזיר סג: ע"ש

שם ט

[שם · תוספתא זבים פ"ב]

שם

[נזיר שם: כל הענין תוס' זבים פ"ב]

[לעיל מ: ע"ש וש"נ]

[נדרים לעיל מט.]

הגהות הב"ח

(א) תוס' ד"ה נטמא וכו' כמו כן שמא מתוך קמצנן כצ"ל:

הגהות הגר"א

[א] רש"י ד"ה בד"א דמשובר ומפורק טהור· נ"ב מילתא דפסיקא נקט אבל בלאמת קאי גם (אשאין לו) [איירן] מקום לעבור:

גליון הש"ס

תוס' ד"ה אלא לפני זריקה יביא שאר קרבנות לא זכיתי להבין הא גם בנטמא אח כזה הוא סותר בטומאה ידוע אבל אם טומאה זבת למפרע בזה אינו סותר ולא וכו' יעיר עיני:

שרידי הכיר בו מי שהרגו: ירוש' בסוף הפ' ר' יוחנן בר מויה בשם ר' פנחס ממה דנן המיי רבנן שולחין סנדליהן תחת' אגף של הר הבית: תאני ר' יהודה מחילות שתחת היכל (קודש) [חול] אמר ריש לקיש ומתני' אמורה נן ומדורה היתה שם ובית כסא של כבוד היה שם וכו' אמר ר' וכי צואה טמאה היא אלא נקיות ויי דא אמ' יוצא והולך לו במסיבה ההולכת תחת הבירה כו': כדי לביישן מפני שפשעו בו ונטמא נטמא והנותר

גמרא

בשני שלה ואחר כך ראתה אינה אוכלת ופטורה מלעשות פסח שני מ"ט לאו משום דמרצה ציץ אמרי לא משום דקסבר ר' יוסי מכאן ולהבא היא מטמאה *והתניא רבי יוסי אומר זב בעל שתי ראיות ששחטו וזרקו עליו בשביעי שלו ואחר כך ראה וכן שומרת יום כנגד יום ששחטו וזרקו עליה בשני שלה ואחר כך ראתה *הרי אלו מטמאין משכב ומושב למפרע [י]ופטורים מלעשות פסח שני אמרי מאי למפרע מדרבנן ואף רבי אושעיא סבר מטמא למפרע מדרבנן *דתניא רבי אושעיא אומר אבל זב שראה בשביעי שלו סותר את שלפניו וא"ל רבי יוחנן לא יסתור אלא יומו ממה נפשך אי קסבר למפרע הוא מטמא אפילו כולהו נסתור אי קסבר מכאן ולהבא הוא מטמא יומו נמי לא נסתור אלא אימא לא יסתור ולא יומו וא"ל רבי יוסי קאי כוותך והא רבי יוסי אומר מטמאין משכב ומושב למפרע אלא לאו שמע מינה מטמא למפרע מדרבנן ש"מ ולר' יוסי השתא דאמר מכאן ולהבא הוא מטמא [למת] בלבד למעוטי מאי נפשוט מינה דבכהן והותרה לו טומאת התהום אמרי לעולם בבעלים ובפסח *וקסבר *אין שוחטין וזורקין על טמאי שרץ ואיצטריך למעוטי אלא לרבי יוסי זבה גמורה היכי משכחת לה בשופעת אי בעית אימא כגון שראתה כל שני בין השמשות בעי רב יוסף כהן המרצה בתמיד הותרה לו טומאת התהום או לא אם תמצא לומר כהן המרצה בקרבנותיהן (של נזיר ועושה פסח) הותרה לו טומאת התהום כהן המרצה בתמיד מאי מי אמרינן כי גמירי טומאת התהום בפסח בתמיד לא גמירי או דילמא יליף תמיד מפסח אמר רבה ק"ו ומה במקום שלא הותרה לו טומאה ידועה הותרה לו טומאת התהום מקום שהותרה לו טומאה ידועה אינו

רש"י

בשני שלה. עדיין ספק הוא שמא תראה יום זה ויצטרף עם אתמול ותראה גם מחר והוו להו שלשה והויא לה זבה גמורה ואם לא תראה תטהר לערב: אינה אוכלת. שהרי צריכה להיות עד מחר שומרת יום כנגד יום: ופטורה מלעשות פסח שני. קס"ד כיון דבשעת שחיטה וזריקה ספק הוי מרצה ציץ מטומאת התהום דזיבה ואע"ג דאיגלאי מילתא למפרע שנטמאה ודאי בטומאת התהום: מכאן ולהבא היא מטמאה. שומרת יום כנגד יום שספרה קצת היום וטבלה טהורה מטומאה של אתמול וכי הדר חזית בו ביום מטמאה מכאן ולהבא ותהיה מחר שומרת יום כנגד יום הלכך בזריקה ושחיטה טהורה מעלייתא הואי ורבנן פליגי עליה ואמרי דכי חזית איגלאי מילתא למפרע דזיבה היא וחדא טומאה היא ובשעת שחיטה ספק הואי וחייבת בפסח שני ולקמיה פריך כיון דלרבי יוסי כל חד וחד טומאה באפי נפשיה הוא היאך מצטרפים לזיבה לעשות זבה גדולה: בעל שתי ראיות. דאילו בעל ג' ראיות לא חזי למיכל לאורתא עד שיביא קרבנותיו בח' ובשמיני נמי לא מצי למיקנק ומיתני ואח"כ ראה מטמא משכב ומושב למפרע דכיון דילא מזיבה ראשונה לשעה שהיא ראויה לקרבן הויא לה הך זיבה אחריתי ומושב ומשכב שמתאמול לאחר טבילה ועד הגה טהורה למפרע אפילו טבלה בז' שחרית: משכבות ומושבות. שלאחר טבילתו טמאין שהרי סתר מנייניו והרי הוא כבתחלתו דכתיב (ויקרא טו) וספר לו שבעת ימים והרי אינן ומקדקי כמי בשומרת יום למפרע אלמא כמי למפרע מטמאה ואפ"ה פטור לה מפסח שני ש"מ טעמא משום דטומאת התהום הוי ומשכבות ומושבות רבותא נקט להו מפני שהן אב הטומאה לטמא אדם ובדבר זה זב חלוק משאר טמאין:מדרבנן. אבל מדאורייתא לא מטמאו אלא מכאן ולהבא לא הזב בז' ולא שומרת יום בשני דמקצת יום עולה להן לספירתן הילכך לגבי פסח טהורין מעליא הוו: אבל הרואה זוב כו'. לא ידענו אהיכא קאי אבל: סותר את שלפניו. כל ספורין שספר וצריך לספור ז' אחרים: וא"ל רבי יוחנן לא יסתור אלא יומו. ויחזור ויספור יום ח' והוינן אמילתיה דר' יוחנן מה נפשך אי למפרע מטמא דאין מקצת היום עולה לו ולא נגמרה ספירתו: כולהו נמי נסתור. דכתיב וספר לו ז' ימים לטהרתו טהרה אחת לכולן שלא תהיה טומאה מפסקת ביניהן במס' נדה (דף לג:) ואם מנה לסירוגין כי הכא שיסתור יומו וישלימו למחר נמצאת הפסקה ביניהם: ואם מכאן ולהבא מטמא. שעלתה לו מקצת היום וגמרו ספורין שלו: יומו נמי לא לסתור. אלא הרי הוא כראיה ראשונה של זיבה אחרת ואין בה אלא טומאת ערב ויטבול לערב ויטהר דקי"ל ראיה ראשונה של זב קרי בעלמא הוא במס' נדה (דף עב:): אלא. ה"ק ר' יוחנן לא יסתור ולא יומו כלומר אפילו יומו לפי שכבר עלתה לו מקצת היום ככולו ושלמו ספורין שלו וילא מכלל זיבה: וא"ל ר' אושעיא לרבי יוחנן: ר' יוסי קאי כוותך. דס"ל נמי מכאן ולהבא הוא מטמא מדפטר ליה לעיל מפסח שני אלמא קסבר ר' אושעיא למפרע דר' יוסי מדרבנן קאמר: והא ר' יוסי כו'. מסקנא דמילתיה הוא ולא משום קשיא מייתי לה:השתא דאמר מכאן ולהבא מטמא. ולא משכחת טומא' התהום בזיבה: בלבד. דקתני לעיל למעוטי מאי ע"כ למעוטי שרץ תוקמא ובכהן כדאמר לעיל דאילו בבעלים לא מהני שרץ דקאמר דבטומאת התהום דמת מיהא הותרה לו: אין שוחטין וזורקין על טמא שרץ. ואשמעינן דטומא' התהום נמי דחיא ליה: היכי משכחת לה. כיון דאית ליה מקצת היום עולה לה לספירתה ומכאן ולהבא מטמאה הו"ל כל יומא טומאה באפי נפשה: בשופעת. כל שלשה רצופין דלא הוה לה מנייחא כלל: אי נמי ברואה שני בה"ש. דכל תחלות הימים היו בטומאה דאין כאן ספירה כלל ובשני בין השמשות סגי דהיכא טומאת ג' ימים רצופין כגון בה"ש של ע"ש יש כאן סוף ערב שבת ותחלת שבת ובין השמשות של מחר שהוא סוף השבת ותחלת א' בשבת הרי ג' ימים רצופין ואין כאן תחלת יום טהור שיעלה לספירה ולפי הדברים למ"ד מקצת היום ככולו תחלת הלילה עולה לספירתה וא"ל עלות השחר מדאיצטריך למנקט בין השמשות ולא נקט משכחת לה בשרואה בלילות:בתמיד. כל השנה ואליבא דמאן דאמר טומאה דחויה היא בציבור קבעי רב יוסף הכי אי איצטריך להדר הכהן טהור משום טומא' התהום אי לא ואליבא דמ"ד לקמן דטומאת התהום מרלי ליץ גבי נזיר ועושה פסח אפי' לכתחלה כגון שנודע לו לפני זריקה: בקרבנותיהן. דנזיר ועושה פסח:במקום שלא הותרה לו טומאה ידועה.כלל כגון נזיר ועושה פסח שהן קרבנות יחיד: מקום שהותרה לו טומאה ידועה. היכא דליכא טהורין: אינו

תוספות

לאו משום דסבר דציץ מרצה. תימה לרשב"א מנ"ל דילמא הא דפטורין היינו משום דסבר דנשים בשני רשות ואור"י דבהדיא מוכח לקמן סוף פרק האשה (דף צא:) דרבי יוסי סבר נשים בשני חובה: קסבר רבי יוסי מכאן ולהבא היא מטמאה. פי' ולכן סבירא לן כרבנן דלמפרע מטמאה וא"ת כי ס"ד נמי דטעמא דרבי יוסי משום דסבר ציץ מרצה מאי פריך לימא דס"ל כרבנן וי"ל שלא רצה לעשות מחלוקת חדשה שלא מצינו תנאים חלוקים בכך אבל בלמפרע הוא מטמא מצינו תנאים בשילהי נדה (דף עב:)[ד]מתני' דטבלה יום שלאחריו ושימשה: אי נמי כגון רואה שני ימים בין השמשות. מדלא משני ברואה בלילות משמע דספירה לילה היא ספירה וכן פי' בקונטרס וקשה לריב"א דתנן פ' שני דמגילה (דף כ.) וכן שומרת יום כנגד יום לא תטבול עד הנץ החמה ומסיק בגמ' קמ"ל כיון דבעי שימור שימור ביממא הוא וכן בשילהי נדה (דף עב:) אמר ושוין ברואה תוך י"א יום וטבלה לערב ושמשה שמטמאים משכב ומושב וחייבין בקרבן משמע אפילו לא ראתה אח"כ ומשום דבלילה לא חשיב שימור וי"ל דודאי ספירת לילה לא הויא ספירה ומ"מ לא מצי לאוקמא ברואה בלילות משום דכיון דסבר רבי יוסי מקצת היום שספרה בשביעי הוי ככולו ה"ה אם פסקה בחלי היום שיעלה לה שימור סוף היום הנשאר לכך מוקי בשופעת שלא היה סוף היום בטהרה אע"ג ברואה שני בין השמשות וליכא למימר שיעלה לה תחלת היום שימור דלא אמר מקצת היום ככולו אלא או תחלתו או סופו אבל אמצע לא וכן איתא בהדיא בנזיר בפ"ב (דף טו:) דקאמר ורבי יוסי זבה גמורה היכי משכחת לה כיון דחזיא פלגא דיומא אידך פלגא סליק לה שימור ומשני כגון דחזיא תלתא יומי סמוך לשקיעת החמה דלא הוה שהות ביום דסליק לה ממנינא ותלתא יומי לאו דווקא דראיה שלישית לא חיישינן שתהא סמוך לשקיעת החמה מאחר שכבר ראתה שני ימים סמוך לשקיעת החמה ובשלישי תראה באיזו שעה שתהיה בלילה ובלבד שתראה קודם היום שלא יעלה לה שימור תחלת יום ג' וא"ת והא אמרינן בפרק בנות כותים (נדה דף לג:) דכותית יום שפוסקת כופרתו למנין שבעה הא רבי יוסי נמי סבר הכא סוף היום ככולו וי"ל דלא אמר סוף היום ככולו בתחלת חשבון אלא דוקא בסוף חשבונו כי הכא כגון זב בשביעי או שומרת יום כנגד יום שאין לה למנות יותר וסוף חשבון מסוף חשבון אית לן למילף ולא מתחלת חשבון ואשכחן חילוק בין תחלת חשבון לסוף חשבון בפ"ק דר"ה (דף י:) דנדה עולה לה סוף היום בתחלתה ואין תחלת היום עולה לה בסופה אע"ג דהתם הוי איפכא מסברתא*:

אמר רבא ק"ו כו' מקום שהותרה לו טומאה ידועה אינו דין שהותרה לו טומאת התהום. וא"ת ונימא דיו מה טומאה ידועה לא הותרה אלא היכא דלא אפשר ה"נ טומאת התהום וי"ל דעדיפא פריך אפילו לר' טרפון דלית ליה דיו היכא דמיפרך ק"ו (ב"ק ד' כה.): לריש

רבינו חננאל

בשני שלה ואחר כך ראתה הרי זו אינה אוכלת ופטורה מלעשות פסח שני ושני' קסבר רבי יוסי טהורה היתה בשעת זריקה ונפטרה ומכאן ולהבא מטמא כלומר משעה שראת היא טמאה אינו דר' יוסי סבר מכאן ולהבא והתניא רבי יוסי אומר זב בעל שתי ראיות ששחטו וזרקו עליו בשביעי שלו וכן שומרת יום כנגד יום ששחטו וזרקו עליה בשני שלה ואחר כך ראתה חוזרין משכב ומושב למפרע ושנינן מאי מטמאין למפרע דקתני מדרבנן והדייק' מדתני ר' אושעיא זב שראה בשביעי שלו סותר את שלפניו וכל מה שנגעו באותן ששה ימים כולן מטמאין ורבי יוחנן אמר לא יסתור אלא יומו אע"פ שלא ראה היום כולו [ס"א בחזקת טומאה] היא מן הבוקר כלו' כל מה שנגע היום כלו נטמאו ואקשי' לר' יוחנן מאי דעתיך אי למפרע הוא מטמא יסתור הימים כולן אי מכאן ולהבא אפילו יומו לא יסתור ושני' כך אמר רבי יוחנן לא יסתור ולא יומו אלא משעה שראה ואמר לו רבי אושעיא הא רבי יוסי קאי כוותך ש"מ דרבי אושעיא סבר דהאי דמטמא בזב בעל שתי ראיות ובשומרת יום כנגד יום למפרע מדרבנן דאי מדאורייתא מהור מעליא הוא ודאמרינן ליה לרבי יוחנן דאמר אינו סותר ולא יומו רבי יוסי קאי כוותך והשתא דאוקימנא דר' מכאן ולהבא היא מטמאה [למת בלבד] למעוטי מאי ופשוט מינה דבכהן הותרה לו טומאת התהום ודחי' לא לעולם בבעלים בפסח וקסבר אין שוחטין וזורקין על טמא שרץ ואיצטריך או בדרך רחוקה דשמעי' מיניה או בדרך רחוקה למעוטי מטומאת התהום ולר' יוסי לא משכחת לה זבה גמורה אלא בשופעת דם בלא הפסקה בין ליום אי נמי ברואה שני בין השמשות כיצד כגון שראתה ערב שבת בין השמשות מחזיקין ראייתה לשני ימים בערב שבת ובשבת ועוד ראתה בשבת בין השמשות מחזיקין ראייתה בין השמשות לשבת וליום ראשון הנה ראתה שלשה ימים זה אחר זה הרי זבה גמורה: בעי רב יוסף כהן המרצה בתמיד הותרה לו טומאת התהום או לא אמר רבה קל וחומר ומה יחיד שלא הותרה לו טומאה ידועה שהיחיד אם נתברדה טומאה

נדחה לפסח שני הותרה לו טומאת התהום כדתנן נטמא טומאת התהום הציץ מרצה צבור שהותרה להם לטומאה ידועה שנאמר איש איש כי יהיה טמא לנפש איש נדחה לפסח שני ואין צבור נדחין לפסח שני אלא עושין

עין משפט נר מצוה

סז א מיי' פ"ז מהל' משכב ומושב הלכה ט:

סח ב מיי' פ"ז מהל' ק"פ הלכה ג:

סט ג מיי' פ"ג מהל' מחוסרי כפרה הלכה א:

מסורת הש"ס

מי' טו:

יתכן להיות דאמר רב אושעיא אבל דלא מצינו רב אושעיא בברייתא בבדיל אף על פי שהוא סידר ברייתות גם ר' יוחנן ספס לא נזכר בברייתא בסוס מקום וכן הגרס בגליון במי' טו:

[לעיל סט. וש"נ]

רש"ל מ"ז

גליון הש"ס

גמ' וקסבר אין שוחטין וזורקין. עיין לקמן צ"ע ע"א תוס' ד"ה קשיא:

[ועיין תוספו' נדה לג: ד"ה ספירתו ועוד שם עב. ד"ה הרואה ותוס' מגילה כ. ד"ה ר"ה י. ד"ה ימים ותוספות נזיר טו: ד"ה זבה]

on her second day, and then she saw [a discharge], may not eat [of the sacrifice] and is exempt from observing the second Passover.[5] What is the reason? Is it not because the headplate propitiates?[1]—I will tell you: It is not so, [the reason being] because R. Jose holds: She is defiled from now and henceforth.[2] But it was taught, R. Jose said: A *zab* of two discharges[3] on whose behalf they slaughtered [the Passover-offering] and sprinkled [its blood] on the seventh day,[4] and then he discharged again;[5] similarly, a woman who watches from day to day on whose second day they slaughtered and sprinkled on her behalf, and then she discharged again,—these defile their couch or their seat retrospectively,[1] and they are exempt from observing the second Passover.[2]—I will tell you: what does 'retrospectively' mean? By Rabbinical law.[3]

Now R. Oshaia too holds [that] he defiles retrospectively by Rabbinical law [only].[4] For it was taught, R. Oshaia said:[5] But a *zab* who saw [a discharge] on his seventh day upsets the preceding [period];[6] whereupon R. Joḥanan said to him: He does not upset [aught] save that day.[7] (What will you? If he holds [that] he defiles retrospectively,[8] let us upset even all of them; while if he holds that he defiles [only] from now and onwards,[9] let him not upset even that day?[10]—Rather say: He does not even upset that day.) Whereupon he [R. Oshaia] said to him [R. Joḥanan], R. Jose agrees with you.[1] Yet surely R. Jose said: They defile their couch and their seat retrospectively? Hence it certainly proves that they defile retrospectively by Rabbinical law [only]. This proves it.

Now according to R. Jose, seeing that he rules [that] he defiles from now and onwards [only], what does '[They spoke of the "uncleanness of the deep"] in respect of a corpse alone' exclude?[2] [Hence] let us solve from this that it refers to the priest, and [thus] the 'uncleanness of the deep' is permitted to him?—I will tell you: After all it refers to the owners and [treats] of the Passover-offering, but he [R. Jose] holds: One may not slaughter [the Passover-offering] and sprinkle [its blood] on behalf of those who are unclean through a reptile, and thus it is necessary to exclude it.[3]

But according to R. Jose, how is a complete *zabah* possible?[4]—When she has a continuous discharge.[5] Alternatively, e.g., if she sees [a discharge] the whole of two [successive] twilights.[6]

R. Joseph asked: The priest who officiates at[7] the continual-offering,[8] is the 'uncleanness of the deep' permitted to him or not? If you should say that the 'uncleanness of the deep' is permitted to the priest who officiates at their sacrifices,[9] what about the priest who officiates at the continual-offering? Do we say, when have we a tradition about 'the uncleanness of the deep', in respect of the Passover-offering, [but] we have no tradition about the 'uncleanness of the deep' in respect to the continual-offering; or perhaps the continual-offering is learned from the Passover-offering?—Said Rabbah: It stands to reason: if where *known* uncleanness was not permitted to him,[1] yet the 'uncleanness of the deep' was permitted to him; then where known uncleanness was permitted

(5) During the eleven days following the seven days of *niddah* (menstruation) which are called the eleven days between the menses, a woman cannot become a *niddah* again, it being axiomatic that a discharge of blood in that period is not a sign of *niddah*, but *may* be symptomatic of gonorrhoea (*zibah*). A discharge on one or two days within the eleven renders her unclean for that day or those days only, but she cannot perform *ṭebillah* (v. Glos.) to become clean until the evening of the following day (for full details v. Nid. 71*b* ff), and she must wait for the third to see whether another discharge will follow, rendering her a *zabah*, or not. Thus on the first or second day of her discharge within these eleven days she is called 'a woman who watches from day to day.' Should another discharge follow on the third day, she cannot regain her cleanness until seven days have passed without any issue at all. (The foregoing is on the basis of the ancient law, but already in the period of the Talmud itself the law was adopted that a single blood issue at any time imposes all the restrictions which necessitate for cleanness a period of seven consecutive clean days.) Now in the present instance the eve of Passover occurred on the second day of her discharge; the sacrifice was offered and its blood was sprinkled on her behalf *before* she had a discharge on that day, so that if she had not discharged later she would have been fit to eat in the evening. Since, however, she subsequently discharged, she cannot eat of the sacrifice, as she cannot perform *ṭebillah* until the following evening.

a (1) For when the blood was sprinkled she was doubtfully unclean, since she might discharge again on that day. Thus she is assumed to be unclean with the 'uncleanness of the deep,' and is exempt from observing the second Passover because the headplate propitiates and makes her sacrifice valid, though she cannot partake of it. (2) If she discharges on one day, waits *part* of the following and performs *ṭebillah*, she is clean, and if she subsequently discharges on the same day she becomes unclean *anew*, but does not continue her previous uncleanness. Hence when the sacrifice was slaughtered she was actually clean, having already performed *ṭebillah*, so that no propitiation is required. (3) When a man suffers three gonorrhoeic discharges within three days or less (in this respect a man differs from a woman, who becomes a *zabah* only if the three discharges are on three consecutive days), he becomes a full *zab*, i.e., he does not regain his cleanness until seven consecutive days pass without a discharge, while during these seven days he is unclean as a *zab*; should he discharge on any of these days, he requires a further seven days, and so on. On the eighth day he brings a sacrifice, and on the evening that follows he may eat of sacred flesh (having performed *ṭebillah* the previous day). If, however, he suffers two discharges only, he is likewise unclean for seven days, but does not bring a sacrifice on the eighth; hence he can partake of sacrifices on the evening following the seventh day. (4) So that if the day passes without a further discharge, he is fit to partake of the Passover-offering in the evening. (5) Lit., 'Saw.' 'Saw' and 'sight' are technical terms denoting the gonorrhoeic discharges of a *zab*.

b (1) Anything upon which they sit or lie, even without actually touching it, becomes unclean, its degree of defilement being that of a 'principal uncleanness' which in turn defiles people or utensils (v. Mishnah *supra* 14*a* and note a.l.).—'Retrospectively' means, since the *ṭebillah* (q.v. Glos.) on the seventh day. Before the *ṭebillah* of course he would in any case be unclean. (2) Thus they are not unclean only for the future, and yet they are exempt from a second Passover; the reason must be because it is an 'uncleanness of the deep' of gonorrhoea, and he holds that the headplate propitiates. (3) But according to Biblical law she was clean during the interval between the *ṭebillah* until the third discharge. (4) I.e., he interprets R. Jose's ruling thus. (5) So cur. edd. But marginal note emends this to, 'For R. Oshaia said', omitting 'it was taught', as we never find his view expressed in a Baraitha, though he was the compiler of a series of Baraithas. (6) I.e., the seven days are nullified and he must count another seven days; v. *supra*, n. a3. Rashi observes that he does not know to what R. Oshaia refers when he says '*But*', which obviously indicates a contrast with some other law. Possibly, however, אבל means here 'indeed', 'in truth', in which case it is an independent statement. (7) Which is disregarded, and he requires only one more day free from discharge in order to regain his cleanness. (8) I.e., from the beginning of the seventh day, the portion of the seventh day during which he had no discharge not being regarded as a complete day, that we should look upon him as having had seven *consecutive* days without an unclean discharge. (9) Not from the beginning of the day, for the part of the day during which he was free from discharge counts as a whole day. (10) For on that view he has enjoyed seven consecutive days of cleanness, which purifies him. The present discharge therefore is as an entirely *new* attack of gonorrhoea which has no connection with the preceding, and when a man has a *single* discharge he is unclean only until the evening, when he performs *ṭebillah* and becomes clean. Why then does he need another day?

c (1) Since he exempts her from observing the second Passover, he too holds that she is not retrospectively unclean. (2) For, as seen above, on the present ruling there is no 'uncleanness of the deep' in connection with gonorrhoea. Hence it must refer to defilement by a reptile and to the priest; v. *supra* 80*b*. (3) The steps of the argument are stated *supra* 80*b*. (4) Since he holds that part of the day is counted as a whole day, and she is unclean only from when she discharges, each day is distinct and she can never be unclean for the three *consecutive* days which are necessary before she becomes a complete *zabaḥ*. (5) For the whole three days. (6) Twilight counts as the end of one day and the beginning of the following. Hence if she discharges right through the twilights of Sunday and Monday, she is regarded as having 'seen' on Sunday, Monday, and Tuesday, and as this includes the *beginnings* of Monday and Tuesday, she is unclean the whole of these days. (7) Lit., 'propitiates with'. (8) During the whole year. (9) V. *supra* 80*b*.

d (1) E.g., a nazirite and one who sacrifices his Passover-offering. The headplate does not propitiate to make the sprinkling permissible.

in this: one Master holds: [80b] Cleanness defers, [whereas] uncleanness does not defer;[3] while the other Master holds: Even uncleanness defers.

It was stated: If a third were *zabin*, a third clean, and a third unclean through the dead,—R. Mani b. Paṭṭish said: Those unclean through the dead observe neither the first [Passover] nor the second. They do not sacrifice on the first, [because] the *zabin* swell the number of the clean[4] who do not sacrifice in uncleanness; [hence] the unclean through the dead are a minority, and a minority do not sacrifice on the first. They do not sacrifice on the second, [because] the *zabin* combine with those who are unclean through the dead who did not sacrifice on the first; [hence] they are a majority, and a majority is not relegated to the second Passover.

MISHNAH. IF THE BLOOD OF A PASSOVER-OFFERING IS
a SPRINKLED AND THEN IT BECOMES KNOWN THAT IT[1] WAS UNCLEAN, THE HEADPLATE PROPITIATES; IF THE PERSON [THE OWNER] BECAME UNCLEAN,[2] THE HEADPLATE DOES NOT PROPITIATE, BECAUSE THEY [THE SAGES] RULED: [IN THE CASE OF] A NAZIRITE, AND HE WHO SACRIFICES[3] THE PASSOVER-OFFERING, THE HEADPLATE PROPITIATES FOR THE UNCLEANNESS OF THE BLOOD, BUT THE HEADPLATE DOES NOT PROPITIATE FOR THE UNCLEANNESS OF THE PERSON. IF HE WAS DEFILED WITH THE 'UNCLEANNESS OF THE DEEP,'[4] THE HEADPLATE PROPITIATES.[5]

GEMARA. Thus it is only because it was [first] sprinkled and it became known afterwards [that it was unclean]; but if it [first] became known and [the blood] was sprinkled afterwards, it does not propitiate. But the following contradicts it: For what does the headplate propitiate? For the blood, flesh, and fat which were defiled, whether in ignorance or deliberately, accidentally or intentionally, whether in the case of an individual or of a community?[6]—Said Rabina: [With regard to] its defilement, whether [it occurred] in ignorance or deliberately, [the offering] is made acceptable;[7] [but as to its] sprinkling, [if done] in ignorance [that the blood was unclean], it is acceptable; if deliberately, it is not acceptable. R. Shila said: [With regard to] its sprinkling, whether [done] in ignorance [that the blood was unclean] or deliberately, it is accepted; [but as to] its uncleanness, [if it occurred] in ignorance, it is acceptable; if [caused] deliberately, it is not acceptable. But surely he states, 'whether in ignorance or deliberately?'—This is what it means: If it was defiled in ignorance, and he [the priest] sprinkled it, whether unwittingly or deliberately, it is accepted. Yet surely it is taught, IF THE BLOOD WAS SPRINKLED AND THEN IT BECAME KNOWN: thus it is only because it was sprinkled [first] and it became known afterwards; but if it became known [first] and it was sprinkled afterwards, it is not so?—The same law holds good even if it became known [first] and it was sprinkled afterwards, and the reason that he states, IF IT WAS SPRINKLED AND THEN IT BECAME KNOWN is because he wishes to teach in the second clause, IF THE PERSON BECAME UNCLEAN, THE HEADPLATE DOES NOT PROPITIATE, where even if it was sprinkled [first] and it became known afterwards [it does] not [propitiate]; therefore he teaches the first clause too, IF IT WAS SPRINKLED AND THEN IT BECAME KNOWN.

IF HE WAS DEFILED WITH THE 'UNCLEANNESS OF THE DEEP' etc. Rami b. Ḥama asked: The priest who propitiates with their sacrifices, is the 'uncleanness of the deep' permitted to him
b or not?[1] Do we say, when have we a tradition about the 'uncleanness of the deep'?[2] [It is] in the case of the owners, but we have no tradition in respect of the priest; or perhaps we have a tradition in respect of the sacrifice,[3] no matter whether the owners or the priest [are thus defiled]?—Said Raba, Come and hear: For R. Ḥiyya taught: They [the Sages] spoke of the 'uncleanness of the deep' in respect of a corpse alone. What does this exclude? Surely it is to exclude 'uncleanness of the deep' caused by a reptile; and to what [then] do we refer? Shall we say, to the owners [who are thus defiled]? Then in the case of whom? If we say, in the case of a nazirite? Does it [a reptile uncleanness] affect him,[4] [seeing that] the Divine Law said, *and if any man die beside him*
c [etc.].[1] Hence it must refer to him who sacrifices the Passover-offering. Now that is well on the view [that] we may not slaughter [the Passover-offering] and sprinkle [its blood] for those who are unclean through a reptile.[2] But on the view [that] we slaughter and sprinkle on behalf of those who are unclean through a reptile, what can be said? Seeing that *known* uncleanness was permitted to him [who sacrifices at Passover], how much the more 'uncleanness of the deep'! Hence it must surely refer to the priest, whence it is proved that 'uncleanness of the deep' was permitted to him!—Said R. Joseph, No: After all it refers to the owners and the Passover-offering, and it excludes 'uncleanness of the deep' of gonorrhoea.[3]

Yet does it [the headplate] not propitiate for the 'uncleanness of the deep' of gonorrhoea? Surely it was taught, R. Jose said: A woman who watches from day to day[4] on whose behalf they slaughtered [the Passover-offering] and sprinkled [its blood] [81a]

(3) I.e., when the sacrifice comes in a state of cleanness, it relegates the unclean to the second Passover; but when it comes itself in a state of uncleanness, it cannot relegate those who are otherwise unclean to the second Passover. (4) Lit., 'they make large.'

a (1) Rashi: The offering—i.e., the flesh—or the blood. In the former case the headplate makes it acceptable only in the sense that the owner is not liable to another offering and the *emurim* are burnt on the altar; yet the flesh itself may not be eaten (Tosaf. on the basis of Rashi's interpretation). Tosaf. itself maintains that the Mishnah refers to the defilement of the blood only. (2) Through the dead. (3) Lit., 'does,' 'prepares.' (4) This is a technical term denoting the hidden uncleanness of a corpse which is now discovered for the first time. E.g., if he was in a house and it is subsequently learned that a corpse had been buried therein. (5) And he is not liable to a second offering. This is a traditional law. (6) V. *supra* 16b. 'In ignorance' and 'deliberately' are assumed to mean respectively: ignorance of the uncleanness of the blood, and deliberately sprinkling it with that knowledge. (7) The headplate propitiates.

b (1) If the priest who offers the Passover sacrifice or the sacrifices of a nazirite on behalf of their owners was defiled with the 'uncleanness of the deep,' does the breastplate propitiate, so that the sacrifice is valid, or not? (2) That the headplate propitiates for it. (3) Viz., that in the case of the Passover-offering and the sacrifice of a nazirite the headplate propitiates for *personal* defilement caused by the 'uncleanness of the deep.' (4) Even if he is *certainly* defiled by a reptile.

c (1) Num. VI, 9; thus his naziriteship is affected only by uncleanness through the dead. (2) V. *supra* 69. Hence R. Ḥiyya can mean that when one is defiled through the 'uncleanness of the deep' of a reptile the Passover-offering must not be sacrificed for him. (3) A *zab* (gonorrhoeist) is unclean seven days and the Passover-offering may not be offered on his behalf. Now, if the eve of Passover marks the seventh day of his uncleanness, he is in a state of a doubt; for if he does not discharge on that day he will be clean in the evening; while if he does discharge he becomes unclean for a further seven days. Thus he too is unclean with the 'uncleanness of the deep,' and R. Ḥiyya teaches that the headplate does not propitiate in his case and the offering must not be killed or its blood sprinkled on his behalf. (4) Lit., 'day against day.'

עין משפט נר מצוה

סב א שם הלכה ו:

סג ב מיי' פ"ד מהל' ק"פ הלכה ב ופ"ו הלכה יב ופ"ד מהלכות ביאת מקדש הל' ו ופ"ו מהל' נזירות הלכה יז:

סד ג מיי' פ"ד מהל' ק"פ הלכה ג:

סה ד מיי' פ"ו מהלכות ביאת מקדש הל' ו:

סו ה מיי' פ"ו מהלכות נזירות הלכה יח:

רבינו חננאל

ישראל היכא דאשתר הכא לא אשתר חשבינן ליה. כאלו כולן זבין: שלישיתן טהורין ושלישיתן טמאי מתים ושלישיתן זבין אותן טמאי מתים בראשון לא עבדו הגדילו זבין על הטהורין והוו להו טמאי מתים מיעוטא ומיעוטא לא נדחין לפסח שני בשני נמי לא עבדי דזבין וטמאי מתים בשני שוין הוו להו רובא ורובא בשני לא עבדי: מתני' הפסח שנזרק דמו ואחר כך [נודע] שהוא טמא הציץ מרצה כו' ופשוטה היא ואסיקנא הוא הדין דאפילו נודע שהוא טמא ואחר כך נזרק הציץ מרצה והאי דקתני נזרק ואחר כך נודע איידי דבעי מתני סיפא נטמא הגוף אין הציץ מרצה דאפילו נזרק ואחר כך נודע לא משום הכי קתני רישא. נזרק ואחר כך נודע: נטמא טומאת התהום הרי זה מרצה: בעי רמי בר חמא כהן המרצה בקרבנותיהן של ישראל הותרה לו טומאת התהום או לא ופשט רבא מהא דתאני רבי חייא לא אמרו טומאת התהום שהציץ מרצה אלא במת בלבד ודייק מדקתני מת בלבד מכלל דטומאת התהום בשרץ לא הותרה אלא לכהן ודחה רב יוסף ואמר לא לע"ל בבעלים דפסח ולמעוטי טומאת התהום בזיבה דלא הותרה להן: ואקשינן וטומאת התהום בזיבה לא (מטמאה) [והציץ] מרצה והתניא רבי יוסי אומר שומרת יום כנגד יום ששחטו וזרקו עליה

גמרא

מטהרה מדחיא טומאה לא מדחיא ומר סבר אפילו טומאה נמי מדחיא איתמר *היו שלישיתן זבין ושלישיתן טהורין ושלישיתן טמאי מתים אמר רבי מני בר פטיש אותן טמאי מתים אינן עושין לא את הראשון ולא השני בראשון לא עבדי הגדילו זבין על הטהורים דלא עבדי בטומאה הוה ליה טמאי מתים מיעוטא ומיעוטא לא עבדי בראשון בשני לא עבדי נצרפו זבין עם טמאי מתים דלא עבדי בראשון הוו להו רובא ורובא לא מדחו לפסח שני: **מתני'** הפסח שנזרק דמו ואח"כ נודע שהוא טמא הציץ מרצה ²נטמא הגוף אין הציץ מרצה *מפני שאמרו הנזיר ועושה פסח הציץ מרצה על טומאת הדם ואין הציץ מרצה על טומאת הגוף נטמא טומאת התהום הציץ מרצה: **גמ'** טעמא דנזרק ואח"כ נודע אבל נודע ואח"כ נזרק לא מרצה ורמינהו *על מה הציץ מרצה על הדם ועל הבשר ועל החלב שנטמא בין בשוגג בין במזיד בין באונס בין ברצון בין ביחיד בין בציבור אמר רבינא *טומאתו בין בשוגג בין במזיד הורצה זריקתו בשוגג הורצה במזיד לא הורצה רבי שילא אמר זריקתו בין בשוגג בין במזיד הורצה טומאתו בשוגג הורצה במזיד לא הורצה אלא הא דקתני בין בשוגג בין במזיד ה"ק נטמא בשוגג וזרקו בין בשוגג בין במזיד הורצה והא דקתני דם שנזרק ואח"כ נודע טעמא דנזרק ואח"כ נודע אבל נודע ואח"כ נזרק לא הוא הדין דאפילו נודע ואח"כ נזרק והאי דקתני נזרק ואח"כ נודע משום דבעי למתני סיפא נטמא הגוף אין הציץ מרצה דאפילו נזרק ואח"כ נודע לא קתני רישא נמי נזרק ואח"כ נודע: נטמא טומאת התהום וכו'. *בעי רמי בר חמא כהן המרצה בקרבנותיהן הותרה לו טומאת התהום או לא מי אמרינן כי גמירי טומאת התהום בבעלים בכהן לא גמירי או דילמא ¹בזבחא גמירי לא שנא בכהן ול"ש בבעלים אמר רבא ת"ש דתני *רבי חייא *לא אמרו טומאת התהום אלא למת בלבד מת למעוטי מאי לאו למעוטי טומאת התהום דשרץ ובמאי עסקינן אי נימא בבעלים ובמאן אי בנזיר מי מהני ביה °כי ימות מת עליו אמר רחמנא אלא בעושה פסח הניחא למאן דאמר *אין שוחטין וזורקין על טמאי שרץ אלא למאן דאמר שוחטין וזורקין על טמאי שרץ השתא טומאה ידועה הותרה לו טומאת התהום לא כל שכן אלא לאו בכהן ושמע מינה הותרה לו טומאת התהום אמר רב יוסף לא לעולם בבעלים ובפסח ולמעוטי טומאת התהום דזיבה וטומאת תהום דזיבה לא מרצה *והתניא רבי יוסי אומר שומרת יום כנגד יום ששחטו וזרקו עליה בשני

(°במדבר ו)

תוספות

בראשון לא עבדי הגדילו זבין על הטהורין כו'. נראה לר"י דס"ל כרב ולא כשמואל דלאמר במועדו מאי עבדת ביה דלדידיה כיון שאין רוב טהורין לא מידחו טמאים לפסח שני: **נזרק** דמו ואח"כ נודע שהוא טמא כו'. פי' בקונטרס שהוא טמא הדם או הבשר וקשה לריב"א דבטומאת בשר ע"כ אין לא מרצה לאכילה אלא לפטור מפסח שני וכמ"ד האין מרצה על אכילות וכר' נתן דלא בעי אלא גברא דחזי וא"כ היכי דייק טעמא דנזרק ואח"כ טודע הא טודע ואח"כ נזרק לא מרצה אין והיינו לפוטרו מפסח שני וע"כ הא דלא מרצי היינו מדרבנן מדמפליג בין שוגג למזיד וכן אמר בהאשה רבה (יבמות דף צ׳ ושם) והיכי מחייבי ליה רבנן בפסח שני כיון דמדאורייתא פטור הוי חולין בעזרה ועוד הא לעיל (דף ע׳:) תנן נטמא בשר וחלב קיים אינו זורק את הדם והיינו מדרבנן דמוקי לה כרבי נתן וא"כ הא דדייק רב לעיל אם זרק הורצה היינו אפילו מדרבנן ונודע קודם זריקה מיירי מדקאמר לא יזרוק ונראה לריב"א דלא מיירי מתני' אלא בטומאת דם והא דדייק בגמ' הא נודע ואחר כך נזרק לא היינו להתיר בשר באכילה אבל פטור מלעשות פסח שני מיהו יש ליישב פירוש הקונטרס דהא דקאמר האין מרצה היינו להקטיר האימורין הא נודע ואח"כ נזרק לא מרצה להקטיר האימורים ופטור מפסח שני: **הוא** הדין נודע ואחר כך נזרק. וא"ת א"כ מאי דוחקיה דר' שילא לחלק בין טומאה לזריקתו כיון דלאו דווקא קתני במתניתין נזרק ואח"כ נודע ואומר ר"י דר' שילא לאו אהך קושיא אמרה אלא אמאי דפריך בהקומץ רבה (מנחות דף כה:) אהך ברייתא דעל מה האין מרצה מברייתא דקתני דם שנטמא וזרקו בשוגג הורצה במזיד לא הורצה והכא אסיק ליה אגב תירוצא דרבינא: **לאו** למעוטי טומאת התהום דשרץ. וא"ת היכי שייך טומאת התהום בשרץ והא לא מטמא אלא במגע וטומאת התהום איכא בגלוי אלא מכוסה וטמון בעפר בתבן או בצרור כדתניא לקמן (דף פא:) ויש לומר כגון שהכניס ידו בעפר ונגע: **אי** בנזיר וכי ימות מת עליו אמר רחמנא. תימה לר"י דילמא לעולם בנזיר ונפקא מינה אם שחט קרבנות ונטמא דלא מרצי אין וכן קשה בסמוך דקאמר אלא למ"ד שוחטין וזורקין כו' הא מכל מקום נפקא מינה °לאם שחט פסחו כדפי' ואומר ר"י דלא בעי למימר הכי דא"כ תיפשוט דבזיבחא גמירי לא שנא בבעלים ול"ש בכהן: לאו

רש"י

תורה אור

מטהרה מדחיא. טומאה לשני כי עבדי ליבור בטהרה: בראשון לא עבדי. דהא טמאי מתים מיעוטא ובשני לא עבדי דהואיל וטהרו זבין עכשיו נמצאו רוב ליבור לריכין לו ורובא דליבור בשני לא עבדי: **מתני'** הפסח שנזרק את דמו ואח"כ נודע שהוא טמא. הפסח או הדם: הציץ מרצה. ופטור מפסח שני: נטמאו. בעליו טומאת הגוף במת: אין הציץ מרצה · וחייב לעשות פסח שני דהא בשעת זריקה לאו בר מיעבד פסח הוא דרחמנא דחייה: הנזיר. דכתיב ביה (במדבר ו) וכי ימות מת וגו' והימים הראשונים יפלו אם נטמא במת קודם הבאת קרבנותיו סותר: הציץ מרצה על טומאת הדם. ותגלחתו כשירה ומותר לשתות יין ולטמאות למתים: ואין הציץ מרצה על טומאת הגוף. ואם *נטמא בעת הבאת קרבנותיו סותר את הכל: נטמא גופו. בטומאת התהום בטומאת ספק כדמפרש בגמרא הרי זה מרצה דהלכה למשה מסיני היא דהותרה טומאת התהום להם כדאמר בגמרא ובתוספתא [א] מפרש לה הכי כילד אמרו לו קבר היה עמך בבית שנכנסת בו תחת האבן שישבת עליה ונודע לו עד שלא עשה פסחו] לריך לעשות פסח שני משעשה אין לריך לעשות פסח שני. וכן נזיר שהיה הולך להביא קרבנותיו אמרו לו מת היה עמך בבית שנכנסת בו ונודע לו בין עד שלא הביא קרבנותיו בין משהביא קרבנותיו לריך להביא קרבן טומאה אבל אמרו לו קבר התהום עמך בבית שנכנסת בו תחת האבן שישבת עליה ונודע לו עד שלא הביא קרבנותיו לריך להביא קרבן טומאה[ב] ומהו קרבן טומאה אשם ושתי תורים ומתחיל למנות נזירות אחרת. בתוספת' דזבחים: **גמ'** בין בשוגג בין במזיד. קס"ד דהכי קאמר שזרקו בין בשוגג בין במזיד ומשני דהאי שוגג ומזיד אטומאה קאי אבל זריקה בעינן שוגג: בקרבנותיהן. דנזיר ועושה פסח הותרה לו אם נטמא גופו בספק טומאה וקרבן יחיד אינו דוחה שבת וטומאה: כי גמירי. דטומאת התהום מותרת להם בבעלים הוא דגמירי אבל בכהן לא: או דילמא בזיבחא גמירי. בקרבנות הללו בפסח ובקרבנות נזיר גמירי דהותרה להם טומאת התהום של גוף הילכך לא שנא בבעלים ולא שנא בכהן: לא אמרו טומאת התהום. דהותרה בנזיר ועושה פסח: אלא במת בלבד. אבל שאר טומאות ספק לא הותרו: ובמאן. במי תארע טומאת התהום זו דשרץ דקאמר לא הותרה: אי בנזיר מי מהניא ביה. אפילו טומאות דשרץ [ודאי] לסתור מנייני והבאת קרבנותיו: וכי ימות עליו כתיב. פתע זה שוגג פתאום זה מזיד בכריתות (דף ט׳): הניחא למאן דאמר. לקמן בפ' האשה (דף צ:):ה"ג אלא לאו בכהן: לעולם בבעלים. ובעושה פסח ודקשיא לך הא לא מהניא ביה טומאה אחריתי איכא טומאת זיבה שהיא שבעת ימים ואין שוחטים וזורקים עליו ואשמעינן רבי חייא דטומאת התהום דזיבה כגון זב בשביעי שלו דספק הוא שמא יראה היום ויסתור כל מה שמנה ספק לא יראה והרי הוא כטמא שרץ דחזי לאורתא והויא לה טומאת התהום ופסלא ביה: בשני

מסורת הש"ס

[פתיח' כתב דל"ל נטמא]

זבחים כג:

לעיל עז: יומא ז' יבמות ל' מנחות כה:

(זבחים מה:) [מנחות שם]

זבחים כג.

[לקמן פח: ע"ש זבחי' כג. ע"ש נזיר סג:]

[לעיל סט: וש"נ]

נזיר טו:

הגהות הגר"א

[א] רש"י ד"ה נטמא כו' ובתוספתא כו' כיצד אמרו לו קבר היה עמך בבית שנכנסת בו או תחת האבן שישבת עליה ונודע לו בין משעשה פסחו בין עד שלא עשה פסחו צריך לעשות פסח שני כו' אבל אמרו לו קבר התהום היה בבית שנכנסת בו או תחת האבן שישבת עליה ונודע לו עד שלא עשה כו' א"ל מת היה בבית שנכנסת בו או תחת האבן שישבת עליה ונודע לו בין כו' הכל א"ל קבר כו' שנכנסת בו או תחת כו' ונודע לו עד שלא הביא קרבנותיו צריך להביא קרבן טומאה משהביא קרבנותיו אין צריך להביא קרבן טומאה ומהו קרבן טומאה כו' נזירות אחרות בתוספתא בפסחים כצ"ל [וכן בתוספתא דנזיר פ"ו]:

גליון הש"ס

תוספו' ד"ה אי בנזיר כו' נ"מ לאם שחט פסחו ק"ל הא לשחוט לטמא כשר ולזריקה ובעלים כהן ומדין הזריקה בטומאה הא זהו האיבעיא ורוצה באמת לפשוט מזה דלכהן הותרה וכדאמרינן אלא לאו בכהן ובודאי אין חילוק בזה אם הזורק כהן הוא הבעלים או כהן אחר ולע"ג:

הגהות מהר"ב רנשבורג

א] רש"י ד"ה נטמא גופו וכו' ונודע לו עד שלא עשה פסחו וכו' · נ"ב בין שעשה פסחו ובין עד שלא עשה פסחו צריך לעשות פסח שני אבל אמרו לו קבר התהום היה עמך בבית שנכנסת בו או תחת האבן שישבת עליה ונודע לו כצ"ל וכ"ה בתוספתא פ"ו דמכילתן וגם בתוספתא פ"ו דנזיר: ב] בא"ד אבל אמרו קבר התהום עמך וכו' ונודע לו עד שלא הביא קרבנותיו צריך להביא קרבן טומאה וכו' · נ"ב משהביא קרבנותיו אין צריך להביא קרבן טומאה כ"ה בתוספתא הנ"ל ·

מסורת הש"ס

עין משפט נר מצוה

נח א מיי׳ פ״א מהל׳ חגיגה הלכה ד׳:
נט ב מיי׳ פ״ב מהל׳ חגיגה הלכה ס׳:
ס ג מיי׳ פ״ו מהל׳ ק״פ הלכה ד׳:
סא ד שם הלכה ס׳:

דברים ט״ז °לא תוכל לזבוח את הפסח באחד שעריך רבי שמעון אומר אפילו שבט אחד טמא ושאר כל השבטים טהורים הללו עושין לעצמן והללו עושין לעצמן מאי טעמא דרבי שמעון קסבר שבט אחד איקרי קהל רבי יהודה אומר *אפילו שבט אחד טמא ושאר כל השבטים טהורין יעשו בטומאה שאין קרבן ציבור חלוק רבי יהודה סבר שבט אחד איקרי קהל והוו להו פלגא ופלגא ואין קרבן ציבור חלוק ועבדי כולהו בטומאה איתמר היו ישראל מחצה טהורין ומחצה טמאין אמר רב *מטמאין אחד מהן בשרץ ואמאי ניעבדו הני לחודייהו והני לחודייהו דהא אמר רב *הללו עושין לעצמןוהללו עושין לעצמן אמרי הכא במאי עסקינן כגון שהיו טמאין עודפין על הטהורין אחד אי הכי הוו להו רובא טמאים ניעבדו כולהו בטומאה סבר לה כר״א בן מתיא דאמר אין היחיד מכריע את הציבור לטומאה אי הכי הדר קושיין לדוכתיה ניעבדו הני לחודייהו והני לחודייהו אלא ה״ק אי איכא תנא דסבר לה כתנא קמא דאמר פלגא ופלגא לא עבדי כולהו בטומאה וסבר לה כרבי יהודה דאמר אין קרבן ציבור חלוק מטמאין אחד מהן בשרץ ועולא אמר משלחין אחד מהן לדרך רחוקה ויטמאנו בשרץ קסבר שוחטין וזורקין על טמא שרץ ויטמאנו במת מדחהו אתה מחגיגתו השתא נמי מדחהו אתה מפסחו אפשר(א) דעביד בשני במת נמי אפשר דעביד בשביעי דהוה ליה שמיני שלו קסבר עולא *כולהו *תשלומין דראשון נינהו ^בדחזי בראשון חזי בכולהו וכל היכא דלא חזי בראשון לא חזי בכולהו אמר להו רב נחמן זילו ואמרו ליה לעולא מאן צייית דעקר סיכיה ומשכניה ורהיט איתמר ^גהיו רובן זבין ומיעוטן טמאי מתים אמר רב אותן טמאי מתים אינן עושין לא בראשון ולא בשני ראשון לא עבדי דהוו מיעוטא ומיעוטא לא עבדי בראשון בשני נמי לא עבדי כל היכא דעבדי ציבור בראשון עביד יחיד בשני כל היכא דלא עבדי ציבור בראשון לא עביד יחיד בשני במדבר ט °ויעשו בני ישראל את הפסח במועדו מאי עבדת זילו אמרו ליה *לאבא ליה אמר להו זילו אמרו ליה כי הוו כולהו זבין מאי עבדת ליה אלא כיון דלא אפשר לא אפשר הכא נמי לא אפשר איתמר היו רובן טמאי מתים ומיעוטן זבין רב הונא אמר ^דאין תשלומין לפסח הבא בטומאה ורב אדא בר אהבה אמר יש תשלומין לפסח הבא בטומאה נימא בהא קמיפלגי דמאן דאמר אין תשלומין לפסח הבא בטומאה קסבר *טומאה דחויה היא בציבור ומ״ד יש תשלומין לפסח הבא בטומאה קסבר טומאה הותרה בציבור אמרי לא דכולי עלמא טומאה דחויה בציבור ובהא פליגי מר סבר טהרה

[לעיל עט: יומא ו: ז: מו: זבחים כג:]

[עי׳ פירש״י ברכות מז ד״ה אלו]

רש"י

לא תוכל לזבוח את הפסח באחד. בשביל יחיד לא תזבחנו שיהא אותו היחיד גורם ומועיל בשחיטתו שום לד טמיה: איקרי קהל · ומילתא מפ׳ בהוריות (דף ה:) דקאמר ליה רחמנא ליעקב גוי וקהל גוים יהיה ממך וכבר נולדו לו כל השבטים חוץ מבנימין הילכך שבט אחד חשוב כציבור ולא מידחי לשני: תורה אור

יעשו בטומאה. אף טהורין אם ירלו: מטמאין אחד מהן. כי היכי דניהוו רוב טמאין ויעבדו כולהו [בטומאה]: שהיו טמאין עודפין על הטהורין אחד. דלא חזו טהורים ברחשון: הדר׳ קושיין לדוכתיה · דהוו להו פלגא ופלגא והללו יעשו לעצמן והללו יעשו לעצמן: אלא ה״ק כו׳. ולעולם מחלה על מחלה דווקא קתני וה״ק רב אי מסכחת תנא דאית ליה כת״ק דאמר פלגא ופלגא לא עבדי טהורין בטומאה כדקתני הללו עושין לעצמן וכרבי יהודה דאמר אין קרבן ליבור חלוק מכי עביד קהל בטומאה ברחשון לא מפליג למיעבד טהורין בטהרה דאסור ליחלק שנגלי הדבר דמוכחא מילתא בהדיא כשנזהרין אלו מאלו: מטמאין אחד מהן בשרץ. ועבדיה כולהו בטומאה: שוחטין וזורקין על טמא שרץ. הואיל וחזי לאורתא הילכך אין מכריע את הציבור לטומאה: מחגיגתו. של מחר שאתה מטמאו כל שבעה: אפשר דעביד. חגיגתו בשביעי של פסח שהוא שמיני שלו דהא כל ז׳ תשלומין אית ליה: קסבר כולן. הימים של רגל תשלומין של ראשון הן ואינן תשלומין זה לזה ופלוגתא היא בחגיגה (דף ט:) ומאן דאית ליה כולן תשלומין לראשון סבר היכא דלא חזי לראשון תו לא חזי: מאן ציית לך. להשתלח לדרך רחוקה: וכי עקר משכניה וסיכיה. אהלו ויתדותיו ורהיט בתמיה מי ישמע לנו להטריח עצמו הילכך הא עדיפא כרב: רובן זבין. דלא מצו למיעבד בראשון: אין תשלומין לפסח הבא בטומאה. ואין הזבין עושין את השני אפילו טהרו: רב הונא סבר טומאה דחויה היא בציבור · ובקושי הותר להקריבו הלכך לא משוינן להו בטהורים למידחי טמאין לשני: ורב אדא סבר היתר הוא בציבור. ומשוינן להו בטהורין ודחו זבין לשני:

טהרה

כדפרישית ומר סבר טומאה נמי מידחיא וקרא משמע הכי איש נדחה ואין ציבור נדחים אלא עבדי בין בטהרה בין בטומאה: בראשון

תוספות

משלחין אחד מהן לדרך רחוקה. פירוש אחד מן הטהורים מדפריך ויטמאנו בשרץ °וקשה לריב״א אדרבה ישלחו אחד מן הטמאים לדרך רחוקה דהשתא הוו טהורין רובא ועבדי בטהרה דבטלה שמעתין אמרינן דמהדרי׳ אטהרה ותירץ דעולא גופיה אמר לקמן במי שהיה טמא (דף צג:) דרך רחוקה לטהור ואין דרך רחוקה לטמא ולא היה מועיל שילוח טמא דלעולם היה מצטרף לאותם שבירושלים ואין נראה לר״י דטעמא דאין דרך רחוקה לטמא לפי שכשהוא בירושלים נמי אינו יכול לעשות פסחו אלא ע״י שילוח(ב) אבל הכא יש דרך רחוקה לטמא כיון דמחלה טמאין ואם היה בירושלים היה יכול בעצמו לעשותו אלא נראה לר״י דמהדרינן שיעשו כולם בראשון ולא ידחו הטמאין:

אתה מדחהו מחגיגתו. ואם תאמר והא קיימא לן בתמיד נשחט (לעיל סב·) ערל וטמא משלחים קרבנותיהן ותירץ ריב״א הואיל והיא חובה לבא ברגל יש לה דין עולת ראייה דדרשינן בפרק קמא דחגיגה (דף ד:) דטמא פטור מן הראייה שנאמר ובאת שמה והבאתם שמה כו׳ וכן איתא בירושלמי דאיתקש לעולת ראייה ואם תאמר השתא כשמשלחהו בדרך רחוקה נמי מדחהו מחגיגתו שאינו יכול לבא ביום טוב מחוץ לתחום וכיון דלא חזי בראשון לא חזי בשני ויש לומר דיכול לבא ולעשות ביום ראשון מה״ת דתחומין דרבנן ועוד נהי דכשישלחהו בדרך רחוקה עד שעת שחיטה שלא יכול לחזור לירושלים מבעוד יום מכל מקום יכול לבא תוך התחום ויכנס למחר ועוד טמא וחיגר דלא חזי בגופו בראשון לא חזי בשני אבל הכא מיחזא חזי אלא שאינו יכול לבוא וכי הוי יום ראשון בשבת אף על גב דלא חזי אמרינן באלו דברים (לעיל דף ע:) דעביד באינך יומי:

עקר משכניה וסיכיה ורהיט · הך פירכא ליתא למאן *דחשיב דרך רחוקה מאיסקופת עזרה ולחוץ ואם תאמר ומה תקנה רואה רב נחמן שיעשו דהא רב נחמן גופיה קסבר בפרק מי שהיה טמא (לקמן צג·) שוחטין וזורקין על טמא שרץ ויש לומר דקסבר דלאו תשלומין דראשון נינהו ויכול לטמאותו במת:

[פסחים צג:]

לימא בהא קמיפלגי מר סבר טומאה דחויה ומר סבר טומאה הותרה. השתא לכולי עלמא טהרה מידחיא ולא טומאה דאיש כי יהיה טמא משמע דהאיש לבדו טמא והציבור טהורים ומאן דסבר טומאה הותרה מיקרו שפיר טהורים ומסיק דלכולי עלמא דחויה מר סבר טהרה מידחיא

הגה״ה

צ״ל דטמאין אין עושין בראשון ולא בשני ובזה אם נשלח הטמא הא בפסח שני שילטרפו הטמאים יחד איכו ושאר הטמאים יהיו לבור דאין עושין פסח שני ול״ע:

[מנחות סו׳]

[לקמן צ:]

[לעיל עט:]

[חגיגה ט׳]

הגהות הב"ח

(א) גמרא אפשר דעביד בשני כ״ב ז״ל דס״ל כמ״ד בסמוך יש תשלומין לפסח הבא בטומאה או דס״ל לחלק בין מי שהיה זב כשהיה בפסח ראשון לבין מי שהיה בדרך רחוקה בפסח ראשון וק״ל: (ב) תוס׳ ד״ה משלחין וכו׳ ע״י שליח אבל הכא:

גליון הש"ס

תוספ׳ ד״ה משלחין וקשה לריב״א. ק״ל

רבינו חננאל

לא תוכל לזבוח את הפסח באחד שעריך וגו׳: **איתמר** היו ישראל מחצה טהורין ומחצה טמאין אמר רב מטמאין אחד מהן בשרץ ואמאי האמר רב הללו עושין לעצמן והללו עושין לעצמן אמרי הכא במאי עסקי׳ כגון שהיו הטמאין עודפין על הטהורים אחד ואם תאמר א״כ הנה הרוב טמאין יעשו בטומאה סבר רב אין היחיד מכריע את הציבור לטומאה כלומר אחד כמי שאינו הוא אי הכי מחצה על מחצה הן ושנינן ליה לרב דאמר מחצה על מחצה כרוב והללו עושין לעצמן [והללו עושין לעצמן] ושנינן הכי אמר רב אי איכא תנא דסבר לה כת״ק דאמר היו הטמאין עודפין על הטהורין אפילו אחד יעשה בטומאה וכרבי יהודה דאמר אין קרבן צבור חלוק מטמאין אחד מן הטהורין בשרץ ונמצאו הטמאין עודפין על הטהורין שנים כיצד כגון שהיו מאה טהורין ומאה טמאים נטמא אחד מן הטהורי׳ נמצאו הטמאין מאה ואחד והטהורין צ״ט ומשכחת לה אפילו לאלעזר בן מתתיה · **עולא** אמר משלחין אחד מן הטהורין לדרך רחוקה ויטמא בשרץ וכו׳ ואסיקנא קסבר עולא כל מי שהיה טהור וראוי לחגיגה ביום ראשון ונאנס ולא חג כגון שהיה בדרך רחוקה ובא במועד וכיוצא בו חוגג והולך כל הרגל אבל אם היה טמא ביום ראשון כבר נדחה ואינו חוגג אותו הרגל כולו מאי טעמא כולהו תשלומין דראשון הוא ותרוייהו רב ועולא סבירא להו שאין מטמאין אחד מהן במת שלא ידחה מחגיגתו · פי׳ סיכי יתדות והלך · איתמר היו רובן טמאי מתים ומיעוטן זבים רב הונא אמר אין תשלום לפסח הבא בטומאה כלומר הזבין אינן עושין לא את הראשון ולא את השני ואתיא כר׳ נתן דאמר כל הזקוק לראשון זקוק לשני כי השני תשלומין דראשון הוא הלכך כשם שהראשון לא עבדו דתנן הפסח שבא בטומאה לא יאכלו ממנו זבין וזבות וכו׳ בשני נמי לא עבדו דטהרה מדחה הטומאה לפסח שני כדתניא אלו עושין את השני הזבין והזבות והנדות

האנוסין והשוגגין והמזידין והמצורעים ובועלי נדות ומי שהיה טמא ומי שהיה בדרך רחוקה א״כ למה נאמר טמא או בדרך רחוקה לפטרן מן ההכרת ומרבינן לזבין איש איש דתניא יכול לא יהו נדחין מן הא׳ ועושין את השני אלא טמא ומי שהי׳ בדרך רחוקה וזבין ומצורעין מנין ת״ל איש איש הלכך כל היכי דעבדי טהורין בראשון עבדו טמאין בשני אבל אי לא עביד הראשון לא עבדי השני שאר טמאין כגון זבין וזבות וכיוצא בהן דטהרה מדחיא אפילו שאר טמאין לשני אבל טומאה לא מדחיא שאר טמאין מן הראשון לשני הלכך לא עבדו בשני כלל: **ורב** אדא בר אהבה אמר יש תשלומין לפסח הבא בטומאה ומי שלא עשה הראשון יעשה השני דטומאה נמי דחיא מאי טעמא טמאי מתים למה עושין השני לפי שלא יכלו לעשות הראשון זבין ומצורעין נמי כיוצא בהן לא יכלו לעשות הראשון יעשו שני וכולי עלמא טומאה דחויה היא בציבור (ד״א) אפילו טומאה מדחיא דכיון דטמאי מתים עבדו הראשון כשהותרו חשיבי כטומאה מן התורה הלכך שאר הטמאים עושין השני: **איתמר** רובן זבין ומיעוטן טמאי מתים אמר רב טמאי מתים אין עושין בראשון דהא מיעוטא נינהו ומיעוטא נדחין לפסח שני בשני נמי לא עבדו דקיימא לן כל היכא דלא עבוד צבור בראשון לא עבוד בשני וכו׳ כתיב ויעשו בני ישראל

to uncleanness, because it is said, [80a] *Thou mayest not sacrifice the passover-offering at one of thy gates.*[6] R. Simeon said: Even if one tribe is unclean and all the other tribes are clean, the former sacrifice by themselves while the latter sacrifice by themselves. (What is R. Simeon's reason?—He holds: One tribe is designated
a a community.)[1] R. Judah said: Even if one tribe is unclean and all the other tribes are clean, let them [all] sacrifice in uncleanness, because a public sacrifice cannot be divided. (R. Judah holds: One tribe is designated a community, so that it is half against half,[2] and [since] a public sacrifice is not divided, they all sacrifice in uncleanness.)

It was stated: If the Israelites were half [of them] clean and half [of them] unclean,—said Rab: we defile one of them with a reptile.[3] But why so: let the former sacrifice by themselves and the latter by themselves, for surely Rab said: These sacrifice by themselves and those sacrifice by themselves?—I will tell you: what do we discuss here? E.g., where the unclean exceeded the clean by one. If so, the majority are unclean, [then] let them all sacrifice in uncleanness?—He holds as R. Eleazar b. Mathia, who maintained: A single individual cannot overbalance the community to uncleanness. If so, our difficulty returns in full force:[4] let the former sacrifice by themselves and the latter by themselves?—Rather this is what he means: If there is a Tanna who agrees with the first Tanna[5] who rules: [When there is] half against half they must not all sacrifice in uncleanness, and [also] he agrees with R. Judah who said: A public sacrifice cannot be divided, then we defile one of them with a reptile.

But 'Ulla maintained: We send away one of them on a *'journey afar off.'*[6] But let us defile him with a reptile?—He holds: We slaughter [the Passover-offering] and sprinkle [its blood] for a man who is unclean through a reptile.[7] Then let us defile him
b through a dead body?—Then you debar him from his *ḥagigah.*[1] But now too you debar him from his Passover-offering?—It is possible to sacrifice at the second [Passover]. Then in the case of [defilement by] a dead body too it is possible to sacrifice [the *ḥagigah*] on the seventh [day of Passover] which would be his eighth [day after defilement]?—'Ulla holds: They are all a compensation for the first [day]:[2] [hence] he who is eligible on the first is eligible [to sacrifice] on all of them, but wherever one is not eligible on the first, he is not eligible on any of them.

R. Naḥman said to them [his disciples], Go and tell 'Ulla: Who will obey you to pull up his tent-pegs and tent and speed away![3]

It was stated: If the majority were *zabin*[4] and the minority unclean through the dead,—Rab said: Those unclean through the dead cannot sacrifice either on the first or on the second. They do not observe the first [Passover], because they are a minority, and a minority do not observe [it] on the first. They cannot observe it on the second either: whenever the community observes [it] on the first, individual[s] observe [it] on the second; [but] whenever the community does not observe it on the first, individual[s] do not observe [it] on the second. Said Samuel to them [his disciples], Go out and say to Abba:[5] How do you dispose of, *Let the children of Israel keep the Passover in its appointed season!*[6]—He [Rab] answered them: Go and say to him: [yet] how do you dispose of it [the verse] when they are all *zabin?*[7] But [you must say] since it is impossible [to carry it out], it is impossible; so here too it is impossible.

It was stated: If the majority were unclean through the dead and a minority were *zabin,*—R. Huna said: There is no compen-
c sation for a Passover-offering which comes in uncleanness;[1] while R. Adda b. Ahabah said: There is compensation for a Passover-offering which comes in uncleanness. Shall we say that they differ in this, viz., he who maintains [that] there is no compensation for a Passover-offering which comes in uncleanness holds: Uncleanness is *overridden* in the case of the community; while he who maintains [that] there is compensation for a Passover-offering which comes in uncleanness holds: Uncleanness is *permitted* in the case of a community![2]—I will tell you. It is not so, for all hold [that] uncleanness is *overridden* in the case of a community, and they differ

(6) Deut. XVI, 5. He translates: you must not sacrifice it on account of one person, i.e., one person has no power to change any of the conditions of the sacrifice.

a (1) V. Hor. 5*b*. Hence it is not relegated to the second. (2) Communities are not regarded numerically. (3) So that there is a majority unclean, and all can now sacrifice in uncleanness. (4) Lit., 'to its place.' (5) In the previously cited Baraitha. (6) Which is tantamount to being unclean (v. Num. IX, 10) and effects the same result. For the definition of a *'journey afar off'*, v. *infra* 93*b*. (7) Since he can have a ritual bath (*tebillah*) and be fit to eat in the evening.

b (1) V. Glos. The reference is to the *ḥagigah* brought on the fifteenth, and he would be debarred from it, since a man defiled by the dead is unclean for seven days. [But when he is sent away on a *'journey afar off'*, he might manage to be back in Jerusalem on the following day to offer the *ḥagigah*, v. Tosaf.] (2) All the days of the Festival, though fit for the sacrificing of the *ḥagigah*, are only regarded as a compensation for the first day, this being the day when it should really be brought. This question is disputed in Ḥag. 9*b*. (3) None will consent to depart on a distant journey! Hence Rab's expedient is preferable. [R. Naḥman must have accepted R. Akiba's definition (v. loc. cit.) of a *'journey afar off'*, v. Tosaf.] (4) Pl. of *zab*, q.v. Glos. They are unclean, but the law that an unclean majority sacrifice in uncleanness applies only to those who are unclean through the dead. (5) Rab. His name was Abba Arika, but he was called Rab (the Master) in the same way that R. Judah ha-Nasi was called Rabbi. (6) Num. IX, 2. (7) When obviously the precept cannot be fulfilled.

c (1) Hence the *zabin* cannot observe the second Passover. (2) V. *supra* 77*a*; hence it is really the same as any other Passover-offering, and therefore permits of compensation.

a majority: the clean observe the first [Passover], [79b] while the unclean observe neither the first nor the second. They cannot sacrifice on the first, because they are not a majority, [while] they a cannot sacrifice at the second because they are not a minority.[1]

We learned: IF THE COMMUNITY OR THE MAJORITY THEREOF WAS DEFILED, OR IF THE PRIESTS WERE UNCLEAN AND THE COMMUNITY CLEAN, THEY MUST SACRIFICE IN UNCLEANNESS. [Thus] it is only the majority that sacrifices in uncleanness, but [when it is] half and half, they do not sacrifice at the first [Passover], which is a difficulty on Rab's view?—Rab can answer you: [When] a majority [is unclean], *all* sacrifice in uncleanness; [whereas where there is] half and half, these observe [the Passover] by themselves, and those observe [it] by themselves. That too is logical, because the second clause states, IF A MINORITY OF THE COMMUNITY WERE DEFILED: THOSE WHO ARE CLEAN OBSERVE THE FIRST [PASSOVER], WHILE THOSE WHO ARE UNCLEAN OBSERVE THE SECOND. [Thus] only a minority sacrifice at the second, but not [when it is] half against half, for then they sacrifice at the first, these sacrificing by themselves and those sacrificing by themselves.

But in that case it is a difficulty on R. Kahana's view?— R. Kahana can answer you: [It states] IF A MINORITY OF THE COMMUNITY WERE DEFILED, THOSE WHO ARE CLEAN OBSERVE THE FIRST [PASSOVER], WHILE THOSE WHO ARE UNCLEAN OBSERVE THE SECOND; hence [when it is] half against half, the clean observe the first, but the unclean observe neither the first nor the second. Now that is well according to the latter version of R. Kahana['s ruling]; but according to the version in which R. Kahana states, 'The clean observe the first and the unclean observe the second,' what is to be said?—R. Kahana can answer you: The same law [holds good] that even half against half, the clean observe the first while the unclean observe the second; yet as to what he [the Tanna] teaches, A MINORITY OF THE COMMUNITY: because he teaches THE MAJORITY in the first clause, he also teaches A MINORITY in the second clause.

It was taught in accordance with Rab; it was taught in accordance with R. Kahana, and as both versions [of his ruling]. It was taught in accordance with Rab: If the Israelites were half [of them] clean and half [of them] unclean, the former sacrifice by themselves and the latter sacrifice by themselves. It was taught as the first version of R. Kahana['s ruling]: Behold, if the Israelites were half [of them] clean and half [of them] unclean, the clean observe the first [Passover] while the unclean observe the second. And it was taught as the second version of R. Kahana['s ruling]: Behold, if the Israelites were half [of them] clean and half [of them] unclean, the clean observe the first, while the unclean observe neither the first nor the second.

Now according to Rab and the second version of R. Kahana['s b ruling], when he[1] teaches, 'The clean observe the first and the unclean [observe] the second,' how do they reconcile it [with their views]?—E.g., if the Israelites were half [of them] clean and half [of them] unclean, with women making up [the number of] the unclean;[2] now he holds: [The observance of the Passover-offering by] women at the first [Passover] is voluntary;[3] [hence] deduct the women from the [number of] unclean, so that the unclean are a minority, and a minority are relegated to the second Passover.

According to Rab and the first version of R. Kahana, as to what was taught, 'The clean observe the first and the unclean observe neither the first nor the second,' how do they reconcile it [with their views]?—Rab reconciles it [thus]: e.g., if the [male] Israelites were half [of them] unclean and half of them clean, with c women as an addition to the clean.[1] Now he holds: [The observance of the Passover-offering by] women at the first [Passover] is a duty, but voluntary at the second. [Hence] they [the unclean] cannot sacrifice at the first, because they are a minority,[2] and a minority do not sacrifice at the first. While they cannot sacrifice at the second, [because] deduct the women from them,[3] so there is half and half, and a half do not sacrifice at the second. While according to R. Kahana who maintained, a half too sacrifice at the second, he explains it thus: e.g., if the Israelites were half [of them] clean and half [of them] unclean, with women making up [the number of] the clean. Now he holds: [The observance of the Passover-offering by] women at the first Passover is a duty, while at the second it is voluntary. [Hence] they cannot sacrifice at the first, because they are half against half, and a half does not sacrifice at the first. At the second too they cannot sacrifice, [because] deduct the women from the clean [and] the unclean are a majority, and a majority do not sacrifice at the second.

Again, according to R. Kahana, as to what was taught, 'Behold, if the Israelites were half [of them] clean and half [of them] unclean, the former sacrifice by themselves while the latter sacrifice by themselves,' how does he explain it?—R. Kahana can answer you: It is [a controversy of] Tannaim: there is a view [that] half against half is as a majority, and there is a view [that] half against half is not as a majority.

[To turn to] the main text:[4] 'Behold, if the Israelites were half [of them] clean and half [of them] unclean, the former sacrifice by themselves and the latter sacrifice by themselves. If the unclean exceeded the clean even by one, they all sacrifice in uncleanness, because a public sacrifice cannot be divided.'[5] R. Eleazar b. Mathia said: A single individual cannot overbalance the community

a (1) Whereas only a minority sacrifices at the second Passover.

b (1) The Tanna of the cited teaching. (2) I.e., there were half unclean only when women are included. (3) They need not observe it all.

c (1) Bringing up the clean to a majority. (2) Since it is obligatory for women they must be counted. (3) *Sc.* the clean; for since it is only voluntary for women at the second they cannot be counted. (4) From which the teaching cited *supra*, is taken. (5) V. *supra* 79a, n. b2.

נה א מיי' פ"ז מהלכות ק"פ הלכה ג:
נו ב מיי' שם פ"ב הלכה ד ופרק ה הלכה ח:
נז ג מיי' פ"ז שם הל' ב:

רבינו חננאל

אין עושין לא [את] הראשון ולא [את] השני וללישנא קמא דרב כהנא אמר לך הוא הדין אפי' פלגא ופלג' טהורין עושין הראשון וטמאין השני ואיידי דתנא רישא רוב הקהל תנא סיפא מיעוט: תניא כותיה דרב ותניא כותיה דרב כהנא כתרי לישני: לרב וללישנא בתרא דרב כהנא הא דתניא טהורין עושין הראשון וטמאין עושין השני היכי מתרצי לה כגון שהיו ישראל מחצה טהורין ומיעוט טמאין ונשים משלימות לטמאין למחצה ונמצאו מחצה טהורין ומחצה עם הנשים טמאין וקסברי נשים בראשון רשות דל נשים מן הטמאין ונמצאו הטמאין מיעוט ומיעוט נדחין לפסח שני והטהורין עושין הראשון בטהרה כי רוב הקהל טהורין הן לרב וללישנא קמא דרב כהנא הא דתניא טהורין עושין את הראשון וטמאין אין עושין לא את הראשון ולא את השני היכי מתרצי לה רב מתרץ לטעמיה כגון שהיו ישראל מחצה טהורין ומחצה טמאין ונשים עודפות על הטהורין וסבר האי תנא נשים בראשון חובה והאנשים והנשים שוים טהורין עושין את הראשון דהא רובא נינהו טמאין אין עושין הראשון דהא מיעוטא נינהו ומיעוט לא עבדי בראשון בשני נמי אין עושין דלנשים מן הטהורין דנשים בשני רשות והוו להו טמאין פלגא ופלגא לא מדחו לפסח שני הלכך טמאין אין עושין לא את הראשון ולא את השני וללישנא קמא דרב כהנא דאמר פלגא ופלגא נמי עבדי בשני מתרץ לטעמיה כגון שהיו ישראל מחצה טהורין ומחצה טמאין ונשים משלימות לטהורין ועודפות עליהן פי' כגון שהיו עשרה טהורין ועשרה טמאין והטהורי' הם ארבעה אנשים ושש נשים הרי עשרה והטמאים הם ששה אנשים וארבע נשים הרי עשרה ומאי עודפות עליהן דקתני דנפישין טהורות מטהורות וקסבר נשים בראשון חובה ובשני רשות טמאים בראשון לא עבדו דהוה להו פלגא ונדחין לפסח שני בשני נמי לא עבדי דנשים בשני רשות ונשים מן הטהורין ומן הטמאין היו בראשון ונמצאו הטמאין ששה והטהורין ארבעה הנה הטמאין רובא ורובא בשני לא עבדי. ורב כהנא הא דתניא כותיה דרב מוקים ליה כתנאי דלא מתרץ ליה: **גופה** היו ישראל מחצה טהורין ומחצה טמאין הללו עושין לעצמן והללו עושין לעצמן ואם היו הטמאין עודפין על הטהורין אפילו אחד יעשה בטומאה אלעזר בן מתיא אומר אין היחיד מכריע צבור לטומאה שנאמר

תוספות

וטמאין אין עושין לא את הראשון ולא את השני · קשה לריב"א אי פלגא מיקרו איש לידחו לפסח שני ואי לא מיקרו איש אלא ליבור ליעביד בטומאה בראשון וליכא למימר דמספקא ליה אי חשיבי איש או ליבור דאם כן ליטמאו אחד מן הטהורים דבשלמא אי לא מספקא ליה אתי שפיר דלמה יטמאו את הטהור לעשות בטומאה כיון שדין של טמאין ליפטר לגמרי ואומר ר"י דלא מיקרו איש ומ"מ לא יעשו הטהורים בטומאה בשביל כיון שאין רוב טמאים ואין עושין נמי אלו לעצמן ואלו לעצמן דקסבר אין קרבן ליבור חלוק אע"ג דלר' יהודה דאית ליה לקמן אין קרבן ליבור חלוק קאמר יעשו כולם בטומאה רב כהנא לית ליה הך סברא אלא קסבר דמהאי טעמא נידחין לגמרי:

קסבר נשים בראשון רשות · משום רב איצטריך למימר הכי דאי בראשון חובה הוה אמרינן דהללו עושין לעצמן כו' אבל לרב כהנא אפילו הוו בראשון חובה אתי שפיר דפלגא בראשון לא עבדי ובשני עבדי כיון דבשני נשים רשות הוו להו טמאים מיעוטא והא דאמר בפר' קמא דסנהדרין (דף יב·) גבי חזקיהו שהשיא את ישראל לעשות פסח שני היכי דמי אמר רב אשי כגון שהיו ישראל מחצה טמאים ומחצה טהורין ונשים משלימות לטהורים ועודפות עליהן מעיקרא סבר נשים בראשון חובה והוו להו טמאים מיעוטא ומידחו לפסח שני ולבסוף סבר נשים בראשון רשות והוו להו טמאים רובא ורובא בשני לא עבדי והשתא לרב וללישנא בתרא דרב כהנא לא הוה צריך למינקט משלימות אלא עודפות עליהן גרידא וללישנא קמא דרב כהנא הוה מצי למינקט משלימות ולא עודפות אלא נקט משלימות ועודפות דהשתא לכולהו לישני עשה שלא כתורה והוה מצי לשנויי דלבסוף סבר נשים בראשון חובה ובשני רשות ולכך לאו שפיר עבד פסח שני אלא משום דהתם אליבא דרבי שמעון קיימינן דאית ליה לקמן בפרק האשה (דף צא:) נשים בראשון רשות אי נמי ניחא ליה למידחי דאף מה שלא עשו בראשון היה שלא כדין:

נשים בראשון רשות · הוה מצי למינקט בברייתא רוב טהורים וע"י נשים היו רוב טמאים נדחין לפסח שני כיון דנשים בראשון רשות והוו להו מיעוט טמאים:

ורב כהנא מתרץ לה הכי כו' · השתא נמי הוה מצי למינקט בברייתא רבותא דאפי' רוב טהורין אין הטמאין עושין את השני כיון שבלא נשים הוו טהורים מיעוטא ומצינו למימר דנקט בכי האי גוונא לאשמועי' דמחצה על מחצ' אינו כרוב:

משלחין

גמרא

וטמאין אין עושין לא את הראשון ולא את השני בראשון לא עבדי דלא הוו רובא בשני לא עבדי דלא הוו מיעוטא תנן נטמא קהל או רובו או שהיו הכהנים טמאין והקהל טהורים יעשה בטומאה רובו הוא דעבדי בטומאה אבל פלגא ופלגא לא עבדי בראשון קשיא לרב לרב אמר לך רב רובא עבדי כולהו בטומאה פלגא ופלגא הללו עושין לעצמן והללו עושין לעצמן ה"נ מסתברא דקתני סיפא נטמא מיעוט הקהל טהורין עושין את הראשון וטמאין עושין את השני מיעוט הוא דעבדי בשני אבל פלגא ופלגא לא ועבדי בראשון והללו עושין לעצמן והללו עושין לעצמן ואלא קשיא לרב כהנא אמר לך רב כהנא נטמאו מיעוט הקהל טהורין עושין את הראשון וטמאין עושין את השני הא פלגא ופלגא טהורין עושין את הראשון אבל טמאין אינן עושין לא את הראשון ולא את השני התינח ללישנא בתרא דרב כהנא אלא להך לישנא דאמר רב כהנא טהורים עושין את הראשון וטמאין עושין את השני מאי איכא למימר אמר לך רב כהנא הוא הדין דאפילו פלגא ופלגא נמי טהורין עושין את הראשון וטמאין עושין את השני והאי דקתני מיעוט הקהל איידי דתנא רישא רובו תנא נמי סיפא מיעוטו תניא כוותיה דרב תניא כוותיה דרב כהנא כתרי לישני תניא כוותיה דרב היו ישראל מחצה טהורין ומחצה טמאין הללו עושין לעצמן והללו עושין לעצמן תניא כלישנא קמא דרב כהנא הרי *שהיו ישראל מחצה טהורין ומחצה טמאין טהורין עושין את הראשון וטמאין עושין את השני ותניא כלישנא בתרא דרב כהנא הרי שהיו ישראל מחצה טהורין ומחצה טמאין טהורין עושין את הראשון וטמאין אינן עושין לא את הראשון ולא את השני לרב וללישנא בתרא דרב כהנא הא דתנא טהורין עושין את הראשון וטמאין את השני היכי מתרצי לה כגון שהיו ישראל מחצה טהורין ומחצה טמאין ונשים משלימות לטמאים וקסבר נשים בראשון רשות דל נשים מטמאין והוו להו טמאין מיעוטא ומיעוטא ידחו לפסח שני לרב וללישנא קמא דרב כהנא הא דתניא טהורין עושין את הראשון וטמאין אין עושין לא את הראשון ולא את השני היכי מתרצי לה רב מתריץ לה *כגון שהיו ישראל מחצה טמאין ומחצה טהורין ונשים עודפות על הטהורים וקסבר *נשים בראשון חובה ובשני רשות בראשון לא עבדי דהוי ליה מיעוט ומיעוטא לא עבדי בראשון ובשני לא עבדי דל נשים מינייהו והוו להו פלגא ופלגא ופלגא לא עבדי בשני ולרב כהנא דאמר פלגא נמי עבדי בשני הכי מתריץ לה כגון שהיו ישראל מחצה טהורין ומחצה טמאין ונשים משלימות לטהורין *וקסבר נשים בראשון חובה ובשני רשות בראשון לא עבדי דהוו להו פלגא ופלגא בראשון לא עבדי בשני נמי לא עבדי דל נשים מינייהו מן הטהורין הוו להו טמאין רובא ורובא לא עבדי בשני ולרב כהנא הא דתניא הרי שהיו ישראל מחצה טהורין ומחצה טמאין הללו עושין לעצמן והללו עושין לעצמן הוכי מתריץ לה אמר לך רב כהנא תנאי היא איכא למ"ד מחצה על מחצה כרוב ואיכא למ"ד מחצה על מחצה אינו כרוב גופא הרי שהיו ישראל מחצה טהורין ומחצה טמאין הללו עושין לעצמן והללו עושין לעצמן ואם היו טמאין עודפין על הטהורין *אפי' אחד יעשו בטומאה *לפי שאין קרבן ציבור חלוק ר"א בן מתיא אומר אין היחיד מכריע את הציבור לטומאה שנאמר

לא

רש"י

וטמאין אין עושין לא את הראשון · דכיון דלאו כרוב לא עבדי בטומאה ובשני נמי לא דלאו מיעוט: יעשו בטומאה · אף הטהורין: רובה הוא כו' · כי איטמי רובה הוא דעבדי טמאין ראשון ובטומאה: אבל פלגא ופלגא לא עבדי · טמאים לראשון כלל: כלהו · אפילו הטהורין אין לריכין להזהר בשמירת טהרה: מסתברא · דפלגא ופלגא נמי טמאין עבדי בטומאה ולא מידחו: לרב · דאמר הללו לעצמן והללו לעצמן: וללישנא בתרא דרב כהנא · דאמר טמאין אין עושין לא זה ולא זה הא דקתני טמאים נדחין לשני היכי מתרצא לה: משלימות לטמאין · דבזכרים הוו טהורים רובא אבל יש מן הנשים טמאות יותר מן הטהורות עד שמשלימות החשבון למחצה על מחצה וקסבר האי תנא נשים בראשון רשות וכ"ש בשני הילכך דל נשים מהכא דאינן מן המניין וזיל בתר זכרים והוו טמאים מיעוטא ומדחו לשני אבל בפלגא ופלגא אי כמר אי כמר: כגון שהיו ישראל · הזכרים מחצה טהורין ומחצה טמאין וכשאתה מונה הנשים עמהן רבין טהורים על הטמאים: בראשון חובה · והרי הן במנין ונמצאו טמאים מיעוטא: ובשני נשים רשות · ותנאי פליגי בהא מילתא בפ' האשה (לקמן דף צא:): בראשון לא עבדי · טמאין דהוה להו מיעוטא: ובשני לא עבדי · דלגבי שני אין הנשים מן המנין למיהוי טהורין רובא הילכך לא הוו טמאים מיעוטא אלא פלגא ולרב מחצה על מחצה כרוב ולא עבדי בשני: ורב כהנא · דאמר פלגא עבדי בשני מתרץ הכי כו': ונשים משלימות לטהורין · שלא היו טהורין מחצה אלא על ידי הנשים ואי אזלינן בתר זכרים הוו טמאין רובא · ועודפות עליהן לא גרסינן: ופלגא בראשון לא עבדי · בטומאה ללישנא קמא דרב כהנא: תנאי היא · האי תנא ותנא דלעיל דקאי כוותיה האי תנא סבר מחצה על מחצה הוי כרוב ותנא דלעיל סבר איתו כרוב: עושין בטומאה · אפילו הטהורין:

לא

[תוספתא פ"ו]

[לקמן צא: סנהדרין יב:]

ס"י ועודפות עליהן היכי דמי כגון דאיכא ד' גברי טהורין ושש נשים טהורו' שיתא גברי טמאין וד' נשים טמאות וקסבר כו' ורש"ל מ"ז:

[מנחות יד: [עו. לעיל ע"ה]]

ואיבעית אימא רב דאמר כר' יהושע *דתניא רבי יהושע אומר (א) כל הזבחים שבתורה בין שנטמא בשר וחלב קיים בין שנטמא חלב ובשר קיים זורק את הדם נזיר ועושה פסח נטמא חלב ובשר קיים זורק את הדם נטמא בשר וחלב קיים אין זורק את הדם ואם זרק הורצה נטמאו הבעלים במת לא יזרוק ואם זרק לא הורצה: במוקדשין אינו כן וכו': מתניתין מני רבי יהושע היא *דתניא רבי יהושע אומר *כל הזבחים שבתורה שנשתייר מהן כזית בשר או כזית חלב זורק את הדם כחצי זית בשר וכחצי זית חלב אין זורק את הדם ובעולה אפילו כחצי זית בשר וכחצי זית חלב זורק את הדם מפני שכולה כליל ובמנחה אע"פ שכולה קיימת לא יזרוק *מנחה מאי עבידתה :זמר רב פפא מנחת נסכים סלקא דעתך אמינא כיון דקא אתיא מכח זבח כגופיה דזבח דמי קמ"ל חלב מנא לן אמר ר' יוחנן משום ר' ישמעאל ומטו בה משום רבי יהושע בן חנניה דאמר קרא °והקטיר החלב לריח ניחוח לה' חלב אע"פ שאין בשר אשכחן חלב יותרת הכבד ושתי כליות מנא לן היכא אמרינן דזרקינן מדקתני ובמנחה אע"פ שכולה קיימת לא יזרוק מנחה הוא דלא אבל יותרת הכבד ושתי הכליות שפיר דמי מנא לן רבי יוחנן דידיה אמר אמר קרא לריח ניחוח כל שאתה מעלה לריח ניחוח ואיצטריך למכתב חלב ואיצטריך למכתב ריח ניחוח דאי כתב רחמנא חלב הוה אמינא חלב אין יותרת הכבד ושתי הכליות לא כתב רחמנא לריח ניחוח ואי כתב רחמנא לריח ניחוח הוה אמינא כל העולין לריח ניחוח ואפי' מנחה כתב רחמנא חלב: **מתני'** ב'נטמא קהל או רובו או שהיו הכהנים טמאים והקהל טהורים יעשו בטומאה נטמא מיעוט הקהל הטהורין עושין את הראשון והטמאין עושין את השני: **גמ'** ת"ר י'הרי שהיו ישראל טמאין וכהנים וכלי שרת טהורין או שהיו ישראל טהורין וכהנים וכלי שרת טמאין ואפילו ישראל וכהנים טהורין וכלי שרת טמאין יעשו בטומאה *שאין קרבן ציבור חלוק אמר רב חסדא ד'לא שנו אלא שנטמא הסכין בטמא מת דרחמנא אמר °בחלל חרב *חרב הרי הוא כחלל וקא מטמא לגברא דמעיקרא כי מיתעביד °בטומאת הגוף דכרת קא מיתעביד ה'אבל נטמא הסכין בטומאת שרץ דבשר הוא דמטמיא ליה לגברא לא מטמיא ליה טהורין עביד טמאין לא עביד מוטב יאכל בטומאת בשר בלאו ואל יאכל בשר בטומאת הגוף שהוא בכרת אלמא קסבר רב חסדא *טומאה דחויה היא בציבור וכן אמר ר' יצחק טומאה דחויה היא בציבור ורבא אמר אפילו טמאין נמי עבדי מאי טעמא דכתיב °והבשר אשר יגע בכל טמא לא יאכל באש ישרף והבשר כל טהור יאכל בשר *כל היכא דלא קרינן ביה והבשר אשר יגע בכל טמא לא יאכל לא קרינן ביה והבשר כל טהור יאכל בשר כל היכא דקרינן ביה והבשר אשר יגע בכל טמא לא יאכל קרינן ביה והבשר כל טהור יאכל בשר *איתמר הרי שהיו ישראל מחצה טהורין ומחצה טמאין רב אמר מחצה על מחצה כרוב ורב כהנא אמר מחצה על מחצה אינו כרוב רב אמר מחצה על מחצה כרוב *והללו עושין לעצמן והללו עושין לעצמן ור"כ אמר מחצה על מחצה אינו כרוב טהורין עושין את הראשון וטמאין עושין את השני איכא דאמרי אמר רב כהנא מחצה על מחצה אינו כרוב טהורין עושין את הראשון וטמאין

רש"י

איבעית אימא רב דאמר · אם זרק הורצה: כרבי יהושע · דאית ליה אכילת פסחים לא מעכבא: שלמי נזיר · תחילתן לאכילה דבעי שילוח שערו תחת הדוד שהשלמים מתבשלין בו כדכתיב (במדבר ו) ולקח את שער ראש נזרו ונתן על האש וגו' ועוד בעי תנופה זרוע בשלה אלמא צריך שיהא בשר תורה אור טהור בשעת זריקה שיהא ראוי למצוה האמורה בו: ואם זרק הורצה · דאכילה לא מעכבא: נטמאו בעלים · במת דלא חזו למיכל לאורתא דטומאתן שבעה: ואם זרק לא הורצה · דאע"ג דאכילתו לא מעכבא גברא דחזי לאכילה בעינן ורחמנא דחייה לטמא נפש לפסח שני ובנזיר נמי כתיב (שם) כי ימות מת עליו וגו' דסותר את נזירותו: חצי זית בשר וחצי זית חלב אין זורק הדם · דאכילת אדם ואכילת מזבח לא מצטרפין: אפי' כולה קיימת לא יזרוק · את הדם עליה: מנחה מאי עבידתיה · בזריקת דם: מנחת נסכים · הבאה עם הזבח מהו דתימא כזבח דמיא ותיהוי במקום זבח להכשיר את הדם: חלב מנא לן · דהוי שיור להכשיר זריקת דם: והקטיר החלב · גבי זריקת דם כתיב דכתיב וזרק הכהן את הדם וגו' עד והקטיר החלב לריח ניחוח: יותרת הכבד ושתי הכליות מנא לן · מדאיצטריך ליה למיתני מנחה לא הויא שיור מכלל דסבירא ליה דהני דגופיה דזבח נינהו הוי שיור: אמר קרא · בהאי קרא גופיה והקטיר החלב לריח ניחוח: **מתני'** יעשו בטומאה · ואפי' טמאין יחידין דהא פסח דטהורין גופיה בטומאה אתי משום כהנים: **גמ'** שאין קרבן צבור · הבא בטומאה חלוק מאחר שקרבן רובן בא בטומאה אף היחיד עושה בטומאה: לא שנו · למשמע משום טומאת כלי שרת עבדי כולהו בטומאה: אלא שנטמאת סכין בטמא מת · שהוא אב הטומאה הדעשה אף הסכין אב הטומאה לטמא אדם: דרחמנא אמר בחלל חרב · למידרש מיניה דכלי מתכת המיטמא במת נעשה כיוצא בזה שנגע בו · טומאה דחויה היא בצבור · בקושי הותרה וכל כמה דאפשר לאהדורי אטהרה או אטומאה קלה מהדרין: קרינא ביה והבשר כל טהור יאכל בשר · ולא טמא: הללו עושין לעצמן · הללו עושין בטומאה · בטהרה והללו עושין לעצמן בטומאה טהורים לא עבדי בטומאה דהוי כרוב ורוב טהורין לא עבדי בטומאה וטמאין לשני לא מידחו משום דהוו כמי רובא ורובא לשני לא מידחו: טהורין עושין הראשון · בטהרה דלאו כמי מיעוטא נינהו אית להו למעבד הראשון בטומאה וכל שכן כי עבדי בטהרה שפיר דמי: וטמאין עושין את השני · דכיון דאינן כרוב נידונין כמיעוט ונידחין לשני:

תוספות

נזיר ועושה פסח נטמא בשר וחלב קיים איט זורק כו' · ריב"א אומר דלא גרס נזיר דאין חילוק בזה בין נזיר לשאר קרבנות ומה שפירש רש"י דבעי שילוח שערו תחת הדוד אין נראה שיהא עיכוב ומה שפי' כמי משום תנופה הא כל שאר שלמים נמי בעו תנופה ולא אשכחן תנא דאית ליה תנופה בנזיר מעכבת אלא ר"א בסוף ג' מינים (נזיר דף מו·) ובתוספתא לא גרס נזיר:

או שהיו כהנים טמאים יעשו בטומאה · אע"פ שיכולין ליזהר שלא יגעו בבשר כיון דאשתראי טומאה אישתראי נמי טומאת בשר דאמר במי שהיה טמא (לקמן דף צ·) כל היכא דאשתראי טומאת הגוף אישתראי טומאת בשר אימורים משמע שהם שוים:

אלא שנטמאת סכין בטומאת מת כו' · תימה א"כ מאי אפי' דקאמר הייטו רישא ממש הוו ישראל טהורים וכהנים וכלי שרת טמאים כיון דמיטמאת גברא מחמת סכין:

בטומאת הגוף דכרת מיתעביד · וא"ת ישחוט בסכין ארוכה ולא יצטרך ליכנס לעזרה א' כמי יאחוז הסכין בפשוטי כלי עץ וישחוט והאמר ר"י דאין פנאי לכל הפסחים לשחוט בענין זה ולאף להביא סכינים אחרים אין פנאי: וטמאין אין היתר מלד טומאת בשר שהוא בלאו רק משום דטומאת גברא דהוא בכרת ואם כן לא תלי כלל ביכולים ליזהר בנגיעת בשר אם לא ואף אם זר ישחוט מכל מקום הזריקה מתעביד בטומאת הגוף דבכרת: שם ד"ה אלא שנטמא וכו' אם כן מאי אפילו. ק"ל הא בדיבור שלאח"ז הקשו דלשחוט בסכין ארוכה וכו' ואם כן זהו גופא החידוש דבכהנים טמאים א"א בלא דחיית כרת דהא יצטרכו לזרוק בטומאה אבל בסכין טמא ס"ד דלא לדחי דהא אפשר בסכין ארוכה והזורק יהיה כהן אחר שהוא טהור מכל מקום דחיא לכרת כתירוצא דתוספות כאן דאין פנאי וצ"ע:

לעיל כב. מז: | זבחים כב. | קמ. מנחות ט. כו. מעילה טו: [בכורות לט:] תוספתא פ"ז תוספתא דזבחים פ"ד | [מנחות כו. כל הסוגיא] | ויקרא ג | [לקמן עמוד ב' מנחות יד: טו.] | במדבר יט | [לעיל יד: וש"נ] | [לקמן פ. יומא ו: ז: מו: זבחים לג.] | ויקרא ז | [לקמן פ.]

הגהות הגר"א

(א) גמ' כל הזבחים כו' זורק את הדם פסח נטמא חלב כו' כצ"ל:

גליון הש"ס

גמ' בטומאת הגוף דבכרת. עי' ר"ש פ"א מ"ד דאהלות: תוס' ד"ה או שהיו וכו' שלא יגעו בבשר. ולא זכיתי לעמוד על עומק דבריהם הקדושים הא

עין משפט נר מצוה

נא א מיי' פ"א מהלכות פסולי מוקדשין הלכה ל:

נב ב ג ד מיי' פ"ז מהלכות ק"פ הלכה א ופ"ד מהלכות ביאת המקדש הלכה יב:

נג ה מיי' פ"ז מהלכות ק"פ הלכה ם:

נד ו שם הלכה כ:

[כל היכא דקרינן ביה והבשר אשר יגע בכל טמא לא יאכל קרינן ביה והבשר כל טהור יאכל בשר וכל היכא דלא קרינן וכו' לא קרינן ביה וכו' כצ"ל וכ"א בילקוט]

רבינו חננאל

ואי בעית אימא רב דאוקמי למתני' לכתחלה אבל דיעבד אם זרק הורצה כר' יהושע דתניא ר' יהושע אומר נזיר ועושה פסח נטמא בשר וחלב קיים אינו זורק את הדם נטמא חלב ובשר קיים זורק את הדם ואם זרק הורצה נטמאו בעלים במת לא יזרוק ואם זרק הורצה. ובמוקדשין אינו כן אע"פ שנטמא בשר וחלב קיים זורק את הדם: תניא ר' יהושע אומר כל הזבחים שבתורה כו'. פשוטה היא [ובמנחה] פי' ובמנחות נסכים הבאה עם הזבח והמנחה כלה קיימת לא יזרוק מהו דתימא כי גופיה דזבח דמיא קמ"ל דלא ואצט' ואי כתב רחמנא לריח ניחוח הוה אמינא כל העולין ואפילו מנחה כתב רחמנא חלב: מתני' נטמאו קהל או רובו או שהיו הכהנים טמאין והקהל טהור יעשה בטומאה כו'. ת"ר הרי שהיו ישראל טמאין וכהנים וכלי שרת טהורין או שהיו ישראל טהורין וכהנים וכלי שרת טמאין יעשו בטומאה שאין קרבן ציבור חלוק אמר רב חסדא לא שנו כלי שרת טמאין יעשו בטומאה אלא בסכין שנטמאת בטמא מת דרחמנא אמר בחלל חרב דהרב הרי הוא כחלל ומטמאה הסכין לאדם דכי קא מתעביד בטומאת הגוף מתעביד דתניא בשאר ספרי דבי רב מגיד שהחרב טמאה טומאת שבעה והנוגע בחרב טמא טומאת שבעה אבל אם נטמא הסכין בטומאת שרץ שאינו מטמא בטומאת סכין אלא הבשר אבל האדם לא דאין כלי הבא מחמת שרץ מטמא אדם וכבר פירשנוה בפ"א: טהורין עושין הפסח טמאין אין עושין מוטב יאכל בטומאת בשר בלאו שנאמר (ויקרא ז יט) והבשר אשר יגע בכל טמא לא יאכל ואל יאכל בטומאת הגוף שהוא בכרת שנאמר (שם ז כ) והנפש אשר תאכל בשר מזבח השלמים אשר לה' וטומאתו עליו ונכרתה הנפש ההיא וגו': אלמא קסבר רב חסדא טומאה דחויה היא בצבור ורבא [אמר] אפילו הטמאים טומאת הגוף נמי עבדי כל היכא דקרינא ביה והבשר אשר יגע בכל טמא לא יאכל הוא דבעינא והבשר כל טהור יאכל בשר כלומר יאכלנו בטהרה ואל יאכלנו בטומאה אבל היכא דהותרה טומאת בשר לא בעינן לדקדק על טומאת הגוף: איתמר הרי שהיו ישראל מחצה טהורין ומחצה טמאין רב אמר מחצה על מחצה כרוב הללו עושין לעצמן בטהרה בראשון והללו עושין לעצמן בטומאה בראשון. רב כהנא אמר מחצה על מחצה אינו כרוב טהורין עושין את הראשון וטמאין עושין את השני איכא דאמרי רב כהנא אמר מחצה על מחצה אינו כרוב טהורין עושין את הראשון וטמאין אינן עושין לא את הראשון ולא את השני ואקשינן עליה דרב מדתנן נטמא קהל או רובו יעשה בטומאה רובו של קהל הוא דעבדו בטומאה אבל פלגא [לא] ומשני רב בזמן שרוב הקהל טמאין עושין הכל בטומאה ואפי' הטהורין אבל בזמן שחצי הקהל טמאין עושין הטמאין בטומאה והטהורין בטהרה ומוקמינן להאי שינויא דודאי [הכי] הוא מדקתני סיפא נטמא מיעוט הקהל טהורין עושין הראשון וטמאין את השני מיעוט עושין את השני אבל חצין של קהל לא אי הכי קשיא לרב כהנא ומשני רב כהנא הכי קתני נטמא מיעוט הקהל טהורין עושין את הראשון וטמאין עושין את השני אבל אם הן מחצה ומחצה טהורין עושין הראשון וטמאין

Continuation of translation from previous page as indicated by ◁

MISHNAH. IF THE COMMUNITY OR THE MAJORITY THEREOF WAS DEFILED, OR IF THE PRIESTS WERE UNCLEAN AND THE COMMUNITY CLEAN, THEY MUST SACRIFICE IN UNCLEANNESS. IF A MINORITY OF THE COMMUNITY WERE DEFILED: THOSE WHO ARE CLEAN OBSERVE THE FIRST [PASSOVER], WHILE THOSE WHO ARE UNCLEAN OBSERVE THE SECOND.

GEMARA. Our Rabbis taught: Behold, if the Israelites were b unclean, while the priests and the service-vessels[1] were clean, or the Israelites were clean while the priests and the service-vessels were unclean, and even if the Israelites and the priests were clean while the service-vessels were unclean, they must sacrifice in uncleanness, because a public sacrifice cannot be divided.[2]

R. Ḥisda said: They learned this only if the [slaughtering] knife became defiled through a person unclean by the dead,[3] because the Divine Law saith, [*and whosoever . . . toucheth*] *one that is slain by the sword,*[4] [intimating,] the sword is [of the same degree of uncleanness] as the slain;[5] hence it defiles the person. Thus from the very beginning when it is sacrificed,[6] it is sacrificed in [a state of] personal uncleanness, which involves *kareth.* But if the knife became unclean with the uncleanness conferred by a reptile, so that it defiles the flesh alone, but does not defile the person, [only] those who are clean sacrifice, but the unclean do not sacrifice, [for] it is better eaten when the *flesh* is unclean, which is subject to a negative injunction, rather than that the flesh should be eaten when the *person* is unclean, which is subject c to *kareth.*[1] This proves that R. Ḥisda holds: Uncleanness is overridden in the case of a community.[2] And thus said R. Isaac [too]: Uncleanness is overridden in the case of a community.

But Raba said: Even the unclean too may sacrifice. What is the reason? Because it is written, *And the flesh that toucheth any unclean thing shall not be eaten; it shall be burnt with fire. And as for the flesh, every one that is clean may eat thereof.*[3] Wherever we read *'and the flesh that toucheth any unclean thing shall not be eaten,'* we [also] read, *'and as for the flesh, every one that is clean may eat thereof;'* and wherever we do not read, *'and the flesh that toucheth any unclean thing shall not be eaten,'* we [also] do not read, *'and as for the flesh, every one that is clean may eat thereof.'*[4]

It was stated: Behold, if the Israelites were half [of them] clean and half unclean,—Rab said: Half against half is as a majority; while R. Kahana said: Half against half is not as a majority. 'Rab said, Half against half is as a majority'; [hence] these sacrifice[5] by themselves, while those sacrifice by themselves.[6] 'While R. Kahana said: Half against half is not as a majority'; [hence] the clean observe the first [Passover], while the unclean observe the second. Others say, R. Kahana said: Half against half is not as

b (1) Used in connection with the sacrifice, the slaughtering knife and basins in which the blood is caught. (2) That some should bring it in a state of cleanness and others in a state of uncleanness. Since the majority bring it in uncleanness, even the minority who are clean bring it in uncleanness too. (3) This is the 'service-vessel' referred to and its degree of uncleanness. (4) Num. XIX, 16. (5) V. *supra* 14*b*. (6) Lit., 'made.'

c (1) V. Misnah *supra* 14a, n. a2 a.l. Now in the first instance the knife bears a principal degree of uncleanness and defiles human beings. Hence the man who kills with it must in any case become unclean, while normally the penalty for eating sacred flesh in this state is *kareth* (v. Lev. VII, 20). But in the second instance the knife is unclean in the first degree only and does not defile the person who handles it, though it defiles the flesh of the animal which is killed with it. Since this is a lower stage, for eating unclean sacred flesh is merely subject to a negative injunction but does not involve *kareth*, we do not permit the greater uncleanness of the person too; hence those who are bodily unclean must observe the second Passover. (2) But not permitted; v. *supra* 77*a*, n. b2. Consequently we seek as far as possible to bring the sacrifice in cleanness or at least with the smallest possible degree of uncleanness. (3) Lev. VII, 19. (4) I.e., the two are interdependent. Since the flesh is now eaten unclean, unclean persons too may eat it. (5) Lit., 'do'. (6) They must all observe the first Passover. The clean must not allow themselves to be defiled, for each half ranks as a majority, and when the majority is clean they must not sacrifice in uncleanness. On the other hand, the unclean half is not relegated to the second Passover, since they too count as a majority.

עין משפט נר מצוה

נא א מיי' פ"ח מהלכות פסולי המוקדשין הלכה ג:
נב ב ג ד מיי' פ"ז מהלכות ק"פ הלכה א ופ"ד מהלכות ביאת המקדש הלכה יב:
נג ה מיי' פ"ז מהלכות ק"פ הלכה ט:
נד ו שם הלכה ב:

מסורת הש"ס

ואיבעית אימא רב דאמר כר' יהושע *דתניא רבי יהושע אומר (א) כל הזבחים שבתורה בין שנטמא בשר וחלב קיים בין שנטמא חלב ובשר קיים זורק את הדם נזיר ועושה פסח נטמא חלב ובשר קיים זורק את הדם נטמא בשר וחלב קיים אין זורק את הדם ואם זרק הורצה נטמאו הבעלים במת לא יזרוק ואם זרק לא הורצה: במוקדשין אינו כן וכו': מתניתין מני רבי יהושע היא *דתניא רבי יהושע אומר *כל הזבחים שבתורה שנשתייר מהן כזית בשר או כזית חלב זורק את הדם כחצי זית בשר וכחצי זית חלב אין זורק את הדם ובעולה אפילו כחצי זית בשר וכחצי זית חלב זורק את הדם מפני שכולה כליל ובמנחה אע"פ שכולה קיימת לא יזרוק *מנחה מאי עבידתה: *אמר רב פפא מנחת נסכים סלקא דעתך אמינא כיון דקא אתיא מכח זבח כגופיה דזבח דמי קמ"ל חלב מנא לן אמר ר' יוחנן משום ר' ישמעאל ומטו בה משום רבי יהושע בן חנניה דאמר קרא °והקטיר החלב לריח ניחוח לה' חלב אע"פ שאין בשר אשכחן חלב יותרת הכבד ושתי כליות מנא לן היכא אמרינן דזרקינן מדקתני ובמנחה אע"פ שכולה קיימת לא יזרוק מנחה הוא דלא אבל יותרת הכבד ושתי הכליות שפיר דמי מנא לן רבי יוחנן דידיה אמר קרא לריח ניחוח כל שאתה מעלה לריח ניחוח ואיצטריך למכתב חלב ואיצטריך למכתב ריח ניחוח דאי כתב רחמנא חלב הוה אמינא חלב אין יותרת הכבד ושתי הכליות לא כתב רחמנא לריח ניחוח ואי כתב רחמנא לריח ניחוח הוה אמינא כל העולין לריח ניחוח ואפי' מנחה כתב רחמנא חלב: **מתני'** נטמא קהל או רובו או שהיו הכהנים טמאים והקהל טהורים יעשו בטומאה נטמא מיעוט הקהל הטהורין עושין את הראשון והטמאין עושין את השני: **גמ'** ת"ר הרי שהיו ישראל טמאין וכהנים וכלי שרת טהורין או שהיו ישראל טהורין וכהנים וכלי שרת טמאין ואפילו ישראל וכהנים טהורים וכלי שרת טמאין יעשו בטומאה *שאין קרבן ציבור חלוק אמר רב חסדא לא שנו אלא שנטמא הסכין בטמא מת דרחמנא אמר °בחלל חרב *חרב הרי הוא כחלל וקא מטמא לגברא דמעיקרא כי מיתעביד *בטומאת הגוף דכרת קא מיתעביד *אבל נטמא הסכין בטומאת שרץ דבשר הוא דמטמיא ליה לגברא לא מטמיא ליה טהורין עביד טמאין לא עביד מוטב יאכל בשר בטומאת בשר בלאו ואל יאכל בשר בטומאת הגוף שהוא בכרת אלמא קסבר רב חסדא *טומאה דחויה היא בציבור וכן אמר ר' יצחק טומאה דחויה היא בציבור ורבא אמר אפילו טמאין נמי עבדי מאי טעמא דכתיב °והבשר אשר יגע בכל טמא לא יאכל באש ישרף והבשר כל טהור יאכל בשר *כל היכא דלא קרינן ביה והבשר אשר יגע בכל טמא לא יאכל לא קרינן ביה והבשר כל טהור יאכל בשר כל היכא דקרינן ביה והבשר אשר יגע בכל טמא לא יאכל קרינן ביה והבשר כל טהור יאכל בשר *איתמר הרי שהיו ישראל מחצה טהורין ומחצה טמאין רב אמר מחצה על מחצה כרוב ורב כהנא אמר מחצה על מחצה אינו כרוב רב אמר מחצה על מחצה כרוב *הללו עושין לעצמן והללו עושין לעצמן ור"כ אמר מחצה על מחצה אינו כרוב טהורין עושין את הראשון וטמאין עושין את השני איכא דאמרי אמר רב כהנא מחצה על מחצה אינו כרוב טהורין עושין את הראשון וטמאין

רש"י

איבעית אימא רב דאמר · אם זרק הורצה כרבי יהושע: דאית ליה אכילת פסחים לא מעכבא: שלמי נזיר · תחילתן לאכילה דבעי שילוח שערו תחת הדוד שהשלמים מתבשלין בו כדכתיב (במדבר ו) ולקח את שער ראש נזרו ונתן על האש וגו' ועוד בעי תנופה זרוע בשלה אלמא צריך שיהא בשר טהור בשעת זריקה שיהא ראוי למצוה האמורה בו: ואם זרק הורצה · דהני לא מעכבי: נטמאו בעלים · במת דלא חזו למיכל לאורתא דטומאתן שבעה: ואם זרק לא הורצה · דאע"ג דאכילתו לא מעכבא גברא דחזי לאכילה בעינן ורחמנא דחייה לטמא נפש לפסח שני ובנזיר נמי כתיב (שם) כי ימות מת עליו וגו' דסותר את נזירותו: חצי זית בשר וחצי זית חלב אין זורק הדם · דאכילת אדם ואכילת מזבח לא מצטרפין: אפי' כולה קיימת לא יזרוק · את הדם עליה: מנחה מאי עבידתיה · בזריקת דם: מנחת נסכים · הבאה עם הזבח מהו דתימא כזבח דמיא ותיהוי במקום זבח להכשיר את הדם: חלב מנא לן · דהוי שיור להכשיר זריקת דם: והקטיר החלב · גבי זריקת דם כתיב דכתיב וזרק הכהן את הדם וגו' עד והקטיר החלב לריח ניחוח: יותרת הכבד ושתי הכליות מנא לן · מדאיצטריך ליה למיתני מנחה לא הויא שיור מכלל דסבירא ליה דהני דגופיה דזבח נינהו הוי שיור: אמר קרא · בהאי קרא גופיה והקטיר החלב לריח ניחוח: **מתני'** יעשו בטומאה · ואפי' טמאין יחידין דהא פסח דטהורין גופיה בטומאה אתי משום כהנים: **גמ'** שאין קרבן צבור · הבא בטומאה חלוק מאחר שקרבן רובן בא בטומאה אף היחיד עושה בטומאה: לא שנו · דמשמע משום טומאת כלי שרת עבדי כולהו בטומאה: אלא שנטמאת סכין בטומאת מת · שהוא אב הטומאה דנעשה אף הסכין אב הטומאה לטמא אדם: דרחמנא אמר בחלל חרב · למידרש מיניה דכלי מתכת המיטמא במת נעשה כיוצא בו: טומאה דחויה היא בצבור · בקושי הותרה וכל כמה דאפשר לאהדורי אטהרה או אטומאה קלה מהדרינן: קרינא ביה והבשר כל טהור יאכל בשר · ולא טמא: הללו עושין לעצמן · הללו עושין לעצמן בטהרה והללו עושין לעצמן בטומאה: טהורים לא עבדי בטומאה דהוי כרוב ורוב טהורין לא עבדי בטומאה וטמאין לשני לא מידחו משום דהוו נמי רובא ורובא לשני לא מידחו: טהורין עושין הראשון · בטהרה דלאו כמי מיעוטא נינהו את להו למעבד הראשון בטומאה וכל שכן כי עבדי בטהרה שפיר דמי: וטמאין עושין את השני · דכיון דאינן כרוב נידונין כמיעוט ונידחין לשני: וטמאין

תוספות

נזיר ועושה פסח נטמא בשר וחלב קיים אינו זורק כו' · ריב"א אומר דלא גרס נזיר דאין חילוק בזה בין נזיר לשאר קרבנות ומה שפירש רש"י דבעי שילוח שערו תחת הדוד אין נראה שיהא עיכוב ומה שפי' נמי משום תנופה הא כל שאר שלמים נמי בעו תנופה ולא אשכחן תנא דאית ליה תנופה בנזיר מעכבת אלא ר"א בסוף ג' מינים (נזיר דף מו:) ובתוספתא לא גרס נזיר:

או שהיו כהנים טמאים יעשו בטומאה · אע"פ שיכולין ליזהר שלא יגעו בבשר כיון דאשתראי טומאת אימורים אישתראי נמי טומאת בשר דאמר במי שהיה טמא (לקמן דף צ:) כל היכא דאשתראי טומאת בשר אישתראי טומאת אימורים משמע שהם שוים:

אלא שנטמא סכין בטמא מת כו' · תימה א"כ מאי אפי' דקאמר דהיינו רישא ממש היו ישראל טהורים והכהנים וכלי שרת טמאים כיון דמיטמאת גברא מחמת סכין:

בטומאת הגוף דכרת מיתעביד · וא"ת ישחוט בסכין ארוכה ולא יצטרך ליכנס לעזרה א"נ כמי יחתוך הסכין בפשוטי כלי עץ וישחוט ואומר ר"י דאין פנאי לכל הפסחים לשחוט בענין זה ואף להביא סכינים אחרים אין פנאי:

הגהות הגר"א

(א) גמ' כל הזבחים כו' זורק את הדם פסח נטמא חלב כו' כצ"ל:

גליון הש"ס

גמ' בטומאת הגוף דכרת. עי' ר"ש פ"א מ"ד דאהלות: תוס' ד"ה או שהיו וכו' שלא יגעו בבשר. ולא זכיתי לעמוד על כוונתו דבכריכה הא קדושים הם:

[כל היכא דקרינן ביה והבשר אשר יגע בכל טמא לא יאכל קרינן ביה והבשר כל טהור יאכל בשר וכל היכא דלא קרינן וכו' לא קרינן ביה וכו' כצ"ל וכ"א בילקוט]

רבינו חננאל

ואי בעית אימא רב דאוקמי למתני' לכתחלה אבל דיעבד אם זרק הורצה כר' יהושע דתניא ר' יהושע אומר נזיר ועושה פסח נטמא בשר וחלב קיים אינו זורק את הדם נטמא חלב ובשר קיים זורק את הדם ואם זרק הורצה נטמאו בעלים במת לא יזרוק ואם זרק הורצה. ובמוקדשין אינו כן אע"פ שנטמא בשר וחלב קיים זורק את הדם: **תניא** ר' יהושע אומר כל הזבחים שבתורה כו'. פשוטה היא [ובמנחה] פי' ובמנחות נסכים הבאה עם הזבח והמנחה כלה קיימת לא יזרוק מהו דתימא כי גופיה דזבח דמיא קמ"ל דלא ואצ"ל ואי כתב רחמנא לריח ניחוח הוה אמינא כל העולין ואפילו מנחה כתב רחמנא חלב: **מתני'** נטמאו קהל או רובו או שהיו הכהנים טמאין והקהל טהור יעשה בטומאה כו'. ת"ר הרי שהיו ישראל טמאין וכהנים וכלי שרת טהורין או שהיו ישראל טהורין וכהנים וכלי שרת טמאין **יעשו** בטומאה שאין קרבן ציבור חלוק אמר רב חסדא לא שנו כלי שרת טמאין יעשו בטומאה אלא בסכין שנטמאת בטמא מת דרחמנא אמר בחלל חרב דחרב הרי הוא כחלל ומטמאה הסכין לאדם דכי קא מתעביד בטומאת הגוף מתעביד דתניא בשאר ספרי דבי רב מגיד שהחרב טמאה טומאת שבעה והנוגע בחרב טמא טומאת שבעה אבל אם נטמא הסכין בטומאת שרץ שאינו מטמא בטומאת סכין אלא הבשר אבל האדם לא דאין כלי הבא מחמת שרץ מטמא אדם וכבר פירשנוה בפ"א: **טהורין** עושין הפסח טמאין אין עושין מוטב יאכל בטומאת בשר בלאו שנאמר (ויקרא ז יט) והבשר אשר יגע בכל טמא לא יאכל ואל יאכל בטומאת הגוף שהוא בכרת שנאמר (שם ז כ) והנפש אשר תאכל בשר מזבח השלמים אשר לה' וטומאתו עליו ונכרתה הנפש ההיא וגו': **אלמא** קסבר רב חסדא טומאה דחויה היא בצבור ורבא [אמר] אפילו הטמאים טומאת הגוף נמי עבדי כל היכא דקרינא ביה והבשר אשר יגע בכל טמא לא יאכל הוא דבעינא והבשר כל טהור יאכל בשר כלומר יאכלנו בטהרה ואל יאכלנו בטומאה אבל היכא דהותרה טומאת בשר לא בעינן לדקדק על טומאת הגוף: **איתמר** הרי שהיו ישראל מחצה טהורין ומחצה טמאין רב אמר מחצה על מחצה כרוב הללו עושין לעצמן בטהרה בראשון והללו עושין לעצמן בטומאה בראשון. רב כהנא אמר מחצה על מחצה אינו כרוב טהורין עושין את הראשון וטמאין עושין את השני איכא דאמרי רב כהנא אמר מחצה על מחצה אינו כרוב טהורין עושין את הראשון וטמאין אינן עושין לא את הראשון ולא את השני ואקשינן עליה דרב מדתנן נטמא קהל או רובו יעשה בטומאה רובו של קהל הוא דעבדו בטומאה אבל פלגא [לא] ומשני רב בזמן שרוב הקהל טמאין עושין הכל בטומאה ואפי' הטהורין אבל בזמן שחצי הקהל טמאין עושין הטמאין בטומאה והטהורין בטהרה ומוקמינן להאי שינויא דודאי [הכי] הוא מדקתני סיפא נטמא מיעוט הקהל טהורין עושין הראשון וטמאין את השני מיעוט השני אבל חצין של קהל לא אי הכי קשיא לרב כהנא ומשני רב כהנא הכי קתני נטמא מיעוט הקהל טהורין עושין את הראשון וטמאין עושין את השני אבל אם הן מחצה ומחצה טהורין עושין הראשון וטמאין

[79a] Alternatively I may answer, Rab ruled as R. Joshua.[5] For it was taught, R. Joshua said: [In the case of] all the sacrifices of the Torah, whether the flesh was defiled while the fat has remained [clean] or the fat was defiled while the flesh has remained [clean], he must sprinkle the blood. [In the case of] a nazirite[6] and one who sacrifices the Passover-offering, if the fat was defiled and the flesh has remained [clean], he must sprinkle the blood; if the flesh was defiled while the fat has remained [clean], he must not sprinkle the blood. Yet if he sprinkled it, it is acceptable.[7] If the owners became unclean through a dead body, he must not sprinkle [the blood], and if he does sprinkle the blood it is not acceptable.[8]

BUT IN THE CASE OF [OTHER] DEDICATED SACRIFICES IT IS NOT SO etc. Who is [the author of] our Mishnah?—It is R. Joshua. For it was taught, R. Joshua said: [With regard to] all the sacrifices of the Torah of which as much as an olive of flesh or an olive of fat has remained [clean], he sprinkles the blood. [If there remains] as much as half an olive of flesh and half an olive of fat, he must not sprinkle the blood. But in the case of a burnt-offering, even [if there remains] as much as half an olive of flesh and half an olive of fat, he sprinkles the blood, because the whole of it is entirely [burnt].[1] While in the case of a meal-offering, even if the whole of it is in existence,[2] he must not sprinkle [the blood]. What business has a meal-offering [here]?[3]—Said R. Papa: [This refers to] the meal-offering of libations.[4] You might have said, Since it comes in virtue of[5] the sacrifice, it is as the sacrifice:[6] hence he informs us [that it is not so].

How do we know [it of] fat?[7] Said R. Joḥanan on R. Ishmael's authority, while it is [ultimately] derived from R. Joshua b. Ḥananiah: Scripture saith, [*And the priest shall sprinkle the blood . . .*] *and burn the fat* [ḥeleb] *for a sweet savour unto the Lord:*[8] the fat [authorizes the sprinkling of the blood] even if there is no flesh. We have thus found [this to hold good of] fat; how do we know it of the lobe above the liver and the two kidneys?[9] [But] where have we said that we do sprinkle?[10] Since he states, 'while in the case of a meal-offering, even if the whole of it is in existence, we do not sprinkle [the blood],' [that implies,] the meal-offering alone is not [sufficient for the sprinkling of the blood], but the lobe above the liver and the two kidneys are well.[11] Whence [then] do we know it?—R. Joḥanan, giving his own [exegesis] said: Scripture saith, *'for a sweet savour'*: whatever you offer up for a sweet savour.[12]

Now, it is necessary that both *'ḥeleb'* and *'for a sweet savour'* be written. For if the Divine Law wrote *'ḥeleb'* [alone], I would say: only 'fat', but not the lobe on the liver and the two kidneys; [therefore] the Divine Law wrote *'for a sweet savour.'* While if the Divine Law wrote *'for a sweet savour'* [alone], I would say: all that ascend for a sweet savour, and even the meal-offering [permit the sprinkling of the blood]; therefore the Divine Law wrote *'ḥeleb.'*

(5) Who does not consider the eating indispensable. (6) Rashi: the peace-offering brought by a nazirite on the completion of his naziriteship (v. Num. VI, 14) is essentially intended to be eaten: hence the eating is indispensable. Tosaf. however maintains that it is not indispensable, and deletes 'nazirite,' adding that it is absent in the Tosef. too; BaḤ also deletes it. (7) Thus the eating is not indispensable. (8) Because though the eating is not indispensable, the people registered for it must be fit to eat, while Scripture itself relegated him to the second Passover (Num. IX, 10f).

(1) Since both the flesh and the fat are food for the altar, they combine. But this does not hold good of other sacrifices. (2) I.e., it is clean. (3) There is no blood to sprinkle in a meal-offering (4) Which accompanied the sacrifice. (5) Lit., 'by the strength of.' (6) Hence if as much as an olive of the flour is clean, and certainly if all is clean, the blood is sprinkled. (7) *Sc.* that the blood may be sprinkled if there is as much as an olive of clean fat? (8) Lev. XVII, 6. (9) That the blood is to be sprinkled if these alone are clean. (10) If these alone are left. (11) I.e., since they are part of the sacrifice itself, the blood is sprinkled if they alone are clean. (12) Authorizes by itself the sprinkling of the blood.

◁ *For the continuation of the English translation of this page see overleaf.*

but not R. Joshua? [78b] Surely you have said, even R. Joshua agrees in the case of a community! Rather [explain it thus:] I agree with the words of R. Eliezer where it was done [offered], and with the words of R. Joshua [where it is] at the very outset. [But] if it was done, even R. Joshua agrees, for it is taught: R. Joshua agrees that if he sprinkled [the blood] it is made acceptable?—One refers to uncleanness; the other to [the case where it] is lost or burnt. [Thus:] when does he teach, R. Joshua agrees that if he sprinkled [the blood] it is made acceptable, where [the flesh] was defiled, but not if it was lost or burnt; [and] when does R. Jose say, I agree with the words of R. Eliezer if it was done, where [the flesh] was lost or burnt.

a *MISHNAH*. IF THE FLESH WAS DEFILED WHILE THE FAT[1] HAS REMAINED [CLEAN], HE MUST NOT SPRINKLE THE BLOOD;[2] IF THE FAT WAS DEFILED WHILE THE FLESH HAS REMAINED [CLEAN], HE MUST SPRINKLE THE BLOOD. BUT IN THE CASE OF [OTHER] DEDICATED SACRIFICES IT IS NOT SO, FOR EVEN IF THE FLESH WAS DEFILED WHILE THE FAT HAS REMAINED CLEAN, HE MUST SPRINKLE THE BLOOD.[3]

GEMARA. R. Giddal said in Rab's name: If he sprinkled [the blood], it [the Passover-offering] is made acceptable.[4] But we require eating?[5]—The eating is not indispensable. But surely it is written, *according to every man's eating [ye shall make your count for the lamb]*?[6]—That is for preference.[7] And is [this] not [to intimate that] it is indispensable? Surely it was taught: *According to the number of* [bemiksath] *the souls:*[8] this teaches that the paschal lamb is killed for none save those who registered for it. You might think that if he killed it for those who are not registered for it, he should be regarded as violating the precept, yet it is fit. Therefore it is stated, '*according to every man's eating . . . ye shall make your count* [takosu]': The Writ reiterated it, to teach that it is indis-
b pensable; and eaters are assimilated to registered persons.[1]—Rather, Rab ruled as R. Nathan, who said: The eating of the Passover-offerings is not indispensable. Which [statement of] R. Nathan [is alluded to]?[2] Shall we say, the following [dictum] of R. Nathan? For it was taught, R. Nathan said: How do we know that all Israel can discharge [their obligation] with one Passover-offering? Because it is said, *and the whole assembly of the congregation of Israel shall kill it at dusk:*[3] does then the whole assembly kill? Surely only one kills! But it teaches that all Israel can discharge [their duty] with one Passover-offering.[4] Perhaps it is different there, because if some withdraw it is fit for the others, and if the others withdraw it is fit for these?[5]—Rather it is this [dictum of] R. Nathan. For it was taught: If one company registered for it, and then another company registered for it, the former, for whom there is as much as an olive [per person], eat it and are exempt from sacrificing a second Passover-offering; the latter, for whom there is not as much as an olive [per person], cannot eat, and they are bound to sacrifice a second Passover-offering. R. Nathan said: Both are exempt from sacrificing a second Passover-offering, because the blood has already been sprinkled.[6] Yet still perhaps it is different there, because if these withdraw it is fit for them [the others]?[5]—If so, let him teach, because it is possible for them[7] to withdraw? Why [state] 'because the blood has already been sprinkled?' That proves that the matter depends [entirely] on [the sprinkling of] the blood, but the eating is not indispensable.

Now, what compels Rab to establish our Mishnah as meaning in the first place [only] and [in accordance with] R. Nathan: let us
c establish it as [agreeing with] the Rabbis, and even if it was done,[1] it is not [fit]?—To Rab our Mishnah presents a difficulty: why does it state, HE MUST NOT SPRINKLE THE BLOOD: let it teach, 'It is unfit'? Hence this proves that he must not sprinkle in the first place [only], but if done it is indeed well.

But on R. Nathan's view, what is the purpose of, '*according to every man's eating?*'—[To teach] that we require men who are fit to eat [to register for it].

Who is the author of the following which our Rabbis taught: If he slaughtered it for those who can eat of it, but sprinkled its blood for those who cannot eat of it, the Paschal-offering itself is fit,[2] and a man discharges his duty therewith? With whom [does this agree]? Shall we say [that] it is [according to] R. Nathan, but not the Rabbis?—You may even say [that it agrees with] the Rabbis: There is no intention of eaters at the sprinkling.[3]

Who is the author of the following which our Rabbis taught: If he was ill at the time of the slaughtering but well at the time of sprinkling, [or] well at the time of slaughtering but ill at the time of sprinkling, one may not slaughter and sprinkle on his behalf, unless he is well from the time of the slaughtering until the time of the sprinkling? With whom [does this agree]? Shall we say [that] it is [according to] the Rabbis but not R. Nathan?—You may even say [that it agrees with] R. Nathan: we require a man who is capable of eating [to be registered for it].

Who is the author of the following which our Rabbis taught: If he slaughtered it in cleanness and then its owners became unclean, he must sprinkle the blood in cleanness,[4] but the flesh must not be eaten in uncleanness? With whom [does this agree]?—Said R. Eleazar: This was taught as a controversy, and it is [the view of] R. Nathan.[5] But R. Johanan said: You may even say [that] it is [the view of] the Rabbis: we treat here of the com-
d munity,[1] who may even sacrifice in [a state of] uncleanness. If it refers to the community, why may the flesh not be eaten in uncleanness?—As a preventive measure, lest the owners[2] become unclean [in a subsequent year] *after* the sprinkling and they argue: Were we not unclean last year, and yet we ate; then now too we will eat! But they will not know that in the previous year the owners were unclean when the blood was sprinkled,[3] whereas this year the owners were clean [when the blood was sprinkled].[4]

a (1) The portions burnt on the altar. (2) Even according to R. Eliezer, because the main purpose of the Passover-offering is that it should be eaten. (3) Even according to R. Joshua, since the fat is clean. (4) And the owner does not bring another. (5) Which is impossible, since the flesh is defiled. (6) Ex. XII, 4. (7) Lit., 'for a precept'. I.e., in the first place the lamb must certainly be brought for this purpose; nevertheless, even when it cannot be eaten the sacrifice is valid. (8) Ibid.

b (1) Just as registration is indispensable, so are eaters, and consequently eating, indispensable. (2) For he does not rule thus *explicitly*, and it must be inferred from some other statement. (3) Ex. XII, 6. (4) Now in that case there is certainly not as much as an olive of flesh for each, which is the minimum to constitute eating. (5) So that virtually it is fit for all, but in the present case it is not fit for any. (6) Which proves that in R. Nathan's view the eating is not indispensable. (7) Lit., 'they are fit, eligible.'

c (1) I.e., even if the blood was sprinkled. (2) This is assumed to mean that it is fit for the sprinkling of its blood and the burning of the fat, but not for eating. (3) V. *supra* 61b. (4) I.e., by ritually clean priests and with clean service vessels. (5) Who maintains that the eating is not indispensable. R. Eleazar holds that he does not require those registered for it even to be fit to eat. Consequently he explains the previous Baraitha as the view of the Rabbis only

d (1) I.e., the whole or the majority of the community became unclean between the killing and the sprinkling, e.g., if the *nasi* died just then. (2) I.e., the community, cf. n. d1. (3) So that it was a Passover-offering sacrificed in uncleanness, which is eaten in uncleanness too. (4) Hence the sacrifice came in a state of cleanness, and may therefore not be eaten now that the owners are unclean.

הא אמרת בציבור אפילו רבי יהושע מודה אלא רואה אני דברי ר"א בדיעבד ודברי ר' יהושע לכתחלה דיעבד אפילו רבי יהושע נמי מודה הוא דקתני מודה רבי יהושע שאם זרק הורצה הא בטומאה הא באבוד ושרוף כי קתני מודה רבי יהושע שאם זרק הורצה בנטמא *אבל באבוד ושרוף לא כי קאמר ר' יוסי רואה אני את דברי ר"א בדיעבד באבוד ושרוף: **מתני'** נטמא בשר וחלב קיים אינו זורק את הדם נטמא החלב והבשר קיים זורק את הדם ובמוקדשים אינו כן אלא אע"פ שנטמא הבשר והחלב קיים זורק את הדם: **גמ'** אמר רב גידל אמר רב אם זרק הורצה והא בעינן *אכילה אכילה לא מעכבא והא כתיב °איש לפי אכלו למצוה ולעכב לא והתניא* °במכסת מלמד שאין הפסח נשחט אלא למנויו יכול שחטו שלא למנויו יהא כעובר על המצוה וכשר ת"ל איש לפי אכלו תכוסו *הכתוב שנה עליו לעכב ואיתקש אוכלין למנויין אלא רב דאמר כרבי נתן דאמר *אכילת פסחים לא מעכבא הי רבי נתן אילימא הא רבי נתן דתניא *רבי נתן אומר מנין שכל ישראל יוצאין בפסח אחד ת"ל °ושחטו אותו כל קהל עדת ישראל בין הערבים וכי כל הקהל שוחטין והלא אין שוחט אלא אחד אלא מלמד שכל ישראל יוצאין בפסח אחד דילמא שאני התם דאי ממשכי הני חזי להני ואי ממשכי הני חזי להני אלא הא ר' נתן דתניא נמנו עליו חבורה אחת וחזרו ונמנו עליו חבורה אחרת ראשונים שיש להן כזית אוכלין ופטורין מלעשות פסח שני אחרונים שאין להם כזית אין אוכלין וחייבין לעשות פסח שני רבי נתן אומר אלו ואלו פטורין מלעשות פסח שני שכבר נזרק הדם אבתי דילמא שאני התם דאי ממשכי הני חזי להו א"כ ליתני הואיל וראויים לימשך מאי שכבר נזרק הדם ש"מ בדם תליא מילתא אבל אכילה לא מעכבא מאי דוחקיה דרב דמוקים לה מתני' לכתחלה ור' נתן נוקמה כרבנן ואפילו דיעבד נמי לא רב מתני' קשיתיה אמאי (תני) אין זורק את הדם ליתני פסול אלא שמע מינה אין זורק לכתחלה אבל דיעבד שפיר דמי ולר' נתן איש לפי אכלו למה לי דבעינן גברא דחזי לאכילה מאן תנא להא דתנו רבנן שחטו לאוכליו *וזרקו דמו שלא לאוכליו הפסח עצמו כשר ואדם יוצא בו ידי חובתו כמאן נימא רבי נתן היא ולא רבנן אפילו תימא רבנן* אין מחשבת אוכלין בזריקה מאן תנא להא דתנו רבנן הרי שהיה חולה בשעת שחיטה וחלים בשעת זריקה חלים בשעת שחיטה וחולה בשעת זריקה אין שוחטין וזורקין עליו עד שיהא חלים משעת שחיטה עד שעת זריקה כמאן נימא רבנן היא ולא רבי נתן אפילו תימא רבי נתן גברא דחזי לאכילה בעינן מאן תנא להא דתנו רבנן שחטו בטהרה ואחר כך נטמאו הבעלים יזרק הדם בטהרה ואל יאכל בשר בטומאה כמאן אמר רבי (אליעזר) במחלוקת שנויה ורבי נתן היא ורבי יוחנן אמר אפילו תימא רבנן היא הכא במאי עסקינן בציבור דאפילו בטומאה נמי עבדי אי בציבור אמאי אין הבשר נאכל בטומאה גזירה שמא יטמאו הבעלים לאחר זריקה ויאמרו אשתקד לא נטמאנו ואכלנו השתא נמי ניכול ולא ידעי דאשתקד כי איזדריק דם בעלים טהורין הוו השתא בעלים טמאים הוו ואיבעית

רש"י

אלא · תרוייהו ביחיד והא לכתחלה והא דיעבד והא דקתני אם זרק הורצה ואוקימנא ביחיד ה"מ דמודה רבי יהושע בדיעבד בנטמא דהא עלה קאי ומשום דאיתיה בעינא אבל באבוד ושרוף לא ור' יוסי אפי' נשרפו או אבדו שיריה קאמר אם הקטיר קומלה כשירה: **מתני'** נטמא בשר וחלב קיים אין זורק את הדם · אפי' לר' אליעזר דעיקר פסח לאכילת אדם קאתי: ובמוקדשין אינו כן · אפילו לר' יהושע שאפילו נטמא בשר וחלב קיים זורק את הדם דהא הדם תרתי אכלה מתיר ושיריים שהדם מתיר אימורין למזבח: **גמ'** הורצה · ופטור מלעשות פסח שני: לא מעכבא · כפרה בדיעבד: אוכלין חולה וזקן: רב · דאית ליה אכילת פסחים לא מעכבא דאמר כר' נתן: יולאין בפסח אחד · ואע"פ שאין בו כזית לכל אחד אלמא אכילה לא מעכבא: דאי מימשכי הני · מה שיש בהן יותר מכזית לכל אחד חזי להני הנשארים: ואי מימשכי הני כו' · אוכלים אחרים דחזו לכולהו דהי מינייהו מפקא הלכך אע"ג דלא אימשיך חד מינייהו פטורין אבל נטמא לא חזי אפילו לאחד: נימנו עליו · עד שהיה כזית לכל אחד: ומאי דוחקיה דרב · לאוקמא למתני' כר' נתן דלא מעכבא ולמימרא דמתני' לכתחלה קאמר הא אם זרק הורצה: נוקמה כרבנן · ונימא דמתני' אפי' בדיעבד פסול: פסח עלמו כשר · קס"ד לזרוק דמו ולהקטיר חלבו אבל לאכילה לא וקתני ואדם יולא בו ידי חובתו: אין מחשבת אוכלין · חולה וזקן בזריקת דם דאיש לפי אכלו לגבי שחיטה כתיב: חלים · בריא: גברא דחזי לאכילה בעי' · דכי כתיב איש לפי אכלו אגברא כתיב דליהוי גברא בר אכילה אבל פסח לא איכפת לן אי לא חזי: יזרק בטהרה · בכהנים ובכלי שרת טהורין: ור' נתן היא · דאמר אכילה לא מעכבא ולא בעי ר' נתן גברא דחזי לאכילה ומתניתא קמייתא מוקי ר' אלעזר כרבנן: הכא במאי עסקינן בציבור · שנטמאו רוב ציבור בין שחיטה לזריקה כגון שמת הנשיא ונטמאו הילכך גברי דחזו לאכילה ניגהו: גזירה שמא · לשנה אחרת יטמאו ציבור אחר זריקה: ויאמרו אשתקד · מי לא היינו טמאין בשעת אכילה ואכלנו ואע"פ ששחיטתו בטהרה השתא נמי אע"פ ששחיטתו וזריקתו בטהרה ניכול בשר בטומאה ולא ידעי דאשתקד בעידנא דהוי זריקת דם טמאין הוו והוה ליה פסח הבא בטומאה:

תוספות

הא אמרת בציבור אפילו רבי יהושע מודה · תימה לרשב"א מאי קושיא דילמא ה"ק רואה אני דברי רבי אליעזר בציבור שאף ר' יהושע לא אמר אלא ביחיד דכי האי גוונא אמרי' פ"ק דחולין (דף יב·) וכמה דוכתי ואומר ר"י דהכא לא שייך למימר הכי דלא קתני בברייתא לא בציבור ולא ביחיד: **כי** מודה בנטמא · משום דלית מרלה: **ולעכב** לא והתניא במכסת נפשות · תימה לר"י והא קרא בשחיטה כתיב ומהתם נפקא למחשבת אוכלין פסלה בשחיטה אבל בזריקה אמרן לעיל דאין מחשבת אוכלין בזריקה והיכי פריך משחיטה לזריקה ואומר ר"י דווקא מחשבת אוכלין ליתא בזריקה אלא בשחיטה אבל כשאין לו אוכלין לגמרי אף בשעת זריקה סברא היא דפסול שהיא עיקר עבודה כיון דבשעת שחיטה הקפיד הכתוב אפילו אמחשבה: **שאני** התם דאי מימשכי הני כו' · תימה לרשב"א והא בשעת זריקה אינם יכולים לימשך ומנלה הפסח לא חזי לאכילה וי"ל דדילמא ר' נתן סבר כר"ש דתנן לקמן בפרק האשה (דף פט·) נמנין ומושכין ידיהם עד שיזרק הדם אי נמי טמאתו מקרקן או שמתו חזי להני: **ולרבי** נתן איש לפי אכלו למה לי דבעינן גברא דחזי לאכילה · וא"ת לרבנן נמי ליפשי הכי לעיל כי פריך ולעכב לא לימא כי אתא קרא לעכב היינו דבעינן גברא חזי לאכילה אבל בשר לא ולאו פירכא היא דרבנן בעו בשר חזי לאכילה כדקתניא לעיל אחרונים שאין להם כזית אינם אוכלין וחייבין לעשות פסח שני והא נמי לא תיקשי אמאי לא מסגי לר' נתן איש לפי אכלו למלוה כדבעי למימר לעיל משום דלא אשכחן תנא דלא מקיש אוכלין למנויין אלא זקני דרום לחודייהו בפרק שני דזבחים (דף כג·) ולמאי דמוקי מתני' כר' נתן נ"ל דיולאין בפסח אחד דקאמר היינו דווקא דיעבד: **לימא** ר' נתן היא כו' · תימה לר"י והיכי מיתוקמא כר' נתן והא ר' נתן ורבנן לא פליגי אלא בבשר אבל בגברא לכ"ע בעינן גברא דחזי לאכילה ועוד א"כ אפילו שחטו שלא לאוכליו נמי ולמאי נקט שחטו לאוכליו ועוד היכי תיסק אדעתיה למימר השתא דיש מחשבת אוכלין בזריקה הא פשוט בכולי גמרא דאין מחשבת אוכלין בזריקה כדמוכח בזבחים (דף ד·) ובתמיד נשחט לעיל (דס"ז·)* ושם הבאתי ונראה לר"י דה"פ נזרק דמו שלא לאוכליו לא שנזרק שלא לשם אוכליו אלא שבשעת זריקה היו הבעלים חולים והשתא קאמר כמאן כר' נתן דמשמע ליה כיון דר' נתן מיקל כולי האי ולא בעי שיהא בשר ראוי לאכילה ה"נ לא חייש אם אין בעלים ראויין בשעת זריקה אבל רבנן דמחמרי ובעו שיהא בשר ראוי לאכילה ה"ה דבעו שיהו הבעלים ראויים לאכילה בשעת זריקה וה"נ סבר ר' אלעזר בסמוך דלא בעי ר' נתן גברא חזי אלא בשחיטה דווקא:

נזיר

עין משפט נר מצוה

מג א מיי' פ"א מהלכות פסולי המוקדשין הלכה לא:
מד ב מיי' פ"ד מהלכות ק"פ הלכה כ:
מה ג מיי' פ"א מהלכות פסולי המוקדשין הלכה לד:
מו ד מיי' פ"ב מהלכות ק"פ הלכה יד:
מז ה מיי' פ"ד מהלכות קרבן פסח הלכה כג:
מח ו מיי' פ"ב מהל' ק"פ הלכה ו:
מט ח שם הלכה ג:
נ ט מיי' פ"ז מהלכות ק"פ הלכה ט:

רבינו חננאל

הא לכתחלה הא דיעבד רואה אני דברי ר' אליעזר דיעבד כיון שיש דם אע"פ שאין בשר כיפר אבל זה שאומר ר' אליעזר אפי' לכתחלה יזרוק הדם אע"פ שאין בשר אין אני רואה דבריו בזה אלא דברי ר' יהושע אני רואה בזה שלכתחלה לא יזרוק אלא אם יש בשר טהור ראוי לאכילה: איני והא מדקתני ומודה ר' יהושע שאם זרק הורצה כלומר בדיעבד אפי' ר' יהושע מודה וזה הוצרך ר' יוסי לומר רואה אני דברי ר' אליעזר בדיעבד והוא דברי הכל הוא אמרינן מודה בדיעבד בנטמא בלבד אבל באבוד ושרוף פליג ר' יהושע דאפילו דיעבד לא הורצה ואאבוד ושרוף אומר ר' יוסי רואה אני דברי ר' אליעזר דאיעבד הורצה וכר' אליעזר ולכתחלה לא יעשה כר' יהושע: אית לן למימר כיון דסוגיא דשמעתין מ"ד דציץ מרצה על אכילות אמאי תני הני חמשה דברים דתנינן במתני' אין נאכלין אית לן למימר הא דאמרי' דציץ מרצה על אכילות לאו להתירן לאכול בטומאה הוא דתנא אלא לדברים אחרים כגון הא דתנינן במנחות נטמאת אחת מן החלות או אחת מן הסדרים ר' יהודה אומר שניהם ישרפו וחכ"א הטמא בטומאתו והטהור יאכל ואמר רב פפא עלה בציץ מרצה על אכילות מפליגי רבנן סברי כיון דאלו נאכל הציץ מרצה עליהן כטהורין חשבינן להו הלכך אותם שלא נטמאו אינן נפסלין בטומאה אלא הטהורין נאכלין והטמאין נשרפין . וסוגיא דשמעתא נמי אהאי ארהא איכא אית לן לאוקמה: נטמא בשר וחלב קיים אינו זורק את הדם נטמא חלב כו' אמר רב אם זרק הורצה ואע"פ שהבשר טמא אכילת פסחים לא מעכבא איני והכתיב איש לפי אכלו למצוה אבל לעכב לא והתניא במכסת מלמד כו' אמר רב דאמר כר' נתן דסבר כל ישראל יוצאין בפסח אחד וכי כל ישראל אכלין מפסח אחד אלא ש"מ אכילת פסחים לא מעכבא ודילמא שאני התם דאי ממשכי הני חזי להני ואי ממשכי הני חזי להני אלא הא ר' נתן דתניא נמנו עליו וחזרו ונמנו עליו ראשונים שיש להם כזית (חייבין לעשו' פסח)

אוכלין ופטורין מלעשות פסח שני האחרונים שאין להם כזית חייבין לעשות פסח שני ר' נתן אומר אלו ואלו פטורין מלעשות פסח שני שכבר נזרק הדם ש"מ לר' נתן אכילת פסחים לא מעכבא ומאי דוחקיה דרב לאוקמה למתני'

מסורת הש"ס

[זבחים ק:]
לעיל סא. ע"ש זבחים כג. ע"ש
[לעיל סא. וש"נ]
[לעיל סט:]
קידושין מא: מג: ובס"ש א"י ר' יונתן]
[צ"ל תנן]
[עי' תוס' לעיל סא. ד"ה שחטו] [לעיל סא:]
[צ"ל אלעזר]

מסורת הש"ס

[לעיל עו.] מנחות כה:

[זבחים כח:]

יומא ד. ח.

[לעיל עז:]

עין משפט נר מצוה

מא א מיי' פ"ד מהל' פסולי מוקדשין הלכה לד:

מב ב מיי' פ"א מהל' עבודת יום הכפורים הלכה ד

[עי' יומא ח.]

הא לא קשיא הא ביחיד והא בציבור · פי' בקונטרס דסבירא לן טומאה הותרה בציבור וקשה דה"ל למימר אלא קסבר רבי יהושע טומאה הותרה בציבור כדמסיק לעיל דקסבר ציץ מרצה על אכילות ועוד היכי קאמר בסמוך נימא דלא כרבי יוסי דאמר אין הציץ מרצה על אכילות מהאי טעמא גופיה דטומאה הותרה בציבור דאוקימנא כרבי יהושע אתי נמי כר' יוסי* כדקאמר נמי לבסוף ונראה לר"י דלעולם סבירא ליה טומאה דחויה אלא דסבירא ליה דהציץ מרצה על אכילות וביחיד לכתחלה לא יזרוק מדרבנן ופסולה דקתני היינו לכתחלה הלכך בציבור באין לכתחלה ואם תאמר ומאי איכא בין ציבור ליחיד הואיל ומדאורייתא ביחיד נמי זורק לכתחלה יש לומר טומאת הגוף איכא בינייהו דבציבור דחיא ביחיד לא דחיא:

מכלל דרבי יוסי כרבי יהושע ס"ל · תימה לרשב"א מנא ליה הא דילמא כר' אליעזר סבירא ליה ואין הציץ מרצה על אכילות נפקא מינה לשתי הלחם:

והא עיקר קראי בזבחים כתיבי · תימה לר"י דלא ניקום לקמן דקאמר במנחות פרק קמא (דף ט:) שירים שחסרו בין קמיצה להקטרה אין מקטיר קומץ עליהן אדרבה קראי במנחות כתיבי דבזבחים כיון שנשתייר כזית בשר זורק את הדם ומשמע התם דטעמיה מקרא דכתיב המנחה מיהו לרבי יוחנן דפליג עליה התם אתי שפיר:

אלא לא קשיא *כאן ביחיד כאן בציבור נימא מתני' דלא כר' יוסי *דתניא ר"א אומר הציץ מרצה על אכילות רבי יוסי אומר אין הציץ מרצה על אכילות קס"ד מדקאמר ר' יוסי אין הציץ מרצה על אכילות כר' יהושע ס"ל דאמר בעינן תרתי נימא השתא מתני' דלא כר' יוסי לא ר' יוסי כר"א ס"ל דאמר דם אע"פ שאין בשר אי הכי למאי הלכתא אין הציץ מרצה על אכילות וליטעמיך ר"א דאמר הציץ מרצה כיון דאמר דם אע"פ שאין בשר הציץ מרצה על אכילות למאי הלכתא אלא למיקבעיה בפיגול ולאפוקי מידי מעילה קמיפלגי רבי אליעזר סבר מרצה ציץ עילויה ומשוי ליה כטהור וקבע ליה בפיגול ומפיק ליה מידי מעילה ור' יוסי סבר לא מרצה ציץ עילויה ולא משוי ליה כטהור ולא קבע ליה בפיגול ולא מפיק ליה מידי מעילה מתקיף לה רב מרי נהי נמי דרבי יוסי סבר כר"א בשלמא זבחים איכא דם עומר נמי איכא קומץ לחם הפנים נמי איכא בזיכין אלא שתי הלחם מאי איכא למימר וכ"ת לקרב עמהן (א)היינו שלמי ציבור א"כ הוו להו ארבעה ואנן חמשה תנן אלא קסבר רבי יוסי טומאה הותרה בציבור והא *תניא אחד זה ואחד זה מזין עליו כל שבעה מכל חטאות שהיו שם דברי רבי מאיר רבי יוסי אומר ב אין מזין עליו אלא שלישי ושביעי בלבד ואי סלקא דעתך קסבר רבי יוסי טומאה הותרה בציבור למה לי הזאה כלל אלא מחוורתא מתני' דלא כרבי יוסי א"ל רב פפא לאביי ורבי יוסי שטרא מזכי לבי תרי הוא דתניא *א"ר יוסי רואה אני את דברי רבי אליעזר בזבחים ודברי רבי יהושע במנחות דברי רבי אליעזר בזבחים שהיה אומר דם אע"פ שאין בשר ודברי רבי יהושע בזבחים שהיה אומר אם אין דם אין בשר אם אין בשר אין דם דברי רבי אליעזר במנחות שהיה אומר קומץ אע"פ שאין שירים ודברי רבי יהושע במנחות שהיה אומר אם אין שם שירים אין קומץ אם אין קומץ אין שירים א"ל מסתברא קאמר כי קאי בזבחים אמר מסתברא כי היכי דפליגי בזבחים פליגי נמי במנחות כי קאי במנחות אמר מסתברא כי היכי דפליגי במנחות פליגי נמי בזבחים א"ל התינח כי קאי בזבחים אמר מסתברא כי היכי דפליגי בזבחים פליגי נמי במנחות דעיקר קראי כי כתיבי בזבחים כתיבי אלא כי קאי במנחות ואמר מסתברא כי היכי דפליגי במנחות פליגי נמי בזבחים והא עיקר קראי בזבחים הוא דכתיבי אלא לא קשיא רואה אני את דברי ר' אליעזר בנטמא ודברי רבי יהושע באבוד ושרוף בנטמא מ"ט משום דמרצי ציץ הא שמעת ליה לרבי יוסי דאמר אין הציץ מרצה על אכילות אלא לא קשיא רואה אני את דברי רבי אליעזר בציבור רואה אני את דברי רבי יהושע ביחיד בציבור מ"ט משום דטומאה הותרה בציבור חדא דשמעת ליה לר' יוסי דאמר טומאה דחויה היא בציבור ועוד אי בציבור רבי אליעזר מכשיר ולא רבי יהושע הא

ביחיד · לכתחלה פסולה ואם זרק הורצה ומתני' בציבור דאין לכתחלה דטומאת ציבור הוא בהיתר: נימא מתני' דלא כר' יוסי · דכיון דא"ר יוסי בעינן תרתי כדמפרש ואזיל מדקאמר רבי יוסי אין הציץ מרצה על אכילות ש"מ כרבי יהושע סבירא ליה דבעי תרתי ואשמעינן הכא דניטמא בשר לא מהני ליה ציץ למהוי כי בשר קיים לזרוק את הדם דאי לא בעי תרתי ריצוי ציץ אאכילות למה לי הא בלאו אכילות נמי מיתכשרא זריקת דם: כרבי אליעזר ס"ל · דבחדא סגיא ולקמן פריך שתי הלחם אפילו חדא ליכא: למאי אין הציץ מרצה על אכילות · למאי מיבעי לן ריצוי ציץ דידהו אלא על כרחיך לרבי אליעזר ריצוי דציץ דאכילות לאו לאכשורי זריקה מיבעי לן לאפוקי בעלים דבלאו אכילות נמי מיתכשר אלא לאכילות גופייהו מיבעי לן: למיקבעינהו בפיגול · דקי"ל אם יש פסול אחר בקרבן שחישב בו מחשבת פיגול אינו נקבע בפיגול להתחייב כרת על אכילתו דאמר מר ירצה כהרצאת כשר כך הרצאת פיגול במסכת מנחות (דף יו:*): ולאפוקי להאי בשר מידי מעילה · דבקדשי קדשים זריקתן משוי בבשרן שעת היתר לכהנים ותו לא קדשי ה' מיקרו ונפקו מידי מעילה: ומשוי לי' כי טהור · ואע"ג דאסור לאוכלו בטומאה מיהו לכל שאר מילי הוי כי טהור ומהניא ליה זריקה למיקבעיה בפיגול כו': ורבי יוסי סבר · נהי דזריקה כשירה היא להוציא את הבעלים ידי נדרן דלא בעינן תרתי מיהו להאי בשר לא מהני ציץ למהוי הך זריקה מהניא ליה למיקבעה בפיגול ולאפוקה מידי מעילה: בשלמא זבחים · דמתני' איכא עולין דמרצי ציץ עלייהו ואיכא תרתי: עומר נמי דאיכא קומץ · דמרצי ציץ עליה וחדא מיהא איכא: ובלחם הפנים איכא בזיכין · שמתירין את הלחם כקומץ למנחה דכתיב ביה (ויקרא כד) והיתה ללחם לאזכרה: בזיכים · לבונה של לחם הפנים וכתיב בקומץ (שם ב) והקטיר הכהן את אזכרתה וציץ מרצי עלייהו דהא עולים נינהו: אלא שתי הלחם · דכולה אכילות ורבי יוסי אין הציץ מרצה על אכילות קאמר מאי איכא למימר: וכי תימא · הא דקתני מתני' שתי הלחם באין בטומאה לאו בשתי הלחם הבאות בפני עצמן כגון שלא היו להן כבשים דאמרינן במנחות (דף מה:) דבאין בפני עצמן ובהנהו לא קאמר מתני' דליתו בטומאה אלא בבאו עם הכבשים ומשום הכבשים הקריבין עמהן ששחיטתן מקדשת את הלחם וזריקת דמם מתרת אותן קאמר מתניתין דבאות בטומאה משום דציץ מרצי עלייהו: הותרה בציבור · ולא בעי' ציץ: אחד זה ואחד זה · אחד כהן השורף את הפרה ואחד כהן גדול ביום הכפורים שטעונין פרישה שבעת ימים: מכל חטאות · מכל אפרי הפרות שהיו במקדש שאפר פרה של משה לא כלתה: כל שבעה · בפ"ק דיומא מפרש טעמא בראשון לפרישתו שמא היום שלישי לטומאתו שמא היום ג' ימים שניטמא במת וחששא בעלמא היא ומעלה וכן שני שמא שלישי ושלישי שמא שלישי (ב) ואיכך מספקינן כל חד וחד בז' לטומאה: הזאה למה לי · הא קרבן דיום הכפורים דציבור הוא ודוחה טומאה אלא ש"מ בקושי נדחית טומאה בקרבנות ובעי ריצוי ציץ וכיון דלא מרצי אאכילות לא מיתוקם שתי הלחם דמתניתין כרבי יוסי ואפילו סבירא ליה דבחדא סגיא דהא אפילו חדא ליכא: שטרא מזכי לבי תרי הוא · בתמיה כלומר מי ראה שטר שמזכה את התובע ואת הנתבע דקאמר רבי יוסי רואה אני את דברי שניהן: מסתברא קאמר · מסתברא דפליגי בתרוייהו קאמר: עיקר קראי · ועשית עולותיך בזבחים כתיבי · ובמנחות לא כתיבי ואיצטריך לאשמעי' דאפ"ה פליגי במנחות: ועוד · בציבור ר' אליעזר הוא דמכשיר ולא ר' יהושע. בתמיה:

הלא

הגהות הב"ח

(א) גמ' וכ"ת לקרב עמהן כי היכי שלמי ציבור: (ב) רש"י ד"ה כל שבעה בפ"ק דיומא דף ח' מפרש וכו' שמא שלישי אפילו לא בעי זריקה ואיכך מספקינן:

רבינו חננאל

נטמאו הכי פליג אליעזר ועוד מתני' דקתני חמשה דברים באין בטומאה לכתחלה משמע אלא לא קשיא כי קתני בדבעי ר' יהושע תרתי בקרבן יחיד אבל בקרבן צבור הוא ומנחות אפילו חדא סגי ליה ובמנחו' קרבן צבור הוא ומנחות קרבן יחיד. ואתינן למימר מתני' דלא כר' יוסי דתני אין הציץ מרצה על אכילות ור' יוסי סבר לה כר' יהושע דאמר תרתי בעינן ודחי' לא לעולם ר' יוסי בהא כר' אליעזר סבירא ליה דאמר דם אע"פ שאין בשר והאי דקא מיפלגי בציץ מרצה על אכילות בהא פליגי ר' אליעזר סבר הציץ מרצה על אכילות וכיון דמרצה לאכילה הוא דקאי והטהור חשוב הוא ואי חשיב עליה לאכילה חוץ לזמנו אע"ג דהוא טמא קבעא לי' מחשבתו בפיגול ואי אכיל ליה מקודם לאו בר מעילה הוא דאכילה מעליא היא ור' יוסי סבר לא מרצה ציץ ולא משוי ליה טהור ולא קבע ליה בפיגול ולא מפיק ליה מידי מעילה ואקשינן נהי נמי דר' יוסי כר' אליעזר סבירא לי' דאמר דם אע"ג שאין בשר (בשלמא) זבחים איכא דם עומר נמי איכא קומץ לחם הפנים נמי איכא בזיכין אלא שתי הלחם מאי איכא וכי תימא איכא נמי להני שלמים הבאין עמהן [אי הכי] היינו זבחי שלמי צבור והוו להו [ארבעה] ואנן חמשה תנן וקשי' אלא קסבר ר' יוסי טומאה הותרה היא בצבור איני דסבר ר' יוסי הותרה היא בצבור והתניא אחד זה ואחד זה מזין עליו כל שבעה מכל חטאות שהיו שם פי' כהן גדול שהוא מרוצה לשמש ביום הכפורים בין כהן השורף את הפרה היו מזין עליהן כל שבעת הימים שהיו מפרישין אותן מכל אפר הפרות שהיו שם שנעשו מימות משה ועד אותו זמן ואסי' בתחלת סדר יומא דר' יוסי טומאה דחויה בצבור הוא דאית ליה ואמרינן אלא מחוורתא מתני' דלא כר' יוסי: ירושלמי בין למאן דאמר הלחם עיקר בין למאן דאמר כבשים עיקר ארבעה אינון ותנא חש להון וקרינן חמשה: ואקשי' היכי קתני ר' יוסי במילתא דפליגי ר' אליעזר ור' יהושע זה פוסל וזה מכשיר ואמר ר' יוסי רואה אני דברי זה ודברי זה כי יש אמת בשני דרכים המכחישין זה את זה ופרקינן האי דקאמר רואה אני לאו משום דקא מודה להו אלא הכי קאמר רואה אני דברי ר' אליעזר בזבחים כלומר טעמיה במנחות כטעמיה בזבחים כי היכי דפליג בהאי פליג בהאי וכן ר' יהושע ונדחה האי שינויא ושני' רואה אני דברי ר' אליעזר בנטמא דהא איתיה והציץ מרצה: איני והתניא ר' יוסי אומר אין הציץ מרצה על אכילות ונפלו הוא דפליג על ר' אליעזר היכי קתני רואה אני דברי ר' אליעזר במאי דפליג עלה אלא רואה אני דברי ר' אליעזר בציבור מאי טעמא משום דטומאה הותרה היא בצבור והא ר' יוסי טומאה דחויה היא שמעי' ליה והדר הכי ר' יהושע פליג עליה והא אוקימ' לעילא דאפילו ר' יהושע מודה בצבור דדם אע"פ שאין בשר ולפיכך איתוקמא מתניתין כותיה אלא לא קשיא

יהא

[78a]—Rather, there is no difficulty: here the reference is to an individual;[10] there [in the Mishnah] the reference is to a community.[11]

Shall we say that our Mishnah does not agree with R. Jose? For it was taught, R. Eliezer said: The headplate propitiates for [the defilement of] eatables; R. Jose said: The headplate does not propitiate for [the defilement of] eatables. Now it was assumed: since R. Jose rules, The headplate does not propitiate for [the defilement of] eatables, he agrees with R. Joshua who maintains: We require both.[1] Shall we now say [that] our Mishnah does not agree with R. Jose?—No: R. Jose agrees with R. Eliezer, who maintained: The blood [is fit] even if there is no flesh. If so, in respect of what law [does he rule]: the headplate does not propitiate for [the defilement of] eatables?[2]—Then on your reasoning, when R. Eliezer rules: The headplate does propitiate [for the defilement of eatables],—since he maintains [that] the blood [is fit] even if there is no flesh, in respect of what law [does the headplate propitiate]?—Rather they differ in respect of branding[3] it with [the unfitness of] *piggul*[4] and excluding it from [the law of] trespass.[5] R. Eliezer holds: The headplate propitiates for it [the defilement of the flesh] and renders it as clean, and so brands it as *piggul*[6] and excludes it from [the law of] trespass; while R. Jose holds: The headplate does not propitiate for it and does not render it as clean; hence it cannot be branded as *piggul*, nor does it exclude it from [the law of] trespass.

To this R. Mari demurred: Even granted that R. Jose agrees with R. Eliezer: as for sacrifices,[7] it is well, [since] there is blood; as for the *'omer*, there is the handful; [in the case of] the shewbread too there are the censers [of frankincense].[8] But [in the case of] the two loaves, what can be said?[9] And should you answer, it is in respect of what is offered together with them,[1] then it is tantamount to the public peace-offerings, [and] if so there are [only] four, whereas we learned FIVE?—Rather, R. Jose holds: Uncleanness was *permitted* in the case of a community.[2]

But surely it was taught: Both [in the case of] the one and the other,[3] we besprinkle them the whole seven [days][4] with [the ashes of] all the purification offerings[5] which were there:[6] this is R. Meir's view. R. Jose said: We besprinkle them on the third day and on the seventh day alone.[7] Now if you should think that R. Jose holds, Uncleanness was permitted in the case of a community, why do I need sprinkling at all?[8] Hence it is clear that our Mishnah does not agree with R. Jose.

R. Papa said to Abaye: And does R. Jose grant the [Court's] document to two![9] For it was taught, R. Jose said: I agree with the words of R. Eliezer in respect to meal-offerings and [animal] sacrifices, and with the words of R. Joshua in respect to sacrifices and meal-offerings. 'The words of R. Eliezer in respect to sacrifices,' for he used to say: The blood [is fit] even if there is no flesh; 'the words of R. Joshua in respect to sacrifices,' for he used to say: If there is no blood there is no flesh, if there is no flesh there is no blood. 'The words of R. Eliezer in respect to meal-offerings,' for he used to say: the handful [is fit] even if there is no remainder [fit for consumption]; 'and the words of R. Joshua in respect to meal-offerings,' for he used to say: if there is no remainder there is no handful, [and] if there is no handful there is no remainder!—Said he to him: He states what appears logical [to him].[1] [Thus:] when he was studying [the subject of] sacrifices[2] he said: It is logical [that] just as they differ in respect to sacrifices, so do they differ in respect to meal-offerings too. [And] when he was studying [the subject of] meal-offerings he said: It is logical [that] just as they differ in respect to meal-offerings, so do they differ in respect to sacrifices too. Said he to him: It is correct [that] when he was studying [the subject of] sacrifices he said: It is logical [that] just as they differ in respect to sacrifices, so do they differ in respect to meal-offerings too, because the verses [on this matter] are written fundamentally in connection with sacrifices.[3] But when he is studying [the subject of] meal-offerings and he says, It is logical [that] just as they differ in respect to meal-offerings, so do they differ in respect to sacrifices too,—but surely, the verses are fundamentally written in connection with sacrifices! —Rather [explain it thus], there is no difficulty: I agree with the words of R. Eliezer, where it [the flesh] was defiled, and with the words of R. Joshua, where it was lost or burnt. Where it was defiled, what is the reason [that he agrees with R. Eliezer]? Because the headplate propitiates! Surely you know R. Jose to maintain [that] the headplate does not propitiate for [the defilement of] eatables!—Rather [explain it thus], there is no difficulty: I agree with the words of R. Eliezer in the case of the community; I agree with the words of R. Joshua in the case of an individual. In the case of the community, what is the reason [that he agrees with R. Eliezer]? Because uncleanness is *permitted* in the case of a community? But one [objection] is that you know R. Jose to maintain [that] uncleanness is *overridden* in the case of a community. Again, if it refers to a community, [does only] R. Eliezer declare it fit,

(10) Then it is unfit in the first place, but valid if done. (11) Which is unclean; then it is permitted at the very outset.

(1) The blood and the flesh. (2) Since you now say that the blood can be sprinkled in any case. (3) Lit., 'appointing.' (4) V. Glos. (5) For *piggul* v. Lev. XIX, 7 (E.V. *vile thing*); mere *intention* renders it *piggul*, and it may then not be eaten even within the permitted precincts or within the permitted time. But a sacrifice cannot become *piggul* unless it is otherwise fit. Again, if one benefits from sacrifices of the higher sanctity (v. 24a, n. a2) before their blood is sprinkled, he is liable to a trespass-offering; if after, he is exempt, for by then the flesh is permitted to priests. (6) For now there is no other disqualification. (7) Mentioned in our Mishnah that they may be offered in uncleanness. (8) All these ascend the altar, and therefore the headplate makes them acceptable. (9) For these consist entirely of eatables, for whose defilement R. Jose holds that the headplate does not propitiate. How then can they be offered in uncleanness?

(1) V. Lev. XXIII, 18f. The slaughtering of these sacrifices sanctifies the loaves, and the sprinkling of their blood permits them for eating; thus the Mishnah teaches that the headplate propitiates for the defilement of the shewbread in so far as the sacrifices can now be brought. (2) So that propitiation is not required at all; v. *supra* 77a, nn. b2 and b3. (3) *Sc.* the priest who burnt the red heifer (Num. XIX, 4ff) and the High Priest. (4) The former, prior to his burning the red heifer; the latter, before the Day of Atonement, when he officiated in the Temple. (5) The red heifer was designated חטאת, i.e., a sin-offering, here translated purification offering, v. ibid. 9. (6) Some ashes were kept of every red heifer killed since Moses. (7) V. Yoma 4a. (8) Seeing that the sacrifices of the Day of Atonement were public offerings. (9) In a lawsuit the court granted a document containing the verdict to the winner. Here R. Jose grants this document to both sides —i.e., he agrees with both R. Eliezer and R. Joshua.

(1) Without expressing agreement either with the one or the other. (2) Lit., 'when he stands at sacrifices.' (3) V. verses quoted *supra* 77a.

Continuation of translation from previous page as indicated by ◁

c —It is according to his view, yet not entirely so.[1] [Thus]: according to the view of R. Joshua, that we require both, yet not entirely so, for whereas R. Joshua ruled [thus] in the case of sacrifices, but he did not rule [thus] in the case of meal-offerings, this Tanna holds [that it is so] even in the case of meal-offerings.

Now who is this Tanna that agrees with him but is more stringent than he?[2] Moreover, it was taught, R. Jose said: I agree with the words of R. Eliezer[3] in respect to meal-offerings and [animal] sacrifices, and with the words of R. Joshua in respect to [animal] sacrifices and meal-offerings. 'The words of R. Eliezer in respect to [animal] sacrifices,' for he used to say: The blood [is fit] even if there is no flesh; 'and the words of R. Joshua in respect to sacrifices,' for he used to say: If there is no blood there is no flesh, and if there is no flesh there is no blood. 'The words of R. Eliezer in respect to meal-offerings': for he used to say: the handful [is fit] even if there is no remainder [for consumption]; 'and the words of R. Joshua in respect to meal-offerings,' for he used to say: if there is no handful there is no remainder, [and] if there is no remainder there is no handful?[4]—Rather R. Joshua holds: The headplate propitiates for [the defilement of] the objects which ascend [the altar] and for eatables.[5] If so, why [do you say,] 'according to the view of R. Joshua it is unfit?'[6]—[That refers] to what is lost or burnt.[7] Then according to whom does he teach, '[If the remainder] was defiled'? according to R. Eliezer? [But] that is obvious; seeing that you say that [even when it is] lost or burnt, where they are [now] non-existent, R. Eliezer declares [the handful] fit, need it [be stated] where it is defiled, when it is in existence! Hence it is obviously [taught] according to R. Joshua, yet he teaches [that] it is unfit?[8] Furthermore, it was taught, R. Joshua said: [In the case of] all the sacrifices of the Torah, whether the flesh was defiled while the fat has remained [clean], or the fat was defiled while the flesh has remained [clean], he [the priest] sprinkles the blood. But not if both were defiled. This proves that R. Joshua holds that the headplate does not propitiate either for [the defilement of] the objects which ascend

d [the altar][1] or for the eatables![2]—Rather [explain it thus:] after all our Mishnah is [the view of] R. Joshua, yet there is no difficulty: here it means in the first place; there it means if it was done [offered]. R. Joshua said [that both are required] only in the first place, but not if it was done.[3] And whence do you know[4] that R. Joshua draws a distinction between [what is required] in the first place and what was done?—Because it was taught: If the flesh was defiled, or disqualified,[5] or it passed without the curtains,—R. Eliezer said: He must sprinkle [the blood]; R. Joshua maintained: He must not sprinkle [the blood]. Yet R. Joshua admits that if he does sprinkle [it], it is accepted.[6] But surely this explanation is not acceptable: firstly, because 'it is unfit'[7] implies [even] where it was done. Moreover,[8] FIVE THINGS MAY COME [IN UNCLEANNESS] implies [even] in the first place![9]

c (1) Lit., 'and not according to his view.' (2) I.e., do we in fact find *any* such Tanna? (3) Lit., 'I see (as right) the words of R. Eliezer.' (4) This Baraitha is explained anon. From it we see that R. Joshua maintained his view even in respect to meal-offerings. (5) Hence our Mishnah can agree with him. (6) Surely the headplate propitiates, i.e., makes the handful fit for burning on the altar, even if the remainder is unclean? (7) If the remainder is *lost* or *burnt* the handful is unfit, for the headplate propitiates only for defilement. (8) On his view this is necessary, as it informs us that he holds the handful unfit not only if the rest is now entirely non-existent, but even if the rest is in existence, but unclean.

d (1) *Sc.* the fat. (2) *Sc.* the flesh. For if the headplate does propitiate, why is it unfit? (3) I.e., R. Joshua holds that in the first place both are required; nevertheless, if only the blood was clean and it was sprinkled, though it should not have been, it is fit. Our Mishnah too means where it was done. (4) Lit., 'say'. (5) By the touch of a *tebul yom*, q.v. Glos.; v. also *supra* 14a Mishnah and note a.l. (6) V. *supra* 34b for the whole passage. (7) In the ruling of R. Joshua where the remainder was defiled, v. *supra*. (8) Even granted that 'it is fit' implied only in the first instance. (9) So that our Mishnah could still not be in accordance with R. Joshua.

לז א מיי' פ"א מהלכות מעשה קרבנות הל"ד:
לח ב מיי' פ"א מהל' פסולי מוקדשין הלכה כ:
לט ג מיי' פ"א מהלכות פסולי מוקדשין הלכה לד:
מ ד ה שם הלכה לא:

רבינו חננאל

בשר שנאמר ודם זבחיך ישפך ומה אני מקיים ועשית עולותיך הבשר והדם ללמד כי הבשר נזרק על גבי המזבח כמו הדם הוי אומר איר יש בין כבש למזבח שאינו יכול לעבור ועומד בכבש וזורק על גבי המזבח והאי דכתיב והבשר תאכל בא ללמד שאין הבשר נאכל אלא אחרי שיזורק דם (המזבח) [הזבח] כדכתיב ודם זבחיך ישפך והדר והבשר תאכל ומדלא כתיב והבשר תאכל ברישא והדר ודם זבחיך ישפך כדכתיב ועשית עולותיך הבשר והדם ש"מ דדם ישפך לעולם מ"מ ואם יש בשר יאכל אחריו ואם אין בשר ראוי לאכילה אינו מעכב הדם ואם נאמר משנתנו לר' [יהושע] (יהודה) היא והנה הוא לית ליה כי הציץ מרצה על אכילות וכמו דאמרן דר' אליעזר לבדו הוא דאית ליה האי סברא היכי אתו הני חמשה דברים בטומאה ואמרינן אפילו תימא ר' יהושע קסבר הציץ מרצה על העולין כלומר אפילו קרבן כשהן טמאין הציץ מרצה בשלמא זבחים איכא אימוריהן שהן עולין אפילו שמאין וגם הדם נזרק והציץ מרצה אלא עומר ושתי הלחם דקתני באין בטומאה ליכא בהו תרתי שהן עולין אמאי באין בטומאה ושני' לא בעי ר' יהושע אלא בזבחים אבל במנחות אית ליה קומץ אף על פי שאין שירים: איני והתנן במנחות פ"ג נטמאו שיריה נשרפו שיריה אבדו שיריה כמדת ר' אליעזר כשרה כמדת ר' יהושע פסולה מכלל דכי היכי דפליגי בזבחים הכי [נמי] פליגי במנחות ומשני' האי תנא דמנחות שנאה כמדת ר' יהושע דבעי תרתי ולא כמדת ר' יהושע דאלו ר' יהושע בזבחים בעי תרתי במנחות לא בעי תרתי ואקשי' ומאן האי תנא דקאי בשיטת ר' יהושע דבעי תרתי ומחמיר טפי מיניה דבמנחות נמי בעי תרתי ועוד תניא א"ר יוסי [רואה אני] דברי ר' אליעזר בזבחים ודברי ר' יהושע בזבחי' דברי ר' אליעזר במנחות ודברי ר' יהושע במנחות [אלמא] כי הנה בהדיא תאני ר' יוסי כי ר' יהושע סבר במנחות אם אין קומץ אין שירים אם אין שירי' אין קומץ [ומשני](ופי') אלא לעולם קסבר ר' יהושע הציץ מרצה על אכילות אי הכי כי הציץ מרצה על האכילות אמאי תנינן כמדת ר' יהושע פסולה (תאכל) כי הציץ מרצה ושני' כי קתני פסולה אאבדו שיריה ונשרפו שיריה דהא ליתנהו אבל נטמאו שיריה יכל כשרה והא הוצרך התנא לפרש כי ר' אליעזר מכשיר בה ודהי' הכי השתא באבדו ונשרפו דליתנהו כלל מכשיר בה ר' אליעזר בנטמאו דאיתנהו והציץ מרצה על אכילות מיבעיא לי' דודאי מכשיר אלא לא הוצרך נטמאו שיריה אלא לר' יהושע קתני לה וקתני פסולה. ועוד תניא ר' יהושע אומר כל הזבחים בין נטמא בשר והלב קיים בין נטמא חלב ובשר קיים זורק הדם הא נטמאו תרווייהו לא אלמא קסבר ר' יהושע אין הציץ מרצה לא על העולין ולא על האכילות ושנינן שינויא כי קא בעי ר' יהושע תרתי לכתחלה כגון דמנחות אבל דאיעבד כגון משנתנו אפי' חדא (לא) [סגי] ותניא הכי דשני ליה לר' יהושע בין לכתחלה ובין דאיעבד דתניא נטמא הבשר או נפסל או יצא חוץ לקלעים ר' אליעזר אומר יזרק ר' יהושע אומר לא יזרק ומודה ר' יהושע שאם זרק הורצה ואקשי' חדא דפסולה דקתני בנטמאו שיריה דאיעבד משמע דהאי נטמאו קתני ואפי' נטמאו

והני תרי קראי למה לי חד בעולה וחד בשלמים וצריכא דאי כתב רחמנא בעולה הוה אמינא עולה היא דחמירא שכן כליל אבל שלמים דלא חמירי אימא לא ואי כתב רחמנא שלמים הוה אמינא אדרבה דאית בהו שתי אכילות אבל עולה דלית בה שתי אכילות אימא לא קמ"ל ור' אליעזר נמי הכתיב והבשר תאכל אמר לך ההוא מיבעי ליה "שאין הבשר מותר באכילה עד שיזרק הדם אי הכי אימא כוליה להכי הוא דאתא דם אע"פ שאין שם בשר מנלן אמר לך אם כן נכתוב רחמנא הבשר תאכל והדר ודם זבחיך ישפך כדכתיב ברישא °ועשית עולותיך הבשר והדם מאי שנא דאקדמיה לדם זבחיך שמע מינה דם אע"פ שאין בשר ושמע מינה שאין הבשר מותר באכילה עד שיזרק הדם ור' יהושע אין הבשר מותר באכילה עד שיזרק הדם *קל וחומר הוא ומה אימורין דכי ליתנהו לא מעכבי כי איתנהו מעכבי דם דכי ליתיה מעכב כי איתיה לא כל שכן דמעכב ורבי אליעזר *מילתא דאתיא בקל וחומר טרח וכתב לה קרא ור' יהושע *כל היכא דאיכא למדרש דרשינן השתא לימא מתני' דלא כרבי יהושע דכיון דאמר בעינן תרתי וציץ אאכילות לא מרצה היכי אתי בטומאה אפילו תימא רבי יהושע אלא קסבר רבי יהושע הציץ מרצה על העולין הא תינח זבחים דאיכא עולין אלא עומר ושתי הלחם דליכא עולין מאי איכא למימר אמרי כי אמר רבי יהושע נמי דבעינן תרתי בזבחים במנחות לא אמר *והתנן נטמאו שיריה אבדו שיריה כמדת רבי אליעזר כשירה כמדת רבי יהושע פסולה כמדת ולא כמדת רבי יהושע דבעינן תרתי ולא כמדת רבי יהושע דאילו רבי יהושע בזבחים אמר במנחות לא אמר ואילו האי תנא סבר אפילו במנחות ומנו האי תנא דקאי בוותיה ומחמיר טפי מיניה ועוד תניא *א"ר יוסי רואה אני את דברי רבי אליעזר במנחות ובזבחים ודברי רבי יהושע בזבחים ובמנחות דברי רבי אליעזר בזבחים שהיה אומר דם אף על פי שאין בשר ודברי רבי יהושע בזבחים שהיה אומר אם אין דם אין בשר אם אין בשר אין דם דברי רבי אליעזר במנחות שהיה אומר קומץ אף על פי שאין שירים דברי רבי יהושע במנחות שהיה אומר אם אין קומץ אין שירים אם אין שירים אין קומץ אלא קסבר רבי יהושע הציץ מרצה על [העולין ועל] האכילות אי הכי אמאי כמדת רבי יהושע פסולה אאבוד ושרוף אלא נטמא למאן קתני לרבי אליעזר פשיטא השתא יש לומר אבוד ושרוף דליתנהו מכשיר רבי אליעזר נטמא דאיתיה מיבעיא אלא פשיטא לרבי יהושע וקתני פסולה ועוד *תניא רבי יהושע אומר *כל זבחים שבתורה *בין שנטמא בשר וחלב קיים ובין שנטמא חלב ובשר קיים זורק את הדם אבל נטמאו תרווייהו לא אלמא קסבר רבי יהושע אין הציץ מרצה (א) על העולין ולא על האכילות אלא לעולם רבי יהושע היא מתני' ולא קשיא כאן לכתחלה כאן דיעבד כי אמר רבי יהושע לכתחלה דיעבד לא ומנא תימרא דשני ליה לרבי יהושע בין לכתחלה לדיעבד *דתניא נטמא בשר או שנפסל או שיצא חוץ לקלעים ר"א אומר יזרק ר' יהושע אומר "לא יזרק ומודה ר' יהושע "שאם זרק הורצה חדא דפסולה דיעבד משמע ועוד חמשה דברים באין לכתחלה משמע
אלא

שאין בשר ניתר באכילה עד שיזרק הדם · תימה לימא דוקא שלמים דאית ביה תרי אכילות אבל עולה מנלן דאימא כי היכי דלית בה מעילה אחר שנזרק הדם כדתנן במעילה בפרק חטאת העוף (דף ט·) לית בה נמי מעילה קודם זריקה דהאי קרא בשלמים כתיב וי"ל דר"א לא חשיב קך חומרא ורשב"א מתרץ דר"א יליף עולה מקל וחומר דר' יהושע ובשלמים טרח וכתב לה קרא כדאמר בסמוך: **עומר** ושתי הלחם דליכא עולין מאי איכא למימר · וא"ת ובשתי הלחם מה שייך בהין בטומאה ויש לומר משום תנופה דאית בהו: **קסבר** ר' יהושע הציץ מרצה על העולין · וא"ת לענין מה מפיק קרא בעולה אם אין בשר אין דם הלא הציץ מרצה ויש לומר לענין אבוד ושרוף דלא מרצה ציץ: **כי** אמר ר' יהושע בזבחים במנחות לא אמר · השתא משתי הלחם לא תירץ כלום ובלאו הכי פריך שפיר: **אלא** פשיטא ר' יהושע קתני לה · תימה לרשב"א אמאי לא משני כדלעיל כמדת ר' יהושע דבעי תרתי ולא כמדת ר' יהושע דאיהו ס"ל הציץ מרצה על אכילות ואנן סבירא לן דלא מרצה:
הא

והני תרי קראי למה לי · לר' יהושע למה לי: וחד בשלמים · וצריך שלמים: שכן כליל · הילכך חשיבא ומחמרינן בה: אם כן · דהוי אתא למימר דדם מתיר בשר באכילה ולאו למימר דם אע"פ שאין בשר: לכתוב ובשר זבחיך תאכל והדר והדם ישפך · והוי משמע נמי והדם ישפך תחלה קודם לאכילה דהא לא כתיב והדם תשפוך מאי שנא דאקדמיה לדם זבחיך ישפך ברישא: ש"מ · למדרש ודם זבחיך ישפך מכ"מ: אימורים דכי ליתנהו לא מעכבי · וכגון נטמאו או אבדו לא מעכבי אכילת בשר כדאמרן בתמיד נשחט (לעיל דף נט:): כי איתנהו מעכבי · אכילת בשר כדאמרן התם: דם דכי ליתיה מעכב. דהא תרווייהו מודו אם אין דם אין בשר דמתחלת הקרבן הן נאכלין וכפרה איכא בהא אלא בדם וכהנים משולחן גבוה קא זכו וכיון דכפרה ליתיה איסורא להיכא אזל: לימא דלא כר' יהושע · אמילתיה קא מהדר דלאמרן לעיל מתני' דלא כר' יהושע: בעינן תרתי · דם ובשר: ואין האכילות לא מרצי · והשתא בשר ליכא אלא דם לחודיה דמרצי אין עלה ה"ל דלא אתו בטומאה: הציץ מרצה על העולין · על טומאת הנקטרין על האשים דהיינו אימורין מודי רבי יהושע דאי איכא כזית חלב לאכילת מזבח זורק את הדם כדאמר לקמן בברייתא בפירקין (ד' עט:) רבי יהושע אומר כל הזבחים שבתורה שנשתייר מהן כזית בשר או כזית חלב זורק הדם: עומר ושתי הלחם דליכא עולין · לבד הקומץ שהוא במנחה כזריקת דם בזבחים אבל בשיריים ליכא הקטרה וכיון דבעי ר' יהושע תרתי צריך להיות קומץ ושיריים קיימין והכא שיריים ליכא ושתי הלחם דכוליה אכילות אפילו חדא נמי ליכא בשלמא לר"א דאית ליה הציץ מרצה על אכילות כולהו כמאן דלא איטמו ניגהו: כי אמר ר' יהושע · דבעינן תרתי: נטמאו שיריה · של מנחה לאחר שנקמצה ועדיין לא נקטר קומצה: כמדת ר' אליעזר · שהיה אומר בזבחים (ד' קד) דם אף על פי שאין בשר כשירה להקטיר קומצה ונפטרו הבעלים: ומאן האי תנא כו' · היכא אשכחן תנא דאמר הכי מילתיה דר' יוסי מיפרשא לקמן בשמעתין: אלא קסבר רבי יהושע הציץ מרצה על אכילות. ומיתוקמא מתני' אליביה דהא איכא תרתי וגבי שתי הלחם נמי כיון דציץ מרצה על אכילות הוה ליה כמעיקרא ומתירין במקדש: אי הכי נטמאו שיריה · (ב) כיון דנטמאו לר' יהושע אמאי פסולין ומשני כי קתני פסולה אאבדו שיריה ונשרפו שיריה: אלא נטמאו שיריה · כיון דרבי יהושע לא עלה פליג: למאן קתני לה לר' אליעזר וכו' · להודיע לנו דברי מי שנאה להודיענו בה דברי רבי אליעזר דלמדתו כשירה בתמיה פשיטא השתא י"ל כו' אלא פשיטא על כרחיך ר' יהושע פליג עלה ולאשמועינן דרבי יהושע פסיל בה תניא ורבותא אשמעינן דאף על גב דאיתא בעינה פסול: ולא על העולין · דהיינו חלב דאי מרצי אחד מינייהו אמאי פסול: אלא לא קשיא · מתני' ודרבי יהושע מתני' דיעבד ודר' יהושע לכתחלה תרתי בעי ואי אייתוה מתכשר דיעבד: נפסל · בטבול יום: חדא דפסולה דיעבד משמע כו' · אתקפתא היא: ועוד · אי נמי משמע פסולה להקטיר קומצה לכתחלה מתני' באין לכתחלה קתני:
ביחיד

לעיל עז: וש"נ
[קדושין ד: חולין קיח:]
מנחות ט. ע"ש
[לקמן פח.]
לקמן עט. [לעיל סג.]
לעיל לד: [זבחים קד.]

הגהות הב"ח

(א) גמ' אין הציץ מרצה לא על העולין: (ב) רש"י ד"ה אי הכי ניטמו שיריה לר' יהושע כצ"ל ותיבות כיון דניטמו נמחק:

a in connection therewith is written, *and thou shalt eat the flesh.*[1] [77b] Then what is the purpose of these two verses?[2]—One refers to the burnt-offering and one refers to a peace-offering, and both are necessary. For if the Divine Law wrote it in connection with a burnt-offering, I would say: It is [only with] the burnt-offering[3] which is stringent, because it is entirely [burnt]; but as for the peace-offering, which is not stringent, I would say that it is not so. Again, if the Divine Law wrote [it of] a peace-offering, I would say: on the contrary [the reason is] because it has two forms of consumption;[4] but [as for] the burnt-offering, where there are not two forms of consumption,[5] I would say that it is not so. Hence we are informed [otherwise].

Now [according to] R. Eliezer too, surely it is written, *'and thou shalt eat the flesh?'*—He can answer you: He utilizes that [to teach] that the flesh is not permitted for eating until the blood is sprinkled. If so, say that the *whole* verse comes for this [purpose], then how do we know [that] the blood [is fit] even if there is no flesh?—He can answer you: If so, let the Divine Law [first] write *'thou shalt eat the flesh,'* and then, *'and the blood of thy sacrifices shall be poured out,'* as is written in the beginning [of the verse], *'and thou shalt offer thy burnt-offerings, the flesh and the blood.'* Why then does [Scripture] place *'the blood of thy sacrifices'* first? Hence infer from it [that] the blood [is fit] even if there is no flesh, and infer from it also that the flesh is not permitted for eating until the blood is sprinkled.[6] And R. Joshua?[7]—[That] the flesh is not permitted for eating until the blood is sprinkled follows *a minori*: if the *emurim*,[8] which when not available[9] are not indispensable [to the eating of the flesh], yet when available are indispensable;[10] then the blood, which if not available is indispensable, if available
b how much the more is it indispensable! And R. Eliezer?[1] [Even] a law which can be inferred *a minori*, the Writ takes the trouble of writing it. And R. Joshua?—Wherever we can interpret, we do interpret.[2] Shall we now say that our Mishnah is not in accordance with R. Joshua, for since he says that we require both,[3] while the headplate does not propitiate for [the defilement of] eatables, how can it come in uncleanness?[4]—You may even say [that it agrees with] R. Joshua, but R. Joshua holds: The headplate propitiates for those that ascend.[5] That is well of sacrifices, where there are objects which ascend [*sc. emurim*]; but what can be said of the *'omer* and the two loaves, where there are no objects to ascend [the altar]?—I will tell you: R. Joshua too said that we require both only in the case of sacrifices; [but] he did not say [it] in the case of meal-offerings.

Yet did he not say [it] in the case of meal-offerings? Surely we learnt: If the remainder thereof[6] was defiled, [or] if the remainder thereof was lost:[7] according to the view of R. Eliezer[8] it [the handful] is fit;[9] according to the view of R. Joshua,[10] it is unfit![11]

a (1) Deut. XII, 27. This proves that the flesh too must be fit for eating. (2) According to R. Joshua, since both teach that the blood and the flesh are interdependent. (3) That both are interdependent. (4) The fat portions are consumed ('eaten') on the altar while the flesh is consumed partly by priests and partly by its owners. (5) The whole being consumed on the altar. (6) The reversed order intimating this additional teaching. (7) How does he know this? (8) V. Glos. (9) E.g., if lost or defiled. (10) The flesh may not be eaten until the *emurim* are burnt on the altar, v. *supra* 59b.

b (1) Does he not accept this argument? (2) The principle that Scripture writes explicitly what can be inferred *a minori* holds good only when the verse cannot be employed for any other purpose. (3) The blood and the flesh. (4) *Sc.* the objects enumerated in the Mishnah. For on the one hand, propitiation is required (v. 77a, n. b2), while on the other there cannot be propitiation for eatables, and according to R. Joshua the eatables and the blood, or in the case of the meal-offering, the handful, are interdependent. (5) The altar, *sc.* the *emurim*; i.e., providing that as much as an olive of the *emurim* ascends the altar, the headplate propitiates for its defilement, and the blood too can be sprinkled. (6) Of the meal-offering, after the handful was removed (v. Lev. II, 9). In the Hebrew the word is in the plural. This remainder would normally be eaten by the priests (ibid. 10). (7) In both cases before the handful was burnt on the altar. (8) That the blood is fit for sprinkling even if the flesh is not available; the handful of a meal-offering is the equivalent of the blood of an animal sacrifice, while the remainder is the equivalent of the flesh. (9) For burning on the altar, and the owner thus discharges his obligation and need not bring another meal-offering. (10) That the blood and the flesh are interdependent. (11) V. Men. 9a. Thus R. Joshua requires both in the case of meal-offerings too.

◁ *For the continuation of the English translation of this page see overleaf.*

עין משפט נר מצוה

לז א מיי' פ"א מהלכות מעשה קרבנות הל"ד:

לח ב מיי' פ"א מהל' פסולי מוקדשין הלכה כ:

לט ג מיי' פ"א מהלכות פסולי מוקדשין הלכה לד:

מ ד ה שם הלכה לא:

גמרא

והני תרי קראי למה לי חד בעולה וחד בשלמים וצריכא דאי כתב רחמנא בעולה הוה אמינא עולה היא דחמירא שכן כליל אבל שלמים דלא חמירי אימא לא ואי כתב רחמנא שלמים הוה אמינא אדרבה דאית בהו שתי אבילות אבל עולה דלית בה שתי אבילות אימא לא קמ"ל ור' אליעזר נמי הכתיב והבשר תאכל אמר לך ההוא מיבעי ליה "שאין הבשר מותר באכילה עד שיזרק הדם אי הכי אימא כוליה לדבי הוא דאתא דם אע"פ שאין שם בשר מנלן אמר לך אם כן נכתוב רחמנא הבשר תאכל והדר ודם זבחיך ישפך כדכתיב ברישא °ועשית עולותיך הבשר והדם מאי שנא דאקדמיה לדם זבחיך שמע מינה דם אע"פ שאין בשר ושמע מינה שאין הבשר מותר באכילה עד שיזרק הדם ור' יהושע אין הבשר מותר באכילה עד שיזרק הדם *קל וחומר הוא ומה אימורין דכי ליתנהו לא מעכבי כי איתנהו מעכבי דם דכי ליתיה מעכב כי איתיה לא כל שכן דמעכב ורבי אליעזר *מילתא דאתיא בקל וחומר טרח וכתב לה קרא ור' יהושע *כל היכא דאיכא למדרש דרשינן השתא לימא מתני' דלא כרבי יהושע דכיון דאמר בעינן תרתי וציץ אאבילות לא מרצה היכי אתי בטומאה אפילו תימא רבי יהושע אלא קסבר רבי יהושע הציץ מרצה על העולין הא תינח זבחים דאיכא עולין אלא עומר ושתי הלחם דליכא עולין מאי איכא למימר אמרי כי אמר רבי יהושע נמי דבעינן תרתי בזבחים במנחות לא אמר *והתנן נטמאו שיריה אבדו שיריה כמדת רבי אליעזר כשירה כמדת רבי יהושע [ב]פסולה כמדת ולא כמדת כמדת רבי יהושע דבעינן תרתי ולא כמדת רבי יהושע דאילו רבי יהושע בזבחים אמר במנחות לא אמר ואילו האי תנא סבר אפילו במנחות ומנו האי תנא דקאי כוותיה ומחמיר טפי מיניה ועוד תניא *א"ר יוסי רואה אני את דברי רבי אליעזר במנחות ובזבחים ודברי רבי יהושע בזבחים ובמנחות דברי רבי אליעזר בזבחים שהיה אומר דם אף על פי שאין שם בשר ודברי רבי יהושע בזבחים שהיה אומר אם אין דם אין בשר אם אין בשר אין דם דברי רבי אליעזר במנחות שהיה אומר קומץ אף על פי שאין שירים דברי רבי יהושע במנחות שהיה אומר אם אין קומץ אין שירים אם אין שירים אין קומץ אלא קסבר רבי יהושע הציץ מרצה על [העולין ועל] האבילות אי הכי אמאי כמדת רבי יהושע פסולה אאבוד ושרוף אלא נטמא למאן קתני לרבי אליעזר פשיטא השתא יש לומר אבוד ושרוף דליתנהו מכשיר רבי אליעזר נטמא דאיתיה מיבעיא אלא פשיטא לרבי יהושע וקתני פסולה ועוד *תניא רבי יהושע אומר [ג]כל זבחים שבתורה *בין שנטמא בשר וחלב קיים ובין שנטמא חלב ובשר קיים זורק את הדם אבל נטמאו תרווייהו לא אלמא קסבר רבי יהושע אין הציץ מרצה (א) על העולין ולא על האבילות אלא לעולם רבי יהושע היא מתני' ולא קשיא כאן לכתחלה כאן דיעבד כי אמר רבי יהושע לכתחלה דיעבד לא ומנא תימרא דשני ליה לרבי יהושע בין לכתחלה לדיעבד *דתניא נטמא בשר או שנפסל או שיצא חוץ לקלעים ר"א אומר יזרק ר' יהושע אומר [ד]לא יזרק ומודה ר' יהושע [ה]שאם זרק הורצה חדא דפסולה דיעבד משמע ועוד חמשה דברים באין לכתחלה משמע אלא

רש"י

והני תרי קראי · לר' יהושע למה לי : וחד בשלמים · זבחיך שלמים : שכן כליל · הילכך חשיבא ומחמרינן בה : אם כן · דכולי אתא למימר דדם מתיר בשר באכילה ולאו למימר דם אע"פ שאין בשר : לכתוב ובשר זבחיך תאכל והדר והדם ישפך · והוי משמע נמי והדם ישפך תחלה קודם לאכילה דהא לא כתיב והדם תשפוך מאי שנא דאקדמיה לדם זבחיך ישפך ברישא : ש"מ · למדרש ודם זבחיך ישפך מכ"מ : אימורים דכי ליתנהו לא מעכבי · וכגון נטמאו או אבדו לא מעכבי אכילת בשר כדאמרן בתמיד נשחט (לעיל דף נט:): כי איתנהו מעכבי · אכילת בשר כדאמרן התם: דם דכי ליתיה מעכב. דהא תרווייהו מודו אם אין דם אין בשר דמתחלת הקדשן הן נאסרין וכפרה אינה באה אלא בדם וכהנים משולחן גבוה קא זכו וכיון דכפרה ליתיה איסורא להיכא אזל : לימא דלא כר' יהושע · אמילתיה קא מהדר דאמרן לעיל מתני' דלא כר' יהושע : בעינן תרתי· דם ובשר : וציץ אאבילות לא מרצי · והשתא בשר ליכא אלא דם לחודיה דמרצי ציץ עלה ה"נ דלא אתו בטומאה : הציץ מרצה על העולין · על טומאת הנקטרין על האשים דהיינו אימורין מודי רבי יהושע דאי איכא כזית חלב לאכילת מזבח זורק את הדם כדאמר לקמן בברייתא בפירקין (ד' עט·) רבי יהושע אומר כל הזבחים שבתורה שנשתייר מהן כזית בשר או כזית חלב זורק הדם : עומר ושתי הלחם דליכא עולין · לבד הקומץ שהוא במנחה כזריקת דם בזבחים אבל בשיריים ליכא הקטרה וכיון דבעי ר' יהושע תרתי צריך להיות קומץ ושיריים קיימין והכא שיריים ליכא ושתי הלחם דכוליה אכילות אפילו חדא נמי ליכא בשלמא לר"א דאית ליה הציץ מרצה על אכילות כולהו כמאן דלא איטמו ניהו : כי אמר ר' יהושע · דבעינן תרתי : נטמאו שיריה · של מנחה לאחר שנקמצה ועדיין לא נקטר קומצה : כמדת ר' אליעזר · שהיה אומר בזבחים (ד' קד) דם אף על פי שאין בשר כשירה להקטיר קומצה ונפטרו הבעלים : ומאן האי תנא כו' · היכא אשכחן תנא דאמר הכי מילתיה דר' יוסי מיפרשא לקמן בשמעתין : אלא קסבר רבי יהושע הציץ מרצה על אכילות · ומיתוקמא מתני' אליביה דהא איכא תרתי וגבי שתי הלחם נמי כיון דציץ מרצה על אכילות הוה ליה כמעיקרא ומתירין במקדש : אי הכי נטמאו שיריה · (ג) כיון דנטמאו לר' יהושע אמאי פסולין ומשני כי קתני פסולה אאבדו שיריה ונשרפו שיריה : אלא נטמאו שיריה · כיון דרבי יהושע לא עלה פליג : למאן קתני לה לר' אליעזר וכו' · להודיע לנו דברי מי שנאה להודיענו בה דברי רבי אליעזר דלמדתו כשירה בתמיה פשיטא השתא י"ל כו' אלא פשיטא על כרחיך ר' יהושע פליג עלה ולאשמועינן דרבי יהושע פסיל בה תניא ורבותא אשמועינן דאף על גב דאיתא בעינה פסול : ולא על העולין · דהיינו חלב דאי מרצי אחד מינייהו אמאי פסול : אלא לא קשיא · מתני' ודרבי יהושע מתני' דיעבד ודר' יהושע לכתחלה תרתי בעי ואי איתיה מתכשר דיעבד : נפסל · בטבול יום : חדא דפסולה דיעבד משמע כו' · אתקפתא היא : ועוד· אי נמי משמע פסולה להקטיר קומצה לכתחלה מתני' באין לכתחלה קתני : ביחיד

תוספות

שאין בשר ניתר באכילה עד שיזרק הדם · תימה לימא דוקא שלמים דאית ביה תרי אכילות אבל עולה מנלן דאימא כי היכי דלית בה מעילה אחר שנזרק הדם כדתנן במעילה בפרק חטאת העוף (דף ט·) לית בה נמי מעילה קודם זריקה דהאי קרא בשלמים כתיב וי"ל דר"א לא חשיב הך חומרא ורשב"א מתרץ דר"א יליף עולה מקל וחומר דר' יהושע ובשלמים טרח וכתב לה קרא כדאמר בסמוך : עומר ושתי הלחם דליכא עולין מאי איכא למימר · וא"ת ובשתי הלחם מה שייך כאן בטומאה ויש לומר משום תנופה דאית בהו : קסבר ר' יהושע הציץ מרצה על העולין · וא"ת לענין מה מפיק קרא בעולה אם אין בשר אין דם הלא הציץ מרצה ויש לומר לענין אבוד ושרוף דלא מרצה ציץ : כי אמר ר' יהושע בזבחים במנחות לא אמר · השתא מעיקרא הלחם לא תירץ כלום ובלאו הכי פריך שפיר : אלא פשיטא ר' יהושע קתני לה · תימה לרשב"א אמאי לא משני כדלעיל כמדת ר' יהושע דבעי תרתי ולא כמדת ר' יהושע דאיהו ס"ל הציץ מרצה על אכילות ואנן סבירא לן דלא מרצה : הא

רבינו חננאל

בשר שנאמר ודם זבחיך ישפך ומה אני מקיים ועשית עולותיך הבשר והדם ללמד כי הבשר נזרק על גבי המזבח כמו הדם הוי אומר איר יש בין כבש למזבח שאינו יכול לעבור ועומד בכבש וזורק על גבי המזבח והאי דכתיב והבשר תאכל בא ללמד שאין הבשר נאכל אלא אחרי שיזרוק דם (האמבה) [הזבח] כדכתיב ודם זבחיך ישפך והדר והבשר תאכל ומדלא כתיב והבשר תאכל ברישא והדר ודם זבחיך ישפך כדכתיב ועשית עולותיך הבשר והדם ש"מ דדם ישפך לעולם ש"מ ואם יש בשר יאכל אחריו ואם אין בשר ראוי לאכילה אינו מעכב הדם ואם נאמר משנתנו לר' [יהושע] (יהודה) היא והנה הוא לית ליה כי הציץ מרצה על אכילות וכמו דאמרן דר' אליעזר לבדו הוא דאית ליה האי סברא היכי אתו הני המשה דברים בטומאה ואמרינן אפילו תימא ר' יהושע קסבר הציץ מרצה על העולין כלומר אפילו קרבן כשהן מאין הציץ מרצה בשלמא זבחים איכא אימוריהן שהן עולין אפילו מאין גם הדם נזרק והציץ מרצה אלא עומר ושתי הלחם דקתני באין בטומאה ליכא בהו תרתי שהן עולין אמאי באין בטומאה ושני' לא בעי ר' יהושע אלא בזבחים אבל במנחות אית ליה קומץ אף על פי שאין שירים : איני והתנן במנחות פ"ג נטמאו שיריה נשרפו שיריה אבדו שיריה כמדת ר' אליעזר כשרה כמדת ר' יהושע פסולה מכלל דכי היכי דפליגי בזבחים הכי [נמי] פליגי במנחות ומשני' האי תנא דמנחות שנאה כמדת ר' יהושע דבעי תרתי ולא כמדת ר' יהושע דאלו ר' יהושע בזבחים בעי תרתי במנחות לא בעי תרתי ואקשי' ומאן האי תנא דקאי בשיטת ר' יהושע דבעי תרתי ומחמיר טפי מיניה דבמנחות נמי בעי תרתי ועוד תניא א"ר יוסי [רואה אני] דברי ר' אליעזר בזבחים ודברי ר' יהושע בזבחי' דברי ר' אליעזר במנחות ודברי ר' יהושע במנחות [אלמא] כי הנה בהדיא תאני ר' יוסי כי ר' יהושע סבר במנחות אם אין קומץ אין שירים אם אין שירי' אין קומץ [ומשני] (ופי') אלא לעולם קסבר ר' יהושע הציץ מרצה על אכילות אי הכי כי הציץ מרצה ושני' כי קתני פסולה (תאכל) כי הציץ מרצה על האבילות אמאי תנינן כמדת ר' יהושע פסולה אאבדו שיריה ונשרפו שיריה דהא ליתנהו אבל נטמאו שיריה דברי הכל כשרה הא הוצרך התנא לפרש כי ר' אליע"ר מכשיר בה ודהי' הכי השתא באבדו ונשרפו דליתנהו כלל מכשיר בה ר' אליעזר בנטמאו דאיתנהו והציץ מרצה על אכילות מיבעיא לי' דודאי מכשיר אלא לא הוצרך נטמאו שיריה אלא לר' יהושע קתני לה וקתני פסולה. ועוד תניא ר' יהושע אומר כל הזבחים בין נטמא בשר והלב קיים בין נטמא חלב ובשר קיים זורק הדם הא נטמאו תרווייהו לא אלמא קסבר ר' יהושע אין הציץ מרצה לא על העולין ולא על האבילות ושנינן שינויא כי קא בעי ר' יהושע תרתי לכתחלה כגון דמנחות אבל דאיעבד כגון משנתנו אפי' הדא (לא) [סגי] ותניא הכי דשני ליה לר' יהושע בין לכתחלה ובין דאיעבד דתניא נטמא הבשר או נפסל או יצא חוץ לקלעים ר' אליעזר אומר יזרק ר' יהושע אומר לא יזרק ומודה ר' יהושע שאם זרק הורצה ואקשי' הדא דפסולה דקתני בנטמאו שיריה דאיעבד משמע דהאי נטמאו קתני ואפי' נטמאו

מסורת הש"ס

דברים יב

נ"א מכ"ל

[לעיל יח: וש"נ] [קדושין ד: חולין קיח:]

מנחות ט. ט: ע"ש

[לקמן פח.]

ס"א לא

לקמן עט. [לעיל סב.]

לעיל לד: [זבחים קד.]

הגהות הב"ח

(א) גמ' אין הציץ מרצה לא על העולין : (ב) רש"י ד"ה אי הכי ניטמאו שיריה לר' יהושע כצ"ל ותיבות כיון דניטמאו נמחק :

שעירי ראשי חדשים איצטריכא ליה סלקא דעתך אמינא הא לא כתיב בהו מועד קמ"ל דראש חדש איקרי מועד כדאביי *דאמר אביי תמוז דהאי שתא מלויי מליוה דכתיב °קרא עלי מועד לשבור בחורי למימרא דכולהו ממועד אתו מנהני מילי *דתנו רבנן °וידבר משה את מועדי ה' מה תלמוד לומר לפי שלא למדנו אלא לתמיד ופסח שנאמר בהו במועדו *ואפילו בשבת במועדו ואפילו בטומאה שאר קרבנות ציבור מניין שנאמר °אלה תעשו לה' במועדיכם מניין לרבות עומר והקרב עמו שתי הלחם והקרב עמם ת"ל וידבר משה את מועדי ה' אל בני ישראל הכתוב קבעו מועד אחד לכולן וכל הני למה לי צריכי דאי כתב רחמנא תמיד הוה אמינא תמיד שכן תדיר וכליל אבל פסח לא קמ"ל ואי כתב רחמנא פסח פסח שהוא ענוש כרת אבל תמיד דאין ענוש כרת אימא לא קמ"ל ואי כתב רחמנא הני תרתי הוה אמינא הני הוא *יש בהן צד חמור תמיד תדיר וכליל פסח שהוא ענוש כרת אבל שאר קרבנות ציבור אימא לא כתב רחמנא אלה תעשו לה' במועדיכם ואי כתב רחמנא אלה תעשו לה' במועדיכם הוה אמינא שאר קרבנות ציבור הבאין לכפר אבל עומר ושתי הלחם דאין באין לכפר אלא להתיר בעלמא נינהו לא קמ"ל ואי כתב רחמנא עומר ושתי הלחם לחודייהו הוה אמינא אדרבה עומר ושתי הלחם דאלימי דבאין להתיר אבל הנך לא קמ"ל סברוה *דלכולי עלמא טומאה דחויה היא בציבור ובעי' ציץ לרצות דליכא תנא דשמעת ליה דאמר טומאה הותרה בציבור אלא רבי יהודה דתניא *ציץ בין שישנו על מצחו ובין שאינו על מצחו מרצה דברי ר"ש ר' יהודה אומר °עודיהו על מצחו מרצה אין עודיהו על מצחו אינו מרצה אמר לו ר"ש כהן גדול ביום הכפורים יוכיח שאינו על מצחו ומרצה אמר לו הנח ליום הכפורים שטומאה הותרה בציבור מכלל דר"ש סבר טומאה דחויה היא בציבור ודכולי עלמא *אין הציץ מרצה על אכילות דליכא תנא דשמעת ליה דאמר *הציץ מרצה על אכילות אלא ר"א דתניא *ר"א אומר הציץ מרצה על אכילות רבי יוסי אומר אין הציץ מרצה על אכילות נימא מתניתין דלא כרבי יהושע °דתניא °ועשית עולותיך הבשר והדם רבי יהושע אומר *אם אין דם אין בשר אם אין בשר אין דם רבי אליעזר אומר דם אף על פי שאין בשר שנאמר °ודם זבחיך ישפך ומה אני מקיים ועשית עולותיך הבשר והדם לומר לך *מה דם בזריקה אף בשר בזריקה הוי אומר *אויר קטן יש בין כבש למזבח ורבי יהושע נמי הכתיב ודם זבחיך ישפך אמר לך הא כתיב גביה והבשר תאכל

והני

תורה אור: איכה א · ויקרא כג · במדבר כט · דברים יב · שם

רש"י

הא לא כתיב בהו מועד · ולא לידחו טומאה דהא כל קרבנות ציבור ממועד נפקי לן כדלקמן : קרא עלי מועד · תמוז דשלוח מרגלים מלויי מליוה וכלו ארבעים דידהו בט' באב בפרק בתרא דתענית והוקבעה להם בו בכיה לדורות ויום עיבור החדש קרי מועד : וידבר משה וגו' · בתורת כהנים הוא גבי עומר ושתי הלחם : שלא למדנו כו' שנאמר בהן מועד · לדחות שבת וטומאה : במועדו · משמע לא יעבור זמנו ואפילו הן טמאין ואפילו הוא שבת : אלה תעשו וגו' · בפרשת פינחס כתיב גבי מוספים : מניין לרבות עומר והקרב עמו · ועשיתם ביום הניפכם וגו' (ויקרא כג) : ושתי הלחם · והכבשים הקרבין עמהן האמור בתורת כהנים ואינם אמורים בפרשת פינחס : ת"ל · בשילהי ההיא פרשתא דשור או כשב או עז וידבר משה וגו' : כל הני למה לי · לכתוב חד וליתי הנך מיניה : שאר קרבנות ציבור · מוספין דעולה מכפרת אעשה כדתניא ביומא (דף לו.) אין עולה באה אלא על עשה ולא תעשה שניתק לעשה : עומר ושתי הלחם אינן באין אלא להתיר · את החדש זה במדינה וזה במקדש : סברוה · התלמידים בני ישיבה היו סבורין כן לפיכך הוצרך להם לישאל הא דבעי לקמיה לימא מתניתין דלא כר' יהושע : דחויה · אף על גב דאכשרה רחמנא למיתי בטומאה לאו היתר גמור הוא אלא היכא דלא מישתכחי טהורין וכיון דלאו היתר גמור הוא בעי' ציץ לרצויי : בין שישנו על מצחו · בשעה שאירעה טומאה בקרבנות : כהן גדול ביום הכפורים יוכיח . בשעת עבודת פנים: שאינו על מצחו · דהא אין נכנס שם בבגדי זהב °כדאמרינן [בראש השנה] (דף כו.) דאין קטיגור נעשה סניגור : ומרצה · אם באו בטומאה דהא קיימא לן כל קרבנות הציבור הקבוע להן זמן דוחין את הטומאה ורבי שמעון אית ליה טומאה דחויה היא בציבור ואי לאו משום דציץ מרצה אטומאה לא הוו מיתכשרי : שטומאה הותרה בציבור · ואין קרבן ציבור צריך ריצוי הציץ אלא קרבן יחיד : ודכולי עלמא · כלומר הנך רבנן דסתם מתניתין סברי אין הציץ מרצה על אכילות על טומאה שנגע בבשר ובשירי מנחה הנאכלים אלא על טומאת הדם וקמצים (ואימורין) : לימא מתניתין . דאמר עומר ושתי הלחם באין בטומאה ואף על גב דבעינן ריצוי ציץ וציץ אאכילות לא מרצי ומנחה שאין כאן שיריים הנראין אלא הקומץ לבדו שהציץ מועיל וכן במיני דמים לא הועיל ציץ לבשר אלא לדם וקתני והדם נזרק : דלא כר' יהושע · דאמר אם אין בשר ראוי אין דם ראוי : אם אין בשר · ראוי כגון שנטמא או שנאבד אין הדם נזרק : גול . אויר יש בין כבש למזבח לא היה ראש הכבש מחובר למזבח שיש אויר מעט בינתים והמסדר את האברים עומד על הכבש וזורקן על מערכת העצים לקיים מצות זריקה : הא כתיב גביה והבשר תאכל · אלמא בשר קיים בעינן :

תוספות

שעירי ראשי חדשים איצטריך ליה · תימה וליתני שעירי ראשי חדשים ולא ליתני איך : סלקא דעתך אמינא הא לא כתיב בהו מועד · ואע"ג דבפרשת פינחס כתיב נמי ראש חדש ה"א דאלה תעשו במועדיכם דכתיב בסוף פרשת פינחס לא קאי אראש חדש אלא אשאר ימים טובים דכתיבי בתריה דאיקרי רגל דהכי נמי לא קאי *אשבת ותמיד ומצרכי' להו קרא בסמוך :

שכן יש בהן צד חמור · פר"ת שכן ישנן לפני הדיבור וכמאן דאמר (חגיגה דף ו:) עולה שהקריבו ישראל במדבר עולת תמיד היא ולחם הפנים אומר ריב"א מדכתיב תמיד ילפינן ליה דמשמע אפילו בשבת ובתורת כהנים איכא מאן דדריש דתמיד דחי שבת מדכתב ביה תמיד ומיהו מתרי מינייהו הוה מצי למילף כולהו *ואומר ר"י דשמא יש שום פירכא דאי לאו הכי אמאי צריך קרא בשאר · וקשה דבפרק קמא דיבמות (דף ה:) בעי למימר עשה דוחה לא תעשה שיש בו כרת מפסח ותמיד ופריך מה לפסח ותמיד שכן ישנן לפני הדיבור ואמאי לא יליף משאר קרבנות ציבור דדחי שבת כדמסקינן הכא* : דלא אשכחן תנא דאית ליה טומאה הותרה אלא ר' יהודה · ואם תאמר מאי אולמא דר"ש טפי מדרבי יהודה אדרבה אשכחן במי שהוציאוהו (עירובין דף מו:) דר' יהודה ור' שמעון הלכה כרבי יהודה וי"ל דאשכחן לקמן (דף עח.) ר' יוסי דכוותיה עמו דסבר טומאה דחויה היא תימה לר"י דבשמעתין משמע דלמאן דאמר טומאה דחויה איכא דחויה אלא על ידי ריצוי ציץ ואמאי הא טומאה דגברא דדחויה בציבור [א] אע"פ שאין הציץ מרצה על טומאת הגוף כדתנן בפירקין (דף פ:) :

רבי אליעזר אומר הציץ מרצה כו'. רבי אליעזר גרסינן ולא ר' אלעזר דלקמן פריך וליטעמיך כיון דאמר ר' אליעזר יש דם אף על פי שאין בשר הציץ מרצה על אכילות למאי הילכתא :

נימא מתני' דלא כר' יהושע · משמע משום דסבירא ליה דבעינן דם ובשר ותימה דאפי' סבירא ליה נמי יש דם אף על פי שאין בשר כיון דס"ד דטומאה דחויה ואין הציץ מרצה על אכילות לא אתיא מתני' כוותיה משום שתי הלחם :

נימא דלא כר' יהושע · תימה לר"י והא ע"כ כרבי יהושע אתיא דקתני סיפא ובמוקדשין אף על פי שנטמא בשר וחלב קיים זורק את הדם משמע הא נטמאו שניהם אינו זורק והיינו כרבי יהושע כדאמר לקמן וי"ל דה"ק נימא דלא כר' יהושע והא ע"כ סיפא אתיא כוותיה ואם כן קשיא סיפא :

אויר קטן היה בין כבש למזבח · °בלא אויר נמי היה יכול לקיים מצות זריקה [ב] אלא לכך היה אויר שע"י כך יזכור לזרוק :

דם אף על פי שאין בשר שנאמר ודם זבחיך וגו' · תימה לרשב"א מנא ליה בעולה דיש דם אף על פי שאין בשר אימא דווקא שלמים אבל עולה כליל אימא אין בשר אין דם יש דם אף על פי שאין בשר [מנא לן] : שאין

עין משפט נר מצוה

לא א מיי' פ"ד מהלכות ביאת מקדש הלכה טו טז :

לב ב שם הלכה ח :

לג ג שם הלכה ז :

ג"י רש"א לא קאי אשבת

לד ד מיי' פ"ו מהלכות פסולי המוקדשין הלכה לד :

לה ה מיי' פ"ז מהלכות מעשה הקרבנות הלכה ד :

לו ו מיי' פ"ב מהלכות בית הבחירה הל' יג :

[וע"ע תוס' כתובות לב. סד"ה שכן ותוס' סנהד' עו: ד"ה משום]

[וביבמות ה: ד"ה ומכולהו כתבו תוספות בשם ר"י תירוץ ע"ז ע"ש]

מסורת הש"ס

שבועות י. תענית כט. · מנחות פב: [ע"ש] · [יומא מו.] · [מנחות לב. סוטה כט: פסחים ד:] · סנהדרין יב: יומא ז: · [מנחות עו. לקמן עח. מנחות כה: · [תוספתא דזבחים פ"ד] זבחים קד. · שם כב: · [לעיל לד. זבחים סב: קד. ע"ש]

רבינו חננאל

שהוא קרבן צבור וקביע ליה מועד לא דחיא טומאה ובכלל זבחי צבור משמע אפילו שעירי רגלים דהא זבחי צבור הן ואפילו שעירי ראשי חדשים כיוצא בשעירי הרגלים הם. מיהו הוצרך להודיע כי ראש חדש נמי איקרי מועד שנאמר קרא עלי מועד : מנא הני מילי דת"ר וידבר משה את מועדי ה' אל בני ישראל מה ת"ל לפי כו' התמיד שכן תדיר שכן כליל . פי' התמיד חובה קבועה בכל יום והוא עולה כליל מה שאין כן בפסח כי הפסח הוא פעם בשנה ונאכל ואין למזבח ממנו אלא האימורין בלבד ויש בפסח מה שאין בתמיד (ש"מ) [שמי] שאינו עושה פסח ענוש כרת שנא' (במדבר ט יג) וחדל לעשות הפסח ונכרתה מה שאין כן בתמיד כי התמיד אין בו עונש כרת לפיכך הוצרך לפרש בזה במועדו ובזה במועדו להיות שניהן (דומין) [דוחין] השבת והטומאה שאין למדין זה מזה [ואי כתיב] הני תרוייהו לא גמרו מינייהו שכן ישנן לפני הדבור כלומר ניתנין לישראל ועשאום קודם מתן תורה פסח עשאוהו במצרים שנאמר (שמות י"ב ו') ושחטו אותו כל קהל עדת ישראל וגו' תמיד דגרסינן בתחלת חגיגה עולה שהקריבו ישראל במדבר עולת תמיד היא ואי כתיב הני לא ילפי האחרים מינייהו דאיכא למיפרך מה להני שכן ישנן לפני הדבור כדאמרן אי נמי שכן יש בהן צד חמור התמיד תדיר כליל הפסח ענוש כרת משא"כ בשאר הנקרבין לפיכך הוצרך לפרש בהן במועדו והני מילי בקרבנות דמכפרי אבל עומר ושתי הלחם דאין באין כפרה אלא להתיר כדגרסי' עומר מתיר במדינה דכיון שקרב העומר בששה [עשר] בניסן מותרין ישראל לאכול (תרומה) [תבואה] חדשה וכיון שהקריבו שתי הלחם בעצרת הותרו ישראל להקריב מנחה מן התבואה חדשה לפיכך הוצרך לכתוב (אחד במועדו) [עיד את מועדי] שיהיו כולן דוחין הטומאה כמו שאמרנו: סברוה דכ"ע טומאה דחויה בצבור ובעי ציץ לרצות דליכא תנא דשמעת ליה דאמר טומאה הותרה היא בצבור אלא ר' יהודה דתניא בין שישנו על מצחו וכו' ודכולי עלמא סברי אין הציץ מרצה על אכילות כגון מי שאכל קדש בטומאה וכיוצא בה אלא ר' אליעזר דתניא ר' אליעזר אומר הציץ מרצה על אכילות ר' יוסי אומר אין הציץ מרצה על אכילות נימא מתני' דקתני חמשה דברים באין בטומאה ואין נאכלין בטומאה דלא כר' יהושע דהא ר' יהושע שמעינן ליה דתרתי הוא דקא בעי דם ובשר דתניא ועשית עולותיך הבשר והדם ר' יהושע אומר אם אין דם אין בשר אם אין בשר אין דם ואקשי' עליה והכתיב ודם זבחיך ישפך על מזבח ה' אלהיך הנה דם אע"פ שאין בשר ומשני הכתיב ביה והבשר תאכל ותרי קראי בחד ענינא לי ומשני האי קרא ודם זבחיך ישפך שלמים הן והאי דכתיב ועשית עולותיך בעולה וצריכין דאי כתב רחמנא בעולה לא אתו שלמים מינה דפרכינן מה לעולה שכן כליל וכו' : ר' אליעזר אומר דם אע"פ שאין בשר

גליון הש"ס

רש"י ד"ה שאינו על מצחו . כדאמרינן בר"ה . תמוה לי וכי צריך ראיה לזה בלא מפורש בכתוב דלפני ולפנים רק בד' בגדים אלא דבר"ה אמרינן טעמא לקרא: תוס' ד"ה אויר. בלא אויר נמי. עי' תשו' ח"צ סי' קנ"ג:

הגהות מהר"ב רנשבורג

[א] תוס' ד"ה דלא וכו'. דדחוי' בציבור וכו'. נ"ב עיין מנחות ע"ו ע"א תוס' ד"ה וככא מאי ציץ וכו' וצ"ע ודו"ק : [ב] שם ד"ה אויר וכו'. יכול לקיים מצות זריקה . נ"ב עיין שו"ת ח"צ סימן קנ"ג :

PEACE-OFFERINGS?—I will tell you: [77a] It is necessary for him [to teach about] the he-goats of New Moons. I might argue, surely *'appointed season'* [mo'ed] is not written in connection therewith;[7] therefore he informs us that New Moon is designated *mo'ed*, in accordance with Abaye's [dictum]. For Abaye said, The Tammuz[8] of that year[9] was indeed made full,[10] as it is written, *He hath proclaimed an appointed time* [mo'ed] *against me to crush my young men.*[11]

Shall we say that all of them[12] are derived from *mo'ed* ['appointed time']? How do we know it? For our Rabbis taught: *And Moses*
a *declared unto the children of Israel the appointed times of the Lord.*[1] For what purpose is this stated?[2] Because we have learnt only of the daily offering and the Passover-offering [that they override the Sabbath and uncleanness], since *'in its appointed time'* is stated in connection with them,[3] *'in its appointed time'* [implying] even on the Sabbath, *'in its appointed time'* implying even in uncleanness. Whence do we know it of other public sacrifices? Because it is said, *These shall ye offer unto the Lord in your appointed times.*[4] Whence do we know to include the *'omer* and that which is offered with it, and the two loaves and that which is offered with them? Therefore it is stated, *'And Moses declared unto the children of Israel the appointed times of the Lord'*: the Writ fixed it as one appointed season for all of them.[5]

Now, what is the purpose of all these?[6]—They are necessary. For if the Divine Law wrote it of the daily offering [alone], I would say: The daily offering [overrides the Sabbath and uncleanness] because it is constant and entirely burnt, but the Passover is not so;[7] hence we are informed [otherwise]. While if the Divine Law wrote it of the Passover-offering, [I would argue that] the Passover-offering [must be offered under all circumstances] because it involves the penalty of *kareth*,[8] but [as for] the continual offering, for [neglect of] which there is no penalty of *kareth*, I would say that it is not [so]; hence we are informed [otherwise]. Again, if the Divine Law wrote it of these two, I would say: These alone [override Sabbath and uncleanness, since they] possess a stringent feature, the continual offering being constant and entirely [burnt], the Passover-offering involving the penalty of *kareth*; but [as for] other public sacrifices, I would say, It is not so. [Hence] the Divine Law wrote, *'These shall ye offer unto the Lord in your appointed times.'* While if the Divine Law [merely] wrote, *'These shall ye offer unto the Lord in your appointed times,'* I would argue: [It refers only to]
b other public sacrifices, which come to make atonement,[1] but [the sacrifices accompanying] the *'omer* and the two loaves, which do not come to make atonement but are merely in order to permit [the new harvest] are not so; hence we are informed [otherwise]. Again, if the Divine Law wrote [about] the *'omer* and the two loaves alone, I would have said: On the contrary, it [applies only to] the *'omer* and the two loaves which are more important, because they come to permit; but these others are not so. Hence we are informed [otherwise].

Now it was assumed that all hold that uncleanness is *overridden* in the case of a community, hence the headplate is required for propitiation.[2] For there is no [other] Tanna whom you know to maintain [that] uncleanness is *permitted* in the case of a community[3] but R. Judah. For it was taught: The headplate, whether it is on his [the High Priest's] forehead[4] or it is not on his forehead, propitiates; this is the view of R. Simeon. R. Judah maintained: If it is still on his forehead, it propitiates; if it is not still on his forehead, it does not propitiate. Said R. Simeon to him: Let the High Priest on the Day of Atonement prove it, for it
c is not on his forehead, and [yet] it propitiates![1]—Leave the Day of Atonement, replied he, because uncleanness is permitted in the case of a community. Whence it follows that R. Simeon holds: Uncleanness is overridden in the case of a community. Again, [it was assumed that all hold,] the headplate does not propitiate for [the defilement of] eatables,[2] for there is no Tanna whom you know to maintain [that] the headplate propitiates for [the defilement of] eatables save R. Eleazar. For it was taught, R. Eleazar said: The headplate propitiates for [the defilement of] eatables; R. Jose said: The headplate does not propitiate for the defilement of eatables.[3] [Accordingly,] shall we say that our Mishnah[4] does not agree with R. Joshua? For it was taught, *And thou shalt offer thy burnt-offerings, the flesh and the blood:*[5] R. Joshua said: If there is no blood there is no flesh, and if there is no flesh there is no blood.[6] R. Eliezer said: The blood [is fit] even if there is no flesh, because it is said, *And the blood of thy sacrifices shall be poured out* [*against the altar of the Lord thy God*].[7] Then how do I interpret,[8] *'and thou shalt offer thy burnt-offerings, the flesh and the blood?'* [It is] to teach you: just as the blood requires throwing,[9] so does the flesh require throwing:[10] hence say, there was a small passage-way between the stairway and the altar.[11] Now [according to] R. Joshua too, surely it is written, *'and the blood of thy sacrifices shall be poured out?'*—He can answer you: surely

(7) Whereas it is from this word that we deduce anon that festival public sacrifices override the Sabbath and uncleanness. (8) The fourth month of the year, generally corresponding to June. (9) In which the spies reconnoitred the Promised Land, with disastrous results, v. Num. XIII. (10) I.e., it consisted of 30 days. When it consists of 29 days it is called defective. Now, as they set out on the 29th of Sivan, the third month (Ta'an. 29a), the 40 days of their mission ended on the ninth of Ab, the fifth month. Thus their weeping on that night (ibid. XIV, 1) became the forerunner of subsequent lamentation on that date for many generations, for it is the anniversary of the destruction of the Temple. (11) Lam. I, 15. Abaye appears to interpret thus: God caused New Moon (i.e., the 'appointed time'—*mo'ed*) of Tammuz in that year to be proclaimed on such a day that their return and the weeping of the people would coincide with the future anniversary of the destruction of the Temple. Hence, on this interpretation, New Moon too is designated *'mo'ed'*. (12) I.e., those mentioned in the Mishnah that may be offered in uncleanness.

a (1) Lev. XXIII, 44. (2) Seeing that all the Festivals are *individually* treated in that chapter. (3) Num. XXVIII, 2; IX, 2. *'In its appointed time'* implies that the sacrifice must be offered in all circumstances, as explained in the text. (4) Ibid. XXIX, 39. This verse ends the section (chs. XXVIII—XXIX) dealing with the public additional sacrifices on New Moon, the Sabbath and Festivals, and its effect is that the whole section is to be so understood as though *'in its appointed season'* were explicitly written in connection with each. (5) V. previous note; the same applies here, and the *'omer* and the two loaves are prescribed in this section (vv. 10f, 17f). (6) Scripture could have written *'appointed season'* in connection with one only, and the rest would follow. (7) It is not constant by comparison. (8) For not bringing it; v. Num. IX, 13.

b (1) The additional sacrifices make atonement for the transgression of affirmative precepts, v. Yoma 36a. (2) I.e., though uncleanness is not a bar when the whole community is unclean, Scripture does not mean that the normal interdict of uncleanness is completely abrogated, so that it is permitted, but merely that the interdict is overridden in favour of the community. Now in Ex. XXVIII, 38 it is stated: *And it* (the headplate) *shall be upon Aaron's forehead, and Aaron shall bear* (i.e., atone for) *the iniquity committed in the holy things* (*sc.* sacrifices) . . . *and it shall always be upon his forehead, that they may be accepted before the Lord* (i.e., that these sacrifices shall be fit). *'The iniquity'* is understood to refer to a case where a sacrifice accidentally became unclean, and the headplate atones for it, so that it remains fit. Since we hold that even in the case of a community uncleanness is merely overridden, but not actually permitted, the headplate is required for propitiation even then. (3) So that the propitiation of the headplate is not required at all. (4) When the sacrifice accidentally becomes unclean.

c (1) On that day he put aside all his usual vestments, which included the headplate, and wore simple linen garments (v. Lev. XVI, 4). Yet if the community was unclean he still offered the sacrifices, and the headplate 'made them acceptable'. (2) I.e., if the flesh or the part of the meal-offering which is eaten is defiled, the sacrifice cannot be proceeded with, the headplate propitiating only if the blood or the handful which is burnt on the altar is defiled. (3) These two assumptions are the necessary premises for the question which follows. (4) Which states that the *'omer*, the two loaves, etc., may be offered in uncleanness, although the plate does not propitiate on the eatable parts of these offerings. (5) Deut. XII, 27. (6) I.e., if either is defiled, the other is unfit for its purpose. (7) Ibid. (8) Lit., 'fulfil'. (9) I.e., dashing against the altar. (10) On to the altar. (11) Consequently a priest standing at the top of the ascent could not *place* the flesh on the altar but had to throw it.

Rab said: [76b] Fat meat of a [ritually] slaughtered [animal] which was roasted together with lean meat of *nebelah*[9] is forbidden. What is the reason? They fatten each other.[10] But Levi maintained: Even lean meat of a [ritually] slaughtered [animal] which was roasted together with fat meat of *nebelah* is permitted. What is the reason? It is a mere smell, and smell is nothing. Levi gave a practical decision[11] at the house of the *Resh Galutha*[12] in the case of a goat and 'something else.'[13]

An objection is raised: One may not roast two Passover offerings together, on account of the mixture. Surely that means, the
a mixture of [the] flavours,[1] which is a difficulty on Levi's view?—No: [it means] the mixture of their carcasses.[2] This too is logical, since the second clause teaches: Even a kid and a lamb. Now it is well if you say [that it is] on account of the carcasses: hence he teaches, 'even a kid and a lamb.'[3] But if you say [that it is] on account of the mingling of [the] flavours, what does it matter whether it is a kid and a lamb or a kid and a kid?—What then? You are bound [to say] that it is forbidden only on account of the mixing of the carcasses, but the mingling of flavours is permitted; shall we say [then] that this is a refutation of Rab?—Said R. Jeremiah: The case we discuss here[4] is e.g., where he roasted them in two pots. [You say] 'In two pots'—can you think so![5] —Rather say, as though [they were roasted in] two pots,[6] and this is what it teaches: One may not roast two Passover-offerings together, on account of the mixture. What mixture? The mixture of the flavours. And even [when roasted] as it were in two pots it is forbidden on account of the [possible] confusing of the carcasses, and even a kid and a lamb [must not be roasted together].

R. Mari said: This is dependent on Tannaim. If a man removes a hot loaf [from the oven] and places it on a wine barrel of *terumah*, —R. Meir forbids it;[7] whereas R. Judah permits it; while R. Jose permits it in the case of [a loaf of] wheat, but forbids it in the case of barley [flour], because barley absorbs. Surely then it is dependent on Tannaim, one Master holding: Smell is nothing; while the other Master holds: Smell is something [substantial]? According to Levi, it is certainly dependent on Tannaim.[8] Shall we say that it is [dependent on] Tannaim according to Rab [too]?—Rab can tell you: All agree that smell is something [substantial]; [and as to the ruling of R. Judah] was it not stated thereon, Rabbah b. Bar Ḥanah said in the name of Resh Laḳish: In the case of a hot loaf and an open barrel, all agree that it is forbidden; in the case of a cold loaf and a closed [stoppered] barrel, all agree that it is permitted. They differ only in the case of a hot loaf and a sealed
b barrel, [or] a cold loaf and an open barrel;[1] and this too[2] is like a hot loaf and an open barrel.[3]

R. Kahana the son of R. Ḥinena the Elder recited: A loaf which was baked together with roast [meat] in an oven may not be eaten with *kutaḥ*.[4] A fish was roasted [i.e., baked] together with meat, [whereupon] Raba of Parziḳia[5] forbade it to be eaten with *kutaḥ*. Mar b. R. Ashi said: Even with salt too it is forbidden, because it is harmful to [one's] smell and in respect of 'something else.'[6]

MISHNAH. FIVE THINGS [SACRIFICES] MAY COME IN UNCLEANNESS, YET MUST NOT BE EATEN IN UNCLEANNESS: THE 'OMER,[7] THE TWO LOAVES,[8] THE SHEWBREAD,[9] THE SACRIFICES OF THE PUBLIC PEACE-OFFERINGS,[10] AND THE HE-GOATS OF NEW MOONS.[11] THE PASCHAL LAMB WHICH COMES IN UNCLEANNESS IS EATEN IN UNCLEANNESS, FOR FROM THE VERY BEGINNING IT CAME FOR NO OTHER PURPOSE BUT TO BE EATEN.

GEMARA. What does 'FIVE' exclude?[12]—It excludes the
c *ḥagigah* [for example] of the fifteenth.[1] For I might argue, since it is a public sacrifice[2] and a season is fixed for it, let it override uncleanness; therefore he informs us [that] since you can make it up the whole seven [days],[3] it does not override the Sabbath,[4] and since it does not override the Sabbath, it does not override uncleanness.

Now, let him [the Tanna] state the he-goats of festivals too?[5] —He does indeed state THE SACRIFICES OF THE PUBLIC PEACE-OFFERINGS.[6] If so, let him not state the he-goats of New Moons either, seeing that he states THE SACRIFICES OF THE PUBLIC

(9) In the same oven on separate spits and not touching. (10) The odour of the fat meat enters the lean meat and makes it fat, and then in turn the odour of the lean meat, which is forbidden, enters the permitted meat and renders it forbidden too.—Hence if the meat of *nebelah* itself is fat, it is certainly forbidden. (11) As distinct from a mere *theoretical* ruling—in accordance with his view. (12) V. Glos. (13) I.e., a swine, which was generally referred to thus; cf. *supra* 3b. These had been roasted together.

a (1) Each absorbs the flavour of the other through its smell, which would thus be enjoyed by those who have not registered for that animal. (2) The animals themselves may be mixed up with each other. (3) Though a mistake is less likely there. (4) In the teaching cited. (5) The Passover-offering may not be roasted in pots at all. (6) A heap of coals or ashes intervening between the two sacrifices. (7) To a lay Israelite, because it has absorbed the odour of the wine. (8) For R. Meir's view certainly contradicts his.

b (1) And it is only in such cases that R. Judah permits. (2) *Sc.* the case disputed by Rab and Levi. (3) Which even R. Judah agrees is forbidden. (4) V. Glos. This contains milk. (5) Obermeyer, p. 227, n. 2 thinks this identical with Perezina (Faransag), near Bagdad. (6) Leprosy. (7) V. Glos. and Lev. XXIII, 10f. (8) V. ibid. 17. (9) V. Ex. XXV, 30. (10) The lambs offered on Pentecost, v. Num. XXVIII, 27. (11) V. ibid. 15—all these are brought even if the community is unclean, which of course makes them unclean too through the handling of the officiating priest; nevertheless, they may not be eaten, for they are brought merely in discharge of public obligations, but their main purpose is not to be eaten. (12) It is assumed that the number has this purpose, for otherwise the Mishnah would simply state, The *'omer* . . . come in uncleanness etc.

c (1) And similarly the *ḥagigah* of any other Festival. (2) In the sense that all Jews must bring a *ḥagigah*. (3) If not brought on the first day it can be brought for a week afterwards, v. Ḥag. 9a. (4) A public sacrifice overrides the Sabbath only when it cannot be offered on any other day. (5) V. Num. XXVIII, 15, 22, 30; XXIX, 5, 16, 38. (6) For the he-goats too are public sacrifices (R. Ḥan).

עין משפט נר מצוה

כד א מיי' פט"ו מהל' מ"א הלכה לג סמג לאוין [קלז] טוש"ע יו"ד סימן קח סעיף א [כב אלפס חולין פ"ז דף רלא. ושם כל הסוגיא הכא ולר"ת כרא"ש פרק כתרא דע"ז סימן ח] :

כה ב מיי' פ"ז מהל' ק"פ הלכה יד :

כו ג ד מיי' פט"ו מהל' תרומות הלכה יג טוש"ע יו"ד סימן קח סעיף ד :

כז ה מיי' פ"ט מהלכות מ"א הלכה כב סמג לאוין קמא טור טוש"ע יו"ד סימן [ו] סעיף ג :

כז [ה] [טוש"ע יו"ד סי' קטז סעיף ב] :

כח ו מיי' פ"ד מהלכות ביאת מקדש הל' יא :

כט ז מיי' פ"ז מהלכות ק"פ הלכה ח :

ל ח מיי' פ"א מהלכות חגיגה הלכה ח :

תוספות

מאי לאו תערובת טעמים · לפי מה שפי' בקונטרס דלוי לא שרי אלא דיעבד קשיא מה פריך דהכא לכתחלה קתני אבל בדיעבד הוה שרי כלוי : **נימא** תהוי תיובתא דרב · תימה מאי קושיא הא דאסר משום תערובת גופים הייתו היכא דשניהם כחושים דליכא תערובת טעמים :

אסרה רבא מפרזיקיא כו' · מכאן פוסק ר"ת כרב ורבא מני דשרי בבת תיהא (ע"ז דף סו:) מלי סבר כוותיה ושם מפורש ובתוספות [גדולים] שלנו נראה דמותר לאפות לחם עם אותו פשטיד"א הואיל ומסוכסת היטב הוי כעין שתי קדרות ואפי' פלדו"ש שיש להרחיק אין נראה לרבי שיהא אסור שיש אויר מרובה בתנור וההבל מתפשט :

קא משמע לן כיון דלא דחיא שבת לא דחיא טומאה · ולא גרס כיון דאית לה תשלומין שאין הטעם תלוי בכך דלעיל בפרק אלו דברים (דף סט:) ילפינן דלא דחיא שבת מוחגותם וגו' · ועוד פסח נמי אית ליה תשלומין בפסח שני ודחי טומאה ועוד חגיגת ט"ו היכא למ"ד *בפירקין דלית לה תשלומין בטומאת בעלים שאם נטמאו בעלים ביום ט"ו ולא חזו ביום קביעת חובתיה כה"ג לית לה תשלומין : [לקמן פ.]

גמרא

בשר שחוטה שמן שצלאו עם בשר נבילה כחוש אסור מאי טעמא מפטמי מהדדי ולוי אמר *א אפילו בשר שחוטה כחוש שצלאו עם בשר נבילה שמן מותר מאי טעמא ריחא בעלמא הוא וריחא לאו מילתא היא עביד לוי עובדא בי ריש גלותא בגדי ודבר אחר מיתיבי *ב אין צולין שני פסחים כאחד מפני התערובת מאי לאו תערובת טעמים וקשיא ללוי לא מפני תערובת גופין הכי נמי מסתברא מדקתני סיפא *אפילו גדי וטלה אי אמרת בשלמא מפני גופין היינו דקתני אפי' גדי וטלה אלא אי אמרת מפני תערובת טעמים מה לי גדי וטלה מה לי גדי וגדי אלא מאי על כרחיך מפני תערובת גופין הוא דאסור אבל תערובת טעמים שרי לימא תיהוי תיובתיה דרב אמר רבי ירמיה הכא במאי עסקינן כגון שצלאו בשתי קדירות בשתי קדירות סלקא דעתך אלא אימא כעין שתי קדירות והכי קאמר אין צולין שני פסחים כאחד מפני תערובת מאי תערובת תערובת טעמים ואפי' כעין שתי קדירות דליכא תערובת טעמים אסור משום תערובת גופין ואפילו גדי וטלה אמר רב מרי כתנאי *הרודה פת חמה ונתנה ע"פ חבית יין של תרומה ר"מ אוסר ורבי יהודה מתיר ורבי יוסי ג מתיר בשל חיטין ואוסר בשל שעורים מפני שהשעורים שואבות מאי לאו תנאי היא דמר סבר ריחא לאו מילתא היא ומר סבר ריחא מילתא היא ללוי ודאי תנאי היא לרב נימא תנאי היא אמר לך רב דכולי עלמא ריחא מילתא היא לאו איתמר עלה דההיא אמר רבה בר בר חנה אמר ריש לקיש ד בפת חמה וחבית פתוחה דברי הכל אסור בפת צוננת וחבית מגופה דברי הכל מותר לא נחלקו אלא בפת חמה וחבית חתומה פת צוננת וחבית פתוחה והא נמי כפת חמה וחבית פתוחה דמיא תני רב כהנא בריה דרב חיננא סבא ה פת שאפאה עם צלי בתנור אסור לאכלה בכותחא ההיא ביניתא דאיטווא בהדי בישרא אסרה רבא מפרזיקיא °למיכליה בכותחא מר בר רב אשי אמר אפי' [ה'] במילחא נמי אסורה משום דקשיא לריחא ולדבר אחר:

מתני' ז חמשה דברים °באין בטומאה ואינן נאכלין בטומאה העומר ושתי הלחם ולחם הפנים וזבחי שלמי צבור ושעירי ראשי חדשים *ט הפסח שבא בטומאה נאכל בטומאה שלא בא מתחילתו אלא לאכילה :

גמ' חמשה למעוטי מאי ח למעוטי חגיגת חמשה עשר דסלקא דעתך אמינא כיון דקרבן ציבור הוא וקביעא ליה מועד תדחי טומאה קא משמע לן כיון דאית ליה תשלומין כל שבעה לא דחיא שבת ומדשבת לא דחיא לא דחיא טומאה וניתני נמי שעירי הרגלים הא תנא ליה זבחי שלמי צבור אי הכי שעירי ראשי חדשים נמי לא ניתני דהא תנא זבחי שלמי צבור אמרי שעירי

רש"י

בשר שחוטה שמן שצלאו · בתנור בשני שפודים זה רחוק מזה אסור שהריח מן השמן נכנס לכחוש ומפטמו וחוזר זה ומוליא ריח גם הוא וכ"ש שחוטה כחושה ונבילה שמינה ורבותא אשמעינן רב דלא נימא נבילה כחושה הואיל ואין ריחה עודף לא אסרה לה לשחוטה ואשמעינן דשומן שחוטה מפטם לנבילה בריחא והדר מפקא איהו ריחא : עבד עובדא · שנצלו בתנור ובא מעשה לפניו והתיר : דבר אחר · חזיר : אין צולין שני פסחים כאחד מפני התערובת · ונמלא פסח נאכל שלא למנויו ואפילו גדי וטלה שאין מתחלפין זה בזה : מאי לאו תערובת טעמים · דמפטמי מהדדי ונמלא פסח נאכל שלא למנויו : לא מפני תערובת גופים · שלא יתערבו זה בזה ואפילו גדי וטלה זימנין דלאו אדעתייהו ואחלופי : אלא מאי על כרחיך · דקתני ביה ואפילו גדי וטלה שמעינן מינה דמפני תערובת גופים קאמר אבל לתערובת טעמים לא חייש נימא תיהוי תיובתא דרב : הכא במאי עסקינן · דקתני גדי וטלה דלא חייש לתערובת טעמים שצלאן בשתי קדירות : שתי קדירות ס"ד · וכי צולין פסח בקדירה : כעין שתי קדירות · שפוד מכאן ושפוד מכאן ותל גדול של גחלים או אפר באמלע : הרודה · מן התנור : אוסר · לזרים מפני שנכנס לה ריח התרומה : שואבות · את הריח : ללוי · דאמר ריחא לאו מילתא היא ודאי מילתיה כתנאי אמרה דעל כרחיך רבי מאיר אית ליה ריחא מילתא היא וכן רבי יוסי ואי איכא דקאי כוותיה רבי יהודה הוא דקאי כוותיה : אלא רב מי לימא תנאי היא · כלום לריך לאוקומי למילתיה כתנאי ולמימר אנא דאמרי כרבי מאיר ורבי יוסי אבל דרבי יהודה לית ליה או דילמא רבי יהודה נמי קאי כוותיה וטעמא דשרי משום דקא סבר לא עייל בה ריחא : אמר לך רב דכולי עלמא ריחא מילתא · וטעמא דרבי יהודה משום דפת צוננת (*וחבית) מגופה היא ולא עייל בה ריחא דמי לאו איתמר עלה כו' ואע"ג דקיימי תנאי כוותיה דרב הילכתא כוותיה דלוי דהא איפליגו בה אביי ורבא גבי בת תיהא במסכת ע"ז (דף סו:) וקם ליה רבא בשיטתיה דלוי ואמר ריחא לאו מילתא היא ואביי ורבא הילכתא כרבא וכן הוא בתשובות הגאונים ואף משמו של רבי אליעזר בן יצחק נאמר לי דלא חייש לה : ביניתא · דג : דאיטוי בהדי בישרא · בתנור אחד : אסרה רבא מפרזיקא למיכלה בכותחא · שיש בו חלב משום דקסבר ריחא מילתא היא : לדבר אחר · לרעת : **מתני'** חמשה דברים באין בטומאה וכו' · אין לך קרבן נאכל אלא אלו וקרבן ציבור דוחה את הטומאה ואשמעינן מתניתין דאף על גב דקרב בטומאה להפוקי ציבור ידי חובתן אין נאכלין בטומאה ולקמיה פריך ליתני נמי שעירי הרגלים : זבחי שלמי ציבור · כבשי עצרת שאין שלמים אחרים לציבור : הפסח שבא בטומאה · כגון רוב ציבור טמאין : שמתחילתו לא בא אלא לאכילה · כשנלטוה עיקר פסח לאכילה נלטוה דכתיב לפי אכלו וכי שרייה רחמנא למיתי בטומאה*) מאיס נדחה ואין צבור נדחין אדעתא למיכליה שרייה* : **גמ'** חמשה למעוטי מאי · מנייתא למה לי ליתני קרבנות ציבור באין בטומאה ואין נאכלין בטומאה : חגיגת חמשה עשר · והוא הדין לעצרת וסוכות אלא חדא מינייהו נקט : כיון דקרבן ציבור הוא · אף על גב דכל יחיד ויחיד מיחייב קרי ליה קרבן ציבור משום דאתיא בכינופיא באסיפת חברים ברגל במסכת יומא בפרק הוציאו לו (דף נא·) : תשלומין כל שבעה · כדנפקא לן בפרק קמא דמסכת חגיגה (דף ט·) וחגותם אותו חג לה' שבעת ימים : הא תני ליה זבחי שלמי ציבור · שהן מיני דמים ואשמעינן דאין נאכלין בטומאה והוא הדין לשאר מיני דמים :

הא

*) [לעיל סו. סז:]

מסורת הש"ס

[תוספתא פ"ט]

[שם וע"ש]

תרומות פ"י מ"ג ע"ה סו:

לעיל סב:

[לקמן לא.]

גליון הש"ס

גמ' למיכליה בכותחא. עי' לעיל ל. תוד"ה ואפי' במלחא: מתני' באין בטומאה. עי' יומא מו ע"א תוד"ה תחלתו דוחה :

רבינו חננאל

פילי ומתבלע אגב חורפא דתבלי בלע כוליה ואסור: **אמר** רב בשר שחוטה שמן שצלאו עם בשר נבלה כחוש אסור דאזיל ריח השחוטה מפטם לנבלה וחוזר ריח נבלה מפטם לשחוטה ולוי מתיר אפילו נבלה שמינה עם שחוטה כחושה סבר ריחא ולא כלום הוא ועבד עובדא והתיר גדי שנפל עם חזיר ואותבינן עליה מיהא אין צולין שני פסחים ואפילו גדי וטלה מפני התערובות ומסתברא דמשום תערובות גופין הוא גזרה גדי וטלה אטו טלה וטלה שאם נתערבו חיישי' שמא תטול חבורה זו פסח שאינו שלה ונמצא אוכלין פסח שאינו שלהם וקשיא לרב דאמר ריחא מילתא היא והריח כעיקר אע"ג דלא מחלפי כיון שהריח כעיקר נמצא עיקר פסח של חבורה זו בפסח של חבורה ז ואסור ומוקים לה רב הכי אין צולין שני פסחים כאחד מפני תערובות טעמים ואפי' כעין שתי קדרות כגון שיש דבר מפסיק הריח ביניהם ואין שם תערובת טעמים אסור משום תערובת גופין ואפילו גדי וטלה דלא מחלפי גזרה אטו גדי וגדי אטו טלה : **אמר** רב מרי כתנאי הרודה פת חמה ונתנה על פי חבית של תרומה ר' מאיר אוסר ור' יהודה מתיר ור' יוסי מתיר בפת של חטים ואוסר בפת של שעורים מפני שהשעורים שואבות ללוי ודאי תנאי היא דהא ר' מאיר אוסר בפי' (והנה ר' יהודה מתיר דלא כרב) והנה גם לרב [מי נימא] תנאי היא אמר לך הא אתמר עלה בפת חמה וחבית פתוחה לדברי הכל אסור ואפילו ר' יהודה אוסר דריחא מילתא היא בפת צוננת וחבית מגופה דברי הכל מותר דליכא חשש לריח היין של תרומה כלל דהא חבית זו מגופה היא לא נחלקו אלא בפת חמה וחבית מגופה פת צוננת וחבית פתוחה והכא גבי בשר שחוטה שנצלה עם בשר [נבלה] כפת חמה וחבית פתוחה הוא לדברי הכל אסור וקיימא לן כרב דאע"ג דלוי מיתוקמא כתנאי ולוי כר' יהודה הא אתמר עלה דחבית פתוחה ופת חמה דברי הכל אסורה ומסתבר טעמא דרב ולא עוד אלא הא תני רב כהנא פת שאפאה בתנור עם בשר צלי אסור לאכלה בכותח כרב ותוב ההיא ביעתא שנצלית עם בשר ואסרה רבא מפרזיקא לאכלה בכותח שיש בו נסיובי דחלבא . מר בר רב אשי אסור לאכלה אפילו במלח משום דסבר דג ובשר להתבשל יחדיו ולהאכל קשו לריחיא ודבר [אחר] פי' נגע צרעת הני כלהו כרב הלכך כרב עבדינן וראינו מי שאמר קיימא לן כלוי ואנן לא סבירא לן כותיה אלא הלכתא כרב : **מתני'** חמשה דברים באין בטומאה ואין נאכלין בטומאה העומר ושתי הלחם ולחם הפנים וזבחי שלמי צבור ושעירי ראשי חדשים הפסח שבא בטומאה נאכל בטומאה שלא בא מתחלתו אלא לאכילה ואמרינן חמשה כלומר מנין חמשה ולא יתר מה בא למעט [בא למעט] חגיגת חמשה עשר [דכיון] דאית לה תשלומין דתנן מי שלא חג ביום טוב הראשון של חג חוגג והולך כל הרגל וכו' אע"פ

שהוא

עין משפט נר מצוה

כא א ב מיי' פ"ט מהל' מ"א הלכה יז סמג לאוין קמג טוש"ע יו"ד סימן צא סעיף ד וסימן קה סעיף ג :

כב ג ד מיי' שם הלכה יח סמג שם טור שו"ע יו"ד סימן צא סעיף ה :

כג ה מיי' שם הלכה יט סמג שם טור שו"ע שם סעיף ז :

מסורת הש"ס

אסור צונן לתוך צונן דברי הכל מותר חם לתוך צונן וצונן לתוך חם רב אמר עילאה גבר ושמואל אמר תתאה גבר תנן נטף מרוטבו על החרס וחזר אליו יטול את מקומו קא סלקא דעתך בחרס צוננת בשלמא לרב דאמר עילאה גבר משום הכי יטול את מקומו דאזל רוטב מרתח ליה לחרס והדר חרס מרתח ליה לרוטב וכי הדר רוטב אפסח קא מטוי פסח מחמת חמימותא דחרס ורחמנא אמר °צלי אש ולא צלי מחמת דבר אחר אלא לשמואל דאמר תתאה גבר חרס כיון דצונן הוא אקורי מיקר ליה לרוטב אמאי יטול את מקומו כדאמר רבי ירמיה אמר שמואל בסולת רותחת הכא נמי בחרס רותח תנן נטף מרוטבו על הסולת יקמוץ את מקומו קא סלקא דעתך בסולת צוננת בשלמא לרב דאמר עילאה גבר משום הכי יקמוץ את מקומו דמרתחא לה לסולת דהדר הודרניה והדרא סולת ומרתחא ליה לדידיה וקא מטוי רוטב מחמת חמימותא דסולת ורחמנא אמר צלי אש ולא צלי מחמת דבר אחר אלא לשמואל דאמר תתאה גבר סולת כיון דצוננת היא אקורי קא מיקר ליה למה לי יקמוץ את מקומו (תסגי ליה ביטול את מקומו) א"ר ירמיה אמר שמואל בסולת רותחת תנן סכו בשמן של תרומה אם חבורת כהנים יאכלו אם של ישראל אם חי הוא ידיחנו אם צלי הוא יקלוף את החיצון בשלמא לרב דאמר עילאה גבר אמטו להכי סגי ליה בקליפה משום דעילאה צונן הוא אלא לשמואל דאמר תתאה גבר כיון דחם הוא מבלע בלע אמאי סגי ליה בקליפה ניתסר לגמרי שאני סיכה דמשהו בעלמא הוא דעבידא תניא כוותיה דשמואל *חם לתוך חם אסור וכן צונן שנתן לתוך חם אסור חם לתוך צונן וצונן לתוך צונן מדיח חם לתוך צונן מדיח כיון דחם הוא אדמיקר ליה אי אפשר דלא בלע פורתא קליפה מיהא ניבעי אלא אימא חם לתוך צונן קולף צונן לתוך צונן מדיח תניא אידך בשר רותח שנפל לתוך חלב רותח וכן צונן שנפל לתוך חם אסור חם לתוך צונן וצונן לתוך צונן מדיח חם לתוך צונן מדיח כיון דחם הוא אדמיקר ליה אי אפשר דלא בלע פורתא קליפה מיהא ניבעי אלא אימא חם לתוך צונן קולף צונן לתוך צונן מדיח אמר מר צונן לתוך צונן מדיח אמר רב הונא לא שנו אלא שלא מלחו אבל מלחו אסור *דאמר שמואל מליח הרי הוא כרותח כבוש הרי הוא כמבושל אמר רבא הא דאמר שמואל מליח הרי הוא כרותח (וכו') לא אמרן אלא שלא נאכל מחמת מלחו אבל נאכל מחמת מלחו לא *ההוא בר גוזלא דנפל לבדא דכמכא שרייא רב חיננא בריה *דרבא מפשרוניא אמר רבא מאן חכים למישרא מילתא כי הא אי לאו רב חיננא בריה *דרבא מפשרוניא דגברא רבה הוא אמר לך כי אמר שמואל מליח הרי הוא כרותח שאין נאכל מחמת מלחו האי נאכל מחמת מלחו הוא והני מילי חי אבל צלי בעי קליפה ולא אמרן אלא דלית ביה פילי אבל אית ביה פילי אסור ואי מתובל בתבלי אסור אמר רב בשר

שמות יב

[תוספתא חולין פ"ח]

חולין צז: קיב. קיב: קיז.

שם קיב.

נ"א רבה מפרשניא

אסור · דבלע היתר מאיסור : עילאה גבר · העליון נוצח הלכך חם לתוך צונן אסור שהעליון מחממו לתחתון והרי שניהן חמין ובלעי מהדדי וצונן לתוך חם מותר שהעליון מצננו לתחתון ולא בלעי : ושמואל אמר תתאה גבר · הלכך חם לתוך צונן מותר וצונן לתוך חם אסור ואף על גב *דהילכתא כרב באיסורי בהא הילכתא כשמואל דהא תניא תרתי מתני' כוותיה כדלקמן : והדר חרס ומחמם ליה לרוטב · דהוי צלי מחמת דבר אחר : אקורי מיקר ליה · ואמאי יטול את מקומו ולא גרסינן בקולף את מקומו סגיא : לסולת דהדר הודרניה · לסולת אשר סביבותיו : הדר הודרניה · לשון סחור סחור (א) ליה : ואמאי יקמוץ · והכא נמי לא גרס ביטול את מקומו סגיא : [צונן הוא] · דאקורי קא מיקר ליה וקליפה מיהא בעיא דאפילו צונן גמור הוא הפסח מאחר שנגלה ויבש שאי אפשר דלא עייל ביה סיכת השמן פורתא : וצונן לתוך חם אסור · אלמא תתאה גבר : עד דמיקר ליה · קודם שיצטנן בלע כל דהו : כבוש · בחומץ : הרי הוא כמבושל · ואם נכבשו איסור והתר יחד (ב) כולן אסורין : שאין נאכל מחמת מלחו · שהמליחו הרבה עד שמקדיח טעמו מחמת מלחו קצת ואינו ראוי לאוכלו אלא אם כן היה מדיחו והאי אין נאכל לאו לגמרי קאמר שאין שום אדם יכול לאוכלו אלא כיון שנתקלקל טעמו אינו נאכל מחמת מלחו קרי ליה ואסור : כמכא · כותח ואית ביה נסיובי דחלבא : מפשרוניא · מקום : ולא אמרן · דלאו בקליפה סגי ליה אלא דלית ליה פילי קרבנ"ש : ואי מיתבל · בר גוזלא בתבלי אסור דתבלי מרככי ליה ומיילי ובלעי לכותחא ובר גוזלא צונן הוה כדמפרש :

[כשרות מט:]

הגהות הב"ח

(א) רש"י ד"ה לסולת וכו' סחור הס"ד ואח"כ מ"ה אקורי קא מיקר ליה ואמאי יקמוץ : (ב) ד"ה הרי הוא וכו' כולן אסור הס"ד :

תנן נטף מרוטבו על החרס כו' · מרישא דקתני נגע בחרסו של תנור יקלוף את מקומו ליכא לאקשויי אפי' למאי דס"ד בחרס צונן דכ"ע מודו דתתאה בלע כדי קליפה וה"ה לאחר שהוחם מעט מבשל בפסח כדי קליפה אי נמי כיון דקתני נגע אין להוכיח אם נגע מלמעלה או מלמטה אבל הכא דקתני נטף משמע למטה אי נמי חרסו של תנור ודאי חם הוא אבל סיפא דקתני על החרס קס"ד בחרס צונן ולא נהירא דמדנקט חרס משמע דבחרס תנור מיירי :

בשלמא למאן דאמר עילאה גבר להכי יטול את מקומו · וא"ת למאן דאמר עילאה גבר למה הפסח אינו נאסר מחמת השפוד ויהיה צריך ליטול את מקומו סביב השפוד ואומר ר"י דאין שפוד של עץ קולט חום כל כך כמו חרס וסולת אי נמי מכפנים אינו רותח כבחוץ · ברוב ספרים ובפירוש ר"ח גרס וכי הדר רוטב אפסח מיטוי פסח מחמת חמימות החרס כו' וקשה דתיפוק ליה שרוטב איסור נבלע בפסח ונראה דהא דקאמר ומיטוי פסח ארוטב קאי מדקאמר מחמת חרס דאי אפסח קאי הוה ליה למימר מחמת רוטב :

אלא למ"ד תתאה גבר אוקורי מיקר ליה · ה"ג בכל הספרים ובפר"ח ביטול את מקומו סגי ורש"י מחקו משום דקשיא ליה כיון דאוקורי מיקר מה איסורא יש ברוטב ודוחק לומר כגון שהסולת של חבורה אחרת ואסור להן הרוטב לפי שאינו מנויו ולר"ת נראה דגרס ליה שפיר דע"כ מיירי כגון שהרוטב לא יצלה כל צרכו והו"ל אברים דבגללה כל צרכו לא הוה תו מפסיל משום צלי מחמת דבר אחר וגללו ואחר כך בישלו דאסור היינו דוקא במים משום ריבויי' דובשל מבושל מכל מקום כדאמר בסוף כל שעה (לעיל דף מא·) אבל בדבר אחר לא ותדע דהכי הוא דבע"א היה אסור לחתוך בסכין פסח בעוד שהוא חם דמחמם ליה לסכין ומחמם לדידיה והוה ליה צלי מחמת דבר אחר אלא בגללה כל צרכו לא מיפסיל משום הכי וא"ת מ"מ למה נאסור הסולת משום זה יאפו אותו ויצלה כמו הרוטב וי"ל דאז הוי צלי מחמת דבר אחר שהרי על ידי חמימות הסולת הוא נצלה ומיהו לפי זה לא הוה צריך לעיל לאסוקי והדר סולת ומרתח ליה לרוטב דמה צריך לאסוקי איסור ברוטב משום צלי מחמת דבר אחר כיון דאית ביה איסור נא ואור"ת דניחא ליה לאסוקי כל איסור שיכול לומר אבל לעיל גבי נטף מרוטבו על החרס לא גרס ביקלוף את מקומו סגי שהרי יכול לגלותו עם הרוטב ובפי' ר"ח ליתיה :

משום הכי סגי ליה בקליפה · וכגון ששכו אחר שגלגו ולא נשתהה בתנור אחר סיכה כלל שאם לא כן ע"י רתיחת התנור היה נבלע אפי' למאן דאמר עילאה גבר :

תניא אידך בשר רותח כו' · תימה הא תו למה לי להביאה ואומר ר"ת דקמ"ל דאפילו חלב שרי דלא"ג דחם לתוך צונן בעי קליפה בדבר שיכול לעשות קליפה בדבר דלא שייך קליפה כמו בחלב מותר מדלא קתני איסורא גבי חלב דקתני קליפה גבי בשר וריב"א חולק בזה ומצריך ששים כדי קליפה :

רבינו חננאל

צונן לתוך צונן דברי הכל מותר חם לתוך צונן וצונן לתוך חם רב אמר עילאה גבר ושמואל אמר תתאה גבר. תנן נטף מרוטבו על החרס וחזר יטול את מקומו קס"ד בחרס צוננת בשלמא לרב דאמר עילאה גבר כיון דרוטב חם הוא בעידנא דנטף על החרס והוא צונן ארתחיה לחרס ונעשו חם וחם והדר חרס אחום ליה רוטב וכי הדר רוטב אבשרא דפסח אשתכח דפסח קא מטוי מחמת חמימה דחרס והו"ל צלי מחמת דבר אחר ורחמנא אמר צלי אש ולא צלי מחמת דבר אחר אלא לשמואל דאמר תתאי גבר כיון דחרס צונן הוא אקוריה קא מיקיר ליה לרוטב אמאי תנינן יטול את מקומו ומשני בחרס רותחת היא מתני' והוא חם לתוך חם : תנן נטף מרוטבו על הסלת יקמוץ את מקומו קס"ד בסלת צוננת וכו' עד לשמואל ביטול את מקומו סגי אמאי יקמוץ ושני ר' ירמיה בסלת רותחת : ת"ש ממתני' סכו לפסח בשמן של תרומה אם חבורת כהנים יאכלו אם חבורת ישראל אם חי הוא ולא נצלה עדיין ידיחנו ואם צלי יקלוף את החיצון מותר אפי' לישראל בשלמא לרב כיון דשמן צונן הוא אקורי קא מיקיר ליה לפסח ובקליפה סגי אלא לשמואל כיון דפסח חם הוא מחמם ליה לשמן ונעשה חם בחם דלדברי הכל אסור אמאי תני יקלוף את החיצון ודחי שאני סיכה דמשהו עבדי וכיון שהוא מועט אינו נבלע אלא בחיצון בלבד : תניא כותיה דשמואל בשר רותח שנפל לתוך חלב רותח וכן צונן לתוך חם אסור חם לתוך צונן קולף צונן לתוך צונן מדיח והא דתני צונן לתוך חם וצונן לתוך צונן לא שנו אלא שאינו מלוח אבל מליח אסור דאמר שמואל מליח הרי הוא כרותח כבוש הרי הוא כמבושל והני מילי דאמר שמואל מליח הרי הוא כרותח מליח שאינו נאכל מחמת מלחו כלומר הוא מלוח הרבה אבל אם נאכל מחמת מלחו [לא] וקי"ל כשמואל דתניא כותיה ורב הונא ורבא דהוא בתרא מפרשי טעמיה ש"מ דהילכתא כותיה רב הונא עבד כשמואל ושרא לבר יונה דנפל בכמכא דהוא כותחא ואית ביה נסובי דחלבא והני מילי בר יונה נא אבל צלי בעי קליפה ואי אית ביה פילי פי' פלחי כמין נטות בלע כוליה ואסור ואי לית ביה פילי

agree [76a] that it is forbidden;[4] cold into cold, all agree that it is permitted.[5] [If] hot [falls] into cold, or cold into hot,—Rab maintained: The upper prevails;[6] while Samuel maintained: The lower prevails.

We learned: IF SOME OF ITS JUICE DRIPPED ON TO THE EARTHEN[WARE] AND DRIPPED BACK ON TO IT HE MUST REMOVE ITS PLACE. It was assumed that this refers to a cold earthenware; now it is well on Rab's view that the upper prevails: consequently he must remove its place, because the juice goes and heats the earthenware and the earthenware in turn heats the juice, and when the juice drips back on to the paschal lamb, the paschal lamb is roasted [at that spot] by the heat of the earthenware, whereas the Divine Law said, *roast with fire*,[7] but not roast with something else. But on Samuel's view that the lower prevails, since the earthenware is cold it actually cools the juice; why then should he remove its place?—As R. Jeremiah said[8] in Samuel's name: The reference is to hot flour; so here too the reference is to hot earthenware.

We learned: IF SOME OF ITS JUICE DRIPPED ON TO THE FLOUR, HE MUST REMOVE A HANDFUL FROM ITS PLACE. It was assumed that this refers to cold flour. It is well on Rab's view that the upper prevails: consequently he must remove a handful from its place, because it heats the flour around it and the flour in turn heats it, and the juice is roast by the heat of the flour, whereas the Divine Law said, '*roast with fire*', but not roast with something else. But on Samuel's view that the lower prevails, since the flour is cold it actually cools it; why then must he remove a handful from its place?—Said R. Jeremiah b. Samuel: This refers to hot flour.

We learned: IF HE BASTED IT WITH OIL OF TERUMAH, IF THEY [WHO REGISTERED FOR IT] ARE A COMPANY OF PRIESTS, THEY MAY EAT [IT]; IF IT BELONGS TO ISRAELITES: IF IT IS [YET] RAW, LET HIM WASH IT OFF; IF IT IS ROAST, HE MUST PARE THE OUTER PART. It is well on Rab's view that the upper prevails: consequently [mere] paring is sufficient, because the
a upper is cold.[1] But on Samuel's view that the lower prevails, since it is hot it certainly absorbs; why then is paring sufficient: let us forbid it entirely?—Basting is different, because a mere trifle is used.

It was taught in accordance with Samuel: [If] hot matter [falls] into hot, it is forbidden; similarly, if he put cold into hot, it is forbidden; hot into cold or cold into cold, he must wash it off. [You say], 'Hot into cold, he must wash it off'; [surely] since it is hot, until it cools it cannot but absorb a little; then it should at least require paring?—Rather say: hot into cold, he must pare it; cold into cold, he must wash it off.

Another [Baraitha] taught: If hot meat fell into hot milk, and likewise if cold fell into hot, it is forbidden. Hot into cold or cold into cold, he must wash [the meat]. 'Hot into cold, he must wash [the meat]'; [surely] since it is hot, until it cools it cannot but absorb a little, then it should at least require paring?—Rather say: hot into cold, he must pare [it]; cold into cold, he must wash [the meat].

The Master said: 'Cold into cold, he must wash the meat'. R. Huna said: They learned this only where he had not [previously] salted it; but if he had salted it, it is forbidden, for Samuel said:
b Salted [matter] is like hot;[1] if preserved [in vinegar], it is like boiled.[2] Raba said: As to what Samuel said, Salted [matter] is like hot,—this was said[3] only where it cannot be eaten through the salt;[4] but if it can be eaten in spite of the salt, it is not so.

A young pigeon fell into a jug of *kamka*,[5] [and] R. Ḥinena the son of Raba of Pashrunia[6] permitted it. Said Raba: Who is so wise as to permit such a thing if not R. Ḥinena the son of Raba of Pashrunia, who is a great man. [For] he can tell you: when did Samuel say, Salted matter is like hot?—Where it cannot be eaten through the salt; whereas this could be eaten in spite of the salt. That is, however, only if it is raw; but if roast, it requires paring. Further, this was said only if it contains no splits;[7] but if it contains splits, it is [altogether] forbidden; and if it is seasoned with condiments, it is forbidden.[8]

(4) Because each absorbs from the other. (5) Because they do not absorb from each other. (6) Thus: if hot falls into cold, the upper heats the lower, and it is tantamount to hot into hot: while if cold falls into hot, it is as cold into cold. (7) Ex. XII, 8. (8) V. *infra*.

a (1) I.e., the oil is cold. Nevertheless paring at least is required, because the oil cannot but soak slightly into the flesh.

b (1) 'Salted', this is soon defined—it is regarded as hot, and necessitates paring. (2) And the whole of the permitted matter rendered forbidden. (3) Lit., 'we said'. (4) Until the salt is washed off. (5) A relish containing milk, among other things. (6) A town in Babylonia. Obermeyer does not identify it. Jast., however, s.v. פרשוניא identifies it with Perishna, which is mentioned *infra* 91a, and Obermeyer, p. 297, n. 1. thinks that the latter is identical with Barus, which was included in the district of Sura for taxation purposes. (7) Then paring is sufficient. (8) In both cases the flesh absorbs more freely than otherwise.

written, [75b] *where the ashes are poured out shall it be burnt?*[9]—I will tell you: that *'shall it be burnt'* is required for what was taught: *'It shall be burnt'*: even if no ashes are there; *'it shall be burnt'*, even if he made the fire catch on to the greater part of it.[10]

a Rabina said:[1] Unite them[2] and learn: 'A burning by *fire'*: I know it only if it was burnt by fire or with a coal;[3] if it was burnt with hot ashes, boiling lime, boiling gypsum or with anything produced by fire, which includes hot water [heated] by the fire, how do we know it? Therefore *'a burning'* is stated twice as an amplification.

Raba pointed out a contradiction: did then Rabbi say [that] coals are designated fire? But the following contradicts it: [*And he shall take a censer full of*] *coals* [of fire]:[4] you might think [that] quenched [smouldering] coals are meant;[5] therefore *'fire'* is stated. If *'fire'*, you might think [that] a flame [must be brought]; therefore *'coals of'* is stated. How then [is it to be understood]? He must bring of the brightly-burning [coals].[6] Now this is self-contradictory: you say: '"*coals,*" you might think [that] quenched coals [are meant],' which proves that brightly-burning [coals] are [termed] fire. Then consider the second clause: 'if "*fire*", you might think [that] a flame [must be brought]; therefore "*coals of*" is stated,' which proves that even brightly-burning [coals] are not fire? Whereupon R. Shesheth answered, This is what he teaches: *coals:* you might think both smouldering and brightly-burning [can be taken]; therefore *'fire'* is stated. If *'fire,'* you might think [that] a flame [must be brought]; therefore *'coals of'* is stated. How then [is this to be understood]? He must bring of the brightly-burning [coals]. Yet at all events coals are not called fire, which is a difficulty according to Rabbi?—Said Abaye, Explain it thus: *coals of:* you might think quenched, but not brightly-burning; therefore *'fire'* is stated; if *'fire,'* you might think, he can bring a flame[7] or a coal, whichever he desires; therefore *'coals of fire'* is stated. How then [is it meant]? He must bring of the brightly-

b burning [coals]. Raba[1] said: [You say] 'He can bring a flame or a coal, as he desires.' [But] how is a flame without a coal possible? [Only] if one smears a vessel with oil and lights a fire in it! [Then] why do I need a verse [to exclude] that? Seeing that you do not do thus before a king of flesh and blood, is it not all the more [forbidden] before the Holy One, blessed be He! Rather said Raba, Explain it thus: *'coals of'*: you might think, quenched but not brightly-burning; therefore *'fire'* is stated; if fire, you might think, let him bring half coal and half flame,[2] so that by the time he carries it within [the Holy of Holies] it is all a coal; therefore it is stated, *'And he shall take a censer full of coals of fire from off the altar'*: at the very time of taking they must be coals.

The Scholars asked: [Is the word] *omemoth* or *'omemoth?*[3]—R. Isaac quoted: *The cedars in the garden of God could not hide it* ['amamuhu].[4]

MISHNAH. IF IT [THE PASCHAL LAMB] TOUCHED THE EARTHEN[WARE] OF THE OVEN, HE MUST PARE ITS PLACE; IF SOME OF ITS JUICE DRIPPED ON TO THE EARTHEN[WARE] AND DRIPPED BACK ON TO IT, HE MUST REMOVE ITS PLACE.[5] IF SOME OF ITS JUICE FELL ON THE FLOUR, HE MUST TAKE A HANDFUL AWAY FROM ITS PLACE. IF HE BASTED IT [THE PASCHAL LAMB] WITH OIL OF TERUMAH, IF THEY WHO REGISTERED FOR IT ARE A COMPANY OF PRIESTS, THEY MAY EAT [IT]; BUT IF ISRAELITES, IF IT IS [YET] RAW, LET HIM WASH IT OFF; IF IT IS ROAST, HE MUST PARE THE OUTER PART. IF HE ANOINTED IT WITH OIL OF SECOND TITHE,[6] HE MUST NOT CHARGE ITS VALUE TO THE MEMBERS OF THE

c COMPANY, BECAUSE SECOND TITHE MUST NOT BE REDEEMED[1] IN JERUSALEM.[2]

GEMARA. It was stated: [If] hot matter [falls] into hot,[3] all

(9) Ibid.
(10) Yet he must not leave it until the whole is burning. This is deduced because *'it shall be burnt'* is repeated at the end of the sentence, which emphasizes that it is to be entirely burnt in all cases.

a (1) In reply to the contradiction pointed out by R. Aḥadboi. (2) Lit., 'wrap'. (3) Coal is included as implied by the term 'fire', and not derived from the repetition of *'a burning'*, as stated in the original version. (4) Lev. XVI, 12. (5) I.e., without a flame, for otherwise they are simply called *'fire'*. (6) Lit., 'whispering,' for when coals are burning brightly they make a slight hissing noise something like a sibilant whisper. (7) Without a coal.

b (1) As emended in margin from Rabbah. (2) E.g., a piece of wood part only of which is well alight. (3) With an *alef* (א) or with an *'ayin* (ע)? (4) Ezek. XXXI, 8; *'amamuhu* is with an *'ayin* (ע), and the root really means to dim, darken, whence E.V. *'hide'*. (5) I.e., the part on to which it dripped. 'Pare' denotes a very thin strip; 'to remove,' the thickness of the finger. The reason is explained in the Gemara. (6) Second tithe was brought to Jerusalem and eaten there by its Israelite owners; if it was too burdensome, they redeemed it and expended the redemption money in Jerusalem, v. Deut. XIV, 22f.

c (1) Var. lec.: sold. (2) Even to eat it in Jerusalem as holy food. If the owner of this oil charges the other members for their share, he virtually redeems or sells it as far as he is concerned. (3) E.g., hot milk into hot meat, or hot forbidden flesh into hot permitted flesh, or *vice versa*. By 'hot', boiling is meant.

טז א מיי' פ"ג מהל' תמידין הלכה ה וס"ד מהל' עבודת יוה"כ הלכה א:
יז ב מיי' פ"ח מהל' ק"פ הלכה יא:
יח ג שם הלכה יב:
יט ד שם הלכה יג:
כ ה ו שם הלכה(יג)יד:
כא [ז] רב אלפס חולין פ"ח דף ש"א: ונרא"ש שם סימן לד]:

°על שפך הדשן ישרף אמרי ההוא ישרף (ויקרא ד) מיבעי ליה לכדתניא ישרף אע"פ שאין שם דשן ישרף אע"פ שהצית האור ברובו רבינא אמר כרוך ותני °מכות אש אין לי אלא (שם יג) שנכוה באש ובגחלת נכוה ברמץ בסיד רותח ובגפסים רותח ובכל דבר הבא מחמת האור לאיתויי חמי האור מנין ת"ל מכוה מכוה ריבה רבא רמי מי אמר ר' גחלים איקרו אש ורמינהי גחלי יכול עוממות ת"ל אש אי אש יכול שלהבת ת"ל גחלי הא כיצד מביא מן הלוחשות (אלמא גחלים לא איקרי אש אמרי) והא גופא קשיא אמרת גחלי יכול עוממות אלמא לוחשות אש נינהו אימא סיפא אי אש יכול שלהבת ת"ל גחלי אלמא אפילו לוחשות לאו אש נינהו ואמר רב ששת הכי קתני גחלי יכול בין עוממות בין לוחשות ת"ל אש אי אש יכול שלהבת ת"ל גחלי הא כיצד מביא מן הלוחשות מ"מ גחלים לא איקרי אש קשיא לרבי אמר אביי תריץ הכי גחלי יכול עוממות ולא לוחשות ת"ל אש אי אש יכול רצה שלהבת יביא רצה גחלת יביא ת"ל גחלי הא כיצד מביא מן הלוחשות אמר *רבה רצה גחלת יביא רצה שלהבת יביא שלהבת בלא גחלת היכי משכחת לה כגון דשפייה למנא משחא ואתלי ביה נורא ההוא למה לי קרא למעוטי *השתא לפני מלך בשר ודם אין עושין כן לפני מלך מלכי המלכים הקב"ה לא כל שכן אלא אמר רבא תריץ הכי גחלי יכול עוממות ולא לוחשות ת"ל אש אי אש יכול יביא מחצה גחלת ומחצה שלהבת אדעייל לגואי הוי כוליה גחלת ת"ל לומר °ולקח מלא המחתה גחלי אש (שם טז) מעל המזבח *משעת לקיחה ניהוי גחלים *איבעיא להו אוממות או עוממות אמר רבי יצחק °ארזים לא עממוהו בגן אלהים (יחזקאל לא): **מתני'** ינגע בחרסו של תנור יקלוף את מקומו ינטף מרוטבו על החרס וחזר אליו יטול את מקומו ינטף מרוטבו על הסולת יקמוץ את מקומו יסכו בשמן תרומה אם חבורת כהנים יאכלו אם של ישראל אם חי הוא ידיחנו ואם צלי הוא יקלוף את החיצון יסכו בשמן של מעשר שני לא יעשנו דמים על בני חבורה שאין (א) פודין מעשר שני בירושלים: **גמ'** איתמר [ו] חם לתוך חם דברי הכל אסור

רש"י

על שפך הדשן ישרף. סיפא דההוא קרא דכתב בהו בהם הוא: אע"פ שאין שם דשן. דלא תימא אדשן קפיד רחמנא לשורפו על מקום שהיו מוליכין שם דשנו של מזבח החיצון כדכתיב (ויקרא ו) והוציא את הדשן אל מחוץ למחנה ואם ניטל הדשן משם לא ישרפו שם קמ"ל ישרף מכל מקום: אע"פ שהצית האור ברובו. יתעסקו בו עד שתגמר שריפה: רבינא אמר. הא דפרכת לעיל לר' מדאיצטריך מכוה מכוה לרבויי גחלת לא תיקשי דמתני' משבשתא היא וגחלת לאו מריבוייא דמכוה אתא לתנא אלא ממשמעותא דאש וכרוך ותני גחלת בהדי אש במשמעות דרישא אין לי אלא אש וגחלת כו' וריבוייא דמכוה מכוה לרמץ וסיד אתא: גחלי. ולקח מלא המחתה גחלי אש וגו' (ויקרא טז) ואם נאמר גחלי ולא נאמר אש יכול גחלים עוממות כבויות אבל לא לוחשות בוערות דהנך לאו גחלים הוא סתמא אלא אש תלמוד לומר אש בתר גחלי להביא את הלוחשות אי נאמר אש ולא נאמר גחלי יכול שלהבת ולא גחלים לוחשות דלאו אש סתמא נינהו תלמוד לומר גחלי אש כי כתבינהו לתרווייהו משמע גחלים שיש להן אש: הא גופא קשיא אמרת גחלי יכול עוממות. ולא לוחשות מדלא משתמע ליה לוחשות מכלל דלוחשות לאו גחלים איקרו ומאי מיקרו ע"כ אש והדר תני אש שלהבת משמע ולא לוחשות: ואמר רב ששת גרסינן: יכול בין עוממות בין לוחשות. איזה שירצה דתרווייהו גחלי מיקרו ת"ל אש בתר גחלי לאפוקי עוממות: ואי אש. בלא גחלי יכול שלהבת דודאי אש סתמא אין גחלים לוחשות במשמע תלמוד לומר גחלי אש להכי כתב תרווייהו: מכל מקום לרבי קשיא · דמדאיצטריך גחלי שמע מינה אש סתמא אין גחלת במשמע: אמר אביי תריץ הכי גחלי יכול עוממות ולא לוחשות. ולוחשות לאו גחלי נינהו אלא אש תלמוד לומר אש דהיינו לוחשות אבל בסיפא לא תימא אי אש יכול שלהבת ולא גחלת אלא אי אש יכול רצה גחלים לוחשות רצה שלהבת בלא גחלים ותרווייהו אש מיקרו ת"ל גחלי אש למעוטי שלהבת גרידתא: מחצה גחלת ומחצה שלהבת. כגון אוד שאוחז האור ברובו יטול ממזבח החיצון דבין גחלת ובין שלהבת מיקרו אש וכי מטי התם ממזבח החיצון לפני ולפנים הוה ליה כולה גחלת דאילו לעיולי הכי לא איצטריך מיעוטא דלפני מלך בשר ודם אין מביאין אוד בשלהבתו מפני שמעלה עשן וכי איצטריך מיעוטא לשעת לקיחה איצטריך: ת"ל כו'. משעת לקיחה להוי גחלי אש ואין שלהבת משמע גחלי אש: ארזים לא עממוהו. לא הכהו את מראיתו לפי שהיה נאה מכל אילנות ועל חירם מלך צור נאמר: **מתני'** נגע בחרסו של תנור וכו'. נגע הפסח בחרסו של תנור: יקלוף. מן הפסח מקום שנגע בתנור כדמפרש בגמ' שנתבשל שם מחום התנור ולא צלי אש הוא כדאמרן לעיל משום שנאמר צלי אש שני פעמים למעוטי תנור שגרפו וחרס הדפנות גרוף ועומד הוא: נטף. בתנור מרוטב על החרס: וחזר אליו. שחזר שומן שנתחמם מן החרס ונבלע בפסח: יטול את מקומו. דלא סגי ליה בקליפה אלא בנטילה יפה יפה בעובי דשומן נבלע בתוכו הרבה ואותו שומן מבושל מן החרס (היה): נטף מרוטבו על הסולת. מפרש בגמ' בסולת רותחת דמטוי רוטבו מחום הסולת והוי צלי מחמת דבר אחר ואסור למיכליה להאי רוטב שבתוך הסולת משום אל תאכלו כי אם צלי אש הילכך יקמוץ את מקומו וישרוף אותו קומץ כשאר קדשים פסולין: אם חי ידיחנו · דלא בלע: צלי. בעי קליפה משום דבלע: אין מוכרין מעשר שני בירושלים. ואפילו לאוכלו שם בקדושה דכי ירבה ממך הדרך ונתתה בכסף כתיב (דברים יד): **גמ'** חם לתוך חם. בשר רותח לתוך חלב רותח או אחד של איסור ואחד של היתר: אסור

תוספות

תלמוד לומר ולקח וגו' משעת לקיחה בעינן דניהוי גחלים · וא"ת אפילו לא כתיב ולקח אלא גחלי אש ידעינן דניהוי גחלים בשעת לקיחה דלעיולי לגיו לא איצטריך דשמעינן ליה מק"ו ומה לפני מלך כו' וע"כ מוקמינן ליה לשעת לקיחה וי"ל דודאי לא צריך קרא משום הכי אלא דאי אפשר לכתוב בע"א אלא ולקח:

יטול את מקומו. ולא סגי ליה בקליפה לפי שהרוטב נבלע יותר בתוכו. ואם תאמר נגע בחרסו של תנור אמאי סגי ליה בקליפה הלא הרוטב שיש בתוכו כדי קליפה נבלע בפסח עד כדי שיטול את מקומו כמו נטף מרוטבו וחזר אליו וכל דבר הנאסר בצלי דקי"ל דאינו נאסר אלא כדי קליפה מחמת הרוטב שבו יאסיר עד כדי שיטול את מקומו ואיכא לאוקמא באין רוטב כי אם מעט ומעט רוטב אינו אוסר כל כך כדאמרינן בגמ' שאני סיכה דמשהו עבדי לה:

ואם צלי הוא יקלוף את החיצון. בכל ענין מיירי בין חם בין צונן °דמתוך שהוא רך בולע אע"פ שאינו חם דדומיא דחי קתני:

לפי שאין מוכרין מעשר שני בירושלים. פירש בקונטרס דכי ירבה ממך הדרך ונתתה בכסף כתיב וקשיא לר"י דהא קרא בפדיון מיירי שמוציאו מקדושתו ומחללו על דבר אחר אבל הכא אפילו לאוכלו בקדושתו כדפי' בקונטרס גופיה והכי נמי משמע לישנא דמוכרין מדלא קתני מחללין ויש ספרים שכתוב בהן שאין פודין אבל רש"י כתב שאין מוכרין ונראה לר"י דבירושלים גזרו מדרבנן מכירה אטו פדייה דאסור מן התורה ולרשב"א נראה דלא אסרו מכירה אלא משום בזיון מצוה כדתנן בריש מסכת מעשר שני (פ"א מ"א) שאין מוכרין אותו ואין ממשכנין אותו ואין שוקלין כנגדו: תנן

רבינו חננאל

רבינא מתרץ אליבא דרבי מכות אש אין לי אלא נכוה באש ובגחלת נכוה ברמץ כו' ש"מ גחלת אש היא: רבא רמי מי אמר רבי גחלת אש היא והתניא ולקח מלא המחתה גחלי אש יכול שלהבת ת"ל גחלי אש הא כיצד כו' מדקתני יכול שלהבת ת"ל גחלי אש מכלל דגחלים לאו אש נינהו ושני' הכי קתני יכול עוממות ולא לוחשות ת"ל אש מכלל דגחלים הלוחשות הן אש שלהבת בלא גחלת כבר פירשנוהו לעלה ואפי' גחלים עוממות מלשון (יחזקאל לא) ארזים לא עממוהו (איכה ד) איכה יועם זהב: נגע בשר הפסח בחרסו של תנור נצלה מן החרס ולא מן האש לפיכך יקלוף אותו מקום: איתמר חם לתוך חם כגון בשר חם בחלב חם דברי הכל אסור:

הגהות הב"ח

(א) גמרא על בני חבורה (שאין פודין) תא"מ ונ"ב ס"א שאין מוכרין:

[נראה דצ"ל רבא]
[שבת עד: יומא מז:]
ברכות נג: [ע"ש] שבת פז: [ע"ש]

גליון הש"ס

תוס' ד"ה ואם צלי. דמתוך שהוא רך · עי' חולין לו: תוס' ד"ה אבל גללם:

לקיוהא דפירא בעיניה הכא ליתא לקיוהא דפירא בעיניה: אין צולין את הפסח וכו': מעשה לסתור חסורי מיחסרא והכי קתני *ואם אסכלא מנוקבת מותר ואמר רבי צדוק מעשה בר"ג שאמר לטבי עבדו צא וצלה לנו את הפסח על האסכלא מנוקבת בעא מיניה רב חיננא בר אידי מרב אדא בר אהבה *תנור שהסיקו בקליפי ערלה וגרפו ואפה בו את הפת לדברי האוסר מהו א"ל הפת מותרת א"ל והאמר רב חיננא סבא אמר רבי אסי אמר רבי יוחנן תנור שהסיקו וגרפו וצלה בו את הפסח אין זה צלי אש שמו' יב שנאמר °צלי אש °צלי אש שתי פעמי' טעמא דגלי רחמנא צלי אש צלי אש שתי פעמים הא לא גלי רחמנא הוי אמינא צלי אש הוא א"ל גלי רחמנא התם וילפינן מינה ואי בעית אימא התם טעמא דכתב רחמנא צלי אש שתי פעמים הא לא כתב רחמנא צלי אש שתי פעמים הוה אמינא אאש קפיד רחמנא ואפילו גרפו נמי צלי אש הוא אבל הכא אעצים דאיסורא קא קפיד רחמנא והא ליתנהו ת"ר חתכו ונתנו על גבי גחלים רבי אומר אומר אני שזה צלי אש רמי ליה רב אחדבוי בר אמי לרב חסדא מי אמר רבי גחלים אש ויקרא יג נינהו ורמינהו °מכות אש אין לי אלא שנכוה באש *נכוה בגחלת ברמץ בסיד רותח בגפסים רותח וכל דבר הבא מן האור לאיתויי חמי האור מניין ת"ל מכוה מכוה ריבה טעמא דרבי רחמנא מכוה מכוה הא לא רבי רחמנא מכוה מכוה גחלים לאו אש נינהו א"ל גחלת של עץ לא איצטריך קרא לרבויי כי איצטריך קרא לגחלת של מתכת וגחלים של מתכת סס כא °לאו אש הוא והא גבי בת כהן דכתיב °באש תשרף *ואמר רב מתנה פתילה של אבר היו עושין לה שאני התם דאמר קרא באש תשרף תשרף לרבות כל שריפות הבאות מן האש וכ"ש אש עצמה ונקוף לה חבילי זמורות ונקלה אתיא שריפה שריפה מבני אהרן מה להלן שריפת נשמה וגוף קיים אף כאן שריפת נשמה וגוף קיים ונעביד לה חמי האור משום דר"נ *דאמר ר"נ אמר קרא סס יט °ואהבת לרעך כמוך ברור לו מיתה יפה וכי מאחר דאיכא רב נחמן גזירה שוה למה לי אמרי אי לאו גזירה שוה ה"א שריפת נשמה וגוף קיים לאו שריפה היא ואי משום דרב נחמן ניפוש לה חבילי זמורות טובא כי היכי דתמות בעגלא קמ"ל ואלא באש ל"ל לאפוקי אבר מעיקרו אמר ליה רבי ירמיה לרבי זירא וכל היכא דכתיב באש תשרף לרבות כל שריפות הבאות מחמת אש הוא והא גבי פרים הנשרפים דכתיב בהו °ושרף סס ד אותו על עצים באש ותניא באש ולא בסיד רותח ולא בגפסים רותח א"ל הכי השתא התם כתיב באש והדר תשרף לרבות כל שריפות הבאות מחמת האש הכא כתיב ושרף אותו על עצים באש לבסוף אש למימרא דאש אין מידי אחרינא לא התם נמי כתיבא שריפה לבסוף דכתיב על

רש"י

לקיוהא דפירא. אגדו"ר טעם הפרי עומד בו שלא הוציאו ממנו כלום ואע"פ שהוחלש מאליו ונתקלקל טעמו מוציא דם שכחו בקרבו: הכא ליתא לקיוהא דפירא בעיניה. שבלעו צלי הראשון: מנוקבת. עשויה כבריחים כעין שלנו ויש חלל גדול בין בריח לבריח ונותן השפוד לרוחבו וכל הטלה נצלה באויר שבין שני בריחים שאין בשרו נוגע בברזל: לדברי האוסר. בפרק כל שעה [כו:] רבי אומר הפת אסורה: מהו. הכא אין שבח עצים בפת: צלי אש. קרינא ביה וגבי עצי איסורא מיהא ניתסר דהתם לא כתיב מיעוטא: אאש קפיד רחמנא. וחום התנור תולדת אש הוא ואם נתן בו בגד נשרף ונעשה פחם ואש: חתכו. לפסח ולא הבדיל אלא חתכו בשנים ושלשה מקומות למהר צלייתו איקר"ביר בלע"ז: ברמץ. אפר רותח: גפסים. מין סיד הוא: מניין. שנידון משום מכוה ולא משום שחין ואף על פי שמכוה ושחין שוין בטומאתן נפקא מינה דאי גריס מכת מכוה מחמת אור ואי גריס נגעת שחין שהוא לקות חום אחר שלא היה מחמת האור אין מצטרפין בהכל שוחטין (חולין דף ח·) מפרש: פתילה של אבר. מתיכו וזורקו לתוך פיה: תשרף. כל מיני שריפה משמע מדלא כתיב באש ונשתוק: וכ"ש אש. לשון קושיא הוא: בני אהרן שריפת נשמה וגוף קיים הוא. בסנהדרין (דף נב·) כמין ב' חוטין של אש נכנסו להן בחוטמיהן: חמי האור. רותחין דהוי נמי שריפת נשמה וגוף קיים: גזירה שוה · מבני אהרן למה לי תיפוק מהכא דלא מקפינן חבילי זמורות דהא ברור ליה מיתה יפה בעינן: אי לאו גזירה שוה הוה אמינא. על כרחך אש ממש כגון להקיף חבילי זמורות בעינן דאילו שריפת נשמה וגוף קיים לאו שריפה היא וקרא שריפה אצרכה ואי משום דרב נחמן דבעינן מיתה יפה ה"א נפיש לה חבילים טובא ירבו לה היסק גדול שתמות מהר: קא משמע לן. גזירה שוה דשריפת נשמה וגוף קיים נמי שריפה היא וכיון דשריפה היא אהני דרב נחמן לאפוקי זמורות ורותחין(א): אלא באש למה לי. כיון דסופיה לרבות כל שריפות: אבר מעיקרו. שמוציאין אותו מן הקרקע רותח הוא בלא תולדת אש: וכל היכא דכתיב אש. וכתב נמי שריפה בהדיה לרבויי כל שריפות אתא בתמיה: הכא. כיון דכתיב שריפה ברישא ומשמע כל שריפות והדר כתב אש משמע דוקא אש קאמר:

על

תוספות

וגרפו ואפה בו את הפת מהו. תימה לריב"א מאי קבעי הא קתני סיפא (ב) בישלה ע"ג גחלים דברי הכל מותרת ואפי' למאן דמוקי התם בגחלים עוממות לא גרע חומו מחום חרס התנור שגרפו ותירץ ר"י שאני גחלים שאין חומן בא מחמת השלהבת אלא מחמת עצמן ועפרא בעלמא הן אבל חום התנור שגרפו מחמת חום שלהבת האבוקה בא שהוא איסור גמור הילכך מיבעי ליה ותימה לר"י כיון דהפת אסור כשהאבוקה כנגדו וחום אבוקה אסור א"כ כשגרפו ואפה בו את הפת נמי יהא אסור הפת ופי' ר"י דאפילו כשהאבוקה כנגדו לא אסור אלא מדרבנן ולא משמע כן בשמעתין וגם לא הוה שייך לפלוגי אי יש שבח עצים בפת אי לא ובירושלמי דייק כשהפסח נצלה בתנור והגחלים תחתיו הלא חום התנור כמו מן מבשלו והוי צלי מחמת דבר אחר ומפרש כי היכא אש האש נוטל כח התנור והתנור מצרף חום הגחלים שלא יתפזר: **אין** לי אלא שנכוה באש מניין כו'. אע"ג דשחין ומכוה שוין לכל דבר דשחין ומכוה מטמאים בשבוע אחד בשיער לבן ובפשיון מ"מ נ"מ לענין צירוף דשחין ומכוה אין מצטרפין: **נכוה** בגחלת בגפסים כו'. תימה מה בין גפסים רותח וסיד לחרסו של תנור דאמרינן לעיל טעמא דכתב רחמנא צלי אש שני פעמים הא לאו הכי צלי אש קרינא ביה והכא איצטריך ריבויא אבל מאש הוה ידענא: **הא** לאו הכי גחלת לא איקרי אש. נראה לרשב"א דהוה מצי למימר גלי רחמנא במכוה וגמרינן מיניה ולא איצטריך לשנויי בע"א אלא משום לשון אחרון דלעיל מיהו תימה אמאי לא משני דרבי איירי בגחלים לוחשות והכא לא איצטריך לרבויי אלא עוממות דלא איקרי אש כדמוכח בסמוך וי"ל נהי דגחלת דקרא היינו עוממות סתם גחלת משמע ודברייתא הוי לוחשות: **באש** תשרף לרבות כל שריפות. דהוה מצי למיכתב באש תמות. הקשה ה"ר יוסף נימא באש פרט תשרף כלל ונעשה כלל מוסף על הפרט ורבי כל מילי ואפילו אבר מעיקרו דלא דמי לפרט וי"ל דכלל דתשרף קאי אפרט כלומר במה תשרף באש הלכך לא מרבינן מתשרף אלא דומיא דאש דקאי עילויה והוי כלל הצריך לפרט דאמרינן בכיסוי הדם (חולין דף פח:) דאין דנין אותו בכלל ופרט ריב"א. והקשה רבינו יעקב דאורליינ"ש מאי איצטריך קרא למעוטי אבר מעיקרו הא שמעינן ליה מדאיצטריך לא תבערו למעוטי שאין שריפת בת כהן דוחה שבת מכלל דאי יכול לשורפה בו בשבת מעיקרו דאי יכול לשורפה בו א"כ פשיטא דלא דחיא שבת כיון דיכול לעשות בלא דחיית שבת ואומר ר"י דלא פירכא היא כלל דלאיצטריך קרא היכא דליכא אבר מעיקרו דאי לא תימא הכי תיקשי אמאי איצטריך קרא דלא דחי שבת כיון שיכול להרתיח פתילה של אבר מערב שבת: [ועיין תוס' יבמות ו: ד"ה טעמא]:

תלמוד

עין משפט נר מצוה

יא א מיי' פ"ח מהל' ק"פ הלכה ט:

יב ב מיי' פי"ו מהלכות מאכלות אסורות הל' כב טוש"ע י"ד סי' קמב סעיף ד:

יג ג ד מיי' פ"ח מהל' ק"פ הלכה י:

יד ה מיי' פ"ה מהל' טומאת צרעת הל' א:

טו ו מיי' פט"ו מהל' סנהדרין הלכה ג:

רבינו חננאל

התם איתא לקיוהא דפירא כו' רבינא אמר אע"ג דלא אסמיק חיליה אסור אי אפשר דלית ביה שורקי דדמא וקיי"ל כרבינא ולחומרא: מתני' אין צולין את הפסח על האסכלה ואם היתה אסכלה מנוקבת מותר ומבעי לן אליבא דמאן דאסר לצלות את הפסח על האסכלה דסבר כיון שאין האש בעצמה סובבת אותו אין צלי אש: תנור שהסיקו בקליפי ערלה שהן איסורי הנאה וגרפו ואפה בו את הפת לדברי האומר צליית הפסח באסכלה מהו אמר ליה רב אדא הפת מותרת · איני והאמר רבי יוחנן תנור שהסיקו וגרפו וצלה בו את הפסח אין זה צלי אש משום שנאמר צלי אש שתי פעמים ודייקי' טעמא דכתיב צלי אש קרינא ביה ושני' גלי רחמנא בצליית אש דלאו אש היא וילפינן מינה אי בעית אימא כו': ת"ר חתכו ונתנו על גבי גחלים רבי אומר אומר אני שזה צלי אש ומי אמר רבי גחלת אש היא והתניא מכות אש אין לי אלא שנכוה באש ופרחה בה נגע הוא שהוא טמא נכוה בגחלת ברמץ כו' מנין ת"ל מכוה מכוה ריבה כלומ' שנה ושלש הכתוב מכוה לרבות כל מכוה מחמת אש מדרבי לגחלת מרבויא דקרא ש"מ גחלת לאו אש היא ושניא כי קא מרבי קרא גחלת של מתכת אבל גחלת [של] עץ ודאי אש היא איני דגחלת של מתכות אינה אש והא בת כהן דכתיב בה באש תשרף [וא"ר מתנה פתילה של אבר ושני' שאני התם דאמר קרא באש תשרף] מדלא כתיב תשרף באש דמשמע אין שריפה עולה לה אלא באש אלא כתב רחמנא באש תשרף לרבות כל שרפה הבאה מכח האש ואע"פ שאינה אש בעצמה אבל פרים הנשרפים דכתיבא האש אחר שריפה שנאמר ושרף אותו על עצים באש אין שריפה עולה לה אלא באש עצמו למעט ציר רותח וגפסים רותחים וכיוצא בהן: פי' הייא מהרה נ"א לעגל והוא מהרה חילקם בלשון אבל הפתרון אחד:

מסורת הש"ס

לעיל כו:

[חולין ח·]

סנהדרין נב·

סנהדרין מה: [וע"ש נ"ל ר"נ אמר רבה בר אבוה]

הגהות הב"ח

(א) רש"י ד"ה קמ"ל וכו' לאפוקי זמורות ורותחין נ"ב נראה לפענ"ד דהאי ליבא דרש"י לגדדין קאי מפרשין וה"ק דהאי גזיפ לאפוקי זמורות ורותחין דמעטינן להו מג"ש ורותחין מדרב נחמן: (ב) תוס' ד"ה וגרפו וכו' קתני בסיפא נ"ב בפרק כל שעה דף כ"ו ע"ב:

be used for 'contracting'?—There [75a] the tartness of the fruit is present in its natural state, whereas here the tartness of the fruit is not present in its natural state.

ONE MAY NOT ROAST THE PASSOVER-OFFERING etc. A story [is quoted] in contradiction?—The text is defective, and it teaches thus: But if it is a perforated grill, it is permitted, and R. ZADOK SAID [LIKEWISE]: IT ONCE HAPPENED THAT R. GAMALIEL SAID TO HIS SERVANT: 'GO OUT AND ROAST US THE PASSOVER-OFFERING ON THE PERFORATED GRILL'.

R. Ḥinena b. Idi asked R. Idi b. Ahabah: If a man fires an oven with the shells of '*orlah*[5] and then sweeps it out and bakes bread in it, what is [the law] on the view that it is forbidden?[6] The bread is permitted, he answered. Said he to him, But R. Ḥinena the Elder said in R. Assi's name in R. Joḥanan's name: If a man fires an oven, sweeps it out, and roasts the Passover-offering in it, that is not '*roast with fire*,' because '*roast with fire*,' is stated twice.[7] [Thus] the reason is that the Divine Law revealed [it by stating] '*roast with fire*' twice; but if the Divine Law had not revealed it,
a I would say, it is '*roast with fire*'?[1]—The Divine Law revealed it there, replied he, and we learn from it [for elsewhere]. Alternatively, there the reason is that the Divine Law wrote '*roast with fire*' twice; but if the Divine Law had not written '*roast with fire*' twice, I would say, the Divine Law insisted on fire, and even if he swept it out, that too is '*roast with fire*';[2] but here the Divine Law objected to forbidden fuel, which is [now] absent.

Our Rabbis taught: If he cut it[3] and placed it on the coals,—Rabbi said: I maintain that this is '*roast with fire*.' R. Aḥadboi b. Ammi pointed out a contradiction to R. Ḥisda: Did then Rabbi rule [that] coals are fire? But the following contradicts it: [*Or when the flesh hath in the skin thereof*] *a burning by fire* [etc.]:[4] I know it only where it was burnt by fire; if it was burnt with coals, hot ashes, boiling lime, boiling gypsum, or anything produced by fire, which includes hot water [heated] by fire, how do we know it?[5] Therefore '*a burning*' is stated twice, as an amplification. [Hence] it is only because the Divine Law amplified [it by writing] '*a burning*' twice, but if the Divine Law had not amplified [it by writing] '*a burning*' twice, [I would say that] coals are not fire?—Scripture does not find it necessary to include a wood coal, he answered him;[6] a verse is necessary only in respect of a coal of metal.

Then are not coals of metal fire? Surely in respect of a priest's daughter [who committed adultery], though it is written, *she shall be burnt with fire*,[7] R. Mattenah said: They made a lead wick for her?[8]—There it is different, because the Divine Law said, '*she shall be burnt with fire*': '*she shall be burnt*' is to include all burnings which come from fire. Then, have more of the fire itself! [If so] let us surround her with bundles of faggots and burn her?—The meaning of '*burning*' is learnt from the children of Aaron: just as there it was a burning of the soul while the body remained intact, so here
b burning of the soul while the body remains intact [is meant].[1] Then let us prepare for her boiling water [heated] by the fire?[2] —[That is ruled out] on account of R. Naḥman'[s dictum]. For R. Naḥman said, Scripture saith, *but thou shalt love thy neighbour as thyself*:[3] choose an easy death for him. Now, since there is R. Naḥman['s deduction], what is the purpose of the *gezerah shawah*?[4] —I will tell you: But for the *gezerah shawah*, I would say [that] the burning of the soul while the body remains intact is not burning,[5] while as for R. Naḥman's [teaching], let us use many bundles of faggots for her, so that she should die quickly. Therefore it [the *gezerah shawah*] informs us [that it is not so]. Then what is the purpose of '[*she shall be burnt*] *with fire*'?[6]—It is to exclude [boiling] lead [drawn straight] from its source.

R. Jeremiah said to R. Zera: Then wherever '*she shall be burnt with fire*' is written, it is to include all burnings which are produced by fire? Surely in respect to the [sacrificial] bullocks which were burnt, though it is written, *and he* [the priest] *shall burn it on wood with fire*,[7] it was nevertheless taught: '*With fire*,' but not with boiling lime or boiling gypsum?—Said he to him, How compare! There '*with fire*' is written [first] and '*she shall be burnt*' after: [hence] it is to include all burnings which are produced by fire;[8] [whereas] here is written, *and he shall burn it on wood with fire*,' '*with fire*' being at the end, to intimate that fire only [is permitted], but not anything else. But there too burning is written at the end, for it is

(5) V. Glos. (6) Where it is not first swept out; v. *supra* 26*b*. Here, however, there is no improvement of the fuel in the loaf; hence the question. (7) Ex. XII, 8, 9. The repetition emphasizes that it must be roast actually over the fire itself.
a (1) Hence in the present case as there is no Biblical intimation, we should regard it as though the fire itself were present, and by corollary, as though the oven were unswept. (2) Since the heat was the result of fire. (3) The Passover-offering; not actually dividing it, but making a number of deep cuts, so that it should roast more quickly. (4) Lev. XIII, 24. (5) That it falls within this particular category of leprosy? V. Ḥul. 8*a*. (6) For that indeed is fire. (7) Lev. XXI, 9. (8) V. Sanh. 52*a*.
b (1) V. Sanh. 52*a*. (2) I.e., let us execute her by scalding. (3) Lev. XIX, 18. (4) V. Glos. I.e., the derivation from the sons of Aaron. R. Naḥman's dictum in itself excludes also burning by faggots. (5) So that the only alternative left is burning by faggots. (6) Since after all the verse is taken to include all burnings which come from fire. (7) Ibid. IV, 12. (8) Since the addition of '*she shall be burnt*', after '*with fire*' has already been stated, it is superfluous.

the place of slaughtering, which is hollow, [74b] [the blood]
a indeed oozes out.[1]

Shall we say that this supports him: The heart must be torn and the blood withdrawn;[2] if he did not tear it [open], he must tear it after it is boiled[3] and it is permitted.[4] What is the reason? Is it not because we say, as it absorbs, so it exudes?[5]—The heart is different, because it is smooth.[6] But surely Rabin the Elder put a paste of dough over a [roasted] pigeon for Rab, and he [Rab] said to him, 'If the paste is good [tasty], give it me and I will eat it?'[7]—That was [done] with [a paste of] fine flour, which is crumbly.[8]

But Raba visited the home of the *Resh Galutha*[9] and they put a paste of dough over a [roasted] duck for him. Said he, 'Had I not seen that it was as clear as white glass, I would not eat of it.' Now should you think, as it absorbs, so it exudes, why particularly when it is clear; [it is permitted] even if not clear?—There it was [prepared] with white flour, so that it [the paste] is compact.[10] Now the law is: [a paste] of finest flour, whether it looks red or does not look red, is permitted;[11] [a paste] of white flour: if it is as clear as white glass, it is permitted, if not, it is forbidden; [a paste] of other flours: if it looks red, it is forbidden, if it does not look red, it is permitted. [As to] a stuffed [lamb], he who forbids [does so] even if the mouth is at the bottom; while he who permits [does so] even if the mouth is on top. Now the law is: a stuffed
b [lamb, etc.] is permitted even if the mouth is on top.[1]

[With regard to] raw meat,[2] eggs,[3] and the jugular veins, R. Aḥa and Rabina differ therein. (In the whole Torah[4] R. Aḥa is stringent while Rabina is lenient, and the law is as Rabina [viz.,] as the lenient [view]; except in these three, where R. Aḥa is lenient and Rabina is stringent, and the law is as R. Aḥa, [viz.,] as the lenient view.) If raw meat turns reddish, if one cuts[5] and salts it, it is permitted even for a pot; if one impales it on a spit [over the fire], it is permitted,[6] [because] it [the blood] certainly oozes out. If he places it on [burning] coals, R. Aḥa and Rabina differ therein; one forbids and the other permits. He who forbids [holds that] it [the fire] binds [the blood],[7] while he who permits [holds] that it draws [the blood] out. And the law is: it does indeed draw [the blood] out. Similarly with eggs: if he cut and salted them, they are permitted even for a pot. If he suspended them from a spit, they are permitted, [because] it [the blood] certainly oozes out. If he laid them on coals, R. Aḥa and Rabina differ therein: one forbids and the other permits them. He who forbids [holds]: it certainly binds [the blood]; while he who permits [maintains]: it draws it out. Similarly with the [throat portion containing the] jugular veins: if he cut and salted it, it is permitted even for a pot; if he suspended it on a spit, the place of the cut[8] being underneath,[9] it is permitted, [because] it does indeed ooze out. If he laid it on coals, R. Aḥa and Rabina differ therein: one forbids and the other permits. He who forbids [holds]: it does indeed bind [the blood]; while he who permits [maintains]: it draws it out. And the law is: it draws it out.

c Raw meat which turns red, its serum is forbidden;[1] if it does not turn red, its serum is permitted. Rabina said: Even if it does not turn red, its serum is forbidden, [for] it cannot but contain streaks of blood. Mar b. Amemar said to R. Ashi: My father did indeed drink it.[2] Others say: R. Ashi himself drank it.

Mar b. Amemar said to R. Ashi: Vinegar which had been used once for contracting [meat],[3] my father would not use it again for 'contracting'.[4] How does it differ from weak vinegar, which may

a (1) The animal being hung throat downwards. (2) Before it is boiled; the heart is full of blood and therefore ordinary salting, as is done with other flesh, is insufficient. (3) Rashi: this is assumed to mean, after it is roasted over an open fire, roasting being occasionally referred to as boiling, v. II Chron. XXXV, 13: *and they boiled* (wa-yebashshelu) *the passover with fire according to the ordinance.* (4) V. Ḥul. 109*a*. (5) The reference is not to the heart absorbing blood from other meat, but to one part of the heart absorbing blood from another, and it is now suggested that it exudes the same blood, since it is roasted over an open fire. (6) Hence it does not absorb, so that even if it were boiled in a pot it would be permitted, though there that it is not directly over the fire we certainly cannot say, so it exudes. (7) Now the paste absorbs blood from the roasted pigeon; since he wanted to eat it, he must have known that it re-exudes it. (8) And so leaves room for the blood to ooze. (9) V. Glos. (10) Which prevents the blood from oozing. (11) Even in the former case we assume that the blood which the paste absorbed certainly oozed out, the redness being a mere hue which it leaves.

b (1) When it is suspended for roasting; though there is no opening for the blood to run out, it nevertheless oozes out through the flesh. (2) *Umẓa* is raw meat, unsalted and unsoaked. Blood in flesh is forbidden only if it travels from one part of the flesh to another. But if it remains in its original place, e.g., when raw meat is pickled dry, it is permitted (Rashi). (3) The eggs of a male. Rashi: the controversy *infra* arises when they look red. Tosaf.: these eggs are covered with a membrane which is forbidden on account of blood, hence the controversy. (4) Where R. Aḥa and Rabina differ. (5) To allow for the blood to flow out. (6) Even if only slightly salted, as one salts ordinary meat when it is to be roasted. (7) Though not before it has time to travel from its place. (8) I.e., the throat. (9) So that the blood can flow out.

c (1) This is R. Aḥa's view; though he permits the meat itself, he agrees that the serum is forbidden. (2) The serum. (3) Meat was washed in vinegar in order to contract the blood vessels and bind the blood. (4) Because after it has been used once the vinegar loses its strength to bind the blood in its place.

ה א מיי׳ פ״ו מהל׳ מאכלות אסורות הלכ׳ ו סמג לאוין קלז טוש״ע י״ד סי׳ עג ס״א: [תרומות פ״י מ״א]

ו ב מיי׳ שם הלכה יא סמג שם טוש״ע י״ד סי׳ עח ס״א:

ז ג מיי׳ שם הלכה יז סמג שם טוש״ע י״ד סי׳ עח ס״א:

ח ד מיי׳ שם הלכה יב סמג שם טוש״ע י״ד סי׳ ס״ה ס״א וסעיף ד וסימן סז סעיף ד:

ט ה מיי׳ שם הלכה יג סמג שם טוש״ע י״ד סי׳ סו ס״ה:

י ו מיי׳ שם טוש״ע שם סעיף ו:

מידב דייבי נימא מסייע ליה* *הלב קורעו ומוציא את דמו לא קרעו קורעו לאחר בישולו ומותר מ״ט לאו משום דאמרינן כבולעו כך פולטו *שאני לב דשיע (איני) והא רבין סבא טפליה ההיא בר גוזלא לרב ואמר ליה אי מעלי טפליה הב לי ואיכול ההיא בסמידא *דמפריר והא רבא איקלע לבי ריש גלותא וטפלו ליה בר אווזא אמר אי לא דחזיתיה דזיג כזווא חיורא לא אכלי מיניה ואי סלקא דעתך כבולעו כך פולטו מאי איריא כי זיג אפילו כי לא זיג נמי התם בחוורתא דשריר והילכתא דסמידא בין אסמיק בין לא אסמיק שריא דחוורתא אי זיג כזווא חיורא שריא אי לא אסיר דשאר קמחים אסמיק אסור לא אסמיק שרי האי מולייתא מאן דאסר אפילו פומא לתחת ומאן דשרי אפילו פומא לעיל והילכתא מולייתא שרי אפילו פומא לעיל *אומצא ביעי ומיזרקי פליגי בה רב אחא ורבינא בכל התורה כולה רב אחא לחומרא ורבינא לקולא והילכתא כרבינא לקולא לבר מהני תלת דרב אחא לקולא ורבינא לחומרא והלכתא כרב אחא לקולא האי אומצא דאסמיק חתכיה ומלחיה אפילו לקדרה שרי שפדיה בשפודא שרי מידב דייב אחתיה אגומרי פליגי בה רב אחא ורבינא חד אסר וחד שרי מאן דאסר מצמית צמית ומאן דשרי מישאב שאיב והלכתא מישאב שאיב וכן ביעי חתכינהו ומלחינהו אפילו לקדרה שריין תלינהו בשפודא שריין מידב דייב אחתינהו אגומרי פליגי ביה רב אחא ורבינא חד אסר וחד שרי מאן דאסר מצמית צמית ומאן דשרי מישאב שאיב וכן מיזורקי חתכיה ומלחיה אפילו לקדרה שרי תלייה בשפודא בית השחיטה לתתאי שרי מידב דאיב אחתיה אגומרי פליגי רב אחא ורבינא חד אסר וחד שרי מאן דאסר מצמית צמית ומאן דשרי מישאב שאיב והלכתא מישאב שאיב *האי אומצא דאסמיק חלייה אסיר לא אסמיק חלייה שרי רבינא אמר אפילו לא אסמיק נמי חלייה אסיר אי אפשר דלית בה שורייקי דמא אמר ליה מר בר אמימר לרב אשי אבא מגמע ליה גמועי איכא דאמרי רב אשי גופיה מגמע ליה גמועי אמר ליה מר בר אמימר לרב אשי אבא *האי חלא דחליט ביה חדא זימנא תו לא תאני חליט ביה מאי שנא מחלא מתמהא דחלטינן ביה התם איתיה לקיוהא

רש״י

מידב דייבי. לפי שכשנתלה בתנור ופי בית שחיטתו למטה הדם יוצא דרך חלל הגוף שקורין פורציל״א ושותת דרך בית שחיטה: לאחר בישולו. קס״ד לאחר בישולו צלי קאמר דצלי נמי קרי בישול כדכתיב בדברי הימים (ב לה) ויבשלו הפסח באש כמשפט: דשיע. ולא בלע ואפילו בקדירה נמי שרי ואף על גב דליכא למימר כך פולטו: טפליה. בעיסה שקורין פשטיד״א: אי מעלי טפליה. אם יש טעם יפה בלחם: הב לי דאיכול. וסייעתא לרבה: בסמידא. בעיסה של סלת ואינה נדבקת כל כך ונפרכת מאליה והדם יוצא ממנה: דמיפריר. לשון פירורין: ואי לאו דחזיא. ללחם: דזיג. (א) לשון זכוכית לבן וצלול מראה מוהל הבשר שזב בלחם: כי זווא חיורא. צרוף שאין בו אדמימות דם ואי לא לא אכל מיניה: בחוורתא. קמח נקייה כעין שלנו שאינה סולת: דשריר. קשה ואינו פולטו: דסמידא. דאמר לעיל דמיפריר: בין אסמיק. מוהל שבתוך הלחם בין לא אסמיק שרי שהדם ודאי יוצא ואודם זה ודאי לא דמות דם הוא: והילכתא מולייתא שריא ואפילו פומא לעיל. כשהיא תלויה בתנור ואע״ג דעכשיו אין נקב לצאת הדם שרי כבולעו בשר החיצון כך פולטו וחום האור שואבו: אומצא ביעי ומיזרקי. אומצא דאסמיק חתיכות בשר אישקנטור״א בלע״ז וכן ביצי זכר דאסמיק וכן מיזרקי חוטין גסין שהן ורידין שבבית השחיטה: פליגי בה. כדמפרש פלוגתייהו לקמיה דאכחיה אגומרי: בכל התורה כולה. כל היכא דחזית פלוגתייהו ואיתמר סתמא חד אמר לקולא וחד אמר לחומרא ולא פירש מי המיקל ומי המחמיר דע שרב אחא לחומרא ורבינא לקולא והלכתא בכולן כדברי המיקל: מידב דייב. ושפיר דמי אף במלח מעט בתורת צלי: צמית. ודמו נבלע בו: שאיבי ליה. שואבים את הדם: חלייה. מוהל היוצא ממנו כשחותכו לישנא אחרינא שחולטין אותו בחומץ לאחר צלייתו ודמו נסחט לתוכו: אסמיק (ב) חלייה אסיר. לא גרס הוא וחלייה ורב אחא קאמר לה דמיקל ובחלייה מודי דאסיר: מגמע לה. להאי חלא: חלא. חומץ דחלט ביה צלי האדינא כדי להוציא דמו לא חליט ביה זימנא אחריתי לפי שאין בו כח עוד מחמתה. חלא מעיקרו דחלטינן ביה: לקיוהא

תוספות

שאני לב דשיע. נראה דכל שכן דמבחוץ הוא יותר שיע ונראה לריב״א דדוקא לגבי דם דסמיך אמרינן דשיע אבל לענין שמנונית דאיסורא לא דמפעפע ולא אמרינן שיע ולהכי גבי לב לא קתני שאוסר ואינו נאסר כדקתני *גבי כבד והתם טעמא לאו משום דשיע אלא איידי שהיא טרודה לפלוט לא בלעה ומיהו אור״י בשם ר״ת דהא דמסקינן שאני לב דשיע דיחויא בעלמא הוא וכרבה פסקינן בסמוך דמולייתא שריא: טפלו ליה בר אווזא. פירש בקונטרס דהיינו פשטיד״א ואומר ר״ת וריב״א דלשון טפל לא משמע הכי דמשמע דהיינו טיחה כמו בנות עשירים טופלות אותן בסולת (לעיל דף מג:) ועוד דבפשטיד״א לא אמרינן כבולעו כך פולטו דחזינן דלא פלטי שמקום מושבם יבש בתנור על כן נראה דהיינו מה שרגילים לטוח בעיסה שבלילתה רכה ורגילים לעשות סביב קורקבנים ובני מעיים שמשימין אותם בשפוד וטחין סביבותן בעיסה רכה כעין פרפיי״ש: מאן דאסר אפילו פומיה לתחת. אף על גב דאמרינן לעיל שאני בית שחיטה דמחלחל ושרי אף על גב דלא אמרינן כבולעו כך פולטו שאני התם שהחלל רחב ביותר ולא דמי לפומא דמולייתא: וכן ביעי. פי׳ בקונטרס דאסמיקו ובחנם פי׳ כן משום דפירש רבינו חננאל דאיכא עלייהו קרמא דאסור משום דמא כדאמרינן בגיד הנשה (חולין צג.) ה׳ קרמי הוו דביעי כו׳ משום דמא: אסמיק חלייה אסור. פירש בקונטרס מוהל היוצא ממנו כשחותכו ולא גרסינן הוא וחלייה וקשה לר״י דהיכי דמי אי נגלה בשר כל צרכו אף המוהל מותר דלא גרע ממלחיה דאמרינן לעיל דאפילו לקדירה שפיר דמי ואי לא נגלה כל צרכו אמאי בשר מותר מדלא גריס הוא משמע דבעי למימר דבשר שרי ותימה למה יהא מותר אע״ג דדם האברים שרי היכא דאסמיק אסור דהא איכא דמ״ד גומרי מצמית למתי אסור על כרחיך צריכין לחלק להסיר משום דאסמיק וע״י חתיכה אי אפשר שהיה יוצא כולו ועוד מדמייתי בסמוך האי חלא דחליט חדא זימנא מכלל דעד השתא איירי בחלא ממש ולשון אחר שפירש חלא שחולטים אותו בו אחר צלייתו והוא נסחט לתוכו קשה דאית לן למימר דאי חלייה אסור איהו נמי אסור כדמסקינן בכל הבשר (שם קיא:) גבי כבד שהבאתי למעלה ועוד דהתם משמע שהחלא מצמית ולא מפליט ונראה לר״י כמו שפירש ריב״א בשם ה״ג דבבשר חי איירי ומנהג הוא כשנותנים בשר חי לתוך החומץ ואינו שוהה בתוכו לא מפליט מידי ונצמת הדם בתוך הבשר והכל מותר דהכתי לא פירש הדם וכי שוהה בתוכו עד דאסמיק נעקר ממנו הדם ונפלט לתוכו והיינו דקאמר אומצא דאסמיק שנשתהה בחומץ עד דאסמיק הוא וחלייה אסור אבל אי לא אסמיק שרי והיא דכל הבשר בדלא אישתהי ורבינא כי לא אסמיק נמי חלייה אסיר סבירא ליה אפילו לא אישתהי בגו חלא אלא פורתא הוא כפלט מחמת השורייקי מיהו לא כ״כ שתהא הבשר נאסר בפליטה מועטת כזו ורב אשי מגמע גמועי כמסקנא דכל הבשר דחלייה נמי שרי: וגרפו

רבינו חננאל

ואתינן לסיועי׳ מסתני׳ דתני נותן את כרעיו ואת בני מעיו לתוכו ודחי׳ שאני התם כיון דמחלחל בית השחיטה מידב דאיב ולא בלע ואתינן נמי לסיוע מהא דתנן הלב קורעו ומוציא את דמו לא קרעו קורעו לאחר בישולו ומותר ודחי׳ שאני לב דשיע כלומר הלב סתום הוא ואינו פולט הדם שבתוכו וכי קרע ליה מאחר בישולו מוצאו בתוכו ומשליכו ומותר׳ ונרסי׳ בכריתות פ׳ דם שחיטה בבהמה אמר רבי זירא אמר רב לא שנו הלב קורעו לאחר בשולו ומותר אלא בלב עוף הואיל ואין בו דם כזית אבל לב בהמה דיש בו כזית אסור וחייבין עליו כרת׳ וקאמר רב בדם דאתי בלב מבחוץ דאמר רבי זירא אמר רב בשעה שהנשמה יוצאה משרף כלומר מנמע כדגרסינן בקיבת עולה כהן שרעתו יפה שורפה היה: ואמרינן איני דמלייתא שריא דאמרי׳ כבולעו כך פולטו והא רבין פי׳ שם חכם טפל בר גוזלא לרב ואמר ליה אי מעלי טפלאיה הב לי ואיכול ודחי׳ התם בסמידי דאיפרר מלשון פירורין והא רב איקלע לבי ריש גלותא וטפלו ליה בר אוזא ואמר אי לאו דחזיתיה דזיג כי זונא חיורא לא אכלה ואי ס״ד אמרי׳ כבולעו כך פולטו מאי אריא זיג אפילו לא זיג נמי ושני׳ התם בחיורתא דקריר הלכך דסמידא בין אסמיק בין לא אסמיק שרי דחיורתא זיג שרי לא זיג אלא יש בו אדמומית אסור שאר קמחי אסמיק אסור לא אסמיק שרי והא מליתא שריא ואפילו פומא לתחת אמרי מידב דאיב והילכתא מליתא שריא ואפילו פומא לעיל ודוקא צלו כעין הפסח בתנור אבל שליק לא: אומצא ביעי ומזרקא פליגי בה רב אחא ורבינא בכל התורה כולה וכו׳ אומצא דאסמיק פי׳ חתיכה של בשר שהאדימה חתכיה ומלחיה אפילו לבשלה בקדרה מותר שפדי בשפודא מידב דאיב אחתיה אגומריה מישב שאיב וכן הלכה׳ ביעי ביצים בקרמיהו חתכינהו ומלחינהו אפילו לקדרה שריאן · חתכנהו ותלנהו בשפודא שריא דמידב דאיבן · אחתינהו אגומרי הילכתא מישב שאיבן ושרו מורקי חתכינה בדופקא ומלחינהו אפי׳ לקדרה שריאן תלנהו בשפודא בית שחיטה לתתאי מידב דאיבן ושרו · האי אומצא אסמיק הוא וחליה אסור לא אסמיק הוא וחליה שרי : אמר מר בר אמימר אבא חלה דהוה חליט חדא זימנא לא הוה חליט ביה זימנא אחרינא ומאי שנא מחלא התם

מסורת הש״ס

חולין קט. [כריתות כב:]

[וע״ע ערוך ערך סמד פי׳ ר״ח מלשון פירורין ואינו שונין דאיפרר בדלי״ת מלשון ויפרדו]

חולין צג.

הגהות הב״ח

(א) רש״י ד״ה אי לאו דחזיא ללחם דזיג כי זווא חיורא לשון זכוכית וכו׳ שזב בלחם צרוף שאין בו כצ״ל והד״א: (ב) ד״ה אסמיק וכו׳ דרב אחא:

גליון הש״ס

גמ׳ שאני לב דשיע. מלשון הכתוב [illegible]

כיצד צולין את הפסח מביאין שפוד של רמון ותוחבו לתוך פיו עד בית נקובתו ונותן את כרעיו ואת בני מעיו לתוכו דברי ר' יוסי הגלילי ר"ע אומר כמין בישול הוא זה אלא תולין חוצה לו: אין צולין את הפסח לא על השפוד ולא על האסכלא א"ר צדוק מעשה ברג שאמר לטבי עבדו צא וצלה לנו את הפסח על האסכלא: **גמ'** וניתי של מתכת אידי דחם מקצתו חם כולו וקמטוי מחמת השפוד ורחמנא אמר צלי אש (שמות יב) ולא צלי מחמת דבר אחר וניתי של דקל אידי דאית ליה שיבי מפיק מיא והוי כמבושל וניתי של תאנה אידי דמחלחל מפיק מיא והוה ליה כמבושל וניתי של אלון של חרוב ושל שקמה אידי דאית ביה קיטרי מפיק מיא של רמון נמי אית ביה קיטרי שיעי קיטרי ואבע"א בנבגא בר שתא דלית ביה קיטרי והא איכא בי פסקיה דמפיק לבי פסקיה לבר מתני' דלא כרבי יהודה דתניא רבי יהודה אומר כשם ששפוד של עץ אינו נשרף כך שפוד של מתכת אינו מרתיח אמרו לו זה חם מקצתו חם כולו וזה חם מקצתו אינו חם כולו: ונותן את כרעיו וכו': תניא רבי ישמעאל קוריהו תוך תוך ר"ט קוריהו גדי מקולס ת"ר איזהו גדי מקולס דאסור לאכול בלילי פסח בזמן הזה כל שצלאו כולו כאחד נחתך ממנו אבר נשלק ממנו אבר אין זה גדי מקולס השתא יש לומר נחתך ממנו אבר דאף על גב דקא מטוי ליה בהדיה אמרת לא נשלק מיבעיא א"ר ששת שנשלקו במחובר אמר רבה האי מולייתא שריא א"ל אביי והא קא בלע דמא א"ל כבולעו כך פולטו נימא מסייע ליה נותן את כרעיו ואת בני מעיו לתוכו מ"ט לאו משום דאמרינן כבולעו כך פולטו אמרי שאני התם כיון דאיכא בית השחיטה דמחלחל

מידב

רש"י

כיצד צולין. שפוד של רמון. טעמא מפרש בגמרא: ונותן את כרעיו כו'. כדכתיב ראשו על כרעיו וגו' כולו כאחד משמע: כמין בישול הוא זה. שמבשל בני מעיו בתוכו כמו בתוך הקדירה: תולין חוצה לו. תוחבן בשפוד למעלה מפיו של טלה: לא על השפוד. של ברזל כדמפרש בגמ' שהמתכת כשמתחמם מקצתו מתחמם כולו ונצלה הפסח מחום השפוד שבתוכו שהפנימי מתחמם ע"י קצתו החיצון והוה ליה פסח צלי מחמת דבר אחר ורחמנא אמר צלי אש: אסכלא. גרדיל"א בלע"ז וכולה חד טעמא: **גמ'** שיבי. קנלי"ר שעשוי שורות שורות: מחלחל. כעץ של ערבה ושל אגוז שיש להן מוח מבפנים: אלון. יוסכ"א שהוא קשה: אידי דאית בהו קיטרי. ובעי למשעינהו בסכינא מפיק מיא דרך מקום חתך הסכין והוה ליה פסח מבושל: שיעי קיטרי. ואין צריך להעביר סכין עליהם: בנבגא בר שתא. נטיעה בת שנתה: והא איכא בי פיסקי. ראש השפוד שהוא מקום חתך ומוציא מים: דמפיק לבי פיסקי לבר. חוץ לפי הפסח דאי מפקי מיא לא עיילי לפסח: כשם שהשפוד של עץ. כשתולין אותו בתנור ומכוסה בטלה אין מה שבתוך הטלה נשרף שהטלה מגין עליו כך שפוד של מתכת אין מה שבתוך הטלה מרתיח מחמת חום מקצתו היוצא חוץ לטלה: אמרו לו. אע"פ שאין פנימי של עץ נשרף אבל פנימי של מתכת מרתיח שזה של עץ חם מקצתו לא חם כולו והוה ליה צלי אש וזה של מתכת חם מקצתו חם כולו ואפילו מה שמכוסה ממנו הלכך הו"ל צלי שפוד: רבי ישמעאל קוריהו תוך תוך. דנותן לתוכו ס"ל וכשמרתיחין ומתבשלין בתוכו נשמע קול רתיחתן תוך תוך כקול הסיר ל"א כתב בספרים ישנים תכבר לשון תוך ובר כלומר ממולא מבפנים ונראה מבחוץ כעין שממלאין גדיין ותרנגולין שלנו ודוגמא גבי אביגיל (שמואל א כה) חמש צאן עשויות ומתרגמינן חמש עאן תכברין משם רבי קלונימוס: מקולס. לשון כובע נחשת דמתרגמינן קולסא דנחשא (שם יז) דסבירא ליה תולין למעלה בראשו ונראים ככובע נחשת על ראש גבור: איזה גדי מקולס. דתנן בפרק מקום שנהגו (ד' נג.) שאסור לאכול צלי (בערבי) פסחים בזמן הזה במקום שלא נהגו: כאחד. דדמי לפסח ונראה כאוכל קדשים בחוצה לארץ: נשלק מיבעיא. קס"ד דנחתך והדר נשלק ומשעה שחתכו קודם צלייתו תו לא הוי מקולס: האי מולייתא. אינפלדור"א בלע"ז כמו שאנו ממלאין הטלאין והתרנגולין בין בשר לעצמות: שריא. ואפילו לא בישלו את הבשר שנותנים לתוכו מותר ואפילו מלחו כמליחת צלי דאי במליחה כל צורך לקדירה פשיטא: והא קא בלע. הטלה דם היוצא מן הבשר הכנוס בתוכו: פולטו. לחוץ ושואבו חום האור:

מידב

תוספות

כיצד צולין. ותוחבו לתוך פיו (א). אומר ר"י מש"ה תוחבו דרך פיו לפי שטוחן הגס שבשפוד למטה כדי שלא יפול הפסח ולא הוי בית השחיטה למטה וקדייב דמא דרך שם: **נחתך** ממנו אבר אין זה מקולס. נראה לר"י דמצוה לקלסו אבל משום הכי לא מיפסיל מדאמר לקמן בפרק האשה (דף פח:) גבי ה' שנתערבו עורות פסחיהן ופריך והא איכא חד דלא נפיק ומשני משום דלא אפשר היכי נעביד נייתי כל חד וניתנו אי דידי בעל מום הוה להוי האי פסח ואי לא להוי שלמים הא איכא חזה ושוק ופריך וניתי כל חד כהן בהדיה והשתא איך יעשו כן והא חזה ושוק לאסורים לזרים אי אפשר ללותן עם הפסח וצריך לחותכן ולא הוי מקולס אלא משום הכי אין נפסל וכן תנא לקמן (דף פה:) חתכו ונתנו על גבי גחלים רבי אומר אני שזה צלי אש משמע חתכו לגמרי מיהו רש"י פירש לקמן חתכו שלא הבדילו אלא (ב) לירמו בשנים ושלשה מקומות: **האי** מולייתא שריא. פי' בקונטרס אע"פ שלא מלחו אלא לצלי ולר"ת נראה דצלי לא בעי מליחה כלל דלא מיבעיא כשנצלה הבשר יפה יפה ונפלט כל הדם דשרי דיותר מפליט ע"י האש מע"י המלח דמעשים בכל יום שמבשלים כבד אחר צלייתו אע"פ שמחמירים לבשלו אחר מליחתו אלא אפילו לא נצלה כל צרכו דלא נפלט כל הדם מותר אע"ג דאמרינן בפ"ק דכריתות (ד ד: ודף כ"א) דאיכא לאו בדם האברים ה"מ דוקא כשפירש אבל כל זמן שלא פירש ולא יצא לחוץ שרי כדמוכח בפ' מפנין (שבת דקכח) (ג) דבשר טפל מותר לטלטלו משום דחזי להומצא אלמא יכול לאוכלו בלא מליחה ועוד דאמר בפ' כל הבשר (חולין דף קי:) דכבד אחר שחלטוהו ברותחין או בחלא מותר לבשלו לפי שמצמיתין הדם בתוכו ואין מניחין אותו לפלוט דקאמר התם רב הונא חלטי ליה בחלא ורב נחמן חלטי ליה ברותחין סבר רב פפא קמיה דרבא למימר חלייה אסור אמר ליה אי חלייה אסור איהו נמי אסור דכי היכי דפליט הדר בלע אלא ודאי חלייה נמי שרי דמצמית הדם ואין מניחו לפלוט ואפ"ה שרי באכילה ואין לאסור צלי שלא נמלח ולא נצלה כל צורכו משום שמחמת האש הדם נפרש מבפנים מצד זה לצד זה דמה שיוצא לחוץ משרק שריק ומה שנשאר בפנים אע"פ שפירש מצד זה לצד זה לא הוי כדם האברים שפירש דהא איכא מאן דאסר במסכת חולין (דף קיא:) לאכול ככר שחתך עליה בשר מפני דם הבשר שנכנס לתוכו ואפילו הכי משמע דבשר עצמו מותר אע"פ שלא יצא כל דמו ודבר תימה הוא לרש"י מה מועלת מליחה מועטת לצלי דאין הבשר יוצא מידי דמו עד שימלחנו יפה יפה אלא ודאי לא בעי מליחה כלל וכן קבל ר"י מר"ת ובהקומץ רבה (מנחות כא.) גבי מליחת קדשים דקאמר כילד (ד) עושה מביא את האבר ונותן עליו מלח וחוזר והופכו ונותן עליו מלח ומעלהו ויש דגרס בתר הכי אמר אביי וכן לצלי לא גרס לצלי אלא וכן לקדירה וכן כתוב ברוב ספרים והא דאמר בפרק קמא דביצה (יא.) ושוין שמולחין עליו בשר לצלי לאו משום דבעי מליחה אלא שמנהג למולחו והא דאמר בכל הבשר (חולין קיג.) רב ששת מלח גרמא גרמא תרי מ"ט לא משום דפריש מהאי ובלע האי חד נמי פריש מהאי גיסא דפריש מהאי גיסא ובלע האי גיסא דקאמר היינו שפירש לגמרי לחוץ אבל מבפנים שרי כדפרישית: **כבולעו** כך פולטו. בפ' כל הבשר (חולין קיא.) (ה) שרי כבדא עילויה בישרא בדיעבד משום דדם מישרק שריק התם לא שייך להזכיר כלל טעם של כבולעו כך פולטו שהדם טופל שם מבחוץ ושריק ואינו נבלע ומטעם כבולעו כך פולטו נמי לא הויא שריא התם גבי כבד אלא בדיעבד ואע"ג דבא למישרי הכא גבי פסח לכתחלה אע"ג דבני מעיו בתוכו ואיכא נמי כבד גבי פסח לא רצו להחמיר משום דכתיב (שמות יב) ראשו על כרעיו ועל קרבו ואפילו מאן דאסר בכבדא עילויה בישרא לא קשה ליה מתניתין דפסח דמדרבנן אסר ובפסח לא החמירו אי נמי הוא יעמיד כגון שמלח בני מעים מליחה גמורה דאפילו לקדירה מתירו ר"ת על ידי מליחה גמורה ואפילו לפי מנהג העולם שאין מבשלים כבד על ידי שום מליחה מכל מקום כיון דנמלח כמליחת קדירה נתמעט דמו ולא הוסר טפי משאר בשר שלא נמלח דבשרא על גבי בשרא שרי לכתחלה לכולי עלמא ויש ללמוד היתר במולייתא אפילו נמלח בשר החיצון ושהה כדי מליחה והפנימי לא נמלח מדמייתי ראיה מטפילת בר גוזלא דשרי מטעם כבולעו כך פולטו אע"פ שמעשים בכל יום שאוסרים בשר שנפל בציר ומלח שנפלט ואין מותר אפילו בצלי ועדיפא מינה היה אוסר ר"ת תרנגולת שנמלחה בקערה אף על פי שלא שהתה שם שיעור צלייה ולא פלטה אפילו חצי דמה ואסרה לאוכלה צלי משום דלא מפליג רבא *גבי אין מולחין בשר אלא בכלי מנוקב בין שהה הרבה לשהה מעט:

שאני

עין משפט נר מצוה

א א ב מיי' פ"ח מהל' ק"פ הלכה י:

ב ג ד שם הלכה ט:

ג ה מיי' פ"ו מהל' מאכלות אסורות הל' יא סמג עשין מא טוש"ע י"ד סימן עו סעיף א:

ד ו מיי' פ"ו מהלכות מאכלות אסורות הלכה' יז סמג לאוין קלז טור ש"ע י"ד סי' ע"ג אלפס חולין פ"ז דף לג: וכן הרא"ש שם סי' י"ג]:

רבינו חננאל

כיצד צולין את הפסח שפוד של רמון כו' ואקשי' ולמה אינו צולהו בשפוד של מתכת ושני' דאידי דחם מקצתו חם כולו וכיון שנתחמם ראש השפוד כולו חמשוקע נמצא חמום השפוד צולה בשר הפסח ורחמנא אמרה צלי אש ולא צלי ברזל ושפוד של דקל אית ביה שיבי כגון שאיבה ומפקי מיא ותאנה איידי דמחלחלא מפקי מיא והאלון והחרוב והשקמה הני כולהו אית בהו קטרי מקום שצומחין ומגדלין אמירין ונצרים וכשחותכין אותן אותו מקום חתך מפקי מיא וכיון דמפקי מיא על הבשר הוה ליה כמבושל לפיכך אין עושין מהן שפוד לצלות בו הפסח: רמון אע"ג דאית ביה קטרי שיעי כלו' פתומין הן ומקום חיתוכו והוא ראשו שפולט מים מוציאו חוץ לבשר: ירושלמי כל העצים יבשים מבחוץ ואין יבשים מבפנים ורמון יבש מבחוץ ויבש מבפנים ורבי יהודה דמכשיר בשפוד של מתכות אוקים' למתני' דלא כותיה: **נותן** את כרעיו ואת בני מעיו לתוכו תניא ר' ישמעאל קוריהו תוך בר כלומר נותן כרעיו שהן מבחוץ בתוכו ר' טרפון קורהו גדי מקולס: **ת"ר** איזהו גדי מקולס פי' שאסור לאכלו בלילי פסחים בזמן הזה דתנן ביום טוב פ"ב ועושין גדי מקולס בלילי פסחים בזמן הזה והלכתא כחכמים כל שצלאו כאחד נחתך ממנו אבר או נשלק ממנו אבר אין זה מקולס ואוקימנא נחתך ממנו אבר נחתך ונתפרק האבר מן הגדי ממש ונשלק דקתני שלא נחתך האבר אלא היה צולהו ושפת קדרה בצדו ונחתך ירך הגדי כמות שהוא בלא חתיכה בתוך הקדרה ונתבשלה אין זה גדי מקולס ומותר בזמן הזה: **אמר** רבה מליתא שריא פי' מליתא עוף או כבש מלא בשר בתוכו תצלה בתוכו ואמר אביי כבולעה כך פולטה כלומר כשם שבולע מן הבשר כך פולט העוף או שבתוך הכבש כך פולטו מבחוץ וקיימא לן דהא מליתא בצליה היא דהא בעלמא הפסח [ואמר] אבל בבישול או בשליקה לא:

[כחולין קיב. ושם איתא שמואל]

מכילתא פ' בא [ברכות לג: עירובין כט:]

[תוספתא ביצה פ"ב]

[בצלי]

[כאוכל קדשים בחוץ כצ"ל ע' תוי"ט פרק ד' מ"ד]

ס"א שריא ואפילו לא מלחו את הבשר שנותנים לתוכו אלא כמליחת צלי. תו"ח

הגהות הב"ח

(א) תוס' ד"ה כיצד צולין וכו' לתוך פיו כ"ב נראה דהא דאמרי' דלפי שהוכה בבית השחיטה הדם יוצא וכו' מזרקים כיון דנא הוי בית השחיטה למטה דם נשאר שם ממזרקים שנתחכו בשחיטה: (ב) בד"ה נחתך וכו' שלא הבדילו אלא חתכו בשנים ושלשה מקומות למאר צלייתו הס"ד: (ג) ד"ה האי וכו' דבשר תפל מותר וכו': (ד) שם כילד הוא עושה מביא: (ה) ד"ה כבולעו וכו' שרינן כבדא:

גליון הש"ס רש"י ד"ה מקולס. דס"ל תולין. עי' רש"י לעיל נג. ד"ה מקולסין וביצה כב: ברש"י ד"ה מקולס:

CHAPTER VII

MISHNAH. [74a] HOW IS THE PASSOVER-OFFERING ROASTED? WE BRING A SPIT OF POMEGRANATE WOOD AND THRUST IT INTO ITS MOUTH [RIGHT DOWN] AS FAR AS ITS BUTTOCKS, AND PLACE ITS KNEES AND ITS ENTRAILS INSIDE IT: THIS IS THE VIEW OF R. JOSE THE GALILEAN. R. AKIBA SAID: THIS IS IN THE NATURE OF SEETHING;[1] BUT THEY ARE HUNG OUTSIDE IT. ONE MAY NOT ROAST THE PASSOVER-OFFERING EITHER ON A [METAL] SPIT OR ON A GRILL.[2] R. ZADOK SAID: IT ONCE HAPPENED THAT R. GAMALIEL SAID TO HIS SERVANT ṬABI, 'GO OUT AND ROAST US THE PASSOVER-OFFERING ON THE GRILL.'

GEMARA. But let us bring [a spit] of metal?—When part of it is hot the whole of it is hot,[3] and so [part of] it is roasted through the spit,[4] whereas the Divine Law saith, *roast with fire*,[5] and not roast through something else. But let us bring [a spit] of palm wood?—Since it has grooves it exudes water [sap], so that it would be like boiled. Then let us bring [a spit] of fig wood?—Since it is hollow,[6] it exudes water, so that it is like boiled. Then let us bring [a spit] of the oak tree, the carob tree or the sycamore tree?—Because it has knots it exudes water. [But the wood] of the pomegranate tree too has knots?—Its knots are smooth.[7] Alternatively, this refers to a shoot of this [i.e., the first] year's growth, which has no knots. But there is the point where it is
b cut?[1]—He causes the point where it is cut to protrude without [the animal].

Our Mishnah is not according to R. Judah. For it was taught, R. Judah said: Just as a wooden spit is not burnt,[2] so a metal spit does not boil [the flesh].[3] Said they to him: This [*sc.* metal], if part of it is hot, the whole of it is hot; whereas the other [wood], if part of it is hot, the whole of it is not hot.[4]

AND WE PLACE ITS KNEES, etc. It was taught: R. Ishmael called it *tok tok*.[5] R. Ṭarfon called it a helmeted goat.[6]

Our Rabbis taught: What is the helmeted goat which it is nowadays forbidden to eat on the nights of Passover?[7] Wherever the whole is roasted in one [piece]. If a limb was cut from it, [or] if a limb of it was boiled, that is not a helmeted goat. Now that you say that if a limb was cut from it, even if he roasted it together with it, it is not [a helmeted goat], [if a limb is] boiled need it [be stated]?[8]—Said R. Shesheth: It means that he boiled it while attached [to the whole animal].

Rabbah said: A stuffed [lamb][9] is permitted. Said Abaye to him: But [the lamb] absorbs the blood?[10] As it absorbs, so it exudes, he answered him.[11] Shall we say that this supports him: AND [WE] PLACE ITS KNEES AND ITS ENTRAILS INSIDE IT: what is the reason? Is it not because we say, as it absorbs, so it exudes?—I will tell you: it is different there, [for] since there is

(1) The entrails inside the animal are like meat in a pot, which is seething, not roasting. (2) This is explained in the Gemara. (3) Metal—iron—being a good conductor of heat. (4) The flesh actually in contact with it is roasted by the heat of the spit, not by the heat of the fire. (5) Ex. XII, 8. (6) Having a marrow-like substance inside. (7) Hence they do not exude sap.

(1) Which naturally exudes moisture. (2) For being inside the lamb it is protected from the fire. (3) Thus he permits the use of a metal spit. (4) Hence there is no analogy between the two. (5) '*Tok*' is the sound of boiling. Thus he held that the knees etc. are placed inside it, so that it emits a sound of boiling. MS.M. reads: R. Ishmael called it a *takbera* i.e., a basket, as the animal was stuffed with the loose pieces, v. Jast. s.v. תכברא. (6) He held that the knees etc. must hang outside, so that it looked like a helmet on the head of a warrior. (7) I.e., after the destruction of the Temple; v. *supra* 53a. (8) Surely it is superfluous. (9) I.e., the lamb being stuffed with meat salted only enough for roasting, which is less than is required by law when it is to be boiled (Rashi). Blood in flesh is forbidden, hence the prescribed process of soaking and salting in order to draw it out. (10) Which exudes from the pieces of meat with which it is stuffed when the whole is roasted. (11) It exudes on the outside the same amount of blood which it first absorbs on the inside.

WITHDRAWN THEIR HANDS etc. [73b] Now it was taught thereon: During the week in such circumstances it must be burnt immediately. Now it is well if you say that it requires abrogation: this is a Passover, and since it has no owners, its disqualification is in itself, [and] for that reason it must be burnt immediately. But if you say that it does not require abrogation, [then] from the
a beginning[1] it is a peace-offering; on account of what [then] is its disqualification? [Presumably] on account of something extraneous, viz., that he slaughtered it after the evening *tamid!*[2] [But] then it requires disfigurement? For it was taught, This is the general rule: Wherever its disqualification is in itself, it must be burnt immediately; [if it is] in the blood or in its owner, [the flesh] must become disfigured and [then] it goes out to the place of burning.[3] —Rather, do not say,[4] 'if he slaughtered it without specifying its purpose, it is fit as a burnt-offering,' but say, If he slaughtered it for the purpose of a burnt-offering, it is fit. This proves that it requires [express] abrogation.

Then according to R. Ḥiyya b. Gamada, who said: It was thrown out from the mouth of the company and they said: [The circumstances are] e.g., that its owners were unclean through a dead body and relegated to the second Passover: [thus] only this requires abrogation, but in general abrogation is not required, what can be said?[5]—Rather, said R. Huna son of R. Joshua, what are we discussing here? E.g., if he separated it [for a Passover] before midday, and the owner died after midday, so that it was eligible and then rejected, and whatever was eligible and then rejected cannot be eligible again.[6]—Is then our reasoning
b [required] for any but Rab,[1]—surely Rab said: Live animals cannot be [permanently] rejected?[2] Rather, said R. Papa, the author of this[3] is R. Eliezer, who maintained: Similarly, if he slaughters other [sacrifices] for the sake of the Passover, they are unfit,][4] so that its disqualification is in itself.[5] But if it is [according to] R. Eliezer, he would rule him liable to a sin-offering, since R. Eliezer rejects [the view that] he who errs in the matter of a precept[6] is exempt![7]—R. Joseph[8] the son of R. Salla the Pious explained it before R. Papa: The author of this is R. Joseph b. Ḥonai. For we learned, R. Joseph b. Ḥonai said: Those [other sacrifices] which are slaughtered for the purpose of a Passover or for the purpose of a sin-offering are unfit.[9] This proves that its disqualification is in itself, and for that [reason] it must be burnt immediately; while in the matter of non-culpability[10] he agrees with R. Joshua.[11]

R. Ashi said, Rab ruled in accordance with R. Ishmael the son of R. Joḥanan b. Berokah. For it was taught, R. Ishmael the son of R. Joḥanan b. Berokah said: If there was sufficient time in the day to ascertain whether the owners had withdrawn their hands or died or become defiled, he is liable,[12] and it [the sacrifice] must become disfigured and [then] go out to the place of burning. What is the reason? Is it not because it does not require abro-
c gation?[1]—Whence [does this follow]: perhaps it is because he agrees with the tanna of the School of Rabbah b. Abbuha, who said: Even *piggul*[2] too requires disfigurement, because we learn the meaning of '*iniquity*' from *nothar*.[3] For if you should not say thus, where the owners become defiled, what can be said, for surely that certainly requires abrogation, for R. Ḥiyya b. Gamada said, It was thrown out from the mouth of the company and they said: [The circumstances are] e.g., that its owners were unclean through a dead body and relegated to the second Passover? Hence it is clear as we answered at first: this is [in accordance with] R. Joseph b. Ḥonai.

a (1) I.e., immediately the owners die or withdraw their hands. (2) V. Glos.; that is when he would naturally slaughter it, thinking that it was still a Passover, whereas as a peace-offering it must be slaughtered before; v. *supra* 59*b*. (3) V. *supra* 34*b* for notes. (4) In the statement of Rab reported by R. Huna. (5) V. *supra* 64*a* for notes. (6) The original version is to be retained, viz., that he slaughtered it without a specified purpose, express abrogation not being necessary. But the reason in the Baraitha is a different one, as stated. Thus: at midday the owner was still alive and therefore it was *immediately* eligible for a Passover offering; the owner's death disqualified it from that purpose, and he holds that it can never be eligible again in such circumstances.

b (1) This explanation is given only in order to reconcile R. Huna's statement in Rab's name with the Baraitha. (2) V. *infra* 98*a*. (3) The Baraitha which was cited commenting on our Mishnah. (4) V. *supra* 62*b*. (5) I.e., it does not require abrogation, so that it is *automatically* a peace-offering; hence by slaughtering it expressly for a Passover he renders it intrinsically disqualified, and therefore on weekdays it must be burnt immediately. (6) V. Mishnah 71*b* and note a.l. (7) Hence in the Mishnah he should be liable for desecrating the Sabbath. (8) So MS.M. omitting 'But' of cur. edd. (9) V. Zeb. 2*a*. (10) When one errs in a matter of a precept. (11) That he is not culpable. (12) For he should have satisfied himself on these things before slaughtering. Therefore he is regarded not as having erred in the fulfilment of a precept but as an unwitting offender (*shogeg*); hence he is liable.

c (1) As above. Thus this supports Rab, who does not accept the view of the Baraitha quoted at the beginning of the page. (2) V. Glos. (3) V. *infra* 82*b*; though *piggul* is certainly intrinsically disqualified.

ותני עלה *בחול כי האי גונא ישרף מיד אי אמרת בשלמא בעי עקירה האי פסח הוא וכיון דלית ליה בעלים הוה ליה פסולו בגופו אמטו להכי ישרף מיד אלא אי אמרת לא בעי עקירה מרישא הוה ליה שלמים פסולו משום מאי משום דבר אחר הוא דקא שחיט ליה אחר תמיד של בין הערבים עיבור צורה בעי *דתניא זה הכלל כל שפסולו בגופו ישרף מיד בדם ובבעלים תעובר צורתו ויצא לבית השריפה אלא לא תימא שחטו סתם כשר לשום עולה אלא אימא *שחטו לשום עולה כשר אלמא בעי עקירה ולרבי חייא בר גמדא *דאמר נזרקה מפי חבורה ואמרי כגון שהיו בעלים טמאי מתים ונדחין לפסח שני האי הוא דבעי עקירה הא בעלמא לא בעי עקירה מאי איכא למימר אלא אמר רב הונא בריה דרב יהושע הכא במאי עסקינן כגון שהפרישו קודם חצות ומתו בעלים אחר חצות דהוה ליה נראה ונדחה וכל הנראה ונדחה שוב אינו חוזר ונראה מידי הוא טעמא אלא לרב הא אמר רב *בעלי חיים אינם נדחים אלא אמר רב פפא הא מני ר' אליעזר היא דאמר וכן השוחט אחרים לשם פסח פסול דהוה ליה פסול בגופו ואי רבי אליעזר היא חטאת נמי מחייב דהא לית ליה לר"א טועה בדבר מצוה פטור אלא תרגמא רב יוסף בריה דרב סלא חסידא קמיה דרב פפא הא מני יוסף בן חונאי היא *דתנן יוסף בן חונאי אומר הנשחטים לשם פסח ולשם חטאת פסולים אלמא פסולו בגופו היא ומשום הכי ישרף מיד ובפטורי סבר לה כר' יהושע רב אשי אמר רב דאמר כר' ישמעאל בנו של רבי יוחנן בן ברוקה *דתניא ר' ישמעאל בנו של רבי יוחנן בן ברוקה אומר אם יש שהות ביום לידע אם משכו בעלים את ידיהם או שמתו או שנטמאו חייב *ותעובר צורתו ויוצא לבית השרפה מאי טעמא לאו משום דלא בעי עקירה ממאי דילמא משום דסבר לה *כתנא דבי רבה בר אבוה דאמר אפילו פיגול נמי בעי עיבור צורה דיליף עון עון מנותר דאי לא תימא הכי נטמאו בעלים מאי איכא למימר הא ודאי בעי עקירה דאמר רבי חייא בר גמדא *נזרקה מפי חבורה כגון שהיו בעלים טמאי מת ונדחו לפסח שני אלא מחוורתא כדשני מעיקרא יוסף בן חונאי היא:

הדרן עלך אלו דברים

ותני עלה · דמתניתין: בחול כי האי גוונא · הואיל ויכול לשורפו: ישרף מיד · ואין צריך להמתין עד שתעובר צורתו ואע"ג דמותר הפסח קרב שלמים ואם היה שוחטו לזה שמתו בעליו לשם שלמים היה כשר עכשיו שלא עקר שם פסח ממנו ישרף מיד דהוה ליה פסח שנשחט שלא למנויו: אי אמרת בשלמא · אע"ג דסתמיה לשם שלמים קאי בעי עקירה וכל כמה דלא עקר הוי שם פסח עליו משום הכי ישרף מיד ולא בעי עיבור צורה דהוה ליה פסולו בגופו שנשחט שלא למנויו: אלא אי אמרת לא בעי עקירה · וסתמיה שלמים הוא פסולו מחמת מאי הוי הואיל ושלמים הוא משום דנשחט אחר תמיד בין הערבים דשחיטת פסח אחר התמיד היא כדאמר בתמיד נשחט (דף נט:) ועבר על עשה דהשלמה: כל שפסולו בגופו · כגון פיגול נותר טמא ויוצא ישרף מיד ואין צריך להמתין: בדם ובבעלים · כגון נשפך הדם וכגון פסח שמתו בעלים או נטמאו אחר זריקה דעכשיו פסח כשר הוא אלא שאין לו אוכלין: תעובר צורתו · ימתין לו עד שתעובר ממנו צורת בשר דכיון דאין פסולו חמור לא שרפינן קדשים בבזיון ועיבור צורה הוא פסול לינה דהוה ליה פסולו בגופו: ולר' חייא בר גמדא · דאמר בתמיד נשחט (דף סד·) גבי מתניתא דקתני התם דפסח בעי עקירה ואוקמה כגון שהיו בעלים טמאי מתים כו': הא · אחר דלאו סתמא קאי לפסח לא בעי עקירה: מאי איכא למימר · כלומר מתני' דהכא תיובתיה דקתני ישרף מיד ולא מיתוקמא אלא משום עקירה: אלא אמר רב הונא בריה דרב יהושע · לעולם כדקאמר שחטו סתם כשר לעולה דכיון דקאי לעולה סתמיה עולה הוא ואע"פ שתחלתו אשם וכן מותר הפסח כיון דלשלמים קאי סתמא כי שחיט ליה שלמים הוא והכא דקתני ישרף מיד לאו משום עקירה אלא כגון שהפרישו קודם חצות וכי מטא חצות קבעתיה חצות שהוא זמן שחיטתו ונראה לפסח: ומתו בעלים אחר חצות · ונדחה מפסח דשוב אינו חוזר ונראה לשלמים והא דקי"ל מותר הפסח אחר הפסח קרב שלמים כגון שאבד קודם חצות ונמצא אחר שחיטת הפסח דלא אתא חצות עליה למיקבעה ולא נראה לשחיטת פסח מעולם: מידי הוא טעמא אלא לרב. האי תירוצא רב מתריץ ליה דאמר לא בעי עקירה: והאמר רב · בפ' שני שעירי: בעלי חיים אינן נדחין · ואין דיחוי אלא בדם או בבעלים כגון שעיר של שם שנשחט וקודם זריקת דמו מת המשתלח ישפך הדם אבל כל זמן שהקרבן חי אינו נפסל משום דיחוי: אלא אמר רב פפא. לעולם לא בעי עקירה וסתמיה שלמים והא דקתני עלה דמתני' בחול ישרף מיד ר' אליעזר הוא ומשום דשלמים הוא וכגון דשחטיה בהדיא לשם פסח ורבי אליעזר לטעמיה דאמר בפ' תמיד נשחט (דף סג:) שלמים ששחטן לשם פסח פסול: ואי רבי אליעזר · אמאי תנן מתני' פטור לחייב משום שבת דהא לית ליה כו': ובפטורי · דטועה בדבר מצוה: סבר לה · רבי יוסף בן חונאי כרבי יהושע: רב אשי אמר רב דאמר · לעיל לא בעי עקירה לית ליה דהאי תנא דאמר בחול ישרף מיד אלא קסבר רב דמתני' לענין נותר כי האי תנא סבר לה דאמר בעי עיבור צורה: אם יש שהות ביום · לזה ששחט פסח זה בשבת לבדוק אם מתו בעלים כו' ולא שאל לא טועה בדבר מצוה הוא אלא שוגג וחייב שוגג קרי את הקרוב לפושע: ותעובר צורתו · אם הוא חול דאילו בשבת לא אצטריך ליה דהא בשבת לא שריף ליה ולמחר ביום טוב נמי לא שריף ליה: מאי טעמא · בעי עיבור צורה: לאו משום דקסבר לא בעי עקירה · וזה סתם נשחט והרי הוא שלמים כשרין אלא שנשחטו אחר התמיד ופסול מחמת דבר אחר הוא: וממאי דילמא · לעולם בעי עקירה ופסולו בגופו והאי דבעי עיבור צורה משום דרבי ישמעאל סבר לה כתנא דבי רבה בר אבוה דאמר אפילו פיגול שפסולו בגופו טעון עיבור צורה ולא איתפרים לי עיקר מילתיה דתנא דרבה בר אבוה היכא אתמר ובכמה מקומות מייתי לה בגמרא: דאי לא תימא הכי · דטעמא משום דקסבר פסול הגוף טעון עיבור צורה אלא משום דלא בעי עקירה הא תינח מתו או נתכפרו אבל נטמאו מי איכא דלא בעי עקירה הא סתמיה לפסח שני קאי ורבי ישמעאל או שנטמאו נמי קתני: אלא מחוורתא · דטעמא דרבי ישמעאל משום דקסבר פסול הגוף טעון עיבור צורה ותנא דישרף מיד סבר לא בעי עיבור צורה ואי לתרוצי בעית דלא תיקשי לרב הכי תרלת דפסול הגוף דידה גבי מתו או משכו ידם משום דשחטיה לשם פסח בהדיא ואיהו להו לשלמים קאי בלא עקירה כרב והוו להו שלמים לשם פסח ופסול הגוף הוא כיוסף בן חונאי:

הדרן עלך אלו דברים

פסולו מחמת מאי הוי ששחטו כו' · וא"ת מאי קמדמי הך עקירה להאיך דלעיל דאשם שכפרו בעליו באחר תו לא חזי לאשם אבל פסח שנטמאו בעליו או משכו ידיהם אכתי חזי לפסח אם ימנו אחרים עליו כדתנן לקמן (דף פט:) נימנין ומושכין ידיהם עד שישחט וי"ל דהני מילי כשנשאר אחר מבני חבורה עליו שאם נשאר לגמרי בלא בעלים תו לא חזי לפסח כדתניא בסוקמי שהיה טמא (לקמן צה:) המפריש פסח ומת אם בנו נמנה עליו יביאנו לשם פסח אין בנו נמנה עליו יביאנו לשם שלמים: **בדם** ובבעלים תעובר · תימה א"כ היכי קתני שחטו ונודע שמשכו בעלים את ידם או שנטמאו בחול ישרף מיד והא בדם ובבעלים בעינן עיבור צורה וליכא למימר כפי' הקונטרס דהך בדם ובעלים מיירי כגון שנטמאו אחר זריקה דעכשיו פסח כשר הוא אלא שאין לו אוכלין דבפרק כיצד צולין (לקמן פב:) מוקמינן לה קודם זריקה דקתני בעלים דומיא דדם ותירץ ר' שמואל בר' שלמה דההיא דלעיל מיירי קודם שחיטה דהוי כמו שחטו שלא לאוכליו דחשיב פסולו בגופו:

האמר רב בעלי חיים אינם נדחין. תימה הא מסקי' בפ' שני שעירי (יומא סד:) אמר לך רב אליבא דר' יהודה לא קאמינא וא"כ לימא דמתניתין רבי יהודה דסבר נדחין וכמה משניות מליט דסברי דבעלי חיים נדחין בפ' מי שהיה טמא (לקמן צה·) ובתמורה (דף כג.) ובשילהי כריתות (דף כח.) דדייק עלייהו שמע מינה בעלי חיים נדחין וצריך לרב לאוקמי' כרבי יהודה ומתני' נמי אמאי לא מוקי כוותיה:

הדרן עלך אלו דברים

נב א מיי' פ"ד מהל' ק"פ הלכה ג:
נג ב מיי' פ"ד מהלכות פסולי מוקדשין הלכה טו:

רבינו חננאל

אשם שניתק לרעיה ושחטו סתם כשר לעולה קסבר לא בעי עקירה אי הכי כי לא ניתק לרעיה נמי ושנינ' גזרה לאחר כפרה קודם שניתק לרעיה להקריבו עולה שמא יראה אחר ויקריב קודם שיתכפרו בעליו יקריב הוא עולה. היכא אמור רבנן ירעה דתניא אשם שמתו בעליו או נתכפרו ירעה עד שיסתאב וימכר ויפלו דמיו לנדבה. ר' אומר ימכר ויביא בדמיו עולה אמאי ניקרבה איהו גופיה עולה אלא ש"מ גזרה לפני כפרה ש"מ: **מותיב** רב חסדא שחטו ונודע שמשכו בעלים את ידם או שנטמאו פטור מפני ששחט ברשות ותאני עלה בחול כי האי גונא ישרף מיד אי אמרת בשלמא בעי עקירה האי פסח הוא וכיון דלית בעלים ולא אפשר למכליה לערב פסולו בגופו הוא אמו הכי ישרף מיד אלא אי אמרת לא בעי עקירה כיון דנודע בעת השחיטה שכבר מתו בעליו נמצא כי שחיטתו ששחט סתם לשם שלמים הוא משום מאי פסלת ליה משום שנשחט אחר תמיד של בין הערבים האי אין פיסולו בגופו אלא פיסולו מחמת דבר אחר הוא תיבעי צורה דתניא זה הכלל כל שפסולו בגופו ישרף מיד כו' ואתינן לתרוצה להא דרב בששחטה לשם עולה ועקר שם אשם מעליו. ואקשי' ומי בעי עקירה (אי הכי) למאן דאמר נזרקה מפי חבורה ואמרו כגון שהיו בעלים טמאי מתים ונדחו לפסח שני דהאי פסח סתמא לשמו קאי למיפק ביה בפסח שני והאי הוא דבעי עקירה אבל זולתי לא בעי עקירה ולעולם הא דרב כגון ששחטו סתם והא דקתני ונודע שמשכו הבעלים את ידם או שמתו כו' כגון שהפרישו לשם פסח קודם חצות ומתו בעלים אחר חצות דהוה ליה נראה לשם פסח ונדחה שוב אינו חוזר ונראה שנמצא פיסולו בגופו לפיכך תני עלה ישרף מיד ואקשי' עלה מידי הוא טעמא דלא בעי עקירה אלא לרב הא בהדיא אמר בעלי חיים אינן נידחין ומשני רב פפא דמתני' ר' אליעזר היא דאמר וכן השוחט אחרים לשם פסח פסולין [ומקשינן אי] דהוו להו כי האי טונא השוחט בשבת כרת הוא דמחייב דהא לית ליה לרבי אליעזר טעה בדבר מצוה פטור ולא הוה ליה למשחט עד דבריר ליה דהאידנא דקא שחיט בעלים אינון חיים והדרינן אוקמינה ליוסף בן חוני דתנן בריש שחיטת קדשים יוסף בן חוני אומר הנשחטין לשם פסח ולשם חטאת פסולין אלמא פיסולו בגופו ובפטורי סבר לה כר' יהושע דתני טעה בדבר מצוה פטור: **רב** אשי אמר רב דאמר לא בעי עקירה כי האי תנא הוא דאמר הכי דתני אם יש שהות ביום כדי לידע שמשכו הבעלים את ידם או שמתו או שנטמאו ולא שאל אלא שחט בשבת חייב ותעובר צורתו כלומר ישאר ימים עד שיבאיש ולא ישאר עליו ארמומית אלא תעשה צורתו כעין ירקרוקת ויצא לבית השרפה ומדקתני תעובר צורתו ש"מ דלאו פיסולו בגופו אלא מחמת דבר אחר ש"מ דהאי תנא לא בעי עקירה וכיון שמתו בעליו או נטמאו או שמשכו את ידם ממילא הוי ליה שלמים ופסולו משום דנשחט אחר תמיד של בין הערבים לפיכך בעי [עיבור] צורה ודחי' ממאי דכי מוקמת לה הכי היא דלמא לעולם פיסולו בגופו הוא דהאי תנא סבר לה כרבה דאמר אפי' פגול שדברי הכל פיסולו בגופו הוא טעון צורה דאי לא תימא הכי דהאי תנא לא תימא ודאי בעי עקירה תינח במי שמתו בעליו או משכו את ידם איכא למימר סתמיה לשלמים קאי אלא נטמאו בעלים מי איכא מאן דאמר לא בעי עקירה והא אמר ר' חייא בר גמדא נזרקה וכו' אלא מחוורתא יוסי בן חוני היא כדשנינן מעיקרא:

הדרן עלך פרק אלו דברים

לעיל דף נט: לקמן דף סב: [תוספתא פ"ט]

[לעיל סד.]

יומא דף סד. לקמן דף צח.

זבחים דף ב. [ע"ש]

[תוספתא פ"ט]

[תוספתא פ"ו] [לעיל לד: לקמן סב: מנחות כ:]

לעיל דף סד. חולין דף ל.

תורה אור

°עבודת מתנה אתן את כהונתכם והזר הקרב יומת עשו אכילת תרומה בגבולין כעבודת ביהמ"ק: שחטו שלא לאוכליו: פשיטא כיון דהתם פסול הכא חייב משום דתנא סיפא פטור תנא רישא חייב והא נמי פשיטא משום דהתם כשר הכא פטור אלא אידי דתנא שחטו שלא לשמו בשבת תנא נמי שלא לאוכליו והיא גופא למה לי משום דקבעי לאיפלוגי ר' אליעזר ור' יהושע א"ל רב הונא בר חיננא לבריה כי אזלת לקמיה דרבי זריקא בעי מיניה לדברי האומר מקלקל בחבורה פטור שחטו שלא לאוכליו חייב מה תיקן תיקן אם עלו לא ירדו שחטו ונמצא בעל מום חייב מה תיקן תיקן בדוקין שבעין ואליבא דר"ע דאמר אם עלו לא ירדו שחטו ונמצא טריפה בסתר פטור *הא בגלוי חייב מה תיקן תיקן להוציא מידי נבילה מתקיף לה רבינא הא *דתניא השוחט חטאת בשבת בחוץ לע"ז חייב עליה ג' חטאות מה תיקן אמר רב עוירא *שמוציאו מידי אבר מן החי: שחטו ונודע וכו': *א"ר הונא אמר רב אשם שניתק לרעיה ושחטו סתם כשר לעולה אלמא קסבר לא בעי עקירה א"ה כי לא ניתק נמי גזירה לאחר כפרה אטו לפני כפרה ומנא תימרא *דתנן אשם שמתו בעליו או שנתכפרו בעליו ירעה עד שיסתאב וימכר ויפלו דמיו לנדבה ר' אליעזר אומר ימות ר' יהושע אומר ימכר ויביא בדמיו עולה בדמיו אין אבל גופו לא דגזר לאחר כפרה אטו לפני כפרה ש"מ איתיביה רב חסדא לרב הונא שחטו ונודע שמשכו בעלים את ידם וכו'

ותני

במדבר יח

רש"י

עבודת מתנה · מתנות כהונה שנתתי לכם הרי הן כעבודה: פשיטא כיון דהתם · בתמיד נשחט (דף סא.) תנן דפסח שלא לאוכליו פסול: הכא · דשבת קאי ממילא שמעינן דחייב: משום דבעי למיתנא סיפא לאוכליו ושלא לאוכליו פטור תנא רישא שלא לאוכליו חייב: לדברי האומר · במס' שבת (דף קו.): מקלקל בחבורה · העושה חבורה בשבת לקלקלה שאינו מתקן פטור ואין חובל חייב משום שבת אלא שוחט שמתקן או חובל בבהמה וצריך לדם להאכילו לכלבו: שלא לאוכליו חייב. דקתני מתני' חייב: מה תיקן · הא פסלי': תיקן · דכל הקרבנות שנפסלו בעזרה תנן במס' זבחים (דף פד.) אם עלו למזבח אימוריהן להקטיר לא ירדו: בעלי מומין. תנן התם אם עלו ירדו שלא היה פסולן בקודש: בדוקין שבעין · טלי"א כגון הנוטה כדוק שמים (ישעיה מ) וגבי קרבן מום הוא דכתיב (ויקרא כא) או דק או תבלול בעינו: ואליבא דר"ע. במס' *זבחים תנן ר"ע מכשיר בבעלי מומין אם עלו ואמרו בגמרא *לא הכשיר ר"ע אלא בדוקין שבעין הואיל וכשירין לכתחלה בעופות: טריפה · אמר התם אם עלתה תרד: מידי נבילה · מלטמא: השוחט חטאת גר' ובשחיטת חולין בפרק שני מפרש אמאי נקט חטאת: ג' חטאות · משום שבת ומשום ע"ז ומשום שחוטי חוץ לעזרה: מה תיקן · הכא אפי' לטהרו מידי נבילה ליכא דתקרובת ע"ז מטמאה אפי' באהל: מידי אבר מן החי. °לבני נח שאם אכלו אינו נהרג: אשם שניתק לרעיה. שמתו בעליו או נתכפרו באחר וחטאת ואשם אינן באין נדבה ומשנתכפרו באחר אין תקנה לזה וגבי חטאת הילכתא גמירי לה (תמורה כא:) דמתה ובאשם גמירי הילכתא (שם יח.) כל שבחטאת מתה באשם רועה ואם ניתקו מעליו והשליכו לאפר לרעות שיסתאב ויפול בו מום שיוכל לפדותו ולהוציאו לחולין וכל הרועים דמיהם טפלים לנדבה ומה היא נדבה ששה שופרות היו במקדש וכתוב עליהן נדבה ושם היו נותנין כל מותר דמי חטאת ואשם ומביאין משם קיץ המזבח עולות בשר לשם ועורות לכהנים שזהו מדרשו של יהוידע הכהן במס' תמורה (דף כג:) וזה לא המתין עד שיומם ומשניתקו לרעייה שחטו סתם כשר לעולת קיץ המזבח הואיל וסוף סוף דמיו לכך היו עומדים: לא בעי עקירה · מאחר שהוא עומד לכך א"צ לעקור שם אשם ממנו: א"ה כי לא ניתק נמי · משעה שנתכפר באחר סתמיה לקיץ המזבח קאי: גזירה לאחר כפרה אטו קודם שנתכפר · דסתמיה לאשם אבל משניתק לא מיחלף: ומנא תימרא · להא מילתא דאמר לך דגזרי' הכי: לנדבה · לשופרות: ר' אליעזר אומר ימות. כל לדבריו של רבי אליעזר היה עושה אשם כחטאת לכל דבר שנאמר (ויקרא ז) כחטאת כאשם וכן *גבי שלא לשמו וכן גבי חטאת שנכנס דמה לפנים במס' זבחים (דף יז:): רבי יהושע אומר ימכר · לאחר שנסתאב: ויביא בדמיו עולה · נדבה לעצמו ובמס' תמורה מסיק להא מילתא והלא אף הנדבה עולה היא מה בין דברי רבי יהושע לדברי חכמים אלא שבזמן שהיא באה לחובתו הוא סומך עליה ושוחטה ונסכיה קריבין משלו וכשהיא באה לנדבת ציבור אינו סומך עליה כו': בדמיו אין · אבל איהו גופיה לא אמר דיקרב עולה ואף על פי שמקריבו לעצמו אלמא גזירה לאחר כפרה שנתכפר באחר אטו לפני כפרה דאי שרית ליה השתא טעי ואי מיצטריך ליה עולה נמי קודם כפרה מקריב ליה להאי והדר מייתי אחר לאשם ואי אפשר לשנות זבח לזבח אחר כ"ז שעומד לשמו:

ותני

תוספות

לדברי האומר מקלקל בחבורה ט' · וא"ת והלא ר' יהודה הוא דפטר מקלקל בחבורה ומתני' דמחייב בשאינן ראויין דהיינו מתעסק שסובר שוחט זבח זה וסבור שהוא אחר לא אתי כר"י דלדידיה מתעסק פטור כדמוכח בפ' ספק אכל (כריתות יט:) דקאמר הגח לתינוקות מתוך שמקלקל בחבורה חייב מתעסק נמי חייב אלמא משמע מאן דפטר מקלקל בחבורה פטור נמי מתעסק וא"כ מתני' לא מתוקמא כמאן דפטר מקלקל בחבורה וי"ל דלדברי האומר מקלקל בחבורה פטור היינו רבי יוחנן אליבא דרבי שמעון דפטר היכא דמקלקל לגמרי דליכא תיקון כלל ולאפוקי מדר' אבהו דבפ' האורג (שבת קו.) תני ר' אבהו קמיה דר' יוחנן כל המקלקלין פטורין חוץ מחובל ומבעיר א"ל פוק תני לברא חובל ומבעיר אינה משנה וא"ת"ל משנה בחובל וצריך לכלבו ומבעיר וצריך לאפרו והיינו אליבא דר"ש מדמפליג בין חובל ומבעיר לשאר מקלקלין אבל מקלקל גמור לא אפי' לר"ש מיהו אכתי קשה לר"י כיון דס"ד דליכא תיקון כלל במתני' א"כ תקשי לכ"ע היכי חייב לר"ש מקלקל בחבורה הא מלאכה שאינה צריכה לגופה היא ופטור אפילו בחבורה כדמוכח בסוף כל כתבי (שבת קכא:) דפטר ר"ש התם הורג נחשים ועקרבים משום מלאכה שאינה צריכה לגופה ובריש הנחנקין (סנהדרין פד:) נמי מסיק מאן שמעת ליה דאמר מקלקל בחבורה חייב ר"ש האמר מלאכה שאינה צריכה לגופה פטור עליה: תיקן להוציאו מידי אבר מן החי · משמע דתקרובת ע"ז מטמאה מדאורייתא מדלא קאמר תיקן להוציאו מידי נבילה ולא מיחייב אהך טומאה אם נכנס למקדש ובע"ז פ' ר' ישמעאל (דף נב.) משמע שהיא מדרבנן דבעי רבי יוחנן תקרובת ע"ז של אוכלין מהו כו' או דילמא איסורא דאורייתא לא בטלה טומאה דרבנן בטלה וי"ל דאיצטריך הכא לשנויי תיקן להוציאו מאמה"ח כי היכי דלא ניפשוט מהך ברייתא דטומאת תקרובת לאו דאורייתא וכן בסוף העור והרוטב (חולין קכט.) דאמר אביי הרי אמרו תקרובת ע"ז של אוכלין מטמא טומאתה לאו דאורייתא דאי דאורייתא מכינו לאוכלין שמטמאת טומאה חמורה ומשני כששימש מעשה עץ שימש התם נמי דיחויא בעלמא הוא*: שחטו ונמצא טריפה בסתר פטור · תימה לר"י אמאי פטור והלא לא עשה מצוה ומתניתין אוקימנא כר"ש דמחייב אפי' לר' יהושע היכא דלא עשה מצוה וליכא למימר דהכא פטור משום דחשבי' ליה כאנוס דע"כ לאו מטעם אנוס פטר ליה אלא משום דטעה בדבר מצוה כדמוכח בגמ' דפריך אי ר' אליעזר חטאת נמי מחייב דהא לית ליה טעה בדבר מצוה פטור ותי' ר"י דכל זה מדברי ר"מ: אשם שניתק לרעיה ושחטו סתם כשר · כל עיקר רעיה מדרבנן דמדאורייתא לא צריך רעיה כלל ולהכי קאמר אלמא לא בעי עקירה א"ה כי לא ניתק נמי אי אמרת בשלמא בעי עקירה א"ש דבעינן ניתק דע"י ניתק יזכור לעוקרו אבל לא ניתק לא דגזרי' עוקרו אטו לא עוקרו אבל השתא דלא בעי עקירה קודם ניתוק נמי ליכשר דליכא למיחש למידי ומשני דקודם ניתוק גזרי' אחר כפרה אטו לפני כפרה ואחר ניתוק נמי דיעבד כשר אבל לכתחלה מיהא גזרי' אטו לפני כפרה ומנא תימרא דתנן אשם כו' בדמיו אין אבל הוא גופיה לא דהא כ"ע מודו דלאחר עקירה וניתוק היה יכול לשוחטו לכתחלה דליכא למיגזר אטו קודם עקירה הואיל ואיכא היכירא דניתוק אי לאו משום דגזרינן לאחר כפרה וניתוק אטו קודם כפרה ומה שפי' ר"י דאי אמרת דבעי עקירה אתי שפיר דגזרו בשלא ניתק דילמא אתי לשחוט בלא עקירה ק' א"כ פסח בשאר ימות השנה דבעי עקירה אמאי לא מצריך רעיה מקשי' דאמר פ"ק דמנחות (דף ד.) א"ר הונא אמר רב אשם שניתק לרעיה ושחטו סתם כשר לעולה ניתק אין לא ניתק לא מ"ט אמר קרא הוא בהוייתו יהא אלמא ניתוק דאורייתא הוא והכא משמע שהוא מדרבנן וגזרי' אטו קודם כפרה ואור"י דה"פ התם אמר קרא הוא בהוייתו יהא קודם כפרה וכיון דמדאורייתא הוי בהוייתו קודם כפרה גזרי' אחר כפרה אטו קודם כפרה ור"ת פי' דה"ק במנחות ניתק אין לא ניתק לא וטעמא כדמפרש הכא דגזרי' אטו לפני כפרה ומסיק מ"ט אמר קרא הוא כלומר מ"ט כשר הלא הלכה למשה מסיני הוא דכל שבחטאת מתה באשם רועה אמר קרא הוא משמע בהוייתו שלבסוף כשיסתאב וימכר שהדמים לנדבה והויא עולה ואתא קרא ללמוד על הלכה דהכי גמרינן דכל שבחטאת מתה באשם קרב עולה א"נ כי גמרי' דבאשם רועה למצוה א"נ דבאשם אזיל לנדבת ציבור ולא ידעי' אי הוא עצמו או דמיו וגלי קרא דהוא עצמו ואי לאו הלכה ה"א הוא בהוייתו דמעיקרא יהא ולא יקרב עולה ורא"י לפי' זה דבתמורה פ' אלו קדשים (דף יח.) גר' בכל הספרים א"ר הונא אשם שניתק לרעיה ושחטו סתם כשר מ"ט אמר קרא הוא בהוייתו יהא ולא גר' התם בשום ספר ניתק אין לא ניתק לא:

עין משפט נר מצוה

מט א מיי' פ"ב מהל' שגגות הלכה י ·
נ ב מיי' פ"ד מהל' שגגות הלכה א ·
נא ג מיי' פ"ד מהל' פסולי מוקדשין הלכה יד:

רבינו חננאל

עבודת מתנה אתן את כהונתכם עשו אכילת תרומה בגבולין כעבודת בית המקדש ועבודת בן גרושה או בן חלוצה רחמנא אכשרה דתניא היה [עומד] ומקריב על גבי המזבח ונודע שהוא בן גרושה או בן חלוצה כל קרבנות שהקריב פסולין ור' יהושע מכשיר מ"ט דכתיב ברך ה' חילו אפי' חולין שבו פועל ידיו תרצה: מתני' שחטו שלא לאוכלין ושלא למנויו לערלים ולטמאים כו'. ואמרי' פשיטא מדתנינן בתמיד [דף ס"א] שחטו שלא לאוכליו ושלא למנויו לערלים ולטמאים פסול מדקתני התם פסול הכא השוחט [בשבת] כי האי גונא כיון דהזובח פסול ודאי הוא חייב אבל לאוכליו ושלא לאוכליו וכו' כיון דהתם כשר הכא ודאי פטור ואסיקנא לעולם לא הוה צריך למתננהו הני כולהי להכא דמטילא שמעינן לה אלא משום דבעי אשמעי' פלוגתא דרבי אליעזר ורבי יהושע בשאר זבחים ששחטן לשם פסח אם אינן ראויין חייב ואם הן ראויין ר' אליעזר מחייב ור' יהושע פוטר: בעו מר' זריקה לדברי האומר מקלקל בחבורה פטור. פי' העושה חבורה בשבת מקלקל הוא ותנן כל המקלקלין פטורין השוחט שלא לשמו ושלא לאוכליו כגון אלו כולן שהזובח פסול מאי תיקן דקתני חייב אמר ליה תיקן שאם עלו למזבח לא ירדו דתנן בשחיטת קדשים פ"ט המזבח מקדש את הראוי לו ר' יהושע אומר כל הראוי לאשים אם עלה לא ירד שנאמר היא העולה על מוקדה ר"ע אומר כל הראוי לא ירד שנאמר העולה על המזבח אין בין דברי ר' יהודה לר"ש אלא הדם והנסכים שר"ש אומר הזבח כשר והנסכים פסולין והנסכים כשרים והזובח פסול אפי' זה וזה פסול הדם לא ירד והנסכים ירדו ותנא כל הזובחים שלא לגבי המזבח אפי' פסלין הרי אלו לא ירדו: שחטו בשבת ונמצא בעל מום חייב מה תיקן דקתני חייב אמר לו כגון שנמצא בעל מום בדוקין שבעין ואליבא דר"ע דתנן בשחיטת קדשים פ"ט ר"ע מכשיר בבעלי מומין ותרסי' בגמ' אמר ר' חייא לא הכשיר ר' עקיבא אלא בדוקין שבעין הואיל וכשירין בעופות שקודם הקדיש: שחטו בשבת ונמצא טרפה בסתר כגון הריאה שניקבה וכיוצא בה פטור הא טרפה שבגלוי כגון שנקב קרום של מוח או שנחתכו רגליו מן הארכובה ולמעלה וכיוצא בה מה תקן להוציאה מידי נבלה ופשוטה היא כי הנבלה מטמאה במשא ובמגע הטרפה שחוטה אינה מטמאה כלל. והתקפה דרבינא דאמר השוחט חטאת בחוץ לע"ז בשבת חייב שלש חטאות משום שוחט קדשים בחוץ ומשום שוחט בשבת ומשום מקריב לע"ז דשחיטה זו לא מטהרה דגרסי' בפ"ק בשחיטת חולין בענין שחיטת נכרי נבלה ומטמאה במשא ותרגמה רבא הכי קתני שחיטת נכרי מטמאה במשא ואינה מטמאה באהל ויש אחרת שמטמאה אפי' באהל ואיזו זו תקרובת ע"ז שמטמא באהל שנאמר ויצמדו לבעל פעור ויאכלו זבחי מתים מה מת מטמא באהל אף תקרובת ע"ז באהל איכא דאמרי אמר רבא זו כטמאה במשא כו' מכל מקום לתרתי לישני דרבא תקרובת ע"ז לא גריעה מנבלה לטמא במשא מה תיקן דקתני חייב שלש חטאות ומשני רב עוירא תיקן להוציאו מידי אבר מן החי שחוטה והוה אכיל מינה אבר אפי' כזית בשר גידים ועצמות חייב משום אבר והשתא דשחטה כמו נבלה היא ולא מחייב עד דאכל מינה כזית בשר: שחטו ונודע שמשכו הבעלים ידם או שמתו כו' אמר [רב הונא] משום רב אשם

[דף סד.] [דף סה:] חולין דף מ. [ע' תוס' חולין ח. ד"ה מותר] זבחים ה: קיב. קטו. מנחות ד. תמורה יח. [מיר כה: ע"ש] תמורה דף כ: שבועות יב. [זבחים ב:]

גליון הש"ס

ברש"י ד"ה מידי אבר מן החי לב"נ. ע' תוס' חגיגה יא: ע"ב ד"ה אין אסור:

to him, 'Behold, it is said, [73a] *I give you the priesthood as a service of* ['abodath] *gift; and the common man that draweth nigh shall be put to death:*[4] [thus] they made the eating of *terumah* in the borders[5] as [equivalent to] the *'abodah* in the Temple.

IF HE SLAUGHTERED IT FOR THOSE WHO ARE NOT ITS EATERS [etc.]. That is obvious: since it is [taught] there[6] [that it is] unfit, he is liable here?[7]—Because the second clause teaches, HE IS NOT LIABLE, the first clause teaches, HE IS LIABLE. But that too is obvious: Since [the sacrifice] is fit there, he is not liable here?—Rather, because he teaches, IF HE SLAUGHTERED IT FOR A DIFFERENT PURPOSE ON THE SABBATH, he also teaches [about] THOSE WHO ARE NOT ITS EATERS. And what is the purpose of that itself?[8]—[He states it] because he wishes to teach the controversy of R. Eliezer and R. Joshua.[9]

R. Huna b. Ḥinena said to his son, 'When you go before R. Zerika, ask him: On the view that he who causes damage through
a a wound is not liable,[1] [when we learned] IF HE SLAUGHTERED IT FOR THOSE WHO ARE NOT ITS EATERS, HE IS LIABLE, what [of positive value] has he effected?—He effected [this, viz.,] that if they [the *emurim*] ascended [the top of the altar], they do not descend.[2] IF HE SLAUGHTERED IT, AND IT WAS FOUND TO POSSESS A BLEMISH, HE IS LIABLE: what [of positive value] has he effected?[3]—He effected [something positive] in the case of cataracts in the eye,[4] this being in accordance with R. Akiba, who maintained: If they [the *emurim*] ascended, they do not descend.[5] IF HE SLAUGHTERED IT AND IT WAS FOUND TO BE ṬEREFAH INTERNALLY, HE IS NOT CULPABLE. Hence if it is in an exposed part, he is culpable; [yet] what has he effected?[6]—He effected its withdrawal from the scope of *nebelah*.[7] Rabina demurred: As to what was taught: He who slaughters a sin-offering on the Sabbath without [the Temple] to an idol, is liable on account thereof to three sin-offerings:[8]—what has he effected?[9]—Said R. 'Awira: Because he withdraws it from [the interdict of] a limb [cut] from a live animal.[10]

IF HE SLAUGHTERED IT AND IT BECAME KNOWN etc. R. Huna said in Rab's name: A guilt-offering which was transferred to pasture and [then] slaughtered without a specified purpose is
b fit for a burnt-offering.[1] This proves that he holds that it does not require [express] abrogation.[2] If so, [even] if it was not transferred too?[3]—[When it is sacrificed thus immediately] after atonement it is preventively forbidden on account of [when it is sacrificed thus even] before atonement.[4] And whence do you rule [thus]?—For we learned: A guilt-offering whose owner died or whose owner [otherwise] obtained atonement must graze until it becomes unfit;[5] then it is sold, and its money falls [is utilized] for a voluntary offering.[6] R. Eliezer said: It is left to die.[7] R. Joshua said: He can sell it and bring a burnt-offering for its money.[8] Thus, only for its money, but not that itself, because he preventively forbids [it when sacrificed] after atonement on account of [when it is sacrificed] before atonement. This proves it.

R. Ḥisda raised an objection against R. Huna: IF HE SLAUGHTERED IT AND IT BECAME KNOWN THAT THE OWNERS HAD

(4) Num. XVIII, 7. *'Service of gift'* refers to the priestly dues, which includes *terumah*, and it is designated here *'abodah*. (5) This is a technical term denoting all places without the Temple. (6) *Supra* 61a. (7) For its unfitness renders his action a desecration of the Sabbath. (8) For seemingly the same principles are involved here too. (9) Lit., 'to make R. Eliezer and R. Joshua dispute'.

a (1) In general, the desecration of the Sabbath involves culpability only when it has a positive, beneficial effect. For causing damage, however, a man is not liable (Shab. 105b); but in respect to damage by wounding there is a controversy ibid. 106a. (2) If a sacrifice becomes unfit in the Temple Court and its *emurim* (v. Glos.) are placed on the altar for burning, they do not descend but must be burnt there. (3) For if the *emurim* of a blemished animal sacrificed unwittingly are laid on the altar, they must be taken down. (4) Which are a blemish in respect to a sacrifice. (5) In this case, since it is a kind of blemish that does not apply to a bird-offering, v. Zeb. 85b. (6) For here too if the *emurim* are taken up to the altar they must go down again. (7) V. Glos. As *nebelah* it would defile, whereas now it does not defile. (8) (i) For slaughtering on the Sabbath: (ii) for sacrificing to an idol: and (iii) for slaughtering a sacrifice without the Temple. (9) Seeing that the slaughtering does not withdraw it from the scope of defilement, since an idol sacrifice becomes a source of defilement! (10) A limb cut from a live animal is forbidden even to a non-Jew. His present action renders that interdict impossible (Rashi). R. Ḥan.: a man is culpable when he eats as much as an olive of the limb of a live animal even if it is made up of flesh, tendons and bones; now, however, it ranks as *nebelah*, and he is liable only when he eats as much as an olive of the flesh, by itself, excluding the tendons and bones.

b (1) A sin-offering and a guilt-offering cannot be brought as votive sacrifices, but only when they are due for transgression. Now, if a man dedicates an animal for one of these, and then dies, or dedicates and sacrifices another animal in its place, then the first, if a sin-offering, must be allowed to perish; if a guilt-offering, it must be put out to pasture until it receives a blemish, when it is redeemed and reverts to *ḥullin* (v. Glos.), while the redemption money is allocated to a special fund for voluntary sacrifices, which take the form of burnt-offerings. Now, if he slaughtered it (in the Temple Court) before it received a blemish, it is valid as a burnt-offering, since that would eventually have been brought in any case. The flesh is then burnt on the altar, while the hide belongs to the priests. (2) Lit., 'uprooting'. Since this is its ultimate destiny, he need not expressly abrogate its status of a guilt-offering. (3) I.e., if it was slaughtered as a burnt-offering immediately its owner died etc., it should be fit. (4) For the two cases may be confused. But once it is actually put out to pasture there is no fear of confusion.—From the text and Tosaf. a.l. it would appear that if he slaughters it as a burnt-offering before transferring it to pasture it is unfit, even if it was done. While even after it was transferred to pasture it is fit for a burnt-offering only if it was thus sacrificed, so that we are faced with a *fait accompli*. But at the outset it may not be sacrificed even after it is transferred to pasture. (5) For a sacrifice by receiving a blemish. (6) I.e., the money is placed in the fund for voluntary sacrifices. (7) For he holds that a guilt-offering is the same as a sin-offering. (8) I.e., the owner brings it as his own sacrifice, and the money does not go into the fund. Thus it is a private sacrifice, so that he himself can slaughter it, he lays his hands upon it (Lev. I, 4), and the accompanying drink-offerings are at his expense. Whereas when the money goes into the fund it is brought as a public sacrifice, and the foregoing are absent.

Continuation of translation from previous page as indicated by ◁

b Lakish said: If a man mistook a spit of *nothar*[1] for a spit of [ordinary] roast meat[2] and he ate it, he is liable.[3] While R. Joḥanan said: If a man had intercourse with his wife, a *niddah*,[1] he is liable; if he had intercourse with his *yebamah*,[1] a *niddah*, he is not liable.[4] Some say, In the former case[5] he is all the more liable, seeing that he did not perform a religious duty [at all].[6] Others say, In the former case he would not be liable. What is the reason? It is only there[7] because he should have asked; but here, that he could not have asked,[8] [he is] not [liable].

Now [according to] R. Joḥanan, wherein does his *yebamah* differ? Because he performed a religious duty! [Then in the case of] his wife too he performed a religious duty.[9]—It refers to his wife when she is pregnant. But there is the pleasure of the periodical visit?[10]—It was not at the time of her periodical visit. But Raba said: A man is bound to please his wife with a good deed?[11]—It was near her [menstruation] date.[12] If so, the same [applies to]
c his *yebamah*?[1]—He is bashful towards his *yebamah*,[2] [but] he is not bashful towards his wife.

Now R. Joḥanan, according to whom [does he give his ruling]? Shall we say, according to R. Jose, for we learned, R. Jose said: If the first festival-day of the Feast[3] fell on the Sabbath, and one forgot [himself] and carried out the palm-branch[4] into the street,[5] he is not liable [to a sin-offering], because he carried it out with permission.[6] But perhaps it is different there, because his time is urgent?[7] Or does it agree with R. Joshua's ruling on sacrifices?—But there too his time is urgent. Again, if [it is] in accordance with R. Joshua's [ruling] on infants,[8] there too his time is urgent?—Rather, it is in accordance with R. Joshua's [ruling] on *terumah*. For we learned: If he [a priest] was eating *terumah* and it became known that he was the son of a divorced woman or of a *ḥaluẓah*,[9] R. Eliezer holds him liable for the principal plus a fifth,[10] while R. Joshua exempts [him].[11] Perhaps [however] this is as R. Bibi b. Abaye, for R. Bibi b. Abaye said: This refers to *terumah* on Passover eve, since its time is urgent?[12] Alternatively, *terumah* is different, as it is designated *'abodah*,[13] and the Divine Law declared *'abodah* valid.[14] For we learned: If he was standing and offering [sacrifices] and it became known that he was the son of a divorced woman or of a *ḥaluẓah*, all the sacrifices which he offered on the altar are invalid; but R. Joshua declares them valid. Now we said, what is R. Joshua's reason? Because it is written, *Bless, Lord, his substance* [ḥelo] *and*
d *accept the work of his hands*.[1] Now where is *terumah* designated *'abodah*? For it was taught: It once happened that R. Ṭarfon had not attended the Beth Hamidrash the previous evening. The [following] morning R. Gamaliel met him and said to him, 'Why did you not attend the Beth Hamidrash last night?' 'I performed an *'abodah*,' replied he. 'All your words are nought but mysteries,'[2] he retorted, 'for whence have we *'abodah* nowadays?'[3] Said he

b (1) V. Glos. (2) Lit., 'a spit of *nothar* was exchanged to him for a spit of roast'. (3) To a sin-offering, which the unwitting consumption of *nothar* involves. The roast meat was that of a sacrifice, while the eating of sacrifices is a religious duty, as it is written, *and they shall eat those wherewith atonement was made* (Ex. XXIX, 33). Thus he rules that he is liable even where he erred in thinking that he was fulfilling a religious duty. (4) As explained below, the first case means immediately prior to her menstruation period, so that he did not fulfil a religious duty. But in the latter case he fulfils a religious duty (v. Deut. XXV, 5). (5) Viz., that dealt with by R. Simeon b. Lakish. (6) Whereas he did perform a religious duty by rendering to his wife her conjugal rights. (7) Viz., where he cohabited with his wife, that he is liable. (8) There was none to ask about the spit. (9) Viz., that of procreation, which is enjoined in Gen. I, 28: *be fruitful, and multiply*. (10) V. Keth. 61b. (11) *Sc.* intercourse, even at other times too. (12) When one must hold aloof from his wife.

c (1) Neither in her case is there any religious obligation when her menstruation date is near? (2) Therefore he could not ask her. (3) 'Feast' (*ḥag*) without a further determinant always means the Feast of Tabernacles. (4) V. Lev. XXIII, 40. (5) Carrying from private into public ground constitutes a forbidden labour on the Sabbath; v. Shab. 2a, 73a. (6) I.e., though his action is forbidden, nevertheless it was done as a religious duty. Thus this is similar to the case dealt with by R. Joḥanan. (7) He must do it within a fixed period; hence his anxiety not to miss that period excuses his forgetfulness. (8) V. *supra* 72a. (9) V. Glos.—whom a priest may not marry (Lev. XXI, 7—a *ḥaluẓah* is forbidden by Rabbinical law only); the issue of such a union is *ḥallal* (profaned) who ranks as a *zar* (lay Israelite) and must not eat *terumah* under the same penalties as a *zar*. (10) Which a *zar* who eats *terumah* unwittingly must pay, v. Lev. XXII, 14. (11) Because he erred in thinking that he was performing a religious duty; v. n. b3; and the same applies to *terumah*. (12) I.e., it was *terumah* of leaven, and so he was in a hurry to consume it (R. Ḥan.). (13) *'Abodah*, lit., 'service', means the *sacrificial* service; it is now stated that the eating of *terumah* is likewise *'abodah*. (14) When performed by a *ḥallal*, though he is not eligible to do it in the first place. Hence though he may not eat *terumah*, he is nevertheless not liable if he does eat it.

d (1) Deut. XXXIII, 11. The verse refers to priests, and *ḥelo* (E.V. *substance*) is derived here from *ḥullin* (non-sacred, profane); thus it is translated, Bless . . . (even) him who is profaned (*ḥallal*) and accept etc., i.e., let his service be valid. (2) Lit., 'words of astonishment'. (3) After the destruction of the Temple.

מג א מיי' פ"ב מהלכות שגגות הלכה טו :
מד ב שם הלכה ח :
מה ג מיי' פ"ט מהל' דעות הל' ד סמג לאוין קכו טוש"ע א"ח סימן רמ סעיף א' :
מו ד מיי' פ"ב מהלכות שגגות הלכה י :
מז ה מיי' פ"ו מהל' תרומות הלכה יב :
מח ו מיי' פ"ו מהלכות ביאת מקדש הל' י :

באשתו נמי קא עביד מצוה · ובסמוך נמי פריך והא איכא שמחת עונה ותימה הא באשתו נדה קיימינן דליכא מצוה ולא שמחת עונה ואומר ר"י דפריך אליבא בתרא דפוטר טעה בדבר מצוה אע"פ שלא עשה מצוה הלכך פריך והא איכא (ד) שמחה וטעה בדבר מצוה ומסיק דהוה ליה לשיולי:

סמוך לווסתה · אין לפרש דיודע שהוא סמוך לווסתה ומספקא ליה אם נדה גמורה היא אם לאו דא"כ ביבמתו אמאי פטור כיון דיודע שהוא סמוך לווסתה וסמוך לווסתה דאורייתא דנפקא לן מוהזהרתם את בני ישראל אלא יש לפרש שאינו יודע אם הוא סמוך לווסתה אם לאו דהוה ליה לשיולה כיון שאינו יודע והא דאמר בפ"ב דנדה (דף טו:) דכל הנשים בחזקת טהרה לבעליהן היינו כשיודע שלא הגיע זמן ווסתה דלא חיישינן שמא שינתה ווסתה וה"ה דהוה מצי למימר שאינו יודע אם היא נדה גמורה או לאו אלא נקט דאפילו יודע שאינה נדה כיון דמספקא ליה אם הוא סמוך לווסתה באשתו חייב ומיהו הוה מצי לאשמועינן במספקא ליה אם היא נדה גמורה ואפי' הכי ביבמתו פטור: לדברי

שלא נתנה שבת לדחות [וסיפא נתנה שבת לדחות אצלו] הכא הרי נתנה שבת לדחות אצל קרבן ציבור א"ל רב אשי לרב כהנא הכא נמי הרי נתנה שבת לדחות אצל תינוקות דעלמא א"ל לגבי דהאי גברא מיהת לא איתיהיב: ושאר כל הזבחים ששחטן לשום פסח אם אינן ראויין חייב ואם ראויין רבי אליעזר מחייב חטאת ורבי יהושע פוטר: מאן תנא דשני ליה בין ראויין לשאינן ראויין ר' שמעון היא דתניא *אחד הזבחים הראויין ואחד זבחים שאינן ראויין וכן השוחט לשם אימורי ציבור פטור דברי ר' מאיר א"ר שמעון לא נחלקו רבי אליעזר ורבי יהושע על שאינן ראויין שחייב על מה נחלקו על הראויין שרבי אליעזר מחייב חטאת ורבי יהושע פוטר אמר רב ביבי אמר רבי אלעזר פוטר היה רבי מאיר אפי' עגל של זבחי שלמים ששחטו לשום הפסח א"ל רבי זירא לרב ביבי והאמר רבי יוחנן מודה היה רבי מאיר בבעלי מומין א"ל בבעלי מומין לא טריד בהו והאי טריד ביה בעא מיניה רבא מרב נחמן חולין לשום פסח מאי לי א"ר מאיר אמר ליה פוטר היה ר' מאיר אפילו חולין לשום פסח והא"ר יוחנן מודה היה ר"מ בבעלי מומין לא מיחלפי הני מיחלפי וטעמא דרבי מאיר משום איחלופי ולא איחלופי והאמר רב ביבי א"ר אלעזר פוטר היה ר' מאיר אפי' עגל של זבחי שלמים ששחטו לשום הפסח אלמא טעמא דר"מ משום דטריד א"ל טריד אע"ג דלא מחלף מחלף אע"ג דלא טריד לאפוקי בעלי מומין דלא איחלופי מחלף ולא מטריד טריד יתיב ר' זירא ורבי שמואל בר רב יצחק אקילעא דר רב שמואל בר רב יצחק ויתבי וקא אמרי א"ר שמעון בן לקיש *נתחלף לו שפוד של נותר בשפוד של צלי ואכלו חייב ור' יוחנן אמר *אשתו נדה בעל חייב *יבמתו נדה בעל פטור איכא דאמרי כ"ש בההיא דמחייב דלא עשה מצוה אית דאמרי בההיא פטור מאי טעמא התם הוא דה"ל לשיולי אבל הכא דלא ה"ל לשיולי לא ור' יוחנן מאי שנא יבמתו דקא עביד מצוה אשתו נמי קא עביד מצוה באשתו מעוברת והא איכא שמחת עונה שלא בשעת עונתה והאמר רבא *חייב אדם לשמח אשתו בדבר מצוה סמוך לווסתה אי הכי אפי' יבמתו נמי יבמתו *בזיז מינה אשתו לא בזיז מינה ור' יוחנן כמאן אילימא כרבי יוסי *דתנן רבי יוסי אומר *יום טוב הראשון של חג שחל להיות בשבת ושכח והוציא את הלולב לרשות הרבים פטור מפני שהוציא ברשות דילמא שאני התם דזמנו בהול ואלא רבי יהושע דזבחים דילמא התם נמי זמנו בהול ואלא כרבי יהושע דתינוקות התם נמי זמנו בהול ואלא כרבי יהושע דתרומה *דתנן *היה אוכל בתרומה ונודע שהוא בן גרושה או בן חלוצה רבי אליעזר מחייב קרן וחומש ר' יהושע פוטר דילמא כדרב ביבי בר אביי דאמר רב ביבי בר אביי בתרומה בערב הפסח דזמנה בהול אי נמי שאני תרומה דאיקרי עבודה ועבודה רחמנא אכשר *דתנן היה עומד ומקריב ונודע שהוא בן גרושה או בן חלוצה *כל הקרבנות כולן שהקריב על גבי המזבח פסולין ור' יהושע מכשיר ואמרינן *מ"ט דר' יהושע *דכתיב °ברך ה' חילו ופועל ידיו תרצה ותרומה היכא איקרי עבודה דתניא מעשה בר' טרפון שלא בא אמש לבית המדרש לשחרית מצאו רבן גמליאל אמר לו מפני מה לא באת אמש לבית המדרש אמר לו עבודה עבדתי אמר לו כל דבריך אינן אלא דברי תימה וכי עבודה בזמן הזה מנין אמר לו הרי הוא אומר עבודת

ואחד זבחים שאינן ראויין · לפסח · פטור · הואיל וטרוד במחשבת לבו מאז הפרישו ויודע שעליו להקריבם טועה ושוחטן לשם פסח : על שאינן ראויין שחייב · דלאו טועה הוא : אפילו עגל · דסד"א ליכא דטעי בה : לא טריד בהו · אין מחשבת הקרבנן בלבו עד הפרשתן : האי טריד ביה · כל ימי הפרשתו בלבו ועסוק ואומר מתי אפנה ואקריבנו : חולין לשם פסח מה לי א"ר מאיר · כלומר מה ר' מאיר אמר לנו בו : מודה היה ר' מאיר בבעלי מומין · הואיל ולאו בני קרבן נינהו לא יכול לומר טועה הוא וחייב הכא נמי חולין לשם פסח יהא חייב הואיל ולאו בני קרבן נינהו : הני מיחלפי · חולין בקדשים מיחלפי ויכול לומר טעיתי סבור הייתי קדשים הן משום הכי פטור : הני לא מיחלפי · בעלי מומין בקדשים לא יכול לומר טעיתי כסבור קדשים הן משום הכי חייב : אלמא טעמא משום טירדא ולאו משום איחלופי וחולין לא טריד בהקרבתן : אקילעא · לפני הבית כעין בית שער וקורין פורי"א : בשפוד של נותר · של קודש הראוי ואכילת קדשים מצוה דכתיב (שמות כט) ואכלו אותם אשר כופר וגו' · חייב · דטעה בדבר מצוה ולא עשה מצוה (א) ונותר חייבים על זדונו כרת ושגגתו חטאת דכתיב (ויקרא יט) ואוכליו עונו ישא : אשתו נדה בעל חייב · כדמוקי לה לקמיה בסמוך לווסתה ובמעוברת דלאו מצוה היא ולקמיה מפרש והזיל אם חלוק הוא על ריש לקיש או מוסיף על דבריו : כל שכן בההוא · (ב) נותר : דמחייב · דאין שם לחלוחית מצוה אבל הכא אע"ג דמעוברת מיהו מצות שמחת אשתו איכא : בשפוד · ליכא למאן (ג) דשייליה : ור' יוחנן מאי שנא יבמתו · דפטור ואע"ג דהוה ליה לשיולי : דקא עביד · מצות יבום בביאה ראשונה קאמר : אשתו · מצות פריה ורביה : עונה · לפי מה שהוא חמר או גמל או טייל או תלמיד כדמפרש בכתובות (דף סא:) : לשמח את אשתו · אפילו שלא בשעת עונתה אם רואה שמתאוה לו : ומשני בסמוך לווסתה · דמוזהרין ישראל לפרוש מנשותיהן סמוך לזמן ווסת כדאמרינן בשבועות (דף יח:) והזהרתם את בני ישראל והדוה בנדתה מכאן אזהרה לבני ישראל שיהו פורשין מנשותיהן כו' : אי הכי יבמתו נמי · סמוך לווסתה לא רמיא מצוה עליה : בזיז מינה · בוש ממנה לשואלה אם סמוך לווסתה הוא : ור' יוחנן · דאמר פטור כמאן : ברשות · של מצוה שהיה טרוד בה : דזמנה בהול · שקבוע לה היום וטרוד באם לא עכשיו אימתי הולך אצל בקי ללמדו : דזבחים · דפטור במתני' בשוחט לשם פסח משום דטעה בדבר מצוה ועשה מצוה : זמנו · של פסח בהול הוא היום למחר פן יעבור זמנו : בן גרושה · כהן חלל זר גמור הוא דכתיב בכהן הנושא גרושה (ויקרא כא) לא יחלל זרעו שמחללו מדין כהונה : קרן וחומש · שהרי אכלה שוגג : ור' יהושע פוטר · שטעה בדבר מצוה : דאיקרי עבודה · אכילתה כדליקמן : ועבודה · של חלל בשוגג רחמנא אכשרה דתנן כו' : ברך ה' חילו · בכהנים כתיב ישימו קטורה באפך וגו' וסמיך ליה ברך ה' חילו חללים שבו : אמש · בערב : עבודת

רבינו חננאל

לתדחות היום כלל לגבי האי גברא לפיכך חייב אבל אימורי צבור ליכא למימר הכי אלא אפי' טעה והקריב כמה בערב שבת לקרבן (שבת) אפי' הכי חייב בשבת להקריב חובות של שבת לעולם וכיון דנתנה שבת לדחות אמרי' טעה בדבר מצוה פטור : מתני' אם אינן ראוין לפסח אותן הזבחים ששחט בשבת לשם פסח חייב ואם הן ראוין ר' אליעזר מחייב חטאת ור' יהושע פוטר אוקימתא כרבי שמעון דתאני לא נחלקו רבי אליעזר ור' יהושע על שאינן ראויין שחייב על מה נחלקו על הראויין שר' אליעזר מחייב חטאת ור' יהושע פוטר אבל ר' מאיר בין ראויין בין אינן ראויין פוטר וכן השוחט לשם אימורי צבור לשם תמידין ומוספין קדשים אחרים בשבת: פוטר היה ר"מ ואפי' [עגל] של זבחי שלמים ששחטו לשם פסח ואפי' אם שחט חולין לשם פסח פוטר רבי מאיר ורבי מאיר תרתי אית ליה משום דמיחלף ומשום דטריד אבל אם שחט בעל מום לשם פסח ודאי חייב הלכך עגל של זבחי שלמים אע"ג דלא מיחלף עגל בכבש טריד ביה והוא קדשים ובעי אקרוביה חולין לשם פסח כלומר כבש של חולין לשם כבש של פסח מיחלף הלכך פטור לאפוקי בעלי מומין שנפסלו מהקרבה דלא טריד להו ומיחלף לא מיחלפי: יתיב ר' זירא ור' שמואל בר רב יצחק וקאמרי אמר ריש לקיש נתחלף לו שפוד של נותר בשפוד של צלי ואכלו חייב ור' יוחנן אשתו נדה בעל חייב יבמתו נדה יבם פטור. איכא דאמרי אם באשתו שעשה מצוה חייב ר' יוחנן כל שכן בנותר דמחייב ר' יוחנן דהא לא עשה מצוה כלל. איכא דאמרי לא מחייב באשתו אלא משום דהוה ליה לשיולי ולא שאל אבל בנותר דלית ליה דמאן דשאיל פטר ופליג על ריש לקיש ואקשי' ור' יוחנן למה מחייב באשתו ופוטר ביבמתו ושנינן יבמתו מצוה קא עביד שנאמר (דברים כה ה) יבמה יבוא עליה ביאתו על אשתו נמי מצוה היא שנאמר (בראשית ט ז) פרו ורבו ושנינן באשתו מעוברת שכבר נתקיימה מצות פריה ורביה והא איכא מצות עונה שנאמר (דברים ה ל) שובו לכם לאהליכם ושני' שלא בשמחת עונה כלומר זו הביאה זולתי העונה האמורה בתורה כדתנן בכתובות פ' אע"פ שהעונה האמורה בתורה הטיילין בכל יום וכו': והאמר רבא חייב אדם לשמח את אשתו בדבר מצוה ודחי' זו הביאה בזמן שבא עליה בעת שחייב להתרחק ממנה והוא בסמוך [לווסתה] דקיי"ל חייבין ישראל להיות מתפרשין מנשותיהן סמוך לווסתן שנאמר והזהרתם את בני ישראל ואקשי' ויבמתו למה הוא פוטר היה לו לשאול אותה ושני' בזיז מינה כלומר כמו מתבייש הוא לשאול אותה דהא לא ניסא ביה עדיין: ואמרי' ר' יוחנן דאמר טעה בדבר מצוה כי האי גוונא פטור כמאן אי כר' יוסי דלולב דלמא שאני התם דזמנו בהול שאם לא יטלנו היום עובר זמנו וכן ר' יהושע דתינוקות התם נמי משום דזמנו בהול אבל ביבמתו דיכול לקיומי הדא מצוה למחר וליומא חרא אינו בהול הוה ליה לשיולי ולא שאיל חייב וכן ר' יהושע דזבחים נמי זמנו בהול אלא ר' יהושע דתרומה דפטר בזמן שנמצא בן גרושה או בן חלוצה דלמא בתרומות חמץ בערב הפסח דזמנה בהול אי נמי משום דאכילת תרומה נקראת עבודה כרבי טרפון דתני עבודת

[תוספתא פ"ה]

הגהות הב"ח

(א) רש"י ד"ה חייב וכו' מצוה דנותר (שמות כט) : (ב) שם ד"ה כל שכן בההוא דנותר : (ג) שם ד"ה בשפוד ליכא למאן דנשייליה : (ד) תוס' ד"ה באשתו וכו' והא איכא שמחת עונה וטעה :

מסכת כלה

[גי' הערוך בענין כו בזיז]

סוכה דף מג:

תרומות פ"ח [מ"א] יבמות דף לד.

[ר"א אומר כל הקרבנות כלי"ל]

[עי' מכות יב.]

קדושין דף סו:

גליון הש"ס

גמרא יבמתו נדה בעל. עי' יבמות ב ע"א תוספות ד"ה ולאחות אשתו :

eve of the Sabbath, [72*b*] so that the Sabbath does not stand to be overridden,[4] whereas in the second clause the Sabbath stands to be overridden by him;[5] [thus] here, [too], surely the Sabbath stands to be overridden in respect of a public sacrifice.[6] R. Ashi said to R. Kahana: But here too [in the first clause] the Sabbath stands to be overridden in connection with infants in general?—Nevertheless it was not given [to be overridden] in connection with this man, he answered him.

WHILE ALL OTHER SACRIFICES WHICH HE SLAUGHTERED AS A PASSOVER, IF THEY ARE NOT ELIGIBLE, HE IS CULPABLE; WHILE IF THEY ARE ELIGIBLE,—R. ELIEZER RULES HIM LIABLE TO A SIN-OFFERING, WHILE R. JOSHUA RULES HIM NOT CULPABLE. Which Tanna draws a distinction between eligible and not eligible? It is R. Simeon. For it was taught: The sacrifices which are eligible [for a Passover] and the sacrifices which are not eligible are as one; and similarly he who slaughters for the sake of public sacrifices is not liable; this is R. Meir's view. R. Simeon said: R. Eliezer and R. Joshua did not differ about those which are not eligible, [agreeing] that he is liable. About what do they differ? About those which are eligible, R. Eliezer ruling him liable to a sin-offering, while R. Joshua declares him not liable.

R. Bibi said in R. Eleazar's name: R. Meir declared him not liable even [if it was] a calf of a peace-offering sacrifice which he
a slaughtered in the name of a Passover-offering.[1] Said R. Zera to R. Bibi, But R. Joḥanan said: R. Meir admitted [that he is liable] in the case of blemished [animals]?[2]—He is not pre-occupied with blemished animals [at all],[3] whereas he is occupied with this [calf],[4] he answered him.

Raba asked R. Naḥman: What is R. Meir's opinion[5] [where a man slaughters] *ḥullin* for the sake of a Passover?[6] Said he to him: R. Meir declared him not liable even [if he slaughtered] *ḥullin* for the sake of a Passover. But R. Joḥanan said: R. Meir admitted [that he is liable] in the case of blemished [animals]?—Blemished [animals] cannot be confused [for these]; these can be confused.[7] Is then R. Meir's reason because they can be confused or they cannot be confused; surely R. Bibi said in R. Eleazar's name, R. Meir declared him exempt even [if it was] a calf of a peace-offering sacrifice which he slaughtered in the name of a Passover-offering,[8] which proves that R. Meir's reason is because he is pre-occupied with the [sacrificing of an animal].[9]—Said he to him, If he is pre-occupied [he is not liable] even if it cannot be confused; if it can be confused [he is not liable] even if he is not pre-occupied [with sacrificing], which excludes blemished [animals], which can neither be confused nor is he indeed pre-occupied [with the sacrificing of them].

R. Zera and R. Samuel b. Isaac were sitting in the hall of R. Samuel b. Isaac['s house], and they sat and said: R. Simeon b.

(4) And he had not yet discovered his mistake when he came to perform circumcision on the Sabbath. Thus, though he thought that he was occupied with a religious duty, and did in fact perform one, he is nevertheless liable, because the Sabbath did not stand to be violated by him, since there was no infant left for whom the Sabbath must be violated. (5) Hence he erred in the matter of a religious duty, and R. Meir holds that such is not liable even if he did not eventually perform a religious duty at all. Thus here too, if he slaughters a private sacrifice as a public sacrifice, the Sabbath did stand to be overridden in respect of a public sacrifice, and even if it had actually been slaughtered already the error is excusable, and he is not culpable. (6) As explained in last note.

a (1) Though I might think that it is impossible to confuse these two. (2) And he assumes that the two cases are alike, since in both an error should be impossible. (3) Since he never dedicated them as sacrifices. (4) Having set it aside for an offering, his mind was pre-occupied with it and he might have erred in offering it for another purpose. (5) Lit., 'what (says) he'? (6) On the Sabbath. No animal may be slaughtered as a sacrifice unless it is first consecrated. (7) A man cannot err in respect of blemished animals, whereas he can forget that an animal has not been consecrated. (8) Though these too cannot be confused. (9) But he is not occupied in sacrificing *ḥullin*.

◁ *For the continuation of the English translation of this page see overleaf.*

עין משפט
נר מצוה

מג א מיי' פ"ב מהלכות שגגות הלכה טו:
מד ב שם הלכה ח.
מה ג מיי' פ"ט מהל' דעות הל' ד סמג לאוין קכו טוש"ע א"ח סימן רמ סעיף א':
מו ד מיי' פ"ב מהלכות שגגות הלכה ה:
מז ה מיי' פ"ו מהל' תרומות הלכה יב:
מח ו מיי' פ"ו מהלכות ביאת מקדש הל' י:

שלא נתנה שבת לדחות [וסיפא נתנה שבת לדחות אצלו] הכא הרי נתנה שבת לדחות אצל קרבן ציבור א"ל רב אשי לרב כהנא הכא נמי הרי נתנה שבת לדחות אצל תינוקות דעלמא א"ל לגבי דהאי גברא מיהת לא איתיהיב: ושאר כל הזבחים ששחטן לשום פסח אם אינן ראויין חייב ואם ראויין רבי אליעזר מחייב חטאת ורבי יהושע פוטר: מאן תנא דשני ליה בין ראויין לשאינן ראויין ר' שמעון היא דתניא *אחד הזבחים הראויין ואחד זבחים שאינן ראויין וכן השוחט לשם אימורי ציבור פטור דברי ר' מאיר א"ר שמעון לא נחלקו רבי אליעזר ורבי יהושע על שאינן ראויין שחייב על מה נחלקו על הראויין שרבי אליעזר מחייב חטאת ורבי יהושע פוטר אמר רב ביבי אמר רבי אלעזר פוטר היה רבי מאיר אפי' עגל של זבחי שלמים ששחטו לשום הפסח א"ל רבי זירא לרב ביבי והאמר רבי יוחנן מודה היה רבי מאיר בבעלי מומין א"ל בבעלי מומין לא טריד בהו והאי טריד ביה בעא מיניה רבא מרב נחמן חולין לשום פסח מאי לי א"ר מאיר אמר ליה פוטר היה ר' מאיר אפילו חולין לשום פסח והא"ר יוחנן מודה היה ר"מ בבעלי מומין בעלי מומין לא מיחלפי הני מיחלפי וטעמא דרבי מאיר משום איחלופי ולא איחלופי והאמר רב ביבי א"ר אלעזר פוטר היה ר' מאיר אפי' עגל של זבחי שלמים ששחטו לשום הפסח אלמא טעמא דר"מ משום דטריד א"ל טריד אע"ג דלא מחלף מחלף אע"ג דלא טריד לאפוקי בעלי מומין דלא איחלופי מחלף ולא מטריד טריד יתיב ר' זירא ורבי שמואל בר רב יצחק ויתבי וקא אמרי א"ר שמעון בן לקיש *נתחלף לו שפוד של נותר בשפוד של צלי ואכלו חייב ור' יוחנן אמר *אשתו נדה חייב °יבמתו נדה בעל פטור איכא דאמרי כ"ש בההיא דמחייב דלא עשה מצוה אית דאמרי בההיא פטור מאי טעמא התם הוא דה"ל לשיולי אבל הכא דלא ה"ל לשיולי לא ור' יוחנן מאי שנא יבמתו דקא עביד מצוה אשתו נמי קא עביד מצוה והא איכא שמחת עונה שלא בשעת עונתה והאמר רבא *חייב אדם לשמח אשתו בדבר מצוה סמוך לווסתה אי הכי אפי' יבמתו נמי יבמתו *בזיז מינה אשתו לא בזיז מינה ור' יוחנן כמאן אילימא כרבי יוסי *דתנן רבי יוסי אומר *יום טוב הראשון של חג שחל להיות בשבת ושכח והוציא את הלולב לרשות הרבים פטור מפני שהוציא ברשות דילמא שאני התם דזמנו בהול ואלא רבי יהושע דזבחים דילמא התם נמי זמנו בהול ואלא כרבי יהושע דתינוקות התם נמי זמנו בהול ואלא כרבי יהושע דתרומה *דתנן *היה אוכל בתרומה ונודע שהוא בן גרושה או בן חלוצה רבי אליעזר מחייב קרן וחומש ר' יהושע פוטר דילמא כדרב ביבי בר אביי דאמר רב ביבי בר אביי בתרומה בערב הפסח דזמנה בהול אי נמי שאני תרומה דאיקרי עבודה ועבודה רחמנא אכשר *דתנן היה עומד ומקריב ונודע שהוא בן גרושה או בן חלוצה *כל הקרבנות כולן שהקריב על גבי המזבח פסולין ור' יהושע מכשיר ואמרינן *מ"ט דר' יהושע *דכתיב °ברך ה' חילו ופועל ידיו תרצה ותרומה היכא איקרי עבודה דתניא מעשה בר' טרפון שלא בא אמש לביהמ"ד לשחרית מצאו רבן גמליאל אמר לו מפני מה לא באת אמש לבית המדרש אמר לו עבודה עבדתי אמר לו כל דבריך אינן אלא דברי תימה וכי עבודה בזמן הזה מנין אמר לו הרי הוא אומר

עבודת

דברים לג

רש"י

ואחד זבחים שאינן ראויין · לפסח: פטור · הואיל וטרוד במחשבת לבו מאז הופרשו ויודע שעליו להקריבם טועה ושוחטן לשם פסח: על שאינן ראויין שחייב · דלאו טועה הוא: אפילו עגל · דסד"א ליכא דטעי בה: לא טריד בהו · אין מחשבת הקרבתן בלבו עד הנה: האי טריד ביה · כל ימי הפרשתן בלבו ועסוק ואומר מתי אפנה ואקריבנו: חולין לשם פסח מה לי א"ר מאיר · כלומר מה ר' מאיר אמר לנו בו: מודה היה ר' מאיר בבעלי מומין · הואיל ולאו בני קרבן נינהו לא יכול לומר טועה הוא וחייב הכא נמי חולין לשם פסח יהא חייב הואיל ולאו בני קרבן נינהו: הני מיחלפי · חולין בקדשים מיחלפי ויכול לומר טעיתי סבור הייתי קדשים הן משום הכי פטור: הני לא מיחלפי · בעלי מומין בקדשים לא יכול לומר טעיתי כסבור קדשים הן משום הכי חייב: אלמא טעמא משום טירדא · ולאו משום איחלופי וחולין לא טריד בהקריבתן: אקילעא · לפני הבית כעין בית שער וקורין פורי"א: בשפוד של צלי · של קודש הראוי ואכילת קדשים מצוה דכתיב (שמות כט) ואכלו אותם אשר כופר וגו': חייב · דטעה בדבר מצוה ולא עשה מצוה (א) ונותר חייבים על זדונו כרת ושגגתו חטאת דכתיב (ויקרא יט) ואוכליו עונו ישא: אשתו נדה בעל חייב · כדמוקי לה לקמיה בסמוך לווסתה ובמעוברת דלאו מצוה היא ולקמיה מפרש והואיל אם חלוק הוא על ריש לקיש או מוסיף על דבריו: כל שכן בההוא · (ב) נותר: דמחייב · דאין שם לחלוקות מצוה אבל הכא אע"ג דמעוברת מיהו מצות שמחת אשתו איכא: בשפוד · ליכא למאן (ג) דמשייליה: ור' יוחנן מאי שנא יבמתו · דפטור ואע"ג דהוה ליה לשיולי: דקא עביד · מצות יבום בביאה ראשונה קאמר: אשתו · מצות פריה ורביה: עונה · לפי מה שהוא חמר או גמל או טייל או תלמיד כדמפרש בכתובות (דף סא:): לשמח את אשתו · אפילו שלא בשעת עונתה אם רואה שמתאוה לו: ומשני בסמוך לווסתה · דמוזהרין ישראל לפרוש מנשותיהן סמוך לזמן ווסת נדותיהן כדאמרינן בשבועות (דף יח:) והזהרתם את בני ישראל והדוה בנדתה מכאן אזהרה לבני ישראל שיהו פורשין מנשותיהן כו': אי הכי יבמתו נמי · סמוך לווסתה לא רמיא מצוה עליה: בזיז מינה · בוש ממנה לשואלה אם סמוך לווסתה הוא: ור' יוחנן · דאמר פטור כמאן: ברשות · של מצוה שהיה טרוד בה: דזמנה בהול · שקבוע לה היום וטרוד באם לא עכשיו אימתי הולך אצל בקי ללמדו: דזבחים · דפטור במתני' בשוחט לשם פסח משום דטעה בדבר מצוה ועשה מצוה: זמנו · של פסח בהול הוא היום למהר פן יעבור זמנו: בן גרושה · כהן חלל זר גמור הוא דכתיב בכהן הנושא גרושה (ויקרא כא) לא יחלל זרעו שמחללו מדין כהונה: קרן וחומש · שהרי אכלה שוגג: ור' יהושע פוטר · שטעה בדבר מצוה: דאיקרי עבודה · אכילתה כדלקמן: ועבודה · של חלל בשוגג רחמנא אכשרה דתנן כו': ברך ה' חילו · בכהנים כתיב ישימו קטורה באפך וגו' וסמיך ליה ברך ה' חילו חללים שבו: אמש . בערב:

עבודת

תוספות

באשתו נמי קא עביד מצוה · ובסמוך נמי פריך והא איכא שמחת עונה ותימה הא באשתו נדה קיימינן דליכא מצוה ולא שמחת עונה ואומר ר"י דפריך אליבא בתרא דפוטר טעה בדבר מצוה אע"פ שלא עשה מצוה הלכך פריך והא איכא (ד) שמחה וטעה בדבר מצוה ומסיק דהוה ליה לשיולי:

סמוך לווסתה · אין לפרש דיודע שהוא סמוך לווסתה ומספקא ליה אם נדה גמורה היא אם לאו דא"כ ביבמתו אמאי פטור כיון דיודע שהוא סמוך לווסתה וסמוך לווסתה דאורייתא דנפקא לן מוהזהרתם את בני ישראל אלא יש לפרש שאינו יודע אם הוא סמוך לווסתה אם לאו דהוה ליה לשיולה כיון שאינו יודע והא דאמר בפ"ב דנדה (דף טו·) דכל הנשים בחזקת טהרה לבעליהן היינו כשיודע שלא הגיע זמן ווסתה דלא חיישינן שמא שינתה ווסתה וה"ה דהוה מצי למימר שאינו יודע אם היא נדה גמורה או לאו אלא נקט דאפילו יודע שאינה נדה כיון דמספקא ליה אם הוא סמוך לווסתה באשתו חייב ומיהו הוה מצי לאשמעינן במספקא ליה אם היא נדה גמורה ואפי' הכי ביבמתו פטור:

לדברי

רבינו חננאל

לדחות היום כלל לגבי האי גברא לפיכך חייב אבל אימורי צבור ליכא למימר הכי אלא אפי' טעה והקריב כמה בערב שבת לקרבן (שבת) אפי' הכי חייב בשבת להקריב חובות של שבת לעולם וכיון דנתנה שבת לדחות אמרי' טעה בדבר מצוה פטור: מתני' אם אינן ראוין לפסח אותן הזבחים ששחט בשבת לשם פסח חייב ואם הן ראוין ר' אליעזר מחייב חטאת ור' יהושע פוטר אוקימתא כרבי שמעון דתאני לא נחלקו רבי אליעזר ור' יהושע על שאינן ראויין שחייב על מה נחלקו על הראויין שר' אליעזר מחייב חטאת ור' יהושע פוטר אבל ר' מאיר בין ראויין בין אינן ראויין פוטר וכן השוחט לשם אימורי צבור לשם תמידין ומוספין קדשים אחרים בשבת: פוטר היה ר"מ ואפי' [עגל] של זבחי שלמים ששחטו לשם פסח ואפי' אם שחט חולין לשם פסח פוטר רבי מאיר ורבי מאיר תרתי אית ליה משום דמיחלף ומשום דטריד אבל אם שחט בעל מום לשם פסח ודאי חייב הלכך עגל של זבחי שלמים אע"ג דלא מיחלף עגל בכבש טריד ביה והוא קדשים ובעי אקרוביה חולין לשם פסח כלומר כבש של חולין לשם כבש של פסח מיחלף הלכך פטור לאפוקי בעלי מומין שנפסלו מהקרבה דלא טריד להו ומיחלף לא מיחלפי: יתיב ר' זירא ור' שמואל בר רב יצחק וקאמרי אמר ריש לקיש נתחלף לו שפוד של נותר בשפוד של צלי ואכלו חייב ור' יוחנן אשתו נדה בעל חייב יבמתו נדה יבם פטור. איכא דאמרי אם באשתו שעשה מצוה חייב ר' יוחנן כל שכן בנותר דמחייב ר' יוחנן דהא לא עשה מצוה כלל. איכא דאמרי לא מחייב באשתו אלא משום דהוה ליה לשיולי ולא שאל אבל בנותר דלית ליה דמאן דשאיל פטר ופליג על ריש לקיש ואקשי' ור' יוחנן למה מחייב באשתו ופוטר ביבמתו ושנינן יבמתו מצוה קא עביד שנאמר (דברים כה ה) יבמה יבוא עליה ביאתו על אשתו נמי מצוה היא שנאמר (בראשית ט ז) פרו ורבו ושנינן באשתו מעוברת שכבר נתקיימה מצות פריה ורביה והא איכא מצות עונה שנאמר (דברים ה ל) שובו לכם לאהליכם ושני' שלא בשמחת עונה כלומר זו הביאה זולתי העונה האמורה בתורה הטיילין בכל יום וכו': והאמר רבא חייב אדם לשמח את אשתו בדבר מצוה ודחי' זו הביאה בזמן שבא עליה בעת שחייב להתרחק ממנה והוא בסמוך [לווסתה] דקיי"ל חייבין ישראל להיות מתפרשין מנשותיהן סמוך לווסתן שנאמר והזרתם את בני ישראל ואקשי' ויבמתו למה היה לו לשאול אותה ושני' בזיז מינה כלומר כמו מתבייש הוא לשאול אותה בענין הזה דהא לא ניסא ביה עדיין: ואמרי' ר' יוחנן דאמר טעה בדבר מצוה כי האי גוונא פטור כמאן אי כר' יוסי דלמא שאני התם דזמנו בהול שאם לא יטלנו היום עובר זמנו וכן ר' יהושע דתינוקות התם נמי משום דזמנו בהול אבל ביבמתו דיכול לקיומי הדא מצוה למחר וליומא חרא אינו בהול הוה ליה לשיולי ולא שאל ר' יהושע דזבחים נמי זמנו בהול אלא ר' יהושע דתרומה דפטר בזמן שנמצא בן גרושה או בן חלוצה דלמא בתרומות חמץ בערב הפסח דזמנה בהול אי נמי משום דאכילת תרומה נקראת עבודה כרבי טרפון דתני

עבודת

מסורת הש"ס

[תוספתא פ"ה]

מסכת כלה

[גי' הערוך בערך בז בזיז] סוכה דף מא:

תרומות פ"ס [מ"ח] יבמות דף לג.

[ר"א אומר כל הקרבנות כלו']

[ע' מכות יב.] קדושין דף סו:

הגהות הב"ח

(א) רש"י ד"ה חייב וכו' מצוה דנותר: (ב) שם ד"ה כל שכן בההוא דנותר: (ג) שם ד"ה בשפוד ליכא למאן דמשייליה: (ד) תוס' ד"ה באשתו וכו' והא איכא שמחת עונה וטעה:

גליון הש"ס

גמרא יבמתו נדה בעל. עי' יבמות ד' נ"ה ע"א תוספות ד"ה ולאות אשתו:

מא א מיי' פט"ו מהל' פסולי המוקדשין הלכה א ופ"ב מהלכות שגגות הלכה יא:

מב ב ג מיי' פ"ב מהל' שגגות הלכה ח

גמרא

במאי עסקינן אילימא בטועה שמעת מינה *עקירה בטעות הויא עקירה אלא בעוקר אימא סיפא ושאר כל הזבחים ששחטן לשום הפסח אם אינן ראויין חייב אם ראויין הן ר' אליעזר מחייב חטאת ור' יהושע פוטר ואי בעוקר מה לי ראויין מה לי שאינן ראויין אלא פשיטא בטועה רישא בעוקר וסיפא בטועה א"ר אבין אין *רישא בעוקר וסיפא בטועה אשכחיה רב יצחק בר יוסף לר' אבהו דהוה קאי באוכלוסא דאינשי א"ל מתניתין מאי א"ל רישא בעוקר וסיפא בטועה תנא מיניה *ארבעין זימנין ודמי ליה כמאן דמנחא בכיסיה תנן א"ר אליעזר מה אם פסח שמותר לשמו כששינה את שמו חייב זבחים שהן אסורין לשמן כששינה את שמן אינו דין שיהא חייב ואם איתא הא לא דמי דרישא בעוקר וסיפא בטועה לר' אליעזר לא שני ליה לר' יהושע דשני ליה (א) לישני ליה הכי הכי קאמר ליה לדידי לא דמי רישא בעוקר וסיפא בטועה לדידך לא אם אמרת בפסח ששינה את שמו לדבר האסור תאמר בזבחים ששינה את שמן לדבר המותר א"ל רבי אליעזר אימורי ציבור יוכיחו שהן מותרין לשמן והשוחט לשמן חייב אמר לו רבי יהושע לא אם אמרת באימורי ציבור שכן יש להן קצבה תאמר בפסח שאין לו קצבה למימרא דכל היכא דאית ליה קצבה מחייב רבי יהושע והרי תינוקות דיש להן קצבה *ותנן מי שהיו לו שני תינוקות אחד למולו אחר השבת ואחד למולו בשבת ושכח ומל את של אחר השבת בשבת חייב אחד למולו בע"ש ואחד למול בשבת ושכח ומל את של ע"ש בשבת רבי אליעזר מחייב חטאת ור' יהושע פוטר א"ר אמי הכא במאי עסקינן כגון שקדם ומל את של ערב שבת בשבת דאיכא הך דשבת דטריד ביה הכא כגון שקדם ושחטינהו לאימורי ציבור ברישא אי הכי רבי מאיר אומר אף השוחט לשם אימורי ציבור פטור אע"ג דקדים ושחטינהו לאימורי ציבור ברישא *והתניא רבי חייא [מאבל ערב] א"ר מאיר לא נחלקו ר' אליעזר ורבי יהושע על שהיו לו שני תינוקות אחד למול ערב שבת ואחד למול בשבת ושכח ומל את של ערב שבת בשבת דחייב על מה נחלקו על שהיו לו שני תינוקות אחד למול אחר השבת ואחד למול בשבת ושכח ומל את של אחר השבת בשבת *דר' אליעזר מחייב חטאת ור' יהושע פוטר ותסברא מה התם דלא עביד מצוה פטר רבי יהושע היכא דקא עביד מצוה מחייב אמרי דבי רבי ינאי רישא כגון שקדם ומל של שבת בערב שבת שלא

רש"י

אי נימא בטועה · כסבור שהוא זבח אחר: שמעת מינה · מדקתני חייב אלמא פסול הוא: עקירה בטעות · שלא נתכוון לעקור שם פסח ממנו הויא עקירה כעוקר מדעת: מה לי שאינן ראויין · עוקר לאו טועה בדבר מצוה הוא ולמאי פטר ליה ר' יהושע בראויין והלא לא טעה בו שיודע שאינו פסח: רישא · הפסח ששחטו: סיפא · ושאר כל הזבחים: אוכלוסא · חבורה גדולה מאד: הא לא דמי · רישא לסיפא דרישא בעוקר ולאו טועה הוא: לר"א · דלאו האי ק"ו לא שאני ליה בין עוקר לטועה: ומקשי' ר' יהושע דשני ליה · לימא ליה דלא דמי טועה לעוקר ואמאי אהדר ליה טעמא משום ששינה בדבר האסור כו': בפסח שאין לו קצבה · אין חשבון לפסחים וזה שמצא טלה זה עומד בעזרה כסבור שהוא אבוד מבעליו ושחטו לשם מי שהוא: תינוקות דיש להן קצבה · מי שיש לו שני תינוקות אחד למול בשבת ואחד למול באחד בשבת יודע הוא שאין לו למול בשבת אלא אחד: ושכח ומל את של אחר השבת בשבת חייב · דטעה בדבר מצוה ולא עשה מצוה הוא דעדיין לא הגיע זמנו ומודה רבי יהושע דחייב: את של ערב שבת בשבת · קסבור שהוא של שבת וזה של ערב שבת היה אתמול מולה אלא שנאנסו ומילה שלא בזמנה אינה דוחה את השבת דהואיל ועבר זמנה ימתין עד למחר: ר' אליעזר מחייב חטאת · דלית ליה טועה בדבר מצוה ועשה מצוה פטור: רבי יהושע פוטר · דטעה בדבר מצוה ועשה מצוה פטור ואע"ג דחילל שבת ועשה שלא כדת מכל מקום מצות מילה קיים והכא נמי אע"ג דאית להו קצבה ליפטר דמכל מקום עשה מצוה דכל הזבחים שנזבחו שלא לשמן כשירין וזה שמצא זבח אחד בעזרה ושחטו לשם תמידי ציבור כשר כשר לזבחו הראשון: הכא במאי עסקינן כגון שקדם ומל את של ערב שבת בשבת · בשעה שמל את זה עדיין שניהן עומדים דמשום הכי פטור דטרוד היה באחד מהן דיודע הוא שהיום חובת האחד עליו ומתני' כגון דקדים ושחטינהו לאימורי צבור דהשתא לא הוה טרוד ועסוק בשחיטתן: ואע"ג כו' · בתמיה: [מאבל ערב · שם מקום]: ושכח ומל את של ערב שבת בשבת דחייב · ואע"ג דעשה מצוה: על מה נחלקו כו' · וקס"ד השתא ברישא מחייב ר' מאיר כשמל את שניהם ע"י [שסבור] שניהן כבר הגיע זמנן ומל של שבת תחלה שזמנו היום ואחר כך מל את של אתמול ואף על גב דעשה מצוה כיון דלא רמיא מידלא עליה בתר דמהליה לשל שבת לאו טועה בדבר מצוה הוא וסיפא פטור משום דטריד בשל שבת והוחלף לו של מחר דהא ודאי לא קאמר שמל את שניהם דהא לא טעי בהכי אלמא היכא דלא טריד האידנא לר"מ חייב: ותסברא · דטעמא משום הכי הוא השתא סיפא דלא עבד מצוה דעדיין לא הגיע זמנו פטור רישא דעבד מצוה מחייב: אמרי דבי ר' ינאי רישא כגון · שנתחלף לו אתמול של שבת בערב שבת ומלו בערב שבת ועדיין לא טודע טעותו וסבור שזה העומד של שבת הוא ואע"ג דטריד ביה דדמיא מצוה עליה כפי מחשבתו וגם עשה מצוה אפילו הכי חייב משום דלא ניתנה שבת לידחות אצלו וסיפא ניתנה שבת לידחות אצל של שבת וטעה בדבר מצוה פטור ואפילו לא עשה מצוה לרבי מאיר פטור והשוחט לשם אימורי צבור ניתנה שבת לידחות אצל קרבן צבור ואע"ג דקדים שחטינהו לאימורי צבור הרי שכח וע"י שטרוד בזבח זה בימים שעברו ויודע שזבח זה עומד ליקרב נבהל ושכח שכבר נשחטו אימורי צבור ושחטן לשמן:

ואחד

תוספות

שמעת מינה עקירה בטעות הויא עקירה. אומר ר"י דפלוגתא היא בהתכלת (מנחות מט:): **הא** לא דמי רישא בעוקר כו' · ומאי קאמר ר' יהושע שכן שינה שמו בדבר האסור אפילו שינה שמו לדבר המותר נמי חייב כיון שהוא עוקר:

לרבי יהושע דשני ליה לימא ליה הכי · תימה לרשב"א הא אפי' אי מוקמי' כולה בטועה ע"כ רבי יהושע לדבריו דרבי אליעזר קאמר דלדידיה רישא אפילו שינה לדבר המותר חייב כיון דלא עשה מצוה דמתני' מוקמי' בגמרא כרבי שמעון דאית ליה היכא דלא עשה מצוה חייב לרבי יהושע בפרק רבי אליעזר דמילה בסופו (שבת קלז·) דאמר רבי שמעון לא נחלקו רבי אליעזר ורבי יהושע על ב' תינוקות אחד למול אחר השבת ואחד בשבת ושכח ומל את של אחר השבת בשבת דחייב משום דלא עשה מצוה א"כ מה שהוצרך לומר דרישא משום דשינה לדבר האסור היינו לדברי רבי אליעזר דלרבי אליעזר בסיפא נמי לא עשה מצוה דפסל נטיל אחרים לשם הפסח ואומר ר"י דבכמה מקומות מצי למימר וליטעמיך ולא קאמר ועוד דלא דמי לתינוקות דהתם ודאי חייב כשמל של אחר השבת בשבת לפי שלא עשה מצוה וגם לא ניתנה שבת לידחות אצל אותו תינוק אבל פסח ששינה לדבר המותר פטור כיון שניתנה שבת לידחות אצל אותו פסח אם היה שוחטו לשמו:

לדידך לא אם אמרת בפסח כו' · תימה לרשב"א מה משיב ר' יהושע לדברי ר' אליעזר תאמר בזבחים ששינה שמן לדבר המותר כיון לר' אליעזר לא שני בין עוקר לטועה מה מועיל מה ששינה לדבר המותר הלא לר' יהושע עוקר לדבר המותר חייב ה"ה טועה לר' אליעזר ומפרש דה"ק ר' יהושע לר' אליעזר נהי דלא שני לך בין עוקר לטועה מ"מ יש לחלק דרישא תרתי לגריעותא עוקר ולדבר האסור וסיפא תרתי לטיבותא דטועה ולדבר המותר:

שקדם ומל של שבת בערב שבת · הוה מצי לפלוגי בדידי' בין קדם ומל ללא קדם אלא דנקט רבותא בסיפא דמל של אחר השבת בשבת פטור אע"ג דלא עשה מצוה כיון שניתנה שבת לידחות ורישא נמי קמ"ל רבותא דנקט ע"ש אף על גב דעשה מצוה חייב כיון שלא ניתנה שבת לידחות:

באשתו

רבינו חננאל

חטאת כו' אוקימנא בעוקר ומפרש אינו שוחטו אלא לשם שלמים והאי דקתני סיפא ושאר כל דובחים ששחטן לשם פסח בשבת שחל להיות בי"ד אם אינן ראויין לפסח כגון שהיו נקבות או זכרים בני שתים חייב ואם ראוין הן ר' אליעזר מחייב חטאת ורבי יהושע פוטר אוקימנא בשטעה כסבור כי הזבח של פסח הוא ששוחט ונמצא שטעה וזבח זבח אחר ועדרה רישא בעוקר שם פסח מעליו ושוחט לשם שלמים וסיפא בטועה [ואמרינן אינו (נ"א איך) תאמר דרישא בעוקר וסיפא בשוגה] והתנן אמר רבי אליעזר ומה אם הפסח שמותר הוא [לעצמו] בעצמו לשוחטו בשבת לשם פסח אלא מפני ששינה שמו ושחטו לשם שלמים חייב שאר זבחים שאסורין לשוחטן בשבת לשמן כששינה את שמן אינו דין שיהא חייב ואם איתא נימא לא דמי רישא בעוקר ולפיכך חייב אי הוה רישא נמי טועה כסיפא לא הוה מחייב מידי ושנינן לר' אליעזר לא שני ליה בין עוקר לטועה לא פריך הכי לר' יהושע שני ליה והכי קאמר ר' יהושע לדידי לא קשיא רישא בעוקר וסיפא בטועה אלא לדידך דלא שני לך בין עוקר לטועה לא אם אמרת בפסח ששינהו לדבר האסור לשחטו בשבת כגון שלמים וכיוצא בהן תאמר בזבחים ששחטן לשם פסח ששינן לדבר המותר לשחטו בשבת והוא הפסח אמר לו ר' אליעזר תמידין ומוספין יוכיחו שמותרין לשחטן בשבת והשוחט זבחים אחרים לשם תמיד בשבת חייב אמר לו ר' יהושע שאני אימורי צבור שכן יש להן [קצבה] כלומר שני תמידין ושני מוספין בכל שבת וכיון שיש להם קצבה מאחר שנשחטו קצבת הרובה השאר עומדין באיסור שבת כשאר שאקראויין לשבת כגון חטאות וכיוצא בהן תאמר בפסח שאין לו קצבה: ואקשי' וכי כל היכא דאית ליה קצבה מחייב ר' יהושע והתנן בפרק ר' אליעזר מי שהיו לו שני תינוקות אחד למול אחר השבת ואחד למול בשבת חייב כו' ומשני ר' אמי כגון שקדם ומל של ערב שבת בשבת ועדיין טריד בהאי דבשבת הכא דקדים שחטינהו לאימורי צבור ברישא דהא ליכא מידי דטריד ביה. אי הכי ר' מאיר אומר אף השוחט לשם אימורי צבור פטור ואע"ג דקדים שחיט לאימורי צבור והא תני ר' חייא אמר ר' מאיר לא נחלקו ר' אליעזר ור' יהושע על שהיו לו שני תינוקות אחד למול ערב וכו' קתני מיהת רישא ושכח ומל של ערב שבת בשבת שחייב נהי נמי דקדים מהליה להאיך דשבת האמר רבי מאיר אע"ג דקדים עבדינהו לאימורי צבור פטור ואמרי' ולטעמיך תקשי לך רישא אסיפא השתא רישא דקתני שכח ומל את של ערב שבת בשבת דטעה בדבר מצוה ועשה מצוה שאפי' עובר זמנו והוא ימים מקום בר מילה הוא ותתקיימה המצוה סיפא דשכח ומל את של אחר שבת בשבת בן שבעת ימים שאע"פ שטעה בדבר מצוה לא עשה מצוה שבן שבעת ימים אינו בר בילה קא פטור ר' יהושע אלא אמרי דבי ר' ינאי רישא דמתני' כגון שקדם ומל את של שבת [בע"ש] דהא לית ליה לשבת הכא דחויה כלל דהא ליכא תורת מילה הכא בשבת כי הדר מהיל ליה להאיך דבערב שבת בשבת לא טועה בדבר מצוה הוא ולא נתנה שבת להדחות

הגהות הב"ח

(א) גמ' לישני ליה הכי קאמר כצ"ל ותיבת הכי נמחק:

[מנחות מט.]
[כריתות כח. וש"נ]
שבת דף קלז. כריתות יט:
שבת שם [ע"ש]
גי' רש"ל
[מכל ביכמות לג.]

GEMARA. [72a] What are we discussing? Shall we say, where he erred?[3] then you may infer from this that abrogation in error constitutes abrogation?[4] Hence it means that he [intentionally] abrogates [its status].[5] Then consider the sequel: WHILE ALL OTHER SACRIFICES WHICH HE SLAUGHTERED AS A PASSOVER, IF THEY ARE NOT ELIGIBLE, HE IS CULPABLE; WHILE IF THEY ARE ELIGIBLE,—R. ELIEZER RULES HIM LIABLE TO A SIN-OFFERING, WHILE R. JOSHUA RULES HIM NOT CULPABLE. But if he abrogates [their status], what does it matter whether they are eligible or they are not eligible?[6] Hence it obviously refers to a man who errs; [then] the first clause refers to a man who abrogates [its status], whereas the second clause refers to him who errs?—Said R. Abin: Yes the first clause refers to a man who abrogates, whereas the second clause refers to him who errs. R. Isaac b. Joseph found R. Abbahu standing in a large concourse of people. Said he to him, How is our Mishnah meant?—The first clause refers to a man who abrogates, whereas the second clause refers to him who errs, he answered him. He learnt it from him forty times, and it seemed to him as though it were lying in his wallet.[7]

We learned: SAID R. ELIEZER: IF THE PASSOVER, WHICH IS PERMITTED FOR ITS OWN PURPOSE, YET WHEN HE CHANGES ITS PURPOSE, HE IS CULPABLE; THEN [OTHER] SACRIFICES, WHICH ARE FORBIDDEN FOR THEIR OWN PURPOSE, IF HE CHANGES THEIR PURPOSE IS IT NOT LOGICAL THAT HE IS CULPABLE. But if this [interpretation] is so, surely they are
a dissimilar,[1] since the first clause refers to a man who *abrogates*, whereas the second clause refers to him who *errs*?—In R. Eliezer's view there is no difference. But according to R. Joshua, who holds that there is a difference, let him answer him thus?—He says thus to him: According to my view, they are dissimilar, [for] the first clause refers to a man who abrogates, whereas the second clause refers to him who errs. [But even] according to you, it IS NOT SO. IF YOU SAY [THUS] OF THE PASSOVER, [HE IS CULPABLE] BECAUSE HE CHANGED IT FOR SOMETHING THAT IS FORBIDDEN; WILL YOU SAY [THE SAME] OF [OTHER] SACRIFICES, WHERE HE CHANGED THEM FOR SOMETHING THAT IS PERMITTED?

SAID R. ELIEZER TO HIM: LET THE PUBLIC SACRIFICES PROVE IT, WHICH ARE PERMITTED FOR THEIR OWN SAKE, YET HE WHO SLAUGHTERS [OTHER SACRIFICES] IN THEIR NAME IS CULPABLE. R. JOSHUA ANSWERED HIM: NOT SO: IF YOU SAY [THUS] OF PUBLIC SACRIFICES, [THAT IS] BECAUSE THEY HAVE A LIMIT; WILL YOU SAY [THE SAME] OF THE PASSOVER, WHICH HAS NO LIMIT? Are we to say that wherever there is a limit R. Joshua holds him culpable? Yet surely infants have a limit,[2] yet we learned: He who had two infants for circumcision, one for circumcision after the Sabbath and the other for circumcision on the Sabbath,[3] and he erred[4] and circumcised the one belonging to after the Sabbath on the Sabbath, he is culpable.[5] [If he had] one for circumcision on the eve of the Sabbath and another for circumcision on the Sabbath, and he erred and circumcised the one belonging to the eve of the Sabbath on the
b Sabbath,—R. Eliezer holds him liable to a sin-offering,[1] but R. Joshua exempts him.[2]—Said R. Ammi: The circumstances here are e.g., that he first circumcised [the infant] of the eve of the Sabbath on the Sabbath, so that there is this [infant] of the Sabbath with whom he is pre-occupied;[3] here e.g., it means that he first slaughtered the public sacrifices at the beginning.[4]

If so, [when] 'R. MEIR SAID: HE TOO WHO SLAUGHTERS [OTHER SACRIFICES] IN THE NAME OF PUBLIC SACRIFICES IS NOT LIABLE'—[he meant] even if he had first slaughtered the public sacrifices at the beginning? Surely it was taught, R. Ḥiyya of Ebel 'Arab[5] said in R. Meir's name: R. Eliezer and R. Joshua did not differ concerning him who had two infants, one for circumcision on the eve of the Sabbath and one for circumcision on the Sabbath, and he erred and circumcised the one belonging to the eve of the Sabbath on the Sabbath, [both agreeing] that he is culpable. About what do they disagree? About a man who had two infants, one for circumcision after the Sabbath and another for circumcision on the Sabbath, and he erred and circumcised the one belonging to after the Sabbath on the Sabbath, R. Eliezer ruling him liable to a sin-offering, while R. Joshua exempts [him].[6]
c Now is that logical?[1] If there [in the second clause], where he did not perform a religious duty,[2] R. Joshua exempts him; then where he did perform a religious duty, he rules him liable![3] Said the School of R. Jannai: The first clause means e.g., that he previously circumcised [the infant] belonging to the Sabbath on the

(3) Thinking that it was a different sacrifice. (4) Lit., 'uprooting'. By slaughtering it for a different purpose he abrogates (lit., 'uproots') its true status; but this matter is disputed in Men. 49a. (5) Thinking, however, that this is permitted. (6) Since he deliberately abrogates its designation, he is certainly not erring in thinking that he is performing a religious act; why then does R. Joshua hold him not liable? (7) I.e., he then knew it perfectly, and was certain that he would not forget it.

a (1) *Sc.* the two cases. (2) I.e., in the case adduced he knows definitely that he has only one infant for circumcision on the Sabbath, and therefore when he circumcises another his error is inexcusable, as explained in the note on the Mishnah. (3) E.g., twins, one being born on the Sabbath late in the day, and the second born after nightfall (or even during twilight). (4) Lit., 'forgot'. (5) For unwittingly desecrating the Sabbath. For since circumcision is not obligatory before the eighth day, this is not circumcision but the mere infliction of a wound, which entails culpability.

b (1) For though he has actually fulfilled a precept, nevertheless circumcision after its proper time does not override the Sabbath. (2) He erred through fulfilling a precept, viz., because he was occupied with the circumcision of the second, which was actually obligatory for that day; and he also did fulfil a precept by circumcising the first, and R. Joshua holds that in such a case he is not culpable. Hence here too, if he slaughtered a private sacrifice for a public sacrifice, he was occupied with a precept, viz., slaughtering a sacrifice, and he did fulfil a precept, for the sacrifice he did actually offer is valid. Hence he should not be liable. (3) When he circumcised the infant whose circumcision was due on the previous day, he had not yet circumcised the other; hence his error arose because he was rightly pre-occupied with the obligation of circumcision on that day. (4) So that his subsequent error was unjustified, since he had no pre-occupation with any obligation of offering sacrifices at all when he made that error, all permitted sacrifices on that day having been disposed of. (5) [In the Gilead district, v. Horowitz, *Palestine*, p. 6.] (6) It is now assumed that in the first clause R. Meir holds him culpable when he circumcised both, because he thought that it was already time for both, and he first circumcised the infant belonging to the Sabbath, which was due for that day, and then circumcised the other. Now though he did actually perform a religious duty, yet since there was no occasion to be further occupied with this one after having circumcised the one belonging to the Sabbath, he is not regarded as having erred in the fulfilment of a precept. Whereas in the second clause he is exempt because he was pre-occupied with the infant belonging to the Sabbath and circumcised the other by mistake; for it is assumed that he certainly did not circumcise both on that day, as he must have known that one was due for the next day. Thus we see that where he has no occasion at all to be occupied at present with a precept, R. Meir rules him liable.

c (1) That the reason is as stated in the last note. (2) The infant not yet being due for circumcision. (3) Surely not!

*the morning:*7 [71*b*] this teaches concerning the *ḥagigah* of the fourteenth, that it may be eaten two days and one night.[8] Yet perhaps it is not so, but [only] one day and one night?[9] When it [Scripture] says, *'the first day,'* the second morning[10] is meant.[11] Yet perhaps it is not so, but the first morning [is meant], and to what do I relate[12] [the case of] the *ḥagigah* which may be eaten two days and one night?[13] [To all other *ḥagigoth*] excepting this? When [Scripture] says thereof, *But if [the sacrifice of his offering be] a vow,*
a *or a freewill-offering,*[1] it teaches concerning the *ḥagigah* of the fourteenth that it may be eaten for two days and one night.[2]

The Master said:[3] 'Yet perhaps it is not so, but the first morning [is meant]'. But you have [already] said, 'When it [Scripture] says, *"the first day,"* the second morning is meant'?—This is what he means: Yet perhaps it is not so, but the Writ speaks of two *ḥagigoth*, one the *ḥagigah* of the fourteenth, and one the *ḥagigah* of the fifteenth, and the former [must not remain] until *its* morning, while the latter [must not remain] until *its* morning?[4] Then he argues, as to our general ruling[5] [that there is] a *ḥagigah* which is eaten two days and one night,[6] if so, in which [case does] *'if . . . a vow or a freewill-offering'* [hold good]? if the *ḥagigah* of the fourteenth, surely a day and a night is written in connection therewith; if the *ḥagigah* of the fifteenth, surely a day and a night is written in connection therewith?[7] But this is in respect of the *ḥagigah* of the fifteenth, while the whole of the other verse is in respect of the *ḥagigah* of the fourteenth [only,] [and thus] it teaches concerning the *ḥagigah* of the fourteenth that it may be eaten two days and one night. Thus the reason is that *'on the first day until the morning'* is written, so that what does *'morning'* mean? the second morning;[8] hence wherever *'morning'* is written without qualification, it means the first morning, even if *'first'*[9] is not written in connection with it.[10]

MISHNAH. IF THE PASSOVER WAS SLAUGHTERED FOR
b A DIFFERENT PURPOSE[1] ON THE SABBATH, HE [THE SLAUGHTERER] IS LIABLE TO A SIN-OFFERING ON ITS ACCOUNT.[2] WHILE ALL OTHER SACRIFICES WHICH HE SLAUGHTERED AS A PASSOVER,[3] IF THEY ARE NOT ELIGIBLE,[4] HE IS CULPABLE; WHILE IF THEY ARE ELIGIBLE,—R. ELIEZER RULES HIM LIABLE TO A SIN-OFFERING, WHILE R. JOSHUA RULES HIM NOT CULPABLE.[5] SAID R. ELIEZER TO HIM: IF THE PASSOVER, WHICH IS PERMITTED FOR ITS OWN PURPOSE, YET WHEN HE CHANGES ITS PURPOSE HE IS CULPABLE; THEN [OTHER] SACRIFICES, WHICH ARE FORBIDDEN [EVEN] FOR THEIR OWN PURPOSE,[6] IF HE CHANGES THEIR PURPOSE IS IT NOT LOGICAL THAT HE IS CULPABLE! R. JOSHUA ANSWERED HIM, NOT SO. IF YOU SAY [THUS] OF THE PASSOVER, [HE IS CULPABLE] BECAUSE HE CHANGED IT FOR SOMETHING THAT IS FORBIDDEN; WILL YOU SAY [THE SAME] OF [OTHER] SACRIFICES, WHERE HE CHANGED THEM FOR SOMETHING THAT IS PERMITTED?[7] SAID R. ELIEZER TO HIM, LET THE PUBLIC SACRIFICES[8] PROVE IT, WHICH ARE PERMITTED FOR THEIR OWN SAKE,[9] YET HE WHO SLAUGHTERS [OTHER SACRIFICES] IN THEIR NAME IS CULPABLE. R. JOSHUA ANSWERED HIM: NOT SO. IF YOU SAY [THUS] OF PUBLIC SACRIFICES, [THAT IS] BECAUSE THEY
c HAVE A LIMIT;[1] WILL YOU SAY [THE SAME] OF THE PASSOVER, WHICH HAS NO LIMIT?[2] R. MEIR SAID: HE TOO WHO SLAUGHTERS [OTHER SACRIFICES] IN THE NAME OF PUBLIC SACRIFICE IS NOT LIABLE.

IF HE SLAUGHTERED IT[3] FOR THOSE WHO ARE NOT ITS EATERS,[4] OR FOR THOSE WHO WERE NOT REGISTERED[5], FOR UNCIRCUMCISED OR FOR UNCLEAN [PERSONS], HE IS CULPABLE; [IF HE SLAUGHTERED IT] FOR ITS EATERS AND FOR THOSE WHO ARE NOT ITS EATERS, FOR THOSE WHO ARE REGISTERED FOR IT AND FOR THOSE WHO ARE NOT REGISTERED FOR IT, FOR CIRCUMCISED AND FOR UNCIRCUMCISED, FOR UNCLEAN AND FOR CLEAN [PERSONS], HE IS NOT LIABLE.[6] IF HE SLAUGHTERED IT, AND IT WAS FOUND TO POSSESS A BLEMISH, HE IS LIABLE. IF HE SLAUGHTERED IT AND IT WAS FOUND ṬEREFAH[7] INTERNALLY,[8] HE IS NOT LIABLE.[9] IF HE SLAUGHTERED IT, AND [THEN] IT BECAME KNOWN THAT ITS OWNERS HAD WITHDRAWN THEIR HANDS
d FROM IT,[1] OR THAT THEY HAD DIED, OR THAT THEY HAD BECOME UNCLEAN, HE IS NOT CULPABLE, BECAUSE HE SLAUGHTERED WITH PERMISSION.[2]

(7) Deut. XVI, 4. (8) Understanding *'morning'* to refer to the *sixteenth* of Nisan. (9) Relating *'morning'* to the *fifteenth*. (10) After it is slaughtered, i.e., the morning of the sixteenth. (11) Lit., 'said'. For *'the first day'* implies that it may be eaten the whole of the first day after it is slaughtered. (12) Lit., 'how do I fulfil?' (13) That there are such *ḥagigoth* (pl. *ḥagigah*) is deduced anon.

a (1) Lev. VII, 16. (2) The verse continues: *it shall be eaten on the day he offereth his sacrifice and on the morrow*. Thus two days are allotted, while *'if a vow'* is regarded as superfluous, and therefore is interpreted as an extension to include the present case. (3) The Talmud now proceeds to elucidate this Baraitha leading up to the explanation of R. Joseph's argument. (4) I.e., the former must not remain until the morning of the fifteenth, while the latter must not remain until the morning of the sixteenth. Then the verse would be translated thus: *'neither shall any of the flesh . . . which thou sacrificest . . . at even'*—*sc.* of the *ḥagigah* of the fourteenth—*'remain all night'*, which naturally means until the morning of the fifteenth; while that *'which thou sacrificest the first day'*, i.e., on the fifteenth, must not *'remain . . . until the morning'* viz., of the sixteenth. (5) Lit., 'what is established to us'. (6) Rashi: but as to our principle that there is a *ḥagigah* apart from this which may be eaten etc. Thus a different meaning is now given to the phrase 'apart from this'. (7) On the present hypothesis. (8) Because of *'the first day'*. (9) ראשית. (10) This is the point of R. Joseph's objection as explained by Raba.

b (1) Lit., not for its name'—e.g., as a peace-offering. (2) For having desecrated the Sabbath unintentionally, as he thought that just as it is permitted for its own purpose so it is permitted for another purpose. (3) I.e., the animals had been consecrated for other sacrifices. (4) For a Passover, e.g., if they are females or two-years old (v. Ex. XII, 5). (5) R. Eleazar holds that even when a man performs a forbidden action while thinking that he is doing a religious deed, he is culpable. R. Joshua, however, maintains that if the action actually performed is a religious deed, even a slight one, he is not liable, as he is regarded not as having unwittingly desecrated the Sabbath, but as having erred in a religious matter. This applies to the present case, for he did offer a sacrifice, and R. Joshua rules *supra* 62*b* that all sacrifices, including the Passover, even if slaughtered for a different purpose, are nevertheless fit. But in the first case he definitely did not perform a religious action, since all know that a female etc. is not eligible for a Passover, and therefore both agree that he is culpable. (6) On the Sabbath. (7) I.e., he slaughtered them as a Passover, which is actually permitted. (8) Rashi: the sacrifices which are prescribed (*amure* fr. *amur*). (9) The daily burnt-offering and the additional offerings of Sabbaths and Festivals override the Sabbath.

c (1) Only a few animals are slaughtered as public sacrifices, and it is easy to avoid the mistake. Therefore when a man slaughters an animal consecrated for a different purpose as a public sacrifice, he cannot be regarded as having erred in a religious act but as one who unwittingly desecrated the Sabbath. (2) An enormous number of animals were slaughtered (cf. *supra* 64*b*)—seemingly limitless. Hence his error is pardonable, and he is regarded as having erred in a religious duty. (3) The Passover offering, on the Sabbath. (4) Such who could not eat of it; e.g., sick or old people. (5) Lit., 'numbered'. (6) In the former case the offering is unfit; hence his act constitutes desecration of the Sabbath; but in the latter case the offering is valid, v. *supra* 61*a*. (7) V. Glos. (8) Lit., 'in a secret part'. (9) A sin-offering is incurred only when a person intends doing what he does, but is unaware that in the circumstances it is forbidden; he is then technically called *shogeg*, an unwitting offender. But if he did not intend doing it at all, he is called *anus*, the victim of an unforeseen accident, and is not liable. Now an external examination of the animal would have revealed its blemish; his neglect to do this renders him *shogeg*, as though he had known that it was blemished, but thought it permitted. But he could not have known here that it was *ṭerefah;* therefore he is regarded as *anus*, and is not culpable.

d (1) I.e., they had re-registered for a different animal before this was slaughtered. (2) He could not have known of this, and therefore he too is regarded as *anus*.

לז א ב מיי' פ"ב מהל' שגגות הלכה יב ופ' ט"ו מהלכות פסולי המוקדשין הלכה יב :
לח ג מיי' פ"ב מהל' שגגות הלכה יג :
לט ד שם הלכה יב :
מ ה שם הלכה י :

לימד על חגיגת י"ד שנאכלת לשני ימים ולילה אחד או אינו אלא ליום ולילה כשהוא אומר °ביום הראשון (לבקר) הרי בקר שני אמור או אינו אלא בקר ראשון ומה אני מקיים חגיגה הנאכלת לשני ימים ולילה אחד חוץ מזו כשהוא אומר בו °אם נדר או נדבה לימד על חגיגת י"ד שנאכלת לב' ימים ולילה א' אמר מר או אינו אלא בקר ראשון הא אמרת כשהוא אומר ביום הראשון (לבקר) הרי בקר שני אמור ה"ק או אינו אלא בשתי חגיגו' הכתוב מדבר אחת חגיגת י"ד ואחת חגיגת ט"ו וזו לבוקרה וזו לבוקרה הדר אמר אלא דקי"ל חגיגה הנאכלת לשני ימים ולילה אחד א"כ אם נדר או נדבה במאי אי חגיגת י"ד הא כתיב בה יום ולילה אי חגיגת ט"ו הא כתיב בה יום ולילה אלא האי לחגיגת ט"ו והאיך כוליה קרא לחגיגת י"ד לימד על חגיגת י"ד שנאכלת לשני ימים ולילה אחד טעמא דכתיב ביום הראשון לבקר דמאי בקר בקר שני הא כל היכא דכתיב בקר סתמא בקר ראשון ואע"ג דלא כתב ביה ראשית:

דברים טז ויקרא ז

מתני' הפסח ששחטו שלא לשמו בשבת חייב עליו חטאת ושאר כל הזבחים ששחטן לשם פסח אם אינן ראויין חייב ואם ראויין הן רבי אליעזר מחייב חטאת ור' יהושע פוטר א"ל ר' אליעזר מה אם הפסח שהוא מותר לשמו כששינה את שמו חייב זבחים שהן אסורין לשמן כששינה את שמן אינו דין שיהא חייב א"ל ר' יהושע לא אם אמרת בפסח ששינהו בדבר אסור תאמר בזבחים ששינן בדבר המותר א"ל ר"א אימורי ציבור יוכיחו שהן מותרין לשמן והשוחט לשמן חייב א"ל ר' יהושע לא אם אמרת באימורי ציבור שיש להן קצבה תאמר בפסח שאין לו קצבה רבי מאיר אומר אף השוחט לשם אימורי ציבור פטור שחטו שלא לאוכליו ושלא למנויו לערלין ולטמאין חייב לאוכליו ושלא לאוכליו למנויו ושלא למנויו למולין ולערלים לטמאין ולטהורין פטור שחטו ונמצא בעל מום חייב *שחטו ונמצא טריפה בסתר פטור שחטו ונודע שמשכו הבעלים את ידם או שמתו או שנטמאו פטור מפני ששחט ברשות: גמ' במאי

לימד על חגיגת י"ד שנאכלת לשני ימים ולילה אחד · תימה לר"י דתניא בסוף פרק כל הפסולים (זבחים לו·) ובשר זבח תודת שלמיו למדנו תודה שנאכלת ליום ולילה מנין לרבות שלמי נזיר ושלמי פסח ת"ל שלמיו ופי' בקונ' התם שלמים הבאים מחמת פסח הייט חגיגת י"ד והשתא ההיא דהכא בריית' כמאן דלהנהא דשמעתין נאכלת לשני ימים ולכן תימא (לעיל ד' ע·) נמי דנאכלת ליום ולילה נפקא ליה מדהוקש לפסח והתם נפקא ליה מדכתיב זבח תודת שלמיו על כן נראה לר"י דשלמים הבאים מחמת פסח דקתני התם הייט מותר הפסח שקרב שלמים והשתא אתי שפיר דלקמן פרק האשה (ד' פט.) אמרינן דמותר הפסח נאכל ליום ולילה ומנא לן אי לא מקרא דהתם ובת"כ בפרשת צו את אהרן משמע בהדיא כפי' ר"י דדריש התם האי קרא דבשר זבח תודת שלמיו לשלמים הבאים מחמת פסח ובתר הכי מייתי ההיא דשמעתין ודריש מלא ילין מן הבשר אשר תזבח בערב וגו' בחגיגה הבאה עם הפסח הכתוב מדבר שתאכל לשני ימים ולילה אחד אלמא משמע דההיא דלעיל איירי במותר הפסח שקרב שלמים:

והאיך כוליה קרא לחגיגת י"ד · תימה לרשב"א כיון דכולי' קרא בחגיגת י"ד איירי ומאי בקר בקר שני א"כ תאכל לשני ימים ושני לילות דקרא משמע שאינה נפסלת עד בקר שני אבל ליל בקר שני נאכלת:

כל היכא דכתב בקר סתמא בקר ראשון · תימה לר"י דבסוף ערבי פסחים (לקמן קכ:) דריש בקר בקר שני אף על גב דכתיב סתמא

שמעת

תורה אור

או אינו אלא ליום ולילה · דהאי בקר בוקרו של ט"ו קאמר : כשהוא אומר ביום הראשון (לבקר) · מכלל דנאכלת כל יום הראשון של יום טוב וקאמר לבקר דלא תלין עד בקר שני : או אינו אלא בקר ראשון · לקמיה פריך היכי תיסק אדעתין למימר תו הא אמרת ביום הראשון חד ולבקר תרי : ומה אני מקיים חגיגה הנאכלת לשני ימים · דנפקא לן מקרא אחרינא דיש חגיגה נאכלת לשני ימים ולקמן מפרש היכא אשכחן ובאיזו חגיגה אני מקיימה באחד חגיגות חוץ מזו : כשהוא אומר אם נדר · באכילת שלמים שני ימים אם נדר או נדבה זבח קרבנו ביום הקריבו את זבחו יאכל וממחרת וגו' הרי שני ימים ולילה שבינתיים והוה ליה למיכתב נדר (א) ונדבה אם נדר למה לי ריבה אף שלמי חובה לאכילת שני ימים : לימד על חגיגת י"ד כו'.(ב) ולקמן מפרש במאי משתמע ליה והשתא מפרש לה למתניתא והדר אסיק אתקפתי' דתנא לבשר לא בעי ראשית : הכי קאמר או אינו · אלא ליום ולילה והאי דכתב ביום הראשון לבוקר מילתא אחריתי היא ובשתי חגיגות דיבר הכתוב חגיגת ארבעה עשר וחמשה עשר זו לבוקרה וזו לבוקרה והכי משמע קרא לא ילין מבשר חגיגת י"ד אשר תזבח בערב וסתם ליניה לבוקרה משמע ומאותה שתזבח ביום הראשון דהיינו חגיגת חמשה עשר לא ילין לבוקר של ששה עשר : הדר אמר · תנא ומה אני מקיים חגיגה הנאכלת לשני ימים חוץ מזו כלומר באיזו חגיגה חוץ מזו אני מקיים את אשר אני מוצא שנאכלת לשני ימים הרי השוויות את כולן והיכן אני מוצא כשהוא אומר אם נדר הרי מצאתי שיש חגיגה נאכלת לשני ימים ואיזו היא על כרחיך לימד על חגיגת י"ד כו' והאיך לימד דעל כרחיך אי נמי אם נדר בחגיגת ט"ו משוית ליה דקילא דאיכא בהא עם הפסח שמעת בה מיהא דנאכלת לשני ימים וביום הראשון לבקר על כרחיך לאו אחגיגת ט"ו קאי אלא אאשר תזבח בערב ולימד שתאכלנה כל יום הראשון עד בקר שני : האי לחגיגת חמשה עשר · אם נדר : והאיך כולי' · ביום הראשון כדפריש' : וטעמא דכתיב כו' · השתא מפרש אתקפתיה דאילו תנא לבשר לא בעי ראשית אי לא כתיב ביום הראשון לבקר דמשמע תרי הוה אמינא בקר בקר ראשון ואע"ג דבבשר קאי דקיל וכל שכן בקר דכתיב גבי חלב חגי דלא בעי ראשית והאי דסמכינהו קרא מילתא אחריתי דרוש בה :

מתני' הפסח ששחטו בשבת שלא לשמו . וכסבור כשם שמותר לשמו כך מותר שלא לשמו : חייב חטאת . שחילל שבת בשוגג : אם אינן ראויין · לפסח כגון עגל או איל בן שתי שנים או נקבה חייב עליו חטאת אם נעלמה ממנו שבת או כסבור שמותר לשחוט אחרים לשם פסח בשבת דהאי לאו טועה בדבר מצוה הוא דהכל יודעין שאין זה כשר לפסח : ואם ראויין הן · כגון שהוא שה בן שנה של שלמים ששחטו לשם פסח דמתוך שטרוד ובהול לשחוט פסחו טעה בזה ולא נזכר שהקדישו לדבר אחר : ר' אליעזר מחייב חטאת · אע"פ שטעה בדבר מצוה : ור' יהושע פוטר · דקסבר טעה בדבר מצוה ועשה מצוה כל דהו פטור מחיוב חטאת שבה וזה עשה מצוה שהקריב קרבן וכל הזבחים שנזבחו שלא לשמן כשירין ואף הנשחטין לשם הפסח ר' יהושע מכשיר להו בפרק תמיד נשחט (ד' סג:) : מה אם פסח שמותר . לשוחטו בשבת לשמו שינה את שמו מודית לי דחייב חטאת כדקתני לעיל : ששינה בדבר האסור · ששחטו לשם קרבנות אחרים שאסורין לשוחטן בשבת : ששינן בדבר המותר · ששחטן לשם פסח שמותר לשוחטו בשבת : אימורי ציבור · קרבנות האמורין בציבור בשבת כגון תמידין ומוספין יוכיחו שמותרין לשוחטן לשמן והשוחט שאר זבחים לשמן בשבת חייב : שיש להן קצבה · שהיה רואה אחרים הרבה עסוקין בשחיטתן וכיון שנשחט התמיד יודע הוא שאין צריך לשחוט עוד הלכך אין זה טועה אלא שוגג דלא היה לו לטעות בדבר : תאמר בפסח שאין לו קצבה · שהכל צריכין לכך והרי הוא רואה את אחרים הרבה עוסקין בכך וטרוד להתעסק במצוה ואפילו שחט הוא פסחו כבר ומצא זבח זה עומד בעזרה וכסבור שהוא פסח ושחטו לשם מי שהוא וטעה על כך הלכך טועה בדבר מצוה הוא : ר' מאיר אומר · השוחט אחרים כל שבתות שנה לשם אימורי ציבור פטור : שחטו בשבת שלא לאוכליו . דפסח פסול הוא ונעלמה ממנו שבת או כסבור שכשר : שלא לאוכליו · לחולה ולזקן חייב חטאת דלא ניתנה לידחות שבת אלא שחיטה זו : לאוכליו ושלא לאוכליו וכו' פטור · דהא פסח כשר הוא כדתנן בתמיד נשחט (ד' סא·) דמקצת אוכלין לא פסלי : שחטו ונמצא בעל מום חייב · דשוגג הוא ולא אנוס דהוה ליה לבקוריה : שמשכו הבעלים את ידם · ממנו קודם שחיטה ומנו על אחר : או שמתו או שנטמאו · דעכשיו לא ניתנה לידחות שבת אלו : פטור · שאנוס הוא דלא היה יודע שכן ולא היה לו לבדוק על כך : גמ' אי

רבינו חננאל

בעי ראשית לרבויי בקר ראשון דתניא בתורת כהנים לא ילין מן הבשר אשר תזבח בערב ביום הראשון לבקר לימד על חגיגת י"ד שנאכלין לשני ימים ולילה אחד כו' : אמר מר או אינו אלא בקר ראשון והא אמרת כשהוא אומר ביום הראשון לבקר הרי בקר שני אמור אמרי הכי קאמר או אינו אלא בקר ראשון ובשתי חגיגות הכתוב מדבר אחד חגיגת ארבע' עשר ואחד חגיגת ט"ו וזו לבוקרה וזו לבוקרה הדר אמר אלא חגיגה דתנינן חגיגה הנאכלת לשני ימים ולילה אחד נימא חוץ מזו ורבינה מנדר אם נדבה הא [במאי] קא פשטת דכתיב בהאי קרא תרתי חגיגות ותרוייהו ליום אחד אלא ודאי האי דכתיב ביום הראשון לבקר לא בא אלא ללמד על חגיגת י"ד שנאכלת לשני ימים ולילה אחד וטעמא דכתב רחמנא ביום הראשון לבוקר דמשמע בקר של יום (שהרי) [שהוא] אחרי יום ראשון [הא לא"ה] הוה אמינא מאי בקר בבקר ראשון ואף על גב דלא כתיב ראשית וקשיא לרב כהנא . אבל שלמים הבאים מחמת פסח אין נאכלין אלא ליום אחד דתניא בתורת כהנים ובשר זבח תודת שלמיו הרי זה בא ללמד שיהא נאכלין ליום אחד אין לי אלא תודה לחמה מנין ת"ל קרבנו ומנין לרבות הולדות ותמורות ת"ל ובשר ומנין לרבות חטאת ואשם ת"ל זבח ומנין לרבות שלמי נזיר ושלמים הבאים מחמת הפסח ת"ל שלמיו : מתני' הפסח ששחטו שלא לשם פסח או לשם שלמים בשבת חייב עליו

הגהות הב"ח
(א) רש"י ד"ה כשהוא אומר וכו' למיכתב נדר או נדבה : (ב) שם ד"ה לימד וכו' לקמיה מפרש כמאי :

[ע' תוס' לקמן עג. ד"ה שחטו]

בשעת שמחה וליכא משום חגיגה הוי דבר שבחובה *וכל דבר שבחובה אינו בא אלא מן החולין לימא מסייע ליה °והיית אך שמח *לרבות לילי י"ט האחרון לשמחה אתה אומר לילי י"ט האחרון או אינו אלא לילי יום טוב הראשון תלמוד לומר אך (שמח) *חלק מ"ט לאו משום דאין לו במה ישמח לא כדתני טעמא *מה ראית לרבות לילי יום טוב האחרון ולהוציא לילי יום טוב ראשון מרבה אני לילי יום טוב האחרון שיש שמחה לפניו ומוציא אני לילי יום טוב ראשון שאין שמחה לפניו מתיב רב יוסף *חגיגת ארבעה עשר יוצא בה משום שמחה ואין יוצא בה משום חגיגה אמאי הא בעינן זביחה בשעת שמחה וליכא אמר רב אידי בר אבין שעיכב ושחטה אמר רב אשי הכי נמי מסתברא דאי לא תימא הכי הא מתניתא מאן קתני לה בן תימא בן תימא הא פסלה לה בלינה ש"מ מתיב רבא *ההלל והשמחה שמנה ואי אמרת בעינן זביחה בשעת שמחה הא זמנין סגיאין דלא משכחת לה אלא שבעה כגון שחל י"ט הראשון להיות בשבת א"ר הונא בריה דרב יהודה משמחו בשעירי הרגלים אמר רבא שתי תשובות בדבר חדא דשעירי הרגלים חי נאכלין צלי אין נאכלין ושמחה בחי ליכא ועוד כהנים אוכלין וישראל במה שמחים אלא א"ר פפא משמחו בכסות נקיה ויין ישן כי אתא רבין א"ר אלעזר °שלמים ששחטן מערב יום טוב יוצא בהן משום שמחה ואין יוצא בהן משום חגיגה משום שמחה יוצא בהן °לא בעינן זביחה בשעת שמחה ולא משום חגיגה הוי דבר שבחובה וכל דבר שבחובה אינו בא אלא מן החולין מיתיבי והיית אך שמח לרבות לילי יום טוב האחרון לשמחה אתה אומר לרבות לילי יום טוב האחרון או אינו אלא לרבות לילי יום טוב הראשון תלמוד לומר אך חלק מאי טעמא לאו משום דאין לו במה ישמח לא כדתניא מה ראית לרבות לילי יום טוב האחרון ולהוציא לילי יום טוב הראשון מרבה אני לילי יום טוב האחרון שיש שמחה לפניו ומוציא אני לילי יום טוב הראשון שאין שמחה לפניו אמר רב כהנא °מנין לאימורי חגיגת חמשה עשר שנפסלין בלינה שנאמר °ולא ילין חלב חגי עד בקר וסמיך ליה ראשית למימרא דהאי בקר בקר ראשון מתקיף לה רב יוסף טעמא דכתב ראשית הא לא כתב ראשית הוה אמינא מאי בקר בקר שני מי איכא מידי דבשר איפסיל ליה מאורתא ואמורין עד צפרא אמר ליה אביי אלמה לא והרי פסח *לרבי אלעזר בן עזריה דבשר איפסיל ליה מחצות ואמורין עד צפרא אמר רבא רב יוסף הכי קא קשיא ליה מי איכא מידי דאלו תנא לבשר לא בעי ראשית ורב כהנא לאימורין בעי ראשית מאי היא דתניא °לא ילין מן הבשר אשר תזבח בערב ביום הראשון לבקר

לימד

(דברים טז · שמות כג · דברים טז)

תוספות

לרבות לילי יום טוב האחרון . נראה לריב"א דהוא הדין ללילות אחרות איצטריך ריבוי משום דאי לאו קרא הו"א דשמחה לפני ה' שבעת ימים דדרשינן מיניה שלמי שמחה ורבינן נמי מיניה בפרק לולב וערבה (סוכה מג.) במקדש לולב שבעת ימים והתם ימים ולא לילות ומיהו לילי יום טוב האחרון איצטריך ריבויא טפי משום דשמיני רגל בפני עצמו הוא וה"א לא יהא מחוייב לזבוח (ד) שמחה ביום שביעי לצורך שמיני כמו שאינו מחוייב בערב יום טוב לצורך הלילה : **או** איטו אלא לילי י"ט הראשון · ולא בא למעוטי שאר לילות אלא לילי יום טוב האחרון : **לאו** משום דאין לו במה ישמח · וא"ת אם כן תיפוק ליה מהיכך קרא דבעינן זביחה בשעת שמחה וי"ל דאי מהתם ה"א דלא בעינן זביחה בשעת שמחה אלא בחגיגה של יום טוב שיכול לשוחטה בו ביום אבל הכא שאין יכול לשוחטה בלילה לא להכי איצטריך אך למעט : **לילי** יום טוב האחרון · פי' בקונטר' דווקא לילה אבל יום שמיני לא וקשה לריב"א דהתנן ההלל והשמחה שמונה וליכא למימר משום ליל שמיני קתני שמונה דליכא שמונה לילות דליל יום טוב ראשון לא קחשיב ועוד דומיא דהלל דעיקרו ביום ועוד דכי פריך לקמן ואם איתא זימנין דלא משכחת לה שמונה כגון שחל להיות יום טוב הראשון בשבת ואי כפירוש הקונט' תיקשי נמי לכולי עלמא דכשחל יום שמיני באחד בשבת אז ליכא אלא שבעה דמתי יוכל לשחוט לליל שמיני שהוא מוצאי שבת דאי שחיט בערב שבת איפסלא לה הלכך נראה לפרש דלילי יום טוב האחרון לאו דווקא דה"ה ביום : **מנין** לאימורי חגיגה שנפסלין בלינה שנאמר ולא ילין כו' · מהכא נפקא בכל אימורין :

רש"י

בשעת שמחה · ביום טוב שהוא זמן שמחה : והיית אך שמח · קרא יתירא הוא דכתיב לעיל מיניה חג הסוכות תעשה לך שבעת ימים וסמיך ליה ושמחת בחגך והדר כתיב שבעת ימים תחוג וגו' והיית אך שמח : לרבות לילי יום טוב האחרון · ואין שמחה אלא באכילת שלמים ויום טוב האחרון גופיה לא דהא תרי זמני שבעת ימים כתיב גבי שמחה כדפרישי' וממילא אימעיט שמיני : או אינו אלא לרבות לילי יום טוב הראשון . ואף על פי שאין קרבן בלילה נלמד שהטעינו הכתוב לשחוט שלמים מערב יום טוב לשמחת לילי יום טוב : אך (שמח) חלק · כל אכין ורקין מיעוטין : מאי טעמא · משמעות מיעוטא ללילי ראשון וריבויא ללילי אחרון ולא אמרינן איפכא לאו משום דאמרינן אין לו במה ישמח דשלמים השחוטין מבערב לאו שמחה היא דבעינן זביחה בשעת שמחה : שיש שמחה לפניו · כל ימות ולילות החג : חגיגת י"ד כו' · קס"ד דרב יוסף בששחטה בארבעה עשר קאמר : הא מתניתא · בן תימא אמרה לעיל ולבן תימא איפסילא לה דהא אמר אין נאכלת אלא ליום ולילה : והשמחה · בשלמים : שחל יום טוב בשבת · ומבערב אין יכול לשחוט דהא בשעת שמחה בעית : אמר רב הונא · ודאי מקרבן שמחה ליכא אלא שבעה אלא הא דקתני השמחה שמונה משמחו בשעירי הרגלים שעיר החטאת האמור בראשון שבכל יום היה שעיר בא משל ציבור וכל חטאות החיצונות נאכלות וכל קרבן ציבור הקבוע דוחה שבת : חי נאכלין · אם בא לאוכלו בשבת לא יאכלנו כי אם חי דאין צלייתו ובישולו דוחה שבת ובשר חי אין כאן שמחה : ועוד · נהי נמי דיש שמחה בבשר חי הרי חטאות אין נאכלות אלא לכהנים והן אוכלין וישראל במה ישמחו : לרבות לילי יום טוב האחרון לשמחה . כשאר לילי החג : או אינו אלא כו' · כדפרישית : לאימורי חגיגת ט"ו שנפסלין בלינה · ואע"פ שזמן אכילת בשרה כל יום המחרת : וסמיך ליה ראשית ביכורי וגו' · ודרוש ביה בקר ראשון(א) : דבשר איפסיל ליה מאורתא · משחשכה ועבר יום ששה עשר ואימורין יכשרו עד בקר שבעה עשר דאי בקר בקר שני בקר של שבעה עשר : ר' אלעזר בן עזריה . בפרק בתרא (דף קכ:) דאמר מדאורייתא אכילת פסח עד חצות ותו לא : הכי (ב) קשיא ליה · אע"ג דאותיב מלתא אחריתי : ומי איכא מידי · כלומר (ג)אפשר להיות משמעות המקרא בקר שני אבל חזינן תנא דמתני' דלקמן דאפי' לבשר שהוא קל מאימורין לא בעי ראשית ובקר דכתיב ביה משמע ליה לתנא בקר ראשון ורב כהנא באימורין דחמירה קדושתיהו לא משמע ליה בקר דכתיב גבייהו בקר ראשון בלא ראשית : אשר תזבח בערב · בחגיגת ארבעה עשר מיירי דנשחטת עם הפסח בערב דהא ליכא למימר בערב של יום טוב הראשון עלמו קאמר קרא דאם כן מאי בערב הלא שחיטתן ביום כולו : *שנאכלת לשני ימים · דהאי בקר בוקרו של ששה עשר קאמר קרא : או

מסורת הש"ס

מנחות דף פב. [חגיגה ז: ח. כולה ים:] · סוכה דף מח. · [לעיל ס. וש"נ] · [סוכה מח:] · [לעיל ע.] · [סוכה מב:] · [לקמן קכ: וש"נ] · שייך לע"ב

הגהות הב"ח

(א) רש"י ד"ה וסמיך ליה וכו' ראשון הס"ד ואח"כ מ"ה מאי בקר בקר שני בקר של שבעה עשר דבשר איפסיל ליה וכו' שבעה עשר הס"ד והשאר נמחק : (ב) שם ד"ה הכי קא קשיא ליה : (ג) שם ד"ה ומי איכא מידי כלומר איך אפשר וכו' שני והא אנן חזינן : (ד) תוס' ד"ה לרבות וכו' לזבוח שלמי שמחה ביום שביעי :

עין משפט נר מצוה

לג א מיי' פ"ו מהל' פסולי המוקדשין הלכה טו :
לד ב מיי' פ"ב מהלכות חגיגה הלכה יא :
לה ג שם הלכה יב :
לו ד מיי' פ"א מהלכות ק"פ הלכה ז סמג לאוין שמח :

רבינו חננאל

שמחה שהשמחה אינה אלא בשמונת ימי החג ויום י"ד אינה חשובה (אלא) מימי השמחה וכתיב וזבחת ושמחת בעינן זביחה בעידן שמחה. ותנא תנא והיית אך שמח לרבות לילי יום טוב האחרון לשמחה כו' דכתיב (ויקרא כ"ג מ') ושמחתם לפני ה' אלהיכם שבעת ימים שבעה ולא שמונה וכתיב והיית אך שמח ואמרי' אך חלק לרבות לילי יום טוב האחרון לשמחה והוציא ליל יו"ט ראשון דאין לו בלילי יום טוב הראשון במה ישמח [שאפילו שחט בי"ד זביחה בעידן שמחה ליכא ודחינן לאו משום דאין לו בלילי יום טוב הראשון במה ישמח] אלא ריבה לילי יום טוב האחרון משום שיש שמחה לפניו ומיעט לילי יום הראשון שאין לו שמח' לפניו כי (יום) [ליל] י"ג וי"ד חול הוא אין בהן שמחה ולעולם חגיגת ארבעה עשר יוצא בה לשם שמחה. ומותיב עלה רב יוסף אהא דתני בן תימא חגיגת י"ד יוצא בה לשם שמחה ואין יוצא בה לשם חגיגה איני והא בעינן וזבחת ושמחת זביחה בעידן שמחה וליכא ופריק רב אידי בר אבין כגון שהפרישת בי"ד ונתעכב ולא שחטה בי"ד ושחטה בט"ו יוצא בה משום שמחה דהא איכא זביחה בעידן שמחה ואין יוצא בה משום חגיגה דהא אינה מן החולין שכבר הפרישה מיום י"ד והקדישה והודה לו רב אשי דודאי נתעכב ושחטה דהא מותבינן עלה מתניתא דבן תימא היא דסבר דחגיגת י"ד כפסח היא לכל מילי ואינה נאכלת אלא לילי ט"ו בלבד ובבוקר נותר הוא ואי ס"ד ששחטה בי"ד אי אכיל ליה לילי ט"ו בלבד הא אוקימנא לילי יום טוב הראשון אין בו שמחה אי שביק למיכלה ביום טוב הראשון הא איפסליה בלינה ואיך יוצא בה משום שמחה והא לא אכיל לה אלא ודאי שנתעכב ושחטה ביום חמשה עשר : מותיב רבא לר' אלעזר מהא דתנן הלל והשמחה שמונה ואי אמרת שלמים ששחטן מערב יום טוב אין יוצא בהן לשם שמחה דבעינן זביחה בעידן שמחה וליכא זמנין דלא משכחת שמחה אלא ששה ולילי יום טוב האחרון הרי שבעה ואנן תנן לעולם שמונה ופריק רב הונא בר יהודה ... בשבת משמח הרגל בבשר שעירי הרגל שהן חטאות ונאכלות . ודחה רבא בשתי תשובות חדא דשעירי הרגלים חי נאכלין ... ואכלו אותם אשר כופר בהם מלמד שהכהנים אוכלין ובעלים מתכפרין ... ושמחה בבשר חי ליכא [ועוד] שעירי הרגלים קדשי קדשים הן הכהנים אוכלין אותן ... והתורה לא הזהירה בשמחה אלא לישראל לכל אחד ואחד . אלא אמר רב פפא משמחו בכסות נקיה ויין ישן ...

אמר רב כהנא מנין לאימורי חגיגת ט"ו שנפסלת בלינה שנאמר לא ילין חלב חגי עד בקר וסמיך ליה ראשית ... ביום ראשון נאכלין בו ביום ... ובשר נאכל ליום ולילה ... ואמורין עד צפרא ... והדחינן ... ואר"ר ... בעי ראשית ... ואמורין ... ראשון ... דלא

בעי

require the slaughtering [71a] at the time of rejoicing,[9] which is absent [here]. 'On account of *ḥagigah'*: this is an obligatory sacrifice,[10] and every obligatory sacrifice comes from nought but *ḥullin.*[11]

Shall we say that [the following] supports him? [For it was taught], *And thou shalt be altogether* [ak] *joyful:*[12] this is to include the night of the last day of the Festival for rejoicing.[13] You say, the night of the last day of the Festival; yet perhaps it is not so, but
a the night of the first day of the Festival?[1] Therefore *'ak'* is stated, dividing it.[2] Now what is the reason?[3] Is it not because he has nought wherewith to rejoice![4]—No: [it is] as it states the reason: Why do you prefer[5] to include the night of the last day of the Festival and to exclude the night of the first day of the Festival? I include the night of the last day of the Festival, because there is rejoicing before it, while I exclude the night of the first day of the Festival, seeing that there is no rejoicing before it.[6]

R. Joseph raised an objection: The *ḥagigah* of the fourteenth, one discharges with it [his duty] on account of rejoicing, but one does not discharge with it [his duty] on account of *ḥagigah.*[7] [Yet] why so?[8] Surely we require slaughtering to be at the time of rejoicing, which is lacking [here]?[9] —Said R. Idi b. Abin: It is meant where he delayed and slaughtered it [on the fifteenth]. R. Ashi observed: This too is logical, for if you should not say thus, who taught this teaching? The son of Tema?[10] But [according to] the son of Tema, surely he has disqualified it through keeping it overnight![11] This proves it.

Raba objected: [The reciting of] *hallel*[12] and rejoicing[13] are [observed] eight [days].[14] Now if you say [that] we require the slaughtering at the time of rejoicing, then there are many occasions when only seven are found, e.g., if the first day of the Festival
b falls on the Sabbath?[1]—Said R. Huna son of Rab Judah: He rejoices with the he-goats of the Festivals.[2] Said Raba: Of this there are two refutations: firstly, because the he-goats of the Festivals can be eaten raw [on the Sabbath], but cannot be eaten roast,[3] and there is no rejoicing in [eating] raw [meat]; moreover, the *Priests* eat it; and wherewith do the Israelites rejoice? Rather, said R. Papa: He rejoices with clean garments and old wine.

When Rabin came, he said in R. Eleazar's name: Peace-offerings which one slaughtered on the eve of the Festival, he discharges therewith [his duty] on account of rejoicing, but he cannot discharge therewith [his duty] on account of *ḥagigah.* 'He discharges [his duty] on account of rejoicing,' [for] we do not require the slaughtering at the time of rejoicing. 'But not on account of *ḥagigah'*; this is an obligatory [sacrifice], and every obligatory [sacrifice] comes from nought but *ḥullin.*

An objection is raised: *'And thou shalt be altogether* [ak] *joyful:'* this is to include the night of the last day of the Festival for rejoicing. You say, to include the night of the last day of the Festival; yet perhaps it is not so, but it is to include the night of the first day of the Festival? Therefore *'ak'* is stated, dividing it. Now what is the reason? Is it not because he has nought wherewith to rejoice!—No: [it is] as it was taught. Why do you prefer to include the night of the last day of the Festival and to exclude the night of the first day of the Festival? I include the night of the last day of the Festival, because there is rejoicing before it; while I exclude the night of the first day of the Festival, because there is no rejoicing before it.

R. Kahana said: How do we know that the *emurim*[4] of the *ḥagigah* of the fifteenth are disqualified through being kept overnight?[5] Because it is said, *neither shall the fat of My feast* [ḥaggi] *remain all*
c *night until morning;*[1] and in proximity thereto *'the first'* [is stated],[2] to intimate that this *'morning'* means the first morning.[3] To this R. Joseph demurred: [Thus] the reason is that *'first'* is written, but if *'first'* were not written I would say, what does *'morning'* mean? the second morning; [but] is there a case where the flesh is disqualified from the evening, whereas the *emurim* [are fit] until morning?[4] Said Abaye to him, Yet why not? Surely there is the paschal offering according to R. Eleazar b. 'Azariah, where the flesh is disqualified from midnight,[5] whereas the *emurim* [are fit] until morning?—Said Raba, This is R. Joseph's difficulty: is there a case where the Tanna does not require *'first'* in respect of the flesh, whereas R. Kahana requires *'first'* in respect of the *emurim?*[6] What is this [allusion]?—For it was taught: *Neither shall any of the flesh which thou sacrificest the first day at even, remain all night until*

(9) Viz., on the Festival itself. (10) Lit., 'a matter of an obligation'. (11) V. 70a, n. d3. (12) Deut. XVI, 15. This is superfluous, since v. 14 states, *And thou shalt rejoice in thy feast.* Hence it is intended as an extension. (13) I.e., the night of the eighth day. Rashi: It cannot mean the eighth day itself, since *'seven'* is twice specified (in v. 13 and v. 15). Tosaf.: 'night' is not meant particularly, as the same applies to the day. By 'rejoicing' is meant the eating of the peace-offering of rejoicing.

a (1) Perhaps one must eat of the peace-offering then? And since sacrifices cannot be slaughtered at night, it would be necessary to slaughter it on the eve of the Festival. (2) *Ak* is always interpreted as a limitation; hence it excludes the first night. (3) That you include the last night and exclude the first; why not reverse it? (4) Since the sacrifice is not to be offered until the following morning. Thus this supports 'Ulla's statement that the peace-offering of rejoicing cannot be offered on the eve of the Festival. (5) Lit., 'what (reason) do you see?' (6) It is more logical to assume that a continuation of rejoicing already begun is included than that the rejoicing must commence before the time actually prescribed. (7) V. *supra* 70a for notes. (8) Why should he discharge with it his duty on account of rejoicing? (9) He understood it to mean that it was actually slaughtered on the fourteenth. (10) As stated *supra* 70a. (11) Since he holds that the *ḥagigah* of the fourteenth may be eaten only a day and a night, i.e., not after the night of the fifteenth, like the Passover. Hence he must have slaughtered it on the fifteenth. (12) 'Praise'—i.e., Ps. CXIII-CXVIII, which are recited on every Festival. (13) With the peace-offerings of rejoicing. (14) The reference is to the Feast of Tabernacles.

b (1) When the peace-offering may not be slaughtered. (2) V. Num. XXVIII, 22, 30; XXIX, 16 et seq. These were public sacrifices, and therefore slaughtered even on the Sabbath. (3) Though they are slaughtered on the Sabbath, their roasting or cooking does not override the Sabbath. (4) V. Glos. (5) Though its flesh may be eaten the whole of the following day too.

c (1) Ex. XXIII, 18; *'ḥaggi'* refers to the *ḥagigah.* (2) ראשית *The first* (E.V. *'choicest'*) *of the fruits* etc. Here, however, it is read with *'morning'*, as explained in the text. (3) I.e., the fat is not to remain until the first morning after the offering is sacrificed. (4) Surely not, for the flesh may be eaten only on the day it is slaughtered and on the following, but not the night after it! (5) V. *infra* 120b. (6) The sanctity of *emurim,* which are burnt on the altar, is naturally greater than that of the flesh, which is eaten, and accordingly the former becomes unfit more easily than the latter. Yet we see anon that the Tanna assumes that *'morning'* written in connection with the flesh must mean the first morning, without having recourse to ראשית *'first'*; why then does R. Kahana require the proximity of ראשית *'first'* in order to establish that 'morning' written in connection with the *emurim* means the first morning?

a came [70b] in large [portions].[1] How can we know?[2]—Rather it means that it came in uncleanness.[3] Yet after all, how could they know?[4]—The *nasi* had died.[5] When did the *nasi* die? Shall we say that he died on the thirteenth,[6] then why was it necessary for the owner to perform *ṭebillah* for the knife?[7] Again, if he died on the fourteenth, wherein does the knife differ, that [we say] he [its owner] gave it *ṭebillah*, and wherein does the chopper differ, that [we assume] he did not give it *ṭebillah?*[8]—This arises only when the *nasi* was in a dying condition on the thirteenth. As for the knife, [concerning] which [there is] one doubt,[9] he would give it *ṭebillah* [on the thirteenth]; the chopper, [concerning] which [there are] two doubts,[10] he would not give it *ṭebillah*.

It was taught: Judah the son of Durtai separated himself [from the Sages], he and his son Durtai, and went and dwelt in the South.[11] '[For,]' said he, 'if Elijah should come and say to Israel,
b "why did you not sacrifice[1] the *ḥagigah* on the Sabbath?" what can they answer him? I am astonished at the two greatest men of our generation, Shemaiah and Abṭalyon, who are great Sages and great interpreters [of the Torah], yet they have not told Israel, The *ḥagigah* overrides the Sabbath.'[2] Rab said, What is the reason of the son of Durtai? Because it is written, *And thou shalt sacrifice the passover-offering unto the Lord thy God, of the flock and the herd:*[3] yet surely the Passover offering is only from lambs or goats? But '*flock*' refers to the Passover offering, [while] '*herd*' refers to the *ḥagigah*, and the Divine Law saith, '*And thou shalt sacrifice the passover-offering*'.[4] Said R. Ashi: And are we to arise and explain the reason of schismatics?[5] But the verse comes for [the exegesis] of R. Naḥman. For R. Naḥman said in Rabbah b. Abbuha's name: How do we know that the left-over of the paschal offering is brought as a peace-offering?[6] Because it is said, *'and thou shalt sacrifice the passover-offering unto the Lord thy God, of the flock and of the herd'*. Now, does then the Passover offering come from the herd: surely the Passover offering comes only from lambs or from goats? But [it means] the left-over of the paschal offering is to be [utilized] for something which comes from the flock and from the herd.[7]

Now according to the Rabbis, what is the reason that it [the *ḥagigah*] does not override the Sabbath, seeing that it is certainly a public sacrifice?—Said R. Illa'a on the authority of R. Judah b. Safra: Scripture saith, *And ye shall keep it a feast* [ḥag] *unto the Lord*
c *seven days in the year.*[1] '*Seven!*' but there were eight?[2] Hence from here [we learn that] the *ḥagigah* does not override the Sabbath.[3] When Rabin came,[4] he said: I stated before my teachers, Sometimes you can only find six, e.g., if the first day of the Feast [of Tabernacles] fell on the Sabbath?[5]—Said Abaye: That Abin the childless should say such a thing! Eight is altogether impossible, [while] seven are found in most years.[6]

'Ulla said in R. Eleazar's name: Peace-offerings which a man slaughtered on the eve of the Festival, he does not discharge therewith [his duty] either on account of rejoicing or on account of *ḥagigah*.[7] 'On account of rejoicing,' because it is written, *and thou shalt sacrifice [peace-offerings . . .] and thou shalt rejoice;*[8] we

a (1) In which case a *ḥagigah* does not accompany it. (2) So MS.M. Cur. edd. 'they know' that a small number had registered for the Passover for which the unknown owner of this chopper was registered. *Aliter:* 'how could they (the owners) know on the thirteenth that only a small number would register for the Passover, so that it would not be necessary to have the chopper immersed in readiness?' V. Rashi. (3) Hence a *ḥagigah* was not possible. (4) How could the owner know on the thirteenth that on the morrow the majority of the community would be unclean? (5) And the whole community would have to take part in his funeral, which would defile them. (6) When the vessels are generally taken for *ṭebillah*. (7) Seeing that the Passover is brought in uncleanness. Hence the finder should *not* be permitted to assume that it is clean, as he might then slaughter the Festival peace-offerings with it, which is forbidden. [Even when the Passover comes in uncleanness, the Festival sacrifices on the following or subsequent days must be brought in cleanness.] (8) He would not have known on the thirteenth, and therefore just as he assumed that a clean knife was necessary for slaughtering the Passover, so he would also assume that a clean chopper would be required for breaking the bones of the *ḥagigah* which would accompany it. (9) Viz., whether the *nasi* would die on the fourteenth or not. (10) (i) Whether the *nasi* would die; and (ii) whether a *ḥagigah* would be brought, for even if he did not die, only a few people might register for that particular paschal offering, in which case it would not be required. (11) Far from Jerusalem, so that he could not be in Jerusalem on Passover and therefore avoid the obligation of bringing a *ḥagigah*. He held that it was obligatory even if only a small number registered for the paschal offering, and even on the Sabbath.

b (1) Lit., 'celebrate'. (2) [Judah b. Durtai is held to have belonged to the Sadducean party, and his son is identified with Dortos (v. Josephus, *Antiquities* XX, 6, 2) who had been captured by Quadratus in Lydda and executed for having incited the Jews in rebellion against the Romans, v. Derenbourg, *Essai*, p. 187 note.] (3) Deut. XVI, 2. (4) I.e., both are called by the same name and therefore the same law applies to both. (5) Though of course the Talmud abounds in controversies, even of one against many, and the views of the minorities too have to be explained, in actual practice the minority always fell in with the final decision of the majority. Hence R. Judah the son of Durtai was unjustified in separating himself, and we have no need to study his view v. Halevi, *Doroth*, I, 5, pp. 206f.—Or perhaps R. Ashi merely meant that since the interpretation of this verse is according to a minority view, it behoves us to know how the verse is interpreted on the view of the Sages. This appears to be the explanation given by R. Ḥan., whose text differs slightly. (6) E.g., if an animal dedicated for a Passover sacrifice was lost, whereupon its owners registered for another animal, and then it was found after the second was sacrificed. Or again, if a certain sum of money was dedicated to buy a paschal lamb, but it was not all expended; then too the surplus must be used for a peace-offering. (7) *Sc.* a peace-offering.

c (1) Lev. XXIII, 41. This treats of Tabernacles, which was observed for eight days, and the verse teaches that a *ḥagigah* was to be brought (v. 69b, n. c4). (2) For the *ḥagigah*, if not brought on the first day of the Festival, could be brought on any other day. (3) And since one of the eight days must be the Sabbath, there are actually only seven days when it can be brought. (4) From Palestine to Babylonia. (5) Why is this too not intimated in Scripture? (6) Therefore there is no need for Scripture to intimate that there may only be six. (7) V. note on Mishnah. (8) Deut. XXVII, 7.

לא א מיי' פ"ד מהל' קרבן פסח הלכה י:
לב ב מיי' פ"א מהל' חגיגה הלכה ח:

הורה אור

במרובה מנא ידעי ואלא שבא בטומאה סוף סוף מנא ידעי דמית נשיא אימת אילימא דמית בשלשה עשר סכין למה לי דמטבליה ואלא דמית בארבעה עשר מאי שנא סכין דמטביל ומאי שנא קופיץ דלא מטביל לה לא צריכא דנשיא גוסס בשלשה עשר סכין דחד ספיקא מטביל לה קופיץ דתרי ספיקי לא מטביל לה תניא יהודה בן דורתאי פירש הוא ודורתאי בנו והלך וישב לו בדרום אמר אם יבוא אליהו ויאמר להם לישראל מפני מה לא חגגתם חגיגה בשבת מה הן אומרים לו תמהני על שני גדולי הדור שמעיה ואבטליון שהן חכמים גדולים ודרשנין גדולים ולא אמרו להן לישראל חגיגה דוחה את השבת אמר רב מ"ט דבן דורתאי דכתיב °וזבחת פסח לה' אלהיך צאן ובקר והלא אין פסח אלא מן הכבשים ומן העזים אלא צאן זה פסח בקר זו חגיגה ואמר רחמנא וזבחת פסח א"ר אשי ואנן טעמא דפרושים ניקו ונפרוש אלא קרא לכדרב נחמן הוא דאתא *דאמר רב נחמן אמר רבה בר אבוה °מניין למותר הפסח שקרב שלמים שנא' וזבחת פסח לה' אלהיך צאן ובקר וכי פסח מן הבקר בא והלא אין פסח בא אלא מן הכבשים ומן העזים אלא מותר הפסח יהא לדבר הבא מן הצאן ומן הבקר ורבנן מ"ט לא דחי שבת הא ודאי קרבן ציבור הוא א"ר אילעא משום רבי יהודה בן ספרא אמר קרא °וחגותם אותו חג לה' שבעת ימים בשנה שבעה שמונה הוו ²אלא מכאן לחגיגה שאינה דוחה את השבת כי אתא רבין אמר אמרתי לפני רבותי פעמים שאי אתה מוצא אלא ששה כגון שחל י"ט הראשון של חג בשבת אמר אביי *אבין תבלא לימא כי הא מילתא שמנה לא משכחת לה כלל שבעה איתא ברוב שנים אמר עולא אמר רבי אלעזר שלמים ששחטן מערב י"ט אינו יוצא בהן לא משום שמחה ולא משום חגיגה משום שמחה דכתיב °וזבחת ושמחת בעינן זביחה בשעת שמחה

דברים טז | ויקרא כג | דברים כז

רש"י

במרובה. בחבורה מועטת שהפסח מרובה להן ולא יביאו חגיגה: מנא ידעי. הבעלים בשלשה עשר שתהא חבורתו מועטת הרי כל שעה באין ונמנין עליו אנשים מעלמא וקונים להן בו חלק מן הבעלים עד שעת שחיטה הלכך לא קים (א) ליה שתהא חבורה מועטת ומטביל לקופיץ שמא יביאו חגיגה וילטרכו לשבירת עלמות: שבא בטומאה. שרוב ליבור טמאין ותנן בזמן שבא בטומאה אין מביאין עמו חגיגה וזה המוגלה טהור ואע"פ שאף הטהורים עושין בטומאה עם הליבור מטבילה לשבר בה עלמות חגיגת חמשה עשר שאינה באה בטומאה: מנא ידעי. הבעלים בשלשה עשר כשמטבילין סכיניהם שיהו רוב ליבור טמאין: דמית נשיא. ומלוה לכל ישראל להתעסק בו: אי נימא בשלשה עשר. קשהו מטהרין כליהם: סכין למה ליה לאטבוליה. למריה הרי היא עתיד ליטמא וזה המוגלה אם טהור הוא למה מחזיקה בטהרה ושוחט בה שלמי חגיגתו בי"ט: אלא דמית בארבעה עשר. וכשהטבילו כליהם בי"ג הלריכין לארבעה עשר לא היו יודעין שיבוא בטומאה הלכך גם את הקופיץ הטביל לשבירת העלמות דחגיגת ארבע' עשר: ומאי שנא סכין. דאמרי' אטבלה מהו מתמול ומאי שנא קופיץ דלא אמרי' אטבלה מהו מתמול: לא לריכא דנשיא גוסס בשלשה עשר. ולא גרסינן ומת בארבעה עשר דמה לי מת ומה לי לא מת: סכין דחד ספיקא הוא. דאיכא למימר שמא ימות הנשיא ויעשו פסח בטומאה משום הכי ספיקא לא אימנע מלאטבולה ואטבלה דחייש שמא לא ימות ויעשה פסח בטהרה: אבל קופיץ דתרי ספיקי. אית ליה מסלקי ליה מתורת טבילה שמא ימות ולא יביאו חגיגות לא בארבעה עשר ולא בחמשה עשר או אפי' לא ימות שמא אני לא אלטרך לחגיגת ארבעה עשר שתהא חבורתי מועטת ויבא פסח במרובה ואי משום חגיגת חג חמשה עשר עדיין יש שהות להטבילה בי"ד הלכך לא אטבלה מהו בשלשה עשר: בן דורתאי פירש. מן החכמים ונבדל מהם מפני שהיו אומרים אין חגיגת ארבעה עשר דוחה שבת: וישב לו בדרום. רחוק מירושלים שלא יהא לריך לעלות לרגל ויתחייב בפסח ובחגיגה דקסבר חגיגה חובה ואפי' במרובה: ואנן טעמא דפרושים וכו'. וכי לכך הולרכנו לדרוש המקראות אחר טעמי המבדילים מן החכמים: מותר הפסח. בין שהפריש פסחו ואבד ונתכפר באחר ואח"כ נמלא או בן שהפרישים מעות לפסחו ונלה קדושת פסח על טלון והותו טלאים וכיותריו מן המעות: שקרב שלמים. בצאן ומן הבקר. הייט שלמים שכשירין לבא מכל צאן ומכל בקר זכר ונקבה: אמאי לא דחיא שבת. ואפילו חגיגת חמשה עשר הא ודאי קרבן ליבור הוא דהא אתי בכינופיא כי פסח וזמן קבוע לה: וחגותם אותו. בחג הסכות כתיב דמשתעי כל שמונה הוי אלא לאו שמע מינה אין לך חגיגה שדוחה שבת הלכך לא משכחת שמונה דתשלומין דידיה כל שבעה כמו שמונה יום הראשון: כגון שחל יו"ט הראשון של חג להיות בשבת. דמעתי נמי שמיני עלרת בשבת דלאין כאן אלא ששה: אבין תבלא. קובר את בניו היה: לימא כי האי מילתא. שאילה שאינה הוגנת:

תוספות

מאי טעמא דבן דורתאי דכתיב וזבחת פסח וכו'. רש"י פי' דבחגיגת י"ד מיירי °ולפי' נ"ל דלבן תימא אע"ג דאית ליה היקשא אחרינא לעיל חגיגת י"ד לא דחיא שבת אע"ג דלכל מילי אקשיה חגיגה לפסח דאפילו לשבירת עלם אקשיה אי לאו דכתב בו מדקאמר רב אשי בסמוך ואנן טעמא דפרושין ניקו וניפרוש ואי בן תימא נמי ס"ל דדחי' שבת לא הוה מתמה טלי האי וטעמא כדילפינן בסמוך מוחגותם אותו וגו' דלא דחיא שבת אע"ג דקרבן ליבור היא ה"נ לבן תימא ואע"ג דקרא וחגותם אותו בחגיגת ט"ו כתיב סברא הוא להשוות החגיגות יחד ולהכי איצטריך לבן דורתאי למילף מוזבחת פסח שהוקשו לענין זביחה ואפי' בשבת לאפוקי שלא נקיש החגיגות יחד ולא מצי למילף מהיקשא דבן תימא כדפי' וקשה דלעיל קאמר רב אשי דאי חובה היא תיתי בשבת משמע דלבן תימא ולתנא דלקמן דאית להו חגיגת ארבעה עשר דאורייתא דחיא שבת א"כ מאי קמתמה רב אשי ואנן טעמא דפרושין ניקו וניפרוש ועוד תיקשי לההוא דאמר בהוציאו לו (יומא נ.) נקוט האי כללא בידך כל שזמנו קבוע דוחה את השבת ואת הטומאה ואפי' דיחיד הא איכא חגיגת י"ד דקבוע לה זמן ולא דחיא לכך נראה לר"י עיקר דהכא איירי בחגיגת ט"ו כדמוכח דמייתי קרא דוחגותם אותו ואתי שפיר דלא קייל בהוציאו לו אלא דבר שקבוע לו זמן יום אחד ולא יותר אבל חגיגת ט"ו לא חשיב כל כך זמן קבוע כיון שיש לה תשלומין כל שבעה ומ"מ פריך שפיר הא ודאי קרבן ליבור הוא דאף חגיגת חמשה עשר חשיבה זמנה קבוע כדאמרינן בפרק ב' דביצה (דף כ:) אמר להן ב"ה אף זו קבוע לה זמן דתנן עבר הרגל ולא חג אינו חייב באחריותו ואין להקשות א"כ אמאי הולרך בן דורתאי לפרוש ולהתרחק כדי שיהיה בדרך רחוקה ויפטר הלא היה יכול להביא חגיגתו כל שבעה כדילפינן בסמוך אומר ר"י דילמא יהודה בן דורתאי ס"ל כמאן דאית ליה חגיגת חמשה עשר לפסח °שמע מינה אין לה תשלומין והא דמוקי בן דורתאי קרא דוזבחת פסח בחגיגת חמשה עשר ולא בחגיגת י"ד משום דסבר דחגיגת י"ד לאו דאורייתא: הא ודאי קרבן ליבור הוא. נקט קרבן ליבור משום דאיכא תנא דתלי בהכי בפ' יש קרבנות (תמורה יד.) דתנן יש בקרבנות ליבור שאין ביחיד שקרבנות ליבור דוחין את השבת ואת הטומאה ומיהו בפרק הוציאו לו (יומא נ.) אמרי' כל שזמנו קבוע דוחה את השבת וטומאה אפילו ביחיד וק"ק דהכא קרו ליה קרבן ליבור משום דאתי בכינופיא וכן ביומא *[אבל בחגיגה] (דף ו.) קרי ליה קרבן יחיד: הא ודאי קרבן ליבור. תימה לרשב"א מה בכך אם הוא קרבן ליבור והא פסח ותמיד ושעירי ר"ח ועומר ושתי הלחם לכולהו מלרכינן קראי בכילד צולין (לקמן עז.) שידחו שבת ואח"כ הכא מנא לן ואורי' דחגיגה (ב) בכלל שאר קרבנות מועדות °דהאי קרא דוחגותם כתיב בסוף פרשת פינחס: שלמים ששחטן מערב יו"ט וכו'. נראה לר"י דלפי' הקדיש לשם חגיגת ט"ו איירי דאי לשם שלמים דעלמא אין יוצא משום חגיגה אפי' שחטן בי"ט דכל דבר שבחובה אין בא אלא מן החולין לכך נראה דהקדישן לשם חגיגה ושחטן לשם חגיגה דהואיל והוי דבר שבחובה וליכא בא אלא מן החולין שלריך להקדיש לשם כך סברא הוא שישחט נמי בשעה הראויה לחגיגה ורלויה לדבר מדאמר לעיל שבעה שמונה לא הוא אלא מכאן לחגיגה וכו' ולא יכול לשוחטה מערב י"ט דאל"כ אכתי שמונה הוו והא קשה ריב"א והא האי קרא דוזבחת שלמים לא כתיב גבי שמחת י"ט והיכי יליף מיניה י"ט וי"ל דאיכא למימר דבכל ענין קאמר קרא דבעינן זביחה בשעת שמחה:

בשעת

לרבות

רבינו חננאל

חגיגה. ודחי' וכי כתנים קסמי אינהו כלומר ראו בדרך מראה חקוסמים החוזים בכוכבים כי הפסח של זו השנה במרובה הוא בא ואין עמו חגיגה לפיכך לא טהרו הקופיץ שלהן אלא כגון שבא הפסח בטומאה שאין עמו חגיגה. ואקשי' וכי כהנים קוסמי נינהו דהוה ידעי דישראל זו השנה רובן טמאין הן והפסח בא בטומאה ואין בו חגיגה ואמרי' כגון שהיה נשיא גוסס בי"ג סכין דחד ספק הוא ספק מת נשיא היום או מחר ספק לא מת בספק אחד חייש ומטהר לסכין דחייש דלמא לא מאית ובעינן סכין טהורה וליכא קופיץ דהוא [תרי ספיקא] חאי ספיקא דאמרי' וספיקא אחרינא נמי דלמא לא מאית נשיא ואתו הפסח במרובה ואין שם חגיגה לא מטהר ליה ולא מתוקמא דמת נשיא (בי"ד) [בי"ג] נטמאו רוב ועבדו בטומאה דאי אתי בטומאה (קופיץ) [סכין] למה ליה טהרה אלא בפסח הבא בטהרה הוא: ת"ר יהודה בן דירתי [פירש הוא ודורתאי בנו] כו' ודייק מדכתי' וזבחת פסח לה' אלהיך צאן ובקר צאן לפסח ובקר לחגיגת ט"ו מכאן לחגיגת ט"ו שדוחה שבת כשם שפסח דוחה שבת כך חגיגה דוחה שבת. אמר רב אשי האי טעמא דפרושים הוא כלומר מדרש פרושים הוא זה אלא טעמי' דהאי קרא הכי הוא וזבחת פסח לה' אלהיך צאן ובקר ואם יותר מן הדמים שהפרשת לקנות בהן פסח הביאהו דבר הבא מן הבקר וכ"ש מן הצאן וכאי ניהו שלמים ורבנן דפליגי על יהודה בן דירתי (דאמר) [ואמרי] אין חגיגת ט"ו דוחה שבת דייקי' כיון דהחג שמונה ימים הוא דהא אתרבו יום טוב האחרון של חג מבחדש השביעי תחגו אותו כאשר הוא מפורש בחגיגה פ"א נמצא החג שמונה וקאמר רחמנא וחגותם אותו חג לה' שבעת ימים מכאן שאין חגיגה דוחה שבת דכתיב שבעה ולא שמונה למעוטי שבת [מחגיגה] וקשו והלא אי מקלעי יום טוב הראשון של חג בשבת יבוא גם יום טוב האחרון שבת ואיתך דהחג אלא ששה ימים בלבד ופריק שבעה איתא ברוב שנים ואי מקלעי במיעוט שנים כי האי נתנא יו"ט הראשון שבת דלא משכחת ימי חגיגה (אבל) [אלא] ששה למיעוט לא היישי' אבל שמונה לעולם לא תמצא ולא משכחת תמניא יומי בלא שבת: אמר ר' אלעזר שלמים ששחטן מערב יום טוב אין יוצא בהן משום חגיגה [דאפילו] בפ"ו חזה שחטן לא היה יוצא בהן ידי חובתו דחגיגה חובה היא וכל חובה אינה באה אלא מן החולין ואלו השלמים קדשים הן לפיכך אין עולין לו משום חגיגה וגם אין יוצא בהן משום שמחה

זבחים ד' [:ז] ע. מנחות דף פג:

חולין קי. [ע"ש]

הגהות הב"ח

(א) רש"י ד"ה מנא ידעי וכו' לא קים להו שתהא: (ב) תוס' ד"ה הא ודאי וכו' ואורי' דחגיגה הוי בכלל:

גליון הש"ס

תוס' ד"ה מאי טעמא וכו' ולפי' צ"ל דלב"ת. עיין לעיל נט ע"ב תוס' ד"ה כ"ד ולקמן קיד ע"ב תוס' ד"ה אחד זכר לפסח: באד"ה מאין לה תשלומין. פי' ע"כ חגיגה ו' ע"ב בתוס' ד"ה יש בשמחה: תוס' ד"ה הא ודאי וכו' דהאי קרא דוחגותם. עיין טורי אבן מגילה ה ע"א ד"ה והגיגה:

לאו חובה היא דאי סלקא דעתך חובה היא תיתי בשבת ותיתי במרובה ותיתי בטומאה ובמועט מידו מ"ט אתיא כדתניא **חגיגה הבאה עם הפסח נאכלת תחילה כדי שיהא פסח נאכל על השבע: ונאכלת לשני ימים וכו': מתני' דלא כבן תימא דתניא בן תימא אומר חגיגה הבאה עם הפסח הרי היא כפסח ואינה נאכלת אלא ליום ולילה וחגיגת חמשה עשר נאכלת לשני ימים ולילה אחד *וחגיגת ארבעה עשר יוצא בה משום שמחה ואין יוצא בה משום חגיגה מ"ט דבן תימא כדמתני רב לחייא בריה °ולא ילין לבקר זבח חג הפסח זבח חג זה חגיגה הפסח כמשמעו ואמר רחמנא לא ילין איבעיא להו לבן תימא נאכלת צלי או אין נאכלת צלי כי אקשיה רחמנא לפסח ללינה אבל לצלי לא או דילמא לא שנא ת"ש *חלילת חזה כולו צלי* ואמר רב חסדא זו דברי בן תימא שמע מינה איבעיא להו לבן תימא באה מן הבקר או אינה באה מן הבקר באה מן הנקבות או אינה באה מן הנקבות באה בת שתי שנים או אינה באה בת שתי שנים כי אקשיה רחמנא לפסח למידי דאכילה אבל לכל מילי לא או דילמא לא שנא ת"ש חגיגה הבאה עם הפסח הרי היא כפסח באה מן הצאן ואינה באה מן הבקר באה מן הזכרים ואינה באה מן הנקבות באה בת שנתה ואינה באה בת שתי שנים ואינה נאכלת אלא ליום ולילה ואינה נאכלת אלא צלי ואינה נאכלת אלא למנויו מאן שמעת ליה דאית ליה האי סברא בן תימא שמע מינה כולהו מילתא בעינן ש"מ איבעיא להו לבן תימא יש בה משום שבירת עצם או אין בה משום שבירת העצם אע"ג דכי אקשיה רחמנא לפסח אמר קרא בו בו ולא בחגיגה או דילמא האי בו *בכשר ולא בפסול הוא דאתא ת"ש *סכין שנמצאת בארבעה עשר שוחט בה מיד בשלשה עשר שונה ומטביל קופיץ בין בזה ובין בזה שונה ומטביל מני אילימא רבנן מאי שנא סכין דמטביל דחזיא לפסח קופיץ נמי הא חזי לחגיגה אלא לאו דבן תימא היא ושמע מינה יש בה משום שבירת העצם לא לעולם רבנן וכגון שבא בשבת והא מדקתני סיפא חל ארבעה עשר להיות בשבת שוחט בה מיד ובחמשה עשר שוחט בה מיד נמצאת קופיץ קשורה לסכין הרי היא כסכין מכלל דרישא לאו בשבת עסקינן ואלא שבא במרובה

שמות לד

רש"י: על השבע. שיהו נהגין באכילתו ותיחשב להן: ונאכלת לשני ימים. חגיגת חמשה עשר דנפקא לן במסכת חגיגה (דף ט.) מותגותם אותו: יוצא בה משום שמחה. אם עיכבה עד למחר ושחטה יוצא בה משום שמחה משום שלמי שמחה ואע"ג שמופרשת ועומדת היא כבר ושלמי שמחה חובה הן והא דקי"ל (לקמן דף עח.) כל דבר שבחובה אינו בא אלא מן החולין כדתניא בסיפרי* וזבחת פסח כו' עד לאן ובקר והלא אין פסח בא אלא מן הכבשים ומן העזים א"כ למה נאמר בקר להקיש כל הבא מלאן ובקר לפסח מה פסח דבר שהוא חובה ואינו בא אלא מן החולין אף כאן שהוא חובה ואינו בא אלא מן החולין הני מילי בחובות דעלמא אבל שלמי שמחה איתרבי במס' חגיגה (דף ח.) מדתניא בסיפרי ושמחת לרבות כל מיני שמחה יכול אף בעופות ומנחות תלמוד לומר בחגך מי שחגיגה באה מהן יצאו עופות מכאן אמרו ישראל יוצאים ידי חובתן בנדרים ונדבות כו' אע"ג דמחויב ועומד הוא: ואין יוצא בה. משום חגיגת חמשה עשר כדאמרן דבר שיש בו חובה אינו בא אלא מן החולין כלומר משלו ולא ממה שהוא מחויב ועומד וזו כבר נתקדשה מאתמול: מאי טעמא. דאמר אין נאכלין אלא ליום ולילה: נאכלת צלי. צריך לאוכלה צלי: חלילת חזה כולו צלי. מתני' היא בפרק בתרא כולו צלי ואפי' החגיגה: למידי דאכילה. דאזהרת לינה לווי אכילה היא: האי סברא. אינה נאכלת אלא ליום ולילה: שמע מינה כולהו אתיין. כולהו מילי דפסח אתיין בחגיגה בההוא היקשא: שוחט בה. פסחו מיד ואין צריך להטבילה זה המולאה דמסתמא הטבילוה בעליה אם טמאה היתה הטבילוה בשלשה עשר כדי שיהא הערב שמש ותהא טהורה בארבעה עשר: שונה ומטביל. כלומר אע"פ שספק שמא הטבילוה הבעלים זה שונה ומטביל מספק שמא עדיין לא הטבילוה שהיה להן שהות ביום להטבילה ולהעריב שמשה: קופיץ. סכין גדול הוא ורובו אין לשחיטה אלא לחיתוך בשר ולשבירת עלמות: בין בזה בין בזה. אפילו נמלאת בארבעה עשר: שונה ומטביל. דמתוך שאין שבירת העלם בפסח אין הבעלים לריכין לה כל ארבעה עשר עד למחר ויש לומר לא הטבילה שהיה לו שהות ביום להטבילה סמוך לבין השמשות לצורך מחר: מני. הא דמשמע דאין שבירת עלמות בערב הפסח: אי נימא רבנן. דלא מקשי חגיגה לפסח ואין בה איסור שבירת עלם: מאי שנא סכין דמטביל. לה בעליה מאתמול ומוקמינן לה השתא בחזקת טהרה למולאה משום דחזיא ליה לבעלים בארבעה עשר לפסח לשחוט הילכך אטבלה מאתמול דניהוי ליה הערב שמש והא לא חיישינן שמא אבדה לו זה ימים רבים דודאי היום נפלה ממנו דמתוך שבשעת הרגל העם רב אין שוהה שם במקום נפילתה שלא תמלא: חזי לחגיגה. לשבירת עלמות ואטבלה מאתמול ואמאי המולאה בארבעה עשר שונה ומטביל: שבא. ערב הפסח בשבת דאין חגיגה באה עמו הלכך לא לריכה לבעלים בארבעה עשר: חל ארבעה עשר להיות בשבת שוחט. בקופיץ זה מיד ואין לריך להטביל דאע"ג דשמא בעלים היה להן סכין לשחוט ולא היתה קופיץ זו להן אלא לשבירת עלמות והיום אין שבירת העלם בשבת אפילו הכי כיון דלריכה להן ביום טוב אחר שבת כבר הטבילוה מערב שבת דהא בשבת לא מלו לאטבולה כדאמרינן במסכת בילה (ד' יז:) חל יום טוב להיות אחר שבת מטבילין את הכל מלפני השבת: ובחמשה עשר. אם מלאה ביום טוב עלמו: שוחט בה. שלמים מיד דודאי הטבילוה בעלים מאתמול: הרי היא כסכין. ואפילו נמלאת בארבעה עשר שחל להיות בחול שוחט בה מיד דודאי הוטבלה עם הסכין בשלשה עשר הואיל וקשורה עמו: מכלל דרישא. דקתני בין בזה בין בזה שונה ומטביל: לאו בשבת עסקינן. דאם לא כן קשיא רישא אסיפא ואפילו הכי קאמר דאין בו שבירת עלמות אלמא אסור לשבור עלמות בחגיגת ארבעה עשר:

תוספות: לאו חובה היא. כלומר אינו חייב מן התורה להביאה דאי ס"ד חובה היא מן התורה שוב אין לנו לומר שיש חילוק בין שבת לחול דהוי קרבן הקבוע לו זמן ותיתי במרובה ובטומאה אלא ודאי לאו חובה היא ואינה באה אלא כדי שיאכל הפסח על השבע ואומר ריב"א דמשמע בירושלמי דהא דפסח נאכל על השבע היינו מדרבנן גזירה משום שבירת עצם שאם לא היתה באה על השבע מתוך שאוא רעב לאכול הבשר שסביב העצמות היה בא לידי שבירתן וקשה לר"י דהשתא משמע דלרבנן דבן תימא דבסמוך הויא חגיגת ארבעה עשר דרבנן ולקמן (דף עא.) משמע שהיא מן התורה דתניא לא ילין מן הבשר וגו' לימד על חגיגת ארבעה עשר שנאכלת לשני ימים ויש לומר דאשכחן בפ"ק דחגיגה (דף ח.) תנא דסבירא ליה שהיא מדרבנן דקאמר רב אשי הא קמ"ל חגיגת חמשה עשר אין חגיגת ארבעה עשר לא אלמא קסבר חגיגת י"ד לאו דאורייתא והשתא לבן *תימא ולתנא דלקמן דאית להו חגיגת ארבעה עשר דאורייתא לחי שבת והשתא אתי שפיר דהיה דריש תמיד נשחט (לעיל נט.) בארבעה עשר שחל להיות בשבת כו':

והא מדקתני סיפא חל י"ד להיות בשבת כו'. וא"ת אמאי לא פריך אי בשבת היכי שרי להטביל כלים הא קיימא לן דלא מזין ויש לומר דהא טובלין ולא פירכא היא דאיכא למימר שונה ומטביל לאחר י"ט וי"ד וי"ג (שחל להיות בשבת) אמליאה קאי: מאי

עין משפט נר מצוה:
כה א מיי' פ"א מהל' ק"פ הלכה ג:
כו ב מיי' פ"ב מהל' חגיגה הלכה י:
כז ג מיי' פי"ג מהל' אבות הטומאה הל' ה:
כח ד שם הלכה ו:
כט ה שם הלכה ס:
[תוספתא פ"ה]
ל ו שם הלכה ז:

רבינו חננאל
דקתני בקופיץ ביום ארבעה עשר שונה ומטביל שאין בארבעה עשר צורך לקופיץ ולא היו בעליו טורחין אותו אלא למחרו היום להשתמש בו למחר ומאן שמעת ליה האי סברא שחגיגת ארבעה עשר כפסח היא בן תימא וש"מ כי לבן תימא אסור לשבר בו עצם לפיכך אין צורך ביום ארבעה עשר לקופיץ דאי רבנן כיון דאמרי חגיגת ארבעה עשר אינה כפסח ומותר לשבר בה עצמות אמאי לא ניטא דהאי קופיץ בארבעה עשר מותר לגמרי הוא ולשבור עצמות החגיגה הוציאו בעליה אלא ש"מ משנה זו אינה לרבנן אלא לבן תימא וש"מ יש לו לבן תימא שחגיגת י"ד אסור לשברבה עצם. ודחי' לא לעולם מתני' רבנן וכגון שחל י"ד להיות בשבת [שאין שם חגיגה כלל. ודחינא להא סברא מסיפא דקתני חל י"ד להיות בשבת] שוחט בה מיד מכלל דרישא לאו שבת הוא אלא בחול עסקי' אלא בפסח שבא במרובה פי' מעט בני אדם נמנו בפסח והוא ואינן צריכין בשר אחר אלא די להם הפסח לבדו לשבוע ממנו דליכא

שקלים פ"ח מ"ג. [ע' תוס' זבחים לה: בד"ה סתם יום]

[לקמן עא.]
לקמן דף קטז. [ע' תוס' שם ד"ה כולו]
[לקמן עב. סד: ע.]
אין בתמאה זמנות סב.]

[70*a*] is not obligatory. For if you should think that it is obligatory, let it come [be sacrificed] on the Sabbath, and let it come [when the Passover sacrifice is divided] in large [portions], and in uncleanness. Nevertheless, what is the reason that it comes [when the paschal lamb is divided] in small portions?—As it was taught: The *ḥagigah* which comes with the Passover is eaten first, so that the Passover be eaten after the appetite is satisfied.

AND IT IS EATEN FOR TWO DAYS etc. Our Mishnah is not in agreement with the son of Tema. For it was taught: The son of Tema said: The *ḥagigah* which comes with the Passover is as the Passover, and it may only be eaten a day and a night, whereas the *ḥagigah* of the fifteenth[2] is eaten two days and one night; again, the *ḥagigah* of the fourteenth, a man discharges therewith [his duty] on account of rejoicing, but he does not discharge therewith [his duty] on account of *ḥagigah*.[3] What is the son of Tema's reason?[4]—As R. Ḥiyya taught his son, *Neither shall the sacrifice of the feast* [zebaḥ ḥag] *of the passover be left unto the morning*:[5] '*zebaḥ ḥag,*' this is the *ḥagigah*; '*the passover*' is what it implies; and the Divine Law saith, '*it shall not be kept overnight*'.[6]

The Scholars asked: According to the son of Tema, is it [the *ḥagigah*] eaten roast or is it not eaten roast?[7] [Do we say,] When the Divine Law compared it to the Passover it was in respect of keeping it overnight, but not in respect of roast; or perhaps there is no difference?—Come and hear: On this night all [must be eaten] roast;[1] and R. Ḥisda said: These are the words of the son of Tema. This proves it.[2]

The Scholars asked: According to the son of Tema, does it [the *ḥagigah*] come from the herd or does it not come from the herd; does it come from females or does it not come from females; does it come a two-year old, or does it not come a two-year old?[3] [Do we say,] when the Divine Law compared it to the Passover it was in the matter of eating,[4] but not in respect of all [other] things; or perhaps there is no difference?—Come and hear: The *ḥagigah* which comes with the Passover is as the Passover: it comes from the flock, but it does not come from the herd; it comes from the males but it does not come from the females; it comes a year old, but it does not come a two-year old, and it may be eaten only a day and a night, and it may be eaten only roast, and it may be eaten only by those who have registered for it. [Now,] whom do you know[5] to hold this view?[6] The son of Tema. This proves that we require everything.[7] This proves it.

The Scholars asked: According to the son of Tema, is it subject to [the prohibition of] breaking a bone, or is it not subject to [the prohibition of] breaking a bone?[8] [Do we say,] though the Divine Law assimilated it to the Passover, yet the Writ saith, '[*neither shall ye break a bone*] thereof,' [implying] '*thereof,*' but not of the *ḥagigah*;[9] or perhaps, this '*thereof*' comes [to teach], of a fit [sacrifice], but not of an unfit one?[10]—Come and hear: If a [slaughtering] knife is found on the fourteenth, one may slaughter with it immediately;[11] [if it is found] on the thirteenth, he must
b repeat the *ṭebillah*.[1] [If he finds] a chopper,[2] whether on the one or on the other,[3] he must repeat the *ṭebillah*.[4] Who [is the authority for this]?[5] Shall we say the Rabbis?[6] wherein does a [slaughtering-] knife differ, that we assume that it had been immersed;[7] because it is fit for [slaughtering] the Passover? Then a chopper too, surely it is fit for [breaking the bones of] the *ḥagigah*?[8] Hence it must be [the view] of the son of Tema, which proves that it is subject to [the prohibition of] breaking a bone!—No: in truth [it is the view of] the Rabbis, and [this was taught] e.g., when it [the Passover] comes on the Sabbath.[9] But since the second clause teaches, If the fourteenth occurred on the Sabbath, he may slaughter with it immediately;[10] and [likewise if he finds it] on the fifteenth, he may slaughter with it immediately;[11] if a chopper is found tied to a knife, it is as the knife,[12] it follows that the first clause[13] does not treat of the Sabbath?—Rather it means that it [the Passover]

(2) V. 69*b*, n. c4. (3) V. note on Mishnah on these two sacrifices. Now the *ḥagigah* of the fourteenth is a voluntary sacrifice (*supra*), and it is a general rule that an animal already dedicated for such cannot be used for an *obligatory* sacrifice, except in the case of the peace-offering of rejoicing, v. *infra*, 71*a*. Hence if the *ḥagigah* dedicated for the fourteenth is not killed on that day, it can be utilized the next day as the peace-offering of rejoicing, but not as the *obligatory ḥagigah* of the fifteenth. (4) That the *ḥagigah* may be eaten only a day and a night. (5) Ex. XXXIV, 25. (6) Referring to the *ḥagigah* too. (7) I.e., must it be eaten roast or not? Similarly the problems which follow.

(1) V. *infra* 116*a*. (2) That the *ḥagigah* too must be roast. (3) V. Ex. XII, 5: *your lamb* (*sc.* the Passover) *shall be . . . a male of the first year; ye shall take it from the sheep, or from the goats*. Does the same apply to the *ḥagigah* or not? (4) I.e., in the conditions under which it must be eaten. (5) Lit., 'hear'. (6) That it may be eaten only a day and a night. (7) I.e., it must be like the Passover in all respects. (8) V. Ex. XII, 46: *neither shall ye break a bone thereof* (*sc.* the Passover). (9) I.e., there is no interdict in its case. (10) If the Passover is unfit its bones may be broken; v. *infra* 83*a*. (11) Without immersing it. For if it were unclean its owner would have immersed it on the thirteenth, so that it should be clean at sunset (v. Num. XIX, 14-19; *shall be clean at even* applies to utensils too), in readiness for slaughtering the Passover on the fourteenth. We disregard the possibility that the owner may have lost it some time ago, for Jerusalem was thronged at Passover and it could not have lain long without being discovered.

b (1) I.e., he must immerse it, though even if it was unclean its owner may already have done so. (2) A large knife used for cutting up meat and breaking the bones, but not as a rule for slaughtering. (3) Viz., the thirteenth or the fourteenth. (4) For since the bones of the Passover sacrifice must not be broken, even if it was unclean its owner may not have troubled to immerse it on the thirteenth but waited for the fourteenth, to have it in readiness for the use of breaking bones on the *following* day, to break the bones of the *ḥagigah* of the *fifteenth* or of the peace-offering of rejoicing. (5) Which implies that there is no breaking of bones on Passover eve. (6) Who do not assimilate the *ḥagigah* of the fourteenth to the paschal sacrifice, and consequently hold that the bones of the former may be broken. (7) On the day before by the owner so that he who finds it need not immerse it. (8) Why then should the finder repeat the immersion? (9) So that a *ḥagigah* cannot be brought at all. As there would be no need for the chopper, the owner, it is to be assumed, did not immerse it. (10) *Sc.* even with the chopper, if he has no knife. For if it were unclean its owner would have performed *ṭebillah* on Friday, to use it on Sunday (v. n. b4), since *ṭebillah* is forbidden on the Sabbath. (11) For the same reason that *ṭebillah* must already have been performed. (12) And even if found on the fourteenth on a weekday he may slaughter with it immediately, for since they are tied together they must both have received *ṭebillah* at the same time. (13) Which requires a second immersion for either.

through a reptile, [69b] and wherever an individual would be relegated [to the second Passover], in the case of the community they keep [it] in uncleanness, and whatever is [obligatory] in the case of a community is [obligatory] in the case of an individual, and whatever is not [obligatory] in the case of a community is not [obligatory] in the case of an individual. [Hence as for the defect of] uncircumcision, where if the whole community are uncircumcised we say to them, 'Arise, circumcise yourselves, and sacrifice the Passover,' then an individual too, we say to him, 'Arise, circumcise yourself, and sacrifice the Passover,' while if he does not circumcise [himself] and [does not] sacrifice he is punished with *kareth*. But [in the case of] uncleanness, where if the whole community is unclean we do not sprinkle [the water of purification] upon them but they keep [it] in uncleanness, [therefore] an individual too is not culpable.[3] R. Huna son of R. Joshua said to Raba: Yet there is the second Passover, which is not [practised] in the case of a community, yet it is [practised] in the case of an individual?—There it is different, replied he, because the community has [already] sacrificed at the first [Pass-
a over].[1]

An objection is raised: You might think that there is no penalty of *kareth* [for neglecting to offer the Passover] except if he [the delinquent] was clean and was not on a journey afar off;[2] how do we know it of an uncircumcised person and one who was unclean through a reptile and all others who are unclean?[3] Because it is stated, *and the man* [*that is clean etc.*].[4] Now, since he seeks [a verse to teach the inclusion of] him who is unclean through a reptile, he [evidently] holds, One may not slaughter [the Passover sacrifice] and sprinkle [its blood] for him who is unclean through a reptile; for if one may slaughter and sprinkle, why seek [a verse] for him, [seeing that] he is indeed [identical with] a clean person?[5] This proves that though he is not fit, the obligation is upon him [to make himself fit], and though this is not [so] in the case of a
b community,[1] yet it is [so] in the case of an individual?—Rather, said Raba: R. Eliezer holds, One may slaughter and sprinkle for a man who is unclean through a reptile, and the same law applies to a man who is unclean through the dead on his seventh day;[2] then for what [purpose] is the *haza'ah?* for the eating[3]— [yet] the eating of the Passover sacrifice is not indispensable.[4] R. Adda b. Abba said to Raba, If so, it is found that the Passover sacrifice is slaughtered for those who cannot eat it?[5] 'For those who cannot eat it' means for the infirm and the aged, he replied, since they are [physically] unfit; but this one is indeed fit, save that he is not made ready.

R. AKIBA STATED A GENERAL RULE etc. Rab Judah said in Rab's name: The *halachah* is as R. Akiba. And we learned similarly in respect to circumcision. R. Akiba stated a general rule: No labour which can be performed on the eve of the Sabbath overrides the Sabbath; circumcision, which cannot be performed on the eve of the Sabbath,[6] overrides the Sabbath; and Rab Judah said in Rab's name: The *halachah* is as R. Akiba. Now [both] are necessary. For if he informed us [this] in connection with the Passover, [I would say,] it is only there that the necessary adjuncts of the precept do not override the Sabbath, because thirteen covenants were not made over it; but as for circumcision, over which thirteen covenants were made,[7] I would say that they [the adjuncts] override [the Sabbath]. While if he informed us [this of] circumcision, [I would argue], it is only there that the necessary adjuncts of the precept do not override the Sabbath, since there
c is no *kareth;*[1] but as for the Passover sacrifice, where there is *kareth*,[2] I might argue, Let the necessary adjuncts override [the Sabbath]. Thus they are necessary.

MISHNAH. WHEN DOES HE[3] BRING A ḤAGIGAH[4] WITH IT [THE PASSOVER SACRIFICE]? WHEN IT COMES DURING THE WEEK, IN PURITY, AND IN SMALL [PORTIONS].[5] BUT WHEN IT COMES ON THE SABBATH, IN LARGE [PORTIONS], AND IN UNCLEANNESS, ONE DOES NOT BRING THE ḤAGIGAH WITH IT. THE ḤAGIGAH WAS BROUGHT OF FLOCKS, HERDS, LAMBS OR GOATS, OF THE MALES OR THE FEMALES, AND IT IS EATEN TWO DAYS AND ONE NIGHT.[6]

GEMARA. What has he taught [previously] that he [now] teaches [about] the *ḥagigah?*[7]—He has taught about carrying it [the paschal lamb on his shoulders] and bringing it, which do not override the Sabbath, so he also teaches about the *ḥagigah* that it [too] does not override the Sabbath, and he states thus: WHEN DOES ONE[8] BRING A ḤAGIGAH WITH IT? WHEN IT COMES DURING THE WEEK, IN PURITY, AND IN SMALL [POR-
d TIONS].[1]

R. Ashi said: This proves that the *ḥagigah* of the fourteenth

(3) This explains why a person who is unclean through a corpse need not purify himself, yet an uncircumcised person must circumcise himself. Thus:—the whole community are not bound to purify themselves by sprinkling, even if the seventh day of their uncleanness falls on the eve of Passover, so that after *haza'ah* they would be clean in the evening, when the Passover is to be eaten. For he holds that if an individual is unclean through a reptile and has not performed *ṭebillah* (q.v. Glos.), though he can do so and be clean in the evening, nevertheless the Passover may not be slaughtered on his behalf; the same applies to him who is unclean through the dead whose seventh day falls on the eve of Passover, though he too would be clean in the evening if he were besprinkled during the day. Thus he must postpone his sacrifice for the second Passover; and therefore by the rule stated, a community in like condition is not bound to purify itself but may sacrifice in uncleanness. Again, since the community need not purify itself by sprinkling, an individual is not obliged to either, for an individual has no obligation which is not likewise binding upon the community; consequently, since an individual is not bound to purify himself, he may not do so on the Sabbath. But if the whole community are uncircumcised, it is their duty to circumcise themselves on the eve of Passover, and therefore it is the duty of an individual too, neglect of which entails *kareth*. Had he, however, held that we do slaughter the Passover for a man who is unclean through a reptile or through a corpse when his seventh day falls on the eve of Passover, then since the individual is not relegated, the community too might not sacrifice in uncleanness but would have to purify itself; and as a corollary, since the community would have to perform *haza'ah*, it would also be an individual's duty, and in consequence it would be permitted on the Sabbath.

a (1) Where, however, the community as a whole did not sacrifice at the first Passover for some other reason of uncleanness than that of corpse uncleanness, there is no second Passover for individuals who are unclean through a corpse. (2) V. Num. IX, 10, 13. (3) In the same way, viz., that they could be clean by the evening, as explained in note a5. (4) '*And*' is an extension, and teaches the inclusion of these. (5) For he could have the animal sacrificed by another and he would be clean in the evening to eat it. Hence he must hold that you cannot sacrifice for him whilst he is unclean, i.e., before he performs *ṭebillah* yet even so he incurs *kareth* since he could have performed *ṭebillah*.

b (1) The community is not bound to perform *haza'ah*, even if it could, but sacrifices in uncleanness. (2) If he held that you may not slaughter etc., then *haza'ah* would certainly be permitted on the Sabbath and obligatory too, notwithstanding that it is not obligatory upon a community. Since he holds the reverse, however, the actual sacrificing is possible without *haza'ah* at all. (3) He cannot *eat* of the Passover sacrifice, as indeed of all sacrifices, without previous *haza'ah*. (4) For the fulfilment of the precept of the paschal sacrifice. Tosaf. in such a case where he could make himself fit for eating but does not. (5) Whereas it is stated *supra* 61a that such a Passover sacrifice is unfit. (6) When the Sabbath is the eighth day from birth. (7) In the passage enjoining circumcision upon Abraham and his descendants (Gen. XVII) '*covenant*' is mentioned thirteen times, which shows its great importance.

c (1) If circumcision is postponed. (2) For not offering it. (3) Var. lec. 'ONE'. (4) Festival sacrifice. Such was obligatory on the first day of all Festivals; hence in the case of Passover, on the *fifteenth* of Nisan. The obligation is deduced in Ḥag. 9a from, *and ye shall keep it a feast* (ḥag) *unto the Lord* (Lev. XXIII, 41), *ḥag* being interpreted as referring to a Festival sacrifice. In this Mishnah, however the reference is to a *ḥagigah* brought on the *fourteenth*, and the Mishnah lays down the conditions when it is brought, it being in addition to the *ḥagigah* of the *fifteenth*. Besides the Festival *ḥagigah*, there was another obligatory sacrifice

וכל שאילו ביחיד נדחה בציבור עבדי בטומאה וכל מילתא דאיתא בציבור איתא ביחיד וכל מילתא דליתא בציבור ליתא ביחיד ערילות דאי כוליה ציבור ערלים נינהו אמרינן להו קומו מהולו נפשייכו ועבידו פסחא יחיד נמי אמרינן ליה קום מהול ועביד פסחא ואי לא מהיל ועביד (א) ענוש כרת טומאה דאי כוליה ציבורא טמאין נינהו לא מדינן עלייהו אלא עבדי בטומאה יחיד נמי פטור א"ל רב הונא בריה דרב יהושע לרבא והרי פסח שני דליתיה בציבור ואיתיה ביחיד א"ל שאני התם דהא עבד ליה ציבורא בראשון מיתיבי *יכול לא יהא ענוש כרת אלא שהיה טהור ושלא היה בדרך רחוקה ערל וטמא שרץ ושאר כל הטמאים מנין ת"ל °והאיש מדקא מהדר אטמא שרץ קסבר אין שוחטין וזורקין על טמא שרץ דאי שוחטין וזורקין על טמא שרץ ל"ל לאהדורי' עליה היינו טהור אלמא אע"ג דלא חזי (ג) חיובא עליה ואע"ג דליתיה בציבור איתיה ביחיד אלא אמר רבא קסבר רבי אליעזר שוחטין וזורקין על טמא שרץ והוא הדין לטמא מת בשביעי שלו הזאה למאי לאבילה *אבילת פסחים לא מעכבא א"ל רב אדא בר אבא לרבא א"כ נמצא פסח נשחט שלא לאוכליו א"ל שלא לאוכליו לחולה ולזקן דלא חזי אבל האי מיחזא חזי תקוני הוא דלא מתקן: כלל אמר ר"ע וכו': *אמר רב יהודה אמר רב [1]הלכה כר"ע ותנן נמי גבי מילה כי האי גוונא *כלל א"ר עקיבא כל מלאכה שאפשר לעשותה מע"ש אינה דוחה את השבת מילה שאי אפשר לעשותה מע"ש דוחה את השבת ואמר רב יהודה אמר רב [1]הלכה כר"ע וצריכא דאי אשמעינן גבי פסח התם *(דהוא מכשירי) מצוה לא דחו שבת משום דלא נכרתו עליה שלש עשרה בריתות אבל מילה דנכרתו עליה שלש עשרה בריתות אימא לידחי ואי אשמעינן מילה התם הוא דמכשירי מצוה לא דחו שבת דליכא כרת אבל פסח דאיכא כרת אימא לידחי צריכא: **מתני׳** [7]אימתי מביא חגיגה עמו בזמן שהוא בא בחול בטהרה ובמועט °ובזמן שהוא בא בשבת במרובה ובטומאה אין מביאין עמו חגיגה חגיגה היתה באה מן הצאן מן הבקר מן הכבשים ומן העזים מן הזכרים ומן הנקבות [ה]ונאכלת לשני ימים ולילה אחד: **גמ׳** מאי תנא דקתני חגיגה תנא *הרכבתו והבאתו דלא דחי שבת וקתני נמי חגיגה דלא דחיא שבת והכי קאמר אימתי מביאין עמו חגיגה בזמן שהוא בא בחול בטהרה ובמועט א"ר אשי שמע מינה *חגיגת ארבעה עשר לאו

---

called the peace-offering of rejoicing, deduced from, *and thou shalt rejoice in thy feast* (Deut. XVI, 14). This is discussed anon. (5) I.e., so many are registered for one paschal lamb that each person can receive but a small portion. (6) The night between the two days. (7) The sudden introduction of the *ḥagigah* is abrupt and irrelevant, unless it has some point in common with the preceding Mishnah. (8) Cf. n. c3.

d (1) While the next clause proceeds to state when the *ḥagigah* does *not* override the Sabbath, and that is the connection with the preceding Mishnah.

מסורת הש"ס

עין משפט נר מצוה

יח א מיי' פכ"ג מהל' שבת הלכה ח:

יט ב מיי' פ"ה מהל' ק"פ הלכה ד:

ור' אליעזר שבות דמצוה עדיף ליה תניא *אמר רבי אליעזר ומה לי אם דחו מכשירי מצוה שלאחר שחיטה את השבת דאיתעביד ליה מצוה לא ידחו מכשירי מצוה שלפני שחיטה את השבת אמר לו ר' עקיבא דמה לי אם דחו מכשירי מצוה שלאחר שחיטה את השבת שהרי דחתה שחיטה את השבת תאמר ידחו מכשירי מצוה שלפני שחיטה את השבת שלא דחתה שחיטה את השבת דבר אחר שמא ימצא זבח פסול ונמצא מחלל את השבת למפרע אי הכי משחט נמי לא נשחט שמא ימצא זבח פסול ונמצא מחלל את השבת למפרע אלא הא אמר ליה ברישא ופרכיה והדר א"ל הך דמה לי אם דחו: השיב ר"ע ואמר הזאה תוכיח וכו': תניא אמר לו ר' אליעזר עקיבא בשחיטה השבתני בשחיטה תהא מיתתו אמר לו ר' *אל תכפירני בשעת הדין כך מקובלני ממך *הזאה שבות היא ואינה דוחה את השבת וכי מאחר דהוא אגמרי' מאי טעמא קא הדר ביה אמר עולא רבי אליעזר כי אגמריה הזאה דתרומה אגמריה דתרומה גופה לא דחיא שבת ר"ע נמי כי אותביה הזאה דתרומה אותביה שהיא מצוה והיא משום שבות והוא סבר הזאה דפסח קא מותיב ליה מתיב רבה השיב ר"ע ואמר הזאת טמא מת תוכיח שחל שביעי שלו להיות בשבת ובערב הפסח שהיא מצוה והיא משום שבות ואינה דוחה את השבת אלא וודאי הזאה דפסח אגמריה וכי מאחר דאגמריה מ"ט קא פריך ליה ר' אליעזר ר' אליעזר גמריה איתעקר ליה ואתא ר"ע לאדכורי גמריה וניממא ליה בהדיא סבר לאו אורח ארעא והזאה מאי טעמא לא דחיא שבת מכדי טלטולי בעלמא הוא ותדחי שבת משום פסח *אמר רבה גזירה שמא יטלנה ויעבירנה ארבע אמות ברשות הרבים ולר' אליעזר ניעברי' דהא א"ר אליעזר מכשירי מצוה דוחין את השבת אמרי הני מילי היכא דגברא גופיה חזי ורמי חובא עליה אבל הכא דגברא גופיה לא חזי לא רמי חובא עליה אמר רבה לדברי ר' אליעזר קטן בריא מחמין לו חמין להברותו ולמולו בשבת דהא חזי ליה קטן חולה אין מחמין לו חמין להברותו ולמולו דהא לא חזי ליה אמר רבא ואי בריא הוא למה ליה חמין להברותו אלא אמר רבא הכל חולין הן אצל מילה אחד קטן בריא ואחד קטן חולה אין מחמין לו חמין להברותו ולמולו בשבת דהא לא חזי איתיביה אביי *ערל שלא מל ענוש כרת דברי רבי אליעזר והא הכא דגברא גופיה לא חזי וקתני ענוש כרת אלמא רמי חובא עליה אמר רבה קסבר רבי אליעזר *אין שוחטין וזורקין על טמא שרץ וכל

[תוספתא פ"ה]

ורבי אליעזר. אמר לך האי לאו קל וחומר הוא דשבות מצוה עדיפא משבות דרשות הלכך יום טוב דשמחתו רשות גזרו על שבות שלו אבל שבת דדחייה מלאכה שבו משום מצוה היא לא גזרו חכמים בה על השבות לדחות את המצוה: שלאחר שחיטה. מיחוי קרביו ואע"ג דאיתעביד ליה צורך גבוה: לא ידחו כו'. בתמיה למיעבד צורכי גבוה: דמה לי. כלומר דין הוא כן ומה לי לתמוה שהרי דחתה שחיטה כבר את שבת במלותה הלכך הואיל וניתנה לדחות כבר לא גזרו בה שוב על שבות הצריך: ברישא. אמר ליה האי טעמא שמא ימצא זבח פסול: ופרכיה. ואמר ליה א"כ משחט נמי לא נשחוט: בשחיטה השבתני. דבר שחוק וגיחוך שאמרת או חילוף ומה אם הזאה שהיא שבות אינה דוחה שחיטה לא כל שכן שלא תדחה ובאת לעקור את מה שכתוב בו במועדו ויודע היית שאין זה ק"ו: אל תכפירני. אל תכפור במה שלימדתני הזאה אע"פ שהיא שבות אינה דוחה ולכך דנתי קל וחומר זה לפניך אע"פ שאינו כדאי אלא כדי שתשים אל לבך אחרי שבא זה לדון שחיטה מהזאה מכלל דהזאה פשיטא ליה דלא דחיא מתוך כך תזכור מה שלימדתני דלא דחיא ותחזור בך ממה שאתה אומר ועליה אני דן: בשעת הדין. בשעה זו שאנו דנין עליה: ומאחר דאגמריה. ר' אליעזר גופיה דלא דחיא מאי טעמא פריך ואמר עליה אני דן: הזאה דתרומה. הבא להזות עליו ליטהר כדי לאכול תרומה אגמריה דלא דחיא שבת דהא הפרשת תרומה גופא לא דחיא שבת: הזאת טמא מת כו'. אלמא דבהזאת פסח השיבו וקאמר אינה דוחה שבת אלמא דאגמריה ר' אליעזר דאינה דוחה מדפשיטא ליה כולי האי: אלא ודאי הזאת פסח אגמריה. ומאי גזירת שבות איכא בהזאה גזירה שמא יעבירנה בידו וכשהיה דן עליה עם ר' עקיבא שכח דבר זה מלמודו והכי נמי אמרינן בע"א בפרק כל הצלמים (דף מו:) ר' אליעזר גמריה איעקר ליה ואתא ר' עקיבא לאדכוריה גמריה: דוחין את השבת. אפי' מלאכה גמורה במס' שבת (דף קל.): היכא דגברא חזי. כגון להביא איזמל למילה דרך רשות הרבים שכבר התינוק ראוי למול אבל היכא דגברא לא חזי כגון האי טמא לא רמיא חובא עליה ואין אלו מכשירי מצוה: אמר רבה לדברי רבי אליעזר. דאמר כל היכא דגברא לא חזי ליכא חובא עליה: קטן בריא. דבלאו רחיצה ראוי למול: מחמין לו חמין. בשבת קודם מילה: להברותו. להיות בריא וחזק: קטן חולה. שכל זמן שלא ירחצוהו בחמין לא יראה למול ואם ירחצוהו יראה למילה: הכל אצל מילה חולין הן. כל זמן שלא נרחצו בחמין ואפילו לרבי אליעזר צריך להיות לו מחמי חמין מערב שבת: איתיביה אביי ערל. גדול שלא מל ערב הפסח: ענוש כרת. בשביל שהיה ראוי לתקן מו' שעות זמן שחיטת הפסח ולמעלה ולא ניתקן ולא דמי לטמא ושהיה בדרך רחוקה שאין יכולין לתקן באותן שש שעות ומיקמי הכי לא רמיא חובא עלייהו אלמא אע"ג דלא חזיא רמיא מצוה עליה היכא דאפשר למיתקן והזאה נמי תדחה שבת דהא מצוה רמיא עליה ליתקן לכך ולי' קשיא הא דקיימא לן (לקמן דף צב.) הפורש מן הערלה כפורש מן הקבר וצריך הזאה שלישי ושביעי ואפילו מל אינו ראוי הא אוקמינן להיא בערל נכרי שנתגייר בפרק האשה: הכי גרסינן אמר רבה קסבר ר' אליעזר אין שוחטין וזורקין על טמא שרץ וכל

אם דחו מכשירי מצוה שלאחר שחיטה (א) השבת כו'. פי' בקונטרס מיחוי קרביו ותימה לר"י מה ראיה מייתי דילמא שאני התם משום דלא אפשר למיעבד מאתמול ונראה לר"י דמכשירי מצוה שלאחר שחיטה דקאמר היינו הקטר חלבים דאפשר להמתין עד הלילה ודחי שבת וכן יש בירושלמי דקא אמר ר' אליעזר אימורי ציבור יוכיחו אע"פ שאפשר להמתין למוצאי שבת מה לי מכשירין שלאחר שחיטה כו' והא דפריך משחט נמי לא לשחוט אע"ג דשחיטה לא אפשר מ"מ פריך משום שכבר הוכיח שאין חילוק בין אפשר ללא אפשר מדשרינן הקטר חלבים:

הזאה דתרומה אגמריה · ולית לן למימר דר' אליעזר הי' סבור דבהזאה דפסח קאמר ר"ע ולכך היה משיב ועליה אני דן שתהא מותרת דהשתא סבירא לן דהזאה דפסח דחיא שבת וקאמר ליה ר"ע (ב) זה חילוף שהיה סבור שר' אליעזר היה טועה במה שלמדו דאינה דוחה:

דתרומה גופה לא דחיא שבת · וא"ת נילף דתידחי שבת מכל הנאו וי"ל משום דיכול לקיים מצות אכילת תרומה אחר השבת:

שמא יעבירנה ארבע אמות · וא"ת ואמאי חיישינן להכי הלא נושא מי חטאת טמא *ויחזור ויטמא את המים ויש לומר דמעביר בכלי אבנים ובכלי גללים דלא מקבלי טומאה:

קטן בריא מחמין כו' דהא חזי · דווקא לר' אליעזר יש חילוק בין חזי ללא חזי אבל ר' עקיבא אינו מחלק כלל דהא קאמר במתני' הזאה תוכיח:

לא שנא חלש ולא שנא בריא אין מחמין לו חמין כו' · וכי אמר רבי אליעזר דמכשירי מילה דחו שבת ה"מ היכא שהוחמו חמין מערב שבת דחזי:

*מדקמהדר אטמא שרץ קסבר אין שוחטין כו'. מכל מקום חייב הוא כרת לפי שהיה יכול לטבול ואז היו שוחטין וזורקין עליו כדאמר לקמן שוחטין וזורקין על טבול יום דשימשא ממילא ערבא:

שוחטין וזורקין כו' · וא"ת אי שוחטי' וזורקי' על טמא שרץ אמאי כתב רחמנא טמא אינו עושה פסח פשיטא דהא כתיב איש לפי אכלו לעכב דבעינן גברא דחזי לאכילה כדמוכח בכילד צולין (לקמן עח:) ונראה לרשב"א דאיצטריך לאשמעינן דחייב בפסח שני דלא נימא דמיפטר משום דשני תשלומין דראשון הוא דחזי בראשון חזי בשני דלא חזי בראשון לא חזי בשני כדאמר לקמן גבי חגיגה בכילד צולין (לקמן פ:) אי נמי איצטריך למימרא דציבור עבדי בטומאה כדדרשינן איש כי יהיה טמא איש נדחה ואין ציבור נדחין: אכילת

רבינו חננאל

לא שמתי עיקר מיהת כי עביד איניש לנפשיה עביד: תניא אמר ר' אליעזר ומה אם דחו מכשירי מצוה של אחר שחיטה כגון מיחוי קרביו והקטרת אימוריו את השבת שכבר נעשת המצוה לא ידחו מכשירי מצוה שלפני שחיטה כגון חתיכת יבלתו וכיוצא בה שעדיין לא נעשת המצוה. אמר ר' (יהושע) [נ"ל ר"ע] מכשירי מצוה דלאחר שבת דחו שבת שכבר נדחית השבת בשחיטת הפסח תאמר במכשירי מצוה שלפני השחיטה שלא נדחה השבת עדיין. ד"א שמא ימצא זבח פסול ונמצא אותם מכשירין שעשה מקודם כי בחלול שבת היו שנתברר כי לא היתה מצוה ראויה ופריך רבי אליעזר אי הכי שחיטה נמי נימא הכי לא נשחט שמא ימצא הזבח טרפה ונמצאת השחיטה באיסור ולא מצא ר' (יהושע) [ר"ע] תשובה. יש מי שאומר זאת התשובה השיב רבי (יהושע) [ר"ע] ברישא ונתפרכה ואח"כ השיב התשובה הראשונה מה לידחו מכשירי מצוה דלאחר שחיט' את השבת כו' שאין בה פירכא: ירושלמי שלש עשרה שנה היה למד ר' עקיבא לפני ר' אליעזר ולא היה משיב לו כלום *תו תחלת תשובותיו שהשיב לו אמר לו ר' יהושע (שופטים ט ל"ח) הלא זה העם אשר מאסת בו צא הלחם בו: מתני' השיב ר"ע הזאה תוכיח שהיא משום מצוה והיא משום שבות כו' אמר ר' אליעזר ועליה אני דן כו' אמר לו הבא לי מועד לאלו כמועד לשחיטה. תניא אמר לו ר' אליעזר עקיבא בשחיטה השבתני בשחיטה תהא מיתתו אמר לו אל תכפירני בשעת הדין כלומר אל תחשדני בכופר על מה שלמדתני אתה למדתני הזאה שבות ואינה דוחה שבת: אמר עולא ר' אליעזר הזאה דתרומה לאו כלומר אם היה כהן טמא מת שחל שביעי שלו להיות בשבת שאין מזין עליו בשבת לאכול בתרומה לערב ומותיב ר' עקיבא מהזאה דתרומה להזאה דפסח ופריך ר' אליעזר אימר דאמרי' דהזאה דפסח דחיא שבת דהא תאמר בהזאה דתרומה שאין תרומה עצמה דוחה שבת. והביא רבא ברייתא מפורשת דר' עקיבא מהזאה דפסח מותיב ודחה דברי עולא ואוקמא לעולם רבי אליעזר לר' עקיבא כי הזאה כדי לעשות הפסח אינו דוחה שבת וכאשר קבל רבי אליעזר השמועה כך מסרה לר"ע ועכשיו שדחה ר' אליעזר והא רבי עקיבא בעקיפין שיזכור דברי ר' אליעזר מתוך דברי ר' עקיבא נמצא שלא לפי שאין דרך תלמיד חכם לומר לרבו

ע"ז דף מו:

סוכה דף מג: ר"ה דף כט: מגילה דף ד: [ביצה דף יז:]

[לקמן דף צד:]

לקמן דף פ: [פס. ל: צד. זבחים כב:]

[לקמן שם]

הגהות הב"ח

(א) תוס' ד"ה אם דחו וכו' שלאחר שחיטה את השבת: (ב) שם ד"ה הזאה וכו' וקאמר ליה ר"ע או חילוף:

גליון הש"ס

תוס' ד"ה שמא. ויחזור ויטמא. עיין פרק י' מ"ו דפרה ובזבחים דף ק"ה תוד"ה מהוסר:

* [הג"ה בירושלמי לפנינו כאן הגי' וזו היה תחילה תשובתו לפני ר' אליעזר אמר לו ר' יהושע הלא זה העם וכו']

the *shebuth* which accompanies it is not permitted! [69a] And R. Eliezer?[3]—In his view the *shebuth* [required] for a precept is more important.[4]

It was taught, R. Eliezer said: I argue,[5] if the necessary adjuncts of the precept which [come] after *shechitah*,[6] when the precept has [already] been performed, override the Sabbath; shall not the necessary adjuncts of the precept which [come] before *shechitah* override the Sabbath! Said R. Akiba: I argue[7] if the necessary adjuncts of the precept which [come] after *shechitah* override the Sabbath, the reason is because the *shechitah* has [already] overridden the Sabbath;[8] will you say that the necessary adjuncts of the precept before the *shechitah* shall override the Sabbath, seeing that the *shechitah* has not [yet] overridden the Sabbath?[9] Another argument is: the sacrifice may be found to be unfit, and thus he will be found retrospectively to have desecrated the Sabbath.[10] If so, let us not slaughter it either, lest the sacrifice be found unfit, and thus it be found that he retrospectively desecrated the Sabbath?—Rather, he first told him this [argument], and he refuted it; and then he told him this 'the reason is' etc.

R. AKIBA ANSWERED AND SAID: LET HAZA'AH PROVE IT etc. It was taught, R. Eliezer said to him: 'Akiba, you have refuted a me by *shechitah*; by *shechitah* shall be his death!'[1] Said he to him, 'Master, do not deny me at the time of argument:[2] I have thus received [the law] from you, [viz.,] *haza'ah* is a *shebuth* and does not override the Sabbath.'[3] Then since he himself had taught it to him, what is the reason that he retracted?—Said 'Ulla: When R. Eliezer taught it to him it was concerning *haza'ah* for [the sake of] *terumah*,[4] since *terumah* itself does not override the Sabbath;[5] [and] R. Akiba too, when he refuted him, refuted him by *haza'ah* for [the sake of] *terumah*, which is [likewise] a religious duty[6] and is [usually forbidden] as a *shebuth;* but he [R. Eliezer] thought that he was refuting him by *haza'ah* for the Passover sacrifice.[7]

Rabbah raised an objection: R. Akiba answered and said, Let the *haza'ah* of a person unclean through the dead prove [refute] it,—when his seventh [day] falls on the Sabbath and on the eve of Passover, so that it is a religious duty[8] and it is [only] a *shebuth*, yet it does not override the Sabbath.[9] Hence he [R. Eliezer] certainly taught him about *haza'ah* for [the sake of] the Passover sacrifice. Then since he [himself] had taught it to him, what is the reason that R. Eliezer rebutted him [thus]?—R. Eliezer had forgotten his own tradition, and R. Akiba came to remind him of his tradition. Then let him tell it to him explicitly?—He thought b that it would not be mannerly.[1]

Now, what is the reason that *haza'ah* does not override the Sabbath; consider, it is mere handling,[2] [then] let it override the Sabbath on account of the Passover sacrifice?—Said Rabbah, It is a preventive measure, lest he take it [the water of purification] and carry it four cubits in public ground.[3] But according to R. Eliezer, let us [indeed] carry it, for R. Eliezer ruled, The necessary adjuncts to a precept override the Sabbath?—I will tell you: that is only when the man himself is fit [to perform the precept] and the obligation lies upon him; but here that the man himself is not fit,[4] the obligation does not lie upon him.

Rabbah said: According to the words of R. Eliezer,[5] [if there is] a healthy infant,[6] one may heat water for him, to strengthen him[7] and to circumcise him on the Sabbath, since it is fit for him. [If there is] a sickly infant,[8] one may not heat hot water for him to strengthen him and to circumcise him, since it is not fit for him.[9] Said Raba: But if he is healthy, why does he need hot water to strengthen him? Rather, said Raba, all are regarded as invalids in respect to circumcision: both in the case of a strong infant or a sickly infant, one may not heat hot water for him to strengthen him and to circumcise him on the Sabbath,[10] since it is not fit for him.

Abaye raised an objection against him: An [adult] uncircumcised person who did not circumcise himself [on the eve of Passover] is punished by *kareth:*[1] this is the view of R. Eliezer. Now here, though the man himself is unfit, yet he states that he is c punished by *kareth*, which proves that the obligation lies upon him.[2]—Said Rabbah: R. Eliezer holds, One may not slaughter [the Passover] and sprinkle [its blood] for him who is unclean

(3) How does he rebut this argument? (4) Hence though a *shebuth* is not permitted on a Festival, it nevertheless overrides the Sabbath when it is necessary for the performance of a precept. (5) Lit., 'and what is to me', this being the ethic dative. (6) I.e., the cleansing of the bowels. (7) Lit., 'for what is it to me'—i.e., I need not wonder at it, for the reason that etc. (8) Therefore it may be overridden again by a *shebuth*. (9) Surely not. (10) For no precept will have been performed.

a (1) I.e., your argument is obviously a humorous one and cannot be taken seriously, since you would thereby eradicate a Scriptural law; v. Mishnah. (2) Rashi; i.e., do not deny what you yourself have taught me—viz., that *haza'ah* does not override the Sabbath. Jast.: do not make me an atonement, (saying, 'may his death be atonement') at the time of judgment—i.e., I need no apology for my attitude; or perhaps, do not be angry with me. (3) Consequently I am justified in using this fact to prove, by a *reductio ad absurdum* (since it would overthrow a Scriptural law), that your argument is fallacious. (4) An unclean priest may not undergo *haza'ah* on the Sabbath in order to eat *terumah* in the evening. (5) *Terumah* may not be separated on the Sabbath. (6) It is the priests' duty to eat *terumah*. (7) Which he holds is permitted on the Sabbath, since otherwise the unclean person is debarred from discharging his obligation. (8) *Haza'ah* will make him fit to partake of the Passover in the evening, which is a religious duty. (9) Thus it is explicitly stated that R. Akiba argued that *haza'ah*, even for the sake of the Passover sacrifice, does not override the Sabbath.

b (1) To tell him plainly; hence he intimated it to him indirectly. (2) It is not a labour. (3) Which is Scripturally forbidden. (4) Since he is unclean. (5) That wherever the man is unfit he has no obligation. (6) To be circumcised on the Sabbath. 'Healthy' means that he is strong enough to be circumcised even without bathing. (7) I.e., to make him even stronger. (8) I.e., one who is too weak to be circumcised in his present state unless he is first bathed. (9) For at present he is too weak; consequently it is not our duty to strengthen him so that he should be immediately liable. Tosaf.: this distinction can be drawn only according to R. Eliezer. But according to R. Akiba it is forbidden in all cases, just as *haza'ah* is forbidden. (10) But the water must be prepared from the previous day.

c (1) Because he could have circumcised himself after midday, when the Passover is obligatory; hence he incurs *kareth* for not partaking of the Passover sacrifice, v. Ex. XII, 48 and Num. IX, 10-13. He is not comparable to an unclean person or one who is on a distant journey, since they could not make themselves fit after midday, while before that there was as yet no obligation. (2) Where it is possible to make the person fit. Hence *haza'ah* too should override the Sabbath, since a man is bound to make himself fit.

[68b] AND THE BURNING OF ITS FAT. It was taught, R. Simeon said: Come and see how precious is a precept in its [proper] time.[9] For lo! the [precept of] burning the fats and limbs and the fat-pieces is valid all night, yet we do not wait for [burning] them until nightfall.[10]

ITS CARRYING AND ITS BRINGING etc. But the following contradicts it: You may cut off a wart [of an animal] in the Temple, but not in the country,[11] and if [it is done] with a utensil [a knife], it is forbidden in both cases?[12]—R. Eleazar and R. Jose b. Ḥanina—one answered, Both refer to [removing the wart] with the hand: one refers to a moist [wart]; the other, to a dry one.[13] While the other maintains, Both refer to a moist [wart], yet there is no diffi-
a culty: one means by hand, and the other means with a utensil.[1]

Now according to him who explained, 'One means by hand, and the other means with a utensil,' why did he not say, Both mean by hand, yet there is no difficulty: one refers to a moist [wart]; the other, to a dry one?—He can answer you: a dry one [just] crumbles away.[2] And according to him who maintained, 'Both mean by hand, yet there is no difficulty: one refers to a moist [wart]; the other to a dry one'; why did he not say: Both refer to a moist [wart], yet there is no difficulty: one means by hand, and the other means with a utensil?—He can answer you: as for a utensil, surely he [the Tanna] teaches there, 'if [it is done] with a utensil, it is forbidden in both cases!'[3] And the other?[4]—That which he teaches [about] a utensil here, [is because] he comes to inform us of the controversy of R. Eliezer and R. Joshua.

SAID R. ELIEZER ... IF SHECHITAH etc. R. Joshua is consistent with his view, for he maintains, Rejoicing on a Festival too is a religious duty.[5] For it was taught, R. Eliezer said: A man has nought else [to do] on a Festival save either to eat and drink or to sit and study. R. Joshua said: Divide it: [devote] half of it to eating and drinking, and half of it to the Beth Hamidrash. Now R. Joḥanan said thereon: Both deduce it from the same verse. One verse says, *a solemn assembly to the Lord thy God*,[6] whereas another verse says, *there shall be a solemn assembly unto you*:[7] R. Eliezer holds: [That means] either entirely to God or entirely to you; while R. Joshua holds, Divide it: [Devote] half to God and half to yourselves.

(Mnemonic: '*aBaM*.)[8] R. Eleazar said: All agree in respect
b to the Feast of Weeks ['*azereth*][1] that we require [it to be] 'for you' too. What is the reason? It is the day on which the Torah was given.[2] Rabbah said: All agree in respect to the Sabbath that we require [it to be] 'for you' too. What is the reason? *And thou shalt call the Sabbath a delight.*[3] R. Joseph said: All agree that on Purim we require 'for you' too. What is the reason? *Days of feasting and gladness*[4] is written in connection therewith.

Mar son of Rabina would fast[5] the whole year,[6] except on the Feast of Weeks, Purim, and the eve of the Day of Atonement. The Feast of Weeks, [because] it is the day on which the Torah was given: Purim, [because] '*days of feasting and gladness*' is written in connection therewith. The eve of the Day of Atonement: for Ḥiyya b. Rab of Difti taught: *And ye shall afflict your souls on the ninth day of the month*:[7] do we then fast on the ninth? Surely we fast on the tenth! But this is to tell you: whoever eats and drinks on the ninth thereof, the Writ ascribes [merit] to him as though he had fasted on the ninth and the tenth.[8]

R. Joseph would order on the day of Pentecost: 'Prepare me a third-born calf,'[9] saying, 'But for the influence of this day,[10] how many Josephs are there in the market place!'[11]

R. Shesheth used to revise his studies every thirty days, and he would stand and lean at the side of the doorway and exclaim, 'Rejoice, O my soul, Rejoice, O my soul; for thee have I read [the Bible], for thee have I studied [the Mishnah].' But that is not so, for R. Eleazar said, But for the Torah, heaven and earth would not endure, for it is said, *If not for my covenant by day and by night, I had not appointed the ordinances of heaven and earth?*[12]—In the first place when a man does it [*sc.* studies] he does so with himself in mind.

R. Ashi said: Yet according to R. Eliezer too, who maintained that [rejoicing on] a Festival is [merely] voluntary, he can be
c refuted:[1] if a Festival, when labour for a voluntary [requirement] is permitted,[2] yet the *shebuth* which accompanies it is not permitted; then the Sabbath, whereon only labour [required for the carrying out of] a precept is permitted, is it not logical that

(9) I.e., as soon as it can be performed, even if it can be postponed. (10) But do it immediately, though it is the Sabbath. (11) *Medinah*, 'province'. This is the technical designation for all places outside the Temple. (12) 'Er. 103a. (13) Our Mishnah refers to a moist wart. Even when it is removed by hand, which is merely a *shebuth*, it is forbidden, since it could have been removed the previous day. But in 'Er. 103a the reference is to a dry one, the removal of which is not even regarded as a *shebuth*.

a (1) The former is permitted, while the latter is forbidden.—This of course is a more lenient explanation. (2) It would not be called cutting at all. (3) Why then should it be repeated in the present Mishnah? (4) Does he not accept the force of this argument? (5) Not merely permitted. (6) Deut. XVI, 8. (7) Num. XXIX, 35. (8) A mnemonic is a word or phrase, whose letters or words respectively each stand for a title or catchword of a subject, strung together as an aid to the memory. Here, '*a* = '*azereth*; *B* = *ShaBBath*; *M* = PuriM.

b (1) Lit., 'the solemn assembly'—without a further determinant this always means the Feast of Weeks. (2) Therefore we must demonstrate our joy in it by feasting. (3) Isa. LVIII, 13. (4) Esth. IX, 22. (5) Lit., 'sat in a fast'. (6) That is if the occasion arose. (7) Lev. XXIII, 32. The punctuation of the E.V. has been disregarded, as is required by the context. (8) Together. (9) I.e., the third calved by its mother. Others translate: (i) in its third year; or (ii) third-grown, i.e., one that has reached a third of its full growth. On all translations this was regarded as particularly choice. (10) Lit., 'if this day had not caused (it).' (11) I.e., I owe my eminence to having studied the Torah, which was given on this day. (12) Jer. XXXIII, 25. I.e., if not for my Torah, which is to be studied by day and by night, heaven and earth would not enjoy permanence. How then could R. Shesheth take such a selfish view of his studies?

c (1) Lit., 'there is a refutation for him'. (2) I.e., *shechitah*, though the eating of meat, which constitutes rejoicing, is voluntary.

עין משפט
נר מצוה

יד א מיי' פ"ד מהל' מעשה קרבנות הל' ג:
טו ב ג מיי' פ"ט מהל' שבת הלכה ח:
ומייר לעיל במשנה סה:]
[תוס' ערכין ספ"ב מנחות עב.

טז ד מיי' פ"ו מהל' י"ט הלכה יט סמג לאוין עה טוש"ע א"ח סי' תקכט סעיף א:
טז [ד] כל זה מן הכל מודים בעצרת עד כאלו התענה: תשיעי ועשירי כרב אלפס ביומא פ"ב סי' תתעה.
יז ה טוש"ע א"ח סי' תרד ס"א:

והקטר חלביו וכו': *תניא אמר רבי שמעון *בא וראה כמה *חביבה מצוה בשעתה שהרי הקטר חלבים ואברים ופדרים כשרים כל הלילה ואין ממתינים להם עד שתחשך: הרכבתו והבאתו וכו': ורמינהו *חותכין יבלת במקדש אבל לא במדינה ואם בכלי כאן וכאן אסור ר' אלעזר ור' יוסי בר חנינא חד אמר אידי ואידי ביד הא בלחה הא ביבשה וחד אמר אידי ואידי בלחה ולא קשיא הא ביד הא בכלי ולמאן דאמר הא ביד הא בכלי מאי טעמא לא אמר אידי ואידי ביד ולא קשיא הא בלחה הא ביבשה אמר לך יבשה מפרך פריכא ולמאן דאמר אידי ואידי ביד ולא קשיא הא בלחה הא ביבשה מאי טעמא לא אמר אידי ואידי בלחה ולא קשיא הא ביד הא בכלי אמר לך כלי הא קתני התם אם בכלי כאן וכאן אסור ואידך הא דקתני כלי הכא פלוגתא דרבי אליעזר ור' יהושע אתא לאשמועינן: א"ר אליעזר ומה אם שחיטה וכו': ר' יהושע לטעמיה דאמר שמחת י"ט נמי מצוה היא *דתניא ר' אליעזר אומר אין לו לאדם בי"ט אלא או אוכל ושותה או יושב ושונה ר' יהושע אומר חלקהו חציו לאכילה ושתיה וחציו לבית המדרש וא"ר יוחנן ושניהם מקרא אחד דרשו כתוב אחד אומר עצרת לה' אלהיך וכתוב אחד אומר עצרת תהיה לכם ר' אליעזר סבר או כולו לה' או כולו לכם ור' יהושע סבר חלקהו חציו לה' וחציו לכם: (עב"ם סימן) א"ר אלעזר [ד'] הכל מודים בעצרת דבעינן נמי לכם מ"ט יום שניתנה בו תורה הוא אמר רבה הכל מודים בשבת דבעינן נמי לכם מ"ט וקראת לשבת עונג אמר רב יוסף הכל מודים בפורים דבעינן נמי לכם מ"ט ימי משתה ושמחה כתיב ביה מר בריה דרבינא כולה שתא הוה יתיב בתעניתא לבר מעצרתא ופוריא ומעלי יומא דכיפורי עצרת יום שניתנה בו תורה פוריא ימי משתה ושמחה כתיב מעלי יומא דכיפורי *דתני חייא בר רב מדפתי ועניתם את נפשותיכם בתשעה לחדש וכי בתשעה (הם) מתענין והלא בעשירי מתענין אלא לומר לך כל האוכל ושותה בתשעה בו מעלה עליו הכתוב כאילו מתענה תשיעי ועשירי רב יוסף ביומא דעצרתא אמר עבדי לי עגלא תלתא אמר אי לא האי יומא דקא גרים כמה יוסף איכא בשוקא רב ששת כל תלתין יומין מהדר ליה תלמודיה ותלי וקאי בעיברא דדשא ואמר חדאי נפשאי חדאי נפשאי לך קראי לך תנאי איני *והא"ר אלעזר אילמלא תורה לא נתקיימו שמים וארץ שנאמר אם לא בריתי יומם ולילה חקות שמים וארץ לא שמתי מעיקרא כי עביד איניש אדעתא דנפשי' קא עביד אמר רב אשי ולמאי דקאמר ר' אליעזר נמי י"ט רשות אית ליה פירכא ומה י"ט שהתיר בו מלאכה של רשות לא התיר שבות שעמה שבת שלא התיר בה אלא מלאכה של מצוה אינו דין שלא תתיר שבות שעמה ורבי

תורה אור: דברים טז; במדבר כט; אסתר ט; ויקרא כג; ירמיה לג

רש"י

כשירין כל הלילה · כדכתיב (ויקרא ו) על מוקדה על המזבח כל הלילה ויכול להקטירן כל הלילה ולהכי אין ממתינין להם עד שתחשך אלא מחללין שבת עליהן כדכתיב (במדבר כח) עולת שבת בשבתו על עולת התמיד אלמא חביב למהר מצוה בשעתה: חותכין יבלת במקדש · דלא גזרו על השבות במקדש: הא והא ביד · שחותכה בידו ולא בסכין דאין בה אלא משום שבות ואפילו הכי אסור בלחה הואיל ומצי למיעבד מאתמול והיינו דעירובין ביבשה דאפילו שבות ליכא וכו' אליעזר לא מצי לאוקמא להאי דעירובין וכי מתה ר' אליעזר היא דאמר במתני' דוחין משום דקתני התם ואם בכלי דהוי מלאכה גמורה כאן וכאן אסור ואי ר' אליעזר היא הא אמר מכשירי מצוה דוחין את השבת אפילו במלאכה גמורה במסכת שבת (דף קל.) דתנן ר' אליעזר אומר אם לא הביא כלי מערב שבת מביאו בשבת: הא · דעירובין ביד ומתניתין בכלי דהוי מלאכה גמורה ובעירובין בפרק בתרא איתא נמי כולה הך סוגיא ומקשינן התם והא גבי שבות תני לה דקתני אלו שמשום שבות לא ידחו כו' אלמא לאו בכלי קאי: מפרך פריכא · ולא קרי לה חתיכה: מאי טעמא לא אמר הא ביד הא בכלי · ותוקמא למתני' דעירובין נמי בלחה: הא קתני התם · בעירובין דאסור ולמה לי למיהדר למסתמא הכא בפסחים: ור' יהושע · דמפיק שמחת יום טוב רשות לפסח אזיל לטעמיה דאמר שמחת יום טוב מצוה היא ואפ"ה לא דחיא שבות הראוי לעשות מבעוד יום: דבעינן נמי לכם · שישמח בו במאכל ומשתה להראות שנוח ומקובל יום זה לישראל שניתנה תורה בו: כל האוכל ושותה כו' · בפ' בתרא דיומא מוקמינן להא דרשה אליבא דמאן דאמר אין אדם מוזהר על תוספת עינוי להתחיל ולהתענות מבעוד יום ואפילו למאן דאית ליה מוסיפין מחול על קודש מקרא אחרינא נפקא ליה מבחריש ובקציר תשבות הילכך כי אתא האי בתשעה לכי אתא והכי קאמר מה שאתם עושים בתשעה הריני מקבלה ושתיה אני קורא עינוי: תילתא · *שליש לבטן ומובחר הוא: עבדי לי · היה מצוה לתקשי ביתו להכין לו סעודה: אי לאו האי יומא · שלמדתי תורה ונתרוממתי הרי אנשים הרבה בשוק ששמן יוסף ומה ביני לבינם: ותלי · נשען: חדאי נפשאי · שמחי נפשי: לך קראי לך תנאי · בשבילך ולצורכך שניתי וקריתי: איני · וכי אין הנאה בתלמוד תורה אלא ללומדיה לבדם: אם לא בריתי · של יומם ולילה דהייתו תלמוד תורה שכתוב בו (יהושע א) והגית בו יומם ולילה: אית ליה פירכא · למילתיה דאמר מכשירי מצוה דוחה כל שכן שבות דמצוה שפיר מהדר ליה ר' יהושע יום טוב יוכיח מקל וחומר ומה שמחת יום טוב שהיא רשות והתרת' בו משום מלאכה לא התרתה בו משום שבות שבת שלא התרתה בה אלא מלאכ' מצוה כגון שחיטת קרבנות לבור אינו דין שלא תתיר שבות אפי' של מצוה: ורבי

תוספות

מפרך פריכא · הילכך ההוא דעירובין ליכא לאוקמא ביבשה דהא קתני סיפא ואם בכלי כאן וכאן אסור ויבשה כיון דמפרכא אפילו בכלי נמי שריא והכי מוכח בפרק בתרא דעירובין (דף קג.): *ומה שחיטה שהיא משום מלאכה דוחה את השבת אלו כו' · תימה לר"י מה קל וחומר הוא זה דלמא שאני הכי משום דלאפשר לעשותן מערב שבת ור' אליעזר גופיה אית ליה זה החילוק ומשום הכי בפ' רבי אליעזר דמילה (שבת קלג.) מצריך תרי קראי חד למילה וחד למכשיריה משום דלאפשר לעשותן מערב שבת דאמר התם מילה וכל מכשיריה דוחין את השבת דברי ר' אליעזר מנא ליה לרבי אליעזר הא דאמר קרא וביום השמיני ביום ואפילו בשבת והדר קאמר ע"כ לא פליגי רבנן עליה אלא במכשירים אבל מילה דברי הכל דחיא מנא לן והשתא מאי קבעי מנא לן תיפוק מההוא קרא דביום דדריש מיניה ר' אליעזר מכשירים אע"כ משום דבעינן תרי קראי למילה ולמכשיריה כדפרישי' ונראה לר"י דוולאי לר' אליעזר לא צריך קרא אלי קל וחומר דהא אפילו מכשירי פסח דהוו מלאכה גמורה דחו שבת אע"ג דלאפשר לעשותן מערב שבת כדקאמר (לקמן סט.) בגמרא וליעבדיה דהא שמעינן ליה לרבי אליעזר דאמר מכשירי מצוה דחו והא דקאמרינן הכא ק"ו לדבריהם דרבנן קאמר כלומר אף על גב דלאפשר לעשותן מערב שבת כיון דליכא אלא שבות בעלמא יותר יש להתיר משחיטה עצמה דהיא מלאכה גמורה אף על גב דלאי אפשר לעשותה מבערב ותימה לר"י מכשירי פסח מנא ליה לרבי אליעזר דדחו שבת דהא גבי מילה מצריך תרי קראי וכי תימא דגמר מסוכה ולולב ומלה ושופר ועומר ושתי הלחם דמוכח התם דדחו מכשיריהם שבת הא איכא למיפרך דמה להנך שכן בשעת דחייתו מיד יכול לקיים מצותן אבל פסח אינו נאכל אלא בלילה ועוד אי מהתם יליף אמאי איצטריך במועדו גבי פסח דקאמר ר' אליעזר עקרת מה שכתוב בתורה במועדו אפי' בשבת: *מה ראיה רשות למצוה · משמע דמכשירי אוכל נפש שאפשר לעשותן מערב יו"ט אסירי לר' אליעזר והקשה ר"ש כהן דבריש חולין (שבת ד' קלז:) אמרינן דרבי אליעזר עדיפא מדר' יהודה ושרי אפי' מכשירי דאפשר מערב יו"ט ותירץ לו ר"י דלא שרי אלא דוקא במשמרת דלא דמיא מלאכה כולי האי: הכל מודים בעצרת דבעינן לכם · תימה לריב"א א"כ מאי קאמר רבי אליעזר מה ראיה רשות למצוה דנימא עצרת תוכיח שהיא מצוה וי"ל דהא דבעי רבי אליעזר בעצרת לכם לאו דוקא מקרא אלא מסברא: אם

רבינו חננאל

כתיב הכא ורעו כבשים כדברם וכתיב התם ירעו בשן וגלעד כימי עולם: **והקטר** חלביו דוחה את השבת תניא אמר ר' שמעון ראה כמה חביבה מצוה בשעתה שהרי הקטר חלבים כשרים כל הלילה ואין ממתינין להם עד שתחשך מ"ש אלא מקטירין אותן בשבת לקיים מצוה בשעתה: **הרכבתו** אינו דוחה השבת. דלא כר' נתן דאמר בפרק המצניע כי החי נושא את עצמו והמוציאו בשבת פטור והני מילי חוץ לירושלים אבל חוץ לעזרה לא: **הבאתו** מחוץ לתחום אין דוחה את השבת כר' עקיבא דאמר בסוטה בפרק [כשם] תחומין דאוריי'. ירושלמי הרכבתו לא אמרו אלא חוץ לירושלים אבל חוץ לעזרה מותר משום שבות שהתירו במקדש: **חתיכת** יבלתו אין דוחה את השבת יבלת לחה או בכלי והא דתנן בסוף עירובין חותכין יבלת במקדש ביבשה וביד: **מתני'** ר' אליעזר אומר דוחין אמר ר' אליעזר ומה אם שחיטה שהוא אב מלאכה דוחה את השבת אלו שמשום שבות לא ידחו את השבת אמר לו ר' יהושע יום טוב יוכיח שהתיר בו כל מלאכה שהיא לצורך אוכל נפש ואוסר בו דבר של שבות כדתנן ביום טוב אלו שהן משום שבות לא עולין באילן ולא רוכבין אמר לו רבי אליעזר יהושע מה ראיה שבות דרשות לא עולין באילן לשבות דמצוה שהיא הבאת הפסח כדי שישהם ור' יהושע אמר לך יום טוב נמי מצוה לשמח בכל מיני מאכל הוא והתרתה לשחוט ולבשל ולא התרתה להביא מחוץ [לתחום] וכיוצא בו ולעשות שמחת יו"ם ור"א אומר יום טוב או כולו לך או כולו לה' כיון דאי בעי למיעבד כולו לה' ולקרות היום כולו הרשות בידו כאלו אין כאן שמחת יום[טוב]: **איכא** למיפרך ומה יום טוב שהתירו בו מלאכה דרשות כגון הא דאמרינן הואיל והותרה הבערה לצורך הותרה נמי שלא לצורך לא התירו שבות לעלות באילן לשוט על פני המים(ולהביא)(ולהוציא) משם אש לבשל אפי' דיום טוב שבת שלא התיר בה אלא כגון שחיטת הפסח וכיוצא בו מלאכה של מצוה בלבד אינו דין שלא נתיר שבות דעמה ור' אליעזר אמר לך אפי' הכי שבות דמצוה עדיפא: **אמר** רבא הכל מודים בשבת דבעי' לכם כלומר אין יישב היום כולו ולקרות ולבטל שמחת שבת דכתיב וקראת לשבת עונג: **מר** בריה דרבינא כוליה שתא הוה יתיב בתעניתא בר מעצרת ופוריא ועי"ב יום הכפורים רב ששת הוה אמר חדאי נפש כלומר שמחי לך קראתי כדי שתהא שוכנת בטח לעולם הבא **ואע"פ** שהעולם **אינו** מתקיים אלא בזכות תופשי התורה שנאמר **אם** לא בריתי יומם ולילה חקות שמים וארץ לא

[קדושין לג. ע"ש] [חולין מד: ע"ש]
עירובין קג. [ע"ש]
ביצה טו:

גליון הש"ס
גמ' ואין ממתינים להם. עי' טורי אבן ר"ה לג: ד"ה נתקלקלו: שם אר"א הכל מודים בעצרת. עי' ר"ה ט: תוספות ד"ה כאילו התענה:

[עי' רש"י עירובין סג. ועי' רש"י סנהדרין סה: ולעיל קוע' תוס' גיטין נו. ורש"י שבת ....]
מדרש לג [וזוגמתו סנהדרין לגו:]

*בועל נדה כטמא מת למאי אילימא לטומאתם האי טומאת שבעה כתיב ביה והאי טומאת שבעה כתיב ביה אלא לאו למחנותם ומדסיפא למחנותם הוי רישא נמי למחנותם מידי איריא הא כדאיתא והא כדאיתא מיתיבי מצורע חמור מזב וזב חמור מטמא מת יצא בעל קרי שטמא מת חמור ממנו מאי יצא לאו יצא מכלל זב ובא לכלל טמא מת דהא טמא מת חמור ממנו ומותר במחנה לויה לא יצא ממחנה טמא מת ונכנס למחנה זב ואע"ג דטמא מת חמור ממנו (*דמותר) במחנה לויה למאי דדמי לי' מדמינן ליה תני תנא קמיה דרב יצחק בר אבדימי °ויצא אל מחוץ למחנה [א] זו מחנה שכינה לא יבא אל תוך המחנה [ב] זו מחנה לויה מכאן לבעל קרי שיצא חוץ לשתי מחנות אמר לי' אכתי לא עיילתיה אפיקתיה לישנא אחרינא אכתי לא אפיקתיה עיילתיה אלא אימא מחוץ למחנה זו מחנה לויה לא יבא אל תוך המחנה זו מחנה שכינה מתקיף לה רבינא אימא אידי ואידי למחנה שכינה ולעבור עליו בעשה ולא תעשה אם כן לימא קרא ויצא אל מחוץ למחנה ולא יבא אל תוך המחנה למה לי שמע מינה ליתן לו מחנה אחרת: ומיחוי קרביו וכו': מאי מיחוי קרביו רב הונא אמר שמנקבן בסכין (רב) חייא בר רב אמר שירקא דמעייא דנפקא אגב דוחקא דסכינא אמר ר' (*אליעזר) מאי טעמא דחייא בר רב דכתיב °וחרבות מחים גרים יאכלו מאי משמע כדמתרגם רב יוסף ונכסיהון דרשיעיא צדיקיא יחסנון °ורעו כבשים כדברם אמר מנשיא בר ירמיה אמר רב כמדובר בם מאי כמדובר בם אמר אביי וחרבות מחים גרים יאכלו אמר ליה רבא בשלמא אי כתיב חרבות כדקאמרת השתא דכתיב וחרבות מילתא אחריתי קאמר אלא אמר רבא כדרב חננאל דאמר רב חננאל אמר רב עתידין צדיקים שיחיו את המתים כתיב הכא ורעו כבשים כדברם וכתיב התם °ירעו בשן וגלעד כימי עולם בשן זה אלישע הבא מן הבשן שנאמר °ויעני יושפט בבשן וכתיב °פה אלישע בן שפט אשר יצק מים על ידי אליהו גלעד זה אליהו שנאמר °ויאמר אליהו התשבי מתושבי גלעד וגו' אמר ר' שמואל בר נחמני א"ר יונתן עתידים צדיקים שיחיו מתים שנאמר °עוד ישבו זקנים וזקנות ברחובות ירושלם ואיש משענתו בידו מרוב ימים וכתיב °ושמת משענתי על פני הנער *) עולא רמי כתיב °בלע המות לנצח וכתיב °כי הנער בן מאה שנה ימות לא קשיא כאן בישראל כאן בעכו"ם ועובדי כוכבים מאי בעו התם דכתיב °ועמדו זרים ורעו צאנכם ובני נכר אכריכם וכורמיכם רב חסדא רמי כתיב °וחפרה הלבנה ובושה החמה וכתיב °והיה אור הלבנה כאור החמה ואור החמה יהיה שבעתים כאור שבעת הימים לא קשיא כאן לעולם הבא כאן לימות המשיח *ולשמואל דאמר אין בין העולם הזה לימות המשיח אלא שיעבוד מלכיות בלבד מאי איכא למימר אידי ואידי לעולם הבא ולא קשיא *כאן במחנה שכינה כאן במחנה צדיקים *רבא רמי כתיב °אני אמית ואחיה וכתיב מחצתי ואני ארפא השתא אחויי מחיי מרפא לא כל שכן אלא אמר הקב"ה מה שאני ממית אני מחיה כמו שמחצתי ואני ארפא *ת"ר אני אמית ואחיה יכול מיתה באחד וחיים באחד כדרך שהעולם נוהג ת"ל מחצתי ואני ארפא מה מכה ורפואה באחד אף מיתה וחיים באחד מכאן תשובה לאומרים אין תחיית המתים מן התורה דבר אחר בתחלה מה שאני ממית אני מחיה והדר מה שמחצתי ואני ארפא:

והקטר

*) [סנהדרין צא:]

רש"י

בועל נדה כטמא מת. סיפא דמתני' דלעיל היא: מצורע חמור מזב. למחנותיו כדאמרן וכן זב מטמא מת: יצא בעל קרי. מפרש ואזיל מאי היא: לא יצא מכלל טמא מת כו'. והכי משמע יצא בעל קרי מכלל זה דהנך לפי חומר טומאתן חומר שלוחן יצא בעל קרי שאע"פ שטמא מת חמור ממנו שהוא טומאת שבעה וזה טומאת ערב אפילו הכי לענין מחנות בעל קרי חמור דעל כרחיך כי כתיב וכל זב לרבויי בעל קרי אתא לכלל זב וכל טמא לרבויי טמא שרץ לכלל טמא מת אתא דכל חד וחד למאי דדמי ליה מדמינן ליה ובעל קרי דומה לזב שהטומאה יוצאה עליו מגופו: ויצא אל מחוץ למחנה. בבעל קרי כתיב כי יהיה בך איש וגו': הכי גרסינן ויצא אל מחוץ למחנה זו מחנה שכינה ולא יבא אל תוך המחנה זו מחנה לויה מכאן שבעל קרי משתלח חוץ לשתי מחנות דקאמר קרא שאם נטמא בעזרה יצא משתיהן: אמר ליה אכתי לא עיילתיה אפיקתיה. עדיין לא הכנסתו למחנה לויה וכבר הוצאתו ממנה דמדקאמרת לא יבא לתוכה מכלל דעומד חוצה לה וקאמר לא יכנס והא אכתי לא אישתעי בזה שיצא ממחנה שכינה ועומד במחנה לויה לשלחו ממנה וקא מזהר ליה שלא יכנס כאילו כבר יצא אכתי לא אעיילתיה כלומר עדיין לא דיבר על כניסתו מה תהא עליה אפיקתיה ודיבר עליו כאילו יצא. ל"א גרסי' אכתי לא אפיקתיה אעילתי' עדיין לא הוצרכתו לצאת ממחנה לויה וכבר הזהרתו שלא יכנס והיינו אעילתיה כבר אתה מדבר בכניסתו: אלא אימא הכי ויצא אל מחוץ למחנה זו מחנה לויה. וכשבא לצאת ממנה אל יכנס במחנה שכינה ואי לא הוו כתיבי שתי מחנות הוה מוקמינא ליה בעומד במחנה שכינה ומצריכו לצאת ממנה אבל עומד במחנה לויה אין משתלח והשתא דכתבינן שתי מחנות על כרחיך הכי תוקמא: אם כן. נימא וישלחו מן המחנה ולא יבא אל תוך ולישתוק: מנקבן בסכין. שיצא הרעי שאם יניחנו בתוכן יסריחו קודם שתחשך ולשון מיחוי שמוציא פרש רכה דנמחת בתוכה דנפי"ר בלע"ז כמו וממחה ושופך (מעשר שני פ"ה מ"א) וכמו המחהו וגמעו (לעיל דף לה.) לישנא אחרינא מיחוי לשון נקיבה וחיבול כמו תמחה את זכר עמלק (דברים כה): שירקא דמעיא. ליחה האדוקה במעים שיוצא מהן בדוחק בסכין ובלע"ז לימו"ן מיחוי לשון דבר בזוי כדמפרש טעמא וחרבות מחים: רשיעא. אלמא דבר רע ושטי הוא: ורעו כבשים כדברם. כבשים ישראל: כמדובר בם. כמה שהובטחו על ידי נביא: מאי כמדובר בם. מה היא אותה הבטחה ומפרש לה סיפא דקרא היינו הבטחה וחרבות מחים גרים יאכלו צדיקים עד הנה כגרים ותושבים: אי כתיב חרבות מחים. ה"א סיפא דקרא פירוש לרישא כדקאמרת אבל השתא דכתב וחרבות לאו פירושא דרישא הוא אלא מילתא אחריתי היא: אלא. כמדובר בם דרישא היינו כרב חננאל כמדובר באליהו ואלישע שהחיו את המתים כך יחיו כל הצדיקים את המתים ירעו ורעו לגזירה שוה: ויעני ושפט בבשן. ושפט הוא אביו של אלישע דכתיב אלישע בן שפט: ושמת משענתי. באלישע כתיב על שהחיה בן השונמית: ובלע המות. יבולע מלאך המות שלא ישלוט בישראל. כתיב ובלע המות וגו': ובושה החמה. שלא תאיר: יהיה שבעתים כאור שבעת הימים. שבעתי' הן ארבעים ותשע וכתיב כאור שבעת הימים ארבעים ותשע כאור שבעת ימים של עכשיו נמצא עודף על אור של עכשיו ג' מאות וארבעים ושלשה: בעולם הבא. וחפרה הלבנה ובושה החמה שלא יהא בעולם אלא זיו זוהר ומראה שכינה: לימות המשיח. יהיה אור הלבנה כאור החמה: ולשמואל. דאמר ימות המשיח אין משתנין משל עכשיו מה הוא מקיים והיה אור הלבנה כאור החמה: כתיב אני אמית ואחיה מחצתי ואני ארפא. כיון שאמר שהמתים הוא מחיה פשיטא דהמחוצים יכול לרפאות אלא הא אתא לאשמועינן דלא תימא אמית ואחיה לאו דמתים חיים קאמר אלא אני אמית את המתים ואני מחיה וזן את החיים ובורא את הנולדים להכי כתיב בתריה מחצתי ואני ארפא כשם שמה שמחצתי אני ארפא דאין רפואה אלא במוכה כך אותו עצמו שאני ממית אני מחיה: מיתה באחד וחיים באחד. אני ממית את המתים ואני מחיה וזן את החיים: הכי גרסינן דבר אחר בתחלה מה שאני ממית אני מחיה והדר מה שאני מחצתי אני ארפא. שכדרך שהן מתים חגרים סומים אלמים כך הן חיין במומן ואחר כך מתרפאים כדכתיב אז ידלג כאיל פסח (ישעיה לה):

כשירין

עין משפט נר מצוה

[יג א ב מיי' פ"ג מהל' ביאת מקדש הלכה ח ועי' בכסף משנה דלהרמב"ם וגם לסמג לא היה הגירסא הא"ל אכתי לא עיילתיה וכו' אלא אימא וכו' ע"ש]:

רבינו חננאל

קרי באונס מטמא: ת"ש מסיפא ובועל נדה כטמא מת למאי אילימא לטומאה הא בהדיא כתיב בתרוייהו טומאת שבעה אלא לאו למחנותם כשם שטמא מת חוץ למחנה אחת כך בועל נדה חוץ למחנה אחת ומדסיפא למחנותם רישא נמי למחנותם קשיא לר' יוחנן ומשני מידי איריא רישא לטומאה סיפא למחנותם: ת"ש מצורע חמור מזב וזב חמור מטמא מת יצא בעל קרי שטמא מת חמור ממנו מאי לאו יצא מכלל זב ונכנס לטומאת מת ואע"פ שטמא מת חמור ממנו מדקתני הכי שמע' מינה שבועל נדה כטמא מת חוץ למחנה אחת ומשני לא יצא ממחנה טמא מת ונכנס למחנה זב להשתלח חוץ לשתי מחנות ואע"ג שטמא מת חמיר ממנו הואיל ובעל קרי טומאה מגופו יוצא לזב מוקמינן ליה: תאני תנא קמיה דרב יצחק ויצא אל מחוץ למחנה זו מחנה שכינה לא יבוא אל תוך המחנה זו מחנה (שכינה) [לויה] אמר ליה אכתי לא אפיקתיה (אלא) עיילתיה פי' מכדי הני קראי בבעל קרי כתיבי ובעל קרי נתרבה מזב דטומאה יוצא מגופו וחוץ לשתי מחנות משתלח כמו הזב ועדיין לא אפיקתיה אלא ממחנה שכינה וצריכת עוד לאפוקיה ממחנה לויה וקודם שתוציאו ממחנה לויה חזרת ואמרת לא יבוא אל תוך המחנה זו מחנה שכינה מכלל דבמחנה לויה נכנס ואתה מזהירו שלא יכנס ממחנה לויה למחנה שכינה עדיין לא יצא ממחנה לויה ואתה צריך להוציאו עוד אלא כך אמור ויצא אל מחוץ למחנה זו מחנה שכינה לא יבוא אל תוך המחנה זו מחנה לויה כלומר לא יבוא ממחנה ישראל לתוך מחנה לויה: ומתקיף רבינא דלמא בעל קרי אינו משתלח אלא חוץ למחנה שכינה והני קראי לחוביה חד קרא בעשה והוא ויצא וחד קרא והוא לא יבוא בלאו ללמד כי בעל קרי הנכנס למחנה שכינה עובר בעשה ולא תעשה ודחי' אם כן נכתוב רחמנא ויצא אל מחוץ למחנה לא יבוא תו אמאי כתיב אל תוך המחנה ללמד שהתורה הזהירה על המחנה אחרת: מיחוי קרביו מנקבן בסכין להוציא הרעי פי' שירקא דמעיא השומן הדומה למוח ודבוק במעים כמו הפרש הדבוק במעים ואינו יתפרק אלא בגרירה אלא בסכין כמו הרשעים שמחזקין בנכסי הטובים כתיב חרבות מחים גרים יאכלו פי' וחרבות נכסי מחים הרשעים גרים יאכלו הצדיקים כלומר נכסי הרשעים הצדיקים יאכלו אותם: אמר רב חיננא עתידין הצדיקים להחיות את המתים כתיב

מסורת הש"ס

[זבים פ"ה מ"א יומא ו.]
[צ"ל ומותר]
דברים כג
[צ"ל אלעזר]
ישעיה ה
שם
מיכה ז
דה"ב כ
מ"ב ג
שם א יז
זכריה ח
מ"ב ד
ישעיה כה
שם סה
שם סא
שם כד
שם ל
ברכות לד: שבת סג. וש"נ
[סנהדרין צא:]
דברים לב
סנהדרין צא: [ע"ש]

גליון הש"ס

גמ' כאן במחנה שכינה. עי' ילקוט תהלים טו בפסוק כי צדיק ה':

Continuation of translation from previous page as indicated by ◁

—Said Abaye: *'And the waste places of the fat ones shall wanderers eat'*. Said Raba to him, If *'the waste places'* were written, it would be well as you say;[9] since, however, *'and the waste places'* is written, this states another thing. Rather, said Raba: [It is to be explained] as R. Ḥananel said in Rab's name. For R. Ḥananel said in Rab's name: The righteous are destined to resurrect the dead. [For] here it is written, *'Then shall the lambs feed* kedobram', while elsewhere
c it is written, *Then shall Bashan and Gilead feed as in the days of old.*[1] [Now] Bashan means Elisha, who came from Bashan, as it is said, *and Janai and Shaphat in Bashan,*[2] while it is written, *Elisha the son of Shaphat is here, who poured water on the hands of Elijah.*[3] [Again,] Gilead alludes to Elijah, for it is said, *And Elijah the Tishbite, who was of the settlers of Gilead, said* [*unto Ahab*].[4]

R. Samuel b. Naḥmani said in R. Jonathan's name: The righteous are destined to resurrect the dead, for it is said, *There shall yet old men and old women sit in the broad places of Jerusalem, every man with his staff in his hand for very age;*[5] and it is written, *and lay my staff upon the face of the child.*[6]

'Ulla opposed [two verses]. It is written, *He will swallow up death for ever;*[7] but it is written, *For the youngest shall die a hundred years old?*[8] There is no difficulty: there the reference is to Israel; here, to heathens. But what business have the heathens there? —Because it is written, *And strangers shall stand and feed your flocks, and aliens shall be your plowmen and your vinedressers.*[9]

R. Ḥisda opposed [two verses]. It is written, *Then the moon shall be confounded, and the sun ashamed;*[10] whereas it is written, *Moreover the light of the moon shall be as the light of the sun, and the light of the sun shall be sevenfold, as the light of the seven days?*[11] There is no difficulty: the former refers to the world to come;[12] the latter to the days of the Messiah.[13] But according to Samuel, who maintained, This world differs from the Messianic age only in respect of the servitude to governments,[14] what can be said?—Both refer to the world to come, yet there is no difficulty: one refers to the camp of the righteous; the other, to the camp of the *Shechinah*.

d Raba opposed [two verses]: It is written, *I kill, and I make alive;*[1] whilst it is also written, *I have wounded, and I heal:*[2] seeing that He even resurrects, how much the more does He heal![3] But the Holy One, blessed be He, said thus: What I put to death I make alive, just as I wounded and I heal [the same person].[4]

Our Rabbis taught: *'I kill, and I make alive'*: You might say, I kill one person and give life to another, as the world goes on.[5] Therefore it is stated, *'I have wounded, and I heal'*: just as the wounding and the healing [obviously] refer to the same person, so death and life refer to the same person. This refutes those who maintain that resurrection is not intimated in the Torah.[6] Another interpretation: At first what I slay I resurrect;[7] and then, what I wounded I will heal.[8]

(9) The second part of the verse being explanatory of the first.
c (1) Mic. VII, 14. (2) I Chron. V, 12. (3) II Kings III, 11. (4) I Kings XVII, 1. Now both Elijah and Elisha resurrected the dead (v. ibid. IV; I Kings XVII, 21 seq.) and *'feed'* is therefore understood to allude to this metaphorically; hence the same meaning is assigned to *'feed'* in the first verse too, *'the lambs'* being the righteous. (5) Zech. VIII, 4. (6) II Kings IV, 29. The staff was employed to revive the child (ibid. seq.), and the same purpose is assumed for it in the first verse. (7) Isa. XXV, 8. (8) Ibid. LXV, 20. (9) Ibid. LXI, 5. (10) Ibid. XXIV, 23. (11) Ibid. XXX, 26. (12) Then the sun and the moon shall be ashamed—i.e., fade into insignificance—because of the light radiating from the righteous (Rashi in Sanh. 91*b*). (13) V. Sanh., 90*a*, n. 3. (14) I.e., delivery from oppression.
d (1) Deut. XXII, 39. (2) Ibid. (3) Why then state it? V. Sanh. 91*b* and notes a.l. in the Sonc. ed.: the point of the difficulty is explained there differently. (4) As explained in the next passage. (5) People dying and others being born. (6) V. Sanh., 90*a*, n. 5. and 90*b*, n. 12. (7) I.e., in the same state. (8) After their resurrection I will heal them of the blemishes they possessed in their former life.

[יג א ב מיי' פ"ג מהל' ביאת מקדש הלכה ח ועי' בכסף משנה דלהרמב"ם וגם לסמג לא היה הגירסא הא"ל אכתי לא עיילתיה וכו' אלא אימא וכו' ע"ש]:

*בועל נדה כטמא מת למאי אילימא לטומאתם האי טומאת שבעה כתיב ביה והאי טומאת שבעה כתיב ביה אלא לאו למחנותם ומדסיפא למחנותם הוי רישא נמי למחנותם מידי איריא הא כדאיתא והא כדאיתא מיתיבי מצורע חמור מזב וזב חמור מטמא מת יצא בעל קרי שטמא מת חמור ממנו מאי יצא לאו יצא מכלל זב ובא לכלל טמא מת דהא טמא מת חמור ממנו ומותר במחנה לויה לא יצא ממחנה טמא מת ונכנס למחנה זב ואע"ג דטמא מת חמור ממנו (*דמותר) במחנה לויה למאי דדמי לי' מדמינן ליה תני תנא קמיה דרב יצחק בר אבדימי °ויצא אל מחוץ למחנה [א] זו מחנה שכינה לא יבא אל תוך המחנה [ב] זו מחנה לויה מכאן לבעל קרי שיצא חוץ לשתי מחנות אמר לי' אכתי לא עיילתיה אפיקתיה לישנא אחרינא אכתי לא אפיקתיה עיילתיה אלא אימא מחוץ למחנה זו מחנה לויה לא יבא אל תוך המחנה זו מחנה שכינה מתקיף לה רבינא אימא אידי ואידי למחנה שכינה ולעבור עליו בעשה ולא תעשה אם כן לימא קרא ויצא אל מחוץ למחנה ולא יבא אל תוך המחנה למה לי שמע מינה ליתן לו מחנה אחרת: ומיחוי קרביו וכו': מאי מיחוי קרביו רב הונא אמר שמנקבן בסכין (רב) חייא בר רב אמר שירקא דמעייא דנפקא אגב דוחקא דסכינא אמר ר' (*אליעזר) מאי טעמא דחייא בר רב דכתיב °וחרבות מחים גרים יאכלו מאי משמע כדמתרגם רב יוסף ונכסיהן דרשיעיא צדיקיא יחסנון °ורעו כבשים כדברם אמר מנשיא בר ירמיה אמר רב כמדובר בם מאי כמדובר בם אמר אביי וחרבות מחים גרים יאכלו אמר ליה רבא בשלמא אי כתיב חרבות כדקאמרת השתא דכתיב וחרבות מילתא אחריתי קאמר אלא אמר רבא כדרב חננאל דאמר רב חננאל אמר רב עתידין צדיקים שיחיו את המתים כתיב הכא ורעו כבשים כדברם וכתיב התם °ירעו בשן וגלעד כימי עולם בשן זה אלישע הבא מן הבשן שנאמר °ויעני יושפט בבשן וכתיב °פה אלישע בן שפט אשר יצק מים על ידי אליהו גלעד זה אליהו שנאמר °ויאמר אליהו התשבי מתושבי גלעד וגו' אמר ר' שמואל בר נחמני א"ר יונתן עתידים צדיקים שיחיו מתים שנאמר °עוד ישבו זקנים וזקנות ברחבות ירושלם ואיש משענתו בידו מרוב ימים וכתיב °ושמת משענתי על פני הנער *) עולא רמי כתיב °בלע המות לנצח וכתיב °כי הנער בן מאה שנה ימות לא קשיא כאן בישראל כאן בעכו"ם ועובדי כוכבים מאי בעו התם דכתיב °ועמדו זרים ורעו צאנכם ובני נכר אכריכם וכורמיכם רב חסדא רמי כתיב °וחפרה הלבנה ובושה החמה וכתיב °והיה אור הלבנה כאור החמה ואור החמה יהיה שבעתים כאור שבעת הימים לא קשיא כאן לעולם הבא כאן לימות המשיח *ולשמואל דאמר אין בין העולם הזה לימות המשיח אלא שיעבוד מלכיות בלבד מאי איכא למימר אידי ואידי לעולם הבא ולא קשיא °כאן במחנה שכינה כאן במחנה צדיקים *רבא רמי כתיב °אני אמית ואחיה וכתיב מחצתי ואני ארפא השתא אחויי מחיי מרפא לא כל שכן אלא אמר הקב"ה מה שאני ממית אני מחיה כמו שמחצתי ואני ארפא *ת"ר אני אמית ואחיה יכול מיתה באחד וחיים באחד כדרך שהעולם נוהג ת"ל מחצתי ואני ארפא מה מכה ורפואה באחד אף מיתה וחיים באחד מכאן תשובה לאומרים אין תחיית המתים מן התורה דבר אחר בתחלה מה שאני ממית אני מחיה והדר מה שמחצתי ואני ארפא:

*) [סנהדרין צא:]

והקטר

[זבים פ"ב מ"א יומא ו.] [צ"ל ומותר] [צ"ל אלעזר] דברים כג / ישעי' ה / מיכה ז / מ"ב ג / שם א יז / זכריה ח / מ"ב ד / ישעי' כה / שם סה / שם סה / שם כד / שם ל / ברכות לד: שבת סג. וש"נ / [סנהדרין צא:] / דברים לב / סנהדרין צא: [ע"ש]

גליון הש"ס גמ' כאן במחנה שכינה. עי' ילקוט תהלים מ' בפסוק כי צדיק ה':

רש"י

בועל נדה כטמא מת. סיפא דמתני' דלעיל היא: מצורע חמור מזב. למחיצותיו כדאמרינן ובן זב מטמא מת: יצא בעל קרי. מפרש ואזיל מאי היא: לא יצא מכלל טמא מת כו'. והכי משמע יצא בעל קרי מכלל זה דהכך לפי חומר חומר טומאתן חומר שלוחן יצא בעל קרי שאע"פ שטמא מת חמור ממנו שהוא טומאת שבעה וזה טומאת ערב אפילו הכי לענין מחנות בעל קרי חמור דעל כרחיך כי כתיב וכל זב לרבויי בעל קרי אתא לכלל זב וכל טמא לרבויי טמא שרץ לכלל טמא מת אתא דכל חד וחד למאי דדמי ליה מדמינן ליה ובעל קרי דומה לזב שהטומאה יוצאה עליו מגופו: ויצא אל מחוץ למחנה. בבעל קרי כתיב כי יהיה בך איש וגו' הכי גרסינן ויצא אל מחוץ למחנה זו מחנה שכינה ולא יבא אל תוך המחנה זו מחנה לויה מכאן שבעל קרי משתלח חוץ לשתי מחנות דקאמר קרא שאם נטמא בעזרה יצא משתיהן: אמר ליה אכתי לא עיילתיה אפיקתיה. עדיין לא הכנסתו למחנה לויה וכבר הוצאתו ממנה דמדקאמרת לא יבא לתוכה מכלל דעומד חוצה לה וקאמר לא יכנס והא אכתי לא אישתעי בזה שיצא ממחנה שכינה ועומד במחנה לויה לשלחו ממנה וקא מזהר ליה שלא יכנס כאילו כבר יצא אכתי לא עיילתיה כלומר עדיין לא דיבר על כניסתו מה תהא עליה אפיקתיה ודיבר עליו כאילו יצא. ל"א גרסי' אכתי לא אפיקתיה עיילתיה עדיין לא הזהרתו לצאת ממחנה לויה וכבר הזהרתו שלא יכנס והיינו עיילתיה כבר אתה מדבר בכניסתו: אלא אימא הכי ויצא אל מחוץ למחנה זו מחנה לויה. וכשבא לצאת ממנה אל יכנס במחנה שכינה ואי לא הוו כתיבי שתי מחנות הוה מוקמינא ליה בעומד במחנה שכינה ומצריכו לצאת ממנה אבל עומד במחנה לויה אין משתלח והשתא דכתבינן שתי מחנות על כרחיך הכי תוקמא: אם כן. לימא וישלחו מן המחנה ולא יבא אל תוך ולישתוק: מנקבן בסכין. שיצא הרעי שאם יניחנו בתוכן יסריחו קודם שתחתך ולשון מיחוי שמוציא פרש רכה דנמחת בתוכה דשנפי"ר בלע"ז כמו וממחה ושופך (מעשר שני פ"ה מ"ח) וכמו המחהו וגמעו (נזיר דף לה.) לישנא אחרינא מיחוי לשון נקיבה ויכול כמו תמחה את זכר עמלק (דברים כה): שירקא דמעיא. ליחה הלזוקה במעים שיוצא מהן בדוחק בסכין ובלע"ז לימו"ן מיחוי לשון דבר בזוי כדמפרש טעמא וחרבות מחים: רשיעא. אלמא דבר רע ושטי הוא: ורעו כבשים כדברם. כבשים ישראל: כמדובר בם. כמה שהובטחו על ידי נביא: מאי כמדובר בם. מה היא אותה הבטחה ומפרש לה סיפא דקרא היינו הבטחה וחרבות מחים גרים יאכלו לדיקים עד הגה כגרים ותושבים: אי כתיב חרבות מחים. ה"א סיפא דקרא פירוש לרישא כדקאמרת אבל השתא דכתב וחרבות לאו פירושא דרישא הוא אלא מילתא אחריתי היא: אלא. כמדובר בם דרישא הייט כרב חננאל כמדובר באליהו ואלישע שהחיו את המתים כך יחיו כל הלדיקים את המתים ירעו ורעו לגזירה שוה: ויעני ושפט בבשן. ושפט הוא אביו של אלישע דכתיב אלישע בן שפט: ושמת משענתי. באלישע כתיב על שהחיה בן השונמית: ובלע המות. יבולע מלאך המות שלא ישלוט בישראל. כתיב ובלע המות וגו': ובושה החמה. שלא תאיר: יהיה שבעתים כאור שבעת הימים. שבעתי' הן ארבעים ותשע וכתיב כאור שבעת הימים ארבעים ותשע כאור שבעת ימים של עכשיו נמלא עודף על אור של עכשיו ג' מאות וארבעים ושלשה: בעולם הבא. וחפרה הלבנה ובושה החמה שלא יהא בעולם אלא זיו זוהר ומראה שכינה: לימות המשיח. יהיה אור הלבנה כאור החמה: ולשמואל. דאמר ימות המשיח אין משתנין משל עכשיו מה הוא מקיים והיה אור הלבנה כאור החמה: כתיב אני אמית ואחיה מחצתי ואני ארפא. כיון שאמר שהמתים הוא מחיה פשיטא דהמחולים יכול לרפאות אלא הא אתא לאשמועינן דלא תימא אמית ואחיה לאו דמתים חיים קאמר אלא אני אמית את המתים ואני מחיה וזן את החיים ובורא את הנולדים להכי כתיב בתריה מחצתי ואני ארפא כשם שמה שמחצתי אני ארפא דאין רפואה אלא במוכה כך אותו עלמו שאני ממית אני מחיה: מיתה באחד וחיים באחד. אני ממית את המתים ואני מחיה וזן את החיים: הכי גרסינן דבר אחר בתחלה מה שאני ממית אני מחיה והדר מה שאני מחלתי אני ארפא. שבדרך שהן מתים חגרים סומים אלמים כך הן חיין במומן ואחר כך מתרפאים כדכתיב אז ידלג כאיל פסח (ישעיה לה):

כשירין

רבינו חננאל

קרי באונס מטמא: ת"ש מסיפא ובועל נדה כטמא מת למאי אילימא לטומאה הא בהדיא כתיב בתרוייהו טומאת שבעה אלא לאו למחנותם כשם שטמא מת חוץ למחנה אחת כך בועל נדה חוץ למחנה אחת ומדסיפא למחנותם רישא נמי למחנותם קשיא לר' יורנן ומשני מידי איריא רישא לטומאה סיפא למחנותם: ת"ש מצורע חמור מזב וזב חמור מטמא מת יצא בעל קרי שטמא מת חמור ממנו מאי לאו יצא מכלל זב ונכנס לטומאת מת ואע"פ שטמא מת חמור ממנו מדקתני הכי שמעי' מינה שבועל נדה כטמא מת חוץ למחנה אחת ומשני לא יצא ממחנה טמא מת ונכנס למחנה זב להשתלח חוץ לשתי מחנות ואע"ג שטמא מת חמור ממנו הואיל ובעל קרי טומאה מגופו יוצא לזב מוקמינן ליה: תאני תנא קמיה דרב יצחק ויצא אל מחוץ למחנה זו מחנה שכינה לא יבוא אל תוך המחנה זו מחנה (שכינה) [לויה] אמר ליה אכתי לא אפיקתיה (אלא) עיילתיה פי' מכדי הני קראי בבעל קרי כתיבי ובעל קרי נתרבה מזב דטומאה יוצא מגופו וחוץ לשתי מחנות משתלח כמו הזב ועדיין לא אפיקתיה אלא ממחנה שכינה וצריכת עוד לאפוקיה ממחנה לויה וקודם שתוציאו ממחנה לויה חזרת ואמרת לא יבוא אל תוך המחנה זו מחנה שכינה מכלל דבמחנה לויה נכנס ואתה מזהירו שלא יכנס ממחנה לויה למחנה שכינה עדיין לא יצא ממחנה לויה ואתה צריך להוציאו עוד אלא כך אמור ויצא אל מחוץ למחנה זו מחנה שכינה לא יבוא אל תוך המחנה זו מחנה לויה כלומר לא יבוא ממחנה ישראל לתוך מחנה לויה: ומתקיף רבינא דלמא בעל קרי אינו משתלח אלא חוץ למחנה שכינה והני קראי לחייביה חד קרא בעשה והוא ויצא וחד קרא והוא לא יבוא בלאו ללמד כי בעל קרי הנכנס למחנה שכינה עובר בעשה ולא תעשה ודחי' אם כן נכתוב רחמנא ויצא אל מחוץ למחנה לא יבוא תו אמאי כתיב אל תוך המחנה ללמד שהתורה הזהירה על המחנה אחרת: מיחוי קרביו מנקבן בסכין להוציא הרעי פי' שירקא דמעיא השמן הדומה למוח ודבוק במעים כמו הפרש הדבוק במעים ואינו נפרק אלא בגרירה אלא בסכין כמו הרשעים שמחזיקן בנכסי הטובים כתיב וחרבות מחים גרים יאכלו פי' וחרבות נכסי מחים הרשעים גרים יאכלו הצדיקים כלומר נכסי הרשעים הצדיקים יאכלו אותם: אמר רב חננא עתידין הצדיקים להחיות את המתים כתיב

An objection is raised: [68a] He who has intercourse with a *niddah*[7] is like he who is unclean by the dead.[8] In respect of what: shall we say, in respect of their uncleanness,—but uncleanness for seven [days] is written in connection with the one, and uncleanness for seven days is written in connection with the other?[9]
a Hence it must surely be in respect of their camp;[1] and since the second clause is in respect of their camps, the first clause too is in respect of their camps?—What argument is this! the one is as stated, and the other is as stated.[2]

An objection is raised: A leper is more stringent than a *zab*,[3] and a *zab* is more stringent than he who is unclean by the dead.[4] A *ba'al ḳeri* is excepted, for he who is unclean by the dead is more stringent than he. What does 'is excepted' mean? Surely [it means], he is excepted from the rule of a *zab* and is included[5] in the rule of him who is unclean by the dead, seeing that he who is unclean by the dead is more stringent than he, and [yet] he is permitted within the Levitical camp?—No: [it means that] he is excepted from the camp of him who is unclean by the dead and is included in the camp of a *zab*; and though he who is unclean by the dead is more stringent than he, and [yet] he may enter the Levitical camp, [nevertheless] we compare him [the *ba'al ḳeri*] to what is like himself.[6]

A tanna recited before R. Isaac b. Abdimi: *Then he shall go abroad out of the camp*:[7] this means the camp of the *Shechinah*;[8] *he shall not come within the camp*:[9] this means the Levitical camp. From this [we learn] that a *ba'al ḳeri* must go without the two camps.[10] Said he to him, You have not yet brought him in that you should [already] expel him![11] Another version: you have not yet expelled
b him, and [already] you [discuss whether] he should enter![1] Rather say: *'abroad out of the camp'*—this is the Levitical camp; *'he shall not come within the camp'*—that is the camp of the *Shechinah*. To this Rabina demurred: Assume that both refer to the camp of the *Shechinah*, [it being repeated] so that he should violate an affirmative command and a negative command on its account?—If so, let Scripture say, *'Then he shall go abroad out of the camp'* and *'he shall not enter'*: what is the purpose of *'within the camp'?* Infer from it that it is to prescribe another camp for him.[2]

AND THE CLEANSING [MIḤUY] OF ITS BOWELS. What is THE CLEANSING OF ITS BOWELS?—R. Huna said: [It means] that we pierce them with a knife.[3] Ḥiyya b. Rab said: [It means the removal of] the viscous substance of the bowels, which comes out through the pressure of the knife. R. Eleazar observed, What is Ḥiyya b. Rab's reason? Because it is written, *and the waste places of the fat ones* [meḥim] *shall wanderers eat*.[4] How does this imply it?—As R. Joseph[5] translated: and the estates of the wicked shall the righteous inherit.[6]

Then shall the lambs feed as in their pasture [kedobram]:[7] Menassia b. Jeremiah interpreted it in Rab's name: As was spoken about them [*kimedubbar bam*].[8] What means 'as was spoken about them'?

(7) V. Glos. (8) This is the conclusion of the Mishnah just quoted, Zab. V, 11. (9) V. Lev. XV, 24; Num. XIX, 11.

a (1) Both are sent out of the camp of the *Shechinah* only. (2) Lit., 'as it is',—i.e., each clause is governed by its own particular requirements. (3) The leper being sent out of all three camps, whereas the *zab* is sent out of two only; *supra 67a*. (4) The last-named being sent out of the camp of the *Shechinah* only. (5) Lit., 'enters'. (6) Viz., a *zab*. Thus the meaning of the Baraitha is this: A leper, a *zab*, and he who is unclean by the dead follow the rule that the more stringent the uncleanness the further away is he sent; but a *ba'al ḳeri* is excepted from this rule, and though his uncleanness is less than that of a person unclean by the dead, he is sent further away, because he must be compared to a *zab*, since both are unclean through bodily discharge. (7) Deut. XXIII, 11; the reference is to a *ba'al ḳeri*. (8) The Sanctuary. (9) Ibid. (10) I.e., if he is in the Temple ('the camp of the *Shechinah*') when he becomes a *ba'al ḳeri*, he must leave both that and the Temple mount ('the Levitical camp'). (11) I.e., since Scripture states that he must not enter the Levitical camp, it follows that he is without: how then say that he is inside? (Rashi).

b (1) I.e., you have not yet ordered him to leave the Levitical camp, and yet you are already forbidding him to enter. (2) From which he must depart. (3) To allow the dung to fall out. (4) Isa. V, 17. (5) [V. Targum Version a.l. The Targum on the Prophets is ascribed by some to R. Joseph. V. B.K., 3b, n. b9.] (6) Thus he translates *'meḥim'* the wicked, i.e., the repulsive; similarly *'miḥuy'* refers to the repulsive matter, viz., the viscous substance. (7) Ibid. One part of the verse having been quoted and translated, the Gemara proceeds to discuss the other half. (8) I.e., in accordance with the promise made: *'lambs'* is understood as meaning Israel.

◁ *For the continuation of the English translation of this page see overleaf.*

since it defiles [even] accidentally?[7]—I will tell you: [67b] To that extent[8] a *zab* too is certainly defiled through an accident, in accordance with R. Huna. For R. Huna said: The first discharge[9] of a *zab* defiles [when it is caused] by an accident.[10]

What is the greater stringency of a leper over a *zab?*[3] Because
a he requires *peri'ah*[1] and rending [of garments], and he is forbidden sexual intercourse.[2] On the contrary, a *zab* is more stringent, because he defiles couch and seat,[3] and he defiles earthen vessels by *hesset?*[4]—Scripture saith, [instead of] 'a leper', '*and every* [kol] *leper'*[5] to include a *ba'al ḳeri;*[6] and a leper is more stringent than a *ba'al ḳeri*, and what is his greater stringency? As we have stated.[7] On the contrary, a *ba'al ḳeri* is more stringent, because he defiles by the smallest quantity [of semen]?[8]—He agrees with R. Nathan. For it was taught, R. Nathan said on the authority of R. Ishmael: A *zab* requires [a discharge of matter] sufficient for the closing of the orifice of the membrum, but the Sages did not concede this to him. And he holds that a *ba'al ḳeri* is assimilated to a *zab*.[9] What is the purpose of '*and every* [kol] *leper'?*[10]—Since '*every one* [kol] *that hath an issue*' is written, '*every* [kol] *leper*' too is written.[11]

Now [as for] R. Judah, [surely] R. Simeon says well?[12]—He requires that[13] for what was taught; R. Eliezer said: You might think, if *zabin* and lepers forced their way through and entered the Temple Court at a Passover sacrifice which came in unclean-
b ness,[1]—you might think that they are culpable; therefore it is stated, ['*Command the children of Israel,*] *that they send out of the camp every leper, and every one that hath an issue* [zab], *and whosoever is unclean by the dead'*: when those who are unclean by the dead are sent out, *zabin* and lepers are sent out; when those who are unclean by the dead are not sent out, *zabin* and lepers are not sent out.

The Master said: '"*And every* [kol] *one that hath an issue*" is to include a *ba'al ḳeri*'. This supports R. Joḥanan. For R. Joḥanan said: The cellars [under the Temple] were not consecrated; and a *ba'al ḳeri* is sent without the two camps.[2]

An objection is raised: *A ba'al ḳeri* is like [a person defiled through] contact with a reptile. Surely that means in respect of their camp?[3]—No: [it means] in respect of their uncleanness.[4] [You say] 'In respect of their uncleanness!' [Surely] uncleanness until evening is written in connection with the one, and uncleanness until evening is written in connection with the other?[5] Hence it must surely mean in respect of their camp!—No: after all [it means] in respect of their uncleanness, and he informs us this: that a *ba'al ḳeri* is like [a person defiled through] the contact of the reptile: just as the contact of a reptile defiles [even] accidentally, so is a *ba'al ḳeri* defiled [when the semen is discharged] accidentally.[6]

(7) I.e., even if it touches the person by accident. But a discharge makes a man unclean as a *zab* only if it issues of its own accord. If, however, it is caused by an 'accident', e.g., physical over-exertion or highly-seasoned food, he is not unclean. (8) Lit., 'in such a manner' as that defilement caused by a reptile. (9) Lit., 'seeing'—of discharge. (10) He is not unclean as a *zab*, for a period of seven days, but only until evening, while a reptile too defiles until evening only.

a (1) Letting the hair grow long and neglected, v. Lev. XIII, 45. (2) V. M.Ḳ. 7b. (3) This is a technical phrase. He defiles that whereon he lies or sits, imposing such a high degree of uncleanness on it that if a man touches it he in turn becomes so unclean as to defile his garments, even if they did not touch it. But a leper, though he too defiles couch and seat, the degree of uncleanness is less, and the man who touches it becomes unclean only in so far that he in turn defiles food and drink, but not his garments, nor can he defile any other utensils by touch.—Rashi. But Maim. and others omit this passage, whence it appears that they do not accept this distinction; v. also Tosaf. a.l. s.v. משכב. (4) Lit., 'shaking'. A *zab* defiles an earthen vessel when he causes it to move through his weight, e.g., if it is standing on one end of a rickety bench and he sits down on the other, causing it to move upwards, as on a see-saw. (5) V. 67a, n. b5. (6) A man who has discharged semen. (7) Rashi understands this as part of the following question: Now what is his greater stringency—as stated? On the contrary etc. (8) Whereas for leprosy there must be at least as much as a bean (*geris*). (9) As it is written, *This is the law of him that hath an issue* (zab), *and of him from whom the flow of seed goeth out* (ba'al ḳeri)—Lev. XV, 32. Thus a *ba'al ḳeri* too requires a certain minimum; hence a leper is more stringent, and therefore a leper is mentioned in order to assign a third camp to him. (10) I.e., the '*kol*' written in connection with a leper. (11) For the sake of parallelism. (12) What then is the purpose of the verse quoted by R. Judah *supra* 67a? (13) *Sc.* the verse employed by R. Simeon for this purpose.

b (1) I.e., when the community as a whole was unclean. (2) Viz., the camp of the *Shechinah* (the place of the Sanctuary) and the Levitical camp, just like a *zab*. R. Joḥanan heard these two teachings from his master (Rashi). (3) I.e., just as a man who is defiled by a reptile is sent out from the camp of the *Shechinah* only, i.e., from the Temple, so is a *ba'al ḳeri*. (4) Neither is unclean for seven days, but only until the evening. (5) V. Lev. XI, 24; XV, 16. Hence the comparison is pointless and unnecessary. (6) V. *supra* 67a bottom and note a.l.

יא א מיי' פ"ב מהלכות מחוסרי כפרה הל"ה:
יב ב שם הלכה ט:
יג ג מיי' פ"ה מהלכות אבות הטומאה הל"ב:

כי האי גוונא זב נמי טמויי מטמי באונס כדרב הונא *דאמר רב הונא *ראיה ראשונה של זב מטמאה באונס מאי חומריה דמצורע מזב שכן טעון פריעה ופרימה ואסור בתשמיש המטה אדרבה זב חמור שכן (א) מטמא משכב ומושב ומטמא כלי חרס בהיסט אמר קרא זב וכל זב לרבות בעל קרי ומצורע חמור מבעל קרי ומאי חומריה כדאמרן אדרבה בעל קרי חמור שכן מטמא במשהו *סבר לה כר' נתן *דתניא ר' נתן אומר משום ר' ישמעאל זב צריך *כחתימת פי האמה *ולא הודו לו חכמים ואיתקש ליה בעל קרי לזב וכל צרוע למה לי *איידי דכתיב כל זב כתיב נמי כל צרוע ורבי יהודה שפיר קאמר רבי שמעון ההוא מיבעי ליה *לכדתניא רבי אליעזר אומר יכול דחקו זבין ומצורעין ונכנסו לעזרה בפסח הבא בטומאה יכול יהו חייבין ת"ל *וישלחו (במדבר ה) מן המחנה כל צרוע וכל זב וכל טמא לנפש בשעה שטמאי מתים משתלחין זבין ומצורעין משתלחין אין טמאי מתים משתלחין אין זבין ומצורעין משתלחין אמר מר זב וכל זב לרבו' בעל קרי מסייע ליה לר' יוחנן *דא"ר יוחנן מחילות לא נתקדשו *ובעל קרי משתלח חוץ לשתי מחנות מיתיבי *בעל קרי כמגע שרץ מאי לאו למחנותם לא לטומאתם האי טומאת ערב כתיב ביה והאי טומאת ערב כתיב ביה אלא לאו למחנותם לא לעולם לטומאתם והא קמשמע לן דבעל קרי כמגע שרץ מה מגע שרץ מטמא באונס אף בעל קרי מטמא באונס מיתיבי בועל

רש"י

זב נמי מטמא באונס. כגון בראיה ראשונה שאין בה אלא טומאת ערב דאיתקש לשכבת זרע דכתיב (ויקרא טו) זאת תורת הזב ואשר תצא ממנו שכבת זרע והיינו ראיה ראשונה דלא מנה ביה בהאי קרא אלא חדא זיבה דאזלינן בתר מניינא דקרא כדאמרינן במגילה (ד' ח:) מנה הכתוב שתים וקראו טמא כו': מטמאה באונס. מהאי היקש גופיה נפקא ליה לרב הונא מה קרי מטמא באונס אם ראה מחמת רוב מאכל ומשתה דגבי קרי לא כתיב מיעוטא אף ראיה ראשונה של זב מטמאה באונס: זוב דומה ללובן ביצה המוזרת שכבת זרע דומה ללובן ביצה שאינה מוזרת: פריעה. פריעת הראש גידול שיער: פרימה. בבגדים: ואסור בתשמיש המטה. כדכתיב (ויקרא יד) וישב מחוץ לאהלו ואין אהלו אלא אשתו למאן דאמר במועד קטן (ד' ז:) ק"ו לימי חלוטו איכא חומרא טובא ולמאן דאמר ימי ספרו דוקא אפ"ה חומרא מיהא היא דאילו זב לא מיתסר מידי בתשמיש: זב. עושה משכבו ומושבו אב הטומאה לטמא אדם הנוגע בו טומאה חמורה לטמא בגדים שעליו אע"פ שלא נגעו הבגדים במשכב אבל מצורע אע"ג דתניא בתורת כהנים עושה משכב ומושב לאו אב הטומאה לטמא אדם לטמא בגדים אלא לטמא אוכלין ומשקין: ומטמא כלי חרס בהיסטו. דכתיב (ויקרא טו) וכלי חרש אשר יגע בו הזב ישבר ותניא בתורת כהנים יכול אפילו נגע בו הזב מאחוריו יהא טמא תלמוד לומר אשר יגע בו ולהלן הוא אומר אשר תבושל בו מה בו האמור להלן מאוירו אף בו האמור כאן אינו מטמא במגע אלא מאוירו אם כן מאחר שלמדנו שמטמא אותו מאוירו מה ת"ל אשר יגע בו פירוש ומה חלק בו ומה הוסיף בו בכלי חרס בטומאת הזב מבשאר טומאות במגעו שהוא ככולו הוי אומר זה היסטו: ומטמינן זב וכל זב לרבות. קרי כזב: וכיון דאיתרבי בעל קרי לישתלח חוץ לשתי מחנות לא איצטריך מצורע דחמור מבעל קרי: ופרכינן מאי חומרא כדאמרן. וכיון דלא איצטריך וכתביה רחמנא ליתן לו מחנה שלישית אדרבה כו': במשהו. כעין חרדל ובפחות מכאן במסכת נדה (ד' מ:) ומצורע שיעורו כגריס בתורת כהנים: כחתימת פי האמה. כדי סתימת נקב פי אמתו ויליף לה מהחתים בשרו את זובו במסכת נדה (דף מג:): ואיתקש בעל קרי לזב. כדכתיב זאת תהיה תורת הזב ואשר תצא ממנו שכבת זרע מה זב צריך כחתימת פי האמה אף בעל קרי אלמא מצורע חמור דהואיל ליה פירכא דכל שהוא וכי איצטריך ליתן לו מחנה שלישית: וכל. דכתיב גבי מצורע מאי (כל) מרבי גבי דין מצורע: שפיר קאמר ר' שמעון. דמפיק ליה מההוא קרא דין שילוחין ולמה לי קרא אחרינא: ההוא. לצרוע וזב לכדרבי אליעזר אתי לאקשינהו לטמא מת לפוטרו מן ההיכרת בפסח הבא בטומאה ואע"ג דלא איפשרי להו לכתחלה בביאת מקדש: אין טמאי מתים משתלחין. כגון פסח הבא בטומאה דאיפשרו (*טמאי מתים לכתחלה כשרוב הציבור טמאי מתים כדכתיב איש וכו') כדלעיל בשמעתין: אין זבין ומצורעין משתלחין. שילוחן הראשון בכרת ומיהו לכתחלה לא איפשרו דהא טמא לנפש גלי רחמנא דאין ציבור נדחין הא בשאר טומאות נדחין מיהו אהני היקישא לפוטרן מן היכרת: מחילות (א) לא נתקדשו. הני תרתי מילי שמעינהו כי הדדי מרביה וכי הדדי אמרינהו מחילות ומערות שלתחת העזרה לא נתקדשו בקדושת עזרה: ובעל קרי משתלח כו'. והיינו כברייתא דהא איתקש לזב: לטומאתן. דאין טמא שבעה כזב וכטמא מת: טומאת ערב בהדיא כתיב ביה. כי תצא ממנו שכבת זרע ורחץ במים וגו' (ויקרא טו): מה שרץ מטמא באונס. אם נפל עליו שרץ מת: מטמא באונס. כגון אם ראה מחמת רוב מאכל ומשתה: בועל

תוספות

כי האי גוונא זב נמי טמויי מטמי באונס. תימה לרשב"א אכתי שרץ חמור שמטמא בכעדשה מה שאין בן בזב דכר' נתן מוקמי' לה דבעי חתימת פי האמה דהוי טפי אפילו מכגריס כדמוכח בסמוך ואור"י דאם היו מפוזרין כעדשה יהיה יותר מחתימת פי האמה ומגרים ודוחק ונראה לתרץ דאיכא למימר טמא מת יוכיח דבכות ופריך בסמוך לדרבה בבעל קרי חמור שכן מטמא במשהו לא שייך טמא מת יוכיח דהא אין משולח אלא חוץ למחנה אחת ושם רוצה שיהא מצורע משתלח חוץ לשתי מחנות כבעל קרי:

שכן טעון פריעה ופרימה. תימה לר"י אמאי לא קאמר נמי שכן מטמא בביאה הבא אל האהל: ואסור בתשמיש המטה. כמאן דאמר בפ"ק דמ"ק (ד' ז:) דמוחלט אסור בתשמיש המטה: שכן עושה משכב ומושב. פירש בקונטרס דהא דתניא בת"כ דמצורע עושה משכב ומושב לא לטמא אדם ובגדים *אלא לטמא אוכלין ומשקין אבל ליכא למימר דהא מיירי במצורע בימי ספרו דאינו עושה משכב ומושב כדקתני בהדיא בת"כ דהא אמר הכא דמשולח חוץ לג' מחנות ובשילהי מסכת נגעים (פי"ד מ"ג) תנן דבימי ספרו הוי כטמא שרץ אלמא אינו משולח אפי' חוץ למחנה לויה והא דקתני נמי התם ונכנס לפנים מן החומה לאו דוקא לפנים מן החומה ועוד דמסיק הכא שכן טעון פריעה ופרימה והיינו במוחלט והקשה הרב משה מפונטייז"א דתניא בתורת כהני' (*אשר ישכב) איש אותה פרט למצורעת ואי מצורע לא מטמא משכב ומושב למ"ל למעוטי מהיכי תיתי שתטמא את בועלה דמנדה לא ילפא שכן מטמאה משכב ומושב אלא ודאי מטמאה משכב ומושב להכי איצטריך קרא למעוטי ויש לומר דאסמכתא בעלמא היא ועוד הקשה מהא דאמר לזכר לרבות מצורע למעיינותיו אקשיה רחמנא לזב מה זב דאיתו מטמא במשא ט' והואיל ואיתקיש אין היקש למחצה ולמשכב ומושב נמי איתקש ולאו פירכא היא דאם כן למחנותם נמי נימא דאיתקש ואם כן מאי פריך הכא והא דתנן בפרק בתרא דמסכת זבין (פ"ה מ"ו) הנוגע בזב ובזבה במצורע כו' אחד הנוגע אחד המסיטו ואחד הנושא ואחד הנישא אלמא משמע דמצורע מטמא בהיסט ובמתניתין משמע דלא מטמא אור"ת דהא דקתני נישא דמשמע דמטמא בהיסט לא קאי אמצורע אלא אשארא*:

ואיתקש בעל קרי לזב. הכא משמע דבעל קרי נמי טמא מטעם ראיה ואומר ר"י דפליגא אההיא דריש המפלת (נדה דף כב.) דקאמר התם בעא מיניה רבא מרב הונא הרואה קרי בקיסם מהו אמר ליה ותיפוק ליה דהוא עצמו אינו מטמא אלא בחתימת פי האמה וקאמר למימרא דנוגע הוי פירוש מדבעי חתימת פי האמה אלמא משמע התם דמטעם נגיעה טמא ובפרק יוצא דופן (שם דף מב:) דקאמר שכבת זרע לרואה במשהו לנוגע בכעדשה פליגא אדשמעתא ודהמפלת: מחילות לא נתקדשו. וא"ת הא אמר בפ"ב דזבחים (דף כד.) נעקרה אבן ונעמד במקומה מהו כו' ומסיק לעולם פשיטא ליה דכי קדיש דוד רצפה עד ארעית תהומא קדיש וי"ל דבכילד צולין (לקמן דף פו.) מסקינן כי א"ר יוחנן בפתוחות לחול אבל פתוחות לקודש קודש: *האי טומאת שבעה כתיב ביה והאי טומאת כו'. הוי מצי לשנויי כדמשני בפ"ק (ב) דיומא (דף ו:) דלעולם לטומאת שבעה וסיפא איצטריכא ליה אלא שחמור הימנו בועל נדה שמטמא משכב ומושב לטמא אוכלין ומשקין: מיפרך

[פי' משנה למלך פ"ג מהלכות ביאת המקדש ה"ג]

[ועי' תוס' יומא ו: ד"ה שמטמא]

נדה לג. | שם מג: | [שם כב.] | [יבמות נד: וש"נ] | [לק' לה:] מנחות לה: | לקמן פו. [תמיד כז:] | זבין פ"ה [מ"ח יומא ו.] | לקמן פו.

הגהות הב"ח

(א) רש"י ד"ה מחילות. נ"ב עי' פ"ס כילד צולין כרש"י: (ב) תוס' ד"ה האי וכו' בפ"ק ל"ב דף ו' וע"ש בתוס' בד"ה סיפא:

הגהות הגר"א

(א) גמ' שכן מטמא משכב ומושב ומטמא כ"ח. נ"ב פרש"י וכל הנוסחים לא גרסי משכב אלא שכן מטמא כלי חרס כו':

גליון הש"ס

גמ' סבר לה כר' נ. עי' בנה כו ע"א תוס' ד"ה תוס' ד"ה שכן עושה וכו' אלא לטמא אוכלין. ועי' פ"ס ו' ע"ב תוס' ד"ה שמטמא: מגילה ח ע"א תוס' ד"ה ומה מצורע. נדה כד ע"ב תוס' ד"ה יכול:

רבינו חננאל

שנא' (דברים ה') שובו לכם לאהליכ' וכן מפורש במשקין [דף ז' ע"ב]: אדרבה זב חמור שכן מטמא משכב ומושב וכלי חרס בהיסט מה שאין כן במצורע ושניג' מכל זב אתה מרבה בעל קרי ששניהם כו' אתן יוצא מטפן ובבעל קרי מצורע חמור שכן טעון פריעה ופרימה ואסור בתשמיש [המטה] וא"ת בעל קרי חמור שמטמא במשהו מה שאין כן במצורע שהמצורע אינו מטמא [אלא] כגריס דתנן נתפו של בהרת כגריס הקילקי מרובע מקום הגריס תשע עדשות מקום עדשה ארבע שערות נמצאו ל"ו שערות זב נמי כר' נתן דאמר צריך כחתימת פי האמה ובעל קרי איתקש לזב דמוכל [של] זב קא מתרבי לשילוח מן המחנה כו': אמרינן ר' יהודה שפיר קאמר ליה ר"ש דלא צריכת לריביי להו שלש מחנות מולא יטמאו את מחניהם מושלחו מן המחנה קא מרבית להי אמר לך האי וישלחו מן המחנה מיבעי ליה לכדתניא ר' אליעזר אומר יכול דחקו זבין ומצורעין ונכנסו לעזרה בפסח הבא בטומאה יכול יהו חייבין ת"ל וישלחו מן המחנה כל צרוע וכל זב וכל טמא לנפש בשעה שטמאי מתים משתלחין זבין ומצורעין משתלחין אין טמאי מתים משתלחין אין זבין ומצורעין [משתלחין]: אמר זב וכל זב לרבות בעל קרי מסייע ליה לר' יוחנן [דאמר] מחילות לא נתקדשו ובעלי קריין משתלחין חוץ לשתי מחנות כמו הזבין ומותבינן עליה מיהא דתנן בסוף מס' זבין בעל קרי כמגע שרץ מאי לאו למחנותם מה טמא שרץ חוץ למחנה אחת קשיא לר' יוחנן דאמר חוץ לשתי מחנות ומשני לאו למחנותיהם איתקש אלא לטומאתן ובא ללמדנו דבעל קרי כמגע שרץ מה מגע שרץ אפי' באונס טמא אף בעל קרי אם ראה קרי

אלא יש לך שעה שזבין ומצורעין משתלחין ואין טמאי מתים משתלחין ואיזה זה פסח הבא בטומאה אמר אביי אי הכי לימא נמי יאמר זב וטמאי מתים ואל יאמר מצורע ואני אומר זב משתלח מצורע לא כ"ש אלא יש לך שעה שמצורעין משתלחין ואין זבין וטמאי מתים משתלחין ואיזה זה פסח הבא בטומאה וכי תימא הכי נמי והתנן *פסח הבא בטומאה לא יאכלו ממנו זבים וזבות נדות ויולדות ואם אכלו פטורין אלא אמר אביי לעולם מקרא קמא אם כן ניכתוב רחמנא איש איש כי יהיה טמא לנפש למה לי וכי תימא האי לנפש להכי הוא דאתא הטמא מת הוא דנדחה לפסח שני אבל שאר טמאין לא *והתניא יכול לא יהו עושין פסח שני אלא טמאי מתים ושהיה בדרך רחוקה זבין ומצורעין ובועלי נדות מניין ת"ל איש איש לנפש דכתב רחמנא למה לי אלא הכי קאמר איש נדחה לפסח שני ואין ציבור נדחה לפסח שני אלא עבדי בטומאה וכי עבדי ציבור בטומאה בטמא מת אבל שאר טומאו' לא עבדי אמר רב חסדא מצורע שנכנס לפנים ממחיצתו פטור שנאמר °בדד ישב מחוץ למחנה מושבו בדד ישב לבדו ישב מחוץ למחנה מושבו הכתוב נתקו לעשה איתיביה *מצורע שנכנס לפנים ממחיצתו בארבעים זבין וזבות שנכנסו לפנים ממחיצתן בארבעים *[ג]וטמא מת מותר ליכנס למחנה לויה ולא טמא מת בלבד אמרו אלא אפילו מת עצמו שנאמר °ויקח משה את עצמות יוסף עמו עמו במחיצתו תנאי היא דתניא בדד ישב לבדו *ישב שלא יהו טמאין אחרים יושבין עמו יכול יהו זבין וטמאי מתים משתלחין למחנה אחת תלמוד לומר °ולא יטמאו את מחניהם *[ג]ליתן מחנה לזה ומחנה לזה דברי רבי יהודה ר"ש אומר אינו צריך הרי הוא אומר °וישלחו מן המחנה כל צרוע וכל זב וכל טמא לנפש (א)יאמר טמאי מת ואל יאמר טמאי זב ואני אומר טמאי מתים משתלחין זבין לא כ"ש למה נאמר זב ליתן לו מחנה שניה ויאמר זב ואל יאמר מצורע ואני אומר זבין משתלחין מצורעין לא כל שכן למה נאמר מצורע ליתן לו מחנה שלישית כשהוא אומר בדד ישב הכתוב נתקו לעשה מאי חומריה דזב מטמא מת שכן טומאה יוצאה עליו מגופו אדרבה טמא מת חמור שכן טעון הזאה שלישי ושביעי אמר קרא טמא וכל טמא לרבות טמא שרץ וזב חמור מטמא שרץ ומאי חומריה כדאמרן אדרבה שרץ חמור שכן מטמא באונס אמרי כי

רש"י

אלמא יש לך שעה שזבין ומצורעין משתלחין. מן העזרה וטמאי מתים נכנסים לתוכה: בטומאה. כשרוב ציבור טמאין במת עושין פסח בטומאה וזבין ומצורעין שבהן נדחין: מצורע חמור מזב. לקמן מפרש חומריה: ואיזה זה כו'. בתמיה: לא יאכלו ממנו. דכי דייקינן איש נדחה ואין ציבור נדחין בטמא נפש הוא דדייקינן גבי איש כי יהיה טמא לא כתיב אלא לנפש ובדידה דייקינן איש ולא ציבור אלמא מהתם יליף דאי מויסלחו כדר"ל זב נמי לישתרי: אלא לעולם מקרא קמא. וכדדייקינן איש נדחה ואין ציבור נדחין ודקשיא לך אימא ציבור כלל לא א"כ דדיוקא דממעטינן ציבור מהאי דינא לחומרא ממעטינן למאי הילכתא כתב לנפש למעוטי זבין ומצורעין לכתוב טומאה סתם דנשמע דבכל טומאות יחיד נדחה לשני וציבור לית להו תקנתא דע"כ לנפש למעוטי זבין ומצורעין אתא ולאחמורי עלייהו ואי לגבי ציבור לא מחמירו עלייהו ולמימר דבטומאת מת הוא דאין ציבור נדחין אלא עושין פסחיהן בטומאה אבל בטומאת זיבה וצרעת אפילו ציבור נמי נדחין לגבי מאן מחמיר עלייהו וה"ת לגבי יחיד מחמיר עלייהו וקאמר טמא נפש הוא דאית ליה תשלומין לשני אבל זב ומצורע אפי' נטהר בשני לית לי' תקנתא בתשלומין והתניא יכול לא יהו חייבין לפסח שני אלא טמא נפש כו': ת"ל איש איש. כי יהיה טמא משמע כל טומאה מדלא כתיב לנפש ברישא א"כ איש כי יגע במת ש"מ למידרשי' באנפיה נפשיה הוא לנפש למה לי אלא ע"כ מיעוטא דציבור לאקולי אתא ולמימרא דאין נדחין אלא עושין בטומאה ומש"ה כתיב לנפש למימר דבטומאת מת הוא דאקיל עלייהו אבל זיבה וצרעת לא: לפנים ממחיצתו. מחיצה שנאסר ליכנס בה דהיינו לפני' מחומת כל ערי ישראל כדאמר לקמן מצורע משתלח חוץ למחנה ישראל: פטור. ממלקות דלא יטמאו את מחניהם: נתקו לעשה. ואע"ג דלאו בתר לאו כתיב ע"כ לנתוקי לאוי אתא דקי"ל לאו שניתק לעשה אין לוקין עליי' ואי לאטעוניה עשה ול"ת הא כתב ביה עשה אחרינא וישלחו מן המחנה אבל זבין וטמאי מתים לא נתקו לעשה ואע"ג דעשה יתירי כתיבי כל חד וחד למילתיה מדריש בספרי ועוד דבהאי כתיב כל ימי אשר הנגע בו וגו' משמע כל ימיו בבדד ישב קאי דאם עבר ונכנס יחזור ויצא ואין בו עונש אחר כדדרשינן כל ימיו דאונס את הנערה במס' מכות (דף טו.) כל ימיו בעמוד והחזר קאי ומנתקינא ליה ללאו: זב. מחילתו הר הבית דאסור לכנס במחנה לויה כדלקמן שכל הטמאין אין משתלחין אלא מן העזרה לבדה חוץ מזב ובעל קרי שמשתלחין אף מהר הבית ומצורע משתלח אף ממחנה ישראל דהיינו כל העיר: מחנה לויה. כל הר הבית חוץ לחומת העזרה: עמו. ומשה לוי היה: תנאי היא. דאיכא תנא דלא מייתי ליה קרא לעשה אלא ליתן לו מחנה שלישית: שלא יהו טמאין אחרים יושבין עמו. כגון זבין וטמאי מתים למדנו לשלוחו של מצורע שהוא חמור מכולן: יכול יהו זבין וטמאי מתים משתלחין למחנה אחת ת"ל ולא יטמאו את מחניהם תן מחנה לזה ומחנה לזה. מדלא כתיב מחנה משמע מחנה לכל אחד ואחד והתם תרתי מחנות כתיבי וישלחו מן המחנה מחוץ למחנה תשלחום והאי מחוץ למחנה דמצורע ליתן לו מחנה שלישית: אינו צריך. האי מחוץ למחנה ליתן לו מחנה שלישית להוציאו דכולהו מהתם נפקי דע"כ כולן חמורים זה מזה בטומאותיהן דאי כולהו שוו לענין מחנות לכתוב שילוח בקל ואנא ידענא כל שכן דחמור בעי שילוח ומדכתבינהו כולהו ש"מ שילוחו של זה לא כשילוחו של זה: זב לא כ"ש. לקמיה פריך מאי חומריה דזב מטמא מת: לרבות טמא שרץ. לשילוח והוא הדין לנוגע בנבילה וכל טמאי מגע וכיון דכתב רבוייא לטמאי מגע לא איצטריך למיכתב זב דחמיר מטמא שרץ שהרי טומאה יוצאה עליו מגופו: זב. אינו מטמא מחמת אונס אם ראה מחמת מאכל ומשתה או חולי או קפילה כדאמר במסכת נדה בפרק בנות כותים (דף לה.) מבשרו ולא מחמת אונסו ומשנינן כי האי גוונא זב טמויי נמי מטמא כגון טומאת טמאי שרץ שאינו אלא טומאת ערב:

תוספות

הכתוב נתקו לעשה. פי' בקו' דכתיב כל ימי אשר הנגע בו משמע דניתוק הלאו הוא כל ימיו בדד ישב שאם עבר ונכנס יחזור ויצא ואין בו עונש אחר כמו לא יוכל לשלחה כל ימיו וקשה לר"י דאם כן ה"ל לאיתויי רישיה דקרא בספרים ועוד הקשה ריב"א דלא דמי דלא יוכל לשלחה כל ימיו משמע דליכא לאו אלא כשמשלחה כל ימיו אבל הכא לא משמע מקרא הכי ואור"י דהאי נתקו לעשה לאו הוי כשאר לאו הניתק לעשה שהעשה כתוב אחר הלאו בסמוך משמע שלתקן הלאו בא כמו לא תותירו ממנו והנותר וגו' (שמות יב) וכמו לא תקח האם על הבנים שלח תשלח (דברים כב) *אלא ה"פ הכתוב נתקו לעשה דכיון דכל הטמאים היו בכלל ולא יטמאו את מחניהם ופרט במצורע בפני עצמו עשה אחת להוציאו מכלל האחרים לנתקו מן הלאו וליתן בעשה אבל היכא שהוא כתוב הלאו אלא על דבר אחד לא מנתקינן את הלאו בעשה אלא הוי בלאו ועשה וקשה דבעל קרי נמי לא לילקי אם נכנס לפנים ממחיצתו שהכתוב נתקו לעשה דכתיב ויצא אל מחוץ למחנה וי"ל דהכא בחד קרא איכא תרי עשה בדד ישב מחוץ למחנה מושבו והאי ניתוק עשה נראה *דלא מהני אלא במחנה שלישית דלא גרע מזב הואיל ואיכא לאוקמי ניתוק למחנה שלישי' ובמחנה שכינה חייב כרת דלא גרע ממחוסר כפורים וכן משמע בפ' כל הפסולים (זבחים דף לב:) דקאמר ואי ביאה במקצת שמה ביאה היכי מטיל ידיה לבהונות אידי ואידי עשה שיש בו כרת הוא ה"ל ומטונך הואיל והותר לצרעתו הותר לקריו והיכא למידחי דהסיה כרבי יהודה דלא חשיב ליה לקמן ניתוק לעשה:

זבין ובועלי נדות שנכנסו כו'. ריב"א לא גרס ובועלי נדות בהדי זבין דהא אמרינן לקמן בועל נדה כטמא מת למחנות ובתוספתא ליתיה:

מאי חומריה דזב שכן טומאה יוצאה עליו מגופו. וה"ה דהוה מצי למימר שכן מטמא משכב ומושב וכלי חרס בהיסט כדלקמן אלא ניחא ליה למינקט חומרי דלא מצי למימר להו בסמוך גבי חומר בזב מבמצורע:

עין משפט נר מצוה

ח א מיי' פ"ג מהלכות ביאת מקדש הל' ח סמג עשין קפד ולאוין רמ: ט ב שם הלכה ד: י ג שם הלכה ג:

[ועי' תוס' שבועות ד. ד"ה מלאות נגעים כו' ואם התרה בו כו' לא אמר כו' וקלא ליש]:

מסורת הש"ס

לקמן נה: [בכורות לג:] כריתות י. — לקמן נג — נזיר מה. סוטה כ: [תוספתא דכלים פ"א ע"ש] — [זבחים קיז.] — [שם]

הגהות הגר"א

(א) גמ' יאמר טמא מת ואל יאמר זב וכו' כצ"ע:

גליון הש"ס

תוס' ד"ה הכתוב נתקו לעשה. אלא ה"פ הכתוב נתקו לעשה כו'. עי' חולין פ"ב ע"ב תוס' ד"ה כגת למעמ"ז:

רבינו חננאל

הא כיצד טמא מת משתלח חוץ למחנה שכינה וטמא שרץ כמותו זב משתלח חוץ למחנה לויה ובעל קרי כמותו מצורע משתלח חוץ למחנה ישראל נמצא המצורע משתלח חוץ לשלש מחנות וזב משתים וטמא מת מאחת וברור הוא: ואתקיף אביי אהא דריש לקיש ואהדר לדרשא דר' יוחנן והכי קאמר לעולם מקרא קמא ונכתוב רחמנא איש איש כי יהיה טמא ולישתוק לנפש למה לי וכי תימא נפש הוא נדחה לפסח שני אבל שאר טמאים לא והתניא יכול לא יהו עושין השני אלא טמאי נפש ומי שהיה בדרך רחוקה זבין ומצורעין ובועלי נדות מנין ת"ל איש איש ואמאי לכל טמאין עושין פסח שני לנפש דכתב רחמנא למה לי אלא הכי קאמר רחמנא איש נדחה לפסח שני ואין צבור נדחין לפסח שני אלא עבדי בטומאה וצבור דעבדו בטומאת מת אבל בשאר טומאות לא: אמר רב חסדא מצורע שנכנס לפנים ממחיצתו פטור ממלקות שנאמר בדד ישב מחוץ למחנה מושבו אחר שכתוב בו לא יטמאו את מחניהם וקבעו בלא [תעשה] העתיקו לעשה וכתב בו בדד ישב מחוץ למחנה מושבו נתקו לעשה לומר שאינו לוקה ומותבינן עליה מצורע שנכנס לפנים ממחיצתו בארבעים וכן זבים וטמאי מתים שנכנסו לפנים ממחיצתן בארבעים וטמא מת מותר להכנס במחנה לויה ואפילו מת עצמו מותר להכניסו במחנה לויה שנאמר ויקח משה את עצמות יוסף עמו במחיצתו קתני מיהא מצורע שנכנס לפנים ממחיצתו בארבעים והיכי פטר ליה רב חסדא ושני' תנאי היא ורב חסדא דאמר כר' שמעון דתניא בדד ישב מחוץ למחנה לבדו ישב שלא יהו טמאין אחרים יושבים עמו יכול יהו זבין וטמאי מתים משתלחין מן המחנה אחת ת"ל ולא יטמאו את מתניהם ליתן מחנה לזה ומחנה לזה דברי ר' יהודה ר"ש אומר אינו צריך הרי הוא אומר וישלחו מן המחנה כל צרוע וכל זב וכל טמא לנפש יאמר טמא נפש ואל יאמר זב ואני אומר טמא מת משתלח זב לא כל שכן מה ת"ל זב ליתן לו מחנה שניה יאמר זב ואל יאמר מצורע נתקו לעשה: מאי חומריה דזב מטמא מת דקתני ואני אומר טמא מת משתלח זב לא כל שכן מכלל שהזב חמור מטמא מת מאי חומריה שכן הזב טומאה יוצאה עליו מגופו אדרבה טמא מת חמור ממנו שטעון הזאה שלישי ושביעי ודחי' מוכל דכתיב בטמא מת מרבינן טמא שרץ דלא כתיב ביה בהדיה להיות טעון שילוח חוץ למחנה ומרבינן טמא שרץ שבאה לו הטומאה מבחוץ שדומה לטמא מת והזב חמור מטומאת שרץ שהזב טומאה יוצאה לו מגופו. ותי אקשי' יש לומר שטומאת שרץ חמור שמטמא אפי' [אם] נפל עליו השרץ באונס מה שאין כן ב'ב שהזב אינו מטמא באונס דתנן בשבעה דרכים בודקין את הזב וכו' ואם נמצא עליו אונס אינו טמא מאותה הראי' שבאונס ושנינן להמצאות הזב בטומאת ערב כטומאת שרץ אפילו אם רא ראיה באונס מטמא טומאת ערב דלא גרע מקרי וכדרב הונא דאמר ראיה ראשונה של זב מטמאה באונס נתברר שהזב חמור הוא מטמא שרץ שנתרבה מטמא מת ועל זה אמר יאמר טמא נפש ולא יאמר זב וכן עוד דתאני זב משתלח לא כל שכן מכלל שמצורע חמור מזב מאי חומריה דמצורע מזב שכן טעון פריעת הראש ופרימת בגדיו ואסור בתשמיש שנאמר (ויקרא י"ד) וישב מחוץ לאהלו ואין אהלו אלא אשתו שנאמר

and lepers![3] [67a] But [it intimates,] there is a time when *zabin* and lepers are sent out, whereas those who are unclean by the dead are not sent out; and when is that? It is [when] the Passover comes [is sacrificed] in uncleanness.

Said Abaye, If so, let us also argue: 'Let [Scripture] state a *zab* and those who are unclean by the dead, and let it not state a leper, and I would argue, If a *zab* is sent out, how much the more a leper; but [the fact that a leper is stated intimates] there is a time when lepers are sent out, whereas *zabin* and those who are unclean by the dead are not sent out, and when is that? It is [when] the Passover comes in uncleanness'? And should you say, That indeed is so—surely we learned: The Passover which comes in uncleanness, *zabin* and *zaboth*, menstruant women and women in childbirth must not eat thereof, yet if they ate, they are not liable [to *kareth*]? Rather, said Abaye, After all, [it is derived] from the first verse;[4] [and as to the question raised,[5] the reply is], If so,[6] let the Divine Law write, *'If any man of you shall be unclean'*: what is the purpose of *'by reason of a dead body'*? And should you say, this [phrase] *'by reason of a dead body'* comes for this [purpose, viz.,] only he who is unclean by reason of a dead body is relegated to the second Passover, but not other unclean [persons], surely it was taught: You might think that only those who are unclean by the dead and he who was on a distant journey keep the second Passover; whence do we know [to include] *zabin* and lepers and
a those who had intercourse with menstruant women?[1] Therefore it is stated, *'any man'*.[2] Then what is the purpose of [the phrase] *'by reason of a dead body'* which the Divine Law wrote? But this is what [Scripture] states: A man [i.e., an individual] is relegated to the second Passover, whereas a community is not relegated to the second Passover, but they keep [the first Passover] in uncleanness. And when do the community keep [the first Passover] in uncleanness? When [they are] unclean by reason of the dead; but in the case of other forms of uncleanness, they do not keep [it thus].

R. Ḥisda said: If a leper entered within his barrier,[3] he is exempt [from flagellation],[4] because it is said, *he shall dwell solitary; without the camp shall his dwelling be:*[5] the Writ transformed it [his prohibition] into a positive command:[6] An objection is raised: A leper who entered within his barrier [is punished] with forty lashes; *zabin* and *zaboth* who entered within their barrier [are punished] with forty lashes; while he who is unclean by the dead is permitted to enter the Levitical camp;[7] and they said this not only [of] him who is unclean by the dead, but even [of] the dead himself, for it is said, *And Moses took the bones of Joseph with him,*[8] *'with him'* [implying] within his barrier [precincts]![9]—It is [a controversy of] Tannaim. For it was taught: *'He shall dwell solitary'*: [that means,] he shall dwell alone so that other unclean persons[10] should not dwell with him.[11] You might think that *zabin* and unclean persons are sent away to one [the same] camp; therefore it is stated, *that they defile not their camps:*[12] [this is] to assign a camp for this one and a camp for that one: this is R. Judah's opinion. R. Simeon said, It is unnecessary. For lo, it is said, '[*Command the children of Israel*] *that they send out of the camp every leper, and everyone that*
b *hath an issue, and whosoever is unclean by the dead*'.[1] Now, let [Scripture] state those who are unclean by the dead and not state *zab*, and I would say, if those who are unclean by the dead are sent out, how much the more *zabin*! Why then is *zab* stated? To assign a second camp to him. And let [Scripture] state *zab* and not state leper, and I would say, if *zabin* are sent out, how much the more lepers! Why then is a leper stated? To assign a third camp to him. When it states, *'he shall dwell solitary'*, the Writ transforms it [the prohibition] into a positive command.[2]

What is the greater stringency of a *zab* over him who is unclean by reason of the dead?[3]—Because uncleanness issues upon him from his own body. On the contrary, he who is unclean by the dead is more stringent, since he requires sprinkling on the third and the seventh [days]?[4]—Scripture saith, [instead of] 'the unclean,' *'and whosoever* [kol] *is unclean,'*[5] to include him who is unclean through a reptile, and a *zab* is more stringent than he who is unclean through a reptile; and what is his greater stringency? As we have stated.[6] On the contrary, a reptile is more stringent,

(3) Their uncleanness is more stringent, since it emanates from themselves. (4) Num. IX, 10. (5) By Resh Laḳish. (6) That the deduction is to be made as R. Simeon b. Laḳish proposes.

a (1) Which act defiles them. (2) Heb. *ish ish:* the doubling indicates extension, and therefore includes these. (3) I.e., into the precincts that are forbidden to him. (4) Though he thereby transgressed the negative injunction, *that they defile not their camp.*—Num. V, 3. (5) Lev. XIII, 46. (6) Only a negative command involves flagellation, but not a positive command. Though a negative command is stated in this connection, this verse teaches that he is regarded as having violated a positive command only. (7) The whole of the Temple Mount outside the walls of the Temple Court is so called. (8) Ex. XIII, 19. (9) Moses was a Levite. (10) E.g., *zabin* and those unclean through the dead. (11) This shows that his uncleanness is greater and stricter than theirs. (12) Num. V, 3: *'camps'*, plural.

b (1) Num. V, 2. (2) Since according to R. Simeon this can have no other purpose; thus we have a controversy of Tannaim. (3) That the former could be deduced as stated *a minori* from the latter. (4) V. Num. XIX, 19. (5) I.e., Scripture employs the second, more-embracing phrase, where the first would suffice. (6) That the uncleanness emanates from himself. Hence the reference to a *zab* is superfluous, and therefore it teaches as above.

it between its horns.' [66b] But he performed work with sacred animals?[4]—[They did] as Hillel. For it was taught: It was related of Hillel, As long as he lived[5] no man ever committed trespass through his burnt-offering.[6] But he brought it unconsecrated [*hullin*] to the Temple Court, consecrated it, layed his hand upon it,[7] and slaughtered it.

[Yet] how might a person consecrate the Passover on the Sabbath? Surely we learned: You may not consecrate, nor make a valuation vow,[8] nor make a vow of *ḥerem*,[9] nor separate[10] *terumah* and tithes. They said all this of Festivals, how much the more of the Sabbath!—That applies only to obligations for [the discharge of] which no time is fixed; but in the case of obligations for [the discharge of] which a time is fixed, you may consecrate. For R. Joḥanan said: A man may consecrate his Passover on the Sabbath, and his Festival-offering [*ḥagigah*] on the Festival.

a But he drives [a laden animal]?[1]—It is driving in an unusual way.[2] [But] even driving in an unusual manner, granted that there is no Scriptural prohibition, there is nevertheless a Rabbinical prohibition?—That is [precisely] what they asked him: An action which is permitted by Scripture, while a matter of a *shebuth* stands before it to render it impossible,[3] such as [an action performed] in an unusual manner [standing] in the way of a precept, what then? Said he to them, 'I have heard this *halachah*, but have forgotten it: but leave [it] to Israel, if they are not prophets they are the sons of prophets.'

Rab Judah said in Rab's name: Whoever is boastful, if he is a Sage, his wisdom departs from him; if he is a prophet, his prophecy departs from him. If he is a Sage, his wisdom departs from him: [we learn this] from Hillel. For the Master said. 'He began rebuking them with words,' and [then] he said to them, 'I have heard this *halachah*, but have forgotten it.'[4] If he is a prophet, his prophecy departs from him: [we learn this] from Deborah. For it is written, *The rulers ceased in Israel, they ceased, until that I arose, Deborah, I arose a mother in Israel;*[5] and it is written, *Awake, awake, Deborah, awake, awake, utter a song.*[6]

Resh Lakish said: As to every man who becomes angry, if he is a Sage, his wisdom departs from him; if he is a prophet, his prophecy departs from him. If he is a Sage, his wisdom departs from him: [we learn this] from Moses. For it is written, *And Moses was wroth with the officers of the host* etc.;[7] and it is written, *And Eleazar the priest said unto the men of war that went to the battle:*
b *This is the statute of the law which the Lord hath commanded Moses* etc.,[1] whence it follows that it had been forgotten by Moses.[2] If he is a prophet, his prophecy departs from him: [we learn this] from Elisha. Because it is written, *'were it not that I regard the presence of Jehoshaphat the king of Judah, I would not look toward thee, nor see thee';*[3] and it is written, *'But now bring me a minstrel.' And it came to pass, when the minstrel played, that the hand of the Lord* [i.e., the spirit of prophecy] *came upon him.*[4]

R. Mani b. Paṭṭish said: Whoever becomes angry, even if greatness has been decreed for him by Heaven, is cast down. Whence do we know it? From Eliab, for it is said, *and Eliab's anger was kindled against David, and he said: 'Why art thou come down? and with whom hast thou left those few sheep in the wilderness? I know thy presumptuousness, and the naughtiness of thy heart; for thou art come down that thou mightest see the battle.'*[5] And when Samuel went to anoint him [*sc.* a king], of all [David's brothers] it is written, *neither hath the Lord chosen this,*[6] whereas of Eliab it is written, *But the Lord said unto Samuel, 'Look not on his countenance, or on the height of his stature; because I have rejected him':*[7] hence it follows that He had favoured him until then.

We have [thus] found that the *tamid* and the Passover override the Sabbath; how do we know that they override uncleanness?[8]—I will tell you: just as he learns the Passover from the *tamid* in respect to the Sabbath, so also does he learn the *tamid* from the Passover in respect to uncleanness. And how do we know it of the Passover itself?—Said R. Joḥanan, Because the Writ saith, *If any man of you shall be unclean by reason of a dead body:*[9] a man [i.e., an individual] is relegated to the second Passover,[10] but a community is not relegated to the second Passover, but they must offer it in [a state of] uncleanness. R. Simeon b. Lakish said to R. Joḥanan: Say, a man is relegated to the second Passover, [whereas] a community has no remedy [for its uncleanness], neither on the first Passover nor on the second Passover? Rather, said R. Simeon b. Lakish, [It is deduced] from here: [*Command the children of Israel,*] *that they send out of the camp every leper, and every*
c *one that hath an issue, and whosoever is unclean by the dead:*[1] let [Scripture] state those who are unclean by the dead, and not state *zabin*[2] and lepers, and I would argue, if those who are unclean by the dead are sent out [of the camp], how much the more *zabin*

(4) Which is forbidden, v. Deut. XV, 19: *thou shalt do no work with the firstling of thine ox*—a firstling being sacred. (5) Lit., 'from his days'. (6) I.e., through making unlawful use of the consecrated animal. (7) V. Lev. I, 4: *and he shall lay his hand upon the head of the burnt-offering.* (8) I.e., vow your own value to the Temple; v. Lev. XXVII, 2-13. (9) A vow dedicating an object for priestly use, ibid. 28 seq. (10) Lit., 'raise', 'lift off'.

a (1) Which is likewise forbidden. (2) Lit., 'as in a back-handed manner'—an idiom connoting an unusual way of doing anything. Sheep and goats are not employed as beasts of burden, hence this is unusual, whereas by Scriptural law work is forbidden on the Sabbath and Festivals only when performed in the usual way. (3) Lit., 'to eradicate it'. (4) Though his rebuke was probably justified and timely, he should not have drawn attention to his own promotion. (5) Judg. V, 7. (6) Ibid. 12; thus after boasting that she was a mother in Israel, she had to be urged to awake and utter song, i.e., prophecy, the spirit having departed from her. (7) Num. XXXI, 14.

b (1) Num. XXXI, 21. (2) Lit., 'it had become hidden from Moses'. (3) II Kings III, 14; this was an expression of anger. (4) Ibid. 15. (5) I Sam. XVII, 28. (6) Ibid. XVI, 8f. *passim.* (7) Ibid. 7. (8) If the larger part of the community is unclean, these offerings are still sacrificed. (9) Num. IX, 10. (10) I.e., in the second month, ibid. 11.

c (1) Num. V, 2. (2) Those who have an issue. Pl. of *zab*, q.v. Glos.

והא קא עביד עבודה בקדשים *כהלל דתניא *אמרו עליו על הלל מימיו לא מעל אדם בעולתו אלא מביאה חולין לעזרה ומקדישה וסומך ידו עליה ושוחטה פסח בשבת היכי מצי מקדיש ליה *והתנן אין מקדישין ואין מעריכין ואין מחרימין ואין מגביהין תרומה ומעשרות כל אלו ביום טוב אמרו קל וחומר בשבת הני מילי בחובות שאין קבוע להן זמן אבל בחובות שקבוע להן זמן מקדישין *דאמר רבי יוחנן מקדיש אדם את פסחו בשבת וחגיגתו ביו"ט והלא מחמר מחמר כלאחר יד מחמר כלאחר יד נמי נהי דאיסורא דאורייתא ליכא איסורא מדרבנן מיהא איכא היינו דקא בעי מיניה דבר שיש לו היתר מן התורה ודבר שבות עומד לפניו לעקרו כלאחר יד במקום מצוה מאי אמר להן הלכה זו שמעתי ושכחתי אלא הניחו להן לישראל אם אין נביאים הן בני נביאים הן: אמר רב יהודה אמר רב *כל המתיהר אם חכם הוא חכמתו מסתלקת ממנו אם נביא הוא נבואתו מסתלקת ממנו אם חכם הוא חכמתו מסתלקת ממנו מהלל דאמר מר התחיל מקנטרן בדברים וקאמר להו הלכה זו שמעתי ושכחתי אם נביא הוא נבואתו מסתלקת ממנו מדבורה דכתיב °חדלו פרזון בישראל חדלו עד שקמתי דבורה שקמתי אם בישראל וגו' וכתיב °עורי עורי דבורה עורי עורי דברי שיר וגו' ר"ל אמר כל אדם שכועס אם חכם הוא חכמתו מסתלקת ממנו אם נביא הוא נבואתו מסתלקת ממנו אם חכם הוא חכמתו מסתלקת ממנו *ממשה דכתיב °ויקצוף משה על פקודי החיל וגו' וכתיב °ויאמר אלעזר הכהן אל אנשי הצבא הבאים למלחמה זאת חוקת התורה אשר צוה ה' את משה וגו' מכלל דמשה איעלם מיניה אם נביא הוא נבואתו מסתלקת ממנו מאלישע דכתיב °לולי פני יהושפט מלך יהודה אני נושא אם אביט אליך ואם אראך וגו' וכתיב °ועתה קחו לי מנגן והיה כנגן המנגן ותהי עליו יד ה' וגו' אמר רבי מני בר פטיש כל שכועס אפילו פוסקין עליו גדולה מן השמים מורידין אותו מנלן מאליאב שנאמר °ויחר אף אליאב בדוד ויאמר למה [זה] ירדת ועל מי נטשת מעט הצאן ההנה במדבר אני ידעתי את זדונך ואת רוע לבבך כי למען ראות המלחמה ירדת וכי אזל שמואל למשחינהו בכלהו כתיב °לא בזה בחר ה' ובאליאב כתיב °ויאמר ה' אל שמואל אל תביט אל מראהו ואל גבה קומתו כי מאסתיהו מכלל דהוה רחים ליה עד האידנא: אשכחן תמיד ופסח דדחו שבת דדחו טומאה מנא לן אמרי כי היכי דיליף פסח מתמיד לענין שבת הכי נמי °יליף תמיד מפסח לענין טומאה ופסח גופיה מנא לן אמר רבי יוחנן דאמר קרא °איש איש כי יהיה טמא לנפש *איש נדחה לפסח שני ואין ציבור נידחין לפסח שני אלא עבדי בטומאה אמר ליה ר"ש בן לקיש לרבי יוחנן אימא איש נדחה לפסח שני ציבור לית להו תקנתא לא בפסח ראשון ולא בפסח שני אלא אמר רבי שמעון בן לקיש מהכא °וישלחו מן המחנה כל צרוע וכל זב וכל טמא לנפש יאמר טמאי מתים ואל יאמר זבין ומצורעין ואני אומר אם טמאי מתים משתלחין זבין ומצורעין לא כל שכן אלא

[נדרים ס:] · ביצה לו: · [דף קנג.] · שבת קמח: · שופטים ה · שם · [נ"ל ליס] · שם · [אדר"נ פ"א] · במדבר לא · שם · מלכים ב ג · שם · שמואל א יז · שם טז · שם · במדבר ט · [חולין כט.] · במדבר ה

תורה אור

רש"י

והא עביד מלאכה בקדשים · ועובר משום לא תעבוד בבכור (דברים טו): דעבדי כהלל · דלא מקדשי לקרבן עד דמייתי להו לעזרה: לא מעל · שלא היה שהות בין הקדישה לשחיטה שיבאו בה לידי מעילה: דתנן לא מקדישין וכו' · במסכת ביצה והיאך הקדישו פסחיהן אלו בשבת: הני מילי · דאין מקדישין: חובות הקבוע להן זמן · לבו ביום שפיר דמי דהואיל ונשחטין היום יכול להקדישן היום: פסחו · ליכא למימר ביום טוב דאין פסח קרב ביום טוב וחגיגה ליכא למימר בשבת: מחמר לא קרי אלא בבהמה הנושאת משוי והוא מנהיגה קרי לי' מחמר ומוזהר עליו בפ' מי שהחשיך*: כלאחר יד · שאין דרך טולה לשאת משוי: שיש לו היתר מן התורה · כגון זה שאינו מחמר גמור אלא כלאחר יד ואין כאן אלא שבות ואפילו שבות דידיה לא חמיר כשאר שבות דכל כלאחר יד לא שכיחא: במקום מצוה · כי האי גוונא דמעכב מפסח: עד שקמתי דבורה · יוהרא שהיתה משפלת המנהיגים שלפניה ומתפארת לעצמה: עורי עורי דבורה · שנסתלקה מחמת סילוק נבואתה: קחו לי מנגן · להעביר כעסו שכעס על יהורם: ותהי עליו יד · מכלל דאסתלק: לא בחר · משמע מעולם אבל מאסתיהו משמע השתא מאסתיהו מפני שהוא רגזן מאסו מכלל שמתחלה נבחר ואע"ג דהאי מעשה דמשיחה קדים לרגזנות מיהו לא מליכו בו דופי אלא זה בלבד ומפני שגלוי לפניו שהוא רגזן מאסו: דדחו טומאה מנא לן · הואיל ומועדו לא משמע (להו) מנא לן דדחו ואנן קיימא לן דדחו טומאה בכיסוי חולין (דף ע:): פסח איקרי קרבן ציבור דאתי בכנופיא באידך פירקין (דף עו:): זבין ומצורעין · חמורין מטמאי מתים שהרי טומאה יוצאה עליהן מגופן אלא על כרחיך כי איצטריך זב ומצורע להיכא דאין טמא מת משתלח איצטריך: אלמא

תוספות

והא קא עביד עבודה בקדשים כהלל · בירושלמי מפרש בענין אחר דכל עבודה של צורך הקרבן אין בו מעילה ויליף מפרה כי היכי דלא חשיב עבודה מידי דלצרכה לפסלה ה"נ לא חשיב עבודה להתחייב במעילה ומייתי הא דתנן במסכת פרה (פ"ב מ"ג) רכב עליה ותלה בזנבה ועבר בה את הנהר קיפל עליה את המוסרה נתן טליתו עליה פסולה אבל קשרה במוסרה עשה לה סנדל בשביל שלא תחליק פירס טליתו עליה מפני הזבובים כשירה זה הכלל כל שהוא לצרכה כשירה: מביאה כשהיא חולין לעזרה. בפ' המוכר את הספינה (ב"ב דף פא:) גבי קונה שתי אילנות פריך ליחוש דילמא לאו בכורים נינהו וקא מעייל חולין לעזרה ובהזרוע (חולין דף קל·) נמי דקאמר טעמא דכ' רחמנא זה הא לאו הכי ה"א חולין חייבין בחזה ושוק הא בעי תנופה והיכי ליעבד ליניפינהו לפני ה' כתיב ואי מגוואי קא מעייל חולין לעזרה התם ודאי אסור שעושה בהן תנופה כדרך שעושה בקרבן אבל הכא שמכניס טלה חולין בעזרה ואינו עושה שום דבר שעושה בקרבנות שריא כמקרי' חולין לגבוה שרי כדאשכחן בהקומץ רבה (מנחות דכ"א:*) שהיו אוכלי' חולין בעזרה כדי לאכול מנחות על השבע: מחמר כלאחר יד הוא·ה"מ לבנויי כשהוא מהלך מניחו עליו וכשהוא עומד נוטלו הימנו דכי האי גוונא שרי בריש מי שהחשיך (שבת ד' קנג·): כלאחר יד נמי אסור מדרבנן · הוי מצי למיפרך הלא משתמש בבעלי חיים דאסור מדרבנן: הנח להן לישראל · ואם תאמר והא במתניתין אסר שבות דרבנן כיון דאפשר לעשות מערב שבת ויש לומר שבות בהמתו קיל משבות עצמו: ואין ציבור נדחין · תימה דהכא לא ממעטינן מאיש אלא רוב ישראל ובפ"ק דסנהדרין (דף יז:) דר שינן והוצאת את האיש ההוא איש ואשה אתה מוציא לשעריך ואי אתה מוציא כל העיר כולה לשעריך ואיכא דממעט התם שבט וי"ל דשאני התם דמלינו שחלק בעיר הנדחת א"כ טובא איש ואשה כתיבי התם*: אלא אמר ר"ש לקיש וישלחו מן המחנה · תימה לרשב"א לדריש לקיש הניחא לרבי יהודה אלא לרבי שמעון דאמר לקמן דלהכי כתב רחמנא טמא מת זב ומצורע לפי שחלוקים בשלוח מחנות פסח דדחי טומאה מנא ליה:

הכתוב

עין משפט נר מצוה

ג א מיי' שם:

ד ב מיי' פכ"ג מהלכות שבת הלכה יד סמג לאוין סה טוש"ע א"ח סימן שלט סעיף ד וסימן תקכ"ד סעיף א:

ה ג מיי' שם הלכה יד ופ"א מהלכות ק"פ הלכה יט סמג עשין רנג:

ו ד מיי' פ"ב מהלכות דעות הלכה ג:

ז ה מיי' פ"א מהלכות תמידין הלכה ז:

[ועי' תוס' ביצה כ: ד"ה והביא ותוס' ב"ב פא: ד"ה ודילמא ותוספות מנחות כא: ד"ה חולין ודף פ: ד"ה וכי ותוס' חולין קל: ד"ה אי ותוס' תמורה כג. ד"ה אוכלין]

גליון הש"ס

גמ' דכתיב ויקצוף משה. עי' תשובת פנים מאירות ח"ב סימן כ"ט:

[וע"ע תוס' חולין כט. ד"ה איש]

רבינו חננאל

נביא נבואתו מסתלקת ממנו מדבורה דכתיב חדלו פרזון בישראל חדלו עד שקמתי דבורה שקמתי אם וגו' וכתיב עורי עורי דבורה עורי עורי דברי שיר וגו': אמר ר"ש בן לקיש כל הכועס אם חכם הוא חכמתו מסתלקת ממנו ממשה דכתיב ויקצוף משה על פקודי החיל וגו' וכתיב ויאמר אלעזר [הכהן] וגו' מכלל דאיעלם ממשה רבינו. אם נביא הוא נבואתו מסתלקת ממנו מאלישע דכתיב לולי פני יהושפט מלך יהודה אני נושא אם אביט אליך ואם אראך וגו' וכתיב ועתה קחו לי מנגן וגו' מכלל שנסתלקה הנבואה מעליו וכן הכועס אפי' [אם] פוסקין לו גדולה מן השמים מורידין אותו ממנו מאליאב אחי דוד שנאמר ויחר אף אליאב בדוד וגו': תניא אמר להם מקובל אני מרבותי שהפסח דוחה השבת ולא פסח ראשון אלא אפילו פסח שני ולא פסח צבור אלא אפילו פסח יחיד אמרו לו מה יהא על העם ששכחו להביא סכינם מאתמול לשחוט פסחיהם כו' וסליקא כיון דפסח חובה הקבוע להם זמן הוא שרי להקדיש ולהקריב בשבת לפיכך מי שהיה פסחו טלה תחב הסכין בצמרו ומי שהיה פסחו גדי תחב הסכין בין קרניו והביאום לעזרה ומקשינן והא עבדין עבודה בקדשים ופרקי' קודם שהקדישום הביאום לעזרה ואח"כ הקדישום שלא יתיראו כעושי מלאכה בקדשים ואע"ג שנראין כמחמר אחר בהמתו בשבת הא אסיקנא כלאחר יד הוא שהוא שלא כדרך המחמרין שכל העושה בשבת דבר שאינו כדרך מלאכה מחמר כלאחר יד מקרי ופטור כדתנן המוציא לאחר ידו או ברגלו כו' ואע"פ שמן התורה פטור מדרבנן אסור הוא. והכי קא מיבעיא להו לבני בתירא ושאלו מהלל דבר המותר מן התורה ודבר שבות כלאחר יד עומד בפניו לעכבו במקום מצוה שרי או לא אמר להם הניחו להן לישראל אם הן אינם נביאים בני נביאים הם ונתברר כי התמיד והפסח מן התורה דחו שבת אבל דדחו טומאה מנא לן אמר ר' יוחנן פסח משום דכתיב איש איש כי יהיה טמא לנפש וגו' איש נדחה לפסח שני ואין צבור נדחין לפסח שני אלא עושין בטומאה ודחה ר"ל להא דר"י ואמר הוא מהכא וישלחו מן המחנה כל צרוע וכל זב וגו' תא

תורה אור

*אמר לו רבי עקיבא או חלוף מה אם הזאה שהיא משום שבות אינה דוחה את השבת שחיטה שהיא משום מלאכה אינו דין שלא תדחה את השבת אמר לו ר' אליעזר עקיבא עקרת מה שכתוב בתורה °במועדו בין בחול בין בשבת אמר לו רבי הבא לי מועד לאלו כמועד לשחיטה *כלל *אמר רבי עקיבא כל מלאכה שאפשר לעשותה מערב שבת אינה דוחה את השבת שחיטה שאי אפשר לעשותה מע"ש דוחה את השבת: **גמ'** תנו רבנן הלכה זו נתעלמה מבני בתירא *פעם אחת חל ארבעה עשר להיות בשבת שכחו ולא ידעו אם פסח דוחה את השבת אם לאו אמרו כלום יש אדם שיודע אם פסח דוחה את השבת אם לאו אמרו להם אדם אחד יש שעלה מבבל והלל הבבלי שמו ששימש שני גדולי הדור שמעיה ואבטליון ויודע אם פסח דוחה את השבת אם לאו שלחו וקראו לו אמרו לו כלום אתה יודע אם הפסח דוחה את השבת אם לאו אמר להם וכי פסח אחד יש לנו בשנה שדוחה את השבת והלא הרבה יותר ממאתים פסחים יש לנו בשנה שדוחין את השבת אמרו לו מנין לך אמר להם נאמר מועדו בפסח ונאמר °מועדו בתמיד מה מועדו האמור בתמיד דוחה את השבת אף מועדו האמור בפסח דוחה את השבת ועוד ק"ו הוא ומה תמיד שאין ענוש כרת דוחה את השבת פסח שענוש כרת אינו דין שדוחה את השבת *מיד הושיבוהו בראש ומינוהו נשיא עליהם והיה (א) דורש כל היום כולו בהלכות הפסח התחיל מקנטרן בדברים אמר להן מי גרם לכם שאעלה מבבל ואהיה נשיא עליכם עצלות שהיתה בכם שלא שמשתם שני גדולי הדור שמעיה ואבטליון אמרו לו ר' שכח ולא הביא סכין מע"ש מהו אמר להן הלכה זו שמעתי ושכחתי אלא הנח להן לישראל אם אין נביאים הן בני נביאים הן למחר מי שפסחו טלה תוחבו בצמרו מי שפסחו גדי תוחבו בין קרניו *ראה מעשה ונזכר הלכה ואמר *כך מקובלני מפי שמעיה ואבטליון אמר מר נאמר מועדו בפסח ונאמר מועדו בתמיד מה מועדו האמור בתמיד דוחה את השבת אף מועדו האמור בפסח דוחה שבת ותמיד גופיה מנלן דדחי שבת אילימא משום דכתיב ביה במועדו פסח נמי הא כתיב ביה במועדו אלא מועדו לא משמע ליה הכא נמי מועדו לא משמע ליה אלא אמר קרא °עולת שבת בשבתו על עולת התמיד מכלל [עולה] דתמיד קרבה בשבת אמר מר ועוד ק"ו ומה תמיד שאין ענוש כרת דוחה את השבת פסח שענוש כרת אינו דין שדוחה את השבת איכא למיפרך מה לתמיד שכן תדיר וכליל ק"ו אמר להו ברישא ופרכוה והדר אמר להו גזירה שוה וכי מאחר דגמר גזירה שוה ק"ו למה לי אלא לדידהו קאמר להו בשלמא גזירה שוה לא גמריתו *דאין אדם דן גזירה שוה מעצמו אלא ק"ו דאדם דן מעצמו איבעי לכו למידן אמרו ליה ק"ו פריכא הוא: אמר מר למחר מי שפסחו טלה תוחב לו בצמרו גדי תוחב לו בין קרניו והא

במדבר ט · במדבר כח · שם

רש"י

אמר לו רבי עקיבא או חילוף · או אני אחליף הדין דפשיטא לי דהזאה מעכבא וילפינן בקל וחומר מינה לשחיטה שתעכב: במועדו · ויעשו בני ישראל את הפסח במועדו: הבא לי מועד לאלו · שיהא זמן קבוע להן כמה שקבוע לשחיטה הילכך כיון דלא קביע להו זימנא ומצי למיעבד להו מאתמול לא דחו והזאה נמי לאו מגופיה דפסח היא ולא כתיב בה מועד: **גמ'** הלכה זו · שפסח דוחה שבת: בני בתירה · נשיאים היו: אמר להן · הלל: וכי פסח אחד יש לנו שדוחה את השבת והלא יותר ממאתים פסחים יש לנו שדוחין את השבת · כלומר יותר ממאתים קרבנו' יש שדוחין שבת בשנה חמשים שבתות השנה בכל שבת ושבת ארבעה כבשים שנים לתמידים ושנים למוספין הרי מאתים לבד שבת שבתוך פסח ובתוך החג שקריבין בהן מוספי היום שבעת עולים בפסח וארבעה עשר לחג: מה מועדו האמור בתמיד · ולקמיה פריך תמיד גופיה מנא להו: והיה יושב ודורש · כדרך שהנשיא עושה: מקנטרן · לשון קינטור ועלבון קונט"כדיר בלע"ז: מהו. הבאת סכין אינה דוחה דהא אפשר למיעבד מאתמול ומה יעשה: שמעתי ושכחתי. לקמן מפרש טעמא: בני נביאים הן · ותראו מה יעשו: למחר · בארבעה עשר בשבת: שפסחו טלה תחב לו בצמרו · את הסכין: ומי שפסחו גדי · שאין לו צמר אלא שיער שאין יכול לתוחבו בצמרו תחב לו בין קרניו ואין זה משאוי לעבור עליו משום שביתת בהמתו דלאו אורחיה בכי האי מלאכה ובענין זה הביאו סכיניהן: ראה · הלל זה המעשה שעשו: ונזכר הלכה · כך שמעתי: כך מקובלני · שכך הלכה כמו שעשו אלו: פסח נמי כתיב ביה במועדו · ולא שמעת לי' מיניה ומתמיד ילפת ליה אלא על כרחיך מדבעית למילף מתמיד לא משתמע להו דחיית שבת דאמרי במועדו דקאמר בזמן התירא קאמר הכא בתמיד נמי לא משמע להו ומנא ליה: אלא אמר קרא · במוספין עולת שבת בשבתו על עולת התמיד לבד מעולת התמיד אלמא תמיד נמי דחי: אמר מר ועוד קל וחומר כו' ופרכוה · מהא פירכא שכן כליל שכן תדיר: וכי מאחר דגמיר · מרבותיו שגזירה שוה זו לכך באה דקיימא לן אין אדם דן גזירה שוה מעצמו אלא אם כן נתקבלה ובאה מסיני דדילמא קרא למילתא אחריתי אתא וכיון דהוא כך קיבל הרי הוא כמו שנכתב בגופו בפירוש ולמה ליה קל וחומר שהוא דבר סברא מדעתו ומלבו: הכי קאמר נהי דגזירה שוה לא גמריתו · מרבותיכם גזירה שוה לריכא רב דאין אדם דן גזירה שוה מעצמו אלא אם כן למדה מרבו אלא קל וחומר כו': אמרו לו קל וחומר · דאית ביה לא דייניגן דפריכא הוא כדאמרן שכן תדיר: והא

תוספות

מה מועדו האמור בתמיד דוחה את השבת. ולקמן יליף מעל עולת התמיד תימה דבשמעתין לא דריש ממשמעות דמועדו וכן הא דפסח דחי טומאה ילפינן לקמן מאיש איש כדחה ואין ליבור נדחין ובתמיד ילפינן מג"ש דמועדו מועדו ובפרק כילד צולין (לקמן דף עז.) משמע דדריש לה ממשמעות דמועדו דתניא וידבר משה את מועדי ה' מה ת"ל לפי שלא מצינו בכל התורה שנאמר בהן מועדו אלא בפסח ותמיד מועדו אפי' בשבת מועדו אפילו בטומאה שאר קרבנות מנין תלמוד לומר אלה תעשו לה' במועדיכם ת"ל וידבר משה ומשמע דממשמעות' דמועדו דריש ועוד דקאמר התם ולריכי דאי כתב רחמנא תמיד שכן תדיר וכליל אבל פסח לא ואי כתיב פסח שכן כרת ואי מגזירה שוה ילפינן מה לריך ללריכותא הא אילטריך מועדו דתמיד משום טומאה ודפסח משום שבת אלא ודאי ממשמעותא דמועדו דריש וע"כ תנאי היא ועוד בפ' ר' ישמעאל במנחות (דף עב.) דריש *שתי הלחם דדחו שבת מתקריב תקריב אפילו בשבת ואפילו בטומאה ולפי שמעתין מצי למילף בג"ש דמועדו מפסח ותמיד או ממשמעותא כמו בכילד צולין (לקמן דף עז.):

תוחב לו בצמרו · וא"ת *והא בעי כלי שרת כדילפינן בפ' דם חטאת (זבחים דף צז:) ויקח את המאכלת וי"ל שהקדישוה השתא משמע בשמעתין דיש איסור רשות הרבים בירושלים וקשה דאמרינן בפ' קמא דעירובין (דף ו:) ירושלים אלמלא דלתותיה ננעלות בלילה חייבין עלי' משום רשות הרבים ולאו דוקא ננעלות אלא ראויות לנעול כדמסיק התם ותירץ ר"י דהכא לאחר שנפרצו בה פרצות וכי האי גוונא משני בפרק בתרא דעירובין (דף קא.) אמילתא אחריתי*:

מה לתמיד שכן תדיר · ותימה ונילף מבינייהו דתמיד ומילה או משתי הלחם (*גרידא) דדחו שבת:

והא

עין משפט נר מצוה

ב א מיי' פ"א מהלכות קרבן פסח הל' יח:

[עי' פרש"י לקמן סח: ד"ה כלל]

לאי דרשה אקירת העומר קאי ע"ש

[עי' תוס' זבחים מז. ד"ה איזהו ותוס' חולין ב. ד"ה כגון]

[ועי"ע תוס' ב"מ ע: ד"ה דנפול]

[משתי הלחם וחד מסך כצ"ל רש"א]

ע"ז מו:

לקמן סט: [שבת קל. יכמות יד. מנחות עב.ט.]

[תוספתא פ"ד]

ב"מ פה.

[סנהד' פב.]

[נדה יט:]

הגהות הב"ח

(א) גמ' והיה יושב ודורש כל היום:

רבינו חננאל

ת"ר הלכה זו נתעלמה מבני בתירא פעם אחת חל ארבעה עשר להיות בשבת אמרו לו להלל הזקן פסח דוחה את השבת או לא אמר להו וכי פסח אחד יש לנו שדוחה את השבת והלא יותר ממאתים פסחים דוחין את השבת כו' ירושלמי אית תנא תני מאה פסחים [אית תנא תני מאתים] אית תנא תני שלש מאות מאן דתני מאה תמידין [של] שבת מאן דתני מאתים תמידין ומוספין של שבתות מאן דתני ג' מאות מוסף של ראשי חדשים ושל ימים טובים וכו': אמר מר נאמר במועדו בפסח ונאמר במועדו בתמיד מה זו דוחה שבת דכתיב עולת שבת בשבתו על עולת התמיד אף פסח דוחה שבת וכו' ועוד קל וחומר וכו' הכי קאמר להו נהי גזרה שוה לא גמיר לכו דאין אדם דן גזרה שוה מעצמו אא"כ [קבל] קבלה מאבותיו אבל היה לכם לדון קל וחומר מעצמו אמרו [לו] ק"ו איכא למיפרך מה לתמיד שכן כליל שכן תדיר. מינהו נשיא עליהן התחיל לקנתרן ומפני שנתיהר נתעלמה ממנו הלכה מכאן אמר רב שכל המתיהר אם חכם הוא חכמתו מסתלקת ממנו מהלל ואם נביא

SAID R. AKIBA TO HIM, OR ON THE CONTRARY: IF HAZA'AH, WHICH IS [FORBIDDEN] AS A SHEBUTH, DOES NOT OVERRIDE
a THE SABBATH,[1] THEN SHECHITAH, WHICH IS [NORMALLY FORBIDDEN] ON ACCOUNT OF LABOUR, IS IT NOT LOGICAL THAT IT DOES NOT OVERRIDE THE SABBATH.[2] AKIBA! SAID R. ELIEZER TO HIM, YOU WOULD ERASE WHAT IS WRITTEN IN THE TORAH, [LET THE CHILDREN OF ISRAEL PREPARE THE PASSOVER SACRIFICE] IN ITS APPOINTED TIME,[3] [IMPLYING] BOTH ON WEEK-DAYS AND ON THE SABBATH. SAID HE TO HIM, MASTER, GIVE ME AN APPOINTED TIME FOR THESE AS THERE IS AN APPOINTED SEASON FOR SHECHITAH![4] R. AKIBA STATED A GENERAL RULE: WORK WHICH COULD BE DONE ON THE EVE OF THE SABBATH DOES NOT OVERRIDE[5] THE SABBATH; SHECHITAH, WHICH COULD NOT BE DONE ON THE EVE OF THE SABBATH, DOES OVERRIDE THE SABBATH.

GEMARA. Our Rabbis taught: This *halachah* was hidden from [i.e., forgotten by] the Bene Bathyra.[6] On one occasion the fourteenth [of Nisan] fell on the Sabbath, [and] they forgot and did not know whether the Passover overrides the Sabbath or not. Said they, 'Is there any man who knows whether the Passover overrides the Sabbath or not?' They were told, 'There is a certain man who has come up from Babylonia, Hillel the Babylonian by
b name, who served[1] the two greatest men of the time,[2] and he knows whether the Passover overrides the Sabbath or not'. [Thereupon] they summoned him [and] said to him, 'Do you know whether the Passover overrides the Sabbath or not?' 'Have we then [only] one Passover during the year which overrides the Sabbath?' replied he to them, 'Surely we have many more than two hundred Passovers during the year which override the Sabbath![3] Said they to him, 'How do you know it?'[4] He answered them, *'In its appointed time'* is stated in connection with the Passover, and *'In its appointed time'*[5] is stated in connection with the *tamid;* just as *'Its appointed time'* which is said in connection with the *tamid* overrides the Sabbath, so *'Its appointed time'* which is said in connection with the Passover overrides the Sabbath. Moreover, it follows *a minori;* if the *tamid,* [the omission of] which is not punished by *kareth,* overrides the Sabbath, then the Passover, [neglect of] which is punished by *kareth,*[6] is it not logical that it overrides the Sabbath! They immediately set him at their head and appointed him *Nasi* [Patriarch] over them,[7] and he was sitting and lecturing the whole day on the laws of Passover. He began rebuking them with words. Said he to them, 'What caused it for you that I should come up from Babylonia to be a *Nasi* over you? It was your indolence, because you did not serve the two greatest men of the time, Shemaiah and Abṭalyon.' Said they to him, 'Master, what if a man forgot and did not bring a knife on the eve of the Sabbath?' 'I have heard this law,' he answered, 'but have forgotten it. But leave it to Israel: if they are not prophets, yet they are the children of prophets!' On the morrow, he whose Passover was a lamb stuck it [the knife] in its wool; he whose Passover was a goat stuck it between its horns. He saw the incident and recollected the *halachah* and said, 'Thus have I received the tradition from the mouth[s] of Shemaiah and Abṭalyon.'

The Master said: '"*In its appointed season*" is stated in connection with the Passover, and "*in its appointed time*" is stated in connection with the *tamid:* just as "*its appointed time*" which is said in connection with the *tamid* overrides the Sabbath, so "*its appointed time*" which is said in connection with the Passover overrides the Sabbath.' And how do we know that the *tamid* itself overrides the Sabbath? Shall we say, because *'in its appointed time'* is written in connection
c with it;[1] then the Passover too, surely *'in its appointed time'* is written in connection with it?[2] Hence [you must say that] *'its appointed time'* has no significance for him [Hillel]; then here too, *'its appointed time'* should have no significance for him?—Rather Scripture saith, *This is the burnt-offering of every Sabbath, beside the continual burnt-offering:*[3] whence it follows that the continual burnt-offering [*tamid*] is offered on the Sabbath.

The Master said: 'Moreover, it follows *a minori:* if the *tamid,* [the omission of] which is not punished by *kareth,* overrides the Sabbath; then the Passover, [neglect of] which is punished by *kareth,* is it not logical that it overrides the Sabbath!' [But] this
d can be refuted: as for the *tamid,* that is because it is constant,[1] and entirely [burnt]?[2]—He first told them the *a minori* argument, but they refuted it; [so] then he told them the *gezerah shawah.* But since he had received the tradition of a *gezerah shawah,* what was the need of an *a minori* argument?—Rather he spoke to them on their own ground: It is well that you do not learn a *gezerah shawah,* because a man cannot argue [by] a *gezerah shawah* of his own accord.[3] But [an inference] *a minori,* which a man can argue of his own accord, you should have argued!—Said they to him, It is a fallacious *a minori* argument.

The Master said: 'On the morrow, he whose Passover was a lamb stuck it in its wool; [he whose Passover was] a goat stuck

a (1) I regard this as certain. (2) This is a *reductio ad absurdum.* (3) Num. IX, 2. (4) *Shechitah* must be done on the fourteenth; have these a similar fixed time?—surely not! (5) Lit., 'every work . . . does not override'. (6) 'The children of Bathyra'—they were the religious heads of Palestine at the time of this incident.—Bathyra is a town of Babylonia. [Their name is, however, generally held to be derived from the colony of that name in Batanea mentioned in Josephus, *Antiquities,* XVII, 2, 2, and established by Herod for the settlement of the Jews who had come from Babylon. For another view, v. Derenbourg, *Essai,* p. 179.]

b (1) I.e., studied under. (2) Lit., 'generation'. (3) I.e., during the year more than two hundred sacrifices are offered on the Sabbath, viz., the two daily burnt-offerings and the two additional sacrifices of every Sabbath, besides the extra sacrifices offered on the Sabbath which occurs in the middle of Passover and the middle of Tabernacles. (4) A question of such importance cannot be decided by a mere argument, however strong, but must have Biblical support, as well as the support of tradition. (5) Num. XXVIII, 2. (6) V. Num. IX, 13. (7) This story of Hillel's rise to eminence contains a number of difficulties particularly (i) the ignorance of Bene Bathyra, the religious heads of the people, and (ii) the fact that there was no *single* head, but the authority lay in the hands of a family. V. Halevi, *Doroth,* I, 3, pp. 37ff, where this is discussed at great length; he maintains that the Great Sanhedrin, which was the ruling authority on all religious matters, had been abolished, and there was no single religious head at the time. [Büchler *Synhedrion* pp. 144ff connects this story with the controversy related *infra* 70b which led to the retirement of Judah b. Durtai to the south.]

c (1) Which implies whenever it is. (2) Then why is it regarded as axiomatic in the case of the former, whereas the latter must be learnt from it? (3) Num. XXVIII, 10.

d (1) Every day; in comparison therewith the Passover, which is only once a year, is not constant. (2) Each of which fact gives it a stronger claim to override the Sabbath. (3) A man must have received a tradition from his teachers that a particular word in the Pentateuch is meant for a *gezerah shawah,* but he cannot assume it himself. Hence the Bene Bathyra, not having received this tradition, could not adduce this *gezerah shawah.*

that maketh atonement by reason of the life:[8] [65*b*] blood wherewith life departs, makes atonement; and blood wherewith life does not depart, does not make atonement?—Rather [reply],[9] R. Judah is consistent with his view, for he maintained: Blood cannot nullify [other] blood.[10]

It was taught, R. Judah said to the Sages: On your view, why did they stop up [the holes in] the Temple Court?[11] Said they to him: It is praiseworthy for the sons of Aaron [the priests] to walk in blood up to their ankles. But it interposed?[12]—It is moist [liquid] and does not interpose. As it was taught: Blood, ink, honey and
a milk, if dry, interpose; if moist, they do not interpose.[1] But their garments become [blood-] stained, whereas it was taught: If his garments were soiled and he performed the service, his service is unfit? And should you answer that they raised their garments.[2] surely it was taught: [*And the priest shall put on*] *his linen measure:*[3] [that means] that it must not be [too] short nor too long?[4]—[They could raise them] at the carrying of the limbs to the [Altar] ascent, which was not a service. Was it not? But since it required the priesthood, it was a service! For it was taught, *And the priest shall offer the whole,* [*and burn it*] *on the altar:*[5] this refers to the carrying of the limbs to the [altar] ascent.—Rather [they could raise them] at the carrying of the wood to the [altar] pile, which was not a service. Nevertheless, how could they walk when carrying the limbs to the [altar] ascent and when carrying the blood? They walked on balconies.[6]

HOW DID THEY HANG UP [THE SACRIFICES] AND FLAY [THEM] etc. THEN HE TORE IT OPEN AND TOOK OUT ITS EMURIM, PLACED THEM ON A TRAY AND BURNT THEM [ON THE ALTAR]. Did he then burn them himself?[7]—Say, To burn them on the altar.

THE FIRST DIVISION WENT OUT etc. A Tanna taught: Each one placed his paschal lamb in its hide and slung it behind him. Said R. 'Ilish: In Arab-like fashion.[8]

CHAPTER VI

MISHNAH. THESE THINGS IN [CONNECTION WITH] THE PASSOVER OFFERING OVERRIDE THE SABBATH: ITS SHECHITAH AND THE SPRINKLING OF ITS BLOOD AND THE CLEANSING OF ITS BOWELS AND THE BURNING OF ITS FAT. BUT ITS ROASTING AND THE WASHING OF ITS BOWELS DO
b NOT OVERRIDE THE SABBATH. ITS CARRYING[1] AND BRINGING IT FROM WITHOUT THE TEḤUM[2] AND THE CUTTING OFF OF ITS WART DO NOT OVERRIDE THE SABBATH. R. ELIEZER SAID: THEY DO OVERRIDE [THE SABBATH]. SAID R. ELIEZER, DOES IT NOT FOLLOW A FORTIORI: IF SHECHITAH, WHICH IS [USUALLY FORBIDDEN] AS A LABOUR, OVERRIDES THE SABBATH, SHALL NOT THESE, WHICH ARE [ONLY FORBIDDEN] AS A SHEBUTH, OVERRIDE THE SABBATH?[3] R. JOSHUA ANSWERED HIM, LET FESTIVAL[S] REBUT[4] IT, WHEREIN THEY PERMITTED LABOUR AND FORBADE A SHEBUTH.[5] SAID R. ELIEZER TO HIM, WHAT IS THIS, JOSHUA, WHAT PROOF IS A VOLUNTARY ACT IN RESPECT OF A PRECEPT! R. AKIBA ANSWERED AND SAID, LET HAZA'AH[6] PROVE IT, WHICH IS [PERFORMED] BECAUSE IT IS A PRECEPT AND IS [NORMALLY FORBIDDEN ONLY] AS A SHEBUTH, YET IT DOES NOT OVERRIDE THE SABBATH;[7] SO YOU TOO, DO NOT WONDER AT THESE, THAT THOUGH THEY ARE [REQUIRED] ON ACCOUNT OF THE PRECEPT AND ARE [ONLY FORBIDDEN] AS A SHEBUTH, YET THEY DO NOT OVERRIDE THE SABBATH. SAID R. ELIEZER TO HIM, BUT IN RESPECT OF THAT [ITSELF] I ARGUE: IF SHECHITAH, WHICH IS A LABOUR, OVERRIDES THE SABBATH, IS IT NOT LOGICAL THAT HAZA'AH, WHICH IS [ONLY] A SHEBUTH, OVERRIDES THE SABBATH! [66*a*]

(8) Ibid. (9) To the question, 'But the draining blood is mixed with it'. (10) Therefore there must be a little of proper (i.e., life-) blood, if spilled in this goblet of mixed blood, and that is sufficient for atonement. (11) On the eve of Passover they stopped up the holes through which the blood of the sacrifices passed out to the stream of Kidron. (12) Between the pavement and their feet, whereas they had to stand actually on the pavement itself, Zeb. 15*b*.

a (1) When a person takes a ritual bath (*tebillah*), nothing must interpose between the water and his skin; if something does interpose, it invalidates the bath. (2) I.e., they made them short, so that they did not reach down to the blood. (3) E.V. *Garment*. Lev. VI, 3. (4) But reach exactly to the ground. (5) Lev. I, 13. (6) Projecting boards alongside the walls. (7) This was not necessarily done by the same priest. (8) In the fashion of Arab merchants, Rashi. Jast.: in the manner of travellers.

b (1) Lit., 'riding'—i.e., carrying it upon one's shoulder. (2) V. Glos. (3) 'Labour' (מלאכה) denotes work regarded as *Biblically* forbidden, whereas a *shebuth* is only a Rabbinical interdict. (4) Lit., 'prove'. (5) Lit., 'they permitted (that which is forbidden on the Sabbath) on account of labour' etc. Slaughtering and cooking, for example, are permitted on Festivals, whereas bringing food from without the *teḥum* which is only a Rabbinical prohibition, is forbidden. (6) *Haza'ah* connotes the sprinkling of the waters of purification (v. Lev. XIV, 7, 16; Num. XIX, 19) upon an unclean person; *zeriḳah*, the sprinkling of the blood of the sacrifice upon the altar. (7) If the seventh day of the unclean person (v. Num. ibid.) falls on the Sabbath, which happens to be the eve of Passover, R. Akiba holds that the *haza'ah* must not be performed, though the man is thereby prevented from joining in the Passover sacrifice.

מסורת הש"ס

עין משפט נר מצוה

נו א מיי' פ"ב מהל' מקוואות הלכה ב סמג לאוין קיא טוש"ע י"ד סי' קלח סעיף טו :

נז ב מיי' פ"א מהל' כלי המקדש הל' ד :

נח ג מיי' פ"א מהל' פסולי מוקדשין הלכה כב :

זבחים עח: [מנחות כב: חולין פז:]

נט ד מיי' פ"א מהל' ק"פ הל' ו :

א ה מיי' פ"א מהל' ק"פ הלכה יח סמג עשין רכג :

שבת קכ: זבחים לה: מנחות כא:

[נ"ל ותניא]

ב ו מיי' פ"ו שם הל' ו:

גמרא

דם שהנפש יוצאה בו מכפר דם שאין הנפש יוצאה בו אינו מכפר אלא ר' יהודה *לטעמיה *דאמר אין דם מבטל דם תניא *אמר להן ר' יהודה לחכמים לדבריכם למה פוקקין את העזרה אמרו לו שבח הוא לבני אהרן שילכו עד ארכובותיהם בדם והא קא חייץ לח הוא ואינו חוצץ כדתניא* הדם והדיו והחלב והדבש יבשים חוצצין לחין אין חוצצין והא קמתווסי מאנייהו (*ותנן) היו בגדיו מטושטשין ועבד עבודתו פסולה וכי תימא דמדלו להו למאנייהו והתניא* מדו בד מדו כמדתו שלא יחסר ולא יותיר בהולכת איברין לכבש דלאו עבודה היא ולא והא מדבעי כהונה עבודה היא דתניא* והקריב הכהן את הכל המזבחה זו הולכת אברים לכבש אלא בהולכת עצים למערכה דלאו עבודה היא בהולכת אברים לכבש ובהולכת דם מיהא היכי אזלי דמסגי אאיצטבי: כיצד תולין ומפשיטין וכו' קרעו והוציאו את אמוריו נתנם במגיס להקטירם: אטו הוא גופיה הוה מקטר להו *אימא להקטירן ע"ג המזבח: יצתה כת ראשונה וכו': תנא כל אחד ואחד נותן פסחו בעורו ומפשיל לאחוריו אמר רב עיליש טייעות:

הדרן עלך תמיד נשחט

אלו דברים בפסח דוחין את השבת שחיטתו וזריקת דמו ומיחוי קרביו והקטרת חלביו אבל צלייתו והדחת קרביו אינן דוחין את השבת *הרכבתו והבאתו מחוץ לתחום וחתיכת יבלתו אין דוחין את השבת ר' אליעזר אומר דוחין *אמר ר"א והלא דין הוא *מה אם שחיטה שהיא משום מלאכה דוחה את השבת אלו שהן משום שבות לא ידחו את השבת א"ל רבי יהושע יום טוב יוכיח שהתירו בו משום מלאכה ואסור בו משום שבות א"ל ר"א מה זה יהושע מה ראיה רשות למצוה השיב רבי עקיבא ואמר הזאה תוכיח שהיא משום מצוה והיא משום שבות ואינה דוחה את השבת אף אתה אל תתמה על אלו שאף על פי שהן משום מצוה והן משום שבות לא ידחו את השבת אמר לו רבי אליעזר ועליה אני דן ומה אם שחיטה שהיא משום מלאכה דוחה את השבת הזאה שהיא משום שבות אינו דין שדוחה את השבת אמר

רש"י

דם שהנפש יוצאה בו . דם קילוח שה' דמים הם בפרק דם שחיטה : אלא רבי יהודה לטעמיה דאמר אין דם מבטל דם . הלכך לא בטיל ההוא דאישתפיך ובכל פורתא דמטי מיניה למזבח זריקה היא ומיתכשר ומילתיה דרבי יהודה בזבחים בפרק כל הזבחים שנתערבו דקתני גבי דם זבחים דם שנתערב במים אם יש בו מראית דם כשר נתערב בדם בהמת חולין או בדם חיה רואין את הפסול כאילו היה מים ואם יש בכשר כדי להיות בהן מראית דם כשר ואם לאו פסול ר' יהודה אומר אין דם מבטל דם : תניא גרסינן : לדבריכם למה פוקקין . את נקב חומת העזרה שהדמים המתערבין באמה יוצאים בו לחוץ *והיו פוקקין אותו בכל ערבי פסחים בשלמא לדידי כדי שלא יצא כל דם הנשפך וכשמילא כוס התערובות נמלא מכולם בתוכו ואם נשפך אחד מהן בלא זריקה נמצא זורק ממנו : והא קא הוי חציצה . בין רגליהן לרצפה דתנן בזבחים (ד' טו:) עומד על הכלי או על גבי רגל חבירו פסול דבעינן לעמוד לשרת ואין זה עמידה : חוצץ . לענין טבילה תנן : מיתווסי . מתלכלכין בדם : מדו . ולבש הכהן מדו בד: כמדתו . שוה לארץ: בהולכת אברים דלאו עבודה · היו מגו מדלן להו ולקמיה פריך ושאר עבודות היכי עביד : זו הולכת אברים · דגבייהו כתיב האי קרא והקרב והכרעים וגו': דמסגו אאיצטבי . איצטבאות של בנין היו שם והרי הן כרצפה : והקטירן סלקא דעתך הוא גופיה מקטר להו . בתמיה והא זר הוא דבזר קיימינן כדתני נותן על כתיפו ועל כתף חבירו ותולה ומפשיט וכהנים לא היו מפשיטין קדשים קלים דמה לי ולהן ואפילו הפשט וניתוח של עולה שהוא מצוה כשר בזר כדאמרינן בשילהי פרק ב' דיומא (ד' כו:) ואית דמפרשי אטו במגס גופיה מקטר להו ולאו מילתא היא דודאי אורחיה למתני הקטרה בכלי שרת : להקטירן · נותנן במגס עד שיבוא הראוי להקטירן ויקטירם : כל אחד ואחד . כשהיו הולכין לבתיהם היה נותן פסחו בעורו ומפשילו לאחוריו : אמר רב עיליש · שם חכם : טייעות . דרך סוחרים ישמעאלים הוא זה :

הדרן עלך תמיד נשחט

אלו דברים דוחין את השבת . לקמיה בגמרא מפרש מנא לן : שחיטתו וזריקת דמו . אי אפשר אלא ביום דכתיב (ויקרא ז) ביום צוותו להקריב את קרבניהם ביום ולא בלילה : מיחוי קרביו . מפרש בגמ' וטעמא שלא יסריחו : צלייתו והדחת קרביו אין דוחין . דאפשר משתחשך : הרכבתו . על כתף האדם להביאו לעזרה דרך רשות הרבים אע"פ שאינו אלא איסור שבות דרבנן דקי"ל חי נושא את עצמו אין דוחה דה"ל למיעבד מאתמול וכן הבאתו מחוץ לתחום : וחתיכת יבלתו . ורוא"ה בלע"ז וחותכה בצפרניו או בשיניו איכא אלא שבות דמלאכה כלאחר יד היא : שחיטה שהיא . אסורה בחולין בשבת משום איסור מלאכה גמורה שהרי באבות מלאכות היא מניה ואעפ"כ דוחה את השבת בפסח : לא ידחו · בתמיה : י"ט יוכיח שהתירו בו . שחיטה ובשול שהוא אב מלאכה ומותרין להדיוט ואסרו בו להביא דבר מחוץ לתחום ולאכלו הואיל והוה אפשר לן מאתמול ואע"ג דתחומין דרבנן : מה ראיה רשות למצוה . אכילת הדיוט רשות היא וצרך גבוה מצוה היא ואם העמידו חכמים איסור שבות שלהן במקום רשות יעמידוהו אף במקום מצוה בתמיה : הזאה תוכיח שהיא מצוה . בטמא מת שחל שביעי שלו להיות בשבת ערב פסח שאם לא יזה לא יעשה פסחו ואפ"ה איכא דוחה *דהכי שמעינן ליה לרבי עקיבא דלא דחיא והזאה שבות הוא דמאי מלאכה היא אלא מתחזי כמתקן גברא: ועליה אני דן . וגם על ההזאה אני חולק ואומר שתדחה ולא תעכבהו מפסח ומקל וחומר זה עצמו : אמר

תוספות

אטו במגס גופיה מקטר ליה . רש"י מוחקו משום דבמנחות לא פריך דתניא בכמה דוכתי ומקטירה בכלי שרת וכן מוחק בפ' שני שעירי (יומא סז:) ואין צריך להגיה הספרים דבריש פר' שני דסוטה (ד' טו·) פריך גבי מנחות כי האי גוונא דקתני התם ומעלה ומקטירה בכלי שרת ופריך ובכלי שרת מקטר ליה אימא להקטירה ומשום דהתם פריך ומשני לא פריך לה במנחות והא דפריך הכא גבי אימורים אע"ג דכבר פריך בפרק שני שעירי (ד' סז:) משום דהתם בפרים והכא בכבשים ומיהו יש ספרים דגרסי בברייתא דסוטה מעלן ומקטירן בכלי שרת ומולחן ונותן ע"ג האשים ופריך מקטירן בכלי שרת ס"ד פי' וכי כמו שהוא בכלי שרת מקטירן והא לא מלחן ומשני להקטירן פירוש אחר מליחה ולפי זה יתכן פרש"י ור"ת מפרש דגבי מנחה לא שייך למיפרך דשייך למיתני ומקטירן בכלי שרת כיון שהיא כבר בכלי שרת שהיא נתונה שם להתקדש אבל נתנם במגס משמע שבא לומר שבתוך המגס מקטירם* : [ע"ע תוס' יומא סז: ד"ה אטו וכו' הארכנו ביתר ביאור]

הדרן עלך תמיד נשחט

אלו דברים . זריקת דמו תנא אגב שחיטתו וקשה לר"י אמאי לא תני נמי הפשט עורו דדחי שבת כדתנן בפירקא דלעיל (ד' סד·) י"ד שחל להיות בשבת מניח ידו כו' ותולה ומפשיט ותירץ ר"י משום דהוי בכלל הקטר חלביו שאינו יכול להפשיט אלא עד החזה לרבי יוחנן בן ברוקה בפ' כל כתבי (שבת ד' קי:) ואפילו רבנן דפליגי עליה לא שרו להפשיט כדרכו אלא עד החזה והשאר מפשיט וחותך בחתיכות קטנות כדאמרינן התם *לא צריכא דשקיל לה בברזי : מה

רבינו חננאל

שהנפש יוצא בו הוא מכפר : **ואסיקנא** דדם לח אינו חוצץ דתניא הדם והדבש והחלב יבשים חוצצין להין אין חוצצין והנה כיון שהוא זה הדם לח אין הוצצין ברגליהן [ומקשינן] הלא מטנפי מן הדם בגדי הכהנים ואמרינן דמדלו להו פי' שהיו מגביהין בגדיהם מעט שלא יטנפו מן הדם איני והתניא מדו בד כמדתו שלא יחסר ולא יותיר ושנינן לא היו מגביהין בגדיהם [אלא] בהולכת אברים לכבש דלאו עבודה היא כו' ואסיקנא בהולכת אברים והולכת דם היו מהלכין על האצטבאות: **כיצד** תולין ומפשיטין אונקלאות של ברזל כו' פי' מגים כמין קערה שנותן בה החלבים כדמתרגמינן קערה מניכתא · תאנא כל אחד נותן פסחו בעורו ומפשילו לאחוריו אמר רב עיליש (כוית) [טייעות] :

הדרן עלך תמיד נשחט

אלו דברים בפסח דוחין את השבת שחיטה וזריקה ומחוי קרביו והקטרת חלביו צלייתו והדחת קרביו כו' פי' מיחוי קרביו היא שירקא דמעייא והוא כמו שומן רך שדומה למוח וקרוב להיות רעי ועל זה השומן שדומה למוח נקרא מיחוי קרביו :

[זבחים לה: עי' נדה ע.]

זבחים יח: [לה:]

[יומא כג:]

סוטה טו: יומא סז:

[לקמן סט: ערכין קג:]

[עי' תוס' לקמן סח: ד"ה ומה שחיטה]

גליון הש"ס

גמ' במגים להקטירם · נ"ל והקטירן

מסורת הש"ס

ועולה גופה מנלן אמר קרא °אל יסוד מזבח העולה אלמא עולה טעונה יסוד: יצתה כת ראשונה וכו': תנא *היא נקראת כת עצלנית והא לא סגי דלאו הכי מאי הוי להו למיעבד אפ"ה איבעי להו לזרוזי נפשייהו כדתני'* רבי אומר אי אפשר לעולם בלא בסם ובלא בורסי אשרי מי שאומנתו בסם אוי לו מי שאומנתו בורסי ואי אפשר לעולם בלא זכרים ובלא נקבות אשרי מי שבניו זכרים אוי לו מי שבניו נקבות: כמעשהו בחול וכו': שלא ברצון מאן אמר רב חסדא שלא ברצון רבי אליעזר דאי רבנן הא אמרי שבות הוא ואין שבות במקדש מאי היא דתניא* אחד °החולב °והמחבץ והמגבן כגרוגרות המכבד והמרבץ והרודה חלות דבש בשוגג בשבת חייב חטאת חזיד ביום טוב לוקה את הארבעים דברי רבי אליעזר וחכמים אומרים °אחד זה ואחד זה אינו אלא משום שבות רב אשי אמר אפילו תימא שלא ברצון חכמים ורבי נתן היא דתניא רבי נתן אומר שבות צריכה התירו שבות שאינה צריכה לא התירו: רבי יהודה אומר כוס היה ממלא וכו': תניא* רבי יהודה אומר כוס היה ממלא מדם התערובות שאם ישפך דמו של אחד מהן נמצא זה מכשירו אמרו לו לרבי יהודה והלא לא נתקבל בכלי מנא ידעי אלא הכי קאמרי ליה שמא לא נתקבל בכלי אמר להן אף אני לא אמרתי אלא בנתקבל בכלי מנא ידע *כהנים זריזין הן אי זריזין אמאי משתפיך אגב זריזותייהו דעבדי משתפיך והלא דם התמצית מעורב בו ולרבי יהודה לטעמיה דאמר דם התמצית דם מעליא הוא דתניא* °דם התמצית באזהרה רבי יהודה אומר בהיכרת *והאמר ר' אלעזר מודה ר' יהודה לענין כפרה שאינו מכפר שנא' °כי הדם הוא בנפש יכפר דם

[תוספתא שבת פ"ט] שבת צה. ביצה ג.

רש"י

ועולה גופה מנלן · שמתן דמה במקום שיש תחתיו יסוד למעוטי מזרח ודרום חוץ מאמה למזרח אצל צפון ואמה לדרום אצל מערב דהכי תנן (מדות פ"ג מ"א) אוכל במזרח אמה אחת ובדרום אמה אחת: אל יסוד מזבח העולה · גבי חטאת [נשיא] כתיב ולקח הכהן מדם החטאת באצבעו ונתן על קרנות מזבח העולה ואת דמו ישפך אל יסוד מזבח העולה וה"ל למיכתב אל יסוד המזבח למה לי דכתיב מזבח העולה אלא הכי קאמר אל יסוד מזבח תעשה העולה: עצלנית · מפני שנתעצלה להיות אחרונה: והא לא סגי דלאו הכי · דמצוה לשלש כתות: לזרוזי נפשייהו · להיות מן הראשונים: שלא ברצון רבי אליעזר · דאמר בעלמא גבי מכבד דהייתו דומיא דהדחה איכא חיוב חטאת הלכך במקדש כסבר נעשה צורך גבוה אסור: החולב · מושך החלב מן הבהמה: מחבץ · מעמיד החלב ועושה ממנו חבילין קורין מטונ"ש: אחד זה ואחד זה · מכבד ומרבץ ורודה אבל מאידך לא קאמרי דתולדות אב מלאכה נינהו כדאמרינן בפרק המצניע רבי אליעזר משום הכי מחייב חולב משום מפרק מגבן משום בונה מחבץ משום בורר בהמצניע ומרבץ ומכבד מפרש התם משום אשווי גומות: ורודה · מדכתיב (שופטים יד) ויטבול אותה ביערת הדבש: רב אשי אמר · לעולם רבנן דאמרי בעלמא כמי שבות הוא ומתני' כר' נתן דאמר שבות שאינה צריכה לא התירו במקדש: שאם נשפך דמו של אחד מהן · לארץ ולא נזרק ממנו למזבח: נמצא כוס זה מכשירו · שהרי מעורב בו מן הנשפך: שמא לא נתקבל בכלי · אותו שאתה רוצה להכשיר שמא לא נתקבל בכלי ותו לא מהניא ליה זריקה דתנן נשפך מצואר בהמה על הרצפה ואספו פסול בזבחים בפרק שני (דף כה:): אף אני לא אמרתי · שיועיל אלא כשנתקבל בכלי: ומנא ידע · רבי יהודה אם נתקבל בכלי והא חששא בעלמא הוא דקאמר שאם ישפך דמו וכיון דלתקוני ספיקי אתא היכי מיתקני בהכי שמא לא נתקבל: כהנים זריזין הן · וליכא למיחש לשמא לא קיבלוהו ליכא אחריתא שמא לא נתקבל בכלי כל זה שאתה שואב מאותו ומלאת זורק דם פסול אף אני לא אמרתי למלאות אלא ממקום שיודעין שנשפכו שם דמים שנתקבלו בכלי ואי משום דמיערב בהו מהאי דלא נתקבל כגון דם התמצית הא קא פריך ליה בסיפא ולאו עיקר: אי זריזין הן היכן נשפכין הא זריזין הן וידעי: אגב זריזותייהו · שממהרים לרוץ ולקרב ולזרוק מישתפיך מידייהו: והלא דם התמצית · של פסחים הרבה מעורב בו ואי נשפך דם של אחד כולו בטל במיעוטו ומה תועיל זריקה שהרי בטל: דם התמצית · של חולין ושל קדשים: באזהרה · בלאו ולא כרת דכתיב כי נפש כל בשר דמו בנפשו הוא וגו' עד כל אוכליו יכרת יצא דם התמצית שאינו דם הנפש ובמסכת כריתות מפרש טעמא מ(ה)שה לאוין כתיבי בדם ומייתר חד לדם התמצית: לענין כפרה · שאינו ראוי לזריקה: דם

תורה אור: ויקרא ד

[זבחים מ' ע"ש] [תוספתא פ"ד] ב"ב טז: סנהדרין ק: קדושין פב: שבת צה: [זבחים לד: ודף פ' ע"ש] [שבת כ"ו ע"ב] [תוס' כריתות פ"ב] כריתות ד: חולין עד: [זבחים לה:]

תוספות

החולב כגרוגרות · הקשה ה"ר אפריס דתנן בפ' המוציא (שבת עו:) דשיעור המוציא חלב כדי גמיאה ושיעורי שבת הן שוים לכל המלאכות הוצאה טחינה וקצירה ותירץ דהתם חלב כדי גמיאה שהוא שיעור גדול אבל הכא בחולב לגבינה דאחשובי אחשביה שיעורו כגרוגרות דזוטר אבל אי כדי גמיאה זוטר צריך לומר דסתם חלב לגבינה ולכך הכא שיעורו כגרוגרת והא דמיחייב בכדי גמיאה היינו במפרש בהדיא לאכילה ולשתיה דאי סתם חולב לאכילה ולשתיה ולא לגבינ' אפילו היה מפרש בהדיא לגבינה היה לו להתחייב בכדי גמיאה דזוטר הואיל וסתמו לאכול ולשתות כדאמרינן בסוף כלל גדול (שבת עו·) המוציא תבן כמלא פי פרה לגמל חייב אף על גב דלגמל לא הוי שיעורא בהכי הואיל וסתמא לפרה מיחייב אשיעורא דפרה ויש מפרש דכשהחלב כבר בעין מיחייב בכדי גמיאה אבל חולב לא מיחייב אלא בכגרוגרת דאין אדם טורח לחלוב בפחות מגרוגרת וכי האי גוונא מפליג בהמוציא (שבת עט·) גבי עור לעשות קמיע*: המכבד והמרבץ · ע"כ לאו פסיק רישיה הוא דפסיק רישיה לא הוה שרי ר"ש לרבנן לכתחלה בשילהי המצניע (שבת צה·) ותימה לר"י דא"כ אמאי מחייב רבי אליעזר כיון דיכול להיות בלא גומות ודוחק לומר דפליגי אי הוי פסיק רישיה אי לא ונראה לר"י דבהא פליגי דר' אליעזר סבר סתם מכבד ומרבץ °מתכוון להשוות גומות אף על פי שא"ל להשוות גומות מחייב לרבי יהודה הואיל והשוה גומות לבסוף ורבנן סברי דאין מתכוון אלא לכבד ולרבנן בעלמא וליכא אלא שבות· תימה לר"י היכי מתוקמא מתניתין כרבי אליעזר והא בעזרה שהיה לה רצפת אבנים לא שייך בה אשווי גומות ואפילו לכתחלה שרי כדאמר בשילהי המצניע (גם זה שם) אמימר שרא זילחא במחוזא אע"ג דגזרינן בבמה מדליקין (שבת דף כט:) עיליתא דשישא אטו עיליתא דעלמא מחוזא היתה כולה רצופה באבנים לא גזרינן אטו דעיר דעלמא ואור"י דבעזרה בין רובד לרובד היו גומות אי נמי דלרבי אליעזר דאיכא איסורא דאורייתא בכיבוד דעלמא גזרינן עזרה אטו כיבוד דעלמא דכמה שבות אסרו במקדש בפ' בתרא דעירובין (דף קב:) אבל לרבנן דאפילו בעלמא ליכא אלא איסורא דרבנן אין שבות כי האי במקדש כיון דליכא איסורא דאורייתא בשום מקום· פסק בהלכות גדולות דכיבוד מותר כדאמרינן בהמצניע (דף צה.) גבי ריבוץ הלכתא קיימא לן כרבי שמעון דשרי לרבנן לכתחלה ואין נראה לר"י דהא מזיז עפר ממקומו אסרינן בכירה (שבת דף לט·) ובביצה (ד' ח·) ועוד בפרק כל הכלים (שבת דף קכד:) אמרינן אמר רבי (אליעזר) [נ"ל אלעזר] אף מכבדות של תמרה מותר לטלטל ופריך אי מחמה לצל בהא לימא רבי (אליעזר) [אלעזר] כו' משמע דפשיטא דהוי מלאכתו לאיסור לטולי עלמא ואף על גב דריבוץ שרי לכתחלה לרבי שמעון בכיבוד אסור דמשוי ביה גומות יותר מריבוץ: שמא לא נתקבל בכלי · פי' בקונטרס ולא תועיל זריקה משום דנשפך מצואר בהמה וקשה לר"י דמ"מ יזרוק דתועיל זריקה לאותו שנשפך אחר שנתקבל ונראה לר"י דהכי פי' שמא לא נתקבל בכלי ואסור להעלות דם פסול על גבי המזבח כדמוכח בכמה דוכתי דדוקא אם עלו דיעבד לא ירדו וקאמר אף אני לא אמרתי אלא בנתקבל דסמכינן אזריזות כהנים כדמסיק ודוקא מדם הראוי להתקבל פריך אבל דם התמצית כמים בעלמא חשיב כיון דלאו ראוי לכיסוי אינו אוסר להעלותו וכי פריך והלא דם התמצית מעורב בו ובטיל ליה ברוב לא פריך מדם הראוי אין מבטלין זה את זה אפי' לרבנן כדאמר בהקומץ רבה (מנחות דף כב:) :

עין משפט נר מצוה

נב א מיי' פ"ח מהל' שבת הלכה ז:

נג ב שם הלכה יא:

נד ג מיי' פכ"א מהל' שבת הלכה ג ו סמג לאוין סה טוש"ע א"ח סי' שכא סעיף יג וסימן שלז סעיף א ב:

נה ד מיי' פ"ו מהל' מאכלות אסורות הלכה ד:

רבינו חננאל

שהיו הכהנים מדיחין העזרה [בשבת] שלא ברצון חכמים· אמרי' מאן חכמים ר' אליעזר אבל חכ"א אין שבות במקדש אלא כל דבר שאיסורו משום שבות מותר הוא במקדש: והדחה מנא לן דמשום שבות היא מיהא החולב בהמה והמגבן והמחבץ כגרוגרת המכבד והמרבץ והרודה חלות דרש רשוו רשרת חייב חטאת במזיד ביום טוב לוקה דברי ר"א וחכמים אומרים אחד זה ואחד זה אינן אלא משום שבות· רב אשי אמר שלא ברצון רבי נתן דתני [שבות] שצריכה התירו שבות שאינה צריכה לא התירו וזו ההדחה אינה צורך עבודה במקדש: תניא רבי יהודה היה אומר כוס היה ממלא מדם התערובות שאם נשפך אחד מהן אחר שנתקבל בכלי זה מכשירו ואף על גב שדם התמצית מעורב בו אין דם התמצית מבטל דם הנפש ולא תימא דדם התמצית לר"י אינו דם אלא דם מעליא הוא דתנן דם התמצית באזהרה רבי יהודה אמר בכרת ואפילו הכי לענין כפרה [מודה] ר' יהודה כי דם הנפש בעינן שנאמר כי הדם הוא בנפש יכפר דם

כריתות כב:

גליון הש"ס

תוספות ד"ה המכבד מתכוון להשוות גומות אף על פי שא"א וכו' לא זכיתי להבין דהא כיון דלא הוי פסיק רישיה א"כ צריך לומר וכעלמא מסכת מכוון ואין צריך מכוון לכבו'

משך הבית אבל לא בשביל פסחים וכן חוסר גומא שמכוון לתקן לצורך העפר אבל לא לשתמש בגומא אבל הכא דשווי בגומות הוא מעשה בנין ואם מתכוון לשוות גומות פי' מתכוון לנוש :

too require [sprinkling against] the base. [65a] And how do we know it of the burnt-offering itself?—Scripture saith, *at the base of the altar of the burnt-offering*:[9] this proves that the burnt-offering requires [sprinkling at] the base.[10]

THE FIRST DIVISION WENT OUT etc. A Tanna taught: It [the third division] was called the slothful division.[11] But it was impossible otherwise? What should they have done!—Even so, they should have hurried themselves, as it was taught: Rabbi said: The world cannot exist without a perfume maker and without a tanner: happy is he whose craft is [that of] a perfume maker, [and] woe to him whose craft is [that of] a tanner. Nor can the world exist without males and females: happy is he whose children
a are males, [and] woe to him whose children are females.[1]

AS HE DID ON WEEK-DAYS etc. Without whose consent?[2]—Said R. Ḥisda, Without the consent of R. Eliezer; for if [the ruling of] the Rabbis [is regarded], surely they maintain that it is a *shebuth*,[3] and a *shebuth* is not [interdicted] in the Temple. What is this [allusion]?—For it was taught: Whether he milks, sets milk [for curdling],[4] or makes cheese, [the standard for culpability is] as much as a dried fig. He who sweeps [the floor], lays [the dust by sprinkling water], and removes loaves of honey, [if he does this] unwittingly on the Sabbath, he is liable to a sin-offering; if he does it deliberately on a Festival, he is flagellated with forty [lashes]: this is R. Eliezer's view. But the Sages maintain: In both cases it is [forbidden] only as a *shebuth*.[5] R. Ashi said: You may even say, [it means] without the consent of the Sages, this agreeing with R. Nathan. For it was taught, R. Nathan said: A *shebuth* that is necessary they permitted [in the Temple]; [but] a *shebuth* which is not necessary they did not permit.

R. JUDAH SAID: HE USED TO FILL A GOBLET etc. It was taught, R. Judah said: He used to fill a goblet with the mingled blood,[6] so that should the blood of one of them be spilled, it is found that this renders it fit. Said they to R. Judah, But surely it [this mingled blood] had not been received in a basin? How do they know?[7] Rather, they said thus to him: Perhaps it was not
b caught in a vessel?[1] I too, he answered them, spoke only of that which was received in a vessel. How does he know?[2] The priests are careful. If they are careful, why was it spilled?—Because of the speed with which they work,[3] it is spilled.

But the draining blood[4] is mixed with it?[5]—R. Judah is consistent with his view, for he maintained, The draining blood is [considered] proper blood. For it was taught: The draining blood is subject to a 'warning';[6] R. Judah said: It is subject to *kareth*.[7] But surely R. Eleazar said, R. Judah agrees in respect to atonement, that it does not make atonement, because it is said, *for it is the blood*

(9) Lev. IV, 7. (10) For in fact the altar was not used for the burnt-offering exclusively, the very sentence quoted treating of a sin-offering. Hence the verse must mean, at the base of the altar, as is done with the burnt-offering. (11) For remaining to the last.

a (1) This was not said in a spirit of contempt for the female sex, but in the realization of the anxieties caused by daughters; v. Sanh. 100b. (2) I.e., on whose view is this wrong? (3) V. Glos. (4) Rashi. Jast.: beats milk into a pulp. (5) Which is only a Rabbinical prohibition, and involves neither a sin-offering nor flagellation, v. Shab. 95a. (6) Lit., 'the blood of those which were mixed'. (7) This is an interjection: how do the Rabbis, who raise this objection, know that it was not caught in a vessel?

b (1) But poured straight from the animal's throat on to the ground. Rashi: in that case sprinkling is of no avail. Tosaf.: sprinkling, if already performed, is efficacious, but such blood must not be taken up to the altar in the first place. (2) That it was caught in a vessel? For R. Judah prescribed this merely because the blood might have been spilled; then how can it be remedied with blood about which there is a doubt? (3) *Zariz* denotes both careful and speedy; they hurried to catch the blood, present it at the altar, and sprinkle it. (4) *Tamẓith* denotes the last blood which slowly drains off the animal, contrad. to the life-blood, which gushes forth in a stream. (5) Whereas the 'life-blood' is required for sprinkling. (6) This is a technical designation for a negative injunction whose violation is punished by lashes. But it involves no *kareth*, as does the consuming of the life-blood (v. Lev. XVII, 10f). (7) Just like life-blood. Hence it is also the same in respect to sprinkling.

Continuation of translation from previous page as indicated by ◁

was not a single Paschal lamb for which more than ten people had not registered; and they called it, 'The Passover of the dense throngs.'

'He took a kidney'! but it required burning [on the altar]?—He burned them subsequently.[3] But it is written, *And [Aaron's sons] shall burn it* etc.,[4] [which intimates] that he must not mix the fat [portions] of one [sacrifice] with [that of] another?—He subsequently burned them each separately. But it was taught:
c *And [the priest] shall burn them:*[1] [this teaches] that all of it must be [burnt] simultaneously.[2] But it was a mere seizure, i.e., he took it from them until they gave him something else.[3]

THE PRIESTS STOOD IN ROWS etc. What is the reason? Shall we say, lest they take [a basin] of gold and return [a basin] of silver;[4] then here too,[5] perhaps they might take [a basin] of two hundred [measures] capacity and return one of one hundred? Rather, [the reason is] that it is more becoming thus.[6]

AND THE BASINS DID NOT HAVE [FLAT] BOTTOMS etc. Our Rabbis taught: None of the basins in the Temple had [flat] bottoms, except the basins of the frankincense for the shew-bread, lest they put them down and they break up the bread.[7]

AN ISRAELITE KILLED AND THE PRIEST CAUGHT [THE BLOOD] etc. Is then an Israelite indispensable?[8]—He [the Tanna] informs us that very fact, viz., that the *shechitah* is valid [when done] by a lay Israelite. AND THE PRIEST CAUGHT [THE BLOOD] informs us this: from the receiving of the blood and onwards it is a priestly duty.

HE HANDED IT TO HIS COLLEAGUE. You can infer from this that carrying without moving the feet is carrying![9]—[No:] perhaps he moved slightly [too]. Then [in that case] what does he inform us?—He informs us this: *In the multitude of people is the king's glory.*[10]

HE RECEIVED THE FULL [BASIN] AND GAVE BACK THE
d EMPTY ONE etc. But not the reverse.[1] This supports R. Simeon b. Laḳish. For R. Simeon b. Laḳish said: You must not postpone the precepts.[2]

THE PRIEST NEAREST THE ALTAR etc. Which Tanna [holds] that the Passover offering requires sprinkling?[3]—Said R. Ḥisda, It is R. Jose the Galilean. For it was taught, R. Jose the Galilean said: *Thou shalt sprinkle their blood against the altar, and thou shalt burn their fat:*[4] 'its blood' is not said, but 'their *blood*'; 'its fat' is not said, but 'their *fat*'.[5] This teaches concerning the firstling, the tithe [of animals] and the Passover offering, that they require the presenting of blood and *emurim* at the altar.[6] How do we know that they require [sprinkling against] the base?—Said R. Eleazar: The meaning of 'sprinkling' is deduced from a burnt-offering.[7] Here it is written, *thou shalt* sprinkle *their blood against the altar*, while there it is written, *And Aaron's sons, the priests, shall* sprinkle *its blood against the altar round about:*[8] just as the burnt-offering requires [sprinkling against] the base, so does the Passover offering

(3) After the event. (4) Lev. III, 5.

c (1) Lev. III, 16. (2) All the parts of the sacrifice which are burnt on the altar (called *emurim*) must be burnt at the same time. Here, however, the kidneys would be burnt separately. (3) The unpopularity of the census (v. *supra*, n. b2) may have necessitated this procedure. (4) Which is 'descending in sanctity', and this must be avoided. (5) I.e., even with the present arrangements. (6) The general beauty and dignity of the proceedings are thereby enhanced. (7) These vessels were kept near the shewbread, and if they were not provided with a base to stand on they might fall against the rows of shewbread and break up their formation. (8) Lit., 'is it not enough that it should not be an Israelite?'—Surely a priest too could kill it! (9) Carrying the blood to be sprinkled was one of the four services (v. *supra* 59b Mishnah), and there is a controversy in Zeb. 14b whether the priest actually had to walk a little for this or not. From the present passage we see that this was unnecessary. (10) Prov. XIV, 28.

d (1) It had to be done in this order. (2) Lit., 'one must not pass by precepts', but must perform them immediately they come to hand. Thus when the full basin is held out, the next priest must accept it immediately, before returning the empty one, as the reception of the full basin on its way to the sprinkling is a religious service. (3) From the distance, and not just pouring out; v. *infra* 121a. (4) Num. XVIII, 17. (5) Though the passage treats of one sacrifice only, viz., the firstling. The *plural* possessive suffix indicates that other sacrifices too are included in this law. (6) These are the only sacrifices in connection with which it is not mentioned elsewhere, hence the plural is applied to them. Furthermore, Scripture states '*thou shalt sprinkle*' (tizroḳ), not 'thou shalt pour out' (*tishpok*). (7) Lit., '"sprinkling", "sprinkling" is deduced from a burnt-offering'. (8) Lev. I, 11.

מה א שם הלכה יז:
מו ב שם הלכה ט:
מז ג שם הלכה י:
מח ד שם הלכה ו:
מט ה מיי' פ"ה מהל' תמידין הלכה ג':
נ ו מיי' פ"ה מהל' מעשה קרבנות הל' יז:
נא ז שם:

אתיא זריקה זריקה מעולה. בפ' איזהו מקומן (זבחים נז:) פריך ונילף מעולה מה עולה שתים שהן ארבע אף פסח כו' ומשני אמר אביי למה לי למיכתב סביב בעולה סביב בחטאת הוו להו שני כתובין הבאין כאחד ואין מלמדין וקשה לר"י דנהי דלא ילפינן משני כתובין הבאין כאחד במה מצינו מדלא כתב בחד מינייהו בכור ומעשר ופסח דליכול גזירה שוה נילף שפיר מעולה דלאין גזירה שוה למחצה ואומר ר"י דע"כ אשם וחטאת דכתיב בהו סביב דלאמדינן התם דהוו שני כתובים ושלשה כתובים ילפינן בג"ש מעולה או עולה ילפא מינייהו והשתא אתי שפיר הא דמסיק הוו להו שני כתובים הבאין כאחד דלמעוטי דלא נילף בגזירה שוה אתו דדומיא דכתב בהו סביב הוא קא ממעט דלאית בהו גזירה שוה כדפרישי':

החולב

תורה אור

שחל להיות בשבת מניח ידו על כתף חבירו ויד חבירו על כתיפו ותולה ומפשיט קרעו והוציא את אימוריו נתנו במגים והקטירן על גבי המזבח *יצתה כת הראשונה וישבה לה בהר הבית שניה בחיל והשלישית במקומה עומדת חשיכה יצאו וצלו את פסחיהן: **גמ'** א"ר יצחק *אין הפסח נשחט אלא בג' כתות של שלשים שלשים בני אדם מ"ט קהל ועדה וישראל מספקא לן אי בבת אחת אי בזה אחר זה הלכך בעינן שלש כתות של שלשים שלשים בני אדם דאי בבת אחת הא איכא ואי בזה אחר זה הא איכא *הלכך בחמשין נמי סגיא דעיילי תלתין ועבדי עיילי עשרה ונפקי עשרה ועיילי עשרה ונפקי עשרה: נכנסה כת ראשונה וכו': איתמר אביי אמר ננעלו תנן רבא אמר נועלין תנן מאי בינייהו איכא בינייהו למסמך אניסא אביי אמר ננעלו תנן כמה דעיילו מעלו וסמכינן אניסא רבא אמר נועלין תנן ולא סמכינן אניסא והא דתנן *א"ר יהודה ח"ו שעקביא בן מהללאל נתנדה שאין עזרה ננעלת על כל אדם בישראל בחכמה וביראת חטא כעקביא בן מהללאל אביי מתרץ לטעמיה ורבא מתרץ לטעמיה אביי מתרץ לטעמיה אין בעזרה בשעה שננעלה על כל אדם בישראל בחכמה וביראת חטא כעקביא בן מהללאל רבא מתרץ לטעמיה אין בעזרה בשעה שנועלין אותה על כל ישראל בחכמה וביראת חטא כעקביא בן מהללאל תנו רבנן מעולם לא נתמעך אדם בעזרה חוץ מפסח אחד שהיה בימי הלל שנתמעך בו זקן אחד והיו קוראין אותו פסח מעוכין תנו רבנן *פעם אחת ביקש אגריפס המלך ליתן עיניו באוכלוסי ישראל אמר ליה לכהן גדול תן עיניך בפסחים נטל כוליא מכל אחד ונמצאו שם ששים ריבוא זוגי כליות כפלים כיוצאי מצרים חוץ מטמא ושהיה בדרך רחוקה ואין לך כל פסח ופסח שלא נמנו עליו יותר מעשרה בני אדם והיו קוראין אותו פסח מעובין: נטל כוליא הא בעי אקטורה דהדר מקטיר להו והכתיב °והקטירו *שלא יערב חלביו של זה בזה דהדר מקטיר להו חדא חדא והתניא *°והקטירם שיהא כולו כאחד אלא תפיסה בעלמא דשקיל מינייהו עד דיהבין ליה מידי אחרינא: כהנים עומדין שורות וכו': מאי טעמא אילימא דילמא שקלי דדהבא ומעיילי דכספא הכא נמי דילמא שקלי בר מאתן ומעיילי בר מאה אלא דהכי שפיר טפי: ולא היו לבזיכין שוליים וכו': תנו רבנן כל הבזיכין שבמקדש לא היו להן שוליים *חוץ מבזיכי לבונה של לחם הפנים שמא יניחום ויפרום הלחם: שחט ישראל וקבל הכהן וכו': לא סגיא דלאו ישראל היא גופא קמ"ל דשחיטה בזר כשירה וקבל הכהן הא קמשמע לן *מקבלה ואילך מצות כהונה נותנו לחבירו שמעת מינה הולכה שלא ברגל הויא הולכה דילמא הוא *נייד פורתא ואלא מאי קמ"ל הא קמשמע לן °ברב עם הדרת מלך: קבל את המלא ומחזיר את הריקן וכו': אבל איפכא לא מסייע ליה לר"ש בן לקיש *דאמר ר"ש בן לקיש אין מעבירין על המצות: כהן הקרוב אצל המזבח וכו': מאן תנא פסח בזריקה א"ר חסדא ר' יוסי הגלילי היא דתניא *ר' יוסי הגלילי אומר °את דמם תזרוק על המזבח ואת חלבם תקטיר דמו לא נאמר אלא דמם חלבו לא נאמר אלא חלבם למד על °בכור ומעשר ופסח שהן טעונין מתן דמים ואימורין לגבי מזבח מנלן דטעונין יסוד אמר רבי אלעזר אתיא זריקה זריקה מעולה כתיב הכא את דמם תזרוק על המזבח וכתיב התם °וזרקו בני אהרן הכהנים את דמו על המזבח סביב מה עולה טעונה יסוד אף פסח נמי טעון יסוד

ויקרא ג | שם | משלי יד | במדבר יח | ויקרא א

ועולה

שחל להיות בשבת. ואינו יכול לתקן המקלות: ידו על כתף חבירו · ותולה אותו בגידי ארכובותיו בזרועו: במגים. קערה: וישבה לה בהר הבית. בשבת קאמר שלא היו יכולין להוליך פסחיהן לבתיהן: בחיל· לפני הסורג הוא בין הסורג לחומת עזרת נשים בתחלת עליית ההר: **גמ'** שלשים בכל כת וכת. קהל עשרה ועדה עשרה וישראל עשרה: מספקא ליה. דילמא בבת אחת לוה לשוחטו ויהיו בה שלשים: או בזה אחר זה. שלש כתות של עשרה עשרה הלכך שלש כתות בעינן דילמא בזה אחר זה קאמר ושל שלשים בעינן דילמא בבת אחת קאמר ואינו יכול לשוחטו בפחות משלשים: בנ' סגי עיילי שלשים. ברישא ושוחטים פסחיהן ונפקי עשרה מינייהו ועיילי י' חדשים לאי בהדדי קאמר הא איכא ואי שלש כתות קאמר הא איכא: ננעלין תנן. מאליהן ומעשה נסים: סמכינן אניסא. וכל זמן שאין ננעלין מאליהן מניחין אותם ליכנס ולא חיישינן דלמא עיילי כולהו ואין כאן שלש כיתות: חס ושלום כו'. במסכת עדיות תנן ארבעה דברים העיד עקביא בן מהללאל כו' וקתני התם הוא היה אומר אין משקין לא את הגיורת ולא את המשוחררת אמרו לו מעשה בכרכמית שפחה שהיתה בירושלים והשקוה שמעיה ואבטליון אמר להם דוגמא השקוה דומין לה היו אותן שהשקוה ונידוהו אמר רבי יהודה חס ושלום שעקביא נתנדה שאין עזרה ננעלת כו' כשהיתה ננעלת על כל אדם בערבי פסחים שהקהל גדול ורב אין בהם אחד בחכמה וביראת חטא כעקביא: פסח מעוכין. על שם שנתמעך: פסח מעובין · עב על שם שהעם רב: והקטירו. משמע לבדן שלא יערב חלבים של קרבן זה בחלבים של קרבן אחר: שיהא כולו כאחד. כל האימורין של קרבן: תפיסה בעלמא. תופס כוליא ומראה לשליח והוא נותן פול או אבן כנגדה: מאי טעמא. שורה שכולה כסף כסף: אי נימא דילמא. כשהוא מחזיר הריקן ומקבל המלא זימנין דמחזיר ריקן של זהב ומקבל מלא של כסף והוה ליה מורידין בקודש: חוץ מבזיכי לבונה של לחם הפנים · שהיו מניחין אותן אצל הלחם על השולחן והתקינו להם מושב שוליים רחב כדי שלא יסמכו על הלחם שאצלם ויפרסו דופנותיו שהיה עשוי דפנות כמין תיבה פרוצה משני רוחותיה: מקבלה ואילך כו'. דכתיב ושחט את בן הבקר והקריבו בני אהרן וגו' ואמר מר במסכת חגיגה (דף יא·) והקריבו זו קבלת הדם לימד על הקבלה שטעונה כהונה: שמעת מינה הולכה שלא ברגל. כי הא הויא הולכה ופלוגתא היא בשילהי פרק קמא דזבחים (דף יד:) ארבע עבודות נאמרו בדם שחיטה וקבלה והולכה וזריקה קבלה והולכה מוהקריבו נפקי בשילהי פרק קמא דחגיגה ומאי אשמעינן מתניתין דאיכפל למיתני סדר הולכתן היאך אי לאו הא אתא לאשמעינן: ברב עם הדרת מלך · שהיו כולן עסוקין בעבודה: אבל איפכא · מחזיר את הריקן ברישא לא דמכי מושיט ליה האי מיד בעי לקבולי דאין מעבירין על המצוה מאחר שבאת לידו: מאן תנא פסח בזריקה. למרחוק ולא בשפיכה בנחת מקריב הכלי לכותל המזבח דאיכא למאן דאמר בפרק בתרא (דף קכא·) פסח בשפיכה ורבי ישמעאל היא דמפיק ליה מודס זבחיך ישפך במסכת זבחים *בפרק בית שמאי אין לך קרבן שצריך מתנה באצבע· אלא חטאת בלבד אבל כל שאר קרבנות מתן דם על ידי זריקת כל הכלי: דמו לא נאמר. בבכור כתיב אך בכור שור וגו': אלא דמם. אלמא אחריני נמי מישתמעי לימד על הפסח ומעשר בהמה שלא מצינו להם מתן דמים בתורה אלא כאן וכתיב תזרק ולא כתיב תשפך:

ועולה

מכילתא פ' בא
ברכות יט. עדיות פ"ה מ"ו:
[תוספת' פ"ד]
מנחות צז:
ת"כ פ' ויקרא
[ברכות נג: וש"נ] זבחים יד:
יומא לג: [וש"נ]
זבחים לז [ס:]
[דף נז:]

רבינו חננאל

אמר רבי יצחק אין הפסח נשחט אלא בשלש כתות של שלשים שלשים בני אדם · מאי טעמא מספקא לן אי כולהו קהל ועדה וישראל בבת אחת נכנסין או בזה אחר זה הלכך עיילי שלשים שלשים ואפי' [בחמשין נמי סגי] משכחת לה כגון דעיילי שלשים עבדי עשרה ונפקי ועיילי עשרה אחריני ועבדי נמי עשרה ונפקי ועיילי עשרה אחריני: יש מי ששונה ננעלו [דלתות העזרה] מעצמם בנס מן השמים ויש מי ששונה נועלין דלתות העזרה כלומר כיון שנתמלאת העזרה נועלין הדלתות דלא לירמסו אהדדי והא דתנן בעדיות [ח"ו] שעקביא בןמהללאל נתנדה שאין העזרה ננעלת על כל אדם בחכמ' וביראת' חטא כעקביא בן מהללאל (וכו') כל השמועה פשוטה היא: והכליות שלקח תפיסה בעלמא עד שיתנו לו דבר אחר כגון צרור או כיוצא בו לעמוד בהן על המנין: מדקתני שחט ישראל ש"מ כי בא התנא להודיענו דשחיטה בזר כשרה: נותנים לחברו וחברו לחברו [ש"מ] דהולכה שלא ברגל כשר' והא דניידי פורתא ותו שמעי' מדקתני קבל המלא מקודם ואחר כך החזיר הריקן הא דאמר ריש לקיש אין מעבירין על המצות אלא מקדים מצוה דפגע ברישא ומיהא דקתני זרקו זריק' אחת כנגד היסוד ש"מ דמתני' רבי יוסי דאמר פסח [בזריקה ונפקא ליה מקרא דאת דמם תזרוק דפסח טעין] מתן דמים על המזבח:

[64b] FELL ON THE SABBATH, HE PLACED HIS HAND ON HIS NEIGHBOUR'S SHOULDER AND HIS NEIGHBOUR'S HAND ON HIS SHOULDER, AND HE [THUS] SUSPENDED [THE SACRIFICE] AND FLAYED [IT].[7] THEN HE TORE IT AND TOOK OUT ITS EMURIM, PLACED THEM IN A TRAY AND BURNT THEM ON THE ALTAR.

THE FIRST DIVISION WENT OUT AND SAT DOWN ON THE
a TEMPLE MOUNT,[1] THE SECOND [SAT] IN THE ḤEL,[2] WHILE THE THIRD REMAINED IN ITS PLACE. WHEN IT GREW DARK THEY WENT OUT AND ROASTED THEIR PASCHAL LAMBS.

GEMARA. R. Isaac said: The Passover offering was not slaughtered except in three divisions each consisting of thirty men. What is the reason? *'Assembly', 'congregation,'* and *'Israel'* [are prescribed, and] we are doubtful whether [that means] at the same time or consecutively.[3] Therefore we require three divisions each consisting of thirty men, so that if [it means] at the same time, they are there; and if consecutively, they are there. Hence fifty [in all] too are sufficient, thirty entering and preparing [their sacrifices], then ten enter and ten leave, [and another] ten enter and [another] ten leave.

THE FIRST DIVISION ENTERED etc. It was stated, Abaye said: We learned, 'They [the doors] locked themselves';[4] Raba said, We learned: THEY LOCKED. Wherein do they differ?—They differ in respect of relying on a miracle. 'Abaye said, We learned, They locked themselves'; as many as entered, entered, and we rely on a miracle.[5] Raba said, We learned, THEY LOCKED, and we do not rely on a miracle. And as to what we learned, R. Judah said: Heaven forfend that Akabia b. Mehalallel was banned! For the Temple Court was never closed upon any man in Israel equal in wisdom and fear of sin to Akabia b. Mehalallel,[6]— Abbaye explains it according to his view, [while] Raba explains it according to his view. Abaye explains it according to his view: there was none in the Temple Court when it closed itself upon every man in Israel like Akabia b. Mehalallel in wisdom and fear of sin. Raba explains it according to his view: There was none in the Temple Court when they closed it on all Israel like Akabia b. Mehalallel in wisdom and the fear of sin.

Our Rabbis taught: No man was ever crushed in the Temple
b Court[1] except on one Passover in the days of Hillel, when an old man was crushed, and they called it 'The Passover of the crushed'.

Our Rabbis taught: King Agrippa once wished to cast his eyes on the hosts of Israel.[2] Said he to the High Priest, Cast your eyes upon the Passover sacrifices. He [thereupon] took a kidney from each, and 600,000 pairs of kidneys were found there, twice as many as those who departed from Egypt, excluding those who were unclean and those who were on a distant journey; and there

(7) But the staves might not be used on that day.

a (1) If the fourteenth fell on the Sabbath, as they could not carry their sacrifices home and had to wait for the evening. (2) A place within the fortification of the Temple (Jast.); v. Mid. I, 5. (3) And each expression denotes a minimum of ten. (4) Or, were locked—miraculously, without human agency. (5) That the doors should shut themselves when sufficient had entered. (6) V. 'Ed. V, 6 for the whole discussion. 'Was never closed'—on the eve of Passover, at the sacrificing of the Paschal lambs.

b (1) In spite of the enormous crowds that thronged it. (2) I.e., to take a census of the Jewish people. This was an unpopular proceeding, as it was regarded as of unfortunate omen; cf. I Chron. XXI. In addition, a census was looked upon with suspicion as being the possible precursor of fresh levies and taxation, and the decision of Quirinius, the governor of Syria, to take a census in Judea (c. 6-7 C.E.) nearly precipitated a revolt; v. Graetz. *History of the Jews* (Eng. translation) II, ch. V. pp. 129 seq. According to Graetz (op. cit. p. 252) the present census was undertaken by Agrippa II in the year 66 C.E. as a hint to the Roman powers not to underrate the strength of the Jewish people, and therefore avoid driving them too far by the cruelty and greed of the Procurator, at that time Gessius Florus. Graetz assumes that an extra large number flocked to Jerusalem on that occasion, and it is then that the old man was suffocated. This however does not agree with the statement that the man was crushed in the days of Hillel, which is a far earlier date, Hillel having flourished or commenced his Patriarchate one hundred years before the destruction of the Temple, i.e., 30 B.C.E.

◁ *For the continuation of the English translation of this page see overleaf.*

מה א שם הלכה יז:
מו ב שם הלכה ט:
מז ג שם הלכה י:
מח ד שם הלכה ו:
מט ה מיי' פ"ה מהל' תמידין הלכה ג':
נ ו מיי' פ"ה מהל' מעשה קרבנות הל' יז:
נא ז שם:

רבינו חננאל

אמר רבי יצחק אין הפסח נשחט אלא בשלש כתות של שלשים שלשים בני אדם. מאי טעמא מספקא לן אי כולהו קהל ועדה וישראל בבת אחת נכנסין או בזה אחר זה הלכך עיילי שלשים ואפי' [בחמשין נמי סגי] משכחת לה כגון דעיילי שלשים עבדי עשרה ונפקי ועיילי עשרה אחריני ועבדי נמי עשרה ונפקי ועיילי עשרה אחריני: יש מי ששונה ננעלו [דלתות העזרה] מעצמם בנס מן השמים ויש מי ששונה נועלין דלתות העזרה כלומר כיון שנתמלאת העזרה נועלין הדלתות דלא לירמסו אהדדי והא דתנן בעדיות [ח"ו] שעקביא בן מהללאל נתנדה שאין העזרה ננעלת על כל אדם בחכמ' וביראת' חטא כעקביא בן מהללאל (וכו') כל השמועה פשוטה היא: והכליות שלקח תפיסה בעלמא עד שיתנו לו דבר אחר כגון צרור או כיוצא בו לעמוד בהן על המנין: מדקתני שחט ישראל ש"מ כי בא התנא להודיענו דשחיטה בזר כשרה: נותנים לחברו וחברו לחברו [ש"מ] דהולכה שלא ברגל כשר' והוא דניידי פורתא ותו שמעי' מדקתני קבל המלא מקודם ואחר כך החזיר הריקן הא דאמר ר"ש לקיש אין מעבירין על המצות אלא מקדים מצוה דפגע ברישא ומיהא דקתני זרקו זריק' אחת כנגד היסוד ש"מ דמתני' רבי יוסי דאמר פסח [בזריקה ונפקא ליה מקרא דאת דמם תזרוק דפסח טעון] מתן דמים על המזבח:

שחל להיות בשבת מניח ידו על כתף חבירו ויד חבירו על כתיפו ותולה ומפשיט קרעו והוציא את אימוריו נתנו במגים והקטירן על גבי המזבח *יצתה כת הראשונה וישבה לה בהר הבית שניה בחיל והשלישית במקומה עומדת חשיכה יצאו וצלו את פסחיהן: **גמ'** א"ר יצחק *[ב]אין הפסח נשחט אלא בג' כתות של שלשים שלשים בני אדם מ"ט קהל ועדה וישראל מספקא לן אי בבת אחת אי בזה אחר זה הלכך בעינן שלש כתות של שלשים שלשים בני אדם דאי בבת אחת הא איכא ואי בזה אחר זה הא איכא [ג]הלכך בחמשין נמי סגיא דעיילי תלתין ועבדי עיילי עשרה ונפקי עשרה עיילי עשרה ונפקי עשרה: נכנסה כת ראשונה וכו': איתמר אביי אמר ננעלו תנן רבא אמר נועלין תנן מאי בינייהו איכא בינייהו למסמך אניסא אביי אמר ננעלו תנן כמה דעיילו מעלו וסמכינן אניסא רבא אמר נועלין תנן ולא סמכינן אניסא והא דתנן *א"ר יהודה ח"ו שעקביא בן מהללאל נתנדה שאין עזרה ננעלת על כל אדם בישראל בחכמה וביראת חטא כעקביא בן מהללאל אביי מתרץ לטעמיה ורבא מתרץ לטעמיה אביי מתרץ לטעמיה אין בעזרה בשעה שננעלה על כל אדם בישראל בחכמה וביראת חטא כעקביא בן מהללאל רבא מתרץ לטעמיה אין בעזרה בשעה שנועלין אותה על כל ישראל בחכמה וביראת חטא כעקביא בן מהללאל תנו רבנן מעולם לא נתמעך אדם בעזרה חוץ מפסח אחד שהיה בימי הלל שנתמעך בו זקן אחד והיו קוראין אותו פסח מעוכין תנו רבנן *פעם אחת ביקש אגריפס המלך ליתן עיניו באוכלוסי ישראל אמר ליה לכהן גדול תן עיניך בפסחים נטל כוליא מכל אחד ונמצאו שם ששים ריבוא זוגי כליות כפלים כיוצאי מצרים חוץ מטמא ושהיה בדרך רחוקה ואין לך כל פסח ופסח שלא נמנו עליו יותר מעשרה בני אדם והיו קוראין אותו פסח מעובין נטל כוליא הא בעי אקטורה דהדר מקטיר להו והכתיב °והקטירו *[ד]שלא יערב חלביו של זה בזה דהדר מקטיר להו חדא חדא והתניא *°והקטירם שיהא כולו כאחד אלא תפיסה בעלמא דשקיל מינייהו עד דיהבין ליה מידי אחרינא: כהנים עומדין שורות וכו': מאי טעמא אילימא דילמא שקלי דדהבא ומעיילי דכספא הכא נמי דילמא שקלי בר מאתן ומעיילי בר מאה אלא דהכי שפיר טפי: ולא היו לבזיכין שוליים וכו': תנו רבנן כל הבזיכין שבמקדש לא היו להן שוליים [ה]חוץ מבזיכי לבונה של לחם הפנים שמא יניחום ויפרוס הלחם: שחט ישראל וקבל הכהן וכו': לא סגיא דלאו ישראל היא גופא קמ"ל דשחיטה בזר כשירה וקבל הכהן הא קמשמע לן *מקבלה ואילך מצות כהונה נותנו לחבירו שמעת מינה הולכה שלא ברגל הויא הולכה דילמא הוא *נייד פורתא ואלא מאי קמ"ל הא קמשמע לן °ברב עם הדרת מלך: קבל את המלא ומחזיר את הריקן וכו': אבל איפכא לא מסייע ליה לר"ש בן לקיש *דאמר ר"ש בן לקיש אין מעבירין על המצות: כהן הקרוב אצל המזבח וכו': מאן תנא פסח בזריקה א"ר חסדא ר' יוסי הגלילי היא דתניא *ר' יוסי הגלילי אומר °את דמם תזרוק על המזבח ואת חלבם תקטיר דמו לא נאמר אלא דמם חלבו לא נאמר אלא חלבם למד על [ו]בכור ומעשר ופסח שהן טעונין מתן דמים ואימורין לגבי מזבח מנלן דטעונין [ז]יסוד אמר רבי אלעזר אתיא זריקה זריקה מעולה כתיב הכא את דמם תזרוק על המזבח וכתיב התם °וזרקו בני אהרן הכהנים את דמו על המזבח סביב מה עולה טעונה יסוד אף פסח נמי טעון יסוד

[במדבר יח: ויקרא ג; ויקרא ג; משלי יד; במדבר יח; ויקרא א]

אתיא זריקה זריקה מעולה. בפ' איזהו מקומן (זבחים נז.) פריך ונילף מעולה מה עולה שתים שהן ארבע אף פסח כו' ומשני אמר אביי למה לי למיכתב סביב בעולה סביב בחטאת הוו להו שני כתובין הבאין כאחד ואין מלמדין וקשה לר"י דהכי דלא ילפינן משני כתובין הבאין כאחד במה מצינו מדלא כתב בחד מינייהו בכור ומעשר ופסח דאיכא גזירה שוה נילף שפיר מעולה דאין גזירה שוה למחצה ואומר ר"י דע"כ אשם וחטאת דכתיב בהו סביב דאמרינן התם דהוו שני כתובים ושלשה כתובים ילפינן בג"ש מעולה או עולה ילפא מינייהו והשתא אתי שפיר הא דמסיק הוו להו שני כתובים הבאין כאחד למעוטי דלא נילף בגזירה שוה אתו דדומיא דכתב בהו סביב קא ממעט דאית בהו גזירה שוה כדפרישי': החולב

שחל להיות בשבת. ואינו יכול לתקן המקלות: ידו על כתף חבירו. ותולה אותו בגידי ארכובותיו בזרועו: במגים. קערה: וישבה לה בהר הבית. בשבת קאמר שלא היו יכולין להוליך פסחיהן לבתיהן: בחיל. לפני הסורג הוא בין הסורג לחומת עזרת נשים בתחלת עליית ההר: **גמ'** שלשים בכל כת וכת. קהל עשרה ועדה עשרה וישראל עשרה: מספקא ליה. דילמא בבת אחת לוה לשוחטו ויהיו בה שלשים: או בזה אחר זה. שלש כתות של עשרה עשרה הלכך שלש כתות בעינן דילמא בזה אחר זה קאמר ושל שלשים בעינן דילמא בבת אחת קאמר ואינו יכול לשוחטו בפחות משלשים: בנ' סגי. עיילי שלשים. ברישא ושוחטים פסחיהן ונפקי עשרה מינייהו ועיילי י' חדשים דאי בהדדי קאמר הא איכא ואי שלש כתות קאמר הא איכא: ננעלין תנן. מאליהן ומעשה נסים: סמכינן אניסא. וכל זמן שאין ננעלין מאליהן מניחין אותם ליכנס ולא חיישינן דלמא עיילי כולהו ואין כאן שלש כיתות: חס ושלום כו'. במסכת עדיות תנן ארבעה דברים העיד עקביא בן מהללאל כו' וקתני התם הוא היה אומר אין משקין לא את הגיורת ולא את המשוחררת אמרו לו מעשה בכרכמית שפחה שהיתה בירושלים והשקוה שמעיה ואבטליון אמר להם דוגמא השקוה דומין לה היו אותן שהשקוה ונידוהו אמר רבי יהודה חס ושלום שעקביא נתנדה שאין עזרה ננעלת כו' כשהיתה ננעלת על כל אדם בערבי פסחים שהקהל גדול ורב אין בהם אחד בחכמה וביראת חטא כעקביא: פסח מעוכין. על שם שנתמעך: פסח מעובין. עב על שם שהעם רב: והקטירו. משמע לבדן שלא יערב חלבים של קרבן זה בחלבים של קרבן אחר: שיהא כולו כאחד. כל האימורין של קרבן: תפיסה בעלמא. תופס כוליא ומראה לשליח והוא נותן פול או אבן כנגדה: מאי טעמא. שורה שכולה כסף: אי נימא דילמא. כשהוא מחזיר הריקן ומקבל המלא זימנין דמחזיר ריקן של זהב ומקבל מלא של כסף והוה ליה מורידין בקודש: חוץ מבזיכי לבונה של לחם הפנים. שהיו מניחין אותן אצל הלחם על השולחן והתקינו להם מושב שוליים רחב כדי שלא יסמכו על הלחם שאלמלא כן ויפרסו דופנותיו שהיה עשוי דפנות כמין תיבה פרוצה משני רוחותיה: מקבלה ואילך כו'. דכתיב ושחט את בן הבקר והקריבו בני אהרן וגו' ואמר מר במסכת חגיגה (דף יא.) והקריבו זו קבלת הדם לימד על הקבלה שטעונה כהונה: שמעת מינה הולכה שלא ברגל. כי הא הויא הולכה ופלוגתא היא בשילהי פרק קמא דזבחים (דף יד:) ארבע עבודות נאמרו בדם שחיטה וקבלה והולכה וזריקה קבלה והולכה מוהקריבו כפקי בשילהי פרק קמא דחגיגה ומאי אשמעינן מתניתין דאיכפל למיתני סדר הולכתן היאך אי לאו הא אתא לאשמעינן: ברב עם הדרת מלך. שהיו כולן עסוקין בעבודה: אבל איפכא. מחזיר את הריקן ברישא לא דמכי מוסיט ליה האי מיד בעי לקבולי דאין מעבירין על המצוה מאחר שבאת לידו: מאן תנא פסח בזריקה. למרחוק ולא בשפיכה בנחת מקריב הכלי לכותל המזבח דאיכא למאן דאמר בפרק בתרא (דף קכא.) פסח בשפיכה ורבי ישמעאל היא דמפיק ליה מודם זבחיך ישפך במסכת זבחים *בפ"ק בית שמאי אין לך קרבן שצריך מתנה באצבע אלא חטאת בלבד אבל כל שאר קרבנות מתן דם על ידי זריקת כל הכלי: דמו לא נאמר. בבכור כתיב אך בכור שור וגו': אלא דמם. אלמא אחריני נמי מישתמעי לימד על הפסח ומעשר בהמה שלא מצינו להם מתן דמים בתורה אלא כאן וכתיב תזרק ולא כתיב תשפך:
ועולה

מכילתא פ' בא, ברכות יט. עדיות פ"ה מ"ו, [תוספתא פ"ד], מנחות צט:, ת"כ פ' ויקרא, [ברכות לג. וש"נ], זבחים יד:, יומא נג: [וש"נ], זבחים לד: [מ:], [דף לז:]

קשיא מליקה אמליקה קשיא הקטרה אהקטרה ולטעמיך תיקשי לך היא גופא דקתני לא אמרו אלא בפסח בלבד והדר תני אחד השוחט ואחד הזורק ואחד המולק ואחד המזה אלא הא והא ר"ש מליקה אמליקה לא קשיא כאן בארבעה עשר כאן בחולו של מועד ואידי ואידי ר"ש היא הקטרה אהקטרה נמי לא קשיא תנאי היא דאיכא דמקיש הקטרה לשחיטה ואיכא מאן דלא מקיש: רבי יהודה אומר אף התמיד וכו': מאי טעמא דרבי יהודה אמר לך °זבחי (שמות כג) זבח המיוחד לי ומאי ניהו תמיד: ר"ש אומר הפסח בארבעה עשר וכו': מ"ט דר"ש דכתיב זבחי זבחי תרי זמני קרי ביה זבח זבחיו למאי הלכתא פלגינהו רחמנא מהדדי ולא כתב זבחיו למימר בזמן דאיכא זבח לא מחייב אזבחיו בזמן דליכא זבח מחייב אזבחיו: ובמועד לשמו פטור וכו': טעמא דשלא לשמו הא סתמא פטור אמאי פסח בשאר ימות השנה שלמים הוי *שמעת מינה פסח בשאר ימות השנה בעי עקירה אמר ר' חייא בר גמדא נזרקה מפי חבורה ואמרו כגון שהיו בעלים טמאי מת ונדחין לפסח שני דסתמיה לשום פסח קאי:

מתני' *הפסח נשחט בשלש כתות שנאמר ושחטו אותו (שם יב) כל קהל עדת ישראל קהל ועדה וישראל נכנסה כת הראשונה נתמלאה העזרה נעלו דלתות העזרה תקעו הריעו ותקעו הכהנים עומדים שורות שורות ובידיהם בזיכי כסף ובזיכי זהב שורה שכולה כסף כסף ושורה שכולה זהב זהב לא היו מעורבין ולא היו לבזיכין שוליים שמא יניחום ויקרש הדם *שחט ישראל וקבל הכהן נותנו לחבירו וחבירו לחבירו ומקבל את המלא ומחזיר את הריקן כהן הקרוב אצל המזבח זורקו זריקה אחת כנגד היסוד יצתה כת ראשונה ונכנסה כת שניה יצתה שניה נכנסה שלישית כמעשה הראשונה כך מעשה השניה והשלישית קראו את ההלל אם גמרו שנו ואם שנו שלשו אע"פ שלא שלשו מימיהם ר' יהודה אומר *מימיהם של כת שלישית לא הגיעו לאהבתי כי ישמע ה' מפני שעמה מועטין כמעשהו בחול כך מעשהו בשבת אלא שהכהנים מדיחים את העזרה שלא ברצון חכמים ר' יהודה אומר *כוס היה ממלא מדם התערובת זרקו זריקה אחת על גבי המזבח ולא הודו לו חכמים כיצד תולין ומפשיטין אונקליות של ברזל היו קבועים בכתלים ובעמודים שבהן תולין ומפשיטין כל מי שאין לו מקום לתלות ולהפשיט *מקלות דקים חלקים היו שם מניח על כתפו ועל כתף חבירו ותולה ומפשיט ר"א אומר י"ד שחל

רש"י

קשיא מליקה אמליקה. דס"ד בארבעה עשר קאמר וקתני דעבר אמליקה דומיא דשאר קרבנות ועוד דקא חשיב ליה כשחיטה: ה"ג ולטעמיך תיקשי לך היא גופא דקתני רישא לא אמרו אלא פסח בלבד. אבל אשאר קרבנות לא מחייב והדר תני אחד המולק ואחד המזה: אלא הא והא. תרוייהו הנך מתניתא רבי שמעון דמתני' דפטר אשאר קרבנות בארבעה עשר ומחייב עלייהו במועד: מליקה אמליקה לא קשיא. קמייתא דפטר בארבעה עשר קאי כדתני בה בהדיא ותנא עוף והוא הדין לשאר זבחים אלא משום דאורחיה לעכוביה בו ביום אחר התמיד נקט ליה ורישא דמתניתא בתרייתא דקתני נמי לא אמרו אלא פסח בלבד רבי שמעון אמרה ואארבעה עשר קאי ואחד השוחט כו' דסיפא בחולו של מועד קאמר ואשמעינן חיובא לזורק ולמולק כשוחט דלא תימא שחיטה דווקא: תנאי היא. הני תרתי סתמי תנאי היא ואליבא דרבי שמעון מר מקיש הקטרה לעבודת הדם הואיל וישנו בהלכת אימורין ומר לית ליה הא היקישא דשחיטה קאמר רחמנא וזריקה דמתרביא בהדיא מדם זבחי אבל הקטרה לא: זבחי זבחי תרי זימני. תרי קראי כתיבי שקיל י' דחד מינייהו ושדי אאידך וקרי ביה זבח דהיינו פסח וקרי ביה זבחיי לשאר זבחים: ואמאי פלגינהו רחמנא · ולא כתב זבחיי בחד קרא והכל במשמע בין בפסח בין בשאר זבחים: לומר לך בזמן דאיכא זבח. דהיינו פסח בארבעה עשר לא מחייב אשאר זבחים: הא סתמא פטור. מלא תשחט דאמרינן כל כמה דלא עקר שם פסח מיניה הוא פסח ושחטו בשאר ימות השנה ופסול ושחיטה שאינה ראויה היא: בעי עקירה. ולא אמרינן סתמיה שלמים הוא ולשון בעיא הוא כלומר פשטינן לה מהכא או לא: מפי חבורה. כולם הודו בדבר זה לאוקומי מתני' דמשמע דבעי למעקר שם פסח מיניה כגון שהיו בעליו טמאין בארבעה עשר דסתמיה לשם פסח שני קאי מש"ה בעי עקירה: **מתני'** הפסח נשחט בשלש כיתות. פסחי צבור בין שהצבור מועטין ויכולין לישחט כולן בבת אחת מצוה ליחלק לשלש כיתות זו אחר זו: בזיכי זהב ובזיכי כסף. כפות גדולות לקבל בהן הדם: שכולה כסף כו'. בגמ' מפרש טעמא: ולא היו לבזיכין שוליים· רחבין מלמטה אלא חדין תחתיהם כדי שלא יוכלו ליתנם על הקרקע: שמא יניחום. כהנים על גבי קרקע עד שיקבלו דם אחר מחמת שהן מרובין ושכחום ויקרש הדם ולא יהא ראוי לזרוק: שחט ישראל. אם ירצה שהשחיטה כשירה בזרים בכל הקרבנות: וקיבל כהן. הדם בבזך מצואר הטלה: נותנו לחבירו. שהרי בשורה הן עומדים עד המזבח: מקבל את המלא. מיד השוחט ומחזיר את הריקן שחזר אליו מיד כהן הזורק: זריקה אחת. בבזך עצמו זורק ולא מתפה באצבע שאין לך קרבן טעון אצבע אלא חטאת לבדה כדכתיב באצבעו: כנגד היסוד. ברוחות שבמזבח שהיה יסוד תחתיהן וזורק לזקיפתו של מזבח והוא נופל ליסוד ולפי שאין היסוד מקיף את המזבח אלא את הצפון ואת המערב כדתנן במסכת מדות (פ"ג משנה א) לכך הוצרך לומר כנגד היסוד: כך מעשה השניה ושלישית. הכל כאשר אמרנו: קראו את ההלל. אכל כיתות קאי: אם גמרו שנו. כשהיו מתחילין לשחוט מתחילין לקרות ואם רבו הפסחים ומשך זמן שחיטתן עד שגמרו ועדיין לא גמרה שחיטת פסחי אותה הכת שנו ואם שנו ועדיין רבים שוחטין חוזרין וקורין שניה: וכן השניה וכן השלישית ואע"פ שלא אירע מעולם ששלשו לפי שהיו שם כהנים מרובין וזריזין במלאכתן: לא הגיעו לאהבתי. אפילו פעם ראשון: אלא שהכהנים מדיחין העזרה. שאמת המים מהלכת בעזרה וכשהן רוצין להדיח העזרה פוקקין את נקב יציאתה והמים פושטין והולכין על גדותיה ומדיחין את כל העזרה שרצפה של שיש היתה כולה. ואחר כך פותחין הנקב והמים יוצאים ובערב הפסח מתוך שהדמים מרובים היו מדיחין אותה והכהנים היו מדיחין אותה בשבת שלא ברצון חכמים: מדם התערובות. המוטל על הרצפה וטעמא מפרש בגמרא: אונקליות. מסמרים שראשיהן כפופין למעלה קרוק"ש בלע"ז: בעמודים. אלו עמודין קטנים הרבה וקרויין ננסין כדאמרינן במס' תמיד (פ"ג משנה ה) דתנן בית המטבחיים היה לצפון של מזבח ועליו שמונה עמודין וקרויין ננסין וקורות של ארז על גביהן ואונקליות של ברזל היו קבועין בהן וג' סדרים שבהן תולין ומפשיטין: וקבועין. בעזרה במקום בית המטבחיים: חלקים. מחולקין מפוצלות קליפתן:

שחל

תוספות

הא והא רבי שמעון. נראה לר"י דההיא קמייתא לא הוה מצי לאוקומי כרבנן משום דקתני בה אבל המולק את העוף בי"ד אינו עובר בולא כלום אמאי נקט עוף אי לאו דאתא למידק דווקא בי"ד אבל בחול המועד אפילו בעוף נמי מיחייב והיינו כר' שמעון ובקונטרס פי' לעיל טעם אחר אמאי נקט עוף:

ואיכא דלא מקיש. חלב לזבח וכהי דלא מקיש להקטרה לענין הכי מקיש דלא אמרינן אפילו אחד בסוף העולם דסברא הוא לאקושי להכי:

טעמא שלא לשמו הא סתמא פטור ש"מ כו'. זאת גירסת רש"י ואין נראה לר"ת דהא איכא למידק מרישא איפכא וגריס ר"ת הכי לשמו אמאי פטור שלמים לשם פסח קשחיט ש"מ בעי עקירה פירוש דאי לא בעי עקירה אפילו שחט לשמו כשר דשלמים לשם פסח כשר דהא מכשיר לעיל ר' יהושע שוחט אחרים לשמו*:

קראו את ההלל. פי' לוים דתניא בתוספתא ישראל שוחטין את פסחיהן ולוים קוראים את ההלל קשה לר"י דאמרינן בפ' אין נערכין בערכין (יא.) ובכילד מברכין (ברכות לה. ושם) אין אומרים שירה אלא על היין והכא חזינן דאיכא שירה בלא נסכים וכן היו *מקדשין העזרות בב' תודות ובשיר ואומר ר"י דה"פ אין אומרים שירה בשעת הקרבת קרבן אלא על היין דמשמח אלהים ואנשים דריש ליה ועיקר שתיה ושמחה היינו בשעת אכילה ודומיא דהכי נמי לגבוה בשעת הקרבת קרבן קאמר דאין אומר שירה אלא על היין אבל שלא בשעת הקרבה היו אומרים שירה שלא על היין בכמה דוכתי:

עין משפט נר מצוה

לו א מיי' פ"א מהל' ק"פ הלכה ט·
לז ב שם הלכה יא:
לח ג שם הלכה יב:
לט ד שם הלכה יג·
מ ה שם הלכה יד:
מא ו שם הלכה טו:
מב ז שם הלכה יא:
מג ח שם הלכה טז:
מד ט שם הלכה יד:

רבינו חננאל

והתם קתני המקטיר את האימורין עובר והמולק אינו עובר: קשיין אהדדי ופרקי' שתי הברייתות לר"ש הן הא דפטרה אמליקה בי"ד והכי קאמר ר' שמעון במתני' ושאר כל הזבחים בי"ד בין לשמן ובין שלא לשמן פטור וכיון דר' שמעון פוטר בשאר זבחים כ"ש אמליקה והא דמחייבת אמליקה בחולו של מועד דבההיא מחייב ר"ש במשנתנו [דתנן] ושאר כל הזבחים במועד בין לשמן ובין שלא לשמן [חייב] ומליקה כשחיטה חשיב לה· הקטרת אימורין יש תנא דמקיש הקטרה לשחיטה ומחייב ויש תנא דלא מקיש ותרווייהו אליבא דר"ש: ואמרינן מאי טעמא דר' שמעון די"ד מחייב השוחט את הפסח לבדו על החמץ ופוטר השוחט שאר הזבחים על החמץ ופוטר השוחט הפסח *לשמו ופשטא טעמא דר"ש משום דכתיבי תרי קראי לא תשחט ולא תזבח ובתרווייהו כתיב זבחי שמע' מתרי זבחי דאינון זבחי וכיון דהוה ליה למכתב זבחיו דמשמע זבחים טובא ופלגינהו וכתב זבחי זבחי ש"מ כל היכא דאיכא זבח והוא זבח חג הבשר שעובר עליו קרינא ביה זבחי אזבח זה חייב ולא אשאר זבחים אבל במועד דליכא זבח חג הפסח קרינא זבחים וחייב אשאר זבחים ודיקי' מדקתני השוחט הפסח על החמץ במועד לשם שלמים חייב דוקא שעקר שם פסח מעליו וקראו שלמים מכלל דבשאר ימות השנה בעי עקירה ופרקי' לעולם אימא לך דלא בעי עקירה ומתני' כגון שהיו בעליו טמאי מתים ונדחו לפסח שני דסתמיה לשם פסח קאי: מתני' הפסח נשחט בשלש כתות שנאמר ושחטו אותו כל קהל עדת ישראל קהל ועדה וישראל:

*) ובמועד אשאר זבחים

מסורת הש"ס

לקמן סג: חולין ג.
זבחים יד:
סוכה מ:
[זבחים לד: מנחות נט:]
שבת קכג:

not violate a negative command. [64*a*] Now [the rulings on] wringing are contradictory, [and the rulings on] burning [the fat] are contradictory?—Then according to your reasoning, let that [Baraitha] itself present a difficulty to you. For it teaches, 'They said [this] of nought except the Passover offering alone'; and then it teaches, 'Whether he slaughters or he sprinkles or he a wrings [a bird's neck] or he sprinkles [the blood of the bird]?[1] [Say] rather, both are [according to] R. Simeon; [the rulings on] wringing are not contradictory: here[2] it refers to the fourteenth,[3] while there[4] it means during the Intermediate Days, and thus both the one and the other are [according to] R. Simeon. [The rulings on] the burning [of fat] too are not contradictory: it is dependent on Tannaim. For some compare burning to slaughtering,[5] whilst others do not compare [them].

R. JUDAH SAID: THE [EVENING] TAMID TOO etc. What is R. Judah's reason?—He tells you: Scripture saith, [*Thou shalt not slaughter the blood of*] *My sacrifice*,[6] [implying] the sacrifice which is particularly assigned to Me; and which is that? the *tamid*.

R. SIMEON SAID: [IF HE SLAUGHTERS] THE PASSOVER SACRIFICE [WITH LEAVEN] ON THE FOURTEENTH etc. What is R. Simeon's reason?—Because '*My sacrifice*,' '*My sacrifice*,' is written twice:[7] read it, 'a sacrifice,' 'My sacrifices'.[8] For what law did the Divine Law divide them from one another and not write 'My sacrifices' [in one word]? To intimate: when there is 'a sacrifice' [viz., the Paschal lamb], you are not liable on account of 'My sacrifices'; when there is no 'sacrifice,' you are liable for 'My sacrifices'.

[BUT IF HE KILLS THE PASSOVER OFFERING WITH LEAVEN] ON THE FESTIVAL, IF FOR ITS OWN PURPOSE, HE IS EXEMPT etc. The reason is that it is for a different purpose,[9] but if it is unspecified, he is exempt. [Yet] why? The Passover offering during the rest of the year[10] is a peace-offering![11] Can you then infer from b this[1] [that] the Passover offering during the rest of the year requires cancellation?[2]—Said R. Ḥiyya b. Gamada: It was thrown out from the mouth of the company[3] and they said: [The circumstances are] e.g., that its owners were unclean by reason of a dead body and relegated to the second Passover,[4] so that while unspecified it [still] stands [to be sacrificed] as a Passover offering.[5]

MISHNAH. THE PASSOVER OFFERING IS SLAUGHTERED IN THREE DIVISIONS,[6] FOR IT IS SAID, AND THE WHOLE ASSEMBLY OF THE CONGREGATION OF ISRAEL SHALL KILL IT:[7] [I.E.,] 'ASSEMBLY,' 'CONGREGATION,' AND 'ISRAEL.'[8] THE FIRST DIVISION ENTERED, THE TEMPLE COURT WAS FILLED, THEY CLOSED THE DOORS OF THE TEMPLE COURT, THEY SOUNDED A TEḲI'AH, A TERU'AH, AND A TEḲI'AH.[9] THE PRIESTS STOOD IN ROWS, AND IN THEIR HANDS WERE BASINS[10] OF SILVER AND BASINS OF GOLD; A ROW WHICH WAS ENTIRELY OF SILVER WAS OF SILVER, AND A ROW WHICH WAS ENTIRELY OF GOLD WAS OF GOLD: THEY WERE NOT MIXED; AND THE BASINS HAD NO [FLAT] BOTTOMS, LEST THEY PUT THEM DOWN AND THE BLOOD BECOME CONGEALED. THE ISRAELITE KILLED [THE LAMB], AND THE PRIEST CAUGHT [THE BLOOD]; HE HANDED IT TO HIS COLLEAGUE AND HIS COLLEAGUE [PASSED IT ON] TO HIS COLLEAGUE; AND HE RECEIVED THE FULL [BASIN] AND GAVE BACK THE EMPTY ONE.[11] THE PRIEST NEAREST THE ALTAR SPRINKLED c IT ONCE OVER AGAINST THE BASE [OF THE ALTAR].[1] THE FIRST DIVISION [THEN] WENT OUT AND THE SECOND ENTERED; THE SECOND WENT OUT AND THE THIRD ENTERED. AS THE MANNER OF THE FIRST [GROUP], SO WAS THE MANNER OF THE SECOND AND THE THIRD. THEY RECITED THE HALLEL;[2] IF THEY FINISHED IT[3] THEY REPEATED, AND IF THEY REPEATED [AND WERE NOT FINISHED YET], THEY RECITED IT A THIRD TIME, THOUGH THEY NEVER DID RECITE IT A THIRD TIME. R. JUDAH SAID: THE THIRD DIVISION NEVER REACHED[4] 'I LOVE THAT THE LORD SHOULD HEAR' [ETC.],[5] BECAUSE THE PEOPLE FOR IT WERE FEW. AS WAS DONE ON WEEK-DAYS SO WAS DONE ON THE SABBATH, SAVE THAT THE PRIESTS SWILLED THE TEMPLE COURT, [BUT] WITHOUT THE CONSENT OF THE SAGES. R. JUDAH SAID: HE [A PRIEST] USED TO FILL A GOBLET WITH THE MIXED BLOOD[6] [AND] HE SPRINKLED IT ONCE ON THE ALTAR; BUT THE SAGES DID NOT AGREE WITH HIM.

HOW DID THEY HANG UP [THE SACRIFICES] AND FLAY [THEM]? THERE WERE IRON HOOKS FIXED IN THE WALLS AND IN THE PILLARS, ON WHICH THEY SUSPENDED [THE SACRIFICES] AND FLAYED [THEM]. IF ANY ONE HAD NO PLACE TO SUSPEND AND FLAY, THERE WERE THERE THIN SMOOTH STAVES WHICH HE PLACED ON HIS SHOULDER AND ON HIS NEIGHBOUR'S SHOULDER, AND SO SUSPENDED [THE ANIMAL] AND FLAYED [IT]. R. ELIEZER SAID: WHEN THE FOURTEENTH

a (1) The last two refer to birds, hence not to the Passover offering, v. 63*b*, n. c7. (2) In the first Baraitha. (3) As is distinctly stated. Then he is exempt, culpability being incurred on that day only for the Paschal lamb. (4) In the second Baraitha. (5) Actually only slaughtering which includes sprinkling is mentioned in Ex. XXXIV, 25. (*Thou shalt not* slaughter the blood of etc.'), but some maintain that burning is the same. (6) Ex. XXIII, 18; XXXIV, 25. (7) In Ex. XXIII, 18 and XXXIV, 25. (8) I.e., by transferring the *yod* (י) from one זבחי to the other, we have זבח, זבחיי, a 'sacrifice' referring to the Paschal lamb, and זבחיי, 'My sacrifices', plural, referring to all others. (9) I.e., he *explicitly* states thus. (10) I.e., at any time other than the eve of Passover. (11) *Automatically*. Why then is an explicit declaration required.

b (1) Viz., that we do nevertheless require this explicit statement. (2) Lit., 'uprooting', 'eradicating'. I.e., it does not become a peace-offering *automatically*, but its character as a Passover offering must be explicitly cancelled. (3) I.e., all the scholars unanimously declared. (4) V. Num. IX, 10ff. (5) In the following month; therefore it is not a peace-offering automatically. But in other cases it is, and an explicit declaration is then unnecessary. (6) Irrespective of the number sacrificing. (7) Ex. XII, 6. (8) Each denotes a separate division. (9) *Teḳi'ah* is a long, straight blast on the *shofar* (ram's horn); *teru'ah* is a series of three short consecutive blasts. (10) To receive the blood. (11) After the blood had been sprinkled. Thus it was worked on the 'endless-chain' system.

c (1) I.e., on the side which has a projecting base, viz., the north and west sides of the altar, v. Mid. III, 1. (2) Lit., 'praise', a liturgical passage at present consisting of Ps. CXIII—CXVIII. This was recited by each group. (3) Before they finished sacrificing. (4) Lit., 'from the days of the third party they did not reach'. (5) Ps. CXVI, 1 seq. (6) The blood of many sacrifices which ran together.

sprinkles [the blood] [63b] or to one of the members of the company,[6] and providing that it [the leaven] is with him in the Temple Court. R. Joḥanan said: Even if it is not with him in the Temple Court.

Wherein do they differ? Shall we say that they differ in whether '*with*' ['al] means 'near,'[7] R. Simeon b. Laḳish holding, '*with*' means 'near', while R. Joḥanan holds, We do not require '*with*' [in the sense of] 'near,'—but surely they have differed in this once [already]?[8] For we learned: If a man slaughters the thanksoffering within [the Temple Court], while its bread is without the wall, the bread is not sanctified.[9] What does 'without the wall' mean?
a R. Joḥanan said, Without the wall of Beth Pagi;[1] but [if] without the wall of the Temple Court, it is sanctified, and we do not require '*with*' [in the sense of] near. R. Simeon b. Laḳish said: Even if without the wall of the Temple Court, it is not sanctified; which proves that we require '*with*' [in the sense of] near!—Rather, they differ over a doubtful warning.[2] But in this too they have already differed once? For it was stated: [If a man declares, 'I take] an oath that I will eat this loaf to-day,' and the day passed and he did not eat it,—R. Joḥanan and R. Simeon b. Laḳish both maintain, He is not flagellated. R. Joḥanan said, He is not flagellated, because it is a negative injunction not involving an action,[3] and every negative command not involving an action, we do not flagellate for it; but a doubtful warning counts[4] as a warning.[5] While R. Simeon b. Laḳish said, He is not flagellated, because it is a doubtful warning, and a doubtful warning does not count as a warning; but as for a negative command not involving an action, we flagellate for it!

I will tell you: After all they differ in whether '*with*' implies near,
b yet it is necessary.[1] For if they differed on the subject of leaven [alone], I would say: It is only there that R. Joḥanan maintains that we do not require '*with*' [in the sense of] near, because it is a prohibited article, and wherever it is, it is; but in the matter of sanctifying the bread, it is not sanctified save within [the Temple Court], [hence] I would assume [that] he agrees with R. Simeon b. Laḳish, that if it is inside it is sanctified, and if not, it is not sanctified, by analogy with service vessels.[2] Thus this [latter case] is necessary. And if we were informed [of this] in the matter of sanctifying the bread, I would say: in this R. Simeon b. Laḳish maintains that we require '*with*' [in the sense of] near, so that if it is inside it is sanctified, [and] if not, it is not sanctified. But in the matter of leaven [I would say that] he agrees with R. Joḥanan that we do not require '*with*' [in the sense of] near, because it is a prohibited article, and wherever it is, it is. Hence they are [both] necessary.

R. Oshaia asked R. Ammi: What if he who slaughters has none, but one of the members of the company has [leaven]?[3]—Said he to him, Is it then written, '*Thou shalt not slaughter* [*the blood of My sacrifice*] *with* thy *leavened bread*'? '*Thou shalt not slaughter* [*the blood of My sacrifice*] *with leavened bread*' is written.[4] If so, he countered, [he is culpable] even if a person at the end of the world [possesses leaven]!—Said he to him, Scripture saith, *Thou shalt not slaughter* [*the blood of My sacrifice with leavened bread*]; *neither shall* [*the sacrifice of the feast of the passover*] *be left overnight unto the morning:* [thus,] '*Thou shalt not slaughter . . . with leavened bread*' [applies to] those who are subject to '*it shall not be left overnight*' on its account.[5]

R. Papa said: As a corollary, the priest who burns the fat [on the altar] violates a negative command, since he is subject to the
c general [interdict of] leaving the *emurim* overnight.[1] It was taught in accordance with R. Papa. He who slaughters the Passover sacrifice with leaven violates a negative command. When is that? When it belongs to him who slaughters or to him who sprinkles [the blood] or to one of the members of the company. If it belonged to someone at the end of the world, he is not tied to him.[2] And whether he slaughters or sprinkles or burns [the fat],[3] he is liable. But he who wrings a bird's neck on the fourteenth[4] does not violate anything.[5] But the following contradicts it: He who slaughters the Passover offering with leaven violates a negative command. R. Judah said: The *tamid* too.[6] Said they to him, They [the Sages] said [thus] of nought except the Passover-offering alone. When is that? When either he who slaughters or he who sprinkles or one of the members of the company possesses [the leaven]. If a person at the end of the world possesses it, he is not tied to him. And whether he slaughters or he sprinkles or he wrings [a bird's neck] or he sprinkles[7] [the blood of the bird], he is liable. But he who takes the handful of the meal-offering[8] does not violate a negative command. He who burns the *emurim* does

(6) Registered for this sacrifice. (7) In Ex. XXXIV, 25, quoted 63*a*, n. b6. (8) Why then repeat the controversy here? (9) The thanksoffering was accompanied by forty loaves. These were verbally sanctified before the sacrifice was actually slaughtered, whereupon they acquired a monetary consecration, which means that they might not henceforth be eaten or put to use until the offering is sacrificed; while if they became defiled, they were redeemed and reverted to *ḥullin*. The slaughtering of the sacrifice conferred intrinsic ('bodily') sanctity upon them; they were more readily disqualified then, and if defiled they had to be burnt. In this connection too '*with*' (על) is written: *then he shall offer with the sacrifice of the thanksoffering unleavened cakes . . . with* (על) *cakes of leavened bread he shall present his offering* (Lev. VII, 12f).—'Not sanctified' means not intrinsically sanctified.

a (1) A fortified suburb of Jerusalem (Jast.), which is the uttermost boundary of the town (Rashi). Its exact spot has not been identified, v. Neubauer, *Géographie*, pp. 247ff. (2) Flagellation, the punishment for violating a negative command, is imposed only if the offender has been duly warned before he sinned. Now, if the leaven is in the Temple Court, he can be warned with the certainty that his proposed action is forbidden. But if it is not in the Temple Court, we are doubtful, as we do not know whether he has leaven at home, and thus it is a doubtful warning. R. Simeon b. Laḳish holds that such is not a valid warning, and flagellation is not thereby incurred; while R. Joḥanan holds that it is a warning, and when we subsequently learn that he had leaven at home, he is flagellated. (3) I.e., he violates the injunction, '*Thou shalt not take the name of the Lord thy God in vain* (Ex. XX, 7) by remaining passive, not by a positive act, v. Shebu. 20*b*. (4) Lit., 'its name is'. (5) For naturally until the last moment of the day only a doubtful warning can be given, as we do not know that he will permit the day to pass without eating it.

b (1) For them to differ in both cases. (2) These sanctify whatever is put into them, but only when they are in the Temple Court (Tosaf.). (3) Resh Laḳish states it (*supra*) as an obvious thing, but R. Oshaia was in doubt. (4) Ex. XXXIV, 25. Hence he is culpable. (5) And that obviously applies to its owners only.

c (1) I.e., if he still has leaven when he burns the *fat*, even if none of the company has any. (2) He has no connection with him,—or, he is not bound to take him into account,—is unaffected thereby. (3) This supports R. Papa. (4) While he still possesses leaven. The reference is to a bird offered as a sacrifice for a man lacking atonement; as stated *supra* 59*a*, it could be brought on the fourteenth after the afternoon *tamid*, i.e., when it is time for the Passover sacrifice to be slaughtered. (5) This is explained anon. (6) V. note on Mishnah. (7) מזה, term used in connection with bird sacrifices, as distinct from זרק, which refers to animal sacrifices. (8) V. Lev. II, 2.

תורה אור

או לאחד מבני חבורה ועד שיהא עמו בעזרה ר' יוחנן אמר *אע"פ שאין עמו בעזרה במאי קמיפלגי אילימא בעל בסמוך קמיפלגי דרבי שמעון בן לקיש סבר *על בסמוך ורבי יוחנן סבר לא בעינן על בסמוך והא איפלגו בה חדא זימנא *דתנן [א]השוחט תודה לפנים ולחומה חוץ לחומה לא קדש הלחם מאי חוץ לחומה רבי יוחנן אמר [ב]חוץ לחומת בית פאגי אבל חוץ לחומת העזרה קדיש ולא בעינן על בסמוך רבי שמעון בן לקיש אמר אפילו חוץ לחומת עזרה לא קדיש אלמא בעינן על בסמוך אלא בהתראת ספק קמיפלגי בהא נמי הא פליגי בה חדא זימנא *דאיתמר שבועה שאוכל ככר זו היום ועבר היום ולא אכלה ר' יוחנן ור"ש בן לקיש דאמרי תרוייהו אינו לוקה [ג]רבי יוחנן אמר אינו לוקה משום דהוה ליה לאו שאין בו מעשה וכל לאו שאין בו מעשה אין לוקין עליו [ד]אבל התראת ספק שמה התראה ור"ש בן לקיש אמר אינו לוקה משום דהוה ליה התראת ספק והתראת ספק לא שמה התראה אבל לאו שאין בו מעשה לוקין עליו אמרי לעולם בעל בסמוך קא מיפלגי *וצריכא דאי איפליגו לענין חמץ הוה אמינא בההוא הוא דקאמר רבי יוחנן דלא בעינן על בסמוך משום דאיסור הוא וכל היכא דאיתיה איתיה אבל לענין מקדש לחם לא קדיש אלא בפנים אימא מודה ליה לר"ש בן לקיש דבעינן על בסמוך דאי איתיה גואי קדיש אי לא לא קדיש מידי דהוה אכלי שרת צריכא ואי אשמעינן לענין מקדש לחם ה"א בהך קאמר ר"ש בן לקיש דבעינן על בסמוך דאי איתיה גואי קדיש אי לא לא קדיש אבל לענין חמץ מודה ליה לרבי יוחנן דלא בעינן על בסמוך דאיסורא הוא וכל היכא דאיתיה איתיה צריכא בעא מיניה רב אושעיא מרבי אמי אין לו לשוחט ויש לו לאחד מבני חבורה מהו אמר ליה מי כתיב לא תשחט על חמצך °לא תשחט על חמץ כתיב (שמות לד) אמר ליה אי הכי אפילו לאחד בסוף העולם נמי אמר ליה אמר קרא לא תשחט ולא ילין לא תשחט על חמץ הנך דקיימי עליה משום לא ילין אמר רב פפא הילכך כהן המקטיר את החלב עובר בלא תעשה הואיל וישנו בכלל הלנת אמורין תניא כוותיה דרב פפא *[ה]השוחט את הפסח על החמץ עובר בל"ת אימתי בזמן שהוא לשוחט או לזורק או לאחד מבני חבורה היה לאחד בסוף העולם אין זקוק לו ואחד השוחט ואחד הזורק ואחד המקטיר חייב אבל המולק את העוף בארבעה עשר אינו עובר בלא כלום ורמינהי השוחט את הפסח על החמץ עובר בלא תעשה ר' יהודה אומר אף התמיד אמרו לו לא אמרו אלא בפסח בלבד אימתי בזמן שיש לשוחט או לזורק או לאחד מבני חבורה היה לאחד בסוף העולם אין זקוק לו ואחד השוחט ואחד הזורק ואחד המולק ואחד המזה חייב אבל הקומץ את המנחה אינו עובר בלא תעשה המקטיר את האימורין אינו עובר בלא תעשה

קשיא

רש"י

בעל בסמוך. כל היכא דכתיב על משמע בסמוך והכא על חמץ כתיב כמו ועליו מטה מנשה (במדבר ב): בפנים · בעזרה: לחמי תודה· משהוקדשו בפה קדשו קדושת דמים ליאסר באכילה ובהנאה אבל לא קדשו קדושת הגוף ואם נטמאו נפדין ויוצאין לחולין ושחיטת הזבח מקדשתן לגופן להיות נפסלין בטבול יום ובמגע מחוסר כפורים ובלינה ואם נטמאו ישרפו כדכתיב על זבח התודה חלות ואמר מר במנחות קרבנו על זבח מלמד שאין הלחם קרוי קרבן אלא בזביחה: לא קדש הלחם. קדושת הגוף: בית פאגי. הייני מקום חיצון שבירושלים התם הוא דחוץ לחומת בית פאגי חוץ לירושלים הוא ואינו מקום אכילת קדשים קלים ואם יצאו שם נפסלין התם ודאי לא מקדשא ליה שחיטה אבל אי חוץ לחומת עזרה קאי אע"ג דלאו גבי זבח קאי בשעת זביחה הואיל ובמקום הכשירו היה עומד שפיר דמי ולא בעינן על בסמוך: אלא. הכא גבי חמץ: בהתראת ספק קא מיפלגי. דמלקות ליתא אלא בהתראה וכי מתרינן ביה לא תשחט על החמץ אי חזינן חמץ גביה ומתרין ביה הויא התראת ודאי ואי לא התראת ספק היא ואפילו אשתכח דהוה ליה בביתיה כיון דאנן לא הוי ידעינן לאו התראה היא ורבי יוחנן סבר התראת ספק שמה התראה ואי אישתכח דהוה ליה מיחייב: פטור ממלקות. דלא תשא: התראת ספק· וכי מתריה ביה אכלהו היום פן תעבור על השבועה שמא יעבור שמא לא יעבור על התראתו דעדיין שהות ביום: וצריכי· לאיפלוגי בחמץ ובלחמי תודה: מידי דהוה אכלי שרת. דמקדשי לגופה כדכתיב כל הנוגע בהם יקדש ואין מקדשין אלא הנכנס לתוכן: רב אושעיא. הא דפשיטא לר"ל לעיל הוא מיבעיא ליה: אפי' לאחד בסוף העולם. שאינו מבני חבורה נמי אם ישנו עמו בעזרה יעבור השוחט הזה עליו אם התרו בו: כל בני חבורה בכלל לא ילין מן הבשר הן בכלל תותירו: לא תשחט ולא ילין. בחד קרא ניהו: המקטיר את החלב · של פסח על החמץ שיש לו בשעת הקטרה אי נמי אם יש לא' מבני חבורה חמץ בשעת שחיטה ויש לו לכהן המקטיר בשעת הקטרה עובר הוא ואע"ג דלא כתיב אלא לא תשחט *וזריקה מתרבית במכילתא מדם אתי נמי הקטרה מדסמכיה ללא ילין כל שישנו בעבודה שלהן באזהרת הלנה ישנו נמי באזהרת חמץ הילכך מקטיר נמי עובר:הואיל וישנו בהלנת אמורין. דכתיב בהו נמי לא ילין חלב חגי: אבל המולק את העוף. של מחוסר כיפורים דאמרן בפירקין (דף נט:) דכשר להקריבה אחר התמיד שהוא זמן שחיטת פסח אינו עובר עליו משום לא תשחט על חמץ ולקמן מוקי לה כר"ש דמחייב נמי אשאר זבחים במועד והכא טעמא' לפטורה משום דבי"ד לא מיחייב עליה אשאר זבחים ועוף דנקט לאו דוקא אלא משום דאין דרך לשחוט שום קרבן בזמן שחיטת פסח דהייט אחר חצות אלא קרבן של מחוסר כיפורים כדי שיאכל פסחו לערב ורובייהו עוף מייתין זב וזבה ויולדת אפי' עשירים ומצורע עני:*אחד השוחט.את הפסח ואחד הזורק את דמו ואחד המולק חטאת העוף דמחוסר כיפורים:ואחד המזה.מדמה כדכתיב והזה מדם החטאת וגו' ובחטאת העוף קאי והך סיפא דמשמע דעובר אף אשאר קרבנות רמי לקמן ארישא דקתני לא אמרו אלא פסח בלבד: אבל הקומץ מנחה.במועד על החמץ: אינו עובר. דקמילה ודאי לאו שחיטה היא:המקטיר את האימורין. בין פסח בי"ד בין במועד אשאר זבחים אינו עובר:

קשיא

תוספות

או לאחד מבני חבורה · אומר ר"י דלא מיחייב בעל החמץ אלא השוחט והזורק דלא תשחט אמר רחמנא ועוד היאך יתחייב לרבי יוחנן הא לאו שאין בו מעשה הוא: לא אמרינן על בסמוך. תימה דבפ' שתי הלחם (מנחות צה·) אמרינן דלכל הפחות בעינן על בסמוך דפליגי תנאי בבזיכי לבונה של לחם הפנים דאיכא למאן דאמר ונתת על המערכת על ממש ואיכא למאן דאמר על בסמוך וכן באלו נאמרין (סוטה לז·) פליגי בקרא דונתת את הברכה על הר גרזים אי על ממש אי בסמוך וי"ל דהתם סברא הוא דהוי בסמוך דהא בשעת הנחת הלחם היו מניחין אותם ובשעת סילוקו נקטרים וכן גבי הר גריזים סברא הוא דלכל הפחות סמוך בעינן דאי לאו הכי למאי כתביה וכן משמע בסמוך דהיכא דסברא הוא לא פליגי דקאמר אבל לענין מקדש הימא מודה ליה לריש לקיש: התראת ספק לא שמה התראה. מתוך פ"ה משמע דלא הוי התראה משום כיון דלא ידעינן לאו התראה היא ולא נהירא לר"י דמה לנו אם ספק למתרה אלא שיהא ודאי למותרה דלא ניתנה התראה אלא להבחין בין שוגג למזיד ולשון הקונטרס נמי יש ליישב דה"ק כיון דאנן לא הוה ידעינן לאו התראה היא שיכול המותר' להכחישנו ולומר שוגג הייתי: לאו שאין בו מעשה לוקין עליו כו'. מפורש בהשוכר את הפועלים (ב"מ צ:): מידי דהוי אכלי שרת. פי' בקונטרס דאין מקדשין אלא מה שבתוכן· וקשה מה שייך זה לשחיטת הזבח שלא יקדש אלא מה שבפנים לעזרה הילכך נראה לפרש מידי דהוה אכלי שרת שאין מקדשין מה שבתוכן אלא כשהן בעזרה וכן משמע בפרק המזבח מקדש* (זבחים פה·) דקאמר כלי שרת אין מקדשין אלא מתוכן ואין מקדשין אלא בפנים וא"ת דתנן בלולב וערבה (סוכה מח:) כמעשהו בחול כך מעשהו בשבת אלא שהיה ממלא חבית של זהב שאינה מקודשת מערב שבת ופריך (שם מט:) ולמאי ניתי מקודשת א"ר זעירי קא סבר אין שיעור למים וכלי שרת מקדשין שלא מדעת פי' ואי מייתי מקודשת איפסיל להו בלינה והשתא אכתי נייתי מקודשת ויניחנה חוץ לעזרה דלא מיקדשה אלא בפנים וי"ל דטוב להביא שאינה מקודשת ויניחנה בפני' ממקודשת ויניחנה בחוץ:

[וע"ע תוספות ד"ה אלא]

הא

עין משפט נר מצוה

לב א ב מיי' פי"ט מה' פסולי מוקדשין הלכה טז:

לג ג מיי' פ"ד מהל' שבועות הלכה כ:

לד ד מיי' פט"ז מהל' סנהדרין הלכה ד סמג עשין קה:

לה ה מיי' פ"א מהל' ק"פ הלכה ה:

רבינו חננאל

בהאי פליגי ריש לקיש סבר כיון דכתיב לא תשחט על חמץ האי על משמע אצלו במקום שחיטה ור' יוחנן סבר כיון דהוא אצלו ברשותו אפי' במקום רחוק כאלו בידו הוא ועל קרינא ביה ואמרינן למה הוצרכו להלוק ע"ז הרי נחלקין עליו במקום אחר דתנן במנחות פרק [התודה] השוחט את התודה בפני' ולחומה חוץ לחומה לא קדש הלחם רבי יוחנן אמר חוץ לחומת בית פאגי במקום שאינו יכול לאכלו שם שהוא רחוק מירוש' דכתי' (ויקר' ז') והקריב על זבח התודה חלות מצות וגו' וחומת בית פאגי רחוק הוא ונמצא זבח בלא לחם כי הוא במקום אחד והלחם במקום אחר אבל לפנים מחומת בית פאגי שאוכלין שם קדשים קלים שפיר דמי כדגרסי' בענין החבוש בבית האסורין אבל אי קאי לפנים מבית פאגי אפשר דמעיילי ליה להתם ואכיל כן גם זה לחם התודה אם הוא בירושלים שהוא מקום אכילת קדשים קלים קדש הלחם דעל זבח קרינא ביה וריש לקיש אמר אפי' חוץ לחומת עזרה לא קדש הלחם דבעינן לחם לזבח באותו מקום שהוא ואמרינן רבי יוחנן וריש לקיש הכא בהתראת ספק פליגי ריש לקיש אמר כשמתרין לשוחט זה לא תשחט על חמץ שכל השוחט על חמץ לוקה אם החמץ עמו בעזרה נמצאת התראת ודאי אבל אם אינו עמו חיישינן שמא נאכל או נשרף נמצא המתרה מתרה אם לא השבת אותו חמץ שהיה לך שראינהו בחצרך אלא הוא קיים עכשיו ואתה שוחט הפסח קודם השבתתו ואתה עובר בלאו נמצאת זו התראת חספק דאיכא למימר דילמא אדם השביתו כבר הלכך ספק הוא והתראת ספק כי האי גונא אינה התרא' ודבר זה מפורש באלו הן הלוקין ובענין השוחט אותו ואת בנו כו' עוד הקשינו גם בזה חלקו במקום אחר · דאיתמר שבועה שאוכל ככר זה היום ועבר היום ולא אכלה רבי יוחנן ורבי שמעון בן לקיש דאמרי תרווייהו אינו לוקה כשמתרין אותו בשעת שבועה אל תשבע שמא לא יזדמן לו לאכלה היום ונמצאת עובר על שבועתך היא התראת ספק כי יתכן לו לאכלה ויקיים שבועתו וכי האי גונא אינה התראה רבי יוחנן אמר התראת ספק שמה התראה אלא למה אינו לוקה משום דהוה ליה לאו שאין בו מעשה כי לא עשה מעשה כלום אלא ישב ולא אכל הנה לא עשה מעשה וכל לאו שאין בו מעשה אין לוקין עליו (ואפי') [ואמרינן] לעולם בעל בסמוך פליגי והאי דאמרת הא איפלגו בה חדא זימנא כלומר נתברר לנו דבריהם במקום אחר ומשם אנו יודעין כי כך דעתם בכל מקום והילכתא כרבי יוחנן אצטריכא צריכה לברר הכא והתם חלוקתם דאי אשמעינן [illegible] ופשוטה היא: בעא מיניה רבי אושעיא מרבי אמי אין לו לשוחט חמץ כלל אבל יש לאחד מבני חבורה [illegible] [איתא] בלא תשחט ודייק מינה רב פפא אפי' אם יש חמץ לכהן המקטיר את האמורין עובר הואיל ואיתיה בהלנת אימורין: תניא כרב פפא השוחט את הפסח על החמץ עובר בלא כו' עד אחד השוחט ואחד הזורק ואחד המקטיר אבל המולק העוף על החמץ בי"ד אינו עובר איני והתניא אחד השוחט ואחד הזורק ואחד המולק ואחד המזה חייב אבל לא הקומץ מנחה והמקטיר את האמורין אינו עובר הכא קתני המולק עובר והמקטיר (אינו) עובר

מסורת הש"ס

[סוטה לז: מנחות כו: סנ' לח· סנהד' יג:]

מנחות עח: [מעילה ט:]

שבועות דף כ: ודף כא· מכות דף טו: תמורה דף ג:

[מנחות עט:]

[תוספת' פ"ד]

[עי' רש"י לעיל נט: ד"ה כגון דקאמר ר"י]

גליון הש"ס

גמ' אף ע"פ שאין עמו בעזרה. עי' ר"ש פ"א מ"ח דכלים וצ"ע: רש"י ד"ה המקטיר וכו' וזריק' מתרבאי במכילתא. עי' יומא דף ס"ג ע"ב תד"ה אזיקת דמים:

כח א מיי' פ"ד מהל' תרומות הל' טו טוש"ע י"ד סימן של"א סעיף מה:
כט ב מיי' פ"ב מהל' שבועות הל' י"א סמג לאוין רמא טוש"ע י"ד סימן רי סעיף א:
ל ג מיי' פי"ז מהלכות פסולי מוקדשין הל"ח:
לא ד מיי' פ"א מהל' ק"פ הל' ס':

לימא קסברי אחרים *אינה לשחיטה אלא בסוף וכדרבא דאמר רבא עדיין היא מחלוקת הילכך הקדים מולין לערלים מולין חיילי ערלים לא חיילי הקדים ערלים למולין ערלים חיילי מולין לא חיילי אמר *רבה לא לעולם קסברי אחרים ישנה לשחיטה מתחלה ועד סוף והכא במאי עסקינן כגון שגמר בלבו לתרוייהו בין למולין בין לערלים והוציא בפיו לערלים ולא הספיק לומר למולין עד שנגמרה שחיטה בערלים ובהא פליגי דר"מ סבר לא בעינן פיו ולבו שוים ורבנן סברי בעינן פיו ולבו שוים וקסבר ר' מאיר לא בעינן פיו ולבו שוין ורמינהו **המתכוין לומר תרומה ואמר מעשר מעשר ואמר תרומה ²או שאיני נכנס לבית זה ואמר לזה שאיני נהנה לזה ואמר לזה לא אמר כלום עד שיהו פיו ולבו שוין אלא אמר אביי רישא דאמר סימן ראשון למולין וסימן שני אף לערלים דבסימן שני נמי פתיכי ביה מולין סיפא דאמר סימן ראשון לערלים סימן שני למולין דבסימן ראשון הא לא פתיכי ביה מולין ור' מאיר לטעמיה דאמר *מפגלין בחצי מתיר ורבנן לטעמייהו דאמרי ³אין מפגלין בחצי מתיר:

מתני׳ ⁴**השוחט את הפסח על החמץ עובר בלא תעשה ר' יהודה אומר אף התמיד רבי שמעון אומר *הפסח בארבעה עשר לשמו חייב ושלא לשמו פטור *ושאר כל הזבחים בין לשמן ובין שלא לשמן פטור *ובמועד לשמו פטור שלא לשמו חייב ושאר כל הזבחים בין לשמן בין שלא לשמן חייב חוץ מן החטאת ששחטו שלא לשמה:

גמ׳ אמר רבי שמעון בן לקיש לעולם אינו חייב עד שיהא החמץ לשוחט או לזורק

וכדרבא. בפ"ב דזבחים(א): עדיין היא מחלוקת. גבי תפוס לשון ראשון דאיפלגי בה ר' מאיר ור' יוסי באומר הרי זו תמורת עולה תמורת שלמים הרי זו תמורת עולה דברי רבי מאיר דתפוס לשון ראשון רבי יוסי אומר דבריו קיימים דאף בגמר דבריו אדם נתפס ואיבעיא להו אמר תהא עולה ותהא שלמים מי מודה בה ר' מאיר או לא מי אמרינן טעמא דרבי מאיר משום דנמלך הוא וכיון דחל שם עולה תו לא פקע אבל כי אמר לתרוייהו ליכא למימר הכי או דילמא כיון דפשטה ביה קדושת עולה ברישא תו לא חיילא קדושת שלמים ואמר אביי בהא ודאי מודי ר"מ ורבא אמר עדיין היא מחלוקת ואותביה רבא לאביי מהשוחט את הזבח לאכול כזית בחוץ כזית למחר דקא פליג ר' יהודה אדרבנן ואמר כר' מאיר תפוס לשון ראשון דקאמר זה הכלל כל שמחשבת זמן קדמה למחשבת מקום פיגול וחייבין עליו כרת לא שנא בעבודה אחת ולא שנא בשתי עבודות חישב בעבודה שניה מחשבת פסול בתר מחשבת פיגול לא מפקע ליה מיד פיגול דתפוס לשון ראשון ורבנן סברי אף בגמר דבריו הוא נתפס והויא לה בחדא עבודה עירוב מחשבות ולא קרב המתיר כמצותו והכא בעינן דלא ליהוי ביה פסול אחרינא והדלאה כתיב ביה אלמא מאן דאית ליה תפוס לשון ראשון אפילו לתרוייהו אית ליה דהא זימי טובה יש בזבח ופליג ר' יהודה ואמר ליה אביי מי סברת אינה לשחיטה אלא לבסוף וחדא מחשבה היא ישנה לשחיטה מתחלה ועד סוף כו' וכגון דאמר סימן ראשון חוץ לזמנו ושני חוץ למקומו ור"מ סבר מפגלין בסימן אחד מכלל דרבא דאותביה מהא ס"ל אליבא דר' מאיר ור' יהודה דאינה לשחיטה אלא לבסוף וכולה מחשבה בסוף שחיטה הואי והוה ליה חדא מחשבה ונמלך ליכא למימר דהא בשני זימים חשיב ואפילו הכי פליג והיינו דאמרינן הכא לימא קסברי אחרים אינה לשחיטה אלא לבסוף וכל מחשבת שחיטה לא מהניא אלא אם כן חישב בגמרה וכדרבא דאמר התם עדיין היא מחלוקת באומר לתרוייהו ועל כרחך אית ליה לרבי מאיר אינה לשחיטה אלא לבסוף ואחרים היינו ר"מ הילכך בגמר שחיטה אין שהות לומר שני דברים והיכא דהקדים מולין לערלים בסוף שחיטה מולין חיילי כולה הקדים ערלים למולין ערלים חיילי כולה והוה ליה כולה ערלה ופסולה: והכא במאי עסקינן. דקתני הקדים ערלים למולין פסול כגון שגמר בלבו להוציא מולין אחר ערלים ואומר לערלים ולמולין כל מחשבה דקדשים מוציא בפיו הוא: לא בעינן פיו ולבו שוין. והלך אחר פיו והיכא כולה ערלה ואע"פ שלא היה בלבו אלא למקצתה: שאיני נהנה לזה. לאיש זה: לא אמר כלום. וסתם משנה היא ור"מ היא: סימן שני אף לערלים גרסינן בסימן ראשון לא היה דעתו אלא למה שהוציא בפיו ובסימן שני היה מוסיף על מחשבתו הילכך כי הקדים ערלים למולין נגמר סימן ראשון בערלים: ור' מאיר לטעמיה דאמר. במנחות מפגלין בחצי מתיר דתנן *פיגל בקומץ ולא בלבונה בלבונה ולא בקומץ כלומר חישב בהקטרת האחד על מנת לאכול מן השיריים למחר ר"מ אומר פיגול וחכ"א אין בו כרת עד שיפגל בכל המתיר: יש פיגול. במחשבת חצי מתיר והאי חצי מתיר הוא דשחיטה בשני הסימנין היא: פתיכי. מעורבין: **מתני׳** השוחט את הפסח על החמץ עובר בלא תעשה. דלא תשחט על חמץ וגו': אף התמיד. של בין הערבים דערב הפסח בי"ד: ר"ש אומר הפסח בי"ד. ששחטו על החמץ וטעמא יליף בגמ': לשמו חייב. משום לא תשחט על חמץ דפסח כשר הוא ושחיטה שחיטה ראויה היא (ושמה שחיטה): ושלא לשמו פטור. דפסול הוא ושחיטה שאינה ראויה לאו שמה שחיטה והכי אית ליה לר"ש בכל דוכתי בכיסוי הדם (חולין דף פה.) ובאותו ואת בנו (דף פה:) ובתשלומי ארבעה וחמשה (ב"ק דף ע:): ושאר כל הזבחים. ששחטן בי"ד לאחר חצות על החמץ בין לשמן ושלא לשמן ואע"ג שכשירין הן כדתנן (זבחים דף ב.) כל הזבחים שנזבחו שלא לשמן כשירין: פטור. כדמפרש בגמ' בעידנא דמחייב אפסח לא מחייב אשאר זבחים: ובמועד. בתוך הפסח אם לשמו שחטו לפסח על החמץ פטור מלא תשחט דפסח שלא בזמנו לשמו פסול והויא לה שחיטה שאינה ראויה: שלא לשמו. אלא לשם שלמים: חייב. דלהכי קאי והויא לה שחיטה ראויה וחייב משום לא תשחט בהדי לאו דלא יראה ולא ימצא ואיכא מלקות כמי דשחיטה: ושאר כל הזבחים. ששחטן במועד על החמץ: בין לשמן בין כו' חייב. דהא כשירין הן ובגמ' מפרש דקרא אשאר זבחים כמי אזהר: חוץ מן החטאת ששחטה שלא לשמה. דפסולה היא כדתנן בזבחים (שם) חוץ מן הפסח והחטאת וטעמא משום דכתיב בשחיטה חטאת היא מעוטא היא ולא הגשחטת שלא לשמה: **גמ׳** עד שיהא החמץ לשוחט כו'. ואע"ג דכתיב על חמץ סתמא אם היה חמץ לאחד שאינו מבני חבורה ואפילו ישנו עמו בעזרה ואלו השוחטין פסחיהן רואין אותו והתרו בהן אין עוברין כדמפרש לקמיה מדכתיב לא תשחט ולא ילין כל שישנו בהלנה ישנו בשחיטה ואם יש לא' מהן טלן עוברין: לזורק. הדם דזריקה נמי איתרביא במכילתא מדם *זבחך: בעל

לימא קסברי אחרים אינה לשחיטה אלא לבסוף וכדרבא וכו'. בפ' שני דזבחים (ד' ל:) פליגי אביי ורבא אליבא דר"מ דלאביי אמר בלתרוייהו מודה ר' מאיר ורבא אמר עדיין היא מחלוקת והתם נמי סבר ר' מאיר תפוס לשון ראשון ולהכי מפרש בקונטרס הכא תמורת עולה והיא תמורת שלמים ונראה כפירוש ר"ח דמפרש להיות לחצי היום יחולו שניהם וקאמר אביי דהתם מודה ר"מ כיון דבשעת אמירה הוא חלים ולחצי היום יחולו שניהם ורבא סבר דאפילו התם פליג רבי מאיר כמו בשחיטה דאינה אלא לבסוף דאין כאן אלא משהו אחד לחול לשניהם ולר' מאיר חייל קמא ולהכי לערלים ולמולים ערלים חיילי דלאמרינן תפוס לשון ראשון אבל אי ישנה לשחיטה מתחלה ועד סוף כיון שיש שהות לשניהם לחול חיילי תרווייהו ולא אמרינן תפוס לשון ראשון אלא דוקא אי אמרינן אינה לשחיטה אלא לבסוף דאין להם שהות לחול לשניהם כדפרי' ולא דמי לתמורת עולה ותמורת שלמים דיותר אמרינן תפוס לשון ראשון כי לא אמר לחצות שיש שהות לשניהם לחול מכי אמר לחצות דהתם כיון דאמר תמורת עולה ואפילו הכי חייל תמורת עולה ואפילו לא חייל תמורת שלמים אבל מולים וערלים כי אמרי ישנה לשחיטה כו' הואיל ויכולים לחול זה אחר זה חיילי תרווייהו אף על גב דסבירא ליה בעלמא תפוס לשון ראשון:

ולא הספיק לומר למולים כו'. תימה לרשב"א א"כ מאי איריא דקתני הקדים מולים לערלים אפילו הקדים ערלים כשר אם הספיק לומר למולים קודם גמר שחיטה:

רבי מאיר סבר לא בעינן פיו ולבו שוין. מכאן מדקדק ר"ח דהא דקרי בכל דוכתי *פיגול פסול מחשבה דלאו דוקא דלאו פיגול עד שיוציא בשפתיו דאי במחשבה תליא מילתא בלא הספיק לומר למולים אמאי פסול לר' מאיר הלא גמר בלבו נמי

המתכוין לומר תרומה כו'. אפילו אי דברים שבלב לא הוו דברים גבי הקדש דבהא לא הוו דברים כי הוה (קדושין דף מט:) דזבין לניכסי' אדעתא למיסק לארץ ישראל ובעידנא דזבין לא אמר התם איכא טעות בדיבורו אבל הכא הכל דברים שבלב הם ומה שהוציא בשפתיו אינו כלום לפי שטעה בדיבורו:

וסימן שני אף לערלים דפתיכי מולין וכו'. ול"ת א"כ אמאי קאמר הקדים מולין אפילו לא הקדים נמי אלא ששחט סימן ראשון למולים ולערלים וכן שני ואומר ר"י דקמ"ל דאפילו לא פירש אף לערלים אלא ששחט סימן ראשון למולים מסתמא אף לערלים קאמר וכן בסיפא דקתני ערלים למולים פסול אפילו הקדים מולין פסול אם פירש שני לערלים דוקא אלא הא קמ"ל דאע"פ ששחט סימן ראשון לערלים סתם לא אמרינן כיון ששחט סימן שני למולים גלי אדעתיה דבסימן ראשון אף לערלים קאמר וכסר:

השוחט פסח על החמץ עובר בלא תעשה. אומר ריב"א דהפסח כשר דהא לא שנה עליו הכתוב לעכב *ובתוספתא דמכילתין (פ"ד) תניא בהדיא השוחט את הפסח על החמץ בי"ד עובר בלא תעשה והפסח עצמו כשר ויוצא בו ידי חובתו בפסח: *[וע"ע תוס' תמורה ד: ד"ה רבא וכו' דבירושל' יש קרא להכשיר]

רבינו חננאל

ערלים למולים פסול נימא קסברי אחרים אינה לשחיטה אלא לבסוף וכי אמר הריני שוחט למולין ולערלים אסוף שחיטה קא מכוין דאמר הריני שוחט ואינה לשחיטה אלא לבסוף ובסוף שחיטה חלו נמולים ולא אשתייר רווחא לערלין למיחל לפיכך הפסח ההוא כשר וכדרבא דאמר עדיין הוא מחלוקת ועיקר דהא שמעתא דרבא בשחיטת קדשים פ"ב דתנן הרי זו תמורת עולה תמורת שלמים הרי זו תמורת עולה דברי ר' מאיר ר' יוסי אומר אם לכך נתכוון וכו' איבעיא להו הרי זו תמורת עולה תמורת שלמים לחצות מאי אמר ר' מאיר מי אמרי' בהא מודי רבי מאיר דכיון דאית ליה רווחא מהשתא ועד לחצות חילן תרוייהו או דלמא בהא נמי פליגי רבי מאיר משום (דלא) איכא חילא לכי מטיא חצות בההיא שעתא חיילא להו תמורת עולה ולית לה לתמורת שלמי' רווחא למיחל: **אמר** רבא לעולם קסברי אחרים ישנה לשחיטה מתחלה ועד סוף ובגמר בלבו למולין ולערלים והוציא בפיו לערלים ולא הספיק לומר למולין עד שנגמרה השחיטה בערלים דרבי מאיר סבר לא בעינן פיו ולבו שוין אלא כיון שהוציא בפיו ערלים לא חיישינן במה שהיה בלבו הילכך פסול ורבנן סברי בעינן פיו ולבו שוין: **ומותיב** אביי המתכוין לומר תרומה ואמר מעשר מעשר ואמר תרומה תמורת עולה ואמר שלמים שאיני נכנס לבית זה ואמר לזה נתכוין לומר שאיני נהנה לזה ואמר לזה לא אמר כלום עד שיהא פיו ולבו שוין קשיא הדא מתני' לרבי מאיר דהא סתמא היא וקיימא לן סתם מתני' רבי מאיר · ופירק אביי רישא כגון ששחט סימן ראשון למולין וסימן שני למולין ולערלים דפתיכי מולין בכולה שחיטה סיפא דאמר סימן ראשון לערלים וסימן שני למולין ורבי מאיר לטעמיה דאמר מפגלין בחצי מתיר וכיון ששני הסימנין מתירין הזבח ואם פיגל באחד מהן שהוא חצי המתיר הרי זה פיגול דתנן פיגל בקומץ ולא בלבונה בלבונה ולא בקומץ רבי מאיר אומר פיגול וחכמים אומרים אין בו כרת עד שיפגל בכל המתיר ורבנן כיון [דפתיכי] מולין בהאי שחיטה אין מפגלין בחצי מתיר: **ירושל'** אין מחשבת אוכלין בהאי

[זבחים ל: חולין לט: ב"ק קמ:] [ער' קמה:] [גי' רש"ל רבא ורב"א גורס רבה] [פרמות ס"ג (מ"א)] [מנחות טו: זבחים קי: מנחות עח:] [פ"י תוס' יומא כב: ד"ה אלא אפילו מולין לי] [דף טז:] [זבח]

הגהות הב"ח (א) רש"י ד"ה וכדרבא בפ"ב דזבחים כ"ל דף ל' ע"א:

גליון הש"ס מתני' השוחט את הפסח על החמץ עי' פ' ובתשובת פני יהושע ח"א סימן י"ג:

בזריקה (דמר לא) [ר' אילא] בשם ר' יוחנן שחטו לאוכליו לזרוק דמו שלא לאוכליו כשר נעשה כמי ששחטו לאוכליו ושלא לאוכליו: **רבי** שמלאי אתא לגבי רבי יוחנן אמר ליה אלפני הגדה אמר ליה מסורת בידינו מאבותינו שלא ללמד הגדה לא לבבליים ולא לבני דרום שהן גסי הרוח מיעוטי התורה ואת נהרדעי ודר בדרום (ועוד מעט קטן): **מתני'** השוחט את הפסח על החמץ עובר בלא תעשה שנא' (שמות כ"ג) לא תזבח על חמץ דם זבחי רבי יהודה אומר אף התמיד מדכתיב זבחי רבי שמעון אומר הפסח בארבעה עשר לשם פסח חייב שלא לשמו כיון שנפסל אינו עובר עליו משום שוחט על חמץ דשחיטתו לאו שחיטה היא וכן שאר דבריו וזה כללם: **אמר** רבי שמעון בן לקיש לעולם אינו חייב עד שיהא חמץ לשוחט או לזורק או לאחד מבני חבורה ועד שתהא החמץ עמו בעזרה: ורבי יוחנן אמר אפילו אין עמו בעזרה חייב ואמרינן בהאי

cised, which is absent? [63a] Shall we [then] say that the 'others' hold, Slaughtering does not count save at the end, and [this is] in accordance with Raba, who said, There is still the controversy. Therefore if he put the circumcised before the uncircumcised, it operates in respect of the circumcised,[2] but it does not operate in respect of the uncircumcised; while if he put the uncircumcised before the circumcised, it operates in respect of the uncircumcised, but it does not operate in respect of the circumcised?[3]—Said Rabbah, Not so: in truth the 'others' hold [that] slaughtering counts from beginning to end, but the case we discuss here is this: e.g., where he mentally determined [it] for both of them, [i.e.,] both for circumcised and for uncircumcised, and he verbally
a expressed[1] [his intention] for uncircumcised, but he had no time to say, 'for the circumcised' before the slaughtering was completed with [the expressed intention of] the uncircumcised [alone], and they differ in this: R. Meir holds [that] we do not require his mouth and his heart [to be] the same [in intention];[2] while the Rabbis hold, We require his mouth and his heart [to be] the same.[3]

Yet does R. Meir hold that we do not require his mouth and his heart [to be] the same, but the following contradicts it: He who intended saying '[Let this be] *terumah*,' but he said 'tithe' [instead], [or, 'let this be] tithe,' and he said '*terumah*,' or, '[I swear] that I will not enter *this* house,' but he said, '*that* [house],' or, '[I vow] that I will not benefit from *this* [person],' but he said
b 'from *that* [person],' he has said nothing,[1] unless his mouth and his heart are alike?[2]—Rather, said Abaye, The first clause means where he stated, '[I cut] the first organ for the circumcised and the second organ for the uncircumcised *too*,' so that at the second organ also circumcised too are included.[3] [But] the second clause means where he stated '[I cut] the first organ for uncircumcised, the second organ for circumcised' so that at the first organ circumcised are not included. Now R. Meir is consistent with his opinion, for he maintained, You can render [a sacrifice] *piggul* at half of that which makes it permitted; while the Rabbis[4] are consistent with their view, for they maintain, You cannot render [a sacrifice] *piggul* at half of that which makes it permitted.[5]

MISHNAH. HE WHO SLAUGHTERS THE PASSOVER OFFERING WITH LEAVEN [IN HIS POSSESSION][6] VIOLATES A NEGATIVE COMMAND.[7] R. JUDAH SAID: [ALSO] THE [EVENING] TAMID TOO.[8] R. SIMEON SAID: [IF HE SLAUGHTERS] THE PASSOVER OFFERING [WITH LEAVEN] ON THE FOURTEENTH FOR ITS OWN PURPOSE, HE IS LIABLE [TO PUNISHMENT]; [IF] FOR A
c DIFFERENT PURPOSE, HE IS EXEMPT.[1] BUT [FOR] ALL OTHER SACRIFICES,[2] WHETHER SLAUGHTERED FOR THEIR OWN PURPOSE OR FOR A DIFFERENT PURPOSE, HE IS EXEMPT. [BUT IF HE SLAUGHTERS THE PASSOVER SACRIFICE WITH LEAVEN] ON THE FESTIVAL, IF FOR ITS OWN PURPOSE, HE IS EXEMPT; IF FOR A DIFFERENT PURPOSE, HE IS LIABLE;[3] BUT [FOR] ALL OTHER SACRIFICES [SLAUGHTERED ON THE FESTIVAL WITH LEAVEN], WHETHER FOR THEIR OWN PURPOSE OR FOR ANOTHER PURPOSE, HE IS LIABLE,[4] EXCEPT [IN THE CASE OF] A SIN-OFFERING WHICH HE SLAUGHTERED FOR A DIFFERENT PURPOSE.[5]

GEMARA. R. Simeon b. Laḳish said: He is never liable unless there is leaven belonging to him who slaughters or to him who

(2) Lit., 'the circumcised fall' (i.e., are counted).—The slaughtering counts as having been performed for the circumcised. (3) When a man would substitute an animal for another *consecrated* animal, both are holy (Lev. XXVII, 33), the former bearing the same holiness as that of the latter, and it must be offered as the same sacrifice. Now if he declares, 'This animal be a substitute for a burnt-offering', 'This (the same) animal be a substitute for a peace-offering', R. Meir rules that it is a substitute for the first only, for only his first words are regarded. R. Jose holds that his last words *too* are regarded, and therefore it is a substitute for both; hence it must be redeemed, and the redemption money expended on *two* animals, one for a burnt-offering and another for a peace-offering. Now a problem is raised in Zeb. 30a: What if he declares, '*Half* of this be a substitute for a burnt-offering, and half be a substitute for a peace-offering'; does R. Meir agree with R. Jose or not? Is R. Meir's reason in the former case because he regards the second statement as a change of mind, which is invalid, since by his first statement it has already become a burnt-offering? But that is obviously inapplicable to the case in question, hence R. Meir will agree. Or perhaps here too R. Meir holds that since the sanctity of the burnt-offering first takes possession of it, as it were, that of the peace-offering cannot operate? Abaye maintains that R. Meir does agree in this case, but Raba holds that there is still the controversy. Thereupon Raba raised an objection to Abaye from this: If a man slaughters a sacrifice with the intention of eating as much as an olive without the permitted area and as much as an olive after the permitted time, R. Judah disagrees with the Rabbis and rules as R. Meir, that only his first statement is counted, hence it is not *piggul*, which applies to the second only, and *kareth* is not incurred for eating it. For R. Judah states this as a general rule: If the intention of an illegitimate time is expressed before the intention of an illegitimate place, it is *piggul*, and *kareth* is incurred for eating it, whether these two intentions are both expressed at the same service or at different services, because the first statement only is regarded. But the Rabbis maintain that his last words too count, so that if both are expressed at the same service there is a mixing of intentions, and it does not become *piggul*, for a sacrifice becomes *piggul* only when the blood has otherwise been properly sprinkled. This proves that the view that the first statement only is regarded is maintained even in respect of halves, for the sacrifice is large enough to permit us to assume that each wrongful intention was expressed with respect to a different part thereof, and yet R. Judah disagrees. To this Abaye answered, Do not think that the slaughtering counts only when it is completed, so that the two intentions come together at the same moment. On the contrary, the slaughtering counts from beginning to end, and in the passage quoted he cut one organ of the animal with the intention of eating it after time, and the second organ with the intention of eating it without the permitted area, R. Meir holding that you can make an animal *piggul* even at one organ only. (Ritual slaughtering—*shechitah*—consists of cutting across the two organs of the throat, viz, the windpipe and the gullet.) This proves that Raba, who raised this objection, holds that in the views of R. Meir and R. Judah slaughtering counts only at the end. Hence the present passage too can be explained on that basis too. Thus: he must express his intention for whom he is slaughtering the Passover sacrifice at the end of the slaughtering, and at that moment there is insufficient time to mention both, and so only the first expression is regarded, the second being entirely disregarded. Therefore if he first mentions the circumcised, it is fit; while if he first mentions the uncircumcised, it is unfit.

a (1) Lit., 'uttered with his mouth'. (2) I.e., we merely regard the *explicit* intention. Hence since he mentioned the uncircumcised only, the sacrifice is unfit. (3) I.e., both are regarded. Therefore the Mishnah *supra* 61a states that if it is sacrificed for both, whatever the order, it is fit.

b (1) I.e., his words are invalid. (2) This is an anonymous Mishnah, and it is a general rule that such reflects R. Meir's view; Sanh. 86a. (3) Hence it is fit. (4) I.e., the view of the Mishnah *supra* 61a. (5) 'That which makes it permitted' (the *mattir*) here is the *slaughtering*; half of that etc., is the cutting of one organ. R. Meir holds that the intention expressed at the cutting of the first organ determines the status of the sacrifice. Hence, if this intention was to eat it after time, it is *piggul;* while in the present case, since it was for the uncircumcised, it is disqualified. The Rabbis, however, hold that an illegitimate intention at the first organ cannot render it *piggul*, and in the same way an intention for uncircumcised at the first organ does not disqualify it. (6) I.e., before the leaven has been destroyed. The phraseology is Biblical: *Thou shalt not slaughter* (E.V. '*offer*') *the blood of My sacrifice with leavened bread* (Ex. XXXIV, 25). (7) V. preceding note. (8) I.e., if he kills the evening *tamid* of the fourteenth before the leaven is destroyed, he violates a negative command.

c (1) In the former case the sacrifice is fit, hence the *shechitah* is duly regarded as *shechitah*. But in the latter the sacrifice is *unfit;* hence R. Simeon does not regard the *shechitah* as *shechitah*, and the verse quoted *supra*, n. b6. does not apply to it. (2) Offered on Passover eve with leaven in his possession. (3) For a Passover offering killed at a time other than its own, viz., the fourteenth, is disqualified if sacrificed as a Passover offering, but fit if sacrificed as a peace-offering. (4) Because they are fit, v. Zeb. 2a. (5) Because it is disqualified, ibid.

say, [62b] in the case of uncleanness of the flesh; where was it permitted? Hence it obviously refers to uncleanness of the person, and where was it permitted? In the case of a community?[8] Thus the first clause refers to uncleanness of flesh, while the second clause refers to the uncleanness of the person?—Yes: he argues from the designation of uncleanness.

Alternatively, the whole refers to uncleanness of the flesh; and [as to the question,] where was it permitted? [It was] in [the case of] the uncleanness of the Paschal lamb. For we learned: The Paschal lamb which comes [if offered] in uncleanness is eaten in uncleanness, for
a at the very outset it did not come for [aught] except to be eaten.[1]

R. Huna son of R. Joshua raised an objection: If a Paschal lamb has passed its year[2] and he [its owner] slaughtered it at its own time[3] for its own purpose;[4] and similarly, when a man kills other [sacrifices] as a Passover offering in its [own] time,—R. Eliezer disqualifies [it];[5] while R. Joshua declares it fit.[6] Thus the reason [that R. Eliezer disqualifies it] is that it is in its own time, but [if it were slaughtered] at a different time[7] it is fit; yet why so? Let us say, *Since* he disqualifies [it][8] in its own time, he also disqualifies it at a different time?[9]—Said R. Papa, There it is different, because Scripture saith, *Then ye shall say, The sacrifice of the Lord's passover* it is:[10] let it retain its own nature:[11] neither may it be [slaughtered] in the name of other [sacrifices], nor may others [be slaughtered]
b in its name; in its time[1] when it is disqualified [if slaughtered] in the name of others, others are disqualified [if slaughtered] in its name; at a different time, when it is fit [if slaughtered] in the name of others, others are fit [if slaughtered] in its name.

R. Simlai came before R. Joḥanan [and] requested him, Let the Master teach me the Book of Genealogies.[2] Said he to him, Whence are you?—He replied, From Lod.[3] And where is your dwelling?—In Nehardea.[4] Said he to him, We do not discuss it[5] either with the Lodians or with the Nehardeans, and how much more so with you, who are from Lod and live in Nehardea![6] But he urged[7] him, and he consented. Let us learn it in three months, he proposed. [Thereupon] he took a clod and threw it at him, saying, If Beruriah, wife of R. Meir [and] daughter of R. Ḥanina b. Teradion, who studied three hundred laws from three hundred teachers in [one] day,[8] could nevertheless not do her duty[9] in three years, yet you propose [to do it] in three months!

As he was going he said to him, Master, What is the difference between [a Passover sacrifice which is offered both] for its own purpose and for a different purpose, and [one that is offered both] for those who can eat it and for those who cannot eat it?[10]—Since you are a scholar, he answered him, come and I will tell you. [When it is killed] for its own purpose and for another purpose, its disqualification is in [respect of] itself;[11] [when he kills it] for those who can eat it and for those who cannot eat it, its disqualification is not in [respect of] itself; [when it is] for its own purpose and
c for another purpose, it is impossible to distinguish its prohibition;[1] [when it is] for those who can eat it and for those who cannot eat it, it is possible to distinguish its interdict.[2] [Sacrificing] for its own purpose and for another purpose applies to the four services;[3] for those who can eat it and for those who cannot eat it, does not apply to the four services.[4] [The disqualification of sacrificing] for its own purpose and for another purpose applies to the community as to an individual;[5] for those who can eat it and for those who cannot eat it, does not apply to the community as to an individual.[6] R. Ashi said: [That] its disqualification is intrinsic and [that] it is impossible to distinguish its prohibition are [one and] the same thing. For why does he say [that][7] its disqualification is intrinsic? Because it is impossible to distinguish its prohibition.

Rami the son of Rab Judah said: Since the day that the Book of Genealogies was hidden,[8] the strength of the Sages has been impaired and the light of their eyes has been dimmed.[9] Mar Zuṭra said, Between '*Azel*' and '*Azel*' they were laden with four hundred camels of exegetical interpretations![10]

It was taught: Others[11] say, If he put the circumcised before the uncircumcised,[12] it is fit; the uncircumcised before the circumcised, it is disqualified. Wherein does [the case where he put] circumcised before uncircumcised differ, that it is fit,—because we require
d [them to be] all uncircumcised:[1] then [where he put] the uncircumcised before the circumcised too, we require all [to be] uncircum-

(8) V. *supra* 61b.

a (1) V. *infra* 76a. (2) It became a year old on the first of Nisan, and was then set aside for the Passover sacrifice. Since a year is the extreme limit for such (v. Ex. XII, 5: *a male of the first year*), it automatically stands to be a peace-offering, being unfit for its original purpose. (3) I.e., on the eve of Passover. (4) *Sc.* as a Passover offering. Thus he killed a peace-offering as a Passover sacrifice. (5) He infers this *a minori:* if an animal set aside for the Passover offering is disqualified if slaughtered in its time (on the eve of Passover) as a peace-offering, though if left until after Passover it must be offered as such; then how much the more is a peace-offering disqualified if killed on the eve of Passover as a Passover offering, seeing that if left over and not brought as a peace-offering at the time appointed for same, it cannot be brought as a Passover offering on Passover eve. (6) For all sacrifices, except the Passover offering and the sin-offering, if sacrificed for another purpose, are fit. He too argues *a minori:* if during the rest of the year, when it is disqualified if slaughtered in its own name (*sc.* as a Passover sacrifice), yet if others (i.e., peace-offerings) are slaughtered in its name they are fit (in accordance with the general rule stated at the beginning of this note); then in its own time, when it is of course fit if slaughtered in its own name, how much the more are others fit if killed in its name! (7) Lit., 'not in its time'. (8) This is the reading in cur. edd. Tosaf.'s reading is preferable: since it is disqualified, etc. (9) Now that R. Ḥisda accepts the argument of 'since' where this results in greater stringency. (10) Ibid. 27. (11) Lit., 'it is in its own being'. *Hu* ('it is') is an emphatic assertion that it must always retain its own peculiar nature, as explained in the text.

b (1) *Sc.* the eve of Passover. (2) A commentary on Chronicles, presumably so called because of the many genealogical lists it contains. (3) Lydda in southern Palestine. [The original home of R. Simlai, v. Hyman, *Toledoth*, p. 1151.] (4) The famous academy town on the Euphrates in Babylonia. It is fully discussed in Obermeyer, *Landschaft*, pp. 244ff. (5) So. cur. edd. Var. lec.: we do not teach it. (6) Probably he was simply putting him off. (7) Lit., 'compelled'. (8) BaḤ (on basis of Var. lec. v. *D.S.*) reads: and in a day of the *Shutha*, i.e., a day when the *Shutha* (a severe south—'Ar. east—wind) blew. This is undoubtedly an exaggeration, but it is interesting to note that a *woman* is cited as an illustration of wide scholarship, thus showing that the Rabbis were by no means averse to women studying as has been commonly supposed; v. Ned., 35b, n. 2. (9) I.e., study it adequately. (10) Why is it disqualified in the first case but fit in the second? (11) The illegitimate intention is in respect of the sacrifice itself.

c (1) I.e., you cannot say this portion of the animal was sacrificed for its own purpose, and that portion for another purpose. (2) It is possible to allocate separately the share for those who cannot eat it. (3) V. Mishnah 58b. (4) An intention with respect to the eaters expressed or conceived at the sprinkling has no effect, v. *supra* 61a, n. b1. (5) I.e., both to private and to public sacrifices. (6) Intention in respect to eaters has effect only in the case of the Passover sacrifice, which is a private one, and in no others. (7) [MS.M.: 'For why is']. (8) This probably means either suppressed or forgotten; perhaps destroyed. (9) Rashi: it contained the reasons for many Scriptural laws which have been forgotten. (10) I.e., on the passage commencing with '*And Azel had six sons*' (I Chron. VIII, 38) and ending with '*these were the sons of Azel*' (Ibid. IX, 44) there were such an enormous number of different interpretations! This too, of course, is not to be understood literally. (11) 'Others' frequently refers to R. Meir, v. Hor. 13b, and does refer to him here, as is evident from the text *infra*. (12) I.e., if he *first* intended it for the former and then for the latter.

d (1) In order to disqualify the sacrifice.

בטומאת בשר היכא הותרה אלא פשיטא בטומאת גברי והיכא הותרה מכללה בציבור רישא בטומאת בשר סיפא בטומאת גברי אין שם טומאה קפריך ואיבעית אימא כולה בטומאת בשר והיכא הותרה בטומאת פסח דתנן *פסח הבא בטומאה נאכל בטומאה שלא בא מתחילתו אלא לאכילה מתיב רב הונא בריה דרב יהושע *הפסח שעברה שנתו ושחטו בזמנו לשמו וכן השוחט אחרים לשם פסח בזמנו ר"א פוסל ורבי יהושע °מכשיר טעמא בזמנו הא שלא בזמנו כשר ואמאי נימא הואיל ובזמנו פוסל שלא בזמנו נמי פוסל אמר רב פפא שאני התם דאמר קרא °ואמרתם זבח פסח הוא הוא בהווייתו לא הוא לשום אחרים ולא אחרים לשמו בזמנו שהוא פסול לשום אחרים אחרים פסולין לשמו שלא בזמנו שהוא כשר לשום אחרים אחרים כשרים לשמו ר' שמלאי אתא לקמיה דרבי יוחנן א"ל ניתני לי מר ספר יוחסין א"ל מהיכן את א"ל מלוד והיכן מותבך בנהרדעא א"ל אין *נידונין לא ללודים ולא לנהרדעים וכל שכן דאת מלוד ומותבך בנהרדעא כפייה וארצי א"ל ניתנייה בג' ירחי *שקל קלא פתק ביה א"ל ומה ברוריה דביתהו דר"מ ברתיה דר"ח בן תרדיון דתניא תלת מאה שמעתתא (א) ביומא מג' מאה רבוותא ואפ"ה לא יצתה ידי חובתה בתלת שנין ואת אמרת בתלתא ירחי (ב) כי שקיל ואזיל א"ל רבי מה בין לשמו ושלא לשמו לאוכליו ושלא לאוכליו א"ל הואיל וצורבא מרבנן את תא ואימא לך לשמו ושלא לשמו פסולו בגופו לאוכליו ושלא לאוכליו אין פסולו בגופו לשמו ושלא לשמו א"א לברר איסורו לאוכליו ושלא לאוכליו אפשר לברר איסורו לשמו ושלא לשמו ישנו בד' עבודות לאוכליו ושלא לאוכליו אינו בארבע עבודות לשמו ושלא לשמו ישנו בציבור כביחיד לאוכליו ושלא לאוכליו אינו בציבור כביחיד רב אשי אמר פסולו בגופו וא"א לברר איסורו חדא מילתא היא דמה טעם אמר פסולו בגופו משום דא"א לברר איסורו אמר רמי בר רב יודא א"ר מיום שנגנז ספר יוחסין תשש כחן של חכמי' וכהה מאור עיניהם אמר מר זוטרא °בין אצל לאצל טעינו ד' מאה גמלי דדרשא תניא *אחרים אומרים הקדים מולים לערלים כשר ערלים למולים פסול מאי שנא מולין לערלים דכשר דכולה ערלה בעינן וליכא ערלים למולין נמי כולה ערלה בעינן וליכא לימא

תורה אור: שמות יב · דה"א ח

רש"י

שמתחלתו לא בא . לא נאמרה הבאת עיקר פסח אלא לאכילה וכי שרייה רחמנא לאיתויי בטומאה ברוב ציבור כדכתיב איש איש כי יהיה טמא וגו' איש נדחה לפסח שני ואין ציבור נידחין אדעתיה לאכילה שרייה : שעברה שנתו . שנולד אשתקד קודם ראש חודש ניסן והפרישו לשם פסח וכי מטא ראש חדש ניסן ועברה שנתו תו לא חזי לפסח דכתיב זכר בן שנה וקאי לשלמים כדילפינן בפירקין דלקמן (ד' עג:) פסח בשאר ימות השנה שלמים הוא : ושחטו בזמנו לשמו גרם דהוה ליה שוחט שלמים לשם פסח בזמנו : ר' אליעזר פוסל . טעמא מפרש בפ"ק דזבחים ומה פסח שמותרו בא שלמים שחטו לשם שלמים בזמנו פסול שלמים שאין מותרן בא פסח שחטן לשם פסח בזמן פסח אינו דין שפסול : ורבי יהושע מכשיר . דכל זבחים שנזבחים שלא לשמן כשירין חוץ מפסח וחטאת ואי משום דנשחטו לשם פסח קל וחומר הוא ומה שלא בזמנו שאינו כשר לשמו אחרים כשירים לשמו בזמנו שהוא כשר לשמו אינו דין שיכשרו אחרים לשמו וכל טעמייהו התם מפרש : שלא בזמנו . לא פסיל ליה רבי אליעזר אם שחטו לשם פסח כדאמר ליה ר' יהושע ומה שלא בזמנו שאינו כשר לשמו אחרים כשירים לשמו ולא מיהדר רבי אליעזר לדידי שלא בזמנו נמי אחרים פסולים לשמו ואמאי לרב חסדא דאמר לחומרא אמרינן הואיל נימא הכא הואיל ואלו זמנו הוה ושחיט לשמו מיפסיל הכא הכי נמי ליפסיל כדקאמר גבי ערל הואיל ואי הוה מל פסיל השתא נמי פסיל : שלא בזמנו שהוא כשר לשם אחרים . דנפקא לן לקמן (ד' ע:) מוזבחת פסח לה' צאן ובקר דפסח שניתותר לאחר הפסח קרב שלמים ואף קודם הפסח נמי כדנפקא לן בפ"ק דזבחים מקרא אחרינא מואם מן הצאן קרבנו לזבח שלמים דבר הבא מן הצאן דהיינו פסח יהא לזבח שלמים: אחרים כשירין לשמו . דהא איתקש פסולו לשם אחרים ופסול אחרים לשמו : ספר יוחסין . מתני' דדברי הימים : אין שונין ספר יוחסין לא ללודים כו' . לדחוייה איכוון ל"א לפי שאינן מיוחסין : לא יצתה ידי חובתה . לא יכלה לשנותה בשלש שנים : שקל קלא . מוט"א : בהדי דקא שקיל ואזיל א"ל . ר' שמלאי לר' יוחנן: מה בין לשמו ושלא לשמו לאוכליו ושלא לאוכליו . מאי שנא דלשמו ושלא לשמו פסול לאוכליו ושלא לאוכליו כשר : פסולו בגופו . מחשבה בגופו של קרבן אבל מחשבת אוכליו פסול דבר אחר הוא: אי אפשר לברר . דמה חלק לשמו ומה חלק שלא לשמו אבל אוכליו אפשר לברר חלק אוכליו לצד זה וחלק חולה וזקן בצד אחר אי נמי לברר אם אמת מחשבתו אם אין בה ממש כגון יאכילנו לראויין ונמלאת מחשבתו בטילה למפרע ולשאינן ראויין יחזור דמיהן וכך שמעתי : אינו בארבע עבודות . דאין מחשבת אוכלין בזריקה: מחשבת אכילה לא שייכא בקרבן ציבור דלא שייכא אלא בפסח : תשש כחן . שנגנזו מהן טעמי תורה שהיו בו : נגנז . נשתכח : מאצל לאצל . שני מקראות הן ופרשה גדולה ביניהן ולאצל ששה בנים וקא חשיב ואזיל הבנים וסיפא דפרשתא אלה בני אצל :

וכדרבה

תוספות

אילימא בטומאת בשר היכא הותרה . ואם תאמר והא ודאי טומאת בשר הותרה לזרוק הדם כדאמרינן בכילד צולין (ד' עז:) גבי חמשה דברים באים בטומאה ואע"ג דלא מישתריא באכילה דבכי האי גוונא הוי השתא הותרה לטומאת גברי לזרוק הדם דלאכתי לא ידע גמרא הא דפסח נאכל בטומאה ויש לומר דה"פ דנין דבר שלא הותרה מכללו בפסח מדבר שלא הותר מכללו בפסח ואל תוכיח טומאה שהותרה מכללה בפסח כי ההיא דלעיל דנין דבר שאינו נוהג בכל הזבחים אלא בפסח מדבר כו' וכי מוקי לה בטומאה דגברי ומאי הותרה מכללה בצבור היינו בפסח כדפירש הקונטרס : ורבי יהושע מכשיר . ואע"ג דליכא מאן דאמר פסח בשאר ימות השנה בעי עקירה בעברה שנתו מודו כ"ע דהיינו עקירתו ושלמים לשם פסח שחיט : לימא הואיל ובזמנו פסול כו' . פי' שיכול להמתין עד זמנו ויפסל ולמאי דמסקינן בריש שני שעירים (יומא סג:) דאין מחוסר זמן לבו ביום לגבי הואיל נרא' לפר' דמבו ביום פריך דשלא בזמנו משמע אפי' בי"ד שחרית ולהכי פריך הואיל בזמנו בו ביום פסול שלא בזמנו נמי פסול : שאני התם דאמר קרא הוא . וא"ת והא מק"ו דריש ליה רבי אליעזר בפ"ק דזבחים (ד' יא:) ומה פסח שמותרו בא שלמים כו' כדמייתי בקונטרס . וי"ל דעי' ק"ו משמע ליה לר' אליעזר דהוא בהווייתו יהא לא הוא לשם אחרים ולא אחרים לשמו ועל ידי כך דריש דשלא בזמנו דכשר לשם אחרים אחרים כשרים לשמו דהא איתקוש אהדדי אבל אי לאו ק"ו לא הוה דרשינן אלא הוא לשם אחרים ותו לא : מה בין לשמו ושלא לשמו לאוכליו ושלא לאוכליו . תימה מאי קא בעי הא גמר לעיל מקרא דמקצת אוכלים לא פסלי ונראה לרשב"א דמיבעיא ליה מאי חזא קרא ליה דמאי לא גמרינן לשמו ושלא לשמו דכשר מלאוכליו ושלא לאוכליו : לשמו ושלא לשמו ישנו בציבור כו' . תימה לר"י מאי איריא דליתו בציבור תיפוק ליה דאפי' ביחיד ליתו נוהג אלא בפסח גרידא : פסולו בגופו ואי אפשר לברר איסורו חדא מילתא היא . דס"ל דאי לאו טעמא דאי אפשר לברר איסורו לא קרי ליה בגופו הואיל ומחשבה היא כדלעיל אבל ר' יוחנן לא דייק בהכי וקרי ליה שפיר פסולו בגופו ושינוי בעלים נמי אי אפשר לברר איסורו ולהכי לא קחשיב ליה לעיל : ערלים למולים נמי ליתיה לכולה ערלה . משמע דהוה ניחא ליה אי הוה תני בתרוייהו כשר וא"ת אדרבה בתרוייהו הוה ליה למיפסל דהא ר"מ אית ליה מפגלים בחצי מתיר ואחרים היינו רבי מאיר וי"ל דלא אמר פיגול בחצי מתיר אלא במפרש סימן ראשון או שני לערלים דהוי דבר מסוים כדמוכח בפ"ב דזבחים (ד' ל.) ובקונטרס הביאה אמר ליה אביי מי סברת איגה כו' ישנה לשחיטה מתחלה ועד סוף דאמר סימן ראשון חוץ לזמנו וסימן שני חוץ למקומו ולמה ליה לפרושי הוה ליה למימר בסתם אלא ודאי לא אמר ר' מאיר מפגלי' בחצי מתיר אלא במפרש ועוד נראה דאפילו אמר בחצי סימן לאו כלום היא אלא דווקא בסימן שלם דפריך התם והרי קמיצה דכי לחצות דמי ופליגי ומשני התם נמי *דאמרי' קומץ דמנחה חוץ לזמנו דלבונה חוץ למקומה והרי קומץ דמנחת חוטא דליכא לבונה ופליגי ומשני לא פליגי כו' ואמאי לא קאמר דפליגי דאמר חצי קומץ חוץ לזמנו וחצי חוץ למקומו אלא על כרחיך דבר המסוים ושלם בעינן :

לימא

עין משפט נר מצוה

כז א מיי' פט"ו מהל' פסו"ה הי"ב :

רבינו חננאל

שהותרה מכללה בפסח שבא בטומאה פריך דתנן פסח הבא בטומאה נאכל בטומאה שלא בא בתחלתו אלא לאכילה : ומותבינן אהא דאמרינן כל הואיל אם הוא לחומרא דברי הכל הוא מיהא הפסח שעברה שנתו שחטו בזמנו בי"ד רבי אליעזר פוסל ורבי יהושע מכשיר אפילו רבי אליעזר דפוסל אינו פוסל אלא השוחט בי"ד לשם פסח אבל בשאר ימות השנה מכשיר ואמאי נימא הואיל ובזמנו פסול כך שלא בזמנו פסול דהא לחומרא הוא ופרקי' שאני התם דרחמנא אכשריה שנא' ואמרתם זבח פסח הוא לה' הוא בהויתו יהא כלו' הפסח הוא ששחט לשם פסח בי"ד לאפוקי קדשים אחרים לשם פסח דלא ולא פסח לשלמים דבעינן הוא בהויתו יהא לשמו בזמנו דהוא אם ישחט לשם אחרים פסול שלמים נמי אם ישחטו לשם פסח פסולין לשמו שלא בזמנו דהוא כשר לשם שלמים גם שלמים לשם פסח כשרים : ניתני לי מר ספר יוחסין · פי' אמר לו למדני ספר דברי הימים: שדא קלא פתיק ביה נטל אבן זרק עליו כלו' נער בו שאלו : מה בין לשמו ושלא לשמו לאוכליו ושלא לאוכליו· שהשוחט לשמו ושלא לשמו פסול והשוחט לאוכליו ושלא לאוכליו כשר אמר ליה שלא לשמו פסולו בגופו שהוא פסח ושחטו לשם שלמים שינה הזבח עצמו במחשבתו לאוכליו ושלא לאוכליו לבריא ולחולה אין הזבח פסולו בגופו כי הזבח בכשרותו עומד לשמו ושלא לשמו אי אפשר לברר איסורו כלומר לא יתכן להודע איזה צד של זבח לשמו ואיזה צד שלא לשמו כדי שתניח האיסור ותאכל המותר' לאוכליו ושלא לאוכליו אפשר לברר איסוריה החולה אסור והבריא מותר לשמו ושלא לשמו ישנו בארבע עבודות לאוכליו ושלא לאוכליו אינו אלא בשחיטה לשמו ושלא לשמו בקרבן צבור כביחיד דבין זה ובין זה שלא לשמו פסול לאוכליו ושלא לאוכליו לא משכחת לה בצבור דליכא בצבור זבחי שלמים אלא שני כבשי עצרת הבאין עם שתי הלחם וכתיב (ויקרא כ"ג) והניף הכהן אותם על לחם הבכורים תנופה על שני וגו' לכהן הם ולא לצבור : אמר רב אשי פסולו בגופו ואי אפשר לברר איסורו דבר אחד הן והכי קאמר מה טעם איסורו בגופו שאי אפשר לברר איסורו : מתני' שחטו למולין ולערלים לטהורין ולטמאין כשר · מפורש בסוף הוריות מאן אחרי' ר' מאיר: תניא אחרי' אומרים הקדים מולים לערלים כשר הקדים

מסורת הש"ס

לקמן עו: · זבחים יא. · ס"א שונין · [ר"ס כסי שבועות יח:] · [מנחות פ"ז] · נ"ל דאמר

הגהות הב"ח

(א) גמ' תלת מאה שמעתתא ביומא דשונות מתלת מאה רבוותא וכו': (ב) שם בתלת ירחי סוס קא שקיל ואזיל:

בהאי קרא קמיפלגי °ונרצה לו לכפר עליו * °עליו ולא על חבירו רבה סבר חבירו דומיא דידיה מה הוא דבר כפרה אף חבירו דבר כפרה לאפוקי האי ערל דלאו בר כפרה הוא ורב חסדא סבר האי ערל נמי כיון דבר חיובא הוא בר כפרה הוא [הואיל] דאי בעי מתקן נפשיה *ומי אית ליה לרב חסדא הואיל והא איתמר *האופה מיו"ט לחול רב חסדא אמר לוקה רבה אמר אינו לוקה אמרינן הואיל ואי מקלעי ליה אורחים חזי ליה השתא נמי חזי ליה ולא לקי רב חסדא אמר לוקה לא אמרינן הואיל בשלמא דרבה אדרבה לא קשיא הכא מחוסר מעשה התם דלא מחוסר מעשה אלא דרב חסדא אדרב חסדא קשיא אמרי כי לית ליה לרב חסדא הואיל לקולא לחומרא אית ליה אמר ליה מר זוטרא בריה דרב מרי לרבינא קתני הואיל וערלה פוסלת וטומאה פוסלת מה טומאה לא עשה בה מקצת טומאה ככל טומאה אף ערלה לא עשה מקצת ערלה ככל ערלה האי טומאה היכי דמי אילימא בטומאת גברי ומאי לא עשה בה מקצת טומאה ככל טומאה דאי איכא ארבעה וחמשה גברי טמאין וארבעה וחמשה גברי טהורין לא פסלי להו טמאין לטהורין גבי ערלה נמי הא לא פסלי דתנן למולין ולערלים כשר מאי שנא טומאה דפשיטא ליה ומאי שנא ערלה דמספקא ליה אלא בטומאת בשר ומאי לא עשה בה מקצת טומאה ככל טומאה [ג]דאילו איטמי חד מאברים האי דאיטמי שרפינן ליה ואידך אכלינן ליה במאי אוקימתא בטומאת בשר אימא סיפא דנין דבר שאינו נוהג בכל הזבחים מדבר שאינו נוהג בכל הזבחים ואל יוכיח זמן שנוהג בכל הזבחים ומאי טומאה אי נימא טומאת בשר אמאי אינו נוהג בכל הזבחים אלא פשיטא בטומאת גברי ומאי אינו נוהג בכל הזבחים [ד]דאילו בכל הזבחים ערל וטמא משלחין קרבנותיהן ואילו בפסח ערל וטמא אין משלחין פסחיהן רישא בטומאת בשר וסיפא בטומאת גברי א"ל אין שם טומאה קא פריך ואיבעית אימא סיפא נמי בטומאת בשר ומאי אינו נוהג בכל הזבחים דאילו *בכל הזבחים בין שנטמא חלב ובשר קיים בין שנטמא בשר וחלב קיים זורק את הדם ואילו בפסח נטמא חלב ובשר קיים זורק את הדם נטמא בשר וחלב קיים אינו זורק את הדם במאי אוקימתא בטומאת בשר אימא סיפא דנין דבר שלא הותר מכללו מדבר שלא הותר מכללו ואל תוכיח טומאה שהרי הותרה מכללה במאי אילימא בטומאת

רש"י

בהאי קרא פליגי. וכשיתכפרו בו ערלים דקאמר שאין מנויין עליו קאמר ומשום מחשבה שלא למנויו קאמרי אבל במנויין עליו ושחטו למולים שהן נמי מנויין לזרוק דמו למנויו ערלים שבהם לבדם דהויא כולה זריקה לערלים מנויין דכולי עלמא פסול ובערלים שאינן מנויין ומשום מחשבה שלא למנויו פליגי והאי קרא דשלא למנויו בזריקה מהכא נפיק בכל הקרבנות לכפר עליו היינו זריקה עליו ולא על חבירו הזורק לשם חבירו: רבה סבר חבירו. דפסול משום שינוי בעלים דומיא דידיה בעינן מה הוא דבר כפרה כו': מתקן נפשיה. מל את עצמו: הואיל ואי מיקלעי ליה אורחים חזי ליה לא לקי. ואע"ג דלאו השתא לא סעד ליה ולא צריך למידי: אלא דרב חסדא קשיא. השתא היכא דלא מחוסר מעשה כגון זימון אורחים דלאו מעשה הוא לית ליה הואיל הכא גבי ערל דמחוסר מעשה אית ליה הואיל: לקולא. לפוטרו ממלקות: לחומרא. לפסול בפסחים: בטומאת גברי. שמנו עליו טמאים וטהורים וכדפרישית לעיל: לא פסלי להו טמאין. לפסח על הטהורין: ערל וטמא משלחין קרבנותיהן. בעזרה חוץ מפסח דבעינן ראוי לאכלו שאכילת בעליו מעכבת בו דכתיב לפי אכלו תכוסו: ואיבעית אימא. לעולם בטומאת בשר ומאי אינו נוהג בכל הזבחים אין מנהגו בשאר זבחים שוה למנהגו בפסח דאילו בשאר זבחים לר' יהושע דאמר בכילד צולין (לקמן דף עז.) אם אין בשר אין דם אם בשר קיים לאכילת אדם או חלב קיים לאכילת מזבח זורק את הדם ואילו פסח לא מהניא אכילת מזבח לזרוק דם עליה אלא אם נשתייר כזית בשר כדתנן בכילד צולין: דנין דבר שלא הותר מכללו. ערלה במקום שאסרה דהיינו בפסח לא הותרה: מדבר שלא הותר מכללו. זמן: *היכא אישתרא. טומאת בשר לאכילה אפילו קרבן ציבור שדוחה טומאה הני מילי להקרבה אבל למיכלה בטומאה לא דתנן בכילד צולין (דף עו:) חמשה דברים באין בטומאה ואין נאכלין בטומאה כו': אלא פשיטא בטומאת גברי. שאפילו פסח שלא הותר ליחיד טמא לשלח פסחו לעזרה לשחוט הותר לציבור להביא פסחיהן בטומאה אם רובן טמאין כגון שהותרה מכלל איסורה: שמתחלתו

תוספות

האי מחוסר מעשה כו'. הקשה ריב"א דבפ' אלו עוברין (דף מז:) מסיק כתישה בי"ט מי שרי משמע אי הוה שרי אמרינן הואיל אע"ג דמחוסר מעשה ותירץ ר"י דהאי מעשה דמילה חשיב טפי: כי לית ליה לקולא וכו'. נראה דרב חסדא לא פליג אלא מדרבנן דמדאורייתא לא שייך לחלק בין לחומרא בין לקולא ומדאורייתא לא אמרינן הואיל כלל אפי' לחומרא וכן מוכח בר"פ שני שעירים (יומא דס"ג:) דקאמר רבינא השתא דאמר ר"ח מחוסר הגרלה כמחוסר מעשה דמי פי' אם שחט שעיר יום הכפורים בחוץ היה פטור משום דמחוסר הגרלה אי לאו משום דחזי לשעיר חיצון שלמים (א) ששחטן קודם פתיחת ההיכל פטור מחוסר פתיחה כמחוסר מעשה דמי אלמא לית ליה הואיל אפילו לחומרא ואין להקשות אי מדרבנן היאך יתחייב פסח אחר הא קמייתי חולין לעזרה לא היא כיון דלא יזרוק הדם אינו יוצא ומותר לאכול באחר וכן מוכח בכילד צולין דאמר רב לא זרק את הדם חייב לעשות פסח אחר כו' *(תימה דהשתא לרב אשי דמחשבת ערלים המנויין לכ"ע תהא את הזריקה והאכילה מנויין איכא מאן דמכשר וסברא משמע איפכא דהשתא כשאינה מנויין לא פסלה כ"ש במנויין):

מאי שנא טומאה דפשיטא ליה ומאי שנא ערלה דמספקא ליה. תימה לרשב"א דלמא טומאה פשיטא ליה משום דילפינן טומאת גברי מטומאת בשר וכי תימא דמשמע ליה דאי פשיטא לן בטומאת גברי דלא עשה בה מקצת טומאה ככל טומאה הוא הדין בערלה משום דמחד קרא דלפי אכלו נפקי ותו לא הוה שייך למילף מזמן מכל מקום מאי קאמר דנין דבר שלא הותר מכללו כו' הא ע"כ איכא למילף טפי טומאת גברי מטומאת בשר דהוי טומאה מטומאה ודמי ליה בכל-לד מדנילף טומאת גברי מזמן דלא דמי ליה כלל וכיון דפשיטא לן בטומאה דגברי פשיטא לן נמי בערלה כיון שיש להשוותם והיכי קבעי למילף ערלה מזמן ואומר ר"י דטומאת גברי נמי איכא למימר דנילף טפי מזמן מדנילף מטומאת בשר משום דדנין פסול מחשבה מפסול מחשבה ולא תוכיח טומאת בשר דלא הוי פסול מחשבה:

ערל משלח קרבנות וטמא משלח כו'. כרבי עקיבא אתיא דמרבי ערל כי טמא בחגיגה (דף ד:) דאי לאו הכי לייתי איהו גופיה קרבנותיו וקשה לר"י (ב) בריש חגיגה (שם) טמא פטור מן הראייה שנאמר ובאת שמה והבאתם שמה כל שישנו בביאה ישנו בהבאה וכל שאינו כו' משמע דטמא אינו משלח שום קרבן דבההוא קרא גופיה כתיבי שאר קרבנות עולותיכם וזבחיכם וגו' ואומר ר"י דמכל מקום דווקא בחגיגה שתלויה בביאה קפיד קרא ואע"ג דכל הקרבנות כתיבי בקרא לא קאי אכולהו דהא מעשרות ותרומה כתיבי נמי התם ועוד קשה לר"י טמא איך משלח קרבנות והא בעי סמיכה ואפילו למאן דאמר ביאה במקצת לא שמה ביאה ליכא למימר אפשר דמעייל ידיה וסמיך דהא בפרק כל הפסולים (זבחים דף לג:) אמרינן כל הסומך ראשו ורובו מכניס מאי טעמא כל כחו בעינן ותירץ ר"י דהכא מיירי בעופות וכן משני בכל הגט (גיטין דף כח:) אי נמי בבכור ומעשר דלא בעי סמיכה כדתנן פרק שתי מדות (מנחות דף צג:) ובקרבן נשים ליכא לאוקמי משום ערל: [וע"ע תוס' יבמות קד: ד"ה דאמר]

עין משפט נר מצוה

כד א מיי' פט"ו מהל' פסולי המוקדשין הלכה ח:

כה ב מיי' פ"ד מהל' ק"פ הלכה ג:

כו ג מיי' פ"ב מהל' ביאת מקדש הי"ב:

מסורת הש"ס

זבחים ד: [ו' א:]

ומה פני פ"ע [לעיל מז: ביצה כא.]

שייך לע"ב

לקמן עט:

הגהות הב"ח

(א) תוס' ד"ה כי לית וכו' ששחטן כשחטן קודם פתיחת ההיכל: (ב) ד"ה ערל וכו' וקשה לר"י דאמר בריש:

רבינו חננאל

בהא פליגי וכפר עליו ואמרינן עליו ולא על חברו רבא דייק עליו ולא על חבירו סבר דיקי' בעינן חברו דפסול דומיא דידיה מה הוא בר כפרה אף חברו דבר כפרה אבל ערל דלאו בר כפרה הוא אם זרק עליו לא פסול ורב חסדא אמר האי נמי בר כפרה הוא הואיל דאי בעי מיתקן נפשיה ומכפר השתא נמי בר כפרה קרינא ביה: ומי אית ליה לרב חסדא הואיל והא איתמר האופה מיום טוב לחול רב חסדא אמר לוקה רבה אמר אינו לוקה הואיל ואי מקלעי ליה אירחין חזי ליה כו' הנה רבה הוא דאית ליה הואיל אבל רב חסדא לית ליה הואיל כו' פי' מחוסר מעשה מילה ופרקי' כי לית ליה לרב חסדא הואיל להקל אבל לחומרא אית ליה: ומתמהי' מאי שנא האי תנא דאי איכא מקצת מבני חבורה טמאין ומקצתן טהורין דפשיטא ליה דלא פסלי הטמאין לטהורין אבל אוכלין הטהורין ולא חיישינן לטומאה ואי איכא מקצת מבני חבורה ערלים ומקצתן מולין דמספקא ואמר ליה רבינא בטומאת בשר היא דאמר כגון שנטמא מקצת אבריו של זבח שהטמאין נשרפין והטהורין נאכלין ולא פסלי הטמאין לטהורין: ומי מצית לאוקמה בטומאת בשר והא תאני סיפא דנין דבר שאינו נוהג בכל הזבחים היינו ערלה מדבר שאינו נוהג בכל הזבחים הטומאה ואי בטומאת בשר אמאי אינה נוהגת בכל הזבחים מי משכחת בשר זבח טמא שהותר אלא בטומאת גברי ומאי אינה נוהגת בכל הזבחים דערל וטמא משלחין קרבנותיהן וקרבין דלא גרע מנכרי ותנן בשקלים נכרי ששלח עולתו ממדינת הים ושלח עמהן נסכין קרבין משלו כו' ותנן נמי בגטין השולח חטאתו ממדינת הים מקריבין אותה בחזקת שהוא קיים כו' ותנן בתורת כהנים ואם האכל יאכל מבשר זבח שלמיו וגו' יכול השוחט לערלים ולטמאים יהא בלא ירצה ת"ל המקריב אותו בלא ירצה ואין השוחט לערלים לטמאין בלא ירצה מכאן שהערל והטמא משלחין קרבנותיהן הכהנים אכלו להו וראויין הן (ואפי') [אבל] בפסח לא ערל ולא טמא אין משלחין פסחיהן דהא איש לפי אכלו תכוסו כתיב והני לאו בני אכילה נינהו ואמר רבינא ש טומאה פריך ולעולם רישא בטומאת בשר סיפא בטומאת גברי איבעית אימא רישא וסיפא בטומאת בשר ואי אינה נוהגת בכל הזבחים [דבכל הזבחים] בין נטמא חלב ובשר קיים ובין נטמא בשר וחלב קיים זורק את הדם כדבעינן למימר קמן ואלו פסח נטמא חלב ובשר קיים זורק את הדם נטמא בשר וחלב כו' ודברים פשוטין הן והאי דפריך ואל תוכיח טומאה שהותרה

said R. Ashi, R. Ḥisda and Rabbah [62a] differ in this verse: *And it shall be accepted for him to make atonement* for him:[3] *'for him'*, but not for his companion.[4] Rabbah holds, His companion must be like himself: just as he is capable of atonement, so must his companion be capable of atonement,[5] thus excluding this uncircumcised person, who is not capable of atonement.[6] But R. Ḥisda holds, This uncircumcised person too, since he is subject to the obligation, he is [also] subject to atonement, since if he wishes he can make himself fit.[7]

Yet does R. Ḥisda accept [the argument of] 'since'?[8] Surely it was stated, If one bakes [food] on a Festival for [use on] a weekday,—R. Ḥisda said: He is flagellated; Rabbah said: He is not flagellated. 'Rabbah said, He is not flagellated': We say, *Since* if guests visited him, it would be fit for him [on the Festival itself], it is fit for him now too.[9] 'R. Ḥisda said, He is flagellated': We do not say, 'since'.[10] As for Rabbah, it is well, [and] he is not self-contradictory: here [in the case of circumcision], an action is
a wanting,[1] whereas there an action is not wanting.[2] But R. Ḥisda is self-contradictory?[3]—I will tell you: when does R. Ḥisda reject [the argument of] 'since'? [where it leads] to [greater] leniency;[4] [but where it results] in stringency, he accepts it.[5]

Mar Zuṭra son of R. Mari said to Rabina: [The Baraitha] teaches: 'since uncircumcision disqualifies, and uncleanness disqualifies, [then] just as uncleanness, part uncleanness was not made tantamount to entire uncleanness, so uncircumcision, part uncircumcision was not made tantamount to entire uncircumcision.' How is this uncleanness meant? Shall we say, it means uncleanness of the person, and what is meant by, 'part uncleanness was not made tantamount to entire uncleanness'? That if there are four or five unclean persons and four or five clean persons,[6] the unclean do not disqualify [the Paschal lamb] for the clean. But then in the case of uncircumcision too they do not disqualify, for we learned, FOR CIRCUMCISED AND UNCIRCUMCISED . . . IT IS FIT: how then is uncleanness different, that he is certain about it, and how is uncircumcision different, that he is doubtful?[7] Hence it must refer to uncleanness of the flesh, and what is meant by, 'part uncleanness was not made tantamount to entire uncleanness'? For where one of the limbs becomes unclean, that which becomes unclean we burn, while the others we eat. To what have you [thus] referred it?[8] To uncleanness of the flesh! Then consider the sequel: 'you judge that which does not apply to all sacrifices by that which does not apply to all sacrifices,[9] hence let not time [dis]prove it, since it applies to all sacrifices'. Now what does 'uncleanness' mean? Shall we say, uncleanness of the flesh,—why does it not
b apply to all sacrifices?[1] Hence it is obvious that it refers to uncleanness of person, and what does 'it does not apply to all sacrifices' mean? For whereas in the case of all [other] sacrifices an uncircumcised person and an unclean person can send their sacrifices,[2] in the case of the Passover offering an uncircumcised person and an unclean person cannot send their Passover offerings. Thus the first clause refers to uncleanness of the flesh, while the second clause refers to uncleanness of the person?—Yes, answered he to him, he argues[3] from the designation of uncleanness.[4]

Alternatively, the sequel too refers to the uncleanness of flesh. Then what is [meant by] 'it does not apply to all sacrifices'? [It means this], for whereas in the case of all [other] sacrifices, whether the fat[5] is defiled while the flesh remains [clean], or the flesh is defiled while the fat remains [clean], he [the officiating priest] sprinkles the blood;[6] in the case of the Passover offering, if the fat[5] is defiled while the flesh remains [clean], he sprinkles the blood; but if the flesh is defiled while the fat remains [clean], he must not sprinkle the blood.[7]

To what have you referred it: to uncleanness of the flesh? Then consider the final clause: 'you judge a thing which was not freed from its general interdict by a thing which was not freed from its general interdict, hence let not uncleanness disprove it, seeing that it was freed from its general interdict.' In which [case]? Shall we

(3) Lev. I, 4. [I.e., by sprinkling, v. *supra* 61*b*, n. b2.] (4) I.e., if the blood is sprinkled on behalf of a different person, the sacrifice is disqualified. (5) Only then does this change of name disqualify the sacrifice. (6) I.e., he is not fit to have the Paschal offering made acceptable on his behalf; cf. loc. cit. Hence the intention that the sprinkling shall be on his behalf does not disqualify it. (7) By circumcision. (8) I.e., does he accept the view that since a different state of affairs is possible, we take it into account as though it were already in existence? (9) Though he has no guests. He is therefore regarded as having baked for the Festival itself. (10) V. *supra* 46*b*.

a (1) Viz., circumcision, before he is fit; hence though he is potentially circumcised, we cannot regard him as actually so. (2) The coming of guests involves no action on his part; hence Rabbah's ruling. (3) As in the case of baking on a Festival for a weekday. (4) If he accepts the argument of 'since' even in the case of circumcision, where an action is wanting, how much the more where no action is wanting! (5) Tosaf.: according to this, R. Ḥisda disqualifies the sacrifice (*supra* 61*a* top) only by Rabbinical law, for in Scriptural law this distinction is unacceptable. (6) Registered for the same Paschal lamb. (7) That the one must be deduced from the other. (8) Lit., 'in what (case) have you established it?' (9) The reference to uncleanness. V. *supra* 61*b*, n. a2.

b (1) It certainly does. (2) To be sacrificed on their behalf, though they cannot partake of them personally. (3) Lit., 'he rebuts'. (4) I.e., from uncleanness as a cause of disqualification, without particularizing the nature of the uncleanness. (5) Which is burnt on the altar. (6) And the sacrifice effects its purpose. (7) For there must be at least as much as an olive of *eatable* flesh before its blood may be sprinkled.

[61*b*] If he slaughtered it for circumcised persons on condition that uncircumcised persons should be atoned for therewith at the sprinkling,[2]—R. Ḥisda said: It [the lamb] is disqualified; Rabbah ruled: It is fit. R. Ḥisda said, It is disqualified: There is [a disqualification in] an intention for uncircumcised at the sprinkling. Rabbah ruled, It is fit: There is no [disqualification in] an intention for uncircumcised at the sprinkling. Rabbah said, Whence do I know it? Because it was taught: You might think that he [an uncircumcised person] disqualifies the members of the company who come with him,[3] and it is logical: since uncircumcision disqualifies, and uncleanness disqualifies, [then] just as with uncleanness, part uncleanness was not made tantamount to entire uncleanness,[4] so with uncircumcision, part uncircumcision was not made tantamount to entire uncircumcision.[5] Or turn this way:[6] since uncircumcision disqualifies, and time disqualifies: then just as with time, part [in respect to] time was made tanta-
a mount to the whole [in respect of] time,[1] so with uncircumcision, part [in respect] to uncircumcision should be made tantamount to the whole [in respect to] uncircumcision. Let us see to what it is similar: you judge [draw an analogy between] that which does not apply to all sacrifices by that which does not apply to all sacrifices,[2] and let not time provide an argument, which operates [as a disqualification] in the case of all sacrifices. Or turn this way: you judge a thing which was not freed[3] from its general rule by a thing which was not freed from its general rule,[4] and let not uncleanness provide an argument, seeing that it was freed from its general rule.[5] Therefore it is stated, *This* [*is the ordinance of the Passover*].[6] What is [the purpose of] *'this'*?[7] If we say, [to teach] that entire uncircumcision disqualifies it [the Paschal lamb], but part thereof[8] does not disqualify it, surely that is deduced from, *and* all *uncircumcised person*[*s*] [*shall not eat thereof*]?[9] Hence he [the Tanna] must have taught thus: Therefore it is stated, *'and* all uncircumcised shall not eat thereof. Entire uncircumcision disqualifies it, [but] part thereof does not disqualify it. And should you say, the same law applies to sprinkling, viz., that entire un-
b circumcision at least does disqualify it:[1] therefore *'this'* is stated, [teaching,] it is only at the slaughtering that entire uncircumcision disqualifies, but [as for] sprinkling, even entire uncircumcision too does not disqualify it.[2] And should you ask, What is the leniency of sprinkling?[3] That there is no intention of eaters in respect to sprinkling.[4]

But R. Ḥisda [maintains,] On the contrary, [the Baraitha is to be explained] in the opposite direction. [Thus:] therefore it is stated, *and all uncircumcised person*[*s*] [*shall not eat thereof*]: if the whole of it [the registered company] is [in a state of] uncircumcision, it disqualifies it, but part thereof does not disqualify it. But [as for] sprinkling, even part thereof disqualifies it.[5] And should you say, the same law applies to sprinkling, viz., that unless there is entire uncircumcision it does not disqualify it, therefore *'this'* is stated, [teaching,] only at the slaughtering does part thereof not disqualify it, but at the sprinkling even part thereof disqualifies it. And should you ask, What is the stringency of sprinkling?[6] [It is] that [the prohibition of] *piggul* cannot be imposed save at the sprinkling.[7]

To this R. Ashi demurred: Whence [do you know] that this [verse] *'and all uncircumcised person*[*s*],' implies in its entirety; perhaps this [verse], *'and all uncircumcised person*[*s*]' implies whatever there
c is of uncircumcision,[1] [and] therefore the Merciful One wrote *'this'* to teach that unless there is an entire [company in a state of] uncircumcision, it does not disqualify it, there being no difference whether [it is] at the slaughtering or at the sprinkling?[2] Rather,

(2) Whether the latter were registered for it or not. ['To be atoned for' here is employed in a technical sense denoting to have the blood sprinkled on behalf of (a person), as there is no question of atonement with the Paschal lamb. The words 'at the sprinkling' are accordingly superfluous, and in fact do not appear in MS.M.] (3) I.e., if he registered together with duly circumcised, all are disqualified from partaking of this lamb. (4) Only if *all* who register are unclean is the sacrifice disqualified, but not if merely some of them are unclean. (5) Hence it is not disqualified. (6) I.e., argue thus.

a (1) I.e., if he expressed an intention of eating even only part of the sacrifice after the time legally permitted, the *whole* sacrifice is *piggul* (q.v. Glos.) and disqualified. (2) Uncircumcision and uncleanness are not disqualifications in the case of other sacrifices, which may be killed on behalf of their owners even if they are uncircumcised or unclean. (3) Lit., 'permitted'. (4) In no case may a sacrifice be eaten by an uncircumcised person or after its permitted time. (5) If the whole community is unclean, the Paschal lamb is sacrificed and eaten by them.—Thus two contradictory arguments are possible. (6) Ex. XII, 43; the passage proceeds to disqualify an uncircumcised person (v. 49), and this word is quoted as teaching that an uncircumcised person does not disqualify others who register with him. *'This'* is a limitation, teaching that the law is exactly as stated, and is not to be extended to others. (7) This is part of Rabbah's argument. How does *'this'* signify that the uncircumcised does not disqualify the members of the company that come with him? (8) I.e., when only some of the registered company are uncircumcised. (9) Ibid. 48, which is thus interpreted: when *all* who have registered for a particular animal are uncircumcised, none must eat thereof. But if only a fraction are uncircumcised, the circumcised may eat thereof. (E.V. *but no uncircumcised person shall eat thereof.*)

b (1) Viz., where he expressed an intention that the sprinkling should make atonement for uncircumcised only. (2) *'This'* implies that uncircumcision disqualifies at one of the four services only, which is assumed to be the slaughtering. This interpretation of the Baraitha supports Rabbah's view. (3) What other leniency do you find in sprinkling, that you assume that the limitation of *'this'* teaches a further leniency in respect to uncircumcision. (4) He need not sprinkle expressly for those who are registered, as the requirement of registration and eaters is stated in connection with slaughtering, v. *supra* 61*a* note on Rabbi's exegesis. (5) As his view *supra*. (6) What other stringency do you find in sprinkling, that you assume that the limitation of *'this'* teaches a further stringency in respect to uncircumcision. (7) An illegitimate intention to partake of the sacrifice after the permitted time, expressed at one of the four services (v. Mishnah *supra* 59*b*) renders it *piggul*, and he who eats it, even within the permitted time, incurs *kareth*, only if the subsequent services are performed without any intention at all or with a legitimate intention or with the *same* illegitimate intention. But if any one of the subsequent services is performed with a *different* illegitimate intention, e.g., to eat it without the permitted boundaries, it ceases to be *piggul* and does not involve *kareth*, v. Zeb. 28*b*. Hence the only service in which it can *definitely* be fixed as *piggul* without possibility of revocation is sprinkling, because that is the last service. That is regarded as a stringency of sprinkling.

c (1) I.e., on the contrary it may imply that even if a single person of those who are registered for the sacrifice is uncircumcised, it is disqualified. (2) For on the present exegesis there is no verse to intimate a distinction.

בג א מיי' שם הל' ו:

רבינו חננאל

לשם חבורה אחרת ושמנא בענין למנויו שנאמר במכסת נפשות תכוסו על השה ואוכליו שנאמר איש לפי אכלו ואיתקש אוכלין למנויין: **אתמר** שחטו למולין על מנת שיתכפרו בו ערלים רב חסדא אמר פסול יש מחשבת אוכלין בזריקה כלומר בענין שחשב בזריקה לאוכליו מכיון שחשב לערלים שאינן יכולין לאכול שנאמר (שמות יב מח) וכל ערל לא יאכל בו פסול רבא אמר כשר בתר שחיטה אזלינן ואין מחשבת אוכלין פוסלין בזריקה כלומר אם זרק שלא לאוכליו לא נפסל הפסח. ירושלמי אמר ר' יוחנן שחטו לאוכליו וזרק דמו שלא לאוכליו כשר אמר רבא מנא אמינא לה דאין מחשבת ערלין בזריקה יכול לפסול בני חבורה הבאין עמו ודין הוא הואיל וטומאה פוסלת שנאמר (במדבר ט ו) ויהי אנשים אשר היו טמאים וגו' וערלה פוסלת שנא' וכל ערל לא יאכל בו מה טומאה לא עשה בה מקצת טומאה ככל הטומאה אף ערלה לא עשה בה מקצת ערלה ככל ערלה[או] כלך לדרך זו הואיל וערלה פוסלת וזמן פוסל מה זמן עשה בו מקצת זמן ככל זמן אף ערלה עשה בה מקצת ערלה ככל ערלה נראה למי דומה דנין דבר שאין נוהג בכל הזבחים [כמו] הערלה שאין ערלה פוסלת אלא בפסח אבל בשאר זבחים לא דקיימא לן ערל וטמא משלחין קרבנותיהן מדבר שאינו נוהג בכל הזבחים [הטומאה] שאין טומאה פוסלת אלא בפסח אבל בשאר זבחים לא דקיימא לן [טמא משלח קרבנותיו] ואל יוכיח זמן שנוהג בכל הזבחים. או כלך לדרך זו דנין דבר שלא הותר מ[כל]לה הערלה מדבר שלא הותר מכללו הזמן ואל תוכיח טומאה שהרי הותרה מכללה בצבור שנאמר (שם ט י) איש איש כי יהיה טמא לנפש איש נדחה לפסח שני ואין צבור נדחה לפסח שני אלא עושה בטומאה ת"ל זאת חקת הפסח ודייק רבה מאי זאת אלא לאו הכי קתני ואל תוכיח טומאה שהותרה מכללה בצבור ת"ל וכל ערל אי איכא כולה ערלות פסלה ואי לא לא פסלה וכי תימא הוא הדין לזריקה דאי אית בה כולה ערלות פסלה ת"ל זאת בשחיטה הוא דפסלה ערלה בזריקה לא פסלה ומאי קולא בזריקה לדחויה דאין מחשבת אוכלין פוסלה בזריקה כדאמרן: **ורב** חסדא אדרבה לאידך גיסא כולה ערלות פסלה בשחיטה מקצתה לא פסלה וכי תימא הוא הדין לזריקה דבזריקה נמי לא פסלה עד דאיכא כולה ערלות ת"ל זאת בשחיטה הוא דבעי כולה ערלות אבל בזריקה אפי' מקצת ערלה פסלה דזריקה חמורה משחיטה דלא מקבע פיגול בשחיטה אלא בזריקה דתנן בזבחים פ"ב [כז.] השוחט [הזבח] לזרוק דמו למחר או מקצת דמו למחר להקטיר אימוריו למחר או מקצתן לאכול כזית מבשרו למחר פיגול וחייבין עליו כרת הנה לא מקבע הפסח פגול אלא מזריקה ואילך אבל בשחיטה לא דאי אפשר לחשב בשחיטה לשחטו למחר דהא היום שחט ליה ובא רב אשי ודחה האי תירוצא לאמר ממאי דהאי וכל דכתיב בערלה כולה משמע דלמא האי וכל כלום משמע דאפילו מקצת ערלה כתב רחמנא זאת עד דאיכא כולה ערלות לא שנא בשחיטה ולא שנא בזריקה וכי פליגי רבא ורב חסדא בהאי

שחטו למולין על מנת שיתכפרו בו ערלים בזריקה *רב חסדא אמר פסול רבה אמר כשר רב חסדא אמר פסול יש מחשבת ערלים בזריקה רבה אמר כשר אין מחשבת ערלים בזריקה אמר רבה מנא אמינא לה דתניא יכול יפסול בני חבורה הבאין עמו ודין הוא הואיל וערלה פוסלת וטומאה פוסלת מה טומאה לא עשה בה מקצת טומאה ככל טומאה אף ערלה לא עשה בה מקצת ערלה ככל ערלה או כלך לדרך זו הואיל וערלה פוסלת וזמן פוסל מה זמן עשה בה מקצת זמן ככל זמן אף ערלה עשה בה מקצת ערלה ככל ערלה נראה למי דומה דנין דבר שאינו נוהג בכל הזבחים מדבר שאינו נוהג בכל הזבחים ואל יוכיח זמן שנוהג בכל הזבחים או כלך לדרך זו דנין דבר שלא הותר מכללו מדבר שלא הותר מכללו ואל תוכיח טומאה שהותרה מכללה ת"ל *זאת (שמות יב) מאי זאת אילימא דכולה ערלה פסלה מקצתה לא פסלה האי מוכל ערל נפקא אלא לאו הכי קתני ת"ל וכל ערל כולה ערלה פסלה מקצתה לא פסלה וכי תימא הוא הדין לזריקה דכולה ערלה מיהא פסלה ת"ל זאת בשחיטה הוא דכולה ערלה מיהא פסלה אבל זריקה אפילו כולה ערלה נמי לא פסלה וכי תימא מאי קולא דזריקה *דאין מחשבת אוכלין בזריקה ורב חסדא אדרבה לאידך גיסא ת"ל וכל ערל כולה ערלה פסלה מקצתה לא פסלה אבל זריקה אפילו מקצתה נמי פסלה וכי תימא הוא הדין לזריקה דעד דאיכא כולה ערלה לא פסלה ת"ל זאת שחיטה הוא דמקצתה לא פסלה אבל זריקה אפילו מקצתה פסלה וכ"ת ומאי חומריה דזריקה דלא מקבע פיגול אלא בזריקה מתקיף לה רב אשי ממאי דהאי וכל ערל משמע כל דהו דילמא האי וכל ערל משמע כל דהו ערלה כתב רחמנא זאת דעד דאיכא כולה ערלה לא פסלה לא שנא בשחיטה ולא שנא בזריקה אלא אמר רב אשי רב חסדא ורבה בהאי

רב חסדא אמר פסול. ואם תאמר מאי שנא משחטו למולים ולערלים תרין דהתם יש מחשבת מולים בשחיטה אבל הכא לא פתיכי מולים בזריקה: **רבה אמר כשר.** תימה לר"י נילף מק"ו דפסול משינוי בעלים דמה הריני שוחט לשם פלוני דכשר לזרוק דמו לשם פלוני פסול שוחט לשם ערלים דפסול אינו דין דלזרוק לערלים נמי פסול וכי האי גוונא עביד בזבחים (ד' י.) קל וחומר אשלא לשמו ותירץ ר"י דשאני הכא דרבה יליף מקרא לקמן ועוד אומר ר"י דאיכא למיפרך מה לשינוי בעלים שכן אם זרק לשם פלוני דפסול תאמר בשוחטו לזרוק לערלים שכן זורק לשם ערלים כשר דאין מחשבת אוכלין בזריקה לכ"ע כדפרישית ואם תאמר היא גופה נילף משינוי בעלים שיהא זורק לשם ערלים פסול ושמא יש מיעוט למעט אוכלים מזריקה ומיהו מתכונו לא משמע שום מיעוט אלא מיעוט אחרינא איכא ועוד איכא למיפרך מה לשינוי בעלים שכן פסול בכל הזבחים: **וכי** תימא ה"ה לזריקה. וכן רב אשי קאמר בסמוך לא שנא שחיטה ולא שנא זריקה תימה לריב"א כיון דזריקה קילא דאין בה מחשבת אוכלין היכי נילף משחיטה ואמאי איצטריך השתא זאת: **דילמא** האי כל ערל אפילו כל דהו. אע"ג דפלוגתא דתנאי הוא בסנהדרין (ד' עח.) גבי הכוהו עשרה בני אדם בי' מקלות בכל נפש אי כולה נפש משמע או כל דהו וכן בבכורות (ד' ג.) גבי כל בכור רב אשי בא לסתור ראייתו של רבה ולהעמיד הברייתא כמאן דאמר כל דהו משמע ועוד כדפי' בקונטרס דברייתא גופה מוכחא דזאת בא להתיר מקצת ערלות ולהכי פריך: **כתב** רחמנא זאת עד דאיכא כולה ערלה. תימה לשתוק מכל ועוד דנימא איפכא דזאת ודאי כולה ערלה משמע כתב רחמנא כל אפילו כל דהו וי"ל דידע בעל הש"ס דאיצטריך כל לשום דרשה אחריתי ואיצטריך זאת לגלויי דלא נדרוש מכל כל דהו אבל אי הוה דרשי' איפכא לא הוה ידעינן כלל זאת למאי אתא: האי

שחטו. להאכילו למולין מנויין אבל יתכפרו בו בזריקתו ערלים או מנויין או שאינן מנויין: **אין מחשבת ערלים בזריקה.** לא מ'תני לפסול וטעמא מפרש לקמיה: **מנא אמינא לה כו'.** רישא דברייתא וכל ערל לא יאכל בו: **יכול יפסול.** ערל: **בני חבורה הבאין עמו.** שאם נמנו עמו עליו מולין וערל שמתו אחיו מחמת מילה ושחטו לשם כולם יכול יפסל: **הואיל וטומאה פוסלת.** אם שחטו לטמאין דבעינן הראוי לאוכלו כדכתיב איש לפי אכלו תכוסו תשחטו ולתנא קמא דלית ליה לשון סורסי בתריה כתיב ושחטו אותו: **וערלה פוסלת.** מהאי טעמא נמי דראוי לאכילה בעינן: **מה טומאה לא עשה בה מקצת טומאה.** כגון לטמאים ולטהורים: **ככל טומאה.** כאילו נשחט כולו לטמאים ולקמן פריך מאי שנא טומאה דפשיטא ליה ומאי שנא ערלה דמספקא ליה: **וזמן פוסל.** שחטו על מנת לאכול הימנו כזית חוץ לזמנו נעשה כולו פיגול והיינו מקצת זמן שלא חישב אלא על כזית הימנו כדכתיב אם האכל יאכל וגו' ותניא בתורת כהנים ובזבחים (דף כט:) כוף אזנך לשמוע במחשב לאכול מזבחו ביום השלישי הכתוב מדבר וכתיב האכל יאכל אכילה בכזית: **ערלה וטומאה** אינה נוהגת בשאר זבחים כפסח שכן ערל וטמא משלחין קרבנותיהן דלא מעכבא בהו אכילת בעלים: **ערלה לא הותרה מכללה.** שאין שום קרבן נאכל לערלים דילפינן ביבמות (דף עג.) דערל אסור בקדשים דאתי בקל וחומר מפסח הקל וזמן נמי לא הותר לשום קרבן לאוכלו חוץ לזמנו וטומאה הותרה מכללה כדמפרש לקמן הפסח שבא בטומאה נאכל בטומאה: [לקמן עז.] **ת"ל זאת.** חקת הפסח וכתיב בההיא פרשתא כל ערל לא יאכל בו: **מאי זאת.** היכי משמע מזאת דאינו פוסל בני חבורה הבאין עמו על כרחך מילתא אחריתי קאמר והכי קאמר ת"ל וכל ערל עד דאיכא כולה ערלות וזאת אתא דלא תימא הוא הדין לזריקה דכולה ערלות מיהא פסלה ביה אם שחטו למולין על מנת לזרוק דמה לערלים לבדם: **תלמוד לומר זאת.** דמשמע בעבודה א' הוא דפסלה ערלות והיינו שחיטה דהיא תחלה לעבודות והיא הוזכרה אצל מנויין ואוכלין כדמפרש: **וכ"ת מאי קולא דזריקה.** דתימא האי זאת אשחיטה קאי ולמעוטי זריקה הייט קולא דהא לא אתרבי מחשבת אוכלין אצל זריקה דשחיטה גלי בה רחמנא הלכך מסתברא דזאת דפסול כולה ערלות אשחיטה קאי ולאו אזריקה וזאת משמע מיעוטא: **ורב חסדא.** דאמר לעיל יש מחשבת (אוכלין) [ערלים] בזריקה אמר לך האי זאת לאו לקולא גבי זריקה הוא אלא לאחמורי עליה אתא והכא קאמר זאת היא דמקצת ערלה לא פסלה בה אבל זריקה אפי' מקצתה פסלה: **וכי תימא מאי חומרא דזריקה.** משחיטה דמוקמית קולא דמקצת ערלה לא פסלה אשחיטה אבל זריקה אפי' מקצתה פסלה הייט חומרא דילה דלא מקיים פיגול אלא בזריקה אם חישב באחת מארבע עבודות על מנת לאכול הימנו כזית חוץ לזמנו פיגול הוא וחייבין עליו כרת אפילו אכל ממנו תוך זמנו כדכתיב (ויקרא ז) והנפש האוכלת ממנו עונה תשא ובלבד שיעשו כל עבודות שלאחריה שלא בפסול אחר אלא או בשתיקה או בכשרות על מנת תוך זמנו או על מנת פיגול כמותה אבל חישב באחת מעבודות שלאחריה פסול אחר כגון חוץ למקומו שוב אין בו כרת כדאמרי' בזבחים (דף כח:) ובמנחות בפ' שני (דף טז:) הרצאה כתיבה בפיגול נאמר לא ירצה בפיגול ונאמר בבשר מיום השמיני והלאה ירצה כהרצאת כשר כך הרצאת פיגול מה הרצאת כשר עד שיקרבו כל מתיריו בכשרות אף הרצאת פיגול עד שיקרבו כל מתיריו או בפיגול או בכשרות אלמא לא מיקבע וודאי של פיגול אלא בזריקה שהיא סוף העבודה דכל שעתא קאי בספק שמא יחשב פסול אחר בעבודה הבאה ויפקיע שם פיגול ממנו: **מתקיף לה רב אשי.** בין לרבה בין לרב חסדא ממאי דהאי וכל ערל עד דאיכא כולה ערלה משמע דנייתי זאת למעוטי זריקה למר לחומרא ולמר לקולא ות"ל זאת דקתני תנא מילתא אחריתי קאמר דילמא זאת דקתני תנא אמילתיה קאי ומינה יליף דאינו פוסל בני חבורה הבאין עמו ומשום דכל ערל כל דהו משמע והכי קאמר יכול יפסול בני חבורה דכל ערל כל דהו משמע ושוב לא יאכל בו שום אדם: **ת"ל זאת.** עבודה שלימה בעינן בערלות ולעולם לא שנא שחיטה ולא שנא זריקה שוין: בהאי

וישנו לאחר מיתה. מת בנו מביא קרבן אביו ואם שחטו שלא לשמו לא עלה לשם חובה ואחריות הקרבן מוטל על בניו המת וצריך להביא אחר וישנו בקרבן צבור כקרבן יחיד: אבל בשינוי בעלים. מחשב בדבר אחר הוא והיינו בארבע עבודות בשאר זבחים דלאו פסח דלאו עיקרן לאכילה אתי אלא לכפרה לא שייך שינוי בעלים אלא בזריקה שאין לו בקרבן אלא כפרתו וכפרה ליתא אלא בזריקה וכי מרבינן שאר עבודות לפסולה בשינוי בעלים בפ"ק דזבחים *לא מרבינן אלא שוחט להתכפר אחר בזריקת דמו או מוליך או מקבל לזרוק לשם אחר או זרק ממנו לשם אחר אבל שוחט לשם אחר שתהא השחיטה לבדה לשם אחרים אבל בשעת שחיטה אין דעתו על הזריקה אלא לבעליו כשר והכי אמרי' התם *אמר רב אשי ק"ו ומה אם במקום שאמר הריני שוחט לשם פלוני דכשר שחטו לזרוק לשם פלוני פסול מקום שאם אמר כו' ש"מ מיהא דאין מחשבת שינוי בעלים בשאר עבודות אא"כ מחשבין באחת מהן על מנת לזרוק אבל בשינוי קודש שחט שלא לשמו פסול דכתיב זבח שלמים זביחה לשם שלמים וכן בחטאת ושחט אותה לחטאת וכן פסח זבח פסח הוא ומיהו ודאי פסח שעיקרו לבעליו ליאכל לא שחטו שלא לשם בעליו להאכילו למנויין אחרים פסול כדקתני מתני' שחטו שלא למנויו פסול וע"כ בחושב על השחיטה לחודה קאמר לא על מנת לזרוק מדאיפלגו בה אמוראי בגמרא שחטו למולין על מנת שיתכפרו בו ערלים מכלל דשחטו לערלים דמתני' אין במחשב על השחיטה קאמר ושלא למנויו דומיא דלערלים דהא גבי הדדי קתני להו: והיינו לאחר מיתה. דאין שם בעליו עליו מאחר שמת ואם שינה שמו כשר: והיינו בצבור. דלשם מי ישנה אותו שלא יהא בעליו אם לשם נכרים לא מיפסיל כדאמרי' התם ולקמן בשמעתין דאין שינוי בעלים פסול אא"כ שינהו למחויב כפרה כמותו דיליף מלכפר עליו ולא על חבירו אלמא שינוי בעלים פסול בחבירו דומיא דידיה ומחויב כפרה כמותו ואי לא לא פסול: ואע"ג דתרתי. מהגך פירכי לאו דווקא. כלומר לאו פירכי נינהו תרתי מיהא דווקא ומפרש ואזיל הי תרתי לאו דווקא: פסול מחשבה לא מיקרי פסול הגוף: ולרב פנחס. בפ"ק דזבחים אמרה: יש בעלים לאחר מיתה. ואם שחטו לשם בעלים אחרים צריך היורש להביא אחר: כמי שאין לו בעלים. כמי ששחטו בזמנו שלא לשם בעלים ואי שמעתי שינוי בעלים אינו בזריקה כדאמרי' אין מחשבת אוכלים בזריקה ואי אפשר לומר כן דמחשבת שלא לאוכליו מנויין עליו ובשחיטה הוא דגלי רחמנא ולא בשאר עבודות אבל מחשבת שלא למנויו דהיינו שינוי בעלים עיקרה בזריקה הוא כדיליף לקמן בשמעתין בזריקה וכפר עליו ולא על חבירו:

מתני' לאוכליו ושלא לאוכליו כשר. דמקצת אוכלין לא פסלי ולקמן מפרש טעמא: ממרס בדמו. שלא יקרוש כדי שיהא ראוי לזריקה: ואם נזרק. קודם לתמיד כשר דאע"ג דאמרן (לעיל ד' נט.) יאוחר דבר שנאמר בו בערב ובין הערבים וגו' לא מיפסיל בהכי:

גמ' מכסת. לשון מנויין כמו את מכסת הערכך (ויקרא כז): סורסי. ארמי חכמי האומות קורין לו לינגא סורייא: כוס. שחוט למימרא דבשעת שחיטה צריך להתכוין למנויו: לפי אכלו. הראוי לאכול פרט לחולה ולזקן ולערל ואפילו הן מנויין שחטו

[דף ד.] | זבחי' דף ד: [פ"ש] [דף ז.] | [לעיל ס. וע"ש פרש"י ותוס'] | יבמות דף לג. | [תוספ' פ"ד] | לקמן דף עח: [פ"ש] זבחים כג. ע"ש | [לקמן עח: יומא לו: לה. יבמות מ. שבועות יד. זבחים כג. מנחות יט:]

וישנו לאחר מיתה וישנו בצבור כביחיד תאמר בשינוי בעלים דאין פסולו בגופו ואינו בארבע עבודות ואינו לאחר מיתה ואינו בצבור כביחיד ואף על גב דתרתי לאו דוקא תרתי מיהא דוקא דמאי שנא שינוי בעלים דלא הוי פסולו בגופו דפסולו מחשבה בעלמא היא שינוי קודש נמי פסולו מחשבה בעלמא היא ותו הא דאמר שינוי בעלים אינו לאחר מיתה ולרב פנחס בריה דרב אמי דאמר יש *שינוי *בעלים לאחר מיתה מאי איכא למימר תרתי מיהת דוקא נינהו אלא אמר רבא *פסח ששחטו בשאר ימות השנה בשינוי בעלים נעשה כמי שאין לו בעלים בזמנו ופסול: **מתני'** *שחטו שלא לאוכליו ושלא למנויו *לערלים ולטמאים פסול לאוכליו ושלא לאוכליו למנויו ושלא למנויו למולים ולערלים לטמאים ולטהורים כשר *שחטו קודם חצות פסול משום שנא' בין הערבים (שמות יב) שחטו קודם לתמיד כשר ובלבד שיהא אחר ממרס בדמו עד שיזרק התמיד ואם נזרק כשר: **גמ'** ת"ר *כיצד שלא לאוכליו לשום חולה או לשום זקן כיצד שלא למנויו נמנו עליו חבורה זו ושחטו לשם חבורה אחרת מנהני מילי *דת"ר במכסת (שם) מלמד שאין הפסח נשחט אלא למנויו יכול שחטו שלא למנויו יהא כעובר על המצוה וכשר ת"ל במכסת תכוסו הכתוב *שנה עליו לעכב ר' אומר לשון סורסי הוא כאדם שאומר לחבירו כוס לי טלה זה אשכחן שלא למנויו שלא לאוכליו מנא לן אמר קרא איש (שם) לפי אכלו תכוסו איתקש אוכלין למנויין

וישנו לאחר מיתה. ושינוי בעלים ליתו לאחר מיתה משום דכתיב לכפר עליו ולא על חבירו ומת ולאו בר כפרה גמורה הוא אלא שנתחייב להביאו והך דשמעתין אתיא להדיא כמ"ד שיעבודא דאורייתא וכרב אסי אמר רב *בפ"ק דקדושין (ד' יג:) דמוקי לה דתנן האשה שמתה יביאו יורשין עולתה אע"פ שלא הפרישתה מחיים אבל לרב יהודה אמר שמואל דאמר והוא שהפרישתה מחיים אבל לא הפרישתה לא משום דשיעבודא לאו דאורייתא לכאורה היינו נפקותא בין שינוי קודש לשינוי בעלים דלאחר מיתה כיון דבשינוי קודש [נמי] אין היורש חייב להפריש אחר תחתיו ומיהו י"ל דכ"מ אם הפרישו בעלים שתי עולות לאחריות שאם תפסל האחת יביא השניה ואם לאו תהא השניה חולין אי נמי שינוי קודש אסור לשנות אחר מיתה דאמר בריש זבחים (ד' ב:) ונדבה מי שרי לשנויי בה אבל שינוי בעלים ליכא אפי' איסור כיון דליתו לאחר מיתה:

נעשה כמי שאין לו בעלים בזמנו ופסול. תימה לר"י ל"ל למימר נעשה כיון דתרתי דוקא ליתא דפסול משום דאין כאן עקירה ואי לא חייש להני פירכי וסבר דדמי לשינוי קודש הואיל ופסלו בזמנו וחשיב עקיר' א"כ אמאי הוי כמי שאין לו בעלים בזמנו הלא בשינוי קודש לא חשבי' משנה כבזמנו לפסול ואור"י דהכי פי' אפי' ליתנהו להנהו פירכי מ"מ לא הוי עקירה דנעשה כפסח בזמנו שמתו בעליו דאמר בסוף אלו דברים (ד' עג:) דבעי עקירה וכששחטו סתם פסול אע"פ שהוא כמפרש שלא לשם בעליו שהרי מתו ה"נ שלא בזמנו שינוי בעלי' לא חשיב עקירה וכן מוכיח הלשון דקאמר שאין לו בעלים ולא קאמר כמי ששחטו בשינוי בעלים: **רבי** אומר לשון סורסי הוא זה. אור"י דרבי לא פליג את"ק ומודה דאיכא עיכובא באוכליו ומנויו ואיתו אלא מפרש דבריו דלא פסלי אוכליו ומנויו אלא בשחיטה וכן משמע בכיצד צולין (ד' עח:) דמסיק רב דאמר אכילה לא מעכבי כרבי נתן ולא קאמר כר' והיינו משום דלפרושי אתא כדפי': **לאוכליו** מנא לן. אור"י דערלים וטמאים כולהו נפקי מהאי קרא דאיש לפי אכלו דכיון דלא מצו אכלי ליה חשיבי כולהו שלא לאוכליו וכן משמע בפ"ב דזבחים (ד' כג:) דקאמר קסברי זקני דרום טמא משלח קרבנותיו פי' פסח והתניא במכסת נפשות מכאן שאין הפסח נשחט אלא למנויו ואיתקש אוכליו למנויו משמע בהדיא דטמא נפקא לן מאיש לפי אכלו: **ואיתקש** אוכליו למנויו. תימה לר"י א"כ מה מנויו פסלי בד' עבודות דהיינו שינוי בעלים אף אוכליו יפסלו בד' עבודות ובשאר קרבנות נמי יפסלו במנויו וי"ל דשלא למנויו אין זה שינוי בעלים דשינוי בעלים לא פסיל אלא בזריקה כגון שוחט או מקבל ומוליך על מנת לזרוק לשם אחרים או זורק לשם אחרים אבל שוחט ומקבל ומוליך לשם אחרים כשר דמוכפר עליו נפקא לן ושלא למנויו היינו שוחט שלא למנויו ולא פסיל אלא בשחיטה דווקא כדכתיב תכוסו ודווקא בפסח ולא בשאר קרבנות וא"ת ונימא הואיל וגלי שלא לאוכליו בשחיטה ה"ה בשאר עבודות כדאי' בפ"ק דזבחים (ד' ז:) פסח שלא לשמו מזבח פסח שאר עבודות מנא לן הואיל וגלי גלי ואור"י דלא דמי כיון דגלי בכל הקרבנות דלא עלו לבעלים לשם חובה וגבי פסח אשכחן פסול בחד מינייהו אין לנו לחלק: **שחטו** למולין על מנת שיתכפרו בו ערלים. אם שחטו למנויו על מנת שיתכפרו בו שאינם מנויו הא פשיטא דפסול לכ"ע דהיינו שינוי בעלים דפסול בפסח ובחטאת ומיהו נראה לר"י דה"ה פליגי בשחט לאוכליו על מנת שיתכפרו שאינם אוכלין כגון חולה וזקן דפסל ביה רב חסדא כמו בערלים אע"ג דקראי דמייתי בערל כתיבי דמחד קרא דלפי אכלו נפקי וילפי מהדדי לכל מילי דהא לאוכליו ושלא לאוכליו דכשר היינו משום דילפי' מנמולים ולערלים ודווקא בשחט למולים ע"מ שיתכפרו ערלים פסל רב חסדא אבל נזרק לשם ערלים אפי' רב חסדא מודה דכשר דאין מחשבת אוכלין בזריקה דהא בכ"מ פשוט זה למסדר הש"ס בכולה שמעתי' ובריש זבחים (ד' ד.) דקאמר אשכחן זביחה שאר עבודות מנלן וכי תימא נילף מזביחה מה לזביחה שכן פסולה שלא לשם אוכלין בפסח משמע דליכא מאן דפליג דאין מחשבת אוכלין בזריקה ועוד דרב אשי מסיק דרבה לא פליג בהא אדרב חסדא ובפ' כיצד צולין (ד' עח.) דתניא שחטו לאוכליו לזרוק דמו שלא לאוכליו פסח עצמו כשר ואדם יוצא בו ידי חובתו לא גרסינן לזרוק דמו אלא וזרק דמו דלא תיקשי לרב חסדא וכן יש במקצת ספרים וריב"א פי' דדוקא נקט על מנת שיתכפרו שחישב להתכפר בו ערלים אבל אם לא חישב להתכפר אלא חישב לזרוק להאכיל הבשר לערלים אפי' רב חסדא מודה דכשר דלא שייך בזריקה מחשבת פסול דאכילה אלא פסול דכפרה ובשחיטה דווקא אם חישב להאכיל שלא לאוכליו ולערלים תפסול דשחיטה ודאי בעינן לשם בעלים הראויים לאוכלו כדכתיב איש לפי אכלו תכוסו והיינו דאין מחשבת אוכלין בזריקה:

רב

עין משפט נר מצוה

יח א מיי' פט"ו מהלכות פסולי מוקדשין הלכה יא:

שם כתוב רב אסי א"ר יוחנן וצריך לעיין אם הוא רבי אסי תלמיד דר' יוחנן או רב אסי תלמיד חבר לרב עי' רש"י שבת קמו: ד"ה רב כהנא ותוס' חולין יט. ד"ה אמר רב הונא

יט ב מיי' פ"ב מהלכות ק"פ הלכה ה:

כ ג מיי' פ"א מהלכות ק"פ הלכה ד ופט"ו מהלכות פסולי מוקדשין הלכה יב:

כא ד מיי' פ"ב מהלכות ק"פ הלכה א:

כב ה שם הלכה ג:

[בזבחים ז: איתא יש בעלים לאחר מיתה וכן עיין רש"י הכא ד"ה יש בעלים כו']

כל מקום שתמצא ערל בזה הענין הוא ישראל שמתו אחיו מחמת מילה ועליו נאמר כל ערל לא יאכל בו

רבינו חננאל

אחר כשר ושינוי קודש עוד ישנו אפי' לאחר מיתת המקדש כגון שהיה עולה ושחטו לשם שלמים לאפוקי שינוי בעלים דאינו אלא מחיים דכיון דמת פקעה רשותיה ודוכרני' מעליה. וישנו בצבור כביחיד כי שנוי קדש פוסל בקרבן הצבור שאם נשחט העולה לשם חטאת או לשם אשם כמו שפוסל בקרבן יחיד כך פוסל בקרבנות צבור ואע"ג דפרכת שינוי קודש דפסולו בגופו ושינוי בעלים אין פסולו בגופו לאו פירכא הוא דתרווייהו פסול מחשבה נינהו ולא שנא ומאי דפרכת נמי יש שינוי קודש לאחר מיתה ואין שינוי בעלים לשם מיתה הרי רב פנחס בריה דרב אמי אמר [דיש] שינוי בעלים לאחר מיתה דגרסינן בתחלת שחיטת קדשים ואמר רבא עולה הבאה לאחר מיתה שחטה בשינוי קדש פסולה בשינוי בעלים כשרה אין בעלים לאחר מיתה ורב פנחס בר רב אמי אומר יש בעלים לאחר מיתה אמר לו רב אשי לרב פנחס דוקא קאמר מר יש בעלים לאחר מיתה והוה ליה כשינוי קדש ובעי איתויי אחריתי או דלמא אמרי' [דאי] איכא גביה כמה עשה ומכפרא ליה א"ל דוקא קא אמינא:וזו השמועה כלה מה לשנוי קדש שכן פסולו בגופו וישנו בארבע עבודות וישנו לאחר מיתה וישנו בצבור כביחיד כולו מפורש בפ"א בשחיטת קדשים פריך מיהא לדברי הכל באחת ולרבא דהוא מרא דשמעתא תרתי מה לשנוי קודש שכן ישנו בארבע כדאמרן וישנו בצבור כביחיד לאפוקי צבור דלא משכחת ליה בשנוי בעלים דהא כל ישראל בעליו הן ופשטה פסח ששחטו בשאר ימות השנה לשם פסח בשנוי בעלים נעשה כמי שאין לו בעלים בזמנו ופסול. תנן בתחלת שחיטת קדשים חוץ מן הפסח ומן החטאת פסח בזמנו שלא לשמו פסול שנאמר ואמרתם זבח פסח הוא לה' דייקינן מינה דבעינן לשמו ותנן נמי [שם מג.] (הפסח) [הזבח] נפסל בארבעה כו' בשחיטה שנאמרה המקריב את זבח השלמים כו' בקבלה שנא' והקריבו זו קבלת הדם בזריקה שנאמר הזורק את דם השלמים בהולכה שנאמר והקריבו הלכה דאפקה רחמנא בלשון הקרבה: **מתני'** שחטו שלא לאוכליו ושלא למנויו כו' ת"ר כיצד שלא לאוכליו שחטו לחולה ולזקן כיצד שלא למנויו ומנו עליו חבורה א ושחטו לשם

in respect of the four services,[5] [61a] and it is [operative] after death,[6] and it is [operative] in the case of the community as in the case of an individual;[7] will you say [the same] of a change of owner, where the disqualification is not intrinsic, and it is not [operative] in respect of the four services,[8] and it is not [operative] after death,[9] and it is not [operative] in the case of the community as in the case of an individual? And though two [of these distinctions] are not exact,[10] two nevertheless are exact. For how is a change of owners different, that [you say] its disqualification is not intrinsic: because its disqualification is merely [one of] intention? Then with a change of sanctity too, its disqualification is merely one of intention. Again, as to what he says, A change of owners is not [operative as a disqualification] after death, then according to R. Phineas the son of R. Ammi who maintained, There is [a disqualification in] a change of owner after death, what is there to be said? Two [of these distinctions] are nevertheless exact! Rather, said Raba: A Paschal lamb which he slaughtered during the rest of the year with a change of owners is re-
a garded as though it had no owners in its proper time,[1] and it is disqualified.

MISHNAH. IF HE KILLED IT FOR THOSE WHO CANNOT EAT IT OR FOR THOSE WHO ARE NOT REGISTERED FOR IT, FOR UNCIRCUMCISED PERSONS OR FOR UNCLEAN PERSONS, IT IS UNFIT. [IF HE KILLED IT] FOR THOSE WHO ARE TO EAT IT AND FOR THOSE WHO ARE NOT TO EAT IT, FOR THOSE WHO ARE REGISTERED FOR IT AND FOR THOSE WHO ARE NOT REGISTERED FOR IT, FOR CIRCUMCISED AND FOR UNCIRCUMCISED, FOR UNCLEAN AND FOR CLEAN PERSONS, IT IS FIT. IF HE KILLED IT BEFORE MIDDAY, IT IS DISQUALIFIED, BECAUSE IT IS SAID, [AND THE WHOLE ASSEMBLY . . . SHALL KILL IT] AT DUSK.[2] IF HE KILLED IT BEFORE THE [EVENING] TAMID, IT IS FIT, PROVIDING THAT ONE SHALL STIR ITS BLOOD UNTIL [THAT OF] THE TAMID IS SPRINKLED;[3] YET IF IT WAS SPRINKLED,[4] IT IS FIT.

GEMARA. Our Rabbis taught: How is 'for those who cannot eat it' meant? [If it was killed] in the name of an invalid or an old man. How is 'for those who were not registered for it' meant? If one company registered for it and he killed it in the name of a different company.

How do we know this? Because our Rabbis taught, [*Then shall he and his neighbour next unto him take one*] *according to the number of* [be-miksath] [*the souls*]:[5] this teaches that the Paschal lamb is not slaughtered save for those who are registered [numbered] for it. You might think that if he slaughtered it for those who were not registered for it, he should be as one who violates the precept, yet it is fit. Therefore it is stated, '*according to the number of* [be-miksath] [*the souls*] . . . *ye shall make your count* [takosu]': the Writ reiterated it, to teach that it is indispensable. Rabbi said, This is a Syriac expression, as a man who says to his neigh-
b bour, 'Kill [*kos*] me this lamb.'[1] We have thus found [it disqualified if killed] for those who are not registered for it; how do we know [the same of] those who cannot eat it? Scripture saith, *according to every man's eating ye shall make your count:* [thus] eaters are assimilated to registered [persons].

(5) V. Mishnah *supra* 59b and note a.l. (6) If the owner of the sacrifice died, his son must bring it, and if the latter slaughters it for a different purpose it is disqualified. (7) A public sacrifice, just like a private sacrifice, is disqualified if offered for another purpose. (8) In the case of sacrifices other than the Passover a change of owner is a disqualification only when it is expressed in connection with the sprinkling of the blood, i.e., he declares that he will sprinkle the blood on behalf of another person. (9) When its owner dies the sacrifice loses his name, and therefore even if it is offered in another man's name it is fit. (10) They are not true distinctions, as shown anon.

a (1) I.e., as though it were slaughtered on Passover eve as a Passover sacrifice, but for no persons in particular. (2) Ex. XII, 6; lit., 'between the evenings'. (3) To prevent it from congealing. (4) Before the blood of the *tamid*. (5) Ex. XII, 4.

b (1) Thus Rabbi connects the word with slaughter. But he also admits its Hebrew connotation of counting, and he thus points out that an intention for those who cannot eat it or who are not registered for it disqualifies the sacrifice only when it is expressed at the killing, but not when it is expressed at one of the other services (Tosaf.).

a disqualified?[1] [60*b*] Hence it surely refers [also] to one service,[2] and since the second clause refers [also] to one service, the first clause too refers [also] to one service!—What argument is this: the one is according to *its* nature, while the other is according to its nature: the second clause refers [also] to one service,[3] while the first clause refers either to one service or to two services.[4]

The scholars asked: What is the law of a Passover sacrifice which he killed at any other time of the year for its own purpose and for another purpose?[5] Does the other purpose come and nullify[6] its own purpose, and [thus] make it fit, or not?—When R. Dimi came,[7] he said, I stated this argument before R. Jeremiah: Since [slaughtering it] for its own purpose makes it fit at its own time, while [slaughtering it] for another purpose makes it fit at a different time,[8] then just as [the slaughtering] for its own purpose, which makes it fit at its own time, does not save[9] it from [the disqualifying effect of] another purpose,[10] so also [the slaughtering] for another purpose, which makes it fit at a different time, does not save it [from the disqualifying effect] of its own purpose, and it is unfit. Whereupon he said to me, It is not so: If you say thus in respect to another purpose,[11] that is because it operates in the case of all sacrifices;[12] will you say [the same where it is slaughtered] for its own purpose, seeing that it does not operate [as a cause of disqualification] in the case of all [other] sacrifices but only in the case of the Passover sacrifice alone?

What is [our decision] thereon?—Said Raba, A Passover sacrifice which he slaughtered at any other time of the year for its own purpose and for another purpose is fit. For it tacitly stands [to be killed] for its own purpose, yet even so, when he b kills it for another purpose[1] it is fit, which proves that the other purpose comes and nullifies its own purpose. Hence, when he slaughters it for its own purpose and for another purpose too, the other purpose comes and nullifies its own purpose. Said R. Adda b. Ahabah to Raba: Perhaps where he states it, it is different from where he does not state it?[2] For [if he kills it] for those who can eat it and for those who cannot eat it, it is fit, yet when he kills it for those who cannot eat it alone, it is disqualified. Yet why so? Surely it tacitly stands for those who can eat it?[3] Hence [you must admit that] where he states it, it is different from where he does not state it; so here too, where he states it, it is different from where he does not state it. Is this an argument? he rejoined. As for there, it is well: there, as long as he does not [expressly] overthrow it at the slaughtering, its tacit [destiny] is certainly to be killed for its own purpose. But here, does it tacitly stand for those who are [registered] to eat it? Perhaps these will withdraw and others will come and register for it, for we learned: They may register and withdraw their hands from it [the Paschal lamb] until he kills it.

The scholars asked: What is the law of a Paschal lamb which was slaughtered during the rest of the year with a change of its c owners?[1] Is a change of owner like a change of sanctity,[2] and it validates it; or not?—Said R. Papa, I stated this argument before Raba: Since a change of sanctity disqualifies it at its own time, and a change of owner disqualifies it at its own time: then just as a change of sanctity, which disqualifies it at its own time, validates it at a different time,[3] so a change of owner, which disqualifies it at its own time, validates it at a different time. But he said to me, It is not so: If you say thus in the case of a change of sanctity, [that is] because its disqualification is intrinsic,[4] and it is [operative]

a (1) Since even if only one desired to eat of it the whole animal must be killed, v. *infra* 61*a*. (2) I.e., *also* to one service. (3) This will not have quite the same meaning as the same phrase used before. There it obviously meant that it treats of one service *only*. Here however the meaning is this: even in the case of one service the sacrifice is fit, this law holding good in the case of both one service or two services. Thus, if this intention, viz., that he was killing it for eaters and non-eaters, was expressed at the slaughtering, the sacrifice is fit, because eaters were included. While it may also refer to two services, as explained on 60*a*, n. c7. (4) V. 60*a*, n. c6. (5) E.g., if a man dedicated a lamb for the Passover sacrifice a considerable time beforehand. Now it is stated *infra* 70*b* that if he kills it as a peace-offering at any time other than the eve of Passover it is fit; if as a Passover offering, it is unfit. (6) Lit., 'exclude from'. (7) From Palestine to Babylon (8) Lit., 'not in its own time'. (9) Lit., 'draw out'. (10) So that if it is killed both for its purpose and for another purpose, it is unfit. (11) That it disqualifies the Passover sacrifice even if it is also killed for its own purpose. (12) All sacrifices, if slaughtered for a purpose other than their own, are disqualified, either wholly, viz., in the case of a sin-offering and the Passover offering, which may then not be eaten, or in part, in the sense that they may be eaten, but their owners have not discharged their obligations and must bring another. Therefore it is logical that its disqualifying power should be so strong as to render of no avail the fact that it was slaughtered for its purpose too.

b (1) Before the eve of Passover. (2) The other purpose can nullify the *tacit* assumption that it stands for its own purpose, but it may be unable to nullify the *explicit* declaration that it is slaughtered for its own purpose too. (3) So that according to your argument it is the same as though he *explicitly* killed it for both.

c (1) The animal was set aside for a certain person and then slaughtered for a different person, but for its own purpose (Rashi). (2) I.e., like slaughtering it as a different sacrifice. (3) The text must be emended thus. (4) I.e., an illegitimate intention is expressed in respect to the sacrifice itself.

אלא לאו בעבודה אחת ומדסיפא בעבודה אחת רישא נמי בעבודה אחת מידי איריא הא כדאיתא והא כדאיתא סיפא בעבודה אחת ורישא או בעבודה אחת או בשתי עבודות איבעיא להו פסח ששחטו בשאר ימות השנה לשמו ושלא לשמו מהו מי אתי שלא לשמו ומפיק ליה מידי לשמו ומכשיר ליה או לא כי אתא רב דימי אמר אמריתא לשמעתא קמיה דר' ירמיה הואיל ולשמו מכשירו בזמנו ושלא לשמו מכשירו שלא בזמנו מה לשמו המכשירו בזמנו אין מוציאו מידי שלא לשמו אף שלא לשמו המכשירו שלא בזמנו אין מוציאו מידי לשמו ופסול ואמר לי לא אם אמרת בשלא לשמו שכן נוהג בכל הזבחים תאמר בלשמו שכן אינו נוהג בכל הזבחים אלא בפסח בלבד מאי הוי עלה אמר רבא פסח ששחטו בשאר ימות השנה לשמו ושלא לשמו כשר דהא סתמו לשמו קאי ואפילו הכי כי שחיט ליה שלא לשמו כשר אלמא אתי שלא לשמו ומפיק ליה מידי לשמו כי שחיט נמי לשמו ושלא לשמו אתי שלא לשמו ומפיק ליה מידי לשמו א"ל רב אדא בר אהבה לרבא דילמא שאני היכא דאמר מהיכא דלא אמר דהא לאוכליו ושלא לאוכליו כשר וכל היכא דשחיט ליה שלא לאוכליו לחודיה פסול ואמאי הא סתמא לאוכליו קאי אלא שאני היכא דאמר מהיכא דלא אמר הכי נמי שאני היכא דאמר מהיכא דלא אמר א"ל *מידי איריא בשלמא התם כמה דלא עקר ליה בשחיטה סתמיה ודאי לשמו קאי אלא הכא סתמיה לאוכליו קאי דילמא מימשכי הני ואתי אחריני ומימני עלויה (אחריני) דתנן *נמנין ומושכין את ידיהם ממנו עד שישחט איבעיא להו פסח ששחטו בשאר ימות השנה בשינוי בעלים מהו שינוי בעלים כשינוי קודש דמי ומכשיר ליה או לא אמר רב פפא אמריתא לשמעתא קמיה דרבא הואיל ושינוי קודש פוסלו בזמנו ושינוי בעלים פוסלו בזמנו מה שינוי קודש שפוסלו בזמנו מכשירו *לאחר זמנו אף שינוי בעלים שפוסלו בזמנו מכשירו *לאחר זמנו ואמר לי לא *אם אמרת בשינוי קודש שכן פסולו בגופו וישנו בארבע עבודות

וישנו

אלא לאו בעבודה אחת. אף בעבודה אחת ומתני' בין בעבודה אחת בין בשתי עבודות קאמר בעבודה אחת כגון בשחיטה מכשר ליה דמשום מקצת אוכלין לא פסלי ובשתי עבודות כגון שחטו לאוכליו וזרק שלא לאוכליו אף על גב דכולה זריקה שלא לאוכליו כשר משום דאין מחשבת אוכלים בזריקה: ומדסיפא אף בעבודה אחת קאמר רישא נמי אף בעבודה אחת קאמר. דלשמו ושלא לשמו פסול דאף בגמר דבריו אדם נתפס ורבי יוסי היא ולא ר' מאיר: סיפא בעבודה אחת. רישא אימא לך אי אף בעבודה אחת ורבי יוסי היא אי בשתי עבודות קאמר ולא בעבודה אחת ור"מ דאי בעבודה אחת כשר בלשמו ושלא לשמו דתפוס לשון ראשון: פסח בשאר ימות השנה. כגון שהפרישו קודם לכן ימים רבים וקיימא לן דכשר לשלמים בפירקין דלקמן (ד' ע:) ואם שחטו לפסח פסול דלאו זמניה ואי לשם שלמים שחטו כשר והיכא דשחטו לשמו ושלא לשמו מהו: אמריתא לשמעתא. למילף מדין בנין אב דפסול: אין מוציאו מידי שלא לשמו. לתפוס לשון אחרון לבדו ולהכשיר הנשחט שלא לשמו ולשמו: אף שלא לשמו כו' אין מוציאו מידי לשמו. לתפוס לשון אחרון ולהכשירו: שכן נוהג. פסולו בכל הזבחים או לפסול לגמרי בפסח וחטאת או לפסול מעולות לבעלים לשם חובה בשאר זבחים כדתנן (זבחים ד' ב.) כל הזבחים שנזבחו שלא לשמן כשרין לזרוק ולהקטיר אימורים ולאכול בשרן ולא עלו לבעלים לשם חובה חוץ מפסח וחטאת שפסולין לגמרי אלמא נוהג בכל הזבחים הלכך לא אתי שלא לשמו ומפיק לה מידיה לגמרי: תאמר. בפסול דלשמו שאינו נוהג אלא בפסח בשאר ימות השנה וכיון דקיל אתי שלא לשמו ומפיק ליה מידיה: מהיכא דלא אמר. דאף על גב דהיכא דלא אמר ברישא לשמו ואמר שלא לשמו כשר היכא דאמר פסול: דהא שלא לאוכליו פסול. ואף על גב דסתמיה לאוכליו קאי אתי שלא לאוכליו ומפיק ליה מסתמיה וכי אמר ברישא לאוכליו והדר שלא לאוכליו לא אתי שלא לאוכליו ומפיק ליה מידי לאוכליו וכשר: הכי השתא. ומי דמי סתמא דלאוכליו לסתמא דלשמו דתילפינהו מהדדי התם סתמא דלשמו אלים טובא דכל כמה דלא איעקר ליה שם פסח מיניה סתמא לשמו קאי ואפילו הכי כי אמר שלא לשמו מפיק ליה מסתמיה הלכך כי אמר לשמו ברישא נמי יליף מיניה דאתי שלא לשמו ומפיק ליה מידיה דלא שאני לן בין היכא דאמר מהיכא דלא אמר אבל לאוכליו מי אלים סתמא דידיה דסתמא ליקו להני אוכלין הא אי בעי מימשכו הני מיניה ומוכרין אותו לחבורה אחרת: דתנן נמנין עליו ומושכין ידיהן ממנו עד שישחט. הבא למנות עליו ימנה והרוצה למשוך ידיו ממנו שכבר נמנה עליו מושך הלכך לא אלים סתמא דלאוכליו ואף על גב דאתיא מחשבת שלא לאוכליו ומפקא ליה מסתמא ופסל ליה שאני לן היכא דאמר לאוכליו ברישא מהיכא דלא אמר דהתם טעמא משום דלא אלים סתמיה הוא ואיכא למימר אימשכו להו קמאי ואימנו עליה חולה וזקן ואישתחיט כוליה שלא לאוכליו וכי אמר לאוכליו ושלא לאוכליו הוו להו מקצת אוכלין ולא פסלי: ה"ג פסח ששחטו בשאר ימות השנה בשינוי בעלים מהו. ול"ג לשמו שחטו סתם בשינוי בעלים של ראובן היה ושחטו לשם שמעון אבל לא עקר שם פסח ממנו: כשינוי קודש. שלא לשמו: שינוי בעלים פוסל. בפסח בזמנו לגמרי וכן בחטאת ובשאר זבחים מונען מלעלות לשם חובה וכל תורת שינוי קודש עליהן בשמעתא קמייתא דזבחים: פסולו בגופו. שמחשבתו על עצמו של קרבן: וישנו בארבע עבודות. שחט או קיבל דמו (או *זרק או הלך) שלא לשמו פסול דבכל ארבע עבודות דם ילפינן ליה לפוסלה בפ"ק דזבחים (ד' ז.) שחיטה מזבח פסח שתהא זביחתו לשם פסח ושאר עבודות מועשית פסח שיהו כל עשיותיו לשם פסח:

וישנו

פסח ששחטו לשמו ושלא לשמו. אומר ר"י דמיבעיא ליה אפי' לר"מ דסבר בעלמא תפוס לשון ראשון דילמא הכא פסול דלשמו דאינו נוהג בכל הזבחים לא חשיב למיחל והוי עקירה או דילמא אפ"ה אמר תפוס לשון ראשון אליבא דר' יוסי הוה מצי למיבעי אפילו בשלא לשמו ולשמו אלא להכי נקט לשמו ושלא לשמו משום דבעיא אפילו אליבא דר"מ:

בשאר ימות השנה. היינו קודם שהגיע זמן הפסח כדפי' בקונטרס ולכך בעי עקירה לפי שעומד לפסח כשיבא ובכולה שמעתא חשיב ליה דקאי לשמו אבל לאחר הפסח משמע לקמן (ד' סד.) דספיקא הוי דקאמרינן ש"מ פסח בשאר ימות השנה בעי עקירה:

הכא נמי אתי שלא לשמו ומפיק מידי לשמו. וא"ת והא לשמו ושלא לשמו כשר לר"מ ולא אמרינן אתי שלא לשמו ומפיק מידי לשמו ושלא לשמו גרידא פסול אע"ג דסתמא לשמו קאי ואור"י דהתם היינו טעמא דהכשר לשמו נוהג בכל הזבחים הילכך כי אמר לשמו אלים למיחל טפי ולא אתי שלא לשמו ומפיק ליה אבל האי פסול דלשמו אינו נוהג בכל הזבחים ולהכי לא מקשה ליה אלא מלאוכליו ושלא לאוכליו דלא שייך אלא בפסח גרידא:

סתמו להני אוכלין קאי הני מימשכי כו'. הקשה ריב"א מה לנו אי לא קאי להני אוכלין מ"מ סתמא לאוכלין קאי או להני או לאחריני דסתמא לא לחולים או לזקנים קאי ואפ"ה שלא לאוכליו מפיק מלאוכליו ושלא לאוכליו נמי אמאי לא עקר לאוכליו דקאמר ברישא ואומר ר"י דכששוחטו לאוכליו ושלא לאוכליו אינו כשר אלא על ידי אותם אוכלין ששחט וחושב עליהן וסתמיה לאו להנהו אוכלין (א) והרי כאילו לא קאי לאוכליו:

וישנו

הפתוך שבסיד כו': איבעיא להו פסח בשאר ימות השנה לשם פסח ולשם שלמים מהו אתי שלא לשמו מפיק ליה מיד לשמו ומכשיר ליה או לא מפורש בתחלת שחיטת קדשים כי שלא לשמו בכל הזבחים פסול שלא עלו לבעלים לשם חובה ולשמו כשר ופסח בשאר ימות השנה שלא לשמו כשר ולשמו פסול זה ביניהם ופשיט ליה רבא מיניה דאתי שלא לשמו מפיק ליה מיד לשמו וכשר ודייק הכי דקאמר (לעולם) [דהא] בסתמא לשמו קאי וכי (מפרש) נשחט בשאר ימות השנה שלא לשמו נדחה לשמו וכשר כאע"פ שהזכיר עכשיו לשמו בא שלא לשמו ודחאו ונמצא הזבח כשר ואקשי' עליה רב אדא והא סתמא לאוכלין קאי ואי פריש שלא לאוכליו בלבד פסול אמאי נימא כאלו לאוכליו ושלא לאוכליו שחטו והיה כשר ודחה רבא ואמר לא דמי בשלמא פסח מעת שהקדישו לשם פסח ודאי נקבע לשם פסח וסתמו שם פסח עליו ואי אפשר לו [להפקיעו] מקדושתו אבל הני אוכלין מדבק דביקי ביה [כי ממשכו] הני ואתו אחרינא ונדחו קמאי לגמרי בערנא דאתו בתראי ופסח ליכא למימר הכי לפיכך שאני: איבעיא להו פסח ששחטו בשינוי בעלים בשאר ימות השנה כגון שהיה פסח זה לראובן ושחטו לשם שמעון מי נחשב זה אותו שינוי בעלים כשינוי קדש דהוה פסח ושינה אותו לשחטו לשם שלמים או לא ופשטי' שינוי קדש פוסל בזמנו. גרסי' בשחיטת קדשים אשכחן שינוי קדש שינוי בעלים מנא לן אמר רב פנחס אמר קרא ובשר זבח תודת שלמיו פי' כשם שאם שחט הפסח לשם שלמים פסול וזהו שינוי קדש הפוסל בזמנו כן אם שחט פסח ראובן לשם שמעון פסול כשם ששינוי קדש מכשירו שלא בזמנו כך שינוי בעלים מכשיר אותו שלא בזמנו. פריך מה לשינוי קדש שכן נפסל בשמו כי היה שמו פסח ונשחט לשם שלמים נמצא כי נשתנה ונעשה שינוי בגופו בזבח עצמו עוד נוהג שינוי קודש בארבע עבודות בשחיטה או בקבלה או בהולכה או בזריקה בכל אחת מאלו נפסל לאפוקי שינוי בעלים דאינו נפסל אלא בשחיטה בלבד כדתנן נמנין ומושכין ידיהן ממנו עד שישחוט אבל אם נשחט לשם בעלים אף על פי (שנשחט) [שנזרק] לשם

[או הלך או זרק כך יתכן להיות ועיין מה שכתבו התי"ט פרק ב' דזבחים מ"ו ד"ה שמחשבתם וכו' דדחוק לומר כפירש"י ותרע"ב דהתם:]

דהכי השתא כצ"ל

לקמן ד' סט: [יומא מט: גיטין כט.]

לשלא בזמנו כצ"ל זבחים דף ד.

הגהות הב"ח

(א) תוס' ד"ה סתמו וכו' לאו להנהו אוכלין קאי והרי:

או דילמא בשתי עבודות תנן ואפי' לר' מאיר דאמר תפוס לשון ראשון הני מילי בעבודה אחת אבל בשתי עבודות מודה דמיפסיל אמרי אהייא אי נימא אשלא לשמו ולשמו בין בעבודה אחת בין בשתי עבודות בין לר' מאיר בין לר' יוסי איפסיל ליה מקמייתא דהא לרבי יוסי *נמי אף בגמר דבריו אדם נתפס [נזיר ט: ע"ש] אית ליה אלא אלשמו ושלא לשמו מאי ת"ש הפסח ששחטו שלא לשמו וקבל והלך וזרק שלא לשמו היכי דמי אי נימא כדקתני למה לי עד דמחשב לכולהו מקמייתא איפסיל ליה אלא לאו הכי קתני *הפסח ששחטו שלא לשמו אי נמי שחטו לשמו וקבל והלך וזרק שלא לשמו אי נמי שחטו וקבל והלך לשמו וזרק שלא לשמו דהויא לה שתי עבודות אימא סיפא לשמו ושלא לשמו היכי דמי אי נימא בשתי עבודות היינו רישא אלא לאו בעבודה אחת ור' יוסי היא דאמר אף בגמר דבריו אדם נתפס לא לעולם בשתי עבודות ורישא דקאי בשחיטה וקא מחשב בשחיטה א"נ קאי בזריקה וקא מחשב בזריקה סיפא דקאי בשחיטה וקחשיב בזריקה דאמר הריני שוחט את הפסח לשמו לזרוק דמו שלא לשמו וקמ"ל דמחשבין מעבודה לעבודה והיינו בעיא דרב פפא ת"ש או שלא לשמו ולשמו פסול היכי דמי אי נימא בשתי עבודות השתא לשמו ושלא לשמו אמרת פסול שלא לשמו ולשמו מיבעיא אלא לאו בעבודה אחת ומדסיפא בעבודה אחת רישא נמי בעבודה אחת לא לעולם בשתי עבודות ובדין הוא דלא איצטריך ליה ואיידי דתנא לשמו ושלא לשמו תנא נמי שלא לשמו ולשמו תא שמע *שחטו שלא לאוכליו [לקמן סא.] ושלא למנויו לערלים ולטמאין פסול הכא פשיטא בעבודה אחת ומדסיפא בעבודה אחת רישא נמי בעבודה אחת מידי איריא הא כדאיתא והא כדאיתא סיפא בעבודה אחת רישא אי בעבודה אחת אי בשתי עבודות תא שמע *לאוכליו ושלא לאוכליו [שם] כשר היכי דמי אי נימא בשתי עבודות וטעמא דחשיב בזריקה דאין מחשבת אוכלין בזריקה הא בעבודה אחת כגון בשחיטה דמהניא ביה מחשבת אוכלין פסול והא קיימא לן מקצת אוכלין לא פסלא

אלא

רש"י

או דילמא בשתי עבודות תנן. אחת חישב לשמו ובשניה שלא לשמו והכא ליכא למימר תפוס לשון ראשון שהרי ארבעתן העבודות חשובות זו כזו ליפסול את הזבח באחת מהן ואפילו לרבי מאיר מיפסיל: ומהדר גמרא אהייא מהני ליפשט דסיפא דמתניתין קיימא קך בעיא: אי נימא אשלא לשמו. ברישא והדר לשמו הא בין לר' מאיר בין לר' יוסי אפילו בעבודה אחת מיפסיל לר' מאיר דהא אמר תפוס לשון ראשון ולרבי יוסי נמי מיפסיל דהא ר' יוסי אף בגמר אית ליה כלומר תחלת דבריו של אדם וסופן בכולן דעתו נתפסת וכולן מתקיימין: אלשמו ושלא לשמו. דאי בעבודה אחת נמי פסול ליה מתני' תו לא מיתוקמא כרבי מאיר דהא אמר תפוס לשון ראשון ולשון אחרון לא חייל: אי נימא כדקתני. שחט וקיבל והלך וזרק כולן שלא לשמו ולאו או קאמר למה לי בכולהו הא בחדא קי"ל בזבחי' בשמעתא קמייתא הזבח נפסל: לעולם. סיפא נמי דקתני לשמו ושלא לשמו בשתי עבודות ודקשיא לך היינו רישא לא תיקשי רישא מיירי דכי שחט חישב בה לשמו וכשזורק חישב בה שלא לשמו וסיפא מיירי דבשעת שחיטה חישב תרתי מחשבות חדא על השחיטה לשמו וחדא על הזריקה שלא לשמו: דאמר הריני שוחט לשמו. על מנת לזרוק שלא לשמו והכא ליכא למימר תפוס לשון ראשון דהא לעבודה אחריתי קאי לשון שני וקא משמע לן מתני' דמחשבין מעבודה לעבודה כלומר דמחשב בשעת עבודה זו על חברתה לעשותה במחשבת פסול נפסל מיד ואפילו לא עשה השניה במחשבת פסול כמו שחיטה: והיינו בעיא דרב פפא. דאמר מחשבים מעבודה לעבודה בשחיטת קדשים בפ"ק (ד' י:) דאמרינן התם מתקיף לה רב פפא דילמא הא קמ"ל דמחשבין מעבודה לעבודה: השתא לשמו ושלא לשמו. דעבודה ראשונה בכשרות אמרת פסול במחשבת עבודה שניה: שלא לשמו ולשמו מיבעיא. דכיון דנפסל בעבודה ראשונה מהיכן יחזור ויוכשר: אלא לאו בעבודה אחת. ותנא שלא לשמו ולשמו לאפוקי מדרבי מאיר דאמר תפוס לשון ראשון ותנא שלא לשמו ולשמו דלא תימא תפוס לשון אחרון דהא הדר ביה מקמא וכי שחיט אהאי בתרא קא שחיט קמ"ל דר' יוסי הוא דאמר בכל דבריו אדם נתפס ולא הדר ביה אלא אתרוייהו איכוון: ומדסיפא. שלא לשמו ולשמו בעבודה אחת קאמר דבשתי עבודות לא איצטריך: רישא. דלשמו ושלא לשמו נמי אף בעבודה אחת ור' יוסי היא: לעולם בשתי עבודות. ודקשי' לך פשיטא הא איפסיל ליה מעבודה קמייתא: איידי דתנא לשמו ושלא לשמו. לאשמעינן דמחשבין מעבודה לעבודה כדלעיל תנא נמי שלא לשמו ולשמו: שלא לאוכליו. לחולה ולזקן שאין יכולין לאכול כזית ואין בו מנויין אחרים אלא הן: פסול. דהא לפי אכלו כתיב (שמות יב) בהראוי לאכול: שלא למנויו. שנימנו עליו חבורה זו ושחטו לשם חבורה אחרת: לערלים. ישראל שמתו אחיו מחמת מילה והן פסולין מלאכול פסח דכתיב כל ערל לא יאכל בו (שם): טמאים. נמי אסורים בקדשים ובכרת הן על אכילתן: הכא פשיטא בעבודה אחת. כלומר אפילו בעבודה אחת ודלא כר' מאיר: מידי איריא. וכי ראיה היא זו: סיפא. דבמחשבה אחת מיירי ליכא לאוקומה אלא בעבודה אחת: רישא. דמיירי בשתי מחשבות איכא לאוקומא אי אף בעבודה אחת ודלא כר' מאיר: אי בשתי עבודות. ולא בעבודה אחת וכר' מאיר: לאוכליו ושלא לאוכליו. כדמפרש ואזיל: היכי דמי אי נימא בשתי עבודות. שחטו לאוכליו ע"מ לזרוק שלא לאוכליו ולטמאים דכשר: וטעמא מאי משום דאין מחשבת אוכלין. אין מחשבת פסול האוכלין כגון חולה וזקן פוסלת בזריקה דבשחיטה הוא דכתיבי אוכלין לפי אכלו תכוסו והיינו תשחטו כדמתרגמי' ושחטו ויכוס: ה"נ בעבודה אחת כגון בשחיטה דמהני' בה מחשבת אוכלין פסול. ואפי' כה"ג דאמר לאוכליו ושלא לאוכליו: והא קיימא לן. לקמן (ד' סא.): מקצת אוכלין. כגון הכא דנימנו בו ראויין לאכול ושחטו לשם כולן כשר דהא כולה שחיטה נמי משום אוכלין לריכה דלאי אפשר לכזית בשר בלא שחיטה ולקמן מפרש מאי שנא לשמו ושלא לשמו פסול ולאוכליו ושלא לאוכליו כשר:

תוספות

אבל בשתי עבודות אפי' ר' מאיר מודה. וא"ת והיכי מיתוקמא מתני' כר' מאיר הא קתני סיפא לטמאים ולטהורים כשר ואמאי נימא תפוס לשון ראשון ובעבודה אחת מיירי דאין מחשבת טמאים אלא בשחיטה וי"ל דמתני' מיירי כגון דקיימי קמיה טמאים וטהורים ואמר הריני שוחט לאלו דבענין אחר לא משכחת מקצת ערלה דלא פסלה לר' מאיר אליבא דניבא דאמר אינה לשחיטה אלא לבסוף:

אי בשתי עבודות היינו רישא. וא"ת ולימא דרישא איירי כששחט סתמא ולכך כשזרק שלא לשמו אמר הוכיח סופו על תחלתו אבל אם אמר בהדיא הריני שוחט לשמו ה"א דלא עקר שלא לשמו אפי' בשתי עבודות להכי איצטריך סיפא וי"ל דסברא הוא דבשתי עבודות אינו מועיל מפרש יותר מסתם:

והיינו בעיא דרב פפא. פי' הקונט' דחוק דנקט רב פפא ולא נקט ר' יוחנן דאמר התם בהדיא מחשבין מעבודה לעבודה ונראה לריב"א דגר' לעיל בעי רב פפא בעבודה אחת תנן ומסיק היינו בעיא דרב פפא פי' שפיר מתוקמא בעיא דרב פפא שאינו יכול לפושט' מן המשנה וכן מלא רבי בספר ישן וכן גר"ח ורשב"א מפרש והיינו בעיא דרב פפא מה ששאל בעבודה אחת תנן או בשתי עבודות הנך שתי עבודו' היינו כגון שוחט לשמו על מנת לזרוק שלא לשמו:

שלא לשמו ולשמו מיבעיא. וא"ת כי נמי אמרי' בעבודה אחת תיקשי ליה הכי השתא לשמו ושלא לשמו פסול שלא לשמו ולשמו מבעיא דאפי' ר' מאיר דפליג בלשמו ושלא לשמו בשלא לשמו ולשמו מודה דלכ"ע תפוס לשון ראשון וי"ל דהאי בעבודה אחת מיירי קא משמע לן כמו שפירש בקונ' דלא אזלינן בתר לשון אחרון [דוקא] לאפוקי מבן ננס דאית ליה בפרק בית שור (ד' קה.) תפוס לשון אחרון לגמרי לבטל הראשון ור"י מפרש דבעבודה אחת אתי שפיר דתני שלא לשמו ולשמו אגב לשמו ושלא לשמו כיון דשניהם בעבודה אחת אבל בשתי עבודות דרישא הפסול בזריקה וסיפא הפסול בשחיטה לא דמו אהדדי ולית ליה למתניי' אגב רישא:

שחטו שלא לאוכליו. פי' רש"י לחולה ולזקן ואין מנויין עליו אלא הן וקשה אם כן מאי איריא שלא לאוכליו אפי' סתם נמי פסול כיון שאין לו אוכלין ונראה דמיירי דיש נמי מנויים אחרים:

אילימא בב' עבודות טעמא דחשיב בזריקה. נראה לר"י דהכא איירי אליבא דרבה דאמר לקמן (ד' סא:) שחטו למולין על מנת שיתכפרו בו ערלים כשר דלרב חסדא דאמר פסול לא מצי מיירי בשתי עבודות מיהו לקמן משמע במסקנא דאף לרבה פסול:

פסח

עין משפט נר מצוה

טז א מיי' פרק ט"ו מהלכות פסולי מוקדשין הלכה א:
יז ב מיי' שם הלכה י:

רבינו חננאל

פסח ולשם שלמים או דלמא בשתי עבודות בשחיטה אמר לשם פסח ובקבלה אמר לשם שלמים. ודברי ר' מאיר דאמר בתחלת דבריו אדם מתפים ור' יוסי הוא דאמר אף בגמר דבריו אדם מתפים מפורשין הן במשנתנו בתמורה פ' חמישי האומר הרי זו תמורת עולה תמורת שלמים הרי זו תמורת עולה דברי ר' מאיר ר' יוסי אומר אם לכך נתכוון בתחלה אע"פ שאי אפשר לקרות שני שמות כאחת דבריו קיימין אם משאמר תמורת עולה נמלך ואמר תמורת שלמים הרי זו תמורת עולה ומפרשא דגמרי' אליבא דרבי מאיר דאמר בתחלת דבריו אדם מתפים לר' יוסי בדקי' ליה [אי] מהדר הוא דקא הדר ביה תפוס לשון ראשון ואי אמר לתמורת שניהם נתכוונתי דבריו קיימין מאי. ת"ש הפסח ששחטו שלא לשמו קבל והלך וזרק שלא לשמו או לשמו ושלא לשמו כו' היכי דמי אי נימא בעבודה אחת כדקתני למה לי עד דמחשב שלא לשמו בכולהו מקמייתא איפסל ליה לדברי הכל אלא לאו הכי קתני הפסח ששחטו שלא לשמו [או ששחטו לשמו] וקבל שלא לשמו כו' דהוה ליה שתי עבודות אחת לשמו ואחת שלא לשמו אי הכי אימא סיפא או לשמו ושלא לשמו ה"ד אי נימא בשתי עבודות היינו רישא למה לי למתני ליה תרי זימני אלא לאו בעבודה אחת שחטו לשם פסח ולשם שלמים ומתני' רבי יוסי היא דאמר אף בגמר דבריו אדם מתפים לפיכך תני פסול אבל לר' מאיר בתחלת דבריו מתפים וכשר ודחי' לא לעולם כולה מתני' בשתי עבודות רישא כגון דשחים ומחשב בשחיטה לשמו ומחשב שלא לשמו קבלה וכן בהולכה וכן בזריקה סיפא כגון דאמר בשחיטה הריני שוחטו לשם פסח לזרק דמו שתים שהן ארבע לשם שלמים שמעינן מינה דמחשבין מעבודה לעבודה והיינו בעיא דרב פפא הא איפשטא: ת"ש או שלא לשמו ולשמו פסול האי מאי אי אמרת דמתני' בשתי עבודות ומחייבי' באחת שלא לשמו ובאחרת לשמו היינו רישא דרישא והיא תחלת משנתנו דאמרי' דברי הכל פסול אי דקאי בעבודה ומחשב בעבודה אחרת היינו רישא אלא לעולם בעבודה אחת רישא נמי לשמו ושלא לשמו בעבודה אחת ובעיא דרב פפא קיימא ודחי' לא לעולם בשתי עבודות ומדין הוא וכו': ת"ש שלא לאוכליו ושלא למנויו לערלים וכו'. ת"ש שחטו לאוכליו ושלא [illegible] יהן עד שישחט כו' ואוקימנא שרין כשר אלא ודאי לעבודה הפתוך בשלג ביין המזוג בשלג והפתוך

לאוכליו וכו' כשר היכי דמי אי נימא בשתי עבודות כגון שחטו לאוכליו וזרק לשמו שלא לאוכליו טעמא דחשיב בזריקה והפיכך הוא כשר דאין מחשבת אוכלין בזריקה דתנן נמנין ומושכין את ידיהן עד שישחט כו' ואוקימנא מחלוקת למשוך אבל לימנות דברי הכל עד שישחט שנא' במכסת נפשות הכתוב הזהיר לשחוט על שנמנין בו הא אלו שוחט לאוכליו ושלא לאוכליו [פסול] והא קי"ל כל היכא דפתיכא פסולין לכשרין כשר אלא ודאי לעבודה כו' ומדסיפא כו' ובעיא דרב פפא לא איפשטא [illegible] בתחלת נגעים [illegible] הפתוך בשלג ביין המזוג בשלג והפתוך

a first expression;[1] [60a] or perhaps we learned [it only] in respect to two services, and even according to R. Meir, who said, 'Seize the first expression,' that applies only in the case of one service, but in the case of two services he agrees that it is disqualified?[2] —I will tell you: to which [case does this problem refer]? Shall we say, to [the case where it was] for another purpose [first] and [then] for its own purpose, then whether it was in connection with one service or in connection with two services, according to both R. Meir and R. Jose it was disqualified by the first [wrongful intention], for according to R. Jose too, he holds that a man is held responsible for his last words *also*?[3]—Rather, [the problem refers] to [where it was done] for its own purpose [first] and then for another purpose: what then?—Come and hear: IF A MAN SLAUGHTERED THE PASSOVER SACRIFICE FOR ANOTHER PURPOSE AND CAUGHT [THE BLOOD], AND WENT AND SPRINKLED IT FOR ANOTHER PURPOSE: how is it meant? Shall we say, [literally] as he teaches it,[4] why must he intend *all* of them [for a wrong purpose]? From the first it is disqualified! Hence he must teach thus: IF A MAN SLAUGHTERED THE PASSOVER SACRIFICE FOR ANOTHER PURPOSE, or even if he slaughtered it for its own purpose, but HE CAUGHT [ITS BLOOD], AND WENT AND SPRINKLED IT FOR ANOTHER PURPOSE,[5] or even if he slaughtered it, caught [its blood], and went [with it] for its own purpose, but SPRINKLED IT FOR ANOTHER PURPOSE, so that it is [a question of] two services.[6] Then consider the second clause: FOR ITS OWN PURPOSE AND FOR ANOTHER PURPOSE: how is it meant? Shall we say, in respect of two services: then it is identical with the first clause! Hence it must surely be in respect of one service, and this agrees with R. Jose, who maintained: A man is held responsible for his last words too!—No. After all
b it refers to two services,[1] but the first clause [discusses] where he is standing at [engaged in] the slaughtering and intends [with due purpose] in respect of the slaughtering, or again[2] he is standing at the sprinkling and intends [for another purpose] in respect of sprinkling.[3] While the second clause means when he is standing at the slaughtering and intends in respect of the sprinkling, when he [for instance] declares, 'Behold, I slaughter the Passover sacrifice for its own purpose, [but] to sprinkle its blood for another purpose'; and he [the Tanna] informs us that you can intend at one service for another service,[4] and that is R. Papa's question.[5]

Come and hear: OR FOR ANOTHER PURPOSE AND FOR ITS OWN PURPOSE, [IT] IS DISQUALIFIED. How is it meant? If we say, in the case of two services, [then] seeing that where [if the first is] for its own purpose and [the second is] for another purpose, you say that it is disqualified, is it necessary [to state it where it is first] for another purpose and [then] for its own purpose?[6] Hence it must surely refer to one service, and since the second clause refers to one service, the first clause too refers [also] to one service!—No, after all it refers [only] to two services, and logically indeed it is not required, but because he speaks of 'FOR ITS OWN PURPOSE AND FOR ANOTHER PURPOSE,' he also mentions 'FOR ANOTHER PURPOSE AND FOR ITS OWN PUR-
c POSE.[1]

Come and hear: If he killed it [the Passover sacrifice] for those who cannot eat it or for those who were not registered for it,[2] for uncircumcised[3] or for unclean persons,[4] it is disqualified. Now here it obviously refers to one service, and since the second clause refers to one service, the first clause too treats [also] of one service![5]—What argument is this? The one is according to *its* nature, while the other is according to *its* nature; the second clause [certainly] refers [only] to one service, while the first clause may refer either to one service or to two services.[6]

Come and hear: [If he killed it] for those who can eat it and for those who cannot eat it, it is fit. How is it meant? Shall we say, at two services:[7] and the reason [that it is fit] is because he intended it [for non-eaters] at the sprinkling, for there can be no [effective] intention of eaters at the sprinkling;[8] hence [if it were] at one service, e.g., at the slaughtering, where an intention with reference to eaters is effective, it would be disqualified,—but we have an established law that if some are eaters it is not

a (1) Where the two parts of a man's statement are mutually exclusive, regard the first only. (2) On the first hypothesis the Mishnah refers even to one service, and will certainly also hold good in the case of two services; while on the second hypothesis the Mishnah refers to two services *only*, but will not hold good in the case of one service; Rashi *infra* 60b. s.v. סיפא בעבודה אחת and as is evident from the context. (3) I.e., they too must be taken into account, but his first words certainly cannot be ignored. (4) Viz., that all four services were performed for another purpose. (5) [The text seems to be in slight disorder, v. D.S. The general meaning is, however, clear.] (6) I.e., this clause states the case of a legal purpose at one service and an illegal purpose at another service.

b (1) And still the two clauses are not identical as it goes on explaining. (2) [MS.M. omits: 'or again'.] (3) ['Slaughtering' and 'sprinkling' are taken merely as examples, the same applying to the other services. Each was performed with the due or undue intention, as the case may be, in respect of itself.] (4) And that such intention is taken into account, so that if it is illegitimate the sacrifice is disqualified. (5) Riba: that is why R. Papa asks his question, because the Mishnah affords no solution. Rashba: R. Papa's question as to whether the Mishnah may refer to two services is in such conditions, viz., where an illegitimate intention for one service is expressed in the course of another service. (6) For the very first intention is illegitimate and disqualifies it; how then is it to regain its validity? The same difficulty arises if the Mishnah refers to one and the same service, but then it can be answered that the Mishnah informs us in the first clause ('FOR ITS OWN PURPOSE AND FOR ANOTHER PURPOSE') that we do not determine the matter *purely* by his first words, and in the second clause ('FOR ANOTHER PURPOSE AND FOR ITS OWN PURPOSE') that the matter is not determined *purely* by his last words, but that due weight must be given to both.

c (1) For the sake of parallelism. (2) Every Paschal lamb required its registered consumers before it was slaughtered, in accordance with Ex. XII, 4. In the present instance he enumerated those for whom he was slaughtering it, all of whom, however, were incapable of eating through old age or sickness (Rashi: none others had registered for it; Tosaf.: others who were capable had also registered for it, but he ignored them in his declaration), or had not registered for this particular animal. (3) 'Uncircumcised' in this connection always means men whose brothers had died through circumcision, and they were afraid of a similar fate. These may not eat thereof, ibid. 48. (4) Who may likewise not eat it, being forbidden all sacred flesh. Lev. XXII, 4ff. (5) The Mishnahs printed on 59b and 61a are actually clauses of the same Mishnah. (6) I.e., either also to one service or exclusively to two services. And the question is, to which? (7) Thus: at the slaughtering he declared that it was for those who can eat, and at the sprinkling he declared that it was for those who cannot eat (R. Ḥan.). (8) I.e., an intention with respect to the eaters expressed at the sprinkling is of no account.

saith, [59b] *And the priest shall [have] offer[ed] the burnt offering,*[3] [implying], that which he has already offered.[4]

R. Shaman b. Abba said to R. Papa: According to you who maintain [that] he takes it up and keeps it overnight on the top of the altar, shall we arise and do a thing to the priests whereby they may come to a stumbling-block, for they will think it is of that day, and thus come to burn it?[5]—The priests are most careful, replied he.

R. Ashi said to R. Kahana—others state, R. Huna the son of R. Nathan [said] to R. Papa: But as long as the *emurim*[6] have not been burnt, the priests may not eat the flesh?[7] For it was taught: You might think that the priests should be permitted [to partake] of the breast and the thigh before the burning of the *emurim:* therefore it is stated, *And the priest shall burn the fat upon the altar,*[8] and then follows, *but the breast shall be Aaron's and his sons'*. And as long as the priests have not eaten [it], the owners obtain no atonement, for it was taught: *And they shall eat those things wherewith atonement was made:*[9] this teaches that the priests eat [it] and the owners obtain atonement!—Said he to him, Since it is im-
a possible,[1] they [the *emurim*] are treated[2] as though they were defiled or lost. For it was taught: You might think that if the *emurim* were defiled or lost, the priests have no right to the breast or the thigh, therefore it is stated, *'But the breast shall be Aaron's and his sons'*, in all cases.

R. Kahana opposed [two verses]: It is written, *neither shall the fat of My feast remain all night until the morning:*[3] [thus] it is only *'until the morning'* that *'it shall not remain all night,'* but it may be kept for the whole night;[4] but it is written, *and he shall burn thereon the fat of the peace-offerings,*[5] [implying,] after it complete all the sacrifices?[6] He raised the difficulty; and he himself answered it: That is where they were left over.[7]

R. Safra pointed out a contradiction to Raba: It is written, *neither shall the sacrifice of the feast of the Passover be left unto the morning:*[8] thus it is only *'unto the morning'* that *'it shall not be left,'* but it may be kept all night;[9] but it is written, *The burnt-offering of the Sabbath* [shall be burnt] *on its Sabbath,*[10] but not the burnt-offering of a weekday on the Sabbath, nor the burnt-offering of a weekday on a Festival?—Said he to him, R. Abba b. Ḥiyya has already pointed out this contradiction to R. Abbahu, and he answered him, We treat here of the case where the fourteenth falls on the Sabbath,[11] for the fats of the Sabbath may be offered on the Festival. Said he to him, Because the fats of the Sabbath may be offered on the Festival, we are to arise and assume that this verse is written [only] in respect of the fourteenth which
b falls on the Sabbath?[1] Leave the verse, he answered, for it is compelled to establish its own [particular] case.[2]

MISHNAH. IF A MAN SLAUGHTERED THE PASSOVER SACRIFICE FOR ANOTHER PURPOSE,[3] AND HE CAUGHT [THE BLOOD] AND WENT AND SPRINKLED IT FOR ANOTHER PURPOSE;[4] OR FOR ITS OWN PURPOSE AND FOR ANOTHER PURPOSE; OR FOR ANOTHER PURPOSE AND FOR ITS OWN PURPOSE;[5] IT IS DISQUALIFIED. HOW IS 'FOR ITS OWN PURPOSE AND FOR ANOTHER PURPOSE' MEANT? IN THE NAME OF THE PASSOVER SACRIFICE [FIRST] AND [THEN] IN THE NAME OF A PEACE-OFFERING. 'FOR ANOTHER PURPOSE AND FOR ITS OWN PURPOSE' [MEANS] IN THE NAME OF A PEACE-OFFERING [FIRST] AND [THEN] IN THE NAME OF THE PASSOVER-OFFERING.

GEMARA. R. Papa[6] asked: Did we learn [of a dual intention expressed even] in respect to one service,[7] or did we learn [only of a dual intention expressed] at two separate services? Did we learn [of a dual intention expressed even] in respect of one service, this being in accordance with R. Jose, who maintained, A man is responsible for[8] his last words too;[9] for if [it agreed with] R. Meir, surely he said, Seize [i.e., determine the matter by] the

(3) Lev. XIV, 20; the bracketed additions show the meaning which the verse is capable of bearing, by treating הֶעֱלָה as a pluperfect, beside its usual and obvious meaning. (4) Hence although the sin-offering should come before the burnt-offering, yet the possible meaning of this verse teaches that even if the order is reversed it is valid. Therefore we can explain the present Baraitha as meaning that he had already sacrificed his burnt-offering. (5) During the night the limbs of the sacrifices of the previous day are burnt, all *before* the *tamid* of the following morning. Here, however, the animal sin-offering which was kept untouched overnight must be burnt *after* the morning *tamid*, whereas the priest may confuse it with the rest and burn it before. (6) V. Glos. (7) And in consequence atonement is incomplete, so that the owner may not partake of the Passover sacrifice in any case, if his sin-offering is left overnight. (8) Lev. VII, 31. (9) Ex. XXIX, 33.

a (1) To burn the *emurim* after the evening *tamid*, on account of the affirmative precept of 'completion'. (2) Lit., 'they (the Sages) treated them'. (3) Ex. XXIII, 18. (4) I.e., the priest has the whole night in which to burn the fat, providing that nothing is left by the morning. (5) Lev. VI, 5. (6) V. *supra* 58*b*. Thus nothing may be done after the evening *tamid*. (7) Of the sacrifices whose blood was sprinkled *before* the evening *tamid*. Immediately the blood is sprinkled the fat etc. is ready for burning on the altar, and therefore even if it is delayed, its ultimate burning during the night is regarded as following the *tamid* of the previous *morning*, not that of the evening. (8) Ex. XXXIV, 25. (9) During which the altar portions of the Passover sacrifice are burnt. Although these, strictly speaking, belong to a sacrifice which has been offered on a weekday, i.e., the fourteenth, yet they may be burnt on the night of the Festival. (10) Num. XXVIII, 10. (11) I.e., only then is the implication of the first verse applicable.

b (1) Surely there is no warrant for this limitation. (2) Since there is a contradiction, the verse itself proves that it can only relate to this particular instance. (3) Lit., 'not for its own name', i.e., as a different sacrifice. E.g., when he killed it he stated that it was for a peace-offering, not for a Passover sacrifice. (4) Slaughtering the sacrifice, catching the blood, going with it to the side of the altar where it is to be sprinkled, and sprinkling it, are regarded as four distinct services, any of which, if performed with an illegal intention, disqualifies the Passover sacrifice. (5) I.e., one of the services was for its own sake and another was for a different purpose, in the order stated. (6) Rashal reads: Raba. (7) I.e., even if he declared at one of the services, e.g., the slaughtering, that he was doing it for its own purpose and for another purpose. (8) Lit., 'seized'. (9) V. *supra* 53*b*. Hence since his last words were illegal, the sacrifice is disqualified.

יא א מיי' פ"ט מהלכות מעשה קרבנות הלכה י"א:
יב ב מיי' פ"י שם הלכה ה:
יג ג מיי' פ"א מהלכות תמידין הלכה ה וס"א מהלכות ק"פ הלכה ח:
יד ד שם הלכה ז:
טו ה מיי' פט"ו מהל' פסולי המוקדשין הלכה ג הלכה יח וס"ד מהל' ק"פ הלכה א:
[טז] [ו] מיי' פרק י"ג מהלכות פסולי מוקדשין הלכה ה' [מהל' נדה]:

עשאום כמי שנטמאו או אבדו · למאן דאמר (לקמן דף עז:) אין הציץ מרצה על העולין ניחא הא דנקט הכא שנטמאו או אבדו אבל בריית' דלקמן (דף פ:) על מה הציץ מרצה על הדם ועל החלב נ"ל הואיל ומדרבנן לא מרצה הוי כאילו אבדו האימורין :

והעלה הכהן את העולה ואת המנחה וגו' · בפר חטאת כתיב ומדהוה ליה למיכתב ואת העולה יעלה וכתיב והעלה משמע אפילו הבאה העולה קודם לחטאת יכפר : דסברי דיומא היא · כשמקטירים כל הלילה אברים שניתותרו מקרבנות שנשחטו ונזרק דמן קודם לתמיד ויראו את האברים הללו יהו

ויקרא יד

והעלה הכהן את העולה שהעלה כבר אמר ליה רב שמן בר אבא לרב פפא לדידך דאמרת מעלה ומלינה בראשו של מזבח קיימין *ועבדינן מילתא לכהנים דאתו בה לידי תקלה דסברי דיומיה הוא ואתו לאקטורי אמר ליה *כהנים זריזין הן אמר ליה רב אשי לרב כהנא ואמרי לה רב הונא בריה דרב נתן לרב פפא והא כמה דלא מתקטרי אמורין כהנים לא מצו אכלי בשר דתניא *יכול יהו כהנים רשאין בחזה ושוק קודם הקטרת אמורין תלמוד לומר והקטיר הכהן את החלב המזבחה והדר והיה החזה לאהרן ולבניו וכמה דכהנים לא אכלי בשר בעלים לא מתכפרי דתניא *ואכלו אותם אשר כפר בהם מלמד שהכהנים אוכלים ובעלים מתכפרין אמר ליה כיון דלא אפשר עשאום כמי שנטמאו או שאבדו דתניא יכול נטמאו אמורין או שאבדו לא יהו כהנים זכאין בחזה ושוק תלמוד לומר והיה החזה לאהרן ולבניו מכל מקום. רב כהנא רמי כתיב לא ילין חלב חגי עד בקר עד בוקר הוא דלא ילין הא כל הלילה כולה ילין וכתיב והקטיר עליה חלבי השלמים *עליה השלם כל הקרבנות כולן הוא מותיב לה והוא מפרק לה בשנתותרו רמי לי' רב ספרא *לרבא כתיב לא ילין לבקר זבח חג הפסח לבקר הוא דלא ילין הא כל הלילה ילין והכתיב *עולת שבת בשבתו ולא עולת חול בשבת ולא עולת חול ביום טוב אמר ליה כבר רמייה ניהליה רב אבא בר חייא לר' אבהו ושני ליה הכא בארבעה עשר שחל להיות בשבת עסקינן *דחלבי שבת קריבין ביום טוב אמר ליה משום דחלבי שבת קריבין ביום טוב אנן ניקו ונימא ליה דהאי קרא בארבעה עשר שחל להיות בשבת הוא דכתיב אמר ליה *שבקיה לקרא דהוא דחיק ומוקים אנפשיה: **מתני'** *הפסח ששחטו שלא לשמו וקבל והלך וזרק שלא לשמו או [ו]לשמו ושלא לשמו או שלא לשמו ולשמו פסול כיצד לשמו ושלא לשמו לשם פסח ולשם שלמים שלא לשמו ולשמו לשם שלמים ולשם פסח: **גמ'** בעי *רב פפא בעבודה אחת תנן או בשתי עבודות תנן בעבודה אחת תנן ורבי יוסי היא דאמר אף בגמר דבריו אדם נתפס דאי ר"מ הא אמר תפוס לשון ראשון או

(ויקרא ו · ויקרא ז · שם ז · שם · שמות כט · ויקרא ז · שמות כג · ויקרא ג · שמות לד · במדבר כח)

יכול נטמאו או שאבדו לא יהו הכהנים כו' · הכי סלקא מסקנא הכא דאי לא אכלי כהנים לא מכפרי בעלים ולא משתרו לאכול בקדשים ומקשה ריב"א דבהאשה רבה (יבמות דף צ.) אמר ת"ש דם שנטמא וזרקו בשוגג הורצה במזיד לא הורצה והא הכא דמדאורייתא לרצויי מרצי כו' ומשני מאי לא הורצה להתיר בשר באכילה אבל בעלים מתכפרין אלמא אף על גב דבשר אינו נאכל בעלים מתכפרין וי"ל דהיכא דחזי לאכילה מדאורייתא מתכפרין והכא בעי למימר דכל כמה דלא חזו כהנים לאכילת בשר (א) לא מתכפרים בעלים ותימה קשה מכמה בשר היאך זורק את הדם הא אין לשער שעת היתר לכהנים ונראה לפרש דכל זמן דחזי בשר לאכילה לא מתכפרי בעלים עד שיאכלו כהנים אבל אם נטמא אחרי כן או יצא או נעשה נותר מתכפרי בעלים :

ולא עולת חול ביו"ט · הקשה ריב"א דהא קרא בשבת כתיב דחמיר אבל ביו"ט דקיל מנא לן דלא קרבה וי"ל דאתיא כרבי עקיבא דאמר בסוף אלו קשרים (שבת דף קיד.) עולת שבת לימד על חלבי שבת שקרבין ביו"ט ומשמע ליה קרא עולת שבת זו בשבת אחרת דהיינו יו"ט של שבת בי"ט מכלל דשל חול בי"ט לא קרבה וקשה לר' עקיבא תיפוק לי' דחלבי שבת קריבין בי"ט מקרא הכא דלא ילין הא כל הלילה ילין שהפסח מיתוקם בארבעה עשר שחל להיות בשבת ותימה לר"י הא קרא בנותר דבשר מיירי דהא לקמן (דף סג:) מחייב שוחט על חמץ אחד מבני חבורה מדכתיב לא ילין בתריה דמשמע הני דקיימין עלי' בלא ילין וכל הלילה ילין כדר' עקיבא אוקימנא לסוגיא דהכא ושמעינן ליה לר' עקיבא דפסח נאכל כל הלילה עד שעת חפזון ואיכא למימר דמשמע ליה למסדר הש"ס דקרא בכל הזבח מיירי בין בבשר ובין באימורין ומדלא כתיב חלב כמו גבי חלב חגי ומדלא כתיב גבי אכילה דואכלו את הבשר כדכתב התם לא תותירו ש"מ דבתרווייהו משתעי:

בארבעה עשר שחל להיות בשבת עסקינן · בירושלמי דייק מקרא דלא ילין חלב חגי כה"ג ומוקי לה נמי ר' אבהו בי"ד שחל להיות בשבת ופריך דלא מצי לאוקמי בשבת דחגי כתיב דהיינו חגיגה הבאה עם הפסח דלא דחיא שבת כדאמר לקמן באלו דברים (דף סט:) ומפרש דה"ק שמרהו שלא יבא לידי בל ילין שיקריבהו מבעוד יום בשעה הראויה לו ותימה על ירושלמי דפריך מינה דהאי קרא דחלב חגי דבחגיגת חמשה עשר מיירי כדמוכח באלו דברים הקשה רשב"א לבן תימא דדריש לקמן באלו דברים (דף ע.) חגיגה הבאה עם הפסח הרי היא כפסח דזבח חג זה חגיגה היכי מיתוק' האי קרא בשבת הא מודה דלא דחיא שבת כדמוכח התם *וי"ל דבן תימא יסבור כר' ישמעאל דאמר באלו קשרים (שבת דף קיד:) דחלבי חול קריבין בי"ט אי נמי בן תימא יפרש שמרהו שלא יבא לידי בל ילין כדמפרש בירושלמי :

דאי ר' מאיר האמר תפוס לשון ראשון · אור"י *דרבא לטעמיה דאית ליה דפליגי בתפוס לשון ראשון דאמרינן בפ"ב דזבחים (דף ל.) עדיין היא מחלוקת פירוש אפילו בתמורת עולה ושלמים פליג ר"מ ובלאו הכי הך דיוקא דהכא לא מיתוקם אלא אליבא דרבא דמייתי לקמן בפירקין (דף סג.) גבי אחרים אומרים הקדים מולים לערלים כו' וסבר איכא לשחיטה אלא לבסוף וכדרבא דאמר עדיין היא מחלוקת ופליגי בתפוס לשון ראשון אפילו בכי האי גוונא אף על גב דאיכא לשחיטה אלא לבסוף וברגע אחרון יש לשניהם להול וסבר ר"מ התם תפוס לשון ראשון אע"פ שלא חל בשעה שאמר דלרבה ואביי דלקמן דסבירא להו דישנה לשחיטה מתחלה ועד סוף חיילי תרווייהו אפילו לר"מ כמו שנאמר לקמן וא"כ לא יכשיר הכא לר"מ לשמו ושלא לשמו אפי' בעבודה אחת :
אבל

סבורין שגם אלה ניתותרו ורואין להקטירם היום ויקטירם ועברי אעשה דהשלמה : זריזין הן · והמעלן שם יודיע לאחיו הכהנים ויזהרו בהן : אמר ליה רב אשי כו' · אדרב פפא פריך דאמר מלינן : מכדי כל כמה דלא מקטרי אמורין · דחטאת כהנים בשר החטאת לא מצי אכלי ובעלים לא הויא להו כפרה ועדיין מחוסר כפורים הוא והיאך יאכל בקדשים : בחזה ושוק · הנתונים לכהנים מן השלמים : ואכלו אותם · במלואים כתיב : אשר כופר בהם · כתב כפרה גבי אכילה למימרא דאף באכילה תלויה כפרה : כיון דלא אפשר . לאקטורינהו האידנא משום עשה דהשלמה עשאום כמי שנטמאו או שאבדו ומשתרו כהנים באכילת בשר והויא כפרה לבעלים : הא כל הלילה ילין · למטה ומעלן ומקטירן כל הלילה ואינו נפסל אלא אם כן מלאן בעלות השחר כשהוא למטה אלמא כל הלילה ראוי להקטיר : והכתיב עליה השלם · דמשמע שלא יתעכב דבר אחר תמיד של בין הערבים : כשנתותרו · מקרבנות שנזרק דמן קודם תמיד ולא הספיקו להקריב דכיון דנראה להקרבה קודם לכן על תמיד של שחר הוא מושלם : הא כל הלילה ילין · ויקטירנו בלילי י"ט ואע"פ שנותר מקרבן של חול דהא י"ד שנזרק דם הפסח בו חול הוא : ואנן ניקו כו' · קושיא היא : שבקי' לקרא דהוא דחיק ומוקי אנפשיה · מדקשו קראי אהדדי על כרחיך קראי גופייהו מוקמי אנפשייהו הכי :

מתני' הפסח ששחטו שלא לשמו · לשם שלמים : או קיבל או הלך או זרק שלא לשמו · שבארבע עבודות הללו הפסח נפסל במחשבתן אם לפסול אם לפגל כדיליף בשמעתא קמייתא דזבחים (דף ד.) : או לשמו ושלא לשמו · בגמרא מפרש אי במחשבת עבודה אחת קאמר אי במחשבת שתי עבודות כגון קיבל לשמו וזרק שלא לשמו : פסול · דכתיב זבח פסח הוא שתהא זביחתו לשם פסח וכתיב הוא למעוטי נשחט שלא לשמו :

גמ' בעבודה אחת תנן · וחישב בה לשמו ושלא לשמו ואפ"ה קתני פסול ור' יוסי היא דאמר במסכת תמורה (דף כה.) אף בגמר דבריו אדם נתפס דבוק : דאי ר' מאיר האמר תפוס לשון ראשון · במס' תמורה (ג"ז שם) גבי האומר הרי זו תמורת עולה תמורת שלמים ר"מ אומר הרי זו תמורת עולה ר' יוסי אומר דבריו קיימים ותרעה עד שתומם ותמכר ויביא בדמי חציה עולה ובדמי חציה שלמי':
או

רבינו חננאל

עמהן וקימא לן דאפילו חטאת העוף קודמת לעולת בהמה ופריק דבא אין כל החטאות קודמות לעולות הבאות עמהן ולפי' עולת מצורע שאם הקדים העולה לחטאת כיפר שנאמר והעלה הכהן את העולה ואת המנחה מאי העולה שהעלה כבר: אמר ליה רב אדא לרב פפא וכי עבידי מילתא דאתי בה לידי תקלה הני אמורין דאמרת מעלן ומלינן על גבי המזבח ניחוש דלמא סברי דיומיה נינהו ואתו לאקטורינהו ופריק כהנים זריזין הן ולא אתו לידי תקלה והא כמה דלא מתקטרי אימורין לא מיתכיל בשר ולא[סלקא] לבעלי' טהרה שנאמר ואכלו אותם אשר כפר בהם מלמד שהכהנים אוכלין ובעלים מתכפרין ופרקי' כיון דלא אפשר להקטיר לאימורין הללו עשאום כמי שנטמאו או שאבדו הכהנים אוכלין ובעלים מתכפרין נטמאו אימורין: רב כהנא רמי כתיב לא ילין חלב חגי עד בקר: [הא] כל הלילה ילין ויקטיר איזו שעה שיודמן לו שיקטיר מן הלילה יקטיר והכתיב

[נ"ל לרבא וכ"ה בילקוט כנהם רמז תתמ"ב ופי' משפטים רמז שנ"ה וידוע דרך ספרא הא"ל רבה משה ספיר דקאמרה שבת קה: וכן בצאר דוכתי וכוה אתי נמי ספיר שכתיב הכא כבר רמייה ניהליה ראב"ח לר' אבהו מאתא"כ רב כיס זמן מוכח קודם לר' אבהו]

[זבחים פט:] [שבת כ. וש"נ] [יבמות צ. יומא סח:] [לעיל נח. יומא לג.] [לקמן סג: שבת כד:] [שבת קיד.] [קדושין מח. נדה נג.] [זבחים יג.] [ועי' תוס' לקמן ע. סד"ה לא] [גי' תוס' זה: בפי' רבא ובן מלאתי בכ"ב וכמהרש"א]

הגהות הב"ח
(א) תוס' ד"ה יכול וכו' י"ל וכו' דכל כמה דלא חזו כהני' לאכילת בשר. נ"ב פי' אפילו מדאורייתא :

גליון הש"ס
גמ' והכתיב עולת שבת. עי' שבת דף כ"ד ע"א תד"ה למאי, וביומא דף מו ע"א תוד"ה אבל ול"ע:

הקטיר עליה חלבי השלמים עליה השלם כל הקרבנות תנא כל הקרבנות עם תמיד של שחר הן קרבים קודם תמיד של בין הערבים ופריק באותן החלבים שנותרו מן היום מקריבין כל הלילה והזהירה תורה לא ילין מכל אותן החלבים עד הבקר : רמי ליה רב ספרא לרבא כתיב לא ילין לבקר זבח חג הפסח לבקר הוא דלא ילין הא כל הלילה כשרין להקרבה והא הפסח נשחט בארבעה עשר הוא וחל הלילה שהוא לילי חמשה עשר יום טוב הוא וכתיב עולת שבת בשבתו ולא עולת חול בשבת ולא עולת שבת בחול ופרקי' האי קרא כתיב לא ילין לבקר זבח חג הפסח ודיקינן מינה לבקר הוא דלא ילין הא כל הלילה ילין כלומר יקריב לילי חמשה עשר אע"פ שהוא יו"ט בארבעה עשר שחל להיות בשבת עסקינן דחלבי שבת קריבין ביו"ט כלומר דברים הנשחטין בשבת וחלביהן קריבין ביום טוב : אמר ליה רבא תיובא ליה לקרא דבארבעה עשר שחל להיות בשבת כתיבת א"ל שבקיה לקרא כיון דלית ליה דרשה אחרינא הוא דחיק ומוקים נפשיה בהכי : מתני' הפסח ששחטו שלא לשמו כו' בעי רב פפא בעבודה אחת מאלו העבודות אמר לשמו

הגהות מהר"ב רנשבורג
רש"י ד"ה והעלה הכהן וכו' בפר חטאת. נ"ל בתר העולה : דתני' יכול נטמאו אמורין. סרמכים בזמנים כרייתא זאם עיין נ"ית דף כ:

*יאוחר דבר שנאמר בו בערב ובין הערבים לדבר שלא נאמר בו בערב אלא בין הערבים בלבד אי הכי קטרת ונרות נמי נקדמו לפסח יאוחר דבר שנאמר בו בערב ובין הערבים לדבר שלא נאמר בו אלא בין הערבים בלבד שאני התם דמיעט רחמנא אותו *דתניא °מערב ועד בקר *תן לה מדתה שתהא דולקת מערב עד בוקר דבר אחר אין לך עבודה שכשירה מערב עד בוקר אלא זו בלבד מאי טעמא אמר קרא °יערוך אותו אהרן ובניו מערב עד בקר אותו מערב עד בוקר ואין דבר אחר מערב עד בוקר ואיתקש קטרת לנרות ותניא כי קושיין *תמיד קודם לקטרת קטרת קודמת לנרות ונרות קודמות לפסח יאוחר דבר שנאמר בו בערב ובין הערבים לדבר שלא נאמר בו אלא בין הערבים בלבד והא כתיב אותו האי אותו מיבעי ליה למעוטי עבודה שבפנים ומאי ניהו קטרת סלקא דעתך אמינא הואיל וכתיב °ובהעלות אהרן את הנרות בין הערבים יקטירנה אימא נדליק נרות ברישא והדר נקטיר קטורת מיעט רחמנא אותו אלא בין הערבים יקטירנה למה לי הכי קאמר רחמנא בעידן דמדלקת נרות תהא מקטרא קטרת תנו רבנן *אין לך דבר שקודם לתמיד של שחר אלא קטרת בלבד שנאמר בה בבקר בבקר ויוקדם קטרת דבר שנאמר בו בבקר בבקר לדבר שלא נאמר בו אלא בקר אחד ואין לך דבר שמתעכב אחר תמיד של בין הערבים אלא *קטרת ונרות *ופסח ומחוסר כפורים בערב הפסח שטובל ואוכל את פסחו לערב רבי ישמעאל בנו של רבי יוחנן בן ברוקא אומר אף מחוסר כפורים בשאר ימות השנה שטובל ואוכל בקדשים לערב °בשלמא לתנא קמא יבא עשה דפסח שיש בו כרת וידחה עשה דהשלמה שאין בו כרת אלא לר' ישמעאל בנו של ר' יוחנן בן ברוקה מאי אולמיה דהאי עשה מהאי עשה אמר רבינא אמר רב חסדא הבא בחטאת העוף עסקינן שאין למזבח אלא דמה רב פפא אמר אפילו תימא בחטאת בהמה *מעלה ומלינה בראשו של מזבח והאיכא אשם בשלמא לרב פפא היינו דמלין לה אלא לרב חסדא מאי איכא למימר אמרי שקרב אשמו והאיכא עולה וכ"ת *עולה לא מעכבא והתניא *ר' ישמעאל בנו של רבי יוחנן בן ברוקא אומר כשם שחטאתו ואשמו מעכבין אותו כך עולתו מעכבתו וכי תימא בשקרבה עולתו ומי קרבה עולתו קודם לחטאתו והתניא °והקריב את אשר לחטאת ראשונה מה תלמוד לומר אם ללמד שתהא קודמת לעולה הרי כבר נאמר °ואת השני יעשה עולה כמשפט אלא זה בנה אב *לכל חטאות שיהו קודמות לכל עולות הבאות עמהן וקי"ל דאפילו חטאת העוף קודמת לעולת בהמה אמר רבא שאני עולת מצורע דרחמנא אמר והעלה

(שמות כז) (שם) (שם ל) (ויקרא ה) (שם)

רש"י

יאוחר דבר כו' · טעמא דרישא קא מפרש תמיד קודם לפסח דדין הוא שיאוחר הפסח שנאמר בו בערב ובין הערבים תזבח את הפסח בערב (דברים טז) ושחטו אותו וגו' (שמות יב) לתמיד שלא נאמר בו אלא את הכבש השני תעשה בין הערבים (במדבר כח): אי הכי קטרת ונרות נמי ליקדמו לפסח · משום האי טעמא גופיה יאוחר דבר כו' דבקטרת ונרות חד בין הערבים כתיב ובהעלות אהרן את הנרות בין הערבים יקטירנה (שמות ל) ובין הערבים אתרוייהו קאי: דמיעט רחמנא. גבי נרות: אותו מערב ועד בקר ואין אחר מערב ועד בקר · ואין לך עבודה כשירה אחריה להתחיל: תן לה מדתה · חצי לוג לכל נר דאין לך ליל ארוך שלא יהא לך בה כשיעור: ואתקש קטרת לנרות · מה נרות אין עבודה כשירה אחריה אף קטרת אין עבודה כשירה אחריה: תמיד קודם לקטרת וקטרת קודם לנרות · טעמא מפרש בסדר יומא בפ' אמר להן הממונה: ההוא למעוטי עבודה שבפנים · ההוא אותו לאו למעוטי פסח אתא שהיא עבודת חוץ דמסתברא דכי קא ממעיט עבודת פנים דכוותה קממעיט נרות עבודת פנים וקטרת עבודת פנים: תהא מיקטרא קטרת · כבר תהא מקוטרת: אין לך כל דבר באשים קודם לתמיד של שחר אלא קטורת שנאמר בה בפרשת ואתה תצוה בבקר בבקר ובתמיד לא כתיב אלא חד בקר: ומחוסר כפורים · כגון מצורע או זב ששכח ולא הביא כפרתו קודם לתמיד ואם לא יביאנה לא יאכל פסח דמחוסר כפורים אסור בקדשים וענוש כרת: שטובל · ואע"פ שטבל אתמול בשביעי שלו צריך לטבול אחר שהביא כפרתו דתנן בחומר בקודש (דף כא:) האונן והמחוסר כפורים צריכים טבילה לקודש: בשאר ימות השנה · אם הביא שלמי נדבה קודם התמיד והוא היה מחוסר כפורים ואם לא יביא כפרתו לא יאכל את שלמיו דכתיב ואכלו אותם אשר כופר בהם אלמא אכילת קדשים עשה היא בין הנאכלים לכהנים בין הנאכלים לישראל: דהשלמה. עליה השלם: האי עשה (*דהשלמה) מהאי עשה (*דאכילת קדשים): הכא · דקא"ר ישמעאל אף מחוסר כפורים במצורע עני קאמר שמביא חטאת העוף ונאכלת לכהנים ואין בה הקטרה ועשה דהשלמה גבי הקטרה כתיב וטהרה של מחוסרי כפרה תלויה בחטאת כדכתיב (ויקרא יב) והקריבו לפני ה' וכפר עלי' ובחטאת קאי ביולדת: מעלה ומלינה בראש המזבח · כדכתיב והקריבו לפני ה' וכפר עליה ולמחר יקטירנה לאחר תמיד של שחר ולינה אינה פוסלת בראש המזבח כדאמר בזבחים בפ' המזבח מקדש (דף פז.) °לד"ה דלא ירדו: והא איכא אשם מצורע · דלא אתי עוף: וכ"ת אשם לא מעכב · לא גר' דהיכי תיסק אדעתין דלא מעכב הרי עיקר טהרה תלויה בו שהרי נותן מדמו על גבי בהונות: בחטאת ואשם פשיטא לן דמעכבי טהרה לאכילת קדשים חטאת כדאשכחן ביולדת אשם שהרי ממנו לבהונות: ואת השני · בתרי' דההוא קרא כתיב בשבועת ביטוי וממילא ידעי' כיון דהאי שני עולה הוי חטאת הוה ראשון: זה בנה אב · הבנין הזה בנה הכתוב אב ללמד לכל חטאות שיקדמו לעולות הבאות עמהן: וקיימא לן · בזבחים בפרק כל התדיר (דף צ.) דהאי בנין אב לא איצטריך אלא לחטאת העוף הבאה עם עולת בהמה כגון יולדת עשירה שמביאה עולתה בהמה וחטאתה עוף שתקדים חטאת לעולה:

תוספות

יאוחר דבר כו' · אע"ג דתמיד תדיר איצטריך למיכתב דה"א שהפסח יקדים משום עליה השלם: קטרת ונרות נקדמו לפסח · הקשה ריב"א והלא בנרות כתיב נמי מערב ועד בקר ומה לי בערב ויש לומר דמערב ועד בקר איצטריך ליתן לה מדתה ולא לאיחור: אין לך דבר שמתעכב כו' אלא קטרת · נראה לר"י דלא גרס ונרות דע"כ לא חשיב אלא מידי דהקטרה דבה הקפידה תורה לאחר כדכתיב והקטיר עליה חלבי וגו' דאי לא תימא הכי ליחשוב נמי ברישא אין לך שקודם לתמיד של שחר אלא קטרת ודישון מזבח הפנימי ושני גזרי עצים והטבת נרות דקודמין לתמיד כל הני כדאמרינן באמר להן הממונה (יומא דף לג.) ובתוספתא נמי ליתא: אתי עשה דפסח דאית ביה כרת ודחי כו' · הקשה ריב"א הא בעידנא דמיעקר עשה דהשלמה לא מיקיים עשה דאכילת פסח דאינה אלא בלילה ותירץ דמיירי שישחטו פסח עליו קודם שידחו עשה דהשלמה דשוחטין וזורקין על טבול יום ומחוסר כפורים לכולי עלמא אפילו לא יאכל לבסוף הואיל ובידו תלוי ופטור מפסח שני אפילו לא אכל הלכך כשהמקריב כפרתו מקיים עשה דפסח דאז הוי ראוי לאכול שאם לא היה יכול להקריב לא יהיה ראוי לאכול לערב והפסח היה פסול ור"י מתרץ דדוקא בלא תעשה דחמיר בעינן בעידנא דמיעקר לאו דלקיים עשה אבל עשה דחמיר דחי עשה הקל בכל ענין אפילו לא מקיים עשה חמור בעידנא דקא עבר אעשה הקל כדמוכח *בהשולח (גיטין דף לח:) גבי רבי אליעזר שיחרר עבדו ובשילוח הקן (חולין דף קמא.) דהוה דחי עשה דמצורע דחמיר לעשה דשילוח הקן אי לאו דאמר רחמנא שלח תשלח אפי' לדבר מצוה*: זה בנה אב לכל חטאות כו' · ואפילו לעכב קאמר דאי למצוה הכתי לימא בשקרבה · הקשה ריב"א דבת"כ משמע דליכא עיכובא דקתני התם גבי יולדת שאם הביאה עולתה תביא חטאתה ממין עולתה ובפרק כל התדיר (זבחים דף צ.) משמע דלא איצטריך האי זה בנה אב אלא לחטאת העוף הבאה עם עולת בהמה וליכא כי אם יולדת עשירה ובמסכת קנים (פ"ב) נמי אמרינן האשה שהביאה חטאתה ומתה מביאין יורשים עולתה כו' עולתה ומתה לא יביאו יורשים חטאתה משמע קצת אם היתה קיימת לא היתה מביאה אלא חטאתה ותירץ רבינו חיים כהן דהא דפריך הכא ואפילו עיכובא יהא היינו דוקא במצורע דכתיב ביה תהיה דמשמע עיכובא כדאמר דריש הקומץ רבה (מנחות דף יט.) ומשני דכתיב והעלה למעוטי מעיכובא*: דכתיב והעלה · ודוקא בדיעבד דהא כתיב בהדיא ואחר ישחט את העולה:

עשאום

והעלה

עין משפט נר מצוה

ג א מיי' פ"ג מהלכות תמידין הלכה יא:
ד ב מיי' פ"א מהלכות ק"פ הלכה ב:
ה ג מיי' פ"ג מהלכות תמידין הלכה ד ה:
ו ד שם הלכה יא ובהל' ק"פ שם:
ז ה מיי' שם ופ"א מהל' תמידין הלכה ד:
ח ו מיי' פ"ג מהלכות פסולי המוקדשין הלכה יא:
ט ז מיי' פ"א מהלכות מחוסרי כפרה הל"ה:
י ח מיי' פ"ג מהלכות תמידין הלכה ו:

מסורת הש"ס

[זבחים יב:]
יומא טו. זבחים יח: מנחות פט. וע"ש בתוס'
[צ"ל דאכילת קדשים] [צ"ל דהשלמה]
ערכין כח. [מיר יח: ע"ש]
[הוריות יג. זבחים צ.]

גליון הש"ס

גמ' בשלמא לת"ק יבא עשה. ע' שבת דף ד ע"א תוספות ד"ה וכי אומרין: רש"י ד"ה מעלה ומלינה וכו' לד"ה לא ירדו. עי' לעיל דף ע"ב תוס' ד"ה ונתקלקלו ומנחות ע"א תוספות ד"ה מאי:

רבינו חננאל

שהתמיד נאמר בו בין הערבים והפסח נאמר בו בין הערבים דכתיב (שמות י"ב ו') ושחטו אותו כל קהל עדת ישראל בין הערבים ונאמר בו בערב שנאמר (דברים ט"ז ו') שם תזבח את הפסח בערב וקטורת לא נאמר בה אלא בין הערבים שנא' (שמות ל' ח') ובין הערבים יקטירנה ונרות נאמר בהן בין הערבים דכתיב (שם) ובהעלות אהרן את הנרות [בין הערבים] וכתיב בהן מערב (שם כ"ז כ"א) שנאמר יערוך אותו אהרן ובניו מערב עד בקר. תניא כי קושיין תמיד קודם לקטורת וקטורת לנרות ונרות לפסח יאוחר דבר שנאמר בו בערב ובין הערבים כו' אסיקנא הכי אמר רחמנא בעידנא דמדלקת נרות תהא מקטרא קטורת זו היא לישנא דיקא דמתניתא: ת"ר אין לך דבר קודם לתמיד של שחר אלא קטורת שנאמר בבקר בבקר ... מעכבין את הכפרה] לפיכך אמר מעלן ומלינן על גבי המזבח כמי שנטמאו או שאבדו ואוכלין הכהנים הבשר ונשלמה הכפרה לבעלים באכילת הכהנים הבשר ... ואימורין של אשם נמי עביד להו כמה דעביד לאימורין של חטאת בהמה אלא לרב חסדא דאוקמא בזב ואפילו במצורע דסבר כל מחוסר כפורים טהור הוא ואי לא עביד פסח חייב כרת הנה מצורע ... ועולתו עופות א"א לו מכבש לאשם והני אימורין [שהן] למזבח היכי עביד וכי תימא הקרבת אשמו אינו מעכבו מלאכול בקדשים והתניא שמעכב וכי תימא בשקרב האשם מקודם התמיד אפילו הכי הא איכא עולת העוף שהולכת במערכה וכי תימא עולתו אינה מעכבתו מלאכול בקדשים והתניא שאפילו עולתו מעכבתו לאכול בקדשים וכי תימא בשקרבה עולתו והתניא זה בנה אב שיהו כל החטאות קודמות לעולות הבאות עמהן

kindling of] the lights; [59*a*] let that in connection with which *ba-'ereb* [at evening] and *ben ha-'arbayim* [between the evenings][11] are said be deferred after that in connection with which *ba-'ereb* is not said, save *ben ha-'arbayim* alone.[12] If so, let [the burning of] the incense [and the kindling of] the lights also take precedence over the Passover offering, [for] let that in connection with which *ba-'ereb* and *ben ha-'arbayim* are stated be deferred after that in a connection with which nought save *ben ha-'arbayim* alone is said?[1] —There it is different, because Scripture expressed a limitation, '*it*'. For it was taught: [*Aaron and his sons shall set it in order, to burn*] *from evening to morning:*[2] furnish it with its [requisite] measure, so that it may burn from evening to morning. Another interpretation: you have no [other] service which is valid from evening to morning save this alone. What is the reason? Scripture saith, '*Aaron and his sons shall set* it *in order, to burn from evening to morning*': '*it*' [shall be] from evening to morning, but no other thing shall be from evening until morning;[3] and [the burning of] the incense is likened to [the kindling of] the lights.[4]

Now it was taught in accordance with our difficulty: The [evening] *tamid* is [sacrificed] before [the burning of] the incense, the incense is [burnt] before [the kindling of] the lamps, and the lamps are [kindled] before [the sacrificing of] the Passover offering: let that in connection with which *ba-'ereb* and *ben ha-'arbayim* are stated be deferred after that in connection with which nought save *ben ha-'arbayim* alone is stated. But '*it*' is written?[5] —That '*it*' is required to exclude a service of the inner [Temple]; and what is it? [The burning of] the incense.[6] You might think that I would say, since it is written, *And when Aaron lighteth the* b *lamps at dusk, he shall burn it,*[1] say, let us first light the lamps and then burn the incense; therefore the Merciful One expressed a limitation, '*it*'. Then what is the purpose of, '*at dusk he shall burn it*'?—This is what the Merciful One saith: When thou lightest the lamps, the incense must [already] be burning.

Our Rabbis taught: There is nothing which takes precedence over the morning *tamid* except [the burning of] the [morning] incense alone, in connection with which '*in the morning, in the morning*' is stated; so let [the burning of the] incense, in connection with which '*in the morning, in the morning,*' is stated, for it is written, *And Aaron shall burn thereon incense of sweet spices, in the morning, in the morning,*[2] take precedence over that in connection with which only one '*morning*' is stated.[3] And there is nothing which may be delayed until after the evening *tamid* save [the burning of] the incense, [the lighting of] the lamps, [the slaughtering of] the Passover sacrifice, and he who lacks atonement[4] on the eve of Passover, who performs ritual immersion a second time[5] and eats his Passover sacrifice in the evening. R. Ishmael the son of R. Joḥanan b. Beroḳa said: He who lacks atonement at any other time of the year too, who performs ritual immersion and eats of sacred flesh in the evening.[6] According to the first Tanna, it is well: let the affirmative precept of [eating] the Passover sacrifice, c which involves *kareth,*[1] come and override the affirmative precept of completion,[2] which does not involve *kareth.*[3] But according to R. Ishmael the son of R. Joḥanan b. Beroḳa, wherein is this affirmative precept stronger than the other affirmative precept? —Said Rabina in R. Ḥisda's name: We treat here of a sin-offering of a bird, the blood of which alone belongs to the altar.[4] R. Papa said: You may even say [that we treat of] an animal sin-offering: he takes it up and keeps it overnight on the top of the altar.[5] But there is the guilt-offering?[6] As for R. Papa, it is well: hence we keep it overnight. But according to R. Ḥisda, what can be said?—I will tell you: It means where he has offered up his guilt-offering.[7] But there is the burnt-offering?[8] And should you answer, The burnt-offering is not indispensable,[9] surely it was taught, R. Ishmael the son of R. Joḥanan b. Berokah said: Just as his sin-offering and his guilt-offering are indispensable for him, so is his burnt-offering indispensable for him. And should you answer, It means where he has offered his burnt-offering; yet can his burnt-offering be offered first before his sin-offering? Surely it was taught: *And he shall offer that which is for the sin-offering first:*[10] for what purpose is this stated? If to teach that it comes before the burnt-offering, surely it is already said, *And he shall prepare the second for a burnt-offering, according to the ordinance?*[11] But this furnishes a general rule for *all* sin-offerings, that they take precedence of all burnt-offerings which accompany them; d and we have an established principle[1] that even a bird sin-offering takes precedence of an animal burnt-offering![2]—Said Raba, The burnt-offering of a leper is different, because the Merciful One

(11) E.V.: '*at dusk*'. (12) This is why the evening *tamid* is before the Passover sacrifice. For in connection with the latter both these expressions are used: Ex. XII, 6: *and the whole assembly . . . shall kill it at dusk* (ben ha-'arbayim); Deut. XVI, 6: *thou shalt sacrifice the passover-offering at even* (ba-'ereb). But in connection with the former only *ben ha-'arbayim* is stated, Num. XXVIII, 4: *and the other lamb shalt thou offer at dusk* (ben ha-'arbayim).

a (1) For only *ben ha-'arbayim* is stated in connection with the former two, Ex. XXX, 7f: *And Aaron shall burn thereon incense of sweet spices . . . And when Aaron lighteth the lamps at dusk* (ben ha-'arbayim), *he shall burn it*, '*ben ha-'arbayim*' applying to both the burning of the incense and the lighting of the lamps. (2) Ex. XXVII, 21. (3) Hence nothing may come after the kindling of the lights, and consequently the slaughtering of the Passover offering must take precedence. (4) Just as no service after the former is valid, so is no service valid after the latter. (5) Implying that nothing must be done after the kindling of the lights. (6) For it is logical that a service similar to itself should be excluded, the kindling of the lamps likewise being a service in the inner Temple, and '*it*' shows that no other inner service may take place after the kindling of the lamp. But the Passover offering was sacrificed in the outer Court.

b (1) Ex. XXX, 7. (2) Ibid.; E.V.: '*every morning*'. The literal translation is given in the text, and the repetition implies an earlier hour. (3) Num. XXVIII, 4: *The one lamb shalt thou offer in the morning*. (4) The technical designation of an unclean person who may not eat holy flesh until he has brought a sacrifice after regaining his cleanliness, viz., a *zab* and a *zabah* (v. Glos.), a leper and a woman after childbirth. If one of these forgot to bring his sacrifice before the evening *tamid* was sacrificed on the eve of Passover, he must bring it after the *tamid*, since otherwise he may not partake of the Passover offering in the evening, which is obligatory. (5) Though he must perform ritual immersion the previous day, this being necessary *before* the purificatory sacrifice may be offered, he nevertheless repeats it before partaking of holy flesh. (6) If he brought a peace-offering that day but forgot to bring his purificatory sacrifice, he must bring it even after the afternoon *tamid*, so that he may eat the flesh of his peace-offering in the evening, R. Ishmael regarding this too as obligatory.

c (1) If unfulfilled, v. Num. IX, 13. (2) V. *supra* 58*b* bottom: 'after it complete all the sacrifices'. (3) Even if a sacrifice is unlawfully brought after the evening *tamid* it is not punished by *kareth*. (4) R. Ishmael, in speaking of one who lacks atonement during the rest of the year, refers to a poor leper, who brought a bird for his sin-offering. This was eaten by the priests, and nothing of it was burnt on the altar, whereas the affirmative precept of 'completion' is written in reference to burning on the altar (v. Lev. VI, 5: *and he shall burn thereon the fat of the peace-offerings*), and hence applies only to animal sacrifices, the fat of which was burnt on the altar. (5) He slaughters the sacrifice after the evening *tamid*, but carries the animal on to the top of the altar and leaves it there overnight, postponing the burning of the fat until after the *tamid* of the following morning. (6) Required by a leper; even if poor, he brought a lamb, v. Lev. XIV, 21. (7) But had forgotten about the sin-offering. (8) Likewise required by a leper, ibid. 19, 22. This of course *was* burnt on the altar (v. n. c4). (9) To the eating of sacred flesh. (10) Lev. V, 8, q.v. (11) Ibid. 10.

d (1) *Binyan Ab*, a building up of a principle (or class), i.e., a conclusion by analogy. (2) V. Zeb. 90*b*.

If we do not fear, let us sacrifice it at six and a half [hours]?[2]—He holds that the [burning of the frankincense in the] censers takes precedence over the additional sacrifices: [hence] he sacrificed the additional sacrifices at six hours, [performed the burning in] the censers at seven, and sacrificed the *tamid* at seven and a half.

To this Rabbah b. 'Ulla demurred: Does he then teach, Just as its order on weekdays [in general], so is its order on the Sabbath which is the eve of Passover: these are the words of R. Ishmael? [Surely] he teaches, 'so is its order on the Sabbath,' without qualification! Rather, said Rabbah b. 'Ulla, this is what he means: Just as its order on a weekday in general, so is its order on the Sabbath in general:[3] these are the words of R. Ishmael. R. Akiba said: Just as its order on the eve of Passover in general, so is its order on the Sabbath in general:[4] [hence] our Mishnah which teaches, WHETHER ON WEEKDAYS OR ON THE SABBATH agrees with all.[5] Wherein do they differ?—They differ as to [whether there is] a preventive measure on account of vows and freewill-offerings. R. Ishmael holds: We enact a preventive measure for the Sabbath on account of weekdays;[6] while R. Akiba holds: We do not enact a preventive measure. If we do not enact a preventive measure, let us sacrifice it at six and a half?[7]—He holds that the additional sacrifices take precedence over [the burning of the frankincense in] the censers: [hence] the additional sacrifices are [offered] at six hours, the [burning in the] censers at seven, and he sacrifices the *tamid* at seven and a half [hours].

An objection is raised: The *tamid*, during the whole year it is offered according to its law, [viz.,] it is slaughtered at eight and a half [hours] and offered at nine and a half hours. But on the eve of Passover it is slaughtered at seven and a half and offered at eight and a half; if it [the eve of Passover] fell on the Sabbath, it is as

a though it fell on a Monday.[1] R. Akiba said: As its order is on the eve of Passover. As for Abaye, it is well;[2] but according to Raba it is a difficulty?[3]—Raba can answer you: Do not say, It is the same as when it falls on a Monday, but say, it is the same as a Monday in general.[4]

An objection is raised: If it falls on the Sabbath, it is as its order during the whole year: these are the words of R. Ishmael.[5] R. Akiba said: It is as its order on the eve of Passover in general.[6] Now as for Raba, it is well;[7] but according to Abaye it is difficult?—Abaye answers you: Do not say, 'It is as its order during the whole year,' but say, It is as its order in all [other] years:[8] these are the words of R. Ishmael. R. Akiba said: It is as the order

b when the eve of Passover falls on the eve of the Sabbath.[1]

Our Rabbis taught: How do we know that there must not be anything before the morning *tamid?*[2] Because it is said, *and he shall lay the burnt-offering in order upon it.*[3] What is the exegesis?[4]—Said Raba: The *burnt-offering* implies the *first* burnt-offering.[5] And how do we know that nothing may be offered after the evening *tamid?* Because it is stated, *and he shall burn upon it the fat of the peace-offerings.*[6] What is the exegesis?[7]—Said Abaye: After *it*[8] [*sc.* the morning *tamid*] [you may sacrifice] peace-offerings, but not after its companion [*sc.* the evening *tamid*] [may you sacrifice] peace-offerings. To this Raba demurred: Say [then], it is only peace-offerings that we may not present,[9] yet we may present burnt-offerings? Rather, said Raba: *Ha-shelamim* implies, upon it complete all the sacrifices.[10]

Our Rabbis taught: The [evening] *tamid* is [sacrificed] before the Passover offering, the Passover offering is [sacrificed] before the [burning of the evening] incense, the incense before [the

(2) Since there are many Passover sacrifices, while there is no need to delay it on account of vows, which are not offered on the Sabbath. (3) In both cases the *tamid* is slaughtered at eight and a half hours, though on the Sabbath no voluntary sacrifices are offered. (4) Viz., in both cases the *tamid* is slaughtered at seven and a half hours. (5) For their controversy does not refer to the eve of Passover at all. (6) If we permit him to slaughter the afternoon *tamid* on Sabbath at seven and a half hours, he may slaughter it at the same hour during the week too, leaving no time for voluntary offerings, which are disqualified if brought after the afternoon *tamid*. (7) For it is a general principle that all precepts must be performed as early as possible.

a (1) Lit., 'the second (day) of the week'—there are no specific names for the days of the week in Hebrew, except, of course, for the Sabbath.—I.e., it is the same as when it falls during the week, Monday being mentioned as an example (Rashi and Tosaf.). (2) For since R. Ishmael says that if it falls on the Sabbath it is the same as when it falls on a Monday, R. Akiba must mean, Just as its order on the eve of Passover which falls on the eve of the Sabbath. (3) For Raba interprets R. Ishmael's statement thus: just as its order on weekdays *in general* etc. But since R. Ishmael concludes, it is the same as when it falls on a Monday, i.e., a weekday in general, it is obvious that he does *not* refer to a weekday in general in the first half of his statement. (4) An ordinary weekday which is not Passover eve when the *tamid* is slaughtered at eight and a half hours, because we fear for the overheating of the flesh. (5) I.e., the *tamid* is slaughtered at eight and a half hours, because we fear for the overheating of the flesh. (6) It is slaughtered at seven and a half hours. (7) For this is exactly as Raba interprets the Baraitha. (8) I.e., just as in all other years when the eve of Passover falls on an ordinary weekday and the *tamid* is slaughtered at seven and a half hours, so likewise when it falls on the Sabbath.

b (1) Viz., the *tamid* is slaughtered at six and a half hours. (2) Rashi: nothing must be burnt upon the wood pile before the morning *tamid*, after the latter has been laid in order upon it. Tosaf.: no voluntary offering may be sacrificed before the morning *tamid*. Tosaf. accepts Rashi's interpretation as an alternative. (3) Lev. VI, 5. This follows, *'and the priest shall kindle wood on it every morning'*, (ibid.) showing that immediately after the wood pile is kindled, the *tamid* is the first thing to be burnt. (4) How is it implied that *'the burnt-offering'* mentioned in the verse refers to the morning *tamid?* (5) The def. art. points to some *particular* sacrifice, viz., the first burnt-offering mentioned in the chapter on sacrifices, Num. XXVIII, which is the daily morning *tamid*, and this verse teaches that it must be the first thing to ascend the altar every day, and nothing else may take precedence over it. (6) Ibid. (7) How is it implied in this verse? (8) Taking עליה (*'upon it'*) in this sense. (9) After the evening *tamid*. (10) V. *supra* 58a, n. b5.

אי לא חיישינן ניעבדיה בשש ומחצה קא סבר מוספין קודמין לבזיכין עביד להו למוספין בשש ובזיכין בשבע ועביד ליה לתמיד בשבע ומחצה מתקיף לה רבה בר עולא מידי כסידרו בחול כך סידרו בשבת בערב הפסח דברי ר' ישמעאל קתני כך סידרו בשבת סתמא קתני אלא אמר רבה בר עולא הכי קתני כסידרו בחול דעלמא כך סידרו בשבת דעלמא דברי ר' ישמעאל ר"ע אומר כסידרו בערב הפסח דעלמא כך סידרו בשבת דעלמא ומתני' דקתני בין בחול בין בשבת דברי הכל היא במאי קמיפלגי בגזרת נדבות ונדרים קמיפלגי ר' ישמעאל סבר גזרינן שבת אטו חול ור' עקיבא סבר לא גזרינן אי לא גזרינן ניעבדיה בו' ומחצה קסבר מוספין קודמין לבזיכין מוספין בשש ובזיכין בו' ועביד ליה לתמיד בז' ומחצה מיתיבי תמיד כל השנה כולה קרב כהלכתו נשחט בשמונה ומחצה וקרב בתשע ומחצה ובערב הפסח נשחט בז' ומחצה וקרב בח' ומחצה חל להיות בשבת כחל להיות בשני בשבת דברי ר' ישמעאל ר"ע אומר כסידרו בערב הפסח בשלמא לאביי ניחא אלא לרבא קשיא אמר לך רבא לא תימא כחל בשני בשבת אלא אימא כשני בשבת דעלמא מיתיבי חל להיות בשבת כסידרו כל השנה כולה דברי ר' ישמעאל ר"ע אומר כסידרו בערב הפסח דעלמא בשלמא לרבא ניחא אלא לאביי קשיא אמר לך אביי לא תימא כסידרו כל השנה אלא אימא כסידרו כל השנים כולן דברי ר' ישמעאל ר"ע אומר כסידרו ערב הפסח שחל להיות בערב שבת

*תנו רבנן מנין שלא יהא דבר קודם לתמיד של שחר תלמוד לומר °וערך עליה העולה ויקרא ו מאי תלמודא *אמר רבא °העולה עולה ראשונה שם ומנין שאין דבר קרב אחר תמיד של בין הערבים ת"ל °והקטיר עליה חלבי השלמים שם מאי תלמודא אמר אביי עליה שלמים ולא על חבירתה שלמים מתקיף לה רבא אימא שלמים הוא דלא נקריב הא עולות נקריב אלא אמר רבא השלמים עליה השלם כל הקרבנות כולן ת"ר תמיד קודם לפסח פסח קודם לקטרת קטרת קודמת לנרות

יאוחר

רש"י

אי לא חייש ניעבדיה בשש ומחצה · דהא הפסחים מרובין ובשבת לא בעי לאיתוריה משום נדרים ונדבות: קסבר מוספין קודמין לבזיכין · ועל כרחך בזיכין בשבע ואין פטיין בה: בעלמא · כל ימות החול בשמונה ומחצה: כך סידרו · בשבתות של כל השנה ואף על גב דליכא נדרים ונדבות חיישינן לסרך נדרים דחול דילמא אתו למסרך ולמיעבד בחול נמי בשבע ומיפסלי נדרים ונדבות של אחריו: ר"ע אומר · כל שבתות השנה הוא נשחט בשבע ומחצה כסידרו ערב הפסח דלא גזרינן משום חול: דברי הכל היא · דר' ישמעאל ורבי עקיבא לא איירי בערב פסח כלל וכמתניתין סבירא להו בין בחול בין בשבת: ניעבדיה בשש ומחצה · דהא זריזין מקדימין למצות: קסבר מוספין קודמין לבזיכין גרסינן: כחל להיות בשני בשבת · ערב הפסח שהתמיד נשחט בשבע ומחצה: בשני בשבת · חד מימות החול נקט ואית דאמרי יומא קמא דשבתא דחזי לארביסר נקט וחד בשבתא לא חזי לארביסר דלא בד"ו פסח ולאו מילתא היא שהרי על פי הראייה היו מקדשין: ור"ע אומר כסידרו ערב הפסח גרסינן ותו לא: בשלמא לאביי ניחא · דמדקאמר רבי ישמעאל חל להיות בשבת כחל להיות בשני בשבת על כרחך כסידרו ערב הפסח דקאמר ר"ע בע"פ שחל להיות בע"ש קאמר: אלא לרבא · דקאמר רבי ישמעאל למיכמר בישרא חייש וכסידרו בחול בעלמא קאמר הא קתני הכא כחל להיות בשני בשבת: אלא אימא כשני בשבת · שאינו ערב הפסח דהייט בשמונה ומחצה דחיישינן למיכמר בישרא: כסדר כל השנה · הייט בשמונה ומחצה דחיישי' למיכמר בישרא: כל השנים · שערב הפסח חל בחול דשחטינהו בשבע ומחצה ור"ע אמר כסידרו ערב הפסח שחל להיות בערב שבת: מניין שלא יהא דבר · נקטר במערכה משנערכה שחרית קודם לתמיד של שחר ת"ל וערך עליה בתר ובער עליה הכהן כתיב דהוא סידור מערכה: מאי תלמודא · דהאי העולה אתמיד של שחר קאי: העולה עולה ראשונה · מדלא כתיב וערך עליה עולה אלא העולה הכי קאמר וערך עליה מיד העולה החשובה האמורה תחלה לכל העולות והייט עולת תמיד דפרשת קרבנות *[בפ' פינחס] דקרבן תמיד כתיב ברישא: והקטיר עליה · אתמיד קאי דסיפיה דקרא הוא וה"ק והקטיר על העולה הזאת כלומר אחריה חלבי השלמים: ואימא שלמים הוא דלא קרבי. אחר תמיד של בין הערבים: השלמים · לשון השלם: תמיד · של בין הערבים קודם לפסח: לקטורת · של בין הערבים וכולהו יליף טעמא: לנרות · להדלקת נרות:

יאוחר

תוספות

דברי הכל היא · ובין בחול ובין בשבת דקתני במתני' לא קאי אריש' אלא אערב הפסח והא דקאמר דברי הכל היא לאו לגמרי קאמר דברי הכל אלא אדברי הכל לפלוגתא דהך ברייתא הייט כלומר דמצית לאוקמי כדברי הכל לפלוגתא דהך ברייתא דקיימינן עלה אבל איכא שני ברייתות דמייתי בסמוך דפליגי בהדיא בשבת דערב פסח ומהנהו ולאי איכא למיפשט דלאו דברי הכל היא:

באילו חל בשני בשבת · אין צריך לפרש דדוקא נקט שני דהוא יומא קמא דמיקלע ביה ארבעה עשר דחד בשבתא לא חזי לארביסר דלא בד"ו פסח דהא ע"כ לרבא דמוקי לה בשני בשבת דעלמא לא הוי שני בשבת דוקא דהא לא בערב הפסח מיירי הוא הדין לאביי אם לא יהיה דוקא אין לחוש ורש"י שהקשה דעל פי הראייה היו מקדשין אין נראה לר"י דאע"ג דהיו מקדשין על פי הראייה היו נזהרין שלא יבאו תרי שבי בהדי הדדי דאמרינן בהדיא פרק קמא דראש השנה (דף כ.) מאיימין על העדים על החדש שנראה בזמנו לומר שלא ראו והא דאמרי' בשילהי אלו קשרים (שבת דף קיג.) חלבי שבת קריבין ביום הכפורים אלמא בהדי הדדי ניהו מוקי לה בהחליל (סוכה דף נד:) כאחרים דאמרי אין בין עצרת לעצרת אלא ד' ימים בלבד:

אלא לרבא קשיא · תימה לרבה בר עולא נמי תיקשי לדבריו לרבי עקיבא מוספין קודמין לבזיכין ולפי מה שהברייתא מכאי' לרבי עקיבא תמיד נשחט בשש ומחצה וא"כ בזיכין קודמין למוספין ותירץ רשב"א דלרבה בר עולא לא קאי ר"ע אלא אריש' דקתני תמיד כל השנה קרב כהלכתו משמע לא שנא חול ולא שנא שבת ועלה פליג ר"ע ואמר דשבת דעלמא כערב הפסח והיינו ממש כרבה בר עולא או יתרץ כרבה:

העולה עולה ראשונה · תימה דבזבחים פ' כל התדיר (דף פט.) מפקינן מקרא אחרינא דתנן התמידין קודמין למוספין שנאמר מלבד עולת הבקר אשר לעולת התמיד וליכא למימר דהתם איצטריך לגבור שאין להן תמידין ומוספין אלא כדי אחד מהם דהא קתני התם דם חטאת קודם לדם עולה ודומיא דזה הוי תמידין ומוספין וליכא למימר נמי דאיצטריך קרא תניא לעכב דבהתכלת (מנחות דף מט:) אמרינן בהדיא דליכא עיכובא וי"ל דהתם איצטריך למוספין דלא קדמי והכא לנדרים ונדבות וצריכי דאי מוספין אמרי שהן קרבן צבור או שמא נדרים ונדבות אמרי שרגילים ומצויים יותר אי נמי קרא דהכא להקדמת הקטרה דבהקטרה כתיב וערך עליה העולה וקרא דכל התדיר להקדמת שחיטה דתעשו את אלה בעשיית הדם כתיב והא דפריך בהתכלת (שם) גבי הא דתנן התמידין אין מעכבין את המוספין וקאמר היכי דמי אילימא דלית ליה ולקדם והתניא מנין שלא יהא דבר ט' ומייתי הא דרבא ולא מייתי קרא דמלבד משום דלשון שלא יהא דבר קודם משמע טפי עיכוב [להכי] אתייה טפי מן המשנה אי נמי למימרא דאפי' בהקטרה דלא תנן בכל התדיר תמיד של שחר קודם אך קשה דאמאי איצטריך העולה ומלבד תיפוק לי' דתמיד קודם למוספין דבתמיד כתיב בבקר ובמוספין כתיב ביום דמשמע בעילומו של יום ולמאי דאמרי' בהתכלת דליכא עיכובא בהקדמה לתמיד אתי שפיר הא דאמרינן בריש עירובין (דף ב.) שלמים ששחטן קודם פתיחת דלתות ההיכל פסולים שנאמר ושחטו פתח אהל מועד בזמן שהן פתוחין ולא בזמן שהן נעולין דמטעם ששחטן קודם תמיד של שחר לא הוו פסולין והא דתני בתוספתא דמכילתין [פ"ד] כל הקדשים שהקריבן קודם תמיד של שחר או שעיכבן אחר תמיד של בין הערבים פסולין שאין לך קודם לתמיד של שחר אלא קטורת ואין לך שמתעכב אחר תמיד של בין הערבים כו' האי פסולין הייט מדרבנן [ועיין תוס' עירובין ב' · ד"ה שלמים ותוס' יומא כט · ד"ה אלא ע"ש היטב שכתבו להדיא אבל לשון התוספתא משמע דאפי' זרק הדם בדיעבד ועשה כל מצות אפ"ה פסולין דקתני שהקריבו ולא קתני ששחטו ואי מדרבנן אמאי פסולין וכו']:

יאוחר

רבינו חננאל

שהשוחטין ליה [לפסח] משעה עשירית ולמעלה ור"ע לא חייש למכמר בישרא. פי' מכמר כגון כימוש כדגרסינן באיזהו נשך בזיתים שכמר עיולי לבי דפא כו': אי לא חייש נעביד ליה לתמיד בשש ומחצה כי דיניה והפסח אחריו ושני ר"ע סבר מוספין קודמין לבזיכין הלכך עביד להו למוספין בשש ולבזיכין בשבע ולתמיד בשבע ומחצה וקרב בשמונה ומחצה והפסח אחריו ודחה רבה בר עולא להא דאביי ולהא דרבא ואמר בשבת דעלמא פליגי ופריש הוא הכי כסדרו בחול דעלמא בשמונה שעות ומחצה כך סדרו בשבת דעלמא בשמונה שעות ומחצה ר"ע אומר כסדרו ערב הפסח בשבע ומחצה [כך סידורו] בשבת דעלמא אבל בערב הפסח שניהם [מודים] שהיו בשבע ומחצה בין בחול בין בשבת ובשבת דעלמא בלבד פליגי ר' ישמעאל סבר גזרינן בשבת להעשות התמיד בח' שעות ומחצה ולא מקדמינן ליה גזרה שלא יבוא להקדימו בחול וישארו הנדרים והנדבות ור"ע סבר לא גזרינן שבת אטו חול הכל יודעין שהשבת אין שם נדרי' ונדבות ומקשינן אי הכי אי לא גזר ר"ע [נקרביה] בשש ומחצה כי דיניה ופרקינן אית ליה מוספין קודמין לבזיכין נמצא לטעמיה דאביי ר' ישמעאל כמתני' ולטעמיה דרבא ר' עקיבא כמתני': מיתיבי חל ערב פסח להיות בשבת כחל להיו' בשני בשבת דברי ר' ישמעאל ור"ע אומר כסדרו ערב הפסח מאי לאו ר' ישמעאל היא דסבר בין בחול בין בשבת בשבע ומחצה דהא בהדיא תני לה חל ערב פסחים להיות בשבת כחל להיות בשני בשבת כתנא דמתני' קשיא לרבא ומשני רבא ואמר מתניתא הכי קתני חל להיות ערב פסחים בשבת דינן כשני בשבת כמו חל דעלמא מה שני בשבת התמיד בשמנה ומחצה אף ערבי פסחים שחל להיות בשבת התמיד נשחט בשמונה ומחצה דלא כמתני' ר"ע אומר כסדרו ערב הפסח מה כל ערב הפסח התמיד בשבע ומחצה כך בשבת בערב הפסח בז' ומחצה כתנא דמתני'. ודיקי' מיניה מדקתני שני בשבת דשביק ליה לאחד בשבת וקתני בשני בשבת מכלל דלא אפשר ערב הפסח שיחול באחד בשבת דאם כן הוא חל פסח בשני בשבת מכאן תשובה לאומרים כי בימי החכמים חל פסח בבד"ו וכי אחרי סתימת התלמוד תקנו לא בבד"ו פסח: תוב מותבי' לאביי מהא דתניא תמיד כל [השנים] קרב כהלכתו חל להיות בשבת כסדר כל השנה דברי ר' ישמעאל ר"ע אומר כסדר ערב הפסח כלומר לא שנא חול ולא שנא שבת(לר"י)[לר"ע] דינם כאחד קשיא לאביי ומשני לא תימא כסדר כל השנה דמשמע בשמונה ומחצה אלא אימא כסדר כל השנים בערב הפסח שחל להיו' [ר"ע אומר כסידרו] ע"ש: ת"ר מנין שלא יהא דבר קודם לתמיד של שחר כו' פשוטה היא: ת"ר תמיד קודם לפסח.

מסורת הש"ס

ב"ק קיא. תמיד כח: מנחות מט: יומא לג: לד. כתובות קו: [ב"מ נה.] זבחים קג.

[פי' בתוס' ב"מ נה. ועי' ברש"י כתובות קו: ד"ה טעולה]

תורה אור

תמיד *נשחט בשמונה ומחצה וקרב בתשעה ומחצה בערבי פסחים נשחט בשבע ומחצה וקרב בשמונה ומחצה בין בחול בין בשבת *חל ערב פסח להיות בערב שבת נשחט בשש ומחצה וקרב בשבע ומחצה והפסח אחריו: גמ' מנא הני מילי אמר ר' יהושע בן לוי דאמר קרא °את הכבש אחד תעשה בבקר ואת הכבש השני תעשה בין הערבים חלקהו לבין שני ערבים ב' שעות ומחצה לכאן שתי שעות ומחצה לכאן ושעה אחת לעשייתו מתיב רבא בערבי פסחים נשחט בשבע ומחצה וקרב בשמונה ומחצה בין בחול בין בשבת ואי סלקא דעתך בשמונה ומחצה דאורייתא היכי מקדמינן ליה אלא אמר רבא *מצותו דתמיד משינטו צללי ערב מאי טעמא דאמר קרא בין הערבי' מעידנא דמתחיל שמשא למערב הלכך בשאר יומות השנה דאיכא נדרים ונדבות דרחמנא אמר °עליה חלבי השלמים ואמר מר (עליה חלבי השלמים) *עליה השלם כל הקרבנות כולם מאחרינן ליה תרתי שעי ועבדינן ליה בשמונה ומחצה בערבי פסחים דאיכא פסח אחריו קדמינן ליה שעה אחת ועבדינן ליה בשבע ומחצה חל ערב פסח להיות ערב שבת דאיכא נמי צלייתו דלא דחי שבת מוקמינן ליה אדיניה בשש ומחצה ת"ר כסידורו בחול כך סידורו בשבת דברי ר' ישמעאל רבי עקיבא אומר כסידורו בערב פסח מאי קאמר אמר אביי הכי קאמר כסידורו בחול בערב הפסח כך סידורו בשבת בערב הפסח דברי רבי ישמעאל רבי עקיבא אומר כסידורו בערב הפסח שחל להיות בערב שבת כך סידורו בשבת ומתני' דקתני בין בחול בין בשבת רבי ישמעאל היא במאי קא מיפלגי במוספין קודמין לבזיכין קמיפלגי רבי ישמעאל סבר* מוספין קודמין לבזיכין עבד להו למוספין בשש ובזיכין בשבע ועביד ליה לתמיד בשבע ומחצה רבי עקיבא סבר בזיכין קודמין למוספין בזיכין בחמש ומוספין בשש ועביד ליה לתמיד בשש ומחצה מתקיף לה רבא מידי רבי עקיבא כסידרו בערב הפסח שחל להיות בערב שבת קתני כסידרו בערב הפסח סתמא קתני אלא אמר רבא הכי קאמר כסידרו בחול דעלמא כך סידרו בשבת בערב הפסח דברי רבי ישמעאל רבי עקיבא אומר כסידרו בערב הפסח ומתני' דקתני בין בחול בין בשבת רבי עקיבא היא במאי קא מיפלגי במכמר בשרא קמיפלגי רבי ישמעאל סבר חיישינן למכמר בשרא ורבי עקיבא סבר לא חיישינן למכמר בשרא אי

במדבר כח · ויקרא ו · ס"א ל"ג

רש"י

תמיד · של בין הערבים : וקרב בתשעה ומחצה · גמר הקרבתו שהיו שוהין שעה אחת בעשייתו ובגמ' מפרש טעמא : ערבי פסחים · מקדמינן ליה משום דבעי למיעבד פסח אחריו בברייתא מפרש בגמ' מנא לן דפסח אחר תמיד : חל ערב פסח בערב שבת · בעינן לאקדומי טפי משום דבעי לשחוט פסח אחריו ולצלותו מבעוד יום : גמ' בין הערבים · משש שעות ולמעלה שהצל נוטה קרינן בין הערבים והוה ליה למכתב בערב ושני דבדוריה וכתב בין הערבים לדרשה חלוק הערב לשני חלקים שתי שעות ומחצה לכאן קודם לעשייתו וב' שעות ומחצה לכאן לאחר עשייתו : אלא אמר רבא · כולה תקנתא דרבנן היא ומדאורייתא כל שש שעות אחרונות כשירות דהיינו מכי ינטו צללי ערב *דהיינו מחצי שבע ואילך שהחמה נוטה למערב והצל למזרח כשאדם עומד כנגד החמה צלו נוטה למזרח אבל שש וחצי שבע היא עומדת באמצע הרקיע ואין צל נוטה אלא לכל אדם תחתיו : ואמר מר · לקמן בהאי פירקא : עליה חלבי השלמים · על תמיד של שחר השלם כל הקרבנות ולא תשלומים על תמיד הערב דלאחר תמיד הערב לא תקריב קרבן לפיכך אף על פי שזריזים מקדימין למצות התקינו לאחרה כדי שיביאו נדריהם ונדבותיהן ויהא כשר להקריבן ובשבת נמי אף על גב דליכא נדרים ונדבות מאחרינן ליה משום *סדר גזירת נדרים ונדבות דחול דכמפרש לקמן : לצליית פסח אינו דוחה שבת · מפני שאורך הדיוט היא ויכול לצלות מבעוד יום : ומוקמינן ליה אדיניה · מכי ינטו הצללים דהיינו בשש ומחצה : כסידרו · של תמיד : כסידרו בערב פסח גרסי' ברבי עקיבא : כסידרו בחול בערב הפסח · דהיינו בשבע ומחצה כך סידרו בשבת בערב הפסח : ר' עקיבא אומר · בשבת של ערב הפסח הוא בשש ומחצה כסידרו בערב הפסח שחל להיות בערב שבת דכיון דבעי למיעבד פסח אחריו ובשבת לא קרבי נדרים ונדבות דנצטריך לאיחוריה מוקמינן ליה אדיניה בשש ומחצה : ומתני' דקתני · ערבי פסחים נשחט בשבע ומחצה בין בחול בין בשבת רבי ישמעאל היא : במאי קא מיפלגי · למאי קא מאחר ליה רבי ישמעאל הא מסתבר טעמא דרבי עקיבא מפני שהפסחים מרובין לשחוט וליקרב אחריו דבשלמא כשהוא חל בחול מאחרינן ליה חדא שעתא משום נדרים ונדבות אבל בשבת למה לי לאחריניהו בשלמא בשאר שבתות לא חיישינן לאקדומי ולשנויי מחול דידיה משום נדרים ונדבות דחול אבל השתא משום פסחים בעינן לאקדומיה : בזיכין · היא לבונה הנתונה בשני בזיכים על שתי מערכות של לחם הפנים ובשבת היו מסלקין הישנה ומסדרין את החדשה כדכתיב ביום השבת יערכנו ומקטיר הבזיכין והן מתירין הלחם לאכילת כהנים (א) והיתה ללחם לאזכרה וחולקין הלחם מיד וצריך שעה אחת להתעסק בכך : ר' ישמעאל סבר מוספין קודמין · לסילוק בזיכין והקטרתן וזמן מוספין אורחייהו בשש דכתיב בהו יום ולא כתיב בהו בקר דכתיב דבר יום ביומו וקיימא לן בסדר יומא בפרק אמר להן הממונה (דף לד·) בקר הוי הקדמה ויום משמע איחור : ובזיכין בשבע · דבעי לאחריניהו דבמוספין כתיב יום ובבזיכין כתיב ביום ביום תרי זימני ומהכא ילפינן טעמא דאמר מוספין קודמין לבזיכין במסכת יומא (שם) מדכתב בהו ביום השבת ביום השבת תרי זימני לאחר ועבדינן ליה בשבע ומחצה והוא הדין דמצי למיעבדיה בתחלת ח' אלא חדא דשמא אין חילוק לחם הפנים כלה בסוף שבעה ועוד כל הני זימני לא משכינן ליה אלא בשש ומחצה כדיניה או בשבע ומחצה כשאר ערבי פסחים : בזיכין קודמין · וטעמא נמי מפרש התם גמר חוקה חוקה מחביתין : מי קתני כו' · במילתי' דרבי עקיבא ולהכי לא פריך ליה אמילתיה דר' ישמעאל דאיהו נמי אמר כוותיה דאביי במקצת ובההוא מקצת פריך ליה רבה בר עולא לקמן : כסידרו · של תמיד : בחול דעלמא · כל ימות השנה דהיינו בשמונה ומחצה כך סידרו בשבת בערב הפסח דלא מקדמינן לי' למהר שחיטת הפסחים אחריו דהואיל ואינו יכול לצלותו עד שתחשך חיישינן שמא יתחמם בשר הפסח ויסריח : ר' עקיבא אומר כסידרו · שאר ערב הפסח מפני שהפסחים מרובים וצריך להקדימם : לא חיישינן למכמר בישרא · חימום הבשר ודומה לו באיזהו נשך (דף עד·) על הכומר של זיתים שמניחין יחד בכלי כדי שיתחממו [ועי' פירש"י בחומש מקץ מ"ג פסוק ל'] : אי

תוספות

תמיד נשחט · מאחרינן ליה תרתי שעי · אבל טפי לא שלא היו רוצין לעשות כל כך באמצע סמוך לחשיכה ורבא דמפרש לקמן מילתיה דר' ישמעאל כסדרו בחול בעלמא כן סדרו בשבת בערב הפסח *(בשמונה) ומחצה הייט בדוחק משום מכמר בישרא :

מוקמינן ליה אדיניה בו' שעות ומחצה . בריש אמר להן הממונה (יומא דף כח:) פריך ונשחטיה מכי משחרי כתלי פי' מתחלת שבע ומשני משום דלא מכווני :

רבי ישמעאל סבר מוספין קודמים לבזיכין · דוקא בשבת דערב הפסח פליגי דאיכא היתירא שמקדמים אותו מפני עשיית הפסח שאחריו ולא שייך למיגזר אטו חול אבל בשבת דעלמא קרב כסדר החול גזירה שבת אטו חול :

וקעבדינן ליה בז' ומחצה · וא"ת וליעבדיה בתחלת שמונה ופי' בקונטרס לפי שאין חלוק הלחם כלה בסוף שבע ואין נראה לר"י דהא לר"ע קאמר בזיכין בחמש ומוספין בשש משמע לר"ע ליכא שהייה בהקטרה וחילוק לחם אלא שעה ונראה לר"י כלשון אחר שפי' בקונטרס :

מידי ר"ע כסדר הפסח שחל להיות ערב שבת קתני · אע"ג דלרבא נמי איכא למיפרך כדפריך בסמוך רבה בר עולא מידי כסדרו בחול בעלמא כן סדרו בשבת בערב הפסח קתני רבא לא חשיב ליה פירכא דהא ר' ישמעאל אמתני' קאי דקתני דערב הפסח שוה בין בחול בין בשבת ועליה פליג רבי ישמעאל ולכך לא היה צריך להזכיר בדבריו ערב הפסח :

חיישינן למיכמר בישרא · הואיל ואין הדחת קרביו דוחה שבת כדאמר בפרק [אלו דברים] (לקמן דף סה:) : דברי

עין משפט נר מצוה

א א ב מיי' פ"א מהל' תמידין הלכה ג ה סמג עשין קנ :

[בעשרה . אולי צ"ל בט']

ב ג מיי' פ"ד שם הל' י"א ופ"ו הל' יא :

רבינו חננאל

תמיד נשחט בשמונה ומחצה וקרב בתשעה ומחצה כו' מה"מ ובא ר' יהושע לפרש כי מן התורה הוא זה השיעור ונדחו דבריו ופשיט רבא מצותו בתמיד של בין הערבים מכי ינטו צללי ערב מאי טעמא בין הערבים משעה שמתחיל היום להעריב משמע דתחלת שעה שביעית הוא בין שני הערבים בין ערב דאתמול לערב דהאידנא שכל הלילה נקרא ערב שנאמר (בראשית א ה) ויהי ערב ויהי בקר ונמצאת מצות התמיד מתחלת שביעית הלכך כל השנה דבעי' להשלי' כל קרבן ואח"כ תמיד של בין הערבים דאמר מר והקטיר עליה חלבי השלמים למה לי וכי אין מקטירין אלא חלבי השלמים והלא חלבי החטאות והאשמות כיוצא בהן אלא לומר לך עליה השלם כל הקרבנות וכיון דאיכא בכל השנה נדרים ונדבות עבדינן להו קודם התמיד של בין הערבים מאחרינן לה לתמיד שתי שעות ומחצה ועבדינן ליה בשמונה ומחצה [בערבי פסחים מקדמינן ליה שעה אחת לעבדינן ליה בשבע ומחצה] כדי שתהא שהות ביום לשחיטת הפסח חל ערב פסחים להיות בערב שבת דאיכא נמי צליית הפסח דבעינן מבעוד יום עבדינן התמיד כדין התורה בשש שעות ומחצה : ת"ר כסדרו בחול כך סדרו בשבת דברי ר' ישמעאל ר' עקיבא אומר כסדרו בערב הפסח ופריש ליה אביי הכי כסדרו בחול בערב הפסח בשבע שעות ומחצה כך סדרו בשבת בערב הפסח דברי ר' ישמעאל נמצאו דברי ר' ישמעאל כמשנתנו דקתני בשבע שעות ומחצה בערב הפסח נשחט התמיד בין בחול בין בשבת ר' עקיבא אומר התמיד של בין הערבים של שבת בערב הפסח היה נשחט בשש שעות ומחצה כסדרו בערב הפסח שחל להיות בערב שבת ובהא פליגי ר' ישמעאל סבר מוספין קודמין לבזיכי לחם הפנים הלכך מוספין בשש כו' ור' עקיבא סבר בזיכין קודמים הלכך בזיכים בחמש ומוספים בשש והתמיד בשש ומחצה ודחי לה רבא להא דאביי הכי [מידי] כסדרו בחול בערב הפסח קתני כסדרו*) בחול סתמא קתני ופריש רבא הכי כסדרו בחול דעלמא בשמונה ומחצה כך סדרו בשבת בערב הפסח ר' עקיבא כסדרו בכל ערב הפסח בשבע ומחצה כך סדרו בשבת למכמר אלא מאחרינן ליה ישחטינן

בערב הפסח כמתניתין דקתני בין בחול בין בשבת בשבע ומחצה ובמכמר בשרא פליגי ר' ישמעאל סבר כיון דלא צלינן ליה עד לערב אי שחטת ליה לפסח משעה תשיעית אתי בשרא

* [נראה כי לפני רבינו היתה גי' אחרת בגמ' דרבא מקשה על אביי דגם בדברי ר"י א"א לפרש כן דמידי כסדרו בחול בע"פ קתני וכו']

מסורת הש"ס

יומא כח:

[לקמן נט: יומא נג.]

[יומא נג. נד.]

הגהות הב"ח

(א) רש"י ד"ה בזיכין וכו' לאכילת כהנים כדכתיב וכו' והיתה :

גליון הש"ס

רש"י ד"ה אלא אמר רבא דהיינו מחצי שבע וכו' עי' בר"י שבת ד"ט ע"ב ד"ה מנחה גדולה וצ"ע מסוגיא דיומא דף כח ע"ב וכו' לקמן דף צג ע"ב ד"ה מילין :

CHAPTER V

a *MISHNAH.* [58*a*] THE [AFTERNOON] TAMID[1] IS SLAUGHTERED AT EIGHT AND A HALF HOURS[2] AND IS OFFERED AT NINE AND A HALF HOURS.[3] ON THE EVE OF PASSOVER[4] IT IS SLAUGHTERED AT SEVEN AND A HALF HOURS AND OFFERED AT EIGHT AND A HALF HOURS, WHETHER IT IS A WEEKDAY OR THE SABBATH. IF THE EVE OF PASSOVER FELL ON SABBATH EVE [FRIDAY], IT IS SLAUGHTERED AT SIX AND A HALF HOURS AND OFFERED AT SEVEN AND A HALF HOURS, AND THE PASSOVER OFFERING AFTER IT.[5]

GEMARA. Whence do we know it?—Said R. Joshua b. Levi, Because Scripture saith, *The one lamb shalt thou offer in the morning, and the other lamb shalt thou offer between the two evenings:*[6] insert[7] it between the two 'evenings', [which gives] two and a half hours before and two and a half hours after[8] and one hour for its preparation.[9]

Raba objected: ON THE EVE OF PASSOVER IT IS SLAUGHTERED AT SEVEN AND A HALF HOURS AND OFFERED AT EIGHT AND A HALF HOURS, WHETHER IT IS A WEEKDAY OR THE SABBATH. Now if you think that [it must be slaughtered] at eight and a half hours according to Scriptural law, how may we
b perform it earlier? Rather, said Raba: The duty of the *tamid*[1] properly [begins] from when the evening shadows begin to fall.[2] What is the reason? Because Scripture saith, '*between the evenings*', [meaning] from the time that the sun commences to decline in the west. Therefore on other days of the year, when there are vows and freewill-offerings,[3] in connection with which the Divine Law states, [*and he shall burn*] *upon it the fat of the peace-offerings* [ha-shelamim],[4] and a Master said, '*upon it*' complete [*hashlem*] all the sacrifices,[5] we therefore postpone it two hours and sacrifice it at eight and a half hours.[6] [But] on the eve of Passover, when there is the Passover offering after it, we advance it one hour and sacrifice[7] it at seven and a half hours. When the eve of Passover falls on the eve of the Sabbath, so that there is the roasting too [to be done], for it does not override the Sabbath,[8] we let it stand on its own law, [viz.,] at six and a half hours.

Our Rabbis taught: Just as its order during the week, so is its order on the Sabbath: these are the words of R. Ishmael. R. Akiba said: Just as its order on the eve of Passover. What does this mean?—Said Abaye, This is what it means: Just as its order on a weekday which is the eve of Passover, so is its order on the Sabbath which is the eve of Passover:[9] these are the words of R. Ishmael. R. Akiba said: Just as its order on the eve of Passover which falls on the eve of the Sabbath, so is its order on the Sab-
c bath;[1] and our Mishnah which teaches, WHETHER ON A WEEKDAY OR THE SABBATH, agrees with R. Ishmael. Wherein do they differ?—They differ as to whether the additional sacrifices[2] take precedence over the [burning of the frankincense in the] censers:[3] R. Ishmael holds, The additional offerings take precedence over the [burning of the frankincense in the] censers: therefore he [the priest] sacrificed the additional sacrifices at six hours, [burned the incense in] the censers at seven, and sacrificed the *tamid* at seven and a half [hours]. R. Akiba holds: [The burning of the frankincense in] the censers takes precedence over the additional sacrifices: [hence] the [burning in the] censers took place at five [hours], the additional offering at six hours, and the *tamid* was sacrificed at six and a half hours.

To this Raba demurred: Does then R. Akiba teach, Just as its order on the eve of Passover which falls on the Sabbath, so is its order on the Sabbath; surely he teaches, 'Just as its order on the eve of Passover,' without qualification? Rather, said Raba, This is what he means: Just as its order on the weekdays in general,[4] so is its order on the Sabbath which is the eve of Passover:[5] these are the words of R. Ishmael. R. Akiba said: Just as its order on the eve of Passover;[6] hence our Mishnah which teaches, WHETHER ON WEEKDAYS OR ON THE SABBATH agrees with R. Akiba.
d Wherein do they differ?—They differ in the heating of the flesh.[1] R. Ishmael holds, We fear for the heating of the flesh; while R. Akiba holds: We do not fear for the heating of the flesh. [58*b*]

a (1) The daily burnt-offering: one was brought every morning and another every afternoon. Num. XXVIII, 4. (2) The day being counted from sunrise to sunset, i.e., about six a.m. to six p.m. (3) The sacrificial ceremonies took an hour. (4) The Heb. is in the plural: on the eves of Passovers. (5) When the eve of Passover falls on a Friday, time must be left for roasting the Passover offering before the Sabbath commences; hence the earlier hour of the *tamid*. (6) Ibid. Literal translation. 'Evening' (ערב *'ereb*) is defined as the whole afternoon until nightfall. (7) Lit., 'divide'. (8) Lit., 'here' . . . 'there'. (9) Thus the 'two evenings' are from midday (= six) until eight and a half hours, and from nine and a half hours until nightfall (= twelve).

b (1) The slaughtering of it. (2) Lit., 'decline'. The sun reaches its zenith at midday and then begins to decline in the west, the decline being perceptible from half an hour after midday, and this is regarded as the falling of the evening shadows. (3) These are two technical terms: a 'vow' is a votive sacrifice, the particular animal having been unspecified when the vow was made; in a freewill-offering a particular animal was specified at the time of the vow. The difference is that in the former case, if the animal which he *subsequently* dedicates dies or is rendered unfit before it is sacrificed, he must bring another; but in the latter case he has no further obligation. (4) Lev. VI, 5. (5) Rashi: upon *it*, *sc.* the *morning tamid*, to which the verse refers, complete etc., i.e., all the sacrifices of the day are to be brought after the *morning tamid*, but not after the afternoon *tamid*, which must be the last of the day. This exegesis connects *shelamim* with *shalem* (whole, complete). Jast. translates: with it (the evening sacrifice) cease all sacrifices (none can be offered after it). This is simpler, but not in accordance with the context. (6) To allow time for the voluntary offerings. (7) Lit., 'make'. (8) Though the roasting is a precept, yet it may not be done on the Sabbath. (9) I.e., in both cases the *tamid* is slaughtered at seven and a half hours.

c (1) Hence in both cases it is slaughtered at six and a half hours. For since no vows are offered on the Sabbath, it is unnecessary to delay the *tamid*, which is therefore sacrificed as early as possible, to leave ample time for the Passover sacrifice. (2) Offered on Sabbaths, New Moons, and Festivals; midday (six hours) was the earliest time when they could be offered.—In memory of these additional sacrifices there is now an Additional Service (*Musaf*) on these days. (3) Two censers of frankincense stood by the rows of shewbread; this shewbread was set on the Table every Sabbath and removed and replaced by fresh bread the following Sabbath. At the same time the frankincense was burnt, and after that the priests ate the shewbread. The removing, replacing and burning of the incense took an hour. (4) During the year. (5) Viz., at eight and a half hours. For the flesh of the Passover sacrifice may not be roasted until evening, therefore it is inadvisable to slaughter it earlier, lest the flesh became overheated and putrid, and consequently the *tamid* is slaughtered at the usual time. (6) Viz., at seven and a half hours, so likewise on the Sabbath. Since many are to be offered, we must start as early as possible.

d (1) V. *supra* n. c5; also perhaps, the shrinking of the flesh caused by overheating; v. Jast. s.v. כמר and Rashi on Gen. XLIII, 30.

day. So he came, [57b] [and] indicated with his hand,[7] 'If the goat were better, let it be offered for the daily sacrifice'. Said the king, 'Since he had no fear of my royal person, let his right hand be cut off.' But he gave a bribe [and] they cut off his left hand [instead]. Then the king heard [of it] and they cut off his right hand [too]. Said R. Joseph: Praised be the Merciful One Who caused Issachar of Kefar Barkai to receive his deserts in this world.

R. Ashi said: Issachar of Kefar Barkai had not studied the Mishnah. For we learned, R. Simeon said: Lambs take precedence over goats in all places.[8] You might think that that is because they are the best of their species, therefore it is stated, *And if he bring a lamb as his offering.*[9] Rabina said: He had not even studied Scripture either, for it is written, *If [he bring] a lamb . . . And if [his offering be] a goat:*[10] if he wishes, let him bring a lamb; if he wishes, let him bring a goat.[11]

(7) I.e., in a contemptuous fashion. (8) Wherever both are mentioned together in the same verse the lamb is stated first. (9) Lev. IV, 32; this is given as an alternative to a goat, which is prescribed *earlier* in the same section in v. 28. (10) Lev. III, 7, 12. (11) And neither is preferable to the other.

אחרי בידיה אי גדיא יאי יסק לתמידא אמר מלכא הואיל ולא הוי ליה אימתא דמלכותא ניפסקו לימיניה יהב שוחד ופסקיה לשמאליה שמע מלכא ופסקיה לימיניה אמר רב יוסף °בריך רחמנא דאשקליה לישכר איש כפר ברקאי *למיטרפסיה מיניה בהאי עלמא אמר רב אשי יששכר איש כפר ברקאי לא תנא מתניתין *דתנן ר"ש אומר כבשים קודמים לעזים בכל מקום יכול מפני שמובחרין במינן ת"ל °אם כבש יביא קרבנו מלמד ששניהן שקולין כאחד רבינא אמ' אפילו מקרא נמי לא קרא דכתיב °אם כבש אם עז אי בעי כבש לייתיה אי בעי עז לייתיה:

הורה אור ויקרא ד שם ג

אחוי בידיה. בלשון לחוק: אימתא דמלכותא. לא דיו שלא אמר כמותי אלא שאמר אף בלשון לחוק: דאשקליה. שהשיא שוט וגמולו: למיטרפסיה גמולו: לא תנא. לא שנה משנה וברייתא: כבשים קודמין לעזים. בכ"מ כתב כבש תחלה: אם כבש יביא לחטאת. כאן הקדים שעירה לכבשה דכתיב בפרשה עליונה והביא את קרבנו שעירת עזים וגו' והדר אם כבש יביא וגו': אם כבש אם עז. *גבי שלמים מדלא הראה לך הכתוב רמז מובחר בזה מזה שמעת מינה ששניהן שוין:

הדרן עלך מקום שנהגו וסליקא לה פסח ראשון

כריתות כח.

[עי' רש"י אם בכריתות]

[פי' גכס דיט ממנו וי"א לשון ארמי הוא ופי' נטל חלקו ונזרז מן העונש כנגד חוטאו. ערוך]

גליון הש"ס

גמ' אמר רב יוסף בריך רחמנא. כעין זה יבמות קב ע"ב:

סדר והלכות קרבן פסח ראשון בקצרה*

מצות עשה לשחוט קרבן פסח בי"ד בניסן אחר חצות בכ"מ בעזרה. ואיש ואשה חייבין במצוה זו*. ובא מן הכבשים או מן העזים זכר בן שנה. ומי שביטלה במזיד והוא טהור ובדרך רחוקה לא היה חייב כרת*: ולא יהיה כזית חמץ בבית שום א' מהמתעסקים ואם היה חמץ ברשות אחד מהם לוקה והפסח כשר*. לכתחילה צריך לשחוט אותו אחר התמיד של בין הערבי' והקטרת והטבת נרות*[א] ובחול נשחט התמיד בז' ומחצה וקרב בח' ומחצה[ב] ובשבת נשחט בו' ומחצה וקרב בז' ומחצה והפסח אחריו*. הפטורין מקרבן ראייה פטורין מפסח* (תוס' פסחים דף ג':) ומצוה לכתחילה להלק כל העם ששחטו הפסחים לג' כתות בעזרה וכל כת לא פחות מל' בני אדם. נכנסה כת ראשונה עד שנתמלאה העזרה ונועלין הדלתות ושוחטין ואם נמצא בעל מום או טריפה שוחטין אחר אפי' בשבת אפי' מאה עד שיכשיר א' או עד שתחשך וידחה לפסח שני שהרי אנוס הוא[ג]. ויהא א' ממרס בדמו שלא יקרוש עד שיזרוק [ד] דם התמיד. והלוים קראו את ההלל בשיר כל זמן שחיטה והקרבה ואם גמרו ההלל ועדיין לא שלמו הכת מלהקריב שונים ואם שנו ולא שלמו מלהקריב משלשין ומעולם לא שלשו. ועל כל קריאה וקריאה תוקעין ג' תקיעות בחצוצרות תקיעה תרועה תקיעה [ועל כל פסח היו ט' תקיעות וב"ין הקריאה והתקיעות מפורש בסוכה נד. ובתוס' ד"ה שייר] והכהנים עומדים שורות שורות ובידיהם מזרקי כסף ומזרקי זהב שורה שכולה כסף כסף ושורה שכולה זהב זהב ולא היו מעורבין משום נוי. ולא היו למזרק שוליים כדי שלא יניחום ויקרוש הדם. שחט השוחט וקיבל הכהן ונותנו לחבירו וחבירו לחבירו עד שיגיע הדם אצל הכהן הקרוב למזבח ושופכו שפיכה אחת כנגד היסוד. חזר וקיבל מזרק א' מלא ואח"כ החזיר הריקן. ואח"כ תולין הבעלים הפסח במסמרות של ברזל שהיו קבועין בכתלים ובעמודין ומי שלא מצא מקום לתלות לוקח ממקלות דקים וחלקים שהיו שם והניחו על כתיפו ועל כתף חבירו ותולה ומפשיט. ומפשיטין את כולו וקורעו וממחה את קרביו עד שמסיר מהן הצואה והפרש ומוציא האימורין והם החלב שעל הקרב ויותרת הכבד וב' כליות והחלב שעליהן והאליה לעומת העצה ונותנם בכלי שרת ומולחן ומקטירן הכהן ע"ג מזבח כל פסח בפני עצמו. ואסור להביא האימורין לידי נותר. נטמא הבשר ונודע לו קודם זריקה אע"פ שהאימורין טהורין לא יזרוק הדם ואם זרק לא הורצה ואם נודע לו אחר הזריקה הורצה. נטמאו האימורין והבשר קיים זורק הדם והבשר נאכל לערב. נטמאו הבעלים כל החבורה אחר שנשחט לא יזרוק ואם זרק לא הורצה וחייבין בפסח שני: כל שפסולו בגופו ישרף מיד. בדם או בבעלים תעובר צורתו ואח"כ ישרף (מיד). שלמו מלהקריב פותחין דלתות העזרה ויוצאת כת ראשונה ונכנסה כת שניה יצאת שניה נכנסה שלישית כמעשה ראשונה כך מעשה שניה ושלישית. שלמה כת ג' ויצאת רוחצים העזרה אפילו בשבת. חל י"ד בשבת מעשהו כמעשהו בחול לפי שקבוע לו זמן וא"א לעשותו קודם השבת אבל מה שהיה אפשר לעשות קודם השבת כגון הבאתו מחוץ לתחום והתיכת יבלתו בכלי אם היבלת לח וכדומה אסור או מה שאפשר לעשות אחר השבת כגון הדחת קרביו וצלייתו וכדומה[ה] אינו דוחה שבת. שכח ולא הביא הסכין בע"ש אם לא הקדישו עדיין יניחנו בין קרני הכבש או בצמרו ומכישו עד שמביאו לעזרה ומקדישו שם הואיל וקבוע לו זמן. ובשבת לבד רשאין להקטיר האימורין כל הלילה לפי שחלבי שבת קרבין בי"ט: שלמו מלהקריב בחול בעל הזבח נוטל פסחו עם העור ומביאו לביתו בירושלים ובשבת לא היו רשאין להוליך פסחיהן לבתיהן אלא כת א' יוצאין בפסחיהן ויושבין בהר הבית וכת ב' יושבת בחיל וכת ג' עומדין במקומן בעזרה ושוהים הכל עד מ"ש:

ואחר שבא לביתו *צולהו וכיצד צולהו נוטל אותו טלו שלא יחסר אבר ממנו ותוחבו מתוך פיו עד בית נקובתו בשפוד של עץ רמון ותולהו לתוך התנור שלא יגע בחרסית התנור והאש למטה וכרעיו ובני מעיו תולה לו ואין צולין אותו בתנור שגרוף האש או ע"ג כלי אבן או כלי מתכת לפי שצריך להיות צלי אש ולא ע"י ד"א ואם היה הכלי מנוקב שבולט בו האור צולין עליו. ואסור לאוכלו חי אפילו חצי צלי ומבושל אפילו לאחר צלייתו ומותר לסוך אותו בשעת צלייתו או לטבל בשעת אכילתו במי פירות חוץ ממים: **ואחר** שצלאו אוכלו לערב וחותך הבשר ואוכל וחותך העצמות מן הפרק ומפרקן אם רצה וכשיגיע לגיד הנשה מוציאו ומניחו עם שאר הגידין והעצמות והקרומות שיוצאין בשעת אכילה. ולא יאכל ממנו כזית צלי מבעו"י. וכל האוכל מן הפסח אינו אוכל אלא בחבורה אחת ואין מוציאין ממנו מן החבורה שיאכל בה (אבל ב' חבורות יכולין לאכול פסח א' בב' מקומות)(כ"ס הכ"מ) ובשר הפסח שהוציאו בעקירה והניחה חוץ לחבורתו מן האגף ולחוץ נאסר באכילה. הפסח אינו נאכל אלא בהיקף מחילה וב' חבורות שאוכלין בבית א' צריכין כל חבורה לעשות היקף מחילה לעצמן ואלו הופכין פניהם לכאן ואלו לכאן שלא יראו מעורבין וכלה מותרת להחזיר פניה ושמש א' שמשמש לשניהם והתחיל לאכול ואוכלו בפיו כשהולך לשמש לחבורה אחרת קופץ פיו ומחזיר פניו עד שמגיע אצל חבורתו נפרצה המחילה אינן אוכלין וכן אם נעשה מחילה בין חבורה א' אינן אוכלין עד שתסתלק: בתחלת הסעודה שנכנסו רק ב' מהחבורה צריכין להמתין על השאר אבל ג' שנכנסו בזמן הסעודה אין צריכין להמתין: נטמא מקצת האברים שורף את הטמאים ואוכל הטהורים. נטמא שלם או רובו שורפין אותו לפני הבירה כדי לביישן שלא נזהרו בו ונשרף מעצי המערכה ואם רצו הבעלים לשורפו בקש ובקנים משל עצמן שורפין. ונטמא מיעוטו והנותר שורפין בחצרותיהן מעצי עצמן. נטמאו הבעלים מקצתן אע"פ שהתחילו כבר לאכול ונטמאו זכו הטהורים בחלקם של טמאים אבל התחילו כולן לאכול ונטמאו מקצתן חלק הטמאים ישרף וה"ה אם מתו. אין הפסח נשחט ונזרק ונאכל אלא למנויו ולנמולים ולטהורים ולשם פסח. המאכיל פסח ראשון או שני למומר או גר תושב ולנכרי אף על פי שנימול מכין אותו מכת מרדות וישראל ערל שאכל פסח חייב מלקות: מילת בניו ועבדיו וטבילת שפחותיו של גדול מעכבתו מלשחט ולאכול הפסח ולא עבדיו ושפחותיו של קטן מעכבים את הקטן. לכתחלה לא ישחוט על יחיד ואם שחט צריך שיהיה ראוי לאכול את כולו וכן אין שוחטין אלא על מי שראוי לאכול כזית ממנו משעת שחיטה עד שעת זריקה. הרבה נמנין על פסח א' עד שיהא כזית לכל א' ונמנין על מוח שבראש אבל לא על הגידין הרכין שסופן להקשות ולא על מוח שבקולית. וכל זמן שלא נשחט עדיין יכולין למנות עליו ולמשוך ידיהן ממנו ואף כולן יכולין למשוך ממנו רק שישאר א' מהם ואין נמנין על שני פסחים כאחד וכשנמנה על שנים יאכל מן הנשחט ראשון. ואין צולין שני פסחים כאחד. אין עושין חבורה נשים ועבדים קטנים ועבדים אבל עושין חבורה כל אחד לעצמן ולכתחילה אין עושין חבורה כולה קטנים או חולים זקנים ואוננים וגרים. שחטו לכשרים ולפסולים כשר אבל זרק הדם לכשרים ולפסולים פסול שהזריקה חמורה שהוא עיקר הקרבן אפי' חישב בשעת שחיטה ע"מ לזרוק לכשרים ולפסולים פסול אבל חישב לזרוק שלא לאוכליו כשר שאין מחשבת אוכלין בזריקה. שוחט אדם בשביל אחרים שהן ברשותו כגון בנו ובתו הקטנים ועבדו ושפחתו הכנענים אפי' שלא מדעתן ומי שאינו ברשותו שוחט עליו מדעתו ממין שטוב לו ואם שינה פסול ובנו ובתו הגדולים ועבדו ושפחתו העברים ואשתו כ"ז שלא מיחו הוי מדעתן. ואין שוחטין על חצי עבד וחצי בן חורין: זמן אכילת הפסח מן התורה כל הלילה ומדרבנן עד חצות ומה שנותר עד הבוקר באש תשרף: טעון הלל בשעת אכילתו. אסור לשבר עצם מפסח טהור שיש עליו כזית בשר או שיש בו מוח אפי' לאחר זמן אכילתו אפי' מפסח שנפסל ובלבד שהיתה לו שעת הכושר בשחיטה וזריקה. לפיכך שורפין עצמות הפסח בכלל הנותר שלא יבוא לידי תקלה. וכל הנאכל בשור הגדול אחר שנתבשל הוא שמותר לאכול כנגדו מן הגדי הרך אחר צלייתו: *כשמקריבין הפסח בחול ובטהרה ובחבורה גדולה שהאוכלים מרובים מקריבין חגיגה עמו כדי שיהא הפסח נאכל על השובע ואוכל מחגיגה תחלה ומברך בא"י אמ"ה אקב"ו על אכילת הזבח ובאחרונה אוכל מגוף הפסח כדי שיהא הפסח גמר שביעה ומברך בא"י אמ"ה אקב"ו על אכילת הפסח ואוכל אפי' כזית מבשר הפסח ואינו טועם אחריו כלום. והחגיגה נאכלת כבשר שלמים. ובשר חגיגה שעלה עם הפסח על השלחן זמן אכילתו כפסח עצמו. מי שאבד פסחו ומצאו אחר שהפריש פסח אחר יקריב איזו שירצה והשני יקריב שלמים. פסח שנתערב בשלמים יקריב כולו שלמים ומעות פסח שנותר יקריב ג"כ שלמים ופסח שלא בזמנו יקריב שלמים. מחוסרי כפורים שחל יום הבאת קרבנותיהן בי"ד שוחטין עליהן ומקריבין קרבנותיהן בי"ד בין קודם שחיטת הפסח בין אחר שחיטתו ואוכלין פסחיהן לערב ואין שוחטין עליהן עד שימסרו קרבנותיהן ביד ב"ד שמא יפשעו: מצורע שחל שמיני שלו בי"ד וראה קרי בו ביום הרי זה טובל ונכנס לעזרת נשים. ישראל ערל שמל בע"פ שוחטין עליו אחר שמל אבל גר שמל וטבל בי"ד אין שוחטין עליו: מי שבא בבית הפרס ה"ז מנפח והולך ואם לא מצא עצם ולא נטמא שוחט ואוכל פסחו וכן בית הפרס שנידוש טהור לעושה פסח: (יתר הלכות הפסח יבואר לקמן דף צה. בהלכות פסח שני)

[לקמן לה:] [לקמן צג:] [לקמן סג.] [לקמן נט.] [לקמן נח.] [לקמן כד.] [לקמן עד.] [לקמן קטו.]

הגהות הגאון מוה' ליב פישלס ז"ל

[א] נ"ל בין בחול בין בשבת. (עיין במשנה תמיד בסתם): [ב] נ"ל ובערב שבת ע"ש. [ג] חסר ונ"ל אם שחטו אחר חצות קודם לתמיד כשר (עיין במשנה דף ס"א ע"א). [ד] חסר ונ"ל ואם זורק קודם לדם התמיד כשר (ע"ש): [ה] חסר ונ"ל מין מקטעל חלבים והאימורין שהכינה מבעי"ו בשבת (עיין דף ס"ח ע"ב):

*FOR THE TRANSLATION OF THIS SECTION, SEE END OF VOLUME

נימא תלתא תנאי הוו לא תרי תנאי הוו ותנא קמא דר' שמעון היינו ר' יוסי ותנא קמא דר' יוסי היינו ר' שמעון ומאי אף אקמייתא ת"ר *בן בוהיין נתן פיאה לירק ובא אביו ומצאן לעניים שהיו טוענין ירק ועומדין על פתח הגינה אמר להם בני השליכו מעליכם ואני נותן לכם כפליים במעושר לא מפני שעיני צרה אלא מפני שאמרו חכמים אין נותנין פיאה לירק למה ליה למימרא להו לא מפני שעיני צרה כי היכי דלא לימרו דחויי קא מדחי לן ת"ר *בראשונה היו מניחין עורות קדשים בלשכת בית הפרוה לערב היו מחלקין אותן לאנשי בית אב והיו בעלי זרועות נוטלין אותן בזרוע *התקינו שיהיו מחלקין אותן מערב שבת לע"ש דאתיין כולהו משמרות ושקלן בהדדי ועדיין היו גדולי כהונה נוטלין אותן בזרוע עמדו בעלים והקדישום לשמים אמרו לא היו ימים מועטים עד שחיפו את ההיכל כולו בטבלאות של זהב שהן אמה על אמה כעובי דינר זהב ולרגל היו מקפלין אותן ומניחין אותן על גב מעלה בהר הבית כדי שיהו עולי רגלים רואין שמלאכתם נאה ואין בה *דלם *תנא אבא שאול אומר קורות של שקמה היו בירחו והיו בעלי זרועות נוטלין אותן בזרוע עמדו בעלים והקדישום לשמים עליהם ועל כיוצא בהם אמר אבא שאול בן בטנית משום אבא יוסף בן חנין אוי לי מבית בייתוס אוי לי מאלתן אוי לי מבית חנין אוי לי *מלחישתן אוי לי מבית קתרוס אוי לי מקולמוסן אוי לי מבית ישמעאל בן פיאבי אוי לי מאגרופן שהם כהנים גדולים ובניהן גיזברין וחתניהם אמרכלין ועבדיהן חובטין את העם במקלות *תנו רבנן ארבע צווחות צווחה עזרה ראשונה צאו מכאן בני עלי שטימאו היכל ה' ועוד צווחה צא מיכן יששכר איש כפר ברקאי שמכבד את עצמו ומחלל קדשי שמים דהוה כריך ידיה בשיראי ועביד עבודה ועוד צווחה העזרה שאו שערים ראשיכם ויכנס ישמעאל בן פיאבי תלמידו של פנחס וישמש בכהונה גדולה ועוד צווחה העזרה שאו שערים ראשיכם ויכנס יוחנן בן נרבאי תלמידו של פנקאי וימלא כריסו מקדשי שמים אמרו עליו על יוחנן בן נרבאי שהיה *אוכל ג' מאות עגלים ושותה ג' מאות גרבי יין ואוכל ארבעים סאה גוזלות בקינוח סעודה אמרו כל ימיו של יוחנן בן נרבאי לא נמצא נותר במקדש מאי סלקא ביה יששכר איש כפר ברקאי אמרי מלכא ומלכתא הוו יתבי מלכא אמר גדיא יאי ומלכתא אמרה אימרא יאי אמרו מאן מוכח כהן גדול דקא מסיק קרבנות כל יומא אתא איהו אחוי

הדרן עלך מקום שנהגו

רש"י

הכי גרסינן נימא תלתא תנאי הוו לא תרי תנאי הוו · תנא קמא דרבי יוסי היינו ר' שמעון ותנא קמא דרבי שמעון היינו רבי יוסי ומאי אף אקמייתא : נימא תלתא תנאי הוו · תנא קמא דר' יוסי ללפת ולכרוב ולא לקפלוט ותנא קמא דרבי שמעון ללפת ולקפלוט ולא לכרוב ורבי יוסי ורבי שמעון כי הדדי סבירא להו דללפת ולכרוב ולקפלוט : לא · ת"ק דר' שמעון הוא ר' יוסי ות"ק דר' יוסי הוא ר' שמעון ומאי אף דקאמרי תרווייהו אקמייתא דתנא קמא דידהו קיימי דהיינו אלפת דקאמר תנא קמא דרבי יוסי ללפת ולכרוב וקאמר ליה רבי יוסי אף לקפלוט כמו ללפת אבל לכרוב לא ותנא קמא דרבי שמעון נמי הכי קאמר ללפת ולקפלוט כרבי יוסי וקאמר ליה רבי שמעון אף לכרוב כמו ללפת אבל לקפלוט לא דהיינו כתנא קמא דר' יוסי : בן בוהיין · שם אביו בוהיין : כפליים במעושר גרסי' אני אתן לכם כפליים שיש לכם עכשיו פיאה אתן לכם חולין מתוקנין ומעושרין: אין נותנין פיאה לירק · משום דמפקע ליה ממעשר דכתיב (דברים יד) ובא הלוי כי אין לו חלק ונחלה עמך מי שאין לו נחלה עמך חייב לעשר יצא פיאה שיש לו נחלה עמך דהפקר נינהו וכן בשביעית דהפקר פטור ממעשר דכתיב (שמות כג) ואכלו אביוני עמך ויתרם תאכל חית השדה מה חיה אוכלת ופטורה ממעשר אף האביונים פטורין מן המעשר : למה ליה למימר להן לא מפני כו' · הא קא יהיב להן כפליים ומיחזא חזו דלא עין רעה היא: דלא נימרו דחויי מדחי לן · ולא יתן לנו כלום דמה לו ליטול זו וליתן פי שנים לפיכך הוצרך לפרש להן טעמא של דבר : עורות קדשים · עור עולה וחטאות ואשמות וקרבנות ציבור שמתחלקין עורות קדשי הקדשים לכהנים כדכתיב (ויקרא ז) עור העולה אשר הקריב וילפינן בזבחים (דף קג:) מעולה כל עורות קדשי קדשים : ולערב · שכל יום היו מחלקין אותן לאנשי בית אב שעבדו היום שהמשמר היה חלוק לששה בתי אבות לששה ימים ומה שהגיע ליומן הן מרובה הן מועט הוא נוטל אע"פ שיש יום שמרבים היחידים להביא ביום זה מחבירו : בעלי זרועות · שהיו בכהנים חזקים מחביריהם:לערב שבת· דכולי משמרה תיהוי התם ולא יניחו לבעלי זרועות ליטול בזרוע : גדולי כהונה · שרים שבהן: עמדו בעלים·כל כהני משמרות יחד והקדישום לבדק הבית : בהר הבית · רחבה פנויה חוץ לעזרה ויש שם מעלות כדאמרינן בפ"ק דיומא (דף טז.): דלם · דופי : קורות · מחוברין עוביו של אילן קרי קורה: בייתוס· כהן גדול היה וכן כולן [והיו להן עבדים המסנין וחובטין את העם]: אלתן · מקלותיהן כמו לא באלה ולא ברומח במסכת שבת (דף סג.): לחישתן· יועצי רע : קולמוסין · שהיו כותבין אגרות לרעה : אמרכלים·אמר כולו על פיו נחתך כל צורך הקדש : שטימאו · כדכתיב (שמואל א ב) אשר ישכבון את הנשים : כריך ידיה בשיראי · וחציצה פוסלת בקדשים דבעינן ולקח הכהן שיקח בעצמו ועוד דבזיון הוא : ישמעאל בן פיאבי · כשר היה אבל אנשי ביתו היו בעלי זרוע : שלש מאות עגלין · שהיה מגדל בביתו כהנים הרבה : מאי סלקא ביה · מה גמול נשתלם : מלכא ומלכתא· מלכי בית חשמונאי: גדיא יאי· גדי טוב לאכול יותר מן הכבש : אחוי

תוספות

אלא מפני שאמרו חכמים אין פיאה לירק · ואם תאמר מכל מקום ליפטר ממעשר מפני שהפקירם והפקר פטור ממעשר וי"ל כב"ה דאמרי במס' פאה [פ"ו מ"א] אינו הפקר עד שיופקר לעניים ולעשירים כשמיטה וילפינן (בירושלמי) משמיטה דכתיב תשמטנה ונטשתה מה ת"ל ונטשתה יש לך נטישה אחרת שהיא כזו ומה היא זו הפקר לעניים ולעשירים א"כ אפילו בית שמאי דילפי מפיאה וסברי דהפקר לעניים הפקר (*הכא מחייבי משום דהפקר בטעות הוה) וטעמא מפרש התם דכתיב בפיאה לעני ולגר מה תלמוד לומר תעזוב אותם יש לך עזיבה אחרת שהיא כזו ומה היא זו לעניים ולא לעשירים *ומיהו בפיאה גופיה כולי עלמא מודו דפטורה כדדרשינן בספרי ובא הלוי כי אין לו חלק ונחלה עמך יצא זה שיש לו ללוי חלק בהן שאם הוא לוי עני נוטל פיאה:

דכריך ידיה בשיראי · פירש בקונטרס וחציצה פוסלת בקדשים דכתיב ולקח הכהן בעינן שתהא לקיחה בעצמו של כהן וא"ת והא גבי לולב לא אמרינן הכי בפרק לולב הגזול (סוכה דף לז:) גבי לא ליכרוך איניש לולבא בסודרא רבא אמר לקיחה על ידי ד"א שמה לקיחה ותירץ ר"י דהתם מיירי באוחז הלולב על ידי סודר כעין לבא כגון שכורך הלולב בסודר ואוחז בסודר שהסודר מסייעו להחזיק וכי האי גוונא לא הויא חציצה וכן משמע בההיא שמעתא דבהכי מיירי דהא קאמר התם לא ליהדוק איניש לוליבא בהושענא דילמא נתרי טרפי והוי כחציצה רבא אמר מין במינו אינו חוצץ משמע דבשאינו מינו חוצץ והיינו משום דההיא הוי כעין דשמעתין דכריך ידיה בשיראי דכי האי גוונא שייכא חציצה*:

רבינו חננאל

ואוקימנא לה לר' יוסי ור' שמעון ומאי אף דקתני הא והא אלפת והכי קתני נותנין ללפת ולכרוב ר' יוסי אומר ואף לקפלוט ר' יוסי הוא התנא קמא דפליג על ר' שמעון ותניא אידך נותנין פאה ללפת ולקפלוט ר' שמעון אומר ללפת אף לכרוב ר"ש הוא התנא קמא דר' יוסי נמצא תנא קמא דר' יוסי ר' שמעון ות"ק דר"ש רבי יוסי ואמאי דקתני ת"ק ראשון מוסיף עליה בר פלוגתיה אף כך וכך : **בן** *) נכי (היין) [היה] נותן פיאה לירק בא אביו ומצאן לעניים טוענין ועומדין בפתח הגנה אמר להם בני השליכו מעליכם [ואני נותן לכם] כפלים מעשר עני לא מפני שעיני צרה אלא מפני שאמרו חכמים אין נותנין פיאה לירק : ת"ר בראשונה היו מניחין עורות קדשים בלשכת הפרוה ולערב היו חולקין אותן והיו בעלי זרועות נוטלין אותן בזרוע הקדיש בעליהם לשמים כו' עד כדי שיהיו עולי רגלים רואין שמלאכתן נאה בלי דלם : **תניא** קורות שקמה היו בירחו והיו בעלי זרועות נוטלין אותן בזרוע עמדו בעליהן והקדישום לשמים עליהם ועל כיוצא בהן אמרו אוי לי מבית חנן אוי לי מלחישתן שהיו רכלין אוי לי מבית ביתוס אוי לי מאלתו' בעלי זרוע אוי לי מבית קתרום אוי לי מקולמוסן שהיו חוקקי און . ישמעאל בן פיאבי הוא היה טוב ובני ביתו היו אגרופין והם כהנים גדולים ובניהם גזברין והתניהן אמרכלין ועבדיהם חובטין העם במקל: **ת"ר** ארבע צווחות צוחה עזרה שתים בכניסה ושתים ביציאה ראשונה צוחה צאו מכאן בני עלי שטמאו היכל ה' ועוד צוחה צא מכאן יששכר איש כפר ברקאי שמכבד עצמו דכריך ידיה בשראי ועביד עבודה ונמצא מבזה קדשי שמים ליגע אותם בידו ועוד צוחה שאו שערים ראשיכם ויכנס ישמעאל בן פיאבי תלמידו של פנחס וישמש בכהונה גדולה : **הדרן עלך פרק מקום שנהגו**

נה א מיי' פ"ה מהלכות מעשה קרבנות הל' כ:

ט"ס פה וצ"ע דסמוך אחר מלות ולא לעשירים יגכון

[בס בתוספתא]

[ועי' תוס' יומא נח. ד"ה מין ותוס' זבחים כד. ד"ה הוליל ותוס' סוכה לז. ד"ה כי]

[תוספתא פי"ג]

[תוספתא דמנחות פי"ג וזבחים פי"א]

[בערוך ערך דלוס פי' דופי]

[פי' שהיו רכלין ערוך ערך לחש]

כריתות כח. [וע"ש]

פי' לו ולאנשי ביתו כי היו לו בני בית לרוב

סי' רש"ל

*) אולי צ"ל בן מביא יין וכ"ה בירושלמי כאן או שסי' גורס בירושלמי בן נכי היין ובתוספתא הגי' מעשה בבן נבו ועי' במלאכת השם כאן .

R. Simeon said: For cabbage too. [57a] Shall we say that there are three Tannaim [in dispute]?—No: there are [only] two Tannaim [in dispute], the first Tanna opposed to[11] R. Simeon being R. Jose, while the first Tanna opposed to R. Jose is R. Simeon. And what does 'too' mean? It refers to the first mentioned.[12]

a Our Rabbis taught: The son of Bohayon[1] gave *pe'ah* from vegetables, and his father came and found the poor laden with vegetables and standing at the entrance to the kitchen garden. Said he to them, 'My sons, cast it from you, and I will give you twice as much of tithed [produce]; not because I begrudge it to you, but because the Sages said, You must not give *pe'ah* from vegetables.' Why had he to say to them, 'Not because I begrudge it to you?' So that they should not say, 'He is merely putting us off.'

Our Rabbis taught: At first they used to place the skins of sacrifices in the chamber of Beth Ha-Parwah.[2] In the evening they used to divide them among the men of the paternal division,[3] but men of violence[4] used to seize [more than their due share] by force. So they enacted that they should divide them every Sabbath eve, so that all the 'wards' came and received their portions together.[5] Yet the chief priests still seized [them] by force; thereupon the owners[6] arose and consecrated them to Heaven.[7] It was related: It did not take long before they covered the whole Temple with gold plaques a cubit square of the thickness of a gold *denar*. And on festivals they used to lay them together[8] and place them on a high eminence on the Temple Mount, so that the Festival pilgrims might see that their workmanship was beautiful,[9] and that there was no imperfection in them.

It was taught, Abba Saul said: There were sycamore tree-trunks in Jericho, and the men of violence seized them by force, [whereupon] the owners arose and consecrated them to Heaven. And it was of these and of such as these that Abba Saul b. Bothnith said in the name of Abba Joseph b. Ḥanin: 'Woe is me because b of the house of Boethus; woe is me because of their staves![1] Woe is me because of the house of Ḥanin, woe is me because of their whisperings![2] Woe is me because of the house of Ḳathros,[3] woe is me because of their pens![4] Woe is me because of the house of Ishmael the son of Phabi,[5] woe is me because of their fists! For they are High Priests[6] and their sons are [Temple] treasurers and their sons-in-law are trustees and their servants beat the people with staves.'[7]

Our Rabbis taught: Four cries did the Temple Court cry out. The first: 'Depart hence, ye children of Eli,' for they defiled the Temple of the Lord. And another cry: 'Depart hence, Issachar of Kefar Barkai, who honours himself while desecrating the sacred sacrifices of Heaven'; for he used to wrap his hands with silks and perform the [sacrificial] service.[8] The Temple Court also cried out: 'Lift up your heads, O ye gates, and let Ishmael the son of Phabi, Phineas's disciple,[9] enter and serve in the [office of the] High Priesthood.' The Temple Court also cried out: 'Lift up your heads, O ye gates, and let Joḥanan the son of Narbai,[10] the disciple of Pinkai,[11] enter and fill his stomach with the Divine sacrifices. It was said of Joḥanan b. Narbai that he ate three hundred calves and drank three hundred barrels of wine and ate forty *se'ah* c of young birds as a dessert for his meal.[1] It was said: As long as Joḥanan the son of Narbai lived,[2] *nothar*[3] was never found in the Temple.

What was the fate of[4] Issachar of Kefar Barkai? It was related: The king and queen[5] were sitting: the king said, 'Goat's [flesh] is better,' while the queen said, 'Lamb is better'. Said they, Who shall decide?[6] The High Priest, who offers up sacrifices every

(11) Lit., 'of'. (12) Thus: the first Tanna states turnips and cabbages, whereupon R. Jose says, for porret too, just as for turnips, but not for cabbages; similarly R. Simeon in the second Baraitha.

a (1) The name of a certain man. (2) Name of a Persian builder and Magian, after whom a compartment in the Temple was supposed to have been named (Jast.). (3) The priests were divided into 'wards', (משמר), each 'ward' officiating a week at a time in the Temple; these were further subdivided into paternal divisions (*beth ab*), of which each officiated one day in the week. (4) Among the priests (Rashi). Lit., 'men of (strong) arms'. (5) Cur. edd.; Rashi's reading seems to be: so that the whole ward (sing.) i.e., all the paternal divisions etc. This is more correct, and if our reading is retained it must also be understood in the same sense.—The larger number present would act as a check. (6) I.e., all the priests of each ward. (7) *Sc.* for the Temple. (8) The word really means 'fold them', but as gold plates of that thickness could hardly be folded, it must be understood as translated. (9) For the sacrifices, with the skins of which these were brought, were mostly offered by the Festival pilgrims.

b (1) With which they beat the people. (2) Their secret conclaves to devise oppressive measures. (3) Supposed to be identical with χανϑηρᾶς, Josephus, *Antiquities* XX, 1, 3. (4) With which they wrote their evil decrees. (5) He himself was religious and held in high repute, as is seen below (v. also Par. III, 5; Soṭ. IX, 5; Yoma 35b), but he did not restrain his sons from lawlessness; in the passage of Josephus too, already cited, reference is only made to his children. (6) The High Priesthood by this time was a source of great political power. Once a man became a High Priest he retained much of his power, and perhaps his title too, even if he was deposed; hence there were often several High Priests at the same time; v. Halevi, *Doroth*, I, 3, p. 445, n. 30; pp. 633f; 718. (7) For this passage cf. Josephus, *Antiquities* XX, 8, 8. (8) This disqualifies the sacrifice. (9) In his zeal for God. (10) [Ananias son of Nebedus. V. Josephus, *Antiquities* XX, 5, 2.] (11) Perhaps this is a nickname formed by a play on words, פינכא (here פינקא) being a meat dish; i.e., the gourmand.

c (1) The marginal note softens this statement by observing that this was eaten by his whole household, which was very numerous. (2) Lit., '(during) all the days of' etc. (3) V. Glos. (4) Lit., 'what happened to?' (5) Hasmonean monarchs. [In Ker. 28b: King Jannai and the Queen. The name Jannai appears in the Talmud as a general name for kings of the Hasmonean dynasty.] (6) Lit., '(from) whom is it proved?'

did not forbid them to do it. [56b] Whom do you know to main- a tain [that] they forbade and did not forbid?[1] R. Judah. Yet he teaches, They reaped with the consent of the Sages?—Then according to your reasoning, [surely] these are four! Rather, delete reaping from this.

'And they permitted the branches of carob and sycamore trees of *heḳdesh*.' They said: Our fathers sanctified nought but tree trunks, hence we will permit [for use] the branches of *heḳdesh* of carob and sycamore trees. Now we discuss the growth which came after that;[2] so that while they held as he who rules, There is no trespass-offering [due] when [one benefits from] what grows, the Rabbis held, Granted that there is no trespass-offering [due], there is nevertheless a prohibition.

'And they made breaches [etc.].' 'Ulla said in the name of R. Simeon b. Laḳish: The controversy is in respect of [the dates of] the upper branches, for the Rabbis held, We forbid them preventively, lest he go up and cut them off, while the inhabitants of Jericho held, We do not forbid them preventively, lest he go up and cut them off. But as for the dates which are among the lower branches, all agree that it is permitted.[3] Said Rabbah to him, b But they are *muḳẓeh?*[1] And should you say, [that is] because they [the dates] were fit for [his] ravens,[2] [I would rejoin],—seeing that that which is ready[3] for man is not ready for dogs, for we learned, R. Judah said, If it was not *nebelah* from the eve of the Sabbath, it is forbidden, because it is not of that which is ready,[4] then shall what is ready for birds be [regarded as] ready for human beings?[5]—Yes, he replied. That which is ready for human beings is not ready for dogs, for whatever is fit for a man, he does not put [it] out of his mind;[6] [but] that which is ready for birds is [also] ready for human beings,[7] [for] his mind is [set] upon it.

When Rabin came,[8] he said in the name of R. Simeon b. Laḳish: The controversy is in respect of [the fallen dates] among the lower branches, the Rabbis holding, That which is ready for birds is not ready for man, while the men of Jericho hold, That which is ready for birds is ready for man. But [the fallen dates] on the upper branches, all agree that they are forbidden; we forbid [them] preventively, lest he ascend and cut off [some dates].

AND THEY GAVE PE'AH FROM VEGETABLES. Yet did not the inhabitants agree with what we learned: They stated a general principle in respect to *pe'ah:* whatever is an eatable, and is guarded, and c its growth is from the earth, and is [all] gathered simultaneously,[1] and is collected for storage,[2] is subject to *pe'ah*. 'Whatever is an eatable' excludes the aftergrowth of woad[3] and madder;[4] 'and is guarded' excludes *hefḳer;*[5] 'and its growth is from the earth' excludes mushrooms and truffles;[6] 'and is [all] gathered simultaneously' excludes the fig tree;[7] 'and is collected for storage' excludes vegetables![8]—Said Rab Judah in Rab's name: The reference is to turnip tops, and they differ [in respect to what] one collects for storing by means of something else:[9] one Master holds, If he takes it in for storage by means of something else it is designated storage; while the other Master holds, What he takes in for storage by means of something else is not designated storage.[10]

Our Rabbis taught: At first they used to leave *pe'ah* for turnips and cabbages. R. Jose said: Also for porret. While another [Baraitha] taught: They used to give *pe'ah* for turnips and porret;

a (1) I.e., who makes this distinction, but not the distinction between with and without their consent. (2) *Sc.* after the trees had been dedicated. (3) *Mekabedoth* are the upper branches on which dates grow; *kipin* are the lower branches where dates do not grow. Rashi: they differ in respect of the dates which fell on the Festival and were caught on these upper branches. Since they are high up, he must climb up to get them, and the Rabbis held that we fear that this will lead him to pull off some dates still on the branches, which is forbidden; while the inhabitants of Jericho held that there was no need to fear this. But all agree that he may take those which had been caught by the lower branches, for no dates grow there in any case, that we should fear that he will pull some off. Tosaf.: the reference is to dates which fell off before the Festival commenced, being caught either by the upper or the lower branches, and then they fell to the ground on the Festival. The Rabbis held that those which had been caught on the upper branches are forbidden, for since they were there at twilight, when the Festival was about to commence, and also there are dates growing on these upper branches, we fear that he might ascend and pluck some; while the inhabitants of Jericho did not thus forbid them preventively, since they were already detached on the eve of the Festival. But all agree that those which had fallen on the lower branches in the first place are permitted now that they have fallen to earth, for since none grow there, there was never any fear that he might go up and cut off the growing dates.—Though this explanation removes several difficulties, Tosaf. observes that it raises a practical difficulty: how is one to distinguish between those which fell down before the Festival and those which fell on the Festival itself, and those which had fallen on the upper branches in the first place and those which had first fallen on the lower branches?

b (1) V. Glos. Rashi: on the eve of the Sabbath or Festival at twilight they were *muḳẓeh* on account of the prohibition of cutting them off then from the tree, and consequently they remain so for the whole day, even after they fall. (*Muḳẓeh* is always determined by the status of an object at twilight of the Sabbath or Festival.) Tosaf.: they were *muḳẓeh* at twilight because one must not make use of a tree on the Sabbath or Festival, e.g., by climbing it, taking articles which had been suspended upon it, etc. (2) If he has ravens at home, they could have eaten these dates on the Sabbath even while they were still on the tree; since they are fit for his birds, they are also regarded as fit for himself too. (3) *Mukan*, a technical term denoting the opposite of *muḳẓeh*. (4) If an animal dies on the Sabbath, the first Tanna holds that the carcass may be cut up for dogs. But R. Judah rules as stated. For while alive it could have been ritually killed and then permitted for human consumption; hence it was ready not for dogs but for human beings, and thus R. Judah holds that its readiness for human beings does not make it ready for dogs too. (5) Surely not! (6) To think of giving it to dogs. (7) Even if it is fit for dogs. (8) From Palestine to Babylonia.

c (1) I.e., the whole of the crop ripens about the same time. (2) Lit., 'he brings it in to keep'. This applies to cereals in general, which are stored in granaries for long periods. (3) ἰσάτις, *isatis tinctoria*, a plant producing a deep blue dye. (4) Both are used as dyes. (5) V. Glos. (6) Though these grow in the earth, they were held to draw their sustenance mainly from the air. (7) Whose fruits do not all ripen at the same time. The same is true of many other trees, which are likewise excluded. (8) Which must be eaten fresh. (9) R. Ḥan.: i.e., by means of pickling. (10) It must be capable of storing in its natural state.

עין משפט
נר מצוה

נד א מיי׳ פ״ב מהל׳ מתנות עניים הלכה א ב:

מאן שמעת ליה דאמר מיחו ולא מיחו רבי יהודה וקתני קוצרין ברצון חכמים וליטעמיך הני ארבעה הוה אלא סמי מיכן קצירה: ומתירין גמזיות של הקדש של חרוב ושל שקמה אמרו אבותינו לא הקדישו אלא קורות ואנו נתיר גמזיות של הקדש של חרוב ושל שקמה ובגידולין הבאין לאחר מכאן עסקינן וסברי לה כמ״ד אין מעילה בגידולין ורבנן סברי נהי דמעילה ליכא איסורא מיהא איכא: ופורצין פרצות: אמר עולא א״ר שמעון בן לקיש מחלוקת בשל מכבדות דרבנן סברי גזרינן שמא יעלה ויתלוש ואנשי יריחו סברי לא גזרינן שמא יעלה ויתלוש אבל בשל בין הכיפין דברי הכל מותר א״ל (א) רבא והא מוקצות נינהו וכי תימא הואיל דחזי לעורבין השתא מוכן לאדם לא הוי מוכן לכלבים *דתנן ר׳ יהודה אומר אם לא היתה נבילה מע״ש אסורה לפי שאינה מן המוכן מוכן לעורבים הוי מוכן לאדם א״ל *אין מוכן לאדם לא הוי מוכן לכלבים דכל מידי דחזי לאיניש לא מקצה ליה מדעתיה מוכן לעורבים הוי מוכן לאדם כל מידי דחזי לאיניש דעתיה עלויה כי אתא רבין א״ר שמעון בן לקיש מחלוקת בשל בין כיפין דרבנן סברי מוכן לעורבים לא הוי מוכן לאדם ואנשי יריחו סברי מוכן לעורבים הוי מוכן לאדם אבל בשל מכבדות דברי הכל אסור גזרינן שמא יעלה ויתלוש: ונותנין פיאה לירק: ולית להו לאנשי יריחו הא *דתנן *כלל אמרו בפיאה כל שהוא אוכל ונשמר וגידולו מן הארץ ולקיטתו כאחת ומכניסו לקיום חייב בפיאה כל שהוא אוכל פרט לספיחי סטים וקוצה ונשמר פרט להפקר וגידולו מן הארץ פרט לכמהין ופטריות ולקיטתן כאחת פרט לתאנים ומכניסו לקיום פרט לירק א״ר יהודה אמר רב הכא בראשי לפתות עסקינן ומכניסו לקיום ע״י דבר אחר קמיפלגי מר סבר מכניסו לקיום ע״י דבר אחר שמיה קיום ומר סבר לא שמיה קיום: ת״ר בראשונה היו נותנין פיאה ללפת ולכרוב ר׳ יוסי אומר אף לקפלוט ותני׳ אידך *היו נותנין פיאה ללפת ולקפלוט ר״ש אומר אף לכרוב נימא

מאן שמעת ליה. דנקט ליתנא דמיחו ולא מיחו ר׳ יהודה היא דשמעת ליה לעיל: וליטעמיך. דסבירא לך הא דלעיל דקתני אלו ואלו שלא ברצון חכמים כו׳ מתרצתא היא דקא רמית אחריתי עליה ליפרכיה מינה ובה דקתני על שלשה לא מיחו וקא חשיב ארבעה מרכיבין וכורכין וקוצרין וגודשין: ובגידולין גרסינן: כמאן דאמר אין מעילה בגידולין. במסכת מעילה (דף יג׳): מחלוקת. דאנשי יריחו ורבנן: בשל מכבדות. כפות תמרים הן בראש הדקל וכפופות זו אצל זו כעין כלי וכשהתמרים נושרין מקבלות אותן וכיון דגבוה וצריך לעלות על הדקל לנטלן חיישינן שמא יתלוש מן המחוברות דהוי אב מלאכה: בשל בין הכיפים. למטה מנופיהן נופות התחתונים וליכא למיחש לתלישה דאין כאן מחוברות: והא מוקצות נינהו. שמערב שבת בין השמשות היו מחוברות וכשנפלו מוקצות מחמת איסור תלישה ומוקצה בין השמשות מוקצה לכל היום: וכי תימא הואיל וחזו. במחובר לעורבים. שיש לו הגדילות בתוך ביתו לגדולה ומותר להעמידם עליהן לאוכלם: נבילה שנתנבלה בשבת היתה עומדת בין השמשות לאדם ולא חשיב לה מוכן לגבי כלבים: ונשמר. שאינו מופקר ומקפידין עליו לשומרו: ומכניסו לקיום. שמתקיים ימים רבים: ספיחי סטים וקוצה. קשין לאכילה אבל סטים וקוצה שאינם ספיחים חזו לאכילה סטים מוריק״א קרו״ג: קוצה. וויישר״א: תאינה אינה מתבשלת כאחת אלא זו גמורה היום ואחרת יוצאה בלידה כל ימות הקיץ: ראשי לפתות. עלי הלפת מכניסין אותן לקיום על ידי האימהות: ללפת. לעלין דבאימהות כולי עלמא מודו דהא מתקיימין הכי

מחלוקת בשל מכבדות. פ״ה כולה שמעתא בנתלשו ביו״ט ודווקא בשל מכבדות דאיכא כמי מחוברות גזרו רבנן שמא יעלה ויתלוש וקשה נהי דלא גזרו בני יריחו בשל מכבדות שמא יעלה ויתלוש תיפוק ליה שמשתמש במחובר דאטו לית להו הא דתנן (ביצה דף לו:) אין עולין באילן וכו׳ ובין הכיפין נמי אמאי ד״ה מותר הא קמשתמש באילן כדאמר בבירה (שבת דף מה׳) אין מניחין נר על גבי דקל שמא ישתמש באילן בשעת נטילתה וכן משמע בעירובין (דף ק׳) ובכמה דוכתי ועוד דלא גרע בין הכיפין מביצה שנולדה שהיא על הקרקע דאסרינן בביצה (דף ג׳) משום פירות הנושרין *וליכא לאוקמה בפחות מג׳ טפחים דמותר להשתמש דמ״מ ה״ל לפלוגי בבין הכיפין בין פחות מג׳ טפחים ליותר ונראה לר״י דשמעתא איירי בתלושין מעי״ט מכבדות וכיפים ומונחים שם בין השמשות וקאמר מחלוקת בשל מכבדות דרבנן אסרי אפילו נפלו לארץ בי״ט כיון דמכבדות איכא נמי מחוברים גזרינן שמא יעלה ויתלוש כיון דבין השמשות היו על האילן אע״פ שהן תלוש ובני יריחו לא גזרו כיון דתלוש מעי״ט אבל בשל בין הכיפין הואיל ולא היו שם מחוברים ליכא למיגזר אטו שמא יעלה ויתלוש ממקום שלא נשרו והבאה א״ש דלא דמי לביצה דהתם שנולד בי״ט גזרינן והכא כיון דנתלשו מעי״ט וקאת תימה איך יכירו בין אותם שנשרו אתמול לאותם שנשרו היום ונשר מן הכיפין לנשר מן המכבדות ופריך והא מוקצה נינהו כיון דהיו בין השמשות על האילן ולא היו ראויות ליטול שלא ישתמש באילן ובירושלמי דס״פ פריך במה אנן קיימין אי בנשרו מעי״ט ד״ה מותרים ואי בי״ט ד״ה אסורים אלא במה קיימין בכתם פי׳ דבכתם לא שייך למיגזר שמא יעלה ויתלוש אלא דוקא בנשרו ולאי בי״ט והיכא דנשרו ולאי בי״ט אפילו בשל בין הכיפין אסור ופריך והא מוקצות נינהו פי׳ ספק מוקצות נינהו אבל מ״מ קשה דתיפוק ליה שמשתמש במחובר:

דתנן רבי יהודה אומר אם לא היתה נבילה מע״ש. תימה הא התם לא הוי מוכן לאדם דאסור לשוחטה בשבת ומפרש ה״ר יוסף דממשכה יתירה דייק דלא ה״ל למיתני לפי שאינה מן המוכן כיון דבדבר תנא היסורא אלא אפילו היה מוכן באין מוקצה מחמת איסור לא הוי מוכן לכלבים ור׳ יהודה מפ״ש מוכן לאדם הייט שעומדת לאכילת אדם ואע״ג דאין ראויה לאדם לאותה שבת הייט מחמת איסור ולא מחמת הקצאה שלא היה רוצה שיהנה בה אדם ולא אמרינן עמידתה לאדם כעמידתה לכלבים שאלו היתה עומדת לכלבים כמו שעומדת לאדם היתה מותרת כשנתנבלה בשבת דלגבי כלבים ליכא מוקצה מחמת איסור כי יש דברים שראוים ליתן לכלבים חיים כגון עופות וכיוצא בהן ולא אמר דהוי מוכן לכלבים אע״ג דלבסוף הוי מוכן לכלבים אלא אדרבה לפי שסתמא עומד לאדם מקצי ליה מכלבים ה״נ מוכן לעורבים לא הוי מוכן לאדם אע״ג דלבסוף הוי מוכן לאדם: מוכן לעורבים. אפילו הי לא שרי הכא אלא למי שיש לו עורבים איצטריך ברים ביצה (דף ג׳) למיסר פירות הנושרין מטעם גזירה שמא יעלה ויתלוש דלא מצי למימר התם איסורא משום מוקצה שהרי מעמיד שם המשנה בתרנגולת העומדת לאכילה א״כ איסור מוקצה לא שייך בה למיגזר אי לאו משום גזרה שמא יעלה ויתלוש:

כלל אמרו בפיאה כו׳. נראה לרבינו תם דמדאורייתא לא מיחייב בפאה אלא זית וכרם ושדה דכתיבי בהדיא בקרא ואחריני תקנתא דרבנן ניהו ושאין מכניסו לקיום לא רצו לתקן פיאה דאינו דבר חשוב ותאינה וכל דדמי לה אף על גב דחשיב איכא בטול עניים לפי שאין לקיטתן כאחד והפסד יתר על הריוח וכמיהין ופטריות הואיל ואין במינו היוצא שאין גדל בקרקע לא תקנו והא דדריש בתורת כהנים יכול שאני מרבה קישואין ודלועין שיהיו חייבין בפיאה תלמוד לומר ובקוצרכם את קציר ארצכם מה קציר שהוא אוכל ונשמר וגידולו מן הארץ אף כל כו׳ יצאו ירקות כו׳ אסמכתא בעלמא היא כמו שדורש שם מקרא מעשר ירק אף על גב דהוי דרבנן:
הלה

מהרש״א מהפך הדברים כך וליכא לאוקמא בתחלה עד ליותר ואח״כ ועוד דלא גרע כו׳ עד פירות הנושרין ואח״כ ונראה לר״י:

רבינו חננאל

מתני׳: מתירין גמזיות של הקדש פי׳ הן נצרים הפרים משרשי אילנות והן קשקשי אילנות והיו אנשי יריחו אומרים אבותינו לא הקדישו אלא הקורות מפני שהיו בעלי בתים נוטלין אותן בורוע קורות הקדש' ואלו לא הקדישו והיו מתירין הגזיות ומיחו בידם חכמים ואמרו נהי דמעילה בגידולין ליכא איסורא מיהא איכא רבנן למעטיהו דפליגי עליה דר׳ יוסי במעילה פ״ד ואמרי הקדיש אילן ואח״כ נשא פירות שדה ואח״כ נתמלאת עשבים מועלין בהן ואין מועלין במה שבתוכן: ואוכלין מתחת הנשרו׳ פי׳ בין הפירות הנובלות מן האילן ומיחו בידם חכמים ואוקימנא בלישנא בתרא מחלוקת בשל בין הכיפים ואנשי יריחו סברי מוכן לעורבים הוה מוכן לאדם ורבנן סברי מוכן לעורבים לא הוה מוכן לאדם אבל התמרים של מכבדות שהן מחוברין אם נשרו דברי הכל אסורין מאי טעמא הרואה כי מחוברין היו ונפלו בשבת ואמרו מותרין הן יעלה ויתלוש: ואקשינן ונותנין פיאה לירק והתנן כלל אמרו בפיאה כל שהוא אוכל ונשמר וכו׳ ואמרינן בסיפא ומכניסו לקיום חייב בפיאה ותאני עלה הירק אע״פ שלקיטתו כאחת אין מכניסו לקיום ושני רב יהודה משמא דרב האי ירק דקתני במתני׳ ראשי לפתות הן דמכניסן לקיום ע״י ד״א בכבישה כדרך כל הכבישין. אנשי יריחו סברי כי האי גונא מכנסו לקיום [מיקרי] ורבנן סברי לא: ת״ר נותנין פיאה ללפת ולכרוב רבי יוסי אומר אף לקפלוט ותניא אידך נותנין פיאה ללפת ולקפלוט רבי שמעון אומר אף לכרוב

מסורת הש״ס

חולין ידי: שבת קטו: ביצה ו: כו:

[ביצה שם]

שבת סח: נדה כ׳ פיאה פ״א [מ״ד]

[תוספתא פ״ג]

הגהות הב״ח

(א) גמרא א״ל רבא והא מוקצות נינהו:

ואוכלין מתחת הנשרים בשבת ונותנין פאה לירק ומיחו בידם חכמים: **גמ׳** *ת"ר ששה דברים עשה חזקיה המלך על שלשה הודו לו ועל שלשה לא הודו לו *גירר עצמות אביו על מטה של חבלים והודו לו כיתת נחש הנחשת והודו לו גנז ספר רפואות והודו לו ועל שלשה לא הודו לו קיצץ דלתות של היכל ושיגרן למלך אשור ולא הודו לו סתם מי גיחון העליון ולא הודו לו עיבר ניסן בניסן ולא הודו לו: מרכיבין דקלים כל היום וכו׳: היכי עבדי ׳אמר רב יהודה מייתי אסא דרא ושיכרא דדפנא וקימחא דשערי דרמי במנא דלא חלפי עליה ארבעין יומין ומרתחי להו ושדו להו לדיקלא בליביה וכל דקאי בארבע אמות דידיה אי לא עבדי ליה הכי צאוי לאלתר רב אחא בריה דרבא אמר מנחי כופרא דיכרא לנוקבתא: וכורכין את שמע: היכי עבדי אמר רב יהודה אומרים °שמע ישראל ה׳ אלהינו ה׳ אחד ולא היו מפסיקין רבא אמר מפסיקין היו אלא שהיו אומרים היום על לבבך דמשמע היום על לבבך *ולא מחר על לבבך: *ת"ר כיצד היו כורכין את שמע אומרים שמע ישראל ה׳ אלהינו ה׳ אחד ולא היו מפסיקין דברי רבי מאיר רבי יהודה אומר מפסיקין היו אלא שלא היו אומרים ברוך שם כבוד מלכותו לעולם ועד *ואנן מאי טעמא אמרינן ליה כדדריש ר׳ שמעון בן *לקיש דאמר רשב"ל °ויקרא יעקב אל בניו ויאמר האספו ואגידה לכם ביקש יעקב לגלות לבניו קץ הימין ונסתלקה ממנו שכינה אמר שמא חס ושלום יש במטתי פסול כאברהם שיצא ממנו ישמעאל ואבי יצחק שיצא ממנו עשו אמרו לו בניו שמע ישראל ה׳ אלהינו ה׳ אחד אמרו כשם שאין בלבך אלא אחד כך אין בלבנו אלא אחד באותה שעה פתח יעקב אבינו ואמר ברוך שם כבוד מלכותו לעולם ועד אמרי רבנן היכי נעביד נאמרוהו לא אמרו משה רבינו לא נאמרוהו אמרו יעקב התקינו שיהו אומרים אותו בחשאי אמר רבי יצחק אמרי דבי רבי אמי משל לבת מלך שהריחה ציקי קדירה אם תאמר יש לה גנאי לא תאמר יש לה צער התחילו עבדיה להביא (א) בחשאי אמר רבי אבהו התקינו שיהו אומרים אותו בקול רם מפני תרעומת המינין ובנהרדעא דליכא מינין עד השתא אמרי לה בחשאי: *תנו רבנן ששה דברים עשו אנשי יריחו שלשה ברצון חכמים ושלשה שלא ברצון חכמים ואלו ברצון חכמים מרכיבין דקלים כל היום וכורכין את שמע וקוצרין לפני העומר ואלו שלא ברצון חכמים גודשין לפני העומר ופורצין פרצות בגנותיהן ובפרדסותיהן להאכיל נשר לעניים בשני בצורת בשבתות ובימים טובים ומתירין גמזיות של הקדש של חרוב ושל שקמה דברי רבי מאיר אמר לו רבי יהודה אם ברצון חכמים היו עושין יהו כל אדם עושין כן אלא אלו ואלו שלא ברצון חכמים היו עושין על שלשה מיחו בידם ועל שלשה לא מיחו בידם ואלו שלא מיחו בידם מרכיבין דקלים כל היום וכורכין את שמע וקוצרין וגודשין לפני העומר ואלו שמיחו בידם מתירין גמזיות של הקדש של חרוב ושל שקמה ופורצין פרצות בגנותיהן ופרדסיהן להאכיל נשר לעניים בשבתות וימים טובים בשני בצורת נותנין פיאה לירק ומיחו בידם חכמים וסבר רבי יהודה קצירה שלא ברצון חכמים היא *והתנן אנשי יריחו קוצרין לפני העומר ברצון חכמים וגודשין לפני העומר שלא ברצון חכמים ולא מיחו בידם חכמים

מאן

לא היו מפסיקין · בין שמע ישראל לשם דמשמע דהומר לשם שישמע ישראל ויענם* : מחלוקת

ואוכלין מתחת הנשרין . תחת הדקל המשיר פירותיו היו אוכלין מן הנושרות וטעמא דכולהו מפרש בגמרא : ונותנין פיאה לירק . והוא פטור מן הפיאה כדמפרש בגמרא : ומיחו בידן . משום דקא מפקעי ליה ממעשר שהיו עניים אוכלין אותה פיאה בטיבלה דסבורין שהיא פיאה גמורה ולקט שכחה ופיאה פטורין מן המעשר משום דהפקר נינהו : **גמ׳** גירר עצמות אביו . משום כפרה ולא קברו בכבוד בדרגש ומטה נאה ומפני קידוש השם שיתגנה על רשעו ויוסרו הרשעים : כיתת נחש הנחשת . לפי שהיו טועים אחריו : וגנז ספר רפואות . כדכתיב והטוב (והישר) בעיניך עשיתי ואמרינן בברכות שגנז ספר רפואות לפי שלא היה לבם נכנע על חולים אלא מתרפאין מיד : סתם מי גיחון . כדכתיב (ד"ה ב לב) למען לא יבאו מלכי אשור ומצאו מים לשתות : ולא הודו לו . שהיה לו לבטוח בהקב"ה שאמר (מלכים ב יט) וגנותי על העיר הזאת להושיעה : עיבר ניסן בניסן . לאחר שנכנס ניסן נמלך ועשאו אדר השני כדכתיב (ד"ה ב ל) ויועץ המלך חזקיה לעשות פסח בחדש השני וגו׳ כי מרבית העם רבים אשר לא הוטהרו עדיין מטומאות שהחזיקו בהן בימי אביו אחז הרשע : ולא הודו לו. כדאמר בסנהדרין* ובברכות [י:] החדש הזה וגו׳ זה ניסן ואין אחר ניסן : אסא דרא. הדס לח : ושיכרא דדפנא. שכר של עץ שקורין לו"ר וגדילין בו פרי שקורין ביי"ש : דלא חלו עליה ארבעין יומי . משנטחנה : ושדו ליה לדקלא בליביה . דקל יש לו לב מתוכו ויש לו מיח לאורכו כמו שיש לעץ שקורין שנבו"ג ולאגוז והמשקה הזה מועיל לדקל להתקיים : וכל . אילן דקאי בארבע אמות דידיה דלא עבדי ליה הכי : לאוי . מתייבש : רב אחא בריה דרבא אמר. לאו הייטו מרכיבין דמתניתין אלא מנחי כופרא דוכרא לנוקבתא מניחין ותוחבין גמזיות רכה בת שנתה שניתוספה באילן בשנה שעברה וקרי ליה כופרא דיכרא על שם שמכניסין אותו בענף האילן שקולץ ענף גדול וסודקו ומשים את זה בתוכו לשון אחר כופרא דיכרא ענף רך של דקל זכר ומרכיבו בסדק של דקל נקיבה מפני שדקל נקיבה אינה עושה פירות והזכרים עושין פירות : ולא היו מפסיקין . בין אחד לואהבת(ב) אע"פ דצריך להאריך באחד ולהפסיק בין קבלת מלכות שמים לדברים אחרים שכל אחד מקבל עליו ואומר אחד הוא אלהינו בפסוק ראשון ופסוק שני לשון צוואה הוא : רבי יהודה אומר מפסיקין היו אלא שלא היו אומרים ברוך שם כבוד מלכותו : וכורכין.כלומר שהיו מדבקין כל הקרייה כמות שהיא ולא היו מוסיפין ואית דגרסי שהיו אומרים ברוך שם כבוד מלכותו פי׳ שהיו אומרים אותו בקול רם : קץ הימין . שיחזיר ימינו לפניו שהשיב אחור ימינו מפני אויב : שמע ישראל . לאביהם היו אומרים : נימריה · להאי ברוך שם כבוד מלכותו בקרית שמע : ציקי קדירה . ארשדור"א : יש לה צער . צער גופה מחמת התאוה : מפני תרעומת המינין . שלא יהו אומרים עלינו שאנו מוסיפין דבר שאינו הגון בחשאי ומאן דגרסי שהיו אומרים ברוך שם כבוד מלכותו לעולם ועד מפרש שהיו אומרים אותו בקול רם כשאר הקרייה וביניהן לא היו מינין : נשר . פירות הנושרין : ה"ג מתירין גמזיות של הקדש של חרוב ושל שקמה . כשהוקדשו הסדנין תחילה ונתוספו הגידולין : קוצרין לפני העומר ברצון חכמים . כלומר לא הקפידו חכמים דאיסורא דאורייתא ליכא דמקום שאי אתה מביא הוא ואיסורא דרבנן נמי ליכא דילמא אתי למיכל מיניה לא גזרו דהא חדש מיבדל בדילי מיניה כולי שתא שאינו נוהג אותו כל השנה : וגודשין שלא ברצון חכמים . כיון דלאו פסידא הוא גזרו רבנן שימתינו משום שמתוך שהוא מתעסק בו אתי למיכל מיניה :

מאן

*) מדברי רבינו ז"ל אלו נראה שהיה גורס בגמ׳ אמר רבי אבהו באושא התקינו וכו׳ ולפיכך נתן טעם משום דבאושא הוו שכיחי מינין .

תורה אור: דברים ו. בראשית מט

ברכות י: [במשנה׳ נדפס כל זה למשנה ועפוי"ש] [סנהדרין מז·] — [דף יב:] — [תוספתא פ"ג] — מנחות עא· תוספת׳ פ"ג — מנחות סא:

נג א מיי׳ פ"א מהל׳ ק"ש הלכה ד סמג עשין יח טוש"ע א"ח סי׳ סא סעיף יג [רב אלפס ברכות פ"ב דף יא.]

[ועי׳ תוס׳ מנחות עא. ד"ה וכורכין]

[עי׳ תוס׳ ע"ז ג׳ ד"ה היום]

פ"א בן פזי

רבינו חננאל

קיימא לן כי הא דאמר מייתו נופרא. פי׳ צאוי יבש׳ מייתו נופרא דיכרא ומעייל ליה בי׳ דנקיבתא: **וכורכין** את שמע קיימא לן כרבי יהודה דאמר לא שהיו כורכין שמע ישראל עם ואהבת את ה׳ אלא לעולם מפסיקין היו אלא שלא היו אומרים ברוך שם כבוד מלכותו לעולם ועד ומאי כורכין דקתני דלא היו מפסקי בדבר אחר בין שמע לואהבת את ה׳: **ואנן** מאי טעמא אמרי׳ ליה כי הא דדרש ר"ש בן פזי ויקרא יעקב אל בניו מלמד שבקש לגלות הקץ לבניו נסתלקה שכינה ממנו אמר דלמא חס ושלום פסול יש במטתי פתחו כלן ואמרו שמע ישראל ה׳ אלהינו ה׳ אחד כיון ששמע להם כך פתח הוא ואמר ברוך שם כבוד מלכותו לעולם ועד התקינו במקום שאין בו מינין לאמרו בחשאי ובמקום שיש בו מינין אומרין אותו בקול [רם] באושא*) הוו שכיחי

הגהות הב"ח

(א) גמרא להביא לה בחשאי: (ב) רש"י ד"ה ולא היו מפסיקין בין אחד לואהבת ר"ל אין מאריכין דצריך להאריך כצ"ל ותיבת אע"פ נמחק:

[56a] AND THEY ATE THE FALLEN FRUIT FROM BENEATH [THE TREE] ON THE SABBATH, AND THEY GAVE PE'AH[8] FROM VEGETABLES; AND THE SAGES FORBADE THEM.[9]

GEMARA. Our Rabbis taught: Six things King Hezekiah did; in three they [the Sages] agreed with him, and in three they did not agree with him. He dragged his father's bones [corpse] on a rope bier,[10] and they agreed with him; he crushed the brazen serpent,[11] and they agreed with him; [and] he hid the book of a remedies,[1] and they agreed with him. And in three they did not agree with him: He cut [the gold off] the doors of the Temple[2] and sent them to the King of Assyria,[3] and they did not agree with him; and he closed up the waters of Upper Gihon,[4] and they did not agree with him;[5] and he intercalated [the month of] Nisan in Nisan,[6] and they did not agree with him.

THEY GRAFTED PALM TREES ALL DAY. How did they do it?—Said Rab Judah: They brought a fresh myrtle, the juice of bay-fruit and barley flour which had been kept[7] in a vessel less than forty days,[8] and boiled them together and injected [the concoction] into the heart of the palm tree; and every [tree] which stands within four cubits of this one, if that is not treated likewise immediately withers. R. Aḥa the son of Raba said: A male branch was grafted on to a female [palm tree].[9]

THEY 'WRAPPED UP' THE SHEMA'. What did they do?—Rab Judah said, They recited, *Hear, O Israel: the Lord our God, the Lord is One*[10] and did not make a pause.[11] Raba said: They did make a pause, but [the meaning is] that they said [*And these words,* b *which I command thee*] *this day shall be upon thy heart,*[1] which implies, this day [shall they be] upon thy heart, but to-morrow [they shall] not [be] upon thy heart.[2]

Our Rabbis taught: How did they 'wrap up' the *shema'?* They recited '*Hear O Israel the Lord our God the Lord is One,*' and they did not make a pause: this is R. Meir's view. R. Judah said: They did make a pause, but they did not recite, 'Blessed be the name of His glorious Kingdom for ever and ever.'[3] And what is the reason that we do recite it?—Even as R. Simeon b. Laḳish expounded. For R. Simeon b. Laḳish said: *And Jacob called unto his sons, and said: Gather yourselves together, that I may tell you* [*that which shall befall you in the end of days*].[4] Jacob wished to reveal to his sons the '*end of the days*',[5] whereupon the *Shechinah* departed from him. Said he, 'Perhaps, Heaven forfend! there is one unfit among my children,[6] like Abraham, from whom there issued Ishmael, or like my father Isaac, from whom there issued Esau.' [But] his sons answered him, 'Hear O Israel, the Lord our God the Lord is One:[7] just as there is only One in thy heart, so is there in our heart only One.' In that moment our father Jacob opened [his mouth] and exclaimed, 'Blessed be the name of His glorious kingdom for ever and ever.' Said the Rabbis, How shall we act? Shall we recite it,—but our Teacher Moses did not say it. Shall we not say it—but Jacob said it! [Hence] they enacted that it should be recited quietly.[8]

R. Isaac said, The School of R. Ammi said: This is to be compared to a king's daughter who smelled a spicy pudding.[9] If she reveals [her desire], she suffers disgrace;[10] if she does not reveal c it, she suffers pain.[1] So her servants began bringing it to her in secret. R. Abbahu said: They [the Sages] enacted that this should be recited aloud, on account of the resentment of heretics.[2] But in Nehardea, where there are no heretics so far, they recite it quietly.

Our Rabbis taught: Six things the inhabitants of Jericho did, three with the consent of the Sages, and three without the consent of the Sages. And these were with the consent of the Sages: They grafted palm trees all day [of the fourteenth], they 'wrapped up' the *shema'*, and they harvested before the '*omer.*[3] And these were without the consent of the Sages: They stacked [the corn] before the '*omer,*[4] and they made breaches in their gardens and orchards to permit the poor to eat the fallen fruit in famine years on Sabbaths and Festivals, and they permitted [for use] the branches of carob and sycamore trees belonging to *heḳdesh:* this is R. Meir's view. Said R. Judah to him, If they did [these things] with the consent of the Sages, then all people could do so! But they did both without the consent of the Sages, [save that] three they forbade them [to do], and three they did not forbid them [to do]. And it is these which they did not forbid them: They grafted palm trees the whole day, and they 'wrapped up' the *shema'*, and they stacked [the corn] before the '*omer*. And it is these which they forbade them to do: They permitted [for use] branches of *heḳdesh* of carob and sycamore trees, and they made breaches in their garden and orchards to permit the poor to eat the fallen fruit in famine years on Sabbaths and Festivals; they gave *pe'ah* from vegetables; and the Sages forbade them.

Yet does R. Judah hold that the reaping was not with the consent of the Sages? Surely we learned: The inhabitants of Jericho reaped before the '*omer* with the consent of the Sages and stacked before the '*omer* without the consent of the Sages, but the Sages

(8) V. Glos. *Pe'ah* is exempt from tithes, and the poor, by eating the vegetables without tithing them in the belief that they were *Pe'ah*, ate *ṭebel* (v. Glos.). (9) For a full discussion of this Mishnah v. Büchler, *Priester* pp. 164ff. (10) Instead of showing him the honour due to a king. He did this in order to effect atonement for him, his father (Ahaz) having been very wicked. (11) Set up by Moses, Num. XXI, 8f; v. II Kings XVIII, 4.

a (1) Because they cured so quickly that illness failed to promote a spirit of contrition and humility. V. Ber. 10*b*. V. Weiss, *Dor*, I, p. 121. (2) Or, he cut down the doors etc. (3) Sennacherib, as a bribe to leave him in peace; v. II Kings XVIII, 16. (4) V. II Chron. XXXII, 1-4. (5) In both cases he should have trusted in God. (6) Ibid. XXX, 1-3. The Talmud holds that he effected this by declaring Nisan an intercalated month, calling it the second Adar, after it (Nisan) had already commenced. (Since the Jewish year which is lunar is some eleven days shorter than the solar year, it is necessary periodically to lengthen it by the intercalation of a second Adar, the last month of the civil year. In ancient times this was done not by mathematical calculation, as nowadays, but according to the exigencies of the moment, but this had to be done before Nisan actually commenced, v. Sanh. 12*b* and Ber. 10*a*). (7) Lit., 'cast'. (8) Lit., 'over which forty days had not passed'. (9) Jast. translates: they put the male flower (scatter the pollen) over the female tree.—But he does not regard the operation described by Rab Judah as grafting. (10) Deut. VI, 4. (11) Before proceeding with the next verse, *And thou shalt love* etc.: '*One*' (Heb. אחד) must be prolonged in utterance, which creates a pause, but they did not do thus (Rashi). Tosaf.: they did not pause between '*Hear O Israel*' and '*the Lord*' etc. thus read together it is a prayer that God may hearken to Israel, which of course gives a completely wrong sense in this instance.

b (1) Deut. VI, 6. Reading it without a pause at 'day' as is indicated in the E.V. (2) [Elbogen, *Gottesdienst*, p. 3ff on the basis of these explanations concludes that the custom among the people of Jericho was for the reader to read aloud the whole section, while the congregation repeated it silently after him, in contrast to the practice in vogue elsewhere for alternating the recitation.] V. Soṭ., 30*b*, n. 11. (3) Before '*and thou shalt love*' etc. (4) Gen. XLIX, 1. (5) The final universal redemption, v. Dan. XII, 13. (6) Lit., 'in my bed'. (7) 'Israel' referring to their father. (8) V. Weiss, *Dor*, I, 236 on another theory for the reciting of this quietly. (9) And conceived a strong desire for it. (10) Through her lack of self-control.

c (1) Through her restraint. (2) Heb. *min*, sectarian. They might think that the Jews were cursing them. (3) V. *supra* 55*b*, n. d6. (4) As it is quite unnecessary, for the produce will not suffer loss if it is left unstacked until after the '*omer*, and while engaged in stacking it, they might come to eat it.

a the Festival, [55b] he may finish it on the fourteenth.[1] When is that? When he began it before the fourteenth; but if he did not begin it before the fourteenth, he must not begin it on the fourteenth, even a small girdle, even a small hair-net. [Thus,] only when required for the Festival, but not when it is not required! —No: the same law holds good that even when it is not required for the Festival we may also finish it, and he informs us this: that even when it is required for the Festival, we may only finish, but not begin.

Come and hear: R. Meir said: Any work which is required for the Festival, he may finish it on the fourteenth; but that which is not required for the Festival is forbidden; and one may work on the eve of Passover until midday where it is customary [to work]. [Thus,] only where it is the custom, but if it is not the custom, it is not [permitted at all]. Hence this proves that when required for the Festival it is [permitted], but when it is not required for the Festival it is not [permitted]. This proves it.

BUT THE SAGES MAINTAIN, THREE CRAFTSMEN [etc.]. A Tanna taught: Tailors, because a layman[2] may sew in the usual way on the Intermediate Days;[3] hairdressers and washermen, because he who comes from overseas and he who comes out of prison may cut their hair and wash [their garments] on the Intermediate Days.[4] R. Jose son of R. Judah said: Shoemakers too, because the Festival pilgrims[5] repaired their shoes on the Intermediate Days. Wherein do they differ?—One Master holds, We learn the beginning of the work from the end of the work;[6] while the other Master holds, We do not learn the beginning of the work from the end of the work.

MISHNAH. ONE MAY SET UP CHICKEN-HOUSES FOR b FOWLS ON THE FOURTEENTH,[1] AND IF A [BROODING] FOWL RAN AWAY,[2] ONE MAY SET HER BACK IN HER PLACE; AND IF SHE DIED, ONE MAY SET ANOTHER IN HER PLACE. ONE MAY SWEEP AWAY FROM UNDER AN ANIMAL'S FEET ON THE FOURTEENTH,[3] BUT ON THE FESTIVAL[4] ONE MAY REMOVE [IT] ON A SIDE [ONLY].[5] ONE MAY TAKE UTENSILS [TO] AND BRING [THEM BACK] FROM AN ARTISAN'S HOUSE, EVEN IF THEY ARE NOT REQUIRED FOR THE FESTIVAL.

GEMARA. Seeing that you may [even] set [the fowls for brooding], is there a question about putting back?[6]—Said Abaye: The second clause refers to the Intermediate Days of the Festival.[7] R. Huna said: They learnt this[8] only [when it is] within three [days] of her rebellion,[9] so that her heat[10] has not yet left her, and after three days of her brooding, so that the eggs are quite spoiled.[11] But if it is after three days since her rebellion, so that her heat has left her, or within three days of her brooding, so that the eggs are still not completely spoiled,[12] we must not put [her] back.[13] R. Ammi said: We may even put her back within [the first] three days of her brooding.[14] Wherein do they differ? —One Master holds, They [the Sages] cared about a substantial loss, but they did not care about a slight loss;[15] while the other Master holds: They cared about a slight loss too.

ONE MAY SWEEP AWAY FROM UNDER [etc.]. Our Rabbis taught: The manure which is in the court-yard may be moved aside; that which is in the stable and in the court-yard may be taken out to the dunghill. This is self-contradictory: you say, The manure which is in the court-yard may [only] be moved aside; then he [the Tanna] teaches, that which is in the stable and in the court-yard may [even] be taken out to the dunghill?—Said Abaye, There is no difficulty: one refers to the fourteenth [of Nisan]; the other, to the Intermediate Days. Raba said: Both refer to the Intermediate Days, and this is what he says: If the court- c yard became like a stable,[1] it may be taken out to the dunghill.

ONE MAY TAKE UTENSILS [TO] AND BRING [THEM BACK] FROM AN ARTISAN'S HOUSE. R. Papa said: Raba examined us. We learned: ONE MAY TAKE [UTENSILS TO] AND BRING UTENSILS FROM AN ARTISAN'S HOUSE, EVEN IF THEY ARE NOT REQUIRED FOR THE FESTIVAL. But the following contradicts it: One may not bring utensils from an artisan's house, but if he fears that they may be stolen, he may remove them into another court-yard?[2] And we answered, There is no difficulty: Here it means on the fourteenth; there, on the Intermediate Days. Alternatively, both refer to the Intermediate Days, yet there is no difficulty: here it is where he trusts him;[3] there, where he does not trust him. And thus it was taught: One may bring vessels from the artisan's house, e.g., a pitcher from a potter's house, and a [glass] goblet from a glass-maker's house; but [one may] not bring wool from a dyer's house nor vessels from an artisan's house.[4] Yet if he [the artisan] has nothing to eat, he must pay him his wages and leave it [the utensil] with him; but if he does not trust him, he places them in a nearby house; and if he is afraid that they may be stolen, he may bring them secretly home.[5] You have reconciled [the contradictions on] bringing; but [the contradictory statements on] taking [the utensils to the artisan's house] present a difficulty, for he teaches, 'One must not *bring* [from the artisan's house]', d hence how much more that we must not *take* [them to his house]![1] —Rather, it is clear [that it must be reconciled] as we answered it at first.[2]

MISHNAH. SIX THINGS THE INHABITANTS OF JERICHO DID: THREE THEY [THE SAGES] FORBADE THEM,[3] AND THREE [THEY] DID NOT FORBID THEM. AND IT IS THESE WHICH THEY DID NOT FORBID THEM: THEY GRAFTED PALM TREES ALL DAY,[4] THEY 'WRAPPED UP' THE SHEMA',[5] AND THEY HARVESTED AND STACKED [THEIR PRODUCE] BEFORE [THE BRINGING OF] THE 'OMER.[6] AND IT IS THESE WHICH THEY FORBADE THEM: THEY PERMITTED [FOR USE] THE BRANCHES [OF CAROB OR SYCAMORE TREES] BELONGING TO HEKDESH,[7]

a (1) Even where it is customary not to do any work. (2) I.e., a man who is not a craftsman in this particular trade. (3) Lit., 'the non-holy (portion) of the Festival'; v. 5a, n. a4. Only professional work is forbidden, but not the work a non-professional does at home. (4) Hence on the fourteenth, which is certainly lighter than the Intermediate Days, these may be done in general, and even by professionals. (5) V. Deut. XVI, 16. (6) Making shoes is the beginning; repairing them is the end. Just as repairing is permitted, so is making them permitted.

b (1) I.e., you may put in eggs for brooding (Jast.). Rashi reads 'and' instead of 'FOR', and renders: One may set up dove-cots *and* fowls (to brood). (2) From its eggs. (3) *Sc*. the dung, and throw it away. (4) Which of course is stricter. (5) But not sweep it altogether away. (6) It is obvious! (7) A fowl may not be set to brood then, but she may be put back. (8) That she may be put back even on the Intermediate Days of the Festival. (9) I.e., of her running away. (10) The desire to hatch. (11) They can no longer be eaten, being too addled. (12) They can still be eaten. (13) In the Intermediate Days. (14) Since the eggs have been slightly spoiled, and not all people would eat them. (15) After three days there is a substantial loss, as the eggs are quite unfit; but within three days the loss is only slight, since some people would eat them.

c (1) It contains so much manure that it cannot be moved aside. (2) Near the artisan's house, where it is better guarded, but he may not take them home if it is a long distance. (3) Either that the artisan will not dispose of them, or that he will not claim payment a second time. (4) The latter two when they are not needed for the Festival. (5) Not publicly, as that would give a too workaday appearance to these days.

d (1) While the question of trusting does not arise here. (2) Viz., that our Mishnah refers to the fourteenth, while the Baraitha refers to the Intermediate Days. (3) Lit., 'stayed their hand'. (4) Of the fourteenth. (5) I.e., they recited it without the necessary pauses, v. Gemara 56a. (6) V. Glos. and Lev. XXIII, 10-14. Rashi deletes HARVESTED, as that was quite permissible as far as Jericho was concerned, since no '*omer* could be brought from Jericho which was situated in a valley. V. Men. 71a, 85a. (7) I.e., the branches which grew after the trees had been vowed to the Sanctuary.

מו א מיי' שם הלכה כא טוש"ע שם סעיף ו:
מז ב מיי' שם טוש"ע שם סעיף ז:
מח ג מיי' שם טוש"ע שם סעיף ח:
מט ד ה מיי' וסמג שם טוש"ע או"ח סימן תקלו סעיף ד:
נ ו ז מיי' שם הלכה יא סמג שם טוש"ע או"ח סי' תקלה סעיף ג:
נא ח מיי' שם הלכה כא סמג שם טוש"ע או"ח סי' תקלט סעיף א:
נב ט מיי' שם הלכה יז סמג שם טוש"ע או"ח סי' תקלד סעיף ג:

גומרה בארבעה עשר. אפילו במקום שלא נהגו לעשות מלאכה: לא נהגו לא. אפילו גמר דהא בגמר קיימי': החייטין. משום הכי שרו בארבעה עשר בכל מקום שכן מלינו בהן קולא משאר אומניות גבי חולו של מועד: שכן ההדיוט תופר כדרכו. משנה היא במועד קטן* הדיוט שאינו אומן בכך הלכך בארבעה עשר דקיל מחולו של מועד אפי' אומן נמי שרי: שכן הבא ממדינת הים וכו'. וכיון דאשכחן בהן היתר קלא בחולו של מועד הלכך בארבעה עשר דקיל שרי לכולי עלמא: תחילת מלאכה. רלענין שעושין מנעלים חדשי': מסוף מלאכ'. תיקון מנעלים:

[דף יח:]

עולי רגלים מתקנים מנעליהן. מהכא משמע בהדיא דאסור לתקן מנעלים בחוה"מ דלא התירו אלא לעולי רגלים דווקא ואין לומר דדבר האבד הוא שמא יקרעו יותר דהא יכול לקטע חדשים ובפרק מי שהפך (מ"ק יג.) מייתי הך ברייתא ופריך אלא מעתה לבלר ליתשרי שכן כותב גיטי נשים ושוברים כדתנן בפרק אלו מגלחים (שם יח:) ומשני ספיר*:

[ועי' תוס' מ"ק י. ד"ס ההדיוט]

ואם מהיירא שמא יגנבו. וכיון שאין יכול להניחם בביתו ולא בבית הסמוך לו לא הזקיקוהו להניח בבית שלישי והתירו להביאם בצינעא בביתו:

גומרה בארבעה עשר אימתי בזמן שהתחיל בה קודם ארבעה עשר אבל לא התחיל בה קודם ארבעה עשר לא יתחיל בה בארבעה עשר אפילו צילצול קטן אפילו שבכה קטנה לצורך המועד אין שלא לצורך המועד לא הוא הדין דאפילו שלא לצורך נמי גמרינן והא קמ"ל דאפי' לצורך המועד מיגמר אין אתחולי לא ת"ש ר' מאיר אומר כל מלאכה שהיא לצורך המועד גומרה בארבעה עשר ושאינה לצורך המועד אסור ועושין מלאכה בערבי פסחים עד חצות במקום שנהגו מקום שנהגו אין לא נהגו לא וש"מ לצורך המועד אין שלא לצורך המועד לא ש"מ: וחכמים אומרים שלש אומניות: תנא *החייטין שכן הדיוט תופר כדרכו בחולו של מועד הספרין והכובסין שכן הבא ממדינת הים והיוצא מבית האסורין מספרין ומכבסין בחולו של מועד רבי יוסי ברבי יהודה אומר אף הרצענין שכן עולי רגלים מתקנין מנעליהן בחולו של מועד במאי קמיפלגי מר סבר למידין תחילת מלאכה מסוף מלאכה ומר סבר אין למידין תחילת מלאכה מסוף מלאכה: **מתני'** *מושיבין שובכין לתרנגולים בי"ד ותרנגולת שברחה מחזירין אותה למקומה ואם מתה מושיבין אחרת תחתיה גורפין מתחת רגלי בהמה בי"ד ובמועד מסלקין לצדדין מוליכין כלים ומביאין מבית האומן אע"פ שאינם לצורך המועד: **גמ'** השתא אותובי מותבינן אהדורי מיבעיא אמר אביי [א] סיפא אתאן לחולו של מועד אמר רב הונא לא שנו אלא [ב] תוך שלשה למרדה דאכתי לא פרח צימרא מינה ואחר שלשה לישיבתה דפסדא לה ביעי לגמרי אבל לאחר שלשה למרדה דפרח לה צימרא מינה ותוך שלשה לישיבתה דאכתי לא פסידי ביעי לגמרי לא מהדרינן רבי אמי אמר אפילו תוך שלשה לישיבתה מהדרינן במאי קמיפלגי מר סבר *להפסד מרובה חששו להפסד מועט לא חששו ומר סבר להפסד מועט נמי חששו: גורפין מתחת: ת"ר *הזבל שבחצר מסלקין אותו לצדדין שברפת ושבחצר מוציאין אותו לאשפה הא גופא קשיא אמרת שבחצר מסלקין אותו לצדדין והדר תני שברפת ושבחצר מוציאין אותו לאשפה אמר אביי לא קשיא כאן בי"ד כאן בחולו של מועד רבא אמר [ג] הא והא בחולו של מועד והכי קאמר 'אם נעשה חצר כרפת מוציאין אותו לאשפה: מוליכין כלים ומביאין מבית האומן: *א"ר פפא בדיק לן רבא תנן מוליכין ומביאין כלים מבית האומן אע"פ שאינן לצורך המועד ורמינהו אין מביאין כלים מבית האומן ואם חושש להן שמא יגנבו מפנן לחצר אחרת ומשנינן לא קשיא כאן בארבעה עשר כאן בחולו של מועד ואיבעית אימא הא והא בחולו של מועד ולא קשיא כאן במאמינו כאן בשאינו מאמינו והתניא *מביאין כלים מבית האומן כגון הכד מבית *הכדר והכוס מבית הזוגג אבל לא צמר מבית הצבע ולא כלים מבית האומן ואם אין לו מה יאכל נותן לו שכרו ומניחו אצלו ואם אינו מאמינו מניחן בבית הסמוך לו ואם חושש שמא יגנבו מביאן בצינעה בתוך ביתו תרצת מביאין מוליכין קשיא דקתני אין מביאין וכ"ש דאין מוליכין אלא מחוורתא כדשנינן מעיקרא: **מתני'** *ששה דברים עשו אנשי יריחו על שלשה מיחו בידם ועל שלשה לא מיחו בידם ואלו הן שלא מיחו בידם מרכיבין דקלים כל היום וכורכין את שמע וקוצרין וגודשין לפני העומר ואלו שמיחו בידם מתירין גמזיות של הקדש ואוכלין

מתני' מושיבין שובכין. כשנותנין בילים תחת תרנגולת להתחמם לגדל אפרוחים קרי מושיבין שובכין: ותרנגולת. המחממת בילים: שברחה. מעליהם מחזירין אותה ובגמ' פריך השתא אותובי מותבינן אהדורי מבעיא ל"א הכי כתיב בסדר משנה מושיבים שובכין ותרנגולת כלומר שובכין ליונים ותרנגולת היו מושיבין להתחמם לגדל אפרוחי' והכי מסתבר' דשובך לא שייך אלא ביונים: גורפין. ומשליכין לחוץ ובמועד שחמור יותר אין משליכין לחוץ אלא מסלקין לצדדים: גמ' סיפא. דקתני מחזירין בחולו של מועד קאמר והכי קאמר מושיבין שובכין בי"ד ותרנגול' שברח' בחולו של מועד מחזירין אותה משום הפסד בילים דדבר האבד מותר: לא שנו. דאף במועד מחזירין אלא תוך שלשה למורדה שעדיין לא עברו שלשה ימים שברחה מעליהן: דאכתי לא פרח צימרא. לא עבר חמימותה ממנה והיא נוחה להחזיר: צימרא. כמו אבתא למירתא (ע"ז דף כח.*): ולאחר שלשה לישיבתה. שכבר ישבה עליהן שלשה ימים קודם שעמדה מעליהן וכבר נשתנו הבילים ואם לא תחזור הרי הן אובדין דאין ראויין לאכילה: אבל לאחר שלשה למרדה. שהיא קשה וטורח גדול להחזיר או אפילו תוך שלשה למרדה אם תוך שלשה עמדה מעליהן דאכתי לא פסדי ביעי שהרי ראויין לאכילה לא מהדרינן: אפילו תוך שלשה לישיבתה. הואיל ונשתנו קצת ואין ראויין לכל אדם אלא למי שדעתו יפה ואינו איסטניס מהדרינן: להפסד מועט. שמוכרים בזול למי שדעתו יפה: לצדדין. ולא לאשפה חוץ לחצר: אם נעשית חצר כרפת. שנתקלקלה כולה ואין מקום לסלק לצדדין מוציאין אותן לאשפה: בדיק לן. מנסה אותנו: לחצר אחרת. אצל האומן אבל לא יביאם לביתו שרחוק מבית האומן מפני הטורח: במאמינו. לאומן שלא ימכרם אין מביאין ל"א מאמינו שלא יתבע שכרו פעם אחרת והוא צריך לשכרו עכשיו: והתניא. בניחותא: כגון כד מבית הכדר וכוס מבית הזוגג. שצריכין למועד: זגג. עושה כלי זכוכית: אבל לא צמר. שאין צורך המועד: ואם אינו מאמינו וכו'. אלמא שאני לן בין מאמינו לשאין מאמינו: תרצת מביאין. דמתני' ואין מביאין דמועד קטן תרוייהו בחולו של מועד ומתניתין דהכא בשלא מאמינו אבל מוליכין קשיא דקתני מתניתין מוליכין והתם מאי אין מאמינו איכא ובההיא קתני אין מביאין וכ"ש דאין מוליכין: מעיקרא. מתניתין בי"ד וההיא בחולו של מועד: **מתני'** ששה דברים עשו אנשי יריחו. היו נוהגין ישראל הדרים ביריחו: מרכיבין דקלים כל היום. של י"ד בלע"ז אינטי"ר: וכורכין את שמע. מפרש בגמרא: וקוצרין לא גרסינן דהא היתר גמור הוא דקיימא לן במנחות בפרק רבי ישמעאל (דף עא.) ממקום שאי אתה מביא אתה קוצר ותבואת יריחו של עמקים היא ואינה כשירה למנחות דתנן (שם פה.) אין מביאין סולת למנחה לא מבית השלחין ולא מבית העמק וכו' ולהכי אינה כשירה לעומר דאין מנחות באה ממנו דבעינן משבח ארץ ישראל דילפינן התם ג"ש ארץ ארץ: מתירין גמזיות. גידולין ענפים שגדלו בחרובין ושיקמין שהקדישו אבותיהן הן היו מתירין ליהנות מן הגידולים דרך חרוב ושקמה לקוצצו לשבע שנים והן חוזרין וגדלין ומיתוספין וקודם קציצתן קרי ליה בתולת שיקמה ומשנקצץ קרי ליה סדן שיקמה והקדישו מתחילה כשהן מקוצצין וניתוסף לאחר מיכן גמזיות: ואוכלין

[מ"ק יג.]

[לעיל כה: שבת סו.]

[לעיל סו: וש"נ]

[תוספתא פ"ג]

מ"ק ג. [עירובין נה. וש"נ]

[מ"ק שם: ע"ש]

[מנחות עא.]

הגהות הגר"א
[א] גמ' סיפא. נ"ב ברישא כרמב"ם ור"ח:
[ב] שם תוך ג' למרדה דאכתי לא פרח צימרא מינה. נ"ב הרי"ף לא גרס לה (וכ"ג ליה) אלא אחר ג' כו' אבל תוך ג' כו'. וכ"ה בר"ח א"ח סוף סי' תקל"ו. ומ"ש כהרי"ף שלא אינו מהרי"ף וכדפי' הר"ן ליתא: [ג] שם הא והא בחולו של מועד. נ"ב הרי"ף לא גרס לה:

נראה דצ"ל הכדר כדל"ת עי' תוס' חולין ס"ד. ד"ה טורח

רבינו חננאל
עשר כלל ואפילו מצי למגמרינהו ומה שהתחיל קודם י"ד אם הוא לצורך המועד יגמור ואי לא לא. ואסיקנא הכי ת"ש ר' מאיר אומר כל מלאכה שהיא לצורך המועד שהתחיל בה קודם י"ד גומרה בי"ד ושאינה לצורך המועד אסור ש"ם לצורך המועד תנן שגומרה בי"ד ש"מ וקיימא לן כותיה. ואין מתחיל בי"ד אפי' צלצול קטן ואפי' סבכה קטנה ואפי' הן לצורך המועד וחכמים אומרים שלש אומניות עושין מלאכה בערבי פסחים החייטין שכן הדיוט תופר כדרכו בחולו של מועד והספרין והכובסין שכן הבא ממדינת הים והיוצא מבית האסורין מותרין לספר ולכבס בחולו של מועד ר' יוסי בר' יהודה אומר אף הרצענין שכן עולי רגלים מתקנין מנעליהן בחולו של מועד ואע"פ שתקנת המנעל סוף מלאכה היא קסבר ר' יוסי ילפינן תחלת מלאכה מסוף מלאכה מה סוף מלאכה מותר אף תחלת מלאכה מותר: מתני' מושיבין שובכין לתרנגולים בי"ד כו' ותרנגולת שברחה מחזירין אותה למקומה ואם מתה מושיבין אחרת תחתיה אמר רב הונא לא שנו שמחזירין אותה בחולו של מועד אלא תוך שלשה ימים למרדה דאכתי לא פרח צמרה עדיין החמימות שיש בה והיא תחמם הביצים ואחר שלשה ימים לישיבתה על הביצים כלומר כיון שעברו אחר שישבה על הביצים התחילו לרקם ואם תניחם נפסדין הביצים לגמרי ואחר ג' ימים לישיבתה שלא הופסדו הביצים לגמרי ואחר ג' ימים למרדה דפרח לה צמרה לא מהדרינן לה בחולו של מועד ר' אמי אמר אפילו תוך ג' ימים לישיבתה כו' ואסיקנא רב הונא סבר להפסד מרובה חששו כלומר במקום שיש הפסד מרובה כי הביצים נפסדין לגמרי חששו ואמרו מחזירין אבל תוך ג' לישיבתה דלא נפסדו אלא שאין אפרוחין אבל ראוין הן לאכילה ואין בהן הפסד אבל דביני ביני הפסד מועט הוא ולהפסד מועט לא חששו ורב אמי סבר אפילו להפסד מועט [חששו] ומחזירין: מתני' גורפין הרעי מתחת רגלי הבהמה בארבעה עשר ובמועד מסלקין אותו לצדדין וכו' ת"ר הזבל שבחצר מסלקין אותו לצדדין שברפת ושבחצר מוציאין אותו לאשפה הא גופה קשיא אמרת שבחצר מסלקין אותו לצדדין והדר תאני ושבחצר מוציאין אותו לאשפה ומשני אביי בארבעה עשר מוציאין אותו לאשפה ובחולו של מועד מסלקין אותו לצדדין רבא אמר לעולם בחולו של מועד והכי קתני אם נעשית החצר כרפת שנתמלאת רעי מוציאין אותו לאשפה: ירושלמי ובלבד שבמבוי מסלקו לצד שברפת ושבחצר מוציאין לאשפה אמר [רבא] הדא דתימא בהצר קטנה אבל בחצר גדולה מסלקה לצדדין והרפת בין קטנה בין גדולה מוציאו לאשפה: אמר רב פפא הוה בדיק לן רבא תנן מוליכין ומביאין כלים מבית האומן ואם חושש להם שמא יגנבו מפנן לחצר אחרת ושנינן לה מתני' דהכא דקתני מוליכין ומביאין כלים מבית האומן בארבעה עשר ומתנתא דקתני אין מביאין בחולו של מועד וכו' סוגיין דשמעתא סלקא ואע"ג דאמרינן מתני' דהכא נמי בחוש"מ ומפני שאינו מאמין בעל הבית כליו לאומן קתני מביאין אפילו כלים שאינן לצורך המועד כדתניא מביאין כלים מבית האומן כגון כוס מבית הזוגג ואסיקנא שנית מביאין כלומר התירו לו להביאן מפני שאינו מאמינו התינח מביאין מוליכין מאי איכא למימר למה מוליכין בחוש"מ ואסיקנא אלא מחוורתא מתני' דקתני מוליכין [ורמינהו אין מביאין כלים מבית האומן] ומביאין בארבעה עשר ומתני' דקתני אין מביאין בחולו של מועד: ומסקנא מקום שנהגו לעשות מלאכה בע"פ עד חצות כו' קיימא לן הכי: ששה דברים עשו אנשי יריחו וכו' אלו שלא מיחו מרכיבין דקלים כל היום

תנא קולי קולי קתני: ובכל מקום ת"ח וכו': *למימרא דרשב"ג סבר לא חיישינן ליוהרא ורבנן סברי חיישינן ליוהרא והא איפכא שמעינן להו דתנן *חתן אם ירצה לקרות קריאת שמע לילה הראשון קורא רשב"ג אומר לא כל הרוצה ליטול את השם יטול אמר ר' יוחנן מוחלפת השיטה רב שישא בריה דרב אידי אמר לא תיפוך דרבנן אדרבנן לא קשיא הכא כיון דכולי עלמא עבדי מלאכה ואיהו לא עביד מיחזי כיוהרא אבל התם כיון דכולי עלמא קרי ואיהו נמי קרי לא מיחזי כיוהרא דר' שמעון בן גמליאל אדרשב"ג לא קשיא התם הוא דבעינן כוונה ואנן סהדי דלא מצי כווני דעתיה מיחזי כיוהרא אבל הכא לא מיחזי כיוהרא אמרי מלאכה היא דלית ליה פוק חזי *כמה בטלני איכא בשוקא: **מתני'** וחכמים אומרים ביהודה היו עושין מלאכה בערבי פסחים עד חצות ובגליל לא היו עושין כל עיקר *הלילה ב"ש אוסרים וב"ה מתירין עד הנץ החמה: **גמ'** מעיקרא תנא מנהגא ולבסוף תנא איסורא אמר ר' יוחנן לא קשיא הא ר' מאיר הא ר' יהודה דתניא אמר ר' יהודה ביהודה היו עושין מלאכה בערבי פסחים עד חצות ובגליל אינן עושין כל עיקר אמר לו ר"מ מה ראייה יהודה וגליל לכאן אלא מקום שנהגו לעשות מלאכה עושין מקום שנהגו שלא לעשות אין עושין מדקאמר ר' מאיר מנהגא מכלל דרבי יהודה איסורא קאמר וסבר ר' יהודה ארבעה עשר מותר בעשיית מלאכה והתניא ר' יהודה אומר המנכש בשלשה עשר ונעקרה בידו שותלה במקום הטיט ואין שותלה במקום הגריד בשלשה עשר אין בארבעה עשר לא מכדי שמעינן ליה לר' יהודה דאמר *כל הרכבה שאינה קולטת לשלשה ימים שוב אינה קולטת ואי ס"ד ארבעה עשר מותר בעשיית מלאכה למה לי שלשה עשר והאיכא ארביסר וחמיסר ומקצת שיתסר אמר רבא בגליל שנו והאיכא ליליא אמר רב ששת כב"ש רב אשי אמר לעולם כב"ה לפי שאין דרכן של בני אדם לנכש בלילה רבינא אמר לעולם ביהודה ובהשרשה חד מקצת היום ככולו אמרינן תרי מקצת היום ככולו לא אמרינן: **מתני'** ר' מאיר אומר כל מלאכה שהתחיל בה קודם לארבעה עשר גומרה בארבעה עשר אבל לא יתחיל בה בתחלה בארבעה עשר אע"פ שיכול לגומרה וחכמים אומרים * ג' אומניות עושין מלאכה בערבי פסחים עד חצות ואלו הן החייטין והספרים והכובסין ר' יוסי בר יהודה אומר אף רצענין: **גמ'** איבעיא להו לצורך המועד תנן אבל שלא לצורך המועד אפילו מיגמר נמי לא או דילמא שלא לצורך המועד תנן אבל לצורך המועד אתחולי מתחלינן או דילמא בין לצורך המועד בין שלא לצורך מיגמר אין אתחולי לא ת"ש אבל לא יתחיל בתחלה בארבעה עשר אפילו *צלצול קטן אפילו שבכה קטנה מאי אפילו לאו אפי' הני דלצורך המועד מיגמר גמרינן אתחולי לא מכלל דשלא לצורך מיגמר נמי לא גמרינן לא לעולם דשלא לצורך מיגמר נמי גמרינן ומאי אפילו אפילו הני נמי דזוטרי נינהו דסלקא דעתך אמינא התחלתן זו היא גמר מלאכתן נתחיל בהו נמי לכתחילה קמשמע לן: תא שמע רבי מאיר אומר כל מלאכה שהיא לצורך המועד גומרה

תנא קולי קולי נקט. כל הני אין בין חד תנא אמרינהו וקולי קולי נקט ברישא הכא אין (א) בין תשעה באב קל מיוה"כ לכתחלה אלא שזה ספיקו כו' וסיפא תנא אין תשעה באב קל מתענית ליבור אלא לענין מלאכה ובחומרי דחמיר תשעה באב מתענית ליבור לא איירי הכא דתידוק מינה זה וזה שוין ולעולם לענין רחילה ט"ב חמיר: ליטול לו את השם. כתר פרישות ויראת חטא שאינו יכול לבטל הימנו מלכות שמים אפילו לילה אחת שאין לב כל הרוצה ליטלו יטלנו דמיחזי כיוהרא ומתחזי בידיה: מוחלפת השיטה. התנא שסידרן טעה באחת מהן והחליף שיטתו: אמרי מלאכה לית ליה. הרואה אותו בטל אומרים אין לו מה לעשות ולא מיחזי כנוהג בו איסור: **מתני'** הלילה. אור לארבעה עשר: **גמ'** מעיקרא תנא מנהגא. תלה במנהג: ולבסוף תנא איסורא. דקתני בית שמאי אוסרין דמשמע בכל מקום: מה ראיה יהודה וגליל לכאן. אף כל מקום שנהגו היתר היתר נהגו איסור איסור: מכלל דר' יהודה איסורא קאמר. דבני יהודה מתירין ובני גליל אוסרין דאי מנהגא קאמר מאי פלוגתיה דר"מ האמר ר' יהודה נמי הכי הוה אמר בגליל היו נוהגין בו איסור שהחמירו על עצמן וביהודה נוהגין בו היתר: וסבר רבי יהודה מותר. דקאמר בני יהודה מתירין: המנכש. מבין תבואות *דגן: בשלשה עשר בניסן. מפרש ואזיל שלשה עשר אמאי נקט: ונעקרה בידו. השבולת עלמה נעקרה בידו שורשה מן הארץ ובא לחזור ולשתלה: שותלה במקום הטיט. שממהר ליקלט קודם העומר שהעומר מתיר את הנשרשין אבל הנשרשין אחר העומר אסורין משום חדש עד שיבא עומר הבא: הגריד. יבש שאינו ממהר לקלוט: מנכש בשלשה עשר קתני מנכש בארבעה עשר לא קתני ומ"ט נקט שלשה עשר ולא קתני ארבעה עשר אי משום דלא מיקלטא לפני העומר הקרב בששה עשר מכדי שמעינן לרבי יהודה כו' בפ"ק דר"ה השנה (דף י:) ואי ארבעה עשר מותר במלאכה ניכנקט ארביסר נמי דהא איכא מקלת ארביסר וחמיסר כוליה ומקלת שיתסר עד שעת הקרבתו: בגליל שנו. שלא היו עושין מלאכה כל עיקר בארבעה עשר ובכן נשנית משנה זו: והא איכא לילה. ומלי למיתני המנכש לילי ארבעה עשר: כב"ש. דמתניתין דתקן הלילה ב"ש אוסרין: ה"ג רבינא אמר לעולם ביהודה. ודקשיא לך ליתני בארבעה עשר ובהשרשה חד מקלת אמרינן תרי מקלת לא אמרינן להשרשה חד מקלת היום ככולו אמרינן אם היה מנכש בין השמשות של כניסת ארבעה עשר הוה אמרינן דקלטה בי"ד שלם ובחמשה עשר שלם ומקלת ששה עשר אבל תרי מקלת כגון מנכש בי"ד דמיבעי לן למימר תרי מקלת לא אמרינן: **מתני'** שלש אומניות עושין מלאכה. בכל מקום וטעמא מפרש בגמרא: רלענין. אושכפין: **גמ'** לצורך המועד תנן. הא דר"מ: או דילמא שלא לצורך המועד תנן. ומשום הכי אין מתחילין אבל לצורך המועד אפילו אתחולי נמי שרי כו': צלצול. בגדי"ל לחגור: שבכה. על הראש: גומרה

קולי קולי קתני. בלא דר' אלעזר דאסר להושיט אצבעו במים נ"ל קולי קולי קתני דהא בתשעה באב לכל הפחות כל גופו אסור אפילו בלונן ובתענית ליבור מותר בלונן כדמוכח בפ"ק דתענית (דף יג.): אמר ר' מאיר מה ראייה יהודה וגליל לכאן. לרבי מאיר דאית ליה דהוי מנהגא קסבר דלא נחלקו ב"ש וב"ה בדבר זה דבמנהגא לא שייך פלוגתא דליהוי הכי נהוג: מדקאמר ר"מ מנהגא מכלל דרבי יהודה איסורא קאמר. ממתניתין ליכא למידק הכי מדקאמר ת"ק מנהגא מכלל דחכמים איסורא קאמרי דלמתני' איכא למימר דתרוייהו סברי מנהגא וה"ק חכמים לת"ק למה אתה סותם דבריך והלא אתה יכול לפרש דבריך ולבאר דבגליל אין עושין וביהודה עושין ובברייתא לא שייך לפרש כן: כל הרכבה שאינה קולטת. וא"ת א"כ למה אינו שותלה במקום הגריד אי קלטה עד שלשה ימים שרי לה עומר ואי לא קלטה שוב לא תקלוט ואינו לריך היתר כמו חיטי דכלא* וי"ל דבמקום הגריד מתחיל לקלוט יותר מג' ימים א"כ יש לחוש כשירחא שלא תקלוט שישתול אותה במקום הטיט אחר העומר: ומאי אפילו אפי' הני נמי דזוטרי. ה"מ למימר לסניי כדבסמוך אפי' הכי נמי דלצורך המועד מיגמר אין אתחולי לא אלא ניחא ליה למידחי שלא יפשוט מינה כלל דהכאה מלי למימר דלצורך המועד אתחולי נמי מתחלינן: עולי

הגהות הב"ח

(א) רש"י ד"ה תנא קולי וכו' תנא אין תשעה באב קל מיוה"כ ותיבת בין נמחק:

גליון הש"ס

תנא קולי קולי קתני. עיין נזיר מז ע"ב תד"ה ת"ש הכניה ועיין מגילה ה ע"ב תד"ה ממעטי:

מסורת הש"ס: ברכות יז. | סס טז: | [לעיל נ:] | [יבמות יג:] | נ"ל דנ"ל דבר שאינו דגן מלאס לא. | שביעית פ"ב [מ"ו] ר"ה י: יבמות פג. | מ"ק יג.

עין משפט נר מצוה

מד א מיי' פ"ד מהל' ק"ש הלכה ז סמג עשין יח טוש"ע א"ח סי' ע סעיף ג:

מה ב ג מיי' פ"ח מהל' יו"ט הלכה יז ובג טוש"ע א"ח סי' תסח סעיף ס:

[ב"מ מ: מנחות סט.]

רבינו חננאל

להושיט אצבעו במים ופרקי' תנא חומרי חומרי קתני פי' תנא אין בין ט' באב ליום הכפורים אלא חמור יום הכפורים מט' באב שיום הכפורים ספקו אסור וט' באב ספקו מותר כדאמרן וכן שנה חמור תענית צבור מט' באב שתענית צבור אסור במלאכה וט' באב מותר במקום שנהגו ויש עוד חומר לט' באב מתענית צבור בט' באב אסור אפי' ברחיצת פניו [ידיו] ורגליו ובתענית צבור אין אסיר אלא כל גופו אבל פניו ידיו ורגליו מותר: ובכל מקום תלמידי חכמים בטלים רשב"ג אומר כל אדם יעשה עצמו תלמיד חכם ורמינן אי משום דחיישי' ליוהרא הא מדתנן לענין החתן איפכא משמע ואמר ר' יוחנן מוחלפת השיטה כלומר הפך דברי ת"ק לרשב"ג ורב שישא אמר לא תפוך והדברים פשוטין הן: וחכמים אומרים ביהודה היו עושין מלאכה בערבי פסחים עד חצות ובגליל לא היו עושין מלאכה כל עיקר ופי' כל היום הלילה בגליל ב"ש אוסרין וב"ה מתירין עד הנץ החמה ואקשי' בתחלת פרקין קתני מקום שנהגו לעשות מלאכה בערבי פסחים מכלל דבמנהגא תליא מילתא והכא קתני ב"ש אוסרין וב"ה מתירין ואפי' לב"ה לאחר הנץ החמה אוסרין מכלל דאיסור איכא ליחזי היכא נהוג ופרקי' לא קשיא מתני' דרישא דתני מנהגא לר' מאיר והאי דתני איסורא לר' יהודה. במאי אוקימתה להא מתני' כר' יהודה וסבר ר' יהודה ארבעה עשר מותר במלאכה כו' דקתני וחכמים אומרים ביהודה היו עושין מלאכה בערבי פסחים עד חצות והתניא ר' יהודה אומר המנכש בשלשה עשר ונעקרה שבולת בידו שותלה במקום הטינא ואין שותלה במקום (הגרד) [הגריד] ואי ס"ד לר' יהודה ארבעה עשר מותר בעשיית מלאכה מכדי על מאי קא מהדר ר' יהודה למפסריה להאי שבולת העומר הקרב בששה עשר בניסן *(אסור באכילה עד שיבוא עומר אחר ויתירנה) ואם ישתלנה במקום (הגדר) [הגריד] שהוא מקום יבש כדגרסי' במשקין בית השלחין אם היתה שדה מטוננת מוהרת ואין משקין שדה גריד במועד כלומר זו השבולת אינה קולטת קודם ששה עשר בניסן ונמצאת כאלו נזרעה אחר העומר והיא אסורה עד ששה עשר בניסן הבא אחר זה ואם היא נשתלת במקום הטינא ביום שלשה עשר בניסן קלטה קודם העומר והעומר מתירה ככל תבואה שבעולם. ואקשי' אמאי פסיק [המנכש בי"ג]ותני בי"ג מכלל די"ד לא אפשר הא שמעי' ליה לר' יהודה דאמר כל הרכבה שאינה קולטת לג' ימים שוב אינה קולטת אפילו השותל בי"ד הא איכא ג' ימים ארביסר וחמיסר ומקצת שיתסר וקיימא לן מקצת היום ככולו ש"מ דלית ליה לר' יהודה עשיית מלאכה בארביסר כלל לפיכך תני היה מנכש בי"ג ופריק רב יוסף [זו] הברייתא אליבא דבני גליל היא שנויה שאין עושין מלאכה ביום י"ד כלל. ואמרי' אפילו לבני גליל אין אוסרין אלא יום י"ד ממש אבל הלילה ב"ה מתירין ולדבריך היה לו לומר המנכש לילי י"ד ופריק רב ששת הא מתניתא אליבא דב"ש שנאה שאוסרין אפי' הלילה: **רב** אשי אמר אפלו תימא אליבא דב"ה ולא שנא אלא דרך שהוא בני אדם ואין דרך בני א"ם לנכש בלילות לפיכך לא תנא המנכש בלילה. רבינא אמר חד מקצת היום ככולו אמרי' תרי לא אמרינן פי' המנכש לילי י"ד או יום י"ד צריכין אנו לומר מקצת היום ככולו ולהשוב יום י"ד כולו ויום ט"ו כולו ומקצת ט"ז עד שעת הקרבת העומר לחשבו ככולו נמצא תרי מקצתו ככולו באלו הג' יום י"ד ויום ט"ו ותרי מקצת לא אמרינן דכי האי גונא לא משתכח אלא שני מקצת ויום אחד בלבד. ויש שמחליפין דברי ר' יהודה לר' מאיר דמעמידין תחלת הפרק כר' יהודה והא דתני מנהג ור' מאיר סבר איסור והפי' במקומו עומד בין לר' יהודה בין לר' מאיר הפי' שפרשנו אליבא דר' יהודה החזירוהו אליבא דר' מאיר. גירסא דמתיבתא דתניא אמר ר' מאיר ביהודה בראשונה היו עושין מלאכה בערבי פסחים עד חצות ובגליל לא היו עושין כל עיקר פי' ר' מאיר סבר אין דבר זה תלוי במנהג אלא אם הלכה כבני (גליל) [יהודה] בני גליל טועים הם ואם הלכה כבני גליל בני יהודה עוברים על האיסור אמר לו ר' יהודה דבר זה במנהג תלוי וכן אמר לו וכי מאי ראיה ליהודה וגליל מעתה אלא מקום שנהגו לעשות עושין שלא לעשות אין עושין ש"מ מדקאמר ר"י מנהג מכלל דר' מאיר אסורה קאמר ומתני' דקתני מנהגא ר' יהודה הוא ור' מאיר פליג ואמר אסורא: **מתני'** ר"מ אומר כל מלאכה שהתחיל בה כו' פשוטה היא ובעינן למפשט טעמא דר' מאיר ופשטי' דאתחולי לא מתחלינן בארבעה עשר

*) מתיבת אסור באכילה עד תי' ויתירנה נראה דמקומו בשורה הבאה אחר תי' במועד וגם צ"ל כן אסור באכילה וכו' ויתירנה כלומר זו השבולת וכו':

man's face, hands, and feet?[5]—Said R. Papa: [55a] The Tanna teaches a series of leniences.[6]

AND IN ALL PLACES SCHOLARS etc. Shall we say that R. Simeon b. Gamaliel holds that we do not fear [the appearance of] conceit, while the Rabbis hold that we do fear [the appearance of] conceit? But we know them [to hold] the reverse! For we learned: A bridegroom, if he wishes to recite the reading of the
a *shema'*[1] on the first night, he may recite it. R. Simeon b. Gamaliel said: Not everyone who wishes to assume[2] the name [reputation] may assume it.[3]—Said R. Joḥanan: The discussion must be reversed. R. Shisha the son of R. Idi said, Do not reverse it. The Rabbis are not self-contradictory: here, since everybody works, while he [alone] does not work, it looks like conceit; but there, since everybody recites [the *shema'*] and he too recites [it], it does not look like conceit. R. Simeon b. Gamaliel too is not self-contradictory: There only, since devotion is required, while we are witnesses that he cannot devote his mind,[4] it looks like conceit. But here it does not look like conceit, [for] people will say, 'It is work that he lacks: go out and see how many unemployed there are in the market place!'

MISHNAH. BUT THE SAGES MAINTAIN,[5] IN JUDEA THEY USED TO DO WORK ON THE EVE OF PASSOVER UNTIL MIDDAY, WHILE IN GALILEE THEY DID NOT WORK AT ALL. [AS FOR] THE NIGHT,[6]—BETH SHAMMAI FORBID [WORK], WHILE BETH HILLEL PERMIT IT UNTIL DAYBREAK.

b *GEMARA.* At first he [the Tanna] teaches custom,[1] and then he teaches a prohibition?—Said R. Joḥanan, There is no difficulty: one is according to R. Meir; the other, according to R. Judah. For it was taught, R. Judah said: In Judea they used to do work on the eve of Passover until midday, while in Galilee they did not work at all. Said R. Meir to him: What proof is Judea and Galilee for the present [discussion]?[2] But where they are accustomed to do work, one may do it, [while] where they are accustomed not to do [work], one may not do it. Now, since R. Meir states [that it is merely a matter of] custom, it follows that R. Judah states [that it is] a prohibition.[3]

Yet does R. Judah hold that work on the fourteenth is permitted?[4] Surely it was taught, R. Judah said: He who weeds on the thirteenth and [an ear of corn] is uprooted in his hand, must replant it in swampy [damp] soil, but must not replant it in a dry place.[5] Thus, only on the thirteenth, but not on the fourteenth.[6] Now consider: we know that R. Judah maintains: Any grafting which does not take root within three days will never take root. Then if you think that work may be done on the fourteenth, why [state] the thirteenth; surely there is the fourteenth, the fifteenth and part of the sixteenth?[7]—Said Raba: We learned [this] of Galilee. But there is the night?[8]—Said R. Shesheth: This is according to Beth Shammai.[9] R. Ashi said: In truth it is as Beth Hillel, [yet the night of the fourteenth is not stated] because it is not the practice of people to weed at night. Rabina said: After all it refers to Judea, but in respect to taking root we do say once that part of the day is as the whole of it, but we
c do not say twice that part of the day is as the whole of it.[1]

MISHNAH. R. MEIR SAID: ANY WORK WHICH HE BEGAN BEFORE THE FOURTEENTH, HE MAY FINISH IT ON THE FOURTEENTH; BUT HE MAY NOT BEGIN IT AT THE OUTSET ON THE FOURTEENTH, EVEN IF HE CAN FINISH IT [ON THE SAME DAY]. BUT THE SAGES MAINTAIN: THREE CRAFTSMEN MAY WORK ON THE EVE OF PASSOVER UNTIL MIDDAY, AND THESE ARE THEY: TAILORS, HAIRDRESSERS, AND WASHERMEN. R. JOSE B. R. JUDAH SAID: SHOEMAKERS TOO.[2]

GEMARA. The scholars asked: Did we learn [that it may be finished] when required for the Festival, but when not required for the Festival he may not even finish it; or perhaps we learned [that he must not begin work] when it is not required for the Festival, but when it is required we may indeed begin it; or perhaps, whether it is needed for the Festival or it is not needed, he may finish but not start?—Come and hear: But he may not begin at the outset on the fourteenth even a small girdle, [or] even a small hair-net. What does 'even' imply? Surely, even these which are required for the Festival, he may only finish, but not begin; whence it follows that where it is not required [for the Festival], we may not even finish!—No: after all, even when it is not required we may indeed finish [the work], and yet what does 'even' connote? Even these too, which are small. For you might argue, their beginning, that is the end of their work;[3] then we should even begin them at the very outset; therefore he informs us [that it is not so].

Come and hear: R. Meir said: Any work which is required for

(5) Which shows that on the Ninth of Ab washing of face and hands and feet is permitted. (6) The whole series of 'there is no difference etc. is taught by the same Tanna, and in each he merely wishes to intimate a point of leniency. Thus he first teaches that the Ninth of Ab is not more lenient than the Day of Atonement save that the doubt of the former is permitted. Then he states that the Ninth of Ab is not more lenient than public fasts save that work is permitted on the former. But he does not refer to the reverse cases where the Ninth of Ab is more stringent; hence you cannot deduce that they are alike in all other matters.

(1) 'Hear'—the passage commencing 'Hear O Israel' etc. (Deut. VI, 4f). This is recited every morning and evening, but a bridegroom is exempt on the evening of his marriage. (2) Lit., 'take'. (3) Unless he has a reputation for great piety, as otherwise it looks like an unwarrantable assumption of piety (Rashi in Ber. 17b). (4) His feelings are obviously such that unless he is extremely pious he cannot recite the *shema'* with proper devotion. (5) This is a continuation of the last Mishnah. (6) Following the thirteenth day of Nisan.

b (1) The preceding Mishnah regards abstention from work a mere custom and in this Mishnah it is treated as a prohibition! (2) I.e., why cite Judea and Galilee? the matter is everywhere determined by local custom. (3) Viz., that in Judea it is held to be permitted, while in Galilee it is held to be definitely prohibited, and not merely dependent on custom. (4) According to the views held in Judea. (5) It takes root in damp soil more quickly. Now the *'omer* (v. Glos. and Lev. XXIII, 10-14) is effective in permitting everything which has taken root before it is waved; hence it is desirable that this should take root before the *'omer* is waved on the sixteenth of the month. (6) For it is obvious that the law is so stated as to give the latest possible time. (7) And it is a principle that part of the day counts as the whole day; thus there is time for it to take root even if it is replanted on the fourteenth. (8) Following the thirteenth, when it is permissible even in Galilee. (9) Who in our Mishnah forbid the night.

c (1) For if he weeds some time on the fourteenth we would have to count the rest of the day as a complete day, and also the beginning of the sixteenth until the waving of the *'omer* as another complete day. (2) These may work everywhere. (3) I.e., they require so little time.

spirits [demons] too. Others say, Also [54b] Adam's raiment.[7]

Our Rabbis taught: Seven things are hidden[8] from men. These are they: the day of death, and the day of comfort,[9] the depth [extent] of judgment;[10] and a man does not know what is in his neighbour's heart; and a man does not know from what he will earn; and when the Davidic dynasty will return;[11] and when the wicked kingdom[12] will come to an end.

Our Rabbis taught: Three things [God] willed to come to
a pass,[1] and if He had not willed them, it would be but right that He should will them. And these are they: Concerning a corpse, that it should become offensive; and concerning a dead person, that he should be forgotten from the heart; and concerning produce, that it should rot;[2] and some say, concerning coins, that they should enjoy currency.[3]

MISHNAH. WHERE IT IS THE CUSTOM TO DO WORK ON THE NINTH OF AB,[4] ONE MAY DO IT; WHERE IT IS THE CUSTOM NOT TO DO WORK, ONE MAY NOT DO IT. AND IN ALL PLACES SCHOLARS CEASE [FROM WORK ON THAT DAY]. R. SIMEON B. GAMALIEL SAID: A MAN MAY ALWAYS MAKE HIMSELF A SCHOLAR.[5]

GEMARA. Samuel said: There is no public fast in Babylonia save the Ninth of Ab alone.[6] Shall we say that Samuel holds, [with regard to] the Ninth of Ab, its twilight is forbidden;[7] but Samuel said: [with regard to] the Ninth of Ab, its twilight is permitted? And should you say, Samuel holds, The twilight of every public fast is permitted,—surely we learned: One must eat and drink while it is yet day. Now what is this to exclude—is it not to exclude twilight?—No: it is to exclude after nightfall.

Shall we say that this supports him? [It was taught:] There is no difference between the Ninth of Ab and the Day of Atonement except that with the latter, its doubt is forbidden, while with the former, its doubt is permitted. What does 'its doubt is permitted' mean? Surely [that refers to] twilight?—No, [but] as
b R. Shisha the son of R. Idi said,[1] It is in respect of the fixing of New Moon; so here too it is in respect of the fixing of the New Moon.[2]

Raba lectured: Pregnant women and suckling women must fast and complete [the fast] on that day [the Ninth of Ab], just as they fast and complete [the fast] on the Day of Atonement; and the twilight thereof is forbidden. And they said likewise in R. Joḥanan's name. Yet did R. Joḥanan say thus? Surely R. Joḥanan said: The Ninth of Ab is not like a public fast. Surely that means in respect of twilight?—No: in respect of work.[3] [You say], 'Work'! we have learned it: WHERE IT IS THE CUSTOM TO DO WORK ON THE NINTH OF AB, ONE MAY DO IT; WHERE IT IS THE CUSTOM NOT TO DO WORK, ONE MAY NOT DO IT. And even R. Simeon b. Gamaliel merely says that if he sits and does not work it does not look like conceit, yet he certainly does not forbid it?—Rather, what does 'is not like a public fast' mean? In respect of the *Ne'ilah* service.[4] But surely R. Joḥanan said: Would that a man would go on praying all day![5]—There it is
c a [statutory] obligation, whereas here it is voluntary.[1] Another alternative [answer] is, 'What does 'it is not like a public fast' mean? In respect of the twenty-four [benedictions].[2]

R. Papa said: What does 'it is not like a public fast' mean? It is not like the first ones but like the last [ones].[3] An objection is raised: There is no difference between the Ninth of Ab and the Day of Atonement except that with the latter, its doubt is forbidden, while with the former, its doubt is permitted. Now what does 'its doubt is permitted' mean? Does it not refer to its twilight?—Said R. Shisha son of R. Idi: No: [It is meant] in respect of the fixing of New Moon.

Hence in all [other] regulations they are alike. This supports R. Eleazar. For R. Eleazar said: A man is forbidden to dip his finger in water on the Ninth of Ab, just as he is forbidden to dip his finger in water on the Day of Atonement. An objection is raised: There is no difference between the Ninth of Ab and a public fast except that on one work[4] is forbidden, while on the other work is permitted, where it is customary. This [implies that] in all [other] matters they are both alike; whereas in respect to a public fast it was taught, When they [the Sages] ruled, Bathing is forbidden, they spoke only of the whole body, but not of a

(7) This probably refers to Gen. III, 21: *And the Lord God made for Adam and for his wife garments of skins, and clothed them* (Rashi). (8) Lit., 'covered'. (9) No man knows when he will be relieved of his anxieties. (10) *Sc.* Divine Judgment (Rashi). (11) This was probably said in order to discourage those who tried to calculate the advent of the Messiah on the basis of Scripture; cf. Sanh. 97*a*. (12) A covert allusion to Rome (Rashi).

a (1) Lit., 'came up in (God's) intention to be created'. (2) If kept too long. This is necessary in order to restrain the producer from withholding supplies and thus artificially raising the prices. (3) For the benefit of the poor who have no other means of obtaining sustenance (v. Marginal Glosses). (4) Which is a fast-day in commemoration of the destruction of the Temple. (5) I.e., he may abstain from work even if he is not a scholar. (6) I.e., if a public fast is proclaimed, it does not commence on the previous evening, nor is work forbidden, even where it is the practice not to work on the Ninth of Ab. (The Day of Atonement, of course, stands in a different category entirely.) In the whole of the subsequent discussion 'public fast' does not mean one of the statutory fasts, but a fast proclaimed on account of drought or disaster etc (7) I.e., it is forbidden to eat at twilight on the eve of the fast, since he regards the twilight as possessing the full rigours of a fast-day. Twilight is a period of doubt, and it is not certain whether it is day or night.

b (1) V. *infra*. (2) E.g., if a man is in the wilderness and does not know what day was fixed as New Moon, he must observe two Days of Atonement (his doubt could only be whether the previous month had consisted of twenty-nine days or thirty days), but only one day as the Ninth of Ab. (3) On the fast-day itself. On a specially proclaimed public fast work is forbidden, whereas on the Ninth of Ab it is permitted. (4) On specially proclaimed public fast-days an extra service was added at the end of the day, called *ne'ilah*, which means 'closing'. R. Joḥanan states that there is no *ne'ilah* on the Ninth of Ab. (5) If a man does not remember whether he has recited his statutory prayers, R. Joḥanan rules that he should recite them now, though there is an opposing view that a man must not pray when in this doubt. Now, since R. Joḥanan holds that a man must pray when in doubt, why should there not be a *ne'ilah* service on the Ninth of Ab, seeing that it is like a specially proclaimed public fast in many respects?

c (1) On a public fast-day *ne'ilah* is obligatory; on the Ninth of Ab a man may recite it if he desires. (2) On public fast-days six benedictions were added to the usual eighteen which constituted the 'Prayer' *par excellence* (Ta'an. 15*a*). R. Joḥanan teaches that these are not recited on the Ninth of Ab. (3) In times of drought three public fasts were proclaimed, which began at daybreak. But if the drought nevertheless continued, another three were proclaimed, and these began the previous evening (v. Ta'an. Mishnah 10*a* and 12*b*). R. Joḥanan thus ruled that the Ninth of Ab begins on the previous evening, and eating is forbidden from twilight. (4) Lit., 'the doing of work'.

מא א ב מיי' פ"ה מהל' תעניות הל' י סמג עשין ג טוש"ע א"ח סי' תקנד סעיף כב:
מב ג מיי' שם טוש"ע שם סעיף ה:
מג ד מיי' שם הלכה ז וסמג שם טוש"ע א"ח סי' תקנג סעיף ב:

בגדו של אדם הראשון ת"ר *שבעה דברים מכוסים מבני אדם אלו הן יום המיתה ויום הנחמה ועומק הדין ואין אדם יודע מה בלבו של חבירו ואין אדם יודע במה משתכר ומלכות בית דוד מתי תחזור ומלכות חייבת מתי תכלה ת"ר ג' דברים עלו במחשבה ליבראות ואם לא עלו דין הוא שיעלו על המת שיסריח ועל המת שישתכח מן הלב ועל התבואה שתרקב וי"א על המטבע שיצא: **מתני'** **מקום שנהגו לעשות מלאכה בתשעה באב עושין מקום שנהגו שלא לעשות מלאכה אין עושין ובכל מקום תלמידי חכמים בטלים רשב"ג אומר לעולם יעשה אדם עצמו תלמיד חכם: **גמ'** אמר שמואל *אין תענית ציבור בבבל אלא תשעה באב בלבד למימרא דסבר שמואל ט' באב בין השמשות שלו אסור והאמר שמואל תשעה באב °בין השמשות שלו מותר וכי תימא קסבר שמואל כל תענית ציבור בין השמשות שלו מותר והאנן *תנן אוכלין ושותין מבעוד יום למעוטי מאי לאו למעוטי בין השמשות לא למעוטי משחשיכה נימא מסייע ליה אין בין תשעה באב ליום הכיפורים אלא שזה ספיקו אסור וזה ספיקו מותר מאי ספיקו מותר לאו בין השמשות לא כדאמר רב שישא בריה דרב אידי לקביעא דירחא הכא נמי לקביעא דירחא דרש רבא עוברות ומניקות מתענות ומשלימות בו כדרך שמתענות ומשלימות ביום הכיפורים ובין השמשות שלו אסור וכן אמרו משמיה דר' יוחנן ומי אמר ר' יוחנן הכי והאמר רבי יוחנן תשעה באב אינו כתענית ציבור מאי לאו לבין השמשות לא למלאכה מלאכה תנינא מקום שנהגו לעשות מלאכה בתשעה באב עושין ובמקום שנהגו שלא לעשות אין עושין ואפילו רשב"ג לא אמר אלא דכי יתיב ולא עביד לא מיחזי כיוהרא אבל מיסר לא אסר אלא מאי אינו כתענית ציבור לתפילת נעילה והאמר ר' יוחנן *ולואי שיתפלל אדם *והולך כל היום כולו התם חובה הכא רשות ואיבעית אימא מאי אינו כתענית ציבור לעשרים וארבעה רב פפא אמר מאי אינו כתענית ציבור אינו כראשונות אלא כאחרונות ואסורה מיתיבי אין בין תשעה באב ליום הכיפורים אלא שזה ספיקו אסור וזה ספיקו מותר מאי ספיקו מותר לאו בין השמשות שלו אמר רב שישא בריה דרב אידי לקביעא דירחא הא לכל (א) דבריהם זה וזה שוין מסייע לרבי אלעזר דא"ר אלעזר אסור לו לאדם להושיט אצבעו במים בתשעה באב כדרך שאסור להושיט אצבעו ביום הכיפורים מיתיבי אין בין תשעה באב לתענית ציבור אלא שזה אסור בעשיית מלאכה וזה מותר בעשיית מלאכה במקום שנהגו הא לכל דבריהם זה וזה שוין ואילו גבי תענית ציבור תניא *כשאמרו אסור ברחיצה לא אמרו אלא כל גופו אבל פניו ידיו ורגליו לא א"ר פפא תנא

רש"י

בגדו של אדם הראשון. שהיו חקוקות בו כל מין חיה ובהמה והוא נמסר לנמרוד על כן יאמר כנמרוד גבור ציד (בראשית י) ועשו הרגו ונטלו לפיכך היה איש ציד והן שכתוב בהן החמודות אשר אתה בבית (שם כז) ואני שמעתי בגדיו של אדם הראשון היינו כתנות עור שהיו לו: ויום הנחמה. של כל אדם מתי יתנחם מדאגתו: ועומק הדין הרבה טועים בו אי נמי עומק הדין העתיד: מלכות חייבת. רומי שכתוב בה גבול רשעה ורשעה היינו חייבת: *עלו במחשבה. ונתקיימו: ואם לא עלו דין הוא שיעלו. דאל"כ לא היה אדם מתקיים: שיסריח. שאל"כ הקרובים היו מצניעין אותו ורואין את צערן תמיד לפניהם: ועל התבואה שתרקב. שאל"כ היו בעלי בתים אוצרין אותה ומביאין רעבון לעולם*: **מתני'** ובכל מקום. בין נהגו בין לא נהגו: תלמידי חכמים בטלין. ממלאכה אותו היום: רבן שמעון כו'. ולא אמרינן מיחזי כיוהרא ואם רצה ליבטל רשאי: **גמ'** אין תענית ציבור בבבל. הואיל ואין צריכין לגשמים אם גוזרין על דבר אחר אין חומר תענית ציבור נוהג בו לאכול מבעוד יום וליאסר במלאכה ושאר חומרי האמורים שם: בין השמשות שלו אסור. באכילה *ובמלאכה דמחמירין על ספיקו כדאמרינן בתענית ציבור ושמואל קא משוי ט' באב כתענית ציבור: מבעוד יום למעוטי מאי לאו למעוטי בין השמשות. ספק: לא למעוטי משחשכה. ודאי אבל על ספיקו לא מחמרינן: אין בין ט' באב ליוה"כ. לכתחילה קאמר אבל דאי עבד טובא איכא זה כרת וזה איסור בעלמא: דרב שישא. לקמן: לקביעא דירחא. לעשות שני ימים כי מספקא לן אם עברו ב"ד חדש שעבר אי לא: מאי לאו. לאכילת בין השמשות: לא למלאכה. של יום עצמו משתחך ואשמעי' דבתענית ציבור אסור ובט' באב שרי: ואפילו לר' שמעון. לאו למיסר אתא אלא אם ירצה מי שאינו תלמיד חכם לעשות עצמו כתלמיד חכם וליבטל במקום העושין רשאי ולא חיישינן דילמא מיחזי כיוהרא: לתפלת נעילה. שבתענית ציבור היו מתפללין תפלת נעילה כדתנן בפ' בתרא דתענית (דף כו.) בג' פרקים בשנה כהנים נושאים כפיהן ד' פעמים ביום שחרית ומוסף ומנחה ונעילה ואלו הן ג' פרקים תענית ומעמדות ויוה"כ: והאמר ר' יוחנן. במסכת ברכות דאין בתפלה יתירה משום ברכה לבטלה: התם דחובה. בתענית צבור חובה מדרבנן ובתשעה באב אשמועינן דלאו חובה הוא ומ"מ אם בא להתפלל כל ימות השנה מותר ולואי: לעשרים וארבעה. דתנן במסכת תענית (דף טו.) שמוסיפין בתענית ציבור שש ברכות על שמונה עשרה: רב פפא אמר. לעולם כדסלקא דעתין מעיקרא דאינו כתענית ציבור דאמר לבין השמשות קאמר ולא תקשי לרבי יוחנן קמייתא דהאי דקאמר אינו כתענית ציבור לחומרא קאמר והכי קאמר אינו כשלש ראשונות שמותר בין השמשות שלהן כדתנן בהו בתענית אוכלין ושותין משחשיכה אלא כאחרונות דתנן בהו אוכלין ושותין מבעוד יום: לאו בין השמשות. וקשיא לרבא ולרבי יוחנן דאמרי בין השמשות שלו אסור: הא לכל דבריהן זה וזה שוין. מילתא באנפי נפשה היא ודייק לה ממתניתין דלעיל דקתני אין בין תשעה באב ליום הכפורים שיהא מותר לכתחלה בזה מה שאסור בזה אלא שזה ספיקו אסור וזה ספיקו מותר: אין בין תענית ציבור לתשעה באב. קס"ד בין להקל בין להחמיר אלמא לא חמיר תשעה באב מתענית ציבור ובתענית ציבור תניא דפניו ידיו ורגליו מותר: תנא

תוספות

אין תענית ציבור בבבל אלא תשעה באב. פ"ה לאכול מבעוד יום ולאסור במלאכה ושאר חומרי האמורים שם וא"ת תשעה באב מי הוי כתענית ציבור לאסור במלאכה וי"ל דה"ק אין תענית ציבור בבבל אפילו במקום שלא נהגו לעשות מלאכה: **אין** בין תשעה באב ליום הכפורים. הא דלא חשיב מלאכה שמותר בתשעה באב במקום שנהגו נראה לר"י משום דבסיפא מסיק לה לשריותא דמלאכה גבי אין בין ט' באב לתענית ציבור והא דלא חשיב תפילת נעילה דליתא בט' באב כדלקמן משום דבברייתא לא איירי אלא במידי דאיסור והיתר: **לאו** דברי בין השמשות דידיה. תימה לר"י אמאי קתני גבי יוה"כ ספיקו הא אפילו ודאי יום אסור דתוספת יוה"כ דאורייתא ותירץ דנקט ספיקו לאשמועינן דבט' באב אפילו ספיקו מותר*: **לקביעא** דירחא. אין לפרש כגון בני בבל שאין יודעים מתי הוקבע החודש בא"י שהיו צריכים לעשות יוה"כ שני ימים דבהדיא אמר בסוף פ"ק דר"ה (דף כא.) שאין עושין אלא יום אחד אלא ה"פ ספיקו אסור אם מסתפק אפילו בא"י מתי הוקבע החודש כגון שמהלך במדבר עושה ב' ימים כדין כל ספיקות דאורייתא דאזלינן לחומרא הקשה רשב"א דמשמע לקביעא דירחא הן חלוקין הא לכל דבריהן שוין והא יום הכפורים תוספתו אסור וט' באב תוספתו מותר ותירץ ר"י דלא מיירי אלא בדברים דשייכי בתענית עצמו: **והאמר** ר' יוחנן ולואי שיתפלל כל היום. אע"ג דר' יוחנן איירי דוקא בספק לא התפלל אבל ודאי התפלל אסור להתפלל כדמוכח במי שמתו (ברכות כא.) דקאמר ספק התפלל ספק לא התפלל אל יתפלל ור' יוחנן אמר ולואי שיתפלל כל היום וקאמר אם התפלל ומצא ציבור מתפללין אם יכול לחדש דבר בתפלתו יחזור ויתפלל ואם לאו אל יתפלל מ"מ פריך שפיר כיון דר' יוחנן על הספק מחייב להתפלל א"כ בתשעה באב דדמי לתענית ציבור בכמה דברים ובתענית ציבור איכא תפלת נעילה בט' באב נמי יתפלל ומשני התם חובה והכא רשות פי' לא לגמרי רשות אלא לאו חובה הוי אלא מצוה מיהא איכא: קולי

רבינו חננאל

ובגדו של אדם הראשון והמזיקין: ת"ר שבעה דברים מכוסין מבני אדם יום מיתה ויום נחמה ועומק הדין ואין אדם יודע מה בלבו של חברו [ואין אדם יודע במה משתכר] ומלכות בית דוד מתי תבוא ומלכו' חייבת מתי תכל': ת"ר שלשה דברים עלו במחשב' ליבראות ואילו לא עלו דין הוא שיעלו המת שיסריח וישתכח מן הלב והתבואה שתרקב ויש אומר' אף על המטבע שיצא: מתני' מקום שנהגו לעשות מלאכה בתשעה באב עושין כו'. אמר שמואל אין תענית צבור בבבל אלא תשעה באב בלבד ופירושה דסבר שמואל אחד תענית צבור ואחד תשעה באב ביה"ש שלו [מותר] ואינן אסורין אלא משחשכה. נימא מסייעא ליה אין בין תשעה באב ליום הכפורים אלא שיום הכפורים ספיקו אסור ותשעה באב ספיקו מותר מאי לאו בין השמשות ודחי' לא לקביעא דירחא כלומר אם מסתפק לך מתי נקבע החדש אתה תופס מספק שני ימים יום כפור ולא שני ימים תשעה באב וכדאמר רב שישא: דרש רבא עוברו' ומניקות מתענות ומשלימות [בו כדרך שמתענות ומשלימות] ביום הכפורים ובין השמשות שלו אסור וכן אמרו משמא דר' יוחנן. *)פי' האלהים לא אמרה הכי בשבועה נשבע רבא דלא אמרה ר' יוחנן ואקשי' ומי אמר ר' יוחנן הכי והאמר ר' יוחנן תשעה באב אינו כתענית צבור מאי לאו לבין השמשות מכלל שבין השמשות שלו מותר ודחי רבא לא למלאכה מותר ואקשי' למלאכ' הא תנינא מקום שנהגו לעשות מלאכה בת"ב עושין דאי ס"ד איסורא היכא דנהגו במקום איסורא שבקי' להו אלא מאי אין תשעה באב כתענית צבור להפלת נעילה כלומר אין מתפללין נעילה בתשעה באב. ומאי איכפת לן והא [אמר] ר' יוחנן ולואי שיתפלל אדם כל היום כולו ופרקי' הכא דאמר ולואי רשות הוא ובתענית צבור תפלת נעילה חובה. ואיצטריך למימר [דת"ב] אינו כתענית צבור*) בתעניות הראשונות דקילי כדתנן אוכלין משחשכה כו' אלא באחרונות דחמירן ובין השמשות שלו אסור ומותבי' על רבא מהא אין בין ט' באב ליוה"כ אלא שיוה"כ ספקו אסור וט' באב ספקו מותר מאי לאו ספקו בין השמשות וקתני מותר ודחי רב שישא מאי ספק קביעא דירחא שיוה"כ תופס שני ימים וט' באב יום אחד דייקי' מינה מדקתני אין ביניהם אלא כך וכך הא לכל דבריהם ט' באב ויוה"כ שוין מסייע ליה לר' אלעזר דאמר אסור לאדם להושיט אצבעו במים בט' באב כדרך שאסור להושיט אצבעו ביוה"כ: מיתיבי אין בין תשעה באב לתענית צבור אלא שתענית צבור אסור בעשיית מלאכה ומפורש בתענית פ"ק וט' באב מותר בעשיית מלאכה במקום שנהגו בו לעשות מלאכה דייקי' מינה הא לכל דבריהם זה וזה שוין אלו גבי תענית צבור תניא כשאמרו אסור ברחיצה לא אמרו אלא כל גופו אבל פניו ידיו ורגליו מותר. והנה הקיש ט' באב לתענית צבור מה תענית צבור פניו ידיו ורגליו מותר אף ט' באב מותר ואיך אמר אסור להושיט

*) נראה מדברי רבינו אלו דהיה גירסא אחרת בסוגיא זו וצ"ע. **) נראה דחסר בדברי רבינו וצ"ל רב פפא אמר מאי אינו כתענית ציבור אינו כראשונות.

מסורת הש"ס

מכילתא פ' בשלח | ע' הגהות רש"ל | ס"א על המטבע שיצא. דאל"כ במה היו עניים מתפרנסין שאין להם עבודת שדה וכרם: | [תענית ל: ברכות יז:] | [ועי' תוס' ר"ה ט. ד"ה ורבי עקיבא] | תענית יא: וע"ש | [עי' רש"י דתענית יג ד"ה כשאמרו כו' והמ"א סי' תקנד סק"ג הניחו בצ"ע] | תענית יב: | ברכות כא. | [בברכות וגם בתוס' דהכא ליתא] | [מ"ק טו: תענית יג.]

הגהות הב"ח

(א) גמ' לכל דבריהם זה וזה שוין:

גליון הש"ס

גמ' בה"ש שלו מותר. עיין עירובין מא ע"א תד"ה אי אתם מודים:

ואיש תבונה ידלנה. הבין מה היה בלבו של עולא שהיה מתכוון בו : ואינהו כמאן סברוה. עולא ורבה שלא רצו להודות לדברי רבי אבא : עמא דבר. נוהג : באור ששבת. שהיה בשבת שדלק היום ומכל מקום ממלאכת עבירה שבת שדלק בהיתר כגון של חיה ושל חולה או נר הדולק מערב יום הכפורים מברכין אף במוצאי יום הכפורים דהשתא ברכה משום דדבר חידוש הוא לו שלא נהנה מן האור היום : באור היוצא מהעצים. דנבראה עכשיו אין מברכין עליו במוצאי יוה"כ אלא במוצאי שבת שאף הוא תחילת בריית אור : רבי מפוזרן. רבי כשראה אור מברך עליו מיד וכשמביאין לו בשמים לסוף שעה מברך עליהן : מכנסן. על הכוס כמו שאנו עושין: באר. באר של מרים סלע שיצאו ממנו המים על ידי משה ועגול כמין כברה היה ומתגלגל עמהן כל מקום שהולכין : כתב. קריאת שם האותיות: המכתב. חקיקתן וצורתן כך שמעתי ולי נראה כתב זו היא חקיקת צורתן והמכתב הוא עט וחרט שנכתב בו חקיקת הלוחות כי ההיא דקדושין (דף כב:) מניין לרבות הסול והסירא והמכתב ונראין דברי דקרייה לא קרי ליה כתב : ומערה שעמד בו משה. ושמתיך בנקרת הצור *עד עברי (שמות לג) וכן באליהו וילך עד הר האלהים חורב ויבא שם אל המערה וילן שם (מלכים א יט) : לבלוע את הרשעים. עדת קרח : והפרד. אין כל חדש תחת השמש ופרד ראשון נברא מן הארץ ולא בא מן הכלאים: האיל. של אברהם : השמיר. כמין תולעת היה ואין כל דבר קשה עומד בפניו שלא יתפרק ובו בנה שלמה את הבית במסכת גיטין (דף סח.) : הצבת. טנליי"ש של ברזל : צבתא. שעושין עכשיו הנפחים : בצבתא מתעביד. על ידי צבת אחרת היא עשויה שאוחזה בצבת ומכה בקורנס עד שנעשית וצבתא קמייתא מאן עבדה : הא לאי. באמת על כרחך בריה בידי שמים היא : יעשנה בדפוס. על ידי יציקה כמו שיוצקין כלי כסף וכלי נחשת: ויקבענה כיון. כולה כאחד מהר : ראשית דרכו. קודם לשאר דרכים והא דאמרן לעיל הכתב בערב שבת בכתבן של לוחות וזו היתה כתובה מתחילה *באש שחורה על גבי לבנה : בטרם הרים יולדו. בראת מדת תשובה : תשב אנוש עד דכא. עד ידכא לבבו לפניך: מקדם. מוקדם לעולם : מאתמול. קודם לעולם: תפתה. שכל המתפתה ביצרו נופל *שם : מרום מראשון. מרום הוא בערבות מראשון מקודם העולם וכן מקום מקדשנו נברא מראשון: חללה. חלל של גיהנם קודם בריית העולם ותירוצא הוא : אין לו כבייה עולמית. שהוא אור של גיהנם : חזר וכללו. לקרותו טוב לפי שהרשעים נידונין בו : אלא. ודאי אור דגיהנם נברא בשני בשבת והא דתניא לעיל אור בערב שבת באור דידן ודתניא בריאה במו"ש לא תיקשי כאן במחשבה כאן ביצירה בערב שבת עלה במחשבה ליבראות ולא נברא עד מוצאי שבת : וטחן. טח והכה ושפשף זו בזו : דורשי חמורות. מקראות סתומים : פסול היה. שאחיו מאמו היה אביו כדמפרש שבא צבעון על אמו והוליד : אלה בני שעיר וגו'. וצבעון וענה אלמא אחי הוו וכתיב אלה בני צבעון ואיה וענה אלמא בנו היה: שמואל קרי ליה רבא שבור מלכא משום דבקי היה בדינין והלכתא כוותיה בדיני כדין היוצא מפי המלך שמתקיים ושבור ממלך פרסיים היה בימי רבא :

תורה אור

ואיש תבונה ידלנה מים עמוקים עצה בלב איש זה עולא ואיש תבונה ידלנה זה רבה בר בר חנה ואינהו כמאן סברוה כי הא דאמר ר' בנימן בר יפת אמר רבי יוחנן *מברכין על האור בין במוצאי שבת בין במוצאי יום הכפורים וכן *עמא דבר מיתיבי אין מברכין על האור אלא במוצאי שבת הואיל ותחילת ברייתו הוא וכיון שרואה מברך מיד רבי יהודה אומר סודרן על הכוס ואמר רבי יוחנן הלכה כרבי יהודה לא קשיא כאן באור ששבת כאן באור היוצא מן העצים ומן האבנים תני חדא *אור היוצא מן העצים ומן האבנים מברכין עליו ותני חדא אין מברכין עליו לא קשיא כאן *במוצאי שבת כאן במוצאי יום הכפורים רבי מפזרן רבי חייא מכנסן אמר רבי יצחק בר אבדימי אע"פ שרבי מפזרן חוזר וסודרן על הכוס כדי להוציא בניו ובני ביתו ואור במוצאי שבת איברי והא תניא *עשרה דברים נבראו בערב שבת בין השמשות אלו הן באר והמן וקשת כתב ומכתב והלוחות וקברו של משה ומערה שעמד בו משה ואליהו פתיחת פי האתון ופתיחת פי הארץ לבלוע את הרשעים רבי נחמיה אומר משום אביו אף האור והפרד ר' יאשיה אומר משום אביו אף האיל והשמיר רבי יהודה אומר אף הצבת הוא היה אומר צבתא בצבתא מתעבדא וצבתא קמייתא מאן עבד הא לאי בריה בידי שמים היא אמר ליה אפשר יעשנה בדפוס ויקבענה כיון הא לאי בריה בידי אדם היא לא קשיא הא באור דידן הא באור דגיהנם אור דידן במוצאי שבת אור דגיהנם בערב שבת ואור דגיהנם בערב שבת איברי והא תניא *שבעה דברים נבראו קודם שנברא העולם ואלו הן תורה ותשובה וגן עדן וגיהנם וכסא הכבוד ובית המקדש ושמו של משיח תורה דכתיב
משלי ח °ה' קנני ראשית דרכו תשובה דכתיב °בטרם הרים יולדו וכתיב °תשב
תהלים צ אנוש עד דכא ותאמר שובו בני אדם גן עדן דכתיב °ויטע ה' אלהים גן
בראשית ב בעדן מקדם גיהנם דכתיב °כי ערוך מאתמול תפתה כסא הכבוד ובית
ישעיה ל
ירמיה יז המקדש דכתיב °כסא כבוד מרום מראשון מקום מקדשנו שמו של משיח
תהלים עב דכתיב °יהי שמו לעולם לפני שמש ינון שמו אמרי חללה הוא דנברא קודם שנברא העולם ואור דידיה בערב שבת איברי והתניא רבי יוסי אומר אור שברא הקב"ה בשני בשבת אין לו כבייה לעולם
ישעיה סו שנאמר °ויצאו וראו בפגרי האנשים הפושעים בי כי תולעתם לא תמות ואשם לא תכבה ואמר רבי בנאה בריה דרבי עולא מפני מה לא נאמר כי טוב בשני בשבת מפני שנברא בו אור של גיהנם ואמר רבי אלעזר אע"פ
בראשית א שלא נאמר בו כי טוב חזר וכללו בששי שנאמר °וירא אלהים את כל אשר עשה והנה טוב מאד אלא חללה קודם שנברא העולם ואור דידיה בשני בשבת ואור דידן במחשבה עלה ליבראות בערב שבת ולא נברא עד מוצאי שבת דתניא ר' יוסי אומר שני דברים עלו במחשבה ליבראות בערב שבת ולא נבראו עד מוצאי שבת ובמוצאי שבת נתן הקב"ה דיעה באדם הראשון מעין דוגמא של מעלה והביא שני אבנים וטחנן זו בזו ויצא מהן אור והביא שתי בהמות והרכיב זו בזו ויצא מהן פרד רבן שמעון
שם לו בן גמליאל אומר פרד בימי ענה היה שנאמר °הוא ענה אשר מצא את הימים במדבר *דורשי *)חמורות היו אומרים ענה פסול היה לפיכך הביא
שם פסול לעולם שנאמר °אלה בני שעיר החורי וכתיב אלה בני צבעון ואיה וענה *אלא מלמד שבא צבעון על אמו והוליד ממנה ענה ודילמא תרי ענה הוו *אמר רבא אמינא מילתא דשבור מלכא לא אמרה ומנו שמואל איכא דאמרי אמר ר"פ אמינא מילתא דשבור מלכא לא אמרה ומנו *רבא אמר קרא הוא ענה דמעיקרא תנו רבנן *עשרה דברים נבראו בערב שבת בין השמשות ואלו הן באר ומן וקשת הכתב והמכתב והלוחות קברו של משה ומערה שעמד בה משה ואליהו פתיחת פי האתון ופתיחת פי הארץ לבלוע את הרשעים ויש אומרים אף מקלו של אהרן שקדיה ופרחיה ויש אומרים אף המזיקין ויש אומרים אף בגדו

*) ועי' תוס' חולין קלד: ד"ה דורשי חמורות מ"ש בשם הערוך.

תוספות

אלה בני שעיר החורי וכו' מלמד שבא צבעון על אמו. תימה דבים נוחלין (ב"ב קטו:) מוכח מהאי קרא דבני בנים כבנים וא"כ מנלן שבא על אמו ועוד לא מלינו בכל התורה שיקראו לבן אשתו בנו והכא אמר דלהכי קרי ליה בנו לפי שנולד מאשתו וי"ל דקרי ליה בנו לפי שהיה בן בנו כדאמרינן בים נוחלין והכא דייק שבא על אמו מדלא כתיב איה שהיה כמו כן בן צבעון ולא כתיב אלא ענה לחודיה ש"מ לפי שהיה כמי בן אשתו של שעיר כתביה קרא הכא עם שאר בני שעיר :

אין

עין משפט נר מצוה

לב א מיי' פכ"ט מהל' שבת הל' כד סמג עשין כט טוש"ע א"ח סי' רצח סעיף א וסי' תרכד סעיף ד: [רב אלפס ברכות פ"ח דף מג:]

לג ב ג מיי' שם הל' כו טוש"ע שם סי' רצח סעיף ח:

מסורת הש"ס

[ברכות נג. וע"ש]

[ושמות כפי שלון]

אבות פ"ה מ"ו [ע"ש] מכילתא פרשת בשלח

נדרים לט:

[כלאי' ירושלמי יס.]

[ברכות כד. חולין קלד:]

ב"ב קטו:

[עי' איכה רבה ועי' שם בפי' הרש"ים]

[אבות פ"ה וע"ש כמה שנוים]

גליון הש"ס

רש"י ד"ה ראשית דרכו כו' כלאם שחורה ע"ג לבנה. עי' ברכ"י שיר השירים בפסוק קווצותיו תלתלים שחורות כעורב:

רבינו חננאל

כמאן סבירא כי הא דאמר משום ר' אלעזר מברכין על האור במוצאי שבתו' ובמוצאי יום הכפורים וכן עמא דבר: ואותבי' עלייהו הא דתניא אין מברכין על האור אלא במוצאי שבתות הואיל ותחלת ברייתו הוא וכיון שרואהו מברך עליו מיד ר' יהודה אומר סודרן על הכוס ואמר ר' יוחנן הלכה כר' יהודה ופרקי' לא קשיא הא דתניא אין מברכין על האור אלא במוצאי שבת באור היוצא מן העצים ומן האבנים והא דאמר משמא דר' אלעזר מברכין אפילו ביוה"כ באור ששבת ממלאכת עבודה. בואלו דברים שבין ב"ש וב"ה בסעודה תניא נמי חבי עששית שהיתה דולקת והולכת בשבת כלו במוצאי שבת מברכין עליה ואקשי' ואור במוצאי שבת איברי והתניא אלו דברים שנבראו [בע"ש] בין השמשות באר שהיתה מהלכת עם ישראל ומן שירד להם וקשת דכתיב (בראשית ט יג) את קשתי נתתי בענן . כתב מכתב פי' כתב צורת האותיות מכתב צירוף האותיות להיות תיבה להקרות במלה ד"א כתב הוא כתב הקודש שהן כ"ב אותיות מכתב הוא שהיה חרות על הלוחות הנקרא סטרגינא מפני שהיה נקרא מארבעה צדדים ולוחות כמשמען וקבר משה רבינו ואליהו ופתיחת פי אתון בלעם ופתיחת פי הארץ לבלוע קרח . ור' יאשיה אמר אף האיל הנאחז בסבך והשמיר שבו בנה שלמה הבית ר' נחמיה אומר משום אביו אף האור והפרד ר' יהודה אומר אף הצבת קתני מיהא ר' נחמיה דאיר בין השמשות נברא ופרקי' האי אור דגיהנם הוא אבל אור דידן במוצאי שבת נברא . ואקשי' איני והא גיהנם אחד משבעה דברים שנבראו קודם בריאת העולם הוא ואלו הן תורה ותשובה גן עדן וגיהנם כסא הכבוד ובית המקדש ושמו של משיח ופרקי' חללה של גיהנם נבראת קודם בריאת העולם אור של גיהנם נברא בשני בשבת אור דידן עלה במחשבה להבראות בערב שבת ולא נברא עד מוצאי שבת . ר' יוסי אומר שני דברי' עלו במחשבה ליבראות בערב שבת ובמוצאי שבת נתן הקב"ה בינה באדם מעין דוגמא של מעלה והביא שתי אבני' וטחנן זו בזו ויצא מהן אור והביא מין סוס ומין חמורה והרכיבן זו על זו ויצא מהן פרד וכו' : ת"ר עשרה דברים נבראו בע"ש ביה"ש ואלו הן מן ובאר וכו' ויש אומר' אף מקלו של אהרן ושקדיה ופרחיה ובגדו

בגדו

Continuation of translation from previous page as indicated by ◁

a garden in Eden from aforetime.[8] The Gehenna, for it is written, *For Tophet* [i.e., Gehenna] *is ordered of old.*[9] The Throne of Glory and the Temple, for it is written, *Thou throne of glory, on high from the beginning, Thou place of our sanctuary.*[10] The name of the Messiah, as it is written, *His* [*sc.* the Messiah's] *name shall endure for ever, and has existed before the sun!*[11]—I will tell you: only its cavity was created before the world was created, but its fire [was created] on the eve of the Sabbath.

Yet was its fire created on the eve of the Sabbath? Surely it was taught, R. Jose said: The fire which the Holy One, blessed be He, created on the second day of the week shall never be
c extinguished,[1] as it is said, *And they shall go forth, and look upon the carcasses of the men that have rebelled against me; for their worm shall not die, neither shall their fire be quenched?*[2] Again, R. Bana'ah son of R. 'Ulla said: Why was *'it was good'* not said concerning the second day of the week?[3] Because the fire of the Gehenna was created thereon. Also R. Eleazar said, Although *'it was good'* was not said in connection with it, yet He re-included it in the sixth, as it is said, *And God saw everything that He had made, and behold, it was very good.*[4]—Rather, the cavity [was made] before the world was created, and its fire on the second day of the week; while as for our fire, on the eve of the Sabbath He decided[5] to create it, but it was not created until the termination of the Sabbath. For it was taught, R. Jose said: Two things He decided to create on the eve of the Sabbath, but they were not created until the termination of the Sabbath, and at the termination of the Sabbath the Holy One, blessed be He, inspired Adam with knowledge of a kind similar to Divine [knowledge],[6] and he procured two stones and rubbed them on each other, and fire issued from them; he also took two [heterogeneous] animals and crossed them, and from them came forth the mule. R. Simeon b. Gamaliel said: The mule came into existence in the days of Anah, for it is said, *This is the Anah who found the mules*[7] *in the wilderness.*[8] Those who interpret symbolically[9] used to say: Anah was unfit,[10] therefore he
d brought unfit [animals][1] into the world, for it is said, *These are the sons of Seir the Horite* [. . . *and Zibeon and Anah*],[2] while it is written, *And these are the children of Zibeon: Aiah and Anah.*[3] Hence it teaches that Zibeon cohabited with his mother and begat Anah by her. But perhaps there were two Anahs? Said Raba: I say a thing which [even] King Shapur could not say, and who is that? Samuel. Others say, R. Papa said: I say a thing which even King Shapur did not say, and who is that? Raba.[4] The Writ saith, that *is Anah* [meaning], that is the original Anah.[5]

Our Rabbis taught: Ten things were created on the eve of the Sabbath at twilight, and these are they: The well, manna, the rainbow, writing, the writing instruments, the Tables, the sepulchre of Moses and the cave in which Moses and Elijah stood, the opening of the ass's mouth, and the opening of the earth's mouth to swallow up the wicked. While some say, Also Aaron's staff, its almonds and its blossoms.[6] Others say, The harmful

(8) Gen. II, 8. (9) Isa. XXX, 33. (10) Jer. XVII, 12. (11) Ps. LXXII, 17.—Thus the Gehenna was created before the world.—The general idea of this Baraitha is that these things are indispensable pre-requisites for the orderly progress of mankind upon earth. The Torah, the supreme source of instruction; the concept of repentance, in recognition that 'to err is human', and hence, if man falls, the opportunity to rise again; the Garden of Eden and the Gehenna, symbolizing reward and punishment; the Throne of Glory and the Temple, indicating that the goal of Creation is that the Kingdom of God (represented by the Temple) shall be established on earth, as it is in heaven; and finally, the name of the Messiah, i.e., the assurance that God's purpose will ultimately be achieved.

c (1) Because it is the fire of the Gehenna. (2) Isa. LXVI, 24. (3) In which the world was created. (4) Gen. I, 31. (5) Lit., 'it came up in (His) intention'. (6) Lit., 'of above'. (7) E.V. *'hot springs'*. (8) Gen. XXXVI, 24. (9) דורשי חמורות Lit., 'those who interpret (Scripture) as jewels', i.e., as ethical teachings. Levi connects the phrase with חומר a beautiful and graceful gazelle, i.e., those who teach with charming and graceful interpretations. Lauterbach in *J.Q.R.* (New Series) Vol. I, p. 509 maintains that it connotes a class of interpreters who sought the significance of the law regarding the *action* it enjoins as symbolic, so that once its significance is understood the performance of the action is not important; v. whole article there pp. 503 seqq. and Kid., 22*b*, n. 10. (10) *Pasul*, i.e., the issue of an incestuous union.

d (1) I.e., the offsprings of heterogeneous breeding—i.e., they saw in this the teaching that evil begets evil (Lauterbach l.c. p. 513). (2) Gen. XXXVI, 20. (3) Ibid. 24. In the first verse Anah appears as Zibeon's brother, whereas in the second he is his son. (4) Shapur I, King of Persia, was a contemporary of Samuel, while Shapur II was a contemporary of Raba. These names are applied here to Samuel and Raba, as indicating their acknowledged authority in learning. V. *MGWJ.* 1936, p. 217. (5) Identical with the first mentioned. (6) V. Num. XVII, 23. This too was ordained at the Creation.

ואיש תבונה ידלנה. הבין מה היה בלבו של עולא שהיה מסתכל בו: ואינהו כמאן סברוה. עולא ורבה שלא רצו להודות לדברי רבי אבא: עמא דבר. נוהג: באור שבת. שהיה בשבת שדלק היום ומכל מקום ממלאכת עבירה שבת שדלק בהיתר כגון של חיה ושל חולה או נר הדולק מערב יום הכפורים מברכין אף במוצאי יום הכפורים דהשתא ברכה משום דבר חידוש הוא לו שלא נהנה מן האור היום: באור היוצא מהעצים. דבראשית עכשיו אין מברכין עליו במוצאי יוה"כ אלא במוצאי שבת שאף הוא תחילת ברייה אור: רבי מפזרן. רבי כשראה אור מברך עליו מיד וכשמבדילין לו בשמים לסוף שפה מברך עליהן: מכנסן. על הכוס כמו שאנו עושין: באר. של מרים סלע שילאו ממנו המים על ידי משה ועגול כמין כברה היה ומתגלגל עמהן כל מקום שהולכין: כתב. קריאת שם האותיות: המכתב. חקיקתן ולורתן כך שמעתי ולי נראה כתב זו היא חקיקת לורתן והמכתב הוא עט וחרט שנכתב בו חקיקת הלוחות כי ההיא דקדושין (דף כה:) מניין לרבות הסול והסירה והמכתב ונראין דברי דקרייה לא קרי ליה כתב: ומערה שעמד בו משה. ושמתיך בנקרת הצור *עד עברי (שמות לג) וכן באליהו וילך עד הר האלהים חורב ויבא שם אל המערה וילן שם (מלכים א יט): לבלוע את הרשעים. עדת קרח: והפרד. אין כל חדש תחת השמש ופרד ראשון נבראה מן הארץ ולא בא מן הכלאים: האיל. של אברהם: השמיר. כמין תולעת היה ואין כל דבר קשה עומד בפניו שלא יתפרק ובו בנה שלמה את הבית במסכת גיטין (דף סח.): הצבת. טנליי"ש של ברזל: צבתא. שעושין עכשיו הנפחים: בצבתא מתעביד. על ידי צבת אחרת היה עשויה שאוחזה בצבת ומכה בקורנס עד שנעשית וצבתא קמייתא מאן עבדה: הא לאו. בתמיה על כרחך בריה בידי שמים היא: יעשנה בדפוס. על ידי יציקה כמו שיוצקין כלי כסף וכלי נחשת: ויקבענה כיון. כולה כאחד מהר: ראשית דרכו. קודם לשאר דרכים והא דאמרן לעיל הכתב בערב שבת נבראת בכתבן של לוחות וזו היתה כתובה מתחילה *באש שחורה על גבי לבנה: בטרם הרים יולדו. בראת מדת תשובה: תשב אנוש עד דכא. עד ידכא לבבו לפניך: מקדם. מוקדם לעולם: מאתמול. קודם לעולם: תפתה. שכל המתפתה בילרו נופל *שם: מרום מראשון. מרום הוא בערבות מראשון מוקדם העולם וכן מקום מקדשנו נבראת מראשון: חללה. חלל של גיהנם קודם בריית העולם ותירוצה הוא: אין לו כבייה עולמית. שהוא אור של גיהנם: חזר וכללו. לקרותו טוב לפי שהרשעים נידונין בו: אלא. ודאי אור דגיהנם נבראת בשני בשבת והא דתניא לעיל אור בערב שבת באור דידן ודתניא בריאה בשני ש"מ לא תיקשי כאן במחשבה כאן ביצירה בערב שבת עלה במחשבה ליבראות ולא נבראת עד מוצאי שבת: וטחנן. טח והכה ושפשף זו בזו: דורשי חמורות. מקראות סתומים: פסול היה. שאחיו מאמו היה אביו כדמפרש שבא צבעון על אמו והוליד: אלה בני שעיר וגו'. ולבעון וענה אלמא אחי הוו וכתיב אלה בני צבעון ואיה וענה אלמא בנו היה: שמואל קרי ליה רבא שבור מלכא משום דבקי היה בדינין והלכתא כוותיה בדיני כדין היוצא מפי המלך שמתקיים ושבור ממלך פרסיים היה בימי רבא:

ואיש תבונה ידלנה מים עמוקים עצה בלב איש זה עולא ואיש תבונה ידלנה זה רבה בר בר חנה ואינהו כמאן סברוה כי הא דאמר ר' בנימין בר יפת אמר רבי יוחנן *מברכין על האור בין במוצאי שבת בין במוצאי יום הכפורים וכן *עמא דבר מיתיבי אין מברכין על האור אלא במוצאי שבת הואיל ותחילת ברייתו הוא וכיון שרואה מברך מיד רבי יהודה אומר סודרן על הכוס ואמר רבי יוחנן הלכה כרבי יהודה לא קשיא כאן באור ששבת כאן באור היוצא מן העצים ומן האבנים תני חדא ג'אור היוצא מן העצים ומן האבנים מברכין עליו ותני חדא אין מברכין עליו לא קשיא כאן ג'במוצאי שבת כאן במוצאי יום הכפורים רבי מפזרן רבי חייא מכנסן אמר רבי יצחק בר אבדימי אע"פ שרבי מפזרן חוזר וסודרן על הכוס כדי להוציא בניו ובני ביתו ואור במוצאי שבת איברי והא תניא *עשרה דברים נבראו בערב שבת בין השמשות אלו הן באר והמן וקשת כתב ומכתב והלוחות וקברו של משה ומערה שעמד בו משה ואליהו פתיחת פי האתון ופתיחת פי הארץ לבלוע את הרשעים רבי נחמיה אומר משום אביו אף האור והפרד ר' יאשיה אומר משום אביו אף האיל והשמיר רבי יהודה אומר אף הצבת הוא היה אומר צבתא בצבתא מתעבדא וצבתא קמייתא מאן עבד הא לאו בריה בידי שמים היא אמר ליה אפשר יעשנה בדפוס ויקבענה כיון הא לאו בריה בידי אדם היא לא קשיא הא באור דידן הא באור דגיהנם אור דידן במוצאי שבת אור דגיהנם בערב שבת ואור דגיהנם בערב שבת איברי והא תניא *שבעה דברים נבראו קודם שנברא העולם ואלו הן תורה ותשובה וגן עדן וגיהנם וכסא הכבוד ובית המקדש ושמו של משיח תורה דכתיב (משלי ח) ה' קנני ראשית דרכו תשובה דכתיב (תהלים צ) בטרם הרים יולדו וכתיב תשב אנוש עד דכא ותאמר שובו בני אדם גן עדן דכתיב (בראשית ב) ויטע ה' אלהים גן בעדן מקדם גיהנם דכתיב (ישעיה ל) כי ערוך מאתמול תפתה כסא הכבוד ובית המקדש דכתיב (ירמיה יז) כסא כבוד מרום מראשון מקום מקדשנו שמו של משיח דכתיב (תהלים עב) יהי שמו לעולם לפני שמש ינון שמו אמרי חללה הוא דנברא קודם שנברא העולם ואור דידיה בערב שבת ואור דידיה בערב שבת איברי והתניא רבי יוסי אומר אור שברא הקב"ה בשני בשבת אין לו כבייה לעולם שנאמר (ישעיה סו) ויצאו וראו בפגרי האנשים הפושעים בי כי תולעתם לא תמות ואשם לא תכבה ואמר רבי בנאה בריה דרבי עולא מפני מה לא נאמר כי טוב בשני בשבת מפני שנברא בו אור של גיהנם ואמר רבי אלעזר אע"פ שלא נאמר בו כי טוב חזר וכללו בששי שנאמר (בראשית א) וירא אלהים את כל אשר עשה והנה טוב מאד אלא חללה קודם שנברא העולם ואור דידיה בשני בשבת ואור דידן במחשבה עלה ליבראות בערב שבת ולא נברא עד מוצאי שבת דתניא ר' יוסי אומר שני דברים עלו במחשבה ליבראות בערב שבת ולא נבראו עד מוצאי שבת ובמוצאי שבת נתן הקב"ה דיעה באדם הראשון מעין דוגמא של מעלה והביא שני אבנים וטחנן זו בזו ויצא מהן אור והביא שתי בהמות והרכיב זו בזו ויצא מהן פרד רבן שמעון בן גמליאל אומר פרד בימי ענה היה שנאמר (שם לו) הוא ענה אשר מצא את הימים במדבר *דורשי *) חמורות היו אומרים ענה פסול היה לפיכך הביא פסול לעולם שנאמר (שם) אלה בני שעיר החורי וכתיב אלה בני צבעון ואיה וענה *אלא מלמד שבא צבעון על אמו והוליד ממנה ענה ודילמא תרי ענה הוו *אמר רבא אמינא מילתא דשבור מלכא לא אמרה ומנו שמואל איכא דאמרי אמר ר"פ אמינא מילתא דשבור מלכא לא אמרה ומנו *רבא אמר קרא הוא ענה דמעיקרא תנו רבנן *עשרה דברים נבראו בערב שבת בין השמשות ואלו הן באר ומן וקשת הכתב והמכתב והלוחות קברו של משה ומערה שעמד בה משה ואליהו פתיחת פי האתון ופתיחת פי הארץ לבלוע את הרשעים ויש אומרים אף מקלו של אהרן שקדיה ופרחיה ויש אומרים אף המזיקין ויש אומרים אף בגדו

*) ועי' תוס' חולין קלד: ד"ה דורשי חמורות מ"ש בשם הערוך.

תוספות

אלה בני שעיר החורי וכו' מלמד שבא לבעון על אמו. תימה דבים נוחלין (ב"ב קטו:) מוכח מהאי קרא דבני בנים כבנים וא"כ מכלן שבא על אמו ועוד לא מליט בכל התורה שיקראו לבן אשתו בנו והכא אמר דלהכי קרי ליה בנו לפי שנולד מאשתו וי"ל דקרי ליה בנו לפי שהיה בן בנו כדאמרינן בים נוחלין והכא דייק שבא על אמו מדלא כתיב איה שהיה כמו כן בן לבעון ולא כתיב אלא ענה לחודיה ש"מ לפי שהיה כמי בן אשתו של שעיר כתביה קרא הכא עם שאר בני שעיר:

עין משפט נר מצוה

לב א מיי' פכ"ט מהל' שבת הל' כד סמג עשין כט טוש"ע או"ח סי' רלח סעיף א וסי' תרכד ס"ד: [רב אלפס ברכות פ"ח דף מג:]

לג ב ג מיי' שם הל' כו טוש"ע שם סי' רלח סעיף ח:

מסורת הש"ס

[ברכות נב: וש"נ]

[ושמתי כפי עליך]

אבות פ"ה מ"ו [ע"ש] מכילתא פרשת בשלח

נדרים לט:

[כדאי' עירובין יט.]

[ברכות כד. חולין קלד:]

ב"ב קטו:

[שם איתא רבה ועי' שם בפי' הרשב"ם] [אבות פ"ה ע"ש] כמה שנוים

גליון הש"ס

רש"י ד"ה ראשית דרכו כו' באש שחורה ע"ג לבנה. עי' ברש"י שיר השירים בפסוק קווצותיו תלתלים שחורות כעורב:

רבינו חננאל

כמאן סבירא כי הא דאמר' משום ר' אלעזר מברכין על האור במוצאי שבתו' ובמוצאי יום הכפורים וכן עמא דבר: ואותבי' עלייהו הא דתניא אין מברכין על האור אלא במוצאי שבתות הואיל ותחלת ברייתו הוא וכיון שרואהו מברך עליו מיד ר' יהודה אומר סודרן על הכוס ואמר ר' יוחנן הלכה כר' יהודה ופרקי' לא קשיא הא דתניא אין מברכין על האור אלא במוצאי שבת באור היוצא מן העצים ומן האבנים והא דאמר משמא דר' אלעזר מברכין אפילו ג' יוה"כ באור ששבת ממלאכת עבודה. באלו דברים שבין ב"ש וב"ה בסעודה תניא נמי עששית שהיתה דולקת והולכת בשבת כלו במוצאי שבת מברכין עליה ואקשי' ואור במוצאי שבת איברי והתניא אלו דברים שנבראו [בע"ש] בין השמשות באר שהיתה מהלכת עם ישראל ומן שירד להם וקשת דכתיב (בראשית ט יג) את קשתי נתתי בענן. כתב מכתב פי' כתב צורת האותיות מכתב צירוף האותיות להיות תיבה להקרות במלה ד"א כתב הוא כתב הקודש שהן כ"ב איתיות מכתב הוא שהיה חרות על הלוחות הנקרא פטרונגנא מפני שהיה נקרא מארבעה צדדים ולוחות כמשמען וקבר משה רבינו ואליהו ופתיחת פי אתון בלעם ופתיחת פי הארץ לבלוע קרח. ור' יאשיה אמר אף האיל הנאחז בסבך והשמיר שבו בנה שלמה את הבית ר' נחמיה אומר משום אביו אף האור והפרד ר' יהודה אומר אף הצבת קתני מ"מ הא ר' נחמיה דאמר בין השמשות נברא ופרקי' האי אור דגיהנם הוא אבל אור דידן במוצאי שבת נברא. ואקשי' איני והא ניהנם אחד משבעה דברים שנבראו קודם בריאת העולם הוא ואלו הן תורה ותשובה גן עדן וגיהנם כסא הכבוד ובית המקדש ושמו של משיח ופרקי' חללה של גיהנם נבראת קודם בריאת העולם אור של גיהנם נברא בשני בשבת אור דידן עלה במחשבה להבראות בערב שבת ולא נברא עד מוצאי שבת. ר' יוסי אומר שני דברי' עלו במחשבה ליבראות בערב שבת ובמוצאי שבת נתן הקב"ה בינה באדם מעין דוגמא של מעלה והביא שתי אבני' וטחנן זו בזו ויצא מהן אור והביא מין סוס ומין חמורה והרכיבן זו על זו ויצא מהן פרד וכו': ת"ר עשרה דברים נבראו בע"ש ביה"ש ואלו הן מן ובאר וכו' ויש אומר' אף מקלו של אהרן ושקדיה ופרחיה ובגדו

deep water; [54a] *but a man of understanding will draw it out.*[5] *'Counsel in the heart of man is like deep water'*— this applies to 'Ulla;[6] *'but a man of understanding will draw it out'*—this applies to Rabbah b. Bar Ḥanah.[7] And in accordance with whom did they hold their view?[8]—In accordance with the following which R. Benjamin b. Japheth said in R. Joḥanan's name: We recite a blessing over light both at the termination of the Sabbath and at the termination of the Day of Atonement, and that is the popular practice.

An objection is raised: We do not recite a blessing over light except at the termination of the Sabbath, since it was then created for the first time; and as soon as he sees [it] he immediately recites a blessing. R. Judah said: He recites them[9] in order over the cup [of wine]. Now R. Joḥanan said thereon: The *halachah* is as R. Judah?—There is no difficulty: here the reference is to light that has burnt over the Sabbath;[10] there it refers to light which issues from tinder and stones.[11]

One [Baraitha] taught: We can recite a blessing over light which issues from tinder and stones; [while] another taught: We cannot recite a blessing over it?—There is no difficulty: one refers to the termination of the Sabbath, [and] the other refers to the termination of the Day of Atonement.

a Rabbi used to 'scatter' them.[1] R. Ḥiyya 'collected' them.[2] R. Isaac b. Abdimi said: Though Rabbi scattered them, he subsequently repeated them in [their] order over the cup [of wine], so as to quit his children and household [of their obligation].[3]

Yet was light created at the termination of the Sabbath? Surely it was taught: Ten things were created on the eve of the Sabbath at twilight. These are they: the well,[4] the manna, the rainbow,[5] the writing[6] and the writing instrument[s], the Tables,[7] the sepulchre of Moses, the cave in which Moses and Elijah stood,[8] the opening of the ass's mouth,[9] and the opening of the earth's mouth to swallow up the wicked.[10] R. Nehemiah said in his father's name: Also fire and the mule.[11] R. Josiah said in his father's name: Also the ram[12] and the *shamir.*[13] R. Judah said: Tongs too. He
b used to say: Tongs are made with tongs;[1] then who made the first tongs? Hence in truth it was[2] a Heavenly creation. Said they to him, It is possible to make it in a mould and shape it simultaneously.[3] Hence in truth it is of human manufacture![4]—There is no difficulty: one refers to our fire, the other to the fire of the Gehenna.[5] Our fire [was created] at the termination of the Sabbath; the fire of the Gehenna, on the eve of the Sabbath.

Yet was the fire of the Gehenna created on the eve of the Sabbath? Surely it was taught: Seven things were created before the world was created, and these are they: The Torah, repentance, the Garden of Eden, Gehenna, the Throne of Glory, the Temple, and the name of the Messiah. The Torah, for it is written, *The Lord made me* [*sc.* the Torah] *as the beginning of his way.*[6] Repentance, for it is written, *Before the mountains were brought forth,* and it is written, *Thou turnest man to contrition, and sayest, Repent, ye children of men.*[7] The Garden of Eden, as it is written, *And the Lord planted*

(5) Prov. XX, 5. (6) Who understood from R. Abba the error of Rabbah b. Bar Ḥanah. (7) He understood why 'Ulla looked at him with displeasure, though he gave no reason. (8) Viz., 'Ulla and Rabbah, who would not accept R. Abba's ruling. (9) Various blessings which are to be recited on the termination of Sabbath. (10) It had burnt during the day. Nevertheless it had observed the Sabbath, as it were, in that it was lit in permitted circumstances, e.g., for an invalid or a woman about to be delivered of child. Or in the case of the Day of Atonement, it had been lit prior to its commencement. There a blessing is recited at the termination of the latter too, because it is as a new thing to the person, since he did not benefit from the light during the day. (11) I.e., which is made now. A blessing over this is recited only at the termination of the Sabbath, when light was likewise created for the first time, but not at the termination of the Day of Atonement.

a (1) Immediately he saw light after the termination of the Sabbath he recited the appropriate blessing. Later, when spices were brought to him, he recited a further blessing over them. Thus the blessings were 'scattered'. (2) He recited both blessings together over a cup of wine, as is the present practice. (3) I.e., he recited the blessings a second time on their behalf. (4) The Well of Miriam which followed the Israelites in the Wilderness; v. Num. XXI, 16-18, which some relate to this. (5) V. Gen. IX, 13f. (6) I.e., the shape of letters. (7) Ex. XXXII, 16. (8) When God allowed them to see His glory; v. Ex. XXXIII, 22; I Kings XIX, 9. (9) Num. XXII, 28. (10) Ibid. XVI, 30. That these last two should happen when the need arose was decreed at the time of the creation. (11) The mule is regarded as a hybrid, as stated *infra.* But according to R. Nehemiah, the first was created directly, and was not the result of cross-breeding. (12) Which Abraham offered as a substitute for Isaac, Gen. XXII, 13; it was ordained at the Creation that the ram should thus be ready to hand. (13) A legendary worm used for the building of the Temple. It was laid upon the stones and cut through them, and so obviated the need for iron tools, in conformity with Ex. XX, 22; v. I Kings VI, 7 and Giṭ. 68*a.*

b (1) The already manufactured tongs must hold the iron on the anvil as it is beaten out into another pair of tongs. (2) Lit., 'was this not etc.?' (3) Without beating it out. (4) For the whole passage v. Ab., chapter V, 5 and notes a.l. — This shows that fire was created already on Sabbath eve. (5) Hell or purgatory. (6) Prov. VIII, 22. (7) Ps. XC, 2f. 'Before' etc. applies to 'repent'.

◁ *For the continuation of the English translation of this page see overleaf.*

so?[3]—Rather say, [53b] It is near to making Israel eat sacred flesh without [the Temple].[4] [Thus,] only a 'helmeted' goat,[5] but not if it is not 'helmeted'?—I will tell you: if it is 'helmeted', there is no difference whether he stated[6] or he did not state; [but] if it is not 'helmeted', if he specified, it is [forbidden]; if he did not specify, it is not [forbidden].

R. Aḥa learned this Baraitha as [the statement of] R. Simeon.[7] To this R. Shesheth demurred: It is well according to him who learns it as [the statement of] R. Jose; then it is correct. But according to him who learns it as [the statement of] R. Simeon, is it correct? Surely we learned, R. Simeon declares him exempt, because he did not make the offering in the way which people make [this] offering![8] Said Rabina to R. Ashi: And is it correct [even] according to him who learns it as [the statement of] R. Jose? Surely Raba said: R. Simeon stated this according to the
a view of R. Jose, who maintained: A man is held responsible[1] for his last words too. Surely then, since R. Simeon agrees with R. Jose, R. Jose also agrees with R. Simeon?[2]—No: R. Simeon agrees with R. Jose, but R. Jose does not agree with R. Simeon.[3]

The scholars asked: Was Thaddeus, the man of Rome, a great man or a powerful man?[4]—Come and hear: This too did Thaddeus of Rome teach: What [reason] did Hananiah, Mishael and Azariah see that they delivered themselves, for the sanctification of the [Divine] Name,[5] to the fiery furnace? They argued *a minori* to themselves: if frogs, which are not commanded concerning the sanctification of the [Divine] Name, yet it is written of them, *and they shall come up and go into thy house . . . and into thine ovens, and into thy kneading troughs:*[6] when are the kneading troughs to be found near the oven? When the oven is hot.[7] We, who are commanded concerning the sanctification of the Name, how much the more so.[8] R. Jose b. Abin said: He cast merchandise into the
b pockets of scholars.[1] For R. Joḥanan said: Whoever casts merchandise into the pockets of scholars will be privileged to sit in the Heavenly Academy, for it is said, *for wisdom is a defence, even as money is a defence.*[2]

MISHNAH. WHERE IT IS THE PRACTICE TO LIGHT A LAMP [AT HOME] ON THE NIGHT OF THE DAY OF ATONEMENT,[3] ONE MUST LIGHT [ONE]; WHERE IT IS THE PRACTICE NOT TO LIGHT [A LAMP], ONE MUST NOT LIGHT [ONE]. AND WE LIGHT [LAMPS] IN SYNAGOGUES, SCHOOL-HOUSES, AND DARK ALLEYS, AND FOR THE SAKE OF INVALIDS.

GEMARA. It was taught: Whether they maintained that we should light [lamps] or they maintained that we should not light [them], both intended [it] for the same purpose.[4] R. Joshua said, Raba lectured: *Thy people also shall all be righteous, they shall inherit the land for ever*: etc.[5] whether they maintained that we should light [lamps] or they maintained that we should not light [them], both intended nought but the same purpose.

Rab Judah said in Samuel's name: We do not recite a blessing over light except at the termination of the Sabbath, since it was then created for the first time.[6] Said a certain old man to him—others state, Rabbah b. Bar Ḥanah—'Well spoken! and thus [too] did R. Joḥanan say.'

'Ulla was going along, riding an ass, while R. Abba proceeded at his right and Rabbah b. Bar Ḥanah at his left. Said R. Abba to 'Ulla: Do you indeed say in R. Joḥanan's name: We do not recite a blessing over light except at the termination of the Sabbath, since it was then created for the first time? 'Ulla turned round and
c looked at Rabbah b. Bar Ḥanah with displeasure.[1] Said he to him, I said it not in reference to that but in reference to this.[2] For a tanna recited before R. Joḥanan, R. Simeon b. Eleazar said: When the Day of Atonement falls on the Sabbath, even where they maintain that we must not light [a lamp], we do light [it] in honour of the Sabbath; which R. Joḥanan followed with the remark,[3] But the Sages forbid it. Said he to him, Let it be this.[4] R. Jose applied to this the verse, *Counsel in the heart of man is like*

(3) Surely the goats were not dedicated as sacrifices. (4) I.e., it is similar to sacrifices. (5) Should be forbidden. (6) That it was for Passover. (7) Not R. Jose. (8) V. Men. 103*a*. If a man declares, 'I vow a meal-offering of barley', the first Tanna rules that he must bring a meal-offering of wheat. For a man's liabilities are determined by his first words only, where these contradict his last words. Thus, when he declared, 'I vow a meal-offering', this is a binding vow; when he adds 'of barley', this is impossible, since only wheat is permitted; therefore his first words are binding. But R. Simeon maintains that he must be judged by his last words too: hence he really meant a meal-offering of barley, thinking that this is permitted; consequently his entire statement is invalid, and he is exempt. Now, in this case, how could it be regarded as near to sacred flesh? He did not consecrate the animal whilst alive, and even if he designated it a Passover-sacrifice at the time of roasting, this is not the way in which people consecrate animals: therefore his words are invalid.

a (1) Lit., 'seized'. (2) That a vow made in an unusual manner is not binding. Hence the same difficulty arises according to R. Jose. (3) He maintains that even when a vow is not made in a usual manner it must be taken into account, because no man speaks without a purpose. Hence though R. Simeon bases his ruling on R. Jose's view, R. Jose himself does indeed hold that a man is held responsible for his last words too, but only when both his first words and his last can take effect (v. Tem. 25*b*); but where his last words would completely nullify his statement, as here, they are disregarded; hence the vower is liable to a wheat meal-offering (Maharsha). So here too, if he declared at the *roasting*, 'This be for a Passover sacrifice', though such a vow is unusual, I would say that he means that a sacrifice shall be bought with its monetary value. Thus it is 'near to sacred flesh' on R. Jose's view. But according to R. Simeon this is a real difficulty, which remains unanswered. (4) Lit., 'a man of fists'.—On what grounds did they refrain from imposing the ban? (5) This is one of the great principles of Judaism: a man must by his actions sanctify the Divine Name, i.e., prove his deep conviction of the truth of Judaism even to the extent of suffering for it, and thereby shed lustre and glory upon it. (6) Ex. VII, 28. (7) And yet at God's command they entered them. (8) This quotation shows that he was a great scholar.

b (1) I.e., he gave them opportunities for trading. (2) Eccl. VII, 12. R. Joḥanan translates: he will enter within the precincts (lit., 'shadow') of wisdom, who brings a scholar within the protection of his wealth. (3) I.e., before it commences, so that it should burn through the night. (4) Viz., to curb their desire for sexual indulgence. The former argued that this would be the better effected by the presence of a lamp, because darkness is generally required; while the latter held that a lamp would strengthen his desire, as he could see his wife by the light. (5) Isa. LX, 21. (6) Lit., 'that was the beginning of its creation'—on the evening of the first day.

c (1) For misrepresenting R. Joḥanan's view. (2) [MS.M.: I did not say this but that.] (3) Lit., 'and R. Joḥanan answered after him'. (4) I admit this to be right.

קרוב להאכיל את ישראל קדשים בחוץ מקולס אין שאין מקולס לא אמרי מקולס *לא שנא אמר לא שנא לא אמר שאינו מקולס פירש אין לא פירש לא רב אחא מתני לה להא מתני' *כר' שמעון מתקיף לה רב ששת בשלמא למאן דתני לה כרבי יוסי ניחא אלא למאן דמתני כר' שמעון מי ניחא *והתנן רבי שמעון פוטר שלא התנדב כדרך המתנדבים אמר ליה רבינא לרב אשי ומאן דמתני לה כר' יוסי מי ניחא והאמר רבא *רבי שמעון בשיטת רבי יוסי אמרה דאמר *אף בגמר דבריו אדם נתפס מאי לאו מדרבי שמעון סבר לה כר' יוסי רבי יוסי נמי סבר לה כרבי שמעון לא רבי שמעון סבר לה כר' יוסי ולא רבי יוסי סבר לה כר' שמעון איבעיא להו תודוס איש רומי גברא רבה הוה או בעל אגרופין הוה ת"ש עוד זו דרש תודוס איש רומי מה ראו חנניה מישאל ועזריה שמסרו [עצמן] על קדושת השם לכבשן האש נשאו קל וחומר בעצמן מצפרדעים ומה צפרדעים שאין מצווין על קדושת השם כתיב בהו °ובאו [ועלו] בביתך [וגו'] ובתנוריך ובמשארותיך אימתי משארות מצויות אצל תנור הוי אומר בשעה שהתנור חם אנו שמצווין על קדושת השם על אחת כמה וכמה רבי יוסי בר אבין אמר מטיל מלאי לכים של תלמידי חכמים היה דאמר ר' יוחנן כל *המטיל מלאי לכיס תלמידי חכמים זוכה ויושב בישיבה של מעלה שנא' °כי בצל החכמה בצל הכסף:

מתני' °מקום שנהגו להדליק את הנר בלילי יום הכפורים מדליקין מקום שנהגו שלא להדליק אין מדליקין °ומדליקין בבתי כנסיות ובבתי מדרשות ובמבואות האפלים ועל גבי החולים:

גמ' תנא *בין שאמרו להדליק ובין שאמרו שלא להדליק שניהן לדבר אחד נתכוונו אמר רב יהושע דרש רבא °ועמך כלם צדיקים לעולם יירשו ארץ וגו' בין שאמרו להדליק ובין שאמרו שלא להדליק שניהם לא נתכוונו אלא לדבר אחד אמר רב יהודה אמר שמואל אין מברכין על האור אלא במוצאי שבת הואיל ותחלת ברייתו הוא ואיתימא רבה בר בר חנה *יישר וכן אמר רבי יוחנן עולא הוה רכיב חמרא ואזיל והוה שקיל ואזיל רבי אבא מימיניה ורבה בר בר חנה משמאליה אמר ליה רבי אבא לעולא ודאי דאמריתו משמיה דרבי יוחנן אין מברכין על האור אלא במוצאי שבת הואיל ותחלת ברייתו הוא הדר עולא חזא ביה ברבה בר בר חנה בישות א"ל אנא לאו אהא אמרי אלא אהא אמרי דתני תנא קמיה דרבי יוחנן ר"ש בן אלעזר אומר °יום הכפורים שחל להיות בשבת אף במקום שאמרו שלא להדליק מדליקין מפני כבוד השבת ועני רבי יוחנן בתריה וחכמים אוסרים א"ל עדא תהא קרי עליה רב יוסף °מים עמוקים עצה בלב איש ואיש

קרוב להאכיל. דומה לקדשים: שאינו מקולס לא. וקשיא לרב דאמר בשר גרידא מיחלף בפסח: ומשני מקולס אע"ג דלא אמר בשר זה לפסח ולא מזכיר עליו את השם אסור אבל שאינו מקולס אמר הרי בשר זה לפסח אסור משום דנראה כקורא שם: רב אחא מתני לה להא מתני'. דתודוס: כר' שמעון. אמר רבי שמעון תודוס איש רומי כו': רבי שמעון פוטר. באומר הרי עלי מנחה מן השעורים דתנן במנחות מביא מן החיטין דכיון דאמר הרי עלי מנחה תפוס לשון ראשון ומנחה אינה באה מן השעורין נדבה הלכך יביא מן החיטין ורבי שמעון פוטר דאמר אף בגמר דבריו אדם נתפס ונדבק ודעתו לכל מה שמוליא בפיו ולמנחת שעורין נתכוין וסבור שאדם יכול להתנדב ולהביא כן ולפיכך אין בדבריו כלום והאי מאכיל גדי מקולס נמי מאי קרוב לקדשים בחוץ איכא הלא מחיים לא קרא עליו שם פסח ואפילו היה קורא לו שם בשעת צלייה שלא כדרך המקדישין הוא ואין השם חל עליו: ר' שמעון. דפטר באומר מנחה מן השעורים ולא חייביה משום תפוס לשון ראשון בשטת רבי יוסי אמרה דאמר במסכת תמורה (דף כה:) אף בגמר דבריו אדם נדבק ונתפס כלומר תופס הוא את גמר דבריו דתנן הרי זו תמורת עולה תמורת שלמים הרי זו תמורת עולה דברי ר"מ דאמר תפוס לשון ראשון רבי יוסי אומר אם לכך נתכוין תחלה הואיל ולא הוה אפשר ליה להוציא שני שמות כאחד ועל כרחו הוציא זה אחר זה דבריו קיימין ותרעה עד שתסתאב ותמכר ויביא בדמי חציה עולה ובדמי חציה שלמים: מאי לאו מדרבי שמעון סבר לה כרבי יוסי. בתפיסת גמר דברים: ר' יוסי סבר לה כר' שמעון. במתנדב שלא כדרך המתנדבים דלא אמר כלום והיא דתודוס לא מתוקמא כר' יוסי: ה"ג לא ר"ש סבר לה כר' יוסי ולא רבי יוסי סבר לה כרבי שמעון. והכי פירושא לא היא כדאמרת אלא רבי שמעון סבר לה כרבי יוסי דאף בגמר דבריו נתפס דעת האדם והוה ליה מתנדב שלא כדרך מתנדבין ורבי שמעון סבר הואיל ושלא כהוגן התנדב אין בדבריו כלום אבל רבי יוסי לא סבר כרבי שמעון במתנדב שלא כדרך המתנדבין דלא אמר כלום אלא חיובי מחייב ליה להביא מנחת חיטין ולאו משום תפוס לשון ראשון אלא משום דאין אדם מוליא דבריו לבטלה וגבי גדי מקולס נמי אע"ג דשלא כדרך המקדישין הוא הוה ליה קרוב להאכיל קדשים בחוץ דאי הוה אמר עליה הרי זה לפסח אמרי לדמי פסח קאמר: גברא רבה הוה. ומפני כבודו לא גזרו עליו נדוי: או בעל אגרופין. ומפני היראה: ועוד זו דרש. אלמא גברא רבה הוה: מה ראו. שלא דרשו (א) ותי בהן ולא שימות בהן: מטיל מלאי. טוען סחורה לתלמידי חכמים להשתכר בה: בצל החכמה. במחילת החכמה יכנס זה שהגהא מנכסיו: **מתני'** מקום שנהגו להדליק את הנר. בגמרא מפרש טעמא: **גמ'** בין שאמרו להדליק. אותן שנהגו להדליק והנוהגין שלא להדליק לא נתכוונו אלא לדבר אחד להפריש עצמו ממשכבי אשה האומרים להדליק משום דאין אדם משמש מטתו לאור הנר והאומרים שלא להדליק סוברים כשהנר דולק רואה את אשתו ומתאוה לה: יישר. שפיר קאמרת וכן א"ר יוחנן ולא גרסינן יישר: ודאי דאמריתו כו'. אמת הדבר ששמעתי עליכם שאתם אומרים משמיה דר' יוחנן הכי: הדר עולא חזא ביה ברבה בר בר חנה בישות. נסתכל בו בפנים זועפות כלומר אתה אמרת בשם רבי יוחנן והוא לא אמר כן אלא אף במוצאי יוה"כ מברכין עליו הואיל ודבר חדש הוא שנאסר בו כל היום ועכשיו נהגה ממנו: אלא אהא אמרי להו. משמיה דרבי יוחנן דענה אחר התנא וחכמים אוסרין להדליק את הנר אף ביום הכפורים שחל להיות בשבת עד מוצאי שבת ולא הזכרתי שמו של ר' יוחנן על אור במוצאי שבת אלא בזו והם סבורים שעל דבר ברכת האור הזכרתי שמו: עדא תהא. זאת תהיה בזו אני מודה שאמרה רבי יוחנן: *) זה עולא. *שהבין מדבריו של רבה בר בר חנה טעות וחזא ביה בישות וסתם דבריו שלא אמר לו כלום והייט עצה בלב איש דנקיט ליה בלביה ולא אמר לו למה אמרת כך:

*) שייך לדף נד ע"א

רבי שמעון בשיטת רבי יוסי אמרה דאמר אף בגמר דבריו וכו'. אע"ג דלר' יוסי חיילי תרוייהו היינו משום דתרי מילי קאמר ואינם פירוש זה לזה אבל הכא מן השעורים הוא פי' מה שאמר הרי עלי מנחה וכיון דאף בגמר דבריו אדם נתפס מבטלים להא דאמר בתחלה הרי עלי מנחה ולפי' אם אמר אילו הייתי יודע שאין נודרין כך לא הייתי נודר כך אלא כך הייתי טעמא דרבנן דאלים להו לשון ראשון ולא הוי נדר ופתחו עמו כי אמר אילו הייתי יודע כו' כדאמרינן בהמנחות והנסכים (מנחות קג.): **מה** ראו חנניה מישאל ועזריה. פ"ה מה ראו שלא דרשו וחי בהם ולא שימות בהם וקשה דהא בפרהסיא הוה ומסקינן בסנהדרין (דף עד.) דלכולי עלמא בפרהסיא חייב למסור עצמו אפילו אמצוה קלה ומפר"ת דלאו זה שעשה נבוכדנצר לאו ע"ז הוה אלא אנדרטא שעשה לכבוד עצמו ולכך קאמר מה ראו וכן משמע מדכתיב לאלהך ליתנא פלחין ולצלם דדהבא לא נסגוד משמע דלאלהא דידיה ולצלמא תרי מילי נינהו ואתי נמי שפיר הא דאמרינן באלו נערות (כתובות לג:) אלמלי נגדו לחנניה מישאל ועזריה פלחו לצלמא ואי ע"ז הוה ח"ו שהיו משתחוים לו ומיהו לשון פלחו לא אתי שפיר ור"י מפרש מה ראו שלא ברחו שהרי קודם המעשה היו יכולים לברוח כמו שעשה דניאל כדאמר בחלק (סנהדרין צג.) ג' היו באותה עלה: **אין** מברכין על האור אלא במוצאי שבת. הקשה ה"ר יוסף למה אין מברכין בכל שעה שנהנה ממנו דלאסור ליהנות מן העולם הזה בלא ברכה ותירץ דה"מ כשגופו נהנה אבל שאר הנאה לא ואף על גב דמברכין על אור השמש בכל יום היינו משום שמתחדש בכל יום:

לה א מיי' פ"ה מהל' מלה הלכה יא ח"מ סי' תמט סעיף א ג: לו ב מיי' פ"ג מהל' שביתת עשור הלכה י טוש"ע א"ח סי' תרי סעיף א: לז ג שם סעיף ג: לח ד מיי' שם טוש"ע שם סעיף א:

מנחות קג. נזיר ט. [ערכין כ.] — [מנחות קג:] — [לקמן נט. ס. נזיר ט.] — פי' שבת סג. וכתובות קיא: — [תוספתא פ"ג] — [שבת סג: וש"נ וכ"ל יישרו כה"א ככרכות מב: ובשבת סג: שבועות מ. מס: חולין יז. סה: יישר כח יודין] — תירה אור — ישעיה ס — קהלת ז — משלי כ — שמות ז

הגהות הב"ח (א) רש"י ד"ה מה ראו וכו' ותי בהם ולא שימות בהם.

[ועי' תוס' כתובות לג: ד"ה אילמלא ותוס' ע"ז ג. ד"ה שלא]

רבינו חננאל

ופרקי' גדי מקולס אפי' בסתמא שלא יזכיר לפסח אסור אבל בשר שאינו מקולס ראשו על כרעיו ועל קרבו אם הזכיר עליו לפסח אסור בסתמא מותר: **אמר** רב פפא דוקא בשר כי האי תנא אסור אבל חטים ואפי' אומר החטים הללו מותרין [לפסח] פ"ש חטים דמנפקו לפסח קאמר. איכא דמתני להא [דרבי יוסי] [מתניתא] הכי קאמר הנהיג תודוס איש רומי לאכול כו' ואתקפי' בשלמא למאן דמתני לה כרבי יוסי [ניחא דחייש] בכל כה"ג אלא למאן דמתני לה כר' שמעון מי חייש ר' שמעון כי האי גונא והתנן בסוף מנחות הרי עלי מנחה מן השעורים יביא מן החטים קמח יביא מן הסלת כו' עד רבי שמעון פוטר שלא התנדב כדרך המתנדבין הנה מי שיאמר כגון זה בשר זה לפסח לא חייש ליה דאין אדם מתנדב בשר לקרבן. מי ניחא והאמר רבא רבי שמעון בשיטת רבי יוסי אמרה דסבר בגמר דבריו אדם מתפיס דתנן הרי זו תמורת עולה תמורת שלמים הרי זו תמורת עולה דברי רבי מאיר אמר רבי יוסי לכך נתכוון מתחלה אע"פ שאי אפשר לקרות שני שמות כאחד דבריו קיימין ואוקי' לרבי יוסי דאמר בגמר דבריו אדם מתפיס לאו מדרבי שמעון סבר לה כר' יוסי ר' יוסי נמי וכו' ואסיקנא תודוס איש רומי חכם היה ומטיל מלאי בכים תלמידי חכמים היה: **מתני'** מקום שנהגו להדליק ביום הכפורים מי שאמר להדליק סבר שאם יהיה הבית אפל ישמש מטתו לפיכך ידליק יתרחק מן העבירה ומי שאמר לא ידליק סבר אין היצר מתאוה אלא מה העין רואה לפיכך לא ידליק שכיון שלא יראה לא יתאוה ושניהם לטובה מתכוונו פי' דבר אחר תשמיש המטה אבל מדליקין בפונדקאות ובבתי המים. אמר רב יהודה אמר שמואל אין מברכין על האור אלא במוצאי שבת ותחלת ברייתו הוא אמר ליה [ההוא סבא] יישר וכן אמר רבי יוחנן: **אמר** ליה רבי אבא לעולא ודאי דאמריתו משמא דרבי יוחנן אין מברכין על האור אלא במוצאי שבתות אהדר ביה (רבי אבא) [עולא ברבה] בר בר חנה בישות והרגיש רבה בר בר חנה אמר ליה לא אמרי הכי אלא הכי אמרי תאני חדא קמיה דרבי יוחנן רבי שמעון בן אלעזר אומר יום הכפורים שחל להיות בשבת אפילו במקום שאמרו שלא להדליק מדליקין מפני כבוד השבת ועני רבי יוחנן בתריה וחכמים אוסרין ודיקי' מינה מאחר שאין מדליקין ביום הכפורים לא ימצא אור ששבת ממלאכת עבודה שמעי' מינה כי אין מברכין על האור במוצאי יום הכפורים אמר ליה עדה תהא כלומר זאת הוא ופי' עדה כדגרסינן בענין בנהיה דרב נחמן [גיטין מה] עדי טברין ותוב עדה סוראה כלן ענין אחד הן וכיון שדרשו שמועה זו כלומר אינה הלכה כמאן

משיגריעו והזיתים משיניצו ושאר כל האילנות משיוציאו *ואמר רב אסי הוא בוסר הוא גירוע הוא פול הלבן פול הלבן סלקא דעתך אלא אימא שיעורו כפול הלבן ומאן שמעת ליה דאמר בוסר אין סמדר לא רבנן וקתני שאר כל האילנות משיוציאו אלא רבי אילעאי *בדניסחני קץ תנו רבנן אוכלין בענבים עד שיכלו דליות של אוכל אם יש מאוחרות מהן אוכלין עליהן אוכלים בזיתים עד שיכלה אחרון שבתקוע ר' אליעזר אומר עד שיכלה אחרון של גוש חלב כדי שיהא עני יוצא ואינו מוצא לא בנופו ולא בעיקרו רובע אוכלין בגרוגרות עד שיכלו פגי בית היני *אמר רבי יהודה לא הוזכרו פגי בית היני אלא לענין מעשר (דתנן) פגי בית היני ואהיני דטובינא חייבין במעשר: אוכלין בתמרים עד שיכלה האחרון שבצוער רשב"ג אומר אוכלין על של בין הכיפין ואין אוכלין על של בין השיצין ורמינהי באוכלין בענבים עד הפסח בזיתים עד העצרת בגרוגרות עד התנוכה בתמרים עד הפורים ואמר רב ביבי ר' יוחנן תרתי בתרייתא מחליף אידי ואידי חד שיעורא הוא ואי בעית אימא הא קתני בהדיא אם יש מאוחרות מהן אוכלין עליהן תניא *רבן שמעון בן גמליאל אומר °סימן להרים מילין סימן לעמקים דקלים סימן לנחלים קנים סימן לשפלה שקמה ואף על פי שאין ראיה לדבר זכר לדבר שנאמר °ויתן המלך את הכסף בירושלים כאבנים ואת הארזים נתן כשקמים אשר בשפלה לרוב סימן להרים מילין סימן לעמקים דקלים נפקא מינה לבכורים דתנן *אין מביאין בכורים אלא משבעת המינין דולא מדקלים שבהרים ולא מפירות שבעמקים סימן לנחלים קנים *נפקא מינה לנחל איתן סימן לשפלה שקמה נפקא מינה למקח וממכר השתא דאתית להכי כולהו נמי למקח וממכר:

מתני' *מקום שנהגו למכור בהמה דקה לנכרים מוכרין *מקום שלא נהגו למכור אין מוכרין ובכל מקום אין מוכרין להם בהמה גסה עגלים וסייחין שלמין ושבורין ר' יהודה מתיר בשבורה *בן בתירא מתיר בסוס המקום שנהגו לאכול צלי בלילי פסחים אוכלין מקום שנהגו שלא לאכול אין אוכלין:

גמ' אמר רב יהודה אמר רב *אסור לו לאדם שיאמר בשר זה לפסח הוא מפני שנראה כמקדיש בהמתו ואוכל קדשים בחוץ אמר רב פפא דוקא בשר אבל חיטי לא דמינטר לפסחא קאמר ובשר לא מיתיבי *אמר ר' יוסי תודוס איש רומי הנהיג את בני רומי לאכול גדיים מקולסין בלילי פסחים שלחו לו אלמלא תודוס אתה גזרנו עליך נדוי שאתה מאכיל את ישראל קדשים בחוץ קדשים סלקא דעתך אלא אימא
קרוב

משיגריעו. משגדלו הענבים קלת ונקראו גירוע ולקמן מפרש שיעורו כפול הלבן: **משיניצו.** משיגדיל הנץ עליהן והוא כעין פרחים ודומה לו בברכות (דף לו:) הפטמה של רימון מלטרף והנץ שלו אינו מלטרף: **הוא בוסר.** דאמר כל היכא דתנן או בוסר או גירוע כולהו חדא נינהו בוסר תנן בגיטין (דף לא:) משעת כניסת המים לבוסר: **פול הלבן ס"ד.** הא בגפנים קיימא: **ומאן.** תנא דשמעת ליה דאמר בוסר הוא דהוי פירי דקתני משיגריעו דהיינו בוסר אבל סמדר לא לאו רבנן היא וקתני דמודו בשאר אילנות הא דרב אסי הוא בוסר הוא גירוע נקט הכא משום דלא תימא גירוע היינו סמדר ורבי יוסי היא: **בדניסחני קץ.** תמרים של דקל זכר ואינן מתבשלין בו עולמית ונודרין אותן בניסן והן מתבשלות מאליהן בכלי כפות תמרים ולעולם הן קטנות הלכך ר' אילעאי לא אפסיד מידי: **אוכל.** מקום כרמים ואית דגרסי של *אבל והוא אבל כרמים: **דליות.** טרייל"ש: **תקוע.** מקום זיתים כדתנן במנחות (דף פה:) תקועה אלפא לשמן ומתוך שהשמן מצוי שם ורגילין בו מצויין חכמים בהן כדכתיב (שמואל ב יד) וישלח יואב תקועה וגו': **גוש חלב.** נמי איכא זיתים טובא והוא בחלקו של אשר דכתיב ביה וטובל בשמן רגלו במנחות (שם): **כדי שיהא עני יוצא כו'.** מותר לאכול מן הכנוסין עד שיכלו בשדה כל כך שיהא עני יוצא לבקש ואינו מוצא כו': **גרוגרות.** תאנים יבשים: **פגי בית היני.** תאנים של אותו מקום: **לא הוזכרו.** בבית המדרש להחשב פירי אלא למעשר: **אהיני.** תמרים: **דטובינא.** מקום ואותן פגים ואותן תמרים לעולם קטנים: **ואמר רב ביבי** גרסינן ולא תיובתא הוא: **תרתי בתרייתא מחליף.** בגרוגרות עד הפורים בתמרים עד חנוכה: **סימן להרים מילין.** עפלין גלי"ש אבל שאר אילנות שבהרים אין יפין ונפקא מינה דלא מייתינן בכורים מיניהו כדלקמן: **דקלים.** תמרים: **שקמה.** אילנא עושה פירי: **שפלה.** ארץ מישור ולקמיה מפרש מאי נפקא מינה: **כשקמים אשר בשפלה.** שמע מינה דרך שפלה לשקמים ומיהו לאו ראיה גמורה היא לידע דאם אין בה שקמים לא תהא קרויה שפלה: **בבכורים** כתיב אשר תביא מארצך ודרשינן במנחות (דף פד:) נאמר כאן ארצך ונאמר להלן ארץ חטה ושעורה וגו' מה להלן שבח ארץ דהא בשבחה הכתוב מדבר אף כאן שבח ארץ וילפינן מינה דאין מביאין אלא משבעת המינין האמורין שם ואין מביאין אלא ממקום משובח ותמרים משבעת המינין הם דכתיב ודבש דהיינו דבש תמרים: **ולא מדקלין שבהרים.** דאינן משובחין אלא דקלים של עמקים: **ולא מפירות.** תבואת דגן שבעמקים שהמים לנים שם ותבואתן*) כמושה ומרקבת: **לנחל איתן.** לעגלה ערופה צריך שיהו קנים גדלים בו ואי לא לא מיקרי נחל: **למקח וממכר.** שפלה אני מוכר לך צריך שיהו בה שקמים: **מתני'** מקום שנהגו שלא למכור. דהחמירו על עצמן דילמא אתי למכור גסה: **ובכל מקום אין מוכרין להן בהמה גסה.** דגזור ביה רבנן משום שאלה ומשום שכירות ומשום נסיוני במסכת ע"ז (דף טו:) וישראל מצווה על שביתת בהמתו בשבת: **עגלים וסייחים.** קטנים ואף על גב דלאו בני מלאכה נינהו מיחלפי במכירת גדולים ושבורים מיחלפי במכירת שלימים: **בשבורה.** דלא משהי לה ושחטו לה הלכך לא חזי ליה ישראל גבי נכרי ולא אתי למישריה מכירה אחריתי: **בן בתירא מתיר בסוס.** לפי שמלאכתו לרכיבה ונסיוני דידיה ליכא למיגזר בהן דאין בה אלא משום שבות דאין רוכבין על גבי בהמה גבי שבות תנן לה במסכת ביצה (דף לו:): **שלא לאכול.** דמיחזי כאוכל פסח בחוץ: **גמ'** בשר זה. ואפילו שחוטה כבר: **אבל חיטי.** לא דמו מידי לקדשים וכי קאמר חיטין אלו לפסח דמנטר לפסח קאמר אצניעו לפסח לאוכלם ולא אמרינן מיחזי כמאן דאמר למוכרן ולקנות פסח בדמיהן: **ה"ג אמר רבי יוסי תודוס איש רומי.** ישראל חשוב שהיה ברומי: **מקולסין.** צלויין ראשו על כרעיו ועל קרבו כצליית הפסח דתניא בכיצד צולין (לקמן עד.) רבי *עקיבא קורהו מקולס לפי שתולה כרעיו חוצה לו בצדו כנושא כלי זיין בצדו כובע נחושת בגלית (שמואל א יז) תרגומו קולסא דנחשא: **אלמלא תודוס אתה.** אדם חשוב:
קרוב

*) בס"י איתא כחושה

מפני שנראה כמקדיש קדשים בחוץ. בכולי שמעתא פירש"י שעכשיו קורא שם ופירש נמי שלא התנדב כדרך המתנדבים היינו דמחיים לא קרא לו שם פסח ואי נמי קרא לו שם בשעת צלייה הוי שלא כדרך המקדישין וקשה דקאמר נראה כמאכיל קדשים בחוץ והלא גם בפנים אין לעשות כן דאינו קדוש אלא לדמיו והוה ליה למימר שהוא קרוב למעילת קדשים ועוד בגדי מקולס לר' שמעון נהי דליכא למיחש שמא הקדישו עכשיו שאין זה כדרך המתנדבים מכל מקום ליתסר למיעבד הכי שלא יאמר מחיים אקדשיה דסופו מוכיח על תחלתו שעשאו מקולס וע"כ טעמא משום הכי הוא דהא מוקמינן לא שנא אמר ולא שנא לא אמר לכך נראה דעל ידי שאומר עכשיו בשר זה לפסח סברי אינשי דמחיים אקדשה ורבי שמעון אפילו אקדשה מחיים [לשחוט] בחוץ לא הוי הקדש משום שלא התנדב כדרך המתנדבים כדמוכח בתוספתא [א] בפרק בתרא דמנחות דקאמר הרי עלי עולה על מנת שאקריבנה בבית חוניו רבי שמעון אומר אין זה עולה וה"נ הוי כמקדיש על מנת להקריב בחוץ הוא דאינו קדוש והא דלא מייתי לה הכא אלא מייתי ההיא דמנחה משום דמפרש בה בהדיא שלא התנדב כדרך המתנדבים:
רבי

עין משפט נר מצוה

כו א מיי' פ"ה מהלכות שמטה הלכה יח:
כז ב מיי' פ"ז מהלכות שמטה הלכה יא:
כח ג מיי' פ"ב מהל' ביכורים הלכה ג:
כט ד שם הלכה ג:
ל ה מיי' פ"כ מהלכות שבת הלכה ה סמג לאוין סה טוש"ע י"ד סי' קנא סעיף ד:
לא ו מיי' שם הל' ג:
לב ז שם הלכה ד:
לג ח מיי' פ"ח מהלכות מלה הלכה יא סמג עשין מא טוש"ע א"ח סי' תעו סעיף א:
לד ט י טוש"ע א"ח סי' תסט:

נדה ח:

נ"א מקום שנהגו שלא למכור

מסורת הש"ס

ברכות לו.

גליון הש"ס גמרא סימן להרים מילין. עי' ת' חכם צבי סי' ל"ג

[תוספתא דשביעית פ"ז]
ערכין כח: [ע"ש ובס ליתא מלת דתנן]
[תוספתא דשביעית פ"ז]
מנחות פד. בכורים פ"א [מ"ג]
ע"ז יד:
שבת לד. בכורות ב.
ברכות יט. ביצה כג. [תוספתא דביצה פ"ב]

הגהות מהר"ב רנשבורג
[א] תוס' ד"ה מפני וכו' כדמוכח בתוספתא בפ' בתרא דמנחות. נ"ל במשנה דמנחות ד' קט.

[לפנינו שם איתא רבי טרפון]

רבינו חננאל

פרי ואמרי' אינו ומי פליגי רבנן עליה בכל האילנות והתנן בשביעית סוף פ"ג מאימתי אין קוצצין את האילנות בשביעית ב"ש אומרים כל האילנות משיוציאו וב"ה אומרים החרובין משישרשו וגפנים משיגריעו והזיתים משיניצו ושאר כל האילנות משיוציאו ואמר רבי אסי הא דתנן הגפנים משיגריעו ופי' בעת שיהא בוסר כשיעור פול הלבן יש לו גרעינין ומאותה העת נקרא פרי ואסור לקצצו ולהפסידו דלאכלה אמר רחמנא ולא להפסדה ש"מ דלהאי תנא בוסר נקרא פרי אבל סמדר אינו פרי מאן שמעת ליה האי סברא רבנן [וקתני] ושאר כל האילנות משיוציאו והנה לא נחלקו רבנן על ר' יוסי אלא על הגפנים בלבד ופרקי' לעולם כל אילן משיוציאו אסור לקצצו ורבי אילא כפנייתא שחנטו קצץ דלדברי הכל אין בהן פרי: ירושלמי בשביעית סוף פ"ד תאני רב הונא הרובין שלשלן היא הנטן גפנים משיגרעו אמר רבי יונה משיזחילו מים דכתיב (איוב לו) כי יגרע נטפי מים. [עוד שם בפ' חמישי] תאני רשב"ג מהוצאת עלין עד הפגים חמשים יום ומן הפגים עד השיתים שלשים יום ומן השיתים [עד התאנים] חמשים יום רבי אומר כולהו מארבעים יום לוקט תאנה ואינו יודע מאימתי חנטה אמר רבי יונה מונה מאה יום למפרע אם חל לתוכן חמשה עשר בשבט הוא יודע מתי חנטה אמרו לו והלא עמו בטבריא בנות שוח ועושות לשנה אחת אמר לו והלא עצכם בציפורי ועושות הן לשלש שנים *): **תנו** רבנן אוכלין בענבים עד שיכלו פגיות של אבל: **אמר** רב יהודה לא הוזכרו פגי ביתוני אלא לענין מעשר פגי ביתוני ואהינא דטובניא פי' ניסואן חייבין במעשר אוכלין בתמרים עד שיכלה האחרון שבצוער וכו' ורמינהי אוכלין בגרוגרות עד החנוכה בתמרים עד הפורים ואמר רב ביבי רבי יונה מהליף אוכלין בגרוגרות עד הפורים בתמרים עד החנוכה ושני' אידי ואידי חד שיעורא הוא כלומר התמרים כלים בצוער בפורים. איבעית אימא הא תנינן בההיא ואם יש מאוחרת מהן אוכלין עליהן כיפין וציצין כבר פירשנום למעלה: **תניא** רבן שמעון בן גמליאל אומר סימן להרים מילין שהן עפץ גדילים בהרים סימן לעמקים דקלים כלומר אין אילן גדילים אלא בעמקים נפקא מינה דאין דקלים טובים אלא בעמקים ומהם ראוי להביא בכורים דתנן אין מביאין בכורים חוץ משבעת המינין ולא מן הדקלים שבהרים ולא מן התמרים שבעמקים פי' ששת המינין הנותרים לא תביא מן העמקים שאינן גדילים כהונן: **מתני'** מקום שנהגו למכור בהמה דקה לנכרים כו' מקום שנהגו לאכול צלי בלילי הפסח אוכלין וכו' אמר רב יהודה אמר רב אסור לאדם שיאמר בשר זה לפסח מפני שנראה כמקדיש בהמתו ונראה אוכל קדשים בחוץ ומותבינן עליה מדרבי יוסי דאמר תודוס איש רומי הנהיג את בני רומי לאכול גדיים מקולסין בלילי פסחים וכו' ופרקי'

*) לפנינו בירושלמי הגי' לשתי שנים.

a from when they form kernels;[1] olive trees, from when they blossom;[2] and all other trees, from when they bring forth. Now R. Assi said thereon: *Boser* [half-ripe fruit], *girua'* [formation of kernels], and the white bean are identical.[3] 'The white bean'—can you think so![4]—Rather, say, its size is that of the white bean. Now, whom do you know to maintain that *boser* is fruit, but not *semadar?* The Rabbis.[5] Yet it is stated, 'and all other trees, from when they bring forth?'[6]—Rather, R. Ilai cut down *nishane.*[7]

Our Rabbis taught: One may eat grapes [of the Sabbatical year] until the espalier branches of okel[8] are finished. If there are later ones than these, one may eat [in reliance] on them.[9] One may eat olives until the last of Tekoa[10] is finished. R. Eliezer said: Until the last of Gush-Ḥeleb[11] is finished, so that a poor man should go out and not find a quarter[12] either on the branches or on the stem. One may eat dried figs until the unripe figs [*pagge*] of Beth Hini[13] are finished. Said R. Judah: The unripe figs of Beth Hini were not mentioned except in connection with tithe, for we learned,[14] The unripe figs of Beth Hini and the dates[15] of Tobanya[16] are subject to tithe.[17]

'One may eat dates until the last in Zoar is finished; R. Simeon b. Gamaliel said: One may eat [in reliance] on those that are among the upper [overarching] branches, but you may not eat [in reliance] on those that are among the single prickly branches.' But the following contradicts this: One may eat grapes until
b Passover; olives until Pentecost; dried figs until Ḥanukkah;[1] [and] dates until Purim.[2] Now R. Bibi said, R. Joḥanan transposes the last two![3]—Both are one [the same] limit. Alternatively, surely it is explicitly taught, 'If there are later ones than these, one may eat [in reliance] on them.'[4]

It was taught, R. Simeon b. Gamaliel said: An indication of mountainous country is [the presence of] *millin;*[5] an indication of valleys is palm trees; an indication of streams is reeds; an indication of lowlands is the sycamore tree. And though there is no proof of the matter, there is an allusion to the matter, for it is said, *And the king made silver to be in Jerusalem as stones, and cedars made he to be as the sycamore trees that are in the lowland, for abundance.*[6]

'An indication of mountainous country is [the presence of] *millin;* an indication of valleys is palm trees.' The practical difference is in respect of first fruits. For we learned: First fruits are not brought of any save the seven species,[7] nor of the palm trees in the highlands nor of the fruits in the valleys.[8] 'An indication of streams is reeds.' The practical difference is in respect of the
c *'rough valley'* [naḥal ethan].[1] 'An indication of lowlands is the sycamore tree.' The practical difference is in respect of buying and selling.[2] Now that you have arrived at this, all the [others] too are in respect of buying and selling.

MISHNAH. WHERE IT IS THE PRACTICE TO SELL SMALL CATTLE[3] TO HEATHENS, ONE MAY SELL; WHERE IT IS THE PRACTICE NOT TO SELL,[4] ONE MAY NOT SELL. AND IN ALL PLACES ONE MAY NOT SELL LARGE CATTLE TO THEM, [NOR] CALVES OR FOALS, WHETHER SOUND OR MAIMED.[5] R. JUDAH PERMITS IN THE CASE OF A MAIMED [ONE].[6] THE SON OF BATHYRA PERMITTED IT IN THE CASE OF A HORSE.[7] WHERE IT IS THE CUSTOM TO EAT ROAST [MEAT] ON THE NIGHT OF PASSOVER, ONE MAY EAT [IT]; WHERE IT IS THE CUSTOM NOT TO EAT [IT],[8] ONE MAY NOT EAT [IT].

GEMARA. Rab Judah said in Rab's name: A man is forbidden to say, 'This meat shall be for Passover,' because it looks as though he is sanctifying his animal and eating sacred flesh without [the Temple]. Said R. Papa: This applies only to meat, but not to wheat, because he means, It is to be guarded [from fermenting] for Passover. But not 'meat'? An objection is raised: R. Jose said,
d Thaddeus of Rome[1] accustomed the Roman [Jews] to eat helmeted goats[2] on the nights of Passover. [Thereupon] they [the Sages] sent [a message] to him: If you were not Thaddeus, we would proclaim the ban against you, because you make Israel eat sacred flesh without [the Temple]. 'Sacred flesh'—can you think

a (1) Or, ovules containing moisture (v. Jast. s.v. גרע, II). (2) I.e., when their blossoms, a calyx-like growth, come forth. (3) Lit., 'that is *boser,* that is' etc. I.e., the three terms indicate the same stage. The Mishnah often speaks of these. (4) We are discussing the vine! (5) For R. Jose maintains that even *semadar,* which denotes an earlier stage, is fruit. (6) Thus they agree with R. Jose in respect to other trees. (7) Stunted dates of palms whose fruit *never* matures. (8) Cur. ed. 'Ar. (also quoted by Rashi) reads: Abel, i.e., the branches of Abel Cheramim (lit., 'the palm of the vine-yards'—v. Jud. XI, 33), situate six or seven Roman miles from Philadelphia (Rabbath-Ammon), and as its name implies, famous for its vineyards; v. *J.E.* s.v. (9) I.e., as long as they are yet on the branches. (10) A city of southern Judea often mentioned in the Bible (e.g., II Sam. XIV, 2f; Amos I, 1; II Chron. XI, 6), and famous for the abundance of its olives, v. Men. 85*b*. (11) Lit., 'fat ground', (Gush-ḥeleb) or Giscala in Galilee, not far from Tyre (Neub. *Géogr.* p. 230), was rich in oil; Josephus, *Vita,* 13; Men. 85*b*; v. *J.E.* s.v. Giscala. (12) I.e., a *log*. (13) Bethania, near Jerusalem; v. Neub. op. cit., 149f. *Pagge* are probably a species of figs that never reach full maturity, but are nevertheless fit for eating. (14) 'We learned' is absent in this passage as quoted in 'Er. 28*b*. [It is a Baraitha (Tosef. Sheb. VII) and not a Mishnah.] (15) *Ahina* (pl. *ahini*) is a species of late and inferior dates. (16) Name of a certain place. (17) But these figs do not determine the time for the removal of figs.

b (1) The Feast of Lights, commencing on the twenty-fifth of Kislev and lasting for eight days. It generally falls in the latter half of December. (2) 'Lots'—the minor Festival in celebration of Haman's downfall. It is held on the fourteenth of Adar, and generally occurs in March. (3) I.e., dried figs until Purim, and dates until Ḥanukkah. By then the various kinds mentioned have disappeared from the field; thus this conflicts with the previous statement. (4) Thus even if these are different time-limits, the later one is stated in accordance with this teaching. (5) *Milla,* pl. *millin,* a species of oak from which the gall-nut is collected (*quercus infectoria*). Jast. (6) I Kings X, 27. (7) Enumerated in Deut. VIII, 8; *a land of wheat and barley, and vines and fig trees and pomegranates; a land of olive trees and honey.* (8) Because these are of inferior quality. The same idea is expressed by R. Simeon b. Gamaliel when he says that palm trees are an indication of valleys, i.e., the best grow in the valleys. His other statements bear a similar meaning.

c (1) V. Deut. XXI, 4. *Naḥal* is a stream which in summer dries up and leaves a valley bed. The presence of reeds along the margin of the valley indicates that this is a fitting place for the purpose. (2) If a man sells a lowland estate it must contain sycamores (Rashi). Or, if a man sells sycamore trees, guaranteeing them to be of the best quality, they must be from lowland country. (3) E.g., sheep and goats. (4) For fear that large cattle too may be sold to them; v. n. c5. (5) Large cattle, because they are thereby deprived of the Sabbath rest (v. A.Z. 15*a*); calves or foals, being the young of large cattle, as a preventive measure; maimed, likewise as a preventive measure on account of whole animals. (6) Because it is unfit for work and will immediately be killed for food. Therefore the Jew will not see it in the heathen's possession, and so will not come to sell him others too. (7) The main use of a horse is for riding, and riding on the Sabbath, even by a Jew, is not regarded as Scripturally forbidden but merely as a *shebuth* (v. Glos.). (8) This means after the destruction of the Temple. While the Temple stood the Passover sacrifice was eaten roast (Ex. XII, 8). Consequently, when the Temple was no more it became the practice to refrain from eating roast meat on the night of Passover, so that it should not appear that a sacrifice was brought without the Temple, which is forbidden.

d (1) Lit., 'a man of Rome'. (2) Goats roasted whole with the entrails and the legs on the head, like a helmet (the verb *kalas* denotes to put on a helmet). That is how the Passover sacrifice was roasted, v. *infra* 74*a*.

Zoar is finished;[3] R. Simeon b. Gamaliel said: [52*b*] One may eat [in reliance] on those that are among the upper [overarching] boughs, but one may not eat [in reliance] on those that are among the single prickly branches.[4]

We learned elsewhere: There are three [separate] districts[5] in respect of removal: Judea, Transjordania and Galilee;[6] and there are three districts in each of them separately.[7] Then why did they say, There are [only] three districts in respect of removal?[8] Because in each one they may eat until it [the produce] has ceased in the
a last [region] thereof.[1] Whence do we know it?—Said R. Ḥama b. 'Uḳba in the name of R. Jose b. Ḥanina, Scripture saith, [*And the sabbath-produce of the land shall be food for you* . . .] *and for thy cattle, and for the beasts that are in thy land:*[2] as long as the [wild] beasts can eat in the field, feed the cattle in the house;[3] when there is no more for the beasts in the field, make an end of it for the cattle in the house;[4] and we have it on tradition that the beasts in Judea do not live on the produce of Galilee, and the beasts in Galilee do not live on the produce of Judea.[5]

Our Rabbis taught: Produce which went from the Land[6] abroad[7] must be removed wherever it is.[8] R. Simeon b. Eleazar said: They must go back to their [original] place and be removed, because it is said, '*in thy land*'. But you have utilized this?[9]—Read therein, 'in the land', '*in thy land*'.[10] Alternatively, [it is deduced] from, '*that are* [asher] *in thy land*'.[11]

R. Safra went from the Land abroad, [and] he had with him a barrel of wine of the Sabbath year. Now, R. Huna the son of R. Iḳa and R. Kahana accompanied him. He asked them, Is there any one who has heard from R. Abbahu[12] [whether] the *halachah* is as R. Simeon b. Eleazar or not?—Said R. Kahana to him: Thus did R. Abbahu say: The *halachah* is as R. Simeon b. Eleazar. R. Huna the son of R. Iḳa [however] said to him, Thus did R. Abbahu say: The *halachah* is not as R. Simeon b. Eleazar. Said R. Safra, Accept this ruling of R. Huna,[13] because he is meticulously careful to learn the laws from his teacher, like Reḥabah of Pumbeditha. For Reḥabah said in Rab Judah's name: The Temple Mount consisted of a double colonnade, [i.e.,] a colonnade within a colon-
b nade.[1] [Thereupon] R. Joseph applied to him [R. Safra] the verse, *My people ask counsel at their stock, and their staff* [maḳḳelo] *declareth unto them:*[2] whoever is lenient [*meḳal*] to him, to him he concedes [right].[3]

R. Elai cut down date-berries of the Sabbatical year.[4] How might he do thus: the Merciful One said, [*It . . . shall be*] *for food*,[5] but not for destruction? And should you answer that is only where it has reached[6] [the stage of] fruit,[7] but not where it has not reached [the stage of] fruit,—surely R. Naḥman said in Rabbah b. Abbuha's name: The calyxes[8] of '*orlah* are forbidden, because they became a guard for the fruits. Now, when is it a guard for the fruits? When they are unripe berries, yet he calls them fruits!—R. Naḥman ruled as R. Jose. For we learned, R. Jose said. The [berries of '*orlah*] in the budding stage [*semadar*] are forbidden, because they count as fruit; whereas the Rabbis disagree with him. To this R. Shimi of Nehardea demurred; yet do the Rabbis disagree with R. Jose in respect to other trees,[9]—surely we learned, From when may you not cut down trees in the Sabbatical year?[10] Beth Shammai maintain: All trees [may not be cut down] from when they bring forth;[11] but Beth Hillel rule: The carob trees from when they form chains [of carobs]; the vine trees, [53*a*]

(3) Dates may be eaten in the whole of Judea until the last palm tree is finished in Zoar, a town near the Dead Sea (Gen. XIII, 10) particularly well-stocked with palm trees (v. Deut. XXXIV, 3, though '*the city of palm trees*' mentioned there refers to Jericho, not Zoar). (4) The lower portion of the palm tree near the roots is surrounded with single prickly, thorn-like branches. Now, when a wind blows, the falling dates are retained both among the ordinary (upper) branches as well as the prickly ones. R. Simeon b. Gamaliel rules that you may eat only as long as there are dates among the higher branches, which are accessible; but those on the prickly branches must be disregarded, since animals cannot take them because of the prickles. In our Mishnah the first Tanna means: When they have *completely* ceased, even from the prickly branches, he must remove them. Whereas R. Judah maintains that unless one can go and bring them, i.e., unless they are accessible, he must remove them, which means even if there are still dates on these thorn branches. (5) Lit., 'countries'. (6) In each the time of removal is when the produce has 'ceased from the field' in that particular district. (7) The produce ceasing in each at a different time. (8) Instead of nine.

a (1) Rashi: until it has ceased in the last subdivision. Tosaf. explains it differently, v. Shebi. IX, 2-3. (2) Lev. XXV, 6f. (3) I.e., domestic animals. (4) I.e., you must no longer keep the produce in the house for your private needs. (5) I.e., they do not stray so far in search of food (Rashi). (6) I.e., Palestine, 'the Land' *par excellence*. (7) Lit., 'to without the Land.' (8) The law of sabbatical produce, being dependent on the soil, is binding in Palestine only, v. Ḳid. 36*b*; yet it is also binding upon Palestine produce, even when transported elsewhere. Nevertheless, he is not bound to take it back to Palestine for removal, but can do it wherever he is. (9) To show that one district cannot rely on another. (10) I.e., Scripture could have written 'in the land', which would suffice for the present exegesis. *In* thy *land* intimates both. (11) *Asher* is superfluous; hence it can be used for this purpose. (12) Who was his teacher. (13) Lit., 'hold . . . in your hand'.

b (1) V. *supra* 13*b* and Beẓah, 11*b*, n. 9. The point of the quotation is not clear. In Ber. 33*b* Rashi explains that Reḥabah was careful to use the word *setaw*, the exact word used by his teacher, though the passage is based on a Mishnah (v. *supra* 11*b*), where the word *iẓtaba* is used. (2) Hos. IV, 12. (3) A humorous play on words, connecting *maḳḳel*, a staff, with *meḳal*, he is lenient. (4) I.e., before they ripened and were fit for food (R. Ḥananel); Rashi: he cut down the palm tree before the dates had ripened. (5) Lev. XXV, 6. (6) Lit., 'descended to'. (7) I.e., when it is ripe. (8) Which surround the date in its early stage. (9) Apart from the vine, to which the above refers. (10) As stated above, they must be used for food, not for destruction. Now the question is: at what stage are their fruits regarded as food, so that the tree must not be cut down, but left until its fruit ripens. (11) Rashi explains here: the first leaves (preceding the fruits); but in Ber. 36*b* Rashi explains: when they bring forth the fruit; Strashun accepts the latter view.

אוכלין על של בין הכיפין ואין אוכלין על שבין השיצין *תנן התם *שלש ארצות לביעור יהודה ועבר הירדן וגליל ושלש ארצות בכל אחת ואחת *ולמה אמרו שלש ארצות לביעור שיהיו אוכלין בכל אחת ואחת עד שיכלה האחרון שבה מנא הני מילי אמר רב חמא בר עוקבא א"ר יוסי בר חנינא *אמר קרא °ולבהמתך ולחיה אשר בארצך *כל זמן שחיה אוכלת מן השדה האכל לבהמה שבבית כלה לחיה אשר בשדה כלה לבהמתך מן הבית וגמירי דאין חיה שביהודה גדילה על פירות שבגליל ואין חיה שבגליל גדילה על פירות שביהודה ת"ר *פירות שיצאו מארץ ישראל לחוצה לארץ מתבערין בכל מקום שהן רשב"א אומר יחזרו למקומן ויתבערו משום שנאמר בארצך הא אפיקתיה קרי ביה בארץ בארצך אי נמי מאשר בארצך רב ספרא נפק מארץ ישראל לחוצה לארץ הוה בהדיה גרבא דחמרא דשביעית לוו בהדיה רב הונא בריה דרב איקא ורב כהנא אמר להו איכא דשמיע ליה מיניה דרבי אבהו הלכה כר"ש בן אלעזר או לא א"ל רב כהנא הכי א"ר אבהו הלכה כר' שמעון בן אלעזר א"ל רב הונא בריה דרב איקא הכי א"ר אבהו אין הלכה כרשב"א אמר רב ספרא נקוט הא כללא דרב הונא בידך *דדייק וגמר שמעתתא מפומיה דרביה כרחבה דפומבדיתא *דאמר רחבה אמר רב יהודה הר הבית סטיו כפול היה סטיו לפנים מסטיו קרי עליה רב יוסף °עמי בעצו ישאל ומקלו יגיד לו כל המיקל לו מגיד לו ר' אילעאי קץ כפנייתא דשביעית היכי עביד הכי °לאכלה אמר רחמנא ולא להפסד וכי תימא הני מילי היכא דנחית לפירא אבל היכא דלא נחות לפירא לא והאמר רב נחמן אמר רבה בר אבוה *הני מתחלי דערלה אסירי הואיל ונעשו שומר לפירי ושומר לפירי אימת הוה בכופרי וקא קרי להו פירי ר"נ דאמר כר' יוסי *דתנן רבי יוסי אומר סמדר אסור מפני שהוא פירי °ופליגי רבנן עליה מתקיף לה רב שימי מנהרדעא ומי פליגי רבנן עליה דרבי יוסי בשאר אילנות והא *תנן מאימתי אין קוצצין את האילנות בשביעי' ב"ש אומרים כל האילנות משיוציאו וב"ה אומרים °החרובין *משישרשרו והגפנים משיגריעו

אוכלין על של בין הכיפין. דרך דקלים להיות בעיקרן קוצים סביב והיינו שיצים ומן הדקל עצמן הן ולמעלה עולין שלו עשויין כסדרן כמין כפות תמרים וכשהרוח מנשב התמרים נופלין ונשארין באותן כיפין ולמטה בשיצין וקאמר רבן שמעון דכל זמן שמצויין בכיפין אוכלין מאותן שבבית אבל אין אוכלין מן הבית על סמך אותן שבשיצין לפי שאין החיה יכולה ליטלן מפני הקוצים ומתניתין הכי קאמר תנא קמא כלה נגמרי אף מבין השיצין חייב לבער אבל כלו מן הכיפין ועדיין יש בשיצין אינו חייב לבער רבי יהודה אומר לא והבא לך אף אתה ממקום הראוי ליטלן ולא תמתין ולאומרת אמרה רבי יהודה: שלש ארצות. בארץ ישראל חלוקות זו מזו לענין ביעור שאין זו סומכת על זו משכלו בה ואע"פ שלא כלו בחבירתה: ושלש ארצות בכל אחת ואחת. שחלוקות במנהג קיום פירותיהן שפירותיהן כלות של זו קודם לזו ואע"פ שעשו כולן אחת לביעור כדמפרש ואזיל: ולמה אמרו שלש ארצות. הואיל ושלש ארצות בכל אחת הרי כאן תשע ארצות למאי הילכתא אמרו שלש ארצות לביעור ותו לא: שיהיו אוכלין בכל אחת. עשאום לשלש שבכל אחת כאילו הן אחת ואוכלין כל אחת ואחת מהשלש החלוקות לביעור עד שיכלה האחרון שבשלש ארצותיה אוכלין ביהודה עד שיכלה אחרון שבשלש ארצותיה וכן בעבר הירדן וכן בגליל: מנא הני מילי. דאוכלין ביהודה עד שיכלה אחרון שבשלש ארצות שבה אבל אין אוכלין ביהודה ע"י אותן שבגליל: וגמירי. מסורת מאבותינו: דאין חיה שביהודה. מתרחקת כל כך לצאת מיהודה לגליל ומגליל ליהודה אבל יוצאה היא מגליל לגליל ומיהודה ליהודה: מתבערין. כשהגיע עונת הביעור שכלו לחיה בכל מקום שהן. ולא מטרחינן ליה להחזירן לארץ לבערן שם: משום שנאמר בארצך. לחיה אשר בארצך וזהו ביעורן שמפקירן במקום דריסת חיה ובהמה: הא אפיקתיה. למעוטי דאין סומכין בני יהודה אלא על ארצם ולא על של גליל: קרי ביה בארץ בארצך. אי הוה כתיב בארץ הוה שמעת מינה חדא מיניהו השתא דכתיב בארצך דרוש בה תרתי: אי נמי. אשר לדרשה: לוו בהדיה. נלוו עמו בחבורה: מיניה דרבי אבהו. תלמידיו היו: דקים ליה דהיאו דייק שמעתא מפומיה דרביה. כשהשמועה יוצאה מפי רבו מדקדק ואומר לרבו לשנותה פעם שנייה ומבחין הימנו או הן או לאו: כרחבה דפומבדיתא. שהיה מדקדק בשמועתו לדעת ממי קיבלה: רבי יהודה. ספק *שמעה מרב יהודה או מר' יהודה נשיאה דהוה נמי בההוא דרא: סטיו כפול היה. איצטבאות סביב לו כפולות זו לפנים מזו סביב: קרי רב יוסף עליה. דרב ספרא: קץ כפנייתא דשביעית. דקל טעון כפניות והן תמרים קטנים שלא בישלו וקצץ הדקל לעצים והפסיד כפניות: דנחת לפירא. פירי שנגמר אסור להפסידו: מתחלי דערלה. שומר הגדל סביבות התמרים בקטנן כעין פקס הגדל סביבות אגוזי יער הדקות: אסירי. משום ערלה דלא הוו כעץ אלא שם פירי עליהם הואיל דנעשו שומר לפירי: ושומר פירי אימת הוי בכופרי. כשהן קטנות וכופרא הוא כפניות וכשגדילין הוא יבש ונופל אלמא כפניות קרויין פירי: רב נחמן. דאמר פירי שלא נגמר קרוי פירי: דאמר כר' יוסי. דאמר משנפל פרח הגפן ונראית צורת הענבים והיינו סמדר אסור משום ערלה מפני שהוא פירי ובלעז קורין אשפני"ר: ופליגי רבנן עליה. במסכת ערלה דקתני רישא העלין והלולבין ומי גפנים וסמדר מותרים משום ערלה ורבי אלעאי דעבד כרבנן: בשאר אילנות. חוץ מגפן: אין קוצצין. לעצים מפני שמפסיד הפירי ורחמנא אמר לאכלה ולא להפסד: משיוציאו. °תחילת העלין בימי ניסן: משישרשרו. משירא בהן כעין *שרשרות של חרובין: משיגריעו

עד שיכלה אחרון שבה. פ"ה עד שתכלה האחרונה שבארצותיה והשלש ארצות שבכל אחת שוות הן ואין נראה דאם כן מה שונה שלש ארצות בכל אחת ועוד קשה לר"י דתנן בפ"ט דשביעית (מ"ב) שלש ארצות לביעור ושלש ארצות בכל אחת עד שיכלה האחרונה שבה ר"ש אומר לא אמרו שלש ארצות אלא ביהודה מכלל דלתנא קמא שלש ארצות חלוקות שכל אחת חלוקה לביעור ור"ש נמי מודה להו ביהודה לכך י"ל דאחרון שבה היינו פירות שבהר עד שיכלה אחרון שבהר ופירות שבעמקים עד שיכלה אחרון שבעמקים וכן שבשפלה עד שיכלה אחרון שבשפלה ובירושלמי יש אמר *ר' חייא בר' עקיבא בשם ר' יוסי בר חנינא שיעור לומר אין חיה שבהר גדילה בעמק וחיה שבעמק אין גדילה בהר ולפי זה משמע דהוי מדאורייתא ולא תיקשי הא דאמרינן בשמעתין דאין חיה שביהודה גדילה על של גליל דמיירי אפי' מהר להר והיינו דמסקינן בשילהי שמעתין דתניא אמר רשב"ג סימן להריס מילין וכו' דנפקא מינה נמי לג' ארצות שביהודה והא דלא קאמר לקמן נפקא מינה לביעור משום דחילוק הר ושפלה ועמק לא שייך אלא ביהודה נגידה כדקתני במסכת שביעית בהדיא אבל ביכורים ונחל איתן שייכים בכל א"י ובגמ' דירושלמי במסכת שביעית עלה דההיא סימן להריס מילין קאמר אית דבעי למימר למידק הדא ליתמר פירוש לענין שלש ארצות נאמר אותו סימן:

מתבערין בכל מקום. פ"ה שנותנין אותן במרמס חיה ובהמה ולא נראה דהא מותרין אחר ביעור לעניים כי דתנן התם (משנה ה) מי שהיו לו פירות שביעית והגיע שעת הביעור מחלקן מזון שלש סעודות לכל אחד עניים אוכלים אחר הביעור ולא עשירים דברי ר' יהודה ר' יוסי אומר אחד עניים ואחד עשירים אוכלים אחר הביעור ובתוספתא קתני מי שיש לו פירות שביעית והגיע שעת הביעור מחלק מהן לשכיניו ולקרוביו ולוודעיו ומוציא ומניח על פתח ביתו ואומר אחינו בית ישראל מי שצריך ליטול יטול וחוזר ומכניס לתוך ביתו והולך ואוכל עד שיכלו ואומר ר"י הא דמשמע בכל מקום לאסור לאכול אחר הביעור היינו כשמשהה בביתו בחזקת שלו אבל אם מפקירו ומוציאו מרשותו שיאכל כל מי שירצה הן אדם והן חיה מותר להכניסו ולאכלו אחר הביעור:

רב ספרא אפיק גרבא דחמרא מא"י לח"ל. הקשה ריב"א דתנן בפ"ו דשביעית (משנה ה) אין מוציאין שמן שריפה ופירות שביעית מן הארץ לח"ל ותירץ דהתם מיירי לאכילה ורב ספרא אפיק לסחורה דיש סחורה שמותרת אי נמי בשוגג הוציאו:

עין משפט נר מצוה

כ א מיי' פ"ז מהלכות שמיטה הל' ט' י':

כא ב שם הלכה א:

כב ג שם הלכה יב:

כג ד מיי' פ"ה מהל' שמיטה הלכה יג:

כד ה מיי' פ"ח מהל' מעשר שני ונטע רבעי הלכה יג:

כה ו מיי' פ"ה מהל' שמטה הלכה יח:

[ובסמ"ג [?]] רב חמא בר עוקבא

מסורת הש"ס

שביעית פ"ט [מ"ב]

[שם מ"ג]

ר"ה דף נב: [פ"ה:] [תענית ז: ע"ש פירש"י]

גליון הש"ס

רש"י ד"ה משיוציאו תחלת העלין. עיין ברש"י ברכות לו ע"ב ד"ה משיוציאו:

[ברכות לג: לח:] [עי' יג:] סוכה מה. [ברכות לג.]

ברכות לג:

שם ערלה פ"א [מ"ז] [קידושין נד:]

ברכות לו: שביעית פ"ד משנה י

ס"א משלשל [?]

[עיין ברש"י דברכות לג: ומגלה [illegible]]

ס"א שלשלות

רבינו חננאל

טעם באחרון מ"מ דרבי (אליעזר) [יהושע] אחרון נותן טעם בראשון:

רבינא אמר בפלוגתא דהני תנאי דתניא אוכלין בתמרים עד שיכלה האחרון שבצוער רשב"ג אומר אוכלין על של בין הכיפים פי' הנסבכין בין האמירין שאיפשר לאדם ללקטן ואין אוכלין על של בין השיצים כגון שנסבכו על קוצין שמכין היד שכל הרואה אותן מתיאש מהן ואין נכשרין אלא לעופות. ת"ק כי הני ור' יהודה אומר אומרים לו צא והבא לך אף אתה ממקום שאתה בו ואם כלה מאותו המקום לא חיישינן מפני ש"ש בצוער: תנן התם שלשה ארצות לביעור כו' ולמה אמרו שלשה ארצות שיהיו אוכלין כל אחת ואחת עד שיכלה אחרון שבה שנאמר ולבהמתך ולחיה אשר בארצך ופשוטה היא: ת"ר פירות שיצאו מארץ לחוץ [לארץ] מתבערין בכ"מ שהן ר"ש בן אלעזר אומר יחזרו למקומן ויתבערו במקומן וטעמא מאי דמשמע שנאמר בארצך תהיה כל תבואתה לאכול ואקשי' והא אפקתיה הא דדרשת ביה ולבהמתך ולחיה אשר בארצך כ"ז שחיה אוכלת בשדה האכל גם אתה לבהמתך מטה שיש לך בביתך וכו' ושני' קרי ביה בארץ כלומר היה לו לומר לחיה אשר בארץ למה כתב בארצך ש"מ תרתי. אי נמי מאשר: ביד רב ספרא נפיק מארץ לחוצה לארץ גרבא דחמרא דשביעית אמר להו לרב כהנא ולרב הונא מי איכא בכו דשמע מר' אבהו אם הלכתא כר' שמעון בן אלעזר דמצריך להחזיר פירות שביעית לארץ ולבערן התם או לא רב הונא בר רב הונא בר אבין אמר הכי אמר ר' אבהו אין הלכה כרבי שמעון בן אלעזר אלא מתבערין בכל מקום שהן ורב כהנא אמר הילכתא כר' שמעון בן אלעזר אמר רב ספרא נקיט דרב הונא בר איקא בידך כלומר זה שאמר רביאבהו אין הלכה כר' שמעון בן אלעזר הוא האמת שמדקדק דברירבותיו ועומד בהן על בוריין כרחבא דהוה דייק בין ר' לרב שלא תתחלף ויאמר אותה בשם זולתי האמרה וכיון שנסתפק לו בעל השמועה מי הוא אם רב יהודה אמרה אם רבי יהודה היה גורסה בשם שניהם דאמר רחבה אמר ראבי יהודה הר הבית סטיו כפול מעוקל היה כו' קרי עליה דרב ספרא עמי בעצו ישאל ומקלו יגיד לו כל המיקל לו מודה לדבריו כלומר כמו רב ספרא שהורה לרב הונא בר איקו ושבחו ואמר האמת עמו מפני שמיקל לו והתיר לו לבער גרבא דחמרא בח"ל ולא המריתו להחזירו לארץ: רבי אילא קץ כפניתא בשביעית פי' אל סלע של שביעית והיכי עביד הכי והא מפסיד פירי שביעית דלא מנח להו עד [שיהיו] נגמרין והתורה אמרה לאכלה ולא להפסד הנה אם פירות שביעית וכי תימא הני מילי פירות הוא דאסור להפסיד אבל כפנייתא עדין אינן פרי והאמר רב נחמן מתחלי דערלה אסירי פי' קצבאן דערלה אסור הואיל ונעשו שומר לפירי והני מתחלי לא לפרי אלא בכופרי דהן אל סלע דאלמא פרי הן דהא קרו להו פרי ושני' רב נחמן כרבי יוסי סבירא ליה דתניא רבי יוסי אומר סמדר אסור מפני שהוא פרי ופליגי רבנן עליה ואמרי כל כי האי גונא אינן פרי

ביישוב לא עבידנא מפני שינוי המחלוקת
במדבר מאי א"ל הכי אמר רב אמי *ביישוב
אסור במדבר מותר רב נתן בר אסיא אזל
מבי רב לפומבדיתא בי"ט שני של עצרת
שמתיה רב יוסף א"ל אביי ולנגדיה מר נגידי
א"ל (א) עדיפא עבדי ליה *דבמערבא *מימנו
אנגידא דבר בי רב ולא מימנו אשמתא א"ד
נגדיה רב יוסף א"ל אביי נשמתיה מר דרב
ושמואל דאמרי תרוייהו 'מנדין על שני ימים
טובים של גליות א"ל ה"מ איניש דעלמא
הכא צורבא מדרבנן הוא דטבא ליה עבדי
דבמערבא מימנו אנגדתא דבר בי רב ולא
מימנו אשמתא: כיוצא בו המוליך פירות
שביעית וכו': ולית ליה לר' יהודה הא דתנן
נותנין עליו חומרי המקום שיצא משם וחומרי
המקום שהלך לשם אמר רב שישא בריה דרב
אידי מילתא אחריתי קאמר ר' יהודה וה"ק או
ממקום שלא כלו למקום שכלו ושמע
שכלו במקומו חייב לבער ר' יהודה אומר
צא והבא לך אף אתה מהיכא דאייתינהו
והא לא כלו להו למימרא דר' יהודה לקולא
קאמר והאמר ר"א לא אמר רבי יהודה אלא
לחומרא אלא איפוך אינו חייב לבער רבי
יהודה אומר צא והבא לך אף אתה מהיכא
דאייתינהו והא כלו להו אביי אמר לעולם
כדקתני וה"ק או ממקום שלא כלו למקום
שכלו והחזירן למקומן ועדיין לא כלו אינו
חייב לבער רבי יהודה אומר צא והבא לך
אף אתה מהיכא דאייתינהו והא כלו להו
מתקיף לה רב אשי לרבי יהודה אטו אגבא
דחמרא קלטינהו אלא אמר רב אשי
בפלוגתא דהני תנאי דתנן *הכובש שלשה
כבשין בחבית אחת ר"א אומר אוכלין על
הראשון ר' יהושע אומר אף על האחרון ר"ג
אומר 'כל שכלה מינו מן השדה יבער מינו
מן החבית והלכה כדבריו רבינא אמר
בפלוגתא דהני תנאי דתנן 'אוכלין בתמרין
עד שיכלה האחרון שבצוער רשב"ג אומר
אוכלין

רש"י

ביישוב לא עבידנא. מלאכה ביום טוב שני הואיל ונהגו בו איסור לא אשנה לעיניהם את המנהג: דעדיפא מינה. החמורה ממנה עבדי ליה. עשיתי לו: מימנו אנגדא דבר בי רב. תלמיד שסרח היו נמנין להלקותו ולא לנדותו משום דשמתא חמורה וחוששין לכבוד התורה: ולית ליה לר' יהודה כו'. דמשמע שיכול לומר לו בן מקום שלא כלו לבן מקום שכלו לא והבא לך אף אתה ממקום שהבאתי ותמצא שלא כלו שם לחיה ואכול מאותן שתביא (ב) ואותה שלך שיש לך בבית אסורין וטעמא משום דגדלו כאן ובזה המקום כלו אבל אני הבאתי את שלי ממקום היתר ואין כאן מחלוקת ולית ליה לר' יהודה לאסור משום חומרי מקום שהלך לשם ואפילו אין שם מחלוקת דהא ממקום שאין עושין למקום שעושין דטעמא לאו משום מחלוקת הוא ואסרינן ליה משום חומרי מקום שיצא משם: הכי גרסינן מילתא אחריתי קאמר. או ממקום שלא כלו למקום שכלו ושמע שכלו במקומן חייב לבער ורבי יהודה אומר לא והבא לך אף אתה מהיכא דאייתינהו והא לא כלו(ג): מילתא אחריתי קאמר. תנא קמא: ושמע שכלו במקומן חייב לבער. ואע"ג דאין כאן חומרי מקום שיצא משם שבשעה שיצא עדיין לא היו נוהגין בהן חומרא: ר' יהודה אומר לא. יכול זה לומר לבני מקומו שיצא משם איני משנה ממנהגכם דהא הולכתים למקום שלא כלו ולא והבא לך משם ותוכל למצוא הרבה: לחומרא אמרה רבי יהודה. הכי הוה גמיר לה ר"א מרביה דרבי יהודה אמר לחומרא: אלא איפוך. תוספת זו שהוסיפו על המשנה ואימא או ממקום שלא כלו למקום שלא כלו ושמע שכלו במקומן אינו חייב לבער דאין כאן משום חומרי מקום שיצא משם שכשהוציאם עדיין לא נאסרו ר' יהודה אומר יש כאן זילזול מקומו דאמרי ליה בני מקומו הראשון לא והבא לך מהיכא דאייתינהו ממקום שהבאתם ותמצא שכבר כלו: לעולם כדקתני. דלא איירי מתניתין במביא ממקומו למקום השוה לו אלא למקום שאין שוה לו: והכי קאמר. מתניתין המוליך פירות שביעית ממקום שכלו למקום שלא כלו או ממקום שלא כלו למקום שכלו חייב לבער החזירן למקומן ועדיין לא כלו אינו חייב לבער ורבי יהודה מחמיר דאמרינן ליה לא והבא לך אף אתה מהיכא דאייתינהו השתא והא כלו להו: גבא דחמרא קלטינהו. גבו של חמור שהכניסן לתוך אותו מקום החמור קלטן בחומרי אותו מקום שלא יוכל להחזירן עוד הא לא גדלו שם ואינו אוכלן שם: הכובש שלשה כבשים. שלשה מיני ירק בחבית אחת של חומץ או של ציר כדי להתקיים: אוכלין. משלשתן: על הראשון. על סמך הראשון המתחיל להיות כלה לחיה מן השדה אחד מכן מן השדה שלשתן אסורין דכבשיהו משוי להו כחד: אף על האחרון. על סמך מין הכלה אחרון ואוכל השלשתן ואע"פ שמין השנים כלה לחיה כבר ותנא דמתני' ור' יהודה בהא פליגי דתנא קמא סבר לה כרבי יהושע דמיקל והכי משתמעא למילתיה ממקום שלא כלו למקום שכלו כולן חייב לבער אבל כלו מקצתן אוכל אף ממין הכלה כר' יהושע דאוכלין אף על האחרון ר' יהודה אומר לא והבא לך אף אתה מאותו המין מן השדה והרי לא תמצא בשדה ואסור כרבן גמליאל: אוכלין בתמרים. בכל ארץ יהודה עד שיכלה דקל האחרון שבצוער שהיא עיר התמרים ותנן לקמן שלש ארצות לביעור שאין בני יהודה אוכלין משכלו בכל ארץ יהודה ואע"פ שלא כלו בגליל אבל אוכלין הן ביהודה ואפילו במקום שכלה עד שיכלה מקום אחרון שבכל ארץ יהודה לפי שחיה כשאינה מוצאת כאן הולכת למקום אחר והיא מתפרנסת שם ורחמנא תלה בה כדלקמן: אוכלין

תוספות

ביישוב לא עבדינן. אפילו בצינעא ואפילו דעתו לחזור דלא אפשר למלאכה בצינעא כמו שאר דברים: *ממקום שכלו למקום שלא כלו חייב לבער. תימה לר"י והלא אסור לשנות מפני המחלוקת אפילו לקולא כדאמר לעיל אין בזה מפני שינוי המחלוקת דמימר אמרי כמה בטלני איכא בשוקא הא לא לאו הא טעמא הוא אסור לשנות מפני המחלוקת ומיהו יש לומר אי מדאורייתא חייב לבער משום מחלוקת לא יעבור על דברי תורה ועוד אור"י דלא שייך מחלוקת אלא בדבר שתלוי בגוף האדם אבל בפירות לא שייך מחלוקת דאמרינן ממקום שכלו כלו: אביי אמר לעולם כדקתני. לדבריו אין חסר כלום מן המשנה דרבי יהודה אדיוקא דמתניתין קאי: הכובש שלשה כבשים. כגון לפת ובצל וקפלוט שאין ביעורן שוה רבי אליעזר אומר אוכלין על הראשון שטעמו אוסר כולם ולא חשיב כמבוער אך לרבי יהושע תימה לר"י איך מותר גוף אותם שכלו ואומר רבינו תם דבתורת כהנים בפרשת בהר סיני פליגי בקרא דתניא מן השדה תאכלו את תבואתה כל זמן שאתה אוכל מן השדה אתה אוכל מן הבית וכו' מכאן אמרו חכמים הכובש שלשה כבשים בחבית רבי אליעזר אומר כיון שכלה אחד מן השדה יבער הכל מן הבית והיינו אוכלין על הראשון דבמשנתין ואם תאמר לר' אליעזר לישתוק קרא מיניה דנפקא לן מולבהמתך וי"ל דסבר ר' אליעזר דאי לאו האי קרא ה"א דאותו המין דוקא יבער ולא יותר אע"פ שטעם האיסור מעורב בהן דלא דמי איסור דביעור לשאר איסורים דהא שרי לעניים וה"א דניחשביה כמבוער כיון שאין כאן אלא הטעם ור' יהושע סבר דודאי הטעם חשיב כמבוער והאי קרא אתי להתיר אף גוף אותו שכלה הואיל ומעורב בהן הטעם המותרין ומן השדה משמע ליה מן דבר שמקצת הטעם ממנו בשדה תאכלו אף האיסור שעמו ורבן גמליאל סבר ממשות של כל אחד שכלה מן השדה אסור אבל הטעם הוא כמבוער ובמגילת סתרים דרבינו נסים פירש דראשון היינו שניתן ראשון בכבוש ואחרון שניתן אחרון בכבוש והכי אמרינן בירושלמי מה טעם דרבי אליעזר הראשון נותן טעם באחרון הלכך אם כלה מן השדה אותו שכבש ראשון אוסר הכל אבל האחרון אינו נותן טעם בראשון ואם כלה מין האחרון מן השדה אינו אוסר אותם שנכבשו קודם וטעם דרבי יהושע אחרון נותן טעם בראשון פי' אף האחרון כדאמר הכל אף על האחרון וקסבר ר' יהושע דמיד כשכלה אחד מהמינים האחרון או הראשון או האמצעי כולן אסורין דנותן טעם זה בזה ורבי יהודה דמתניתין לחומרא כותיה ורבן גמליאל סבר כדפרישית דהגוף שכלה אסור והטעם הוי כמבוער: עד

רבינו חננאל

בישוב לא עבידנא במדבר ארץ ישראל מהו לעשות ביום שהוא ברור לי שהוא חול מי אמור רבנן בכי הא מילתא במדבר ארץ ישראל נותנין עליו חומרי מקום שיצא משם או לא אמר ליה הכי אמר ר' אמי בישוב אסור במדבר מותר: והא דשמתיה רב יוסף לרב נתן בר אסיא משום דאתא מבי רב לפומבדיתא ביום טוב שני דעצרת ואמר ליה אביי ולינגדיה מר אמר ליה רב [יוסף] דעדיפא מינה עבדי ביה כלומר השמתא חמורה מן המלקות דבמערבא מימני אנגדא דבר בי רב פי' מתקבצין אצל הרב ואין מלקין עד שיסכימו בהכאתו ולא מימנו אשמתא למה שלא תהיה שמתא אלא על דבר חמור ובדבר חמור אין חולקין כבוד לרב אלא משמתין אותו מיד לפיכך השמתא עדיפא היא מן המלקות: איכא דאמרי נגדיה ר' [יוסף] ואמר דטבא ליה עבדי ליה דהי המלקות קלה היא מן השמתא דגרסי' באלו מגלחין בהאי עניינא דלא מימנו אשמתא דבר בי רב מאי שמתא אמר רב שם מיתה ושמואל אמר (שמיה) [שממה] יהא. אמר רב יוסף שרי שמתא ארנבי דכלבא והיא דידה עבדא ודברים ברורין הן. כיוצא בו המוליך פירות שביעית כו' ואקשינן ולית ליה לר' יהודה נותנין עליו חומרי מקום וכו' ואמר רב שישא לעולם אית ליה ומלתא אחריתי קאמר במתני' דלא איתמרא בהדיא דמאחר שהורה שהמוליך ממקום שכלו למקום שלא כלו וממקום שלא כלו למקום שכלו הוצרך עוד לפרש המוליך פירות שביעית ממקום שלא כלו למקום שלא כלו ושמע שכלו מאותו מקום שהביאם ואתא לאוקמה דרבי יהודה לקולא ונדחה ואפיכנא למתני' ואוקימנא רבי יהודה לחומרא חייב לבער ות"ק לקולא אינו חייב לבער והכי פירושו ת"ק סבר כיון דאייתינהו ממקום שלא כלו למקום שלא כלו נתלקו פירות אותו מקום שהביאו משם מעליו ואע"ג דכלו התם השתא כיון דלא כלו הכא אין חייב לבער. ור' יהודה אומר לו צא והבא ממקום שהבאת אותם וכיון שאין שם מי יביא חייב לבער וכאלו הביאם עכשיו ממקום שכלו למקום שלא כלו שנותנין עליו חומרי מקום שיצא משם לפיכך חייב לבער: והא דאמר אביי ממקום שלא כלו למקום שכלו והחזירן למקומן שלא כלו ת"ק סבר הרי הן בחזקתן ור' יהודה סבר כיון דעיילינהו למקום [שכלו] נאסרו ואתקפתא דרב אשי פשוטין הן. ואוקמה רב אשי בפלוגתא דהני תנאי דתנן הכובש שלשה כבשין בחבית אחת ר' אליעזר אומר אוכלין על הראשון פי' אותו הכבוש שכבש מתחלה ור' יהושע אומר אף על האחרון כו' והכי קתני במתני' וכן הכובש שלשה כבשין בחבית אחת ולא כלה הכל אלא אפי' נשאר אחד מהן אינו חייב לבער רבי אליעזר אומר כיון שכלה אחד מהן חייב לבער שאומר לו צא והבא לך אף אתה וכיון שאינו מוצא להביא חייב לבער נמצא רבי יהודה דמחמיר כרבי אליעזר. וגרסי' בירושלמי מאי טעמא דר' אליעזר הראשון נותן טעם

עין משפט נר מצוה

יד א מיי' פ"ט מהל' יו"ט הלכה כ טוש"ע א"ח סי' תצו סע"ג:
שייך למתניתין
טו ב מיי' פ"ז מהלכות ת"ת הלכה א סמג לאוין רח טוש"ע י"ד סי' שלד סעיף מג:
טז ג מיי' פ"ו מהלכות ת"ת הלכה יד סמג שם טוש"ע שם סעיף מג:
יז ד מיי' פ"א מהלכות יו"ט הלכה כב סמג לאוין עה טוש"ע א"ח סי' תצו סעיף א:
יח ה מיי' פ"ז מהלכות שמיטה הלכה ו סמג עשין קמה:
יט ו שם הלכה יא:

מסורת הש"ס

מ"ק יז: [פי' מתקבצין אצל הרב ואין מלקין עד שיסכימו בהכאתו ולא מימנו לשמתא אלא על דבר חמור ובדבר חמור אין חולקין כבוד לרב. לפיכך השמתא עדיפא מן המלקות. ערוך]

שביעית פ"ט משנה ס

הגהות הב"ח

(א) גמרא דעדיפא עבדי ליה: (ב) רש"י ד"ה ולית ליה לר' יהודה וכו' מאותן שתביא ואותן שלך שיש לך: (ג) ד"ה הכי גרסינן וד"ה מילתא אחריתי וכו' רבי יהודה סד"א:

a art] of fixing the New Moon,[1] [52a] in inhabited places I do not work,[2] because it is a change [which would lead to] strife. [But] how is it in the wilderness?—Said he to him, Thus did R. Ammi say: In inhabited regions it is forbidden; in the desert it is permitted. R. Nathan b. Asia went from Rab's academy [in Sura][3] to Pumbeditha on the second Festival day of Pentecost, [whereupon] R. Joseph put him under the ban. Said Abaye to him, Yet let the master punish him with lashes?—Said he to him, I have treated him more severely, for in the West [*sc.* Palestine] they take a vote for punishing a disciple with lashes, yet they do not take a vote on the ban.[4] Others say, R. Joseph had him lashed. Said Abaye to him, Yet let the Master ban him, for Rab and Samuel both said: We impose the ban for [the violation of] the two Festival days of the Diaspora?—Said he to him, That refers only to an ordinary person, but here it is a scholar, so I did what was better for him, for in the West they take a vote for punishing a disciple with lashes, yet they do not take a vote on the ban.

SIMILARLY, HE WHO TRANSPORTS SABBATICAL-YEAR PRODUCE etc. Does then R. Judah not accept what we learned, WE LAY ON HIM THE RESTRICTIONS OF THE PLACE WHENCE HE DEPARTED AND THE RESTRICTIONS OF THE PLACE WHITHER HE HAS GONE?—Said R. Shisha the son of R. Idi, R. Judah says[5] a different thing, and this is its meaning: or from a place where it has not ceased to a place where it has not ceased, and then he heard that it had ceased in his town, he is bound to remove it.

b R. Judah said: [He can say,][1] 'Do you too go out and procure [produce] for yourself from the place whence I have obtained it', since it has not ceased for them.[2] Shall we say that R. Judah [thus] rules leniently? But surely R. Eleazar said, R. Judah did not rule otherwise than stringently?[3] Rather, reverse it: He is not bound to remove it.[4] R. Judah said: [His townspeople can say to him], 'Do you too go out [now] and obtain [produce] from the place whence you brought it [the produce you possess], and lo! it has ceased'.[5] Abaye said: In truth it is as taught,[6] and this is what he states: Or from a place where it has not ceased to a place where it has ceased, and [then] he brought it back to its place, and it has still not ceased [there], he is not bound to remove it. R. Judah said: [They can say to him,] 'Go out and do you too bring [produce] from the place whence you have [now] brought it, and lo! it has ceased [there]'. To this R. Ashi demurred: According to R. Judah, has he then caught them [these restrictions] up on the back of an ass![7] Rather, said R. Ashi, [This enters] in the controversy of the following Tannaim. For we learned: If a man preserves three [kinds of] preserves in one barrel,[8]—R. Eliezer said: One may eat [in reliance] upon the first [only];[9] R. Joshua said: Even [in reliance] upon the last;[10] R. Gamaliel said: Whatever kind has ceased from the field, he must remove that kind from c the barrel, and the *halachah* is as his ruling.[1]

Rabina said, [It enters] into the controversy of the following Tannaim. For we learned:[2] One may eat dates until the last in

a (1) By Biblical law Festivals are holy on the first and the seventh days only (Pentecost one day altogether). But owing to uncertainty in early time about the exact day of New Moon, i.e., when the month began, it became a binding practice in the Diaspora to observe two days instead of one, and this remained binding even when New Moon was ascertained by mathematical calculation, which obviated all doubt. (2) On the second day of Festivals. [I.e., when I happen to be in Babylon, v. *infra* p. 52a.] (3) [Var. lec. 'Biram' on the West bank of the Euphrates. V. Asheri and MS.M. In Biram, which was the home of R. Nathan b. Asia, only a one day Festival was observed, v. R. H., 23b, n. 2. and Obermeyer, p. 99]. (4) As the ban would damage his prestige more than corporal punishment. This proves that the ban is a severer punishment. (5) [Var. lec. omit 'R. Judah' the reference being to the first Tanna, v. Rashi.]

b (1) To the people of the place whence he came. (2) Thus, he does not regard the practice of his own town, since they too can do as he. (3) In this connection. (4) I.e., insert the addition in the Mishnah thus: Or if he goes from a place where it has not ceased to a place where it has not ceased, and he then learns that it has ceased in his own town, he is not bound to remove it, as one cannot speak of the restrictions of the place whence he came, for when he left it there were as yet no restrictions. (5) I.e., the fact remains that by now it has ceased in your own town, and the resultant law applies to yourself too just as to us. (6) It refers to two *dissimilar* places, not to two similar places. (7) So that he brings them back with him! The produce has neither grown in that second town nor does he consume it there: how then can he be subject to the restrictions of that place? (8) I.e., three different vegetables. These may 'cease from the field' at different times—the reference is to the Sabbatical year. (9) As soon as the first kind 'ceases from the field', he must declare the whole free to all, because their being preserved together makes them as one. (10) He may go on eating of all three until the last kind has ceased from the field.

c (1) Now in the Mishnah there is the same controversy. The first Tanna agrees with R. Joshua's lenient view, and this is what he means: If a man carries various kinds of produce from a place where they have not ceased to a place where *all of them* have ceased, he is bound to remove them. But if only some kinds have ceased, he may eat even of the kind which has ceased. R. Judah rules, One can say to him, 'Go out and do you too bring of that kind from the field', i.e., you will not find of that kind, and therefore you must remove it in accordance with R. Gamaliel. (2) [The teaching that follows is not a Mishnah but a Baraitha, Tosef. Sheb. VII. Read accordingly with MS.M.: 'It has been taught'.]

a garden, [51b] and he took the aftergrowth of the cabbage[1] and ate it, and he gave [some] to me and said to me, 'My son, in my presence you may eat,[2] when not in my presence, you may not eat [it]. I who saw R. Simeon b. Yoḥai eat [it],—R. Simeon b. Yoḥai is [great] enough to rely upon in his presence and not in his presence; [but] you may eat in my presence, but do not eat [when] not in my presence'.[3] What is [this reference to] R. Simeon?—For it was taught, R. Simeon said: All aftergrowths are forbidden,[4] except the aftergrowth of the cabbage, because there is none like them among the vegetables of the field;[5] but the Sages maintain, All aftergrowths are forbidden. Now, both [state their views] on the basis of R. Akiba. For it was taught: *Behold, we may not sow, nor gather in our increase.*[6] R. Akiba said: Now, since they do not sow, whence can they gather?[7] Hence it follows that the aftergrowth is forbidden.[8] Wherein do they differ?—The Rabbis hold, We preventively forbid the aftergrowth of cabbage on account of other aftergrowths in general; whereas R. Simeon holds: We do not preventively forbid the after-
b growth of cabbage on account of [other] aftergrowths in general.[1]

HE WHO GOES FROM A PLACE etc. As for [teaching], HE WHO GOES FROM A PLACE WHERE THEY DO WORK TO A PLACE WHERE THEY DO NOT WORK... WE LAY UPON HIM THE RESTRICTIONS OF THE PLACE WHITHER HE HAS GONE, AND A MAN MUST NOT ACT DIFFERENTLY, ON ACCOUNT OF THE QUARRELS, that is well, and he must not work. But [if he goes] FROM A PLACE WHERE THEY DO NOT WORK TO A PLACE WHERE THEY DO WORK... A MAN MUST NOT ACT DIFFERENTLY, BECAUSE OF THE QUARRELS,—[that is] he is to work? But you say, WE LAY UPON HIM THE RESTRICTIONS OF THE PLACE WHITHER HE HAS GONE AND THE RESTRICTIONS OF THE PLACE WHENCE HE HAS DEPARTED!—Said Abaye: It refers to the first clause.[2] Raba said: After all it refers to the second clause, but this is its meaning: This does not come within [the scope of] differences which cause quarrels. What will you say: He who sees will say, '[He regards] work as forbidden?'[3] [No:] they will indeed say, 'How many unemployed are there in the market place!'[4]

R. Safra said to R. Abba:[5] For instance I,[6] who know [the

a (1) Rashi: It was in a Sabbatical year, and after the time when provisions must be removed from the house; v. 50b, n. a1. Tosaf. maintains that 'and he took' implies that he pulled it out of the earth; thus it was still available for cattle, and therefore it was before the time of removal. (2) Because you can rely upon me. (3) Whereas Rabbah b. Bar Ḥanah told his son not to rely upon him even in his presence. (4) After the time of removal (Rashi); v. however next note. (5) Rashi offers two explanations, the first of which he rejects. The second, about which he is also doubtful, is this: cabbages remain in the ground right through winter, whereas the aftergrowths of other vegetables are consumed earlier: hence we are more lenient with cabbages, because we can never apply to them the principle, 'when it ceases for the beasts in the field, it must cease for (i.e., be removed from) the man in the house'. V. *infra*, n. b1, for a different interpretation. (6) Lev. XXV, 20. (7) Then why state '*nor gather in our increase*'? (8) And to this they refer.

b (1) R. Tam: the reference is to the time *before* the removal. Both R. Simeon and the Rabbis accept R. Akiba's view that the aftergrowth is Scripturally forbidden, but only that aftergrowth which is similar to sowing (seeds), for the verse, '*we may not sow, nor gather in our increase*', implies that '*our increase*', which refers to the aftergrowth, is similar to what '*we may not sow*'; but the cabbage plant has more affinity to trees then to seeds (v. Keth. 111b), hence it is not forbidden by Biblical law. This view is held by both, and they differ whether the cabbage aftergrowth is *Rabbinically* forbidden as a preventive measure or not. Another explanation is given in Tosaf. on quite different lines. (2) I.e., HE MUST NOT ACT DIFFERENTLY if he goes FROM A PLACE WHERE THEY DO WORK TO A PLACE WHERE THEY DO NOT WORK. (3) Though we permit it; do you fear that this will lead to strife? (4) Raba explains the Mishnah thus: IF A MAN GOES FROM A PLACE WHERE THEY DO NOT WORK TO A PLACE WHERE THEY WORK... WE IMPOSE UPON HIM THE RESTRICTIONS OF THE PLACE WHENCE HE HAS DEPARTED. For the general principle that a man MUST NOT ACT DIFFERENTLY from the rest of the people was only ON ACCOUNT OF THE QUARRELS, whereas here we have no fear. (5) Var. lec. Raba. (6) [So Tosaf. and MS.M., cur. edd. 'we'.]

[כרכות פ"א הלכה ט]

יב א מיי' פ"ד מהל' שמיטה הלכה ג:
יג ב מיי' פ"ח מהלכות י"ט הלכה כ סמג לאוין עה טוש"ע או"ח סי' תסח סעיף ד:

ונטל ספיחי כרוב ואכל ונתן לי ואמר לי בני בפני אכול שלא בפני לא תאכל אני שראיתי את ר"ש בן יוחי שאכל כדי הוא ר' שמעון בן יוחי לסמוך עליו בפניו ושלא בפניו אתה בפני אכול שלא בפני לא תאכל מאי ר"ש *דתניא רבי שמעון אומר כל הספיחים *אסורין חוץ מספיחי כרוב שאין כיוצא בהן בירק השדה וחכ"א *כל הספיחין אסורים ותרוייהו אליבא דר' עקיבא דתניא°הן לא נזרע ולא נאסוף את תבואתנו א"ר עקיבא וכי מאחר שאין זורעין מהיכא אוספין מכאן *לספיחין שהן אסורין במאי קא מיפלגי רבנן סברי גזרינן ספיחי כרוב אטו שאר ספיחי דעלמא ור"ש סבר לא גזרינן ספיחי כרוב אטו ספיחי דעלמא: ההולך ממקום וכו': בשלמא ההולך ממקום שעושין למקום שאין עושין נותנין עליו חומרי מקום שהלך לשם ואל ישנה אדם מפני המחלוקת ולא ליעביד אלא ממקום שאין עושין למקום שעושין אל ישנה אדם מפני המחלוקת ונעביד הא אמרת נותנין עליו חומרי מקום שהלך לשם וחומרי מקום שיצא משם אמר אביי ארישא רבא אמר לעולם אסיפא והכי קאמר ^באין בזו מפני שינוי המחלוקת מאי קא אמרת הרואה אומר מלאכה אסורה *מימר אמרי כמה בטלני הוי בשוקא א"ל רב ספרא לרבי אבא °כגון אנן דידעינן בקביעא דירחא ביישוב

תורה אור: ויקרא כה [מנחות ה:]

ונטל ספיחי כרוב. בשביעית לאחר זמן הביעור: כדי. ראוי: בפני אכול. בפני אתה יכול לסמוך עלי אוכל וראיתי את ר"ש שאכל והיינו פלוגתא דידיה דלעיל אמר לא תאכל אפי' בפני והכא קאמר דאע"ג דלאו בר סמכא הוא ולאו מגמריה ומסבריה קא שרי ליה סמכינן עליה מיהא בפניו משום דחזיא לגברא רבה דאכיל: כל הספיחין אסורין. בשביעי' מזמן הביעור ואילך: חוץ מספיחי כרוב. עלין היוצאין מקלח הכרוב: שאין כיוצא בהן בירק השדה. משרשים הן גדלין והרי הן כאילן שמוסיף ענפים על ענפים ולאו בכלל שאר ספיחים נינהו וכל שאר ספיחים מזרע הנחבט ונופל לארץ הוא אבל ספיחי כרוב אינו כן אלא עלין גדילין בענפים ולא אסר' תורה אלא ספיחים מעין זריעה כדכתיב הן לא נזרע וגו' כך שמעתי וקשיא לי חדא דכי האי גוונא לא קרי ספיחים אלא הגדילים מזרע הנחבט ונופל לארץ קודם לקיטה ועוד אילנות בשביעית מי לא נהגא בהן נמי קדושה ונראה בעיני דטעמא משום דכרוב אינו כלה לחיה כל ימות החורף וגימגום: א"ר עקיבא. למה נאמר ולא נאסוף מאחר שאין אנו זורעין מה יאספו לימד על הספיחים שאסורין וה"ק הן לא נזרע והגדילין מאיליהן לא נאסוף: גזרינן ספיחי כרוב אטו ספיחין דעלמא. דאע"ג דאין ביעור לכרוב דהא מתקיים כל ימות הגשמים ספיחין דידיה אסורין דלא לימא טעמא משום דאין בספיחי' איסור שביעית ואתו למישרי שאר ספיחים: ארישא. ואל ישנה דמתני' ארישא קאי ההולך ממקום שעושין למקום שאין עושין: רבא אמר לעולם אסיפא. והכי משמע מתני' או ממקום שאין עושין למקום שעושין נותנין עליו חומרי מקום שיצא משם ולא ליעבד דהא דקי"ל בעלמא אל ישנה אדם ממנהג העיר אינו אלא מפני המחלוקת וכאן אין מחלוקת(א): דמאי אמרת. הרואה אותו בטל יאמר זה אומר שהמלאכה אסורה וחלוק על כולנו לא יאמר הכי אלא יאמר מלאכה אין לו שהרי כמה בטלנין יש בשוק כל ימות השנה:

ביישוב

אני ראיתי את ר"ש שאכל. תימה לר"י דאמר בירושלמי* ר"ש חזא להההוא גברא מלקט ספיחי כרוב בשביעית א"ל מאי הא לאו הא לאו את הוא דשרית א"ל ולאו חבראי פליגי עלי קרי עליה פורץ גדר ישכנו נחש וכן הוות ליה והשתא כיון שבעלמו היה אוכל למה היה כועס על אחרים שהיו אוכלין וסומכין על הוראתו וי"ל דמ"מ לא היה רוצה שעמי הארץ יסמכו עליו כל זמן שלא פסקו הלכה כמותו:

כל הספיחים אסורין חוץ מספיחי כרוב. פי' רש"י לאחר ביעור מיירי ואין ביעור נוהג בכרוב לפי שאין השורש כלה בארץ ולא קרינן ביה כלה לחיה מן השדה וקשה לר"י א"כ אמאי איצטריך קרא דלא נאסוף תיפוק ליה דכתיב ולבהמתך ועוד מאי שנא דלא מפיק אלא ספיחי כרוב ה"ל למעוטי כל הני דפ"ז דשביעית (משנה ב) דתנן עיקר הלוף (ב) השוטה *וכרבינה אין להן ביעור ועוד מאי שנא דרבנן גזרי הכא ספיחי כרוב אטו שאר ספיחים ובכל הנהו דהתם לא גזרי ועוד הקשה ריב"א דלעיל קתני ונכנסתי לגינה אחריו ונטל ספיחי כרוב ואכל משמע שתלשן מן הקרקע והי' מהן הרבה מחוברין וא"כ איירי קודם ביעור ועוד הקשה ר"ת דאמרינן בפ"ק דמנחות (דף ה:) (ג) מה למנחת העומר שכן מתיר חדש בשביעי' ספיחים כר"ע דאמר ספיחי' אסורים ובפסח של שביעית היא קודם ביעור שאז תבואה אינה כלה בשדה ואדרבה היא במילואה וביעור לא היה אלא בשמינית כשהיא כלה לחיה מן השדה ועוד דקאמר ותרוייהו אליבא דר"ע (ד) ורבנן נמי לא פליגי אדרשה דכלה לחיה בשדה ומודו רבנן דספיחים אסורים אחר ביעור דבספרי קאמר אמילתא דרבנן דפליגי אדר' עקיבא אמרת לנו לא זרענו ומה שאנו אוספים אין מכניסו לקיום פי' שאסור אחר ביעור אמרת לנו בערו מה אנו אוכלין מן הביעור ואילך °לכך נראה לר"ת דבשביעית קודם ביעור מיירי כדמשמע קרא דלא נאסוף דמייתי דכתיב ביה מה נאכל בשנה השביעית ודריש ר"ע מהאי קרא דספיחים אסורים בשביעית ורבנן פליגי עליה ודרשי לא נאסוף להכניסו לקיום ולא אסרי אלא אחר ביעור ור"ש ורבנן פליגי הכא אליבא דר"ע ומתיר ר"ש ספיחי כרוב דלא אסרה תורה אלא ספיחים דומיא דזריעה דכתיב הן לא נזרע אבל ספיחי כרוב דמו לאילן כדאמר (כתובות קיא:) כרוב הניח לנו אבא והיינו עולים (ה) בו בסולם ולא גזרינן אטו שאר ספיחים ורבנן גזרי ודוקא אליבא דר"ע דאיסור ספיחים מדאורייתא פליגי אבל לרבנן דפליגי עליה דר"ע וסברי איסור ספיחים דרבנן ליכא למיגזר (ו) הקשה רבינו נסים גאון דאיפכא שמעינן להו במסכת שביעית בפ"ט (משנה א) דקתני התם ר"ש אומר כל הספיחים מותרין חוץ מספיחי כרוב שאין כיוצא בהן בירק השדה וליכא למיגרס התם אסורין דבירושלמי מוכח בהדיא דגרס התם מותרין ותירץ דהתם מיירי בספיחים שגדלו בששית בהיתר ונכנסו בשביעית ונשתהו עד לאחר הביעור ולכך שאר ספיחים שרו דלא אתו לאיחלופי בהנהו שגדלו בשביעית דשל ערב שביעית גדולים ושל שביעית קטנים אבל של כרוב שגדילים הרבה בזמן מועט אין היכר בין הגדל בערב שביעית לגדל בשביעית וכן איתא בירושלמי א"ר ינאי כל ירק אתה יכול לעמוד עליו בין חדש ובין ישן ברס הכא פי' ספיחי כרוב שלא ילך ויביא מן האיסור ויאמר מן האמהות הבאתי והך דשמעתא איירי בשביעית עצמה כדמפר"ת ורבינו נסים פי' נמי שמעתא בע"א ופי' דהכא בספיחים של שביעית שיצאו למוצאי שביעית דאסורין מדרבנן עד כדי שיעשו כיוצא בהן וסבר ר"ש ספיחים אסורין במוצאי שביעית דכשיראו אותם גדולים יסברו שלקטן בשביעית אבל ספיחי כרוב שאין כיוצא בהן בירק השדה לא גזרו בהן אטו שאר ספיחים דכשיראו אותם גדולין לא יסברו שלקטן בשביעית דדרכם ליגדל הרבה בזמן מועט וכשאכל ר"ש בן [רבי] יוסי בן לקוניא ספיחי כרוב במוצאי שביעית הוה דאכל כר"ש בן יוחי (ז) ולא משמע הכי ורבנן גזרי היתירא אטו איסורא וכולן אסורין ובגמרא דדמאי בפרק שני גרס לענין ספיחים מר"ה ועד חנוכה איסור ספיחים ומחנוכה ועד ר"ה היתר ספיחים ותניא בתוספתא בפ"ה בצלים שיצאו משביעית למוצאי שביעית אם עשו כיוצא בהן מותרין ואם לאו אסורין ותרוייהו אליבא דר"ע דאסר ספיחים מדאורייתא בשביעית אבל לרבנן דפליגי עליה ליכא למיגזר ומה שפי' רבינו נסים דמה שגדל בששית ונכנסה לשביעית היכא דאיכא למיטעי שמא גדל בשביעית אסור קשה לרשב"א דתניא בפ"ק דר"ה (דף טו.) ר"ש בן יהודה משום ר"ש אומר אתרוג בת ששית שנכנסה בשביעית פטור מן המעשר ומן הביעור והשתא ביעור לא הוי אלא בזמן שהפירות כלים ואפ"ה קאמר פטור מן הביעור ואע"ג דאיכא למיטעי ולמימר שזה האתרוג גדל בשביעית וי"ל דהתם מיירי מדאורייתא א"נ כשלקטן בתחילתה של שביעית דליכא למיטעי מיהו הא קשיא לר"י דבשמעתא משמע לכ"ע דירקות הגדילין בשביעית אסורין באכילה ובמסכת שביעית משמע דשרו דתנן (פ"ט מ"ד) האומר לפועל הילך דינר זה ולקט לי בו ירק היום ובפרק בתרא דע"ז (דף סב.) מייתי לה ותירץ ר"י דבשל ערב שביעית מיירי ומה שיש בהן דין שביעית לענין סחורה ושאר דינים לפי שנלקט בשביעית דבירק אזלינן בתר לקיטה:

כגון אנא דידענא בקביעא דירחא. ולא בסוד העיבור קאמר דהא בני בבל בקיאי בעיבורא דירחא כדאמרינן בריש ביצה (דף ד:) ועבדי תרי יומי אלא מפרש ר"ת שהיה במקום ששלוחי בית דין מגיעין ושם אין עושין אלא יום אחד והיינו בקביעא דירחא שהיה יודע מתי נקבע החודש דהתם ליכא למיגזר שמא יעשה מלאכה בי"ט ששומעין קידוש החודש*:

ביישוב

רבינו חננאל

יונתן בן אלעזר דאיהו ר' שמעון בן יוסי בן לקוניא שנטל ספיחי כרוב ואכל ונטל ונתן לי אמר אני שראיתי את ר' שמעון בן יוחאי שאכל ספיחי כרוב בשביעית כדי הוא לסמוך עליו בפניו ושלא בפניו אתה בפני אכול שלא בפני אל תאכל וס"ל פליגי דידיה אדידיה: מאי ר' שמעון דתנן בתרומות פ"ט ר' שמעון אומר כל הספיחי' אסורין חוץ מספיחי כרוב שאין כיוצא בהן בירקות השדה וחכמים אומרים כל הספיחים אסורין ר' שמעון וחכמים אית להו האי דר' עקיבא דתניא הן לא נזרע ולא נאסוף את תבואתנו א"ר עקיבא מאחר שאין זורעין מהיכן אוספין מכאן לספיחים שאסורין פי' הן לא נזרע ומאי שאינו זורע ודאי שאינו אוסף אלא אפי' הספיחים שצמחו לא נאסוף אותם מכאן לספיחים שאסורין לאוספן בשביעית וכולי עלמא ספיחים אסורין ובספיחי כרוב פליגי רבנן סברי גזרינן ספיחי כרוב אטו שאר ספיחים חשיבי דאם נתיר ספיחי כרוב שמא יתירו הן שאר ספיחים יאמרו מאי שנא ספיחי כרוב משאר כל הספיחים חדא הוא ור' שמעון סבר לא גזרינן דהא אין כיוצא בהן בירקות השדה דנימא אתי לאחלופי בהו הני בהני הלכך לא גזרינן. ומצינו במשנה ר' שמעון אומר כל הספיחין אסורין חוץ מספיחי כרוב שאין כיוצא בהן בירקות שדה מכלל שספיחי כרוב מותרין וגרסי' בגמרא ר' חמא בר עוקבא בשם ר' יוסי בר חנינא אומר מפני שדרכן לגדל אמהות יהו אסורין. אמר ר' שמואל כל ירק אתה יכול לעמוד בין חדש בין ישן ברם הכא שלא ילך ויביא מן האיסור ויאמר מן האמהות הבאתי לכאורה ר' שמעון אומר כל הספיחי' מותרין משמע. ותו גרסינן ר' שמעון בן יוחאי הוה עבר בשמטוניתא חמא חד מלקט שביעית אמר ליה אסור אמר ליה ספיחין אינון ולית אנת דשרי אמר ליה ולית חברי חלוקין עלי וקרא עליו ופורץ גדר ישכנו נחש ואע"ג דאיכא לשנויי כי ספיחי כרוב היו מיהו כי מעיינת ביה בקצירת ספיחים חלקו כדתניא ספיחי שביעית אין תולשין אותן ביד אבל חורש כדרכו ובהמה רועה כדרכה מר סבר גזרינן ומר סבר לא גזרינן: מתני' ההולך ממקום שעושין למקום שאין עושין כו' אקשינן אהא דתנן ואל ישנה אדם מפני המחלוקות וכי ממקום שאין עושין למקום שעושין אל ישנה אלא עושה והא אנן תנן נותנין עליו חומרי מקום שיצא לשם ובאותו מקום אין עושין ומשני אביי הא דתנן אל ישנה ארישא דקתני ההולך ממקום שעושין למקום שאין עושין אל ישנה ממנהג המקום שבא בו אלא ישב ולא יעשה. רבא אמר לעולם אסיפא ההולך ממקום שאין עושין למקום שעושין נותנין עליו חומרי מקום שיצא משם ויושב ולא יעשה ואם תאמר אל ישנה מפני המחלוקות שיבאו לומר כי הוא שישב בטל סבור הוא כי המלאכה אסורה והללו שעושין עוברין ואתו לאינצויי הכי רוצה לומר אין בזה מחלוקות כי יש לומר הרואה אותו יושב ובטל אומר אין לו מלאכה לעשות ולאו משום שאומר שהמלאכה אסורה הלא תראה כמה בני אדם יושבין ובטלין מאנשי המקום בעצמו אומר פוק חזי כמה בטלני איכא בשוקא ולאו משום דמלאכה אסורה סבירא להו דקאמרי דבטל: אמר ליה רב ספרא לר' אבא כגון אנא דידענא בקביעא דירחא ובני מקומי עושין שני ימים כי בעינא למיסק לארץ ישראל דלא עבדי אלא יום אחד בישוב

שביעית פ"ט מ"א ושם הגי' מותרין [ועי' מה שתירצו תוס' ד"ה כל הספיחים כו' על סתירה זו ועי' תוס' ר"ה יד: ד"ה ולשביעי' ותוס' בכורות כב: ד"ה תירוס]

[לקמן נה. ברכות יז:]

הגהות הב"ח

(א) רש"י ד"ה רבא וכו' ד"ה דמאי הד"א: (ב) תוס' ד"ה כל הספיחים כו' עיקר הלוף והשוטה: (ג) בא"ד בפ"ק דמנחות תיתי ממנחת העומר מה למנחת העומר שכן מתיר חדש בשביעי' שביעי' נמי שכן מתרת ספיחים כר"ע דאמר וכו' של שביעית עדיין הוא קודם ביעור שאז התבואה כו': (ד) בא"ד אליבא דר"ע הא רבנן נמי לא וכו' אחר ביעור דבתורת כהנים קאמר אמילתא וכו' אמרת לנו בערוהו ומה אנו אוכלין: (ה) בא"ד והייט עולים ויורדים בו בסולם: (ו) בא"ד הקשה רבינו נסים. נ"ב עי' רפ"ק דקדושין ד' ג' ד"ה אתרוג: (ז) בא"ד דאכל כרשב"י (ולא משמע הכי) תא"מ ונ"ב כ"ל דהגה"ס הוא מגליון תוס':

[ועי' תוס' סוכה מג. ד"ה לא ידעינן]

גליון הש"ס גמ' כגון אנן דידעינן בקביעא דירחא. עי' מהרש"א ולענ"ד י"ל דהא במקום דמגיעים ג"כ שלוחי תשרי והלך בניסן למקום דמגיעים שם שלוחי ניסן ולא שלוחי תשרי והם צריכים לעשות ב' ימים כדאי' דר"ה: תוס' ד"ה כל הספיחים. לכך נראה לר"ת דבשביעית קודם ביעור. עיין תענית י"ט ע"ב תד"ה רשב"ג:

אי אתה רשאי להתירן בפניהם אמר לו ולאו מי איתמר עלה אמר רב חסדא בכותאי כותאי מאי טעמא משום דמסרכי מילתא הנך אינשי נמי סרכי מילתא אלא אמר רב אשי חזינן אי רובן אורז אכלי לא ניכלה זר באפייהו דילמא משתכחא תורת חלה מינייהו ואי רובן דגן אכלי ניכלה זר באפייהו דילמא אתי לאפרושי מן החיוב על הפטור ומן הפטור על החיוב גופא דברים המותרין ואחרים נהגו בהן איסור אי אתה רשאי להתירן בפניהן אמר רב חסדא בכותאי עסקינן וכ"ע לא והתניא רוחצין שני אחין כאחד ואין רוחצין שני אחין בכבול *ומעשה ביהודה והלל בניו של רבן גמליאל שרחצו שניהם כאחד בכבול ולעזה עליהן כל המדינה אמרו מימינו לא ראינו כך ונשמט הלל ויצא לבית החיצון ולא רצה לומר להן מותרין אתם יוצאים בקורדקיסון בשבת ואין יוצאין בקורדקיסון בשבת בבירי *ומעשה ביהודה והלל בניו של רבן גמליאל שיצאו בקורדקיסון בשבת בבירי ולעזה עליהן המדינה ואמרו מימינו לא ראינו כך ושמטום ונתנום לעבדיהן ולא רצו לומר להן מותרין אתם ויושבין על ספסלי נכרים בשבת ואינן יושבין על ספסלי נכרים בשבת בעכו *ומעשה *בר"ש בן גמליאל שישב על ספסלי נכרים בשבת בעכו ולעזה עליו כל המדינה אמרו מימינו לא ראינו כך נשמט על גבי קרקע ולא רצה לומר להן מותרין אתם בני מדינת הים נמי כיון דלא שכיחי רבנן גבייהו ככותים דמו בשלמא ספסלי נכרים משום דמחזי כמקח וממכר בקורדקיסון נמי דילמא משתלפין ואתי לאיתויינהו ארבע אמות ברשות הרבים אלא רוחצין מאי טעמא לא כדתניא *עם הכל אדם רוחץ *חוץ מאביו וחמיו ובעל אמו ובעל אחותו ור' יהודה מתיר באביו מפני כבוד אביו והוא הדין לבעל אמו ואתו אינהו וגזור בשני אחין משום בעל אחותו תנא *תלמיד לא ירחץ עם רבו ואם רבו צריך לו מותר כי אתא רבה בר בר חנה אכל דאייתרא עול לגביה רב *עוירא סבא ורבה בריה דרב הונא כיון דחזינהו כסייה מינייהו אתו ואמרו ליה *לאביי אמר להו שווינכו ככותאי ורבה בר בר חנה לית ליה הא דתנן נותנין עליו חומרי המקום שיצא משם וחומרי המקום שהלך לשם *אמר אביי הני מילי מבבל לבבל ומארץ ישראל לא"י אי נמי מבבל לא"י אבל מא"י לבבל לא כיון דאנן כייפינן להו עבדינן כוותייהו רב אשי אמר אפילו תימא מא"י לבבל *הני מילי היכא דאין דעתו לחזור ורבה בר בר חנה דעתו לחזור הוה א"ל רבה בר בר חנה לבניה בני לא תאכל לא בפני ולא שלא בפני אני שראיתי את ר' יוחנן שאכל כדי הוא ר' יוחנן לסמוך עליו בפניו ושלא בפניו אתה לא ראית אותו לא תאכל בין בפני בין שלא בפני ופליגא דידיה אדידיה דאמר רבה בר בר חנה סח לי רבי יוחנן בן אלעזר פעם אחת נכנסתי אחר ר"ש בן רבי יוסי בן לקוניא לגינה ונטל

דסרכי מילתא. של קולא ומזלזלין יותר: הנך אינשי נמי. כיון דלא גמרי: סרכי מילתא. קושיא היא דאתו לאימנועי מחלה אף מדגן: המפריש מן האורז על הדגן אוכל טבלים דלא חל השם על האורז ולא ניתקן הדגן והמפריש מן הדגן על האורז מאכיל טבל לכהן שאין השם חל על הדגן בשביל האורז שהרי אינו מחוייב ונמצא שאין זו חלה אלא טבל: רוחצין שני אחים כאחד. ואין כאן משום פריצות דנימא מתוך שמלוין יחד ועכשיו רוחצין ערומים זה את זה נותנין עין איש באחיו למשכב זכור: ואין רוחצין כו'. כלומר אין נוהגים שני אחים לרחוץ כאחד: בכבול. מקום: קורדקיסון. אשקפונ"ש רחבים ולא חייכין דילמא משתלפי ואתי לאיתויינהו ארבע אמות ואין דרך בני בירי לצאת בקורדקיסון שכן נוהגין בהן איסור: ספסלי נכרים. שכן מוכרין בהן סחורה ולא חיישינן לחשדא: ככותאי דמי. דכיון דלא גמירי ולאו מקום תורה הוא סרכי מילתא: מאביו וחמיו. מתוך שרואהו ונזכר מקום שיצא נותן לבו להרהור וכן בחמיו נותן לבו שילתה אשתו מכאן וכן בבעל אחותו נמי איכא הירהורא: מפני כבוד אביו. שמשמשו במרחץ: ואתו אינהו. בני כבול: תלמיד לא ירחץ עם רבו. שצריך להתבייש מכבודו וממוראו: ואם היה רבו צריך לו. שישמשו במרחץ: אכל דאייתרא. חלב שבכפיפת הקיבה שהקיבה כפופה ועשויה כקשת ואותו חלב שבמקום היתר אוכלין בני ארץ ישראל ובני בבל נוהגין בו איסור: שוינכו ככותאי. דאמרינן לעיל דברים המותרים ואחרים נהגו בהן איסור אי אתה רשאי להתירן בפניהן ואוקמה רב חסדא בכותאי: הני מילי מבבל לבבל. מעיר בבבל לעיר בבבל דכיון דלא כייפי להדדי אם ישנה מנהגן לעיניהן יש כאן מפני המחלוקת וכל שכן מבבל לארץ ישראל אל ישנה את מנהג המקום מפני המחלוקת: אבל מארץ ישראל לבבל. אם ישנה את המנהג בבבל אין כאן מחלוקת דהא כייפינן לבני א"י דאינהו סמיכי ובבבל לא סמיכי: עבדינן כוותייהו. כלומר אם באין משם לכאן אין להם לשנות מנהגם אלא עושין כמקומן: אפילו תימא מארץ ישראל לבבל. אל ישנה: לא תאכל. דאייתרא: ונטל

אי אתה רשאי להתירן בפניהן. תימה א"כ היאך התיר ר' בית שאן בפ"ק דחולין (דף ו:) ותירץ רבינו נסים במגילת סתרים דהאי דברים המותרים ואחרים נהגו בהן איסור היינו שיודעים שהן מותרים והם רוצים להחמיר על עצמן וכן משמע לישנא דברים המותרים אבל דברים שנוהגים מחמת טעות שסבורים שהוא אסור והוא מותר יכול להתיר בפניהם וכן משמע בהדיא בירושלמי *וא"ת א"כ אמאי קאמר דילמא אתי לאפרושי מן הפטור על החיוב כיון דידעי שהוא פטור וי"ל דלאו כ"ע ידעי וא"ת דמשמע דווקא בבני המדינה או בכותאי אינו רשאי להתיר אבל בפני חכמים או שלא בפניהם מותר ואמאי והא תנן נותנין עליו חומרי מקום שיצא משם ושהלך לשם ואור"י דמתניתין איירי במנהג חשוב שהנהיגו ע"פ ת"ח והכא מיירי שנהגו בני המדינה מעצמם וכן הנהו דמייתי ודאייתרא דלקמן קים ליה דהוי מנהג חשוב ור"י מסתפק במנהג שאינו חשוב דיכולין להתיר בפני ת"ח אם יכול להתיר להם כדמשמע לקמן ולא רצו לומר להם מותרים אתם משום דבני המדינה חשוב להו ככותאי אבל לתלמידים משמע שהיו אומרים מותרין אתם או דילמא יכול להתיר לעצמו בפניהם אבל להם אינו יכול להתיר וה"ק לא רצה לומר להם מותרים אתם ומה שהחמרתם לא מחמת איסור אלא מחמת מנהג שטות ולתלמידים היה מתיר לעצמו בפניהם אבל לא להם ורשב"א אומר דלא קשה ממתני' דרב אשי דמוקי מתני' באין דעתו לחזור ובכותאי אפילו דעתו לחזור אסור ולאביי דמוקי ה"מ מבבל לא"י אבל מא"י לבבל עבדינן כוותייהו ובכותאי אפילו מא"י לבבל אסור והנהו נמי דמייתי הוו מא"י לבבל:

כיון דאנן כייפינן להו וכו'. קשה לר"ת דבפ"ק דסנהדרין (דף ה.) אמר פשיטא מהכא להתם מהני דהכא שבט והתם מחוקק משמע דבני בבל עדיפי ותירץ דה"מ לאפקועי ממונא אבל לענין איסור והיתר וסמיכה בני א"י עדיפי שלומדים תורה ברבים ואמרינן (ב"ב דף קנח:) אוירא דארץ ישראל מחכים*:

עבדינן כוותייהו. לא עבדי (א) כוותייהו ה"ל למימר ומשום פ"ק דחולין (דף יח:) נקט הכי דקאמר התם כי סליק רבי זירא אכל מוגרמת דרב ושמואל ופריך ולית ליה לרבי זירא נותנין עליו חומרי מקום וכו' ומשני אביי הני מילי וכו' אבל מבבל לארץ ישראל כיון דאנן כייפינן להו עבדינן כוותייהו:

רבה בר בר חנה דעתו לחזור הוה. ובחולין נמי מתרץ רבי זירא אין דעתו לחזור הוה קצת קשה דהשתא לגדדין קתני (ב) וחומרי מקום שיצא משם בדעתו לחזור וחומרי מקום שהלך לשם באין דעתו לחזור:

אני

ט א טוש"ע אה"ע סי' כג סעיף ו בהג"ה:
י ב מיי' פ"ה מהל' ת"ת הלכה ו טוש"ע י"ד סי' רמב סעיף טז:
יא ג מיי' פ"ח מהלכות י"ט הלכה כ סמג לאוין עה טוש"ע א"ח סי' תסח סעיף ד:

[וע"ע תוספות ערכין קה: ד"ה רבי יוסי]

ס"א ברבן גמליאל

[וע"ע תוס' חולין יח: ד"ה כיון]

[תוספתא ד"ק פ"ב]

[תוספתא דמ"ק שם]

[ג"ז שם]

[כמס' שמחות פי"ב]

[כהלפס הגי' איא ובר"ח הגי' עויא]

לאבוה רש"ל

חולין יח:

הגהות הב"ח

(א) תוס' ד"ה עבדי' כוותייהו לא עבדי כוותן ה"ל למימר: (ב) ד"ה רבה וכו' וחומרי מקום:

רבינו חננאל

ואסקינ' אמר רב אשי חזינן אי רובא דבני הוזאי אורז אכלי לא ניכלה זר באנפייהו כי היכי דלא תשתכח תורת חלה מינייהו ואי רובא חיטי ושערי אכלי ניכלה זר להאי חלת האורז באפייהו כדי שיתברר להם שאין בה תורת חלה דחיישינן דלמא אתו לאפרושי חלה מן עיסה של אורז על עיסה של חטין דאתו למימר כיון שכלן חייבין בחלה מין אחד מהן זה פוטר את זה: גופה דברים המותרים ואחרים נהגו בהן איסור אי אתה רשאי להתירן בפניהם אוקמה רב חסדא בכותאי מאי טעמא משום דסרכי אומרין הלא דבר פלוני היינו נוהגין בו איסור והיה מותר כן גם דבר זה מותר הוא ויבואו להתיר האיסור לפיכך כל דבר שנהגו בו איסור אין מתירין אותו להם ולאו כותאי בלבד אלא אפי' מקום שאינן בני תורה וחיישינן כי האי תנא אין מתירין להם כגון כבול שנהגו שלא לרחוץ שני אחים כאחד ונכנסו יהודה והלל בני ר"ג לרחוץ כאחד ולעזה עליהם כל המדינה אמרו לא ראינו כך מימינו ונשמט הלל ויצא לבית החיצון ולא רצה לומר מותרים אתם וכן בבירי נהגו שלא לצאת בשבת בקורדקיסן פי' מנעל שאין לו עקב והוא סנדל ויצאו יהודה והלל בקורדקייסן בשבת ולעזות המדינה עליהם כו' וכן בעכו נהגו שלא לישב על ספסלי גוים בשבת ונזדמן לרשב"ג וישב בשבת בעכו על ספסלי גוים שיש להם בחנויות ולעזה עליו המדינה וכו' הנה אלו כלן לא רצו לומר להם מותרין אתם ושני' בני מדינות נמי כיון דלא שכיחי רבנן גבייהו אתו למסרך ולהתיר כמו שאמרנו על הכותים. שני אחים מאי טעמא כדתניא עם הכל אדם רוחץ חוץ מאביו וחמיו ובעל אמו והוא הדין לבעל אחותו וגזרו על שני אחים כאחד משום בעל אחותו: תנא תלמיד לא ירחוץ עם רבו ואם רבו צריך לו מותר. ירושלמי ר' אלעזר בשם ר' אבון כל דבר שאינו יודע שהוא מותר וטעה בו באיסור נשאל ומתירין לו וכל דבר שיודע שמותר ונהג בו באיסור נשאל ואין מתירין לו. כל הדברים תלוי אותן במנהג נשים דנהגן דלא למעבד עובדא ביומא דירחא מנהגא דלא עבדי באפוקי שבתא עד דתתפני סדרא ובשני ובחמישי עד דתתפני תעניתא מנהגא: כי אתא רבה בר בר חנה בבבל אכל השומן דאייתרא דנהגו בבבל איסור כדגרסינן באלו טרפות [דף נ:] דאקשתא של קיבה כ"ע לא פליגי דאסור והוא החלב שעליה שלמעלה דאייתרא אויא א"ר אמי מקמצין והכא בבבל נהגו בו איסור שמעיה דר' חנינא הוה קאי קמיה[דר' חנינא] אמר קטוף (יהבו ליה) [והב לי] דאיכול חזייה דהוה מחסם א"ל בבלאי את (פום) [תפום] שדי עול לגבי רבה בר בר חנה רב אויא ורבה בר נתן כדחזנהו כסייה להא דאיתרא דהוה אכיל ליה אמר להו אביי כותאי שויניכו שאין מתירין בפניהם דברים שנהגו בהן איסור ורבה בר בר חנה היכי עביד הכי והתנן נותנין עליו חומרי מקום שהלך לשם והנה בבבל שהוא שם עתה איסור היו נוהגין בה ופריק רב אשי דעתו לחזור הוה ומי שדעתו לחזור אין נותנין עליו חומרי אותו מקום שהלך לשם. אמר ליה רבה בר בר חנה לבריה אני שראיתי את ר' יוחנן דאכל דאיתרא כדאי הוא ר' יוחנן למסמך עליו בפניו ושלא בפניו אתה לא תאכל לא בפני ולא שלא בפני מכלל שהבא מכח אחר שיראה מי שעשה מעשה אע"פ שהוא עושה כמותו אחרים אין סומכין עליו בפניו וכל שכן שלא בפניו. איני והא איהו דאמר סח לי

treat them as forbidden,[3] [51a] you may not permit it in their presence? Said he to him, Yet was it not stated thereon, R. Ḥisda said: This refers to Cutheans.[4] What is the reason in the case of Cutheans? Because they confound one thing [with another]![5] Then these people too [being ignorant] confound one thing [with another]?—Rather, said R. Ashi, we consider: if most of them eat rice [bread], a lay Israelite must not eat it [the *ḥallah*] in their presence, lest the law of *ḥallah* be [altogether] forgotten by them; but if most of them eat corn [bread], let a lay Israelite eat it in their presence, lest they come to separate [*ḥallah*] from what is liable upon what is exempt, and from what is exempt upon what is liable.[6]

[It was stated in] the text: 'Things which are permitted, yet others treat them as forbidden, you may not permit it in their presence. Said R. Ḥisda: This refers to Cutheans'. Yet not [to] all people? Surely it was taught: Two brothers may bathe together,[7] yet two brothers do not bathe [together] in Cabul.[8] And it once happened that Judah and Hillel, the sons of R. Gamaliel, bathed together in Cabul, and the whole region criticized them, saying, 'We have never seen such [a thing] in [all] our days;' whereupon Hillel slipped away and went to the outer chamber,[1] but he was unwilling to tell them, 'You are permitted [to do this]'. [Again,] one may go out in slippers on the Sabbath,[2] yet people do not go out in slippers in Beri.[3] And it once happened that Judah and Hillel, the sons of R. Gamaliel, went out in slippers on the Sabbath in Beri, whereupon the whole district criticized them, saying, 'We have never seen such [a thing] in [all] our days'; so they removed them and gave them to their [non-Jewish] servants, but they were unwilling to tell them, 'You are permitted [to wear these].' Again, one may sit on the stools of Gentiles on the Sabbath,[4] yet people do not sit on the stools of Gentiles on the Sabbath in Acco.[5] And it once happened that R. Simeon b. Gamaliel sat down on the stools of Gentiles on the Sabbath in Acco, and the whole district criticized him, saying, 'We have never seen such [a thing] in [all] our days'. [Accordingly] he slipped down on to the ground, but he was unwilling to tell them, 'You are permitted [to do this]'.[6]—The people of the coastal region, since Rabbis are not common among them, are like Cutheans.[7]

As for [not sitting on] Gentiles' stools, that is well, [the reason being] because it looks like [engaging] in buying and selling. [That they do not go out] in slippers too [is understandable], lest they fall off and they come to carry them four cubits in the street. But what is the reason that [brothers] do not bathe [together]?—As it was taught: A man may bathe with all, except with his father, his father-in-law, his mother's husband and his sister's husband.[8] But R. Judah permits [a man to bathe] with his father, on account of his father's honour,[1] and the same applies to his mother's husband. Then they [the people of Cabul] came and forbade [it] in the case of two brothers on account of [bathing with] his sister's husband.[2]

It was taught: A disciple must not bathe with his teacher, but if his teacher needs him, it is permitted.

When Rabbah b. Bar Ḥanah came,[3] he ate of the stomach fat.[4] Now, R. 'Awira[5] the Elder and Rabbah son of R. Huna visited him; as soon as he saw them, he hid[6] it [the fat] from them. When they narrated it to Abaye he said to them, 'He has treated you like Cutheans'. But does not Rabbah b. Bar Ḥanah agree with what we learned: WE LAY UPON HIM THE RESTRICTIONS OF THE PLACE WHENCE HE DEPARTED AND THE RESTRICTIONS OF THE PLACE WHITHER HE HAS GONE?—Said Abaye: That is only [when he goes] from [one town in] Babylonia to [another in] Babylonia, or from [a town in] Palestine to [another in] Palestine, or from [a town in] Babylonia to [another in] Palestine; but not [when he goes] from [a place in] Palestine to [another in] Babylonia, [for] since we submit to them,[7] we do as they.[8] R. Ashi said: You may even say [that this holds good when a man goes] from Palestine to Babylonia; this is, however, where it is not his intention to return; but Rabbah b. Bar Ḥanah had the intention of returning.

Rabbah b. Bar Ḥanah said to his son: My son, do not eat [this fat], whether in my presence or not in my presence. As for me who saw R. Joḥanan eat [it], R. Joḥanan is sufficient [an authority] to rely upon in his presence and not in his presence. [But] you have not seen him [eat it]; [therefore] do not eat, whether in my presence or not in my presence. Now, [one statement] of his disagrees with [another statement] of his. For Rabbah b. Bar Ḥanah said: R. Joḥanan b. Eleazar related to me: I once followed R. Simeon son of R. Jose b. Lakunia into a kitchen

(3) Lit., 'practise a prohibition in connection with them'. (4) The people whom Shalmaneser settled in Samaria after the deportation of the Ten Tribes. They formally accepted Judaism, but as they retained many heathen practices, their religious status fluctuated, until they were finally declared heathens. In the present passage they are treated as Jews, but so lax as to require special laws. (5) If they were treated with leniency in one case, their laxity in general would increase. (6) *Ḥallah* can be separated from one piece of dough upon another piece, providing that both are liable; but if one is liable while the other is not, the separated piece is not *ḥallah*, while the other remains forbidden as *ṭebel*. Hence if they separate *ḥallah* from rice dough, which is really exempt, upon dough of wheat, which is liable, the latter remains *ṭebel*, and by eating it they transgress. Again, if they separate *ḥallah* from wheat dough upon itself and upon a rice dough, the former is not *ḥallah* but likewise *ṭebel*, and when it is given to the priest he eats *ṭebel*. (7) Lit., 'as one'—without fear that this may induce a desire for pederasty. (8) A place south-east of Acco. Though the fear of pederasty may seem far-fetched, this is not so when its prevalence in the Roman Empire is remembered; v. Weiss, *Dor*, II, 21f.

a (1) Of the baths. (2) Though they are loose-fitting; we do not fear that they may fall off and the wearer will thus come to carry them in the street, which of course is forbidden. (3) A town in Galilee. (4) When they are engaged in business, and we do not fear that the Jew who sits down there will be suspected of doing the same. (5) A town and harbour on the coast of Phoenicia. (6) In all these instances Jews are referred to, yet we see that this law holds good. (7) In that leniency may lead to laxity, where there is none to show them the difference between what is mere stringency and what is really prohibited by law. (8) In their case this may lead to impure thoughts.

b (1) He can perform some services for him and help him. (2) Lest the latter be thought permitted too. (3) From Palestine to Babylonia. (4) The stomach is partly curved, like a bow, and partly straight, like the string of a bow, which is the meaning of the present word. The fat on the straight part of the stomach is really permitted, but in Babylonia it was treated as forbidden. (5) Alfasi and Rosh read: 'Awia. (6) Lit., 'covered'. (7) We accept their jurisdiction. (8) I.e., a Palestinian going to Babylonia may retain his home practice, for this cannot give rise to quarrels.

Continuation of translation from previous page as indicated by ◁

Our Rabbis taught: He who looks to the earnings of his wife or of a mill will never see a sign of blessing. 'The earnings of his wife' means [when she goes around selling wool] by weight.[3] '[The earnings of] a mill' means its hire.[4] But if she makes [e.g., woollen garments] and sells them, Scripture indeed praises her, for it is written, *she maketh linen garments and selleth them*.[5]

Our Rabbis taught: He who trades in cane and jars will never see a sign of blessing. What is the reason? Since their bulk is large, the [evil] eye has power over them.

Our Rabbis taught: Traders in market-stands[6] and those who breed small cattle,[7] and those who cut down beautiful trees,[8] and those who cast their eyes at the better portion,[9] will never see a sign of blessing. What is the reason? Because people gaze at them.[10]

Our Rabbis taught: Four *perutoth* never contain a sign of blessing:[11] the wages of clerks, the wages of interpreters,[12] the profits
d of orphans,[1] and money that came from oversea countries. As for the wages of interpreters, that is well, [the reason being] because it looks like wages for Sabbath [work]; orphans' money too, because they are not capable of renunciation;[2] money which comes from overseas, because a miracle does not occur every day.[3] But what is the reason for the wages of writers?—Said R. Joshua b. Levi: The men of the Great Assembly[4] observed twenty-four fasts so that those who write Scrolls, *tefillin* and *mezuzoth*[5] should not become wealthy, for if they became wealthy they would not write.

Our Rabbis taught: Those who write Scrolls, *tefillin*, and *mezuzoth*, they, their traders and their traders' traders,[6] and all who engage [in trade] in sacred commodities,[7] which includes the sellers of blue wool,[8] never see a sign of blessing. But if they engage [therein] for its own sake,[9] they do see [a sign of blessing].

The citizens of Beyshan[10] were accustomed not to go from Tyre to Sidon[11] on the eve of the Sabbath. Their children went to R. Joḥanan and said to them, For our fathers this was possible; for us it is impossible. Said he to them, Your fathers have already taken it upon themselves, as it is said, *Hear my son, the instruction of thy father, and forsake not the teaching of thy mother*.[12]

The inhabitants of Ḥozai[13] were accustomed to separate *ḥallah*
e on rice.[1] [When] they went and told it to R. Joseph he said to them, Let a lay Israelite eat it in their presence:[2] Abaye raised an objection against him: Things which are permitted, yet others

(3) Jast.; i.e., trading in wool, but not making it up; this realizes very little profit and is not a dignified occupation for a woman. (4) But trading in mills, buying and selling them, is profitable. (5) Prov. XXXI, 24. This occurs in the description of the 'woman of valour'. (6) [Heb. *Simṭa*. Tosef. Bek. II has *Shemiṭṭah*, the Sabbatical year when trading with produce is forbidden.] (7) Sheep, goats, etc. (8) To sell for their timber. (9) When sharing with their neighbour. (10) Market traders are exposed to the public gaze, and so to the evil eye, which was regarded as a potent source of misfortune. The other three incur the ill-will of people, the first because breeding small animals was generally frowned upon. (11) *Peruṭah* was the smallest coin. I.e., the monies earned by the four things enumerated. (12) Officials who spoke the Sabbath lectures of the Sages to the congregation; the Sage whispered his statements to the interpreter, and he explained them to the people. Also, those who publicly interpreted and translated the weekly readings of the Law on the Sabbath.

d (1) Orphans' money was sometimes entrusted to people to trade with, and they kept half the profit for themselves for their labour. (2) He may take more than his due, and a minor cannot legally renounce it in his favour. (3) Considerable danger attended the transport of freights at sea, and one might very easily suffer loss. (4) A body of one hundred and twenty men founded by Ezra, regarded as the bearers of Jewish teaching and tradition after the Prophets; v. Ab. I, 1. (5) V. Glos. (6) All who trade in these, whether directly or indirectly. (7) Lit., 'work'. (8) Wool dyed blue for insertion in garments as fringes; v. Num. XV, 38. (9) To benefit the community, profit being a secondary consideration. (10) Beyshan (Scythopolis) in Galilee (Jast.). [Beyshan was, however, far too distant from Tyre to enable its inhabitants to go there and back in one day. It must therefore be located in the neighbourhood of Tyre and it is identified with the village at Abasiya, N.E. of Tyre (Hurwitz, *Palestine*, p. 112).] (11) On the coast of Palestine. Friday was market day at Sidon (Rashi). (12) Prov. I, 8. (13) Known to-day as Khuzistan, in S. W. Persia; Obermeyer, pp. 204ff.

e (1) Which is unnecessary by law. (2) *Ḥallah* may be eaten by a priest only. Thus he intimated that this was not *ḥallah*.

עין משפט נר מצוה

ב א מיי' פ"ו מהל' שמטה ויובל הל' יג:

ג ב טוש"ע או"ח סי' רנא סעיף א:

[נ"ל דרבה]

ד ג ד מיי' פ"ג מהל' ת"ת הל' ה ופ"י מהל' ת"ת הל' יד טוש"ע או"ח סי' רנא סעיף א וטוש"ע י"ד סי' רמו סעיף כא:

ה ה מיי' פכ"ו מהל' שבת הלכה ה סמג עשין כט טוש"ע או"ח סי' רנא סעיף י:

ו ו מיי' פ"ג מהלכות תענית הלכה ד טוש"ע או"ח סי' תקעה סעיף ג:

[עי' תוס' תענית ז. ד"ה וכל העוסק ותוס' ברכות יז. ד"ה העושה]

ז ז מיי' פ"ג מהל' ת"ת הלכה ה ופ"י מהלכות תשובה הלכה ה סמג עשין יג טוש"ע יו"ד סי' רמו סעיף כ:

ז [ו] [מיי' פ"ב מהל' שבת הלכה יג טוש"ע או"ח סי' רמח סעיף א]:

ח ח טוש"ע יו"ד סי' ריד סעיף א ב:

תוספות

העושה מלאכה במוצאי שבתות. אור"י דאיתא בירושלמי הכי הני נשי דנהיגי דלא למעבד עבידתא באפוקי שבתא לאו מנהגא עד דיתפני סידרא מנהגא פי' (ג) שישלים התפלה מנהג כשר ובהא איירי נמי הכא: **וכאן** בעושים שלא לשמה וכדרב יהודה. תימה (דרב) גופיה אמר בפ"ב דברכות (ד' יז.) כל העוסק בתורה שלא לשמה נוח לו שלא נברא ואור"י דהתם מיירי כגון שלומד כדי להתייהר ולקנטר ולקפח את חביריו בהלכה ואינו לומד ע"מ לעשות אבל הכא מיירי דומיא דהאי דלעיל יש שפל ונשכר דלא עביד כוליה שבתא ולא במעלי שבתא שאין מתכוון לשום רעה אלא מתוך עצלות אפ"ה גדול עד שמים חסדו*: **מתקולתא**. מטוה לכך קורא אותה מתקולתא לפי שנשכרת לשיעור משקל מטוה כדתנן בכתובות (ד' סד:) כמה היא עושה לו משקל ה' סלעים ופר"ח שהיא מתבזה על כך שהיא מגלה זרועותיה בשעת טוויה: **ומגדלי** בהמה. וקשה לר"ת דאמר (בחולין ד' פד:) הרוצה שיתעשר יעסוק בבהמה דקה ואמר נמי עשתרות שמעשרות את בעליהן וי"ל דהתם בחורשין: **כותבי** ספרים. אור"י בשם ריב"א דדוקא הכותבים כדי למכור עליהן בקשו דלעולם ימצאו לוקחין כדקתני הן ותגריהם אבל על המשכירים עצמן לבעלי בתים לא בקשו שלא היו מקפחים פרנסתן שלא ימצאו כל כך להשתכר: **די**"מא אתי לאפרושי מן הפטור על החיוב. וא"ת והיכי אתי למיטעי תיפוק ליה דמפריש ממין על שאין מינו וי"ל דבבלול איכא למיטעי דלית ביה משום מין על שאין מינו כדפי' בפ' כל שעה (לעיל לה.) ואיכא למיחש שתהא עיסה רובה אורז במקום אחד ויפריש מאותו צד על צד אחר: אי

גמרא

ואל ישנה אדם מפני המחלוקת כיוצא בו *המוליך פירות שביעית *ממקום שכלו למקום שלא כלו או ממקום שלא כלו למקום שכלו חייב לבער ר' יהודה אומר צא והבא לך אף אתה: **גמ'** *מאי איריא ערבי פסחים אפילו ערבי שבתות וערבי ימים טובים נמי דתניא [ו]העושה מלאכה בערבי שבתות וימים טובים מן המנחה ולמעלה אינו רואה סימן ברכה לעולם התם מן המנחה ולמעלה הוא דאסור סמוך למנחה לא [ו]הכא מחצות אי נמי התם סימן ברכה הוא דלא חזי אבל שמותי לא משמתינן ליה [ו]הכא שמותי נמי משמתינן ליה גופא העושה מלאכה בערבי שבתות ובערבי ימים טובים מן המנחה ולמעלה [ו]ובמוצאי שבת ובמוצאי יו"ט ובמוצאי יום הכפורים ובכל מקום שיש שם נידנוד עבירה [ו]לאתויי [א] תענית ציבור אינו רואה סימן ברכה לעולם: ת"ר *יש זריז ונשכר ויש זריז ונפסד יש שפל ונשכר ויש שפל ונפסד זריז ונשכר דעביד כולי שבתא ולא עביד במעלי שבתא זריז ונפסד דעביד כולי שבתא ועביד במעלי שבתא שפל ונשכר דלא עביד כולי שבתא ולא עביד במעלי שבתא שפל ונפסד דלא עביד כולי שבתא ועביד במעלי שבתא אמר רבא *הני נשי דמחוזא אע"ג דלא עבדן עבידתא במעלי שבתא משום מפנקותא הוא דהא כל יומא נמי לא קא עבדן אפילו הכי שפל ונשכר קרינן להו רבא רמי כתיב °כי גדול עד שמים חסדך וכתיב °כי גדול מעל שמים חסדך הא כיצד כאן בעושין לשמה וכאן בעושין שלא לשמה וכדרב יהודה (א) *דאמר רב יהודה אמר רב [ו]לעולם יעסוק אדם בתורה ומצות אף על פי שלא לשמה שמתוך שלא לשמה בא לשמה: תנו רבנן המצפה לשכר אשתו וריחים אינו רואה סימן ברכה לעולם שכר אשתו מתקולתא ריחייא אגרתא אבל עבדה ומזבנה אישתבוחי משתבח בה קרא דכתיב °סדין עשתה ותמכור: ת"ר המשתכר בקנים ובקנקנים אינו רואה סימן ברכה לעולם מאי טעמא כיון דנפיש אפחזייהו שלטא בהו עינא: תנו רבנן *תגרי סימטא ומגדלי בהמה דקה וקוצצי אילנות טובות [ו]ונותנין עיניהן בחלק יפה אינו רואה סימן ברכה לעולם מאי טעמא דתהו ביה אינשי: ת"ר ד' פרוטות אין בהן סימן ברכה לעולם שכר כותבין ושכר מתורגמנין ושכר יתומים ומעות הבאות ממדינת הים בשלמא שכר מתורגמנין משום דמיחזי כשכר שבת ומעות *יתומים נמי לאו בני מחילה נינהו מעות הבאות ממדינת הים משום *דלאו כל יומא מתרחיש ניסא אלא שכר כותבין מאי טעמא א"ר יהושע בן לוי כ"ד תעניות ישבו אנשי כנסת הגדולה על כותבי ספרים תפילין ומזוזות שלא יתעשרו *שאילמלי מתעשרין אין כותבין: ת"ר *כותבי ספרים תפילין ומזוזות הן ותגריהן ותגרי תגריהן וכל העוסקין במלאכת שמים לאיתויי מוכרי תכלת אינן רואין סימן ברכה לעולם ואם עוסקין לשמה רואין: בני ביישן [ו] נהוג דלא הוו אזלין מצור לצידון במעלי שבתא אתו בנייהו קמיה דר' יוחנן אמרו לו אבהתין אפשר להו אנן לא אפשר לן (ג) אמר להו [ו]כבר קיבלו אבותיכם עליהם שנאמר °שמע בני מוסר אביך ואל תטוש תורת אמך: בני חוזאי נהגי דמפרשי חלה מארוזא אתו ואמרו ליה לרב יוסף אמר להו ניכלה זר באפייהו איתיביה אביי *°דברים המותרים ואחרים נהגו בהן איסור אי

רש"י

ואל ישנה אדם. בגמרא פריך ממקום שאין עושין למקום שעושין והיינו נמי אל ישנה וליעבד והא אמרת נותנין עליו חומרי מקום שיצא משם: המוליך פירות שביעית ממקום שכלו. לחיה מן השדה וחייבין בני המקום לבער מן הבית והוליכן זה למקום שלא כלו תורה אור ובני אותו מקום עדיין אוכלין הכנוסין בבית: חייב לבער. משום חומרי מקום שיצא משם: צא והבא לך אף אתה. מפרש בגמרא: **גמ'** מאי איריא ערבי פסחים. דקתני עד חצות במנהגא מכלל דמחלוקת ולהכן אסור ולמה ליה למיתני חצות לאשמעינן הך דיוקא הא כל ערבי ימים טובים אסירי: מן המנחה. תשע שעות ומחצה: סמוך למנחה. קודם לכן: נידנוד עבירה. רמז עבירה: תענית צבור. אסור במלאכה במסכת תענית (דף יב:) כשהיו מתענין על הגשמים אבל שאר תענית ציבור לא כדאמר שמואל אין חומר תענית ציבור בבבל (לקמן דף נד:): במוצאי שבתות. משום כבוד שבת שמוסיפין מחול על הקדש: זריז. בעל מלאכה: שפל ונשכר דלא עביד כוליה שבתא ולא במעלי שבתא. ואע"ג דלאו לשום מצוה מיכוין מצוה שלא לשמה מיהא הויא דאמרינן לקמן יעסוק אדם במצוה ואפי' שלא לשמה: ה"ג ואע"ג דהאי דלא קעבדן כו': עושין לשמה. מעל שמים ושלא לשמה עד לשמים דמצוה מיהא קא עביד כדרב יהודה: מתקולתא. טוטלת מחזיקים בידה ומהלכת בשוק להשכירן לכל הצריכין דשכר מועט הוא ומתבזה אשה על שכר מועט: אגרתא. שכר ריחיים שמשכירין מורת גדול ושכר מועט הוא אבל קונה ריחיים ומוכרן הרי הוא כשאר פרקמטיא: בקנים. כל מקלות דקים קרי קנים שעושין מהן גדרות ומחיצות: אפחזייהו. נפח שלהן: תגרי סימטא. יושבין ומוכרין בשוק ועין שולטת בהן ומגדלי בהמה דקה. הכל צווחין עליהן: וקוצצי אילנות טובות למוכרן לעצים הכל תמיהים ומלעיזין עליהם ומתוך כך עין שולטת בהן ולעקת בני אדם: ונותנין עיניהם בחלק יפה. כשחולקים עם אחרים תמיד מקפידין ליטול חלק יפה: מתורגמנין. שעומדין לפני החכם בשבתות ושומעין מפיו ומשמיעין לרבים: ומעות יתומין. למחלה שכר: ממדינת הים. משלח ספינותיו תמיד ממקום סכנה: תכלת. לציצית: אינן רואין. כדאמרן שאם יתעשרו לא יהו עסוקין: ואם עוסקין לשמה. להיות המצוה מצויה לצריכין לה רואין. דהואיל ולשמה עושין לא יניחו בשביל עשרן: מצור לצידון. יום השוק של צידון בע"ש והם מחמירים על עצמן שלא להיבטל מלרכי שבת הוה אפשר להו. להמנע מן השוק שעשירים היו: מארוזא. אורז דסרכי

[מיוחס' לקמן נג. ד"ה ממקום]

[עי' תוס' לקמן נה: ד"ה מאן איריא]

[תוספתא דיבמות פ"ד]

[שבת לג:]

סנהדרין קה. ערכין טז: סוטה כב: מז. הוריות י: נזיר כג:

[תוספתא דבכורים פ"ב ושם הגירסא שמיטה]

[ב"מ כב:]

[מגילה ז:]

[תוספתא דבכורים פ"ב]

[עי' תוס' מגילה כא. ד"ה אלמין]

נדרים טו. פא: [מגילה ה:]

סייך לקמן

תהלים קח / תהלים נז

משלי לא

משלי א

הגהות הב"ח

(א) גמרא וכדרב יהודה אמר רב דאמר רב יהודה: (ב) שם לא אפשר לן מאי אמר להו: (ג) תוס' ד"ה העושה וכו' פי' עד שישלים:

הגהות הגר"א

[א] גמרא לאתויי תענית. נמחק כל"ז:

רבינו חננאל

ברכה לעולם ושני' התם עד המנחה ולמעלה הכא מחצות אי נמי התם ברכה לא חזי הכא בערב הפסח העושה מלאכה מחצות היום ולמעלה זולתי שהתירו להם חכמים משמתינן ליה: **גופא** העושה מלאכה בערבי שבתות ובערבי ימים טובים ובמוצאי שבתות ובמוצאי ימים טובים מן המנחה ולמעלה ובתענית צבור אינו רואה סימן ברכה לעולם. תוספתא בתחלת יבמות יש זריז ונשכר דעביד מלאכה כל יום ואינו עושה שבת מן המנחה ולמעלה זריז ומפסיד שעושה כל השבוע ובערב שבת שפל ונשכר שאינו עושה מלאכה לא בכל השבוע ולא בערב שבת שפל ומפסיד כל השבוע יושב ובטל ובערב שבת עושה מלאכה: **גדול** מעל שמים חסדך אלו העושין לשמה כי גדול עד שמים חסדך אלו העושין שלא לשמה שאע"פ שעושין שלא לשמה יש להם חסד כדרב יהודה אמר רב דאמר רב לעולם יעסוק אדם בתורה ובמצות אפי' שלא לשמה שמתוך שלא לשמה בא לשמה: **המצפה** לשכר אשתו כדי להתפרנס ממנו.פי' מתקן משקל המטוה שטווה בכל יום ושכר הרחים שכירות מפני שהוא דבר מועט אינו רואה סימן ברכה בזה הדרך: **ת"ר** ארבע פרוטות הן אין בהן ברכה שכר ברכה שבקשו עליהן אנשי כנסת הגדולה מלפני הקב"ה שלא יתעשרו שכר מתורגמנין הדרשנין שדורשין בשבת לצבור ועושין להן פסיקה נראה כאלו שכר שבת הוא והנושא והנותן במעות של יתומים קרוב לשכר ורחוק להפסד פעמים שאינו מדקדק היטב היטב ויתמי לאו בני מחילה נינהו ומעות הבאות ממדינת הים פעמים שילך [לאבוד] הכל בבת אחת כגון שנטבעה הספינה: **ת"ר** כותבי ספרים תפלין ומזוזות הן ותגריהן ותגרי תגריהן וכל העוסקין במלאכת שמים לאתויי מוכרי תכלת אין רואין סימן ברכה ואם עוסקין לשמה מתברכין: **בני** בישן נהוג שלא לילך בצידן בערב שבת ובאו בניהן ואמרו לו לר' יוחנן אבותינו היו עשירים ולא היו צריכים לעשות מלאכה בערב שבת ואנו עניים מהו לילך ולישא וליתן אמר להם כבר קבלו אבותיכם עליהם דכתיב ואל תטוש תורת אמך ופי' בירושלמי כי לפרש בים שאלוהו ואסר להם משום דסבר אסור לפרש בים הגדול אבל זה אפי' נדר נשאל ומתירין לו ולא אסר אלא דסבר אסור לפרש בים: **בני** בי חוזאי נהגו להפריש חלה מן האורז שאינו חייב בחלה ואסקינן

גליון הש"ס גמ' ונותנין עיניהן בחלק יפה. עיין מ"ק כ"ח ע"ב תד"ה וליטול:

PLACE WHITHER HE HAS GONE; [50b] AND A MAN MUST NOT ACT DIFFERENTLY [FROM LOCAL CUSTOM] ON ACCOUNT OF THE QUARRELS [WHICH WOULD ENSUE]. SIMILARLY, HE WHO TRANSPORTS SABBATICAL YEAR PRODUCE FROM A PLACE WHERE IT HAS CEASED TO A PLACE WHERE IT HAS NOT CEASED OR FROM A PLACE WHERE IT HAS NOT CEASED TO A PLACE
a WHERE IT HAS CEASED,[1] IS BOUND TO REMOVE IT.[2] R. JUDAH SAID: 'DO YOU TOO GO OUT AND BRING [PRODUCE] FOR YOURSELF'.[3]

GEMARA. Why particularly THE EVE OF PASSOVER? Even on the eve of Sabbaths and Festivals too? For it was taught: He who does work on the eve of Sabbaths or Festivals from *minḥah*[4] and onwards will never see a sign of blessing?[5]—There
b it is forbidden only from *minḥah* and onwards, but not near to[1] *minḥah*; [whereas] here it is [forbidden] from midday. Alternatively, there he merely does not see a sign of blessing,[2] yet we do not place him under the ban; [whereas] here we even place him under the ban.

[To turn to] the main text: He who does work on the eve of the Sabbath and on the eve of Festivals from *minḥah* and onwards, and at the termination of the Sabbath or at the termination of a Festival, or at the termination of the Day of Atonement, or wherever there is the [least] suspicion of sin,[3] which is to include a public fast,[4] will never see the sign of a blessing.

Our Rabbis taught: Some are industrious and profit [thereby,] while others are industrious and suffer loss; some are indolent[5] and profit [thereby], while others are indolent and suffer loss. An industrious man who profits,—he who works the whole week but does not work on the eve of the Sabbath. An industrious man who suffers loss,—he who works the whole week and works on the eve of the Sabbath. An indolent man who profits,—he who does not work the whole week and does not work on the eve of the Sabbath.[6] An indolent man who suffers loss,—he who does not work the whole week but works on the eve of the Sabbath. Raba said: As to these women of Maḥuza,[7] though they do not work on the eve of the Sabbath, it is because they are used to indulgence [indolence], seeing that they do not work every day either. Yet even so, we call them, 'an indolent person who profits'.[8]

Raba opposed [two verses]. It is written, *For thy mercy is great* unto *the heavens;*[9] whereas it is also written, *For thy mercy is great* above *the heavens?*[10] How is this [to be explained]? Here it refers
c to those who perform [God's behest] for its own sake;[1] there it refers to those who perform [it] with an ulterior motive.[2] And [this is] in accordance with Rab Judah. For Rab Judah said in Rab's name: A man should always occupy himself with Torah and good deeds, though it is not for their own sake, for out of [doing good] with an ulterior motive there comes [doing good] for its own sake.

a (1) The law concerning produce of the Sabbatical year is this: as long as there is produce in the field available for animals, a man may keep produce at home as his private property; but when the produce in the field has ceased, the animals having consumed it, he must carry out the produce from his home and declare it free for all. Having done this, he may then take back into the house whatever he needs for his private use (Tosaf. 52b, s.v. מתבערין). (2) I.e., place it at everybody's disposal. (3) This is explained in the Gemara. (4) The afternoon service, and the time for same—beginning generally two and a half hours before nightfall. (5) I.e., the money earned then will not be profitable.

b (1) I.e., before. (2) I.e., it is inadvisable. (3) As he may continue work after the Sabbath or Festival has actually commenced; or begin before they have quite terminated. (4) Proclaimed on account of rain, when work was forbidden, Ta'an. 12b. On other fast-days work is permitted. (5) Lit., 'low'. (6) Though his abstention then is due to indolence, not to respect for the Sabbath, he is nevertheless rewarded, since in fact he does abstain. (7) V. 5b, n. c5. (8) [Var. lec. (v. Rashi); These women of Maḥuza, although the reason they do no work . . . Sabbath is that they are used . . , yet even so are called etc.] (9) Ps. LVII, 11. (10) Ibid. CVIII, 5.

c (1) Lit., 'name'. To them His mercy is great above the heavens. (2) Lit., 'not for its own name'.

◁ *For the continuation of the English translation of this page see overleaf.*

ב א מיי' פ"ח מהל' שמטה ויובל הל' יב:
ג ב טוש"ע או"ח סי' רנא סעיף א:
ד ג ד מיי' פ"ח מהל' י"ט הל' יז ופ"ג מהל' ת"ת הל' ה טוש"ע או"ח סי' תסח סעיף א וטוש"ע י"ד סי' רמו סעיף כא:
ה ה מיי' פכ"ג מהל' שבת הלכה ה סמג עשין כט טוש"ע או"ח סי' רנא סעיף ב:
ו ו מיי' פ"ג מהלכות תענית הלכה ז טוש"ע או"ח סי' תקעה סעיף ג:
ז ז מיי' פ"ג מהל' ת"ת הלכה ה ופ"י מהלכות תשובה הלכה ה סמג עשין יב טוש"ע י"ד סי' רמו סעיף כ:
ח [ז] מיי' פ"ו מהל' ת"ת הל' יד טוש"ע או"ח סי' רמח סעיף ח:
ט ח מ טוש"ע י"ד סי' ריד סעיף א ב:

תוספות

העושה מלאכה במוצאי שבתות. אור"י דאיתא בירושלמי הכי הני נשי דנהיגי דלא למעבד עבידתא באפוקי שבתא לאו מנהגא עד דתיתפני סידרא מנהגא פי' (ג) שישלים התפלה מנהג כשר ובהא איירי נמי הכא: **וכאן** בעושים שלא לשמה וכדרב יהודה. תימה (דרב) גופיה אמר בפ"ב דברכות (ד' יז.) כל העוסק בתורה שלא לשמה נוח לו שלא נברא ואור"י דהתם מיירי כגון שלומד כדי להתיהר ולקנטר ולקפח את חביריו בהלכה ואינו לומד ע"מ לעשות אבל הכא מיירי דומיא דההיא דלעיל יש שפל ונשכר דלא עביד כוליה שבתא ולא במעלי שבתא שאין מתכוון לשום רעה אלא מתוך עצלות אפ"ה גדול עד שמים חסדו*: **מתקולתא**. מטוה לכך קורא אותה מתקולתא לפי שנשכרת לשיעור משקל מטוה כדתנן בכתובות (ד' סד:) כמה היא עושה לו משקל ה' סלעים ופר"ח שהיא מתבזה על כך שהיא מגלה זרועותיה בשעת טוויה: **ומגדלי** בהמה. וקשה לר"ת דאמר (בחולין ד' פד:) הרוצה שיתעשר יעסוק בבהמה דקה ואמר נמי עשתרות שמעשרות את בעליהן וי"ל דהתם בחורשין: **כותבי** ספרים. אור"י בשם ריב"א דדוקא הכותבים כדי למכור עליהן בקשו דלעולם ימצאו לוקחין כדקתני הן ותגריהם אבל על המשכירים עצמן לבעלי בתים לא בקשו שלא היו מקפחים פרנסתן שלא ימצאו כל כך להשתכר: ***דילמא** אתי לאפרושי מן הפטור על החיוב. וא"ת והיכי אתי למיטעי תיפוק ליה דמפריש ממין על שאין מינו וי"ל דבכלל איכא למיטעי דלית ביה משום מין על שאין מינו כדפי' בפ' כל שעה (לעיל לה.) ואיכא למיחש שתהא עיסה רובה אורז במקום אחד ויפריש מאותו לד על לד אחר:
אי

גמרא

ואל ישנה אדם מפני המחלוקת כיוצא בו *המוליך פירות שביעית *ממקום שכלו למקום שלא כלו או ממקום שלא כלו למקום שכלו חייב לבער ר' יהודה אומר צא והבא לך אף אתה: **גמ'** *מאי איריא ערבי פסחים אפילו ערבי שבתות וערבי ימים טובים נמי דתניא העושה מלאכה בערבי שבתות וימים טובים מן המנחה ולמעלה אינו רואה סימן ברכה לעולם התם מן המנחה ולמעלה הוא דאסור סמוך למנחה לא הכא מחצות אי נמי התם סימן ברכה הוא דלא חזי אבל שמותי לא משמתינן ליה הכא שמותי נמי משמתינן ליה גופא העושה מלאכה בערבי שבתות ובערבי ימים טובים מן המנחה ולמעלה ובמוצאי שבת ובמוצאי יו"ט ובמוצאי יום הכפורים ובכל מקום שיש שם נידנוד עבירה לאתויי [א] תענית ציבור אינו רואה סימן ברכה לעולם: ת"ר *יש זריז ונשכר ויש זריז ונפסד יש שפל ונשכר ויש שפל ונפסד זריז ונשכר דעביד כולי שבתא ולא עביד במעלי שבתא זריז ונפסד דעביד כולי שבתא ועביד במעלי שבתא שפל ונשכר דלא עביד כולי שבתא ולא עביד במעלי שבתא שפל ונפסד דלא עביד כולי שבתא ועביד במעלי שבתא אמר רבא *הני נשי דמחוזא אע"ג דלא עבדן עבידתא במעלי שבתא משום מפנקותא הוא דהא כל יומא נמי לא קא עבדן אפילו הכי שפל ונשכר קרינן להו רבא רמי כתיב °כי גדול עד שמים חסדך וכתיב °כי גדול מעל שמים חסדך הא כיצד כאן בעושין לשמה וכאן בעושין שלא לשמה וכדרב יהודה (א) *דאמר רב יהודה אמר רב לעולם יעסוק אדם בתורה ומצות אף על פי שלא לשמה שמתוך שלא לשמה בא לשמה: תנו רבנן המצפה לשכר אשתו וריחים אינו רואה סימן ברכה לעולם שכר אשתו מתקולתא ריחייא אגרתא אבל עבדה ומזבנה אישתבוחי משתבח בה קרא דכתיב °סדין עשתה ותמכור: ת"ר המשתכר בקנים ובקנקנים אינו רואה סימן ברכה לעולם מאי טעמא כיון דנפיש אפחזייהו שלטא בהו עינא: תנו רבנן *תגרי סימטא ומגדלי בהמה דקה וקוצצי אילנות טובות °ונותנין עיניהן בחלק יפה אינו רואה סימן ברכה לעולם מאי טעמא דתהו ביה אינשי: ת"ר ד' פרוטות אין בהן סימן ברכה שכר כותבין ושכר מתורגמנין ושכר יתומים ומעות הבאות ממדינת הים בשלמא שכר מתורגמנין משום דמיחזי כשכר שבת ומעות *יתומים נמי לאו בני מחילה נינהו מעות הבאות ממדינת הים משום *דלאו כל יומא מתרחיש ניסא אלא שכר כותבין מאי טעמא א"ר יהושע בן לוי כ"ד תעניות ישבו אנשי כנסת הגדולה על כותבי ספרים תפילין ומזוזות שלא יתעשרו *שאילמלי מתעשרין אין כותבין: ת"ר *כותבי ספרים תפילין ומזוזות הן ותגריהן ותגרי תגריהן וכל העוסקין במלאכת שמים לאיתויי מוכרי תכלת אינן רואין סימן ברכה לעולם ואם עוסקין לשמה רואין: בני בייישן [י] נהוג דלא הוו אזלין מצור לצידון במעלי שבתא אתו בנייהו קמיה דר' יוחנן אמרו לו אבהתין אפשר להו אנן לא אפשר לן (ב) אמר להו כבר קיבלו אבותיכם עליהם שנאמר °שמע בני מוסר אביך ואל תטוש תורת אמך: בני חוזאי נהגי דמפרשי חלה מארוזא אתו ואמרו ליה לרב יוסף אמר להו ניכלה זר באפייהו איתיביה אביי *°דברים המותרים ואחרים נהגו בהן איסור
אי

רש"י

ואל ישנה אדם. בגמרא פריך ממקום שאין עושין למקום שעושין ואיהו נמי אל ישנה וליעבד והא אמרת נותנין עליו חומרי מקום שיצא משם: **המוליך** פירות שביעית ממקום שכלו. לחיה מן השדה וחייבין בני המקום לבערן מן הבית והוליכן זה למקום שלא כלו ובני אותו מקום עדיין אוכלין הכנוסין בבית: **חייב** לבער. משום חומרי מקום שיצא משם: **צא** והבא לך אף אתה. מפרש בגמרא: **גמ'** מאי איריא ערבי פסחים. דקתני עד חצות במנהגא מכלל דמחצות ולהלן אסור ולמה ליה למיתני חצות לאשמעינן הך דיוקא הא כל ערבי ימים טובים אסירי: **מן** המנחה. תשע שעות ומחצה: **סמוך** למנחה. קודם לכן: **נידנוד** עבירה. רמז עבירה: **תענית** צבור. אסור במלאכה במסכת תענית (דף יב:) כשהיו מתענין על הגשמים אבל שאר תענית ציבור לא כדאמר שמואל אין חומר תענית ציבור בבבל (לקמן דף נד:): **במוצאי** שבתות. משום כבוד שבת שמוסיפין מחול על הקדש: **זריז**. בעל מלאכה: **שפל** ונשכר דלא עביד כולה שבתא ולא במעלי שבתא. ואע"ג דלאו לשום מצוה מיכוין מצוה שלא לשמה מיהא הויא דאמרינן לקמן יעסוק אדם במצוה ואפי' שלא לשמה: ה"ג ואע"ג דהאי דלא קעבדן כו': **עושין** לשמה. מעל שמים ושלא לשמה עד לשמים דמצוה מיהא קא עביד כדרב יהודה: **מתקולתא**. נוטלת מאזנים בידה ומהלכת בשוק להשכירן לכל הצריכין דשכר מועט הוא ומתבזה אשתו על שכר מועט: **אגרתא**. שכר ריחיים שמשכירין טורח גדול ושכר מועט אבל קונה ריחיים ומוכרן הרי הוא כשאר פרקמטיא: **בקנים**. כל מקלות דקים קרי קנים שעושין מהן גדרות ומחיצות: **אפחזייהו**. נפח שלהן: **תגרי** סימטא. יושבין ומוכרין בשוק ועין שולטת בהן: **ומגדלי** בהמה דקה. הכל צווחין עליהן: **וקוצצי** אילנות טובות. למוכרן לעצים הכל תמהים ומלעיזין עליהם ומתוך כך עין שולטת בהן ולעקת בני אדם: **ונותנין** עיניהם בחלק יפה. כשחולקים עם אחרים תמיד מקפידין ליטול חלק יפה: **מתורגמנין**. שעומדין לפני החכם בשבתות ושומעין מפיו ומשמיעין לרבים: **ומעות** יתומין. למחלית שכר: **ממדינת** הים. משלח ספינותיו תמיד במקום סכנה: **תכלת**. לצילית: **אינן** רואין. כדאמרן שאם יתעשרו לא יהו עסוקין: **ואם** עוסקין לשמה. להיות המצוה מצויה לצריכין לה: **רואין**. דהואיל ולשמה עושין לא יניחו בשביל עשרן: **מצור** לצידון. יום השוק של צידון בע"ש והם מחמירים על עצמן שלא להיבטל מצרכי שבת: **הוה** אפשר להו. להמנע מן השוק שעשירים היו: **מארוזא**. אורז:
דסרכי

הגהות הב"ח

(א) גמרא וכדרב יהודה דאמר רב יהודה: (ב) שם לא אפשר לן מאי אמר להו: (ג) תוס' ד"ה העושה וכו' פי' עד שישלים:

הגהות הגר"א

[א] גמרא לאתויי תענית צבור כצ"ל:

רבינו חננאל

ברכה לעולם ושני' התם עד המנחה ולמעלה הכא מחצות אי נמי התם ברכה לא חזי הכא בערב הפסח העושה מלאכה מחצות היום ולמעלה זולתי שהתירו להם חכמים משמתינן ליה: **גופא** העושה מלאכה בערבי שבתות ובערבי ימים טובים ובמוצאי שבתות ובמוצאי ימים טובים מן המנחה ולמעלה ובתענית צבור אינו רואה סימן ברכה לעולם. תוספתא בתחלת יבמות יש זריז ונשכר דעביד מלאכה כל יום ואינו עושה שבת מן המנחה ולמעלה זריז ומפסיד שעושה כל השבוע ובערב שבת שפל ונשכר שאינו עושה מלאכה לא בכל השבוע ולא בערב שבת שפל ומפסיד כל השבוע יושב ובטל ובערב שבת עושה מלאכה: **גדול** מעל שמים חסדך אלו העושין לשמה כי גדול עד שמים חסדך אלו העושין שלא לשמה שאע"פ שעושין שלא לשמה יש להם חסד כדרב יהודה אמר רב דאמר לעולם יעסוק אדם בתורה ובמצות אפי' שלא לשמה שמתוך שלא לשמה בא לשמה: **המצפה** לשכר אשתו כדי להתפרנס ממנו. פי' מתקן משקל המטוה שטווה בכל יום ושכר הרחים שכירות מפני שהוא דבר מועט אינו רואה סימן ברכה בזה הדרך: **ת"ר** ארבע פרוטות הן אין בהן ברכה שכר ברכה שבקשו עליהן אנשי כנסת הגדולה מלפני הקב"ה שלא יתעשרו שכר מתורגמנין הדרשנין שדורשין בשבת לצבור ועושין להן פסיקה נראה כאלו שכר שבת הוא והנושא והנותן במעות של יתומים קרוב לשכר ורחוק להפסד פעמים שאינו מדקדק היטב היטב ויתמי לאו בני מחילה נינהו ומעות הבאות ממדינת הים פעמים שילך [לאבוד] הכל בבת אחת כגון שנטבעה הספינה: **ת"ר** כותבי ספרים תפלין ומזוזות הן ותגריהן ותגרי תגריהן וכל העוסקין במלאכת שמים לאיתויי מוכרי תכלת אין רואין סימן ברכה ואם עוסקין לשמה מתברכין: **בני** בישן נהוג שלא לילך בצידן בערב שבת ובאו בניהן ואמרו לו לר' יוחנן אבותינו היו עשירים ולא היו צריכים לעשות מלאכה בערב שבת ואנו עניים מהו לילך ולישא וליתן אמר להם כבר קבלו אבותיכם עליהם דכתיב ואל תטוש תורת אמך ופי' בירושלמי כי לפרש בים שאלוהו ואסר להם משום דסבר אסור לפרש בים הגדול אבל זה אפי' נדר נשאל ומתירין לו ולא אסר אלא דסבר אסור לפרש בים: **בני** בי חוזאי נהגו להפריש חלה מן האורז שאינו חייב בחלה ואסקינן

גליון הש"ס

גמ' ונותנין עיניהן בחלק יפה. עיין מ"ק כ"ח ע"ב תד"ס וליטול:

א א מיי' פ"ח מהל' י"ט הל' יז סמג לאוין עה טוש"ע או"ח סי' תסח סעיף ג ד:

*כאיסורו מה איסורו בכזית אף חזרתו בכזית תניא ר' נתן אומר זה וזה כשתי ביצים ולא הודו לו חכמים °והיה ביום ההוא לא יהיה אור יקרות וקפאון מאי יקרות וקפאון א"ר אלעזר זה אור שיקר בעולם הזה וקפוי לעולם הבא ר' יוחנן אמר אלו נגעים ואהלות שיקרין הן בעוה"ז וקפויין הן לעולם הבא ור' יהושע בן לוי אמר אלו בני אדם שיקרין הן בעולם הזה וקפויין הן לעוה"ב *כי הא דרב יוסף בריה דר' יהושע בן לוי חלש ואיתנגיד כי הדר אמר ליה אבוה מאי חזית אמר ליה עולם הפוך ראיתי עליונים למטה ותחתונים למעלה אמר לו בני עולם ברור ראית ואנן היכי התם כי היכי דאיתו אנן הכא הכי איתינן התם ושמעתי שהיו אומרים *אשרי מי שבא לכאן ותלמודו בידו ושמעתי שהיו אומרים הרוגי מלכות אין אדם יכול לעמוד במחיצתן (ומאן) ניניהו אילימא ר"ע וחבריו משום הרוגי מלכות ותו לא אלא הרוגי לוד [צ"ל כאן] °ביום ההוא יהיה על מצלות הסוס קדש לה' מאי מצלות הסוס א"ר יהושע בן לוי עתיד הקב"ה להוסיף על ירושלים עד שהסוס רץ ומציל תחתיו ר' אלעזר אמר כל מצילות שתולין לסוס בין עיניו יהיה קדש לה' ור' יוחנן אמר כל ביזה שבוזזין ישראל עד שעה שהסוס רץ ומציל יהיה קדש לה' בשלמא למאן דאמר כל ביזה שבוזזי ישראל היינו דכתיב °והיה הסירות בבית ה' כמזרקים לפני המזבח אלא למ"ד בהנך תרתי מאי והיה הסירות בבית ה' מילתא אחריתי קאמר דמתעתרי ישראל ומתנדבי ומייתי בשלמא למ"ד ביזה היינו דכתיב °ולא יהיה כנעני עוד בבית ה' צבאות אלא למ"ד הנך תרתי מאי ולא יהיה כנעני א"ר ירמיה °אין כאן עני וכנעני מנלן *דאיקרי תגר דכתיב °וירא שם יהודה בת איש כנעני מאי כנעני אילימא כנעני ממש אפשר בא אברהם והזהיר את יצחק בא יצחק והזהיר את יעקב ויהודה אזיל ונסיב אלא אמר רבי שמעון בן לקיש בת גברא תגרא דכתיב °כנען בידו מאזני מרמה ואיבעית אימא מהכא °אשר סוחריה שרים כנעניה נכבדי ארץ: °והיה ה' למלך על כל הארץ ביום ההוא יהיה ה' אחד ושמו אחד אטו האידנא לאו אחד הוא אמר רבי אחא בר חנינא לא כעולם הזה העולם הבא העולם הזה *על בשורות טובות אומר ברוך הטוב והמטיב ועל בשורות רעות אומר ברוך דיין האמת לעולם הבא כולו הטוב והמטיב ושמו אחד מאי אחד אטו האידנא לאו שמו אחד הוא א"ר נחמן בר יצחק לא כעולם הזה העולם הבא העולם הזה נכתב ביו"ד ה"י ונקרא באל"ף דל"ת אבל לעולם הבא כולו אחד *נקרא ביו"ד ה"י ונכתב ביו"ד ה"י *סבר רבא למדרשה בפירקא א"ל ההוא סבא לעלם כתיב ר' אבינא רמי כתיב °זה שמי לעלם *וזה זכרי לדור דור אמר הקב"ה לא כשאני נכתב אני נקרא נכתב אני ביו"ד ה"א ונקרא אני באל"ף דל"ת:

הדרן עלך אלו עוברין

*מקום *שנהגו לעשות מלאכה בערבי פסחים עד חצות עושין מקום שנהגו שלא לעשות אין עושין ההולך ממקום שעושין למקום שאין עושין או ממקום שאין עושין למקום שעושין *נותנין עליו חומרי מקום שיצא משם וחומרי מקום שהלך לשם ואל

רש"י

כאיסורו. של חמץ ובשר קודש נמי משנפסל ביוצא אסור באכילה: יקרות וקפאון. אוידי דאיירי בירושלים ביוצאות שעריה דקתני וכן מי שיצא מירושלים כו' פתח בהא פרשתא דבעינן למימר קמן שעתיד הקב"ה להוסיף על ירושלים: אור שיקר בעולם הזה. כשחמה מאירה בגבורתה ואורה גדול והוא תורה אור חשוב ויקר שלא יהא קפוי וקל לעולם הבא כל דבר קל קרי קפוי לף על המים ויצף הברזל מתרגמינן וקפא פרזלא (מלכים ב ו): בני אדם שיקרים. עשירים וחשובים ואינן טובים למקום: איתנגיד. גוע ופרחה רוחו: עליונים למטה. אותן שהיו כאן חשובים ראיתי קלים: ואנן. תלמידי חכמים היכי איתינן התם: הרוגי מלכות ותו לא. לא היתה בהן מעלה אחרת שיחשבו עליה אלא זו בלבד: הרוגי לוד. שני אחים היו שמסרו עצמן *על ישראל שהודו על עצמן הריגת בת מלך שהיו מטילין אותה על כל ישראל: עד שעה שהסוס רץ ומציל. כשיעור מרוצת הסוס עד חצי היום ולשון מציל שצילו תחתיו שכל שעות היום חמה נוטה לצדדין וצל האדם וצל הבהמה נוטה לצידו כשחמה במזרח צל האדם למערב אבל בחצי היום חמה עומדת באמצע הרקיע בראש כל האדם וצל הסוס תחתיו בפי' ר' מכיר ז"ל מצאתי: כל מצילות. כלומר שתולין לסוס לנוי ולקשקש לשון מצלתים (ד"ה א יג): יהיה קודש לה'. שיתנדבו ישראל נדבותיהן למקדש כל ביזה שיבוזו ישראל. מן הנכרים ביום אחד עד חצות יהיו קודש לה' שיביאום נדבה למקדש: הסירות כמזרקים. אף הסירות יהיו של כסף ושל זהב שתהא שם ביזה רבה להקדש: מאי והיה הסירות כמזרקים. הא במצילות הסוס ליכא הקדש כולי האי: דמיתעתרי ישראל. יתעשרו ישראל ובשורה אחרת היא: כנעני. לא יהיו צריכין גזברין לעשות סחורה בנכסי הקדש לפי שיהא שם עושר גדול מן הביזה: בא אברהם והזהיר את יצחק. שהשביע לאליעזר לא תקח אשה לבני מבנות הכנעני (בראשית כד): ויצחק את יעקב. לא תקח אשה מבנות כנען (שם כח): כולו הטוב והמטיב. שאין שם בשורה רעה: למידרשיה בפירקא. קרייה דיו"ד ה"י דארבע אותיות דרשיה וטעמיה התלויים בו: לעלם כתיב. זה שמי לעלם חסר וי"ו לשון העלמה: כתיב זה שמי לעלם. בהעלמה וכתיב זה זכרי דמשמע קרייה ולא העלמה לשון אחר כיון דכתב זה שמי פשיטא דזה זכרי היאך יקרא אלא בשמו: לא כשאני נכתב. שני שמות לימדו שם הכתיבה ושם הקרייה:

הדרן עלך אלו עוברין

מקום שנהגו. עד חצות. חצי היום: שלא לעשות. כדי שלא יהא טרוד במלאכה וישכח ביעור חמצו ושחיטת הפסח ותקון מצה לצורך הלילה דמצוה לטרוח מבעוד יום כדי להסב מהר כדאמר בפ' בתרא (דף קט.) חוטפין מצה בלילי פסחים בשביל תינוקות שלא ישנו: ואל

תוספות

מקום שנהגו. אור"י בשם ריב"א דמפרש בירושלמי מאי שנא ערבי פסחים משאר י"ט משום דזמן הפסח מחצות ואילך ואף יחיד קאמר התם בשאר ימות השנה ביום שמביא קרבן אסור במלאכה ופריך אם כן יהא כל היום אסור כמו יחיד שמביא קרבן ומפרש התם משום דראוי להקריב משחרית אבל פסח אינו יכול להקריבו אלא אחר חצות כדנפקא לן מבין הערבים ופריך אם כן קרבן תמיד שהוא לכל ישראל וקרב בכל יום יהא בכל יום אסור במלאכה ומשני שאני תמיד שהתורה הוציאה מן הכלל דכתיב ואספת דגנך ואם כל ישראל יושבים ובטלים מי יאסוף להן דגן ומשמע התם דמדאורייתא אסורה ונראה דאף בזמן הזה דליכא הקרבה כיון שנאסר אז אסור לעולם: העושה

מסורת הש"ס

[לקמן קכא.] ב"ב י: [תענית יח:] [מ"ק כח. כתובות עז:] ב"ב י. [ב"ב עה.] [ברכות נד.] [נכתב ביו"ד ה"י ונקרא ביו"ד ה"י כך הוא נכון וכ"ה בילקוט שמות רמז קע"]] יבמות יג: חולין [קיז.]

זכריה יד; זכריה יד; דה"ב; זכריה יד; בראשית לח; הושע יב; ישעיה כג; זכריה יד; שמות ג; קדושין עא.; ס"א וכתיב

גליון הש"ס

גמ' א"ר י' אין כאן עני. עי' שבת סג ע"א רש"י ד"ה לא יחדל:

רבינו חננאל

כנותר מה נותר איסורו בכזית דאכילה כתיב ביה אף חזרתו: וכיון שהזכיר אם לא עבר הצופים חוזר דש"מ עד הצופים מירושלים הוא חשוב הוצרך מהאי קרא והיה ביום ההוא יהיה על מצלות הסוס קדש לה' ואמר ר' יהושע בן לוי עתיד הקב"ה להוסיף על ירושלים עד שעה שהסוס רץ ומציל פי' חצי היום שהצל של סוס תחתיו ומפני זה פתח והיה ביום ההוא לא יהיה אור יקרות וקפאון פי' ר' אלעזר אור שהוא יקר בעולם הזה כלו כדכתיב (משלי ו כג) כי נר מצוה ותורה אור וכתיב (שמואל א ג א) ודבר ה' היה יקר בימים ההם קפוי הוא מצוי לעולם הבא וכל דבר מצוי ביד הרבים בזול הוא דכתיב (יואל ג א) ביום ההוא אשפוך את רוחי על כל בשר ונבאו ריש לקיש דרשו בתלמוד נגעים ואהלות שהוא יקר עכשיו כו' ור' יוחנן אמר אלו בני אדם שנראין בעולם הזה יקרים ונכבדים קפויים הם לעולם הבא כי הא דיוסף בריה דר' יהושע בן לוי חלש כאלו פרחה נשמתו איתפח אמר ליה אבוה מאי חזית אמר ליה עולם הפוך ראיתי עליונים למטה כלומר היקרים החשובים בעולם הזה כדכתיב (ישעיה יג יב) אוקיר אנוש מפז ואדם מכתם אופיר ראיתי אותם תחתונים במדרגה התחתונה והיורדים בעולם הזה ראיתי בעליה למעלה מאלו אמר ליה בני עולם ברור ראית כלומר האמת שם הוא שהוא לשם עליון הוא העיקר אמר ליה ואנו אנה מקומנו אמר ליה אנו חשיבותינו התם כי הכא ושמעתי אשרי מי שיבא לכאן ותלמודו בידו יש מי שאומר שגורס על פה כי הלך וגרסתו עמו ויש מי שמפרש מי שיבא בכאן ומעשיו מיסדים ותלמודו שקיים כל מה שלמד נמצא כאלו הביא ראיותיו עמו והרוגי מלכות אין כל בריה ולשון יכולה במחיצתן ואסיקנא לאו ר"ע וחבריו דהללו מעלתן גדולה זולתי מצות הריגתם אלא שני אחים שהיו בלוד בשעה שנמצאת בת קיסר הרוגה ובקשו להרוג כל יהודי בשבילה ואמרו שני האחים אנו הרגנוה כדי להציל כל ישראל ונהרגו הן וכו': והיה ה' למלך [על כל הארץ] ביום ההוא יהיה ה' אחד ושמו אחד [יהיה] ה' אחד שאין שם בשורה רעה שצריך לומר ברוך דיין האמת אלא הטוב בכל שהכל טוב שאין שם רע ושמו אחד כר"נ בר יצחק דאמר בעולם הזה שמי נכתב ביוד הא ונקרא באלף דלת אבל בעולם הבא כולו אחד כשאני נכתב כך אני נקרא: רבה סבר למדרשה בפירקא ולגלותו א"ל ההוא סבא זה שמי לעלם חסר ו' כתיב כלומר עלמיה [וזה] זכרי כשאני נקרא עכשיו באלף דלת ובעולם [הבא] בשמי שנא' זה שמי לעולם:

הדרן עלך ואלו עוברין

מקום שנהגו לעשות מלאכה בערבי פסחים עד חצות עושין כו' ומתמהי' מאי אריא ערבי פסחים אפי' כל ערובה נמי דתניא העושה מלאכה בערבי שבתות ובערבי ימים טובים מן המנחה ולמעלה אינו רואה סימן ברכה

as much as an egg. While R. Judah holds, Its return [50a] is like its prohibition: just as its prohibition is for as much as an olive,[2] so its return is for as much as an olive.

It was taught, R. Nathan said: Both[3] have the standard of two eggs; but the Sages did not agree with him.

And it shall come to pass in that day that there shall not be light, but heavy clouds [yeḳaroth] *and thick* [we-ḳippa'on];[4] what does *yeḳaroth we-ḳippa'on* mean?—Said R. Eleazar: This means, the light which is precious [*yakar*] in this world, is yet of little account [*ḳapuy*][5] in the next world.[6] R. Joḥanan said: This refers to Nega'im and Ohaloth,[7] which are difficult [heavy] in this world yet shall be light [easily understood] in the future world. While R. Joshua b. Levi said: This refers to the people who are honoured in this world, but will be lightly esteemed in the next world. As was the case of R. Joseph the son of R. Joshua b. Levi, [who] became ill and fell into a trance. When he recovered, his father asked him, 'What did you see?' 'I saw a topsy-turvy world', he replied, 'the upper [class] underneath and the lower on top', he replied: 'My son', he observed, 'you saw a clear world.[8] And how are we [situated] there?' 'Just as we are here, so are we there. And I heard them saying, "Happy is he who comes hither with his learning in his hand". And I also heard them saying, "Those martyred by the State, no man can stand within their barrier"'.[9] Who are these [martyrs]? Shall we say, R. Akiba and his companions?[10] Is that
a because they were martyrs of the State and nothing else?[1] Rather [he meant] the martyrs of Lydda.[2]

In that day there shall be upon the bells of the horses [meẓiloth ha-sus]: HOLY UNTO THE LORD.[3] What does '*meẓiloth ha-sus*' [intimate]?—Said R. Joshua b. Levi: The Holy One, blessed be He, is destined to add to Jerusalem as far as a horse can run and cast its shadow [*maẓẓil*—under itself].[4] R. Eleazar said: All the bells which are hung on a horse between its eyes shall be holy unto the Lord.[5] While R. Joḥanan said: All the spoil which Israel shall take spoil [from morning] until a horse can run and cast its shadow [under itself] shall be holy unto the Lord. As for him who explains it [as referring to] all the spoil which Israel shall take spoil, it is well: hence it is written, *and the pots in the Lord's house shall be like the basins before the altar*.[6] But according to those who give the [other] two explanations, what is [the relevance of] '*and the pots in the Lord's house shall be*' [etc.]?—[The verse] states another thing, viz., that Israel will become wealthy, make votive offerings, and bring them [to the Temple]. As for him who says [that it means] spoil, it is well: that is what is written, *and in that day there shall be no more a trafficker in the house of the Lord of hosts*.[7] But according to those who give the [other] two explanations, what does *and there shall be no more a trafficker* [kena'ani] [etc.] mean?—Said R. Jeremiah: No poor man shall be here.[8] And how do we know that [*kena'ani*] connotes a merchant?—Because it is written, *And*
b *Judah saw there the daughter of a certain Canaanite* [kena'ani]:[1] what does '*kena'ani*' mean? Shall we say, literally a Canaanite: is it possible that Abraham came and admonished Isaac, Isaac came and admonished Jacob,[2] and then Judah went and married [a Canaanite]! Rather, said R. Simeon b. Laḳish: [It means] the daughter of a merchant, as it is written, *As for the trafficker* [kena'an], *the balances of deceit are in his hand*,[3] Alternatively, I can quote this: *Whose merchants are princes, whose traffickers* [kin'anehah] *are the honourable of the earth*.[4]

And the Lord shall be King over all the earth; in that day shall the Lord be One, and His name one:[5] is He then not One now?—Said R. Aḥa b. Ḥanina: Not like this world is the future world. In this world, for good tidings one says, 'He is good, and He doeth good', while for evil tidings he says, 'Blessed be the true Judge';[6] [whereas] in the future world it shall be only 'He is good and He doeth good'.[7] '*And His name one*': what does '*one*' mean? Is then now His name not one?—Said R. Naḥman b. Isaac; Not like this world is the future world. [In] this world [His name] is written with a *yod he*[8] and read as *alef daleth;*[9] but in the future world it shall all be one: it shall be written with *yod he* and read as *yod he*. Now, Raba thought of lecturing it at the session, [whereupon] a certain old man said to him, It is written, *le'alem*.[10] R. Abina pointed out a contradiction: It is written, *this is my name, to be hidden;* [and it is also written],[11] *and this is my memorial unto all generations?*[12] The Holy One, blessed be He, said: Not as I [i.e., My name] am written am I read: I am written with a *yod he*, while I am
c read as *alef daleth*.[1]

CHAPTER IV

MISHNAH. WHERE IT IS THE CUSTOM TO DO WORK ON THE EVE OF PASSOVER UNTIL MIDDAY ONE MAY DO [WORK]; WHERE IT IS THE CUSTOM NOT TO DO [WORK], ONE MAY NOT DO [WORK]. HE WHO GOES FROM A PLACE WHERE THEY WORK TO A PLACE WHERE THEY DO NOT WORK, OR FROM A PLACE WHERE THEY DO NOT WORK TO A PLACE WHERE THEY DO WORK, WE LAY UPON HIM THE RESTRICTIONS OF THE PLACE WHENCE HE DEPARTED AND THE RESTRICTIONS OF THE

(2) V. 49b, n. c12. (3) The leaven and the holy flesh. (4) Zech. XIV, 6. (5) Lit., 'light', 'floating'. (6) For the light of this world will pale into insignificance before the greater light of the next. He translates the verse: *And it shall come ... the light will not be precious but* (only) *of small account*. (7) The laws of leprosy and the defilement of tents through a dead body. (8) In which people occupy the positions they merit. (9) They occupy such an exalted position in the next world that they are unapproachable. (10) Who were executed or martyred by the Roman State at various times for their insistence on teaching the Torah in spite of the Roman interdict. A passage describing the death of great scholars, ten in number, is found in the liturgies for the Day of Atonement and the Fast of Ab. Some of the most famous of them were R. Gamaliel, R. Judah b. Baba and R. Akiba.
a (1) Surely they had other claims to eminence too! (2) Two brothers, Lulianus and Papus, who took upon themselves the guilt for the death of the Emperor's daughter, so as to save the people as a whole; v. Ta'an. 18b. Lydda was a district in Asia Minor, to which belonged the city Laodicea, which city it denotes here. (3) Zech. XIV, 20. (4) Rashi: i.e., as far as a horse can run from the morning until midday, when its shadow (*ẓel*) is directly beneath it. (5) I.e., they shall be votive offerings to the Sanctuary. (6) Ibid. Even the pots shall be of gold and silver, owing to the abundance of spoil. (7) Ibid. 21. The Temple Treasurers will not need to buy or sell for the Temple, on account of the great wealth of the spoil. (8) Reading *kena'ani* as *kan 'ani*, here is a poor man.
b (1) Gen. XXXVIII, 2. (2) Not to marry a Canaanite; v. Ibid. XXIV, 3; XXVIII, 1. (3) Hos. XII, 8. (4) Isa. XXIII, 8. (5) Zech. XIV, 9. (6) V. Ber. 54a. (7) For there will never be any evil tidings there. (8) YHWH = *yod he waw he*, the letters of the Tetragrammaton. (9) *Adonay* = *alef daleth nun yod*. (10) To hide it. This is explained anon. (11) The bracketed word is added in var. lec. (12) Ex. III, 15. The actual reading is: *this is my name for ever* (le'olam, לעולם); but it is written, *to be hidden* (le'alem, לעלם). Thus this indicates that God's name must be kept secret; whereas '*this is my memorial*' etc. implies that He is to be known by this name. Another version, accepting the reading *le'olam* (*for ever*) explains the difficulty thus: since God states *this is my name*, it is obvious that He is to be known by it: why then add, '*and this is my memorial*' etc.?
c (1) The importance attributed to the Divine Name was owing to the fact that it was not regarded simply as a designation, but was held to express the essence of the Godhead. The right way of pronouncing the Tetragrammaton was not generally known, being preserved as an esoteric teaching. Cf. Kid., 71a, n. 6 and Sanh., 60a, n2.

thorn bush, [which is] a repulsive [49b] and unacceptable thing.

Our Rabbis taught: Let a man always sell all he has and marry
a the daughter of a scholar. If he does not find[1] the daughter of a scholar, let him marry the daughter of [one of] the great men of the generation.[2] If he does not find the daughter of [one of] the great men of the generation, let him marry the daughter of the head of synagogues. If he does not find the daughter of the head of synagogues,[3] let him marry the daughter of a charity treasurer. If he does not find the daughter of a charity treasurer, let him marry the daughter of an elementary school-teacher, but let him not marry the daughter of an *'am ha-areẓ*, because they are detestable and their wives are vermin, and of their daughters it is said, *Cursed be he that lieth with any manner of beast.*[4]

It was taught, Rabbi said: An *'am ha-areẓ* may not eat the flesh of cattle, for it is said, *This is the law* [Torah] *of the beast, and of the fowl:*[5] whoever engages in [the study of] the Torah may eat the flesh of beast and fowl, but he who does not engage in [the study of] the Torah may not eat the flesh of beast and fowl.

R. Eleazar said: An *'am ha-areẓ*, it is permitted to stab him [even] on the Day of Atonement which falls on the Sabbath. Said his disciples to him, Master, say to slaughter him [ritually]?—He replied: This [ritual slaughter] requires a benediction, whereas that [stabbing] does not require a benediction.[6]

R. Eleazar said: One must not join company with an *'am ha-areẓ* on the road, because it is said, *for that* [the Torah] *is thy life, and the*
b *length of thy days:*[1] [seeing that] he has no care [pity] for his own life,[2] how much the more for the life of his companions! R. Samuel b. Naḥmani said in R. Joḥanan's name: One may tear an *'am ha-areẓ* like a fish! Said R. Samuel b. Isaac: And [this means] along his back.

It was taught, R. Akiba said: When I was an *'am ha-areẓ*[3] I said: I would that I had a scholar [before me], and I would maul him like an ass. Said his disciples to him, Rabbi, say like a dog! The former bites and breaks the bones, while the latter bites but does not break the bones, he answered them.

It was taught, R. Meir used to say: Whoever marries his daughter to an *'am ha-areẓ* is as though he bound and laid her before a lion: just as a lion tears [his prey] and devours it and has no shame, so an *'am ha-areẓ* strikes and cohabits and has no shame.

It was taught, R. Eliezer said: But that we are necessary to them for trade, they would kill us. R. Ḥiyya taught: Whoever studies[4] the Torah in front of an *'am ha-areẓ* is as though he cohabited with his betrothed in his presence,[5] for it is said, *Moses commanded us a law, an inheritance* [morashah] *of the congregation of Jacob:*[6] read not *morashah* but *me'orasah* [the betrothed].[7] Greater is the hatred wherewith the *'amme ha-areẓ* hate the scholar than the hatred wherewith the heathens hate Israel, and their wives [hate even] more than they. It was taught: He who has studied and then abandoned [the Torah] [hates the scholar] more than all of them.[8]

Our Rabbis taught: Six things were said of the *'amme ha-areẓ:* We do not commit testimony to them; we do not accept testimony from them; we do not reveal a secret to them; we do not appoint
c them as guardians for orphans; we do not appoint them stewards[1] over charity funds; and we must not join their company on the road. Some say, We do not proclaim their losses too.[2] And the first Tanna?[3]—Virtuous seed may sometimes issue from him, and they will enjoy[4] it, as it is said, *He will prepare it, and the just shall put it on.*[5]

SIMILARLY, HE WHO WENT OUT OF etc. Shall we say that R. Meir holds, only as much as an egg is of importance, whereas R. Judah holds, Even as much as an olive too is of importance?[6] But the following contradicts it: For what [minimum] quantity[7] must they recite grace in common?[8] Until as much as an olive.[9] R. Judah said: Until as much as an egg!—Said R. Joḥanan: The discussion[10] must be reversed. Abaye said, After all you need not reverse [it]: there they differ in [the interpretation of Scriptural] verses, [whereas] here they differ in a matter of logic. 'There they differ in [the interpretation of] verses': R. Meir holds: *And thou shalt eat,*[11] this refers to eating; *and be satisfied*, this means drinking, and eating is [constituted] by as much as an olive.[12] While R. Judah holds: '*And thou shalt eat and be satisfied*' [implies] eating in which there is satisfaction [of one's hunger], and what is that? As much as an egg. 'Here they differ in a matter of logic',
d for R. Meir holds: Its return is like its defilement:[1] just as its defilement requires as much as an egg, so does its return require

a (1) I.e., cannot obtain. (2) *Gedole ha-dor*, title probably designating the civil leaders of the community, v. Büchler, *Sepphoris*, p. 9. (3) [The *archi synagogos*, the supreme authority over the synagogues in the town; v. Sot. 41a, n. 5.] (4) Deut. XXVII, 21. (5) Lev. XI, 46. (6) These and the following dicta show that a strong antipathy existed between the scholar and the *'am ha-areẓ*. Nevertheless, it is perfectly obvious that a statement like the present one is merely humorous and no more than a *jeu d'esprit*, and many others must be similarly understood. V. Lazarus, M. *Ethics of Judaism*, Appendix pp. 258ff; also *J.E.* art. *'Am Ha-areẓ*.

b (1) Deut. XXX, 20. (2) In that he forsakes the Torah. (3) R. Akiba was a poor, illiterate shepherd before he became a scholar; v. Ned. 50a. (4) Lit., 'engages in'. (5) So great is the affront which the *'am ha-areẓ* feels when Torah is studied in his presence, v. Rashi. (6) Ibid. XXXIII, 4. (7) Thus the Torah is as the bride of the whole of Israel. (8) More than any *'am ha-areẓ* hates the scholar.

c (1) The Heb. is the same as in the previous phrase. *Epitropos* is a steward who looks after another person's estates, etc. (2) He who finds lost property is bound to proclaim it; if the owner is an *'am ha-areẓ*, he is not bound to proclaim it. (3) Why does he omit this? (4) Lit., 'eat'. (5) Job XXVII, 17. (6) I.e., worthy of being taken into account. (7) Lit., 'how far?' (8) When three or more people dine together they must recite grace in common, prefacing it with the statement, 'Let us say grace', and they must not separate before this is done, even if each intends reciting grace alone. Here the question is: what is the minimum meal for which this is necessary? (9) That is the minimum. Until (*'ad*) is meant in a diminishing sense. (10) I.e., the opinions. (11) Deut. VIII, 10. (12) This is the minimum called eating, e.g., for eating this quantity of forbidden food liability is incurred; the command to eat unleavened bread on the first night of Passover means at least as much as an olive. The verse continues: *and thou shalt bless the Lord thy God*—i.e., recite grace.

d (1) I.e., the same quantity of leaven which is subject to defilement as an eatable necessitates returning in order to remove it.

ואינו מתקבל: תנו רבנן ^א^לעולם ימכור אדם כל מה שיש לו וישא בת תלמיד חכם לא מצא בת תלמיד חכם ישא בת גדולי הדור לא מצא בת גדולי הדור ישא בת ראשי כנסיות לא מצא בת ראשי כנסיות ישא בת גבאי צדקה לא מצא בת גבאי צדקה ישא בת מלמדי תינוקות ולא ישא בת עמי הארץ מפני שהן שקץ ונשותיהן שרץ *ועל בנותיהן הוא אומר °ארור שוכב עם כל בהמה תניא ר' אומר עם הארץ אסור לאכול בשר (בהמה) שנאמר °זאת תורת הבהמה והעוף כל העוסק בתורה מותר לאכול בשר בהמה ועוף וכל שאינו עוסק בתורה אסור לאכול בשר בהמה ועוף: אמר רבי אלעזר עם הארץ מותר לנוחרו ביום הכיפורים שחל להיות בשבת אמרו לו תלמידיו ר' אמור לשוחטו אמר להן זה טעון ברכה וזה אינו טעון ברכה: אמר רבי אלעזר עם הארץ אסור להתלוות עמו בדרך שנאמר °כי היא חייך ואורך ימיך על חייו לא חס על חיי חבירו לא כל שכן אמר רבי שמואל בר נחמני אמר רבי יוחנן עם הארץ מותר לקורעו כדג אמר רבי שמואל בר יצחק ומגבו: תניא אמר רבי עקיבא °כשהייתי עם הארץ אמרתי מי יתן לי תלמיד חכם ואנשכנו כחמור אמרו לו תלמידיו רבי אמור ככלב אמר להן זה נושך ושובר עצם וזה נושך ואינו שובר עצם: תניא היה רבי מאיר אומר כל המשיא בתו לעם הארץ כאילו כופתה ומניחה לפני ארי *מה ארי דורס ואוכל ואין לו בושת פנים אף עם הארץ מכה ובועל ואין לו בושת פנים: תניא רבי אליעזר אומר *אילמלא אנו צריכין להם למשא ומתן היו הורגין אותנו תנא רבי חייא כל העוסק בתורה לפני עם הארץ כאילו בועל ארוסתו בפניו שנאמר °תורה צוה לנו משה מורשה אל תקרי מורשה אלא *מאורסה גדולה שנאה ששונאין עמי הארץ לתלמיד חכם יותר משנאה ששונאין עובדי כוכבים את ישראל ונשותיהן יותר מהן: תנא שנה ופירש יותר מכולן: תנו רבנן ששה דברים נאמרו בעמי הארץ ^ב^אין מוסרין להן עדות ואין מקבלין ממנו עדות ואין מגלין להן סוד ^ג^ואין ממנין אותן אפוטרופוס על היתומים ואין ממנין אותן אפוטרופוס על קופה של צדקה ואין מתלוין עמהן בדרך ויש אומרים אף אין מכריזין על אבידתו ותנא קמא *זמנין דנפיק מיניה זרעא מעליא ואכיל ליה שנאמר °יכין וצדיק ילבש: וכן מי שיצא וכו': *למימרא דרבי מאיר סבר כביצה הוא דחשיב ורבי יהודה סבר כזית נמי חשיב ורמינהי *עד כמה הן מזמנין ^ד^עד כזית ורבי יהודה אומר עד כביצה אמר רבי יוחנן מוחלפת השיטה אביי אמר לעולם לא תיפוך התם בקראי פליגי הכא בסברא פליגי התם בקראי פליגי רבי מאיר סבר °ואכלת זו אכילה ושבעת זו שתיה *ואכילה בכזית ורבי יהודה סבר ואכלת ושבעת אכילה שיש בה שביעה ואיזו זו בכביצה הכא בסברא פליגי דרבי מאיר סבר חזרתו *כטומאתו מה טומאתו בכביצה אף חזרתו בכביצה ור' יהודה סבר חזרתו כאיסורו

ואינו מתקבל. לשומעים: גדולי הדור. אנשי מעשה ולדיקים: בת גבאי לדקה. שאין ממנין אלא אם כן טובים ונאמנין: נשותיהן שרץ. שאינן זהירות במצות: עם כל בהמה. שדומות לבהמה שאין להן לב להבין: כי היא חייך ואורך ימיך על חייו לא חס. ללמוד תורה ולחיות: על חיי חבירו לא כל שכן. ויש לדאג שמא יהרגנו: ומגבו. דתו לא חיי כדאמרינן בשחיטת חולין (דף כא:) קרעו כדג מטמא באהל מיד ואף על גב שמפרפר ואמר רבי שמואל בר רב יצחק ומגבו: אילמלא צריכין אנו להם. למזונותיהן ולעזרתם היו הורגין אותנו: כאילו בא על ארוסתו בפניו. שמביישו: מאורסה. לכל קהילות יעקב: שנה ופירש. תלמיד ששנה ופירש מן התורה ויודע כמה תלמידי חכמים מגנים את עמי הארץ וכמה הם שפלים בעיניהם שונא יותר מכולם: אין מוסרין לו עדות. אין מזמנין אותו לשמוע דבר להעיד עליו: ואין מגלין לו סוד. שום דבר סתר לפי שהולך רכיל ומגלה: על היתומין. שחשוד על הגזל: המולא אבידה חייב להכריז. כדאמרי' באלו מציאות (ב"מ כח.) ועם הארץ לאו אחיך הוא דאינו עושה מעשה עמך: מזמנין. שלשה שאכלו כאחת דתנן חייבין לזמן ואין רשאין ליחלק: ואכלת ושבעת. מהאי קרא נפקא לן ברכת (הזימון) בברכות (דף מח:): חזרתו. ומדרבנן היא ואשיעור טומאתו אסמכוה וטומאת אוכלין בכביצה: כאיסורו

אמר רב כהנא אי לאו דנסיבי כהנתא לא גלאי. משמע שלא היה כהן והא דאמרינן בפ"ק דקדושין (דף ח.) רב כהנא שקל סודרא בפדיון הבן בשביל אשתו היה לוקח כדאמרינן בפ' הזרוע (חולין דף קלב.) רב כהנא הוה אכיל בשביל אשתו והא דאמר בפרק ערבי פסחים (לקמן קיג.) א"ל רב לרב כהנא פשוט נבילתא בשוקא ושקול אגרא ולא תימא כהנא [וגברא] רבא אנא לא בשביל שהיה כהן אלא שכך היה שמו: **לא** מצא בת גבאי לדקה ישא בת מלמדי תינוקות. משמע דגבאי לדקה עדיפי ממלמדי תינוקות והא דאמר בפרק השותפין (ב"ב ה:) והמשכילים יזהירו כזוהר הרקיע אלו גבאי לדקה ומלדיקי הרבים ככוכבים אלו מלמדי תינוקות ל"ל דזוהר הרקיע עדיף מזוהר כוכבים: **מה** ארי דורס ואוכל. פר"ת דורס ואוכל ואין ממתין עד שתמות אף עם הארץ אינו ממתין עד שתתפייס*: **ויש** אומרים אף אין מכריזין על אבידתו. וא"ת מאין יודע שהיא של ע"ה *ואור"י כגון שיירא של ע"ה עוברת ורואינו שנפל מהם והשתא משמע דדוקא אין מכריזין על אבידתו אבל לגזול בידים לא אע"ג דלית ליה האי סברא דבסמוך אפשר דנפיק מיניה ברא מעליא ותימה לר"י אמאי ממונו אסור השתא גופו מותר שמותר לקורעו כדג ממונו לא כל שכן דכה"ג אמר בהגוזל בתרא (ב"ק קיט.) ובע"ז (דף כו.) גבי מוסר לאמן דלית ליה סברא דאפשר דנפיק מיניה ברא מעליא וגו' לר"י דלעיל מיירי במכיר וכופר להכעיס דה"ל הריגתו כמו פיקוח נפש שהוא לסטין וחשוד על הדמים דאי לאו הכי היאך מותר להורגו ביום הכפורים שחל להיות בשבת הלא אפילו נכרי אסור וכן משמע הלשון על חייו אינו חס דמכיר וכופר דיש הרבה עניני ע"ה כדמוכח בסוטה בפ' היה נוטל (דף כב.) ואור"י דמה שאנו מקבלים עדות מע"ה כדאמר בפרק חומר בקדש (חגיגה כב.) כמאן מקבלים האידנא סהדותא מע"ה כרבי יוסי: **ואכלת** זו אכילה. נראה דהני שיעורי כזית וכביצה דלא הוי אלא אסמכתא וכן פ"ה בפרק מי שמתו (ברכות כ:) גבי הא דאמר בן מברך לאביו ומוקי לה כגון דאכל האב שיעור דרבנן ופ"ה שם דהיינו כזית וכביצה דמדאורייתא בעינן שביעה גמורה וכן מוכח התם דקאמר לא אשא פנים לישראל שכתבתי להם ואכלת ושבעת וברכת והן מדקדקים על עצמם בכזית וכביצה וקשה דבפרק ג' שאכלו (שם מח.) אמר ינאי מלכא ומלכתא כרכי ריפתא בהדי הדדי אמר מאן יהיב לן גברא דמברך לן אייתוהו לרבי שמעון בן שטח וכו' שתה ובריך להו וקאמר רבי שמעון בן שטח לגרמיה הוא דעבד דלעולם אינו מוציא אחרים ידי חובה עד שיאכל כזית דגן משמע דאם אכל כזית דגן היה מוציא אחרים ואי כזית דרבנן היכי מפיק להו הא אמר דלא אתי דרבנן ומפיק דאורייתא ואור"י דהיינו דוקא קטן אינו מוציא אותו שאכל שיעור דאורייתא אבל גדול אפילו לא אכל כלל יכול להוציא אחרים מדאורייתא: הדרן עלך אלו עוברין

נב א מיי' שם הל' לב טוש"ע שם ס"ו:
נג ב מיי' פי"א מהל' עדות הלכה ב סמג לאוין ריד טור ש"ע ח"מ סימן לד סעיף יז:
נד ג מיי' פ"י מהל' נחלות הלכה ו סמג עשין לו טוש"ע ח"מ סי' רל סעיף ב:
[וע"ע תוס' קדושין ח. ד"ה ר"כ וב"ב קי. ד"ה ולא ובחולין קלב. ד"ה ר"כ]
נה ד מיי' פ"ה מהלכות ברכות הל' ח סמג עשין כז טוש"ע א"ח סי' קפד סעי' ו וסי' קנו ס"ד:
[וע"ע תוס' חולין סא. ד"ה הדורס ותוס' ב"ק עז: ד"ה דרס]
[וע' תוס' ב"מ כב: ד"ה אי דליכא]
[אולי צ"ל אלמלי ביו"ד עי' תוס' מגילה כח. ד"ה אלמלא]

דברים כז | ויקרא יא | דברים ל | דברים לג | [ערכין טו:] | [המזון צ"ל] | [סנהדרין נ: ע"ש] | דברים לג [ברכות ח. סנהדרין נט.] | [ב"ק קיט.] | איוב כז | [ברכות מט:] | ברכות דף מט: יומא דף עט: | דברים ח | [יומא פא.] | [לקמן קכא.]

גליון הש"ס
גמ' אמר ר"ע כשהייתי ע"ה. עי' כתובות סב: ע"ב תוס' ד"ה דהוה נגוע

רבינו חננאל
ובר מרקיד בי טבא ובר מלחך פנכי ובר מן רבעי: **תניא** ר' אומר עם הארץ אסור לאכול בשר שנאמר זאת תורת הבהמה. אמר ר' אלעזר עם הארץ מותר לנוחרו ביום הכפורים שחל להיות בשבת אמרו לו תלמידיו כו' ואסור להתלוות עמו בדרך: **ת"ר** גדולה שנאה ששונאין עמי הארץ תלמידי חכמים כו' ונשותיהן כו' שנה ופירש יתר מכולן: **ת"ר** ששה דברים נאמרו בעמי הארץ אין מוסרין להם עדות ואין מקבלין מהן עדות ואין מגלין להם את הסוד ואין ממנין מהם אפוטרופין על היתומים ואין ממנין אותן אפוטרופין על קופה של צדקה ואין מתלוין עמהן בדרך ויש אומרים אף אין מכריזין על אבדתן ות"ק זימנין דנפיק מיניה זרעא מעליא יכין וצדיק ילבש:
מתני' וכן כי שיצא מירושלים ונזכר שיש בידו בשר קדש אם עבר צופים שורפו כו' פי' שם מקום שעומד שם וצופה בכל צד שורפו במקום שנזכר ואם לא עבר הצופים חוזר כו' עד כמה חוזרין ר"מ אומר בזה ובזה בכביצה ר' יהודה אומר זה וזה בכזית והחכמים אומרים בשר קדש כזית וחמץ (כביצה) [ואקשי' ורמינהי] (כותבת) עד כמה מזמנין עד כזית ר' יהודה אומר עד כביצה מכלל דלר"מ כזית חשוב ולר' יהודה כביצה ומשני' ר' יוחנן מוחלפת השיטה כלומר הפך דברי ר' מאיר לר' יהודה ודברי ר' יהודה לר' מאיר כי תני מדברים על דבריהם. אביי אמר לעולם לא תיפוך והתם בענין זימון בקראי פליגי ר"מ סבר ואכלת זו אכילה ושבעת זו שתיה ומצינו אכילה בכזית ור' יהודה סבר לא בענין אכילה שיש בה שביעה ולא תהיה פחות מכביצה והכא בסברא פליגי ר"מ מקיש ליה לטומאה מה טומאה בכביצה אף חזרתו בכביצה ר' יהודה אומר כנותר

תורה אור

מתני׳ *ארבעה עשר שחל להיות בשבת מבערין את הכל מלפני השבת דברי ר"מ וחכמים אומרים בזמנו ר"א בר צדוק אומר תרומה מלפני השבת וחולין בזמנן: גמ׳ *תניא ר"א בר צדוק אומר פעם אחת שבת אבא ביבנה וחל ארבעה עשר להיות בשבת ובא זונין ממונה של ר"ג ואמר הגיע עת לבער את החמץ והלכתי אחר אבא וביערנו את החמץ: מתני׳ [א]ההולך לשחוט את פסחו ולמול את בנו ולאכול סעודת אירוסין בבית חמיו ונזכר שיש לו חמץ בתוך ביתו אם יכול לחזור ולבער ולחזור למצותו יחזור ויבער ואם לאו מבטלו בלבו להציל מן *הנכרים ומן הנהר *ומן הלסטים ומן הדליקה ומן המפולת יבטל בלבו ולשבות שביתת הרשות יחזור מיד *וכן מי שיצא מירושלים ונזכר שיש בידו בשר קדש אם עבר צופים שורפו במקומו ואם לאו חוזר ושורפו *לפני הבירה מעצי המערכה ועד כמה הן חוזרין ר"מ אומר זה וזה בכביצה ר' יהודה אומר זה וזה בכזית וחכמים אומרים בשר קדש בכזית וחמץ [ג] בכביצה: גמ׳ ורמינהו ההולך לאכול סעודת אירוסין בבית חמיו ולשבות שביתת הרשות יחזור מיד א"ר יוחנן לא קשיא הא ר' יהודה הא רבי יוסי דתניא סעודת אירוסין רשות דברי ר' יהודה רבי יוסי אומר מצוה והשתא דאמר רב חסדא מחלוקת בסעודה שניה אבל בסעודה ראשונה דברי הכל מצוה אפילו תימא הא והא ר' יהודה ולא קשיא הא בסעודה ראשונה הא בסעודה שניה תניא אמר רבי יהודה אני לא שמעתי אלא סעודת אירוסין אבל לא סבלונות אמר לו ר' יוסי אני שמעתי סעודת אירוסין וסבלונות תניא רבי שמעון אומר [ד]כל סעודה שאינה של מצוה אין תלמיד חכם רשאי להנות ממנה כגון מאי א"ר יוחנן כגון בת כהן לישראל ובת תלמיד חכם לעם הארץ דא"ר יוחנן בת כהן לישראל אין זווגן עולה יפה מאי היא אמר רב חסדא או אלמנה או גרושה או זרע אין לה במתניתא תנא קוברה או קוברתו או מביאתו לידי עניות אני והא א"ר יוחנן הרוצה שיתעשר ידבק בזרעו של אהרן כל שכן שתורה וכהונה מעשרתן לא קשיא *הא בת"ח הא בעם הארץ ר' יהושע נסיב כהנתא חלש אמר לא ניחא ליה לאהרן דאדבק בזרעיה דהוי ליה חתנא כי אנא רב אידי בר אבין נסיב כהנתא נפקו מיניה תרי בני סמיכי רב ששת בריה דרב אידי ור' יהושע בריה דרב אידי אמר ר"פ *אי לא נסיבנא כהנתא לא איעתרי אמר רב כהנא אי לא נסיבנא כהנתא לא גלאי אמרו ליה והא למקום תורה גלית לא גלאי כדגלי אינשי אמר רבי יצחק כל הנהנה מסעודת הרשות לסוף גולה שנא׳ °ואוכלים כרים מצאן ועגלים מתוך מרבק וכתיב לכן עתה יגלו בראש גולים: ת"ר כל ת"ח המרבה סעודתו בכל מקום סוף מחריב את ביתו ומאלמן את אשתו ומייתם את גוזליו ותלמודו משתכח ממנו ומחלוקות רבות באות עליו ודבריו אינם נשמעים ומחלל שם שמים ושם רבו ושם אביו וגורם שם רע לו ולבניו ולבני בניו עד סוף כל הדורות מאי היא אמר אביי קרו ליה בר מחים תנורי רבא אמר בר מרקיד בי כובי רב פפא אמר בר מלחיך פינכי רב שמעיה אמר בר מך רבע: ת"ר לעולם ימכור אדם כל מה שיש לו וישא בת ת"ח שאם מת או גולה מובטח לו שבניו ת"ח ואל ישא בת ע"ה שאם מת או גולה בניו ע"ה ת"ר לעולם ימכור אדם כל מה שיש לו וישא בת ת"ח וישיא בתו לת"ח משל לענבי הגפן בענבי הגפן דבר נאה ומתקבל ולא ישא בת עם הארץ משל לענבי הגפן בענבי הסנה דבר כעור ואינו

עמוס ו

[לעיל דף יג. ודף כ:]
[תוספתא פ"ג]
ס"א הגיים
ס"א לג
[לקמן דף פא: [illegible]]
[פי' פירש"י לקמן דף פא: ד"ה נטמאה וכו' לפני הבירה וכו']
[פי' תוס' לקמן דף קיג. ד"ה אמר]
[ברכות נט.]

רש"י

מתני׳ מבערין את הכל. בין חולין בין תרומה חוץ מכדי אכילתו לשבת אבל כל מה שעתיד לבער יבער: תרומה מלפני השבת. שאינו יכול להאכילה לא לזרים ולא לבהמת זרים והשתא אי אפשר אבל חולין אין צריך לבער אלא בזמנו שיכול למצוא להן אוכלים הרבה: גמ׳ שבת. נשתהה שם שבת אחת: מתני׳ ההולך. בארבעה עשר: אם יכול. שיש שהות ביום: להציל מן הנכרים. את ישראל הנרדפין: יבטל בלבו. ולא יחזור ואפי׳ יש שהות דמדאורייתא סגי ליה בביטול בעלמא: לשבות שביתת הרשות. שהיה הולך להחשיך על התחום לקנות שביתה שם כדי שיהא לו משם ולהלן אלפים לילך למחר שם לדבר הרשות יחזור מיד אבל לקנות שביתת מצוה כגון שילך מחר חוץ לתחום לבית האבל או לבית המשתה היינו כהולך לשחוט את פסחו: שיש בידו בשר קודש. עמו בדרך ונפסל ביוצא שמחיצת קדשים קלים חומת ירושלים: אם עבר צופים. שם כפר שיכול לראות בית המקדש משם: שורפו במקומו. ולא הטריחוהו לחזור: ואם לאו חוזר ושורפו כו׳. כדאמרן בכל שעה (לעיל כד.) בקודש באש תשרף דבמקום אכילתו שריפתו: זה וזה. חמץ דאמרן לעיל ונזכר שיש לו חמץ בביתו ובשר קודש שעמו: בכביצה. אבל בפחות גבי חמץ יבטל בלבו וגבי בשר קודש שורפו במקומו: גמ׳ סעודה שניה. כך הוא דרך החתנים לאחר סעודת אירוסין חוזר ומשגר סבלונות לארוסתו וסועד שם: אני לא שמעתי. שתהא מצוה אלא סעודת אירוסין לבדה אבל לא סעודת סבלונות: סבלונות. דורונות כלים נאים: בת כהן. צריכה להינשא לכהנים ולא לפגום משפחתה להינשא לישראל: אין זווגן עולה יפה. במזל טוב: מאי היא. מה עולה בידן: או אלמנה או גרושה או זרע אין לה. כדכתיב (ויקרא כב) ובת כהן כי תהיה לאיש זר וסמיך ליה ובת כהן כי תהיה אלמנה וגרושה וזרע אין לה וגו׳: או קוברה. בלא זמן: תלמיד חכם. (א) הוא שבח לו אבל עם הארץ ואינו כהן גנאי הוא לו לאהרן ונעשים: לא גלאי. רב כהנא גלה מבבל לא"י כדאמר בהגוזל ומאכיל (ב"ק קיז.): לא גלאי כדגלו אינשי. שאר תלמידים יוצאין מדעתן ואני יצאתי על כרחי מחמת מרדין ואימת מלכות: ומאלמן את אשתו. שמבקש לימודו ואי אפשר לו וגולה למזונות והרי אשתו באלמנות חיות: גוזליו. יתומין: ותלמודו משתכח. שאינו עסוק לחזור עליו: ומחלוקות רבות באות עליו. מחמת ששכח תלמודו או הקפות שמקיף מחנוכין לסעודותיו: קרו ליה. לבנו: מרקיד בי כובי. כדרך הליצנים שמשחקין ומרקדין בחנויות להשקותן בשכרן: מלחיך פינכי. קערות: מך רבע. מקפל לבושו ורובץ וישן כך דרך המשתכרין אינו מספיק לילך לביתו ולשכב על מטתו אלא מקפל לבושו תחתיו וישן: מך. כמו בר חמרא מוך שקיך וגני (*תענית דף ו:): ואינו

תוספות

לשבות שביתת הרשות. פ"ה שהיה הולך להחשיך על התחום לקנות שביתה שם ולילך ד' אלפים לדבר הרשות וקשה א"כ תיקשי למ"ד בפ' בכל מערבין (עירובין לא.) אין מערבין אלא לדבר מצוה וכו' לר"י דה"פ לשבות שביתת הרשות שהולך לשמוח בפסח בבית אוהבו או קרובו: אם עבר צופים. פי' בקונט' שם כפר וקשה לר"י א"כ ה"ל למימר וכמדתו לכל רוח כדתניא בפ' מי שהיה טמא (לקמן צג:) איזו דרך רחוקה מן המודיעין ולחוץ וכמדתה לכל רוח ואור"י דבתוספתא דמכילתין מפרש בהדיא איזהו צופים הרואה ואין מפסיק פי' כל מקום סביב ירושלים שיכול לראותו משם: ושורפו לפני הבירה. פ"ה כדאמר פ' כל שעה (דף כד.) בקודש באש ישרף במקום אכילתו שריפתו וקשה לר"י אי דאורייתא הוא מה לי עבר צופים ומ"ל לא עבר צופים וי"ל דמן התורה יכול לשורפה בכ"מ שירצה דבפרק כל שעה (ג"ז שם) לא מרבינן אלא פסולי קדשי קדשים ואימורי קדשים קלים אבל שאר קדשים שנאכלים לזרים לא מרבינן ומה שהצריכו חכמים לשרוף הני דהכא לפני הבירה היינו גזירה אטו קדשי קדשים: לפני הבירה. בזבחים בפ' טבול יום (דף קד:) פליגי מאי בירה אמר רבה בר בר חנה א"ר יוחנן מקום יש בהר הבית ובירה שמו ר"ל אמר כל הבית כולו קרוי בירה שנאמר *אל הבירה אשר הכינותי: וחכמים אומרים בשר קודש בכזית וחמץ בכביצה. אומר ריב"א דמפרש בירושלמי משום דבשר קודש לית ליה תקנה בביטול החמירו בכזית אבל חמץ אית ליה תקנה בביטול לא החמירו עד כביצה: תניא א"ר יהודה. תימה אמאי לא מייתי תניא כמי הכי מהך דהכא לרב חסדא: אמר

[נ"א ולכנסת]

עין משפט נר מצוה

מז א מיי׳ פ"ג מהל׳ חמץ הלכה ג סמג עשין לט טוש"ע א"ח סי׳ תמד סעיף א:

מח ב מיי׳ שם הל׳ ט טוש"ע שם סעיף ז:

מט ג מיי׳ פרק יט מהלכות פסולי המוקדשין הלכה ח:

מט [נ] [מיי׳ פ"ג מהל׳ חמץ הל׳ ט טוש"ע א"ח סי׳ תמד סעיף ז]:

נ ד מיי׳ פ"ה מהלכות דעות הלכה ב:

נא ה מיי׳ פכ"א מהל׳ איסורי ביאה הלכה לב סמג לאוין קכו טור ש"ע אה"ע סי׳ ב ס"ח:

רבינו חננאל

כר׳ מאיר דשנת לן תנא בלשון דחכמים: מתני׳ ארבעה עשר שחל להיות בשבת מבערין הכל מלפני השבת דברי ר׳ מאיר ר׳ אליעזר אומר תרומת מלפני השבת וחולין בזמנן וקיי"ל כר׳ אלעזר בר׳ צדוק: תניא ר׳ אלעזר ברבי צדוק אומר פעם אחת שבת אבא ביבנה וחל ארבעה עשר להיות בשבת כו׳: מתני׳ ההולך לשחוט את פסחו ולמול את בנו ולאכול סעודת אירוסין בבית חמיו ונזכר כו׳ ורמינהי ההולך לאכול סעודת אירוסין בבית חמיו ולשבות שביתת הרשות יחזור מיד והא קתני במתני׳ יבטל בלבו מכלל שאין מחייבין אותו לחזור ושנינ׳ מתני׳ ר׳ יוסי היא דסבר סעודת אירוסין מצוה וביעור חמץ נמי מצוה מידי ביעור חמץ אפשר לקיימה בביטול חמץ וישלים סעודת אירוסין שנמצא מקיים שתיהן ובריית׳ ר׳ יהודה דסבר סעודת אירוסין רשות כגון שביתת הרשות ולדברי הכל חייב לחזור מיד דתניא סעודת אירוסין רשות דברי ר׳ יהודה ר׳ יוסי אומר מצוה והשתא דאמר רב חסדא מחלוקת בסעודה שניה אבל בסעודה ראשונה אפי׳ ר׳ יהודה מודה דמצוה אפי׳ תימא מתני׳ ר׳ יהודה ובסעודה ראשונה שהיא מצוה ברייתא בסעודה שניה שהיא רשות:

הגהות הב"ח

(א) רש"י ד"ה תלמיד חכם שבח הוא לו:

תניא אמר ר׳ יהודה אני לא שמעתי אלא סעודת אירוסין בלבד אמר ר׳ יוסי אני שמעתי סעודת אירוסין וסבלונות: ירושלמי לשבות שביתת הרשות לשבות אצל ר׳ או מי שהוא גדול ממנו אמר ר׳ יוסי בר בון גדול השלום שהוקש לשני דברים שחייבין עליהן כרת מילה ושחיטת פסח: תניא א"ר אלעזר כל סעודה שאינה של מצוה אין תלמיד חכם רשאי ליהנות ממנה כגון מאי א"ר יוחנן כגון בת כהן [לישראל] או בת תלמיד חכם אצל עם הארץ לפי שאין זיווגן עולה יפה כדכתיב ובת כהן כי תהיה אלמנה וגרושה וזרע. אמר רב כהנא אי לא נסיבנא כהנתא לא גלאי ומעשה דרב כהנא מפורש בהגוזל בתרא כי שמטיה לקועיה להוא גברא ועריק לארץ ישראל: אמר ר׳ יצחק כל הנהנה מסעודת הרשות לסוף גולה שנא׳ אוכלים כרים מצאן ועגלים מתוך מרבק וכתיב בתריה לכן עתה יגלו בראש גולים: ת"ר תלמיד חכם המרבה סעודתו בכ"מ לסוף שהריב את ביתו ומאלמן את אשתו ומייתם גוזליו ותלמודו משתכח ומחלוקות רבות [באות] עליו ודבריו אין נשמעין ומחלל שם שמים ושם אביו ושם רבו וגורם שם רע לו ולבניו עד סוף כל הדורות וקרו לו בר מיחם תנורא ובר

Continuation of translation from previous page as indicated by ◁

Said R. Jose to him: I have heard of [both] the feast of betrothal and [that] of espousal gifts.

It was taught, R. Simeon said: Every feast which is not in connection with a religious deed, a scholar must derive no enjoyment thereof.[4] What, for instance?—Said R. Joḥanan: E.g., [the feast at the betrothal of] the daughter of a priest to an Israelite,[5] or the daughter of a scholar to an ignoramus. For R. Joḥanan said: If the daughter of a priest [marries] an Israelite, their union will not be auspicious. What is it?[6] Said R. Ḥisda: [She will be] either a widow or a divorced woman, or she will have no seed [children].[7] In a Baraitha it was taught: He will bury her or she will bury him, or she will reduce him to poverty. But that is not so, for R. Joḥanan said: He who desires to become wealthy, let him cleave to the seed of Aaron, [for it is all the more] that the Torah and the priesthood will enrich them?—There is no difficulty: one refers to a scholar;[8] the other refers to an *'am ha-areẓ*.[9]

R. Joshua married a priest's daughter. Falling sick, he said, Aaron is not pleased that I should cleave to his seed [and] possess a son-in-law like myself. R. Idi b. Abin married a priest's daughter, and there came forth from him two ordained sons—R. Shesheth the son of R. Idi and R. Joshua the son of R. Idi. R. Papa said: Had I not married a priest's daughter, I would not have become
c wealthy.[1] R. Kahana said: Had I not married a priest's daughter, I had not gone into exile.[2] Said they to him, But you were exiled to a place of learning!—I was not exiled as people are [generally] exiled.[3]

R. Isaac said: Whoever partakes of a secular feast eventually goes into exile, for it is said, *and* [ye that] *eat the lambs out of the flock, and the calves out of the midst of the stall;* and it is written, *therefore now shall they go captive at the head of them that go captive.*[4]

Our Rabbis taught: Every scholar who feasts much in every place, eventually destroys his home, widows his wife, orphans his young, forgets his learning,[5] and becomes involved in many quarrels;[6] his words are unheeded, and he desecrates the Name of Heaven and the name of his teacher and the name of his father, and he causes an evil name for himself, his children, and his childrens' children until the end of time.[7] What is it?[8] Said Abaye: He is called, a heater of ovens. Raba said: A tavern dancer! R. Papa said: A plate licker. R. Shemaiah said: A folder [of garments] and a man who lies down [to sleep].[9]

Our Rabbis taught: Let a man always sell all he has and marry the daughter of a scholar, for if he dies or goes into exile, he is assured that his children will be scholars. But let him not marry the daughter of an *'am ha-areẓ*, for if he dies or goes into exile, his children will be *'amme ha-areẓ*.

Our Rabbis taught: Let a man always sell all he has and marry the daughter of a scholar, and marry his daughter to a scholar. This may be compared to [the grafting of] grapes of a vine with grapes of a vine, [which is] a seemly and acceptable thing. But let him not marry the daughter of an *'am ha-areẓ;* this may be compared to [the grafting of] grapes of a vine with berries of a

(4) I.e., must not partake of it. (5) I.e., a non-priest. She blemishes her family by marrying beneath her. (6) In what respect will it be unfortunate? (7) Rashi: because it is written, *And if a priest's daughter be married unto a common man*, which is followed by, *But if a priest's daughter be a widow, or divorced, and have no child* (Lev. XXII, 12f).—Hence such a union was looked upon with disfavour, and R. Joḥanan maintains that the feast is not a true religious one. (8) If a scholar marries into a priestly family he brings honour upon it. (9) V. Glos.

c (1) He was a wealthy brewer. (2) From my home in Babylonia to Palestine; v. B.Ḳ. 117*a*. (3) Voluntarily; but I had to flee. (4) Amos VI, 4, 7. (5) Lit., 'his learning is forgotten from him'. (6) Lit., 'come upon him'. (7) Lit., 'until the end of all generations'.—His fondness for feasting elsewhere leads him to do the same in his own home, and to make it possible he must sell his furniture, etc. Seeing himself on the road to ruin, he wanders into exile, leaving his wife and children widowed and orphaned. He wastes his time, so forgets his learning. This involves him in disputes on learning. Or, his poverty involves him in disputes with tradesmen because he cannot settle his bills. Again, the banqueting table itself is a fruitful source of quarrels (Rashi and Maharsha). (8) How does he bring his name etc., into contempt? (9) Where he is, being too drunk to go home.—Or, the son of a heater of ovens etc., with reference to his children. The translation follows Maharsha, *bar* (בר) being understood as 'a man who'. The alternative is Rashi's.

מתני׳ *ארבעה עשר שחל להיות בשבת מבערין את הכל מלפני השבת דברי ר"מ וחכמים אומרים בזמנו ר"א בר צדוק אומר תרומה מלפני השבת וחולין בזמנן: גמ׳ *תניא ר"א בר צדוק אומר פעם אחת שבת אבא ביבנה וחל ארבעה עשר להיות בשבת ובא זונין ממונה של ר"ג ואמר הגיע עת לבער את החמץ והלכתי אחר אבא וביערנו את החמץ: מתני׳ "ההולך לשחוט את פסחו ולמול את בנו ולאכול סעודת אירוסין בבית חמיו ונזכר שיש לו חמץ בתוך ביתו אם יכול לחזור ולבער ולחזור למצותו יחזור ויבער ואם לאו מבטלו בלבו להציל מן *הנכרים ומן הנהר *ומן הלסטים ומן הדליקה ומן המפולת יבטל בלבו ולשבות שביתת הרשות יחזור מיד *וכן מי שיצא מירושלים ונזכר שיש בידו בשר קדש אם עבר צופים שורפו במקומו ואם לאו חוזר ושורפו *לפני הבירה מעצי המערכה ועד כמה הן חוזרין ר"מ אומר זה וזה בכביצה ר' יהודה אומר זה וזה בכזית וחכמים אומרים בשר קדש בכזית וחמץ [ג] בכביצה: גמ׳ ורמינהו ההולך לאכול סעודת אירוסין בבית חמיו ולשבות שביתת הרשות יחזור מיד א"ר יוחנן לא קשיא הא ר' יהודה הא רבי יוסי דתניא סעודת אירוסין רשות דברי ר' יהודה רבי יוסי אומר מצוה והשתא דאמר רב חסדא מחלוקת בסעודה שניה אבל בסעודה ראשונה דברי הכל מצוה אפילו תימא הא והא ר' יהודה ולא קשיא הא בסעודה ראשונה הא בסעודה שניה תניא אמר רבי יהודה אני לא שמעתי אלא סעודת אירוסין אבל לא סבלונות אמר לו ר' יוסי אני שמעתי סעודת אירוסין וסבלונות תניא רבי שמעון אומר "כל סעודה שאינה של מצוה אין תלמיד חכם רשאי להנות ממנה כגון מאי א"ר יוחנן כגון בת כהן לישראל ובת תלמיד חכם לעם הארץ דא"ר יוחנן בת כהן לישראל אין זווגן עולה יפה מאי היא אמר רב חסדא או אלמנה או גרושה או זרע אין לה. במתניתא תנא קוברה או קוברתו או מביאתו לידי עניות איני והא א"ר יוחנן הרוצה שיתעשר ידבק בזרעו של אהרן כל שכן שתורה וכהונה מעשרתן לא קשיא "הא בת"ח הא בעם הארץ ר' יהושע נסיב כהנתא חלש אמר לא ניחא ליה לאהרן דאדבק בזרעיה דהוי ליה חתנא כי אנא רב אידי בר אבין נסיב כהנתא נפקו מיניה תרי בני סמיכי רב ששת בריה דרב אידי ור' יהושע בריה דרב אידי אמר רב פפא *אי לא נסיבנא כהנתא לא איעתרי אמר רב כהנא אי לא נסיבנא כהנתא לא גלאי אמרו ליה והא למקום תורה גלית לא גלאי כדגלי אינשי אמר רבי יצחק כל הנהנה מסעודת הרשות לסוף גולה שנא׳ °ואוכלים כרים מצאן ועגלים מתוך מרבק וכתיב לכן עתה יגלו בראש גולים: ת"ר כל ת"ח המרבה סעודתו בכל מקום סוף מחריב את ביתו ומאלמן את אשתו ומייתם את גוזליו ותלמודו משתכח ממנו ומחלוקות רבות באות עליו ודבריו אינם נשמעים ומחלל שם שמים ושם רבו ושם אביו וגורם שם רע לו ולבניו ולבני בניו עד סוף כל הדורות מאי היא אמר אביי קרו ליה בר מחים תנורי רבא אמר בר מרקיד בי כובי רב פפא אמר בר מלחיך פינכי רב שמעיה אמר בר מך רבע: ת"ר לעולם ימכור אדם כל מה שיש לו וישא בת ת"ח שאם מת או גולה מובטח לו שבניו ת"ח ואל ישא בת ע"ה שאם מת או גולה בניו ע"ה ת"ר לעולם ימכור אדם כל מה שיש לו וישא בת ת"ח וישיא בתו לת"ח משל לענבי הגפן בענבי הגפן דבר נאה ומתקבל ולא ישא בת עם הארץ משל לענבי הגפן בענבי הסנה דבר כעור ואינו

תורה אור — עמוס ו

רש"י

מתני׳ מבערין את הכל. בין חולין בין תרומה חוץ מכדי אכילתו לשבת אבל כל מה שעתיד לבער יבער: תרומה מלפני השבת. שאינו יכול להאכילה לא לזרים ולא לבהמת זרים ולהשהותה אי אפשר אבל חולין אין צריך לבער אלא בזמנו שיכול למצוא להן אוכלים הרבה: גמ׳ שבת. נשתהה שם שבת אחת: מתני׳ ההולך. בארבעה עשר: אם יכול. שיש שהות ביום: להציל מן הנכרים. את ישראל הנרדפין: יבטל בלבו. ולא יחזור ואפי׳ יש שהות דמדאורייתא סגי ליה בביטול בעלמא: לשבות שביתת הרשות. שהיה הולך להחשיך על התחום לקנות שביתה שם כדי שיהא לו משם ולהלן אלפים לילך למחר שם לדבר הרשות יחזור מיד אבל לקנות שביתת מצוה כגון שילך מחר חוץ לתחום לבית האבל או לבית המשתה היינו כהולך לשחוט את פסחו: שיש בידו בשר קודש. עמו בדרך ונפסל ביוצא שמחיצת קדשים קלים חומת ירושלים: אם עבר צופים. שם כפר שיכול לראות בית המקדש משם: שורפו במקומו. ולא הטריחוהו לחזור: ואם לאו חוזר ושורפו כו׳. כדאמרן בכל שעה (לעיל כד.) בקודש באש תשרף דבמקום אכילתו שריפתו: זה וזה. חמץ דאמרן לעיל ונזכר שיש לו חמץ בביתו ובשר קודש שעמו: בכביצה. אבל בפחות גבי חמץ יבטל בלבו וגבי בשר קודש שורפו במקומו: גמ׳ סעודה שניה. כך הוא דרך החתנים לאחר סעודת אירוסין חוזר ומשגר סבלונות לארוסתו וסועד שם: אני לא שמעתי. שתהא מצוה אלא סעודת אירוסין לבדה אבל לא סעודת סבלונות: סבלונות. דורונות כלים נאים: בת כהן. צריכה להינשא לכהנים ולא לפגום משפחתה להינשא לישראל: אין זווגן עולה יפה. במזל טוב: מאי היא. מה עולה בידן: או אלמנה או גרושה או זרע אין לה. כדכתיב (ויקרא כב) ובת כהן כי תהיה לאיש זר וסמיך ליה ובת כהן כי תהיה אלמנה וגרושה וזרע אין לה וגו׳: או קוברה. בלא זמן: תלמיד חכם. (א) הוא שבח לו אבל עם הארץ ואינו כהן גנאי הוא לו לאהרן ונעכשים: לא גלאי. רב כהנא גלה מבבל לא"י כדאמר בהגוזל ומאכיל (ב"ק קיז.): לא גלאי כדגלו אינשי. שאר תלמידים יוצאין מדעתן ואני יצאתי על כרחי מחמת מרדין ואימת מלכות: ומאלמן את אשתו. שמבקש לימודו ואי אפשר לו וגולה למזונות והרי אשתו באלמנות חיות: גוזליו. יתומין: ותלמודו משתכח. שאינו עסוק לחזור עליו: ומחלוקות רבות באות עליו. מחמת ששכח תלמודו או הקפות שמקיף מחנוכין לסעודותיו: קרו ליה. לבנו: מרקיד בי כובי. כדרך הליצנים שמשחקין ומרקדין בחנויות להשקותן בשכרן: מלחיך פינכי. קערות: מך רבע. מקפל לבושו ורובץ וישן כך דרך המשתכרין אינו מספיק לילך לביתו ולשכב על מטתו אלא מקפל לבושו תחתיו וישן: מך. כמו בר חמרא מוך שקיך וגני (*תענית דף ו:): ואינו

תוספות

לשבות שביתת הרשות. פ"ה שהיה הולך להחשיך על התחום לקנות שביתה שם ולילך ד׳ אלפים לדבר הרשות וקשה א"כ תיקשי למ"ד בפ׳ בכל מערבין (עירובין לא.) אין מערבין אלא לדבר מצוה וכו׳ לר"י דה"פ לשבות שביתת הרשות שהולך לשמוח בפסח בבית אוהבו או קרובו: אם עבר צופים. פי׳ בקונט׳ שם כפר וקשה לר"י א"כ ה"ל למימר וכמדתו לכל רוח כדתניא בפ׳ מי שהיה טמא (לקמן צג:) איזהו דרך רחוקה מן המודיעין ולחוץ וכמדתה לכל רוח ואור"י דבתוספתא דמכילתין מפרש בהדיא איזהו צופים הרואה ואין מפסיק פי׳ כל מקום סביב ירושלים שיכול לראותו משם: ושורפו לפני הבירה. פ"ה כדאמר פ׳ כל שעה (דף כד.) בקודש באש ישרף במקום אכילתו שריפתו וקשה לר"י אי דאורייתא הוא מה לי עבר צופים ומ"ל לא עבר צופים וי"ל דמן התורה יכול לשורפה בכ"מ שירצה דבפרק כל שעה (ג"ז שם) לא מרבינן אלא פסולי קדשי קדשים ואימורי קדשים קלים אבל שאר קדשים שנאכלים לזרים לא מרבינן ומה שהצריכו חכמים לשרוף הכי דהכא לפני הבירה היינו גזירה אטו קדשי קדשים: לפני הבירה. בזבחים בפ׳ טבול יום (דף קד:) פליגי מאי בירה אמר רבה בר בר חנה א"ר יוחנן מקום יש בהר הבית ובירה שמו ר"ל אמר כל הבית כולו הוי בירה שנאמר *אל הבירה אשר הכינותי: וחכמים אומרים בשר קודש בכזית וחמץ בכביצה. אומר ריב"א דמפרש בירושלמי משום דבשר קודש לית ליה תקנה בביטול החמירו בכזית אבל חמץ אית ליה תקנה בביטול לא החמירו עד כביצה: תניא א"ר יהודה. תימה אמאי לא מייתי תניא כמי הכי מהך דהכא לרב חסדא:

עין משפט נר מצוה

מו א מיי׳ פ"ג מהל׳ חמץ הלכה ג סמג עשין לט טוש"ע א"ח סי׳ תמד סעיף א:

מז ב מיי׳ שם הל׳ ט טוש"ע שם סעיף ז:

מח ג מיי׳ פי"ח מהלכות פסולי המוקדשין הלכה ח:

מט [נ] [מיי׳ פ"ג מהל׳ חמץ הל׳ ח טוש"ע א"ח סי׳ תמד סעיף ז]:

נ ד מיי׳ פ"ה מהלכות דעות הלכה ב:

נא ה מיי׳ פכ"א מהל׳ אסורי ביאה הלכה לב סמג לאוין קכו טור ש"ע אה"ע סי׳ ב ס"ח:

מסורת הש"ס

[לעיל דף יג. ודף כ:]

[תוספתא פ"ג]

ס"א הנכרים ס"א לג

לקמן דף פח: כריתות דף טו:

[עי׳ פירש"י לקמן פ"א: ד"ה נטמא וכו׳ לפני הבירה וכו׳]

[נ"ע ולבנת]

הגהות הב"ח

(א) רש"י ד"ה תלמיד חכם שבח הוא לו:

[עי׳ תוס׳ לקמן דף קיג. ד"ה אמר]

[כתובות נט.]

רבינו חננאל

כר׳ מאיר דשנה לן תנא בלשון דחכמים: מתני׳ ארבעה עשר שחל להיות בשבת מבערין הכל מלפני השבת דברי ר׳ מאיר ר׳ אליעזר אומר תרומה מלפני השבת וחולין בזמנן וקיי"ל כר׳ אלעזר בר׳ צדוק: תניא ר׳ אלעזר ברבי צדוק אומר פעם אחת שבת אבא ביבנה וחל ארבעה עשר להיות בשבת כו׳: מתני׳ ההולך לשחוט את פסחו ולמול את בנו ולאכול סעודת אירוסין בבית חמיו ונזכר כו׳ ורמינהו ההולך לאכול סעודת אירוסין בבית חמיו ולשבות שביתת הרשות יחזור מיד והוא קתני במתני׳ יבטל בלבו מכלל שאין מחייבין אותו לחזור ושנינ׳ מתני׳ ר׳ יוסי היא דסבר סעודת אירוסין מצוה וביעור חמץ נמי מצוה מיהו ביעור חמץ אפשר לקיימה בביטול חמץ וישלים סעודת אירוסין שנמצא מקיים שתיהן וברייתא ר׳ יהודה דסבר סעודת אירוסין רשות כגון שביתת הרשות ולדברי הכל חייב לחזור מיד דתניא סעודת אירוסין רשות דברי ר׳ יהודה ר׳ יוסי אומר מצוה והשתא דאמר רב חסדא מחלוקת בסעודה שניה אבל בסעודה ראשונה אפי׳ ר׳ יהודה מודה דמצוה אפי׳ תימא מתני׳ ר׳ יהודה ובסעודה ראשונה שהיא מצוה ברייתא בסעודת שניה שהיא רשות:

תניא אמר ר׳ יהודה אני לא שמעתי אלא סעודת אירוסין בלבד אמר ר׳ יוסי אני שמעתי סעודת אירוסין וסבלונות: ירושלמי לשבות שביתת הרשות לשבות אצל ר׳ או מי שהוא גדול ממנו אמר ר׳ יוסי בר בון גדול השלום שהוקש לשני דברים שחייבין עליהן כרת מילה ושחיטת פסח: תניא א"ר אלעזר כל סעודה שאינה של מצוה אין תלמיד חכם רשאי ליהנות ממנה כגון מאי א"ר יוחנן כגון בת כהן [לישראל] או בת תלמיד חכם אצל עם הארץ לפי שאין זיווגן עולה יפה כדכתיב ובת כהן כי תהיה אלמנה וגרושה וזרע. אמר רב כהנא אי לא נסיבנא כהנתא לא גלאי ומעשה דרב כהנא מפורש בהגוזל בתרא כי שמטיה לקועיה להוא גברא ועריק לארץ ישראל: אמר ר׳ יצחק כל הנהנה מסעודת הרשות לסוף גולה שנא׳ אוכלים כרים מצאן ועגלים מתוך מרבק וכתיב בתריה לכן עתה יגלו בראש גולים: ת"ר תלמיד חכם המרבה סעודתו בכ"מ לסוף מחריב את ביתו ומאלמן את אשתו ומייתם גוזליו ותלמודו משתכח ומחלוקות רבות [באות] עליו ודבריו אין נשמעין ומחלל שם שמים ושם אביו ושם רבו וגורם שם רע לו ולבניו עד סוף כל הדורות וקרו לו בר מיחם תנורא ובר

MISHNAH. [49a] IF THE FOURTEENTH [OF NISAN] FALLS ON THE SABBATH, EVERYTHING MUST BE REMOVED[4] BEFORE THE SABBATH:[5] THIS IS R. MEIR'S VIEW; WHILE THE SAGES MAINTAIN: [IT MUST BE REMOVED] AT ITS [USUAL] TIME;[6] R. ELEAZAR B. ZADOK SAID: TERUMAH [MUST BE REMOVED] BEFORE THE SABBATH,[7] AND ḤULLIN AT ITS [USUAL] TIME.[8]

GEMARA. It was taught, R. Eleazar b. Zadok said: My father once spent a week in Yabneh,[9] when the fourteenth fell on the Sabbath, and there came Zonin, R. Gamaliel's deputy,[10] and announced: 'The time has come to remove the leaven', and I followed my father and we removed the leaven.

MISHNAH. HE WHO IS ON HIS WAY[11] TO SLAUGHTER HIS PASSOVER SACRIFICE OR TO CIRCUMCISE HIS SON[12] OR TO DINE AT A BETROTHAL[13] FEAST AT THE HOUSE OF HIS FATHER-IN-LAW, AND RECOLLECTS THAT HE HAS LEAVEN AT HOME, IF HE IS ABLE TO GO BACK, REMOVE [IT], AND [THEN] RETURN TO HIS RELIGIOUS DUTY,[14] HE MUST GO BACK AND REMOVE [IT]; BUT IF NOT, HE ANNULS IT IN HIS HEART. [IF HE IS ON
a HIS WAY] TO SAVE [PEOPLE] FROM HEATHENS[1] OR FROM A RIVER OR FROM BRIGANDS[2] OR FROM A FIRE OR FROM A COLLAPSE [OF A BUILDING], HE ANNULS IT IN HIS HEART.[3] [BUT IF] TO APPOINT A SABBATH STATION FOR A VOLUNTARY [SECULAR] PURPOSE,[4] HE MUST RETURN IMMEDIATELY. SIMILARLY, HE WHO WENT OUT OF JERUSALEM AND RECOLLECTED THAT HE HAD HOLY FLESH WITH HIM,[5] IF HE HAS PASSED SCOPUS,[6] HE BURNS IT WHERE HE IS;[7] BUT IF NOT, HE RETURNS AND BURNS IT IN FRONT OF THE TEMPLE[8] WITH THE WOOD OF THE [ALTAR] PILE.[9] AND FOR WHAT [QUANTITY] MUST THEY RETURN? R. MEIR SAID: FOR BOTH,[10] WHEN THERE IS AS MUCH AS AN EGG; R. JUDAH SAID: FOR BOTH, WHEN THERE IS AS MUCH AS AN OLIVE; BUT THE SAGES RULE: HOLY FLESH, [THE STANDARD IS] AS MUCH AS AN OLIVE; WHILE LEAVEN, [THE STANDARD IS] AS MUCH AS AN EGG.[11]

GEMARA. But the following contradicts it: He who is on his way to partake of a betrothal feast in his father-in-law's house or to appoint a Sabbath station for a voluntary purpose must return immediately?—Said R. Johanan, There is no difficulty: one is [according to] R. Judah: the other is [according to] R. Jose. For it was taught: The betrothal feast is a voluntary [function]; this is R. Judah's view. R. Jose said: It is a religious [function]. But now that R. Ḥisda said: The controversy is in respect of the second
b feast,[1] but in respect to the first feast all agree that it is a religious [function], you may even say [that] both are [according to] R. Judah, yet there is no difficulty; one refers to the first feast, while the other refers to the second feast.

It was taught, R. Judah said: I have heard only of the betrothal feast,[2] but not of [the feast in connection with] espousal gifts.[3]

(4) I.e., destroyed. (5) Save what is required for the Sabbath itself. (6) On the morning of the fourteenth. (7) Because if any is left over none can eat it; neither *zarim* nor cattle. (8) Because it is easy to find eaters for it. (9) The famous town to the north-west of Jerusalem, seat of R. Joḥanan b. Zakkai's academy and Sanhedrin after the destruction of Jerusalem. (10) The superintendent of the Academy. (11) Lit., 'is going'. (12) In ancient days and until comparatively recently this was done in the Synagogue. (13) *Erusin* denotes the first stage of marriage, v. Glos. (14) He himself being the bridegroom. A 'betrothal feast' is considered a religious duty, v. Gemara.

a (1) Rashi: Jews who are being pursued. (2) Var. lec.: a robber band. (3) If 'robber band' is read before, this must be deleted. Even if there is time to return, he must not go back. (4) On the Sabbath a man must not go more than two thousand cubits beyond the town boundary; this outside limit is called the *teḥum*. But before the Sabbath commences he can appoint any spot within the *teḥum* as the station where he will spend the Sabbath, and then he may proceed two thousand cubits beyond that spot; he does that by taking some food to the place, which he will eat on the Sabbath. (5) Holy flesh, if taken without Jerusalem, becomes unfit and must be burnt. (6) An eminence north-east of Jerusalem, whence the Temple can be seen. To-day it is the site of the Hebrew University. (7) And need not return to Jerusalem. (8) [*Birah*. This is variously explained in Zeb. 104*b* as the Temple Mount itself, a place in the Temple Mount, and a tower in the Temple Mount.] (9) I.e., wood arranged in a pile for use on the altar.—V. *supra* 24*a*. (10) *Sc.* leaven and sacred flesh. (11) These are the minima for which one must return.

b (1) After the betrothal the bridegroom (*arus*) sent gifts to his bride, in connection with which there was a second feast at the father-in-law's house. (2) As being a religious function. (3) *Siblonoth*.

◁ *For the continuation of the English translation of this page see overleaf.*

it is likewise in respect of *ḥallah*.[5] But we learned: [48b] Slightly more than five quarters[6] of flour are subject to *ḥallah?*[7]—This is what he says: A *ḳab* of Meloga too is the equivalent of this quantity.

R. Joseph said: Our women are accustomed to bake a *ḳapiza*[8] at a time on Passover. Said Abaye to him, What is your intention? To be stricter![9] [But] it is strictness which leads to [unwarranted] leniency, as [the woman] exempts it from *ḥallah?*[10]—Said he: They do as R. Eliezer. For we learned, R. Eliezer said: If he removes [loaves from the oven] and places [them] in a basket, the basket combines them in respect of *ḥallah;*[11] whereon Rab Judah said in Samuel's name: The *halachah* is as R. Eliezer. Said he to him, But it was stated thereon, R. Joshua b. Levi said: They taught this only of Babylonian loaves, which cleave to each other,[12] but not
a [of] cracknels?[1]—Surely it was stated thereon, R. Ḥanina said: Even cracknels.

R. Jeremiah asked: What of a board which has no ledges?[2] Do we require the *inside* of a vessel, which is absent here; or perhaps we require the air space of a vessel, which is present? The question stands.

It was taught: R. Eliezer said: The basket [only] combines them; R. Joshua said: The oven combines them;[3] R. Simeon b. Gamaliel said: Babylonian loaves which cleave to each other combine.[4]

MISHNAH. R. GAMALIEL SAID: THREE WOMEN MAY KNEAD AT THE SAME TIME[5] AND BAKE IN ONE OVEN, ONE AFTER THE OTHER. BUT THE SAGES RULE: THREE WOMEN MAY BE ENGAGED ON DOUGH AT THE SAME TIME,[6] ONE KNEADING, ANOTHER SHAPING AND A THIRD BAKING.[7] R. AKIBA SAID: NOT ALL WOMEN AND NOT ALL KINDS OF WOOD AND NOT ALL OVENS ARE ALIKE.[8] THIS IS THE GENERAL PRINCIPLE: IF IT [THE DOUGH] RISES, LET HER WET[9] IT WITH COLD WATER.[10]

GEMARA. Our Rabbis taught: Having kneaded [the dough] she forms it [in shape], while her companion kneads in her place; having formed [the dough] she bakes it, and her companion shapes [the dough] in her place, while the third [woman] kneads. [The first] having baked, she kneads [again], and her companion bakes in her place, while the third shapes [her dough]. And thus
b the round revolves.[1] As long as they are engaged [in working] on the dough, it does not come to fermentation.

R. AKIBA SAID: NOT ALL WOMEN etc. It was taught, R. Akiba said: I discussed [the matter] before R. Gamaliel: Let our Master teach us: Does this[2] refer to energetic women or to women who are not energetic; to damp wood or to dry wood; to a hot oven or to a cool oven? Said he to me, You have nought else save what the Sages learned: IF IT RISES, LET HER WET IT WITH COLD WATER.

MISHNAH. SI'UR[3] MUST BE BURNT, WHILE HE WHO EATS IT IS NOT CULPABLE; SIDDUḲ[4] MUST BE BURNT, WHILE HE WHO EATS IT [ON PASSOVER] IS LIABLE TO KARETH. WHAT IS SI'UR? [WHEN THERE ARE LINES ON THE SURFACE] LIKE LOCUSTS' HORNS;[5] SIDDUḲ IS WHEN THE CRACKS HAVE INTERMINGLED WITH EACH OTHER: THIS IS THE VIEW OF R. JUDAH. BUT THE SAGES MAINTAIN: REGARDING THE ONE AND THE OTHER,[6] HE WHO EATS IT IS LIABLE TO KARETH.[7] AND WHAT IS SI'UR? WHEN ITS SURFACE IS BLANCHED, LIKE [THE FACE OF] A MAN WHOSE HAIR IS STANDING [ON END].

GEMARA. Our Rabbis taught: What is *si'ur?* Whenever its surface is blanched, like [the face of] a man whose hair is standing on end; *sidduḳ* is [when there are lines on the surface] like locusts' horns: this is R. Meir's view. But the Sages maintain: What is *si'ur?* [When the lines on its surface are] like locusts' horns; *sidduḳ* is when the cracks have intermingled with each other; and in both cases, he who eats it is liable to *kareth*. But we learned: SI'UR MUST BE BURNT, WHILE HE WHO EATS IT IS NOT CULPABLE.. THIS IS THE VIEW OF R. JUDAH?—Say according to R. Meir,
c in both cases,[1] he who eats it incurs *kareth*.[2] Raba said: What is R. Meir's reason? There is not a single crack on the surface for which there are not many cracks below [the surface].[3]

(5) That is the smallest quantity subject to *ḥallah*. (6) Lit., 'five quarters and more'. I.e., quarters of a *ḳab*, = one and one fourth logs. (7) V. Ḥal. II, 6. (8) A measure = three fourths of a *ḳab;* v. Obermeyer, p. 241, n. 1. (9) For the permitted quantity is larger. (10) If she baked a *kab* of Meloga at a time, she would have to separate *ḥallah*, whereas now she is exempt. (11) I.e., they are counted as one, if together they make up the minimum quantity. (12) Lit., 'bite of each other'. They were wide, and when set in the oven they stuck to each other, owing to lack of space; therefore they all count as one.
a (1) A kind of narrow roll. (2) Does it combine the loaves placed upon it? (3) If they are baked together in an oven, even if they are not subsequently placed together in a basket, they are all counted as one in respect of *ḥallah*. (4) But not cracknels. (5) Lit., 'as one'. (6) Not all *kneading* at the same time, which would necessitate too long a wait when they come to bake it after each other. (7) V. Gemara. (8) Hence the views of R. Gamaliel and the Sages are unacceptable. (9) Lit., 'polish'. (10) Which retards fermentation.
b (1) This is the explanation of the Sage's ruling: THREE WOMEN MAY BE ENGAGED ON DOUGH AT THE SAME TIME. (2) *Sc.* the ruling that three women may knead or may be working on dough at the same time. (3) V. *supra* 43*a*. (4) Dough, the surface of which is cracked through fermentation. This is completely leaven. (5) I.e., small lines are just beginning to appear. (6) I.e., both stages as defined by R. Judah. (7) Even at the earlier stage it is no longer *si'ur*.
c (1) *Sc.* both *si'ur* and *sidduḳ* as defined by R. Judah. (2) Because he regards both as *sidduḳ*. (3) Hence even when the cracks on the surface are still separate, they already cross below the surface.

מא א מיי' פ"ו מהל' ביכורים הלכה טו סמג עשין קמא טוש"ע י"ד סי' שכד סעיף א:

[וע"ע תוס' שבת טו. ד"ה רבי יוסי אומר ובעירובין פג: ד"ה שבעת]

מב ב מיי' פ"ה מהל' חלה הלכה יא סמג לאוין עט טור ש"ע א"ח סי' תנז ס"א:

מג ג ד טוש"ע א"ח סי' תנז ס"א:

מד ה ו מיי' פ"ו מהל' ביכורים הלכה טז יז סמג עשין קמא טוש"ע י"ד סי' שכה סעיף א:

מה ז מיי' פ"ה מהל' חמץ הלכה יג סמג לאוין עט טור ש"ע א"ח סי' תנט סעיף ג:

מו ח טור ש"ע שם:

חמשת רבעים קמח. רש"י לא גרס ועוד משום דחמשה לוגין ציפוריים בלמוס הוי כעיסת מדבר ור"ת מפרש דהיינו כר' יוסי דאמר בפ"ק דשבת (דף טו.) חמשה פטורים חמשה ועוד חייבין והיינו טעמא דר' יוסי דלאחר הפרשת חלה בעינן שיעור עריסותיכם*:

לא שנו אלא ככרות שנושכות זו את זו. תימה דלא משמע הכי במסכת חלה (פ"ב משנה ד) דתנן העושה עיסתו קבין פטור מן החלה עד שישוכו רבי אליעזר אומר אף הרודה וכו' אלמא לא בעי ר' אליעזר שישוכו ואי לא גרס אף אתי שפיר דמצי למימר דבעי תרתי שישוכו ויתנם לסל:

לשבות

חמשת רבעים קמח ועוד חייבין בחלה הכי קאמר קבא מלוגנאי נמי אהאי שיעורא קאי אמר רב יוסף הני נשי דידן נהוג למיפא קפיזא קפיזא לפיסחא א"ל אביי מאי דעתיך לחומרא חומרא דאתי לידי קולא הוא דקא מפקע לה מחלה א"ל דעבדן כר' אליעזר (*דתניא) *רבי אליעזר אומר הרודה ונותן לסל הסל מצרפן לחלה ואמר רב יהודה אמר שמואל הלכה כרבי אליעזר א"ל והא איתמר עלה אמר רבי יהושע בן לוי לא שנו אלא ככרות של בבל שנושכות זו מזו אבל כעכין לא הא איתמר עלה א"ר חנינא אפי' כעכין בעי ר' ירמיה טבלא שאין לה לבזבז מהו תוך כלי בעינן והא ליכא או דילמא אויר כלי בעינן והא איכא תיקו: תניא ר' אליעזר אומר הסל מצרפן ר' יהושע אומר תנור מצרפן רבן שמעון בן גמליאל אומר ככרות[א] של בבל שנושכות זו מזו מצטרפות: **מתני' רבן גמליאל אומר שלש נשים לשות כאחת ואופות בתנור אחד זו אחר זו וחכמים אומרים שלש נשים עוסקות בבצק כאחת אחת לשה ואחת עורכת ואחת אופה ר' עקיבא אומר *לא כל הנשים ולא כל העצים ולא כל התנורים שוין זה הכלל תפח תלטוש בצונן: **גמ'** ת"ר לשה היא מקטפת וחבירתה לשה תחתיה מקטפת היא אופה וחבירתה מקטפת תחתיה והשלישית לשה חבירתה אופה היא לשה וחבירתה אופה תחתיה והשלישית מקטפת וחוזרת חלילה כל זמן שעוסקות בבצק אינו בא לידי חימוץ: ר"ע אומר לא כל הנשים וכו': תניא אמר רבי עקיבא דנתי לפני רבן גמליאל ילמדינו רבינו בנשים זריזות או בנשים שאין זריזות בעצים לחים או בעצים יבשים בתנור חם או בתנור צונן אמר לי אין לך אלא מה ששנו חכמים זה הכלל תפח תלטוש בצונן: **מתני'** שיאור ישרף *והאוכלו פטור סידוק ישרף והאוכלו חייב כרת איזהו שיאור כקרני חגבים סידוק שנתערבו סדקין זה בזה דברי רבי יהודה וחכמים אומרים זה וזה האוכלו חייב כרת ואיזהו שיאור כל שהכסיפו פניו כאדם שעמדו שערותיו: **גמ'** תנו רבנן *איזהו שיאור כל שהכסיפו פניו כאדם שעמדו שערותיו סידוק כקרני חגבים *דברי ר' מאיר וחכמים אומרים איזהו שיאור כקרני חגבים סידוק שנתערבו סדקין זה בזה וזה וזה האוכלו חייב כרת והאנן תנן שיאור ישרף והאוכלו פטור דברי רבי יהודה אימא לרבי מאיר זה וזה האוכלו חייב כרת אמר רבא מאי טעמא דר' מאיר אין לך כל סדק וסדק מלמעלה שאין לו כמה סדקים מלמטה:

מתני'

חמשת רבעים. לוגין ציפוריים שהן שבעה ועוד מדבריים שזה הוא שיעור העומר שהיתה עיסת מדבר שנאמר גבי חלה (במדבר טו) ראשית עריסותיכם כדי עריסותיכם דהיינו עיסת מדבר שהוא עומר לגולגולת והוא עשירית האיפה והאיפה שלש סאין וסאה ששה קבין מדבריות חשוב עישור שבהן ותמצא שבעת רבעי קב וביצה וחומש ביצה כיצד חלק שלש סאין שהן שמונה עשרה קבין ועשה מהן רבעי קב הייטו לוגין ותמצא בהן שבעים ושנים לוג טול עישור של שבעים הרי שבעה והשנים הנשארים שתים עשרה ביצים הן עישור שלהן ביצה וחומש ביצה הרי שבעת רבעים ועוד דהוא ביצה וחומש ביצה ובירושלים הוסיפו על המדות שתות מלבר שהוא חומש מלגו שנתנו ששה מן הראשונים בתוך חמשה האחרונים הרי ששת רבעים הראשונים נעשו חמשה והרובע וביצה וחומש הנשארים נעשו רובע שהרובע שש ביצים עשה מהן חמש ביצים גדולות והביצה וחומש ביצה נעשית ביצה גדולה שניתוסף עליה חומשה מלגו דהוא שתות מלבר הרי שש ביצים גדולות דהוא רובע קב גדול הרי עומר המדבר ששה רבעים ירושלמיים וסאה ציפורית עודפת על ירושלמית שתות מלבר כדאמר בעירובין (דף פג.) הרי עומר שהיה ששה רבעים ירושלמיים נכנס בחמש ציפוריים: נהוג למיפא. בפסחא קפיזא קפיזא שלשת לוגין לחומרא לשומרו מן החימוץ: אמר ליה. כר' אליעזר סבירא לן דהסל מצרפן לחלה לאחר אפייתן והאידנא קיימא לן כר' אליעזר בחלה של חוץ לארץ דלאין שורפין קדשים ביום טוב ולהפרישה אי אפשר ומשיקרא עליה שם אסור לאפותה דהא לאו לאכילה היא ולא קרינן עלה שם אלא עושה חררה קטנה אבל גדולה ואופה שתיהן וכשהוא רודה נותנן לכלי והוא מצרפם ונוטל הקטנה וקורא שם ומברך ומצניעה ושורפה משתחשך או למחר וכן הורה לנו רבינו יעקב בן יקר: שנושכות זו את זו. שהן רחבות ועגולות כעין שלט וכשמדביקין זו אצל זו בתנור נושכות זו מזו הלכך חדא היא: אבל כעכין. קויילו"ש בלע"ז ארוכין וקצרין ואין נושכין זה מזה: טבלא שאין לה לבזבז. מסגרת ושפה סביב לה ורדה פת לתוכה מן התנור: מהו. שתצטרף לר' אליעזר: תנור מצרפן. [ב] אף תנור מצרפן אף על פי שלא נתנן לסל: ככרות של בבל כו'. אבל כעכין לא: **מתני'** רבן גמליאל אומר שלש נשים לשות כאחת. כל אחת מלא התנור ואין כאן חימוץ אף על פי שהאחת ממתנת עד שיאפו השתים: וחכמים אומרים. אין להקל כל כך שיהו לשות כאחת אלא שלש נשים עוסקות כל אחת בבצק שלה: אחת לשה. האחרונה לשה כשחבירתה האמצעית מקטפת והשלישית שלשה תחלה אופה וסידרא מפרש בגמרא: לא כל הנשים. יש עצלניות ומתמילות אם ישהו כל כך ויש תנור שאינו חם מהר ויש עצים שאינם נבערים מהר: זה הכלל תפח. הבצק בידה שהיא רואה שרוצה לתפוח: תלטוש. ידיה במים צונן והקטפנה ותצטנן: **גמ'** תנא לשה היא מקטפת. אדרבנן קאי הראשונה שקדמה ללוש מלא התנור קטן שלהן תחלה כשהיא מקטפת דהייט עריכה שקורין אנטוורטי"ר וחברתה מתחלת ללוש עיסה שלה: מקטפת היא אופה. וזו הראשונה שהיתה מקטפת עכשיו וגמרה קיטופה היא אופה ונותנת לתנור וחבירתה שהיתה לשה מקטפת תחתיה והשלישית לשה וכשגמרה ראשונה לאפות גמרה אמצעית לקטף ואחרונה ללוש הרי האמצעית המקטפת אופה וחבירתה האחרונה מקטפת תחתיה והראשונה חוזרת ולשה שהיו תנורין קטנים ולא היתה מספקת [אלא] כמלא תנור: וכן חוזרות חלילה. חלילה לשון מחול סביב סביב: דנתי לפני רבן גמליאל. שהיה אומר כלל דבר בכל שלש נשים לשות כאחת וממתנת האחת עד שיאפו השתים: **מתני'** שיאור. שלא החמיץ כל צרכו: סידוק. כשהוא מחמיץ נעשין בו סדקין: קרני חגבים. סדק לכאן וסדק לכאן: זה וזה האוכלו בכרת. דקרני חגבים נמי סידוק הוי: ואיזהו שיאור. שפטור זה שאין בו סדק אבל הכסיפו פניו כאדם שעמדו שערותיו ומתוך פחד ורעת פניו מכסיפין: **גמ'** חכמים דברייתא הוא ר' יהודה דמתני' וחכמים דמתני' הוא ר' מאיר: ה"ג בברייתא וחכמים אומרים אי זהו שיאור כקרני חגבים סידוק שנתערבו סדקין זה בזה וזה וזה האוכלו בכרת: והא אנן תנן. דר' יהודה פטר בשיאור דידיה דהע"ג דאמר ישרף לא מיחייב עלה לא מלקות ולא כרת: אימא לרבי מאיר זה וזה. בין שיאור דרבי יהודה דקרני חגבים בין סידוק חייבין כרת דתרווייהו לרבי מאיר סידוק נינהו: כמה סדקין מלמטה. בתוכו הלכך כי הוי למעלה כקרני חגבים הוי למטה כנתערבו סדקין:

מתני'

רבינו חננאל

חמשת רבעים ועוד והן שיעור הקמח להוציא מהן חלה: **אמר** רב יוסף הני נשי דידן. כלומר בני בתאי נהגו למיפא **קפיזא** קפיזא בפסח שהוא מקבא מלוגנאה ואמר להו אביי נתרחקו מאיסור דחמץ ואפקעו תורת חלה: אמר ליה לא מפקעינן מחלה אלא עבדין כר' אליעזר דתנן ר' אליעזר אמר הרודה ונותן לסל הסל מצרפן לחלה ואמר רב יהודה אמר שמואל הלכה כרבי אליעזר בככרות שנושכות זו את זו ונראות כאלו נכנסות זו בתוך זו ואפי' בענין שאין נושכות הסל מצרפן: **בעי** ר' ירמיה טבלא שאין לה לבזביז. פירוש לבזביז מסגרת מהו מי מצרפן לחלה דאויר כלי מצרף והא איכא אויר או דלמא תוך כלי מצרף והא לית ליה תוך ועלתה בתיקו: **תניא** רבי אליעזר אומר הסל מצרפן לחלה וקיימ' לן כותיה ר' יהושע אומר תנור מצרפן רשב"ג אומר ככרות נושכות זו את זו מצטרפות: **מתני'** ר"ג אומר שלש נשים לשות כאחת ואופות בתנור אחד זו אחר זו וזו אחר זו ואע"פ שכולן (לשו) [יאפו] בתנו' אחד אחת מסיקה התנור ואופה והשניה אחריה והשלישי' אחריה וקס"ל אע"פ שיהא הבצק שוהה כדי שלשה הסקות ושתי אפיות אינו בא לידי חמוץ וטוב לעשות כך אבל ארבע נשים ללוש כאחת לא נחברר כי התיר רשב"ג ללוש לקטף ולאפות אשה אחת והאחרת שלשה עמה ממתנת לה: **וחכמי'** אומרים שלש נשים עוסקות בבצק אחת לשה וכשתתחיל לערוך אחרת לשה וזה שעורכת מסיקה ואופה וזו שלשה אחריה עורכ' וכשתתחיל הראשונה לאפות והשני' לערוך מתחלת השלישית ללוש נמצאת בבת אחת הראשונה אופה והשניה עורכת והשלישית לשה ואין אחת מהן ממתנת לחברתה אלא כולן עוסקות וזו היא ששנינו בחיצונה לשה היא מקטפת וחברתה לשה תחתיה מקטפת היא אופה וחברתה מקטפת תחתיה [והשלישית לשה] אופה היא לשה וחברתה אופה תחתיה [והשלישית מקטפת] וחוזרות חלילה כל זמן שעסוקות בבצק אינו בא לידי חמוץ: **ר'** עקיבא אומר לא כל הנשים ולא כל העצים ולא כל התנורים שוין זה הכלל תפח תלטוש בצונן ויש אומרים תפח: שיאור ישרף והאוכלו פטור סדוק ישרף והאוכלו חייב כרת כו' במשנתנו שנה לנו דברי ר' מאיר בלשון חכמים ובברייתא שנה לנו דברי ר' מאיר בלשון חכמים לרבי יהודה השיאור כקרני חגבים והסדוק שנתערבו סדקיו זה בזה ולר' מאיר שיאור שהכסיפו פניו כאדם שעמדו שערותיו סידוק כקרני חגבים מ"ט שאין לך סדק שלמעלה שאין בו כמה סדקין מלמטה ובתרווייהו האוכלו חייב כרת נמצא שיאור דר' יהודה סידוק לר' מאיר: ת"ר אי זהו (סידוק) [שיאור] כקרני חגבים סידוק שנתערבו סדקיו זה בזה וזה וזה האוכלו חייב כרת ואקשי' מאן שמעת ליה דאית ליה האי סברא ר' יהודה וקי ר' יהודה מחייב אקרני חגבים כרת והתנן שיאור ישרף והאוכלו פטור דברי יהודה ושני' אימא זה וזה כלומר בין סידוק כקרני הגבים בין סידוק שנתערבו סדקיו זה בזה לר' מאיר אחד הוא כל סדק זה וזה חייב כרת וקי"ל כר'

שבת טו: [חלה פ"ב מ"ו] עדיות פ"א [מ"ב]

[נ"ל דתנן נדה ח. [חלה פ"ב מ"ד]

לעיל מג.

מכילתא פ' בא

[לעיל מג. מנחות נג. חולין כג.]

הגהות הגר"א

[א] גמ' רשב"ג אומר ככרות כו'. נ"ב וכוה תנור וכוה דברי ת"ק דמתני' דחלה: [ב] רש"י ד"ה תנור מצרפן אף תנור כו'. נ"ב בירושלמי (פ"ב דחלה) איתא דוקא תנור ולא סל:

גליון הש"ס

גמ' מהו תוך כלי בעינן. עיין טורי אבן חגיגה כד ע"א ד"ה לרוייה: מתני' לא כל הנשים. כעין זה יבמות קכ ע"ב:

מן המאתים. על כרחיך אנסכים קאי וקאמר הביאו הנסכים עליו מן המאתים שישתיירו מאתים בבור היין: מכאן לערלה שבטלה במאתים. דאי לאו בשאיסור מעורב בו קאי אמאי מצריך מאתים ובעלמא בסיפרי נפקא לן שפיר דערלה וכלאי הכרם בטילין במאתים והאי מכאן לאו דוקא אלא אף כאן אתה יכול לסמוך קצת: איסור דבר אחר. שבת: הא את הוא דאמרת · באלו הן הלוקין (מכות דף כא:): חילוק מלאכות לשבת · שאם עשה שתים בהעלם אחד או [אחת] בשתי העלמות חייב שתים: ואין חילוק מלאכות ליום טוב. שאם עשה שתי מלאכות במזיד אינו לוקה שתים

והכא ביום טוב קיימינן ומחייבת ליה משום י"ט תרתי משום מוקצה ומשום מבשל גיד ביום טוב: אמר רמי בר חמא הא דרבה ורב חסדא· דאיפליגו גבי יום טוב אי שרינן ליה משום הואיל או לא: מחלוקת רבי אליעזר ור' יהושע היא דרבי אליעזר סבר אמרינן הואיל · אע"ג דסופו להפריש אחת מהן לחלה ונמצא שטרח בדבר שאינו ראוי לאכילה אפי' הכי אמרינן הואיל ואי בעי לא מפריש חדא לחלה אלא בלע מכל חדא וחדא ואיכא למימר בכל חדא חזיא ליה ומותר לאפותה: ור' יהושע סבר לא אמרינן הואיל. כדי להתיר מלאכות יום טוב והאי הואיל ואי בעי מיתשיל עלה דלעיל לא קאי רמי בר חמא אלא אהואיל דאיסור מלאכת יום טוב: אלא דבעידנא דעיילי לה. איכא למימר בכל חדא וחדא חזיא ליה בלאו הואיל דבכל חדא איכא למימר א לא תהא לחלה: אבל הכא דלאורחין הוא דחזיא. והרי עדיין לא זימן לית ליה הואיל למישרייה לרבי אליעזר: דלא חזיא לא לדידיה ולא לאורחים · (א) והרי סופו ליטול אחת לחלה שאין דרך לבלוע מכל אחת: אבל הכא. דכולהו חזו לאורחין ואורחין שכיחי אמרינן הואיל למישרייה ואי קשיא הא דאמר ר' יהושע לא זהו חמץ שמוזהרין כו' אלמא לית ליה הואיל ואי בעי מיתשל עלה אפילו לחומרא וכל שכן הואיל דהכא לקולא לא דמי דהפסח מיהא לאו דידיה הוא וכך שמעתי ומגמגם לבי עלה ונראה בעיני דאין הואיל בזה בדבר שאינו שלו דכיתא הואיל ואי בעי מייתי ליה ברשותיה דאם כן הקדש דקיימא לן אבל אתה רואה של גבוה ולא פליג ר"א הא אי בעי פריק ליה והוי דידיה ואף סוגיא דשמעתא לא מייתבא שפיר וכמדומה דפירוש הכתוב ברישא דשמעתא הואיל ואי בעי מיתשיל עליה לא גרי הכי גר' ר' אליעזר סבר אמרי' הואיל ור' יהושע סבר לא אמרינן הואיל והכי פירושא ר' אליעזר סבר שרי לאפותה ואע"ג דסוף סוף איכא חדא דלא חזיא ליה אין כאן איסור מלאכה הואיל וכל חדא וחדא חזיא ליה דמצי למשקל מכל חדא פורתא ור' יהושע סבר לא אמרינן הואיל דהא סופו ליטול אחת מהן לחלה הלכך כיון דטובת הנאה איכא ממון ולא עבר עלה מנחתה עד הערב וישרפנה: אמרוה. להא דרמי בר חמא: מילתא דקשיא לן כו'. דבטובת הנאה ממון ליכא לאוקמי פלוגתייהו לחוד דהכי נמי דטובת הנאה ממון לר' אליעזר אפילו הכי השתא נמי עובר משום לא תעשה כל מלאכה ומוטב לעבור על בל יראה מאליו ואינו עושה מעשה בידים מלעבור על לא תעשה כל מלאכה ועושה מעשה בידים: טעמא דידי משום הואיל. ואין כאן חילול: אהדר ליה במכילתא אחריתא. ואיכא למימר דבתרוייהו פליגי ר' אליעזר סבר טובת הנאה ממון הלכך אי מחמלה גביה עבר עלה ולאפותה קודם לכן אין כאן איסור דאמרי' הואיל ואיכא למימר בכל חדא חזיא ליה ור' יהושע סבר ליכא ממון הלכך לא זהו חמץ שמוזהרין עליו וכי אפי לה עבר עלה דלא אמרינן הואיל והא דתריגלא לעיל דכולי עלמא טובת הנאה איכא ממון לכתי לא שמיע לן הא דלהדר ליה ר' אליעזר לר' יהושע הרי הוא עובר בבל יראה: הלכה כבן בתירא. קטיל לגונן: שיעור עיסה. ללוש בפסח ולא יותר שיכול לשומרה מידי חימוץ: חילוף הדברים. שהשעורין קרובין להחמיץ יותר מן החיטים: הא בחסיכתא הא במעלייתא. קמייתא במעלייתא בתרייתא בחסיכתא ששלש שלהן אינן אלא כקביים טובות: שמע מינה. לענין מקח וממכר גריעין חיטי חסיכתא ממעלייתא טפי ממאי דגריען שערי חסיכתא ממעלייתא. דאילו בחיטי קתני דטובות קביים וברעות שלשה קבים אלמא גרעי תילתא ואילו בשעורין הטובות שלשת קבין והרעות ארבעה אלא ריבעא: קבא מלוגנאה. קב של אותו מקום: לפיסחא. שלא ללוש יותר כדי שיוכל לשומרו מן החימוץ: וכן לחלה. בכך שיעור עיסה נמי כל ימות השנה להתחייב בחלה:

תורה אור

יחזקאל מה °מן המאתים ממותר שתי מאות שנשתיירו בבור מכאן ^א לערלה שבטילה במאתים ממשקה ישראל *מן המותר לישראל מכאן אמרו ^ב אין מביאין נסכים מן הטבל יכול לא יביא מן המוקצה אמרת מה טבל מיוחד שאיסור גופו גרם לו אף כל שאיסור גופו גרם לו ^ג יצא מוקצה שאין איסור גופו גרם לו אלא איסור דבר אחר גרם לו ואי אמרת איסור מוקצה דאורייתא מה לי איסור גופו מה לי איסור דבר אחר ועוד הא את הוא דאמרת *^ד חילוק מלאכות לשבת ואין חילוק מלאכות ליו"ט אלא אפיק הבערה ועייל עצי אשירה ואזהרה מהכא דברים יג °ולא ידבק בידך מאומה מן החרם אמר ליה רב אחא בריה דרבא לאביי ונלקי נמי משום שם ז °ולא תביא תועבה אל ביתך אלא אפיק הבערה ועייל עצי הקדש ואזהרה מהכא שם יב °ואשירידם תשרפון באש לא תעשון כן לה' אלהיכם אמר רמי בר חמא הא דרב חסדא ורבה מחלוקת דר"א ורבי יהושע היא דר"א סבר אמרינן הואיל ורבי יהושע סבר לא אמרינן הואיל אמר רב פפא ודילמא עד כאן לא קאמר ר"א התם דאמרינן הואיל אלא דבעידנא דקא עיילי לתנורא כל חדא וחדא חזיא ליה לדידיה אבל הכא הלאורחין הוא דחזי לדידיה לא חזי אימא הכי נמי דלא אמרינן הואיל אמר רב שישא בריה דרב אידי ודילמא לא היא עד כאן לא קאמר רבי יהושע התם דלא אמרינן הואיל אלא דאיכא חדא דלא חזיא לא לדידיה ולא לאורחין אבל הכא דחזי מיהת לאורחין אימא הכי נמי אמרינן הואיל אמרוה [רבנן] קמיה דרבי ירמיה ור' זירא ר' ירמיה קיבלה ר' זירא לא קיבלה א"ל רבי ירמיה לרבי זירא מילתא דקשיא לן ואתיא כמה שני במאי פליגי ר"א ור' יהושע השתא אמרוה משמיה דגברא רבה ולא ניקבלה אמר ליה היכי אקבלה דתנינא אמר ליה רבי יהושע לדבריך הרי הוא עובר משום * שמות כ °לא תעשה כל מלאכה ושתיק ליה ואי איתא לימא ליה טעמא דידי משום הואיל א"ל וליטעמיך הא דתנינא בברייתא אמר לו ר"א לדבריך הרי הוא עובר משום בל יראה ובל ימצא ושתיק ליה ה"נ דלא אהדר ליה הא קא מהדר ליה במתני' דתנן לא זהו חמץ שמוזהרין עליו משום בל יראה ובל ימצא אלא שתיק ליה בברייתא ומהדר ליה במתני' ה"נ אימור שתיק ליה במתני' ואהדר ליה במכילתא אחריתי תניא רבי אומר הלכה כר"א ור' יצחק אמר הלכה כבן בתירא וכמה שיעור עיסה רבי ישמעאל בנו של רבי יוחנן בן ברוקה אומר בחיטין קבין ובשעורין שלשת קבין ר' נתן אומר משום ר"א חילוף הדברים והתניא רבי ישמעאל בנו של ר' יוחנן בן ברוקה אומר בחטין שלשת קבין ובשעורין ארבעה קבין לא קשיא הא בחסיכתא הא במעלייתא אמר רב פפא שמע מינה גריעין חיטי חסיכתא מחיטי מעלייתא טפי מדגריען שערי חסיכתא משערי מעלייתא דאילו התם תילתא והכא ריבעא אמר רב קבא מלוגנאה לפיסחא וכן לחלה (*והתניא) חמשת

רבי אומר הלכה כר' אליעזר. ה"ר יוסף פסק כרבי משום דקיימא לן* טותיה מחבירו וכן מנהג ור"י דוחה דשמא לא קאמר הלכה כרבי מחבירו דהא איפליגו רבה ורב חסדא בהכי והא דהלכה כרבי מחבירו היינו היכא דליכא פלוגתא דאמוראי:

המגה

הא מפריש כל חדא וחדא חזיא ליה ושרי ליה למיפה לפניך לא תקרא לה שם עד שתאפה ור' יהושע סבר לא אמרינן הואיל וכיון דאיכא חדא דלא חזיא ליה [illegible]

*) נראה דיש טעות סופר בדבריו וכצ"ל טעמא דר"א ואי אכריע דכשאני אופה נמצאתי עובר על כל מלאכה לא יעשה בהם ועושה כו'.

רבינו חננאל

מן המאה מותר שתי מאות שנשתיירו בבור כלומר אפי' ערלה שהיא חמורה מן הכלאים עלתה (ונשתיירו) [ואם נשתיירו] מאתים מותרין הן מכאן לערלה שבטלה (במאה) [במאתים] ממשקה ישראל מן היין המותר לישראל מכאן אמרו אין מביאין נסכים מן הטבל יכול לא יביא מן המוקצה אמרת (יביא) [illegible] גמרי' מטבל מה טבל מיוחד שאיסור גופו גרם לו יצא מוקצה שאין איסור גופו גרם לו [illegible] אלא איסור הכנה בא להרחיק ואי סיד מוקצה אסור מן התורה [illegible] ושני אפיק הבערה ועייל עצי אשרה ואזהרתיה ולא ידבק בידך מאומה מן החרם כו' ואוקימנא אלא עייל עצי הקדש כו': אמר רמי בר חמא מחלוקת ר' אליעזר ור' יהושע במתני' בהואיל ופליגי בדרבה ורב חסדא ר' אליעזר סבר הואיל ואי בעי מפריש ואי בעי [illegible] חמשת

לז א מיי' פט"ו מהל' מאכלות אסורות הלכה יד:
לח ב מיי' פ"ה מהל' איסורי מזבח הל"ט:
לט ג שם הלכה י:
מ ד מיי' פ"ה מהל' יו"ט הלכה ג:
[לעיל כו.]

[מנחות ס. חולין ... תמורה כט.]
[מכות כא:]

הגהות הב"ח
(א) רש"י ד"ה דלא חזיא וכו' דהכי סופו:

[כך קרא בשבת כתיב ואולי צ"ל כל מלאכה לא יעשה בהם דכתיב גבי חג פסח שמות יב טז]
[צ"ל והתניא]

tithe;[7] *of the flock*, this is to exclude a *palges;*[8] [48*a*] *out of the two hundred*, [i.e.,] out of the residue of the two hundred which was left in the vault, whence we learn that *'orlah* is nullified in [an excess of] two hundred;[9] *from the well-watered pastures of Israel:* from that which is permitted to Israel. Hence it was said, One may not bring drink-offerings from *ṭebel.*[10] You might think, he must not bring [them] from *mukẓeh* [either], then say: just as *ṭebel* is dis-
a tinguished in that its intrinsic prohibition causes it,[1] so everything whose intrinsic prohibition causes it [may not be used], thus *mukẓeh* is excluded, because not its intrinsic prohibition causes it, but a prohibition of something else causes it.[2] Now if you say that the prohibition of *mukẓeh* is Scriptural, what does it matter[3] whether it is an intrinsic prohibition or a prohibition through something else? Moreover, it was you who said, There is separation of labours on the Sabbath,[4] but there is not separation of labours on a Festival![5]—Rather, delete lighting and substitute the wood of the *asherah*,[6] while its 'warning' [injunction] is [learnt] from here, [viz.,] *And there shall cleave nought of the accursed thing to thy hand.*[7] R. Aḥa son of Raba said to Abaye, Then let him be flagellated on account of, *And thou shalt not bring an abomination into thy house*[8] too?—Rather, delete lighting and substitute the wood of *hekdesh*, while the 'warning' is [learnt] from here, [viz.,] *and ye shall burn their Asherim with fire . . . ye shall not do so unto the Lord your God.*[9]

Rami b. Ḥama said: This [controversy] of R. Ḥisda and Rabbah is the controversy of R. Eliezer and R. Joshua.[10] For R. Eliezer holds, We say, 'since',[11] while R. Joshua holds, We do not say 'since'. Said R. Papa: Yet perhaps R. Eliezer rules that we say 'since', there only, because when they go into the oven, each one is fit for himself;[12] but here that it is fit for visitors only, but it is
b not fit for himself,[1] perhaps it is indeed [the fact] that we do not say 'since'? R. Shisha son of R. Idi said: Yet perhaps it is not so:[2] R. Joshua may rule that we do not say, 'since', only there, where there is one [*mazzah*] that is not fit either for himself or for visitors; but here that it is at least fit for visitors, perhaps it is indeed [the fact] that we say 'since'?

The Rabbis reported this [Rami b. Ḥama's statement] before R. Jeremiah and R. Zera. R. Jeremiah accepted it: R. Zera did not accept it. Said R. Jeremiah to R. Zera: A matter which has been a continual difficulty to us for many years, [viz.,] wherein do R. Eliezer and R. Joshua differ, now [that] it has been explained in the name of a great man, shall we then not accept it? Said he to him, How can I accept it? For it was taught, R. Joshua said to him: According to your words,[3] he transgresses on account of *thou shalt not do any manner of work*,[4] and he was silent before him. But if this[5] is correct, let him answer him, My reason is on account of 'since'?—Then on your view, replied he, as to what was taught in a Baraitha, R. Eliezer said to him: According to your words, behold, he violates, '*it shall not be seen*' and '*it shall not be found*', and he was silent before him; could he indeed not answer him; surely he answers him in the Mishnah, for we learned: NOT THIS IS LEAVEN ABOUT WHICH WE ARE WARNED, 'IT SHALL NOT BE SEEN', AND 'IT SHALL NOT BE FOUND'. But [what we must say is that] he was silent before him in the Baraitha, yet he answered him in our Mishnah. So here too, say that he was silent before him in a teaching,[6] yet he answered him in another collection [of Baraithas].

It was taught, Rabbi said: The *halachah* is as R. Eliezer; while R. Isaac said: The *halachah* is as the Son of Bathyra.

And what[7] is the standard of dough?[8]—R. Ishmael the son of R. Joḥanan b. Berokah said: In the case of wheat, two *kabs;* in the case of barley, three *kabs*. R. Nathan said on R. Eleazar's
c authority: The rulings are [to be] reversed.[1] But it was taught, R. Ishmael son of R. Joḥanan b. Berokah said: In the case of wheat, three *kabs*, and in the case of barley, four *kabs?*—There is no difficulty: one refers to inferior [corn]; the other to superior corn.[2] R. Papa observed: This proves, Poor wheat is more inferior to good wheat than poor barley is inferior to good barley, for whereas there [there is a difference of] a third, here [there is a difference of] a quarter.

Rab said: A *kab* of Meloga[3] [is the standard] for Passover,[4] and

(7) I.e., the tithe of animals cannot be dedicated for a daily burnt-offering. '*One*' implies that it stands by itself, whereas the tithe is one out of ten. (8) A sheep beyond the age of כבש (lamb) and below that of איל (ram).—Jast.; i.e., a sheep in its thirteenth month. '*Of*' is partitive and implies limitation. (9) '*Out of the two hundred*' is unintelligible in itself. Hence the Talmud assumes that it refers to the wine of the drink-offering (libation) which accompanied the continual burnt-offering (Num. XXVIII, 7f), and the meaning is this: if one part of forbidden wine, *sc.* wine of '*orlah*, as much as is required for the drink-offering, becomes mixed with two hundred times as much permitted wine, so that when the required quantity is removed from the wine-vault there still remains two hundred times as much, then it may be used, the '*orlah* having been nullified by the excess.—This is actually deduced from elsewhere (in Sifre), and this verse is merely quoted as support. (10) V. Glos.

a (1) I.e., *ṭebel* is unfit for drink-offerings because it is forbidden in itself. (2) I.e., it is not forbidden in itself, save that its owner has voluntarily put it out of use for the time being. (3) Lit., 'what is it to me?' (4) If a man performed two labours on the Sabbath in one state of unawareness, or one labour twice, each time having been unaware of the Sabbath (though he was reminded in the interval), he is liable on account of each separately. (5) Yet here, where we treat of a Festival, you rule that he is separately culpable for *mukẓeh* and for boiling the sinew. (6) V. Glos. He used that for fuel, and is flagellated on that account. (7) Deut. XIII, 18. (8) Ibid. VII, 26. (9) Ibid. XII, 3f. (10) In the Mishnah *supra* 46*a*. (11) Though he will eventually separate one *mazzah* for all, and that is not fit for eating, yet if he wishes he can take a piece from each *mazzah*, and so he will have baked every one for eating. Hence we say, since it would be permitted in the latter case, it is also permitted in the former. (12) As explained in n. a11.

b (1) As far as he is concerned he is definitely baking it for the week, while he has not invited visitors. (2) This too is a criticism of Rami b. Ḥama's statement. (3) I.e., if he does as you say. (4) Ex. XX, 10. (5) Rami b. Ḥama's explanation. (6) Mathnitha, especially collection of Mishnah not embodied in the Mishnah of R. Judah, as Baraitha, Tosaf. etc., contrad. to Mathnithin, *our* Mishnah (Jast.). (7) Lit., 'how much?' (8) Which one can knead on Passover and keep it from fermenting.

c (1) Three in the case of wheat, and two in the case of barley, for barley ferments more quickly. (2) Two *kabs* of superior wheat is the equivalent of three *kabs* of inferior wheat; while three *kabs* of superior barley is the equivalent of four *kabs* of inferior barley. (3) Supposed to be a place in Babylon. (4) One must not knead more dough than that.

[47b] and it is the seventh year, on a Festival, [and he is] a priest and a nazirite, [while this furrow is] in unclean ground.[6] Now if we say 'since', let him not be liable for ploughing [on the Festival], *since* it is fit for covering the blood of a bird?[7]—Said R. Papa b. Samuel: The reference is to smooth, round stones.[8] [But] they are fit for crushing?[9]—Is then crushing permitted on the Festival?[10] But they are fit for crushing in an unusual manner?[11]—The reference
a is to rocky ground.[1] Is then rocky ground capable of being sown? —It is rocky ground above, but powdered [loose] earth beneath. Then deduce it [that he is not culpable] because of the loose earth?[2] But said Mar the son of R. Ashi: The reference is to clayey earth.[3] And is clayey earth capable of being sown?—It refers to swampy earth.[4]

Abaye raised an objection against him:[5] He who cooks the thigh sinew[6] on a Festival and eats it is flagellated five times. He is flagellated on account of cooking the sinew on a Festival;[7] he is flagellated on account of eating the sinew; he is flagellated for cooking meat in milk; he is flagellated for eating meat [cooked] in milk;[8] and he is flagellated on account of lighting [a fire].[9] But if we say, 'since', let him not be liable on account of lighting, *since* it is fit for him for his [legitimate] needs?—Said he to him, Omit lighting and substitute the thigh sinew of a *nebelah*.[10] But R. Ḥiyya taught: He is flagellated twice for his eating and thrice for his cooking; now if this is correct,[11] he should say, thrice for his eating?—Rather, omit lighting and substitute the wood of *mukẓeh*.[12] And is *mukẓeh* a Scriptural [interdict]?—Yes, he replied, for it is written, ***And it shall come to pass on the sixth day that they shall prepare that which they bring in;***[13] and its 'warning' [injunction] is [learnt] from here, [viz.,] from, ***thou shalt not do any manner of***
b ***work.***[1] Said he to him, But it was you who said, I asked of R. Ḥisda, —others state, I asked of R. Huna: What if he brought a lamb from the meadow[2] and slaughtered it as a continual burnt-offering[3] on a Festival?[4] And you said to us: He answered me, [It is written], ***And a lamb,***[5] [implying], but not a firstling;[6] ***one,*** but not the

(6) V. Mak., 21*b*, nn. 1–9. (7) When a bird is slaughtered its blood must be covered, v. Lev. XVII, 13. This ploughing crushes the earth and makes it fit for that purpose, and *since* a bird might be slaughtered on the Festival, that too would be necessary. (8) The ploughing breaks up the earth into smooth, round lumps; these are not fit for covering the blood, for which crushed, dust-like earth is required. Rashi, however, merely reads: stones; v. Tosaf. s.v. באבנים מקורזלות. (9) And then be used for covering the blood. (10) Surely not. (11) Lit., 'as with the back of the hand'. Such a crushing is not Scripturally forbidden but merely as a *shebuth* (v. Glos.). That being so, flagellation, which is administered for the violation of a *Scriptural* prohibition, should not be incurred.

a (1) Harder than ordinary stones; this cannot be crushed. (2) This makes his action non-punishable. (3) With which blood may not be covered. (4) Which is fit for sowing, yet cannot be crushed into dust for covering blood. (5 Against Rabbah. (6) Which may not be eaten, v. Gen. XXXII, 32. (7) Which is a forbidden labour, since it is not the preparation of food which may be eaten. (8) These are two separate offences. (9) Which is likewise prohibited on a Festival, save when required for cooking permitted food, v. Beẓ. 12*a*. (10) I.e., it was the thigh sinew of a *nebelah*, and he is flagellated for eating *nebelah*. (11) *Sc.* the proposed emendation. (12) V. Glos. This may not be handled on Festivals.—He is thus flagellated not for lighting but for putting it to use. (13) Ex. XVI, 5. This teaches that only what is 'prepared', as opposed to ***mukẓeh***, may be handled on Sabbaths and Festivals.

b (1) Ex. XX, 10. Flagellation is administered only for the violation of a ***negative*** injunction, not an affirmative precept. The first verse quoted belongs to the latter category, hence the second verse must be added. Thus, since the use of ***mukẓeh*** is forbidden by the first verse, making a fire with it is an ordinary labour forbidden by the second.—Though the second verse refers to the Sabbath, whereas we are here treating of the Festival, these two are alike in respect to work, save that the preparation of food is permitted on Festivals, but not on the Sabbath. Once however it is shown that a particular action is forbidden, it does not matter whether it is the Sabbath or a Festival. (2) Outside the town. Animals that graze there are brought home (i.e., into town) only at intervals, not every evening, and therefore they are ***mukẓeh***, and may not be slaughtered on Festivals unless designated for that purpose on the eve of the Festivals. (3) V. Num. XXVIII, 3. (4) May it be offered? (5) Ezek. XLV, 15, whence the whole verse which follows is quoted. (6) A ***'lamb'*** implies both male and female, whereas a firstling applies only to males.

לה א מיי' פט"ו מהל' מעשה קרבנות הלכה טו :
לו ב מיי' פ"א שם הלכה יד :

ושביעית ביום טוב כהן ונזיר אבית הטומאה ואי אמרינן הואיל °אחרישה לא ליחייב הואיל וחזי לכיסוי דם ציפור א"ר פפא בר שמואל באבנים מקורזלות ראויות לכותשן וכתישה ביום טוב מי שרי ראויות לכותשן כלאחר יד בצונמא צונמא בר זריעה מלמעלה ועפר תיחוח מלמטה ותיפוק ליה משום עפר תיחוח אלא אמר מר בר רב אשי בטינא וטינא בר זריעה הוא במתנתא איתיביה אביי *המבשל גיד הנשה בחלב בי"ט ואוכלו לוקה חמש לוקה משום מבשל גיד ביום טוב ולוקה משום אוכל גיד ולוקה משום מבשל בשר בחלב ולוקה משום אוכל בשר בחלב ולוקה משום הבערה ואי אמרינן הואיל אהבערה לא ליחייב הואיל דחזי ליה לצרכו אמר ליה אפיק הבערה ועייל גיד הנשה של נבילה והתני רבי חייא לוקין שתים על אכילתו ושלש על בישולו ואי איתא שלש על אכילתו מיבעי ליה אלא אפיק הבערה °ועייל עצי מוקצה ומוקצה דאורייתא הוא א"ל אין דכתיב °והיה ביום הששי והכינו את אשר יביאו ואזהרתה מהכא °לא תעשה כל מלאכה א"ל והא את הוא דאמרת בעאי מיניה מרב חסדא ואמרי לה בעאי מיניה מרב הונא הביא שה מאפר ושחטו תמיד ביו"ט מהו *ואת אמרת לן (אמר לי) עלה שה ולא הבכור אחת *ולא מעשר מן הצאן °ולא הפלגם מן

תורה אור
[ביצה יב. [ע"ש] תמו' כא: [ע"ש]]
[שמות טז]
[שם כ]
[ס"א א"ל שה]

ושביעית. דעובר משום שדך לא תזרע וחורש תולדה דזורע כגון חורש לכסות את הזריעה : ובכלאים בכרם. דבהדי דקא חרש מחפה בכלאים והמחפה בכלאים לוקה הרי חמשה וי"ט הרי ששה ושבת לא תנא משום דלאו שניתן לאזהרת מיתת ב"ד הוא דאין לוקין עליו : וכהן ונזיר אבית הטומאה. שזה בית הקברות והוא כהן ונזיר ויש כאן לאו דכהן לנפש לא יטמא ולאו דנזיר על נפש מת לא יבוא : אחרישה. משום לאו די"ט לא לילקי : דם לפור. הואיל ואי מזדמני ליה לפרים וחיות טובא : באבנים. דלא חזו לכיסוי : ראויות לכותשן. קושיא היא : כלאחר יד. ע"י שינוי דשבות בעלמא הוא וכיון דמדאורייתא שרי פקע ליה מלקות : טינא. טיט לח ובלול : מתונתא. ארץ לחה ראויה לזריעה ואינה נעשית עפר אם בא לכותשה היא מדבקת ונגבלת : לוקה משום מבשל גיד בי"ט. בישול שאינו ראוי ולוקה משום מבשל בשר בחלב אפילו הוא חול וקסבר יש בגידים בנותן טעם ובשר הם : משום הבערה. שלא לצורך דהבערה מלאכה לעצמה ובישול מלאכה לעצמו : גיד הנשה של נבלה. דלוקה על אכילתו משום נבילה : שתים על אכילתו. אוכל גיד ואוכל בשר בחלב : שלש על בישולו. משום הבערה די"ט ומשום בישול די"ט ומשום מבשל בשר בחלב אפילו בחול : ועייל עצי מוקצה. דהשתא ליכא למימר הואיל דמדאורייתא אסור להשתמש בהם מוקצה בי"ט: מוקצה דאורייתא. בתמיה : והכינו. במזומן שמזמן כל צורכו היום ויאמר דבר זה לצורך היום דמשום טורח מלאכה שבת לא צריך דהכתיב את אשר תאפו אפו ואת אשר תבשלו בשלו וכיון דלאו מזומן הוא והכתוב קראו הכנה הויא לה מלאכה ועובר עליה משום לא תעשה כל מלאכה : בעאי. שאלתי : מאפר. אחו ומוקצה הוא שאינו נכנס לייִשוב ימים רבים : תמיד. עולה של ציבור : מהו. ליקרב : שה ולא את הבכור. מתניתא היא ודרשה קרא דיחזקאל (מה) גבי קרבנות ושה אחת מן הצאן מן המאתים ממשקה ישראל: שה ולא את הבכור. דשה משמע שיהא ראוי להיות בין זכר בין נקבה דכולן בכלל שה ובכור אינו אלא זכר : ולא מעשר. למעשר בהמה אינו ראוי להקדישו לקרבן אחר והכי משמע אחד שיהא לבד ולא זה שאינו בא אלא מכלל עשרה : מן הצאן. ולא כל הצאן מיעוטא הוא להוציא פלגס יצא מכלל כבש ולכלל איל לא בא והיינו כל חודש שלשה עשר דכבש בן שנה הוא ואיל משנכנס לשנה שניה חודש שלם והכי מפרש לה במס' פרה (פ"א משנה ג) :

אפילו ע"י ד"א אין מעשרין מזה על זה תירוש ודגן דגן ודגן שהן כלאים ע"י דבר אחר וכו' ע"י ד"א דקאמר לא קאי אדגן ודגן דבלאו דבר אחר מיחייב בחטים ושעורים לחוד וטעמא דר' יאשיה דכלאים בכרם לא מיחייב אלא בשלשה מינין ובכלאי זרעים מיחייב בב' מינין מפר"י דזריעת כלאים משמע בב' מיני זרעים וחרנן לאו מין זריעה הוא אבל אין לפרש משום דמשמע לא תזרע בהדי כרמך כלאים אבל שדך בלא שום זרע קרוי שדה דהא לא שייך לפרש כן גבי בהמתך ולפירוש ר"י קשה אמאי נקט שור וחמור בשור לחודי' ה"מ לאשכוחי כלאים בשור פסולי המוקדשים כדאמר בפ' בתרא דמכות (דף כב.) דאמר רבי יצחק המנהיג בשור פסולי המוקדשים דלוקה משום דעשאו הכתוב ב' גופים דאיתקש לצבי ואיל ולפ"ה ניחא דליכא בפסולי המוקדשי' לאו דמעילה ולפר"י י"ל דמשום דעיקר כלאים בשור ובחמור כתיב נקט שור וחמור : **ושביעית**. למ"ד בפ"ק דמועד קטן (דף ג.) חורש בשביעית אינו לוקה מוקי הך דהכא בחורש ומחפה דמחפה חייב משום זורע : **אחרישה** לא ליחייב הואיל וחזי לכיסוי דם ציפור. אם היה דם ציפור במקום חרישה ובכה"ג שאם היה מבקש עפר אחר יגנב הדם או יטשטש ע"י מים ולא יקיים מצות כיסוי וגם מיירי שאין יכול לקפלו וליטלו דאם לא כן לא שייך כאן דלידחי עשה לא תעשה כדאמר ר"ל [בשבת] (דף קלג:) כל מקום שאתה מוצא עשה ולא תעשה אם אתה יכול לקיים שניהם מוטב אם לאו ידחה עשה לא תעשה : **באבנים** מקורזלות. פי' רכות שהן ראויות לזריעה מיהו לא חזי לכיסוי עד שיכתוש וגבי בית הכסא כמי לפי שהן רכות ראויות יותר לקינוח מכשהן קשים ולא כפ"ה דפי' התם בפ' כירה (שבת מג:) מקורזלות חדות דהכא לא א"ש ורש"י מחקו כאן מן הספרים* : **כתישה** בי"ט מי שרי. הקשה ריב"א מאי פריך הא ודאי שרי כמו חרישה דשרי משום הואיל הכא נמי כתישה ועוד תימה היכי פריך הכא דליתי עשה דכיסוי וידחה לאו די"ט הא אין י"ט נדחה מפני עשה דהא תנן בכילד צולין (לקמן פג:) אין שריפת קדשים דוחה י"ט ובפ' במה מדליקין (שבת כד:) יליף מקראי או משום כדמסיק רב אשי התם די"ט עשה ולא תעשה הוא ואין עשה דוחה לא תעשה ועשה ומפרש רשב"ם הואיל וחזי לכיסוי דם ציפור לא משום דחיה קאמר אלא משום דאז לא צריך לחרישה אלא לעפרה ופטור *דהחופר גומא ואינו צריך אלא לעפרה פטור משום דהוי מלאכה שאין צריכה לגופה והשתא פריך שפיר כתישה בי"ט מי שרי דכתישה הוי כטחינה וצריכה לגופה הוא שמתכוון לעשות עפר לכסות ולא משתרי לצורך כיסוי דאין עשה דוחה לא תעשה ועשה וקשה לר"י הא דחופר גומא פטור היינו דוקא בבית דמקלקל הוא כדמוכח בפ"ק דחגיגה (דף י.) והכא בשדה דלזריעה קיימא שמשביח את השדה בחרישה ואפילו אי הוה התם דם ציפור הוה חייב אי חריש בארעא דיליה ואי הוי מלאכה שאין צריכה לגופה פטור השתא נמי פטור א"כ ביטלת כל מלאכת שבת ור"ת מפרש דבחרישה דכלאים קאי דליכא אלא לאו גרידא אבל איום טוב לא קאי וכגון שאם היה הולך לבקש עפר אחר היה הדם נבלע בקרקע ומסיק כתישה בי"ט מי שרי טפי כיון דמשום י"ט אסור דמשום דאית ביה עשה ולא תעשה גם משום כלאים לא שייך למיפטר בהואיל דאפילו אם היה שם דם ציפור אסור ובתחלה נמי הוה מצי לשנויי חרישה בי"ט מי שרי אלא דמשני ליה בע"א משום יגדיל תורה ויאדיר* : **ולוקה** משום הבערה. בפ"ק דביצה (דף יב:) אמר הא מני ב"ש היא דלית להו מתוך אבל לבית הלל שרי אע"ג דצריך שיהא לצורך היום הא נמי חשיב לצרך היום אע"פ שאין ראוי לאוכלו אלא באיסור : **אהבערה** לא ליחייב. מכאן מוכיח ריב"א דרבה דאמר הואיל היינו אפילו לבית שמאי אמר : **הואיל** וחזי לצורכו. בלא האי פירכא נמי קאמר במכות אפיק הבערה משום דקשיא ליה הא דקאמר רבה חילוק מלאכות לשבת ואין חילוק מלאכות לי"ט : **ועייל** עצי מוקצה. תימה לר"י מ"מ ליתני גיד הנשה של נבילה ולילקי נמי משום נבילה : **שה** ולא הבכור. פירש בקונט' דשה משמע בין זכר ובין נקיבה ותימה דהא בעולה איירי דאין באה נקבה וא"ת אמאי אילטריך קרא שאין תמיד בא מבכור ומעשר תיפוק ליה שאין מתנותיהן שוות וי"ל דהא אמר* כל הניתני' במתן ד' שנתנו במתנה אחת כיפר וע"ק היאך יעשה תמיד מבכור הא קעבר משום כל שממנו לאשים הרי הוא בבל תקטירו (יבמות דף ק.) וי"ל כיון דמסיק ליה לשם עולה דינו כדין עולה ומהאי טעמא נמי ניחא לענין מתנה ור"י פירש דהאי קרא מישתעי בפסח דכתיב ביה שה תמים (א) וקאמר שלא יביאהו לא דבכור ולא דמעשר וא"ש השתא דמתנותיהן שוות ולא תיקשי כל שממנו לאשים : **שה** ולא בכור. וא"ת בפרק קמא דחגיגה (דף ה.) דנפקא לן ממסכת ידך לכל דבר שבא חובה אין בא אלא מן החולין וי"ל דהכא אסמכתא בעלמא היא ומן המאתים שערלה בטילה במאתים נמי אסמכתא היא אך קשה דממשקה ישראל מן המותר לישראל דרשה גמורה היא דמהאי קרא יליף בפ"ק דמנחות (דף ה:) דטריפה אסורה לגבוה :
רבי

מו

[וע"ע תוס' סוכה לו: ד"ה מקורזלות]
[שבת פג:]
[עיין תוס' חולין קמא. ד"ה לא ליחייב וכו' ובתוס' ריב"א]
[זבחים נו:]

הגהות הב"ח
(א) תוס' ד"ה שה ולא הבכור וכו' ור"י פי' דהאי קרא מישתעי בפסח דכתיב ביה שה תמים א"ח קרא שיביאו פסח מדבר שיכול להיות אחד מהן נקבה דהיינו חולין ולא בכור ושה אחת כתיב וקאמר ופי' :

גליון הש"ס
גמ' אחרישה לא ליחייב. עי' טורי אבן חגיגה באבני מלואים דף יח ד"ה וכלל : שם ועייל עצי מוקצה. עי' מג"א סי' שכ"ס סק"ס :

רבינו חננאל
וכלאים בכרם אחת והוא בשביעית ויו"ט שתים. כהן ונזיר אבית הטומאה שתים הרי ה' לאוין ואי ס"ד אמרי' הואיל אחרישה ביום טוב לא ליחייב הואיל וראוי לכסות באותה החפירה דם צפור ודחי' איתו מקום שיורש בו אבנים מקורזלות הם דלאו בני כסוי נינהו. אמרי' והא ראוי לכותשן כלאחר יד כו' ואוקמה רב אשי בטינא פי' קרקע שיש בו לחלוחית ואינו ראוי לכסות בו ויש בו שאור מים יבש: ומותיב אביי המבשל גיד הנשה בחלב ביו"ט ואכלו לוקה חמש כו' ואי אמרינן הואיל אהבערה לא ניחייב הואיל והוי ליה לצרכיה לבשל ולאכול ושני' אפיק הבערה ועייל גיד של נבלה. איני והתנן ר' חייא אומר לוקה שתים ושלשה על בישולו ואלו הן לוקה משום מבעיר אש שלא לצורך אכילה ולוקה משום מבשל גיד ביום טוב שאינו בר אכילה וכן משום בשר בחלב הרי שלשה בבישול ושתים באכילה משום או"ל גיד הנשה ומשום אוכל בשר בחלב ואם תוציא הבערה ותכניס גיד הנשה של נבלה ומשום אכילת נבלה יבואו שלשה על האכילה ושתים על הבישול והדר ומשני אפיק הבערה ועייל עצי מוקצה ואקשי' וכי מוקצה מדאורייתא הוא שלוקין עליו כו' והא את הוא דאמרת בעי מרב הונא ואמרי לה מרב חסדא הביא שה מן האפר פי' מן המדבר מקום המרעה ושחט תמיד ביום טוב מהו מי יש מוקצה לגבוה או לא ואמרת פשטה לן מהאי קרא ושה אחת מן הצאן [מן המאתים] ממשקה ישראל שה ולא בכור אחת ולא מעשר מן הצאן ולא מן הפלגם הפלגם כלומר הפלגם פסול שאינו לא כבש ולא איל ומפורש במס' פרה

*נאכל לתשעה לעשרה ולאחד עשר לא פחות ולא יותר כיצד כדרכו לתשעה נאפה בערב שבת נאכל בשבת לתשעה חל יום טוב להיות בע"ש נאכל לשבת לעשרה שני ימים טובים של ראש השנה נאכל לשבת לאחר עשר *לפי שאינו דוחה לא את השבת ולא את הי"ט ואי אמרת צורכי שבת נעשין בי"ט אמאי לא דחי י"ט א"ל *שבות קרובה התירו שבות רחוקה לא התירו ולרשב"ג דאמר *משום רבי שמעון בן הסגן דוחה את י"ט ואינו דוחה את יום צום מאי איכא למימר בהא פליגי מר סבר שבות קרובה התירו שבות רחוקה לא התירו ומר סבר שבות רחוקה נמי התירו מתיב רב מרי *שתי הלחם אינן נאכלות לא פחות משנים ולא יותר על שלשה כיצד נאפות ערב יום טוב נאכלות ליום טוב לשנים חל י"ט להיות אחר השבת נאכלות לי"ט לשלשה 'לפי שאינה דוחה לא את השבת ולא את הי"ט ואי אמרת צורכי שבת נעשין בי"ט השתא דשבת בי"ט שרי דיום טוב ביום טוב מיבעיא שאני התם דאמר קרא לכם *לכם ולא לגבוה ולרשב"ג דאמר משום ר"ש בן הסגן דוחה את יום טוב מאי איכא למימר סבר לה כאבא שאול דאמר *לכם לכם ולא לנכרים שלח ליה רב חסדא לרבה ביד רב אחא בר רב הונא מי אמרינן הואיל והא תנן *יש חורש תלם אחד וחייבין עליה משום שמונה לאוין החורש בשור וחמור והן מוקדשים וכלאים בכרם ושביעית

רש"י

נאכל לתשעה. ליום תשיעי לאפייתו: נאפה בערב שבת. זו מסדרין אותן למחר ולשבת הבאה מסלקים אותו הרי הוא נאכל לשבת הבאה ליום תשיעי לאפייתו: חל י"ט בערב שבת. ולא היו יכולין לאפות דבר שלא לצורך י"ט ואפאוהו מערב י"ט שהוא חמישי בשבת נאכל לשבת שניה דהיינו בעשרה: שני ימים של ר"ה. חלו בחמישי וששי כגון שבאו עדים מן המנחה ולמעלה דתנן (ר"ה דף ל:) נוהגים אותו היום קודש ולמחר קודש נאפה ברביעי בשבת ונאכל בשבת שניה לאחד עשר והוא שבת לאו יום טוס הוא דכשהיו באים עדים לאחר המנחה היו עושין אלול מעובר ומונין מיום שני כדאמרינן שלא היו מקבלין את העדים לקדש בו ביום אא"כ באים קודם המנחה וא"כ הוי יום טוב מאי אכיל ליה לאורתא דהוי נאכל ליום ולילה והקדשים לילה הולכת אחר היום ושני ימים טובים של ר"ה דוקא נקט דבזמן לחם הפנים לא היו שני ימים טובים של גליות: שאינו דוחה. באפייתו: לחם הפנים. צרכי שבת הוא שמסלקין ואוכלין אותו בשבת ואי מדאורייתא נעשין בי"ט בגבולין ומדרבנן הוא דאסור הא במקדש קיימא לן דלא גזרו על השבות ואמאי אינו דוחה: לעולם צרכי שבת. בי"ט אין בהן אלא משום שבות ודקא קשיא לך הכא ליתסרי דאין שבות במקדש: שבות קרובה. של י"ט עצמו או של אותה שבת עצמה שצריכה לבו ביום במקדש התירו: שבות רחוקה. לדחות שבות י"ט זה בשביל שבת שניה לא התירו במקדש: ואינו דוחה את יום צום הכפורים. באפייתו דאיסורא דאורייתא הוא דלא הותר בו אוכל נפש אבל יו"ט הותר בו אוכל נפש והאי אוכל נפש הוא ואע"ג דאינו צורך לי"ט הרי צורך לשבת דהוא נמי י"ט הלכך בעלמא איסור שבות הוא ובמקדש לא גזור ואע"ג דרחוקה היא: שתי הלחם. הבאין בעצרת: לשלשה. לפי שאפאום מערב שבת: ביום טוב מיבעיא. אי נמי לא חזו השתא הא חזו לבו ביום ומי גרעי מצרכי שבת של מחר דלכל האי יומא לא חזי ליה דהא שעד כבר אלא לאו שמע מינה אין מותר בי"ט מן התורה אלא דבר הראוי לו אותה שעה וצרכי שבת טעמייהו משום הואיל דאורחים ובהני ליכא למימר הואיל משום דההיא שעתא לא חזי עד שישחטו כבשים עליהן ויזרוק דמן וכיון דהוה אפשר למיעבד מאתמול לא דחי ליה לי"ט מידי דלא חזי ליה: רבן שמעון כו'. לא גרסי' ביה ואינו דוחה יום צום דמה ענין יום צום סמוך לעצרת: כאבא שאול. במס' ביצה (דף כ:): לכם ולא לנכרים. אבל לגבוה שרי: ביד רב אחא. הטעימו תשובה זו לאומרה לרבה משמו: החורש בשור וחמור. משום לא תחרוש וגו': והן מוקדשין. עובר על השור שהוא קדשי מזבח משום לא תעבוד בבכור שורך וכל הקדשים כבכור ועל החמור שהוא קדשי בדק הבית משום לאו דהזיד במעילה דאמרן בפ' כל שעה (לעיל לג.) הזיד במעיל' באזהר' וגמר חטא חטא מתרומה הרי שלשה לאוין חלוקין ולא חשיב אלא לאוין חלוקין: ושביעית

תוספות

נאכל לאחד עשר יום. כגון שבאו עדים מן המנחה ולמעלה ביום חמישי דנוהגין אותו היום קודש ולמחר קודש כי היכי דלא נזלזלו ביה לשנה הבאה כשיבאו העדים קודם המנחה כדמוכח בריש ביצה (דף ה:) ובתרא עיקר ומיניה מנינן יוה"כ ויהא יוה"כ ביום א' ואז נאכל לי"א אבל אם באו עדים קודם המנחה א"כ למחר ביום ו' חול גמור הוא ויכולין לאפות לחם אחר ביום ו' ולחם הראשון יפדה דאין התנור מקדש כיון דקסבר דאינו דוחה לא שבת וי"ט כדפרישית לעיל:

ואי אמרת צורכי שבת נעשים בי"ט. תימה לר"י מאי פריך והא רב חסדא לא פליג עליה דרבה אלא שמתיר לבשל בי"ט לשבת כמו שמותר לבשל לבו ביום דקדושה אחת היא כדפ"ה אבל בכה"ג דמייתי אפי' לבו ביום אסורה כדקתני סיפא גבי שתי הלחם ובהא לא אמר רב חסדא שיעשו בי"ט יותר מרבה ונראה לר"י דה"פ לעיל צרכי שבת נעשים בי"ט לאו משום דקדושה אחת היא אלא כלומר הואיל שהיא מצות שבת אם לא יעשנה בי"ט שוב לא יעשנה חשיב כמו אוכל נפש די"ט והשתא פריך שפיר בשלמא לדידי דלא שריא בי"ט לשמחת י"ט אלא בכה"ג שיהא עיקרו משום שמחת י"ט והכא ליכא שמחת י"ט וגבי שתי הלחם נמי אין עיקרו לשמחת י"ט אלא עיקרו משום זבח אלא לדידך דאמרת צורכי שבת נעשים בי"ט וכל דבר שהוא מצוה וצריך לעשות בי"ט שאין לו זמן אחר הכא אמאי לא דחי י"ט וכן נראה לקמן גבי שתי הלחם ורש"י פי' גבי שתי הלחם דלרבה א"ש דלא שייכא הואיל משום דההיא שעתא לא חזו עד שישחטו עליהם כבשים ויזרוק דמן וקשה לר"י לפירושו כיון דהגמרא אינה יודעת חילוק בין גבוה להדיוט וכי בשביל שלא יהא עכשיו ראוי אע"פ שיהא ראוי לבו ביום יהא אסור הלא כשאופה העיסה לאורחים אינה ראויה עד שאפאה ושלמי חגיגה שמותר לשוחטן אע"פ שהכורים עד שיזרוק דמן ושחט בהמתו נמי בשעת שחיטה אינה ראויה אלא כיון שמותר אחר זמן לבו ביום לאו חסרון הוא וא"כ תיקשי נמי לרבה ומיהו י"ל לפ"ה דשתי הלחם אין להם שום חסרון בגופו:

ולר"ש ב"ג דאמר דוחה י"ט. בשלמא לדידי דאמינא דסבירא ליה לת"ק דצורכי שבת אינן נעשים בי"ט איכא למימר דבהא פליגי ולא איירי אלא בדאורייתא וקשה לך מת"ק אי נמי אומר רשב"א דאיכא למימר דפליגי דמר סבר אמרי' הואיל ויכול לפדותו ומר סבר לא אמרי' הואיל דלא שכיח כדפרי' לעיל אלא לדידך דאמרת דטעמא דת"ק משום שבות רחוקה בהא ליפלוג עליה רשב"ג:

לכם ולא לגבוה. פי' אף ולא לגבוה ודרשינן נמי ולא לנכרי כדמוכח בביצה (דף כ:) דמאן דסבר נדרים ונדבות אין קריבין בי"ט דריש נמי לכם ולא לנכרי גבי אמרו להם בית שמאי לבית הלל והלא כבר נאמר לכם ולא לגבוה:

ומוקדשין. פ"ה דבמוקדשין איכא תרתי בשור עובר משום לא תעבוד בבכור שורך וחמור שהוא קדשי בדק הבית חייב משום מעילה ובחנם דחק דבשור גופיה מיחייב משום מעילה אם הוא עולה או חטאת וקשה לר"י דבפרק בתרא דמכות (דף כב.) אמר מידי דאיתא בשאלה לא קתני ופריך והרי הקדש ומשני בבכור ופריך והרי נזיר והשתא מחמור הוה ליה לאקשויי לפ"ה כיון דאיירי בחמור הקדש וע"ק לפי' ליחשוב נמי כלאי זרעים ולוקמא כגון שזורע הרבה מינין בכרם דכי האי גוונא פריך במסכת מכות (דף כא.) לחשוב כמה לאוי °ונראה לר"י דלא חשיב לאוי דלקי עלייהו אחרישה כל שהוא אבל אלאו דמעילה לא לקי עד שיחרוש בשוה פרוטה וכלאי הכרם מפרש ר"י דחשיב תרי לאוי משום כלאי זרעים ומשום כלאי הכרם וכן משמע כפי' מדלא קתני כלאי הכרם אלא כלאים בכרם והא דאמר רבי יאשיה אינו חייב עד שיזרע חטה ושעורה וחרצן במפולת יד לאו משום דלית ליה כלאי זרעים אלא אינו חייב משום כלאי הכרם קאמר וכן משמע בירושלמי דקאמר על דעתיה דר' יאשיה כתיב שדך לא תזרע כלאים לאיזה דבר נאמר לא תזרע כרמך כלאים פי' כיון דבלא חרצן מיחייב משום שדך ומשני שאם התרו בו משום שדך לוקה ומשום כרמך לוקה וכן משמע בפ' אותו ואת בנו (חולין פב.) דקאמר הזורע כלאים כלאים לוקה ופריך כלאים כלאים למה לי ומסיק מילתא אגב אורחיה קמשמע לן דאיכא תרי גווני כלאים לאפוקי מדרבי יאשיה דאמר עד שיזרע חטה וכו' וקא משמע לן דכי זרע חטין וחרצן ושעורה וחרצן נמי חייב ומדלא נקט חטה ושעורה אלא חטה וחרצן משמע דרבי יאשיה מודה בחטה ושעורה דלוקה משום כלאי זרעים והא דאמרינן בפרק בתרא דבכורות (דף נד.) דתירוש ויצהר אין תורמין מזה על זה מדכתיב כל חלב יצהר וכל חלב תירוש ודגן תן חלב לזה וחלב לזה אשכחן תירוש ויצהר תירוש ודגן דגן ודגן מנין אמרת קל וחומר וכו' ולרבי יאשיה מייתי לה הכי מה תירוש ויצהר שאינם כלאים זה עם זה
אפילו

עין משפט נר מצוה

לג א מיי' פ"ה מהל' תמידין הלכה י סמג עשין קצ:
לד ב מיי' פ"ח שם הל' ח סמג עשין רה:

רבינו חננאל

קודם שתמות נבלה ואי אפשר לכות בשר בי"א שהיפה וכי קא שהיס לאכילה קא שריס ואקשי' אהא דאמרי' מדאורייתא יום טוב מכין לשבת אינו והתנן במנחות פי"א לחם הפנים נאכל לתשעה לעשרה לאחד עשר לא פחות ולא יותר כו' וקתני סיפא לפי שאינה דוחה לא את השבת ולא את יום טוב ופריק שבות קרובה התירו שבות רחוקה לא התירו כלומר יום טוב מכין לשבת שהוא אחריו אבל בלחם הפנים אינו מותר באכילה אלא לשבת הבאה שהיא שבת רחוקה לא התירה תורה ולרשב"ג דאמר משום ר' שמעון בן הסגן לחם הפנים דוחה יום טוב ואינו דוחה את יום צום כלומר אם חל יום הכפורים ערב שבת אינו דוחה אפיית לחם הפנים יום צום כמו שדוחה יום טוב קסבר אפי' שבת רחוקה התירו. ומותיב רב מרי משתי הלחם ואי אמרת יום טוב מכין לשבת יום טוב ליום טוב אמאי אינו מכין דתנן בשתי הלחם לפי שאינן דוחות לא את שבת ולא יו"ט ושני' שאני קדשים דאמר קרא יעשה לכם לכם ולא לגבוה ור"ש בן הסגן [סובר] לכם מותר ק"ו לגבוה ופשוטה היא: שלח רב חסדא לרבה (בר) [ביד] רב אחא בר הונא ומי אמרינן הואיל והתנן בפ' ואלו הן הלוקין יש חורש תלם אחד וחייב עליו שמונה לאוין ואלו הן החורש בשור וחמור [והן השור והחמור] מוקדשין חייב בשור אחת ובחמור אחר' כל אחת בפני עצמו

מסורת הש"ס

מנחות ק: ערכין ח:
[שבת קיד.]
[מנחות ק.]
ג"ש שם ערכין ח:
[ביצה כ:]
[ביצה כ. כח:] [מגילה ז:]
מכות כא:

גליון הש"ס

תוס' ד"ה ומוקדשין. ונראה לר"י. עיין בכורי אכן ר"ה דף ד ד"ה נדקות:

[47a] is eaten on the ninth, the tenth, or the eleventh [day],[10] a neither earlier nor later.[1] How so? Normally it is eaten on the ninth [day]: it is baked on the eve of the Sabbath [and] eaten on the Sabbath [of the following week], [which is] on the ninth. If a Festival occurred on the eve of the Sabbath, it is eaten on the Sabbath, on the tenth.[2] [If] the two Festival days of New Year[3] [occurred before the Sabbath], it is eaten on the Sabbath on the eleventh day, because it [the baking of the shewbread] does not override either the Sabbath or the Festival. Now if you say [that] the requirements of the Sabbath may be prepared on a Festival, why does it not override the Festival?[4]—Said he to him, A near *shebuth* they permitted; a distant *shebuth* they did not permit.[5] Then according to R. Simeon b. Gamaliel, who said on the authority of R. Simeon the son of the *Segan:*[6] It overrides the Festival, but it does not override the fast-day,[7] what is to be said?[8]—They differ in this: one Master holds, They permitted a near *shebuth*, [but] a distant *shebuth* they did not permit; while the other Master holds: a distant *shebuth* too they permitted.[9]

R. Mari raised an objection: The two loaves[10] are eaten neither less than two [days after baking] nor more than three [days after baking].[11] How so? They were baked on the eve of the Festival [and] eaten on the Festival, [i.e.,] on the second [day]. If the b Festival fell after the Sabbath,[1] they are eaten on the Festival, on the third [day], because it [the baking] does not override either the Sabbath or the Festival.[2] But if you say [that] the requirements of the Sabbath may be prepared on the Festival, seeing that [those] of the Sabbath are permitted on the Festival, is there a question about [those] of the Festival on the Festival!—There it is different, because Scripture saith, [*Save that which every man must eat, that only may be done*] for you:[3] '*for you*', but not for the Most High.[4] Then according to R. Simeon b. Gamaliel who said on the authority of R. Simeon the son of the *Segan:* It overrides the Festival, what is there to be said?—He holds as Abba Saul, who interpreted: '*for you*', but not for Gentiles.[5]

R. Ḥisda sent to Rabbah by the hand of R. Aḥa son of R. Huna: But do we say 'since'? Surely we learned: One may plough one furrow, and be culpable for it on account of eight negative injunctions. [Thus:] he who ploughs with an ox and an ass [together], which are sacred, [and the furrow consists of] *kil'ayim* in a vineyard,

(10) After it is baked. The shewbread was generally baked on Friday, placed on the Table in the Temple on the Sabbath, and removed the following Sabbath and eaten; when it was removed it was replaced by fresh bread.

a (1) Lit., 'less' ... 'more'. (2) For it would have to be baked on Thursday. (3) Even in Palestine, where all festivals were kept one day only, in accordance with Scripture, New Year was sometimes kept two days v. R.H. 30b. (4) Since baking on a Festival for the Sabbath (without an '*erub*) is thus but a Rabbinical prohibition (a *shebuth*; v. Glos.) and as such does not apply to the Temple. (5) I.e., they permitted the abrogation of the *shebuth* in the Temple when it was shortly required, viz., for that same Sabbath, but not when it would only be required a week later. (6) V. *supra* 14a, n. a1. (7) *Sc.* the baking of the shewbread. The Fast-day is the Day of Atonement. (8) Why may it not be baked on the Festival? Tosaf.: On my view, says Rabbah, there is no difficulty, as I maintain that this is precisely the point of the controversy: the first Tanna holds that the requirements of the Sabbath may not be prepared on a Festival, while R. Simeon b. Gamaliel holds that they may be prepared. But on your view that the first Tanna too holds that the requirements of the Sabbath may be prepared on a Festival, but that here it is forbidden as a distant *shebuth*, R. Simeon b. Gamaliel should merely state that even a distant *shebuth* is permitted. (9) And that is what R. Simeon b. Gamaliel really means. (10) Which were brought on Pentecost, v. Lev. XXIII, 17. (11) The figures are inclusive of the day on which they were baked.

b (1) I.e., on Sunday, so that they would be baked on the previous Friday. (2) Hence they could not be baked on the Festival itself and eaten on the same day. (3) Ex. XII, 16. (4) The two loaves, as well as the shewbread, are sacred, and regarded as being 'for the Most High'. (5) Lit., 'strangers', v. Beẓ 20b.

a WATER.[1] SAID R. JOSHUA: [46b] THIS IS NOT THE LEAVEN CONCERNING WHICH WE ARE WARNED WITH [THE INJUNCTIONS], 'IT SHALL NOT BE SEEN', AND 'IT SHALL NOT BE FOUND',[2] BUT HE SEPARATES IT AND LEAVES IT UNTIL THE EVENING, AND IF IT FERMENTS IT FERMENTS.[3]

GEMARA. Shall we say that they differ in respect of goodwill benefit, R. Eliezer holding, Goodwill benefit is considered money, while R. Joshua holds, Goodwill benefit is not money?[4]—No: all hold [that] goodwill benefit is not money, but here they differ in respect to 'since'. For R. Eliezer holds: We say, *since* if he desires, he can have it [*sc*. the designation of *ḥallah*] revoked,[5] it is his property.[6] While R. Joshua holds: We do not say, *since*.[7]

It was stated: [With regard to] one who bakes [food] on a Festival for [consumption on] a weekday,—R. Ḥisda said: He is flagellated; Rabbah said: He is not flagellated. 'R. Ḥisda said, He is flagellated': We do not say, Since if guests visited him it would b be fit for him [on the Festival itself].[1] Rabbah said: He is not flagellated: we say, 'since'. Said Rabbah to R. Ḥisda, According to you who maintain, We do not say, 'since', how may we bake on a Festival for the Sabbath?[2]— On account of the *'erub*[3] of dishes, he answered him. And on account of an *'erub* of dishes we permit a Biblical prohibition!—Said he to him, By Biblical law the requirements of the Sabbath may be prepared on a Festival, and it was only the Rabbis who forbade it, lest it be said, You may bake on a Festival even for weekdays;[4] but since the Rabbis necessitated an *'erub* of dishes for it,[5] he has a distinguishing feature.[6]

He [Rabbah] raised on objection against him: [In the case of] an animal at the point of death,[7] he must not slaughter it[8] save when there is time to eat as much as an olive of it roast before night.[9] [Thus, it states when] he is able to eat [thereof], [that is] even if he does not wish to eat. Now according to me, who maintain that we say, 'since', it is well: *since* if he desires to eat, he is able to eat, for that reason he may slaughter. But according to you who maintain, we do not say, 'since', why may he slaughter?—Said he to him, On account of the loss of his money. And on account of the loss of his money we permit a Biblical prohibition!—Yes, he replied: on account of the loss of his money he determined in his heart to eat as much as an olive, and as much as an olive of flesh is impossible [to obtain] without slaughtering.

He [Rabbah] raised an objection against him: The shewbread

a (1) I.e., the *ḥallah* must be separated from the dough in the usual way and placed in cold water until evening, to prevent it from fermenting. (2) I.e., even if it does turn leaven it is not subject to these prohibitions. The Gemara explains the reason. (3) It does not matter. (4) Goodwill benefit is a man's right to dispose of property to whomever he desires, though he may not keep it, and it is disputed whether such a right is accounted as of monetary worth. Naturally, even if it is, its value is small. Thus an Israelite must separate *ḥallah*, but he can give it to any priest he desires, and a friend of a particular priest might pay him a trifle to give it to that priest. Now, it has been stated *supra* 5*b* that the interdict against leaven being seen or found in the house applies only to one's own leaven. Now if goodwill benefit ranks as money, the *ḥallah* is accounted the Israelite's property, and therefore it is subject to this interdict: hence R. Eliezer holds that the dough must first be baked. But if goodwill benefit does not rank as money, the *ḥallah* is not accounted the Israelite's property, and therefore it is separated from the dough, and it does not matter if it turns leaven. (5) When a man declares anything sacred, as *ḥallah*, it is really the equivalent of a vow that this shall be sacred, and therefore he can be absolved of it, whereby his declaration is annulled, just as in the case of other vows. (6) Until he gives it to the priest. Therefore it is subject to these injunctions. (7) We disregard this possibility, since in fact he has not revoked it. Hence it is not his property. But v. *infra* 48*a*.

b (1) Therefore his action is not culpable. (2) But that we use this argument: *since* it is fit (of use) for him on that same day if he is visited by guests. (3) V. Glos. (4) Which is definitely forbidden. (5) I.e., for cooking on a Festival for the Sabbath. (6) Which makes it clear to him that cooking on Festivals is not permitted indiscriminately, but only for the Festival or the Sabbath. (7) Lit., 'in danger'—of death. Hence the owner wishes to slaughter it before it dies, which would render its flesh *nebelah* (v. Glos). (8) On a Festival. (9) Lit., 'while it is yet day',—i.e., on the Festival itself.

ל א מיי׳ פ״ה מהלכות י״ט הלכה טו סמג לאוין עה טוש״ע או״ח סי׳ תקו סעיף ה:
לא ב מיי׳ פ״ג מהלכות י״ט הלכה א:
לב ג מיי׳ פ״ו שם הלכה יב סמג שם טוש״ע או״ח סי׳ תלה סעיף ו:

לא זה הוא חמץ שמוזהרין עליו בבל יראה ובבל ימצא אלא מפרישתה ומניחתה עד הערב ואם החמיצה החמיצה: **גמ׳** *לימא בטובת הנאה קמיפלגי דר׳ אליעזר סבר טובת הנאה ממון ור׳ יהושע סבר טובת הנאה אינה ממון לא דכולי עלמא סברי טובת הנאה אינה ממון והכא בהואיל קמיפלגי [א] דר׳ אליעזר סבר אמרינן הואיל ואי בעי איתשיל עלה ממוניה הוא ור׳ יהושע סבר לא אמרינן הואיל *איתמר האופה מיום טוב לחול רב חסדא אמר לוקה רבה אמר *אינו לוקה רב חסדא אמר לוקה לא אמרינן הואיל ומיקלעי ליה אורחים חזי ליה רבה אמר אינו לוקה אמרינן הואיל אמר ליה רבה לרב חסדא לדידך דאמרת לא אמרינן הואיל היאך אופין מיום טוב לשבת א״ל משום עירובי תבשילין ומשום עירובי תבשילין שרינן איסורא דאורייתא אמר ליה מדאורייתא צורכי שבת נעשין בי״ט ורבנן הוא דגזרו ביה גזירה שמא יאמרו אופין מי״ט אף לחול וכיון דאצרכוה רבנן עירובי תבשילין אית ליה היכירא איתיביה *בהמה המסוכנת לא ישחוט אלא כדי שיכול לאכול הימנה כזית צלי מבעוד יום יכול לאכול אע״ג דלא בעי למיכל בשלמא לדידי דאמרי הואיל ואי בעי למיכל מצי אכיל משום הכי ישחוט אלא לדידך דאמרת לא אמרינן הואיל אמאי ישחוט אמר ליה משום הפסד ממונו ומשום הפסד ממונו שרינן איסורא דאורייתא אמר ליה אין משום הפסד ממונו גמר בלבו לאכול כזית ואי אפשר לכזית בשר בלא שחיטה איתיביה לחם הפנים נאכל

רש״י

לא זהו חמץ שמוזהרין עליו. כדמפרש בגמ׳ דלאו דידיה הוא לאחר שקרא עליה שם וקרא כתיב שלך אי אתה רואה וזה אינו שלך ולא של חבירך דלאכתי לא מטא ליד כהן: **גמ׳** טובת הנאה. דבר מועט דהנאה (כתובות דף כז:) רשאי ישראל לומר לחבירו הילך סלע ותן כל תרומותיך לבן בתי כהן והיינו טובת הנאה שיש לו לישראל בחלה זו שרשאי לתתה לכל כהן שירצה וליטול דבר מועט מאוהבו של כהן בשביל שיתנה לו ר׳ אליעזר סבר טובת הנאה ממון והויא הך חלה כדידיה ועבר עלה אי מחמיצה גביה הלכך אפי׳ לה ברישא ור׳ יהושע סבר טובת הנאה אינה ממון ולאו דידיה הוא ולאו מוזהר עליה ומשום פקדון נמי ליכא דלאכתי לא מטא לידא דכהן: לא דכולי עלמא טובת הנאה אינה ממון והכא בהואיל קא מיפלגי. ר׳ אליעזר סבר עבר עליה משום הואיל ואי בעי מיתשיל עלה והדרה לטיבלא ודידיה היא דעל כל נדר והקדש ותרומה הקדוש בא לאמירת פה יכול לישאל לחכם ולעקור דבורו הלכך ממוניה הוא ועבר עליה ומלאכת אפייתה נמי בי״ט כי לא קרא עליה שם ואע״ג דאיכא חדא דלא חזיא משתריא דכל חדא וחדא איכא למימר הא לאו חלה היא ואי נמי קרא עליה שם מצי למיפא לה הואיל ואי בעי מיתשיל עלה מיהו כיון דאית (א) לר״א הסל מצרפן לחלה הכי שפיר טפי שתאפה תחלה משום רווחא דמילתא וכל כמה דאפשר למיעבד שפיר בלא שום הואיל ניחא למיעבד: לא אמרינן הואיל. הלכך על חימוצה אינו עובר אבל על אפייתה עובר דאיכא חדא דלא חזיא ליה: האופה מי״ט לחול. לאחר שאכל וגמר סעודתו דפשיטא לן דלא חזיא ליה מידי האידנא עד אורתא שהוא חול: לוקה. משום לא תעשה כל מלאכה: הואיל ואי מיקלעי ליה אורחין. שיהו צריכין לפת זה היום: היאך אופין מי״ט לשבת. אי לאו דאמרי׳ הואיל אי מיקלעי ליה אורחין חזי ליה כוליה ליום טוב: מדאורייתא צורכי שבת נעשין ביו״ט. דכתיב (שמות יב) אך אשר יאכל לכל נפש ושבת ויו״ט חדא קדושה היא דתרווייהו שבת איקרו וכי היכי דמותר לבשל לבו ביום מותר לבשל למחר: ורבנן הוא דגזור. כי לא אותיב עירוב תבשילין כדי שלא יאמרו אופין אף לחול: בהמה מסוכנת. ורוצה לשוחטה ביום טוב שלא תמות ויפסידנה: כזית צלי. זהו קל בבישולים: כדי שיכול לאכול. שיהא שהות ביום כדי להפשיט ולחתוך כזית ולצלות ולאכול ואי איכא שהות כי האי שרי ואע״ג דלא אכיל מינה: אמאי שחיט. הא לא צריך למיכל שכבר אכל: משום הפסד ממונו. (ב) ויודע הוא שאינו מותר בלא אכילה גמר בלבו לאנס את עצמו ולעבור על דעתו ולאכול כזית והוה ליה כצריך לזית בי״ט ומשום ההוא זית בעיא למישחטיה לכולה דאי אפשר לכזית בשר בלא שחיטה אבל הכא דליכא למימר גמר בלבו לאנס עצמו משום הואיל לא שרינן איסורא דאורייתא כיון דלא צריך למידי: לחם הפנים. כל שבת ושבת נאכל

תוספות

הואיל ואי בעי מיתשיל עליה. הקשה בקונטרס א״כ יקרא לה שם ואח״כ תאפה מטעם הואיל ואי בעי מיתשיל עלה (ג) ואור״י כיון שיכול לעשות בלא הואיל אין לנו לעשות ע״י הואיל וא״ת א״כ אמאי שרי ר׳ אליעזר לאפות משום הואיל דכל חדא וחדא חזיא ליה כדלקמן בלא הואיל יכול לעשות ע״י הטלה לצונן ואור״י דהכי עדיף טפי מהטלה לצונן דאיכא למיחש שלא תזהר יפה ויבא לידי חימוץ ועוד י״ל הואיל ואי בעי מיתשיל עלה לא שכיח לא אמר להתיר כדמוכח לקמן גבי לחם הפנים ושתי הלחם דלאין דאפייתן דוחה יו״ט אע״ג דאיכא למימר הואיל ואי בעי פריק ליה שאין התנור מקדש שאם היה מקדש א״כ יפסלו בלינה כיון דאופין אותן קודם יו״ט וכן מוכח במנחות (דף עב:) דמ״ד אין אפייתן דוחה י״ט קסבר דאין התנור מקדשן ורשב״א פירש כי נ״ל שדעת רש״י כיון שהסל מצרפן וסופו ליטול אחת על כולן נמצא שטרח בדבר שאין ראוי לאכילה אלא מטעם הואיל שרי דאי בעי לא מפריש חדא לחלה אלא בלע פורתא מכל חדא וחדא וכל חדא וחדא חזיא ליה וכיון דכי נמי לא תקרא לה שם עד שתאפה לא שרי אלא על ידי הואיל ואם יקרא לה שם קודם שתאפה הוו תרי הואיל ותרי הואיל לא אמרינן וקשה לרשב״א לפירושו כיון דאם יבלע מכל חדא וחדא יהא מותר בלא הואיל היאך שרו רבנן למיעבד ע״י הואיל כיון דאפשר בלא הואיל ותירץ שלא הטריחו חכמים לבלוע מכל אחת ואחת ור״י מקשה דהא כי נמי בלע מכל חדא וחדא אסור לאפות כדמוכח בפ״ב דבילה (דף כב.) דאמר עיסה של נכרי ושל ישראל אסור לאפות בי״ט כיון דאפשר למיפלגה בלישה ונראה לרשב״א לחלק דדוקא בעיסת נכרי אסרו מדרבנן אבל גבי חלה לא אסרו משום תיקון חלה ואין נראה לריב״א מה שמשמע מתוך פ״ה דאע״פ שהיה בהן כדי חיוב חלה מתחלה בעינן צירוף סל להפריש אחת על כולן וכן משמע בפסק שלו לקמן דלא בעינן צירוף סל לר׳ אליעזר אלא כשלא היה בתחלה שיעור חלה דהאכי מייתי לה לקמן *בשמעתין והכי תניא בהדיא במס׳ חלה (פ״ב משנה ד) דתנן העושה עיסתו קבין קבין (ד) פטור מן החלה עד שישוכו ר׳ אליעזר אומר אף הרודה ונותן לסל וכו׳ משמע בהדיא דמיירי היכא דלא היה שיעור חלה אבל היכא דיש שיעור חלה לא בעינן צירוף סל להפריש מזה על זה אלא הקפה בעלמא כדי לתרום מן המוקף כמו בתרומה ומעשר דלא בעינן צירוף סל להפריש מזה על זה אלא הקפה מיהו נראה לר״י דעם נתינה לסל בעינן נמי נגיעה בהדי הדדי משום נטילת חלה מן המוקף וכדאמר ר׳ אליעזר גופיה בפ׳ כשם (סוטה ל.) שתי עיסות אחת טהורה ואחת טמאה נותן פחות מכביצה באמצע כדי ליטול מן המוקף מדלא שרי על ידי צירוף סל משמע דבעי נמי נגיעה:

הואיל אי בעי מיתשיל עלה. תימה לרשב״א אמאי אמר בפרק כל שעה (לעיל דף לח.) דמצת מעשר שני אין יוצא בה בפסח לר״מ דסבר מעשר שני ממון גבוה הוא ולא חשיב מצתכם הא הואיל אי בעי מיתשיל עלה מחשבינן [ליה] כשלו ועוד דאמר לעיל (דף ה:) אבל אתה רואה של אחרים ושל גבוה והא של גבוה נמי חשיב כשלו הואיל אי בעי מיתשיל עליה ותי׳ ר״י דשאני הנהו דכתיב בהו *לה׳ [ב] אע״ג דאי בעי מיתשיל עלה חשבם הכתוב של גבוה ועוד תי׳ ר״י היכא דאתא הקדש ליד הגזבר לא אמרי׳ הואיל אי בעי מיתשיל עלה והואיל אי בעי פריק נמי לא אמרינן דאם כן היה קונה אותו דאטו נחשוב חמץ של נכרי כשלו הואיל אי בעי קני ליה ועוד תירץ כיון שנתחמץ שוב אדם לא יפדנו וצ״ע בההוא הואיל דכל שעה (ג״ז שם) הואיל ולא קרא לה שם:

רבה אמר אינו לוקה. וא״ת דאמר בהמצניע (שבת צה.) המכבד (ה) והרודה חלות דבש שגג בשבת חייב חטאת הזיד ביום טוב סופג את הארבעים דברי רבי אליעזר וחכמים אומרים אין כאן אלא שבות ואמאי לוקה לר׳ אליעזר לימא הואיל ומיקלעי ליה אורחים ואפי׳ רבנן לא פטרי אלא משום דלא חשיבי דבש בכוורתו מחובר ויש לומר כגון שהדביש הדבש ואינה ראויה לאכול ואפי׳ אי מיקלעי ליה אורחים לא חזי להו אי נמי ברודה סמוך לשקיעת החמה שאפילו יבואו אורחים אין שהות ביום לאוכלו ובהאי שינויא א״ש מה שהקשה ריב״א דשמעינן ליה לרבה דאית ליה הכנה בריש מסכת בילה (דף ב:) ובריש בכל מערבין (עירובין לח:) דאמר אין יום טוב מכין לשבת אי אמרת הואיל היכא משכחת לה דאין יום טוב מכין לשבת והשתא משכחת לה סמוך לשקיעת החמה כדפרישית ואם תאמר אי אמרינן הואיל א״כ בטלת כל מלאכת שבת הואיל וראוי לחולה שיש בו סכנה וי״ל כיון דלא שכיח כלל לא אמרינן הואיל: נאכל

רבינו חננאל

ביום טוב כו׳ לימא בטובת הנאה קא מיפלגי פי׳ אותה הנאה שיש לו לישראל לתת חלתו לאיזה כהן שירצה אע״פ שעיקר חלה חייב ליתנה לכהן אבל יש לו לבחור כהן לתתה לו שיחזיק לו טובת אותה הנאה ממון הוא ור׳ אליעזר אומר דממונו הוא והוא חייב עליה בבל יראה ובל ימצא ור׳ יהושע אומר אינו ממונו דאי מקדש בה אשה אינה מקודשת לפיכך אינו חייב עלי׳ כלל ודחי׳ לא כ״ע טובת הנאה אינה ממון ובהואיל פליגי ר׳ אליעזר סבר הואיל אי בעי מתשיל עליה ומפריש עליה כלומר הולך אצל חכם ואומר טעיתי שקריתי עליה שם חלה ומתירה לו החכם ויוצאת לחולין ונעשית ממונו לפיכך עכשיו נמי חייב עליה ור׳ יהושע סבר לא אמרי׳ הואיל השתא מיהא לא איתשל עלה מי יימר דמיתשיל עלה: איתמר האופה מיום טוב לחול רב חסדא אמר לוקה דהא לא חזי ליה רבה אמר אינו לוקה הואיל ואי מקלעי ליה אורחים חזי ליה השתא נמי לא לקי אמר ליה רבה לרב חסדא בשלמא לדידי דאית לי הואיל לפיכך אופין מיום טוב לשבת אלא לדידך דלית לך הואיל איך אופין מיום טוב לשבת אמר ליה משום עירובי תבשילין אמר ליה משום עירובי תבשילין שרינן איסורא דאורייתא שלוקין עליה אמר ליה מדאורייתא יום טוב מכין לשבת ורבנן הוא דגזרו כו׳ שלא יאמרו מיום טוב לשבת אסור קל וחומר מיום טוב לחול וכיון דתקנו עירובי תבשילין אית ליה הכירא ואותבי׳ עליה דרבה הא דתנן בהמה המסוכנת לא ישחוט וכו׳ ושני משום הפסד ממונו גמר בלבו לאכול כזית ואי אפשר לכזית בשר בלא שחיטה ונאכל

מסורת הש״ס

קדושין נח. נדרים פד: ב״מ יא: חולין קלא.
ביצה כא. לקמן סב:
ביצה כה. [ע״ש אבל גרסא דהכא היא דמיימ׳]
[קדש עיין קדושין נג.]

הגהות הב״ח

(א) רש״י ד״ה לא דכ״ע וכו׳ דאיכא חדא וחדא כו׳ דאית ליה לר׳ אליעזר: (ב) ד״ה משום הפסד ממונו דיודע: (ג) תוס׳ ד״ה הואיל וכו׳ ואי בעי מיתשיל עלה ותירץ וכיון שיכול כו׳ ותיבת ואור״י נמחק: (ד) בא״ד במס׳ חלה כו׳ עיסתו קבין קבין ונגעו זה בזה פטורין מן החלה: (ה) ד״ה רבה וכו׳ המכבד והמרבץ והרודה:

הגהות מהר״ב רנשבורג

[א] בגמ׳ דר״א סבר אמרינן הואיל ואי בעי מיתשיל עלה ממוניה הוא. כ״כ ואע״ג דר״א כב״ש ס״ל דטעות הקדש הקדש ואין נשאלין עליו עיין מ״ש בזה הרמ״ע מפאנו סי׳ ס״ב וצ״ע בלשון רש״י כאן בד״ה לא דכ״ע וכו׳ שאין תירוצו דהרמ״ע מספיק לדבריו ועיין בתי״ט במשנתנו בד״ה ר״א וכו׳ ועי׳ תוס׳ חדשים סוף הסדר מועד: [ב] בתוס׳ ד״ה הואיל תימה לרשב״א וכו׳ ותירץ ר״י דשאני הנהו דכתיב בהו לה׳. נ״ב ר״ל דכתיב בהו קודש לה׳ בסוף פ׳ בחקתי אבל חלה דאמר הש״ס הכא הואיל ואי בעי מיתשל עלה שאני דל״כ בה קודש כדמשני הש״ס בקדושין דף נ״ג ע״א ישוב״ה ודוק. אחרי שנים רבות שכתבתי זה יצא לאורה ס׳ מעין החכמה להגאון מוהרמ״ה וראיתי פ״ז ע״א בד״ה ומאורהו של הרמב״ן וכו׳ ישוב אחר בזה על התוס׳ והנלענ״ד כתבתי והוא אמת נכון יותר:

לענין צירוף טומאה בפסח ובשאר ימות השנה איכא פלוגתא היכי דמי כגון *דאיכא פחות מכביצה אוכלין ונגעו בהאי בצק בפסח דאיסורו חשוב מצטרף בשאר ימות השנה דבקפידא תליא מילתא אם מקפיד עליו מצטרף אם רוצה בקיומו הרי הוא כעריבה מתקיף לה רבא מי קתני מצטרף והא חוצץ קתני אלא אמר רבא וכן להעלות טהרה לעריבה היכי דמי כגון דאיטמי הך עריבה ובעי לאטבולי בפסח דאיסורו חשוב חוצץ ולא סלקא לה טבילה בשאר ימות השנה בקפידא תליא מילתא אי מקפיד עליו חוצץ ואם רוצה בקיומו הרי הוא כעריבה מתקיף לה רב פפא מי קתני וכן לענין טהרה הא לענין טומאה קתני אלא אמר רב פפא וכן לענין להוריד טומאה לעריבה היכי דמי *כגון דנגע שרץ בהאי בצק בפסח דאיסורו חשוב הוציץ ולא נחתה לה טומאה בשאר ימות השנה דבקפידא תליא אם מקפיד עליו חוצץ אם רוצה בקיומו הרי הוא כעריבה:

מתני׳ בצק החרש אם יש כיוצא בו שהחמיץ הרי זה אסור: **גמ׳** אם אין שם כיוצא בו מהו א״ר אבהו אמר ר׳ שמעון בן לקיש כדי שילך אדם ממגדל נוניא לטבריא מיל *ונימא מיל *הא קמ״ל דשיעורא דמיל כממגדל נוניא ועד טבריא *א״ר אבהו אמר רבי שמעון בן לקיש לגבל ולתפלה ולנטילת ידים ארבעה מילין אמר רב נחמן בר יצחק אייבו אמרה וארבעה אמר בה והדא מינייהו עבוד דתנן *וכולן שעיבדן או שהילך בהן כדי עבודה טהורין חוץ מעור האדם וכמה כדי עבודה א״ר (אינייא) א״ר ינאי כדי הילוך ארבעה מילין א״ר יוסי ברבי חנינא *לא שנו אלא לפניו אבל לאחריו אפילו מיל אינו חוזר אמר רב אחא ומינה מיל הוא דאינו חוזר הא פחות ממיל חוזר:

מתני׳ כיצד מפרישין חלה בטומאה ביו״ט ר״א אומר לא תקרא לה שם עד שתאפה בן בתירא אומר תטיל בצונן א״ר יהושע לא

רש״י

לענין צירוף טומאה. כדמפרש ואזיל דבפסח תליא מילתא בשיעוריה ובשאר ימות השנה איכא פלוגתא. חילוק בין מקפיד לשאינו מקפיד והיינו דתנא סיפא אם מקפיד עליו: דאיכא פחות מכביצה אוכלין דנגעו בהאי בצק. הדבוק בעריבה ונגעה בהן טומאה ואיטמי והדר נגעו בהן אוכלים טהורים: בפסח. דאיסור חמץ מחשבו ועושהו חשוב אוכל וכזית הזוכר להיחשב לענין איסור חמץ דלא בטיל לגבי עריבה כדתניא רישא הפסח לענין טומאה נמי לא בטיל לגבי עריבה ומצטרף להשלים לכביצה ואע״ג דאין מקפיד עליו ומטמאת את אחרים: בשאר ימות השנה. דליכא למימר איסורו חשובו בקפידא תליא מילתא אם מקפיד עליו מצטרף חשיב אוכלא אוכל וסופו ליטלו: וכן להעלות לה טהרה לעריבה. תליא נמי בשיעורא ולא שיעורא בפסח ואם מקפיד עליו קאי אשאר ימות השנה כגון דאיטמי וקא מטביל לה וקאמר דבפסח חוצץ וכזית עובר עליה ובדפנות איסורו חושבו דעל כרחו צריך ליטלו וחייץ דלא הוי כעריבה ואפי׳ אינו מקפיד עליו(א): אבל בשאר ימות השנה. בין מרובה בין מועט בקפידא תליא מילתא: וכן להוריד טומאה לעריבה. על ידי בצק זה תליא נמי בימות הפסח בשיעורא ולאו שיעורא ואם מקפיד עליו אשאר ימות השנה קאי: ה״ג והיכי דמי כגון דנגע שרץ בהאי בצק: בפסח. דכזית איסורו חשובו חייץ ולא הוי כעריבה ולא נחתא לה שום טומאה לעריבה ואפילו אין מקפיד עליו ובפחות מכזית כי אינו מקפיד עליו לא(ב): ובשאר ימות השנה. אם מקפיד עליו אפילו בפחות מכזית חוצץ: ואם רוצה הוא בקיומו הרי הוא כעריבה. והוי כאלו נגע שרץ בעריבה ממש:

מתני׳ בצק החרש. שאין ניכר אם החמיץ אם לאו משמשנה הוא כחרש הזה שיש לו אזנים ואינו ניכר אם שומע אם לאו דאין אדם עומד על בירורו ועל דעתו ליבקא אחריתא בצק החרש קשה כחרש ואינו ניכר שהחמיץ ר״ל שהכסיפו פניו ואין סידוק לסימן החימוץ: אם יש כיוצא בו שהחמיץ. אם יש עיסה אחרת שנילושה בשעתה וכבר החמיצה: **גמ׳** ממגדל נוניא לטבריא. דהיינו מיל: לגבל ולתפלה כו׳. מאום דרבי אבהו אמר ריש לקיש נקט לה: לגבל. המגבל עיסה אחרים בשכר וכלי בעל הבית טמאים עד ארבע מילין הטריחוהו חכמים לילך למקוה לטבול כליו וכן לתפלה אם מהלך אדם בדרך ובא עת לנון ולהתפלל אם יש בית הכנסת לפניו ברחוק ארבע מילין הולך ומתפלל שם וכן לנטילת ידים לאכילה אם עתיד למצוא מים לפניו בד׳ מילין הולך לשם ונוטל את ידיו: ר׳ אייבו אמרה. להא מילתא משמיה דריש לקיש ולא ר׳ אבהו אמרה: וארבעה מילי אמר בה. לשיעור ארבע מילין הייט תלת וחדא מוסיף(ג): ומאי היא עבוד. שיעור עבוד של עור רך המטמא כבשר כגון הכך דחשיב בהעור והרוטב ארבע מילין הוא לבטלו מתורת בשר מחמת עיבודו: כולן. כל אלו שמנו חכמים בהעור והרוטב שעורותיהן מטמאין כבשרן מפני שהוא רך ודרכו לאכול: שהילך בהן. דרך עורות לשוטחן לפני דריסת רגלי אדם וזהו תחילת עיבודן: אלא לפניו. אנטילת ידים ותפלה דמהלך בדרך קאי דאילו גבל יליך עד ד׳ מילין דמה יש לו להפסיד: ומינה. מהא דר׳ יוסי בר חנינא דאמר בהדיא אפי׳ מיל אינו חוזר דוקא מיל קאמר הא פחות ממיל חוזר: **מתני׳** כיצד מפרישין חלה בטומאה. בנטמאת העיסה ושוב אין חלה הניטלת ממנה ראויה לאכילת כהן כיצד מפרישין אותה ביום טוב של פסח הרי אין יכול לאפותה מאחר שאינה ראויה לאכילה ולשהותה לשורפה לערב אי אפשר שלא תחמיץ ולשורפה או להאכילה לכלבים אי אפשר שאין שורפין קדשים ביום טוב: רבי אליעזר אומר לא תקרא לה שם. חלה: עד שתאפה. תחלה דהכי כל חדא וחדא חזיא ליה דמפריש מכל חדא פורתא ולאחר אפייה אם רצה יפריש חלה שלימה על כולן כדתניא בגמרא דקסבר רבי אליעזר הסל שהוא רודה מן התנור להוכו מצרפו לחלה:

תוספות

לגבל. פי׳ בערוך דבחדא מהלך בדרך מיירי דומיא דתפלה דאם יש גבל העושה עיסתו בטהרה ברחוק ד׳ מילין ימתין עד שיגיע לאותו גבל והשתא א״ש דלא שנו אלא לפניו קאי אכולהו: **ולתפלה.** נראה כפירוש הקונטרס ולא כערוך דפירש לתפלה היינו לרחוץ ידיו להתפלל דהיכי דמי אי בעידנא דצלותא הא אמרינן בברכות (דף טו.) (*אביי) לייט אמאן דמהדר אמיא בעידן צלותא דכתיב ארחץ בנקיון כפי ואי שלא בזמן תפלה מאי איריא ד׳ מילין אפי׳ טובא נמי: **לא** תקרא לה שם עד שתאפה. שאם היה (ד) קורא לה שם לא היה יכול לאפותה ולא לשורפה דאין שורפין קדשים ביו״ט כדיליף בבמה מדליקין (שבת כד:) והיינו נמי טעמא הא דתנן התם אין מדליקין בשמן שריפה ביו״ט ותימה בשלמא פסול קודש אין שורפין ביו״ט שאין יכול להנות ממנה בשעת שריפה אבל תרומה טמאה שיכול להנות ממנה בשעת שריפה אמאי אין שורפים כמו שמותר להדליק בשמן של חולין להנאתו כך ישרוף תרומה טמאה להנאתו וכי מפני שמצוה לשרוף מיגרע גרע ותירץ ריב״א דשמן של חולין מותר להדליק להנאתו כמו שמותר לאכול אבל תרומה טמאה דאסורה בכל ההנאות נמצא שההבערה אינה להנאה אלא לשם מצות שריפה אלא שהתורה לא הקפידה אם יהנה ממנה בשעת שריפה לכך אין דוחה יו״ט כשאר שריפת קדשים מידי דהוי אנדרים ונדבות למ״ד אין קרבים ביו״ט (ביצה דף יט.) אע״פ שיש בהן היתר לאכילת אדם כיון דעיקרו לגבוה וכהנים משולחן גבוה קזכו אסור לשוחטן ולמ״ד קרבים קסבר עיקר שחיטה לצורך אדם אבל שריפת תרומה טמאה אינה לשם הנאה מדאסר כל שאר הנאות אלא ודאי לשם מצות ביעור הוא ור״י פי׳ דודאי מותר לשרוף ביו״ט תרומה לצורך אוכל נפש דלא שייך למימר משולחן גבוה קא זכו אלא דגזרינן לצורך אטו שלא לצורך דשלא לצורך אסור מן התורה דגמרינן מקדשים שאין שורפין ביו״ט*: **עד** שתאפה. אומר ר״י אנן שרינן לקרות לה שם קודם אפייה אע״ג דפסקינן כר״א דהא אי איכא כהן קטן חזיא ליה כדאמר בפרק עד כמה (בכורות כז.) אין תרומת ח״ל אסורה אלא למי שטומאה יוצאה עליו מגופו וכן פסק בה״ג בסדר פסח בשם רב כהן צדק דיש מתיבתא ואפי׳ ליכא כהן קטן אי איכא כהן גדול שרי דחזיא ליה ע״י ביטול ברוב כדאמר התם רבה מבטל לה ברוב ואכיל לה בימי טומאתו ואמאי לא שרינן לאפות חלה טמאה מטעם דאמר (ר״א בר׳ שמעון) בפ״ב דביצה (דף יז.) אף ממלאה אשה תנור פת אע״פ שאינה צריכה אלא לככר אחד מפני שהפת נאפה יפה כשהתנור מלא ואמר (רבה) התם הלכה *כר״א ברבי שמעון ואפילו נאמר דאסור לאפות שאסור לטלטלה מכל מקום כי לא קרא לה שם אמאי צריך לטעמא דהואיל ואי״ נ דטעמא [דאמרינן] בביצה לא שייך אלא בתנור אבל כשאופה אחת אחת גחלים לא: **תטיל** בצונן. אור״י דר״א ורבי יהושע לא פליגי אבן בתירא שלא הועיל הטלה לצונן והיכא שאירע שקרא לה שם אור״ח תטיל בצונן:

רבינו חננאל

צירוף טומאה וכי קתני לענין טומאה בפסח ובשאר ימות השנה איכא פלוגתא כיצד כגון דאיכא פחות מכביצה אוכלין בהאי עריבה ואית בה כזית בצק ונגעי בה בפסח דאיסורא חושבו להאי בצק ולמשקליה קאי מצטרף ואי נגעה בה טומאה איטמי אבל בשאר ימות השנה אם מקפיד עליו ובעי למשקליה מצטרף ואי לא לא אלא הרי הוא כעריבה דלא מצטרף ודחי רבא אי הכי מצטרף מיבעי ליה למתני במתני׳ אלא הכי קתני וכן להעלות טהרה לעריבה כגון שזו העריבה טמאה היא והטבילה ונמצא בה בצק בסדקיה בפסח דאיסורא חושבו וחייב לבערו הוצץ ולא עלתה לה טבילה בשאר ימות השנה אם רוצה בקיומו הרי בצק זה כעריבה ועלתה לו טבילה ואינו חוצץ ואוקמה רב פפא אלא הכי וכן לענין טומאה להוריד טומאה לעריבה היכי דמי כגון דדביק בצק בהאי עריבה ונגע שרץ בבצק בפסח דחייב לבערו לאו כגופה דעריבה דמי ולא נטמאת העריבה בשאר ימות השנה אי מקפיד לקלפו ולא נחתה לה טומאה לעריבה ואם רוצה בקיומו הרי הוא כעריבה וכאלו נגע השרץ [בעריבה] ונטמאת: **בצק** החרש אם כיוצא בו שהחמיץ. כלומר אם יש מי שלש בבת אחת עמו והחמיץ אותו הבצק גם זה אסור שחמץ הוא ואע״פ שהוא חרש ואין אדם יכול להרגיש בו אין שם כיוצא בו אם שהה משעה שנגמר הלישה כשעור הליכת מיל אסור שודאי החמיץ: **אמר** ר׳ אבהו אמר ריש לקיש לגבל כגון שיש לפניו המגבל בטהרה ולתפלה כגון שצריך להתפלל ויש לפניו מים ליטול ידיו ולנטילת ידים רוצה לאכל ואין לו מים ליטול ידיו ארבעת מילין פי׳ אם יש גבל העושה עיסתו בטהרה או אם יש מים ברחוק ארבעת מילין לפניו ימתין עד שיגיע לגבל ההוא שעושה בטהרה ויעשה לו עיסתו בטהר׳ וכן לא יתפלל ולא יאכל עד שיגיע למים ויטול ידיו: **והני** מילי דבעינן ד׳ מילין לפניו אבל לאחריו אפי׳ מיל אחד אין מטריחין אותו לחזור אלא עושה עיסתו במה שמזומן לו ומקנח ידיו ומתפלל וגם אוכל בבלאי חמתות בלא נטילה. וכן עבודת העור בהלוך ארבעת מילין נקרא עבודה ונפטר העבודת העור בהלוך מפורש בפרק העור והרוטב (דף קכב): **מתני׳** כיצד מפרישין חלה בטומאה

מסורת הש״ס

[פי׳ תוס׳ שבת לה. ד״ה אי לענין טומאה]

[מגילה ה:] חולין קכב.

שם נדה נח.

[נ״ל אייבו]

ברכות טו. חולין קכב.

הגהות הב״ח

(א) רש״י ד״ה וכן להעלות וכו׳ אבל בשאר וכו׳ ד״ה בפסח וכו׳ (ב) בשאר וכו׳: (ג) ד״ה וחדא וכו׳: (ד) תוס׳ ד״ה לא תקרא וכו׳ שאם היה קורא לה שם לא היה יכול לאפותה וכו׳

גליון הש״ס

גמרא כגון דאיכא פחות מכביצה. עיין שבת לה ע״א תוס׳ ד״ה אי לענין: שם הא קמ״ל דשיעורא דמיל. עיין טורי אבן מגילה ג ע״ב ד״ה הא קמ״ל:

עין משפט נר מצוה

כד א מיי׳ פ״ד מהל׳ כלים הלכה ט:

כה ב מיי׳ פ״ה מהל׳ חמץ הלכה יג סמג לאוין עה טוש״ע או״ח סי׳ תנט סעיף ב:

כו ג מיי׳ פ״ה מהל׳ ביכורים הל׳ יא:

[נ״ל רב חסדא]

כז ד מיי׳ פ״א מהל׳ שאר אבות הטומאות הלכה ב:

כח ה מיי׳ פ״ד מהל׳ תפלה הלכה ב סמג עשין יט טוש״ע או״ח סי׳ צב סעיף ד וסימן קסג סעיף א:

כט ו מיי׳ פ״ב מהלכות י״ט הלכה ט סמג לאוין עה טוש״ע או״ח סי׳ תנז סעיף ב וסי׳ תקו סעיף ד:

[ועי׳ תוס׳ שבת כד: ד״ה לפי ותוס׳ ביצה כז: ד״ה ועל החלה]

[נ״ל שמעון בן אלעזר]

[נ״ל רבא]

נ״ל כר״ש בן אלעזר

thus: AND IT IS LIKEWISE [46a] IN RESPECT TO combining for UNCLEANNESS on Passover, whereas during the rest of the year there is a distinction. How is that? E.g., if there are eatables less than an egg in quantity,[2] and they were in contact with this dough: on Passover, when its prohibition renders the dough important,[3] it combines.[4] [But] during the rest of the year, when the matter is dependent on [his] objecting, IF HE OBJECTS TO IT,[5] it combines; [while] IF HE DESIRES ITS PRESERVATION, IT IS LIKE THE KNEADING-TROUGH. To this Raba demurred: Does he then teach, It combines; surely he teaches, IT INTERPOSES! Rather, said Raba: [The meaning is], AND IT IS LIKEWISE IN RESPECT TO cleaning[6] the kneading-trough. How is that? E.g., if this kneading-trough became unclean, and he wishes to immerse it. On Passover, when its interdict [renders it] important, IT INTERPOSES, and the immersion is not efficacious for it. But during the rest of the year the matter is dependent on his objecting: IF HE OBJECTS TO IT, IT INTERPOSES, WHILE IF HE DESIRES ITS PRESERVATION, IT IS LIKE THE KNEADING-TROUGH. To this R. Papa demurred: Does he teach, And it is likewise in respect to cleanness? Surely he teaches, AND IT IS LIKEWISE IN RESPECT TO UNCLEANNESS! Rather, said R. Papa: [The meaning is], AND IT IS LIKEWISE IN RESPECT TO causing UNCLEANNESS to descend upon the kneading-trough. How so? E.g., if a *sherez* touched this dough: on Passover, when its interdict [renders it]
a important, IT INTERPOSES,[1] and uncleanness does not descend upon it;[2] [but] during the rest of the year, when the matter is dependent on [his] objecting, IF HE OBJECTS TO IT, IT INTERPOSES; WHILE IF HE DESIRES ITS PRESERVATION, IT IS LIKE [i.e., identical with] THE KNEADING-TROUGH.[3]

MISHNAH. [REGARDING] 'DEAF' DOUGH,[4] IF THERE IS [A DOUGH] SIMILAR TO IT WHICH HAS BECOME LEAVEN,[5] IT IS FORBIDDEN.

GEMARA. What if there is no [dough] similar to it?—Said R. Abbahu in the name of R. Simeon b. Lakish: [The period for fermentation is] as long as it takes a man to walk from the Fish Tower [Migdal Nunia] to Tiberias, which is a *mil*.[6] Then let him say a *mil*?—He informs us this, [viz.,] that the standard of a *mil* is as that from Migdal Nunia to Tiberias.[7]

R. Abbahu said in the name of R. Simeon b. Lakish: For kneading, for prayer, and for washing the hands, [the standard is] four *mils*.[8] R. Naḥman b. Isaac said: Aibu stated this,[9] and he stated
b four [laws] about it,[1] and one of them is tanning. For we learned: And all these, if he tanned them or trod on them to the extent of tanning,[2] are clean,[3] excepting a man's skin. And how much is 'the extent of tanning'?—Said R. Aibu in R. Jannai's name: The extent of walking four *mils*. R. Jose son of R. Ḥanina said: They learned this only [about going on] ahead: but [as for going] back, he need not return even a *mil*.[4] Said R. Aḥa: And from this [we deduce]: it is only a *mil* that he need not go back, but less than a *mil* he must go back.

MISHNAH. HOW DO WE SEPARATE ḤALLAH ON THE FESTIVAL [FROM DOUGH WHICH IS] IN [A STATE OF] UNCLEANNESS?[5] R. ELIEZER SAID: IT MUST NOT BE DESIGNATED WITH THE NAME [OF ḤALLAH] UNTIL IT IS BAKED.[6] THE SON OF BATHYRA SAID: LET IT [THE DOUGH] BE CAST INTO COLD

(2) This being the minimum standard which can defile. (3) Lit., 'its prohibition is important'. (4) With the eatables. I.e., the dough, if an olive in quantity, is important in so far as its prohibition necessitates its removal, and owing to this it combines with the eatables to the standard of an egg, whereby if unclean they can together defile other food. (5) Which gives it an importance. (6) Lit., 'bringing it up'—from its uncleanness.

a (1) Between the *sherez* (v. Glos.) and the trough. (2) The trough does not become unclean, for we do not regard the *sherez* as having touched it. (3) So that the trough becomes unclean through the contact of the *sherez* with the dough. (4) An idiomatic expression: dough in which it is doubtful whether leavening has set in or not. Another reading: 'potsherd' dough, i.e., dough whose surface has gone hard and smooth and contains no splits, which are the usual signs of fermentation, and thus there is doubt. (5) I.e., dough which was kneaded at the same time. (6) Two thousand cubits. This is generally regarded as an eighteen minutes' walk. If it is eighteen minutes since the dough was kneaded (before being set in the oven), it is leaven. (7) I.e., that they are a *mil* apart. (8) A paid kneader must go four *mils* to immerse the kneading vessels, if they are unclean. A man on a journey, when he wishes to stop for the night, must go on another four *mils* if there is a synagogue within that distance, to pray there. Similarly, he must go on four *mils* ahead to procure water for washing his hands prior to eating; but if no synagogue or water is available within that distance, he is not bound to undertake a longer journey. (9) In the name of R. Simeon b. Lakish, and not R. Abbahu.

b (1) Not three; i.e., the three already mentioned and another. (2) Hides were spread out to be trodden on, and this was part of the tanning process. (3) In Ḥul. 122a a number of animals are enumerated whose skins are the same as their flesh in respect of defilement, as they are likewise accounted as eatables (several animals unfit for food are included in the list). But if he tanned them, etc., they are clean, i.e., they lose the status of flesh and thus become clean. (4) E.g., to procure water, etc. (5) The reference is to Passover. Unclean *ḥallah* may not be eaten by the priest. Now this *ḥallah* may not be baked, since it cannot be eaten, and only the preparation of food is permitted on a Festival; it cannot be kept until evening, as it may turn leaven; nor may it be burnt or given to dogs, for sacred food must not be destroyed thus on a Festival.—The actual Festival days are meant, i.e., the first and the last days (outside Palestine, the first two and the last two), but not the Intermediate Days, which possess only a semi sanctity. (6) I.e., the dough must first be baked, and then all the unleavened *mazzoth* are put in a basket, and one *mazzah* or so is declared *ḥallah* for all. Usually *ḥallah* must be separated from the dough, but when this is impossible, or if it was not done, it is separated from the baked bread.

of a kneading trough, where it serves for reinforcing, [45*b*] it does not interpose, and he does not transgress; [if it is] in a place where it does not serve for reinforcing, it interposes, and he transgresses. When is this said? When there is less than an olive; but if there is as much as an olive, even in a place where it serves for reinforcing, it interposes, and he transgresses. Then these are contradictory?—Said R. Huna: Delete the more lenient [Baraitha]
a in favour of[1] the more stringent. R. Joseph said: You quote Tannaim at random![2] This is a controversy of Tannaim. For it was taught: If a loaf went mouldy, he is bound to remove it, because it is fit to crumble and leaven many other doughs with it. R. Simeon b. Eleazar said: When is this said? If it is kept for eating. But a mass[3] of *se'or* which he put aside for sitting, he has nullified it.[4] Now, since R. Simeon b. Eleazar said, 'He has nullified it', it follows that the first Tanna holds that he has not nullified it. This proves that he holds, wherever there is as much as an olive, even if he nullifies it, it is not nullified. Said Abaye to him: You have reconciled it where there is as much as an olive; [yet] have you reconciled it [where there is] less than an olive? Rather both the one and the other are [the rulings of] R. Simeon b. Eleazar, yet there is no difficulty: one [is taught where it is] in the place of
b kneading; the other, where it is not in the place of kneading.[1] R. Ashi said: Do not assume that 'not in the place of kneading' means on the back of the trough [only], but [it means even] on the [upper] rim of the trough. That is obvious?—You might say, it sometimes splashes up and reaches there:[2] hence he informs us [otherwise].

R. Naḥman said in Rab's name: The *halachah* is as R. Simeon b. Eleazar. Yet that is not so, for R. Isaac b. Ashi said in Rab's name: If he plastered its surface[3] with clay, he has nullified it. [Thus,] only if he plastered it, but not if he did not plaster it?[4]—He who recited this did not recite that.[5] Others state, R. Naḥman said in Rab's name: The *halachah* is not as R. Simeon b. Eleazar, for R. Isaac b. Ashi said in Rab's name: If he plastered its surface with clay, he has nullified it etc.

c R. Naḥman said in Samuel's name: [If there are] two half olives[1] and a thread of dough joining[2] them, we see: wherever if the thread were taken up these would be carried with it, he is bound to remove [them];[3] but if not, he is not bound to remove [them]. Said 'Ulla: This was said only of [dough in] a kneading trough; but [if they are] in the house, he is bound to remove [them].[4] What is the reason? Because he may sometimes sweep them and they will fall together.

'Ulla said: They asked in the West [Palestine]: What of a room[5] and an upper storey; what of a room and the [entrance] hall; what of two rooms, one within the other?[6] The questions stand.

Our Rabbis taught: If a loaf went mouldy and it became unfit for human consumption, yet a dog can eat it, it can be defiled with the uncleanness of eatables, if the size of an egg, and it may be burnt together with an unclean [loaf] on Passover.[7] In R. Nathan's name it was ruled: It cannot be defiled [as an eatable]. With whom agrees the following which we learned: A general principle was stated in respect to the laws of [ritual] cleanness: Whatever is set aside for human consumption is unclean,[8] until it becomes unfit for a dog to eat? With whom [does this agree]? It is not in accordance with R. Nathan.

Our Rabbis taught: [With regard to] the trough of tanners[9] into which he put flour,[10] [if] within three days [before Passover], he is bound to remove it;[11] [if] before three days, he is not bound to remove it.[12] Said R. Nathan: When is this said? If he did not put hides into it; but if he put hides into it, even [if it is] within
d three days, he is not bound to remove [the flour].[1] Raba said: The *halachah* is as R. Nathan, even [if it is] one day, and even one hour [before Passover].

AND IT IS LIKEWISE IN RESPECT TO UNCLEANNESS: IF HE OBJECTS TO IT, IT INTERPOSES; BUT IF HE DESIRES ITS PRESERVATION, IT IS LIKE THE KNEADING-TROUGH. How compare: there the matter is dependent on the quantity [of the dough], [whereas] here the matter is dependent on [his] objecting [to it]?—Said Rab Judah, Say: But in respect to uncleanness it is *not* so. Said Abaye to him, But he states, AND IT IS LIKEWISE IN RESPECT TO UNCLEANNESS? Rather, said Abaye, He means it

a (1) Lit., 'before'. (2) There is no reason for assuming that both Baraithas represent the view of the same Tanna. (3) *Kopeth* really means a low seat or block. (4) I.e., he gave up the nominal use of it as *se'or* and hence it no longer counts as leaven.

b (1) In the second Baraitha, 'where it does not serve for reinforcing', refers only to a place where no kneading is done at all, e.g., at the upper edge; but dough in the cracks at the sides is regarded as reinforcing the trough, and hence it must be removed. But the first Baraitha holds that even in the latter case it does not reinforce it, though kneading is done there, while 'where it serves for reinforcing' refers to the bottom only. Hence this is what the first Tanna states: Where it serves for reinforcing, e.g., at the bottom, he does not transgress even if there is as much as an olive. Where it does not serve for reinforcing (i.e., to support the water), e.g., in the sides, which is a place for kneading yet not a place for the water, if there is as much as an olive, it interposes, and he transgresses. But if there is less than an olive, even if it is in the sides it does not interpose, for since it does help somewhat to support the dough which is kneaded there (viz., that it should not sink into the crack), it is nullified. But this Tanna does not discuss dough which is not in the place of kneading, viz., at the upper rim, and he would admit in that case that even if there is less than an olive it is not nullified. While the second Tanna rules thus: If it is in the place where it affords support to the dough, i.e., in the sides, if there is less than an olive it does not interpose; if there is as much as an olive, it interposes, and this is the view of the first Tanna too. While where it is not made for reinforcing (or, supporting), i.e., at the upper rim, even less than an olive interposes, and this too agrees with the first Tanna. (2) So that the rim is regarded as a place of kneading and must be removed, even if less than an olive. [MS.M. omits 'and reaches there'. V. also Rashi.] (3) *Sc.* that of the mass of *se'or* which he set aside for sitting. (4) Whereas R. Simeon b. Eleazar holds that it is nullified in any case. (5) There are two opposing views on Rab's ruling.

c (1) I.e., two pieces of dough, each the size of half an olive.—The reference is to the cracks in the kneading trough. (2) Lit., 'between'. (3) Because it is all one. (4) Even if they are not thus united by a thread of dough. (5) *Bayith* in the Talmud often has the meaning of a room in a house. (6) I.e., if there is half an olive in one and half in the other: do we fear here too that they may be swept together? (7) V. *supra* 15*b*. (8) I.e., subject to defilement as an eatable. (9) Into which they put hides for tanning. (10) Which is used in the tanning process. (11) Because it is still regarded as flour, and of course it is leaven. (12) Because by Passover it will be so spoiled through the odour of the trough, even if there are no hides in it, that it will not be regarded as flour.

d (1) Because the hides utterly spoil it.

יח א מיי' שם הל' ט' טוש"ע שם סעיף יא:

יט ב ג ד מיי' שם הל' טו טוש"ע שם סעיף ח:

כ ה שם ס"כ וסעיף ט:

כא ו מיי' פ"ב מהל' טומאת אוכלין הלכה יח:

כב ז ח מיי' פ"ד מהל' חמץ הל' ט סמג עשין לט טוש"ע א"ח סי' תמב סעיף א:

[וע' תוספות סנהדרין מח: ד"ה נתנן]

כג ט מיי' פ"ח מהל' מקוואות הלכה יב סמג עשין רמח:

כופת שאור שייחדה לישיבה בטלה. אע"פ שראוי לאכילה כיון שאין מקיימין אותו לאכילה בטלה כמו לענין טומאה דאמרינן בהעור והרוטב (חולין דף קכט.) דבטלה אע"פ שראוי לאכילה כדאמרינן התם בית שסיככו בזרעים טהרו וטומאתו לאו דאורייתא דלאו דאורייתא א"כ מינו אוכלים דמטמאי טומאה חמורה ומשני כשעשה מעשה עץ שימש משמע דמיירי בראוי לאכילה ונראה לר"י דכי היכי דפליגי לענין טומאה בפרק במה בהמה (שבת דף נב:) דרבנן סברי דכל הכלים עולין מטומאתם בשינוי מעשה ורבי יהודה סבר דלא אמרינן שינוי מעשה לתקן אלא לקלקל הכי נמי פליגי גבי *חמץ לענין ... אינו חוצץ. אם נטמאת ובא להטבילה דבטיל לגבי עריבה: ואינו עובר. לענין חמץ בפסח: במה דברים אמורים. דבמקום שאין עשוי לחזק עובר בכזית והיינו כלישנא קמא דאוקמה למתני' בשאין עשוי לחזק קתני בה נמי הכי דבכזית עובר ובפחות מכזית בטל אבל אי עשוי לחזק אפילו כזית בטל: קילתא מקמי חמירתא. קמייתא דאיכא משנה: רב יוסף אמר תרוייהו איתנו בי מדרשא ומשנה הן ותנאי נינהו ופליגי בהכי: תנאי שקלת לך מעלמא. דלא משכחת תנאי דפליגי בהכי דקאמרת סמי דאיכא משנה: כופת. מטו"ן: שייחדה לישיבה גרסינן וכופת שם דבר הוא ובסדר טהרות טובא איכא כופת של עץ וכופת של אבן: בטלה. אלמא איכא דסבירא ליה אפי' כזית מכי מבטיל לה בטל ומתני' קמייתא דקתני נמי במקום העשוי לחזק אפילו כזית בטל רבי שמעון בן אלעזר היא דכיון דאינה מקויימת לאכילה בטלה: תרלת כזית. שבמקום העשוי לחזק דר"ש היא: פחות מכזית. במקום שאין עשוי לחזק דקשו נמי אהדדי דקמייתא תני אף במקום שאין עשוי לחזק אין חייב לבער ובתרייתא תני חייב במקום שאין עשוי לחזק מי קא תרלת הא לא שמעינן ליה לרבי שמעון דמיקל אלא בשאינה מקויימת לאכילה אבל במקויימת לאכילה לא שמעינן דשני ליה בין כזית לפחות מכזית: אלא הא והא רבי שמעון בן אלעזר ולא קשיא כאן במקום לישה כאן שלא במקום לישה. מתניתין בתרייתא לא קרי מקום שאין עשוי לחזק אלא מקום שאינו מקום לישה כלל כגון שפה העליונה אבל דפנות קרי מקום העשוי לחזק וקמייתא קרי אף דפנות מקום שאין עשוי לחזק ואף על גב דבמקום לישה הוא ומקום העשוי לחזק קרי שוליים והכי קאמר תנא קמא במקום העשוי לחזק כגון שוליים שמקבלין את המים אפילו כזית אינו עובר מקום שאינו עשוי לחזק מים כגון דפנות דמקום לישה הוא ולאו מקום מים חוצץ ועובר ופחות מכזית אפילו בדפנות נמי אינו חוצץ

אינו חוצץ ואינו עובר במקום שאין עשוי לחזק חוצץ ועובר במה דברים אמורים בפחות מכזית אבל בכזית אפילו במקום העשוי לחזק חוצץ ועובר קשיין אהדדי אמר רב הונא סמי קילתא מקמי חמירתא *רב יוסף אמר תנאי שקלת מעלמא תנאי היא דתניא הפת שעיפשה חייב לבער מפני שראוי לשוחקה ולחמע בה כמה עיסות אחרות רבי שמעון בן אלעזר אומר במה דברים אמורים במקויימת לאכילה אבל *כופת שאור שייחדה לישיבה בטלה מדאמר ר' שמעון בן אלעזר בטלה מכלל דתנא קמא סבר לא בטלה אלמא קסבר כל כזית אע"ג דמבטל לא בטיל אמר ליה אביי תרצת בכזית פחות מכזית מי תרצת אלא הא והא ר' שמעון בן אלעזר היא ולא קשיא הא במקום לישה הא שלא במקום לישה אמר רב אשי לא תימא שלא במקום לישה אגבה דאגנא אלא אשיפתא דאגנא פשיטא מהו דתימא זמנא דאטיף ומטי להתם קא משמע לן א"ר נחמן אמר רב הלכה כר' שמעון בן אלעזר איני והאמר רב יצחק בר אשי אמר רב *אם טח פניה בטיט בטלה טח אין לא טח לא מאן דמתני הא לא מתני הא איכא דאמרי אמר רב נחמן אמר רב אין הלכה כר' שמעון בן אלעזר דאמר רב יצחק בר אשי אמר רב אם טח פניה בטיט בטלה וכו' אמר רב נחמן אמר שמואל *שני חצאי זיתים וחוט של בצק ביניהן רואין כל שאילו ינטל החוט ונוטלין עמו חייב לבער ואם לאו אינו חייב לבער אמר עולא לא אמרן אלא בעריבה אבל בבית חייב לבער מאי טעמא דזימנין דכניש להו ונפלי גבי הדדי אמר עולא בעו במערבא בית ועלייה מהו בית ואכסדרא מהו שני בתים זה לפנים מזה מהו תיקו *ת"ר הפת שעיפשה ונפסלה מלאכול לאדם והכלב יכול לאוכלה מטמאה טומאת אוכלין בכביצה ונשרפת עם הטמאה בפסח משום ר' נתן אמרו אינה מטמאה כמאן אזלא הא דתנן *כלל אמרו בטהרות כל המיוחד לאוכל אדם טמא עד שיפסל מלאכול לכלב כמאן דלא כר' נתן תנו רבנן *עריבת העבדנין שנתן לתוכה קמח תוך שלשה ימים חייב לבער קודם שלשה ימים אינו חייב לבער אמר ר' נתן במה דברים אמורים שלא נתן לתוכה עורות אבל נתן לתוכה עורות אפילו תוך שלשה אין חייב לבער אמר רבא *הלכה כר' נתן אפילו יום אחד ואפילו שעה אחת: וכן *לענין טומאה אם מקפיד עליו חוצץ ואם רוצה בקיומו הרי הוא כעריבה: מי דמי התם בשיעורא תליא מילתא הכא בקפידא תליא מילתא אמר רב יהודה אימא ולענין הטומאה אינו כן א"ל אביי הא וכן לענין טומאה קתני אלא אמר אביי הכי קאמר וכן לענין

[שבת נב: עירובין לב: ביצה יט: סנהדרין מח:]

[חולין קכט.]

[תוספתא פ"ב]

לעיל מו:

טהרות פ"ח מ"ו

[כריתות כא:] [תוספ' פ"ג]

דכיון דמהני פורתא לחזק עיסה כשמשפשפין ולשין שם בטיל ובשלא במקום לישה כגון שפה עליונה לא איירי האי תנא מידי ומודה הוא בה דאפילו פחות מכזית לא בטיל ביה ותנא בתרא הכי קאמר מקום העשוי לחזק עיסה כגון דפנות אינו חוצץ בפחות מכזית והכי נמי אמרן בקמייתא מקום שאין עשוי לחזק כגון שפה העליונה חוצץ ואף על גב דליכא כזית על גב דליכא כזית והכי נמי אמרן בקמייתא וכזית אפילו בדפנות חוצץ והכי נמי תניא בקמייתא: לא תימא שלא במקום לישה. דלאמרן ביה דאפילו בליר מכזית חוצץ היינו גבה דאגנא מבחוץ אבל שיפתא דאגנא קרי מקום לישה ובטיל ביה פחות מכזית: אלא שיפתא דאגנא. נמי קרי שלא מקום לישה ולא בטיל ביה בליר מכזית: כללא דתרוייהו תנאי ספה עליונה אפילו פחות מכזית אינו עובר דפנות כזית עובר פחות מכזית אינו עובר שוליים אפילו כזית אינו עובר: זימנין דאטיף. פעמים שהיא לשה על ספה עליונה והוי מקום לישה: כרבי שמעון בן אלעזר. דכיון דבטלה בטלה ואפילו טובא: טח פניה. של כופת שאור לתקנה לישיבה: מאן דמתני הא. מילתא דרב לא מתני הא ולאמוראי נינהו ולליבא דרב: שני חצאי זיתים. בסידקי העריבה: חייב לבער. דחוט מלרפן והוי כזית במקום אחד ובדפנות קאי: לא אמרן. דאם אין ניטלין עמו אינו חייב לבער אלא בעריבה דקביעי בה: אבל בבית. אפילו שני חלאי זיתים שאין חוט מלרפן חייב לבער: זימנין דכניש להו. מכבד הבית ונפלי אהדדי: בית ועלייה. חלי זית בבית וחלי זית בעלייה מי חיישינן לכנושי דילמא כניש להו ומחברן או לא ואם תמלא לומר בית ועלייה לא חיישינן דהא לא מקרי דלי כפול כהוי מכוון כנגד התחתון בית ואכסדרה מהו ואם תמלא לומר בית ואכסדרה שדרך האכסדרה ככנסים ויולאין לבית תמיד ואין מחילות שלימות סובבות ביניהם שיש חלונות ופתחים לאכסדרה הרבה מכל לד והוי כחד ביתא וחיישינן דכניש כיבודי בית ואכסדרה: שני בתים זה לפנים מזה. וככנסין לפנימי דרך החיצון אבל אין תשמישן שוה תדיר מזה לזה כבית ואכסדרה מהו מי חיישינן דכניש כיבודי בית זה בזה או לא: ונפסלה מלאכול לאדם וכלב אוכלה בעיפושה ממאכל אדם: מטמאה טומאת אוכלין. דכל זמן שהיא ראויה לכלב לא פקע תורת אוכל מינה: ונשרפת עם הטמאה בפסח. אם תרומה טהורה היא דכיון דלא חזיא לאדם מותר לטמאה בידים ואפילו לרבי יוסי דאמר בפרק קמא (דף יד.) זו לטהרה וזו לטומאה: המיוחד לאוכל אדם ואל עליו שם אוכל לעולם ואפילו נתקלקל מאכילת אדם עד שיפסל מאכילת כלב: העבדנין. שנותנין בה עורות לעבד ונותנין שם קמח: תוך שלשה ימים. לפסח נתן קמח לתוכה עדיין שם חמץ עליה וכשבא הפסח חייב לבער ואפילו היו בה עורות: קודם שלשה ימים. כבר נתקלקלה ע"י ריח הכלי ואף על פי שלא נתן לתוכה עורות: רבי נתן אומר. לא נתן לתוכה עורות מודיגא לך דתוך שלשה ימים חייב לבער ואחר שלשה ימים לא שנתקלקלה מריח הכלי אבל נתן לתוכה עורות בקמח ביטלה מתורת חמץ: אם מקפיד עליו. שעתיד ליטלו חוצץ ואין טבילה עולה לה: בקיומו. שמקיים בסדקו לסתום: מי דמי. דקתני וכן התם גבי פסח בשיעורא בכזית ופחות מכזית תליא מילתא והכא תליא מילתא בקפידא לא שנא פורתא ולא שנא טובא: לענין

רבינו חננאל

שעשוי לחזק שנעשה כעץ אבל כזית אפילו במקום העשוי לחזק אסור וחייב לבער וכן במקום שאין עשוי לחזק אפי' כל שהוא אסור. תניא כלישנא קמא תניא כלישנא בתרא קשיין אהדדי אמר רב הונא סמי קמייתא דקילתא היא מקמי בתרייתא דהיא חמירתא ורב יוסף אמר תנאי היא דתניא פת שעפשה חייב לבער מפני שיכול לשוחקה ולחמע בה כמה עיסות אחרות ר' שמעון בן אלעזר אומר בד"א במקויימת לאכילה אבל כופת שאור וייחדה לישיבה בטלה מכלל דת"ק סבר כל זית כזית אע"ג דמבטל ליה לא בטל *) דת"ק סבר כל כזית דתניא כלישנא קמא. אמר ליה אביי לרב יוסף שנית כזית פחות מכזית מאי אלא הא והא ר' שמעון הא דתניא כזית במקום העשוי לחזק חוצץ ועובר במקום לישה אבל פחות מכזית לא והתניא כזית במקום העשוי לחזק אינו חוצץ ואינו עובר שלא במקום לישה וכל שכן פחות מכזית שאפי' במקום שאין עשוי לחזק אינו עובר: **אמר** רב אשי לא תימא שלא במקום לישה אחורי אגנא כגון ספל שלשין בה אלא אף שפת אגנא הוא שלא במקום לישה ומדחי' רב אשי דאביי ש"מ דהילכתא כותיה: **אמרי** משמיה דרב הלכה כר' שמעון בכופת שאור והוא דטח פניה בטיט: שני חצאי זיתים חמץ וחוט של בצק ביניהן רואין כל שאילו ינטל החוט ניטלין עמו כלומר חוט זה יש עמו כזית הוא חייב לבער מוקמינן לה [דמיירי] במקום העשוי לחזק (אפילו) ובמקום לישה דפחות מכזית אינו עובר אבל כזית עובר ואם החוט מצרפן נמצא כזית במקום אחד וחייב. אמר עולא לא אמרו אם ניטלין עם החוט אלא בעריבה אבל בבית אפי' אין ביניהם חוט חייב לבער מאי טעמא זמנין דכניש ונפלי אהדדי והוו

להו כזית במקום אחד: **איבעי'** להו בית ועלייה בית ואכסדרה שני בתים זה לפנים מזה מהו ועלו בתיקו ניתיק לחומרא: **ת"ר** פת שעפשה ונפסלה מלאכול אדם והכלב יכול לאכלה מטמאה טומאת אוכלין בכביצה ונשרפת עם הטמאה בפסח. משום רבי נתן אמרו אין מטמאה וקיימא לן כת"ק דתנן כוותיה כלל אמרו [בנותרות] [בטהרות] כל המיוחד לאכל אדם טמא עד שיפסל מלאכול הכלב: **ת"ר** עריבת העבדנין [שנתן] לתוכה קמח בשלשה עשר או בשלשה חייב לביער בארבעה עשר ...ש מקדם לו לשלשה ימים אינו חייב לבער וכן הלכה: **תוספתא** הקילורי והאספלנית והרטיה שנתן לתוכן קמח אין צריך לבער ... ולענין הטומאה אם רוצה בקיומו כי צריכה לה אין חוצצת שאם ... צריכה לו כו' וכן הלכה ... הסדק סתום הרי הוא כעריבה ואינו חוצץ ואקשינן ... ולענין טומאה ... בקפידא ... בשיעור תליא ... וכן לענין צירוף

*) נראה דצ"ל דסב"א כלישנא בתרא ות"ק דסבר דכל כזית לא בטיל היינו כלישנא קמא.

משום דהוה נזיר וחטאת *שני כתובין הבאין כאחד ואין מלמדין נזיר הא דאמרן חטאת מאי היא *דתניא °כל אשר יגע בבשרה יקדש וגו' יכול אפילו לא בלעה ת"ל בבשרה (יקדש) *עד שיבלע בבשר יקדש *להיות כמוה שאם פסולה היא תיפסל ואם כשירה היא תאכל כחמור שבה ורבנן נמי ניהוי נזיר וחטאת שני כתובין הבאין כאחד ואין מלמדין אמרי הנהו מיצריך צריכי ור"ע מאי צריכי בשלמא אי כתב רחמנא בחטאת לא גמר נזיר מינה *דחולין מקדשים לא גמרינן אלא לכתוב רחמנא בנזיר ותיתי חטאת ותגמור מיניה דהא כל איסורין שבתורה קא גמר מנזיר ורבנן אמרי לך* מיצרך צריכי חטאת להיתר מצטרף לאיסור וחולין מקדשים לא גמר ומשרת ליתן טעם כעיקר ומכאן אתה דן לכל התורה כולה ור' עקיבא תרוייהו להיתר מצטרף לאיסור והוו להו שני כתובין הבאין כאחד וכל שני כתובין הבאין כאחד אין מלמדין א"ל רב אשי לרב כהנא אלא הא דתניא °מכל אשר יעשה מגפן היין מחרצנים ועד זג *לימד על איסורי נזיר שמצטרפים זה עם זה השתא לר"ע איסור והיתר מצטרפין איסור ואיסור מיבעיא אמר ליה איסור והיתר בבת אחת *איסור ואיסור בזה אחר זה:

מתני' *בצק שבסדקי עריבה אם יש כזית במקום אחד חייב לבער ואם (*לא) בטל במיעוטו וכן לענין הטומאה אם מקפיד עליו חוצץ ואם רוצה בקיומו הרי הוא כעריבה:

גמ' אמר רב יהודה אמר שמואל לא שנו אלא במקום שאין עשויין לחזק אבל במקום שעשויין לחזק אינו חייב לבער מכלל דפחות מכזית אפי' במקום שאין עשוי לחזק אינו חייב לבער איכא *דמתני לה אסיפא ואם לאו בטל במיעוטו אמר רב יהודה אמר שמואל לא שנו אלא במקום העשוי לחזק אבל במקום שאין עשוי לחזק חייב לבער מכלל דכזית אפילו במקום העשוי לחזק חייב לבער תניא כלישנא קמא תניא כלישנא בתרא תניא כלישנא קמא בצק שבסידקי עריבה במקום העשוי לחזק אינו חוצץ ואינו עובר ובמקום שאין עשוי לחזק חוצץ ועובר במה דברים אמורים בכזית אבל בפחות מכזית אפילו במקום שאין עשוי לחזק אינו חוצץ ואינו עובר ותניא כלישנא בתרא *בצק שבסידקי עריבה במקום העשוי לחזק אינו

רש"י

משום. דבדוכתא אחריתי נמי כתבה רחמנא ושני כתובין הבאין כו' אבל לרבנן דמוקי ליה לטעם כעיקר לא הוו שני כתובין הבאין כאחד כדמפרש לקמיה: כל אשר יגע בבשרה. בשר חולין או שלמים שזמן אכילתו מרובה מחטאת ונגע בחטאת יקדש כדמפרש להיות כמוה שאם פסולה היתה החטאת כגון פיגול או פסול אחר תיפסל אף זו שבלעה ממנה ואם כשירה היא החטאת מהכיא לבולעת הימנה לאסור באכילה אלא כחומר שבה כחומר החטאת שנבלע בה לפנים מן הקלעים ולזכרי כהונה וליום ולילה אחד: יכול אפילו לא בלעה. הנוגעת בה ממנה קאמר רחמנא יקדש ת"ל כו': תאכל. הבולעת כחומר שבה שהרי יש בה ב' מינין אחד חמור ואחד קל וכולה הולכת אחר החמור אלמא היתר מצטרף לאיסור: מיצרך צריכי. תרוייהו כדמפרש לקמיה ולא הוו שני כתובין הבאין כאחד דחד מחבריה לא מצי יליף דנימא מהדדר כתביה לאידך ולא ילפה מחבריה ש"מ דווקא הכי *) קאמר: חולין. להחמיר לא גמרי מדין קדשים דדין קדשים להיות חמורין: ה"ג ורבנן אמרי לך מיצרך צריכי חטאת לשמועינן משום דהיתר מצטרף לאיסור (א)ולאי נמי לא איבלע בכולה אי אכל חצי זית פיגול וחצי זית היתר בבת אחת ניגמור מינה דבקדשי' ניחייב ומיהו בשאר איסורין לא אמרינן הכי ואפילו בנזיר דחולין מקדשים לא גמרינן ומשרת לאו לאגמורי היתר מצטרף לאיסור אתא בנזיר אלא ליתן טעם כעיקר דמגיעולי נכרים לא יליף חידוש הוא ולאצריך למכתביה בנזיר ומכאן אתה דן לכל התורה: ור' עקיבא. אית ליה גיעולי נכרים לאו חידוש הוא (ב) דלא אצריך קרא לטעם כעיקר הלכך לר"ע כיון דשמעת ליה דמפיק משרת להיתר מצטרף לאיסור על כרחיך תרוייהו הכי להיתר מצטרף לאיסור אתו והוה ליה חטאת קרא יתירה דמצי למיגמר מנזיר והוו להו שני כתובין הבאין כאחד ומש"ה פשיטא ליה לרבי יוחנן דר"ע לא גמר שאר איסורין מנזיר דהא לא מצי דשני כתובין ניהו והא ליכא למימר משרת להיתר מצטרף לאיסור וחטאת לטעם כעיקר דגיעולי נכרים חידוש הוא ולא מצי גמר חטאת מינייהו ואין כאן שני כתובין דא"כ טעם כעיקר בשאר איסורין מנא ליה מגיעולי נכרים לא גמרינן מקדשים נמי לא גמרינן ורבנן דפליגי עליה דר"א בכותח הבבלי אלמא לית להו טעם כעיקר דאורייתא מפקי להאי משרת להיתר מצטרף לאיסור כר"ע ובגיעולי נכרים סבירא להו דחידוש הוא כרבנן והכי אמרינן נמי בכל הבשר דאיכא למאן דאמר טעמו ולא ממשו דרבנן: לימד על איסורי נזיר כו'. מדכייליהו לחרצנים וזגין בחדא אכילה לימד שמצטרפין: השתא לרבי עקיבא. ל"ל דכתב רחמנא קרא להכי השתא איסור והיתר מצטרפין כו': מתני' וכן לענין הטומאה. מפרש בגמ': גמ' ה"ג ל"ש אלא במקום שאין עשוי לחזק אבל במקום העשוי לחזק אינו חייב לבער מכלל דפחות מכזית אפילו במקום שאין עשוי לחזק אינו חייב לבער ופירש לא שנו דכזית במקום אחד חייב לבער אלא שאין הסדקין בשולי עריבה מקום הלקת מים שיהא בצק זה מועיל לעריבה לחזק המים אלא בדפנותיהן מקום שאין עשוי לחזק אבל אם במקום העשוי לחזק הן בטלו לגבה והוו כגון דמסתמא בטליניהו האי גברא להתם ואפילו כזית אינו חייב לבער(ג): מכלל דפחות מכזית כו'. ותלמודא דייק ממילתא דשמואל דאוקמה למתני' במקום שאין עשוי לחזק וקתני מתני' בפחות מיכן בטל במיעוטו שמע מינה דפחות מכזית לא חשיב ואע"ג דאיכא בה פלגי זיתא טובא הואיל ולאו במקום אחד ניהו לא חשיבי: ה"ג איכא דמתני לה אסיפא פחות מיכן בטל במיעוטו אמר רב יהודה אמר שמואל לא שנו אלא במקום העשוי לחזק אבל במקום שאין עשוי לחזק חייב לבער מכלל דכזית אפילו במקום העשוי לחזק חייב לבער. ואע"ג דודאי מבטיל ליה אפילו הכי כיון דחשיב לא בטיל ולישנא בתרא חמיר מקמא: אינו

תוספות

משום דהוי נזיר וחטאת שני כתובין הבאין כאחד. תימה לרשב"א אמאי לא קאמר נזיר וחמץ דר"ע דריש כל בפ' התערובת (זבחים דף פב.): ר"ח גרס כחומר שבהן ומיירי בחטאת ושלמים ואם נבלע החטאת בשלמים שנשחטו אתמול נאכל כחומר השלמים ולינו נאכל בלילה ואם נבלע החטאת בשלמים שנשחטו היום נאכל כחומר החטאת ולינו נאכל למחר ולשון הברייתא קשה דקאמר עד שיבלע בבשרה משמע דאיירי בהיתר שנבלע באיסור והדר קאמר יקדש להיות כמוה משמע שהאיסור נבלע בהיתר: ורבנן אמרי לך חטאת להיתר מצטרף לאיסור. אור"י דבנזיר בפ' ג' מינין (דף לז:) משמע נזיר וחטאת לרבנן תרוייהו לטעם כעיקר דקאמר התם אצטריך דאי כתב רחמנא חטאת חולין מקדשים לא גמרינן ואי כתב רחמנא נזיר חטאת מנזיר לא ילפינן דחמיר איסוריה דאפילו חרצן אסיר ליה: בשמעתין משמע דטעם כעיקר דאורייתא דילפינן מנזיר דלאו אסמכתא היא מדר"ע דאמר לקי אהיתר מצטרף לאיסור בנזיר משמע לרבנן וקשה מפ' כל הבשר (חולין דף קח.) וממסכת ע"ז (דף סז:) ושם מפורש: כאן שלא במקום לישה. פ"ה דשלא במקום לישה עובר בפחות מכזית וקשה דאמר לקמן לא אמרן אלא בעריבה אבל בבית חייב לבער משום דזימנין (ד)דמיכנף ונפלי אהדדי ולפ"ה תיפוק ליה דפחות מכזית חייב לבער שלא במקום לישה ונראה לר"י דמקום העשוי לחזק היינו את הכלי בין במקום לישה ובין שלא במקום לישה עושין לחזק אף במקום לישה יש להחמיר יותר שיש לחוש שידבק מאותה עיסה לעיסה אחרת על ידי לישה או תבלע מן הטעם ולכך כזית במקום לישה אפילו עשוי לחזק עובר אף על גב דודאי מבטלו כיון דאיכא תרתי לריעותא כזית ובמקום לישה ופחות מכזית אפילו במקום לישה אי עשוי לחזק לא גזרו ביה רבנן דכיון שהוא דבר מועט יכול לשמור שלא ילוש עליו וכן כזית שלא במקום לישה אי עשוי לחזק אין עובר אבל פחות מכזית ושלא במקום לישה אפילו אין עשויה לחזק מותר: כופת

עין משפט נר מצוה

יד א מיי' פ"ח מהל' מעשה קרבנות הלכה טז:
טו ב שם הלכה טו:
טז ג ד מיי' פ"ה מהל' נזיר הלכה ג:
יז ה ו מיי' פ"ג מהל' חמץ הל' טו סמג עשין לט טוש"ע א"ח סי' תמב סעיף ז:

מסורת הש"ס

[לעיל כו' וש"נ] נזיר לז: זבחים צז: שם חולין צט. [שבועות כג:] [נזיר לז: ע"ש] צ"ל כבי [צ"ל לאו] [תוספ' פ"ג]

הגהות הב"ח

(א) רש"י ד"ה ה"ג ורבנן וכו' לאיסור ולאי נמי: (ב) ד"ה ור' עקיבא וכו' ולא אצריך: (ג) ד"ה ל"ש וכו' לבער: (ד) תוספות ד"ה כאן וכו' דזימנין דמיכנף להו ונפלי:

רבינו חננאל

מצטרף לאיסור ומכאן אתה דן לכל התורה כלה ודחי' משום דהאי נזיר וחטאת שני כתובין הבאין כאחד ואין מלמדין נזיר הא דאמרן חטאת דתניא כל אשר יגע בבשרה יקדש יכול אע"פ שלא בלע ת"ל בבשרה עד שיבלע בבשרה יקדש להיות כמוה שאם פסולה היא תפסל ואם כשרה היא תאכל כחומר שבה פי' החטאת נאכלת ליום ולילה והשלמים לשני ימים ולילה אם ניתז*) (מדם) החטאת שנשחטה היום על חתיכת בשר שלמים שנשחטו מאתמול נאכל הבשר בתורת שלמים בו ביום בלבד אבל לא בלילה כבשר החטאת ואם נשחטו שניהם היום נאכל בתורת חטאת היום והלילה בלבד אבל לא למחר כשאר בשר שלמים הנה ההיתר נצטרף לאיסור וזהו פי' נאכל כחמור שבהן פעמים נאכל בתורת שלמים ופעמים נאכל בתורת חטאת כי השלמים שנשחטו מאתמול היום מותר ובלילה אסור באכילה והחטאת שנשחטה היום מותרת באכילה כל הלילה נמצאו השלמים בזה חמורין מן החטאת: ורבנן כי אמרי' שני כתובין הבאין כאחד היכא דתרווייהו חולין או תרווייהו קדשים ניניהו אבל חד חולין והוא הנזיר וחד קדשים והוא חטאת מצרך צריכי ולא קרינן בהו שני כתובין הבאין כאחד ונדרש

חזור ואמרו חטאת להיתר מצטרף לאיסור ומשרת ליתן טעם כעיקר ומכאן אתה דן לכל התורה כלה איסור שבתורה **)בין בזה ובין בזה ור"ע תרתמה ליתן טעם כעיקר [גמרינן] מגיעולי נכרים חטאת ונזיר תרווייהו מצטרף לאיסור והוו להו שני כתובין הבאין כאחד ואין מלמדין ומקשי' רב אשי אליבא דרבי עקיבא הא דתניא מכל אשר יעשה מגפן היין מחרצנים ועד זג לימד על איסור נזיר כגון חצי זית חרצן וחצי זית זג שמצטרפין זה עם זה השתא לרבי עקיבא חצי זית פת שהוא היתר וחצי זית יין מצטרפי חרצן [וזג] ששניהן אסורין לנזיר מיבעיא ושני' פת ויין ביחד אבל זה בעצמו וזה בעצמו לא מצטרפי חרצן וזג אפילו זה אחר זה מצטרפי: מתני' בצק שבסדיקי ערבה אם יש כזית במקום אחד חייב לבער ואוקי' רב יהודה הא דתנן כזית במקום אחד ***) במקום שיש בו סדק או נקב ונתן זה הבצק לסתמו שנמצא עושה מלאכה ובמקום שהוא כזית ש"מ דפחות מכזית אפילו במקום שאין עשוי לחזק אינו חייב לבער: ואיכא דמתני לה לדרב יהודה אסיפא דקתני ואם לאו בטל במיעוטו ודייקינן לא שנו פחות מכזית בטל אלא במקום שעשוי

*) נראה דצ"ל מרוטב החטאת. **) נראה דר"ל דאמר לכל התורה כולה כוונתו בין בקדשים בין בחולין אבל עדיין לשונו צריך ביאור וכנגס. ***) נראה דחסר כאן ואולי צ"ל כזית במקום אחד במקום שאין עשוי לחזק אבל במקום וכו' מלאכה בבצק בטל אע"פ כו'.

a conclusion for the whole Torah?[3]—Said he to him, [45a] Because a nazirite and a sin-offering are two verses with the same teaching,[4] and they do not illumine [other cases].[5] 'A nazirite', that which we have stated. What is the reference to the sin-offering?—For it was taught: *whatsoever shall touch in the flesh thereof shall be holy:*[6] you might think, even if it did not absorb [of the flesh of the sin-offering]; therefore it is stated, 'in *the flesh thereof*'.[7] Only when it absorbs in the flesh?[8] '*Shall be holy*', to be as itself, so that if it [the sin-offering] is unfit, that [which touches it] becomes unfit; while if it is fit, that may be eaten [only] in accordance with its stringencies.[9] Then according to the Rabbis too, let a nazirite and a sin-offering be two verses with the same teaching and they do not illumine [other cases]?—They can answer: these are indeed [both] neces-
a sary.[1] And R. Akiba?[2]—How are they [both] necessary? It is well [to say] that if the Merciful One wrote it in respect to a sin-offering, [the case of] a nazirite could not be derived from it, because we cannot derive *ḥullin* from sacred sacrifices.[3] But let the Merciful One write it in respect to a nazirite, and then the sin-offering would come and be derived from it, seeing that all the prohibitions of the Torah are learnt from a nazirite. But the Rabbis can answer you: they [both] are indeed required; the sin-offering, to [show that] the permitted combines with the forbidden, while *ḥullin* cannot be deduced from sacred sacrifices; and '*an infusion*', to intimate that the taste is as the substance itself, and from this you may draw a conclusion for the whole Torah. But R. Akiba maintains: both [are required] for [teaching] that the permitted combines with the forbidden, so that they are two verses with the same teaching, and all [instances of] two verses with the same teaching do not illumine [other cases].

R. Ashi said to R. Kahana: Then as to what was taught, [*All the days of his Naziriteship shall he eat*] *nothing that is made of the grape vine, from the husks to the kernels:*[4] this teaches concerning a nazirite's prohibited commodities, that they combine with each other;—seeing that according to R. Akiba [even] the forbidden with the permitted combine, is it necessary [to state] the forbidden with the forbidden?[5]—Said he to him: The forbidden with the permitted [combine only when eaten] together; the forbidden with the forbidden, [even when eaten] consecutively.[6]

MISHNAH. [WITH REGARD TO] THE DOUGH IN THE CRACKS OF THE KNEADING TROUGH, IF THERE IS AS MUCH AS AN OLIVE IN ONE PLACE, HE IS BOUND TO REMOVE [IT]; BUT IF NOT, IT IS NULLIFIED THROUGH THE SMALLNESS OF
b ITS QUANTITY.[1] AND IT IS LIKEWISE IN THE MATTER OF UNCLEANNESS: IF HE OBJECTS TO IT, IT INTERPOSES;[2] BUT IF HE DESIRES ITS PRESERVATION,[3] IT IS LIKE A KNEADING-TROUGH.[4]

GEMARA. Rab Judah said in Samuel's name: They learned this[5] only of a place where it [the dough] does not serve[6] for reinforcing [the trough]; but where it serves for reinforcing [it], he is not bound to remove it.[7] Hence it follows that [where there is] less than an olive, even if it does serve for reinforcing [it], he is not obliged to remove it. Others recite it in reference to the second clause: BUT IF NOT, IT IS NULLIFIED THROUGH THE SMALLNESS OF ITS QUANTITY. Said Rab Judah in Samuel's name: They learned this only where it serves for reinforcing [the trough]; but where it does not serve for reinforcing [it], he is bound to remove it. Whence it follows that if there is as much as an olive, even where it serves for reinforcing [it], he is bound to remove it.

It was taught as the former version; it was taught as the latter version. It was taught as the former version: Dough in the cracks of the kneading trough, where it serves for reinforcing, it does not interpose,[8] and he [its owner] does not transgress.[9] But [if it is] in a place where it does not serve for reinforcing, it interposes, and he transgresses. When is this said? Where there is as much as an olive. But if there is less than an olive, even where it does not serve for reinforcing, it does not interpose, and he does not transgress.

Again, it was taught as the latter version: Dough in the cracks

(3) Then why did R. Joḥanan (*supra* 43b bottom) limit this principle to a nazirite, seeing that his statement is in accordance with R. Akiba? (4) Lit., 'which come as one'. (5) V. *supra* 26a, n. c2. (6) Lev. VI, 20. '*Holy*' means 'forbidden', in the sense that any other flesh which touches this flesh of the sin-offering becomes subject to the same laws and limitations as those to which the sin-offering is subject. (7) Literal translation. I.e., it is forbidden only if it absorbs some of the sin-offering within itself. (8) [The text of cur. edd. is difficult. A better reading is preserved in the Sifra a.l. 'till it absorbs', omitting the words 'in the flesh', and the deduction being from the word '*thereof*'.] (9) A sin-offering must be eaten within the sacred precincts, by male priests, and for one day and night only; similarly the food which absorbs some of it.—Thus here too the permitted flesh combines with the forbidden, and all is regarded as forbidden.

a (1) And where that is so, they do illuminate other cases, since neither could be deduced from the other. (2) Does he not admit this? (3) The latter being naturally more stringent. Hence the fact that there the permitted combines with the forbidden does not prove that it will also do so in the case of *ḥullin*, where the interdicted food is not sacred. (4) Num. VI, 4. (5) Surely it is obvious; why then is the verse required? (6) For further notes on the whole discussion beginning with R. Abbahu's dictum in the name of R. Joḥanan on page 43b, v. Nazir, 35b–36a

b (1) I.e., he has abandoned the normal use of the dough in favour of the trough. (2) V. *infra* n. b8; if he objects to it, it is regarded as a foreign body. (3) I.e., he wants the dough to be there to close the crack. (4) And it does not interpose. (5) That if there is as much as an olive in one place it must be removed. (6) Lit., 'it is not made for'. (7) E.g., if the crack is at the bottom of the trough, and the dough fills it and so prevents the water from running out. It is then regarded as part of the trough, not as dough, and therefore it need not be removed. But if the crack is high up, it does not serve this purpose and must be removed. (8) When a utensil is ritually unclean and cleansed in a ritual bath, nothing must interpose between the utensil and the water of the bath (called a *miḳweh*); otherwise the ablution is invalid. This dough, since it reinforces the trough, is counted as part of itself and not as a foreign body, and therefore it is not an interposition between the trough and the water; hence the ablution is valid. (9) The law of Passover by leaving it there and not removing it.

[this is] to intimate that the taste is as the substance itself, so that if he [the nazirite] steeped grapes in water and it possesses the taste of wine, he is culpable.[3] From this you may draw a conclusion for the whole Torah.[4] For if a nazirite, whose prohibition is not a permanent prohibition, and his prohibition is not a prohibition of [general] use,[5] and there is a release for his prohibition,[6] yet [Scripture] made the taste tantamount to the substance in his case; then *kil'ayim*, the prohibition of which is a permanent prohibition, and whose prohibition is a prohibition of [general] use, and there is no release from its prohibition, is it not logical that the taste should be treated as tantamount to the substance itself? And the same applies to *'orlah* by two [arguments]![7]—The authority for this is the Rabbis, while R. Joḥanan[8] stated [his ruling] in accordance with R. Akiba.

Which [ruling of] R. Akiba [is alluded to]? Shall we say, R. Akiba of our Mishnah, for we learned: 'R. Akiba said: If a nazirite soaked his bread in wine, and it contains sufficient to combine as much as an olive, he is culpable'? But whence [do you know that he means sufficient] of the bread and the wine; perhaps [he means] of the wine alone?[9] And should you say, [if] of the wine alone, why state it? He informs us thus: [He is culpable] although
a it is a mixture![1]—Rather it is R. Akiba of the Baraitha. For it was taught, R. Akiba said: If a nazirite soaked his bread in wine and ate as much as an olive of the bread[2] and the wine [combined], he is culpable.

Now [according to] R. Akiba, whence do we know that the taste [of forbidden food] is like the substance itself?[3]—He learns it from [the prohibition of] meat [seethed] in milk; is it not merely a taste,[4] and it is forbidden? so here too[5] it is not different. And the Rabbis?[6]—We cannot learn from meat [seethed] in milk, because it is an anomaly.[7] Yet what is the anomaly? Shall we say because this [*sc.* meat] by itself is permitted, and that [*sc.* milk] by itself is permitted, while in conjunction they are forbidden,—but [with] *kil'ayim* too, this [species] by itself is permitted, and that species] by itself is permitted, yet in conjunction they are forbidden?—Rather [the anomaly is] that if he soaked it all day in milk it is permitted,[8] yet if he but seethed it [in milk] it is forbidden. Then R. Akiba too? [The prohibition of] meat [seethed] in milk is certainly an anomaly?[9]—Rather he learns it from the vessels of Gentiles.[10] The vessels of Gentiles, is it not merely a flavour [which they impart]? Yet they are forbidden; so here too it is not different. And the Rabbis?[11]— The vessels of Gentiles too are an anomaly, for whatever imparts a deteriorating flavour is permitted,[12] since we learn it from *nebelah*,[13] yet here it is for-
b bidden.[1] But R. Akiba [holds] as R. Ḥiyya the son of R. Huna, who said: The Torah prohibited [it] only in the case of a pot used on that very day, hence it is not a deteriorating flavour.[2] And the Rabbis?—A pot used on that very day too, it is impossible that it should not slightly worsen [the food cooked in it].

R. Aḥa son of R. 'Awia said to R. Ashi: 'From the Rabbis let us learn the view of R. Akiba. Did not the Rabbis say, "*An infusion*": [this is] to intimate that the taste is tantamount to the substance itself. From this you may draw a conclusion for the whole Torah?' Then according to R. Akiba too [let us say]: '*An infusion*': this is [to intimate] that the permitted commodity combines with the forbidden commodity. From this you may draw

(3) For drinking it. (4) I.e., that the taste of all forbidden food is forbidden just as the substance itself. [That is provided the forbidden substance consisted originally of the size of an olive. This requirement distinguishes this principle from that of R. Joḥanan, in virtue of which what is permitted combines with what is forbidden, even though the latter is less in size than an olive's bulk.] (5) Though he may not *eat* grapes or drink wine, etc., he may *benefit* from them. (6) He can be absolved of his vow, whereupon it all becomes permitted. (7) Rashi: *'orlah* too is forbidden for use and there is no release for its prohibition. The third argument however cannot be applied here, as *'orlah* is not permanently forbidden, since it is permitted after three years. Tosaf. explains it differently.—But incidentally we see that '*an infusion*' is required for a different purpose. (8) *Supra* 43*b* bottom. (9) Viz., that the bread had soaked up that quantity of wine. Yet the term 'combine' is applicable, because the wine is not separate now but is spread through the bread.

a (1) Of bread and wine, the wine not standing alone. (2) The wine had not soaked through the whole olive-bulk of the bread, so that part of the bread is by itself; and the only reason for culpability must be the principle enunciated by R. Joḥanan. (3) Since he utilizes '*an infusion*' for the purpose just stated. (4) Which the meat has received from the milk. (5) I.e., in respect of all other forbidden food. (6) Why cannot they learn it in the same way? (7) Lit., 'a new law', i.e., it is peculiarly different from other laws, and therefore does not provide a basis for analogy. (8) By Scriptural law, even to eat it; Scripture forbids it only when cooked in milk. (9) How then can he derive it thence? (10) Lit., 'the exudings (from the vessels) of Gentiles', i.e., vessels in which Gentiles cooked food. These must be purged with boiling water (this is called *hage'alah*) before they may be used, because they exude a flavour of the food which was boiled in them. (11) V. n. a6. (12) I.e., when the imparted flavour spoils the taste of the permitted food. (13) Deut. XIV, 21: *Ye shall not eat of any thing that dieth of itself* (nebelah); *thou mayest give it unto the stranger*. Hence whatever is fit for a stranger is designated *nebelah*, but what is unfit is not designated *nebelah*, in the sense that if it imparts a deteriorating flavour it does not render the food forbidden.

b (1) They assume that the flavour exuded by the vessel has a deteriorating effect. (2) Because it is still fresh.

*ליתן טעם כעיקר שאם שרה ענבים במים ויש בהן טעם יין חייב מכאן אתה דן לכל התורה כולה ומה נזיר שאין איסורו איסור עולם ואין איסורו איסור הנאה ויש היתר לאיסורו עשה בו טעם כעיקר כלאים שאיסורו איסור עולם ואיסורו איסור הנאה ואין היתר לאיסורו אינו דין שיעשה טעם כעיקר והוא הדין לערלה בשתים הא מני רבנן היא ורבי יוחנן דאמר כרבי עקיבא הי ר"ע אילימא ר"ע דמתני' דתנן *רבי עקיבא אומר *נזיר ששרה פתו ביין ויש בו לצרף כזית חייב ומאי דמפת ומיין דילמא מיין לחודיה וכי תימא מיין לחודיה מאי למימרא הא קמ"ל דאע"ג דתערובת אלא ר"ע דברייתא דתניא ר"ע אומר נזיר ששרה פתו ביין ואכל כזית מפת ומיין חייב ור"ע טעם כעיקר מנא ליה יליף מבשר בחלב לאו טעמא בעלמא הוא ואסור הכא נמי לא שנא *ורבנן מבשר בחלב לא גמרינן דחידוש הוא ומאי חידוש אילימא דהאי לחודיה והאי לחודיה שרי ובהדי הדדי אסור כלאים נמי האי לחודיה והאי לחודיה שרי ובהדדי אסור אלא דאי תרו ליה כולי יומא בחלבא שרי בשיל ליה בשולי אסור ור"ע נמי בשר בחלב ודאי חידוש הוא אלא יליף מגיעולי נכרים גיעולי נכרים לאו טעמא בעלמא הוא ואסור הכא נמי ל"ש ורבנן גיעולי נכרים נמי חידוש הוא דהא כל נותן טעם לפגם מותר דגמרינן מנבילה והכא אסור ורבי עקיבא כדרב *חייא בריה דרב הונא דאמר לא אסרה תורה אלא *בקדירה בת יומא הלכך לאו נותן טעם לפגם הוא ורבנן קדירה בת יומא נמי לא אפשר דלא פגמה פורתא א"ל רב אחא בריה דרב אויא לרב אשי מדרבנן נשמע לרבי עקיבא מי לא אמרי רבנן משרת ליתן טעם כעיקר מכאן אתה דן לכל איסורין שבתורה לרבי עקיבא נמי משרת להיתר מצטרף לאיסור מכאן אתה דן לכל איסורין שבתורה כולה א"ל
משום

רש"י

ליתן טעם כעיקר. לעשות טעמו של איסור כעיקרו וממשו: ויש בהן. במים טעם יין: חייב. בכזית מהן והא לאו משום היתר מצטרף לאיסור הוא אלא משום דאיתעביד ליה טעם כעיקר אבל היתר מצטרף לאיסור לא ילפינן מינה: לכל התורה כולה. שיהא טעמו של איסורין כממשו: שאין איסורו איסור עולם. אלא כמה שפירש ואם סתם שלשים יום וענבים ויין מותרין לו בהגלחה: ויש לו היתר לאיסורו. אף תוך זמנו על ידי (הפרת) חכם: כלאים. כלאי הכרם: איסור עולם. זרע חטה וחרצן הכל אסור לעולם: והוא הדין לערלה בשתים. ק"ו זה אתה דן לערלה בשתי דרכים דאיסורו איסור הנאה ואין היתר לאיסורו בתוך שלש מה שאין כן בנזיר ואיסור עולם ליכא למימר בה דלאחר שלש מותרות: הא מני. דלפיקתיה להאי קרא לטעם כעיקר רבנן דפליגי אדר"ע בהיתר מצטרף לאיסור ולקמיה מפרש מאי היא: הי ר"ע. מהי מילתא דר"ע שמעינן היתר מצטרף לאיסור: דילמא מיין לחודיה. ולירוף שייך למימני בה משום דנבלע בתוך הפת והיאך משערין כזית יין ממלא כלי מפה לפה ומביא זית ונותן לתוכו והיין היוצא הוא כזית יין וכן הוא בתוספתא דנזיר: תערובת. שאינו בעין שנבלע בפת: מפת ומיין חייב. ופליגי רבנן עליה דלית להו היתר מצטרף לאיסור ואילו פשט היין בכל הפת לא הוו פליגי רבנן עליה דהא אית להו טעם כעיקר ואיתעביד ליה פת גופיה איסור ובהא מיהא פליגי עליה דטעמא דר"ע משום לירוף הוא וא"כ לא נסרית כל הפת ביין מצטרף נמי היתר לאיסור לחובה: ור"ע. כיון דמפיק ליה להאי משרת להיתר מצטרף לאיסור: טעם כעיקר. היכא דליכא מידי עיקר אלא טעם כגון שרה ענבים במים מנא ליה: בשר בחלב. בשר שנתבשל בחלב והבשר בעיניה אלא שטעם החלב נבלע בו: חידוש הוא. כל איסורו תימה הוא ודבר חידוש שאינו מצוי (א) בינינו בשאר איסורין לא גמרינן חומרא דידיה אשאר איסורין דכי היכי דשאר חידושין דידיה לא הוו בשאר איסורין האי דטעם כעיקר נמי לא תיגמר מיניה: ומאי חידושיה. משאר מילי: אילימא היינו חידושיה. דשני דברים המותרים הם וכשנתערבו נאסרין מה שאין כן בשאר דברים: הא כלאים נמי. דוגמתן: תרי ליה. שורהו בחלב כל היום שרי כלומר מותר לשרותו בתוכו ואינו עובר עליו אפילו על אכילתו דלא אסרה תורה אלא דרך בישול ואפילו יהיב ביה טעמא ומיהו מדרבנן אסור: בשיל ליה בשולי אסור. עובר על בישולו ועובר על אכילתו: גיעולי נכרים. קדירה שבישל בה הנכרי וכשחוזר ישראל ומבשל בה היא מגעלת בליעתה לתוך של ישראל גיעול לשון מקיא ופולט והתורה אסרתו במעשה מדין כל דבר אשר יבא באש (במדבר לא) דהיינו יורות וקומקמוסין וכיוצא בהן שמרתיחין אותן על האור: דגמרינן מנבילה. דכתיב לא תאכלו כל נבילה לגר וגו' (דברים יד) הראויה לגר קרויה נבילה שאינה ראויה לגר אינה קרויה נבילה: והכא אסור. דהאי נמי לפגם הוא דאותה בליעה משהתה בדופנו של כלי לילה אחת הופג טעמו ונתקלקל ותו לא משבחת לאוכל שהיא נפלטת לתוכו: בת יומא. שבישל בה הנכרי בו ביום: דלא פגמה פורתא. מטעם הכלי נפגמה הבליעה: מדרבנן נשמע לר"ע. לרבי יוחנן פריך דאמר לעיל כל איסורים שבתורה אין היתר מצטרף לאיסור חוץ מאיסורי נזיר ואוקימנא כר"ע מכדי לר"ע שמעינן ליה דאמר באיסורי נזיר היתר מצטרף לאיסור ובשאר איסורי לא איירי מידי ור' יוחנן אמאי לא אמר דכי היכי דאית ליה באיסורי נזיר אית ליה נמי בשאר איסורי הא ממאי דשמעינן להו לרבנן בטעם כעיקר מלינן למשמע מינה נמי דעתיה דר"ע בהיתר מצטרף לאיסור: לאו אמרי רבנן כו'. וקא אמרי נמי הכי בשאר איסורי לר"ע נמי דמפיק לה להיתר מצטרף לאיסור איכא למימר נמי דאית ליה מכאן אתה דן לכל התורה כולה: אמר ליה. כיון דמוקי ליה ר"ע להיתר מצטרף לאיסור לא מלינן למימר מכאן אתה דן:
משום

תוספות

והוא הדין לערלה בשתים. וכן אמרינן בפ"ק דקדושין (דף לח.) גבי חדש ופ"ה דערלה אין איסורו איסור עולם דלאחר שלש מותר וקשה מה שמותר אחר שלש היינו האילן והאילן לא נאסר מעולם רק הפרי והפרי אין לו היתר ור"ת פי' הוא הדין לערלה בשתים היינו בשנת ארבע דיש היתר לאיסורו על ידי פדייה או להביא לירושלים ור"י מפרש בנזיר וחדש אין איסורן איסור עולם שהגדל מן הגפן אחר השלמת נזרו לא חל עליו איסור וכן חדש היוצא מקמה השיבולת אחר הבאת העומר לא חל עליו איסור כיון שהשרישו קודם העומר וכן ערלה אחר ג' שנים היוצא ממנו אין איסור חל עליו ויש היתר לאיסורו יש לפרש כפ"ה שנזיר תוך זמנו יש לו היתר על ידי שאלה וחדש נמי לר' יהודה דאמר *יום הנף כולו אסור יש לו היתר תוך זמנו על ידי עומר וערלה אין לה היתר תוך זמנה וילדה בזקינה דבטלה אין זה אילן דערלה דפנים חדשות באו לכאן ועוד מפר"י שהפרי של חדש שנאסר כבר וכן היוצא מן הגפן קודם השלמת נזירות יש להן היתר בהשלמת זמן האיסור אבל ערלה וכלאים הפרי שנאסר אין לו היתר ופירוש זה נראה עיקר דאין צריך להעמיד כר' יהודה ואין להקשות לפי' זה אמאי לא חשיב יש היתר לאיסור בשאלה ובעומר ויהא ג' בערלה דיש לומר דלא סבר כר' יהודה אלא האיר המזרח מתיר ונזיר נמי אי מתשיל אין זה היתר לדבר שנאסר שהחכם עוקר הנדר מעיקרו ונמצא שלא נאסר מעולם אבל לפי' קמא ה"מ לאחשובי מה שהפרי עצמו נאסר לעולם והיה מותר בערלה שלש:

ודילמא מיין לחודיה. ולשון לצרף אתי שפיר כלומר לצרף היין הבלוע בתוכו:

ורבנן מבשר בחלב לא גמרינן דחידוש הוא. תימה לרשב"א התינח לרבא אלא לאביי דאית ליה בפרק כל הבשר (חולין דף קח.) דבשר בחלב לאו חידוש הוא אמאי איצטריך למילף מנזיר לטעם כעיקר*):

אלא יליף מגיעולי נכרים. הקשה ה"ר יוסף היכי יליף רבי עקיבא טעם כעיקר בנזיר מגיעולי נכרים הא נזיר קל מכל איסור שבתורה שאין איסורו איסור עולם ויש היתר לאיסורו ותי' דבמדין נמי היו כליהן בלועות מיין ואסורים לנזיר:

ורבנן קדירה בת יומא נמי אי אפשר דלא פגמה פורתא. ואפ"ה אסר הכתוב אם כן ליכא לאיפלוגי בין בת יומא לשאין בת יומא וכולהו אסורים ור"ע סבר קדירה בת יומא לא פגמה כלל אבל שאין בת יומא דפגמא שרי דנ"ט לפגם מותר דגמר מנבילה וה"נ סבר ר"ש בפרק בתרא דמסכת ע"ז (דף סז:) ור"מ פליג עליה התם וסבר נ"ט לפגם אסור דגמר מגיעולי נכרים דאסר הכתוב אע"ג דנ"ט לפגם הוא דאפילו קדירה בת יומא אי אפשר דלא פגמה פורתא וגיעולי נכרים לאו חידוש הוא ומה שהתיר הכתוב נבילה מוקי לה בסרוח מעיקרא ולרבי מאיר מצי למילף נמי מגיעולי נכרים לטעם כעיקר כיון דלאו חידוש הוא ואיכא השתא שלש מחלוקות בדבר:
משום

*) [ועי' תוס' חולין קח. ד"ה מבשר וכו' כתבו דלאביי חזר בו]

עין משפט נר מצוה

יג א ב מיי' פ"ה מהל' נזיר הל' ג:

רבינו חננאל

לכדתניא משרת ליתן טעם כעיקר שאם שרה ענבים במים ויש בהן טעם יין אסור ומכאן אתה דן לכל התורה כולה ומה נזיר שאין איסורו איסור עולם אלא עד מלאת ימי נזרו בלבד ואין הנאת היין עליו אסורה אלא שתייתו בלבד [ויש היתר לאיסורו] ואפי' זה היין בעצמו שנאסר לו אחר מלאת ימי נזרו הוא מותר בו שנא' (במדבר ו' כ') ואחר ישתה הנזיר יין עושה משרת ענבים שאין בו אלא טעם יין כענבים עצמן כלאים שאיסורן איסור עולם שנא' (ויקרא י"ט י"ט) את חקותי תשמרו חקים שחקקתי לך כבר כי באיסורן הן לעולם ואיסורן איסור הנאה דכתיב (דברים כ"ב ט) פן תקדש המלאה הזרע ודרשי' לה תוקדש תוקד אש ואין היתר לאיסורו דלשריפה אזיל אינו דין שיהיה בו טעם כעיקרו והוא הדין [לערלה] בשתים שאיסורן איסור הנאה שנא' (ויקרא י"ט כ"ג) ערלים לא יאכל ודרשי' ביה אחד איסור הנאה ואחד איסור אכילה ואין היתר לזה האילן באלו שני ערלה כלל לא בו ולא בפירותיו אבל אחר כן מותר הפירות והאילן והרי משרת להכי הוא דאתא ומשני רבי יוחנן זו הברייתא לרבנן היא ואני לא אמרתי אלא אליבא דרבי עקיבא דתניא רבי עקיבא אומר אפילו שרה פתו ביין ואכל כזית מפת ומיין חייב אבל הא דתנן ר' עקיבא אומר אפי' שרה פתו ביין ויש בו כדי לצרף כזית אסור דהויה היא ודחי' ממאי דחצי זית פת וחצי זית יין עליו דמצטרפי ואסור דלמא כזית מיין לחודיה קאמר וקמ"ל אע"ג דליתיה להודיה במקום אחד כיון דאית ביה שיעור לאצטרופי כזית אסור: ואמרי' ורבי עקיבא דמפיק כל משרת להיתר מצטרף לאיסור ליתן טעם כעיקר מנא ליה ואמר מבשר וחלב שאין בחלב אלא טעם בשר וכן בבשר טעם חלב ואסירי כך כל איסור טעם כעיקר אסור ורבנן האי חידוש הוא דאי תרו לבשר כולי יומא בחלב שרי ואי מבשל להו בהדי הדדי אסירי ומאי שנא בישול משריה אלא חידוש הוא ור' עקיבא מחידוש היכי גמר ואמרי' אלא רבי עקיבא מגיעולי נכרים גמר לכל התורה כולה דהא גיעולי נכרים טעמא בעלמא הוא וכתיב (במדבר ל"א כ"ג) כל דבר אשר יבא באש תעבירו באש ותניא דברים שנשתמשו בהן על ידי חמין כגון יורות וקומקמוסין ומיחמי חמין מגעילן ומטבילן כו' וקתני בסיפא וכולן שנשתמשו בהן עד שלא הגעיל ולא ליבן אסור ואוקימנא למאן דתאני נותן טעם לפגם אסור . ורבנן בכל התורה כולה נותן טעם לפגם שרי דילפינן מנבלה דכתיב בה (דברים יד כ"א) תתננה ואכלה וכתיב בטריפה (שמות כ"ב ל') לכלב תשליכון אותו ודייקי' מינה אם נפסלת מלאכול הכלב היא פרחה ממנה תורת נבלה וגיעולי נכרים כיון דנותן טעם לפגם הוא ומותר והכא כתיב אסור אמרי' חידוש הוא ורבנן לא גמרי' ורבי עקיבא גמר מינה דהא לא פגם אלא כדרב חייא בריה דרב הונא דאמר לא אסרה תורה אלא קידרה בת יומא דנותן טעם לשבח הוא ורבנן אפילו קדרה בת יומא אי אפשר דלא פגמה פורתא ומפורש בע"ז : ותוב אקשי' ורבי עקיבא למה לי דלא אסרה תורה כולה מיהא נמי הכי משרת להיתר מצטרף

מסורת הש"ס

[נ"ל הפרת]

נזיר [לז:] לד' שטשש כב:

מנחות סה.

חולין קח.

ע"ז סו: אימה ר"ח בריה דרב חייא [ע"ז עה: נזיר לז: ע"ש]

הגהות הב"ח

(א) רש"י ד"ה חידוש הוא וכו' שאינו מצוי כצ"ל ונשאר:

לענין חמץ בפסח נמי אין הכי נמי ולאפוקי *מדאביי דאמר יש הקטרה לפחות מכזית קמשמע לן *דהקטרה לאו לפחות מכזית יתיב רב דימי וקאמר לה להא שמעתא אמר ליה אביי לרב דימי וכל איסורין שבתורה אין היתר מצטרף לאיסור והתנן *המקפה של תרומה והשום והשמן של חולין ונגע טבול יום במקצתן פסל את כולן *המקפה של חולין והשום והשמן של תרומה ונגע טבול יום במקצתן לא פסל אלא מקום מגעו בלבד והוינן בה מקום מגעו אמאי פסולה הא בטלי להו ברוב ואמר רבה בר בר חנה *מה טעם הואיל וזר לוקה עליהן בכזית היכי דמי לאו משום דהיתר מצטרף לאיסור לא מאי כזית דאיכא כזית בכדי אכילת פרס וכזית בכדי אכילת פרס דאורייתא היא *א"ל אין אי הכי אמאי פליגי רבנן עליה דר"א בכותח הבבלי אלא מאי משום דהיתר מצטרף לאיסור סוף סוף אמאי פליגי רבנן עליה דר"א בכותח הבבלי אלא הנח לכותח הבבלי דלית ביה כזית בכדי אכילת פרס אי בעיניה *דקשריף וקאכיל ליה *בטלה דעתיה אצל כל אדם ואי משטר קשטר ואכיל לית ביה כזית בכדי אכילת פרס איתיביה שתי קדירות אחת של חולין ואחת של תרומה ולפניהן שתי מדוכות אחת של חולין ואחת של תרומה ונפלו אלו לתוך אלו מותרין שאני אומר תרומה לתוך התרומה נפלה וחולין לתוך חולין נפלו ואי אמרת כזית בכדי אכילת פרס דאורייתא אמאי אמרינן שאני אומר תרומה לתוך כו' א"ל הנח לתרומת תבלין דרבנן איתיביה *שתי קופות אחת של חולין ואחת של תרומה ולפניהם ב' סאין אחת של חולין ואחת של תרומה ונפלו אלו לתוך אלו מותרין שאני אומר חולין לתוך חולין נפלו תרומה לתוך תרומה נפלה ואי אמרת כזית בכדי אכילת פרס דאורייתא אמאי אמרינן שאני אומר אמר ליה *הנח לתרומה בזמן הזה דרבנן והאי משרת להכי הוא דאתא *האי מיבעי ליה לכדתניא משרת ליתן

[כתובות לג: וש"נ] [נזיר לו: ע"ש]

רש"י

אפילו חמץ נמי. דהא אמרינן על עירובו בלאו והיינו נמי היתר מצטרף לאיסור: ומשני אין הכי נמי. דחמץ בפסח היתר מצטרף לאיסור והאי דנקיט שאור לאפוקי מדאביי דאמר במנחות בפ' כל המנחות באות מצה יש הקטרה בפחות מכזית וחייב בהקטרת שאור כל דהו ולא בעי צירוף ומתרץ לברייתא דלעיל הכי אין לי אלא כזית חצי זית מנין ת"ל כל ויליף מינה דיש הקטרה לפחות מכזית קא משמע לן דאין הקטרה ואי איכא צירוף אין ואי לא לא: להא שמעתא. דר' יוחנן: המקפה. תבשיל קפוי ועב של תרומה כגון דייסא והשום והשמן הנתונין בו לתבלין היו של חולין: פסל. את כל הקדירה דמקפה עיקר וטבול יום פוסל את התרומה: מקום מגעו אמאי פסל הא בטלו להו תבלין ברובא. דקא ס"ד דימוע מדרבנן הוא דאסור: ואמר רבה בר בר חנה. דימוע מדאורייתא הוא וזר לוקה עליו בכזית משום דיש שם תרומה עלה הלכך לגבי טומאה נמי שם תרומה עלה ומיהו לא חמירא כתרומה עצמה ליפסול את כולן ומ"ט זר לוקה עליו בכזית משום זרות הא לא אכל כזית תרומה לאו משום דהיתר מצטרף לאיסור: ומשני מאי לוקה בכזית דקאמר כזית בכדי אכילת פרס שאם אכל פרס ממנו שיעור ארבעה ביצים יש בו כזית תרומה וקי"ל דכל שיעורי אכילת איסור בין כזית של חלב ודם ובין כותבת דיום הכפורים מצטרפין אכילת השיעור בכדי שהייה זו שאם אכל כחרדל חלב וחזר ואכל כחרדל עד שהשלים לכזית אם אין מתחילת האכילה ועד סופה יותר משהיית כדי אכילת פרס באכילה בינונית מצטרף והוי כמו שאכלו בבת אחת וחייב והכא נמי יש כאן תרומה כדי להצטרף כזית באכילת פרס ממנו: וכזית בכדי אכילת פרס דאורייתא. בתמיה הא דאמור רבנן כזית מצטרף כשיעור שהיית אכילת פרס מי הוי מדאורייתא הלכה למשה מסיני כשאר שיעורין דקא אמרת לוקה ומתרצת משום דהכיל כזית מאיסור בר מהיתר: אמאי פליגי רבנן עליה דר' אליעזר בכותח. נהי נמי דלא דרשי כל לרבות עירובו הא אכיל מיהא מאיסור כזית בכדי אכילת פרס: ואלא מאי. סבירא לך האי לוקה דרבה משום דהיתר מצטרף לאיסור ובחד כזית קאמר דלקי: סוף סוף אמאי פליגי רבנן עליה. יצטרף היתר לאיסור וליחייב: אלא גרס: הנח לכותח הבבלי. דלא אכיל כזית מן החמץ כשיעור שהיית אכילת פרס דהא כותח אינו עשוי לאכול אלא לטבל ואי מתרמי ואכיל ליה ממש דהשתא איכא כזית ממהר להצטרף כשיעור אכילת פרס ממנו: בטלה דעתו. ולאו אכילה היא לחובי עלה: ואי מישטר קא שטר. מטבל בתוכו כדרכו ליכא כזית מן החמץ בכדי שהיית אכילת פרס שכשאכל כדי אכילת פרס ממה שטיבל בתוכו לא אכל מן הכותח אלא מעט או שני זיתים או ארבעה ובההוא פורתא ליכא מן החמץ כזית ושכר המדי נמי אף על גב דשתי ליה בעיניה מיהו אין לך שותה ב' וג' כוסות שלא יפסיק וישהה בינתיים הלכך בכדי שהיית אכילת פרס לא שתי כזית מן החמץ לבד מן המים ושאר התערובת שבתם שכר עיקרו מן התמרים או מתאנים אלא שבמדי מערב עמהם מי שעורין קצת: פרס. הוא חצי ככר שיעורו בו עירובי תחומים שהוא מזון שתי סעודות וחציו לבית המנוגע לטמא בגדים אם ישהה בו כדי אכילתו שנתנה תורה שיעור שהייתו כדי סעודה דכתיב (ויקרא יד) והאוכל בבית יכבס את בגדיו והלכה למשה מסיני דחצי ככר של שמונה ביצים הוא סעודה: שתי מדוכות. שהתבלין נידוכין בתוכן פלפלין וזנגביל: אלו לתוך אלו. ממדוכות לתוך הקדירות: מותרין. קדירות חולין לזר: היכי אמרינן שאני אומר. ותלינן לקולא בעון מיתה ודילמא תרומה לתוך חולין נפל וכי אכיל לה איכא כזית תרומה באכילת פרס אלא שמע מינה אי נמי ודאי נפל לא מיחייב משום כזית בכדי אכילת פרס אלא מדרבנן וכי מספקא לן תלינן לקולא: במסכת נזיר גרסינן ואלא מאי היתר מצטרף לאיסור היכי אמר שאני אומר אלא הנח לתרומת תבלין דמדרבנן דראשית דגנך תירושך ויצהרך כתיב: קופות. גדולות ובתוכן דגן דהויא תרומה דאורייתא:

ליתן

תוספות

לענין חמץ בפסח נמי. לר' יוחנן לא מצי פריך דהיא לא דריש כל ואם תאמר והא בפרק בתרא דיומא (דף עד.) דריש רבי יוחנן מכל חלב לחצי שיעור אסור מן התורה ואור"י דלא דריש אלא לאיסורא אבל להתחייב מלקות כמו בכשיעור לא וכן גבי חמץ*:

מקום מגעו אמאי פסל הא בטיל ברובא. ופירש בקונטרס דס"ד השתא דדימוע דרבנן וקשה לריב"א דמשמע שהשום והשמן בעין מדקתני נגע במקצתן ולא קתני במקצתה ועוד דתני סיפא אימתי בזמן שהן גוש בקערה אבל אם היה מפוזר טהור ואי פסיל מקום מגעו משום מדומע אדרבה כי הוי מפוזר יש לו להיות מדומע יותר ועוד אמאי פסיל מקום מגעו ותו לא כיון דחשיב כמו כולה תרומה על ידי דימוע יפסל הכל או לא יפסל אפילו מקום מגעו דבהדיא איתא הא פלוגתא במסכת טבול יום בעיסה מדומעת ומי שפוסלה פוסלה לגמרי ומי שמכשיר מכשיר לגמרי ונראה לר"י כפירוש ר"ת דפירש דמתניתין איירי שהשום והשמן בעין וכדגרס בכל הספרים מקום מגעו אמאי פסל והא לא הוי כבילה והואיל דלא מקבל טומאה אלא מדרבנן אית לן למימר דבטלי אגב מקפה כדפרישית בפרק כל שעה (לעיל דף לג:):

לאו משום דהיתר מצטרף לאיסור. ומטעם הואיל אם היה מלקט מן השום או מן השמן כזית וילקה עליו לית לן למימר שלא תבטל אגב מקפה כיון שאין דרך אכילה בכך:

דאיכא כזית בכדי אכילת פרס. מקשין דבהשוחט (חולין דף לד:*) אמרינן הנח לנזיד הדמע דלית ביה כזית בכדי אכילת פרס משמע דבסתמא לא הוי כזית בכדי אכילת פרס ויש לומר דהכא קים ליה דעסקינן בדאית ביה כזית בכדי אכילת פרס ולפירוש ר"ת דמוקי שהשום והשמן בעין אתי שפיר דאי הוי מעורב לא הוי כזית בכדי אכילת פרס:

[גירסת ב"ח כת"י]

אלא מאי היתר וכו'. נראה דלא גרס ליה דאי גרס ליה א"כ מאי ס"ד דאביי לאקשויי כיון דלדידיה נמי קשה אלא לאביי א"ש דפליגי עליה רבנן דלר"ע דווקא אית ליה היתר מצטרף לאיסור בכל התורה דגמר מנזיר אבל לרבנן דמוקמי משרת לטעם כעיקר לית להו היתר מצטרף לאיסור בשום מקום ועוד דבנזיר בפ' ג' מינים (דף לז:) גרסינן גבי שתי קופות דבסמוך בשלמא לדידי דאמינא היתר מצטרף לאיסור דנפישי חולין כו' לאביי הא דהיתר מצטרף לאיסור היינו כשיש מן האיסור יותר מן ההיתר או שניהם בשוה אבל כשהיתר רבה על האיסור אין מצטרף ולרב דימי אין היתר מצטרף לאיסור בשום מקום כדמסיק לקמן דהוי חטאת ונזיר שני כתובים הבאים כאחד ואין מלמדין וה"פ א"ה אמאי פליגי רבנן כו' בשלמא לדידי פליגי רבנן משום דר' אליעזר דריש כל ואתא כל לרבות אפילו כשהאיסור מועט ורבנן לא דרשי כל דכשהאיסור מועט אין מצטרף כמו בעלמא אלא לדידך אמאי פליגי וכן גבי קופה ומדוכות אתי שפיר לאביי:

הנח לתרומת תבלין דרבנן. קשה לרשב"א כיון דתרומת תבלין דרבנן גבי שום אמאי פסל מקום מגעו ויש לחלק:

איתיביה שתי קופות. ואם תאמר מאי פריך אמאי אמרינן שאני אומר והא פשיטא דבכל מקום מדאורייתא מין במינו בטל ברוב והכא איירי שרבו חולין על התרומה כיון דסבר השתא דמיירי בתרומה דאורייתא דבדאורייתא בעי רבייה אפילו לר' יוחנן בהערל (יבמות דף פב.) ואור"י דבעי למימר בכל ענין אפילו מין בשאינו מינו כגון קמח חיטין בקמח שעורין שאינו ניכר:

והוא

עין משפט נר מצוה

ז א מיי' פ"ה מהל' איסורי מזבח הלכה כג:

[ועי' תוספות שבועות כא: ד"ה כרבי שמעון]

ח ב מיי' פ"ח מהל' טומאת אוכלין הל' יב:

ט ג שם הל' יג:

י ד מיי' פ"ד מהל' מאכלו' אסורו' הל' כב:

יא ה מיי' פ"ה מהל' תרומות הל' כו סמג עשין קלג טוש"ע יו"ד סימן שלא סעיף כ:

יב ו מיי' פ"ה מהלכות נזיר הלכה ד*:

מסורת הש"ס

מנחות כו: נח: [מיר לו.]

טבול יום פ"ב [מ"ג נזיר לו.]

[ע"ש]

[פי' שגומע ואוכל כמו בורקא ערוך ... ע"ז כט: ע"ש נזיר לו:]

לעיל מ: יבמות פב. נזיר לז: [תוספתא דתרומות פ"ו וכה דלא כפי ממשנה דתרומות פ"ז מ"ע פ"ט פ"ב] [שם]

רבינו חננאל

כותח הבבלי לרבי אליעזר היתר מצטרף לאיסור והוה ליה לזעירי למיתנינהו לכלהו ושנינן אין הני כלהו היתר מצטרף לאיסור נינהו מיהו לא הזכיר זעירי השאור לבדו אלא לאפוקי מדאביי דאמר יש הקטרה בפחות מכזית אתא זעירי לאשמועינן דאין הקטרה בפחות מכזית ובעי צירוף להשלימו: אקשי' לר' אבהו ולר' יוחנן ליכא מידי אחריני דהיתר מצטרף לאיסור והתניא מקפה של חולין והשום והשמן של תרומה ונגע טבול יום במקצתו לא פסל אלא מקום מגעו והוינן בה מקום מגעו במקפה אמאי פסל ואמר משמי' דר' יוחנן הואיל וזר לוקה על המקפה בכזית מאי לאו משום דמקפה שהיא היתר מצטרף לאיסור לשום ולשמן שהן איסור ונעשית המקפה כלה איסור לפיכך זר האוכל ממנה לוקה אלמא לרבי יוחנן איכא דברים דהיתר מצטרף לאיסור מדאורייתא ושנינן לעולם לית ליה והכא כגון דאיכא במקפה שאכל הזר יש באותה אכילה כזית מן השום והשמן של תרומה ונצטרף השום והשמן ונעשו כזית ולפיכך לוקה שאינו לוקה אלא על התרומה ולא על המקפה ושיעור אכילה שמצטרפת מעט מעט עד שמצטרפין לכזית בכדי אכילת פרס דתני' אכל וחזר ואכל אם יש מתחלת אכילה ראשונה עד סוף אכילה אחרונה שיעור כדי אכילת פרס מצטרפי' וכמה היא כדי אכילת פרס מצאנו ששיער ר' חצי פרס שתי ביצים ואחד מעשרים בביצה נמצא הפרס ארבעה ביצים ואחד מעשרה בביצה ומפורש בעירובין פרק כיצד משתתפין בתחומין ואקשי' אי הכי בכותח הבבלי נמי נימא איכא כזית אוכל מקומניתא דאומא בכדי אכילת פרס ואמאי פליגי רבנן ואמרי בולא כלום ואמרינן שאני כותח הבבלי דלא משכחת בי' כזית בכדי אכילת פרס אי דקא גריף ואכיל כותח כגון אכילת הביצה בטלה דעתו כלומר אין זה דרך ארץ ואי דקא שטר ואכיל שהוא כעין טבילת פת במרק ליכא כזית מקומניתא דאומא כשיעור שעה כדי שיאכל אדם פרס ואם הוא יותר מזה השיעור אין מצטרפין וראשון ראשון בטל: ומותבינן מיהא שתי קדירות אחת של חולין ואחת של תרומה ולפניהם שתי מדוכות באחת תבלין של תרומה כו' ושנינן הנח לתרומת תבלין דאינה מן התורה לפי שאינם מיני תבואות ומותבי' תוב שתי קופות של חולין ושל תרומה ולפניהם שתי סאין אחת של חולין ואחת של תרומה ונפלו אלו לתוך אלו מותרין שאני אומר חולין לתוך חולין נפלו ואי כזית בכדי אכילת פרס מדאורייתא מצטרף כל ספק דאורייתא לחומרא אמאי תאני שאני אומר חולין לתוך חולין נפלו נמצא מיקל ומשני' כי תניא ההיא בתרומה בזמן הזה שהיא מדרבנן ואקשינן מדרך אחרת ומשרת להיתר מצטרף לאיסור הוא דאתא ההוא מיבעי ליה לכדתניא

If so, [44a] in the matter of leaven too?[10]—That indeed is so; yet
a this[1] is to reject [the ruling] of Abaye, who said, There is burning [on the altar] in respect of less than an olive;[2] therefore he informs us that there is no burning for less than an olive.

R. Dimi sat and reported this discussion. Said Abaye to R. Dimi: And [in] all [other] prohibitions of the Torah, does not a permitted commodity combine with a prohibited [commodity]? Surely we learned: If the *mikpeh*[3] is of *terumah*, while the garlic and the oil are of *ḥullin*, and a *ṭebul yom* touched part of it, he disqualifies all of it.[4] If the *mikpeh* is of *ḥullin*, while the garlic and the oil is of *terumah*, and a *ṭebul yom* touches part of it, he disqualifies only the place which he touches. Now we pondered thereon: why is the place where he touches unfit? Surely the seasoning[5] is nullified in the greater quantity?[6] And Rabbah b. Bar Ḥanah answered: What is the reason? Because a lay Israelite is flagellated on its account for [eating] as much as an olive.[7] How is that conceivable?[8] Is it not because the permitted [commodity] combines with the forbidden [commodity]?—No: what does 'as much as an olive' mean: that there is as much as an olive within the time of eating half [a loaf].[9] Is then 'as much as an olive within the time of eating half [a loaf]' a Scriptural [standard]?[10] Yes, he answered him. If so, why do the Rabbis disagree with R. Eliezer in reference to Babylonian *kutaḥ*?[11]—What then: [the reason is] because the permitted [commodity] combines with the prohibited commodity? Then after all why do the Rabbis differ from R. Eliezer in the
b matter of Babylonian *kutaḥ*? But leave Babylonian *kutaḥ* alone,[1] because it does not contain as much as an olive within the eating of half [a loaf]. [For] if [it is eaten] in its natural state,[2] so that he gulps it down and eats it, we disregard such a fancy as being exceptional.[3] While if he dips [bread] into it[4] and eats it, it does not contain as much as an olive within the time of eating half [a loaf].

He raised an objection against him: If there are two [stew] pots, one of *ḥullin* and the other of *terumah*, and in front of them are two mortars, one containing [condiments of] *ḥullin* and the other containing *terumah*, and the latter fell into the former, they are permitted,[5] for I assume: the *terumah* fell into the *terumah*, and the *ḥullin* fell into the *ḥullin*. Now if you say that as much as an olive within the [time of] eating half [a loaf] is a Biblical [standard], why do we say, 'for I assume, the *terumah*' etc.?[6]—Leave the *terumah* of condiments alone, he replied, which is [only] Rabbinical.[7]

He raised an objection against him: [If there are] two baskets, one containing *ḥullin* and the other containing *terumah*, and in front of them are two *se'ah* [of provisions], one of *ḥullin* and the other of *terumah*, and these fell into those, they are permitted, for I assume: the *ḥullin* fell into *ḥullin*, [and] the *terumah* fell into the *terumah*. Now if you say that as much as an olive within the eating of half [a loaf] is a Scriptural [standard], why do we say, 'because I assume' [etc.]?[8]—Leave the *terumah* [set aside]
c at the present time[1] he answered him, which is only Rabbinical.

Now does this [law of] the infusion [of grapes] come for this purpose?[2] It is required for what was taught: '*An infusion*': [44b]

(10) There too he learns that there is a negative injunction in respect of the mixture of leaven; hence he should likewise assume that it refers to half an olive of each.

a (1) *Sc.* the particular mention of the burning of leaven on the altar. (2) Even if one burns less than an olive of leaven on the altar, he is culpable, since the leaven itself, whatever its quantity, involves punishment. (3) Jast.: a stiff mass of grist, oil and onions. (4) A *ṭebul yom* (v. Glos.) disqualifies *terumah*. Since the main part of the dish is *terumah*, even the *ḥullin* too becomes unfit, because it is subsidiary to the *terumah*. (5) I.e., the garlic and oil. (6) As explained in n. a4, it is merely subsidiary to the main dish. (7) Hence it is not regarded as nullified, in spite of its subsidiary nature. (8) When a lay Israelite eats as much as an olive of that dish, he has not eaten that quantity of *terumah*. Why then is he flagellated? (9) I.e., if he eats as much as half a loaf of eight average eggs in size, this half constituting an average meal, within the time that the normal eater requires for a meal, he will have eaten as much as an olive of *terumah*, and for that he is culpable. [According to Maim. *Yad 'Erubin*, half a loaf is equivalent to three average eggs]. (10) That flagellation is incurred.—Flagellation is only imposed for the violation of a law of Scripture. (11) Even if flagellation is not incurred on account of the mixture, yet there too in a quantity of four eggs of *kutaḥ* there is as much as an olive of leaven, and for that he should be liable.

b (1) I.e., do not ask a question from it. (2) I.e., by itself, and not as a relish with something else. (3) Lit., 'his mind is nullified by the side of every man'. It is not considered eating, and therefore does not involve punishment.—Punishment is incurred only when forbidden food is eaten in the normal way. (4) Rashi; Jast.: if he spreads it (on bread). (5) The pot of *ḥullin* is permitted to a lay Israelite. (6) For of course it might have been the reverse; how then can we make this lenient assumption when there is a doubt of a *Scriptural* prohibition? (7) By Scriptural law no *terumah* is required for these; hence the entire prohibition in this case is only Rabbinical. (8) V. n. b6.

c (1) After the destruction of the Temple. (2) V. *supra* 43b bottom.

It is necessary: [43b] you might argue, since it is written, *Thou shalt eat no leavened bread with it; seven days shalt thou eat unleavened bread therewith:*[7] whoever is subject to 'arise, eat unleavened bread', is subject to '*thou shalt eat no leavened bread*'; hence these women, since they are not subject to, 'arise, eat unleavened bread', because it is an affirmative precept limited to time,[8] I would say that they are also not subject to, '*thou shalt eat no leavened bread*'. Hence it [the verse] informs us [otherwise].

And now that they have been included in [the injunction of] '*thou shalt eat no leavened bread*', they are also included in respect of eating unleavened bread, in accordance with R. Eleazar. For R. Eleazar said: Women are subject to the [precept of] eating unleavened bread by the law of Scripture, for it is said, *Thou shalt eat no leavened bread with it; [seven days shalt thou eat unleavened bread [therewith]*: whoever is subject to '*thou shalt eat no leavened bread*', is subject to the eating of unleavened *bread;* and these women, since they are subject to [the injunction of] '*thou shalt eat no leavened bread*', are [also] subject to, 'arise, eat unleavened bread'.

a And why do you prefer[1] [to assume] that this '*whosoever*' is to include women, while you exclude its mixture; say that it is to include the mixture?[2]—It is logical that when treating of eaters [Scripture] includes eaters; [but] when treating of eaters, shall it include things which are eaten?[3] To this R. Nathan the father of R. Huna demurred: Then wherever [Scripture] treats of eaters does it not include things eaten? Surely it was taught: *For whosoever eateth the fat* [ḥeleb] *of the beast, of which men present an offering [made by fire unto the Lord, even the soul that eateth it shall be cut off from his people]*:[4] I only know it of the *ḥeleb* of unblemished [animals], which are fit to be offered [as sacrifices]; whence do we know it of the *ḥeleb* of blemished animals? Therefore it is stated, '*of the beast*'.[5] Whence do we know it of the *ḥeleb* of *ḥullin?* Because it is stated, '*For whosoever*'.[6] Thus here, though [Scripture] treats of eaters, yet it includes things eaten?—Since there are no eaters there [to be included],[7] it includes things eaten. Here, however, that there are eaters [to be included],[8] he cannot abandon eaters and include things eaten.

Now as to the Rabbis who do not accept the view [that a negative injunction is violated through] a mixture, they do not interpret '*whosoever*' [as an extension]. But then how do they know [that] women [are liable to *kareth*]?[9]—They do not interpret '*whosoever*' [as an extension], but they do interpret 'for *whosoever*' [as such].[10] Then [according to] R. Eliezer, say that '*whosoever*' is to include women; 'for *whosoever*' is to include the mixture [of

b leaven]?[1] And should you answer, R. Eliezer does not interpret 'for *whosoever*' [as an additional extension], surely it was taught: *For ye shall not burn any leaven . . . [as an offering made by fire unto the Lord]*:[2] I only know it of the whole of it;[3] whence do I know [even] part of it?[4] Because '*any*' [kol] is stated. Whence do we know [that] its mixture[5] [is forbidden]? Because it is stated *for any* [ki kol]. Whom do you know to interpret *kol* [as an extension]? R. Eliezer; and he [also] interprets '*for any*' [ki kol]. This is [indeed] a difficulty.

R. Abbahu said in R. Joḥanan's name: In all the prohibitions of the Torah, a permitted [commodity] does not combine with a prohibited [commodity],[6] except in the [case of the] prohibitions of a nazirite, for lo! the Torah said, *[any] infusion [of grapes]*.[7] While Ze'iri said: Also 'ye shall not burn any leaven'.[8] With whom [does this agree]? With R. Eliezer, who interprets *kol*.[9]

(7) Deut. XVI, 3. (8) Lit., 'caused by the time'. I.e., it is performed at certain times or seasons, and it is shown in Ḳid. 29a that women are exempt from such.

a (1) Lit., 'what (reason) do you see?' (2) While the limitation excludes women. (3) Surely not. (4) Lev. VII, 25. (5) Implying whether it is fit for sacrificing or not. (6) Which is an extension. (7) For the inclusion of women in the prohibition and penalty follows from Rab's dictum *supra* 43a bottom. (8) Viz., women, as explained *supra*. (9) For eating leaven. For R. Eliezer interprets '*whosoever*' in both cases, one as including a mixture, and the other as including women. But since the Rabbis do not interpret '*whosoever*' as an extension, there is nothing to intimate the inclusion of women. (10) Written in connection with *kareth*, Ex. XXI, 15 and 19.

b (1) Teaching that *kareth* is involved, and not merely a negative precept. (2) Lev. II, 11. *For . . . any* (E.V. *For ye shall make no . . .*) is *ki . . . kol*, the same words which are translated '*for whosoever*' in the previous verses. (3) I.e., where the whole of that which is burnt on the altar consists of leaven. (4) Leaven must not even be used as part of the offering. (5) I.e., anything containing a mixture of leaven. (6) The minimum quantity to involve punishment is as much as an olive. Now, if a man eats half that quantity of *ḥeleb* together with half that quantity of permitted meat simultaneously, the latter does not combine with the former, that it should be regarded as though he had eaten the full quantity of prohibited food. (7) Num. VI, 3: *neither shall he drink any infusion of grapes*. By this the Talmud understands that he must not eat bread steeped in wine. Now bread itself is permitted, yet Scripture forbids the combination of bread and wine as though that also were forbidden, and if the *two together* amount to an olive, punishment is involved. For if Scripture refers to a case where the wine itself contains that quantity, why state it at all; obviously the wine is not less prohibited merely because it has been absorbed by the bread? (8) Cf. Lev. I, 11. Rashi: if the priest put half an olive of leaven and half an olive of *mazzah*, not mixed together but each separately distinguishable, upon the altar, he incurs punishment. Tosaf. explains it differently. (9) *Supra:* 'whence do I know (even) part of it' etc. He understands this to mean that there is half an olive of each.

ה א מיי' פ"ו מהלכות מצה הלכה י סמג עשין מ טוש"ע או"ח סי' תעב סעיף יד:

ו ב מיי' פ"ה מהלכות איסורי מזבח הלכה א סמג לאוין שמ:

סלקא דעתך אמינא הואיל וכתיב °לא תאכל עליו חמץ שבעת ימים תאכל עליו מצות כל שישנו בקום אכול מצה ישנו בבל תאכל חמץ והני נשי הואיל וליתנהו בקום אכול מצה דהויא ליה מצות עשה שהזמן גרמא (היא) אימא בבל תאכל חמץ נמי ליתנהו קמ"ל והשתא דאתרבו להו בבל תאכל חמץ איתרבי נמי לאכילת מצה כרבי (*אליעזר) דאמר ר"א* *נשים חייבות באכילת מצה דבר תורה שנא' לא תאכל עליו חמץ וגו' כל שישנו בבל תאכל חמץ ישנו באכילת מצה והני נשי נמי הואיל וישנן בבל תאכל חמץ ישנן בקום אכול מצה ומאי חזית דהאי כל לרבויי נשים ומפקת עירובו אימא לרבויי עירובו מסתברא קאי באוכלין קאי באוכלין מרבה אוכלין מרבה נאכלין מתקיף לה רב נתן אבוה דרב הונא (*בריה דרב נתן) וכל היכא דקאי באוכלין לא מרבה נאכלין והא תניא °כי כל אוכל חלב מן הבהמה אשר יקריב אין לי אלא חלב תמימין שראוי ליקרב חלב בעלי מומין מנין ת"ל מן הבהמה חלב חולין מניין ת"ל כי כל והא הכא דקאי באוכלין וקא מרבה נאכלין ההם דליכא אוכלין מרבה נאכלין הכא דאיכא אוכלין לא שביק להו לאוכלין ומרבה נאכלין ורבנן דלית להו עירוב כל לא דרשי אלא נשים מנא להו כל לא דרשי כי כל דרשי ור"א אימא כל לרבות את הנשים כי כל לרבות את עירובו וכי תימא כי כל ר"א לא דריש והתניא °שאור בל תקטירו אין לי אלא כולו מקצתו מניין ת"ל כל עירובו מניין ת"ל כי כל מאן שמעת ליה דדריש כל רבי אליעזר וקא דריש כי כל קשיא *א"ר אבהו אמר רבי יוחנן כל איסורין שבתורה אין היתר מצטרף לאיסור חוץ מאיסורי נזיר שהרי אמרה תורה °משרת וזעירי אמר אף שאור בבל תקטירו כמאן כר"א דדריש כל אי הכי

לענין

תורה אור: דברים טז | ויקרא ז | ויקרא ב | במדבר ו

רש"י

מצות עשה שהזמן גרמא. נפקא לן בפ"ק דקדושין (דף כט.) דנשים פטורות: קמ"ל. דהאי כל למוזהרות על החמץ וכיון דמוזהרות על לאו דחמץ חייבות בעשה דאכילת מצה לילה הראשון ואע"ג דזמן גרמא כר' אליעזר הואיל וישנן בבל תאכל חמץ דנפקא לן מכל אוכל חמץ ישנן בקום אכול מצה: קאי באוכלין. כל דגבי כרת באוכלי חמץ כתיב אבל כל דאזהרה בנאכל כתיב כל מחמצת: קאי באוכלין מרבה נאכלין. בתמיה: אשר יקריב. משמע קדשים ושיהו תמימים: התם דליכא לרבויי אוכלין. דהא נשים מדרב יהודה נפקי(א) השוה הכתוב אשה לאיש לכל עונשין שבתורה: הכא דאיכא לרבויי אוכלין. דנשים באיסור חמץ דלא נפקי לן מדרב יהודה כדאמרן לעיל לא שביק אוכלין ומרבה נאכלין: ופרכינן ורבנן. דפליגי אדר"א בעירוב דחמץ כיון דלית להו לאו בעירוב פשיטא כל דכתיב גבי אזהרה דכל מחמצת לא דרשי והשתא על כרחך כל דגבי כרת לרבויי נשים נמי לא דרשי ואלא נשים מנא להו: כל. דגבי אזהרה דלא כתיב כי בהדיה לא דרשינן לרבויי נאכלין דעירובו אבל גבי כרת דאוכלין כתיב כי כל אוכל דרשינן ליה: ומקשינן ור"א אימא כל. דכרת לרבויי נשים כי כל דכרת לרבויי עירובו נמי לכרת דכיון דליכא תו אוכלין לרבויי מרבינן ביה נאכלין כדאמרן גבי חלב ואימא על עירובו בכרת: אין לי אלא כולו. בזמן שכל ההקטר מן השאור: מקצתו. חצי זית שאינו הקטר שלם דאין הקטרה פחותה מכזית: עירובו מניין. (ב)כשאינו בעין אלא מעורב ובלול עם מנחה הוגנת של מצות לאחר שפתתן דאינן בעין: אין היתר מצטרף לאיסור. אכל חצי זית חלב וחצי זית בשר בבת אחת אין היתר משלים את שיעור האיסור לחייבו חוץ מאיסורי נזיר שאם אכל חצי זית ענבים וחצי זית לחם בבת אחת חייב שהרי אמרה תורה משרת ענבים לא ישתה חייב על שריית פתו ביין ואי איכא מיין לחודיה כזית למה לי קרא וכל משרת לא גרסינן ואית דגרסי ליה ומפרשי דאפילו לרבנן דלא דרשי כל וכל דרשי ולא היא דהא פרכינן לקמן האי מיבעיא ליה לכדתניא משרת ליתן טעם כעיקר ואם איתא נימא ליה הא טעמא דידי מוכל אלא ממשמעותא דמשרת נפקא ליה וכל לא דריש: אף שאור בל תקטירו. נמי היתר מצטרף לאיסור חצי זית קומץ דשאור וחצי זית דמצה ואינן מעורבין אלא כל אחד ניכר: כר"א דדריש כל. לעיל ומהתם נפקא ליה כדאמרן לעיל מקצתו מניין ת"ל כל ודריש ליה הכי מקצתו מניין חצי זית שאור וחצי זית מצה עמו:

אפילו

תוספות

סלקא דעתך אמינא כל שישנו בקום אכול מצה. תימה לר"י היכי סלקא דעתך למידרש הכי אדרבה איפכא יש לדרוש דלתומרא מקשינן ואור"י דס"ד דאורחיה דקרא דסיפא מפרש לרישיה משום הכי אמר דבאכילת מצה תלוי דהתיבה בסוף ועוד יש לומר דהכא יש לדרוש יותר היתר לנשים משום ג"ש דט"ו מחג הסוכות והוו מיפטרי ממצה כמו מסוכה דפטר להו בהדיא בפ' הישן (סוכה כח.) מהלכה למשה מסיני יש מקשים למה נשים אין חייבות בכלאי' משום דכל שישנו בלבישת שעטנז ישנו בגדילים כדדרשינן בערכין (דף ג:) גבי כהנים ולפירוש ר"י דפי' דמסיפא לרישא סברא לדרוש קשה להפך שלא יהו נשים חייבות בכלאים וכי תימא ה"נ והא בפ"ק דבילה (דף יד:) משמע דכלאים לא חזו למידי*: אין לי אלא כולו מקצתו מנין. בפרק כל המנחות באות מצה (מנחות נח.) מפרש אביי אינלי אלא כולו דהיינו כזית מקצתו חצי זית מניין ורבא אמר התם דה"ק אין לי אלא קומץ כולו מקצת קומץ מניין ומסיק התם דאיכא בינייהו דאביי סבר דיש קומץ בפחות מב' זיתים דהיינו כזית לכך מפרש כולו כזית וסבר נמי דיש הקטרה בפחות מזית ואע"ג דבפ' כילד צולין (לקמן עט.) א"ר יהושע כל הזבחים שבתורה שנשתייר מהן כזית בשר וכזית חלב זורק את הדם משמע דאין הקטרה בפחות מכזית הכא היינו טעמא משום דסבר דיש קומץ בפחות מב' זיתים א"כ כשריבה הכתוב חצי קומץ ע"כ ריבה חצי זית ורבא סבר אין קומץ בפחות מב' זיתים ואין הקטרה בפחות מזית: מאן שמעת ליה דדריש כל ר' אליעזר. אף על גב דר"ע נמי דריש כל בפ' התערובות (זבחים פב.) גבי כל חטאת *לא קשה דאפילו יהא כר"ע מ"מ לא מישתמיט תנא למימר (שיסבור) שיהא תערובת חמץ בכרת ועוד נראה לר"י דאפילו לרבנן דלא דרשי הכא כל דרשי בעלמא בריש מרובה (ב"ק סג.) דאמר כל רבויא הוא ובפ' שני דסוכה (דף כח.) גבי כל האזרח ודווקא הכא לא דרשי בדבר שאין סברא לרבות כגון עירובו וכגון נשים משום היקשא וכגון מקצת דבל תקטירו וה"פ כמאן כר"א דדריש כל אפילו לדבר שאין סברא לרבות כגון עירובו וכגון נשים והא קאמר נמי דרבנן לא דרשי כל: חוץ מאיסורי נזיר. אע"ג דחטאת נמי קאמר לקמן לרבי יוחנן היתר מצטרף לאיסור הכא לא חשיב חטאת דבקדשים לא קמיירי: כמאן כר"א דדריש כל. נראה לר"י דזעירי משמע ליה דשאור היתר מצטרף לאיסור מדקתני עירובו מניין ת"ל כי כל ומדרבי עירובו א"כ היתר מצטרף לאיסור והיינו כדרבא דלדידיה ה"פ מקצתו מניין היינו זית שלם אבל לאביי דמפרש מקצתו מניין חצי זית לא שייך היתר מצטרף לאיסור דאמשהו דאיסור לחודיה מיחייב והא דמרבה עירובו היינו כשמתערב לגמרי ולא אמר שיתבטל האיסור אגב ההיתר והא דקאמר כמאן כר"א דדריש כל משום דלרבנן אף על גב דדרשי כי כל לא מוקמא ליה לרבות עירובו אלא לרבות מקצתו ורש"י פירש דזעירי משמע ליה מקצת היינו חצי זית קומץ דשאור וחצי זית דמצה ואין מעורבין אלא כל אחד ניכר וק"ל לפירושו טובא חדא דלא הוי זעירי לא כאביי ולא כרבא ועוד מאי קאמר כמאן כר"א הא כרבנן נמי אתיא דהא כי כל דרשי ומוקמי ליה אמקצתו דהיינו היתר מצטרף לאיסור לפ"ה ועוד בחמץ מנ"ל תערובת כיון דלריך קרא להיתר מצטרף לאיסור ועוד דלפ"ה נ"ל מקצתו מניין פי' חצי זית איסור וחצי זית היתר שאינם מעורבים יחד דאי לאו הכי היינו עירוב ולקמן גבי חטאת משמע דאי: היתר מצטרף לאיסור אם לא שיתערב האיסור וההיתר יחד דהא אמר עד שיבלע בבשרה:

רבינו חננאל

ראיה מדלא כתיב אוכל כל מחמצת ונכרתה אלא כתיב כי כל אוכל מחמצת ונכרתה ש"מ לאוכלין קא מזהיר ואפילו נשים חייבות באכילת חמץ ומוזהרות באכילת מצה בפסח: ואמרי' מאי חזית דהאי כל דכרת מרבית לנשים בכרת וממעט עירוביו בכרת ואמרי' מסתברא קאי באוכלין מרבה אוכלין כלומ' כתב כל אוכל לרבות כל אדם האוכל ואפילו נשים וכתיב כל מחמצת לרבות כל המתחמץ ואפילו ע"י תערובת בלאו אבל לית ליה אורחא דקרא כדקאי באוכלין למשבק אוכלין לרבויי נאכלין ואמרינן איני דכל היכא דקאי באוכלין לא מרבה נאכלין והתניא כי כל אוכל חלב מן הבהמה אשר יקריבו ממנה קרבן לה' אין לי אלא חלב תמימים הראויה ליקרב חלב בעלי מומין מנין ת"ל מן הבהמה: חלב חולין מנין ת"ל כי כל והא הכא כי כל אוכל כתיב דמשמע אוכלין וקאי באוכלין וקא מרבי חלב חולין הנאכלין ושני' היכא דליכא אוכלין מרבה נאכלין אבל היכא דאית ליה לרבות אוכלין כגון הנשים לא שבק אוכלין ומרבה נאכלין ורבנן דלית בעירוביו משום דלא דרשו כל אם כן נשים שחייבות בכרת מנא להו ושני' כל לא דרשי כי כל דרשי ובכרת כתיב כי כל אוכל מחמצת ונכרתה: ואקשי' לר' אליעזר נימא כל לרבות נשים כי כל לרבות בכרת דתניא שאור לא תקטירו אין לי אלא כולו מקצתו מנין ת"ל כל שאור פי' כלום משאור. אפי' מקצתו. עירובו מנין ת"ל כי כל שאור לרבות עירובו מאן שמעת ליה דדרש כל ר' אליעזר ודרש כי כל עירוביו ועלתה בקשיא: אמר ר' אבהו א"ר יוחנן אין היתר מצטרף לאיסור חוץ מאיסורי נזיר שהרי אלו אמרה תורה משרת ענבים הייתי למד שמשרת ענבים אסור למה כתב כל לאסור עירוביו: זעירי אמר אף שאור בבל תקטירו היתר מצטרף לאיסור ואם יש מקצת שאור ומצה משלים לכזית חייב כמאן כר' אליעזר דמרבה עירוביו מכל אקשי' אם כן הוא כי זעירי אליבא דר' אליעזר [קאמר] אמאי אמר שאור ותו לא אפי' כותח

[צ"ל אליעזר]

[ועי' תוס' יבמות ד. ד"ה דכתיב ותוס' שבועו' כ: ד"ה כל ותוס' מנחות צג. ד"ה ור"ש ותוספות ערכין ג: ד"ה הכל]

[ועי' תוס' זבחים פב. ד"ה ת"ל ותוס' מנחות יא: ד"ה קומץ עוד שם כו: ד"ה אמר]

לקמן מג:

[יש למחוק כמו שמוחק הרש"ק]

בכורות ס: גבי רב תחליפא אבוה דרב הונא בר תחליפא ועי' לקמן קז: וזבחים פ"]

מנחות נח.

נזיר לה:

הגהות הב"ח

(א) רש"י ד"ה דהא נשים וכו' נפקי השוה: (ב) ד"ה עירובו וכו' דאיתו כעין:

מסורת הש"ס

[א] מנחות פו' רש"י שקורין גליסמא

שם מנחות פו. מגילה יג.

[לקמן מח:]

[לקמן מח: מנחות נג. חולין כג:]

לעיל כח.

סוכה כח. יבמות פד. ב"ק טו. תמורה ב: נדה מח: [קדושין לה.]

עין משפט נר מצוה

ד א מיי' פ"א מהלכות חמץ הלכה ו סמג לאוין עו:

שבת פ. מו"ק ט: [נזיר נט:]

[ותוס']

[לעיל כח: וכן דליקא ליתא להא דמחמצת רש"י לעיל כח: חמץ אין לי אלא שנתחמץ מאליו]

[אשה לאיש]

גמרא

תורה אור

*שהגיעו לפרקן ולא הגיעו (א) לשנים בנות עניים טופלות אותן בסיד בנות עשירים טופלות אותן בסולת בנות מלכים בשמן המור שנא' °ששה חדשים בשמן המור *מאי שמן המור רב הונא בר ירמיה אומר סטכת רב ירמיה בר אבא אמר שמן זית שלא הביא שליש תניא ר' יהודה אומר אנפיקנין שמן זית שלא הביא שליש ולמה סכין אותו מפני שמשיר את השיער ומעדן את הבשר: זה הכלל כל שהוא ממין דגן: תניא א"ר יהושע וכי מאחר ששנינו כל שהוא מין דגן הרי זה עובר בפסח למה מנו חכמים את אלו כדי שיהא רגיל בהן ובשמותיהן כי הא דההוא בר מערבא איקלע לבבל הוה בישרא בהדיה אמר להו קריבו לי מתבילתא שמע דקאמרי קריבו ליה כותח כיון דשמע כותח פירש: הרי אלו באזהרה: מאן תנא דחמץ דגן גמור ע"י תערובות ונוקשה בעיניה בלאו אמר רב יהודה אמר רב ר"מ היא דתניא שיאור ישרף ונותנו לכלבו והאוכלו בארבעים הא גופא קשיא אמרת שיאור ישרף אלמא אסור בהנאה והדר תני ונותנו לפני כלבו אלמא מותר בהנאה הכי קאמר שיאור ישרף *דר"מ לר' מאיר דר' יהודה לר' יהודה ונותנו לפני כלבו דר' מאיר לר' יהודה והאוכלו בארבעים אתאן לר' מאיר שמעינן ליה לרבי מאיר נוקשה בעיניה בלאו וכל שכן חמץ דגן גמור על ידי תערובת רב נחמן אמר ר"א היא דתניא *על חמץ דגן גמור ענוש כרת על עירובו בלאו דברי ר' אליעזר וחכמים אומרים על חמץ דגן גמור ענוש כרת על עירובו בלא כלום ושמעינן ליה לר' אליעזר דאמר חמץ דגן גמור על ידי תערובת בלאו וכל שכן נוקשה בעיניה ורב נחמן מ"ט לא אמר כרב יהודה אמר לך דילמא עד כאן לא קאמר ר"מ התם אלא נוקשה בעיניה אבל חמץ דגן גמור על ידי תערובת לא ורב יהודה מ"ט לא אמר כרב נחמן אמר לך עד כאן לא קאמר ר"א התם אלא חמץ דגן גמור ע"י תערובת אבל נוקשה בעיניה לא אמר תניא כוותיה דרב יהודה °כל מחמצת לא תאכלו לרבות כותח הבבלי ושכר המדי וחומץ האדומי וזיתום המצרי יכול יהא ענוש כרת ת"ל °כי כל אוכל חמץ ונכרתה על חמץ דגן גמור ענוש כרת ועל עירובו בלאו מאן שמעת ליה דאמר על עירובו בלאו ר"א היא ואילו נוקשה בעיניה לא קאמר ש"מ נוקשה לר"א לית ליה ור"א עירובו בלאו מנא ליה דכתיב כל מחמצת לא תאכלו אי הכי כרת נמי לחייב דהא כתיב כי כל אוכל מחמצת ונכרתה ההוא מיבעי ליה *לכדתניא (*מחמצת) אין לי אלא שנתחמץ מאליו מחמת ד"א מניין ת"ל כל (ב) מחמצת ונכרתה אי הכי דלאו נמי להכי הוא דאתא אלא טעמא דר"א מכל התם נמי הכתיב כל ההוא מיבעי ליה לרבות את הנשים נשים מדרב יהודה אמר רב נפקא *דאמר רב יהודה אמר רב וכן תנא דבי ר' ישמעאל אמר קרא °איש או אשה כי יעשו מכל חטאת האדם השוה הכתוב *איש לאשה לכל עונשין שבתורה איצטריך

אסתר ב · שמות יב · שם · במדבר ה

סלקא

רש"י

שהגיעו לפרקן ולא הגיעו לשנים · שיש להן שערות כאילו הגיעו לפרקן והן לא הגיעו לכלל שנים ובושות על כך: עשירות טופלות אותן בסולת · ומשיר את השער: אנפיקינון · במנחות תנן אנפקינון לא יביא ומפרש ר' יהודה אנפקינן הוא שמן זית כו': סטכת · לא איתפרש*: ומעדן את הבשר · אשקלייר"א: שיהא בקי בהן · שידע ממה הן עושין אותו שיהא נזהר בהן כשיביאו לו כותח ידע שיש חלב ויש שם חמץ אם פסח הוא: מתבילתא · שום לפתן ללפת בו את הפת: כיון דשמע · שקראו שמו כותח: פירש · שבקי היה וידע שיש שם חלב: מאן תנא · דמתני' דאית ליה חמץ דגן גמור שנתערב במין אחר ואינו בעין שנימוח אי נמי חמץ נוקשה רע ואיתיה בעיניה מוזהרין על אכילתו בלאו דקתני מתניתין כותח הבבלי ושכר המדי חמץ דגן גמור אלא שנתערב בדבר אחר ותכשיטי נשים בעיניה הוא אבל נוקשה הוא דאינו ראוי לאכילה וקתני באזהרה דעובר עליהן בלאו: שיאור · שלא נתחמץ כל צרכו שיאור פליגי במתני'* ר"מ קרי שיאור את שהכסיפו פניו וזהו תחלת חימוצו ולר' יהודה הוי שיאור שהתחיל ליסדק כבר סדקין דקין כקרני חגבים אחד לכאן ואחד לכאן אבל שהכסיפו פניו לרבי יהודה מצה היא ולר"מ קרני חגבים חמץ גמור הוא והכא הכי קאמר שיאור ישרף לאסור בהנאה שיאור דר"מ הכסיפו פניו ישרף לר"מ ושיאור דרבי יהודה ישרף לרבי יהודה וסיפא דקתני ונותנו לפני כלבו אליבא דרבי יהודה קאמר ליה ואשיאור דר"מ קאי והאוכלו בארבעים אהאן לר"מ כלומר לר"מ האוכלו לשיאור זה שרבי יהודה מתיר בהנאה סופג את הארבעים אלמא שמעינן ליה לר"מ דאית ליה חדא מהני תרתי דמתני' דקאמר נוקשה בעיני' בלאו כגון שיאור דנוקשה הוא דאינו ראוי לאכילה הואיל והחמיץ קצת ולא גמר והחמיץ עיסות אחרות כשאור נמי לא חזי וקאמר בלאו וכ"ש חמץ גמור ע"י תערובת דקסבר רב יהודה ע"י תערובת חמיר מנוקשה בעין והאי לאו דנוקשה נפקא ליה מכל מחמצת לא תאכלו כל רבויא הוא כדלקמן: ועל עירובו בלאו. מכל מחמצת כדלקמן: מ"ט לא אמר כדרב יהודה. דמוקי מתניתין כר"מ: רב נחמן ס"ל נוקשה בעיניה חמור מחמץ גמור ע"י תערובת: תניא כוותיה דרב יהודה. דאמר חמץ גמור בתערובת חמור: לענין כרת לא כתיב כל מחמצת אלא כל אוכל חמץ ולקמן מפרש ליה: כותח ושכר וחומץ וזיתום כולן חמץ גמור מעורב בהן כותח איכא פת והנך תלתא איכא שערי וכולהו בני אכילה ושתיה נינהו אבל זומן ועמילן וקולן דנוקשה הוא ובעיניה הואיל ולאו בני אכילה נינהו לא תנינהו והיינו כדרב יהודה דאמר מודה היה ר"א בנוקשה בעיניה דפטור: ור"א עירובו בלאו מנא ליה. פשיטא מדאפקיה בלשון מחמצת וגבי כרת נמי מחמצת כתיב: ההוא. מחמצת דגבי כרת לאו לעירובו אתא אלא לנתחמץ מחמת דבר אחר: אי הכי. האי דגבי לאו נמי אימא לאזהורי אנתחמץ מחמת דבר אחר אתא ואזהרה דתערובת מנא ליה: התם נמי. גבי כרת הא כתיב כל אוכל מחמצת ונכרתה: לכל עונשין. מכאן שהנשים חייבות על כל לא תעשה שבתורה שהרי עונשן מלקות:

מלות

תוספות

למה מנו חכמים את אלו · תימה לרשב"א הא איצטריך למתנא לאשמועינן שהן בלאו ולא בכרת ותירץ ר"י דלא הוה ליה לאשמועינן אלא תרי מינייהו חד לנוקשה בעיניה וחד ע"י תערובת ועוד הקשה דת"ק שמנאם לית ליה האי כללא דהא איכא תכשיטי נשים שהן מין דגן ואין עובר בפסח אלא רבי אליעזר הוא דקאמר לה:

מאן תנא חמץ גמור ע"י תערובת ונוקשה בעיניה בלאו · משמע בשמעתין דאי לאו דאיתרבי חמץ נוקשה למלקות אפילו איסור לא היה בו ותימה לר"י דבפ"ק דחולין (דף כג:) בעי רבי זירא הרי עלי לחמי תודה מן החמץ או מן המצה והביא שיאור מהו שיאור דמאן אי דר"מ לר"מ מלקי עליה חמץ הוא והשתא מנא ליה דהוי חמץ לענין תודה דילמא שאני חמץ בפסח דרבייה קרא למלקות (גרידא) ואור"י דהתם נמי איכא שום קרא דמרבינן מיניה חמץ נוקשה והא דתניא בפרק כל המנחות באות מצה (מנחות דף נג:) אין מחמילין בתפוחים דהוי חמץ נוקשה כדמשמע התם הייט לכתחילה אבל בדיעבד כשר:

ואילו נוקשה בעיניה לא קתני · וא"ת וניטא דמשום הכי לא חשיב ליה משום דכ"ש הוא כדאמר רב נחמן וי"ל דאי כ"ש הוא הוה ליה למיתני לאשמועינן דלית ביה כרת:

ונותנו לפני כלבו דר"מ לרבי יהודה · מדאורייתא אפי' באכילה שרי כדאמרינן בפ"ק דחולין (דף כג:*) דמצה מעלייתא היא אלא מדרבנן אסור:

ההוא כל לאתויי נשים · תימה לר"י הא תרי כי כל כתיבי גבי כרת כי כל אוכל חמץ ונכרתה וכי כל אוכל מחמצת ומרבינן עירובו לכרת ואפילו לרבנן דלא דרשי כל כי כל דרשי ואור"י דפשיטא ליה לגמרא דאתא לנשים דרשא:

סלקא

הגהות הב"ח

(א) גמ' שהגיעו לפרקן ולא הגיעו בנות כו' ותיבת לשנים נמחק ונ"ב ע"י פ' המוליא יין דף פ' ע"ב: (ב) שם דבר אחר מנין ת"ל כל אוכל מחמצת:

רבינו חננאל

תניא אמר ר' יהושע וכי מאחר ששנינו כל שהוא מין דגן הרי זה עובר בפסח למה מנו חכמים את אלו כותח הבבלי ושכר המדי ושאר המנויין במשנה והלא בכלן יש בהן מין דגן אלא כדי שיהא בקי בהן ובשמותיהן כי ההוא דאמר להו הבו לי מידי למכלא ביה רפתא שמע דקאמרי הבו ליה כותחא הוה בהדיה בשרא כיון דשמע כותח פירש דידע דאית ביה נסיוביה דחלבא: **הרי** אלו באזהרה ואין בהן משום כרת. אמרינן מאן האי תנא דאית ליה חמץ דגן גמור על ידי תערובות כגון כותח הבבלי וכיוצא בו ונוקשא בעיניה כגון עמילן של טבחים וזומן של צבעין וקולן של סופרים בלאו אמר רב יהודה אמר רב ר"מ הוא דתניא שיאור ישרף וכו' ואוקימנא [דשיאור] דקרי ליה ר"מ שיאור והוא הכספת פנים וכן שיאור דקרי ליה ר' יהודה שיאור והוא כקרני חגבים תני ישרף ושיאור דר' מאיר דהוא הכספת פנים כגון נוקשא בעלמא הוא אומר ר' יהודה נותנו לפני כלבו כלומר מותר בהנאה. ור' מאיר אומר האוכלו בארבעים מיהא שמעינן לר' מאיר דאמר נוקשה בעיניה בלאו פי' נוקשה שאינו חמץ גמור וכל שכן חמץ על ידי תערובות. רב נחמן אמר מתני' ר' אליעזר היא דתניא על חמץ דגן גמור ענוש כרת ועל עירובו בלאו דברי ר' אליעזר וחכמים אומרים על עירובו בולא כלום שמעי' ליה לר' אליעזר דאמר חמץ דגן גמור על ידי תערובת בלאו וכש"כ נוקשא בעיניה רב יהודה לא אמר כרב נחמן אמר לך רב יהודה ר' אליעזר לא אמר אלא ע"י תערובות שהוא בלאו אבל נוקשא בעיניה לא: **תניא** כרב יהודה כל מחמצת לא תאכלו לרבות כותח הבבלי ושכר המדי וחומץ האדומי יכול יהא ענוש כרת ת"ל כי כל אוכל מחמצת לא תאכלו על חמץ דגן גמור ענוש כרת ועל עירובו בלאו מאן שמעת ליה בהדיא על עירובו בלאו ר' אליעזר ואלו הני דפשיטנא דאינון נוקשא בעיניה זומא של צבעין ועמילן של טבחים וקולן וזיתום שיירינהו ש"מ דלית ליה לר' אליעזר נוקשה בעיניה בלאו ואיתוקמא דמתני' ר"מ היא. ואפי' הכי דרשינן טעמא דר' אליעזר עירובו בלאו מנא ליה ופשטי' מרוקיא דקרא מדהוה ליה למכתב מחמצת לא תאכלו וכתב כל מחמצת לא תאכלו ואפי' ע"י תערובות בלאו ואם תאמר אי הכי אפי' כרת נמי ליחייב דהא כתיב מחמצת ונכרתה ודחי' ההוא (מחמץ) [מחמצת] דכרת מיבעי ליה להכין אין לי חמץ שנתחייב עליו [כרת] אלא חמץ שנתחמץ מאליו נתחמץ ע"י ד"א כגון ע"י שאור וכיוצא בו מנין ת"ל כי כל אוכל מחמצה ונכרתה לרבות את שנתחמץ מחמת ד"א אי הכי מחמצת דלאו נמי להכי הוא דאתא ושנינן טעמא דר' אליעזר דדריש מכל מחמצת ואפילו עירובו אי הכי כרת נמי הכתיב ביה כל ההוא כל לרבות הנשים שחייבות בחמץ ודייקי' דוקיא דהני קראי בלאו דחמץ כתיב כל מחמצת לא תאכלו כתב כל כחמצת לרבות כל המחמיצין ואפי' ע"י תערובת לא תאכלו לאוקמיה בלאו. יכרת דחמץ כתיב ביה (לא תאכל) [כי כל אוכל] מחמצת בא ללמד לכל בני אדם שהן האוכלין שנאמר כי כל אוכל מחמצת ונכרתה (ולא) [ועוד] כתיב כי כל אוכל מחמצת ונכרתה חד כתיבא לרבות כי כל מי שיא.ל ואפי' נשים

וראיו

of Israel [43a] who have attained maturity but have not attained [their] years,[5] the daughters of poor men plaster them [the unwanted hairs] with lime; the daughters of wealthy men plaster them with fine flour; while royal princesses, with oil of myrrh, as it is written, *six months with oil of myrrh*.[6] What is oil of myrrh?—R. Huna b. Jeremiah said: *Saṭkath*.[7] R. Jeremiah b. Abba said. Oil of olives which were not a third grown. It was taught, R. Judah said: *Anpiḳanin*[8] is oil of olives which were not a third grown. And why do [women] rub it in [their skin]? Because it removes the hair and rejuvenates the skin.

THIS IS THE GENERAL RULE: WHATEVER IS OF THE SPECIES OF CORN. It was taught, R. Joshua said: Now since we learned, WHATEVER IS OF THE SPECIES OF CORN MUST BE REMOVED ON PASSOVER, why did the Sages enumerate these? So that a one should be familiar with them and with their names.[1] As it once happened that a certain Palestinian[2] visited Babylonia. He had meat with him and he said to them [his hosts], Bring me a relish.[3] He [then] heard them saying, 'Take him *kutaḥ*'. As soon as he heard *kutaḥ*, he abstained.[4]

THESE ARE SUBJECT TO A 'WARNING'. Which Tanna [holds] that real leaven of corn in a mixture, and spoiled leaven[5] in its natural condition, is subject to a negative injunction?[6]—Said Rab Judah in Rab's name: It is R. Meir. For it was taught: *Si'ur*[7] must be burnt, and he may give it to his dog, and he who eats it is [punished] by forty [lashes].[8] Now this is self-contradictory. You say, '*si'ur* must be burnt': this proves that it is forbidden for use. Then it is stated, 'and he may give it to his dog', which proves that it is permitted for use! This is its meaning: *Si'ur* [i.e., what is *si'ur*] according to R. Meir [must be burnt] in R. Meir's opinion, and [what is *si'ur*] according to R. Judah [must be burnt] in R. Judah's opinion. And he may give it to his dog, [i.e., what is *si'ur*] according to R. Meir [may be given to a dog] in R. Judah's opinion. And he who eats it is [punished] by forty [lashes]—this agrees with R. Meir.[9] [Thus] we learn that R. Meir holds that spoiled [leaven] in its natural state[10] is subject to a negative injunction, and all the more real leaven of corn in a mixture.[11]

R. Naḥman said, It is R. Eliezer. For it was taught: For real leaven of corn there is the penalty of *kareth;* for a mixture of it [one is subject to] a negative injunction: this is the view of R. Eliezer. But the Sages maintain: For real leaven of corn there is b the penalty of *kareth;* for the mixture of it there is nothing at all.[1] [Thus] we learn that R. Eliezer holds that real leaven of corn in a mixture is subject to a negative injunction, and all the more spoiled [leaven] in its natural state.[2] Now R. Naḥman, what is the reason that he does not say as Rab Judah?—He can tell you: perhaps R. Meir rules [thus] only there, [in respect of] spoiled [leaven] in its natural state, but not [in the case of] real leaven of corn in a mixture. And Rab Judah: what is the reason that he does not say as R. Naḥman? He can tell you: [Perhaps][3] R. Eliezer rules [thus] only there, [in respect of] real leaven of corn in a mixture, but not [in the case of] spoiled [leaven] in its natural state.

It was taught in accordance with Rab Judah:[4] *Ye shall eat nothing leavened:*[5] this is to include Babylonian *kutaḥ* and Median beer and Idumean vinegar and Egyptian *zithom*. You might think that the penalty is *kareth;* therefore it is stated, *for whosoever eateth that which is leavened shall be cut off:*[6] for real leaven of corn there is the penalty of *kareth*, but for the mixture of it [you are subject] to a negative injunction. Now, whom do you know to maintain [that] for the mixture of it [you are subject] to a negative injunction? It is R. Eliezer. Yet he does not state[7] spoiled [leaven] in its natural state. This proves that R. Eliezer does not hold [that] spoiled [leaven is subject to a negative injunction].

Now R. Eliezer, whence does he know that the mixture of it involves a negative injunction: because it is written, '*ye shall eat nothing leavened*'? If so, let him [the offender] be liable to *kareth* too, since it is written, '*for whosoever eateth that which is leavened . . . shall be cut off*'?—He requires that for what was taught: ([*Ye shall* c *eat nothing*] *leavened*):[1] I only know [that it is forbidden] where it turned leaven of itself; if [it fermented] through the agency of another substance, how do we know it? Because it is stated, *for whosoever eateth that which is leavened shall be cut off*. If so, [the teaching] of the negative injunction too comes for this purpose?[2] Rather, R. Eliezer's reason is [that he] deduces from '*whosoever*'.[3] [But] there too[4] '*whosoever*' is written?—He requires that to include women.[5] But women are deduced from Rab Judah's [dictum] in Rab's name. For Rab Judah said in Rab's name, and the School of R. Ishmael taught likewise: *when a man or woman shall commit any sin that men commit:*[6] the Writ assimilated woman to man in respect of all the penalties which are [decreed] in the Torah?—

(5) I.e., they have grown the hair which is the evidence of maturity before the usual age, which is twelve years and a day. They would normally be ashamed and wish to remove it. Tosaf. in Shab. 80*b* s.v. שהגיעו omits 'years' and seems to translate: 'who have reached their time (for marriage), and yet have not attained it', so that they wish to make themselves more beautiful. (6) Est. II, 12 q.v. (7) Jast.: oil of myrrh or cinnamon. (8) It is stated in Men. 86*a* that *anpiḳanin* must not be brought with a meal-offering. R. Judah explains what this is.

a (1) That all may know that their use is forbidden on Passover. (2) Lit., 'son of the West'. (3) To go with the meat. (4) He knew that it contains milk, whilst they did not. (5) '*Nuḳsheh*', a leavened substance unfit for food. (6) Babylonian *kutaḥ* and Median beer both contain real leaven, but mixed with other substances; while women's paste is simply flour, unmixed, but spoiled and unfit for food. (7) This is dough which is beginning to ferment, i.e., semi-leaven. At that stage it is unfit for eating, and therefore the same as spoiled leaven; v. *infra* 48*b*. (8) This is the punishment for violating a negative injunction. (9) V. *infra* 48*b* for the controversy between R. Meir and R. Judah as to what constitutes *si'ur*, semi-leaven. Now both R. Meir and R. Judah hold that use of *si'ur*, as each defines it respectively, is forbidden, and hence it must be burnt. But *si'ur*, as defined by R. Meir, is in R. Judah's opinion *mazzah* (unleavened bread), but as it is not fit for eating, it must be given to a dog. The final clause teaches this: according to R. Meir, he who eats *si'ur*, as defined by himself, is flagellated, though R. Judah holds that at that stage it is *mazzah* and may be eaten. (10) Such as *si'ur*. (11) Rab Judah being of the opinion that real leaven in a mixture is more stringent leaven than spoiled leaven in its natural state.

b (1) No penalty is incurred. (2) Thus R. Naḥman holds that spoiled leaven unmixed is more stringent than real leaven in a mixture. (3) [Added with MS.M.] (4) That real leaven mixed is the more stringent. (5) Ex. XII, 20. (6) Ibid. 19. (7) I.e., include.

c (1) The bracketed passage is omitted in some edd. as well as *supra* 28*b* in the quotation of this Baraitha. (2) That a negative injunction is involved even in respect of that which is made leaven through a foreign substance. How then do we know that even for a mixture a negative injunction is transgressed? (3) Heb. *kol*. This is an extension, and so teaches even the inclusion of a mixture. (4) In reference to *kareth*. (5) That they too are subject to the penalty of *kareth*. (6) Num. V, 6.

a White[1] bread, fat meat, and old wine. White bread, [42b] of fine meal. Fat meat, of a goat which was not opened.[2] Old wine: very old.[3] Everything that is beneficial for the one is harmful for the other,[4] and what is harmful for one is beneficial for the other, save moist *zangebila*,[5] long peppers, white bread, fat meat and old wine, which are beneficial for the whole body.

MEDIAN BEER. Because barley water is mixed into it.

IDUMEAN VINEGAR. Because barley is cast into it. R. Naḥman [b. Isaac] said:[6] In former times, when they used to bring [wine] libations from Judah, the wine of Judah did not turn vinegar unless barley was put into it, and they used to call it simply vinegar.[7] But now the wine of the Idumeans does not turn vinegar until barley is put into it, and it is called 'Idumean vinegar', in fulfilment of what is said, [*Tyre hath said against Jerusalem . . .*] *I shall be replenished, now that she is laid waste:*[8] if one is full [flourishing] the other is desolate, and if the other is full the first is desolate.[9] R. Nahman b. Isaac quoted this: *and the one people shall be stronger than the other people.*[10]

It was taught, R. Judah said: Originally, he who bought vinegar from an *'am ha-areẓ*[11] did not need to tithe it, because it was a presumption that it was produced from nought but *tamad*.[12] But now, he who buys vinegar from an *'am ha-areẓ* must tithe it.[13] Now does R. Judah hold [that] *tamad* is not liable to tithing, but we learned: He who makes *tamad*, pouring water on by measure,
b and [then] he finds the same quantity, is exempt [from tithing]:[1] but R. Judah declares him liable?[2]—This is what he says: The *'amme ha-areẓ* were not under suspicion in connection with *tamad*.[3] Alternatively, they were under suspicion, yet there is no difficulty: the one refers to [*tamad* made with] the straining bag; the other refers to [*tamad* made of] kernels.[4]

AND EGYPTIAN ZITHOM. What is EGYPTIAN ZITHOM?—R. Joseph learned: [A concoction made of] a third part barley, a third part safflower, and a third part salt. R. Papa omitted barley and substituted wheat. And your token is '*sisane*'.[5] They soaked them [these ingredients], then roasted them, ground them and then drank them. From the [Passover] sacrifice[6] until Pentecost, they who are constipated are relieved, while they who are diarrhoeic are bound. [But] for an invalid and a pregnant woman it is dangerous.[7]

AND DYER'S BROTH. Here it is explained: Bran water, with which *lacca*[8] is primed.

AND COOK'S DOUGH. A loaf [i.e., dough] made of corn less than a third grown, which she places on the mouth of the pot and it absorbs the froth.

AND SCRIBES' PASTE. Here it is explained: Shoemaker's paste.[9] R. Shimi of Hozae[10] said: It is a toilet paste used by the daughters of rich men, of which they leave [some] for the daughters of poor men.[11] But that is not so, for R. Ḥiyya taught: They are four
c commodities of general use[1] and three manufacturing commodities.[2] Now if you say that it is a toilet paste used by the daughters of rich men, what manufacturing commodities are there?[3] What then; [it is] shoemaker's paste? Then why does he call it SCRIBES' PASTE; he should say, cobbler's PASTE?—Said R. Oshaia to him: In truth it is shoemaker's paste; yet why does he call it: SCRIBES' PASTE? Because scribes too stick their papyruses together with it.

R. ELIEZER SAID: WOMEN'S ORNAMENTS TOO etc. WOMENS' ORNAMENTS! can you think so![4] Rather, say, WOMEN'S cosmetics TOO. For Rab Judah said in Rab's name: [As to] the daughters

a (1) Lit., 'clean'. (2) I.e., which has not given birth to young. (3) Rashi: three years old.—But it is doubtful if this would be called very old. (4) I.e., what is beneficial for the heart is harmful to the eyes, etc. (5) Zingiber, an Arabian spice plant, prob. ginger (Jast.). (6) The Yalkuṭ omits b. Isaac; the text *infra* supports this omission. (7) The wine was so good that without barley it would never turn sour. (8) Ezek. XXVI, 2. (9) Tyre—here represented as synonymous with Edom—and Jerusalem can neither both flourish simultaneously nor both be desolate simultaneously.—True religion and paganism are irrevocably opposed to each other, and the triumph of one must involve the defeat of the other. (10) Gen. XXV, 23. (11) V. Glos. (12) An inferior wine made from the husks of grapes steeped in water. But it was definitely not from wine, for the wine was too good to turn into vinegar. (13) Because it is probably from wine, which is nowadays of a poorer quality and readily turns vinegar. Of course, the *'am ha-areẓ* himself should have tithed it, but they were suspected of neglecting tithes, and therefore the purchaser had to render tithe; v. Glos. s.v. *Demai*.

b (1) Because it is mere water, though it has slightly absorbed the appearance and taste of wine from the husks and kernels. (2) Because its appearance and taste determine its status as wine. (3) Because it was so cheap that even they would not grudge its tithes. (4) When *tamad* is made by pouring water over the lees in the strainer, it is wine, and is subject to tithes. But *tamad* made with kernels is merely coloured water, and is not subject to tithes at all. (5) 'Twigs'. R. Joseph (יוסף) included barley (שעורי), both words containing an *S* (ס and ש) and the two ס in '*sisane*' serve as mnemonic for this. (6) I.e., from Passover. (7) Because its laxative properties are too great. (8) So the reading in Maim. and Jast. *Lacca* is the juice of a plant, used for dyeing. (9) *Perura* is a paste made of crumbs. (10) The modern Khuzestan. (11) It is a depilatory made of fine flour, and wealthy women give the leavings to their poorer sisters, the daughters of scribes, who were generally poor.

c (1) Lit., 'for the country'. (2) Thus he sums up the seven things mentioned in the Mishnah. (3) This is not an article used in manufacture. (4) They have nothing to do with leaven.

ג א מיי' פ"ב מהלכות מעשר הלכה ו:

דסמידא בשר שמן דצפירתא דלא אפתח יין ישן עתיק עתיקי כל מילי דמעלי להאי ודקשה להאי מעלי להאי בר מזנגבילא רטיבא ופילפלי אריכתא ופת נקייה ובשר שמן ויין ישן דמעלי לכולי גופיה: שכר המדי: דרמו ביה מי שערי: וחומץ האדומי: דשדו ביה שערי אמר רב נחמן *(בריצחק) בתחלה כשהיו מביאין נסכים מיהודה לא היה יינם של יהודה מחמיץ עד שנותנין לתוכן שעורין והיו קורין אותו חומץ סתם ועכשיו אין יינם של אדומיים מחמיץ עד שנותנין לתוכן שעורין וקורין אותו חומץ האדומי לקיים מה שנאמר °אמלאה החרבה *אם מלאה זו חרבה זו ואם מלאה זו חרבה זו רב נחמן בר יצחק אמר מהכא °ולאם מלאם יאמץ תניא אמר רבי יהודה בראשונה *הלוקח חומץ מעם הארץ אינו צריך לעשר מפני שחזקה אינו בא אלא מן התמד ועכשיו הלוקח חומץ מעם הארץ צריך לעשר שחזקתו אינו בא אלא מן היין וסבר רבי יהודה תמד לאו בר עשורי הוא והא (*תניא) **המתמד ונתן מים במדה ומצא כדי מדתו פטור ורבי יהודה מחייב הכי קאמר לא נחשדו עמי הארץ על התמד אי בעית אימא נחשדו ולא קשיא הא *בדרווקא הא בדפורצני: וזיתום המצרי וכו': מאי זיתום המצרי *תנא רב יוסף תלתא שערי תלתא קורטמי ותלתא מלחא רב פפא מפיק שערי ומעייל חיטי וסימניך סיסני תרו להו וקלו להו וטחני להו ושתו להו *מדיבחא ועד עצרתא דקמיט מרפי ליה ודרפי מקמיט ליה לחולה ולאשה עוברה סכנתא: וזומן של צבעים וכו': הכא תרגימו מיא דחיורי דצבעי בהו לבא*: ועמילן של טבחים וכו': פת תבואה שלא הביאה שליש שמניחה על פי קדירה ושואבת הזוהמא: וקולן של סופרים וכו': הכא תרגומא פרורא דאושכפי רב שימי מחוזנאה אמר זה טיפולן של בנות עשירים שמשיירות אותו לבנות עניים איני והא תנא רבי חייא ארבעה מיני מדינה ושלשה מיני אומנות ואי אמרת טיפולן של בנות עשירים מאי מיני אומנות איכא ואלא מאי פרורא דאושכפי אמאי קרי ליה האי קולן של סופרים קולן של רצענין מיבעיא ליה אמר רב אושעיא לעולם פרורא דאושכפי (א) ומאי קרי ליה קולן של סופרים דסופרים נמי מדבקין בהו ניירותיהן: רבי אליעזר אומר אף תכשיטי נשים וכו': תכשיטי נשים סלקא דעתך אלא אימא אף טיפולי נשים דאמר רב יהודה אמר רב בנות ישראל שהגיעו

רש"י

דסמידא. סולת: דלצפירתא דלא אפתח. עז שלא ילדה: עתיק עתיקי. ישן של שלש שנים: כל דמעלי. לחולי זה קשה לזה המועיל ללב קשה לעינים או לאחד מתחלואי שאר האברים: זנגבילא. זינזיבר"א: דרמו ביה מי שערי. שמטילין לתוכו מי שעורין כגון שכר שלנו ועושין אותו במדי: שכר המדי. לפי שבאותן הימים אין נוהגין לעשות שכר אלא מתמרים ובמדי עושין שכר ממי שעורין כעין אותן שלנו קרי ליה שכר המדי: דשדו ביה שערי. *ביין נותנין שעורין שלמים כדי להחמיצו לפי שיינם טוב ואינו בא לידי חימוץ עד שנותנין לתוכו שעורין: בתחילה. כשבית המקדש קיים היו מביאין נסכים מיהודה ובזכות הנסכים היה טעם ביינם ולא היה מחמיץ כו': אמלאה החרבה. רישא דקרא יען אמרה צור לירושלים האח וגו' אתמלא מן חורבנה של ירושלים וצור מאדום היא: ולאם מלאם יאמץ. כשעשו גבור יעקב חלש אין מלכות שניהם מתקיים יחד: תמד. בופי"ט לפי שהיין היה טוב ואינו מחמיץ וסתם חומץ שלהם מן תמד היה בא: ועכשיו. בטל טעם היין וממהר להחמיץ: פטור. מלעשר שהרי אין כאן אלא מים שלא מצא אלא כדי מדתו ואע"ג דחזותיה וטעמא חמרא קיוהא דפירא בעלמא הוא דעייל ביה: ורבי יהודה מחייב. דאזיל בתר חזותא וטעמא: הכי קאמר. מתניתא קמייתא לא נחשדו עמי הארץ מלעשר את התמד לפי שאינו חשוב בעיניהם לפיכך הלוקחו ממנו פטור מן הדמאי: ואי בעית אימא נחשדו. ורבי יהודה במתניתא קמייתא טעמיה משום דפטור אפי' ממעשר ודאי ובתמד דפורצני קאמר שנותנין מים בחרצנין והוא מחמיץ ומרתיח לאחר זמן כיין התוסס והיינו תמד ולית ביה אלא קיוהא דפירא והא דקתני ר' יהודה מחייב בדרווקא שנותנין בשמרים מים והוא נמי תמד בההוא מחייב ר' יהודה אע"ג דלא מצא אלא כדי מדתו לפי שהיין של שמרים מעורב בו ומן המים נשאר בשמרים: קורטמי. מוריק"א קרו"ג: וסימניך. שלא תטעה מאן אמר חיטי ומאן אמר שערי: סמ"ך. רב יוסף שיש סמ"ך בשמו אמר שערי לישנא אחרינא וסימניך סיסני כלי ששמו כן כדאמרינן (בכתובות) (ב"מ דף סז:) ואי אגבינהו בסיסני קנה ושם כלי זה יהא סימן לגירסא זו דרב יוסף אמר שערי שני סמכי"ן יחד: תרו להו. שורין אותן יחד: מדבחא ועד עצרתא. מפסח ועד עצרת: דקמיט. עצור מנקביו: מרפי ליה. משלשלו: ודרפי קמיט ליה. למי שיש לו שילשול מעצרו: סכנתא. שמשלשל יותר מדאי: מיא דחיורא. מי סובין: דצבעו בהו לבא. סרכ"א: פירורא דאושכפי. גלו"ד והרצענים מדבקין בו את העור כשמתחלק לשתים או מדבקין שתי עורות יחד לעשותן עבה ודרכן לתת בה קמח של שיפון ולקמיה מפרש מאי של סופרים: טיפולן של בנות עשירים. שהיא של סולת משיירות משיוריהן לבנות סופרים מלמדי תינוקות שהן עניים ומטיפולן של בנות עניים לא מצי למימר דעניות אין להן סולת אלא סיד טיפול לשון מטפל ומדביק אותו דבר או סיד או סולת על בשרן להסיר השער: והא תני ר' חייא. ויהיב סימנא בהני דמתני' ואמר ארבע מיני מדינה שנינו בהם הצריכין לכל אדם בין אומן בין לא אומן שהרי למאכל או לרפואה עשויין כותח שכר וחומץ וזיתום אבל זומן אינו ראוי אלא לצבעים וקולן של סופרים ועמילן של נחתומין (ב) כייר עשוי מעשבים ע"י דבק שקורין גלו"ד: תכשיטי נשים. הוא כחל ושרק ובשמים שתולות בצואריהן להריח ומאי חמץ איכא: שהגיעו

תוספות

הא בדרווקא והא בדפורצני. והא דאמרינן שחזקתו מן התמד היינו מתמד דפורצני אבל דרווקי טוב מאד ואינם נעשים לעולם חומץ: **וסימניך** סיסני. בבמה אשה יוצאה (שבת סו:) גבי הקיטע יוצא בקב שלו רבי יוסי אוסר גרסינן וסימניך סמ"ך סמ"ך הוא סימן טוב יותר והכא לא מצי למימר הכי משום דשערי בשי"ן כתיב: **טיפולן** של בנו' עשירי'. וא"ת א"כ היינו (ג) תכשיטי נשים ותירץ הר"י דאורלינ"ש דהכא מיירי בפנים של מעלה (ד) דלא מאיס כל כך כשטופלים על פניהם ותכשיטי נשים היינו בפנים של מטה שטופלים להסיר השער דמאיס טפי: למה

רבינו חננאל

ספסקא פסולת הסלת פת קיבר צפירתי דלא אפתח יש מי שאומר שעירה שעדיין לא ילדה כלומר לא נפתחה רחמה ויש אומר עופות צפרים שמנות שלא ילדו: שכר המדי רמי ביה שערי וחומץ האדומי אין יינם של אדום מחמיץ עד שנותנים בו שעורים. פי' תמד דפורצני אחר שסוחטין הענבים נותני' שם על החרצנים שנים שלש' ימים ואחר כן סוחטין אותן והמים היוצאת מהן נקראת תמד דפורצני והנותן מים בשמרי יין וסוננן היוצא מהן נקרא תמד דרדוקא: זיתום המצרי משום שערי דאית ביה: זומא של צבעין. משום מיא דחיורא: עמילן של טבחים. הפת ששורין לשאוב הזוהמא של בשר נקרא עמילן של טבחים: קולן של סופרים. ויש מי שאומר קולה הדבר אחר הוא חצא אל נשי שמדבקין בו הסופרים ניירותיהם. אלו כולן השנויי' במשנתנו במקום שיש בתוכן מים אבל אין בהן מים הא קיי"ל מי פירות אין מחמיצין ומצאנוהו מפורש בתלמוד ארץ ישראל אלו עוברין בפסח וכו' אמר ר' מונא ובלבד על ידי מי': כותח הבבלי הוא דיהיב בגויה קמחא דשערי. תאני ר' חייא שלשה מיני מדינה הן הכותח והשכר והחומץ וארבעה מיני אומנות זיתום מעשה אומנות הרופאים וזומא של צבעים ועמילן של טבחים וקולן של סופרים. ר' אליעזר אומר אף תכשיטי נשים תריצנא טיפולי נשים: תנאי

תורה אור: יחזקאל כו; בראשית כה

[ילקוט פרשת תולדות וכן ביחזקאל כו רמז שסה לא נזכר בר יצחק וכנה א"א נסמן]

[צ"ל תנן]

[פי' תוס' ע"ז לד. ד"ה דורדיא ותוס' ב"ב צז: ד"ה אין הלכה]

[עי' תוספות לעיל לג: ד"ה מי סירוס]

מגילה ו.

[תוספתא דמאי רפ"א ע"ש]

ב"ב צו. חולין כה: מעשרות פ"א [מ"ו]

שבת קי. [ע"ש גרש"י]

[שבת קמז:]

[לבא כ"ה בפי' המשניות להרמב"ם ובפי' רש"י פ"ב דחולין כח. לבא לבע עור אדום ע"ש]

הגהות הב"ח

(א) גמ' לעולם פרורא דאושכפי ואמאי קרי: (ב) רש"י ד"ה והא תני רבי חייא וכו' ועמילן של טבחים כייר: (ג) תוס' ד"ה טיפולן וכו' היינו תכשיטי נשים: [אין לומר] דהקושיא היא דהוה ליה למימר טיפולי נשים ...

אלא קשיא להו דהי טיפולן כו' היינו תכשיטי נשים אם כן מאי קאמר ר"א אף תכשיטי נשים ... קאמר תכשיטי נשים ועיקר קושית התוס' הוא דה"ל לפרש במאי דפליגי ותירץ הר"י כו' דהכא ... של מעלה ובלבע בעל פניהם וכדתניא בפרק המצניע אשה לא העביר סרק על פניה מפני שאוב ... הפנים גם אם לא היתה טופלת ולכך [לא קרי לה] תכשיטי נשים אבל מה שטופלת בפנים ש... השער דמאוס טפי אם לא היתה טופלת קרי לה תכשיטי נשים דכיון דבזה מעביר המיאוס א"כ ...

רבי יהודה היא. דאמר לאו הבא מכלל לאמור לאו הוא: שרוע. הוא שאחת מעיניו גדולה ואחת קטנה וכן שאר אברים: קלוט. שפרסותיו קלוטות: נדבה תעשה אותו. לדמיו הקדישהו לבדק הבית ולנדר להעלות קרבן לא ירצה וכתב אותו אותו בעל מום אתה מתפיס לקדושת בדק הבית ואין אתה מתפיס תמימים הראויין למזבח לבדק הבית: וידבר ה' וגו'. בתחלת הפרשה כתיב: לא נאמר בדברים. נוטריקון לאמר: לאו אמור. אמור להן שיש איסור לאו בדברים והכא גבי פסח נמי כתיב בתחלת הפרשה ויאמר ה' אל משה ואל אהרן לאמר: האישבורן. לשון תורה אור שבירה שמשתבר הקרקע ויש בקעים שהמים נאספים ושוהין בתוכן ואין נבלעין ומחמיצין: הכי גרסינן הא דנפישי דקוו הא דלא נפישי דלא קוו. כשהן מרובות הן נקוות אל מקום אחד ואין נבלעות מהר ומחמיצות וכשהן מועטות לא קוו: שלנו. בלילה מפני שבימי ניסן המעיינות חמין שעדיין ימות הגשמים הן כדאמרינן במי שהיה (לקמן נד:) בימות הגשמים חמה מהלכת בשיפולו של רקיע לפיכך כל העולם צונן ומעיינות חמין הלכך מלינן בלילה ומצטננין: דרשה רב מתנה. ובלשון הקודש היו דורשין וכסבורין השומעין שמים שלו הוא אומר: דביתו. תרגום של לנו (דביתו): לא בחמה. לפי שחום השמש מחממת: ולא בחמי חמה. במים שהוחמו בחמה וכ"ש בחמי האור: הגרופים מן המולייר. דוד גדול של נחושת ותלוי על האור כל שעה ונחושתו עבה ואפי' כשאין שם אור מים שבשוליו חמים או פושרין: גרופים. לשון שירייס שממלין מנחושתו של שוליו: ואל תגביה ידה מן התנור. כלומר תהא עוסקת בבצק כל שעה: שמקטפת בו. טחה פני החררה במים: שמצננת בו ידיה. דאותן שמקטפת בהן מתחממות מחום ידיה והעיסה: עברה ולשה. בחמין: לא נתבקעו מותרות. ואע"ג דתנא אין לותתין הכא נמי לי"ש הואיל ואנו רואין שלא החמיץ שאין שם לא סימני שיאור ולא סימני סידוק: מחיתא מחיתינהו. כולם אריגה אחת אריגת' משום דבחדא איסורא דרבנן תנא אם עבר מותר באכילה בעית למימר נמי בכולהו: היכא דאתמר. בהדיא דלא קנסינן ליה אתמר והיכא דלא אתמר לא אתמר והלכך עברה ולשה בחמין קרובה למזיד היתה ואסור ולא דמי לבליקות של נכרים דאמרינן (לעיל דף מ.) (א) ממלא אדם כריסו מהן דהכא בעינן למיקנסה דעברה אדרבנן. מעשה אורג מתרגמינן עובד מחי (שמות כח):

הדרן עלך כל שעה

ויקרא כב | רבי יהודה היא *דתניא °שור ושה שרוע וקלוט נדבה תעשה אותו *אותו אתה מתפיס לבדק הבית ואי אתה מתפיס תמימים לבדק הבית מכאן אמרו כל המתפיס תמימים לבדק הבית עובר בעשה אין לי אלא בעשה בלא תעשה מנין ת"ל °וידבר ה' אל משה לאמר לימד על כל הפרשה כולה שהיא בלא תעשה דברי רבי יהודה *אמר לו רבי לבר קפרא מאי משמע אמר לו דכתיב לאמר לא נאמר בדברים בי רב אמרי לאמר לאו אמור: [ג]מי תשמישו של נחתום וכו': תני חדא שופכין במקום מדרון ואין שופכין במקום האישבורן ותניא אידך שופכין במקום האישבורן לא קשיא הא דנפישי דקוו הא דלא נפישי דלא קוו אמר רב יהודה אשה לא תלוש אלא במים שלנו דרשה רב מתנה בפפוניא למחר אייתו כולי עלמא חצבייהו ואתו לגביה ואמרו ליה הב לן מיא אמר להו אנא [ג]במיא דביתו אמרי *דרש רבא [ד]אשה לא תלוש בחמה ולא בחמי חמה ולא במים הגרופין מן המולייר °ולא תגביה ידה מן התנור עד שתגמור את כל הפת (וצריך*) שני כלים אחד שמקטפת בו ואחד שמצננת בו את ידיה איבעיא להו עברה ולשה מהו [ו]מר זוטרא אמר מותר רב אשי אמר אסור אמר מר זוטרא מנא אמינא לה דתניא *אין לותתין השעורין בפסח ואם לתת נתבקעו אסורים לא נתבקעו מותרין ורב אשי אמר *אטו כולהו חדא *מחיתא מחיתינהו היכא דאיתמר איתמר והיכא דלא איתמר לא איתמר:

הדרן עלך כל שעה

ואלו [ח]עוברין בפסח כותח הבבלי ושכר המדי וחומץ האדומי וזיתום המצרי וזומן של צבעים ועמילן של טבחים וקולן של סופרים ר"א אומר אף תכשיטי נשים זה הכלל כל שהוא ממין דגן הרי זה עובר בפסח [ט]הרי אלו באזהרה ואין בהן משום כרת: **גמ'** ת"ר שלשה דברים נאמרים בכותח הבבלי מטמטם את הלב ומסמא את העינים ומכחיש את הגוף מטמטם את הלב משום נסיובי דחלבא ומסמא את העינים משום מילחא ומכחיש את הגוף משום קומניתא דאומא *ת"ר ג' דברים מרבין הזבל וכופפין את הקומה ונוטלין *אחד מחמש מאות ממאור עיניו של אדם אלו הן *פת קיבר ושכר חדש וירק *חי ת"ר שלשה דברים ממעטין את הזבל וזוקפין את הקומה ומאירין את העינים אלו הן פת נקייה בשר שמן ויין ישן פת נקייה דסמידא

לאמר לימד על כל הפרשה שהיא בלאו [א]. נראה לר"י דהייט דוקא בהנך דברים דאית בהו לאו הבא מכלל עשה אבל שאר דברים לא:

הדרן עלך כל שעה

ואלו עוברין בפסח. פ"ה לעבור עליהן בבל יראה ובבל ימצא וגם ריב"א מדקדק מלשון עוברים דמשמע (ב) עוברין מן העולם ואין נראה לר"ת דמשמע דכל הנך מרבינן מכל מחמצת לא תאכלו ואפילו באכילה לא הוה מיחייב אי לאו דרבייא קרא ומהיכי תיתי בל יראה ובל ימצא ונראה לר"ת דאלו עוברין (ג) פי' האוכלין ועוברין הייט מעל השולחן דלאו בני מיכל נינהו אבל בל יראה ליכא: **רבי** אליעזר אומר אף תכשיטי נשים. הייט (ד) חמץ נוקשה ואפילו הוי חמץ דגן גמור על ידי תערובות מ"מ מדקאמר אף משמע דמודה לת"ק ובגמרא אמרי' דרבי אליעזר סבר נוקשה בעיניה בלא כלום לכך נראה דגרס רבי אליעזר בחד מינייהו או במתני' או בגמרא: הא

ואלו עוברין. עליהן בבל יראה ובבל ימצא וכולהו מפרש להו בגמרא זיתום וזומן וקולן ועמילן: תכשיטי נשים. בגמרא מפרש: מין דגן. חמשה מינין חיטין ושעורין וכוסמין ושבולת שועל ושיפון: ואין בהן כרת. אם אכלן אבל לאו יש באכילתן ובגמרא יליף לה כולה: **גמ'** מטמטם. לשון סתימה: מסמא את העינים משום מילחא. מלח סדומית יש שמסמא את העינים כשנוגע במלח וחוזר ונוגע בעין: נסיובי דחלבא. מישג"א: קומניתא דאומא. עיפושא פת שמתעפש לאחר זמן בתוך הכותח: וכופפין את הקומה. כלומר מתישין כוחו: ירק חי. כגון כרישין ובצלים וחזרין כשאוכל מהן הרבה תמיד: דסמידא

תמורה ז: | שם | [שם] | [נ"ל ביתו] | יומא כח: | [נ"ל וצריכה] | [לעיל מ. ברכות כד. וש"נ] | עירובין נה: | [ברכות מג: שבת קיג: תענית י:] | [חולין מח: פרש"י כביאור נכון] | [פי' פסולי' הסולת. ערוך] | [בעירובין ליתא מלת חי]

עין משפט נר מצוה

קפו א מיי' פ"ו מהל' ערכין הלכה ו :

קפז ב מיי' פ"ה מהל' חמץ הלכה טו סמג לאוין עט טור ש"ע או"ח סימן תנג סעיף ד:

קפח ג מיי' שם הלכה יא טור ש"ע או"ח סימן תנה סעיף א:

קפט ד מיי' שם הלכה יב טוש"ע או"ח סימן תנה סעיף א :

קצ ה מיי' שם טוש"ע שם סעיף ג :

קצא ו מיי' שם טוש"ע שם סעיף ג :

קצב ז מיי' שם טוש"ע שם סעיף ה :

א ח מיי' פ"ד מהלכות חמץ הלכה ח סמג לאוין עט טוש"ע או"ח סימן תמב סעיף א :

ב ט מיי' פ"א מהלכות חמץ הלכה ו :

רבינו חננאל

דמאכילתו בלילה שהוא עשה הבאתה לא תאכל ביום שהוא לאו וכל כי האי גונא עשה הוא ואין לוקין על עשה. אמר רב חסדא זו הברייתא לר' יהודה היא דתניא ושור ושה שרוע וקלוט נדבה תעשה אותו פי' אותו שהוא בעל מום אתה מתפיס נדבה לבדק הבית ואי אתה מתפיס תמימים לבדק הבית אלא לנדר מתפיס תמימין מכאן אמרו כל המתפיס תמימים לבדק הבית עובר בעשה דלאו הבא מכלל עשה עשה הוא ואין לי אלא בעשה בלא תעשה מנין ת"ל וידבר ה' אל משה לאמר לימד על הפרשה כולה שהיא בלאו דברי ר' יהודה א"ל ר' לבר קפרא והיכן אתה מוצא בזה הפסוק לאו אמר ליה דכתיב לאמר לא יומרו דברים מכאן למדנו כל התימר ממה ואפילו עשה עובר בלאו שהרי התמיר דבי רב אמרי כן פרשו לאמר לא אמר כלומר על כל מצוה שבתורה גזר עליהן בלאו: מי תשמישו של נחתום ישפכו מפני שהן נקיין ומחמיצין פירורי העיסה הנגררים מן הכלים שנשתמש בהן כמו שרוחץ אותם נקיין ומחמי ואוקימ' אי נפישי דקוו וקימו נשפכין במקום מדרון ואי לא נפישי אלא נבלעין ממקומן שופכין אפילו במקום האשבורן. אמר רב יהודה אין לשין אלא במים שלנו מאתמול ולנו בלילה דאינון מיא ביתו ונצטננו הרבה: דרש רבא אין לשין בחמה ולא בחמי חמה פי' במים שהוחמו בחמה ולא בחמין ולא אפילו במים הגרופין ולא במים הנרופין מן מושכין דכתיב (שופטים ה' כ"א) נחל קישון נרפם כלומר משכם ולא תגביה היד מן התנור כלומר לא תניח הפת מוטל ותתעסק בדבר אחר עד שתגמור את הפת ויש אומרים לא תגביה ידה מן הפת עד שתדבקהו בתנור וצריכה שני כלים במים אחד שמקטפת בו הפת בתוך התנור ואח' שמצננת ידיה עברה ולשה בחמין או במים נרופין או באלו כלן מאי ופשט רב אשי עברה ולשה אסור וקיימא לן כותיה: הדרן עלך כל שעה:

פ"ג ואלו עוברין בפסח כותח הבבלי ושכר המדי וכו' כותח הבבלי אסור בפסח משום קומניתא דאומא דהיא חמץ פת ניקודים ואסור לאכלו בבשר משום נסיובי דחלבא פי' נסיובא פי' ריפתא

הגהות הב"ח

(א) רש"י ד"ה היכא דאיתמר וכו' דאמרן לעיל דף מ ממלא אדם כריסו מהן :

גליון הש"ס

(ב) תוס' ד"ה ואלו וכו' מלשון עוברים דמשמע. כ"כ פירוש מדלא קאמר עוברין עליהם : (ג) בא"ד ונראה לר"ת דאלו עוברין פי' (האוכלין) תו"מ וכ"כ ס"א האוכלין : (ד) ד"ה ר' אליעזר וכו' הייט חמץ נוקשה. כ"כ ולפי זה מוסיף ר"א דלת"ק [דוקא נוקשה] בעיניה ולר"א אף נוקשה [ע"י תערובות] ואי הוי חמץ דגן גמור ע"י תערובות [מוסיף] ר"א דאפילו תכשיטי נשים [דלא] הוי ראויים לאכילה :

הגהות מהר"ב רנשבורג [א] תוס' ד"ה לאמר לימד על כל הפרשה שהיא בלאו. כ"ב עיין מנחות דף כ"א בתוס' ד"ה אף כאן וכו' ודוק :

—Said R. Ḥisda, The author of this [42a] is Rabbi Judah. For it was taught: *Either a bullock or a lamb that hath anything superfluous or lacking in its parts,* that *mayest thou offer for a freewill-offering; [but for a vow it shall not be accepted]*:[5] that thou mayest dedicate[6] for the Temple repair,[7] but thou mayest not dedicate unblemished [animals] for the Temple repair.[8] Hence it was said, Whoever dedicates unblemished [animals] for the Temple repair transgresses an affirmative precept. I only know [that he transgresses] an affirmative precept: whence do we know [that he transgresses also] a negative injunction? Because it is stated, *And the Lord spake unto Moses, saying* [lemor]:[9] this teaches concerning the whole section that it is subject to a negative injunction: this is R. Judah's view.[10] Rabbi asked Bar Ḳappara: How does that imply it? Said he to him, Because it is written, *'lemor'*: a 'not' [*'lo'*] was stated
a in [these] matters.[1] The School of Rab interpreted: *Lemor*, a negative injunction [*law*] was stated.

THE WATER USED BY A BAKER etc. One [Baraitha] taught: You must pour [it] out on a slope, but you may not pour [it] out on broken [ground].[2] While another [Baraitha] taught: You may pour [it] out on broken ground?—There is no difficulty: here it means that it [the water] is abundant, so that it collects;[3] there it means that it is not abundant, so that it does not collect.

Rab Judah said: A woman must knead [unleavened bread] only with water which was kept overnight.[4] R. Mattenah taught this [in a public lecture] at Papunia.[5] On the morrow all took their pitchers and repaired to him and demanded of him, 'Give us water'. Said he to them, 'I meant with water which has been kept overnight'.

Raba lectured: A woman may not knead in the sun, nor with water heated by the sun, nor with water collected[6] from the caldron;[7] and she must not remove her hand from the oven until she has finished all the bread;[8] and she requires two vessels, one with which she moistens [the dough], and the other wherein she cools her hands.[9]

The scholars asked: What if she transgressed and kneaded [in warm water]?—Mar Zuṭra said: [The bread] is permitted; R. Ashi
b said: It is forbidden. Mar Zuṭra said, Whence do I know[1] it?—Because it was taught: One may not wash barley on Passover; and if one did wash [them], if they split they are forbidden; if they did not split, they are permitted.[2] But R. Ashi says: Will you weave all these things in one web?[3] Where it was stated,[4] it was stated; and where it was not stated, it was not stated.

CHAPTER III

MISHNAH. NOW THE FOLLOWING [THINGS] MUST BE
c REMOVED[1] ON PASSOVER: BABYLONIAN KUTAḤ,[2] MEDIAN BEER, IDUMEAN VINEGAR, EGYPTIAN ZITHOM,[3] THE DYER'S BROTH,[4] COOK'S DOUGH,[5] AND THE SCRIBES' PASTE.[6] R. ELIEZER SAID: WOMEN'S ORNAMENTS TOO.[7] THIS IS THE GENERAL RULE: WHATEVER IS OF[8] THE SPECIES OF CORN[9] MUST BE REMOVED ON PASSOVER. THESE ARE SUBJECT TO A 'WARNING',[10] BUT THEY DO NOT INVOLVE KARETH.

GEMARA. Our Rabbis taught: Three things were said of Babylonian *kutaḥ*: it closes up the heart,[11] blinds the eyes, and emaciates the body. It closes up the heart, on account of the whey of milk; and it blinds the eyes, on account of the salt; and it emaciates the body, on account of the stale crusts.[12]

Our Rabbis taught: Three things increase one's motion, bend the stature, and take away a five hundredth part of a man's eyesight. They are these: Coarse black bread, new beer, and raw vegetables.

Our Rabbis taught: Three things decrease one's motion, straighten the stature, and give light to the eyes. These are they:

(5) Lev. XXII, 23. (6) Lit., 'cause to be seized'—with sanctity. (7) I.e., it must be redeemed and the redemption money devoted to the general needs of the Temple, as apart from sacrifices. (8) Since they are fit for the higher sanctity of sacrifices. (9) Ibid. 1. (10) Ex. XII, 8, which is now being discussed, has likewise the same superscription in v. 1, q.v.
a (1) *'Lemor'* is treated as contraction of *'lo amur'*. I.e., the laws contained in this section are subject to the admonition, 'do not violate them'. (2) Rashi: Broken ground contains shallows and cavities where the water will gather, instead of soaking in, and will thereby cause fermentation. Jast.: the place where water poured out would remain stagnant. (3) Hence it may not be poured out there. (4) Because in Nisan the water in the wells is warm (v. *infra* 94b), which hastens fermentation. Therefore it must be drawn the evening before it is required, so that it can cool off. (5) A town between Bagdad and Pumbeditha, and included in the juridical district of the latter. Obermeyer, *Landschaft*, p. 242.—He lectured in Hebrew, using the actual words *'mayim shelanu'*, which may also mean, water belonging to us.—This suggests that Hebrew was sufficiently well known by the masses to make public lectures in that language possible. (6) Lit., 'swept out'. (7) The last-named is generally warm, and heat hastens fermentation. (8) I.e., she must work on the dough all the time until it is baked. (9) Her hands too, if heated, induce fermentation.
b (1) Lit., 'says'. (2) V. *supra* 40a. Thus though it may not be done in the first place, if done it is permitted as long as there are no signs of leavening, and the same applies here. (3) You surely cannot bring all cases into one category. (4) That it is permitted if done.
c (1) I.e., they must not be used; lit., 'they must pass away' (R. Tam. and Jast.). Rashi: (On account of) the following things you transgress the injunctions, (leaven) *'shall not be seen'* and (leaven) *'shall not be found'* (in the house). (2) V. *supra* 21b, nn. c7 and 8. (3) A kind of beer. (4) Made of bran, to keep the dye fast. (5) Which is placed over the pot to absorb the froth. (6) With which they paste strips of parchment etc. together. All these are forbidden because they contain the product of cereals which turn leaven. (7) This is explained in the Gemara. (8) I.e., contains. (9) As enumerated in the Mishnah *supra* 35a. (10) This is a technical term, denoting a negative injunction, the violation of which is punished by flagellation. (11) Probably, makes its action sluggish. (12) Jast.: the decay of the flour-substance.

Raba said: If he ate it semi-roast, [41b] he is flagellated twice;[7] if he ate it boiled, he is flagellated twice;[8] [if he ate] semi-roast and boiled, he is flagellated thrice. Abaye said: We do not flagellate on account of an implied prohibition. Some maintain: He is not
a indeed flagellated twice,[1] but he is nevertheless flagellated once.[2] Others say, He is not even flagellated once, because [Scripture] does not particularize its interdict, like the interdict of muzzling.[3]

Raba said: If he [a nazirite] ate the husk [of grapes], he is flagellated twice; if he ate the kernel, he is flagellated twice; [for] the husk and the kernel, he is flagellated thrice.[4] Abaye maintained: We do not flagellate on account of an implied prohibition. Some say: He is indeed not flagellated twice, but he is nevertheless flagellated once.[5] Others maintain: He is not even flagellated once, because [Scripture] does not particularize its interdict, like the interdict of muzzling.

Our Rabbis taught: If he ate as much as an olive of semi-roast [paschal offering] before nightfall,[6] he is not culpable; [if he ate] as much as an olive of semi-roast flesh after dark, he is culpable. If he ate as much as an olive of roast meat before nightfall, he does not disqualify himself from [being one of] the members of the company;[7] [if he eats] as much as an olive of roast meat after
b dark,[1] he disqualifies himself from [being one of] the members of his company.

Another [Baraitha] taught: You might think that if he ate as much as an olive of semi-roast before nightfall he should be culpable; and it is a logical inference: if when he is subject to [the precept] 'arise and eat roast [flesh]',[2] he is subject to [the interdict] *'do not eat it semi-roast'*; then when he is not subject to [the precept], 'arise and eat roast', is it not logical that he is subject to [the interdict] *'do not eat it semi-roast?'* Or perhaps it is not so:[3] when he is not subject to [the precept], 'arise and eat roast', he is subject to, *'do not eat it semi-roast'*, [while] when he is subject to [the precept], 'arise and eat roast', he is not subject to [the interdict] *'do not eat it semi-roast'*, and do not wonder [thereat], for lo! it was freed[4] from its general interdict in respect to roast.[5] Therefore it is stated, *'Eat not of it semi-roast, nor boiled at all* [bashel mebushshal] *with water, but roast with fire'*. Now, *'but roast with fire'* should not be stated;[6] then why is *'but roast with fire'* stated? To teach you: When he is subject [to the command], 'Arise and eat roast', he is [also] subject to *'Eat not of it semi-roast'*; when he is not subject to [the command], 'Arise and eat roast', he is not subject to, *'Eat not of it semi-roast'*.[7]

Rabbi said: I could read *'bashel'*; why is *'mebushshal'* stated [too]? For I might think, I only know it[8] where he boiled it after nightfall. Whence do we know it if he boiled it during the day?[9] Therefore it is stated, *'bashel mebushshal'*, [implying] in all cases. But Rabbi has utilized this *'bashel mebushshal'* in respect of [flesh]
c roast[ed] in a pot and [flesh boiled] in other liquids?[1]—If so,[2] let Scripture say either *bashel bashel* or *mebushshal mebushshal:*[3] why *'bashel mebushshal'?* Hence you infer two things from it.

Our Rabbis taught: If he ate roast [paschal offering] during the day, he is culpable; and [if he ate] as much as an olive of semi-roast after nightfall, he is culpable. [Thus] he teaches roast similar to half-roast: just as semi-roast [after nightfall] is [interdicted] by a negative injunction, so is roast [before nightfall] subject to a negative injunction. As for half-roast, it is well: it is written, *'Eat not of it semi-roast'*. But whence do we know [the negative injunction for] roast? Because it is written, *'And they shall eat the flesh in that night'*: only at night, but not by day. But this is a negative injunction deduced by implication from an affirmative command, and every negative injunction deduced by implication from an affirmative command is [technically] an affirmative command?[4]

(7) Once on account of the injunction against semi-roast, and again because of the interdict, *'Eat not . . . but roast with fire'*. (8) On account of the injunction against boiled flesh, and again as in the case of semi-roast meat.

a (1) Since he is flagellated on account of the direct prohibition, *'Eat not of it semi-roast'*, or, *'nor boiled'*, he is not flagellated on account of the implied interdict too. (2) Rashi: E.g., he who boils it in the hot springs of Tiberias. Since there is no *explicit* injunction, we fall back upon the *implied* injunction. Tosaf.: If he was merely warned against violating the injunction, *'Eat not of it . . . but roast with fire'*. (3) V. Deut. XXV, 4. This is an interdict explicitly forbidding a particular action, and this is the model of all interdicts the disregard of which involves flagellation, since it immediately follows the law of flagellation (ibid. v. 3). But the interdict of *'eat not of it . . . but roast with fire'* does not particularize any method of preparation as forbidden. (4) V. Num. VI, 4: *All the days of his naziriteship he shall eat nothing that is made of the grape vine, from the kernels even to the husk*. According to Raba, the kernels and the husk are explicitly prohibited, while they are also included in the *implied* prohibition of *'he shall eat nothing that is made of the grape vine'*, and the offender is flagellated on account of each. (5) Rashi: E.g., if he ate the leaves of the vine; cf. n. a2. (6) Lit., 'while it was yet day'—on the fourteenth of Nisan. (7) Each paschal offering had to be eaten by one company, the members of which had registered for that particular animal. It might not be eaten by two companies, while on the other hand no man might eat in two separate places. It is now taught that if he eats some roast meat *before* nightfall, he is not disqualified from eating elsewhere with his company after nightfall, the earlier eating not being regarded as eating of the paschal offering in this sense.

b (1) Not in the company where he registered. (2) I.e., after nightfall. (3) I.e., perhaps a different argument is to be used. (4) Lit.. 'permitted'. (5) For even roast paschal offering is not permitted before nightfall, as it is written, *'and they shall eat the flesh* in that night, *roast with fire'*, which implies, but not before; at night this implied prohibition is lifted. Hence we might argue: granted that the general interdict is not lifted at the outset in respect of semi-roast too, yet if he ate it he is not liable to punishment. (6) For the previous verse states: *And they shall eat the flesh in that night, roast with fire*. (7) I.e., flagellation for eating semi-roast meat of the paschal offering is incurred only on the evening of the fifteenth, when one is bidden to eat the roast of the Passover sacrifice, but not on the day of the fourteenth, before the obligation commences. (8) That boiled paschal offering flesh must not be eaten. (9) That even then it may not be eaten at night.

c (1) *Supra 41a*. (2) That that is its only teaching. (3) Granted that the repetition is necessary, the same grammatical form could be repeated. (4) Which does not involve flagellation.

מסורת הש"ס

עין משפט נר מצוה

תורה אור

לוקה שתים מבושל לוקה שתים נא ומבושל לוקה שלש *אביי אמר אין לוקין על לאו שבכללות איכא דאמרי *תרתי הוא דלא לקי חדא מיהת לקי איכא דאמרי חדא נמי לא לקי דלא מייחד לאויה *כלאו דחסימה *רבא *אמר ב אכל זג לוקה שתים זג וחרצן לוקה שלש אביי אמר אין לוקין על לאו שבכללות איכא דאמרי תרתי הוא דלא לקי חדא מיהת לקי איכא דאמרי חדא נמי לא לקי דלא מייחד לאויה כלאו דחסימה ת"ר אכל כזית נא מבעוד יום פטור כזית נא משחשיכה חייב אכל כזית צלי מבעוד יום לא פסל עצמו מבני חבורה כזית צלי משחשיכה פסל עצמו מבני החבורה תניא אידך יכול אכל כזית נא מבעוד יום יהא חייב ודין הוא ומה בשעה שישנו בקום אכול צלי ישנו בבל תאכל נא בשעה שאינו בקום אכול צלי אינו דין שישנו בבל תאכל נא או לא בשעה שאינו בקום אכול צלי ישנו בבל תאכל נא בשעה שישנו בקום אכול צלי אינו בבל תאכל נא ואל תתמה שהרי הותר מכללו אצל צלי תלמוד לומר °אל תאכלו ממנו נא ובשל מבושל במים כי אם צלי אש שאין תלמוד לומר כי אם צלי אש ומה תלמוד לומר כי אם צלי אש לומר לך *בשעה שישנו בקום אכול צלי ישנו בבל תאכל נא בשעה שאינו בקום אכול צלי אינו בבל תאכל נא *רבי אומר אקרא אני בשל מה ת"ל מבושל שיכול אין לי אלא שבישלו משחשיכה בשלו מבעוד יום מנין תלמוד לומר בשל מבושל מכל מקום והאי בשל מבושל אפקיה רבי לצלי קדר ולשאר משקין אם כן לימא קרא או בשל בשל או מבושל מבושל מאי בשל מבושל שמעת מינה תרתי תנו רבנן ד אכל צלי מבעוד יום חייב וכזית נא משחשיכה חייב קתני צלי דומיא דנא מה נא בלאו אף צלי בלאו בשלמא נא כתיב אל תאכלו ממנו נא אלא צלי מנלן דכתיב °ואכלו את הבשר בלילה הזה *בלילה אין ביום לא ה והאי לאו הבא מכלל עשה הוא וכל לאו *הבא מכלל עשה עשה אמר רב חסדא הא מני רבי

שמות יב

שם

לוקה שתים · משום לא תאכל נא ומשום לא תאכלו כי אם צלי אש דכי אם צלי אש נמי אלאו דלא תאכלו קאי : מבושל לוקה שתים · משום מבושל ומשום לא תאכלו כי אם צלי אש : לאו שבכללות הוא · דכולל בו כל מיני בשולים שאינן צלייה לאסור : איכא דאמרי תרתי הוא דלא לקי. כיון שהוא לוקה משום נא [או]משום מבושל תו לא לקי משום כי אם צלי אש: אבל חדא מיהא לקי· כגון המבשל בחמי טבריא ואכלו דאין כאן מלקות דבישול ולא מלקות של נא לוקה משום כי אם צלי אש : ואיכא דאמרי חדא נמי לא לקי· משום כי אם צלי אש דלא מיוחד לאויה דידיה כלאו דחסימה שהוא מפרש איסורו וסמיכא ליה פרשת מלקות לעיל מיניה : אכל זג לוקה שתים · נזיר שאכלו משום זג לא יאכל ומשום מכל אשר יעשה מגפן היין מחרצנים וגו' דלא יאכל קאי נמי אמכל אשר יעשה: לאו שבכללות· אין לוקין על מכל אשר יעשה דלאו שבכללות הוא שכולל חרצנים וזגים וענבים לחים ויבשים ועלים ולולבין : תרתי לא לקי · היכא דאכל זג או חרצן ולקי עלייהו לא לקי תו משום מכל אשר יעשה ומודה אביי דאם אכל זג וחרצן לוקה שתים דכיון דמפורש כל אחד לעצמו קאי נמי אלאו דלא יאכל והוי כמאן דכתב לאו אכל חד וחד והכי מוכח במסכת נזיר דלא פליג אביי אלא אמלקות דמכל אשר יעשה: חדא מיהא לקי· אם אכל עלין ולולבין דאין כאן מלקות דזג וחרצן לקי משום לאו דמכל אשר יעשה:אכל כזית נא מבעוד יום פטור· טעמא מפרש לקמיה מקרא:לא פסל את עצמו מבני חבורה· דאמרי' לקמן (דף פו·) אין הפסח נאכל לא בשתי חבורות כאחד ואין האוכל אוכל בשני מקומות ונפקא לן מבבית אחד יאכל ומתרגמינן בחבורא חדא יתאכל ואכילה דמבעוד יום לאו אכילה היא ומותר לאכול משתחשך עם בני חבורה שנמנה עמהן : כזית צלי משחשיכה · מפסח שנמנה עליו: פסל עצמו מבני חבורה· כדפרישית שאין האוכל מותר לאכול הימנו בשני מקומות : בשעה שאינו בקום אכול צלי · דאין לו היתר אכילת צלי אינו דין שישנו בלאו דלא תאכל נא : או לא · או לא נאמר כן אלא בענין אחר בשעה שישנו בקום אכול צלי דהיינו בלילה דכתיב ואכלו את הבשר בלילה הזה אינו בבל תאכל נא : ואל תתמה שהרי הותר מכללו אצל צלי · דהא אפילו צלי היה אסור לאכול ביום כדכתיב ואכלו את הבשר בלילה הזה ולא ביום וכשחשכה הותר מכלל איסור עשה דצלי ונימא נמי נהי דלא הותר לכתחלה אכל נא מיהו לא לחייב עליה אם אכלו : שאין תלמוד לומר כי אם צלי אש · דהא כתיב לעיל מיניה צלי אש ומצות וגו' : אקרא אני בשל · דייך הוה ליה בקריאת בשל : אין לי · שיתחייב על אכילת בשר אלא אם כן בישלו משחשיכה שהוא עיקר זמנו : בישלו מבעוד יום. ואכלו משתחשך מנין : והא אפקיה · רבי גופיה דרשיה לעיל לשאר משקין ולצלי קדר : בשל מבושל · מדשני בדבוריה דריש ביה דרשה אחריתי נמי : כזית צלי מבעוד יום חייב · מפרש ליה לקמיה : קתני · חיובא דצלי דמבעוד יום דומיא דחיובא דנא משחשיכה :

דבי

אבל כזית נא לוקה שתים משום נא ומשום כי אם צלי אש דהוי כאילו כתיב אל תאכלו כי אם צלי אש · הקשה הרר"י דאורליינ"ש אמאי חשבי' בריש אלו נערות (כתובות דף ל·) בעולה לכהן גדול בעשה גרידא דכי אם בתולה מעמיו כתיב הא כי היכי דחשבינן הכא כי אם צלי אש בלאו ה"נ ה"ל לאיחשובי בעולה לכהן גדול בלאו דהוי כאילו כתיב לא יקח כי אם בתולה וי"ל דכי אם בתולה לא חשיב לאו משום דסיפא דקרא מוכח עליו דהוי עשה דכתיב כי אם בתולה מעמיו יקח אשה : **איכא** דאמרי חדא מיהא לקי· פ"ה בחי וחמי טבריא חייב משום כי אם צלי אש וקשה לר"ת א"כ בין לאביי בין לרבא תיקשי להו ברייתא דלעיל דתניא נא ומבושל אמרתי לך ולא חי אלמא לא לקי על חי ועוד דאמר בפ' המקבל (ב"מ דף קטו:) אפלוגתא דרב הונא ורב יהודה בחובל ריחים ורכב דרב יהודה אמר לוקה שתים ורב הונא אמר לוקה שלש ומסיק רבא אנא דאמרי אפילו כרב יהודה עד כאן לא קאמר רב יהודה התם אלא דכי נפש הוא חובל לדברים אחרים הוא דאתא אבל הכא כי אם צלי אש למאי אתא זלפ"ה הא איצטריך לחי ולחמי טבריא לכ"ע לר"ת דחי לא לקי לכו"ע דכי אם צלי אש לא משמע דאתא למלקות אלא לעשה דכי אם צלי אש תאכלו ולא דמי לכי נפש הוא חובל דבההוא מודו כו"ע דלוקה אשאר דברים כדקתני התם בהדיא בברייתא חבל זוג של ספרים וצמד של פרות לוקה שתים דכי נפש הוא חובל משמע שפיר בלשון לאו שהוא נתינת טעם כל שהוא דבר נפש לא תחבול ואתא שפיר הא דקאמר רבא התם דכי נפש הוא חובל אתא לשאר דברים אבל כי אם צלי אש לא אתא אלא לעשה ונא ומבושל דווקא פליגי דרבא סבר להכי סמכיה לאו ללקות עליו על נא ומבושל שהם בני מילקא ואביי אמר אין לוקין על לאו שבכללות והא דקאמר חדא מיהת מילקא לקי הכי פי' אם התרו בו משום כי אם צלי אש לבדו אבל על מלקות נא ומבושל לא ילקה דלהכי מהני מה שכתבו בלשון כלל ומיהו לבדו מיהא לקי שסמכו לאו שהם בני מלקות : **אמר** רבא אכל זג לוקה שתים · הא פלוגתא דאביי ורבא איתמר איפכא בפ' שלשה מינין (נזיר דף לה:) וכהנה רבות בגמרא* : **שאין** ת"ל כי אם צלי אש · אע"ג דאיצטריך להלקות עליו משום כי אם צלי אש היינו נמי משום דסמכיה לנא ומבושל : **אם** כן לימא קרא בשל בשל או מבושל מבושל · הכא משמע דאורחיה דקרא לכפול תיבה אחת בענין אחד טפי מבשני עניינים וכן במרובה (ב"ק דף סה·) גבי המצא תמצא ובהחובל (שם דף פה:) גבי ורפא ירפא וקשה דבריש היו בודקין (סנהדרין ד"מ:) קאמר מדהוי ליה למיכתב דרוש תדרוש או חקור תחקור וכתב היטב שמע מינה לאפנויי משמע דאי הוה כתב הכי לא הוה מופנה ושמא התם לא חש לדקדק בלשון רק להוכיח דמופנה* : לאמר

קפב א מיי' פ"ח מהל' ק"פ הלכה ד ופ' י"ח מהלכות סנהדרין הלכה ג :

קפג ב מיי' פ"ה מהל' נזיר הלכה ח :

קפד ג מיי' פ"ח מהל' ק"פ הלכה ד :

קפה ד ה שם הלכה ה :

רבינו חננאל

אכל נא לוקה שתים אחת משום נא ואחת משום צלי אש אכלו מבושל לוקה שתים נא ומבושל לוקה שלש ואביי אמר אין לוקין על לאו שבכללות כלומר לאו אחד כולל האוכל נא והאוכל מבושל שנא' אל תאכלו ממנו נא ובשל מבושל במים וגו': **איכא** דאמרי לאביי אכל נא ומבושל חדא מיהא לקי איכא דאמרי לא לקי כלל עד דמיחד לאויה כלאו דחסימה : **אמר** רבא נזיר שאכל זג לוקה שתים אחת משום שנאמר (במדבר ו' ד') מחרצנים ועד זג וגו' ואחת משום שנא' (שם) מכל אשר יעשה מגפן היין חרצן לוקה שתים זג וחרצן לוקה שלש אביי אמר אין לוקין וכו' : **ת"ר** אכל כזית נא מבעוד יום פטור מאי טעמא אל תאכלו ממנו נא ובשל מבושל במים כי אם צלי אש בשעה שישנו בקום אכול צלי שהוא בלילה דכתיב ואכלו את הבשר בלילה הזה ישנו בבל תאכל נא מבעוד יום שאינו בבל תאכל צלי אינו חייב אם אכל נא אכל כזית נא משחשכה חייב שהרי ישנו בקום אכול צלי אכל כזית צלי מבעוד יום לא פסל עצמו מבני חבורה שאינה אכילת כזית צלי משחשכה פסל עצמו מבני חבורה וסוגיא דשמעתא כולה בענין הזה ואקשי' אהא דתניא אכל כזית צלי מבעוד יום חייב אמאי לאו הבא מכלל עשה הוא האיך שנא' (שמות יב ח) ואכלו את הבשר בלילה הזה צלי אש בלילה אכול אותו ולא ביום וזהו לאו הבא מכלל עשה

[הכיאו הוס' מנחות נח: בפרוטרוט כד"ה ואיכא]

מנחות נח:

[שם]

[מכות יג: טו.]

[נ"ל אמר רבא עי' תוס' דסכת ד"ה אמר רבה אנוס גי' הכ"מ בפ"ה מהלכות נזירות אמר אביי אכל זג וכו' רבא אמר אין לוקין על לאו שבכללות]

ב"מ קטו.

מכילתא פ' בא

[לקמן קב:]

יבמות נד: ע. סה. עג: זבחים לד. חולין פא.

[וע"ע תוס' כתובות לג: ד"ה אין ותוס' ב"ק סה. ד"ה לכתוב ותוס' מנחות יז: ד"ה לכתוב]

אחרוסת קאמר מר או אחרדל קאמר מר א"ל למאי נפקא מינה לדרב כהנא דאמר רב כהנא מחלוקת לתוך החרדל אבל לתוך החרוסת דברי הכל ישרף מיד א"ל *לא שמיע לי כלומר לא סבירא לי א"ר אשי כוותיה דרב כהנא מסתברא מדאמר שמואל *אין הלכה כרבי יוסי מאי לאו(א) צמותי הוא דלא צמית הא חמועי מחמעא לא דילמא לא מצמת צמית ולא חמוע מחמע: אין מבשלין וכו': ת"ר °במים אין לי אלא במים שאר משקין מניין אמרת קל וחומר ומה מים שאין מפיגין טעמן אסורין שאר משקין שמפיגין טעמן לא כ"ש רבי אומר במים אין לי אלא מים שאר משקין מניין °ת"ל °ובשל מבושל מ"מ מאי בינייהו איכא בינייהו צלי קדר ורבנן האי בשל מבושל מאי עבדי להו מבעי ליה לכדתניא *בשלו ואח"כ צלאו או שצלאו ואח"כ בשלו חייב בשלמא בשלו ואח"כ צלאו חייב דהא בשליה אלא צלאו ואח"כ בשלו הא צלי אש הוא אמאי אמר רב כהנא הא מני רבי יוסי היא *דתניא יוצאין ברקיק השרוי ובמבושל שלא נימוח דברי ר"מ רבי יוסי אומר יוצאין ברקיק השרוי אבל לא במבושל אע"פ שלא נימוח עולא אמר אפילו תימא ר"מ שאני הכא דאמר קרא *ובשל מבושל מ"מ ת"ר °יכול צלאו כל צורכו יהא חייב ת"ל °אל תאכל ממנו נא ובשל מבושל במים נא ובשל מבושל אמרתי לך ולא שצלאו כל צורכו היכי דמי אמר רב אשי °דשויא חרוכא תנו רבנן °יכול אכל כזית חי יהא חייב תלמוד לומר אל תאכלו ממנו נא ובשל נא ובשל אמרתי לך ולא חי יכול יהא מותר תלמוד לומר °כי אם צלי אש היכי דמי נא אמר רב כדאמרי פרסאי אברנים *אמר רב חסדא °המבשל בחמי טבריא בשבת פטור פסח שבשלו בחמי טבריא חייב מאי שנא בשבת דלא דתולדות אש בעינן וליכא פסח נמי לאו תולדות אש הוא אמר רבא °מאי חייב °דקתני דקא עבר משום צלי אש רב חייא בריה דרב נתן מתני לה להא דרב חסדא בהדיא א"ר חסדא המבשל בחמי טבריא בשבת פטור ופסח שבשלו בחמי טבריא חייב שעבר משום צלי אש אמר *רבא *אכלו נא לוקה

שמות יב

רש"י

אחרוסת קאמר · מי איכא לך דרבנן נמי אחרוסת פליגי: לא סבירא לי · אלא בחרוסת נמי שרו והלכה כמותן: כוותיה דרב כהנא מסתברא · דאמר רבנן אחרוסת לא פליגי וכי אמר שמואל הלכה כחכמים אחרדל קאמר: אין הלכה כרבי יוסי · דאמר לעיל חומץ צומתן: מאי לאו · מדלא צמית חטין שהתחילו ליבקע כבר אלמא (ב) בשאר משקין הוא אחמועי נמי מחמע את העיסה מתחלה לתוכו כדרב כהנא אלמא שמואל כרב כהנא סבירא ליה וכי קאמר שמואל הלכה כחכמים אחרדל קאמר ולא אחרוסת: לא צמית · את שהתחיל להחמיץ ולא מחמע נמי את הניתן לתוכו דלא הוי כמים: במים · ובשל מבושל במים: שמפיגין טעמן · שנותנין בו טעם שלהן: ובשל מבושל · רבויא הוא דהוה ליה למיכתב נא ומבושל: צלי קדר · שמבשלין אותו בקדירה בלא מים ובלא שום משקה אלא מים הנפלטין משמנו למאן דיליף לה מק"ו הכא שרי לרבי דיליף מרבויא האי נמי בשל מבושל הוא: חייב · מלקות על אכילתו: ר' יוסי היא · דאמר בישול לאחר אפיה בישול הוא: יוצאין · ידי חובת מצה ברקיק השרוי בתבשיל לאחר אפייתו ואף על פי שמתמסמס לחם הוא כל זמן שהוא קיים שלא נימוח לגמרי וכן במבושל: אבל לא במבושל · דלאו לחם קרינא ביה ואע"פ שכבר נאפה בתנור הואיל וחזר ובישלו ביטלו מתורת לחם: שאני הכא דרבייה קרא · ובשל מבושל דהוי ליה למכתב נא ומבושל וגזירת הכתוב הוא בפסח: יכול צלאו כל צורכו · ואח"כ בשלו יהא חייב והאי תנא הוא דאמר לעיל צלאו ואח"כ בישלו חייב ליכא אחריני יכול צלאו כל צורכו דשויא חרוכה כדמפרש יהא חייב דלאו צלי אש הוא אלא קלי אש ושרוף וזה עיקר ולאשון אינו כלום דההוא תנא דרבי קרא צלאו ואחר כך בישלו מה לי שויה חרוכה מה לי לא שויה חרוכה: חרוכה · שרוף: חי · לגמרי שלא נצלה כלל: נא · צלי ואינו צלי: יכול יהא מותר. לאכול ממנו חי לכתחלה דלאפי' איסורא נמי ליכא תלמוד לומר אל תאכלו ממנו נא כי אם צלי אש ולא זה אלא בצלי והויא לאו שבכללות והאי תנא סבר אין לוקין על לאו שבכללות: כדאמרי פרסאי · אברנים · שבלשון פרסי קרויה אברנים בלשון הקודש קרי נא: חמי טבריא · מעינות רותחין: פסח שבישלו בחמי טבריא חייב · על אכילתו וקא סלקא דעתך משום דלא תאכל מבושל: דלאו תולדות אש היא · הלכך לאו בישול הוא דליהוי חייב משום אב מלאכה: משום צלי אש · לאו דלא תאכל כי אם צלי אש איכא ולא לאו דבישול וסבר לוקין על לאו שבכללות: בהדיא · דחייב רב חסדא משום צלי אש ולאו משום בישול: לוקה

תוספות

לא שמיע לי כלומר לא סבירא לי · אף על גב דהוא כוותיה קסבר מתניתין פליגא:

מדאמר שמואל אין הלכה כרבי יוסי · השתא מדמי חומץ לחרוסת וע"כ נראה לר"י דעולא דאמר לעיל בין כך ובין כך אסור משום לך לך אמרינן נזירא סחור סחור לכרמא לא תקרב פליג אדרב כהנא דהא רב כהנא דאמר אבל לתוך חרוסת לדברי הכל ישרף ולעולא לא אסר אלא משום לך לך אמרינן:

מאי לאו מדלא צמית מחמע · קשה לר"י דלעיל קאמר י"א אף נותן את החומץ ואח"כ וכו' ופריך וקמה כר' יוסי דאמר שורן בחומץ וחומץ צומתן משמע דתנא קמא דיש אומרים היינו ת"ק דר' יוסי דלית ליה דחומץ צמית ואפילו הכי קאמר נותן הקמח ואח"כ נותן את החומץ אלמא קסבר דאע"ג דלא צמית חמועי נמי לא מחמע ואור"י דלעיל איירי לפי המסקנא דהכא:

אין מבשלין את הפסח לא במשקין וכו' · תימה למה שנאו כאן כאן אי משום דתנא ירקות שלוקות ומבושלות א"כ מיד היה לו לשנות בסמוך אחריה:

איכא בינייהו צלי קדר · פי' אי לוקה עליו אי לא אבל לכולי עלמא פסול הוי ועשה נמי איכא ביה דצלי מחמת ד"א הוא כדאמרינן בריש כילד צולין (לקמן עה:) נטף מרוטבו על החרס וחזר עליו יטול את מקומו וכן נגע בחרסו של תנור יקלוף את מקומו וכן שאר משקין לא איצטריך למילף אלא לענין מלקות אבל פשיטא לכלל הפסול איכא עשה דכי אם צלי אש וא"ת והיכי יליף שאר משקין מק"ו והא אין מזהירין מן הדין ויש לומר דהאי קל וחומר אינו אלא מגלה דבישול דקרא איירי אף בשאר משקין:

אמר רב כהנא הא מני ר' יוסי היא · תימה דרב כהנא דמוקי לה כרבי יוסי לרבנן האי בשל מבושל מאי עבדי להו דלאו ולאחר כך בישלו לא צריך קרא דמסברא ידעינן דבישול מבטל הצליה כדאמר רבי יוסי גבי מצה ויש לומר דרב כהנא סבר דרבי יוסי יליף מבטל מבושל דבישול מבטל אפייה:

אבל לא במבושל · פ"ה דבישול מבטל ליה מתורת לחם ולפי' מיירי בבלילתו רכה דבלילתו עבה לא נפיק מתורת לחם כדפירש לעיל ור"י מפרש דמיירי בבלילתו עבה ופסולה משום מצה עשירה ומייתי דכי היכי דסבר רבי יוסי דבישול מפיק ליה מתורת אפייה לשוויה מצה עשירה כאילו לא נאפה ה"נ גבי פסח עקר מיניה בישול שם צליה:

עולא אמר אפי' תימא ר' מאיר וכו' · הכא מדמי פסח לבישול מצה והיינו דלא כמסקנא דכילד מברכין (ברכות דף לח:) דקאמר התם עולא משמיה דר' יוחנן שלקות מברכין עליהם שהכל לרבי יוסי דאית ליה הכא גבי מצה דבישול מבטל האפיה ה"נ בישול מבטל מהם שם ירק ודחי ע"כ לא קאמר רבי יוסי אלא דבעינן טעם מצה ועולא לטעמיה דלא בעי לדחויה הכא טעמא דרבי יוסי דבעינן טעם מצה והתם נמי קאמר דלרבי יוסי מברך שהכל: אכל

עין משפט נר מצוה

קעז א ב מיי' פ"ח מהל' ק"פ הלכה ז ח סמג לאוין שנ:

קעח ג מיי' פ"ז מהל' חמץ הלכה ו טור שו"ע או"ח סימן תסא סעיף ד:

קעט ד ה ו מיי' פ"ח מהלכות ק"פ הל' ו סמג לאוין שנ:

קפ ז מיי' פ"ע מהלכות שבת הלכה ג:

קפא ח מיי' פ"ח מהל' ק"פ הלכה י:

רבינו חננאל

במשקין ולא במי פירות אבל סכין אותו ומטבילין אותו בהם: ת"ר ובשל מבושל במים אין לי אלא במים שאר משקים מנין אמרת קל וחומר ומה מים שאין מפיגין טעם הבשר אסור שאר משקין שמפיגין טעמו של בשר אינו דין שאסור. ר' אומר במים אין לי אלא במים שאר משקין כמים מי פירות מנין ת"ל ובשל מבושל במים מכל מקום לר' דמפיק ליה מלשון בשול אפי' צלי קדר כיון שהוא עשוי כמין בשול אסור הוא ות"ק דמטעם מכח הפגת הטעם צלי קדר מותר שאינו מפיג טעמו ות"ק דמייתי ליה לשאר משקין בק"ו ובשל מבושל מאי עביד ליה מבעי ליה דאפילו אם בשלו אחר שצלאו או צלאו אחר שבשלו חייב וכר' יוסי דתאני יוצא ברקיק השרוי אבל לא במבושל ואע"פ שלא נימוח הרי לר' יוסי אע"פ כי רקיק זה אפוי הוא כיון שבשלו יצא מתורת אפוי והרי הוא כמבושל כך זה הבשר אע"פ שצלאו כיון שבשלו יצא מתורת צלי והרי הוא כמבושל. צלאו כל צרכו כגון דשויא חרוכא פטור כי אינו חייב אלא על נא ועל מבושל פי' נא אברנים כגון שנצלה מעט אבל בשר חי לגמרי דלא עבר באש כלל אינו חייב: אמר רב חסדא המבשל בשבת בחמי טבריא פטור דלאו תולדות אור הן פסח שבשלו בחמי טבריא פטור אמר רבא ועובר משום דבעינן צלי אש וליכא: אמר רבא

[ג"י סה"מ בפרק ח' מהלכות ק"פ דין ד' אמר אביי אכל נא לוקה וכו' רבא אמר אין לוקין על לאו שבכללות וכ"כ סה"מ עוד בפרק י"ח מהלכות סנהדרין דין ג' וע"ע מ"ש הכ"מ פ"ס מהלכות מזוזת דין ח' ורא"ש לגירסתם מ"ש תוס' שבת דף כג: ד"ה גזירה ועוד שם ע: ד"ה נודע וכו' דאין מהדרך שלא מצינו בכל הש"ס שקבע להקדים רבא לאביי וכ"כ בשאר דוכתי וכ"כ הרא"ש פ"ד דב"מ סימן י"ט שלא מצינו בכל הש"ס שקבע דברי רבא קודם וכו' ע"ש.]

מסורת הש"ס

[עירובין קב: וש"נ]

[לעיל מ.]

[תוספתא פ"ה]

ברכות לח:

[עי' תוס' חולין קטו. ד"ה שאין]

שבת מ:

[יותר נכון לגרוס מאי חייב דקאמר]

ב"מ קטו:

הגהות הב"ח

(א) גמ' אין הלכה כרבי יוסי מאי לאו מדלא צמית חמועי נמי מחמעא כצ"ל ותיבות צמותי הוא ותיבת הא נמחק: (ב) רש"י ד"ה מאי לאו וכו' אלמא בשאר משקין אחמועי כצ"ל ותיבת הוא נמחק:

R. Naḥman b. Isaac to R. Huna the son of Rab Judah: [41a] Do you[2] say it in reference to *ḥaroseth*,[3] or do you say it in reference to mustard? What is the practical difference? asked he.—In respect to R. Kahana's [dictum]. For R. Kahana said: The controversy is [about putting flour] into mustard; but [if it was put] into *ḥaroseth*, all agree that it must be burnt immediately.[4] I have not heard it, he replied to him, as if to say, I do not agree with it. R. Ashi said: Logic supports R. Kahana, since Samuel said: The *halachah* is not as R. Jose.[5] Surely then, since it [vinegar] does not bind, it does indeed cause fermentation?[6]—No: perhaps it neither binds nor promotes fermentation.

ONE MAY NOT BOIL etc. Our Rabbis taught: [*Eat not of it raw, nor boiled at all*] *with water:*[7] I only know [that it may not be boiled] in water; whence do we know [it of] other liquids? You can answer, [it follows] *a minori:* if water, which does not impart its taste,[8] is forbidden; then other liquids, which impart their taste, how much more so![1] Rabbi said: '*With water*': I only know it of water; whence do we know [it of] other liquids? Because it is stated, '*nor boiled at all*',[2] [implying] in all cases.[3] Wherein do they differ?—They differ in respect of [that which is] roasted in a pot.[4] And the Rabbis: how do they utilize this [phrase] '*nor boiled at all*'?—They employ it for what was taught: If he boiled it and then roasted it, or roasted it and then boiled it, he is liable.[5] As for 'if he boiled it and then roasted it, he is liable,' that is well, seeing that he boiled it.[6] But if he roasted it and then boiled it, surely it is '*roast with fire*'; why [then is he liable]?—Said R. Kahana: The author of this is R. Jose. For it was taught: The law[7] is complied with by [eating] an [unleavened] wafer that is soaked[8] or boiled, but not dissolved: this is the view of R. Meir. R. Jose said: The law is complied with by [eating] a wafer that is soaked, but not with one that is boiled, even if not dissolved.[9] 'Ulla said: You may even say [that it agrees with] R. Meir;[10] here it is different, because Scripture saith, '*nor boiled at all*', [implying] in all cases.[11]

Our Rabbis taught: You might think that if he roasted it as much as it needs,[12] he should be liable. Therefore it is stated: *Eat not of it semi-roast nor boiled at all with water:* semi-roast or boiled did I forbid[13] thee, but not that which is roasted as much as it needs.[14] How is that meant?—Said R. Ashi: That he rendered it charred meat.

Our Rabbis taught: You might think that if he ate as much
b as an olive of raw meat,[1] he should be liable; therefore it is stated, *Eat not of it semi-roast* [na] *nor boiled at all* [*with water*]: semi-roast and boiled did I forbid thee, but not raw. You might think that it is permitted; therefore it is stated, '*but roast with fire*'. How is '*na*' understood?—Said Rab: as that which the Persians call *abarnim*.[2]

R. Ḥisda said: He who cooks [food] in the hot springs of Tiberias on the Sabbath is not culpable;[3] if he boiled the Passover sacrifice in the hot springs of Tiberias, he is culpable. Wherein does the Sabbath differ, that [he is] not [culpable]? Because we require the product of fire,[4] which is absent! Then [in respect to] the Passover sacrifice too it is not a product of fire?—Said Raba, What is the meaning of his statement,[5] 'he is culpable'? That he transgresses on account of '[*Thou shalt not eat* . . .] *but roast with fire*'.[6] R. Ḥiyya son of R. Nathan recited this [dictum] of R. Ḥisda explicitly. [Thus:] R. Ḥisda said: He who cooks in the hot springs of Tiberias on the Sabbath is not culpable; but if he boiled the Passover sacrifice in the hot springs of Tiberias, he is culpable, because he transgressed on account of '*but roast with fire*'.

(2) Lit., 'does the Master'. (3) That the paps ferment also with *ḥaroseth*. (4) Do you too accept this, or do you maintain that there is a controversy in respect of *ḥaroseth* too? (5) *Supra* 40a, q.v. in reference to vinegar. (6) Which is the reason that flour must not be put into *ḥaroseth*, since it contains vinegar, and it further follows that if put into it, it is forbidden. Hence when Samuel said that the *halachah* is as the Sages, that it is permitted, he must have referred to mustard, but not to *ḥaroseth*. (7) Ex. XII, 9. (8) Lit., 'which does not lose its taste' (to the substance boiled in it).

(1) Since the sacrifice now has a foreign flavour. (2) The emphatic '*at all*' is expressed in Hebrew by the doubling of the verb. (3) In whatever it is boiled. (4) Without any liquid, save its own juice. If we deduce the interdict of other liquids *a minori*, this however is permitted. But when we learn it from the emphatic doubling of the verb, even this is forbidden.—The Passover sacrifice was roasted on a spit directly over the fire. (5) To flagellation for eating it. (6) In the first place. It can never be subsequently regarded as '*roast with fire*'. (7) Relating to the eating of unleavened bread on Passover. (8) In another dish. (9) Because it is not called bread, notwithstanding that it was previously baked in an oven. Similarly, if the Passover is boiled after being roasted, it is no longer regarded as '*roast with fire*'. (10) Viz., that once baked it retains its name as bread. (11) Even after roasting. This answers the question, 'And the Rabbis: how do they utilize this (phrase), "*nor boiled at all*"?'. (12) I.e., he overroasted it, thus burning it. I might think that this is not called '*roast with fire*' but 'burnt with fire', and therefore he incurs flagellation for eating it. (13) Lit., 'tell'. (14) No interdict is violated by eating it thus.

b (1) Of the Passover sacrifices. (2) Half-done meat. V. Jast. s.v. אברנים. (3) For the desecration of the Sabbath, because this is not really cooking. (4) Before it can be called cooking. (5) Lit., 'which he states'. (6) He is not culpable on account of, *Thou shalt not eat of it . . . boiled with water*' because this is not designated boiling. But the other portion of the verse, '*but roast with fire*', is an implied negative injunction, the command being that you must not eat anything which is not roast, and what is boiled in the springs of Tiberias is therefore forbidden by implication. He thus holds that a man is flagellated for an *implied* negative injunction, i.e., one which is not explicitly stated.

from beginning to end. Mar the son of Rabina, [40b] his mother
a stored [grain] for him in a trough.[1]

A certain ship of grain foundered in Ḥishta,[2] [whereupon] Raba gave permission to sell [the grain][3] to Gentiles. Rabbah b. Lewai[4] raised an objection against Raba: [With regard to] a garment wherein *kil'ayim*[5] is lost,[6] he must not sell it to a Gentile,[7] nor may he make a saddle-cloth for an ass;[8] but it may be made into shrouds for a corpse.[9] What is the reason [that it may] not [be sold] to a Gentile? Surely it is because he might resell it to an Israelite?[10] Subsequently Raba said, Let them sell it to Israelites, a *kab*[11] at a time,[12] so that it should be consumed before Passover.

Our Rabbis taught: One may not mash a dish on Passover;[13] and he who wishes to mash, must put in the flour and then add the vinegar.[14] But some say, He may even put in the vinegar [first] and then add the flour.[15]

Who is 'some say'? Said R. Ḥisda, It is R. Judah. For we learned: [In the case of] a stew pot or a boiling pot[16] which he removed seething [from the fire],[17] he must not put spices therein,[18] but he
b may put [spices] into a dish or a tureen.[1] R. Judah said: He may put [spices] into anything except what contains vinegar or brine.[2] Yet let us establish it as R. Jose, for it was taught, R. Jose said: He can soak them in vinegar, and the vinegar binds them?[3] —We know R. Jose [to rule thus] only when it is by itself, but not when it is in a mixture. 'Ulla said: Both the one and the other are forbidden,[4] because, 'Go, go, thou nazirite', say we, 'take the most devious route, but approach not the vineyard'. R. Papa permitted the stewards[5] of the house of the *Resh Galutha*[6] to mash a dish with parched grains. Said Raba: Is there anyone who permits such a thing in a place where slaves are found?[7] Others say, Raba himself mashed a dish with parched grains.

MISHNAH. FLOUR MAY NOT BE PUT INTO ḤAROSETH[8] OR INTO THE MUSTARD,[9] AND IF HE DID PUT [IT], IT MUST BE EATEN IMMEDIATELY;[10] BUT R. MEIR FORBIDS [IT]. ONE MAY NOT BOIL THE PASSOVER SACRIFICE, NEITHER IN LIQUIDS NOR IN FRUIT JUICE,[11] BUT ONE MAY BASTE AND DIP IT IN THEM.[12] THE WATER USED BY A BAKER MUST BE POURED OUT, BECAUSE IT PROMOTES FERMENTATION.

GEMARA. R. Kahana said: The controversy is [about putting flour] into mustard; but [if it was put] into *ḥaroseth*, all agree that it must be burnt immediately. And it was taught likewise: Flour must not be put into *ḥaroseth*, and if he did put [it], it must be burnt immediately. [If put] into mustard,—R. Meir said: It must be burnt immediately; but the Sages rule: It must be eaten im-
c mediately.[1]

R. Huna the son of Rab Judah said in R. Naḥman's name in Samuel's name: The *halachah* is as the words of the Sages. Said

a (1) For use on the night of Passover. Thus this too was guarded from the beginning. (2) A canal in Babylonia. This happened before Passover. (3) Which became leaven. (4) Or, the Levite. (5) V. Glos. (6) I.e., a thread of the forbidden material was woven in the cloth, and its place is not known. (7) For the latter may resell it to a Jew who will wear it in ignorance of the fact that it contains *kil'ayim*. (8) Lest he subsequently remove it and sew it into a garment. (9) Because it can henceforth not be used for any other purpose, since the raiment of the dead is forbidden for general use. On the other hand, the corpse is not subject to any of the laws of the Torah, v. Shab. 30a. (10) Then the same should apply here. (11) A measure of capacity = one sixth of a *se'ah*. (12) I.e., not selling a large quantity to any single person. (13) I.e., make a mash of flour and vinegar in the usual way, which is to put in the vinegar first and then add the flour. This is forbidden, because it easily ferments and becomes leaven. (14) The vinegar prevents fermenting. (15) Although the vinegar becomes mixed with the rest of the dish when it is put in first, it can still prevent the fermenting of the flour. (16) The first means a tightly covered pot. (17) At twilight on Friday. (18) After the Sabbath commences. The pot is a 'first vessel', i.e., it was used directly on the fire, and its contents, as long as they are seething, cause any condiments put therein to boil likewise. This of course is forbidden on the Sabbath.

b (1) Containing a hot stew. The dish or the tureen is a 'second vessel', i.e., it was not used directly on the fire, and cannot make the spices boil. (2) Being sharp, they cause them to boil, though the vinegar or brine is mixed with the rest of the dish. By causing them to boil they prevent fermentation, and the same applies here. (3) Which prevents fermentation. (4) Whichever is put first. This was proverbial: a man must not venture into temptation, and a nazirite, who must not eat grapes, must not even go near a vineyard. Similarly, if a man is permitted to make the mash in one way, he will make it in the other way too. (5) Jast. s.v. אכונגר conjectures that בורדיקי is a corruption of that word. (6) Exilarch, the official title of the head of Babylonian Jewry. (7) As in the house of the Exilarch. They are very lax in any case, and such leniency will lead to even greater laxity. (8) A pap made of fruits and spices with wine or vinegar, used for sweetening the bitter herb on Passover night (Jast.). (9) Lest the flour become leaven. (10) Before it can ferment. (11) Though Scripture only mentions water, v. Ex. XII, 9. (12) I.e., the flesh may be greased with these liquids when it is being roasted, and the roasted meat may be dipped into liquids at the time of eating.

c (1) The greater strength of mustard retards fermentation, hence the controversy. But it ferments very quickly in *ḥaroseth*.

מנקטא ליה אימיה בארבי: ההוא ארבא דחיטי דטבעא בחישתא שריא רבא לזבוני לנכרים איתיביה רבה בר לוואי לרבא *בגד שאבד בו כלאים הרי זה *לא ימכרנו לנכרי ולא יעשה (א) בו מרדעת לחמור אבל עושין אותו תכריכין למת לנכרי מאי טעמא לא לאו משום דהדר מזבין ליה לישראל הדר אמר רבא ג'לזבינהו קבא קבא לישראל כי היכי דכליא קמי פיסחא תנו רבנן אין מוללין את הקדירה בפסח והרוצה שימלול נותן את הקמח ואח"כ נותן את החומץ ויש אומרים אף נותן את החומץ ואח"כ נותן את הקמח *מאן י"א א"ר חסדא רבי יהודה היא *דתנן ד'האילפס והקדירה שהעבירן מרותחין לא יתן לתוכן תבלין אבל נותן לתוך הקערה או לתוך התמחוי רבי יהודה אומר לכל הוא נותן חוץ מדבר שיש בו חומץ וציר ונוקמה כר' יוסי *(דתנן) ר' יוסי אומר שורן בחומץ וחומץ צומתן כי אשמעינן ליה לרבי יוסי הני מילי דאיתיה בעיניה אבל על ידי תערובת לא עולא אמר ו'אחד זה ואחד זה אסור משום *לך לך אמרינן נזירא סחור סחור לכרמא לא תקרב רב פפי שרי ליה *לבורדיקי דבי ריש גלותא ה'למימחה קדירה בחסיסי אמר רבא איכא דשרי כי האי מילתא בדוכתא דשכיחי עבדי א"ד רבא גופא מחו לה קידרא בחסיסי: **מתני'** אין נותנין קמח לתוך חרוסת או לתוך החרדל ואם נתן יאכל מיד ורבי מאיר אוסר *אין מבשלין את הפסח לא במשקין ולא במי פירות ז'אבל סכין ומטבילין אותו בהן מי תשמישו של נחתום ישפכו מפני שהן מחמיצין: **גמ'** אמר רב כהנא מחלוקת לתוך החרדל אבל לתוך חרוסת דברי הכל ישרף מיד ותניא נמי הכי ח'אין נותנין קמח לתוך החרוסת ואם נתן ישרף מיד לתוך החרדל ר' מאיר אומר ישרף מיד ט'וחכמים אומרים יאכל מיד אמר רב הונא בריה דרב יהודה אמר רב נחמן אמר שמואל הלכה כדברי חכמים א"ל רב נחמן בר יצחק לרב הונא בריה דרב יהודה

אחרוסת

מנקטא ליה אימיה · חיטין מתחלת קציר לצורך הפסח ועבדה להו שימור מעיקרא : בארבי · מלא עריבה או עריבות הרבה ומלגימתן לבדם לצורך הפסח : חישתא · שם הנהר . טבעה קודם הפסח והיו בה חיטין : שאבד בו כלאים · שנארג בו חוט של כלאים ואינו ניכר : הרי זה לא ימכרנו לנכרי · דהואיל ואין כלאים שבו ניכרים אתי לזבוני האי נכרי לישראל ולביש להו ישראל ולאו אדעתיה : ולא יעשנו מרדעת לחמור · דילמא הדר שקיל ליה מהתם ותופרו באחד מבגדיו : אבל עושה אותו תכריכין למת · דמהתם תו לא שקיל ליה דבגדי המת אסורין בהנאה ומת אין מצות נוהגות בו דכתי' במתים חפשי כיון שמת אדם נעשה חפשי מן המצות (שבת ל·) והני חיטי כיון דלא מינכר חימוץ דידהו אתי האי נכרי והדר מזבין להו לישראל : קבא קבא · קב לזה וקב לזה ולא הרבה לאיש א': מוללן · בקמח קרי מלילה כשנותנין קמח לתבשיל : ואחר כך נותן את החומץ · דאין החומץ מניחו להחמיץ לפי שמבשלו : ויש אומרים אף נותן חומץ תחלה. דאף על גב דחומץ כבר מעורב בתבשיל הוא מבשל את הניתן בתוכו: שהעבירן מעל האור. מרותחין ערב שבת עם חשיכה: לא יתן לתוכן תבלין · דכלי ראשון מבשל ונמצא מבשל תבלין בשבת : לתוך הקערה · דכלי שני אינו מבשל : לכל הוא נותן · לכל מיני מאכל הוא נותן תבלין בכלי שני חוץ מדבר שיש בו חומץ וציר שהחומץ מבשלן ואע"ג שקדם : הני מילי בעיניה · כשהחומץ בעין אבל כשהוא מעורב בתבשיל אין כחו חזק: אחד זה ואחד זה · בין חומץ תחלה בין חומץ בסוף אסור : לבורדקאי · נחתומין : בחסיסי · קמחא דאבשונא : בדוכתא דשכיחי עבדי · כגון בי ריש גלותא שהעבדים מזלזלין בדבר איסור יותר ויותר: **מתני'** חרוסת · איינגרו"ס ויש בו חומץ ועשוי לטבל בו בשר ורגילים לתת בו קמח וכל דבר שמקהה את טעמו וקמח לאחר זמן מחמיץ ומקהה את הטעם : אין מבשלין · דכתיב (שמות יב) אל תאכלו ממנו נא ובשל מבושל וגו': לא במשקין · אע"ג דכתיב במים וטעמא מפרש בגמרא: סכין · בשעת צלייתו : ומטבילין · בשעת אכילתו : מי תשמישו של נחתום · שמצנן בו ידיו בשעה שהוא עורך ומקטף את המלה ישפכו : **גמ'** מחלוקת · דשרי ליה תנא קמא לאוכלו מיד בנותן קמח לתוך החרדל לפי שהוא חזק ואין מניחו מהר להחמיץ :

אחרוסת

לא יעשנו מרדעת לחמור . אומר ר"י דדוקא בכלאים דאורייתא אסור לעשות מהן מרדעת שמא יעשנו טלית על גבו ולא יזהר נמי שלא יגע בבשרו אבל בכלאים דרבנן שרי כדאמרי' במסכת כלאים (פ"ט מ"ד) מרדעת החמור אין בה משום כלאים ומותר לעשות מהן כר וכסת ובלבד שלא יגע בבשר אע"ג דאמרינן בפ"ק דביצה (דף יד:*) אפי' עשר מצעות זו על גב זו אסור שמא תכרך לו נימא על בשרו שמא כר וכסת ומרדעת אין רגילין ליכרך כל כך : **אבל** עושהו תכריכין למת · וא"ת והא איכא לועג לרש וגו' ובפרק התכלת (מנחות דף מא·) אמר רב טובי בר קיסנא אמר שמואל כלי קופסא חייבין בציצית (אמר רב) ומודה שמואל בזקן שעשאה לכבודו שפטורה וההיא שעתא ודאי רמינן ליה משום לועג לרש ומהאי טעמא נמי לא יעשה כלאים למת ואומר ר"ת דציצית שקולה כנגד כל המצות לכך איכא לועג לרש טפי כדאמרינן בהתכלת (שם דף מג:) וזכרתם את כל מצות ה' מלמד ששקולה ציצית כנגד כל המצות והא דאמר בפ' מי שמתו (ברכות דף יח·) רבי חייא ורבי יונתן הוו שקלי ואזלי בבית הקברות הוי שדיא תכלת דרבי יונתן אמר ליה ר' חייא דלייה שלא יאמרו למחר באים אצלנו והיום מלעיגים אותנו ואף על גב דמתים נמי יש להם ציצית אומר ר"ת דמכל מקום שייך בהן ליעוג לפי שמראין עצמן כמצווין במצות והן אינן מצווין ואינו דומה מצווה ועושה למי שאין מצווה ועושה ומה שמסירים בזמן הזה מטליתות של מתים סומכין אהא דתניא במסכת שמחות (פי"ב) אבא שאול בן בטנית צוה לבניו *קברוהו תחת מרגלותיו של אבא והתירו תכלת מפליוני ובכמה דברים אנו סומכין על ספרים חיצונים ומניחין גמרא שלנו דבפרק בתרא דמגילה (דף לא:) אמרי' ראש חודש אב שחל להיות בשבת מפטירין חדשיכם ומועדיכם דהיינו חזון ישעיה* ואנו מפטירין השמים כסאי וכן הוא בפסיקתא ובפר' ויחל אנו קורין בתענית שלנו אע"ג דתנן במגילה (גם זה שם) שקורין בתענית בקללות וברכות ואנו סומכין על מס' סופרים (פי"ז ה"ז)* : **האילפס** והקדירה שהעבירן מרותחין לא יתן לתוכן תבלין · מכאן אין להוכיח דעירוי ככלי שני מדלא אשמעינן רבותא שלא יערה (ב) על הקערה שהתבלין בתוכה דאדרבה דוק מסיפא איפכא דקתני אבל נותן הוא לתוך הקערה ולא קתני אבל מערה על הקערה שיש בה תבלין ונראה דאפילו שמואל דאית ליה תתאה גבר ותניא כוותיה (לקמן דף עו·) כוותיה אפ"ה מבשל העירוי כדי קליפה דאמר התם תניא כוותיה דשמואל חם לתוך צונן קולף צונן לתוך צונן מדיח ואם עירו רותחין על התרנגולת צריך קליפה וכלי שנשתמשו בכלי ראשון לא יוכל להגעילו ע"י עירוי דאין מבשל אלא כדי קליפה והוא בלע יותר מכדי קליפה והא דאמרינן בפרק כירה (שבת דף מב·) דשרי חם לתוך צונן יש לומר כיון שאינו מבשל אלא כדי קליפה הואיל והצונן של מטה מים שהוא דבר המתערב אינו יכול להתבשל מחמת צינת המים אבל דבר שאינו מתערב לא ובשילהי ע"ז (דף עו·) אמר *מר עוקבא זבן יורה מנכרי והדר ליה גדנפא וכו' ומסיק כבולעו כך פולטו מה בולעו בניצוצות אף פולטו בניצוצות ואי עירוי ככלי ראשון הוא מאי איריא משום דבלע בניצוצות אפילו בלע בליעה גמורה פליט בניצוצות דהיינו עירוי אלא ודאי לא בשיל אלא כדי קליפה והא דתנן בפרק חבית (שבת דף קמה:) כל שלא בא בחמין לפני השבת מדיחין אותו בחמין בשבת וכו' צריך לאוקמא בכלי שני דבכלי ראשון אפילו הדחה אסורה וקשה דקתני דוקא מדיחין אבל שורין לא והכא גבי תבלין קתני אבל נותן לתוך הקערה או לתוך התמחוי דהיינו אפילו שורין ואומר ר"י דהתם מיירי במידי דבר בישול וכששורין אותו אפילו בכלי שני מיחזי כמבשל אבל תבלין עשויין למתק הקדירה ולא מיחזי כמבשל ובירושלמי בפרק כירה בעי מהו ליתן תבלין מלמטה ולערות עליהן מלמעלה ר' יונה אומר אסור דעירוי ככלי ראשון הוא חיליה דר' יונה מן הדא וכלי חרש אשר תבושל בו ישבר א' שבישל בו וא' שעירה לתוכו רותח ודחי ר' אסי תמן כלי חרס בולע תבלין אינו מבשל התיב ר' אסי בר בון והתניא אף בכלי נחשת כך אית לך למימר כלי נחשת בלע בתמיה: **רבא** מחו ליה קידרא בחסיסי · פ"ה קימחא דאבישונא וקשה דהא לעיל (דף לט:) אסרינן וליכא מאן דפליג ונראה לר"י כדפירש בערוך בחסיסי קמח של עדשים דאין דרכם לבא לידי חימוץ כל כך :

לא

קע א מיי' פ"י מהלכות כלאים הלכה כו טוש"ע יו"ד סימן שא סעיף ח :

[וביומא סט.]

ע"ז סה: נדה סא:

קעא ב מיי' פ"ה מהל' חמץ הלכה ט טוש"ע או"ח סימן תסז סעיף א :

קעב ג מיי' פכ"ב מהל' שבת הלכה ו טור שו"ע או"ח סימן שיח סעיף ט :

קעג ד ה מיי' פרק ה מהלכות מצה הלכה ה טוש"ע או"ח סימן תסג סעיף ג :

שבת מב:

קעד ו מיי' פ"ח מהל' ק"פ הלכה ז סמג לאוין שנ :

קעה ז שם הלכה ח :

קעו ח ט מיי' פ"ה מהלכות מצה הלכ' יט טוש"ע או"ח סימן תסד :

[נ"ל קברו אותי]

[עי' תוס' מגילה לא: ד"ה ר"ח אב וכו' וקל"ע ועי' תרומת הדשן סי' יט]

[וע"ע תוס' ברכות יח. ד"ה למחר ובב"ב עד. ד"ה פסקי ובע"ז סס: ד"ה אבל ובנדה כא: ד"ה אבל]

[עי' תוספות חולין לב. סד"ה ובנמצא]

[עמ"ש תוס' ב"ב נג: ד"ה מאן]

[נ"ל דתניא]

[שבת יג. ע"ש לב. ע"ז יז. נח. נט.]

[גי' הערוך למרדק]

[עי' תוספות לקמן מא. ד"ה אין מבשלין]

נ"ל רב עוקבא

הגהות הב"ח

(א) גמ' בר ליואי לרבא בגד שאבד וכו' לא יעשנו מרדעת לחמור כצ"ל : (ב) תוס' ד"ה האילפס וכו' שלא יערה בקערה כצ"ל ותיבת על נמחק :

רבינו חננאל

היתה משמרת אותם לשם מצה מתחלה: **ההיא** ארבא דטבעא בחישתא. כלומר טבעא ספינה בנהר התיר רבא למכור החטים שבספינה לנכרים ומותבינן ליה [מהא דתניא] הבגד שאבד בו כלאים הרי זה לא ימכרנו לנכרי חיישי' שמא יחזור הנכרי וימכרם לישראל אחר ולא יעשנו מרדעת לחמור אבל עושין אותו תכריכין למת הדר ביה דבא ושרנהו לזבונינהו קבא קבא לישראל כי היכי דניכלו קמי פסחא : **ת"ר** אין מוללין את הקדרה בפסח. פי' מלילות הקמח בקדרה והרוצה שימלול נותן הקמח ואח"כ החומץ ויש אומרים נותן החומץ נותן הקמח ואוקימ' יש אומרים ר' יהודה הוא דתאני בענין נתינת תבלין בשבת ר' יהודה אומר לכל הוא נותן חוץ מדבר שיש בו חומץ וציר כלומר החומץ והציר מבשל ומדלענין שבת מבשל לענין חמץ בפסח שרי דקדים ומבשיל ליה ולא אתי לידי חימוצא ונקמה מאן יש אומרים ר' יוסי דאמר שורן בחומץ וחומץ צומתן ודחי' אימור דאמר ר' יוסי בחומץ לבדו שצומת אבל על ידי תערובת וחומץ מי קאמר עולא אמר בין החומץ מקודם בין אחרי כן הכל אסור למלול משום הרחק איסור כמו שאמר לנזיר התרחק מן הכרם שלא תאכל מן הענבים ר' אבא מיחי ליה בחסיסי כעין ותיקא ולא על רב פפי דשרי לדבי ריש גלותא אלא משום דעבדי דלא מעלי ועבדי איסורא : **אין** נותנין קמח לתוך החרוסת ולא לתוך החרדל ואם נתן לתוך החרדל יאכל מיד ור"מ אוסר אבל לתוך חרוסת דברי הכל ישרף מיד . תניא נמי הכי אין נותנין קמח לתוך חרוסת ואם נתן ישרף מיד לתוך החרדל ר' מאיר אומר ישרף מיד וחכמים אומרים יאכל מיד ואמר רב נחמן אמר שמואל הלכה כחכמים : **אין** מבשלין במשקין

תרי חיטי בהדי הדדי דילמא אזלא חדא ויתבה בציריא דחברתה ולא סליק להו דיקולא דמיא מארבע רוחתא ואתי לידי חימוץ ואמר אביי לא ליהרוך איניש תרי שבולי בהדי הדדי דילמא נפקי מיא מהאי ובלע אידך ואתיא לידי חימוץ אמר לי' רבא א"ה אפילו חדא נמי דילמא נפיק מהאי רישא ובלע אידך רישא *אלא אמר רבא מי פירות נינהו *ומי פירות אינן מחמיצין והדר ביה אביי מהההיא דכל אגב מדלייהו לא מחמצי דאמר אביי האי חצבא דאבישנ' סחיפא שרי זקיפא אסור רבא אמר אפילו זקיפא נמי שרי מי פירות נינהו ומי פירות אינן מחמיצין ת"ר ׳אין לותתין *שעורין בפסח ואם לתת נתבקעו אסורות לא נתבקעו מותרות ר' יוסי אומר שורן בחומץ וחומץ צומתן *אמר שמואל אין הלכה כר' יוסי א"ר חסדא אמר מר עוקבא ׳לא נתבקעו ממש אלא כל שאילו מניחן על פי חבית והן נתבקעות מאיליהן ושמואל אמר נתבקעו ממש עבד שמואל עובדא בדורא דבי בר חשו נתבקעו ממש אמר רבה בעל נפש לא ילתות מאי איריא בעל נפש אפילו כולי עלמא נמי דהא תניא אין לותתין שעורין בפסח הכי קאמר ׳בעל נפש אפי' חיטין דשרירי לא ילתות א"ל ר"נ מאן דציית ליה לאבא אכיל נהמא דעיפושא דהא בי רב הונא בר אבין לתתי ובי רבא בר רב הונא לתתי ורבא אמר אסור ללתות אלא הא דתניא אין לותתין שעורין בפסח שעורין הוא דלא הא חיטי שרי לא מיבעי' קאמר לא מיבעיא חיטין כיון דאית ביה ציריא עיילי בהו מיא אבל שערי דשיעי אימא שפיר דמי קמ"ל הדר אמר רבא *מותר ללתות *דתניא יוצאין בפת נקיה והדראה ואי אפשר נקיה בלא לתיתה איתיביה רב פפא לרבא הקמחין והסלתות של נכרים של כפרים טהורים ושל כרכין טמאין דכפרים מ"ט לאו משום דלא לתתי וקא קרי ליה סולת תרגומא אקמחא בתר דנפיק אמר מ"ט לא אימא ליה מהא *דאמר רבי זירא אמר רב ירמיה אמר שמואל חיטין של מנחות אין לותתין אותם וקא קרי להו סולת הדר אמר רבא מצוה ללתות שנאמר °ושמרתם את המצות אי לא דבעי לתיתה שימור למאי אי שימור דלישה לאו שימור הוא דאמר רב הונא בצקות של נכרים אדם ממלא כריסו מהן ובלבד שיאכל כזית מצה באחרונה באחרונה אין בראשונה לא מ"ט משום דלא עבד בהו שימור ולעביד ליה שימור מאפייה ואילך אלא לאו שמע מינה שימור מעיקרא בעינן וממאי דילמא שאני התם דבעידנא דנחית לשימור לא עבד לה שימור אבל היכא דבעידנא דנחית לשימור עביד לה שימור הכי נמי דשימור דלישה הוי שימור ואפ"ה לא הדר ביה רבא דאמר להו להנהו דמהפכי כיפי כי מהפכיתו הפיכו לשום מצוה ׳אלמא קסבר שימור מעיקרא מתחלתו ועד סופו בעינן מר בריה דרבינא

מנקטא

תורה אור: °שמות יב

תוספות

ה"ג ר"ח **כל** שאילו מניחן על פי אבוב של קלאים והם מתבקעות · פירוש כלי שבעלי קליות עושין בו קליות והוא מנוקב כדאמרינן בפרק ר' ישמעאל (מנחות דף סו·) מניחין בתוך אבוב של קלאים כדי *שתגמור האור בכולו והם מתבקעות מכח האור וכן מצא ר"י בספר ישן בשם רבינו תם :

תרגומא אקמחים · תימה השתא אמאי תני סלתות ויש לומר דלגלדין קתני :

כי מהפכיתו כיפי הפכיתו לשם מצה · וא"ת כיון דסבירא ליה דבעי שימור בשעת היפוך אם כן היכי מוכח דמצוה ללתות דילמא לאו מצוה היא אלא דצריך שימור מתחלתו ועד סופו ויש לומר דעיקר שימור כדי שלא תחמיץ וסבר רבא אי לאו שיש שימור מחמץ בשעה שהוא עדיין דגן כגון לתיתה לא היה מצריך שימור בשעת כי דרי מתחילת הדגון :

רש"י

תרתי חיטי · גרעיני חיטין אלא חדא חדא ליטחנה: דילמא אתיא חדא ויתבה בציריא דחברתה · בסדק של חברתה : דיקולא דמיא · רתיחת המים : ציריא · סדק כמו (א) טיילא חריפא דמגלי זיקי דמסכת ע"ז (דף ל·) : אי הכא אפילו חדא · שבולתא נמי לא ליהרוך : דילמא נפקי מיא · מחוטי דבריתא חדא ובלעי חטים דאידך רישא : ה"ג והדר ביה אביי דכל אגב מדלייהו לא מחמצי · כל דרך כפילתם לא מחמצי : חצבא דאבישונא · כד שמייבשין בתוכו קליות בתנור : סחיפא שרי · אם פיו כפוי למטה שיהו המים הנפלטין מן הקלי על ידי חום האור זבין ויוצאין לחוץ שרי : זקיפא · שהיא זקוף כדרכו אסור שהמים נפלטין וחוזרין ונבלעין ומדאמר אביי סחיפא שרי משום דדייבי אבראי שמע מינה הדר ביה מהאי דאמר לעיל לא ליהרוך איניש תרתי שיבולי דהכי נמי דייבי מיא ושרקי ונפלי ולא מיבלעי באידך : נתבקעו · מחמת הניפוח שמחמת המים אסורות דודאי ממהרות להחמיץ : שורן בחומץ · אם רוצה שנופחות שורן בחומץ : וחומץ צומתן · לאשטרייג"ר בלע"ז ולא מניחן להחמיץ : וכן מתבקעות מאליהן · שאין יכולות לעמוד מפני ריח היין : בדורא דבי בר חשו · בכפר של אותו האיש : נתבקעו ממש · כלומר דאין אסורות אלא נתבקעו ממש ואותן לא מבוקעות ממש היו והתירן : אמר רבה גרסינן : בעל נפש · חסיד : הכי קאמר אפילו חיטי · שהן קשין משעורין ואין ממהרין להחמיץ בעל נפש לא ילתות אבל דלאו (ב) בעל נפש דלא מחמיר על נפשיה כולי האי : דשריקן · קשים : לאבא (ג) · רבה הכי קרי ליה לשון רבנות : מאן דציית ליה לאבא יאכל לחם עיפושא · כלומר לא תהא סולתן נקיה : דהא בי רב הונא לתתי · כולה רב נחמן אמר לה : ורבא אמר אסור ללתות לכולי עלמא : דשיעי · שחלקין הן : והדראה · קיבר : של כפרים טהורים · לפי שאין מקפידין על סולתן לעשותן נקיה כל כך ולא לתתי לחיטי דידהו ונמצא שלא הוכשרו וקא קרי להו סולת אלמא אפשר לנקיה בלא לתיתה : בתר דנפק · רבא מבי מדרשה : אמר · רב פפא נלטער בעצמו מדוע לא נזכרתי להשיב לו מהא דאמר ר' ירמיה כו' : ואי לאו · לתיתה דעכשיו בעי שימור שלא יחמיצו שימור למה לי : לאו שימור הוא · אי לא עבד ליה שימור מקמי הכי : דאמר רב הונא גרסינן : בצקות של נכרים שמכיר בהן שלא החמיצו שאין שם לא קרני חגבים ולא הכסיפו פניו דהוא הוי סימן סידוק וסימן שיאור כדלקמן : שיאכל כזית מצה באחרונה · דבהא לא נפיק ידי חובת מצה משום דלא הוי לה שימור לשם מצה ואף על פי שאנו רואין שאין כאן חימוץ ומיהו למצה של מצוה שימור לשמה בעינן : באחרונה ·(ד) היא מצות אכילתה שעם הפסח היא חובת אכילתה דכתיב קרא (שמות יב) על מצות ומרורים יאכלוהו ופסח נאכל על השובע כדתנן (לקמן דף קיט:) אין מפטירין אחר הפסח אפיקומן : בראשונה לא · כלומר באכילה ראשונה שאכל מבצקות של נכרים לא נפיק : הכי גרסינן מאי טעמא דלא עבד לה שימור ולא גרסינן אי נימא דהא ודאי טעמא משום הכי הוא : מאפייה ואילך · משמע משמתקנה לאפייה כגון עריכתה וקיטוף שלה ונתינתה לתנור : וממאי דילמא · לעולם שימור דלישה שימור הוא ואע"ג דלא אילטריך שימור מקמי הכי והכא מאי טעמא לא נפיק משום דמשעת נתינת מים לקמח שזה דבר המחמצת הויא צריכה שימור וזו לא נעשה לה שימור מההיא עידנא דנחית לתורת שימור דהיינו מנתינת מים : ואפילו הכי · דלא אשכח רבא סייעתא למילתיה לא הדר ביה ממאי דאמר בעינן שימור קודם לישה : מהפכי כיפי · העמרין וקושרין את העמרים בימות הקציר :

מנקטא

עין משפט נר מצוה

קסז א מיי' פ"ה מהל' חו"מ הלכה ד טוש"ע א"ח סי' תס"ג סעיף א :

קסח ב ג ד מיי' פ"ה מהלכות מצה הל' ו ז טוש"ע או"ח סימן תנג סעיף ה :

קסט ה מיי' שם הלכה ח ט טוש"ע או"ח סימן תנג סעיף ד :

רבינו חננאל

תרתי חיטי בהדי הדדי כו' אלו הן כגון קליות והא דאמר אביי לא נהריך איניש תרתי שבלי בהדי הדדי לית הלכתא כותיה אלא כרבא דאמר מי פירות אין מחמיצין וכן חצבא דאבישנא שהן שיבולי דשערי דמיבתא אמר אביי כשנותנין זה החצבא בתנור בימות הפסח ופיה למטה כל זיעה שיוצא מאותן השעורים נשפכין בתנור (ואם לאו) אסורין אלא אם ישארו אותן המים היוצאין מהן בחצבא מחמיץ ולית הלכתא כאביי וקיימא לן כל מי פירות אין מחמיצין : ת"ר אין לותתין את השעורין בפסח ואם לתתן נתבקעו אסורות לא נתבקעו מותרות ואמרי' לא נתבקעו ממש אלא כל שמניחן על פי הביב של קלאים והן כלים מאליהם וכן הלכתא ור' יוסי דאמר שורן בחומץ מפני שהחומץ צומתן לית הלכתא כותיה דהא בהדיא אמר שמואל אין הלכה כר' יוסי והא דעביד שמואל עובדא נתבקעו ממש לא סמכינן עליה . אמר רבה בעל נפש כלומר המתרחק מריח עבירה ומדקדק הרבה על עצמו לא ילתות אפילו חטין דשריקן פי' שהן חזקים מן השעורים ולא אתי לידי חימוץ הא לא ילתות כל שכן שעורים: אמר רב נחמן מאן דצאית לרבה איכל פת מעופשת. פי' כגון פת קיבר שאין בה סלת דהא (בר) [בי] רב הונא ובי רבה בר אבוה לתתי ורבה אמר אסור ללתות. ומותבינן עליה אין לותתין את השעורים בפסח הא חטין שרי כו' . פי' צריא כגון סדק באמצעה של חטה אבל השעורים שייעי אין בהן סדק : איכא דאמרי אמר רבא מותר ללתות דתנן יוצאין בפת נקיה והדראה ואי אפשר לפת נקיה בלא לתיתה כלומר אם אין שורין את החטים לא יצא מהם סלת ומותיב רב פפא מהא דתאני הקמחין והסלתות של נכרים של כרכים טמאים ושל כפרים טהורים ש"מ מדקתני טהורין מכלל דלא הוכשרו וקרי להו סלתות הנה סלת בלא לתיתה ודחי רבא האי דקתני של כפרים טהורין אקמחים בלבד ולא אסלתות והא דאמר רבא אי אפשר לפת נקיה בלא לתיתה דחויה היא דהא משמא דשמואל אמרו חטים של מנחות אין לותתין וקרי להו התורה סלת הנה נמצאת בלא לתיתה . הדר אמר רבא מצוה ללתות דכתיב ושמרתם את המצות ואין שמור אלא שמור דחטים בלתיתה [דשימור דלישה לאו] שימור מדרב הונא דאמר הבצקות של נכרים אדם ממלא כריסו מהם ובלבד שיאכל כזית מצה באחרונה ואי הוה שמור דלישה שמור היה עושה שימור לבצק של נכרי ואינו צריך כזית אחר ודחי' הני בצקות של נכרים משום דלא אתחיל בהו ישראל בשמור דנכרי לאו בר שימור הוא אבל ישראל דבר שימור הוא אם התחיל מתחלה להשמר אפילו שימור דלישה הוי שימור אפילו הכי לא הדר ביה רבא דאמר רבא להנהו דהוו מהפכי לנוץ והן העומרין הפכו לשם מצה כלומר הזהרו מהכשרת המים והפיכו להו למקום שאין בו הכשרת המים שיהיה שימור לשמו לשם מצה : מר בריה דרבינא מנקטא ליה בארבי . פי' בעיקריתם היתה

מסורת הש"ס

[לעיל לה. נזיר לז:]

[לקמן מב.]

[לקמן מא.]

ס"א ירא שמים המחמיר על נפשו

[סנהדרין כ:]

לעיל לו:

לעיל לו.

הגהות הב"ח

(א) רש"י ד"ה ציריא סדק כמו טיילא כו' נ"ב לשון יון : (ב) ד"ה הכי קאמר וכו' דלאו בעל נפש לא מחמיר : (ג) ד"ה לאבא וכו' וד"ה מאן דציית : (ד) ד"ה באחרונה מצות וכו' כצ"ל ותיבת היא נמחק :

R. Joseph said: A man must not scald [40a] two grains of wheat together, lest one becomes wedged in the cleft of the other, so that the column of water will not surround it on all[3] sides, and [thus] it will come to fermentation. And Abaye said: A man must not singe two ears of corn together, lest sap [water] issue from one and the other absorb it, and [thus] it will come to fermentation. Said Raba to him: If so, [forbid] even one also, lest it [the sap] issues from one end and the other end absorbs it? But, said Raba: It is sap [water] of fruit,[4] and sap of fruit does not cause fermentation. Now Abaye retracted from that [view], because as long as they [the grains] absorb [liquid], they do not ferment.[5] For Abaye said: The jar for roasting [ears of corn]: if it is inverted, it is permitted;[6] if upright, it is forbidden.[7] Raba said: Even if upright it is still permitted, [because] it is the sap of fruit, and the sap of fruit does not cause fermentation.

Our Rabbis taught: One may not wash[8] barley on Passover; and if one did wash [them] and they split, they are forbidden;[9] if they did not split, they are permitted. R. Jose said: He can soak them in vinegar, and the vinegar binds them.[10] Samuel said: The *halachah* is not as R. Jose. R. Ḥisda said in Mar 'Uḳba's name: It does not mean literally split, but [if they reach] such [a condition] that if placed on the mouth of a [wine] cask they will split of themselves.[11] But Samuel said: It means literally split. Samuel acted in the vicinity of the home of Bar Ḥashu [on the view that] 'split' is meant literally.[1]

Rabbah said: A conscientious man should not wash [corn].[2] Why particularly a conscientious man: even any other man[3] too, for surely it was taught: One may not wash barley on Passover?—He says thus: He should not wash even wheat, which is hard.[4] Said R. Naḥman to him: He who will heed Abba[5] will eat mouldy bread.[6] For surely the household of R. Huna washed [it], and the household of Raba b. Abin washed [it]. But Raba said: It is forbidden to wash [wheat]. But what of what was taught: You may not wash barley on Passover, [implying] barley only may not [be washed], but wheat is permitted?—He leads to a climax![7] It is unnecessary [to teach about] wheat, for since it has splits, the water enters it;[8] but barley, which is smooth, I would say that it is allowable. Therefore he informs us [otherwise]. Subsequently Raba said: It is permitted to wash [wheat]. For it was taught: One can discharge [the obligation] with fine bread and with coarse bread.[9] Now fine bread is impossible without washing [the grain].

R. Papa raised an objection against Raba: [With regard to] the flours and fine meals of Gentiles, those of villages are clean, while those of towns are unclean. What is the reason that those of villages [are clean]? Is it not because they do not wash [the grain],[10] yet he calls it 'fine meal'?[11]—Explain [this[12] as referring to] 'flour'. After he [Raba] departed, he [R. Papa] said [to himself], Why did I not cite him [an objection] from what R. Zera said in R. Jeremiah's name in Samuel's name: The wheat for meal-
b offerings must not be washed; yet he calls it fine meal?[1] Subsequently Raba said: It is obligatory to wash [the grain],[2] for it is said, *And ye shall guard the unleavened bread.*[3] Now, if not that it requires washing, for what purpose is the guarding?[4] If guarding for the kneading,[5] the guarding of kneading is not guarding,[6] for R. Huna said: The doughs of a heathen,[7] a man may fill his stomach with them,[8] providing that he eats as much as an olive of unleavened bread at the end. [Thus] only at the end, but not at the beginning:[9] what is the reason? Because he had not afforded it any guarding. Then let him guard it from the baking and onwards?[10] Hence this surely proves that we require guarding from the beginning. Yet whence [does this follow]: perhaps it is different there, because when guarding became necessary,[11] he did not guard it;[12] but where he did guard it when guarding became necessary, it may indeed be that the guarding at the kneading is [truly] considered 'guarding'.

Yet even so,[13] Raba did not retract. For he said to those who handled sheaves,[14] Handle them for the purpose of the precept.[15] This proves that he holds [that] we require guarding *ab initio*,

(3) Lit., 'four'. (4) I.e., produce. (5) MS.M. reads: as long as they (the liquids) are in motion (boiling), they do not create fermentation. (6) As the sap which is exuded runs out and is not re-absorbed by the other ears.—Therefore the same will hold good when he singes two ears of corn together, which on this view must be permitted. Thus he retracted from his former view. (7) Because the sap is retained in the vessel. (8) The verb connotes to moisten the grain before grinding. (9) Because then they turn leaven very quickly. (10) Prevents fermentation. (11) Then they are forbidden.

a (1) And since those about which he was consulted were not actually split, he ruled that they were permitted. (2) V. *supra*, n. c8. (3) Lit., 'the whole world'. (4) And consequently is slower to ferment than barley. Others who are not so conscientious may moisten wheat, for only barley is forbidden in the Baraitha. (5) Lit., 'father'—a title of respect. (6) I.e., unclean bread, since the wheat was not washed. (7) Lit., 'he states, it is unnecessary "(to teach etc.)"'. (8) And certainly causes it to ferment. (9) V. *supra* 37a. (10) And eatables cannot become unclean unless moisture has previously been upon them. (11) Which shows that fine bread is possible without washing. (12) The reference to villages.

b (1) Such is prescribed in Scripture for meal-offerings, v. Lev. II, 1. (2) For preparing the unleavened bread. (3) Ex. XII, 17. (4) For the grain cannot ferment unless there is moisture upon it. (5) I.e., that when it is kneaded care must be taken that it does not turn leaven. (6) This verse implies that at a certain stage of its manufacture the unleavened bread must be guarded for the express purpose of fulfilling the law prescribing the eating of unleavened bread. Hence, if a man eats on the first night of Passover only unleavened bread which was not guarded expressly for that purpose, he does not do his duty. Now Raba states that the guarding that is given to it at the stage of kneading is not considered 'guarding' in this respect. (7) Which one recognizes as not having turned leaven. (8) On the first night of Passover. (9) I.e., the law is complied with only with this unleavened bread which he eats at the end, but not with the heathen's dough which he eats at the beginning. The unleavened bread eaten in fulfilment of the precept comes at the end of the meal with the Paschal lamb, v. *infra* 119b. (10) I.e., from when it is prepared for baking, viz., when it is shaped, moistened and put into the oven. (11) Lit., 'when it entered upon (the need for) guarding'.—I.e., at the beginning of the kneading process—from the moment when water was added to the flour making fermentation possible. (12) Though it nevertheless remained unleavened. (13) Though Raba's proof was refuted. (14) At harvest time, gathering and tying them. Lit., 'turned about'. (15) Bear in mind that they may be used for that purpose. R. Ḥan. reads: for the sake of unleavened bread—i.e., take care that no water falls on them and do not store them in a damp place.

learned it: [39b] A garden-bed which is six handbreadths square, may be sown with five species of seeds, four on the four sides of the bed and one in the middle![4]—You might say that this applies only to seeds [cereals], but not to vegetables;[5] therefore he[6] informs us [otherwise]. Shall we [then] say that vegetables are stronger than seeds?[7] But surely we learned: All species of seeds may not be sown in one garden-bed [together], [yet] all species of vegetables [herbs] may be sown in one seed-bed?[8]—You might say, This *maror*[9] is a species of seed [cereal]; hence he informs us [that it is not so].[10] [You say], 'Seeds'!—Can you think so! But surely we learned, HERBS; and Bar Ḳappara [also] taught, 'Herbs'; and the School of Samuel [also] taught 'Herbs'?[11]—He needs [to state it about] lettuce:[12] I might argue, since it is destined to harden,[13] we must allow it more space. [For] did not R. Jose b. R. Ḥanina say: If the cabbage stalk hardens, more room is given to it [up to]
a a *beth roba'*?[1] This proves that since it is destined to harden, we allow it more space: so here too we should give it more space. Hence he[2] informs us [otherwise].

THE LAW IS COMPLIED WITH BY [EATING THEM] BOTH MOIST [FRESH] OR DRY etc. R. Ḥisda said: They learned this only of the stalk; but in the case of the leaves, only moist [fresh] ones, but not dry ones. But since a later clause states, WITH THEIR STALK, it follows that the first clause [refers to] leaves?—[That clause] indeed gives an explanation: when does he [the Tanna] teach, BOTH MOIST AND DRY? In reference to the stalk.

An objection is raised: One can discharge [the obligation] with them and their stalks, both moist and dry: this is R. Meir's view. But the Sages maintain: One can discharge [the obligation] with moist [fresh] ones, but one cannot discharge [the obligation] with dry ones. And they agree that one can discharge [the obligation] with them [when] withered,[3] but not [when] preserved, stewed or boiled. This is the general principle of the matter: Whatever has the taste of *maror*, one can discharge the obligation with it; but whatever does not possess the taste of *maror*, one cannot discharge the obligation with it![4]—Explain it[5] [as referring] to the stalk.

Our Rabbis taught: One cannot discharge [the obligation] with them [when] withered. In the name of R. Eleazar b. R. Zadok it was said: One can discharge [the obligation] with them [when] withered.

Rami b. Ḥama asked: How about a man discharging his obligation with second tithe *maror* in Jerusalem? On R. Akiba's view,[6] there is no question: seeing that he discharges his obligation [therewith] in the case of unleavened bread, [the tithing of] which is [enjoined] by Scripture, need you ask about *maror*, which is [only]
b Rabbinical.[1] The question arises on the view of R. Jose the Galilean. What then? Is it only with unleavened bread, which is [tithed] by Scriptural law, that he cannot discharge his obligation, but with *maror*, which is [tithed] by Rabbinical law [only], he discharges his obligation; or perhaps whatever [measure] the Rabbis enacted, they enacted it similar to a Scriptural law?[2]—Said Raba: It is logical [that] unleavened bread and *maror* [are assimilated].[3]

MISHNAH. ONE MAY NOT SOAK BRAN FOR FOWLS, BUT ONE MAY SCALD IT. A WOMAN MAY NOT SOAK BRAN TO TAKE WITH HER[4] TO THE BATHS,[5] BUT SHE MAY RUB IT ON HER DRY SKIN. AND A MAN MAY NOT CHEW WHEAT AND PLACE IT ON HIS WOUND, BECAUSE IT TURNS LEAVEN.

GEMARA. Our Rabbis taught: These are the things which cannot come to fermentation: That which is baked,[6] boiled, and that which is scalded, having been scalded in boiling water. 'That which is boiled'? But while it is being boiled it turns leaven!—Said R. Papa: He means: baked [*mazzah*] which was [then] boiled. It was taught, R. Jose b. R. Judah said: Flour into which there fell a dripping [of water], even all day, does not come to fermentation.[7] Said R. Papa: Provided that it acted drop after drop.[8] The School of R. Shila said: *Wattiḳa*[9] is permitted. But it was taught: *Wattiḳa* is forbidden?—There is no difficulty: here it is such as is prepared with oil and salt;[10] there it is prepared with water and salt.[11]

Mar Zuṭra said: A man must not line a pot with flour of roast
c grain, lest it had not been properly baked[1] and it comes to leaven.[2]

(4) V. Shab. 84b (Sonc. ed.) note a.l. Then what does Rab add? (5) Because they draw their sustenance more vigorously, hence from a wider area. (6) Rab. (7) In drawing from the ground. (8) Cereal seeds must not be sown within this area, and the statement that five species of seeds may be sown in a plot six handbreadths square applies to vegetables (herbs) only. (9) I.e., the species enumerated *supra* in our Mishnah and Gemara. (10) This answer abandons the previous answer. Seeds (cereals) in fact require more space, for their drawing power is greater, and Rab informs us that *maror* belongs to the species of herbs, not seeds, and therefore the more lenient law applies to them. (11) All these authorities describe *maror* as herbs; how then could it be assumed that *maror* belongs to the class of cereals? (12) The last reply to the question, 'What does Rab add', being untenable, another answer is offered. (13) Its stalk becomes hard and thick.

a (1) A piece of ground of the capacity of one *roba'* (quarter of a *ḳab*) of seed. (2) Rab. (3) This is not the same as dry. (4) Here too R. Meir seems to state that both the herbs themselves (i.e., the leaves) and the stalks may be fresh or dry. And the Mishnah too evidently agrees with R. Meir, since the Rabbis maintain that dried herbs cannot be eaten. (5) The statement permitting its use dried. (6) V. *supra* 36a.

b (1) By scriptural law vegetables need not be tithed at all; hence Biblically speaking this *maror* is not second tithe. (2) So that *maror* is the same as unleavened bread. (3) V. *supra* 39a, n. b6. (4) Lit., 'in her hand'. (5) A bran paste was used as a depilatory or cosmetic. (6) Once unleavened bread is baked it can never turn leaven. (7) The incessant dripping prevents fermentation. (8) Without an appreciable interval between them. (9) Name of a certain pastry or tart made of flour. (10) Oil does not cause fermentation. (11) Then it is forbidden.

c (1) Lit., 'boiled'. (2) Though roast grain is baked, and therefore can never become leaven, yet we fear that it may not have been fully baked, and when the dish is put into the pot with the water this flour will ferment.

קנח א מיי' פ"ד מהל' כלאים הלכה ט טוש"ע י"ד סי' רצז סעיף לד:
קנט ב מיי' שם הלכה יג טוש"ע שם סעיף לז:
קס ג מיי' פ"ז מהלכות מצה הלכה יג ס:ג עשין מא טוש"ע א"ח סי' תעג סעיף ה:
קסא ד מיי' פ"ה מהל' חמץ הלכה יז סמג לאוין עט טוש"ע א"ח סי' תנד סעיף ג וסי' תסה סעיף א:
קסב ה מיי' שם הל' יט טוש"ע שם סעי' ב:
קסג ו מיי' וסמג שם טוש"ע א"ח סי' תסו סעיף א:
קסד ז ח מיי' שם הל' י טוש"ע שם סעיף ו:
קסה ט מיי' שם הלכה ד טוש"ע א"ח סי' תסג סעיף ב:
קסו י מיי' שם הל' ה טוש"ע שם סעי' ג:

ערוגה בת ו' טפחים זורעין לתוכה ה' זרעים · וא"ת הואיל ורחוק ג' טפחים לא ינקי מהדדי דהא אמצעית אינה רחוקה מן האחרות אלא ג' טפחים דבפרק ר' עקיבא (שבת דף פה:) משמע דד' מארבע רוחות הערוגה לא בקרנות אלא באמצע הרוחות א"כ יזרע לתוכה ט' זרעים ג' שורות של ג' ג' ויהא רחוקים זה מזה ג' טפחים ואומר ר"י דהכא אינה משום יניקה אלא משום עירבוב לאחר שיהיו גדולים ולא רצו חכמים להתיר יותר ותדע דאפי' חמשה לא היו מתירים אי לאו דנפקא לן בשבת בפרק ר' עקיבא (ג"ז שם) בהדיא מקרא אע"ג דקים להו לרבנן דחמשה בשיתא לא ינקי והיינו משום דאיכא למיחש לערבוביא ואם תאמר ואיך זורעים בתוכה חמשה זרעונים והא אין רחוק זה מזה שלשה טפחים דהא איכא מקום זריעה ותירץ ר"ת דטפחים של כלאים שוחקות כדמוכח בריש עירובין (דף ד:) ור"י אומר דגמירי דבהכי לא ינקי אע"פ שיש מקום זרעים:

לא שלוקין ולא מבושלין. משמע דשליקה הוי טפי מבישול דאי לאו הכי הוי זו ואין צריך לומר זו וכן משמע בכמה דוכתין והא דתנן בפרק ג' מינים (נזיר דף מה:) היה מבשל השלמים או שולקן אע"ג דשליקה הוי טפי מבישול לא הוי התם זו ואין צ"ל זו דקמ"ל דבשליקה אינו יוצא מתורת בישול*:
ה"ג

*ערוגה שהיא ששה על ששה טפחים זורעין בתוכה חמשה זרעונין ארבע על ארבע רוחות הערוגה ואחת באמצע מהו דתימא הני מילי בזרעין אבל בירקות לא קמ"ל למימרא דירקות אלימא מזרעים *והתנן ג כל מיני זרעים אין זורעין בערוגה אחת כל מיני ירקות זורעין בערוגה אחת מהו דתימא הני מרור מין זרעים נינהו קמ"ל זרעים סלקא דעתך והא תנן ירקות ותני בר קפרא ירקות ותני דבי שמואל ירקות חזרת איצטריכא ליה ס"ד אמינא הואיל וסופה להקשות ניתיב לה רווחא טפי לאו א"ר יוסי בר' חנינא קלח של כרוב שהוקשה מרחיבין לו בית רובע אלמא כיון דסופו להקשות יהבינן ליה רווחא טפי ה"נ ניתיב לה רווחא טפי קמ"ל: יוצאין בהן בין לחין בין יבשין כו': א"ר חסדא ד לא שנו אלא בקלח אבל בעלין לחין אין יבשין לא והא מדקתני סיפא בקלח שלהן מכלל דרישא עלין פרושי קא מפרש כי קתני בין לחין בין יבשין אקלח מיתיבי *יוצאין בהן ובקלח שלהן בין לחין בין יבשין דברי ר' מאיר וחכ"א לחין יוצאין בהן יבשין אין יוצאין בהן ושוין שיוצאין בהן כמושין אבל לא כבושין ולא שלוקין ולא מבושלין כללו של דבר כל שיש בו טעם מרור יוצאין בו וכל שאין בו טעם מרור אין יוצאין בו תרגומא אקלח ת"ר אין יוצאין בהן כמושין משום ר"א בר' צדוק אמרו יוצאין בהן כמושין בעי רמי בר חמא מהו שיצא אדם ידי חובתו במרור של מעשר שני בירושלים אליבא דר' עקיבא *לא תיבעי לך השתא במצה דאורייתא נפיק במרור דרבנן מיבעי' כי תיבעי לך אליבא דר' יוסי הגלילי *מאי במצה דאורייתא הוא דלא נפיק אבל מרור דרבנן נפיק או דילמא *כל דתקינו רבנן כעין דאורייתא תקון אמר רבא מסתברא מצה ומרור: מתני' ה אין שורין את המורסן לתרנגולים אבל חולטין ו האשה לא תשרה את המורסן שתוליך בידה למרחץ אבל שפה היא בבשרה יבש *ז לא ילעוס אדם חיטין ויניח על מכתו מפני שהן מחמיצות: גמ' תנו רבנן אלו דברים שאין באין לידי חימוץ האפוי והמבושל והחלוט שחלטו ברותחין מבושל אדמבשל ליה מחמע אמר רב פפא ח האפוי שבישלו קאמר תניא רבי יוסי ברבי יהודה אומר ט קמח שנפל לתוכו דלף אפילו כל היום כולו אינו בא לידי חימוץ אמר רב פפא י והוא *דעביד טיף להדי טיף אמרי דבי ר' שילא ותיקא שרי והתניא ותיקא אסור לא קשיא הא דעבדיה במישחא ומילחא הא דעבדיה במיא ומילחא אמר מר זוטרא לא לימחו איניש קדרא בקמחא דאבישנא דילמא לא בשיל שפיר ואתי לידי חימוץ אמר רב יוסף לא ליהלוט איניש תרי

אבל בירקות לא. דירקות יניקי טפי: למימרא דירקות אלימא. לינק טפי מזרעים דאיצטריך ליה למימר דאף ירקות נזרעין חמשה מינין בערוגה של ששה: כל מיני זרעים אין נזרעין בערוגה אחת. אפילו בשיעור הזה משום דיניקי טפי והא דתנן זורעין בתוכה חמשה זרעונין בירקות קאמר דנזרעים כהלכתן: מהו דתימא הני דמרור מין זרעים נינהו. ולא יזרעו בערוגה אחת קמשמע לן רב דמין ירקות נינהו ונזרעים: זרעים סלקא דעתך. היכי תיסק אדעתין דזרעים נינהו והא כולהו תנאי ירקות קרי להו: חזרת איצטריכא ליה. לאשמועינן דנזרעת כשאר ירקות בערוגה עם ארבעה זרעונין: להקשות. קלח שלה נעשה עב: מרחיבין לו. מקום עד בית רובע שלא יזרעו אצלו מין אחר: בית רובע. מקום זריעת רובע הקב אצל המשכן היה שיעור לבית סאתים וכל בית כור ובית סאה ובית רובע שבגמרא לפי אותו חשבון: לא שנו. דיבש יש לו טעם מרור אלא קלח דמתוך שהוא עב אינו מתייבש שיפסיד טעמו אבל עלין יבשין הרי הן כעפר בעלמא: מכלל דרישא בעלין. קא פסיק ותנא בהו בין לחים בין יבשים: כמושין. פלאישטר"ו בלע"ז: כללו של דבר כו'. קתני מיה' בדר' מאיר יוצאין בהן ובקלחין שלהן בין לחין בין יבשין ומתני' נמי מדמכשר ביבשים רבי מאיר היא ושמע מינה בעלין נמי מכשר: תרגומא. להא דקתני בדר' מאיר יבשין אקלח קאמר: השתא מצה. דמעשר דידה דאורייתא והיכא למיפסלה משום דאין לה היתר במושבות קאמר ר"ע דנפיק הואיל ואי מטמיא פריק לה ואית לה היתר: מרור. דמעשר ירק מדרבנן הוא ומדאורייתא אית ליה היתר במושבות מיבעיא: כעין דאורייתא תקון. ואין לו היתר במושבות ומרור איתקש למצה מה מצה בעינן נאכלת בכל מושבות אף מרור נמי בעינן יש לו היתר. ליכא אחריתא מצה בזמן הזה דאורייתא ומרור מדרבנן בפרק בתרא (דף קכ.) וזה שמעתי וקשיא לי בזמן הזה מי מסקי מעשר שני לירושלים ואי למאן דאמר קדושה ראשונה קידשה לשעתה וקידשה לעתיד לבוא בהדיא איבעי ליה לפרושי בזמן הזה: מצה ומרור. הוקשו יחד וכי היכי דמצה יש עליה שם מעשר שני ולא נפיק ביה אף מרור נמי שיש עליה שם מעשר שני לא נפיק ביה:

מתני' חולטין. ברותחין שאין מניחין אותו להחמיץ: לא תשרה המורסן. לשוף בה בשרה מפני שמחמיץ בשרייתו: אבל שפה היא. מורסן יבש בבשרה ואע"פ שמים שופכין על בשרה: לא ילעוס. לא יכוס: גמ' האפוי. לאחר שנאפה כל מה ששוריהו במים אינו מחמיץ: אדמבשל ליה מחמע. בעוד שהמים פושרים קודם שירתיחו הוא מחמיץ ובדשדי ליה לתוך רותחין ליכא לאוקומה דהא בהדיא תני לה וחלוט שחלטו ברותחין: אפוי שבשלו. כלומר אפוי אפילו הוא מבשלו לאחר אפייה אינו מחמיץ: דלף. מן הגג: אינו בא לידי חימוץ. שטירוד הדלף הנופל תמיד אינו מניחו להחמיץ: טיף להדי טיף. שנופלין טיפה אחר טיפה סמוך ותכף ואין שהות בינתים: ותיקא. מאכל קמח: מישחא ומילחא. בקימחא שרי דמי פירות אין מחמיצין: לא לימחי איניש קדרא. שמטבין תבשיל הקדירה על ידי שממחין קמח לתוכו ואפילו בקמחא דלאבישונא שנתייבשה וניקלית בתנור כשהיא לחה עושין אותה קלי בתנור והרי היא כאפויה אפילו הכי לא ליעביד: דילמא לא בשיל שפיר. לא נעשית קלי כל צורכה בתנור ומחמצת בתבשיל וכשהוא טורפה בקערה היא מחמצת (ועוד) שאין דרך נתינתה לתוך תבשיל רותח: לא ליהלוט. ברותחין:
תרתי

כלאים פ"ג [מ"א] שבת דף פד: [קידושין לט:]
כלאים שם [מ"ב]
[ברכות ד' לח:]
[לעיל לו.]
[שם]
[לעיל לו: וש"נ]
כתובות דף קב: ס"א בפסח
[ע"ז לג:]

הגהות מהר"י לנדא
א] אמר רב פפא האפוי שבשלו וכו'. חסר בליוני עין משפט מיי' פ"ה מהלכות חמץ הלכה ג:

[ועי' תוס' זבחים לו: ד"ה ללוין ועי' ברש"י ור"ן ורא"ש נדרים מט. ד"ה הנודר]:

רבינו חננאל
היא מנין לערוגה שהיא ששה על ששה טפחים שזורעין בתוכה חמשה זרעונים כו' ודחי' מהו דתימא הני מילי זרעים אבל ירקות בעו טפי ואקשי' וכי ירקות אלימי מזרעים והא איפכא תנן כל מיני זרעים אין זרעין בערוגה וזורעין כל מיני ירקות בערוגה מהו דתימא הני מרורים כולן ששנינו מיני זרעים ניתהו ואין זורעין אותן בערוגה בא רב להודיענו כי ירקות הן ונזרעין בערוגה אחת. ואקשי' והא מתני' ירקות קתני כל תנא תנא נמי ירקות קתני וליכא תנא דתני זרעים חזרת שסופה להקשות איצטריכא ליה סד"א ניתיב ליה רווחא טפי משאר ירקות כמו קלה של כרוב שהוקשה כלומר שגדל ונעשה קשה שמרחיבין לו בית רובע מכל צדדין פי' אין מניחין סביבותיו זרע כדי שישלח שרשיו לכל צד מפני שגדול הוא נעשה גם כך לחזרת קמ"ל דלא: יוצאין בהן באלו הירקות בין לחין בין יבשין. אמר רבא לא שנו יבשין אלא קלח אבל עלין לחין אין יבשין לא. ורב חסדא פרק תרגומא אקלח אבל עלין אין יוצאין בהן אלא לחין ושוין שיוצאין בהן כמושין אבל לא כבושין ולא מבושלין זה הכלל כל שיש בו טעם מרור יוצאין בו: בעי רמי מהו שיצא אדם במרור של מעשר שני אליבא דר' עקיבא ופשטה רבה כשם שיוצאין במצה שהיא מדאורייתא כך יוצאין במרור שהוא מדרבנן: מתני' אין שורין את המורסן לתרנגולין אבל חולטין: ת"ר דברים שאין באין לידי חימוץ אזיקנא כנון אפוי שבשלו וחלוט שחלטו ברותחין תניא רבי יוסי ברבי יהודה אומר קמח שנפל לתוכו דלף דעביד טיף כנגד טיף אפילו כל היום כולו אינו בא לידי חימוץ ותיקא דהוא כגון שתיתא דעביד במשחא ובמלחא בקמחא שרי פירש כי השמן מי פירות הוא ומי פירות אין מחמיצין אבל במיא ומלחא וקמחא אסור לא לימחי איניש קדירה בקמחא דאבשינא דלא בשיל שפיר ואתי לידי חימוצא. הא דאמר רב יוסף לא נחלוט איניש תרתי

מתני' אלו ירקות שאדם יוצא בהן ידי חובתו בחזרת ובתמכא ובעולשי' ובחרחבינא ובמרור. כולהו מפרש בגמ': כבושין. בחומץ: שלוקין. מבושלין הרבה מאד עד שנימוחין: מבושלין. כדרך בישול: ומצטרפין לכזית. אם אין לו מאחד מהן כזית אבל יש לו מזה חצי זית ומזה חצי זית מצטרפין זה עם זה כדי לצאת ידי חובתו: ובדמאי ובמעשר ראשון כו'. אבל בטבל לא ואף על גב דמעשר ירק דרבנן הויא לה מצוה הבאה בעבירה דומיא דעלין שאינו נקוב דאמרן בפירקין*: גמ' חסא. ליטוגא: הינדבי. עשב שקורין קרישפל"א: תמכתא. מרובי"א: אצוותא דדיקלא. סיב הגדל ונכרך סביב לדקל שקורין ווידיל"א: מרירתא. אמירפויי"ל והיא פופרץ: חרחלין. לא איתפרש שמו: ובחורין. חזרת: עולשי שדה. אע"ג דיש להן שם לווי הרי הן כעולשי גינה: עסווס וטורא ומר ירואה. מיני ירקות: הירדופנין. יש מפרשין אלויינ"א: חזרת גליס. שם לווי הוא: ערקבלין. מפרש בסוף פ' שני דעירובין *אצוותא חרזייתא הוא סיב גדול ועב ומין לעצמו הוא: וחזרתי על כל תלמידיו. של ר' אליעזר ובקשתי לי חבר לסייעני ששמע דבר זה מפיו ולא מצאתי: שרף. *כשסוחטין אותו במקום חיתוכו יוצא ממנו שרף לבן כחלב וקורין לייטו"ן: מכסיפין. אינו ירק מאד ככרתי אלא פלדש: כל ירק מר. תרווייהו אית ליה יש לו שרף ופניו מכסיפין והן הן סימני מרור: מדברי כולן. כל המפרשין שמות הירקות כגון מתני' ותנא דבר קפ"א ורבי יהודה ור' מאיר ותנא דבי שמואל מכולן למדנו שהמרור יש לו שרף ופניו מכסיפין שבכל הירקות הללו רואין אנו בהן הסימנין הללו: אמררייתא. פופרץ: והא. אנן רישא דכולהו חזרת תנן: ותנא דבי שמואל. נמי חזרת תנא ברישא אלמא היא קדמי לכולהו: מצוה בחזרת. כדמפרש טעמא כדרבא ור' יונתן: מאי חסא. מאי טעמא קרינן ליה חסא משום דזכר הוא דחס רחמנא עלן אלמא להכי קיימא: למה נמשלו כמרור. דכתיב (שמות א) וימררו את חייהם: תחילה רכה. בתחילה נשתעבדו להן ע"י שכר שהיו שוכרין אותן: מרור סופו קשה. הקלח שלו מתקשה כעץ: הדרי בי. לא אוסיף עוד: מרירתא דכופיא. מרה של דג ששמו כן: כי מנה. שהרי הוקשו: הירדוף. עץ שהמתיק בו משה את מי מרה ואמרינן (בסוטה) (מכילתא פרשת בשלח) נס בתוך נס שהוא היה מר והוא הירדוף: הרזיפו. מין זרע וסם המות לבהמה הוא: הרזיפו אינו ניקח בכסף מעשר דאינו פרי מאכל ואכן אוכלא בעינן דומיא דיין ושכר ובקר וצאן כדכתיב (דברים יד) ונתתה הכסף בכל אשר תאוה נפשך וגו': ואימא מרור חד. מינא הוא מהנך ירקות ולאו כל הני אלא מר שבכולן: כרישין. כרתי כרישין של גינה: כרשי שדה. שלווי"ש: והרמוצה. מין דלעת הוא ובמסכת נדרים (דף נא.) מפ' קרא קרקוזאי: אינן כלאים זה בזה. אע"ג שיש שם לווי לאחד אינו כלאים בחבירו: חזרת בחזרת גלין. וכן עולשין בעולשי השדה (זוגות זוגות כמו שהן שנויין): וכי תימא כולהו בהדי הדדי קתני. דבכל הני קאמר דאינן כלאים זה בזה חזרת עולשין וכרישין: זוגות זוגות. חזרת וחזרת גלין או עולשין ועולשי שדה וכן כולן שנינו דאין כלאים זה בזה אבל חזרת בעולשין לא: מאי. כולן נזרעין בערוגה אחת דאמר רב לעיל נזרעין כהלכתן קא אמר כדי שלא ייכנו זה מזה כגון חמשה זרעונין בערוגה של ששה על ששה טפחים כדתנן במסכת שבת (דף פד:): אבל

מתני' *ואלו ירקות שאדם יוצא בהן ידי חובתו בפסח בחזרת בתמכא ובחרחבינא ובעולשין ובמרור *יוצאין בהן בין לחין בין יבשין אבל לא כבושין ולא שלוקין ולא מבושלין ומצטרפין לכזית ויוצאין בקלח שלהן ובדמאי ובמעשר ראשון שנטלה תרומתו ומעשר שני והקדש שנפדו: **גמ'** חזרת חסא עולשין הינדבי תמכא אמר רבה בר בר חנה תמכתא שמה חרחבינא אמר רשב"ל אצוותא דדיקלא ובמרור מרירתא תני בר קפרא אלו ירקות שאדם יוצא בהן ידי חובתו בפסח בעולשין ובתמכא בחרחלין בחרחבינין ובחורין רב יהודה אומר אף עולשי שדה ועולשי גינה וחזרת עולשי גינה וחזרת הא תנא לה רישא הכי קאמר אף עולשי שדה כעולשי גינה וחזרת רבי מאיר אומר אף עסווס וטורא ומר ירואר א"ל ר' יוסי עסוס וטורא *אחד הוא ומר זה הוא ירואר תני דבי (ר') שמואל אלו ירקות שאדם יוצא בהן ידי חובתו בפסח בחזרת בעולשין ובתמכא ובחרבינין ובחרגינין ובהרדופנין ר' יהודה אומר אף חזרת יולין וחזרת גלין כיוצא בהן *ר' אילעא אומר משום ר"א אף ערקבלים וחזרתי על כל תלמידיו ובקשתי לי חבר ולא מצאתי וכשבאתי לפני ר"א בן יעקב הודה לדברי *ר' יהודה אומר כל שיש לו שרף ר' יוחנן בן ברוקה אומר כל שפניו מכסיפין אחרים אומרים [כל] ירק מר יש לו שרף ופניו מכסיפין א"ר יוחנן מדברי כולן נלמד ירק מר יש לו שרף ופניו מכסיפין אמר רב הונא הלכה כאחרים רבינא אשכחיה לרב אחא בריה דרבא דהוה מהדר *אמרירתא א"ל מאי דעתיך דמרירין טפי והא חזרת תנן ותנא דבי שמואל חזרת וא"ר אושעיא מצוה בחזרת ואמר רבא מאי חזרת חסא מאי חסא דחס רחמנא עילוון ואמר ר' שמואל בר נחמני א"ר יונתן למה נמשלו מצריים כמרור לומר לך מה מרור זה שתחילתו רך וסופו קשה אף מצריים תחילתן רכה וסופן קשה א"ל הדרי בי א"ל רב רחומי לאביי ממאי דהאי מרור מין ירק הוא אימא מרירתא דכופיא דומיא דמצה מה מצה גידולי קרקע אף מרור גידולי קרקע ואימא הירדוף דומיא דמצה מה מצה מין זרעים אף מרור מין זרעים ואימא הרזיפו דומיא דמצה מה מצה שניקחת בכסף מעשר אף מרור שניקח בכסף מעשר א"ל רבה בר רב חנין לאביי אימא מרור חד מרורים כתיב ואימא מרורים תרי דומיא דמצה מה מצה מינין הרבה אף מרור מינין הרבה אמר רבה בר רב הונא אמר רב ירקות שאמרו חכמים שאדם יוצא בהן ידי חובתו בפסח כולן נזרעין בערוגה אחת דלית בהו משום כלאים מתיב רבא *חזרת וחזרת גלין עולשין ועולשי שדה כרישין וכרישי שדה כוסבר וכוסבר שדה חרדל וחרדל מצרי ודלעת המצרי והרמוצה אינם כלאים זה בזה חזרת וחזרת גלין אין חזרת ועולשין לא וכי תימא כולהו בהדדי קתני להו והא אמר רב זוגות זוגות קתני מאי נזרעין דאמר רב נזרעין כהלכתן תנינא ערוגה

אצוותא דדיקלא. נ"ל דהוי מין זרעים דהא לקמן אמרינן מה מצה מין זרעים אף מרור מין זרעים*:

ואימא הירדוף כי מנה וכו'. בפ' לולב הגזול (סוכה דף לג:) פריך גבי הדס ואימא הירדוף אמר אביי דרכי' דרכי נועם ופ"ה דלא הוי נועם כיון דהוי סם המות לבהמה הכא נמי ה"מ לשנויי הכי אלא דמשני שפיר טפי אבל קשה לרשב"א דלעיל אמר דהירדופני כשר למרור ובפרק אלו טרפות (חולין דף נח:) משמע דהוי סם המות לבהמה דאמר בהמה שאכלה הירדופני כשירה ופריך היינו הירדפוני היינו סם המות ומשני תרי גווני סם המות:

ערוגה

קנו א ב מיי' פ"ו מהל' חמץ ומצה הלכה יג סמג עשין מא טוש"ע א"ח סי' תעג סעיף ה:

קנז ג מיי' פ"ג מהל' כלאים הלכה ג סמג לאוין רעג טוש"ע י"ד סי' רצז סעיף יד:

[וע"ע תוס' סוכה לג: ד"ה נסיב ועוד שם תוס' יג. ד"ה אפקותא]

ס"א חד הוא ומר זהו וזהו מר ירואר רש"ל

[לעיל דף לה:]

[ברכות לט.]

[דף כח: וש"נ בפרש"י וליע קלא]

נ"ל כשסוחטין

עירובין כח.

[תוספתא פ"ב ע"ש]

[פי' תוס' סוכה יג: ד"ה מררית ותוס' חולין נח: ד"ה עיקרא]

כלאים פרק א. [מ"ב]

רבינו חננאל

מתני' אלו ירקות שאדם יוצא בהן ידי חובתו וכו'. חזרת חסא עולשין הנדבי תמכא כך שמה חרחבינא אצוא דדיקלא ומרור מרירתא: אמר רבי יוחנן מדברי כולן נלמוד ירק מר יש לו שרף ופניו מכסיפין אמר רב הונא הלכה כאחרים דאמרי ירק מר ופניו מכסיפין ויש לו שרף והוא מרור רב אחא בריה דרבא הוה מהדר אמררייתא דדברא אמר ליה רבינא מאי דעתיך דמרירן טפי והא אנן חזרת תנן וכן תאני בר קפרא ור' שמואל חזרת ואמר ר' אושעיא מצוה בחזרת וכו' אמר ליה (אמרי בי) [הדרי בי] ש"מ דכולי עלמא מצוה בחזרת דהיא חסא: **אימא** מרורתא דכופיא יש מי שאומר תמרה של בהמה ויש מי שאומר מרה של דג ששמו כופיא והיא שיבוטא והוא קולים האספנין ודחי' בעינן מרור גידולי קרקע כמצה דהא הקישו הכתוב (במדבר ט י"א) על מצות ומרורים פי' הרדוף חרופא ואסיקנא מרורים כתיב מינין הרבה: **אמר** רבה בר רב הונא אמר רב ירקות ששנינו כגון חזרת ועולשין ותמכה והרחבינה וכיוצא בהן שאדם יוצא בהן ידי חובתו בפסח משום מרור כולן נזרעין בערוגה אחת דוקנן מינה כי אלו כולן מין אחד הן ואין בהן משום כלאים ומותיב רבא עליה חזרת וחזרת גלין עולשין ועולשין שדה כרישין כו' ואמרינן בסופה כולן נזרעין בערוגה אחת ודייקי' דוקא חזרת וחזרת גלין דתרוייהו מין חזרת נינהו הני הוא דליתנהו כלאים בהדי הדדי הא חזרת ועולשין אע"ג דתרווייהו מין מרור אינון כלאים הוו וכי תימא הכי קתני כל מין חזרת וכל מין עולשין וכל מין כרישין וכל מין כוסבר וכל מין חרדל וכל מין דלעת אלו כולן ביחד נזרעין בערוגה והא רב הוא דאמר זוגות זוגות שנינו כלומר חזרת וחזרת גלין הנה זוג עולשין ועולשי שדה זוג אחד כרישין וכרישי שדה זוג אחד כי האי גונא זוגות זוגות בפני עצמן אינן כלאים הא כולהו בהדדי כלאים נינהו ושני' מאי נזרעין דקאמר רבה בר רב הונא כהילכתן כלומר אם בא לזרען בערוגה אחת נותן לכל אחד כדי עבודתו שלא יהא זרע אחד יונק מגבול חברו ואמרינן הא פשיטא מתני'

יזא

MISHNAH. [39a] AND THESE ARE THE HERBS WITH WHICH A MAN DISCHARGES HIS OBLIGATION ON PASSOVER:[2] WITH LETTUCE [ḤAZERETH], WITH TAMKA,[3] WITH ḤARḤABINA,[4] WITH ENDIVES ['ULSHIN] AND WITH MAROR.[5] THE LAW IS COMPLIED WITH BY [EATING THEM] BOTH MOIST [FRESH] AND DRY, BUT NOT PRESERVED [IN VINEGAR], NOR STEWED NOR BOILED.[6] AND THEY COMBINE TO THE SIZE OF AN OLIVE.[7] AND YOU CAN DISCHARGE [YOUR OBLIGATION] WITH THEIR STALK[S], AND WITH DEMAI, AND WITH FIRST TITHE THE TERUMAH OF WHICH HAS BEEN SEPARATED, AND WITH HEKDESH AND SECOND TITHE WHICH HAVE BEEN REDEEMED.[8]

GEMARA. ḤAZERETH is *ḥassa* [lettuce]; 'ULSHIN is *hindebi* [endives]. TAMKA: Rabbah b. Bar Ḥanah said: It is called *temakta*.[9] ḤARḤABINA: R. Simeon b. Lakish said: [It is] the creeper of
a the palm tree. AND WITH MAROR: *merirta*.[1]

Bar Kappara taught: These are the herbs with which a man discharges his obligation on Passover: with endives, with *tamka*, with *ḥarḥallin*,[2] with *ḥarḥabinin*,[3] and with lettuce. R. Judah said: Also with wild [field] endives and with garden endives and with lettuce. 'Garden endives and lettuce': but that is taught in the first section?[4]—This is what he says: Wild endives too are like garden endives and lettuce. R. Meir said: Also with *'aswaws*, and *ṭura* and *mar yero'ar*.[5] Said R. Jose to him: *'Aswaws* and *ṭura* are one; and *mar* is *yero'ar*.[6]

The School of Samuel taught: These are the herbs with which a man discharges his obligation on Passover: With lettuce, with endives, with *tamka*, with *ḥarḥabinin*, with *ḥarginin*,[7] and with *hardofannim*.[8] R. Judah said: *Ḥazereth yolin* [thistles] and willow lettuce too are like them. R. Il'ai said in R. Eliezer's name: *'Arkablin* too,[9] but I went about to all his [*sc*. R. Eliezer's] disciples and sought a companion[10] but did not find one, but when I came before R. Eleazar b. Jacob he agreed with my words. R. Judah said: Whatever [plant which] contains an acrid [pungent] sap. R. Joḥanan b. Berokah said: Any [plant] the leaves of which look faded [bleached]. Others say: Every bitter herb contains an acrid sap and its leaves are faded. R. Joḥanan said: From the words of all of them we may learn [that every] bitter herb contains an acrid sap and its leaves are faded.[11] R. Huna said: The *halachah* is as the 'Others'.

Rabina found R. Aḥa son of Raba going in search of *merirta*. Said he to him, What is [in] your mind: that it is more bitter? But we learned ḤAZERETH; and the School of Samuel taught, *Ḥazereth;* while R. Oshaia said: The obligation is properly [fulfilled with] *ḥazereth*. And Raba said: What is *ḥazereth? Ḥassa*. What does *ḥassa* [symbolize]? That the Merciful One had pity [*ḥas*] upon us. Further, R. Samuel b. Naḥmani said in R. Jonathan's
b name: Why were the Egyptians compared to *maror?*[1] To teach you: just as this *maror*, the beginning of which is soft while its end is hard,[2] so were the Egyptians: their beginning was soft [mild], but their end was hard [cruel]![3]—Then I retract, he replied.

R. Reḥumi said to Abaye: How do you know that this *'maror'*[4] means a kind of herb; say that it is the gall of *Kufia?*[5]—It is like unleavened bread:[6] just as unleavened bread is a product of the earth, so *'maror'* means a product of the earth. Then say it is *hirduf?*[7]—It is like unleavened bread: just as unleavened bread is a species of plant, so *'maror'* means a species of plant. Then say it is *harzipu?*[8]—It must be like unleavened bread: just as unleavened bread is that which can be bought with second tithe money, so *'maror'* is that which can be bought with second tithe money.[9]

Rabbah son of R. Ḥanin said to Abaye: Say that *maror* means one [herb]?[10]—*Merorim* [plural] is written. Then say that *merorim* means two?—It is like unleavened bread: just as unleavened bread [can be of] many species,[11] so [can] *maror* [be of] many species.

Rabbah son of R. Huna said in Rab's name: [Regarding] the herbs whereof the Sages ruled that a man can discharge his duty with them on Passover, they all may be sown in one garden bed. Is this to say that they are not [forbidden] on account of *kil'ayim?*[12] Raba objected: [Lettuce] and willow lettuce, [garden] endives and wild endives, [garden] leeks and wild leeks, [garden] coriander and wild coriander, mustard and Egyptian mustard [and] the Egyptian gourd and the bitter gourd,—all these are not *kil'ayim*
c with one another.[1] [Thus] only lettuce with willow lettuce, but not lettuce with endives?[2] And should you answer, They are all taught together, surely Rab said: He teaches them in pairs?—What did Rab mean by 'they are sown'? They are sown according to their law.[3] [You say], 'According to their law'! but we [already]

(2) Bitter herbs are eaten on the first two (in Palestine one) nights of Passover, v. Ex. XII, 8. (3) A kind of cheveril (Jast.). (4) A kind of creeper. (5) Lit., 'bitter' (herb). A plant, prob. Cichorium Itybus, Succory (Jast.). (6) *Shelukin* means boiled to a pulp; *mebushalin*, boiled in the usual manner. (7) That is the minimum quantity which must be eaten; and it can be made up of all these. (8) V. *supra* 35a, n. b1. (9) Rashi: marrubium, hoarhound (Jast.).

a (1) The Aramaic for *maror*. (2) A prickly plant, thistles. (3) Pl. of *ḥarḥabina*. (4) What does R. Judah add? (5) Names of bitter herbs. V. next note. (6) Jast. *ferule*. Rashal reads: *'Aswaws* and *ṭura* are one, and it is bitter (*mar*), and that is (what is called) *mar yero'ar*. (7) Jast.: garden ivy. (8) Wall ivy. (9) Jast.: prickly creepers on palm trees, palm ivy. (10) To support me, that he too had heard it from R. Eliezer. (11) I.e., all the herbs mentioned by the foregoing teachers possess these two features.

b (1) In Ex. I, 14 where the Hebrew for *embittered* is from the same root as *maror*. (2) The top is soft, while the stalk hardens like wood. (3) At first they dealt mildly with the Israelites, but subsequently treated them with great cruelty.—All this was adduced by Rabina, to show that *merirta* was not preferable. (4) Prescribed in Ex. XII, 8. *Merorim*, pl. of *maror*, is the actual word used there. (5) Name of a fish, supposed to be identical with colias. (6) To which it is placed in juxtaposition, ibid. (7) Jast.: a shrub or tree with bitter and stinging leaves, supposed to be rhododaphne, oleander. (8) Name of a bitter herb, not generally eaten. (9) This excludes *harzipu*, for only what is generally eaten can be bought; v. Deut. XIV, 26: all the things enumerated there are normal victuals. (10) Viz., the most bitter of all. (11) V. Mishnah *supra* 35a. (12) V. Glos.

c (1) Kil. I, 2. (2) I.e., these *are* heterogeneous. (3) I.e., on the contrary, care must be taken not to sow them together, and when they are in one garden-bed the proper space must be left between the separate species.

Rabbah, Because Scripture saith, [38b] *And ye shall guard the unleavened bread:*[7] [it must be] unleavened bread which is guarded for the sake of [the precept of eating] unleavened bread, thus excluding this, which is guarded not for the sake of unleavened bread but for the sake of a sacrifice. R. Joseph said, Scripture saith, *seven days shall ye eat unleavened bread:*[8] [that implies] unleavened bread which may be eaten seven days, thus excluding this, which is not eaten seven days but [only] a day and a night.[9] It was taught in accordance with Rabbah; it was taught in accordance with R. Joseph. It was taught in accordance with Rabbah: You might think that he can discharge his obligation with the loaves of the thanksoffering and the wafers of a nazirite, therefore it is stated, '*And ye shall guard the unleavened bread*', teaching [that it must be] unleavened bread which is guarded for the sake of [fulfilling the obligation of eating] unleavened bread, thus excluding this which is guarded not for the sake of unleavened bread but for the sake of a sacrifice. It was taught in accordance with R. Joseph: You might think that a man can discharge his obligation with the loaves of the thanksoffering and the wafers of a nazirite; therefore it is said, '*seven days ye shall eat unleavened bread*', implying, unleavened bread which may be eaten seven days, thus excluding this, which may not be eaten seven days but [only] a day and a night.

Yet deduce it from [the fact that it is designated], '*the bread of affliction*', teaching, [it must be] that which may be eaten in grief, thus excluding this, which is not eaten in grief but [only] in
a joy?—He holds as R. Akiba, who said, "*ani*' is written.[1] Then let him deduce it [from the fact] that it is rich unleavened bread?[2]—Said R. Samuel b. R. Isaac: There is [only] a *rebi'ith* [of oil], and it is divided among many loaves.[3] Yet deduce it [from the fact] that they might not be eaten in all habitations?[4]—Said Resh Laḳish: This proves that the loaves of the thanksoffering and the wafers of the nazirite could be eaten in Nob and Gibeon.[5]

It was taught, R. Il'ai said: I asked R. Eleazar, How about a man discharging his obligation with the loaves of the thanksoffering and the wafers of a nazirite? I have not heard, replied he. [So] I went and asked it before R. Joshua. Said he to me, Surely they [the Sages] said: [AS TO] THE [UNLEAVENED] LOAVES OF THE THANKSOFFERING AND THE WAFERS OF A NAZIRITE, IF HE MADE THEM FOR HIMSELF, HE CANNOT DISCHARGE HIS OBLIGATION WITH THEM; IF TO SELL IN THE MARKET, HE CAN DISCHARGE HIS OBLIGATION WITH THEM. When I went and discussed the matter before R. Eleazar, he said to me, By the covenant! These are the very words which were stated to Moses at Sinai. Others state: By the covenant! Are these the very words
b which were stated to Moses at Sinai? And is not a reason required?[1] And what is the reason?—Said Rabbah: Whatever is for market, he may change his mind [about it], and he says, 'If it is sold, it is sold; if it will not be sold, I will discharge my duty with it'.

(7) Ex. XII, 17. E.V. translates differently. (8) Ibid. 15. (9) V. Lev. VII, 15.
a (1) V. *supra* 36a for this passage. (2) Since he follows the written text, "*ani*', viz., poverty; for the unleavened cakes brought with a sacrifice were kneaded with oil, which makes them 'rich' bread (*supra* 36a). (3) Only a quarter *log* of oil was used in the kneading of twenty large loaves: this would not make it rich *maẓẓah*. (4) I.e., outside the walls of Jerusalem; v. *supra* 36a. (5) Before the building of the Temple, Israel sacrificed at the 'high places', altars being erected at Nob and Gibeon, amongst other places. Resh Laḳish observes that since we do not deduce the present law from the fact that these loaves might not be eaten in all 'habitations', it follows that there was a time when they *were* eaten without Jerusalem, viz., during the period of the high places at Nob and Gibeon, v. Zeb. 112b. There is an opposing view, that of R. Simeon, that the thanksoffering and the sacrifices of a nazirite could not be offered at the high places, v. Meg. 9b.
b (1) Do you claim a divine origin for them that you draw this distinction without stating its grounds?

שמות יג °ושמרתם את המצות מצה המשתמרת לשם מצה יצתה זו שאין משתמרת לשם מצה אלא לשום זבח רב יוסף אמר אמר קרא °שבעת ימים מצות תאכלו מצה הנאכלת לשבעת ימים יצתה זו שאינה נאכלת לשבעת ימים אלא ליום ולילה תניא כוותיה דרבה ותניא כוותיה דרב יוסף תניא כוותיה דרבה יכול יצא ידי חובתו בחלות תודה ורקיקי נזיר תלמוד לומר ושמרתם את המצות מצה המשתמרת לשם מצה יצתה זו שאינה משתמרת לשם מצה אלא לשום זבח תניא כוותיה דרב יוסף יכול יצא אדם ידי חובתו בחלות תודה ורקיקי נזיר תלמוד לומר שבעת ימים מצות תאכלו מצה הנאכלת לשבעה יצתה זו שאינה נאכלת לשבעה אלא ליום ולילה ותיפוק ליה מלחם עוני *מי שנאכל באנינות יצא זה שאינו נאכל באנינות אלא בשמחה סבר לה כר' עקיבא דאמר עני כתיב ותיפוק ליה דהוה ליה מצה עשירה אמר שמואל בר רב יצחק רביעית היא ומתחלקת היא לכמה חלות ותיפוק ליה דאינן נאכלות בכל מושבות אמר ריש לקיש זאת אומרת חלות תודה ורקיקי נזיר נאכלין בנוב וגבעון *תניא אמר ר' אילעאי שאלתי את ר' אליעזר מהו שיצא אדם בחלות תודה ורקיקי נזיר אמר לי לא שמעתי באתי ושאלתי לפני ר' יהושע אמר לי הרי אמרו חלות תודה ורקיקי נזיר שעשאן לעצמו אין אדם יוצא בהן למכור בשוק יוצא בהן כשבאתי והרציתי דברים לפני ר' אליעזר אמר לי ברית הן הן הדברים שנאמרו לו למשה בסיני איכא דאמרי ברית הן הן הדברים שנאמרו לו למשה בסיני ולא טעמא בעיא וטעמא מאי אמר רבה כל לשוק אימלוכי מימלך אמר אי מזדבן מזדבן אי לא מזדבן איפוק בהו אנא:

מתני'

ושמרתם את המצות עביד לה שמירה לשם מצה. כל שימור שאתה משמרה שלא תחמיץ התכוון לשם מצה של מצוה: יצאת כו'. דלאו לשם מצה של מצות פסח עביד לה אלא לשם מצה של זבח: שאינה נאכלת לשבעה. דלאחר יום ולילה הויא נותר כדכתיב (ויקרא ז) תורה אור ובשר זבח תודת שלמיו ביום קרבנו וגו' והיכא דלא נשחט עליהן הזבח אע"ג דעכשיו יש לה היתר לשבעה מיהו כי עבדה לאו לשם מצה הראויה למצוה איתכוון דכי עבדה אדעתא לאיפסולי ביום ובלילה עבדה ואית ליה לרב יוסף הא דרשה (דרבה*) דבעינן שימור לשם מצוה ואההוא קרא סמיך ובהא פליג דאי נמי איכוין לה נמי לשימור מצת מצוה למיפק בה משום תודה ומשום מצה לא נפיק דבעי' שימור לשום מצה כל שבעה: ותיפוק ליה דאינה נאכלת לאונן. ולמה לי קרא אחרינא דכל קדשים אסורין לאונן ביבמות (דף עג:) אתיא לן בק"ו מה מעשר הקל אמרה תורה לא אכלתי באוני בשר קודש חמור לא כל שכן: סבר לה כרבי עקיבא דאמר · לעיל (דף לו.) במצה של מעשר שני נפיק ואע"ג דאסור לאונן דלא דריש עוני לשון אוני אלא עני כמשורת: ותיפוק ליה. כיון דדריש עני הא לאו מצה ענייה היא דהא נילושה בשמן: רביעית היא. חצי לוג שמן מביא לתודה וחולקו חציו לעשר חלות ועשר רקיקין וחציו לרבוכה במסכת מנחות בפרק שתי מדות (דף פט.) ובנזירות לא היתה רבוכה אלא חלות ורקיקין ולא היה מביא אלא רביעית כדאמרינן נמי התם הלכך רביעית שמן לעשרים חלות גדולות שנעשות משבע עשרונות פחות שליש עשרון שזה הוא שיעורן כדאמרינן התם בהתודה* אין כאן עושר: ותיפוק ליה דאינן נאכלות בכל מושבות. אלא בירושלים דמחיצת קדשים קלים לפנים מן החומה כדכתיב (דברים יב) ואכלת לפני ה' וגו' וכל נדריך אשר תדור ואם יצאו נפסלין דכתיב (שמות כב) ובשר בשדה טרפה וגו' כיון שיצא בשר חוץ למחיצתו נאסר: זאת אומרת. מדלא נפקא ליה מבכל מושבותיכם קסבר חלות תודה ורקיקי נזיר נאכלות בנוב וגבעון ודלא כר"ש דאמר בפ"ק דמגילה (דף ט:) דלא קרב בנוב וגבעון דהייט במה גדולה אלא פסחים וחובות הקבוע להן זמן אבל חובות שאין להן זמן קבוע לא ודלא כמ"ד בפרק בתרא דזבחים (דף קיז.) כאן וכאן במה גדולה דנוב וגבעון ובמה קטנה שהיה עושה בראש גגו לא קרבו ליחיד אלא עולה ושלמים ועל אותן שקרבו בנוב וגבעון הוצרך להביא ראיה מושמרתם את המצות וממצות תאכלו וגו' דלא נפקי מבכל מושבותיכם דאית להו היתר בכל מושבות שהיו יכולין להוליכן בכל מקום שירצו בתוך זמן אכילתן דתנן בפרק בתרא דזבחים (דף קיב:) באו לנוב וגבעון הותרו הבמות קדשי קדשים נאכלין לפנים מן הקלעים קדשים קלים ומעשר שני בכל ערי ישראל עד שלא הוקם המשכן היו במות מותרות ועבודה בבכורות משהוקם המשכן עבודה בכהנים ונאסרו הבמות עברו את הירדן והוקבעו בגלגל ז' שכיבשו וז' שחילקו היו הבמות מותרות באו לשילה לאחר שחילקו והוקבע משכן שם נאסרו הבמות וכולהו מפרש מקראי בפרק בתרא דזבחים חרבה שילה בימי עלי כשנשבה הארון בארץ פלשתים באו להן לנוב ולא היה שם משכן אלא בית של אבנים היה והוקבע שם מזבח הנחשת אבל ארון לא היה שם שכשהחזירוהו פלשתים עמד בקרית יערים עשרים שנה עד שמלך דוד והביאו לציון ובציון עמד עד שבנה שלמה בית המקדש כדכתיב (מ"א ח) ויביאו הכהנים את ארון ברית ה' וגו' ומזבח הנחשת היה בנוב כל ימי שאול ושמואל כדכתיב (ש"א כא) ויאמר אין לחם חול אל תחת ידי כי אם לחם קודש [וגו'] המוסרים מלפני ה' חרבה נב על דבר זה שהרגם שאול מפני שנתנו לחם לדוד ובאו להם לגבעון וניתן שם מזבח הנחשת עד שבנה שלמה הבית כדכתיב בדברי הימים (א כא): ברית. שבועה: ואיכא דאמרי. בתמיה אמר ליה וכי הן הדברים כו' דלא בעי טעמא כהלכה למשה מסיני: וטעמא מאי. גמרא בעי לה וטעמא מאי שעשאן למכור בשוק לצורכי תודה יוצא בהן אם לא מכרן הרי לא נשתמרה לשם מצה אלא לשם זבח: איפוק בהו אנא. ידי חובת מצה:

מתני'

זאת אומרת חלות תודה ורקיקי נזיר. פ"ה דלא אתי כר"ש דאמר בפ"ק דמגילה (דף ט:) לא קרבו אלא פסחים וחובות הקבוע להם זמן אבל שאין קבוע להם זמן לא וכפירושו משמע בפרק בתרא דזבחים (דף קיז.) דקאמר התם כל הנידר ונידב קרב בבמה ושאין נידר וכו' דברי ר' מאיר וחכמים אומרים לא קרבו אלא עולות ושלמים בלבד רבי שמעון אומר אף ציבור לא הקריבו אלא חובות הקבוע להן זמן משמע דמודה ר' שמעון לחכמים דלא קרבו מנחה ונזירות בבמה וקשה דבפ"ק דמגילה (דף ט:) תנן אין בין במה גדולה לבמה קטנה אלא פסח זה הכלל כל שנידר ונידב קרב בבמה שאין נידר וכו' ואמר בגמרא מני כר"ש היא א"כ לר' שמעון קרבה מנחה בבמה דנידר ונידב הוא ונזירות נמי קרב לדידיה בבמה דהא ר"מ דקתני בהאי לישנא כל שנידר ונידב קרב בבמה וסבר רקיקי נזיר איכא בבמה דאמר התם מאי טעמא דר"מ אמר קרא לא תעשון ככל אשר אנחנו עושים וגו' אמר להו משה כי עליתון לארץ ישרות אקריבו חובות לא אקריבו ומנחה ונזירות ישרות נינהו דנזירות גופייהו נידר ונידב הוא אע"ג דהקרבנות חובה ורבנן מפרש התם דסברי אין מנחה בבמה ונזירות אע"ג דנידר הוא מ"מ הקרבן חובה ונראה לר"י דה"פ דמתניתין דמגילה דאין חילוק בין במה גדולה לבמה קטנה אלא פסחים זה הכלל כל הנידר ונידב הקרב בבמה גדולה קרב בבמה קטנה וכל שאין נידר וכו' ולא נחית אלא לפרש מה ששוה הגדולה לקטנה אבל יש נידר ונידב כמו מנחה ונזירות שאינן קריבין לא בזו ולא בזו: **נאכלים** בנוב וגבעון. הקשה רבינו נסים א"כ היכי ממעט ביכורים מבכל מושבות והא ביכורים הוו חובה הקבוע להן זמן בזמן שמחה דמעצרת עד החג מביא וקורא א"כ קריבים בנוב וגבעון כמו פסחים שהיו קריבים לכ"ע ויש לומר דביכורים הואיל ויש להם זמן גדול כל כך לא חשיב זמן קבוע ורשב"א מפרש דמשום הכי הוו ביכורים חובה שאין להן זמן קבוע כיון שאם אין לו פירות לא יביא ביכורים:

אגוותא

ושמרתם את המצות מצה המשתמרת לשם מצה יצתה זו כו' דברי רבה ורב יוסף פשוטין הן התורה כתבה (ויקרא ז' ט"ו) ביום זבחכם יאכל וכן כל הלחם הקרב עמהואמרי' פשיטא דהא אין נאכלות באנינות ודהי' מתני' ר' עקיבא היא דאמר עני כתיב למעוטי מצה עשירהותיפוק לי' דחלות תודה על ידי משקה עשויות ושנינן רביעית שמן היא ומתחלק לכמה חלות: **ברית** הן הן הדברים שנאמרו למשה בסיני · כלומר ודאי ברית פי' נשבע לו בשבועה הן הן הדברים למשה בסיני אע"פ כן לאו טעמא בעיא: **אמר** רבא כל לשוק אימלוכי מימלך אי מזדבני מזדבני ואי לא אפיק בהו אנא ש"מ שכל הדברים המפורשים במשנה הלכה למשה מסיני הן ואע"פ שהן שנויין סתמא. ללישנא קמא ר' אליעזר אמר לר' אילעאי [ברית] הן הן הדברים וללישנא בתרא ר' יהושע עצמו הוא שאמר ברית הן הן הדברים:

נ"ל דרבא · [לעיל לו.] · תוספתא דחלה פ"א · [דף מה.]

מצות של מעשר שני לדברי ר' מאיר אין אדם יוצא בה ידי חובתו בפסח לדברי חכמים יוצא בה ידי חובתו בפסח אתרוג של מעשר שני לדברי ר' מאיר אין יוצא בו ידי חובתו ביום טוב לדברי חכמים אדם יוצא בו ידי חובתו ביום טוב מתקיף לה רב פפא בשלמא עיסה דכתיב עריסותיכם משלכם אתרוג נמי דכתיב ולקחתם לכם לכם משלכם יהא אלא מצה מי כתיב מצתכם אמר רבא ואיתימא רב יימר בר שלמיא אתיא לחם לחם כתיב הכא לחם עוני וכתיב התם והיה באכלכם מלחם הארץ מה להלן משלכם אף כאן משלכם לימא מסייע ליה עיסה של מעשר שני פטורה מן החלה דברי ר"מ וחכמים אומרים חייבת לימא מסייע היינו הך הכי קאמר (ליה) לימא מדפליגי בעיסה בהנך נמי פליגי או דילמא שאני התם דכתיב עריסותיכם תרי זימני בעי ר' שמעון בן לקיש מהו שיצא אדם ידי חובתו בחלה של מעשר שני בירושלים אליבא דר' יוסי הגלילי לא תיבעי לך השתא בחולין לא נפיק בחלתו מיבעיא כי תיבעי לך אליבא דר' עקיבא בחולין הוא דנפיק דאי מיטמו יש להן היתר במושבות אבל חלה דאי מטמיא לית לה היתר במושבות ולשריפה אזלא לא נפיק או דילמא אמרינן הואיל ואילו לא קרא עליה שם ואיטמי אית לה היתר במושבות ונפיק בה השתא נמי נפיק איכא דאמרי הא ודאי לא תיבעי לך דודאי אמרינן הואיל כי תיבעי לך חלה הלקוח בכסף מעשר שני ואליבא דרבנן לא תיבעי לך כיון דאמרי יפדה היינו מעשר כי תיבעי לך אליבא דר' יהודה דאמר יקבר דתנן הלקוח בכסף מעשר שני שנטמא יפדה ר' יהודה אומר יקבר מי אמרינן הואיל ואי לא לקוח הוי והואיל ולא קרא עלי' שם ואיטמי יש לו היתר במושבות ונפיק בי' השתא נמי נפיק ביה או דילמא חד הואיל אמרינן תרי הואיל לא אמרינן אמר רבא מסתברא שם מעשר חד הוא: חלות תודה ורקיקי נזיר וכו': מנה"מ אמר רבה דאמר קרא ושמרתם

אתיא לחם לחם. הקשה הר"י דאורליינ"ש כיון דילפינן לחם לחם דבעינן מצה שלכם אמאי איצטריך לעיל למעוטי שלא נאכלה בטבל ומי שאיסורו משום בל תאכל חמץ כו' תיפוק ליה דבעי' שלכם וטבל אינו שלכם דהא אתרוג של דמאי דמכשרי ב"ה בלולב הגזול (סוכה דף לה:) מפרש התם משום דאי בעי מפקר לנכסיה והוי עני וחזי ליה השתא נמי שלכם הוא וקרינן ביה משמע דטבל גמור לא חשיב שלכם ותי' ר"י אתרוג של טבל לא חשיב שלו כיון שצריך ליתן ממנו לכהן וללוי ובעינן שיהא כל האתרוג שלו אבל מצה שאם אכל כל כך שאם היה טחן ממנו תרומה או מעשר ממה שאכל אכתי אכל שיעור מצה חשיב שפיר שלו ורשב"א תירץ דאיצטריך לעיל קרא להיכא שמה שיפרים יהיה שלו [א] כגון אם הוא כהן או לוי או ישראל עני ונטל ממנו *כבר תרומה ומעשר ראשון דשלכם קרינן ביה*: **אבל** חלתו דאי מטמיא. זו הסוגיא כמ"ד (מכות דף כ.) מחילה לקלוט דאורייתא דאי מדרבנן יש לה היתר מושבות דאי יצאה חוץ למחילה נפדית אפילו טהורה אי נמי כיון דמדרבנן אין להם פדייה לא חשיב נאכל בכל מושבות: **או** דילמא הואיל ואילו לא קרי לה שם. תימה לר"י אי אמרת הואיל א"כ בכורים נמי נאכלין בכל מושבותיכם הואיל ולא קרי ליה שם וי"ל דלא דמי דשם בכורים אינו נאכל בכל מושבותיכם אבל הכא שם חלה נאכל בכל מושבותיכם וכן שם מעשר נמי לחודיה נאכל בכל מושבותיכם הלכך בחלת מעשר אמר שפיר הואיל ולא קרי לה שם ועוד הקשה אי אמרת הואיל מעשר שני נמי נאכל בכל מושבותיכם הואיל ולא העלהו לירושלים ומאי איצטריך לאוקמה לעיל (דף לו.) כרבי אלעזר וי"ל דאי לאו משום דר' אלעזר לא חשיב שם מעשר שני נאכל בכל מושבותיכם משום דהואיל ולא העלהו לירושלים כמו שאין לומר הואיל ולא קרא לו שם מעשר: **רבי** יהודה אומר יקבר. טעמיה דר' יהודה משום דדריש כסף ראשון ולא כסף שני ולכך אינו נפדה לקוח טהור ברחוק מקום וה"ה שאין נפדה טמא בקרוב מקום דתרוייהו מחד קרא נפקי מלא תוכל שאתו ורבנן לא דרשי כסף ראשון ולא כסף שני וסברי דלקוח טהור נפדה ברחוק מקום וה"ה טמא בקרוב מקום וקשה לרשב"א דבריש איזהו מקומן (זבחים דף מט.) פריך ולא מליט שטפל חמור מן העיקר והרי מעשר הוא נפדה ולקוח אינו נפדה דתנן הלקוח שנטמא יפדה נטמא אין לא נטמא לא והייט ברחוק מקום דכה"ג מעשר עלמו נפדה ובע"א לא הוי טפל חמור מן העיקר *אלמא לקוח לרבנן נמי אינו נפדה טהור ברחוק מקום ותירץ ר"י דהתם מיירי מדרבנן: **חלות** תודה ורקיקי נזיר. נראה לר"י כפ"ה דמיירי שלא נשחט עליהם הזבח ולא הוקדשו דאי הוקדשו תיפוק ליה דבעינן מצתכם דגמרינן לעיל לחם לחם ועוד דקאמר למכור בשוק יוצאין בהן משמע דבלא הוקדשו מיירי וה"פ מצה המשתמרת לשם מצה יצאה זו שמשתמרת לשם זבח כשיקדישנה וכן שאין נאכלין אלא ליום אחד אקרא *דמשתמרת סמיך דבעינן שתהא נשמרת לשם שבעה והא דפריך ותיפוק ליה שאין נאכלין באנינות ושאין נאכלין בכל מושבות ה"פ שאין נעשה לאכול בכל מושבותיכם ולאכול באנינות והא דלא פריך שאין נעשה להיות מצתכם אלא לגבוה כיון דלא כתב בהדיא פסול דמצתכם לא שייך למיפרך הכי:

ומלה של מעשר שני לדברי ר"מ אין אדם יולא בה. ואפילו לא דריש עוני לשון אנינות בעינן מלה שלו ולא של גבוה ולקמן פריך מי כתיב מלתכם: הכי קאמר. לימא מסייעא הא נכל מילתיה דרב אסי דמדהא פליגי באתרוג נמי פליגי: תרי זימני. אבל התם לכם למעוטי שאול וגזול אבל אתרוג של מעשר שני הוי דאתחזיה ליה לאכילה נפיק ביה ואפילו לר"מ: דרבי יוסי הגלילי. דאמר לעיל ילא זה שאינו נאכל באנינות: בחולין. לאחר שנטמא חלתו לא נפיק בחולין דידיה: כי תיבעי לך לר"ע. דלא דריש אוני ומיהו היתר מושבות בעי כדמיטעט לעיל בכורים מהאי טעמא ומעשר שני ריבה מושבות דאית ביה היתר מושבות אפי' לאחר שנכנס לירושלים אם נטמא כרבי אלעזר: לשריפה אזלה. דתרומה טמאה אסורה באכילה ובעודה טהורה אין לה היתר במושבות משום דמעשר שני הוא ובתר דקלטתה מחילות ליתא ליה פדייה: או דילמא הואיל ואילו לא קרא עליה שם חלה אית לה היתר במושבות. אם נטמא ונפיק השתא נמי לא פקע תורת מלה מינה משום קריאת שם חלה דהא חלה בעלמא לא נפקא מכלל מלה כדתנן מתניתין והכהנים בחלה אלא הא לא לחודה משום דאסורה ליה במושבות ואמרינן הואיל ונפיק: הלקוח בכסף מעשר שני. בירושלים דכתיב ונתתה הכסף בכל אשר תאוה נפשך וגו': ואליבא דרבנן. דפליגי עליה דרבי יהודה ואמרי לקוח בכסף מעשר שנטמא יפדה דאלימא לאיתפסא פדיונו לא תיבעי לך דאף על גב דהך חלה לית לה היתר במושבות לכל זמן שלא נטמא אין לה פדייה בירושלים ומשנטמאה שוב אין לה היתר אכילה דהא חלה היא אפילו הכי אמרינן הואיל ואילו לא קרא עליה שם הוה לה היתר במושבות על ידי טומאה דנפיק בה אף בירושלים השתא נמי נפיק כדאמרן במעשר גופיה: יקבר. כל לקוח בכסף מעשר שני שנטמא משום דקלישא קדושתיה ולא אלים למיתפס פדיוניה ואי נמי לא קרא עליה שם חלה לא הוה ליה היתר במושבות: מאי מי אמרינן הואיל ואי לאו לקוח הוא. כלומר הואיל ומעשר שני גופיה דאתי האי מחמתיה וקיל האי מיניה נפקינן במלה דידיה דאית ליה היתר במושבות על ידי טומאה והא דלית ליה היתר להאי לאו חומרא הוא לגביה אלא קולא הוא משום דלא אלים למיתפס פדיונו הלכך לא חמיר כדמעיקרא ואי משום דחלה הוא ובלאו לקוח נמי לית ליה היתר הכא נמי נימא הואיל אחריתא הואיל ואילו לא קרא עליה שם ולא לקוח הוא: או דילמא חד הואיל אמרינן. כגון חלת מעשר גופיה דלא נפקי בה אלא ע"י הואיל ואי לא קרא עליה שם אי נמי חולין של לקוח לא נפקי בה אלא ע"י הואיל ואי לאו לקוח הוא התם אמרינן הואיל ושרי אבל חלת לקוח דבעי תרי הואיל לא אמרי' וא"ת בחלת מעשר גופיה נמי תרי הואיל איכא הואיל ואי לא קרא עליה שם והואיל ואי מיטמא פריק לה ואית ליה היתר במושבות הכא לא קרינא הואיל דבר שיש בידו לעשות לגרום לה טומאה מיד ופריק: מסתברא שם מעשר חד הוא. וכי היכי דנפיק במעשר גופיה נפיק בחלתו הואיל ושם חלה לא נפיק בעלמא מכלל מלה ונפיק נמי בחלת הלקוח דהא מכח מעשר באה ולא מחמרינן ליה מיניה: ושמרתם

רבינו חננאל

וכן מצה של מעשר שני וכן אתרוג של מעשר שני אין יוצאין בהן ידי חובה ודייק מהא עיסה של מעשר שני פטורה מן החלה דברי ר' מאיר וחכמים אומרים חייבת נימא מדבהא פליגי בהני נמי פליגי ודחי' דלמא לעולם לא פליגי ושאני הכא דכתיב עריסותיכם תרי זימני ואמרי' מדכתיב תרי זימני בעינן עיסה שלכם שתהיה שלכם ממש של חולין ולא של מעשר שני דהא אינו שלכם אלא חשוב הוא כשלמים שהן קדשים והותרו לבעלים לאכלן בירושלים אבל אתרוג אע"ג דכתיב ולקחתם לכם למעוטי שאול וגזול הוא דאתא ולא למעוטי אתרוג של מעשר שני מצה נמי לא כתיב מצתכם ולחם לחם מחלה לא יליף: **בעי** ריש לקיש מהו שיוצא אדם בחלה של מעשר שני בירושלים אליבא דר' עקיבא דאמר אדם יוצא ידי חובתו במעשר שני בירושלים מי אמרינן בחולין דמעשר שני נפיק דאי מטמאי פריק להו לרבי אלעזר דאמר מנין למעשר שני שנטמא שפודין אותו ואפילו בירושלים שנאמר כי לא תוכל שאתו ואין שאת אלא אכילה שנאמר וישא משאת מאת פניו אלי' אבל חלה דאי מטמאי נשרפה לא נפיק בה או דלמא הואיל ואלו הוה מטמאי מקמי דנקרי עלה שם חלה הוה נפיק בה השתא (הוה) [נמי] נפיק בה: **איכא** דאמרי הא נמי לא תבעי לך דבודאי אמרי' נפיק בה דאמרי' הואיל וכי לא נטמא נפיק בה כי נטמא נמי נפיק בה כי תיבעי לך בחלת לקוח כלומר קנה חטים מכסף מעשר שני ועשה מהן עיסה והוציא חלה ואליבא דרבנן דאמרי לקוח שנטמא יפדה לא תיבעי לך דבודאי נפיק דהיינו מעשר כי תיבעי לך אליבא דר' יהודה דאמר יקבר דתנן במעשר שני פ' שלישי לקוח במעות מעשר שני שנטמא יפדה ר' יהודה אומר יקבר מאי מי אמרי' הואיל ואי [לא] היה לקוח והואיל ולא היה קורא עליהן שם חלה הוה נפיק בחולין דמעשר שני השתא נמי נפיק או דלמא חד הואיל אמרי' תרי הואיל לא אמרינן אמר רבא מסתברא שם מעשר חד הוא כלומר כיון שאומר הואיל במעשר לא שנא חד ולא שנא תרי: **וסוגיא** דשמעתין סלקא דאין קרוי לחם אלא האפוי בתנור אבל מעשה אילפס פטור מן החלה ואין מברכין עליו המוציא ואין אדם יוצא בהן ידי חובתו בפסח ואשכחן בתלמוד ארץ ישראל בחלה אמר ר' יוחנן ובלבד במעשה אילפס על ידי משקה והא דתאני יוצאין בסופגנין שנעשו על ידי האור מוקים לה ריש לקיש כשהאור מהלך עליהם מן הצד ובהאור מהלך על תחתיהן הרתיח ובסוף הדביק שלא על ידי משקה לחם קרי ליה. ירושלמי בתחלת חלה ר' שמואל בר נחמן שמע להון כלהון מן הדין קרא ושם חטה שורה ושעורה נסמן וגו' חטה כמשמעה שורה זו שבולת שועל ולמה נקרא שמה שורה שהיא עשויה כשורה ושעורה כמשמעה נסמן זה השיפון וכוסמת אלו כוסמין גבולתו עד כאן גבולתו וכי למדין מדברי קבלה אמר ר' סימון מדכתיב (ישעיה כח כו) ויסרו למשפט אלהיו יורנו כמי שהוא דבר תורה: **חלות** תודה ורקיקי נזיר עשאן לעצמו אין יוצא בהן מנא לן אמר רבא ושמרתם

קנא א מיי' פ"ו מהל' מלה הלכה ח:

קנב ב מיי' פ"ח מהל' לולב הלכה ב:

קנג ג מיי' פ"ו מהל' מלה הל' ו טוש"ע א"ח סי' תנד סעיף ד:

קנד ד מיי' פ"ו מהל' מעשר שני הל' יא:

קנה ה ו מיי' פ"ו מהל' מלה הלכה ט:

נ"ל כבר

[וע"ע תוס' סוכה לה. ד"ה דאי בעי]

[סוכה דף לה:]

[סוף כז:וש"נ]

סנהדרין קיב: [סוכה לה:]

[לעיל לו.]

[שם]

ב"מ דף נג: סנהדרין קיב. מ"ש פ"ג[מ"י] זבחים מט.

גליון הש"ס

תוס' ד"ה ר"י אומר כו' אלמא לקוח לרבנן כ"ע אינו נפדה. תמוה לי דלמאי צריך לזה הוכחה. הא מפורש כן בהך מתני' עלמה דקתני בסיפא א"ל לא אם אמרת במעשר שכן עלמו נפדה ברחוק מקום תאמר בלקוח שאינו נפדה בטהור ברחוק מקום ומוכח דרבנן מודו לו כוס:

הגהות מהר"ב רנשבורג

[א] בתוס' ד"ה אתיא לחם וכו' ורשב"א תירץ דאילטריך לעיל קרא להיכא שמה שיפרים יהיה שלו. נ"ב עיין ש"ות שאגת ארי' דף פ"ה עמוד דני"ת שזהו עד ש"ס דחולין דף קל"א ע"א שאפילו מעני שבישראל מוליאין את המעשר עני ול"ע:

ḥallah. [38a] [As to] unleavened bread of second tithe, according to R. Meir, a man cannot discharge his obligation therewith on Passover; according to the Sages, a man can discharge his obligation therewith on Passover. [With regard to] a citron[5] of second tithe, according to R. Meir he cannot discharge his obligation therewith on the Festival; according to the Sages, a man can discharge his obligation therewith on the Festival. R. Papa demurred: as for dough, it is well, because it is written, *of the first of* your *dough*,[6] [implying] of your own.[7] The citron too [is likewise], for it is written, *and ye shall take unto* yourselves,[8] [implying] it shall be of your own. But as for unleavened bread, is then '*your* unleavened bread' written?[9]—Said Raba—others state, R. Yemar b. Shalmia: [The meaning of] '*bread*' [here] is derived from '*bread*' [elsewhere]. Here it is written, *the* bread *of affliction*,[10] while there it is written, *then it shall be, that, when ye eat of the* bread *of the land [ye shall offer up an heave offering unto the Lord. Of the first of your dough* etc.]:[11] just as there [it means] of your own, so here too [it must be] of your own.

Shall we say that [the following] supports him: Dough of second tithe is exempt from *ḥallah:* this is the view of R. Meir; but the Sages maintain, It is liable? [You say], 'Shall we say that this supports him': this is the identical statement!—This is what he says: Shall we say that since they differ in the case of dough, they
a differ in respect to those too;[1] or perhaps it is different there, because 'your *dough*' 'your *dough*' is written twice?[2]

R. Simeon b. Lakish asked: Can a man discharge his obligation[3] with the *ḥallah* of second tithe in Jerusalem? On the view of R. Jose the Galilean[4] there is no problem; seeing that he does not fulfil his obligation with *ḥullin*,[5] can there be a question about its *ḥallah?* Your question arises on the view of R. Akiba:[4] is it only with *ḥullin* that he can discharge his obligation, because if it is defiled it is permitted in [all] 'habitations',[6] but with *ḥallah*, which if defiled, is not permitted in [all] the 'habitations' and is consigned to the fire,[7] he cannot discharge his obligation: or perhaps we say, since if he had not designated it with the name [of *ḥallah*] and it became defiled, it would be permitted in [all] the 'habitations', and he could discharge [his obligation therewith], then now too he can discharge [his obligation with it]?[8]

Others state, this is certainly no question, for we certainly say 'since'.[9] Your question arises in respect of *ḥallah* which was bought with the money of second tithe.[10] Now, on the view of the Rabbis there is no question, for since they say that it[11] is to be redeemed,
b it is [identical with] the tithe [itself].[1] Your question arises on the view of R. Judah who said, It must be buried. For we learned: If that which was bought with second tithe money was defiled, it must be redeemed: R. Judah said, It must be buried.[2] Do we say, *since* if it were not purchased, and *since* if he had not designated it with the name [of second tithe] and it became defiled, it would be permitted in [all] 'habitations', and he could discharge his duty therewith, he can [therefore] discharge his duty therewith now too;[3] or perhaps we say one 'since',[4] but we do not say 'since' twice?[5]—Said Raba: It is logical that the name of tithe is one.[6]

THE UNLEAVENED LOAVES OF THE THANKSOFFERING AND THE WAFERS OF A NAZIRITE etc. Whence do we know it?—Said

(5) One of the four species which are taken on the Feast of Tabernacles. (6) Num. XV, 20. (7) And whereas according to R. Meir second tithe is not 'your own'. (8) Lev. XXIII, 40. (9) Surely not! Therefore even if second tithe is not 'yours' according to R. Meir, the law is still complied with by eating second tithe unleavened bread. (10) Deut. XVI, 3. (11) Num. XV, 19.

a (1) *Sc.* the citron and unleavened bread. (2) Which lays particular emphasis on 'your', as explained above. (3) Relating to the eating of unleavened bread. (4) V. *supra 36a.* (5) I.e., with ordinary second tithe after the *ḥallah* has been separated. (6) This is a technical term denoting all places outside Jerusalem. I.e., when defiled it can be redeemed even after it has entered Jerusalem and then eaten anywhere. The fact that it might be eaten anywhere strengthens the reason for assuming that one can discharge his obligation with it, v. *supra 36b.* (7) *Ḥallah* is like *terumah*. Now when the *ḥallah* of second tithe is clean it must be eaten in Jerusalem, like all second tithe, while if it is defiled it may not be eaten at all, like all unclean *terumah*. Thus it can never be eaten without Jerusalem. (8) For the mere fact that it is *ḥallah* is no drawback, as stated in the Mishnah *supra 36a*, while its being second tithe is not a drawback either, on R. Akiba's view. Why then should it be unfit if it is *ḥallah* of second tithe? (9) I.e., this last argument is certainly valid. (10) I.e., second tithe was redeemed, flour was bought with the money, and now *ḥallah* was separated from the dough. (11) I.e., that which was purchased with second tithe money and which in turn became defiled, v. *infra*.

b (1) And the same law applies. (2) Its sanctity is too slight to permit of redemption, while it may not be eaten on account of its uncleanness. (3) I.e., the food that is purchased with second tithe money cannot be more stringently regarded than second tithe itself. For the fact that it cannot be redeemed is not due to its greater sanctity but on the contrary because its sanctity is too slight to be capable of transference. (4) I.e., in the case of *ḥallah* set aside from the second tithe. (5) I.e., in the case of *ḥallah* set aside from that which has been purchased with second tithe money. (6) Whether it is actual tithe or bought with tithe money. Hence they are alike, and therefore he can fulfil his obligations with the *ḥallah* set aside from either.

offer one [37*b*] *out of each oblation,*[6] '*one*' [intimating] that he should not take a broken-off piece, whereas here it is as broken off:[7] therefore he informs us [that it is not so].

An objection is raised: The *me'isah,*[8] Beth Shammai exempt it [from *ḥallah*], while Beth Hillel hold it liable [thereto]. The *ḥaliṭah,*[9] Beth Shammai hold it liable [to *ḥallah*], while Beth Hillel exempt [it]. Which is '*me'isah*' and which is '*ḥaliṭah*'?. '*Me'isah*' is flour [poured] over boiling water; '*ḥaliṭah*' is boiling water [poured] over flour. R. Ishmael b. R. Jose ruled in his father's name [that] both are exempt—others state, that both are liable. But the Sages maintained: Both the one and the other, if prepared in an *ilpes*, each is exempt; in an oven, each is liable. Now according to the first Tanna, wherein does *me'isah* differ from *ḥaliṭah?*[10]—Said Rab Judah in Samuel's name, and thus did R. Joḥanan—others state, R. Joshua b. Levi—say: Just as there is a controversy in respect of the one so is there a controversy in respect of the other, and they [the two clauses] are contradictory, he who learnt the one not having learnt the other.[1] Now it is at all events taught, 'But the Sages maintain: Both the one and the other, if prepared in an *ilpes*, each is exempt; in an oven, each is liable', which is a refutation of R. Joḥanan?—R. Joḥanan can answer you, It is dependent on Tannaim. For it was taught: You might think that *me'isah* and *ḥaliṭah* are liable to *ḥallah*, therefore '*bread*' is stated. R. Judah said: Nought is bread save that which is baked in an oven. Now R. Judah is identical with the first Tanna? Hence surely they differ over that which is prepared in an *ilpes:* the first Tanna holds, That which is prepared in an *ilpes* is liable; while R. Judah holds, That which is prepared in an oven is exempt!—No: All (agree) that what is prepared in an *ilpes* is exempt, but they differ here, e.g., where he rebaked it in an oven,[2] the first Tanna holding [that] since he rebaked it in an oven, it is called '*bread*'; while R. Judah holds, Nought is bread save that which is baked in an oven from the very beginning, and since this was not baked in an oven from the very beginning, we do not call it '*bread*'. Raba said, What is R. Judah's reason?—Because it is written, *ten women shall bake your bread in* one *oven:*[3] bread which is baked in *one* oven is called bread, but that which is not baked in one oven is not called bread.[4]

Rabbah and R. Joseph were sitting behind R. Zera, and R. Zera was sitting in front of 'Ulla. Said Rabbah to R. Zera, Ask 'Ulla: What if he placed [the dough] within,[5] and boiled it up[6] from without?[7] What shall I ask him, he replied, for if I ask him he will say to me, That then is the [very] preparation of an *ilpes!*[8]—R. Joseph [then] said to R. Zera, Ask 'Ulla: What if he placed [the dough] inside and the flame is opposite it?[1] What shall I ask him, he replied, for if I ask him he will reply, Most poor people do thus.[2]

R. Assi said: Dough of second tithe, according to R. Meir,[3] is exempt from *ḥallah;* according to the Rabbis,[4] it is liable to

(6) Ibid. 14. (7) Since it is not completely baked. (8) A paste made of flour poured over boiling water, contrad. to *ḥaliṭah*, where the boiling water is poured over flour, as explained in the text. (9) V. preceding note. (10) The Mishnah is first discussed and explained, and then the point of the objection is stated.

a (1) *Me'isah* and *ḥaliṭah* are alike in law. One Tanna holds that in both Beth Hillel are more lenient, while another holds that Beth Shammai are more lenient in both. (2) *Sc.* that which was prepared in an *ilpes* in the first place. (3) Lev. XXVI, 26. (4) Hence this excludes the case where it is first treated in an *ilpes*. (5) Rashi: in an *ilpes*. Tosaf: in an oven. (6) I.e., heated it. (7) Rashi: He placed a bread dough in an *ilpes*, baking it with an outside fire: is it bread or not? Tosaf: He placed in an *oven* such dough as is generally prepared in an *ilpes:* does this render it bread or not? (8) Which is a point of issue between R. Joḥanan and Resh Laḳish.

b (1) The flame itself bearing directly on the *ilpes*, which causes it to bake more quickly. (2) They cannot afford much fuel, and so they have the flame directly opposite it. Hence this cannot change its status. (3) Who holds in Ḳid. 54*b* that second tithe is *sacred*, not secular property, but that the Almighty favoured the Israelite by permitting him to eat it himself. (4) Who hold that it is secular property.

קמח א מיי' פ"ט מהל' מעשה קרבנות הלכה כב:

קמט ב מיי' פ"ו מהל' בכורים הל' יב טוש"ע י"ד סי' שכט סעיף ח:

קנ ג מיי' שם הל' ד:

אחד מכל קרבן *אחד *שלא יטול פרוס והכא כמאן דפריסא דמיא קמ"ל *מיתיבי המעיסה בית שמאי פוטרין וב"ה מחייבין החליטה בית שמאי מחייבין ובית הלל פוטרין איזהו המעיסה ואיזהו החליטה המעיסה קמח שעל גבי מוגלשין החליטה מוגלשין שעל גבי קמח ר' ישמעאל ב"ר יוסי אומר משום אביו זה וזה לפטור ואמרי לה זה וזה לחיוב וחכמים אומרים אחד זה ואחד זה עשאן באילפס פטור בתנור חייב ותנא קמא מאי שנא המעיסה ומאי שנא חליטה אמר רב יהודה אמר שמואל וכן א"ר יהודה* ואיתימא ר' יהושע בן לוי כמחלוקת בזו כך מחלוקת בזו *ותברא מי ששנה זו לא שנה זו קתני מיהת וחכמים אומרים אחד זה ואחד זה שעשאן באילפס פטור בתנור חייב תיובתא דר' יוחנן אמר לך ר' יוחנן תנאי היא דתניא יכול יהא מעיסה והחלוטה חייבין בחלה ת"ל לחם ר' יהודה אומר אין לחם אלא האפוי בתנור ר' יהודה היינו תנא קמא אלא לאו מעשה אילפס איכא בינייהו תנא קמא סבר מעשה אילפס חייבין ור' יהודה סבר מעשה אילפס פטורין לא דכולי עלמא מעשה אילפס פטורין והכא כגון שחזר ואפאו בתנור קא מיפלגי דתנא קמא סבר כיון שחזר ואפאו בתנור לחם קרינן ביה ור' יהודה סבר אין לחם אלא האפוי בתנור מעיקרא וכיון דמעיקרא לאו בתנור אפייה לאו לחם הוא אמר רבא מאי טעמא דר' יהודה דכתיב °ואפו עשר נשים לחמכם בתנור אחד לחם (ויקרא כו) האפוי בתנור אחד קרוי לחם ושאין אפוי בתנור אחד אין קרוי לחם יתיב רבה ורב יוסף אחוריה דרבי זירא ויתיב ר' זירא קמיה דעולא אמר ליה רבה לר' זירא בעי מיניה מעולא הדביק מבפנים והרתיחה מבחוץ מהו אמר ליה מאי איבעיא ליה דאי אמינא ליה אמר לי הי ניהו מעשה אילפס א"ל רב יוסף לרבי זירא בעו מיניה מעולא הדביק מבפנים ואבוקה כנגדו מהו אמר ליה מאי איבעיא ליה דאי אמינא ליה אמר לי רוב עניים עושין כן אמר רב אסי *עיסה של מעשר שני לדברי ר' מאיר פטורה מן החלה לדברי חכמים 'חייבת בחלה

מצות

תורה אור

אחד מכל קרבן. תרומה לה' לכהן הזורק וגו' ארבעת מינין היו בה של עשר עשר חלות ומכל מין ומין נותן אחד לכהן והשאר לבעלים וכתיב אחד שלא יתן לו פרוסה: המעיסה. החליטה: פוטרין. מן החלה: מוגלשין. רותחין: ותנא קמא כו'. ברישא מהדר גמרא לפירושא דברייתא דלא תהוי משבשתא והדר מסיים מילתיה ומותיב תיובתא מינה לרבי יוחנן: כמחלוקת בזו. כלומר המחייב בזו מחייב בזו והפוטר בזו פוטר בזו ורישא דמפיך פלוגתייהו לאו חדא תנא אמרינהו וקשיין אהדדי ומי ששנה זו לא שנה זו האי תנא אית לי' דמחומרי בית שמאי ומקולי בית הלל היא ותנא חליטה והוא הדין למעיסה והאי אית ליה דמקולי בית שמאי וחומרי בית הלל היא ותנא המעיסה והוא הדין לחליטה: תברא. קשיין אהדדי: תנא קמא סבר מעשה אילפס חייבין. והכי קאמר יכול תהא המעיסה והחליטה חייבין בחלה ת"ל לחם והני לאו לחם נינהו דקודם לישתן מבושלין ברותחין הן אבל מעשה אילפס שלא נאפו אלא על האור קרובין הן למעשה תנור ולחם נינהו וחייב ואפי' הדביק ולבסוף הרתיח ואמר ליה ר' יהודה מעשה אילפס נמי פטורין דאין לחם אלא האפוי בתנור: שחזר ואפאן בתנור. למעשה אילפס והכי קאמר תנא קמא ת"ל לחם והני לאו לחם נינהו דמבושלים במים הן והוא הדין למעשה אילפס נמי שהדביק ולבסוף הרתיח נמי לאו לחם נינהו אבל חזר ואפאו בתנור לחם קרינא ביה: ור' יהודה סבר. אפוי בתנור אחד בעינן ולא בשני תנורים כגון אילפס ותנור: הדביק מבפנים. הלחם באילפס: והרתיח מבחוץ. שנתנה על האור כמו שאנו עושים: מהו. מי הוי לחם: הי ניהו. אלו הן מעשה אילפס שנחלקו בו חכמים ר' יוחנן וריש לקיש: ואבוקה כנגדו. מלמעלה וחום האש לוהט באילפס וממהר אפייתו מהו מי הוי כעין תנור או לא: רוב עניים עושין. כל מעשה אילפס כן שאין להם עצים ובכך הוא ממהר לאפות: לדברי רבי מאיר. דאמר בפרק שני דקדושין (דף נד:) מעשר ממון גבוה הוא פטורה מן החלה כדמפרש דעריסותיכם כתיב ולא של גבוה:

ומלה

[מנחות עו: נדרים יב:] [חלה פ"א מ"ו] [עדיות פ"ה מ"ב]

[נ"א ר' יוחנן]

[פי' תוס' כתובות עה: ד"ה תברא]

סוכה לה.

ותנא קמא מאי שנא החליטה. תימה לר"י מאי קבעי מינה נימא דמר סבר עילאה גבר ומר סבר תתאה גבר ותירץ ר"י דקפסיק ותני אע"ג דלית ביה אלא שיעור חלה מצומצם ולהכי קבעי מ"ש דבין עילאה גבר ובין תתאה גבר אי אפשר שלא יתבשל מעט ממנו וחסר ליה משיעוריה: אמר לך רבי יוחנן תנאי היא דתניא. לא איצטריך לאשכוחי תנאי אלא ללישנא דאמרי לה זה וזה לפטור אבל ללישנא דזה וזה לחיוב איכא תנאי בהך ברייתא גופא דע"כ הא דמחייבא היינו באילפס דאי בתנור אבל באילפס פטור א"כ ר' ישמעאל ברבי יוסי היינו חכמים: דכולי עלמא מעשה אילפס פטורים. פסק ר"ח כר"ל מדקאמר דכולי עלמא מעשה אילפס פטורין ועוד דיתיב רבה ורב יוסף אחוריה דר' זירא אליבא דר"ל מיירי ולר"י נראה דכר' יוחנן קי"ל מדלא חשיב לה בהחולץ (יבמות לו.) בהדי ג' דהלכה כריש לקיש לגבי רבי יוחנן ואומר ר"י דעל ידי משקה מודה ר' יוחנן דמעשה אילפס פטור' ואין מברך עליו המוציא כדמוכח בירושלמי דמסכת חלה בפרק קמא דחלה אמר ר' יוחנן כל שהאור מהלך תחתיו חייב בחלה ומברכין עליו המוציא ואדם יוצא בה ידי חובתו בפסח ריש לקיש אמר אינו חייב בחלה ואין מברכין עליו המוציא ואין אדם יוצא בו ידי חובתו בפסח ואמר ר' יוחנן ובלבד שיהא על ידי משקין ואומר רבינו תם דדווקא בבלילתו רכה פליגי דר' יוחנן סבר אפייתו באילפס עושהו לחם וחייב בחלה ור"ל סבר אין עושהו לחם ופטור אבל בלילתו עבה כולי עלמא מודו דחייב בחלה אפי' על ידי משקה דהא חיוב חלה הוי משעת גלגול כדמוכח בכמה דוכתי וכן משמע במס' חלה (פ"א מ"ה) דתנן עיסה שתחלתה וסופה סופגנין פטורה מן החלה תחלתה סופגנין וסופה עיסה תחלתה עיסה וסופה סופגנין חייבת בחלה ונראה לרבינו תם דהכי נמי מברכין עליו המוציא נמצא ראיה ממנחות (דף עה:) ומכילד מברכין (ברכות לז:) דאמר היה עומד ומקריב מנחה בירושלים אומר שהחיינו נטלו לאוכלו אומר המוציא וקפסיק ותני כל המנחות אפי' מנחת מחבת ומרחשת אע"פ שמטוגנת בשמן ואין סברא לחלק בין מים לשמן א"כ על לפנצול"ו ופניטלט"ו אומר בורא מיני מזונות ועל גלטונ"ו וירבל"ו מברך המוציא ועל אופלטק"ו נראה שאין מברך המוציא אף על פי שעושין אותו בלא משקה דאין עליהם תוריתא דנהמא תדע שהרי אין מפרישין ממנו חלה אפילו יש הרבה בסל אחד כשיעור חלה אע"פ שהסל מצרפן לחלה ואע"ג דטריתא אמרינן בכילד מברכין (שם) דחייב בחלה ומברכין עליו בורא מיני מזונות ההוא כדמפרש התם דגובלא בעלמא הוא ואינו סועד הלב ורבינו תם היה אומר דאף על גרימזל"ו אין מברך המוציא דלית בהו תוריתא דנהמא אף על גב דמסתמא חייב בחלה: לחם שאין אפוי בתנור אחד. ואם תאמר מנלן לחלק בין בלילה רכה ובין בלילה קשה והלא אינו תלויה לר' יהודה אלא באפוי בתנור אחד ואומר רבינו תם דהכי פירושו לר' יהודה לחם האפוי בתנור וכו' לחם שרגילין לאפות בתנור היינו בלילתו קשה: הדביק מבפנים והרתיח מבחוץ מהו. לפ"ה דמפרש דמיירי באילפס תימה אם כן במאי סבר רבה דפליגי רבי יוחנן וריש לקיש ע"כ בהדביק מבפנים והרתיח מבפנים אם כן מאי מיבעיא ליה לרב יוסף בתר הכי הדביקה מבפנים ואבוקה כנגדו מהו ונראה לר"י דהכא בהדביק בתנור מיירי ומיבעיא ליה כיון דתנור הוא לא חשיב מעשה אילפס או דילמא לא שנא ולרב יוסף מיבעיא כשהדביק בתנור ולא הסיקו אלא מתבשל מהיסק שכנגדו וכן פירש רבינו חננאל:

התיא

רבינו חננאל

תודה: ת"ש המעיסה שהיא קמח על גבי מונלשים [פי' מונלשים] מים רותחים בית שמאי פוטרים וב"ה מחייבים החליפה שהיא מונלשים על גבי הקמח ב"ש מחייבים ב"ה פוטרים ר' ישמעאל אומר משום אביו כו' קתני מיתת וחכמים אומרים בין מעיסה בין החליפה עשאן באילפס פטורים בתנור חייבים קש"א לר' יוחנן אמר לך ר' יוחנן תנאי היא וכך סידורא במסקנא המעיסה ב"ש פוטרים וב"ה מחייבים והוא הדין לחליפה ותנא אחר שונה החליפה ב"ש מחייבים וב"ה פוטרים והוו פי' תברא מי ששנה זו לא שנה זו אלא תרי תנאי וכל חד מינייהו רישא וסיפא חדא קתני לה ופשוטה היא ודחי' לא כולי עלמא מעשה אילפס פטורה והכא בשחזר ועשאן בתנור ת"ק סבר כיון שחזר ואפאו בתנור לחם קרינא ביה ור' יהודה סבר אין לחם אלא האפוי בתנור בלבד מעיקרא: אמר רבא מאי טעמיה דר' עקיבא כו' ואסיקנא הדביק מבפנים והרתיח מבחוץ היינו מעשה אילפס הדביק מבפנים ואבוקה כנגדו רוב עניים עושין כן: אמר ר' אסי עיסה של מעשר שני לדברי ר' מאיר פטורה מן החלה לדברי ר' יהודה חייבת בחלה

וכמה פת עבה טפח. ואפי' הכי שרו בית הלל אבל טפי מטפח לא: שכן מצינו בלחם הפנים. שהוא אסור לבא חמץ כדאמרינן במנחות (דף נז.) כל המנחה אשר תקריבו וגו' לרבות לחם הפנים לחימוץ לאזהרה שלא יחמיצו ואפילו הכי עובי דפנותיו טפח דהיינו לחם שהיו לו פנים ואין פנים פתוחין *מטפח: הם אמרו. והתירו עובי טפח: לזריזין. כהנים שבקיאין בשימורו שלא יחמיץ יתירו לכל אדם שאינן זריזין: בפת עמילה. שאינה ממהרת להחמיץ שעמילתה מעכבתה עמילה ברייר"א כדתנן (מנחות דף עו:) כל המנחות טעונין שלש מאות שיפה וחמש מאות בעיטה: בתנור חם. בכל יום תמיד היו מסיקין תנור של מקדש לאפיית מנחות ולחמי תודה ושל מתכת היה כדאמר בזבחים בפ' דם חטאת (דף צה:): בעצים יבשים. שהיו מביאים אותן מימות החמה כדאמרינן בתענית (דף לא.) מחמשה עשר באב ואילך תשש כחה של חמה ולא היו כורתין עצים למערכה: פת מרובה. הרבה חררין ביחד ולאו משום חימוץ נקט לה ובחררין דקים קאמר ומשום דקא טרח טירחא דלא צריך הוא: ביחוד. בינו לביני רביה דר' ירמיה רב רביה דרב רבינו הקדוש לישנא אחרינא בייחוד בברור כמו וידעו ביחוד ששם ארון נגנז (יומא דף נד.): בלישה. כשלשין אותה עבה היא העיסה כשהיא כולה ביחד: הכי גרסינן תניא נמי הכי ב"ש אומרים. אין אופין פת עבה בי"ט ולא גרסינן בפסח: תניא נמי הכי. דלאו משום חמץ נקט אלא משום טירחא דהא הכא לא תנא פסח: ובסריקין המצויירים. מצות המצויירות ואע"פ שאמרו לכתחלה אסור דיעבד שפיר דמי: שוהה עליהן. לציירן ואין נותנין מהר לתנור ומחמיצין: אפשר יעשה. הצורה בדפוס ויקבענה בסריק: כיון. כלומר מהר בדחיפה אחת: יאמרו כל הסריקין אסורין ושל בייתוס מותרין. שהרי רוב נחתומין אין להן אותו דפוס: לא של כל אדם אמרו. לאסור דבעל הבית העושה אותן לעצמו אינו חושש לייפותן כל כך ואינו שוהה עליהן: אלא של נחתומין. העושין למכור ומקפידין על נויין ושוהין על ציורן: איכא דאמרי לא של נחתומין אמרו. לאסור שרגילין ובקיאין בדבר ויש להן דפוסין: עושין סריקין. מצויירין כמין רקיקין ובלבד שיהו דקין וקלושין דאין ממהרין להחמיץ אבל לא מציירין את העבים כגלוסקאות דמתוך עוביין מחמיצין בשהייה מועטת: הסופגנין. עשויין כספוג: והדובשנין. מטוגנין בדבש וכולן מין לחם: והאיסקריטין. עשויין כלפיחית דמתרגמינן איסקריטון (שמות טז) שלשין עיסתן רכה מאד: המסרת. תרגום של מחבת: ופטורין מן החלה. דכתיב (במדבר טו) באכלכם מלחם הארץ והני לאו לחם נינהו ולקמיה מפרש טעמא: והמדומע. חולין שנפלה תרומה לתוכן פטור דתרימו תרומה כתיב ולא שכבר היה תרומה: חלוט של בעלי בתים. אינו נעשה כתקון לחם: ריש לקיש אכולהו קאי ולאו לאפלוגי אדר' יהושע בן לוי אתא: מעשה אילפס הן. לפיכך לאו לחם הוא דקא סבר אין לחם אלא האפוי בתנור כדכתיב לחמכם בתנור אחד (ויקרא כו): והללו. להכי פטורין לפי שעשאן בחמה ולא באור: שהרתיחו. האילפס ואחר כך הדביק בה הלחם דהוה ליה כעין מעשה תנור הלכך חייבין: הינא. אינה אפויה כל צרכה לשון אל תאכלו ממנו נא (שמות יב): העשויה באילפס. ואע"ג דלחם בעינן כדכתיב לחם עוני (דברים טז): מאי מצה הינא. כלומר כמה תאפה ויהא יוצא בה: שפורסה. שמשברה לשון פרוסה: וכן לענין לחמי תודה. אם שחט הזבח עליהן מאחר שנאפת כענין הזה קידש הלחם והתודה כשירה דהואיל וקרמו פניה דתנן במנחות כי האי גוונא בעינן: אחד

ובית הלל מתירין וכמה פת עבה א"ר הונא טפח שכן מצינו בלחם הפנים טפח מתקיף לה רב יוסף *אם אמרו בזריזין יאמרו בשאינן זריזין אם אמרו בפת עמילה יאמרו בפת שאינו עמילה אם אמרו בעצים יבשין יאמרו בעצים לחים אם אמרו בתנור חם יאמרו בתנור צונן אם אמרו בתנור של מתכת יאמרו בתנור של חרס אמר ר' ירמיה בר אבא שאילית את רבי ביחוד ומנו רב איכא דאמרי *רב ירמיה בר אבא אמר רב שאילית את רבי ביחוד ומנו רבינו הקדוש מאי פת עבה פת מרובה ואמאי קרו ליה פת עבה משום דנפישא בלישה ואי בעית אימא באתריה דהאי תנא לפת מרובה פת עבה קרו ליה מאי טעמא אי משום דקא טרח טירחא דלא צריך מאי איריא בפסח אפילו בי"ט נמי אין הכי נמי והאי תנא ביום טוב של פסח קאי תניא נמי הכי בית שמאי אומרים אין אופין פת *עבה ביום טוב ובית הלל מתירין *ת"ר יוצאין בפת נקיה *ובהדראה ובסריקין המצויירין בפסח אע"פ שאמרו אין עושין סריקין המצויירין בפסח אמר רב יהודה דבר זה שאל ביתוס בן זונין לחכמים מפני מה אמרו אין עושין סריקין המצויירין בפסח אמרו לו מפני שהאשה שוהה עליה ומחמצתה אמר להם אפשר יעשנה בדפוס *ויקבענה כיון *אמרו לו יאמרו כל הסריקין אסורין וסריקי בייתוס מותרין אמר רבי אלעזר בר צדוק פעם אחת נכנסתי אחר אבא לבית רבן גמליאל והביאו לפניו סריקין המצויירין בפסח אמרתי אבא לא כך אמרו חכמים אין עושין סריקין המצויירין בפסח אמר לי בני לא של כל אדם אמרו אלא של נחתומין אמרו איכא דאמרי הכי קאמר ליה לא של נחתומין אמרו אלא של כל אדם א"ר יוסי עושין סריקין *כמין רקיקין ואין עושין סריקין *כמין גלוסקאות (א) *ת"ר הסופגנין והדובשנין ואיסקריטין וחלת המסרת והמדומע פטורים מן החלה מאי חלת המסרת אמר רבי יהושע בן לוי זה חלוט של בעלי בתים אמר ריש לקיש הללו מעשה אילפס הן ורבי יוחנן אמר מעשה אילפס חייבין והללו שעשאן בחמה מיתיבי הסופגנין והדובשנין והאיסקריטין עשאן באילפס חייבין בחמה פטורין תיובתיה דרבי שמעון בן לקיש אמר עולא אמר לך רבי שמעון בן לקיש הכא במאי עסקינן שהרתיחו ולבסוף הדביק אבל הדביק ולבסוף הרתיח מאי הכי נמי דפטורין אדתני סיפא עשאן בחמה פטורין ליפלוג וליתני בדידה בד"א כגון שהרתיחו ולבסוף הדביק אבל הדביק ולבסוף הרתיח פטורין חסורי מחסרא והכי קתני בד"א שהרתיחו ולבסוף הדביק אבל הדביק ולבסוף הרתיח נעשה כמי שעשאן בחמה ופטורין ת"ש *יוצאין במצה הינא ובמצה העשויה באילפס הכא נמי שהרתיחו ולבסוף הדביק מאי מצה הינא אמר רב יהודה אמר שמואל כל שפורסה ואין חוטין נמשכין הימנה אמר רבא *וכן לחמי תודה פשיטא הכא לחם כתיב והכא לחם כתיב מהו דתימא הואיל וכתיב °והקריב ממנו אחד

ובית הלל מתירין. טעמא דבית הלל כדאמרינן (ביצה דף יז.) מערמת אשה וממלאה תנור מלא ככרות אע"פ שאין צריכה רק לככר אחד אבל למלאות התנור פעם אחרת ליכא מאן דשרי*: תנא בפסח קאי. תימה דלא משני הכי בריש ערבי פסחים (לקמן צט:) דפריך מאי איריא ערבי פסחים וכו' וי"ל דהתם פריך משבת דהוי בכל שבוע ולא שייך לשנויי דנקט ערבי פסחים משום דהכא בפסח קאי*: ותנא

[סוכה ה.]

מלה אמר חסר פי' ביצה כב:

[ביצה אי' מרובה]

[מ"ק יד. חולין קו:]

ג"י הערוך מין תלה פ"א [מ"ד]

מנחות עח: [ע"ש]

[שם]

הגהות הב"ח

(א) גמ' כמין גלוסקאות תנן הסופגנין והדובשנין וכן גי' הר"ן:

גליון הש"ס

גמ' ויקבענה כיון. וכן במתני' פ"ו דתמיד מ"א פותח כיון. וכן במכ' כלה עמד ונפל על פניו וכיון אגב:

קמ א ש"ע או"ח סי' תס סעיף ה:

קמא ב ג מיי' פ"ג מהל' י"ט הל' ח טוש"ע או"ח סי' תקז סעיף ו:

קמב ד מיי' פ"ו מהל' מצה הל' ה סמג לאוין עט טוש"ע או"ח סי' תנד סעיף א:

קמג ה מיי' פ"ה מהל' מצה הל' טו סמג שם טוש"ע או"ח סי' תס סעיף ד:

[ועי' תוס' ביצה כב: ד"ה דנפישי]

קמד ו מיי' פ"ו מהל' בכורים הלכה יב סמג עשין קמא טוש"ע י"ד סי' שכט סעיף א:

קמה ז מיי' פ"ו מהל' מצה הלכה ו טוש"ע או"ח סי' תסא סעיף ג:

[וע"ע תוס' לקמן נט: ד"ה מאי]

קמו ח מיי' שם טוש"ע שם סעיף ג:

קמז ט מיי' פי"ב מהל' פסולי המוקדשין הלכה יז:

לקמן מ.

[ג"י הערוך בע' כד הדראה פי' לחם עב ובלשון לע"ז סוא אדר"ז]

רבינו חננאל

ת"ר אין אופין פת עבה בפסח וב"ה מתירין. ופרחי' לאוקמה במצה בפסח וכמה עבה טפח כעובי לחם הפנים שהיה מצה והיה עביו טפח ודחי' ואסקי' האי פת עבה פת מרובה היא ומשום טירחא ובכל יום טוב הוא ואמאי תנא בפסח משום דבעניינא דפסח הוה קאי: תניא נמי הכי ב"ש אומר אין אופין פת עבה ביום טוב וב"ה מתירין: ת"ר יוצאין בפת הדראה ובסריקין המצויירין ואף על פי שאמרו אין עושין סריקין המצויירין בפסח ואמרי' מאי טעמא מפני שהאשה שוהה עליהן ומחמצתן ויעשו בדפוס ודחו ואמרו אפי' בדפוס אין עושין וסריקי ר"ג אמר ר' (יצחק) [צדוק] לר' אלעזר בנו לא של כל אדם אמרו אין עושין אלא של נחתומין דבעו מסקי ליה טפי שהו עלייהו. איכא דאמרי הכי אמר ליה לא של נחתומין אמרו דפקיעי ועבדו לעגל אלא של כל אדם אמר ר' דלא פקיעי דבי ר"ג נפקיעי ר' יוסי אומר עושין סריקין כמין רקיקין ואין עושין סריקין כמין גלוסקאות: ת"ר הסופגנין והדובשנין והאסקריטין וחלת המשרת והמדומע פטורין מן החלה מאי חלת המשרת זה חלוט של בעלי בתים שאמרנו למעלה והן חלות אפויות במסרת על ידי טנן ומפני שאינן אפויות בתנור אלא במסרת נקראו חלת המסרת פי' מדומע פירות שנתקנו ונפלה בהן תרומה נקרא דמוע. מאי טעמא הללו פטורין מן החלה ריש לקיש אמר מפני שהן מעשה אלפס ואינו קרוי לחם אלא האפוי בתנור ור' יוחנן אמר אפי' מעשה אלפס חייב בחלה והללו לא נעשו באלפס על ידי אור אלא בחמה ומותבינן לריש לקיש הסופגנין והדובשנין והאסקריטין עשאן באלפס חייבין בחמה פטורין ומשני כגון שהרתיח האלפס ובסוף הדביק הסופגנין הללו באלפס חייבין [והכין קתני בד"א בשהרתיח האלפס ולבסוף הדביק] שנמצאת אפייתן [כמעשה תנור] אבל הדביק ולבסוף הרתיח נעשה [כמי שעשאן] בחמה ופטור והא נמי דתני יוצאים במצה נא ובמצה העשויה באלפס אוקמ' בשהרתיח ולבסוף הדביק ומצה נא כל שפורסה ואין חוטין נמשכים הימנה ואילו נגרי מינה חוטי בצק הוא עדיין ואסירי דבעינן לחם וליכא וכן לענין לחמי תודה

this is the view of Beth Shammai; [37a] but Beth Hillel permit it. And how much is a thick loaf?[8]—Said R. Huna, A handbreadth, because thus we find in the case of the shewbread [that it was] a handbreadth.[9] To this R. Joseph demurred: If they [the Sages] said [this] of men of care,[10] did they say [it] of those who are not careful?[11] If they said [this] of well-kneaded bread, did they say [it] of bread that is not well-kneaded? If they said [this] of dry *logs*, did they say [it] of damp *logs?* If they said [this] of a hot oven, did they say [it] of a cool oven? If they said [this] of a metal oven, did they say [it] of an earthen oven?[12] Said R. Jeremiah b. Abba, I asked my teacher in private, and who is it? Rab—others state, R. Jeremiah b. Abba said in Rab's name, I asked my teacher in a private, and who is it? Our holy Teacher.[1] What is [meant by] a thick bread? Bread in large quantity.[2] And why is it called a thick bread? Because it is much in kneading.[3] Alternatively, in the locality of this Tanna bread in large quantity is called thick bread.

[Then] what is the reason:[4] if because he takes unnecessary trouble,[5]—why particularly on Passover: even on any [other] festival too [it is forbidden]?—That indeed is so, but this Tanna was engaged on[6] the festival of Passover. It was taught likewise:[7] Beth Shammai maintain: One may not bake thick bread on a festival,[8] while Beth Hillel permit it.

Our Rabbis taught: You discharge [your obligation] with fine bread,[9] with coarse bread,[10] and with Syrian cakes shaped in figures, although they [the Sages] said, Syrian cakes shaped in figures must not be made on Passover. Rab Judah said: This thing Boethus b. Zonin asked the Sages: Why was it said [that] Syrian cakes shaped in figures must not be made on Passover? Said they to him, Because a woman would tarry over it and cause it to turn leaven. [But], he objected, it is possible to make it in a mould, which would form it without delay.[11] Then it shall be said, replied they, [that] all Syrian cakes [shaped in figures] are forbidden, but the Syrian cakes of Boethus are permitted![12]

R. Eleazar b. Zadok said: I once followed[13] my father into the house of R. Gamaliel, and they placed[14] before him Syrian cakes shaped in figures on Passover. Said I, 'Father, did not the Sages say thus, One may not make Syrian cakes shaped in figures on Passover?' 'My son', he replied, 'they did not speak of [the cakes of] all people, but only of those of bakers'.[15] Others say, he said thus to him: 'They did not speak of those of bakers, but [only] b of those of private people'.[1]

R. Jose said: One may make Syrian cakes like wafers, but one may not make Syrian cakes like rolls. We learned elsewhere:[2] Sponge cakes,[3] honey cakes, paste-balls,[4] cakes made in a mould, and mixed dough[5] are exempt from *ḥallah*.[6] What are cakes made in a mould?—Said R. Joshua b. Levi: That is *ḥaluṭ*[7] of private people.[8] Resh Laḳish said: These are prepared in an *ilpes*.[9] While R. Joḥanan maintained: Those which are prepared in an *ilpes* are liable [to *ḥallah*], but these [are exempt] because they were prepared in the sun.

An objection is raised: Sponge cakes, honey cakes, and paste-balls: if prepared in an *ilpes*, they are liable [to *ḥallah*]; if in the sun, they are exempt. This is a refutation of R. Simeon b. Laḳish?—Said 'Ulla, R. Simeon b. Laḳish can answer you: The case we treat of here is where he [first] heated [the *ilpes*] and then placed [the dough in it].[10] But what [is the law] if he [first] placed [the dough] and then heated it? Are they indeed exempt! Then instead of teaching [in] the second clause, 'if prepared in the *sun*, they are exempt', let him draw a distinction in that itself and teach: When is that? E.g., if he heated [it] and then placed [the dough]; but if he [first] placed [the dough] and then heated it, they are exempt?—There is a lacuna [in this teaching], and it was thus taught: When is that? If he heated [it] and then placed [the dough]; but if he first placed [the dough] and then heated it, it becomes as though he prepared it in the sun, and they are exempt.

Come and hear: You discharge your duty with partially baked unleavened bread and unleavened bread which was prepared in an c *ilpes?*[1]—Here too it means that he [first] heats it and then places [the dough]. What is partially baked unleavened bread?[2]—Said Rab Judah in Samuel's name: Whatever can be broken without threads dragging from it.[3]

Raba said: And the same [rule applies to] loaves of the thanks-offering.[4] That is obvious: '*bread*' is written here and 'bread' is written there?[5]—You might say, since it is written, *and he shall*

(8) Which Beth Hillel permit. (9) Though the shewbread was unleavened (Men. 27a). (10) *Sc.* the priests. (11) Unleavened bread for Passover is made by all, and many cannot exercise sufficient care to prevent the dough from fermenting when it is so thick. (12) In the preparation of the shewbread all these conditions would be observed; but they might be absent in a private home.

a (1) Viz., R. Judah ha-Nasi. (2) Though baked in thin wafers. (3) I.e., when sufficient dough is kneaded for many wafers. (4) That Beth Shammai forbid it, seeing that we are actually dealing with thin wafers. (5) In kneading so much at a time. Though food may be prepared on Festivals, unnecessary trouble is forbidden. (6) Lit., 'standing at'. (7) That it is forbidden because of the unnecessary labour. (8) Here Passover is not mentioned. (9) Bread made of fine meal. (10) 'Ar.: thick bread. (11) Lit., 'immediately'. (12) Which is absurd. Most bakers lack these moulds! (13) Lit., 'entered after'. (14) Lit., 'brought'. (15) Who bake for sale. They are more particular for the shape to be exactly right and so may take too long over it. But private people are not so particular.

b (1) Because professionals are more expert; also they may have moulds, and so can make them more quickly. (2) This is the reading of Ran, and it is so emended here by BaḤ. (3) Cakes made from a spongy dough. (4) A kind of cake made of very loose dough. (5) A dough of *ḥullin* into which there fell dough of *terumah*. (6) V. Glos. (7) V. 36b, n. a14. (8) I.e., home-made pancakes. They are not made like bread, and only dough made for bread is subject to *ḥallah*. (9) Jast.: a tightly covered stew pot. I.e., it is not bread at all, Resh Laḳish holding that only that which is baked in an oven is bread to be subject to *ḥallah*. (10) When the *ilpes* is first heated it is similar to an oven.—*Hidbiḳ* (הדביק) lit., 'to cause to cleave', the cake being pressed to the side of the pot, which was the ancient method of baking.

c (1) Which proves that what is baked in an *ilpes* is bread, thus refuting R. Simeon b. Laḳish. (2) What is the minimum? (3) It must be baked at least as much as that. (4) The thanksoffering was accompanied by forty loaves, which were sanctified by the killing of the sacrifice. As soon as the loaves have arrived at this stage of baking as defined by Rab Judah, they become sanctified by the slaughtering of the sacrifice, and the sacrifice itself valid. (5) Obviously then the same definition applies to both. *Ḥallah: when ye eat of the bread of the land* (Num. XV, 19); the thanksoffering: Lev. VII, 13: *with cakes of leavened bread* etc.

[36*b*] [and] I will [thus] exclude wheat and barley, which species are subject to first fruits? Hence [the repetition,] '*unleavened bread*', '*unleavened bread*',[3] is stated as an extension. If [the repetition,] '*unleavened bread, unleavened bread*' is an extension, then even first fruits too [may be included]?—R. Akiba retracted.[4] For it was taught: You might think that a man can discharge his obligation with first fruits. Therefore it is stated, '*in all your habitations shall ye eat unleavened bread*', teaching, [it must be] unleavened bread which is eaten in all your habitations, thus excluding first fruits, which may not be eaten in all your habitations save in Jerusalem [alone]. You might think that I exclude second tithe too,[5] but [the repetition] '*unleavened bread*', '*unleavened bread*', is stated as an extension. But what [reason] do you see to include second tithe and exclude first fruits?—I include second tithe because it can be permitted [to be eaten] in all habitations,[6] in accordance with R. Eleazar, and I exclude first fruits, for which there is no permission in all habitations. For R. Eleazar said: Whence do we know in the case of second tithe that became defiled, that we can redeem it even in Jerusalem? From the verse, *when thou art not able* se'etho [*to bear it*].[7] Now *se'eth*[8] can only refer to eating, as it is said, *And he took and sent* mase'oth [*messes*] *unto them from before him*.[9] Now, whom do you know to
a maintain that he fulfils his obligation with second tithe? R. Akiba.[1] Yet he excludes first fruits through [the phrase] '*in all your habitations*'.[2] This proves that he retracted.

And R. Jose the Galilean, let him deduce it from [the phrase] '*the bread of affliction* ['oni]', implying, that which can be eaten in grief, thus excluding this [*sc.* first fruits], which can be eaten only in rejoicing?[3]—He holds as R. Simeon, For it was taught: First fruits are forbidden to an *onen*;[4] but R. Simeon permits [them]. What is the reason of the Rabbis?[5]—Because it is written, *Thou mayest not eat within thy gates* [*the tithe of thy corn . . . nor the heave-offering of thy hand*],[6] and a Master said: '*The heave-offering of* [terumoth] *thy hand*' means first fruits. Thus first fruits are assimilated to tithe: just as tithe is forbidden to an *onen*,[7] so are first fruits forbidden to an *onen*. And R. Simeon?[8]—The Divine Law designated them '*terumah*', [hence they are] like *terumah*: just as *terumah* is permitted to an *onen*, so are first fruits permitted to an *onen*. Now R. Simeon: granted that he does not accept the *hekkesh*,[9] yet 'rejoicing' is nevertheless written in connection therewith, for it is written, *and thou shalt rejoice in all the good* etc.?[10]—That comes for the *time* of rejoicing.[11] For we learned: From Pentecost until the Festival [of Tabernacles] he [the Israelite] brings [the first fruits] and recites [the 'confession'];[12] between the Festival and Ḥanukkah[13] he brings [the first fruits] but does not recite [the 'confession'].

Our Rabbis taught: '*Bread of poverty*', this excludes *haluṭ*[14] and
b *ashishah* [pancake].[1] You might think that a man can discharge his obligation only with coarse bread;[2] therefore [the repetition] '*unleavened bread*', *unleavened bread*', is stated as an extension, [intimating] even [if it is] like the unleavened bread of Solomon.[3] If so, why is '*bread of poverty*' stated? To exclude *haluṭ* and pancakes. And where is it implied that this [word] '*ashishah*' denotes something of value?[4]—Because it is written, *And he dealt among all the people, even among the whole multitude of Israel, both to men and women, to every one a cake of bread, and a good piece of flesh* [eshpar] *and an* ashishah,[5] whereon R. Ḥanan b. Abba said: '*Eshpar*' means one sixth [*eḥad mishshishah*] of a bullock [*par*]; *ashishah* means [a cake made with] one sixth of an *ephah* [of flour].[6] Now he differs from Samuel, for Samuel said: *Ashishah* is a cask of wine, for it is written, *and love casks of* [ashishe] *grapes*.[7]

Our Rabbis taught: One may not bake a thick loaf on Passover:

(3) V. *supra* 35*b* and note a.l. (4) From the view that unleavened bread and bitter herbs are assimilated in this respect, and he accepts the deduction of R. Jose the Galilean. (5) In Jerusalem, since it may not be eaten outside Jerusalem. (6) When it becomes defiled as explained below. (7) Deut. XIV, 24; the next verse states, *then thou shalt turn it into money*. (8) שאת, *to bear*. (9) Gen. XLIII, 34. Thus he translates the first verse: *If thou art not able to eat it*—being defiled—*then thou shalt turn it into money*—i.e., redeem it.

a (1) *Supra* 36*a*. (2) Not by assimilating unleavened bread and bitter herbs. (3) V. *supra* 36*a*. Why then does he deduce it from, '*in all your habitations*'? (4) V. *supra* 36*a*, n. a4. (5) I.e., the first view, which forbids. (6) Deut. XII, 17. (7) V. Deut. XXVI, 14. (8) How does he justify his view? (9) V. Glos. I.e., even if he rejects the comparison of first fruits and tithe. (10) Ibid. 11; this refers to first fruits. Since rejoicing is required, an *onen* is automatically excluded. (11) I.e., to teach that the first fruits must be brought to the priest, and the passage relative thereto, called the 'confession', recited at a time of natural rejoicing, viz., during the months of harvesting and collecting the produce from the fields. (12) *Sc.* Deut. XXVI, 3-10. (13) V. Glos. It generally falls towards the end of December. (14) A rich bread made of dough prepared by stirring the flour with hot water.

b (1) Where the dough is made compact and substantial by pressing (Jast.). (2) Which is really '*bread of poverty*'. (3) I.e., made of the finest flour. (4) Viz., a rich food. (5) II Sam. VI, 19. (6) E.V.: *a cake of raisins*. (7) Hos. III, 1; i.e., of wine. E.V.: *cakes of raisins*.

[מהרש"א גורס ול"ת אם כן כו' ולאו לחם בעינן כו' ועי' רש"ל]

קלד א מיי' פ"ג מהל' מעשר שני הל"ג

קלה ב מיי' פ"ג מהל' בכורים הלכה ו:

קלו ג מיי' פ"ג מהל' מעשר שני הל' ה:

קלז ד מיי' פ"ד מהל' בכורים הלכה יג:

קלח ה מיי' פ"ה מהל' מלה הל' ג טוש"ע או"ח סי' תנד סעיף ג:

קלט ו מיי' פ"ו מהל' מלה הל' ה טוש"ע או"ח סי' תנד סעיף א:

אוציא חיטין ושעורין שיש במינן ביכורים ת"ל מצות מצות ריבה אי מצות ריבה אפילו ביכורים נמי הדר ביה רע"ק דתניא יכול יצא אדם ידי חובתו בביכורים ת"ל בכל משבותיכם תאכלו מצות מצה הנאכלת בכל מושבות יצאו ביכורים שאינן נאכלין בכל מושבות אלא בירושלים יכול שאני מוציא אף מעשר שני תלמוד לומר מצות מצות ריבה ומה ראית לרבות מעשר שני ולהוציא ביכורים מרבה אני מעשר שני שיש לו היתר בכל מושבות כדר' (אליעזר) ומוציא אני ביכורים שאין להן היתר בכל מושבות *דא"ר (אליעזר) *מנין למעשר שני שנטמא שפודין אותו אפי' בירושלים ת"ל כי לא תוכל שאתו ואין שאת אלא אכילה שנאמר וישא משאת מאת פניו מאן שמעת ליה דאמר במעשר שני נפיק ביה רבי עקיבא וקממעט להו לביכורים מבכל מושבותיכם שמע מינה הדר ביה ור' יוסי הגלילי תיפוק לי' מלחם עוני מי שנאכל באוני יצא זה שאין נאכל אלא בשמחה סבר ליה כרבי שמעון *דתניא ביכורים אסורין לאונן ור' שמעון מתיר מאי טעמא דרבנן דכתיב לא תוכל לאכול בשעריך ואמר מר *תרומת ידך אלו ביכורים דאיתקש ביכורים למעשר מה מעשר אסור לאונן אף ביכורים אסור לאונן ורבי שמעון תרומה קרינהו רחמנא כתרומה מה תרומה מותרת לאונן אף ביכורים מותר לאונן ורבי שמעון נהי דהיקיש לית ליה שמחה מיהא מיכתב כתיבא בהו דכתי' ושמחת בכל הטוב ההוא לזמן שמחה הוא דאתא *דתנן מעצרת ועד החג מביא וקורא מהחג ועד חנוכה מביא ואינו קורא תנו רבנן לחם עוני פרט לחלוט ולאשישה יכול לא יצא אדם ידי חובתו אלא בפת הדראה ת"ל מצות ריבה ואפילו כמצות של שלמה א"כ מה ת"ל לחם עוני פרט לחלוט ולאשישה ומאי משמע דהאי אשישה לישנא דחשיבותא דכתיב ויחלק לכל העם לכל המון ישראל למאיש ועד אשה לאיש חלת לחם אחת ואשפר אחד ואשישה אחת וגו' ואמר רב חנן בר אבא אשפר אחד משישה בפר אשישה אחד משישה באיפה ופליגא דשמואל דאמר שמואל אשישה גרבא דחמרא דכתיב ואהבי אשישי ענבים ת"ר *אין אופין פת עבה *(ביום טוב) בפסח דברי בית שמאי ובית

(שמות יב; דברים יב; בראשית מג; דברים יב; דברים כו; ש"ב ו; הושע ג)

רש"י

הדר ביה ר' עקיבא. מקל הקישא דמצה ומרור ויליף ביכורים מבכל מושבותיכם: אף מעשר שני. בירושלים הוא ואינו נאכל בכל מושבות מעתה משהכניסו לירושלים שוב אינו יכול לחלל לאכול בחוץ כדאמרינן במסכת מכות (דף כ.) מחילה לקלוטו מדרבנן תורה אור דמשקלטוהו מחילות שוב אינו נפדה: כר' אליעזר. דאם נטמא פודין אותו ואוכלין אותו בכל מקום הלכך כי לא ניטמא נמי ולא נפדה נפיק ביה: שאתו. כשלא תוכל לאוכלו כגון זה שניטמא ונתת בכסף: מאן שמעת ליה כו' ר' עקיבא. לעיל בברייתא קמייתא וקממעט להו לביכורים מבכל מושבותיכם ולא מהקיש מצה ומרור: ור' יוסי. למה ליה למילף ביכורים מבכל מושבותיכם תיפוק ליה מלחם עוני מהיכא דנפקא ליה מעשר שני בשלמא ר' עקיבא לא פירש אוני: ואמר מר. במסכת מכות (דף יז.): אלו ביכורים. דכתיב בהו יד ולקח הכהן הטנא מידך (דברים כו): תרומה מותרת לאונן. ביבמות בהערל נפקא לן מוכל זר יתירא זרות אמרתי לך ולא אנינות: ה"ג שמחה כתיב בהו ושמחת בכל הטוב: זמן שמחה. בזמן קצירה ולקיטה שאדם לוקט תבואתו ולבו שמח הצריכו הכתוב קרייה דארמי אובד אבי: מעצרת. דתנן במנחות (דף כח:) אין מביאין ביכורים קודם לעצרת משתי הלחם של עצרת מתירין הבאת ביכורין דביכורים איקרו דכתיב וביום הביכורים בהקריבכם מנחה חדשה וגו': ועד החג. שבסוף הזמן הזה זמן לקיטה ושמחת במעשיו: מהחג ועד חנוכה. אינו זמן שמחה ואינו קורא ומילך אינו זמן הבאה דתניא בספרי אשר תביא מארצך כל זמן שמצויין על פני ארצך שלא כלו לחיה מן השדה: חלוט. איסקלדי"ר וחשיבות הוא: אשישה. גלוסקא גדולה: הדראה. שניטל כל הדרה דהיינו פת קיבר: של שלמה. שהיה מעונג כלומר סלת נקייה: גרבא דחמרא. איפה של יין: וכמה

תוספות

אוציא חטין ושעורין שיש במינן ביכורים. (א) *ה"ל אם כן תליא כל חמשת המינין שיש במינן ביכורים דלאו לחם בעינן דממעטינן לעיל אורז ודוחן:

אי מצות מצות ריבה אפי' ביכורים נמי. תימה לר"י דנימא להכי ריבוי לרבות יש במינו ביכורים ולהכי מיעוט למעט ביכורי' ויש לומר דסברא הוא אי מרבינן הא מרבינן נמי הא:

דאמר ר' אליעזר. נראה לר"י דהא דאיצטריך למימר כר' אליעזר היינו אי מחילה לקלוט דאורייתא אבל אי מחילה לקלוט דרבנן לא צריך דר' אליעזר דהא נאכל בכל מושבות שיכול להוציאו חוץ לירושלים ולפדותו ומיהו רבי אליעזר מצי סבר מחילה לקלוט דרבנן ואיצטריך קרא לנטמא שיכול לפדותו אפי' בירושלים ואם תאמר והא מעשר שני נאכל בכל ערי ישראל בנוב וגבעון כדתנן בפרק בתרא דזבחים (דף קיב:) באו לנוב וגבעון הותרו הבמות קדשי קדשים נאכלין לפנים מן הקלעים קדשים קלים ומעשר שני נאכלין בכל ערי ישראל ולקמן *חשבינן הא נאכלין בכל מושבות גבי חלות תודה ורקיקי נזיר דקאמר ריש לקיש חלות תודה ורקיקי נזיר נאכלין בנוב וגבעון ולכך מפיק להו מקרא אחרינא מושמרתם ולא מצי מפיק להו מבכל מושבותיכם וביכורים נמי נאכלין בנוב וגבעון ובכל ערי ישראל דמאי שנא והיכי ממעטינן להו מבכל מושבותיכם ויש לומר דהכא לא ממעטינן להו מבכל מושבותיכם אלא לזמן בית עולמים ולא לזמן נוב וגבעון ולקמן גבי חלות תודה ורקיקי נזיר איצטריך למידרש מושמרתם לזמן נוב וגבעון ולא לזמן בית עולמים*:

מאן שמעת ליה דאמר מעשר שני נפיק ביה ר' עקיבא. אע"ג דכמה תנאי דרשי מסורת ולא מקרא ולדידהו נפיק במעשר שני דלא דרשינן אוני מ"מ אע"ג דס"ל דמסורת עיקר א"א דלא דרשי המקרא לשום דרשה:

ורבי יוסי הגלילי תיפוק לי' שאינן נאכלין לאונן. ואם תאמר לר' יוסי הגלילי מעשר שני תיפוק ליה מבכל מושבותיכם כמו ביכורים וי"ל דאי לאו עוני ה"א דמושבותיכם אתא דוקא לביכורים אבל מעשר שני שיכול להיות לו היתר בכל מושבות אם נטמא כר"א ה"א מצות מצות ריבה:

מה תרומה מותרת לאונן אף ביכורים. תימה לר"י דבפרק בתרא דמכות (דף יז.) קתני ותרומת ידך אלו הביכורים אמר ר' שמעון וכי מה בא זה ללמדך אם לאכלן חוץ לחומה פירוש דכתיב ברישא דקרא לא תוכל לאכול בשעריך קל וחומר ממעשר הקל וכו' והשתא נימא דאיצטריך קרא דאי לאו קרא הוה אמינא דלא נילף ממעשר הקל דתרומה קרינהו רחמנא כדאמרינן הכא ונראה לרשב"א דלענין חוץ לחומה איכא למילף ממעשר טפי לפי ששניהן ענין אחד הן ששניהן טעונין קריאה והבאת מקום:

פרט לחלוט. משמע דחלוט הוי לחם אלא דלא הוי לחם עוני והא דאמרינן בסמוך מאי חלות המסרת חלוט של בעלי בתים משמע דלא הוי לחם מדפטר מן החלה לקמן מיירי בבלילתו רכה כמו שאפרש לפנים אי נמי הכא בדהדר אפייה בתנור אך קשה דאמרי' בהחולץ (יבמות מ.) אע"ג דחלטיה מעיקרא כיון דהדר ואפייה בתנור או באילפס לחם קרי' ביה ואדם יוצא ידי חובתו בפסח ואומר רבינו תם דהתם נמי מיירי בבלילתו רכה דקודם אפייה לאו לחם הוא כלל ואחר אפייתו הוא דחשיב לחם וחשיב נמי לחם עוני כיון שבלילתו רכה:
ובית

[צ"ל אליעזר]

ב"מ נג: מכות יט: סנהדרין קיב:

[צ"ל אליעזר]

[דף לח:]

[בכורים פ"ב מ"ב] יבמות עג.

[יבמות סס: מכות יז. חולין קכ: מגילה טו:]

[ועי' תוס' זבחים קיח. ד"ה כאן]

[בכורים פ"א מ"ו]

ביצה כב: ושם ליתא תיבת ביו"ט

הגהות הב"ח

(א) תוס' ד"ה אוציא וכו' בכורים ואין לומר א"כ וכו' דאכן לחם בעינן:

רבינו חננאל

ואקשי' אי הכי דמי שהוכשר למרור הוא שהוכשר למצה יש לומר [אי מה מרור] אין במינו בכורים כי ירק הוא ואין בכל מיני ירק בכורים ואף מצה בעינן דבר שאין במינו בכורים אוציא חטים ושעורים שיש במינן בכורים דתנן אין מביאי' בכורים חוץ משבעת המינים. ופרשי' בגמ' דהני שבעת המינים הן חטה ושעורה גפן ותאנה ורמון זית ותמרים ת"ל מצות מצות ריבה אפי' בכורים יוצא אדם בהן והדר ביה ר' עקיבא והודה לר' יוסי הגלילי דקא ממעט לבכורים מבכל מושבותיכ' דתניא יכול יהא אדם יוצא בבכורים ת"ל בכל מושבותיכם תאכלו מצות מצה הנאכלת בכל מושבות יצאו בכורים שאין נאכלים בכל מושבות וכו' ואוקימנא לר' עקיבא מדקא ממעט לבכורים ממושבות ש"מ הדר ביה מההיא דתניא מצות מצות ריבה חטים ושעורים אע"פ שיש במינן בכורים: מאי טעמא דרבנן דפליגי על ר' שמעון דאמרי בכורים אסורים לאונן ואמרי' דכתיב לא תוכל לאכול בשעריך מעשר דגנך וגו' ואמר מר ותרומת ידך אלו הבכורים הקישן הכתוב למעשר ובמעשר כתיב (דברים כו יד) לא אכלתי באוני ממנו מה מעשר אסור לאונן אף בכורים אסורין לאונן. ור' שמעון אמר לך התורה קרנהו תרומה מה תרומה מותרת לאונן דתניא בהדיא בגמרא יבמות פ' הערל אונן אסור במעשר ומותר בתרומה ובפרה טבול יום אסור [illegible] ומותר בפרה ובמעשר כו' אף בכורים מותרין לאונן [והא] דכתיב בבכורים ושמחת בכל הטוב וגו' לאו למעוטי אונן הוא דאתא אלא ללמדך שאין מביאין בכורים [וקורין] אלא עד זמן שמחה והן ימי החג: ת"ר לחם עוני פרט לחלוט ולאשישה יכול לא יצא אלא בפת הדראה בלבד כלומר פת סובין שאוכל העני ת"ל מצות מצות ריבה אפי' כמצת שלמה שהיתה סלת יוצא בה לא טיעשה התורה אלא מצה עשירה כגון חלוט [illegible] ותני מילי בלילה הראשון דגרסי' בירושלמי אר"י בן לוי אותו כזית שאדם יוצא בו ידי חובתו בפסח צריך שלא יהא בו משקין. ר' ירמיה אומר למצוה ר' יהודה בן פזי אומר לעיכוב התיב [ר' בון בר חייא] [illegible] חלות תודה ורקיקי נזיר יוצאין בהן והא אית בהו משקין אמר ר' יוסי תמן רביעית היא ומתחלקת לכמה מינין: יוצאין בפסח במצה עבה עד טפח כלחם הפנים ובמצה נא עד כדי שתפרס ולא תעשה [illegible]

האוכל נבלה ביום הכפורים פטור רבינא אמר אפילו תימא רבנן מי שאיסורו משום בל תאכל חמץ בלבד יצא זה שאין איסורו משום בל תאכל חמץ בלבד אלא אף משום בל תאכל טבל *מידי בלבד כתיב אלא מחוורתא כדרב ששת ת"ר יכול יוצא אדם ידי חובתו במעשר שני בירושלים ת"ל לחם עוני (א) *מה שנאכל באנינות יצא זה שאינו נאכל באנינות אלא בשמחה דברי *ר' יוסי הגלילי ר' עקיבא *אומר *מצות מצות ריבה אם כן מה ת"ל לחם עוני פרט לעיסה שנילושה ביין ושמן ודבש מאי טעמא דר' עקיבא מי כתיב לחם עוני עני עני כתיב ור' יוסי הגלילי מי קרינן עני עוני קרינן (ב) ור' עקיבא האי דקרינן ביה עוני כדשמואל *דאמר שמואל לחם עוני לחם שעונין עליו דברים הרבה וסבר ר"ע עיסה שנילושה ביין ושמן ודבש לא והתניא אין לשין עיסה בפסח ביין ושמן ודבש ואם לש רבן גמליאל אומר תשרף מיד וחכמים אומרים *יאכל ואמר רבי עקיבא שבתי היתה אצל רבי אליעזר ורבי יהושע ולשתי להם עיסה ביין ושמן ודבש ולא אמרו לי דבר ואף על פי שאין לשין בו מקטפין בו אתאן לתנא קמא וחכמים אומרים את שלשין בו מקטפין בו ואת שאין לשין בו *אין מקטפין בו ושוין שאין לשין את העיסה בפושרין לא קשיא הא ביום טוב ראשון הא ביום טוב שני כדאמר להו ר' יהושע (ג) לבניה יומא קמא לא תלושו לי בחלבא מכאן ואילך לושו לי בחלבא *והתניא אין לשין את העיסה בחלב ואם לש כל הפת אסורה מפני הרגל עבירה אלא הכי קאמר יומא קמא לא תלושו לי בדובשא מכאן ואילך לושו לי בדובשא ואיבעית אימא לעולם בחלבא כדאמר רבינא כעין תורא שרי הכא נמי כעין תורא: ושוין שאין לשין את העיסה בפושרין: מאי שנא ממנחות *דתנן *כל המנחות נילושות בפושרין *(ומשתמרין) שלא יחמצו אם אמרו בזריזין יאמרו בשאין זריזין אי הכי מילתת נמי לתית אלמה *אמר רבי זירא אמר רבה בר ירמיה אמר שמואל *חיטין של מנחות אין לותתין אותן לישה בזריזין איתא לתיתה ליתא בזריזין ולישה מי איתא בזריזין והכתיב *ויצק עליה שמן וגו' והביאה *אל הכהן *מקמיצה ואילך מצות כהונה לימד על יציקה ובלילה שכשירה בכל אדם לישה נהי דבזריזין ליתא במקום זריזין איתא דאמר מר בלילה כשירה בזר *חוץ לחומת עזרה פסולה לאפוקי לתיתה דאינה בזריזין ולא במקום זריזין ומאי שנא ממנחת העומר דתניא *מנחת העומר לותתין אותה וצוברין אותה צבור שאני: תנו רבנן יכול יוצא אדם ידי חובתו בבכורים *תלמוד לומר *בכל מושבותיכם תאכלו מצות מצה הנאכלת בכל מושבותיכם יצאו בכורים שאין נאכלין בכל מושבותיכם אלא בירושלים דברי רבי יוסי הגלילי רבי עקיבא אומר מצה ומרור מה מרור שאינו בכורים אף מצה שאינה בכורים אי מה מרור שאין במינו בכורים אף מצה שאין במינה בכורים

אוציא

דברים טז | ויקרא ב | שמות יב

רש"י

האוכל נבילה ביום הכפורים. שוגג: פטור. מחטאת דאין איסור יום הכפורים חל על איסור נבילה ואם בו ביום נתנבלה אפילו הכי היתה אסורה קודם יום הכפורים משום אבר מן החי: מידי בלבד כתיב. קרא משמע דכל מי שאיסור חמץ נוהג בו אתה יוצא בו משום מצה: מי שנאכל באנינות. שמותר לאוכלו כשהוא אונן דרוש ביה לחם אוני ומעשר שני אינו נאכל באנינות דכתיב (דברים כו) לא אכלתי באוני ממנו: מי כתיב עוני. בוי"ו דתשמע מיניה אוני: שעונין עליו דברים. שגומרים עליו את ההלל ואומרים עליו הגדה: אין לשין את העיסה. של מצות ביין ושמן ודבש מפני שקרובה וממהרת להחמיץ ואין אדם יכול לשומרה לפיכך אם לש תשרף מיד ובמועד קאמר ולא ביום טוב דהבערה שלא לצורך היא *(ולר' יוחנן) דאמר לעיל מי פירות אין מחמיצין לא קשיא הך דאיהו אין חייבין על חימוצו כרת קאמר ולא הוי חמץ גמור אלא חמץ נוקשה הוי כלומר רע ואותו חימוץ הן ממהרין להחמיץ ואי אפשר לשומרן: וחכמים אומרים תאכל. דקסברי אפשר לשומרה והכא לא גרסינן מיד דמשנאפה לא תחמיץ: שבתי היתה. שביתתי היתה רגל פסח אחד אצל ר' אליעזר ור' יהושע: מקטפין. טחין פניה לאחר עריכתה: פושרין. ממהרין להחמיץ: יום ראשון. לילה הראשון שהמצה חובה בעינן לחם עוני: אין לשין עיסה בחלב. כל ימות השנה שלא יאכל בשר עמה: כעין תורא. מעט כעין של שור מותר ללוש בחלב דאכיל ליה מיד בבת אחת ולא משהי ליה דליכשל שנילוש בחלב: ומאי שנא ממנחות. דתנן בהו דבאות מצות ואפילו הכי נלושות בפושרין ומשמרן שלא יחמיצו: הכי גרסינן כהנים זריזין הם: לתיתה. לשורן במים מעט ולכותשן במכתשת להסיר מורסנן כדי שתהא סולתן נקיה: לתיתה ליתא בזריזין. כשמביאה הזר כבר היא סולת: לישה. כגון מנחת מחבת ומרחשת ומנחת מאפה תנור שאופין אותה תחילה עשר חלות ואחר כך פותתין אותן עד שמחזירן לסלתן כדכתיב (ויקרא ב) פתות אותה פתים ואחר כך נותן שמן ובוללה ויוצק וקומץ וכשאפאה תחילה נילושה בפושרין: לימד על יציקה ובלילה כו'. והני במנחת מאפה תנור לאחר לישה ואפייה ופתיתה ניהנהו: במקום זריזים איתא. בעזרה שהמחבת והמרחשת כלי שרת הן וכן תנור של מקדש וכיון דבעזרה איתא חזו לה כהנים ומלמדין אותו להיזהר בה: ומאי שנא. שאר מנחות דקאמר שמואל אין לותתין אותם ממנחת העומר דתנן בה לותתין אותה וצוברין אותה שיזובו מימיה: ציבור שאני. מנחת העומר קרבן ציבור היא וכל עסקין שלה נעשין על פי בית דין קצירתה והיבהוב שלה ולתיתה הכל בבית דין ובזריזין הוא ואיכא דאמרי לבור שאני דהואיל וצוברין אותה מימיה זבין ואין מחמיצין ולאו מילתא היא חדא דבתוספתא קתני לה ולא קתני וצוברין אלא ובוררין ועוד אי איכא תקנתא בצבור (של) חיטים של מנחות נמי נילתתינהו ונצברינהו: בבכורים. כגון כהן שהביאו לו חיטין בכורים בירושלים: בכורים אין נאכלין אלא בירושלים. שנאמר לא תוכל לאכול בשעריך וגו' ואמר מר (מכות דף יז.) ותרומת ידך אלו בכורים: מצה ומרור. הקישן הכתוב על מצות ומרורים: מרור אינו בכורים. דתנן (בכורים פ"א מ"ג) אין מביאין בכורים אלא מז' מינין דכתיב מארצך משבח ארצך במנחות בפ' כל קרבנות (דף פד.) ולקמן במקום שנהגו (דף נג.):

הדר

תוספות

האוכל נבילה ביום הכפורים. פ"ה אפילו נתנבלה ביום הכפורים לא חיילא עלה איסור יוה"כ דהרי הוה עלה איסור אבר מן החי וקשה לר"י דהא כי פקע איסור אבר מן החי יחול עלה איסור יום הכפורים ונבילה בבת אחת דמודה רבי שמעון באיסור בבת אחת ומיהו י"ל אפילו נתנבלה ביום הכפורים לא חייל עלה איסור יום הכפורים דאיסור שאין זבות הוא ביה נמי מעיקרא ואכתי לא פקע מיניה*:

עוני קרינן ביה. והא דגבי לולב (סוכה דף לב.) כ"ע מודו דכפת כתיב ולא אמר כפות קרינן וילפינן שני לולבים ליטול אור"י משום דהתם סמכינן אקרא פרי עץ הדר דלא משמע אלא חד לכך מודו התם כ"ע דדרשינן מסורת*:

במקום זריזים איתא. וא"ת והא הכא במנחת מאפה תנור מיירי שהיתה נילושה בפושרים ואותה מכלן שנבללת בעזרה ושאר מנחה שנבללת בעזרה לפי שהבלילה היתה בכלי שרת וי"ל דגם מאפה תנור היו לשין בעזרה סמוך להנור של קודש שלא תחמיץ ורבינו אפרים בר אפרים הגבור מפרש דע"כ היו לשין אותה בעזרה לפי שהיו מודדין אותה בעשרון של קודש כדתנן בפרק שתי מדות (מנחות פז.) עשרון מה היה משמש בו מודד לכל המנחות*:

מה מרור שאין ביכורים. וליכא למימר מרור היינו זית שהוא מר כדדרשינן (*סנהדרין דף קח:) והנה עלה זית טרף בפיה אמרה יונה יהא מזונותי מרורים כזית וכו' דלקמן (דף לט.) אמר מרור דומיא דמצה מה מצה מין זרעים אף מרור כן ועוד שזית האילן מר ולא הפרי כדמשמע עלה זית ואמרינן נמי (מכילתא פ' בשלח) ויורהו ה' עץ זהו זית שאין מר באילנות כזית*:

הוגיה

עין משפט נר מצוה

קכה א מיי' פ"ו מהל' מלה הלכה ח:

קכו ב ג מיי' שם הל' ה סמג לאוין עט טוש"ע או"ח סי' תסב סעיף א:

קכז ד מיי' שם פ"ה הלכה ב ג טוש"ע שם סעיף ד בהג"ה:

[וע"ע תוס' חולין לג. ד"ה השתא ותוס' שבועות כד. ד"ה האוכל ע"ש]

קכח ה מיי' פי"ב מהל' מעשה קרבנות הלכה כא:

קכט ו מיי' שם הל"כ:

[וע"ע תוס' סוכה ו: ד"ה ור"ש ועוד שם לב. ד"ה כפת שכתבו דלר"ע דעמא וע"ע תוס' סנהדרין ד. ד"ה כולהו ותוס' זבחים מ. ד"ה לא נלמוד ותוס' נדה טו. ד"ה לא]

קל ז מיי' שם הל' כג ופי"א מהל' פסולי המוקדשים הלכה ז:

קלא ח מיי' שם הל' ו:

קלב ט מיי' פ"ב מהל' מעשה קרבנות הלכה כ:

קלג י מיי' פ"ו מהל' מלה הלכה ח:

[ועי' תוס' סוכה מ. ד"ה ואיתא ותוס' מנחות ה: ד"ה ריש לקיש]

[ערובין יח:]

[וע"ע תוס' עירובין יח: ד"ה מרורין]

[נ"ל ומשמרן]

מנחות ט. יח.

מסורת הש"ס

קדושין עז: שבועות כד. נזיר ד. [כריתות כג.]

[לקמן לח.]

[שם. לט:]

[לעיל לה:]

[נ"ל ולריש לקיש]

לקמן קטו:

הגהות הב"ח

(א) גמ' לחם עוני מי שנאכל: (ב) שם קרינן ביה ור' עקיבא: (ג) שם ר' יהושע בן לוי לבניה:

לעיל ל. ב"מ לא. זבחים לד:

מנחות נה.

לקמן מ. ע"ש

[והביאה אל בני אהרן הכהנים וקמץ כצ"ל]

גליון הש"ס

גמ' מידי בלבד כתיב. עיין בכה"ג ס"א מ"ג דטהרות ועי"ש

רבינו חננאל

שבל דתניא האוכל נבלה ביום הכפורים פטור ולא אתי איסור יום הכפורים חייל אאיסור נבלה: **ת"ר** יכול יוצא אדם ידי מצה בפסח במעשר שני בירושלים ת"ל לחם עוני כי בעינן לחם הנאכל באוני יצא זה שאינו נאכל באוני אלא בשמחה דברי ר' יוסי הגלילי כדתנן בס"פ מעשר שני במנחה ביום טוב היו מתודים כיצד היה וידוי בערתי הקדש מן הבית זה מעשר שני וכו' עד לא אכלתי באוני ממנו אם אכלו באנינה לא היה יכול להתודות: **ר' עקיבא** אומר מצות ריבה אם כן מה ת"ל לחם עוני פרט למצה עשירה ואסיקנא לר' עקיבא כתיב עני למעוטי מצה עשירה וקרינן עוני כשמואל דאמר לחם שעונין אחריו דברים ואקשי' אני דר' עקיבא אוסר לאכול בפסח מצה עשירה והתניא אין לשין את העיסה ביין ושמן ודבש ואם לש ר"ג אומר תשרף מיד וחכמים אומרים תאכל מיד פי' אם אפאה אמר ר' עקיבא שבתי היתה אצל ר' אליעזר ור' יהושע ולשתי להם עיסה ביין ושמן ודבש ולא אמרו לי דבר ושנינן הא דאסר מצה עשירה ביום טוב ראשון בלבד בזמן שעונין אחריו דברים והן ההגדה שאמר מצה זו שאנו אוכלין על שום מה וכו' אסור אותו זמן לאכול מצה עשירה דבעינן עוני ולשתי להם עיסה ביין ושמן ודבש בשאר הימים ויש לומר כי דבר מועט לש להם כגון בני ר' יהושע שלשו כחלב בעין תורא שהוא דבר מועט וביום הראשון [אזור] ובשאר הימים מותר. ונתברר לנביני מדע דסוגיא דברייתא הכי הוא אין לשין את העיסה ביין ושמן ודבש ואע"פ שאין לשין מקטפין בהן והכמים אומרים אין לשין ואם לא מקטפין ואם לש או קיטף ר"ג אומר תשרף מיד ואפי' אפאה וחכמים אומרים תאכל מיד דברי הכל זו הברייתא בשאר ימות הפסח היא שנויה זולתי יו"ם ראשון ומראין הדברים שהת"ק שאמר אע"פ שאין לשין בו מקטפין בו כך פי' דבריו אע"פ שאין לשין בסים ושמן ואם לשו במים ושמן מכלל שהלישה שאסר שמן על ידי מים הוא שאסר בלישה ומה שהתיר בקיטוף וחכמים אסרו זה וזה הלישה והקיטוף ע"י מים הכל אסור וקיי"ל כחכמים שאפי' אם לש במים לקטף בשמן כלל וכל שכן שאין לשין בסים ושמן כלל: ושוין שאין לשין את העיסה בפושרין. ואמרי' אמאי לא והא כל המנחות מצה הן ותנן כל המנחות נילושות[בפושרין]ומשמרן שלא יחמיצו ורחי' אם שהן זריזין ומשמרין העיסה שלא תחמיץ ומשום זריזותן התירו להן יתירו לכל אדם ודחי' לתיתה פעמים שתהיה שלא על ידי כהן והא לישה נמי יתכן שתהיה שלא על ידי כהן דהא מקמיצה ואילך מצות כהונה ולישה קמי הכי הוא דהויא ואפילו [הכי] לישה כי ליתא בכהנים אינה אלא בעזרה מקום שהכהנים רואים אותה אבל חוץ לחומת העזרה פסולה לתיתה אינה לא בכהנים ולא בעזרה לפיכך לא התירוה: **ת"ר** יכול יוצא אדם ידי חובתו בבכורים כו' בא ר"ע למעט הבכורים ממצה ומרור ואמר בעינן מצה כמרור מה מרור אין מביאין ממנו בכורים כי ירק הוא ולא פירי כך מצה אין מביאים מן הבכורים ואקשי'

prohibition.[15] For it was taught, R. Simeon said: [36a] He who eats *nebelah* on the Day of Atonement is not liable [to a sin-offer-
a ing].[1] Rabina said, You may even say [that it agrees with] the Rabbis: [the meaning is] that the interdict which is on account of '*thou shalt not eat leavened bread with it*' alone, thus this is excluded, for its interdict is not on account of '*thou shalt not eat leavened bread with it*' alone, but also on account of 'thou shalt not eat *ṭebel*'. Is then 'alone' written?[2]—Rather, it is clearly as R. Shesheth [stated].

Our Rabbis taught. You might think that a man can discharge his obligation with second tithe in Jerusalem; therefore it is stated, *the bread of affliction* ['oni],[3] teaching, [it must be] that which may be eaten in grief [*aninuth*],[4] thus this is excluded, which is not eaten in grief but [only] in joy:[5] this is the view of R. Jose the Galilean. R. Akiba said: [The repetition of] '*unleavened bread*', '*unleavened bread*', is an extension.[6] If so, what is taught by '*bread of affliction*' ['oni]? It excludes dough which was kneaded with wine, oil, or honey.[7] What is R. Akiba's reason?—Is then *leḥem* [bread of] *'oni* [grief] written? Surely *'ani* [poverty] is written.[8] And R. Jose the Galilean?[9]—Do we then read it *'ani?* Surely we read it *'oni*. And R. Akiba?—The fact that we read it *'oni* [is explained] as Samuel's [dictum]. For Samuel said: Bread of *'oni* [means] bread over which many words are recited [*'onin*].[10]

Yet does R. Akiba hold [that] dough which was kneaded with wine, oil, or honey is not [fit]? Surely it was taught: Dough must not be kneaded on Passover with wine, oil, or honey; and if one
b did knead it,—R. Gamaliel said: It must be burnt immediately;[1] while the Sages say: It may be eaten. Now R. Akiba related: I was staying [one Passover] with R. Eliezer and R. Joshua, and I kneaded dough for them with wine, oil or honey, and they said nothing to me. And though one may not knead, yet one may smooth the surface with them,—this is according to the first Tanna. But the Sages maintain: With that with which one may knead, one may smooth, while with that with which one may not knead, one may not smooth. And they all agree that dough may not be kneaded with lukewarm [water]![2]—There is no difficulty: the one refers to the first day of the Festival; the other, to the second day of the Festival.[3] As R. Joshua b. Levi said to his sons: For the first day[4] do not knead [it] for me with milk;[5] from then onwards knead it for me with milk. But it was taught: Dough must not be kneaded with milk, and if one does knead it, the whole loaf is forbidden, because it leads to sin?[6]—Rather, he said this: For the first day do not knead it for me with honey; from then onwards knead [it] for me with honey. Alternatively I can say: After all it means with milk, [but] as Rabina said, [When made] like the eye of an ox, it is permitted;[7] so here too, [it was] like the eye of an ox.

'And they all agree that dough may not be kneaded with lukewarm [water]'. Why is it different from meal-offerings: for we learned: All meal-offerings[8] are kneaded with lukewarm water, and he [the official in charge] guards them that they should not become leaven?—If this was said of [very] careful men [priests], shall it
c [also] be said of those who are not careful?[1] If so, let it also be permitted to wash [the grain];[2] why did R. Zera say in the name of Rabbah b. Jeremiah in Samuel's name: The wheat for meal-offerings must not be washed?—The kneading was done by careful men, but the washing would not be done by careful men.[3] Yet must the kneading be done by careful men [priests]; surely it is written, *and he shall bring it to Aaron's sons the priests: and he shall take thereof his handful:*[4] from the taking of the handful and onwards is the duty of the priesthood; this teaches concerning the pouring [of oil] and the mixing,[5] that it is valid [when done] by any man?—The kneading, granted that it is not [done] by careful men, yet it is [done] in the place of careful men.[6] For a Master said: The mixing is valid [if done] by a lay Israelite; [but if done] without the wall[s] of the Temple Court, it is invalid. Thus this excludes washing, which is not [done] by careful men nor in the place of careful men. And wherein do they [all other meal-offerings] differ from the meal-offering of the *'omer*,[7] for it was taught: The meal-offering of the *'omer* is washed and heaped up?[8]—A public [offering] is different.[9]

Our Rabbis taught: You might think that a man discharges his duty with first fruits,[10] therefore it is stated, *in all your habitations shall ye eat unleavened bread,*[11] teaching, [it must be] unleavened bread which is eaten in all your habitations, thus excluding first fruits, which may not be eaten in all your habitations save in Jerusalem [alone]: this is the view of R. Jose the Galilean. R. Akiba said: Un-
d leavened bread and bitter herbs [are assimilated]:[1] just as bitter herbs which are not first fruits [are required],[2] so unleavened bread which is not first fruits [must be eaten]. If so, just as bitter herbs of a species not subject to first fruits [are required], so unleavened bread of a species [of grain] not subject to first fruits [is meant],

(15) I.e., when a thing is already forbidden on one score, another interdict cannot become operative at the same time. Thus here the prohibition of *ṭebel* is earlier; consequently the fact that it subsequently became leaven too is ignored, and it is regarded as prohibited on account of *ṭebel* only.

a (1) Which eating on the Day of Atonement usually incurs, the reference being to eating in ignorance. The reason is that since it is forbidden on the score of *nebelah*, the interdict of the Day of Atonement cannot take effect. Thus the same applies here. (2) Surely not! Scripture does not imply this at all. (3) Deut. XVI, 3. (4) Connecting *'oni* (עני) with *anah* (אנה) to mourn or grieve, though the former is spelled with an ע, while the latter is with an א, these letters often being interchangeable in Semitic languages.—*Aninuth* denotes the state of grief between the death of a near relative, e.g., one's father, and his burial, the bereaved person then being called an *onen*. (5) An *onen* (v. preceding note) may not eat second tithe, cf. Deut. XXVI, 14: *I have not eaten thereof* (*sc.* second tithe) *in my mourning*. (6) V. *supra* 35b and note a.l. Thus it includes second tithe. (7) Which makes it into 'rich' *mazzah*. The phrase is now translated: bread of poverty, from *'ani* (עָנִי) poor. (8) Though the word is read *'oni*, as though spelled with a *waw* (עוני), it is actually written *'ani* (עני), without a *waw*. (9) How does he rebut this? (10) A long liturgical service—called the *haggadah*—is read in connection with the eating of unleavened bread on the night of Passover.

b (1) R. Gamaliel holds that it ferments too quickly, and so to prevent it from becoming leaven it must be burnt immediately. But the Sages hold that it can be baked before it is leaven. (2) This causes fermentation very quickly. (3) On the night of the first day the *mazzah* must be '*bread of poverty*', whereas this is a rich *mazzah;* hence it cannot be used. But on the second night any *mazzah* is permissible. (4) I.e., Passover night. (5) This too makes a 'rich' bread. (6) One may come to eat it with meat. This refers to the whole year. (7) I.e., when made very small, so that it is at once entirely eaten up, and nothing is left for later. (8) Which were offered unleavened.

c (1) This is the answer. The preparing of unleavened bread for meal-offerings was in the hands of priests, who were very careful and could be relied upon not to permit it to ferment. But unleavened bread for Passover is made in every home, and the people could not be trusted to take so much care. (2) I.e., to soak it slightly in water and then pound it so as to remove the bran and make a fine flour. (3) This was not the priest's duty. (4) Lev. II, 2. (5) Which preceded the taking of the handful; v. ibid. 1, 2. (6) I.e., in the Temple Court, which is frequented by priests, and these would take heed that whoever kneaded it should not permit fermentation. (7) V. Glos. (8) For the water to drain off. (9) This was a public offering, and everything in connection with it, right from the harvesting of the grain, was done under competent guidance and vigilance. (10) E.g., a priest to whom an Israelite brought the first fruits of his wheat harvest. (11) Ex. XII, 20.

d (1) Num. IX, 11: *they shall eat it with unleavened bread and bitter herbs*. (2) For only the seven species enumerated in Deut. VIII, 8, ('*a land of wheat and barley, and vines and fig trees and pomegranates; a land of oil olive and honey*') are subject to the law of first fruits.

a fruit juice,[1] [35b] and fruit juice does not cause fermentation.[2]

AND THEY DISCHARGE THEIR OBLIGATION WITH DEMAI AND WITH THE FIRST TITHE etc. DEMAI? But it is not fit for him?[3] —Since if he wishes he can renounce his property, become a poor man, and eat *demai*,[4] it is fit for him now too. For we learned: The poor may be fed with *demai*, and [Jewish] troops [in billets] [may be supplied] with *demai*.[5] And R. Huna said, It was taught: Beth Shammai maintain: The poor may not be fed with *demai*, nor troops in billets; but Beth Hillel rule: The poor may be fed with *demai*, also troops in billets.

FIRST TITHE WHOSE TERUMAH HAS BEEN SEPARATED. That is obvious? Since its *terumah* has been separated, it is *ḥullin*?[6]—It is necessary [to teach it] only where he anticipated it [in setting it aside[7] while the corn was still] in the ears, and *terumah* of the tithe was taken from it, but the great *terumah* was not taken from it,[8] this being in accordance with R. Abbahu. For R. Abbahu said in the name of Resh Laḳish: First tithe which he anticipated [the setting aside thereof] in the ears is exempt from the great *terumah*, for it is said, *then ye shall offer up an heave offering of it for the Lord, a tithe of the tithe:*[9] I ordered thee [to offer] '*a tithe of the tithe*', but not the great *terumah* plus the *terumah* of the tithe '*of the tithe*'. Said R. Papa to Abaye: If so, even if he anticipated it in the stack too,[10] let it be exempt?—For your sake Scripture writes, *out of all your gifts ye shall offer every heave offering of the Lord*,[11] he answered
b him. And what [reason] do you see [to interpret thus]?[1]—The one has become corn [*dagan*], while the other has not become corn.[2]

THE SECOND TITHE AND HEḲDESH WHICH HAVE BEEN REDEEMED etc. That is obvious?—We treat here of a case where he assigned[3] the principal but did not assign the fifth:[4] and he [the Tanna] informs us that the fifth is not indispensable.[5]

AND PRIESTS [DISCHARGE THEIR OBLIGATION] WITH ḤALLAH AND TERUMAH etc. This is obvious?—You might say, We require unleavened bread that is equal[ly permitted] to all men. Therefore he informs us, [the repetition] '*unleavened bread*', '*unleavened bread*',[6] is an extension.

BUT NOT WITH ṬEBEL etc. That is obvious?—It is necessary [to teach it] only of *ṭebel* made so by Rabbinical law, e.g., if it was sown in an unperforated pot.[7]

NOR WITH FIRST TITHE WHOSE TERUMAH HAS NOT BEEN SEPARATED. That is obvious?—It is necessary [to state it] only where it had been anticipated [and set aside] in the pile.[8] You might argue as R. Papa proposed to Abaye;[9] hence he [the Tanna] informs us [that it is] as Abaye answered him.

NOR WITH SECOND TITHE OR HEḲDESH WHICH HAVE NOT BEEN REDEEMED etc. That is obvious?—It is necessary only where they have been redeemed; and what does they 'HAVE NOT BEEN REDEEMED' mean? That they have not been redeemed with their
c regulations.[1] [Thus:] it is second tithe which he redeemed with uncoined metal,[2] for the Divine Law states, *And thou shalt bind up* [we-ẓarta] *the money in thine hand*,[3] [implying], that which bears a figure [*ẓurah*].[4] [Again it is] *heḳdesh* which was secularized[5] by means of land,[6] for the Divine Law stated, Then he shall give the money and it shall be assured to him.[7]

Our Rabbis taught: One might think that a man can discharge his obligation with *ṭebel* which was not made ready.[8] (But surely all *ṭebel* indeed has not been made ready!—Rather say, with *ṭebel* which was not made ready with all its requirements, the great *terumah* having been separated from it whereas the *terumah* of tithe was not separated from it; [or] the first tithe, but not the second tithe, or even the poor tithe).[9] Whence do we know it?[10] Because it is stated, *thou shalt not eat leavened bread with it:*[11] teaching, [you must eat of] that the interdict of which is on account of '*thou shalt not eat leavened bread with it*', thus this is excluded, for its interdict is not on account of '*thou shalt not eat leavened bread with it*' but on account of 'thou shalt not eat *ṭebel*'.[12] Yet whither has the interdict of leaven gone?[13]—Said R. Shesheth, The author of this is R. Simeon, who maintained, A prohibition cannot fall[14] upon another

a (1) *Sc.* wine, oil or honey, date-honey being meant. (2) I.e., 'leavening'. (3) *Demai* may not be eaten until the tithe has been separated. (4) A poor man need not separate tithe on *demai*. (5) They too are regarded as poor, since they are not at home. (6) I.e., permitted for food. (7) *Sc.* the separation of the first tithe. (8) The great *terumah* is a portion of the produce, unspecified by Scripture (the Rabbis prescribed from one fortieth to one sixtieth, according to the owner's generosity), which is the priest's due; for *terumah* of tithe v. note on Mishnah *supra* 35a. The great *terumah* must be separated first, and then the first tithe. But here the order was reversed and the Israelite separated his tithe while the grain was yet in the ears. (9) Num. XVIII, 26. (10) I.e., when it is no longer in the ears but piled up in stacks. (11) Ibid. 29; i.e. '*all*' is an extension, and shows that the offering is due even in such a case.—'For your sake' or, 'concerning you'—to refute this possible view.

b (1) To apply the limitation of the first verse to the one case and the extension of the second to the other—perhaps it should be reversed? (2) The priestly due, i.e., the great *terumah*, is '*the firstfruits of thy corn*' (Deut. XVIII, 4). Hence once it is piled up as corn it is due, and the Israelite cannot then evade his obligations by reversing the order. But before it is piled up there is no obligation for the great *terumah;* therefore if the Levite receives his first tithe then he is not defrauding the priest. (3) Lit., 'gave'—for redemption. (4) When a man redeemed second tithe or *heḳdesh* he added a fifth of its value. (5) To the validity of the redemption, and the redeemed produce may be consumed anywhere, even though the fifth has not been added. (6) This may refer either to Deut. XVI, 4, 8, or in general to the fact that '*unleavened bread*' is repeated several times. (7) According to Scriptural law such is not *ṭebel* at all, and therefore I would think that a man discharges his obligation therewith. (8) The tithe having been separated but not the great *terumah*. (9) That it is exempt, *supra*.

c (1) Lit., 'laws'. (2) V. B.M. 47b for the meaning of *asimon*. (3) Deut. XIV, 25. (4) The image stamped on the coin. This connects *ẓarta* with *ẓurah*. (5) I.e., redeemed, whereby the *heḳdesh* assumes an ordinary, non-holy character. (6) I.e., land was given for its redemption. (7) I.e., it can be redeemed by money, but not by land. Actually there is no such verse, but v. B.M., 54a, n. c1. (8) For eating, by separating the priestly and the Levitical dues. (9) In the first, second, fourth, and fifth years after the 'years of release' (*shemiṭṭah*) the first and second tithes were separated. In the third and sixth years, the first and third tithes were separated, the latter being a poor tithe, i.e., it belonged to the poor. (10) That he cannot discharge his obligation therewith. (11) Deut. XVI, 3. (12) I.e., the unleavened bread which one must eat must be such that, if leavened, it would be forbidden because it is leavened. But in the case of *ṭebel*, if it were leavened it would be forbidden because it is *ṭebel*. (13) Surely it is still forbidden on account of leaven, *ṭebel* merely being an *additional* prohibition? (14) I.e., become operative.

ומי פירות אין מחמיצין: יוצא בדמאי ובמעשר וכו': דמאי *הא לא חזי ליה כיון דאי בעי מפקר לנכסיה הוי עני ואוכל דמאי השתא נמי חזי ליה *דתנן מאכילין את העניים דמאי ואת אכסניא דמאי ואמר רב הונא תנא בית שמאי אומרים אין מאכילין את העניים דמאי ואת האכסניא דמאי ובית הלל אומרים מאכילין: מעשר ראשון שנטלה תרומתו וכו': פשיטא דכיון שנטלה תרומתו חולין הוי לא צריכא שהקדימו בשיבלים ונטלה הימנו תרומת מעשר ולא נטלה הימנו תרומה גדולה וכדרבי אבהו דאמר ר' אבהו אמר רבי שמעון בן לקיש *מעשר ראשון שהקדימו בשיבלים פטור מתרומה גדולה שנאמר והרמותם ממנו תרומת ה' מעשר מן המעשר מעשר מן המעשר אמרתי לך ולא תרומה גדולה ותרומת מעשר מן המעשר אמר ליה רב פפא לאביי אלא מעתה אפילו *הקדימו בכרי נמי ליפטר א"ל עליך אמר קרא מכל מתנותיכם תרימו את כל תרומת ה' ומה ראית האי אידגן והאי לא אידגן: מעשר שני והקדש שנפדו וכו': פשיטא הכא במאי עסקינן שנתן את הקרן ולא נתן את החומש וקא משמע לן דאין חומש מעכב: והכהנים בחלה ובתרומה וכו': פשיטא מהו דתימא מצה שוה לכל אדם בעינן קמ"ל *מצות מצות ריבה: אבל לא בטבל וכו': פשיטא לא צריכא בטבל טבול מדרבנן שזרעו בעציץ שאינו נקוב: ולא במעשר ראשון שלא נטלה תרומתו: פשיטא לא צריכא שהקדימו בכרי מהו דתימא כדאמר ליה רב פפא לאביי קא משמע לן כדשני ליה: ולא במעשר שני והקדש שלא נפדו וכו': פשיטא לעולם דנפדו ומאי לא נפדו שלא נפדו כהלכתן מעשר שני שפדאו על גב אסימון דרחמנא אמר וצרת הכסף *דבר שיש לו צורה והקדש שחיללו על גבי קרקע דרחמנא אמר *ונתן הכסף וקם לו תנו רבנן יכול *יוצא אדם ידי חובתו בטבל שלא נתקן כל טבל נמי הא לא נתקן אלא בטבל שלא נתקן כל צורכו שנטלה ממנו תרומה גדולה ולא נטלה ממנו תרומת מעשר [מעשר] ראשון ולא מעשר שני ואפילו מעשר עני מנין תלמוד לומר לא תאכל עליו חמץ מי שאיסורו משום בל תאכל חמץ יצא זה שאין איסורו משום בל תאכל חמץ אלא משום בל תאכל טבל ואיסורא דחמץ להיכן אזלא אמר רב ששת הא מני ר' שמעון היא דאמר אין איסור חל על איסור דתניא ר' שמעון אומר האוכל

רש"י

דמאי הא לא חזי ליה · ואמרינן לקמן מי שאיסורו משום בל תאכל חמץ לבדו אתה יוצא בה לשום מצה יצא מי שיש לו איסור אחר א"נ הויא לה מצוה הבאה בעבירה: השתא נמי חזי ליה. דתומרא דרבנן בעלמא הוא דרוב עמי הארץ מעשרין הן: אכסניא. חיילות מלכי ישראל המוטלין על בני העיירות לזונן להגין עליהם מאויביהן וישראלים הן והרי הן כעניים הואיל ואינן במקומן: שהקדימו בשיבלים. את המעשר הקדים לתרומה גדולה קודם מירוח דמן התורה תרומה קודמת למעשר דראשית קרי' רחמנא ומן הנותר הוא נותן מעשר ראשון ללוי ועכשיו הקדים הלוי וקידמו כדי שלא יחסרנו הכהן אחד מחמשים ונטלה הימנו תרומת מעשר כדינו אבל תרומה גדולה הראשונה לא נטלה הימנו ואשמעינן מתני' דמותר כרבי אבהו: מכל מתנותיכם. בלוים כתיב: את כל תרומת ה'. אפילו תרומה גדולה: ומה ראית. דאוקמת קרא לחיוב' כשהקדימו בכרי וקרא דפטורא כשהקדימו בשיבלין: האי. דנתמרח בכרי אידגן וכיון דנקרא דגן נעשה טבל לתרומה כדכתיב ראשית דגנך: האי לא אידגן · וכי שקליה לוי עדיין לא הוה טבול לתרומה: טבול מדרבנן. ואפ"ה מצוה הבאה בעבירה היא חשיב לה ולא דמי לדמאי וכדאמרן דהתם אשכחן ביה היתירא לכתחילה הלכך הכא בדיעבד נפיק: ולא במעשר ראשון שלא נטלה תרומתו. קא ס"ד בתרומת מעשר קאמר וקא פריך פשיטא: לא צריכא שהקדימו בכרי. והאי תרומתו דקתני תרומה גדולה דהוי חזי לאפרושי מינה מעיקרא קאמר: כדאמר ליה רב פפא לאביי. לעיל בשמעתין: אסימון. מטבע בלא צורה פלאט"ה בלע"ז: ונתן הכסף וקם לו. במקדיש שדה כתיב ויסף חמישית כסף ערכך וגו': כל טבל נמי לא איתקן. קושיא היא: או אפילו (אכילת) מעשר עני. שאין בו שום קדושה דאילו מעשר ראשון אית ביה תרומת מעשר שהיא קדושה ומעשר שני כולו קדוש: מי שאיסורו משום בל תאכל חמץ. אתה יוצא בו ידי מצה בפסח אם עשאו מצה: האוכל

תוספות

ומי פירות אין מחמיצין. היינו להתחייב כרת כדאמרינן בהדיא אין חייבין על חימוצו כרת אבל לאו איכא ביה ובסמוך נמי אמרינן* אין לשין ביין ושמן ודבש ואם לש תשרף מיד וחכמים נמי דאמרי תאכל היינו משום שיכולין לשומרו מן החמוץ כשאר עיסה אבל לכולי עלמא מחמיצין וקשה דלקמן (דף מ.) מסקינן גבי *קימחא דאבישונא אבל מי פירות שרי דמי פירות אין מחמיצין משמע דשרינן לגמרי וכן פי' ר"ת דאין מחמיצין כל עיקר והא דאמר תשרף מיד כשעירב עמהן מים דאז ממהרות יותר להחמיץ ועל הא אמר דאין בהן כרת אבל לאו איכא ביה אבל היכא דלית ביה תערובת מים כגון יין ושמן ושאר מי פירות שרו לגמרי וכן מוכח בסוף כל המנחות באות מצה (מנחות דף נז: ושם) דאמר אשר תקריבו לרבות מנחת נסכים לחימוץ דברי רבי יוסי הגלילי ופריך מנחת נסכים מי פירות הן ואין מחמיצין אמר ריש לקיש אומר היה רבי יוסי מנחת נסכים מגבלה במים והיא כשירה והשתא אי סלקא דעתיך דריש לקיש ורבי *יוחנן מיירי הכא בלא מים כלל ואפילו הכי כרת ליכא אבל מלקות איכא דחמץ נוקשה הוי אמאי איצטריך למימר התם מגבלה במים בלא גיבול מים נמי איצטריך קרא שלא תאפה חמץ דהוי חמץ נוקשה וחמץ נוקשה פסול למנחה כדמשמע התם במנחות (דף נג:) דקאמר התם שיאור דר' יהודה לרבי יהודה דפסול למנחות אלא ודאי היכא דליכא מים אינו מחמיץ כלל וקשה לרשב"א דחומץ האדומי חשיב ליה בפרק אלו עוברין (לקמן דף מג.) חמץ דגן גמור ע"י תערובת ואמאי והא חומץ האדומי מפרש התם* דרמו ביה שעורים פי' משימין השעורים ביין כדי שיחמיץ היטב והא מי פירות אין מחמיצין ואפילו אם משימין מים עמהן אכתי לא הוי אלא חמץ נוקשה ואומר ר"י שהשעורים שורין במים קודם שמשימין ביין ובמי ביצים נסתפק רש"י אי חשיב מי פירות או לא ולפי שאנו רגילים שהעיסה נעשה עבה בהן יותר ממים אבל ר"ת נהג היתר בדבר והיה נוהג לאכול בערב הפסח אחר ארבע שעות עוגה שנילושה בביצים והא דקאמרינן *בירושלמי האוכל מצה בערב פסח קודם זמנה כאילו בועל ארוסתו בבית חמיו היינו מצה הראויה לצאת בה ידי חובה וזו מצה עשירה היא:

יוצאין בדמאי. מסופק ר"י אי בעי למימר יוצא דוקא דיעבד כדאמרינן הואיל ומפקיר לנכסיה וחזי ליה מכל מקום עדיין לא מפקיר להו אי נמי יוצאים אף לכתחלה הואיל ושרי לעניים ואכילת מצה נמי נקרא אכילת עניות: אכסניא · מפרש בירושלמי נכרים: שחילל על גב קרקע דרחמנא אמר ונתן הכסף. תימה אי כסף משמע ליה דווקא נימעוט שוה כסף ואי יליף מישיב דשוה כסף ככסף אפילו קרקע נמי ונראה לר"י דילפינן בכלל ופרט וכלל ויסף חמישיתו כלל כסף פרט והיה לו חזר וכלל מה הפרט מפורש דבר המטלטל וגופו ממון וכו' יצאו קרקעות ועבדים ושטרות וכן מוכח בפרק יש בכור (בכורות דף נא.) דתנן אין פודין לא בעבדים ולא בשטרות ולא בקרקעות ולא בהקדשות ומפרש התם בגמרא ולא הקדשות בכל אלו ובכור יליף התם בכלל ופרט וכלל *וכן נמי יש לפרש הקדשות ומיהו תימה מאי מיבעי ליה בפ' הזהב (ב"מ דף נד.) חומש מהו שיתחלל ע"ג קרקע והא עיקר המיעוט בחומש כתיב ויסף חמישית כסף ערכך (ויקרא כז):

עין משפט נר מצוה

קיח א מיי' פ"ה מהל' חמץ הלכה ב סמג לאוין שם טוש"ע שם: [לקמן לו.]

[תוס' דאבישונא כצ"ל]

שבת קכו: ברכות מו. סוכה לה: עירובין לה.

קיט ב מיי' פ"ו מהל' חמץ הלכה ז:

קכ ג מיי' פ"י מהלכות מעשר הלכה יא:

קכא ד מיי' פ"ג מהל' תרומות הל' יג טור ש"ע י"ד סי' שלא:

קכב ה מיי' פ"ו מהל' מצה הלכה ח:

קכג ו ז שם הלכה ז:

קכד ח מיי' פי"ו מהל' איסורי ביאה הל' ח ופ"ד מהל' מאכלות אסורות הלכה יח:

[נפסינו בסוגי' לא נמצא רבי יוחנן רק ר"ל]

[דף מג:]

ונתן הכסף לא כתיב ע"י תוס' שבת קכח. ד"ה ונתן

[וע"ע תוס' מנחות נג: ד"ה אין מחמיצין כו']

מסורת הש"ס

[לקמן פ' מנחות מז:] · דמאי פ"ג [מ"א] עירובין יז: · [כריתות מז: שבת קכו: עירובין לה: ביצה יג:] · תמורה ס: · [לקמן לו:] · [ב"מ נג:] · [פי' תוס' סוכה ל: ד"ה משום] · דברים טז

גליון הש"ס

גמרא לא צריכא בטבל טבול מדרבנן. עיין לקמן קיד ע"ב תוס' ד"ה דמאי:

רבינו חננאל

במי פירות ומי פירות אין מחמיצין · ירושל' אין לשין עיסה במשקין אבל מקטפין אותה במשקין אמר רבי עקיבא מעשה שהייתי עם רבי אליעזר ורבי יהושע בספינה ולשתי מצתם במשקין · אין לשין בחמין מפני שחולטין ולא בפושרין מפני שהן מחמיצין: דמאי כב"ה דאמר מאכילין את העניים דמאי וכיון דחזו לעניים יוצא אדם בו בפסח וכבר פרשנוהו בכמה מקומות דדמאי הוא הלוקח פירות מעם הארץ ואינו יודע אם הן מעושרין אם לאו נותן מהם חלק אחד ממאה לכהן והן תרומת מעשר שחייב הלוי ליתן לכהן מעשר מן המעשר אבל תרומה גדולה אחד מחמשים ודאי הן מפרישים ואפילו עמי הארץ וכן מי שהפריש עשיר אחד מעשרה ונתנו לכהן קודם שיעשנו טרן וקודם שיוציאו ממנו תרומה גדולה לכהן ונתן הלוי ממנו תרומת מעשר והוא מעשר ואע"פ שתרומה גדולה לא נתן לכהן מותר ללוי אותו מעשר שלא נתחייב הלוי בתרומה גדולה אלא אם קבל הלוי מעשר מן הגורן אחר שהעמיד ישראל כרי אם הפריש ממנו מעשר ונתנו ללוי מקודם בתרומות וחייב בתרומת מעשר הלוי ופשטא היא והיא מפורשת בסוטה פרק אחרון: ובמעשר שני והקדש שנפדו אם נתן הקרן אע"פ שלא נתן עדיין החומש כבר שלו הוא וכן החלה והתרומה לכהנים שלישראל אסורה מצות מצות ריבה. טבל הוא שלא הורמה ממנו התרומה והמעשר ואע"פ שהיא תבואה שנזרעה בעציץ שאינו נקוב ואינה תרומת הארץ אלא תבואה זרועה בכלי מדאוריי' פטור מדרבנן חייב תרומה ומעשר לפיכך אינו מותר ואינו ראוי לאכילה וכ"ש טבל דאוריי': ולא במעשר ראשון שלא נטלה תרומתו כגון שהקדים בכרי ונתן אחד מעשרה בו ללוי ונמצא במעשר שלקח הלוי אחד מחמשים לכהן גדולה וחייב עוד אחרי כן לתת לכהן מן הנשאר בידו חלק אחד מעשרה והיא תרומת מעשר ואפילו אם נתן תרומת מעשר ולא נתן התרומה גדולה אין יוצא בו ידי חובתו בפסח וכן במעשר והקדש שנפדו על מעות שאין בהן צורה כלומר לא נטבעו במטבע אלא התולק בלא צורה כאלו לא נפדו דפדיה כי האי גונא לא שמה פדיה משם דאין מתחלל אלא על כסף שיש עליו צורה שנאמר וצרת הכסף בידך ודייקינן וצרת עליו צורה למעוטי אסימון שאין עליו צורה: ת"ר יכול יוצא אדם בטבל שלא תקנו כהלכתו כגון שהפריש כל מה שחייב להפריש חוץ מדבר אחד ואפי' מעשר עני שמוציא בשנה השלישית ת"ל לא תאכל עליו חמץ משום לא תאכל חמץ יצא זה שאיסורו משום לא תאכל טבל פי' כל תבואה שלא נתקנה כהלכתה נקראת טבל ואקשי' עליה ואיסורא דחמץ היכא אזיל ודחי' הא מתניתא ר' שמעון היא דסבר אין איסור

אלא מעלה. בעלמא הוא מדרבנן שהחמירו בכלי ולסמכוה רבנן אקרא: הכא נמי מעלה. בעלמא הוא דאין זריקה לתרומה ולמעשר מלאכול: תניא. דעבוד רבנן מעלה בקדשים אפילו מדאורייתא: בקדשים לא. אם טומאה דבת כפרה היא כגון זב וזבה ויולדת: והבשר. כל טהור יאכל וגו' וי"ו יתירה לרבות עצים ולבונה של קודש לטומאה וקאי אדלעיל והבשר אשר יגע בכל טמא לא יאכל והבשר: איטמויי ניטהו. בתמיה הא לאו אוכל ניהו: מתני' אלו דברים שאדם יוצא בהן ידי חובתו. משום חובת מצה בלילה ראשונה שהוא מחוייב לאכול מצה דכתיב (שמות יב) בערב תאכלו מצות: שיבולת שועל. אבייא"ה שיבולת שלה עשוי כזנב שועל: שיפון. סיגל"א: יוצאין בדמאי: תבואה הנלקחת מעם הארץ והיא נקראת דמאי ספק עישרה ספק לא עישרה וחייבו חכמים להפריש מעשרותיה מספק ואם אכל מצה ממנה ולא הפריש מעשר ממנה יצא: ובמעשר ראשון. של לויים: שנטלה תרומתו. תרומת מעשר לכהן ומכאן ואילך המעשר מותר לזרים: והכהנים בחלה ובתרומה. אבל ישראל בתרומה לא כדיליף לקמן לא תאכל עליו חמץ שבעת ימים תאכל עליו מצות מי שאינו מוזהר על חימוצו אלא משום חמץ אתה יוצא בו ידי חובת מצה יצא זה שאסור מחמת איסור אחר: ולא במעשר שני. חוץ לירושלים: עשאן לעצמו. לחם תודה ונזיר: אין יוצא בהן. ואפילו לא שחט הזבח עליהן ולא קרא שם עליהן אלא שעשאן לדעת כן וטעמא מפרש בגמ': למכור בשוק. לצורכי לחמי תודה ונזירות יוצא בהן אם לא מכר להן וטעמא מפרש בגמרא: גמ' מין חיטין. לענין תרומה דאין תורמין ממין על שאינו מינו ותורמין חיטין על כוסמין: דישרא. שיגל"א: גולבי. איספילטא בלע"ז: שבילי תעלא. אבייצ"א תעלא תרגום של שועל: דברים הבאין לידי חימוץ אדם יוצא בהן. משום מצה אם עשאן מצה: אורז ודוחן. אין עושין חמץ ואם מחמיצין אותן מסריחין: אוסר באורז ודוחן. לאכול הימנו תבשיל בפסח יש מפרשים למנחות משום דכל המנחות באות מצה ושיבוש הוא דאין מנחה באה אלא חטים דכתיב (שמות כט) סולת חטים תעשה אותם חוץ ממנחת העומר שאינה באה אלא שעורין [וכן] מנחת סוטה ופשיטא דדוחן לא ומאן פליג עליה דרבי יוחנן בהא ומי מתיר: שקרוב לחימוץ. אלמא בא לידי חימוץ ולדידיה יוצאין בו משום מצה: חמץ גמור לא הוי. ונפקא מינה דאין ענוש כרת ואם אכלו בשוגג אין מביא קרבן: קרמית. מפרש לקמיה: חייבת בחלה. דמין דגן הוי ואע"ג דחלה לחם כתיב בה וגמר לחם לחם מלחם עוני במנחות בפרק רבי ישמעאל (דף ע:) אורז [א] נמי לחם הוא: שיצניתא. קלא שקורין כייל"א בלע"ז עגול הוא כעין דוחן ושחור לישנא אחרינא שמעתי אשדרכיל"א ונמצאת בשיפון: כלניתא. מק' בלע"ז: ביין ובשמן. דלא נתן בה מים: אין חייבין על חימוצו כרת. דמי פירות אין מחמיצין כדלקמן: מצה עשירה. ורחמנא אמר לחם עוני: המחהו וגמעו. אשום לחם דמין דגן קאי ולאשמעינן דגמיעה כאכילה לחייבו: המחה. דישטנפרי"ר בלע"ז שהמחהו במים: אין אדם יוצא בה ידי חובתו. דלאו דרך אכילה קאכיל ליה:

כוסמין מין חיטין שיבולת שועל ושיפון מין שעורין. רש"י פירש לענין דאין תורמין ממין על שאינו מינו ור"י אומר דבמנחות בפרק ר' ישמעאל (דף ע:) מוכח בהדיא דברייתא לענין חלה מייתי' יש מקשין דתנן במסכת חלה (פ"ד מ"ב) החיטה אינה מצטרפת עם הכל חוץ מן הכוסמין והשעורין מצטרפין עם הכל חוץ מן החיטין אלמא כוסמין בהדי שעורין שפיר דמי ואומר ר"י דכוסמין מין חיטין כלומר אף מין חיטין וכל שכן מין שעורין שיבולת שועל ושיפון מין שעורין ולאו מין חטין והא דתניא התם בריש המסכת חמשה דברים חייבין בחלה החיטין והשעורין והכוסמין ושיבולת שועל ושיפון הרי אלו חייבין בחלה ומצטרפין זה עם זה אומר ר"י דמשני בירושלמי כאן בנשוך וכאן בבלול פי' בנשוך שכל אחת ואחת נעשה עיסה בפני עצמה ואחר כן נשכו ונתחברו יחד התם ודאי אין מצטרפין כולם אלא כמו שמפורשין בבלול שכל הקמחים נילושים יחד ועשו מהן עיסה בההיא טלס מצטרפים דחשבינן כולם כאחד: ומי

אלא מעלה הכא נמי מעלה אמר רב שימי בר אשי אף אנן נמי תנינא *טבל ועלה *אוכל במעשר העריב שמשו אוכל בתרומה בתרומה אין בקדשים לא אמאי טהור הוא אלא *מעלה ה"נ מעלה אמר רב אשי אף אנן נמי תנינא והבשר *לרבות את העצים ולבונה עצים ולבונה בני איטמויי נינהו אלא *מעלה הכא נמי מעלה: **מתני'** אלו דברים שאדם יוצא בהן ידי חובתו בפסח בחטים בשעורים בכוסמין ובשיפון ובשיבולת שועל ויוצאין בדמאי ובמעשר ראשון שנטלה תרומתו ובמעשר שני והקדש שנפדו והכהנים בחלה ובתרומה אבל לא בטבל ולא במעשר ראשון שלא נטלה תרומתו ולא במעשר שני והקדש שלא נפדו חלות התודה ורקיקי נזיר עשאן לעצמו אין יוצא בהן עשאן למכור בשוק יוצאין בהן: **גמ'** *תנא *כוסמין מין חיטין שיבולת שועל ושיפון מין שעורין כוסמין גולבא שיפון דישרא שיבולת שועל שבילי תעלא הני אין אורז ודוחן לא מנהני מילי *אמר רבי שמעון בן לקיש וכן תנא דבי רבי ישמעאל וכן תנא דבי ר' אליעזר בן יעקב אמר קרא °לא תאכל עליו חמץ שבעת ימים תאכל עליו מצות דברים הבאים לידי חימוץ אדם יוצא בהן ידי חובתו במצה יצאו אלו שאין באין לידי חימוץ אלא לידי סירחון מתניתין דלא כרבי יוחנן בן נורי דאמר אורז מין דגן הוא וחייבין על חימוצו כרת *דתניא רבי יוחנן בן נורי אוסר באורז ודוחן מפני שקרוב להחמיץ איבעיא להו שקרוב להחמיץ דקדים ומחמיץ או דילמא קרוב להחמיץ הוי חמץ גמור לא הוי תא שמע דתניא *אמר רבי יוחנן בן נורי אורז מין דגן הוא וחייבין על חימוצו כרת ואדם יוצא בו ידי חובתו בפסח וכן *היה רבי יוחנן בן נורי אומר קרמית חייבת בחלה מאי קרמית אמר אביי שיצניתא מאי שיצניתא אמר רב פפא שיצניתא דמשתכחא ביני כלניתא אמר רבה בר בר חנה אמר ריש לקיש 'עיסה שנילושה ביין ושמן ודבש אין חייבין על חימוצה כרת יתיב רב פפא ורב הונא בריה דרב יהושע קמיה דרב אידי בר אבין ויתיב רב אידי בר אבין וקא מנמנם א"ל רב הונא בריה דרב יהושע לרב פפא מאי טעמא דריש לקיש א"ל דאמר קרא לא תאכל עליו חמץ [וגו'] דברים שאדם יוצא בהן ידי חובתו במצה חייבין על חימוצו כרת והא הואיל ואין אדם יוצא בה ידי חובתו 'דהויא ליה מצה עשירה אין חייבין על חימוצה כרת איתיביה רב הונא בריה דרב יהושע לרב פפא *המחהו וגמעו אם חמץ הוא ענוש כרת ואם מצה הוא אין אדם יוצא ידי חובתו בפסח והא הכא דאין אדם יוצא ידי חובתו במצה וחייבין על חימוצו כרת איתער בהו רב אידי בר אבין אמר להו *דרדקי היינו טעמא דריש לקיש משום דהוו להו מי פירות ומי

קיב א מיי' פ"ב מהל' מעשר שני הל' ד סמג לאוין רסד:
קיג ב מיי' פ"ה מהל' תרומות הלכה ב סמג לאוין רנ:
קיד ג מיי' פ"ו מהל' איסורי מזבח הלכה ח:
קטו ד מיי' פ"ה מהל' חו"מ הל' א ופ"ו הלכה ד סמג לאוין עט טוש"ע א"ח סי' תנג סעיף א:
קטז ה מיי' שם ופ"ו מהל' ביכורים הלכה ג טוש"ע שם וטוש"ע יו"ד סי' שכב סעיף א:
קיז ו ז מיי' פ"ה מהל' חו"מ הל' ב ופ"ו הלכה ה סמג לאוין עט טוש"ע א"ח סימן תסב סעיף א:

[מנחות ע:]

רבינו חננאל

תנן אלמא (עיקרן) [דעקירין] מן המעין הן ותלושי' נינהו והדר קרי להו מים חיים אל כלי אלמא מחוברים נינהו אלא מעלה עשו בהן דאע"ג דהן בכלי והן בתוך המעין (נקראים) [ונקראים] חיים וכי האי גונא בחולין (דלא) [לא] מטמאי' דכתיב (ויקרא יא) אך מעין ובור מקוה מים יהא טהור והכא במי חטאת כיון שהן בכלי מיטמאין ואין חבורן במעין *) מטהרן הנה מעלה: רב שימי אמר מהא טבל ועלה אוכל במעשר העריב שמשו אוכל בתרומה **) אמאי בעי הערב שמש והא טהור הוא אלא מעלה. רב אשי אמר מהא והבשר לרבות עצים ולבונה עצים ולבונה בני קבולי טומאה נינהו אלא מעלה עשו הכא נמי מעלה עשו: מתני' אלו דברים שאדם יוצא בהן ידי חובתו בפסח בחטים בשעורים כו' הני אין אבל אורז ודוחן אם יעשה מהן מצה אינו יוצא בהן ידי מצת מדאורייתא מנא לן ושמעינן [ליה] מהאי קרא לא תאכל עליו חמץ שבעת ימים תאכל עליו מצות לחם עוני וגו' דברים שיתכן לבוא לידי חימוץ אותם הזהירה תורה שלא תניחם להחמיץ אלא תאכלם מצה אבל אלו שאין באים לידי חימוץ לעולם אלא לידי סרחון גם אם תאכלם במי

מצה אינה חשובה מצה. ואוקימנא למתני' דלא כרבי יוחנן בן נורי דאמר כי האורז קרוב להחמיץ. פשטנא שמחמיץ הוא כלומר במהרה מדקתני וחייבין על חימוצו כרת: קרמית. עשב כדאמרינן קודמי דאגמא: אמר ריש לקיש עיסה שנילושה ביין ושמן ודבש אין חייבין על חימוצה כרת קס"ד משום דהוה מצה עשירה ואותבי' עליה המחהו פי' המחהו לככר במשקה וגמעו אם חמץ הוא ענוש כרת ואם מצה היא אין אדם יוצא בה ידי חובתו בפסח דכיון שפתתו כמין שתיתא יצא מתורת לחם והא הכא הפת המחוי אין יוצא בה ידי חובתו בפסח וחייבין על חימוצו כרת ושני' לא תימא משום דהויא מצה עשירה אלא משום דנילושה במי

*) פירש רבינו בכאן הוא כפי' התוס' לעיל לד ע"ב ד"ה ונתן ודו"ק. **) מלשון רבינו נראה דגי' אחרת היה לו בד' הגמ' כאן דהרא"ה היא מתרומה עצמה דעשה בה התורה מעלה.

מס"ק פח: יבמות עה: [מעילה סוף פ"ג]

חולין לג: [לעיל כד: ע"ש זבחים לד: מז:]

[ע"ע תוספות זבחים לד: ד"ה ואם ותוס' מנחות כה: ד"ה יצאו]

[עי' תוס' לעיל יז: ד"ה אלמא ויותר מבואר בתוס' חגיגה כג: ד"ה והא]

מנחות ע.

[פי' בפירש"י דהכא ד"ה מין חיטין וכו' ופי' בפרש"י מנחות דף ע: ד"ה כוסמין]

[ברכות לז: לקמן קיד:]

גם זה שם

[תוספתא דחלה פרק א']

חולין קכ.

[עיין פרש"י שבת קמה:]

גליון הש"ס
גמרא אלא מעלה. עיין משנה למלך פ"ג הלכה יז מהלכות פסולי המוקדשין:

הגהות מהר"ב רנשבורג [א] רש"י ד"ה חייבת בחלה וכו' אורז נמי לחם הוא. נ"ל קרמית נמי לחם הוא:

that it is detached, but surely this is attached![10] [35a] but it is a
a higher standard; so here too it is a higher standard.[1] R. Shimi b. Ashi said, We too learned thus: When he [an unclean person] has a ritual bath, he may eat tithe; when the sun sets,[2] he may eat *terumah*. [Thus] only *terumah*, but not sacred food.[3] Yet why so? He is clean? But [you must say] it is a higher standard; so here too it is a higher standard. R. Ashi said, we too learned [thus]: *And the flesh:*[4] this is to include fuel and frankincense.[5] Are then fuel and frankincense capable of being defiled?[6] But [you must say] it is a higher standard;[7] so here too it is a higher standard.

MISHNAH. THESE ARE THE COMMODITIES WITH WHICH A MAN DISCHARGES HIS OBLIGATION ON PASSOVER:[8] WITH WHEAT, WITH BARLEY, WITH SPELT, WITH RYE,[9] AND WITH OATS. AND THEY DISCHARGE [IT] WITH DEMAI,[10] WITH FIRST TITHE WHOSE TERUMAH HAS BEEN SEPARATED, AND WITH
b SECOND TITHE OR HEKDESH WHICH HAVE BEEN REDEEMED;[1] AND PRIESTS [CAN DISCHARGE THEIR OBLIGATION] WITH ḤALLAH AND TERUMAH. BUT [A MAN CAN]NOT [DISCHARGE HIS OBLIGATION] WITH ṬEBEL, NOR WITH FIRST TITHE WHOSE TERUMAH HAS NOT BEEN SEPARATED, NOR WITH SECOND TITHE OR HEKDESH WHICH HAVE NOT BEEN REDEEMED. [AS TO] THE [UNLEAVENED] LOAVES OF THE THANKSOFFERING[2] AND THE WAFERS OF A NAZIRITE,[3] IF HE MADE THEM FOR HIMSELF,[4] HE CANNOT DISCHARGE [HIS OBLIGATION] WITH THEM; IF HE MADE THEM TO SELL IN THE MARKET, HE CAN DISCHARGE [HIS OBLIGATION] WITH THEM.

GEMARA. A Tanna taught: *Kusmin* [spelt] is a species of wheat; oats and rye are a species of barley; *kusmin* is *gulba; shipon* is *dishra; shiboleth shu'al* is foxears.[5]

Only these[6] [are fit],[7] but not rice or millet. Whence do we know it?—Said R. Simeon b. Lakish, and thus the School of R. Ishmael taught, and thus the school of R. Eliezer b. Jacob taught, Scripture saith, *Thou shalt eat no leavened bread with it; seven days shalt thou eat unleavened bread therewith:*[8] [with regard to] commodities which come to the state of leaven, a man discharges his obligation with unleavened bread [made] thereof; thus these are excluded, which do not come to the state of leaven but to the state of decay.

Our Mishnah does not agree with R. Joḥanan b. Nuri, who maintains: Rice is a species of corn, and *kareth*[9] is incurred for [eating it in] its leavened state. For it was taught: R. Joḥanan b. Nuri prohibits [the use of] rice and millet, because it is near to turn leaven. The scholars asked: does 'because it is near to turn leaven'
c mean that it quickly becomes leaven,[1] or perhaps it is *near* to leaven, but is not completely leaven?[2]—Come and hear: For it was taught, R. Joḥanan b. Nuri said: Rice is a species of corn and *kareth* is incurred for [eating it in] its leavened state, and a man discharges his obligation with it on Passover. And thus R. Joḥanan b. Nuri used to say, *Karmith* [cow-wheat] is subject to *ḥallah*. What is *karmith?*—Said Abaye: *Shezanitha* [weed]. What is *Shezanitha?*—Said R. Papa: A weed found among *kalnitha*.[3]

Rabbah b. Bar Ḥanah said in the name of Resh Lakish: [As to] dough which was kneaded with wine, oil or honey, *kareth* is not incurred for [eating it in] its leavened state.[4] Now, R. Papa and R. Huna son of R. Joshua sat before R. Idi b. Abin, while R. Idi b. Abin was sitting and dozing. Said R. Huna son of R. Joshua to R. Papa: What is Resh Lakish's reason?—He replied, Scripture saith, *Thou shalt eat no leavened bread with it* etc.: [In the case of] the commodities with which a man discharges his obligation in respect of unleavened bread, *kareth* is incurred for [eating them in] their leavened state; but [with regard to] this [dough], since a man cannot discharge his obligation therewith, because it is rich *mazzah*,[5] *kareth* is not incurred for its leaven. R. Huna son of R. Joshua objected to R. Papa: If he dissolves it[6] and swallows it, if it is leaven, he is punished with *kareth;* while if it is unleavened bread, he does not discharge his obligation therewith on Passover.[7] Now here, though a man does not discharge his obligation therewith as unleavened bread, yet *kareth* is incurred for its leaven? —[Thereupon] R. Idi b. Abin awoke [and] said to them, Children! This is the reason of Resh Lakish, because they are

(10) The passage is rather difficult. Rashi: '*And he shall put*' implies that Scripture refers to detached water, i.e., water which does not form part of a stream but has been detached and collected in a vessel, whence it is poured into a second vessel containing the ashes. But when the Mishnah states that the running must be direct into the vessel, it insists on attached water, i.e., water forming part of the stream. This must be because the Rabbis set a higher standard. Tosaf.: '*and he shall put*' implies that the water is regarded as detached water, which can be defiled, though actually it is running water, as stated, and consequently this proves that by Scriptural law sacred water cannot be made clean by 'levelling' (v. 34*b*, n. b4), for levelling only renders it as attached water, whereas we see here that even when attached it is regarded as detached. And just as Scripture thus sets a higher standard for sacred water, so did the Rabbis set a higher standard for *terumah*.—Maharsha observes (on Rashi's explanation) that he does not see how this proves that the Rabbis set a higher standard *even when they were verbally sanctified*.

a (1) *Sc.* that the resowing of *terumah* does not permit it to be eaten (*supra* 34*a*). (2) Lit., 'his sun makes evening'. (3) If his uncleanness requires a sacrifice, e.g., in the case of a *zab*, he may not eat sacred food until he has brought the sacrifice, though he is completely clean. (4) Lev. VII, 19. (5) V. *supra* 24*b* and notes a.l. (6) Surely not, as they are not eatables! (7) Though fuel and frankincense cannot usually be defiled, a higher standard is set when they are to be used in the sacred service. (8) Unleavened bread is obligatory on the first night of Passover, as it is written, *on the fourteenth day of the month at even ye shall eat unleavened bread* (Ex. XII, 18). The Mishnah enumerates the species of corn with which this unleavened bread, eaten as an obligation, can be made. (9) Jast.: others: oats. (10) V. Glos.

b (1) One tenth (tithe) of the produce, called the first tithe, was given to the Levite, and he in turn gave a tenth thereof, called the *terumah* of tithe, to the priest. Another tenth of the produce, called the second tithe, was eaten by its owners (Israelites, as opposed to Levites and priests) in Jerusalem, or redeemed and the redemption money was expended in Jerusalem. *Hekdesh* (q.v. Glos.) could be similarly redeemed. The second tithe reference in the Mishnah is to places outside Jerusalem. (2) The thanksoffering was accompanied by forty loaves, thirty of which were unleavened. (3) V. Num. VI, 15. (4) For his own sacrifice. (5) Ears of corn foxtailed in shape.—The other words are the Aramaic in general use. (6) Enumerated in our Mishnah. (7) For making unleavened bread as defined *supra*, n. a8. (8) Deut. XVI, 3. (9) V. Glos.

c (1) And therefore it is altogether forbidden on Passover, as it turns leaven before it can be baked. (2) I.e., it can never become completely leaven. Hence R. Joḥanan b. Nuri prohibits its use *on the first night* for the fulfilment of one's obligations. (3) *Papaver Spinosum* (Jast.). (4) If no water at all was used in kneading it. (5) Unleavened bread made with wine etc., is a rich confection, whereas Scripture prescribes '*bread of poverty*' (E.V. *affliction*—Deut. XVI, 3). (6) *Sc.* bread. (7) Because swallowing soaked bread is not eating.

Wherever its disqualification is in itself, it must be burnt immediately; [if it is] in the blood[10] or in its owner,[11] [the flesh] must become disfigured and [then] it goes out to the place of burning.—Said he to him: This tanna is a tanna of the School of Rabbah b.
a Abbuha[1] who maintained: Even *piggul*[2] requires disfigurement.[3]

He [R. Joḥanan] raised an objection to him: If the flesh became unclean or disqualified, or if it passed without the curtains,[4] R. Eliezer said: He [the priest] must sprinkle [the blood];[5] R. Joshua said: He must not sprinkle [the blood].[6] Yet R. Joshua admits that if he does sprinkle [it], [the sacrifice] is accepted.[7] Now, what does 'disqualified' mean? Is it not through mental neglect?[8] Now, it is well if you say that it is a disqualification of uncleanness, then it is conceivable that the headplate makes it accepted.[9] But if you say that it is an intrinsic disqualification, why is it accepted?[10]—What does 'disqualified' mean? It was disqualified by a *ṭebul yom*.[11] If so, it is identical with 'unclean?'—There are two kinds of uncleanness.[12]

When Rabin went up,[13] he reported this teaching[14] with reference to the *terumah* plants before R. Jeremiah, whereupon he observed: The Babylonians are fools. Because they dwell in a land of dark-
b ness[1] they engage in dark [obscure] discussions.[2] Have you not heard this [dictum] of R. Simeon b. Laḳish in R. Oshaia's name: If the water of the Festival was defiled[3] and he made level contact and then sanctified it, it is clean; if he sanctified it and then made level contact, it is unclean.[4] Now consider: this is 'sowing';[5] what does it matter whether he made level contact and then sanctified it or he sanctified it and then made level contact? This proves that 'sowing' has no effect upon *heḳdesh*;[6] so here too sowing has no effect upon *terumah*.[7]

R. Dimi sat and reported this teaching.[8] Said Abaye to him, Does he [R. Oshaia] mean [that] he sanctified it in a vessel, but if [merely] verbally the Rabbis did not set a higher standard;[9] or perhaps for verbal [sanctification][10] too the Rabbis set a higher standard?—I have not heard this, he replied, [but] I have heard something similar to it. For R. Abbahu said in R. Joḥanan's name: If grapes were defiled and he trod them and then sanctified them,[11] they are clean;[12] if he sanctified them and then trod them, they are unclean. Now grapes are [a case of] verbal sanctification, yet
c even so the Rabbis set a higher standard![1]—Said R. Joseph: You speak of grapes! We treat here of grapes of *terumah*,[2] their verbal sanctifications being tantamount to the sanctification of a vessel.[3] But those that require a vessel [for sanctification,[4] where they are sanctified] verbally [maybe] the Rabbis did not set a higher standard.

'If he trod them'—[does that mean] even in great quantity? But did R. Joḥanan say thus? Surely R. Joḥanan said: If grapes are defiled, he may tread them out less than an egg in quantity at a time?[5]—If you wish I can say that here too [it means] less than an egg at a time. Alternatively, I can answer: There the case is that they [the grapes] had come into contact with a first degree [of uncleanness], so that they [the grapes] are a second. But here they come into contact with a second degree, so that they are a third.[6]

Raba said: We too learned [thus]:[7] *And he shall put thereto running* [living] *water in a vessel:*[8] [this teaches] that its running must be [directly] into a vessel.[9] *'And he shall put'*—this proves

(10) E.g., if the blood was spilled before it could be sprinkled. (11) E.g., if he became unclean before the Passover could be eaten and there were no others available to eat it, as the Passover may be eaten only by those who registered for it.

a (1) [R. Ḥananel seems to omit 'is a . . . who'. R. Simeon b. Laḳish could certainly not refer to the School of Rabbah b. Abbuha, who was a disciple of Rab.] (2) V. Glos. There the flesh itself is certainly disqualified. (3) 73*b*. (4) The partitions of the Temple corresponding to those of the Tabernacle (Jast.). Thus 'without the curtains' means without the enclosures of the Temple Court. This refers to sacrifices of the higher sanctity (v. *supra*, 24*a*, n. a2), whose flesh might not be eaten without these enclosures. (5) He holds that the blood must be sprinkled even when there is no flesh. (6) He holds that the blood is dependent on the flesh. (7) This is a technical term denoting that the sacrifice fulfils its purpose. (8) For there is no other disqualification, since defilement is stated separately. It cannot mean a disqualification through an illegitimate intention, e.g., if the officiating priest expressed his intention to eat the flesh outside the boundaries or after the time allotted for its eating, for then the blood too is disqualified and can certainly not be sprinkled. (9) The headplate worn by the High Priest makes atonement in such a case, even if the flesh is definitely unclean; v. *supra* 16*b*. Nevertheless R. Joshua rules that the blood must not be sprinkled at the outset, for he holds that the acceptability conferred by the headplate is only if it was sprinkled, but it may not be sprinkled in the first place in reliance on the headplate. (10) For the headplate cannot make atonement for such a disqualification. (11) V. Glos. His touch disqualifies it, as he is not really clean until evening falls. (12) V. Mishnah *supra* 14*a* and note a.l. (13) From Babylonia to Palestine. (14) *Sc.* of R. Shesheth.

b (1) Babylonia is possibly so called on account of the Parsees (fire-worshippers), who forbade the Jews to have any light in their dwellings on their (the Parsees') festivals. (2) I.e., they discuss laws without knowing their true meanings. (3) 'Festival' without a further determinant always means the Feast of Tabernacles. The 'water of the Festival' is that used for libations each day which was drawn the previous evening with great ceremony and joy. Here the reference is to the water for the Sabbath libation; fresh water could not be brought on the Sabbath, and therefore this water had to be made clean. (4) Unclean water can be purified by placing it in a vessel and immersing the vessel in a *miḳweh* (ritual bath) until the water in the vessel is level with and just touches the water of the *miḳweh*. This is called *hashshaḳah* (lit., 'kissing') and the unclean water thereby becomes one with the *miḳweh*, which of course is clean.—The water for libation was sanctified by formal dedication, or by being poured into a sacred service vessel. (5) The process of levelling is regarded as 'sowing', as though the water were sown in the *miḳweh*, just as unclean produce becomes clean if it is resown in the earth. (6) Lit., 'there is no sowing for *heḳdesh*'—to make it clean. The reason is because a higher standard of purity is required in the case of *heḳdesh*. (7) Hence the plants remain unclean in so far that they are forbidden to be eaten. (8) Of. R. Oshaia. (9) I.e., by formal dedication, v. n. b4. (10) In which case levelling would not be effective. (11) For its wine to be used for libations. (12) V. *supra* 33*b*, where R. Joḥanan holds that the expressed juice of unclean grapes is clean.

c (1) In declaring the expressed juice unclean, whereas it would be clean if it were not sanctified. (2) The sanctification referred to is not as previously assumed (cf. *supra*, n. b11) for libations but for purposes of *terumah*. (3) Since *terumah* can only be verbally sanctified, there being no sacred vessels to sanctify them. (4) Such as wine for libations. (5) V. *supra* 33*b* notes. (6) V. *supra* 14*a*, n. a2. When the grapes are unclean in the second degree they render the juice unclean in the *first* degree, it being a general rule that whatever disqualifies *terumah*, i.e., eatables unclean in the second degree, defiles liquids in the first degree (*supra* 14*b*). But when they are unclean in the third degree they cannot defile liquids. Hence if he first trod them, even in great quantity, they remain clean. But if he first sanctified them, the expressed juice is unclean, because the Rabbis set a higher standard for *terumah*. (7) Viz., that the Rabbis set a higher standard for sacred objects, even when they were verbally sanctified. (8) Num. XIX, 17. (9) In which it is sanctified with the ashes of the red heifer, but it must not be collected in another vessel and then poured over into this.

קח א מיי' פ"ד מהל' ק"פ הלכה ג:
קט ב מיי' פי"ח מהל' פסולי המוקדשין הלכה כא:
קי ג מיי' פ"ז מהלכות איסורי מזבח הל' א:
קיא ד שם הלכה ט:
קיב [ה מיי' פי"ב מהל' תרומות הלכה יא]

*כל שפסולו בגופו ישרף מיד בדם ובבעלים תעובר צורתן ויוצאין לבית השריפה א"ל האי תנא תנא דבי רבה בר בר אבוה הוא *דאמר אפילו פיגול טעון עיבור צורה *איתיביה נטמא או שנפסל הבשר או שיצא חוץ לקלעים רבי אליעזר אומר יזרוק ומודה רבי יהושע שאם זרק הורצה מאי נפסל לאו בהיסח הדעת אי אמרת בשלמא פסולי טומאה הוי היינו דמשכחת לה דמרצי ציץ אלא אי אמרת פסול הגוף הוי אמאי הורצה (ציץ) מאי נפסל נפסל בטבול יום אי הכי היינו טמא תרי גווני טמא כי סליק רבין אמרה לשמעתיה קמיה דר' ירמיה *ואמר בבלאי טפשאי משום דיתבי בארעא דחשוכא אמריתון שמעתתא דמחשכו לא שמיע לכו הא דרבי שמעון בן לקיש משמיה דר' אושעיא מי החג שנטמאו השיקן ואחר כך הקדישן טהורין הקדישן ואח"כ השיקן טמאים מכדי זריעה נינהו מה לי השיקן ואח"כ הקדישן מה לי הקדישן ואחר כך השיקן אלמא דאין זריעה להקדש הכא נמי אין זריעה לתרומה יתיב רב דימי וקאמר לה להא שמעתא אמר ליה אביי הקדישן בכלי קאמר אבל בפה לא עבוד רבנן מעלה או דילמא בפה נמי עבוד רבנן מעלה אמר ליה זו לא שמעתי כיוצא בה שמעתי דאמר ר' אבהו אמר רבי יוחנן ענבים שנטמאו דרכן ואח"כ הקדישן טהורים הקדישן ואח"כ דרכן טמאין והא ענבים דקדושת פה נינהו ואפילו הכי עבוד רבנן מעלה אמר רב יוסף ענבים קאמרת הכא [ד] בענבים של תרומה עסקינן דקדושת פה דידהו כקדושת כלי דמיא אבל הני דבעי כלי בפה לא עבוד רבנן מעלה דרכן ואפילו טובא ומי אמר רבי יוחנן הכי והאמר רבי יוחנן *ענבים שנטמאו דורכן פחות פחות מכביצה איבעית אימא הכא נמי פחות פחות מכביצה ואבע"א התם דנגעו להו בראשון דהוו להו שני הכא דנגעו בשני דהוו להו שלישי [א] אמר רבא אף אנן נמי תנינא °ונתן עליו מים חיים אל כלי *שתהא חיותן בכלי ונתן בכלי אלמא תלושין נינהו והא מחוברין נינהו אלא

כל שפסולו בגופו. פסול ודאי ובבשר עצמו ישרף מיד: בדם. כגון נשפך הדם: ובבעלים. כגון נטמאו בעלים והפסח קיים ואין כאן מי שיאכלנו ודם אע"פ שפסול גמור הוא אפילו הכי הואיל ואינו כבשר עצמו בעי עיבור צורה: תנא דבי רבה בר אבוה. עיקר מילתא לא ידענא היכא וטעמא למילתיה בכילד צולין: אפילו פיגול. שפסול הגוף הוא טעון עיבור צורה והכא לא מצי לשנויי כדמשני לקמיה מאי פסולי טומאה הגוף שנפסל בטבול יום דהיינו טומאה וטורה למה לי: רבי אליעזר אומר יזרוק. את הדם ר' אליעזר לטעמיה דאמר בכילד צולין דם אף על פי שאין בשר: רבי יהושע אומר לא יזרוק · ר' יהושע לטעמיה דאמר אם אין בשר אין דם ויוצא חוץ לקלעים בבשר קדשי הקדשים קאמר שמחיצה שלהן חומת עזרה כדכתיב בחצר אהל מועד יאכלוה ואם יצאה נפסלת כדילפינן בכילד צולין מאל הקודש פנימה: מאי נפסל לאו בהיסח הדעת. בתמיה דכיון דתנא נטמא ויוצא מאי פסול איכא תו אי נפסל בעבודת דם כגון במחשבת חוץ למקומו וחוץ לזמנו לא קרי נפסל בשר שהרי אף הדם נפסל ובהא לא נימא ר' אליעזר יזרוק: אי אמרת בשלמא. פסול חשש טומאה הוא משום הכי מודה רבי יהושע שאם זרק הורצה דאפילו נטמא ודאי ואע"ג דטומאה פסול הגוף הוי מרצה ציץ ולכתחלה לא יזרוק דקא סבר ריצוי ציץ בדיעבד הוא ויוצא אע"ג דלא מהני ליה ציץ הורצה בדיעבד דאע"ג דרבי יהושע בעי תרתי דם ובשר מיהו הואיל והבשר בעין ופסול יוצא פסול מחמת דבר אחר הוא חשבינן ליה פסול חסרון מחיצות בפרק קמא דמנחות בסופו איכא למימר בדיעבד הורצה: אלא אי היסח הדעת פסול הגוף הוא· וציץ נמי לא מרצי עליה אמאי הורצה: ה"ג אלא אי אמרת פסול הגוף הוי אמאי הורצה. ולא גרסינן פסול הגוף מי קא מרצי ציץ דהא פסול יוצא נמי לא מרצי ציץ כדאמרינן בפרק קמא (דף טז:) הא איהו טמא אלא עון כמדברטומאה: נפסל בטבול יום. וטעמא משום ציץ: אמרה קמיה דר' ירמיה. הא דרב ששת לעיל דאסורין מלאכול משום היסח הדעת הוא: שמעתתא דמחשכן. כשאין יודעין טעמו של דבר בודין מלבם טעם שאינו: אתרא דמחשכא. בבל עמוקה: לא שמיע לכו כו' · ומכאן יכולין ללמוד טעמה של משנה דאסורין מלאכול משום מעלה דאף על גב דמהניא זריעה לחולין עבוד רבנן מעלה דלא תהני לתרומה להעלות לה טהרה גמורה להיתר אכילה ומיהו מלטמא טהרו דהא לא עבוד מעלה: מי החג. כגון של ניסוך המים דשבת שבתוך החג היו ממלאין אותן מערב שבת וכשנטמאו אין יכולין לילך ולמלאות מן השילוח בשבת וטורח הוא למלאות מבור הגדול בגלגל והלך והשיקם באמת המים שבעזרה ומים סלקא להו השקה דזו היא זריעתן שמעברו עליהן מי המקוה ונעשה חיבור ובטלו: ואח"כ הקדישן. לא קידשו בכלי שרת טהורין: אין זריעה להקדש. לטהרו בכך דמעלה עשו בקדשים הכא נמי אין זריעה לתרומה דמעלה עשו: להא שמעתא. דרבי אושעיא: הקדישן בכלי שרת קאמרת. דכיון דקדושין הן קדושת המקדש עבדינהו להו רבנן מעלה אבל משום קדושת פה דממלאן בכלי חול לשם חג לא עבדי להו מעלה ומהניא להו השקה: זו לא שמעתי. במעלה זו דזריעה לא שמעתי · אם בפה אם בכלי אבל במעלה אחרת שמעתי דאף בקדושת פה עבדו רבנן והיכא למילף מינה דהוא הדין לכל מעלות שבקודש: דרכן ואחר כך הקדישן טהורות: לנסכים ור' יוחנן לטעמיה דאמר לעיל משקין מיפקד פקידי ולא קבילי טומאה ולקמיה מפרש היכי דריך להו: הקדישן ואח"כ דרכן טמאות. קא ס"ד הקדיש יינן לנסכים: דעבוד רבנן מעלה בקדשים דמיטמא משקה עם האוכל ולא אמרינן בהו משקין מיפקד פקידי והא ענבים קדושת פה הן דהא נמי נתנן לכלי אין כלי מקדשין דאין כלי שרת מקדשין אלא דבר הראוי לו כדילפינן בשחיטת קדשים* גבי מזבח שנאמר כל הנוגע במזבח יקדש שומע אני בין ראוי בין שאינו ראוי תלמוד לומר עולה מה עולה ראויה וכלי שרת דומיא דמזבח דמזבח נפקא לן התם: בענבים של תרומה. והאי הקדישן קדושת תרומה קאמר דבתרומה לא שייכא קדושת כלי לא ביין ולא בענבים: אבל הכי: דרכן ואפילו טובא. לעיל קמהדר אמרת דרכן ואחר כך הקדישן טהורות ואפילו טובא בבת אחת בתמיה והא אמרת לעיל פחות פחות מכביצה דלא יותר הא איטמו משקין בכביצה מיעלה טיפה ראשונה טומאת האוכל שהרי יש בה כשיעור: הכי גרסינן אי בעית אימא הכא נמי בפחות מכביצה ואי בעית אימא התם דבעינן פחות מכביצה שנגעו ענבים בראשון · כגון טמא מת שרץ או טמא נבילה וכל שכן טמא מת דכיון דהוו ענבים שני טימאו את המשקין בכביצה משלאת טיפה ראשונה ואף על פי שהן חולין דכל הפוסל את התרומה מטמא משקין להיות תחלה ושני עושה שלישי בתרומה לא גרסינן דהא בחולין עסקינן דאי בתרומה הא אמרן דעבוד מעלה שמטמאה משקה עם האוכל: הכא דנגעו. ענבים בשני דהוו להו שלישי הלכך דרכן ואחר כך הקדישן שקרא להן שם תרומה טהורין ואפילו דרך הרבה יחד שהאוכל שלישי לא עשה למשקה כלום ומתחלה לא נטמאו עם האוכל דקודם קריאת שם לא עבוד מעלה הקדישן לתרומה ואח"כ דרכן טמאין דמקריאת שם חלה המעלה עליהן ונעשה המשקין כאוכל הכל אחד: אף אנן נמי תנינא. דעבוד רבנן מעלה בקדשים ואפילו בקדושת פה: שתהא חיותן בכלי. באותו כלי עצמו שהוא מקדש בו מי חטאת באפרן צריך למלאותו מן המעין ולא ימלאם בכלי אחר ויערה לתוך זה וכתב ונתן דמשמע תלושין דמותר למלאותו בכלי אחר ויערה לתוך זה: אלא

שאם זרק הורצה. אף על גב דאין ציץ מרצה על היוצא רבי יהושע סבר זריקה מועלת ליוצא כרבי עקיבא דריש מעילה (דף ז:) דאמר זריקה מועלת להוציא בשר מידי מעילה וכל שכן להרצאה דהא רבי אליעזר דאמר הכא יזרוק קאמר התם דלהוצאה ממעילה לא מהניא:

ונתן אלמא תלושין והא מחוברין נינהו. פירוש דונתן משמע דחשיב להו תלושין והיינו לענין קבלת טומאה אף על פי שהן מחוברין והשתא מייתי ראיה דאין השקה להקדש מן התורה וכן בתרומה נמי עבוד רבנן מעלה *ופ"ה דחוק:

רבינו חננאל

השרפה וכיון שנפסל הסיח דעתו ממנו הניחא לדידי דאמינא פסול טומאה הוא מש"ה בעי עיבור צורה אלא לדידך דאמרת פסול הגוף הוא למה לי עיבור צורה והתנן זה הכלל כל שפסולו בגוף ישרף מיד בדם ובבעלים תעובר צורתו כלומר כל זמן שיתכן שיאכל מניחין אותו שמא יבוא אליהו ויתירנו באכילה עד שיסריח וישנה מצורת בשר שאי אפשר להאכל כלל ויצא לשרפה קתני מיהא כל שפסולו בגופו ישרף מיד ושני' האי תנא סבר אפילו פגול שאינו מרצה לעולם והוא ודאי פסול הגוף טעון עיבור צורה דיליף עון עון מנותר: ותוב מותיב עליה מהא [דתני'] נטמא הבשר או נפסל או יצא הו"קלעי' כו' קתני מיהא אם זרק הורצה וכי פסול הגוף בר הרצאה הוא ומשני' רבי שמעון בן לקיש מאי נפסל דקתני נפסל בטבול יום דלא מסח דעתיה ותרי גוני טומאה קתני: ר' ירמיה פשיט ליה לבעיא דרבה בר מתנה מהא דאמר ריש לקיש מי החג שנטמא השיקן ואחר כך הקדישן טהורין הקדישן ונטמאו ואחר כך השיקן טמאין פי' כיצד משיקן נותן בכלי גללים או בכלי אבנים או בכלי אדמה וממלא אותו הכלי מן המים ומטבילן במי מקוה כדי שיהיו מי מקוה צפין עליו ועלתה להם טהרה והיינו השקתן וכבר פירשנוה ביום טוב · פי' הקדיש מים לנסך אותם בחג ונטמאו והשיקן פי' ושקען במי מקוה לטהרן אע"פ שנכנסו תחת המים שנמצאו כאלו זרועים הם במקוה לא עלתה להם טהרה שאין הזריעה מטהרת בהקדש כך שתילי תרומה אע"פ ששקען וזרען בקרקע לא עלתה להם (התרה) [טהרה] ומאי אסורה אסורה לכהנים: א"ל לרב דימי בקדושת כלי קאמרת כגון אלו ימי החג וכיוצא בהן שנקדשו בכלי הקדש עבדו בהן רבנן מעלה שאין זריעה מטהרת בהקדש שנקדש בכלי הקדש אבל אם הקדישה קדושה בפה שאמר זה קדש ועדיין לא בא בכלי קדש הא מיבעיא לי יש לו זו המעלה שהרי כבר נקדש או לא אמר לו זו בהדיא לא שמעתי כיוצא בה שמעתי דאמר רבה בר בר חנה אמר ר' יוחנן ענבים שנטמאו דרכן ואח"כ הקדישן טהורין הקדישן ואח"כ דרכן טמאין הרי ענבים הללו קדושת פה נינהו שעדיין לא באו בכלי ואינם יין לנסך ואפילו הכי עבוד להו מעלה ודחי רב יוסף ואמר הני ענבים דאמר רבי יוחנן ענבים דתרומה הן דקדושת הפה (נינהו) [דידהו] קדושה גמורה היא וכיון שאמר הרי אלו תרומה כקדושת כלי דמיא קדושתן אבל קדש דבעו כלי כגון ניסוך המים וכיוצא בו בכה בלא קדושת כלי לא עשו בהן מעלה ואקשי' אהא ומי אמר ר' יוחנן ענבים שנטמאו דורכן כלו טהורים והא איהו דאמר סוחטן פחות פחות מכביצה ושני' הכי נמי מאי דרכן דקתני נמי פחות פחות מכביצה · איבעית אימא התם דאמר רבי יוחנן פחות פחות מכביצה דנגעי בשרץ והוו להו ענבים ראשון דמטמו אחריני והכא דקתני כגון שנטמאו במים שנטמאו בשרץ דהוו להו שני ואין שני עושה שני ואין שני עושה שלישי בחולין ואי תרומה נינהו דנגעי בולד שני דהוו להו ענבים שלישי ואין שלישי עושה רביעי בתרומה: אמר רבא אף אנן נמי תנינא דבקדושת כלי עבדו בהן מעלה דכתיב ונתן עליו מים חיים אל כלי שתהא חיותן בכלי מדקאמר תתן

*בשליקתא ומאיסתא הכא נמי בשליקתא ומאיסתא והיכא איתמר דרב אשי אהא דאמר רבי אבין בר רב אחא א"ר יצחק אבא שאול גבל של בית רבי היה והיו מחמין לו חמין בחיטין של תרומה טמאה ללוש בהן עיסה בטהרה אמאי ניחוש דילמא אתי בהו לידי תקלה א"ר אשי בשליקתא ומאיסתא אביי בר אבין ורב חנניא בר אבין תנו תרומות בי רבה פגע בהו רבא בר מתנה אמר להו מאי אמריתו בתרומות דבי מר אמרו ליה ומאי קשיא לך אמר להו *תנן "שתילי תרומות שנטמאו ושתלן (א) טהורים מלטמא ואסורין מלאכול (בתרומה) וכי מאחר דטהורין מלטמא אמאי אסורין מלאכול אמרו ליה הכי אמר רבה מאי אסורין אסורין לזרים ומאי קמ"ל גידולי תרומה תרומה *תנינא "גידולי תרומה תרומה וכי תימא גידולי גידולין ומאי קמ"ל בדבר שאין זרעו כלה *הא נמי תנינא "הטבל גידוליו מותרין בדבר שזרעו כלה אבל בדבר שאין זרעו כלה אפי' גידולי גידולין אסורין באכילה אישתיקו א"ל מידי שמיע לך בהא אמר להו הכי אמר רב ששת מאי אסורין "אסורין לכהנים הואיל ואיפסילו להו בהיסח הדעת הניחא למ"ד היסח הדעת פסול הגוף הוי שפיר אלא למ"ד היסח הדעת פסול טומאה הוי מאי איכא למימר דאתמר היסח הדעת רבי יוחנן אמר "פסול טומאה הוי ורבי שמעון בן לקיש אמר פסול הגוף הוי רבי יוחנן אמר פסול טומאה הוי שאם יבא אליהו ויטהרנה שומעין לו רבי שמעון בן לקיש אומר פסול הגוף הוי שאם יבא אליהו ויטהרנה אין שומעין לו איתיביה רבי יוחנן לרשב"ל *ר' ישמעאל בנו של רבי יוחנן בן ברוקא אומר *לול קטן היה בין כבש למזבח במערבו של כבש ששם היו זורקין פסולי חטאת העוף ותעובר צורתן ויוצאין לבית השריפה אי אמרת בשלמא פסול טומאה הוי משום הכי בעי עיבור צורה שמא יבא אליהו ויטהרנה אלא אי אמרת פסול הגוף למה לי עיבור צורה *והתנן *זה הכלל כל

בשליקתא ומאיסתא. לאחר שנטמאו שולקן ואח"כ זורקן לבין העלים והן נמאסות ורב הונא חייש דלמא אכיל לה מקמי דלישלקינהו או בשעה ששולקן: והיו מחמין לו חמין בחיטין של תרומה טמאה. שהיו לוקחין אותם מכהנים בזול: ללוש בהן עיסה בטהרה. כלומר אע"פ שרבי אוכל חולין בטהרה היה לא חייש דילמא נגעו הני חטים טמאים בעיסה דבטלו להו מתורת אוכל ולא מטמאו: תנו תרומות. מס' תרומות: מאי אמריתו. חידוש וטעמא בתרומות שאתם שונים בבית אדם גדול כרבה: שתילי תרומה. כגון שתילי כרוב וכרישין: טהרו מלטמא. אחרים שחיבורן לקרקע בטלן מתורת אוכל: ואסורין מלאכול. וקא ס"ד משום טומאה ולכהנים: אסורים לזרים. דלא אמרינן פקע שם תרומה מינייהו: ומאי קא משמע לן גידולי תרומה כתרומה. אפילו בדבר שזרעו כלה כגון חיטין או לגלות שומין הניכר: וכי תימא. האי אסורין מלאכול בדבר שאין זרעו כלה קאמר כגון בצלים דקים שקורין ליבו"ש וכשמוציאים אחת אחת לבדה הן נוספות ומתחברות שתה ו' יחד והיינו גידולי גידולין אותן הנוספות עליהן שלא היו תרומה מעולם וגידולין עצמן כגון שתילי כרוב שמולבים ומרחיבין העלין הראשונים ועדים החדשים העולין בקלח הוו גידולי גידולים: הטבל גידוליו מותרין. אע"פ שנתמרח בכרי והוקבע למעשר וחל עליו שם טבל וזרעו ולא הפריש מעשרותיו תחלה ולמח ונגמר וקצרו מותר לאכול עראי עד שימרח בכרי ואף על גב דגידולי תרומה תרומה מדרבנן הוא ולהומרה שלא להפסיד את הכהנים אבל גידולי טבל חולין הן והרי הן כשקולין כשאר תבואה ואוכל מהן עראי עד שימרחם: בהיסח הדעת. כשנטמאו מתחלה הסיח דעתו מהם שוב מלאוכלן ונפסלין בהיסח הדעת דכתיב גבי תרומה (במדבר יח) את משמרת תרומותי עביד לה שימור ולא תסיח דעתך: פסול הגוף הוי. מעלה היא בקדשים שנפסלין בכך ושם פסול הוא לעצמו ואפילו יבוא אליהו ויאמר שלא נטמאו כל אותן הימים שהסיח דעתו מהן אין שומעין לו: שפיר. משום הכי אסורין שאין שתילתן מועלת להן להסיר שם פסול מעליהן: אלא למ"ד. כל מה שקדשים נפסלין בהיסח הדעת אינו אלא משום חשש טומאה שמא ע"י שהסיח דעתו משמירתן נגעה בהן טומאה ואינו יודע: מאי איכא למימר. הני אמאי מיפסלי משום חשש טומאה הא אפי' טומאה ודאית שבהן טיהרתם שתילתן: ויטהרנו. ויאמר שלא נגעה בו טומאה כל ימי היסח: לול קטן. כמין גומא חלולה עשויה בבנין הרצפה: בין כבש למזבח. כלומר בקרן זוית סמוך לכבש וסמוך למזבח במקום שהם מתחברים: במערבו של כבש. אצל שפת מערבית של כבש: ששם זורקין פסולי חטאת העוף. לפי שהיא נעשית בקרן מערבית דרומית למטה וכשאירע פסול בה שאינו פסול הגוף ממש ואין יכול לשורפה מיד משום בזיון קדשים נותנין אותה שם: ותעובר צורתה. היינו פסול לינה עיבור צורת מראית בשר בלינת לילה אחד הוא וכיון שלנה בלילה הרי היא נותר וטעון שריפה ונשרף ועל כרחך מדבעינן העברת צורה לאו כשפיגל בה או נטמאת או יצתה או מלקה שלא כמצותה קמיירי דהא פסול מעליא הוא ולמה לן לאהדורי אפסול לינה ואין לנו דניבעי לינה אי לאו פסול היסח הדעת וא"א פסול חשש טומאה הוא היכא למימר דהאי פסול בהיסח הדעת קאמר וכיון דלא חזינן ליה דאיטמי אלא חששא בעלמא הוא בעי עיבור צורה דלא מצינן למשרפה להדיא שמא יבוא אליהו אחרי כן ויאמר טהורה היתה ונמצאת ששרפנו קדשים טהורין אלא אם שם פסול הוא לעצמו אפי' לא נטמא למה לי עיבור צורה:

בשליקתא ומאיסתא. קצת נראה דוקא שהן כבר מאוסות מותר להשהותן אבל לאחס אסור דבתוך כך אתי ביה לידי תקלה כמו בדריכת ענבים דבפרק הלוקח בהמה (בכורות דף כב:) אמרינן סאה תרומה טמאה שנפלה לתוך מאה חולין טהורים ר"א אומר תרום ותרקב ובמס' תרומות בפ"ה גרסינן תרום ותשרף ואומר ר"ת דבמאיסתא תשרף ויהנה ממנו בשעת שריפה: מחמין לו חמין בחיטין של תרומה. אור"ת דלכהנים של בית רבי היו עושין דלישראל לא שריא אלא הנאה שאינה של כילוי כמו עירוב דמערבין לישראל בתרומה אבל הנאה של כילוי כגון להאכיל לבהמתו או להדליק אסור לישראל כדאמרינן בפ"ק דמס' ע"ז (סו.*) כהן ששכר פרה מישראל לא יאכילנה כרשיני תרומה ובמסכת תרומות (פי"א משנה י') נמי אמרי' מדליקין בבתי כנסיות ובבתי מדרשות בשמן של תרומה שנטמא ברשות כהן פירוש אם יש שם כהן דנר לאחד נר למאה ור"י אומר טעמא משום דדרשינן משמרת תרומותי מה תרומה טהורה וכו' ומה טהורה דוקא לכהן אף טמאה דוקא לכהן ובטמאה ליכא אלא הדלקה*: טהרו מלטמא. תימה לר"י דבפ' קמא דשבת (דף טז:) מסקינן דהיינו טעמא דגזרו גידולי תרומה תרומה משום תרומה טמאה ביד כהן פי' שלא ישהה אותה לזריעה והשתא כיון דטהרו ישהה אותה לזריעה כדי לטהרה ואומר ר"י דמשום ריוח פורתא לא ישהה אותה מאחר שעדיין היא תרומה ולא נעשית חולין הקשה רבינו נסים גאון דתניא בתוספתא* גידולי תרומה ומעשר שני הרי הן כחולין ומאי תירוץ בירושלמי דמסכת תרומות דהרי הן כחולין היינו להתחייב בלקט ושכחה ופאה ועניי ישראל ועניי כהנים מלקטין אותן אלא שאסורין לזרים והיינו דתניא עניי ישראל מוכרין את שלהן לכהנים בדמי תרומה וטעמא לפי שמדאורייתא אין תרומה ומעשר חייבין בלקט שכחה ופאה ולא אתי גזירה דרבנן ומפקע ליה ועוד הקשה הר"ר משה נבריי"ש דתנן במסכת בכורים (פ"ב מ"ב) יש במעשר ובכורים מה שאין כן בתרומה שהמעשר ובכורים גידולן אסורים מלאכול בירושלים אף לזרים ולבהמה משא"כ בתרומה משמע דגידולי תרומה שרו לזרים מיהו בלאו הכי לא א"ש לישנא אף לזרים דאדרבה אף לכהנים מיבעי ליה למימר ונראה דזרים דהתם *היינו נכרים וכן משמע בירושלמי: גידולי גידולין. פירש ריב"א דגידולים היינו גידולי ראשון מן הזרע ואח"כ חזר ונטע אותן גידולים זהו גידולי גידולין ומביא ראיה מירושלמי דמסיק התם אגידולי גידולין משיעשו שני גורנות דהיינו בכה"ג שנזרע ונלקט שתי פעמים ולפ"ה הכל הוי גידול ראשון ומה שפ"ה דשומין הוי דבר שזרעו כלה לא משמע הכי דבמסכת תרומות תנן בפ"ט (מ"ו) איזהו דבר שאין זרעו כלה הלוף והשום והבצלים: פסול הגוף הוי. תימה דלעיל (דף כ:) אמרינן אם היתה במקום המוצנע יניחנה במקום התורפה ואמרי' גרמא אין בידים לא ואמאי אין מותר לשורפה מיד כשמסיח דעתו ממנה: למה לי עיבור צורה. קשה לר"י דילמא האי פסול היינו בדם ובבעלים דבעי עיבור צורה וי"ל מ"מ אחר שנזרק בלול יש בו היסח הדעת הר"ר אלחנן:

[פי' תוספות ב"ק קטו: ד"ה אתי לידי תקלה וכו' דבר נמי מודה בזה]

תרומות פ"ט משנה ז

ר"מ מוחק זה

[שבת יז: תרומות פ"ט מ"ד נדרים.]

ג"ז שם

תוספתא זבחים פ"ז

[צ"ל והתניא]

קב א מיי' פי"א מהל' תרומות הל' כג:

קג ב שם הלכה כא* ו:

קד ג מיי' פ"ו מהל' מעשר הלכה ו"ד:

קה ד מיי' פי"א מהל' תרומות הלכה כב:

קו ה מיי' פי"ט מהל' פסולי מוקדשין הלכה ד*:

קז ו מיי' פ"ב מהל' בית הבחירה הל' יד:

[וכן במשנה תרומות פי"א משנה ט]

[ועיין תוספות יבמות סו: ד"ה לא וכו' מבואר באורך ועיין לעיל ט: ד"ה כדי ותוס' שבת כו: ד"ה אין מדליקין ותוס' מנחות סו: ד"ה כדי שתהא]

[דטהרות פ"א]

[לקמן עו: וש"נ]

[תוספתא פ"ו]

הגהות הב"ח

(א) גמרא ושתלן טהרו מלטמא וכו'. ס"א כצ"ל:

רבינו חננאל

חיטי שליקתא ומאיסתא שרי לארלוקי בהו אבל חיטי שפירן וכיוצא בהן דחיישי' דלמא אכיל להו ואתי לידי תקלה לא משהינן להו וכן אבא שאול גבל של בית רבי היה מחמם חמין בחיטין שליקתא של תרומה [טמאה] ומאיסתא כדי ללוש עיסה בטהרה: בעי רבה בר מתנה מאביי ורב חנניה בר אבין הא דתנן פ"ט דתרומה שתילי תרומה שנטמאו ושתלן טהרו מלטמא ואסו' מלאכול עד[שינום] את האוכל וכיון שטהרו [מלטמא] אמאי אסורין לאכול א"ל הכי אמר רבה אסורה לזרים כלומר תרומה הי יכן ישתן קיימי אמרו לו מאי קמ"ל דגידולי תרומה תרומה הן תנינא גידולי תרומה תרומה וכ"ת בגידולי גידולין עסקינן ובדבר שאין זרעו כלה הא נמי תנינא *) דתנן גידולי תרומה תרומה וגידולי גידולין חולין ואקשינא בדבר שזרעו כלה אבל בדבר שאין זרעו כלה אפי' גידולי גידולין אסורין אשתיקו פי' דבר שאין זרעו כלה כגון הלוף והשום והבצלים אמר להו הכי א"ר ששת אסור לכהנים מ"ט הואיל ונפסלו בהיסח הדעת כלו' כיון שנטמאו הסיח דעתו מהן ונפסלו . ואמרי' הניחא למאן דאמר היסח הדעת פסול הגוף הוא כלו' הרי הוא כבשר המת שאין לו היתר לעולם אלא למאן דאמר היסח הדעת פסול טומאה הוא לא יהא הפסל חמור מן העיקר כיון שעתלן אכרת טהרו מטומאתן ולמה לא יהו מותרין מפסול (טומאה) [היסח הדעת] ונדחו גם דבריו וחזרו לברר מחלוקת ר' יוחנן ור"ל דאיתמר היסח הדעת [ר"ל אמר פסול הגוף הוי] שאם יבוא אליהו ויטהרנה אין שומעין לו ומו ;יב עליה ר' יוחנן מהא דתניא בסוף תמורה ר' ישמעאל בנו של ר' יודנן בן ברוקא אומר לול קטן [היה] בין כבש למזבח למערבו של כבש ששם היו זורקין פסולי חטאת העוף שתעובר צורתן ויוצאו לבית השרפה

*) גי' אחרת הי' לו לרבינו ז"ל כאן דמייתי מתרומה גופה שם במשנה ד' והיא יותר מחוורת מגי' דידן .

[34a] It refers to boiled [grains], so that they are repulsive; so here too it refers to boiled [grains], which are repulsive.[8]

And where was R. Ashi's [explanation] stated? In reference to what R. Abin son of R. Aḥa said in R. Isaac's name: Abba Saul was the baker[9] in Rabbi's house, and they used to heat him hot water with wheat of defiled *terumah*, wherewith to knead dough in purity. But why? Let us fear lest he come to a stumbling-block through it?[10]—Said R. Ashi: It refers to boiled [grains], which are repulsive.

Abaye b. Abin and R. Ḥanania b. Abin studied Terumoth[11] at Rabbah's academy. Rabbah b. Mattenah met them [and] asked them, What have you discussed in Terumoth at the Master's academy?—Said they to him, But what is your difficulty? He replied, We learned: Plants of *terumah*[12] which were defiled, and he [their owner] replanted them, are clean in that they do not defile
a [other eatables],[1] but they are forbidden to be eaten [as *terumah*].[2] But since they are clean in that they do not defile, why are they forbidden to be eaten?—Said they to him, Thus did Rabbah say: What is meant by 'forbidden'? They are forbidden to lay Israelites. Now what does he inform us? That that which grows of *terumah* is [itself] *terumah!* [But] we have [already] learned it [elsewhere]: That which grows of *terumah* is *terumah?*[3] And should you answer: It refers to the second growth,[4] and what does he inform us? [That this law holds good] in respect of that whose seed[5] is not destroyed?[6] But surely we learned this too: [In the case of] *ṭebel*, that which grows out of it is permitted in a species whose seed is destroyed,[7] but in the case of a species whose seed is not destroyed, even its second growth[8] is forbidden for eating![9]—They were silent. Said they to him, Have you heard anything about this? Thus did R. Shesheth say, he answered, What does 'forbidden' mean? They are forbidden to priests, since they became unfit [for eating] through [his] mental neglect.[10] That is correct
b on the view that mental neglect is an intrinsic disqualification,[1] then it is well. But on the view that mental neglect is a disqualification of defilement,[2] what can be said?[3] For it was stated, [As to] mental neglect: R. Joḥanan said, It is a disqualification of defilement; while R. Simeon b. Laḳish said, It is an intrinsic disqualification.[4] 'R. Joḥanan said, It is a disqualification of defilement', for if Elijah should come and declare it clean,[5] we heed him.[6] 'R. Simeon b. Laḳish said, It is an intrinsic disqualification', for if Elijah should come and declare it clean, we do not heed him. R. Joḥanan raised an objection to R. Simeon b. Laḳish: R. Ishmael son of R. Joḥanan b. Beroḳa said: There was a small passage between the stairway and the altar at the west of the stairway, whither they used to throw disqualified bird sin-offerings until [the flesh] became disfigured[7] and then they passed out to the place of burning.[8] Now it is well if you say that [mental neglect] is a disqualification of uncleanness: therefore it requires disfigurement, lest Elijah may come and declare it clean.[9] But if you say that it is an intrinsic disqualification, what is the need of disfigurement? Surely it was taught, This is the general rule: [34b]

(8) When thrown among the wood. (9) Lit., 'mixer' (of dough). (10) If the unclean wheat is kept for that purpose, as above. (11) The Tractate on the laws of *Terumah*. (12) E.g., cabbages and leeks which were separated as *terumah*.

a (1) Because the planting in the ground removes their uncleanness. (2) Maharam deletes the bracketed passage.—It is now assumed that the prohibition refers to priests, and they may not be eaten because they are defiled *terumah*, v. Ter. IX, 7. (3) Even in the case of a species whose original seed rots away in the earth. (4) Lit., 'what is grown of what is grown'. (5) I.e., the original stock. (6) E.g., an onion, the original stock of which remains when it is planted. Now its original leaves grow larger, and this is referred to as the growth. But in addition it sends our fresh shoots altogether, which never were *terumah:* these are referred to as the second growth, and we are informed that even these are *terumah*. (7) E.g., if *ṭebel* of wheat is sown the crop is not *ṭebel*. Before produce becomes *ṭebel* one may make a light meal of it though he has not yet rendered the tithe and *terumah;* but nothing whatsoever may be eaten of it when it reaches the stage of *ṭebel*. Though that which grows from *terumah* remains *terumah* even if its seed is destroyed, that is merely a Rabbinical stringency, lest the priestly dues are thus evaded. But that which grows of *ṭebel* is not *ṭebel* but ordinary produce of which a light meal may be enjoyed until it becomes *ṭebel*, which happens when it is heaped up in a stack. (8) As explained in n. a7. (9) Because it retains the same status as that of its parent stock. The same logically applies to *terumah* that is sown. (10) And not because it is defiled *terumah*. The priest must always keep the *terumah* in mind; v. Num. XVIII, 8: *behold, I have given thee the charge of mine heave offerings*—*'charge'* implies that he must think of it. The *terumah*, having once become defiled, however, the priest would dismiss it from his mind, as he would abandon the hope of using it.

b (1) I.e., sacred food, even if proved *not* to have been defiled, becomes unfit thereby, because this neglect is in itself a disqualification. (2) I.e., it is not a disqualification in itself, but merely because while the priest was not thinking about it it might have become defiled. (3) For it has now been established that even when it is certainly unclean it regains its cleanliness when replanted. (4) [This question remains unanswered, v. R. Ḥananel.] (5) Elijah was regarded as the future resolver of all doubts; cf. B.M., 3a, n. a2. (6) Declaring the *terumah* fit to be eaten. (7) I.e., by being kept overnight and thus becoming *nothar* (v. Glos.) (8) The reference is to the offerings disqualified through mental neglect. (9) In which case it should not have been burnt. But when it is disfigured it must be burnt in any case.

When R. Huna the son of R. Joshua came,[10] [33b] he said, Scripture saith, *The firstfruits* [*of thy corn* etc.], [implying] that its residue is distinct [in that it becomes permitted] to the Israelite,[11] [thus] this[12] is excluded, since its residue is not [so] distinct.[13]

R. Aḥa b. R. 'Awia sat before R. Ḥisda and he sat and said in R. Joḥanan's name: If grapes are defiled, one may tread them out less than an egg in quantity at a time, and their wine is fit for libations.[14] This proves that he holds that the juice is indeed stored up;[15] [consequently] when is it [the juice] defiled? When he expresses it; [but] when he expresses it, its standard quantity
a [for defiling] is absent.[1] If so, [he can tread] as much as an egg too, for we learned: If a man unclean through a corpse squeezes out olives or grapes exactly as much as an egg in quantity, they are clean?[2]—There it is [thus] if he did it;[3] here it is in the first instance [when he must not tread as much as an egg] for fear lest he come to tread[4] more than an egg.[5] Said R. Ḥisda to him, Who heeds you and R. Joḥanan your teacher: whither then has their uncleanness[6] gone? This proves that he holds that the juice is indeed absorbed,[7] and since the [solid] eatable is defiled, the juice too is defiled. And do you not hold that the juice is stored up? he replied. Surely we learned: If he who is unclean through a corpse squeezes out olives and grapes exactly as much as an egg in quantity, they are clean. Now it is well if you say that the liquid is stored up: for that reason it is clean. But if you say [that] it is absorbed, why is it clean?—Said he to him: We discuss here grapes which were not made fit;[8] when [then] do they become fit? when he squeezes them;[9] but when he squeezes them the standard quantity [for defilement] is diminished.[10] For if you should not say thus, [then] when it was taught, 'To what is this like? To *terumah* of mulberries and grapes which were defiled, which is not permitted to him either for eating or for burning,'[11]—but surely it may be eaten too, for if he wishes, he can tread them
b out less than an egg at a time?[1]—Said Raba: It is a preventive measure,[2] lest he come to a stumbling-block through them.[3] Abaye said to him, Yet do we fear a stumbling-block? Surely it was taught: One may light [a fire] with bread or oil of *terumah* which was defiled![4]—The bread he casts among the wood, he replied, and the oil of *terumah* he pours into a repulsive vessel.[5]

[It was stated in] the text: 'One may light [a fire] with bread or oil of *terumah* which was defiled'. Abaye said in Hezekiah's name, and Raba said, The School of R. Isaac b. Martha said in R. Huna's name: They learned this of bread only, but not of wheat, lest he come to a stumbling-block through it.[6] But R. Joḥanan said: Even wheat.[7] But why? Let us fear lest he come to a stumbling-block through it?—As R. Ashi said [elsewhere],

(10) [Var. lec. omit, 'came', v. Rashi.] (11) I.e., by giving the firstfruits, viz., the *terumah* to the priest, the residue becomes permitted to the Israelite. (12) Leaven separated as *terumah* during Passover. (13) The residue, being leaven, remains forbidden to the Israelite. (14) On the altar. Unclean food less than an egg in quantity cannot defile other eatables. Hence when he treads out the grapes in such small quantities, there is never enough to defile the exuded juice, and the wine manufactured therefrom is clean, and consequently fit for libations on the altar, for which, of course, only undefiled wine is valid. (15) It is not joined, as it were, to the outer skin and part of it, but like a liquid that is kept in a vessel. For if it were held to be absorbed and part of the skin, it would become unclean simultaneously with the skin.

a (1) As explained *supra*, n. b14. (2) This person defiles food, and the food in turn, if not less than an egg in quantity, defiles liquids. Here the man does not touch the expressed juice. Now after the first drop issues the residue is less than the necessary minimum and therefore it does not defile the liquid that follows. (3) If he squeezed as much as an egg, it is clean. (4) I.e., tread out. (5) If he comes to ask what to do, he is told to tread it less than an egg at a time. For if he is permitted to tread out exactly as much as an egg, he may exceed it, thus rendering the whole unclean. (6) Of the grapes. (7) As part of the grape, and does not stand separate. (8) To become unclean. Before an eatable can become unclean it must have had moisture upon it. (9) I.e., the first drop which exudes and touches the outer skin makes the grapes fit to become unclean. (10) For after the first drop has oozed out, less than an egg in quantity is left. (11) V. *supra* 32a.

b (1) If we assume that the liquid is merely stored up. Hence it follows that the liquid is absorbed and is unclean simultaneously with the outer skins of the mulberries and grapes. (2) *Sc.* thus denying him the right to squeeze them out in such small quantities. (3) He may eat them whilst treading them. (4) And we do not fear that he may come to eat it. (5) So that in both cases he is not likely to eat it. (6) Even if wheat is thrown among wood it does not become repulsive. (7) Is permitted.

אמר אמר קרא °ראשית *ששיריה ניכרין יצתה זו שאין שיריה ניכרין יתיב רב אחא בר רב עויא קמיה דרב חסדא ויתיב ואמר משמיה דר' יוחנן *ענבים שנטמאו °דורכן פחות פחות מכביצה ויינן כשר לנסכין אלמא קסבר משקין מיפקד פקידי לאימת קא מיטמאי לכי סחיט להו לכי סחיט להו ליתיה לשיעוריה אי הכי כביצה נמי *דהתנן °טמא מת שסחט זיתים וענבים כביצה מכוונת טהורין התם דאי עבד הכא לכתחלה גזירה דילמא אתי למיעבד יותר מכביצה א"ל רב חסדא *מאן צייית לך ולרבי יוחנן רבך וכי טומאה שבהן להיכן הלכה אלמא קא סבר משקין מיבלע בליעי וכיון דאיטמו ליה אוכלא איטמו ליה משקין אמר ליה ואת לא תיסברא דמשקין מיפקד פקידי והתנן טמא מת שסחט זיתים וענבים *מכוונת כביצה טהורין אי אמרת בשלמא מיפקד פקידי משום הכי טהורין אלא אי אמרת מיבלע בליעי אמאי טהורין א"ל הכא במאי עסקינן בענבים שלא הוכשרו לאימת מתכשרי לכי סחיט להו *כי סחיט להו בציר להו שיעורא דאי לא תימא הכי הא דתניא *הא למה זה דומה לתרומת תותין (זיתים) וענבים שנטמאה שאין לו בה לא היתר אכילה ולא היתר הסקה הא היתר אכילה נמי אית ביה דאי בעי דריך להו פחות פחות מכביצה אמר רבא גזירה *דילמא אתי בהו לידי תקלה *אמר ליה אביי ומי חיישינן לתקלה והא תניא מדליקין בפת ובשמן של תרומה שנטמאת אמר ליה °פת זריק ליה בין העצים שמן של תרומה רמי ליה בכלי מאוס גופא מדליקין בפת ובשמן של תרומה שנטמאת אביי אמר משמיה דחזקיה ורבא אמר דבי רבי יצחק בר מרתא אמר רב הונא לא שנו אלא פת אבל חיטי לא שמא יבא בהן לידי תקלה ורבי יוחנן אמר °אפילו חיטי ואמאי ניחוש דילמא אתי בהן לידי תקלה כדאמר רב אשי בשליקתא

דאמר קרא ראשית. משמע שתהא היא ראשית ואלו שיריים ניכרים שתהא היא מתירתן לישראל ואי במפריש תרומת חמץ מה היתר יש בשיריה שתהא ראשית עושה שיריים כי הוו מעיקרא טבל הוו שרו בהנאה ואסורין באכילה השתא נמי שרו בהנאה ואסורין באכילה משום חמץ ולענין מאי הוו שיריים: פחות מכביצה. אוכל טמא אין מטמא אחרים: ויינן כשר לנסכים. דלאו מטמא: קסבר משקין מיפקד פקידי. מופקדין הן בתוך הזג ואין חיבור לו אלא כמי שמונחין בכלי וכשנטמא הזג לא נטמא משקה בכלל זג טומאת אוכלין דלאו אוכל דכוותיה חשיבי בהדייהו וטומאת משקין נמי לא נטמאו ואע"פ שמשקה מקבל טומאה בכל שהוא דלא היה שם משקה עליו מעולם ואין צירוף חבירו עמו דהא זה לא נגע במשקין שבחבירו: לאימת מיטמו. משקין לכי סחיט להו והכשתא נוגעין לכל הזגים יחד וכי סחיט להו ליתיה לשיעוריה דאין בזגין כביצה ליתן טומאה דהא פחות מכביצה דרך: כביצה נמי. דהא כי נפיק משקין מינייהו חסר ליה שיעוריה. אוכל ומשקה מקבל טומאה בכל שהן אבל אין מטמא אחרים אלא אוכל כביצה ומשקה ברביעית והכי תניא בתורת כהנים מכל האוכל מלמד שמטמא בכל שהוא יכול יטמא לאחרים בכל שהוא ת"ל אשר יאכל אוכל הנאכל בבת אחת והיינו כביצה כדאמרינן בפרק יוה"כ (יומא פ.) אין בית הבליעה מחזקת יותר מביצת תרנגולת ואני שמעתי דאף לקבל טומאה בעי כביצה: טמא מת שסחט זיתים וענבים כביצה מכוונת טהור. וכדמסיק מילתא במסכת טהרות ובלבד שלא יגע במשקה וכגון שדרכן בפשוטי כלי עץ שאין מטמאין שאין כאן מטמא משקה אלא הזגין שנגע בהן הטמא קודם לכן בידים שהוא לא נזהר אלא משילא משקה וכשהמשקין נוגעין בזגין כבר חסר שיעור כביצה ויותר מכביצה כל דהו קתני התם בהדיא טמא שכיון שיצא טפה ראשונה נטמאת הטפה בכביצה שעדיין היה באוכל כביצה אע"ג דאין משקה הנבלע באוכל מקבל טומאה עמו משלים הוא את שיעורו דכוותה תנן התם טובא ובמנחות (דף נד:) נמי מייתי לה בגמרא כביצה אוכלין שהניחו בחמה ונתמעטו טהורין וכן כזית חלב ופיגול ונותר חזר והניחן בגשמים ותפחו טמאין וחייבין עליהן משום פיגול ונותר וחלב ואע"ג דגשמים הנבלעין בתוכו לאו חלב נינהו דאי סחיט להו ושתי מינייהו כזית פטור אפילו הכי כל כמה דבגווה נינהו משלמי לשיעוריה וטמא מת דוקא נקט שאינו מטמא בהיסט והוא הדין לטמא שרץ וכל טומאת מגע ורישא דכולהו נקט אבל זב שמטמא בהיסט שסחט אפילו גרגיר יחידי תנן התם דמטמא אפילו בפשוטי כלי עץ דכיון דיצאת טפה ראשונה *ונטבל העץ והגביהו נטמאו משקין שעל העץ במשא דמשקה מקבל טומאה בכל שהוא וכשחזר ונתנו לתוכו נתערב טמא בטהור והכל טמא: התם דאי עביד קאמר. שסחט אבל הכא בבא לימלך מה יעשה נימא ליה דרוך פחות מכביצה אבל כביצה לא דילמא אתי למיעבד יותר מכביצה כל שהוא וכשיוצאה טפה ראשונה עדיין יש באוכל כביצה ונטמאת הטפה וחוזרת ומתערבת במשקין: טומאה שבהן. שקיבלו תחלה עם האוכל כשנטמאו הענבים: משקין בליעי. באוכל הן בלועין מכל דפנותיו וחיבור הן לו ונטמאו עמו: אמאי טהורין. הרי נטמאו הענבים במגע טמא מת ואע"פ שלא נגע במשקה נטמא: כי סחיט להו ליתיה לשיעוריה. וכשנוגע באוכל הנגוב ודוחהו אל תחת המדוך אין בהן שיעור כדי לקבל טומאה והוא זהיר מליגע במשקה כדקתני בהדיא ובלבד שלא יגע במקום המשקה: דאי לא תימא הכי. דמשקין בליעי ואיטמאו אלא מיפקד פקידי ואין מטמאין בנגיעת טומאה באוכל: הא דתניא. לעיל כו' לתרומת תותים וענבים דמשמע שנטמאו תותים וענבים קודם דריכה וקתני אין לו בה היתר אכילה הא היתר אכילה נמי אית בה דאי בעי דריך לה פחות פחות מכביצה: לידי תקלה. כשהוא דורכן שמא יאכל מהן: מדליקין בפת ובשמן כו'. והא ודאי בחד שעתא לא מדליק שמן כולה אלא לזמן מרובה ולא חיישינן דילמא אכיל מיניה: אלא פת. דכי זריק ליה ממאיסא ותו לא אתי למיכליה: אבל חיטי. אי נמי זריק להו לא ממאיסי: בשליקתא

אמר קרא ראשית ששיריה ניכרים. ואם תאמר והא שיריה ניכרים דמעיקרא הוא אסירא בהנאה של כילוי כגון הדלקה וכיוצא בו מידי דהוה אטבל טמא דאין מדליקין בו ומשעת הרמה ואילך מדליקין בו וי"ל דדוקא בטבל טמא אין מדליקין כדדרשינן *את משמרת תרומותי בשתי תרומות הכתוב מדבר מה תרומה טהורה אין לך בה אלא משעת הרמה ואילך אף תרומה וכו' אבל בטבל של חמץ מדליקין דלא איירי אלא בשתי תרומות:

לאימת מתכשרי לכי סחיט להו וכי סחיט להו בציר ליה שיעוריה. מכאן מקשה ר"ת לפ"ה דפירש דכל שהוא מקבל טומאה מן התורה דהא מכי נפיק מיגה פורתא מתכשרי ומיד מקבל טומאה כל הנשאר דמשקין מיבלע בליעי וה"ר יוסף תירץ דאע"פ שאוכל מקבל טומאה בפחות מכביצה *אין מקבל הכשר בפחות מכביצה ואומר ר"י דהיינו טעמא דמאשר יאכל נפקא ליה לטמא אחרים בכביצה אוכל הנאכל בבת אחת ועלה קאי אשר יבא עליו מים אלמא לא מקבל הכשר בפחות מכביצה ועוד מקשה ר"ת דאמרינן בפ' אלו עוברין (לקמן מד.) השום והשמן של תרומה ומקפה של חולין ונגע טבול יום במקצתו לא פסל אלא מקום מגעו וכתב בכל הספרים והוינן בה מקום מגעו אמאי פסול והא לא הוי כביצה אלמא לא מקבל טומאה בכל שהוא ורש"י מוחק שם מן הספרים ומפרש בדוחק ועוד ה"ר אליהו מביא ראיה מת"כ דדרשינן גבי כלי חרס דכתיב ואותו תשברו אותו אתה שובר לטהרתו ואי אתה שובר אוכלין לטהרתן ואי מקבלין טומאה בכל שהוא פשיטא דלא מהני להו שבירה והיא דת"כ שהביא רש"י שאוכל מטמא בכל שהוא אסמכתא היא ומילי טובא מפיק מקרא בת"כ וליתנהו אלא אסמכתא ורש"י בעצמו חזר בו בפ' אותו ואת בנו (חולין דף פב.) בשמעתא דפרה מטמא טומאת אוכלים דהקשה למה לה קבלת טומאה היא גופה מטמא אדם ובגדים ותירץ רש"י דכי האי גוונא מפרש בכריתות בפ' דם שחיטה (דף כא.) כגון שחיפוה בפחות מכביצה בצק אי משוית ליה אוכל מצטרף ליה בהדי בצק ומקבל האי בצק טומאה אם יגע בטומאה ומטמא שאר אוכלין ואי לאו אוכל הוא לא מקבל האי בצק טומאה דלית בה שיעור וכי נגעי ביה אוכלין אחריני טהורין הן שאין נוגעין בכביצה אלא בבצק לשון רש"י: [וע"ע תוס' שבת לה. ד"ה אי לענין ותו' זבחים לא: ד"ה אמר]: בשליקתא

עין משפט נר מצוה

צט א מיי' פי"ב מהל' תרומה הלכה יא ופ"ו מהל' איסורי מזבח הלכה ז:

ק ב מיי' פ"ט מהלכות טומאת אוכלין ה"ב: [שבת כו.]

קא ג ד מיי' פי"ב מהלכות תרומה הלכה יב:

רבינו חננאל

מדרשא כואתי: רב הונא בריה דרב יהושע אמר בעינן ראשית ששיריה מותר לישראל יצאת תרומת חמץ בפסח ששיריה אסורה לישראל: אמרי משמיה דר' יוחנן ענבים שנטמאו דורכן פחות פחות מכביצה ויינם כשר לנסכים אלמא קסבר משקין מיפקד פקיד בזוגין ולא נגע בהו טומאה אימת איטמו לכי סחיט להו בתר דסחיט להו ליכא אוכל כביצה דלטמא להו להני משקין ואקשי' אי הכי לדרכינון אפי' כביצה נמי דהא תנן בטהרות פ"ג טמא מת שסחט זיתים וענבים כביצה מכוונת משקה הנסחט מהן טהור ובלבד שלא יגע במקום המשקה יתר מכביצה טמא שמכיון שיצאת טיפה ראשונה נמצאת מכביצה ושני' מתני' התם משום דאיעבד וסחט אבל לכתחלה לא שרינן ליה דאי שרינ' כביצה חיישי' דלמא אתי למעבד הוא ביותר מכביצה ותנן יתר מכביצה טמא שמכיון שיצאת טיפה ראשונ' נטמאת מכביצה לפיכך לא שרינן אלא פחות פחות מכביצה: אמר רב חסדא והלא ענבים הללו שנטמאו קתני מכלל דטמאין הם ואם כן טומאה שלהם להיכן הלכה דיינן כשר לנסכים ודייקי' מדבריו דאמר אנה הלכה טומאתן מכלל דקסבר הוא משק' בענבים מבלע בליעי וכיון שנטמאו הענבים הן והמשקין שבהן נטמאו ביחד וכיון שנטמאו יחד אנה הלכה טומאתן ואקשי' איני שאם נטמאו הענבים נטמאו גם המשקין והא טמא מת שנגע בענבים טמאן ותנן טמא מת שסחט ענבים כביצה מכוונת טהור אע"פ שנגע בהן וטמאן ואי אמרת נטמאו גם המשקין אמאי תנן טהור ושני' אליבא דרב חסדא בשלא הוכשרו ולא טמאן מגע טמא מת איטמת מטמו לכי מתכשרו מן המשק' דמסחטי מינייהו בתר דסחטו מינייהו כל דהו בצר ליה שיעורו דביצה דהא כביצה מכוונת הוי וכיון דבצרו מכביצה לא מטמו אבל הני ענבים דאמר ר' יוחנן הוכשרו דהא נטמאו קאמר דאי לא תימא הכי דמשקה בענבים בליע הא דתניא הא למה זה דומה לתרומת תותים וענבים שנטמאת שאין לה היתר אכילה ולא היתר הסקה כלל אמאי לית ליה והא אי דרך להו פחות פחות מכביצה שרו בשתיה. אמר רב פפא ההיא גזירה היא משום דחיישי' דלמא אתי לידי תקלה כלומר כמות שהם או יסחטם יותר מכביצה: מותיב עליה אביי מדליקין בפת ובשמן של תרומה שנטמאת ואי חיישינן דלמא אתי לידי תקלה היכי שרינן ליה ושני' פת זורקה לבין העצים שמן נמי רמי ליה בכלי מאוס וכיון דמאיס לא אתי למיכל מיניהו וכן חיטי

מסורת הש"ס

[ערכין לג: חולין קלו:]

[לקמן לד: עי' תוס' חולין קיז: ד"ה ולא שומר]

שבת קמה: טהרות פ"ג [מ"ג]

[נדרים נח. שבועות י: מעילה יב.]

[נ"ל כביצה מכוונת]

[עי' תוס' כריתות יג. ד"ה כיון דקיי']

ס"א לצ"ע

[לעיל כ: וש"נ]

ס"א ונתנו בתוכו

גליון הש"ס

גמ' יצתה זו שאין שיריה נכרין. תמוה לי דה"ל לא תליא כלל בתרומת אם סאה חמץ או לא ותלי בכל...

בשיריים דמסכתא דמפריש תרומת חמץ כיון שיש לו סאה חמץ וט' סאין שאינן חמץ דיכול לקרות לסאה חמץ תרומה על הט' סאין דהא שיריה נכרין ובסיפוך אם הט' סאין חמץ וסאה שאין חמץ אי להפריש סאה זו על הט' סאין דאין שיריה נכרין: שם דורכן פחות. עיין חולין קי"ז ע"ב תוס' ד"ה ולא שומר: שם א"ל אביי ומי חיישינן לתקלה. ק"ל דאיך סבר אביי דלא חיישי' לתקלה... בלועי וטמאים מ"מ הא חזי לזילוף אע"כ דחיישי' לתקלה וכמ"ש רש"י לעיל דף לב ע"א וצ"ע: בתוס' ד"ה לאימת וכו' אין מקבל הכשר. עיין כריתות יג ע"א תוס' ד"ה כיון

תורה אור

הזיד במעילה במיתה רבי היא דתניא *הזיד במעילה רבי אומר במיתה וחכמים אומרים *באזהרה מאי טעמא דרבי אמר רבי אבהו *גמר חטא חטא מתרומה מה תרומה במיתה אף מעילה במיתה ומינה מה תרומה בכזית אף מעילה בכזית ומתקיף לה רב פפא ממאי דרבי כרבנן סבירא ליה דילמא כאבא שאול סבירא ליה דאמר יש בה שוה פרוטה אע"ג דלית בה כזית והא רב פפא הוא דאמר דאבא שאול תרתי בעי אלא ש"מ הדר ביה מר בריה דרבנא אמר הכי קאמר לא אם אמרת בשאר מצות שלא עשה בהן שאין מתכוין כמתכוין שאם נתכוין לחתוך את התלוש וחתך את המחובר שפטור תאמר במעילה שאם נתכוין להתחמם בגיזי חולין ונתחמם בגיזי עולה שמעל רב נחמן בר יצחק אמר הכי קאמר לא אם אמרת בשאר מצות שכן לא מתחייב בהן שאין מתעסק כמתעסק שאם נתכוין להגביה את התלוש וחתך את המחובר שפטור תאמר במעילה שאם הושיט ידו לכלי ליטול חפץ וסך ידו בשמן של קודש שמעל אמר מר בד"א במפריש תרומה והחמיצה אבל הפריש חמץ תרומה דברי הכל אינה קדושה מנא הני מילי *אמר רב נחמן בר יצחק אמר קרא °תתן לו ולא לאורו מתיב רב הונא בריה דרב יהושע *[ב]אין תורמין מן *הטמאה לטהורה ואם תרם בשוגג תרומתו תרומה ואמאי לימא לו ולא לאורו לא קשיא התם היתה לו שעת הכושר הכא לא היתה לו שעת הכושר ודלא היתה לו שעת הכושר היכי דמי כגון דאהמיץ במחובר אבל אחמיץ בתלוש הכי נמי דקדשה א"ל אין °בגזירת עירין פתגמא *ובמאמר קדישין שאילתא וכן מורין בבי מדרשא כוותי כי אתא רב הונא בריה דרב יהושע אמר

דברים יח | דניאל ד

רש"י

הזיד. בהנאת קדש שבשגגתה מעילה: ר' אומר במיתה. כדמפרש גמר חטא חטא הנאת קדש מאכילת תרומה כתיב הכא וחטאה בשגגה וכתיב בתרומה לא ישאו עליו חטא ומתו בו וגו' (ויקרא כב): וחכ"א באזהרה. רבנן נמי אית להו גזירה שוה דר' דהא עיקר מילתא דמעילה בהא גזירה שוה גמרי בפרק חמישי דמעילה (דף יח:) בברייתא גבי פגם ונהנה ובדבר שפגם נהנה ובתלוש מן הקרקע ובשליח שעשה שליחותו כל הני מתרומה גמרי בה ואזהרה נמי מתרומה גמרי מה אכילת תרומה הזהיר דכתיב (א) לא יאכל קודש אף הנאת הקדש דמעילה הזהיר ומיהו מיתה לא גמרינן מינה כדמפרשי רבנן טעמייהו בסנהדרין דמיעט רחמנא בתרומה ומתו בו והאי בו מיעוטא בו ולא במעילה וכן עיקר: מאי טעמא דרבי גרסינן: ומינה. היינו נרגא כלומר וכיון דמיתה מהכא נפקא לן על כרחיך הכי תילף ומינה מה תרומה מיתה הכתובה בה אאכילה כתובה דהוא כזית אף מעילה אין מיתה עד דאיכא כזית וליכא למימר דתנא הכי תאמר במעילה שחייב בה מיתה בפחות מכזית: ומתקיף לה רב פפא. להכי דשדו ביה נרגא: ממאי דרבי. בתרומה כרבנן דפליגי אדאבא שאול סבירא ליה דבעו כזית בתרומה דילמא כאבא שאול סבירא ליה ושפיר מצי למילף מינה מיתה במעילה דהיא בשוה פרוטה מתרומה אפילו לפחות מכזית: מר בריה דרבנא אמר. הא מתניתא דלעיל בשיבושא איתני בבי מדרשא והכי קאמר סיפא לא אם אמרת בשאר מצות שכן לא חייב בהן קרבן בשוגג (ב) שאין מתכוין לאותה מלאכה כשוגג שמתכוין לאותה מלאכה: שאם נתכוין לחתוך את התלוש. שהוא מתכוין לדבר המותר וחתך את המחובר שאפילו בשבת פטור דמלאכת מחשבת בעינן שיתכוין לחתיכת מחובר ומיהו שגג בשבת שאינו יודע שהוא שבת או אינו יודע שהמלאכה זו אסורה: תאמר במעילה שאם נתכוין כו' שמעל. כגון היו כאן גיזי חולין וגיזי עולה ונתכוין ליטול של חולין והלכה ידו על של עולה ומכיר הוא מי עולה ומי חולין אלא שנסתכל במקום אחר דהיינו שאין מתכוין למעשה זה וחייב מעילה דוחטאה בשגגה כל דהו כתיב ולא כתב בה מיעוטא כדכתיב בשבת מלאכת מחשבת וכתיב בשאר מצות אשר חטא בה פרט למתעסק והיינו מתעסק שמתעסק בדבר אחר ובא זה לידו: ר"נ בר יצחק אמר. הא לא הוה ליה למיתני דהא בשאר מצות נמי אם היה מתעסק בחתיכה ואפי' בשל היתר ועלתה בידו חתיכת איסור ואע"ג דאין מתכוין לזו מלאכת מחשבת היא וחייב אלא הכי קאמר לא אם אמרת בשאר מצות שכן לא חייב בהן שאין מתעסק בדבר היתר ושגג באיסור כיוצא בו כמתעסק בדבר היתר ועלה בידו איסור: שאם נתכוין להגביה את התלוש. דהיינו אין מתעסק בחתיכה לגמרי ואפי' בשל היתר וחתך מחובר שפטור ולא עשאו כמתעסק לחתוך תלוש וחתך מחובר: תאמר במעילה שאם הושיט ידו כו'. ולא היה מתעסק בשום סיכה ואפילו בשל היתר וסך ידו בשמן של קודש שמעל: אמר מר במה דברים אמורים כו' דברי הכל. קאמר ואפי' למאן דשרי הנאת חמץ בפסח קאמר: תתן לו. בתרומה כתיב ראשית דגנך וגו': ולא לאורו. אפי' היא ראויה להסיק הואיל ואינה ראויה לאכילה: אין תורמין מן הטמא על הטהור. לכתחלה שמפסיד את הכהן: בשוגג. שלא ידע שטבל זה טמא: שהיתה לו שעת הכושר. שנראית כבר לתרומה קודם שנטמא והא דלעיל בחמץ שלא היתה לו שעת הכושר לתרום ממנו דקודם שחל הפסח היה מחובר והחמיץ במחובר וכל זמן חיבורו לא היה ראוי לחול שם תרומה עליו דראשית דגנך כתיב משנדגן ודיגון לשון אסיפה והעמדת כרי הוא: עירין. מלאכים כלומר תלמידי חכמים שהם כמלאכי השרת אמרי בבית המדרש כמותי דהא דקתני לעיל אינה קדושה בשהחמיץ במחובר קאמר: ובמאמר קדישין שאילתא. מקרא הוא בדניאל: מורין. מורין הוראה: כוותי. כמותי: רב הונא בריה דרב יהושע אמר. אפילו בשהחמיץ בתלוש נמי קאמר דאינה קדושה: דאמר

תוספות

ומינה מה תרומה בכזית. אע"ג דבסוף כל התדיר (זבחים נא:) ובפרק בתרא דמנחות (דף קי.) איכא למ"ד דרבי סבר דון מינה ואוקי באתרה הכא אין לומר אוקי באתרה מה מעילה דממון שוה פרוטה אף מעילה דאכילה כן דהא אכילה דהקדש מאכילה דתרומה יליף והיאך יהיה בו מיתה אם לא כשיעור אכילת תרומה דבשאר נהנה ליכא מיתה אלא אאכילה אפילו לרבי דומיא דתרומה ואם תאמר אמאי אין מפרש לא אם אמרת בשאר מצות שלא חייב מיתה עד דהוי כזית בכדי אכילת פרס תאמר במעילה דאפי' בעינן כזית הא תנן בפרק הנהנה (מעילה יט:) לירך את המעילה אפי' לזמן מרובה וי"ל דליכא נמי למיפרך דניליף מתרומה שלא ילטרף: **אף** מעילה בכזית. תימה לר"י דהכא משמע דמאן דיליף חטא חטא סבירא ליה דמעילה בכזית כמו תרומה וכולהו אית להו גזירה שוה דפרק הנהנה (גם זה שם) יליף מעילה מתרומה למילי טובא ורבנן לא פליגי ארבי אלא לענין מיתה משום דכתיב בו ולא במעילה ואם כן מ"ט דרבנן דלעיל דאמרי לא אמר שוה פרוטה אלא לענין מעילה אבל בתרומה עד שיהא בו כזית: **נתכוין** לחתוך את התלוש וחתך את המחובר. ר"ת מפרש כגון שהוא מחובר דאי נתכוון לחתוך תלוש זה וחתך מחובר אחר מאי איריא נתכוון לתלוש אפילו נתכוון לחתוך מחובר זה וחתך מחובר אחר פטור הואיל ולא איתעבידא מחשבתו דתניא בהדיא בפרק ספק אכל (כריתות כ:) היו לפניו שתי נרות ונתכוון לכבות את זה וכבה את זה פטור: **תתן** לו ולא לאורו. אור"י דלא איצטריך למידרש מלו אלא לר' יוסי הגלילי דאית ליה חמץ מותר בהנאה °דלהנך תנאי דאסרי חמץ בהנאה נפקא לן מוגתן לכהן את הקודש דבר הראוי להיות קודש או מתתן לחודיה שאין ליתן אלא מידי דשרי בהנאה לכל הפחות דשייכא ביה נתינה ולכך משמע ליה למידרש מתתן לו דבר הראוי לאכילה ולא דבר שאין ראוי אלא לאורו והיינו תרומה טמאה דלא חזיא אלא לאורו דאיסור הנאה מהתם נפקא ואם תאמר ובעל הגמרא דבעי מנהני מילי והא הנך תנאי דהך ברייתא דהפריש חמץ תרומה ד"ה אינה קדושה כיון דסבירא להו דאסור בהנאה דבר פשוט הוא דאינו קדוש ומאי קבעי ליה יש לומר דפשיטא ליה לגמרא דלא איצטריך למיתני בברייתא ד"ה אלא לרבי יוסי הגלילי דמשום דהנך דאסירי בהנאה לא איצטריך למיתני ולהכי בעי מנהני מילי לרבי יוסי הגלילי אי נמי רב נחמן גופיה דמפרש לו ולא לאורו קאמר מה"מ לפי שהיה פשוט לו דאליבא דכ"ע קתני הכי וכה"ג איכא בכמה דוכתי*: אמר

עין משפט נר מצוה

צז א מיי' פ"א מהל' מעילה הלכה ג:
צח ב מיי' פ"ה מהל' תרומות הלכה ח:

מסורת הש"ס

סנהדרין [פג.] פד.

[קדושין מב: סנהדרין פד. זבחים מה. תמורה ג. מעילה יח:]

שבת כה:

מנחות כה: תרומות פ"ב מ"ב יבמות פט.

[מן הטמא על הטהור כנ"ל]

[ומאמר קדישין כנ"ל]

[עי' תוס' כילה לח. ד"ה וא"ר יוחנן יומא עו. ד"ה הני ה' ענויין ב"מ כא. ד"ה וכמה ב"ב כב: ד"ה וכמה ובכורות כט. סוף ד"ה היכי ובנזיר ל. ד"ה פשיטא]

הגהות הב"ח

(א) רש"י ד"ה וחכמים וכו' הזהיר דכתיב וכל זר לא יאכל: (ב) ד"ה מר בריה כו' בשוגג כשאין מתכוין:

גליון הש"ס

תוס' ד"ה תתן לו: דלהנך תנאי דאסרי חמץ בהנאה. יש לעיין דלהאורה לא צריך קרא כלל דהא אין יכול לקרות שם תרומ' דאיסורי הנא' לאו דידי' הוי כדאמרינן ב' דברים עשאן הכתוב כו' ועי' כריתות דף כד ע"א:

רבינו חננאל

מקדשי ה' וכתיב בתרומה ולא תשא עליו חטא בהרימכם את חלבו ונדחה ולא אשכחן מאן דאמר הזיד במעיל' במיתה אלא רבי דתניא הזיד במעילה ר' אומר במיתה וחכמים אומרים באזהרה ואמרינן מאי טעמא דרבי גמר חטא חטא מתרומה מה תרומה במיתה דכתיב ומתו בו כי יחללוהו אף מעילה במיתה ומינה מה תרומה בכזית חייב פחות מכזית פטור אף מעילה כך. ואסיקנא דודאי רב פפא דאמר אבא שאול בעי תרתי כזית ושוה פרוטה הדר ביה: **מר** בריה דרבנא אמר לא הכי קתני לא אם אמרת בשאר מצות שכן לא עשה בהן שאין מתכוין כמתכוין שאם נתכוין לחתוך את התלוש בשדה וחתך את המחובר שפטור תאמר במעילה שאם נתכוון להתחמם בגיזי חולין ונתחמם בגיזי עולה שמעל. ורב נחמן בר יצחק אמר שאם נתכוון להגביה התלוש וחתך המחובר פטור תאמר במעילה שאם נתכוון להושיט ידו לחביות ליטול הפך וסך ידו בשמן של תרומה: **בד"א** במפריש תרומה והחמיצה אבל הפריש חמץ תרומה דברי הכל אינה קדושה דא"ק ראשית דגנך תתן לו כלומר תתן לו תרומה מה שהן ראויה לו לאכילה ולא מה שאין ראוי לו ואע"פ שראוי לאורו בעינן לו ממש ומותבינן מדתנן בתרומות פ"ב אין תורמין מן הטמא על הטהור ואם תרם בשוגג תרומתו תרומה אמאי והא אינה ראויה לו ופרקי' שאני הכא דהיתה לה שעת הכושר קודם שתטמא אבל הא דתניא הפריש חמץ תבואה בפסח דברי הכל אינה קדושה כגון שהוכשר החטים והחמיצו והן מחוברין קודם קצירתן שלא היתה להם שעת הכושר כלל. ואמרי' מכלל דאי היתה לה שעת הכושר כגון דהחמיצה אחר תלישה הכי נמי דקדשה. אמר ליה רב נחמן בר יצחק אין הכי נמי בגזירת עירין פתגמא ובמאמר קדישין שאלתא וכך מורין בבי מדרשא

maintain? [33a] If he deliberately transgressed in respect of a trespass-offering,[6] [he is punished] by death? It is Rabbi. For it was taught: If he deliberately transgressed in respect of a trespass-offering,—Rabbi said: [He is punished] by death; while the Sages maintain: By a warning.[7] What is Rabbi's reason?—Said R. Abbahu: He derives identity of law from the fact that *'sin'* is written here and in the case of *terumah:*[8] just as *terumah* involves death, so trespass involves death. And from that [it also follows]: just as *terumah* [involves punishment] for as much as an olive, so trespass
a [involves punishment] for as much as an olive.[1] Now R. Papa demurred:[2] How do you know that Rabbi holds as the Rabbis;[3] perhaps he agrees with Abba Saul, who said: If it possesses the worth of a *peruṭah*, even if it does not contain as much as an olive?[4] But surely it was R. Papa who said [that] Abba Saul requires both? Hence this proves that he retracted.

Mar the son of Rabbana said, This is what he[5] means: No: if you say thus of other precepts, where the unintentional is not treated as intentional, for if he intended cutting what was detached but cut what is attached, he is not culpable;[6] will you say [the same] in the case of trespass, where if he intended to warm himself with wool shearings of *ḥullin* but warmed himself with the wool shearings of a burnt-offering, he is liable to a trespass-offering?

R. Naḥman b. Isaac said: He means this: If you say thus in the case of other precepts, that is because he who is not engaged therein is not declared culpable like he who is engaged therein, for if he intended picking up that which was detached but he plucked[7] that which is attached [instead], he is not culpable;[8] will you say [the same] of trespass, where if he stretched out his hand to take a vessel and [incidentally] anointed his hand with holy oil,[9] he is liable for trespass?

The Master said: 'When is this said? When he separates *terumah* and it became leaven. But if he separates *terumah* of leaven on Passover, all agree that it is not holy.' Whence do we know this?—Said R. Naḥman b. Isaac, Scripture saith, [*The firstfruits of thy corn, of thy wine, and of thy oil . . .*] *shalt thou give* to him:[10] but not
b for its light.[1] R. Huna son of R. Joshua objected: One must not separate *terumah* from unclean [produce] for clean; yet if he separates [thus] unwittingly, his *terumah* is valid. Yet why? Let us say, *'for him,* but not for his light'?—There is no difficulty: There it enjoyed a time of fitness,[2] whereas here[3] it did not enjoy a time of fitness.[4] And how is it conceivable that it had no time of fitness? E.g., if it became leaven whilst attached [to the soil].[5] But if it became leaven when detached,[6] would it indeed be holy?[7]—Yes, he replied: *'the sentence is by the decree of the watchers, and the matter by the word of the holy ones'*;[8] and thus do they rule[9] in the academy in accordance with my view.

(6) I.e., he deliberately transgressed where an unwitting transgression involves a trespass-offering. (7) I.e., flagellation. This is a technical term to denote that he has infringed an ordinary negative injunction, for which he is flagellated. (8) Trespass: *If a soul commit a trespass, and* sin *through ignorance in the holy things of the Lord* (Lev. V, 15); *Terumah: Lest they bear* sin *for it, and die therefor* (Ibid. XXII, 9).

a (1) This is the 'axe': according to this R. Ḥiyya b. Abin is obviously wrong. (2) In objection to 'those who swung the axe'. (3) That as much as an olive is the minimum to involve payment or punishment in the case of *terumah*. (4) Hence the same applies to trespass too, and thus R. Ḥiyya b. Abin's answer is correct. (5) The Tanna of the cited teaching. (6) This refers to the Sabbath, when one must not cut or pluck produce growing in the soil ('attached'). In the present case he is not liable to a sin-offering, which is only due when a man sins in ignorance, i.e., where he intended to do what he did, but did not know that it was forbidden. (7) Lit., 'cut'. (8) Here he was not engaged in plucking or cutting at all. (9) There too he was not engaged in anointing at all. (10) Deut. XVIII, 4.

b (1) I.e., the priest must be able to consume it himself and not have to burn it for its heat or light. Hence if it is separated in a state in which it cannot be eaten, as here, it does not become *terumah*. (2) Before it became unclean it was fit to be separated as *terumah*. (3) In the case of the leaven *terumah*. (4) It was not fit to be *terumah* before Passover as it goes on explaining. (5) Whilst before it is harvested it cannot be declared *terumah*. (6) I.e., before Passover, so that it was fit to be *terumah* before the Festival. (7) If separated as *terumah* during Passover. (8) Dan. IV, 14; i.e., this is the view of great teachers. (9) מורין implies to give a practical, as opposed to a mere theoretical, ruling.

[32b] Abaye said: R. Eliezer b. Jacob, R. Akiba and R. Joḥanan
a b. Nuri all[1] hold [that] leaven during Passover is forbidden for use, and they differ in this, viz., R. Akiba[2] holds: He must pay according to value;[3] while R. Joḥanan b. Nuri holds: He must pay according to quantity. That is obvious?—You might say, R. Joḥanan b. Nuri also holds as R. Akiba [that] he must pay according to value, but the reason that he declares him liable there is this, [viz.,] because he agrees with R. Jose the Galilean who maintained, Leaven is permitted for use on Passover: [therefore] he informs us [that it is not so]. Yet perhaps that indeed is so?—If so, let R. Joḥanan b. Nuri answer R. Akiba just as R. Eleazar Ḥisma answered R. Eliezer b. Jacob.

Our Rabbis taught: He who eats as much as an olive of *terumah*[4] must pay the principal plus a fifth. Abba Saul said: [He is not liable] unless it has the worth of a *peruṭah*.[5] What is the first Tanna's reason?—Scripture saith, *And if a man* eat *of the holy thing unwittingly*[6] and eating [requires] as much as an olive.[7] And Abba Saul: what is [his] reason?—Scripture saith, *and he shall* give [*unto the priest the holy thing*],[6] and giving is not less than the worth of a *peruṭah*. And the other too, surely '*eat*' is written? That comes [to teach],
b excluding him who destroys [*terumah*].[1] And the first Tanna, surely it is written, '*and he shall give*'?—He requires that [to intimate that he must return] something which is fit to be holy.[2]

Our Rabbis taught: He who eats less than an olive of *terumah* must pay the principal, but he does not pay the [additional] fifth. How is it meant? If it is not worth a *peruṭah*, let him not pay the principal either; while if it is worth a *peruṭah*, let him pay a fifth too?—After all it means that it is worth a *peruṭah*, yet even so, since it was less than an olive he pays the principal but does not pay the fifth. The Rabbis stated this before R. Papa: This is not according to Abba Saul, for if according to Abba Saul, surely he says, since it is worth a *peruṭah*, even if it is less than an olive [the law applies]!—Said R. Papa to them: You may even say [that it agrees with] Abba Saul. Abba Saul requires both.[3] Yet does Abba Saul require both? Surely we learned, Abba Saul said: For that which possesses the worth of a *peruṭah* he [the eater] is liable for payment; [for] that which does not possess the worth of a *peruṭah* he is not liable for payment. Said they [the Sages] to him. The worth of a *peruṭah* was stated in connection with a trespass-offering only;[4] but for *terumah* he is not liable unless it contains as much as an olive. Now if this is correct,[5] they should have stated, 'once it contains as much as an olive'?[6] This is a refutation.

Now, R. Papa too retracted,[7] for it was taught: [*If any one commit a trespass,*] *and sin unwittingly:*[8] this excludes deliberate [trespass]. But does this not follow *a fortiori:* if other precepts, for
c [the transgression of] which one is liable to *kareth*,[1] yet [Scripture] exempts the deliberate offender in their case;[2] [with regard to] trespass, which does not involve *kareth*, does it not follow that the deliberate transgressor is exempt? No: if you say [thus] in the case of other precepts, that is because he is not liable to death on their account; will you say [the same] of trespass, for which death is incurred?[3] Therefore '*unwittingly*' is stated, excluding deliberate [transgression]. Now R. Naḥman b. Isaac said to R. Ḥiyya b. Abin: This Tanna, at first, regards *kareth* as severer, while subsequently he regards death [at the hands of Heaven] as more severe?[4] And he answered him, This is what he means: No; if you say [thus] in the case of other precepts, that is because he is not liable to death on their account for less then an olive; will you say [the same] of trespass, where death is incurred for less than an olive. Whereon he said to him, Thy mind be at rest, because thou hast set my mind at rest. Said he to him, What satisfaction [is there in this answer], seeing that Rabbah and R. Shesheth have swung an axe at it:[5] Whom do you know to

a (1) Rashi omits 'R. Eliezer b. Jacob' and 'all'. (2) And likewise R. Eliezer b. Jacob. (3) And since it has no value, the eater is exempt. (4) This refers to the rest of the year. (5) The smallest coin. (6) Lev. XXII, 14. (7) This is the smallest quantity to which the term 'eating' can be applied.

b (1) Without eating it; this law of the extra fifth does not apply in his case. (2) I.e., the return must be made in kind, which can itself be holy (viz., *terumah*), not in money, which cannot be *terumah*. (3) It must be worth not less than a *peruṭah* and be not less than an olive in size. (4) If he unwittingly converts *hekdesh* (q.v. Glos.) to secular use he is liable to a trespass-offering, providing the object so misappropriated is worth at least a *peruṭah*. (5) That Abba Saul requires both. (6) Since he too agrees to this, their view must be: once it contains the size of an olive he is liable even if it is not worth a *peruṭah*. (7) From his view that Abba Saul requires both. (8) Lev. V, 15: the passage deals with the trespass-offering for the misappropriation of *hekdesh* and the restitution of the principal plus a fifth.

c (1) V. Glos. E.g., if one consumes blood or forbidden fat (*ḥeleb*). (2) From a sacrifice, which is due only for an unwitting offence. (3) Surely not. By 'death', death at the hands of Heaven is meant. (4) This follows from a comparison of the two halves of the argument. (5) I.e., proved it to be incorrect.

צה א מיי' שם הל' כו: צו ב ג מיי' שם הל' ג:

תורה אור

אמר אביי רבי אליעזר בן יעקב ורבי עקיבא ור' יוחנן בן נורי כולהו סבירא להו חמץ בפסח אסור בהנאה ובהא פליגי דרבי עקיבא סבר *לפי דמים משלם ורבי יוחנן בן נורי סבר לפי מדה משלם פשיטא מהו דתימא רבי יוחנן בן נורי נמי כרבי עקיבא סבירא ליה דאמר לפי דמים משלם והתם היינו טעמא דקא מחייב משום דסבר לה כר' יוסי הגלילי דאמר *חמץ בפסח מותר בהנאה קמ"ל ואימא הכי נמי אם כן נהדר ליה רבי יוחנן בן נורי לר' עקיבא כי היכי דמהדר ליה רבי אלעזר חסמא לר' אליעזר בן יעקב: ת"ר [ג]האוכל כזית תרומה משלם קרן וחומש אבא שאול אומר עד שיהא בו שוה פרוטה מ"ט דתנא קמא אמר קרא °ואיש כי יאכל קדש בשגגה ואכילה בכזית ואבא שאול מאי טעמא אמר קרא ונתן ואין נתינה פחות משוה פרוטה ואידך נמי הא כתיב יאכל ההוא *פרט למזיק הוא דאתא ותנא קמא הכתיב ונתן ההוא מיבעי ליה לדבר הראוי להיות קדש (פרט לאוכל תרומת חמץ בפסח): ת"ר [ד]האוכל תרומה פחות מכזית משלם את הקרן ואינו משלם את החומש היכי דמי אי דלית ביה שוה פרוטה קרן נמי לא לישלם ואי דאית בה שוה פרוטה חומש נמי לישלם לעולם דאית בה שוה פרוטה ואפילו הכי כיון דלית ביה כזית משלם את הקרן ואינו משלם את החומש אמרוה רבנן קמיה דרב פפא הא דלא כאבא שאול דאי כאבא שאול כיון שיש בה שוה פרוטה אע"ג דלית ביה כזית אמר להו רב פפא אפילו תימא אבא שאול תרתי בעי ומי בעי אבא שאול תרתי והא *תנן אבא שאול אומר את שיש בו שוה פרוטה חייב בתשלומין את שאין בו שוה פרוטה אינו חייב בתשלומין אמרו לו לא אמרו שוה פרוטה אלא לענין מעילה בלבד אבל לתרומה אינו חייב עד שיהא בו כזית ואם איתא כיון שיש בו כזית מיבעי ליה תיובתא ואף רב פפא הדר ביה דתניא °וחטאה בשגגה פרט למזיד והלא דין הוא ומה שאר מצות שחייב בהן כרת פוטר בהן את המזיד מעילה שאין בה כרת אינו דין שפטר את המזיד לא אם אמרת בשאר מצות שכן לא חייב בהן מיתה תאמר במעילה שחייב בה מיתה ת"ל בשגגה פרט למזיד ואמר ליה רב נחמן בר יצחק לרב חייא בר אבין האי תנא מעיקרא אלימא ליה כרת ולבסוף אלימא ליה מיתה ואמר ליה הכי קאמר לא אם אמרת בשאר מצות שכן לא חייב בהן מיתה בפחות מכזית תאמר במעילה שחייב בה מיתה בפחות מכזית ואמר ליה *תנוח דעתך שהנחת את דעתי וא"ל מאי ניחותא דרבה ורב ששת שדו ביה נרגא מאן שמעת ליה דאמר

הזיד

ויקרא כב

ואין נתינה פחות משוה פרוטה. ורבנן נמי לא פליגי אלא משום דכתיב אכילה ולא"ה והא קיימא לן (חולין דף קלג:) דחטה אחת פוטרת את הכרי אע"ג דכתיב בה נתינה דכתיב תתן לו ובהזהב (ב"מ מז.) אמר קונין בכלי אע"פ שאין בו שוה פרוטה אע"ג דכתיב ונתן לרעהו וגבי גט נמי אמרינן (גיטין דף כ.) כתבו על איסורי הנאה כשר אע"ג דכתיב ונתן בידה ויש לומר דהכא ודאי בעינן שוה פרוטה דנתינה קיימא אתשלומין והוי כמו השבת גזילה שאין בפחות משוה פרוטה ולהכי משום דכתיב ונתן משמע שפיר נתינה חשובה אבל שאר מילי אע"ג דכתיב בהן נתינה לא בעינן שוה פרוטה מיהו קשה לר"י דרבי יהודה דריש בכריתות (דף ו:) ואשר יתן ממנו על זר בכזית ויליף נתינה נתינה מתרומה ואדיליף מתרומה בכזית ליליף מכל נתינה לחומרא דסגי בכל שהוא כגון מתן דמים ומתן בהונות שאין בהן שיעור והוי נמי דומי' דסיכה דסגי בכל שהוא ולמ"ד התם נתינה בכל שהוא א"ש*: **ההוא** מיבעיא ליה לדבר הראוי להיות קודש. ולא"ג דמאת הקודש דרשינן דבר הראוי להיות קודש אצטריך נמי ונתן דאי כתב את הקודש לחודיה ה"א דלא אתא למעוטי אלא מעות אבל כל פירות ישלם להכי כתב ונתן דמשמע שהפירות של נתינה בעינן ראוי להיות קודש: **מעילה** שלא חייב בה כרת אינו דין שפטר בה את המזיד. תימה נימא היא הנותנת דשאר מצות שכן חמורות שהן בכרת אין לזדונה כפרה אבל מעילה שהיא קלה שאין בה כרת יש לזדונה כפרה וכה"ג איכא בריש מכות (דף ב:) דקאמר ק"ו ומה הוא שעושה מעשה במזיד אינו גולה עדים שלא עשו מעשה אינו דין שלא יגלו היא הנותנת הוא שעשה מעשה במזיד לא יגלה כי היכי דלא תיהוי ליה כפרה הן שלא עשו מעשה יגלו דתיהוי להו כפרה ועוד ארבעה המביאין על הזדון כשגגה יוכיחו דאין בהן כרת וחייבין על זדונם הבא על שפחה חרופה ונזיר טמא ושבועת העדות והפקדון *(תוספתא דכריתות פ"א) ואומר ר"י דשפיר פריך בלאו הכי לא אם אמרת וכו' ומיהו קשה לר"י אמאי איצטריך בכריתות (דף ט.) בשפחה חרופה אשר חטא לרבות זדון וגבי נזיר נמי דריש מפתאום לרבות זדון דאי משום דלא נילף ממעילה דלמעוט מזדון אדרבה משבועת העדות והפקדון אית לן למילף דלחומרא מקשינן: ומינה

[ועי' תוספות גיטין כ. ד"ה דילמא כו' שייכו קושיא זו ועי' תוס' מנחות ס. ד"ה מי בעינן ותוס' ב"מ מז. ד"ה קונים בכלים]

רש"ל מ"ז

[וכ"ה להדיא במשנה דכריתות ח: ד' מביאין על הזדון כשגגה ומפרש שם (ט.) במשנה עצמה אלו מביאין כו']

אמר אביי ר' עקיבא ור' יוחנן בן נורי. אע"ג דלאו חייב בתשלומין סבירא להו דאין לו דמים ובהא פליגי רבי עקיבא ור' יוחנן בן נורי: א"כ. דסבירא ליה מותר ניהדר ליה ר' יוחנן לרבי עקיבא אף לזה יש לו היתר הסקה: כזית תרומה. בשאר ימות השנה קאי: פרט למזיק. תרומה של כהן אפי' בשוגג שאינו משלם חומש אלא קרן כשאר מזיק חולין: ההוא מיבעי ליה לדבר הראוי להיות קדש. וכוליה קרא משום סיפא אצטריך: דאית בה שוה פרוטה. וליכא כזית כגון שנת בצורת: כיון דלית בה כזית כו'. דאכילה כתיבא בה: אמרוה רבנן קמיה דרב פפא. דקדקו מלבן ואמרו לפניו דהא מתני' דקפדה אכזית דלא כאבא שאול דהא שמעינן לי' דקפיד אפרוט' ולא אכזית: תרתי בעי. שיהא בו כזית דהא אכילה כתיבא ביה ושיהא בדמיו פרוטה דהא כתיב ונתן: חייב בתשלומין. אתרומה שוגג קאי וקרן וחומש קאמר: לענין מעילה. בנהנה מהקדש גבוה דהתם לא כתיב אכילה אבל לתרומה אפי' יש בו שוה פרוטה אין חייב חומש עד שיהא בו כזית. מכלל לאבא שאול אע"ג דליכא כזית דאם איתא דתרתי בעי וכיון בו כזית קאי אבא שאול וקאמר דאע"ג דאית ביה כזית בעינן פרוט' הכי הוה להו למימר כיון דיש בו כזית חייב: וחטאה בשגג'. במעיל' דהקדש כתיב: והלא דין הוא. דמזיד פטור מקרבן ולמה לי קרא: שחייב בהן הכתוב כרת. כגון חלב ודם: פטר בהן את המזיד. מקרבן דגבי חטאת שגגה כתיב: לא חייב בהן מיתה. בידי שמים אבל מעילה חייב על זדונה מיתה דלכדמן ודילמא מיתה חמירא מכרת: ואמר ליה רב נחמן גרסינן האי תנא אלימא ליה כרת ממיתה מעיקרא דקתני מעילה שלא חייב בה כרת אלא מיתה כו' אלמא כרת חמירא ולבסוף אלימא לי' מיתה דקתני תאמר במעילה כו': וא"ל. רבי חייה לעולם כרת אלימא ליה והך סיפא דמתני' הכי קאמר לא אם אמרת בשאר מצות שהרי לא חייב בהן אפילו מיתה בפחות מכזית תאמר במעילה שחייב בה מיתה אפי' בפחות מכזית בכולהו גרסינן ואמר ליה ומתקיף ליה רב פפא כו' עד הדר ביה: ומאי ניחותא. איכא דהא רבה ורב ששת שדו ביה נרגא בהאי פירושא דתרוייהו ומקשו הכי. היכי אמרי' דתנא לפחות מכזית מחייב מיתה: מאן שמעת ליה דאמר מעילה זדונה מיתה רבי. ועל כרחך מתרומה גמר לה כדמפרשינן. וכיון דמתרומה גמר לא משכח בה מיתה אלא בכזית כתרומה דתרומה גבי מיתה כתיב בה אכילה דמיתה דתרומה נפקא לן מדסמיך וכל זר לא יאכל קדש גבי ומתו בו כי יחללוהו כדאמרינן בסנהדרין (דף פג:)

הזיד

[לעיל כג. כה:]

[יומא פ: פא. ב"מ נה: מעילה יט.]

[תוספתא דתרומות פ"ז ע"ש וגי' והתניא]

[שבת קנב: יומא סו: סנהדרין ל: מנחות צה. ק.]

רבינו חננאל

עקיבא ור' יוחנן בן נורי ור' אליעזר בן יעקב יש לומר כי כולהו סבירא להו חמץ בפסח אסור בהנאה ובהא פליגי מאן דפטר סבר לפי דמים משלם וחמץ בפסח אין לו דמים לפיכך פטור ומאן דמחייב סבר לפי מדה משלם ואע"פ שאין לו דמים כיון שאינו משלם אלא לפי מדה חייב לשלם ולית לן למימר סמאי (דר' יוחנן בן נורי) [דסבר לפי מדה משלם דלמא סבירא ליה כר' יה(ו)גלילי] ונמצא דחמץ בפסח מותר בהנאה סבירא ליה דאי הכי הוי ליה לרבי יוחנן בן נורי לאהדורי לר' עקיבא אף חמץ בפסח יש לו היתר שאם רצה מסיקה או מריצה לפני כלבו כי היכי דמהדר ר' אלעזר חסמא ש"מ: ת"ר אכל כזית תרומה משלם קרן וחומש מ"ט דכתיב ואיש' כי יאכל קדש בשגגה חמישיתו עליו ואכילה בכזית אכילה היא אבא שאול אומר אינו משלם עד שיהיה בה שוה פרוטה מאי טעמא דכתיב ונתן לכהן את הקדש ואין נתינה בפחות משוה פרוטה. תנא אכל פחות מכזית תרומה משלם קרן ואינו משלם חומש ואוקימנה דלא כאבא שאול דאי אבא שאול כיון דאית ביה שוה פרוטה אע"ג דלא הוי כזית ואמר רב פפא אפי' תימא אבא שאול [אבא שאול] תרתי בעי שיהיה בו כזית פרוטה. איני דאבא שאול לא בעי אלא אם יש כזית והתניא אבא שאול אומר כל שיש בו שוה פרוטה חייב בתשלומין וכל שאין בו שוה פרוטה אינו חייב אמרו לו לא אמרו שוה פרוטה אלא לענין מעילה אבל לענין תרומה עד שיהא בה כזית מכלל דהשתא*) לאבא שאול לא מחייב ואם איתא דאבא שאול לא הוה מחייב עד דאית ביה כזית חייב הוה להו למימר ועלתה בתיובתא לרב פפא: ואף רב פפא הדר ביה דתניא נפש כי תמעול מעל וחטאה בשגגה מקדשי ה' פרט למזיד שאינו מביא קרבן והלא דין הוא ומה שאר מצות שחייב בהן כרת פטר המזיד מקרבן מעילה שלא חייב בה כרת אינו דין שיפטר המזיד לא אם אמרת בשאר מצות שכן לא חייב בהן מיתה כו' וקשיא לן האי תנא מעיקרא אלימא ליה כרת ויליף מעילה שהוא במיתה מחייבי כריתות בקל וחומר והדר פריך תאמר במעילה שחייב בה מיתה שהמיתה חמורה מן הכרת ושנינן לעולם כרת חמורה כי פריך בפחות מכזית פריך דליתא בחייבי כריתות ואיתא במעילה שהיא במיתה ויליף חטא חטא מתרומה כתיב במעילה ונפש כי תמעול מעל וחטאה בשגגה מקדשי

*) אולי צ"ל מכלל דבש"ס לבד לאבא שאול ג"כ חייב דאם איתא וכו'.

עין משפט נר מצוה

צב א מיי' פ"ב מהל' גזילה הל' ב סמג עשין עג טוש"ע ח"מ סי' שסב סעיף ב:
צג ב מיי' פ"י מהל' תרומות הלכה ו:
צד ג שם הלכה ס:

מסורת הש"ס

ב"ק צג: וש"נ

עירובין כט:

[לעיל כג. כח:]

לעיל כט. [וש"נ]

[תוספתא פ"א]

[לקמן לג:]

ואחד הסך אחד תרומה טמאה ואחד תרומה טהורה משלם חומש וחומשא דחומשא איבעיא להו כשהוא משלם לפי מדה משלם או לפי דמים משלם כל היכא דמעיקרא שויא ארבעה זוזי ולבסוף שויא זוזא לא תיבעי לך דודאי כדמעיקרא משלם לפי דמים *דלא גרע מגזלן דתנן **כל הגזלנין משלמין כשעת הגזלה כי תיבעי לך דמעיקרא שויא זוזא ולבסוף שויא ארבעה מאי לפי מדה משלם דא"ל גריוא אכל גריוא משלם או דילמא לפי דמים משלם בזוזא אכל בזוזא משלם אמר רב יוסף תא שמע *אכל גרוגרות ושילם לו תמרים תבא עליו ברכה אי אמרת בשלמא לפי מדה משלם אמטו להכי תבא עליו ברכה דאכיל גריוא דגרוגרות דשויא זוזא וקא יהיב גריוא דתמרים דשויא ארבעה אלא אי אמרת לפי דמים משלם אמאי תבא עליו ברכה בזוזא אכל בזוזא קא משלם אמר אביי לעולם לפי דמים משלם ואמאי תבא עליו ברכה דאכל מידי דלא קפיץ עליה זבינא וקא משלם מידי דקפיץ עליה זבינא: תנן האוכל תרומת חמץ בפסח בשוגג משלם קרן וחומש אי אמרת בשלמא לפי מדה משלם שפיר אלא אי אמרת לפי דמים משלם חמץ בפסח בר דמים הוא אין הא מני ר' יוסי הגלילי היא דאמר *חמץ בפסח מותר בהנאה אי הכי אימא סיפא במזיד פטור מן התשלומין ומדמי עצים אי ר' יוסי הגלילי אמאי פטור מן התשלומין ומדמי עצים סבר לה כר' נחוניא בן הקנה דתניא *רבי נחוניא בן הקנה היה עושה את יום הכפורים כשבת לתשלומין וכו' כתנאי **האוכל תרומת חמץ בפסח פטור מן התשלומין ומדמי עצים דברי רבי עקיבא ר' יוחנן בן נורי מחייב אמר לו רבי עקיבא לר' יוחנן בן נורי וכי מה הנאה יש לו בה אמר לו ר' יוחנן בן נורי לר"ע ומה הנאה יש לאוכל תרומה טמאה בשאר כל ימות השנה שמשלם אמר לו לא אם אמרת בתרומה טמאה בשאר ימות השנה שאע"פ שאין לו בה היתר אכילה יש לו בה היתר הסקה תאמר בזה שאין לו בה לא היתר אכילה ולא היתר הסקה *הא למה זה דומה לתרומת תותים וענבים שנטמאה שאין לו בה לא היתר אכילה ולא היתר הסקה בד"א במפריש תרומה והחמיצה אבל מפריש תרומת חמץ דברי הכל אינה קדושה תניא אידך °ונתן לכהן את הקדש (ויקרא כב) דבר הראוי להיות קדש פרט לאוכל תרומת חמץ בפסח שפטור מן התשלומים ומדמי עצים דברי ר' אליעזר בן יעקב ור"א חסמא מחייב אמר לו ר"א בן יעקב לר"א חסמא וכי מה הנאה יש לו בה אמר לו ר"א חסמא לר"א בן יעקב וכי מה הנאה יש לו לאוכל תרומה טמאה בשאר ימות השנה שמשלם אמר לו לא אם אמרת בתרומה טמאה בשאר ימות השנה שאע"פ שאין לו בה היתר אכילה יש לו בה היתר הסקה תאמר בזו שאין לו בה לא היתר אכילה ולא היתר הסקה אמר לו אף בזו יש לו בה היתר הסקה שאם רצה הכהן *מריצה לפני כלבו או מסיקה תחת תבשילו

אמר

רש"י

גמ' ואחד הסך. דאמרי' בפ' בתרא דיומא (דף עו:) סיכה כשתיה ושתיה בכלל אכילה והכא כתיב כי יאכל קדש בשגגה דאילו גזלה והשליכה לנהר לפי' בשוגג דלא ידע שהיה תרומה אינו משלם חומש אלא קרן כשאר מזיק חולין דעלמא דאמר מר (לקמן ע"ב) כי יאכל פרט למזיק: וחומש חומשא. שהתשלומין נעשין תרומה ואם חזר ואכל בשוגג אותו חומש ראשון חוזר ומשלם חומשו עליו: איבעיא להו. כיון דגבי תרומה בשוגג קפיד רחמנא אתשלומי פירות ולא מעות דכתיב ונתן לכהן את הקודש לפי מדה משלם או לפי דמים משלם בגזלן דחולין שוגג או מזיד וכן גזלן דתרומה מזיד לא איבעיא לן כיון דלא קפיד רחמנא אתשלומין דידהו דאמר יסיב לרבות אפילו שוה כסף ואפילו סובין ודאי לפי דמים משלם אבל בתרומה שוגג איבעיא לן הואיל וקפידה התורה לשלם פירות: כל היכא דמעיקרא. כשאכלה הויא שויא הך גריוא ד' זוזי והשתא כשמשלם שויא זוזא ותו לא לא מיבעיא לן נהי נמי דאיכפר ליה אכילת תרומה בתשלומי מדה מיהו ממונא דכהן [אוכל] (ממונא) הוא ולא גרע משאר ממונא דחולין שהדיינין גובין ממנו כשעת גזילה דכתיב (ויקרא ה) אשר גזל כמה שגזל: גריוא משלם. ולעו"ג דשויא השתא טפי או דילמא לפי דמים משלם דאע"ג דהקפידה התורה לשלם פירות לא הקפידה אלא לפי הדמים כשאר תשלומין ומה שישלם ישלם בפירות: גרוגרות. תאנים יבשים: תמרים. חשובין מתאנים ודמיהן מרובים: אכל גרוגרות. דתרומה שוגג: זבינא. לוקחים: אימא סיפא במזיד פטור מן התשלומין ואי ר' יוסי הגלילי אמאי פטור. אי אמרת בשלמא דכבן וטעמא דרישא משום דלפי מדה משלם סיפא דאינו אלא כשאר גזלן דמשלם מעות ולפי דמים פטור מן התשלומין דחמץ בפסח לאו בר דמים הוא אלא אי אמרת ר' יוסי הגלילי ובר דמים הוא אמאי פטור: כרבי נחוניא בן הקנה. דאמר המתחייב כרת פטור מן התשלומין ויליף טעמא מאסון אסון והוא הדין למתחייב מיתת שמים כגון אוכל תרומה מזיד וסיפא דמתני' בהזיד בתרומה ולא בחמץ ופטור משום מיתה ובדין הוא דליתני במזיד דתרומה דעלמא דלאו חמץ בפסח דפטור מתשלומין משום מיתה ומשום רישא נקט מילתא בחמץ בפסח דאשמועינן דהיכא דשגג בשתיהם חייב דחמץ בר דמים הוא ושוגג דרישא דשגג בשתיהן דאי שגג בחמץ והזיד בתרומה מאי חומש איכא ואי שגג בתרומה והזיד בחמץ אמאי משלם הא איחייב ליה כרת וסיפא אשמועינן דהזיד בתרומה אפילו שגג בחמץ פטור דמיתה בידי שמים כי כרת דאי הזיד בחמץ והא דפטר ליה משום כרת הוא דפטר ליה לשמעי' כולה מתני' בחמץ חולין של חבירו וניתני שוגג חייב ומזיד פטור משום כרת: כתנאי. לפי מדה או לפי דמים: פטור מתשלומין. בין שוגג בין מזיד: מה הנאה יש לו. לכהן בה ומה הפסידו זה הרי אסור בהנאה: ומה הנאה יש לו. לכהן בתרומה טמאה שאסורה באכילה לכהן ואי אכלה זר שוגג משלם קרן וחומש דליכא למאן דפליג אסתמא דתנן לעיל אחד תרומה טהורה ואחד תרומה טמאה וטעמא משום דלפי מדה משלם ואע"ג דלאו בר דמים הוא: היתר הסקה. דכתיב (במדבר יח) ואני הנה נתתי לך את משמרת תרומותי שתי תרומות במשמע אחת טהורה ואחת טמאה וכתיב לך תהיה להסקה: תרומת תותים וענבים. משקה הן ואינן ראויין להסקה ולזלף נמי לא כדאמרינן בפ"ק (דף כ:) משום תקלה ובההוא נמי סבירא ליה דזר האוכלה פטור מלשלם ור' יוחנן בן נורי מחייב דקסבר לפי מדה משלם: בד"א. דמשכחת תרומת חמץ בפסח דקדשה בהפריש תרומה והחמיצה והוא הדין להפרישה חמץ קודם הפסח: אבל מפריש תרומת חמץ. בפסח כגון חטים שהחמיצו דברי הכל אפי' לרבי יוסי הגלילי דשרי חמץ בפסח בהנאה וחזיא ליה להסקה אינה קדושה ולקמן מפרש טעמא בשילהי שמעתין: את הקדש. משמע את הקדש שאכל אלמא ראוי להיות קדש היה שכשישלם דוגמתו יהא שם קדש חל עליו: פרט לאוכל תרומת חמץ בפסח. שכשמשלם דוגמתו אין שם קדש חל עליו: וכי מה הנאה יש לו. לכהן בה ומה הפסידו נהי נמי דלית לך הא דרשה מיהו מה ישלם הואיל ואין לו דמים:

אמר

תוספות

דבר הראוי להיות קודש פרט לאוכל תרומת חמץ. פי' הפסוק משמע שיתן לו דבר הראוי להיות קודש כמו שאכל וא"כ מה שאכל בעינן דבר הראוי להיות קודש וחמץ בפסח אינו ראוי להיות קודש כדתניא לעיל אבל מפריש (א) חמץ ד"ה אין קדוש *לע"ג דבכל ענין פטור הכא מתשלומין אפי' שהיה לה שעת הכושר ולקמן מוקמינן הא דלד"ה אין קדוש היינו שלא היה לה שעת הכושר אור"ת היינו לרבי יוסי הגלילי אבל לרבא"י הואיל וסבירא ליה דחמץ בפסח אסור בהנאה אפילו היה לה שעת הכושר אין ראוי להיות קודש דאין כאן נתינה והיינו דקאמר ליה רבא"י מה הנאה יש לו בה כלומר הואיל ואין לו הנאה בה אית ליה למעוטי מקרא כדפרישית: ואין

ענין פטור הכא מתשלומין. ק"ל למאי נקטו קושייתם בדרך דמסתמא קאמ' בכל ענין הלא א"א כלל בגוונא אחרינא דהא אכל תרומת חמץ א"כ כמאכל היה לה שעת הכושר דהל"כ לא משכחת שהיא תרומה וצ"ע:

רבינו חננאל

משלם קרן וחומש אחד האוכל ואחד השותה ואחד הסך אחד אוכל תרומה טהורה ואחד אוכל תרומה טמאה משלם חומשא וחומש חומשא והוא חומשא מלבר כדקתני בהדיא שיהא הוא וחומשו חמשה שנאמר ויסף חמישיתו עליו דברי ר' יאשיה: איבעיא להו לפי מדה משלם קב אכל קב וחומשו משלם או לפי דמים משלם. כלומר כפי שהיה שוה בשעה שאכלו וכל היכא דהויא שויא ארבעה זוזי בעידן אכילתה והשתא שויא זוזא לא מיבעיא לן דודאי ארבעה זוזי משלם דלא גרע מגזלה דתנן כל הגזלנין משלמין כשעת הגזלה כי תיבעי לן דמעיקרא הוית שויא זוזא והשתא שויא ארבעה מאי ואתא רב יוסף למפשט לפי מדה משלםמיהא אכל גרוגרו' ושלם לו תמרים תבוא עליו ברכה כלומר שאכל קב גרוגרות שדמיהם זוזא ושלם קב תמרים ששוים ארבעה זוזי ודחה אביי לעולם לפי דמים משלם ואמאי תבוא עליו ברכה ואי אית למימר וכי כל המשלם דבר שחייב בו מחזיקין לו טובה ומברכים אותו יש לך לומר לאו משום דקא משלם[יותר]אלא משום דמשלם דבר מעולה דקפיץ עליה זיבונא ואקשי' על אביי ממתני' דקתני האוכל תרומת חמץבפסח בשוגג משלם כו' ואי אמרת לפי דמים משלם חמץ בפסח בר דמים הוא ומשני' מתני' ר' יוסי הגלילי היא דאמר חמץ בפסח מותר בהנאה סיפא דקתני במזיד פטור סבר לה ר' יוסי הגלילי כר' נחוניא בן הקנה דפוטר חייבי כריתות מן התשלומים: כתנאי יש תנא שאומ' לפי דמים משלם ויש תנא שאומר לפי מדה משלם דתניא האוכל תרומת חמץ בפסח בשוגג משלם קרן וחומש במזיד פטור מן התשלומים ומדמי העצים דברי ר' עקיבא ר' יוחנן בן נורי מחייב אמר לו ר' עקיבא לר' יוחנן בן נורי מה הנאה יש לו שמשלם כו' עוד השיבו ר' עקיבא לא אם אמרת בתרומה טמא' בשאר ימות השנה שאע"פ שאין לו בה [היתר אכילה יש לו בה]היתר הסקה תאמר בחמץ בפסח שאין לו בה היתר הנאה כלל לא באכילה ולא בהסקה חמץ בפסח למה הוא דומה לתרומת תותים וענבים שנטמאת שאין לה היתר אכילה כלל ולא היתר הסקה דלאו בני הסקה נינהו בד"א במפריש תרומה והחמיצה אבל המפריש תרומת חמץ דברי הכל אינה קדושה: תניא אידך ונתן לכהן את הקדש דבר הראוי להיות קדש פרט לאוכל חמץ תרומה בפסח שפטור דברי ר' אליעזר בן יעקב ר' אלעזר חסמא מחייב אמר לו ר' אליעזר בן יעקב וכי מה הנאה יש לו וכו' עד אמר לו ר' אלעזר חסמא אף חמץ בפסח יש לו היתר שאם רצה מסיקה תחת תבשילו או מריצה לפני כלבו ודאי ר' אלעזר חסמא אית ליה כי חמץ בפסח מותר בהנאה אבל ר' עקיבא

הגהות הב"ח

(א) תוס' ד"ה דבר וכו' לעיל אבל מפריש תרומת חמץ וכו' ולקמן מוקמי'. נ"ב בדף לג סוף ע"א:

[עי' תוס' ביצה כז: ד"ה ועל]

גליון הש"ס

גמ' דלא גרע מגזלן. ק"ל הא מ"מ נ"מ דאם אינו חייב רק מדין גזלן יכול לשלם חד גריוא בפירות דאתי לידי כפרה והשאר משלם במעות והכהן יכול למחול וגם החומש הוא רק על חד גריוא. אבל אם לפי דמים צריך לשלם ד' גריוא וחומש' מפירי והכהן אינו יכול למחול: תוד"ה דבר כו' לע"ג דבכל

drinks, [32a] or anoints [therewith]; whether it was defiled or undefiled *terumah*, he must pay a fifth and a fifth of the fifth.[6] The scholars asked: When he repays, does he repay according to quantity[7] or according to value?[8] Where it was originally worth four *zuz* while subsequently it was worth a *zuz*,[9] there is no question, for he must certainly repay on the original [price],
a according to its value,[1] because it is no worse than a robber, for we learned: All robbers repay as at the time of the robbery.[2] The question arises where it was originally worth a *zuz* while subsequently it was worth four. What then? Must he repay according to quantity, for he [the priest] can say, He ate a *griwa*,[3] he must repay a *griwa;* or perhaps he repays according to the value: he ate [the worth of] a *zuz*, he repays [the worth of] a *zuz?*—Said R. Joseph, Come and hear: If he ate figs [of *terumah*] and repaid him dates, blessings be upon him! It is well if you say that he must repay according to quantity: therefore 'blessings be upon him,' because he ate a *griwa* of dried figs, which is worth a *zuz*, and he returns [him] a *griwa* of dates, which is worth four. But if you say that he pays according to its value, why should 'blessings be upon him': he ate for a *zuz* and he returns [as much as] for a *zuz?*—Said Abaye, Indeed he pays according to value, yet why should 'blessings come upon him'? Because he ate something for which buyers are not eager,[4] and he pays [with] something for which buyers are eager.[5]

We learned: HE WHO EATS TERUMAH OF LEAVEN ON PASSOVER UNWITTINGLY, MUST PAY [TO THE PRIEST] THE PRINCIPAL PLUS A FIFTH. It is well if you say that he must pay according to quantity: then it is right. But if you say that he must pay according to the value, has then leaven on Passover any value?—Yes: the author of this is R. Jose the Galilean, who maintained: Leaven on Passover is permitted for use. If so, consider the second clause: IF DELIBERATELY, HE IS FREE FROM PAYMENT AND FROM [LIABILITY FOR] ITS VALUE AS FUEL. But if [the author is] R. Jose the Galilean, why is he free from payment and from [liability for] its value as fuel?[6]—He holds as R. Neḥunia b. ha-Ḳanah. For it was taught: R. Neḥunia b. ha-Ḳanah used to treat the Day of Atonement as the Sabbath in regard to payment, etc.[7]

b This[1] is dependent on Tannaim: He who eats *terumah* of leaven on Passover is free from payment and from [liability for] the value of the fuel: this is R. Akiba's ruling. R. Joḥanan b. Nuri declares him liable. Said R. Akiba to R. Joḥanan b. Nuri: What benefit then has he [the priest] therein?[2] R. Joḥanan b. Nuri retorted to R. Akiba: And what benefit has [the priest therein] that he who eats unclean *terumah* during the rest of the year must pay?[3] Not so, replied he: if you speak of unclean *terumah* during the rest of the year, [that is] because though he [the priest] does not enjoy the right to eat it, yet he enjoys the right to use it as fuel.[4] Will you say the same of this, in which he does not enjoy the right of eating or the right to use it as fuel? Hence, to what is this like: to *terumah* of mulberries and grapes which was defiled, in which he does not enjoy the right of eating or the right to use it as fuel.[5] When is this said?[6] When he separates *terumah* and it became leaven. But if he separates *terumah* of leaven [on Passover], all agree [that] it is not holy.[7]

Another [Baraitha] taught: [*And if a man eat of the holy things unwittingly, then he shall put the fifth part thereof unto it,*] *and shall give unto the priest the holy thing:*[8] [that implies,] something which is fit to be holy, thus excluding him who eats *terumah* of leaven on Passover, [teaching] that he is free from payment and from [liability for] its value as fuel: this is the view of R. Eliezer b. Jacob; but R. Eleazar Ḥisma declares him liable. Said R. Eliezer b. Jacob to R. Eleazar Ḥisma: Yet what benefit has he [the priest] therein? R. Eleazar Ḥisma replied to R. Eliezer b. Jacob: And what benefit has he [therein] that he who eats unclean *terumah* during the rest of the year, must pay? Not so, answered he: if you speak of unclean *terumah* during the rest of the year, [that is] because though he [the priest] does not enjoy the right to eat it, yet he enjoys the right to use it as fuel; will you say [the same] of this, in which he does not enjoy the right of eating or the right to use it as fuel? Said he to him, In this too he has the right to use it as fuel, for if the priest wishes, he can place it before his dog or burn it under his pot.

(6) The first fifth becomes the same as the original *terumah*, and if he ate it, he must restore that fifth and a fifth thereof. (7) Lit., 'measure'. (8) The question arises because since he must repay in kind it is possible that the quantity is the deciding factor, as explained in the text. (9) 'Originally' and 'subsequently' mean when he ate it and when he makes restoration respectively.
(1) Thus he must return quantitively four times as much, and the fifth in addition. (2) B.Ḳ. 93*b*; i.e., what its value was then. (3) A dry measure equal to one *se'ah*. (4) *Sc.* 'dried figs'. Lit., 'buyers do not leap upon it'. (5) *Sc.* dates. (6) Seeing that it has a monetary value. (7) V. *supra* 29*a* and note a.l. The same holds good when one incurs 'death at the hands of heaven', which is the penalty for eating *terumah* deliberately. According to this, the first clause, UNWITTINGLY, must now mean that the eater knew neither that it was *terumah* nor that it was leaven; for if he knew that it was leaven he is liable to *kareth*, which frees him from payment.
b (1) Whether payment is to be made according to quantity or value. (2) Seeing that it is forbidden to him for use, he suffers no loss. (3) I.e., what benefit can a priest derive from unclean *terumah*, seeing that it must not be eaten. Yet if a lay Israelite eats it, all agree that he must pay. The text is in disorder, cf. Rashi and Tosef. Pes. I. (4) Lit., 'though he has not in it a permission of eating, yet he has in it a permission of heating'. The other passages below have the same literal meanings. (5) Strictly speaking, he enjoys the latter right, but it is unfit for fuel on account of the juice. (6) When is it conceivable that *terumah* of leaven should possess sanctity during Passover? (7) Even according to R. Jose the Galilean, though he permits general benefit from leaven on Passover. The reason is given below. (8) Lev. XXII, 14.

the circumstances here [in both clauses] are that he [the borrower] deposited it [the leaven] with him, and they differ in R. Isaac['s dictum]. For R. Isaac said: Whence do we know that the creditor
a acquires a title to the pledge?[1] Because it is said, [*Thou shalt surely restore to him the pledge when the sun goeth down . . .*] *and it shall be righteousness unto thee:*[2] if he has no title thereto, whence is his righteousness?[3] Hence it follows that the creditor acquires a title to the pledge. Now the first Tanna holds, That[4] applies only to an Israelite [taking a pledge] from an Israelite, since we read in his case, '*and it shall be righteousness unto thee*'; but an Israelite [taking a pledge] from a Gentile does not acquire a title.[5] While R. Meir holds, [It follows] *a fortiori;* if an Israelite acquires from an Israelite, how much the more an Israelite from a Gentile! But if a Gentile lent [money] to an Israelite on his leaven, after Passover all agree that he transgresses: there the Gentile certainly does not acquire a title from the Israelite.[6]

We learned: IF A GENTILE LENT [MONEY] TO AN ISRAELITE ON HIS LEAVEN, AFTER PASSOVER IT IS PERMITTED FOR USE. Now even granted that he deposited it with him, surely you said that a Gentile does not acquire a title from an Israelite?—There is no difficulty: there [in the Mishnah] it means that he said to him, 'From now';[7] here [in the Baraitha] it means that he did not say to him, 'From now'.[8] And whence do you assume that we draw a distinction between where he said 'from now' and where he did not say 'from now'?—Because it was taught:
b If a Gentile deposited with an Israelite large loaves as a pledge,[1] he [the Israelite] does not transgress; but if he said to him, 'I have made them yours,'[2] he transgresses. Why is the first clause different from the second? This surely proves that where he says to him, 'from now,' it is different from where he does not say, 'from now'. This proves it.

Our Rabbis taught: A shop belonging to an Israelite and its wares belong to an Israelite, while Gentile workers enter therein, leaven that is found there after Passover is forbidden for use, while it need not be stated for eating. A shop belonging to a Gentile and the wares belong to a Gentile, while Israelite workers go in and out, leaven that is found there after Passover may be eaten, while it is unnecessary to state [that] benefit [is permitted].[3]

MISHNAH. IF RUINS COLLAPSED ON LEAVEN, IT IS REGARDED AS REMOVED.[4] R. SIMEON B. GAMALIEL SAID: PROVIDED THAT[5] A DOG CANNOT SEARCH IT OUT.

GEMARA. R. Ḥisda said: Yet he must annul it in his heart.[6]

A Tanna taught: How far is the searching of a dog? Three handbreadths.[7] R. Aḥa the son of R. Joseph said to R. Ashi: As to what Samuel said, Money can only be guarded [by placing it] in the earth[8]—do we require [it to be covered by] three handbreadths or not?—Here, he replied, we require three hand-
c breadths on account of the smell [of the leaven];[1] but there [it is put into the earth] in order to cover it from the eye; therefore three handbreadths are not required. And how much [is necessary]?—Said Rafram of Sikkara:[2] one handbreadth.

MISHNAH. HE WHO EATS TERUMAH OF LEAVEN ON PASSOVER UNWITTINGLY, MUST REPAY [TO THE PRIEST] THE PRINCIPAL PLUS A FIFTH;[3] IF DELIBERATELY,[4] HE IS FREE FROM PAYMENT AND FROM [LIABILITY FOR] ITS VALUE AS FUEL.[5]

GEMARA. We learned elsewhere: He who eats *terumah* unwittingly must restore the principal plus a fifth; whether he eats,

a (1) That whilst in his possession it is his, and he is responsible for all accidents. (2) Deut. XXIV, 13. (3) There is no particular righteousness in returning what does not belong to one. (4) The dictum of R. Isaac. (5) Therefore he does not transgress in respect of the leaven. (6) Hence the leaven stood in the ownership of the Israelite. (7) When he deposited the leaven with him he said to him, 'If I do not repay by the stipulated time, the leaven is yours *from now*'. Hence the leaven stands in the lender's ownership, whether Jew or Gentile. (8) Therefore, where the Gentile lent to the Jew, all agree that even if the debt was not repaid, the leaven may not be used, because during Passover it was definitely in the Jew's ownership, notwithstanding that it was deposited with the Gentile, because he does not acquire a title from a Jew. But the dispute arises only where the Israelite lent to the Gentile.

b (1) *Purni* was a large oven in which large loaves were baked. 'Large loaves' are mentioned as a natural thing, since only such are sufficiently valuable to be a pledge. (2) From now, if I do not repay at the proper time. (3) In both cases we assume that the leaven was of the stock, and did not belong to one of the workers. (4) Since it is inaccessible. (5) Lit., 'whatever'. (6) Lest the débris be removed during the festival. (7) The leaven must be covered by not less than three handbreadths of débris; otherwise a dog can search it out, and it would therefore be necessary to remove the débris and destroy the leaven. (8) That is the only way in which a bailee can carry out his charge; otherwise he is guilty of negligence and liable for theft.—In ancient days there was probably no other place as safe, but nowadays it suffices if the bailee puts the money in the place where he keeps his own (Asheri, B.M. 42*a*).

c (1) If the leaven is covered by less, a dog can smell it. (2) A town S. of Maḥuza. (3) I.e., he did not know that it was *terumah*, even if he knew that it was leaven. Though leaven has no value during Passover, yet here he must make the usual restoration of the principal plus a fifth (v. Lev. XXII, 14), not in money but in kind, the same as he ate, v. *infra* 32*a*. (4) I.e., he knew that it was *terumah*, even if he did not know that it was leaven. (5) If the *terumah* was unclean, when it has no other value, since unclean *terumah* may not be eaten. The reason is this: the law of restoring the principal plus a fifth, in kind, holds good only when the *terumah* is misappropriated unwittingly, the restoration being for the purpose of atonement. But when one appropriates it deliberately his act constitutes larceny, and he must return its value in money, not in kind, as in all cases of larceny. Leaven during Passover, however, has no monetary value, all benefit thereof being interdicted: hence he is free from payment.

פה א מיי' פ"י מהלכות שכירות הלכה א סמג עשין לד טוש"ע ח"מ סי' עב סעיף ב:

פו ב מיי' פ"ד מהלכות חמץ הל' ה טוש"ע או"ח סי' תמח סעיף א:

פז ג טוש"ע או"ח סי' תמו:

פח ד ה מיי' פ"ג מהל' חמץ הל' יא טוש"ע או"ח סי' תלג סעיף ח:

פט ו ז מיי' פ"ד מהל' שאלה ופקדון הלכה ד סמג עשין פח טוש"ע ח"מ סי' רצא סעיף (יח) [טו]:

צ ח מיי' פ"י מהלכות תרומות הל' א:

צא ט שם הל' ב:

ב"מ פב. גיטין לז. שבועות מד. [קדושין ח:]

[תוספתא פ"ב ע"ש]

ב"מ מב. לעיל ח.

ב"מ שם

תרומות פ"ו [מ"א] ב"מ נד:

תורה אור: דברים כד

אלא הכא במאי עסקינן כגון שהרהינו אצלו וקמיפלגי בדר' יצחק *דא"ר יצחק "מנין לבעל חוב שקונה משכון שנאמר °ולך תהיה צדקה אם אינו קונה משכון צדקה מנין מכאן לבעל חוב שקונה משכון ת"ק סבר הני מילי ישראל מישראל הוא דקרינא ביה ולך תהיה צדקה אבל ישראל מנכרי לא קני ור"מ סבר קל וחומר ישראל מישראל קני ישראל מנכרי לא כל שכן אבל נכרי שהלוה את ישראל על חמצו אחר הפסח דברי הכל עובר התם ודאי נכרי מישראל לא קני תנן נכרי שהלוה (א) ישראל על חמצו אחר הפסח מותר בהנאה נהי נמי דהרהינו אצלו הא אמרת נכרי מישראל לא קני לא קשיא "הא דאמר ליה מעכשיו הא דלא אמר ליה מעכשיו ומנא תימרא דשני ליה בין היכא דאמר מעכשיו ובין היכא דלא אמר מעכשיו דתניא נכרי שהרהין פת פורני אצל ישראל אינו עובר ואם אמר לו הגעתיך עובר מאי שנא רישא ומאי שנא סיפא אלא לאו שמע מינה שאני היכא דא"ל מעכשיו להיכא דלא אמר ליה מעכשיו שמע מינה ת"ר *"חנות של ישראל ומלאי של ישראל ופועלי נכרים נכנסין לשם חמץ שנמצא שם אחר הפסח אסור בהנאה ואין צריך לומר באכילה חנות של נכרי ומלאי של נכרי ופועלי ישראל נכנסים ויוצאין לשם חמץ שנמצא שם אחר הפסח מותר באכילה ואין צריך לומר בהנאה: מתני' *"חמץ שנפלה עליו מפולת הרי הוא כמבוער רבן שמעון בן גמליאל אומר כל שאין הכלב יכול לחפש אחריו: גמ' אמר רב חסדא "וצריך שיבטל בלבו תנא כמה חפישת הכלב שלשה טפחים אמר ליה רב אחא בריה דרב יוסף לרב אשי הא דאמר שמואל *"כספים אין להם שמירה אלא בקרקע מי בעינן שלשה טפחים או לא אמר ליה הכא משום ריחא בעינן שלשה טפחים התם משום איכסויי מעינא הוא ולא בעי שלשה וכמה 'אמר רפרם בר פפא מסיכרא טפח: מתני' האוכל תרומת חמץ בפסח בשוגג משלם קרן וחומש במזיד פטור מתשלומין ומדמי עצים: גמ' תנן התם *"האוכל תרומה בשוגג משלם קרן וחומש "אחד האוכל ואחד השותה ואחד

רש"י

אלא. רישא וסיפא כשהרהינו אבל בלא הרהינו דכולי עלמא מכאן ולהבא הוא גובה: קונה משכון. כל ימי הלואה המשכון קנוי לו ואם נאנס חייב באונסין שאינו עליו לא כשומר חנם ולא כשומר שכר שפטורין באונסין אלא כולו ברשותיה ובשמירתו עומד: ולך תהיה צדקה. בהשבת העבוט כתיב אי אמרת קונה משכון איכא צדקה בהא שכיבה ששכב בשמלתו שהשאיל לו זה דבר הקנוי לו ואם אינו קונה צדקה בהשכבה זו מניין על שלו שכב: אבל ישראל מנכרי לא. הלכך לא עבר עליה דאמר מר (לעיל דף כט.) אבל אתה רואה של אחרים: תנן נכרי שהלוה וכו'. ואותיבנא לרבא לעיל ושנינן כשהרהינו אצלו והא אמרת השתא דברי הכל נכרי מישראל לא קני: לא קשיא. מתניתין דאמר ליה כשהרהינו אצלו אם לא אתן לך עד יום פלוני יהא שלך מעכשיו הלכך נכרי שהלוה את ישראל קם ליה חמץ ברשות נכרי וישראל שהלוה את הנכרי קם ליה ברשות ישראל ברייתא דלא אמר ליה מעכשיו אלא כשאר משכון נתנו לו וקבע לו זמן שאם לא יפרע לו יגבה חובו ממשכונו וישום אותו בדמים הלכך בנכרי שהלוה לישראל דברי הכל אפילו לא פרע ליה אסור לישראל ליהנות ממנו דכל ימות הפסח של ישראל היה דמכאן ולהבא הוא גובה ואי משום דהרהינו נכרי מישראל לא קני וישראל שהלוה פליגי מאן דאסר סבר כיון שהרהינו בעל חוב קונה משכון וליכא למימר הכא מכאן ולהבא גובה ומאן דשרי קסבר ישראל מנכרי ליכא צדקה ולא קני משכון: ומנא תימרא. דאפילו כשהרהינו שאני לן בין אמר מעכשיו ללא אמר מעכשיו: פת פורני. פת גדולה האפויה בתנור גדול כעין תנורים שלנו שהתנורים שלהם היו קטנים ומיטלטלין ופיהם למעלה ומדביקין הפת בדפנות שאין אופין בה אלא פתים קטנים ואורחא דמילתא נקט דאיידי דחשיבי שקיל ליה במשכון: אינו עובר. בפסח דקסבר ישראל מנכרי לא קני משכון: הגעתיך. מעכשיו קאמר אם לא אפרע לך עד יום פלוני עובר ואף על פי שלא הגיע הזמן שמא כשיגיע לא יפרע ונמצא עובר למפרע בבל יראה: מאי שנא רישא כו'. אי הגעתיך לאו מעכשיו הוא מאי קא מהני בלאו הגעתיך נמי כי מטא זמניה ולא פרע שקיל ליה בחובו: ומלאי של ישראל. פת ויין הנמכר בתוכה: אסור בהנאה. דלא תלינן ליה בפועלין אלא מן של מלאי היה ושל ישראל הוא: גמ' צריך שיבטל בלבו. שמא יפקח הגל במועד ונמצא עובר עליו: כספים. של פיקדון אין להם שמירה אלא בקרקע ואם לא נתנן בקרקע ואבדו פשיעה היא אצלו וחייב דשומר חנם חייב בפשיעה: משום ריחא. שהכלב מריחו ומחטטו ומוציאו: מסיכרא. מקום: מתני' בשוגג. ששגג בתרומה ואפילו הזיד בחמץ משלם קרן וחומש ואף על גב דלא הוה שויא מידי דחמץ בפסח אסור בהנאה מיהו שוגג דתרומה דכתיב ביה וחמישיתו יוסף עליו ונתן לכהן את הקודש דבר הראוי להיות קודש שאינו יכול לשלם לו המעות אלא הפירות והתשלומין נעשין תרומה כדלקמן לאו לפי דמים משלם אלא לפי מדה משלם הלכך לאו בתר דמים אזלינן: במזיד. שהזיד בתרומה אפילו שגג בחמץ פטור מן התשלומין: ומדמי עצים. אם תרומה טמאה היא אין משלם לו דמי עצים שהיתה ראויה להיסק תחת תבשילו משום דתרומה מזיד אין בה חומש ואין תשלומיה לכפרה ואין נעשין תרומה דגבי חומש בשגגה כתיב אבל מזיד אינו אלא כשאר גזלן בעלמא ומשלם מעות ולפי דמים ולא לפי המדה וחמץ בפסח לאו בר דמים דאסור בהנאה ואף להיסק לא הוי חזי ליה ולאו מידי אפסדיה:

ואחד

תוספות

אלא הב"ע שהרהינו אצלו וקמיפלגי בדרבי יצחק. תימה לריב"א לאביי היאך יתרץ הך דע"כ בדרבי יצחק קמיפלגי וסיפא דקתני נכרי שהלוה את ישראל על חמצו אמאי דברי הכל עובר אע"ג דלא קנה כיון דלמפרע הוא גובה ורישא נמי אמאי אינו עובר למ"ד כיון דלמפרע הוא גובה ומפרש ריב"א דהשתא כי מוקי פלוגתא בדרבי יצחק מיירי שלא בא ישראל לידי גבייה שפדאו נכרי לבסוף דלא שייך השתא פלוגתא דאביי ורבא כלל אלא בהא קמיפלגי דלמאן דאמר עובר ס"ל דקני ליה ישראל מנכרי וה"ל ברשות ישראל ומ"ד אינו עובר ס"ל דלא קני ליה והרי לא היה ברשותו ובסיפא ד"ה עובר דלא קני ליה נכרי לכ"ע והרי היה ברשות ישראל ומיהו מתניתין דקתני נכרי שהלוה וכו' מותר בהנאה מיירי שלא פדאו ישראל דאי פדאו אע"ג דמוקי לה בסמוך בדאמר ליה מעכשיו מכל מקום מאי מהני: בדרבי יצחק קמיפלגי. תימה הא ר' יצחק לא קאמר דקני משכון אלא שלא בשעת הלואה כדמוכח בהאומנין (בבא מציעא פב.) והכא ישראל שהלוה לנכרי על חמצו תנן דמשמע בשעת הלואה כדמשמע בהאומנין* דקתני הלוהו [דף פח:] על המשכון שומר שכר והתניא שומר חנם ומשני הא דמשכנו בשעת הלואתו והא שלא בשעת הלואתו ופריך והא אידי ואידי על המשכון קתני ויש לומר דהכי פירושו כיון דשלא בשעת הלואה קונה לגמרי כדרבי יצחק א"כ לענין חמץ יש לנו לחושבו כאילו הוא שלו לעבור בבל ימצא אף בשעת הלואה דחשבינן ליה מלוי וכן יש לפרש בהשולח (גיטין לז.) גבי המלוה על המשכון אינו משמט מדרבי יצחק כיון דקני ליה שלא בשעת הלואה בשעת הלואה נמי מיקרי של אחיך בידך: שקונה משכון. פ"ה קונה משכון לענין חיוב אונסין ור"י אומר דבהאומנין (ב"מ פב.) משמע דלא הוי אלא שומר שכר דהלוהו על המשכון שומר שכר בעי למימר התם בגמרא דסבר לה כרבי יצחק וכולה שמעתא חמצו של נכרי ביד ישראל איירי שלא קבל עליו ישראל אחריות דאי קבל הרי הוא שלו ועובר עליו כדמוכח בפ"ק (דף ה:): ואם אמר הגעתיך עובר. לאביי רישא מיירי כשפדאו וסיפא כי אמר הגעתיך הייטו שאינו רוצה לפדותו:

דבר

רבינו חננאל

היא ואוקימנה בשהרהינו אצלו ואמר לו קנה מעכשיו וכדר' יצחק דאמר בעל *)חוב קונה משכון ופליגי ת"ק לית ליה הא דר' יצחק ור' מאיר אית ליה ומתמהי' וכי דר' יצחק תנאי היא ושני' [דכ"ע] אית להו דר' יצחק והכא בהא קא מיפלגי ת"ק סבר ישראל מישראל דבר צדקה הוא קני אבל משכון דנכרי דלאו בר צדקה הוא לא קני ור' מאיר סבר ק"ו משכון דישראל קני ליה המלוה משכון דנכרי לא כל שכן אבל נכרי שהלוה את ישראל על חמצו וקבע לו זמן לפרעו אחר הפסח דברי הכל עובר דלא קני הנכרי חמצו של ישראל אלא ברשות ישראל קאי ועובר עליו ומקשי' תנן נכרי שהלוה את ישראל על חמצו אחר הפסח מותר בהנאה והאמרת נכרי מישראל לא קני ואפי' הרהינו אצלו ושני' משנתינו בשפירש לו קני מעכשיו כדתניא נכרי שהרהין פת פורני אצל ישראל אינו עובר בפסח ואם אמר לו הגעתיך כלומר קני מעכשיו עובר וכך סוגיא דשמעתא יו סלקא והוא כגון הא דתנן (ב"מ דף סה) הלוהו על שדהו ואמר לו אם איני מביא לך עד שלש שנים הרי הוא [שלך] מעכשיו**) כו': ת"ר חנות של נכרי ומלאי של נכרי. כלומר הסחורה שבתוך החנות לנכרי ופועלי ישראל נכנסין לשם ועושין מלאכתן חמץ שנמצא שם אחר הפסח אסור בהנאה ואין צריך לומר באכילה כלומר חמץ של ישראל הוא וכן חנות של ישראל ומלאי של ישראל ופועלי נכרים נכנסין שם חמץ שנמצא שם אחר הפסח מותר באכילה ואין צריך לומר בהנאה כללא דמילתא בתר פועלין אזלינן אם פועלין ישראל הן חמצן הוא ואסור ואם של נכרים מותר: חמץ שנפלה עליו מפולת ונטמן בעפר אם הוא טמון שלשה טפחים בכדי שאין הכלב יכול לחפש אחריו כלומר אינו מריח ריח החמץ הרי הוא כמבוער ואין חייב להפור ולהוציאו ולשרפו אבל צריך לבטלו ולא תימא אפי' בשמירת הפקדון כך כי הא דאמר שמואל כספים אין להם שמירה אלא בקרקע ולא בעינן כולי האי אלא טפח בלבד סגי דכיון דמשום אכסויי מעינא הוא דיו דהא משום ריחא לא חיישי' הלכך אפי' הוא טמון בקרקע טפח סגי ליה: מתני' האוכל תרומת חמץ בפסח בשוגג משלם קרן וחומש במזיד הואיל וחייב כרת פטור מן התשלומי' ומדמי העצים פי' לא תאמר חשוב זו התרומה שאכלת אתה כאלו שרפת אותה ונהנת ממנה ואתה חייב לשלם כפי הנאתך אלא אפי' כעצים העומדין לשרפה אין חייב לשלם שהחמץ בפסח איסורי הנאה הוא ולית ליה לכהן לשרפה וליהנות ממנה אי הכי אפי' בשוגג יהא פטור מן התשלומי' דהא לית דמים דאיסורא הנאה הוא ואמרי' מתני' ר' יוסי הגלילי הוא דאמר והמה על עצמך האיך חמץ אסור בהנאה כל שבעה כדבעי' למימר קמן: תנן התם בתרומה פ"ו האוכל תרומה שוגג משלם

*) משמע דרבינו הי' לו גי' אחרת בגמ' דמעיקרא ס"ד דפליגי בדר' יצחק גופא אי ב"ח קונה משכון או לא.

**) במשנה שם לא הוזכר דמיירי מעכשיו אבל בג"ס שם ד' סו ע"ב מוקמינן דאמר ליה קני מעכשיו.

הגהות הב"ח

(א) גמ' שהלוה את ישראל על חמצו:

תורה אור

ואתי מלוה ופריק *דתנן "מוסיף עוד דינר ופודה את הנכסים האלו כי פליגי דזבין מלוה וקדיש מלוה אביי אמר למפרע הוא גובה כיון דמטא זמניה ולא פרעיה איגלאי מילתא למפרע דמעיקרא ברשותיה הוה קאי ושפיר אקדיש ושפיר זבין ורבא אמר מכאן ולהבא הוא גובה כיון דאילו הוו ליה זוזי הוה מסליק להו בזוזי אישתכח דהשתא קא קני ומי אמר רבא הכי *והאמר רמי בר חמא "ראובן שמכר שדה לשמעון באחריות וזקפן עליו במלוה ומת ראובן ואתא בעל חוב דראובן וטריף ליה משמעון ואתא שמעון ופייסיה בזוזי דינא הוא דאתו בני ראובן ואמרי ליה לשמעון אנן מטלטלי שבק אבון גבך ומטלטלי דיתמי לבעל חוב לא משתעבדי ואמר רבא אי פיקח שמעון מגבי להו ארעא והדר גבי לה מינייהו *דאמר רב נחמן "יתומים שגבו קרקע בחובת אביהם בעל חוב חוזר וגובה אותה מהן אי אמרת בשלמא למפרע הוא גובה אמטו להכי חוזר וגובה אותה מהן דכמאן דגבו מחיים דאבוהון דמי אלא אי אמרת מכאן ולהבא הוא גובה אמאי חוזר וגובה אותה מהן הא הוי כמאן דזבין יתמי נכסי דמי ואילו קני יתמי נכסי מי קא משתעבדי לבעל חוב שאני התם דאמר להו כי היכי דמשתעבדנא ליה לאבוכון משתעבדנא נמי לבעל חוב דאבוכון מדר' נתן *דתניא רבי נתן אומר "מנין לנושה בחבירו מנה וחבירו בחבירו שמוציאין מזה ונותנין לזה ת"ל "ונתן לאשר אשם לו: תנן נכרי שהלוה את ישראל על חמצו אחר הפסח מותר בהנאה אי אמרת בשלמא למפרע הוא גובה אמטו להכי מותר בהנאה אלא אי אמרת מכאן ולהבא הוא גובה אמאי מותר בהנאה ברשותא דישראל הוה קאי הכא במאי עסקינן כשהרהינו אצלו לימא כתנאי ישראל שהלוה לנכרי על חמצו לאחר הפסח אינו עובר משום רבי מאיר אמרו עובר מאי לאו בהא קמיפלגי דמר סבר למפרע הוא גובה ומר סבר מכאן ולהבא הוא גובה ותסברא אימא סיפא אבל נכרי שהלוה לישראל על חמצו לאחר הפסח דברי הכל עובר והא איפכא מיבעי ליה למאן דאמר התם אינו עובר הכא עובר למאן דאמר התם עובר הכא אינו עובר אלא

במדבר ה

רש"י

ואתי מלוה ופריק. מן ההקדש בדבר מועט כדי שלא יאמרו הקדש יוצא בלא פדיון וגובה חובו כדתנן בערכין בפרק שום היתומים הקדיש בתשעים מנה והיה חובו מאה מנה מוסיף מלוה זה על הלואתו דינר ופודה את הנכסים הללו מיד הקדש בדינר זה ונוטלן בחובו ודינר דיהיב מפרש טעמא התם שלא יאמרו הקדש יוצא בלא פדיון ואף על גב דאמר רבא (כתובות דף נט:) הקדש חמץ ושיחרור מפקיעין מידי שיעבוד דוקא קדושת הגוף קאמר רבא כגון קונמות או בהמה לקרבן או בגד שפירסו על המת כי ההיא דיבמות (דף סו:) גבי איצטלא דמילתא דפירסוה יתמי אמיתנא דהוה משתעבד לכתובת האשה דאמר רבא קנייא מיתנא אבל קדושת דמים לא אמרינן: כי פליגי דאקדיש מלוה. בתוך הזמן את הקרקע המשועבד לו ולא הקדיש את החוב אלא הקרקע והשתא כשהגיע הזמן ולא פרעו זה והוא בא לגבותה מן הלוה חוזר בו מן ההקדש: כיון דאילו הוה ליה זוזי. ללוה ביום הזמן הוה מסלק ליה למלוה מן הקרקע בזוזי אישתכח שלא היה הקרקע קנוי לו עדיין אלא עכשיו כשהוא גובה אותה בחובו היא נקנית לו: באחריות. שמא יטלנה בעל חוב דראובן משמעון בשביל חוב ששיעבדה לו ראובן שישלם לו ראובן זה מעותיו לשמעון ולא היו לו נכסים עוד על דבר אחריות זה: וזקפן עליו במלוה. שלא היו מעות לשמעון שפסק על שדה זו וכתב לראובן שטר עליהן ושיעבד נכסיו לו עליהן: ומת ראובן. המוכר ובא בעל חובו וטורפה משמעון ועדיין לא נתן שמעון המעות לראובן ולא ליתומיו ופייסיה שמעון לבעל חוב דראובן באותן המעות: דינא הוא. אע"ג דאבוהון קביל עליה אחריות מכירה זו אפילו הכי יכולין בני ראובן לבא על שמעון ולומר אנן מטלטלי שבק אבון גבך לא היית חייב עליו אלא מעות ולא היה לך ליתנן לבעל חוב ולא לעכבן בשביל אחריות מכירתך דמטלטלי דיתמי לא שיעבדום חכמים לבעל חוב דקרקע של יתומים הוא דאמרינן בעל חוב גובה אותה בחובו משום דמחיים חל שיעבודא עליהן אבל על מעות שלא היו בעין לא חייל שיעבודו מחיים עליהן וכשהן בעין אין כאן לוה ולבעלי המעות דהיינו יתומים לא הלוה זה כלום: ואמר רבא גרסינן: אי פיקח. זה שמעון יטעון ויאמר להם אין לי מעות לפרוע לכם אלא קרקע יש לי ונותנה להם בחובותם וחוזר וגובה אותם מהם בשביל אחריות מכירה שקבל אביהן עליו דהשתא כי אגבי להו הא ארעא איגלאי מילתא דלאו מטלטלי הוא דשביק גביה אלא קרקע: בעל חוב. אחר של אביהן חוזר וגובה אותה מהן אלמא אמרינן הגוטל קרקע בחובו מאותה שעה שנתן לו המעות נקנית לו: אא"ב. אמרינן איגלאי מילתא למפרע שהיתה קנויה לאביהן קרקע זה שגבו בחוב אביהן משום הכי בע"ח אחר של אביהן חוזר וגובה אותה מהן דכמאן דגבי לה מחיים דאבוהון דמי: אלא אי אמרת. כל הגובה קרקע בחובו אינה קנויה לו אלא מגבייה ואילך אמאי בעל חוב אחר חוזר וגובה אותה מהן לא יהא דבר זה אלא כמי שקנו יתומים קרקע במעות שלהן מי הוה משתעבדא לבעל חוב: שאני התם דאמר להו כי היכי דמשתעבדנא לאבוכון משתעבדנא נמי לבעל חוב דאבוכון מדרבי נתן. לעולם מכאן ולהבא הוא גובה ומאי דאמר רב נחמן בעלמא בעל חוב חוזר וגובה אותה מהן משום דאמר להן בעל חוב ליתומים מכח מי באתם וגביתם קרקע זו מכח שיעבוד של אביכן וכי היכי דמשתעבדא לאבוכון קרקע זו של לוה שלוה מאביכם משתעבדא נמי לדידי שהייתי מלוה של אביכן והמחויב לו כלום משועבד לי מדרבי נתן הלכך קדם שיעבודי עליה אפי' אלל לוה שהיתה ברשותו ושמעון נמי אמר להו לבני ראובן כי היכי דהוי נכסיי משועבדין לאביכם בשביל חובו היו משועבדין גם לעצמי מכח אביכן שהיה לוה אלי מחמת אחריות המכירה מדר' נתן דמה לי אני מה לי אחר הלכך אע"פ שלא היתה קנויה לאביכם מחיים חל שיעבודי עליה אלל עצמי: לאשר אשם לו. לאשר הלוהו לו לא נאמר אלא לאשר אשם לו לאשר הקרן שלו בבבא קמא *אמרינן אשם זה קרן: תנן נכרי שהלוה כו'. קס"ד השתא בשלא מסרו לו אלא שיעבדו לו כשאר לווים שאם לא אתן לך עד יום פלוני בא לביתי וגבה מחמץ זה: כשהרהינו אצלו. בביתו של נכרי נתנו קס"ד השתא דטעמא משום דהוה ליה תורת משכון ובעל חוב קונה משכון: ישראל שהלוה את הנכרי על חמצו. קודם הפסח לאחר הפסח אינו עובר אם נהנה ממנו: מאי לאו. בשלא הרהינו ובהא קמיפלגי דת"ק סבר מכאן ולהבא הוא גובה כו': אימא סיפא דברי הכל עובר. ואי טעמא משום להבא ולמפרע הוא איפכא הוה לן לאפוכי פלוגתייהו בהא ולא לאשויי דעתייהו דלמאן דאמר לעיל ברישא עובר אלמא למפרע הוא גובה הכא הוה ליה למימר אינו עובר משום דבשעת הלואה קם ליה ברשות נכרי ולמאן דאמר התם כו':

אלא

תוספות

באחריות. שלא באחריות פשיטא דיתן ליורשיו אפילו לא זקפן עליו במלוה אבל באחריות קמ"ל דה"א יעכבם לעצמו דה"ל כתופס מחיים קמ"ל דלא חשיב ליה כתופס מחיים כיון דזקפן עליו במלוה: ופייסיה בזוזי. רבותא נקט אף על פי שנתן מעות לא מצי למימר המעות שנתחייבתי לאביכם נתתי לו:

משתעבדנא לב"ח דאבוכון מדרבי נתן. וא"ת גבי מטלטלים נמי נימא הכי ונראה לר"י דדוקא גבי קרקע שייך למימר הכי דבת שיעבוד היא דכשהקרקע זו משועבדת לראובן חשבינן ליה כאילו היא בידו דהא אם מכרה או משכנה חוזר ראובן וגובה אותה ולכך משועבדת נמי לבע"ח אבל מטלטלים אין להחשיבם כאילו הם ביד ראובן כיון שאילו מכרם או משכנם אין גובה מהן ומכאן יש להוכיח דהלכה כרבי נתן דהא רבא קאי כוותיה בשמעתין:

אלא

עין משפט נר מצוה

פא א מיי' פ"ז מהלכות ערכין הלכה טז:
פב ב מיי' פי"א מהל' מלוה הלכה י סמג עשין לד:
פג ג מיי' שם הלכה ט וסמג שם טוש"ע ח"מ סי' קז סעיף א:
פד ד מיי' פ"ב שם הלכה ו סמג עשין נג טוש"ע ח"מ סי' פו סעיף א:

מסורת הש"ס

ערכין כג:
כתובות נג.
ב"ק מג. כתובו' צב. קי. ב"ב קכה.
קדושין טו. כתובות יט. ופס. גיטין לז. ב"ק מ:
[דף קי.]

רבינו חננאל

אקדיש לוה אתי מלוה ופריק להנהו נכסי דתנן בערכין פ"ו מוסיף עוד דינר ופודה את הנכסים האלו ומקשי' ומי אמר רבא הכי והאמרי' ראובן שמכר שדה לשמעון באחריות וזקפן עליו במלוה ומת ראובן ואתי בעל חוב לטרוף משמעון ופייסיה שמעון בזוזי דינא הוא דלימרו בני ראובן אנן מטלטלי שבק אבון גבך כלומר האי מלוה דאית לאבונא גבך מטלטלי הוא ומטלטלי לבעל חוב לא משתעבדי אמר רבא ואי שמעון פקח הוא מגבי להו ליתמי קרקע בחובייהו והדר שמעון תבע להו באחריות דקבל עליה אבוהון וטרף ליה להאי ארעא מדרב נחמן דאמר יתומים שגבו קרקע בחובות אביהם בעל חוב חוזר וגובה מהן אי אמרת בשלמא רבא סבר למפרע הוא גובה שפיר דאמרינן מחיי אבוהון הות קניא הא ארעא דגבו להו בניה אלא אי אמרת מכאן ולהבא הוא גובה וכאלו זבני יתמי האידנ' ארעא [ומי] משתעבדא לבעל [חוב] דאבוהון ושני' הכא טעמא אחרינא היא דאמר להו שמעון ליתמי דראובן בההיא שעתא דזקפי עלי אבוכון מלוה כי היכי דאשתעבדי לאבוכון הכי אשתעבדי לבעל חוב דיליה כדר' נתן דתני מנין שמוציאין מן הלוה של ראובן ונותנין למלוה של ראובן שנאמר ונתן לאשר אשם לו ואקשי' לרבא מסתני' דקתני נכרי שהלוה את ישראל על חמצו כו' אי אמרת למפרע הוא גובה היינו דמותר בהנאה דאמרי' מההיא שעתא דיזיף ישראל מנכרי על חמצו [לאו] ברשו' ישראל קאי וחמץ של נכרי קרינא ביה לפיכך שרי אלא אי אמרת מכאן ולהבא וכו' ושני' בשהרהינו אצל הנכרי: נימא כתנאי ישראל שהלוה את נכרי על חמצו וקבע לו זמן לפרעו אחר הפסח אינו עובר עליו משום ר' מאיר אמרו עובר מאי לאו בהא קא מיפלגי וכו' ופשוטה

it,[8] [31a] and the creditor can come and redeem it,[9] for we learned: He adds another *denar* and redeems this property.[10] They differ where the *creditor* sold or dedicated [it].[11] Abaye said: 'He collects retrospectively'; since the time [for payment] came and he did not repay him, the matter was retrospectively revealed that from
a the [very] beginning it stood in his[1] possession, and he rightly dedicated or sold [it]. But Raba ruled: 'He collects from now and onwards'; since if he [the debtor] had money, he could have quitted him with money, it is found that he [the creditor] acquires it only now.

Yet did Raba say thus? Surely Rami b. Ḥama said: If Reuben sold his estate to Simeon with security,[2] and he [Simeon] set it [the money] up as a loan against himself,[3] then Reuben died, and Reuben's creditor came and seized [the estate] from Simeon, whereupon Simeon went and satisfied him with money, it is by right that the children of Reuben can go and say to Simeon, 'As for us, we [maintain that] our father left [us] movables in your possession, and the movables of orphans are not under lien to a creditor.'[4] Now Raba said: If Simeon is wise, he lets them seize the land, and then he reclaims it from them.[5] For R. Naḥman said: If orphans seize land for their father's debt,[6] a creditor [of their father] can in turn seize it from them. Now, if you agree that he [a creditor] collects retrospectively, it is right: for that reason he in turn can seize it from them, because it is just as though they had seized it in their father's lifetime. But if you say that he collects it from now and henceforth, why can he in turn seize it from them: surely it is as though the orphans had bought [immovable] property,[7] and if orphans buy [immovable] property, is it then under a lien to [their father's] creditor?—There it is differ-
b ent, because he can say to them, just as I was indebted[1] to your father, so I was indebted to your father's creditor. [This follows] from R. Nathan['s dictum]. For it was taught, R. Nathan said: How do we know that if one man claims a *maneh* from his neighbour, and his neighbour [claims a like sum] from another neighbour, that we collect from the one [the last] and give to the other [the first]? From the verse, *and he shall give it unto him to whom he is indebted.*[2]

We learned: IF A GENTILE LENT [MONEY] TO AN ISRAELITE ON HIS LEAVEN, AFTER PASSOVER IT IS PERMITTED FOR USE. It is right if you say that he collects retrospectively: therefore it is permitted for use. But if you say that he collects from now and henceforth, why is it permitted for use? [Surely] it stood in the possession of the Israelite!—The circumstances here are that he deposited it with him.[3]

Shall we say that it is dependent on Tannaim: If an Israelite lent [money] to a Gentile on his leaven, after Passover he does not transgress.[4] In R. Meir's name it was said: He does transgress. Now do they not differ in this, viz., one Master holds [that] he collects retrospectively, while the other Master holds [that] he collects from now and onwards.[5]—Now is that logical! Consider the second clause: But if a Gentile lent [money] to an Israelite on his leaven, after Passover he transgresses on all views. But surely the reverse [of the rulings in the first clause] is required: according to the view there [in the first clause] that he does not transgress, here he does transgress; [while] according to the view there that he does transgress, here he does not transgress![6] [31b] Rather

(8) From the purchaser, without compensation. (9) From *hekdesh*, at a mere trifle, not at its full value, so that some *form* of redemption may be observed. (10) 'Er. 23*b*. If the debtor dedicates to *hekdesh* property worth ninety *manehs*, while his debt is one hundred *manehs*, the creditor adds (i.e., gives) just one *denar* as a formal redemption and seizes it. Thus in both cases they agree that the pledge belonged retrospectively to the creditor. (11) Before he actually foreclosed.

a (1) The creditor's. (2) A guarantee to indemnify S. against loss if a creditor of R. should seize it for debt. (3) S. could not pay for the field, so he gave him an IOU for the sum, pledging his own property as security. (4) Although their father had given security for this transaction, yet the orphans can plead, we inherited movables from our father which were in your possession, i.e., you merely owed him money, the field actually being yours; hence you should not have given that money to the creditor, because movables inherited by orphans are not subject to any lien; nor had you the right to withhold payment. Hence you still owe us the money. (5) I.e., he pleads that he has no money; hence they must take the field in payment. This will prove retrospectively that they had inherited land, not movables. Then he can demand its return, since their father had indemnified him against loss. (6) I.e., for a debt owing to their father. (7) I.e., with the money owing to them they *now* purchased this estate.

b (1) Lit., 'pledged'. (2) Num. V. 7, translating: and he (the third) shall give it unto him (the first) to whom he (the second) is indebted. (3) It is now assumed that he deposited it with the Gentile as a pledge, and the Gentile acquires a title to it as such. (4) If he takes the leaven for the debt and uses it. (5) It being now assumed that he did not deposit his leaven with the Gentile. (6) Since the case is reversed, the Gentile having lent money to the Jew, obviously the rulings too should be reversed, if they are dependent on whether the creditor collects retrospectively or from now and onwards.

[30b] one must not grease an oven with fat, and if he does grease it, all the bread [baked therein] is forbidden until the oven is refired. Which [implies], if the oven is refired it is nevertheless permitted? This is a refutation of Raba b. Ahilai!—[It is indeed] a refutation.

Rabina said to R. Ashi: Now since Raba b. Ahilai was refuted, why did Rab say, Pots must be broken on Passover?[6]—There it was a metal oven, replied he, [whereas] here an earthen pot [is referred to]. Alternatively, both refer to earthenware: this [the oven] is fired from the inside;[7] while the other [the pot] is fired on the outside. And should you say, here too let him burn it [the pot] out from within,—he would spare it, lest it burst.[8] Therefore a tiled pan,[9] since it is burnt from without,[10] is forbidden; but if he filled it with coals,[11] it is permitted.

Rabina asked R. Ashi: What does one do about the knives on Passover?—I provide [make] new ones for myself, he replied. That is well for you, who can [afford] this, said he to him, [but] what about one who cannot [afford] this? I mean *like* new ones, he answered: [I thrust] their handles in loam and their blades in
a fire, and then I place their handles in boiling water.[1] But the law is: both the one and the other[2] [need only be put] into boiling water, and in a 'first' vessel.[3]

R. Huna the son of R. Joshua said: A wooden pot ladle must be purified[4] in boiling water and in a 'first' vessel. [Thus] he holds, as it absorbs, so it exudes.[5]

Meremar was asked: Glazed vessels, may they be used on Passover? About green ones there is no problem, as they are certainly forbidden;[6] the question is, how about black ones and white ones? Again, if they have splits there is no question, as they are certainly forbidden;[7] the question is, what about smooth ones? Said he to him: We see that they exude,[8] which shows that they absorb; hence they are forbidden; and the Torah testified concerning an earthen vessel that it [the absorbed matter] never passes out from its sides.[9] And what is the difference in respect of wine of *nesek*,[10] that Meremar lectured: Glazed vessels,[11] whether black, white, or green, are permitted?[12] And should you answer, [the interdict of] wine of *nesek* is [only] Rabbinical, [whereas that of] leaven is Scriptural,—surely whatever the Rabbis enacted, they enacted similar to Scriptural law?—Said he to him: This is used with hot [matter], while the other is used with cold.[13]

Raba b. Abba said in R. Hiyya b. Ashi's name in Samuel's name: All utensils which were used with leavened matter [*hamez*], cold, may be used with unleavened bread [*mazzah*], except a
b container of *se'or*, because it is strongly leaven.[1] R. Ashi said: And a *haroseth*[2] container is like a container of *se'or*, because it is strongly leaven. Raba said: The kneading basins of Mahuza,[3] since leaven is continually kneaded in them and leaven is kept in them, are like a container of *se'or*, which is strongly leaven. That is obvious?—You might say, since they are wide, the air acts on them and they do not absorb. Therefore he informs us [otherwise].

MISHNAH. IF A GENTILE LENT [MONEY] TO AN ISRAELITE ON HIS LEAVEN,[4] AFTER PASSOVER IT IS PERMITTED FOR USE. WHILE IF AN ISRAELITE LENT [MONEY] TO A GENTILE ON HIS LEAVEN, AFTER PASSOVER IT IS PROHIBITED FOR USE.[5]

GEMARA. It was stated: [In the case of] a creditor,—Abaye said: He collects retrospectively;[6] while Raba said: He collects from now and onwards.[7] Now, where the debtor sanctified [the pledge] or sold [it], all agree that the creditor can come and seize

(6) For we see that greased ovens (these were generally of earth) can be re-heated and then used, the heat expelling the traces of fat. Then let the pots too be subjected to fire, which would likewise expel the absorbed leaven. (7) Which is efficacious to expel absorbed matter. (8) Hence if he is told to burn it from within, he will burn it from without and think that enough. (9) A kind of plaque made of tiles upon which bread was baked. (10) The coals being under it and the bread on top. (11) On top.

a (1) This process frees them from their absorbed leaven. (2) *Sc.* the handle and the blade. (3) A 'first' vessel means the vessel in which the water was boiled, while it is still at boiling point; a 'second' vessel is that into which the water is poured from the 'first'. (4) *Hag'alah* is the technical term for ridding a utensil of the forbidden matter which it has absorbed. (5) I.e., the same conditions are necessary to make it exude as those whereby it absorbed. Since the ladle absorbs the leaven from a 'first' vessel, for it is used for stirring the contents of the pot on the fire, it exudes only when likewise placed in a first vessel.

(6) These were made from an earth containing alum crystals and absorbed freely. (7) The splits permitting them to absorb. (8) I.e., they are porous. (9) Hence once forbidden they remain so for all time. (10) *Nesek*, lit., 'libation', is wine handled by a heathen. It is forbidden, because he may have dedicated it as a libation for his deity. (11) Which had contained wine of *nesek*. (12) For use, in spite of the wine which they had absorbed. (13) And of course it has greater powers of absorption in the former case.

b (1) And though the *se'or* placed therein was cold, yet it infects the vessel which in turn imparts a flavour of leaven to anything placed therein. (2) A paste made of flour and vinegar, used as a sauce or relish. (3) V. *supra* 5b, n. c5. (4) The leaven being a pledge; the loan was made before Passover. (5) In both cases the leaven was seized for payment after Passover. V. *infra* Gemara. (6) I.e., if the creditor has to exact the pledge in repayment of the loan, the pledge is regarded as having retrospectively belonged to him from the time of the loan. (7) It is regarded as having belonged to him only from the moment he actually seized it.

עג א מיי' פ"ה מהל' מ"א הל' כג טוש"ע א"ח סי' תנא ס"א:
עד ב מיי' פ"ה מהל' חו"מ הל' כד סמג לאוין עח טוש"ע א"ח סי' תנא סעיף ג:
עה ג מיי' שם הל' כה טוש"ע שם סעיף כב:
עו ד מיי' פי"א מהל' מאכלות אסורות הל' יט סמג לאוין קמח טוש"ע יו"ד סי' קלה סעיף ו:
עז ה ו מיי' פ"ה מהל' חמץ הל' כה סמג לאוין עח טוש"ע א"ח סי' תנא סעיף כג:
עח ז מיי' שם טוש"ע שם סעיף יז:
עט ח מיי' פ"ד מהלכות חמץ הל' ה טוש"ע א"ח סי' תמא ס"א:
פ ט שם סעיף ג:

שם איתא רמי

כיון דלכלי מכר"ס

אין משיחין את התנור באליה ואם טש כל הפת כולה אסורה עד שיסיק את התנור הא הוסק התנור מיהא שרי תיובתא דרבא בר אהילאי תיובתא אמר ליה רבינא לרב אשי וכי מאחר דאיתותב רבא בר אהילאי אמאי קאמר רב קדירות בפסח ישברו אמר ליה התם תנור של מתכת הכא בקדיר' של חרס ואיבעית אימא הא והא בשל חרס וזה הסיקו מבפנים וזה הסיקו מבחוץ וכי תימא ה"נ ליעבד ליה הסקה מבפנים *חיים עליה משום דפקעה הלכך האי *בוכיא הסיקו מבחוץ הוא ואסור ואי מלייה גומרי שפיר דמי א"ל רבינא לרב אשי הני סכיני (א) בפסחא היכי עבדינן להו אמר ליה לדידי חדתא קא עבדינן אמר ליה תינח מר דאפשר ליה דלא אפשר ליה מאי אמר ליה אנא כעין חדתא קאמינא קתייהו בטינא ופרזלייהו בנורא והדר מעיילנא לקתייהו ברותחין והלכתא אידי ואידי ברותחין ובכלי ראשון אמר רב הונא בריה דרב יהושע עץ פרור מגעילו ברותחין ובכלי ראשון קסבר כבולעו כך פולטו *בעו מיניה (ב) מאמימר הני מאני דקוניא מהו לאישתמושי בהו בפסחא ירוקא לא תיבעי לך דודאי אסירי כי תיבעי לך אוכמי וחיורי מאי והיכא דאית בהו קרטופני לא תיבעי לך דודאי אסירי כי תיבעי לך דשיעי מאי א"ל חזינא להו דמידייתי אלמא בלעי ואסירי (ג) והתורה העידה על כלי חרס שאינו יוצא מידי דופיו לעולם ומאי שנא *לענין יין נסך דדריש מרימר מאני דקוניא בין אוכמא בין חיורי ובין ירוקי שרי וכי תימא יין נסך דרבנן חמץ דאורייתא (ד) *כל דתקון רבנן כעין דאורייתא תקון אמר ליה זה תשמישו על ידי חמין וזה תשמישו על ידי צונן אמר רבא בר אבא אמר רב חייא בר אשי אמר שמואל *כל הכלים שנשתמשו בהן חמץ בצונן משתמש בהן מצה חוץ מן בית שאור הואיל שחימוצו קשה אמר רב אשי ובית חרוסת כבית שאור שחימוצו קשה דמי אמר רבא הני אגני דמחוזא הואיל ותדירי למילש בהו חמירא ומשהו בהו חמירא כבית שאור שחימוצו קשה דמי פשיטא מהו דתימא כיון דרויחא שליט בהו אוירא ולא בלעי קמ"ל: **מתני' נכרי שהלוה את ישראל על חמצו אחר הפסח מותר בהנאה וישראל שהלוה את נכרי על חמצו אחר הפסח אסור בהנאה: **גמ'** איתמר בעל חוב אביי אמר למפרע הוא גובה ורבא אמר מכאן ולהבא הוא גובה כל היכא דאקדיש לוה וזבין לוה כולי עלמא לא פליגי דאתי מלוה וטריף ואתי

והלכתא אידי ואידי ברותחין. תימה דתניא בתוספתא דע"ז הסכין והשפוד והאסכלא מלבנן באור ובפרק קמא דחולין (דף ח: ושם) אמר כגון שליבנה באור אלמא צריך ליבון ותירץ ר"ת דהתם בירושלמי דמיירי בסכינים ארוכים שצולין בהם בשר דומיא דשפוד וכן ההוא דחולין ועוד יש לחלק בין היתירא בלע ובין איסורא בלע כדמחלק רב אשי בשילהי מסכת ע"ז והא דמצריך להו רב אשי הכא ליבון מחמיר על עצמו היה: **התורה** העידה על כלי חרס שאינו יוצא מידי דופיו לעולם דכתיב ביה ישבר. וא"ת תיפוק ליה דחזינן להו דמידייתי והיינו אחר הגעלה דאי לפני הגעלה אטו כלים נמי מידייתי וי"ל דלעולם מיירי קודם הגעלה וכמו שפ"ה בע"ז (דף לד.) דמידייתי בחוץ וכיון דמדייתי מבחוץ בלעי טפי וא"ת והלא יוצא מידי דופיו ע"י כבשונות דבזבחים בפ' דם חטאת (דף צו. ושם) פריך וליהדריהו לכבשונות ואמאי קדירות במקדש ישברו ומשני לפי שאין כבשונות בירושלים הא יש כבשונות שרו בחזרה לכבשונות וכן לעיל אמר (אבל) קדירה לא דלמא חיים עלה הא לאו הכי שרי קדירות בהיסק מבפנים וכן אמר אי מליה גומרי שפיר דמי ואור"ת דזה לא חשיב יוצא מידי דופיו דכיון שהסיקו נעשה ככלי חדש שכן דרך כלי חרס כשעושין אותו נותנו אותו בכבשן להסיקו וא"ת והיכי מייתי ראיה מדכתיב ישבר דילמא גזירת הכתוב הוא דאפי' תלאו באויר התנור בעי התם *רבא בר חמא אי קפיד רחמנא אבישול בלא בלוע או לא וי"ל *דלכלי נחושת מועיל שטיפה ומריקה אפילו בבישול ובלוע א"כ מה שהקפיד בכלי חרס אבישול בלא בלוע היינו לפי שעשאו כבישול וכבלוע ולר"ת יש להקשות תנור שנטמא אמאי חולקין לשלשה כיון דחשיב כאחד א' [א] ליעבד ליה היסק ותו לא ונראה לרשב"א *דמיירי בקדרה שאין דרכה להסיק כשמחזירין אותה לכבשונות אז פנים חדשות באו לכאן אבל תנור כל שעה ושעה מסיקו מבפנים ולאו כפנים חדשות דמי וצריך שבירה באחריות:

י"ג דדווקא

טשין. לשון טח: מאחר דאיתותב רבא בר אהילאי. ושמעינן דהיסק מועיל לכלי חרס קדירות בפסח אמאי ישברו יסיקם ויתלבנו: א"ל. רב מוקים ליה להוא דקתני עד שיוסק דמשמע הא הוסק שרי בתנור של מתכת אבל של חרס התורה העידה עליו שאינו יוצא מידי דופיו לעולם: חיים עלייהו. ולאו שרית ליה על ידי היסק פנים מורה היתירא וסמיך אהיסק בחוץ: בוכיא. כלי שהוא מרעפים שקורין טייל"ש ואופין ומטגנין בו ככר: לדידי חדתא עבדא. לצורכי עושין סכינים חדשים: למר אפשר ליה. שהרי עשיר אתה: קתייהו בטינא. להגן עליהם שלא ישרפס האור: והלכתא. לא צריך לאותביניהו בנורא אלא פרזלייהו כי קתייהו נמי סגי להו בהגעל' ברותחין: עץ פרור. שמגיסין בו הקדרה: כבולעו כך פולטו. כבולעו מתוך כלי ראשון כך פולטו בכלי ראשון: קונייא. פלומי"ר בלע"ז ושל חרס הוא וטוח באבר: ירוקי. עשויין מקרקע שחופרים ממנה צריף אלו"ם בלע"ז והוא עז ובולע לעולם: ה"ג ירוקי לא תיבעי לך דודאי אסירי דמצרפי ובלעי. דמצרפי צריף: קרטופני. בקעים: כי תיבעי לך דשיעי. שהן חלקים: דמידייתי. פולטין המשקין מדופנן החיצון ובלע"ז טרשטדט"ש וכיון דמידייתי ודאי בלעי והואיל ובלעי שוב אינן פולטין שהתורה העידה על כלי חרס שכיון שבלע אינו יוצא מידי דופיו לעולם שהרי בכלי עץ ומתכות כתב לך ישטף תעבירו באש ומורק ושוטף אבל בכלי חרס ישבר: חמץ. תשמישו ע"י חמין כל השנה אבל יין נסך לא נשתמש בו אלא צונן: בית חרוסת. כלי שנותנין בו חומץ וכל דבר שיש לו קיהוי ורגילין ליתן בו קמח ועשוי לטבל בו בשר כל ימות השנה והקמח מתחמץ מחמת הקיהוי ולשון חרוסת קיהוי אייגרו"ש בלע"ז: בית שאור. כלי שהאשה שורה ומנחת בו את השאור ונותנתו בעיסה ופעמים שהוא שוהה שם בלילה: אגני. עריבות מיי"ן: **מתני'** נכרי שהלוה את ישראל. מעות על חמצו קודם הפסח ועבר עליו הפסח מותר בהנאה ולקמיה בגמרא מוקי לה כשהרהינו אצלו בביתו ושוהה אצל הנכרי כל ימות הפסח דכיון דמטא זמניה ולא פרעיה ומחוסר גוביינא נמי לא הוה שהרי אצלו נתון איגלאי מילתא למפרע דמשעה שהרהינו אצלו הוה דידיה: ישראל שהלוה את הנכרי כו'. נמי כיון דהרהינו אצלו ומטא זמניה ולא פרעי' מהיא שעתא דאוזפיה קם ליה ברשותיה: **גמ'** בעל חוב. המלוה את חבירו ושיעבד לו נכסיו שאם לא אפרע לך עד יום פלוני גבה מנכסי והגיע זמן ולא פרע: אביי אמר למפרע הוא גובה. גבייתו שגבה עכשיו איגלאי מילתא דמשעה שהלווהו עמדו נכסיו הללו בחזקתו: ורבא אמר. אינן בחזקתו אלא מיכן ולהבא ולקמיה מפרש למאי נפקא מינה: כל היכא דאקדיש לוה. נכסיו בתוך הזמן: או זבין לוה. מוכרן לאחרים: כולי עלמא לא פליגי. אפילו לרבא דאמר עד עכשיו היו ברשות לוה מודה הוא דאין מכירתו לאחרים מכירה ואין הקדישו הקדש שהרי ממושכנין הן למלוה ואף על גב שהן שלו אינן ברשותו ורחמנא אמר (ויקרא כז) ואיש כי יקדיש את ביתו קדש מה ביתו ברשותו אף כל ברשותו: דאתי מלוה וטריף. מן הלקוחות בחנם: ואתי

[עי' תוס' ב"ב קי. ד"ה כשוע]

[וכ"ה בערוך אמנם בזבחים אי' בוכיא וכ"ה בשאלתות פ' מטות סי' קלו וכ"ס בפריש' ביו"ד סי' צ]

ע"ז לג: כתובות קז:

[ע"ז שם]

[לקמן לט: קמו: יומא לא. יבמות יא. גיטין סד: סה. ע"ז לג. כתובות מ.]

הגהות הב"ח

(א) גמרא סכי סכיני דפסחא: (ב) שם בעו מיניה ממרימר הני מאני: (ג) שם בלעי ואסירי פ"ס והתורה העידה: (ד) שם חמץ דאורייתא והא כל דתקון:

הגהות מהר"ץ לגנא

[א] תוס' ד"ה התורה העידה וכו' כיון דחשיב כאחד. נ"ב כיון דחשיב כאחר:

הגהות מהר"ב רנשבורג

[א] תוס' ד"ה התורה העידה כו' כיון

גליון הש"ס גמ' אין טשין. ועי' ב"ב קי ע"א תוד"ה כשוע: דחשיב כאחד. נמחק מלת כאחד וכ"ב צ"ל כאחר ור"ל דחשיב ע"י ההיסק ככלי אחר וכ"ה בתוס' זבחים צ ע"א יש"ש:

רבינו חננאל

בחלב מפני הרגל עבירה כלומר שלא יאכל הפת ההוא בבשר ואם לש כל הפת אסורה כיוצא בו אין (שפין) [טשין] את התנור באליה מפני הרגל עבירה שלא יאכל הפת בחלב ואם (שש) [טש] כל הפת שאפה באותו תנור אסורה עד שיוסק התנור ש"מ שאם הוסק מותר ועלתה בתיובתא (לרבא) [לרבה] בר אהילאי: ואקשי' לרב נמי נסקינהו להני קדרות מבפנים וניבשל בהו ומשני תנור היינו דרך תשמישו והסיקו מבפנים אבל קדרות דלאו היינו אורחייהו ואי אמרת לי' לאסוקינהו מבפנים חאיס עלייהו חאיס דלמא פקעי ולא עביד הלכך גזרי' בהו. פי' בוכיא כגון מגן של חרס שאופין עליו עוגו' אי מלייה גחלי' ואורחתח שפיר דמי לשוייא עליה מצה ואסקנא הסכינין הלכתא ברותחין בכלי ראשון פי' בירה מלאה מים רותחין והיא על גבי כירה וכן עץ פרור והוא התרווד שמנער בו הקדרות רותחו' דקיימ' לן כבולען כך פולטן כשם שבליעתן ברותחין כך פליטתן ברותחין ואסיקנא הני מאני דקוניא פי' כלי חרס שנשתמש בהן נכרי אפי' בשאר ימות השנה אסירי לאשתמושי בהו ישראל בין אוכמי בין חיוארי וכל שכן ירוקא ולא תימא הני דאית בהו קרטופני כגון סדקין [אלא] אע"ג דשיעי כיון דמדייתו כלומר *) נשחורים משחל שחלי וכלהו אסירי להשתמש בהן כל ימות השנה וכל שכן בפסח אבל הני מאני דקוניא דאשתמשו בהו נכרים ביין נסך שרו כדדריש מרימר ואע"ג דחמץ דאורייתא ויין נסך דרבנן וכל דתקון רבנן כעין דאורייתא תקון חמץ בפסח תשמישו בחמין הלכך לעולם אסור אבל יין נסך תשמישו בצונן **) ובהרתחה סגי להו: **אמר** רב זביד הלכתא משמיה דשמואל כל הכלים של חרש שנשתמשו בהן בצונן משתמש בהן בפסח חוץ מבית שאור והוא כלי חרש שמצניעין בו שאור מפני שחימוצו קשה ונבלע כח החימוץ בכלי ובית חרוסת דינו כבית שאור דאסור: **אמר** רבא אגאני דמשהו בהו חמירא אע"ג דרויחי ושליט בהו אוירא כבית שאור דמי ואסירי ולא שרינן מאני דקוניא אלא החדשים וכל שכן כלי חרס אחרים דלא שרו אלא חדשים: **מתני'** נכרי שהלוה את ישראל על חמצו לאחר הפסח מותר בהנאה אוקימנה בשהרהינו אצלו להאי חמץ אצל הנכרי והוא אצל הנכרי וקבע לו זמן קודם הפסח דכיון דעבר הזמן קנייה הנכרי ונעשה כחמצו של נכרי: **איתמר** בעל חוב אביי אמר למפרע הוא גובה משעת ההלואה ואם מכר המלוה או הקדיש נכסיו של לוה והגיע הזמן ולא פרעו נתברר כי מאותה העת של מלוה היה ומה שעשה מאותה העת עשוי ורבא אמר מכאן ולהבא הוא גובה ומה שהקדיש או מכר המלוה לא עשה כלום שלא היו שלו הלא תראה שאלו היה לו מעות ללוה היה מסלקו במעות ולא היה יכול לומר לו הקרקע הוא קנוי לו ונמצא כי עכשיו קנה הנכסים אבל אם מכר הלוה הכל מודים דאתי מלוה וטריף ואי אקדיש

*) תיבות אלו משוללי הבנה ואולי דצ"ל פי' כמו משחילין (כלים ד' לה) ומשחל שחלי (כיומא ד' עח) כצ"ל.

**) נראה דמפרש דמיירי בכלים שמכניסין לקיום וכו'. כן מהא דאמר רבא בע"ז דף עד ע"ב נעוה ארתחו ויותר נראה דע"ס יש כאן וצ"ל וכהדחה סגי להו ועי' היטב בב"י יו"ד סי' קל"ה וסי' קל"ח ודו"ק.

אמר רבא הלכתא "חמץ בזמנו בין במינו בין שלא במינו אסור במשהו כרב [ב]שלא בזמנו בין במינו בין שלא במינו מותר כרבי שמעון ומי אמר רבא הכי והאמר רבא *רבי שמעון קנסא קניס הואיל ועבר עליו בבל יראה ובל ימצא הני מילי בעיניה אבל על ידי תערובת לא ואזדא רבא לטעמיה דאמר רבא כי הוינן בי רב נחמן כי הוו נפקי שבעה יומי דפסחא אמר לן פוקו וזבינו חמירא דבני חילא: *אמר רב קדירות בפסח ישברו ואמאי לשהינהו אחר הפסח וליעבד בהו שלא במינן גזירה דילמא אתו למיעבד בהו במינו ושמואל אמר [ג]לא ישברו אבל משהי להו לאחר זמנו ועביד בהו בין במינו בין שלא במינו ואזדא שמואל לטעמיה דאמר שמואל להנהו דמזבני כנדי אשוו זביני אכנדיכי ואי לא דרשינא לכו כרבי שמעון ולידרוש להו דהא שמואל כרבי שמעון סבירא ליה אתריה דרב הוה *ההוא תנורא דטחו ביה טיחיא אסרה רבא בר אהילאי למיכלי' לריפתא אפי' במילחא לעולם דילמא אתי למיכליה בכותחא מיתיבי *°[ד]אין לשין את העיסה בחלב ואם לש כל הפת כולה אסורה מפני הרגל עבירה כיוצא בו

אין

רש"י

אמר רבא הלכתא כו'. ש"מ דפסק רבא הלכתא דכל איסורין שבתורה במינן במשהו ולא שני לן בין חמץ לשאר איסורי אלא בהא מילתא דגזר שלא במינן אטו מינן שמעינן מינה חלב שנפל לקדירה אוסר במשהו וכן הלכה והא דקי"ל כל איסורין שבתורה בששים בשלא במינן הוא: שלא בזמנו בין במינו בין שלא במינו מותר. אפילו בנותן טעם: אבל ע"י תערובת לא. ואפי' שהייה בעיניה ועבר עליה לא קנים למיסר תערובת דיליה: ואזדא רבא. דאמר הלכה כר' שמעון לטעמיה דאמר נמי בעלמא חמץ של נכרי שעבר עליו הפסח מותר אף באכילה הואיל וליכא למיקנס ביה מידי ואי רבי יהודה חמץ סתמא קאמר ואפילו דנכרי: בני חילא. נכרים אע"פ °שאופיהו יום זה שעבר והוא פסח: אמר רב קדירות בפסח ישברו. רב לטעמיה דאמר חמץ אף לאחר זמנו אסור בהנאה כר' יהודה ואית ליה במשהו וקסבר נותן טעם לפגם אסור ולית הלכתא כוותיה מתרי טעמי חדא דאוקי רבא הלכתא דתערובת לאחר זמנו מותר כר"ש והאי פחות מתערובת הוא ועוד דקי"ל נותן טעם לפגם מותר וזה משעברו עליו ימי הפסח הופג טעמו בדופני הכלי: וליעבד בהו שלא במינו. דהא מודי רב לעיל דחמץ שלא בזמנו שלא במינו במשהו מותר והאי משהו חשיב להו: כנדי. קדרות לאחר הפסח: אשוו זביניכו. אל תעלו דמיהן יותר משוויי': כר"ש. דמותרות הקדרות הישנות לאחר הפסח: כר"ש ס"ל. כדאמרן לעיל: דטחו ביה טיחיא. שומן נתנו בו בקרקעיתו ונותן טעם בלחם: לעולם. אפילו חזר והוסק: אפילו במילחא. להכי נקט אפילו במילחא שאין דרך לאכול פת בלא מלח או ליפתן:

טשין

תוספות

אמר רבא הלכתא חמץ בזמנו בין במינו ובין שלא במינו אסור בכל שהוא כרב. פסק רש"י בחולין דמין במינו במשהו כרבי יהודה דאמר בפ' כל הבשר (חולין קט.) מין במינו לא בטיל ואף רבי קאמר התם נראין דברי רבי יהודה מכלל דהלכתא הכי ועוד הביא ראיה מהא דפליגי אביי ורבא בפרק בתרא דע"ז (דף סו.) אלא דחמרא וחלא דשיכרא חמירא דחיטי וחמירא דשערי רבא אמר במשהו אביי אמר בנותן טעם משום דמר סבר בתר שמא אזלינן ומר סבר בתר טעמא אזלינן אלמא בין לאביי בין לרבא מין במינו במשהו ועוד פסק רבא בשמעתא מין במינו במשהו כרב ור"ת אומר דכל אלו אינם ראיות דאין הלכה לא כר' יהודה ולא *כרבי והביא דפ' בתרא דמס' ע"ז פלוגתא דאביי ורבא אלי למימר דחמירא וחלא לטבל ויין נסך דמודו ר' יוחנן ור"ל שהם במשהו ושמעתא אי גר' במשהו כרב י"ל שפוסק בחמץ כרב ולא מטעמי' דרב דס"ל בכל איסורין שבתורה במינו במשהו ורבא לית ליה אלא דוקא בחמץ בפסח משום חומרא דחמץ וגם רב יהודאי גאון פסק כן דדוקא בחמץ פסק רבא כרב דשאלו מקמיה כל איסורין שבתורה במשהו כרב או בנותן טעם כר"ש והשיב מדאמר רבא חמץ בזמנו בין במינו בין שלא במינו במשהו א"כ בהא [מיהו] הלכה כרב במשהו אבל בשאר איסורין בנ"ט כר' יוחנן וכר"ל ועוד אומר ר"ת דלא גרסי' במשהו כרב וכן משמע בה"ג דלא גרס ליה וסבר רבא גם בחמץ כר' יוחנן והא דלא פסק בהדיא הלכה כר' יוחנן משום דה"א דלא פסק כוותיה אלא בזמנו אבל שלא בזמנו לא דלא תקשי דרבא אדרבא דהא אמר רבא קנסא הוא דקניס ר' שמעון כדפרי' להכי איצטריך לפרש ומביא ר"ת ראיה דבהדיא סבירא ליה לרבא בפ' גיד הנשה (חולין צז: ושם) מין במינו בס' דקאמר אמרו רבנן בטעמא וכו' מין במינו דליכא למיקם אטעמא אי נמי מין שלא במינו וליכא קפילא בס' ואין לדחות דמיירי בחמרא חדתא ועינבי דהוי טעמא אחד והוי בס' משום דרבא בתר שמא אזיל ולא חשיב מינו דא"כ אמאי קרי ליה מין במינו ובהקומץ רבה (מנחות כג. ושם) משני רבא דסבר ר' יהודה מין במינו וד"א וכו' מכלל דאיהו לית ליה ובפ' התערובת (זבחים עט. ושם) קסבר ר"א בן יעקב מין במינו בטל וסתמא דגמרא קאמר בשילהי מסכת ביצה (ד' לט: ושם) שפיר עבוד דאחיכו עליה חיטי בחיטי נהי דלרבי יהודה לא בטל לרבנן מיבטל בטיל מכלל דהכי הלכתא ורש"י גופיה פסק בפרק בתרא דמס' ע"ז (ד' סו.) גבי פלוגתא דאביי ורבא דהלכתא כרבי יוחנן דסבר בנ"ט ובה"ג של אספמיא פסק דאתיכה באתיכות בנ"ט ומייתי מדרבא בפ' גיד הנשה (חולין צז.) ויין נסך דקאמר התם במשהו אומר ר"ת דוקא כשנתנסך לפני ע"ז דלמתני' קאי דבעי תרתי דבר שבמנין ואיסורי הנאה °אבל סתם יינן דשרי בהנאה בס' ובתשובת הגאונים שכתב רבינו יוסף טוב עלם מצא ר"ת יין נסך שנתנסך ממנו לפני ע"ז אסור בהנאה ואינו בטל אפילו באלף כמו ששנינו *אלו אסורין ואיסורן איסור הנאה בכל שהוא יין נסך וכו' מכלל דשאר איסורין וסתם יינן חוץ מטבל ויין נסך בין במינו ובין שלא במינו בנ"ט ובחמץ בפסח לא עשה ר"ת מעשה אע"ג דבשאלתות דרב אחאי* נמי איתא דרבא אית ליה גם בחמץ בנ"ט: [וע"ע תוס' חולין צז. ד"ה אמר רבא]:

אמר רב קדירות בפסח ישברו. בפ' בתרא דמס' ע"ז (דף סח: ושם) גבי עכברא בשיכרא מספקא ליה אי קסבר רב נותן טעם לפגם אסור או מותר ועכבר' בשיכרא אשבוחי משבח ואי ס"ל מותר אפ"ה קאמר הכא שפיר ישברו דנ"ט לפגם דוקא בדיעבד שרי אבל לכתחלה אסור דגזרינן שאינו בת יומא אטו בת יומא ועוד דהתם שרי לפי שפוגם טעמו כמו שהוא בעין אבל הכא אינו פוגם אלא מחמת ששהה בדופני הכלי: לשהינהו עד אחר הפסח וליעבד בהו שלא במינן. תימה לר"י נהי דסבירא לן דטעמא דחמץ בקדירה חשיב משהו שאין רגילין להשתמש הרבה ביחד מ"מ הא תנן אין מבטלין איסור לכתחלה ואפי' איסורא דרבנן אין מבטלין דאם לא כן מה הועילו חכמים בתקנתם שאסרו עד ששים הואיל שיכול להוסיף ולבטל האיסור ולא דמי לעצים שנשרו מן הדקל לתנור בי"ט שמרבה עליהן עצים מוכנים ומסיקן (ביצה ד' ד:) דהתם איסור מוקצה אין לו שורש מן התורה אבל מידי דאית לי' שורש מן התורה לא ומפרש ה"ר יוסף הואיל ואיכא תרתי לטיבותא שהוא נותן טעם לפגם ומשהו שלא במינו בכה"ג מבטלין ולדבריו נ"ל דה"פ וליעבד שלא במינו אי ס"ל לרב נותן טעם לפגם מותר ור"י מפרש דכיון שהקדירות של חרס הן אם יהיו אסורין ואין להם תקנה זה חשוב דיעבד ואע"ג דלענין איסור קדירה שאין בת יומא אסרינן לה אע"פ שאין לה תקנה משום דהתם בלע איסור הרבה אבל הכא ליכא אלא משהו והואיל ושלא במינו הוא יכול לבטל וכדיעבד דמי: דילמא אתי למיעבד במינו. לעיל לא גזר שלא במינו אטו מינו דהא לא שכיח שיתערב לו חמץ אבל הכא להתיר לבשל בהן איכא למיגזר: ואפילו במלחא. והא דאמר בכיצד צולין (לקמן עו:) פת שאפאה עם הצלי בתנור אסור לאוכלו בכותח אבל במלח שרי התם לא אסירא אלא מטעם ריח דליכא איסור כולי האי: דילמא אתי למיכליה בכותח. ותימה וליכליה בכותח דהא נותן טעם בנ"ט הוא כדאמר בפ' כל הבשר (חולין קיא: ושם) דגים שעלו בקערה מותר לאוכלן בכותח וי"ל דקאמר התם נמי צנון שחתכו בסכין אסור לאוכלו בכותח ופרש"י משום חורפא דצנון בלע טפי מדגים רותחים שעלו בקערה ולפי זה דגים שנתבשלו בקדירה אסור לאוכלן בכותח דע"י בישול בלעי יותר מדאי וכן נמי הכא מחום התנור בלעי טפי ולפי' אחר שפ"ה שם דצנון אסור לפי שפעמים שהשמנונית קרוש על הסכין ואינו ניכר ואיכא בצנון טעם בשר ממש קשה הכא כיון שנתקנח התנור יפה או הוסק פעם אחרת אמאי אסור לאוכלו בכותח וי"ל דשומן שעל החרס אינו יכול °לקנח יפה:

והלכתא

רבינו חננאל

בין במינו בין שלא במינו מותר כר' שמעון: אמר רבא הלכתא חמץ בפסח שהוא זמן איסורו בין במינו בין שלא במינו אסור במשהו כרב לאחר הפסח שלא בזמנו בין במינו בין שלא במינו מותר כר' שמעון דהא רב ושמואל ור' יוחנן שלא בזמנו כולן שוין בזה שמותר. ואקשינן ומי אמר רבא הכי והא רבא הוא דאוקימתא' כר' שמעון דאמר אע"ג דסבר ר' שמעון דחמץ לאחר הפסח שרי קנס משום דעבר עליה בבל יראה ובל ימצא ושני' אין ר' שמעון לעולם קנים לאחר הפסח מידו לא קנים אלא היכא דאיתיה לחמץ שעבר עליו הפסח בעיניה אבל על ידי תערובות אפי' במינו לא קנים: ואזדא רבא לטעמיה דאמר כי הוינא בי רב נחמן כי הוו נפקו יומי דפסחא הוה אמר לן פוקו אייתו חמירא דבני חילא מראין הדברים דחמירא *) דא דבני חילא ברשות ישראל הות ואע"ג דכדידהו הות דמיא הוה שרי רב נחמן דהא על ידי תערובות היא: אמר רב קדרות בפסח ישברו חיישינן לשהויינהו לאחר הפסח ולבשל בהו שלא במינן גזרה דלמא אתי לבשל בהו במינן ושמואל אמר אחר זמנן מותר לבשל בהו בין במינן בין שלא במינן ואזדא שמואל לטעמיה דאמר שמואל להני דמזבני כנדי פי' כנדי כגון אנני דפחרא אשוו זבינו כלומר מכרו בזול ולא תמכרו ביוקר ואי לא דרשינא לכו כר' שמעון דשרי בישינים לאחר הפסח בין במינו בין שלא במינן והאי דלא דרש להו דמשום אתריה דרב [הוה] ולא הוה בעי לאורוי קמיה דרב וקיי"ל בהא כשמואל: ההוא תנורא דטחיה בשומן של בשר אסריה (רבא) [רבה] בר אהילאי למיפא ביה פת לעולם אע"פ שמסיקין אותו חייש דלמא אתו למיכל הפת ההוא בחלב ומותבינן עליה אין לשין העיסה בחלב

*) עיין לעיל דף כ ע"ב א"ל רבא לבני מחוזא בעירו חמירא דבני חילא וכו' וע"ע היטב בהשגות הראב"ד כפ"ד מהל' חו"מ הלכה ג' ובכ"מ ובלח"מ שם ועי' בח"י סי' ת"מ סק"ד בשם הירושלמי ודו"ק.

עין משפט נר מצוה

סט א מיי' פ"א מהל' חמץ הל' ה ופט"ו מהל' מאכלות אסורות הל' ט סמג לאוין עח טוש"ע א"ח סי' תמז סעיף א:

ע ב מיי' שם טוש"ע שם סעיף יא:

עא ג מיי' פ"ה מהל' חו"מ הל' כה סמג שם טוש"ע א"ח סי' תנא סעיף א:

עב ד מיי' פ"ט מהל' מאכלות אסורות הל' כב סמג לאוין קמא טוש"ע יו"ד סימן צז סעיף א:

י"ג מרכ

[ע"ז עד. ע"ש]

[פ' לו סי' ס]

מסורת הש"ס

[לעיל כט.]

זבחים לה:

[עס]

לקמן לו. זבחים לה: ב"מ לא.

גליון הש"ס

גמ' אין לשין את העיסה בחלב. עי' שבת עח ע"ב תד"ה תחת איסטוגי: רש"י ד"ה בני חילא כו' שאופיהו. עי' ב"י יו"ד סי' קיג: תוס' ד"ה אמר רבא אבל סתם יינם דשרי בהנאה כו'. לא סתם יינם אסור בהנאה כדמוכח בכמה דוכתי במס' ע"ז ושם ובחולין מתכני הו' סתם אסור סתם יינם בטל בס'. וכן נלע"ד דע"ס הוא כתוס: תוס' ד"ה דלמא אתי כו' אינו יכול לקנח יפה. עי' מ"ק דף יז ע"א ברש"י ד"ה ומכניס כי שמיא:

[30a] Raba said: The law is: Leaven, in its time, whether [mixed] with its own kind or with a different kind, is forbidden [even] when there is a minute quantity, in accordance with Rab; when not in its time, whether [mixed] with its own kind or with a different kind, it is permitted, in accordance with R. Simeon. Yet did
a Raba say thus?[1] Surely Raba said, R. Simeon does indeed penalize him, since he transgressed *'there shall not be seen'* and *'there shall not be found'* with it?[2]—That is only in its natural state, but not when it is in a mixture.[3] Now Raba[4] is consistent with his view, For Raba said: When we were at R. Naḥman's house, when the seven days of Passover were gone he would say to us, 'Go out and buy leaven from the troops.'[5]

Rab said: Pots must be broken on Passover.[6] Why so? Let them be kept until after Passover and used with a different kind?[7]—Lest he come to use it with its own kind. But Samuel maintained: They need not be broken, but can be kept until after its period and [then] used with their own kind[8] or with a different kind. Now Samuel is consistent with his view. For Samuel said to the hardware merchants:[9] Charge an equitable price for your pots, for if not I will publicly lecture [that the law is] in accordance with R. Simeon.[10] Then let him lecture [thus] to them [in any
b case], seeing that Samuel holds as R. Simeon?[1]—It was Rab's town.

A certain oven was greased with fat.[2] [Thereupon] Raba b. Ahilai forbade for all time[3] the bread [baked therein] to be eaten even with salt, lest he come to eat it with *kutaḥ*.[4] An objection is raised: One must not knead dough with milk, and if he does knead it, the whole loaf is forbidden, because it leads to sin.[5] Similarly,

a (1) That the leaven mixture is permitted after Passover. (2) V. *supra* 29a. (3) Even if he kept it in its natural, unmixed state during Passover and then it became mixed with other food, R. Simeon does not penalize him by disqualifying the mixture. (4) Who accepts the ruling of R. Simeon. (5) Gentile troops quartered in the town, though they had baked it on Passover.—Their leaven was permitted after Passover since no transgression had been committed with it.—In the Diaspora Passover is kept for *eight* days, not seven. Raba probably mentions 'seven' loosely, using the Biblical phraseology, while meaning eight; v. S. Strashun. R. Ḥan. simply reads: 'when the days of Passover etc.'. V., however, Obermeyer, p. 99. (6) Pots in which leaven is cooked absorb and retain some of the leaven. Now Rab holds that *all* leaven kept over Passover is forbidden after Passover, which includes absorbed leaven. Further, when other food is cooked in it after Passover the absorbed leaven imparts a flavour, and though it has a deteriorating effect, Rab holds that even such disqualifies the food. Thus the pots cannot be used after Passover; hence they must be broken. (7) For only a very minute quantity is absorbed, and such, even according to Rab, does not disqualify a different kind. (8) I.e., the same kind of leaven which was cooked in them before Passover. (9) Lit., 'sellers of pots'. (10) People did break their pots before Passover, and the merchants took advantage of the increased demand after Passover to raise prices. Thereupon Samuel threatened them that he would publicly lecture that leaven kept over Passover is not forbidden, so that people need not break their pots.

b (1) As stated *supra*. (2) Lit., 'grease'. (3) Even if the oven should be fired and burnt through again. (4) A preserve consisting of sour milk, bread-crusts and salt (Jast.). The bread of course receives the flavour of the fat, and must not be eaten with anything containing milk or a milk product. (5) One may come to eat it with meat.

R. Aḥa b. Raba recited [29b] this discussion in R. Joseph's name in the following version: All agree that one may not redeem sacred food in order to feed it to dogs, but here they differ in this, viz., whether that which has indirect monetary value[2] is as money. He who says [that] he commits trespass holds, That which has indirect monetary value is as money; while he who maintains [that] he does not commit trespass holds, That which has indirect monetary value is not as money.[3] R. Aḥa b. Jacob said: All agree that that which has indirect monetary value is as money, but here they differ in the controversy of R. Judah and R. Simeon. He who says [that] he is not liable for trespass holds as R. Judah;[4] while he who rules [that] he is liable for trespass
a agrees with R. Simeon.[1] But it was R. Aḥa b. Jacob himself who said that R. Judah learns *se'or* of 'eating' from *se'or* of 'seeing'?[2] —Hence R. Aḥa b. Jacob retracted from that [statement].

R. Ashi said: All hold that we may not redeem [etc.], and that which has indirect monetary value is not as money. But here they differ in the controversy of R. Jose the Galilean and the Rabbis. He who rules [that] he is liable to trespass holds as R. Jose;[3] while he who rules [that] he is not liable for trespass agrees with the Rabbis.

Rab said: Leaven, in its time,[4] whether [mixed] with its own kind or with a different[5] kind, is forbidden; when not in its time, [if mixed] with its own kind, it is forbidden; [if with] a different kind, it is permitted. What are we discussing: Shall we say, where it imparts [its] taste [to the mixture], then [how state] when not in its time, if [mixed] with a different kind it is permitted? Surely it imparts taste![6]—Rather it refers to a minute quantity [of leaven]:[7] 'leaven in its time, whether [mixed] with its own kind or with a different kind, is forbidden', Rab being consistent with his view. For Rab and Samuel both said: All forbidden things of the Torah, [if mixed] with their own kind, [render forbidden the mixture even] when there is a minute quantity; [if] with a different kind, [only] when [the forbidden element] imparts its taste. Now Rab forbade leaven in its time [when mixed] with a different kind on account of [a mixture with] its own kind. When not in its period [and mixed] with its own kind, it [the mixture] is forbidden in accordance with R. Judah: but [when mixed] with a different kind it is permitted, because [to forbid it] when not in its time and [mixed] with a different kind on account of [a mixture] with its own kind,—to that extent we do not enact
b a preventive measure.[1]

Samuel said: Leaven, in its time, [if mixed] with its own kind, is forbidden; if with a different kind, it is permitted. When not in its time, whether [mixed] with its own kind or with a different kind, it is permitted. 'Leaven, in its time, [if mixed] with its own kind, is forbidden.' Samuel is consistent with his view. For Rab and Samuel both said: All prohibited things of the Torah, [if mixed] with their own kind, [render forbidden the mixture even] when there is a minute quantity; [if mixed] with a different kind, [only] when [the forbidden element] imparts [its] flavour. Now he does not forbid [leaven mixed] with a different kind on account of [a mixture with] its own kind. 'When not in its time, whether [mixed] with its own kind or with a different kind, it is permitted,'—in accordance with R. Simeon.

While R. Joḥanan said: Leaven, in its time, whether [mixed] with its own kind or with a different kind, is forbidden when it imparts [its] taste; when not in its time, whether [mixed] with its own kind or with a different kind, it is permitted. 'Leaven, in its time, whether [mixed] with its own kind or with a different kind, [is forbidden] when it imparts [its] taste.' R. Joḥanan is consistent with his view. For R. Joḥanan and Resh Laḳish both maintain: All forbidden things in the Torah, whether [mixed] with their own kind or with a different kind, [render forbidden the mixture only] when they impart [their] taste.' 'When not in its time, whether [mixed] with its own kind or with a different kind, it is permitted,'—in accordance with R. Simeon.

(2) Lit., 'a thing which leads to money'. (3) On this version both Tannaim agree with R. Simeon. Thus it has no present value at all, save an indirect value, since it can be used after Passover, and they disagree as to whether this deferred value can be regarded as immediate value. (4) That all benefit is forbidden to an Israelite even after Passover, so that the leaven has no monetary value at all; nor has it any indirect monetary value, since it cannot be redeemed to feed it to dogs by selling it to a non-Jew for the purpose.

a (1) That it is permissible for general use after Passover, even to an Israelite, and that it has a monetary value. (2) Whereby leaven of *hekdesh* is permitted for use during Passover even according to R. Judah. (3) That benefit is permitted even during Passover. This leaven could be redeemed and used as fuel. (4) V. *supra* 28b, n. b4. (5) Lit., 'not with its kind'—and similarly in the whole passage. (6) It is a general principle that if something forbidden is mixed with something permitted and imparts its taste thereto, the whole mixture is prohibited. (7) Insufficient to impart a flavour to the other.

b (1) *Gazar* means to enact a preventive measure, i.e., to forbid one case which should be permitted because it might otherwise be thought that another case, which is actually forbidden, is permitted too.

פו א מיי' פ"ו מהלכות מאכלות אסורות הל' ז ... ח"מ סי' ... סעיף א:
פח ב מיי' פ"ו מהל' מאכלות אסורות הלכה ו סמג לאוין קמא טוש"ע י"ד סימן ... סעיף א:

לדהא שמעתא משמית דרב יוסף בהא לישנא דכולי עלמא אין פודין את הקדשים להאכילן לכלבים והכא בהא קמיפלגי בדבר הגורם לממון כממון דמי מאן דאמר מעל *קסבר *דבר הגורם לממון כממון דמי ומאן דאמר לא מעל קסבר דבר הגורם לממון לאו כממון דמי רב אחא בר יעקב אמר דכולי עלמא דבר הגורם לממון כממון דמי והכא בפלוגתא דרבי יהודה ורבי שמעון קמיפלגי מאן דאמר לא מעל כרבי יהודה ומאן דאמר מעל כר"ש והא רב אחא בר יעקב הוא דאמר דר' יהודה יליף שאור דאכילה משאור דראייה אלא הדר ביה רב אחא בר יעקב מההיא רב אשי אמר דכולי עלמא אין פודין ודבר הגורם לממון לאו כממון דמי והכא בפלוגתא דרבי יוסי הגלילי ורבנן קמיפלגי מאן דאמר מעל כרבי יוסי ומאן דאמר לא מעל כרבנן: אמר רב חמץ בזמנו בין במינו בין שלא במינו אסור שלא בזמנו במינו אסור שלא במינו מותר במאי עסקינן אילימא בנותן טעם שלא בזמנו שלא במינו מותר הא יהיב טעמא אלא במשהו חמץ בזמנו בין במינו בין שלא במינו אסור רב לטעמיה *דרב ושמואל דאמרי תרוייהו כל איסורין שבתורה במינן במשהו שלא במינן בנותן טעם רב גזר חמץ בזמנו שלא במינו אטו מינו ושלא בזמנו במינו אסור כרבי יהודה ושלא בזמנו שלא במינו מותר ד"שלא בזמנו ושלא במינו אטו מינו כולי האי לא גזרינן שמואל אמר חמץ בזמנו במינו אסור שלא במינו מותר שלא בזמנו בין במינו בין שלא במינו מותר חמץ בזמנו במינו אסור שמואל לטעמיה דרב ושמואל דאמרי תרוייהו כל איסורין שבתורה במינן אסורין במשהו שלא במינן בנותן טעם שלא במינן אטו מינן לא גזר שלא בזמנו בין במינן בין שלא במינן מותרין כר' שמעון ורבי יוחנן אמר חמץ בזמנו בין במינו ובין שלא במינו אסור בנותן טעם שלא בזמנו בין במינו בין שלא במינו מותר חמץ בזמנו בין במינו בין שלא במינו בנותן טעם ר' יוחנן לטעמיה *דר' יוחנן וריש לקיש דאמרי תרוייהו °כל איסורין שבתורה בין במינן בין שלא במינן בנותן טעם שלא בזמנו בין במינן בין שלא במינן מותרין כר' שמעון

אמר

להא שמעתא. דרב יוסף: דכולי עלמא אין פודין. ואליבא דר' שמעון הוא דפליגי דשרי ליה לאחר פסח אף לאכילת ישראל ובהא פליגי מאן דאמר מעל סבר אף על גב דהשתא לא חזי הואיל ולקמיה גורם לממון הוא כממון דמי: הכי גרסינן רב אחא בר יעקב אמר דכולי עלמא כממון דמי: ומאן דאמר לא מעל. כרבי יהודה דאמר אף לאחר הפסח אסור בהנאה וכל שכן בפסח עצמו הלכך לאו ממון איכא דלישראל לא חזי ולאו גורם לממון איכא שאם יפדה לא יהנה ממנו ולנכרי לא מזדבן דאין פודין את הקדשים להאכילן לכלבים: ומ"ד מעל כר"ש. דאמר ראוי הוא לאחר הפסח אף (לאדם) [לישראל] והו"ל גורם לממון: משאור דראייה. ושל הקדש אף בפסח מותר והכא אמר לרבי יהודה לא מעל: הכי גרסינן רב אשי אמר דכולי עלמא אין פודין ודבר הגורם לממון לאו כממון דמי. כלומר דכולי עלמא לנכרי לא מזבנינן ליה בפסח ומשום דלאחר הפסח דחזי לישראל לא מחייבי ליה דדבר הגורם לממון לאו כממון דמי והכא טעמא דמעילה משום דסבר לה כרבי יוסי הגלילי דאמר אף תוך זמנו מותר בהנאה הלכך חזי למפרקיה ולהסיקו תחת תבשילו ומאן דאמר לא מעל כרבנן דאמרי חמץ בפסח אסור בהנאה ואי משום דמלי לשהויי לאחר זמן כר"ש השתא מיהא לאו ממון הוא: חמץ בזמנו וכו'. מפרש כוליה לקמיה: אי נימא בנותן טעם שלא בזמנו שלא במינו מותר. בתמיה הא יהיב טעמא ורב מדקאמר שלא בזמנו במינו אסור גלי דעתיה דכר' יהודה סבירא ליה דאמר אף לאחר הפסח אסור: שלא במינו. נמי בזמנו אסור ואע"ג דלית ליה לרב בכל איסורין שלא במינו בנותן טעם רב גזר בחמץ בזמנו הואיל ובכרת הוא שלא במינו אטו מינו ואע"ג דבחלב ודם לא גזר שלא במינו אטו מינו התם הוא דבדילי מיניה אבל חמץ לא בדילי מיניה הואיל ואוכלו כל ימות השנה: שלא בזמנו במינו אסור כרבי יהודה. דאמר לאחר הפסח דאורייתא הלכך אף תערובת אסור: שלא במינו מותר. דשלא בזמנו דאינו בכרת שלא במינו אטו מינו לא גזר כי היכי דלא גזר בבשר בחלב ובשאר איסורין: ושמואל אמר כו'. במשהו עסקינן שלא במינו מותר כשאר איסורין דלא גזר שמואל בחמץ שלא במינו אטו מינו: כרבי שמעון. דלאחר זמנו שרי ואפי' בנותן טעם נמי שרי ולקמן פריך והא אסר ליה ר' שמעון משום קנסא:

אמר

לפדותו ומותר בהנאה ויש לומר דכיון דכמו שהוא עכשיו לא שוי מידי לא שייכא ביה מעילה והיינו נמי טעמא דכל איסורי הנאה אין מקדשין בהן דאשה אע"ג דכל הנשרפין אפרן מותר ואפילו אי דבר הגורם לממון כממון דמי ומעל לא דמי דהתם חזי לאחר הפסח שהוא כמו בעין ועוד יש לומר הא דאין מקדשין באיסורי הנאה היינו היכא דלית ביה שוה פרוטה לכשיהא אפר ולתירוץ קמא קשה (א) הא חזי בעיניה שלא כדרך הנאה*: **הדר** ביה רב אחא. תימה דבפרק קמא דחולין (דף ד:) אמר סברוה הא מני ר' יהודה דאמר חמנן של עוברי עבירה לאחר הפסח מותר מיד מפני שמחליפים והכא מסקינן לר' יהודה אפילו חמץ של נכרי אסור אחר הפסח ויש לומר דהתם סברוה כס"ד דהכא לרב אחא מעיקרא ורבינו תם מפרש לאו דווקא מיד דהא צריך שיהא שיעור להחליף והוא הדין שיהא חמץ זה ראוי לעשות אחר הפסח: **רב** אשי אמר דכולי עלמא. וקשה לר"י היכי גרסינן אי גרסינן דכולי עלמא פודין אם כן לרבנן אמאי לא מעל אף על גב דלישראל אסור בהנאה מכל מקום ימכרנו לנכרי ההקדש עצמו ואי גרים אין פודין אפילו לרבי יוסי הגלילי אמאי מעל ויש לומר דגרסי' אין פודין ואף על גב דאין פודין להאכיל לכלבים מכל מקום שרי להסיק תחת תבשילו *וכפרישית דהכא דקדושת דמים אין פודין מדרבנן ולא גזרו רבנן אלא שלא להאכילו לכלבים אבל היכא דאין פודין מדאורייתא דהיינו היכא דאיכא קדושת הגוף אין פודין אפי' להסיק דהא תניא (*בפ"ק) דבכורות (דף טו.) אם מתו יקברו וקאמר התם ממאי דהאי אם מתו יקברו משום דבעי העמדה והערכה דילמא משום דאין פודין הקדשים להאכילן לכלבים והשתא אי טעמא משום דאין פודין אמאי יקברו והא ראוי להסיקו תחת תבשילו אלא ודאי מדאורייתא אין חילוק וכן לעיל (דף כב.) דרשינן ואי אתה מוליך לכלב כל איסורין שבתורה ואסירי אפילו להסקה אלמא מדאורייתא אין לחלק בהנאה ואם תאמר לרבנן אמאי לא מעל הלא הקדש יכול למכור לנכרי על מנת שיסיקנו לפניו ויש לומר דגזרינן שמא יאכלנו הנכרי וכהאי גוונא אמר במסכת ע"ז (דף טו.) אין מוכרין בהמה לנכרי על מנת לשוחטה וכו' ומכאן מוכיח ר"י שהמשהה חמץ בפסח ודעתו לבערו אינו עובר באותה שהייה דלאי אמרת עובר אכתי אמאי מעל לרבי יוסי הא מיד כשיפדה אותו הוא שלו ומודה רבי יוסי דשלך אי אתה רואה אלא ודאי לא עבר וטעמא משום דלא ירחה *ניתק לעשה ולכך אינו עובר כשמבערו לבסוף:

אמר

[וע"ש תוס' קדושין מ: ד"ה כמקדש וכו']

[ועי' תוס' ב"ק עג: ד"ה לענין כלים]

[צ"ל בפ"ב]

[לעיל ט: כתובות לד. ב"ק עא: [קה.] שבועות לב. לג.]

ע"ז עג:

[פי' לקמן ל. תד"ה כפרטיה]

הגהות הב"ח

(א) תוס' ד"ה אין פודין וכו' ולתירוץ קמא קשה. נ"ב עיין בתוס' פ' האשה מקדש דף נ ע"ב ד"ה המקדש בערלה:

רבינו חננאל

פי' דבר הגורם לממון כגון מי שגזל חמץ זה של הקדש אם הוא בעינו מחזירו לו לנגזל ופטור דתנן גזל חמץ ועבר עליו הפסח אומר לו הרי שלך לפניך וכיון שאכלו נתחייב הגזלן לשלם לו ממון ואע"פ שהחמץ בפסח אינו ממון השבתתו גורם ממון. רב אחא בר יעקב אומר כולי עלמא דבר הגורם לממון לאו כממון דמי והכא בפלוגתא דר' שמעון ורבנן פליגי ת"ק כר' שמעון דאמר תוך זמנו הוא דעבר עליו בלאו לאחר זמנו אינו עובר עליו בלא כלום וממון מעליא הוא לפיכך מעל ויש אומרים כר' יהודה דאמר אפי' לאחר זמנו עובר בלאו ואמרינן והא רב אחא הוא דאמר דר' יהודה יליף שאור דאכילה משאור דראיה מה שאור דראיה של גבוה מותר בראיה כך שאור דאכילה של גבוה מותר לאחר זמנו אפי' באכילה ולמה לא מעל אלא ודאי הדר ביה: **רב** אשי אמר כולי עלמא אין פודין קדשים להאכילן לכלבים ודבר הגורם לממון לאו כממון דמי והכא בפלוגתא דר' יוסי הגלילי ורבנן קא מיפלגי ת"ק כר' יוסי הגלילי דקתני ותמה על עצמך האיך חמץ אסור בהנאה כל שבעה ויש אומרים כרבנן. ירושלמי מתני' דקתני חמץ של נכרי שעבר עליו הפסח מותר בהנאה במקום שלא נהגו לאכול פת של נכרים אבל במקום שנהגו לאכלו מותר אפי' באכילה פי' כגון שהיה ישראל רואהו ומסייעו באפיית אותה הפת וקיי"ל בזמן שישראל רואהו כגון תבצקת של נכרים דאמור רבנן אדם ממלא כרסו מהן אלו וכיוצא בהן: **אם** היה גגו של נכרי סמוך לגגו של ישראל הרי זה דוחפו בקנה היתה שבת או יום טוב כופה עליו כלי. רב אמר צריך שיאמר בשעה שיבער בא"י אמ"ה אקב"ו על בעור חמץ וצריך נמי שיאמר כל חמץ שישנו ברשותי ואיני יודע בו יהא בטל: **אמר** רב חמץ בזמנו בין במינו בין שלא במינו אסור אפי' במשהו רב לטעמיה דאמר כל איסורין שבתורה במינו במשהו וגזרה שלא במינו אטו במינו. שלא בזמנו כלומר אחר הפסח במינו אסור במשהו סבר לה כר' יהודה שלא במינו לאחר הפסח מותר דלא גזר. ושמואל אמר חמץ בפסח במינו אסור במשהו שמואל לטעמיה דאמר כל איסורין שבתורה במינן במשהו שלא במינו שרי ולא גזר שלא במינו אטו מינו שלא בזמנו בין במינו בין שלא במינו מותר כר' שמעון. ור' יוחנן אמר חמץ בפסח בין במינו בין שלא במינו אסור בנותן טעם ר' יוחנן לטעמיה דאמר כל איסורין שבתורה

בין

מסורת הש"ס

עין משפט נר מצוה

טו א מיי' פ"א מהלכות חמץ הל' ד סמג לאוין עו:

דישראל נמי מישרא קא שרי ואי ר' יוסי הגלילי אפי' תוך זמנו נמי מישרא קא שרי בהנאה אמר רב אחא בר יעקב לעולם ר' יהודה היא ויליף שאור דאכילה משאור דראייה מה שאור דראייה *שלך אי אתה רואה אבל אתה רואה של אחרים ושל גבוה אף שאור דאכילה שלך אי אתה אוכל אבל אתה אוכל של אחרים ושל גבוה ובדין הוא דאיבעי ליה למיתנא דאפי' באכילה נמי שרי ואיידי דתנא דישראל אסור בהנאה תנא נמי דנכרי מותר בהנאה ובדין הוא דאיבעי ליה למיתנא דאפילו בתוך זמנו מותר בהנאה ואיידי דתנא דישראל לאחר זמנו תנא נמי דנכרי לאחר זמנו רבא אמר לעולם רבי שמעון היא *ורבי שמעון *קנסא קניס הואיל ועבר עליה בבל יראה ובל ימצא בשלמא לרבא היינו דקתני של ישראל אסור משום שנאמר לא יראה אלא לרב אחא בר יעקב משום לא יאכל חמץ מיבעי ליה מי סברת אסיפא קאי ארישא קאי והכי קאמר חמץ של נכרי שעבר עליו הפסח מותר בהנאה משום שנאמר לא יראה לך שלך אי אתה רואה אבל אתה רואה של אחרים ושל גבוה ויליף שאור דאכילה משאור דראייה ואזדו לטעמייהו דאיתמר האוכל שאור של נכרי שעבר עליו הפסח לדברי ר' יהודה רבא אמר לוקה ורב אחא בר יעקב אמר אינו לוקה רבא אמר לוקה לא יליף רבי יהודה שאור דאכילה משאור דראייה ורב אחא בר יעקב אמר אינו לוקה יליף שאור דאכילה משאור דראייה והדר ביה רב אחא בר יעקב מההיא דתניא האוכל חמץ של הקדש במועד מעל ויש אומרים לא מעל *מאן יש אומרים אמר רבי יוחנן רבי נחוניא בן הקנה היא *דתניא ר' נחוניא בן הקנה היה עושה את יום הכפורים כשבת לתשלומין מה שבת מתחייב בנפשו ופטור מן התשלומין אף יום הכפורים מתחייב בנפשו ופטור מתשלומין רב יוסף אמר בפודין את הקדשים להאכילן לכלבים קמיפלגי מאן דאמר מעל קסבר *פודין את הקדשים להאכילן לכלבים ומאן דאמר לא מעל קסבר *אין פודין רב אחא בר רבא תנא לה להא

[לעיל ה:] [לקמן ל.] [בכורות טו: תמורה יז. לא. לג:] [בכורות טו. שבועות יא: תמורה יז. לג:]

דישראל נמי מישרא שרי. בהנאה לאחר זמנו: לעולם ר' יהודה היא. ולאו"ג דנפקא ליה מקראי דלאחר זמנו אסור קרא בשאור דישראל קאמר אבל דנכרי שרי: ויליף שאור דאכילה. כלומר חמץ דגבי לא יאכל משאור דראייה ומותר חמצו של נכרי אף באכילה ואפי' בפסח מן התורה: לעולם ר' שמעון היא. דאמר מדאורייתא לא מיתסר חמץ אחר זמנו הלכך דנכרי שרי ומיהו דישראל אסור מקנסא דקנסוהו רבנן משום דעבר בבל יראה: בשלמא לרבא. דאמר טעמא דאסור בהנאה משום קנסא דעבר בבל יראה היינו דתנא מתני' אסור משום לא יראה לך: ואזדו לטעמייהו. רבא ורב אחא בר יעקב: מעל. חייב קרבן מעילה דקסבר חמץ הקדש בפסח בר דמים הוא ולפסדיה להקדש כר' שמעון דאמר חמץ לאחר הפסח מותר ואע"ג דקנסא קניס ה"מ בחמצו של הדיוט הואיל ועבר עליו בבל יראה אבל האי דבהדיא שהיי' גביה דאמר מר (לעיל דף ה:) אבל אתה רואה של אחרים ושל גבוה אחר הפסח הוה מזבין ליה גיזבר לישראל ואכלי ליה: ויש אומרים לא מעל. כדמפרש דהואיל ונתחייב כרת משום אכילה פטור מן התשלומין כרבי נחוניא ובמקום שאין קרן אין חומש ואין מעילה: את יוה"כ כשבת. המדליק גדיש ביוה"כ ומתחייב כרת פטור מן התשלומין כאילו הדליקו בשבת שהוא מתחייב בנפשו מיתת ב"ד דפשיטא לן דפטור מלשלם כדכתיב (שמות כא) ולא יהיה אסון ענוש יענש הא אם אסון יהיה לא יענש שאף יוה"כ שמיתתו בידי שמים שכורתים חייו ובניו אסון הוא קרוי שנא' (בראשית מב) וקראהו אסון הלכך פטור מלשלם והכי פרשינן לה באלו נערות ויש מועטים דקשיא להו כי פטר ר' נחוניא במזיד פטר דבר כרת הוא והכא בשוגג עסקינן מדקתני מעל ושוגג לאו בר כרת הוא וטעות הוא זה דגבי חמץ מזיד הוא וגבי הקדש שוגג הוא דלא ידע שהוא של הקדש: ורב יוסף אמר. לא הוה סבירא להנך תנאי כרבי שמעון דאמר תוך זמנו נמי אסור בהנאה דכולי עלמא מודו דפטור הואיל והשתא מיהא לא חזי ולאו ממונא הוא ואע"ג דסופו גורם הוא לממון לאחר הפסח אלא אליבא דר' יוסי הגלילי פליגי דאמר תוך זמנו נמי שרי בהנאה ובפודין קדשים להאכילן לכלבים קא מיפלגי מאן דאמר מעל סבר דראוי היא באותה שעה לפדות לאכילת כלבים ובר דמים הוא ודר' נחוניא לית ליה: ומאן דאמר לא מעל סבר אין פודין. הלכך לא חזי ופלוגתא דתנאי היא בתמורה (דף לא.) תזבח ולא גיזה בשר ולא חלב ואכלת ולא לכלבים מכאן שאין פודין ואיכא דדריש תזבח ואכלת אין לך בהן היתר אכילה אלא לאחר זביחה למעוטי גיזה וחלב אבל לא לכלביך לא דריש: להא

בדין הוא דאפי' תוך זמנו מותר. פרש"י מותר באכילה וקשה דאי אפשר אם לא יהא שלו בשעת אכילה דאם נתן לו הנכרי הרי הוא שלו ואם גזל מנכרי הרי חייב באחריותו ולא גרע מחמץ שחייב באחריותו דהוי כשלו ועוד לקמן דקאמר ואזדו לטעמייהו דפליגי בחמץ שעבר עליו הפסח ליפלגו בפסח גופיה ונראה לריב"א דהא דקאמר אפי' תוך זמנו מותר היינו בהנאה והא דקאמר אבל אתה אוכל של אחרים לאו דוקא אי נמי אחר זמנו קאמר ומיהו בשל גבוה קשה לפרש בתוך הפסח דאם לא פדאו אסור בהנאה ואם פדאו הרי הוא שלו ושמא י"ל אבל אתה נהנה משל גבוה שלא יהא איסור חמץ אבל איסור הקדש יש: מאן יש אומרים ר' נחוניא. תימה לר"י דמאן דיליף אסון אסון בריש אלו נערו' (כתובו' ל.) (א) ואית ליה מיתה בידי שמים פטור מן התשלומים לר' נחוניא אם כן לרבי דאמר לקמן (דף לג.) הזיד במעילה במיתה אמאי פוטר כרת מתשלומים והא אע"ג דבעלמא פוטר מיתה מתשלומין הכא לא פטר דגלי לן קרא דבשוגג חייב וה"ה כרת אע"ג דבכרת הוא במזיד בשוגג יתחייב ואור"י דבמיתה דגלי לן קרא דלא פטרה הכא מתשלומים גלי בכרת דלא גלי לא גלי וא"ת והא אמר לקמן (דף לא:) האוכל תרומת חמץ בפסח בשוגג משלם קרן וחומש ומוקמי' לה כר' נחוניא ואפ"ה מיחייב בתשלומין משום דכי היכי דלא מיפטר מתשלומין משום חיוב מיתה דתרומה הכי נמי לא מיפטר משום כרת של חמץ ואור"י דתשלומי תרומה מחמת כפרה הם כדמוכח במסכת תרומות (פ"ו מ"א) דתנן אם רצה כהן למחול אינו יכול למחול וכיון דכפרה הוא אין כרת פוטרו משום קם ליה בדרבה מיניה ותדע דהא מאן דלא יליף אסון אסון ולא פטר מיתה בי"ש מתשלומין אם כן אוכל תרומת חמץ אמאי משלם דלא שייך למימר כיון שמיתה אינה פוטרת ה"ה כרת דהא מיתה לא פטרה בשום מקום אלא ע"כ מטעם כפרה הוא ועוד אור"י דהכא אתי אליבא דרבנן דאמרי הזיד במעילה באזהרה*: רבי נחוניא היא. אע"ג דהכא בשוגג איירי מדקתני מעל ולא מעל מ"מ קיימא לן כחזקיה דאמר* חייבי מיתות שוגגין פטורים מן התשלומין וה"ה כרת לר' נחוניא הקשה ריב"א אמאי פטורין הכא מקרבן מעילה משום דקם ליה בדרבה מיניה הא אמר בהמצניע (שבת צג:) המוציא אוכלים בכלי שגג באוכלים והזיד בכלי חייב על האוכלים חטאת ועל הכלי סקילה אלמא קם ליה בדרבה מיניה לא פטר מקרבן ותירץ כיון דפטר מקרן וחומש פטר נמי מקרבן שאין אשם מעילות בא אלא כשיש קרן וחומש: אין פודין את הקדשים וכו'. הקשה הר"ח דבפ"ב דבכורות (דף יד:) משמע דלא פליגי אלא היכא שקדם הקדישן למומן אבל קדם מומן להקדישן הואיל ומעולם לא קדשו קדושת הגוף כ"ע מודים דפודים והכא משמע דפליגי אפי' בקדושת דמים ותי' ר"י דה"ק אין פודין מדרבנן ואין לתמוה אטו משום חששא דרבנן נפקיע מעילה דאורייתא דכיון דאמרו רבנן אין פודין לא שויא מידי והא דאמר בהתערובות (זבחים עא.*) נתערבו בשור שנעבדה וכו' בכלאים וטריפה ירעו עד שיסתאבו וימכרו והשתא ע"כ יאכיל לכלבים דלישראל טריפה אסורה ליה אתי שפיר אפילו למאן דאמר אין פודין דהא דאין פודין היינו היכא דלא חזו לאכילה אבל הכא חזו לאדם אם היו ניכרים דהא רבי עקיבא שרי בבכורות (דף לג:) לזמן נכרי על הבכור ובזבחים בפ' טבול יום (דף קד.) *מוכח שר' עקיבא אוסר בכור טריפה בעל מום להאכיל לכלבים שאפילו העור אסור כשנמצא טריפה קודם הפשט והיכא דשרי לישראל איתקש לצבי ולאיל: אין פודין. תימה לר"י אע"ג דאין פודין נמעול דהא לאחר שנשרף ונעשה אפר יכול לפדותו

הגהות הב"ח

(א) תוס' ד"ה מאן וכו' בריש אלו נערות. נ"ב וע"ש בדף ל תוס' בד"ה זר שאכל:

כתובות ל. שבועות לג. לקמן לב. [מגילה ז:] תוספתא ב"ק פ"ט]

[וע"ע תוס' כתובות לג ד"ה זר]

[כתובות לה.]

[וע"ע תוס' ד"ה ובטריפה]

[וע"ע תוס' ד"ה אמר ר' עקיבא]

רבינו חננאל

ומנו דישראל נמי שרי בהנאה אי ר' יוסי הגלילי כו' ואוקמה רב אחא בר יעקב כר' יהודה' ואמר דר' יהודה יליף שאור דאכילה שנאמר (שמות יב יט) שבעת ימים שאור לא ימצא בבתיכם כי כל אוכל מחמצת וכתיב (שם טו) תשביתו שאור מבתיכם כי כל אוכל חמץ וגו' ויליף האי שאור דאכילה משאור דראיה שנאמר ולא יראה לך שאור ומפרש בשאור דראית לך ודרשי' ביה שלך אי אתה רואה אבל אתה רואה של אחרים ושל גבוה ובדין הוא דליתני במתני' הכי חמץ של נכרי שעבר עליו הפסח מותר באכילה ובתוך זמנו נמי מותר בהנאה ואיידי דבעי מיתנא סיפא ושל ישראל אסור דאפי' בהנאה נמי חמץ ישראל שעבר עליו הפסח אסור תנא רישא נמי של נכרי שעבר עליו הפסח מותר בהנאה. רבא אמר מתני' ר' שמעון היא דסבירא ליה דלפני זמנו ולאחר זמנו אינו עובר עליו בלא כלום ומתני' דקתני ושל ישראל אסור לאחר זמנו קנסא הוא דקנים ליה משום דשהיי' גביה ועבר עליה על לא יראה ועל לא ימצא בשלמא לרבא דאוקמה למתני' לר' שמעון ומשום דעבר על לא יראה קנסוהו היינו דקתני במתני' ושל ישראל אסור משום שנאמר לא יראה לך אלא לרב אחא דמוקים כר' יהודה משום לא תאכל מבעי ליה למיתנא ומשני רב אחא בר יעקב מי סברת אסיפא דקתני ושל ישראל אסור קאי לא ארישא קאי והכי קתני חמץ של נכרי מותר שנאמר לא יראה לך שאור ויליף שאור דאכילה משאור דראיה כדאמרן: ואזדו לטעמייהו דאיתמר האוכל חמץ של נכרי שעבר עליו הפסח לדברי ר' יהודה רבא אמר לוקה דהא סתמא קתני לא שנא דישראל ולא שנא דנכרי חמץ לפני זמנו ולאחר זמנו עובר בלאו ואמרי' מאי טעמיה דר' יהודה תלתא קראי כתיבי חד לפני זמנו שנאמר לא תאכל עליו חמץ והוא משעה ששית עד שהיטת הפסח וחד לאחר זמנו לא יאכל חמץ וחד תוך זמנו שחייב לאו וכרת שנאמר כי כל אוכל מחמצת ונכרתה וגו' ולא יליף שאור דאכילה משאור דראיה רב אחא בר יעקב אומר אינו לוקה יליף שאור כו': והדר ביה רב אחא בר יעקב דתניא האוכל חמץ של הקדש במועד מעל ויש אומרים לא מעל מאן יש אומרים א"ר חסדא ר' נחוניא הוא דפטר מחויב כרת מן תשלומין כמחויב מיתת ב"ד וכיון שאוכל חמץ בפסח חייב כרת הוא ופטור מלשלם קרבן מעילה: רב יוסף אמר בפודין קדשים להאכילם לכלבים פליגי. פי' החמץ אע"פ שהוא קדש בין בפסח בין לאחר הפסח אסור באכילה מיהו פודין אותו להאכילו לכלבים והרי ממון הוא והנהנה ממנו של הקדש מעל ת"ק סבר פודין ולפיכך מעל ויש אומרים סבר אין פודין את הקדשים להאכילן לכלבים:

if R. Simeon, [29a] even that of an Israelite is indeed permitted.[2] While if [it is] R. Jose the Galilean, even during its time it is indeed permitted for [general] use?—Said R. Aḥa b. Jacob: In truth it is R. Judah, and he learns *se'or* [leaven] of 'eating' from *se'or* of 'seeing':[3] just as [with] the *se'or* [stated in connection] with 'seeing', 'you must not see your own, but you may see that belonging to others or to the Most High',[4] so [with] the *se'or* [written in connection] with 'eating', you must not eat your own, but you may eat that belonging to others or to the Most High;[5] and logically he [the Tanna of our Mishnah] ought to teach that it[6] is permitted even for eating, but because he teaches that that of an Israelite is forbidden for use, he also teaches that that of a Gentile is permitted for use. Again, logically he ought to teach that even during its period it[6] is permitted for use, but because he mentions after its period in connection with that of an Israelite, he also teaches about that of a heathen after its period.

Raba said: In truth it[7] is R. Simeon; but R. Simeon does indeed penalize him, since he transgresses *'there shall not be seen'* and *'there shall not be found'* therewith.[8] As for Raba, it is well: hence it is taught, BUT THAT OF AN ISRAELITE IS FORBIDDEN [FOR GENERAL USE], BECAUSE IT IS SAID, NEITHER SHALL THERE LEAVEN BE SEEN WITH THEE.[9] But according to R. Aḥa b. Jacob, he should state, because [it is said], *there shall no leavened*
a *bread be eaten?*[1]—Do you think that that[2] refers to the second clause? [No,] it refers to the first clause, and he states thus: LEAVEN BELONGING TO A GENTILE OVER WHICH PASSOVER HAS PASSED IS PERMITTED FOR USE, BECAUSE IT IS SAID, NEITHER SHALL THERE BE LEAVEN SEEN WITH THEE, [implying], thine own thou must not see, but thou mayest see the leaven of strangers or of the Most High; and *se'or* of 'eating' is learnt from *se'or* of 'seeing'.

Now they[3] are consistent with their views. For it was stated: If one eats *se'or* belonging to a heathen over which Passover has passed, according to R. Judah's view,—Raba said: He is flagellated; while R. Aḥa b. Jacob said: He is not flagellated. Raba said, He is flagellated: R. Judah does not learn *se'or* of 'eating' from *se'or* of 'seeing'. While R. Aḥa b. Jacob, said, He is not flagellated: he learns *se'or* of 'eating' from *se'or* of 'seeing'.

But R. Aḥa b. Jacob retracted from that [view]. For it was taught: He who eats leaven of *hekdesh*[4] during the Festival [Passover] commits trespass; but some say, He does not commit trespass.[5] Who is [meant by] 'some say'?—Said R. Joḥanan, It is R. Neḥunia b. ha-Kanah. For it was taught: R. Neḥunia b. ha-Kanah used to treat the Day of Atonement as the Sabbath in regard to payment: just as [with] the Sabbath, he forfeits his life and is exempt from [payment], so [with] the Day of Atonement, he forfeits his life and is exempt from payment.[6] R. Joseph said: They differ as to whether sacred food can be redeemed in order to feed dogs therewith. He who says [that] he commits trespass holds, One may redeem sacred food in order to feed dogs therewith; while he who rules [that] he does not commit trespass holds,
b One may not redeem [etc.].[1]

(2) For general use, after its time. (3) I.e., he learns the prohibition of *eating se'or* from that of *seeing se'or*. (4) V. *supra* 5b. (5) I.e., when R. Judah teaches *supra* 28b that leaven even after its period is forbidden, this analogy shows that that applies to leaven belonging to a Jew only. (6) The leaven of a Gentile. (7) Our Mishnah. (8) Thus the Mishnah states the Rabbinic law, while in the Baraitha the Scriptural law is stated. (9) I.e., as a penalty for violating this injunction.

a (1) That being the verse quoted by R. Judah *supra* 28b. (2) The verse quoted in the Mishnah. (3) *Sc.* Raba and R. Aḥa b. Jacob. (4) V. Glos. (5) On committing trespass, v. *supra* 26a n. a6. The first Tanna holds that leaven belonging to *hekdesh* has a value even during Passover. For he agrees with R. Simeon that leaven kept during Passover is Biblically permitted after Passover, and though R. Simeon penalizes its owner, that does not apply to *hekdesh*, since leaven of *hekdesh* falls within the permissive law, 'but thou mayest see that of Heaven'. Thus this man, by eating it, has caused loss to the Temple treasury, and therefore he is liable to a trespass-offering. But the second Tanna, while admitting this, holds that since he incurs *kareth* for the eating of leaven, he is free from any lesser penalty, as explained in the Text. (6) It is a principle that if a man commits an act involving the death penalty and a monetary compensation, he is exempted from the latter owing to the greater punishment; this holds good even if he is not actually executed. E.g., if he sets fire to another man's property on the Sabbath, since his violation of the Sabbath involves death, he is not liable for the damage. Now R. Neḥunia b. ha-Kanah holds that it is the same if his act involves *kareth* instead of death: e.g., if he sets fire to another man's property on the Day of Atonement, the violation of which is punishable by *kareth*.—Thus in the present case he need not indemnify *hekdesh* for the leaven, in view of the *kareth* involved, and where that is so, there is no trespass-offering.

b (1) If these Tannaim held with R. Simeon that during Passover it is forbidden for general use, they would agree that he is not liable for trespass, since it was valueless when he actually ate it, notwithstanding that it would become valuable after Passover. But they hold with R. Jose the Galilean that leaven is permitted for use during Passover. Now, the only use to which leaven can be put then is to give it to dogs. This may be done with ordinary leaven, but there is a controversy in respect of sacred leaven. The first Tanna holds that it can be redeemed for that purpose: hence the leaven is valuable, and therefore the eater commits trespass. But the others ('some say') hold that sacred leaven may not be redeemed for dogs. Consequently it has no value, and the eater does not commit trespass.

and [commits a sin subject to] *kareth*.[4] [28*b*] R. Simeon said: [As to] leaven, before and after its time, he does not transgress anything at all on its account; during its time, he transgresses on its account [an interdict subject to] *kareth* and a negative command. And from the hour that it is forbidden for eating, it is forbidden for [general] use; this agrees with the first Tanna. R. Jose the Galilean said: Wonder at yourself! How can leaven be prohibited for [general] use the whole seven [days]? And how do we know of him who eats leaven from six hours and onwards that he transgresses a negative command? Because it is said, *Thou shalt eat no leavened bread with it:*[5] this is R. Judah's opinion. Said R. Simeon to him: Is it then possible to say thus, seeing that it is already stated, *Thou shalt eat no leavened bread with it; seven days shalt thou*
a *eat unleavened bread therewith?*[1] If so, what does '*thou shalt eat no leavened bread with it*' teach? When he is subject to [the injunction], 'arise, eat unleavened bread,'[2] he is subject to [the prohibition], 'do not eat leavened bread'; and when he is not subject to, 'arise, eat unleavened bread,' he is not subject to, 'do not eat leavened bread.'

What is R. Judah's reason?—Three verses are written: *There shall no leavened bread be eaten;*[3] *Ye shall eat nothing leavened;*[4] and *Thou shalt eat no leavened bread with it.* One refers to before its time; another to after its time; and the third to during its time.[5] And R. Simeon?[6]—One refers to during its time. '*Ye shall eat nothing leavened*' he requires for what was taught: *Ḥameẓ:*[7] I only know [that it is forbidden] where it turned leaven of its own accord; if [it turned leaven] through another substance, how do we know it? Therefore it is stated, *Ye shall eat nothing leavened.*[8] '*There shall no leavened bread be eaten*' he requires for what was taught: R. Jose the Galilean said: How do we know that at the Passover of Egypt its [prohibition of] leaven was in force one day only? Because it is said, '*There shall no leavened bread be eaten*', and in proximity thereto [is written], *This day ye go forth.*[9] And R. Judah: how does he know [that it is prohibited when made leaven] through another substance?—Because the Divine Law expressed it in the term *maḥmeẓeth*.[10] How does he know R. Jose the Galilean's [deduction]?—I can either say, because '*this day*' is stated in proximity thereto.[11] Alternatively, he does not base interpretations on the proximity
b of verses.[1]

The Master said: 'And how do we know of him who eats leaven from six hours and onwards that he transgresses a negative command? Because it is said, *Thou shalt eat no leavened bread with it:* this is R. Judah's opinion. Said R. Simeon to him: Is it then possible to say thus, seeing that it is already stated, *Thou shalt eat no leavened bread with it; seven days shalt thou eat unleavened bread therewith?*' Now as to R. Judah, R. Simeon says well to him?—R. Judah can answer you: [The purpose of] that [verse] is to make it a statutory obligation even for nowadays.[2] And R. Simeon? Whence does he know to make it a statutory obligation [even nowadays]!—He deduces it from, *at even ye shall eat unleavened bread.*[3] And R. Judah?—He requires that in respect of an unclean person or one who was on a distant journey. I might say, since he cannot eat the Passover sacrifice, he need not eat unleavened bread or bitter herbs either. Hence we are informed [that it is not so]. And R. Simeon?—For an unclean person or one who was on a distant journey no verse is required,[4] because he is no worse than an uncircumcised person and an alien,[5] for it is written, *but no uncircumcised person shall eat thereof:*[6] '*thereof*' he shall not eat, but he eats of unleavened bread and bitter herbs. And R. Judah? It is written in the case of one,[7] and it is written in the case of the other.[8]

c Now, who is [the authority for] our Mishnah?[1] If R. Judah, he states leaven without qualification, even that of a Gentile. And

(4) During its (forbidden) time means during Passover. Before its time, from six hours (mid-day) on the fourteenth of Nisan until evening, when Passover commences; after its time, after Passover—i.e., leaven which was kept from before until after Passover. He transgresses by eating it. (5) Deut. XVI, 3. '*It*' refers to the Passover sacrifice, which was offered on the fourteenth of Nisan from mid-day and onwards; and the verse is interpreted: You are to eat no leavened bread at the time that you must offer the Passover sacrifice.

a (1) Now, unleavened bread (*maẓẓah*) was not eaten before evening; hence '*therewith*' must mean when the Passover sacrifice is *eaten*, viz., in the evening, and '*with it*' must bear the same meaning in the first half of the verse. (2) I.e., in the evening. (3) Ex. XIII, 3. (4) Ibid. XII, 20. (5) On the meaning of these terms v. *supra*, n. b4. (6) How does he interpret these verses? (7) In Ex. XIII, 3 and Deut. XVI, 3 (E.V. *leavened bread*). (8) Heb. *maḥmeẓeth*. This implies even if fermentation was induced by something else. (9) Ex. XIII. 4. He translates: *There shall no leavened bread be eaten* (on) *this day* (that) *ye go forth*. (10) 'Leavened'; v. n. a8. This implies an additional teaching, for otherwise the three verses should use the same term, viz., *ḥameẓ*. (11) Thus this too conveys an additional teaching.

b (1) And thus he rejects the view that at the Exodus the prohibition of leaven was for one day only. (2) The verse does not assimilate the prohibition of leavened bread to the precept of eating unleavened bread, in the sense that the former is valid only when the latter is, but the reverse: the latter is assimilated to the former. As long as leaven is prohibited, there is an obligation to eat unleavened bread, i.e., even nowadays, after the destruction of the Temple and the cessation of sacrifices. For I might think, since it is written, *they shall eat it* (*sc.* the Passover sacrifice) *with unleavened bread and bitter herbs* (Num. IX, 11), the obligation to eat unleavened bread holds good only as long as the Passover sacrifice is offered. Hence this verse teaches that it is not so. (3) Ex. XII, 18. This is otherwise superfluous, since it is stated in v. 8, *and they shall eat the flesh in that night . . . and unleavened bread.* (4) That he has to eat unleavened bread. (5) V. Ex. XII, 43. According to the Talmud, Shab. 87*a* this means a Jew whose acts have alienated him from Heaven, i.e., a nonconformist. (6) Ibid. 48. (7) *Sc.* an uncircumcised person and an 'alien'. (8) *Sc.* an unclean person and one who was on a distant journey; v. *infra* 120*a*, n. b6. Hence Deut. XVI, 3 is still required to show that the eating of unleavened bread is a permanent obligation.

c (1) Here the Talmud reverts to its original question (*supra a* bottom), which was interrupted for a discussion of the various opinions quoted.

עין משפט נר מצוה

סד א מיי' פ"א מהל' חמץ הל' ד:

סה ב מיי' שם הלכה ו סמג לאוין עו:

[עי' בהרא"ש דאסברא פסי דמוקמינן לה כר"ש לכך מתני' כדף כ:]

רבינו חננאל

מני אי ר' יהודה חמץ סתמא קתני דאסור ואפי' דנכרי אי ר' שמעון הא אמר לאחר

גמרא

רבי שמעון אומר חמץ לפני זמנו *ולאחר זמנו אינו עובר עליו בלא כלום תוך זמנו עובר עליו בכרת ובלאו ומשעה שאסור באכילה אסור בהנאה אתאן לתנא קמא *ר' יוסי הגלילי אומר תמה על עצמך היאך חמץ אסור בהנאה כל שבעה ומנין לאוכל חמץ משש שעות ולמעלה שהוא עובר בלא תעשה שנאמר (דברים טז) לא תאכל עליו חמץ דברי רבי יהודה אמר לו ר' שמעון וכי אפשר לומר כן והלא כבר נאמר לא תאכל עליו חמץ שבעת ימים תאכל עליו מצות אם כן מה ת"ל לא תאכל עליו חמץ בשעה שישנו בקום אכול מצה ישנו בבל תאכל חמץ ובשעה שאינו בקום אכול מצה אינו בבל תאכל חמץ מ"ט דר' יהודה תלתא קראי כתיבי (שמות יג) לא יאכל חמץ (שמות יב) וכל מחמצת לא תאכלו לא תאכל עליו חמץ חד לפני זמנו וחד לאחר זמנו וחד לתוך זמנו ורבי שמעון חד לתוך זמנו וכל מחמצת מבעי ליה *לכדתניא (א) *אין לי אלא שנתחמץ מאליו מחמת דבר אחר מנין תלמוד לומר כל מחמצת לא תאכלו לא יאכל חמץ מיבעי ליה *לכדתניא רבי יוסי הגלילי אומר מנין לפסח מצרים שאין חימוצו נוהג אלא יום אחד תלמוד לומר לא יאכל חמץ וסמיך ליה (שמות יג) היום אתם יוצאים ור' יהודה מחמת דבר אחר מנא לי' מדאפקיה רחמנא בלשון מחמצת ודר' יוסי הגלילי מנא ליה אי בעית אימא מדסמיך ליה היום אי בעית אימא *סמוכין לא דריש אמר מר ומנין לאוכל חמץ משש שעות ולמעלה שהוא עובר בלא תעשה שנאמר לא תאכל עליו חמץ דברי רבי יהודה אמר לו ר' שמעון וכי אפשר לומר כן והלא כבר נאמר לא תאכל עליו חמץ שבעת ימים תאכל עליו מצות ורבי יהודה שפיר קאמר ליה רבי שמעון ורבי יהודה אמר לך ההוא לקובעו חובה אפילו בזמן הזה הוא דאתא ור' שמעון לקובעו חובה מנא ליה נפקא ליה (שמות יב) *מבערב תאכלו ור' יהודה *מיבעי לי' לטמא ושהיה בדרך רחוקה סלקא דעתך אמינא הואיל ובפסח לא יאכל מצה ומרור נמי לא ניכול קמ"ל ור' שמעון טמא ושהיה בדרך רחוקה לא איצטריך קרא דלא גרע מערל ובן נכר דכתיב (שמות יב) *וכל ערל לא יאכל בו *בו הוא אינו אוכל אבל אוכל הוא במצה ובמרור ורבי יהודה כתיב בהאי וכתיב בהאי מני מתניתין אי רבי יהודה חמץ סתמא קאמר אפילו דנכרי ואי רבי שמעון דישראל

רש"י

ומשעה שאסור באכילה. היינו משש שעות ולמעלה דאמרן לפני זמנו בלאו והא מילתא רבי יהודה קאמר לה כדמפרש בגמרא אתאן לתנא קמא: תמה על עצמך וכו'. דאפילו בתוך המועד קאמר דמותר בהנאה וקא מתמה אהכי דאסרי: לא תאכל עליו. משעת שחיטה דהיינו משש שעות ולמעלה שחמה נוטה להעריב: הכי גרסינן חמץ אין לי אלא שנתחמץ מאליו: מנין לפסח מצרים. שלא נהגו בו איסור חמץ אלא יום אחד: ת"ל לא יאכל חמץ וסמיך ליה היום אתם יוצאים. לא יאכל חמץ היום: ואי בעית אימא סמוכין לא דריש רבי יהודה אלא במשנה תורה לחוד והכי שמעינן ליה בפרק קמא דיבמות (ד' ד.*) הלכך לית ליה דרבי יוסי הגלילי: לקובעו חובה. האי שבעת ימים (ב) תאכלו מצות ולאו לאקושי איסור חמץ למצות אכילת מצה אתא אלא לאקושי אכילת מצה לאזהרת חמץ לקבוע אכיל' מצה חובה לדורות כל זמן שהוא מוזהר על החמץ ואפילו בזמן שאין פסח דלא תימא על מצות ומרורים יאכלוהו כתיב ואי ליכא פסח מיחייב באכילת מצה ואי לא לא: בערב תאכלו מצות. קרא יתירה הוא דהא כתיב על מצות ומרורים יאכלוהו: לטמא ושהיה בדרך רחוקה. שאף על פי שאינו עושה פסח חייב באכילת מצה: לא ניכול. לא נחייביה: ערל. שמתו אחיו מחמת מילה: בן נכר. מי שנתנכרו מעשיו לאביו שבשמים ולא לכל התורה: כתיב בהאי. ערל ובן נכר וכתיב טמא ושהיה בדרך רחוקה דליכול מצות ואף על גב דמצי יליף מיניה הלכך איצטריך היקשא לקובעו חובה ומקראי אחריני טובא כגון שבעת ימים מצות תאכלו וכגון מצות יאכל את שבעת הימים לא נפקא ליה קביעות חובה דהנהו לאו חובה ניהו אלא מצות יאכל ולא חמץ ואם רצה ליזון שלא מחמץ ושלא ממצה הרשות בידו ודע דהא בכולהו כתיב את שבעת הימים וחובת מצה אינו אלא לילה הראשון כדילפינן בפרק בתרא* אבל מההוא *קרא נפקא לן חובת לילה הראשון מדכתיב להיקשא גבי פסח ולכדכתיב תאכל עליו מצות כי פסח לילה הראשון אף היקישא שלא בזמן פסח ללילה ראשונה והכי היקישא לקובעו חובה בזמן הזה והאי עליו למימרא דקביעת חובה דהיקישא לאו לכל שבעה אלא ללילה הראשון:

דישראל

תוספות

רבי שמעון אומר חמץ לפני זמנו ולאחר זמנו אינו עובר עליו בלא כלום. נראה דלרבי שמעון נהי דאין עובר עליו בלאו דחמץ לפני זמנו מודה הוא דאסור באכילה משש שעות ולמעלה מדאמרינן בפ"ק (לעיל דף יד.) אין שורפין תרומה טהורה עם *הטמאה משמע הא לבדה שורפין בשש ואי מותרת לאכול יאכלנה עד הלילה ועוד דקאמר משעה שאסור באכילה אסור בהנאה אתאן לת"ק מכלל דלרבי שמעון אסור באכילה אע"פ שאינו אסור בהנאה דהיינו אחר שש ונראה דנפקא ליה מתשביתו ומאך חלק ומשמע תשביתו שלא כדרך הנאה דהיינו אכילה אבל להסיקו תחת תבשילו מותר לרבי שמעון וא"ת למה שורפין בשש לרבי שמעון יסיקנו עד הלילה מעט מעט תחת תבשילו וי"ל דגזרינן שמא יאכלנו וכן לרבי יוסי הגלילי דשרי חמץ להסיקו תחת תבשילו היינו הכל ביחד אבל מעט מעט לא שמא יאכלנו דמסתמא אית ליה אור לארבעה עשר בודקין וכו':

אם כן מה תלמוד לומר לא תאכל עליו. הלשון דחוק ונראה לרשב"א דהכי פירושו והלא כבר נאמר תאכל עליו מצות וההוא עליו ע"כ אאכילת פסח קאי הכי נמי לא תאכל עליו חמץ קאי כמו אשעת אכילת פסח וקשה אמאי איצטריך קרא להכי מהיכא תיתי שיהא בבל תאכל חמץ בי"ד דהא כולהו קראי מרבינן לקמן אליבא דרבי שמעון:

וחד לפני זמנו. וא"ת ולחזקיה מכנן איסור הנאה לפני זמנו דליכא אלא חד לא יאכל והוה מסברא מוקמינן לתוך זמנו ואור"י כיון דחד מהנהו קראי משמע איסור הנאה לא נחלק ביניהם:

מחמת דבר אחר. פי' ריב"א מחמת דבר אחר דלאו מינו דעל ידי שאור מיקרי חמץ טפי משנתחמץ מאליו כדמוכח בפרק כל המנחות (מנחות נג:) אלא כגון שנתחמץ על ידי שמרי יין שמייבשין השמרים בתנור כאשר עושין בארץ אשכנז ול"ד לעיסה שנילושה ביין דלית ביה כרת ויש בה לאו:

ואידך נפקא לה מבערב תאכלו מצות. תימה לר"י דבפ' קמא דקדושין (ד' לז:) נפקא לן דזמן הזה ממושבותיכם דכתיב גבי מצה והיינו לחלכד ועוד תימה לרב אחא בר יעקב דאית ליה בשילהי ערבי פסחים (לקמן קכ.) מצה בזמן הזה דרבנן ודריש התם לכולהו קראי דלא ככל התנאים*:

כל ערל לא יאכל בו וכל בן נכר לא יאכל בו בו הוא אינו אוכל אבל אוכל הוא במצה ומרור. תימה גבי בן נכר שהוא אומר אמאי איצטריך קרא פשיטא שחייב לאכול מצה דהא חייב בכל מצות האמורות בתורה ואי קמשמע לן דמצי אכיל מצה אע"ג דאסור בפסח הא נמי פשיטא דלאו מצה קדושה אית בה וי"ל דאיצטריך להיכא דנשחט הפסח כשהיה מומר ועשה תשובה דאף על גב דלא אכיל בפסח דאין נאכל אלא למנויו מכל מקום חייב לאכול מצה ומרור*:

ערל. פי' הקונטרס שמתו אחיו מחמת מילה ולפירושו פסול כמו בתרומה דבהערל (יבמות ע. ושם) יליף תרומה מפסח בגז"ש דתושב ושכיר והא דמיבעיא לן התם (דף עא.) ערל קטן מהו לסוכו שמן של תרומה ערלה שלא בזמנה פוסלת או לא יש לחלק בין שלא בזמנה דקטן שאין חייב למול כיוצא בו למתו אחיו מחמת מילה דכיוצא בו חייבין ודע דהא טומטום אינו אוכל בתרומה בפרק הערל (שם עב.) אף על גב דמסברא אין חיוב לקרוע הוא ה"ה מתו אחיו מחמת מילה דאינו אוכל אף על גב דאינו חייב למול:

מסורת הש"ס

[לעיל כג. לקמן לג:] [וכן בכריתות כה:] לקמן מג. לקמן מ: [ברכות כה: יבמות ד. סנהדרין פו:] [קכ.] לקמן קכ. לקמן ע. וקכ. יבמות עא. [וע"ע תוס' לקמן קכ. ד"ה רב אחא בר יעקב] [וע"ע תוס' לקמן קכ. ד"ה כל בן נכר]

הגהות הב"ח

(א) גמרא לכדתניא חמץ אין לי וכו': (ב) רש"י ד"ה לקובעו וכו' שבעת ימים תאכל עליו מצות לאו:

בדין

מסורת הש"ס

עין משפט נר מצוה

נח א מיי' פ"ג מהלכות חמץ הלכה יא סמג עשין לט טוש"ע א"ח סימן תמה סעיף א:
נט ב מיי' פ"ח מהלכות ע"ז הלכה ו טוש"ע י"ד סי' קמו סעיף יד:
ס ג מיי' שם הל' ו ופ"ג מהל' חמץ הלכה יא סמג עשין לט טוש"ע א"ח סי' תמה סעיף א:
סא ד מיי' פ"ד מהלכות חמץ הלכה ב טוש"ע א"ח סי' תמח סעיף א:
סב ה מיי' פ"א מהל' חמץ הל' ד סמג לאוין עו טוש"ע שם סעיף ג:
סג ו מיי' שם הלכה ח:

חזר רבי יהודה ודנו דין אחר נותר ישנו בבל תותירו וחמץ בבל תותירו מה נותר בשריפה אף חמץ בשריפה אמרו לו אשם תלוי וחטאת העוף הבא על הספק לדבריך יוכיחו שהן בבל תותירו שאנו אומרים בשריפה ואתה אומר בקבורה שתק ר' יהודה אמר רב יוסף היינו דאמרי אינשי כפא דחטא נגרא בגווה נשרוף חרדלא (*אמר אביי) סרדנא בסדני יתיב מדויל ידיה משתלים רבא אמר גירא בגירי מקטיל מדויל ידיה משתלים: וחכ"א *מפרר וזורה וכו': איבעיא להו היכי קאמר מפרר וזורה לרוח ומפרר ומטיל לים או דילמא מפרר וזורה לרוח אבל מטיל לים בעיניה *ותנן נמי גבי ע"ז כי האי גוונא ר' יוסי אומר שוחק וזורה לרוח או מטיל לים ואיבעיא להו היכי קאמר שוחק וזורה לרוח ושוחק ומטיל לים או דילמא שוחק וזורה לרוח אבל מטיל לים בעיניה אמר רבה מסתברא ע"ז דלים המלח קא אזלא לא בעי שחיקה חמץ דלשאר נהרות קאזיל בעי פירור א"ל רב יוסף אדרבה איפכא מסתברא ע"ז דלא ממיסה בעי שחיקה חמץ דממיס לא בעי פירור תניא כוותיה דרבה תניא כוותיה דרב יוסף תניא כוותיה דרבה היה מהלך במדבר מפרר וזורה לרוח היה מהלך בספינה מפרר ומטיל לים תניא כוותיה דרב יוסף היה מהלך במדבר שוחק וזורה לרוח היה מהלך בספינה שוחק ומטיל לים שחיקה קשיא לרבה פירור קשיא לרב יוסף שחיקה לרבה לא קשיא הא לים המלח הא לשאר נהרות פירור לרב יוסף לא קשיא הא בחיטי הא בנהמא: **מתני'** *חמץ של נכרי שעבר עליו הפסח מותר בהנאה ושל ישראל אסור בהנאה שנאמר °לא יראה לך שאור: **גמ'** מני מתניתין לא רבי יהודה ולא רבי שמעון ולא רבי יוסי הגלילי מאי היא דתניא חמץ בין לפני זמנו בין לאחר זמנו עובר עליו בלאו תוך זמנו עובר עליו בלאו וכרת דברי רבי יהודה רבי

[נד.] [דילמא אביי אמר] [נד.] ע"ז מג: רש"ל [עירובין סד:] °שמות יג

רש"י

חמץ ישנו בבל תותירו. לא יראה ולא ימצא: אשם תלוי. בא על ספק כרת כגון חלב ושומן לפניו ושגג באחד מהן ואינו יודע איזה מהן אכל ואם נודע לו שחטא ואירע בו פסול או נותר פליגי ר' יהודה ורבנן בשילהי פרק בתרא דתמורה* לר' יהודה בקבורה לרבנן בשריפה: חטאת העוף הבא על הספק. כגון הפילה ספק ולד ספק אינו ולד אינה אוכלת בקדשים שמא ולד הוא עד שתביא כפרתה עולה באה על תנאי אם ילדתי הרי היא לחובתי ואם לאו הרי היא נדבה וחטאת העוף מביאתו על הספק ואין כהן משום חולין בעזרה דמקראי נפיק במסכת נזיר בפרק מי שאמר (דף כט.) ואסורה באכילה שמא חולין היא ומליקתה שויה נבילה ופליגי בה רבי יהודה ורבנן בפרק בתרא דתמורה* חטאת העוף הבאה על הספק תשרף רבי יהודה אומר יטילנה לאמה: ואתה אומר בקבורה. ואשם תלוי קאי דקאמר ר' יהודה יקבר ואף ע"ג שהנותר ממנו אסור באכילה ובהנאה וענוש כרת והוא בבל תותירו: כפא דחטא נגרא. כף בזך שחקק האומן בתוכו ישרוף את לשונו ואת חכו בחרדל לישנא אחרינא ישרוף הומי"ר בלע"ז כמו שורפה חיה בע"ז (דף כט:): סדנא. נגר עושה סד לשום בו רגלי אסירים כמו ותשם בסד רגלי (איוב יג): מדויל ידיה משתלים. מהרמת ידו וממלאכתו משתלם שכרו כשגמלא גנב: גירא. עושה חצים: או דילמא. לרוח הוא דבעי פירור שמא יזרקנו שלם וימצאנו אחר ויאכלנו אבל לים מטיל בעיניה דממים ונימוק מאליו. לשון שחיקה שייך במתכת ולשון פירור שייך בפת: ים המלח. [הנקרא מי"ר בטי"ה] אין ספינה עוברת בו: בעי פירור. שמא תפגע בו ספינה ותטלנו ולאו אדעתייהו: לא ממסה. אין המים ממסות אותו: תניא כוותיה דרבה. דחמץ בעי פירור: תניא כוותיה דרב יוסף. דע"ז בעי שחיקה: בחיטי. שהחמיצו בעי פירור כלומר פיזור שלא יתנם בשק ויזרקם אלא יפזרם על פני המים שלא יוכל אדם ללקטן מעל פני המים: **מתני'** משום שנאמר לא יראה לך. בגמרא מפרש לה משום קנסא דעבר עליה משום בל יראה: **גמ'** בין לפני זמנו. משש שעות עד שתחשך: (א) לאחר זמנו. משעבר הפסח עובר עליו בלאו ואם אכלו אינו ענוש כרת ולקמן מפרש ללאו: תוך זמנו. במועד: ומשעה

הגהות הב"ח

(א) רש"י ד"ה בין לפני וכו' משתחשך בין לאחר זמנו כצ"ל והד"א: (ב) תוס' ד"ה ע"ז וכו' צמחים והכי אמרינן התם:

תוספות

חזר ר' יהודה ודנו דין אחר. הא דקרי ליה השתא דין אחר טפי מהכי דלעיל אומר ריב"א משום דהשתא אין צריך לאיסור אכילה והנאה וענוש כרת אלא בלא דבל תותירו לחודיה מצינו למילף דליתיה בכולהו הרי הוא בבל תותירו. תימה לר"י היכי עביד לעיל קל וחומר ומותר שאינו בבל יראה ובל ימצא והא חשיב הכא בל תותירו כמו בל יראה ואומר ר"י דמכל מקום נראה דעביד שפיר קל וחומר דנותר אינו בבל יראה דמיד שהותיר עובר ושוב אינו עובר אבל חמץ אפי' לאחר שהותיר עובר בכל שעה בבל יראה: אמרו לו אשם תלוי יוכיח. תימה לרשב"א לדבריהם דרבנן דאמרו שהם בשריפה אמאי לא ילפינן חמץ מנותר שהוא בשריפה ואומר ר"י דמשמע להו* הנותר בשריפה ולא כל איסורין שבתורה בשריפה ואפי' חמץ: ואתה אומר בקבורה. טעמא דר' יהודה דליש בה"כ מכי קדש הוא הוא בשריפה ולא חטאת עוף ואשם תלוי בשריפה: ותנן נמי גבי ע"ז. אומר ר"י דרבנן דמתניתין היינו רבי יוסי דפרק כל הצלמים (ע"ז מג:) אי נמי מתני' דהכא א"ש כרבנן דהתם דאמרו לו אף היא נעשה זבל ומגדל צמחים ורחמנא אמר לא ידבק בידך וגו' והא דשרו הכא היינו משום דבחמץ כתיב לא יאכל ואינו אסור אלא כדרך הנאה וכי האי גוונא לאו דרך הנאה היא אבל בע"ז לא כתיב אכילה ואסור אפי' שלא כדרך הנאה: חמץ דלשאר נהרות. דלא מצינו שהיה שונה בשום מקום גבי חמץ ים המלח אבל גבי ע"ז אשכחן בכמה דוכתין כי האי דלעיל יוליך הנאה לים המלח הלכך סתם ים דתני גבי ע"ז הוי ים המלח מיהו לרבה מועלת שחיקה בשאר נהרות כדקאמר בסמוך כאן בים המלח כאן בשאר נהרות: איפכא מסתברא. לשון איפכא אינו מיושב דמה שייך איפכא כיון שרבה משוה אותם לכתורה: ע"ז דלא ממיסה בעי שחיקה. ויש להקשות אמאי קאמר רב יוסף דבעי שחיקה אפילו בים המלח דמסתמא אמאי דקאמר רבה אין צריך שחיקה דהיינו בים המלח קאמר רב יוסף דבעי שחיקה ועוד אי בשאר נהרות דוקא קאמר רב יוסף דבעי שחיקה ולא בים המלח ילא פליג ארבה בע"ז אלא בחמץ א"כ מאי קאמר תניא כוותיה דרב יוסף ומאי קאמר כמי שחיקה קשיא לרבה ולפי זה לרב יוסף בשאר נהרות לא מהני שחיקה מדקמצריך להוליך לים המלח ואין נראה דהא ר' יוסי מייתי ראיה מויזר על פני המים משמע דמהניא שחיקה בשאר נהרות ועוד דבכל מקום דמזכיר ים המלח בע"ז ובשאר דוכתין לא מזכיר שחיקה ובכמה דוכתין מצינו דקתני ים המלח ואפי' הכי מהני בשאר נהרות דבסוף כל הצלמים (ע"ז מט:) תנן ר' אליעזר אומר יוליך הנאה לים המלח ואמרינן התם בגמרא גבי חבית שקול ד' זוזי ושדי לנהרא וכן בנזיר (דף כד.) ובמעילה (דף יח.) תנן גבי מפריש מעות לנזיר ומת יוליך לים המלח ובערכין (דף כט.) אמרינן גבי הקדש שקול ארבעה זוזי ושדי בנהרא לכך נראה דגם לרב יוסף לא בעי שחיקה אלא בשאר נהרות כמו לרבה אלא דרבה סבירא ליה דמטיל לים סתם דע"ז היינו ים המלח ובלא שחיקה כדתנא רישא גבי צורת לבנה וצורת חמה ובכמה דוכתי יוליך לים המלח ורב יוסף מוקי לה בשאר נהרות ועל ידי שחיקה מדלא תני בהדיא יטיל לים המלח וליכא בין רבה לרב יוסף אלא חמץ בשאר נהרות וא"ת לרבנן דלית להו בע"ז (מפרר) [שוחק] וזורה לרוח מה יעשו מע"ז אטו כל שעה יוליך לים המלח דלרבנן לא מהני שחיקה בשאר נהרות דקתני התם אמרו לו משם ראיה הרי הוא אומר ויזר על פני המים לא נתכוין משה אלא לבודקן כסוטה ומדאיצטריך להאי טעמא מכלל דלא מהני שחיקה בשאר נהרות וטעמא לפי שהמים מוליכים אותו על ידות הנהר ויש לומר דלרבנן מפרר וזורה לרוח במקום שאין מגדל צמחים (ב) וכן אמרינן התם:

רבי

[לעיל כד.]

רבינו חננאל

חזר ר' יהודה ודנו דין אחר נותר הרי הוא בבל תותירו וחמץ הרי הוא בבל תותירו מה נותר טעון שריפה אף חמץ טעון שריפה אמרו לו חטאת העוף הבאה על הספק ואשם תלוי לדבריך יוכיחו שהן בבל תותירו כדכתיב (ויקרא ז טו) לא יניח ממנו עד בקר ואנו אומרים בשריפה ואתה אומר בקבורה דתנן בסוף תמורה אשם תלוי ישרף [ר"י אומר יקבר] חטאת העוף הבא על הספק ישרף ר' יהודה אומר יטילנה לאמה ותניא כיצד אמר רבי יהודה יטילנה לאמה מנתחה אבר אבר ומשליכה לפני אמה ומתגלגלת ויורדת לנחל קדרון: ת"ר אשם תלוי וחטאת [העוף] הבאה על הספק וחולין שנשחטו בעזרה ר' יהודה אומר יקברו ר' שמעון אומר ישרפו שתק ר' יהודה. ירושלמי אשם תלוי בשיטתך יוכיח שאסור באכילה ובהנאה וחייבין עליו ויש בו זמן ואתה אומר בקבורה ולא בשריפה פירושו אשם תלוי שנודע לו אחר שחיטה וחטאת העוף הבאה על הספק שנודע לו אחר מליקתה דתנן בכריתות פ'[המביא אשם(ד' כה)] חטאת העוף הבאה על הספק אם משנמלקה נודע לו הרי זו תקבר: שתק ר' יהודה היינו דאמרי אינשי כפא דחטם נגרא כו' פירוש כמו משל אומרין בני אדם הכף שחטטו בני אדם וחקקו כי חטט וחקק אחד הוא כגון החוטט בגדיש לעשות לו סוכה בתוכו שורפין חרדל שלו כלומר שאלו לא מצא הכף שחקקו לא היו שורפין החרדל שלו וכן היה ר' יהודה אומר אילולי לא השיבהו מדבריו לא היו משתקין אותו: פי' סרנא כמו היה יושב בספינה או באסרא והם כבלים שנותנין ברגלי הכלאים בבית הכלא: גיראה האומן העושה החצים: וחכמים אומרים מפרר וזורה לרוח או מטיל לים ותנן נמי גבי ע"ז כי האי גוונא ר' יוסי אומר שוחק וזורה לרוח ומטיל לים [ואיבעיא לן היכי קאמר מפרר ושוחק וזורה לרוח או מפרר ושוחק ומטיל לים] או כשמטיל לים לא בעי לא פרירה ולא שחיקה ופשיט רבה כי החמץ דאזיל לשאר נהרות לעולם צריך פירור אבל ע"ז דלים המלח הוא דאזיל לא בעי פירור ואקשי' עלה והתניא היה מהלך במדבר שוחק וזורה לרוח היה מהלך בספינה שוחק ומטיל לים ומשני האי דתניא שוחק בשאר נהרות כי קאמינא אנא דע"ז לא צריכה שחיקה שמשליכה לים הגדול רב יוסף אמר חמץ כשמשליכין אותו לים לא בעי פירור אבל לעולם בעי שחיקה ואקשי' עלה והתניא היה מהלך בספינה מפרר ומטיל לים ומשני' הא דתניא מפרר בחטים כי קאמינא דלא בעי פירור בנהמא והלכתא כרבה דאמר חמץ בעי פירור: מתני' חמץ של נכרי שעבר עליו הפסח מותר כו' מני מתני' לא ר' יהודה ולא ר' שמעון ולא ר' יוסי הגלילי מאי היא דתניא חמץ לפני זמנו ולאחר זמנו וכו'

מפי

require burning. [28a] R. Judah argued again [with] another argument: *Nothar* is subject to *'ye shall let nothing of it remain,'*[4] and leaven is subject to *'ye shall let nothing of it remain'*:[5] just as *nothar* [is disposed of] by burning, so is leaven [disposed of] by burning. Said they to him, Let the guilt-offering of suspense[6] and the sin-offering of a bird which is brought for a doubt,[7] on your view,[8] prove it: for they are subject to *'ye shall let nothing of it remain,'*[9] and we maintain that they require burning, while you say [it is disposed of] by burial.[10] [Thereupon] R. Judah was silent. Said R. Joseph: Thus people say, The ladle which the artisan hollowed out, in it [his tongue] shall be burnt with mus-
a tard.[1] Abaye said: When the maker of the stocks sits in his own stock, he is paid with the clue which his own hand wound.[2] Raba said: When the arrow maker is slain by his own arrows, he is paid with the clue which his own hand wound.

BUT THE SAGES MAINTAIN: HE CRUMBLES AND THROWS IT etc. The scholars asked: How is it meant: He crumbles and throws it to the wind, or he crumbles and throws it into the sea; or perhaps, he crumbles and throws it to the wind, but he may throw it into the sea whole [without crumbling]? And we learned similarly in connection with an idol too: R. Jose said: He crushes and throws it to the wind or casts it into the sea. And the scholars asked: How is it meant: He crushes and throws it to the wind, or he crushes and casts it into the sea; or perhaps, he crushes and throws it to the wind, but he may cast it into the sea whole [without crushing?]—Said Rabbah: It is logical that an idol, which goes into the Dead Sea, need not be crushed;[3] leaven, which goes into other streams, needs crumbling. Said R. Joseph to him, On the contrary, the logic is the reverse: An idol, which does not dissolve, needs crushing; leaven, which dissolves, does not need crumbling.

It was taught in accordance with Rabbah;[4] it was taught in accordance with R. Joseph.[5] It was taught in accordance with Rabbah: If he was walking in a wilderness, he crumbles it [the leaven] and casts it to the wind; if he was travelling in a ship, he crumbles it and casts it into the sea. It was taught in accordance with R. Joseph: If he was travelling in the desert, he crushes [the idol] and throws it to the wind; if he was travelling in a ship, he crushes and casts it into the sea. [The teaching requiring] 'crushing' is a difficulty according to Rabbah, [while the teaching requiring] 'crumbling' is a difficulty according to R. Jose? 'Crushing' is not a difficulty according to Rabbah: one means into the Dead Sea,[6] the other means into other waters. 'Crumbling' is not a difficulty
b according to R. Joseph: One refers to wheat [grains],[1] the other refers to bread.

MISHNAH. LEAVEN BELONGING TO A GENTILE OVER WHICH PASSOVER HAS PASSED[2] IS PERMITTED FOR USE; BUT THAT OF AN ISRAELITE IS FORBIDDEN FOR USE, BECAUSE IT IS SAID, NEITHER SHALL THERE BE LEAVEN SEEN WITH THEE.[3]

GEMARA. Who is [the authority of] our Mishnah: it is neither R. Judah nor R. Simeon nor R. Jose the Galilean. What is this [allusion]?—For it was taught: [As to] leaven, both before its time and after its time, he transgresses a negative command on its account; during its time, he transgresses a negative command

(4) Ex. XII, 10. (5) Since leaven must not be seen or found in the house after midday on the fourteenth of Nisan, it may obviously not remain there until then. (6) I.e., doubt. When a man is in doubt whether he has committed a transgression for which, if certain, a sin-offering is due, he brings a guilt-offering of suspense. (7) E.g., when a woman miscarries, and it is not known whether the fetus was viable or not. (8) V. Tem. 34a. The Rabbis hold that this bird sin-offering must be burnt, while R. Judah maintains that it is cast into a water-duct which carries it off. (9) In common with all sacrifices. (10) This refers to the guilt-offering of suspense.

a (1) Or, from it he shall swallow mustard. (2) Jast. Rashi, he is paid by the uplifting—i.e., the work—of his own hand. (3) For the Dead Sea is unnavigable; hence none will pick it up. (4) That leaven requires 'crumbling'. (5) That an idol requires 'crushing'. (6) The idol need not be crushed before it is thrown thither.

b (1) Which had turned leaven. These must be crumbled, i.e., scattered into the sea. But they may not be tied in a sack and thrown into the sea, lest someone finds the sack. (2) I.e., it had been kept over Passover. (3) Ex. XIII, 7.

R. Papa: When the flame is opposite it.[2] [27b] Whence it follows that the Rabbis who disagree with him permit it even when the flame is opposite it; then how is forbidden fuel conceivable according to the Rabbis?[3]—Said R. Ammi b. Ḥama: In the case of a stool.[4]

Rami b. Ḥama asked R. Ḥisda: If an oven was heated with wood of *hekdesh*[5] and bread is baked therein, what [is the law] according to the Rabbis who permit in the first case?[6]—The bread is forbidden, he replied. And what is the difference between this and *'orlah?*—Said Raba: How compare! *'Orlah* is annulled in two hundred [times its own quantity]; *hekdesh* is not annulled even in one thousand [times its quantity].[7] But said Raba, If there is a difficulty, this is the difficulty: Surely he who fires [the oven] commits trespass, and wherever he who fires [the oven] commits trespass, it [the fuel] passes out to *ḥullin?*[8]—Said R. Papa: We treat here of wood of peace-offerings,[9] and in accordance with R. Judah, who maintained: *Hekdesh*, if [misappropriated for secular use] unwittingly, becomes *ḥullin;* if deliberately, it does not become *ḥullin*. Now what is the reason that if deliberately it does not [be-
a come *ḥullin*]? Since it does not involve a trespass-offering,[1] it does not pass out to *ḥullin;* so peace-offerings too, since it [the misappropriation of this type of sacrifice] does not involve a trespass-offering, it does not pass out to *ḥullin*.

Yet whenever he that fires [the oven] commits trespass, it [the fuel] passes out to *ḥullin?* But it was taught: [In the case of] all which are burnt,[2] their ashes are permitted [for use], except the wood of an *asherah*, while the ashes of *hekdesh* are forbidden for ever?[3]—Said Rami b. Ḥama: E.g., if a fire fell of its own accord on wood of *hekdesh*, so that there is no man to be liable for trespass.[4] R. Shemaiah said: It[5] refers to those [ashes] which must be hidden,[6] for it was taught: *And he shall put them* [the ashes][7]—gently; *and he shall put them*—the whole thereof; *and he shall put them* [means] that he must not scatter them.[8]

R. JUDAH SAID: THERE IS NO REMOVAL etc. It was taught, R. Judah said: There is no removal of leaven save by burning, and logic impels this: if *nothar*, which is not subject to *'there shall not be seen'* and *'there shall not be found'*, requires burning, then leaven, which is subject to *'there shall not be seen'* and *'there shall not be found'*, how much the more does it require burning! Said they to him: Every argument that you argue [which] in the first place is stringent yet in the end leads to leniency is not a [valid] argument: [for] if he did not find wood for burning, shall he sit and do nothing, whereas the Torah ordered, *Ye shall put away leaven out of your houses,*[9] [which means] with anything wherewith you can put it away? R. Judah argued again [with] another argument.[10] *Nothar* is forbidden for eating and leaven is forbidden for eating: just as *nothar* [is disposed of] by burning, so is leaven
b [destroyed] by burning. Said they to him, Let *nebelah* prove [it][1] for it is forbidden for eating yet does not require burning. Said he to them, There is a difference:[2] *nothar* is forbidden for eating and for [all] use, and leaven is forbidden for eating and for [all] use: just as *nothar* requires burning, so does leaven require burning. Let the ox that is stoned[3] prove it, they replied: it is forbidden for eating and for [all] use, yet it does not require burning. Said he to them, There is a difference: *Nothar* is forbidden for eating and for [all] use, and he [who eats it] is punished with *kareth*, and leaven is forbidden for eating and for [all] use, and he is punished with *kareth:* just as *nothar* [must be destroyed] by burning, so is leaven [destroyed] by burning. Said they to him, Let the *ḥeleb* of the ox that is stoned prove it, which is forbidden for eating, for [all] use, and involves the penalty of *kareth*, yet it does not

(2) Directly opposite the bread through the oven mouth. (3) I.e., when do they prohibit benefit from forbidden fuel? (4) Made of forbidden wood. One must not sit upon it, because he thereby benefits from the wood while it is yet fully in existence. (5) V. Glos. (6) *Sc.* where it is heated with *'orlah* or *kil'ayim*. (7) If *'orlah* is accidentally mixed with two hundred times its own quantity of permitted produce and cannot be removed, it is annulled, and the whole is permitted. But *hekdesh* in similar circumstances is never annulled: thus its interdict is obviously more stringent. (8) When one misappropriates *hekdesh* for secular use, he commits trespass and is liable to an offering for having withdrawn it from sacred ownership. Thus by this very act he converts it into *ḥullin*, and therefore the bread should be regarded as having been baked with ordinary fuel, hence permitted. This principle holds good of all *hekdesh* save animals dedicated for sacrifices and the service utensils in the Temple. (9) I.e., wood dedicated for peace-offerings, which means that it is to be sold and peace-offerings bought with the money. Peace-offerings belong to the category of 'sacrifices of lower sanctity', and do not involve a trespass-offering; nevertheless they are forbidden for secular use.

a (1) Sacrifices were brought only for *unwitting* transgressions. (2) Viz., leaven on Passover, unclean *terumah*, *'orlah* and *kil'ayim* of the vineyard. Tem. 33*b*. (3) V. Tem. 34*a*. (4) Only then are the ashes of *hekdesh* for ever forbidden. (5) The teaching cited. (6) Viz., the censerful of ashes hidden at the base of the altar, v. *supra* 26*a*. Only these are for ever forbidden. (7) Lev. VI, 3. (8) V. *supra* 26*a*. (9) Ex. XII, 15. (10) Not on the basis of an *a minori* argument, but a *gezerah shawah*, the conclusion of which is accepted irrespective of the result.

b (1) I.e., refute the argument. (2) Between *nebelah* on the one hand and *nothar* and leaven on the other. (3) V. Ex. XXI, 28.

נו א מיי' פ"ח מהלכות ע"ז הל' יד טוש"ע י"ד סי' קמב סעיף ח :

נז ב ג מיי' פי"ט מהל' פסולי המוקדשין הלכה יג :

מכלל דרבנן דפליגי עליה שרו אפי' כשאבוקה כנגדו אלא עצים דאיסורא לרבנן היכי משכחת להו א"ר אמי בר חמא בשרשיפא בעא מיניה רמי בר חמא מרב חסדא תנור שהסיקו בעצי הקדש ואפה בו הפת לרבנן דשרו בקמייתא מאי א"ל הפת אסורה ומה בין זו לערלה אמר רבא הכי השתא ערלה בטילה במאתים הקדש אפילו באלף לא בטיל אלא אמר רבא אי קשיא ליה הא קשיא והלא מעל המסיק וכל היכא *דמעל המסיק נפקו להו לחולין אמר רב פפא הכא בעצי שלמים עסקינן ואליבא דר' יהודה דאמר הקדש בשוגג מתחלל במזיד אינו מתחלל מאי טעמא לא כיון דלאו בר מעילה הוא לא נפיק לחולין שלמים נמי כיון דלאו בר מעילה נינהו לא נפקא לחולין והא *תניא כל הנשרפין אפרן מותר *חוץ מעצי אשירה ואפר הקדש לעולם אסור אמר רמי בר חמא כגון שנפלה דליקה מאיליה בעצי הקדש דליכא איניש דנמעול רב שמעי' אמר באותן שטעונין גניזה *דתניא °ושמו (ויקרא ו) בנחת ושמו כולו ושמו שלא יפזר: ר' יהודה אומר אין ביעור וכו': תניא *א"ר יהודה אין ביעור חמץ אלא שריפה והדין נותן ומה נותר שאינו בבל יראה ובל ימצא לא כל שכן שטעון שריפה אמרו לו °כל דין שאתה דן תחלתו להחמיר וסופו להקל אינו דין לא מצא עצים לשורפו יהא יושב ובטל והתורה אמרה °תשביתו (שמות יג) שאור מבתיכם בכל דבר שאתה יכול להשביתו חזר ר' יהודה ודנו דין אחר נותר אסור באכילה וחמץ אסור באכילה מה נותר בשריפה אף חמץ בשריפה אמרו לו נבילה תוכיח שאסורה באכילה ואינה טעונה שריפה אמר להן הפרש נותר אסור באכילה ובהנאה וחמץ אסור באכילה ובהנאה מה נותר טעון שריפה אף חמץ טעון שריפה אמרו לו שור הנסקל יוכיח שאסור באכילה ובהנאה ואינו טעון שריפה אמר להן הפרש נותר אסור באכילה ובהנאה וענוש כרת וחמץ אסור באכילה ובהנאה וענוש כרת מה נותר בשריפה אף חמץ בשריפה אמרו לו חלבו של שור הנסקל יוכיח שאסור באכילה ובהנאה וענוש כרת ואין טעון שריפה חזר

תוספות

מכלל דרבנן שרו כשאבוקה כנגדו . ואם תאמר לרבנן הואיל ואבוקה כנגדו חשיב כמו שלהבת באה מן הגחלים מאי פריך בסוף לולב הגזול (סוכה מ.) ובהגוזל עצים (ב"ק קא:) והא איכא עצים דמשחן שהנאתן וביעורן שוה הא בשעת הנאה מבוערין הן כבר במקום השלהבת ויש לומר משום [א] דשיעור כזה לא חשיב הנאה אחר ביעורן לענין שביעית שהרי באכילה דמינה ילפינן התם ליכא לגמרי הנאה וביעורן שוה ולא ממעטינן אלא שאר עצים שאין הנאתן אלא אחר שנעשו גחלים לגמרי ולרבי עצים דלא משחן נמי הוה ליה למיסר דלדידיה כשאבוקה כנגדו הנאתן וביעורן שוה ואיכא למימר הואיל ורוב הנאה אחר ביעור איכא לן למימר דלא אסרה תורה בכהן אבל תימה למאן דאמר לוחשות לרבי אסורים אמאי לא אסר בכל עצים בשביעית שהרי הנאתן וביעורן שוה הואיל ולא חשיב להו מבוערות כשהן לוחשות דבזתן הוי עיקר הנאה :

הקדש אפי' באלף לא בטיל. תימה מה חומר היא זו הלא הקדש דבר שיש לו מתירין הוא ע"י חילול ומטעם זה אין דינו להיות בטל אפילו באיסור קל אפילו מדרבנן כדאמרינן בריש ביצה (דף ד.) :

בעצי שלמים. ה"מ לאוקמי בעצי הקדש ובמזיד ואליבא דרבי יהודה אלא דלאו אורחא דמלתא לעבור במזיד :

ורמינהו כל הנשרפין וכו'. ה"מ לאוקמי בעצי שלמים :

חוץ מעצי אשירה. תימה לרשב"א היאך יהיו כעבודת גלולים שנשברה מאליה דשריא כדאמרינן בפרק כל הצלמים (ע"ז מח:) ואין לומר דהכא מיירי באשירה של ישראל דאין לה ביטול עולמית דהא בסוף תמורה (ד' לד.) מפרש דלהכי לא עריב ותני אפר הקדש ואשירה לעולם אסורין משום דאשירה יש לה היתר אם שורפה עו"ג דבטלה:

אין ביעור חמץ אלא שריפה. נראה דהלכה כרבי יהודה דסתם לן תנא כותיה בפרק בתרא דתמורה (ד' לג:) וא"ת א"כ בהא דאמר *ר' יהודה סוכה אינה נוהגת אלא בארבע מינין שבלולב יהא נמי הלכה כמותו דהתם נמי לא פליגי רבנן אלא מטעם דכל דין שתחלתו להחמיר וסופו להקל [ב] אין דין ובפ"ק דסוכה (ד' יא.) סתם לן תנא כרבנן דקתני הדלה עליה את הגפן ואת הדלעת אם קצצן כשירה וי"ל דהכא קיימא לן כרבי יהודה משום דין אחר דיליף במה מצינו אף על גב דאמרו לו חטאת העוף ואשם תלוי יוכיחו ושתיק מ"מ לדידן סבירא לן כרבנן דאמרי חטאת ואשם בשריפה וליכא תוכיח : [סוכה לו: ע"ש]

מה נותר בשריפה אף חמץ בשריפה . וא"ת למאן דדריש לעיל (ד' כד.) הנותר בשריפה ואין דבר אחר בשריפה היכי יליף רבי יהודה חמץ בשריפה מנותר ותירץ רשב"א דלית לן למעוטי מנותר אלא שאר איסורין אבל חמץ דדמי לנותר בכרת ובבל תותירו לא ממעטינן וא"ת לעיל היכי יליף שאר אסורין באם אינו ענין טקי קרא בחמץ בפסח דוקא דדמי ליה טפי וי"ל דלחמץ בפסח לא צריך [קרא] דמצי למילף במה מצינו :

חלבו של שור הנסקל יוכיח. הקשה ריב"א היא גופה נילף מנותר שיהא בשריפה דדמי ליה ותירץ דלא דמי ליה בבל תותירו :

רש"י

עצים דאיסורא. דמסרי בהנאה לרבנן היכי משכחת להו : בשרשיפא. כסא לישב עליו או להדום לרגליו דהנאתן כשהן בעין ועל ידי ממש אבל הנאת היסק אין הנאתו אלא לאחר ביעורו או בשעת ביעורו : בטילה במאתים. הלכך לא חמירא משכלה ונבער איסורו : והלא מעל המסיק. וחייב קרבן מעילה וכל דבר שאין בו קדושת הגוף כגון בהמה שאינה של קרבן וכלי שאינו כלי שרת כיון שמעל בו יצא לחולין דתנן (מעילה דף יט:) אין מועל אחר מועל במוקדשין אלא בהמה וכלי שרת בלבד אבל כל מידי אחרינא ממעילה ראשונה נפקא לחולין דקי"ל אין מעילה בכ"מ אלא שינוי שנשתנה מקדושתו ולמאי פת אסורה הא קודם שנתנו הפת היה ההיסק חולין : בעצי שלמים. שהפרישן לדמי שלמים למוכרן וליקח בדמיהן שלמים וקדשים קלים הם אין להם מעילה דלאו קדשי ה' קרינן ביה שכולן לבעלים ואין לגבוה בהן אלא לאחר זריקת דמים את האימורין ואיסורא מיהא רכיבה עלייהו וממעילה הוא דאימעיטו במסכת מעילה : ואליבא דרבי יהודה. פשט ליה רב חסדא בקדושין בפ"ב (דף נה.) דאמר הקדש במזיד אין מתחלל אם נהנה ממנו במזיד לא יצא לחולין הלכך בשלמים שוגג דידהו כמזיד דהקדש דהא לאו בני מעילה נינהו והכי נמי הוה מצי למימר הכא כשהסיקו מזיד עסקינן מיהו כשהסיקו משמע שוגג ומזיד וכיון דמצי לאוקמה בין בשוגג בין במזיד אוקמה : כל הנשרפין. בשילהי פרק בתרא דתמורה מפרש אלו נשרפין ואלו נקברין : ואפר הקדש לעולם אסור. להכי נקט גבי הקדש לעולם וגבי אשירה לא נקט לעולם משום דאשירה יש לה היתר אם שורפה עו"ג ובטלה אבל הקדש אין בו ביטול והכי מפורש בשילהי תמורה : רמי בר חמא ורב שמעיה. אאפר הקדש לעולם אסור מהדרי באותו אפר שטעון גניזה. קאמר לעולם אסור וזהו אפר של תרומת הדשן שלא היתה מעילה בהסיקו : כל דין שאתה דן. שמתחלתו אתה דנו כדי להחמיר עליו שהרי חמור הוא ואתה מביא לו חומר אחר כדקאמרת חמץ שהוא בבל יראה אין דין שטעון שריפה וסופו נמצא שחומר שאתה מוסיף עליו גורם לו להקל : איט דין. שהרי הדין מלמד שיהא חמור והרי הוא מקילו : שאם לא מצא עצים ישב ויבטל. בתמיה ואף על גב דאמרי' בפרק קמא (דף יב:) לרבי יהודה אבל בשעת ביעורו השבתתו בכל דבר גבי פלוגתייהו מיהא קולא היא במי שהוא רוצה לצאת בשיירא או בתוך שלשים דאמרינן *זקוק לבער וכשאין עצים לשורפו יהא יושב ובטל ולא יבערנו : ודנו דין אחר. שאינו קל וחומר אלא גזירה שוה ובין לקולא ובין לחומרא בתרה אזלינן דגזירת הכתוב הוא ואין להשיב עליו תחלתו להחמיר וסופו להקל :

רבינו חננאל

משכחת לה ושני' בשאבוקה כנגדה ומכח האבוקה נאפת ורבנן דשרי אפי' כשאבוקה כנגדו עצי איסור היכי משכחת לה ושני' בשרשפא פי' כסא לשבת בו כגון זה אסרה תורה: **בעי** מיניה רמי בר חמא מרב חסדא תנור שהוסק בעצי הקדש ואפה בו פת לר' המתיר [מהו] וא"ל הפת אסורה ומה בין עצי הקדש לעצי ערלה אמר רבא משום דערלה בטלה במאתים והקדש אפי' באלף לא בטיל קשיא ליה לרבא והא קיי"ל כי המסיק בעצי הקדש מעל וכיון דמעל נפקי להו העצים לחולין [ואמאי] הפת אסורה ומשני רב פפא בעצי הקדש שאמרנו במאי עסקינן כגון שהקדישם בתורת שלמים וכר' יהודה [דתני] בקדושין פ"ב הקדש בשוגג מתחלל במזיד אינו מתחלל מאי טעמא אינו מתחלל משום דלאו בר מעילה הוא הכא נמי בעצי הקדש המוקדשים בתורת שלמים כיון דשלמים לאו בני מעילה נינהו לא נפקי לחולין ומקשי' וכל היכי דמעל המסיק נפקי לחולין והתניא כל הנשרפין אפרן מותר חוץ מעצי אשרה ואפר הקדש דלעולם אסור ואי אמרת מעל המסיק ונפקי לחולין אמאי אסור ושניה כגון שנפלה דליקה מאיליה דליכא איניש דלימעול לפיכך תאני אפר הקדש לעולם אסור. רב שמעיה אמר האי דקתני אפר הקדש לעולם אסור כגון תרומת הדשן שטעון גניזה ושמועה זו תרומת הדשן שהוא טעון גניזה בסוף תמורה כדתניא ושמו אצל המזבח ושמו בנחת ושמו כלו (בנחת) ושמו שלא יפזר : ר' יהודה אומר אין ביעור חמץ אלא שריפה. תניא אמר ר' יהודה אין ביעור חמץ אלא שריפה והדין נותן ומה נותר שאינו בבל יראה ובבל ימצא וכו' עד

[עיין כוס מעי' ר"ס כח.]

תמורה לד.

שם לעיל ט. [ע"ש]

[לעיל ה: יב: כא. תמור' לד.]

[לעיל ו.]

הגהות הב"ח

(א) תוס' ד"ה מכלל וכו' ויש לומר משום שיעור כזה לא חשיב : (ב) ד"ה אין ביעור וכו' ושוב לפסל איט דין :

גליון הש"ס

גמ' כל דין שאתה דן תחלתו להחמיר. עי' שבת קלב ע"ב תוס' ד"ה דאתיא ובזבחים יב ע"ב תד"ה בן שמי :

עד שיהא בו כדי להחמיץ ואמר אביי לא שנו אלא שקדם וסילק את האיסור אבל לא קדם וסילק את האיסור אסור אלמא *זה וזה גורם אסור וממאי דטעמא דר' אליעזר כאביי דילמא טעמא דר' אליעזר משום דאחר אחרון אני בא לא שנא לא קדם וסילק את האיסור לא שנא קדם וסילק את האיסור אבל בבת אחת ה"נ דשרי אלא ר' אליעזר דעצי אשירה *דתנן נטל הימנה עצים אסורין בהנאה הסיק בהן את התנור חדש יותץ ישן יוצן אפה בו את הפת אסורין בהנאה נתערבה באחרות ואחרות באחרות כולן אסורין בהנאה רבי אליעזר אומר *יוליך הנאה לים המלח (אמר) לו אין פדיון לע"ז אימור דשמעת ליה לר' אליעזר בע"ז דחמיר איסורה בשאר איסורין שבתורה מי שמעת ליה אלא אם כן אמאן תרמייה ועוד הא תניא בהדיא וכן היה ר' אליעזר אוסר בכל איסורין שבתורה אמר אביי אם תמצא לומר זה וזה גורם אסור רבי היינו ר' אליעזר ואם תמצי לומר זה וזה גורם מותר והכא משום דיש שבח עצים בפת הוא [ב]הני קערות וכוסות וצלוחיות אסירי כי פליגי בתנור וקדירה למ"ד זה וזה גורם אסור למאן דאמר *זה וזה גורם מותר שרי איכא דאמרי אפי' למ"ד זה וזה גורם מותר [ג]קדירה אסורה דהא קבלה בישולא מקמי דניתן עצים דהתירא א"ר יוסף א"ר יהודה אמר שמואל תנור שהסיקו בקליפי ערלה או בקשין של כלאי הכרם חדש יותץ ישן יוצן אפה בו את הפת רבי אומר הפת מותרת וחכמים אומרים הפת אסורה והתניא איפכא שמואל איפכא תני ואב"א בעלמא קסבר שמואל *הלכה כרבי מחבירו ולא מחביריו ובהא אפי' מחביריו וסבר אתנייה איפכא כי היכי דניקום רבנן לאיסורא: בישלה על גבי גחלים דברי הכל הפת מותרת: (אמר) רב יהודה אמר שמואל ור' חייא בר אשי א"ר יוחנן חד אמר לא שנו אלא גחלים עוממות אבל גחלים לוחשות אסורין וחד אמר [ד]אפילו גחלים לוחשות נמי מותרין בשלמא למ"ד לוחשות אסורין משום דיש שבח עצים בפת אלא למ"ד אפילו לוחשות מותרות פת דאסר דיש שבח עצים בפת לרבי היכי משכחת ליה א"ר פפא כשאבוקה כנגדו מכלל

לא שנו. דאחר אחרון אני בא ואם נפל היתר בסוף מותר אלא שקידם את האיסור וסילקו מכיון שנפל בו היתר מיד דהוציא וסילקו ועדיין לא החמיץ בטל והלך לו ואע"ג דהועיל בה קצת שיכול זה האחרון לגמור חימוץ על ידו אעפ"כ כבר בטל לו ושוב אין חוזר וניעור בו אבל לא קדם וסילק ונגמר על ידי שניהם ואינו יכול ליבטל אסור אלמא זה וזה גורם אסור: דאחר אחרון אני בא. וטעמא משום דאזל בתר גמר מעשה גמרו בהיתר מותר ואפי' לא קדם וסילק דאיכא זה וזה גורם גמרו באיסור אסור (ואפילו קדם וסילק את האיסור): אבל בבת אחת. אם נפלו כאחת דליכא גמרו באיסור הכי נמי דשרי דזה וזה גורם מותר: הימנה. מן האשירה: יוליך הנאה לים המלח. דמי עצים מכל מקום שמעינן ליה כל כמה דלא ממטי הנאה לים המלח מודה הוא לת"ק בין אחדש יותץ בין אישן יוצן בין אאיסור פת אלמא כיון דקתני חדש יותץ אית ליה זה וזה גורם אסור והא דתניא לעיל חדש יוצן רבנן היא דפליגי עליה דר' ואמרי הפת מותרת משום דלא חשיבא להו הנאת היסק ואפילו בגורם אחד לבדו משום דליתיה לאיסורא בעיניה וכל שכן בתנור שאינו נאכל הוא בעצמו ואין הנאתו בגורם אחד לבדו אלא בשני גורמים שלו ושל היתר ואם תאמר לרבנן יוצן למה לי הא שרו לפת האפויה בהיסק איסור הני מילי דיעבד אבל לכתחלה לא קא שרו לאפות בהיסק איסור ולקמן פריך עלים דאיסור לרבנן היכי משכחת לה לאסירי מדאורייתא והוא הדין דמצי לאוקמא להא דחדש יותץ דלעיל כתנא קמא דר' אליעזר אלא משום דלא ידעינן מנו וניחא ליה למינקט ר' אליעזר והוא ומחלוקתו קאמר: א"כ דפרכת דילמא שאני ליה אמאן תרמייה להא דתניא לעיל גבי ערלה יותץ על כרחיך כיון דלא משכחת תנא דאמר זה וזה גורם אסור אלא רבי אליעזר ומחלוקתו במסכת ע"ז וחזינא סתמא דתני בשאר איסורי נמי הכי רבי אליעזר קאמר לה ולא שני ליה: אמר אביי אם תמצי לומר. ברייתא מפורשת הכי דכי היכי דאסר רבי בפת הכי נמי אסר בתנור ואע"פ שאין עצמו נאכל דאית ליה זה וזה גורם אסור וקישא דברייתא דלעיל דערלה רבי קאמר לה כולה: היינו ר' אליעזר. בניחותא וליכא למיבעי מידי: ואם תמצי לומר. דסבירא ליה זה וזה גורם מותר וקישא דההוא לאו רבי הוא אלא רבי אליעזר הוא והתם בפת הוא דאסר רבי משום דיש שבח עצים בגופה ונמלא כשאוכלה גופו הוא הנהנה מן האיסור בגורם אחד אבל בתנור חדש וליכנו שרי: הני קערות כוסות וצלוחיות. של חרס שצרפן בעצי אשירה אסירי אפילו לרבי דהא יש שבח עצים בהן והנאתן בלא גורם שני הוא ועל ידי גורם ראשון הוא משתמש בהן הנאת גופו ולא דמו לתנור דלא מטיא הנאה לגוף מיניה עד דאיכא גורם שני: כי פליגי. רבי דלא אסר אלא בפת ור' אליעזר אית ליה זה וזה גורם אסור בתנור וקדירה שאין הגוף נהנה מהן עד שיבא גורם שני והוא של היתר: קדירה. שצרפה כשהיא חדשה בעצי איסור דהא מקבלה בישולה. ואיכא הנאת תשמיש שמשתמש בה בלא גורם אחר אבל תנור אין נותנין בו פת אלא לאחר הסיקה של גורם היתר: איפכא תני לה. להא ברייתא דלעיל ואיפכא אתנייה: ואי בעית אימא. שמואל נמי הכי אתנייה ואית ליה דר' אסר ורבנן שרו ואיהו הפך לה כדי שלא ילכו בני אדם אחרי רבים להתיר דבעלמא במחלוקות אחרות שנחלקו רבים על רבי סבירא ליה לשמואל דאע"ג דהלכה כרבי מחבירו במקום יחיד אין הלכה כמותו מחביריו כלומר במקום רבים ובהא סבירא ליה דהלכה כמותו ואע"ג דרבים פליגי עליה: אפכה ואשנינה כי היכי דתיקו הא מילתא דאיסורא בשם רבנן ויעשו בני אדם כמותן שהכל הולכין אחרי רבים שאם אני אומר הלכה כרבי שהוא יחיד לא יאמינו לי: גחלים עוממות. כבויות כדכתיב (יחזקאל לא) ארזים לא עממוהו ומתרגמינן כהה עמיא: לוחשות. גחלים בוערות נראות כמתנענעות ולוחשות זו לזו: אסורין. לרבי: כנגדו. כנגד הפת מבעיר העצים בפי התנור:
עצים

עד שיהא בו כדי להחמיץ. פי' באיסור דאי יש באיסור וגם בהיתר כדי להחמיץ נראה לרשב"א דשרי דהא בפ' בתרא דמסכת ע"ז (דף סח.) תניא שאור של חולין ושל תרומה שנפלו לעיסה ובזה כדי להחמיץ ובזה כדי להחמיץ וחימצו אסור ור' שמעון מתיר והשתא הוי ר' שמעון כרבנן *דהכא והא דתנן בסוף פ"ק דתמורה (דף יב.) אין מחמץ אחר מחמץ [אוסר] אלא לפי חשבון שבה שאם נפל שאור של תרומה בעיסה וחימצה וחזרה ונפלה לעיסה אחרת גדולה מזאת אם יש בשאור כדי להחמיץ השניה אסורה אע"פ שנתחמצה על ידי שאור של איסור ועל ידי עיסה ראשונה שהיה של היתר ומוקמינן לה התם כרבנן דהכא אור"י מצי למימר דהתם מיירי כגון שאין בעיסה כדי להחמיץ ובשאור של תרומה יש כדי להחמיץ: נתערבו באחרות. אור"ת דלא גרסי' ואחרות באחרות דבסדר המשנה לא גרס ליה לא במסכת ע"ז ולא בסדר זרעים*: וכן היה רבי אליעזר אוסר בכל איסורין שבתורה. השתא משמע דבכל מקום אית ליה לרבי אליעזר דזה וזה גורם אסור ותימה לרשב"א דתיקשי מהכא לרב הונא בר חיננא דתניא בתמורה בפרק כל האסורין (דף ל: ושם) כל האסורין לגבי מזבח ולדותיהן מותרין ותניא עלה ר"א אוסר וקאמר רב הונא בר חיננא מחלוקת כשעיברו ולבסוף נרבעו דרבי אליעזר סבר עובר ירך אמו הוא אבל נרבעו ולבסוף עיברו ד"ה מותרין אלמא לרבי אליעזר זה וזה גורם מותר*: ובהא אפילו מחביריו. וטעמא דרבי משום דיש שבח עצים בפת ולא מטעם דזה וזה גורם דשמואל פסיק בהדיא בפרק כל הצלמים (ע"ז מט.) הלכה כר' יוסי דזה וזה גורם מותר:
מכלל

[סנהדרין פ. וש"נ]
רש"ל מוחק זה
ע"ז מט:
[נ"ל אמרו]
[ע"ז מט. סנהדרין פ. חולין נח. תמורה לג.]
[עירובין מו: כתובות נא. נא. ב"ב קכד:]
[נראה שהוא טעות הדפוס]

נג א מיי' שם טוש"ע שם:
נד ב מיי' פט"ז מהל' מאכלות אסורות הל' כג טוש"ע שם סעיף ה:
[ועי' תוס' ע"ז סח: ד"ה רבי שמעון]
נה ג ד מיי' שם הלכה כד טוש"ע שם סעיף ו ז:
[ועי' תוס' ע"ז מט. ד"ה נתערבו]
[ועי' תמורה ל: מה שתירצו תוס' ד"ה אבל]

רבינו חננאל

אומרים בין שנפל בתחלה בין שנפל בסוף לעולם אין אסור עד שיהא בשאור של תרומ' כדי לחמץ ואמר אביי לא שנו שאם יהיה האחרון שאור של חולין שהעיסה מותרת אלא שקדם וסלק את האיסור שיחמיץ אבל לא קדם וסלק את האיסור אע"ג שהאחרון חולין אסור ש"מ לר' אליעזר זה וזה גורם אסור ודחי' וממאי דכדאביי היא דלמא טעמא דר' אליעזר דסבר הכל אחר גמרו אי גמר באיסורא אסור אי גמר בהיתרא מותר בין סלקו בין לא סלקו לא שנא לפיכך שנה אחר אחרון אני בא אבל הכא שנתערבו שבח עצים ושבח תנור ובבת אחת הן באין על הפת דברי הכל שרי אלא הא ר' אליעזר דתנן בע"ז פ"ג נטל הימנה מן האשרה עצים והסיק בה התנור (כו') עד ר' אליעזר אומר יוליך הנאה לים המלח כו' פי' כשיעור שכר אפיית הפת יפרה הפת יוליך דמיה לים המלח קתני מיהת הפת אסורה ש"מ לר' אליעזר זה וזה גורם אסור ודחי' שאני התם משום חומרא דע"ז. אם כן הערלה וכלאי הכרם לאיזה איסור נדמה אותם ועוד תניא בהדיא וכן היה ר' אליעזר אוסר בכל איסורין שבתורה אליבא דמאן דאמר דלרבי זה וזה [גורם] מותר והכא בפת אמאי אסר משום דיש שבח עצים בפת סבירא ליה ומש"ה קתני הפת אסורה. קערות וכוסות וקיתונות וצלוחיות שנתבשלו בעצים של איסור דברי הכל אסורות דחד גורם הוא בתנור וקדרה פליגי כי התנור אינו אופה אלא ע"י הדלקת עצים וכן הקדרה אינה מבשלת אלא בעצים שנמצאו התנור והקדרה איסור והעצים שמדליקין בהן תוך התנור ותחת הקדרה של היתר והרי שניהם גורמין לאפיית הפת ולבישול מאן דאמר זה וזה גורם מותר גם אלו מותרות ומאן דאמר אסור גם אלו אסורות: איכא דאמרי בקדרה דברי הכל אסור מאי טעמא דהא קדים עייל בישולא שבח הקדרה מקמי דניתי כח עצים: שמואל הוה מהפיך דברי רבי לרבנן ואמר וחכמים אומרים הפת אסורה וגם הברייתא דתניא וחכמים אומרים הפת מותרת הוה מהפיך לה ותאני וחכמים אומרים הפת אסורה כי היכי דתיקום דרבנן לאיסורא וקיימא לן הכי: בשלה על גבי גחלים דברי הכל הפת מותרת יש מי שאומר לא שנו אלא גחלים עוממות קרובות לכבוי מלשון (יחזקאל ל"א ח') ארזים לא עממוהו וכמוהו (איכה ד' א') איכה יועם זהב דהא קלי ליה איסורא אבל גחלים לוחשות הפת אסורה ויש מי שאומר אפי' לוחשות הפת מותרת אי הכי לרבי קסבר יש שבח עצים בפת היכי
משכחת

[27a] unless it[7] contains sufficient to induce fermentation.[8] Now Abaye said: They learned this[9] only where he anticipated and removed the forbidden matter; but if he did not anticipate and remove the forbidden matter, it is forbidden:[10] this proves that the product of two causes is forbidden. Yet how do you know that R. Eliezer's reason is as Abaye [states it]: perhaps R. Eliezer's reason is because I follow the last, there being no difference whether he anticipated and removed the forbidden matter or he did not anticipate and remove the forbidden matter;[11] but [if they fell
a in] simultaneously, then indeed it may be permitted?[1]—Rather it is R. Eliezer'[s ruling] on the wood of the *asherah* [which is alluded to]. For we learned: If he took wood from it [*sc.* the *asherah*], benefit thereof is forbidden. If he fired an oven with it, if new, it must be destroyed; if old, it must be allowed to cool. If he baked bread in it, benefit thereof is forbidden; if it [the bread] became mixed up with others, and [these] others [again] with others,[2] they are all forbidden for use. R. Eliezer said: Let him carry the benefit [derived thence][3] to the Dead Sea.[4] Said they to him: You cannot redeem an idol. Granted that you hear R. Eliezer [to rule thus] in the case of idolatry, whose interdict is [very] severe; do you know him [to rule likewise] in respect of other interdicts of the Torah?—Then if so, to whom will you ascribe it?[5] Moreover, it was explicitly taught: And thus did R. Eliezer declare it forbidden in the case of all interdicts in the Torah.

Abaye said: Should you say that the product of two causes is forbidden, then Rabbi is identical [in view] with R. Eliezer.[6] But should you say, The product of two causes is permitted,[7] while here [Rabbi forbids the bread] because there is the improvement of the fuel in the bread, then plates, goblets, and
b flasks[1] are forbidden.[2] They differ only in respect of an oven and a pot.[3] On the view [that] the product of two causes is forbidden, these are forbidden; on the view [that] the product of two causes is permitted, these are permitted. Others state: Even on the view [that] the product of two causes is permitted, the pot is forbidden, for it receives the stew before the permitted fuel is placed.[4]

R. Joseph said in Rab Judah's name in Samuel's name: If an oven was fired [heated] with shells of *'orlah* or with stubble of *kil'ayim* of the vineyard, if new, it must be demolished; if old, it must be allowed to cool. If he baked bread in it,—Rabbi said: The bread is permitted; but the Sages maintain: The bread is forbidden. But the reverse was taught![5]—Samuel learned it the reverse. Alternatively, in general Samuel holds [that] the *halachah* is as Rabbi as against his colleague, but not as against his colleagues, but here [he holds], even against his colleagues, and so he reasoned, I will recite it reversed, in order that the Rabbis may stand [as ruling] stringently.[6]

'If he baked it upon the coals, all agree that the bread is permitted'.[7] Rab Judah in Samuel's name, and R. Ḥiyya b. Ashi in R. Joḥanan's name [differ therein]: one says, They learned [this] only of dying coals, but live[8] coals are forbidden;[9] while the other maintains, Even live coals too are permitted. As for the view that live [coals] are forbidden, it is well, [the reason being] because there is the improvement of the fuel in the bread.[10] But on the view that even live [coals] are permitted, then how is the bread which is forbidden because there is the improvement
c of the fuel in the bread conceivable according to Rabbi?[1]—Said

(7) The *se'or* of *terumah*, v. Tosaf. (8) If forbidden matter falls into permitted, it does not render it forbidden unless it imparts its taste to it. The *se'or* imparts its taste to the dough when it makes it leaven.—*Se'or* of *terumah* is designated forbidden matter, since it is forbidden to a lay Israelite. (9) *Sc.* R. Eliezer's view. (10) R. Eliezer holds that if the *hullin* fell in last, the dough is permitted. This is only if he removed the *terumah* immediately the *ḥullin* fell in, and before the dough was leavened. Though the *terumah* must have helped slightly in the leavening, yet since it is no longer there when the dough really becomes leaven, it is disregarded. But if the *terumah* was left there, the dough becomes forbidden even if the *ḥullin* fell in last. (11) The reason being that he regards that which completes the leavening as having produced the whole of it.

a (1) Because R. Eliezer permits the product of two causes. (2) 'And (these) others' etc. is absent in the Mishnah in A.Z. 49*b*, and R. Tam deletes it here too. (3) I.e., the value of the wood. (4) But R. Eliezer admits that if the benefit is not thrown into the Dead Sea, the new oven must be destroyed, which proves that he holds that the product of two causes is forbidden (v. *supra*, 26*b*, n. b3). (5) Lit., 'upon whom will you cast it?' This is the answer: there is none other to whom the Baraitha *supra* 26*b* can be ascribed. Hence it must be assumed that R. Eliezer draws no distinction between idolatry and other interdicts. (6) I.e., if the Baraitha *supra* 26*b* is to be explained thus: just as Rabbi forbids the bread baked by the heat of the nutshells of *'orlah*, so he also forbids the new oven that is fired by same, because he holds that the product of two causes is forbidden. Hence the whole Baraitha states Rabbi's ruling, his view being identical with R. Eliezer's. Consequently the problem which he proceeds to state does not arise. (7) Hence the first clause stating that a new oven must be destroyed cannot agree with Rabbi, but only with R. Eliezer.

b (1) Of earthenware, which received their final hardening in a kiln heated by forbidden fuel. (2) On all views. For they have been made fit for use and will be used without any further improvements, and there is direct benefit from forbidden matter. (3) Both of which must be heated again before food is cooked or baked in them. (4) The food for stewing is placed in the pot before the heat is applied to it. The mere placing is regarded as benefit, and this was made possible solely by the forbidden fuel. (5) *Supra* 26*b*. (6) And so that people might accept the stringent ruling. (7) V. *supra* 26*b*. (8) Lit., 'whispering'. When the coals are burning brightly they seem to be moving and whispering to each other (Rashi). (9) I.e., the bread is forbidden in Rabbi's view. (10) For the fuel is regarded as still in existence and directly baking the bread.

c (1) For obviously the bread does not bake until the fuel burns up, and by then it is a mass of coals.

so, even in the first clause too [the same applies]? [26b]—This can only be compared to the following: If a bird rested upon it [the red heifer], it remains fit;[2] but if it copulated with a male, it is unfit. What is the reason?—Said R. Papa: If it were written "*abad*'[3] and we read it "*abad*', [I would say, It becomes unfit] only if he himself wrought with it. While if "*ubad*'[4] were written and we read it "*ubad*,' [it would imply] even if it were of itself.[5] Since, however, it is written "*abad*' [active], whilst read "*ubad*' [passive], 'it was wrought with' must be similar to 'he wrought [with it]':[6] just as 'he wrought [with it]' must mean that he approved of it, so also 'it was wrought with' refers only to what he approved.[7]

Come and hear: He may not spread it [viz.,] a lost [raiment][8] upon a couch or a frame for his needs, but he may spread it out upon a couch or a frame in its own interests. If he was visited by guests, he may not spread it over a bed or a frame, whether in its interests or his own![9]—There it is different, because he may
a [thereby] destroy it,[1] either through an evil eye or through thieves.

Come and hear: Clothes merchants sell in their normal fashion, providing that they do[2] not intend [to gain protection] from the sun in hot weather[3] or from the rain when it is raining;[4] but the strictly religious[5] sling them on a staff behind their back.[6] Now here, though it is possible to do as the strictly religious, yet when he has no intention [of benefiting], it is permitted; this is a refutation of him who learns Raba's first version?[7] This is [indeed] a refutation.

AND ONE MAY NOT FIRE etc. Our Rabbis taught: If an oven was fired with the shells of '*orlah*[8] or with the stubble of *kil'ayim* of the vineyard, if new, it must be demolished; if old, it must be allowed to cool.[9] If a loaf was baked in it,—Rabbi said: The loaf is forbidden;[10] but the Sages maintain: The loaf is permitted.[11] If he baked[12] it upon the coals, all agree that it is permitted.[13] But it was taught: Whether new or old, it must be allowed to cool?—There is no difficulty: one agrees with Rabbi, the other with
b the Rabbis.[1] Granted that you know Rabbi [to rule thus] because the benefit[2] of the fuel lies in the loaf; do you know him [to maintain this ruling] where two things produce [the result]?[3]—Rather, [reply thus:] There is no difficulty: one is according to R. Eliezer, the other according to the Rabbis. Which [ruling of] R. Eliezer [is alluded to]? Shall we say, R. Eliezer['s ruling] on *se'or?*[4] For we learned: If *se'or* of *ḥullin* and [*se'or*] of *terumah* fall into dough, and neither is sufficient to make [it] leaven, but they combined and made [it] leaven,—R. Eliezer said: I regard[5] the last;[6] but the Sages maintain: whether the forbidden matter falls in first or the forbidden matter falls in last, it never renders it forbidden

(2) It is not disqualified because it has been put to some use. The red heifer had to be one '*upon which never came yoke*' (Num. XIX, 2), i.e., it had not been put to service. (3) Active: 'with which he (the owner) had (not) wrought'. (4) Passive: 'was (not) wrought with'. (5) I.e., even if it were wrought with entirely without the owner's volition. (6) I.e., though it may have been put to work without the knowledge of its master, it shall nevertheless be only such work as its master would have approved. (7) Now, if a bird rests on it, the master does not approve, since he does not benefit; but he does benefit from its copulation. Similarly, if he takes the heifer into the team and it accidentally threshes, he does not benefit thereby, as the team itself would have sufficed. Therefore it is not made unfit, unless that was his express purpose.—Though one passage refers to the beheaded heifer, while the other deals with the red heifer, it is deduced in Soṭ. 46a by a *gezerah shawah* (v. Glos.) that they are alike in law. (8) Which he has found, and awaiting the owner to come and claim it. (9) Thus, though he must spread it out, yet since he intends to benefit himself, it is forbidden.

a (1) Lit., 'burn it'. (2) Lit., 'he does'. The singular taken in the distributive sense. (3) Lit., 'in the sun'. (4) The reference is to garments containing the forbidden mixture of wool and linen (v. Deut. XXII, 11), sold to heathens. Merchants slung their wares across their shoulders for display, and though it is like wearing them, and some protection is afforded thereby, it is permitted. (5) Lit., 'the modest'. (6) So that they do not actually lie upon them. (7) V. *supra* 25b. (8) I.e., the shells of nuts of '*orlah*. (9) 'New' means that the oven has never been used yet. Before it is fit for use it must be burnt through so as to harden it, and if this was done with the shells of '*orlah*, the oven must be demolished, since it was made fit with prohibited fuel. But if it had been used before, the only benefit is that it is now hot: hence that benefit must be forfeited by allowing the oven to cool without using its heat. (10) He holds that the benefit of the forbidden fuel is contained directly in the loaf. (11) In their view the benefit of the forbidden fuel is not actually contained in the loaf, for the flame of the burning shells is not identical with the shells themselves. By the same reasoning they reject the ruling that if new, the oven must be destroyed, holding it sufficient that it should be allowed to cool. (12) Lit., 'boiled'. (13) When the nutshells or stubble are burnt through and a mass of coals, they are regarded as already destroyed and not in existence. Consequently, if he bakes the bread upon them, the bread is not regarded as having benefited directly from them, and even Rabbi admits that it is permitted.

b (1) V. *supra*, n. a11. (2) Lit., 'improvement'. (3) For when the new oven is fired, bread is not baked in it yet, and it will have to be fired a second time. Thus the bread that is baked will be the product of two things: the forbidden fuel and the permitted fuel. We do not find Rabbi holding that this too is forbidden, and if it is not, there is no need to demolish the oven. (4) *Se'or* is leaven with which other dough is made leaven. *Ḥameẓ* is leavened bread. (5) Lit., 'come after'. (6) The status of the dough is determined by which fell in last: if *ḥullin*, the dough is permitted to a lay Israelite; if *terumah*, it is forbidden.

עין משפט נר מצוה

מז א מיי' פ"א מהל' פרה הלכה ז:

מח ב מיי' פי"ג מהל' אבידה הל' יד סמג עשין עד טוש"ע חו"מ סי' רסז סעיף יז:

מט ג מיי' פי' מהל' כלאים הל' טו סמג לאוין רעג טוש"ע י"ד סי' שא סעיף ז:

נ ד מיי' פט"ז מהלכות מאכלות אסורות הלכה כב טוש"ע י"ד סי' קמב סעיף ד:

נא ה מיי' שם הל' כד טוש"ע שם סעיף ו:

נב ו ז מיי' שם הל' כב ופ"ו מהלכות ע"ז הל' יב טוש"ע שם סי' ד:

הא לא דמיא אלא להא שכן עליה עוף. מייתי לה משום דרב פפא אמר מילתיה עלה לפי שהיא משנה:

עלה עליה זכר פסולה. וא"ת אמאי פסולה הא ודאי לא ניחא ליה להפסיד פרה שדמיה יקרים בשביל דבר מועט וי"ל דאפס נאמר כשירה הוה ניחא ליה ולכך אין להכשירה וא"ת הכניסה לרבקה ודשה אמאי כשירה נו"ש מעלה עליה זכר דפסולה וי"ל דהתם לא ניחא ליה דבישתה שאין מרויח כלום בדישתה דבלאו הכי נידושה התבואה וה"ר יהודה פירש דהתם פרה בחורה היא ומסתמא אין אדם רוצה להטריחה וא"ת והא דתנן* פרה מעוברת ר' אליעזר מכשיר וחכמים פוסלין והכא אמר עלה עליה זכר פסולה וי"ל דהכא כחכמים דפוסלין דה"כ ר' יהודה פליג ואמר דווקא העלה עליה זכר אבל עלה מעצמו כשירה אי נמי הא דאמר הכא פסולה היינו כשרוצה בשעת עלייה וניחא ליה כדאמר גבי הכשר (בפ"ק דחולין) (*דף יג.) עודהו הטל עליהן ושמח הרי זה בכי יותן נגבו אינן בכי יותן דבעינן יותן דומיא דיתן אף על פי שאם היה יודע בעוד הטל עליהן היה שמח והא דאמרינן בפרק עגלה ערופה(סוטה מו.) עול פוסל בין בשעת עבודה ובין שלא בשעת עבודה שאר דברים אינן פוסלין אלא בשעת עבודה מה שהזכר משמש בה חשוב עבודה:

מגוד. פירש ר"ח כמו נגוד ליה גלימא (*עירובין ד' נד.):

חדש יותן. קסבר יש שבח עצים בפת וה"ה יש שבח עצים בתנור וזה וזה גורם אסור ויש שבח עצים בפת היינו העצים שהן גורמים אפיית הפת כשאבוקה כנגדו ורבנן סברי אין שבח עצים בפת אף על פי שהאבוקה כנגדו דשלהבת אינה באה מן העצים אלא מחמת משהו הנשרף וא"כ היא כמו נחלת דאין האיסור בעין וכן פירש"י הקשה ה"ר אהרן *לרבי הא דאמר (תרומה פ"ב מ"ג) המבשל בשבת בשוגג יאכל ואפילו בשבת ואמאי נימא יש שבח מוקלה בפת דגחלים מוקצין הן ואומר ר"י דלא שייך אלא באיסורי הנאה דווקא וכן פי' הקונטרס בפרק בתרא דע"ז (דף סו. ושם) גבי תנור שהסיקו בכמון של תרומה:

בישלה על גבי גחלים. בישלה דווקא דיעבד אף על גב דכל הנשרפין אפרן מותר* אפילו לכתחלה יש לחלק בין אפרן לגחלים:

בין חדש בין ישן יותן. דזה וזה גורם מותר אף על גב דזה וזה גורם דווקא בדיעבד מותר כדמוכח בסוף פרק כל הצלמים (ע"ז מט:) דאמר רבי יוסי אין נוטעין אגוז של ערלה ומודה ר' יוסי שאם נטע שהוא מותר וחשיב ליה זה וזה גורם דהכא הוי כדיעבד דאם נאמר חדש יותן יפסיד התנור:

בין חדש ובין ישן יותן. ואף על גב דזה וזה גורם מותר מ"מ ישן כיון דסגי ליה בליבון ולא מפסיד מידי אלא איסור הגלה לאודה לכך צריך ליבון:

הא לא דמיא אלא להא **שכן עליה עוף כשירה עלה עליה זכר פסולה מ"ט אמר רב פפא אי כתיב °עבד וקרינן עבד עד דעביד בה איהו אי כתיב עובד וקרינן עובד אפילו ממילא נמי השתא דכתיב עבד וקרינן עובד עובד דומיא דעבד מה עבד דניחא ליה אף עובד דניחא ליה ת"ש *אבידה לא ישטחנה לא על גבי מטה ולא על גבי מגוד לצורכו אבל שוטחה לצורכה על גבי מטה ועל גבי מגוד נזדמנו לו אורחין לא ישטחנה לא על גבי מטה ולא על גבי מגוד בין לצורכה בין לצורכו שאני התם דקלי לה אי משום עינא בישא אי משום גנבי ת"ש *מוכרי כסות מוכרין כדרכן ובלבד שלא יתכוין בחמה מפני החמה ובגשמים מפני הגשמים והצנועין מפשילין לאחוריהם במקל והא הכא דאפשר למעבד כצנועין וכי לא מכוין שרי תיובתא למאן דמתני לישנא קמא דרבא תיובתא: ולא יסיק בו וכו': *ת"ר תנור שהסיקו בקליפי ערלה או בקשין של כלאי הכרם חדש יותץ ישן יוצן אפה בו את הפת רבי אומר °הפת אסורה וחכמים אומרים הפת מותרת °בישלה על גבי גחלים דברי הכל מותר והא תניא 'בין חדש ובין ישן יוצן לא קשיא הא רבי והא רבנן והא רבנן אימור דשמעת ליה לרבי 'משום דיש שבח עצים בפת זה וזה גורם מי שמעת ליה אלא לא קשיא הא ר' אליעזר הא רבנן הי רבי אליעזר אילימא רבי אליעזר דשאור *דתנן שאור של חולין ושל תרומה שנפלו לתוך עיסה ואין בזה כדי להחמיץ ואין בזה כדי להחמיץ ונצטרפו וחמצו רבי אליעזר אומר אחר אחרון אני בא וחכמים אומרים בין שנפל איסור *לכתחלה ובין שנפל איסור לבסוף לעולם אינו אוסר עד

הא לא דמיא. תירוצא הוא: שכן עליה עוף. בפרה אדומה קאי שפרח ונח על גבה אע"ג דכתיב לא עלה עליה עול דמשמע עליה אפילו עליה בעלמא ואי משום דכתיב עול הא מרבינן ביה שאר עבודות במסכת סוטה (דף מו.) אפ"ה בהא עלייה כשרה דלא ניחא ליה והוא הדין להכניסה לרבקה ודשה: עלה עליה זכר פסולה. דניחא ליה והוא הדין לתינק ותידוש: עובד. משמע ממילא עבד משמע בידים ואף על גב דהאי בעגלה כתיב תרוייהו ילפינן מהדדי בגזרה שוה דעול עול במסכת סוטה (דף מו.): לא ישטחנה. במולא בגד אבודה קאי: מגוד. קבילי"א: לצורכה. כדי שלא יתלכלו עש: נזדמנו לו אורחין וכו'. אלמא אף על גב דלצורכה הוא והיינו לא אפשר הואיל ומתכוין להתכבד בשל חבירו באורחין חשיב ליה גזל ואסור: ומשני לאו משום כוונה הוא אלא משום דבשטיחה זו קלי לה כלומר מאבדה בידים אי משום עינא בישא אי משום דלמא אורחין גנבי ניהו וגנבי לה: מוכרין כדרכן. מעוטפין בכסות כלאים דאין מתכוין להנאת לבישה: והצנועים. פרושים שמתרחקין מן הכיעור ומן הדומה לו: לישנא קמא דרבא. אפשר ולא מתכוין אסור אפילו לרבי שמעון דא"כ הא מני: יש שטוענין שמקשין על משנה זו אותה ששנינו בגד שאבד בו כלאים לא ימכרנו לנכרי אלמא כלאים אסור למכור וטעות בידם דהתם אבד דווקא שמא יחזור נכרי וימכרנו לישראל ולא יכיר שיש בו כלאים וילבשנו אבל כלאים הניכר מותר בכל הנאות מכירה: בקליפי ערלה. קליפי אגוזים ורמונים שאף הם בכלל פרי ואסורין משום ערלה וכן קשין של כלאי הכרם הכל אסור דבכלאים לא כתיב פרי: חדש יותץ. שהרי על ידי היסק זה של ערלה נגמר ומתקיים כולו: ישן. שאין היסק זה מועיל לו אלא לאפיה בו פת: יוצן. שלא יאפה בו פת בהיסק זה: אפה בו פת. בהיסק זה לקמן מוקי לה כשאבוקה כנגדו דכל שעה שהיתה פת בתנור היה דולק האור ואופהו שהיה נהנה מן האיסור בשעה שהאיסור בעין: רבי אומר הפת אסורה. דיש שבח עצי איסור בפת: וחכמים אומרים הפת מותרת. (דהא) סברי אין שבח עצים בפת ממש והוא הדין דלית להו נמי חדש יותץ אלא יוצן והכי אמרי' בשמעתין: בישלה על גבי גחלים. דברי הכל הפת מותרת ואפילו לרבי דכי איתיהבי פת מאיסור כבר כלה ובטל וגחלים אילטריכא ליה דלא תימא הכא איסורא בעיניה וכל שכן בתנור גרוף ואין אבוקה כנגדו: הא רבי. דקתני חדש יותץ רבי היא דאמר הפת אסורה משום דגמרה באיסור והוא הדין לתנור חדש שנגמר נמי ע"י האיסור: אימור דשמעת ליה לרבי דיש שבח עצים בפת. כי שמעת ליה דפליג רבי אדרבנן בשבח עצים בפת לחודה הוא דשמעת ליה דרבנן הוו מקילי טפי וסברי אפי' פת נאכל דאמרי אין שבח עצים בה אלא שבח היסק ואיסור (א) שבה כבר כלה הוא ורבי סבר הואיל ואבוקה כנגדו יש שבח עצים ואיסור גמור בה וגבי תנור חדש נמי דיש שבח עצים בו מיהו הוא עצמו אין נאכל אלא להסיק אחר עומד ויאפו בו ונמצאת פת נגמרת ע"י איסור והיתר עליו איסור שנגמרו (בו) את התנור ועצי היתר שנגמרו את הפת והיכא סתמינן ליה לאסור רבי: הא ר' אליעזר. דסתמינן ליה זה וזה גורם אסור דבר שאיסור והיתר גרמו לו ביבא אסור בהנאה: לתוך עיסה. של חולין: אחר אחרון אני בא. אם סילק את הראשון כדמתרך ליה לאביי: לא

מסורת הש"ס

פרה פ"ב מ"ד

דברים כא

ב"מ ל. [ע"ש]

שבת כט: מו. כלאים פ"ט משנה ה

לקמן עה.

ע"ז מט. עג: תמורה לד. ערלה פ"ב מי"א

צ"ל בתחלה וכ"א במשנה

[כפ"ב דב"מ כב.]

[ויותר מפורש בכורות מד:]

רש"ל גורס לר"י ועי' רש"א

[צ"ל דהסם]

[תמורה לד. וע"ש]

(ע"ז מה:)

הגהות הב"ח

(א) רש"י ד"ה אימור וכו' היסק ואיסור שבה:

גליון הש"ס

גמ' בישלה על גבי גחלים. עי' לקמן דף עה ע"א תוס' ד"ה וגרפו ובתשובת פני יהושע סי' י"א:

רבינו חננאל

ת"ש כסות המופקדת אצלו לא ישטחנה לא על גבי מטה ולא על גבי מגוד לצורכו אבל שוטח' לצרכה נזדמנו לו אורחין בין לצורכו בין לצרכה לא ישטחנה הנה אפי' לצרכה אסור ושנינן שאני התם דקא קלא ליה כלומר כיון שרואין אותה האורחין באין בלילה ונוטלין אותה נמצא כששטחה כאלו שורפה באש: ת"ש הכניסה לפרה אדומה בנוקבה לרבקה. פי' לפסוס' מלשון (ירמיה יו כא) עגלי מרבק ודשה כשרה בשביל שתינק והחדש פסולה הנה כיון שנתכוין לדוש פסלה ואוקימ' מה עבד דניחא ליה אף עובד דניחא ליה [אע"פ שעובד בה מלאכה שלא על ידיו אלא ניחא ליה עבודה היא ונפסלת בה

ת"ש מהא דתנן בפ"ט דכלאים מוכרי כסות מוכרין כדרכן כלומר נישאין בגדי כלאים על כתפיהן ומהלכין מהן ובלבד שלא יתכוין בחמה מפני החמה ובגשמים מפני הגשמים והצנועין מפשילין לאחוריהן במקל והא הכא דאפשר למעבד כצנועין ואע"ג דלא עביד כצנועין כי לא מיכוין שרי ותיובתא למאן דאתני לישנא קמא דרבא תיובתא וקיימא לן אפי' אפשר ולא קא מיכוין שרי: **ולא** יסיק בו תנור וכירים. ת"ר תנור שהסיקו בקליפי ערלה או בקשין של כלאי הכרם חדש יותץ ישן יוצן אפה בו את הפת ר' אומר הפת אסורה וחכמים אומרים הפת מותרת בשלה על גבי גחלים דברי הכל מותר (*פי' יוצאי מותר עצים) איני והתניא אחד ישן ואחד חדש יוצן ושנינן הא דתני [אפילו חדש] יוצן רבנן והא דתני [חדש] יותץ רבי. ואקשי' אימור דשמעת ליה לר' דיש שבח עצים בפת כלומר שבח עצי האיסור שרוי בפת והוא אפיית הפת הוה ידוע בפת לפיכך שנה הפת אסורה אבל עצי היתר שנצטרפו עצים של היתר בתנור [בתנור של איסור] התנור חדש אסורה הפת [של איסור] [שמעון] נתיצה גורמין אפיית הפת [מי] שמעת לרבי שאור בזה ואתינן לאוקמיהו לר' אליעזר ורבנן דפליגי בשאור של חולין ושל תרומה שנפלו בעיסה ואין באחד מהן שיעור להחמיץ הוא לבדו העיסה ונצטרפו וחימצו ר' אליעזר אומר אחר אחרון אני בא וחכמים אומרים

* דברי רבינו אלו מבולבלי הכונה הם ואולי צ"ל: ע"ש נפל בדבריו.

עין משפט נר מצוה

לז א מיי' פי"ד מהל' מאכלות אסורות הל' יב [רב אלפס כאן ובע"ז פ"ד דף שלה:]
לח ב מיי' פ"ה מהלכות מעילה הלכה ה:
לט ג מיי' פ"ז מהלכות בית הבחירה הל' כג:
[ועי' תוס' ע"ז מח: ד"ה לא ישב]
מ ד מיי' פ"ה מהלכות מעילה הל' יו סמג עשין רי:
מא ה מיי' פ"ב מהל' כלי המקדש הל' י:
מב ו שם הלכה ט:
מג ז מיי' פ"ה מהלכות מעילה הלכה טז:
מד ח מיי' פ"ב מהל' תמידין ומוספין הלכה טו:
מה ט מיי' פ"ח מהל' כלי המקדש הל' ס:
מו י מיי' פ"א מהלכות פרה הלכה ז:

ורבא *אמר לך עד כאן לא קאמר ר' יהודה שאין מתכוין כמתכוין אלא לחומרא אבל מתכוין כשאין מתכוין לקולא לא אמר אביי מנא אמינא לה דתניא אמרו עליו על רבן יוחנן בן זכאי שהיה יושב בצילו של היכל ודורש כל היום כולו והא הכא דלא אפשר ומיכוין ושרי ורבא אמר שאני היכל דלתוכו עשוי אמר רבא מנא אמינא לה (דתניא) *גלולין היו פתוחין בעליית בית קדשי הקדשים שבהן משלשלין את האומנים בתיבות כדי שלא יזונו עיניהם מבית קדשי הקדשים והא הכא דלא אפשר וקא מיכוין ואסור ותסברא *והאמר ר' שמעון בן פזי א"ר יהושע בן לוי משום בר קפרא קול ומראה וריח אין בהן משום מעילה אלא מעלה עשו בבית קדשי הקדשים איכא דאמרי אמר רבא מנא אמינא לה דתניא אמר ר' שמעון בן פזי אמר ר' יהושע בן לוי משום בר קפרא קול ומראה וריח אין בהן משום מעילה מעילה הוא דליכא הא איסורא איכא מאי לאו לאותן העומדין בפנים דלא אפשר וקא מיכוין ואסור לא לאותן העומדין בחוץ גופא א"ר שמעון בן פזי אמר ריב"ל משום בר קפרא קול ומראה וריח אין בהן משום מעילה וריח אין בו משום מעילה והא תניא *המפטם את הקטורת להתלמד בה או למוסרה לציבור פטור להריח בה חייב והמריח בה פטור אלא שמעל אלא אמר רב פפא קול ומראה אין בהן משום מעילה לפי שאין בהן ממש וריח לאחר שתעלה תמרתו אין בו משום מעילה הואיל ונעשית מצותו למימרא דכל היכא דנעשית מצותו אין בו משום מעילה והרי תרומת הדשן דנעשית מצותה ויש בה משום מעילה דכתיב °ושמו אצל המזבח *שלא יפזר ושמו שלא יהנה משום דהוו תרומת הדשן ובגדי כהונה שני כתובין הבאין כאחד וכל שני כתובין הבאין כאחד אין מלמדין תרומת הדשן הא דאמרן בגדי כהונה דכתיב °והניחם שם °מלמד *שטעונין גניזה הניחא לרבנן דאמרי מלמד שטעונין גניזה אלא לר' דוסא (א) דפליג עלייהו דאמר אבל ראויין הן לכהן הדיוט ומאי והניחם שם שלא ישתמש בהם ביום כפורים אחר מאי איכא למימר משום דהוו תרומת הדשן ועגלה ערופה שני כתובין הבאין כאחד *וכל שני כתובין הבאין כאחד אין מלמדין הניחא למ"ד אין מלמדין אלא למאן דאמר מלמדין מאי איכא למימר תרי מיעוטי כתיבי כתיב ושמו וכתיב °הערופה ת"ש *הכניסה לרבקה ודשה כשירה בשביל שתינק ותדוש פסולה והא הכא דלא אפשר וקא מיכוין וקתני פסולה שאני התם דכתיב אשר לא עובד בה מכל מקום אי הכי אפילו רישא נמי הא

רש"י

ורבא אמר לך עד כאן. לא שמעת ליה לרבי יהודה דלא אזיל בתר כוונה אלא דלא פטר ליה משום אין מתכוין בדאפשר דמתכוין אסור לדברי הכל ומשוי שאין מיכוין כמתכוין לחומרא לאסור אבל דלא חשיבא ליה כוונה דמשוי מכוין כשאין מתכוין לקולא כגון דלא אפשר בשאין מתכוין שרי ונישרי נמי רבי יהודה במתכוין דלא חשיב כוונה כלל הא לא שמעת ליה: ההיכל גובהו מאה אמה ונראה הולך למרחוק מאד ברחוב שלפני הר הבית ומתוך שרחוב גדול היה ומחזיק בני אדם הרבה היה דורש שם מפני החמה שאין לך בית המדרש מחזיקן: דלא אפשר. מלדרוש לרבים הלכות החג: וקא מיכוין. ליהנות מצל הקודש: דלתוכו עשוי. ואין הנאה זילו נאסרה דאין זה דרך הנאתו: לול. ארובה שבעלייה היורדת לבית קרי לול: האומנין. כשיש בדק בחומת בית קדשי הקדשים: יזונו. לשון הנאה כמזונות שמשביע עצמו ממראית נוי המלאכה ונהנה: והא הכא דלא אפשר. שלא ירדו לתקן ואפילו הכי צריך לתת אותן בתיבות שלא יוכלו להסתכל אנה ואנה דילמא מיכווני ליהנות ואסור: קול. של כלי שיר שהן הקדש: וריח. הקטורת: אין בהן משום מעילה. דאורייתא הואיל ואין בהם ממש וכיון דמדאורייתא שרו כי לא אפשר כגון הכא אמאי אטרחינהו רבנן אלא מעלה בעלמא הואי: העומדים בפנים. לשמש דלא אפשר מלעמוד שם ואסור להו להיות מתכוונים: לאותן העומדים בחוץ. קאמר אין מעילה הא איסורא איכא אבל לעומדין בפנים אפילו איסורא ליכא: המפטם את הקטורת. קטורת זרה שאינה של ציבור: אם להתלמד בה או למוסרה. אחר פיטומה לציבור פטור מכרת אבל אם דעתו להצניע לצורכו להריח בה ועשאה בסממנין הכתובים חייב כרת דכתיב (שמות ל) איש אשר יעשה כמוה להריח בה ונכרת: והמריח בה. בקטורת של ציבור פטור מכרת ומחטאת דלא חייבה תורה אלא מפטם להריח: אלא שמעל. שנהנה מן הקודש ומביא אשם מעילות: קול ומראה. אין בהם ממש ופטורים לעולם: וריח. יש בו ממש בסממנין לפיכך חייב ודקא אמר רבי יהושע פטור לאחר שתעלה תמרתו במקדש קאמר דמשום דנעשית מצותו ואין צורך גבוה עוד בה יצאה מכלל קדשי ה' ובריתא במריח בה בביתו שנותן ממנה על הגחלים: תמרתו. עמוד עשנו: תרומת הדשן. בכל יום היה נוטל מלא מחתה ונותנה אצל המזבח והיא נבלעת במקומה כדכתיב והרים את הדשן וגו' ואסורה בהנאה ומועלין בה כדכתיב ושמו אצל המזבח אלמא טעונה גניזה: ובגדי כהונה. ארבעה בגדי לבן שכהן גדול נכנס בהם לפני ולפנים ביום הכפורים דאסורין שוב להשתמש בהן כדכתיב והניחם שם: הא ניחא לרבנן. פלוגתייהו במסכת יומא (דף כד:): כשירין הם לכהן הדיוט. כל השנה שהן הן הבגדים הראויין לשימוש הדיוט כתונת ומכנסים ומצנפת ואבנט: עגלה ערופה. כתיב שם דמשמע שם תהא קבורתה: אלא למ"ד מלמדין. ר' יהודה במסכת סנהדרין בשלהי ארבע מיתות (סז:): הכא מיעוטי כתיבי. בהני למימרא דלא תיגמר מינייהו ושמו לזה ולא לאחר הערופה ולא לדבר אחר: הכניסה לרבקה. עגלה ערופה רבקה קופל"א בלע"ז שקושרין ארבע פרות ביחד: ודשה. תבואה עם חברותיה: כשירה. שלא נתכוין לכך ולאו עבודה היא: ואם נתכוין שתינק ותדוש פסולה. והכא לא אפשר שלא יכניסנה שתינק וכי מתכוין שתינק ותדוש פסולה: אשר לא עובד בה מכל מקום. דאע"ג דבעלמא לא מיתסר הכא אסור:
הא

תוספות

שאני היכל דלתוכו עשוי. פ"ה ואין הנאת צילו נאסרת שאין זה דרך הנאתו וא"ת והא לא כתיב אכילה ואפילו שלא כדרך הנאה יהא אסור וי"ל דמעילה ילפינן *חטא חטא מתרומה ובתרומה כתיב אכילה והא דאסר בפ' כל הצלמים (ע"ז מח:) לישב תחת אשירה משום דאשירה לצל עשויה והיא דרך הנאה ועוד דגבי ע"ז לא כתיב אכילה*: והא הכא דלא אפשר וקמיכוין ואסור. ה"מ אביי לאוקמא כרבי שמעון דאליבא דרבי יהודה פליגי:

ותסברא והאמר רבי שמעון בן פזי קול ומראה וריח אין בהן משום מעילה. פ"ה וכיון דמדאורייתא שרי כי לא אפשר אמאי אטרחוה רבנן וקשה לר"י הא בגרירה דליכא איסורא דאורייתא ופליג רבא ואסר בלא אפשר ומיכוון ומאי קא מוכיח אביי לרבא וי"ל דה"פ כיון דלא אסירי אלא מדרבנן א"כ כשהוא לצורך כגון לתקן בית קדשי הקדשים סברא הוא דאפילו איסורא דרבנן ליכא:

מעילה הוא דליכא הא איסורא איכא. תימה דבפרק החליל (סוכה נג. ושם) תניא אשה בוררת חטים לאור של בית השואבה והשמן והפתילה היו של קודש כדתנן התם ובירושלמי דייק מינה דקול ומראה וריח אין בהן משום מעילה:

לאותן העומדים בחוץ. ליכא איסורא אלא שלא יקרבו עצמן לעזרה כדי להריח יותר דהא אמרינן (יומא דף לט:) לא היתה כלה צריכה להתבשם בירושלים מפני ריח הקטורת:

כתיב הכא ושמו וכתיב התם הערופה. תימה לר"י אמאי איצטריך תרי מיעוטי בחד סגי דלהכי כתביה דלא למילף מינייהו* וי"ל דאי לא כתיב אלא חד מיעוטא לא הוה מצי למעוטי אלא מילתא דלא דמי כל כך למיסר אבל מילתא דדמי למיסר לא להכי איצטריך תרווייהו:

הכניסה לרבקה. בתוספתא תני ליה גבי פרה:
הא

[בתוספות חולין קיז: ד"ה עיין כו' עוד שם קיז: וכן בזבחים מו. הניחו דבר זה בתימה אמנם במעילה יח. תירצו בשם ה"ר פרץ עי"ש וכן ביומא ס. הארכתי בגיליון זה]

רבינו חננאל

וסמיך אביי אהא דרבן יוחנן בן זכאי שהיה יושב ודורש כל היום בצלו של היכל ודחי' רבא שאני התם דהיכל לתוכו עשוי ואין קדושה בצלו רבא אמר מהא דתנן לולין היו פתוחין בעליית קדשי קדשים שבהן היו משלשלין האומנין בתיבות כדי שלא יזונו עיניהםמבית קדשי הקדשים ש"מ דהנאה הבאה לו לאדם בעל כרחו אסור. ודחי אביי מעלה עשו דהא קול ומראה וריח אין בהן משום מעילה. איכא דאמרי רבא הוה מסתייע מזה דהוה דאיק אין בהן משום מעילה הא איסורא איכא מאי לאו באותם העומדים בפנים דלא אפשר וכיון דמכוני אסיר ודחינן לא באותן העומדים בחוץ דאפשר שלא יעמדו ולפיכך מעילה (איכא) [ליכא] איסורא איכא. ואיני דריח אין בו מעילה [והא תנן] המפטם קטרת להתלמד בה [או] למוסרה לצבור [פטור] להריח בה חייב המריח פטור אלא שמעל ושני' הא דתני ריח אין בו מעילה לאחר שתעלה תמרתו היא שניה מאי טעמא דהא אתעבידא מצותה והא דתני המריח פטור אלא שמעל בשלא עלתה תמרתו: איני והרי תרום' הדשן דאתעבידא מצותה ומועלין בה ושני' משום דכתיב בתרומת הדשן ושמו אצל המזבח ובבגדי כהונה נמי אחר שנעשה מצותן [יש בהם מעילה] כדכתיב והניחם שם לאו משום דטעונין גניזה הוא [ולמ"ד דראוים הם לכהן הדיוט] מפיק בגדי כהונה ומעייל עגלה ערופה כתיב וערפו שם את העגלה בנחל ולמאן דאמר מלמדין מיעט רחמנא בגדי כהונה ושמו אצל המזבח זה טעון גניזה ולא זולתו ובעגלה ערופה כתיב וערפו שם את העגלה הני אין מידי אחרינא לא:

מסורת הש"ס

[נ"ל דתנן מדות לז. [פ"ד מ"ה]
כריתות ו.
תמורה לד. לקמן כז: [ע"ש] וגי' רש"ל ושמו אצל המזבח שלא ימעלו בה אחרים אלא שיהא כולו אצל המזבח משום דהוי:
כריתות ו. חולין קיז. מעילה יא: זבחים כו. יומא יב. כד. ס.
[לקמן מה. יומא ס. קדושין כד. לה. לז: מב: מג. נח. גיטין עו. מיר לז: ע"ז כד: סנהדרין מה: סז: עב: שבועות כו: זבחים כד. מו. מ. בכורות מט. ערכין יד: חולין סא: קיג: קיז. כריתות ו. מעילה יא:

הגהות הב"ח

(א) גמ' דפליג שלייהו ואמר אבל:

גליון הש"ס

תוס' ד"ה שאני. חטא חטא מתרומה. עי' שאגת אריה סי' עו ובתוס' ר"פ כל הצלמים ד"ה ימותו:

says thus: R. Judah rules that the unintentional is the same as the intentional only in the direction of stringency, but he did not rule that the intentional is the same as the unintentional where it is in the direction of leniency.

Abaye said: Whence do I know it? Because it was taught: It was related of R. Joḥanan b. Zakkai that he was sitting in the shadow of the Temple and teaching all day.[1] Now here it was impossible [not to lecture], and he intended [to benefit from the shade], and it is permitted?[2] But Raba said: The Temple was different, because it was made for its inside.[3]

Raba said: Whence do I know it? Because we learned: There were passage ways opening in the upper chamber to[4] the Holy of Holies, through which the artisans were lowered in boxes,[5] so that they might not feast their eyes on the Holy of Holies. Now here it was impossible [to avoid going there], and he [the workman] intended [to gaze at the Holy of Holies], and it was forbidden. But is that logical? Surely R. Simeon b. Pazzi said in R. Joshua b. Levi's name on Bar Ḳappara's authority: Sound, sight, and smell do not involve trespass?[6] Rather, they set up a higher standard for the Holy of Holies.[7]

Others state, Raba said: Whence do I know it? Because it was taught, R. Simeon b. Pazzi said in R. Joshua b. Levi's name on Bar Ḳappara's authority: Sound, sight, and smell do not involve trespass. [Thus] they merely do not involve trespass, but there is an interdict. Is that not for those who stand inside [the Temple],[1] so that it is impossible [to avoid it], while there is an intention [to enjoy], and it is forbidden?—No: it refers to those standing outside.[2]

[It was stated in] the text, 'R. Simeon b. Pazzi said in R. Joshua b. Levi's name on Bar Ḳappara's authority: Sound, sight, and smell do not involve trespass.' But, does not smell involve trespass? Surely it was taught: He who compounds incense in order to learn [the art thereof] or to give it over to the community[3] is exempt; [if] in order to smell it,[4] he is liable; while he who smells it[5] is exempt, but that he commits trespass![6] Rather, said R. Papa: Sound and sight do not involve trespass, because they are intangible; and smell, after its smoke column has ascended,[7] does not involve trespass, since its religious service has been performed.[8]

Shall we say that wherever the religious service has been performed no trespass is involved? But what of the separation of the ashes,[9] though its religious service has been performed, yet it involves trespass, for it is written; *and he shall put them* [the ashes] *beside the altar,*[10] [which means] that he [the priest] must not scatter nor use [them]?[11]—Because [the references to] the separation of the ashes and the priestly garments are two verses c written with the same purpose,[1] and the teaching of two such verses does not illumine [other cases].[2] 'The separation of the ashes': that which we have stated. 'The priestly garments,' as it is written, *and he shall leave them there:*[3] this teaches that they must be hidden.[4] That is well on the view of the Rabbis who say, This teaches that they must be hidden. But according to R. Dosa who disagrees with them and maintains: But they are fit for an ordinary priest, while what does '*and he shall leave them there*' mean? that he [the High Priest] must not use them on another Day of Atonement, what can be said?—Because the separation of ashes and the beheaded heifer[5] are two verses with the same teaching, and such two verses do not illumine [other cases]. That is well according to him who maintains, They do not illumine [other cases]; but on the view that they do illumine,[6] what can be said?—Two limitations are written: it is written, '*and he shall put* them [the ashes]'; and it is written, [*over the heifer*] *whose neck was broken* [etc.].[7]

Come and hear: If he took it [the heifer] into the team[8] and it [accidentally] did some threshing, it is fit;[9] [but if it was] in order that it should suck and thresh, it is unfit. Now here it is impossible d [to do otherwise],[1] and he intends [to benefit], and he [the Tanna] teaches that it is unfit!—There it is different, because Scripture saith, '*which hath not been wrought with,*' [implying] in all cases. If

whether it is avoidable or not; therefore if it is unavoidable it is permitted.

(1) He was lecturing on the laws of Festivals to the masses, this being within thirty days before a Festival; v. *supra 6a* and *b*. As his own school-house was too small for the large number who wished to hear him, he taught in the open, choosing this site on account of the shade afforded by the high walls of the Temple. (2) Though one must not derive any benefit from the Temple. (3) It was normally used inside; hence the shade was not forbidden at all. (4) Lit., 'the loft of'; v. Mid. IV, 5. (5) I.e., closed lifts. When they had to pass there for making repairs. (6) He who benefits from sacred things (*hekdesh*) commits trespass and is liable to a sacrifice. But no trespass is involved when he benefits by sound, sight or smell, e.g., when he hears the music in the Temple, sees the beauty of the Temple, or smells the frankincense. Consequently, even if workmen did look upon the Holy of Holies it would not really matter. (7) Forbidding even that which the law permitted.

(1) I.e., those engaged on some Temple service. (2) Who can avoid enjoying these things. (3) For use in the Temple. (4) I.e., he intends keeping it for smelling. (5) *Sc.* the incense belonging to the community and in use in the Temple. (6) The reference is to Ex. XXX, 33: *Whosoever compoundeth any like it, or whosoever putteth any of it upon a stranger, he shall be cut off from his people* (*kareth*). In the first case he is exempt from *kareth*, in the second he is liable, while in the third he is exempt from *kareth* but liable to a trespass-offering. This contradicts R. Simeon b. Pazzi. (7) The incense was thrown upon burning coals, which caused a cloud or a column of smoke to ascend. This constituted its sacred service. (8) The incense then does not count as the sacred things of the Lord, and it is to this case that R. Simeon b. Pazzi refers. But before the smoke has ascended trespass is involved, because the smell, being directly caused by the spices with which the incense is compounded, is regarded as tangible. (9) A censerful (Yoma 24a) of the ashes of the daily burnt-offering was taken every day and placed at the side of the altar, where the earth absorbed it. (10) Lev. VI, 3. (11) Rashal reads: (teaching) that others must not commit trespass therein, but all of it must be beside the altar.—'All of it' refers to the censerful.

c (1) Lit., 'which come as one'. (2) This is a general principle of exegesis. When a law is taught in one case it may be extended to other cases too by general analogy. But when it is taught in two cases it cannot be extended; for if it were intended to illumine others too, it would be written in one instance only, and the second, together with all others, would follow from it. (3) Lev. XVI, 23. This refers to the additional garments worn by the High Priest on the Day of Atonement when he entered the Holy of Holies. (4) And all use is forbidden. Here too they had fulfilled their religious purpose. (5) V. Deut. XXI, 1-9. There too it is written, '*and shall break the heifer's neck* there *in the valley*' (v. 4). '*There*' indicates that it must remain there and all benefit thereof is forbidden, though its religious purpose had already been fulfilled. (6) R. Judah holds his view: v. Sanh. 67b. (7) Lit., '*the* one who is neckbroken'. Ibid. 6. '*The*' too is a limitation and the combined effect of the two limitations is to exclude all other cases from the operation of this law, which forbids benefit even after the religious requirements have been carried out. (8) Of three or four cows used for threshing; his purpose was that it should suck. (9) To make atonement for a murder by an unknown person; v. Deut. ibid. The heifer was to be one '*which hath not been wrought with, and which hath not drawn in the yoke*' (v. 3). Though this heifer had threshed, it remains fit, because it had been taken into the team to feed, not to thresh.

d (1) It must be taken into the team to suck.

with all [forbidden] things, except idolatry, incest,[3] [25b] and murder.[4] Idolatry, as we have stated.[5] Incest and murder, as it was taught: Rabbi said: *For as when a man riseth against his neighbour, and slayeth him, even so is this matter.*[6] Now, what connection has a murderer with a betrothed maiden? Thus this comes to throw light, and is itself illumined.[7] The murderer is compared to a betrothed maiden: just as a betrothed maiden must be saved [from dishonour] at the cost of his [her ravisher's] life, so [in the case of] a murderer, he [the victim] must be saved at the cost of his [the attacker's] life. Conversely, a betrothed maiden [is learned] from a murderer: just as [in the case of] murder, one must be slain rather than transgress, so a betrothed maiden must be slain yet not transgress.[8] And how do we know it of murder itself?[9] It is common sense. Even as one who came before Raba and said to him: The governor of my town has ordered me, 'Go and kill So-and-so; if not, I will kill you.' He answered him: 'Let him kill you rather than that you should commit murder; what [reason] do you see [for thinking] that your blood is redder? Perhaps his blood is redder.'[10]

Mar son of R. Ashi found Rabina rubbing his daughter with undeveloped olives of *'orlah*.[11] Said he to him: 'Granted that the Rabbis ruled [thus][12] in time of danger; was it [likewise] ruled when there is no danger?' 'This inflammatory fever is also like a time of danger,' he answered him. Others say, he answered him: 'Am I then using it in the normal manner of its usage?'

It was stated: [As to forbidden] benefit that comes to a man against his will,—Abaye said: It is permitted; while Raba maintained: It is forbidden. Where it is possible [to avoid it], while he intends [to benefit], or if it is impossible [to avoid it], yet he intends [to benefit], none dispute that it is forbidden. If it is impossible [to avoid it], and he does not intend [to benefit], none dispute that it is permitted. They differ where it is possible [to avoid it] and he does not intend [to benefit]; now, on the view
a of R. Judah, who ruled, That which is unintended is forbidden,[1] none dispute that it is forbidden. Where do they differ? On the view of R. Simeon, who maintained: That which is unintended is permitted. Abaye rules as R. Simeon. But Raba [argues]: R. Simeon rules thus only where it is impossible [to do otherwise], but not where it is possible.[2]

Others state: If it is possible [to avoid it], and he does not intend [to benefit], that is [the case of] the controversy between R. Judah and R. Simeon.[3] If it is impossible [to avoid it], and he does not intend [to benefit], none dispute that it is permitted. When do they differ? Where it is impossible [to avoid it] and he intends [to benefit]. Now, on the view of R. Simeon, who regards the intention,[4] none dispute that it is forbidden. Where do they differ? On the view of R. Judah, who maintained: It makes no difference whether he intends or does not intend, if it is possible [to avoid it] it is forbidden. Abaye rules as R. Judah.[5] [26a] Raba

(3) Which includes adultery. (4) Lit., 'bloodshed'. (5) Viz., the interdict of the wood of the *asherah*. (6) Deut. XXII, 26. This refers to the ravishing of a betrothed maiden. (7) I.e., the verse shows that the case of a murderer throws light upon that of a betrothed maiden, but is also itself illumined thereby. (8) She should rather suffer death than dishonour. (9) That one must allow oneself to be slain rather than commit murder. (10) You have no right to murder him to save yourself; his life is no less valuable than your own. (11) For a remedy. (12) That anything may be used for a remedy.

a (1) V. Shab. 22a. (2) The controversy of R. Judah and R. Simeon is with respect to dragging a bench over an earthen floor on the Sabbath, because it is needed in another part of the room. The dragging may make a rut in the earth, which is forbidden. Now in Abaye's view, R. Simeon permits the unintentional even when the whole act is avoidable, e.g., the bench is light enough to be carried. But in Raba's view R. Simeon permits it only when the bench is too heavy for this, so that the dragging is unavoidable.—An action is regarded as unavoidable when its purpose—here to have the bench elsewhere—is permissible or necessary. Similarly below, lecturing to the masses is regarded as unavoidable. (3) Raba too admits this. (4) As the determining factor. (5) Since R. Judah rules thus, we see that the matter always depends on

תורה אור

ושפיכות דמים ע"ז הא דאמרן גילוי עריות ושפיכות דמים דתניא *ר' אומר °כי כאשר יקום איש על רעהו ורצחו נפש כן הדבר הזה וכי מה ענין רוצח אצל נערה המאורסה *הרי זה בא ללמד ונמצא למד מקיש רוצח לנערה המאורסה מה נערה המאורסה ניתן להצילה בנפשו *אף רוצח ניתן להצילו בנפשו ונערה המאורסה מרוצח °מה רוצח יהרג ואל יעבור אף נערה המאורסה תהרג ואל תעבור ושפיכות דמים גופיה מנלן סברא הוא *כי ההוא דאתא לקמיה דרבא א"ל מרי דוראי אמר לי זיל קטליה לפלני' ואי לא קטלינא לך א"ל ליקטלוך ולא תיקטול מאי חזית דדמא דידך סומק טפי דילמא דמא דההוא גברא סומק טפי מר בר רב אשי אשכחיה לרבינא דשייף לה לברתיה בגוהרקי דערלה אמר ליה 'אימור דאמור רבנן בשעת הסכנה שלא בשעת הסכנה מי אמור א"ל האי אישתא צמירתא נמי כשעת הסכנה דמיא איכא דאמרי א"ל °מידי דרך הנאה קא עבידנא איתמר הנאה הבאה לו לאדם בעל כרחו אביי אמר מותרת ורבא אמר אסורה אפשר וקא מיכוין לא אפשר וקמיכוין כולי עלמא לא פליגי דאסור לא אפשר ולא מיכוין כולי עלמא לא פליגי דשרי °כי פליגי דאפשר ולא מיכוין ואליבא דר' יהודה דאמר *דבר שאין מתכוין אסור כולי עלמא לא פליגי דאסור כי פליגי אליבא דר"ש דאמר דבר שאין מתכוין מותר אביי כרבי שמעון ורבא אמר עד כאן לא קא א"ר שמעון אלא היכא דלא אפשר אבל היכא דאפשר לא איכא דאמרי אפשר ולא מיכוין היינו פלוגתייהו דר' יהודה ור' שמעון לא אפשר ולא קא מיכוין כולי עלמא לא פליגי דשרי כי פליגי דלא אפשר וקא מיכוין ואליבא דר' שמעון דאזיל בתר כוונה כולי עלמא לא פליגי דאסור כי פליגי אליבא דר' יהודה דאמר לא שנא מתכוין ולא שנא שאין מתכוין אפשר אסור אביי כרבי יהודה

ורבא

דברים כב

ושפיכות דמים . כגון אמרו לו הרוג ישראל חבירך ואם לאו תיהרג : מה למדנו מרוצח לנערה המאורסה . והלא פירש בה אונס פטור כדכתיב ולנערה לא תעשה דבר אלא נראה כמי שרוצה בא ללמד כאן ונמצא שהוקש כאן להיות למד מכאן והכי קאמר כרוצח כנערה שניהן שוין כמו והיה כעם ככהן (ישעיה כד) ולא נאמר והיה העם ככהן : ניתן להצילה . ניתן רשות לרוצח שהוא רודף אחריה שיצילנה ממנו בנפשו של רודף כדכתיב (דברים כב) ואין מושיע לה הא אם יש מושיע צריך להושיעה בכל אשר יכול אפילו בהריגתו אם אין יכול להציל באחד מאבריו יהרגנו : יהרג . אם אמר לו עו"ג הרוג או תיהרג יהרג ואל יעבור עבירה זו : מרי דוראי . מושל עירי : מאי חזית דדמא דידך סומק . כלומר כלום באתה לישאל על כך אלא מפני שאתה יודע שאין מצוה עומדת בפני פיקוח נפש וסבור אתה שאף זו תדחה מפני פיקוח נפשך אין זו דומה לשאר עבירות דמ"מ יש כאן אבוד נפש והתורה לא התירה לדחות את המצוה אלא מפני חיבת נפשו של ישראל וכאן עבירה נעשית ונפש אבודה מי יאמר שנפשך חביבה לפני המקום יותר משל זה דילמא של זה חביבה טפי עליו ונמצא עבירה נעשית ונפש אבודה : שייף . מושח : גוהרקי דערלה . בוסר זיתים קטנים משום רפואה דקסבר מותר להתרפאות באיסורי הנאה : אישתא צמירתא . חולי שקורין מלוי"ש צמירתא חם כמו דאמרה למורי בבבא קמא (דף ס.) : דרך הנאתו . לאחר שיתבשלו ויוצא שמנן בבית הבד מותרת . אין צריך לפרוש הימנה כדמפרש : הכי גרסינן אפשר וקא מיכוין לא אפשר וקא מיכוין כולי עלמא לא פליגי דאסיר . אפשר לו ליבדל וקא מיכוין להתקרב כדי ליהנות כגון ריח של ע"ז או אפילו אי אפשר לו ליבדל ומיהו מתכוין הוא וחביב הוא לו ליהנות : לא אפשר . לו ליבדל ולא קא מיכוין ליהנות דאיכא תרתי להיתר לכ"ע שרי : כי פליגי דאפשר . לו ליבדל ולא נבדל ומיהו לא קא מיכוון : פלוגתא דרבי יהודה ורבי שמעון במסכת שבת (דף כב.) בגרירת מטה וכסא וספסל ובמסכת בילה (דף כג:) : דלא אפשר . כגון שצריך לאותן כלים ואין יכול להגביהן על כתיפו ואביי סבר בקטנים נמי שרי רבי שמעון אע"פ שאפשר להגביהן על כתיפו והכי אמרינן במס' שבת* ולרבא לא שרי ר' שמעון אלא בגדולים : איכא דאמרי . מודה רבא היכא דלא קא מיכוין אע"ג שאפשר שרי ר' שמעון דבהכי פלוגתייהו דר' יהודה ור' שמעון ובין לאביי ובין לרבא לר' יהודה אסור לרבי שמעון שרי : כולי עלמא . אביי ורבא לא פליגי דשרי ואפי' לרבי יהודה : כי פליגי דלא אפשר וקא מיכוין . ומיהו אליבא דר' שמעון דחשיבא ליה כוונה דמתיר אפי' בדאפשר הואיל ולא קא מיכוין אלמא אכוונה קפיד היכא דקא מכוין אע"ג דלא אפשר אסור : ה"ג כי פליגי אליבא דר' יהודה דאמר לא שנא מתכוין ולא שנא אין מתכוין אפשר אסור . ולא גרסינן ולא אפשר שרי דהא לא שמעינן ליה דאמר הכי דאי שמעינן ליה הכי היכי פליג רבא למיסר : אביי כר' יהודה . דקסבר כיון דאסר רבי יהודה בדאפשר אע"ג דלא קא מיכוין שמע מינה לא חשבינן ליה כוונה אלא בדאפשר ולא אפשר תליא טעמא הלכך היכא דלא אפשר אע"ג דקא מיכוין לא איכפת ליה לרבי יהודה :

ורבא

אף נערה המאורסה יהרג ואל יעבור . פי' הבועל אבל היא תיבעל ולא תיהרג דקרקע עולם היא כדאמר בבן סורר ומורה (סנהדרין עד:) ובריש כתובות (דף ג:) כמי פריך ולידרוש להו לאונס שרי ור"י אומר דשפיר גר' תיהרג דהא דמשמע בבן סורר ומורה ובריש כתובות דאונס שרי היינו היכא שהיא קרקע עולם ולא עבדה מעשה אבל לעשות מעשה כגון שאומר לה שתביא הערוה עליה תיהרג ואל תעשה מעשה דמרוצח ילפינן ורוצח לא מיחייב למימסר נפשיה אלא כשאומר לו להרוג בידים אבל אם אומר הנח לזרוק עצמך על התינוק או תיהרג אינו חייב למסור עצמו כדי להציל חבירו דאדרבה איכא למימר מאי חזית דדמיה דחבריה סומק טפי דילמא דמא דידי סומק טפי ומיהו לדידיה אם אומרים לו הנח לתקוע אותך בערוה יהרג ואל יעבור דלא מצי למימר לא עבידנא מעשה דכיון שתוקעין אותו ואין קישוי אלא לדעת כדאמרי' בריש הבא על יבמתו (יבמות נג.) ומה שהוא מתקשה הוי מעשה* :

לא אפשר ולא מיכוין כולי עלמא לא פליגי . לישנא קמא נראה לפרש דכ"ע קאי אאביי ורבא ולא פליגי דשרי היינו לרבי שמעון דרבי יהודה אסר דהא רבא מוקי פלוגתא דרבי יהודה ור' שמעון בלא אפשר ולא מיכוין דלאפשר קאמר דמודה רבי שמעון דאסור ולאיכא דאמרי לא אפשר ולא מיכוין לכולי עלמא דשרי האי כולי עלמא היינו ר' יהודה ור' שמעון ואע"ש דלאיכא דאמרי לא הדר וקיט אלא מה שמשנה מלשון ראשון ולהכי לא נקט בדאיכא דאמרי אפשר ומיכוין לכ"ע אסור ומיירי כגון דלא הוי פסיק רישיה דבפסיק רישיה מודה רבי שמעון וליכא למימר דאפילו בפסיק רישיה שרי הכא ר' שמעון משום דהכא מיירי בגרירה דכלים דליכא אלא איסורא דרבנן שהוא חופר כלאחר יד כדאמר *בבמה מדליקין (שבת כט) דהא בשמעתא מייתי עלה מידי דאורייתא כגון מעילה וכלאים ופסול פרה וי"ל דכל הנהו דמייתי לא הוי פסיק רישיה ולא אפשר דכולי שמעתא נראה לר"י דלא אפשר כדרכו אלא בטורח גדול דהא שילשול האומנין בקופות חשיב לא אפשר והא דאמרינן בכתובות (דף ה:) גבי מהו לבעול בתחלה בשבת דקאמר לר' יהודה דאסור משום דבר שאין מתכוון אע"ג דהוי לא אפשר ולא מיכוין וצריך לומר דההיא סוגיא כרבי ירמיה דבמה מדליקין *דאסר לר' יהודה לא אפשר ולא מיכוין אע"ג דאיתותב במאי דאמר קטנים אסורים אפילו לר"ש (איתותב) מ"מ במאי דאסר אפילו בגדולים לר' יהודה לא איתותב :

אביי כרבי יהודה . נראה דסבר אביי הואיל ואפשר ולא מיכוין אסור ובלא אפשר ולא מיכוין שרי אלמא דאיסור משום דאפשר הוא ומה שהיה בספרים בבמה מדליקין (שבת כט:) ופליגא דעולא דאמר עולא מחלוקת בקטנים אבל בגדולים ד"ה אסור שיבוש הוא דבכולי שמעתא שרי טפי לא אפשר מהיכא דאפשר וגדולים היינו לא אפשר אלא גרס ד"ה מותר והיינו כלישנא בתרא דהכא דבלא אפשר ולא מיכוין כ"ע ל"פ דשרי :

שאני

[וביומא פב. הארינו תוס' טובא. ועי' תוס' יבמות נג: ד"ה אין אונס]

לד א מיי' פ"א מהל' רוצח הל' ו ז סמג לאוין קסד :

לה ב מיי' פ"ה מהלכות יסודי התורה הל' ז סמג עשין ה טוש"ע י"ד סימן קנז סעיף א :

לו ג ד מיי' שם הלכה ח סמג שם טוש"ע יו"ד סי' קנה סעיף ג [ורב אלפס כאן ובמסכת ע"ג פ"ב דף שלח:] :

רבינו חננאל

ושפיכות דמים ע"ז הא דאמרן עריות ושפיכות דמי' מנא לן כדתניא רבי אומר [כתיב] אין לנערה חטא מות כי כאשר יקום איש על רעהו רצחו נפש וכי מה למדנו לרוצח מעתה וכי יש לומר אם יקום על רעהו ורצחו אין לו דין מות כמו זו הנערה שכתוב בה אין לנערה חטא מות אלא הרי זו הנערה באת ללמד לאחרים ונמצאת היא למדה הוקשה זו הנערה לרוצח מה רוצח יהרג ואל יעבור כך נערה המאורסה אם יאמר לה הישמעאלי השמעי לי ואם לאו הנני הורגך תהרג ואל תשמע לו ואם תפסה ונתחזק עליה אין לה חטא מות ורוצח גופיה שלמדה ממנו הנערה מנא לן דדינו ליהרג ואל יהרוג סברא [הוא] כההוא דאתא קמי' דרבא א"ל אמר לי מרי דוראי זיל קטליה לפלניא ואי לא קטלינא לך וכו' : מר בר רב אשי הוה שאיף נרקי דערלה. פי' גרגרים של ערלה לברתיה דהוה בה אישתא צמירתא ואמר ליה האי אישתא צמירתא סכנה היא ובמקום סכנה שרי. איכא דאמרי מידי דרך הנאתן קא עבידנא ושלא כדרך הנאתן שרי : איתמר הנאה הבאה לו בעל כרחו כגון שהיה עובר והריח ריח בשמים של ע"ז אביי אמר מותר רבא אמר אסור . כל היכא דאפשר פי' יש דרך אחרת ואפשר לו שלא יעבור דרך שם ומתכוין לעבור שם כדי ליהנות מן הריח של ע"ז כולי עלמא לא פליגי דאסור כי פליגי דאפשר לו שלא יעבור שם וכשעובר שם אינו מתכוין ליהנות ועלתה זו בתיובתא דרבא אבל אי לא אפשר ומתכוין קיימא לן דאסור כרבא

[יומא פב. סנהדרין עד.]

[שם חולין כח. קיז. ערכין כט:]

סנהדרין עד. יומא פב:

שבת מא: [ג. פא: קלג. קיא. כג. יומא לד: כתובות ו: ב"ק קיג. כריתות כ:]

[דף כט:]

גליון הש"ס

גמ' מידי דרך הנאה קעבידנא. עי' ב"ק קא. תוס' ד"ה ולא יצבע: שם כי פליגי דאפשר ולא מיכוין. עי' בחידושי הרמב"ן ע"ג ד"ה י"א אהא דאמר דמי' שם ממתכוי מרית ע"ז :

תורה אור

מה לערלה שכן לא היתה לה שעת הכושר תאמר בבשר בחלב שהיתה לו שעת הכושר חמץ בפסח יוכיח שהיה לו שעת הכושר ואסור בהנאה מה לחמץ בפסח שכן ענוש כרת תאמר בבשר בחלב שאינו ענוש כרת כלאי הכרם יוכיחו שאין ענוש כרת ואסור בהנאה ואם איתא ניפרוך מה לכלאי הכרם שכן לוקין עליהן אפילו שלא כדרך הנאתן ואביי תאמר במאי תאמר בבשר בחלב שאין לוקין עליו אלא דרך הנאתו *אטו בבשר בחלב אכילה כתיבה ביה ואידך דקא מותיב לה סבר להכי קא גמר מנבילה מה נבילה דרך הנאתה אף בשר בחלב דרך הנאתו ואביי להכי לא כתב אכילה בגופו לומר שלוקין עליו אפי' שלא כדרך הנאתו וליפרוך מה לכלאי הכרם שכן לא היתה לו שעת הכושר א"ר אדא בר אהבה זאת אומרת כלאי הכרם עיקרן נאסרין הואיל והיתה להן שעת הכושר קודם השרשה מתיב רב שמעיה *המעביר עציץ נקוב בכרם אם הוסיף מאתים אסור הוסיף אין לא הוסיף לא אמר רבא תרי קראי כתיבי כתיב *°הזרע וכתיב המלאה הא כיצד ג זרוע מעיקרו בהשרשה זרוע ובא הוסיף אין לא הוסיף לא א"ר יעקב א"ר יוחנן בכל מתרפאין חוץ מעצי אשירה היכי דמי אי נימא דאיכא סכנה אפילו עצי אשירה נמי ואי דליכא סכנה אפילו כל איסורין שבתורה נמי לא לעולם דאיכא סכנה ואפי' הכי עצי אשירה לא *דתניא ר' אליעזר אומר אם נאמר °בכל נפשך למה נאמר בכל מאודך ואם נאמר בכל מאודך למה נאמר בכל נפשך אלא לומר לך אם יש אדם שגופו חביב עליו מממונו לכך נאמר בכל נפשך (א) ויש אדם שממונו חביב עליו מגופו לכך נאמר בכל מאודך כי אתא רבין אמר רבי יוחנן ד בכל מתרפאין *חוץ מע"ז וגילוי עריות ושפיכות

(דברים כב) (שם ו)

רש"י

ערלה לא היתה לה שעת הכושר. שהפרי הזה חנט באיסור ונגמר באיסור תאמר בבשר בחלב שיש לו שעת הכושר קודם שניתן בחלב: כלאי הכרם יוכיחו. ובשחיטת חולין פריך ונימא ערלה תוכיח וחזר הדין והתם מתרץ לה בכל הבשר ולקמן פריך ונימא מה לכלאי הכרם שכן לא היתה להם שעת הכושר: ואם איתא. דכלאי הכרם חלוקין להחמיר משאר איסורין ליפרוך הכי: ואביי. אמר לך היכי ניפרוך היכי נסיימה למילתיה דלא נילף בשר בחלב מיניה נימא תאמר בבשר בחלב כו' אטו בשר בחלב אכילה כתיבה ביה התם נמי לוקין עליו אפי' שלא כדרך הנאתה: מנבילה. ונבילה אכילה כתיבא ביה נבילה לאו דוקא קאמר דהא מטריפה גמרינן לה ויש מפרשים דמשום דהאי טריפה דקרא איירי באבר ובבשר המדולדל בה ושחטה כדאמרינן בבהמה המקשה לילד (חולין עג:) קרי ליה נבילה דדמי לנבילה דלא מישתרו בשחיטה ואין נראה לי דטריפה נמי לא מישתריא בשחיטה ואי משום דלא מיטמיא הנך נמי לא מיטמאו: ואידך. אביי אמר לך להכי לא כתיב אכילה בגופו ללמדך שלוקין כו' הלכך לא מצי פריך תאמר בבשר בחלב כו': וליפרוך מה לכלאי הכרם שכן לא היתה להם שעת הכושר. וקא סלקא דעתך שאין נאסרין אלא גידוליהן ולכן לא היתה להן שעת הכושר: זאת אומרת. מדלא פריך הכי שמע מינה כלאי הכרם עיקרן נאסר אף עיקר הזריעה עצמה נאסרה וזריעה היתה לה שעת הכושר כל ימיה עד שנשרשה י"מ דהאי מקשה נמי ידע שאף הזריעה נאסרת אלא סבור שמשעת זריעה נאסרת וכך שמעתי אבל א"א להעמידה דמיבעי לן לפרושי הכי מה לכלאי הכרם שכן לא היתה להן שעת הכושר משעה שבאו לכלל כלאים תאמר בבשר בחלב שהיתה לו שעת הכושר משעה שבא לכלל זה דאם שורהו כל היום בחלב אינו נאסר בכך ומשני עיקרן נאסרו משנשרשו ולא משנזרעו וכמה גמגומים יש בה חדא דטעמא דלא מיתסר °משום דאכתי לא בשר בחלב חשיב ליה והרי הוא כאילו זה לבד וזה לבד וכן כלאים כ"ז שלא נשרשו הרי הן כמונחין בכדא ועוד כי אמר לעיל חמץ בפסח יוכיח מיבעי ליה למימר שהיה לו שעת הכושר משנקרא חמץ בפסח והא ליתא ועוד מדמותיב רב שמעיה הוסיף אין לא הוסיף לא מכלל דליכא מאן דסליק אדעתיה משעת זריעה אלא הוה סלקא דעתיה תוספת אין עיקר לא ולשון עיקרן משמע כדפרישית דללישנא בתרא הכי הוה ליה למימר זאת אומרת כלאי הכרם בהשרשה נאסרו: המעביר עציץ נקוב בכרם. וזרעים בתוכו שכבר נמחו הוסיף הצמח בכרם מאתים אחד מן המאתים שיש בו עכשיו שמתחלה היו בו קנ"ט שיעורים כתוספת זו ועכשיו יש בו מאתים אסורין לפי שאין בהיתר הראשון כדי לבטל התוספת האסור שהערנה וכלאים אין בטלין אלא במאתים של היתר לבד האיסור לא הוסיף מאתים אלא פחות כל שהוא מותר דיש בו כדי להעלות באחד ומאתים ובספרי יליף ליה מתרומה שעולה באחד ומאה וכלאים שכפל את אסוריו שאסורין בהנאה כפל את עלייתן ודוקא נקט נקוב דיונק מקרקע דרך אויר: לא הוסיף לא. אלמא אין הזריעה נאסרת: מליאה. גידולין: הזרע. הראשון: זרוע מעיקרו. בכרם בהשרשה כדכתיב הזרע משמע שאף הזריעה נאסרת מיהו קודם השרשה כמאן דמנחא בכדא דמי: זרוע ובא. קודם לכן הוסיף אין לא הוסיף לא דכתיב מלאה: בכל מתרפאין. אפילו באיסורי הנאה: למה נאמר בכל מאודך. יאמר החביב משניהן ודיו ומפרש לפי שפעמים שזה חביב ופעמים שזה חביב לכך הוצרכו שניהן לומר אהוב את בוראך יותר מן החביב עליך והמתרפא בעצי אשירה נראה כמודה בה:

תוספות

מה לערלה שכן לא היתה לה שעת הכושר. הקשה ריב"א נילף מערלה שהיתה לה שעת הכושר כגון נטל ענף מאילן של היתר שלא עמדו פירותיו והרכיבו או נטעו ואומר ר"י דאינו אוסר אלא מה שגדל אחר שהרכיבו או נטעו וזה לא היה לו שעת הכושר והענף עצמו אינו נאסר אלא מפני תערובת האיסור ואם היה יכול להבדיל אותו הענף ממה שגדל אחרי כן היה מותר וכן כלאי הכרם אי לא היה עיקרו נאסר או מעביר עציץ נקוב חשוב לא היה לו שעת הכושר שהאיסור הגדל אחרי כן לא היה לו מעולם שעת הכושר: מה לחמץ בפסח שכן ענוש כרת. ומשור הנסקל לא מצי למימר יוכיח דמה לערלה ולשור הנסקל שכן לא היה להם שעת הכושר לאכילה: כלאי הכרם יוכיחו. בפ' כל הבשר (חולין קטו:) פריך ונימא ערלה תוכיח ומשני ונראה לר"י דהוה מצי למילף במה מצינו מכלאי הכרם לחודייהו דמה כלאי הכרם שכן נעבדה בו עבירה ואסורה באכילה ובהנאה אף אני אביא בשר בחלב וכו' אלא ניחא ליה למילף מכל הני בק"ו דאלים טפי: מה לכלאי הכרם שכן לוקים עליו שלא כדרך כו'. תימה לרשב"א היא גופא נילף במה מצינו מכלאי הכרם שילקו על בשר בחלב שלא כדרך הנאה ואומר ר"י דליכא למילף דאיכא למימר דשור הנסקל וחמץ שעבר עליו בבל יראה יוכיח שנעבד בו עבירה ואסור באכילה ואינו אסור אלא כדרך הנאתו דאכילה כתיב בהו: עיקרן נאסרין. אומר ר"י שגם הגבעולים והקש שגדל ממנו נאסר כדאמרינן לקמן (ד' כו:) תנור שהסיקו בקליפי ערלה או בקשין של כלאי הכרם חדש יותץ וקשה לר"י דבפרק האשה שנפלו (כתובות דף פ. ושם) גבי מוציא הוצאות על נכסי אשתו וכו' מפרש רב יהודה אפי' לא אכל אלא חבילי זמורות רב יהודה לטעמיה דאמר אכלה ערלה וכלאים ושביעית הוי חזקה פי' אע"פ שבכל אלו אין יכול לאכול רק העלים שהפירות אסורין אלמא עלי כלאים שרו ואומר ר"ת דהתם מיירי באותן עלים שהיו קודם זריעת כלאים וקודם שהוסיף מאתים אבל אותן שגדילין אחרי כן אסורין מאחר שהוסיף מאתים: הואיל והיתה לו שעת הכושר קודם השרשה. והא דאמרינן בפ"ק דמנחות (דף ו. ושם) גבי טריפה דכלאים לא היה להם שעת הכושר התם קאי על משקה ישראל ומשקה לא היה לו לעולם שעת הכושר: חוץ מעצי אשירה. נראה לר"י דמיירי כגון שאין יכול להתרפא משאר עצים אלא בזה כגון על ידי שדים או שום דבר אחר משום דאתי למיטעי בתר ע"ז וגבי בן דמא בע"ז פרק שני (דף כז: ושם) שנשכו נחש ובא יעקב איש כפר סכניא לרפאותו ולא הניחו ר' ישמעאל משום דאפיקורסות משכא ומפרש בירושלמי בפ' שמנה שרצים שהיה רוצה ללחוש לו בשם זר אבל ע"י תחבושת שרי כדאמרי' התם (דף כח.) דר' אבהו רמא ליה יעקב אפיקורסא סמא אשקיה:

אף

ושפיכות

עין משפט נר מצוה

ל א מיי' פי"ד מהלכות מאכלות אסורות הל' ד ה ו טוש"ע שם:

לא ב מיי' פ"ה מהל' כלאים הל' יג טוש"ע י"ד סי' רצו סעיף ט:

לב ג מיי' שם הל' כג טוש"ע שם סעיף יז:

לג ד מיי' פ"ה מהלכות יסודי התורה הל' ו סמג עשין ה טוש"ע י"ד סי' קנה סעיף ג [רב אלפס כאן ובע"ז פ"ב ד' שלט]:

רבינו חננאל

מהא ברייתא דמייתי איסור בשר בחלב בק"ו מערלה ודחי' מה לערל' שכן וכו' חמץ בפסח יוכיח ופרכי' מה לחמץ שכן ענוש כרת כלאי הכרם יוכיחו ואם איתא נפרוך מה לכלאי הכרם שכן לוקין עליהן אפי' שלא כדרך הנאתן ופריק אביי הכי בשר בחלב נמי לוקה עליו אפי' שלא כדרך אכילתו דהא לא כתיבא ביה אכילה. (ואיסי)[ואידך] אמר לך כיון דבשר בחלב איתקש לנבלה שנאמר כי עם קדוש אתה לה' אלהיך לא תבשל גדי בחלב אמו וכתי' ואנשי קדש תהיון לי [ובשר בשדה טרפה לא תאכלו] הנה נאמר בכאן כי עם קדוש ונאמ' להלן ואנשי קדש תהיון לי וכתיב בטרפה לא תאכלו הרי אכילה כתיבא ביה בשר בחלב [נמי כאלו] אכילה כתיב' ביה ואביי אדרבה ניסא להכי לא כתיב ביה אכילה בגופו לומר שלוקה שלא כדרך הנאתו ונפרוך מה לכלאי הכרם שכן לא היתה להם שעת הכושר תאמר בבשר בחלב שאם שרה בשר בחלב היום כולו מותר ואינו אסור אלא בישולו ודחי' כלאי הכרם נמי מדלא פריך הכי שמע' מינה דהיתה להם שעת הכושר משעת זריעה עד שעת השרשה *כי לא נאסר אלא עיקרן ומהאי [טעמא] דייק רב אדא בר אהבה ואמ' זאת אומר' כלאי הכרם עיקרן נאסרו: אני דכלאי הכרם בהשרשה נאסרין והתניא המעביר עציץ נקוב בכרם אם הוסיף מאתים אסור. כלומר אם הוסיף עציץ זה בכרם כשיעור שיש בו חלק אחד במאתים חלקים כמה שיש בו נאסר דייק' מינה מדקתני הוסיף נאסר מכלל שאם לא הוסיף אפי' השריש לא נאסר ופריק רבא כתיב המלאה וכתיב הזרע הא כיצד אם היה זרוע עד שילא כדכתי' המלאה לא היה זרוע אלא עכשיו נזרע בהשרשה בעת שנזרע הזרע בהשרשה נאסר שנאמר הזרע: אמר רבי יוחנן בכל מתרפאין חוץ מע"ז וגילוי עריות

מסורת הש"ס

חולין קטו. כלאי' פ"ו מ"ח

[המלאה תכתיב הזרע וכן איתא בחולין קיו. וכ"כ בפירש"י דהכא]

ברכות סא: יומא פב. סנהדרין עד.

[פי' תוס' סוטה י: ד"ה טוח]

הגהות הב"ח

(א) גמ' ואם יש אדם שממונו חביב:

גליון הש"ס

ברש"י זאת אומרת. משום דאכתי לאו בב"ח כו'. עי' מנחות קג: ברש"י ד"ה סולת ובתוספ' שם ד"ה פיגול:

* דברי רבינו הוא כפי' י"מ שהובא ברש"י כאן ד"ה זאת אומרת ואולי דרש"י כיון בזה על דברי ר"ח ז"ל אלו

it not logical that they are forbidden for use? [25a] [This can be refuted]. As for *'orlah*, [that may be] because it had no period of
a fitness;[1] will you say [the same of] meat and milk [seethed together], seeing that they had a period of fitness? Then let leaven during Passover prove it: though it had a period of fitness, it is forbidden for use. [This again can be refuted]. As for leaven during Passover, [that may be] because he [the offender] is punished with *kareth*;[2] will you say [the same] of meat [seethed] in milk, where he is not punished with *kareth?* Then let *kil'ayim* of the vineyard prove it: though he [the offender] is not punished with *kareth*, yet it is forbidden for use. Now if this is so,[3] let us refute [it thus]: as for *kil'ayim* of the vineyard, [that may be] because we flagellate on its account even [when he does] not [use it] in the normal manner of its usage? And Abaye?[4]—[He can answer]—'will you say'—with what?[5] 'Will you say [the same] of meat [seethed] in milk, for which we do not flagellate save [when it is eaten] in the normal manner of its use'—is then 'eating' written in connection with meat [seethed] in milk?[6] And the other who raises the objection holds: for that purpose[7] it is deduced from *nebelah*:[8] just as *nebelah* [must be enjoyed] in the normal manner of its usage,[9] so [must] meat [seethed] in milk, in the normal manner of its usage. And Abaye?—[He argues]: for that reason 'eating' is not written in its own case,[10] to teach that we flagellate on its account even [when one does] not [enjoy it] in the normal manner of its usage.

But let us refute it [thus]: as for *kil'ayim*, [that may be] because it had no period of fitness?[11]—Said R. Adda b. Ahabah: This[12] proves that [in] *kil'ayim* of the vineyard, their very stock is for-
b bidden,[1] [and so we cannot refute it thus] since it had a time of fitness before taking root.[2]

R. Shemaiah objected: If one sets a perforated pot in a vineyard,[3] if one two-hundredth part is added, it is [all] forbidden:[4] thus, only if there is added, but not if there is not added?[5]—Said Raba, Two verses are written: *'the fulness'* is written, and *'the seed'* is written.[6] How is this [to be reconciled]? That which is sown[7] from the very outset [becomes forbidden] on taking root;[8] that which was sown when [partly] grown,[9] if it increased it is [forbidden];[10] if it did not increase, it is not [forbidden]![11]

R. Jacob said in R. Joḥanan's name: We may cure ourselves with all things, save with the wood of the *asherah*.[12] How is it meant? If we say that there is danger,[13] even the wood of the *asherah* too [is permitted]; while if there is no danger, even all [other] forbidden things of the Torah too are not [permitted]?—After all [it means] that there is danger, yet even so the wood of the *asherah* [must] not be used. For it was taught, R. Eliezer said: If *'with all thy soul'* is said, why is *'with all thy might'* said? Or if *'with all thy might'* is said, why is *'with all thy soul'* said?[14] But it is to teach you: if there is a man to whom his person is dearer than
c his wealth, therefore, *'with all thy soul'* is stated;[1] and if there is a man to whom his wealth is dearer than his person, therefore *'with all thy might'* [i.e., substance] is stated. When Rabin came,[2] he said in R. Joḥanan's name: We may cure [i.e., save] ourselves

a (1) From the time of its planting it was never fit for food. (2) For eating it. (3) *Sc.* Abaye's statement *supra* 24*b*. (4) How will he meet this question? (5) I.e., how would you conclude this refutation? (6) It is not! Hence this last assumption would be unwarranted, and could not overthrow the argument. (7) The prohibition of meat seethed with milk. (8) I.e., from Ex. XXII, 30; v. next note. (9) Before a penalty is incurred. *Nebelah* is employed here loosely, as in fact we learn from *ṭerefah* (v. Glos.), which is the subject dealt with in Ex. XXII, 30 (Rashi). (10) I.e., in connection with milk seethed with meat. (11) It is now assumed that when two diverse species are planted together, the interdict of *kil'ayim* applies only to what grows after they are planted or sown, but not to the stock itself. Thus this added growth was never at any time fit for eating. (12) *Sc.* that we do not refute it thus.

b (1) *Sc.* that which was already grown before they were planted as *kil'ayim*. (2) The stock itself becomes forbidden, but only after it takes root. (3) The pot contains cereals, and being perforated it draws its sustenance from the soil of the vineyard, which renders it (the pot) forbidden as *kil'ayim*. (4) One two-hundredth part is inclusive, i.e., the addition is one two-hundredth of the present total, so that the original is only one hundred and ninety-nine times as much. If *kil'ayim* is mixed with permitted eatables, it is all forbidden unless the latter is two hundred times as much as the former. (5) Though it struck root; which shows that the original stock is not forbidden. (6) Deut. XXII, 9: *lest the fulness of the seed which thou hast sown be forfeited. 'The fulness'* implies the additional growth only, while *'the seed'* implies the original stock. (7) In a vineyard. (8) Since it begins to grow under forbidden circumstances. Nevertheless, before it strikes root it is just as though it were lying in a jug. (9) Lit., 'sown and coming'. (10) *Sc.* the increase. (11) The stock remaining unaffected. (12) A tree or grove devoted to idolatry. (13) In the person's illness. (14) V. Deut. VI, 5: *And thou shalt love the Lord thy God with all thy heart, and with all thy soul, and with all thy might.*

c (1) I.e., one should love God even to the extent of giving his soul (life) in His service. (2) From Palestine to Babylon.

is flagellated five times; [24b] [for] a hornet, he is flagellated six times?[5]—Said he to him: Wherever we can interpret we do interpret,[6] and do not apply it to additional injunctions.

Now what is the purpose of *'and the flesh'* [*that toucheth any unclean thing shall not be eaten*][7] of the commencement of the verse?[8]

a —It is to include wood and frankincense.[1] What is the purpose of, *'And as for the flesh, every one that is clean shall eat thereof'* of the end [of the verse]?[2]—It is to include *emurim*.[3] [But] *emurim* are learnt from elsewhere, for it was taught: *But the soul that eateth of the flesh of the sacrifice of peace-offerings, that pertain unto the Lord* [*having his uncleanness upon him*]:[4] this is to include the *emurim*?[5] —There [the reference is to] the uncleanness of the *person*, [which is punishable] with *kareth*, [whereas] here [we treat of] the uncleanness of the *flesh*, [which is subject to] a negative injunction.[6]

R. Abbahu said in R. Joḥanan's name: [With regard to] all the prohibited articles of the Torah, we do not flagellate on their account save [when they are eaten] in the normal manner of their consumption. What does this exclude?—Said R. Shimi b. Ashi: It is to exclude [this, viz.,] that if he ate raw *ḥeleb*, he is exempt [from punishment]. Others say, R. Abbahu said in R. Joḥanan's name: [With regard to] all the prohibited articles of the Torah, we do not flagellate on their account save [when they are used] in the normal manner of their usage. What does this exclude?—Said R. Shimi b. Ashi: It is to exclude [this, viz.,] if he applied the *ḥeleb* of the ox which is stoned[7] upon his wound, he is exempt;[8] and all the more so, if he eats raw meat, he is exempt. It was stated likewise: R. Aḥa b. R. 'Awia said in R. Assi's name in R. Joḥanan's name: If he applies the *ḥeleb* of the ox which is stoned upon his wound he is exempt, because [in the case of] all the interdicts of the Torah, we do not flagellate on their account save [when they are used] in the normal manner of their usage.

R. Zera said, We too learned [thus]: 'One does not receive

b forty [lashes][1] on account of *'orlah*,[2] save for that which issues from olives or from grapes alone': but [for that which issues] from mulberries, figs and pomegranates [there is, as implied,] no [flagellation]. What is the reason? Is it not because he does not eat them in the normal manner of their usage?[3] Said Abaye to him: That were well if he informed us[4] of the fruit itself, where he did not eat it in the normal manner of its usage; but here [the reason[4] is] because it[5] is mere moisture.[6]

Abaye said: All agree in respect of *kil'ayim*[2] of the vineyard, that we flagellate on its account even [when one does] not [enjoy it] in the normal manner of its usage. What is the reason? Because 'eating' is not written in connection therewith. An objection is raised: Issi b. Judah said: How do we know that meat and milk [seethed together] are forbidden?[7] It is stated here, *for thou art a* holy people [. . . *thou shalt not seethe a kid in its mother's milk*],[8] and it is stated elsewhere, *And ye shall be* holy men *unto me;* [*therefore ye shall not eat any flesh that is torn of beasts in the field; ye shall cast it to the dogs*]:[9] just as there it is forbidden,[10] so here too it is forbidden. Again, I know it only of eating; how do I know it of [general] use? I will tell you: [it follows] *a minori*. If *'orlah*, though no sin was committed therewith,[11] is forbidden for use, then meat and milk [seethed together], wherewith a sin was committed, is

(5) In Lev. XI, 43, it is stated: *Ye shall not make yourselves detestable with any swarming thing that swarmeth, neither shall ye make yourselves unclean with them*. This is a twofold injunction, and since it does not specify *'that swarmeth* upon the earth', it applies to both water reptiles and land reptiles. Further v. 11, referring to unclean fish, states: *and they shall be a detestable thing unto you; ye shall not eat of their flesh*. This is a third injunction against water reptiles. And finally, in Deut. XIV, 10, there is a fourth injunction: *and whatsoever hath not fins and scales ye shall not eat*. The ant is a land reptile ('swarming thing'); hence the two injunctions of Lev. XI, 43 apply to it. There are also the following three: (i) Lev. XI, 41: *And every swarming thing that swarmeth upon the earth . . . shall not be eaten;* (ii) ibid. 42: *even all swarming things that swarm upon the earth them ye shall not eat, for they are a detestable thing;* and (iii) ibid. 44: *neither shall ye defile yourselves with any manner of swarming thing that moveth upon the earth*. The hornet is a *'winged swarming thing'* and also moves upon the earth. Hence it is subject to these five injunctions and also to that of Deut. XIV, 19: *And all winged swarming things are unclean unto you: they shall not be eaten*. Thus eating one forbidden thing can involve more than one penalty, and the same may apply here. (6) As applying to another subject. (7) Lev. VII, 19. (8) Seeing that the verse does not bear upon its own subject at all, why specify *'the flesh'*? Scripture could say, and that which toucheth etc.

a (1) Used in the sacrificial service: though these are not eatables, they nevertheless become unclean. (2) The question is only in respect of *'and as for the flesh'*, the rest of the verse being utilized in Men. 25b. (3) V. Glos. Teaching that if they are defiled and a priest eats them he transgresses the injunction against unclean flesh. The verse accordingly is read thus: *and the flesh that toucheth any unclean thing shall not be eaten . . . and the flesh*, viz., the *emurim*.—Since the *emurim* must be offered on the altar, the priest is a *zar* ('stranger') in relation thereto, and he transgresses on that account also. (4) Lev. VII, 20. (5) Which *'pertain unto the Lord'*. (6) The inclusion of *emurim* in the former would not prove its inclusion in the latter case, since the former is a graver offence, as proved by the greater penalty attaching to it. (7) V. 22b. (8) Because *ḥeleb* is generally used for lighting and softening hides.

b (1) I.e., flagellation. Actually only thirty-nine were given. (2) V. Glos. (3) For they are not generally pressed for their juice. (4) That there is no flagellation. (5) That which issues from mulberries, etc. (6) Lit., 'sweat'. I.e., he did not eat fruit of *'orlah* at all. Thus this does not support R. Joḥanan. (7) The prohibition of seething a kid in its mother's milk (Deut. XIV, 21) is understood by the Talmud as a prohibition of seething any meat and milk together. The question here is how do we know that if seethed together they are forbidden to be eaten. (8) Ibid. (9) Ex. XXII, 30. (10) I.e., *'holy man'* etc. introduces a prohibition of eating. (11) When it was planted.

כד א מיי' פ"ו מהלכות איסורי מזבח הלכה ח ופ"ח מהל' פסולי המוקדשין הלכה יב :
כה ב שם הלכה יח :
כו ג שם הלכה יב :
כז ד מיי' פ"ד מהל' מאכלות אסורות הל' י טוש"ע יו"ד סי' קפה סעיף ג :
כח ה מיי' פ"י שם הלכה כב :
כט ו מיי' פ"ד שם הלכה י טוש"ע יו"ד סי' קפה סעיף ג :

לירעה. שרץ העוף היא וגם שורצת על הארץ ויש בה אלו חמש לאוין ומוסיף עליה לאו דשרץ העוף במשנה תורה (יד) וכל שרץ העוף טמא הוא לכם לא יאכלו שרץ לשון רחוש ונענע ואינו נראה ואין בהמה וחיה הגבוהין מן הארץ בכלל שרץ הלכך לא תשקצו את נפשותיכם בבהמה ובעוף וגו' דכתיב בקדושים תהיו אינו מן המנין דלאו בשרצים כתיב : והבשר למה לי. השתא דאמר קרא לאו לגופיה אתא אלא לאו הוא ענין הוא ואשר יגע בכל טמא לא יאכל והבשר למה לי ומשני לרבות עצים ולבונה לקבל טומאה ואע"ג דלאו אוכלא הוא : והבשר כל טהור יאכל למה לי. והבשר יתירה מבעיא ליה דאילו כל טהור יאכל בשר דריש ליה במנחות (ד' כה:) כל טהור יאכל בשר והנפש אשר תאכל בשר וגו' הניתר לטהורין חייבין עליו משום טומאה יצא בשר שנטמאת לפני זריקת דם לשון אחר בין ברישא בין בסיפא ו' יתירה מיבעי' ליה : לרבות את האימורין. שאם נטמאו ואכלן טהור שיעבור עליהן משום ב' לאוין לאו דזרות שאף הכהן זר אצלם ולאו דטומאת בשר ואהדליט קאי והכי קאמר לא יאכל והבשר נמי שנטמאת לא יאכל : אשר לה'. קרא יתירה הוא דה"ל למכתב מזבח השלמים וטומאתו עליו וכתיב אשר לה' לרבות אף בשר הקרב לה' שאם אכלו בטומאה ענוש כרת : ומשני התם בטומאת הגוף איירי (ג) והאי וטומאתו עליו מוקמינן לה בזבחים בפרק ב"ש (דף מג:) בטומאת הגוף הכתוב מדבר והכא רבינהו לאזהרת טומאת בשר כשנטמאו הם והוא טהור שיהא מוזהר עליהן והכא ליכא כרת אלא לאו דאימעט מכרת בזבחים בפרק ב"ש : אלא דרך אכילתן. אלא אם כן אכלן דרך אכילתן : איכא דאמרי. הא דרבי אבהו איתמר והנך דאסירי בהנאה : חלב. אין דרך הנאתו אלא בהבערה ולמשוח עורות ולא לרפואה וכ"ש אוכל חלב חי : אין סופגין את הארבעים כו'. גבי משקין קתני במסכת תרומות וקאמר דאין כל מי פירות קרויין משקין אלא אלו בלבד. אין סופגין את הארבעים על שום מי פירות של ערלה משום דכולהו שלא כדרך הנאתן הוא אלא אלו : בשלמא אי אשמעינן בפרי גופא. דאי אכיל שלא כדרכו כגון שבישל אגוזים או אפרסקין ואכלן ואשמעינן דלא מחייב : שפיר. שמעינן מינה דאין לוקין אלא כדרך אכילתן אבל השתא טעמא דפטור משום דלאו פרי אכל : כלאי הכרם. כתיב (דברים כב) פן תקדש המלאה דמשמע לא תהנה ממנו אלא תשרפנו ופן לאו הוא : שהוא אסור. באכילה : ערלה שלא נעבדה בה עבירה. בנטיעותה : בשר בחלב שנעבדה בו עבירה. כשבישלו ועבר עליו על לאו לא תבשל :
ערלה

צירעה לוקה שש א"ל כל היכא *דאיכא למדרש דרשינן ולא מוקמינן בלאוי יתירי °והבשר אשר יגע בכל טמא לא יאכל דרישי' (א) למה לי *לרבות עצים ולבונה והבשר כל טהור יאכל בשר דסיפיה למה לי לרבות אימורין אימורין מהתם נפקא *דתניא °והנפש אשר תאכל בשר מזבח השלמים אשר לה' לרבות את האימורין "התם טומאת הגוף בכרת "הכא טומאת בשר בלאו א"ר אבהו א"ר יוחנן *כל איסורין שבתורה אין לוקין עליהן אלא דרך אכילתן למעוטי מאי אמר רב שימי בר אשי למעוטי שאם אכל חלב חי שפטור איכא דאמרי א"ר אבהו אמר ר' יוחנן "כל איסורין שבתורה אין לוקין עליהן אלא דרך הנאתן למעוטי מאי אמר רב שימי בר אשי למעוטי °שאם הניח חלב של שור הנסקל על גבי מכתו שהוא פטור וכל שכן אוכל חלב חי שהוא פטור אתמר נמי אמר רב אחא בר *עויה אמר רב אסי א"ר יוחנן הניח חלב של שור הנסקל על גבי מכתו פטור לפי שכל איסורין שבתורה אין לוקין עליהם אלא דרך הנאתן אמר ר' זירא אף אנן נמי תנינ' *"אין סופגין את הארבעים משום ערלה אלא על היוצא מן הזיתים ומן הענבים בלבד ואילו מתותים תאנים ורמונים לא מאי טעמא לאו משו' דלא קאכיל להו דרך הנאתן אמר ליה אביי בשלמא אי אשמעינן פרי גופא דלא קאכיל ליה דרך הנאתו שפיר אלא הכא משום דזיעה בעלמא הוא אמר אביי *"הכל מודים בכלאי הכרם שלוקין עליהן אפילו שלא כדרך הנאתן מאי טעמא משום דלא כתיב בהו אכילה מיתיבי איסי בן יהודה אומר *מנין לבשר בחלב שהוא אסור נאמר כאן °כי עם קדוש אתה ונאמר להלן °ואנשי קדש תהיון לי מה להלן אסור אף כאן אסור ואין לי אלא באכילה בהנאה מנין אמרת ק"ו ומה ערלה שלא נעבדה בה עבירה אסורה בהנאה בשר בחלב שנעבדה בו עבירה אינו דין שיהא אסור בהנאה
מה

צירעה לוקה שש. פ"ה דהא (ג) דכתיב בקדושים אל תשקצו את נפשותיכם בבהמה ובעוף ובכל אשר תרמוש האדמה וגו' לא חשיב ליה דבגדולים מיירי דלא כתיב (ד) שרץ ולשון שרץ דבר שהוא כד בארץ ואינו נראה אלא ע"י שירוצו מפני קטנו וקשה דבפ' ד' מיתות (סנהדרין נט:) דרשינן וכל חיה הרומשת זה הנחש משמע דרמישה היה נמי בדבר הרוחש כמו נחש שהולך על גחונו ותי' הר"י דאורלינ"ש דההוא קרא איירי בח' שרצים דאמרינן במעילה בפרק קדשי מזבח (דף טז: ושם) במובדלים ממך דיבר הכתוב דכתיב בסיפא דקרא אשר הבדלתי לכם לטמא והיינו ח' שרצים שהן טמאים : **לרבות את האימורים.** דסד"א אין חייבין עליהם משום טומאה הואיל ואין ניתרים ודרשינן במנחות בפרק הקומץ את המנחה (דף כה:) הניתר לטהורי' חייבים עליהם משום טומאה להכי איצטריך לרבוייהו מיהו קשה דבמעילה בפ' חטאת העוף (דף י:) דריש התם מאשר יקרב בכל הקדשים הכתוב מדבר ויליף התם אימורים *וכל שאין ניתר לטהורים ורבינו שמשון תירץ דאיצטריך לרבויי דסד"א דלא יבא איסור טומאה ויחול על איסור חלב : **פרט** לאוכל חלב חי. והא דאמר בגיד הנשה (חולין קכ:) אכל צפור טהורה בחייה בכל שהוא במיתתה בכזית שאני עוף שהוא רך וחזי לאומצא וחשיב כדרך הנאתו והא דאמר בהקומץ רבה (מנחות כא.) דם שבשלו אינו עובר עליו ופריך אביי מהא דתניא הקפה את הדם ואכלו או שהמחה את החלב וגמעו חייב ומשני כאן שהקפה באור וכאן שהקפה בחמה ולפי הך דהכא נ"ל שהברייתא לצדדים קתני הקפה את הדם בחמה ואת החלב באור דאי בחמה חי הוא ופטור : **אלא** הכא משום דזיעה בעלמא הוא. תימה לר"י דבהעור והרוטב (חולין קכא. ושם) יליף מקרא דאין חייב משום ערלה אלא על היוצא מזיתים וענבים דגמר ערלה פרי פרי מבכורים ובכורים מתרומה ובתרומה כתיב תירוש ויצהר אם כן אמאי איצטריך למימר הכא זיעה בעלמא הוא °וי"ל דהא דאיצטריך למילף התם פרי פרי מבכורים לאו למעוטי שאר משקין איצטריך דמן הדין אפילו תירוש ויצהר לא היה (ה) ליחשב למשקין פרי דזיעה בעלמא הוא כדאמרינן הכא והתם איצטריך למילף שנחשוב משקה של תירוש ויצהר כמו הפרי והשתא א"ש הא דאמר בשמעתין דזיעה בעלמא הוא דמהאי טעמא הוא דשמעינן דמשקה אינו כפרי מיהו תימה אמאי אמר דזיעה בעלמא הוא והא טעם כעיקר דאורייתא : **אמרת** קל וחומר. תימה היכי אתיא ק"ו לאפוקי מג"ש דיליף מנבילה בג"ש שלא תאסר בהנאה כמו נבילה ובפרק כל הבשר (חולין קטז.) איכא תנא דיליף הכי וסבר דבשר בחלב לא אסור בהנאה ואור"ת דבההוא קרא דאנשי קדש כתיב ביה נמי איסורי הנאה דמבשר בשדה דרשינן *קדשים שיצאו חוץ למחילה וגלי לן ק"ו דגמרינן מקדשים ולא (*מנבילה) וא"ת בלא ק"ו נמי מקשינן לחומרא וי"ל דהכא ס"ד לאקשויי לקולא משום דמפורש בהדיא בקרא היתר הנאה דכתיב לכלב תשליכון אותו הקשה הר"י דאורלינ"ש אמאי לא ילפינן מנותר איסור אכילה ואיסור הנאה מקדש קדש דמההוא קדש דנותר דריש ג"ש בפ' לולב וערבה (סוכה מח.) ובפרק כל הזבחים (זבחים כח:) וי"ל דהכא עם קדוש מאנשי קדש דרשי' שהן ענין אחד דקיימא קדושה אגברי אי נמי דנין חולין מחולין ואין דנין חולין מקדשים* : **הכל** מודים בכלאי הכרם. הא דלא קאמר הכל מודים בחולין שנשחטו בעזרה משום דכתיב בהו אכילה דמזבחת ואכלת נפקא לן ועוד דאיכא מאן דאמר לאו דאורייתא °והא דלא קאמר הכל מודים בבשר וחלב שמא משום דאין מזהירין מן הדין : **אמרת** ק"ו. איסור אכילה לא מצי למילף בק"ו מערלה כדאמר בכל הבשר (חולין קטו:) משום דאיכא למימר חורש בשור וחמור וחוסם פי פרה יוכיח דנעבדה בהו עבירה ושרו באכילה אבל השתא דיליף מקרא איסור אכילה ליכא למימר תוכיח דהנהו שרו באכילה:
מה

רבינו חננאל

לוקה שש הכא נמי לוקה על שני לאוין והא דאביי מפורש בפ' אלו הן הלוקין פוטיתא הוא דג טמא וכתיב בדגים (ויקרא יא יא) ושקץ יהיו לכם מבשרם לא תאכלו *וכתיב (עוד לכל השרץ השורץ לא יאכל כי שקץ הם) ועוד כתיב (שם מג) אל תשקצו את נפשותיכם בכל השרץ השורץ ולא תטמאו בהם נמצאו ארבעה לאוין באוכל שרץ סתם ולא פירש באחד מהם בארץ ודרשי' הלאוין בכל שרץ בין שרץ של ים ובין שרץ של יבשה לפיכך אמר אביי אכל פוטיתא שהיא שרקהים לוקה עליה הללו ארבעה לאוין כלם. אכל נמלה שהיא שקץ היבשה עובר **בארבעה לאוין הללו והוסיפה התורה על שקץ של יבשה לאו חמישי שנא' (שם מד) ולא תטמאו את נפשותיכם בכל השרץ השורץ על הארץ הלכך לוקה חמש אכל צרעה שהיא שרץ העוף עובר על חמשה לאוין הללו הוסיפה עליו התור' לאו אחד שנא' [דברים יד יט] וכל שרץ העוף טמא הוא לכם לא (יאכלו) [יאכל] הלכך לוקה שש מלקיות ופרקי' הני מילי דמוקמי' ליה בלאו יתירי היכא דליכא מידי למדרש [אבל אי איכא למדרש] כי האי תנא דרשי' : **מכדי** כתיב ואם האכל יאכל מבשר זבח השלמים וגו' והבשר אשר יגע בכל טמא למה לי לרבות עצים ולבונה שאם נטמאו ישרפו והבשר כל טהור יאכל בשר תוב למה לי לרבות אימורין שנטמאו סד"א כל טהור יאכל בשר כתיב מידי דכהן טהור מצי למיכליה אם אכלו בטומאה חייב אבל חלבים דלא יכול למיכלינהו אפי' הוא טהור אימא לית להו חיוב משום טומאה קמ"ל. שנינו בתוספתא פ' הזרוע הלחיים והקבה נוהגין בכלאים כו' ואסיקנא מהאי קרא דכתיב והנפש אשר תאכל בשר מזבח השלמים אשר לה' ונכרתה ואמרי' לה' לרבות האוכל אימורין בטומאת הגוף שהוא בכרת ובא הבשר אשר יגע בכל טמא לא יאכל לרבות בשר קדש שנטמא אכלו כהן טהור בלאו : **אמר** רבי אבהו אמר רבי יוחנן כל איסורין שבתורה אין לוקין עליהן אלא דרך הנאתן וכל שכן דרך אכילתן למעוטי אכל חלב חי ודרך הנאתן למעוטי [אם הניח] חלב של שור הנסקל על מכתו שפטור : **אמר** ר' זירא אף אנן נמי תנינא אין סופגין ארבעים משום ערלה אלא על היוצא מן הזיתים ומן הענבים הא מן התותים ומן הענבים לבד משום דאינו דרך הנאתן . ושני אביי שאני התם דזיעה בעלמא הוא : **אמר** אביי הכל מודים בכלאי הכרם כיון דלא כתיב בהו אכילה לוקה עליהן אפי' שלא כדרך הנאתן ומותיב עליהן איסי בן יהודה מהא

[בכורות ו:]
[לקמן לה. וש"נ ע"ש בפירש"י]
[זבחים לו: כריתות כג: לקמן לו.]
[עי' תוס' ע"ז יב: ד"ס אלא]
וכל שאין לו מתירין כצ"ל רש"ל
[בר רב עויא וכ"א לקמן לג:]
[עי' תוס' ע"ז יב: ד"ה אלא וכו' דלאסור דה"ה בע"ן לוקין אפי' שלא כדרך הנאתן ע"ש]
[מכות יח.]
[מחרפה כצ"ל]
[וע"ע תוס' בכורות י. ד"ס מס לכלן]

הגהות הב"ח

(א) גמרא לא יאכל דרישיה דקרא למה לי : (ב) רש"י ד"ה ומשני וכו' איירי דהכא : (ג) תוס' ד"ה צירעה וכו' פ"ה דהא. נ"ב עיי' פ' כל מערבין דיכה:(ד) בא"ד דלא כתיב בהו שרץ ולשון שרץ וכו' ואינו נראה מפני קוטנו אלא על ידי שירוצו וכו' וקשה כצ"ל: (ה) ד"ה אלא וכו' היה ליה ליחשב:

* דברי רבינו תמוהים דהא בהאי קרא כתיב בהדיא לכל השרץ השורץ על הארץ וגו' ובאמת הרי"ף סו"פ אלו טרפות ונרש"י כאן ובמכות ע"ז הביאו ללאו ד' הך קרא, דמשנה תורה וכל אשר אין לו וגו'.
** גם זה צ"ע דקרא דושקץ יהיה לכם מבשרם לא תאכלו כתיב רק בשרץ המים ושרץ הארץ לא נכלל כלל בהך קרא ועי' ברי"ף וברש"י ודברי רבינו מצוה ליישב .

גליון הש"ס גמ' שאם הניח חלב של שור הנסקל . עיין נדה לב ע"א תד"ה וכסמן . עיי' בספר כתנות אור להגאון בעל פנים מאירות סוף פ' ברכאית : **תוס'** ד"ה אלא וי"ל כו' דהא דאיצטריך למילף . עי' ע"ז יב ע"ב תד"ה אלא וצע"ק : **תוס'** ד"ה הכל מודים . והא דלא קאמר וכו' משום דאין מזהירין מן הדין .

ואם אינו ענין לאכילה תנהו ענין לאיסור הנאה אי מה כאן בשריפה אף כל איסורין ויקרא ו שבתורה בשריפה אמר קרא °בקדש באש תשרף בקדש בשריפה ואין כל איסורין שבתורה בשריפה והאי בקדש באש תשרף להכי הוא דאתא האי מיבעי ליה לכדרבי שמעון *דתניא רבי שמעון אומר בקדש באש תשרף לימד על חטאת ששורפין אותה בקדש ואין לי אלא זו בלבד פסולי קדשי קדשים ואמורי קדשים קלים מנין *תלמוד לומר (וכל) בקדש באש תשרף אמר ליה רבי יונתן רבך שמות כט מהאי קרא קאמר לה °ואם יותר מבשר המלואים ומן הלחם עד הבקר וגו' שאין תלמוד לומר לא יאכל ומה תלמוד לומר לא יאכל אם אינו ענין לגופיה דהא כתיב שם °ושרפת את הנותר באש תנהו ענין לשאר איסורין שבתורה ואם אינו ענין לאכילה תנהו ענין לאיסור הנאה אי מה כאן בשריפה אף כל איסורין שבתורה בשריפה אמר קרא ושרפת את הנותר נותר בשריפה ואין כל איסורין שבתורה בשריפה והאי לא יאכל להכי הוא דאתא האי מיבעי ליה לכדרבי אלעזר *דאמר ר' אלעזר *לא יאכל כי קדש הוא [כ]כל שבקדש פסול בא הכתוב ליתן לא תעשה על אכילתו אמר אביי לעולם מקרא קמא ואיפוך דליכתוב באש תשרף ולא בעי לא תאכל מה תלמוד לומר לא תאכל אם אינו ענין לגופו דנפקא ליה מדרבי אלעזר תנהו ענין לכל איסורין שבתורה ואם אינו ענין לאכילה תנהו ענין לאיסור הנאה אי מה כאן בשריפה אף כל איסורין שבתורה בשריפה אמר קרא הנותר הנותר בשריפה ואין כל איסורין שבתורה בשריפה אמר ליה רב פפא לאביי ואימא ליחודי ליה לאו לגופיה הוא דאתא דאי מדרבי ויקרא ז אלעזר *אין לוקין על לאו שבכללות אלא אמר רב פפא מהכא °והבשר אשר יגע בכל טמא לא יאכל באש ישרף שאין תלמוד לומר לא יאכל מה תלמוד לומר לא יאכל אם אינו ענין לגופו דהא נפקא ליה מקל וחומר דברים כו ממעשר הקל °ומה מעשר הקל אמרה תורה °לא בערתי ממנו בטמא בשר קדש חמור לא כל שכן וכי תימא *אין מזהירין מן הדין °היקישא היא דברים יב דכתיב °לא תוכל לאכול בשעריך מעשר דגנך תירושך ויצהרך ובכורות בקרך וגו' מה תלמוד לומר לא יאכל אם אינו ענין לגופו תנהו ענין לכל איסורין שבתורה ואם אינו ענין לאכילה תנהו ענין להנאה אי מה כאן בשריפה אף כל איסורין שבתורה בשריפה אמר קרא הנותר הנותר בשריפה ואין כל איסורין שבתורה בשריפה אמר לי' רבינא לרב אשי ואימא לעבור עליו בשני לאוין לאו מי *אמר אביי [ג]אכל פוטיתא לוקה ארבע נמלה לוקה חמש צירעה

רש"י

ואם אינו ענין. לאוסרם באכילה דהא איסור אכילה בגופייהו כתיב עו מדה בתורה דבר שלא הולרך לגופו תנהו ענין לענין אחר ותלמוד דבר לדבר אחר וכל המדות הלכה למשה מסיני: לימד על חטאת. פסולה שבריפתה בקדש בעזרה דמוהגה שורף לא הוה שמעינן מקום שריפתה היכן: פסולי. כל שאר קדשי קדשים כגון מנחה ועולה ואשם שנטמאו או שנשפך דמן ומנחה שלא נקטר קומלה ואימורי קדשים קלים שנטמאו ודוקא נקט הכי שמחילתן בתוך חומת העזרה אבל פסולי בשר קדשים קלים שאכילתן בכל העיר אף שריפתן אם נפסלו חוץ לעזרה הן והכי נמי תנן באלו עוברין (לקמן מט:) שורפין לפני הבירה והיינו חוץ לעזרה ושם היה בית הדשן לכך וכן מפורש בזבחים בפ' טבול יום (ד' קד:): אמר ליה. ההוא מרבנן לרבי שמואל בר נחמני דאקשי ליה האי קושיא רבי יונתן רבך נמי לא הוה מייתי איסור הנאה לכל איסורין מבקדש באש תשרף דמבעי ליה לכדאמרת שתשרף בעזרה אלא מהאי קרא אמר להו: דהא כתיב ושרפת. אלמא לאו בר אכילה הוא: לכל איסורין. דוגמתן שנאמר בהן לאו באכילתן: ואם אינו ענין לאכילה. דהא בגופייהו כתיב תנהו ענין להנאה: אמר קרא והנותר. דהוה ליה למכתב ושרפתו באש: מיבעי ליה לכדרבי אלעזר. ליתן לא תעשה דאי מושרפת לא הוה ידעינן ביה איסור לאו למלקות: כל שבקודש פסול. מדכתיב כי קודש הוא יתירה לרבות על שאר פסולי קדשי קדשים בלאו כגון פיגול ויוצא ונשפך דמו: מקרא קמא. וכל חטאת ולאו מבאש תשרף דאיצטריך לומר שישרף בעזרה אלא מלא תאכל ליכתוב באש תשרף אלמא לאו בר אכילה הוא וממילא נפקא לן ביה נמי איסור לאו מהאי דרבי אלעזר דמפיק מלא יאכל כי קודש הוא כל פסולי קדשים: לאו שבכללות. כגון זה שנכלל כל הפסולין יחד: לא בערתי. אזהרה נפקא לן ביה ביבמות בהערל (דף עג:): אין מזהירין. מדין קל וחומר אף על פי שאדם דן קל וחומר מעצמו אינה אזהרה ללאו במסכת מכות (דף ה:) נפקא לן: היקישא הוא. ולאו קל וחומר דאיתקש נדריך ונדבותיך דהיינו שלמים למעשר דגן דכתיב ביה לא בערתי ממנו בטמא ותייתי לן מינה דאף קדשים לא יאכלו בטומאה ולא בערתי ממנו בטמא אע"ג דוידוי בעלמא הוא ואינו לאו הא נפקא לן ביה איסור לאו ביבמות בהערל מהאי קרא דלא תוכל לאכול בשעריך ולהלן הוא אומר בפסולי המוקדשים שנפדו (דברים טו) בשעריך תאכלנו הטמא והטהור יחדיו טמא וטהור אוכלין בקערה אחת יש כאן טומאת בשר לטהור וטומאת הגוף לטמא וקא אמר רחמנא גבי מעשר וקדשים ההוא בשעריך דשראי לך ב'יה טומאה התם בפסולי המוקדשין הכא לא תאכל: אכל פוטיתא. שרץ המים: לוקה ארבע. חד לאו בשרץ המים בתורת כהנים דהוא ספר ויקרא וחד במשנה תורה ושני לאוין כתובים בתורת כהנים בשקצים סתם (א) לא תשקצו את נפשותיכם בכל השרץ השורץ ולא תטמאו בהן והכא לא כתיב על הארץ ומשמע בין שרץ המים ובין שרץ הארץ הרי ארבע: נמלה. שהוא שרץ הארץ: לוקה חמש. הני תרי דסתם שרצים וחד וכל השרץ השורץ על הארץ שקץ הוא לא יאכל וחד לכל השרץ השורץ על הארץ לא תאכלום כי שקץ הם וחד ולא תטמאו את נפשותיכם בכל השרץ הרומש על הארץ:

לרעה

תוספות

ואם אינו ענין לאכילה. לא תני שפיר דהיכי מצי לאוקמי' באיסור אכילה דהא כתיב באש תשרף: הא אין לוקין על לאו שבכללות. הקשה הר"ר אליעזר ממיץ דבלאו הכי הלוקין (מכות יג.) אמר דלאו דנותר ופיגול הוה בכלל הלוקין ואמאי והא לאו שבכללות הוא ותירץ דלגבי נותר שמפורש בהדיא דכתיב ושרפת את הנותר באש לא יאכל כי קדש הוא לא חשיב לאו שבכללות ופיגול נמי גמרינן עון עון מנותר אך קשה דבפרק בתרא דמכות (דף יז: יח.) גבי זר שאכל עולה לפני זריקה לוקה חמש פריך ולילקי נמי מדרבי אלעזר דאמר כל שבקודש פסול ומאי קושיא והא לאו שבכללות הוא: אם אינו ענין לגופו דאתי בקל וחומר ממעשר. ואם תאמר והא איצטריך לרביעי בקודש כדאמרינן בפרק קמא (דף יט.) וי"ל דלא ליכתוב לא יאכל אלא ישרף: היקישא הוא. תימה אמאי קרי ליה היקישא תיפוק ליה דקודש כתיב בהדיא בקרא ובכורות בקרך ולאכך ואזהרה למעשר נמי יליף מהאי קרא וי"ל דצריך היקישא משום איסור הנאה דלא תוקי קרא דוהבשר לאיסור הנאה שיהא בלאו דבפ' שני דשבת (דף כה.) לא ילפי' איסור הנאה בשמן קדש שנטמא אלא ממעשר: דכתיב לא תוכל לאכול בשעריך. האי לא חשיב לאו שבכללות מדלא כתיב מעשר דגנך ובכורות בקרך לא תוכל לאכלם ש"מ ליחודי לאו אתא חד דכתי' בקרא אחא:

לירעה

עין משפט נר מצוה

כא א מיי' פי"ט מהל' פסולי המוקדשין הלכה א ב:

כב ב מיי' פי"ח שם הלכה ג ד:

כג ג מיי' פ"ב מהלכות מאכלות אסורות הל' כג [רב אלפס חולין סוף פ"ג דף רפ"ב: תהרי"ף בפירושו]

[ועי' תוס' יומא לו: ד"ה לאו ותוס' מכות יג. ד"ה מגן]

מכות יח. מעילה יט.

[שבת כה.]

[יבמות כב: מכות ה:]

מסורת הש"ס

לקמן מט:

[במכות יג. ובמעילה יז. ליתא אליעזר בר"ו ודע עוד דבמעילה ברייתא היא דתניא ר"א אומר לא יאכל כו']

[לקמן מה: חולין לה: ב"מ קטו: סנהדרין פג. מנחות ה: תמורה ז: כריתות ד. ה.]

מכות טז: עירובין כח.

הגהות הב"ח

(א) רש"י ד"ה לוקה ארבע וכו' בשקצים סתם לא תשקצו:

גליון הש"ס

גמרא היקשא הוא. עיין זבחים לד ע"א תד"ה והבשר:

רבינו חננאל

שבתורה שיהו אסורין אפי' בהנאה ואם תאמר כל איסורין שבתורה בשרפה תלמוד לומר [בקדש] באש תשרף כל פסול שהוא בקדש בשרפה ולא שאר איסורין שבתורה: והאי בקדש מבעי ליה לכדתניא בקדש באש תשרף לימד על חטאת כו' והא דאמר ר' יונתן ואם יותר מבשר המלואים וגו' נדחו דבריו ותרצה אביי לעולם מקרא קמא והוא וכל חטאת אשר יובא מדמה אל אהל מועד וא"כ נימא קרא בקדש באש תשרף ותשתוק לא תאכל למה לי אם אינו ענין לגופיה דנפק' ליה מדר' אלעזר דאמר לא יאכל כי קדש הוא כל שבקדש פסול ליתן לא תעשה על אכילתו תנהו ענין לשאר איסורין שבתורה ודחי' תוב ואימא ליחודי ליה לאו לגופיה דאי מדר' אלעזר הוה ליה לאו שבכללות כדפירש כל שבקדש כלל כל פסולין שבקדש [וכל לאו] שבכללות אין לוקין עליו אלא א"ר פפא מהכא והבשר אשר יגע בכל טמא לא יאכל שאין ת"ל (באש ישרף) [לא יאכל] כו' עד וכי מזהירין מן הדין ודחי' הקישא הוא כלומר התורה הקישה הקדש למעשר שנאמר לא תוכל לאכול בשעריך מעשר דגנך תירושך ויצהרך ובכורות בקרך וצאנך וגו' וכל נדריך אלו קדשים ... אמר ליה רבינא לרב אשי ואימא לעבור עליו בשני לאוין כלומר ... לא תוכל לאכול בשעריך לא יאכל עוד למה בא לחייבו בשני לאוין מי לא אמר אביי אכל פוטיתא לוקה ארבע נמלה לוקה חמש צרעה ... לוקה

its teaching to all [other] prohibitions of the Torah;[7] [24a] and if it is irrelevant in respect of eating,[8] apply the matter to the prohibition of benefit.[9] If so, just as there [it must be destroyed] by burning, so all prohibited things of the Torah [must be destroyed] by burning?—Scripture saith, *'in the holy place . . . it shall be burnt with fire'*: [that which is forbidden] in the holy place requires burning, but all the [other] forbidden things of the Torah do not require burning. But does this [phrase,] *'in the holy place . . . it shall be burnt with fire,'* come for this [teaching]? Surely it is required for R. Simeon's [dictum]! For it was taught, R. Simeon said: *'In the holy place . . . it shall be burnt with fire'*: this teaches concerning the sin-offering[10] that we burn it in the holy place.[11] Now, I only know this alone; how do we know it of the unfit of the [other]
a most sacred sacrifices and the *emurim*[1] of the lesser sacrifices?[2] Therefore it is stated, *in the holy place . . . it shall be burnt with fire!*[3] —Said he to him,[4] R. Jonathan thy teacher deduced it[5] from this verse: *And if aught of the flesh of the consecration, or of the bread, remain unto the morning, then thou shalt burn the remainder with fire; it shall not be eaten, because it is holy.*[6] Now *'it shall not be eaten'* need not be stated:[7] then why is *'it shall not be eaten'* stated? If it is irrelevant in respect of itself, seeing that it is written, *'then thou shalt burn the remainder with fire'* apply its teaching to the other interdicts of the Torah. And if it is irrelevant in respect of eating, apply its teaching to the prohibition of benefit. If so, just as here [it must be destroyed] by burning, so all the forbidden things of the Torah [must be destroyed] by burning?—Scripture saith, *'then thou shalt burn the* [nothar] *remainder: nothar* requires burning, but all [other] forbidden things of the Torah do not require burning.

Yet does this [verse] *'it shall not be eaten'* come for this [teaching]? Surely it is required for R. Eleazar's [dictum]! For R. Eleazar said: *'it shall not be eaten, because it is holy'*: whatever of holy [flesh, etc.] that is unfit, the Writ comes to impose a negative injunction against eating it?[8]—Said Abaye: After all [it[9] is deduced] from the first verse,[10] but reverse [the argument]: for let Scripture write, *'it shall be burnt with fire,'* so that *'it shall not be eaten'* will be superfluous; why then is *'it shall not be eaten'* written? If it is irrelevant for itself, seeing that it is deduced by R. Eleazar's [exe-
b gesis],[1] apply its teaching to all [other] interdicts of the Torah. And if it is irrelevant in respect of eating, apply its teaching to the prohibition of benefit. If so, just as here [it must be destroyed] by burning, so all the forbidden things of the Torah [must be destroyed] by burning?—Scripture saith, *'the* [*nothar*] remainder'; *'nothar'* requires burning,—but all [other] forbidden things of the Torah do not require burning. R. Papa said to Abaye: Yet say that it[2] comes to assign a negative injunction [specifically] for itself? For if [we learn] from R. Eleazar ['s dictum], we do not flagellate for an implied negative injunction![3]—Rather, said R. Papa: [It[4] is deduced] from this: *And the flesh that toucheth any unclean thing shall not be eaten; it shall be burnt with fire.*[5] Now, *'shall not be eaten'* need not be stated: why then is *'shall not be eaten'* stated? If it is irrelevant for itself, seeing that it may be deduced *a minori* from tithe, which is lighter, [thus:] if tithe, which is light, yet the Torah said, *neither have I put away thereof, being unclean,*[6] how much the more sacred flesh, which is more stringent! And should you say, We cannot give a warning [of flagellation] as a result of an *ad majus* conclusion,[7] but this is a *hekkesh*,[8] for it is written, *Thou mayest not eat within thy gates the tithe of thy corn, or of thy wine, or of thine oil, or the firstlings of thy herd or of thy flock, nor any of thy vows*
c *which thou vowest, nor thy freewill-offerings*, etc.[1] Then why is *'shall not be eaten'* stated? If it is irrelevant in its own case, apply its teaching to all [other] prohibitions of the Torah. And since it is irrelevant in respect of eating, apply it to benefit. If so, just as here [it must be destroyed] by burning, so all the forbidden things of the Torah require burning?—Scripture saith, *'the* [*nothar*] remainder': *nothar* requires burning, but all [other] forbidden things of the Torah do not require burning.

Rabina said to R. Ashi: Yet perhaps [it teaches that] he transgresses two negative injunctions on its account?[2] Did not Abaye say: If he ate *puṭitha*[3] he is flagellated four times;[4] [for] an ant, he

(7) This is a principle of Talmudic exegesis: when a statement or verse is superfluous in its own connection, it is applied to other laws. (8) It certainly cannot teach that, since each prohibition of eating is stated separately. (9) For *'it shall be burnt'* shows that all benefit is forbidden, and this has now been applied to all other prohibitions. (10) Rendered unfit. (11) For *'and, behold, it was burnt'* (v. n. b6) does not teach where it must be burnt.

a (1) Lit., 'devoted objects'; those portions of the sacrifices offered on the altar. (2) Sacrifices were divided into two categories; (i) most sacred; these included the sin-offering, meal-offering, burnt-offering and guilt-offering. (ii) Sacrifices of lesser sanctity, e.g., the peace-offering and the thanksoffering. The question is: how do we know that if these are defiled or their blood is spilled, thus rendering them unfit, they must be burnt in the Temple Court? The flesh of the lesser sacrifices is not mentioned, for this was eaten outside the Temple precincts and consequently when unfit was burnt without the Temple Court, v. *infra 49a*. (3) I.e., whatever would normally be consumed or otherwise disposed of in the holy place must now be burnt there. (4) Viz., this scholar to R. Samuel b. Naḥmani. (5) The prohibition of benefit as applied to other forbidden things in the Torah. (6) Ex. XXIX, 34. (7) Since we are told that it must be burnt. (8) *'Because it is holy'* is unnecessary, and therefore R. Eleazar utilizes it thus. Hence its transgression involves flagellation. (9) The teaching of R. Joshua b. Levi. (10) Viz., *'and every sin offering'*, etc.

b (1) Without R. Eleazar's deduction, *'it shall not be eaten'* would be necessary in spite of the statement *'it shall be burnt with fire'*, to show that it is subject to a negative injunction, which involves flagellation. But now that R. Eleazar has deduced a negative injunction in respect of *all* unfit sacrifices from *'it shall not be eaten because it is holy'*, this is superfluous. (2) The verse *'it shall not be eaten'* written here. (3) I.e., where the action is not explicitly forbidden but only by an injunction stated in general terms, which includes a number of other actions too. (4) V. *supra*, n. a9. (5) Lev. VII, 19. (6) Deut. XXVI, 14, q.v. This refers to the second tithe, which was eaten by its Israelite owner in Jerusalem, and who had to declare that he had not eaten it *'being unclean'*, which shows that this was forbidden. The sanctity of tithes is of course lighter than that of sacrifices. (7) This is a general principle. Hence this argument does not suffice to make it an offence punishable by flagellation, and so *'shall not be eaten'* is here required. (8) V. Glos., an analogy between two laws which rests on a Biblical intimation (as Lev. XIV, 13) or on a principle common to both (Jast.). Flagellation is inflicted on the basis of a *hekkesh*.

c (1) Deut. XII, 17. *'Vows'* and *'freewill-offerings'* are sacrifices, and Scripture, by coupling these with tithes, shows that they are the same. (2) And is flagellated for each separately. In that case the verse is not superfluous. (3) A small water reptile (*sherez*), a young eel, v. Mak., 16b, n. 8. (4) I.e., four flagellations of the prescribed number of lashes.

uncleanness and cleanness. [23b] Surely then they differ in this, [viz.,]: R. Jose the Galilean holds, *'ye shall not eat'* connotes both a prohibition of eating and a prohibition of benefit, and when the verse comes to permit *nebelah*, it comes in respect of benefit. While R. Akiba holds: It connotes a prohibition of eating, [but] does not connote a prohibition of benefit, and for what [purpose] does the verse come? In respect of uncleanness and cleanness!—No: all hold that *'ye shall not eat'* connotes both a prohibition of eating and a prohibition of benefit, but here they differ in this: R. Jose the Galilean holds, when *nebelah* was permitted,[3] it [alone] was permitted, [whereas] its fat [*ḥeleb*] and its sinew[4] were not permitted, and [therefore] for what purpose is the verse required? It is in respect of permission for use. But R. Akiba holds: when *nebelah* was permitted, its fat [*ḥeleb*] and its sinew too were permitted; hence for what purpose is the verse necessary? It is in respect of uncleanness and cleanness.

Now as to R. Jose the Galilean, we have found that the Divine Law permits *ḥeleb* for use; but as for the sinew, let us say that it is forbidden?—If you wish I can say that it is in fact forbidden. Alternatively, it is adduced *a minori:* if *ḥeleb*, for which there is a penalty of *kareth*, is permitted for use, how much the more the sinew, for which there is no penalty of *kareth*. But R. Simeon, who forbids it, [argues]: This can be refuted. As for *ḥeleb*, that is because it is freed from its general [prohibition] in the case
a of a beast;[1] will you say [the same] of the sinew, which was not freed from its general [prohibition] in the case of a beast?[2] And the other?—We are speaking of cattle[3] [*behemah*]; [and] in the case of cattle at all events it [*sc. ḥeleb*] was not permitted.

Consider: we have raised objections from all these verses and answered them; [then] wherein do Hezekiah and R. Abbahu differ?—In respect of leaven during Passover, on the view of the Rabbis,[4] [and] in respect of the ox that is stoned, and this on the view of all:[5] Hezekiah deduces it[6] from *'shall not be eaten'*, while R. Abbahu learns it from *nebelah*.[7] Consider: according to both Masters they are forbidden for use: [then] wherein do they [practically] differ?—They differ in respect of *ḥullin* which was slaughtered in the Temple Court:[8] Hezekiah holds, *'shall not be eaten'*[9] is to exclude these,[10] while *'it'*[11] is to exclude *ḥullin* which was slaughtered in the Temple Court.[12] R. Abbahu[13] holds: *'it'* is to exclude these, while *ḥullin* which was slaughtered in the Temple Court is not forbidden [for use] by Scriptural law.

One of the scholars sat before R. Samuel b. Naḥmani, and he sat and said in R. Joshua b. Levi's name: How do we know of all prohibitions in the Torah, that just as they are forbidden for food, so are they also forbidden for use, and which are they? Leaven [*ḥamez*] during Passover and the ox that is stoned? ([You ask,] 'How do we know'!—learn it from *'it shall not be eaten'?*—To him[14] *'it shall not be eaten'* implies a prohibition of eating, but it does not imply a prohibition of benefit. Then let him deduce it
b from *nebelah?*[1]—He agrees with R. Judah, who maintained: The words are as they are written. If he agrees with R. Judah, let him deduce it whence R. Judah deduces it, [viz.] from *'ye shall cast it to the dogs'?*[2]—He holds that *ḥullin* which was slaughtered in the Temple Court is [forbidden for use] by Scriptural law.[3] Whence then do we know it?)—From the verse, *And no sin-offering, whereof any of the blood is brought into the tent of meeting to make atonement in the holy place, shall be eaten: it shall be burnt with fire.*[4] Now, *'it shall be burnt with fire'* need not be stated;[5] then what is the purpose of *'it shall be burnt with fire'?* If it is unnecessary in its own connection, seeing that it is written, *and, behold, it was burnt,*[6] apply

(3) In respect of benefit. (4) The thigh sinew.
a (1) The *ḥeleb* of a *ḥayyah* (wild or semi-wild animal) is permitted. (2) The prohibition of a thigh sinew applies also to a beast. (3) The text under discussion speaks of the fat of an ox or lamb, v. Lev. VII, 23. (4) Who hold that benefit thereof is forbidden. (5) V. *supra* 22b. (6) That these are forbidden for use. (7) V. Glos. (8) On the view of R. Judah who maintains: the words are as written, so that *nebelah* can serve as basis of deduction for other prohibitions, v. *supra* 21b-22a. (9) Written in connection with leaven and the ox that is stoned. (10) *Sc.* the two just mentioned. (11) Written in connection with *nebelah*, v. *supra* 22a. (12) Showing that benefit thereof is *Scripturally* forbidden, v. *supra*. (13) Who makes no distinction between the passive and active forms in which the prohibition is expressed. (14) R. Joshua b. Levi.
b (1) As above. (2) Ex. XXII, 30. (3) Deducing it from *'it'*: hence it cannot be utilized for these two. (4) Lev. VI, 23. (5) As shown below. (6) Lev. X, 16, q.v. Moses upbraided the sons of Aaron for burning it, observing, *'Behold, the blood of it was not brought into the sanctuary within'* (v. 18). This proves that when it is brought within, the sacrifice must be burnt; hence the present verse is superfluous.

מאי לאו בהא קמיפלגי דר' יוסי הגלילי סבר לא תאכלו משמע בין איסור אכילה בין איסור הנאה וכי אתא קרא למישרייה לנבילה בהנאה הוא דאתא ורבי עקיבא סבר איסור אכילה משמע איסור הנאה לא משמע וכי אתא קרא לטומאה וטהרה לא דכ"ע לא תאכלו משמע בין איסור אכילה בין איסור הנאה והכא בהא קמיפלגי רבי יוסי הגלילי סבר כשהותרה נבילה היא הותרה חלבה וגידה לא הותרו וכי איצטריך קרא להיתר הנאה הוא דאתא ורבי עקיבא סבר *כשהותרה נבילה חלבה וגידה נמי הותרו וכי איצטריך קרא לטומאה וטהרה ור' יוסי הגלילי אשכחן חלב דשרייה רחמנא בהנאה *אלא גיד נימא דאסור איבעית אימא הכי נמי דאסור איבעית אימא מייתי לה בק"ו ומה חלב שענוש כרת מותר בהנאה גיד שאינו ענוש כרת לא כל שכן ור"ש דאסר איכא למיפרך *מה לחלב שכן הותר מכללו אצל חיה תאמר בגיד שלא הותר מכללו אצל חיה ואידך בבהמה מיהת לא אישתרי מכדי אותבינהו כל הני קראי ושנינהו חזקיה ורבי אבהו במאי פליגי בחמץ בפסח ואליבא דרבנן בשור הנסקל ואליבא דדברי הכל חזקיה נפיק ליה מלא יאכל ורבי אבהו נפיק ליה מנבילה מכדי בין למר ובין למר אסורין בהנאה מאי בינייהו איכא בינייהו חולין שנשחטו בעזרה חזקיה סבר לא יאכל למעוטי הני אותו למעוטי חולין שנשחטו בעזרה רבי אבהו סבר אותו למעוטי הני *חולין שנשחטו בעזרה לאו דאורייתא נינהו יתיב ההוא מרבנן קמיה דרבי שמואל בר נחמני ויתיב וקאמר משמיה דר' יהושע בן לוי מנין לכל איסורין שבתורה דכי היכי דאסורין באכילה הכי נמי אסורין בהנאה ומאי ניהו חמץ בפסח ושור הנסקל מנין תיפוק ליה מלא יאכל לא יאכל איסור אכילה משמע ליה איסור הנאה לא משמע ליה תיפוק ליה מנבילה סבר לה כר' יהודה דאמר *דברים ככתבן אי סבר לה כר' יהודה תיפוק ליה מהיכא דנפקא ליה לר' יהודה °מלכלב [שמות כב] תשליכון אותו קסבר חולין שנשחטו בעזרה דאורייתא מנין דכתיב °כל חטאת אשר יובא [ויקרא ו] מדמה וגו' שאין ת"ל באש תשרף ומה ת"ל באש תשרף אם אינו ענין לגופו דכתיב °והנה שורף [שם י] תנהו ענין לכל איסורין שבתורה

ואם

רש"י

חלבה וגידה לא הותרו. דחלב אינו בכלל בשר הלכך לא הוה במשמע תתננה ואכלה וגבי נוגע בנבלתה נמי לאו חלב במשמע הלכך יעשה לכל מלאכה לא הוצרך לטהרו אלא להתירו מכלל הנאות לא תאכל חלב: ורבי עקיבא סבר. חלב בכלל נבילה בין להיתר הנאה בין לטמא הלכך כי איצטריך קרא לטהרו איצטריך: ורבי שמעון. דאמר לעיל גיד אסור בהנאה משום דסבירא ליה אין בגידין בנותן טעם ולא הותר בכלל נבילה מאי טעמא לא מייתי ליה כרבי יוסי להתיר הנאה מקל וחומר מחלב: מכללו. אף באכילה: ואידך. רבי יוסי אמר לך אנא בחלב בהמה קא מייתינא קרא להתיר בהנאה דקרא בחלב שור וכשב קאי וקא שרי ליה בהנאה ובבהמה לא הותר מכללו באכילה הלכך אתי גיד הנשה מיניה: מכדי אותבינהו כל הנך קראי. דכל איסורין שנאמ' בהן לא תאכל ומותרין בהנאה: ושנינהו. רבי אבהו ואשכח בהו פרטא להיתר לא מצינו באחד מכולם שהחמיר בו רבי אבהו ויאמר שאסור בהנאה ולחזקיה ישתרו אלא דבר האסור אסור לדברי שניהן והמותר מותר לדברי שניהן: במאי פליגי. דאין לך איסורי הנאה בדבר שנאמר בו לאו באכילתו שלא נאמר בו פרט להתיר אלא הנך שני דברים דכתיב בהן לא יאכל כגון שור הנסקל וחמץ בפסח ובין למר ובין למר אסורין: ואליבא דרבנן. דפליגי עליה דרבי יוסי דאמר לעיל חמץ בפסח מותר בהנאה: מנבילה. מדאיצטריך קרא למישרי נבילה ואי הוה כתיב לא תאכל נמי הוה מיתסרי: איכא בינייהו חולין שנשחטו בעזרה. ואליבא דר' יהודה דאמר מנבילה לא מצי למיגמר דלדברים ככתבן אתא דחזקיה סבר הני תרי מדשני בדיבוריה איתסר ולכלב תשליכון אותו לא הוצרך למעט את אלו ולאוסרן בהנאה וכי אתא למעוטי חולין שנשחטו בעזרה אתא וכדפרישית לעיל ורבי אבהו סבר אין חילוק בין לא יאכל בין לא יֵאָכֵל ואצטריך אותו למעוטי הני והכי משמע טריפה אף על גב שכתבתי לך לאו באכילתה אני מתיר לך הנאתה אבל לא חמץ ושור הנסקל שלא פרטתי לך בהן היתר: חולין בעזרה לאו דאורייתא. וכי אמר רבי אבהו לא יאכל איסור הנאה משמע אליבא דרבי מאיר אמרה דלית ליה לדברים ככתבן ומדאיצטריך למישרי נבילה מכלל דשאר איסורין כגון חמץ ושור הנסקל אסירי ולאו משום שינוי הלשון שאין חילוק בין לא יאכל ללא יאכל לרבי אבהו אלא מדאיצטריך למישרי נבילה ואותו לר"מ למעוטי חולין בעזרה: ה"ג ומאי ניהו חמץ בפסח ושור הנסקל: ותיפוק ליה מהיכא דנפקא ליה לרבי יהודה. לעיל אליבא דרבי אבהו דמייתי ליה מאותו אתה משליך לכלב ואי אתה משליך שאר איסורין: קא סבר. האי תנא: חולין שנשחטו בעזרה. אסורין בהנאה מדאורייתא ונפקא ליה מאותו ומיבעי ליה קרא אחרינא לשאר איסורין: כל חטאת אשר יובא מדמה. לאו בחטאות הפנימיות שהובא דמן כמצוותן לפנים כתיב דהא בהדיא כתיב בהן בפר כהן משיח והעלם דבר שריפתן מחוץ למחנה אלא ללמד על חטאת החיצונה דאם הכניס דמה לפנים פסולה: אם אינו ענין לגופו דהא כתיב והנה שורף. בשעיר נחשון בויהי ביום השמיני וקאמר להו משה למה שרפתם אותו הן לא הובא את דמה אל הקדש פנימה מכלל דאם הובא שפיר עבוד דשרפוה אלמא בת שריפה היא: לכל איסורין. שנאמר בהן לאו באכילתן כזה ועל כרחיך לא מייתי אלא חמץ בפסח ושור הנסקל דבשאר איסורים כתיב פרטא להיתירא:

ואם

תוספות

ומה חלב שענוש כרת מותר בהנאה. וא"ת לימא שור הנסקל ושאר איסורי הנאה יוכיחו שאינן בכרת ואפ"ה אסורין בהנאה וי"ל דה"פ ומה חלב (א) שענוש כרת ואסור באכילה ומותר בהנאה כמו נבילה עצמה גיד שאין ענוש כרת לכ"ש שיהא בכלל היתר נבילה והשתא לא שייך למימר תוכיח ולא מצי למיעבד נמי ק"ו מדם דדם אינו בכלל נבילה ואפילו טומאה אינבו מטעם נבילה כדפרישי' לעיל (דף כב.) אבל חלב הוה שפיר בכלל נבילה דלטומאה לא הוה צריך קרא דאדרבה לטהרו מידי נבילה מצריך קרא והא דקאמר היא הותרה וחלבה לא הותרה לאו משום דלא הוי בכלל נבילה אלא משום דלא הותרה בנבילה אלא מה שהותר בטהורה באכילה והשתא א"ש הא דקאמר ואידך אגן בבהמה קיימינן דלא ילפינן אלא שיהא בכלל היתר נבילה אבל בעלמא מודה דפריך שפיר*: בבהמה מיהא לא אישתרי. [פי' תוס' חולין קב. ד"ה חלב] אין להקשות דגיד חיה מיהא ליתסר דכיון דשל בהמה לא מיתסר בהנאה אם כן לא יאכל דכתיב גבי גיד הנשה באכילה דוקא קאמר ומהיכא תיתי לן לאסור של חיה בהנאה: מאי בינייהו. תימה לרשב"א לימא דאיכא בינייהו חמץ נוקשה וחמץ דגן גמור ע"י תערובות דמרבינן בריש אלו עוברין (לקמן מג.) מכל מחמצת לא תאכלו דלחזקיה מותר בהנאה ולרבי אבהו כל מקום שנאמר לא תאכלו משמע איסור הנאה וכי תימא כיון דמרבינן ליה לאכילה ה"ה להנאה אם כן כרת נמי ליחייב: דכתיב והנה שורף. פרש"י בשעיר נחשון ובת"כ דריש בהדיא אשעיר דראש חודש מדכתיב ואותה נתן לכם וגו' והיינו של ר"ח דמכפר עון (ב) על טומאת מקדש וקדשיו*): דהא כתיב והנה שורף. פרש"י ואמר להו משה הן לא הובא את דמה אל הקדש פנימה מכלל דאם הובא שפיר עבוד דשרפוה הקשה הרב רבינו שלמה מדרויש הא על כרחיך לאו שפיר עבוד דשרפוה דהא שרפוה בלא עיבור צורה ואמר בפרק כיצד צולין (לקמן פב:) כל שפסולו בגופו ישרף מיד בדם ובבעלים תעובר צורתו ויצא לשריפה וקרא ה"ק מדוע לא אכלתם את החטאת הן לא הובא את דמה הא אם הובא שפיר עבוד דלא אכלוה ואומר ר"י דה"פ אם אינו ענין לגופה דהא קיי"ל בפרק כיצד צולין (גם זה שם) כל שפסולו בקדש בשריפה וחטאת דאהרן משום מעשה שהיה תנהו לכל איסורים:

ואם

רבינו חננאל

בהנאה נמצא חזקיה כר' עקיבא ור' אבהו כר' יוסי הגלילי לא לעולם ר' עקיבא נמי לא תאכלהו איסור הנאה נמי משמע ולמה דרש הפסוק לטומאה וטהרה משום [דהיתר הנאה] כבר (למה)[למר] מנבלה קסבר כשהותרה הנבלה הבשר והחלב והגידים הותרו מ"ט שנא' ואכלה כולה משמע כמות שהיא ולא איצטריך קרא אלא לטהרה וטומאה ור' יוסי הגלילי סבר היא הותרה חלבה וגידה לא הותרו כו': ואמרינן מכדי אותבי' כל הני תיובתא ושני כל חד לנפשיה חזקיה ור' אבהו .מאי פליגי ואמרינן פליגי בחמץ בפסח ואליבא דרבנן דאסרי אפילו בהנאה ולא כר' יוסי הגלילי דשרי ובשור הנסקל ואליבא דדברי הכל כו': תוב אמרי' מכדי חזקיה ור' אבהו בחמץ בפסח ובשור הנסקל מיסר אסרי בין באכילה בין בהנאה מאי בינייהו ואמרי' איכא בינייהו חולין שנשחטו [בעזרה] דקיי"ל אמרה תורה שחוט חולין [בחוץ וקדשים בפנים וזה פירש שחוט שלי כלומר שחוט חולין] במקדש בגבולך מה קדשים בחוץ אסורין אפילו בהנאה אף חולין בפנים כך אסורין חזקיה סבר איסו' חמץ בפסח ואיסו' שור הנסקל ששניהם אסורין בהנאה מלא יאכל נפקא והנבלה לדברים ככתבן הוא דאתי בא אותו למעוטי חולין שנשחטו בעזרה שיהיו אסורין בהנאה דדרשינן הכי אותו ובשר טריפה אתה משליכו לכלבך ונהנה בו ואי אתה משליך חולין שנשחטו בעזרה ור' אבהו סבר בין לא יאכל בין לא תאכל [בין לא תאכלו] כולו אחד הוא ובא לא תאכלו כל נבלה למעוטי שאר אסורין ובא אותו למעוטי חמץ בפסח ושור הנסקל אבל חולין שנשחטו בעזרה איסורן לאו דאורייתא ור' אבהו לא סבר לה כר' מאיר דאמר חולין שנשחטו בעזרה דאורייתא: יתיב ההוא מרבנן וקאמר מנין לחמץ ושור הנסקל שאסורין בהנאה ואמרי' ותיפוק ליה מלא יאכל כחזקיה קסבר לא יאכל ולא תאכל ולא תאכלו חד הוא ותיפוק ליה מנבלה כר' אבהו סבר לה כר' יהודה דאמר (ארבעה) דברים ככתבן ותיפוק ליה מאותו כר' יהודה קסבר חולין שנשחטו בעזרה מדאורייי' ואלא מנא ליה ופרשי' מדכתי' וכל חטאת אשר יובא מדמה אל אהל מועד לכפר בקדש לא תאכל באש תשרף שאין ת"ל באש תשרף דנפקא ליה מוהנה שורף דכתיב (ויקרא י יז) מדוע לא אכלתם את החטאת במקום הקודש (שם יח) הן לא הובא את דמה אל הקודש פנימה ודאי בת שריפה היא מה ת"ל באש תשרף אם אינו ענין לגופו תנהו ענין לכל איסורין

מסורת הש"ס

[לעיל כב.]

[חולין קכ.]

[לעיל כב. וש"נ]

[לעיל כא. וש"נ]

הגהות הב"ח

(א) תוס' ד"ה ומה חלב וכו' וי"ל דה"פ ומה חלב שענוש: (ב) ד"ה וכו' דכתיב דמכפר על עון טומאת כצ"ל:

גליון הש"ס

גמ' אלא גיד נימא דאסור. עי' ק"ל לפמ"ש תוס' חולין ק"ב ע"ב ד"ה דחלב הוא דהדרים גרמי דכתי' חלב שור אבל גיד אל מיד א"כ י"ל דדוקא בחלב לא"ח כשותרה דהא מכתת לה הקרא לגר אשר תתננה דעוקלו כולו עם החלב כגון שנסילה בהמה דליכא איסור חלב אבל גיד דל"ש כן י"ל דאמרינן כשהותרה ועי':

*) [וכן הוא בהדיא בשבועות ט: ובפרש"י שם וכן בזבחים קא: וכן פירש"י בחומש להדיא אבל ר"ח וכן פירש"י לקמן פב: ד"ה לכך נאמר וכ"כ רש"י יומא ה: ד"ה כאשר צוה וכ"כ רש"י חולין סח: ד"ה הכל היו]

לרבים רבי יהודה אומר להוציא את הנטוע לרבים מאי טעמא דתנא קמא דכתיב ונטעתם ליחיד משמע לרבים לא משמע כתב רחמנא לכם להביא את הנטוע לרבים ורבי יהודה ונטעתם משמע בין לרבים בין ליחיד ולכם בין יחיד בין רבים משמע הוי רבוי *אחר רבוי ואין רבוי אחר רבוי אלא למעט והרי תרומה דרחמנא אמר °וכל זר לא יאכל קדש ותנן *מערבין לנזיר ביין ולישראל בתרומה אמר רב פפא שאני התם דאמר קרא °תרומתכם שלכם תהא ואידך תרומתכם דכל ישראל קאמר והרי נזיר דרחמנא אמר °מחרצנים ועד זג לא יאכל ותנן מערבין לנזיר ביין אמר מר זוטרא שאני התם דאמר קרא נזרו שלו יהא רב אשי אמר °קדוש יהיה גדל פרע שער ראשו *גידולו קדוש ואין דבר אחר קדוש מידי ואין דבר אחר כתיב אלא מחוורתא כדמר זוטרא והרי חדש דרחמנא אמר °לחם וקלי וכרמל לא תאכלו עד עצם היום הזה ותנן *°קוצר לשחת ומאכיל לבהמה אמר רב שמעיה שאני התם דאמר קרא קצירכם קצירכם שלכם יהא ואידך קצירכם דכל ישראל משמע והרי שרצים דרחמנא אמר °שקץ הוא לא יאכל ותנן *°ציידי חיה ועופות ודגים שנזדמנו להם מינין טמאין מותרין למוכרן לנכרים שאני התם דאמר קרא לכם שלכם יהא אי הכי אפי' לכתחלה נמי שאני הכא דאמר קרא יהיו בהוייתן יהו ולחזקיה למה לי למיכתב לא יאכל ומייתי לכם למישרייה לא לכתוב רחמנא לא יאכל ולא בעי לכם אמר לך חזקיה טעמא דידי נמי מהכא והרי חמץ דרחמנא אמר לא יאכל חמץ ותניא *ר' יוסי הגלילי אומר °תמה על עצמך היאך חמץ אסור בהנאה כל שבעה שאני התם דאמר קרא °ולא יראה לך שאור שלך יהא ורבנן *שלך אי אתה רואה אבל אתה רואה של אחרים ושל גבוה ואידך תרי לך כתיבי ואידך חד בנכרי שכיבשתו וחד בנכרי שלא כיבשתו ואידך תלתא לך כתיבי ואידך חד בשאור וחד בחמץ וצריכי לימא כתנאי °יעשה לכל מלאכה מה ת"ל לכל מלאכה שיכול למלאכת גבוה יהא מותר למלאכת הדיוט יהא אסור תלמוד לומר לכל מלאכה דברי רבי יוסי הגלילי רבי עקיבא אומר שיכול למלאכת הדיוט יהא טהור למלאכת גבוה יהא טמא תלמוד לומר לכל מלאכה ורבי יוסי הגלילי לטומאה ולטהרה לא איצטריך קרא כי איצטריך קרא לאיסור ולהיתר ורבי עקיבא איסור והיתר לא צריך קרא כי איצטריך קרא לטומאה ולטהרה מאי

תורה אור: ויקרא כב — במדבר יח — שם ו — שם — ויקרא כג — שם יא — שמות יג — ויקרא ז

רש"י

לרבים. לצורך רבים כגון באמצע הדרך לכל עובר: ונטעתם ליחיד משמע. דאין דרך רבים לנטוע ולכל חד וחד קאמר ונטעתם: מערבין לנזיר. עירובי תחומין ביין אע"פ שסעודה שאינה ראויה לו היא הואיל ואי מתשיל אנזירותיה שריא ליה מערבין וכן לישראל בתרומה דאי בעי מיתשל עליה דתרומה טעות אינה תרומה והדרה לטיבלה והדר מפריש עלה מינה ובה: תרומתכם. ונחשב לכם תרומתכם ובתרומת מעשר דמפרשי לוים כתיב ותרומה גדולה איתקש בההוא קרא כדכתיב כדגן מן הגורן דהיינו תרומה גדולה: ואידך. חזקיה דאמר לא תאכלו לא משמע הנאה האי תרומתכם לאו למישרי הנאה אתא אלא תרומתכם דכל ישראל קאמר ואורחיה דקרא לאישתעויי הכי ישראל לאו דוקא דהא בלוים כתיב: גידולו. שיער שלו אסור בהנאה וטעון שריפה כדכתיב ונתן על האש אשר תחת זבח השלמים: מידי ואין דבר אחר כתיב. דילמא גידולו והוא הדין לדבר אחר דמאי מיעוט כתב הכא: חדש. לפני העומר: קוצר לשחת. אע"ג דכתיב עומר ראשית קצירכם אל הכהן דמשמע דאסור לקצור לפני העומר מותר לקצור לשחת כשהוא עשב דלאו קציר הוא: ומאכיל לבהמה. אף חיטין גמורין על ידי קיטוף מכל מקום חדש מותר בהנאה: ואידך. חזקיה דלא נפקא ליה הנאה מלא תאכלו ולא איצטריך קצירכם למישרי אמר לך קצירכם דכל ישראל קאמר ואורחיה דקרא לאישתעויי הכי: שנזדמנו. דווקא שנזדמנו דלא מצרכינן להו להפקירן אבל לכתחלה אסור לחזר אחריהן כדתנן התם במס' שביעית (פ"ז מ"ג) אין עושין סחורה לא בנבילות וטריפות ולא בשקצים ורמשים: יהיו. ושקץ יהיו לכם: ולחזקיה למה לי למכתב לא יאכל ומייתי לכם למישרייה. בשלמא לרבי אבהו לא מצינו לאקשויי בכל הנך דכתיב בהו לא תאכל והדר כתיב בו היתר הנאה דאיצטריך לא תאכלו לאכילה ואיצטריך היתירא להנאה אלא לחזקיה כיון דסוף סוף שרי ליה רחמנא בהנאה למה לי קרא דשני בדיבורא וכתב לא יאכל דמשמע הנאה ואיצטריך לכם למישרייה בהנאה ליכתוב לא תאכל ותו לא איצטריך לכם: טעמא דידי. דאמינא לא יאכל משמע הנאה מהא נפקא לי (א) ואי לאו האי קרא דכתיב לא יאכל ותו כתב לכם למישרייה לא הוה ידענא דלא יאכל איסור הנאה הוא וכל הנך קראי דהיתר הנאה דכתיבי גבי לא תאכל הא דרשינהו חזקיה למילתא אחרינא כדאמרן לעיל תרומתכם קצירכם דכל ישראל: תמה על עצמך היאך נאסר חמץ בהנאה. דס"ל מותר בהנאה כל שבעה וכ"ש לאחר הפסח ופליגא דרבי יהודה דאמר חמץ שעבר עליו הפסח אסור בהנאה לקמן בפירקין (דף כח:): תלתא לך כתיבי. לא יראה לך חמץ ולא יראה לך שאור בכל גבולך ועוד קרא אחרינא ולא יראה לך שאור בכל גבולך שבעת ימים: וצריכי. דאי כתב שאור משום דחימוצו קשה אבל חמץ אימא מותר ואי כתב חמץ משום דראוי לאכילה אבל שאור דלא אתי למיכליה אימא לא עבר עליה הכי מפרש להו בפ"ק דביצה (דף ז:): לימא כתנאי. לא תאכל דרבי אבהו: יעשה למלאכה. הוה מצי למיכתב גבי חלב דנבילה: שיכול. אי לא הוה כתב לכל הוה אמינא למלאכת גבוה יהא מותר אם צריך למשוח ממנו עורות למלאכת בדק הבית יהא מותר דהא מישתרי חלב באכילה לגבי גבוה למזבח אבל למלאכת הדיוט יהא אסור שהרי נאמר בו לא תאכלו ואיסור הנאה במשמע ת"ל לכל מלאכה: רבי עקיבא אומר כו'. כלומר לא הוצרך הכתוב להתיר דלא הוה ס"ד לאיסור ולא בא אלא לטהרו מכלל טומאת הבשר ולומר שאין חלב בכלל נבילה ואינו חושש לטומאה אלא מותר לישתמש טהרות בעור המשוח בחלב נבילה ואם לא ריבה לכל מלאכה הייתי אומר למלאכת הדיוט יהא טהור להשתמש בו חולין אבל למלאכת גבוה להשתמש קדשים יהא טמא:

מסורת הש"ס: [ב"ק מה:] — עירובין כו: [כח.] — קדושין נז: — מנחות עא. — שביעית [פ"ז מ"ד] — [לקמן כח: נב.] — [לעיל ה: וש"נ] — [עי' תוס' לעיל כ. ד"ה ור' שמעון]

תוספות

נטוע לרבים. ברה"י לצורך רבים ולא כמו שפ"ה באמצע הדרך דקתני במסכת ערלה (פ"א מ"ב) הנוטע לרבים חייב ורבי יהודה פוטר והדר קתני הנוטע ברה"ר והנכרי שנטע והגוזל כו' מדקתני בתרי בבי ש"מ תרי מילי נינהו:

מערבין לנזיר ביין. בפ' בכל מערבין (עירובין כח.) מפרש טעמא משום דאע"ג דלא חזי להאי חזי להאי ולא פריך הכא אליבא דמ"ד (שם דף לא.) אין מערבין אלא לדבר מצוה ומלות לאו ליהנות ניתנו:

נזרו שלו יהא. תימה לחזקיה נזרו למאי אתא ואית ספרים דגרסינן על נזרו מגלח °ואינו מגלח על נזירות אביו:

קוצר לשחת ומאכיל לבהמה. אף על גב דהא דקוצר לשחת היינו דווקא לבהמה כדמוכח במנחות בפ' רבי ישמעאל (ד' עא:) מ"מ ומאכיל לבהמה לא משמע ליה דקאי אקוצר לשחת דא"כ לא פריך מידי דחדש שאסר הכתוב היינו תבואה גמורה אלא מאכיל לבהמה היינו אפילו חיטין גמורין ועל ידי קיטוף כפ"ה ועוד דקתני סיפא רבי שמעון אומר יקצור ויאכיל אף משהביא שליש*:

קצירכם שלכם יהא. תימה לרשב"א מנ"ל דאתא להכי הא איצטריך לכדדרשינן במנחות בפרק ר' ישמעאל (דף סב: ושם) קצירכם ולא קציר מצוה וחזקיה נמי לישני הכי וי"ל מדלא כתב ראשית קציר והוי מצי למיכתב קצירך וכתב קצירכם שמע מינה תרתי:

אמר קרא יהיו בהוייתן יהו. וא"ת א"כ סוסים וחמורים היכי זבנינן וי"ל דבמידי דאכילה מיירי דווקא ובירושלמי דמסכת שביעית ספ"ח פריך והרי חמור וגמל ומשני למלאכתן הן גדילים וא"ת דאמרי' במרובה (ב"ק פב: שם) אסור לישראל לגדל חזירים תיפוק ליה דמדאורייתא אסור וי"ל דנפקא מינה למיקם בארור אי נמי הא דאסור מדאורייתא היינו להשתכר ולמכור לנכרי לאכול אבל להשתכר בשומנן או בעורן לא או שמגדל שלא למכור אלא למשוח ולהדליק אפילו הכי בחזירים אסור א"נ בנזדמנו לו כגון שנפלו בירושה אין לגדלן:

שאני התם דאמר קרא לא יראה לך. תימה דליכתב לא יאכל לחזקיה ולא בעי לך: ומה

עין משפט נר מצוה

יח א מיי' פ"א מהלכות עירובין הל' יד סמג עשין דרבנן א טוש"ע או"ח סי' שפו סעיף ח:
יט ב מיי' פ"ג מהלכות תמידין הלכה טו:
כ ג מיי' פ"ח מהלכות מאכלות אסורות הל' יז סמג לאוין קלט טוש"ע י"ד סימן קיז:

רבינו חננאל

הנטוע לרבים שחייב בערלה ר' יהודה אומר לכם פרט לנטוע לרבים: והרי תרומה דכתיב וכל זר לא יאכל קדש ותנן מערבין לנזיר ביין ושנינן שאני התם דכתי' תרומתכם שלכם תהא: והרי נזיר דכתיב מחרצנים ועד זג לא יאכל ותנן מערבין לנזיר ביין ושנינן שאני התם דכתיב נזרו נזרו שלו יהא כו': והרי חדש דכתיב ולחם וקלי וכרמל לא תאכלו ותנן קוצר לשחת ומאכיל לבהמה (נהנה בזמן אכילתו ומותר בהנאתו) [ואף שנהנה באכילתה אלמא דמותר בהנאה] ושנינן שאני התם דכתיב קצירכם [שלכם] יהא להתיר בהנאה: והרי שרצים דכתיב בהו וכל השרץ השורץ על הארץ לא יאכל ותנן בשביעי' פ"ז ציידי חיה עופות ודגים (שנתמנו) [שנזדמנו] להם מינין טמאין מותר למכרן וקשיא לתרוייהו ושני' שאני התם דכתי' לכם להתיר בהנאה אי הכי אפי' לכתחלה אמאי תאני שנתמנה דאיעבד אפי' לכתחלה יהיו מותרין לצודן ודחי' אמר קרא שקץ הוא בהוייתו יהא ואקשי' לחזקיה למה לי למכתב בשרצים לא יאכל דמשמע אפילו איסור הנאה והוצרך לכתוב לכם להתיר בהנאה היה כותב ולא יאכל ולא יכתוב לכם להתיר ואנא ידענא דכל היכא דכתי' לא יאכל מותר בהנאה ואמר חזקיה אדרבה טעמא דידי מהכא מדאצטריך קרא למכתב לכם להתירו בהנאה ש"מ דכל היכא דכתיב לא יאכל אחד איסור אכילה ואחד איסור הנאה במשמע: והרי חמץ דכתיב לא יאכל ואמר ר' יוסי הגלילי תמה על עצמך היאך חמץ אסור בהנאה כל שבעה ודחי' שאני התם דכתיב לך שלך יהא כו': נימא כתנאי וחלב נבלה וחלב טרפה יעשה לכל מלאכה [מה ת"ל לכל מלאכה] ר' יוסי הגלילי אומר בין למלאכת גבוה בין למלאכת הדיוט מותר שנאמר לכל מלאכה ר' עקיבא אומר שיכול למלאכת הדיוט הוא טהור למלאכת גבוה יהא טמא ת"ל לכל מלאכה יהא טהור אם לגבוה הוא [טהור]* קל וחומר להדיוט דיקי' מדדרש ר' עקיבא לקרא בטומאה וטהרה מכלל דפשיטא ליה דמותר

גליון הש"ס

גמ' תמה על עצמך היאך חמץ. היינו היאך אתה אומר חמץ אסור בהנאה וכן תמה על עצמך האיך הופשת בנדה

הגהות הב"ח

(א) רש"י ד"ה טעמא דידי וכו' דאי לאו:

סה ע"א תוס' שם ד"ה כך אמרו בסד"ה: תוס' ד"ה נזרו. ואינו מגלח על נזירות אביו. ק"ל הא לר"י ור"מ דס"ל בספ"ד דנזיר דבכל ענין מגלח על נזירות אביו א"כ יהא מוכח מדאיצטריך נזרו דלא יאכל איסור הנאה במשמע וא"כ איך אמרי' דא"ב חולין שנשחטו בעזרה לר"י ור"ש:

*[נראה דחסר כאן איזה תיבות ואולי דקאי על הא דאמרינן ור"י הגלילי לטומאה ולטהרה לא איצטריך קרא ודו"ק].

'Unto you': this is to include what is planted [23a] for the public. R. Judah said: It is to exclude what is planted for the public. What is the reason of the first Tanna? Because it is written, *'and ye shall have planted'*; [this] implies [a law] to the individual, but it does not imply [a law] for the public;[6] [therefore] the Merciful One wrote, *'unto you'*, to include what is planted for the public. While R. Judah [argues]: *'and ye shall have planted'* implies [a law] both to the public and to the individual, and *'unto you'* [too] implies both for the public and for the individual: thus it is an extension after an extension, and an extension after an extension has no [other significance] save to limit.[7]

But there is *terumah*, of which the Merciful One saith, *There*
a *shall no common man*[8] *eat of the holy thing:*[9] yet we learned: An *'erub*[1] may be made for a nazirite with wine, and for a [lay] Israelite with *terumah?*[1]—Said R. Papa: There it is different, because Scripture saith, your *heave-offering:*[2] it shall be yours. And the other?[3]—It means, *'your heave-offering,'* [viz.,] that of all Israel.[4]

But what of a nazirite, though the Merciful One saith, *from the kernels even to the husk, he shall not eat,*[5] yet we learned: An *'erub* may be made for a nazirite with wine?—Said Mar Zuṭra, There it is different, because Scripture saith, [*All the days of*] his *naziriteship:*[5] it shall be his.[6] R. Ashi said: *He shall be holy, he shall let the locks of the hair of his head grow long:*[7] his [hair] growth is holy,[8] but nothing else is holy. Is then 'and nothing else' written?[9] But it is clearly as Mar Zuṭra [stated].

But what of *ḥadash,*[10] where the Merciful One saith, *And ye shall eat neither bread, nor parched corn, nor fresh ears, until this selfsame day;*[11] yet we learned: He may cut [the corn] for fodder and feed his cattle?[12]—Said R. Shemaiah, There it is different, because Scripture saith, [*ye shall bring the sheaf of the firstfruits of*] your *harvest:*[13] [implying,] it shall be yours.[14] And the other?[15]—*'Your harvest'* implies that of all Israel.

But what of creeping things, where the Merciful One saith, *It is a detestable thing; it shall not be eaten;*[16] yet we learned: Hunters of beasts, birds, and fish, who chance upon unclean species, are permitted to sell them to Gentiles?—There it is different, because Scripture saith, [*they are a detestable thing*] unto you:[17] it shall be yours. If so, [it should be permitted] at the very outset too?[18]—Here it is different, because Scripture saith, and they shall be
b [*a detestable thing*]:[1] [meaning,] they shall be in their [forbidden] state. Now according to Hezekiah, for what purpose is *'shall not be eaten'* written—so that *'unto you'* is adduced to teach that it is permitted; let the Merciful One not write *'shall not be eaten,'* so that *'unto you'* will be unnecessary?—Hezekiah can answer you: My opinion[2] is indeed [deduced] from this.[3]

But what of leaven, though the Merciful One saith, *there shall no leavened bread be eaten,*[4] yet it was taught, R. Jose the Galilean said: Wonder at yourself! how can leaven be prohibited for [general] use the whole seven [days]?—There it is different, because Scripture saith, *neither shall there be leaven seen* unto thee:[5] [this implies,] it shall be thine. And the Rabbis?[6]—Thine own thou must not see, but thou mayest see that belonging to others and to the Most High. And the other?[7] *'Unto thee'* is written twice.[8] And the other?—One refers to a heathen whom you have conquered, and the other refers to a heathen whom you have not conquered.[9] And the other?[10]—*'Unto thee'* is written three times.[11] And the other?—One refers to leaven [*se'or*], and one refers to leavened bread [*ḥameẓ*], and they are [both] necessary.[12]

Shall we say that it[13] is dependent on Tannaim? [*And the fat of that which dieth of itself, and the fat of that which is torn of beasts,*] *may be used for all service* [: *but ye shall in no wise eat of it*].[14] Why is *'for* all *service'* stated? For I might think, for the service of the Most High let it be permitted, but for secular service let it be for-
c bidden;[1] therefore it is stated, *'for* all *service'*: this is the view of R. Jose the Galilean. R. Akiba said: For I might think, for secular service let it be clean, [but] for service of the Most High let it be unclean;[2] therefore it is stated, *'for* all *service'*. Now R. Jose the Galilean [holds] that in respect of uncleanness and cleanness a verse is not required, a verse being required only in respect of what is forbidden and what is permitted. While R. Akiba [maintains]: [in respect of] what is forbidden and what is permitted no verse is required, a verse being required only in respect of

(6) Since the public do not plant. (7) This is a principle of exegesis. Cf. the inverse principle of the English language: a double negative is a positive. (8) I.e., an Israelite who is not a priest. (9) Lev. XXII, 10.
a (1) Though these may not be eaten by each respectively.—Thus a non-priest may *benefit* from *terumah*. (2) Num. XVIII, 27. (3) Hezekiah: what is the purpose of *'your heave-offering*? Cf. 22b, n. b10. (4) I.e., it is merely the idiomatic usage of the language. (5) Num. VI, 4. (6) I.e., the things which he may not eat are nevertheless available for his use in other ways. (7) Ibid. 5. (8) In the sense that he must not benefit from it. (9) There is nothing to warrant this inference. (10) V. Glos. (11) Lev. XXIII, 14, q.v. (12) With this *ḥadash*, though he may not eat it himself. Thus benefit is permitted. (13) Ibid. 10. (14) Available for your benefit. (15) Hezekiah: what is the purpose of *'your harvest'* according to him? Cf. 22b, n. b10. (16) Lev. XI, 41. (17) Ibid. 10. (18) To hunt unclean animals, whereas the Mishnah merely permits selling if they *happened* to trap them.
b (1) Lev. XI, 11. (2) Lit., 'reason'. (3) The very fact that *'unto you'* is required shows that elsewhere *'shall not be eaten'* includes the prohibition of benefit in general. (4) Ex. XIII, 3. (5) Ibid. 7. (6) Who hold that benefit is forbidden: how do they interpret *'unto thee'*? (7) R. Jose: how does he know this? (8) *And there shall no leavened bread be seen* unto thee, *neither shall there be leaven seen* unto thee. (9) I.e., whether the heathen is a Jewish subject or not, his leaven may be seen in a Jewish house. (10) How does he know this? (11) The third is in Deut. XVI, 4 q.v. (12) If leaven (*se'or*) alone were written, I might argue that it is forbidden because its degree of leaven is very strong, but leavened bread (*ḥameẓ*) which is not so strong, is permitted. And if leavened bread (*ḥameẓ*) were written, I would say that that is forbidden because it is fit to be eaten, but not so leaven (*se'or*), which cannot be eaten.—Beẓ. 7b. (13) *Sc.* R. Abbahu's ruling. (14) Lev. VII, 24.
c (1) Since we find fat (*ḥeleb*) used in the service of God, the fat of a sacrifice being burnt on the altar. (2) E.g., if leather was softened with *ḥeleb*, sacred food must not be placed on it, for it will thereby be defiled.

[22b] Now according to Hezekiah, in respect of what law is blood likened to water?[10]—For [the law of] R. Ḥiyya b. Abba in R. Joḥanan's name. For R. Ḥiyya b. Abba said in R. Joḥanan's name: How do we know that the blood of sacrifices does not make [anything] fit [to be defiled]? Because it is said, *thou shalt pour it out upon the earth as water:* blood which is poured out as water renders fit; blood which is not poured out as water does not render fit.

But what of the limb of a living animal, though it is written,
a *thou shalt not eat the life with the flesh,*[1] yet it was taught, R. Nathan said: How do we know that a man must not hold out a cup of wine to a nazirite or the limb of a living animal to the children of Noah?[2] Because it is stated, *thou shalt not put a stumbling-block before the blind.*[3] This implies that [giving] to dogs is permitted?[4]—The limb of a living animal is different, because it is assimilated to blood, as it is written, *Only be steadfast in not eating the blood; for the blood is the life.*[5] Then according to Hezekiah, in respect of what law is the limb from a living animal assimilated to blood?[6]—He can answer you: It is blood which is assimilated to the limb from a living animal:[7] just as a limb from a living animal is forbidden,[8] so is the blood from a living animal forbidden,[9] and which [blood] is that? The blood of arteries with which life goes out.[10]

But what of the ox that is stoned, though the Divine Law saith, *its flesh shall not be eaten,*[11] yet it was taught: From the implication of the verse, *the ox shall be surely stoned,*[12] do I not know that it is *nebelah*, and *nebelah* is forbidden as food? Why then is it stated, *'and its flesh shall not be eaten'?* The Writ informs us that if it was [ritually] slaughtered after its trial was ended,[13] it is forbidden. I only know this in respect of eating; how do we know it in respect of benefit? From the verse, *but the owner of the ox shall be clear.* How is this implied? Simeon b. Zoma said: As a man may say to his friend, 'So-and-so has gone out clear from his property, and has no benefit whatsoever from it.' Thus the reason is that *'but the owner of the ox shall be clear'* is written; for if [we deduced] from *'it shall not be eaten'* [alone], that would imply a
b prohibition of eating, but not a prohibition of benefit?[1]—In truth *'it shall not be eaten'* implies a prohibition of eating and a prohibition of benefit, and as to *'but the owner of the ox shall be clear,'* that is stated[2] in respect of the use of its skin;[3] and it is necessary: you would think that I might argue, *'his* flesh *shall not be eaten'* is written, [thus] only his flesh [is forbidden], but not his skin; therefore we are informed [otherwise]. But according to those Tannaim who employ this verse for a different exegesis, [viz.,] for half ransom and damages for children,[4] how do they know [that] the use of the hide [is forbidden]?—They infer it from *eth besaro* [*his flesh*], meaning, that which is joined to its flesh.[5] And the other?[6]—He does not interpret *eth*.[7] As it was taught, Simeon Imsoni[8]—others state, Nehemiah Imsoni—interpreted every *eth* in the Torah;[9] [but] as soon as he came to, *thou shalt fear* [eth] *the Lord thy God,*[10] he desisted.[11] Said his disciples to him, 'Master, what is to happen with all the *ethin*[12] which you have interpreted?' 'Just as I received reward for interpreting them', he replied, 'so will I receive reward for retracting'.[13] Subsequently[14] R. Akiba came and taught: *Thou shalt fear* [eth] *the Lord thy God* is to include scholars.[15]

c But there is *'orlah,*[1] whereof the Merciful One saith, *Three years shall it be forbidden unto you: it shall not be eaten;*[2] yet it was taught: *'It shall be as forbidden unto you: it shall not be eaten'.* [Thus] I only know the prohibition of eating; whence do we know that a man may not benefit from it, that he may not dye or light a lamp with it? From the verse, *then ye shall count* [*the fruit thereof*] *as forbidden:* [*three years shall they be*] *as forbidden* [*unto you*]: *it shall not be eaten;*[2] which is to include all of them.[3] Thus the reason is that Scripture wrote, *'then ye shall count the fruit thereof as forbidden . . . they shall be as forbidden';* but if it were not so, I would say, it implies a prohibition of eating, [but] it does not imply a prohibition of benefit?—In truth *'it shall not be eaten'* implies both a prohibition of eating and a prohibition of benefit, but there it is different, because it is written, *'unto you'*, and thus it is necessary: I might argue, since it is written, *'unto you,'* [that implies] it shall be yours;[4] hence we are informed [that it is not so]. Then now that these verses[5] are written, what is the purpose of *'unto you'?*—For what was taught:

(10) Since he holds *supra* 21b that only the passive form, *'shall not be eaten'*, implies a prohibition of all benefit, but not the active *'thou shalt not eat'*, benefit from blood is permitted in any case, for the prohibition is not expressed in the passive. Then what is the purpose of assimilating blood to water?

a (1) Deut. XII, 23. This is interpreted as an injunction against eating a limb torn from a living animal. (2) The technical designation for all but Jews. A nazirite must not drink wine, nor may non-Jews eat of the limb of a living animal. (3) Lev. XIX, 14. This is understood metaphorically: do not lead anyone to sin. (4) Though this is benefit. (5) Deut. XII, 23. (6) V. *supra*, n. b10; the same applies here. (7) And not the reverse, as the order indicates. (8) With the prohibition that is stated in its case, i.e., for eating only. (9) With the prohibition relevant to blood, viz., an injunction which involves *kareth* (q. v. Glos.). (10) V. Ker. 22a. (11) Ex. XXI, 28. Thus it is expressed in the passive, which on all views intimates that general benefit is forbidden. (12) Ibid. (13) I.e., after sentence.

b (1) Cf. *supra*, n. a11. (2) Lit., 'comes'. (3) Teaching, even that is forbidden. (4) Ransom, v. Ex. XXI, 28-30, 35f; it might be thought, by comparing these verses, that half ransom is payable in this case. (Damages for child, v. ibid. 22). I might think that the same holds good when the damage is done by a man's ox Therefore *'but the owner of the ox shall be clear* (E.V. *quit*)' teaches that he is free from both. (5) Interpreting *'eth'*, the sign of the acc., as an extending particle. (6) What does *'eth'* teach on his view? (7) As indicating extensions or having any particular significance apart from its grammatical one. (8) Jast. conjectures that it may mean from Amasia, in Pontus. (9) As an extending particle. (10) Deut. VI, 13. (11) Holding it impossible that this fear should extend to another. (12) Pl. of *eth*. (13) Lit., 'separating' (myself from them). Since the *eth* in one verse does not signify extension, it cannot do so elsewhere. (14) Lit., 'until'. (15) Who are the depositaries of God's word; hence the verse exhorts obedience to religious authority.

c (1) V. Glos. (2) Lev. XIX, 23. (3) I.e., the repetition of *'forbidden'* is an extension. (4) Viz., you may use it, though not eat it. (5) Repeating the phrase *'forbidden'* to extend the prohibition to general benefit.

עין משפט נר מצוה

יג א סמג לאוין קסח: [ע"ש בתוס' ד"ה מנין]
יד ב מיי' פ"ו מהלכות מאכלות אסורות הל' ג סמג לאוין קלז:
טו ג מיי' פ"ד שם הל' כב סמג לאוין קלה:
טז ד מיי' פ"י שם הל' ט סמג לאוין קמד טוש"ע י"ד סימן רלד סעיף א:
יז ה שם סעיף כה:

גמרא

ולחזקיה למאי הלכתא איתקש דם למים
לכדר' חייא בר אבא דאמר ר' חייא בר אבא
א"ר יוחנן *מנין לדם קדשים שאינו מכשיר
שנאמר °לא תאכלנו על הארץ תשפכנו (דברים יב)
כמים דם שנשפך כמים מכשיר שאינו נשפך
כמים אינו מכשיר והרי אבר מן החי דכתיב
°לא תאכל הנפש עם הבשר ותניא *רבי נתן (שם)
אומר *מנין שלא יושיט אדם כוס יין
לנזיר ואבר מן החי לבני נח ת"ל °ולפני עור (ויקרא יט)
לא תתן מכשול הא לכלבים שרי שאני
אבר מן החי דאיתקש לדם דכתיב °רק חזק (דברים יב)
לבלתי אכול הדם כי הדם הוא הנפש
ולחזקיה למאי הלכתא איתקש אבר מן
החי לדם אמר לך דם הוא דאיתקש לאבר
מן החי מה אבר מן החי אסור אף דם מן החי
אסור ואי זה זה דם הקזה שהנפש יוצאה
בו והרי שור הנסקל דרחמנא אמר °לא (שמות כא)
יאכל את בשרו *ותניא ממשמע שנאמר
°סקול יסקל השור איני יודע שהיא נבלה (שם)
ונבלה אסורה באכילה ומה ת"ל לא יאכל
מגיד לך הכתוב שאם שחטו לאחר שנגמר
(את) דינו אסור אין לי אלא באכילה בהנאה
מנין ת"ל °ובעל השור נקי מאי משמע (שם)
שמעון בן זומא אומר כאדם שאומר לחבירו
יצא פלוני נקי מנכסיו ואין לו בהם הנאה של
כלום טעמא דכתב ובעל השור נקי דאי
מלא יאכל איסור אכילה משמע איסור
הנאה לא משמע לעולם לא יאכל איסור
אכילה ואיסור הנאה משמע ובעל השור
נקי להנאת עורו הוא דאתא ואיצטריך ס"ד
אמינא לא יאכל את בשרו כתיב בשרו אין
עורו לא קמ"ל ולהנך תנאי דמפקי ליה
להאי קרא לדרשה אחרינא לחצי כופר
ולדמי וולדות הנאת עורו מנא להו נפקא
להו מאת בשרו את הטפל לבשרו ואידך
*את לא דריש *כדתניא שמעון העמסוני
ואמרי לה נחמיה העמסוני *היה דורש כל
אתים שבתורה כיון שהגיע °לאת ה' אלהיך (דברים י)
תירא פירש אמרו לו תלמידיו רבי כל אתים
שדרשת מה תהא עליהן אמר להם כשם
שקבלתי שכר על הדרישה כך אני מקבל
שכר על הפרישה עד שבא ר"ע ודרש את
ה' אלהיך תירא לרבות תלמידי חכמים
והרי ערלה דרחמנא אמר °ערלים לא יאכל (ויקרא יט)
ותניא *ערלים לא יאכל אין לי אלא איסור
אכילה מנין שלא יהנה ממנו שלא יצבע בו
ולא ידליק בו את הנר ת"ל וערלתם ערלתו
ערלים לא יאכל לרבות את כולם טעמא דכתב רחמנא וערלתם ערלתו ערלים
הא לאו הכי הוה אמינא איסור אכילה משמע איסור הנאה לא משמע לעולם
לא יאכל משמע בין איסור אכילה בין איסור הנאה ושאני התם דכתיב לכם
ואצטריך סלקא דעתך אמינא הואיל וכתב לכם שלכם יהא קמשמע לן ואלא
השתא דכתיבי הנך קראי לכם למה לי לכדתניא לכם לרבות את הנטוע
לרבים

רש"י

ולחזקיה. דאמר לעיל איסור הנאה דחמץ מלא יאכל הא לא תאכל ולא תאכלו לא משמע ליה הנאה: למאי הלכתא איתקש דם למים. למשרייה בהנאה ומהיכא תיתי לך דניתסרו ומנבילה לא אותביניה לחזקיה למאי איצטריך קרא למשרייה דאי כר' יהודה סבר לדברים ככתבן הוא דאתא ואי כר"מ סבר לה אצטריך להקדים נתינה דגר למכירה דנכרי: לא תאכל הנפש עם הבשר. בעוד שהנפש בו: בני נח נאסר להם אבר מן החי דכתיב (בראשית ט) אך בשר בנפשו דמו לא תאכלו: לפני עור. אלמא לא מיתסר אלא משום לפני עור לא תתן מכשול אבל בהנאה אחריתי כגון לכלב שרי: לבלתי אכול הדם. סיפיה דקרא לא תאכל הנפש וגו': מה אבר מן החי אסור. באיסור האמור בו אף דם מן החי אסו' באיסו' האמור בו כלומר כרת משום דם גמור מהו דתימא רק חזק לבלתי אכול הדם אוזבחת מבקרך ומצאנך דכתיב לעיל קאי ודם זביחה הוא דאסור אבל דם הקזה מותר: ואיזה זה. כלומר על איזה דם מן החי אסור משום דם הא דם הנפש כתיב על דם הקזה של בהמה שהנפש יוצאה בו יש ד' מיני דמים בהיקז כדאמרינן בכריתות (דף כב.) בתחלה שותת ולבסוף מקלח ואח"כ משחיר וסופו שותת יש מהן שאין הנשמה יוצאה בו ויש מהן שהנשמה יוצאה בו והתם תניא איזהו דם היקז שהנשמה יוצאה בו כל זמן שמקלח כו': שאם שחטו כו'. והכי אמר קרא סקול יסקל השור ואי לא סקלו אעפ"כ לא יאכל את בשרו: איסור הנאה לא משמע. וקשיא אפילו לחזקיה וכ"ש לרבי אבהו: ולהנך תנאי. דבב"ק פ' שור שנגח (דף מב: ומג.) דמפקי ליה להאי נקי לדרשה אחרינא לאשמעי' דתם פטור מחצי כופר דקאמר נקי מחצי כופר אם המית איש דאילו מועד משלם כופר שלם והתם אפי' חצי כופר לא משלם והיכא דמפיק ליה לדמי וולדות אם נגח אשה הרה ויצאו ילדיה: ואידך. דנפקא ליה הנאת עור מנקי: את לא דריש. לריבויא דסבר לה כשמעון העמסוני שפירש כל אתים שבתורה לרבות כיון שהגיע לאת ה' אלהיך תירא אמר מה ארבה לירא עמו פירש מכולן וחזר בו מכל ריבויין שדרש דמדהא לאו לרבויי אתא כולהו נמי לאו לרבויי אתו: לרבות תלמידי חכמים. שיהא מורא רבך כמורא שמים: ולא יצבע בו. כגון בקליפי אגוזים שהשומר אסור משום ערלה כפרי עצמו: ולא ידליק בו את הנר. כגון בשמן של ערלה: והשתא דכתיבי הני קראי. לאסריה לכם. דמשמע היתירא למאי אתא:

לרבים

מסורת הש"ס

חולין [נג.]לד: לעיל טו. [כ.]
ע"ג ו.
ב"ק מא. קדושין נז.
ב"ק מא. קדושין נז. בכורות ו: [ע"ש]
קדושין נו: ב"ק קא.

תוספות

ואבר מן החי לבני נח. תימה כיון דבאבר מן החי של נכרי מיירי כדאמר בפ"ק דמסכת ע"ג (דף ו:* ושם) מדקתני לא יושיט ולא קתני לא יתן א"כ היכי דייק דשרי בהנאה אי לאו לפני עור וי"ל דכיון דבשכר היה אסור להושיט דאסור להשתכר באיסורי הנאה אף על גב דדיעבד שכרו מותר כדמשמע בפ' בתרא דמס' ע"ז (דף סב.) מכל מקום אסור לכתחלה ובחנם נמי אסור דמה שמחזיק לו העכו"ם טובה חשיב כמשתכר והא דאמר בסוף אלו מציאות (ב"מ לב:) גבי אם היתה טעונה יין נסך אין זקוק לה ואי אמרת צער בעלי חיים דאורייתא אמאי אין זקוק לה אע"ג דחשיב כמשתכר באיסורי הנאה ואסור אפילו בחנם מ"מ כיון דאינו מתכוון שיחזיק לו טובה ומשום צער בעל חיים חשיב כמו *לא אפשר ולא מיכוון דשרי א"נ אין זקוק לה משמע ליה אפילו שלא בפני נכרי דאין מחזיק לו טובה: [לקמן כה:]

סלקא דעתך אמינא בשרו אין עורו לא. וא"ת ליפתוק מעורו ומבשרו וי"ל דאיצטריך בשרו אע"ג דעבדיה כעין בשר ומאן דלית ליה הא דרשה בפ' שור שנגח ד' וה' (ב"ק מא.) אתא לדרשה אחרינא*: [ע"ג לד:]

מנין שלא יצבע. וא"ת כיון דנפקא לן דאסור בהנאה אמאי איצטריך לאסור צביעה והדלקה ואור"י דס"ד דצביעה לא חשיב הנאה דלא הוי אלא חזותא בעלמא כדאמר בהגוזל (שם קא. ושם) אהך מילתא גופא וכן הדלקה סלקא דעתך דשריא כיון דהוי דרך ביעורו ולמ"ד *אין שבח עצים בפת דשרי עצים בהדלקה הא דאסר קרא הכא היינו בשמן דהוי בעין כשדולק בנר אבל עצים נעשה גחלים והשלהבת בא מן הגחלים ואם תאמר אמאי איצטריך קרא גבי תרומה טמאה להתיר דדרשי' *לך שלך תהא להסיקה תחת תבשילך דהכא איצטריך קרא למיסר ויש לומר דסלקא דעתך דנילף ממעשר הקל דאסר ביה הבער' דכתיב לא בערתי ממנו כדאמר בפ' במה מדליקין (שבת כה. ושם) ומה מעשר הקל אמרה תורה וכו': [לקמן כו:] [שבת כה.]

לכם למ"ל לכדתניא. הקשה הר"י מקורבל אמאי איצטריך ג' ערלים ליכתוב תרי ערלים לצביעה והדלקה ועל כרחך אתי' לכם לנטוע לרבים דאי להיתר הדלקה אתא לא לכתוב לכם ולא חד מהנך ערלים ולאסור מלא יאכל הנאה ומחד ערלים לצביעה ולהדלקה אין קרא לאסור ואין לומר דמלא יאכל משמע לאסור אפילו לצביעה והדלקה ואי הוה כתיב לא יאכל וחד ערלים הוה אסרינן מלא יאכל כל הנאה וערלים לשום דרשה והא דמצרכי' קראי לצביעה והדלקה היינו משום דכתב לכם דלכם משמע להתיר כל הנאה ולהכי אי הוה כתיב תרי ערלים ולכם הוה שרינן הדלקה אי אפשר לומר כן דמלא יאכל לא שמעינן צביעה דהא חזותא בעלמ' הוא כדאמר בהגוזל (ב"ק קא. ושם): [חגיגה יב.] [קדושין מ. מיר סה: סוטה יז. ב"ק מח: מנחות יח: בכורות ו: נדה לה:]

כנוטע

רבינו חננאל

ולחזקיה דאמר כל איסור דלא כתיב ביה לא יאכל מותר בהנאה הרי דם דלא כתיב בהו לא יאכל למה לי למתני כמים למשריה הא שרי וקאי ושני' לא אתא למשרי לדם בהנאה דהא פשיטא ולא צריך קרא ולא אתא לאשמעי' אלא האי מנין לדם קדשים שאינו מכשיר שאין אני קורא בו תשפכנו כמים אלא על המזבח: הרי אבר מן החי שנא' לא תאכל הנפש עם הבשר ותניא ר' נתן אומר מנין שלא יושיט אדם כוס לנזיר ואבר מן החי לבני נח וכו' ולחזקיה למאי הלכתא איתקש לדם אמר לך חזקיה הדם למד מן אבר [מן] החי שנאמר רק חזק לבלתי אכול הדם כי הדם הוא הנפש ולא תאכל הנפש עם הבשר מה אבר מן החי אסור אף דם מן החי אסור להאכילו לבני נח ואיזה זה דם הקזה שהנשמה יוצא בו ועניש כרת: הרי שור הנסקל דכתיב ולא יאכל את בשרו וטעמא דכתיב ובעל השור נקי לאסור אפי' בהנאה מכלל דלא יאכל איסור הנאה לא משמע וקשיא לחזקיה ושנינן לעולם מלא יאכל נפקא לן אפילו איסורי הנאה והאי ובעל השור נקי מבעי ליה דאסור אפי' להנאת עורו כו' והרי ערלה דכתיב ערלים לא יאכל כו' וקשיא לחזקיה ושני' לעולם לא יאכל אחד איסור אכילה ואחד איסור הנאה במשמע ואצטריך סלקא דעתך אמינא הואיל וכתב שלש שנים יהיה לכם ערלים לא יאכל הוי אמינא שלכם הוא ומותר בהנאה קמ"ל הני קראי לכם למה לי לכדתניא לכם לה"ש

*אותו אתה משליך לכלב ואי אתה משליך לכלב כל איסורין שבתורה [א] ור' מאיר אותו אתה משליך לכלב ואי אתה משליך לכלב חולין שנשחטו בעזרה ואידך *חולין שנשחטו בעזרה לאו דאורייתא היא מתיב רבי יצחק נפחא והרי גיד הנשה דרחמנא אמר °על כן לא יאכלו בני ישראל את גיד הנשה *ותנן שולח אדם ירך לנכרי וגיד הנשה בתוכו מפני שמקומו ניכר קסבר ר' אבהו *כשהותרה נבילה היא וחלבה וגידה הותרה הניחא למאן דאמר יש בגידין בנותן טעם אלא למאן דאמר אין בגידין בנותן טעם מאי איכא למימר מאן שמעת ליה דאמר אין בגידין בנותן טעם רבי שמעון דתניא *האוכל מגיד הנשה של בהמה טמאה רבי יהודה מחייב שתים ורבי שמעון פוטר רבי שמעון הכי נמי דאסר בהנאה דתניא גיד הנשה מותר בהנאה דברי רבי יהודה ורבי שמעון אוסר והרי דם דרחמנא אמר °כל נפש מכם לא תאכל דם ותנן *אלו ואלו מתערבין באמה ויוצאין לנחל קדרון ונמכרין לגננין לזבל ומועלין בו שאני דם דאיתקש למים דכתיב °לא תאכלנו על הארץ תשפכנו כמים מה מים מותרין אף דם מותר ואימא כמים המתנסכים על גבי המזבח אמר רבי אבהו כמים רוב מים מידי רוב מים כתיב אלא אמר רב אשי כמים הנשפכין ולא כמים הניסכין ואימא כמים הנשפכין לפני ע"ז התם נמי ניסוך איקרי דכתיב °ישתו יין נסיכם ולחזקיה

רש"י

אותו אתה משליך כו' כל איסורין. שנאמר בהן לא תאכל כגון זה ומדאיצטריך קרא למשריה לא מצי למילף טעמא דלאו אותו הוה אמינא קרא למעוטיה איצטריך שאין הקב"ה מקפח שכר כל בריה ונאמר במצרים לא יחרץ כלב לשונו (שמות יא) לפיכך הקפידה תורה ליתן שכרו וככבד [שכר] הכלב מן העובד כוכבים שהנבלה ימכור לנכרי וטרפה לכלב: ור"מ. דנפקא ליה איסור הנאה בשאר איסורים מדפרט בנבילה בשלמא פרט היתר דטרפה לגופיה איצטריך למיפרט בה היתר משום דלאו דפרט ביה הוה אמינא ליתסר בהנאה אלא אותו למה לי ומשני לאיסור הנאה חולין שנשחטו בעזרה דנפקא לן *בהו איסור אכילה מדכתב (דברים יב) כי ירחק ממך המקום וזבחת ואכלת בריחוק מקום דהיינו חוץ למחנה שכינה אתה זובח ואוכל ואי אתה זובח ואוכל בקרוב מקום *ומשום דלאו מפורש בהן לאו בהדיא בהכילה איצטריך למילף להו איסור הנאה מהכא והכי משמע אותו שנאסר משום חוץ למחילה אתה משליך לכלב דהא מהאי קרא ובשר בשדה טרפה נפקא לן איסור מחילה כגון הושיט העובר את ידו בשעת שחיטה בפרק בהמה המקשה לילד (חולין סח.) אבל יש לך אחר הנאסר משום מחילה ואי אתה משליכו לכלב ואיזה זה חולין שנשחטו בעזרה: חולין שנשחטו בעזרה. דאסירי בהנאה לאו דאורייתא בפרק שני דקדושין (דף נח.) איפליגו בה: שולח אדם ירך לנכרי. ולא מצרכינן ליטול גידה ולא גזרינן שמא יראה ישראל חבירו כשיתננה לו וילך ויקנה אותה מן הנכרי וכסבור שניטל גידה הואיל ומתחת יד ישראל יצתה ויאכלנה בגידה: מפני שמקומו ניכר. אם הוא נטול ואם לאו שמעינן מינה מיהא דגיד מותר בהנאה וקשיא לר' אבהו: היא וחלבה וגידה הותרה. לפיכך כל חלב וכל גיד מותרין בהנאה שהן בכלל לגר אשר בשעריך תתננה ואכלה שגם הן קרויין עמה נבלה והרי לך היתר הנאה בלאו דגיד ל"ש נבילה ול"ש כשירה: הניחא למ"ד יש בגידין. טעם בשר הרי הוא בכלל נבילה: אלא למ"ד אין בגידין. דאיסור נותן טעם בשר אם נתבשלו עם הבשר אלמא לאו טעם בשר אית בהו ולאו נבילה מיקרו אלא כעצמות דהן עץ בעלמא ולא אישתרי בכלל נבילה ועץ הוא והתורה חייבה עליו מאי איכא למימר ופלוגתייהו בגיד הנשה (חולין צט:): ור"ש פוטר. לגמרי מבהמה טמאה פטור דקסבר אין בגידין בנותן טעם בשר ומגיד נמי פטור דכי אזהריה רחמנא אגיד היכא דבשרה מותר דהיינו בהמה טהורה דהכי משמע גיד לא תאכל הא בשר אכול אבל טמאה לא הזהיר על גידה והכי מפרשי' לה בגיד הנשה (שם קא.) ולרבי שמעון הכי נמי דאסור גיד דטהורה אפילו בהנאה דלמא לא תאכלו איסור הנאה משמע וכשהותרה נבילה בהנאה היא לא הותרה לר"ש דלאו בכלל נבילה היא אבל לרבי יהודה מותר משום דקסבר יש בגידים בנותן טעם כדקתני רבי יהודה מחייב שתים הלכך גיד בכלל בשר וכשהותרה נבילה הותרה גם היא: אלו ואלו. שירי דם חטאות הפנימית הנשפכין על יסוד מערבי של מזבח החיצון ושירי דם חטאות החיצונות הנשפכין על יסוד דרומי יוצאין מן היסוד לרצפה דרך שני נקבים קטנים ומתערבין באמה סילון שהיה עובר בעזרה: ויוצאין לנחל קדרון. כמו לנחל איתן (דברים כא) עמק: לגננים. בעלי גנות לזבל: ומועלין בהן. כלומר אסור להנות מהן בלא דמים מפני שהן של הקדש מכל מקום דם מותר בהנאה: כמים המתנסכין. שאסורות בהנאה שהרי קדש הן שקדשו בכלי שרת וכתיב (שמות ל) כל הנוגע בהם יקדש: ולחזקיה

תוספות

אותו אתה משליך. פ"ה דבלאו אותו לא מצי למידרש מגופיה דקרא דאיצטריך שאין הקב"ה מקפח שכר כל בריה והר"ר דאורלינ"ש מפרש דאיצטריך למישרי עובר שהוציא את ידו משום דמקרא דבשר בשדה טרפה דריש נמי קדשים שיצאו חוץ למחיצתן בריש בהמה המקשה (חולין סח.) והוה אסרינן יד העובר בהנאה מדאיתקש לקדשים דאסור בהנאה כדאמר *כל שבקודש פסול בא"ש תשרף ולכך איצטריך אותו לכל איסורים: חולין שנשחטו בעזרה לאו דאורייתא. פ"ה איסור הנאה ולא משמע פשט ההלכה כן אלא לגמרי קאמר לאו דאורייתא וכן בסוף שמעתא גבי הא דאמר איכא בינייהו חולין שנשחטו בעזרה אי אפשר לפרש בענין אחר *ובפרק מי שאמר הריני נזיר ושמע חבירו ואמר ואני (נזיר כט. ושם) פריך למ"ד כדי לחנכו במצות הא קמייתי חולין לעזרה ומשני קסבר חולין שנשחטו בעזרה לאו דאורייתא ואי לענין איסור אכילה הוו דאורייתא אכתי תיקשי ליה היאך הקרבן נאכל דמשמע התם שנאכל וקשה לרשב"א דבת"כ בפ' צו גבי נותר דרש רבי יהודה לא יאכל כי קודש הוא יכול חטאת העוף הבא על ספק והאשם תלוי וחולין שנשחטו בעזרה ישרפו ת"ל הוא מדאיצטריך למעוטי שאינם בשריפה מכלל דאסירי בהנאה מדאורייתא: ורבי שמעון נמי מיסר אסר בהנאה. משמע דההיא דהשולח ירך לנכרי אתיא כר' יהודה. הק' ריב"א דהא רבי יהודה אית ליה בפ"ק דמס' ע"ז (דף כ. ושם) דאסור ליתן להם מתנת חנם וי"ל דהא אמר התם* אם היה שכינו מותר מפני °שהוא כמוכרו לו הקשה הר"י דאורלינ"ש °היכי מצי אתי כר' יהודה ורבי יהודה אית ליה בפ' גיד הנשה (חולין ק:) דגיד הנשה אסור לבני נח וקעבר משום לפני עור לא תתן וגו' ואומר ר"י דלא קשה מידי דלא קאסר אלא לבני יעקב דוקא דקודם מתן תורה איקרו בני נח דהא לא ניתנית בסיני וא"ת תיקשי לחזקיה מרבי שמעון דסבירא ליה דלא תאכלו איסור הנאה משמע מדאסר גיד הנשה וי"ל כיון דסבר אין בגידין בנ"ט סברא הוא דכי אסור בהנאה נמי אסור דלא שייכא ביה אכילה °א"נ חזקיה לא סבר כרבי שמעון אלא כרבי יהודה דלכאורה נמי לא אתיא חזקיה כרבי מאיר דלרבי מאיר פשיטא לן לעיל מדאיצטריך למישרי נבילה דכל איסורים אסורים בהנאה וכן לקמן (דף כג:) גבי יתיב ההוא מרבנן פשיטא ליה לגמרא דלרבי מאיר גמר מנבילה והא דקאמר לקמן *לימא כתנאי היינו לרבי אבהו דחזקיה לא מצי אתי ככ"ע: והרי דם דרחמנא אמר. משמע דדם לא הוי בכלל בהמה מדלא משני כשהותרה בהמה דמה נמי הותרה וקשה לר"ת דאמר בהמוציא יין (שבת עז. ושם) דם נבילה ב"ה מטמא וקאמר התם ר' יוסי (כרבי) יהודה דלא מטמא ב"ה אלא כשיש רביעית דם הואיל ויכול לקרוש ולעמוד על כזית אלמא חשיב ליה כבשר ותי' ר"י דהתם לאו משום דחשיב ליה כבשר אלא יש שום פסוק דדרשינן מיניה דדם נבילו' טמא ומסברא משערינן ברביעי' כדאמר התם אבל בלא ריבוי לא חשבינן דם כבשר ובמעילה (דף יז. ושם) נמי מפיק דם השרץ מזה לכם הטמא ומשרץ גופיה לא ידעינן ליה*: מועלין בהן. מדרבנן ולא מדאורייתא דבסוף הוציאו לו (יומא נט: ושם) אמר אין לך דבר שנעשה מצותו ומועלים בו ואור"י דבמעילה בפרק ולד חטאת (דף יא.) ת"ר מועלים בדמים דברי רבי מאיר ורבי שמעון וחכמים אומרים אין מועלין ופלוגתייהו אחר שיצא לנחל קדרון דקודם זריקה קתני ר"ש התם דאין מועלין בו והיה שם בספרים מאי טעמא דמ"ד אין מועלין ול"ג דמ"ד דא"כ הוה משמע דלרבי מאיר ורבי שמעון מועלין בו מן התורה אלא ה"ג מאי טעמא אין מועלין ואמתני' קאי דקתני דם בתחלה אין מועלין בו: מה מים מותרים אף דם מותר. אף על גב דדם קדשים שאין נשפך כמים לא הוקש למים מ"מ כיון דמשמע קרא בדם חולין דשרי בהנאה ולא תאכל דידיה היינו אכילה ולא הנאה הוא הדין לדם קדשים ואף על גב דאיכא תרי לאוי חד לדם חולין וחד לקדשים מ"מ גילוי מילתא בעלמא הוא דכולהו לאוי דדם הוי איסור אכילה דוקא*: ואימא כמים הניסכים על גבי המזבח. לא פריך למילף שיהא דם אסור בהנאה דממילא ידעינן מלא תאכל אלא כלומר מהכא לא מצי למילף דשרי בהנאה: ואבר

עין משפט נר מצוה

ח א מיי' פ"ב מהלכות שחיטה הלכה כ:
ח א מיי' פ"ח מהלכות מאכלות אסורות הל' יד סמג לאוין קלז טוש"ע י"ד סי' סה סעיף יא:
ט ב מיי' פ"ט שם הל' יד סמג שם טוש"ע שם סעיף ט:
י ג מיי' פ"ד שם הלכה יח ופ"ח הלכה ה:
יא ד מיי' פ"ח שם הל' (טו) [יד] טוש"ע שם ס"י:
יב ה מיי' פ"ב מהלכות מעילה הלכה יא:

מסורת הש"ס

קדושין נח. | [לקמן כג: קדושין נח. נזיר כט. ב"ק עב] | [קדושין נז:] | [לקמן כג.] | חולין ק: | ע"ז מד. יומא נח: | חולין צג: | [וע"ע תוס' מנחות קד ד"ה הואיל] | [וע"ע תוס' חולין נג. ד"ה דם]

רבינו חננאל

אתה משליכו לכלבך ואינך משליך שאר איסורין שבתורה מיהא שמעינן לכל שאר איסורין דאסורי ואפילו בהנאה וקרא דנבלה הוא דאתי לאו למימר שאר אסורין אפילו בהנאה ור' יהודה אמר חולין שנשחטו בעזרה אינו מן התורה: ומותבינן לר' אבהו הרי גיד הנשה דכתיב ביה לא יאכל והוא מותר בהנאה דתנן שולח אדם ירך שגיד הנשה בתוכה וכו' ושנינן קסבר ר' אבהו כשהותרה הנבלה היא וחלבה וגידה הותרה כי הנבלה כמות שהיא בחלבה ובגידה הותרה להמכר לנכרי ואקשי' איני שהגידים הותרו בנבלה והא ואכלה כתיב לא הותר אלא מידי דבר אכילה וגידים לאו בני אכילה נינהו דלית בהו בנותן טעם (איני) והתנן ירך שנתבשל בה גיד הנשה וכו' ואמרינן מאן אית ליה האי סברא דאין בגידין בנותן טעם ר"ש ר"ש הכי נמי דאוסר בהנאה דתניא גיד הנשה מותר בהנאה דברי ר' יהודה ור' שמעון אוסר: הרי דם דכתיב לא תאכל דם ומותר בהנאה [דתנן] ונמכרין לזבל ומועלין בהן ודחי' שאני דם דאיתקש למים שנאמר על הארץ תשפכנו כמים כו'

גליון הש"ס

גמ' ור"מ אותו אתה משליך לכלב. תמוה לי דלמא מה דאמר ...

סד ע"ב תוס' ד"ה ולמדנו: בא"ד היכי מצי אתיא כר"י. תמוה לי הא זהו ליכא קושי' כ"כ די"ל דמתני' דירך ס"ל כר"י בזה דג"ה מותר בהנאה אבל בזה לא ס"ל כר"י דמבני יעקב נאסר. ואמאי לא האלימו קושיתם יותר דאיך ס"ל לר"י דכשהותרה נבילה היא וחלבה וגידה הותרו הא ע"כ דלגר אשר בשעריך לא קאי אגיד דהא אסור משום לפני עור וצ"ע: בא"ד א"נ חזקיה לא סבר כר"ש. עי' חולין ל"ס ע"ב מש"ס:

in the field;] *ye shall cast it to the dogs:*[8] [22a] '*it*' you may cast to dogs, but you may not cast to dogs all [other] things forbidden a in the Torah.[1] And R. Meir?[2]—[He interprets:] '*it*' you may cast to dogs, but you may not cast to dogs *ḥullin* killed in the Temple Court.[3] And the other?[4]—[Benefit from][5] *ḥullin* killed in the Temple Court is not [forbidden] by Scriptural law.

R. Isaac of Nappaḥa[6] objected: But what of the *nervus ischiadicus*, though the Divine Law saith, *Therefore the children of Israel eat not the sinew of the thigh-vein*,[7] yet we learned: A man may send the thigh [of an animal] to a heathen with the *nervus ischiadicus* in it, because its place is distinguishable![8]—R. Abbahu holds, when *nebelah* was permitted [by the Torah], it, its forbidden fat, and its thigh sinew were permitted.[9] This is well on the view that the sinews possess the power of imparting a taste.[10] But on the view that the sinews possess no power of imparting a taste,[11] what can be said?—Whom do you know to maintain [that] the sinews have no power to communicate taste? R. Simeon. For it was taught: He who eats of the thigh sinew of an unclean animal,—R. Judah declares him liable on two [accounts],[12] while R. Simeon holds him non-culpable.[13] [According to] R. Simeon, it is indeed forbidden for use too. For it was taught: The thigh sinew is permitted for use; this is R. Judah's view; but R. Simeon forbids it.

But what of blood, of which the Divine Law saith, *No soul of* b *you shall eat blood*,[1] yet we learned, Both these and those[2] mingled in the duct and passed out to the brook of Kidron,[3] and they were sold to gardeners as fertilizers, and trespass is committed in respect of them?[4]—Blood is different, because it is likened to water, for it is written, *Thou shalt not eat it; thou shalt pour it out upon the earth as water:*[5] just as water is permitted, so is blood permitted. Yet say, like water poured out as libations upon the altar?[6]—Said R. Abbahu: '*as water*' [means] like *most* water. Is then 'most water' written?—Rather, said R. Ashi: 'as water' which is poured out,[7] but not as water offered as a libation. Yet say, like water which is poured out in idol worship?[8]—There too it is designated a libation, as it is written, *They drank the wine of their drink offering* [libation].[9]

(8) Ex. XXII, 30.

a (1) I.e., you may not derive any benefit from them. (2) What is the purpose of '*it*', which expresses a limitation, seeing that he learns this from *nebelah?* (3) This may not be eaten, and R. Meir deduces here that all benefit is forbidden, v. Ḳid. 57*b*. (4) R. Judah: how does he know this? (5) So Rashi, v. however Tosaf. s.v. חולין. (6) Or, the smith. Many Rabbis were workers or tradesmen. (7) Gen. XXXII, 33. (8) The Jew need not remove the *nervus ischiadicus* before sending it, for fear that another Jew, seeing that the heathen had received it from a Jew, may think that the nerve has been removed and that it is all permitted, because one can easily recognize whether the *nervus ischiadicus* has been removed or not. Giving anything to a heathen is regarded as benefit, and we thus see that the benefit of this sinew is permitted, which conflicts with R. Abbahu's statement *supra* 21*b*. (9) Therefore benefit from all forbidden fat and all sinews is permitted. (10) E.g., if forbidden sinews are boiled together with meat, they impart a flavour to the meat, which renders that too forbidden, unless it is sixty times as much as the sinews. On that view the sinews are as flesh, and therefore when *nebelah* was permitted it included the sinews. (11) Because they are not flesh, being merely like wood, and nevertheless they are prohibited: hence they cannot be included in the permission granted for *nebelah*. (12) (i) Because it is of an unclean (i.e., forbidden) animal; (ii) because the thigh sinew itself is forbidden. (13) He is not culpable on account of the unclean animal, because he holds that there is no taste in the sinew. Nor is he liable on account of the sinew, for this involves liability only when the flesh of that animal is permitted, but not when the flesh too is forbidden.

b (1) Lev. XVII, 12. (2) The residues of the blood of the 'inner' sin-offerings, which were poured out on the western base of the outer altar, and the residues of the blood of the 'outer' sin-offerings, which were poured out on the south base of the altar. These passed out through two small holes and mingled in a duct which ran through the Temple Court. (3) Near Jerusalem. (4) I.e., one may not benefit from them without paying. V. Yoma 58*b*.—Yet we see that benefit may be derived from blood in general. (5) Deut. XII, 24. (6) Benefit of which is forbidden. (7) As indicated by the words '*thou shalt pour it out*'. (8) Such water too is forbidden. (9) Ibid. XXXII, 38.

sell it. [21b] R. Judah b. Bathyra said: *Kutaḥ*[7] and all kinds of *kutaḥ*[8] may not be sold thirty days before Passover.[9]

AND BENEFIT THEREOF IS PERMITTED. That is obvious?[10]—It is necessary [to teach it] only where he charred it [in the fire] a before its time,[1] and he [the Tanna] informs us [that the law is] as Rabbah. For Rabbah said: If he charred it [in the fire] before its time, benefit [thereof] is permitted even after its time.[2]

WHEN ITS PERIOD HAS PASSED, BENEFIT THEREOF IS FORBIDDEN. That is obvious?—It is necessary [to state this] only in respect of the hours [when leaven is interdicted] by Rabbinical law.[3] For R. Gidal said in the name of R. Ḥiyya b. Joseph in R. Joḥanan's name: He who betroths from the sixth hour and onwards, even with wheat of Cordyene, we have no fear of his betrothal.[4]

AND HE MAY NOT FIRE AN OVEN OR A POT-RANGE WITH IT. That is obvious?—This is necessary only according to R. Judah, who maintained: There is no removal of leaven save by burning. You might argue, since R. Judah said, Its precept demands burning, then while he is burning it let him benefit from it. Hence we are informed [that it is not so].

Hezekiah said: How do we know that leaven during Passover is forbidden for [general] use?[5] Because it is said, *there shall no leavened bread be eaten:*[6] [meaning,] there shall not be in it permission [i.e., the right] of eating.[7] [Thus] the reason is because the Divine Law wrote, *'there shall no leavened bread be eaten'*; but if *'shall not be eaten'* were not written, I would say, prohibition of eating is implied, [but] prohibition of benefit is not implied. Now he differs from R. Abbahu, for R. Abbahu said: Wherever it is said, *'It shall not be eaten,' 'thou shalt not eat,' 'ye shall not eat,'* the prohibitions of both eating and benefit [in general] are understood, unless the Writ expressly states [otherwise], as it does in the case of *nebelah*.[8] For it was taught: *Ye shall not eat of* [nebelah] *anything that dieth of itself: thou mayest give it unto the stranger* [ger] *that is within thy gates, that he may eat it; or thou mayest sell it unto a* b *foreigner:*[1] I know only that it may be *'given'* to a stranger[2] or *'sold'* to a foreigner [heathen]; how do I know [that] selling to a stranger [*ger*] [is permitted]? Therefore it is stated, *'thou mayest give it unto the stranger* [ger] *that is within thy gates ... or sell.'*[3] How do we know [that] giving to a foreigner [is permitted]? Because it is stated, *'thou mayest give it, that he may eat it, or thou mayest sell it unto a foreigner'*;[4] thus the result is[5] that [to] a stranger [*ger*] and a foreigner [heathen] alike, both selling and giving [are permitted]: this is R. Meir's view. R. Judah said: The words are as they are written, [viz.,] to a *ger* it must be given and to a heathen it must be sold. What is R. Judah's reason? If you should think as R. Meir says, let the Divine Law write, *thou mayest give it unto the stranger* [ger] *that is within thy gates, that he may eat it,* and *thou mayest sell it:* why state *'or'?* Infer from this that the words are as they are written. And R. Meir?[6]—*'Or'* is to show that giving to a *ger* takes precedence over selling to a heathen. And R. Judah?—No verse is required for this: since you are commanded to maintain a *ger*, but you are not commanded to maintain a heathen,[7] a verse is not required, [for] it stands to reason.

On the view of R. Meir who maintained, [to] a *ger* and a heathen alike, both selling and giving are permitted, it is well: since a verse is required to permit benefit from a *nebelah*, it follows that all other things forbidden in the Torah are forbidden in respect of both eating and [general] benefit. But according to R. Judah, who maintained, it comes from [the purpose of teaching that] the words are as they are written, whence does he know that all [other] things forbidden in the Torah are forbidden in respect of benefit? He deduces it from, [*ye shall not eat any flesh that is torn of beasts*

(7) Jast.: a preserve consisting of sour milk, breadcrusts, and salt. V. Perles *Et. St.* p. 85; Fl. to Levy, *Talm. Dict.* II, p. 459*b*. (8) In Shab. 19*a* the reading is: Babylonian *kutaḥ* and all kinds of *kutaḥ*. This makes better sense, and the same may be understood here. (9) It is used as a sauce or relish, and hence lasts a long time. It was customary to give popular lectures about Festivals thirty days before, and therefore from that time one might not sell his *kutaḥ* to a Gentile. (10) For feeding cattle with it is benefit, and it is already stated that this is permitted.

a (1) I.e., before it becomes forbidden. It was so charred that it neither tastes nor looks like leaven. (2) And the Mishnah too refers to this. (3) I.e., in the sixth hour. (4) V. *supra* 7*a* for notes. (5) And not merely as food. (6) Ex. XIII, 3. (7) Rashi: the use of the passive intimates that no benefit which may lead to eating is permitted, i.e., no benefit whatsoever, for generally the monetary value of any benefit is expended on food. (8) V. Glos.

b (1) Deut. XIV, 21. (2) A resident-alien who is a semi-proselyte in so far that he has abjured idolatry. (3) Treating *'stranger'* as the indirect object of both *'give'* and *'sell'*. (4) Treating 'foreigner' as the indirect object of both *'give'* and *'sell'*. (5) Lit., 'it is found saying'. (6) How does he answer this? (7) In a technical sense only: nevertheless Judaism teaches that the poor among heathens must be helped just as the Jewish poor, v. Giṭ. 61*a*.

עין משפט נר מצוה

ג א מיי' פ"ג שם הלכה יא סמג שם טוש"ע א"ח סי' תמח ס"ב וסי' תמב סעיף ט:
ד ב מיי' פ"א שם הל' ט סמג שם טוש"ע א"ח סי' תמג סעיף א:
ה ג מיי' שם הלכה ב:
ו ד מיי' פ"ח מהלכות אסורות הל' טו סמג לאוין קלט:
ז ה מיי' פ"י מהל' ע"ז הלכה ד:

מסורת הש"ס

ר' יהודה בן בתירא אומר כותח וכל מיני כותח אסור למכור שלשים יום קודם לפסח: ומותר בהנאה: פשיטא לא צריכא שחרכו קודם זמנו וקמ"ל כדרבא (א) דאמר רבא *חרכו קודם זמנו מותר בהנאה אפילו לאחר זמנו: עבר זמנו אסור בהנאתו: פשיטא בלא צריכא לשעות דרבנן *דאמר רב גידל אמר רב חייא בר יוסף א"ר יוחנן המקדש משש שעות ולמעלה אפילו בחיטי קורדניתא אין חוששין לקדושין: ולא יסיק בו תנור וכירים: פשיטא לא צריכא (ב) לר' יהודה דאמר אין ביעור חמץ אלא שריפה סלקא דעתך אמינא הואיל ואמר ר' יהודה מצותו בשריפה בהדי דקא שריף ליה °ליתהני מיניה קמ"ל: אמר חזקיה גמנין לחמץ בפסח שאסור בהנאה שנאמר °לא יאכל חמץ (שמות יג) לא יהא בו היתר אכילה טעמא דכתב רחמנא לא יאכל חמץ הא לא כתב לא יאכל הוה אמינא איסור אכילה משמע איסור הנאה לא משמע ופליגא דר' אבהו *דא"ר אבהו דכל מקום שנאמר לא יאכל לא תאכל לא תאכלו אחד איסור אכילה ואחד איסור הנאה (*משמע) עד שיפרט לך הכתוב כדרך שפרט לך בנבילה °דתניא °לא תאכלו (דברים יד) כל נבלה לגר אשר בשעריך תתננה ואכלה או מכור לנכרי וגו' אין לי אלא לגר בנתינה ולנכרי במכירה לגר במכירה מנין ת"ל לגר אשר בשעריך תתננה או מכור לנכרי בנתינה מנין תלמוד לומר תתננה ואכלה או מכור לנכרי נמצאת אומר אחד גר ואחד נכרי בין במכירה בין בנתינה דברי ר' מאיר *ר' יהודה אומר הדברים ככתבן לגר בנתינה ולנכרי במכירה מאי טעמא דרבי יהודה אי סלקא דעתך כדאמר ר' מאיר ליכתוב רחמנא לגר אשר בשעריך תתננה ואכלה ומכור או למה לי שמע מינה לדברים ככתבן ור' מאיר או להקדים נתינה דגר למכירה דנכרי ורבי יהודה הא לא *צריך קרא כיון דגר אתה מצווה להחיותו ונכרי אי אתה מצווה להחיותו לא צריך קרא סברא הוא בשלמא לר' מאיר דאמר אחד גר ואחד נכרי בין במכירה בין בנתינה מדאיצטריך קרא למישרא נבילה בהנאה הא כל איסורין שבתורה אסורין בין באכילה בין בהנאה אלא לרבי יהודה דאמר לדברים ככתבן הוא דאתא הא כל איסורים שבתורה מנא ליה דאסורין בהנאה נפקא ליה °מלכלב תשליכון אותו (שמות כב) אותו

רש"י

ר' יהודה אומר כותח. נותנין בו פירורי לחם ואסור משום חמץ: שלשים יום. דס"ל כב"ש וזה אינו נאכל מהר שאין אוכלין אותו אלא מטבילין בו והני שלשים יום משעה שחל עליו חובת ביעור משהשואלין בהלכות הפסח: ומותר בהנאתו. קס"ד לאשעה שמותר לאכול קאי:

תורה אור

פשיטא. דהא אמרת מאכיל ומוכר היינו הנאה: לא צריכא כו'. והאי מותר אלאחר זמן קאי וכגון שחרכו באור יפה קודם זמנו שבטל טעמו ומראיתו: עבר (ג) זמנו אסור בהנאה לשעות דרבנן ה"ג ולא גרסי' פשיטא דהא אפי' בפסח הוצריך לאשמעי' דהא איכא רבי יוסי הגלילי דשרי בהנאה כל שבעה לקמן: לשעות דרבנן. כלומר האי זמנו זמן אכילתו משמע ואפילו שעה ששית שאין איסורו אלא מדרבנן הוי אסור אף בהנאה: משש שעות. על כרחך מתחלת שש משמע דאי לאחר שש לאסור מדאורייתא מאי אתא לאשמעינן פשיטא דאין מקדשין באיסורי הנאה: חיטי קורדניתא. קשות הן ואפ"ה אם באו לחשש חמץ כגון שנפלו עליהן מים אסור: פשיטא. דהא אמרת אסור בהנאתו: לא יאכל. מדקרינא לא *יאכל משמע לא יהא בו היתר המביא לידי שום אכילה וסתם הנאות לידי אכילה הם באות שלוקח בדמים דבר מאכל: עד שיפרוט לך הכתוב בו. היתר הנאה כדרך שפרט לך בנבלה שלא היה כתוב בה אלא לא תאכלו והוצרך להתירה בהנאה כדכתיב או מכור לנכרי לגר בנתינה לנכרי במכירה לא גרסינן אלא ה"ג כדרך שפרט לך בנבלה דתניא וכו': ת"ל לגר תתננה ואכלה או מכור. דרוש ליה אגר וכן גבי לנכרי נמי דרוש תתננה ואכלה או מכור לנכרי: דברים ככתבן. כך מצותה לא יתננה לנכרי ולא ימכרנה לגר: או. לשון חילוק ואי כר' מאיר קאמר קרא דתרווייהו אגר ותרווייהו אנכרי לא נכתוב או: להקדים נתינה דגר למכירה דנכרי. אם יש גר ליתנה לו נתינתו קודמת למכירתה לנכרי והאי גר בגר תושב קאמר שקיבל עליו שלא לעבוד עכו"ם ואוכל נבלות: גר אתה מצווה להחיותו. דכתיב (ויקרא כה) גר ותושב וחי עמך: סברא היא. מסברא אנו יודעין שנתינה לגר קודמת דחיות הגר מצוה אבל מכירה לנכרי מאי מצוה איכא ואיצטריך קרא לחלק ולאסור ליתן במתנה לנכרי ולמכור נבלה לגר: בשלמא. לר' אבהו אליבא דר"מ מאי למילף מדאיצטריך קרא למישרי נבלה הא כל איסורין שבתורה דכתיב בהו לא תאכל כי הכא אי לא הדר פריט בהו היתרא אסורין הן באכילה ובהנאה: אלא. לר' אבהו אליבא דרבי יהודה מנא ליה דילמא האי פרט דנבלה לאו למשרייה בהנאה אתא דלא איצטריך אלא להחמיר ולומר דלנכרי במכירה ולגר בנתינה דאי לא כתביה הוה אמינא כל הנאות מותרות בה: נפקא ליה. לרבי אבהו ואליבא דרבי יהודה מדכתב בטרפה לא תאכלו ומיעט בה לכלב תשליכון אותו: אותו

תוספות

רבי יהודה אומר כותח וכל מיני כותח. אור"י בשם ר"ת דר"י אתי כב"ה ואסר בכותח משום דשם בעליו עליו ויודעים שהוא כותח של פלוני ויסברו שמכרו בפסח ע"י נכרי אי נמי יסברו שבפסח מכרו ישראל לנכרי ולכן אוסר ר' יהודה למכור כותח לנכרי וא"ש אף לר"ת דמפרש בריש אלו עוברים (לקמן מב.) דמותר להשהות כותח בפסח:

חרכו קודם זמנו מותר בהנאה אף לאחר זמנו. וכגון שנפסל מלאכול לכלב דבענין אחר לא הוי שרי דומיא דפת שעיפשה בפ"ק (דף טו:): עבר זמנו אסור בהנאה פשיטא. רש"י ל"ג פשיטא דהא רבי יוסי הגלילי פליג ושרי חמץ בהנאה כל שבעה ואין לפרש פשיטא דאסור בהנאה מדיוקא דרישא °דדרך התנא בכמה מקומות לכפול את דבריו ועוד דלא משני שפיר ונראה דפריך פשיטא משום דתנא בפ"ק (דף יא:) דשורפין חמץ אלמא אסור בהנאה דלר' יוסי הגלילי א"כ לשורפו אלא ירילנו לפני כלבו או ימכרנו לנכרי:

בהדי דקשריף ליה ליתהני מיניה. משום דלר' יהודה דאמר חמץ בשריפה אפרו מותר דתניא בפ' בתרא דתמורה (ד' לד.*) כל הנשרפין אפרן מותר וקס"ד בהדי דקשריף ליה ליתהני מיניה אבל לרבנן דאין מצותו בשריפה והוי מן הנקברים דאמרינן בפרק בתרא דתמורה אפרן אסור ופשיטא לדידהו דבהדי דקשריף ליה אסור ליהנות ממנו:

כל מקום שנאמר לא יאכל. וא"ת יהא נהנה מחמץ בפסח בכרת דהא כתיב כי כל אוכל חמץ ונכרתה וכי תימא אין הכי נמי א"כ לקמן (דף כג:) דבעי מאי איכא בין חזקיה לר' אבהו לימא דאיכא בינייהו הא ואור"י דלא יאכל ולא תאכל ילפינן מלא תאכלו אבל כי כל אוכל לא ילפינן מלא תאכלו:

ליכתוב רחמנא תתננה ואכלה ומכור. משמע דאי הוי כתב הכי לא הוה דרשינן אלא כר"מ וכן באיהו נשך (ב"מ סא.) גבי נשך ותרבית והא דאמרי' בקדושין (ד' לג:) ורבנן אי ס"ד כרבי יוסי הגלילי ליכתוב רחמנא מפני שיבה תקום והדרת פני זקן היינו משום דלשון והדרת לא שייך אמפני ולשון פני לא שייך אתקום והנך קראי דאין להן הכרעה שאת ארור מחר משוקדים וקם (יומא ד' נב.) אין ענינם לכאן דהתם מני קאי אדלעיל או אלתחת אבל הכא תרווייהו לא מצי קיימי אגר לחודיה או אנכרי לחודיה ובפ"ב דזבחים (ד' כה.) פליגי תנאי גבי ולקח הכהן מדם החטאת באצבעו ונתן איכא דמוקי אצבעו אלקיחה ולא אנתינה משום דפשטיה דקרא קאי אלקיחה דלפניו ואיכא דמוקי לה אנתינה דלאחריו ולא אלקיחה משום דמסכתת בדוכתא אחרינא ולקחת מדם הפר ונתת על קרנות המזבח באצבעך דקאי אצבע אנתינה ואיכא דמוקי לה אתרווייהו משום דמשמע ליה אלקיחה כפשטא דקרא ואנתינה נמי כדמוכח בקרא אחרינא*):

בשלמא לרבי מאיר. תימה לר"מ נמי יקשה דהא איצטריך לאקדומי נתינה דגר ותי' ר"י דודאי אי לא הוה כתב קרא כל עיקר הוה ידעינן מסברא לאקדומי אבל השתא דכתב נתינה תתננה ואכלה ומכור אי לא הוה כתב או ה"א דאתא למידרש שאין צריך להקדים וצריך ליכתב נמי גר ונכרי דאי לא הוה כתב אלא גר הוה אמינא דאתא למעוטי נתינה דנכרי ואי הוה כתוב נכרי לחודיה הוה אמינא דאתא למעוטי מכירה דגר:

*) [וע"ע תוס' יומא נה: נב: ב"מ סא. ע"ז כ. חולין קיד:]

[ולקמן כו:]

קדושין נו: [ע"ש] ב"ק מא. [ע"ש] חולין קיד: [ע"ש]

[*צ"ל במשמע וכן איתא בב"ק מא.]

לעיל ו.

יֵאָבֵל

ע"ז כ:

שם [לקמן כג:]

[ועי' בתוס' שבועות כב: ד"ה איבעית אימא]

רבינו חננאל

בן בתירא אומר כותח וכל מיני כותח אסור למכור שלשים יום קודם לפסח: והלכתא כסתמא דמתני' ואם חרכו לפני זמנו מותר בהנאתו אפי' לאחר זמן איסורו: עבר זמנו אסור בהנאתו אוקימנא בזמן איסורו משש שעות ולמעלה. תנן סתמא כרב המקדש משש שעות ולמעלה [בחיטין שנתן בהן מים] אפילו בחיטי קרדניתא שהן חזקות ולא מחמעי היא אין חוששין לקדושין: אמר חזקיה מנין לחמץ שאסור בהנאה שנאמר לא יאכל חמץ לא יהא בו היתר אכילה ומתוך דבריו שמענו דכל איסורא דלא כתיב בהו לא יאכל מותרים בהנאה ופליגא דר' אבהו דאמר כל היכא דכתיב לא יאכל לא תאכל לא תאכלו אסור בין באכילה בין בהנאה עד שיפרט לך הכתוב כדרך שפרט בנבלה לגר אשר בשעריך תתננה ואכלה וחלוק במקרא הזה ר' מאיר אומר אחד גר ואחד נכרי בין במכירה בין בנתינה ר' יהודה אומר דברים ככתבן כלומר דכתיב קרא לגר במתנה ולנכרי במכירה ואמרינן לר' מאיר דאמר הנכרי והגר דינם אחד הוא התורה התירה לך אמרי' מדאצטריך קרא למישרא נבלה בהנאה מכלל דשאר איסורין שבתורה אסורין אפילו בהנאה אלא לר' יהודה דאמר דברים ככתבן בלומר לא איצטריך קרא [אלא] למיסר מתנה דנכרי ומכירה [דגר] ולנפשיה הוא דאתי שאר אסורין שבתורה מנא ליה דאסירי בהנאה ואצרינן מהאי קרא נפקא ליה ובשר בשדה טרפה לא תאכלו לכלב תשליכון אותו ודייקינן אותו אתה משליך לכלב פי' זה מותר לך בהנאה שהרי אתה

הגהות הב"ח

(א) גמ' כדרבא דאמר רבא חרכו קודם זמנו: (ב) שם לא צריכא אלא לר' יהודה: (ג) רש"י ד"ה עבר זמנו וכו' דרבנן ה"ג ולא גרסינן כצ"ל:

גליון הש"ס

גמ' ליתהני מיניה קמ"ל. עי' לעיל דף ה' ע"ב תד"ה ואומר: תוס' עבר זמנו וכו' דדרך התנא. עי' עירובין נ"ג ע"ב תד"ה וליפרוש עליה. ועיין לקמן ל"ה ע"ב ול"ש

אין הכרעת שלישית מכרעת. אמר ר' יוסי בר חנינא *מחלוקת שנפלה לפחות ממאה סאה חולין טמאין אבל נפלה למאה חולין טמאין דברי הכל תרד ותטמא ואל יטמאנה ביד תניא נמי הכי חבית שנשברה בגת העליונה ותחתיה מאה חולין טמאין מודה רבי אליעזר לרבי יהושע שאם יכול להציל ממנה רביעית בטהרה יציל ואם לאו תרד ותטמא ואל יטמאנה ביד האי מודה רבי אליעזר לרבי יהושע מודה רבי יהושע לר' אליעזר מיבעי ליה אמר רבא איפוך רב הונא בריה דרב יהושע אמר לעולם לא תיפוך הכא במאי עסקינן בכלי שתוכו טהור וגבו טמא מהו דתימא ניגזור דילמא נגע גבו בתרומה קמ"ל:

הדרן עלך אור לארבעה עשר

כל שעה *שמותר לאכול מאכיל לבהמה לחיה ולעופות ומוכר לנכרי ומותר בהנאתו עבר זמנו אסור בהנאתו ולא יסיק בו תנור וכירים *ר' יהודה אומר אין ביעור חמץ אלא שריפה [ג] וחכמים אומרים *אף מפרר וזורה לרוח או מטיל לים: **גמ'** כל שעה שמותר לאכול מאכיל הא כל שעה שאינו מותר לאכול אינו מאכיל לימא מתני' דלא כר' יהודה דאי ר' יהודה הא איכא חמש דאינו אוכל ומאכיל *דתנן ר' מאיר אומר אוכלין כל חמש ושורפין בתחלת שש רבי יהודה אומר אוכלין כל ארבע ותולין כל חמש ושורפין בתחלת שש ואלא מאי ר' מאיר היא האי כל שעה *שמותר לאכול מאכיל כל שעה שאוכל מאכיל מיבעי ליה אמר רבה בר עולא מתניתין רבן גמליאל היא *דתנן רבן גמליאל אומר חולין נאכלין כל ארבע תרומה כל חמש ושורפין בתחלת שש והכי קאמר כל שעה שמותר לאכול כהן בתרומה ישראל מאכיל חולין לבהמה לחיה ולעופות למה לי למיתנא בהמה למה לי למיתנא חיה צריכא דאי תנא בהמה דאי משיירא חזי לה אבל חיה דאי משיירא קמצנעא לה אימא לא ואי תנא חיה משום דאי משיירא מיהת מצנעא אבל בהמה זימנין דמשיירא ולא מסיק אדעתיה וקאי עליה בבל יראה ובבל ימצא אימא לא צריכא עופות ל"ל איידי דתנא בהמה וחיה תנא נמי עופות: ומוכרו לנכרי: פשיטא לאפוקי מהאי תנא *דתניא ב"ש אומרים לא ימכור אדם חמצו לנכרי אא"כ יודע בו שיכלה קודם פסח וב"ה אומרים [ג]כל שעה שמותר לאכול מותר למכור

רבי

רש"י

אין הכרעת שלישית מכרעת. דעת שלישית היא זו שבית שמאי ובית הלל לא הזכירו לגלות דעתם דניחוי חייסינן לתקלה כלל דאי הוו אמרו הכי ב"ש אומרים בין בבית בין בשדה תשפך (א) וב"ה אומרים בין בבית בין בשדה תיעשה זילוף ואתה בא להכריע ולומר בבית כב"ה בשדה כבית שמאי הויא הכרעה אבל השתא דלא הזכירו בית ושדה טעמא אחרינא הוא ולאו משום תקלה ור' ישמעאל חייש לתקלה והיינו תנאי: מחלוקת. ר' אליעזר ור' יהושע שנפלה לפחות ממאה חולין טמאים שיש בגת התחתונה פחות ממאה חולין טמאים דאין תרומה בטילה בהן ופסדי לגמרי דתרומה צריך אחד ומאה לבטלה אבל היו בתחתונה מאה חולין מאה חביות כמו זו של תרומה דברי הכל לא יטמאנה ביד הואיל ולא פסדי חולין דתרומה עולה בהן וחזו בימי טומאה כדמעיקרא לזר: מודה ר' אליעזר כו'. קס"ד אמסקנא קאי אאם לאו דהא פלוגתייהו באם לאו הוא ולהכי פריך מודה ר' יהושע דאמר לעיל יטמאנה ביד לר' אליעזר דאמר לא יטמאנה ביד מיבעי ליה למיתני: בכלי שתוכו טהור וגבו טמא. והאי מודה לאו אסיפא קאי אלא ארישא דקתני אם יכול להציל רביעית בטהרה יציל ואפי' כלי זה שהוא בא להציל רביעית זו בתוכו תוכו טהור וגבו טמא ואשמעינן ליה לר' אליעזר דאמר אל יטמאנה ביד מודה הוא דמותר להציל בזה ולא חיישינן דילמא נגע גבו בתרומה ומטמא לה בידים ובכלי שנטמא במשקין דטומאתן דרבנן היא דמשכחת לה כדתניא כלי שנטמאו אחוריו במשקין אחוריו טמאין תוכו אוגנו אזנו ידיו טהורין:

הדרן עלך אור לארבעה עשר

כל שעה שמותר לאכול מאכיל. לדוקייא איצטריך דתידוק הא משעה שאינו מותר לאכול אינו מותר להאכיל: ולא יסיק בו תנור וכירים. בגמרא פריך פשיטא הא נמי הנאה היא: **גמ'** כל שעה שאוכל מאכיל מבעי ליה. אבל השתא דנקט לה בתרי לישני משמע דאתרי גברי קאי והא ליכא למימר דהכי קאמר כל שעה שמותר לאכול מן התורה מאכיל אפילו מדרבנן ותיתוקם אליבא דר' יהודה דהא איכא שם דמותר לאכול מן התורה ואסור להאכיל לדברי הכל: אלא הכי קאמר כל שעה. שיש היתר לשום אדם לאכול מאכיל אף האסור לאכול לבהמתו כו': בהמה אי משיירא חזי ליה. שאין דרכה להצניע אבל חיה כגון חולדה ונמיה ותתול דרכן להצניע: ואי תנא חיה. הוה אמינא היא עדיפא משום דאי משיירא מצנעא לה *ולא עבר עליה בבל יראה: ולאו אדעתיה לבטלו: קודם. שיבוא הפסח דקסברי מצוה עליו לבערו מן העולם ולא שיהא קיים:

ר'

תוספות

אין הכרעת שלישית מכרעת. פ"ה הואיל ולא הזכירו בית שמאי ובית הלל בית ושדה א"כ טעמא אחרינא הוא ולא משום תקלה ולר"י נראה אע"ג דטעמא דבית שמאי משום תקלה לא חשיב הכרעה לפי שלא גילו הראשונים דעתן לחלק בין בית לשדה שלא הזכירו בדבריהם אחד בית ואחד שדה וכן פ"ה לעיל *גבי ר"ג לאו מכריע הוא והיא דקולי מטלניות בין מן המוכן ובין שלא מן המוכן טמא דברי ר"א ר' יהושע אומר בין מן המוכן ובין שלא מן המוכן טהור ר"ע אומר מן המוכן טמא שלא מן המוכן טהור וחשיב ליה בפ' כירה (שבת לט: ושם) הכרעה שהרי גילו ר' אליעזר ור' יהושע דשייך לחלק בין מן המוכן ובין שלא מן המוכן והיא דפ' כילד מברכין (ברכות מג:) דקאמר ב"ש מברכים על השמן וקאמר ר"ג אני אכריע שמן זכינו לריחו וזכינו לסיכתו הדס לריחו זכינו לסיכתו לא זכינו וקאמר רבי יוחנן הלכה כדברי המכריע לאו משום דמכריע גמור הוא אלא אלא מפרש ונותן טעם לדבריו ותדע דאי מכריע הוא למה הוצרך לפסוק הלכה כמותו הא כבר א"ר יוחנן בפרק כירה הלכה כדברי המכריע וק"ק לפי' זה דהכא מאי איריא הכרעה שלישית שאין הכרעה תיפוק ליה דהכרעת תלמיד לאו הכרעה היא כדאמר בפ' כירה (שבת לט:) ארבי עקיבא ור"ח פי' הכרעת שלישית דור שלישי דהיינו הכרעת תלמיד כדאמר בפ' כירה*:

[עי' תוס' זבחים נ. ד"ה רבי וע"ע תוס' מנחות נח. ד"ה דתניא]

הדרן עלך אור לארבעה עשר

כל שעה. עבר זמנו אסור בהנאה. ואסור למכור ואם מכר דמיו מותרין דאין תופס את דמיו כדתנן בפ"ב דקדושין (דף נו:) מכרן וקידש בדמיהן מקודשת: **לימא** מתניתין דלא כר' יהודה. °אף לפי המסקנא לא אתיא כר' יהודה אלא הכי קאמר לימא מתני' דלא כר' יהודה אלא כר' מאיר ומסיק דכר' מאיר נמי לא אתי: **ואי** אשמעינן חיה משום דמצנעא לה. ואין עובר משום בל יטמין דבל יטמין נפקא לן מלא ימצא ואין זה מצוי כיון שאין ידוע היכן הוא וכן משמע בפ"ק (דף ו:) דפריך וכי משכחת לה ליבטלה משמע דבכל כמה דלא משכחת לא עבר בבל יראה הק' רשב"א היכי שרי להאכיל לחיה שדרכה להטמין הא תנן בפ"ק (דף ט:) מה שמשייר יניחנו בצינעא כדי שלא תטול חולדה בפניו ויהא צריך בדיקה אחריו וכ"ש שאסור ליתן בפניהם ויש לחלק בין חיה לחולדה המגדלים בבתים דההיא לא מצנעא כולי האי כמו חולדה הטומנת בחורים ובסדקין: **וקאי** עליה בבל יראה. פי' אם לא ביטלו והוא הדין דהוה מצי למימר דילמא אתי למיכל מיניה:

רבי

עין משפט נר מצוה

קלה א מיי' פי"ב מהל' תרומות הלכה ה:

א ב מיי' פ"א מהלכות חמץ הלכה י סמג לאוין עו טוש"ע או"ח סי' תמג סעיף א:

ב [ג] מיי' פ"ג שם הלכה יא טוש"ע או"ח סי' תמה סעיף א:

ג ג מיי' שם פ"ג הלכה יא טוש"ע או"ח סי' תמ"ג ס"א וסי' תמה סעיף ג:

מסורת הש"ס

שבת לט. מיר נג. חולין קלו. [ב"ק קטז.] | [דף יג.] | לעיל יג. | תמורה לד. [לעיל יג: לקמן כז:] [כרכ אלפס ובהרא"ש ליתא מלת אף ועיין מג"א ריש סימן תמה:] | לעיל ד: יא: | [לעיל יג.] | [לעיל יא:] | שבת יח:

ס"א נהי דעבר בבל ימצא בבל יראה לא עבר

הגהות הב"ח

(א) רש"י ד"ה אין הכרעת וכו' בין בשדה תשפך הכל וכו'

גליון הש"ס

בתוס' ד"ה לימא. אף לפי המסקנא. עי' מיר דף כ' ע"ב תד"ה לימא:

רבינו חננאל

לאכרועי על ב"ה והא שאמר אין הכרעת שלישי מכרעת ושמועה זו בהגזול זוטא ופרקי' בפ' ראשית הגז תנא ר' ישמעאל בר' יוסי משום אביו ארבע שנאמר וארבע צאן תחת השה תניא אמר רבי אלמלא דבריהם דברי תורה ודברי ברבי קבלה אנו דברי ברבי שומעין וכל שכן שדבריהם דברי קבלה ודברי ברבי דברי תורה והאמר מר אין הכרעת שלישית מכרע' אמר ר' יוחנן מפי שמועה אמורה מפי חגי זכריה ומלאכי: ור' האי ז"ל היה אומר בקבלה כי אינה הכרעה אלא בזמן ששנים חלוקים ואחד מכריע כאחד מהן שנמצאו שנים ואחד מכריע והלכה כרבים אבל בזמן שאומר חצי דברי זה וחצי דברי זה אין זה מכריע טעם שלישי הוא ולפיכך כשאמר ר' ישמעאל בבית תעשה זילוף כב"ה בשדה תשתפך הכל כב"ש אמרו לו הכרעה שלישית היא זו ואין הכרעה שלישי' מכרע': ועוד אמר ר' יוסי בר חנינא מחלוקת שנפלה לפחות ממאה חולין דקא פסדי חולין לגמרי אבל נפלה למאה חולין דלא פסדי להו לחולין דהא תרומה לדברי הכל עולה לאחד ומאה דברי הכל תרד ותטמא ואל יטמאנה ביד ותניא הכי דתניא חבית שנשברה בגת העליונה ותחתיה מאה חולין טמאין מודה ר' אליעזר לר' יהושע שאם יכול להציל רביעית בטהרה יציל ואם לאו תרד ותטמא ואל יטמאנה בידים ומקשינן הא ר' יהושע הוא דתני אף יטמא ביד והוא היה צריך עכשיו להודות לר' אליעזר שלא יטמא ביד והיכי קתני דר' אליעזר הוא שמודה לר' יהושע ואמר רב פפא אפיך ואימא מודה ר' יהושע לר' אליעזר. רב הונא בריה דרב יהושע אמר לעולם לא תפיך והכא בבא להציל רביעית בטהרה בכלי שגבו טמא ותוכו טהור מהו דתימא גזר ר' אליעזר להציל בכלי שגבו טמא כי ההיא דתנן כלי שנטמא אחוריו במשקה תוכו ואגנו ואזנו וידיו טהורין

כ"ג דתימא גזר ר' אליעזר דלמא אתי למנגע בהו בתרומה ויטמא קמ"ל מודה ר' אליעזר שמציל רביעית בטהרה בכלי שתוכו טהור וגבו טמא ולא חייש ר' אליעזר דלמא נגע גבו שהוא טמא ונמצא כאלו מטמא התרומה בידים: הדרן עלך אור לארבעה עשר: כל שעה שמותר לאכול מאכיל לבהמה ולחיה וכו' מתני' דלא כר' יהודה דאי ר' יהודה התנן ר' יהודה אומר אוכלין כל ארבע ותולין כל חמש ושורפין בתחלת שש והא איכא שעה חמישית שהוא אינו אוכל ומאכיל לבהמה ומותר בהנאתו אלא מאי ר' מאיר היא דקתני אוכלין כל חמש אי הכי כל שעה שאוכלין מאכיל מבעי ליה למתנא ולא עמדה לא זו ולא זו ואוקמינן לר"ג דתאני בפ"ק ר"ג אומר חולין נאכלין כל ארבע ותרומה כל חמש ושורפין בתחלת שש והכי קתני כל שעה שכהן מותר לאכול תרומה מאכיל ישראל חולין לבהמה ולחיה כו': ומוכרו לנכרי פשיטא. כלומר מאחר דקתני ומותר בהנאתו מוכרו לנכרי למאי אתא ואוקימנא לאפוקי מהני תנאי דתניא בסוף פ' יציאות השבת ב"ש אומר לא ימכור אדם חמצו לנכרי אלא אם כן יודע שכלה קודם הפסח ב"ה אומר כל שעה שמותר לאכול מותר למכור ר' יהודה

כן

to him: [21a] The compromise of a third [view] is not a compromise.[11]

a R. Jose son of R. Ḥanina said: The controversy[1] is where it falls into less than one hundred *se'ahs* of unclean *ḥullin;*[2] but if it falls into one hundred [*se'ahs*] unclean *ḥullin*, all agree that it must descend and be defiled, and he must not defile it with [his own] hands.[3] It was taught likewise: If a cask [of clean *terumah*] was broken in the upper vat, and beneath it there is one hundred [times as much] unclean *ḥullin*, R. Eliezer concedes to R. Joshua that if he can save a *rebi'ith* thereof in purity he must save it, but if not, let it descend and be defiled, but he must not defile it with [his own] hands. [But instead of] this [phrase], 'R. Eliezer concedes to R. Joshua', 'R. Joshua concedes to R. Eliezer' is required?[4]—Said Raba: Reverse it. R. Huna the son of R. Joshua said: After all you need not reverse it: what case do we discuss here? That of a vessel, the inside is clean while its outside[5] is unclean; you might say, Let us enact a preventive measure lest its outside touch the *terumah*. Therefore he informs us [otherwise].[6]

CHAPTER II

MISHNAH. THE WHOLE TIME THAT ONE IS PERMITTED
b TO EAT [LEAVEN], ONE MAY FEED IT TO CATTLE, BEASTS,[1] AND BIRDS, AND HE MAY SELL IT TO A GENTILE, AND BENEFIT THEREOF IS PERMITTED. WHEN ITS PERIOD HAS PASSED, BENEFIT THEREOF IS FORBIDDEN, AND HE MAY NOT FIRE AN OVEN OR A POT RANGE WITH IT. R. JUDAH SAID: THERE IS NO REMOVAL OF LEAVEN SAVE BY BURNING; BUT THE SAGES MAINTAIN: HE ALSO[2] CRUMBLES AND THROWS IT TO THE WIND OR CASTS IT INTO THE SEA.

GEMARA. THE WHOLE TIME THAT ONE IS PERMITTED TO EAT [LEAVEN] ONE MAY FEED etc. Hence the whole time that one is not permitted to eat it, he may not feed [cattle, etc., therewith]: shall we say that our Mishnah is not according to R. Judah; for if R. Judah, surely there is the fifth hour when he may not eat, yet he may feed. For we learned: R. Meir said: One may eat [leaven] the whole of the five [hours] and must burn [it] at the beginning of the sixth. R. Judah said: One may eat the whole of the four [hours], keep it in suspense the whole of the fifth, and must burn it at the beginning of the sixth![3]—What then? It is R. Meir! [Then instead of] this [phrase], 'THE WHOLE TIME THAT ONE IS PERMITTED TO EAT, ONE MAY FEED,' THE WHOLE TIME THAT ONE eats, he MAY FEED is required?[4]—Said Rabbah b. 'Ulla: Our Mishnah agrees with R. Gamaliel, For we learned: R. Gamaliel said: *Ḥullin* may be eaten the whole of the four [hours] and *terumah* the whole of the five, and we burn [them] at the beginning of the sixth. And this is what he [the Tanna] states: THE WHOLE TIME THAT IT IS PERMITTED to a priest to eat *terumah*, a [lay] Israelite MAY FEED HIS CATTLE, BEASTS AND BIRDS with *ḥullin*.

For what purpose does he state, CATTLE and for what purpose does he state BEASTS?—They are necessary: for if he stated CATTLE, [I might say,] that is because if they leave over it is fit
c for them;[1] but [as for] BEASTS, which if they leave over hide it,[2] I would say [that it is] not [so]. While if he stated BEASTS, [I might say], that is because if they leave over they at least hide it;[3] but as for cattle, sometimes they leave over and he [the owner] may not think about it,[4] and so transgress[5] *'it shall not be seen'* and *'it shall not be found'* on its account, [and therefore] I might say [that it is] not [so]: thus they [both] are necessary. What is the purpose of BIRDS?—Because he states CATTLE and BEASTS, he also states BIRDS.

AND HE MAY SELL IT TO A GENTILE. That is obvious?[6]—It is to reject [the view of] this Tanna. For it was taught: Beth Shammai maintain: A man must not sell his leaven to a Gentile, unless he knows thereof that it will be consumed before Passover; but Beth Hillel say: So long as he [the Jew] may eat it, he may

(11) Since Beth Shammai and Beth Hillel mention nothing about a house or a field, new or old, this is not a compromise but an independent view altogether; cf. *supra* 13a, n. a5.

(1) Between R. Eliezer and R. Joshua. (2) The *terumah* in the upper vat being a *se'ah*. If *terumah* falls into one hundred times as much *ḥullin* it is nullified and permitted to a lay Israelite; if less, it is not nullified. (3) Since it will still be fit for a lay Israelite. (4) It is R. Eliezer who holds that he must never defile deliberately, while it is *R. Joshua* who permits deliberate defilement in other circumstances (v. *supra* 20b). (5) Lit., 'back'. (6) Thus 'R. Eliezer concedes to R. Joshua' applies not to the second clause but to the first, where it is stated that if he can save a *rebi'ith* in purity he must do so. Thereupon we are told that even if the outside of the vessel in which it is to be saved is unclean, so that there is the slight possibility of the *terumah* falling thereon and becoming contaminated, yet R. Eliezer, who rules that in no circumstances is deliberate defilement permitted, admits that he may use this for saving the *terumah*. If unclean liquid falls on the outside of a vessel it contaminates the outside, but not the inside, since the uncleanness of a vessel through liquids is by Rabbinical law only.

b (1) *Behemah* refers to domesticated animals; *ḥayyah* to wild or semi-wild animals. (2) 'Also' is absent in Alfasi and Asheri. (3) 'Keeping it in suspense' means that animals may be fed with it, but it may not be eaten. (4) The impersonal form used in the Mishnah implies that as long as one person may eat, *another* may feed his cattle.

c (1) Later; they leave it on the ground and eat it later. (2) With the result that the leaven may remain in his possession during Passover. (3) So that it is not seen. (4) To annul it before Passover, thinking it was already eaten. (5) Lit., 'stands'. (6) Surely this is no worse than any other benefit.

clean] earthen vessel: [20b] therefore it is stated, *whatsoever is in it shall be unclean*, and in proximity thereto, *all food therein which*
a *may be eaten:*[1] food becomes unclean through the air space of an [unclean] earthen vessel, but no utensils become unclean through the air space of an [unclean] earthen vessel.[2]

R. Ḥisda opposed two teachings of Passover, and reconciled [them]. Did R. Joshua say, Both of them [may be burnt] together?[3] But the following contradicts it: R. Jose said [to R. Meir]: The conclusion is not similar to the premise. For when our Masters testified, concerning what did they testify? If concerning flesh which was defiled through a derivative uncleanness, that we burn it together with flesh which was defiled through a father of uncleanness, [then] this is unclean and that is unclean. If concerning oil which was rendered unfit by a *ṭebul yom*, that it is lit in a lamp which was defiled by one unclean through a corpse,—one is unfit and the other is unclean. So too do we admit in the case of *terumah* which was defiled through a derivative uncleanness, that we may burn it together with *terumah* which was defiled through a 'father' of uncleanness. But how can we burn even that which is doubtful together with that which is unclean: perhaps Elijah will come and declare it clean![4] And he answered: one[5] agrees with R. Simeon, and in accordance with R. Joshua, while the other agrees with R. Jose, and in accordance with R. Joshua.[6] For it was taught: If the fourteenth falls on the Sabbath, everything [*sc.* leaven] must be removed before the Sabbath, and *terumoth*, unclean, doubtful, and clean are burnt [together]: this is R. Meir's view. R. Jose said: The clean [*terumah* must be burnt] separately, the doubtful [*terumah*] separately, and the unclean separately. Said R. Simeon: R. Eliezer and R. Joshua did not differ concerning clean and unclean, that they must not be burnt [together], and concerning doubtful [*terumah*] and clean [*terumah*] that they may be burnt [together]. Concerning what did they differ? Concerning doubtful [*terumah*] and unclean [*terumah*], R. Eliezer maintaining: This must be burnt separately, and this separately; while R. Joshua ruled: Both of them [may be burnt] together. But our
b Mishnah is according to R. Jose?[1]—R. Jose says thus to R. Meir: Even R. Simeon, who in stating R. Joshua's opinion is lenient, is lenient only in respect of doubtful [*terumah*] and unclean [*terumah*], but not in the case of clean and unclean.

R. Jose son of R. Ḥanina opposed *terumah* to Passover, and reconciled them. Did then R. Joshua say, Both together: But the following contradicts it: A cask of *terumah* wherein a doubt of uncleanness is born, R. Eliezer said: If lying in an exposed place, it must be laid in a hidden place; and if it was uncovered, it must be covered. R. Joshua said: If it is lying in a hidden place, one may lay it in an exposed place, and if it is covered, it may be uncovered.[2] Thus only an indirect action [is permitted], but not [defiling] with [one's own] hands?[3]—And he answered: One agrees with R. Simeon and according to R. Joshua's view, while the other agrees with R. Jose and according to R. Joshua's view.[4]

R. Eleazar opposed two teachings of *terumah* and reconciled them. Did R. Joshua say, only an indirect action [is permitted], but not with [one's own] hands? But the following contradicts it: If a cask of [wine of clean] *terumah* is broken in the upper vat, while [in] the lower there is unclean *ḥullin:* R. Eliezer and R. Joshua agree that if a *rebi'ith* thereof can be saved in purity, one must save it. But if not,—R. Eliezer ruled: Let it descend and be defiled, yet let him not defile it with [his own] hands; R. Joshua said: He may even defile it with his own hands?—And he answered: There it is different, because there is the loss of *ḥullin*. To this Raba demurred: In our Mishnah too there is the loss of wood? —Said Abaye to him: They cared about a substantial loss, but
c not about a slight loss.[1] And whence do you know that they cared about a substantial loss but not about a slight one? Because it was taught: If a cask of oil of [clean] *terumah* was broken in the upper vat, while in the lower is unclean *ḥullin:* R. Eliezer concedes to R. Joshua that if a *rebi'ith* thereof can be saved in purity, one must save it. But if not, let it descend and be defiled, yet let him not defile it with [his own] hands.[2] Why is oil different: because it is fit for lighting? Then wine too is fit for sprinkling?[3] And should you answer, sprinkling is of no account,—surely, Samuel said in R. Ḥiyya's name: You drink [wine] at a *sela'* per *log*, whereas you sprinkle [with wine] at two *sela's* per *log*?[4]—It refers to new [wine].[5] But it is fit for ageing?—One will come to a stumbling-block through it.[6] Then oil too, one will come to a stumbling-block through it?—He pours it into a dirty[7] vessel.[8] Wine too can be poured into a dirty vessel?—Seeing that it is required for sprinkling, will he pour it into a dirty vessel!

Now a stumbling-block itself is dependent on Tannaim.[9] For it was taught: A cask of wine of *terumah* which was defiled,—Beth Shammai maintain: It must be poured out all at once; while Beth Hillel rule: It may be used for sprinkling. R. Ishmael son of R. Jose said: I will make a compromise. [If it is] in the field, it must be poured out all at once;[10] in the house, it can be used for sprinkling. Others state: In the case of new [wine], it must be poured out all at once; in the case of old, it can be used for sprinkling. Said they

a (1) Lev. XI, 33f. (2) But if the *sherez* were regarded as completely filling the oven, utensils therein too should be unclean, for direct contact therewith does defile them. (3) *Sc.* unclean *terumah* and doubtful *terumah*. (4) V. *supra* p. 15*a* for notes. (5) Our Mishnah. (6) I.e., R. Simeon and R. Jose differ on R. Joshua's opinion.

b (1) How then can it be said to represent the view of R. Simeon? (2) V. *supra* 15*a* for notes. (3) Though it is doubtful. (4) Who says, how can we burn even doubtful *terumah* together with unclean *terumah*? Thus he will certainly not permit more than indirect action.

c (1) V. *supra* 15*a* and *b* for notes. (2) All agree on this, because the loss of *ḥullin* is only slight, since the defiled *terumah* can be used for lighting. (3) In a room, for its aroma. Hence here too there is only a slight loss. (4) Thus it is even more important. (5) Which lacks aroma. (6) While it is ageing he may forget that it is unclean and drink it. (7) Lit., 'repulsive'. (8) So that it will not be fit for drinking. (9) I.e., whether we fear it or not. (10) Because there is no sprinkling in the field, nor may he bring it home, lest it become a stumbling-block in the meanwhile.

קלא א מיי' פ"ה מהל' טומאת מת הל' ו וס"ג מהל' כלים הל' ג:
קלב ב שם הלכה ג:
קלג ג ד מיי' פי"ב מה' תרומות הלכה ה:
קלד ה שם הלכה יב:

מי אמר ר' יהושע שתיהן כאחת ורמינהו חבית. אומר ר"י הא דלא משני פסח שאני דמשמע ליה דפסח לא מעלה ולא מוריד מדשרי בתלויה ואסר בטהורות א"כ מה שהיא תלויה הוי הטעם: **הא** ר' שמעון אליבא דר' יהושע. תימה לר"י לר' שמעון כיון דשרי תלויה לטמא ביד א"כ שרי לשורפו ואמאי קרי ליה תלויה דתלויה היינו לא אוכלין ולא שורפין וי"ל דתלויה לר"ש היינו דלא מחייב לשורפו: **ראוי** לזילוף. אף על גב דתרומה טמאה בשריפה כיון דמסקינן בפ' בתרא דתמורה (דף לג.) הראוי לשריפה שרפה הראוי לקבורה קבורה והוא הדין בכי האי גוונא הואיל וראוי לזילוף* אין

[וע"ע תוס' שבת דף כה. ד"ה כך]

ת"ל *כל אשר בתוכו יטמא וסמיך ליה מכל האוכל *אוכל מטמא מאויר כלי חרס *ואין כל הכלים מטמאין מאויר כלי חרס: רב חסדא רמי פיסחא אפיסחא ומשני מי א"ר יהושע שתיהן כאחת ורמינהו *א"ר יוסי אין הנדון דומה לראיה כשהעידו רבותינו על מה העידו אם על הבשר שנטמא בולד הטומאה ששורפין אותו עם הבשר שנטמא באב הטומאה זה טמא וזה טמא אם על השמן שנפסל בטבול יום שמדליקין אותו בנר שנטמא בטמא מת זה פסול וזה טמא אף אנו מודים בתרומה שנטמאת בולד הטומאה ששורפין אותה עם התרומה שנטמאת באב הטומאה אבל היאך נשרוף אפילו תלויה עם הטמאה שמא יבא אליהו ויטהרם ומשני הא ר"ש ואליבא דר' יהושע הא ר' יוסי ואליבא דר' יהושע *דתניא י"ד שחל להיות בשבת מבערין את הכל מלפני השבת ושורפין תרומות טמאות תלויות וטהורות דברי ר' מאיר ר' יוסי אומר טהורה בפני עצמה ותלויה בפני עצמה וטמאה בפני עצמה אמר ר"ש לא נחלקו ר' אליעזר ור' יהושע על הטהורה ועל הטמאה שאין שורפין על התלויה ועל הטהורה ששורפין על מה נחלקו על התלויה ועל הטמאה שר' אליעזר אומר תישרף זו בעצמה וזו בעצמה ור' יהושע אומר שתיהן כאחת והא מתניתין ר' יוסי היא הכי קאמר ר' יוסי לר' מאיר אפילו ר"ש ואליבא דר' יהושע דמיקל כי מיקל בתלויה וטמאה אבל בטהורה וטמאה לא: רבי יוסי בר' חנינא רמי תרומה אפיסחא ומשני מי אמר ר' יהושע שתיהן כאחת ורמינהו *חבית של תרומה שנולד בה ספק טומאה רבי אליעזר אומר אם היתה מונחת במקום התורפה יניחנה במקום המוצנע ואם היתה מגולה יכסנה רבי יהושע אומ' אם היתה מונח' במקום המוצנע יניחנה במקום התורפה ואם היתה מכוסה יגלנה גרמא אין בידים לא ומשני הא רבי שמעון אליבא דר' יהושע הא ר' יוסי אליבא דר' יהושע ר' אלעזר רמי תרומה אתרומה ומשני מי אמר ר' יהושע גרמא אין בידים לא ורמינהו *חבית של תרומה שנשברה בגת העליונה ותחתיה חולין טמאין מודה ר' אליעזר (*לר') יהושע שאם יכול להציל ממנה רביעית בטהרה יציל ואם לאו ר' אליעזר אומר תרד ותטמא ואל יטמאנה ביד *ר' יהושע אומר יטמאנה ביד ומשני שאני התם דאיכא הפסד חולין מתקיף לה רבא מתני' נמי איכא הפסד עצים א"ל אביי *להפסד מרובה חששו להפסד מועט לא חששו ומנא תימרא דלהפסד מרובה חששו ולהפסד מועט לא חששו דתניא *חבית של שמן תרומה שנשברה בגת העליונה ובתחתונה חולין טמאין מודה ר' אליעזר לר' יהושע שאם יכול להציל ממנה רביעית בטהרה יציל ואם לאו תרד ותטמא ואל יטמאנה ביד *מ"ש שמן דראוי להדליק יין נמי ראוי לזילוף וכ"ת זילוף לאו מילתא היא והאמר שמואל משום ר' חייא שותין מלוג בסלע ומזלפין מלוג בשתים בחדש והא ראוי לישנו *אתי ביה לידי תקלה שמן נמי אתי ביה לידי תקלה *דרמי ליה בכלי מאוס יין נמי רמי ליה בכלי מאוס לזילוף קא בעי ליה בכלי מאוס רמי ליה *ותקלה עצמה תנאי היא דתניא חבית של יין של תרומה שנטמאת ב"ש אומרים תשפך *חבל ובית הלל אומרים תעשה זילוף אמר רבי ישמעאל ברבי יוסי אני אכריע בשדה תשפך חבל בבית תעשה זילוף איכא דאמרי בחדש תשפך חבל בישן תעשה זילוף אמרו לו אין

ת"ל וסמיך ליה מכל האוכל. כלומר האי כל אשר בתוכו שאמרתי לך באוכל אמרתי לך ולאו כמאן דמלי טומאה חשיב ליה לחיצון כמלאת טומאה נוגעת בגבו של כלי שטף וכלי שטף מטמא מגבו אלא שמע מינה כל אשר בתוכו יטמא מחמת כלי הוא דמטמא ואשמעינן קרא דאוכלין ומשקין הוא דמקבלי טומאה מולד הטומאה אבל כלי לא ומהאי פירוקא נפקא לן בכל דוכתא הא דאשכחן דאין כלי ראשון מטמא כלי ואין אוכלין ומשקין מטמאין כלי כדיליף לעיל מק"ו ואדם נמי שאינו אב הטומאה כגון נוגע בטומאת נבלה ובשרץ לא מטמא כלי דכתיב והנוגע בנבלתם יטמא ולא כתיב כבוס בגדים אבל גבי נושא גזירת הכתוב היא בטומאת משא שמטמא אדם לטמא בגדים שעליו בשעת משא ולא בגדים הבאין לאחר מכאן אלמא ולד הטומאה לא מטמא כלי חוץ מטמא מת שהוא אב הטומאה וכן אדם לא מצינו לו טומאה בכל התורה אלא מאב הטומאה כגון ע"י שרץ ונבלה ושכבת זרע ועל ידי זב ומעיינותיו ומדרסו ועל ידי נדה ומעיינותיה ומדרסה וע"י טמא מת: שתיהן כאחת. בתלויה וטמאה בחמץ בפסח: ורמינהו כו'. וקתני היאך ישרף אפילו תלויה עם הטמאה: מתני' ר' שמעון היא ואליבא דרבי יהושע. וברייתא רבי יוסי אמרה כדקתני אמר ר' יוסי אין הנדון כו' ולקמן פריך והא מתני' ר' יוסי נמי קאמר לה דתנן א"ר יוסי אינה היא המדה: ושורפין תרומה תלויה וטמאה וטהורה. הכל ביחד ר' מאיר לטעמיה דאמר מדבריהם למדנו ששורפין תרומה טהורה עם הטמאה בפסח: ה"ג לא נחלקו רבי אליעזר ורבי יהושע על טהורה ועל טמאה שאין שורפין על התלויה ועל הטהורה ששורפין. דהואיל ולא הוחזק טומאה אין נראה כמטמא בידים: על מה נחלקו על התלויה ועל הטמאה. דהואיל ואין לה טומאה ודאית הרי היא מטמא בידים לר' אליעזר ור' יהושע סבר כיון דתלויה היא אי אתה מוזהר על שמירתה: רמי תרומה אפיסחא. תרומה דעלמא אתרומה דפיסחא: ומי א"ר יהושע שתיהן כאחת. דמותר לטמא תלויה בידים: בידים לא. ואע"ג דתלויה היא: הא. דקתני בידים לא ר' יוסי היא ואליבא דר' יהושע דגבי תלויה דפיסחא נמי הכי אמר ואנן היאך נשרוף אפילו תלויה עם הטמאה: מתני' נמי איכא הפסד עצים. ואמאי קאמר רבי יוסי אליבא דרבי יהושע דלא: מודה רבי אליעזר כו'. אמסקנא קאי אאם לאו תרד ותטמא ולקמן פריך מודה רבי יהושע לרבי אליעזר מבעי ליה מכל מקום קתני גבי שמן דכולהו מודו שלא יטמאנה בידים משום הפסד חולין דשמן חולין שנתערב תרומה בהן יאסרו לכהן ולזר משום טומאה דתרומה משום דהפסד מועט הוא כדמפרש דראוי להדליק: לאו מילתא היא. לא חשיב והרי הפסידו: שותין מלוג. שנמכר בסלע ומזלפין מלוג הנמכר בשתים טוח לקנות לוג בשתי סלעים לזילוף מלקנותו לשתיה ומי שאינו עשיר יקח יין בזול לשתייתו לוג בסלע ויין ביוקר לזילוף: בחדש. דאין ריחו נודף ואין ראוי לזילוף: אתי ביה לידי תקלה. אם ישהנו אצלו עד שיתיישן אתי למשתי מיניה: לזלוף קבעי ליה. וצריך שיהא לו ריחו טוב ובכלי מאוס רמי ליה בתמיה: ותקלה עצמה. אי חיישינן לה ואסור לשהויי אי לא תנאי היא: תשפך חבל (א). לשון חבילה כלומר תשפך יחד ולא לזלף דילמא אדמזלף קלי קלי אפי' בו ביום אתי למשתיה: בשדה תשפך חבל. שאין מזלפין בשדה והא לא אמרינן שיביאנה בבית לזלפו דאדהכי אתי ביה לידי תקלה: ואיכא דאמרי. לשהייה מועטת (לא חיישינן) כי הא מן השדה לבית לא חיישינן אלא בחדש תשפך חבל כו' (ב): *אמר רבי ישמעאל ברבי יוסי. כמה שנים אחר בית הלל וב"ש היה: אמרו לו. בני דורו: אין

הגהות הב"ח

(א) רש"י ד"ה תשפך חבל. נ"ב ובב"ק דף קטו גרס הכל וכן נ"ל נכון: (ב) רש"י ד"ה ולאיכא דאמרי וכו' חבל וכו' הס"ד ואח"כ מ"ה אמרו לו לאו ב"ש וב"ה קאמרי דהא ר' ישמעאל בר' יוסי כמה שנים אחר ב"ה וב"ש היה אלא אמרו לו בני דורו וכו' כצ"ל והד"א:

[נ"ל דזה הדבור הוא מיותר. מראה אש]

רבינו חננאל

אמר ליה לא אמרינן כמאן דמלי שרצים ונימ' כאלו השרץ עצמו נגע בפת ותהוי הפת תחלה דתניא יכול יהו הכלים מטמאין מאויר כלי חרס ת"ל מכל האוכל אשר יאכל אוכלין ומשקין מטמאין מאויר כלי חרס ואין כלים מטמאין מאויר כ"ח ואי ס"ד דאמרינן כמאן דמלי [שרצים] דמי הא קא נגעי שרצי' בכלים אמאי לא מטמו אלא כיון דלא מיטמו הכלים מאויר כלי חרס ש"מ דלא אמרי' כמאן דמלי שרצים דמי. אחרי כל הדברים הללו חזרנו למשנתנו: רב חסדא רמי פסחא אפסחא תנן במתני' כי אמר ר' יוסי על התלויה ועל הטמאה נחלקו ר' אליעזר אומר תשרף זו בעצמה וזו בעצמה ר' יהושע אומר שתיהן כאחת איני והתניא אומר ר' יוסי אין הנדון דומה לראיה כו' אבל היאך נשרוף אפי' תלויה עם הטמאה שמא יבוא אליהו ויטהרנו פי' התלויה ומשני משנתנו כר' שמעון דמתני ששורפין התלויה והטמאה יחדו דברי יהושע וברייתא דקתני אבל היאך נשרוף אפילו תלויה וטמאה כאחת שמא יבא אליהו ויטהרנו ר' יוסי אליבא דר' יהושע ומקשי' והא ר' יוסי היא דקתני במתני' כי ר' יהושע אומר התלויה והטמאה שתיהן כאחת ואיך מוקמת לה לברייתא כר' יוסי דתניא אבל היאך נשרוף אפי' תלויה וטמאה ושנינן הכי קאמר ליה ר' יוסי לר' מאיר לדידי אפי' תלויה עם הטמאה אין שורפין אלא אפי' לר' שמעון אליבא דר' יהושע דמיקל לא מיקל אלא בתלויה וטמאה אבל טהורה וטמאה לא שרפינן: ר' יוסי בר' חנינא רמי תרומה אפסח ומשני איך אתה שונה שר' יהושע אומר שתים כא' שנמצא מטמא התלויה בידים והלא בחבית של תרומה שנולד בה ספק טומאה לא התיר לטמאותה בידים אלא ע"י גרמא ומשני כרב חסדא כי זה ששנינו במשנה ר' יוסי אפי' לר' שמעון שמיקל אליבא דר' יהושע חשיב לר' מאיר. ומשנה דתרומה אליבא דר' יהושע שנאה ר' יוסי אליבא דידיה דמחמיר: ר' אלעזר רמי תרומה אתרומה ומשני אני דלא התיר ר' יהושע בתלויה לטמא בידים והא בחבית של תרומה שנשברה בגת העליונה תחתונה יש בה חולין טמאה אמר ר' יהושע אף יטמאנה ביד. ומשני שאני התם דאיכא הפסד כלומר כיון שהגת התחתונה בתוכה חולין טמאים אם הוריד התרומה עליהם יפסידם. ואקשינן והא מתני' דאיכא הפסד עצים שאתה מצריכו לעשות שתי מדורות ולשרוף הטהורות באחת והטמאות [באחת] ולא חייש אלא אמר זו לעצמה וזו לעצמה ושנינן להפסד מרובה כגון הפסד של חולין חששו אבל הפסד מועט שהוא של עצים לא חששו ושמעינן האי סברא מהא דתניא חבית של שמן של תרומה שנשברה בגת העליונה והתחתונה טמאה ולא התיר ר' יהושע לטמאה ביד כדרך שהתיר ביין אלא אמר תרד ותטמא ואל יטמא ביד לאו מכלל דכיון שאינו הפסד מרובה בשמן דהא ראוי להדליק לא חששו ואמרינן למה בשמן אינו הפסד מרובה משום דראוי להדליקו בנר ובין שמן העומד לאכילה לשמן העומד להדלקה הפסדו מועט גם היין הטמא נמי ראוי לזלף בו כשמן ולא עוד אלא שהיין הטוב הוא הנמכר לזילוף ואין בו הפסד דהא אמרי' שותין מלוג בסלע אבל לזילוף אין מזלפין אלא מן המובחר הנמכר לוג בשני סלעים. ודחי' זה היין חדש הוא שאינו ראוי לזילוף כשמן ואמרי' יניחנו עד שתישן ודחינן חיישינן דלמא אינשי ושתי ליה אי הכי שמן נמי ניחוש דלמא אכיל ליה ודחי' שמן רמי ליה בכלי מאוס אבל יין דבעי ליה לזילוף וריחו הוא דבעיא אי רמי ליה נמר ריחו חיים ולא שדי ליה ואתי ביה לידי תקלה ותקלה תנאי היא דתניא חבית של יין של תרומה שנטמא ב"ש אומר תשפך הכל וחייש לתקלה וב"ה אומר תעשה זילוף ולא חייש לתקלה והלכה כב"ה ואע"ג דאמר ר' ישמעאל בר' יוסי אני אכריע וקיימא לן כל מקום ששנים חלוקים ואחד מכריע הלכה כדברי המכריע ר' ישמעאל תלמיד הוא ולא חשיב ר' ישמעאל בר' יוסי לאכרועי דהא ר' יוסי אביו של ר' ישמעאל שאמר שמועה זו משמו תלמיד שלישי לגבי ב"ה וב"ש הוא לכשתחשוב מרבן יוחנן בן זכאי שהוא תלמיד להלל עצמו עד ר' יוסי אתה מוצא אותם שלשה ר' יהושע ור' עקיבא ור' יוסי ולא עדיף ר' ישמעאל לאכרועי

נשאלין עליה אפילו בכלי המונח על גבי קרקע כדבר שיש בו דעת לישאל והבשר טמא האי בשר דאיתכשר במאי אי נימא דאיתכשר בדם והא *א"ר חייא בר אבא א"ר יוחנן מנין לדם קדשים שאינו מכשיר שנאמר °לא תאכלנו על הארץ תשפכנו כמים דם שנשפך כמים מכשיר ושאינו נשפך כמים אינו מכשיר ואלא דאיתכשר במשקי בית מטבחיא והא א"ר יוסי בר' חנינא *משקי בית מטבחיא לא דיין שהן דכן אלא שאין מכשירין ואלא דאיתכשר בחיבת הקודש אימור דמהניא ליה חיבת הקודש לאיפסולי גופיה למימנא ביה ראשון ושני נמי תיפשוט *דבעי ריש לקיש צריד של מנחות *מונין בו ראשון ושני או לא *אמר רב יהודה אמר שמואל כגון שהיתה פרה של זבחי שלמים והעבירה בנהר ושחטה ועדיין משקה טופח עליה נמצאת בפרש הכל טהור ונהדר פרש וניטמייה לבשר אמר רב אדא בר אהבה בפרש עבה רב אשי אמר אפי' תימא בפרש רכה *משום דהוי משקה סרוח תני תנא קמיה דרב ששת שרץ מטמא את המשקין ומשקין מטמאין את הכלי וכלי מטמא את האוכלין והאוכלין מטמאין את המשקין ולמדנו שלש טומאות בשרץ הני ארבעה הן גוז משקין דסיפא לא אשכחן תנא דאמר משקין מטמאין כלי אלא רבי יהודה והדר ביה וסימניך נזייתא *תנן התם שרץ שנמצא בתנור הפת שבתוכו שניה מפני שהתנור תחלה אמר ליה רב אדא בר אהבה לרבא וניחזי להאי תנור כמאן דמלי טומאה דמי ותיהוי האי פת ראשונה אמר ליה לא סלקא דעתך *דתניא יכול יהו כל הכלים מטמאין מאויר כלי חרס ת"ל

תורה אור: דברים יב

לא דיין שהן דכן אלא שאין מכשירין. לא בעי לשנויי תרגומא אלא דס דלעיל* תירץ כן מחמת דוחק וזה שאין מכשירין משום דס"ל דתלושים לא מכשירין דדריש יטמא דכתי' גבי משקין יטמא ממש ולא הכשר וליכא אלא חד קרא בהכשר וס"ל לאוקמי טפי במחוברין מבתלושין: **אלא** דאיתכשר בחיבת הקודש. וא"ת אי חיבת הקודש מהניא למימני ביה ראשון ושני מאי נפקא מינה דהאי משקין בית מטבחיא דכן ואין מכשירין ואור"י דאיצטריך לכמה דברים שמצויין בעזרה דלא שייך בהו חיבת הקודש כגון ביכורים או חולין שאוכלין בעזרה כדי לאכול המנחה והזבח על השובע כדאיתא בהקומץ רבה (מנחות כא:)*: **ובשעת** שחיטה עדיין משקה טופח עליה. פירש הקונטרס דאי אפשר שלא יפול מן העור על הבשר ואין נראה דאם כן הוי ליה תלושין ותלושין לא מכשירין כיון דדריש שמחובר יטמא ממש וליכא אלא חד קרא בהכשר והוא מוקי לה במחוברים ולהכי נקט והעבירה בנהר משום דבעי הכשר מן הנהר שהוא מחובר ואומר ר"י דעל ידי העור הוכשר הבשר דהעור והרוטב (חולין קיח:) פליגי אי יש יד להכשיר אבל לכולי עלמא יש שומר להכשיר וכל העור בא מים בעודם מחוברים: מי

נשאלין עליה. כלומר חשבינן לה לטמא אותה כאילו יש בה דעת לישאל לשון אחר כשאלין לב"ד מה תהא עליו (א) וזו עיקר כשאלין עליה בעלים יהו כשאלין בעל כרחן בשבילה לב"ד מה תהא עלה: ואפילו הוא כלי מונח על גבי קרקע. כלומר אע"ג דכלי טהור זה שנולד בו הספק אין בו דעת לישאל וכו לא היה אדם עוסק שיהא מוליכו ומביאו בידו אבל אדם עסוק בטומאה שהיה נושא שרץ בידו ספק נגע בכלי ספק לא נגע אם רה"י הוא ספיקו טמא: האי בשר דאיתכשר במאי. ה"כ מאי בעי אקרא והבשר אשר יגע בכל טמא במאי איתכשר והיכא למימר בשר דקרא פשיטא דאיירי הכשר טובא דבשר של שלמים נאכל בכל העיר ולכל אדם ושם מדיחין אותו ומבשלין אותו ואיכא הכשר טובא אבל בהמה זו שנמצאת בבשרה מחט בעזרה במקום שחיטה ומהיכן קבל הבשר הכשר דמה אינו מכשיר מדר' חייא בר אבא א"ר יוחנן כו': משקה בית מטבחיא. שהודאה בכן אינו מכשיר: אלא דאיתכשר בחיבת הקודש. חיבת הקודש מכשרתה לבוא לידי טומאה דקיימא לן בפרק שני דשחיטת חולין חיבת הקודש משוה לה אוכל לקבולי טומאה: למימני ביה ראשון ושני. שיהא הוא מטמא אחרים דקתני הבשר טמא ולא קתני הבשר פסול: נמי. בתמיה א"כ תיפשוט מדקתני טמא משמע מטמא אחרים משום הכשר חיבת הקודש תיפשוט דבעי ריש לקיש בשחיטת חולין: צריד של מנחות. יבש של מנחות מקום שלא נגע שם שמן: צריד. לשון יבש ודומה לו גבי שופר (ר"ה ד' כז:) היה קולו דק או עבה או צריד. להכי נקט פרה של זבחי שלמים לפי שהעור והבשר לבעלים ומתעסק ליפות העור והבשר ומעבירה בנהר סמוך לשחיטה ומשקין אותה כדי שתהא נוחה להפשיט כדאמרינן בסוטה דבילה*: ועדיין משקה טופח עליה. ואי אפשר שלא יפול מן המשקה על הבשר כל שהוא בשעת הפשט: ונהדר פרש. דקא סלקא דעתך תורת משקה עליו שהרי בשעה זו השקה אותה: בפרש עבה. דלאו משקה הוא: שרץ מטמא את המשקין. מקל וחומר מכלי כדלעיל ומשקין שבאו מחמת שרץ מטמאין כלי כדיליף מבכל כלי יטמא וקא סבר יטמא הכלי מן המשקה כדהוה דריש לה ר' יהודה מיקמי דהדר ביה ודריש ביה נמי להאי יטמא יטמא ויליף מיניה דחוזר כלי זה ומטמא את האוכלין כדאשכחן בהו דכלים מטמאין (ג) מכל אשר בתוכו יטמא מכל האוכל משמע שנטמא האוכל מאויר כלי חרס והאוכלין את המשקין כו' ומיהו לא מיתרצא היא דהאי אוכל הבא מחמת כלי דקאמר קרא דמטמא משקה לאו מכלי הבא מחמת משקה קאי אלא בבא מחמת שרץ ותנא תני למדנו שלש טומאות בשרץ דמשמע דטומאה הולכת מזה לזה ומזה לזה ומהכא הוה מלינו למיפרכיה למילתיה אלא דאקשי ליה קושיא אחריתי מפורשת טפי דקתני שלש וקא חשיב ארבע והיא היא: והאוכלין מטמאין את המשקין. דדריש יטמא דגבי אוכלין יטמא לטמא אוכלין המשקין כדדריש ליה ר"ע והוא הדין דמלי למיתני וכלי מטמא את המשקין ומשקין מטמאין אוכלין כיון דאית ליה יטמא יטמא אלא חדא מינייהו נקט ותרווייהו לא מצי למיתני דנימא כלי מטמא את האוכלין ואוכלין את המשקין ומשקין שבאו מן האוכלין מטמאין את האוכלין דהא ליתא בקרא אפי' לר' עקיבא דהוה ליה שלישי עושה רביעי דוכל משקה אשר ישתה אתוכו דכלי חרס קאי שקיבל המשקה הזה טומאה מן הכלי וכי דרשת יטמא יטמא אכתי שני עושה שלישי משכחת מיניה אבל שלישי עושה רביעי לא ילפת מיניה: הני ארבעה הוין. שלישי עושה רביעי לא משכחת ליה בקרא דכי כתיב אוכל הבא מחמת כלי מטמא משקה לאו בכלי הבא מחמת משקה כתיב אלא בכלי הבא מחמת שרץ ותנא גופיה חשיב ארבע ותני שלש: גוז משקין דרישא. מתוך משקין הראשונים ואימא שרץ מטמא את הכלי והכלי את האוכל ואוכל את המשקה וכן הן סדורין במקרא ור' עקיבא הוא דדריש יטמא יטמא ושני עושה שלישי והוא הדין דמלי למיתני נמי שרץ כלי וכלי משקה ומשקה אוכל וחדא מינייהו נקט כדפרשינן דתרווייהו לא מצי למתני והא אתא לאשמעינן דשני עושה שלישי בחולין: אדרבה גוז משקין דסיפא. ואימא שרץ משקה ומשקה כלי מבכל כלי יטמא כדהוה דריש ליה ר' יהודה וכלי אוכל דרוש ביה להאי יטמא דכלי יטמא ומשקין דסיפא לא תיתני משום דרביעי לא כתיב ואע"ג דאוכל ודאי מטמא משקה הכא לא תתנייה דהאי אוכל דהכא שלישי הואי: אמר ליה לא אשכחן תנא כו'. ואי הכי תדרוש כמאן תוקמיה: וסימניך. שלא תטעה בסדרן: נזייתא. סדר מטילי שכר שעורין תחלה נותנין כלי ואח"כ אוכל ואח"כ משקה: שרץ שנמצא בתנור. ולא נגע בפת הפת שבתוכו שני לטומאה ואינם מטמאים חולין לרבנן מפני שהתנור תחלה התנור קיבל טומאה מן השרץ והפת מן התנור: וליחזייה להאי תנור כמאן דמלי טומאה. כיון דקיימא לן אויר כלי חרס מטמא מן השרץ אף על פי שלא נגע אלמא כמאן דמלי טומאה הוא דהא לא נגע בו ומטמאו ותיהוי נמי פת כאילו נוגעת בשרץ: יכול יהו כל הכלים. אם כלי שטף נתון בתוך כלי חרס ושרץ באויר החיצון יכול יהא כלי עץ או כלי מתכת שבתוכו טמא משום דכתיב כל אשר בתוכו יטמא:

ת"ל

רבינו חננאל

דעת להשאל [דמין] כר' יוחנן דאמר נשאלין עליה אפילו בכלי המונח על [גבי] קרקע ולפיכך אמר ברשות הרבים ספיקו טהור ברשות היחיד כי האי נתא ספיקו טמא והאי ספק טומאה ברשות הרבים ספיקו טהור ברשות היחיד ספיקא טמא גמרי' לה מסוטה דכתיב בה (במדבר ה יג) ונסתרה והיא נטמאה הנה כיון שנסתרה ספיקא הוא אלא כיון שברשות היחיד נסתרה אמרה תורה נטמאה וכו' ופשוטה היא וכבר פרשנוה בכמה מקומות לפיכך לא הארכנו בה: והקשי' זה הבשר היאך נטמא בלא הכשר משקה הא אוקימנ' לדם קדשים ולמשקה בית מטבחיא דלא מכשרי היכן הוכשר שנטמא ושני' דאיתכשר בחיבת הקדש כלומר תאות אדם לקדש משוה הדבר שמקדיש אע"פ שלא הוכשר במים כאלו הוכשר. ואמרי' אימור דמהניא חיבת הקדש כו' ואמרינן אי הכי תפשוט בעיא דריש לקיש דבעי צריד של מנחות פי' שהוא פסולת הסלת כגון המורסן וכיוצא בו מונין בו ראשון ושני או לא כלומר אם נגע השרץ בהאי צריד שלא הוכשר במים ונטמא אם יגע הוא באחרים מטמא או לא ולא איפשטא וכיון דלא איפשטא לא איתברר לן דמטמא ושני' דרך אחרת כגון בהמה של זבחי שלמים והעבירה בנהר ועדיין היה משקה טופח עליה ונשחטה והוכשר הבשר באותו משקה הטופח שהיה בעור נמצאת המחט בפרש הכל טהור אוקימ' אפי' בפרש רך שהוא כמים כיון דהוה ליה משקה סרוח אינו מטמא ואפילו למאן דאית ליה טומאה למשקין נהי דמטמא משקין הראויין לשתיה דאינן מקרי משקין אבל הני דסרוחין נינהו לא: תאני תנא הא דתנינן בתורת כהנים שהן דברי ר' עקיבא היה התנא שונה סתם השרץ מטמא את המשקה והמשקה את הכלי והכלי את האוכל והאוכל את המשקה למדנו שלש טומאות בשרץ אמר ליה רב ששת הני לפי מה שפירשת משקה וכלי ואוכל ומשקה ארבעה טומאות הן אלא גוז משקה דרישא כלומר העבר אותו ולא תאמר משקה מטמא את הכלי ולמען שלא יתחלף לך שים לך סימן נזייתא פי' המשקה שאמרת מטמא הכלים שהן נזייתא כדגרסינן בע"פ תמרי לבי נזייתא ארהים ועוד גרסי' מסדרביא דנזייתא סמי אותן דלא אשכחן תנא דאמר משקה מטמא כלי אלא ר' יהודה והדר ביה כדפרשינן לעילא: תנן התם השרץ שנמצא בתנור הפת שבתוכו שניה שהתנור תחלה ואמר ליה רב אדא בר אהבה לרבא זה השרץ לא נגע בכותלי התנור אלא נתלה באוירו ואתה רואה אותו כאלו נגע בכותלי התנור וטמאתו כן נחזייה להא תנור כמאן דמלי שרצים ונימא כאלו השרץ עצמו נגע בפת ותהוי הפת תחלה

שמו

עין משפט נר מצוה:

קכח א מיי' פ"ח מהל' אבות הטומאה הלכה ג:
קכט ב ג מיי' פ"י מהל' טומאת אוכלין הלכה יז:
קל ד מיי' פי"א מהל' אבות הטומאה ה"ב:

מסורת הש"ס:

[לעיל טז. (וש"נ)]
[לעיל טז. חולין לו:]
חולין לו. מנחות קב:
חולין לו:
[לעיל יח.]
שבת קלה: כלים פרק ח משנה ה
שבת קלה:
[דף מ.]

הגהות הב"ח

(א) רש"י ד"ה נשאלין וכו' מה תהא עליה וזו: (ב) ד"ה השרץ וכו' מטמאין אותן מכל אשר בתוכו:

we inquire about it,[7] even in the case of a utensil lying on the ground, just as though it were an object which has the understanding to be questioned.

'While the flesh is unclean'. By what was this flesh made fit?[8] Shall we say that it was made fit by the blood?—surely R. Ḥiyya b. Abba said in R. Joḥanan's name: How do we know that the blood of sacrifices does not make [anything] fit [to be defiled]? Because it is said, *thou shalt pour it out* [*sc.* the blood] *upon the earth as water:*[9] blood which is poured out as water renders fit; blood which is not poured out as water does not render fit.[10] Again, if it was made fit by the liquids of the slaughter-house,[11]—surely R. Jose b. R. Ḥanina said: The liquids of the [Temple] slaughter-house, not enough that they are clean, but they cannot even make [eatables] fit? Again, if it was made fit through the prizing of sacred objects,[12]—say that the prizing of sacred objects is efficacious in rendering that itself unfit, is it also [sufficient] that
a first and second degree should be counted therein?[1] [In that case] you may solve what Resh Lakish asked: The dry portion of meal-offerings,[2] do we count first and second degrees therein or not?[3] —Said Rab Judah in Samuel's name: E.g., if it was an animal for a peace-offering and it was led through a river and then slaughtered, and the water is still dripping upon it.[4]

'If found in the excrements, it is all clean.' But let the excrements defile the flesh in their turn?[5] Said R. Adda b. Ahabah: It refers to thick [solid] excrements.[6] R. Ashi said: You may even say that it refers to loose [fluidlike] excrements, [its non-defilement being] because it is a noisome liquid.[7]

A tanna recited before R. Shesheth: A *sherez* defiles liquids, and the liquids defile a utensil, and the utensil defiles eatables, and the eatables defile liquids,[8] and [thus] we learn three [stages of] uncleanness in the case of a *sherez*. But there are four?—Delete liquids in the first clause. On the contrary, delete liquids in the last clause?—We find no other Tanna who maintains [that] liquids defile utensils save R. Judah, and *he* retracted.[9] And your sign [for remembering the order] is the brewing process.[10]

We learned elsewhere: If a creeping thing is found in an oven, the bread therein is a second, because the oven is a first.[11] R. Adda b. Ahabah said to Raba: Let us regard this oven as though it were filled with uncleanness,[12] and let the bread be a first?—Said he to him, You cannot think so, for it was taught: You might think that all utensils become unclean through the air space of an [un-

(7) Rashi: its owners must consult Rabbinic authority about it—i.e., it is not automatically clean. (8) To contract defilement. A foodstuff is subject to defilement only after moisture has fallen upon it. (9) Deut. XII, 24. (10) V. *supra* 16*a* and *b* for notes. (11) E.g., the water with which it was washed down. (12) Sacred objects were prized so highly that they were fit to become unclean even without a liquid having been upon them.

a (1) For 'the flesh is unclean' implies that it can defile other flesh too (v. 14*a*, n. a2). (2) That which has not been touched by oil. (3) But if the prizing of sacred objects is so efficacious, obviously we do. (4) That water makes it fit to contract uncleanness.—The animal was led through the water immediately prior to its slaughter in order to facilitate flaying, v. Bez. 40*a*. (5) Lit., 'go back'. It is assumed that the excrements rank as a fluid, since the animal was watered immediately before slaughter (v. Bez. 40*a*). The needle should therefore defile the excrements, and that in turn should defile the flesh. (6) This is not a liquid. (7) V. *supra* 18*a*. (8) I.e., each in turn defiles the other. (9) Hence if we retain liquids in the first clause, there is no authority for the second clause, 'and liquids defile a utensil'. By deleting it, however, the reading becomes: a *sherez* defiles utensils. (10) First there is the vessel; an eatable (*sc.* dates) is put therein, whence the liquid (*sc.* beer) is manufactured. (11) The *sherez* touches the oven, which in turn touches the bread, Kelim VIII, 5. (12) For immediately the *sherez* enters the air space of the oven, even before it actually touches it, it defiles; hence one should regard the *sherez* as though completely filling it.

Then let him say, There is no uncleanness of the hands or of utensils
a in the Temple?[1]—Said Rab Judah in Rab's name,—others state, R. Jose son of R. Ḥanina: Hands were taught before the enactment concerning utensils.[2] Raba asked: Surely both were enacted on that self-same day, for we learned: [The following render *terumah* unfit . . .] a Book,[3] the hands,[4] a *ṭebul yom*, and eatables or utensils which were defiled by a liquid?[5] But, said Raba: Leave the uncleanness of the knife, for even in the case of *ḥullin* it would not be unclean. [For] what did this knife touch [that it should be unclean]: shall we say that it touched the flesh,—surely food cannot defile utensils; and if it touched the needle,—surely one utensil cannot defile another utensil.[6]

What is the condition of this needle?[7] Shall we say that it is a doubtful needle?[8] Surely it was stated, R. Eleazar and R. Jose son of R. Ḥanina,—one said, They did not decree [uncleanness] for doubtful saliva in Jerusalem;[9] while the other said: They did not decree [uncleanness] for doubtful utensils in Jerusalem?[10]—Said Rab Judah in Rab's name: E.g., if one lost a needle [unclean through] a person defiled by the dead,[11] and he recognized it in the flesh. R. Jose son of R. Abin said: E.g., if the cow was muzzled
b and came from without Jerusalem.[1]

The [above] text [states]: 'R. Eleazar and R. Jose son of R. Ḥanina,—one said: They did not decree [uncleanness] for doubtful saliva in Jerusalem; while the other said: They did not decree [uncleanness] for doubtful utensils in Jerusalem.' [But] we have learned [about] saliva, [and] we have learned [about] utensils?[2] We have learned [about] saliva, for we learned: All saliva found in Jerusalem is clean, save that of the upper market![3]—It is necessary only [to state] that [this is so] even though a *zab* was known [to have passed there].[4] 'We have learned [about] utensils,' for we learned: 'All utensils which are found in Jerusalem on the way of the descent to the ritual bath-house are unclean',[5] hence those [found] elsewhere are clean!—Then according to your reasoning, consider the second clause: '[those found] on the way of the ascent [*from* the bath] are clean', hence those [found] anywhere else are unclean?[6] Rather, the first clause is exact, whereas the second is not exact,[7] and it is to exclude the narrow paths.[8]

Now according to Rab who said, 'E.g., if one lost a needle [unclean through] a person defiled by the dead, and he recognized it in the flesh?—[But] surely since a Master said, The [verse] '*one slain by the sword*' [teaches that] the sword is as the slain,[9] let
c it defile human beings and utensils too?[1]—Said R. Ashi: This proves that the Temple Court ranks as public ground; so that it is a doubt of uncleanness[2] in public ground, and every doubt of uncleanness in public ground, the doubt is clean. But in private ground,[3] its doubt is unclean?[4] Consider: this needle is an object which has no understanding to be questioned, and everything which has no understanding to be questioned, both in public and in private ground, its doubt is clean?[5]—Because it is a doubt of uncleanness which arises through a person,[6] and R. Joḥanan said: A doubt of uncleanness which arises through a person, [20a]

Temple, and this is all to the good, as sacrifices are thereby saved from defilement.

a (1) I.e., where the uncleanness is Rabbinical only. For we see that the knife too is clean, though if this happened without the Temple it would be unclean by Rabbinical enactment, v. *infra*. (2) The enactment that hands are unclean preceded the other; and when this testimony was given, the latter was not yet in existence at all. (3) Any of the Books of the Bible. (4) Before washing. (5) And all these were of the 'eighteen measures' enacted in the upper chambers of Ḥananiah b. Hezekiah of Garon, v. Shab. 13*b*. (6) Unless the former is a 'father' of uncleanness (v. 14*a*, n. a2. These hold good even by Rabbinical law, which enacted only that a *liquid* defiles utensils. (7) That the flesh is unclean. (8) I.e., we do not know whether it is clean or not. (9) If saliva is found and we do not know whose it is, though it might be that of a *zab* or a *zabah*, which by Scriptural law is a 'father' of uncleanness and defiles human beings and utensils. (10) Which includes a needle. (11) I.e., the needle had been defiled by him. The person is a 'father' of uncleanness, and the needle is likewise, because metal in such a case has the same degree of uncleanness as that which defiles it; v. *supra* 14*b* top. V. however, *infra*.

b (1) Hence it must have swallowed it outside, where a doubtfully unclean utensil is unclean, and it remains so even when it enters Jerusalem. (2) What do they add? (3) Which was specially frequented by the unclean, to avoid defiling others, v. Sheḳ. VIII, 1. (4) Where the saliva was found. Even then it is clean, and we would not have known this from the Mishnah. (5) One went down by one road and left by another. Hence it is assumed that those found there were being taken for a ritual bath and dropped on the way. V. Sheḳ. VIII, 2. (6) Which is in contradiction to the inference from the first clause? (7) I.e., not to be taken in the sense that *only* these are clean. And this fact follows from the statement of R. Eleazar or R. Jose b. R. Ḥanina, without which we might have assumed the reverse. (8) In the vicinity of the two main roads. These were used indifferently for both descent and ascent, hence utensils found there were declared unclean, since they were *certainly* unclean in the first place, and our only doubt is whether they were lost on the way *to* the baths or on the way *from* the baths. But utensils found in the rest of Jerusalem, where it is not known whether they had been unclean at all, are clean. (9) V. *supra* 14*b* top.

c (1) *Sc.* the priest and the knife. (2) It is doubtful whether the priest or knife have touched the needle. (3) I.e., if the Temple Court ranked as private ground. (4) And the priest and knife would be unclean. (5) V. Soṭ. 28*b*. (6) A man has been engaged about this animal, and if the knife had touched the needle it would have been through him.

קבה א מיי' פ"ט מהל' אבות הטומאה הלכה ג:
קבו ב מיי' שם פ"ט הלכה ב:
קבז ג שם הלכה ו':

בפסח ידים והנה ידים לכל הפוסל התרומה מטמא ידים להיות שניות אינו אלא לקדשים כדמוכח בחגיגה ותירץ ר"י דהך גזירה ולאי אינה הויא דחגיגה אלא משמתה כשגזרו אמסס ידים שיהיו שניות (א) גזרו כמו כן משמתה על ידים הנוגעות בראשון שיהיו שניות הלכך

זכות וטובה וריוח ותקנה היא לנו מהפסד קדשים שלא נגזרה גזרת ידים במקדש ליטמא בדבר שאין מטמא אדם דהאי מחט מוקמי ליה דלאו בר טמויי אדם הוא דאילו חוץ למקדש מטמאים ידים בטומאה כל דהו אפילו סתמן משום ידים עסקניות: ונימא. נמי זכינו שאין טומאת כלים במקדש מדרבנן בדבר

ונימא שאין טומאת ידים וכלים במקדש אמר רב יהודה אמר רב ואיתימא ר' יוסי בר' חנינא ידים קודם גזירת כלים נשנו אמר רבא והא תרווייהו בו ביום גזרו *דתנן הספר והידים והטבול יום והאוכלין והכלים שנטמאו במשקין אלא אמר רבא הנח לטומאת סכין דאפי' בחולין נמי לא מטמא האי סכין דנגע במאי אילימא דנגע בבשר הא אין אוכל מטמא כלי ואלא דנגע במחט והא *אין כלי מטמא כלי האי מחט מאי עבידתיה אי נימא ספק מחט והא איתמר ר' אלעזר ור' יוסי בר' חנינא חד אמר לא גזרו על ספק הרוקין שבירושלים וחד אמר לא גזרו על ספק הכלים שבירושלים אמר רב יהודה אמר רב כגון שאבדה לו מחט טמא מת והכירה בבשר ר' יוסי ברבי אבין אמר כגון שהיתה פרה חסומה ובאה מחוץ לירושלים: גופא ר' אלעזר ור' יוסי בר' חנינא חד אמר לא גזרו על ספק הרוקין שבירושלים וחד אמר לא גזרו על ספק הכלים שבירושלים רוקין תנינא כלים תנינא רוקין תנינא *דתנן כל הרוקין הנמצאין בירושלים טהורין *חוץ משל שוק העליון לא צריכא אף על גב דאיתחזק זב כלים תנינא *דתנן כל הכלים הנמצאים בירושלים דרך ירידה לבית הטבילה טמאין הא דעלמא טהורין ולטעמיך אימא סיפא דרך עליה טהורין הא דעלמא טמאין אלא רישא דוקא וסיפא לאו דוקא ולאפוקי גזייתא ולרב דאמר כגון שאבדה לו מחט טמא מת והכירה בבשר כיון דאמר מר *בחלל חרב חרב הרי הוא כחלל אדם וכלים נמי ליטמא אמר רב אשי זאת אומרת *עזרה רשות הרבים היא והוה ליה ספק טומאה ברשות הרבים וכל ספק טומאה ברשות הרבים ספיקו טהור הא ברשות היחיד ספיקו טמא הוא מכדי האי מחט דבר שאין בו דעת לישאל הוא *וכל דבר שאין בו דעת לישאל בין ברה"י בין ברה"ר ספיקו טהור משום דהוי ספק טומאה הבאה בידי אדם ואמר רבי יוחנן *ספק טומאה הבאה בידי אדם נשאלין

הני ידים שנגעו במחט שהוא ראשון היה להם להיות שניות אלא דאין טומאת ידים במקדש: **ונימא** אין טומאת ידים וכלים במקדש. תימה לר"י ממה היה לו לכלי ליטמא אי ממשקין הא משקין בית מטבחיא דכן וי"ל דר"ע היא דאמר טומאת משקין לטמא אחרים דאורייתא א"כ לית ליה שיהא דכן וזה אין נראה לו דלר' עקיבא יהיו דכן מלטמא כלים וא"ת דילמא כי אמר ר"ע עדיין לא נגזרה גזירה דכלים וגזירה דידים לקדש כבר גזרה כדאמרינן בפ"ק דשבת (ד' טו. וסס) דשלמה גזר לקודש והיינו גזרו לתרומה וי"ל דגזירה דכלים היינו בי"ח דבר וא"ת דבר קדמו לר"ע וא"ת מנא ליה לגמרא שאין טומאת כלים במקדש אף דילמא בי"ח דבר גזרו על כלים אף במקדש והא דקתני שהסכין טהור הויא נשנית קודם י"ח דבר שהיה מעמדו של ר' חנינא סגן הכהנים וי"ל דאם איתא דגזרו בי"ח דבר טומאה על הכלים במקדש ה"ל למיתני בהדיא בשום מקום לאשמעינן דהויא דקתני שהסכין טהור קודם גזירה נשנית: **תרווייהו** בו ביום גזרו. תימה דידים לקודש *שלמה גזר וי"ל דר"ע אי"ח דבר קאי שהיתה מחדש וה"ק בי"ח דבר כשעסקו בדיני ידים לא רצו לגזור טומאת ידים במקדש*: **האי** סכין דנגע במאי. וס"ל דמיירי בלא משקין: **אין** כלי מטמא כלי. ולית ליה דרב יהודה דמוקי לה במחט טמא מת דהשתא כלי מטמא כלי אלא כרבי יוסי דאמר כגון שהיתה פרה חסומה: **הא** ברשות היחיד ספיקו טמא. תימה הא איצטריך לאוקמא ברשות הרבים משום ידים דספיקו ברה"י טמא: **מכדי** האי מחט דבר שאין בו דעת לישאל הוא. פי' האי מחט כלי שנגע במחט דבטומאה לא בעינן שיהא בו דעת לישאל אלא המיטמא לחודיה דאם לא כן כל טומאת מת ושרץ אפילו ברה"י יהא ספיקו טהור: **ואמר** רבי יוחנן וכו'. ה"מ לאתויי דזעירי דמשני (נדה ד' ה:) דמעת לעת שבנדה עושה משכב ומושב לאע"ג דמשכב ומושב אין בו דעת לישאל כשחברותיה נושאות אותה במטה: לא

טומאת כלים במקדש מדרבנן בדבר שאין מטמא מן התורה דאילו בחולין גזור רבנן ביה טומאה ואף על גב דמדאורייתא טהור כדתנן גבי י"ח דבר והאוכלים והכלים שנטמאו במשקין והכא קתני סכין טהור: ידים קודם גזירת כלים נשנו. ליטמא מדרבנן וכשהעידו עדות זו עדיין לא נגזרה גזירת חכמים על טומאת כלים דרבנן לפיכך לא יוכל לומר זכינו שאין טומאת כלים במקדש דהאיא שעתא אפי' בעלמא נמי לא הואי: בו ביום. בעליית חנניה בן חזקיה בן גרון ביליאות השבת דתנן אלו פוסלין את התרומה: הספר. והתם מפרש טעמא משום תקנת ספרים שהיו מניחין את הספרים עם התרומה ועכברים אוכלים אותם: והידים. אפילו סתמן אם נגע בתרומה בלא נטילת ידים: והטבול יום. והתם פריך הא דאורייתא היא ומשני סמי מכאן טבול יום: אלא אמר רבא. ודאי כבר נגזרה על הכלים מדרבנן שיטמאו במשקין ומיהו הכא ליכא משקין והנח לטומאת סכין דאפילו בחולין שלא חשו להפסידן לא שייכא בהו הכא טומאה לסכין דהאי סכין דנגע במאי שיטמאוהו לא בשר ולא מחט אין יכולין לטמאו דאין אוכל ולא כלי שאינו אב הטומאה מטמאין כלים אפילו מדרבנן ולא גזרו חכמים מדבריהם טומאה על הכלים אלא שיטמאו מן המשקין ומשום משקה זב וזבה: מאי עבידתיה. דמטמא בשר: ספק מחט. לא ידעינן אי טמא אי טהור ושל מי היתה: על ספק הרוקין. לומר שמא של זב או של נדה הן ורוקין אב הטומאה הן לטמא אדם דכתיב (ויקרא טו) וכי ירוק הזב: מחט של טמא מת. שהוא אב הטומאה והמחט עצמו אב הטומאה דחרב הרי הוא כחלל ולקמיה פריך אמאי הסכין והידים טהורין אף גופו של כהן טמא הוא וצריך טבילה והערב שמש דאורייתא: רבי יוסי בר' אבין אמר. לעולם ספק מחט וכגון שהיתה פרה חסומה ובאה מחוץ לירושלים דודאי מעלמא אתי דמשנכנסה לשם לא בלעתה דהוו להו ספק כלים של מקומות אחרים: של שוק העליון. שם היו מתקבלין טמאין שלא לטמא את חביריהם: ואע"ג דאיתחזק זב. שרגילותו עובר בשוק זה שנמצא בו רוק אשמעינן דלא גזרו דכולי האי לא שמעינן ממתני': בדרך אחת היו יורדין לבית הטבילה. ועולין בדרך אחרת הנמצאין בדרך הירידה טמאין דמאי בעו התם אלא טמאין היו והיה רוצה להטבילן ונפלו ממנו: דרך עליה טהורים. שהטבילום: ולטעמיך אימא סיפא כו'. ומהא ליכא למשמע מינה דאיכא למידק מרישא הכי ומסיפא הכי ואשמעינן הנך אמוראי דלעיל דלאמרי לא גזרו דרישא דוקא דקתני בדרך ירידה הוא דמטמאין הא דכל העיר טהור וסיפא דקתני דרך עליה טהורין לא תידוק מינה הא דכל העיר טמאין אלא לאפוקי גזייתא מבואות קטנים שהיו סמוך לדרך ירידה ועליה ופעמים שהיו יורדין דרך אותן מבואות ופעמים עולים והנהו טמאין מספק שהרי מתחלה טמאין היו ספק נפלו בירידה ספק בעליה ומספקא לא נפקי מטומאה אבל שאר כלים ספק נטמאו ספק לא נטמאו לא גזרו עליהן מספק: כיון דאמר מר חרב הרי הוא כחלל. וזו נגעה בטומאת מת שהוא אב הטומאה ונעשה גם המחט אב הטומאה ואמאי הסכין והידים טהורות: אדם וכלים נמי ליטמא. דכל אב הטומאה מטמא אדם וכלים בין כלי את כלי בין אדם את אדם בין אדם כלי וכלי אדם בפרשה זאת חקת התורה בספרי: עזרה רשות הרבים היא. לטומאה ואדם וסכין ספק נגעו במחט זה ספק לא נגעו והויא לה ספק טומאה ברה"ר דספיקו טהור: ופרכינן הא רה"י הוי ספיקו טמא. הא דבר שאין בו דעת לישאל הוא הסכין ול"ג האי מחט אלא מכדי דבר שאין בו דעת לישאל הוא ואי גרסי' ליה הכי מפרשינן מכדי האי עדות דמחט דבר שאין בו דעת לישאל הוא הסכין וכל מי שאין בו דעת לישאל כו' דכל ספק טומאה מסוטה גמרי' מה סוטה רה"י ועל הספק טמאה אף כל ספק טומאות ברשות היחיד ספיקו טמא ומינה מה סוטה יש בה דעת לישאל אם נטמאה אם לאו אף כל שיש בו דעת לישאל כגון אדם ספק נגע בשרץ ספק לא נגע דיש בו דעת שיכולין לשואלו אם נגע והוא אינו יודע ספיקו טמא: הבאה בידי אדם. אדם היה עסוק בה ואם נגע בו הסכין במחט על ידי אדם נגע בו הלכך אם עזרה רשות היחיד ספיקו טמא: נשאלין

רבינו חננאל

על הידים טומאה במקדש אקשי' עלה והא על הסכין נמי קתני טהור ליתני ר"ע זכינו שאין טומאה במקדש לא לידים ולא לכלים ודחי' בעת שנשנית משנה זו לא גזרו רבותינו טומאה על הכלים ואפילו בחוץ והכלים בכל מקום טהורים היו אם נגעו במשקין טמאין וכל שכן במקדש אבל הידים שבחוץ טמאות הוצרך ר"ע לומר כי במקדש לא גזרו עליהן טומאה ואתקיף עלה רבא והא אשכחן דידים וכלים כאחת גזרו עליהן דתנן (י"ד) [י"ח] דבר גזרו בו ביום ומהן הידים וטבול יום והאוכלין והכלים שנטמאו במשקין ומשני רבא הנח לסכין דאפי' בחולין לא מטמא כי מאין תרד טומאה בסכין בו אם מנגיעת הבשר בסכין הא קיימא לן אין אוכל מטמא כלי והסכין כלי הוא ואם נאמר כיון שנגע בה המחט טמא הסכין מן המחט המחט כלי ואין כלי מטמ' כלי ועמדו דברי רבא: ובאנו לחקור על זה המחט מאיזה דרך טמאה הבשר ואמרנו אם המחט עצמה מטמאתה ספק דחיישי' שמא מחט זו טמאה היתה הא אמרי' לא גזרו על ספק כלים הנמצאים בירושלים ואוקמה רב יהוד' במחט ידועה שנטמאה בטמא מת ונמצא עכשיו בבשר שאינה ספק אלא ודאי ור' יוסי בר אבין אוקמא בפרה חסום ובאה מחוץ לירושלים שנתברר כי זו המחט מחוץ לירושלים בלעתה וכי לא גזרו טומאה על ספק כלים הני מילי בירושלים אבל חוץ לירושלים גזרו וזו המחט מחוץ לירושלים היא. וחזרנו לדקדק על מי שאמר לא גזרו על ספק הרוקין שבירושלים למה הוצרך לומר זה והלא שנינו כל הרוקין הנמצאים בירושלים כו' ופשוטה היא ועוד הא דאמרי' לא גזרו על ספק כלים הנמצאים בירושלים למה הוצרך לאמרו והרי משנה שלימה שנינו בשקלים פ"ח כל הכלים הנמצאים בירושלים דרך ירידה לבית הטבילה טמאים ודייקינן הני ודאי טמאים דמוכחא מילתא דלאטבולינהו בעי הא ספק טהורין ואמרינן אדרבה דייק מסיפא דקתני דרך עליה טהורין דמוכחא מילתא דודאי הטבילן הא אחרים כולהי דאיכא למיחש שמא טמאין הן טמאין ואסקינן לעולם רישא דוקא וסיפא למעוטי גזייתא פי' הכלים הנמצאים דרך מעבר בבית הטבילה דלא ידיע דרך עליה או דרך ירידה היא ואתיא סיפא לאשמעינן שהן טמאים וכי אינן טהורין אלא הנמצאין דרך עליה בלבד. ופי' גזייתא כדכתיב (נחום א' י"ב) וכן נגוזו ועבר וכדמתרגמינן עברו גזו והני מילי בבית הטבילה בלבד אבל בירושלים הכל טהור וגם מי שאמר לא גזרו על ספק כלים שבירושלים דוקא דהא מתניתין קמ"ל: וחזרנו להקשות כי מחט זו אם מחט טמא מת היא ודאי אי הכי אדם וכלים נמי תטמא דהא קיימא לן בחלל חרב חרב הרי הוא כחלל וכבר פי' למעלה בענין נר של מתכת שהוא טמא מת ודחי' רב אשי עזרה כרשות הרבים היא והתנן בטהרות פ"ד ספק טומאה ברשות הרבים טהור עד שיאמר נגעתי ואקשינן עליה מכלל דברשות היחיד כי האי גונא טמא והתנן בפ"ג חרש שוטה וקטן שנמצאו במבוי שיש בו טומאה הרי זו בחזקת טהרה וכל הפקח בחזקת טומאה וכל שאין בו דעת לישאל ספקו טהור והא חרש שוטה וקטן מפני שאין בו דעת להשאיל ספקו טהור וכל שכן מחט ומשני כיון שהיא ספק טומאה הבאה בידי אדם פי' שהמתעסק בבשר הרי פקח הוא כמי שיש בו דעת

שבת יג: [זבים פ"ה מ"ב] | [ברכות נב: חגיגה כ.] | שקלים פ"ח מ"א | שם [מ"ב] | [לעיל יד: וש"נ] | [סוטה כח: נדה ד: ה:] | נדה ה:

הגהות הב"ח

(א) תוס' ד"ה שאין וכו' אמסס ידים שיהיו שניות לתרומה גזרו כמו כן משמתה על ידי' הנוגעי' בראשון שיהיו שניות לתרומה כבר הלכך כני ידים שנגעו בכבר שהוא ראשון

עין משפט נר מצוה

קבא א מיי' פי"א מהל' אבות הטומאה הלכה ד:

קבב ב ג מיי' פ"ב מהלכות אבות הטומאה הלכה יא:

קבג ד מיי' פ"י מהל' טומאת אוכלין הלכה יו:

קבד ה מיי' פ"ח מהל' אבות הטומאה הלכה ו:

גמרא

בכל טמא לא יאכל *מי לא עסקינן דנגע בשני רביעי מקל וחומר כדאמרינן ואי ס"ד סבר כר"ע ניתני נמי רביעי בתרומה וחמישי בקודש אלא ר"ע לא סבר כר' יוסי מנלן א"ל דלא לישתמיט תנא וליתני רביעי בתרומה וחמישי בקודש ונימא ר"ע היא ואנן אהכי ניקום ונסמוך נפק רב אשי ואי תימא רב כהנא דק ואשכח הא *דתנן הכלי מצרף את מה שבתוכו לקודש אבל לא לתרומה והרביעי בקודש פסול והשלישי בתרומה ואמר רבי חייא בר אבא א"ר יוחנן מעדותו של ר"ע נשנית משנה זו (*דתניא) *הוסיף ר"ע הסולת והקטורת והלבונה והגחלים שאם נגע טבול יום במקצתן פסל את כולן רביעי אין חמישי לא שלישי אין רביעי לא אלמא קסבר צירוף דרבנן ופליגא דרבי חנין דאמר צירוף דאורייתא שנאמר כף אחת עשרה זהב מלאה קטרת הכתוב עשה כל מה שבכף אחת *תנן התם על מחט שנמצאת בבשר שהסכין והידים טהורות והבשר טמא נמצאת בפרש הכל טהור אמר רבי עקיבא זכינו שאין טומאת ידים במקדש ונימא

רש"י

בכל טמא מי לא משמע נמי דאי נגע בשני. דהא שני נקרא טמא כל אשר בתוכו יטמא והאוכל דשמעינן ליה לר' יוסי בשלישי לתרומה ולא רביעי ורביעי לקודש ולא חמישי על כרחיך לית ליה שני עושה שלישי בחולין ולא דריש יטמא יטמא דאי אית ליה לייתיה לרביעי בתרומה בק"ו מטבול יום ומה טבול יום שמותר בחולין פסול בתרומה שלישי שפסול בחולין אינו דין שיעשה רביעי בתרומה ודיו ליכא למימר דא"כ מפריך ק"ו דהא שלישי לתרומה נפקא לן מקרא כי היכי דנפקא לן שלישי בחולין ורביעי בקל וחומר וחמישי בקודש בק"ו ממחוסר כפורים אלא ודאי לית ליה לרבי יוסי שני עושה שלישי בחולין: אלא רבי עקיבא לא סבר לה כר' יוסי מנלן. דילמא ר"ע אית ליה נמי ק"ו דר' יוסי ומייתי ליה בהאי ק"ו רביעי בתרומה וחמישי בקודש: א"ל. אם איתא דיש חולקים בדבר הזה וכי לא לישתמיט שום תנא וליתני רביעי בתרומה בחד דוכתא וכי תיקשי לך מני נימא ר"ע היא אלא ודאי לית ליה לר"ע ק"ו דר"י משום פירכא דדור אחרון כדאמר במסכ' סוטה (דף כז:) עתיד דור אחרון לטהר את השלישי בתרומה שאינו מטמאין אותו בקל וחומר מטבול יום ודור אחרון פריך מה לטבול יום שכן אב הטומאה הלכך לר"ע נמי דאית ליה שלישי בחולין לא מייתי שום מעלה ספי לתרומה בק"ו מטבול יום משום הא פירכא ושלישי בין בתרומה בין בחולין נפקא לן מקרא בהדיא דדריש יטמא יטמא ורביעי בקודש נמי מוהבשר אשר יגע בכל טמא מי לא עסקינן דנגע בשלישי דהא לר"ע הואיל ודריש יטמא יטמא משכחת לה דאתי קודש לידי רביעי הכי שרץ טימא כלי וה"ל ראשון וכלי אוכל ואוכל משקה ומשקה אוכל דהא לר"ע טומאת משקין דאורייתא וחמישי בקודש לא מייתי בק"ו ממחוסר כפורים דליכא למיפרך מה למחוסר כפורים שכן אב הטומאה ומבעיא לן לר"מ ור"א דאמרו בהדיא דמשקין אין מטמאין דבר אחר מן התורה ולרבי יוסי נמי דאוקימנא דליה לא ס"ל כי היכי משכחת קודש בא לידי רביעי שרץ כלי הוי ראשון וכלי אוכל הוי שני ואוכל משקה הוי שלישי והיאך יבא לידי רביעי וכ"ל דעל כרחיך לא משכחת לה אלא מדרבנן ותדע דקתני לה גבי מעלות דחומר בקודש: דקי"ל התם (חגיגה כ:) דכולהו מדרבנן ניכהו וזהו מחמש מעלות האחרונות היא ואמר התם ה' אחרונות לית להו דרכא דטומאה דאורייתא ובמסכת סוטה נמי סוגיא דשמעתא דרבי יוסי מדרבנן אזלא ואוכל שלישי לר' יוסי בקודש דקאמר לעיל ולמדנו שלישי בקודש מן התורה מהיכן קיבלה הואיל ואין משקה מטמא אוכל על כרחיך מאוכל קיבלה וס"ל טומאה עושה כיוצא בה בקדשים ואוכל דמטמא משקה כיון דלא דרשי יטמא יטמא לא ידענא מהיכא נפקא להו אי לאו מהאי קרא וכי יותן מים על זרע וגו' ודרשינן הוא טמא ואינו עושה כיוצא בו ומדאיצטריך קרא למעוטי כיוצא בו מכלל דמטמא אחרים וכ"ת טמא הוא הרי הוא טמא ואינו מטמא אחרים א"כ לשתוק קרא מיניה ולכתוב טמא ומהיכא תיתי לן טומאה לאחרים ואי קשיא הואיל ומשקין לא מטמאי אחריני לרבי יוסי תו לא מיתוקמא מתני' כתרלתא דתריץ ר' ירמיה לעיל ואזדא ר' יוסי לטעמיה והדר קושיין לדוכתא אמאי אינה היא המדה מדה ומדה היא לא תיקשי דכי אוקימנא ואזדא רבי יוסי לטעמיה בתר טעמא דהא מתני' דר' יוסי אליבא דר"ע אוקימנא דדריש יטמא יטמא דהא מהא מייתינן סייעתא עליה ואני שמעתי דר' יוסי אית ליה יטמא יטמא גבי משקין והא דאמר לא ס"ל בההיא דאוכלין דר"ע אמרן לענין טומאה עושה כיוצא בה ועכשיו אתה בא לידי רביעי שרץ כלי כלי אוכל ואוכל משקה ומשקה אוכל ואי אפשר להעמידו מפני כמה תשובות ומיהו לר"מ דאמר בהדיא טומאת משקין לטמא אחרים לאו דאורייתא לא משכחת לה רביעי אלא מדרבנן: ואנן אהכי נסמוך. משום דלא אשכחן תנא כימא דר"ע לית ליה ק"ו: דק ואשכח. בהדיא דאמר ר"ע רביעי ולא חמישי: הכלי מצרף מה שבתוכו. עריבה ארוכה ובה אוכלי קודש מכאן ואוכלי קודש מכאן ואין נוגעין זה בזה ונגע טמא באוכלין שבראש אחד ובכלי לא נגע ואוכל אין מטמא כלי אפי' מדרבנן ואפ"ה האוכלין שבשני ראשיה טמאים שהכלי מצרפן: מעדותו. ע"י עדותו: הוסיף ר"ע. בעדות: לבונה וגחלים. אע"ג דלאו אוכלין ניכהו חיבת הקודש מכשרתן ומשויא להו אוכל בפ' כל שעה (לה.): פסל את כולן. אלמא מצרף כלי מה שבתוכו דאי משום דנגעי אהדדי נהי דגחלת שנגע בה מטמא את חברתה אבל חברתה תו לא מטמיא דא"כ ה"ל ששי ושביעי עד ק' ומאותו עדות נשנית משנה זו דהכלי מצרף וקתני בהדיא רביעי בקודש פסול אלמא דר"ע חמישי לית ליה שלישי בתרומה אין רביעי לא אלמא לית ליה לר"ע ק"ו דר' יוסי בלשון אחר שמעתי יורד לעמקי תהום וא"א להעמידו: אלמא קסבר צירוף דרבנן. מילתא באנפי נפשה היא מדא"ר יוחנן מעדותו של ר"ע נשנית אלמא קסבר ר' יוחנן צירוף דכלי לקודש דקתני גבי מעלות לאו דאורייתא הוא אלא מדרבנן מעדותו של ר"ע דמדרבנן הוא דגחלים ולבונה לאו בני קבולי טומאה ניכהו אלא מדרבנן ואע"ג דאמר מר והבשר לרבות עצים ולבונה אמרי' בכל שעה (שם) דמעלה מדרבנן היא: ופליגא. דר' יוחנן אדר' חנין: כף אחת. בקטורת כתיב דקודש הוא: תנן התם. בעדיות ועל המחט העיד עם אחר עדיות שאם נמצאת בבשר קודש שהסכין נוגע בה והידים של כהן שנגעו בה טהורין והבשר טמא ולקמיה מפרש הא מחט מאי טומאה הוא ביה: זכינו.

תוספות

ניתני נמי רביעי בתרומה. וה"ה דהוה מצי למימר אי סבר לה כר"ע אמאי איצטריך לאיתויי בקל וחומר רביעי בקודש ממחוסר כפורים תיפוק ליה דקרא שמעינן ליה כיון דשלישי טמא בחולין קרי כאן והבשר אשר יגע בכל טמא וגו' כי היכי דדרשינן השתא לענין שלישי: לא לישתמיט תנא וליתני רביעי בתרומה וחמישי בקודש. פ"ה דלמ"ד טומאת משקין לטמא אחרים דרבנן לא משכחת רביעי בקודש אלא מדרבנן ועל ידי עצים ולבונה משכחת לה שפיר כדפי' לעיל ור"ל דמיבעיא ליה אי מהני חיבת הקודש למימני ביה ראשון ושני ויסבור דאוכל מטמא אוכל ומה שפ"ה מדקתני לה גבי מעלות בפרק חומר בקודש (חגיגה כג: ושם) אם כן דרבנן היא אין נראה לר"י דהא אוקמא כר"ע ואיהו דריש יטמא יטמא וע"כ רביעי בקודש דאורייתא דקרי כאן והבשר אשר יגע וגו' ולירוף נמי דאורייתא לרבי חנין והא דאמר בחגיגה (שם כה:) חמש מעלות אחרונות לית להו דרכא טומאה דאורייתא רבינו חננאל לא גרס דאורייתא ואפילו אי גרס ליה ה"פ לית להו דרכא טומאה דאורייתא שלא היה לכתוב לטמאה לפי שהן רחוקין מן הטומאה דמן הדין היה להם להיות טהורים ועוד פ"ה דמאן דלא דריש יטמא יטמא נפקא ליה דאוכל מטמא אחרים מדאיצטריך טמא הוא למעוטי שאין טומאה עושה כיוצא בה אור"י הניחא לאביי ולרב אדא בר אהבה אבל לרבינא דאמר מקרא מלא דבר הכתוב דילמא אתא הוא לקדשים דה"א עושין כיוצא בהן מוהבשר אשר יגע בכל טמא: אלמא קסבר צירוף דרבנן. יש פי' מרש"י שמפרש דדייק לר"ע דצירוף דרבנן מדאורייתא אין טומאה ללבונה וגחלים דהא לאו אוכל ניכהו דמעלה דרבנן היא מה שמקבלין טומאה ובפ' כל שעה (לקמן לה.) קרי לה מעלה ואין זה ראיה דהתם נמי קרי לה מעלה להביא כפרתו אוכל בקדשים אף על גב דהוי דאורייתא כדדריש בפרק הערל (יבמות עד:) ועוד דבהדיא מוכח בפרק שני דחולין (דף לו:) דוהבשר לרבות עצים ולבונה ולאו אסמכתא היא דמוכח התם מינה חיבת הקודש מכשר דאורייתא*) ונראה לר"י כמו שהוגה בפי' דדייק דצירוף דרבנן מהא דקתני רישא על אפר חטאת שאם נגע טמא במקצת טימא את כולו והוי מדרבנן שאפר חטאת אינו קודש אלא חול כדמוכח בפרק התכלת (מנחות כב. ושם) שאין מועלין באפר פרה וקתני הוסיף ר"ע משמע דהוי דרבנן כמו רישא: שאין טומאת ידים במקדש. תימה לר"י אמאי היה להם להיות טמא הא אין בהן היסח הדעת ואי משום דאמר בפ' בתרא דחגיגה (דף כד. ושם) כל הפוסל התרומה מטמא ידים להיות שניות א"כ מאי קא פריך תרווייהו בו ביום גזרו והא הנהו ידים שפוסלות התרומה איירי בסתם

רבינו חננאל

וכתיב לא יאכל הנגע בזה הטמא. הנה שלישי מן התורה רביעי מקל וחומר כדאמרן ומה מחוסר כפורים שמותר בתרומה כו' ואי ס"ד דר' יוסי סבר לה כר' עקיבא דאית ליה שלישי בחולין ליתני רביעי בתרומה וחמישי בקדש דהא מעלה לכל אחד ואחד ניניהו מכאן למדנו דר' יוסי לית ליה הא דר"ע ותו אשכחנן בהדיא במסכת סוטה דר' יוסי סבר אין (שלישי) [שני] עושה שלישי בחולין ור' עקיבא נמי לית ליה הא דר' יוסי דתאני ר' יוסי שלישי שפסול בתרומה אינו דין שיעשה רביעי בקדש דאי ס"ד דאית ליה כיון דאית ליה לר' עקיבא דשני עושה שלישי בחולין כמפורש בתורת כהנים נימא שלישי שפסול בחולין אינו דין שיעשה רביעי בתרומה וכי האי דינא ניתי חמישי בקדש ולימא ר' יוסי אליבא דר' עקיבא רביה אמרה מדלא אשכחן תנא דתני הכי ש"מ דאפילו ר' עקיבא לית ליה רביעי בתרומה ולא חמישי בקדש ולית ליה האי דינא דדיין ר' יוסי ומתמהי' וכי אהאי סברא נסמוך ודק רב כהנא ואשכח הא דתניא במס' חגיגה הכלי מצרף מה שבתוכו לקדש אבל לא לתרומה הרביעי בקדש והשלישי בתרומ' ואמרי' מעדותו של ר' עקיבא נשנית משנה זו דתנן הוסיף ר' עקיבא הסלת והקטורת והלבונ' והגחלים שנגע טבול יום במקצת פסל את כלן כלומר אם נגע טבול יום במקצת הסלת נפסלה כולה וכן הלבונה והקטורת כיוצא בה. ויש אומרים פי' אחר אם נגע טבול יום בסלת נעשה תחלת הסלת ראשון והקטורת שני והלבונה שלישי והגחלי' רביעי עד כאן של תורה פי' והוא דנגעי אהדדי אבל אי לא נגעי אהדדי או אם יש שם עוד חמישי והכלי הוא דמצרפן מדרבנן הוא דפסלו: ופליגא דר' חנן דאמר צרוף דאורייתא דכתיב כף אחת עשרה זהב עשה הכתוב כל מה שבכף אחד וקתני סיפא דהא דדייקינן עלה מעדותו של ר' עקיבא נשנית הרביעי בקדש פסול רביעי ולא חמישי: תנן התם בעדיות פ"ב ועל המחט שנמצאת בבשר שהסכין והידים טהורות מכלל שלא גזרו

מסורת הש"ס

חגיגה כ: [מנחות כד.]

חגיגה כג: יומא מה. עדיות פ"ח מ"א

[חגיגה שם]

[עדיות פ"ב משנה ג]

גליון הש"ס

גמ' כל מה שבכף אחת. עי' חולין נו ע"א תוס' ד"ה צריך:

*) [וע"ע תוס' חגיגה כג: ד"ה והא ותוס' זבחים לו. ד"ה ואפי' ככי ותוס' מנחות כב. ד"ה ילאו ותוס' חולין לו: ד"ה נ לך]

any unclean thing [19a] *shall not be eaten:*[5] do we not treat even [of a case] where it touched a second?[6] 'While a fourth [is learned] *a minori*', as we have stated. Now, if you should think that he holds as R. Akiba, let him also state a fourth in the case of *terumah* and a fifth in the case of sacred food.[7] But how do we know that R. Akiba does not agree with R. Jose?[8]—Said he to him, Because a Tanna could not completely refrain from teaching [that there is] a fourth in the case of *terumah* and a fifth in the case of sacred food, and we would say that it agrees with R. Akiba.[9] And shall we arise and rely upon this?[1] [Thereupon] R. Ashi—others say, R. Kahana—went out, searched, and found the following which we learned: A utensil unites its contents in the case of sacred food,[2] but not in the case of *terumah*, and a fourth degree is unfit in the case of sacred food, but not in the case of *terumah*. Whereon R. Ḥiyya b. Abba said in R. Joḥanan's name: This Mishnah was learned as a result of R. Akiba's testimony. For we learned, R. Akiba added[3] the fine meal, incense, frankincense, and the burning coals, that if a *ṭebul yom* touches part thereof he renders all unfit.[4] Thus there is a fourth [in sacred food], but not a fifth; a third [in the case of *terumah*], but not a fourth.[5]

This proves that he holds that [the power of] uniting is Rabbinical.[6] Now he differs from R. Ḥanin who maintained: [The power of] uniting is Biblical, for it is said, *one golden pan of ten shekels, full of incense:*[7] the Writ rendered everything in the pan one.

We learned elsewhere: [He testified] concerning an [unclean] needle which is found in the flesh [of a sacrifice], that the knife[8] and the hands[9] are clean, while the flesh is unclean; if found in the excrements,[10] it is all clean. R. Akiba said: We have been favoured in that there is no uncleanness of the hands in the Temple.[11] [19b]

(5) Lev. VII, 19. (6) For a 'second' is called unclean; thus Scripture intimates that a second makes a third in sacred food. (7) For if he holds that there is a third in the case of *ḥullin*, he can deduce these *a minori*. Thus: if a *ṭebul yom* (v. Glos.), though permitted to eat *ḥullin*, is unfit to eat *terumah*, then surely a third, which is unfit in the case of *ḥullin*, creates a fourth in the case of *terumah*. And we cannot refute this by the principle that it is sufficient for what is learned *a minori* to be like its premise, for in that case the deduction is superfluous, for a third in the case of *terumah* is learned direct from Scripture from the same source whence we learn a third in the case of *ḥullin* (v. *supra* 18a). Hence the deduction *a minori* must be in respect of a fourth, while a *fifth* would then follow on the same lines from one who lacks atonement. (8) In the validity of this argument. (9) For R. Akiba must hold thus if he accepts R. Jose's argument. Surely then in the whole of the Talmud this view would have found expression somewhere!

(1) This is merely a *negative* argument? (2) If two pieces of sacred food are lying in a vessel, not touching each other, and an unclean object touches one piece, the other is defiled too, because the vessel makes them both as one. (3) In his testimony on 'that day', v. 16a, n. a3. (4) This must be because the vessel which contains them makes the various particles one, and not just because they touch each other, for in that case we would have to go in order to render all the particles unfit even beyond a fifth. V. 'Ed., chapter VIII, notes. (5) Thus we have a *positive* proof that R. Akiba does not hold that there are a fourth and a fifth in the case of *terumah* and sacred food respectively. (6) Since R. Joḥanan states that this Mishnah was taught as a result of R. Akiba's testimony, referring as it does to frankincense and live coals, is only Rabbinical, for they are subject to defilement only by Rabbinical, not by Scriptural law (Rashi). Tosaf. offers another explanation. (7) Num. VII, 14. (8) Wherewith the animal was slaughtered. (9) Of the priest who touched the animal. (10) Inside the animal. (11) The uncleanness of the hands in general is only Rabbinical, and R. Akiba maintains that this enactment never applied to the

[18*b*] Are they not [rather] inferred *a minori:* if liquids which are unclean through a utensil defile, how much the more liquids which are unclean through a *sherez!* [Then] it is sufficient that that which is deduced by [this] argument shall be as its premise.[5]

How does he interpret *'shall be unclean'* of the first part?—*'All food therein which may be eaten, that on which water cometh* [yiṭma] *shall be unclean'*: 'it shall defile [*yeṭamme*]' in respect of defiling liquids. You say, to defile liquids; yet perhaps it is not so, but rather to defile utensils? You can answer, it follows *a minori:* if a liquid, which defiles an eatable, cannot defile a utensil; then an eatable, which cannot defile an eatable, surely cannot defile a utensil! Hence how do I interpret,[6] *'shall be unclean'?* That it defiles liquids, which are ready to contract uncleanness. Why particularly apply it to liquids, because they are ready to contract uncleanness? Deduce it from the fact that there is nothing else [left]?[7]—This is what he means: And should you argue, an eatable is more stringent [than liquid], since it defiles liquids,[8] [and therefore] let it defile
a utensils [too]; [hence we are told that] that[1] is a [greater] stringency of liquids, because liquids are ready to contract uncleanness. And what is their readiness? Because they contract uncleanness without being made fit.[2]

'[*It*] *shall be unclean,*' [teaching] that it cannot render something similar to itself [unclean]![3]—But is it deduced from here? Surely it is deduced from elsewhere, [viz.,] *But if water be put upon the seed, and aught of their carcass fall thereon, it is unclean unto you:*[4] it is unclean, but it cannot create a similar uncleanness?[5]—One treats of liquids unclean[6] through a *sherez,* and the other treats of liquids unclean through a utensil; and [both] are necessary. For if we were informed [this] of liquid which is unclean through a utensil, [I would say,] that is because it is not stringent; but in the case of liquid unclean through a *sherez,* which is stringent, I might argue that it creates uncleanness similar to its own. Then let us be told [this] about liquid defiled by a *sherez,* and how much the more liquid unclean through a utensil?—That which may be inferred *a minori,* Scripture takes the trouble of writing it [explicitly].

Rabina said to R. Ashi: But Raba said, R. Jose does not agree with R. Akiba, nor does R. Akiba agree with R. Jose?[7]—Said he to him: R. Jose stated it in accordance with the opinion of R. Akiba his teacher, but he himself does not hold thus.[8]

R. Ashi said to R. Kahana: As for R. Jose not agreeing with R. Akiba, that is well, for it was taught: R. Jose said: How do we know that a fourth degree in the case of sacred food is unfit?
b Now this follows *a minori:* if he who lacks atonement,[1] though permitted to partake of *terumah,* is unfit in respect of sacred food, then[2] a third, which is unfit in the case of *terumah,*[3] is it not logical that it makes a fourth in sacred food! And we learn a third in the case of sacred food from Scripture, and a fourth *a minori.*[4] 'A third from Scripture', for it is written, *And the flesh that toucheth*

(5) Not stricter. Scripture does not state that water defiled by a *sherez* can contaminate something else, but it is merely deduced, as shown in the text. (6) Lit., 'fulfil'. (7) Everything else having been excluded. (8) Which a liquid cannot do.

a (1) The exposition of the verse to the effect that eatables defile liquid. (2) For uncleanness, in contrast to eatables, which may become unclean only after moisture has fallen upon them. (3) As Rabina deduces from the verse itself. (4) Lev. XI, 38. (5) I.e., it cannot make something like itself unclean, which is the actual reading *supra* 14*a*. (6) Lit., 'which come'. (7) *Infra.* Thus R. Jose holds that liquid can defile other liquid, and he must interpret Lev. XI, 33 accordingly. Now the eatable or liquid is a second (v. 18*a*, n. a5), and on this interpretation it makes a third: thus there is a 'third' in the case of *ḥullin.* (8) Viz., the interpretation of *yiṭma,* 'it shall be unclean,' as *yeṭamme,* 'it shall defile'. Since R. Jose himself rejects this exegesis, there is nothing to teach that a second renders a third in the case of *ḥullin.*

b (1) I.e., one who after performing *ṭebillah* (q.v. Glos) must bring an offering before he may partake of the flesh of sacrifices; viz., a *zab* and a *zabah* (v. Glos.), a woman after confinement and a leper. (2) These facts are learned in Yeb. 74*b* from Scripture. (3) I.e., if something unclean in the second degree touches *terumah* it renders it unfit, the *terumah* now being called a third; v. Soṭ. 29*a*. (4) This is added in order to answer the possible objection that what is deduced *a minori* cannot be more stringent than its premise, and since sacred food is thus deduced from *terumah,* it cannot go beyond a third, just as in the case of *terumah.* Hence it is pointed out that a *third* in the case of sacred food does not require an argument *a minori,* for that follows directly from Scripture; hence the deduction *a minori* must refer to a fourth, as otherwise it teaches nothing, and it is stated in B.Ḳ. 25*a* that in such a case we abandon the principle that what is deduced *a minori* does not go beyond its premise.

תורה אור

ולאו מקל וחומר קאתי ומה משקין הבאין מחמת כלי מטמאין משקין הבאין מחמת שרץ לא כל שכן דיו לבא מן הדין להיות כנדון יטמא דרישא היכי דריש מכל האוכל אשר יאכל אשר יבא עליו מים יטמא יטמא לטמא את המשקין אתה אומר לטמא את המשקין או אינו אלא לטמא את הכלי אמרת ק"ו ומה משקה שמטמא אוכל אינו מטמא כלי אוכל שאין מטמא אוכל אינו דין שלא יטמא כלי הא מה אני מקיים יטמא לטמא את המשקין שהן עלולין לקבל טומאה מאי איריא משקין משום דעלולין לקבל טומאה תיפוק ליה משום דליכא מידי אחרינא ה"ק וכ"ת אוכל חמור דמטמא משקין ניטמייה לכלי ההוא חומרא דמשקין הוא משום דמשקין עלולין לקבל טומאה ומה היא עלילתן שמקבלין טומאה שלא בהכשר יטמא דאין עושה כיוצא בה מהכא נפקא מהתם נפקא *°וכי יותן מים על זרע ונפל מנבלתם (ויקרא יא) עליו טמא הוא הוא טמא ואין עושה טומאה כיוצא בה חד במשקין הבאין מחמת שרץ וחד במשקין הבאין מחמת כלי וצריכי דאי אשמועינן במשקין הבאין מחמת כלי משום דלא חמירי אבל במשקין הבאין מחמת שרץ דחמירי אימא עושה טומאה כיוצא בה ולשמעינן משקין הבאין מחמת שרץ וכ"ש משקין הבאין מחמת כלי *מילתא דאתיא בקל וחומר טרח וכתב לה קרא א"ל רבינא לרב אשי והא אמר רבא לא ר' יוסי סבר כר' עקיבא ולא ר"ע סבר כר' יוסי אמר ליה רבי יוסי בשיטת ר"ע רבו אמרה וליה לא ס"ל אמר ליה רב אשי לרב כהנא בשלמא ר' יוסי לא סבר לה כר"ע *דתניא א"ר יוסי מניין לרביעי בקודש שהוא פסול ודין הוא ומה מחוסר כפורים שמותר בתרומה פסול בקודש שלישי שפסול בתרומה אינו דין שיעשה רביעי בקודש ולמדנו שלישי בקודש מן התורה ורביעי מקל וחומר שלישי מן התורה דכתיב °והבשר אשר יגע (שם ז) בכל

רש"י

ומשני משקין הבאין מחמת שרץ מי כתיבי. באורייתא ממשקין מחמת כלי הוא דאתו ומה כו' וכיון דמייתיהו הוא דילפי דיו למשקין שנגעו בשרץ הבאין מן הדין דמשקין שנגעו בכלי להיות כנדון מה אלו אין מטמאין כלי אף אלו אין מטמאין כלי: יטמא דרישא. גבי אוכל היכי דריש ליה ר"ע: משקה שמטמא אוכל. כדאמרן לעיל אינו מטמא כלי כדאמרן אוכל שאין מטמא אוכל דאין טומאה עושה כיוצא בה אינו דין כו' והוא הדין דמצי למימר נמי קל וחומר מיניה וביה כדאמרן גבי משקין דנימא הכי מה כלי שמטמא את האוכל הזה אינו מטמא כלי אוכל שבא מחמת כלי כו' אלא משום דהדר אצטריך ליה למימר כדלעיל ואימא הני מילי אוכל הבא מחמת כלי אבל אוכל הבא מחמת שרץ לטמא כלי וניחא ליה למילף ממשקה דאוקימנא בהו דלא שנא נגעו בשרץ לא שנא ניטמאו מן הכלי לא מטמאו כלי: וכי יטמא אוכל חמור. ממשקה דאילו משקה אין מטמא משקה ואילו אוכל קאמרת מטמא משקה הלכך אע"ג דאין משקה מטמא כלי יהא אוכל מטמא כלי: ההוא. דאוקימנא האי יטמא דאוכל לטמא משקה חומרא דמשקין היא דעלולין לקבל טומאה: יטמא דאין עושה כיוצא בה. כלומר השתא דרשינן יטמא יטמא והאי דקרינן בתרוייהו (א) יטמא ללמדך מיעוט דאין מטמא כיוצא בו כגון אוכל אוכל ומשקה משקה: הוא. מיעוטא ואוכל דכוותיה קא ממעט: חד. (ב) למעוטי משקין הבאין מחמת שרץ אע"ג דלא כתיבי בהאי קרא משקין דכי יותן מים על זרע וגו' דמשמע אפילו שנגע בהן שרץ לאחר שניגבו מיהו גלי באוכל והוא הדין למשקה: וחד במשקין הבאין מחמת כלי. ההוא יטמא דלעיל איירי בבאין מחמת כלי: והא אמר רבא לא רבי יוסי. דלקמן דדריש ק"ו ממחוסר כפורים סבר לה כר' עקיבא שיהא שני עושה שלישי בחולין ולא רבי עקיבא סבר לה כרבי יוסי במאי דמייתי לקמן רביעי בקודש מקל וחומר ממחוסר כפורים ומילתיה דרבא פרשוה רב אשי ורב כהנא לקמן בסמוך וכיון דאית ליה לרבי יוסי משקין מטמאין אחרים דאורייתא לא משכח ראיה אלא מיטמא דדריש יטמא על כרחך אית ליה שני עושה שלישי בחולין דהא בין יטמא דאוכלין בין יטמא דמשקין אשני כתיבי: בשיטת רבי עקיבא רבו אמרה. להא דאמר טומאת משקין לטמא אחרים דאורייתא מיבעי ליה למדרש יטמא יטמא אליבא דר"ע אמרה דדריש ליה גבי אוכלין וקא"ל ר' יוסי הואיל ודריש ר"ע יטמא יטמא אית ליה דמשקין מטמאין אחרים דאורייתא אבל רבי יוסי לא סבירא ליה טומאת משקין לטמא אחרים דאורייתא ולא דריש יטמא יטמא: בשלמא רבי יוסי לא סבר ליה כר"ע. דשני עושה שלישי בחולין: דתניא אמר רבי יוסי מניין לרביעי בקודש שפסול ודין הוא מה מחוסר כפורים שמותר בתרומה. כדילפינן ביבמות פרק הערל (ד' עד:) מקראי טבל ועלה אוכל במעשר הערב שמשו אוכל בתרומה כדכתיב ובא השמש וטהר ואחר יאכל מן הקדשים: אסור בקודש. כדיליף התם מוכפר עליה הכהן וטהרה מכלל שהיא טמאה עד עכשיו: שלישי שפסול בתרומה. לרבנן דפליגי אדר' עקיבא ונפקא לן בקל וחומר מטבול יום ומה טבול יום דמותר בחולין אסור בתרומה שני שפסול בחולין אינו דין שיעשה שלישי בתרומה במסכת סוטה בפרק כשם שהמים בודקין* ובקודש דין הוא שיעשה בה רביעי מקל וחומר ממחוסר כפורים: ולמדנו שלישי בקודש מן התורה. ודלא תימא דיו לבא מן הדין להיות כנדון מה תרומה עושה שלישי ותו לא אף זה קודש יעשה שלישי ותו לא דמשום שלישי לא אצטריך לן קל וחומר דמן התורה למדנו שלישי וכי אתא ק"ו לרביעי הוא דאתא דקיימא לן בב"ק פ' שני (ד' כה.) דהיכא דמיפרך ק"ו לא אמרינן דיו:

תוספות

ולאו מק"ו קאתי ומה משקין הבאין מחמת כלי. וא"ת נילף מק"ו דאוכל ומה אוכל הבא מחמת שרץ מטמא משקין שרץ גופיה לא כל שכן והשתא נימא דבין משקין ובין אוכל מטמא כלי וי"ל דע"כ אין אוכל מטמא כלי אפילו בא מחמת שרץ מק"ו דמשקין הבאין מחמת כלי שמטמא אוכל ואין מטמא כלי אוכל הבא מחמת שרץ שאין מטמא אוכל [מהוא טמא] אינו דין שלא יטמא כלי: דיו לבא מן הדין להיות כנדון. הקשה הרב רבי יעקב דאורליינ"ש אם כן יהיו משקין הבאין מחמת שרץ שניים כמשקין הבאין מחמת כלי והכי קל וחומר דמטמו והכי דיו דהוו שניים דכה"ג אמרינן בכילד הרגל (ב"ק כה:) גבי קל וחומר דמפץ במת לימא הכי קל וחומר לטומאת ערב והכי דיו לאפוקי מטומאת ז' וגבי קרן בחצר הניזק* אמרינן נמי הכי קל וחומר לנזק שלם והכי דיו לגופו ואומר ר"י דלא קשה דהכא לא אשכחן מידי שנגע בשרץ שלא יהיה ראשון הלכך אין לחלק אבל גבי מת אשכחן דבר הנוגע בו שלא יהיה אלא ראשון כגון אוכלים וכלי חרס ונזק שלם מגופו הרי מילי ניכהו אבל אין לתרץ משום דאיכא למימר ק"ו הכי ומה אדם וכלים שאין מיטמאין מאויר כלי חרס מיטמא מאויר כלי חרס לא כל שכן משקין שמיטמאין מאויר כלי חרס והשתא נמי איכא למימר דיו כדמוכח בכילד הרגל (שם): וכי תימא אוכל חמור דמטמא משקין. הוי מצי למילף דאין אוכל מטמא כלי מקל וחומר ומה כלי שמטמא אוכל אין מטמא כלי אוכל שאינו מטמא אוכל אינו דין שלא יטמא כלי: ומהו עלילותן שמקבלין טומאה בלא הכשר. תימה לר"י דלהכתי לא הוי קל וחומר דהא עלילותן לא מהני להו לקבל טומאה ממשקין ולענין אוכל מהני להו א"כ אוכל חמור ולעיל דיליף דמשקה לא מטמא כלי לא מצי למילף בק"ו מאוכל שמטמא משקה ואין מטמא כלי משקה דלא מטמא משקה לא כ"ש דהיא גופה מנלן דאוכל לא מטמא כלי ועוד דמשקין חמור מאוכל דמטמא אוכל והכא לא מצי למיעבד ק"ו כדלעיל דמה כלי שמטמא אוכל אין מטמא כלי אוכל הבא מחמת כלי לא כ"ש דמ"מ אוכל הבא מחמת שרץ מנלן: ומה מחוסר כפורים. אפי' מאן דלית ליה דיו אפילו היכא דמיפרך קל וחומר הכא מודה דבמה מצינו ילפינן שלישי ממחוסר כפורים דמחוסר כפורים כשלישי הוא שאינו עושה כלום בתרומה ופוסל בקודש והוא הדין בכל שלישי הלכך אליס קל וחומר דהכא ולא שייך למימר דיו מה התם שלישי ותו לא אף כאן שלישי ותו לא: למדנו שלישי מן התורה. ניחא ליה להביא מקרא וה"מ למידרש שלישי לקודש קל וחומר מטבול יום ורש"י פירש דלהכי איצטריך למימר למדנו שלישי מן התורה דלא תימא דיו אבל השתא דלמדנו מן התורה לא אמרינן דיו משום דמיפרך קל וחומר:

ניתני

רבינו חננאל

מחמת הכלי אין מטמאין את הכלי כדקאמרת משקין הבאין מחמת שרץ אמאי לא יטמא את הכלי ודחי' וכי תמצא מן התורה בפי' כתוב שהשרץ מטמא משקין מק"ו מייתינן ליה הכי ומה כלי הבא מחמת שרץ מטמא את המשקין דתנינן בתורת כהנים אם כן למה נאמר משקה בכל כלי יטמא מלמד שהכלים מטמאין את המשקה שרץ שמטמא את הכלי אינו דין שיטמא משקין וכיון דטומאת משקין מחמת שרץ בק"ו גמר מן הכלי אמרי' דיו לבא מן הדין הן משקין הבאין מחמת שרץ להיות כנדון והוא הכלי מה כלי אין מטמא כלי שאין טומאה עושה כיוצא בה אף משקין הבאין מחמת שרץ לא יטמאו את הכלי: יטמא דרישא לטמא האוכל את המשקה ואימא לטמא האוכל את הכלי אמרת ק"ו ומה משקה המטמא אוכל אין מטמא אוכל שאין מטמא אוכל כיוצא בו אינו דין שלא יטמא כלי הא מה אני מקיים יטמא דרישא דקרא לטמא את המשקין שהן עלולים לקבל טומאה ואמרינן לא צריך לכולי האי חדא דליכא מידי אחרינא לרבוייה כי (מה יטמא) [שיטמאו] כלים מן אוכל הרי דחינום מק"ו שלא יטמאו מן האוכל וכל שכן אדם לא נשאר אלא אוכלין ומשקין אוכלין ליכא למימר דהא אין טומאה עושה כיוצא בה לא נשארו אלא המשקין ותו מפני שהן עלולין לקבל טומאה שלא בהכשר ואין טומאה עושה כיוצא בה מהתם נפקא וכי יתן מים על זרע וגו' הוא טמא ואין עושה כיוצא בה ואוקמ' חד למשקין הבאין מחמת שרץ וחד למשקין הבאין מחמת כלי וצריכא וכו' וזהו כלו לדברי ר' יוסי ור' שמעון דאמרי לאוכלין טמאין לכלים טהורין ואסקי' ר' יוסי בשיטת ר' עקיבא אמרה ולא סבירא ליה טותיה דיש טומאה שלישית בחולין כמו שדרש ר' עקיבא בו ביום וכן ר' עקיבא לא סבירא ליה כר' יוסי דתניא ר' עקיבא אומר למד על ככר שני שהוא עושה שלישי בחולין ור' יוסי תני בתוספתא בסוף חגיגה מנין לרביעי בקודש שפסול ודין הוא ומה מחוסר כפורים שמותר בתרומ' כדקיימ' לן טבל ועלה אוכל במעשר העריב שמשו אוכל בתרומה הביא כפרתו אוכל בקדשים נמצא מעורב שמש מחוסר כפורים טהור בתרומה פסול בקדש שלישי שפסול בתרומה אינו דין שיעשה רביעי בקדש למדנו שלישי לקדש מןהתורה שנאמר והבשר אשר יגע בכל טמא לא יאכל בטמא לא נאמר אלא בכל טמא אלו נאמר [בטמא] הייתי אומר זה טמא ראשון ולמה נאמר בכל טמא להוסיף טמא אחר זה טמא שני

לעיל יד.

[לקמן עז: יומא מג. יבמות כב: קדושין ד: סוטה כט. ב"מ לד: סנהדרין מח. זבחים סב: קי: חולין קיח:]

סוטה כט: חגיגה כד. [תוספתא דחגיגה פ"ג]

דף כט.

הגהות הב"ח

(א) רש"י ד"ה יטמא דאין וכו' דקרינן בתרווייהו יטמא. ל"ב כלומר מדלא קרינן יטמא: (ב) ד"ה חד למעוטי משקין וכו' משמע אפילו:

בטלו במעיה ואי סלקא דעתך מכלים הוא
דהדר ביה אבל באוכלין כר' יוסי ור' שמעון
סבירא ליה אמאי בטלו במעיה לגמרי נהי
דטומאה חמורה לא מטמאו טומאה קלה
מיהא ניטמאו מאי בטלו במעיה נמי בטלו
מטומאה חמורה אבל טומאה קלה מטמאו
מכלל דתנא קמא סבר טומאה חמורה נמי
מטמאו הא בשרה טמא קתני כולה ר' יהודה
היא וחסורי מיחסרא והכי קתני פרה
ששתתה מי חטאת בשרה טמא בד"א טומא'
קלה אבל טומאה חמורה לא שרבי יהודה
אומר בטלו במעיה רב אשי אמר לעולם
בטלו במעיה לגמרי *משום דהוה ליה
משקה סרוח ר' יוסי ורבי שמעון אומרים
לאוכלין טמאין לכלים טהורים אמר רבה
בר בר חנה אמר ריש לקיש רבי יוסי בשיטת
ר"ע רבו אמרה דדריש יטמא יטמא *דתנן
(ויקרא יא) בו ביום דרש ר"ע °וכל כלי חרש אשר
יפול מהם וגו' אינו אומר טמא אלא יטמא
יטמא אחרים לימד על ככר שני שעושה
(שם) שלישי בחולין והכא היכי דריש °וכל משקה
אשר ישתה בכל כלי יטמא יטמא לטמא
טומאת אוכלין אתה אומר לטמא טומאת
אוכלין או אינו אלא לטמא טומאת משקין
אמרת לא כך היה מאי לא כך היה אמר רב
פפא לא מצינו טומאה שעושה כיוצא בה
רבינא אמר מגופיה דקרא נמי לא מצית
אמרת יטמא לטמא טומאת משקין דאי
סלקא דעתך יטמא דסיפא לטמא טומאת
משקין יטמא דרישא נמי לטמא טומאת
(שם) משקין ניערבינהו וניכתבינהו °מכל האוכל
אשר יאכל אשר יבא עליו מים וכל משקה
אשר ישתה בכל כלי יטמא תרי יטמא למה
לי אלא יטמא דרישא לטמא טומאת משקין
יטמא דסיפא לטמא טומאת אוכלין ואימא
לטמא את הכלים ולאו ק"ו הוא ומה כלי
שמטמא משקה אין מטמא משקין
הבאין מחמת כלי אינו דין שלא יטמאו את
הכלים ואימא כי לא מטמאו משקין הבאין
מחמת כלי אבל משקין הבאין מחמת שרץ ה"נ
דמטמאו משקין הבאין מחמת שרץ מי כתיבי
ולאו

רש"י

בטלו במעיה. דאינן ראויין למי חטאת ואין עוד שם עליהן ואי אית ליה לרבי יהודה משקין בעלמא מטמאו אוכל כהי דבטלי מתורת מי חטאת לענין דלא הוי טמא אב הטומאה לטמא אדם וכלים שם משקה טמא מי ליכא עלייהו כשאר משקין לטמא בשר זה שהוא אוכל ולמאי בטלו במעיה לגמרי אפילו מלטמא בשר זה דהיינו טומאת אוכלין קלה כהי דטומאה חמורה לא מטמאו אם נגעו אדם וכלים בהן בתוך המעים דהא אין שם מי חטאת עליהן טומאה קלה כגון את הבשר לטמאו דהא משקין בעלמא נינהו ושם טומאה לא פקע מינייהו דניטמאו מחמת עצמן דאין נגיעה גדולה ממה שהן נוגעין בעצמן וכי אזיל שם מי חטאת מינייהו הוו להו משקין שנגעו במי חטאת אלא ש"מ מכולהו הדר ביה וכיון דבחוץ לא מטמאו משקין אוכלין אלא מדרבנן הכא דמילתא דלא שכיחא לא גזור: טומאה חמורה. אדם וכלים טומאה קלה אוכלין: והא בשרה טמא קאמר. דלא טימא אלא את הבשר ולא תנא אדם וכלים הנוגעין בהן טמאין: אבל טומאה חמורה. שיהא עדיין שמן עליהן לטמא אדם הנוגע בהן לא מטמאי שר' יהודה אומר בטלו במעיה מתורת מי חטאת: רב אשי אמר לעולם לגמרי. דאפי' שם משקה בעלמא ליכא עלייהו דה"ל משקה סרוח ותניא בת"כ וכל משקה אשר ישתה בכל כלי יטמא פרט למשקה סרוח: ר' יוסי תלמידו של ר' עקיבא היה כדתניא ביבמות בהבא על יבמתו (דף סב:) והיה העולם שמם עד שבא ר"ע אצל רבותינו שבדרום ושנאה להם ואלו הן ר"מ ורבי יהודה ור' יוסי ור"ש ור"א בן שמוע: דדריש יטמא. דכתיב גבי אוכלין טמאין יטמא ואיהו נמי דריש יטמא דכתיב גבי משקין טמאין יטמא: בו ביום. ביום שמינו את ר"א בן עזריה לנשיאות: אשר יפול מהם אל תוכו. ותניא בהכל שוחטין (חולין כד:) אע"פ שלא נגע אלא נתלה באוירו ה"ל כלי ראשון וכתיב כל אשר בתוכו יטמא מחמת הכלי ה"ל אוכל שני ואינו אומר טמא אלא יטמא לדרוש ביה יטמא: לימד על ככר שני. דהא קרא משתעי באוכלין דכתיב בתריה מכל האוכל אשר יאכל והוא היה בתוך הכלי יטמא אלמא ככר שני עושה שלישי ואף בחולין דקרא סתמא כתיב והא ליכא למימר דאוכלין שבו מקבלין טומאה מן השרץ דליהוי אויר כלי כמאן דמלי טומאה וליהוו אוכל ראשון דא"כ אף כלים שבאוירו יטמאו ובפרקין מפרשינן לה בהדיא דעל כרחך שני הוא ומן הכלי הוא מקבלה שמטמא את השלישי ואני שמעתי ככר עושה כיוצא בו ואית ליה לר"ע אוכל מטמא אוכל וא"א לומר כן משום דלא אשכחן לה בהדיא וע"י הדחק נאמר וא"כ כי אקשי לעיל והא אין אוכל מטמא אוכל ודחיק נפשיה ואוקמה מדרבנן טמא כר"ע ס"ל דהא ר"ע גופיה איירי ביה והוסיף עדות על עדותו ולקמן דקאמר לא כך היה ולא מצי לדחויה אלא ע"י טעם זה לא מצינו טומאה עושה כיוצא בה הרי מצינו לר"ע ועוד בהדיא אמר לקמן בההוא יטמא לטמא את המשקין ולא אוכל כיוצא בו: והכא. גבי יטמא דמשקין דקאמר רבי יוסי דמטמא אוכל היכי דריש ליה רבי יוסי דמוקי ליה לטמא אוכל ולא לטמא משקה כיוצא בו ולא כלי: וכל משקה אשר ישתה בכל כלי. אם היה המשקה הזה בתוכו של כלי חרס דהא עלה קאי יטמא ודריש ביה יטמא לטמא את האוכל: לא מצינו טומאה שעושה כיוצא בה. כדאמרינן לקמן דלהכי קרינא יטמא למימר דהוא טמא ואין עושה כיוצא בו: ואי ס"ד. האי יטמא דכתיב במשקה בסיפיה דקרא לטמא משקים קאמר ויטמא דרישא דכתיב גבי אוכל ע"כ לטמא משקין מוקמי ליה לקמיה [א] דהכתיב לעיל מהאי קרא טמא הוא ואמרינן הוא טמא ואין עושה כיוצא בו ומדאיצטריך למעוטי אוכל מכלל דמשקין מטמאי א"כ יטמא יטמא למה לי ניערבינהו וניכתבינהו כו': ואימא. יטמא דסיפא לטמא את הכלים ואמאי קאמר רבי יוסי לכלים טהור: ומה כלי. שטימא את המשקה הזה לא יוכל לטמא את הכלי כדאמר לקמן כל אשר בתוכו יטמא מכל האוכל אוכלין ומשקין מיטמאים מאויר כלי חרס ואין כלים מיטמאים מאויר כלי חרס משקין אלו שבאין מחמת כלי אינו דין כו': ואימא כי לא מטמאו משקין הבאים מחמת כלי. דבהאי קל וחומר הוא נפקא לן דאין משקה מטמא כלי *(אימא כי לא מטמאו משקין כלי) הני מילי משקין הבאין מחמת כלי אבל משקין שנגעו בשרץ יטמאוהו:
ומשני

תוספות

הא בשרה טמא קתני. משמע דוקא בשרה אבל אדם וכלים לא והיינו משום דנפסלו בהיסח הדעת ואם תאמר כיון דפרחה מהן טומאה חמורה אפי' טומאה קלה לא לטמאו דהא אמרי' בפ' בא סימן (נדה נא.) ובפ' טבול יום (זבחים קה.) כל שסופו לטמא טומאה חמורה לא בעי הכשר שרץ וחשיב כאילו נגע בשרץ והיינו דוקא בעוד שסופו לטמא טומאה חמורה אבל כשאין ראוי כבר לטמא טומאה חמורה בעי הכשר כדאמרינן בפרק בהמה המקשה (חולין עג:) גבי בשר הפורש מאבר מן החי דלא מהני ליה *מה שסופו לטמא טומאה חמורה כשהיה עם אביו לשויה מוכשר כיון דלאחר שפירש ממנו אין ראוי לטמא טומאה חמורה וי"ל דשאני התם כששימש מעשה עץ שימש כדאמרינן בהעור והרוטב (שם דף קכט.) ולכך כשפירש מאביו בעי הכשר אבל מי חטאת צריך שיהו ראויין מתחלה לשתיה ונמצא טומאה חמורה שלהן אינו מעשה עץ אלא מטעם שיהיו ראויין לשתיית אדם דבע"א לא היו ראויין להזאה ולכך אף כשנפסלו לא פרחה טומאת משקין:

בטלו במעיה. אבל בעודם בפיה לא בטלו אע"ג דאמרינן במסכת פרה (פ"ט מ"ג) דכל העופות פוסלין מי חטאת אור"י דהתם מיירי קודם קדוש ונפסלים כדפ"ה*) בהנזקין (גיטין נג) דבעינן שתהא חיותן בכלי או משום מלאכה **) והכא איירי לאחר קידוש מדחשיב להו סופו לטמא טומאה חמורה ומלאכה אינה פוסלת אחר קידוש כדתנן במסכת פרה (פ"ד מ"ד) מים מלאכה פוסלת בהן עד שיתן לתוכן אפר (*ובסיפא) יליף לה מדכתיב למי נדה וכבר הם למי נדה ובטלו במעיה משום היסח הדעת ובתוספת' (דמקוואות פ"ז) מפרש טעמ' דר"י משום דכתיב למשמרת יצאו אלו שאינם למשמרת הואיל ששתתה מהן הפרה:

לא מצינו טומאה עושה כיוצא בה. פי' הקונט' כדדרשינן לקמן יטמא שאין טומאה עושה כיוצא בה ואית ספרים דל"ג לקמן ולשון לא מצינו לא משמע כן דמשמע דמעלמא נפקא לן ממשמעות ומפר"י לא מצינו טומאה עושה כיוצא בה כדדרשינן לעיל (דף יד.) מטמא הוא:

*רבינא אמר מגופיה דקרא לא מצית אמרת דאי ס"ד לטומאת משקין לא לכתוב אלא חד יטמא תרי זימני למה לי למעוטי שאין טומאה עושה כיוצא בה:

ומה כלי שמטמא משקין. וא"ת משקין הבאין מחמת אוכל לא יטמאו אוכל מהאי ק"ו וכן אוכל הבא מחמת משקין לא יטמא משקין וי"ל דהכא עביד שפיר ק"ו דמה כלי שאין מטמא כלי משום שהוא קל שאינו אב הטומאה דכשהוא אב הטומאה מטמא כלי וכ"ש משקין הבאים מחמת כלי דקילי טפי אבל מה שאין אוכל מטמא אוכל היינו לפי שאין עושה כיוצא בו וא"ת משקין הבאים מחמת כלי שנגע במת מנלן דלא מטמאו כלי דמק"ו דכלי לא אתי דכלי שנגע במת מטמא כלי וי"ל דהאי קרא בשרץ כתיב אבל משקין שנגעו במת לא כתיב:
ולאו

מסורת הש"ס

[לקמן כ.]
חולין לג: סוטה כז:
[illegible]

הגהות מהר"ב רנשבורג

[א] רש"י ד"ה ואי ס"ד וכו' דהכתיב לעיל מהאי קרא. מלת לעיל נמחק ונ"ב צ"ל בתר האי קרא:

רבינו חננאל

למשקין באוכלין וכי בהא כר' יוסי ור' שמעון סבירא ליה נהי דלא מטמא טומאה חמורה כאב לטמא במשא כאשר עקר מי חטאת ותורתם שהן מאבות הטומאה מטמא אדם וכלים כדתנן למעלה מהן נבלה ומי חטאת שיש בהן כדי הזיה שמטמא האדם במשא לטמא בגדים טומאה קלה מטמא: והא ת"ק נמי בשרה טמא קתני ולא (היא) טומאת מי חטאת עצמן שהן טומאה חמורה אלא טומאה קלה והיא טומאת אוכלין הוא דמטמאה ואי הכי מאי בינייהו ואמרינן חסורי מחסרי והכי קתני בשרה טמא טומאה קלה אבל טומאת מי חטאת שהיא חמורה שמטמ' במשא לא דברי ר' יהודה שר' יהודה אומר בטלו במעיה ולעולם באוכלין ר' יהודה כר' יוסי ור' שמעון סבירא ליה: רב אשי אמר לעולם בטלו לגמרי משום דהוי משקה סרוח: אמר מר ר' יוסי ור"ש אומרים [לאוכלים טמאים]כו'. אמרי' ר' יוסי ור"ש בשטת ר' עקיבא אמרה שהחשיב משקין מטמ' האוכלין דדריש יטמא יטמא הנוגע בו דתנן בסוטה פ"ה בו ביום דרש ר' עקיבא וכל כלי חרש וגו' וכוותיה דרש הכא ר' יוסי וכל משקה אשר ישתה בכל כלי יטמא האוכל הנוגע במשקה הזה יטמא אתה אומר אוכל מטמא מן המשקה או אינו אלא המשקה מטמא מן המשקה ולא האוכל מן המשקה אמרת לא כך היה כלומר אין טומאה עושה כיוצא בה ומאי היא אין מטמא משקה ממשקה אלא האוכל הוא מטמא מן המשקה: רבינא אמר אין טומאה עושה כיוצא בה מרישא דקרא נפקא מכל האוכל אשר יאכל אשר יבא עליו מים יטמא טמא לא אמר אלא יטמא ללמדך כי הוא טמא וגם הנוגע בו יטמא ואי ס"ד כל האוכלין לעולם אין מטמאין (את) [מן] המשקין וכי יטמא דכתיב הכא במשקה אשר ישתה שיהיו לטמא את המשקין באו הוה לי' לקרא למכתב חד יטמא תרי למה לי אלא יטמא דכתיב באוכל לטומאת משקין וטומאה דכתיב במשקין אשר ישתה לטומא' אוכלין: ואימא יטמא דכתיב במשקה אשר ישתה לטמא כלי' הוא דאתי ולא לטומאת אוכלין ודחי' ומה כלי המטמא את המשקה אינו מטמא כלי שאין כלי מטמא כלי דקיימא לן שאין טומאה עושה כיוצא בה משקין הבאין מחמת כלי דתנינן בספרא שהכלי' מטמאין את המשקין שנאמר וכל משקה אשר ישתה בכל כלי יטמא: התינח משקין הבאין

*) [לא מצאתי שם רק בהמגרש פו: רש"י ד"ה מפני שמוללת משמע כן. אמנם ברש"י חולין ע: ד"ה אם מבואר כן להדיא]
**) [וע"ע תוספות גיטין פו: ד"ה כל ותוס' חולין ע: ד"ה אם יכולה]

R. Judah said: [18a] It [the water] is nullified in its bowels.[8] Now if you think that he retracted [only] from [his ruling on] utensils, yet in [respect to] eatables he holds as R. Jose and R. Simeon, why is it completely nullified in its bowels: granted that it cannot defile [with] the graver uncleanness,[9] yet it can at least defile [with] the lighter uncleanness?[10]—What does, 'it is nullified in its bowels' mean? It is indeed nullified from [imposing] grave uncleanness, but it does defile [with] light uncleanness. Hence it follows that the first Tanna holds that it is unclean even with the graver uncleanness; but surely he states, 'Its *flesh* is unclean?'[11]—The whole is R. Judah, but the text is defective, and it was thus taught: If a cow drinks the water of lustration, its flesh is unclean. When is that said? In respect of light uncleanness, but not in respect of grave uncleanness, for R. Judah maintained: It is nullified in its bowels. R. Ashi said: In truth it is completely nullified
a in its bowels, because it is [now] noisome liquid.[1]

'R. Jose and R. Simeon maintained: In respect of eatables they are unclean; in respect of utensils they are clean.' Rabbah b. Bar Ḥanah said in Resh Laḳish's name: R. Jose stated this in accordance with the opinion of R. Akiba his teacher,[2] who interprets *yiṭma* [it shall be unclean] as *yeṭamme* [it shall defile]. For we learned: On that very day[3] R. Akiba lectured: *And every earthen vessel, wherein any of them* [*sc.* creeping things] *falleth, whatsoever is in it shall be unclean* [yiṭma]:[4] it does not state *ṭame* [unclean] but *yiṭma*, [intimating that] it defiles [*yeṭamme*] others, [thus] teaching that a loaf of the second degree produces a third in the case of *ḥullin*.[5] And how does he interpret [it] here?[6]—*And all drink that may be drunk in every such vessel* [yiṭma] *shall be unclean*:[7] it 'shall defile' [*yeṭamme*] in respect of defiling eatables.[8] You say, 'In respect of defiling eatables': yet perhaps it is not so, but rather in respect of defiling liquids?—You can answer, it was not thus. What does 'it was not thus' mean?—Said R. Papa: We do not find that uncleanness renders that which is similar to itself [unclean].[9] Rabina said: From the verse itself too you cannot say 'it shall defile' is in respect of defiling liquids. For if you should think that '*it shall be unclean*' of the second part [of the verse] is in respect of defiling liquids, [while] '*it shall be unclean*' of the first part is also in respect of defiling liquids,[10] then let it [the Torah] combine them and write them [together], *All food therein which may be eaten, that on which water cometh, and all drink that may be drunk in every such vessel shall be unclean*: what is the purpose of '*shall be unclean*' twice? Hence '*shall be unclean*' of the first part is in respect of defiling liquids, [while] '*shall be unclean*' of the second part is in respect
b of defiling eatables. Yet perhaps it is in respect of defiling vessels?[1]—Does it [the reverse] not follow *a minori*: if a utensil, which defiles liquids, cannot defile [another] utensil,[2] then how much the more should liquids which are unclean[3] through a utensil not defile utensils! Yet perhaps, they do[4] not defile [utensils] [when they are] liquids unclean through a utensil; but liquids which are unclean through a *sherez* do indeed defile [utensils]?—Are then liquids which are unclean through a *sherez* written [in Scripture]?

(8) Because it is no longer fit for its purpose, and ceases to be regarded as water of purification. (9) I.e., it cannot defile human beings and vessels. (10) I.e., foodstuffs, *sc.* this flesh. For the water is at least the same as any other liquid and is therefore unclean, for it is regarded as though it touched itself while it was yet the water of purification, and in turn it should defile the flesh. (11) But he does not maintain that the water defiles even human beings and vessels.
a (1) And undrinkable, whereas only drinkable water defiles. (2) But it is not his own view, v. Tosaf. *supra* 15b s.v. ר׳ יוסי. (3) V. 16a, n. a3. (4) Lev. XI, 33. (5) For the *sherez* (creeping thing) is a 'father' of uncleanness; hence it renders the vessel a derivative or a 'first' degree, and that in turn makes the food in it a second, and since the verse teaches that it defiles others, without specifying *terumah*, it follows that this makes a third even in respect of *ḥullin*. (6) In respect of liquids. (7) Ibid. 34. (8) But not liquids. Consequently they only mention eatables in their ruling, but not liquids. (9) V. *infra*. Hence an unclean liquid can defile an eatable, but not another liquid. (10) V. *infra* 18b.
b (1) *Sc.* the second '*shall be unclean*'—why then does R. Jose rule that it is clean in respect of vessels? (2) As shown *infra*. (3) Lit., 'come'. (4) Lit., 'when do they not ...?'

ground, are clean; [17*b*] R. Simeon said: In vessels, they are unclean; in the ground, they are clean.[4]

R. Papa said: Even on the view that the uncleanness of liquids is Biblical, [the non-defilement of] the liquids of the slaughter-house is a traditional law. Said R. Huna the son of R. Nathan to R. Papa: Then when R. Eliezer said, 'Liquids have no uncleanness at all; the proof is that Jose b. Jo'ezer of Zeredah testified that the fluids in the [Temple] slaughter-house are clean,'—but if it is a traditional law, can we learn from this?[5]

Rabina said to R. Ashi: But surely R. Simeon maintained [that] the uncleanness of liquids is Biblical, for it was taught, R. Jose and R. Simeon maintain: In respect of utensils they are clean; in respect of eatables they are unclean;[6] yet here R. Simeon rules: In vessels, they are unclean; in the ground, they are clean. But if it is a traditional law, what is the difference whether they are in vessels or in the ground?—This is a difficulty.

R. Papa said: As to what you say, 'In the ground, they are clean', this was taught only of water, but not of blood. And even of water too we said this only when there is a *rebi'ith*, so that
a needles and hooks can be bathed therein;[1] but if less than a *rebi'ith*, it is unclean.[2]

The Master said: 'R. Judah said: It is unclean in respect of everything.' Shall we say [that] R. Judah holds [that] the uncleanness of liquids, in respect of defiling utensils, is Biblical?[3] Surely we learned:[4] In the case of all utensils which have an outside[5] and an inside, e.g., cushions, feather-beds, sacks and packing bags, if the inside is defiled, the outside is defiled [too]; if the outside is defiled, the inside is not defiled. R. Judah said: When is that said? Where they are defiled by a liquid; but if they are defiled by a *sherez*, if the inside is defiled the outside is defiled, [and] if the outside is defiled the inside is defiled.[6] Now if you think that the uncleanness of liquids in respect of defiling utensils is Biblical, what is the difference whether it was defiled through liquids or through a *sherez?*—Said Rab Judah in Samuel's name: R. Judah retracted.[7] Rabina said: In truth he did not retract: one refers
b to liquids which are unclean[1] through the hands,[2] the other to liquids which are unclean through a *sherez*. If so, instead of stating, 'When is that, when they are defiled by liquids,' let him draw a distinction in that itself: [thus:] when is it said? In the case of liquids unclean through the hands; but in the case of liquids defiled by a *sherez*, if the inside is defiled the outside is defiled, [and] if the outside is defiled the inside is defiled. Hence it is clear as we first answered: R. Judah retracted.

The scholars asked: Did he retract [only] from [his ruling on] utensils, but in [the matter of] eatables he holds as R. Jose and R. Simeon;[3] or perhaps he completely retracted, in accordance with R. Meir['s views]?[4]—Said R. Naḥman b. Isaac, Come and hear: If a cow[5] drinks the water of lustration,[6] its flesh is unclean.[7]

(4) V. *infra*. (5) Surely this does not afford proof, if these liquids stand entirely in a separate category. (6) V. *supra* 16*a*.

a (1) If they are unclean, the *rebi'ith* of water in the ground serving as a ritual bath, as it can do by Biblical law, though the Rabbis enacted that forty *se'ahs* is the minimum capacity. Still, since by Biblical law it constitutes a *mikweh* itself, the water cannot be defiled. A *rebi'ith* is the minimum which may constitute a *mikweh*. (2) Hence according to R. Simeon, R. Joseph b. Jo'ezer's testimony was only in respect of water, not blood. (3) V. 16*a*, n. c11. (4) So cur. edd., the reference being to the Mishnah in Kel. XXV, 1. But the reading there is different, and R. Samson of Sens quotes the present passage as a Baraitha. R. Ḥan. too introduces it by the phrase 'it was taught'. (5) Lit., 'back'. (6) 'Utensils which have a back (outside) and an inside' are those which can be used on both sides. A cushion, feather-bed, etc. had a definite side for use, nevertheless they could be turned inside out and used; similarly, sacks and packing bags could be turned inside out and used, and they are therefore treated like other vessels which require only rinsing in order to become clean (v. Ḥul. 25*a*) so that if the inner side is defiled the whole is unclean, but not the reverse. Thus the first Tanna. R. Judah, however, draws a distinction between liquids and a *sherez* as the contaminating object; in the first case this law holds good, because liquid defiles by Rabbinical law only, and therefore the extent of its defilement was lessened, so that it might be known that it does not defile by Biblical law. Hence if it touches *terumah* the *terumah* must not be burnt, as it would be if it were unclean by Scriptural law. But if a *sherez*, which defiles by Biblical law, contaminates them, they are altogether unclean, no matter where they are touched. (7) From the view that it is unclean in respect of everything.

b (1) Lit., 'which come'. (2) By a Rabbinical enactment a person's hands are generally considered unclean in the second degree; further, they defile liquids and render them unclean in the first degree. It is between such liquids and a *sherez* that R. Judah draws a distinction. (3) That liquids contaminate them Biblically. (4) That liquids do not contaminate them even Rabbinically. (5) Whether sanctified or not. (6) V. Num. XIX, 9 (it is there translated: water of separation). (7) If it is slaughtered while the water is yet within it, for the water of purification defiles human beings and vessels, v. ibid. 21.

(רבן) שמעון אומר בכלים טמאין בקרקע טהורין א"ר פפא אפילו למ"ד טומאת משקין דאורייתא משקי בית מטבחיא (א) הלכתא גמירי לה א"ל רב הונא בריה דרב נתן לרב פפא ואלא הא דאמר ר"א *אין טומאה למשקין כל עיקר תדע שהרי העיד (יוסף) בן יועזר איש צרידה על משקי בית מטבחיא דכן ואי הלכתא גמירי לה מי גמרינן מינה א"ל רבינא לרב אשי והא ר"ש דאמר טומאת משקין דאורייתא *דתניא ר' יוסי ור' שמעון אומרים לכלים טהורין לאוכלין טמאין והבא קאמר (רבן) שמעון בכלים טמאין בקרקע טהורין ואי הלכתא היא מה לי בכלים מה לי בקרקע קשיא אמר רב פפא הא דאמרת בקרקע טהורין לא שנו [א] אלא מים אבל דם לא ומים נמי לא אמרן אלא דהוי רביעית *דחזי להטביל ביה מחטין וצינורות אבל *לא הוי רביעית טמאין: אמר מר רבי יהודה אומר לכל טמא למימרא דסבר רבי יהודה טומאת משקין לטמא כלים דאוריית' *והתנן *כל הכלים שיש להן אחורים ותוך כגון הכרים והכסתות והשקין והמרצופין נטמא תוכו נטמא גבו נטמא גבו לא נטמא תוכו א"ר יהודה *במה דברים אמורים שנטמאו מחמת משקין אבל נטמאו מחמת שרץ נטמא תוכו נטמא גבו נטמא גבו נטמא תוכו ואי סלקא דעתך טומאת משקין לטמא כלים דאורייתא מה לי נטמא מחמת משקין מה לי נטמא מחמת שרץ אמר רב יהודה אמר שמואל חזר בו ר' יהודה רבינא אמר לעולם לא הדר הא במשקין הבאין מחמת ידים הא במשקין הבאין מחמת שרץ אי הכי אדתני במה דברים אמורים שנטמאו מחמת משקין ליפלוג וליתני בדידה במה דברים אמורים במשקין הבאין מחמת ידים אבל במשקין הבאין מחמת שרץ נטמא תוכו נטמא גבו נטמא גבו נטמא תוכו אלא מחוורתא כדשנין מעיקרא חזר בו רבי יהודה איבעיא להו מכלים הוא דהדר ביה אבל באוכלין כרבי יוסי ורבי שמעון סבירא ליה או דילמא לגמרי הדר ביה כרבי מאיר אמר רב נחמן בר יצחק תא שמע *פרה ששתתה מי חטאת בשרה טמא* רבי יהודה אומר בטלו

רש"י

(רבן) שמעון אומר בכלים טמאין. (רבן) שמעון לטעמיה דאמר לעיל טומאת משקין דאורייתא ואפי' לטמא אחרים כדתניא גבי ספק משקה לטמא אחרים (רבן) שמעון אומר באוכלין טמא הלכך במשקי בית מטבחיא לא מצו רבנן לטהורינהו: בקרקע טהורין. ולקמן מתרגם ליה אמים ודאיכא רביעית דאיכא תורת מקוה עלה למחטין וציגורות דמדאורייתא לא מקבלי טומאה כדכתיב (ויקרא יא) מקוה מים יהיה טהור ורביעית הויא מקוה מדאוריית' דכי כתיב ארבעים סאה באדם הוא דכתיבי דנפקא לן *מאת. כל בשרו מים שכל גופו עולה בהן אבל לכלים קטנים אין צריך אלא כדי שיתכסו במים ובציר מרביעית גמרא גמירי לה דלא חשיב למיהוי מקוה וכיון דבעלמא מדאורייתא לא מיטמו ורבנן הוא דבטלו רביעית דמקוה שלא יטבילו כלים בפחות מארבעים סאה כדאמרינן בנזיר (דף לח.) עשר רביעיות הן ופרכינן והא איכא רביעית דמקוה ומשנינן בר מינה דההיא דבטלו רבנן בפרק שלשה מינין ותניא נמי* זה הכלל כל שאדם טובל בו ידים וכלים טובלי' בו וגזרו טומאה אף על המשקין שבקרקע כל כמה דהוי בציר מארבעים סאה והכא גבי מטבחיא אוקמוה אדאורייתא וטהורים: הלכתא גמירי לה. מסיני דלא מיטמאו: מי גמרינן מינה. דטומאת שאר משקין לאו דאורייתא הא אמרת אפילו היא דאורייתא גמירי בהני דטהורין והיכי מייתי רבי אליעזר טעם למילתיה מהכא: והא רבי שמעון. דמשום דסבירא ליה טומאת משקין דאורייתא קאמר הכא בכלים טמאין משום דבשאר משקין דאורייתא ובקרקע הוא דטהורין משום דגבי שאר משקין דרבנן אלמא לאו הלכה למשה מסיני הוא וקשיא לרב פפא דאי הלכתא היא מה לי בכלים דגבי שאר משקין דאורייתא מה לי בקרקע: קשיא. גרסינן הא דרב פפא לאו מילתא היא וכי אמרה לאו אדעתיה ולא היה זכור למשניות הללו: א"ר פפא הא דאמרת. לרבי שמעון בקרקע טהורין לא שנו אלא מים דאיכא שם מקוה עליהן במחובר: אבל דם. אין בו חילוק בין קרקע לכלים דטומאה דידיה דאורייתא אף בקרקע ולר"ש כי איתמר דכן דיוסף בן יועזר אמים לחודייהו איתמר דהוי רביעית כדפרשינן: צינורות. שטווין בהם זהב: אבל לית בהו רביעית. דמדאורייתא לא חזו למקוה ומדאוריי' טמאין אף במחובר ה"נ טמאין ודקיימא לן שיעור טומאת משקין ברביעית *הני מילי לטמא אחרים אבל לעצמן טמאין בכל שהן כדתנן בטהרות (פ"ג מ"ג) ומייתינן לה בגמרא דכל שעה (דף לג:) טמא מת שסחט כו' כיון שילתה טפה ראשונה נטמאת בכבילה: אמר מר רבי יהודה אומר. גבי ספק משקה לטמא אחרים לכל טמא ואפילו לכלים אלמא ודאי נגיעתן מטמא כלים מדאורייתא מדמטמינן ספק דידהו: שיש להם אחורים ותוך. שראויין להשתמש בהן בתוכן ובאחוריהן: מרצופין. של עור: שנטמאו (א) במשקין. דטומאתן לאו דאורייתא לכלים ורבנן הוא דגזור בהו משום משקה זב וזבה שהן אב הטומאה ועבדי בה רבנן היכירא שאם נטמא גבו לא נטמא תוכו הכי לידעו דהך טומאה לאו דאורייתא דלא לשרפו עליה תרומה וקדשים כדאמרינן בבכורות (דף לח.) בעדותו של חזקיה אבי עקש: אבל מחמת שרץ. דטומאתן דאורייתא: חזר בו ר' יהודה. מההיא דלעיל: הא במשקין הבאין מחמת ידים. שגזרו חכמים טומאות סניות על ידים סתם וגזרו עליהן שיטמאו משקין להיות תחלה והיא דרבנן הוא: אי הכי. הא דתני אבל נטמאו מחמת שרץ וכו' לא תיסכה נטמא גבו נטמא תוכו אלא לגמרי באוכלין. כרבי יוסי ורבי שמעון סבירא ליה דמשקין טמאין טומאת עצמן בשרץ עצמו לא ישמעינן אפילו משקין: אבל באוכלין. כרבי יוסי ורבי שמעון סבירא ליה למשקין מטמאין אוכלין מדאורייתא: כרבי מאיר. דאמר לא מיטמא אפי' אוכלין אלא מדרבנן: פרה. של זבח או של חולין: ששתתה מי חטאת. ושחטה בתוך עונתן במעיה: בשרה טמא. שמקבלת טומאה מהן דמי חטאת מטמאין אפי' אדם וכלים כדכתיב (במדבר יט) והנוגע במי הנדה וגו': בטלו

תוספות

אבל דם לא. יוה"ח דהרבה בדם יש לטהר טפי אפי' בכלים דדם קדשים לא איתקש למים כדאמרי' לעיל שאינו כשפך כמים אין מכשיר וי"ל דהכי פי' אבל דם, היכא דמטמא כגון דם חולין או בעלי מומין או זבח שנפסל לו: אלא דהוי רביעית דחזי להטביל בהו מחטין וצינורות. מכאן אומר ר"י שיש לדקדק דמקוה שכולו שאוב אינו פסול אלא מדרבנן דמשקין בית מטבחיא שהן דכן ע"כ הן שאובין מדמפליג בין דם למים ולא מפליג בין שאובין למחוברין ואמר דחזי להטביל בהו מחטין וצינורות ועוד תניא בתוספתא דמסכת מקוואות (פ"ב) מקוה שהניחו ריקן ומצאו מלא כשר והיינו משום דספיקא דרבנן לקולא וריקן נמי משמע שלא היה בו כלום מדלא קאמר שהניחו חסר והא דתניא בת"כ אך מעין ובור יכול אפילו מלא בכתף תלמוד לומר מעין מה מעין בידי שמים אף מקוה בידי שמים נ"ל דאסמכתא בעלמא הוא ואם תאמר כיון דכולו שאוב כשר מדאורייתא אמאי גזרו רבנן בשאיבה כלל ויש לומר דגזרו שאיבה אטו דילמא אתי לאטבולי במנא דבתוך הכלי ודאי אסור לטבול מדאורייתא *ואור"י דכי נמי בטלו רביעית דמקוה *מכל מקום כל שהוא דמעין לא בטלו מדתנן בת"כ אך מעין מטהר בכל שהוא והמקוה בארבעים סאה והא דמקוה במ' סאה היינו לבתר דביטלו רביעית ואפילו הכי קתני דמעין מטהר בכל שהוא הקשה ר"י בשם הרב רבינו שלמה דאמר בפרק חומר בקודש (חגיגה כג.) גבי מקוה שחלקו בסל תדע דבעי' כשפופרת הנוד דהא ארעא חלחולי מחלחלא ובעינן ארבעים סאה במקום אחד וארעא חלחולי מחלחלא לא שייך אלא במעין ובעינן ארבעים סאה במקום אחד והתם מיירי בדבר שכל גופו עולה בפחות דהא לא כן מה ראיה צריך: נטמא (ה"ג) תוכו נטמא גבו נטמא גבו לא נטמא תוכו. וכן גרס רש"י ואף על גב דכל כלי שטף נמי דינו כן מכל מקום נקט כרים וכסתות ושקין ומרצופין משום דרבי מאיר פליג בהני דווקא דקתני סיפא רבי מאיר אומר כל שיש לו תוברואות יש לו אחורים ותוך ושאין לו תוברואות וכו' תוברואות פירושו תפירות שפה לפיהן סביב כעין מכנסים דאז אין מהפכין אותן להשתמש בצד אחר ויש לו דין אחורים ותוך לענין שאם נטמא גבו לא נטמא תוכו כמו שאר כלי שטף: הא

רבינו חננאל

נטמאו בכלים טמאין [בקרקע טהורין] סוגיא דשמעתא רב פפא סבר עיקר טומאת משקה מדרבנן ומשקה בית מטבחיא אוקמינהו אדאורייי' והכין ממש לא גזרו בהו כלל ושמואל אמר טומאת משקין לעצמן מדאורייתא לטמא אחרים מדרבנן ובמשקה בית מטבחיא לא גזרו לטמא אחרים: אמר רב פפא אפילו למאן דאמר טומאת משקין דאורייתא משקה בית מטבחיא דכן הלכתא גמירי לה הכי ואקשי' עליה רב הונא בריה דרב נתן מדר' אליעזר דאמר אין טומאה למשקין כל עיקר תדע שהעיד ר' יוסי ואי הלכתא היא מהלכתא מי גמרינן ולא מצא רב פפא תשובה ולא דחינן ליה להא לא עלתה בתיובתא אבל הא דא' רבינא האמר ר'שמעון טומאת משקין דאורייתא דתני' ר' יוסי ור' שמעון אומר לאוכלין טמאים לכלים טהורין וקתני הכא בכלים טמאים בקרקע טהורים ואי הלכתא גמירי לה מה לי בכלים מה לי בקרקע* ואו קושי' רב פפא ואמר הא דאמר ר' שמעון בקרקע טהורין לא אמרן אלא במים שיש בהן כדי רביעית דחזו לאטבולי בהו מחטין וצינורות כגון מקוה מים שהוא טהור אבל אין בהן כדי רביעית לא והוו שאמר רב פפא בזבחים דגרסי' בשחיטת קדשים פ"ב מקוה שיש בו ארבעים סאה מכוונות ונתן סאה ונטל סאה הרי זה כשר ואמר משמיה דר' יוחנן עד רובו אמר רב פפא ואם קרה ממנו רביעית מטבילין בו מחטין וצינורות דמהכשרא דמקוה קא אתו: אמר מר ר' יהודה אומר לכל טמא כלומר בין לטמא בין לכלים בין לאוכלין ואקשי' וכי ר' יהודה אית ליה טומאה למשקין מדאורייתא כלל** והא תניא כל הכלים שיש להם אחורי' ותוך כגון הכרים והכסתות והמרצופין שיש להם אחורים שפעמים שמשתמשין עליהם ויש להם תוך שפעמים שנותנין בתוכם כגון אלו נטמא גבן נטמא תוכם נטמא תוכם נטמא גבן אמר ר' יהודה במה דברים אמורים בטומאת משקין כלומר שהוא מדרבנן ואין טומאת שרץ נטמא תוכו נטמא גבו נטמא גבו [נטמא תוכו] הא אשכחן לר' יהודה דשני ליה בין טומאת משקה לטומאת שרץ ואי טומאת משקין דאורייתא היא מה לי טומאת שרץ כולה טומאה דאורייתא היא ואמרינן חזר בו ר' יהודה ואמר אין למשקין טומאה דאורייתא ואע"ג דאמר רבינא לעולם לא הדר ביה ר' יהודה ואוקמה במשקין הבאין מחמת שרץ והא דתני נטמא גבו לא נטמא תוכו במשקין הבאים מחמת ידים אבל באוכלין כר' יוסי ור' שמעון סבירא ליה או דלמא לגמרי הוא דהדר כר' מאיר ת"ש פרה ששתתה מי חטאת בשרה טמא ר' יהודה אומר בטלו במעיה

* מדברי רבינו נראה דלא גרס כגמ' קשיא ולספר דלזה רמז רש"י קשיא גרסינן לאפוקי מגי' הר"ח.
** ר"ל לטמא את הכלים וכן במסקנא דאמר דחזר בו ר"י ואמר דאין למשקין טומאה דאורייתא ר"ל לטמא את הכלים.

עין משפט נר מצוה

קיח א מיי' פ"י מהל' טומאת אוכלין הלכה טו: ב מיי' פ"ז מהלכות טומאת אוכלין הלכה ג:
קיט ב ג מיי' פכ"ח מה' כלים הל' ב:
קכ ד מיי' פט"ו מהל' פרה אדומה הל' ו:

מסורת הש"ס

[נ"ל רבי] [נ"ל רבי] [נ"ל רבי] [לקמן קט.] [נ"ל ר' יוסי] [לעיל טז.] [נ"ל רבי] תוספתא מקוות פ"א [עי' תוס' ע"ז עה: ד"ה מים שהכנס כו'] כלים פכ"ה משנה א עי' ר"ש שם

הגהות הב"ח

(א) רש"י ד"ה מרצופין של עור שנטמאו מחמת משקין:

גליון הש"ס

ברש"י ד"ה אבל לית בהו רביעית וכו' הכ"נ טמאין. עי' לעיל יד ע"ב תוד"ה דאיכא: תוס' ד"ה אבל דם לא.

ואמר רב אישתבש כהני מידי הוא טעמא אלא לרב רב משקי בית מטבחיא תני אבל משקי בי מדבחיא מטמא גופא רב אמר אישתבש כהני ושמואל אמר לא אישתבש כהני רב אמר אישתבש כהני רביעי בקדש בעא מינייהו ואמרו ליה טהור ושמואל אמר לא אישתבש כהני חמישי בקדש בעא מינייהו ואמרו ליה טהור בשלמא לרב היינו דכתיב ארבעה °לחם ונזיד ויין ושמן אלא לשמואל חמשה מנא ליה מי כתיב ונגע כנפו °ונגע בכנפו כתיב במה שנגע בכנפו תא שמע °ויאמר חגי אם יגע טמא נפש בכל אלה היטמא ויענו הכהנים ויאמרו יטמא בשלמא לשמואל מדהכא לא אישתבש התם נמי לא אישתבש אלא לרב מאי שנא הכא דאישתבש ומאי שנא התם דלא אישתבש אמר רב נחמן אמר רבה בר אבוה בקיאין הן בטומאת מת ואין בקיאין הן בטומאת שרץ רבינא אמר התם רביעי הכא שלישי ת"ש °ויען חגי ויאמר כן העם הזה וכן הגוי הזה לפני נאם ה' וגו' בשלמא לרב היינו דכתיב טמא אלא לשמואל אמאי טמא איתמוהי קא מתמה והא וכן כל מעשה ידיהם כתיב אמר מר זוטרא ואיתימא רב אשי מתוך שקלקלו את מעשיהם מעלה עליהם הכתוב כאילו הקריבו בטומאה גופא רב תני משקי בית מטבחיא ולוי תנא משקי בי מדבחיא ללוי הניחא אי סבירא ליה כשמואל דאמר *דכן מלטמא טומאת אחרים אבל טומאת עצמן יש להן משכחת לה דנגעי כולהו בראשון אלא אי סבר לי' כרב דאמר דכן ממש היכי משכחת לה על כרחך כשמואל סבירא ליה ולשמואל הניחא אי סבר לה כרב דתני משקי בית מטבחיא אבל משקי בי מדבחיא אחריני נמי מיטמאו רביעי הוא דלא עביד חמישי הא שלישי עביד רביעי אלא אי סבר ליה כלוי דתני משקי בי מדבחיא מאי איריא רביעי דלא עביד חמישי אפילו שני ושלישי נמי לא עבדי על כרחיך כרב סבירא ליה תניא כוותיה דרב תניא כוותיה דלוי תניא כוותיה דרב הדם והיין והשמן והמים משקי בי מדבחיא שנטמאו בפנים והוציאן לחוץ טהורין נטמאו בחוץ והכניסן בפנים טמאין איני והאמר רבי יהושע בן לוי משקי בי מדבחיא לא אמרו דכן אלא במקומן מאי לאו למעוטי נטמאו בפנים והוציאן לחוץ לא למעוטי נטמאו בחוץ והכניסן בפנים והא במקומן קאמר הכי קאמר לא אמרו דכן אלא שנטמאו במקומן תניא כוותיה דרב הדם והמים משקי בית מטבחיא שנטמאו בין בכלים בין בקרקע טהורין רבן

רש"י

ואמר רב. לקמן: אישתבש כהני. שטהרו רביעי בקודש אלמא יין ושמן דמשקי בית מטבחיא נינהו ומיטמאו ואי טומאת משקין דרבנן הא אמרת דלא גזור עלייהו ואי נמי בטומאות דרבנן קא בדיק להו חגי לכהני וכבר נגזר טומאה על המשקין בימי חגי הנביא שהיה מאנשי כנסת הגדולה קשיא לרב דהא אמר דכן ממש וכ"ש אי בדאורייתא קא משתעי קשיא לרב והא ליכא למימר מדרבנן ודלא כיוסף בן יועזר דהקרא לא פליג דמשמע דלית עלייהו טומאה אי דאורייתא אי דרבנן: מידי הוא טעמא אלא לרב. כלום אתה מקשה אלא לרב לא קשיא ליה הא לעולם חגי בדרבנן בדיק להו וכבר נגזרה גזירת טומאה על המשקין ולרב אליבא דיוסף בן יועזר לא תיקשי דרב משקי בי מטבחיא תני בעדותו של יוסף משקה המטבחים דם ומים אבל משקה מדבחיא היין והשמן שהם משקה המזבח גזרו רבנן טומאה עלייהו והיינו דבסדר טומאות דהאי קרא איכא אוכל מטמא אוכל ומשק' מטמא משקה דמדרבנן טומאה עושה כיוצא בה: מי כתיב ונגע כנפו. אל הלחם דמשמע שהשרץ נגע בלחם דלחם הוי ראשון מה שנגע בכנפו נגע ללחם דה"ל לחם שני: טמא נפש. קס"ד טמא מת שהוא אב הטומאה כשרץ: בכל אלה. כסדר שפירשנו טמא מת בלחם ולחם בנזיד וכו': מדהכא לא אישתבש. דאמרו ליה רביעי טמא כדכתיב ויאמרו יטמא הכא נמי לא אישתבש והיכי במה שנגע בכנפו אמר להו דה"ל שמן חמישי ומשום הכי אמרי ליה טהור אלא לרב דאמר גבי שרץ נמי רביעי בעא מינייהו מאי שנא דאמרו ליה טהור: בקיאין הן בטומאת מת. ויודעים שהשלישי עושה בה רביעי ולא היו בקיאין בטומאת שרץ וסבורין שאין שלישי עושה בה רביעי: רבינא אמר. לא היו בקיאין ברביעי בקודש כלל וגבי מת שלישי בקודש בעא מינייהו דהאי טמא נפש דקרא לאו טמא מת אלא מת ממש כלומר טומאה נפש ומת הוי אבות ולחם אב ונזיד ראשון ויין שני ושמן שלישי: ויען חגי ויאמר וגו'. סיפיה דקרא וכן כל מעשה ידיהם ואשר יקריבו שם טמא הוא: בשלמא לרב. דאמר אישתבש כהני היינו דקרי למעשה ידיהם טמא: איתמוהי קא מתמה. מאחר שבקיאין הן בהלכות טומאה וכי כל מעשה ידיהם טמא הוא: וכן. לאו תמיהה משמע: שקלקלו מעשיהם. לאחר זמן היה מתנבא שקלקלו מעשיהן בבית שני בשאר עבירות: ולוי. דתני מדבחיא והכא כתיב יין ושמן דמטמאו הא ניחא אי סבר ליה בהא מילתא כשמואל דדכן דיוסף בן יועזר דכן מלטמא אחרים הן אבל טומאת עצמן יש בהן משכחת לה להאי דכתיב אם יגע טמא נפש בכל אלה דקאמר יטמא דנגעו כולהו בראשון ולאו אסדרא קמא נקט ולא אישתבש כהני שבתחלה שאלם על הסדר ואמרו לו על האחרון לא יטמא מפני שהיין לא יכול לטמאו לשמן שאין משקין בי מדבחיא מטמאין שום דבר ולבסוף שאלם אם יגע הטמא עצמו בכל אלה כלומר או בזה או בזה ואמרו ליה יטמא: אלא אי סבר ליה כרב דאמר דכן ממש היכי משכחת לה. להאי יטמא דקרא בשלמא לרב גופיה לא קשיא דאיהו תני מטבחיא אלא ללוי קשיא: ולשמואל. דאמר לא אישתבש ופריש למילתיה משום דחמישי הוה השמן דמה שנגע בכנפו כתיב הא אי רביעי הוה האי שמן הוה טמא ואע"ג דמן היין קבלה אלמא משקין מטמאין אחרים: הא ניחא. אי תנא בעדותו של יוסף משקה מטבחיא אבל משקה מדבחיא אפי' אחריני נמי מטמאו היינו דפריש למילתיה לעיל ואמר האי דלא הוי שיבוש משום דחמישי הוה והיין שהוא רביעי לא עביד ליה חמישי הא אי הוה יין שלישי הוה עביד ליה רביעי אלא אי תנא מדבחיא כלוי מאי איריא דפריש לעיל משום דחמישי הוה אפילו אי הוה יין שני שלישי לשמן לא עביד: משקי בי מדבחיא. כלומר כל אלו של קודש נקראין על שם מזבח כגון דם לזריקה ומים ויין לנסך ושמן למנחות: שנטמאו בפנים. בעזרה והוציאן לחוץ ונפסלו ביוצא שאין ראויין עוד למזבח: טהורין. מלטמא אחרים שהרי לא ירדה להן תורת טומאה מתחלה לטמא אחרים והן עצמן ודאי טמאין כנבואת חגי: אבל נטמאו בחוץ. קודם שיהא שם מדבחיא עליהן והכניסן לפנים טמאין ואפילו לטמא אחרים דטומאתן כבר ירדה בהן ומי הפקיעה: איני. ארישא פריך דקתני הוציאן לחוץ טהורין ולא אמרינן תחול טומאתן למפרע: אלא במקומן. בפנים: לא למעוטי נטמאו בחוץ והכניסן לפנים. כדמתרץ לישנא בסיפא דמילתא דהכי משמע אלא כשנטמאו במקומן ומשום דלא סיימיה לפרושא דמילתא פריך ליה והא במקומן קאמר דמשמע כל זמן שהן במקומן טהורין ותו לא: רבן

תוספות

רביעי בקודש בעא מינייהו. פ"ה דנגע בכנפו היינו שרץ אל הלחם והלחם אל הנזיד וכו' וקשה לר"ת דמאי שנא דואל כל מאכל יהיה פירוש או אל כל מאכל יותר מכולם ועוד למה דחק שמואל לתרץ במה שנגע בכנפו לימא אל כל מאכל דוקא ועוד למה קורא הכתוב לשרץ כנף ועוד דמפרש רבינא התם רביעי בקדש הכא שלישי שהלחם נעשה אב הטומאה כשנוגע במת °והא קיימא לן בהמפלת (נדה כח:*) דכל דבר שאין לו טהרה במקוה אינו נעשה אב הטומאה °מיהו יש לומר דאין נעשה אב הטומאה היינו דווקא לטמא אדם וכלים אבל לאוכלין ומשקין נעשה אב הטומאה ומפר"ת דהשרץ נגע בכנף ונעשה ראשון והכנף אל הלחם או אל הנזיד וחד מהנך אל היין או אל השמן הרי שלשה ואל כל מאכל הרי ארבעה ונקט סדר כנף מאכל משקה מאכל דלא בעי למינקט שיעשה כיוצא בו ולשמואל דייק מדכתיב בכנפו הרי חמש והשתא אתי שפיר לרבינא דאמר הכא שלישי שהכנף נעשה אב הטומאה כדין כל הכלים כשנוגע במת: אבל

רבינו חננאל

ונו' ואמר רב (אשי) אשתבש כהני כלומר טעו הכהנים באמרם כי אלו כלם הוטרים לא נטמאו מכלל דטמאין הן מכלל דרב סבר כי היין והשמן שהן משקין וטמ' ואיך אמר דכן ממש ופרק' מידי הוא טעמא אלא לרב(כלומר) [כלום] תקשה אלא דרב אדרב הא בהדיא תני רב משקה בית מטבחיא דכן והן המים והדם כדבעינן למימר קמן אבל משקה בית מדבחי' כגון היין שנסכין על המזבח והשמן שמקריבין עם המנחות (טמא) לא אמר רב שהן דכן אלא מטמא וטעו הכהני' שאמרו אין מטמא וכשהזכרנו דברי רב דאמר אשתבש כהני הוצרכנו לבאר טעמו לפיכך אמרנו גופא רב אמר אשתבש כהני שהשיבו על מגע רביעי בשלישי בקדשים שהוא טהור ואינו אלא פסול ושמואל אמר חמישי בקדש בעא מינייהו חגי הנביא והשיבו כהלכה טהור: בשלמא לרב משכחת לה מן המקרא כי רביעי שאל חגי הנביא מן הכהנים שנאמר הן ישא איש בשר קדש בכנף בגדו שנגע בו שרץ ונגע הבשר בכנף בגדו הטמא ונגע עוד הבשר בלחם או בנזיד או ביין או בשמן ונגעו אלו אל כל מאכל נמצא הכנף של בגדו שנגע בשרץ ולד ראשון כי השרץ הוא אב ונמצא הנוגע בו ולד ראשון והבשר שנגע בכנף ולד שני ואלו הלחם והנזיד והמשקין הללו שנגעו בבשר ולד שלישי והמאכל שנגע באלו נמצא ולד רביעי ושאל ואמר להם היקדש המאכל או לאו וטעו והשיבו לא קדש כלומר לא נפסל המאכל והמוכיח שעל המאכל לבדו שאלם באמרו היקדש לשון יחיד ולא אמר היקדשו דמשמע דברים הרבה ושמואל אמר חמישי שאלן ודייק מזה הכתוב שכתב בכנפו שמביא מגע דבר אחר באמצע יתר מאלו הארבעה שהזכרנו שנמצא ה' דברים ולדברי הכל החמישי בקדש טהור ולפיכך אמר לא אשתבש כהני: ומותבינן מהאי קרא ויאמר חגי אם יגע טמא נפש בכל אלה היטמא ויענו הכהנים ויאמרו יטמא פי' אלו כולן באו מכח כנף הבגד שנטמא בשרץ וחזר שאלן אם תהיה הכנף טמאה טומאת נפש ונגע בו ונעש' בשר ולד ראשון* כי הטומאת נפש אב דתנן אבות הטומאות השרץ ושכבת זרע וטמא מת וכו' ונגעו הלחם והנזיד ושאר המשקין בבשר ונגע המאכל בלחם או באלו המשקין שנמצא הבשר ולד ראשון והלחם והללו ולד שני והמאכל ולד שלישי נמצאו כמו שאמר רבינא בטמא מת שלישי בעא מינייהו ולשמואל שאמר במה שנגע כנפו שמכנים בין הכנף לבשר

[לעיל טו.]

גליון הש"ס

תוס' ד"ה רביעי בקודש וכו' והא קיי"ל בהמפלת. שם לא נזכר כלום מזה וצ"ע כדמוכח סוף ערובין קד ע"ב פי' ב"ק כה ע"ב תוס' ד"ה וקמייתי: באד"ה מיהו י"ל. פי' טורי אבן חגיגה כג ע"א ד"ה מה פתות:

דבר אחר הנה ארבעה ולדות ואמרו טמא נמצא לדברי שמואל דלא אשתבש בתהוויהו אלא לרב אמאי טעו בראשון ולא [טעו] באחרון ופריק בקיאין הן בטומאת מת כי הרביעי בטמא מת פסול הוא בקדש ואין בקיאין הן בטומאת שרץ: בשלמא לרב דאמר אשתבש כהני היינו דאמר חגי ויען חגי ויאמר כן העם הזה ואשר יקריבו שם טמא הוא כלומר מקריבין הטמא שהוא טהור הוא ואתם יודעים כי טמא [illegible] חס ושלום אינו טמא ואקשי' [illegible] ומצאנו בתלמוד ארץ ישראל [illegible] בשר קדש וגו' כנף תחלה [illegible] נפש ונגעה בכל אלו יטמא [illegible] שהוא טהור: משקה בית [illegible] שונה דברי יוסף בן יועזר [illegible] למאכל דאמרו הכהנים לחגי [illegible] אומר דכן ממש וזה אומר דכן [illegible] שמעם: תניא כלוי הדם [illegible] כלים טהור ר' שמעון אומר נטמאו

*דברי רבינו ז"ל הם גם כשאלה זו של רביעי בקדש [illegible]

[17a] Whereon Rab said: The priests erred?[6]—Is this view [propounded] against any but Rab? Rab learned, 'the liquids of the slaughter-house'; but the liquids of the altar[7] can be defiled.[8]

[To turn to] the main text: 'Rab said: The priests erred; but Samuel maintained, The priests did not err'. 'Rab said, The priests erred'; he asked them about a fourth degree in respect of holy foodstuffs, and they answered him that it was clean. 'But Samuel maintained, The priests did not err'; he asked them about a fifth degree in respect of holy foodstuffs, and they answered him, It is clean. As for Rab, it is well: hence four are written, 'bread, pottage, wine, and oil'; but according to Samuel, whence does a he know five?—Is it then written, 'and his skirt[1] touch [the bread]'? Surely it is written, *and touch with [that] [by] his skirt*,[2] [meaning that it touched] that which was touched by his skirt.[3]

Come and hear: *Then said Haggai, If one that is unclean by a dead body touch any of these, shall it be unclean? And the priests answered and said, It shall be unclean.*[4] As for Samuel, it is well: since they did not err here, they did not err there [either]; but according to Rab, why did they err here yet did not err there?—Said R. Naḥman in Rabbah b. Abbuha's name: They were well-versed in the uncleanness of a corpse, but not well-versed in the uncleanness of a *shereẓ*.[5] Rabina said: There it was a fourth degree; here it was a third.[6]

Come and hear: *Then answered Haggai and said, So is this people, and so is this nation before me, saith the Lord: and so is every work of their hands: and that which they offer there is unclean.*[7] As for Rab, it is well: hence '*unclean*' is written.[8] But according to Samuel, why was it unclean?—He indeed wondered.[9] But it is written, and b so *is every work of their hands?*[1]—Said Mar Zuṭra, others state, R. Ashi: Because they perverted their actions the Writ stigmatizes them as though they offered up [sacrifices] in uncleanness.

[To turn to] the main text: 'Rab learned, The liquids of the slaughter-house;[2] while Levi learned: The liquids of the altar'. Now according to Levi, it is well if he holds as Samuel, who said, They are clean [only] in so far that they cannot defile other [objects], but nevertheless they are unclean in themselves: then it is possible where they all touched the first.[3] But if he holds as Rab, who maintained [that] they are literally clean, how is it conceivable?[4]—You are compelled [to say that] he holds as Samuel. And according to Samuel, it is well if he holds as Rab who learned, 'The liquids of the slaughter-house', but the liquids of the altar can even defile others: [hence] it is only a fourth degree which cannot make a fifth, but a third can make a fourth.[5] But if he holds as Levi who learned, 'The liquids of the altar', why particularly [ask about] a fourth, which cannot make a fifth; they cannot even make a second or a third?[6]—You are compelled [to say that] he holds as Rab.

It was taught in accordance with Rab; it was taught in accordance with Levi. It was taught in accordance with Levi: Blood, wine, oil and water, the liquids of the altar, which were defiled within[7] and carried without,[8] are clean.[9] If they were defiled c without[1] and [then] brought within, they are unclean.[2] But that is not so? For R. Joshua b. Levi said: 'They did not rule that the liquids of the altar are clean save in their place': is that not to exclude [the case where] they were defiled within and carried without!—No: it is to exclude [where] they were defiled without and [then] taken within. But he states, 'in their place'?[3]—This is what he states: They did not rule [that these liquids] are clean save when they were defiled in their place [*sc.* within].

It was taught as Rab: Blood and water, the liquids of the slaughter-house, which were defiled, whether in vessels or in the

(6) *Ḳodesh* is here translated unclean, from its root idea of 'separation', 'keeping at a distance from', and Haggai was examining the priests in the knowledge of the laws of uncleanness. The exact point of his question is disputed *infra*, but according to Rab it was this: the unclean flesh was a *shereẓ* ('creeping thing'), which bears a principal degree of uncleanness; this *shereẓ* (being held in the skirt of the garment is now designated by the term 'skirt', the mention of which would otherwise be pointless) touched the bread, the bread touched the pottage, the pottage touched the wine, and the wine touched the oil or any other foodstuff, and the question was whether this last would be unclean, i.e., whether there is a 'fourth' degree in the case of holy food, to which this refers. So Rashi. R. Tam: the *shereẓ* touched the skirt, which became a first, the skirt touched the bread or the pottage, which became a second, then one of these touched wine or oil, which became a third, and the wine or oil touched some other eatable. Actually there is a fourth degree and since the priests replied in the negative, they erred (v. 14a, n. a2). Thus we see that wine and oil are unclean, though they are the liquids of the Temple, which contradicts Rab. Now, if the uncleanness of liquids is Rabbinical, it has been stated that the Rabbinical decree did not apply to the Temple. And even if Haggai was examining them on points of Rabbinical law, this still contradicts Rab, who states that they are literally clean. The previous answer that Rabbinical uncleanness only is discussed here, while this does not agree with R. Joseph b. Jo'ezer of Zeredah, is impossible in the present instance, for he obviously cannot disagree with Scripture. (7) In the Aramaic, 'slaughter-house' and 'altar' differ in one letter only. (8) Blood and water are the liquids of the slaughter-house, but wine and oil are liquids of the altar.

a (1) I.e., the *shereẓ* which was in his skirt. (2) So literally. (3) I.e., the *shereẓ* in the skirt touched something which in turn touched the bread, which is therefore a second degree; hence the oil would be a fifth (v. Rashi). (4) Hag. II, 13. (5) Thinking that where the originating uncleanness is a *shereẓ* it does not go beyond the third degree. (6) They were quite unaware that there is a fourth degree, but his second question related to the third degree, Rabina translating thus: If the uncleanness of a dead body touch etc. Since a corpse is a super principal (father of fathers) of uncleanness, the oil would be a third, and of this they knew. (7) Ibid. 14. (8) In their ignorance their work would be as unclean. (9) Seeing that they know the laws so well, can their work be unclean?

b (1) This is a positive statement. (2) In the testimony of R. Joseph b. Jo'ezer of Zeredah. (3) Thus: in the first question Haggai asked about successive stages of defilement, and they answered that the oil is clean, since it touched the wine, which as a liquid of the altar can be defiled (i.e., made unfit) but cannot contaminate. But in the second question each touched the first mentioned, viz., '*one that is unclean by a dead body*', and they rightly answered that they are unclean. (4) That the wine and the oil should be unclean. One cannot raise the objection against Rab himself, since he reads, the liquids of the slaughter-house, i.e., blood and water, but not wine and oil. (5) And for that reason Haggai put his question as to whether the wine, a fourth, could render the oil unfit as a fifth degree of uncleanness, and they rightly gave a negative reply. (6) Wine and oil, whatever their uncleanness, cannot defile others. (7) The Temple Court. (8) Through this act they are henceforth unfit for the altar. (9) In that they cannot defile others, because when they became unclean in the first place they were true 'liquids of the altar', and as such could not contaminate others.

c (1) Before they were ever taken within, so that they were not yet 'liquids of the altar', and they contracted a degree of defilement which contaminates others. (2) I.e., they retain the power to contaminate.—Thus this Baraitha speaks of liquids of the altar. (3) Which is within.

blood which is poured out as water[8] makes fit; [16b] blood which is not poured out as water[9] does not make fit. To this R. Samuel b. Ammi demurred: Behold the last-drained blood,[10] which is
a poured out like water,[1] yet it does not make fit?—Said R. Zera to him, Leave the last-drained blood alone, which does not make fit even in the case of *ḥullin*. R. Samuel b. Ammi received it [the reason] from him, because the Divine Law saith, *Only be sure that thou eat not the blood; for the blood is the life:*[2] blood wherewith life goes out is called blood; blood with which life does not go out is not called blood.[3]

Come and hear: If blood became unclean and he [the priest] sprinkled it unwittingly, it [the sacrifice] is accepted; if deliberately, it is not accepted?[4]—It was Rabbinically [unclean], this not being in accordance with R. Jose b. Jo'ezer of Zeredah.[5]

Come and hear: For what does the headplate propitiate?[6] For the blood, flesh, and the fat which were defiled, whether in ignorance or deliberately, accidentally or intentionally,[7] whether in the case of an individual or of the community.[8] [It was defiled] by Rabbinical law [only], this not being in accordance with Jose b. Jo'ezer of Zeredah.[9]

Come and hear: *And Aaron shall bear the iniquity of the holy things:*[10] now what iniquity does he bear? If the iniquity of *piggul*,[11] surely it is already said, *it shall not be accepted?*[12] If the iniquity of *nothar*,[11] surely it is already said, *neither shall it be imputed [unto him that*
b *offereth it]*?[1] Hence he bears nought but the iniquity of defilement, which is inoperative[2] in opposition to its general rule, in the case of a community.[3] Does that not mean the defilement of the blood? —Said R. Papa: No: the defilement of the handfuls.[4]

Come and hear: *If one bear unclean* [ḳodesh] *flesh in the skirt of his garment, and with his skirt do touch bread, or pottage, or wine, or oil, or any meat, shall it be defiled? And the priests answered and said, No.*[5]

(8) I.e., the blood of non-sacrifices. (9) I.e., the blood of sacrifices, which is sprinkled on the altar. (10) I.e., the blood which flows out slowly after the first violent rush. The life and vitality pass out with the first blood, not with the last.

a (1) It is not fit for sprinkling. (2) Deut. XII, 23. (3) And consequently not in category of liquids (v. Rashi). (4) Lit. 'make acceptable'. The language is the Biblical, cf. Lev. I, 4: *and it shall be accepted for him to make atonement for him*—i.e., the sacrifice is efficacious for its purpose. Now by Biblical law it is accepted whether the sprinkling was done deliberately or in ignorance of its uncleanness, and the flesh may be eaten by the priests, but the Rabbis penalized the priests by not permitting the flesh to be eaten in the former case, though another sacrifice is not required (v. Giṭ. 54*a*). Incidentally we see that blood can become unclean, and thus liquids in general, which contradicts Rab. (5) Who testified that the Rabbinical decree of uncleanness was not applied to the liquids of the Temple slaughter-house. This Tanna obviously holds that it was. (6) The reference is to Ex. XXVIII, 38, q.v. '*That they may be accepted before the Lord*' is understood to mean that the headplate makes sacrifices acceptable and procures atonement in spite of certain irregularities. (7) This appears to contradict the preceding statement, but v. *infra* 80*b* on the discussion of this passage. (8) Thus here too it is stated that the blood becomes defiled. (9) V. n. a5. (10) Ibid. '*Shall bear*' means shall make atonement for. (11) V. Glos. (12) Lev. XIX, 7.

b (1) Lev. VII, 18. (2) Lit., 'permitted'. (3) Public sacrifices, or private sacrifices which the entire community had to bring, e.g., the Passover, were permitted even in defilement. For notes v. Yoma, 6*b*, notes. (4) Of meal which where burnt on the altar, v. Lev. II, 2. This burning was the equivalent of the sprinkling of the blood in the case of an animal sacrifice, atonement being dependent thereon. (5) Hag. II, 12.

קיז א מיי' פ"י מהל' טומאת אוכלין הל' ב:

דם שאינו נשפך כמים אינו מכשיר מתקיף לה רב שמואל בר אמי הרי דם התמצית דנשפך כמים ואינו מכשיר אמר ליה ר' זירא הנח לדם התמצית *דאפי' בחולין נמי לא מכשיר קבלה מיניה רב שמואל בר אמי דאמר רחמנא °רק חזק לבלתי אכול הדם כי הדם הוא הנפש דם שהנפש יוצאה בו קרוי דם דם שאין הנפש יוצאה בו אינו קרוי דם תא שמע *דם שנטמא וזרקו בשוגג הורצה במזיד לא הורצה (א) מדרבנן ודלא כר' יוסי בן יועזר איש צרידה ת"ש *על מה הציץ מרצה על הדם ועל הבשר ועל החלב שנטמא בין בשוגג בין במזיד בין באונס בין ברצון בין ביחיד בין בצבור מדרבנן ודלא (כיוסף) בן יועזר איש צרידה ת"ש °ונשא אהרן את עון הקדשים *וכי איזה עון הוא נושא אם עון פיגול הרי כבר נאמר °לא ירצה אם עון נותר הרי כבר נאמר °לא יחשב הא אינו נושא אלא עון טומאה שהותרה מכללה בציבור מאי לאו טומאת דם אמר רב פפא לא טומאת קמצים תא שמע °הן ישא איש בשר קדש בכנף בגדו ונגע בכנפו אל הלחם ואל הנזיד ואל היין ואל שמן ואל כל מאכל היקדש ויענו הכהנים ויאמרו לא (יקדש) ואמר

דברים יב | שמות כח | ויקרא ז | ויקרא יט | חגי ב

רש"י

דם התמצית. אינו ראוי לזריקה דכתיב* כי הדם הוא (הנפש) בנפש יכפר דם שהנפש יוצאה בו מכפר ושאין הנפש יוצאה בו אינו מכפר אלמא נשפך כמים אינו מכשיר כדברי יוסי בר חנינא: דאפי' בחולין לא מכשיר. כדמפרש טעמא: קיבלה מיניה ר' שמואל. לפירושא דהאי טעמא מרבי זירא דאמאי לא מכשיר דם התמצית לפי שאינו קרוי דם והקרוי דם קרוי משק' כדכתיב (במדבר כג) ודם חללים ישתה ומכשיר כדכתיב וכל משקה וגו' ואוקימנא להכשר ושאינו קרוי דם אינו קרוי משקה: הורצה. קרבן לבעלים דמרצה ציץ כדלקמן: במזיד לא הורצה. להיות בשר קרבן נאכל לכהנים דקנסא הוא אבל בעלים נתכפרו כדאמרינן ביבמות בהאשה רבה (ד' צ.) דכיון דמדאורייתא מרצי נמי אמזיד לא מצו רבנן למימר ליה זיל אייתי חולין לעזרה קתני מיהת דם שנטמא אלמא דם קדשים שהוא משקין בית מטבחיא מקבל טומאה אלמא משקין טומאת עלמא דאורייתא ודכן דיוסף בן יועזר מלטמא אחרים הוא וקשיא לרב: ומשני לעולם טומאת משקין דרבנן. והך טומאת דם דרבנן היא ודקשיא לך הא העיד יוסף בן יועזר דגזירת רבנן לא גזור אמשקי בית מטבחיא האי תנא לית ליה דיוסף בן יועזר: על הדם ועל הבשר ועל החלב. בין שנטמא הדם בין שנטמא הבשר בין שנטמא החלב הציץ מרצה ולא שיהא בשר טמא נאכל דאין ציץ מטהר ודוחה לא תעשה דוהבשר אשר יגע בכל טמא לא יאכל אלא לר' יהושע איצטריך דאמר בכילד צולין (לקמן עז.) אם אין בשר אין דם וקאמר הכא ה"מ כשיצא בשר חוץ למחיצתו שאין ציץ מרצה על היוצא או שאבד הבשר אבל נטמא בשר קודם זריקת דם הציץ מרצה עליו להתיר דם לזריקה: בין בשוגג בין במזיד. והאי דתני לעיל בשוגג הורצה במזיד לא הורצה בכילד צולין* פליגי בה אמוראי חד אמר טומאתו בין בשוגג בין במזיד אבל זריקתו בשוגג אין במזיד לא וחד אמר איפכא: בין ביחיד. בקרבן יחיד מזיד ורצון אחד הוא אבל גבי שוגג שייך מזיד וגבי אונס שייך רצון ושוגג ואונס תרי מילי נינהו וקתני מיהת על הדם אלמא דם קדשים מקבל טומאה וש"מ טומאת משקין דאורייתא ולא רצו רבנן לטהר משקי בית מטבחיא וקשיא לרב: מדרבנן. וקסבר האי תנא דאמשקי בית מטבחיא נמי גזור ודלא כיוסף: ונשא אהרן. בציץ כתיב: את עון הקדשים. פסול הקרבן יכשיר וירצה ואינו מכפר על האוכלין אותו טמא דעון הקדשים כתיב ולא עון הכהנים: איזה עון הוא נושא. איזה פסול הוא מכשיר אם עון פיגול הרי כבר נאמר לא ירצה גרסי' בת"כ ואם עון נותר הרי כבר נאמר לא יחשב והכי פי' אם עון פיגול והוא מחשבת חוץ למקומו שנקראת פיגול כדכתיב בקדושים תהיו ואם האכל יאכל ביום השלישי פגול הוא לא ירצה ומוקמינן לה בזבחים בפ"ב (דף כח:) אם אינו ענין לחוץ לזמנו תנהו ענין לחוץ למקומו הרי כבר נאמר לא ירצה בקדושים תהיו כדפרשינן ואם עון נותר מחשבת נותר ששחטו על מנת להותיר ולאכלו חוץ לזמנו הרי כבר נאמר לא יחשב ואם האכל יאכל מבשר זבח שלמיו ביום השלישי וגו' בפרשת צו את אהרן ואמרינן בזבחים ובתורת כהנים במחשב לאכול שלא בזמנו ביום השלישי הכתוב מדבר וכתיב לא יחשב לו אלמא לית ליה תקנתא ורובא גרסי איפכא אם עון פיגול הרי כבר נאמר לא יחשב ומוקמינן ליה לפיגול חוץ לזמנו שכן לשונו בכל הגמרא ואם עון נותר הרי כבר נאמר לא ירצה ומוקמי' ליה בנותר ממש ולא יתכן חדא דלא כתב לא ירצה אלא במחשבת חוץ למקומו וחוץ לזמנו ועוד אי נותר ממש למאי לא ירצה אי לאכשורי קרבן הרי כשר ועומד הוא משעה שנעשו עבודות דמו בהכשר כדאמרינן בתורת כהנים *או אינו אלא באוכל מזבחו ביום השלישי הכתוב מדבר וכי אפשר לומר כן מאחר שהוכשר חוזר ויפסל ואם לא ירצה לא יתכפר האוכל נותר קאמר וכי יש כפרה לחייבי כריתות ועוד לא ירצה הקרבן משמע ותו מי איצטריך למימר דציץ לא מכפר על המחייב כרת והא עון הקדשים כתיב ולא עון האוכלים וכלישנא קמא גרסי' בתורת כהנים ועיקר הוא והאי דקרי ליה להאי פיגול ולהאי נותר משום דתורת כהנים מדרש הוא ונקט לישנא דקרא: הא. כמו הרי כלומר הרי יש לך להבין על כרחך שאין לך עון הקדשים שיוכל ציץ לרצות עליו אלא עון טומאה ומאי שנא טומאה מפסול יוצא ושאר הפסולין: שהותרה מכללה בצבור. דנדחית מפני קרבן צבור דכתיב במועדו ואפי' בטומאה וכיון דהיקלתה אצלה לכך היקלתה אף ביחיד שלא הותרה אצלו לכתחלה בלא ציץ ירצה הציץ עליה: מאי עון טומאה. לאו טומאת דם דאין מציץ רצוי אלא א"כ נטמא דם שהכפרה תלויה בו אלמא דם מקבל טומאה: לא טומאת קמצים. שהקומץ מתיר את המנחה כדם המתיר את הזבח וכל הכפרה תלויה בו והוא הדין דמצי לשנויי לא בטומאת בשר וחלב ואליבא דר' יהושע בעי ציץ דאמר אם אין בשר אין דם אלא ניחא ליה לאוקמיה כדברי הכל: בשר קדש. שרץ לשון קדש היה בארץ (מלכים א יד) טומאה והיה חגי הנביא בודק את הכהנים בשנת שתים לדריוש שהיה בבנין בית שני לידע אם בקיאין בהלכות טומאה לפי שנשתכח מהן בגולה שלא נתעסקו בה בקדשים: ונגע בכנפו. באותו כנף שהשרץ בו כלומר השרץ עצמו ועל כרחך הכי הוא דאי משום כנף שהוא ראשון כוליה בגד נמי ראשון הוי ומאי איריא דנקיט כנף אלא משום שרץ שהשרץ עצמו נגע אל הלחם והלחם אל הנזיד והנזיד אל היין והיין אל השמן או אל כל מאכל היקדש כלום נטמא האחרון הזה שהוא רביעי בקודש דלחם ראשון ונזיד שני ויין שלישי ושמן רביעי נזיד תבשיל כמו ונזיד עדשים (בראשית כה) יין ושמן של נסכים:

ואמר

תוספות

דם שאינו נשפך כמים אינו מכשיר. הקשה ה"ר יעקב דאורליינ"ש א"כ דם חיה ועוף דטעונים כיסוי לא יהיו מכשירים דכיון דטעונים כיסוי לא חשיב נשפך כמים דאמרינן בפ' כיסוי הדם (חולין פד: ושם) אמריתו חיה בכלל בהמה לסימנים אימא נמי בהמה בכלל חיה לכיסוי ומשני אמר קרא על הארץ תשפכנו כמים אלמא דם חיה לא חשיב נשפך כמים ולאו פירכא היא דכל דם הנשפך כמים לארץ ואין צריך לקבלו בכלי כגון דם חיה הוקש למים לענין הכשר וגם לענין כיסוי היה ראוי להקישו כמים אי לאו דגלי קרא להדיא: מדרבנן ודלא כר' יוסי בן יועזר. ה"מ לאוקמא מדאורייתא וכמ"ד טומאת משקין דאורייתא אלא ניחא לאוקמא מדרבנן וסבר האי תנא מאי נטמא הכשר כמו שאמר רב: על הבשר. בפ' כילד צולין (לקמן עח.) אמרינן לר"א דאמר יש דם אע"פ שאין בשר הציץ מרצה על האכילות למאי הלכתא לאקבועי בפגול ולאפוקי מידי מעילה ודלא כפ"ה דפי' דלא את' אלא כר' יהושע: הא ר"א אם עון פיגול הוא נושא הרי כבר נאמר לא יחשב ואם עון נותר הרי כבר נאמר לא ירצה. דהכי איתא במסקנא בהדיא בפ"ב דזבחים דדריש תרוייהו מחד קרא אריכא דפרשת צו ורישיה דקרא דכתיב ביום השלישי מוקי למחשב לאוכלו חוץ לזמנו וסיפא במחשב לאוכלו חוץ למקומו ובת"כ אהאי קרא דצו איתא האי גירסא ורש"י הגיה איפכא על פי ת"כ דפרש' קדושים דהתם ודאי דריש מקרא זוטא ואותה ברייתא' נשנית לפי מה שרצה הגמרא בזבחים בתחל' ללמוד חוץ למקומו מקרא זוטא דקדושים ולכל הפי' ק"ק אמאי נקט עון פיגול ברישא *: הא אינו נושא אלא עון טומאה שהותרה מכללה. תימה לר"ת למ"ל שהותרה מכללה תיפוק ליה דליכא לאוקמא לקרא אלא בהכי כדמפרש אי עון פיגול וכו' ואור"ת משום דקרא משמע דלא מרצה אלא דבר שיש לו היתר בשום מקום דכתיב בסיפא דקרא לרצון להם ופיגול ונותר נמי הותרו מכללם במנחת כהנים ובמנחת נסכים דתנן בפ' ב"ש (זבחים מג: ושם) דאין חייבים עליהם משום פיגול ועוד דפיגול חוץ למקומו הותר מכללו בבמה וכן משמע בהקומץ רבה (מנחות כה.) דפריך אימא עון שמאל שהותר מכללו ביום הכפורים אמר קרא עון עון שהיה בו ודחיתיו והיינו משום דאלרצון סמיך וה"ק עון שהוא לרצון וא"ת דהתם פריך נמי ואימא עון יוצא דהותר מכללו בבמה ומשני לרצון להם לפני ה' עון דלפני השם הוא נשא ולא יוצא וא"כ בפיגול דחוץ למקומו נמי נימא הכי ומאי קאמר אם עון פיגול וכו' וי"ל דיוצא ודאי אינו לפני ה' אבל מחשב להוציא לפני השם קרינן ביה:

רביעי

רבינו חננאל

האי קרא דכתיב בכל כלי יטמא לתלושין מן הקרקע ותחתים בכלי דמכשרי והאי קרא דכתיב אשר יבוא עליו מים יטמא להמחוברין בקרקע דמכשרי כגון המעינות והנהרות והבורות וכיוצא בהן תרויהו וכו': ת"ש אך מעין ובור מקוה מים יהיה טהור הא תלושין מטמאו והדר' מאי יהיה טהור הבין פירושיה דקרא כל כלי יטמא שיבוא במעין ובור מקוה מים יהיה טהור מטומאתו ואקשי' נמי לרב דאמר כי כתיב אפילו משקה בית מטבחיא מכשרי והאמר ר' יוסי בר' חנינא משקה בית מטבחיא לא דיין שהן דכן אלא שאינן מכשירין ושני' הדם אינו מכשיר כר' יוחנן דאמר דם הנשפך כמים מכשיר אבל דם קדשים שאינו נשפך כמים אלא מתקבל בכלי אינו מכשיר: והרי דם התמצית שאין מתקבל. כלומר שאין מכפרין בו ואינו מכשיר ואקשי' הנח לדם התמצית שאינו דם שנאמר כי הדם הוא הנפש דם שהנפש יוצא בו הוא קרוי דם ואמרינן התם איזהו דם הנפש כל זמן שמקלח ויוצא דם התמצית שהוא שותת ואע"ג דתנן ר' יהודה מחייב בדם התמצית הרי אמרינן עלה מודה היה ר' יהודה לענין כפרה שאינו מכפר והא לא דיין שהן דכן תנינן כלומר לשון משקין הרבה הוא ואיך תאמר תרומה אלא לבדו ועלו' בקשיא: ת"ש דם שנטמא וזרקו בשוגג הורצה במזיד לא הורצה אלמא הדם מטמא ושני' טומאת הדם מדרבנן היא ולא כיוסף בן יועזר [illegible]: ת"ש על מה הציץ מרצה [illegible] ת"ש ונשא אהרן את עון הקדשים [illegible] מאי לאו טומאת דם [illegible] לא טומאת קמצים כלומר [illegible] נטמא הקומץ והקריבו הציץ מרצה יצא והקריבו אין הציץ מרצה: ת"ש הן ישא איש בשר קדש בכנפו

מסורת הש"ס

ויקרא יז

יומא ז. יבמות צ. גיטין נד. זבחים מה. מנחות כה.

[יומא ויבמות שם] [לקמן פ:] [מנחות כה:]

[נ"ל כר' יוסי]

יומא ז. זבחים כג. מנחות כה.

[ותוס' יומא ז: תירלו ב' תירוצי' על זה ובזבחים כג: וכן במנחות כה. כתבו תירוץ אחר]

[וכן בזבחים כט.]

הגהות הב"ח

(א) גמ' מדרבנן ודלא כר' יוסף בן יועזר איש צרידה כצ"ל וכן לקמן:

ספק משקין ליטמא טמא לטמא אחרים טהור דברי ר"מ וכן היה רבי אלעזר אומר כדבריו רבי יהודה אומר לכל טמא רבי יוסי ור"ש אומרים לאוכלין טמאין לכלים טהורין וסבר רבי אלעזר משקין אית להו טומאה בעולם והתניא ר"א אומר אין טומאה למשקין כל עיקר תדע שהרי העיד (יוסף) בן יועזר איש צרידה על איל קמצא דכן ועל משקין בית מטבחיא דכן הניחא לשמואל דאמר דכן מלטמא טומאת אחרים אבל טומאת עצמן יש להן שפיר אלא לרב דאמר דכן ממש מאי איכא למימר אמר ר"נ בר יצחק אחרא והא כדבריו קאמר דנפישי ועוד והא וכן קתני קשיא גופא רב אמר דכן ממש ושמואל אמר דכן מלטמא טומאת אחרים אבל טומאת עצמן יש להן רב אמר דכן ממש קסבר טומאת משקין דרבנן וכי גזרו רבנן במשקין דעלמא ובמשקין בית מטבחיא לא גזור ושמואל אמר דכן מלטמא טומאת אחרים אבל טומאת עצמן יש להן קסבר טומאת משקין עצמן דאורייתא לטמא אחרים דרבנן וכי גזור רבנן במשקין דעלמא במשקין בית מטבחיא לא גזור וכי לא גזור רבנן לטמויי אחרים אבל טומאת עצמן יש להן א"ל רב הונא בר חיננא לרבא כי עיילת לקמיה דרב פפא רמי ליה מי אמר שמואל דכן מלטמא טומאת אחרים אבל טומאת עצמן יש להן קרי כאן (ויקרא ז) והבשר אשר יגע בכל טמא לא יאכל אמר רב שישא בר' דרב אידי מידי דהוה ארביעי בקדש מתקיף לה רב אשי רביעי בקדש לא איקרי טמא האי איקרי טמא קשיא ת"ש (שם יא) וכל משקה אשר ישתה בכל כלי יטמא מאי יטמא הכשיר הכשר מרישא דקרא שמעת ליה מכל האוכל אשר יאכל וגו' חד בתלושין וחד במחוברין וצריכי דאי אשמעינן בתלושין משום דאחשבינהו אבל מחוברין אימא לא ואי תנא מחוברין משום דקיימי בדוכתייהו חשיבי אבל תלושין אימא לא צריכי ת"ש (שם) אך מעין ובור מקוה מים יהיה טהור מאי יהיה טהור מטומאתו ותלושין מי מכשירין והאמר ר' יוסי בר' חנינא משקין בית מטבחיא לא דיין שהן דכן אלא שאין מכשירין תירגמא על דם דאמר ר' חייא בר אבא א"ר יוחנן מנין לדם קדשים שאינו מכשיר שנא' (דברים יב) על הארץ תשפכנו כמים דם שנשפך כמים מכשיר דם

[נ"ל רבי יוסי]

רש"י

ספק משקה ליטמא טמא לטמא אחרים טהור. כשנולד ספק במשקה בתחילת טומאתו כגון טמא שפשט רגלו במשקין טהורין ספק נגע ספק לא נגע וזהו ספק משקה ליטמא שנולד לו ספק טומאה טמא מן הספק דקסבר טומאת משקין טמאין לאורייתא היא דכתיב וכל משקה אשר ישתה וגו' הלכך הויא ליה ספיקא דאורייתא ולחומרא ספק משקה לטמא אחרים כגון (א)היה מקל בידו ובראשו משקין טמאין וזרקה לבין הככרות טהורין ספק נגעה ספק לא נגעה זה הוא ספק משקה לטמא אחרים כך היא שנויה במסכת טהרות: טהור. אותן הככרות טהורות הן דקסבר משקין לטמא אחרים לאו מדרבנן הוא ולא מדאורייתא ולא דורש יטמא דכתיב גבי משקין בלשון יטמא הלכך הויא ליה ספיקא דרבנן ולקולא וגירסא הכי איתא ספק משקה ליטמא טמא לטמא אחרי' טהור: רבי אלעזר גרסי': לכל טמא. אספק משקה לטמא אחרים קאי כשנולד ספק נגיעת שום דבר טהור במשקין טמאין בין שנולד ספק זה בכלים בין שנולד באוכלין הרי הוא טמא מספק דקסבר משקין מטמאין כלים מן התורה ויליף טעמא מאשר ישתה בכל כלי יטמא ודריש יטמא ומדסמכיה לכלי משמע יטמא את הכלי והכי דרשינן ליה בתורת כהנים הלכך כי הוי ספק הוי ליה ספיקא דאורייתא וברה"י ספיקו טמא: ר' יוסי ור' שמעון אומרים לאוכלין טמאין. אם נולד ספק זה באוכלים כגון משקין טמאין שנשפכו לבין הככרות ספק נגעו ספק לא נגעו טמאין דקא סברי משקין מטמאין אוכלין מדאורייתא הלכך ספק נמי ברשות היחיד טמא: לכלים טהורים. אבל אם נולד ספק זה בכלים כגון משקין טמאין שנשפכו לבין הכלים ספק נגעו ספק לא נגעו טהורין דקסברי משקין אין מטמאין כלי אלא מדרבנן ועל ספיקו לא גזרו ורבי יוסי ור"ש דרשי יטמא כרבי יהודה ומיהו כלים לא כדיליף בפירקין יטמא לטמא את האוכלים או אינו אלא לטמא את הכלי אמרת לא כך היה: טומאה בעולם. מדאורייתא ואפילו לטומאת עצמן: ר' אלעזר אומר אין טומאה למשקין. מן התורה כל עיקר ואפילו לטומאת עצמן והאי כל משקה אשר ישתה מוקי לה לקמן לענין הכשר בשמעתין: תדע. דאין להם טומאה מן התורה כל עיקר ואפילו לטומאת עצמן: שהרי העיד יוסף בן יועזר על איל קמצא דכן. מין חגב שמו איל קמצא דכן שהוא טהור וכשר לאכילה: ועל משקה בית מטבחיא דכן. על משקין של בית המטבחים שבעזרה כגון הדם והמים שהן דכן שאינן מקבלין טומאה אלמא טומאת משקין דרבנן ובהני לא גזרו משום הפסד קדשים דאי דאורייתא היכי מצו רבנן לטהרינהו: הא ניחא. הא דאמרת לר' אלעזר יש להן טומאה לשמואל דאמר האי דכן דיוסף בן יועזר דכן מלטמא אחרים קאמר אבל טומאת עצמן יש בהן מצית לתרוצי דהאי אין טומאה למשקין דקאמר רבי אלעזר לטמא אחרים קאמר דהא מעדותו דיוסף בן יועזר מביא ראיה לדבריו ויוסף בן יועזר לטמא אחרים קאמר: אלא לרב דאמר דכן ממש. קאמר יוסף בן יועזר ואפי' מטומאת עצמן על כרחך רבי אלעזר כמי מטומאת עצמן קאמר: אחרא. הא דקאמר ר' אלעזר כדבריו דרבי מאיר אלטמא אחרים טהור דרבי מאיר קאי אבל ליטמא טמא לא סבירא ליה כוותיה: ה"ג והא כדבריו דנפישי קאמר ועוד הא וכן קתני קשיא. דנפישי כלומר כדבריו לשון דברים רבים משמע: קסבר. יוסף בן יועזר טומאת משקין אפילו לטומאת עצמן דרבנן: ושמואל אמר כו'. קסבר יוסף בן יועזר טומאת משקין דאורייתא לעצמן מן וכל משקה אשר ישתה אבל לטמא אחרים דרבנן וכי גזור רבנן לטמא אחרים במשקין בעלמא אבל משקין בית מטבחיא לא גזור לטמא אחרים אבל טומאת עצמן יש בהן דהא מדאורייתא רמיא עלייהו ולא מצו רבנן למשקליה: קרי כאן והבשר אשר יגע כו'. והני דמשקין לא מטמאו אוכלין דחולין מיהו גבי קדשים אשר יגע בכל טמא כתיב וכיון דאמר משקין מטמאין מדאורייתא לעצמן בשר קודש הנוגע בהן הרי נגע בטמא: מידי דהוה ארביעי בקודש. דהוא עצמו פסול ואינו מטמא קודש: רביעי בקודש לא איקרי טמא. ומק"ו הוא דנפיק לן ביה פסולה לקמן* הלכך כי נגע ביה קודש לא קרינן ביה הבשר אשר יגע בכל טמא: ת"ש וכל משקה אשר ישתה כו'. דקא משתעי בכלי חרס שקיבל טומאה מן השרץ וכתב כל אשר בתוכו יטמא מכל האוכל וגו' וכל משקה אשר ישתה בכל כלי יטמא וגו' וקס"ד דהכי קאמר אחד אוכלין שבתוכו ואחד משקין שבתוכו יטמאו וכי דלא דרשת יטמא יטמא מיהו טומאת עצמן מיהא מיטמו: מאי יטמא הכשר. והכי קאמר כל אשר בתוכו יטמא מכל האוכל אשר יבא עליו מים או שיבא עליו כל המשקה אשר ישתה בכל כלי הוו הכשר ויטמא האוכל מחמת אויר כלי חרס טמא: בכל כלי. היינו משקין תלושין: דאחשבינהו. הואיל ומלאן גילה דעתו שהוא לריך להם וזהו חשיבתן: אך מעין ובור יהיה טהור. דאשמעינן הואיל ומחוברין נינהו לא מיטמו הא תלושין מקבלין טומאה וקשיא לרב: יהיה טהור מטומאתו. והכי קאמר אם יבא הטמא במעין ובור מקוה מים יהיה טהור הואיל וטבל הא שאובין לא מטהרי ליה: ותלושין מי מכשרי. אמים הוא דמתמה משום דמים תלושין לא חשיבי אבל אשאר משקין לא מתמה דכולהו תלושין נינהו: אלא שאין מכשירים. אלמא הכשר תלושין דרבנן הוא דאי מדאורייתא מאן שקליה ממשקי בית מטבחיא דלא ליכשרו: תירגמא. להא דקתני אין מכשירין אדם דמשקה בית מטבחיא ולא אמים ודם קדשים רחמנא אפקיה דלא ליכשר כדרבי חייא: שנשפך כמים. דם חולין שאין חשין לקבלו בכלי מכשיר דאיתקש למים אבל דם קדשים מתקבל בכלי ולריך ממנו למזבח ואינו נשפך לאיבוד כמים אינו מכשיר דלא איתקש למים: דם

דף יז

הגהות הב"ח

(א) רש"י ד"ה ספק משקה וכו' כגון היה מקל בידו:

תוספות

קשה במה חולקין כיון דר' יוסי אליבא דרבי עקיבא אומר וכי אינו מודה ר' מאיר דלר' עקיבא משקין לטמא אחרים דאורייתא הא ר' עקיבא דריש בהדיא יטמא יטמא בההיא דבו ביום דרש ר' עקיבא* ותי' ה"ר יוסף מירושלים דסבירא לי' לר' מאיר דיטמא דכתיב גבי משקין הייני הכשר ומשקה דמקבל טומאה נפקא ליה מדדריש ר' עקיבא גבי חולין יטמא דשני עושה שלישי ובחולין לכ"ע אין אוכל מטמא אוכל שלישי ע"כ הייני משקין:

בשלמא לשמואל דאמר דכן מלטמא אחרים. אע"ג דרבי אלעזר קאמר אין להן טומאה כל עיקר הייני משום דקאי בת"כ אמילתיה דר' שמעון דאמר לאוכלין טמא לכלים טהור:

חד בתלושין וחד במחוברין. והא דכתיב (ויקרא יא) וכי יותן מים על זרע הא אמרינן בפ"ב דחולין (ד' לו: ושם) דחד במת וחד בשרץ וצריכי וכיון דגלי לן קרא בחד מינייהו דאין חילוק בין תלושין ובין מחוברים ה"ה באידך ומחוברים פי' ריב"א דבשעת חיבורן נדבקו באוכל והעלה האוכל מן המים אבל אם נגע בעודו במים אינו מוכשר דתנן במסכת מכשירין (פ"ד מ"ו) כגון במערה כדה מדיחתו והוא טהור העלתו כל שהוא מן המים טמא:

תירגמא אדם. בפ"ב דחולין (דף לו:) פריך אהא שינויא והא משקי קאמר ביו"ד דמשמע ב' משקין והכא לא חייש אהאי פירכא משום דמצי לשנויי מאי משקי משקה דעלמא כדאמר (קדושין ד' סד:) בוגרות דעלמא והתם פריך משום דאית ליה שינויא אחרינא: דם

עין משפט נר מצוה

קיד א מיי' פי"ד מהל' אבות הטומאה הלכה ז: לקמן יח

קטו ב ג ד מיי' פ"י מהלכות טומאת אוכלין הלכה טז:

קטז ה מיי' פ"א מהל' פסולי המוקדשין הלכה לו:

רבינו חננאל

היא היא המדה ששורפין תרומה טהורה עם הטמאה ופריק ר' ירמיה הכי מתני' בבשר שנטמא בספק משקין הבאין מחמת שרץ שהוא ולד שאביו ספק כדתנן בטהרות פ"ד ר' יוסי אומ' ספק משקין לאוכלין טמאין לכלים טהורין (ר' מאיר) כיצד שתי חביות אחת טמאה ואחת טהור' עשה עיסה מאחת מהן ואין ידוע באיזה מהן עשה זהו ספק משקין לאוכלין טמאין לכלים טהורין ואודא ר' מאיר לטעמיה דשמעינן ליה דאמר ספק משקה הוא טמא אבל לטמא אחרים טהורים וכיון שזה הבשר ששינו במשנתנו ולד הטומאה שנטמא בספק משקה הוא אמר ר' מאיר זה טהור מאחר ששורפין אותו עם הבשר שנטמא באב הטומאה כך מותר לשרוף התרומה הטמאה והטהורה יחדו ואמר ליה ר' יוסי לא כי אלא ולד שנטמא מספק משקין לאוכלין טמא מן התורה הוא ונמצאת משנתנו לר' מאיר(היא) טמא וטהור לר' יוסי טמא וטמא לפיכך השיב ר' יוסי לטעמיה אינה היא המדה שזה טמא וטמא וזה טמא וטהור ונמצאת לטעמא דר' מאיר מדה ולטעמא דר' יוסי אינה היא מדה: ואקשי' אהא דתניא ספק משקין ליטמא טמא לטמא אחרים טהור דברי ר' מאיר וכן היה ר' אליעזר אומר כדבריו איני דר' אליעזר כר' מאיר סבירא ליה דאמר משקה ליטמא טמא לטמא אחרים טהור והתניא ר' אליעזר אומר אין טומאה למשקין כל עיקר תדע שהרי העיד יוסף בן יועזר איש צרדה על משקה בית מטבחיא דכן תניחא לשמואל דאמר דכן מלטמא אחרים אבל טומאת עצמן יש בהן היינו דר' מאיר אלא לרב דאמר דכן ממש היכי אמרי' ר' אליעזר כר' מאיר סבירא ליה דסבר ליטמא טמא אבל טומאת עצמן יש בהן ופרקי' אליבא דרב מאי כדבריו אחרא פי' דמודה ר' אליעזר לר' מאיר אסיפא דאמר לטמא אחרי' טהור ופליג עליה ארישא דאמר ליטמא טמא והא דרבינא דאמר וכן היה ר' אליעזר אומר כדבריו דנפשיה שאין טומאה למשקין כלל עלתה בקשיא: אמר מר ועל משקה בית מטבחי' דכן רב אמר דכן ממש קסבר טומאת משקין מדרבנן היא ובמשקה בית מטבחיא לא גזרו ושמואל אמר דכן שאין מטמאין אחרים אבל הן עצמן מטמאין דקסבר טומאת משקין לעצמן היא מדאורי' ולטמא אחרים דרבנן וכי גזור רבנן לטמא אחרים זולת משקה בית המטבחים וקשיא לאליבא דשמואל דאמר טומאת משקין עצמן יש בהן ואינן אחרים מדאורייתא והכתיב והבשר אשר יגע בכל טמא לא יאכל הנה כלל הכתוב כל מגע טמא לא יאכל ואיך אמר שמואל הן עצמן טמאין והן דכן מלטמא אחרים ושני' עשאוהו כרביעי שהוא עצמו פסול [...] טהור ודחי' רביעי לא איקרי הא איקרי טמא פסול איקרי טמא ועלתה בקשיא לשמואל: וחזרנו להקשות לרב דאמר דכן ממש ת"ש וכל משקה אשר ישתה בכל כלי יטמא הנה משמע מטמא ושניה מאי [...] דכתיב בהאי קרא יכשיר והאוכל זה המשקה שנפל עליו לקבל טומאה ודחי' ההכשרה של אוכלין כבר למדנו מרישיה דקרא דכתיב מכל האוכל אשר יאכל אשר יבוא עליו מים יטמא ושני' לעולם תרוייהו להכשיר יתאי

taught: [16a] Doubtful [cases of uncleanness with] fluids,[9] in respect of becoming unclean themselves, are unclean; in respect of defiling others,[10] they are clean; this is R. Meir's view, and thus did R. Eleazar too rule as his words. R. Judah said: It is unclean in respect of everything. R. Jose and R. Simeon maintain: In respect of eatables, they are unclean; in respect of utensils they are clean.[11]

But does R. Eleazar hold that liquid is at all susceptible to
a uncleanness,[1] surely it was taught: R. Eleazar said: Liquids have no uncleanness at all [by Scriptural law]; the proof is that Jose b. Jo'ezer of Zeredah[2] testified[3] that the stag-locust[4] is clean [fit for food], and that the fluids[5] in the [Temple] slaughter-house are clean.[6] Now, there is no difficulty according to Samuel's interpretation that they are clean [only] in so far that they cannot defile other [objects], but that nevertheless they are unclean in themselves, then it is well; but according to Rab who maintained that they are literally clean,[7] what can be said?—Said R. Nahman b. Isaac: [He refers] to one [ruling only].[8] But he states: 'as his words', implying that they are many; moreover, he teaches, 'and thus [etc.]'?[9] That is [indeed] a difficulty.

The [above] text [states]: 'Rab said, They are literally clean; while Samuel maintained, They are clean [only] insofar that they cannot defile other [objects], but nevertheless they are unclean in themselves'. 'Rab said: They are literally clean'. He holds that the uncleanness of liquids is Rabbinical, and when did the Rabbis decree thus? [Only] in respect of liquids in general, but there was no decree in respect of the liquids of the slaughter-house.[10] 'While Samuel maintained, They are clean [only] in so far that they cannot defile other [objects], but nevertheless they are unclean in themselves'. He holds that the uncleanness of liquids themselves is Scriptural, [but] in respect of defiling others, Rabbinical; and when did the Rabbis decree? In respect of liquids in general, but in respect of the liquids of the slaughter-house there was no decree; again, when did the Rabbis refrain from decreeing [concerning the liquids of the slaughter-house]? In respect to the defiling of other [objects], but they possess uncleanness in them-
b selves.[1]

R. Huna b. Hanina said to his son: When you come before R. Papa, point out a contradiction to him: Did then Samuel say, 'They are clean in so far that they cannot defile other [objects], but nevertheless they are unclean in themselves',—read here, *and the flesh that toucheth any unclean thing shall not be eaten?*[2]—Said R. Shisha the son of R. Idi: Let it be compared to the fourth degree in the case of sacred [food].[3] To this R. Ashi demurred: A fourth degree in the case of sacred [food] is not designated unclean, [whereas] this is designated unclean?— This is a difficulty.

Come and hear: *And all drink that may be drunk in any vessel shall be unclean?*[4]—What does *'it shall be unclean'* mean? It makes [solid foodstuffs] fit [to become unclean].[5] [You say], 'It makes [solids] fit'; this you know from the beginning of the verse: *All food which may be eaten [that on which water cometh, shall be unclean]?*—One refers to detached [liquid], and the other to attached [liquid],[6] and both are necessary: for if we were informed of detached, that is because he [the owner of the eatables] assigned importance to
c them;[1] but as for attached, I would say that it is not so. And if we were informed of attached, [that may be] because it [the liquid] stands in its place it has value; but as for detached, I would say that it is not so. Thus they are necessary.

Come and hear: *Nevertheless a fountain or a pit wherein is a gathering of water shall be clean?*[2]—What does *'shall be clean'* mean? From his [or, its] uncleanness.[3]

But can detached [liquid][4] make [eatables] fit [to become unclean]; surely R. Jose b. R. Hanina said: The liquids of the [Temple] slaughter-house, not enough that they are clean, but they cannot [even] make [eatables] fit [to become unclean]?[5]—Interpret this as referring to the blood,[6] for R. Hiyya b. Abin said in R. Johanan's name: How do we know that the blood of sacrifices does not make [anything] fit [to become defiled]? Because it is said, *thou shalt pour it out* [*sc.* the blood] *upon the earth as water:*[7]

(9) E.g., if an unclean person, whose touch defiles liquids, puts his hand into a vessel, and it is not known whether he actually touched the liquid there or not. (10) E.g., if unclean liquid fell near food and it is unknown whether it actually touched it or not. (11) The general principle is this: when a doubt arises in a *Scriptural* law, we are stringent; in a *Rabbinical* law, we are lenient. Now liquid can become defiled by Scriptural law (Lev. XI, 34), hence in doubt it is unclean. But there is a controversy as to whether it can defile other objects by Scriptural law. R. Meir holds that it cannot defile either food or utensils; R. Judah that it defiles both; while R. Jose and R. Simeon hold that it defiles food but not utensils.

a (1) Even in respect of itself. (2) V. Cambridge Bible I Kings XI, 26. (3) On the historic occasion when as a result of a dispute between R. Gamaliel and R. Joshua the former was deposed from the Patriarchate and R. Eliezer b. 'Azariah appointed in his stead. An examination was then made of scholars' traditions, and they were declared valid or otherwise; v. 'Ed., Introduction, xi. (4) Heb. *ayil*, of doubtful meaning. (5) *Sc.* blood and water. (6) Even by Rabbinical law. This postulates that the general uncleanness of liquids is Rabbinical only, and it was therefore not imposed in the Temple, so as not to defile the flesh of sacrifices.—The language of this Mishnah is Aramaic whereas all other laws in the Mishnah are couched in Hebrew. Weiss, *Dor*, I, 105 sees in this a proof of its extreme antiquity. (7) Even in respect of themselves. (8) R. Eleazar agrees with R. Meir that it is clean in respect of other objects, but not that it is unclean in respect of itself. (9) Both imply that he fully agrees with R. Meir. (10) V. n. a5.

b (1) I.e., the Rabbis could not free them from the uncleanness which they bear by Scriptural law. (2) Lev. VII, 19. Hence if the liquid is unclean, the sacrificial flesh which touches it may not be eaten. (3) I.e., sacrifices. V. *supra* 14a, n. a2. Thus there too it is unfit itself through defilement, yet cannot defile other flesh of sacrifices. (4) Lev. XI, 34. This shows that liquids contract defilement. (5) For solids cannot be defiled unless moisture has previously been upon them. The words, *'it shall be unclean'* thus refer to 'of all *the food* etc.' with which the verse begins. (6) If rain falls upon produce it renders it susceptible to defilement only if the owner of the produce desired it to fall upon something. E.g., if he put out a basin so that the rain should wash it, and subsequently produce fell into the water, it is henceforth susceptible. We are informed here that whether the water is detached from the soil, i.e., whether the rain falls into something detached from the soil, e.g., a bath (as denoted by the words *'in any vessel'*), or into something attached, i.e., forming part of the soil, e.g., a pit, and then eatables receive moisture from that rain, they are now ready to be defiled. In the latter case the produce is rendered susceptible only if it comes into contact with the water with the owner's desire; in the former, even against the owner's desire. V. Hul. 16a and Rashi a.l. s.v. לענין הכשר.

c (1) By the mere fact that he desired that the water should fall there or by pouring it into the vessel. (2) Lev. XI, 36. This shows that only attached water is clean, but not detached. (3) The verse refers to one who is unclean, and states that if he takes a ritual bath (*tebillah*) in the water of a fountain or a pit he shall be clean, but not in the water of a bath (technically called 'drawn water'). But it does not refer to the cleanness of the water itself. (4) Rashi: this difficulty refers to water, which can be attached too. But all other liquids are essentially detached. (5) This proves that the power of detached liquids in this respect is only Rabbinical; for if it were Scriptural, the Rabbis have no power to make an exception in this case. (6) But not the water. (7) Deut. XII, 24.

a declare it [the former] clean![1] [15*b*] As to ***piggul***,[2] ***nothar***,[3] and unclean [sacrificial flesh],—Beth Shammai maintain: They must not be burnt together;[4] while Beth Hillel rule: They may be burnt together.[5] Now if you think that R. Meir argues from the words of R. Joshua, why does R. Jose answer him from [the view] of R. Ḥanina, the *Segan* of the Priests?—Said R. Naḥman to him: R. Jose did not comprehend his [R. Meir's] reasoning, for he thought [that] R. Meir was arguing from R. Ḥanina, the *Segan* of the Priests, thereupon he said to him, I state [this law by deduction] from R. Joshua. But he answered him, Even on R. Joshua's [view] this is no true analogy, for R. Eliezer and R. Joshua admit that one must burn this separately and that separately. Yet why is this not a [true] analogy. Surely it is a perfect analogy?[6]—There it is different, because there is a loss of *ḥullin*.[7] To this R. Jeremiah demurred: [Surely] in our Mishnah too there is the loss of wood?[8]—Said a certain old man to him: They cared about a substantial loss, but they did not care about a slight loss.

R. Assi said in R. Joḥanan's name: The controversy is [only] in respect of the sixth [hour], but in the seventh all agree[9] that we burn them [together].[10] R. Zera said to R. Assi: Shall we [then] say that R. Joḥanan holds that our Mishnah treats of a principal uncleanness according to Scripture and a derivative uncleanness by Rabbinical law, and that what 'FROM THEIR WORDS' means is from the words of R. Ḥanina, the *Segan* of the

b Priests?[1]—Yes, he replied. It was stated likewise: R. Joḥanan said: Our Mishnah refers to a principal uncleanness according to Scripture and a derivative uncleanness by Rabbinical law, and what does 'FROM THEIR WORDS' mean? From the words of R. Ḥanina, the *Segan* of the Priests; and the controversy is [only] in respect of the sixth [hour], but in the seventh all agree that we burn them together.

Shall we say that we can support him: As to ***piggul***, ***nothar*** and unclean sacrificial [flesh]—Beth Shammai maintain: They must not be burnt together; while Beth Hillel rule: they may be burnt together?[2]—There it is different, because they possess uncleanness by Rabbinical law. For we learned: ***Piggul*** and ***nothar*** defile the hands.[3]

Shall we say that this supports him: If a loaf goes mouldy and is unfit for human consumption, yet a dog can eat it, it can be defiled with the uncleanness of eatables, if the size of an egg,[4] and it may be burnt together with an unclean [loaf] on Passover?[5]—[No]: there it is different because it is merely dust.[6]

c If so,[1] what does [THEY] ADMIT mean?[2]—R. Jose says thus to R. Meir: Even according to R. Joshua, who is lenient, he is lenient only in connection with doubtful and unclean [*terumah*],[3] but not in the case of clean and unclean.[4] If so,[5] why is it not a true analogy? Surely it is a perfect analogy?[6]—Said R. Jeremiah: Here[7] we treat of flesh which was defiled by a liquid which was defiled through a creeping thing, and R. Meir is consistent with his view, while R. Jose is consistent with his view: R. Meir [is consistent] with his view, for he maintains, The uncleanness of liquids in respect of defiling others is [only] Rabbinical; while R. Jose [is consistent] with his view, for he maintains: The uncleanness of liquids in respect of defiling others is Scriptural.[8] For it was

a (1) How then may we defile them with our hands by burning them together? (2) Lit., 'abomination'. The flesh of a sacrifice which the priest offered with the express intention of consuming it after the permitted time. (3) 'Left over',—flesh not consumed within the permitted period. (4) Because the first two, though forbidden, are not unclean Biblically, and when they are burnt together they become defiled. (5) This last portion of the Baraitha dealing with *piggul*, etc., is irrelevant, and is quoted merely in order to complete the Baraitha. (6) For the wine in the cask is quite clean, yet since it is fated to be lost we may deliberately defile it. (7) If the *terumah* is not deliberately defiled and allowed to flow into the lower part of the vat, v. *supra* 15*a*, n. a2. (8) For fuel, if two fires must be made instead of one. (9) Even R. Jose. (10) Since they are then Scripturally forbidden, even the clean *terumah* is certainly the same as unclean.

b (1) Thus: just as that which is only Rabbinically unclean may be burnt together with what is *Scripturally* unclean, so in the sixth hour, the *terumah* of leaven is then only *Rabbinically* forbidden, and may be burnt with unclean *terumah* which is *Scripturally* forbidden. This seems to be R. Ḥan.'s interpretation. Rashi and Tosaf. on the basis of another reading explain it rather differently. (2) This teaching was cited by R. Jose in his argument with R. Meir, he apparently agreeing with the view of Beth Hillel (v. *supra* and notes). Thus since *piggul* and *nothar* are Scripturally forbidden, they may be burnt together with unclean flesh, though they are thereby contaminated; and the same applies to clean *terumah* of leaven in the seventh hour. (3) I.e., Rabbinically, v. *infra* 120*a*. (4) Since it was once fit for *human* food, it can be defiled as food unless it becomes unfit even for a dog. (5) I.e., even if it is *terumah*. Now this must certainly be R. Jose's view, for R. Meir permits them to be burnt together even if the loaf is fresh. This proves that R. Jose agrees where it is quite unfit for human consumption, and the same applies to clean *terumah* of leaven in the seventh hour. (6) When it is unfit because of its mouldiness, it is worse than unclean, having no intrinsic value whatsoever.

c (1) That R. Meir learns from R. Ḥanina. (2) Surely R. Jose's argument that R. Eliezer and R. Joshua admit etc., is irrelevant, seeing that R. Meir is not concerned with them at all? (3) In the two cases cited *supra* 15*a*. (4) With which R. Meir deals. (5) Again, that R. Meir learns from R. Ḥanina. (6) For in the sixth hour the leaven is Rabbinically forbidden, and on R. Joḥanan's view, there is no difference according to R. Jose between what is unclean and what is forbidden for any other reason (since he maintains that in the seventh hour R. Jose agrees that they may be burnt together because both are then Scripturally forbidden) and the same principle should apply equally to R. Meir. (7) In our Mishnah. (8) Hence according to R. Meir this flesh is clean by Scriptural law, yet it is burnt together with flesh Scripturally unclean, and by analogy the same applies to *terumah*. But in R. Jose's view this flesh too was of uncleanness, and therefore it cannot be compared to *terumah* in the sixth hour, when it is only Rabbinically forbidden.

הפיגול והנותר והטמא בית שמאי אומרים אין נשרפין כאחת וב"ה אומרים *נשרפין כאחת ואי סלקא דעתך ר"מ מדברי רבי יהושע קאמר אמאי מהדר ליה ר' יוסי מדר' חנינא סגן הכהנים א"ל רב נחמן רבי יוסי לאו אדעתיה דהוא סבר ר"מ מדרבי חנינא סגן הכהנים קא"ל וא"ל אנא מדר' יהושע קאמינ' וא"ל ואפילו לרבי יהושע נמי אינה היא המדה דהא מודה ר"א ורבי יהושע ששורף זו בפני עצמה וזו בפני עצמה ואמאי אינה היא המדה מדה ומדה היא שאני התם דאיכא הפסד חולין מתקיף לה רב ירמיה מתניתין נמי איכא הפסד דעצים א"ל ההוא סבא *להפסד מרובה חששו להפסד מועט לא חששו א"ר אסי א"ר יוחנן מחלוקת בשש *אבל בשבע דברי הכל שורפין א"ל רבי זירא לר' אסי נימא קסבר רבי יוחנן מתני' באב הטומאה דאורייתא וולד הטומאה דרבנן ומאי מדבריהם מדברי רבי חנינא סגן הכהנים א"ל אין איתמר נמי אמר רבי יוחנן מתניתין באב הטומאה דאורייתא וולד הטומאה דרבנן ומאי מדבריהם מדברי רבי חנינא סגן הכהנים ומחלוקת בשש אבל בשבע דברי הכל שורפין לימא מסייע ליה הפיגול והנותר והטמא ב"ש אומרים אין נשרפין כאחת וב"ה אומרים נשרפין כאחת שאני התם דאית להו טומאה מדרבנן *דתנן הפיגול והנותר מטמאין את הידים לימא מסייע ליה *הפת שעיפשה ונפסלה מלאכול לאדם והכלב יכול לאכלה מטמאה טומאת אוכלין בכביצה ונשרפת עם הטמאה בפסח שאני התם דעפרא בעלמא הוא אי הכי מאי מודה הכי קא"ל ר' יוסי לר"מ אפי' לר' יהושע דמיקל כי מיקל בתלויה וטמאה אבל בטהורה וטמאה לא אי הכי אמאי אינה היא המדה מדה ומדה היא א"ר ירמיה הכא בבשר שנטמא במשקין שנטמאו מחמת שרץ ואודא ר"מ לטעמיה ורבי יוסי לטעמיה ר"מ לטעמיה דאמר *טומאת משקין לטמא אחרים דרבנן ור' יוסי לטעמיה דאמר *טומאת משקין לטמא אחרים דאוריי' דתניא

ספק

רש"י

הפיגול. לא צריך הכא אלא משום הבריית' : הפיגול והנותר. של קדשים : והטמא. בשר קודש שנטמא דקיימא לן בפ' אחרון (ד' קכ:) דגזרו עליהן שיטמאו את הידים ואע"ג שאין אוכל מטמא אדם גזרו עליהן לטמא מיהת את הידים ולא לטמא את הגוף משום חשדי כהונה ועצלי כהונה כדמפרשינן התם ואפילו הכי דאית עלייהו טומאה דרבנן אמרי ב"ש דאין שורפין פיגול ונותר שאין טמאים מן התורה עם הטמאה שהוא טמא מן התורה וכ"ש בתרומה טהורה וטמאה ואפי' ב"ה לא קשרי אלא משום דאית לפיגול ונותר טומא' דרבנן : וא"ל. רבי יוסי לרבי מאיר כי ילפת ליה מדרבי יהושע נמי אינה היא המדה דמודין הן בזו ולקמ' פריך אמאי אינה היא המדה: מדה ומדה היא. דהא טהורה גמורה היא התבית הזאת ומשום דסופה לאיבוד שרי לטמויי בידים: דעצים. שצריך להיסק שתי היסקות: מחלוקת בשש. שעדיין אין על הטהורה אלא איסור דרבנן אבל בשבע שנאסרה כבר מן התורה אין לך טומאה גדולה מזו ודברי הכל אף לר' יוסי שורפין: נימא קסבר ר' יוחנן. דמתני' דרבי חנינא בולד הטומאה דרבנן ור"מ מיניה יליף ודוקא נקט שש רבי יוחנן ומשום דאית עליה איסור דרבנן הוא טעמא דר' מאיר אבל אם בא לשורף' בחמש וארבע מודה רבי מאיר דאין שורפין ואע"ג דסופה לאיבוד דלאו מדרבי יהושע קא יליף דטעמי' דרבי יהושע התם משום הפסד חולין או דילמא לר' יוחנן נמי ר' מאיר מדרבי יהושע יליף וטעמא דרבי מאיר לאו משום איסורא דרבנן הוא דהוא הדין נמי לחמש וארבע והאי דקאמר ר' יוחנן שש אורחא דמילתא נקט : א"ל אין. ודווקא שש קאמר ולקמן פריך אמאי קאמר ר' יוסי אינה היא המדה : נימא מסייע ליה. דבשבע מודה ר' יוסי : הפיגול ונותר כו'. רבי יוסי א"ל לעיל וקאמר ליה לר' מאיר בהא הוא דאמרי בית הלל נשרפין כאחת משום דפיגול ונותר אסירי מדאורייתא אבל באיסורא דרבנן לא שרו לטמויי בידים שמעינן מינה מיהא דבאיסור דאורייתא מודה רבי יוסי ואע"ג דליכא שם טומאה עליה : שאני התם כו'. מהא לא מיסתייעא לר' יוחנן ואפי' בשבע אימא לך דפליג ר' יוסי ואע"ג דאסירא הואיל ואין עליה שם טומאה לא מטמינן ליה והא דמודה בפיגול ונותר משום דאית עלייהו שם טומאה דרבנן : מטמאה טומאת אוכלין. הואיל ומתחלה נראית לאדם ירדה לה תורת טומאה ואין עולה ממנה עד שתפסל מאכילת כלב : ונשרפת עם הטמאה בפסח. ואפילו היא תרומה טהורה והא ודאי ר' יוסי קאמר לה דאי ר' מאיר אפילו פת מעלייתא שרי וש"מ דמודה ר' יוסי היכא דלאו בת אכילה היא והוא הדין לפת מעלייתא בשבע שעות : אי הכי. דרבי מאיר מדרבי חנינא יליף מאי מודה ר' אליעזר דקאמר ליה ר' יוסי הא קא יליף רבי מאיר מדרבי חנינא מהדר ליה איהו מדרבי אליעזר ורבי יהושע : הכי קאמר ליה. הא דקא ילפת מדרבי חנינא אינה היא מן המדה כדמפרש לקמיה ואפילו לרבי יהושע נמי דשמעינן ליה דמיקל טפי גבי חבית דקאמר יטמאנה ביד מודה בשריפה בפסח דאין שורפין דהתם משום הפסד חולין הוא וכי איכא למימר דמיקל בשריפה בתלויה וטמאה הוא דאיכא למימר דמיקל כדשמען ליה גבי חבית שנולד לה ספק טומאה דאמר יגלנה ותנא גרמא והוא הדין בידים אבל בטהורה ליכא למימר דמיקל : אי הכי. דרבי מאיר מדרבי חנינא יליף אמאי אינה היא המדה מדה ומדה היא דהא בשש איכא איסורא דרבנן על הטהורה כי התם דאיכא טומאה דרבנן והא ר' יוסי לא שני ליה בין שם טומאה לשם איסור דהא אמרת דמודה רבי יוסי בשבע הואיל ואיכא איסור דאורייתא ואע"פ דליכא עלה שם טומאה אלמא לא שני ליה וכיון דלא שני ליה שפיר יליף רבי מאיר מדרבי חנינא דאמר דמטמאינן טומאה מדרבנן בטומאה דאורייתא הכא נמי מטמינן איסור דרבנן בטמא טומאה דאורייתא : א"ר ירמיה הכא. בבשר שנטמא בוולד הטומאה דקתני כגון שנטמא במשקין שנטמאו בשרץ : ואזדא ר' מאיר לטעמיה. דאמר משקין אין מטמאין אחרים ואפילו אוכלין אלא מדרבנן והוה ליה מדאורייתא טהור מעליא ושרפי ליה בהדי בשר שנטמא באב הטומאה דטמא מדאורייתא וגבי תרומה טהורה בשש דאיכא נמי איסור דרבנן עלה לא שנא : ורבי יוסי לטעמיה. דמשקין טימאוהו לבשר זה מדאורייתא הלכך אינה היא מן המדה דטמא וטמא הוא ולר' ירמיה איכא לאקשויי א"כ בין לר"מ בין לר' יוסי מאי מוסיפין לו טומאתו קא מסהיד ר' חנינא מעיקרא בראשון נגע וה"ל שני והשתא נמי בהדי ראשון שרפינן להו ונראה בעיני דרבי ירמיה אוולד וולד דקאמר רב יהודה סמיך ולא חש למידק כולי האי ונקט מילתיה בתר ליטנא דמתני' דתני בוולד הטומאה ולעולם בבשר שנטמא במשקין שנטמא בכלי שנטמא בשרץ דהוו להו משקין שניים והוא שלישי ואשמעינן דשלישי מותר לעשותו שני ואכתי איכא לאקשויי סוף סוף כיון דאין אוכל מטמא אוכל אלא מדרבנן מאי קא מהני ליה האי בשר ראשון לבשר שלישי אי לשוויה שני מדרבנן מעיקרא נמי שני מדרבנן הוה דאילו משקין שנגע בהן תחלה היו מדרבנן דהא נגע בראשון ואפי' ע"י שני הן נעשין תחלה אלא על כרחך ר' ירמיה כרב אדא או כאביי ס"ל דאמרי קדשים עושין טומאה כיוצא בהן ואשמעינן ר' חנינא דשני דרבנן עבדינן ליה שני דאורייתא ולר' מאיר שמעינן מינה דשני דרבנן דהוא טהור מעליא דאורייתא מותר לעשותו שני דאורייתא והוא הדין לתרומה טהורה שנשרפת עם הטמאה ולר' יוסי אשמעינן דשני דרבנן דהוא שלישי דאורייתא עבדינן שני דאורייתא הלכך אינה היא מן המדה ורבינא דאית ליה מקרא מלא דבר הכתוב לא ס"ל דרבי ירמיה ומוקי לה להוספת טומאה דרבנן דמתניתין כדאוקימנא בריטא ומאי מדבריהם מדברי ר' אליעזר ורבי יהושע :

ספק

תוספות

ולא ידעינן אי לא נגע אי נגע וקשה לריב"א אי ברה"י ספיקו טמא ואי ברה"ר ספיקו טהור ונראה לר"י לפרש כגון שתי חביות ברה"י ונגע באחת מהן ואינו יודע באיזה מהן נגע דהשתא שתיהן תלויות דבר תורה דלא ילפינן מסוטה לרשות היחיד ספקו טמא אלא דבר שיכול להיות אמת כעין סוטה אבל הכא דודאי אחת מהן טהורה אין לטומאות שתיהן מספק כדתנן בפרק שני נזירים (נזיר ד' נז.) ב' נזירים שאמר להם אחד ראיתי אחד מכם שנטמא מביאין קרבן טומאה וטהרה ומפרש בגמ' דהוי ספק טומאה ברה"ר ואפ"ה לא אמרי' דכל אחד יביא קרבן טומאה משום דודאי לא נטמא רק אחד מהן : נימא קסבר ר' יוחנן כו' מדברי ר' חנינא. פ"ה דמשמע ליה מדקאמר מחלוקת בשש דאי מדרבי יהושע מאי איריא בשש אפי' בד' וה' נמי כיון דאזיל לאיבוד ואין נראה לר"י דדילמא הא דנקט שש לאו למעוטי ד' וה' אלא משום דבעי למימר אבל בז' ד"ה שורפין ועוד דבד' וה' לא אזיל לאיבוד דכיון דשרי באכילה ימלא להן אוכלין הרבה ונראה לר"י דדייק מדקאמר אבל בז' ד"ה שורפין ואי מדברי רבי יהושע קאמר א"כ מנלן דבז' שורפין לרבי יוסי כיון דסבירא ליה דהתם שאני דאיכא הפסד חולין אבל בעלמא לא אע"ג דאזיל לאיבוד א"כ אפי' בז' לא ישרפו עם הטמא וא"ת הא דבז' שורפין אפילו לרבי יוסי משום דיליף מדברי רבי עקיבא דשרי לשרוף פסול עם הטמא וי"ל כיון דמדרבי יהושע יליף ולא מלינו דר"מ יליף איסור מטומאה מסברא אין לנו ללמוד איסור מטמא אבל אי מדבריה' היינו מדברי רבי חנינא ויליף ר"מ איסור מטמא ורבי יוסי דאמר אינה היא המדה משום דסבירא ליה ולד טומאה דאורייתא ולא ילפינן מיניה איסור דרבנן דהיינו בשש אבל בז' איסור דאורייתא ילפינן מיניה : **ונשרפת** עם הטמאה. נראה לו לדמות האי דאזיל לאיבוד לז' אבל כו' אין שורפין כיון דלא אזיל לאיבוד אלא משום גזירה דרבנן : **רבי** יוסי לטעמיה. קשה רבי יוסי גופיה אית ליה לקמן (דף יח:) טומאת משקין לטמא אחרים דרבנן והא דאית ליה הכא דאורייתא בשיטת ר' עקיבא רבו אמר *ואין זה לטעמיה ועוד

קשה

עין משפט נר מצוה

קיא א מיי' פי"ט מהל' פסולי המוקדשין הלכה ה :
קיב ב מיי' פ"ג מהל' חמץ ומצה הל' ד :
קיג ג מיי' פ"ו מהל' אבות הטומאה ה"א:

רבינו חננאל

הטומאה כו' ואי ס"ד ר' מאיר מדברי ר' יהושע קאמר היכי מהדר ליה ר' יוסי מדברי ר' חנניה סגן הכהנים וכו' ופרקי' טעה ר' יוסי דהוה סבר דר' מאיר מדברי ר' חנניה דייק ואמר ליה ר' מאיר מדברי ר' יהושע קאמינא והדר אמר ליה ר' יוסי גם לדברי ר' יהושע אינה היא המדה [ופריך הרי] מדה אחת היא שהרי ר' יהושע בהדיא אמר יטמאנה ביד ודחי' שאני התם דאיכא הפסד חולין כלומר כיון שתנת התחתונה יש בה יין שהוא חולין ואם תרד התרומה הוו עליהן תפסד לגמרי שאינו שמן שראוי להדלקה לפיכך אמר ר' יהושע יטמאנה ביד ואקשי' מתני' נמי אית בה הפסד כי אם תשרף כל אחת במדורה בפני עצמה צריכות עצים הרבה ודחי' הפסד של חולין שהוא מרובה חששו להפסד מועט כגון הפסד של עצים לא חששו: אמר ר' אסי אמר ר' יוחנן מחלוקת בשעה ששית שהיא גזירה מדרבנן דמדאורי' שעה ששית שרי באכיל' אבל בשבע שהוא איסור מן התורה דברי הכל שורפין הכל כאחת לפי שהכל איסורא מדאורי' היא ומאי מדבריה' מדברי ר' חנניה סגן הכהנים ומתני' באב הטומאה דאורייתא ולד הטומאה דרבנן : נימא מסייע לי' הפיגול והנותר והטמא ב"ש אומרי' אין נשרפין כאחת וב"ה אומרים נשרפין כאחת דייקי' מדברי ב"ה כיון דמאמר דכולן השתא אסורין מדאורי' הן אע"ג דהפיגול והנותר טהורין הן נשרפין כאחד אף הני בעידן איסורא מדאורי' והיא משעה שביעית ולמעלה נשרפין כאחד ודחי' לעולם לא מסייע ליה ושאני פיגול ונותר דאית בהו מיהו טומאה מדרבנן דתנן הפיגול והנותר מטמאין הידים. ואתינן תוב לסיועיה מהפת שעפשה שהיא טהורה ונשרפת עם תרומה טמאה בפסח ודחי' שאני פת שעפש' דכעפרא בעלמא היא: ואקשי' לר' יוחנן דאמר ר' מאיר מדברי ר' חנניה סגן הכהנים קאמר אי הכי אמאי אמר לו ר' יוסי לר' מאיר מודה ר' אליעזר ור' יהושע נימא ליה אנא אמינא לר' חנניה סגן הכהנים ואת אמרת לי מדברי ר' יהושע ושנינן הכי קאמר לו ר' יוסי לר' מאיר לא מבעי' הני דמחמרי אלא אפי' ר' יהושע דמיקל לא מיקל אלא בתלויה וטמאה אבל טמאה וטהורה לא: אי הכי כי ר' מאיר מדברי ר' חנניה סגן הכהנים אמר לר' יוחנן דאמר אב הטומאה דאורייתא ולד הטומאה מדרבנן הוא טמא אבל מדאורייתא טהור הוא אמאי אמר ר' יוסי אינה היא המדה הא האב טמא [דאורייתא] והולד מדאורייתא טהור ואמר ר' חנניה לא יגעו לשורפן כאחת

מסורת הש"ס

[שבת קנד:] לקמן כ: נה: נדה נו. ב"ק קיז. ב"מ לח:
לקמן סה. קכב:
לקמן סג:
[לעיל יד:]
ומיהו ...לר"מ מר' חנינא ור"י יליף ספר צריך לטעמיה כיון דעלייהו קיימי ועוד כו' בספק מחלוקת גרסאו:

ומאי מדבריהם מדברי ר' חנינא סגן הכהנים אמר ריש לקיש משום בר קפרא מתניתין באב הטומאה דאורייתא וולד הטומאה דאורייתא ומאי מדבריהם מדברי ר"א ורבי יהושע הי ר' יהושע אילימא הא רבי יהושע דתנן *חבית של תרומה שנולד לה ספק טומאה רבי אליעזר אומר אם היתה מונחת במקום התורפה יניחנה במקום המוצנע ואם היתה מגולה יכסנה רבי יהושע אומר אם היתה מונחת במקום המוצנע יניחנה במקום התורפה ואם היתה מכוסה יגלנה מי דמי התם גרמא בעלמא הכא בידים אלא הא ר' יהושע דתנן *חבית של תרומה שנשברה בגת העליונה ותחתונה חולין טמאין מודה ר"א ורבי יהושע *שאם יכול להציל ממנה רביעית בטהרה יציל ואם לאו ר"א אומר תרד ותטמא ואל יטמאנה ביד *רבי יהושע אומר אף יטמאנה ביד אי הכי האי מדבריהם מדבריו מיבעי ליה ה"ק ממחלוקתן של ר"א ור"י למדנו דיקא נמי דקתני מודה ר"א ור' יהושע ש"מ וכן א"ר נחמן אמר רבה בר אבוה מתני' באב הטומאה דאורייתא וולד הטומאה דאורייתא ומאי מדבריהם מדברי ר"א ורבי יהושע איתיביה רבא לרב נחמן *אמר רבי יוסי אין הנדון דומה לראיה שכשהעידו רבותינו על מה העידו אם על הבשר שנטמא בוולד הטומאה ששורפין אותו עם הבשר שנטמא באב הטומאה זה טמא וזה טמא אם על השמן שנפסל בטבול יום שמדליקין אותו בנר שנטמא בטמא מת זה פסול וזה טמא אף אנו מודים בתרומה שנטמאת בוולד הטומאה ששורפין אותה עם התרומה שנטמאת באב הטומאה אבל היאך נשרף התלויה עם הטמאה שמא יבא אליהו ויטהרנה

הפיגול

רש"י

ומאי מדבריהם. דר' מאיר: מדברי ר' חנינא. דתרומה טהורה בשש שעות דמיא להאי שלישי דטהור דאורייתא וטמא דרבנן והא נמי שריא מדאורייתא עד תחילת שבע ואסירא מדרבנן וכיון דאשמעינן ר' חנינא דמטמינן טומאה דרבנן בטומאה דאורייתא דמטמא ליה מדרבנן דאין אוכל מטמא אוכל מטמינן נמי תרומה טהורה דאסירא מדרבנן בטומאה דתרומה טמאה דאורייתא דלא מטמיא לה אלא מדרבנן דאין אוכל מטמא אוכל אלא מדרבנן: ארשב"ל. לא תדחק לאוקמא הכי דמאי מדבריהם דקאמר מדברי רבי אליעזר ורבי יהושע קאמר ולאו אמתני' קאי ר"מ אלא בעלמא קאי והכי קאמר מדברי סופרים שמענו ששורפין כו' ומאן ניהו סופרים רבי אליעזר ור' יהושע והאי עדות דר' חנינא ורבי עקיבא לא שייך גבי פסח ואיידי דבעי לאורויי ששורפים קדש טהור עם טמא נקט לה: שנולד. שאירע כגון שנכנס אדם טמא לשם ספק נגע בה ספק לא נגע: התורפה. הפקר: יניחנה במקום המוצנע. עדיין מוזהר על שמירתה וטעמא מפרש בבכורות בפ' (*עד כמה) את משמרת תרומותי שתים במשמע אחת טהורה ואחת תלויה ואמר רחמנא עביד לה שימור: יניחנה במקום התורפה. כלומר אם רצה יכול לגרום לה טומאה דקסבר יש אם למסורת ותרומותי כתיב אלמא שמעינן ליה לרבי יהושע דכיון דאינה ראויה אלא להדלקה יכול לגרום לה טומאה והא נמי אפי' טהורה בת ביעור היא ומטמאין אותה: חבית של תרומה בגת העליונה. היינו עדשים של גת שקורין מייט"ש שכונסין בתוכה: והתחתונה. היינו בור שהיין יורד לתוכו: טמאין. חולין טמאין יש בה ורגילין בימי טומאתן או למי שאינו אוכל חולין בטהרה ואם תפול תרומה זו לתוכו ה"ל מדומע טמא ולא חזי לישראל משום תרומה ואפי' טהורה ולא למכור לכהן דכיון דטמאה היא אסורה ביבמות בהערל (דף עג:) נפקא לן שהאוכל תרומה טמאה עובר בעשה בשעריך תאכלנו לזה הטמא והטהור יחדו ולא לאחר: מודה ר"א ור' יהושע. אע"פ שנחלקו באין יכול בסיפא מודין ושוין בכך שאם יכול להציל ממנה רביעית בטהרה אם יכול לחזר אחר כלים טהורין ולקבל קודם שתרד כולה לתוך הטמאין ויקבל הימנה רביעית הלוג: יציל. יחזר אחריהן ולא יקבלנה בכלים טמאין כדי להציל את החולין שלא יתערב ממנה בהן ויאסרו ואע"פ שבתוך כך ירד ממנה לתוכם ויפסדם לא מטמאינן לה לתרומה משום הצלת חולין: ואם לאו. שלא ימלא כלי טהור וסוף סוף טומאה אזלא כולה בזו נחלקו רבי אליעזר ור' יהושע דר' אליעזר אומר אעפ"כ תרד ותטמא מאליו ויפסיד החולין ואל יטמאנה ביד כדי להצילן ר' יהושע אומר יטמאנה ביד אלמא לרבי יהושע כיון דסופה לאיבוד שרי לטמוייה ביד ובפסח נמי לא שנא ור' מאיר מדרבי יהושע יליף: ממחלוקתן למדנו. שהרי הלכה כרבי יהושע בטהרות דרבי אליעזר נמנו עליו שלא לקבוע הלכה כמותו מפני תנורו של עכנאי בב"מ (דף נט:): דיקא נמי. דר"מ מדרבי יהושע יליף מדקא מהדר ליה רבי יוסי אינה היא מן המדה דמודה ר"א ורבי יהושע בזו ש"מ מינייהו הוה יליף לה ולקמיה פריך ממאי אינה היא המדה: א"ר יוסי. לר"מ אין הנדון דומה לראיה נדון שריפת חמץ בפסח שאתה דן ולמד מאלו אינו דומה לדברים שאתה מביא ראיה מהן עליו על מה העידו שתוכל ללמוד מהן: זה טמא וזה טמא. שלישי בקודש טמא הוא והראשון שהוא נשרף עמו טמא הוא: שמא יבא אליהו. לאחר זמן ויאמר טהורה היתה ונמצא למפרע שטימאנו תרומה בידים אף על פי שהיא טעונה שריפה מפני איסור חמץ אסור לטמאה בידים:

הפיגול

תוספות

באב הטומאה דאורייתא. נראה לר"י דלהכי נקט דאורייתא משום דאיכא אב הטומאה דרבנן כגון מעת לעת שבנדה ובית הפרס וארץ העמים והרבה כיוצא בהן והא דנקט דאורייתא לא נפקא מינה מידי דלמ"ד אין אוכל מטמא אוכל דמ"מ לא מטמא אלא מדרבנן ולא נקט דאורייתא אלא משום דבעי למימר ולד טומאה דרבנן דהוי דווקא דרבנן:

ולד טומאה דרבנן. פ"ה כגון כלי שנטמא במשקין והק' ה"ר יעקב דאורלינ"ש א"כ היכי יליף רבי מאיר מדברי ר' חנינא הא בשר קודש שנטמא מכלי שנטמא במשקין אינו נשרף אלא בעיבור צורה כדמוכח במס' חגיגה (דף כב. ושם) ובפ' על אלו מומין (בכורות דף לד. ושם) דקאמר כלי שנטמא במשקין מאחוריו תוכו ואוגנו ואזנו וידיו טהורין דעבוד בהו רבנן היכרא דלא לישרוף עליה תרומה וקדשים ומאחר שנטמ' נותר אפי' היה טהור לגמרי מותר לשורפו עם הטמא' כדמוכח לקמן (-"ב) מיהו אי עיבור צורה היינו לינה בעלמא אע"ג דלא הוי נותר לא קשה מידי ולפרש"י אינה היא מן המדה דר' יוסי היינו דלא מדמינן איסור דרבנן לטומאה דרבנן ונראה לר"י דוולד טומאה דרבנן היינו כדמפרש ר' ירמיה הכא בבשר שנטמא במשקין ור' מאיר לטעמיה וכו' ור' יוסי לטעמיה דאמר טומאת משקים לטמא אחרים דאורייתא אע"ג דבכלי שנטמא במשקין אין שורפין קדשים אלא בעיבור צורה בשאר טומאה דרבנן שורפין דלא כל הטומאות שוות ואור"י דלמ"ד אוכל מטמא אוכל לא איצטריך לאוקמא לעיל בולד ולד אלא לרבי יוסי דאמר (א) משקין לטמא אחרים דאורייתא והוי ולד טומאה דאורייתא אבל לרבי מאיר דהוי ולד טומאה דרבנן בלא ולד ולד איכא תוספת טומאה דמעיקרא טמא דרבנן והשתא כששורפין טמא דאורייתא הקשה ר"י למ"ד אין אוכל מטמא אוכל מדאוריי' א"כ לר' יוסי לא משכחת שלישי דאורייתא אלא שנגע שלישי במשקין שנגעו באוכל ראשון א"כ מאי תוספת טומאה איכא כששורפו עם הבשר שנטמא באב הטומאה דכיון דאין אוכל מטמא אוכל לא הוי שני אלא מדרבנן ובלאו הכי הוי שני דרבנן כיון שנטמא מן המשקין דהוי תחלה ואור"י דאכתי לא נגזרה גזירה דכל הפוסל התרומה מטמא משקין להיות תחלה כדפי' לעיל א"כ דהאי שלישי נטמא בעלים ולבונה כדפירש ר"ת לקמן גבי רביעי בקדש וסבירא ליה השתא דחיבת הקודש מהני למימני ביה ראשון ושני אע"ג דר"ל בעי לה (לקמן דף כ.) ולא איפשיט:

דמדאורייתא טהור מעליא הוא. הקשה ר"י הניחא למ"ד אוכל מטמא אוכל יליף שפיר איסור דרבנן לעשותו שני משלישי מדרבנן אע"ג דאיסור הוי כמו פסול ולעיל משמע דטמא ופסול איכא שוין דחשיב ליה הוסיף מ"מ בטומאה דרבנן לא משמע ליה לחלק אלא למאן דסבר אין אוכל מטמא אוכל מדאורייתא מאי קסבר אי קסבר דיש להשוותם א"כ בלא שום ראיה יהא איסור דרבנן מותר לעשותו שני דרבנן ואי קסבר דאין להשוותם אם כן היכי יליף משלישי וי"ל דלא יליף טפי אלא מכיון דחזינא דשלישי שהוא מקולקל דרבנן מותר לעשותו שני א"כ אין לחלק בין דרבנן לדאורייתא וילפינן איסורא דרבנן מפסול דאורייתא לרבי עקיבא דמותר לעשותו טמא ואור"י דהא דשרי ר' יהושע במתני' לשרוף תלויה עם הטמאה לר' יוסי היינו תלויה דאורייתא לדידיה שלישי דרבנן אסור לעשות שני:*

ולד טומאה דאורייתא. הכא דקיימינן אליבא דר"ל לא אשכחן שלישי דאורייתא למ"ד אין אוכל מטמא אוכל אלא ע"י משקין ולא הוי שני דרבנן ומאי תוספת איכא וי"ל דלא נגזרה גזרה עדיין דכל הפוסל וכו' כדפי' וע"י עלים ולבונה ליכא לאוקמא דר"ל הוא דבעי בפ"ב דחולין (דף לו.) אי מהני חיבת הקודש למימני ביה ראשון ושני והא דנקט ר"ל ולד טומאה דאורייתא כלומר אפי' אם נאמר בולד טומאה דאורייתא איכא לפרושי מדבריהם דר' אליעזר ור' יהושע א"נ נקט דאורייתא לאוקמא אפי' לר"א אבל לר' יהושע אפי' שלישי דרבנן מותר לעשותו שני וכן חמץ בשש שעות שהוא איסור דרבנן יליף ר"מ מדבריו של רבי יהושע:

מדברי ר"א ור' יהושע. והא דתני במתני' מילתיה דר' חנינא ור"ע משום דר' יוסי קטעי וסבר דר"מ מר' חנינא סגן הכהנים קאמר דקאמר בסמוך:

חבית שנולד לה ספק טומאה. פירש הקונטרס כגון שנכנס שם אדם טמא ולא

מסורת הש"ס

לקמן כ: בכורו' לג: תרומו' פ"ח [מ"ח]

תרומות שם [מ"ט] [לקמן כ:] מנחות מח.

[כך דר' יהושע ליתא במשנה ע' בתרומות ועי' ר"ש שם]

לקמן כ: תוספתא פסחים פ"א ה"ס

עין משפט נר מצוה

קי א ב מיי' פי"ב מהל' תרומות הלכה ד:

רבינו חננאל

דמתני' סבר שיש לאדם לטמא התרומה הטהורה בידים לא שנא אב הטומאה ולא שנא ולד הטומאה הכל מדאוריי' ומאי מדבריהם מדברי ר' יהושע דחבית של תרומה שנולד בה ספק טומאה ואמר ר' יהושע אם היתה מונחת במקום מוצנע יניחנה במקום תורפה ואם היתה מכוסה יגלנה כלומ' יעשה אלו הדברים אולי יפול בה שרץ או יבא אדם טמא ויגע בה ותטמא כדי ליהנות ממנה כדכתיב (במדבר יח ח) ואני הנה נתתי לך את משמרת תרומותי בשתי תרומות הכתוב מדבר אחת תרומה טהורה ואחת תרומה טמאה וכתיב ונתתי לך בשתיהן הכתו' מדבר ומפורש ביבמות בפ' הערל דאמר ר' אבהו כתיב לא בערתי ממנו בטמא ממנו אי אתה מבעיר אבל אתה מבעיר בשמן של תרומה שנטמא ודחי' אימור דאמר ר' יהושע לגרום לו טומאה בעלמ' אבל לטמא' בידים מי אמר אלא הא רבי יהושע דתני בחבית של תרומה שנשברה בגת העליונה והתחתונה טמאה [רבי יהושע אומר] אף יטמאנה ביד ודחי אי הכי מדבריו היה צריך לשנות התנא כלומר שהוא ר' יהושע לבד למה שנה מדבריה' וקשיא לן ולמה לא דחה בזו התשובה בתיובתא דאותבי' למעלה מזו (אלא פרק לו כגון שנולד בה ספק טומאה) ואית לן לשנויי לפי שכך דרך התלמוד כל מקום שיש ראיות לדחות דברי המקשה שתים שלש דוחה באחת מהן ואע"פ שיש אחרות וכשישתבר אחת ישיב אחרת ופרקי' עכשיו בזו הכי קאמר ממחלוקתן של ר' אליעזר ור' יהושע שמעי' הכי ואמרי' דיקא נמי דקתני מודה ר' אליעזר ורבי יהושע ש"מ: וכן אמר רב נחמן מתני' באב הטומאה דאורייתא ולד הטומאה דאורייתא ותרווייהו טמאת דאורייתא היא ומאי מדבריהם מדברי ר' אליעזר ור' יהושע: איתיביה רבא אמר ר' יוסי אין הנדון דומה לראיה שכשהעידו רבותינו לא העידו אלא על הבשר שנטמא בולד הטומאה ששורפין אותו עם הבשר שנטמא באב

הגהות הב"ח

(א) תוס' ד"ה ולד טומאה דרבנן וכו' לר' יוסי דאמר טומאת משקין:

ע"כ שייך לעיל ע"ב

[15a] and what does FROM THEIR WORDS mean? From the words of R. Ḥanina, the *Segan* of the Priests?[2]—Said Resh Laḳish in Bar Ḳappara's name: Our Mishnah treats of a principal uncleanness according to Scripture and a derivative uncleanness according to Scripture;[3] and what does FROM THEIR WORDS mean? From the words of R. Eliezer and R. Joshua.[4] Which [teaching of] R. Joshua? Shall we say, the following [teaching of] R. Joshua? For we learned: In the case of a cask of *terumah* wherein a doubt of uncleanness is born,[5]—R. Eliezer said: If it is lying in an exposed place it must be laid in a hidden place, and if it was uncovered, it must be covered.[6] R. Joshua said: If it is lying in a hidden place, one may lay it in an exposed place, and if it is covered it may be uncovered![7] How compare: there it is mere indirect action, whereas here it is [defiling] with [one's own] hands?—Rather it is this [ruling of] R. Joshua. For we learned: If a cask of [wine of clean] *terumah* in the upper part is broken,[8] while [in] the lower part there is unclean *ḥullin*, R. Eliezer and R.
a Joshua agree that if a *rebi'ith*[1] thereof can be saved in purity, one must save it. But if not, R. Eliezer ruled: Let it descend and be defiled, yet let him not defile it with [his own] hands: R. Joshua said: He may even defile it with his own hands.[2] If so, [instead of] this [phrase] 'FROM THEIR WORDS,' he should state, 'FROM his WORDS'?—This is what he means: 'From the controversy of R. Eliezer and R. Joshua we learn [etc.]'. This may be proved too,[3] because he states [further]: R. ELIEZER AND R. JOSHUA AGREE [etc.].[4] This proves it. And thus said R. Naḥman in Rabbah b. Abbuha's name [too]: Our Mishnah refers to a principal uncleanness according to Scripture and a derivative uncleanness according to Scripture, and what does FROM THEIR WORDS mean? From the words of R. Eliezer and R. Joshua.

Raba raised an objection to R. Naḥman: R. Jose said [to R. Meir]: The conclusion[5] is not similar to the premise. For when our Masters testified, about what did they testify? If about flesh which was defiled through a derivative uncleanness, that we burn it together with flesh which was defiled through a principal uncleanness, [then] this is unclean and that is unclean![6] If about oil which was rendered unfit by a *ṭebul yom*,[7] that it is lit in a lamp which was defiled by one unclean through the dead, one is unfit and the other is unclean. So we too admit in the case of *terumah* which was defiled through a derivative uncleanness, that we may burn it together with *terumah* which was defiled by a principal uncleanness. But how can we burn that which is in suspense together with that which is unclean? Perhaps Elijah will come and

(2) And the analogy is thus: just as Rabbinically unclean flesh may be burnt together with Scripturally unclean flesh, though the former is Scripturally clean, so may clean *terumah* be burnt together with unclean *terumah* during the *sixth* hour, though the former is then only *Rabbinically* forbidden, since by Scriptural law the interdict of leaven does not commence until the *seventh* hour, while the latter is already *Scripturally* forbidden for use on account of its defilement. (3) The other hypothesis being a forced one. (4) Thus R. Meir does not refer to the Mishnah at all but to the rulings of some other Sages. Strictly speaking therefore this Mishnah is irrelevant in its present position, but it is included because the subject of burning unclean together with clean is dealt with there. (5) E.g., if there is a doubt whether an unclean person touched it. (6) In spite of the doubt one must still protect it from certain defilement. (7) I.e., since a doubt has arisen you are no longer bound to protect it and may even place it where the risk of contamination is greater than at present. Thus R. Joshua holds that since it is only fit for lighting one may cause it to become unclean, and this furnishes the basis for R. Meir's analogy. (8) And the contents thereof are running down into the lower part of the vat.

a (1) A quarter of a *log*. (2) If the clean *terumah* runs into the *ḥullin*, it becomes unclean too, and then the mixture is forbidden to priest and lay Israelite alike, unless there is one hundred times as much *ḥullin* as *terumah*. In the present case only *unclean* vessels are ready to hand to catch the *terumah*, which would save the *ḥullin* below. Both agree that if there is time to go, procure *clean* vessels and save at least a *rebi'ith* of the *terumah*, this must be done, though in the meantime some *terumah* will descend and render all the *ḥullin* forbidden. But where there is no time to save even a *rebi'ith*, we have a controversy. R. Eliezer holds that even so it must be permitted to descend, though it will thereby be defiled in any case, rather than that we should deliberately defile it by catching it in unclean vessels. But R. Joshua maintains that since it will all be defiled in any case, we may defile it ourselves, in order to save the *ḥullin* below. R. Meir's ruling in the Mishnah is based on R. Joshua's. (3) That R. Meir refers to R. Eliezer and R. Joshua. (4) This would be irrelevant if he had not already referred to them. (5) R. Meir's. (6) Whereas R. Meir deals with unclean and clean. (7) V. Glos.

[14b] [*And whosoever . . . toucheth*] *one that is slain by the sword*,[4] [which intimates], the sword is as the slain;[5] hence it is a principal defilement, and he [R. Akiba] thus holds that a third may be raised to a first.[6] Yet what compels Rab Judah to relate it to a metal lamp? Let him relate it to an earthen lamp, and [as to the question], what does he [R. Akiba] add? [We can reply], For whereas there [in the first clause] it was unclean and is [now] unclean, here it was unfit and is [now] unclean?[7]—Said Raba, Our Mishnah presents a difficulty to him: Why does it particularly state, A LAMP WHICH HAD BEEN MADE UNCLEAN BY THAT WHICH WAS UNCLEAN THROUGH A CORPSE? Let it state, which
a had been defiled by a *sherez*![1] Now what thing is there whose uncleanness is differentiated between the uncleanness of a corpse and [that of] a *sherez*? Say, that is metal.[2]

Raba said: This proves that R. Akiba holds, The uncleanness of liquids in respect of defiling others is Scriptural; for if you should think that it is Rabbinical [only], then consider: how does this lamp affect the oil? If by rendering that itself unfit, surely it is already unfit?[3] Whence [does this follow]: perhaps [it affected it by enabling it] to defile others by Rabbinical law?[4]—If by Rabbinical law [only], why particularly [state when it was defiled] by a principal uncleanness? Even if [it was defiled] by a first or second degree it is still a first.[5] For we learned: Whatever renders *terumah* unfit defiles liquids, making them a first, except a *ṭebul yom*?[6] Hence this must prove that it is *Scriptural*.

SAID R. MEIR: FROM THEIR WORDS WE LEARN etc. From whose words? Shall we say, from the words of R. Ḥanina, the *Segan* of the Priests,—are they alike? There it is unclean and unclean, whereas here it is clean and unclean. Again, if from the words of R. Akiba,—are they then alike? There it is unfit and unclean, whereas here it is clean and unclean? Must we [then] say[7] that R. Meir holds [that] our Mishnah treats of a principal uncleanness according to Scripture and a derivative uncleanness
b by Rabbinical law,[1] which by Scriptural law is completely clean;

(4) Num. XIX, 16. (5) In its degree of defilement. For otherwise, why specify how the person was slain? This is then understood as a general law that any metal vessel or utensil which becomes defiled through a corpse, whether at first hand or not, bears the same degree of defilement as that which contaminates it. (6) For the oil, by contact with the lamp, is raised from a third to a first. (7) V. 14a, n. a2. The flesh, even in a third degree, being sacred, was definitely *unclean*, since there can be a fourth degree. But the oil of *terumah* was only unfit, without power to contaminate, whereas now by being raised to a second degree it becomes unclean. Thus this statement goes beyond R. Ḥanina's.—The reference must be to oil of *terumah*. For though there was also sacred oil, viz., the oil used in meal-offerings, and there a third degree is *unclean* in that it defiles by contact, nevertheless when unclean it cannot be used for lighting but must be burnt, like all other sacrifices which had been invalidated for any reason, so that by burning it together with the derivative of uncleanness and rendering it thereby second, he does not increase the power of defilement.

a (1) Lit., 'a creeping thing'. This too is a principal defilement, just like a man defiled by a corpse. Rashi omits 'by a *sherez*', the question being, what need is there for the Mishnah to define at all the source of principal defilement from which the lamp became contaminated. (2) The rule that a metal vessel bears the same degree of defilement as that which contaminated it applies only to corpse defilement. (3) And what does it matter whether it is of the third degree or of the first? Hence we must assume that it can now contaminate even by Scriptural law, which it could not do before. (4) Which power it previously lacked. (5) Lit., 'beginning'—another designation for a first degree. (6) 'What renders *terumah* unfit' is anything which is unclean in the second degree. By Rabbinical law this in turn defiles liquids and actually inflicts a higher degree of uncleanness than that borne by itself, rendering them unclean in the first degree. Thus if R. Akiba were treating of *Rabbinically* enhanced contamination, it would be unnecessary to speak of the lamp, which bears a principal degree of uncleanness, but of anything which bears even a second degree of uncleanness. (7) Since R. Meir derives his law from the preceding statements.

b (1) E.g., if a utensil was defiled by a liquid and in its turn defiled flesh. The second defilement is only Rabbinical, for by Scriptural law liquid cannot defile a utensil.

עין משפט נר מצוה

קח א מיי' פ"ז מהלכות אבות הטומאה הלכה ה:

קט ב מיי' פ"י שם הלכה ג:

[דהוי ליה לכתוב בחלל כמו לפעל' הנוגע בעצם או בחלל אלא הכי כתב דחרב מיותר להורות דחרב הרי הוא כחלל ערוך ערך חל]

גמרא

°בחלל חרב *חרב הרי הוא כחלל והויא ליה אב הטומאה וקסבר שלישי מותר לעשותו ראשון ומאי דוחקיה דרב יהודה לאוקמיה בנר של מתכת נוקמיה בנר של חרס ומאי הוסיף דאילו התם טמא וטמא ואילו הכא פסול וטמא אמר רבא מתניתין קשיתיה מאי איריא דתני נר שנטמא בטמא מת ניתני שנטמא בשרץ אלא איזהו דבר שחלוקה טומאתו בין טומאת מת לשרץ הוי אומר זה מתכת °אמר רבא ש"מ קסבר ר"ע *טומאת משקין לטמא אחרים דאורייתא דאי ס"ד דרבנן מכדי האי נר מאי קא מתניא להאי שמן אי לאיפסולי גופי' הא פסיל וקאי ממאי דילמא לטמא אחרים מדרבנן אי מדרבנן מאי איריא באב הטומאה אפילו בראשון ושני נמי תחלה הוי *דתנן °כל הפוסל את התרומה מטמא משקין להיות תחלה °חוץ מטבול יום אלא ש"מ דאורייתא היא: א"ר מאיר מדבריהם למדנו וכו': מדבריהם דמאן אילימא מדברי ר' חנינא סגן הכהנים מי דמי התם טמא וטמא הכא טהור וטמא ואלא מדברי ר"ע מי דמי התם פסול וטמא הכא טהור וטמא נימא קסבר רבי מאיר מתניתין באב הטומאה דאורייתא וולד הטומאה דרבנן דמדאורייתא טהור מעליא ומאי

תוספות

ואילו הכא פסול וטמא *ואע"ג דשלישי של תרומה מטמא הקודש כמו שלישי דקודש דתנן במסכת טהרות (פ"ב משנה ז) שלישי שבכולן מטמא משקה קודש ופוסל אוכלי קודש והתרומה קאי ש"מ אור"י דמגע טבול יום לא חשיב כשלישי דאפילו בקודש גופיה לא מטמא דכמטילה בפ' חטאת העוף (דף ח.) תנן חטאת העוף מועלין בה משהוקדשה נמלקה הוכשרה ליפסל בטבול יום ודייק בגמרא לאיפסולי אין לטמויי לא והכי סבר רבי עקיבא לקמן (דף יח.) בהסולת והקטורת והלבונה וכו' מיהו תימה דשלישי דטבול יום יעשה רביעי בקודש מק"ו ממחוסר כפורים כדמסיק רבי יוסי שלישי דטבול יום ספסל בתרומה אינו דין שיעשה רביעי בקודש ואם יש שום מיעוט בשלישי דטבול יום א"כ כי עביד לקמן ק"ו נימא שלישי דטבול יום יוכיח ובירושלמי במסכת חגיגה פריך לה:

אפילו בראשון ושני נמי תחלה הוי. מכאן משמע דשמן חשוב משקה ולקמן (דף יז.) גבי משקה בית מטבחייא וכן בכמה דוכתי והא דתנן (טהרות פ"ג משנה ב) ר"מ אומר שמן תחלה לעולם וחכ"א אף הדבש ור"ש שזורי אומר היין פירוש דווקא יין אבל הנך לא ופסקינן בהקומץ רבה (מנחות לא.) דהלכתא כוותיה אור"ת דהתם מיירי בנקרש ואחר כך נמוח כדמשמע בתוספתא* דקאמר התם במה אמרו שמן תחלה לעולם בנקרש ואחר כך נמוח ובלא נקרש משמע דכ"ע מודו וכן משמע בריש פ"ג דמסכת טהרות (משנה א) דקתני התם הרוטב והגריסין וחלב ושמן שהן משקה טופח הרי הן תחלה קרשו ואח"כ נימוחו הרי הן שניים ובתר הכי קתני ר"מ אומר השמן תחלה לעולם והיינו לעולם אפי' קרשו והא קאי ר"ש שזורי והכא משמע ליה בלא נקרש*:

הכא טהור וטמא. הקשה ר"י לוקמ' בו' דאסור מדאורייתא והיינו מדבריהם כי היכי דשלישי דאורייתא מותר לעשותו שני ה"נ איסור דאורייתא ורבי יוסי דאמר איכה היא המדה אית ליה דליכא לן למילף איסור מטומאה כמו שמפרש לקמן לר"ל משום בר קפרא דלא ילפינן איסור מטומאה ואור"י דלא בעי לאוקמה בשבע דשורפין תרומה טהורה עם הטומאה משמע ליה כדרך שבני אדם רגילין לשרוף והיינו בשש: **התם** פסול וטמא והכא טהור וטמא. וקשה לר"י בשלמא למ"ד אוכל מטמא אוכל א"ש דלא יליף איסורא דרבנן בשעה ששית מפסול דאורייתא אבל למ"ד אין אוכל מטמא אוכל מדאורייתא אמאי לא יליף שפיר כמו שמותר לעשות מפסול דאורייתא ראשון דאורייתא ה"נ מותר לעשות מאיסורא דרבנן שני דרבנן כדקמדמי בסמוך דקאמר נימא דקסבר ר"מ כו' ואור"י דלא דמי דמקלקול דאורייתא שיכול לקלקלו עוד יותר אין ללמוד שיוכל לקלקל קלקול דרבנן יותר אפי' בקלקול דרבנן אבל בסמוך מדמי שפיר קלקול איסור דרבנן לקלקול שלישי דרבנן תדע דהא ר' יוסי דס"ל לקמן (פז.) טומאת משקין לטמא אחרים דאורייתא וה"ל וולד טומאה דר' חנינא דאורייתא לא יליף מיניה איסורא דרבנן שיהא מותר לעשותו שני דרבנן דלמ"ד אין אוכל מטמא אוכל כששורפו עם טמאה לא הוי אלא שני דרבנן וא"ת למאי דמוקים לה בולד טומאה דרבנן °ר' חנינא נמי מוסיף אדר' עקיבא דמר"ע דאמר פסול מדאורייתא מותר לעשותו ראשון לא שמעינן שיהא שלישי דרבנן מותר לעשותו שני ובירושלמי פריך לה וקאמר למ"ד בולד טומאה דרבנן לא בא ר"ע אלא לפחות תיפתר בטבול יום דבית הפרס שהוא מדבריהם אך שמחליף דברי רבי יוחנן לבר קפרא:

רש"י

בחלל חרב. הקיש חרב לחלל מתכת שנגע במת הרי הוא אבי אבות הטומאה כמת עצמו ונגע בטמא מת הרי הוא אב הטומאה כמוהו גזירת הכתוב הוא במתכת אבל טומאת מת ולא אצל שאר טומאות: וה"ל. כר אב הטומאה וכשנותן שמן שלישי לתוכו נעשה ראשון: תורה אור טוקמה בנר של חרס. דאינו אלא ראשון כנוגע בטמא מת ולאשמעינן ר"ע דשלישי מותר לעשותו שני ודקאי' לך מאי הוסיף אדר' חנינא הוסיף טובא דאילו התם גבי בשר קדשים כי שריף שלישי בהדי ראשון ועשהו שני טמא היה מתחלה לטמא אחרים שהשלישי עושה רביעי בקודש ועכשיו כשהוא שני הוי טמא כלומר לא נשתנה שמו לקלקול יותר מברתחלה ואלו גבי עדותו של ר"ע גבי תרומה קאי דאילו שמן קודש אינו אלא של מנחות ובהיכל הוא ואינו ראוי להדליק נר ואם נטמא אותו קודש שנתנו במנחה משקדש בכלי אין לו היתר לכהנים ונשרף בקודש בבית הדשן כשאר פסולי קדשי קדשים אבל שמן תרומה שנטמא כהנים מדליקין בו דכתיב כתתי לך את משמרת תרומותי בשתי תרומות הכתוב מדבר אחת תרומה טהורה ואחת תרומה טמאה ואמר רחמנא שלך תהא להסיק' תחת תבשילך ביבמות בפ' הערל (דף עד.) ושמן שלישי של תרומה אינו טמא לטמא אחרים אלא פסול דאין שלישי עושה רביעי בתרומה וכי הדר עביד ליה שני ה"ל טמא: מתני' קשיתיה. לרב יהודה מאי איריא דתני טמא מת אי בנר של חרס קאי וכראשון עסקינן למה לי דנקט שקיבל טומאה זו מאב הטומאה' של מת ליתני שנטמא בשרץ דהוי נמי אב הטומאה ומה לי אב הטומאה דמת מה לי אב הטומאה דשרץ אלא מדנקט מת ש"מ בנר של מתכת עסקינן דיש חילוק בו בין נגיעת אב הטומאה דמת לאב הטומאה דטמאה ולאשמעי' דבנר שהוא עצמו אב הטומאה קאמר: ש"מ. מדקאמר הוסיף ר"ע קסבר טומאת משקים לטמא אחרים דאורייתא היא ודלא כהני תנאי דפירקין דלאמרי לקמן* שאין משקין מטמאין אחרים אלא מדרבנן דאי ס"ד דאין משקין מטמאין אחרים אלא מדרבנן מאי הוספה דאוסיף ר"ע דאמר שהשמן שהיה שלישי עשאוהו ראשון ומה בכך האי נר אב הטומאה כי עשאו ראשון להאי שמן מאי מהני ליה אחרי שלא יטמא אחרים: לאפסולי גופיה. הוא דמהני ליה הא פסול וקאי: דילמא. אהני ליה שיטמא אחרים מעכשיו מדרבנן: אי. תוספת דרבנן אתא לאשמעי' מאי איריא דנקט שמדליקין אותו בנר אב הטומאה שעושין אותו להאי שמן ראשון דאורייתא א"נ אשמעינן שמדליקין אותו בראשון לטומאה או בשני לטומאה נמי תחלה הוי כלומר איכא נמי תוספת מדרבנן כי ההיא שנעשה ראשון מדרבנן ומטמא עוד שני ושלישי דהא גזור רבנן על המשקין שאפילו נגעו משקין בשני יעשו ראשונים: דתנן כל הפוסל את התרומה. כל האי דמייתינן בפ' יציאות השבת (דף יג:) גבי שמונה עשר דבר שגזרו עליהם תורת שניים לפסול את התרומה מטמאין משקין אפילו חולין להיות תחלה חוץ מטבול יום שפוסל לתרומה מן התורה וגזירת הכתוב היא ומ"מ איקלישא טומאה דידיה ולא גזרו ביה לעשות משקין תחלה דאין דברי תורה לריכין חיזוק ומשום דמשקין עלולים לקבל טומאה ומה היא עלילתן שמקבלין טומאה שלא בהכשר גזרו עליהן חומר הרבה שיהו כהנים זהירין לשומרן: אלא ש"מ. מדמהדר למעבדיה ראשון דאורייתא ש"מ לטמויי אחרים ולעשותן שני דאורייתא קאמר כל סדר טומאה דאב עושה ראשון ראשון שני בחולין ותו לא ושני שלישי בתרומה ושלישי רביעי בקודש כולה מדאורייתא הוא בפירקין: נימא קסבר ר"מ. מדיליף מדבריהן קסבר מתני' דר' חנינא בשר שנטמא באב הטומאה דקתני באב הטומאה דאורייתא דכל אב הטומאה דאורייתא הוא אבל בשר שנטמא בוולד הטומאה דקתני כגון שנטמא בוולד הטומאה דרבנן כגון כלי שנטמא במשקין דמדאורייתא אין אוכלין ומשקין מטמאין כלי שאין אוכל נעשה אב הטומאה ורבנן גזרו שיהיו משקין מטמאין כלי משום משקה זב וזבה שהן אב הטומאה כגון רוקו ומימי רגליו בפ"ק דנדה (ד:) והאי בשר נטמא באותו כלי דהוי וולד וולד דרבנן שהמשקין היו וולד הטומאה והכלי היא וולד וולד דרבנן ומדאורייתא טהור הוא והאי בשר שנעשה שלישי על ידו טהור גמור מן התורה הוא ואשמעינן ר' חנינא דכיון דאיכא עלה טומאה דרבנן מטמאין לה בראשון דאורייתא:

ומאי

רבינו חננאל

סגן הכהנים ומוקים רב יהודה למתני' בנר של מתכת דרחמנא אמר בחלל חרב ודייק' מדהו' ליה למכתב בחלל כדכתי' [במדבר יט יח] ועל הנגע בעצם או בחלל וכתי' וכל אשר יגע על פני השדה בחלל חרב או במת שמעי' מינ' דלא כתבו אלא ללמד כי החרב הרי הוא כחלל ותניא בספרי דבי רב בחלל חרב בא הכתוב ולמד על החרב שמטמא טומאת שבעה והנוגע בו טמא טומאת שבעה הא למדנו לכלים ולאדם וגו' ונרסי' בתחלת שחיטת חולין בענין טמא השוחט בקדשים האי טמא דאיטמי במאי אי נימא דאיטמי במת בחלל חרב כתיב וילפינן חרב הרי הוא כחלל אב הטומאה [הוא] מטייה לסכין תיול סכין תטמיה לבשר נתברר כי כל כלי מתכת הנוגעים בטמא מת הן אב הטומאה הן והשמן שהיה שלישי עכשיו בנגיעתו בנר שנטמא בטמא מת נעשה ולד ראשון וקאמ' לן ר' עקיב' שלישי מותר לעשותו ראשון וכבר פרשנוהו בתחלת שחיט' חולין. וראינו לרבותינו הגאונים שהעמידו זה הנר שנהרג בו אדם הוא מכלל שאם לא נהרג בו איזוה הדין עליו ונתקש' לנו שיש שמועות מוכיחות כאשר פירשנו ונדחק רב יהוד' ואמר נר של מתכת ולא אמר נר של חרש שאע"פ שהנר של חרש הנוגע בטמא מת טמא הוא והרי הוסיף ר"ע על ר' חנניה סגן הכהנים דר' חנניה לא אמר אלא טמא שלישי מותר לעשותו שני אבל טמא ופסול לא אמר ואלו ר' עקיבא הוסיף אפי' פסול[מותר] לעשותו טמא. מתני' קשית' מאי איריאמתני' נר שנטמא בטמא מת: **אמר** רבא ש"מ מדר' עקיבא דקתני הוסיף דטומאת משקין כגון השמן וכיוצא בו לטמא אחר דאורייתא היא דאי ס"ד מדרבנן הוא אבל מדאורייתא טמא הוא אותו המשקה ואינו מטמא אחרים כל שאינו מטמא פסול הוא הגה הטומאה השניה לא הוסיפה לו ולשמן כלום פסול היה מקודם ועכשיו פסול הוא ואלא מאי לטמא אחרים מדאוריי' הוא מכדי משקה לא שנא כי נגעו באב הטומאה ולא שנא כי נגעו בראשון ובשני אינהו שני עבדי דתנן בפ"ח [דפרה] כל הפוסל בתרומה מטמא משקין להיות תחלה חוץ מטבול יום למה לי למתני בנר שנטמא בטמא מת ולאוקמא בנר של מתכת ליתני בנר ואפי' בנר של חרש שמעינן מינה שלישי

מסורת הש"ס

[לקמן יט: פח. שבת קלו. פ"ד: חולין ג.]

[לקמן טז:]

פרה פ"ח [מ"ז] [חולין לג.]

דף פח.

גליון הש"ס

תוס' ד"ה ואילו הכא וכו' ואע"ג דשלישי. עיין חולין לו ע"ב תוד"ה משקה טבול יום: **בא"ד** א"ר דמגע טב"י. עיין חגיגה כ ע"ב תוד"ה ראשון: **גמ'** אמר רבא ש"מ קסבר ר"ע. עיין סוטה דף כט ע"ב: **מתני'** מיהו אלם ע"ב דף יט ע"ב: **תוס'** ד"ה התם פסול וכו' ר"מ נמי מוסיף. עיין זבחים דף ג ע"ב תוד"ה כבותו:

שתי פרות היו חורשות בהר המשחה כל זמן ששתיהן חורשות כל העם אוכלין ניטלת אחת מהן תולין לא אוכלין ולא שורפין ניטלו שתיהן התחילו כל העם שורפין:

מתני' *רבי חנינא סגן הכהנים אומר *מימיהם של כהנים לא נמנעו מלשרוף את הבשר שנטמא בוולד הטומאה עם הבשר שנטמא באב הטומאה אע"פ שמוסיפין טומאה על טומאתו הוסיף ר' עקיבא *ואמר מימיהם של כהנים לא נמנעו מלהדליק את השמן שנפסל בטבול יום בנר שנטמא בטמא מת אף על פי שמוסיפין טומאה על טומאתו אמר רבי מאיר מדבריהם למדנו ששורפין תרומה טהורה עם הטמאה בפסח א"ר יוסי אינה היא המדה ומודים ר' אליעזר ורבי יהושע ששורפין זו לעצמה וזו לעצמה על מה נחלקו על התלויה ועל הטמאה שר' אליעזר אומר תשרף זו לעצמה וזו לעצמה ור' יהושע אומר שתיהן כאחת:

גמ' מכדי בשר שנטמא בוולד הטומאה מאי הוי שני כי שריף ליה בהדי בשר שנטמא באב הטומאה מאי הוי שני ושני הוא מאי מוסיף לו טומאה על טומאתו איכא אמר רב יהודה הכא בוולד וולד עסקינן דהוי ליה שלישי וקסבר שלישי מותר לעשותו שני והא אין אוכל מטמא אוכל דתניא יכול יהא אוכל מטמא אוכל ת"ל °וכי יתן מים על זרע ונפל מנבלתם עליו טמא הוא טמא הוא ואין עושה כיוצא בו טמא הניחא לאביי דאמר לא שנו אלא בחולין אבל בתרומה וקדשים עושה כיוצא בו ולרב אדא בר אהבה משמיה דרבא נמי דאמר לא שנו אלא חולין ותרומה אבל בקדשים עושה כיוצא בהן שפיר אלא לרבינא משמיה דרבא דאמר מקרא מלא דיבר הכתוב לא שנא חולין לא שנא תרומה לא שנא קדשים אינו עושה כיוצא בו מאי איכא למימר הכא במאי עסקינן דאיכא משקין בהדי בשר דקא מיטמא מחמת משקין אי הכי האי עם הבשר שנטמא באב הטומאה עם הבשר ומשקין מיבעי ליה אלא נהי דאין אוכל מטמא אוכל מדאורייתא מדרבנן מיהו מטמא: הוסיף ר' עקיבא מימיהן של כהנים לא נמנעו מלהדליק כו': מכדי שמן שנפסל בטבול יום מאי הוי שלישי וכי מדליק ליה בנר שנטמא בטמא מת מאי הוי שני מאי קמ"ל שלישי מותר לעשותו שני היינו הך אמר רב יהודה הכא בנר של מתכת עסקינן דרחמנא אמר בחלל

עדיות פ"ב [מ"א] | נ"י שם | [ויקרא יא]

רש"י

שתי פרות היו חורשות. לומר היום לסימן: בהר המשחה. הוא הר הזיתים: **מתני'** מימיהם של כהנים. הכא נקט לה משום סיפא דקתני מדבריהן למדנו ששורפין תרומה כו': מלשרוף את הבשר שנטמא בוולד הטומאה. שנגע בבשר קודש זה בראשון לטומאה וה"ל איהו שני ולא נמנעו מלשורפו עם חמור ממנו ממי שנגע באב הטומאה דהוא"ל ואף זה הקל לשריפה עומד לא חשו אם מטמאין אותו יותר ממה שהי' ובגמרא פריך מאי תוספת טומאה איכא הלא גם בראשונה בוולד טומאה נגע ועכשיו חוזר ונוגע בוולד הטומאה: מלהדליק שמן. של תרומה: שנפסל בטבול יום. והוא שלישי דטבול יום פוסל את התרומה מן התורה ביבמות פרק הערל (דף עה.) מכלל קודש לא תגע ויולדת מטבלה לסוף ימי טומאה עד מלאת ימי טהרה שלה טבולת יום הוא ארוך היא שהרי אינה ראויה להביא כפרה עד יום שמונים ואחד אלמא לא הוי הערב שמש דילה עד שקיעת החמה דשמונים: בנר שנטמא בטמא מת. טמא מת אב הטומאה הוא ומטמא כלים דכתיב (במדבר יט) וכל אשר יגע בו הטמא יטמא והנפש הנוגעת תטמא עד הערב בפרשת פרה גבי טומאת מת אלמא טמא מת מטמא אדם ועשאו הכתוב אב הטומאה כשרץ ונבילה שמטמאין אדם ולא כנוגע בהן שאין מטמא אלא אוכלין ומשקין כדכתיב בשרצים (ויקרא יא) כל אשר בתוכו יטמא מכל האוכל אשר יאכל אשר יבוא עליו מים יטמא וכל משקה אשר ישתה בכל כלי יטמא אלמא לא מקבל טומאה מן הכלי שקיבל טומאה מן השרץ אלא אוכל ומשקה בלבד ולא אדם וכלים והאי נר הוי ראשון ועכשיו יש כאן תוספת טומאה שמתחלה היה שמן זה שלישי וחוזר ונעשה שני ע"י הנר דהוא"ל ויש טומאה עליו לא חיישינן ליה ומותר להוסיף בידים: מדבריהן למדנו ששורפין תרומה טהורה עם הטמאה בפסח. עם זמן הביעור דהוא"ל והולכת לאיבוד אף הטהורה ואסורה מדאורייתא לא חיישינן לשמירתה ולעג"ש שמוזהרין אנו לשומרה בטהרה דכתיב (במדבר יח) את משמרת תרומותי: אינה היא המדה. אי אתה יכול ללמוד את זו מדבריהן ובגמרא מפרש אמאי אינה היא המדה: ומודים ר"א כו'. רבי יוסי קאמר לה דלא"ג דאיפלוג ר"א ורבי יהושע בשריפת תרומה בהא מודו ששורפין זו לעצמה וזו לעצמה: **גמ'** שני ושני הוא. מתחלה היה שני ועדיין שני הוא: הכא בוולד וולד עסקינן. האי בוולד הטומאה דקתני מתני' וולד וולד קאמר דהיינו שני ובשר שנגע בו הוה שלישי וכי הדר שרפי ליה בהדי בשר שנטמא באב הטומאה שהוא ראשון חוזר ונעשה שלישי זה שני: והא אין אוכל מטמא אוכל. וכיון דלא מטמא ליה מאי תוספת איכא: ואין עושה כיוצא בו. ואין מטמא אוכל כיוצא בו: הוא טמא. משמע מיעוטא: אבל תרומה וקדשים עושה כיוצא בה. דילפינן מנבואת חגי לחם וכזיד יין ושמן (חגי ב): שפיר. דמתני' בקדשים קיימי': מקרא מלא. לא הוציא ממשמעו לא תרומה ולא קדשים אלא דבר שלם דיבר דאין אוכל מטמא אוכל לעולם ונבואת חגי טומאות דרבנן ניכהו וכבר נגזרו כדלקמן אבל דאורייתא לא מטמא אלא אוכל משקה ומשקה אוכל לקמן בפירקין (דף יח.) יליף לה דאוכל מטמא משקה ומשקה אוכל: דאיכא משקין בהדי בשר. כשנגע באב הטומאה היה משקה טופח עליה ונטמא עמה והוה אף המשקה ראשון וכששורפה עדיין הוא עליה ומטמא הבשר שנשרף עם זה מחמת המשקין ונעשה שלישי שני: מדרבנן מטמא. וקא מוספי ליה טומאה מדרבנן: מאי הוי שני. דנר הוי ראשון: היינו הך. דר' חנינא דתרילנא בהכי ומאי הוסיף ר"ע דמשמע דהוסיף עדות חידוש על חידוש:

בחלל

תוספות

שתי פרות היו חורשות. בירושלמי דייק ירושלים לא מקום שנהגו בו שלא לעשות מלאכה כלומר סברא הוא לנהוג שם איסור כיון שמתקבלין שם אף ממקומות שנהגו בהן איסור ומשני נראות כחורשות: **אבל** תרומה וקדשים עושין כיוצא בהן. פירש בקונטרס דנפיק מקרא דחגי אל הלחם ואל הנזיד ולר"ת דמפרש לקמן [ד' יז.] או אל הנזיד אור"י דנפקא ליה מוהבשר אשר יגע בכל טמא לא יאכל (ויקרא ז') אפי' באוכל ותרומה נפקא לן כיון דלא מצינו למימר מקרא מלא דבר הכתוב דהא איכא קדשים דעושין כיוצא בהן נוקי קרא בדדמי טפי דהיינו חולין: **דאיכא** משקין בהדי בשר. מכאן מדקדק ריב"א *°דמשקין מטמא בפחות מרביעית דסתם משקין דבהדי בשר לית בהן רביעית ולקמן (דף יז: *) נמי אמרו גבי מים אבל פחות מרביעית טמאים והא דאמר בפרק אין מעמידין (ע"ז דף לח. ושם) גבי יין נסך דמטמא טומאת משקין ברביעית ובפ"ב דנדה (דף יט:) גבי דם הירוק ובכמה דוכתין אומר ריב"א דבפסול גוייה איירי דשיעורו ברביעית כדאמר במעילה בפרק קדשי מזבח (דף יז:) דכל המשקים מצטרפין לפסול הגוייה ברביעית ור"י מפרש דהא דבעינן רביעית היינו בהנך דעיקר טומאה לאו דאורייתא כגון סתם יין כותים ודם הירוק דאפי' ביותר מרביעית לא מטמא מדאורייתא אבל שאר משקין מדאורייתא בכל שהוא ור"ת אומר דמדאורייתא בעינן רביעית לטמא אחרים אבל מדרבנן מטמא אחרים בכל שהוא ולפי' נ"ל דהשתא לא מסיק אדעתיה שאוכל יטמא אוכל אפילו מדרבנן מדאיצטריך לאוקמא במשקין ומדרבנן ולא מוקי כמסקנא דאוכל מטמא אוכל מדרבנן ואף על גב דאין אוכל מטמא אוכל אפילו מדרבנן מכל מקום משכחנא שלישי ע"י עלים ולבונה או על ידי משקין דהכתי לא גזרו דכל הפוסל את התרומה מטמא משקין להיות תחלה: **עם** בשר ומשקין מיבעי ליה. וא"ת אמאי לא פריך מאי איריא שנטמא באב הטומאה אפי' בראשון ושני נמי כדפריך לקמן על ר"ע וי"ל משום דרבי חנינא קאמר מימיהם של כהנים משמע שמעולם כך הוא אף קודם י"ח דבר דגזרו דכל הפוסל התרומה מטמא משקין להיות תחלה דבפ"ק דשבת (דף יד: ושם) מוקי האוכלין והכלים שנטמאו במשקין במשקין הבאים מחמת ידים ולפי שגזרו דידים פוסלין התרומה עושין המשקין שנגעו בהן תחלה: **מאי** קא משמע לן דשלישי מותר לעשותו שני היינו הך. למ"ד אין אוכל מטמא אוכל מדאורייתא לא פריך דלדידיה הוסיף דמותר לעשות אף שני דאורייתא:

ואילו

עין משפט נר מצוה

קג א מיי' פי"ט מהל' פסולי מוקדשין הל' י:

קד ב ג מיי' פ"ג מהל' חמץ ומצה הל' ד:

קה ד מיי' פי"ט מהל' פסולי מוקדשין:

קו ה מיי' פ"ו מהלכות אבות הטומאה הל' א סמג עשין רמח:

קז ו מיי' פי"ט מהלכות פסולי מוקדשין הל' ז:

[ועי' תוס' עירובין לס. ד"ה היה אוכל ותוס' יומא פ: ד"ה ותליה ובחולין סו: ד"ה כל משקה וכריתות יג: ד"ה ותלב]

רבינו חננאל

שאול אומר שתי פרות היו חורשו' בהר המשחה כו': **מתני'** אמר רבי חנניה סגן הכהנים מימיהן של כהנים לא נמנעו מלשרוף הבשר שנטמא בולד הטומאה עם הבשר שנטמא באב הטומאה כו' נקוט האי כללא בידך השרץ כיוצא בו הוא אב הטומאה כדתנן אבות הטומאה השרץ ושכבת זרע וטמא מת כו' והנוגע בהן נקרא ולד ראשון והנוגע בולד נקרא ולד שני והנוגע בולד [שני] נקרא ולד שלישי אקשי' אמתני' מכדי בשר שנטמא בולד הטומאה ולד שני הוא כי שריף ליה בהדי בשר שנטמא באב הטומאה הלא נעשה הנוגע באב הטומאה ולד ראשון כי נגע באחר משוי ליה ולד שני כי בבשר שהיה ולד שני לא הוסיף לו טומאה ולד שני הוה וגם עתה כשנגע בו הולד הראשון נעשה ולד שני מה הוסיף לו דקתני במתני' אע"פ שמוסיף לו טומאה על טומאתו ופריק רב יהודה ולד דמתני' ולד שני שעשה הבשר שנגע בו ולד שלישי עשאו שני הנה הוסיף לו טומאה שעד עתה היה ולד שלישי ועכשיו נעשה שני ואקשי' היאך הבשר שהוא אוכל יטמא אוכל כיוצא בו והתניא יכול יהא אוכל מטמא אוכל ת"ל וכי יותן מים על זרע ותנ' הוא טמא ואין עושה טמא כיוצא בו הניחא למאן דאמר בחולין אינו עושה ולמאן דאמר בחולין ובתרומה נמי אין עושה אבל בקדשים עושה טומאה כיוצא בה שפיר דהני קדשים נינהו אלא לרבינא דאמר אפילו קדשים אין עושה אוכל טמא כיוצא בו מאי איכא למימר ופריק רב נחמן בר יצחק מהא דתנן [פרה פ"ח] אין כלי חרס מטמא (חבית) [חבירו] אלא במשקה נטמא המשקה מטמאהו הכא נמי כגון דאיכא משקין בהדי האי בשרא דמטמ' הבשר מחמת משקין ונדחה (ואפי') [אלא נהי] דאין אוכל מטמא אוכל מדאורייתא ומתני' דקתני בשר מטמא בשר אחר מדרבנן: **מתני'** הוסיף ר' עקיבא מימיהן של כהנים כו'. אקשי' מכדי שמן שנפסל בטבול יום מאי הוא שלישי כי הטבול יום פוסל ואינו מטמא והשלישי פוסל ואינו מטמא דתנן בתרומות פ"ב הראשון והשני שבתרומה טמא ומטמא והשלישי פסול ולא מטמא דתנן בטבול יום פ"ב המקפה של תרומה והשום והשמן של חולין ונגע טבול יום במקצתו פסל את כלן נמצא זה השמן פסו' והוא כמו שלישי כדנגע ביה בזה השמן הנר שנטמא מת שני הוא כי הנר הוא ולד ראשון והשמן שנגע בנר נעשה ולד שני מאי קמ"ל ר' עקיבא שלישי מותר לעשותו שני היינו דר' חנינה

סגן

גליון הש"ס

תוס' ד"ה דאיכא. דמשקין מטמא בפחות מרביעית כו'. עי' כרתי' לקמן דף יז ע"ב ד"ה אבל לית בהו רביעית:

It was taught, Abba Saul said: [14a] Two cows used to plough on the Mount of Anointing:[5] as long as both were ploughing, all the people ate; when one was removed, they kept [the leaven] in suspense, neither eating nor burning [it]; when both were removed, all the people began burning [their leaven].

a *MISHNAH*. R. ḤANINA, THE SEGAN[1] OF THE PRIESTS, SAID: DURING THE DAYS OF THE PRIESTS THEY NEVER REFRAINED FROM BURNING [SACRIFICIAL] FLESH WHICH HAD BEEN DEFILED BY A DERIVATIVE UNCLEANNESS WITH FLESH WHICH HAD BEEN DEFILED BY A PRINCIPAL UNCLEANNESS, THOUGH UNCLEANNESS IS ADDED TO ITS UNCLEANNESS.[2] R. AKIBA ADDED AND SAID: DURING [ALL] THE DAYS OF THE PRIESTS THEY DID NOT REFRAIN FROM LIGHTING OIL[3] WHICH HAD BEEN RENDERED UNFIT[4] BY A ṬEBUL YOM[5] IN A LAMP WHICH HAD BEEN MADE UNCLEAN BY THAT WHICH [OR, ONE WHO] IS UNCLEAN THROUGH A CORPSE, THOUGH UNCLEANNESS IS ADDED TO THEIR UNCLEANNESS.[6] SAID R. MEIR: FROM THEIR WORDS WE LEARN THAT WE MAY BURN CLEAN TERUMAH TOGETHER WITH UNCLEAN TERUMAH ON PASSOVER.[7] R. JOSE SAID: THAT IS NOT AN ANALOGY.[8] AND R. ELIEZER AND R. JOSHUA ADMIT THAT EACH IS BURNT SEPARATELY; WHERE DO THEY DIFFER? IN RESPECT OF DOUBT-
b FUL [TERUMAH][1] AND UNCLEAN [TERUMAH], R. ELIEZER RULING, EACH MUST BE BURNT SEPARATELY, WHILE R. JOSHUA RULES, BOTH TOGETHER.

GEMARA. Consider: Flesh which was defiled by a derivative uncleanness, what is it? A second degree. When it is burnt together with flesh which was defiled by a principal defilement, what is it? A second degree:[2] [thus] it was a second degree [before] and [is] a second degree [now], then what adding of uncleanness to its uncleanness is there?—Said Rab Judah: We treat here of the derivative of a derivative, so that it[3] is a third degree, and he holds that a third may be raised to a second. But food cannot defile food, for it was taught: You might think that food should defile food, therefore it is stated, *But if water be put upon the seed, and aught of their carcase fall thereon, it is unclean:*[4] *it* is unclean, but it does not render that which is similar thereto unclean?[5] Now it is well according to Abaye who maintained: They learned this only of *ḥullin*, but in the case of *terumah* and sacred food they can render what is similar thereto [unclean]. And also according to R. Adda b. Ahabah in Raba's name, who maintained: They learned this only of *ḥullin* and *terumah*, but in the case of sacred food it does render its like [unclean], it is correct. But according to Rabina in Raba's name, who said: The Writ states an unqualified law,[6] there is no difference whether it is *ḥullin*, *terumah*, or sacred food, it cannot render its like [unclean], what is there to be said?—We treat here of a case where there is liquid together with the flesh, so that it is defiled on account of the liquid.[7] If so, [instead of] this [phrase] 'TOGETHER WITH FLESH WHICH HAD BEEN DEFILED WITH A PRINCIPAL UNCLEANNESS,' he should state, 'TOGETHER WITH FLESH and liquid' [etc.]?—Rather, [reply] granted that food cannot defile food by Scriptural
c law, by Rabbinical law it can nevertheless defile [it].[1]

R. AKIBA ADDED AND SAID: DURING [ALL] THE DAYS OF THE PRIESTS THEY DID NOT REFRAIN FROM LIGHTING, etc. Consider: When oil is rendered unfit through [contact with] a *ṭebul yom*, what is it? A third degree [of defilement]; and when it is lit in a lamp which was defiled by that which [or, one who] was defiled through a corpse, what does it become? A second degree.[2] [Thus] what he does inform us is that a third degree may be raised to a second; then it is the identical [teaching]?[3]—Said Rab Judah: We treat here of a metal lamp, for the Divine Law said,

(5) I.e., the Mount of Olives.

a (1) Chief of the priests and deputy High-Priest, v. Sanh., 19a, n. 1. (2) The following degrees of defilement are distinguished: (i) The super principal (lit., 'father of fathers' of) defilement, which is that borne by a corpse; (ii) principal (lit., 'the father of') defilement, which is that of a human being or a utensil defiled by a corpse; (iii) derivative (lit., 'offspring of') defilement, borne by a human being, utensil or food which is contaminated by a principal defilement—this is also known as the first degree or 'beginning' of defilement; (iv) the second degree of defilement, which is that of food contaminated by a principal defilement. In *ḥullin* there is nothing further, and if *ḥullin* comes into contact with something unclean in the second degree it remains clean. *Terumah*, however, is liable to (v) a third degree, but no further. Sacred food, i.e., the flesh of sacrifices, is liable to (vi) a fourth degree of defilement. Third degree *terumah* and fourth degree sacred flesh are called 'unfit' but not unclean, because they cannot communicate uncleanness to their own kind, i.e., to *terumah* and sacred flesh respectively. (3) Of *terumah*. (4) V. n. a2. (5) V. Glos. (6) In all these cases something of a lower degree of uncleanness comes into contact with something else of a higher degree of uncleanness when they are burnt together, and their own uncleanness is increased, as explained in the Gemara. (7) I.e., on the eve of Passover, when leaven must be burnt. R. Meir reasons that since a higher degree of uncleanness may be imposed upon *terumah* and sacred flesh when they must be burnt in any case, the same holds good for leaven, even if one is not unclean at all. (8) You cannot deduce one from the other.

b (1) Lit., 'in suspense'. (2) For the latter is a first degree and its contact renders this flesh a second degree. (3) The flesh which is defiled thereby. (4) Lev. XI, 38. (5) Then what increase of uncleanness can there be in the Mishnah? (6) Lit., 'a full verse'. (7) When the flesh was defiled there was water upon it, which is still there when it is burnt with the flesh defiled in a lower degree. The uncleanness of the latter is raised through contact with the water.

c (1) Thus the Mishnah likewise treats of a Rabbinically enhanced defilement. (2) The lamp being unclean in the first degree. (3) Of R. Ḥanina.

in R. Joḥanan's name: They learned this only [13b] when there is the normal rate of decrease; but when [the loss] exceeds the normal rate of decrease, [all agree that] he must sell it by a court order. How much more so here that it is entirely lost.[6]

R. JUDAH SAID FURTHER: TWO [UNFIT] LOAVES, etc. A Tanna recited before Rab Judah: on the top [*gab*] of the [Temple] *iẓṭaba*.[7] Said he to him: Does he then need to hide them?[8] Learn: on the roof of the [Temple] *iẓṭaba* [portico]. Reḥaba said in R. Judah's name:[9] The Temple Mount consisted of a double colonnade.[10] It was taught likewise: The Temple Mount consisted of a double colonnade. R. Judah said: It was called *isṭewawnith*,[11] [being] a colonnade within a colonnade.

UNFIT etc., why UNFIT?—Said R. Ḥanina: Since they were many they became unfit through being kept overnight. For it was taught: A thanksoffering may not be brought during the Feast of Unleavened Bread on account of the leaven therein.[1] But that is obvious?—Said R. Adda b. Ahabah: We treat here of the fourteenth, and he [the Tanna] holds: Sacred food may not be brought to unfitness.[2] Hence everybody brought it on the thirteenth, and since they were numerous they became unfit through being kept overnight. In R. Jannai's name it was said: They were fit, yet why are they called unfit? Because the sacrifice had not been slaughtered for them.[3] Then let us slaughter [it]?—The sacrifice was lost. Then let us bring another sacrifice and slaughter [it]?—It is a case where he [the owner] had declared: 'This [animal] is a thanksoffering and these are its loaves,' this being in accordance with Rabbah. For Rabbah said: If the loaves are lost, other loaves may be brought. If the thanksoffering is lost, another thanksoffering may not be brought. What is the reason? The loaves are subsidiary to[4] the thanksoffering, but the thanksoffering is not subsidiary to the loaves. Then let us redeem and free them as *ḥullin*?[5]—But in truth it is a case where the sacrifice was slaughtered for them, but the blood was poured out.[6] And with whom [does this agree]? With Rabbi, who said: The two things which permit, promote [to sanctity] without each other.[7] For it was taught: The lambs of Pentecost[8] sanctify the loaves only by *shechitah*.[9] How so? If he kills them for their own purpose[1] and sprinkles their blood for their own purpose, he [thereby] sanctifies the loaves. If he kills them for a purpose that is not theirs and sprinkles their blood for a purpose that is not theirs, he does not sanctify [thereby] the loaves. If he kills them for their own purpose but sprinkles their blood for a purpose that is not theirs, the bread is sanctified and not sanctified;[2] this is Rabbi's ruling. R. Eleazar b. R. Simeon said: The bread always remains unsanctified until he kills [the lambs] for their own purpose and sprinkles their blood for their own purpose.[3]—[No,] you may even say [that it agrees with] R. Eleazar son of R. Simeon; but the case we discuss here is where the blood was caught in a goblet and then spilled, while R. Eleazar son of R. Simeon holds as his father, who maintained: That which stands to be sprinkled is as though it were sprinkled.[4]

A Tanna taught: In R. Eleazar's name it was said: They [the loaves] were fit. As long as they [both] lay [there], all the people ate [leaven]; when one was removed, they kept [the leaven] in suspense, neither eating nor burning [it]; when both were removed, all commenced burning [their leaven].

(6) If unsold before it becomes interdicted. (7) The word may denote a bench or a portico. The reading 'on the top' (*gab*) implies the former rendering. Hence the question that follows, v. Rashi. (8) Surely they are intended to be exposed for public gaze. (9) V. Bez., 11a, n. 9 (10) [στοα. For a description of the Temple porticoes v. Josephus, *Wars* V, 5.3 v. also Derenbourg, *Essai* p. 51.] (11) Lit., 'a double colonnade'. [סטיו כפול = διπλαῖ αἱ στοαί of Josephus, *Wars* V, 5.2, v. Hollis, F. J. *Herod's Temple* p. 15.]

a (1) Forty loaves accompanied the offering, ten of which were leaven. (2) A thanksoffering may be eaten on the day that it is brought and the following night. But if it is brought on the fourteenth of Nisan the loaves of leaven may be eaten only until noon, and this Tanna holds that a sacrifice may not be brought at a time when the normal period for its consumption is lessened, so that it is likely to become unfit. (3) I.e., we need not assume that the reference is to loaves which were in fact unfit through having been kept overnight, but even if the sacrifice had not been slaughtered they are also so designated, because the loaves may not be eaten until the thanksoffering is killed on their behalf. (4) Lit., 'on account of'. (5) For the loaves in that case can be redeemed. (6) The loaves cannot be redeemed then. (7) The slaughtering and the sprinkling of the blood are both required before the loaves may be eaten; on the other hand, one alone suffices to promote them to that degree of sanctity ('intrinsic' sanctity, as opposed to 'monetary' sanctity) from which they cannot be redeemed. (8) Lit., 'the solemn assembly'—the term without further qualification always refers to Pentecost. (9) V. Glos. It is stated in Lev. XXIII, 19f: *And ye shall offer . . . two he-lambs . . . and the priest shall wave them with the bread of the firstfruits* (i.e., the 'two wave loaves' mentioned in v. 17, q.v.) *for a wave offering before the Lord, with the two lambs: they shall be holy to the Lord for the priest.* In Men. 46a it is shown that these loaves are sanctified only by the ritual slaughter of the sacrifice.

b (1) Lit., 'for their name'—i.e., as the Pentecost sacrifices. (2) The loaves are sanctified in that they become unfit if taken without the sacred precincts and that they cannot be redeemed, for they are now intrinsically holy. Yet they are unsanctified in the sense that they may not be eaten. (3) Thus the statement that our Mishnah refers to a case where the offering had been slaughtered but its blood was not sprinkled and thereby the loaves were sanctified, would appear to agree with Rabbi only. (4) In the sense that the animal is unfit as a *sacred* offering which has become unfit. Yet it may not be eaten unless the blood is sprinkled.

צח א מיי' פ"ה מהל' בית הבחירה הל' ח :
צט ב ג מיי' פ"ב מהל' חגיגה הל' יג :
ק ד מיי' פי"ב מהלכות פסולי מוקדשין הל' יא:
קא ה מיי' פי"ז שם הלכה יח :
קב ו [מיי' פ"ג שם הל' יח ופ"ו מהל' איסורי מזבח הל' ד ס] :

בכדי חסרונן אבל יותר מכדי חסרונן מוכרן בבית דין וכל שכן הכא דהא פסידי לגמרי: ועוד אמר ר' יהודה שתי חלות כו': תני תנא קמיה דרב יהודה על גב האיצטבא א"ל וכי להצניען הוא צריך תני על גג האיצטבא *אמר רחבא אמר ר' יהודה *הר הבית סטיו כפול היה* תניא נמי הכי הר הבית סטיו כפול היה רבי יהודה אומר איסטוונית היתה נקראת סטיו לפנים מסטיו: פסולות וכו': אמאי פסולות אמר רבי חנינא מתוך שהיו מרובות נפסלות בלינה דתניא *אין מביאין תודה בחג המצות מפני חמץ שבה פשיט' אמר רב אדא בר אהבה הכא בי"ד עסקינן וקסבר *אין מביאין קדשים לבית הפסול וכולי עלמא בשלשה עשר מייתי להו ומתוך שהן מרובות נפסלות בלינה משום ר' ינאי אמרו כשירות היו ואלא אמאי קרי להו פסולות שלא נשחט עליהן הזבח ונשחוט שאבד הזבח ונייתי זבח אחר ונשחוט דאמר זו תודה וזו לחמה וכדרבה דאמר רבה* אבד הלחם מביא לחם אחר אבדה תודה אין מביא תודה אחרת מ"ט לחם גלל תודה ואין תודה גלל לחם וניפרקינהו ונפקינהו לחולין אלא לעולם שנשחט עליהן הזבח ונשפך הדם וכמאן כרבי דאמר רבי *שני דברים המתירין מעלין זה בלא זה דתניא *כבשי עצרת אין מקדשין את הלחם אלא בשחיטה כיצד שחטן לשמן וזרק דמן לשמן קידש הלחם שחטן שלא לשמן וזרק דמן שלא לשמן לא קידש הלחם שחטן לשמן וזרק דמן שלא לשמן לחם קדוש ואינו קדוש דברי רבי ר' אלעזר בר"ש אומר לעולם אינו קדוש הלחם עד שישחוט לשמן ויזרוק דמן לשמן אפי' תימא ר' אלעזר ברבי שמעון הכא במאי עסקינן כגון שנתקבל הדם בכוס ונשפך ור"א בר"ש סבר ליה כאבוה *דאמר כל העומד לזרוק כזרוק דמי תנא משום רבי אלעזר אמרו כשירות היו כל זמן שמונחות כל העם אוכלין ניטלה אחת מהן תולין לא אוכלין ולא שורפין ניטלו שתיהן התחילו כולן שורפין תניא אבא שאול אומר
שתי

בכדי חסרונן. כשאין נחסרין אלא כדרך חסרון של פירות הקלוט בב"מ בהמפקיד (ד' מ.) לחטין ולאורז תשעה חצאי קבין לכור: דקא פסיד לגמרי. שנאסרים בהנאה: על גב האיצטבא. על הכסא ממש: וכי להצניעם הוא צריך. והלא למראה העין הם ניתנות שם: גג האיצטבא. גג היה בנוי למעלה מפני הגשמים: סטיו כפול היה. האיצטבא סביב סביב מקפת ובתוך אותו הקף עוד אחר: מתוך שהן מרובות. לחמי תודה בשלשה עשר בניסן שכל מי שיש לו להביא תודה ברגל מביאה בשלשה עשר: נפסלות בלינה. לבוקרו של י"ד לחמי תודה מ' חלות וי' מהן חמץ שנא' (ויקרא ז) על חלות לחם חמץ: אין מביאין קדשים לבית הפסול. אין מביאין קרבן ביום שיתמעט זמן אכילתו שקבעה לו תורה וגמלא בא לידי נותר ותודה נאכלת ליום ולילה ואם יביאום בי"ד אינן נאכלות של חמץ אלא עד שש שעות: וכולי עלמא בי"ג מייתי להו. כל מי שעליו תודה מביאה בי"ג לפי שלא יקריבנה למחר וכ"ש בפסח: נפסלות בלינה. שאין להם אוכלין כל כך ומשום דפסולות ועומדו' היו ניתנין שם דאם היו כשירות לא היו נותנין אותן שם כדי לפוסלן בידים שמונחות שם עד זמן הביעור ונשרפות: כשירות היו. כלומר אפילו לא היה להן פסול גדול כלינה שהן כבר לשריפה אפ"ה מאחר שאין להם תקנה ליאכל ואפילו הן עדיין טעונות עיבור צורה יהבינן להו התם והיכי דמי כגון שלא נשחט עליהן הזבח ויש להן קדושת דמים משהוקדשו ואין להן היתר עד שישחט עליהן הזבח ויזרק הדם דלחמי תודה אין קדושין קדושת הגוף אלא בשחיטת הזבח כדתניא במנחות על חלות לחם חמץ יקריב קרבנו על זבח מלמד שאין הלחם קדוש אלא בזביחת התודה והאי קדוש קדושת הגוף קאמר דהא משעה שאמר הרי (עלי*) לתודתי חל עליהם שם הקדש אבל אין קדושות ליפסל בלינה ובטבול יום ואם נטמאו נפדין ויוצאין לחולין עד שישחט הזבח עליהן וכשם שהזבח מקדשן כך בזריקת הדם ניתרין הם לאכילה כבשר התודה עצמו דהואיל ותלויין בה הרי היא כמוה וזריקת הדם מתרת קדשים דכתיב ודם זבחיך ישפך והדר והבשר תאכל: אין מביא תודה אחרת. על אותו לחם ופודין אותו ויוצא לחולין דלחם גלל תודה וכיון דהוקבע לזו פסול לאחרת אבל בדמים יקח תודה או לחם תודה אחרת: ואין תודה גלל לחם. שהיא עיקר: ונפרקינהו. דכל זמן שלא קידשו לגופן יש להם פדיון והואיל ויש להם תקנה בכך למה אנו מפסידין קדשים: אלא לעולם שנשחט עליהן הזבח. דשוב אין להן תקנה: וכגון שנשפך הדם. ומיהו עדיין אינן טעונות שריפה וצריכות לעבר צורתן דתנן בכילד צולין (לקמן פב.*) כל שפסולו בגופו ישרף מיד בדם ובבעלים תעובר צורתו ויצא לבית השריפה ואפ"ה מזלזלינן בהו ויהבינן להו התם: כמאן. קאמרת דבשחיטה לתודה קדוש גופו שלא לפדות עוד: שחיטה וזריקה. הן מתירין את הזבח ואת התלוי בו: מעלין. מעלין אותו מעלה אחת ליקדש בגופו ואע"פ שאינו ניתר עד שתבוא השניה: שתי הלחם של עצרת תלויין בשני כבשי שלמים דכתיב (ויקרא כג) ושני כבשים בני שנה לזבח השלמים והניף הכהן אותם על לחם הבכורים תנופה לפני ה' וגמרינן להו מלחמי תודה שאין קדושים אלא בזביחתה במנחות בפרק התכלת*: קדוש. ליפסל ביוצא ושלא יפדה עוד: ואינו קדוש. ואינו ניתר באכילה ואף על פי שהכבשים עצמן מותרין דקיימא לן כל הזבחים שנזבחו שלא לשמן כשירין אלא שלא עלו לבעלים לשם חובה ותניא בפרק שני דבילה (ד' כ:) כבשי עצרת ששחטן שלא לשמן הדם יזרק והבשר יאכל איכהו הוא דמתאכלי כשלמים בעלמא אבל לחם כיון דכבשים אין שמן עליהן דהא לא עלו לשם חובה אלא לשם שלמי נדבה עליהן מי יתירנו: כאבוה. בב"ק בפרק מרובה (ד' עו:): העומד ליזרוק. שאינו מחוסר אלא זריקה: כזרוק דמי. לחול עליו כל שם פסול קדשי קדשים אבל לאישתרויי לא מישתרי עד דזריק:
שתי

בכדי חסרונן. פ"ה כדרך חסרונם של פירות וקשה לר"י א"כ מ"ט דרשב"ג דאמר מוכרן בב"ד ואור"י דמיירי דנחסר בחדש אחד יותר ממה שחסרון עולה לחדש וקרי בכדי חסרונן לפי שעדיין לא נתחסרו יותר מכדי חסרון העולה לשנה כדמפרש' בהמפקיד (ב"מ מ.) לחטין ולאורז תשעה חצאי קבין לכור אבל אם נחסרו יותר ד"ה מוכרן בב"ד:

אמר רחבא אמר רבי יהודה. לפי שהיה רבו מובהק קרי לי' ר':

אין מביאין תודה אחרת. פ"ה ואותו לחם פודים ויוצא לחולין ויקח בדמים תודה אחרת או לחם לתודה אחרת ואין נראה כיון דלחם גופיה לא חזי לתודה אחרת דמים נמי לא חזו לתודה אחרת דמאי שנא ובפרק התודה (מנחות פ.) אמר בהדיא הפריש מעות ללחמי תודה ונותרו אין מביא בהן תודה אחרת ואע"ג דהדמים אסורים פריך שפיר וניפרקינהו דשמא תמצא תודה שאבדה א"נ ניפרקינהו בשוה פרוטה דלכתחלה יכול לחלל שוה מנה על פרוטה כשאין הפסד להקדש כדמוכח בערכין (ד' כט.) :

אלא לעולם שנשחט עליהן הזבח. אומר ריב"א דהשתא הדר ביה ממה שאמר כשירות היו דבי"ג איירי שנשחט הזבח כדאמר לעיל אין מביאין תודה בי"ד והשתא מיפסלו טפי שנשפך הדם וגם נפסלו בלינה ולכך מעמיד כשנשפך הדם שהטעם הראשון שאמר רבי חנינא מתוך שהן מרובות נפסלות בלינה נראה לו דוחק דאיך יתכן דמפני ריבוי שלהן לא ימצא אוכלים אלא מותרין לזרים ובירושלמי רבי חנינא גופיה משני האי סוגיא דגרס התם רבי חנינא אומר פסולות היו מפני שהיו ממהרים להביא תודותיהן מפני חמץ שבתודות ואי אפשר שלא ישפך דמה של אחת מהן והן נפסלות מדקאמר מפני שממהרין משמע דבי"ג מיירי דכולם היו מביאין:

שחטן שלא לשמן וזרק דמן שלא לשמן. נראה דזרק דמן שלא לשמן לאו דוקא דהוא הדין אם נזרק לשמן:

הלחם קדוש. בהתכלת (מנחות ד' מז:) איכא מאן דאמר קדוש לתפוס פדיונו ולא בעי למימר שילא לחולין אלא תופס פדיונו ואינו יוצא לחולין דאל"כ אכתי תיקשי וליפרקינהו:

כל העומד ליזרק כזרוק דמי. וא"ת זרק דמן שלא לשמן נימא נמי כזרוק דמי ואמאי קאמר רבי אלעזר ב"ר שמעון דאינו קדוש וי"ל כיון דנעקרן מלשמן גרע מנשפך הדם ואיגליא מלתא דלא הוי כזרוק בשעת קבלה וקשה דבפרק המנחות והנסכים (מנחות קב.) אמר פיגל בזריקה מטמא טומאת אוכלים לר"ש משום דכל העומד ליזרוק כזרוק דמי ודוחק לחלק בין פיגול לשלא לשמו וי"ל דלגביה גופיה דזבח חשיב כזרוק אע"ג דפיגל בזריקה אבל לגבי דברים המתקדשים עם הזבח כגון לחם לא חשיב כזרוק כשנעשה הזריקה שלא בהכשר:

כשירות היו. וא"ת מאחר דכשירות היו אמאי משהין אותן עד שעת איסור וי"ל דהיינו (כרשב"ג) דאמר לעיל (ד' יא:) תרומה כל חמש ולחמי תודה כתרומה והיו נוטלים האחרונה בסוף חמש וכן משמע בירושלמי :
שתי

[סטיו לפנים מסטיו כצ"ל]

לקמן נג: סוכה מה. ברכות נג:
ביצה יט:
[ביצה שם: [לקמן לז:] זבחים עה: בכורות ס: נדה ע:]
מנחות פ. ופ"ש שנ"ל ר' אבא
[מנחות עח.]
יבמות קד: מנחות מו. ודף עב: (יבמות קה:)
אלו
ב"ק עו: [מנחו' עט: קב: כריתות כד: תמורה כג:]
[ולקמן לד:]
דף מ.

רבינו חננאל

אמרו רבנן לא יגע בהן כר' יוחנן דאמר מחלוקת אם אבד בכדי חסרונן אבל יתר מכדי חסרונן אפי' רבנן מודו שמוכרין אותן וכל שכן הכא בפסח שאם ישארו יפסדו לגמרי וכבר פרשנוהו בגמ' במקומו באר היטב: מתני' ועוד אמר ר' יהודה שתי חלות של תודה פסולות כו' תאני תנא ע"ג האצטבא אמר ליה רב יהודה וכי להצניען היא צריך שמניח בתוך הבית תני על גג האצטבא שיהו הכל מביטין עליהן: למה פסולות מפני שיש בחלות של תודה חמץ לפיכך אין מביאין תודה בחג המצות ואפילו בארבעה עשר אין מביאין שכיון שאין התודה נאכלת אלא ליום ולילה ובארבעה עשר אין מותר לאכלן אפילו בו ביום כלו אין מביאין אותו להפסל לפיכך מקדימין ומביאין הכל ביום שלשה עשר ומפני שהיו באות הרבה היו נותרות ונפסלות. והאי דר' ינאי דאמר כשרות היו נדחו ואוקימנא בשנשחט עליהן הזבח ועדיין לא נזרק הדם וכדר' דאמר שני דברים המתירין והן שחיטה וזריקה שמתירין חלבים למזבח והבשר לאכילה מועלין זה בלא זה כלומר מקדיש האחד בלא חבירו והנהנה ממנו כנהנה מן ההקדש שחייב קרבן מעילה ור' (מאיר) [מאי] היא דתניא כבשי עצרת אין מקדשין אלא בשחיטה כיצד שחטן לשמן וזרק דמן (שלא) לשמן קדש הלחם שחטן שלא לשמן וזרק דמן שלא לשמן לא קדש הלחם שחטן לשמן וזרק דמן שלא לשמן הלחם קדוש ואינו קדוש דברי רבי ר' אלעזר בר' שמעון אומר לעולם אינו קדוש עד שישחוט לשמן ויזרוק דמן לשמן ואמרי' אפי' תימא רבי אלעזר בר' שמעון כגון דקבלה לדם ואשתפיך וסבר לה כר' שמעון אבוה דאמר כל העומד לזרוק כזרוק דמי: משום ר' אלעזר אמרו כשירות היו כל זמן ששתיהן מונחות הכל אוכלין וכו'. תניא אבא

רבן גמליאל לאו מכריע הוא. וקשה לר"י דלימא הלכה כר"ג דסתם לן תנא כוותיה בפ' כל שעה (לקמן כח.) מדקתני מותר ואפי' אם מספקא ליה אם יש לדקדק בלשון מותר אם לאו מ"מ נימא הלכה כר' מאיר או כרבן גמליאל דממה נפשך ההיא דכל שעה כחד מינייהו אתו וי"ל דאליבא דרבי יהודה אימא סמיך ודין הכרעה אפרש בסוף פירקין בע"ה:

ושורפין תרומות טמאות ותלויות וטהורות. אפילו אם נאמר דאסור לשרוף טהורות משום דכתיב (במדבר יח) את משמרת תרומותי כמו שאסור לטמאות הכא שרי אע"ג דמדאורייתא בביטול בעלמא סגי ואין צריך לשורפה מכל מקום כיון דסופה ליאסר ולילך לאיבוד שרי לשורפה כמו לטמאותה דשרי ר' מאיר בסוף פירקין לשרוף טמאה עם הטהורה:

ומשיירין מזון שתי סעודות. וכ"ש בחולין שאוכליהן מרובין דמשיירין כדמשמע בתוספתא [פ"ג]*:

מאי לאו לנכרים. להכי משמע לנכרים דאי לישראל ליסקול לנפשיה כדפריך אביי בסמוך. בירושלמי גרס לא מוכרה בבית דין בשוק משמע אע"פ שנתן לו רשות רבי שהיה אב"ד למכור אפי' הכי צריך ב"ד בשעת מכירה כדי לשומן וא"ת מ"ש מאלמנה דמוכרת לאחרים שלא בב"ד ובב"ד יכולה לעכב אפילו לעצמה דאמר בכתובות (ד' נח. ושם) אלמנה ששמה לעצמה לא עשתה ולא כלום דאמר מאן שם ליך משמע דבבית דין יכולה לשום וקאמרינן כמי התם ההוא גברא דאפקידו גביה כיסתא דיתמי אזל שמה לנפשיה לסוף אייקר אמר ליה מאן שם ליך וי"ל דמוכרת שלא בבית דין משום חינא וגבי כיסתא דיתמי דיכול לעכב לעצמו היינו דוקא בדיעבד א"נ גבי יתמי בית דין עצמן הן המפקידים ולכך יכול לעכב לעצמו על פיהם אבל פקדון של אחרים לא והא דאמר באלו מציאות (ב"מ כה:*) שם דמיהם ומניחן) גבי מציאה התם ליכא חשד שהרי הוא מחזיר אבידה:

תורה אור

בתוך הנ"ץ החמה בגילויי' הוה קאי והדרורי בעלמא הוא דחזא קא משמע לן אמר רב נחמן אמר רב הלכה כרבי יהודה אמר ליה רבא לרב נחמן ונימא מר הלכה כר' מאיר דסתם לן תנא כוותיה דתנן *כל שעה שמותר לאכול מאכיל ההיא לאו סתמא הוא משום דקשיא *מותר ונימא מר הלכה כרבן גמליאל דהוה ליה מכריע א"ל רבן גמליאל לאו מכריע הוא טעם דנפשיה קאמר ואיבעי' אימא רב דאמר כי האי תנא *דתני' ארבעה עשר שחל להיות בשבת מבערין את הכל מלפני השבת ושורפין תרומות טמאות תלויות וטהורו' ומשיירין מן הטהור' מזון שתי סעודות כדי לאכול עד ד' שעות דברי רבי אלעזר בן יהודה איש ברתותא שאמר משום ר' יהושע אמרו לו טהורות לא ישרפו שמא ימצאו להן אוכלין אמר להן כבר בקשו ולא מצאו אמרו לו שמא חוץ לחומה לנו אמר להם לדבריכם אף תלויות לא ישרפו שמא יבא אליהו ויטהרם אמרו לו *כבר מובטח להן לישראל שאין אליהו בא *לא בערבי שבתות ולא בערבי ימים טובים מפני הטורח אמרו לא זזו משם עד שקבעו הלכה כרבי אלעזר בן יהודה איש ברתותא שאמר משום רבי יהושע מאי לאו אפילו לאכול אמר רב פפא משמיה דרבא לא לבער ואף ר' סבר להא דרב נחמן דאמר רבין בר רב אדא מעשה באדם אחד שהפקיד דיסקיא מלאה חמץ אצל יוחנן *חקוקאה ונקבוה עכברי' והיה חמץ מבצבץ ויוצא ובא לפני רבי שעה ראשונה אמר לו המתן שניה אמר לו המתן שלישית אמר לו המתן רביעית אמר לו המתן חמישית א"ל צא ומכרה בשוק מאי לאו לנכרים כרבי יהודה אמר רב יוסף לא לישראל כרבי מאיר אמר ליה אביי אי לישראל נישקלי' לנפשיה משום חשדא *דתניא גבאי צדקה שאין להם עניים לחלק פורטין לאחרים ואין פורטין לעצמן גבאי תמחוי שאין להם עניים לחלק מוכרין לאחרים ואין מוכרין לעצמן משום שנאמר והייתם נקיים מה' ומישראל אמר ליה רב אדא בר מתנה לרב יוסף בפירוש אמרת לן צא ומוכרן לנכרים כרבי יהודה אמר רב יוסף כמאן אזלא הא שמעתא דרבי כרשב"ג *דתנן המפקיד פירות אצל חבירו אפילו הן אבודין לא יגע בהן רשב"ג אומר מוכרן בב"ד מפני השבת אבידה אמר ליה אביי ולאו איתמר עלה אמר רבה בר בר חנה א"ר יוחנן לא שנו אלא בכדי

הלכה כר' יהודה. דתולין כל חמש: ונימא הלכה כר' מאיר. דאוכלין כל חמש דהא סתם לן תנא כוותיה דתנן כל שעה שמותר לאכול מאכיל לבהמה לחיה ולעופות דמשמע כשאינו מותר לאכול אינו מאכיל ואי רבי יהודה הא איכא חמש דאינו אוכל ומאכיל אלא ר' מאיר היא דאמר אוכל עד תחלת שש ומשעה שאינו אוכל אין מאכיל: משום דקשיא מותר. בפרק כל שעה מקשינן כל שעה שאוכל מאכיל מיבעי ליה ומותר משמע כל שעה שמותר אדם אחר לאכול מאכיל זה האסור לאכול ומדוחקא דהא קושיא אוקימנא כרבן גמליאל והכי קאמר כל שעה שמותר כהן לאכול בתרומה מאכיל ישראל חולין לבהמה אלמא סתמא לאו כר"מ היא: כרבן גמליאל. במתני': לאו מכריע הוא. כדפרישית לקמן בפירקין (ד' כא.) דאין הכרעת דעת שלישית מכרעת והא הכרעת דעת שלישית היא דהא ר"מ ורבי יהודה לא איירי דניהוי שייך חילוק בין זמן תרומה לזמן חולין כלל דאי הוה תנן ר"מ אומר אחד חולין וא' תרומה כל חמש ר' יהודה אומר א' חולין ואחד תרומה כל ארבע ורבן גמליאל אומר חולין כל ארבע תרומה כל חמש הויא הכרעה אבל השתא דאינהו לא אדכור תרומה וחולין כלל ולא גלו דעתם שיהא שום רמז דין לחלק ביניהם לאו הכרעה היא אלא דעת שלישית: ה"ג ואיבעית אימא רב דאמר כי האי תנא. דקבע הלכתא כרבי אלעזר ברבי יהודה דאמר אפי' תרומה כל ארבע ותו לא דקתני דקבעו הלכה כמותו: תלויות. ספק טמאות ספק טהורות: מזון שתי סעודות. ולא שלש דכל שלש סעודות דשבת ערבית שחרית ומנחה וערב פסח אסור לאכול מן המנחה ולמעלה: טהורות לא ישרפו. כלל הואיל ולא הגיע זמנן לבער ואע"פ שיש לו שיור(א) כדי לאכסני ביתו של כהן שמא ימצא כהנים אורחים שיאכלום ולא נפסיד תרומה בידים ואם לא ימצא יאכילום למחר לכלבי כהנים או יבטלם בלבו: כבר בקשו ולא מצאו. כלומר כל מה שיש לו לבקש כבר ביקש דהא בשבת לא יבואו אורחים וכבר יודע ובקי הוא באותן שבעיר מי יבואו אללו: לנו. לשון מלון שמא בתוך התחום לנים כהנים אורחים הלילה ויבואו למחר: אף לדבריכם. דחיישינן לשמא אמאי לא פליגיתו אלא בטהורות אף תלויות לא ישרפו קודם זמנן שמא יבוא אליהו היום או מחר קודם זמן ביעורן ויטהרם ויאמר לא נגע בהן טומאה ויאכלום: לא בערבי שבתות כו'. והיום ערב שבת ולמחר ערב יום טוב: מפני הטורח. שיש להן לעסוק בסעודות שבת ויטרדו בו: מאי לאו אפי' לאכול. בכל דבריו קבעו כמותו ואף במה שקבע זמן האכילה עד ד' שעות ואפי' בתרומה: לא לבער. הא דקבעו כמותו לא איירי באכילה אלא בביעור שהיו חביריו חלוקין עליו שלא יבערו טהורות עד למחר קבעו דשורפין מערב שבת בשלשה עשר אבל בשיור לעולם אימא לך כדי לאכול עד חמש שעות והיא בכלל: דיסקייא. שתי מלות מורכבות שני שקים אמתחת של עור: ונקבוה עכברים. והיה נחסר וארבעה עשר בניסן היה וחמץ בזול ובא לפני רבי לידע אם ימכרוהו מפני חסרונו של מפקיד: המתן. שמא יבא ויאכל בעליו: חמישית. דמהשתא תו לא אכיל ליה: אמר לו צא ומוכרן בשוק. בעוד שהוא מותר בהנאה: לא לישראל. וכרבי מאיר והכי קאמר ליה אי שהייתו הא שעתא לא משכחת ישראל דזבין ליה: נישקליה לנפשיה. ויאכלנו ויתן דמיו לבעלים למה לו לטרוח ולילך בשוק אחרי שנותן לו רשות למכור: פורטין. פרוטות של נחשת שגבו לצדקה וכשמשהין אותם מחלידות צריך לפורטן בכסף: תמחוי. מאכל לחם ומיני מאכל שגובין לחלק: ואין מוכרין לעצמן. שמא יחשדום שלקחום בזול: בפירוש אמרת לן כו'. *רב יוסף חלה ושכח תלמודו ולאחר זמן כשהיה מחליף דבריו היו מזכירין אותו תלמידיו כך לימדתנו בראשונה: כמאן אזלא הא דרבי. שהורה למכור פקדון מפני שאבד: אבודין. נחסרין והולכין:

לקמן כח. | [שם] | (לקמן כא.) | עירובין מג: | [עי' תוס' עירובין מג: ד"ה הא מכולל דלא כפירש"י דהכא] | [עי' תוס' לעיל י: ד"ה חקוקאה] | ב"מ לח. ב"ב ח: | ב"מ שם

הגהות הב"ח

(א) רש"י ד"ה טהורות וכו' שיור לאכסני ביתו של כהן דשמא כצ"ל ותיבת כדי נמחק: (ב) תוס' ד"ה מאי לאו וכו' שם דמיהם ומניחן גבי מציאה ליכא חשד כצ"ל:

צד א מיי' פ"ג מהל' חמץ ומצה הל"ג ד סמג עשין לט טוש"ע א"ח סי' תמג סעיף א: צה ב ג מיי' פ"ו מהל' שאלה הל' ג' וטוש"ע א"ח סי' תמג סעיף ב וטוש"ע ח"מ סי' רצב סעיף יט: [רב אלפס ב"מ פ"ג דף פ"א]: צו ד מיי' פ"ט מהלכות מתנות עניים הלכה יא סמג עשין קסב טוש"ע י"ד סי' רנז סעיף ג: צז ה ו מיי' פ"ו מהל' שאלה הלכה ה סמג עשין פח טוש"ע ח"מ סי' רצב סעיף טו:

רבינו חננאל

אמר רב נחמן אמר רב הלכה כר' [יהודה] ואע"ג דלאכילת חמץ משמע כיון דאמרי' כמחלוקת בעדות כך מחלוקת בחמץ ושינויא דשנינן שינויא הוא מכלל שמעי' דהלכתא נמי כר' יהודה בעדות: אמר ליה רבא ונימא מר הלכה כר' מאיר שהרי שנינו סתמא כל שעה שמותר לאכול מאכיל כוותיה דר' מאיר אמר ליה לא עמדה ההיא סתמא כר' מאיר דאי הות כר' מאיר כל שעה שאוכל מאכיל מבעי לי' למיתנא ונדחת ור"ג נמי לאו מכריע הוא דהא ר"ג קדים טובא ואין ראשון מכריע לדברי אחרונים ועוד אינו ר"ג ור"מ דבריהם שונין דהא ר"ג לא התיר בחמץ אלא (התרו) [התרומה] הלכך לא אמרינן מכריע הוא לדחות דברי ר' יהודה ולקיים דברי ר' מאיר אלא טעמא דנפשי' קאמר: איבעית אימא רב דאמר כי האי תנא דתאני ארבעה עשר שחל להיות בשבת כו' ומשיירין בטהורות מזון שתי סעודות כדי לאכול עד ארבע שעות דברי ר' אלעזר בן יהודה איש ברתותא וכו' ודחה רב פפא משמא דרבא ואמר לא קבעו הלכה כמותו אלא בלבער בלבד שאמר מבערין את הכל מלפני השבת. ואמרי' אף רבי סבר דהלכתא כר' יהודה מהא מעשה דאפקיד ההוא גברא דיסקיא מלאה חמץ אצל ר' יוחנן חקוקאה ולא התיר לו ר' למכרה אלא שעה חמישית ואסקינן משמא דרב יוסף כי שעה חמישית התיר לו למכרה לגוים כר' יהודה: והא דרבי כרשב"ג הוא דתנן המפקיד פירות אצל חבירו אפילו הן אבודין לא יגע בהן רשב"ג אומר ימכרם בב"ד מפני השב אבדה לבעלים ודחי' לא כי

ג יון הש"ס

גמ' אמר ר"ס משמיה דרבא לא לבער. כעין ז: תענית י"ח ע"א מנחות ל"ג ע"א:

testified to the same thing, while he who said [that it was] [13a] during sunrise was standing in the glow [before sunrise] and what he saw was merely the glare; hence he informs us [that it is not so].

a R. Naḥman said in Rab's name: The *halachah* is as R. Judah.[1] Said Raba to R. Naḥman, Yet let the Master say [that] the *halachah* is as R. Meir, since a Tanna taught anonymously in agreement with him. For we learned: As long as it is permitted to eat [leaven] he may feed [animals with it]?[2] That is not anonymous, because there is the difficulty of 'it is permitted'.[3] Then let the Master say [that] the *halachah* is as R. Gamaliel, since he makes a compromise?[4]—R. Gamaliel does not make a compromise but states an independent view.[5] Alternatively, Rab rules as this Tanna. For it was taught: If the fourteenth falls on the Sabbath, everything [*sc.* leaven] must be removed before the Sabbath, and *terumoth*,[6] whether unclean, or in suspense,[7] or clean, are burnt, and of the clean [*terumah*] food for two meals is left over, so as to eat until four hours:[8] this is the ruling of R. Eleazar b. Judah of Bartotha[9] which he stated in R. Joshua's name. Said they to him: Clean [*terumoth*] should not be burnt, in case eaters may be found for them?[10]—He replied: They have already sought [eaters] but not found [them].[11] They may have spent the night without the [city] wall? said they to him.[12]—Then on your reasoning, he retorted, even those in suspense should not be burnt,
b lest Elijah come and declare them clean?[1]—Said they to him, It has long been assured to Israel that Elijah will come neither on the eve of the Sabbath nor on the eve of Festivals, on account of the trouble.[2] It was said:[3] They did not stir thence until they decided the *halachah* in accordance with R. Eleazar b. Judah of Bartotha which he stated in R. Joshua's name. Does that not mean even in respect of eating?[4] Said R. Papa in Raba's name: No, [only] in respect of removing.[5]

Now Rabbi too holds this [view] of R. Naḥman. For Rabin son of R. Adda related: It once happened that a certain man deposited a saddle-bag full of leaven with Joḥanan of Ḥukok,[6] and mice made holes in it, and the leaven was bursting out. He then went before Rabbi.[7] The first hour he said to him, 'Wait';[8] the second, he said to him, 'Wait'; the third he said to him, 'Wait'; the fourth he said to him, 'Wait'; at the fifth he said to him, 'Go out and sell it in the market'. Does that not mean to Gentiles, in accordance with R. Judah?[9]—Said R. Joseph: No, to an Israelite, in accordance with R. Meir.[10] Said Abaye to him: If to an Israelite, let him take it for himself?—[He could not do this] because of suspicion.[11] For it was taught: When the charity overseers have no poor to whom to distribute [their funds], they must change the copper coins with others, not themselves.[12] The overseers of the soup kitchen,[13] when they have no poor to whom to make a distribution, must sell to others, not to themselves, because it is said, *and ye shall be guiltless towards the Lord, and towards*
c *Israel.*[1] R. Adda b. Mattenah said to R. Joseph:[2] You explicitly told us [that he said], 'Go out and sell it to Gentiles,' in accordance with R. Judah.

R. Joseph said: With whom does this ruling of Rabbi agree?[3] With R. Simeon b. Gamaliel. For we learned: If a man deposits produce with his neighbour, even if it is suffering loss,[4] he must not touch it. R. Simeon b. Gamaliel said: He must sell it by order of the court, on account of returning lost property.[5] Said Abaye to him, Yet was it not stated thereon, Rabbah b. Bar Ḥanah said

a (1) In our Mishnah. (2) Conversely, when he may not eat leaven he may not feed his cattle with it. But in R. Judah's view he may not eat it during the fifth hour, and yet he may give it to his cattle. Hence this must agree with R. Meir.—It is a general principle that an anonymous Mishnah states the *halachah*. (3) V. infra 21a. In order to answer that difficulty the Mishnah is explained as being R. Gamaliel's view. (4) V. Mishnah on 11b. It is a general rule that the view representing a compromise is the *halachah*. (5) Lit., 'a reason of his own'. R. Gamaliel's view would be a compromise if R. Meir and R. Judah mentioned *terumah* and *ḥullin*, R. Meir *explicitly* stating that even *ḥullin* may be eaten the whole of the five hours, and R. Judah stating that even *terumah* may only be eaten up to four hours. This would show that they recognize that in logic a distinction might be drawn between *ḥullin* and *terumah*. R. Gamaliel, in thus making the distinction, would be effecting a compromise. But they do not rule thus: hence his distinction is an entirely independent one. (6) Plur. of *terumah*. (7) I.e., when it is in doubt whether they are clean or unclean. (8) I.e., one meal Friday evening and one Saturday morning. (9) In Upper Galilee. (10) E.g., guests who are priests may arrive. (11) I.e., it is impossible to have unexpected guests, for these cannot arrive from without the town on the Sabbath, while one knows who is in town. (12) And thus arrive unexpectedly.

b (1) One of the functions ascribed to Elijah was the clearing up of all doubts. (2) His coming then would be inopportune. (3) Lit., 'they said'. (4) And he states that leaven may be eaten until four hours, even if it is *terumah*. This is the basis of Rab's ruling, the question being a rhetorical one. (5) Viz., that even the clean *terumoth* must not be kept for Sabbath morning but must be burnt before the Sabbath. But it is possible that *terumah* may be eaten until the fifth hour. (6) In Northern Palestine. (7) It was Passover eve. (8) The owner may come. (9) Who holds that it is forbidden to Jews then. (10) Who holds that a Jew may eat it during the fifth hour. (11) E.g., that he had undervalued it. (12) Copper coins were unsuitable for keeping a long time, being liable to tarnish and mould. Therefore they would be exchanged for silver ones. (13) תמחוי; actual food was collected for this purpose, not money, and it was distributed to those in immediate need of a meal. V. B.B. 8b.

c (1) Num. XXXII, 22. I.e., one must avoid even the appearance of suspicion. (2) R. Joseph had forgotten his learning owing to an illness, and his disciples would often have to remind him of his teachings, v. Ned. 41a. (3) Lit., 'as whom does it go'? (4) Through mildew or mice. (5) I.e., it is like returning lost property to its owner.

give them more at the beginning, [12b] but that people do not err between day and night; and logically we should give them more at the end,[1] but that in the fifth hour the sun is in the east while in the seventh the sun is in the west.[2]

We learned: R. MEIR SAID: ONE MAY EAT [LEAVEN] THE WHOLE OF THE FIVE [HOURS] AND MUST BURN [IT] AT THE BEGINNING OF THE SIXTH. R. JUDAH SAID: ONE MAY EAT THE WHOLE OF THE FOUR [HOURS], KEEP [IT] IN SUSPENSE THE WHOLE OF THE FIFTH, AND MUST BURN [IT] AT THE BEGINNING OF THE SIXTH. Now according to Abaye who maintains that on R. Meir's view a man does not err at all, let us eat [leaven] for the whole of the six [hours]?[3] And even on the version which asserts [that] a man may err slightly, let us eat until the end of the sixth hour?[4] And according to Abaye on R. Judah's view, who maintains [that] a man may err in half an hour, let us eat [leaven] until half of the sixth hour; and even on the version in which you say, A man may err in an hour and a trifle, let us eat until the end of the fifth hour?—Said Abaye: Testimony is committed to careful men,[1] [whereas] leaven is committed to all.[2] Now according to Raba who maintains [that] on R. Meir's view a man may err in two hours less a trifle, let us not eat [leaven] from the *beginning* of the fifth [hour]?—In the fifth [hour] the sun is in the east, while in the seventh the sun is in the west.[3] If so, let us eat during the sixth [hour] too?—Said R. Adda b. Ahabah: In the sixth the sun stands in the meridian.[4] And according to Raba who maintains on R. Judah's view [that] a man may err in three hours less a trifle, let us not eat from the beginning of the fourth [hour]?—In the fifth [hour] the sun is in the east, while in the seventh it is in the west, and all the more so in the fourth. If so, let us also eat in the fifth [hour]?—Abaye answered this on Raba's view: Testimony is committed to men of care, [whereas] leaven is committed to all.[5] But Raba said: Now this is not R. Judah's reason, but R. Judah follows his opinion, for he maintains, There is no removal of leaven save by burning; the Rabbis therefore gave him one hour in which to collect fuel.[6]

Rabina raised an objection to Raba: R. Judah said: When is this?[7] before[8] the time of removal;[9] but at the time of removal its 'putting away' is with anything.[10] Rather said Raba: It is a preventive measure on account of a cloudy day.[11] If so, let us not eat even during the four hours?—Said R. Papa: The fourth [hour] is the general mealtime.[12]

Our Rabbis taught: The first hour [of the day] is the mealtime for gladiators;[1] the second is the mealtime for robbers;[2] the third is the mealtime for heirs;[3] the fourth is the mealtime for labourers;[4] the fifth is the mealtime for scholars; the sixth is the general mealtime.[5] But R. Papa said: The fourth [hour] is the general mealtime?—Rather reverse it: The fourth is the general mealtime; the fifth is for labourers; and the sixth is for scholars. After that it is like throwing a stone into a barrel.[6] Abaye said: That was said only if nothing at all is eaten in the morning; but if something was eaten in the morning, we have nought against it.

R. Ashi said: As there is a controversy in respect of testimony, so is there a controversy in respect of leaven.[7] But it is obvious? That is precisely what we have said![8]—This is what he informs us: the answers which we gave are [correct] answers, and you need not say that it is dependent on Tannaim.[9]

R. Simi b. Ashi said: They learned this[10] only in respect of hours;[11] but if one testified [that the crime was committed] before sunrise and the other testified after sunrise, their testimony is void. That is obvious? — Rather [say] if one testified [that it was] before sunrise and the other testified during sunrise, their testimony is void. That too is obvious? — You might say, Both

a (1) Lit., 'forward'. (2) According to R. Meir: if A testified that the crime was committed in the second hour, and B that it took place in the third, their testimony is valid (v. *supra* 11b), unless they are rebutted over the whole period in which an error is possible. Thus A, if rebutted, can plead that he erred, and that the crime actually took place either in the first hour or in the third or fourth. He should also be able to plead that it took place within the hour before sunrise, since R. Meir allows for an error of nearly two hours, but that he would never mistake night for day. Similarly B, if rebutted, can plead that he erred, and that the crime took place at any time between the first and the fifth hour. Hence they are liable to be rebutted over the *whole* of this time; i.e., C and D testify that they were elsewhere from the first until the fifth hour, and such rebuttal is designated a rebuttal in respect of hours, and therefore the evidence, if unrefuted, is valid. By the same reasoning, according to R. Judah, who allows for a margin of nearly three hours' error, the period is from the first until the sixth hour, the seventh being disregarded, as explained in the Gemara.—This wide latitude is granted only in so far that the witnesses will not be subject to retaliation (v. 12a, n. a4) otherwise, but the evidence none the less may be void. E.g., if it is necessary to assume that B erred in two hours and that he really meant the fifth hour, A's testimony cannot be reconciled with it on any reasoning, and as we are left with one witness only the accused cannot be condemned. (3) I.e, right until midday, when it is forbidden by Scriptural law. (4) I.e., until just before midday.

b (1) A man does not come to testify without being very careful on the question of time, as he knows that he will be cross-examined. (2) Every man uses his own judgment, and therefore a far wider margin of error is possible. (3) And the interdict of leaven commences in the seventh only; hence there is no possibility of error. (4) Lit., 'between the corners',—equidistant from the east and the west, and so an error is possible. (5) Hence in the matter of leaven people may err between the fifth and the seventh hours, in spite of the difference in the sun's position. Nevertheless, they would not err from the fourth to the seventh. (6) Hence the fifth hour is kept in suspense, for if one were permitted to eat then he might forget about collecting fuel. (7) That burning is the only form of removal. (8) Lit., 'not at'. (9) I.e., during the sixth hour, before there is the Scriptural injunction to put away leaven. (10) It can be destroyed in any fashion.—Then why keep it in suspense? If he forgets to collect fuel he can destroy it in another way. (11) When the position of the sun cannot be clearly ascertained. (12) Hence everybody knows it.

c (1) Whose diet requires special attention (Jast.); or perhaps, circus attendants. (2) Rashi: Both are rapacious, hence they eat so early; but robbers, being awake all night, sleep during the first hour of the day. (3) Not having to earn their living, they have their main meal earlier than others. (4) In the field. (5) Lit., 'the mealtime of all (other) men'. (6) No benefit is derived. (7) Just as R. Meir and R. Judah differ in the possible errors of time in respect to evidence, so in respect of the prohibition of leaven. (8) The whole of our discussion assumes that the two subjects are completely analogous. (9) For though the views of R. Meir and R. Judah are apparently self-contradictory, they have been reconciled. R. Ashi informs us that it is unnecessary to assume that they actually represent irreconcilable opinions, there being a controversy of Tannaim as to the views of R. Meir and R. Judah. (10) That a margin of error, perhaps up to nearly three hours, is allowed in testimony. (11) I.e., when the witnesses state the hour of the day.

צא א מיי' פ"א מהל' חמץ הלכה ט:
צב ב טוש"ע א"ח סי' תמג:
צג ג מיי' פ"ב מהלכות עדות הלכה ה סמג לאוין טו:

אלא בין יממא לליליא לא טעו אינשי ובדין הוא דניתיב לקמיה טפי אלא שבה' חמה במזרח ובז' חמה במערב תנן ר"מ אומר אוכלין כל ה' ושורפין בתחלת ו' רבי יהודה אומר אוכלין כל ד' ותולין כל ה' ושורפין בתחלת ו' לאביי אליבא דר"מ דאמר אין אדם טועה ולא כלום ניכול כולה שית ולהך לישנא נמי דאמר אדם טועה משהו ניכול עד סוף שית ואביי אליבא דר' יהודה דאמר אדם טועה חצי שעה ניכול עד פלגא דשית ולהך לישנא נמי דאמרת אדם טועה שעה ומשהו ניכול עד סוף ה' (אלא) אמר אביי עדות מסורה לזריזים חמץ לכל מסור ורבא אליבא דר"מ דאמר אדם טועה שתי שעות חסר משהו מתחילת ה' לא ניכול ה' חמה במזרח וז' חמה במערב אי הכי בשית נמי ניכול אמר רב אדא בר אהבה שית יומא בקרנתא קאי ורבא אליבא דר' יהודה דאמר אדם טועה ג' שעות חסר משהו מתחילת ד' לא ניכול ה' חמה במזרח ושבע חמה במערב וכל שכן ד' אי הכי בה' נמי ניכול *תרגמה אביי אליבא דרבא עדות מסורה לזריזים חמץ לכל מסור ורבא אמר לאו היינו טעמא דרבי יהודה אלא רבי יהודה לטעמי' דאמר *אין ביעור חמץ אלא שריפה ויהבו ליה רבנן שעה אחת ללקוט בה עצים איתיביה רבינא לרבא א"ר יהודה אימתי שלא בשעת ביעורו אבל בשעת ביעורו השבתתו בכל דבר אלא אמר רבא *גזירה משום יום המעונן אי הכי אפילו בארבע שעות נמי לא ניכול אמר רב פפא ד' זמן סעודה לכל היא ת"ר *שעה ראשונה מאכל לודים שניה מאכל ליסטין שלישית מאכל יורשין רביעית מאכל פועלין חמישית מאכל כל אדם תלמידי חכמים ששית מאכל כל אדם והאמר רב פפא רביעית זמן סעודה לכל היא אלא איפוך ירביעית מאכל כל אדם חמישית מאכל פועלים ששית מאכל תלמידי חכמים מכאן ואילך כזורק אבן לחמת אמר אביי לא אמרן אלא דלא טעים מידי בצפרא אבל טעים מידי בצפרא לית לן בה אמר רב אשי כמחלוקת בעדות כך מחלוקת בחמץ פשיטא היינו הך דאמרינן הא קא משמע לן *שינויי דשנינן שינויא הוא ולא תימא תנאי היא *אמר רב שימי בר אשי לא שנו אלא בשעות אבל אחד אומר קודם הנץ החמה ואחד אומר אחר הנץ החמה עדותן בטילה פשיטא אלא גאחד אומר קודם הנץ החמה ואחד אומר בתוך הנץ החמה עדותן בטילה הא נמי פשיטא מהו דתימא תרווייהו חדא מילתא קאמרי והא דקאמר בתוך

ניכול כולה שית. לאו דוקא כולה שית דהא צריך לשרוף תוך שש: **ולהך** לישנא דאדם טועה שעה ומשהו ניכול עד סוף חמש. אפי' טעה בשתי שעות היה יכול להקשות ניכול עד סוף חמש שבחמש חמה במזרח ובשבע חמה במערב:

בשית חמה בי קרנתא קאי. הקשה ריב"א לאביי דאמר לר' יהודה דאמר אדם טועה חצי שעה ותלינן הטעות בשניהן אם כן אחד אומר בה' ואחד אומר בשבע אמאי עדותן בטלה כיון דאין הכירא בתחילת שש לז' נימא האי דקאמר ה' בסוף ה' והאי דקאמר ז' בתחילת ז' ועובדא הוה בפלגא דשית וטעה כל אחד חצי שעה וי"ל דהא דקאמר שית חמה בי קרנתא קאי וטעו בין תחילת שש לז' היינו חמץ דלכל מסור אבל עדות מסורה לזריזין אי נמי הך שינויא דקאמר בי קרנתא קאי לית ליה לאביי:

אימתי שלא בשעת ביעורו. פירש הקונטרס שלא בשעת ביעורו בשש ובשעת ביעורו מכאן ואילך ופריך הואיל ובשעת ביעורו השבתתו בכל דבר ימתין עד שבע וקשה לר"ת היכי ימתין עד שבע לבערו הא אסקינן לעיל (ד' י:) דגזר ר' יהודה בשעת איסורו לבדוק דילמא אתי למיכל מיניה ועוד שעת ביעורו דמתני' היינו בשש ועוד דמותר יליף ר' יהודה *דחמץ [לקמן כז:] בשריפה ונותר אחר שיעורו טעון שריפה וכמו כן חמץ ומפר"ת דשלא בשעת ביעורו היינו אחר שש שרוב העולם מבערין בשש כתיקון חכמים (ד) וטעם משום דיליף מנותר *והיינו [שם] לאחר איסורו אבל בשעת ביעורו דהיינו בשש כיון שאיכה מצוה לבערו אלא מדרבנן השבתתו בכל דבר וכן איתא בירושלמי פ"ק כל שעה:

ארבע זמן סעודה לכל היא. לא שייך האי טעמא אלא לענין אכילה אבל לענין עדות לא: ר"ג

אלא בין יממא לליליא לא טעו אינשי. ולבתריה יהבינן ליה רביעית חמישית וששית ולבעל חמש יהבינן לקמיה רביעית ושלישית ושניה ולבתריה ששית ולאכתי הוה לן למיתב ליה אלא הא פריש רבי יהודה בהדיא דבין חמש לשבע לא טעו שבחמש חמה במזרח ובשבע במערב וכל הנך טעותא דיהבינן להו ה"מ לאצוליניהו ולמפטרינהו מקטלא אבל מ"מ משעה שהוזם אחד מהן באותה שעה לבדה ובטל אחריה מיד בטלה העדות ואפי' לא הוזם בטעות שלפניו דהא כי אמרו ליה לבעל ג' שלישית ורביעית וחמישית עמנו הייתם והוצרך לומר בשניה היה אלא שטעיתי הרי נחלקה עדותן שאם בשניה היה המעשה אין כאן אלא עד אחד דהא חבירו אמר בחמש ובין שנייה לחמישית לא טעו: ניכול עד סוף שית. דהא מן התורה אינו אסור אלא משעברו שש ורבנן למה(א) הוא דעבוד הרחקה במידי דלא טעו אינשי ביה: עדות מסורה לזריזים. אין אדם בא להעיד על הנפש אא"כ בקי בשעות לפי שיודע הוא שסופו להדרש בדרישה וחקירה אבל חמץ על הכל מוטל ושאינו בקי בשעות טועה בהן: בחמש חמה במזרח ובשבע במערב. וחמץ אינו אסור אלא בשבע ואין טעות בין חמש לשבע: אי הכי בשש נמי ניכול. דהא בשש עדיין לא נטתה חמה לצד מערב אלא באמצע הרקיע וזריחתה תחתיה בראש כל אדם ואין צל נוטה לא לכאן ולא לכאן אלא תחתיו: יומא. חמה: בי קרנתא קאי. באמצע הרקיע קרובה לנטות למזרח וקרובה לנטות למערב ואין עומדין עליה ולהכי נקט לישנא דבי קרנתא ולא נקט בי מילעי דדרום קאי לפי שגלגל חמה שחמה סובבת בו עגול הוא ודבר עגול אין חילוק ארבע רוחות ניכר בו ומזרחו מתעגל עד חצי דרומו וחצי לפונו ומיחזי פלגי דרום בסוף מזרח וראש מערב: מתחילת ארבע לא ניכול. דהא טעי שש וחמש וארבע: ומשני שמעי' ליה לרבי יהודה דאמר בין חמש לשבע לא טעו וכ"ש ארבע: עדות מסורה לזריזין. והילכך מודי בה רבי יהודה דלא טעו בין חמש לשבע אבל חמץ לכל מסור וטעו מיהו כולי האי לא טעו ואע"ג דטעו בין תחילת שלש לסוף חמש דהיינו שלש שעות לא טעו בין סוף ארבע לתחיל' שבע לאסריניהו בד' משום שבע אע"ג דאיכא בציר מג' משום דאיכא היכירא בחמה: ורבא אמר. טעמא דר' יהודה בחמץ לאו משום טעותא היא דלא טעו אינשי בין חמש לשבע כדקאמר חמש חמה במזרח כו' והאי דקאמר תולין כל חמש ר' יהודה לטעמיה דאמר באידך פירקין (דף כא.) אין ביעור חמץ אלא שריפה הילכך אסרו רבנן באכילתו כדי שיהא לו פנאי ללקט עצים בינתיים ואי שרית ליה כל חמש אינו נזכר אבל עכשיו דתלי ליה רמי אנפשיה ומדכר ללקט: אימתי. אני אומר אין ביעור חמץ אלא שריפה: שלא בשעת ביעורו. בתחילת שש וכל שש דהאכתי מדאורייתא שרי (ב) אבל בשעת ביעורו בשבע שהוא מוזהר מן התורה השבתתו בכל דבר וטורח זה למה אם אין לו עצים ימתין עד שעת ביעורו וישביתנו בכל דבר: יום המעונן. שאין חמה זורחת ואין יכולין לבדוק בחמה: זמן סעודה לכל היא. והכל בקיאים בה: לודים ולסטים רעבתנים הן אלא שהליסטים נעורין כל הלילה וישנים שחרית שעה ראשונה ואוכלין בשניה: יורשין. לאו משום רעבתנות אלא הואיל ולא עמלו בו: כמחלוקת. דרבי מאיר ור' יהודה בעדות משום דלרבי יהודה טעי אינשי טפי ובין לר' מאיר ובין לר' יהודה כך מחלוקת במתניתין נמי בחמץ משום דלר' יהודה טעי אינשי טפי ובין לר' מאיר ובין לר' יהודה דלא מרחקי כולי טעותא כדאמרן בעדות למר שתי שעות ולמר שלש שעות (ג): משום שינויא דשנינן. חמץ לכל מסור דלא תימא תנאי היא כי קשיא לך מתני' דסנהדרין ומתני' דהכא לא תימא תנאי היא אליבא דר' מאיר ור' יהודה דתנא דמתני' סבר לר' מאיר אדם טועה שעה אחת ולר' יהודה אדם טועה שתים ותנא דסנהדרין סבר לר"מ אדם טועה שתים ולר' יהודה שלש אלא ודאי כאותו מחלוקת של שם כך הוא כאן אלא משום דחמץ לכל מסור הוא א"נ כי קשה לך לר' יהודה דאמר התם אין טעות בין חמש לשבע משום חמה והכא אמר טעו לא תימא תנאי היא אלא כטעמו שם כך טעמו כאן אלא שבחמץ לכל מסור אי נמי משום יום המעונן: לא שנו. הך דסנהדרין אלא שהעידו על השעות אבל הוציאו בפיהם שם הנץ החמה אין כאן טעות אלא כוז: בתוך הנץ. כשמתחיל הנץ:
הלכה

[שבת נג: וש"נ] [לקמן כא. כז: תמורה לד.] שבת י. [ע"ש] [כתובות לה:] סנהדרין מ.

הגהות הב"ח
(א) רש"י ד"ה ניכול וכו' ורבנן למאי הוא דעבוד: (ב) ד"ה אימתי וכו' מדאורייתא שרי הס"ד: (ג) ד"ה כמחלוקת וכו' משום הס"ד: (ד) תוס' ד"ה אימתי וכו' חכמים וטעמא משום:

רבינו חננאל
המזמין שיתו עמהן [כדי] שיתכן שימעו אבל אם יעידו בשעה ה' אין נותנין שלש שעות שהן ה' וששית ושביעית במעותם למה שבחמש חמה במזרח ובשבע חמה במערב ואין אדם טעה בזה וכענין הזה נותנין למעיד בשעה שביעית ולא יוזמו אלא אם כן יעידו עליהם כי עמנו הייתם משעה שביעית עד שעה עשירית ואם יטעו בשעה ס' לא יוזמו אלא עד שיעידו שהיו עמהם משעה שביעית עד שעה י"א ולמה שנינו אחד אומר יששתי שעות ולא שנינו אחד אומר בשעה ראשונה לפי ששעה ראשונה שהוא שחרית ושעה י"ב שהוא ערבית אין אדם טועה בהן ודייקי' הני מילי מדקתני ר' יהודה אחד אומר בג' ואחד אומר בה' עדותן קיימת ואמר רבא מעשה כי הוה בתחלת ג' שעות הוה ופעי האי דאמר ה' ג' שעות(הוה ופעי האי ה' ג' שעות)חסר משהו אי בסוף ה' הוה מעשה והאי(דקתני)[דקאמר]ג' טעי ג' שעות חסר משהו לפניו ומצטרפי ש"מ דטעי אדם זה השיעור לפניו ולאחריו.וכענין הזה אליבא דר' מאיר שתי שעות חסר משהו זולתי השעות שאין בן אדם טועה בהן שעה ראשונה שאין אדם טועה בה שהיא ג' וכ"ש ד' וכיוצא בה: ואקשינן מתני' אמאי תאני ר' מאיר אוכלין כל חמש ושורפין בתחלת שש לאביי דאמר אין אדם טועה ולא כלום יאכל עד סוף שש דהא קיימא לן אך חלק מחצי היום איסורו של חמץ וללישנא אחרינ' דאביי כו' ולרבא אליבא דר' מאיר דאמר אדם טועה שתי שעו' מתחלת חמש לא יאכל למה אמר רבי מאיר אוכלין כל ה' וכן לר' יהודה מתחלת ד' ופרקי' בהא אליבא דר' יהודה הא אוקימ' לגבי עדות דלא טעי אינש בין שעה ה' לז' דבה' חמה במזרח ובז' חמה במערב וכל שכן ד' דודאי לא טעי בו' ואסיקא תרגמה אביי בין לרידיה בין אליבא דרבא עדות מסורה לזריזין חמץ לכל מסור ולפיכך עבדו רבנן הרחקה ואתא רבא לאוקומי טעמא דר' יהודה משום דקסבר אין ביעור חמץ אלא שריפה ונדחו דבריו ואוקמה גזרה משום יום המעונן. אסקינן במחלוקת דר' מאיר ור' יהודה בעדות דמשום מעותן היא כך מחלוקת בחמץ קאמר לן דשניא דשנינן שנויי ניניהו וסמכינן עליהו. **אמר** רב שימי בר אשי לא שנו דטעו אלא בשעו' כלומר אחד [אומר] כך וכך שעה ביום אבל אחד אומר קודם הנץ החמה ואחד אומר אחר הנץ החמה עדותן בטלה כי עדות מכחשת היא וכענין הזה פירשנו למעלה כי בכל מקום שהכחשות דחויה העדות בטלה היא:

פט א מיי' פ"א מהלכות עדות הלכה ד סמג עשין קט:
צ ב מיי' פ"ב מהלכות עדות הלכה א:

וחד מינייהו קטעי שעה ומשהו אזל רב הונא בריה דרב יהודה אמרה לשמעתתא קמיה דרבא אמר ומה אילו דייקינן בהני סהדי דהאי דקאמר שלש בתחילת שלש והאי דקאמר חמש בסוף חמש והויא עדות מוכחשת ולא קטלינן ואנן ניקום ונקטיל מספקא ורחמנא אמר °ושפטו העדה והצילו העדה [במדבר לה] אלא אמר רבא לדברי רבי מאיר אדם טועה שתי שעות חסר משהו לדברי רבי יהודה אדם טועה שלש שעות חסר משהו לדברי רבי מאיר אדם טועה שתי שעות חסר משהו מעשה כי הוה או בתחלת שתים או בסוף שלש וחד מינייהו קטעי ב' שעות חסר משהו לדברי רבי יהודה אדם טועה שלש שעות חסר משהו מעשה כי הוה או בתחלת שלש או בסוף חמש וחד מינייהו קטעי שלש שעות חסר משהו *תנן היו בודקין (א) אותו בשבע חקירות באיזו שבוע באיזו שנה באיזה חדש בכמה בחדש באיזה יום באיזו שעה באיזה מקום *(ותניא) *מה בין חקירות לבדיקות חקירות אמר אחד מהן איני יודע עדותן בטילה בדיקות אפילו שניהם אומרים אין אנו יודעים עדותן קיימת והוינן בה מאי שנא חקירות ומאי שנא בדיקות ואמרינן חקירות אמר אחד מהן איני יודע עדותן בטילה דהויא לה עדות שאי אתה יכול להזימה בדיקות עדות שאתה יכול להזימה היא ואי אמרת טעי איניש כולי האי חקירות דאיזו שעה נמי עדות שאי אתה יכול להזימה היא דאמרי מטעי קטעינן דיהבינן להו כולי טעותייהו לרבי מאיר יהבינן להו מתחילת שעה ראשונה עד סוף חמש ובדין הוא דניתיב להו [ד"א מעיקרא אמר כנ"ן] מעיקרא טפי אלא בין יממא לליליא לא טעו אינשי ולרבי יהודה יהבינן להו מתחילת שעה ראשונה ועד סוף ששית ובדין הוא דניתיב להו מעיקרא טפי אלא

רש"י

שלש. והאי דאמר בתחילת חמש טעי שעה רביעית ומשהו של סוף שלש אי נמי בתחילת חמש הוה והאי דאמר בסוף שלש טעה שעה רביעית ומשהו: לשמעתתא. דאביי: אמר. רבא וכי אפשר לומר שאין תולין טעות אלא משהו לר' מאיר ושעה ומשהו לר' יהודה א"כ היכך אתה מצרף עדותן מי אמר לך שזה המקדים נתכוין לסוף השעה והמאחר נתכוין לתחילת השעה כדי לקרבן זה אצל זה ולצרף עדותן שלא תהא ביניהן אלא שיעור טעות האדם ומה אילו דייקינן בהני סהדי לחלק עדותן מצית למימר האי דאמר שלש בתחלת שלש והאי דאמר חמש בסוף חמש ויש חילוק ביניהן שלש שעות חסר משהו וכיון דאין אדם טועה כל כך נחלקה עדותן והויא מוכחשת ולא קטלינן ליה להאי ואנן ניקום ונקרב עדותן כדי שיהרג זה(): והא רחמנא אמר והצילו העדה. את הרוצח דמחפשין לזכות אלא ודאי מדקאמר עדותן קיימת ש"מ דסבירא להו דאפי' אתה מחלקן כמו אשר תוכל ולומר שהמוקדם נתכוין לתחלת השעה והמאוחר לסופה יש לך לתלות בטעות ואיך יכול להכחישם שאדם טועה בכל זאת: אלא אמר רבא לר' מאיר (ג) אדם טועה. כל מה שאתה יכול לחלק את אלו שהיה מקיים עדותן דהיינו שתי שעות חסר משהו ומשום הכי עדותן קיימת דכי נמי אמרת זה שאמר שתים בתחלת שתים וזה שאמר שלש בסוף שלש כל רגעים שביניהם שאירע המעשה בהן יש לתלות לטעות ולומר כמו שאמרו: מעשה כי הוה או בסוף שלש או בתחלת שתים. כלומר לא מיבעיא אם היה המעשה בסוף שתים או בתחילת ג' דטעות מועטת הוא דאי נמי *נאמר האי בתחילת שתים אין כאן טעות אלא שעה והאי כנ"ן אי נמי אמר בסוף שלש אין כאן טעות אלא שעה אלא אפילו הוה מעשה בתחילת שתים והאי דאמר שלש בסוף שלש ויש כאן טעות שתי שעות חסר משהו אפי' הכי אין כח לנו לבטלן שאף בכך אדם טועה (ד) ולר' יהודה נמי כו' ובהאי עניינא דפרישית דכי נמי מרחקת להו בכל היכולת אכתי טעו בהכי דהיינו שלש שעות חסר משהו מעשה כי הוה כו' כלומר בכל מה שאתה יכול להרחיק אפי' האחד אמר שבאותה שעה היה המעשה אין עד הרחוק ממנו מוכחש דטעו בהכי: היו בודקין אותו (ה). לעדי נפשות: בשבע חקירות. מקראי נפקא לן בסנהדרין בההוא פירקא (ד' מ.): שבוע. שמיטה באיזו שמיטה של יובל שיש בו שבע שמיטות: באיזו שנה. של שמיטה: באיזה חודש. בשנה: בכמה ימים. בחודש: באיזה יום. בשבת באחד בשבת או בשני בשבת או בשלישי בשבת או א' מן האחרים: (ותניא) מה בין חקירות לבדיקות. דקתני התם מכירין אתם אותו התריתם בו במה הרגו בסייף הרגו או באריכן הרגו כליו שחורים או לבנים וכל המרבה בבדיקות הרי זה משובח ומה בין חקירות הנך שבע קמייתא לבדיקות אוחרנייתא: חקירות אמר אחד (ו) איני יודע. באחת מהן ואפי' *בשעות אומר איני יודע עדותן בטילה: דהויא ליה עדות שאי אתה יכול להזימה. דרחמנא אמר *ודרשו השופטים היטב והנה עד שקר העד וגו' ועשיתם לו כאשר זמם לעשות וגו' עדות שאתה יכול לקיים בה תורת הזמה הוי עדות ואי לא לא והזמה אינה אלא בעמנו הייתם באותו היום ובאותה שעה שאתם אומרין שראיתם עדות זו במקום זה הייתם עמנו במקום פלוני וכי אמרי באחת מהן אפי' בחקירות דאיזו שעה איני יודע שוב איך יכול לומר לו עמי היית באותה שעה וא"ת אתה יכול להזימה ע"י היום אם יבואו עדים ויאמרו כל היום הייתם עמנו מיהא בצרה להו תורת הזמה מן חקירות השעות ורחמנא רבי שבע חקירות בגזרה שוה דהיטב היטב בסנהדרין: בדיקות. כי אמרי אין אנו יודעין עדות שאתה יכול להזימה היא שאין ההזמה תלויה בהן אלא בחקירות דמה עמנו הייתם יש לומר בכלים שחורים או לבנים: ואי אמרת טעי איניש כולי האי חקירות דאיזו שעה נמי. אין לך בה הזמה אפי' כי לא אמר איני יודע דהא כי אמר בחמש ואמרי ליה בחמש עמנו היית יכול לומר בארבע היה אבל טעיתי: ומשני דיהבינן להו כולי טעותייהו. ואם יש מזימין כאן יכולין להזים ע"י שעה וטעותה ולומר לו כל השעה וטעותה היית עמנו: לרבי מאיר. דאמר אדם טועה ב' שעות יהבינן להו להני דשתים וג' מתחילת שעה ראשונה עד סוף חמש בין שניהן להאי דשתים יהבינן ליה שעה ראשונה ושניה ושלישית ורביעית ולהאי דג' יהבינן ליה עוד חמישית ותו לא דכי אמרי ליה להאי דשתים בשניה עמנו היית יש לומר טעיתי שתי שעות לאחוריי ומעשה היה בראשונה ועוד היה לו לומר מעשה היה קודם לראשונה שעה אחת אלא בין יממא לליליא לא טעו אינשי וכי אמרי ליה ראשונה ושניה עמנו היית יש לו לומר טעיתי ב' שעות לפני שלישית ורביעית ואי אמרי ליה כל ארבע שעות עמנו היית הרי הוזם ולבעל שלש נמי יהבינן לקמיה ראשונה ושניה ולבתריה יהבינן רביעית וחמישית ואי מזמי ליה לכולהו חמש הרי הוזם: ולרבי יהודה. דאמר אדם טועה ג' שעות יהבינן להו להנך דשלש וחמש דאיירי ר' יהודה בהן מתחילת שעה ראשונה ועד סוף שית ולבעל שלש יהבינן לקמיה ראשונה ושניה ודין הוא דניתיב ליה טפי: אלא

תוספות

אלא אמר רבא לדברי ר' מאיר אדם טועה ב' שעות חסר משהו. ואם תאמר א"כ אחד אומר בג' ואחד אומר בה' אמאי עדותן בטילה נימא דעובדא ברביעית הוה וי"ל דסבר רבא דאין לתלות הטעות בשניהם אלא יש להקשות אחד אומר בג' ואחד אומר בה' אמאי עדותן בטילה אילו דייקינן בהני סהדי דילמא האי דקאמר בג' בסוף ג' וי"ל דאין לומר להחמיר ולקיים עדותן לא בדקינן להו:

באיזה יום. תימה כיון דככר כיוונו יום אחד לחדש למה למשיילינהו באיזה יום והלא אפי' לא כיוונו איזה יום ה"ל חוזרין ומגידין ואין יכולין לחזור בהם אחר כדי דבור וי"ל לומר כיון דז' חקירות ילפינן מקראי בפרק היו בודקים (סנהדרין דף מ'.) לכך צריך שיכחישו זה את זה ושלא יכחישו את עצמן א"נ נפקא מינה לאחד אומר בג' בחודש ואחד אומר בג' כדפרישית:

לרבי מאיר יהבינן להו מתחילת שעה ראשונה עד סוף ה'. הקשה ריב"א אמאי לא נתלה הטעות במזימים וכשאומרים המזימים עמנו הייתם עד סוף ה' נאמר שטעו וקרו לד' ה' והמעשה היה בה' ולא יהיו מוזמים בכך והני שהעדות מוכחשת היא שהרי אותו שאמר שתים לא היה יכול לטעות עד ה' מ"מ מוזמים לא יהיו ואור"י דלא תלינן הטעות כלל בשני עדים כדפרישית לעיל:

רבינו חננאל

לדברי ר' מאיר אדם טועה משהו ולדברי ר' יהודה אדם טועה שעה ומשהו ובא רבא ודחה לתרי לישני דאביי ופשוטות נינהו וארקעי' רבא הכי לדברי ר' מאיר אדם טועה שתי שעות חסר משהו ומעשה כי הוה פירוש השעה שראו העדות או בתחלת שעה שנייה היה וזה שאמר שנים שפיר אמר והאי שאמר שלש טעה שתי שעות חסר משהו לפיכך אמר עדותן קיימת או בסוף שלש היה המעשה והאי דקאמר בשתי שעות טעה שתי שעות חסר משהו והאי דקאמר שלש שפיר אמר לדברי ר' יהודה אדם טועה ג' שעות חסר משהו מעשה כי היה בתחלת שעה ג' והאי דקאמר ה' טועה ב' שעות חסר משהו או בסוף ה' היה המעשה והאי דקאמר ג' טועה ג' שעות חסר משהו ואקשי' על הא דרבא תנן היו בודקין אותן בשבע חקירות ואחת מהן באיזו שעה וקתני מה בין חקירות לבדיקות חקירות אמר אחד איני יודע עדותן בטלה בבדיקות אמר אחד איני יודע ואפי' שנים אומרים אין אנו יודעין עדותן קיימת והוינן בה מכדי חקירות ובדיקות תרווייהו מדאורייתא נינהו דכתיב (דברים יג טו) ודרשת וחקרת ושאלת היטב מה לי חקירות מה לי בדיקות ואמרי' חקירות כי אמר איני יודע הויא לה עדות שאי אתה יכול להזימה וכל עדות שאינך יכול להזימה אינה עדות ואי ס"ד טעי איניש כולי האי חקירות שעה נמי עדות שאינך יכול להזימה היא שאם יבואו שני העדים ויעידו בשעה ג' ויזומו בשעה ג' יאמרו טעינו שעה ה' היה המעשה וכיון שאמרת יתכן שיטעו זה השיעור הדין עמהם (על זה הדין) נמצא כי בטלה תורת חקירות ואיזה שעה היא לדברי הכל בין לת"ק דאמר שבע חקירות הן בין לר' יוסי דאמר שש חקירות הן איזה יום איזו שעה איזה מקום מ"מ לדברי הכל איזו שעה מן החקירות שהיא ופריק רבא דיהבינן להו כולהי טעותייהו פי' כל עדות שיעיד אדם משעה שניה של יום עד שעה ששית ומשעה שביעית עד שעה י"א של יום יהבינן להו לר' מאיר שתי שעות חסר משהו

ולר' יהודה שלש שעות חסר משהו כיצד לר' יהודה אם יעידו בשעה שנייה של יום צריכין המזימין להעיד בו עמנו הייתם משעה שנייה עד שעה רביעית ואם יעידו בשלישית יאמרו עמנו הייתם ... ואם יעידו בשעה ד' יאמרו עמנו הייתם משעה שנייה עד שעה ששית כשם שיש לומר טעו לפניהם ב' שעות חסר משהו כך י"ל שטעו לאחור וכל היכא דאיכא למתלי בטעות תלינן ולא קטלינן אלא אם יעידו המזימין

הגהות הב"ח

(א) גמ' בודקין אותו בשבע: (ב) רש"י ד"ה אמר רבא וד"ה והא רחמנא: (ג) ד"ה אלא אמר רבא לר' מאיר שהיה מקיים עדותן אדם טועה וכו' לא אלו דהיינו שתי שעות כנ"ל: (ד) ד"ה מעשה וכו' ולר' יהודה כו' כנ"ל: (ה) ד"ה היו בודקין אותו: (ו) ד"ה חקירות אמר אחד מהן איני:

סנהדרין מ.
[סס]
[ותנן]
[נ"א כשם שאומ' אני יודע]

ginning of the fifth, [12a] and one of them erred in just over an hour.

R. Huna the son of R. Judah went and reported this discussion before Raba. Said he: now what if we carefully examined these witnesses [and found] that the one who testified [that it took place] in the third [hour] meant at the *beginning* of the third hour, while he who testified [that it took place] in the fifth [meant] at the *end* of the fifth, so that it would be a confuted testimony and we would not execute [the accused]; shall we then arise and execute him through a doubt,[3] whereas the Merciful One has ordered, *then the congregation shall judge . . . and the congregation shall* deliver?[4] Rather said Raba: On R. Meir's ruling a man may err in two hours less a trifle, while on R. Judah's ruling a man may err in three hours less a trifle. On R. Meir's ruling a man may err in two hours less a trifle: the incident happened either at the beginning of the second or at the end of the third [hour], and one of them erred in two hours less a trifle. On R. Judah's ruling a man may err in three hours less a trifle: the incident occurred either at the beginning of the third or at the end of the fifth [hour], and one of them erred in three hours less a trifle.

a We learned: They[1] were examined with seven *ḥakiroth:*[2] In which septennate [was the crime committed], in which year, in which month, on what day of the month, on what day [of the week], at which hour and in which place? And we [further] learned: What is the difference between *ḥakiroth* and *bedikoth?*[3] In *ḥakiroth*, if one of them [the witnesses] replied, 'I do not know', their testimony is null; in *bedikoth*, even if both declare, 'We do not know', their testimony is valid. Now we questioned this: Wherein this difference between *ḥakiroth* and *bedikoth?* And we answered: In *ḥakiroth*, if one declares, 'I do not know', their testimony is null, because it is a testimony which cannot be rebutted;[4] whereas with respect to *bedikoth* it is [still] a testimony which can be rebutted.[5] Now if you say that a man may err in so much, then the *ḥakiroth* of which hour also [leaves] testimony which cannot be rebutted, for they can assert, 'We did indeed err'?—We allow them [the benefit of] the whole of their [possible] error: according to R. Meir we allow them from the beginning of the first hour until the end of the fifth; and logically we should give them even more at the beginning, but that people do not err between day and night. While according to R. Judah we allow them from the beginning of the first hour until the end of the sixth; and logically we should

(3) I.e., just because we do *not* examine the witnesses to find out exactly what they meant. (4) Num. XXXV, 24, 25; i.e., the accused must be given the benefit of doubt.

a (1) The witnesses in a murder trial. (2) Lit., 'searching questions'. Two types of questions were asked, called *ḥakiroth* and *bedikoth* (examinations); v. Sanh. 40a. (3) As stated, *ḥakiroth* dealt with time and place; *bedikoth* dealt with accompanying circumstances of the crime, e.g., the weapon, the clothes worn, etc. (4) The Hebr. word הזמה used always denotes rebutting by proving that the *witnesses themselves* were elsewhere at the time of the alleged crime, in which case the law of retaliation applies that the witnesses are subject to the punishment which they sought to fasten upon the accused; v. Deut. XIX, 18f. This is obviously impossible unless the witnesses state the exact time and place, whereas the possibility of rebuttal is essential for the validity of testimony. (5) Even if the witnesses are not clear on the accompanying circumstances.

blemish upon it?—There, because one is excited [11b] about his property, if you permit him [to bleed it] in a place where a blemish is not inflicted, he will come to do it in a place where a blemish is inflicted. But the Rabbis [argue]: if you do not permit him at all, he is all the more likely to come to act [thus].

Yet do we say according to R. Judah, A man is excited over his property? Surely we learned: An animal may not be curried on Festivals, because it makes a bruise [wound], but you may scrape it; but the Sages maintain: It may neither be curried nor scraped. Now it was taught: What is currying and what is scraping? Currying is with a small-toothed strigil, and it makes a wound;
a scraping is with a large-toothed strigil and does not make a wound?[1] —There, since it will die if left alone, we say, a man is excited about his property; here, if he leaves it there is merely discomfort, we do not say, a man is excited about his money. Now as to R. Judah; wherein is the difference that he preventively prohibits in the case of leaven but does not preventively forbid in the case of scraping?—One bread can be mistaken for another bread, [but] currying cannot be mistaken for scraping.

MISHNAH. R. MEIR SAID: ONE MAY EAT [LEAVEN] THE WHOLE OF THE FIVE [HOURS] AND MUST BURN [IT] AT THE BEGINNING OF THE SIXTH. R. JUDAH SAID: ONE MAY EAT THE WHOLE OF THE FOUR [HOURS], KEEP IT IN SUSPENSE THE WHOLE OF THE FIFTH, AND MUST BURN IT AT THE BEGINNING OF THE SIXTH.[2] R. JUDAH SAID FURTHER: TWO UNFIT LOAVES OF THE THANKSOFFERING USED TO LIE ON THE ROOF[3] OF THE [TEMPLE] IZṬABA:[4] AS LONG AS THEY LAY [THERE] ALL THE PEOPLE WOULD EAT [LEAVEN]; WHEN ONE WAS REMOVED, THEY WOULD KEEP IT IN SUSPENSE, NEITHER EATING NOR BURNING [IT]; WHEN BOTH WERE REMOVED, ALL THE PEOPLE COMMENCED BURNING [THEIR
b LEAVEN].[1] R. GAMALIEL SAID: ḤULLIN MAY BE EATEN THE WHOLE OF THE FOUR [HOURS] AND TERUMAH THE WHOLE OF THE FIVE [HOURS], AND WE BURN [THEM] AT THE BEGINNING OF THE SIXTH [HOUR].[2]

GEMARA. We learned elsewhere: If one [witness] deposes [that it took place] on the second day of the month,[3] and another deposes, on the third of the month, their testimony is valid, because one knows of the intercalation of the [preceding] month[4] while the other does not know of the intercalation of the month.[5] If one deposed, on the third, while the other deposed, on the fifth, their testimony is null. If one said: During the second hour, and the other said: During the third hour, their testimony is valid.[6] If one said, during the third hour, and the other said, during the fifth, their testimony is null: this is R. Meir's view. R. Judah maintained: Their testimony stands. If one deposed, during the fifth [hour], while the other deposed, during the seventh, their testimony is null, because during the fifth [hour] the sun is in the east, whereas in the seventh it is in the west. Abaye observed: When you examine the matter, you find that on R. Meir's ruling a man does not err [in the time] at all, [while] on R. Judah's ruling a man may err in half an hour. [Thus:] on R. Meir's ruling a man does not err at all: the event [to which they testify] happened at the end of the second and the beginning of the third [hour], and when one says, during the second, [he means] at the end of the second [hour], and when the other says, during the third hour, [he means] at the beginning of the third
c hour.[1] On R. Judah's ruling a man may err in half an hour: the event happened in the middle of the fourth hour, and he who says in the third hour [meant] at the end of the third hour, and he errs in [being] half an hour before; while he who testified, in the fifth hour, [meant] at the beginning of the fifth hour, and he errs in half an hour behind.

Others say, Abaye observed: When you examine the matter, you find that on R. Meir's ruling a man may err in [just] a little, while on R. Judah's ruling a man may err in slightly more than an hour.[2] On R. Meir's ruling a man may err in [just] a little: the event occurred either at the end of the second or at the beginning of the third [hour], and one of them erred a little. On R. Judah's ruling a man may err in slightly more than an hour: the event happened either at the end of the third or at the be-

a (1) The animal is scraped to free it of mud, mire, etc. Thus R. Judah does not argue that if you permit one the other will be used, because a man is anxious to keep his property in good condition. (2) V. *supra* 4b for notes. (3) This is the reading of MS.M. and in the printed edd. of the Mishnah. (4) V. Gemara.
b (1) Forty loaves were brought with a thanksoffering, ten of which were leaven; two leaven loaves which had become unfit (the Gemara discusses how) were publicly exposed on the portico and served as a signal. (2) By Biblical law leaven is permitted until midday. But people often erred in the matter of time (there were, of course, no clocks or watches in those days), and the controversy here is in respect of the extent of possible or likely errors. (3) E.g., a murder. (4) I.e., that it consisted of thirty days. The thirtieth day is said to be intercalated. (5) Thinking that it consisted of twenty-nine days. This holds good only when they agree on other matters, including what day of the week it was. (6) Because one can err in an hour.
c (1) Thus there is no contradiction at all. But if it is shown that there is a contradiction, even in half an hour, one is assumed to be false and their evidence is null. (2) Lit., 'an hour and a little'.

על ממונו אמרינן אי שרית ליה במקום שאין עושין בו מום אתי למעבד במקום שעושין בו מום ורבנן כל שכן דאי לא שרית ליה כלל אתי למעבד ומי אמרינן לרבי יהודה אדם בהול על ממונו *והתנן ר' יהודה אומר אין °*(מקדרין) הבהמה בי"ט מפני שהוא עושה חבורה אבל מקרצפין וחכ"א אין מקדרין אף אין מקרצפין *ותניא איזהו קידור ואיזהו קרצוף קידור קטני' ועושין חבור' קרצוף גדולים ואין עושין חבורה התם דאי שביק לי' מיית אמרינן אדם בהול על ממונו הכא אי שביק לי' צערא בעלמא הוא לא אמרי' אדם בהול על ממונו ור' יהודה מאי שנא גבי חמץ דגזר *ומאי שנא גבי קרצוף דלא גזר לחם בלחם מיחלף קידור בקרצוף לא מיחלף:

מתני' *ר"מ אומר אוכלים כל חמש ושורפין בתחלת שש רבי יהודה אומר *אוכלין כל ארבע ותולין כל חמש ושורפין בתחלת שש ועוד א"ר יהודה שתי חלות של תודה פסולות מונחות על *גב האיצטבא כל זמן שמונחות כל העם אוכלין ניטלה אחת תולין לא אוכלין ולא שורפין ניטלו שתיהן התחילו כל העם שורפין *ר"ג אומר חולין נאכלין כל ארבע ותרומה כל חמש ושורפין בתחלת שש: [שם]

גמ' *תנן התם [סנהדרין מ. [סג.]] אחד אומר בשנים בחדש ואחד אומר בשלשה (א) עדותן קיימת שזה יודע בעבורו של חדש וזה אינו יודע בעבורו של חדש אחד אומר בשלשה ואחד אומר בה' עדותן בטלה אחד אומר בשתי שעות ואחד אומר בשלש שעות עדותן קיימת אחד אומר בשלש ואחד אומר בחמש עדותן בטלה (ב) דברי רבי מאיר רבי יהודה אומר עדותן קיימת אחד אומר בחמש ואחד אומר בשבע עדותן בטלה שבחמש חמה במזרח ובשבע חמה במערב אמר אביי כשתמצא לומר לדברי רבי מאיר אין אדם טועה ולא כלום לדברי רבי יהודה אדם טועה חצי שעה לדברי ר"מ *אין אדם טועה ולא כלום מעשה כי הוה במיפק תרתי ומעייל תלת והא דקאמר שתים בסוף שתים והא דקאמר שלש בתחלת שלש [סנהדרין מ:] לדברי רבי יהודה אדם טועה חצי שעה מעשה כי הוה בפלגא דארבע הוה והאי דקאמר שלש בסוף שלש וקטעי פלגא דשעתא לקמיה והאי דקאמר חמש בתחלת חמש וקטעי פלגא דשעתא לאחוריה איכא דאמרי אמר אביי כשתמצא לומר לדברי רבי מאיר אדם טועה משהו לדברי רבי יהודה אדם טועה שעה ומשהו לדברי ר"מ אדם טועה משהו מעשה כי הוה או בסוף שתים הוה או בתחלת שלש וחד מינייהו טועה משהו לדברי רבי יהודה אדם טועה שעה ומשהו מעשה כי הוה או בסוף שלש או בתחלת חמש וחד

רש"י

על ממונו. כהן זה בהול על הבכור שלא ימות: כ"ש. הואיל ובהול הוא אי לא שרית ליה במקום שאינו עושה בו מום עובר על דבריך ועושה ושוב אין נזהר בין מקום מום לשלא במקום מום דסבור שהכל שוה: מקדרין. אשטרלי"ר: מקרצפין. כדפרשינן בכלי שפיו גסות ואינו עושה חבורה דהוכל בבעלי חיים אב מלאכה היא קתני מיהת אבל מקרצפין אלמא לא גזר מתוך שאדם בהול אי לא שרית ליה קירצוף עביד קידור לפי שהטיט מכחיש את הבהמה ומצערה: לא מיחלף. ורבנן סברי מיחלף: **מתני'** ושורפין בתחלת שש. ואע"ג דכל שעה ששית מדאורייתא שריא גזור רבנן עלה דילמא טעי וסבור על השביעי' שהיא ששית אבל אחמישי' לא טעי למימר על השביעית שהיא חמישית ומותר: תולין כל חמש. ואינו אוכל דטעי וסבור על שביעית שהיא חמישית ומיהו לשרוף אינו צריך ומאכיל לבהמתו אבל ששית אף בהנאה אסור מדרבנן גזירה משום שביעית: שתי חלות. של חמץ: של תודה פסולות. ובגמרא מפרש מאן פסלינהו: היו מונחות. בכל ערב פסח: על גב האיצטבא. סטיו שהיה בהר הבית ששם מתקבצין ויושבים בני אדם והיו רואין אותן לסימן: ניטלה אחת מהן. בתחלת חמש בא שליח בית דין ונוטל האחת: ותרומה כל חמש. דאסור להפסיד קדשים בידים כל זמן שיכול לאוכלן: ושורפין בתחלת שש. דהא ודאי רובא טעו בין שש לשבע: **גמ'** אחד אומר בשנים בחדש. הרג זה את הנפש ואחד מן העדים אומר בשלשה בחדש עדותן קיימת ובית דין היו בודקין אותן בשבע חקירות כדלקמן וכיון דהוחשו שניהן לומר בשלישי או ברביעי וכשבדקום איזה יום בחדש אמר זה בשני וזה אמר בשלישי שניהן על יום אחד העידו אלא שזה ידע בעיבורו של חודש שחודש שעבר מלא והוקבע ר"ח ביום שלשים ואחד וזה שאמר בשנים בחדש ידע בו וזה שאמר שלשה סבור שהוקבע החדש ביום שלשים והואיל ויש טועין בכך אע"פ שמכוונין אנו לחלק את עדותן כדי שתתבטל להציל את הנפש אין בידינו כח לחלקו: עדותן בטלה. דבהא ליכא למטעי וקרא כתיב (דברים יג) ודרשת וחקרת והנה אמת נכון שתהא עדותן מכוונת ואי לא לא קטלינן והוא והן פטורים דאין עדים נהרגין אלא על ידי הזמה: אחד אומר בשתי שעות כו' עדותן קיימת. דטועה אדם בכך: אחד אומר בחמש ואחד אומר בשבע עדותן בטלה. אפילו לרבי יהודה דבחמש חמה במזרחו של רקיע ויכול להבין על ידי הצל כשנותן ידו כנגד המזרח הוה הצל לצד מערב: ובשבע חמה במערב. והצל לצד מזרח: כשתמצא לומר. כשתדקדק בדבריהם ותעמוד על מכוונו תמצא לדברי רבי מאיר דמקיים עדות דב' וג' ומבטל של ג' ושל ה' אין אדם טועה ולא כלום ולדברי רבי יהודה דמקיים אף שלש וחמש אדם טועה חצי שעה לרבי מאיר אין אדם טועה (ג) כלום והטועה שקרן הוא והאי דמקיים רבי מאיר עדות של שתים ושלש משום ששניהם העידו על רגע אחד דמעשה כי הוה במיפק תרתי ומעייל תלת ביציאתה של שניה כשהשלישית נכנסת ושניהן כך העידו דהאי דאמר שתים בסוף שניה קאמר והאי דקאמר כו' ולקמן פריך מי יודע שכוונתן לכך היתה דילמא האי דקאמר שתים בתחלת שתים קאמר ויש חילוק ביניהן והואיל ולר"מ אין תולין בטעות הרי הן שקרנין: ולדברי רבי יהודה תולין בטעות חצי שעה. הילכך כי אמר האי בשלש והאי בחמש עדותן קיימת דמעשה כי הוה בפלגא דארבע כו' וזה אמר בסוף שלש וזה בתחלת חמש וכל אחד מהן טעה מן המעשה חצי שעה ולקמיה פריך ליה היכי מהדרינן לגרופי עדותן הוה לן למימר דהאי בתחלת ג' קאמר והאי בסוף חמש קאמר ויש חילוק גדול ביניהן וכולי האי לא טעו ותחלק עדותן ונציל את הנפש: וחד מנייהו קא טעי משהו. אם בסוף שתים הוה האי דקאמר שלש בתחלת שלש וקא טעי משהו ואי בתחלת שלש האי דקאמר שתים בסוף שתים וקא טעי משהו: לדברי רבי יהודה. מעשה הוה בסוף שלש

תוספות

זה ידע בעיבורו של חדש. וה"ה דה"מ למימר זה ידע בחסרונו של חדש וזה לא ידע דחדש שעבר חסר היה והקשה ריב"א ומה אלו דייקינן בהכי שהדי דתרווייהו ידעי בעיבורו של חדש וה"ל עדות מוכחשת ולאו דניקום וניקטול מספיקא דהכי פריך בסמוך ואע"ג דבפ' בן סורר (סנהד' סט.) דייק מהכא דרובא דאינשי עבידי דטעי בעיבורא דירחא מ"מ מה נפסיד אם נדקדק בהם וי"ל דהכא דייקינן בהו שפיר כיון דשייל' להו באיזה יום וקמיכווני ליום אחד ש"מ שזה לא ידע ומ"מ שפיר מוכיח בבן סורר (שם) מהכא דאזלינן בתר רובא בדיני נפשות דרובא טעי בעיבורא דירחא דאי לא אזלי' בתר רובא כיון שזה אומר בשנים וזה אומר בשלשה מיד ה"ל מוכחשין וכי הדר מכוונים ליום אחד הוה ה"ל חוזר ומגיד תדע דהא אחד אומר בב' ואחד אומר בה' עדותן בטלה אע"פ שמכוונים ליום אחד ולא אמרינן דטעו בשני עיבורים דבתרי עיבורי לא טעו אינשי וחשבינן להו חוזר ומגיד: **אחד** אומר בשתי שעות. וא"ת אמאי עדותן קיימת אילו דייקינן בהכי שהדי הא דקאמר שתים בתחלת שתים וה"ל קודם הנץ החמה ועדותן בטלה כדאמר לקמן דתחלת שעה שניה קודם הנץ החמה הוא דמהלך אדם ביום עשר פרסה שהן מ' מילין ומעלות השחר עד הנץ החמה מהלך ה' מילין כדאמר במי שהיה טמא (לקמן צג:) וזה עולה לשעה ומחצה וי"ל כשזה אומר קודם הנץ החמה וזה אומר לאחר הנץ החמה למדקדקין בהכן לא טעו אינשי אבל הכי לא דקדקו אלא בשעות ואין בני אדם בקיאין בשעות וסבורין שהשניה התחילה אחר הנץ החמה: אלא

עין משפט נר מצוה

פו א מיי' פ"ח מהל' חמץ ומצה הלכה ט סמג לאוין עו טוש"ע או"ח סי' תמג סעיף א:

פז ב מיי' פ"ב מהלכות עדות הל' ד טוש"ע ח"מ סי' ל סעיף ז:

פח ג שם הלכה ה:

[נ"ל מקדרין וכ"ה בעדיות פ"ג מי"ב וכן בביצ' כג. במשנה ובגמ' וכןבערוך וכ"ה בתוספת' דביצה פ"ב וכ"ה בתוי"ט]

רבינו חננאל

ולרבי יהודה מי אמרינן אדם בהול על ממונו דאי שרית ליה בחדא אתי למעבד טובא והתנן ביום טוב בפ"ב ר' יהודה אומר אין מקדרין ביום טוב מפני שעושה חבורה אבל מקרצפין וחכמים אומרים אין מקדרין אף לא מקרצפין והתניא איזהו קידור קטנים ועושין חבורה ואיזהו קרצוף גדולים ואין עושין חבורה פי' קידור כמו תולעים והן רמש כנון אינבא שנושכין בבשר הבהמה ואין מפרידין הקטנים מבשר הבהמה אלא בעשיית חבורה כנון האלכא שאין שולפין אותה מן השער אלא בקושי אבל הפרדת העדולים נקראת קרצוף והנה התיר ר' יהודה הקרצוף ולא (התיר) [חשש] מתוך שזה בהול על ממונו כיון שתתיר לו הקרצוף שמא יעשה הוא קירוד ופרקי' התם גבי קירוד דלא מתה הבהמה מנשיכת הרמש הזה אבל צערא בעלמא הוא דאית ליה לא גזר רבי יהודה הקרצוף אטו קירוד דקירוד נמי אפשר דעביד ליה לאורתא אבל הכא גבי בכור אי שרית ליה במקום שאין עושין בו מום כיון שהוא בהול על ממונו אתי למעבר במקום שעושין בו מום וחמץ נמי דמיחלף במצה דכולה פת היא גזר ר' יהודה קרצוף בקירוד דלא מיחלף דהני גדולי' והני קטנים לא גזר: מתני' ר' יהודה אומר אוכלין כל ארבע ותולין כל חמש ושורפין בתחלת שש. פי' חייש ר' יהודה דילמא אתי למטעי בין שעה רביעית לששית: תנן התם בסנהדרין פ"ה אחד אומר בשתים בחדש ואחד אומר בשלשה עדותן קיימת פי' שניהם ביום אחד מעידין אלא שהאומר בשנים יודע שהחדש שיצא מעובר היה והאומר שלשה לא היה יודע שהחדש שיצא מעובר היה אלא מחשב לו יום שלשים מהחדש שנכנס ולפיכך אמר שלשה אחד אומר בשתי שעות ביום ואחד אומר בשלש עדותן קיימת אחד אומר בשלש ואחד אומר בחמש עדותן בטלה ר' יהודה אומר עדותן קיימת ואתי אביי ואוקמינהו ללישנא קמא דידיה לדברי ר"מ אין אדם טועה ולא כלום לדברי ר' יהודה אדם טועה חצי שעה וללישנא בתרא לדברי

מסורת הש"ס

ביצה כג. [עדיות פ"ג מי"ב]

ביצה שם. [תוספתא דביצה פ"ב]

לעיל ד: לקמן כא.

[במשנה שבמשניות ליתא גב וכן גרס התוי"ט]

הגהות הב"ח

(א) גמ' בשלשה בחדש עדותן קיימת: (ב) שם ואחד אומר בחמש עדותן בטלה ר' יהודה אומר כצ"ל ותיבות דברי ר' מאיר נמחק: (ג) רש"י ד"ה כשתמצא לומר וכו' טועה ולא כלום והטועה שקרן:

גליון הש"ס

גמ' ומ"ש גבי קרצוף. ק"ל הא קידור הוא רק דרבנן דהא אינו מתכוין ולא הוי פ"ר כמבואר להדי' בביצה דאמר ר"י לטעמיה דדשא"מ אסור וא"כ הוי רק איסור דרבנן דהא בשבת דף מא ע"ב בתו' ד"ה מיחם כתבו דלר"י דבר שאינו מתכוין בשבת הוי דרבנן וכ"כ תוס' ביומא דף לד ע"ב וכ"כ רש"י בשבת דף קכא ע"ב ד"ה לפי תומו ואם כן מש"ה לא גזר קירצוף אטו קידור דקידור גופיה הוא דרבנן אבל בחמץ גזרינן שמא יאכל דהוי דאורייתא ועי"ג. אח"ז מצאתי בעזה"י שהקשו כן בתוס' ישנים יומא דף לד ע"ב:

שלא ברצון חכמים (הן עושין) דברי ר"מ רבי יהודה אומר ברצון חכמים היו עושין ולא קא גזר ר' יהודה דילמא אתי למיכל מיניה אמר (א) *רבא שאני חדש מתוך שלא התרת לו אלא על ידי קטוף הוא זכור א"ל אביי תינח בשעת קטיפה טחינה והרקדה מאי איכא למימר הא לא קשיא טחינה ברחיא דיד הרקדה ע"ג נפה אלא הא דתנן *קוצרין בית השלחים ושבעמקים אבל לא גודשין ואוקימנא כרבי יהודה מאי איכא למימר אלא אמר אביי חדש בדיל מיניה חמץ לא בדיל מיניה אמר רבא דרבי יהודה אדרבי יהודה קשיא דרבנן אדרבנן לא קשיא (ב) דר' יהודה אדר' יהודה לא קשיא כדשנינן דרבנן אדרבנן נמי לא קשיא הוא עצמו מחזר עליו לשורפו מיכל קאכיל מיניה רב אשי אמר דר' יהודה אדר' יהודה לא קשיא קמח וקלי תנן (ג) הא דרב אשי *בדותא היא התינח מקלי ואילך מעיקרא עד קלי מאי איכא למימר וכי ת"ל על ידי קיטוף כדרבא אלא קוצרין בית השלחין ושבעמקים ואוקימנא כרבי יהודה מאי איכא למימר אלא דרב אשי בדותא היא וכל היכא דלא בדיל מיניה מי גזר רבי יהודה *והתנן *לא יקוב אדם שפופרת של ביצה וימלאנה שמן ויתננה בצד הנר בשביל שתהא מנטפת ואפי' היא של חרס ור' יהודה מתיר התם משום חומרא דשבת מבדל בדילי ורמי דשבת אשבת *דתניא חבל דלי שנפסק לא יהא קושרו אלא עונבו רבי יהודה אומר כורך עליו פונדא או פסקיא ובלבד שלא יענבנו קשיא דרבי יהודה אדרבי יהודה קשיא דרבנן אדרבנן דרבנן לא קשיא שמן בשמן מיחלף עניבה בקשירה לא מיחלף דרבי יהודה אדר' יהודה לא קשיא טעמא דרבי יהודה לאו משום דגזר עניבה אטו קשירה אלא משום דקסבר עניבה גופה קשירה היא ורמי רבנן אדרבנן *דתנן *קושרין דלי בפסקיא אבל לא בחבל ורבי יהודה מתיר חבל דמאי אילימא חבל דעלמא ורבי יהודה מתיר קשר של קיימא הוא דוודאי אתי לבטולי אלא פשיטא דגרדי וגזרו רבנן חבל דגרדי אטו חבל דעלמא אין חבל בחבל מיחלף עניבה בקשירה לא מיחלפא וכל היכא דבדיל מיניה לא גזר רבי יהודה (ד) והתניא *בכור שאחזו דם אפי' הוא מת אין מקיזין לו דם דברי ר' יהודה וחכ"א *יקיז ובלבד שלא יטיל בו מום התם מתוך שאדם בהול

על

שלא ברצון חכמים. דאיכא למיגזר דילמא כי מעסקי ביה אתי למיכל מיניה: ר' יהודה אומר כו' מתוך שלא התרתיה לו. קצירה כדרך כל השנה אלא בידים קוטפין המלילות מן הקרקע דהא אסור לקצור לפני העומר דכתיב (ויקרא כג) עומר ראשית קצירכם אל הכהן שהוא תחלה לקצירה זכור הוא את איסור החדש על ידי שינוי המעשה לא אתי למיכל: טחינה והרקדה. שהרי קמח תנינא דהיה בידם וכשטחנוהו והרקידוהו איזה שינוי היה שם דלא ליתי למיתב לפומיה: ומשנינן טחינה. לא היו טוחנין אותו ברחים של מים אלא ברחים של יד דהוי שינוי לזכרון: על גבי נפה. לגב תחתון של נפה הופך הנפה על פניה: אלא הא דתנן. במנחות קוצרין בית השלחין כדרך חול קודם לעומר: ושל בית העמקים. תבואה הגדילה בין העמקים וטעמא מפרש התם כתוב אחד אומר וקצרתם את קצירה והבאתם אלמא מותר לקצור קודם לעומר וכתוב אחד אומר עומר ראשית קצירכם דמשמע שהוא קודם לכל קציר הא כיצד ממקום שאתה מביא עומר אי אתה קוצר קודם לו וממקום שאי אתה מביא עומר אתה קוצר ותנן בפרק כל הקרבנות (מנחות סה.) אין מביאין סולת למנחה לא מבית הזבלין ולא מבית השלחין ולא מבית העמקים מפני שתבואה שלהן אינה מן המובחר: מאי איכא למימר. הא ליכא התם שינוייא דהא קוצרין קתני ובמגל ולא גזרינן דילמא אתי למיכל ואוקימנא להסיא כר' יהודה במסכת מנחות בפרק ר' ישמעאל (דף עא.) מדקתני סיפא אנשי יריחו קוצרין לפני העומר כו' ולא מיחו בידם חכמים ואמרינן מאן שמעת ליה דאמר מיחו ולא מיחו ר' יהודה: חדש מבדל בדילי מיניה. שהרי לא הורגלו לאוכלו כל השנה ואין למודין לפשוט יד להושיט לפיהם אבל חמץ למודין הן בכך כל השנה: דרבנן אדרבנן לא קשיא. בתמיה דלא משנית אלא לר' יהודה והא דרבנן נמי קשיא דבמתני' לא גזרינן והתם קתני שלא ברצון חכמים דמשמע דגזר ר' מאיר דהוא מבני פלוגתיה דילמא אתי למיכל: הוא עצמו מחזר עליו לשורפו. אע"ג דבעלמא גזרינן בדבר שעסוק בו שלא יושיט לפיו הכא בבדיקת חמץ ליכא למיגזר דהוא עצמו כל עסקו זה בחמץ אינו אלא מחזר עליו לשורפו אין לך זכרון לאיסור גדול מזה: ומיכל קא אכיל מיניה. בתמיה: קמח וקלי תנן. ואין אלו ראויין לאכילה: מקלי ואילך. לאחר שנתייבש בתנור אין ראוי לאכול: מעיקרא. בעודו רך בקליות קודם שיתייבש מאי איכא למימר: וכי תימא. זכור הוא ע"י הקיטוף כדשני רבא לעיל בית השלחים דליכא קיטוף מאי איכא למימר: אלא בדותא. וטעמא דרבי יהודה משום דבדילי מיניה וחמץ לא בדיל מיניה שרגיל בו כל שעה: כל נר שבגמ' היינו הכלי קרויסו"ל: מנטפת. טיפין דקות כשהפתילה מבערת: ואפי' היא של חרס. אותה שפופרת דמאיסא אפ"ה אסור דילמא אתי למיכל מינה ותניא *המותן שמן לנר חייב משום מבעיר והמסתפק ממנו חייב משום מכבה: ורבי יהודה מתיר. ואע"ג דשמן הכל מדירין בו ודרבנן אדרבנן ליכא לאקשויי דהא אוקימנא טעמא בחמץ משום דהוא עצמו מחזר עליו לשורפו: קשר של קיימא. שהוא עשוי שלא להתירו לעולם הוי אב מלאכה במסכת שבת: לא יהא קושרו. דהוי קשר של קיימא אלא עונבו ולא גזרי' עניבה אטו קשירה: כורך. כריכה בעלמא: פונדא. אזור חלול: פסקייא. פיישל"א שכורכין סביבות שוקיים: שלא יענבנו. גזירה משום קשירה הואיל ועסוק בכך: קשיא דרבנן. דשפופרת אדרבנן דחבל: שמן. זה בשמן דכל שנה מיחלף ואתי למיכליה: קושרין דלי בפסיקייא. דלאו קשר שעשוי להתקיים הוא דאינו מפסיד פסיקייא שלו בכך: אבל לא בחבל. שמא יניחנו שם עולמית: אי נימא חבל דעלמא. שתשמישו לכך ואיכא למיחש שמא יניחנו שם: חבל דגרדי. שאינו ראוי למילוי מים תמיד ורבי יהודה מתיר ולא גזר גבי שבת כדאוקימנא טעמא דמשום חומרא דשבת פרשי אינשי מאיסורא דיליה ומזכרין הן אבל דרבנן דהכא אדרבנן דעניבה קשיא: ומשנינן חבל בחבל מיחלף כו'. והשתא איתרצו כולהו דרבנן גזרו כל היכא דמיחלף בין בשבת בין בשאר איסורי הילכך בחדש לפני העומר גזרו וכן בשפופרת וכן בחבל אבל (ה) בחמץ לא משום דמוזהר עליו לשורפו ובעניבה נמי לא משום דלא מיחלפא ורבי יהודה גזר בכל מילי דלא בדילי מיניה ובמידי דבדילי מיניה לא גזר הילכך בחמץ גזר אבל בחדש בדילי מיניה ובכל הנך דשבת משום דבדילי מינייהו ודקא מחמיר בעניבה משום דקסבר היא גופה קשירה היא: בכור. אסור להטיל בו מום ואפי' לגרום כדתניא מום לא יהיה בו אין לי אלא שלא יפיל בו מום מניין שלא יגרום לו ת"ל כל מום במסכת ביצה (ד' כז:): אין מקיזין דם. אפי' במקום שאינו עושה בו מום דהיינו בכל מקום שבו אם אינו חותך ממנו עצם או פוגם שפתו או אזנו וכל דבר שאינו חוזר לקדמותו הוי מום אידך לא הוי מום וקא גזר רבי יהודה אטו מקום שעושה בו מום ואע"ג דקדשים הכל בדילין מהן מחלוקת רבי שמעון ורבי יהודה בתורת כהנים*:

על

קוצרין בית השלחין. פירש רש"י ממקום שאי אתה מביא אתה קוצר וכו' ובית השלחין וכל הנהו אע"ג דפסיל בפרק כל הקרבנות (מנחות דף סה.) אם הביא כשר כיון דלכתחלה לא יביא חשבינן ליה ממקום שאי אתה מביא ואין לתמוה מי איכא מידי דמדאורייתא לכתחלה אסור ובדיעבד שרי דהיכא מילי טובא דבפרק שישנה הכתוב עליו לעכב כגון קדשים: אבל לא גודשין. דבגדישה ליכא פסידה אם יתעכב אחר העומר דדוקא משום פסידה התירו קצירה שממהרין ליקצר משאר פירות ואי לא קצרי להו פסדי והא דשרי רבי יהודה קמח וקלי לעיל יש לומר משום שעולי רגלים הקילו ור' מאיר אוסר בקמח ושרי קצירה לקמן בפ' מקום שנהגו (דף נ.) דקתני במילתיה קוצרין ברצון חכמים והיינו משום פסידה וכן פי' הקונטרס במנחות ואם תאמר א"כ מאי פריך דילמא הכא שרי רבי יהודה משום פסידה אבל גבי חמץ גזרינן ויש לומר משום מצות ביעור יש להתיר כמו משום פסידה: כורך עליו פונדא. לאו דוקא כורך דאפילו לקשור יכול דלא מבטל ליה ובלבד שלא יענבנו אחבל קאי: כל היכא דבדיל מיניה לא גזר ר' יהודה. דר' מאיר אדר"מ לא רצה להקשות דלעיל גזר גבי חדש וגבי בכור לא גזר דבפרק כל פסולי המוקדשין (בכורות לג: ושם) תניא בכור שאחזו דם מקיזין לו במקום שאין עושין לו מום דברי ר' מאיר ורבי יהודה אומר וכו' משום דאיכא לשנויי שאני בכור דאיכא פסידא:

זה

עין משפט נר מצוה

פג א מיי' פ"ה מהל' שבת הלכה יב סמג לאוין סה טוש"ע א"ח סי' רפ סעיף א:

פד ב מיי' פ"י מהלכות שבת הלכה ג סמג לאוין סה טוש"ע א"ח סי' שיז סעיף ד:

פה ג מיי' פ"ב מהלכות בכורות הל' יג סמג לאוין שמג טוש"ע י"ד סי' שיג סעיף ו:

רבינו חננאל

שבא לדלוק. ואקשי' ומי גזר ר' יהודה והתנן במנחות פ'[ר"י] שקרב העומר יוצאין ומוצאין שוקי ירושלים מלאין קמח וקלי שלא ברצון חכמים דברי ר' מאיר ר' יהודה אומר ברצון חכמים היו עושין דאלמא מתעסקין היו בחדש בזמן איסורו ולא גזר ר' יהודה ש"א יאכל ממנו ופריק רבא שאני חדש הואיל ולא התירו חכמים לקצור כדרכו. אלא בקטוף כדכתיב (דברים כג כו) וקטפת מלילות זכור הוא כי אסור לאכול מן החדש וכן בטחינה לא התירו לטוחנו אלא ברחים של יד והרקדה ע"ג נפה כיון דחזי כל הני שינויי אתי למדכר ולאימנועי. ואקשי' בית השלחין דתנן קוצרין בית השלחין מה איכא למימר הנה קוצרין בלא שינוי ופריק אביי חדש בדיל מיניה פי' מובדל הוא ממנו ואינו אוכלו אלא עד שיראה שהותר אבל החמץ שאינו מובדל ממנו כלל אלא אוכלו יתראה לו פי פתתירו עומד ויבא לאכול ממנו לפיפפוהו עליו. אמרי' עלה והא דקשיא ר' יהודה אדר' יהודה שנינן כאביי והא דתנינן במתנית' בלשון חכמים הוא ר' מאיר קשיא דר' מאיר אדר' מאיר אמאי בחמץ לא גזר ובחדש גזר משנינן (הנה נמי) [הוא עצמו] מחזר על (הפסח) [החמץ] לשרפו ואל אותו לפיכך לא גזרו אבל החדש דלא מתעסק ביה כדי לשרפו אלא כדי לאכלו מתעסק ביה גזרינן ביה ובא רב אשי לפרש שאני חדש דקמח וקלי תנן כלומר לא התירו לו אלא על ידי קליה ודחי' לה הכי הא בדותא היא כלומר חיצונה היא ולא נשנית בין החכמים ואקשי' אפירוקא דאביי וכללא הוא דכל היכא דלא בדיל מינה גזר ביה ר' יהודה והתנן לא יקוב אדם שפופרת של ביצה כו' ור' יהודה מתיר הנה השמן לא בדיל מיניה ולא גזר ר' יהודה שמא יסתפק מן השמן שבשפופרת של ביצה ושנינ' שאני שבת דחמיר ליה: אינו והא קשירות דלי בחבל דבשבת היא וחכמים מתירין לענבו ור' יהודה אוסר קשיא דרבנן אדרבנן ודר' יהודה אדר' יהודה ושני' רבנן אסרי בשפופרת דכיון דלא מאיפא אתי לאסתפוקי מיניה דשמן בשמן מיחלף כלומר [הרואה] אותך אוכל שמן

מסורת הש"ס

[במנחות סז: פיסקא רבה]

מנחות עא.

[ביצה כב.]

[ועי' בכורות לג:]

הגהות הב"ח

(א) גמ' אמר רבא שאני חדש: (ב) שם דרבנן אדרבנן לא קשיא אלא אמר רבא דר' יהודה אדרבי יהודה: (ג) שם וקלי תנן הא דר' אשי וכו' על ידי קיטוף כדרבא אלא: (ד) שם והתניא בכור שאחזו דם: (ה) רש"י ד"ה ומשנינן וכו' בחמץ לא משום דמחזר עליו לשורפו:

לא יקשור דאתי למימר אלו היתה קשירה מותרת לא היה עונב אלא קושר לפיכך לא גזרו בו ור' יהודה לא אלא משום דגזר עניבה אטו קשירה אלא משום דאמר העניבה קשירה מעליא היא והא דרבנן אדרבנן קושרין דלי בפסקיא אבל לא בחבל כו' ור' יהודה אומר בהדיא כל קשר שאינו של קיימא מותר וכן הא דרמינן אדר' יהודה והתניא בכור שאחזו דם כו' דברים פשוטין הן:

Jerusalem filled with flour and parched corn,[6] [11a] [but] not with the consent of the Sages:[7] this is R. Meir's opinion. R. Judah said: They acted with the consent of the Sages.[8] Thus R. Judah did not preventively forbid lest one come to eat thereof?—Said Raba:[9] *Ḥadash*[5] is different: since you permit it to him only by means of plucking,[10] he remembers.[11] Said Abaye to him: That is well at the time of plucking, [but] what can be said of the grinding and sifting?[12]—That is no difficulty: grinding [is done] with a handmill; sifting [is done] on top of the sieve.[13] But as to what we learned: 'One may reap an artificially irrigated field and [the corn] in the valleys,[14] but one may not stack [the corn]',[15] and we established this as [agreeing with] R. Judah, what can be said?[16]
a —Rather, said Abaye: From *ḥadash* one holds aloof[1] but one does not hold aloof from leaven.[2] Raba demurred: R. Judah is self-contradictory, while the Rabbis are not self-contradictory?[3] —Rather, said Raba: R. Judah is not self-contradictory, as we have answered. The Rabbis too are not self-contradictory: he himself is seeking it in order to burn it, shall he then eat thereof![4] R. Ashi said: R. Judah is not self-contradictory, [for] we learned,[5] 'flour and parched corn'.[6] But this [answer] of R. Ashi is a fiction:[7] this is well from [the time when it is] parched ears and onwards; but from the beginning until it is parched corn, what can be said?[8] And should you answer, [It is gathered] by plucking,[9] as Raba [answered], then what can be said of [what we learnt that] 'One may reap an artificially irrigated field and [the corn in] the valleys', which we established as [agreeing with] R. Judah?[10] Hence R. Ashi's [answer] is a fiction.

But, wherever one does not [normally] hold aloof, did R. Judah preventively forbid? Surely we learned: A man may not pierce an eggshell, fill it with oil, and place it over the mouth of a [burning] lamp, in order that it should drip,[11] and even if it is of earthenware; but R. Judah permits it![12]—There, on account of the strictness of the Sabbath he will indeed keep aloof. Then [one ruling] of the Sabbath can be opposed to [another ruling] of the Sabbath. For it was taught: If the cord of a bucket is broken, one must
b not tie[1] it [together] but merely make a loop [slip-knot]; whereas R. Judah maintains: He may wind a hollow belt or a fascia[2] around it, providing that he does not tie it with a slip-knot.[3] [Thus] R. Judah's [views] are self-contradictory, and similarly the Rabbis'?—The Rabbis' [views] are not self-contradictory: oil [from one source] can be interchanged with oil [from another];[4] whereas looping cannot be mistaken for[5] knotting. R. Judah's [views] are not self-contradictory; R. Judah's reason is not that he forbids looping on account of knotting, but because looping itself is [a form of] knotting. Now, the Rabbis may be opposed to the Rabbis. For we learned: A bucket [over a well] may be tied with a fascia but not with a cord;[6] but R. Judah permits it.[7] Now what cord is meant: Shall we say an ordinary [bucket] cord: [how does it state] 'R. Judah permits it',—surely it is a permanent knot, for he will certainly come to abandon it?[8] Hence it is obvious that a weaver's [rope[9] is meant], and [yet] the Rabbis preventively forbid a weaver's cord on account of an ordinary cord?—Even so: one rope may be mistaken for another, [whereas] looping cannot be mistaken for knotting.

But, wherever one [normally] holds aloof from it, does not R. Judah preventively forbid? Surely we learned: If a firstling is attacked with congestion, even if it should die [otherwise], we must not bleed it: this is R. Judah's view;[10] but the Sages rule: He may bleed [it], providing that he does not inflict a [permanent]

(6) Of the new harvest; v. Lev. XXIII, 9—14. Of course, in order to have it ready for sale on the same day the vendors must have prepared it before, and thus they handled it while it was yet prohibited. (7) Lest they eat of it while preparing it. (8) V. Men. 67*b*. (9) BaḤ emends to Rabbah, which is the reading in Men. 67*b*. (10) The new corn may not be reaped at all before the bringing of the *'omer*, but must be plucked by hand. (11) That it may not be eaten. (12) There is nothing to remind him then of the interdict. (13) The sieve is reversed. The unusual ways in which these are done serve as reminders. (14) In the usual way, before the *'omer*. (15) V. Men. 71*a*. (16) There is nothing there to remind one of the prohibition.
a (1) As it is forbidden at all times until the *'omer*, when it ceases to be *ḥadash*. Thus he is accustomed to abstain from it and is not likely to forget himself. (2) During the year, and thus may possibly eat of it when the prohibition is already in force. (3) That you seek to reconcile R. Judah's views only. Yet surely the Rabbis too need harmonizing, for whereas the Rabbis do not preventively forbid in the case of leaven, they do so here, as R. Meir states, 'They did not act with the consent of the Sages'. (4) Surely we need not entertain that fear. (5) In the above cited Mishnah. (6) Which are not fit for eating. (7) בדותא V. B.M., 9*a*, n. c1. (8) In the intermediate stages it is fit for eating! How could it then be handled. (9) Which serves as a reminder. (10) Though there is nothing there to serve as a reminder, v. *infra*. (11) And replenish the contents of the lamp during Sabbath. (12) The reason of the Rabbis is lest he take the oil for eating, which constitutes extinguishing. R. Judah permits it, though one does not normally abstain from oil, v. Shab. 29*a*.
b (1) The tying of a permanent knot constitutes one of the thirty-nine principal classes of forbidden work on Sabbath. (2) A band or fillet. (3) V. Shab. 113*a*. (4) Just as he consumes oil from elsewhere, so may he come to draw supplies from this eggshell, seeing no difference. (5) Lit., 'interchanged with'. (6) On the Sabbath. The first is certainly only temporary, but the second may be left there, and thus a permanent knot will have been tied on the Sabbath. (7) V. Shab. 113*b*. (8) I.e., leave it there as a thing having no other purpose than this. (9) Which is not usually used for drawing water, and will not consequently be left there. (10) One must not inflict a permanent blemish on a firstling. R. Judah rules that the animal must not be bled even without inflicting a permanent blemish upon it, lest one come to do so even by making a permanent blemish. Thus R. Judah forbids preventively, though people do hold aloof from sacred animals, to which category a firstling belongs.

the Sages maintain: It is all *ḥullin*. [10*b*] If a man left [leaven] in this corner and finds [leaven] in another corner, there is a controversy of R. Simeon b. Gamaliel and the Rabbis. For it was taught: If an axe is lost in a house, the house is unclean, for I assume: An unclean person entered there and removed it. R. Simeon b. Gamaliel said: The house is clean, for I assume, He lent it to another and forgot, or he took it from one corner and placed it in another corner and forgot. Who mentioned anything about a corner?[6] The text is defective, and is thus taught: If an axe is lost in a house, the house is unclean, for I say: An unclean person entered there and took it. Or if he leaves it in one corner and finds it in another corner the house is unclean, for I assume, An unclean person entered there and took it from one corner and placed it in another corner. R. Simeon b. Gamaliel said: The house is clean, for I say, He lent it to another and forgot, or he took it from one corner and placed it in another corner and forgot.[7]

Raba said: If a mouse enters [a room] with a loaf in its mouth and he [the owner] enters after him and finds crumbs, a [fresh] search is necessary,[8] because it is not a mouse's nature to make
a crumbs.[1] Raba also said: If a child enters [a room] with a loaf in his hand, and he [the owner] enters after him and finds crumbs, a [fresh] search is not necessary, because it is a child's nature to make crumbs.

Raba asked: What if a mouse enters with a loaf in its mouth, and a mouse goes out with a loaf in its mouth: do we say, the same which went in went out; or perhaps it is a different one? Should you answer, the same which went in went out,—what if a white mouse entered with a loaf in its mouth, and a black mouse went out with a loaf in its mouth? Now this is certainly a different one; or perhaps it did indeed seize[2] it from the other? And should you say, Mice do not seize from each other,—what if a mouse enters with a loaf in its mouth and a weasel goes out with a loaf in its mouth? Now the weasel certainly does take from a mouse; or perhaps it is a different one, for had it snatched it from the mouse, the *mouse* would have [now] been found in its mouth? And should you say, had it snatched it from the mouse, the *mouse* would have been found in its mouth, what if a mouse enters with a loaf in its mouth, and then a weasel comes out with a loaf and a mouse in the weasel's mouth? Here it is certainly the same; or perhaps, if it were the same, the loaf should indeed have been found in the *mouse's* mouth; or perhaps it fell out [of the mouse's mouth] on account of [its] terror, and it [the weasel] took it? The question stands over.

Raba asked: If there is a loaf on the top rafters, need he [take] a ladder to fetch it down or not? Do we say, our Rabbis did not put him to all this trouble, [for] since it cannot descend of its own accord he will not come to eat it;[3] or perhaps it may fall down and he will come to eat it? Now should you say, it may fall down and he will come to eat it,—if there is a loaf in a pit, does he need a ladder to fetch it up or not? Here it will certainly not happen that it will ascend of its own accord; or perhaps he may happen to go down to perform his requirements and come to eat it? Should you say that he may happen to go down for his purposes and come to eat it,—if a loaf is in a snake's mouth, does he need a snake-charmer to take it out or does he not need [one]? [Do we say,] our Rabbis put him to *personal* trouble, but they did not put him to trouble with his money; or perhaps there is no difference? The questions stand over.

MISHNAH. R. JUDAH SAID: WE SEARCH [FOR LEAVEN]
b ON THE EVENING OF THE FOURTEENTH, AND[1] IN THE MORNING OF THE FOURTEENTH, AND AT THE TIME OF REMOVAL. BUT THE SAGES MAINTAIN: IF HE DID NOT SEARCH IN THE EVENING OF THE FOURTEENTH, HE MUST SEARCH ON THE FOURTEENTH; IF HE DID NOT SEARCH IN [THE MORNING OF] THE FOURTEENTH, HE MUST SEARCH AT THE APPOINTED TIME;[2] IF HE DID NOT SEARCH AT THE APPOINTED TIME, HE MUST SEARCH AFTER THE APPOINTED TIME.[3] AND WHAT HE LEAVES OVER[4] HE MUST PUT AWAY IN A HIDDEN PLACE, SO THAT HE SHOULD NOT NEED SEARCHING AFTER IT.

GEMARA. What is R. Judah's reason?—R. Ḥisda and Rabbah son of R. Huna both say, It [the threefold searching] corresponds to the three 'puttings away' mentioned in the Torah: *and there shall no leavened bread be* seen *with thee, neither shall there be leaven* seen *with thee;*[5] *seven days shall there be no leaven* found *in your houses;*[6] and *even on the first day shall ye* put away *leaven out of your houses.*[7] R. Joseph objected: R. Judah said: He who has not searched at these three periods can no longer search, which proves that they
c differ only in respect of from now and henceforth![1] Mar Zuṭra recited it thus: R. Joseph objected: R. Judah said: He who has not searched at *one* of these three periods can no longer search, which proves that they differ in [whether] he can no longer search?—Rather R. Judah too means, where he has not searched,[2] and here they differ in this: one Master[3] holds, only before it is forbidden;[4] but not after it is forbidden, as a preventive measure, lest he come to eat of it; while the Rabbis hold that we do not preventively forbid. But did R. Judah preventively forbid lest he come to eat thereof,—surely we learned: As soon as the *'omer*[5] has been offered, they used to go out and find the markets of

(6) We are discussing the case where it is *lost*. (7) Thus here too, according to the Rabbis we fear that mice have been about, and consequently we also fear that the leaven he now finds is not the same which he left, so that a re-search is required. But on R. Simeon b. Gamaliel's view we do not fear this. (8) To find leaven with which the mouse was seen to enter.

a (1) Therefore these are not merely the loaf crumbled up. (2) Lit., 'throw'. (3) Therefore he may leave it there, and merely annul it.

b (1) So presumably; v. Gemara. (2) *Sc.* of removal, i.e., in the sixth hour (11 a.m.—noon). (3) From noon until nightfall (Rashi). Tosaf. explains differently: 'within the *mo'ed*', from noon on the fourteenth until the end of Passover, translating *mo'ed* as festival, which meaning it generally bears; 'after the *mo'ed*', after Passover, for leaven kept in the house during Passover is forbidden after Passover. (4) 'After the search in the evening, for the following morning's meal' (R. Nissim). (5) Ex. XIII, 7. (6) Ibid. XII, 19. (7) Ibid. 15.—*'Seen' 'found'* and *'put away'* all mean in practice that the leaven must be put away, and corresponding to each expression there must be a search.

c (1) I.e., after the time of removal, R. Judah holding that there is no searching then, while the Sages maintain that there is. But before that all agree that only *one* search is necessary. R. Judah meaning *either* in the evening *or* in the morning etc., the *waw* (translated 'AND' in the Mishnah) being disjunctive, *or*. (2) In the evening; then he must search in the morning. (3) R. Judah. (4) Must one search then. (5) V. Glos.

הניח בזוית זו ומצא בזוית אחרת פלוגתא דרשב"ג ורבנן דתניא קרדום שאבד בבית הבית טמא שאני אומר אדם טמא נכנס לשם ונטלו רשב"ג אומר הבית טהור שאני אומר השאילו לאחר ושכח או שנטלו מזוית זו והניח בזוית האחרת ושכח זוית מאן דכר שמיה חסורי מחסרא והכי קתני *קרדום שאבד בבית הבית טמא שאני אומר אדם טמא נכנס לשם ונטלו או שהניחו בזוית זו ומצאו בזוית אחרת הבית טמא שאני אומר אדם טמא נכנס לשם ונטלו מזוית זו והניחו בזוית אחרת רשב"ג אומר הבית טהור שאני אומר השאילו לאחר ושכח או שנטלו מזוית זו והניח בזוית זו ושכח אמר רבא עכבר נכנס וככר בפיו ונכנס אחריו ומצא פירורין צריך בדיקה מפני שאין דרכו של עכבר לפרר ואמר רבא תינוק נכנס וככר בידו ונכנס אחריו ומצא פירורין א"צ בדיקה מפני שדרכו של תינוק לפרר בעי רבא עכבר נכנס וככר בפיו ועכבר יוצא וככר בפיו מהו מי אמרינן היינו האי דעל והיינו האי דנפק או דילמא אחרינא הוא אם תמצא לומר היינו האי דעל והיינו האי דנפק עכבר לבן נכנס וככר בפיו ועכבר שחור יוצא וככר בפיו מהו ודאי האי אחרינא הוא או דילמא ארמויי ארמיה מיניה ואת"ל עכברים לא שקלי מהדדי עכבר נכנס וככר בפיו וחולדה יוצאה וככר בפיה מהו חולדה ודאי מעכבר שקלתיה או דילמא אחרינא הוא דאם איתא דמעכבר שקלתיה עכבר בפיה הוה משתכח ואת"ל אם איתא דמעכבר שקלתיה עכבר בפיה הוה משתכח עכבר נכנס וככר בפיו וחולדה יוצאה וככר ועכבר בפי חולדה מהו הכא ודאי איהו הוא או דילמא אם איתא דאיהו ניהו ככר בפי עכבר משתכח הוה בעי אישתכוחי או דילמא משום ביעתותא הוא נפל ושקלתיה תיקו בעי רבא ככר בשמי קורה צריך סולם להורידה או אין צריך מי אמרינן כולי האי לא אטרחוהו רבנן כיון דלא נחית מנפשיה לא אתי למיכלה או דילמא זימנין דנפל ואתי למיכלה ואם תמצי לומר זימנין דנפל ואתי למיכלה ככר בבור צריך סולם להעלותה או אין צריך הכא ודאי דלא עבידא דסלקה מנפשה או דילמא זימנין דנחית למעבד צורכיה ואתי למיכליה את"ל זימנין דנחית לצורכיה ואתי למיכלה ככר בפי נחש צריך חבר להוציא או אין צריך בגופיה אטרחוהו רבנן בממוניה לא אטרחוהו רבנן או דילמא לא שנא תיקו: **מתני'** *ר' יהודה אומר בודקין אור י"ד ובי"ד שחרית ובשעת הביעור וחכ"א לא בדק אור י"ד יבדוק בי"ד לא בדק בי"ד יבדוק בתוך המועד [א] לא בדק בתוך המועד יבדוק לאחר המועד (ומה *)שמשייר יניחנו בצינעא כדי שלא יהא צריך בדיקה אחריו: **גמ'** מ"ט דרבי יהודה רב חסדא ורבה בר רב הונא דאמרי תרוייהו כנגד שלש השבתות שבתורה לא יראה לך חמץ ולא יראה לך שאור שבעת ימים שאור לא ימצא בבתיכם אך ביום הראשון תשביתו שאור מבתיכם מתיב רב יוסף רבי יהודה אומר כל שלא בדק בשלשה פרקים הללו שוב אינו בודק אלמא במכאן ואילך הוא דפליגי מר זוטרא מתני הכי מתיב רב יוסף רבי יהודה אומר כל שלא בדק באחד משלשה פרקים הללו שוב אינו בודק אלמא בשוב אינו בודק הוא דפליגי אלא רבי יהודה נמי אם לא בדק קאמר והכא בהא קמיפלגי מר סבר מקמי איסורא אין בתר איסורא לא גזירה דילמא אתי למיכל מיניה ורבנן סברי לא גזרינן ומי גזר ר' יהודה דילמא אתי למיכל מיניה והא *תנן משקרב העומר יוצאין ומוצאין שוקי ירושלים שהם מלאים קמח וקלי שלא

*) [לשון הכ"ץ הניחו תוי"ט ומה שמשייר בלילה לצרכו שיאכל בלילה גם כבוקר]

הבית טמא. כל כלי הבית טמאין שאני אומר אדם טמא נכנס לשם ומשמש בכל כלי הבית: זוית מאן דכר שמיה. פתח באבדו וסיים בנמלא בזוית אחרת: חסורי מיחסרא והכי קתני. שאני אומר אדם טמא נכנס לשם ולקחו לאבוד וגבי מלא בזוית אחרת שמא אדם טמא הניחו שם רבן שמעון כו' וגבי חמץ נמי לרבנן חוששין שמא עכבר עשה וכיון דחוששין לעכבר יש לחוש נמי לא זהו אלא אחר ולרבן שמעון תולין באדם עלמו שהוא עשה ושכח וא"ל בדיקה: ונכנס אחריו ומלא פירורין לריך בדיקה. ואין תולין הככר בו שאין דרכו של עכבר לפרר ולא זהו ככר שהכניס העכבר: אם תמלא לומר היינו האי כו'. דאי פשטת ליה דחיישינן דילמא אחרינא הואי תו לא לריכנא למיבעי שחור ולבן אבל אי פשטת ליה דלא חיישינן אכתי שחור ולבן מיבעיא לן: ארמוייה. השליכו ממנו ונטלו הוא וחבירו בחגיגה (ד' טו:) אי נקטיה ביד מאן מרמי ליה מן ידי: לדידיה הוה שקיל ליה. את העכבר עלמו היה מניח: ככר ועכבר בפי חולדה. עכבר נכנס וככר בפיו וחולדה יולא' כשנכנס בו לבדוק ובפיה ככר מכאן ועכבר מכאן: ככר בפי נחש. בעיא באפי נפשה היא ולא דמי להנך דלעיל ול"ג את"ל: לא אטרחוהו. ויבטל בלבו: בממוניה. לשכור חבר: **מתני'** בתוך המועד. בשעה ששית שהוא מועד הביעור: לאחר המועד. משש שעות ולמעלה עד שתחשך*: **גמ'** שלש השבתות. שלש לשונות של השבתה ראייה מליאה והשבתה: אלמא במכאן ואילך הוא דפליגי. ולאו במידי אחרינא דרבי יהודה לא מלריך שלש בדיקות אלא הכי קאמר או אור לארבעה עשר או שחרית או בשעה ששית ורבנן אמרי אם לא בדק בתוך המועד יבדוק לאחריו: ומר זוטרא מתני. בהדיא באחד משלשה פרקים: לבתר איסורא. לא יבדוק דגזרינן דילמא איידי דעסיק ביה אתי למיכל מיניה: משקרב העומר. בו ביום יולאים ומולאים שוקי ירושלים מלאים קמח וקלי מן החדש למכור וקודם י"ט נקטף ונטחן ונתייבש הקלי בתנור: שלא

הניח בזוית זו ומלא בזוית אחרת פלוגתא דרבן שמעון בן גמליאל ורבנן. דלרבנן לריך בדיקה דחוששין שמא עכבר עשה ולא זהו שהניח ולית להו לרבנן הוא שאבד הוא שנמלא אלא כרשב"ג דאמר תיבדק כל השדה כולה אי נמי אתי אפי' כר' ומיירי כגון שאין יודע כמה ככרות הניח ולריך בדיקה שמא לא מלא כולם:

שאני אומר אדם טמא נכנס לשם. וא"ת דהכא ובפרק קמא דחולין (דף ט:) גבי ללוחית תלינן באדם טמא ובפרק קמא דנדה (דף ד.) גבי ככר הנתון על גבי הדף ומדף טמא מונח תחתיה תלינן באדם טהור ותירץ ר"ת דאמר בפ"ק דשבת (דף ט:) גזרו על ספק כלים הנמלאים ולא גזרו על ספק אוכלין הנמלאים אי נמי גבי ככר רגלים לדבר שטהור הסירו שלא יפול על המדף ויטמא*:

מפני שדרכו של תינוק לפרר. ומיירי שיש פירורין כדי כל הככר ולכך אין לריך בדיקה ואפי' לרבן שמעון בן גמליאל דאמר תיבדק כל השדה כולה הכא רגלים לדבר יש שהפרורים מן הככר שהרי מיד נכנס אחריו:

מי אמרינן היינו הא דעל היינו הא דנפק. ואפילו לרשב"ג דאמר תיבדק כל השדה כולה הכא רגלים לדבר שהרי הוא עם הככר:

או דילמא אחרינא הוא. ואפי' לר' דאמר הוא שנמלא הוא שנאבד הכא חיישינן דמסתמא הראשונה נשאר בבית וזהו אחר שילא:

בממוניה לא אטרחוהו רבנן. פי' הכא דוק' דשמא יוליאנה או יאכלנה אבל היכא דאיכא חמץ אמר לעיל (דף ד:) דניחא ליה לאינש דליעבד מלוה בממוניה:

ואם לא בדק בתוך המועד. פי' הקונטרס בשעה ששית וקשה דלרבי יהודה קרי ליה שעת הביעור ולמה שינה לשונו אלא בתוך המועד היינו מתחלת שבע עד סוף הפסח ולאחר המועד יבדוק כדי שלא יתערב לו חמץ של איסור בשל היתר ויאכלנו ורש"י לא רלה לפרש כן מפני שפירש במשנה דבודקים שלא יעבור בבל יראה: קולרין

[ועי' תוס' חולין ט: ד"ה אני]

עין משפט נר מצוה

עו א מיי' פי"ב מהל' משכב ומושב הל' טו ופ"ב מהל' חמץ הל' יב טוש"ע או"ח סי' תלט סעיף ד:

עז ב ג מיי' פ"ב מהל' חמץ הל' ח ט טוש"ע או"ח סי' תלח סעיף א:

עח ד ה ו ז מיי' שם הל' יג וטור שם:

עט ח ט מיי' שם הל' יד וטוש"ע שם ס"ב:

פ י מיי' שם הל' יג:

פא כ מיי' פ"ג מהל' חו"מ הל' ה סמג עשין לט טוש"ע או"ח סי' תלה:

פב ל מיי' שם הל' ג וסמג שם טוש"ע או"ח סי' תלד סעיף א:

רבינו חננאל

אומרים הכל חולין כלומר אותם המאתים של מעשר שני נלקחו וזה המנה אחר הניחו וחולין הן הניח בזוית זו ומצא בזוית אחרת חלוקת רשב"ג ורבנן וקיימא לן כרבנן דאמרי הבית טמא שאני אומר אדם טמא נכנס לבית ונטלו מזוית זו והניחו בזוית אחרת: **אמר** רבא עכבר נכנס וככר בפיו נכנס אחריו ומצא פירורין צריך בדיקה שאין דרך עכבר לפרר אלא העכבר עם הככר שנטל הלך לו ואלו הפירורין אינן ממנו לפיכך צריך לבדוק אבל אם נטל תינוק ככר ונכנס לבית ונכנס אחריו ומצא פירורין אין צריך בדיקה שכן דרך התינוק לפרר: **בעי** רבא עכבר נכנס וככר בפיו ועכבר יוצא וככר בפיו כו' בעי רבא ככר בשמי קורה צריך סולם להורידו או לא כו' בעי רב אשי ככר בפי נחש צריך חבר להוציאו או לא כו' אלו כולן עלו בתיקו: **מתני'** ר' יהודה אומר בודקין אור ארבעה עשר ובארבעה עשר בשעת הביעור. ירושלמי בשעת הביעור שעה חמישית וחכמי' אומרים לא בדק באור ארבעה עשר יבדוק בי"ד כו' כלומר אין צריך [אלא] לבדוק שחרית בי"ד אם לא בדק באור י"ד אבל אם בדק אור י"ד אין צריך אחרי כן בדיקה כלל. פריש רב חסדא טעמא דר' יהודה דבעי שלש בדיקות כנגד שלש אזהרות שהזהירה תורה על השבתת חמץ ומותבינן עליה מהא דר' יהודה אומר כל שלא בדק אחד משלשה פרקים הללו שוב אינו בודק אלמא ר' יהודה חדא זימנא בעי ואוקימנא לעולם חדא זימנא בעי ובהא פליגי ר' יהודה סבר עד שעת ביעור בודק שאם ימצא חמץ ישרפנו אבל אחר זמן ביעורו אינו בודק חיישינן דילמא אתי למיכל מיניה פי' כגון שהיה במדינת הים ובא במועד ולאחר המועד שחייב כל זמן

מסורת הש"ס

[עי' פירש"י מנחות סז: ד"ה ובשעת]

הגהות מהר"ב רנשבורג

א] מתני' לא בדק כו' לאחר המועד. עי' ערוך ערך מעד ודו"ק:

[לעיל ב: מנחות סז:]

[לעיל ה: וערש"י שם] שמות יג

שם יב שם

מנחות סז:

*בתרומה דרבנן בחמץ דאורייתא מי אמרינן אטו בדיקת חמץ דאורייתא דרבנן היא *דמדאורייתא בביטול בעלמא סגי ליה *צבור אחד של חמץ ולפניו ב' בתים בדוקין ואתא עכבר ושקל ולא ידעינן אי להאי על אי להאי על היינו שני שבילין *דתנן שני שבילין א' טמא וא' טהור והלך באחד מהן ועשה טהרות ובא חבירו והלך בשני ועשה טהרות רבי יהודה אומר אם נשאלו זה בפני עצמו וזה בפני עצמו טהורין שניהן בבת אחת טמאין רבי יוסי אומר בין כך ובין כך טמאין אמר רבא ואיתימא רבי יוחנן בבת אחת דברי הכל טמאין בזה אחר זה דברי הכל טהורין לא נחלקו אלא בבא להשאל עליו ועל חבירו רבי יוסי מדמי ליה לבת אחת ורבי יהודה מדמי ליה לזה אחר זה ספק על ספק לא על היינו בקעה ובפלוגתא דר"א ורבנן *דתנן הנכנס לבקעה בימות הגשמים וטומאה בשדה פלונית ואמר אחד הלכתי במקום הלז ואיני יודע אם נכנסתי באותה שדה ואם לא נכנסתי ר"א מטהר וחכמים מטמאין שהיה ר"א אומר ספק ביאה טהור ספק מגע טומאה טמא על ובדק ולא אשכח פלוגתא דר"מ ורבנן *דתנן היה ר"מ אומר כל דבר שבחזקת טומאה לעולם הוא בטומאתו עד שיודע לך הטומאה היכן היא וחכמים אומרים בודק עד שמגיע לסלע או לקרקע בתולה על ובדק ואשכח פלוגתא דר' ורשב"ג *דתניא שדה שנאבד בה קבר הנכנס לתוכה טמא נמצא בה קבר הנכנס לתוכה טהור שאני אומר קבר שאבד הוא קבר שנמצא דברי ר' רשב"ג אומר תיבדק כל השדה כולה הניח ט' ומצא י' פלוגתא דר' ורבנן *דתניא הניח מנה ומצא מאתים חולין ומעשר שני מעורבין זה בזה דברי ר' וחכ"א הכל חולין הניח י' ומצא תשע היינו סיפא *דתניא הניח מאתים ומצא מנה מנה מונח ומנה מוטל דברי ר' וחכ"א הכל חולין הניח

בתרומה דרבנן. בזמן הזה: ולא ידעינן אי להאי על ואי להאי על. אי מצריכנן בדיקה לתרוייהו אי לא: היינו שני שבילין. מהא דתנן גבי שני שבילין מצינו למיפשט: אחד טמא. קבר מוטל בו לרחבו וממלא את כולו ואין עובר בו שלא יאהיל: והלך ועשה טהרות. נגע בטהרות אח"כ: והלך בשני. יודעין הן שבשביל שהלך זה לא הלך זה השתא ודאי אחד מהן טמא: אם נשאלו. כל א' לחכם ספקו בפני עצמו טהור ואין ב"ד יכול לטמאו כדקיימא לן בספק טומאה ברה"ר ספקו טהור ואם באו בבת אחת הואיל ובהוראה אחת יש לנו לומר טמאין או טהורין אי אפשר לנו לומר להם טהורים אתם שהרי האחד ודאי טמא רבי יוסי אומר בין כך ובין כך טמאין גרס: בזה אחר זה דברי הכל טהורין. אע"פ שכל אחד אומר לפניו כך היה המעשה שלי ושל חבירי אבל איני נשאל אלא על עצמי מה תהא עלי: עליו ועל חבירו. מה תהא על שנינו ר' יוסי מדמי להו לבת אחת ואע"פ שאין שניהן לפניך צריך אתה הוראה אחת לשניהן או טמאין אתם או טהורין אתם והרי אין אתה יכול לומר טהורין אתם: ר' יהודה מדמי להו לזה אחר זה. הואיל ואין כאן שואל אלא אחד משיבין לו טהור אתה שהרי ספק ביאה הוא ומעצמו יבין שאף חבירו כמוהו אבל כששניהן שואלין בתוך כדי דיבור צריך אתה להשיב לשניהן כאחד וגבי בתים נמי אם באו לשאול זה לעצמו וזה בפני עצמו אמרינן ליה לכל חד אי אתה צריך לבדוק דכיון דבדיקת חמץ דרבנן תלינן לקולא ואמרינן ספקו מותר ואי בבת אחת באו שניהן צריכין בדיקה: ספק על ספק לא על. ראה עכבר שנטל חמץ בחצר והבית בדוק ואין יודע אם נכנס או לא נכנס: בקעה. הרבה שדות הסמוכים יחד קרי בקעה: בימות הגשמים. הויא בקעה רשות היחיד לטומאה מפני שכבר צמח הזרע ואין רשות לכל אדם ליכנס לה וקי"ל ספק טומאה ברשות היחיד ספקו טמא: בשדה פלונית. כלומר באחת השדות ויודעין אנו באיזו היא וכל שדה ושדה מסויימת במצריה: במקום הלז. בבקעה זו: וחכמים מטמאין. דהויא ליה ספק טומאה ברה"י ור"א לא חשיב לה ספק טומאה אא"כ נכנס לשדה אבל אינו יודע אם האהיל אם לא אבל השתא הוה ליה ספק ספיקא וגבי בתים אפילו רבנן מודו דכיון דבדיקת חמץ דרבנן תלינן לקולא: על. העכבר נכנס לבית לפניו ובדק בעל הבית אחריו ולא אשכח: כל דבר שבחזקת טומאה. במסכת נדה גל טמא שנתערב עם שני גלין טהורין בדקו אחד מהן ונמצא טהור הוא טהור ושנים טמאים שנים ומצאן טהורין הן טהורין והשלישי טמא שלשתן ומצאן טהורים כולן טמאים שהיה ר"מ אומר כל דבר שבחזקת טומאה לעולם היא בטומאתה עד שיודע לך טומאה היכן היא וחכמים אומרים בודק בקרקע וחופר עד שיגיע לסלע או לקרקע בתולה שלא זזה ממקומה לעולם ואם לא מצא תולין ואומרים בא עורב ונטלה וגבי בדיקת חמץ אפילו לר"מ אמרינן עכבר אכלה דבדיקת חמץ דרבנן: על ובדק ואשכח. נכנס העכבר בפניו ובדק בעל הבית אחריו ואשכח פרוסה ואינו יודע אם זו היא אם לאו: אבד בה קבר. אין ידוע היכן מקומו: נמצא בה קבר. לאחר זמן ואין ידוע אי זהו קבר האבוד בה: הניח מנה. של מעשר שני: מעורבין. ומביא סלעים בשוה מנה ואומר כ"מ שהן מעות מעשר שני הרי הן מחוללים על הסלעים הללו ומעלה הסלעים לירושלים: הכל חולין. שהמנה נטל ואלו הובאו אחרי כן וגבי חמץ נמי לרבנן הט' (נמי) שהניח אינן כאן וצריך לבדוק כל הבית שמא גררום חולדות והעשר הנמצאות איש אחר הביאן כאן: היינו סיפא. לרבי (מאיר) [דאמר] זה הנמצא זהו א' מן הראשונים הכא נמי א"צ לבדוק ולחזור אלא על הפרוסה האבודה ולרבנן צריך לחזור אחר כולן שאין כאן א' מן הראשונים:
הבית

הלך באחד מהן ועשה טהרות. הא דנקט טהרות ולא קאמר אדם טהור משום דלגברי אע"ג דמוקמינן לה בחזקת טהורים מצריכין להו טבילה והאשה שלא יגעו שניהם בתרומה דאי התרומה טמאה ודאית והאוכל במיתה ואם נגעו שניהם באחד ונכנס למקדש חייב*: בבת אחת ד"ה טמאים. נראה דהיינו מדרבנן דמדאורייתא אפי' בבת אחת טהורים: ספק על ספק לא על היינו בקע'. תימה לר"י מה שייך לדמויי לבקעה דהכא אפי' ליכא אלא ספק אחד אוקמא אחזקת בדוק כדאמרינן לעיל ולעיל דימה אותו לספק טומאה ברשות הרבים והכא מדמי לספק טומאה ברשות היחיד: ספק ביאה טהור. פר"י דבספק ספיקא פליגי וכן פר"ת במסכת ע"ז פרק בתרא (ד' ע.) אבל רש"י פירש שם בע"א ונראה לר"י דטעמא דרבי אליעזר דמטהר בספק ספיקא משום דלא גמרינן מסוטה לטמא ברשות היחיד אלא ספיקא אחת כסוטה אבל תרי ספיקי לא ורבנן סברי כיון דמן הדין אפי' בספיקא אחת היה לטהר דאוקמא אחזקת טהרה ואפ"ה טמא הוא הדין אפילו בתרי ספיקי*: על ובדק ולא אשכח פלוגתא דר' מאיר ורבנן. תימה אפי' לר"מ דאמר לעולם היא בחזקת טומאה וכו' ונפקא מינה לטהרות שנגעו על גביו הכא גבי בדיקה כיון שבדק ולא מצא מה יעשה אם יצריכוהו לבדוק פעם שניה נמי לא ימצא ורש"י פירש דאפי' לר' מאיר אמר אימור עכבר אכליה דבדיקת חמץ אינו אלא מדרבנן וקשה דהא בהדיא אמר פלוגתא דר' מאיר ורבנן וי"ל דמיירי בגלא בטלה וקאמר דלר' מאיר לא סגי בבדיקה כיון דלא אשכח והוי בספק לאו דלא ימצא וצריך לבטלו וסגי אפילו לרבי מאיר דלא איירי אלא בספק טומאה דאורייתא אבל הכא בדבדיקת חמץ דרבנן שרי: חולין ומעשר שני מעורבים זה בזה. פ"ה מביא סלעים בשוה מנה ואומר כל מקום שהוא מעות מעשר שני יהיו מחוללים על מעות הללו ובחנם פירש כן דמינייהו גופייהו היה יכול ליקח שיעור מעות מעשר ואומר אם אלו מעות מעשר הרי טוב ואם לאו כל מקום שהן הרי הן מחוללין על אלו וריב"א הקשה לפרש"י דאיך יכול לחלל אסלעים ובפרק הזהב (ב"מ ד' מה.) אמר טיבעא אטיבעא לא מחללין ושם פי' *): הניח עשר ומצא תשע פלוגתא דרבי ורבנן. דר' לטעמיה דאמר הוא קבר שאבד הוא קבר שנמצא וכיון שמצא אחד א"צ לבדוק ולרבנן עד שמצא עשר כדפ"ה ומיירי שכל הככרות קשורים זה בזה דומיא דפלוגתא דרבי ורבנן דפ"ק דביצה (דף י:) אמר מחלוקת בכיסים קשורים אבל כשאין קשורים דברי הכל חולין ומע"ש מעורבין זה בזה ואף על גב דהשתא אין לתלות בעכברים תלינן בקטנים:
הניח

*) [עי' תוס' ב"מ מה. ד"ה ליפלוג ותוס' ביצה י: ד"ה חולין ועי' שם היטב גם ברש"י דסתליפו שיטתייהו]

עא א מיי' פ"ב מהל' חמץ הל' יא סמג לאוין לט טוש"ע או"ח סי' תלט סעיף ב:

[וע"ע תוס' כתובות כז. ד"ה והלך]

עב ב ג מיי' פי"ט מהל' אבות הטומאה הלכה ג:

עג ד מיי' שם פ"כ הל' ט ופ"ב מהל' חמץ הלכה יב:

עד ה ו מיי' שם הלכה יא ופ"ט מהלכות טומאת מת הל"י טוש"ע או"ח סי' תלט ס"ב:

עה ז ח מיי' פ"ו מהל' מעשר שני הלכה ג ופ"ב מהל' חמץ ומצה הלכה יב טוש"ע או"ח סי' תלט סעיף ג:

רבינו חננאל

נפלו בדרבנן [וכן] אוקמי' להא בהדיא בפ' ואלו עוברין [דף מד.] בפסח בתרומה בזמנהזה שהיא מדרבנן: צבור אחד חמץ ושני בתים בדוקין ושקל עכבר ככר אחד מהן ולא ידעינן בהי מינייהו על פשטינן להא משני שבילין וקיי"ל כר' יוחנן דאמר הכל מודים שאם נשאלו לחכם שניהם ביחד דברי הכל טמאים נשאלו בזה אחר זה דברי הכל טהורין לא נחלקו אלא בבא לשאול עליו ועל חברו רבי יהודה מדמה ליה לבת אחת ושניהם טמאים ור' יוסי מדמה לה לזה אחר זה ושניהן טהורין וכן אם באו אלו הבעלי בתים ושאלו שניהם ביחד צריכין בדיקה בזה אחר זה אין אחד מהן צריך בדיקה בא אחד [מהם] לשאל על ביתו ועל בית חברו הלכה כר' יוסי ואליבא דר' יוחנן: ספק על ספק לא על פשטי' לה מבקעה בימות הגשמים שהיא רשות היחיד וחלקו בו ר' אליעזר וחכמים והלכה כחכמים שמטמאין כן בכאן צריך לבדוק על בדק ולא אשכח פשטי' לה מדרבנן דאמרי בודק עד שמגיע לסלע או לבתולה פי' ארץ בתולה על בדק ואשכח פשטי' לה חלוקת ר' ורשב"ג ר' אומר הקבר שנמצא הוא הקבר שאבד רשב"ג אומר תבדק כל השדה כולה: הניח תשע ומצא עשר חלוקת ר' ורבנן דתניא הניח מנה ומצא מאתים חולין ומעשר שני מעורבין כלומר המנה שהניח היה מעשר שני ובא אחר והוסיף עליו מנה אחר של חולין וחכמים אומרים הכל חולין כלומר אותו המנה של מעשר ניטל ואלו אדם אחר הניחם וכולן חולין הם: הניח עשר ומצא תשע חלוקת ר' ורבנן דתניא הניח מאתים ומצא מנה מנה מונח ומנה מוטל דברי רבי כלומר אדם בא ונטל חצים והניח חצים והמנה הנמצא מעשר שני הוא וחכמים

[עי' תוס' ביצה י: ד"ה הכל]
[לעיל ד:]
כתובות כז. טהרות פ"ה [מ"ה]
בבא בתרא נה: ע"ז עה. טהרות פ"ו [מ"ה]
בכורות כה: נדה סח.
בכורות כה:
ביצה י: [תוספתא מ"ש פ"ד]
ביצה שם

we say 'I assume' [10a] in the case of *terumah* [only], which is
a merely Rabbinical;[1] but do we say thus in the case of leaven, which is Scriptural?[2]—Is then the searching for leaven Scriptural; surely it is [only] Rabbinical, for by Scriptural law mere annulment is sufficient.[3]

If there is one package of leaven, and in front of it are two houses which have been searched, and there came a mouse and seized it, and we do not know whether it entered this [house] or that, that is [similar to] the case of two paths. For we learned: If there are two paths, one clean and the other unclean,[4] and a person went through one of them and then touched[5] clean [food], and then his neighbour came and went through the other and he touched clean [food],—R. Judah said: If they each enquire separately, they are clean;[6] if both together, they are unclean. R. Jose said: In both cases they are unclean. Raba—others say, R. Joḥanan—said: If they came together, all agree that they are unclean; if consecutively, all agree that they are clean. They differ only where one comes to enquire about himself and his neighbour: R. Jose compares it to [both coming] together,[7] while R. Judah likens it to each coming separately.[8]

If it is doubtful whether it [the mouse] entered or not,[9] that is [similar to] the case of a plain, and [there we are involved] in the controversy of R. Eleazar and the Rabbis.[10] For we learned: If a man enters a plain[11] in winter,[12] and there is uncleanness[13] in a
b particular field,[1] and he states: I walked in that place, but do not know whether I entered that field or not,—R. Eleazar declares him clean, while the Sages declare him unclean. For R. Eleazar ruled: If there is a doubt about entering, he is clean: if there is a doubt of contact with uncleanness, he is unclean.[2]

If it [the mouse] entered [with the leaven], and he [the master] searched but did not find it, [in like case] there is a controversy of R. Meir and the Rabbis. For we learned: R. Meir used to say: Everything which is in the presumption of uncleanness always [remains] in its uncleanness until it is known to you whither its uncleanness is gone; while the Sages rule: One searches until he reaches a rock or virgin soil.[3]

If it [the mouse] entered [with leaven] and he searched and found [leaven],[4]—[in like case] there is a controversy of Rabbi and R. Simeon b. Gamaliel. For it was taught: If a grave was lost in a field,[5] he who enters therein is unclean. If a grave is [subsequently] found in it, he who enters therein is clean, for I assume: the grave which was lost is the same grave which was found: this is Rabbi's view. R. Simeon b. Gamaliel said: The whole field must be examined.[6]

If a man left nine [pieces of leaven] and found ten, there is a controversy of Rabbi and the Rabbis. For it was taught: If he
c left a *maneh*[1] and found two-hundred [*zuz*],[2] *ḥullin* and second tithe are intermingled,[3] this is Rabbi's view. But the Sages maintain: It is all *ḥullin*.[4] If he left ten and found nine, that is [analogous to] the second clause. For it was taught: If he deposited two-hundred and found one *maneh*, [he assumes], one *maneh* was left lying and one *maneh* was taken away:[5] this is Rabbi's view. But

a (1) Nowadays. (2) When doubt arises in a Rabbinical law we are naturally lenient; but where the law is Scriptural we are strict. (3) *Supra 4b*. (4) E.g., there is a lost grave in one of them, but we do not know in which. (5) Lit., 'made'. (6) Each is given the benefit of the doubt; consequently the food remains clean. (7) Since the question is asked on behalf of both. (8) Since there is only one man asking.—It is a principle that if a doubt of uncleanness arises in public ground, it is clean; if in private ground, it is unclean. Here the paths are public ground; hence when they come separately each is declared clean. But we cannot rule thus when they come together, since one is certainly unclean. The same principles apply *mutatis mutandis* to the searched houses. (9) A mouse was seen to take a package of leaven, but we do not know whether or not it entered a room already searched. (10) [This clause is omitted in MS.M., cf. *infra*, n. b2] (11) Many fields together constitute a plain. (12) It is then private ground, because the seed has already started sprouting. (13) I.e., a grave.

b (1) The field is known. (2) For in the first case there is really a double doubt: firstly, whether he entered the field at all, and secondly, even if he did enter, whether he passed over the grave.—In our problem, however, even the Rabbis agree that a re-search is not necessary; since the search is only Rabbinical, we make the more lenient assumption (Rashi). [Apparently Rashi did not read, 'and in the controversy . . . Rabbis', cf. *supra*, n. a10.] (3) If a pile or heap contains a portion of a corpse, so that it is unclean, while there are two other clean piles, and we do not know now which is which; if one is examined and found to be clean, that is clean, while the others are treated as unclean; if two are found to be clean, they are clean and the third is unclean; but if the three are examined and found to be clean, they are all *unclean* in R. Meir's opinion, unless we know definitely whither the defilement has disappeared. But the Sages maintain that he examines the ground until he reaches a rock or virgin soil which has obviously never been touched, and if it is not found we assume that a bird has flown off with it.—But in the present problem even R. Meir agrees that we are lenient, since the search is only a Rabbinical requirement (Rashi). V. however Tosaf. (4) But he does not know whether it is the same. (5) We do not know where it is. (6) It may not be the same grave.—Here too, presumably, even R. Simeon b. Gamaliel is lenient; cf. n. b3.

c (1) Of second tithe. (2) I.e., two *manehs*. (3) We assume that the original *maneh* was left and an unknown person added another. It will therefore be necessary to redeem one *maneh* by exchanging it for another. (4) For the original *maneh* may have been taken away. The Rabbis will make a similar assumption here and therefore the house must be searched for the nine pieces. (5) Hence the present *maneh* is treated as second tithe.

pit, [9b] and a priest came and looked down it to see whether it was a male or a female;[8] and when the matter came before the a Sages they declared him[1] clean, because weasels and martens[2] were to be found there.[3] Now here, she had certainly thrown it in, while it is doubtful whether they had dragged it away or not by that time, yet the doubt comes and negatives the certainty? —Do not say that she threw a premature child into a pit, but say, 'she threw something like a premature child into a pit', so that it is a doubt against a doubt.[4] But it states: 'In order to see whether it was a male or a female'?[5]—This is what it says: To know whether she had aborted wind[6] or a premature child; and should you say that it was a premature child, to see whether it was a male or a female. Alternatively, there it is a certainty against a certainty; since weasels and martens are to be found there they had certainly dragged it away by that time; [for] granted that they may have left over,[7] yet they certainly had dragged it away by that time.

But do we say, we have no fear that a weasel may have dragged [leaven], etc.? Surely the second clause states:[8] What he leaves over[9] he must put away in a hidden place, so that it should not require a search after it?[10]—Said Abaye, There is no difficulty: the one [refers to a search] on the fourteenth; the other, on the thirteenth. [If one searches] on the thirteenth, when bread is [yet] to be found in all houses, it [a weasel] does not hide [leaven]; on the fourteenth, when bread is not to be found in all houses, it does hide [it]. Said Raba: Is then a weasel a prophet to know that it is the fourteenth now and people will not bake until the evening, so that it should leave [some] over and hide [it]? Rather said Raba: What one leaves over he must put away in a hidden place lest a weasel seize it in his presence and it require a search after it. It was taught in accordance with Raba: If one wishes to eat leaven after the search, what shall he do? Let him put it away in a hidden place, lest a weasel come and seize it in his presence and it require a search after it. R. Mari said: It is for fear that he b may leave ten[1] and [only] find nine.[2]

If there are nine packages of *mazzah* and one of leaven, and a mouse comes and steals [a package], and we do not know whether it took *mazzah* or leaven,[3] that is [similar to the case of] nine shops.[4] If [one package] was separated[5] and a mouse came and stole it, that is [similar to] the second clause. For it was taught: If there are nine shops all selling meat of [ritually] slaughtered [animals], and there is one shop selling meat of *nebelah*,[6] and a man buys [meat] from one of them, but he does not know from which [shop] he bought, the [meat in] doubt is prohibited; but in the case of [meat] found, we follow the majority.[7]

If there are two packages, one of *mazzah* and the other of leaven, and before them are two rooms, one searched and the other unsearched, and two mice came, one took *mazzah* and the other took leaven, and we do not know which [mouse] entered which [room], that is the case of two baskets. For we learned: If there are two baskets, one containing *hullin*[8] and the other containing *terumah*,[8] and in front of them are two *se'ahs* [of provisions], one of *hullin* and the other of *terumah*, and these fell into those, they [*sc*. the contents of the baskets] are permitted, for I assume: The *hullin* fell into *hullin* and the *terumah* fell into *terumah*.[9] Perhaps

(8) To decide the period of the slave's uncleanness (v. Lev. XII, 4, 5). A heathen slave in a Jewish house was a semi-Jew, and bound to observe all the religious obligations of a Jewess.

a (1) The priest. (2) Heb. *Bardelles*. (3) They may have dragged the body into one of their holes, leaving the pit itself empty. Had it been there the priest would have been defiled through stooping over it, even though he did not touch it. (4) For the body may not have been formed yet, in which case it does not contaminate. (5) Which implies that the body was fully formed and the mother was unclean, as after a proper birth, save that the sex had been overlooked. (6) I.e., an unformed body. (7) I.e., not eaten it. (8) *Infra* 10b. (9) After the search, for the following morning's meal. (10) For otherwise a weasel may drag it away.

b (1) E.g., rolls. (2) For then it would be certain that one had been removed, and this would necessitate a further search. (3) V. *supra* 9a, n. c3. If *mazzah*, no further search is required; if leaven, it is required. (4) Explained *infra*. (5) But we do not know whether this separated package was leaven or *mazzah*. (6) V. Glos. (7) And assume it to have come out of one of the nine. In the first instance the forbidden meat is in a fixed place; technically this is called *kabu'a* (fixed), and it is shown in Sanh. 79b that we must then regard the doubt as equally balanced, i.e., as though there were an *equal* quantity of both, and we are therefore stringent. But in the second case the forbidden meat has left its fixed place and is somewhere in the street; the ordinary rule is then followed that the majority decides. (8) V. Glos. (9) By a similar assumption the house already searched does not need to be searched anew.

ובא כהן והציץ בו לידע אם זכר הוא אם נקבה היא ובא מעשה לפני חכמים וטיהרוהו מפני שחולדה וברדלס מצויין שם והא הכא דודאי הטילה וספק גררוהו וספק לא גררוהו ההיא שעתא וקאתי ספק ומוציא מידי ודאי *לא תימא שהטילה נפל לבור אלא אימא שהפילה כמין נפל לבור והוי ספק וספק והא לידע אם זכר הוא אם נקבה היא קתני הכי קאמר לידע אם רוח הפילה אם נפל הפילה ואם תמצא לומר נפל הפילה לידע אם זכר הוא ואם נקבה היא ואיבעית אימא התם ודאי ודאי הוא כיון דחולדה וברדלס מצויין שם ודאי גררוהו בההיא שעתא נהי דשיורי משיירא מיגרר מיהת ודאי גרום בההיא שעתא (לישנא אחרינא נהי דודאי אכלום לא אמרינן ודאי גררוהו לחורייהו אמרינן) ומי אמרינן אין חוששין שמא גררה חולדה והא קתני סיפא *מה שמשייר יניחנו בצנעה שלא יהא צריך בדיקה אחריו אמר אביי לא קשיא הא בארבעה עשר הא בשלשה עשר בשלשה עשר דשכיח ריפתא בכולהו בתי לא מצנעא בארבעה עשר דלא שכיחא ריפתא בכולהו בתי מצנעא אמר רבא וכי חולדה נביאה היא דידעא דהאידנא ארביסר ולא אפי עד לאורתא ומשיירא וממטמרא אלא אמר רבא מה שמשייר [1]יניחנו בצנעה שמא תטול חולדה בפנינו ויהא צריך בדיקה אחריו תניא כוותיה דרבא הרוצה לאכול חמץ אחר בדיקה כיצד יעשה מה שמשייר יניחנו בצנעה שלא תבוא חולדה ותיטול בפנינו ויהא צריך בדיקה אחריו רב מרי אמר גזירה [ב]שמא יניח עשר וימצא תשע: [ג]תשע ציבורין של מצה ואחד של חמץ ואתא עכבר ושקל ולא ידעינן אי מצה שקל אי חמץ שקל היינו תשע חנויות פירש ואתא עכבר ושקל היינו סיפא *דתנן *[ד]תשע חנויות [ה]כולן מוכרין בשר שחוטה ואחת מוכרת בשר נבלה ולקח מאחת מהן ואינו יודע מאיזה מהן לקח ספיקו אסור ובנמצא הלך אחר הרוב [ו]שני ציבורין אחד של מצה ואחד של חמץ ולפניהם שני בתים אחד בדוק ואחד שאינו בדוק ואתו שני עכברים אחד שקל מצה ואחד שקל חמץ ולא ידעינן הי להאי עייל והי להאי עייל היינו שתי קופות *)דתנן [ז]שתי קופות אחת של חולין ואחת של תרומה ולפניהם שני סאין אחד של חולין ואחד של תרומה ונפלו אלו לתוך אלו מותרין שאני אומר חולין לתוך חולין נפלו ותרומה לתוך תרומה נפלה אימור דאמרינן שאני אומר בתרומה

ובא כהן והציץ . על שפת הבור : לידע אם זכר אם נקבה . וכהן קרוב או מבני הבית היה ושלחוהו שם להגיד לאמו מה טיבו ותבחין בין טומאת וטהרת זכר לימי טומאת וטהרת נקבה ולא כזכר* אותו כהן על אזהרת לנפש לא יטמא והציץ בו בבור והנפל לא ראה וטיהרוהו ממאהיל על המת: שחולדה וברדלס מצויין שם . וספק חור חולדה וברדלס פותח טפח הוא וגיררוהו לחורן ולא האהיל : רוח הפילה . ספיר אלא רוח ואם תמצא לומר נפל היה כלומר לכל אלה הולרך שמא רוח הוא ולהגיד ואין כאן לא טומאת זכר ולא טומאת נקבה ואם תראה שהוא וולד לריכי לראות אם זכר אם נקבה: ודאי גררוהו . מוחזקין הן בכך ולא דמי למתניתין דקתני הא חזינא חיישינן דנהי דודאי אכלה לא אמר אבל גירגרוהו לחור שלהן אמר: ברדלס. בלעז פוטוייס"י : ומה שמשייר . אחר בדיקה *מאכילתו יניחנו בצנעה: בשלשה עשר . רישא דקתני אין חוששין בבודק בשלשה עשר שמלוי פת הרבה לחולדה בתוך הבתים ואינה חוששת לשייר וסיפא בהדיא תנן בה בי"ד וכיון דלא חזיא החולדה פת הרבה בבתים כמות שהיא רגילה משיירא : וכי חולדה נביאה היא . לתת לב על כך ולראות את הנולד וידועת שלא יאפו עוד היום : ותיטול בפנינו . והיכא דחזינן על כרחך חיישינן : וימלא תשע . דתכא ודאי איכא למיחש דהא מוכחא מילתא שנטלה פרוסה אחת : תשע ליבורין כו' . פיסקי הלכות הן : ואתא עכבר ושקל. ונכנס לבית בפנינו ולא דעינן אי חמץ שקל וכיון דחזינא לריכין אנו לבדוק או דילמא מלה שקל : היינו תשע חנויות . דקיימא לן בהו לקמיה דכל קבוע שנטלו ממקום קבוע אין הולכין בו אחר הרוב אלא הרי הוא כמחלה על מחלה וספק איסורא לחומרא: פירש . פרוסה מאחת מן הליבורין לאח' מן הזוית ולא ידעינן מהי מינייהו פירש ואתא עכבר ושקליה ונכנס לבית : היינו סיפא. *דמתני' דתשע חנויות דהיכא דלא לקחו במקום קבועו הולכין בו אחר הרוב : ולקח מאחת מהכה . בתוך החנות ספקו אסור דכל קבוע כמחלה על מחלה נידון דנפקא לן מן וארב לו וקם עליו (*בפ' בתרא דיומא) (פד:) ובפ"ק דכתובות (טו:) ובנמלא . בשר הנמלא בקרקע בין החנויות הלך אחר הרוב דכל דפריש מרובה פריש דכיון דפריש אין כאן תורת קבוע: שתי קופות . דבר זה אנו יכולין ללמוד ממשנת שתי קופות דתלינן לקולא: ולפניהן שני סאין . של פירות : ונפלו אלו לתוך אלו . הסאין לתוך אלו הקופות וידוע לנו שהאחד נפל בזו ואחד בזו ואין ידוע אי זה בזו ואי זה בזו : הרי אלו מותרין . פירות של קופות החולין מותרין לזר כבתחלה אפי' אין בקופה כדי להעלות הסאה באחד ומאה שאנו אומרים חולין לתוך חולין נפלו אלמא תלינן לקולא היתר בהיתר ואיסור באיסור ואע"ג דאיכא למימר איפכא הכא נמי לקולא תלינן ואמרינן החמץ נכנס לשאינו בדוק והמלה לבדוק :

בתרומה

ספק גררוהו ההיא שעתא . ואם תאמר האי בור היכא קאי אי ברשות הרבים אפי' בספיקא אחת טהור ואי ברשות היחיד מאי משני שהטילה כמין נפל לבור והתנן (טהרות פ"ו מ"ד) כל ספיקות וספיקי דספיקות שאתה יכול להרבות ברשות היחיד טמא ויש לומר דגרירת חולדה וברדלס הוי ספק הרגיל כדפי' לעיל ואומר ר"י דל"ל דרגלי הכהן היו ברשות הרבים דע"כ בחורייהו ליכא פותח טפח דאי איכא פותח טפח (מפני) מה מועלת גרירה והא פותח טפח מביא את הטומאה ואי רגליו ברשו' היחיד ניחוש שמא גררוהו כנגד רגליו וטומאה בוקעת ועולה ועוד י"ל דרגלי כהן ברשות היחיד היו וגררוהו ואכלוהו הוי ספק הרגיל :

ולא חיישינן לחולדה. הא לא פריך דניחוש לחולדה אפילו מבית לבית דא"כ אין לדבר סוף דאי אפשר שלא יבדוק אחד קודם חבירו ואיכא למיחש שמא הביאה חולדה מבית שאין בדוק לבדוק אלא ממקום למקום פריך דהיינו באותו הבית עצמו כלומר ולא חיישינן לחולדה באותו בית עצמו :

בשלשה עשר לא משיירא . פי' פעם שאינה משיירת ולהכי היכא דלא חזינן לא חיישינן כיון דאפי' גררה פעם שאין משיירת אבל היכא דחזינן חיישינן כיון דפעמים משיירת ובי"ד לעולם משיירת ואפי' לא חזינן חיישינן וגבי בשר אפילו חזינן לא חיישינן דלעולם לא משיירת ולא"ש אביי כרבי זירא :

היינו תשע חנויות . לפי מה שפ"ה לענין בדיקה לא נהירא לר"י דהיכי מייתי ראיה מתשע חנויות דהוי ספיקא דאורייתא ואזלינן לחומרא והכא ספיקא דרבנן הוא כדאמרינן בסמוך מיהו י"ל דאיירי כגון שלא ביטל ועוד קשה דגבי תשע חנויות ליכא חזקת היתר אבל הכא הוקמא אחזקת בדוק דהא בבדוק מיירי דאי לאו הכי פשיטא דבעי בדיקה ונראה לר"י דלענין שהביא עכבר לבית ונמלא קבעי אי שרי לאכילה אי לאו ואם תאמר כי אתא עכבר ושקל מהכי ליבורין אמאי חשיב ליה קבוע מאי שנא נמלא כפי עכבר מנמלא ביד נכרי דבפ' גיד הנשה (חולין צה. ושם) פריך לרב דאמר בשר שנתעלם מן העין אסור מבנמלא הלך אחר הרוב ומשני שנמלא ביד נכרי ואומר ר"י דהכא מיירי כשראינו שלקח מן הקבוע שנולד הספק במקום קביעות אבל אם לא ראינו הוה ליה כפירש ואזלינן בתר רובא והא דפריך בתערובות (זבחים דף עג:) גבי זבחים שנתערבו בחטאות המתות או בשור הנסקל אמאי ימותו כולם כשכבישינהו ונייידינהו ונימא כל דפריש מרובא פריש אע"פ שכבר נולד הספק במקום קביעות שאני התם דלא הוי קבוע גמור שהאיסור מעורב בהיתר ואינו ניכר ומדרבנן אסרו בקבוע זה דמדאורייתא לא חשיב קבוע אלא כשהאיסור ידוע במקומו ולהכי נמי גזרינן התם טפי שמא יקח מן הקבוע מבנמלא כיון שאין האיסור ידוע : **היינו** שתי קופות . הך סוגיא דמדמה בדיקת חמץ לשתי קופות לא אתי כר"ל דמוקי בשילהי הערל (יבמות פב.) להך דשתי קופות כשרבו חולין על התרומה אלא כר' יוחנן דלא בעי התם רבייה דלדידיה א"ש דמדמי חמץ להכיא וכולה שמעתא מיירי שהככר כל כך גדול דליכא למימר אכלתיה :

הלך

עין משפט
נר מצוה

סה א מיי' פ"ט מהל' טומאת מת הי"א :
סו ב מיי' פ"ב מהלכות חמץ ומצה הלכה ז וס"ג הלכה ב סמג עשין לט טוש"ע א"ח סי' תלד סעיף א וסי' תלט ס"ב :
סז ג מיי' שם פ"ב הל"י וסמג שם טוש"ע א"ח סי' תלט סעיף א :
סח ד מיי' פ"ח מהל' מאכלות אסורות הל' יא סמג לאוין קמא טור שו"ע י"ד סי' קי סעיף ג :
סט ה מיי' פ"ב מהל' חמץ ומצה הל' יא סמג עשין לט טוש"ע א"ח סי' תלט סעיף ב :
ע ו מיי' פי"ג מהלכות תרומות הל' יד טוש"ע יו"ד סי' קיא סעיף א :

רבינו חננאל

ובא כהן והציץ בו לידע מה הפילה וטהרוהו חכמים מפני שחולדה וברדלס מצוין בבור דאמרינן שמא גררוהו בחור שלהם ולא היה שם בעת שהציץ ולא האהיל עליו ופרקי' לא תימא שהטילה נפל אלא אימא כמין נפל דהוה ספק וספק כו' ושמא גררה חולדה לא חיישי' והתנן מה שמשייר יניחנו במקום מוצנע מאי לאו דחיישי' כי האי גונא וקתני שלא יהיה צריך בדיקה מכלל שאם לא יניח במקום מוצנע צריך בדיקה אמר רבא הכי תנן במתניתין יניחנו במקום מוצנע שמא תטול חולדה בפנינו ויהא צריך בדיקה אחריו תניא כותיה וכן הלכה : תשע צבורין של מצה ואחד של חמץ ושקל עכבר חד מינייהו היינו תשע חנויות דתניא תשע חנוי' כלן מוכרו' בשר שחוטה ואחת מוכרת בשר נבל' [ולקח] ואינו יודע מאיזה מהן לקח ספיקו אסור: פירש אם נפל ככר תפלו עכבר והכניסו לבית היינו סיפא ובנמצא הלך אחר הרוב הלכך אם הרוב מצה מן הבית אינו צריך בדיקה ואם הרוב חמץ צריך בדיקה וכן מניא דהדין שמעתא כולה:[היינו]דתנן שתי קופות אחת של חולין וא' של תרומה ולפניהם שני סאין א' חולין [ואחד תרומה] ונפלו אלו לתוך אלו מותרות שאני אומר חולין לתוך חולין נפלו כו' כך בכאן העכבר שנטל המצה הוא שנכנס בבית הבדוק ואינו צריך בדיקה אחרת ואמרי' איסור דאמרי' שאני אומר חולין לתוך חולין

מסורת הש"ס

נ"ל מאי

[נ"ל ואכילתו]

פ"א ל"ג

[לקמן יג:]

[דתניא כצ"ל]

כתובות טו. חולין צה. נדה יח.

[בפ"ק דסנהד' עט: כצ"ל]

לקמן מד. יבמות פב. נזיר לז: תוספתא דתרומות פ"ה

---

*) [נ"ל דתניא והא דלא מייתי מבנה דתרומות פ"ז מ"ה עי' פי' ר"ש שם וכן בתוס' יבמות פב. ד"ה שתי]

מתני׳ *אין חוששין שמא גוררה חולדה מבית לבית וממקום למקום דא״כ מחצר לחצר ומעיר לעיר אין לדבר סוף: גמ׳ טעמ׳ דלא חזינא דשקל הא חזינא דשקל חיישינן ובעי בדיקה ואמאי נימא אכלתיה מי לא תנן *מדורו׳ העכו״ם טמאים וכמה ישהה במדור ויהא המדור צריך בדיקה ארבעים יום ואע״פ שאין לו אשה *וכל מקום שחולדה וחזיר יכולין להלוך א״צ בדיקה א״ר זירא לא קשיא הא בבשר והא בלחם בבשר לא משיירא בלחם משיירא אמר רבא האי מאי בשלמא התם אימור הוה אימור לא הוה ואם תמצא לומר הוה אימור אכלתיה אבל הכא דודאי דחזינא דשקל מי יימר דאכלתיה הוי ספק וודאי *ואין ספק מוציא מידי ודאי ואין ספק מוציא מידי ודאי והא *תניא חבר שמת והניח מגורה מליאה פירות ואפילו הן בני יומן הרי הן בחזקת מתוקנין והא הכא דודאי טבילי הני פירי וספק מעושרין וספק לא מעושרין וקאתי ספק ומוציא מידי ודאי התם ודאי וודאי הוא דודאי מעשרי כדר׳ חנינא חוזאה *דא״ר חנינא חוזאה חזקה על חבר שאין מוציא מתחת ידו דבר שאינו מתוקן ואי בעית אימא ספק וספק הוא דילמא מעיקר׳ אימור דלא טבילי כר׳ אושעיא דא״ר אושעיא *מערים אדם על תבואתו ומכניסה במוץ שלה כדי שתהא בהמתו אוכלת ופטורה מן המעשר ואין ספק מוציא מידי ודאי והתניא אמר ר׳ יהודה *מעשה בשפחתו של מציק אחד ברימון שהטילה נפל לבור ובא

רש״י

מתני׳ אין חוששין שמא גיררה חולדה כו׳. אין חוששין כשבדק זוית זו ובא לבדוק זו שמא בתוך שבא לבדוק זו גיררה חולדה חמץ למקום הבדוק וצריכא לחזור ולבדוק: שאם כן. שבאת לחוש לכך הרי גם מחצר לחצר יש לומר כך אני בדקתי קודם לחבירי ולאחר בדיקתי הביאה חולדה חמץ מחצר חבירי לחצרי ואין לדבר סוף ולאו חצר ממש קאמר אלא כל בתי החצר קרוי חצר: גמ׳ הא חזינן. שהביאתו לכאן חיישינן שמא עדיין הוא כאן וצריך לבדוק ולמאי נימא אכלתיה: מי לא תנן. במסכת אהלות מדורות העובדי כוכבים טמאין מפני שקוברין נפליהם בבתיהם והעכו״ם מטמאין במיתתן אף באהל לרבנן *ולר״ש בן יוחי כמי דאמר קברי העובדי כוכבים אינם מטמאין במגע ומשא מודה הוא דלא אימעוט אלא מטומאת אהל דלא מקרו אדם: וכמ׳ ישהה העכו״ם במדור ויהא המדור צריך בדיקה לנשיאת העכו״ם וירצה ישראל לדור בו: מ׳ יום. כדי יצירת הולד: ואע״פ שאין עמו אשה. לפי שחשוד הוא על הזנות: וכל מקום שחזיר וחולדה יכולין להלוך אין צריכין בדיקה. שאם הושלך שם חטטוהו ואכלוהו: הא. דאהלות בבשרא מיירי הלכך ודאי אכלוה דלא משתיירא: האי מאי. כלומר מאי קושיא א״כ אורחא דמשייר׳ בבישרא ליכא לן למיחש התם מידי דהתם חששא בעלמא הוא אימור הוה אימור לא הוה הלכך היכא דשכיחא חולדה תלינן לקולא ואמרי׳ אם תמצא לומר הוה אימור אכלתיה וספק אכילה יכול להוציאנו מידי ספק השלכה אבל הכא גבי חמץ דקשיא לך היכא דחזינן דגררה נמי נימא אכלתיה ודאי הוה. מי יימר דאכלתיה. הוי ספק ביעור ודאי חמץ היה כאן ואין ספק היתר מוציא את הבית הזה מידי ודאי איסור: מגורה. גורן: בני יומן. דנכרין הן שהיום נתמרחו: והא הכא. דכיון דממורחין הן והרי הן בבית דכל מגורה בבית היא: ודאי טבילי. דהא נגמרה מלאכתן וראו פני הבית וחל שם טבל עליהן משעה שראה פני הבית ספק עישרן חבר זה ספק לא עישרן ואתי ספק זה ומוציא פירות הללו מידי ודאי טבל: התם ודאי וודאי הוא. משום דרוב חברים מעשרין הם מיד קודם שיניחם מתחת ידו: כי היכי דפשיטא לן דטבילי מעיקרא הכי נמי פשיטא לן דעשרינהו ואין גמגום והילוך אחר הרוב בדבר אלא חזקה ודאי על כל החברים: ואי בעית אימא ספק וספק הוא. כי היכי דמספקא לן אי עשרינהו אי לא עשרינהו הכי נמי איכא לספוקי אי חל עלייהו שם טבל מעולם אי לא ומעיקרא אימור לא טבול ואע״פ שהן ממורחין ובתוך הבית אימור עבד להו כדר׳ הושעיא שהכניסה לבית במוץ שלה ואחר כך דש וממרח וחובת הטבל הלה בראיית פני הבית בבבא מציעא בהשוכר (דף פח:) וזה בראיית פני הבית לא נגמרה מלאכתן לחול עליו שם טבל וכשנגמר מלאכתן כבר בתוך הבית הוא ואין אלו פני הבית אלא כשנכנס דרך פתחים כדתניא *חסידים הראשונים היו מכניסים פירותיהן דרך טרקסמון כדי לחייבן במעשר עכשיו מכניסין דרך גגות דרך אלירות וקרפיפות לבית כדי לפוטרן הלכך לא חייל עלייהו שם טבל ומותר היורש הזה לאוכלן אכילת קבע ולא תימא נהי דלא חייל עלייהו טיבלא לאכילת עראי אכילת קבע מיהא ליתסרו דהא דמיתסרא אכילת קבע קודם קביעות גורן וגמר מלאכה מדרבנן הוא וגבי איסור דרבנן סמכינן אחזקת חבר שעישרן: כדי שתהא בהמתו אוכלת. ואפילו קבע דכל זמן שאין שם גורנו של טבל עליו אינו אוסר באכילת עראי וכל אכילת בהמה לא גזרו עלה משום אכילת קבע דתנן במסכת פאה (פ״א מ״ו) מאכיל לבהמה ולחיה ולעופות ופטור מן המעשרות עד שימרח אבל למאכל אדם נהי דלא טביל מדאורייתא מיהו אפילו קודם מירוח אסרו לאכול קבע בכולי גמרא: מציק. איניש אלמא וישראל הוה:

ובא

תוספות

אין חוששין שמא גיררה חולדה. ואם תאמר והא תריצנא שמעי׳ דקתני כל מקום שאין מכניסין בו חמץ אין צריך בדיקה תרוצ׳ דהוה מוקמינן בשאין חולדה וברדלס יכולין להלך שם:

כל מקום שחולדה וברדלס וחזיר מצויין שם אין צריך בדיקה. אומר ר״י דהכהנים מותרין ליכנס בבתי עובדי כוכבים אפי׳ אין חזיר וחולדה מצויין שם משום דתניא בתוספתא *דאין מדורות העובדי כוכבים בחוצה לארץ:

בבשר לא משיירא. אומר ר״ת דהיינו דוקא בשר נפלים דרכיך דהא בפרק [שני] דב״ק (דף יט. ושם) חשיב חזיר שאכל בשר אכילה על ידי הדחק: ואם תמצא לומר הוה אימור אכלתיה. וא״ת והא מדורות העובדי כוכבים רשות היחיד הן ותנן במסכת טהרות (פ״ו מ״ד) כל מקום שאתה יכול להרבות ספיקות וספיקי ספיקות ברשות היחיד טמא וי״ל דלא דמי הך ספיקא לשאר ספיקי דלאו איכא לן למימר שיהא בו נפל ודמי לספק ביאה א״נ אימור אכלתיה עדיף משאר ספיקות דספק הרגיל הוא וקרוב לודאי ותדע דאפילו מידי ודאי בעי למימר שיוצא זה הספק:

כדי שתהא בהמה אוכלת. ותימה דמ״מ הוי ודאי טבל מדרבנן לענין אכילת קבע אפי׳ הכניסה במוץ שלה כדאמר כדי שתהא בהמה אוכלת משמע אבל הוא עצמו אסור ובתוספתא תניא ומייתי לה בפ״ק דביצה (דף יג.) הכניסם לבית שבולין לעשות מהן עיסה אוכל מהן עראי ופטור וקאתי ספק ומוציא מידי ודאי דרבנן וחשיב להו בחזקת מתוקנים גבי חמץ ואמאי לא אתי ספק ומוציא מידי ודאי בדיקה דרבנן דמדאורייתא בביטול בעלמא סגי ואומר ר״י דמתני׳ איירי בשלא ביטלו דהוי ודאי דאורייתא ועוד אומר ר״י דהא דקאמר הרי הן בחזקת מתוקנין היינו בהכך דלא חזו אלא לבהמה והא דפריך במנחות בפרק רבי ישמעאל (דף סז: ושם) ואמאי דקאמר מירוח הנכרי אינו פוטר משום בעלי כיסין פירות עשירים שמוכרין תבואתן לנכרי קודם מירוח וחוזרין וקונין מהן אחרי מירוח תרומה נמי אפשר דעביד כרבי אושעיא וכו׳ משמע לגמרי פטור ה״פ עביד להו כרבי אושעיא ובמידי דמאכל בהמה מה הועילו חכמים בתקנתן: כדי שתהא בהמה אוכלת. משמע דבטבל שראה פני הבית אפילו בהמה נמי לא אכלה ותימה לר״י מאי שנא משאר הנאה דשרי דלא מצינו טבל שהוא אסור בהנאה ויש לומר דדרשינן בבמה מדליקין (שבת כו: ושם) גבי אין מדליקין בטבל טמא משום דכתיב את משמרת תרומותי בשתי תרומות הכתוב מדבר אחת טהורה ואחת טמאה מה טהורה אין לך בה אלא משעת הרמה ואילך אף טמאה כן והיינו הדלקה והדר גמר טהורה מטמאה מה טמאה דמיתסר בהדלקה קודם הרמה אף טהורה וכן להאכיל לבהמה וכל הנאה של כילוי ומהכא נמי ידעינן דאין ישראל מאכיל לבהמתו כרשיני תרומה ור״ש לא פי׳ כן בשבת*:

בשפחתו של מציק ובא כהן והציץ לידע אם זכר אם נקבה. מכאן אין להוכיח דשפחה מטמאה בלידה דשמא של גבירתה היה מיהו בת״כ אמרינן בהדיא דבר אל בני ישראל אין לי אלא בני ישראל מנין לרבות גיורת ושפחה משוחררת ושאין משוחררת ת״ל אשה והא דפריך בפ׳ הערל (יבמות עד: ושם) מי מלית אמרת תרומה כתיב הכא והתניא דבר אל בני ישראל גיורת ושפחה משוחררת מנין ת״ל אשה הא דנקט התם משוחררת לאו למעוטי שאין משוחררת אלא קיצר הברייתא משום דלא פריך אלא ממשוחררת כדמפסיק ואי ס״ד לתרומה משוחררת בנות מיכל תרומה ניהו ושאין משוחררת אכלה שפיר אם היה של *כהן ואומר ר״י דכהן שוטה היה דאפילו אם לא נאמר של גבירתה היה והכהן זה קרוב היה לא היה לו ליטמא דאמרינן בתורת כהנים דאין כהן מטמא לנפלים דדומיא דאביו ואמו בעינן בני קיימא ועוד דכאן לא היה לצורך המת:

ספק

עין משפט נר מצוה

ס א מיי׳ פ״ב מהלכות חמץ ומצה הלכה ז סמג עשין לט טוש״ע או״ח סי׳ תלג סעיף ח.

סא ב מיי׳ פי״א מהל׳ טומאת מת הלכה ח:

סב ג שם הלכה ח:

סג ד שם הלכה ט:

סד ה מיי׳ פ״ב מהלכות מעשר הלכה ג וסמג עשין קלג טוש״ע יו״ד סי׳ שלא סעיף סד:

רבינו חננאל

אין חוששין שמא גררה חולדה מבית לבית. חששא הוא דלא חיישי׳ הא אי חזינן לחולדה דשקלא נהמא קמן צריך לבדוק עד דמשכח לה ואמאי נימא אכלתיה כדתנן בסוף אהלות בענין מדורות העובדי כוכבים טמאים וכו׳ כ״מ שחולדה וחזיר יכולין להלך אין צריך בדיקה דאמרי׳ כל (שרץ) שהיה שם הללו אכלוהו ופריק ר׳ זירא מתני׳ דאהלות בבשר (שרץ) דלא משיירא לפיכך לא חיישי׳ מתני׳ דהכא בלחם משום דמשיירי רבא אמר התם באהלות ספק וספק הוא אמרינן שמא שרץ היה שם [שמא לא היה] ואם היה שמא אכלוהו הכא ודאי היה שם פת ומשמא אכלוהו לא שרינן ליה דאין ספק דוחה הודאי ומתמהי׳ ולא והתניא חבר שמת והניח מגורה מלאה פירות וכו׳ ודחי׳ התם נמי ודאי הוא שעשרן דחזקה הוא על החבר שאין דבר יוצא מתחת ידו שאינו מתוקן. ירושל׳ ובלבד שמת ביישוב הדעת אי נמי דלמא [לא] טבילי וכר׳ אושעיא עביד דאמר מערים אדם על התבואה ואינו עושה אותה גורן אלא מכניסה במוץ שלה כדי שתהא בהמתו אוכלת המוץ ופטור מן המעשר בחזקת מתוקן אבל אם נתברר דודאי טבילי לא אמרינן בחזקת מתוקנין: ולא והתניא מעש׳ בשפחתו של מציק אחד ברימון. פי׳ שם מקום שהטילה נפל לבור

מסורת הש״ס

אהלות פי״ח מ״ז

[שם מ״ח]

[יבמות סא.]

[יבמו׳ יט: לח.: ע״ז מא: חולין י.]

לעיל ד: ע״א מה: נדה טו:

[עירובין לב.]

כתובות נה. מנחות סז: נדה טו:

שם ע״ז מב. [תוספתא דאהלות פט״ו]

[ברכות לה:]

[וע״ע תוספות לקמן לד. ד״ה מתמין]

[וע״ע בתוספות יבמות עד: ד״ה ושפחה מנין]

MISHNAH. [9a] WE HAVE NO FEAR THAT A WEASEL MAY HAVE DRAGGED [LEAVEN] FROM ONE ROOM TO ANOTHER OR FROM ONE SPOT TO ANOTHER,[3] FOR IF SO, [WE MUST ALSO FEAR] FROM COURT-YARD TO COURT-YARD AND FROM TOWN TO TOWN, [AND] THE MATTER IS ENDLESS.

GEMARA. The reason is that we did not see it take [leaven]; but if we saw it take [it] we do fear, and it requires a [re-]search, yet why so; let us assume that it ate it? Did we not learn: The dwellings of heathens are unclean,[4] and how long must he [the heathen] stay in a dwelling so that it should need searching?[5] Forty days, even if he has no wife. But in every place where a weasel or a swine can enter no searching is required![6]—Said R. Zera, There is no difficulty: one treats of flesh, the other of bread: in the case of flesh it [the weasel] leaves nothing, [whereas in the case of bread it does leave [something]. Raba said: How compare! As for there, it is well: it is [a case of mere] 'say': say that there was [a burial there], say that there was not.[7] And if you assume that there was, say that it [e.g., a weasel] ate it. But here that we see for certain that it has taken [leaven], who is to say that it ate it? Surely it is a doubt [on the one hand] and a certainty [on the other], and a doubt cannot negative a certainty. But cannot a doubt negative a certainty? Surely it was taught:
a If a *ḥaber*[1] dies and leaves a store-house full of produce [crops], even if they are but one day old, they stand in the presumption of having been tithed.[2] Now here these crops were certainly liable to tithe, and there is a doubt whether they have been tithed or not tithed, yet the doubt comes and negatives the certainty?—There it is one certainty against another certainty, as [we presume that] they have *certainly* been tithed, in accordance with R. Ḥanina of Hozae.[3] For R. Ḥanina of Hozae said: There is a presumption concerning a *ḥaber* that he does not let anything untithed[4] pass out from under his hand. Alternatively: it is a doubt [on the one hand] and a doubt [on the other]; perhaps from the very beginning say that it was not liable to tithe, in accordance with R. Oshaia. For R. Oshaia said: One may practise an artifice with his produce and take it in in its husks, so that his cattle may eat thereof and it be exempt from tithes.[5]

But cannot a doubt negative a certainty? Surely it was taught, R. Judah said: It once happened that the bondmaid of a certain oppressor[6] in Rimon[7] threw her premature-born child into a

(3) I.e., after a room has been searched and cleared of leaven a weasel may have brought leaven into it from elsewhere. (4) Because they used to bury their premature births in their houses. (5) For a buried body, before a Jew may live there. (6) If a baby were thrown there these would eat it, Oh. XVIII, 7.—Thus the same should apply to leaven. (7) I.e., the presence there of a dead child is merely conjectured as a possibility.

a (1) V. Glos. (2) V. *supra* 4b. (3) A province of S. W. Persia, now known as Khuzestan; Obermeyer, pp. 204ff. (4) Lit., 'unprepared'. (5) Produce is not liable to tithes unless it is taken into the house through the front door when its work is completed, not through the roof or the backyard. If grain is brought in in its husks its work is not complete, as this is still to be separated, and it is not liable to tithe, and need not be tithed by Scriptural law; a human being may then make a light meal of it, while cattle may eat their fill. Thus there it may never have become liable to tithe at all. Though a human being may not make a meal of it, that is only a Rabbinical law and is certainly nullified here by the presumption that the *ḥaber* had tithed it. But in its essence we see that it is doubt against doubt; the doubt whether it was liable to tithe at all offset by the doubt that it may have been tithed. (6) A powerful Jew (Rashi) who wielded his power oppressively. (7) A town originally belonging to the tribe of Zebulun, on the north-east frontier (Josh. XIX, 13). It may correspond to the present Al-Rummanah, on the southern edge of the plain of Al-Battof, about ten kilometres north of Nazareth.

the future world,'[3] [8b] he is completely righteous.[4]—Perhaps after he searched [for the leaven] he will come to look for it. R. Naḥman b. Isaac said: [It means] on account of the danger of Gentiles, this agreeing with Pelimo. For it was taught: [In the case of] a hole between a Jew and a Syrian [i.e., a Gentile], he must search as far as his hand reaches, and the rest he annuls in his heart. Pelimo said: He does not search it at all, on account of the danger. [Now] what is the danger? Shall we say, the danger of witchcraft,[5]—then when he used it, how did he use it?—There when he used it, it was day and there was light, therefore [the Gentile] would not suspect anything;[6] but here it is night and a lamp [is used]; hence he will suspect. But R. Eleazar said: Those sent [to perform] a religious duty do not suffer harm?[7]—Where the injury is probable it is different, for it is said, *And Samuel said, How can I go? if Saul hear it, he will kill me. And the Lord said, Take a heifer with thee*, etc.[8]

Rab was asked: Scholars who reside out of town, can they come in the early morning or after nightfall to the academy?[9]—He replied: Let them come, [the risk be] upon myself and my neck. What about returning?[10]—I do not know, he answered them. It was stated: R. Eleazar said: Those sent [to perform] a religious duty will not suffer hurt, neither in their going nor in their returning. With whom [does this agree]?—With this Tanna: for it was taught, Issi b. Judah said: Seeing that the Torah said, *no man shall desire thy land [when thou goest up to appear before the Lord*
a *thy God*...],[1] it teaches that your cow will graze in the meadow and no [wild] beast will hurt it; your fowl will go scratching in the dungheap and no weasel will injure it. Now does this not furnish an argument *a minori?* If these, whose nature it is to be hurt, will not be hurt; then human beings, for whom it is not natural to be hurt, how much more so![2] I know it only in respect of going: how do I know it of returning? Because it is stated, *and thou shalt turn in the morning, and go [back] unto thy tents:*[3] this teaches that you will go and find your tent in peace. But since [he is safe] even on [his] return, why [intimate it] in respect of going?[4]—[That is necessary] for R. Ammi's [teaching]. For R. Ammi said: Every man who owns land must make the Festival pilgrimage; but he who does not own land need not make the Festival pilgrimage.[5]

R. Abin son of R. Adda said in R. Isaac's name: Why are there no fruits of Gennesaret[6] in Jerusalem? So that the Festival pilgrims should not say, 'Had we merely ascended in order to eat the fruits of Gennesaret in Jerusalem it would have sufficed us,' with the result[7] that the pilgrimage would not be for its own sake. Similarly R. Dosethai son of R. Jannai said: Why are the thermal springs of Tiberias not [found] in Jerusalem? So that the Festival pilgrims should not say, 'Had we merely ascended in order to bathe in the thermal springs of Tiberias, it would have sufficed us,' with the result that the pilgrimage would not be for its own sake.

THEN IN WHAT CASE DID THEY RULE, TWO ROWS OF THE WINE CELLAR [etc.]? Who has mentioned anything about a wine cellar?—This is what he [the Tanna] says: EVERY PLACE WHEREIN NO LEAVEN IS TAKEN DOES NOT REQUIRE SEARCHING, and stores of wine and stores of oil do not require searching either. THEN IN WHAT CASE DID THEY RULE, TWO ROWS OF THE WINE CELLAR [MUST BE SEARCHED]? [CONCERNING] A PLACE WHEREIN LEAVEN MAY BE TAKEN, which is one whence [private] supplies are drawn.

BETH SHAMMAI MAINTAIN: TWO ROWS, etc. Rab Judah said: The two rows which they [Beth Shammai] specified [mean] from
b the ground up to the very ceiling;[1] but R. Joḥanan said: [It means] a single row in the shape of a right angle.[2] It was taught in accordance with Rab Judah; [and] it was taught in accordance with R. Joḥanan. It was taught in accordance with Rab Judah: Beth Shammai maintain: Two rows over the front [surface] of the whole cellar, and the two rows which they specified [means] from the ground up to the very ceiling. It was taught in accordance with R. Joḥanan: Two rows over the face of the whole cellar, [i.e.,] the outer one which looks upon the door, and the upper one which faces[3] the ceiling; but that which is within this and below this does not require searching.

BETH HILLEL MAINTAIN: THE TWO OUTER ROWS, WHICH ARE THE UPPERMOST. Rab said: [That means,] the upper row and the one beneath it;[4] while Samuel said: [That means] the upper row and the one on the inside of it. What is Rab's reason? —Because he emphasizes: OUTER. But it [also] teaches: UPPERMOST?—That is to exclude those beneath the lower one.[5] While Samuel says: 'The upper row and the one on the inside of it'. What is the reason? Because he emphasizes: UPPERMOST. But it [also] states: OUTER?—That is to exclude the inner of the
c inner.[1] R. Ḥiyya taught in accordance with Rab, while all tannaim recited as Samuel. And the law is as Samuel.[2]

(3) Lit., 'that I may be a son of the future world'. On the 'future world' v. Sanh., 90a, n. 3. (4) In respect of his action, notwithstanding his selfish motives. Hence in the case under discussion the same holds good. (5) *Sc.* the Gentile may suspect him of witchcraft when he sees him rummaging in the hole. (6) Lit., 'bring it up on his mind'. (7) To be the object of these suspicions is to suffer harm. (8) I Sam. XVI, 2. Thus Samuel was afraid though engaged on a Divine mission, because it was *naturally* dangerous. (9) Do they run a risk in going over the fields at such times? (10) After nightfall.

a (1) Ex. XXXIV, 24. (2) They are certainly immune from danger when going to carry out a religious duty, to which the present verse refers. (3) Deut. XVI, 7. (4) Surely that follows *a fortiori*. (5) This follows from the fact that the Almighty assures the pilgrim that his land will be safe in his absence, which proves that the command refers only to those who possess land. (6) A lake so named from the fertile plain lying on its western side. In the O.T. it is called Yam Kinnereth or Kinneroth; Num. XXXIV, 11; Josh. XII, 3. On its western shore lay Tiberias.—Its fruit was particularly delicious. (7) Lit., 'and it would be found'.

b (1) I.e., the two outer rows of barrels from top to bottom, over their entire area. (2) *Gam*, the shape of the Grk. *Gamma* Γ. I.e., the front row and the whole of the upper layer. (3) Lit., 'sees'. (4) In the outermost row facing the door. (5) I.e., all rows from the third from the top and downwards.

c (1) Those within the second row of the top layer. (2) From the fact that all post-Talmudic authorities accept Rab's view, however, it would appear that this passage was absent from their texts; [v. Tosaf. Yom Tob on our Mishnah and MS.M. R. Ḥananel, however, has this passage and accepts Samuel's ruling.]

עין משפט נר מצוה

נז א מיי' פ"ג מהלכות חמץ ומצה הל' ה סמג עשין לט טוש"ע או"ח סי' תלג סעיף ז:
נח ב מיי' שם טוש"ע שם סעיף ג:
נט ג מיי' שם הלכה ו טוש"ע שם סעיף ט:

הרי זה צדיק גמור דילמא בתר דבדק אתי לעיוני בתרה ר"נ בר יצחק אמר משום סכנת הנכרים ופלימו היא דתני' חור שבין יהודי לארמאי בודק עד מקום שידו מגעת והשאר מבטלו בלבו פלימו אמר *כל עצמו אינו בודק מפני הסכנה מאי סכנה אי נימא סכנת כשפים כי אישתמיש היכי אישתמיש התם כי אישתמיש יממא ונהורא ולא מסיק אדעתיה הכא ליליא ושרגא הוא ומסיק אדעתיה והאמר רבי אלעזר *שלוחי מצוה אינן ניזוקין היכא דשכיח היזיקא שאני שנאמר °ויאמר שמואל איך אלך ושמע שאול והרגני ויאמר ה' עגלת בקר תקח בידך וגו' בעו מיניה מרב הני בני בי רב דדיירי בבאגא מהו למיתי קדמא וחשוכא לבי רב אמר להו *ניתו עלי ועל צוארי ניזיל מאי אמר להו לא ידענא איתמר א"ר אלעזר שלוחי מצוה אינן ניזוקין לא בהליכתן ולא בחזירתן כמאן כי האי תנא דתניא איסי בן יהודה אומר כלפי שאמרה תורה °ולא יחמוד איש את ארצך מלמד שתהא פרתך רועה באפר ואין חיה מזיקתה תרנגולתך מנקרת באשפה ואין חולדה מזיקתה והלא דברים ק"ו ומה אלו שדרכן לזוק אינן ניזוקין בני אדם שאין דרכן לזוק על אחת כמה וכמה אין לי אלא בהליכה בחזרה מנין תלמוד לומר °ופנית בבקר והלכת לאהליך מלמד שתלך ותמצא אהלך בשלום וכי מאחר דאפילו בחזירה בהליכה למה לי לכדר' אמי דא"ר אמי כל אדם שיש לו קרקע עולה לרגל °ושאין לו קרקע אין עולה לרגל א"ר אבין בר רב אדא אמר ר' יצחק מפני מה אין פירות גינוסר בירושלים כדי שלא יהו עולי רגלים אומרים *אלמלא לא עלינו אלא לאכול פירות גינוסר בירושלים דיינו נמצאת עלייה שלא לשמה כיוצא בו אמר ר' דוסתאי בר' ינאי מפני מה אין חמי טבריא בירושלים כדי שלא יהו עולי רגלים אומרים *אלמלא לא עלינו אלא לרחוץ בחמי טבריא דיינו ונמצאת עלייה שלא לשמה: ובמה אמרו ב' שורות וכו': מרתף מאן דכר שמיה [a]הכי קאמר כל מקום שאין מכניסין בו חמץ אין צריך בדיקה ואוצרות יין ואוצרות שמן נמי אין צריך בדיקה ובמה אמרו שתי שורות במרתף מקום שמכניסין בו חמץ ובמסתפק: בש"א שתי שורות וכו': אמר רב יהודה שתי שורות שאמרו מן הארץ ועד שמי קורה ורבי יוחנן אמר שורה אחת כמין *גאם תניא כוותיה דרב יהודה תניא כוותיה דרבי יוחנן תניא כוותיה דרב יהודה בית שמאי אומרים שתי שורות על פני כל המרתף ושתי שורות שאמרו מן הארץ ועד שמי קורה תניא כוותיה דרבי יוחנן שתי שורות על פני כל המרתף חיצונה רואה את הפתח ועליונה רואה את הקורה שלפנים הימנה ושלמטה הימנה אין צריך בדיקה: בית הלל אומרים שתי שורות החיצונות שהן העליונות: אמר רב °עליונה ושלמטה הימנה ושמואל אמר עליונה ושלפנים הימנה מאי טעמא דרב דייק חיצונות והא עליונות קתני למעוטי תתאי דתתייתא ושמואל אמר עליונה ושלפנים הימנה מאי טעמא דייק עליונות והא חיצונה קתני למעוטי גוייאתא דגוייאתא רבי חייא תני כוותיה דרב וכולהו תנאי תנו כוותיה דשמואל והלכתא כוותיה *דשמואל:

מתניתין

רש"י

הרי זה צדיק גמור. בדבר זה ולא אמרינן שלא לשמה עושה אלא קיים מצות בוראו שצוהו לעשות צדקה ומתכוין אף להנאת עצמו שיזכה בה לעולם הבא או שיחיו בניו: בתר דבדק. וגמר את כל המצוה אתי לעיוני בתרה: כל עצמו אינו בודק. כל עצמו של חור אינו בודק שלא יאמר הנכרי כשפים עשה לי: ולאו אדעתיה. דנכרי לשום אל לבו עלילה זו: איך אלך. למשוח את דוד ואע"פ ששלוחו של מקום היה הרי היה ירא: בני בי רב. תלמידים הצריכים לרבם עדיין קרו בני בי רב: דדיירו בבאגי. בכפרים שבבקעה ובלע"ז קנפי"א: מהו למיתי קדמא וחשוכא. השכם והערב קודם עלות השחר ומשתחשך כלום יש להם לירא מן המזיקים: ועל צוארי. יהא עונש הזיקן דולאי לא יוזקו שהמצוה מגינה עליהם: ניזיל. לאושפיזא משתחשך מאי כלום יכולין לסמוך על המצוה אף בחזרה או לא: כלפי שאמרה תורה. מתוך שאמרה תורה כך אנו למדין שהבטיחו הכתוב שלא יוזק ממונו וכל שכן גופו דאין דרכו לזוק דאדם אית ליה מזלא ואינו מהיר להיות ניזק בגופו: כדרבי אמי. קרא קמא לכדר' אמי אתא: פירות גינוסר. מתוקין מאד כדאמרי' בברכות (דף מד.) והיינו כינרת שם מדינה בארץ ישראל: מרתף מאן דכר שמיה. לפוטרו מן הבדיקה דקא מתמה תנא קמא ואמר ובמה אמרו הכי קאמר. דקתני רישא כל מקום שאין מכניסין כו' ואמרי' לעיל כל מקום לאיתויי מאי לאיתויי אוצרות יין ושמן ומשום הכי אמרי' ובמה אמרו לקמן לריך בדיקה ומפרש במקום שמכניסין בו חמץ והיכי דמי כגון במסתפק: שתי שורות שאמרו. בית שמאי (אומרים) מן הארץ ועד שמי קורה דרך האוצרי יין לסדר חביותיהן שורות שורות עד שממלאין כל קרקע המרתף וחוזרין ומניחין חבית על חבית בשורות התחתונות עד הקורה ואמרי בית שמאי שאותן שתי שורות חיצונות אותה שרואה את הפתח על פני רוחב כל המרתף והשורה שלאחריה צריך לבדוק מן הארץ עד התקרה: שמי קורה. כמו שמי השמים (תהלים קמח): ור' יוחנן אמר. שתי שורות שאמרו בית שמאי היא שורה חיצונה מן הארץ ועד תקרה וחוזר ובודק כל החביות העליונות על פני כל ארכו ורחבו של מרתף שאף היא נקראת שורה אם באת למנות מלמעלה למטה: גאם. היא *גימ"ל יוונית ועשויה כמין כף שלנו פתוחה שורה אחת כמין גאם היינו שורה בזקיפה ושורה עליונה בשכיבה כאדם הבודק כותל הבית מבחוץ והגג: הרואה את הקורה. דהיינו כל גג השורות: שלפנים הימנה. של חיצונה: ושלמטה הימנה. של עליונה אינה צריכה בדיקה: בית הלל אומרים כו'. מתני' קא נסיב: עליונה ושלמטה הימנה. האי עליונה לא כל גג השורות באורך המרתף קאמר כדאמר רבי יוחנן אליבא דבית שמאי אלא שורת חבית אחת על פני רוחב כל המרתף ולא מן הארץ ועד הקורה אלא אותה שורה הרואה את הפתח ואת הקורה: ושלמטה הימנה. ועוד שורת חבית אחת למטה מן העליונה היא משורה הזקופה כנגד הפתח והאי פתח לאו כנגדו ממש קאמר אלא הכותל שהפתח בו קרי הכי: עליונה ושלפנים הימנה. בגג החבית בודק שתי שורות על פני כל המרתף: מאי טעמא דרב. דלא בעי למימר עליונה ושלפנים הימנה כמשמעותיה דמתניתין דהא מתניתין עליונות קתני: דייק חיצונות. ואותה שלפנים לאו חיצונה היא וקא סבר רב דתנא דמתני' בחיצונות דק בלישניה אבל בעליונות לא דק בלישניה: תתאי דתתייתא. כגון שלישית ושתחתיה: ושמואל דייק עליונות. והא של מטה לאו עליונה היא:

מתני'

תוספות

שיזכה לעולם הבא הרי זה צדיק גמור. והדתנן (אבות פ"א מ"ג) אל תהיו כעבדים המשמשין את הרב על מנת לקבל פרס היינו בכה"ג שאם לא תבוא לו אותה הטובה שהוא מלפה תוהא ומתחרט על הצדקה שעשה אבל מי שאינו תוהא ומתחרט ה"ז צדיק גמור וכן משמע בריש מסכת ר"ה (דף ד.) ובפ"ק דב"ב (דף י: *): מלמד שתהא פרתך רועה באפר. ומאת קדריש את ארצך הטפל לארצך: לכדרבי אמי. ואם תאמר והשתא את למה לי למידרש בהליכה ואור"י דלא נכתב אלא °משום דבר שנתחדש בה משום חדוש דארצך כתב נמי את למדרש אע"ג דלא איצטריך: רב דייק חיצונות. נראה לר"י דרב סבר דאיכא למידק טפי מחיצונות משום דתנן ברישא ושמואל סבר דמעליונות איכא למידק כיון דעליונות אחיצונות קאי ומפרש מה הן חיצונות:

אין

רבינו חננאל

לכן. ואמרינן וכה"ג לאו מצוה היא והתניא האומר סלע זו לצדקה בשביל שיחיה בני בשביל שאזכה לעולם הבא הרי זה צדיק גמור ופרקי' חיישינן דלמא מסח דעתיה מבדיקת המקלגמרי ואינו מחפש אלא על המחם שאין שם מצוה להגן עליו: רב נחמן בר יצחק אמר משום סכנת שכט נכרי שלא יחשדוהו ויאמר היהודי שכני כשפים עושה לי בכותל ויסכנהו ואע"ג דקי"ל שלוחי מצוה אינן ניזוקין היכא דקביעא היזקא שאני דכתיב איך אלך ושמע שאול והרגני והא שמואל לקיים דבר ה' שהיא מצוה היה הולך אלא במקום שיש היזק קבוע לא סמכינן אהאי שנא' ויאמר ה' עגלת בקר תקח בידך: בעו מרב הני בי רב ששוכנים בשדות מהו שיבאו בלילה בשחר ליכנס לבהמ"ד ויחזרו משחשכ' הוששין מהיזק או לא אמר להם יבאו עלי ועל צוארי כלומר יבואו ואני ערב להם שלא יהיה בהם היזק לא בביאתן ולא בחזירתן כמאן כי האי תנא דתניא איסי בן יהודה אומר כלפי שאמרה תורה ולא יחמוד איש את ארצך בעלותך: מפני מה אין פירות גינסר בירושלים שלא יאמרו עולי רגלים אלו לא עלינו אלא לאכול פירות הללו דיינו ונמצאת עלייה שלא לשמה ומפני מה אין חמי טבריא בירושלים וכו': למה אמרו שתי שורות. אקשי' מי הזכיר בכאן מרתף כלל עד שיאמר למה אמרו שתי שורות במרתף ופרקי' כיון דתנא כל מקום שאין מכניסין בו חמץ אין צריך בדיקה ממילא שמעי' דמרתף אין צריך בדיקה אם כן למה אמרו שתי שורות במרתף מקום שמכניסין בו חמץ היכי דמי במסתפק ממנו: אמר רב יהודה שתי שורות שאמרו מן הארץ ועד שמי קורה ר' יוחנן אמר שורה א' כמין גמא כלומר ממשש המרתף השורה החיצונה הרואה את הפתח והעליונות הרואות את הקורות זהו כמין גמא יווני ותניא כתרוייהו: ב"ה אומר שתי שורות החיצונות שהן העליונות. פי' כל השורות שבמרתף ראשיהם של כלם רואות את הקורות וצדי כל השורות רואות את הפתח לפיכך אמר רב עליונה ושלמטה הימנה דדייק חיצונות ואע"פ שכל השורות ראשיהם שכנגד הפתח כלן חיצונות אינך מוצא שתים חיצונות כאחת אלא אם תפשים ותקח השורה העליונה ושלמטה הימנה כי אם תקח שורה אחת מן הארץ ועד שמי קורה שבפנים ממנה פנימית נקראת ודייק רב חיצונות ממש ומשום זה קתני שהן עליונות ללמדך כי מטעלה מתחיל ושמואל ושלפנים הימנה דהוא דייק עליונות כלומר העליונות דוקא ולא תמצא שתים עליונות אלא כי האי גונא ומפני מה קתני חיצונות למעוטי מן השורה השלישית ולפנים שדברי הכל אין צריך בדיקה. תאני ר' חייא כוותיה דרב וכלהו תנאי תנו כשמואל ואע"ג דקיימא לן הלכתא כרב באיסורי וזו איסור היא כאן דכולהו תנאי תנו כשמואל הלכתא כוותיה הלכך בית שהוא מלא חביות של יין מן הקצה אל הקצה ומקרקע הבית עד שמי קורה זהו מרתף בודק השורה הרואה את הפתח ושלפנים הימנה אלו שניהן בודק משמי קורה ועד הקרקע ודיו:

מסורת הש"ס

יומא יא. קידושין לט: חולין קמב.

שמואל א טז

[ע"י ז.]

שמות לד

דברים טז

[עי' תוס' מגילה כא. ד"ה אלמלא]

[ערוך ערך גם פי' כמין ד' הפוכה]

[מכל הפוסקים ראשונים ואחרונים דפסקו כרב מוכח דלא היה בגירסתם והלכתא כוותיה דשמואל. וכ"כ התוי"ט ד"ה שתי]

גליון הש"ס

גמ' ושאין לו קרקע. וכן איתא בירושלמי ספ"ג דפאה: תוס' ד"ה לכדר"א וכו' משום דבר שנתחדש. כדאיתא שבועות יט ע"א כל פרשה שנאמרה ונשנית לא נשנית אלא בשביל דבר שנתחדש בה:

מפני שאור הנר יפה לבדיקה ואע"פ שאין ראיה לדבר זכר לדבר שנאמר °שבעת ימים שאור לא ימצא בבתיכם ואומר °ויחפש בגדול החל ואומר °בעת ההיא אחפש את ירושלים בנרות ואומר °נר ה' נשמת אדם חופש כל חדרי בטן האי אור החמה היכי דמי אי נימא בחצר האמר רבא ^א^חצר אינה צריכה בדיקה מפני שהעורבין מצויין שם אלא באכסדרה האמר רבא ^ב^אכסדרה לאורה נבדקת לא צריכא לארובה דבחדר ודהיכא ^ג^אי להדי ארובה היינו אכסדרה אלא לצדדין ואבוקה לא והאמר רבא מאי דכתיב °ונוגה כאור תהיה קרנים מידו לו ושם חביון עוזו *למה צדיקים דומין בפני שכינה כנר בפני האבוקה ואמר רבא *אבוקה להבדלה מצוה מן המובחר אמר רב נחמן בר יצחק זה יכול להכניסו לחורין ולסדקין וזה אינו יכול להכניסו לחורין ולסדקין רב זביד אמר זה אורו לפניו וזה אורו לאחריו רב פפא אמר האי בעית והאי לא בעית רבינא אמר האי משך נהורא והאי מיקטף איקטופי: כל מקום שאין מכניסין בו כו': כל מקום לאתויי מאי לאתויי הא דתנו רבנן ^ה^חורי בית העליונים והתחתונים ^ו^וגג היציע וגג המגדל ^ז^ורפת בקר ולולין ומתבן ^ח^ואוצרות יין ואוצרות שמן אין צריכין בדיקה רשב"ג אומר מטה החולקת בתוך הבית ומפסקת צריכה בדיקה ורמינהו ^ט^חור שבין אדם לחבירו זה בודק עד מקום שידו מגעת וזה בודק עד מקום שידו מגעת והשאר מבטלו בלבו ר' שמעון בן גמליאל אומר מטה החולקת בתוך הבית ועצים ואבנים סדורים תחתיה ומפסקת אינה צריכה בדיקה קשיא מטה אמטה קשיא חורין אחורין חורין אחורין לא קשיא הא בעילאי ובתתאי והא במיצעי מטה אמטה לא קשיא הא דמידליא הא דמיתתאי ואוצרות יין אין צריך בדיקה והתניא אוצרות יין צריך בדיקה הכא במאי עסקינן במסתפק אי הכי שמן נמי שמן יש קבע לאכילה יין אין קבע לשתיה תני רבי חייא עשו אוצרות שכר בבבל כאוצרות יין בארץ ישראל במסתפק אמר רב חסדא בי דגים אין צריך בדיקה והתניא צריכין בדיקה לא קשיא הא ברברבי הא בזוטרי אמר רבה בר רב הונא בי מילחי ובי קירי צריך בדיקה אמר רב פפא בי ציבי ובי תמרי צריך בדיקה תנא אין מחייבין אותו להכניס ידו לחורין ולסדקין לבדוק מפני הסכנה מאי סכנה אי נימא מפני סכנת עקרב כי משתמש היכי אישתמש ^י^לא צריכא דנפל אי נפל למה לי בדיקה והתנן *חמץ שנפלה עליו מפולת הרי הוא כמבוער התם שאין הכלב יכול לחפש אחריו הכא כשהכלב יכול לחפש אחריו והא אמר ר' אלעזר *שלוחי מצוה אינן ניזוקין אמר רב אשי שמא תאבד לו מחט ואתי לעיוני בתרה וכה"ג לאו מצוה הוא והתניא *האומר סלע זו לצדקה בשביל שיחיו בני או שאהיה בן העוה"ב הרי

תורה אור

שמות יב | צפניה א | משלי כ | חבקוק ג

רש"י

מפני שאור הנר יפה לבדיקה. לקמיה מפרש מאי מעליותא מאבוקה: לאורה נבדקת. לאור שלה נבדקת ואין צריך להביא לה אור הנר בלילה אלא בודקה ביום: ודהיכא. באיזה מקום בחדר לא סגיא לה לאור הארובה: אי נימא להדי ארובה. נגד האור ממש אמאי לא היינו אכסדרה: לצדדין. ונוגה. של עתיד לצדיקים כאור של שבעת ימי בראשית יהיה: קרנים. מלשון כי קרן עור פניו (שמות לד) והאורין מיד הקב"ה לו לצדיק מזיו של הקב"ה ילכו והאורין להקרין פני הצדיקים ולא יהיה אורם שוה לאורו אלא כנר בפני האבוקה: אורו לאחריו. והאדם האוחזו לפניו הוא בודק הלכך אין יפה לבדיקה: בעית. מתירא שלא יבעיר את הבית ואין לבו על הבדיקה יפה: האי משיך נהוריה. אור הנר נמשך ומאריך במקומו ואינו דולק בקפיצות אלא נח במקום אחד: מיקטף איקטופי. נפסק וקופץ תמיד לשון הקוטפים מלוח (איוב ל): כל לאיתויי מאי. דלא תנא מקום *שמכניסין בו כו': חורי. שבכותל: העליונים והתחתונים. הגבוהים יותר מדאי והנמוכים יותר מדאי ואין נוחין להשתמש אין צריך לבדוק: וגג היציע. אע"פ שהוא נמוך הואיל ומשופע אין צריך לבדוק אבל שאר גגין שלהן לא היו משופעין: יציע. אנפריי"ן: גג המגדל. משטיי"ר של עץ שנותנים לתוכו כלים ואוכלים תוכו צריך בדיקה ולא גגו: ורפת בקר. שאם היה שם חמץ הבהמות אכלוהו: ולולין. מקום דירת תרנגולין: ומתבן. בית התבן דמה דרכו של חמץ שם וכן אוצרות יין ושמן: החולקת. מעמידין אותה במקום מחיצה לחלק תשמישי הבית ואורחא דמילתא נקט: ומפסקת. יש הפסק בין שוליה לקרקע כגון שרגליה גבוהים למטה: עד מקום שידו מגעת. כגון שהכותל עב הרבה: ומפסקת. יש אויר בין שוליה לעלים: קשיא חורין אחורין. דקא תני הכא חורין צריכין בדיקה: הא דקתני לעיל אין צריכין בעילאי ותתאי שאין נוחה תשמישתן כדקתני בהדיא והא במלמעלי שנוחים להשתמש: דמדליא. שגבוהה הרבה ויש אויר תחתיה הרבה נוחה תשמישתה: דמיתתאי. אף על פי שיש קצת אויר אין נוחה תשמישתה: במסתפק. אוצר שמסתפק הימנו יין לשולחנו צריך בדיקה פעמים שהשמש נכנס להביא יין כשהוא כלה על השולחן ופתו בידו: יש קבע לאכילה. יודע הוא כמה שמן צריך לכך וכך בני אדם ומביאו קודם סעודה ואין צריך לעמוד מן השלחן ולהביא אבל יין אין קבע לשתיה פעמים ששתיית סעודה [זו] מרובה משל אתמול ואין השמש בקי בדבר: עשו אוצרות שכר בבבל. להצריך בדיקה במסתפק כאוצרות יין בארץ ישראל דכיון דרגילין בו אין קבע לשתייתו: הא ברברבי. אין צריך בדיקה שיש להם קבע ואומד ואין צריך לעמוד ולהביא באמצע הסעודה: זוטרי. אין להם קבע ואומד וצריך לעמוד ולס"א: בי מלחי: בית המלח: ובי קירי. שעוה צריך בדיקה לפי שעומד מתוך הסעודה להביא מלח ונרות: דנפל. אם נפל הבנין אין מחייבין אותו לבדוק את גל אבנים אלא למראית העין אבל לא להכניס ידו ביניהן ומתחלה כשהיה הכותל קיים נשתמש בחוריו ועכשיו נפל ויש שם סכנת עקרבים שדרכן לימצא באשפות ובגלין: בשאין הכלב יכול לחפש אחריו. הכי מפרש לה *ר"ש בפ"ב *ותניא כמה חפישת הכלב שלשה טפחים: שמא תאבד לו מחט. קודם לכן ואתי השתא לעיוני בתרה וכיון דמתכוין אף למחט לאו שליח מצוה הוא וניזוק: וכה"ג. דמתכוין למצוה ולצרכו לאו שליח מצוה הוא בתמיה:

ר"ה שאין לקמן קג: | נה: כ"מ מג. | לקמן: וכ"מ | יו"ד | [לקמן לא:] [נ"ל רשב"ג]

תוספות

מטה החולקת בתוך הבית ומפסקת. פרש"י דלענין תחתיה מיירי וקשה דלפי' לא ה"ל למימר החולקת אלא מפסקת ותו לא אלא י"ל חולקת בתוך הבית ומפסקת היינו שמונחת באמצע הבית וחולקת היינו שמגעת מכותל לכותל ואינו יכול לעבור מצד אחר אלא על גבי המטה או ישוח ויעבור תחתיה וקאמר דאין צריך בדיקה לצד הפנימי וכן משמע בירושל' ובתוספתא* [ס"א] דקאמר רשב"ג אומר מטה שהיא חוצצת החולקת בתוך הבית ועלים ואבנים מונחים תחתיה בודק לצד החיצון ואינו בודק לצד הפנימי ומתוך הירושלמי משמע דברייתא דקתני בה עלים ואבנים גרס אין צריך בדיקה והא דלא משני הכא שיש עלים ואבנים משום דלא משמע ליה שבשביל כך אין צריך בדיקה [אלא] משום דאין דרך לשוח ולעבור תחת המטה ומשני הא דמידליא התם צריך בדיקה לפי שרגליה גבוהין ויכול לעבור תחתיה בלא שחייה אי נמי במידליא א"נ דלא ניחא לעלות על גבה ולעבור וי"ס דגרסי אין צריך בקמייתא ובבתרייתא צריך ולפי גירסא זו נקט עלים ואבנים סדורים תחתיה לרבותא ור"ח גרס בתרווייהו אין צריך ופריך מהא דבקמייתא לא בעינן עלים סדורים ובבתרייתא בעינן: **הכא** כשהכלב יכול לחפש אחריו. ולכך אינו פטור אלא מפני הסכנה והא דמשמע גבי מפולת דאם הכלב יכול לחפש אינו כמבוער וצריך לבערו ולא מיפטר מפני סכנת עקרב אור"י שאני התם דודאי איכא חמץ הטריחוהו חכמים *להשכיר פועלים במרא וחצינא אבל הכא שאין החמץ ידוע לא הטריחוהו: שיזכה

[לקמן לא: ע"ש]

רש"ל

[פי' אורה מידו של הקב"ה לו לצדיק כמו כי קרן עור פני משה והם חביון עוזו לפי' מעט"ש אלא המקום עוזו כלומר תוקף האור הגדול אצל הקב"ה יותר מאצל הצדיקים ערוך כערך קרן]

עין משפט נר מצוה

מט א מיי' שם הל' ד טוש"ע שם סעיף ו:
נ ב ג מיי' שם טוש"ע שם סעיף ח:
נא ד מיי' שם הלכה ו טוש"ע שם סעיף ד:
נב ה מיי' שם טוש"ע שם סעיף ט:
נג ו מיי' שם טוש"ע שם סעיף י:
נד ז מיי' שם טוש"ע שם סעיף ג:
נה ח מיי' שם הלכה ט טוש"ע שם סעי' ו:
נו ט מיי' שם טוש"ע שם סעיף ט:

רבינו חננאל

הנר מפני שאור הנר יפה לבדיקה. ואע"ג דקי"ל חצר אין צריכה בדיקה הואיל ועורבין מצויין שם ואכסדרה לאורה נבדקת (אתא) ולא לאור החמה [אתא] לאשמעינן שהבודק ביום בזמן שהחמה מצויה בעולם כשהוא בודק בבית אינו בודק אלא בנר וכן באבוקה אע"ג שהאבוקה להבדלה מצוה מן המובחר אין בודקין אלא בנר דמשיך נהוריה ואורו לפניו ויכול להכניסו בחורין ובסדקין: תנו רבנן חורי הבית העליונים כו'. פי' העליונים שאין יד מגעת להשתמש בהן וכן התחתונים עם הקרקע והגג שאין בני אדם משתמשין בו וכן היציע וזה היציע יש לו שלש שמות יציע צלע והתא יציע דכתיב (מ"א ו ו) היציע התחתונה וצלע ומפרש בפ' המוכר את הבית בתחלתו וכן הרפת דכתיב (חבקוק ג יז) ואין בקר ברפתים ולולין דכתי' (מ"א ו ח) ובלולים יעלו. ומתבן כמשמעו. ואוצרות יין ושמן שאין מסתפקין מהן ואין נכנסין בהם בכל שעה דליכא למיחש שמא נכנס אדם שם בפת שבידו ושכחו כל אלו אין צריכין בדיקה וכן מטה החולקת בבית אם היא מושלת בקרקעית הבית ומפסקת כלומר היא מיושבת מן הכותל של בית עד הכותל שכנגדו ואין אדם יכול לעבור לא מתחתיה ולא מצדדיה כל הבית שהוא אחורי המטה אין צריך בדיקה ואם מטה זו מידליא עד שיהיו עצים ואבנים סדורין תחתיה שאין מי שיכול לעבור תחתיה ואם הם אוצרות יין ושמן במסתפק מהן וכן אוצרות שכר בבבל ובי דגים קטנים ובי ציבי ובי תמרי ובי מלחי ובי קירי כולן צריכין בדיקה. פי' קירי שעוה: תנא אין מחייבין אותו להכניס ידו לחור שנפל עכשיו ואע"ג שהכלב יכול לחפש אחריו דחיישינן לסכנת עקרב ואע"ג דאמר ר' אלעזר שלוחי מצוה אין ניזוקין חיישינן שמא יתכוין לחפש אגב חיפוש החמץ על מרם שאבדה לו קודם לכן

save by the light of a lamp, [8a] because the light of a lamp is suitable for searching. And though there is no proof of the matter yet there is a hint of it, for it is said, *'seven days shall there be no leaven found [in your houses]'*; and it is said, *'and he searched, and began at the eldest,* [etc.]', and it is said, *'and it shall come to pass at that time, that I will search Jerusalem with lamps'*; and it is said, *'The soul of man is the lamp of the Lord, searching all the innermost parts of the belly'*.

This light of the sun, where is it meant? Shall we say, in a court-yard,—but Raba said: A court-yard does not require searching, because birds frequent it.[3] While if in a hall,[4]—but Raba said: A hall is searched by its own light?—This is meant only in respect of a skylight in a room. But [then] what part of it? If [that which is] opposite the skylight, then it is the same as a hall?—Rather, it means [the part of the room] at the sides.

And not [by the light of] a torch? Surely Raba said, What is the meaning of the verse, *And his brightness was as the light; he had rays coming forth from his hand: and there was the hiding of his power?*[5] To what are the righteous comparable in the presence of the *Shechinah?* To a lamp in the presence of a torch.[6] And Raba also
a said: [To use] a torch for *habdalah*[1] is the most preferable [way of performing this] duty?—Said R. Naḥman b. Isaac: The one[2] can be brought into holes and chinks [in the wall], whereas the other[3] cannot be brought into holes and chinks. R. Zebid said: The one[2] [throws] its light forward, whereas the other[3] [throws] its light behind.[4] R. Papa said: Here [with a torch] one is afraid, whereas there [with a lamp] one is not afraid.[5] Rabina said: The light of the one[2] is steady, whereas that of the other[3] is fitful.[6]

EVERY PLACE WHEREIN LEAVEN IS NOT TAKEN, etc. What does EVERY PLACE add?—It adds the following taught by our Rabbis: The topmost and the nethermost holes of a room,[7] the roof of the verandah,[8] the roof of a turret,[9] a cow's stable, hen-coops, a shed for straw, and store-houses of wine and oil do not need searching.[10] R. Simeon b. Gamaliel said: A bed which makes a division in a room[11] and leaves a space[12] needs searching. But the following contradicts it: A hole [lying] between a man and his neighbour,[13] this one searches as far as his hand reaches and that one searches as far as his hand reaches,[14] and the rest he annuls in his heart. R. Simeon b. Gamaliel said: A bed which makes a division in a room, timber and stones being arranged under it, and it leaves a space,[15] does not require searching. Thus [the rulings on] a bed are contradictory and [those on] holes are contradictory?—[The rulings on] holes are not contradictory: the one
b refers to the topmost and the nethermost;[1] the other to [holes in] the middle [of the wall]. [The rulings on] a bed are not contradictory: here it is raised; there it is low down.[2]

But, do not store-houses of wine require searching? Surely it was taught, Store-houses of wine need searching; stores of oil do not need searching?—The case we discuss here is where one draws his [immediate] supplies [from it].[3] If so, oil too?—As for oil, there is a limit to eating; but [in respect to] wine, there is no limit to drinking.[4] R. Ḥiyya taught: Stores of beer in Babylonia were made the same as stores of wine in Palestine, where one draws his supplies from them.[5]

R. Ḥisda said: A fish pantry does not require searching. But it was taught [that] they require searching?—There is no difficulty: the one treats of large [fish]; the other of small.[6] Rabbah son of R. Huna said: Salt sheds and wax sheds[7] need searching.[8] R. Papa said: Storehouses for fuel[9] and storehouses for dates need searching.

A Tanna taught: We do not oblige him to insert his hand into holes and chinks and search [there], on account of the danger. Which danger? Shall we say, the danger of a snake,—then when he used it, how could he use it?—This arises only where it [the wall] collapsed.[10] But if it collapsed, why do I need searching [at all]? Surely we learned: If ruins collapsed on leaven, it is regarded as removed?—There [the circumstances are] that a dog cannot search it out; here, that a dog can search it out. But R. Eleazar said: Those sent [to perform] a religious duty do not suffer harm? —Said R. Ashi: He may have lost a needle and come to look for
c it.[1] But is it not [regarded as the fulfilment of] a religious duty in such a case? Surely it was taught: If one declares, 'This *sela'*[2] be for charity in order that my son may live,' or, 'that I may merit

(3) And eat up all crumbs. (4) אכסדרה is a pillared hall or a piazza, open on top, running in front of large houses. (5) Hab. III, 4. (6) Even as the light of a lamp pales before that of a torch, so does the light of the righteous before that of the Almighty. Thus a torch gives more light, and therefore it is even better than a lamp.

a (1) V. Glos. A blessing is pronounced over fire for which a light must be kindled. (2) A lamp. (3) A torch. (4) Therefore it is not suitable for searching. (5) The great flame of a torch may set fire to the house; therefore his preoccupation with this fear will hinder a man from a proper search. (6) A torch throws an unsteady, wavering light. (7) I.e., those which are very high up or very low down in the wall, so that it is inconvenient to use them. (8) A balcony with a sloping roof, which could not be used; other parts of the house had a flat roof. (9) A kind of safe in which food and utensils were kept. The inside had to be searched but not the roof. (10) No leaven is taken into any of these. (11) I.e., it stands in the centre, dividing the room into two parts used for separate purposes. (12) There is a space between it and the floor, as it stands on legs. (13) I.e., in a wall separating two rooms or houses tenanted by different people, the hole passing right through from one side of the wall to the other. (14) E.g., when the wall is very thick. (15) Between the bottom of the bed and the timber.

b (1) V. *supra*, n. a7. (2) If the bottom of the bed is well raised from the ground the space beneath it can be used quite easily. But if it is low down, even if a space is left it is not easy to use it, hence it need not be searched. (3) E.g., a private wine cellar. The servant may enter to take wine for the table while holding bread in his hand. (4) How much oil is to be consumed at a meal can be gauged beforehand, and further supplies will not be required. But one cannot determine beforehand how much wine will be drunk. (5) They must be searched. (6) If large fish are stored there it will be unnecessary to bring more to the table during the meal; but in the case of small fish this may be necessary, and so it must be searched. (7) I.e., the places where these are kept. (8) Salt and candles being sometimes unexpectedly required during the meal. (9) Wood-chips, twigs, etc. (10) Snakes are often found among debris, hence only the top of the ruins must be searched, but one need not investigate below the surface.

c (1) While searching for the leaven. He is, not being exclusively engaged on a religious task, exposed to danger. (2) A coin.

a in the future.[1] [7b] They differ only in respect of 'concerning the removal': one Master holds that it implies in the past;[2] while the other Master holds: It implies in the future.

An objection is raised: 'Blessed [art Thou] . . . who hast sanctified us with Thy commandments and hast commanded us concerning circumcision'?[3]—How [else] should he say [it] there? Shall he say, 'to circumcise'—is it imperative that *he* should circumcise?[4] Then what can be said of the father of the infant?[5]—Then indeed it is so.[6]

An objection is raised: 'Blessed [art Thou] . . . who hast sanctified us with Thy commandments and hast commanded us concerning *shechitah*'?[7]—There too, how [else] shall he say it: shall he say 'to slaughter,'—is it imperative that *he* should slaughter? Then what can be said of the Passover sacrifice and [other] sacrifices?[8]—[There] indeed it is so.[9]

An objection is raised: If one prepares a *lulab*[7] for himself, he recites the blessing, '. . . who hast kept us in life and hast preserved us and hast suffered us to reach this season'. When he takes it in order to fulfil his obligation therewith,[10] he recites:' . . . who hast sanctified us with Thy commandments and hast commanded b us concerning the taking of the *lulab?*'[1] There it is different, because in the [very] moment that he lifts it up his duty is fulfilled.[2] If so, [instead of stating] 'in order to fulfil his obligation therewith,' he should say, 'having fulfilled his obligation therewith?'—That indeed is so, but because he desires to teach 'to sit in the *sukkah*'[3] in the second clause, he also states in the first clause, 'to fulfil his obligation therewith'. For he teaches in the second clause: He who makes a *sukkah* for himself recites: 'Blessed art thou, O Lord . . . who has kept us in life and hast preserved us and hast enabled us to reach this season'. When he enters to sit therein he recites: 'Blessed [art Thou]... who hast sanctified us with Thy commandments and hast commanded us to sit in the *sukkah*.'[4] And the law is: [He recites,] 'concerning the removal of leaven'.[5]

Now incidentally all agree that we must recite the benediction beforehand:[6] how do we know it?—Because Rab Judah said in Samuel's name: For all precepts a benediction is recited prior ['*ober*] to their being performed. Where is it implied that this [word] '*ober* connotes priority?—Said R. Naḥman b. Isaac, Because Scripture saith, *Then Ahimaaz ran by the way of the Plain and overran* [wa-ya'abor] *the Cushite*.[7] Abaye said, [It follows] from this: *and he himself passed over* ['abar] *before them;*[8] alternatively, from this: *and their king is passed on* [wa-ya'abor] *before them, and the Lord at the head of them*.[9]

The School of Rab said: Except [for] a ritual bath and *shofar*.[10] As for a ritual bath, it is well, because the person is not yet fit;[11] but what is the reason for the *shofar?* And should you say, because c he may sound the blast [*teki'ah*] incorrectly;[1] if so, the same applies even to *shechitah* and circumcision too? Rather, said R. Ḥisda: Except for a ritual bath alone was stated. It was taught likewise: When one has a ritual bath and ascends [from the bath], on his ascending he recites: 'Blessed [art Thou]... who hast sanctified us with Thy commandments and hast commanded us concerning *ṭebillah*'.

BY THE LIGHT OF A LAMP, etc. How do we know this?—Said R. Ḥisda: By deriving [the meaning of] 'finding' from 'finding', and 'finding' from 'searching', and 'searching' from 'searching', and 'searching' from 'lamps', and 'lamps' from 'lamp':[2] [Thus:] 'finding' from 'finding': here it is written, *seven days shall there be no leaven* found *in your houses*,[3] while elsewhere it is written, *and he searched, and began at the eldest, and left at the youngest: and the cup was* found [*in Benjamin's sack*].[4] 'Finding' [is learned] from 'searching' [mentioned] in its own connection.[5] And 'searching' from 'lamps', as it is written, *And it shall come to pass at that time, that I will* search *Jerusalem with* lamps.[6] And 'lamps' from 'lamp', for it is written, *The soul of man is the* lamp *of the Lord, searching all the innermost parts of the belly*.[7]

The School of R. Ishmael taught: In the evening of the fourteenth leaven is searched for by the light of a lamp. Though there is no proof of this, there is an allusion to it, because it is said, '*seven days shall there be no leaven* [*in your houses*]'; and it is said, '*and he searched, and began at the eldest, and left at the youngest: and the cup was found* [*in Benjamin's sack*]'; and it is said, '*And it shall come to pass at that time, that I will search Jerusalem with lamps*'; and it is said, '*The soul of man is the lamp of the Lord, searching* [*all the innermost parts of the belly*]'. What is the purpose of the additional quotations?[8]—And should you answer, this '*at that time*' is a statement of lenient treatment by the Merciful One, [viz.,] 'I will not search Jerusalem with the light of a torch, which gives much light, but only with the light of a lamp, the light of which is much smaller, so that great wrongdoing will be found out but petty wrongdoing will not be d found out,[1]—then come and hear! '*The soul of man is the lamp of the Lord,* [searching, etc.]'.[2]

Our Rabbis taught: One may not search either by the light of the sun or by the light of the moon, or by the light of a torch,

a (1) I.e., it implies that the removal is still to be done. This phraseology is therefore certainly admitted, because a benediction is always recited *prior* to the actual performance of the precept to which it refers. (2) I.e., the removal has already been done. Hence this formula is inadmissible. (3) Not, 'to circumcise'. (4) Lit., 'is there no way that he should not circumcise'?—i.e., the obligation does not rest primarily upon the circumciser, but upon the father, whereas if the former said 'to circumcise', it would imply that it is his personal duty in every case. (5) What if the *father* circumcises? (6) He must say 'to circumcise'. (7) V. Glos. (8) Lit., 'sacred (animals)'. The obligation of slaughtering a sacrifice rests primarily upon its owner. (9) He must say 'to slaughter'. (10) V. Lev. XXIII, 40.

b (1) But not 'to take the *lulab*'. (2) Hence he is reciting the blessing after performing the precept, and so he cannot say 'to take'; v. *supra*. (3) V. Glos. (4) And there the future is required because it is an obligation during the whole week of Tabernacles. (5) That too implies the future. Consequently this form is used by all in circumcision and *shechitah*. (6) Before actually performing the precept. (7) II Sam. XVIII, 23. I.e., he passed in front of him, and similarly '*ober*, which is derived from the same root as *wa-ya'abor*, means in front of, i.e., prior to. (8) Gen. XXXIII, 3. (9) Mic. II, 13. (10) V. Glos. Here the benediction is recited *after* the fulfilment of the precept. (11) E.g., one who is unclean through nocturnal pollution may not recite a blessing; hence he is obviously unfit to recite the blessing until *after* the ritual bath, and all others requiring a ritual bath were treated likewise (Rashi).

c (1) In which case the obligation is not fulfilled and the benediction was unnecessarily recited, which is prohibited. (2) As explained in the text. (3) Ex. XII, 19. (4) Gen. XLIV, 12. (5) I.e., in the verse just quoted 'finding' and 'searching' are linked together. (6) Zeph. I, 12. (7) Prov. XX, 27. By comparing all these verses we learn that in order that leaven may not be found in the house it must be searched out by lamplight. (8) Lit., 'what is (the purpose of) "and it is said"?'

d (1) But this verse does not prove that the searching for leaven too may be carried out merely with a lamp—perhaps a torch is required. (2) Thus a single lamp suffices for a search.

עין משפט נר מצוה

מד א מיי' פ"ג מהלכות חמץ ומצה הלכה ו סמג לאוין לט טוש"ע א"ח סי' תלב סעיף א:

מה ב מיי' פ"א מהלכות ברכות הל' ג ופי"א הלכה ג ופ"ד מהלכות תפילין הלכה ז סמג עשין כג [טוש"ע א"ח סימן כה סעיף ח וסי' קנח סעיף יא רב אלפס בהל' תפילין דף עג:]:

מו ג מיי' פי"א מהלכות ברכות הל' ז סמג עשין כז טוש"ע י"ד סי' רסח סעיף ב:

מז ד מיי' פ"ב מהלכות חמץ ומצה הלכה ד סמג עשין לט טוש"ע א"ח סי' תלג סעיף א:

מח ה מיי' שם טוש"ע א"ח שם סעיף ב:

רבינו חננאל

אמר רב יהודה הבודק צריך שיברך קודם שיתחיל לבדוק מאי מברך ואסיקנא והלכתא אקב"ו על ביעור חמץ וכל המצות כולן מברך עליהן קודם עשייתן חוץ מן הטבילה בלבד כדתניא טבל ועלה בעלייתו אומר אקב"ו על הטבילה יש מי שאומר דבטבילה דגר בלבד הוא זה הדבר דתנן עלה וב"ה אמר הפורש מן הערלה כפורש מן הקבר אבל שאר חייבי טבילות מברכין ואחר כך טובלין דגרסי' נדה קוצה לה חלה ויש אומרין כל טמא אינו מברך אלא אחר הטבילה דתנן בתרומות פ"א חמשה לא יתרומו ואם תרמו תרומתן תרומה האלם והשכור והערום והסומא ובעל קרי ואמרי' בגמ' הללו חמשה אין תורמין לכתחלה יש מהם מפני הברכה והוא האלם והערום ובעל קרי מפני שאינן יכולין לברך ולהתרום ויש מהן שאין מכוונים את המובחר והן הסומא והשכור: **שתוי** אל יתפלל ואם התפלל תפלתו תחנונים כלומר ידי תפלה יצא שכור אל יתפלל ואם התפלל תפלתו גידופין איזהו שתוי זה ששתה רביעית שכור ששתה יותר מרביעית. ר' זירא בעי קמיה דר' אסי שכור מהו לברך א"ל ואכלת ושבעת אפי' מרומדם וכו': **אמר** רב חסדא למדנו מציאה ממציאה הכא כתיב שאור לא ימצא והתם כתיב ויחפש בגדול החל וגו' והכא כתיב מציאה בחפוש וכתיב קרא אחרינא בעת ההיא אחפש את ירושלים בנרות נמצאת זו המציאה בשאור כאלו כתיב בה חפוש בנר ואם [תאמר] חפוש ירושלים בנרות קולא הוא כלומר שבנר אינו חפוש יפה הנה הפסוק אמר נר ה' נשמת אדם וגו' כלומר הנר חופש כל מה שבחדרים: **ת"ר** אין בודקין לא לאור החמה ולא לאור הלבנה ולא לאור האבוקה אלא לאור

כי פליגי בעל ביעור מר סבר לשעבר משמע. פירש ר"ת לשעבר משמע טפי מלהבא אבל מ"מ משמע נמי קצת להבא דאי לא משמע כלל להבא אלא לשעבר א"כ היכי קאמר בסמוך נימא למול לא סגי דלאו איהו מהיל וכי בשביל שאין אנו יודעין לתקן יאמר שקר:

לא סגי דלאו איהו מהיל. דעל האב מוטל כדפירש הקונטרס אבל המל גריס מברך למול את הגרים *שהמברך חייב למול כמו האב המל: **בעידנא** דאגבהה נפיק ביה. וא"ת כיון דנפק הילך יברך והלא צריך לברך עובר לעשייתו *ואומר ר"י דע"כ דנפק אכתי עוסק במצוה שצריך לנענע בקריאת הלל (סוכה לז:): **לצאת** יצא מיבעי ליה. ולאו משמע שלא יצא עדיין באותה נטילה ומשכחת לה כשהפכו כדאמרי' בסוכה (ד' מב.) דאינו יוצא אלא דרך גדילתו או שנטלו שלא לצאת בו באותה נטילה וכשחוזר ונוטל לולב אין צריך להופכו כדפי' ר"י כיון שצריך לנענע בהלל או משום שאינו רוצה לצאת באותה נטילה: **והלכתא** על ביעור חמץ. יכול הוא לומר כן שאף זה הלשון משמע להבא או שמא דוקא על ביעור חמץ ויש טעם בברכות ור"י לא מצא טעם לכל הברכות: **על** הטבילה. אומר ר"ח בשם הגאון דוקא בטבילת גר דלא חזי קודם טבילה דלא מצי למימר וצונו דאכתי נכרי הוא אבל שאר חייבי טבילה כגון בעל קרי וכיוצא בו מותר לברך כדאמרינן בפ' מי שמתו (ד' כב.) נהוג עלמא כתלתא סבי כר' יהודה* בבעל קרי שיכול להתפלל ולברך וללמוד קודם טבילה *אעפ"כ אומר ר"י דאין לגעור בנשים שמברכות אחר הטבילה כיון דאיכא טבילת גר דלא מצי לברך לא חילקו וכן בנטילת ידים לא חילקו בין נטילה של אחר בית הכסא דלא מצי לברך קודם מיהו בנטילה יש טעם אחר לברך אחר נטילה קודם ניגוב כדאמרינן (סוטה ד' ד:) האוכל לחם בלא ניגוב ידים כאילו אוכל לחם טמא וי"מ דבכל טבילות קאמר דגברא לא חזי דקודם שירד למים אינו צריך לברך דילמא משום ביעתותא דמיא מימנע ולא טביל ואחר שירד אז הוא ערום ואסור לברך משום דלבו רואה את הערוה*: **ונרות** מנר. וקשה דהוה ליה למימר חיפוש מנר ולא הוה לקי אלא נר לכך יש לפרש דיליף חיפוש דנר מחיפוש דירושלים שהיא בנרות ולהכי נרות מנר ולא שפיר דהשתא צריך להוי קרא דחיפוש נרות ולא הוי סגי בקרא דנר ה' נשמת אדם וגו':

תורה אור

כי פליגי בעל ביעור מר סבר מעיקרא משמע ומ"ס להבא משמע מיתיבי ברוך *אשר קדשנו במצותיו וצונו על המילה התם היכי נימא נימא למול לא סגיא דלאו איהו מהיל אבי הבן מאי איכא למימר אין הכי נמי מיתיבי ברוך אשר קדשנו במצותיו וצונו על השחיטה התם נמי היכי נימא נימא לשחוט לא סגיא דלאו איהו שחט פסח וקדשים מאי איכא למימר אין הכי נמי מיתיבי *העושה לולב לעצמו מברך שהחיינו וקימנו והגיענו לזמן הזה נטלו לצאת בו אומר אשר קדשנו במצותיו וצונו על נטילת לולב שאני התם דבעידנא דאגבהה נפק ביה אי הכי לצאת בו יצא בו מיבעי ליה אין הכי נמי *ומשום דקא בעי למיתנא סיפא לישב בסוכה תנא רישא נמי לצאת בו דקתני סיפא *העושה סוכה לעצמו אומר ברוך אתה ה' שהחיינו וקימנו והגיענו לזמן הזה נכנס לישב בה אומר ברוך אשר קדשנו במצותיו וצונו לישב בסוכה *והלכתא על ביעור חמץ דכולי עלמא מיהא מעיקרא בעינן לברוכי מנלן דאמר רב יהודה אמר שמואל *כל המצות מברך עליהן עובר לעשייתן מאי משמע דהאי עובר לישנא דאקדומי הוא אמר ר"נ בר יצחק דאמר קרא °וירץ אחימעץ דרך הככר ויעבר את הכושי אביי אמר מהכא °והוא עבר לפניהם ואבע"א מהכא °ויעבר מלכם לפניהם וה' בראשם בי רב אמרי חוץ מן הטבילה ושופר בשלמא טבילה דאכתי גברא לא חזי אלא שופר מ"ט וכי תימא משום דילמא מיקלקלא תקיעה אי הכי אפילו שחיטה ומילה נמי אלא אמר רב חסדא *חוץ מן הטבילה בלבד איתמר תניא נמי הכי *טבל ועלה בעלייתו אומר ברוך אשר קדשנו במצותיו וצונו על הטבילה: **לאור הנר וכו':** מנא הני מילי אמר רב חסדא למדנו מציאה ממציאה ומציאה מחיפוש וחיפוש מחיפוש וחיפוש מנרות ונרות מנר מציאה ממציאה כתיב הכא °שבעת ימים שאור לא ימצא בבתיכם וכתיב התם °ויחפש בגדול החל ובקטן כלה וימצא ומציאה מחיפוש דידיה וחיפוש מנרות דכתיב °בעת ההיא אחפש את ירושלים בנרות ונרות מנר דכתיב °נר (אלהים) [ה'] נשמת אדם חופש כל חדרי בטן *תנא דבי ר' ישמעאל לילי י"ד בודקים את החמץ לאור הנר אף על פי שאין ראיה לדבר זכר לדבר שנאמר שבעת ימים שאור לא ימצא ואומר ויחפש בגדול החל ובקטן כלה* ואומר בעת ההיא אחפש את ירושלים בנרות ואומר נר (אלהים) [ה'] נשמת אדם חופש מאי ואומר וכי תימא האי בעת ההיא קולא הוא דקאמר רחמנא לא בדיקנא לה בירושלים בנהורא דאבוקה דנפיש נהורא טובא אלא בנהורא דשרגא דזוטר נהורא טפי דעון רבה משתכח ועון זוטר לא משתכח תא שמע נר ה' נשמת אדם: **תנו רבנן** אין בודקין לא לאור החמה ולא לאור הלבנה ולא לאור האבוקה אלא לאור הנר מפני

(שמואל ב יח) (בראשית לג) (מיכה ב) (שמות יב) (בראשית מד) (צפניה א) (משלי כ)

מעיקרא משמע. על ביעור שביערתי והרי עדיין לא בדיק דהא ברכה קודם בדיקה היא ביעור הייט נמי בדיקה: **נימא למול.** בתמיה משמע דלאותו רופא המל את כל בני העיר (צוה) למול את התינוק הזה: **וכי לא סגי דלאו איהו מהיל.** עליו המצוה מוטלת והלא על אביו מוטל כדאמרן בקדושין פרק קמא (*קרוב לסופו) אבל ביעור מצוה על בעל החמץ מוטלת וכל איש ואיש בודק ביתו והיכא דיכול לומר לבער לא נימא על ביעור: **ופרכינן** אבי הבן מאי איכא למימר. אי על המילה לשעבר משמע וזה אפשר לו לומר למול מאי איכא למימר היכי שרינן ליה למימר על המילה: **אין הכי נמי.** לריך לומר למול: **פסח וקדשים.** הבעלים גלטוו דכתיב (ויקרא א) וסמך ידו ושחט: **נפק ביה.** ומברך על שעבר: **והלכתא על ביעור.** נמי להבא משמע וגבי מילה נמי לא שנא אבי הבן מאיגש דעלמא דהא להבא משמע ועל מילה נמי כלמול דמי: **עובר.** קודם כמו ויעבר את הכושי קדמו במיתת אבשלום: **ויעבר מלכם לפניהם.** יקדים ילך בראש: **דאכתי גברא לא חזי.** כגון טבילת בעלי קרי דקיימא לן בברכות (ד' כ:) שאסור בדברי תורה ובברכה דעזרא תיקן טבילה לבעלי קריין לדברי תורה ומשום ההוא טבילה תקון בכל הטבילות ברכתן לבסוף: **למדנו מציאה.** האמורה בחמץ ממציאה האמורה בגביע דבנימין: **ומציאה מחיפוש.** כלומר ואותה מציאה של בנימין מחיפוש האמור אצלה דמה מציאה של גביע ע"י חיפוש אף מציאת חמץ ע"י חיפוש: **וחיפוש מחיפוש וחיפוש מנרות.** לאחר שלמדת שהיא ע"י חיפוש חזור ולמוד זה החיפוש מחיפוש שכתוב בירושלים שהוא בנרות כדכתיב בעת ההיא אחפש את ירושלים בנרות: **ונרות מנר.** דכתיב בנר יחידי נר (אלהים) נשמת אדם חופש כל חדרי בטן ולקמיה מפרש הא למה לי: **זכר לדבר.** כדפרשינן והשתא מפרש קראי היכא וראיה ממש ליתא אלא אסמכתא בעלמא *דדברי תורה מדברי קבלה ניהו: **קולא הוא.** דאקיל רחמנא גבי ירושלים דלא נבדקיה באבוקה אלא באור קטן הילכך לא ילפינן חמץ מיניה להקל: **תא שמע.** מהאי קרא דבדיקה מעלייתא היא דכתיב חופש כל חדרי בטן:

מפני

[דף כט.] [שבת קלז: מנחות מב.] סוכה מו. [תוספתא ברכות פ"ו ע"ש] [שבת ל. וש"נ] [מנחות מב.] לקמן קיט: מנחות לה: מגילה כא: סוכה לט. נדה סג. [ס'] כצ"ל ברכות כב. [לעיל ג. ע"ש] [ויומא]

גליון הש"ס

רש"י זכר לדבר. דל"ח מד"ק ניטו כדאי' בחגיגה י ע"ב

וניבטליה בשית כיון דאיסורא דרבנן עילויה כדאורייתא דמיא ולאו ברשותיה קיימא ולא מצי מבטיל *דאמר רב גידל אמר ר' חייא בר יוסף אמר רב המקדש משש שעות ולמעלה אפילו בחיטי קורדניתא אין חוששין לקידושין ולבתר איסורא לא מצי מבטיל ליה והא תניא היה יושב בבית המדרש ונזכר שיש חמץ בתוך ביתו מבטלו בלבו אחד שבת ואחד יום טוב בשלמא שבת משכחת לה כגון שחל ארבעה עשר להיות בשבת אלא יום טוב בתר איסורא הוא אמר רב אחא בר יעקב הכא בתלמיד יושב לפני רבו עסקינן ונזכר שיש עיסה מגולגלת בתוך ביתו ומתיירא שמא תחמיץ קדים ומבטיל ליה מיקמי דתחמיץ דיקא נמי דקתני היה יושב בתוך בית המדרש שמע מינה: אמר רבה בר רב הונא אמר רב הפת שעיפשה כיון שרבתה מצה מותרת היכי דמי אילימא דידע בה דחמץ היא כי רבתה מצה מאי הוי אלא דלא ידעינן בה אי חמץ הוא אי מצה הוא מאי איריא כי רבתה מצה אפילו כי לא רבתה מצה נמי ניזיל בתר בתרא מי לא תנן *מעות שנמצאו לפני סוחרי בהמה לעולם מעשר בהר הבית חולין בירושלים בשעת הרגל מעשר בשאר ימות השנה חולין ואמר רב שמעיה בר זירא מאי טעמא הואיל ושוקי ירושלים עשויין להתכבד בכל יום אלמא אמרי' קמאי קמאי אזלי ליה והני אחריני נינהו הכא נמי נימא קמא קמא אזיל והאי דהאידנא הוא שאני הכא דעיפושה מוכיח עילויה אי עיפושה מוכיח עילויה כי רבתה מצה מאי הוי אמר רבה לא תימא שרבתה מצה אלא אימא שרבו ימי מצה עילויה אי הכי פשיטא לא צריכא דעיפושה מרובה מהו דתימא כיון דעיפושה מרובה אינגליא מילתא דודאי חמץ מעליא הוא קא משמע לן כיון שרבו ימי מצה עילויה אמרינן כל יומא ויומא נהמא חמימא אפה ושרא עילויה ועפשא טפי ומי אזלינן בתר בתרא והא תניא ר' יוסי בר יהודה אומר תיבה שנשתמשו בה מעות חולין ומעות מעשר אם רוב חולין חולין אם רוב מעשר מעשר ואמאי ליזיל בתר בתרא אמר רב נחמן בר יצחק הבא במאי עסקינן כגון שנשתמשו בה מעות חולין ומעות מעשר ואין יודע איזה מהן בסוף רב זביד אמר כגון שנשתמשו בה ציבורין ציבורין רב פפא אמר כגון דאשתכח *בגומא: אמר רב יהודה הבודק צריך שיברך מאי מברך רב פפי אמר משמיה דרבא (אומר*) לבער חמץ רב פפא אמר משמיה דרבא על ביעור חמץ בלבער כולי עלמא לא פליגי דודאי להבא משמע כי

רש"י

וניבטליה בשית. ליתקנו רבנן לכל אדם דהשתא לא פשע דאיכא זכרון טובא שהרי עסוק בשריפתו: כיון דאיסורא דרבנן. דמשעברו חמש אסור בחמץ לדברי הכל כדאורייתא דמי ואינו שלו ולא מצי מבטל ליה בלבו וכיון דחס עליה ומשהי ליה פורתא עבר עליה: המקדש. אשה: משש שעות ולמעלה. מתחלת שש דאיסורא דרבנן הוא: אפילו בחיטי קורדנייתא. הגומחים בהרי אררט קשין הם מאד ואפילו הכי אין חוששין לקדושין אם באו עליהם מים ואף על גב דאתי איסור הנאת חמץ דרבנן דשש ומפקע קידושי תורה ושרי אשת איש לעלמא הא מתרלינן* בכמה דוכתין כל דמקדש אדעתא דרבנן מקדש והפקר ב"ד הפקר והם הפקירו ממונו: עיסה מגולגלת. שלא החמילה ומפני אימת כבוד רבו אין יכול לקום ולילך ולאפותה: דקדים ומבטל לה. בלבו דעדיין היא ברשותו שלא נאסרה עליו: דיקא נמי. דעדיין לא החמילה דקתני היה יושב בבית המדרש דמשמע מפני שאין יכול לקום ולילך משם הוא מבטלה בלבו ואי בחמץ גמור למה לי יושב בבית המדרש ואפילו אם היה פנוי מה בידו לעשות יותר השבתה בלב זהו ביעורו אלא ודאי כשיש בידו לתקן קאי ובידו לאפותה אם היה פנוי הואיל ולא החמילה עדיין ומשום יום טוב נקט יושב בבית המדרש ושבת מתוקמא בחמץ גמור ובארבעה עשר שחל להיות בשבת: כיון שרבתה מצה. קס"ד אם נשתמשו בתיבה זו מצה יותר מחמץ אזלינן בתר רובא ומותרת: רוב אוכלי בשר בירושלים כל ימות השנה ממעות מעשר שני הן לפי שלא היו מספיקין לאכול כל מעות מעשר שני שלהן ברגל ונותנין אותם לבני העיר בטובת הנאה והן אוכלים אותם בקדושתן ועיקר אכילת מעות מעשר שלמים היו מביאין מהן כדקיימא לן במנחות (דף פב.) הלכך לוקחין מהן בהמות דכל זמן שיש לו מעות מעשר אינו מוציא מעות חולין ואע"ג דאיכא למימר שמא מיד המוכר נפלו ומעות חולין הן ספק איסורא לחומרא: בהר הבית לעולם חולין. ואפילו בשעת הרגל שיש מעות מעשר מרובין בירושלים ממעות חולין לא מספקינן להו במעשר דאזלינן בתר רובא דשתא ואמרינן לאו האידנא נפול אלא קודם הרגל ובירושלים בשאר ימות השנה חולין דרוב מעות העיר חולין ובשעת הרגל מעשר כדמפרש טעמא מה טעם בשעת הרגל מעשר ולא אמרי' קודם הרגל נפול כדאמרן בגמלאין בהר הבית הואיל ושווקי ירושלים עשויים להתכבד בכל יום מפני הטיט ואי נפול קודם הרגל הוו משתכחי בשעת כיבוד אבל הר הבית מתוך שהוא משופע והרוח מכבדתו מעפרו ועוד שאין אדם נכנס באבק שעל גבי רגליו ואינו עשוי להתכבד אלמא בכל דבר העשוי להתכבד אמרינן קמאי קמאי אזדו וכתם תיבות שמשתמשין בהן אוכלין נוטלין ראשון ראשון כדי שלא יתעפשו וכל שכן דמסתמא בדקה זה אור לארבעה עשר והאי דבתרא היא ומצה היא: מוכיח עליה. שהרי הוא זה ימים רבים וחמץ הוא: שרבו ימי המצה. ורחוי להיות מעופש משנכנס הפסח: אי הכי פשיטא. אפי' ספק ליכא דמסתמא ודאי בדקה והא מצה היא: אם רוב חולין. כשתמשו בה חולין אלמא בתר רובא אזלינן ולא בתר בתרא: ציבורין ציבורין. של מעשר בזוית זו ושל חולין בזוית זו וביום א': בגומא. דליכא למימר זיל בתר בתרא דקמאי הא שקלינהו משום דיש לחוש שמא בגומא נטמן ולא ראוהו: בלבער כולי עלמא לא פליגי דלהבא משמע. ושפיר דמי דברכה קודם עשיית המצוה בעינן כדלקמן:

מעיקרא

תוספות

לפני סוחרי בהמה לעולם מעשר. פ"ה אע"פ דאיכא למתלי במוכר כמו בלוקח מספיקא תלינן לחומרא ואין נראה לר"י דסמוך מיעוטא לחולין דשאר מעות לפלגא דמוכר וה"ל רובא להיתר ואור"י דלוקחים הוו רובא דכמה בני אדם עומדים על בהמה אחת לקנות: בהר הבית לעולם חולין. מקשה ר"י היאך נמצאו שם הא אמר בפ' הרואה (ברכות סג:) לא יכנס בהר הבית במעות הצרורות בסדינו ואור"י דאינו אסור אלא היכא דנושאן בפרהסיא בסדינו דגנאי הוא דנראה כהולך שם לסחורה אבל בצינעא לא*:

עשויין להתכבד בכל יום. קשה לר"י דמסקי' בפרק דם הנדה (נדה נז: ושם) גבי שרץ שנמצא במבוי אין חזקתו מתכבד אלא על ידי בדיקה ותירץ דשרץ שהוא בכעדשה אין חזקתו כל כך מתכבד כמו במעות*:

בלבער כ"ע לא פליגי דלהבא משמע. מכאן היה מצריך רשב"א לברך לפני המילה להכניסו דאי לאחר המילה ישקר בברכתו דלהכניסו להבא משמע ועוד שצריך לברך עובר לעשייתו ולא נראה לר"ת דבפרק ר' אליעזר דמילה (שבת דף קלז: ושם) תניא המל אומר אקב"ו על המילה אבי הבן אומר להכניסו משמע לאחר המילה מקומו אע"ג דלהכניסו משמע להבא לא קשה דלא על זאת הנעשה עכשיו מברך אלא משבח ומודה להקב"ה שצונו על המילה כשתבא לידו ותיקנוה כאן לגלות ולהודיע שזו המילה נעשה לשם יוצרנו ולא לשם ע"ג ולא לשם מורגא ולא לשם הר גרזים ואין צריך לברך עובר לעשייתו אלא במקום שהעושה המצוה הוא מברך אבל כשמברך אחר לא ותדע שהרי ברכת אירוסין אינו מברך אלא אחר אירוסין:

כי

עין משפט נר מצוה

לט א מיי' פ"ה מה' אישות הלכה א סמג עשין מח טוש"ע אה"ע סי' כח סעיף כא:

מ ב מיי' פ"ג מהלכות חמץ ומצה הלכה י טוש"ע או"ח סי' תמד סעיף ח:

מא ג מיי' פ"ו מהלכות מ"ש ונ"ר הלכה י:

מב ד ה טוש"ע או"ח סי' תמו סעיף ד:

מג ו מיי' פ"ו מהלכות מ"ש ונ"ר הלכה יא:

[וע"ע תוס' ב"מ כו. ד"ה בכר]

רבינו חננאל

וניבטליה בשעה ששית למה בזמן הביעור כו' פשוט' היא. פי' קורדניאתא חטים חזקים ואין מחמיצין (היא) אפי' אלו כיון שהוכשרו במים איסורי הנאה הן כחמץ גמור ואקשי' וכי בתר איסורא לא מצי מבטל ליה והתניא היה יושב בבית המדרש ונזכר שיש לו חמץ בביתו מבטלו בלבו אחד שבת ואחד יום טוב והנה יום טוב לא משכחת לה אלא בתר איסורא וקתני דמבטל ושנינן לא בתלמיד חכם שיש לו עסה מגולגלת בביתו ביום טוב ומתירא שמא תחמיץ שמקדים ומבטלה קודם שתחמיץ דיקא נמי מדקתני היה יושב בבית המדרש ש"מ: פת שעיפשה ולא ידע אי מצה אי חמץ הוא אם רבו ימי מצה מותרת היא פי' אחר הפסח: ואקשי' וניזל בתר בתר' כלומר כמעו' מעשר כיון שעכשיו כל הפת שעושין מצה היא [גם זו] מצה היא שהחמץ כבר עבר מי לא תנן [בפ"ז דשקלי'] מעות שנמצא לפני סוחרי בהמה לעולם מעשר כלומר במעות מעשר שני קונין בהמה כדכתיב (דברים יד כו) ונתתה הכסף בכל אשר תאוה נפשך וגו' ואמרי' מה טעם הואיל ושוקי ירושלים עשוין להתכבד בכל יום אלמא אמרי' אינהו אזלו והני אחריני נינהו וכו' אקשי' ומי אזלינן אחר האחרון והתניא ר' יוסי אומר תיבה שנשתמש בה חולין ומעשר אם רוב חולין חולין ואם רוב מעשר מעשר ולא קתני אחר אחרון ופרקי' בדלא ידעינן איזה מהן אחרון או כגון שנשתמשו צבורין צבורין כלומר צבור מכאן וצבור מכאן ושניהן כאחד ואין אחד מהן אחרון או נמצא בגומא דאיכא למימר לא ראה אותה:

he may transgress and not annul it. [7a] Then let him annul it in the sixth [hour]?[8]—Since the Rabbinical interdict is upon it,[9] it is like a Scriptural [interdict] and does not stand in his ownership, hence he cannot annul it. For R. Gidal said in R. Ḥiyya b. Joseph's name in Rab's name: He who betroths from the sixth hour and onwards, even with wheat of Cordyene,[10] we have no fear of his betrothal.[11]

But, is he unable to annul it after the prohibition [commences]? Surely it was taught: If he is sitting in the Beth Hamidrash and recollects that he has leaven at home, he annuls it in his heart, whether it is the Sabbath or the Festival. Now as for the Sabbath, it is well: this is possible where the fourteenth [of Nisan] falls on
a the Sabbath;[1] but the Festival is after the prohibition [commences]?[2]—Said R. Aḥa b. Jacob: We treat here of a disciple sitting before his master, and he recollects that he has a rolled dough[3] at home and fears that it may turn leaven; [therefore] he anticipates and annuls it before it turns leaven. This may be proved too: for it states, 'If he is sitting in the Beth Hamidrash'.[4] This proves it.

Rabbah the son of R. Huna said in Rab's name: If a loaf went mouldy, if *mazzah*[5] exceeds it [in quantity], it is permitted.[6] How is it meant? Shall we say that he [the owner] knows that this [loaf] is leaven, what then matters it if the *mazzah* does exceed it?[7] Again if we do not know whether it is leaven or *mazzah*, then why particularly if the *mazzah* exceeds it; even if the *mazzah* does not exceed it too, let us go after the last?[8] Did we not learn: Money found in front of cattle dealers at all times is [accounted as] tithe; on the Temple Mount, it is *ḥullin*;[5] in [the rest of] Jerusalem, at any other part of the year, it is *ḥullin*; at the Festival season, it is tithe.[9] And R. Shemaia b. Zera observed thereon: What is the
b reason? Because the streets of Jerusalem[1] were swept daily. This proves that we assume: the earlier [losses] have gone, and these [coins] are different ones. So here too let us say: the earlier [bread] has gone and this is of the present?[2]—Here it is different, because its mouldiness proves its status.[3] If its mouldiness proves its status, what does it matter if the *mazzah* exceeds it?—Said Rabbah, Do not say, 'if the *mazzah* exceeds it', but say, 'many days of *mazzah* have passed over it'.[4] If so, it is obvious?—This is necessary only where it is very mouldy; you might argue, since it is very mouldy it is clear that it is certainly true leaven; therefore he informs us that since many days of *mazzah* have passed over it we say: every day hot *mazzah*[5] was baked and thrown thereon, and that made it very mouldy.

Yet do we follow the last? Surely it was taught, R. Jose b. Judah said: If a chest was used for money of *ḥullin* and money of tithe,[6] if it was mostly *ḥullin*, it [the money found therein] is *ḥullin*; if mostly tithe, it is tithe. But why so? let us go after the last?—Said R. Naḥman b. Isaac: Of what do we treat here? E.g., where it was used for money of *ḥullin* and money of tithe, and one does not know which was last. R. Zebid said: E.g., where it was used for separate packages.[7] R. Papa said: E.g., if it was found in a pit.[8]

Rab Judah said: He who searches [for leaven] must pronounce a benediction. What benediction does he pronounce? R. Pappi said in Raba's name: '[... who hast commanded us] to remove leaven'. R. Papa said in Raba's name: '[... who hast commanded us] concerning the removal of leaven'. As for [the phrase] 'to remove,' there is no disagreement at all that it certainly implies

(8) He is not likely to forget it then, since he is engaged in burning it. (9) On all views, v. *supra* 4b. (10) A district lying to the east of the river Tigris, south of Armenia.—That wheat is very hard and does not easily become leaven; nevertheless if moisture had fallen upon it after being harvested it is regarded as leaven. (11) The betrothal is definitely invalid, because the wheat has no value because of the Rabbinical interdict, whereas for betrothal something of value is required (v. Ḳid. 2a).— Thus although the interdict at that hour is only Rabbinical, the leaven is regarded as completely valueless; hence not under his ownership.
a (1) And he recollects before the sixth hour. (2) How can he annul it then? (3) I.e., a dough kneaded but not baked. He cannot leave the Beth Hamidrash to attend to it out of respect to his Master. (4) If it is already leaven, what does it matter where he is; even if he were at home he could do nothing else? (5) V. Glos. (6) This is now assumed to mean: if there is more *mazzah* in the bin than this mouldy loaf, the whole is permitted. (7) Surely a loaf known to be leaven cannot be permitted on that account? (8) I.e., let us assume that this loaf is of the latest batch which was put there, i.e., it is *mazzah*, since a bread bin is cleared out every day, in order to prevent the bread from going mouldy—a necessary precaution in the hot eastern countries—and particularly so in this case, when there had been a search for leaven before the Festival. (9) Shek. VII, 2. If money is found in Jerusalem, the question arises, what is its status—is it ordinary secular coins (*ḥullin*) or tithe money? This was because the second tithe (v. Deut. XIV, 22ff: this was designated second-tithe) had to be eaten in Jerusalem or its monetary equivalent expended there, which money likewise was governed by the law of second tithe. Now, most of the flesh eaten in Jerusalem was bought with second-tithe money, and generally took the form of peace-offerings; when one could not stay long enough in Jerusalem to expend all his tithe money, he would distribute it among the poor or give it to his friends in Jerusalem. Consequently, if money is found in front of cattle dealers, whatever the time of the year, it is assumed to be of the second tithe. On the other hand, if it is found on the Temple Mount, we assume it to be *ḥullin*, even at Festival time, when most of money handled is tithe, because the greater part of the year is not Festival, and then ordinary *ḥullin* is in circulation and this money might have been lost before the Festival. But if found in the streets of Jerusalem, a distinction is drawn, as stated in the text.
b (1) But not the Temple Mount. (2) I.e., unleavened. (3) It must have been there a considerable time, hence it is leaven. (4) I.e., several days of Passover have gone, and so this had had time to go mouldy even if baked as *mazzah* at the beginning of the Festival. (5) Lit., 'bread'. (6) And now we find money in it and do not know which it is. (7) Of money, some being *ḥullin* and others tithe, and both were there on the same day. (8) We cannot assume that the earlier coins had been removed while these were of the most recent deposit, because it might have been overlooked in a pit.

weeks. What is the reason of the first Tanna? [6b] Because lo! Moses was standing on the First Passover and giving instructions
a about the Second Passover,[1] as it is said, *Moreover, let the children of Israel keep the passover in its appointed season;*[2] and it is written, *And there were certain men, who were unclean by the dead body of a man.*[3] And R. Simeon b. Gamaliel?[4]—He answers you: Because he was engaged in the laws of Passover, he instructed them[5] in all the laws of Passover. What is R. Simeon b. Gamaliel's reason? Because lo! Moses was standing at the beginning of the month and giving orders about the Passover, as it is said, *This month shall be unto you the beginning of months: it shall be the first month of the year to you.*[6] And it is written, *Speak ye unto all the congregation of Israel, saying, In the tenth day of this month they shall take to them every man a lamb, according to their father's houses,* etc.[6] But how do you know that he was standing at the beginning of the month; perhaps he was standing on the fourth or the fifth of the month? Rather, said Rabbah b. Shimi in Rabina's name, [It is deduced] from here: *And the Lord spake unto Moses in the wilderness of Sinai, in the first month of the second year;*[7] and it is written, *Moreover let the children of Israel keep the passover in its appointed season.*[8] But here too, how do you know that he was standing at the beginning of the month: perhaps he was standing on the fourth or the fifth of the month? —Said R. Naḥman b. Isaac: [The implication of] '*wilderness*' [here]. is learned from '*wilderness*' [elsewhere]. Here it is written, '*in the* wilderness *of Sinai*'; while there it is written, *And the Lord spake unto Moses in the* wilderness *of Sinai, in the tent of meeting, on the first day of the second month:*[9] just as there [it was] at the beginning of the month, so here too at the beginning of the month.

Now, let [the events of] the first month be written first, and
b then that of the second month?[1]—Said R. Menasia b. Taḥlifa in Rab's name: This proves that there is no chronological order[2] in the Torah. R. Papa observed: This was said only of two subjects; but in the same subject what is earlier is earlier and what is later is later. For should you not say thus, [how, then, apply the principle that] when a general proposition is followed by a particular specification the general proposition comprises only what is contained in the particular specification; perhaps it is a particular specification followed by a general proposition! Moreover, [it is a principle that] when a particular specification is followed by a general proposition, the generalization becomes an addition to the specification,[3] [here too] perhaps it is a generalization followed by a particularization! But if so, the same [question] applies even to two subjects? Now, that is well on the view that [when] a generalization and a specification [are] at a distance from each other, we do not interpret[4] them as a generalization followed by a specification, then it is correct. But on the view that we do interpret [them thus], what can be said?[5]—Even on the view that we do interpret, that is only [when they occur] in the same subject; but [when] in two subjects we do not interpret [them thus].

Rab Judah said in Rab's name: He who searches [for leaven] must [also] declare it null.[6] What is the reason? Shall we say [it is] because of crumbs[7]—but they are of no value?[8] And should you answer, since they are guarded in virtue of his house,[9] they are of account, surely it was taught: [If there are in a man's field] late figs, while he guards his field on account of the grapes; or if there are late grapes, while he guards his field on account of his cucumbers and gourds,[10] when the owner is particular about them, they are forbidden [to a stranger] as theft and are subject to tithes; when the owner is not particular about them, they are not for-
c bidden as theft and are exempt from tithe![1]—Said Raba: It is a preventive measure, lest he find a tasty loaf[2] and [set] his mind upon it.[3] Then let him annul it when he finds it?—He may find it after the interdict [commences], and then it does not stand in his ownership and [so] he cannot annul it. For R. Eleazar said: Two things are not in a man's ownership, yet the Writ regarded them as though they were in his ownership. And these are they: a pit in public ground[4] and leaven from six hours[5] and onwards.[6] Then let him annul it at the fourth or the fifth [hour]?[7]—Since it is neither the time of the prohibition nor the time of searching,

a (1) I.e., the Passover celebrated on the fourteenth of the *second* month by those who were unable to celebrate it at the proper time. (2) Num. IX, 2. (3) Ibid. 6. The narrative relates how Moses gave instructions about the second Passover, vv. 9 seq. (4) How does he refute this proof? (5) Lit., 'completed for them'. (6) Ex. XII, 2f. (7) Num. IX, 1. (8) And from the beginning of the month until Passover is two weeks. (9) Num. I, 1.

b (1) Num. I, 1ff is chronologically a month later than IX, 1ff; why is it not written in that order? (2) Lit., 'earlier and later'. (3) So as to include all things implied in the generalization. (4) Lit., 'judge'. (5) V. B.Ḳ. 85a. (6) I.e., of no account and valueless and free to all. (7) Which may escape his search. (8) They are therefore null in any case. (9) When he guards his house he *ipso facto* guards these crumbs. (10) The late figs and grapes which remain after the harvest never fully ripen. Here they are in a field which is guarded from intruders not for their sake but because it contains other crops yet to be gathered.

c (1) Because they are regarded as ownerless, and such are exempt from tithe. Thus though they are incidentally guarded, that does not give them any value, and the same should apply here. (2) גלוסקא, a loaf made from a special brand of white flour. (3) To keep it until after Passover. (4) He who digs a pit in public ground is responsible for any damage it may cause, as though it were his property, though actually it is not. (5) I.e., noon. (6) One is culpable for its presence in his house then, though technically speaking it is no longer his. (7) I.e., any time in the morning before noon, when it is still his. Why particularly the preceding evening, when he is making the search?

לו א מיי' פ"ג מהלכות חמץ ומצה הלכה ז סמג עשין לט טוש"ע א"ח סי' תלד סעיף ב:
לז ב מיי' פ"א מהלכות מעשר הלכה יב:
לח ג מיי' פ"ג מהלכות חמץ ומצה הלכה ז ח סמג עשין לט טוש"ע א"ח סימן תלד סעיף ג:

שהרי משה עומד בפסח ראשון ומזהיר על הפסח שני שנאמר *ויעשו בני ישראל את הפסח במועדו וכתיב ויהי אנשים אשר היו טמאים לנפש אדם ור' שמעון בן גמליאל אמר לך איידי דאיירי במילי דפסחא מסיק להו לכל מילי דפסחא מאי טעמא דרשב"ג שהרי משה עומד בראש החדש ומזהיר על הפסח שנאמר החדש הזה לכם ראש חדשים וכתיב דברו אל כל עדת ישראל לאמר בעשור לחדש הזה ויקחו להם איש שה לבית אבות וגו' ממאי דבריש ירחא קאי דילמא בארבעה בירחא או בחמשה בירחא קאי אלא אמר רבה בר שימי משמיה דרבינא מהכא וידבר ה' אל משה במדבר סיני בשנה השנית בחדש הראשון וכתיב ויעשו בני ישראל את הפסח במועדו הכא נמי ממאי דבריש ירחא קאי דילמא בארבעה בירחא או בחמשה בירחא קאי אמר רב נחמן בר יצחק אתיא מדבר ממדבר כתיב הכא במדבר סיני וכתיב התם וידבר ה' אל משה במדבר סיני באהל מועד באחד לחדש השני מה להלן בראש חדש אף כאן בראש חדש וניכתוב ברישא דחדש ראשון והדר ניכתוב דחדש שני אמר רב מנשיא בר תחליפא משמיה דרב זאת אומרת אין מוקדם ומאוחר בתורה אמר רב פפא לא אמרן אלא בתרי ענייני אבל בחד עניינא מאי דמוקדם מוקדם ומאי דמאוחר מאוחר דאי לא תימא הכי כלל ופרט אין בכלל אלא מה שבפרט דילמא פרט וכלל הוא ותו פרט וכלל נעשה כלל מוסף על הפרט דילמא כלל ופרט הוא אי הכי אפילו בתרי ענייני נמי הניחא למאן דאמר *כלל ופרט המרוחקין זה מזה אין דנין אותו בכלל ופרט שפיר אלא למאן דאמר דנין מאי איכא למימר אפילו למ"ד דנין הני מילי בחד עניינא אבל בתרי ענייני אין דנין: אמר רב יהודה אמר רב *הבודק צריך שיבטל מאי טעמא אי נימא משום פירורין הא לא חשיבי וכי תימא כיון דמינטר להו אגב ביתיה חשיבי *והתניא סופי תאנים ומשמר שדהו מפני ענבים סופי ענבים ומשמר שדהו מפני מקשאות ומפני מדלעות בזמן שבעל הבית מקפיד עליהן אסורין משום גזל וחייבין במעשר בזמן שאין בעל הבית מקפיד עליהן מותרין משום גזל ופטורין משום מעשר אמר רבא גזירה שמא ימצא גלוסקא יפה ודעתיה עילויה וכי משכחת ליה לבטליה דילמא משכחת ליה לבתר איסורא ולאו ברשותיה קיימא ולא מצי מבטיל דא"ר אלעזר *שני דברים אינן ברשותו של אדם ועשאן הכתוב כאילו ברשותו ואלו הן בור ברשות הרבים וחמץ משש שעות ולמעלה וניבטליה בארבע וניבטליה בחמש כיון דלאו זמן איסורא הוא ולאו זמן ביעורא הוא דילמא פשע ולא מבטל ליה וניבטליה

שהרי משה רבינו עומד בפסח ראשון. ודורש בהלכות פסח השני דהיינו שלשים יום שהוא בארבעה עשר באייר: מה להלן ראש חדש. דכתיב ביה באחד לחדש השני: וניכתוב ברישא כו'. לא אשמעתין פריך אלא אסדר פרשיות קפריך מכדי פרשת פסח נאמרה תחלה שהרי בחדש הראשון נאמר כדכתיב בחדש הראשון לאמר ופרשת פקודים נאמרה באייר ומאי טעמא אקדמה לאהי בראש הספר ופרשה זו בפרשת בהעלותך: אין מוקדם ומאוחר בתורה. לא הקפידה תורה על סדר מוקדם ומאוחר ופרשיות דנאמרו תחלה הקדימו המאוחרות לה: בתרי ענייני. בשתי פרשיות: בחד עניינא. במקראות הסדורות בפרשה אחת: דאי לא תימא הכי. דבסדר כתיבתן נאמרו הא דקיימא לן כל כלל ופרט אין בכלל אלא מה שהוא בפרט לפי שבא הפרט ופרט שזהו הכלל היכי סמכינן עלה דילמא פרט וכלל הוא: נעשה כלל מוסף על הפרט. שלא תאמר אין כאן אלא פרט או כיוצא בו כגון בדינו בבנין אב לכך הוסיף הכתוב כלל אחריו להביא כל דבר ואפילו אינו דומה לפרט: אי הכי. קשיא לך אפילו בתרי ענייני תיקשי לך דהא דיינינן כלל ופרט כשנאמר אחד מהן בפרשה זו ואחד מהן בפרשה אחרת: הא ניחא. דלא קשיא לך: למאן דאמר כלל ופרט המרוחקין אין דנין כו'. ופלוגתא היא במנחות בפרק המנחות באות מצה (דף נה:) ובבבא קמא בהחובל (דף פה.): הבודק צריך שיבטל. בלבו סמוך לבדיקה מיד ואומר כל חמירא דאיכא בביתא הדין ליבטיל: מאי טעמא. הרי מבער כל הנמצא: וכי תימא כיון דמנטר לאו אגב ביתיה. עם שאר ממונו הוא משמרן שכשהוא נוטל ביתו לשומרו נמצא משמר כל מה שבתוכו הלכך חשיבי ושימור דלאו לדעתא דידיה הוא מי מחשיב ליה: והתניא סופי תאנים. סוף לקיטת תאנים כשמתחילין להתבשל כל התאנים שאינן מתבשלות כל צרכן עולמית: ומשמר שדהו מפני ענבים. ובעל הבית זה משמר שדה זו שלא יכנסו בני אדם לתוכה ואין דעתו מפני התאנים אלא מפני שיש בה ענבים שעדיין לא הגיע עת הבציר או סופי ענבים שלא יתבשלו עולמית ובעל הבית משמר שדהו זו שהן בתוכה ולא בשבילן אלא מפני מדלעות ומקשאות שבה: קשואין ודלועין שם הפרי עצמו. מקשאות ומדלעות קרי כל האילנות: וחייבין במעשר. אם ליקטן בעל הבית או נתנן לאחר: ופטורין מן המעשר. דהפקר פטור מן המעשר: ודעתו עליה. חשובה היא בעיניו ואם עליה לשורפה ומשהה אפילו רגע אחד ונמצא עובר עליה בבל יראה ובבל ימצא אבל משבטלה אינו עובר דלא כתב אלא תשביתו: דלאו ברשותיה הוא. אינו שלו: דאמר ר' אלעזר ב' דברים אינן שלו ועשאן הכתוב כאילו הן ברשותו. להתחייב עליהן: בור ברשות הרבים. הפותחו חייב בניזקין ואין הבור שלו אלא של הפקר שהרי ברשות הרבים הוא ואף על פי שכרהו אין רשות הרבים קנויה לו: וניבטליה בארבע. כלומר למה הוצרכו לבטל בלילה ליתקנו רבנן לכל אדם שיבטל קודם איסורו: פשע. ישכח ויבא לידי פשיעה שעל ידי מה יזכר אבל עכשיו שעסוק בבדיקתו יזכר: וניבטליה

*) [ועי' תוס' חולין ד': ד"ה מותר מיד וכו' דכשעות דרבנן ותמן דרבנן דחוששין לקדושין מ"מ מקודשת גמורה לא הויא דאם בא אחר וקדשה חוששין לקידושי שניהן וע"ע תוספות קדושין נח. ד"ה אלמא]

שנאמר ויהי אנשים. והא דאמר בהניזקין (גיטין ד' ס. ושם) שמונה פרשיות נאמרו ביום שהוקם המשכן והיינו בראש חדש ניסן פרשת טמאים לא כפ"ה דפי' פרשת טמאים ויהי אנשים דזו הפרשה נאמרה בערב הפסח כדמשמע הכא אלא פרשת טמאים טומאת תרומה וקדשים:

ומזהיר על פסח שני. אע"ג שעל ידי שאילתו הוזקק לומר להן מ"מ לא היה צריך להאריך אלא אל תעשו פסח ותו לא:

ממאי דבריש ירחא קאי. תימה דשבת בפ"ר עקיבא (דף פו: ושם) קאמר *(רבה) דכ"ע בר"ח אתו למדבר סיני כתיב הכא ביום הזה באו מדבר סיני וכתיב התם החדש הזה וגו' מה להלן ר"ח אף כאן ראש חדש אלמא פשיטא דהחדש הזה נאמר לו בר"ח והיינו משום דאמר בהקומץ רבה (מנחות כט.) שנתקשה משה רבינו בראיית הלבנה עד שאמר לו הקב"ה כזה ראה וקדש ותי' ר"ת אע"ג שאמר הקב"ה למשה בריש ירחא דילמא משה לא אמר להם לישראל אלא בג' או בד' בירחא ומסיק דיליף מדבר ממדבר דבההיא דבאחד לחדש השני אמירת הקב"ה ואמירת משה הוי בריש ירחא דכתיב *באחד לחדש השני ויתילדו וגו' ור"י מפרש אע"ג דהחדש הזה הוה בריש ירחא מיהו דילמא הא דקאמר דברו אל כל עדת ישראל לא הוה בריש ירחא ואם תאמר אמאי לא יליף התם מדבר ממדבר כי הכא וי"ל דמדבר ממדבר לא ילפינן:

אבל בחד עניינא מאי דמוקדם מוקדם. היינו דוקא היכא דליכא דרשה וטעם דהא תנן בפ' נגמר הדין (סנהדרין מה. ושם) דדחיית הנסקל קודם לסקילתו אע"ג דסקילה כתיב ברישא דכתיב כי סקל יסקל או ירה יירה היינו משום דכתיב במקום אחר סקילה בגמר מיתה דכתיב וסקלתם באבנים ומתו:

אבל בתרי ענייני אין דנין. והא דפריך בסוף הפרה (ב"ק ד' נד: ושם) ולימא בהמתך דדברות ראשונות כלל שור וחמור פרט *בהמתך דדברות האחרונות חזר וכלל אע"ג דמרוחקין טובא היינו משום דעשרת הדברות חשיבי כחד עניינא דבדיבור אחד נאמרו:

ודעתיה עילויה. פירוש ולא בטל מאליו כמו פירורין ועל פ"ה קשה מאי פריך כי משכחת ליה ניבטלה הא פי' ודעתיה עילויה שחס עליה לבטלה:

*משש שעות ולמעלה. פ"ה מתחלת שש ולא נהירא לר"ת דע"כ הא דאמר לעיל חמץ מו' שעות ולמעלה אסור היינו מסוף שש ופר"ת דמסוף שש קאמר ומייתי ראיה מחיטי קורדנייתא שהן קשין והוה חמץ נוקשה שאינו אסור כמי אלא *) מדרבנן לפני

רבינו חננאל

שואלין בהלכות הפסח קודם לפסח שלשים יום שנאמר ויהי אנשים אשר היו טמאים לנפש אדם וגו' דהא משה עומד בפסח ראשון ומזהיר על פסח שני רשב"ג אמר שתי שבתות שנאמר וידבר ה' אל משה במדבר סיני בשנה השנית לצאתם מארץ מצרים בחדש הראשון לאמר ויעשו בני ישראל את הפסח במועדו וגמר במדבר במדבר גזרה שוה שנא' וידבר ה' אל משה במדבר סיני באחד לחדש השני וגו' מה במדבר הזה אחד בחדש הזה אף במדבר האמור בענין פסח אחד בחדש הזה קאי באחד לחדש ומזהיר בפסח שתי שבתות: ואקשי' מעשה דניסן הוה ליה למכתב ברישא למה פתח תחלת הספר בחדש השני ולאחר כמה ענינים הזכיר מעשה דניסן ואמר משמיה דרב אין מוקדם ומאוחר בתורה והני מילי בתרי עניני כגון האי במדבר סיני באחד לחדש השני הכתוב בתחלת הספר שהוא ענין שאו את ראש כל עדת בני ישראל וזה במדבר סיני בשנה השנית שהוא בחדש הראשון הכתוב אחרי כמה פרשיות והוא ענין הפסח כי האי גונא אומר אין מוקדם ומאוחר בתורה אלא אע"פ שזה כתב אחר זה באמירה ובצואה ענין הפסח שהיא בחדש הראשון הוא נאמר תחלה ואחריו נאמר ענין הפקודים אבל בחד ענינא מאי דמוקדם מוקדם ומאי דמאוחר מאוחר דאי לא תימא הכי המדות שהתורה נדרשת בהן באות להתחלף כי מה שאתה דן אותו בכלל ופרט כגון (ויקרא א ב) אדם כי יקריב מכם קרבן לה' מן הבהמה זה כלל מן הבקר ומן הצאן פרט ואין בכלל אלא מה שבפרט בקר וצאן אין מידי אחרינא לא ואם תאמר אין מוקדם ומאוחר שמא מן הבקר ומן הצאן תקריבו נאמר תחלה בצואה ואחר כן נאמר מן הבהמה שנמצא פרט וכלל וקיימא לן פרט וכלל נעשה הכלל מוסף על הפרט ואתרבו להו כל מילי לפיכך אמרנו לעולם בחד ענינא המוקדם מוקדם והמאוחר מאוחר. ואקשי' אי הכי דחיישינן כל האי גונא אפי' בתרי עניני נמי משכחת לה דאי לא דנין כלל ופרט מתהפך לפרט וכלל כאשר כבר אמרנו בחד ענינא הוא הניחא לר' דאמר כלל ופרט המרוחקין זה מזה אין דנין אותו בכלל ופרט כגון (שמות כא כה) כויה תחת כויה כלל אפילו כויה שאין בה חבורה כא חבורה תחת חבורה ופרט שהכויה יש בה חבורה והם כלל ופרט המרוחקין זה מזה אין דנין אותו בכלל ופרט אלא לבן עזאי דאמר אפי' כי האי גונא דנין אותו בכלל ופרט [מאי איכא למימר ושנינן לבן עזאי נמי דאמר דנין לא אמר אלא בענין אחד דשתיהן הכויה והחבורה ענין הכאת הגוף וצער הן אבל בתרי עניני לא אמר והלוקת ר' ובן עזאי מפורשת בפ' החובל בחבירו בתחלתו [ד' פ"ה]: אמר רב יהודה הבודק אחר שיבער הכל צריך שיבטל בלבו מה שאינו ידוע לו עכשיו ודייקי' מאי טעמא אי משום פרורין אע"פ שלא בטלן כמו בטלי הן דהא לא קפיד עלייהו ואע"ג (דלא מינטרי) [דמנטרי] אגב בית לא חשיבי כדתניא אסיפת תאנים ומשמר שדהו מפני ענביו כו' עד בזמן שאין בעל הבית מקפיד עליהן מותרין משום גזל ופטורין מן המעשר פי' אסיפת תאנים שכבר אספו התאנה ונשתיירו בה שתים שלש תאנים והסיח דעתו מהן ואינו שומר אלא הענבים כו' ופירש רבא למה צריך לבטל לאו משום פירורין אלא גזירה שמא ימצא גלוסקא דדעתיה עלה ואקשי' למה צריך לבטל אור ארבעה עשר בשעת הבדיקה עד שימצאנה יבטלנה ודחי' שמא ימצאנה אחר זמן איסורה וביטולו אותו העת אינו מועיל כלום כי אין א"ם מבטל אלא דבר שלו והחמץ בזמן איסורו יוצא מרשותו ואינו קרוי חמצו אלא להתחייב בו בראייתו ובהיותו מצוי ברשותו בלבד כדאמר ר' אלעזר משום ר' ישמעאל שני דברים אינן ברשותו של א"ם ועשאן הכתוב כאלו הן ברשותו ונתחייב בהן ואלו הן בור ברשות הרבים וחמץ משש שעות ולמעלה:

תורה אור: ויעשו את הפסח במועדו (במדבר ט) · החדש הזה לכם (שמות יב) · וידבר ה' אל משה במדבר (במדבר ט) · וידבר ה' אל משה במדבר סיני (במדבר א)

גליון הש"ס

גמ' זאת אומרת אין מוקדם. עיין ברש"י בחומש בראשית ו' ג' · שם וכי משכחת ליה לבטלה. עיין לקמן דף ט"ו תד"ה ולא אשמעי' · שם וניבטליה בד'. כו' (בכ"מ) הגי' ונבטליה באחד וכו'

[ב"ק כט. מנחות נה: נזיר ס"ח.] · [ב"ק נט: לה:]

היינו דאיצטריך לא ימצא אלא למאן דאמר כממון דמי לא ימצא למה לי איצטריך סלקא דעתך אמינא הואיל וכי איתיה הדר בעיניה לאו ברשותיה קאי קמשמע לן בעו מיניה מרבא בהמת ארנונא חייבת בבכורה או אין חייבת בבכורה כל היכא דמצי מסלק ליה בזוזי לא קא מיבעיא לן דחייב כי קא מיבעיא לן היכא דלא מצי מסלק ליה בזוזי מאי אמר להו פטורה והתניא חייבת התם דמצי מסלק ליה איכא דאמרי אמר רבא *בהמת ארנונא פטורה מן הבכורה ואע"ג דמצי מסלק ליה עיסת ארנונא חייבת בחלה ואע"ג דלא מצי מסלק ליה מאי טעמא בהמה אית לה קלא עיסה לית לה קלא: תנו רבנן *נכרי שנכנס לחצירו של ישראל ובציקו בידו אין זקוק לבער הפקידו אצלו זקוק לבער יחד לו בית אין זקוק לבער שנא' לא ימצא מאי קאמר אמר רב פפא ארישא קאי והכי קאמר הפקידו אצלו זקוק לבער שנאמר לא ימצא רב אשי אמר לעולם אסיפא קאי והכי קאמר יחד לו בית אין זקוק לבער שנאמר לא ימצא בבתיכם והא לאו דידיה הוא דנכרי כי קא מעייל לביתא דנפשיה קא מעייל למימרא דשכירות קניא *והתנן אף במקום שאמרו להשכיר לא לבית דירה אמרו מפני *שמכניסין לתוכו ע"ג ואי סלקא דעתך דשכירות קניא כי קא מעייל לביתיה דנפשיה קא מעייל שאני הכא דאפקיה רחמנא בלשון לא ימצא מי שמצוי בידך יצא זה שאינו מצוי בידך אמר רב יהודה אמר רב המוצא חמץ בביתו ביום טוב *כופה עליו את הכלי אמר רבא אם של הקדש הוא אינו צריך מאי טעמא מיבדל בדילי מיניה ואמר רב יהודה אמר רב חמצו של נכרי עושה לו מחיצה עשרה טפחים משום היכר ואם של הקדש הוא אינו צריך מאי טעמא מיבדל בדילי אינשי מיניה ואמר רב יהודה אמר רב *המפרש והיוצא בשיירא קודם שלשים יום אין זקוק לבער תוך שלשים יום זקוק לבער אמר אביי הא דאמרת תוך שלשים יום זקוק לבער לא אמרן אלא שדעתו לחזור אבל אין דעתו לחזור אין זקוק לבער ואי דעתו לחזור אפילו מראש השנה נמי אלא אמר רבא הא דאמרת קודם שלשים יום אין זקוק לבער לא אמרן אלא שאין דעתו לחזור אבל דעתו לחזור אפילו מראש השנה זקוק לבער ואזדא רבא לטעמיה דאמר רבא העושה ביתו אוצר קודם שלשים יום אין זקוק לבער תוך שלשים יום זקוק לבער וקודם שלשים נמי לא אמרן אלא שאין דעתו לפנותו אבל דעתו לפנותו אפילו קודם שלשים יום נמי זקוק לבער הני שלשים יום מאי עבידתייהו *כדתניא שואלין ודורשין בהלכות הפסח קודם הפסח שלשים יום ר' שמעון בן גמליאל אומר שתי שבתות מאי טעמא דתנא קמא
שהרי

להכי איצטריך לא ימצא. משום דבעלמא לאו כממון דמי איצטריך קרא למימר לגבי חמץ מיהא מתסר: הואיל וכי איתיה הדר. הוא גופיה למריה בעיניה וזה עדיין לא נאבד וכי אמרה ר' שמעון להאי היכא דליתיה בעין כגון גבי גונב קדשים שהיו הבעלים חייבין באחריותן אמר רבי שמעון אף על פי שאין כפל להקדש דכתיב לרעהו ולא להקדש הכא חייב דכיון דזה חייב באחריותן רעהו קרינא ביה דהא גרם לו להתחייב ממון: ארנונא. המלך נוטל עישור מן הבהמה ומן התבואה: חייבת בבכורה. דקיימא לן *כל שיד נכרי באמצע פטורה מן הבכורה שנאמר (במדבר ג) לי כל בכור בישראל אבל לא באחרים ועדר זה בעישורו של מלך בתוכו חייבת בבכורה לתת לכהן הבכורות שלהם או לא: דמלי מסלק ליה. לנכרי במעות: לא תיבעי לן. כיון דהכתי לא זכה נכרי בהן ודינו אינו קבוע בהן יותר ממעות היכא למימר לא יתן לו בהמות אלא מעות: ואע"ג דמלי מסלק ליה. דכל כמה דלא סלקיה ידו שייכא בבהמות: עיסת ארנונא חייבת. ואע"ג דעיסת נכרי פטורה ואוכל ישראל בלא חלה דהא עריסותיכם כתיב זו חייבת דלית לה קלא והרואה אומר שלו היא ואוכלה בלא חלה אבל בבהמה אית לה קלא והדתניא חייבת בעיסה הוא דתניא: אין זקוק לבער. לא הזקיקוהו להוציא את הנכרי מן הבית כדאמרן אבל אתה רואה של אחרים: הפקידו אצלו. וקיבל עליה אחריות כדמפרש ואזיל זקוק לבער: יחד לו בית. כלומר לא קיבלו עליו אלא אמר ליה הרי הבית לפניך הנח באחת מן הזויות אין זקוק לבער: מאי קאמר. היכי יליף מלא ימצא: לעולם אסיפא. ולא ימצא משמע המצוי בידך לכל חפצך היינו דקיבל עליה אחריות דהוי כדידיה: אף במקום שאמרו להשכיר. בפ"ק דע"ז תנן אין משכירין בתים לנכרים בארץ ישראל אבל בסוריא משכירין וכל שכן בחוצה לארץ ואף במקום שהתירו להשכיר לא לבית דירה התירו אלא להעמיד בו בהמות ועצים ולא שידור הוא בה: שאין מצוי בידך. שהרי אותה זוית מסורה לנכרי: כופה עליו את הכלי. דהא לא חזי לטלטולי ולאפוקי ומיהא בבל יראה לא עבר דהא בטליה בליביה מאתמול כדאמרינן לקמן הבודק צריך שיבטל בלבו אלא משום שלא ישכח ויאכלנו צריך כפיית כלי: מיבדל בדילי מיניה. אפילו בחול למוד הוא לפרוש ממנו: חמצו של נכרי. המופקד אצלו ולא קיבל עליו אחריות דמותר לשהותו: עושה לו מחיצה. בארבעה עשר משום היכר שלא ישכח ויאכלנו ולא סגי ליה בכפיית כלי כל שבעה שהכלי ניטל לצורך ומיהו ההוא דלעיל לא אפשר ליה במחיצה ומשום חד יומא סגי ליה בכפיית כלי ובלילה יבערנו: המפרש. מן היבשה לים: בשיירא. למקום רחוק: קודם שלשים יום. לפסח ולקמן מפרש כנגד ששואלין בהלכות הפסח קודם הפסח שלשים יום ומאז חל עליו להיזהר בצרכי הפסח: דעתו לחזור. בימי הפסח: אפילו מראש השנה נמי. דכי הדר ביה בימי הפסח עבר עליה וההיא שעתא לאו ברשותיה היא דליבטליה שהרי איסור הנאה הוא ואינו שלו וכראהו עובר עליה: אוצר. שהכניס שם תבואה ותחתיה חמץ ואמרינן לקמן *חמץ שנפלה עליו מפולת הרי הוא כמבוער: תוך שלשים זקוק לבער. דלכתחלה לא זהו ביעורו: קודם שלשים. לא חלה חובת ביעור עליו וכי מטי ההיא שעתא לא מחוייב כדאמרן דהא נפלה עליו מפולת:
שהרי

התם דמלי מסלק ליה. הק' ר"י דבפ' איזהו נשך (ב"מ דף ע: ושם) אמר המקבל צאן ברזל מן הנכרי הוולדות פטורים מן הבכורה אף על גב דמלי מסלק ליה לנכרי בזוזי כדאמר התם כיון דאלו בעי נכרי זוזי ולא משכח שקיל בהמה ותי' ר"י דשאני התם *שמתחלה היתה הבהמה של נכרי וכיון דאי בעי זוזי ולא משכח שקיל בהמה לא נפקא מרשותיה אבל כשהבהמה של ישראל ומלי מסלק ליה לנכרי בזוזי לא נכנסה לרשותו: בהמת ארנונא פטורה מן הבכורה אע"ג דמלי מסלק ליה. והא דתניא חייבת פ"ה דגבי עיסה תניא וק' לרשב"א דהא גבי בהמה תניא בהדיא בתוספתא *דחייבת בבכורה וכן גבי עיסה תניא* עיסת ארנונא חייבת בחלה אע"ג דלא מלי מסלק ליה ואית ספרים דגרסי בהמת ארנונא פטורה והוא דלא מלי מסלק ליה ולפי זה מתיישבות שתי הברייתות: יחד לו בית. פ"ה דלא קיבל עליו אחריות אלא אמר ליה הרי הבית לפניך וק' לר"י מאי איריא יחד אפילו לא יחד נמי והכי נמי מסיק בסמוך למימר דשכירות קניא ופר"ת דאפילו באחריות איירי ומשום הכי מפיק מלא ימצא דלא חשיב מצוי כיון שיחד לו בית ורב פפא אית ליה מסברא כיון שיחד לו בית הוי כאלו קיבל עליו אחריות על חמצו של נכרי בביתו של נכרי*: כופה עליו כלי. אע"ג דאיכא למ"ד בפ' כירה (שבת מג.) אין כלי ניטל אלא לדבר הניטל איכא לאוקמי בצריך למקומו אי נמי הכא שרי משום דילמא אתי למיכליה:
שנאמר

רבינו חננאל

בהמת ארנונא. פי' בהמה שיש בה שותפות לנכרי פטורה מן הבכורה דבהדיא קי"ל כל יד נכרי באמצע פטור מן הבכורה ואע"ג דמצי מסלק ליה לנכרי בדמי מ"מ בהמה אית לה קלא כלומר דהאי בהמה דנכרי היא ולא אתו למימר דישראל היא וקא אכיל בוכרי אבל עיסת ארנונא אע"ג דלא מצי מסלק ליה לנכרי מינה חייבת בחלה דהא לית לה קלא: ת"ר נכרי שנכנס להצרו של ישראל ובצק בידו אין זקוק ישראל להוציאו מידו של נכרי ולבערו הפקידו אצלו חייב לבער אלא אם יחד ליה בית ולאו ברשותיה דישראל קאי: למימרא דשכירות קניא והתנן בע"ז סוף פ"ק אף במקום שאמרו להשכיר לא לבית דירה אמרו מפני שמכניס לתוכו עבודת כוכבים וכתיב (דברים ז כו) לא תביא תועבה אל ביתך ואי ס"ד דשכירות קניא לאו ביתךהוא ושני' לעול' שכירות לא קניא ושאני הכא דכתיב לא ימצא כל חמץ שמצוי בידך אסרה תורה והאי כיון דיחד לו בית יצא מידו זה החמץ ואינו מצוי בידו: אמר רב המוצא חמץ ביו"ט שאינו יכול לבערו כופה עליו את הכלי חיישנן שמא יאכלנו בגיו ואם של הקדש אינו צריך מ"מ מיבדל בדילי אינשי מיניה מקמי הכי ולא אתו לטיכליה דחמיר עלייהו איסוריה וחמץ של נכרי צריך מחיצה עשרה טפחים כדי שיצא מרשות ישראל לגמרי: וכן המפרש בים או היוצא בשיירא תוך שלשים יום זקוק לבער (לאחרי כן יבער) קודם שלשים יום אין זקוק לבער בד"א בשאין דעתו לחזור אבל כשדעתו לחזור אפי' מתחלת השנה חייב לבער וכן דין העושה את ביתו אוצר תוך שלשים יום זקוק לבער קודם שלשים יום אין זקוק לבער במה דברים אמורים בשאין דעתו לפנותו קודם הפסח אבל דעתו לפנותו חייב לבער: והני שלשים יום מאי עבידתייהו דתניא

עין משפט נר מצוה

כח א מיי' פ"ד מהל' בכורות הלכה א סמג עשין מח טוש"ע יו"ד סי' שכ סעיף ה:
כט ב מיי' פ"ו מהלכות ביכורים הל' יב סמג עשין קמא טוש"ע יו"ד סי' של סעיף ג:
ל ג ד מיי' פ"ד מה' חמץ ומצה הלכה ב טוש"ע או"ח סימן תמ סעיף ג:
לא ה מיי' פ"ו מהלכות ע"ז הל' ד סמג לאוין מח טוש"ע יו"ד סי' קנא סעיף י:
[בכורות פ"ב]
תוספתא דחלה פ"א
לב ו מיי' פ"ג מהלכות חמץ ומצה הלכה ח סמג לאוין עט טוש"ע או"ח סי' תמו סעיף א:
לג ז מיי' פ"ד שם הל' ב סמג שם טוש"ע או"ח סי' תמ סעיף ג:
לד ח ט מיי' פ"ב שם הלכה יג סמג שם טוש"ע או"ח סימן תלו סעיף א ב:
לה כ טור ש"ע או"ח סי' תכט סעיף א:
[ועי' תוס' ב"מ פא: ד"ה והא]

מסורת הש"ס

[בכורות ג.]
[תוספתא פ"ב]
ע"ז כא. ושו.
[צ"ל שמכניס]
[עי' תוספות כתובות ז. ד"ה מתוך]
[תוספתא פ"א]
מגילה כט: סנהדרין יב: ע"ז ה: [ר"ה ז. בכורות נח. תוספתא מגילה פ"ג]
[דף ח.]

גליון הש"ס

גמ' בהמת ארנונא. עיין נדרים סב ע"ב ברש"י ד"ה והלך זו ארנונא: תוס' ד"ה התם. שמתחלה היתה הבהמה. עי' ב"ב נ"ע: תוס' ד"ה קסבר:

causes [liability] for money is not as money: [6a] hence *'there shall not be found'* is necessary. But on the view that it is as money, what is the purpose of *'there shall not be found'*?[4]—It is necessary: you might argue, since if in existence it is returned as it is,[5] it does not stand in his possession.[6] Hence he informs us [otherwise].

Raba was asked: Is cattle liable to *arnona*[7] subject to the law of firstlings or not?[8] Wherever one can put him off with money,[9] we do not ask, for he is [certainly] liable.[10] Our problem arises where he cannot put him off with money: what then? He replied: It is not subject [thereto]. But surely it was taught: It [the animal] is subject [thereto]?—There it is a case where he can put him off with money. Others state, Raba said: Cattle liable to *arnona* is not subject to the law of firstlings, even when he can put him off with money.[11] A dough [made of flour] liable to *arnona*[12] is subject to *ḥallah*.[13] What is the reason? [The facts about] cattle are generally known;[1] [the facts about a dough] are not generally known.[2]
a

Our Rabbis taught: If a Gentile enters an Israelite's court-yard with [leavened] dough in his hand,[3] he [the Israelite] is not obliged to remove it;[4] if he deposits it with him, he is obliged to remove it;[5] if he assigns a room to him [for the dough], he is not obliged to remove it, because it is said, '[*Leaven*] *shall not be found*'. What does he [the Tanna] mean?[6]—Said R. Papa: He refers to the first clause, and says thus: If he deposits it with him, he is obliged to remove it, because it is said, '[*Leaven*] *shall not be found*'. R. Ashi said: After all it refers to the second clause, and he says thus: If he assigned a room to him he is not obliged to remove it, because it is said, '[*Leaven*] *shall not be found in* your *houses,*' and this is not his [house], for when the Gentile carries in [the leaven], he carries it into his own house. Shall we say that renting confers a title?[7] But surely we learned: Even in the place where they [the Sages] permitted renting [to a heathen], they did not permit [renting] for a dwelling-house, because he [the heathen] introduces [his] idols therein.[8] Now if you should think that renting confers a title, when he introduces [the idols] he introduces [them] into his own house?—Here it is different, because the Divine Law expresses it in the form of *'there shall not be found'*, [implying] that which is found in your hand [is forbidden], which excludes this [case], since it is not found in your hand.

Rab Judah said in Rab's name: If one finds leaven in his house during the Festival, he overturns a vessel upon it.[9] Raba said: If
b it is of *heḳdesh*,[1] this is unnecessary. What is the reason? He does indeed hold aloof from it.[2]

Rab Judah also said in Rab's name: Leaven belonging to a Gentile,[3] he [the Israelite] must set up a partition of ten handbreadths around it as a distinguishing mark;[4] but if it belongs to *heḳdesh* this is unnecessary. What is the reason? People hold aloof from it.

Rab Judah also said in Rab's name: He who sets sail, and he who sets out in a [caravan] company, before thirty days [prior to Passover], is not bound to remove [the leaven]; if within thirty days, he is bound to remove [it]. Abaye observed: When you say, if within thirty days he is bound to remove it, we said this only where his intention is to return [during Passover]; but if it is not his intention to return, he is not bound to remove [it]. Said Raba to him: But if his intention is to return, even [if he sets out] on New Year too?[5] Rather, said Raba: When you say, if before thirty days he is not bound to remove it, we said this only where it is not his intention to return; but if his intention is to return, even [if he sets out] on New Year too. Now Raba is consistent with his view. For Raba said: If one turns his house into a granary[6] before thirty days [prior to the Passover], he is not bound to remove [the leaven];[7] if within thirty days, he is bound to remove it;[8] and even before thirty days too, we said this only when it is not his intention to clear it [the store of provisions] away; but if his intention is to clear it away, even before thirty days too he is bound to remove it.

What business have these thirty days?[9]—As it was taught: Questions are asked and lectures are given on the laws of Passover for thirty days before Passover. R. Simeon b. Gamaliel said: Two

(4) It is obviously forbidden, since it is just like his own! (5) I.e., not lost or stolen or destroyed. (6) In regard to the prohibition *'there shall not be found'*. (7) Tax from crops and cattle paid in kind. (8) Where a non-Jew has a share in an animal it is definitely not subject thereto; the question here is as explained in the text. (9) I.e., the king, to whom the tax is payable, will accept money instead of the animal. (10) The owner is bound to render it as a firstling. (11) Because until he does pay him off the non-Jew has a claim upon it. (12) I.e., a dough from which *arnona* is paid. (13) V. Glos. and Num. XV, 20f: *Of the first of* your *dough ye shall offer up a cake for an heave-offering . . . Of the first of* your *dough ye shall give unto the Lord an heave-offering throughout your generations.* Here too *'your'* excludes dough partly owned by a non-Jew; nevertheless this dough is subject to *ḥallah*, as explained in the text.

a (1) Lit., 'an animal has a sound (voice)'—i.e., it will be known that it belongs to a herd liable to *arnona*. (2) The onlooker does not know that the dough is made of flour subject to *arnona* and may suspect him of violating the law. (3) On the fourteenth of Nisan after noon, when leaven is forbidden. (4) Since it is not his, v. *supra* 5*b*. (5) Where he accepts responsibility for same. (6) If anything the quotation intimates the reverse. (7) So that the house becomes legally the non-Jew's. (8) A.Z. 21*a*. (9) It must not be handled and carried out, because it is *mukẓeh* (v. Glos.), since it cannot be put to any use, all benefit from leaven being forbidden during Passover. He therefore covers it over with a vessel and burns it in the evening on the termination of the Festival.

b (1) V. Glos. (2) In any case, since it is *heḳdesh*. (3) In a Jew's house. (4) The reference here is to the fourteenth, and the partition is needed lest he forget himself and eat it. The overturning of a vessel upon it does not suffice here lest he might remove it in the course of the seven days. (5) He must still remove it, since he will be in the house on Passover. (6) I.e., he stores provisions in it, and under them lies leaven. (7) By being buried under his provisions it is as though it were removed. (8) Because the obligation to remove it becomes operative in this period, and one cannot remove it thus at the very outset. (9) Why is the matter dependent on this period?

Said Raba: [5b] Three things may be inferred from R. Akiba:
a [i] There is no [other] removal of leaven save [by] burning.[1] [ii] Kindling was singled out to indicate separation.[2] [iii] We do not say, since kindling was permitted when it is necessary [for the preparation of food], it was also permitted when it is unnecessary.[3]

Our Rabbis taught: *Seven days shall there be no leaven found in your house:*[4] why is this stated, seeing that it is already said, *and there shall no leavened bread be seen unto thee, neither shall there be leaven seen unto thee, in all thy borders?*[5] Because it is said, *Neither shall there be leaven seen unto thee*, [implying] thine own thou must not see, yet thou mayest see that belonging to others and to the Most High.[6] One might think that one may hide [leaven] or accept bailments [of leaven] from a Gentile:[7] therefore it is stated, *it shall not be* found [*in your houses*].[8] Now, I know this only of a Gentile who is not in your power[9] or does not dwell with you in the [same] court-yard; how do I know it of a Gentile who is in your power and dwells with you in the [same] court-yard? Because it is stated, [*leaven*] *shall not be found in your houses*. I know this only of that which is your houses; how do I know it of [leaven] in pits, ditches
b and cavities?[1] Because it is stated, [*neither shall there be leaven seen with thee,*] *in all thy borders*.[2] Yet I might still argue, [Indeed on account of leaven] 'in *houses*' one transgresses the injunction against it being seen, found, and against hiding it and receiving [it as] bailments from a Gentile; whereas in [respect to leaven in] '*thy borders*' [we say,] thine own thou must not see, yet thou mayest see that belonging to others and to the Most High. How do we [however] know to apply that which is stated in this [verse] to the other, and *vice versa?*[3] Therefore leaven is stated twice[4] for a *gezerah shawah*.[5] [Thus:] leaven is stated in connection with houses: '*no* leaven *shall be found in your houses*'; and leaven is stated in connection with the borders; '*neither shall there be* leaven *seen with thee* [*in all thy borders*]': just as with the leaven which is stated in connection with houses, one transgresses the injunctions, it shall not be seen, it shall not be found, it shall not be hidden nor accepted as bailments from Gentiles, so with the leaven which is stated in connection with the borders, one violates the injunctions, it shall not be seen, it shall not be found, it shall not be hidden nor accepted as bailments from a Gentile. And just as with the leaven which is stated in connection with the borders, [only] thine own thou must not see, but thou mayest see that belonging to others and to the Most High, so with the leaven which is stated in connection with the houses, [only] thine own thou mayest not see, but thou mayest see that belonging to others and to the Most High.

The Master said: 'I know this only of a Gentile who is not in your power or does not dwell with you in the [same] court-yard; how do I know it of a Gentile who is in your power or who dwells with you in the [same] court-yard? Because it is stated, [*Leaven*] *shall not be found* [*in your houses*].' Whither does this tend?[6]—Said Abaye: Reverse it. Raba said: In truth you must not reverse it, but it refers to the first clause: 'Thine own thou mayest not see, yet thou mayest see that belonging to others and to the Most High.' I know this only of a Gentile who is not in your power or
c who does not dwell with you in the [same] court-yard.[1] How do I know it of one who is in your power or who dwells with you in the [same] court-yard? Because it is stated, *'there shall not be found'*. But this Tanna seeks permission yet cites a verse intimating a prohibition?[2]—Because *'unto thee' 'unto thee'* is stated twice.[3]

The Master said: 'One might think that one may hide [leaven] or accept bailments [of leaven] from a Gentile; therefore it is stated, [*leaven*] *shall not be* found [*in your houses*].' But you said in the first clause, 'thine own thou mayest not see, yet thou mayest see that belonging to others and to the Most High?'—There is no difficulty: the one is meant where he [the Israelite] accepts responsibility [for same]; the other, where he does not accept responsibility.[4] Just as Raba said to the townspeople of Maḥuza:[5] Remove the leaven belonging to the troops from your houses: since it stands in your possession if lost or stolen, and you must
d requite [the loss], it is as yours and is forbidden.[1] Now, that is well on the view that that which causes [liability] for money is as money.[2] But on the view that it is not as money, what can be said?—Here it is different, because Scripture saith, *'There shall not be found'*.[3] Others say, That is well on the view that that which

a (1) For if it can be destroyed in any other way, his proof falls to the ground. (2) In Ex. XX, 10 work is forbidden on the Sabbath; this is repeated in XXXV, 2 and 3, with a special prohibition against kindling a fire. Now, kindling is prohibited by the general law of Ex. XX, 10: why then is it singled out? There are two views on this: (i) In order to teach that whereas other labours are punishable by death, this is merely punishable like any other negative precept, viz., by flagellation. (ii) To teach that if one does a number of separate acts on the Sabbath, e.g., seething, reaping, and threshing, they are accounted as separate offences, just as kindling was stated as a separate offence, and a sacrifice must be offered on account of each. Now the first view postulates that kindling is not a principal labour like the rest (v. Mishnah on Shab. 73a); hence R. Akiba must agree with the second view. (3) There is such a view in Beẓ. 12b; if R. Akiba held it, his argument would lose its basis. (4) Ex. XII, 19. (5) Ex. XIII, 7. Though this is in a further chapter, the phrase, 'seeing that it is *already* said', is employed because it is a Talmudic principle that the written order of the Torah is not necessarily chronological. (6) I.e, the sanctuary, this being the meaning of '*unto thee*' (E.V.: *with thee*). (7) For in the former case it cannot be *seen*, while in the latter it is not his property. (8) It must not be there at all. (9) Lit., 'whom you have not subjugated'.

b (1) Different shaped pits are connoted by these three words. (2) Ex. XIII, 7. (3) '*For there shall not be found*' is written only in connection with '*your houses*', while '*unto thee*' is mentioned only in connection with '*borders*'; how do we know that the implications of the one verse hold good in respect of the other? (4) Lit., 'leaven, leaven'. (5) V. Glos. (6) Or, towards the tail! I.e., when you say that you must not accept deposits from a Gentile, obviously he who is in your power or who lives with you in the same court-yard is more likely to be meant than he who is independent or living away from you, since the former is more like yourself. Whereas here the latter is taken for granted, while proof is sought for the former.

c (1) He certainly comes under the category of 'others'. (2) According to Raba's explanation, when the Tanna says, 'how do I know', etc., his purpose is to show that there too it is permitted; while '*there shall not be found*' intimates a more extended prohibition. (3) Rashi: '*Unto thee*' is written twice, once in the verse already quoted, and once in Deut. XVI, 4: *and there shall be no leaven seen unto* (E.V. *with*) *thee in all thy borders seven days*. Here too '*unto thee*' is linked with seeing; since, however, it is superfluous in this connection, on account of the verse first quoted, it is applied to '*there shall not be found*', which is made to read: *there shall not be found unto thee*, '*unto thee*' being a permissive limitation, and it is this which the Tanna quotes.—It is a principle of exegesis that if a word or phrase is superfluous in its own context, it is applied elsewhere. (The fact that '*unto thee*' is written twice in Ex. XIII, 7 is not counted, since one refers to leaven and the other to leavened bread.—V. Beẓ. 7b.) R. Ḥan. interprets it differently and more simply. (4) If the Jew accepts responsibility for the bailment and must indemnify the owner against loss, it is as his own and must not be found in his house. (5) A large Jewish commercial town on the Tigris, where Raba had his academy; v. Obermeyer, pp. 169ff.

d (1) Gentile troops were billeted in Jewish houses together with their food stores, for which the Jews were responsible. (2) Hence though the leaven does not belong to the Jew, yet since it throws a financial responsibility upon him it is regarded as his, i.e., as his money or property. (3) Which implies even if it is not his own and it can be applied only to such a case, since '*unto thee*' excludes leaven in which he has no financial interest at all.

עין משפט
נר מצוה

כו א מיי' פ"א מהלכות חמץ ומצה הלכה ב ופ"ד הלכה א ב סמג לאוין עט:
כז ב ג ד מיי' פ"ד שם הלכ' ב ג ד סמג שם טוש"ע א"ח סי' תמ סעיף א:

מסורת
הש"ס

שמע מינה מדרבי עקיבא תלת שמע מינה *אין ביעור חמץ אלא שריפה ושמע מינה *הבערה לחלק יצאת ושמע מינה לא אמרינן הואיל והותרה הבערה לצורך הותרה נמי שלא לצורך: ת"ר (שמות יב) שבעת ימים שאור לא ימצא בבתיכם מה ת"ל והלא כבר נאמר (שם יג) לא יראה לך שאור [ולא יראה לך *חמץ] בכל גבולך לפי שנא' לא יראה לך שאור *שלך אי אתה רואה אבל אתה רואה של אחרים ושל גבוה *יכול יטמין ויקבל פקדונות מן הנכרי ת"ל לא ימצא אין לי אלא בנכרי שלא כיבשתו ואין שרוי עמך בחצר נכרי שכיבשתו ושרוי עמך בחצר מנין ת"ל לא ימצא בבתיכם אין לי אלא שבבתיכם בבורות בשיחין ובמערות מנין ת"ל בכל גבולך ועדיין אני אומר בבתים עובר משום בל יראה ובל ימצא ובל יטמין ובל יקבל פקדונות מן הנכרי בגבולין שלך אי אתה רואה אבל אתה רואה של אחרים ושל גבוה מניין ליתן את האמור של זה בזה ושל זה בזה ת"ל שאור שאור לגזרה שוה נאמר שאור בבתים שאור לא ימצא בבתיכם ונאמר שאור בגבולין לא יראה לך שאור מה שאור האמור בבתים עובר משום בל יראה ובל ימצא ובל יטמין ובל יקבל פקדונות מן הנכרי אף שאור האמור בגבולין עובר משום בל יראה ובל ימצא ובל יטמין ובל יקבל פקדונות מן הנכרי ומה שאור האמור בגבולין שלך אי אתה רואה אבל אתה רואה של אחרים ושל גבוה אף שאור האמור בבתים שלך אי אתה רואה אבל אתה רואה של אחרים ושל גבוה: אמר מר אין לי אלא בנכרי שלא כיבשתו ואין שרוי עמך בחצר נכרי שכיבשתו ושרוי עמך בחצר מנין ת"ל לא ימצא כלפי *לייא אמר אביי איפוך רבא אמר לעולם לא תיפוך ורישא קאי שלך אי אתה רואה אבל אתה רואה של אחרים ושל גבוה אין לי אלא בנכרי שלא כיבשתו ואין שרוי עמך בחצר [ב]נכרי שכיבשתו ושרוי עמך בחצר מנין ת"ל לא ימצא והאי תנא מיהדר אהיתירא ונסיב לה קרא לאיסורא *משום שנאמר לך לך תרי זימני: אמר מר יכול יטמין ויקבל פקדונות מן הנכרים תלמוד לומר לא ימצא הא אמרת רישא שלך אי אתה רואה אבל אתה רואה של אחרים ושל גבוה לא קשיא *הא דקביל עליה אחריות הא דלא קביל עליה אחריות כי הא דאמר להו רבא לבני מחוזא *בעירו חמירא דבני חילא מבתייכו כיון דאילו *מיגנב ואילו מיתביד ברשותייכו קאי ובעיתו לשלומי כדילכון דמי ואסור הניחא למאן דאמר *דבר הגורם לממון כממון דמי אלא למאן דאמר לאו כממון דמי מאי איכא למימר שאני הכא דאמר לא ימצא איכא דאמרי הניחא למאן דאמר דבר הגורם לממון לאו כממון דמי היינו

רש"י

ש"מ. מדלא נפקא ליה דהאי יום הראשון ערב יום טוב הוא אלא משום דאסור להבעיר ביום טוב שמע מינה סבירא ליה כר' יהודה דאמר לקמן בפרק כל שעה [כח. וכז:] אין ביעור חמץ אלא שריפה ויליף לה מנותר דאי השבתתו בכל דבר סבירא ליה לוקמיה ביו"ט ויבערנו בדבר אחר יאכילנו לכלבים או ישליכנו לים: וש"מ. מדקאמר שהוא אב מלאכה סבירא ליה כר' נתן דאמר הבערה לחלק יצאתה דתניא (שבת דף ע.) הבערה ללאו יצאת שהיתה בכלל לא תעשה כל מלאכה חזר והוציאה מכללו ופרט בה לאו לעצמה לומר לך שאינה במיתת בית דין כשאר מלאכות אלא בלאו זה לבדו רבי נתן אומר לחלק יצאתה שלא תאמר העושה ארבעה או חמשה אבות מלאכות בשוגג בשבת אינו חייב אלא אחת דהא חד לאו איכא בכולהו וחד כרת לפיכך פרט בה בפני עצמה להקיש אליה מה היא מיוחדת שהיא אב מלאכה וחייבין עליה לעצמה כו' אלמא לר' יוסי לאו אב מלאכה היא: והלא כבר נאמר ולא יראה לך שאור בכל גבולך. הרי בתים במשמע: לפי שנאמר ולא יראה לך. דמדכתב לך משמע מינה שלך אי אתה רואה אבל אתה רואה בגבולין של אחרים כגון נכרי ושל גבוה אם הקדישם לבדק הבית: יכול. נלמוד ממקרא זה שיטמין את שלו *ביד שלא יראנו ודיו דהא לא יראה כתיב: ויקבל פקדונות מן הנכרי. דהא כתיב לך: ת"ל לא ימצא. אסר לך הטמנה שאף היא בכלל מציאה ואסר לך של אחרים דהכא לא כתיב לך: אין לי. מלא ימצא לאסור אלא נכרי שלא כבשתו תחת ידיך ואינו שרוי עמך בחצר ולקמיה פריך איפכא מסתברא: נכרי שכיבשתו תחת ידך. דהוי ממונו כממונך או שלא כיבשתו אבל שרוי בחצרך מנין תלמוד לומר לא ימצא לקמיה מפרש לה: ואין לי אלא בבתים. כלומר ואם נאמר זה ולא נאמר ולא יראה לך שאור הייתי אומר אין לי שאסור לשהות חמץ אלא בבתים מפני שהוא מצוי אצלו תמיד דהא בהאי קרא בתים הוא דכתיב: תלמוד לומר בכל גבולך. בקרא דלא יראה כתיב: ועדיין. אע"פ שנאמר שניהם יש לי לומר בבתים עובר בכל אלו דהא לא ימצא דמשמע אפילו הטמנה לא כתב אלא בבתים ולא כתב בהו נמי לך להוציא של אחרים אבל בגבולין בורות שיחין ומערות כתב לך ואני אומר אבל אתה רואה בהן של אחרים מנין ליתן קולו של זה בזה וחומרו של זה בזה ת"ל כו' ולקמיה פריך מאי קאמר דמייתי לה של אחרים ושל גבוה לאיסורא ולהתירא הכא והכא: כלפי לייא. שתי מלות כלפי היכן נוטה דבר זה הא איפכא מסתברא נכרי שכבשתו מסתברא לאסור מפי: לייא. היכן וחבירו בברכות בפרק הרואה (דף נח.) אזלי לנהרא כגני לייא חרסים סבורים להיכן הולכין: איפוך. אין לי לאסור אלא בנכרי שכיבשתו דהוי דומיא דשלך נכרי שלא כיבשתו מניין תלמוד לומר לא ימצא ולא כתב לא תמצא אבל לא ימצא לגמרי משמע: ורישא קאי. להיתירא אין לי דמותר לראות של אחרים בדלא קביל עליה אחריות כדלקמיה אלא שלא כיבשתו נכרי שכיבשתו מנין דמותר ת"ל לא ימצא: ופרכינן לרבא תנא מהדר אהיתירא ונסיב לה למילתיה קרא לאיסורא ומשני להיתירא קא נסיב לה משום שנאמר בגבולין בשאור לך לך תרי זימני לא יראה לך שאור בכל גבולך שבעת ימים בפרשת ראה וכתיב לא יראה לך חמץ ולא יראה לך שאור בכל גבולך בפרשת בא ואם אינו ענין להאי לך בגבולין גבי ראייה דהא כבר אמור תניהו ענין ללא ימצא ודרוש ביה לא ימצא לך אף במצוי אצלך והיינו שרוי עמך קאמינא לך דאין חמץ אסור אלא אם כן שלך אבל אתה מוצא את שלו והיא לך דחמץ לא קחשיב דשאור וחמץ מילרך צריכי כדאמר בבילה (דף ז:) דחד מחבריה לא יליף: מחוזא. עירו של רבא: דבני חילא. גייס של בית המלך ומטילין תיקון טורח מזונותיהן על העיירות: הניחא. הא דאמרינן דמשום אחריות אסור: למאן דאמר כו'. רבי שמעון קאמר ליה בבבא קמא (דף עא:) קדשים שחייב באחריותן חייב:
להכי

תוספות

לחלק יצאת. מדקרי לה אב מלאכה ועוד אומר ריב"א דלמ"ד ללאו יצאתה *לא היה אסור ביו"ט כיון *דאין שם מלאכה עליה: לא אמרינן מתוך. דאי אמרינן מתוך שרי אע"ג דבעינן צורך היום קצת הכא מה שמבער הוי צורכו: אבל אתה רואה של אחרים ושל גבוה. הקשה הרב ר' יעקב דאורליי"נש דהכא לא מצריך תרי קראי למעוטי נכרי וגבוה דמחד לך ממעטינן תרוייהו אע"ג דתלתא לך כתיבי ובפ' כל שעה (לקמן כג.) משמע דצריכי כולהו ובמנחות בפרק רבי ישמעאל (דף סז. ושם) קאמר תרי עריסותיכם כתיבי חד למעוטי נכרי וחד למעוטי הקדש ומיהו בספרים מדויקים גרס חד כדי עריסותיכם פירוש כשיעור עיסת מדבר וחד לעיסת הקדש וכן נראה דבראשית הגז (חולין קלה:) דרשינן מעריסותיכם כדי עיסתכם: משום דכתיב לך לך תרי זימני. פ"ה כיון דמייתר לך שדייה אלא ימצא וקשה לרשב"א דמיותרא דלך גופיה אפילו בלא [לא] ימצא מצינו למעוטי נכרי שכיבשתו ואור"י דאי לאו מלא ימצא מלך לא ממעטינן נכרי שכיבשתו דהוא כמי לך חשיבא וה"א דאתי לדרשה אחרינא אבל השתא דשדינא אלא ימצא ממשמעותיה ממעטינן נכרי שכיבשתו דלא ימצא לך משמע אפילו במצוי בעינא לך אבל עוד קשה לו כיון דשדינא אלא ימצא אמאי איצטריך ליה לעיל למדרש מה שאור האמור בגבולים וכו' אף שאור האמור בבתים שלך אי אתה רואה וכו' ותירץ ר"י דאי לאו דרשה דשאור שאור הוה מוקי לה למעוטי של אחרים ושל גבוה בבתים כמו בגבולים ולא למעוטי נכרי שכיבשתו ודוחק הקשה רבינו תם דבשום דוכתא לא מצריכנא תרי קראי לכיבשתו ושלא כיבשתו בראשית הגז (חולין קלה:) גבי ביתך דגנך שדך וטובא דמייתי התם בכולהו לא מצריך אלא חד קרא לכיבשתו ולשלא כיבשתו ותי' רשב"א דכיון דגלי לן הכא נכרי שכיבשתו לא חשיב שלך בשום דוכתא תו לא צריך תרי קראי וממעטינן תרוייהו מחד קרא וכן יש לתרץ מה שהקשה ה"ר יעקב דאורליינ"ש מעריסותיכם:
התם

תורה אור

[ולא יראה לך שאור כצ"ל וכ"א בילקוט]

רבינו חננאל

אמר רבא ש"מ מדר"ע תלת ש"מ אין ביעור חמץ אלא שרפה דאי ס"ד בלא שרפה ישביתהו אפילו ביו"ט שלא בשרפה ושמעי' מינה הבערה לחלק יצאתה דאי ס"ד ללאו יצאתה תיתי עשה דהשבתת חמץ לידחי לאו דהבערה וש"מ לא אמרינן מתוך שהותרה הבערה לצורך הותרה נמי שלא לצורך: ת"ר שבעת ימים שאור לא ימצא בבתיכם מה ת"ל והלא כבר נאמר לא יראה לך שאור בכל גבולך שבעת ימים וכו' עד מנין ליתן את האמור של זה בזה ואת האמור של זה בזה ת"ל שאור שאור לגזרה שוה נאמר שאור בבתים שבעת ימים שאור לא ימצא בבתיכם ונאמר שאור בגבולך לא יראה לך שאור בכל גבולך מה שאור האמור בבתים כיון שהוא מצוי בביתו עובר בבל יראה ובבל ימצא ובבל יטמין ובבל יקבל פקדונות מן הנכרי' שאילו כולן נכנסין בכלל דבר המצוי בביתו שאין אדם רואה בביתו אלא דבר המצוי בביתו וכן כלם אף שאור האמור בגבולין כן ומה שאור האמור בגבולין כתיב ביה לא יראה לך שלך אי אתה רואה אבל אתה רואה של אחרים ושל גבוה אף שאור האמור בבתים של אחרים ושל גבוה מותר: אמר מר יכול יטמין ויקבל פקדונו' מן הנכרי' ת"ל לא ימצא אין לי אלא נכרי שלא כבשתו ואין שרוי עמך בחצר בוא שלא ימצא אצלך לא ממון ולא פקדון נכרי שכבשתו ושרוי עמך מנין ת"ל לא ימצא ואקשי' (כלפיא) [נראה דצ"ל כלפי אליה] כלומר דברים מהופכין הן כמו שהאליה הפוך מן הראש שכל המהלך בדרך מהלכין הולך ראשו לפנים וזנבו לאחריו והמהופך הולך זנבו לפנים והראש אחריו כך גם זה כלומר אם אסרה לך התורה בנכרי שלא כבשתו עאכ"ו בנכרי שכבשתו שהוא כמו שלך שהוא אסור: אמר אביי איפוך. כלומ' נכרי שכבשתו ושרוי עמך בחצר כמו שלך הוא חשוב ואסור אלא מנין שאף נכרי שלא כבשתו ואינו שרוי עמך בחצר שהוא אסור ת"ל לא ימצא כלל: רבא אמר לעולם לא תיפוך ורישא קאי. כלומר בתחלת הענין הדברים אמורים שלך אי אתה רואה אבל אתה רואה של אחרים ושל גבוה אין לי אלא שמותר לך לראות חמצו של נכרי אלא בנכרי שלא כבשתו ואין שרוי עמך שאין בך יכולת למנעו נכרי שכבשתו ושרוי עמך בחצר מנין שאע"פ שיש בך יכולת למנעו שמותר שנא' לא יראה לך שלך אי אתה רואה אבל אתה רואה של אחרים ואקשי' האי תנא מהדר אהתירא כלומר ממשמע הני קראי מראין הדברים שמותר לראות חמצו של נכרי שלא כבשתו ונסיב לה קרא לא ימצא בבתיכם דמשמע לאיסורא ופרקי' הייתה אומר אשר שנא' לא ימצא מכל מקום קמ"ל לא יראה לך חמץ ולא יראה לך שאור לך לך תרי זימני דאפי' נכרי שכבשתו שרי דקרינא ביה שלך אי אתה רואה אבל אתה רואה של אחרים ושל גבוה הני מילי דלא קביל עליה ישראל אחריות אבל קבל עליה אחריות אסור כדרבא דאמר לבני מחוזא בערו חמירא דבני חילא פי' הנכרים בני החיילות היו מפקידין את החמץ שלהן בבתי ישראל והיו נותנין לחם קצוב ואמרין להם עשו לנו לחם ואפילו אם אבד אותו הלחם באונס אין משגיחין אלא מענישין אותם נמצא אותו לחם כל זמן שהוא אצלם כאלו שלהם הוא ואע"ג דאמרינן דבר הגורם לממון הוא כלומר לכשיאבד אני אשלם ואותה העת נמצא כאלו ממונו אבד אבל כל זמן שהוא ממון הוא"א נכרי הוא קמ"ל דכיון כך ובין כך אסור:

גליון הש"ס

גמ' משום שנאמר לך לך תרי זימני. עי' בריטב"א קדושין לח ד"ה ביובל: תוס' ד"ה לחלק וכו' לא היה אסור ביו"ט. עיין ביצה דף כ"ג ע"א תוס' ד"ה על גבי חרס:

דהא איתקש השבתת שאור לאכילת חמץ
ואכילת חמץ לאכילת מצה השבתת שאור
שמות יב לאכילת חמץ דכתיב °שבעת ימים שאור
לא ימצא בבתיכם כי כל אוכל מחמצת
ונכרתה ואכילת חמץ לאכילת מצה דכתיב
שם °כל מחמצת לא תאכלו בכל מושבותיכם
שם תאכלו מצות (וגו') וכתיב ביה במצה °בערב
תאכלו מצות ואימא לרבות ליל י"ד לביעור
ביום כתיב ואימא מצפרא *אך חלק דבי
רבי ישמעאל תנא מצינו י"ד שנקרא ראשון
שם שנאמר °בראשון בארבעה עשר יום לחדש
רב נחמן בר יצחק אמר ראשון דמעיקרא
איוב טו משמע דאמר קרא °הראשון אדם תולד אלא
ויקרא כג מעתה °ולקחתם לכם ביום הראשון הכי נמי
ראשון דמעיקרא משמע שאני התם דכתיב
ושמחתם לפני ה' אלהיכם שבעת ימים מה
שביעי שביעי לחג אף ראשון ראשון לחג
שמות יב הכי נמי כתיב °אך ביום הראשון תשביתו
שבעת ימים מצות תאכלו אם כן נכתוב
קרא ראשון הראשון למה לי שמע מינה
[לקמן כח:] לכדאמרן אי הכי התם נמי הראשון למה לי
ויקרא כג ותו התם דכתיב °ביום הראשון שבתון וביום
השמיני שבתון אימור ראשון דמעיקרא משמע
שאני התם דאמר קרא וביום השמיני שבתון
מה שמיני שמיני דחג אף ראשון ראשון דחג
הראשון למה לי למעוטי חולו של מועד
חולו של מועד מראשון ושמיני נפקא
איצטריך סד"א הואיל דכתב רחמנא וביום
השמיני *וי"ו מוסיף על ענין ראשון דאפילו
בחולו של מועד קמ"ל ולא לכתוב רחמנא
שם לא וי"ו ולא ה"א ותו התם דכתיב °ביום
הראשון מקרא קדש יהיה לכם ראשון
דמעיקרא משמע אלא הני שלשה ראשון
מיבעי ליה לכדתני דבי רבי ישמעאל דתנא
דבי ר' ישמעאל בשכר שלשה ראשון זכו
לשלשה ראשון להכרית זרעו של עשו
לבנין בית המקדש ולשמו של משיח להכרית
בראשית כה זרעו של עשו דכתיב °ויצא הראשון אדמוני
כולו כאדרת שער ולבנין בית המקדש
ירמיה יז דכתיב °כסא כבוד מרום מראשון מקום
ישעיה מא מקדשנו ולשמו של משיח דכתיב °ראשון
שמות לד לציון הנה הנם רבא אמר *מהכא °לא תשחט
על חמץ דם זבחי לא תשחט הפסח ועדיין
חמץ קיים ואימא כל חד וחד כי שחיט
שחיטה אמר רחמנא תניא נמי הכי אך
ביום הראשון תשביתו שאור מבתיכם
מערב יום טוב או אינו אלא ביום טוב עצמו
ת"ל לא תשחט על חמץ דם זבחי לא תשחט
את הפסח ועדיין חמץ קיים דברי רבי ישמעאל רבי עקיבא אומר אינו צריך
שם יב הרי הוא אומר °אך ביום הראשון תשביתו שאור מבתיכם וכתיב כל מלאכה
לא (תעשו) ומצינו להבערה שהיא אב מלאכה [א] רבי יוסי אומר אינו צריך
הרי הוא אומר אך ביום הראשון תשביתו שאור מבתיכם מערב יום טוב
או אינו אלא בי"ט תלמוד לומר אך חלק ואי ביום טוב עצמו מי שרי הא
איתקש השבתת שאור לאכילת חמץ ואכילת חמץ לאכילת מצה אמר רבא
שמע

רש"י

השבתת שאור לאכילת חמץ. משעה שהוזהר שלא לאכול חמץ הוזהר להשבית השאור דכתיב שאור לא ימצא בבתיכם כי כל אוכל (חמץ): ואכילת חמץ לאכילת מצה. משעה שחייב לאכול מצה הוזהר שלא לאכול חמץ דכתיב כל מחמצת לא תאכלו בכל מושבותיכם תאכלו מצות וכתיב בערב תאכלו מצות אלמא זמן אכילת מצה ואיסור חמץ והשבתת שאור מתחילה: אך חלק. אכין ורקין מיעוטין אלמא מקצת היום מותר ומקצתו אסור ומעתה יש לנו לחלק חציו לאיסור וחציו להיתר ואיכא דאמר אך הוא חק בגימטריא* דאח"ס בט"ע ג"ך דכ"ץ ותופס ח' תחת אל"ף ולד"י במקום כ': ראשון דמעיקרא משמע. בלאו רומיא דקרא אהדדי משמע ראשון במשמעות דקרא שהוא יום קודם לכל שבעה דקרא כיון דכתיב שבעת ימים מצות תאכלו אך ביום הראשון ראשון קודם למעשה קאמר: הראשון אדם תולד. הקודם לאדם הראשון תולדת: הכא נמי הא כתיב. בההוא קרא גופיה שבעת ימים ודרוש נמי ראשון דומיא דשביעי: התם נמי. גבי לולב ה' דהראשון למה לי: מראשון ושמיני נפקא. מדכתיב בההוא שבתון מכלל דאיך לאו שבתון נינהו: על ענין ראשון. על ימים הקדומים לו דהיינו חולו של מועד: לא לכתוב רחמנא לא וי"ו. דמשמע ריבויא דהו איצטריך ה"א למיעוט: אלא מהני שלשה ראשון. דכתיב במקרא קודש דפסח ומקרא קודש דסוכות ומצות לולב לא תותב לרב נחמן דהכי ראשון דכתיב בהו לאו למשמעותייהו קאתו אלא שמא בעלמא הוא דנקראו ראשון וכדתנא דבי ר' ישמעאל: בשכר ג' ראשון. שביתת הרגל דפסח ושביתת הרגל דחג ונטילת לולב שנקראו ראשונים זכו לשלשה ראשון: לא תשחט על חמץ וגו'. ושחיטת פסח זמנה מתחלת שבע שהוא בין הערבים שכבר נוטה חמה ללד שקיעתה והכי אמרינן בפ' אמר להן הממונה (יומא כח:) לנוטים דאברהם מכי משחרי כותלי דהיינו מחצות ואילך וגמרינן מינה דשחיטת התמיד מתחלת שבע וקשיא לן התם מתני' דתמיד נשחט בשמנה ומחצה ומשני לן שלאני כותלי בית המקדש דלא מכווני רחבין מתחתיהן מאד ולא משחרי עד שש ומחצה: ואימא כל חד וחד. יבער סמוך לשחיטתו מעט ואם שהה עד תשע יבערם בתשע: זמן שחיטה קאמר רחמנא. לא חלקה תורה לישראל לזה זמנו ולזה זמנו הואיל וקבע לו זמן ואיסורו שוה בכל לכולם זמן אחד קבע: שהיא אב מלאכה. וזו הבערה שלא לצורך היא והכתוב אסר מלאכה ביו"ט הלכך האי ראשון בארבעה עשר קאמר: אך חלק. הוציא לך הכתוב לשהותו מקצת יום ביעורו ואי יום ביעורו ביום טוב מי שרי לשהוייה כלל הא איתקש כו' ואכילת מצה מתחילה ועל כרחך השבתת שאור בתחלתה ואם כן לא משכחת אך חלק דלאו לאו אך איכא למימר ביום הראשון בין השמשות שהוא התחלת היום אבל השתא על כרחך בתוך יום ביעורו שרי ליה קרא לשהוייה:

תוספות

דהא איתקש השבתת שאור לאכילת חמץ וכו'. בפרק כל שעה (לקמן כח:) יליף ר' יהודה לאכול חמץ מו' שעות ולמעלה שהוא בלא תעשה ור' שמעון פליג עליה ומהכא לא מצי למילף מידי דלא הוקשה אכילת חמץ להשבתת שאור משעת שש ולמעלה אלא להשבתת שאור של שבעת ימים וקשה לרשב"א אמאי לא יליף כרת להשבתת שאור מדאיתקש לאכילת חמץ: למעוטי חולו של מועד. אתרווייהו קאי דלולב איתו ניטל במדינה אלא יום אחד: כדתנא דבי ר' ישמעאל. אע"ג דכתיבי טובא בהנך ג' מצות כתיבי כולהו וכל הכתוב במצוה אחד חשיבי חדא ואין להקשות מנלן דמהני ג' ראשון דרשינן ואך ביום הראשון לכדדרשינן דילמא הוה איכתיב להך דרשה דמשתכחא דמהני דכתיבי במקרא קודש דרשי' כולהו להך דרשה: לא תשחט את הפסח ועדיין חמץ קיים. הקשה רשב"א היכי יליף מהכא דחמץ אסור מו' שעות ולמעלה והא זמן שחיטת הפסח אחר התמיד הוי ותמיד נשחט לפני חלות פסול וא"כ זמן שחיטה לא הוי מיד אחר חלות עד כדי שהיית הקרבת תמיד וי"ל כיון דיעבד אם שחט הפסח קודם תמיד כשר כדתנן התם *חשיב זמן שחיטה מחלות ואילך: זמן שחיטה קאמר רחמנא. אע"ג דאמת הוא דלא תשחט על חמץ כל חד וחד כי שחיט דאמרינן בפרק תמיד נשחט (לקמן סג. ושם) השוחט את הפסח על החמץ עובר בלאו מ"מ כיון דאשכחן דהזהיר על ההשבתה והזהיר שלא לשחוט פסח על חמץ סברא הוא שבזמן שחיטה הזהיר על השבתה: דברי ר' ישמעאל. תימה לר"י דתנא דבי רבי ישמעאל נפקא ליה מקרא אחרינא ובכמה דוכתין* פריך מר' ישמעאל אתנא דבי רבי ישמעאל: (ואומר) כל מלאכה לא תעשו. אע"ג דכשישרף ויעשה גחלים הנאתו מותר כדאמר בפרק כל שעה (לקמן כו:) גבי ערלה בישלה על גבי גחלים דברי הכל הפת מותר וה"ה חמץ והא דתנן בפ' כל שעה (ד כח.) לא יסיק בו תנור וכירים היינו מדרבנן אור"י דסברא הוא דקרא דתשביתו מיירי בכל ענין אפילו אינו צריך לגחלתו אי נמי כיון דמתחלת הבערה אינו יכול להנות ממנו אע"ג שיהא לו הנאה ממנו אחר כך אסור כמו נדרים ונדבות שאין קריבין בי"ט למ"ד (ביצה דף יט כ.) אף על פי שיש בהן מאכל הדיוט לבסוף ומאן דשרי שרי מלהטות°:
לחלק

מסורת הש"ס

[מחמצת]
[פי' שבת קד.]
[לקמן עא. עירובין קה. יומא סה: סוכה מח. ב"ק יא: שבועות יג. מנחות לז: כשרות מו. כריתות ז. פסחים כה.]
[יבמות ט. קדושין יד: ב"מ לה. שבועות י. זבחים מח. [חולין עח.] כריתות כב:]
[מגילה כג. זבחים נב.]
[וכתיב]
[יעשה בהם]

עין משפט נר מצוה

כה א מיי' פ"א מהל' חמץ ומצה הל' ח:

רבינו חננאל

ואימא מצפרא ביה ופרקינן אך חלק כדקיימא לן אכין ורקין למעט ובא זה אך וחלק גם י"ד חציו מותר וחציו אסור: רב נחמן בר יצחק אמר אך ביום הראשון של יום טוב ראשון משמע כלומר קודם יום טוב ודייק מהא דכתיב הראשון אדם תולד (איוב טו ז) כלומר הראשון של אדם הראשון נולדת ולפני גבעות חוללת ואקשי' עליה אלא מעתה ולקחתם לכם ביום הראשון הכי נמי וכו': רבא אמר מהכא לא תשחט על חמץ דם זבחי וגו' לא תשחט את הפסח ועדיין חמץ קיים ושחיטת הפסח מן התורה וזמן שחיטת הפסח שהוא משעה ששית ולמעלה קאמר: תניא כרבא ואליבא דר' ישמעאל ר"ע אומר הרי הוא אומר כל מלאכה לא יעשה ומצינו הבערה שהיא אב מלאכה לפיכך כיון שפטנו שרפה אי אפשר להשבתת שאור ביו"ט אלא מערב יו"ט:

הגהות מהר"י לנדא

א] גמ' רבי יוסי אומר אינו צריך וכו'. נ"ל רבי יוסי הגלילי:

גליון הש"ס

תוס' ד"ה וכתיב כל מלאכה בסוף הדבור שרי מלהטות. נ"ל מלס':

unnecessary, [5a] for the putting away of leaven is assimilated to [the prohibition of] eating leavened bread,[2] and the eating of leavened bread to the [precept of] the eating of unleavened bread. The putting away of leaven [is assimilated] to [the prohibition of] the eating of leavened bread, for it is written, *seven days shall there be no leaven in your houses; for whosoever eateth that which is leavened, that soul shall be cut off.*[3] And [the prohibition of] the eating of leavened bread [is likened] to the [precept of] eating unleavened bread, because it is written, *Ye shall eat nothing leavened; in all your habitations shall ye eat unleavened bread;*[4] and in respect to unleavened bread it is written, *at even ye shall eat unleavened bread.*[5] Yet perhaps it is to include the *night* of fourteenth [as the time] for removal?[6]—'*The day*' is written. Then say [that it must be removed] from the morning?[7]—'*Ak*' divides [it].[8]

The School of R. Ishmael taught: We find that the fourteenth is called the first, as it is said, *On the first, on the fourteenth day of the month.*[9] R. Naḥman b. Isaac said: 'The first'[10] [*rishon*] means the preceding, for the Writ saith, *Wast thou born before* [rishon] *Adam?*[11] If so, *and ye shall take you on the first* [rishon] *day,*[12]— does '*rishon*' here too mean the preceding?—There it is different, because it is written, *and ye shall rejoice before the Lord your God seven*
a *days:*[1] just as the seventh [means] the seventh of the Festival, so the first [means] the first of the Festival. [But] here too it is written, *even the first day* [rishon] *ye shall put away leaven out of your houses. Seven days shall ye eat unleavened bread?*[2]—If so, let Scripture write '*first*' ['rishon']; why 'the *first* [ha-*rishon*]'? Infer from this [that it is required] for what we have stated. If so, there too[1] what is the purpose of 'the *first*' ['ha-*rishon*']? Moreover, when it is written there, *on the first day shall be a solemn rest, and on the eighth day shall be a solemn rest,*[3] say that *rishon* implies the preceding?—There it is different, because Scripture saith, '*and on the eighth day shall be a solemn rest*': just as '*eighth*' means the eighth of the Festival, so '*first*' means [the] first of the Festival. [But still] what is the purpose of 'the *first*' [ha-*rishon*]?[1]—In order to exclude the Intermediate days of the Festival.[4] [But the exclusion of] the Intermediate days of the Festival is derived from '*first*' and '*eighth*'?—It is [nevertheless] required: you might argue, since the Divine Law writes, and *on the eighth day*, the *waw* ['and'] indicates conjunction with the preceding subject, so [as to include] even the Intermediate days of the Festival too;[5] hence ha-*rishon* informs us [otherwise]. Then let Scripture write neither the *waw* nor the *heh?*[6] Moreover, when it is written there, *In the first day* [ha-*rishon*] *ye shall have an holy convocation,*[7] does '*rishon*' mean the preceding?[8] Rather, these three [instances of] '*rishon*' ['first'] are necessary for what the School of R. Ishmael taught. For the School of R. Ishmael taught: As a reward for [the observance of] the three 'firsts'[9] they [Israel] merited three firsts:[10] to destroy[11] the seed of Esau; the building of the Temple; and the name of the Messiah. 'To destroy the seed of Esau,' of whom it is written, *And the*
b first *came forth red, all over like an hairy garment;*[1] and 'the building of the Temple', whereof it is written, *A glorious throne, set on high from the* first[2] *is the place of our sanctuary;*[3] 'and the name of Messiah,' for it is written, First *unto Zion, behold, behold them.*[4]

Raba said, [It[5] is deduced] from here: *Thou shalt not offer the blood of my sacrifice with leavened bread:*[6] [that means,] thou shalt not kill the Passover sacrifice while leavened bread is still in existence.[7] Then perhaps each person [must remove his leaven] when he kills [his sacrifice]?[8]—Scripture meant the time for killing.[9]

It was taught likewise: '[*Even*] *the first day ye shall put away leaven out of your houses*': [this means] on the eve of the Festival. Yet perhaps that is not so, but [rather] on the Festival itself?—Therefore it is stated, '*thou shalt not offer the blood of my sacrifice with leavened bread,*' [i.e.,] thou shalt not kill the Passover sacrifice while leavened bread still exists [in thy house]: that is R. Ishmael's view. R. Akiba said, That is unnecessary: lo, it is said, '*Even the first day ye shall put away leaven out of your houses*', and it is written, *no manner of work shall be done in them;*[10] while we find that kindling is a principal labour.[11] R. Jose said, It is unnecessary: lo, it is said, '*Even* [ak] *on the first day ye shall put away leaven out of your houses*': [that means,] from the eve of the Festival. Or perhaps it is not so, but rather on the Festival? Therefore is stated, '*Ak*', which serves to divide;[12] hence if [it means] on the Festival itself, can [part of it] be permitted? Surely the putting away of leaven is likened to [the prohibition of] eating leavened bread, while the prohibition of eating leavened bread is likened to [the duty of] eating unleavened bread.[13]

(2) Immediately the latter comes into force the former is obligatory. (3) Ex. XII, 19. (4) Ibid. 20. Hence from the very moment that the latter is operative the former is too, and consequently by then the leaven must already be removed. (5) Ibid. 18. Hence no verse would be necessary to show that as soon as evening commences the leaven must be put away; therefore the verse quoted *supra* can only refer to the fourteenth. (6) Since we see that leaven is to be removed on the fourteenth, perhaps it must be done at the beginning of the fourteenth, *sc.* in the evening. (7) As soon as day commences, not from midday. (8) It is a general principle in Talmudic exegesis that *ak* and *rak* (only) imply limitations: thus *ak* divides the day, showing that the putting away takes place in the middle of the day, not at the beginning. (9) Ibid. (10) In verse 18. (11) Job. XV, 7 (E.V.: *Art thou the first man that was born*). Hence Ex. XII, 15 is translated: *yet on the preceding day*—i.e., the fourteenth—*ye shall put away*, etc. (12) Lev. XXIII, 40.

a (1) Lev. XXIII, 40. (2) By the same argument '*rishon*' means first, not preceding.—Actually the order is reversed in Scripture. (3) Ibid. 39. (4) Lit., 'the weekday (portion) of the Festival'. It teaches that these days enjoy semi-sanctity only, and work of an urgent nature is permitted. (5) That work thereon is forbidden. (6) The *heh* is the def. art. '*the*' (*ha*). According to the present argument the *heh* (*ha*) merely neutralizes the possible teaching of the *waw*: then both should be omitted. (7) Ibid. 7; the reference is to Passover. (8) Surely not. (9) The '*first*' of Passover, the '*first*' of Tabernacles, and the taking of the four species (v. 40) on the '*first*' day of Tabernacles. (10) Three things in connection with which '*first*' is written. (11) Lit., 'cut off'.

b (1) Gen. XXV, 25. (2) E.V. *beginning*. (3) Jer. XVII, 12. (4) Isa. XLI, 27. (5) *Sc.* that leaven is forbidden from midday on the fourteenth. (6) Ex. XXXIV, 25. (7) And since the sacrificing commences immediately after noon, it follows that the leaven must already be removed by then. (8) Thus if he kills it at 4 p.m., leaven is permitted to him until that hour. (9) When it is time to kill the sacrifice there must be no leaven in the house, as it is inconceivable that there should be no fixed hour applicable to all. (10) Ibid. XII, 16. (11) Forbidden on the Sabbath, and likewise on Festivals, save when required for the preparation of food. The leaven was burnt. (12) V. *supra* n. b8. (13) *Supra*.

they believed? [4b] Is it not because it stands in the presumption of having been searched, [the Tanna] holding, All are *haberim*[4] in respect to the searching of leaven.[5] For it was taught: If a *haber* dies and leaves a store-house full of produce [crops], even if they are but one day old,[6] they stand in the presumption of having been tithed.[7] How so: perhaps it is different here[8] because they [the woman, slave or minor] state it?—Has then the statement of these any substance?[9] What then [will you assume]? It stands, in the presumption of having been searched? Then it should state, 'All houses stand on the fourteenth in the presumption of having been searched'?—What then [will you assume]? It is because of the statement of these[10] [that the house is assumed to have been searched], but if these did not say [that it had been searched], it is not so? Then solve from this [teaching] that it does not stand in the presumption of having been searched!—No. In truth I may tell you [that generally][11] it does stand in the presumption of having been searched; but what we discuss here[8] is a case where we know for certain that he [the owner] did not search, but these[10] affirm, We searched it. You might say, Let not the Rabbis believe them. Therefore it informs us [that] since the search for leaven is [required only] by Rabbinical law, for by Scriptural law mere nullification[12]
a suffices for it, the Rabbis gave them[1] credence in [respect to] a Rabbinical [enactment].

The scholars asked: What if one rents a house to his neighbour in the presumption of its having been searched, and he [the tenant] finds that it has not been searched? Is it as an erroneous bargain[2] or not?—Come and hear! For Abaye said: It is unnecessary [to say] of a town, where payment is not made [to others] for searching, that a person is pleased to fulfil a precept personally;[3] but even in a town where payment is made for searching [it is not an erroneous bargain], because [it is to be assumed that] one is pleased to fulfil a precept with his money.[4]

We learned elsewhere: R. Meir said: One may eat [leaven] the whole of the five [hours,][5] and must burn [it] at the beginning of the sixth.[6] R. Judah said: One may eat until four [hours],[7] hold it in suspense the whole of the fifth,[8] and must burn it at the beginning of the sixth.[9] Thus incidentally all agree that leaven is [Scripturally] forbidden from six hours [i.e., noon] and onwards: whence do we know it?—Said Abaye, Two verses are written: *Seven days shall there be no leaven found in your houses;*[10] and it is written, *even* [ak] *the first day ye shall put away leaven out of your houses:*[11] how is this [to be understood]?[12] It must include the *fourteenth* [as the day] for removal.[13] Yet say that it includes the night of the fifteenth [as the time] for removal; for one might argue, *'days'* is written, [implying] only days but not nights: hence it [the verse] informs
b us that even nights [are included in the interdict]?[1]—That is

(4) Plur. of *haber*; lit., 'associates'. It denotes members of an association (*haburah*) who undertake to be very scrupulous in their religious observance, particularly in regard to uncleanness and tithes. (5) I.e., all men are regarded as *haberim* in the matter under discussion, as it was universally observed. (6) Only that day had they arrived at the stage when tithing etc. is obligatory. The stage is reached when the harvested produce is stacked up. (7) Lit., 'properly prepared'—it may be assumed that the priestly and Levitical dues have been rendered. Similarly it is to be presumed that the landlord had searched the house before renting it. (8) In the cited teaching. (9) Their testimony is invalid where testimony is required. (10) I.e., the woman, slave or minor. (11) I.e., in a case such as submitted to R. Naḥman b. Isaac. (12) A declaration by the owner that all leaven in the house is null and has no value whatsoever in his eyes.

a (1) I.e., the woman, slave or minor. (2) On the strength of which the tenant can retract. (3) There the tenant is certainly unable to retract, as it is assumed that he, like all the others, is glad of this opportunity to fulfil personally a religious obligation. (4) And even had he known beforehand that the house was not searched he would not have refrained from renting it; hence he cannot retract now. (5) I.e, until 11 a.m. (6) But may not wait until the end of the sixth, i.e., noon (by which time it is Scripturally forbidden to have leaven in the house), because one can err in the time. (7) Until 10 a.m. (8) I.e., in that hour it may neither be eaten, nor need it be burned, but it can be given to animals. (9) V. *infra* 11b. (10) Ex. XII, 19. (11) Ibid. 15. (12) If the leaven is only put away on the first day, as the latter verse implies, there are not seven *full* days without leaven, as is intimated by the former verse. (13) I.e., 'first' must mean the first (immediately) *preceding* day before the seven; cf. *infra* 5a.

b (1) Thus *'yet at the first day'*, etc., may mean that at the very beginning of the seven days, i.e., on the evening of the fifteenth, all leaven must be removed, but there is no prohibition for any part of the fourteenth.

לאו משום דחזקתו בדוק דקסבר הכל חברים הם אצל בדיקת חמץ *דתניא *חבר שמת והניח מגורה מליאה פירות אפי' הן בני יומן הרי הן בחזקת מתוקנים וממאי דילמא שאני הכא משום דקאמרי הני אטו אמירה דהני מידי משמשא אית ביה אלא מאי דחזקתו בדוק האי הכל נאמנים כל הבתים בחזקת בדוקין בארבעה עשר מיבעי ליה אלא מאי משום אמירה דהני הא לא אמרי הני לא תפשוט מיניה דאין חזקתו בדוק לא לעולם אימא לך ג חזקתו בדוק והכא במאי עסקינן דמוחזק לן דלא בדק וקאמרי הני דבדקיניה מהו דתימא לא להימנינהו רבנן קמ"ל כיון דבדיקת חמץ מדרבנן הוא *דמדאורייתא בביטול בעלמא סגי ליה הימנוהו רבנן בדרבנן: איבעיא להו המשכיר בית לחבירו בחזקת בדוק ומצאו שאינו בדוק מהו מי הוי כמקח טעות או לא תא שמע דאמר אביי ד לא מיבעיא באתרא דלא יהבי אגרא ובדקו דניחא ליה לאיניש לקיומי מצוה בגופיה אלא אפילו באתרא דיהבי אגרא ובדקו *דניחא ליה לאיניש לקיומי מצוה בממוניה: *תנן התם ר"מ אומר אוכלין כל חמש ושורפין בתחלת שש ר' יהודה אומר אוכלין כל ארבע ותולין כל חמש ושורפין בתחלת שש דכולי עלמא מיהא חמץ משש שעות ולמעלה אסור מנלן אמר אביי תרי קראי כתיבי כתיב °שבעת ימים שאור לא ימצא בבתיכם (שמות יב) וכתיב °אך ביום הראשון תשביתו שאור מבתיכם (שם) הא כיצד °לרבות ארבעה עשר לביעור ואימא לרבות לילי חמשה עשר לביעור דסלקא דעתך אמינא ימים כתיב ימים אין לילות לא קא משמע לן אפילו לילות ההוא לא איצטריכא ליה
דהא

רש"י

דקסבר. האי תנא: הכל חבירין אצל בדיקה. ואפילו עם הארץ ובדבר שהוא מוחזק חבר מחזקין ליה שלא עבר זמנו עד שעשאוהו: דתניא חבר. הנאמן על המעשרות ומת והניח מגורה מליאה פירות אפילו הן בני יומן שנתמרחו היום הרי הן בחזקת מתוקנים דודאי לא יצא מתחת ידו עד שגמר כל מצותו והכא נמי כיון דאף עמי הארץ חבירין הן על הבדיקה חזקתן שבדקוהו: וממאי. דהא דקתני נאמנין טעמא משום דהכל חבירים הם אצל בדיקה דלמא אין עמי הארץ חבירים על כך וטעמא משום דקאמרי הני אנו ראינו שבדקו: כל הבתים בחזקת בדוקים מיבעי ליה למיתני. ולא הוה למיתליה באמירה דהני ומקשינן אלא מדתלא באמירה ודאי איכא למידק הא לא אמרי לא אם כן מאי קא מיבעיא לך תיפשוט מינה דאין חזקתו בדוק ומשני מהא ליכא למידק למיפשט מידי דאיכא לאוקמא להא כגון דמוחזק לן בהאי דלא בדק כגון שראינוהו טרוד ויצא מבעוד יום לדרך ואמרי הני אנחנו בדקנוהו: בביטול בעלמא. דכתיב תשביתו ולא כתיב תבערו והשבתה דלב היא השבתה: בדרבנן. הימנוהו רבנן בחיובה דליתה אלא מדרבנן דהם הצריכו והם התירו לסמוך באמירתן של אלו וכח בידיהם להאמינם במידי דלאו דאורייתא: מי הוי מקח טעות. ואם בא השוכר לחזור בו על ידי עלילותיו ולומר לא כך שכרתי ואין תנאי שלנו קיים מהו לחזור: לא מבעיא היכא דלא יהבי אגרא. לאחרים ובדקי אלא כל איש ואיש בודק את ביתו דלא מצי למימר ליה מקח טעות דאם הייתי יודע שאינו בדוק לא הייתי שוכרו דודאי ניחא לאיניש למעבד מצוה בגופיה ואי נמי הוה ידע דלא בדיק לא היה מניחו בכך: אלא אפילו באתרא. דנהיגי כל בני העיר לשכור בודקין כל איש בביתו דאיכא השתא חסרון כיס אפילו הכי אי ידע ביה אתמול דלא בדיק לא הוי הדר ביה דניחא ליה כו' והאי דקא הדר ביה משום מלתא אחריתי היא דאשכח ביתא אחריתי דשפירא מינה: תנן התם גרסינן ואף על גב דבפירקין היא: ושורפין בתחלת שש. ולא ימתין עד תחלת שבע שהוא אסור מן התורה לפי שאדם טועה *בשעות: ר' יהודה אומר. טועה אדם יותר מכאן וצריך להתרחק מן העבירה יותר ולא יאכל מסוף ארבע ולמעלה: תולין. לא אוכלין ולא שורפין כלומר אין צריך לשרוף ומאכיל הוא לבהמתו כל חמש אבל הוא לא יאכל: דכולי עלמא מיהא חמץ משש שעות ולמעלה אסור. מן התורה דאי לא מיתסר עד אורתא לא הוו גזרי ביה דבין יממא לליליא לא טעו אינשי: שבעת ימים שאור לא ימצא בבתיכם. אפילו שעה אחת בתוך השבעת ימים וכתיב אך ביום הראשון תשביתו הרי שהה בו שעה אחת: הא כיצד לרבות כו'. דעל כרחיך האי הראשון ראשון קודם לכל שבעה קאמר דהיינו ארבעה עשר: ואימא לרבות ליל חמשה עשר. שלא ימתין עד הבוקר והכי קאמר אך בכניסת יום הראשון מיד תשביתו דאי משבעת ימים הוה אמינא ימים אין לילות לא:
השבתת

תוספות

לאו משום דחזקתו בדוק. תימה מאי ס"ד דאי בחזקתו בדוק אם כן מה לריך לאמירה דהני כלל ואומר ר"י דמיירי כגון שבעל הבית בעיר אע"ג דחזקתו בדוק כיון דאיתיה בעיר לריך לישאל הימנו ולהכי מהני אמירה דהני דלא שאלינן אע"ג דגבי טבל סמכינן אחזקת חבר ואין לריך אפילו לישאל היינו משום דכיון שסגולת לו לאכול מסתמא תיקנה שלא יבא לידי מכשול אבל גבי בדיקה אפילו לא יהיה בדוק לא יהיה כל כך מכשול לכך לריך לישאל אם הוא בעיר ומסיק אי חזקתו בדוק כל הבתים בחזקת בדוקין מיבעי ליה וממילא ידעינן דלאמירה דהני מהני ואין לריך לישאל הימנו אפילו אם הוא בעיר ועוד פירש ר"י דס"ד דאיירי דאמרי הני לא היה בדוק ולכן בדקנו דאי חזקתו בדוק מהימני מגו דאי בעי שתקי אבל אי אין חזקתו בדוק אמאי מהימני ופריך אי הכי כל הבתים בחזקת בדוקין מיבעי ליה דממילא ידעינן דמהימני במגו: מדאורייתא בביטול בעלמא סגי. פי' בקונטרס מדכתיב תשביתו ולא כתיב תבערו אלמא השבתה בלב היא וקשה לר"י דהאי השבתה הבערה היא ולא ביטול דתניא בשמעתין רע"א אין לריך הרי הוא אומר תשביתו ומלינו להבערה שהיא אב מלאכה ועוד דתשביתו אמרינן לקמן מאך חלק שהוא משש שעות ולמעלה ואחר איסורא לא מהני ביטול ואומר ר"י דמדאורייתא בביטול בעלמא סגי מטעם דמאחר שביטלו הוי הפקר ויצא מרשותו ומותר מדקאמרינן אבל אתה רואה של אחרים ושל גבוה והא דאמרינן בנדרים (דף מה.) הפקר בפני שלשה מדאורייתא אין לריך: הימנוהו רבנן בדרבנן. אף על גב דכל דבר שהוא בידם מהימנינן להו לנשים ועבדים ואפילו מדאורייתא דמעשים בכל יום שאנו מאמינים לאשה ועבד על השחיטה ועל הניקור ובפ' המדיר (כתובות עב. ושם) גבי מאכילתו שאינו מעושר משמע שסומך עליה לענין חלה ומעשר מכל מקום גבי בדיקת חמץ אע"ג דבידם מ"מ אי הוי מדאורייתא לא מהימנינן להו משום דאיכא טירחא יתירתא ולריך דקדוק גדול כדמוכח בירושלמי שמפרש מפני שנשים עצלניות הן ותחומין דרבנן מהימנינן להו לאשה ועבד ולא קטן מדתניא בפ' כילד מעברין (עירובין נח: ושם) אפילו עבד ואפילו שפחה נאמנת לומר עד כאן תחום שבת אבל קטנים לא דגריעי טפי מדחשיב להו בשמעתין בסוף ובפרק שני דכתובות (דף כח: ושם) אלו נאמנים להעיד בגודלן מה שראו בקוטנן עד כאן היינו מהלכין בשבת משמע אבל בקוטנן לא היינו משום דתחומין אין בידם כלל לכך אין נאמנים כמו בבדיקת חמץ:* המשכיר בית לחבירו בחזקת שהוא בדוק. נראה לרשב"א דבשלשה עשר איירי דבארבעה עשר על המשכיר לבדוק: וכתיב אך ביום הראשון תשביתו. פי' הקונטרס מדמחייב ביום הראשון להשבית מכלל דמקלתו מותר ואין נראה לר"י דהא תשביתו הבערה היא ולא נוח הכתוב לשורפו אלא לאחר איסורו ועוד אי ממשמעות דיום ראשון משמע מקלת מותר מה לריך לאך חלק מיהו ללישנא שני שפירש הקונטרס דא"ך ח"ן באח"ס בט"ע אתי שפיר ונראה לר"י דמייתורא דקרא קדריש ועוד מדכתיב אך ודרשינן לקמן אך חלק פריך: ואימא לרבות ליל חמשה עשר לביעור. *הוי מצי לשנויי ביום כתיב כדמשני בסמוך וכי נמי משני דאיתקש השבתת שאור לאכילת חמץ לא לריך לקרא דמייתי שבעת ימים שאור לא ימצא דמדאיתקש השבתת שאור לאכילת חמץ יכול לדרוש הכל כמו שדורש רבי יוסי (הגלילי) לקמן*:
דהא

עין משפט נר מצוה

כא א מיי' פ"י מהלכות מעשר הל' ב:
כב ב מיי' פ"ב מהל' חמץ ומצה הל' יז סמג עשין לט טוש"ע או"ח סי' תלז סעיף ב:
כג ג מיי' שם הל' יח טוש"ע או"ח שם סעיף ד:
כד ד מיי' שם הלכה יח טוש"ע או"ח שם סעי' ג:

רבינו חננאל

לאו משום דחזקתו בדוק וקסבר הכל חברין אצל ביעור חמץ ותניא חבר שמת והניח מגורה מליאה פירות אפילו הן בני יומן הרי הן בחזקת מתוקנין ודחי' לא אלא משום דאמרי הני והדרינן ומוקמינן לעולם כי האי תנא חזקתו בדוק והא דתניא הכל נאמנין על ביעור חמץ כגון דמוחזק לן בהאי ביתא דלא בדיק ואמרי הני דבדיק (נימני') [צ"ל נאמנין] כיון דבדיקת חמץ מדרבנן היא דאי מדאורייתא בביטול בעלמא סגי לה הימנינהו רבנן להני נשי ועבדים וקטנים במילתא דהיא מדרבנן ונדחית: המשכיר בית לחבירו בחזקת בדוק ונמצא שאינו בדוק כי האי גונא מקח טעות הוא או לא ופשטה אביי דלא הוי מקח טעות דניחא ליה לאיניש למעבד מצוה בממוניה וכל שכן בגופיה: וכולי עלמא חמץ בי"ד משש שעות ולמעלה אסור מדאוריית' מנא לן ופשיט לה אביי הכן בהאי טעמא והאי דאביי שייכא בדר' יוסי הגלילי כדבעינן למימר קמן שנאמר (שמות יב) שבעת ימים מצות תאכלו וגו' ואי אפשר לומר זה ביום הראשון ביום טוב הראשון הוא וביום ההוא אתה אוכל מצה ומשבית שאור שנאמר שבעת ימים שאור לא ימצא בבתיכם ואי אפשר לומר נמי השבתת שאור לילי ט"ו הוא משום דביום הראשון תשביתו שאור כתיב ולא בלילה שמעי' דזה ביום הראשון קודם יום טוב הראשון הוא ותוב איתקש השבתת שאור לאכילת (מצה) [צ"ל חמץ] שנאמר שבעת ימים שאור לא ימצא בבתיכם וגו' ומשעה שנאסר באכילת חמץ [ביום] הזהר לאכילת מצה שנאמר כל מחמצת לא תאכלו וגו' וכתיב בערב תאכלו מצות וגו' ש"מ דבענין השבתת שאור ביום קודם חיוב אכילת מצה וכיון דחיוב אכילת מצה ליל ט"ו הוא נמצא חיוב השבתת שאור שהוא בי"ד:

מסורת הש"ס

לקמן ט. ע"ז מח: נדה טו:
[לקמן י:]
[ב"מ כט: בכורות יח:, נה.]
לקמן יא: ודף כח.
[בשעה]
[וע"ע תוספות עירובין לה: ד"ה כאן ועוד שם נט. ד"ה ותחומין]
עיין מהרש"ל
[דף ה.]

גליון הש"ס גמ' דניחא ליה לאיניש לקיומי מצוה בממוניה. עי' לקמן דף י ע"ב תוס' ד"ה בממונים: שם לרבות י"ד לביעור. עי' תשובת הר"ן סימן ל"ג:

*רב בר אחוה דר' חייא ובר אחתיה כי סליק להתם אמר ליה איבו קיים *אמר ליה אימא קיימת אמר ליה אימא קיימת אמר ליה *איבו קיים אמר ליה לשמעיה ׳חלוץ לי מנעלי והוליך כלי אחרי לבית המרחץ שמע מינה תלת ש"מ ׳אבל אסור בנעילת הסנדל ושמע מינה ׳שמועה רחוקה אינה נוהגת אלא יום אחד ושמע מינה *׳מקצת היום ככולו ההוא דאמר דונו דיני אמרי שמע מינה מדן קאתי דכתיב °דן ידין עמו כאחד שבטי ישראל [בראשית מט] ההוא דהוה קא אזיל ואמר אכיף ימא אסיסני ביראתא בדקו ואשכחוהו דמזבולן קאתי דכתיב °זבולן לחוף ימים ישכון: [שם] והשתא דקיימא לן דלכולי עלמא אור אורתא הוא מכדי בין לרבי יהודה ובין לר' מאיר חמץ אינו אסור אלא משש שעות ולמעלה ונבדוק בשית *וכי תימא *זריזין מקדימין למצות נבדוק מצפרא דכתיב °וביום השמיני ימול בשר ערלתו [ויקרא יב] ותניא *כל היום כולו כשר למילה אלא שזריזין מקדימים למצות [יומא דף כח:] שנאמר °וישכם אברהם בבקר [בראשית כב] אמר רב נחמן בר יצחק בשעה שבני אדם מצויין בבתיהם ואור הנר יפה לבדיקה אמר אביי ׳הילכך האי צורבא מרבנן לא לפתח בעידניה באורתא דתליסר דנגהי ארבסר דלמא משכא ליה שמעתיה ואתי לאימנועי ממצוה בעו מיניה מרב נחמן בר יצחק המשכיר בית לחבירו בארבעה עשר על מי לבדוק על המשכיר לבדוק דחמירא דידיה הוא או דלמא על השוכר לבדוק דאיסורא ברשותיה קאי *ת"ש ׳המשכיר בית לחבירו על השוכר לעשות לו מזוזה התם הא אמר רב משרשיא *מזוזה חובת הדר היא הכא מאי אמר להו רב נחמן בר יצחק תנינא °המשכיר בית לחבירו אם עד שלא מסר לו מפתחות חל ארבעה עשר על המשכיר לבדוק ואם משמסר לו מפתחות חל ארבעה עשר על השוכר לבדוק בעו מיניה מרב נחמן בר יצחק המשכיר בית לחבירו בארבעה עשר חזקתו בדוק או אין חזקתו בדוק למאי נ"מ ׳לישייליה דליתיה להאי דלשיוליה לאטרוחי להאי מאי אמר להו רב נחמן בר יצחק תניתוה הכל נאמנים על ביעור חמץ אפילו נשים אפילו עבדים אפילו קטנים מאי טעמא מהימני
לאו

רש"י

רב *בר אחוה ובר אחתיה דר' חייא הוה. איבו אביו של רב אחיו של ר' חייא היה מן האב כדאמרינן בפ"ק דסנהדרין (דף ה:) איבו וחנא ושילא ומרתא ור' חייא כולהו בני דר' אחא מכפרי הוו ואימא שהיתה אמו של רב אחותו של רבי חייא היתה מן האם: כי סליק. רב מעירו מבבל לארץ ישראל שהיה ר' חייא שם: אמר. ר' חייא לרב איבו אביך הוא קיים: א"ל. רב: אימא קיימת. בלשון שאלה כלומר עד שאתה משאיל על אבי שאל על אמי שאף היא אחותך: אמר לו. עוד ר' חייא לרב ואימא אחותי קיימת: אמר ליה. רב: איבו קיים. ואבי כלום קיים הוא עדיין לא השיבותיך עליו ומתוך הבין ר"ח בכינויתא היה משיבו רב על מה שהוא שואל כדי שיבין מן הכלל וקשה בעיני לומר שיוציא רב דבר שקר מפיו: חלוץ לי מנעלי. להתאבל על אחי ואחותי: והוליך כלי אחרי לבית המרחץ. ללמד הלכה לתלמידים נתכוון שאין שמועה רחוקה שלאחר שלשים יום נוהגת אלא יום אחד ומקצתו ככולו ואינו צריך לישב כל היום כולו מדאמר ליה והוליך לי כלי אחרי לבית המרחץ ולא המתין עד למחר אלמא שעה אחת די: ההוא דהוה קאמר דונו דיני. בכל דבר משא ומתן שהיה לו עם אדם היה אומר תמיד בא לדין ואינו נשמע לדבר אדם אלא על פי דיין: אכיף ימא אסיסני ביראתא. אתקן בירוגות אם היו לי פלטין לבנות לא הייתי קובעם אלא על שפת הים ותמיד היה משתבח בשפת הים ובתשובות הגאונים מצאתי אכיף ימא אסלא ברוראתא ופירוש כך היה משתבח בשפת הים ואומר תמיד סנאים שעל שפת הים ברושים הם במקומות אחרים ולשון זה הגון סנה בלשון ארמי אסנה ברוש ברותא: בין לר' מאיר בין לרבי יהודה. דאיפליגו במתניתין *בהרחקה דעבוד רבנן לאורייתא חמץ אינו אסור מן התורה בבל יראה ובאכילה אלא משש שעות משעברו שש שעות כדיליף לקמן* מן אך חלק ומן לא תשחט על חמץ: נבדוק. חמץ בתחלת שש וקודם איסורו יבערנו למה לי לאקדומי כולי האי דבשלמא אי אור יממא הוא איכא לתרוצי דמתניתין נמי בשש קאמר אבל השתא תקשה: נבדוק מצפרא. דאיכא הקדמה לזריזים כדאשכחן גבי מילה ובזריזותיה דאברהם שנאמר וישכם אברהם בבקר שלא המתין עד הנץ החמה ומכל מקום בלילה לא הקדים: ואור הנר יפה לבדיקה. בלילה אבל ביום מחשיך ואם תאמר יבדוק לאור היום הא ילפינן לקמן* מחיפוש שמצותו בנר: לא יפתח בעידנא. לא יתחיל בגירסא אם קבע עת לתורה בלילות לא יתחיל להתעסק בשמעתתא: באורתא דתליסר נגהי ארבסר. ליל יציאת שלשה עשר שהוא כניסת ארבעה עשר והוא ליל בדיקת חמץ: דחמירא דידיה הוא. החמץ שבבית שלו הוא: ברשותיה קאי. שהרי עתה הבית שלו: לעשות לו מזוזה. אלמא מידי דמצוה עליה רמיא: חובת הדר. לפי שהיא משמרתו וכתיב ביתך ביאתך נכנס ויוצא בה אבל הכא בדיקת חמץ דרבנן דאי משום בל יראה ובל ימצא הא אמר לקמן דסגי ליה בבטול בעלמא אי מסיח דעתיה מיניה ומשוי ליה כעפרא ואמר כל חמירא דבביתא הדין כו' ורבנן הוא דאצרוך בדיקה והשתא כי האי גוונא מיבעיא לן טורח זה על מי מוטל: מסירת מפתח. הוא קנין השכירות ואם עד שלא מסר המפתח נכנס ליל ארבעה עשר חלה חובת הבדיקה על המשכיר שעדיין היתה ברשותו ואף על פי שמסר לו ביום כבר חלה חובה עליו: בארבעה עשר. שחרית מי מחזקינן ליה להאי משכיר דודאי בדקו אמש כמצות חכמים אי לא: למאי נפקא מיניה ליבעיליה. להאי אם בדקו אם לאו: כגון דליתיה להאי. משכיר למישייליה ומיבעי לן לאטרוחי להאי שוכר לבדוק מספק מאי: נאמנין על ביעור חמץ. להעיד בארבעה עשר שבדקו בעליו אמש: מאי טעמא נאמנין. הא לאו בני אסהודי נינהו לאו משום דבלאו אמירה דידהו נמי מחזקינן ליה בדוק דודאי לא עבר זה על דברי חכמים ואפי' הוא עם הארץ לשאר דברים חבר הוא לענין בדיקה דהכל זריזין:
דקסבר

תוספות

אבא קיים א"ל אבא קיים אימא קיימת א"ל אימא קיימת. זאת גירסת פר"ח פי' ר' חייא שאל על אביו אם הוא קיים ורב השיב לו שאביו של רב קיים וכן באם ולפי גירסת הספרים ר' חייא שאל על אביו אם הוא קיים והשיב לו רב אימא קיימת פי' אימא של רב היא קיימת ולא רצה להשיב אבא קיים שלא יטעה רבי חייא ויסבור שמשיבו על מה ששאלו דקרי איכשי לאבי אבא אבא לכך פירש הגמרא דרב בר אחוה ובר אחתיה דר' חייא הוה לפרש טעמא למה משיב כן: שנאמר וישכם אברהם בבקר. ואם תאמר והיכי מוכח מהאי קרא דזריזין מקדימין למצות ואין מקדימין טפי מצפרא והא בפרק גיד הנשה (חולין צא.-שם) יליף ר' אבהו מהאי קרא דתלמיד חכם לא יצא יחידי בלילה ויש לומר דהכא מוכח מקרא דעקידה דלא היה נמנע אברהם מלצאת יחידי בלילה דשלוחי מצוה אינן ניזוקין ועוד דשני נעריו היו עמו והתם מוכח מוישכם אברהם בבקר דכתיב גבי סדום דלא היה מצוה ויחידי היה שלא רצה שיראו במפלתן של סדום*: על המשכיר לבדוק דחמירא דידיה הוא. אין לפרש הטעם כיון דשלו הוא ואין אדם יכול לבטל אלא הוא חייב לבדוק דא"כ אמאי נקט משכיר לחברו בי"ד אפילו בי"ג יתחייב המשכיר מהאי טעמא לבדוק לכך מפרש ר"י דחמירא דידיה הוא וחל עליו חיוב בדיקה שעה אחת קודם שהשכירה ומייתי ראיה ממזוזה דאע"פ דחל חיוב קודם שהשכיר על השוכר לעשות מזוזה ודחי דמזוזה חובת הדר הוא כלומר אפי' לא היה משכירה היה יכול ליפטר ממזוזה שלא היה דר ומשתמש בבית אבל גבי חמץ [אילו] לא ישכיר לאחר יצטרך לבדוק: אם משמסר המפתח. פירש"י דמסירת המפתחות קונה ואין נראה לר"י דהא אמר במרובה (ב"ק עט.) כשם שקרקע נקנית בכסף בשטר ובחזקה כך שכירות [קרקע] נקנה בכסף וכו' ולא אמרי' דמהני מסירת המפתח הלא כמאן דאמר לך חזק וקני כדאמרינן בהפרה (ב"ק נב. ושם) ומפרש ר"י דהכא שמסר לו המפתח ולא החזיק ומי שיש בידו מפתח כשחל י"ד חייב לבדוק דאותו שאין בידו מפתח איך יכנס ויבדוק מיהו אם הפקיד אדם מפתח ביתו אצל אדם אחר אינו חייב הנפקד לבודקו אלא דוקא כשרוצה להחזיק בבית ולקנותו*:
[וע"ע תו' ב"ק נב. ד"ה כיון ותו' ב"ב נב: ד"ה נעל]
לאו

[וע"ע תוס' יומא כח. ד"ה אמר ותוס' ב"ק פ: ד"ה לעולם ותוס' לעיל ג. ד"ה יכנוס]

עין משפט נר מצוה

יב א טוש"ע יו"ד סי' שמ סעיף יב:
יג ב שם סעיף יב:
יד ג מיי' פ"ה מהלכות אבל הלכה ה סמג עשין מדרבנן שם טוש"ע יו"ד סי' שצ סעיף א:
טו ד ה מיי' פי"ג שם הל' ב סמג שם טוש"ע יו"ד סי' תב סעיף א:
טז ו מיי' פ"א מהלכות מילה הל' ח סמג עשין כח טוש"ע יו"ד סי' רסב סעיף א:
יז ז מיי' פ"ב מהל' חמץ ומצה הל' ג סמג עשין לט טוש"ע או"ח סי' תלג סעיף א:
יח ח מיי' פ"ה מהלכות מזוזה הל' יא סמג עשין כג טוש"ע יו"ד סי' רצא סעיף ב:
יט ט מיי' פ"ב מהלכות חמץ ומצה הלכה יח סמג עשין לט טוש"ע או"ח סי' תלז סעיף ג:
כ י טור ש"ע או"ח שם סעיף ב:

רבינו חננאל

רבי חייא שאל לרב בן אחיו שהוא בן אחותו כשעלה לארץ ישראל אמר ליה אבא קיים כלומר אבי חי הוא לא בקש רב לומר לו כי מת או לא אמר לו אבי שלי חי כלומר אביך אינו חי וכן השיב לו על אמו כענין הזה: ולמדנו ממנו שלשה דברים שאבל אסור בנעילת הסנדל וכי מקצת היום ככולו וכי שמועה רחוקה אינה נוהגת אלא יום אחד: ולמה שנינו אור ארבעה עשר בודקין את החמץ. כלומר למה אין בודקין ביום אלא בלילה ואוקימנא בשעה שבני אדם מצויין בבתיהם מפני שביום טרודין הן בשוק ובערב באין לבתיהן וכן בלילה יפה אור הנר לבדוק בו כי ביום אינו מאיר וכן אמר רב הונא בתלמוד ארץ ישראל כדהוינן ערקין באלין בתותה דסדרא רובא היינו מדליקין כשהיו כהים הינו יודעין שהוא יום וכד הוו מבהיקין הינו יודעין שהוא לילה: המשכיר בית לחברו השוכר חייב במזוזה שהמזוזה חובת הדר היא: המשכיר בית בארבעה עשר בניסן על מי לבדוק ופשטנא על המשכיר לבדוק דתניא המשכיר בית לחברו אם עד שלא חל י"ד מסר לו המפתח על השוכר לבדוק ואם משחל י"ד מסר לו המפתח על המשכיר לבדוק שכבר נתחייב מבערב. ועלה בעינן המשכיר בית לחבירו בי"ד הילך חזקתו בדוק או לא ופשטינן לה מהא דתניא הכל נאמנין על ביעור חמץ אפי' נשים ואפילו עבדים ואפילו קטנים מאי טעמית

מסורת הש"ס

[סנהדרין ה.] מ"ק כ.
[במ"ק כ: פי' אבא כצ"ל ע"י' קדושין לא: ופור ש"ע יו"ד סי' רמ ס"כ]
[לקמן נה. מ"ק טו: יט: כ: נזיר ס: ו. טו: כשרות כ: כה. נדה לג.]
[ר"ה לב:] בהריף גורס ת"ת זריזין מקדימין למצות כדכתיב וביום השמיני ימול מלמד שכל היום כשר למילה אלא שזריזין מקדימין למצות שנא' וישכם אברהם בבקר ונבדוק מצפרא אמר רנב"א בשעה שבנ"א כו'
[ב"מ קב.] [לקמן יא:] ע"ז כא: ב"מ קא: [דף ה:] [דף ז:]

גליון הש"ס

רש"י ד"ה רב בר אחוה כו'. בני דר"א מכפרי. בסנהדרין שם איתא בני אחא כרסלא מכפרי:

[4a] Rab was the son of R. Ḥiyya's brother and the son of his sister.[6] When he went up thither[7] he [R. Ḥiyya] asked him, 'Is Aibu alive?' '[Ask me whether] my mother is alive,' he replied. 'Is your mother alive?' asked he. 'Is then Aibu alive?' he replied.[8] [Thereupon] he [R. Ḥiyya] said to his servant, 'Take off my shoes and carry my [bathing] things after me to the baths.' From this three [laws] may be inferred: [i] A mourner is forbidden to wear shoes; [ii] on a delayed report [of death][9] it [*sc.* mourning] is observed for one day only;[10] and [iii] part of the day is as the whole of it.[11]

A certain man used to say, 'Judge my case'.[12] Said they, This proves that he is descended from Dan, for it is written, *Dan shall judge his people, as one of the tribes of Israel.*[13] A certain man was wont to go about and say, 'By the sea shore thorn-bushes are fir-trees.'[14] They investigated and found that he was descended from Zebulun, for it is written, *Zebulun shall dwell at the haven of the sea.*[15]

And now that it is established that all agree that 'OR' means
a evening,—consider: according to both R. Judah and R. Meir,[1] leaven is forbidden from six hours[2] and onward only, then let us search in the sixth [hour]? And should you answer, The zealous are early [to perform] religious duties, then let us search from the morning? For it is written, *and in the eighth day the flesh of his foreskin shall be circumcised,*[3] and it was taught: The whole day is valid for circumcision, but that the zealous are early [to perform] their religious duties, for it is said, *And Abraham rose early in the morning!*[4]—Said R. Naḥman b. Isaac: [It was fixed] at the hour when people are found at home, while the light of a lamp is good for searching.[5] Abaye observed: Therefore a scholar must not commence his regular session in the evening of the thirteenth breaking into the fourteenth, lest his studies absorb him[6] and he come to neglect his religious duty.

R. Naḥman b. Isaac was asked: If one rents a house to his neighbour from the fourteenth, upon whom [rests the duty] to make the search? [Does it rest] upon the landlord, because the leaven is his; or perhaps upon the tenant, because the forbidden matter exists in his domain? Come and hear: If one rents a house to his neighbour, the tenant must affix a *mezuzah!*[7]—There, surely R. Mesharsheya said: The *mezuzah* is the inhabitant's obligation; but how is it here?—Said R. Naḥman b. Isaac to them, We learned it: If one rents a house to his neighbour, if the fourteenth occurs before he delivers him the keys, the landlord must make the search; while if the fourteenth occurs after he delivers the keys, the tenant must make search.

R. Naḥman b. Isaac was asked: If one rents a house to his neighbour on the fourteenth, does it stand in the presumption of having been searched or not? What difference does it make? Let us ask him!—He is not present to be asked: hence what about troubling
b this one [the tenant]?[1]—Said R. Naḥman b. Isaac to them, We have a teaching:[2] All are believed concerning the removal of leaven, even women, even slaves, even minors.[3] Now why are

(6) Aibu, his father, was R. Ḥiyya's paternal brother, while Rab's mother was R. Ḥiyya's sister on his mother's side. (7) To Palestine. (8) Thus he intimated that they were both dead (Rashi). Tosaf. explains it differently on the strength of a different reading. (9) I.e., which one receives after thirty days. (10) Instead of the usual seven. (11) The latter two follow from his order to take his bathing things to the baths. Thus he intended to observe mourning for a short while only and then proceed to the baths. (12) In every dispute he insisted on going to law. (13) Gen. XLIX, 16. Perhaps it is here translated: Dan shall enter into judgment with his people. (14) Even the thorn-bushes there are as valuable as fir-trees elsewhere—an exaggerated way of expressing his love for the coast. Rashi offers another explanation: By the sea-shore would I build my palaces. (15) Ibid. 13.

a (1) V. Mishnah *infra* 11b. (2) The day was reckoned from sunrise to sunset, hence six hours was about noon. (3) Lev. XII, 3. (4) Gen. XXII, 3. (5) Hence the evening was appointed instead of the morning. (6) Lit., 'draw him away'. (7) V. Glos. Presumably the same principle applies here!

b (1) Must we put him to the trouble of making a search? (2) Lit., 'we have learned it'. (3) Their testimony that the owner duly made a search is accepted.

made them ride upon an ass?[12]—There [3b] it was natural on account of his sons. But it is written, *And it was so, as she rode on her ass?*[13]—There it was natural through fear of the night. Alternatively, there was no fear of the night, but there was fear of David. Another alternative: there was no fear of David either, but there was the fear of the mountain.

a Yet is not 'unclean' written in Scripture?[1] Rather wherever they are equal[ly convenient], [Scripture] discourses in a refined language; but wherever more words would be required, the shorter phraseology is employed. As R. Huna said in Rab's name—others say, R. Huna said in Rab's name on R. Meir's authority: One should always teach his pupil in concise terms. And where they are equal he discourses in refined speech? Yet surely *'riding'* [rokebeth] and *'sitting'* [yoshebeth] are alike [in length], yet *'riding'* [rokebeth] is stated?—*Rakebeth* is stated.[2]

Two disciples sat before Rab. One said, This discussion has made us [as tired] as an exhausted swine;[3] while the other said, This discussion has made us [as tired] as an exhausted kid; and Rab would not speak to the former.

There were two disciples who sat before Hillel, one of whom was R. Joḥanan b. Zakkai—others state, before Rabbi, and one of them was R. Joḥanan: One said, Why must we vintage [grapes] in cleanness, yet need not gather [olives] in cleanness? While the other said: Why must we vintage in cleanness, yet may gather [olives] in uncleanness?[4] I am certain that the latter will be an authorized teacher[5] in Israel, he observed; and it did not take long before[6] he was an authorized teacher in Israel.

There were three priests: one said, I received as much as a bean [of the shewbread]; the second said, I received as much as an olive; while the third said, I received as much as a *halta'ah's* tail.[7] They investigated his pedigree[8] and found a blemish of

b unfitness in him.[1] But we learned: One must not investigate from the altar and above?[2]—Do not say, a blemish of unfitness, but a baseness which made him unfit.[3] Alternatively, there it was different, because he impaired his status himself.

A certain Syrian [i.e., non-Jew] used to go up and partake of the Passover sacrifices in Jerusalem, boasting: It is written, *there shall no alien eat thereof . . . no uncircumcised person shall eat thereof,*[4] yet I eat of the very best. Said R. Judah b. Bathyra to him: Did they supply you with the fat-tail? No, he replied. [Then] when you journey up thither say to them, Supply me with the fat-tail. When he went up he said to them, Supply me with the fat-tail. But the fat-tail belongs[5] to the Most High![6] they replied. Who told you [to do] this? they enquired. R. Judah b. Bathyra, answered he. What is this [matter] before us? they wondered. They investigated his pedigree, and discovered that he was a Syrian, and killed him.[7] Then they sent [a message] to R. Judah b. Bathyra: 'Peace be with thee,[8] R. Judah b. Bathyra, for thou art in Nisibis[9] yet thy net is spread in Jerusalem.'

R. Kahana fell sick. [So] the Rabbis sent R. Joshua son of R. Idi, instructing him, Go and find out what is wrong with him.[10] He went and found him dead.[11] Thereupon he rent his garment and turned the rent behind him[12] and went along weeping. He has died? asked they of him. I have not said it, he answered, *'for he that uttereth evil tidings is a fool'.*[13]

c Joḥanan of Hukok[1] went out to some villages.[2] On his return he was asked, 'Has the wheat crop been successful?'[3] 'The barley crop has been successful,' he replied.[4] 'Go out and tell it to horses and asses,' they retorted, 'for it is written, *Barley also and straw for the horses and swift steeds.*'[5] What then should he have said?—Last year the wheat crop was successful; or, the lentil crop is successful.

(12) Ex. IV, 20. (13) I Sam. XXV, 20.

a (1) It occurs many times. The circumlocution employed in the cited instances merely serves to indicate that delicate phraseology is a matter which must also enter into consideration, v. Rashi. (2) I.e., *rokebeth* is written defectively, without a *waw*, which makes it shorter than *yoshebeth. Yoshebeth* could not be written defectively, as the defective form of *yoshebeth* has always a special meaning (Tosaf.). R. Ḥan. reverses it: the full form of *yoshebeth* is required, as a particular deduction is made from it. (3) Lit., 'something else'—the unmentionable. The rendering 'exhausted' is Rashi's. R. Ḥan. renders differently. (4) V. Shab. 17*a* and notes a.l. The point here is that one scholar avoided the use of the word 'uncleanness', while the other did not. (5) Lit., 'he will give teaching'. (6) Lit., 'it was not few days until'. (7) This is a gross expression. *Halta'ah* is a species of lizard (Jast.). (8) Lit., 'after him'.

b (1) They discovered that his genealogy was impure and that he was unfit to serve in the Temple. (2) Once a priest has officiated at the altar the purity of his descent must be assumed, as priests were not allowed to officiate without full investigation in the first place. (3) They found his own character too vile for officiating on the altar. According to this emendation, the literal translation 'after him' must be retained in the text. (4) Ex. XII, 43, 48. (5) Lit., 'goes up'. (6) I.e., it is burnt on the altar. (7) For a non-Jew might not even penetrate beyond a certain point within the Temple precincts on pain of death, and a public notice gave due warning of this. Josephus *Ant.* XV, 11, § 5. (8) This is the customary greeting in Hebrew. (9) In the north-east corner of Mesopotamia; it contained an important Jewish community. V. Obermeyer, p. 128-130. (10) Lit., 'what is his sentence?' (11) Lit., 'his soul had repose.' (12) So that it should not be immediately perceptible—this was to lessen the shock. (13) Prov. X, 18. E.V. . . . *uttereth slander*, etc.

c (1) In Northern Palestine; v. Josh. XIX, 34. (2) To inspect the crops. (3) Lit., 'comely'. (4) By which they might understand that the former was not. He was unwilling actually to state the bad news. (5) I Kings V, 8.

עין משפט נר מצוה

י א מיי' פ"ב מהלכות דעות הלכה ד :

יא ב מיי' פ"כ מהלכות א"ב הלכה ג טוש"ע אה"ע סי' ב :

יב ג מיי' פ"א מהלכות מעשה הקרבנות הלכה יח :

משום בניו אורחא הוא והכתיב °והיא רוכבת על החמור התם משום ביעתותא דליליא אורחא הוא ואיבעית אימא משום ביעתותא דליליא ליכא משום ביעתותא דדוד איכא ואיבעית אימא ביעתותא דדוד נמי ליכא משום ביעתותא דהר איכא ובאורייתא מי לא כתיב טמא אלא כל היכא דכי הדדי נינהו משתעי בלשון נקיה כל היכא דנפישין מילי משתעי בלשון קצרה כדאמר רב הונא אמר רב ואמרי לה אמר רב הונא אמר רב משום ר"מ *ילעולם *ישנה אדם לתלמידו דרך קצרה וכל היכא דכי הדדי נינהו משתעי בלשון כבוד והא רוכבת ויושבת דכי הדדי נינהו וקאמר רוכבת רכבת כתיב הנהו תרי תלמידי דהוו יתבי קמיה דרב חד אמר שויתינן האי שמעתא כדבר אחר מסנקן וחד אמר שויתינן האי שמעתא כגדי מסנקן ולא אישתעי רב בהדי דהאיך הנהו תרי תלמידי דהוו יתבי קמיה דהלל וחד מינייהו רבן יוחנן בן זכאי ואמרי לה קמיה דרבי וחד מינייהו רבי יוחנן חד אמר מפני מה בוצרין בטהרה ואין מוסקין בטהרה וחד אמר מפני מה בוצרין בטהרה ומוסקין בטומאה אמר מובטח אני בזה שמורה הוראה בישראל ולא היה ימים מועטים עד שהורה הוראה בישראל הנהו תלתא כהני חד אמר להו הגיעני כפול וחד אמר הגיעני כזית וחד אמר הגיעני כזנב הלטאה בדקו אחריו ומצאו בו שמץ פסול והא (תניא) *באין בודקין מן המזבח ולמעלה לא תימא שמץ פסול אלא אימא שחץ פסול ואי בעית אימא שאני התם דאיהו דארע נפשיה ההוא ארמאה דהוה סליק ואכיל פסחים בירושלים אמר כתיב °כל בן נכר לא יאכל בו °כל ערל לא יאכל בו ואנא הא קאכילנא משופרי שופרי אמר ליה רבי יהודה בן בתירא מי קא ספו לך מאליה אמר ליה לא כי סלקת להתם אימא להו ספו לי מאליה כי סליק אמר להו מאליה ספו לי אמרו ליה *גאליה לגבוה סלקא אמרו ליה מאן אמר לך הכי אמר להו רבי יהודה בן בתירא אמרו מאי האי דקמן בדקו בתריה ואשכחוהו דארמאה הוא וקטלוהו שלחו ליה לרבי יהודה בן בתירא שלם לך ר' יהודה בן בתירא דאת בנציבין ומצודתך פרוסה בירושלים רב כהנא חלש שדרוה רבנן לר' יהושע בריה דרב אידי אמרו ליה זיל בדוק מאי דיניה אתא אשכחיה דנח נפשיה קרעיה ללבושיה ואהדריה לקרעיה לאחוריה ובכי ואתי אמרו ליה נח נפשיה אמר להו אנא לא קאמינא °ומוציא דבה הוא כסיל יוחנן חקוקאה נפק לקרייתא כי אתא אמרו ליה חיטין נעשו יפות אמר להם שעורים נעשו יפות אמרו ליה צא ובשר לסוסים ולחמורים דכתיב °השעורים והתבן לסוסים ולרכש מאי הוי ליה למימר אשתקד נעשו חיטין יפות אי נמי עדשים נעשו יפות :

רב

(שמואל א כה; שמות יב; שם; משלי י; מלכים א ה)

תוספות

כל היכא דכי הדדי וכו' · ולכך עקם הכתוב ללמדנו שלעולם יספר אדם בלשון נקיה ואם לא היה עוקם אם כן מהיכא תיתי אפילו היכא דכי הדדי נינהו : רכבת כתיב · וא"ת לכתוב נמי ישבת ואומר ר"י דלא מצי למיכתב ישבת דכל היכא דכתב ישב בלא וי"ו אתא לדרשה כדדרשינן ולוט ישב בשער סדום אותו היום מינוהו שופט (בראשית רבה פרשה נ) : אין מוסקין בטהרה. מפרש ה"ר יוסף דטעמא דבצירה דפ"ק דשבת (ד' יז. ושם) לא שייכי במסיקה דשמא יבצרנו בקופה מזופפת והוה נמי פעמים שאדם הולך לכרמו ורואה אשכול שבכרה סוחטו ומזלפו ע"ג ענבים ובשעת בצירה עדיין משקה טופח עליהן דבזיתים אינו רגיל לעשות כן שאינו משקה ואינו חשוב כדאמר התם ואינו רוצה בקיומה : שמץ פסול. פירש רבינו חננאל דבר עבודת כוכבים כדכתיב (שמות לב) לשמצה בקמיהם ופסול לכהונה כדתנן במסכת מנחות (דף קט.) כהנים ששמשו בבית חוניו לא ישמשו במקדש ואין צ"ל לדבר אחר פירוש לע"ז שנאמר אך לא יעלו כהני הבמות אל מזבח ה' : ואנא אכילנא משופרי שופרי. מכאן אין ראיה שנאמנין לכל הבא לפנינו ואומר ישראל אני דשאני הכא דרוב ישראל היו ואזלינן בתר רובא אך יש להביא ראיה מפרק החולץ (דף מה. ושם) דאמר ליה זיל גלי או נסיב בת מינך וכן *מההוא דאתא לקמיה דרבי יהודה ואמר נתגיירתי ביני לבין עצמי אמר ליה נאמן אתה לפסול את עצמך ואי אתה נאמן לפסול את בניך והיינו משום דמצי למימר ישראל אני והא דאמר בהחולץ (דף מו:) מי שבא ואמר גר אני יכול נקבלנו תלמוד לומר אתך במוחזק לך התם מיירי במוחזק לן באבהתיה שהם נכרים דאי לאו הכי נאמן במיגו דאי בעי אמר ישראל אני* : מאליה מי קספו לך. אע"ג דגדי אין אליתו קריבה רוב פסחיהם היה טלה או שמא הגיד לו ורבי יהודה בן בתירא שלא עלה לרגל (א) י"ל שלא היה לו קרקע או זקן היה שאינו יכול להלך ברגליו דפטור מפסח כמו מראיה א"נ נציבין חו"ל היא כדמוכח בסיפרי בפ' ראה ועוד בתרגום ירושלמי (בראשית י) וארך ואכד וכלנה בארץ שנער מתרגם והדס ונציבין וקטיספי* : חקוקאה. פי' רבינו חננאל סופר ור"י פירש מעיר חקוקה היא בספר יהושע (יט):

אבא

[פי' תוס' יבמות מז: ד"ה במוחזק]

רש"י

משום בניו . שהן זכרים כתב לשון רכיבה : דכי הדדי נינהו . שאין אורך בלשון זה מן המגונה משתעי בלשון כבוד : וכל היכא כו' . והכי דלעיל עיקם ללמדך שצריך לחזור אחר לשון נקי ובשאר מקומות כתיב לשון מגונה וקצר ללמדך שישנה אדם לתלמידו לשון קצרה לפי שמתקיימת גירסא שלה יותר מן הארוכה : רכבת כתיב . ואע"ג דמצי למיכתב נמי ישבת חסר מיהו כל חסירות שבתורה לדרוש הן באין ולכאן למדך בחסרון זה שתתפוס לשון קצרה ואפילו הוא מגונה שהרי כאן תפס לשון מגונה וקצר : כגדי מסנקן . *כגדי עייף סינוק לשון עייפות ודומה לו גד גדי וסינק לא בגמרא דשבת בפרק במה אשה יוצאה (דף סז:) התגבר מזלי ואל תהי עייף : מפני מה בוצרים בטהרה . בכלים טהורים : ואין מוסקין בטהרה . בזיתים קא קרי מסיקה ואין צריך למוסקן בטהרה כדאמר במסכת שבת בילאות שבת (ד' יז.) דלא חשיב מוהל היוצא מהן להכשיר שאינו שמן גמור אלא היוצא ע"י הבד אבל יין הזב על הענבים מכשירן דניחא ליה ביה : הגיעני כפול . מלחם הפנים לחלקי : שמץ פסול . פסול כהונה חלל : אין בודקין . לענין יוחסין לישא אשה : מן המזבח ולמעלה . אם שימש במזבח אין צריך לבדוק למעלה הימנו דאם לא היה ראוי לכהונה לא היו מניחין אותו לשמש כדתנן במסכת מדות (פ"ה מ"ד) לשכת הגזית שם היו יושבים ב"ד ומיחסי כהונה ונויה כל כהן שנמצא בו פסול כשהיה רוצה להתחנך לעבודה לובש שחורים ויוצא : שחץ פסול . הוא עצמו היה גס רוח ומבזה קדשי שמים ואין ראוי לשמש כדקיימא לן [במנחות] (דף יח:) עבודה המסורה לבני אהרן כהן שאינו מודה בכולן אף במגונה שבהן אין לו חלק בכהונה : דארע אנפשיה . והצריך בדיקה אחריו וגלה שלא בדקוהו יפה מתחלה : מי קא ספו לך . כלום נותנין לך מן האליה לאכול אין נותנין לך אלא מן הכחוש שבו ונתכוון להטעותו לכשילך עוד ישאל מן האליה וביד ר' יהודה בן בתירא לא היה להורגו : ספו לי מאליה . הלעיטוני מן האליה וכבש היה ואלייתה קריבה לגבוה דכתיב בכבש (ויקרא ג) האליה תמימה : ר' יהודה בן בתירא . קאמר לי שאין אתם נותנים לי חלק יפה אלא מן הכחוש ואני נתתי דמים כמו כן : מאי דקמן . מה הדבר הזה שבא לפנינו : נציבין . שם עירו האי עובדא נקט הכא משום ההוא דלעיל דגרמו שניהם לבדוק אחריהם וההוא נקט משום לשון מגונה : בדוק מאי דיניה . בדוק ודע מה נהייתה בו : אהדרי' לקרעיה לאחוריה . שלא יבינו מהר להדיא ויצא לנבס : חקוקאה . כינוי השם : לקרייתא . לכפרים לראות בתבואות : שעורין נעשו יפות . ומכלל דבריו משמע שהחטים לא נעשו יפות ולא היה רוצה להוציא דבר קללה מפיו : עדשים נעשו יפות . מאכל אדם :

רב

מסורת הש"ס

חולין סג.

[תנן] קדושין פו.

[לקמן סד:]

גליון הש"ס

רש"י ד"ה כגדי מסנקן. כגדי עיף. עי' בהרע"ב רפ"ב דמסכת תמיד ·

רבינו חננאל

טמא מי לא כתיב בתורה ופרקינן אלא כל היכא דכי הדדי נינהו משתעי דרך כבוד אלא במקום טמא שצריך לומר לא טהור שזה שלש אותיות וזה שש אותיות משתעי דרך קצרה : יאמרינן וכל היכא דכי הדדי נינהו משתעי בלשון כבוד והא רוכבת ויושבת דכי הדדי נינהו ילא משתעי דרך כבוד ופרקינן רכבת כתיב פי' יאם י"ל נכתוב ישבת חסר וי"ו כל יושבת מלא נכתב כגון (איכה ד כא) יושבת בארץ עוץ (שופטי' ד' ה) והיא יושבת תחת תומר ובשמחסירו למדרש מחסירו ואין שם מדרש: כגדי מסנקן. פי' כגדי שמן מלא בכל אבריו כלומר נתמלאו מלא מעים שלנו מזו ההלכה שבענו ממנה כדתנן בתמיד (ד' כח) האברים והפדרים שלא נתאכלו מערב סונקין אותן בצדי המזבח וי"א גדי שנתפשם במים ומתחבט לצאת משם ואינו יכול וזה שאמר כדבר אחר מסנק ולא אשתעי בהדיה רב לפי שדבר על עצמו גנאי יפי' דבר אחר כמו חזיר: בוצרין בטהרה. כלומר נזהרין על בצירת ענבים ומסקי במסיקת זיתים אינן נזהרין כל כך פי' הענבים עלולים לקבל טומאה מפני שהמשקה שבהן מצוי להיות שותת בשעתו מה שאינו כן בזיתים ואע"פ ששניהן מכשירין כדתנן שבעה משקין הן הטל והמים והיין והשמן והדם והחלב ודבש דבורים ; ושבח לזה שאמר מפני מה אין מוסקין בטהרה דלא הוציא טומאה מפיו : וזה שאמר הגיעני כזנב הלטאה שהיא שרץ: ומצא בו. שמץ פסול פי' ע"ז כדכתי' (שמות לב כה) לשמצה בקמיהם*) שניה' פסולין לכהונה כי הכהנים ששמשו לע"ז פסולין כדתנן בסוף מנחות כהנים ששמשו בבית חוניו לא ישמשו במקדש בירושלים ואין צריך לומר לדבר אחר שנאמר (מלכים ב כג ט) אך לא יעלו כהני הבמות אל מזבח ה' כלומר בבית חוניו פסול וכל שכן ע"ז עצמה ואקשינן והתנן במסכת קדושין אין בודקין לא מן המזבח ולמעלה ולא מן הדוכן ולמעלה כלומר כל מי שהוחזק להקריב למזבח ובן לוי שהוחזק לדוכן אין צריכין לדקדק אחריו שלא עלה למזבח ולא לדוכן עד שבדקו והכשירוהו יושבי לשכת הגזית כדתנן בסוף מדות לשכת הגזית שם היתה סנהדרי גדולה יושבת ודנה את הכהונה כהן שנמצא בו פסול כו' ושנינן לא תימא שמץ פסול אלא שחץ פסול פי' שחץ פסול פסולות גסות הרוח ולעיגת לשון כדאמרינן במסכת שבת פרק במה אשה אנשי ירושלים אנשי שחץ היו : רבי יהושע בריה דרב אידי לא בקש לומר דנח נפשיה דרב כהנא דאמר ומוציא דבה הוא כסיל: חקוקאה פי' סופר כדכתיב (ישעיה י' א) הוי החוקקים :

*) עיין בערוך ערך שחן

(א) [עי' מ"ש במשנה למלך בפ"א מהל' ק"פ וסיים בזה"ל סוף דבר דברי תוס' אלו מתחלתם ועד סופם צריכים אלי תלמוד]

*המפלת אור לשמונים ואחד בית שמאי פוטרין מקרבן ובית הלל מחייבים אמרו (להן) בית הלל לבית שמאי מאי שנא אור שמנים ואחד מיום שמנים ואחד אם שוה לו לטומאה לא ישוה לו לקרבן מדקאמר ב"ה לב"ש מאי שנא אור שמונים ואחד מיום שמונים ואחד שמע מינה אור אורתא הוא שמע מינה מיתיבי *יכול יהא נאכל אור לשלישי ודין הוא זבחים נאכלים ליום אחד ושלמים נאכלים לשני ימים מה להלן לילה אחר היום אף כאן לילה אחר היום ת"ל °ביום זבחכם יאכל וממחרת והנותר עד יום °בעוד יום הוא נאכל ואינו נאכל לאור שלישי יכול ישרף מיד ודין הוא זבחים נאכלין ליום ולילה אחד ושלמים נאכלין לשני ימים ולילה אחד מה להלן תיכף לאכילה שריפה אף כאן תיכף לאכילה שריפה תלמוד לומר °והנותר מבשר הזבח ביום השלישי באש ישרף °ביום אתה (שורף) ואי אתה שורפו בלילה מדקאמר יהא נאכל אור לשלישי אלמא אור אורתא הוא שמע מינה תא שמע *אור של יום הכפורים מתפלל שבע ומתודה שחרית מתפלל שבע ומתודה במוסף מתפלל שבע ומתודה במנחה מתפלל שבע ומתודה *בערבית מתפלל מעין שמונה עשר ר' חנינא בן גמליאל אומר משום אבותיו °מתפלל שמונה עשר שלימות מפני שצריך לומר הבדלה בחונן הדעת אלמא אור אורתא הוא שמע מינה תא שמע *דתני דבי שמואל לילי ארבעה עשר בודקין את החמץ לאור הנר אלמא אור אורתא הוא ולא פליגי *מר כי אתריה ומר כי אתריה באתריה דרב הונא קרו *נגהי ובאתריה דרב יהודה קרו לילי ותנא דידן מאי טעמא לא קתני לילי *לישנא מעליא הוא דנקט וכדר' יהושע בן לוי דאמר ר' יהושע בן לוי לעולם אל יוציא אדם דבר מגונה מפיו °שהרי עקם הכתוב שמונה אותיות ולא הוציא °דבר מגונה מפיו שנאמר °מן הבהמה הטהורה ומן הבהמה אשר איננה טהורה רב פפא אמר תשע שנאמר °כי יהיה בך איש אשר לא יהיה טהור מקרה לילה רבינא אמר עשר וי"ו דטהור רב אחא בר יעקב אמר שש עשרה שנאמר °כי אמר מקרה הוא בלתי טהור הוא כי לא טהור תניא דבי רבי ישמעאל לעולם יספר אדם בלשון נקיה שהרי בזב קראו מרכב ובאשה קראו °מושב ואומר °ותבחר לשון ערומים ואומר °ודעת שפתי ברור מללו מאי ואומר וכי תימא הני מילי בדאורייתא אבל בדרבנן לא תא שמע ואומר ותבחר לשון ערומים וכי תימא הני מילי בדרבנן אבל במילי דעלמא לא *ואומר ודעת שפתי ברור מללו ובאשה לא כתיב בה מרכב והכתיב °ותקם רבקה ונערותיה ותרכבנה על הגמלים התם משום ביעתותא דגמלים אורחא היא והכתיב °ויקח משה את אשתו ואת בניו וירכיבם על החמור התם משום

המפלת אור לשמונים ואחד. בכריתות בפרק קמא דקיימא לן זאת תורת היולדת מלמד שמביאה קרבן אחד על ולדות הרבה יכול שתביא על לידה שלפני מלאות ועל הלידה שלאחר מלאות קרבן אחד ולא יותר תלמוד לומר זאת שאם ילדה לאחר מלאות כגון שטבלה לסוף שבועיים של נקבה ונתעברה והפילה אם תוך מלאות הפילה נפטרת בקרבן אחד ואם לאחר מלאות הפילה כבר נתחייב' בקרבן הראשון קודם לידה שניה ולסוף מלאות של לידה שניה תביא שתי קרבנות ואם הפילה ליל של כניסת שמונים ואחד שכבר עברה מלאות שלה אבל עדיין אינה ראויה להבאת קרבן שאין קרבן נשחט בלילה: בית הלל מחייבי. שתי קרבנות דלאחר מלאות קרינא ביה ובית שמאי פוטרין אותה בקרבן אחד כדמפרש טעמייהו: מאי שנא אור שמונים ואחד מיום שמונים ואח'. הלא אתם מודים לנו שאם הפילה בלילה והפילה למחר שחייבת אף כשהפילה אור לשמונים ואחד תתחייב שהרי לכל דבר זמן היום והלילה שוים: אם שוה לו לטומאה לא ישוה לו לקרבן. בתמיה ועוד ראיה אחרת דהאיל ושוה לו לטומאה שעד שקיעת החמה של שמונים דמיה טהורים ואם תראה לאחר שקיעת החמה דמיה טמאין כאילו היא רואה למחר ולמה לא ישוה לו אף לקרבן שכשם שאם תפיל למחר תתחייב כך תתחייב על הוולד של לילו ותשובת בית שמאי במסכת כריתות היא שנויה לא אם אמרתם ביום שמונים ואחד שכן יצאתה לשעה הראויה להביא בה קרבן לפיכך נתחייבה בקרבן הראשון ושוב אין לידה השניה נפטרת בו תאמרו במפלת אור לשמונים ואחד שלא יצאתה מידי וולד הראשון לשעה הראויה לקרבן והדמים שאתם אומרים אינן מוכיחים שהרי הפילה תוך מלאות דמיה של לידה טמאין ופטורה מן הקרבן: אור לשלישי. לאור כניסתו של שלישי ה"ג גרסינן אור לשלישי ושלמים קאי דכתיב בהו ביום זבחכם יאכל וממחרת והוה לשורפו לבוקרו של שלישי יכול יהא נאכל ליל שלפניו: זבחים נאכלים ליום אחד. תודה דכתיב ביום קרבנו יאכל ושלמים נאכלים לשני ימים מה להלן לילה אחר היום דכתיב בגופיה דקרא לא יניח ממנו עד בוקר הא כל הלילה אוכל וכן פסח לא תותירו ממנו עד בוקר אף כאן לילה אחר הימים הכתובים בה: ת"ל וממחרת והנותר עד יום. בעוד שהוא יום ממחרת אכול ולא משתחשך: מה להלן תיכף לאכילה שריפה. כשכלה זמן אכילתן מתחיל זמן שריפתו כדכתיב והנותר ממנו עד בקר באש תשרופו: אף כאן. זמן אכילתו כלה ערבית כדאמר וישרף בלילה: תלמוד לומר. בלו את אהרן ביום השלישי באש ישרף כאן לא נאמר עד יום אלא ביום משום דהאי קרא לא איירי בזמן אכילה אלא בשריפה להורות שביום הוא נשרף ולא בלילה וקרא דלעיל בקדושים תהיו: באתריה דרב הונא קרו. לאורתא נגהי: מאי טעמא לא תני לילי. כדתנא דבי שמואל ומשני אלישנא מעליא קא מיהדר שמלוה ודרך נקיי הדעת לספר בלשון נקיה: דבר מגונה. לאו משום דלילי דבר מגונה הוא והא דר' יהושע בן לוי בעלמא איתמר ומיהו שמעינן מינה לשון חכמים לחזר אחר לשון נקי: אשר איננה טהורה. ולא כתיב הבהמה הטמאה כי אורחיה הרי שמונה אותיות עקם הטמאה חמש אותיות הן אשר איננה טהורה שלש עשרה אותיות ואע"ג דבאורייתא כתיב טמא שני אורחיה בחד דוכתא ללמדך לחזר על לשון נקיה: אשר לא יהיה טהור. הוה ליה למיכתב איש טמא וכי נמי משוית לטהור חסר ו' איכא עיקום תשע שהרי שתים עשרה יש וטמא אינו אלא שלש: ו' דטהור. דהא לא חסר הוא: כי אמר מקרה. טמא הוא לכתוב ולשתוק ויש כאן עיקום י"ו אותיות: בזב כתיב (ויקרא טו) וכל המרכב אשר ירכב ובאשה כתיב (שם) או על הכלי אשר היא יושבת לפי שאין הגון להזכיר רכיבה באשה ופיסוק רגלים באשה ואע"פ שהמרכב והמושב שוין בשניהם: ותבחר לשון ערומים. מלוה עליך כך: ברור מללו. ל' נקי ומבורר: מאי ואומר. למה לו ואומר הא נפקא ליה מקמא: ה"ק וכי תימא ה"מ בדאורייתא. תורה הקפידה בלשונה שילאתה מפי הגבורה אבל חכמים במשנה ובברייתא אין להקפיד על לשונם: ת"ש ותבחר לשון ערומים. שמעינו שהערומים בוחרי לשון הם: משום ביעתותא דגמלים. שהוא גבוה ומתיירא שלא תפול אורחא דאשה לרכוב כדי שתהא מחזקת בו בידים ורגלים:

אם שוה לו לטומאה. חזרו ב"ה מזה הטעם מתשובתם של ב"ש וטעמייהו כדקאמר פ"ק דכריתות (דף ח.) אלו לבת לרבות אור לשמונים ואחד: תלמוד לומר ביום. תימה אמאי איצטריך עד יום תיפוק ליה דאינו נאכל אור לשלישי מדאיצטריך ביום דאי ס"ד דנאכל פשיטא דאינה נשרפת באותו לילה דתיכף לאכילה שריפה ויש לומר דאי לאו עד יום ה"א נאכל ואיצטריך ביום למעוטי שלא ישרף בלילה של אחרי כן: שהרי בזב קראו מרכב וכו'. מרכב ומושב אין דינו שוה דנוגע במרכב אין טעון כבוס בגדים כדמוכח בתורת כהנים ובריש מסכת כלים* והשתא קשה לר"י היכי קאמר דבאשה קרוי מושב אם ר"ל אפי' אוכף שיש לו דין מרכב אף באשה שינה הכתוב לקרותו מושב לדבר דרך כבוד דהא לקמן משני משום ביעתותא דגמלא אורחא הוא אלמא לשנות הדבר ממה שהוא אין לכתוב דרך כבוד ונראה לר"י דה"פ ובאשה קראו מושב מרכובה דקרא למושב דהכי איתא בתורת כהנים אשר היא יושבת עליו זה מושב כלי זה מרכב לימדנו הכתוב לספר בלשון נקיה שלא כתבו בהדיא כמו בזב דכל

רבינו חננאל

דתנן בכריתות פ' המפלת לאור שמונים ואחד ב"ש פוטרין מן הקרבן וב"ה מחייבין כו' פי' יולדת נקבה שטבלה לאחר י"ד ושמשה ונתעברה והפילה לילי פ"א כלומר שלמו פ' יום ימי טוהר ובמוצאי פ' בלילה לילי פ"א הפילה ב"ש פוטרין מן הקרבן על זה הנפל שהיו אומרים הקרבן שהיא מביאה על הלידה פוטר זה הנפל שהרי ביום פ"א נתחייבה בקרבן הלידה וכל מה שהיה מקודם אותו הקרבן פוטרם זה הקרבן וב"ה [מחייבין דהלילה] כיום פ"א הוא חשוב הלא אם ראת דם לילי פ"א דם נדה הוא ולא דם טוהר פירוש הנה הלילה והיום שוין לטומאה כי ראיתה לילי פ"א וראיתה יום פ"א שוין לטומאה נדה היא בין ביום בין בלילה כך אם הפילה לילי פ"א כאלו יום פ"א הפילה וכשם שחייבת קרבן אחר המפלת יום פ"א כך חייבת קרבן המפלת לילי פ"א ומדקאמרי ב"ה מאי שנא [אור] פ"א מיום פ"א ש"מ אור אורתא הוא ש"מ: [ועוד] ת"ש דתניא יכול יהא זבח השלמים נאכל לאור שלישי ודין הוא וכו' תסיב ליה תלמודא ת"ל והנותר מבשר הזבח ביום השלישי באש ישרף ביום אתה שורפו ואי אתה שורפו בלילה ש"מ אור אורתא הוא ש"מ. פשוטה היא מיהו אנו מפרשי' ראש דברים התודה והנותר בבקר נשרף שנאמר ובשר זבח תודת שלמיו ביום קרבנו יאכל וגו' דינה להאכל יום שנשחטה וכל הלילה ובקר שהוא תכף לאכילתה כלומר עכשיו כשנאמר באכילתה תהיה שרפתה וזהו זבחים נאכלין ליום אחד כך זבח השלמים נאכלין לשני ימים ולילה אחד שנאמר ביום הקריבו את זבחו יאכל וממחרת נאכלין בו ביום שנשחטו ובלילה ומחר וכיון שחשך נאסר באכילתן הייתי אומר ישרפו אותה הלילה ותהא שריפתן תיכף לאיסור אכילתן ת"ל והנותר ביום השלישי באש ישרף ביום ישרף ולא בלילה ש"מ אור אורתא הוא ש"מ: ת"ש אור יום הכפורים מתפלל שבע ומתודה וכו' ועוד תא שמע לילי ארבעה עשר בודקין את החמץ לאור הנר ש"מ אור אורתא הוא שמע מינה. ותנא דידן אמאי קרי ללילה אור ואמרינן לישנא מעליא כלומר לא בעי לטיתנא לילה שהוא חשך אלא קראו לחשך אור כגון דקרו לסמיא סגיא נהורא וכדאמרינן אל יוציא אדם דבר מגונה מפיו שהרי עקם הכתוב שמונה אותיות שנאמר הבהמה אשר איננה טהורה שהן י"ג אותיות ואלו כתב בה"א הטמאה היה די לו ומפני מה הוסיף שמונה אותיות משום שלא להזכיר שם טומאה. ודברי רב פפא ורבינא ורב אחא כענין הזה ופשוטין הן: בזב קראו מרכב שנאמר וכל המרכב אשר ירכב עליו יטמא ובאשה כתיב (ויקרא טו כ) וכל אשר תשב עליו יטמא ומפני מה לא הזכיר באשה מרכב שהמרכב הוא בפיסוק רגלים והוא דרך גנאי באשה ופיסוק תלים במקום שאפשר לו לאיבורו בלשון שבח אבל ברכיבת הגמל וכיוצא בה משום פחד שמתיראה לרטב דרך ישיבה שלא תפול אי אפשר שלא להזכיר רכיבה אין עליו כלום. ואקשינן אמר

[פי' כנוי הוא כמו שקורין לסומא סגי נהור והניקר בה מן אור יגה שביב אשו (איוב יח) ערוך]

ה א מיי' פ"א מהלכות מחוסרי כפרה הלכה ה סמ"ג עשין רי"ח:
ו ב מיי' פ"י מהלכות מעשה הקרבנות הל' ו':
ז ג מיי' פי"ט מהלכות פסולי המוקדשין הלכה ד:
ח ד מיי' פ"ב מהלכות תפלה הלכה ז [וע"ע מהל' תשובה פ"ב ה"ז טור או"ח סי' תרי"ע]:
ט ה מיי' שם הלכה ד טוש"ע א"ח סי' תרכב סעיף א:

[משנה ג.]

כריתות ז: עדיו' פ"ד מ"י [להם]
זבחים נו: [ע"ש כמה שינוים]
[שורפו]
יומא פז: נדה ח:
ביומא ובנדה הגי' בנעילה מתפלל שבע ומתודה
[לקמן ז: ע"ש]
[שבת קנג. ביצה טו. יומא נח. נדרים מט. נב: ב"מ ח. קיז. ב"ב יב. מנחות קו: בכורות לג. חולין סו.]
*ברכות יא: יומא עה. יבמות יא: קג. כתובות יג. סה: גיטין עו: פ: ב"מ לא. סנהד' נד. תמורה ל.]
[ת"ש ואומר כצ"ל]

גליון הש"ס

גמ' שהרי עקם הכתוב. עי' מדרש רבה ריש פ' אמור:

Mar Zuṭra raised an objection: [3*a*] If a woman miscarries on the evening [*or*] of the eighty-first day: Beth Shammai exempt her from a sacrifice, whereas Beth Hillel declare her liable.[4] Said Beth Hillel to Beth Shammai: Wherein does the evening ['*or*'] of the eighty-first differ from the day of the eighty-first; seeing that it was assimilated thereto in respect of uncleanness,[5] shall one not assimilate it thereto in respect of sacrifice? Now since Beth Hillel say to Beth Shammai, 'Wherein does the evening [*or*] of the eighty-first differ from the day of the eighty-first,' it follows that '*or*' is evening. This proves it.

a An objection is raised: One might think that it[1] may be eaten on the evening ['*or*'] of the third day [from sacrifice], and it is logical: Sacrifices[2] are eaten on one day,[3] while peace-offerings are eaten on two days: just as there the night follows the day,[4] so here too the night should follow the day. Therefore it is stated, *It shall be eaten the same day ye offer it, and on the morrow: and if aught remain until the third day* [*it shall be burnt with fire*]:[5] teaching, it may be eaten only during the day, but it may not be eaten during the evening ['*or*'] of the third day. One might think that it must be burnt immediately;[6] and this is logical: Sacrifices[2] may be eaten one day and one [*sc.* the following] night, while peace-offerings may be eaten two days and one [*sc.* the intermediate] night: just as there, immediately after [the time allowed for] eating there is burning, so here too immediately after [the time allowed for] eating there is burning. Therefore it is stated, *But that which remaineth of the flesh of the sacrifice, on the third day it shall be burnt with fire:*[7] teaching, you must burn it by day, but you must not burn it by night. Since he states, '. . . it may be eaten in the evening ['*or*'] of the third day,' it follows that '*or*' is evening. This proves it.

Come and hear: On the evening ['*or*'] of the Day of Atonement one recites seven [benedictions] and confesses; in the morning service he recites seven and confesses; in the additional service[8] he recites seven and confesses; at *minḥah*[9] he recites seven and confesses; (at *ne'ilah*—the concluding service—he recites seven and confesses);[10] in the evening service he recites [one benediction] embodying the eighteen; R. Ḥanina b. Gamaliel said on the authority of his fathers: He must recite the eighteen [benedictions] in full, because he must pronounce *habdalah*[11] in [the
b benediction] 'Thou dost graciously grant knowledge'.[1] This proves that '*or*' is evening. This proves it.

Come and hear: For the School of Samuel[2] learned: 'In the evening[3] of the fourteenth leaven is searched for by the light of a lamp'; thus proving that '*or*' is evening![4] The fact is both R. Huna and Rab Judah are alike, agreeing that '*or*' is evening, and there is no controversy: each Master [speaks] in accordance with his locality. In R. Huna's town they called it *naghe*,[5] while in Rab Judah's town it is called night [*lele*].

And our Tanna why does he not employ *lele?*[6]—He employs a refined expression, and in accordance with R. Joshua b. Levi. For R. Joshua b. Levi said: One should not utter a gross expression with his mouth, for lo! the Writ employs a circumlocution of eight letters[7] rather than utter a gross expression, for it is said, *Of every clean beast . . . and of the beasts that are not clean.*[8] R. Papa said: Nine, for it is said, *If there be among you any man, that is not clean by reason of that which chanceth by night.*[9] Rabina said: Ten,
c [including] the *waw* of *ṭahor.*[1] R. Aḥa b. Jacob said: Sixteen, for it is said, *for he thought, Something hath befallen him, he is not clean; surely he is not clean.*[2]

The School of R. Ishmael taught: One should always discourse in decent language, for lo! in the case of a *zab*[3] it is called riding, while in connection with a woman it is called sitting;[4] and it is said, *and thou shalt choose the tongue of the subtle;*[5] and it is said, *and that which my lips know they shall speak purely.*[6] Why [quote] 'and it is said [etc.]'?[7]—[For] should you object, that is only in the case of Scripture,[8] but not in the case of Rabbinical [discussions],—then come and hear, 'and it is said, *and thou shalt choose the tongue of the subtle*'.[9] Yet should you [still] object, that is only in reference to Rabbinical [discussions] but not secular matters,—then come and hear, 'and it is said, *and that which my lips know they shall speak purely*'.

Now, is riding not written in connection with a woman, but surely it is written, *And Rebekah arose, and her damsels, and they rode upon the camels?*[10]—There it was natural through fear of the camels.[11] But it is written, *and Moses took his wife and his sons, and*

(4) A woman must bring a sacrifice eighty-one days after the birth of a daughter (v. Lev. XII, 2-6). This sacrifice suffices also for a miscarriage within the eighty days, i.e., before it was due, but not for a miscarriage (or viable birth) from the eighty-first day and onwards, since by then it was already due on account of the first birth. Now, by the *evening* of the eighty-first day eighty days have already passed; on the other hand, since there are no sacrifices at night, she could not offer hers until the following morning. Beth Shammai and Beth Hillel accordingly differ as to whether that miscarriage entails a sacrifice or not. (5) A discharge of blood on the eighty-first, whether in the evening or during the day, renders her unclean,—this is agreed by all.—A discharge between the fifteenth and the eightieth inclusive does not make her unclean; v. ibid. 5.

a (1) *Sc.* the flesh of a peace-offering. (2) Viz. the thanksoffering. (3) I.e., only on the day they are brought. (4) The thanksoffering may be eaten during the night following the day in which it is sacrificed. (5) Lev. XIX, 6. (6) After the expiration of the time allowed for its eating, i.e., on the evening of the third day. (7) Lev. VII, 17. (8) There is an additional service (*musaf*) on all Sabbaths and Festivals, corresponding to the additional sacrifices of those days. (9) V. Glos. (10) The bracketed passage is absent in our text but is supplied from Yoma 87*b* and Nid. 8*b*. (11) V. Glos.

b (1) The 'Prayer' *par excellence* on weekdays comprises eighteen (subsequently increased to nineteen) statutory benedictions; on Sabbaths and Festivals the first three and the last three only are recited, the intermediate twelve being omitted and replaced by one bearing on the nature of the day. A feature of all the services on the Day of Atonement is the 'confession', a recital of sins committed, not necessarily by the individual but by the people as a whole, for which reason it is couched in the plural—'we have sinned'. The evening following the Day of Atonement is of course non-holy, but the first Tanna permits one benediction comprising the eighteen to be recited. Each of the benedictions bears a name, indicating its main subject: the fourth is designated, 'Thou dost graciously grant knowledge', as it is a prayer for knowledge and understanding, and on the termination of Sabbaths and Festivals *habdalah* is inserted in this benediction. For a full discussion of these benedictions v. *J.E.* art. *Shemoneh 'Esreh*; v. also Elbogen, *J.G.*, 149f. (2) The reading *infra* 7*b* is: the School of R. Ishmael. (3) *Lele*—the very term employed by Rab Judah to define '*or*' in our Mishnah. (4) In refutation of R. Huna. (5) Jast.: 'night-break'. Margin: light employed as a euphemism for darkness in the same way that a blind person is called a man with too much light. (6) V. n. b3. (7) I.e., uses eight letters more than is necessary. (8) Gen. VII, 2; a single word, 'unclean', would save eight letters in the Hebrew text. (9) Deut. XXIII, 11. Here too a single word 'unclean' would save nine letters in the Hebrew text.

c (1) *Ṭahor* (טהור) is written plene, i.e., with a *waw*, and that makes a difference of ten letters. (2) I Sam. XX, 26. (3) V. Glos. (4) The reference is to Lev. XV, 9 and 20: *And what saddle* (or, carriage) *soever he that hath issue rideth upon shall be unclean. Everything also that she sitteth upon shall be unclean.* Actually the conditions of defilement are the same in both cases; nevertheless, Scripture did not speak of a woman's riding, because sitting is a more modest and decent conception. (5) Job. XV, 5. (6) Ibid. XXXIII, 3. (7) What is the purpose of the additional quotations, seeing that the first verse proves his statement? (8) Owing to its great sanctity. (9) This is regarded as a positive injunction to speak subtly, i.e., with a due sense of the proprieties. (10) Gen. XXIV, 61. (11) A woman would ride properly, not merely sit on the side, through fear of falling down from the camel's high back.

since he states, *'and in the night he is as a thief,'* it follows that *'or'* is day?—The meaning there is this: if the matter is as clear as light to you that he [the thief] comes [even] to take life, he is a murderer, and he [the victim] may be saved at the cost of his [the thief's] life; but if you are doubtful about it, like [the darkness of] the night, you must regard him [only] as a thief, and he [the victim]
a must not be saved at the cost of his life.[1]

An objection is raised: *Let the stars of the twilight thereof be dark: let him look for light* [or], *but have none; neither let it behold the eyelids of the morning.*[2] Since he says, *'let him look for light, but have none,'* it follows that *'or'* is day?—There Job indeed curses his destiny[3] and exclaims, Heaven grant that that man [*sc.* himself] look for light, but have none.[4]

An objection is raised: *If I say, Surely the darkness shall overwhelm me, and the light* [or] *about me shall be night:*[5] this proves that *'or'* is day?[6]—There David said thus: I thought, surely darkness shall overwhelm me in the future world, which resembles day; but now, even this world, which resembles night,[7] is light about me.

An objection is raised: R. Judah said: We search [for leaven] in the evening [*'or'*] of the fourteenth, in the morning of the fourteenth, and at the time of removal:[8] Now since R. Judah says, 'We search in the evening [*'or'*] of the fourteenth and in the morning of the fourteenth,' it follows that *'or'* is evening. This proves it.

An objection is raised: From when is work forbidden on the fourteenth [of Nisan]? R. Eliezer b. Jacob said: From the time of the *'or'*;[9] R. Judah said: From the [first] sparklings of the [rising] sun. Said R. Eliezer b. Jacob to R. Judah: Where then do we find a day during part of which work is forbidden while during [the other] part it is permitted? He replied, Let that [day] itself prove [this possibility], for during part of it the eating of leaven
b is permitted, whereas during the other part it is forbidden.[1] Now since R. Judah maintains, From the [first] sparklings of the [rising] sun, it follows that by *'or'* R. Eliezer b. Jacob means evening?—No; what does *'or'* mean? The morning dawn. If so, when he says to him, 'Where then do we find a day during part of which work is forbidden while during [the other] part it is permitted,' let him answer himself: surely there is the night, which is permitted?[2]—R. Eliezer b. Jacob argues thus: As for my view, it is well; we find that the Rabbis drew a distinction between night and day, for it was taught in respect of a public fast: Until when may one eat and drink? Until the commencement[3] of dawn: this is R. Eliezer b. Jacob's view. R. Simeon maintained: Until cockcrow.[4] But on your view: where do we find that the Rabbis drew a distinction in the day itself? [To which] he replied, Let that [day] itself prove it, for during part thereof the eating of leaven is permitted while during part thereof it is forbidden? R. Judah answers R. Eliezer rightly?[5]—R. Eliezer says thus to him: I speak to you of work, which is [prohibited] by the Rabbis, while you answer me about leaven [on the fourteenth day], which is [prohibited] by Scripture; thus far[6] the Divine Law permits, and from then Scripture forbids. And the other?[7]—The [additional] hours are Rabbinical.[8] And the other?—The Rabbis [merely] erected a safeguard for a Scriptural law.[9]

An objection is raised: Bonfires are lit only for a new moon that is visible in its [due] time, in order to sanctify it.[10] And when were the bonfires lit? On the evening [*'or'*] following the inter-
c calated day.[1] This proves that *'or'* is evening. This proves it.

An objection is raised: If he [the priest] was standing all night and offering [the fats of sacrifices] on the altar, at daybreak [*orah*] he must wash his hands and feet:[2] this is Rabbi's view?[3]—*Orah* is [a] different [word].

a (1) V. Ex. XXII, 1; the present verse lays down the conditions for the law stated there to be applicable. (2) Job. III, 9. (3) *Mazzal* is the constellation which controls one's destiny. (4) But 'light' there is not parallel to or synonymous with morning. (5) Ps. CXXXIX, 11. (6) Since it is *contrasted* with night. (7) By contrast, with the next; but not absolutely, Judaism being far too robust and optimistic a religion for such a view; cf. Hertz, *Genesis, Additional Note A*, III, p. 57. (8) When the leaven must be destroyed. (9) But even if it is the practice in a community to cease work earlier, this has no binding force; v. *infra* 50*a*.

b (1) V. *infra* 11*b*. (2) Though night is part of the day. (3) Lit., 'ascending'. (4) The prohibition of work on the fourteenth is likewise merely Rabbinical. (5) Surely he must have perceived the answer himself! (6) Up to a certain hour. (7) Does he not admit the distinction? (8) V. *infra* 11*b* Mishnah. Thus they permit the first four hours and forbid the following two. (9) Lest the day is cloudy and one does not know exactly when it is midday; therefore they added two hours. But when the law is *entirely* Rabbinical, they would not apply it to part of the day only. (10) The Jewish month, which is lunar, consists of either twenty-nine or thirty days. During the early Talmudic age New Moon was fixed by direct observation, not calculation, and communities at a distance from Jerusalem were informed by bonfires. These were lit only if the New Moon appeared 'in its (due) time,' i.e., it was fixed for the thirtieth day, the previous month thus consisting of twenty-nine days only; in that case too Beth Din formally sanctified this day. But if observation fixed it for the thirty-first day, no bonfires were lit, since the absence of bonfires on the previous day would be a sufficient signal; further, New Moon was not formally sanctified by Beth Din (Rashi).

c (1) The additional day is the thirtieth, whereby the month is full; the bonfire is lit on the evening of the thirty-first. (2) Lit., 'he needs the sanctification of his hands and feet (from the laver)', v. Ex. XXX, 17. (3) Thus *'orah'* denotes daybreak, and it is now assumed that *'or'* and *'orah'* are identical.

עין משפט נר מצוה

ב א מיי' פ"ח מהלכות יו"ט הלכה יח: [סמג לאוין עה]

ג ב מיי' פ"א מהלכות תענית הלכה ח סמג עשין דרבנן ג טוש"ע א"ח סי' תקסד:

ד ג מיי' פ"ה מהלכות ביאת מקדש הל' ח:

[ר"ה טו: ועי' תוס' שם ד"ה וכי]

רבינו חננאל

תא שמע בודקין אור ארבעה עשר ובארבעה עשר שחרית ובשעת הביעור מדקתני ובארבעה עשר שחרית מכלל דאור אורתא הוא ש"מ. וכיון שנתברר כי זה האור ששנינו במשנתנו אורתא הוא למה לי למימר עוד ת"ש. יש לומר כי לא מזו המשנה לבדה שמענו כי אור אורתא הוא אלא גם יש לנו ללמוד מזו האחרת: **מאימתי** ארבע' עשר אסור בעשיית מלאכה ר' אליעזר בן יעקב אומר משעת האור ר' יהודה אומר משעת הנץ החמה ש"מ מדקאמר ר"י משעת הנץ החמה מכלל דאור דקאמר ר' אליעזר בן יעקב אורתא הוא ודחי' מאי משעת האור דקאמר ר' אליעזר בן יעקב משיעלה עמוד השחר ויאיר אור היום והכי קאמר ליה בשלמא לדידי דאמינא בלילי י"ד שרי למיעבד מלאכה וביממא אסור אשכחן דשרו בליליא ואסרו ביממא כי האי גונא בתענית דתניא עד מתי אוכל ושותה עד שיעלה עמוד השחר אלא לדידך היכא אשכחן משיעלה עמוד השחר עד הנץ החמה מותר ושאר היום אסור אמר ליה ר' יהודה הוא עצמו ערב הפסח יוכיח שהוא מותר באכילת חמץ עד ארבע שעות ומכאן ולהלן אסור ודחי ר' אליעזר שאני חמץ דהוא מדאורייתא והתורה התירה מקצת היום ואסרה מקצת היום ולא שמעי' אסור מדרבנן [דהיינו] המלאכה בארבעה עשר שהיא מדרבנן מן אכילת חמץ שהיא מן התורה אסורה ור' יהודה אמר לך אנא נמי לא אמרי אלא בשעה ששית שאיסורה מדרבנן שמן התורה אכילת חמץ מותר עד חצי היום דקיימא לן אך חלק ביום הראשון אך חלק הנה מצאנו לרבנן ביום אחד שאסרו מקצתו ודחי ר' אליעזר לאו משום איסורא הוא אלא הרחקה עבוד כו': **תא** שמע אין משיאין משואות אלא על החדש שנראה בזמנו לקדשו ואימתי משיאין עליו לאור עבורו ש"מ אור אורתא הוא ועוד יש משנה אחרת כי אור אורתא הוא

תוספות

אי פשיטא לך דלנפשות קאתי · אומר ר"י וריב"א דהאי קרא באב על הבן מיירי דסתם אב מרחם על הבן ולא יהרגנו אם יעמוד נגדו להציל ממונו ולכך לא ניתן להצילו בנפשו אלא כשיודע בברור שלהורגו בא כדמוכח בפרק בן סורר (דף עב: ושם) דמוקי הברייתא דתניא אם זרחה עליו השמש וכי עליו בלבד זרחה אלא אם ברור לך כשמש שאין לו שלום עמך הרגהו ואם לאו אל תהרגהו באב על הבן והיא דתניא אם ברור לך שיש לו שלום עמך אל תהרגהו מוקי בבן על האב: **מאימתי** י"ד אסור בעשיית מלאכה · פירש רש"י אסור בעשיית מלאכה במקום שנהגו ואין נראה לר"י דבפ' מקום שנהגו (דף נה.) מוכח בהדיא דרבי יהודה אית ליה איסורא ולא מנהגא ועוד תני* הכא איסורא ולא אמרת מנהגא ועוד ניחזי היכי נהוג לכך נראה דבאיסור ודאי פליגי ובגליל כי היכי דפליגי התם במתני' ב"ש וב"ה: **רבי** אליעזר ב"י אומר משעת האור · למאי דמסקינן אור ממש נקט ר' אליעזר בן יעקב שיעור למילתיה בתחלת היום ור' יהודה נקט הנץ החמה משעת כניסת פועלים למלאכה שהוא אחר זריחת השמש כדאמר בהשוכר את הפועלים (דף פג: ושם) פועל בכניסתו משלו ביציאתו משל בעה"ב פי' ביציאתו מביתו למלאכה כדכתיב (תהלים קד) תזרח השמש יאספון וגו' יצא אדם לפעלו ולא הוי ר"א בן יעקב לא כב"ש ולא כב"ה דבית שמאי אוסרין הלילה וב"ה מתירין עד הנץ ולמאי דס"ד דאור אורתא כב"ש יאמר רבי אליעזר בן יעקב לא נחלקו ב"ש וב"ה בדבר הזה: **היכן** מצינו יום שמקצתו אסור ומקצתו מותר · פי' היכא דליכא סברא כי הכא וכן חמץ דלקמן דלקי ליה מיניה אבל היכא דליכא סברא כגון *לא יאכל אדם מן המנחה ולמעלה (לקמן צט:) משום תיאבון ויוצא בו לא מיירי: אם

גמרא

הא מדקאמר ובלילה יהי כגנב אלמא אור יממא הוא התם הכי קאמר אי פשיטא לך מילתא כנהורא דאנפשות קאתי רוצח הוא וניתן להצילו בנפשו ואי מספקא לך מילתא כליליא יהי בעיניך כגנב ולא ניתן להצילו בנפשו מיתיבי (איוב ג) יחשכו כוכבי נשפו יקו לאור ואין ואל יראה בעפעפי שחר מדקאמר יקו לאור ואין אלמא אור יממא הוא התם מילט הוא דקא לייט ליה איוב למוליה אמר יהא רעוא דליצפיה הך גברא לנהורא ולא לישכחיה מיתיבי (תהלים קלט) ואומר אך חשך ישופני ולילה אור בעדני אלמא אור יממא הוא התם הכי קאמר דוד אני אמרתי אך חשך ישופני לעוה"ב שהוא דומה ליום עכשיו העולם הזה שהוא דומה ללילה אור בעדני מיתיבי *ר' יהודה אומר בודקין אור (לארבעה) עשר ובארבעה עשר שחרית ובשעת הביעור מדקאמר רבי יהודה בודקין אור ארבעה עשר ובארבעה עשר שחרית אלמא אור אורתא הוא ש"מ מיתיבי *מאימתי ארבעה עשר אסור בעשיית מלאכה ר' אליעזר בן יעקב אומר משעת האור רבי יהודה אומר *משעת הנץ החמה אמר ליה ר"א בן יעקב לרבי יהודה וכי היכן מצינו יום שמקצתו אסור בעשיית מלאכה ומקצתו מותר בעשיית מלאכה אמר ליה הוא עצמו יוכיח שמקצתו מותר באכילת חמץ ומקצתו אסור באכילת חמץ מדקאמר רבי יהודה משעת הנץ החמה אלמא אור דקאמר ר"א בן יעקב אורתא הוא לא מאי אור עמוד השחר אי הכי דקאמר ליה היכן מצינו יום שמקצתו מותר בעשיית מלאכה ומקצתו אסור בעשיית מלאכה *נימא איהו לנפשיה הא איכא לילה דקא שרי ר"א בן יעקב ה"ק בשלמא לדידי אשכחנא דקא פלגי רבנן בין יממא לליליא (דתנן) *גבי תענית צבור עד מתי אוכל ושותה עד שיעלה עמוד השחר דברי ר' אליעזר בן יעקב ר' שמעון אומר עד קרות הגבר אלא לדידך היכא אשכחנא יממא גופיה דפלגי ביה רבנן אמר ליה הוא עצמו יוכיח שמקצתו מותר באכילת חמץ ומקצתו אסור באכילת חמץ שפיר קאמר ליה ר' יהודה לר"א הכי קאמר ליה רבי אליעזר אמינא לך אנא מלאכה דרבנן ואת אמרת לי חמץ דאורייתא דעד הכא אסר רחמנא ועד הכא שרא רחמנא ואידך שעות דרבנן ואידך הרחקה הוא דעבוד רבנן לדאורייתא *מיתיבי אין משיאין משואות אלא על החדש שנראה בזמנו לקדשו ואימתי משיאין משואות לאור עבורו אלמא אור אורתא הוא ש"מ מיתיבי *היה עומד כל הלילה ומקריב על המזבח לאורה טעון קידוש ידים ורגלים דברי רבי אורה שאני: מיתיב מר זוטרא

המפלת

רש"י

מדקאמר ובלילה יהי כגנב · מכלל דאור דרישיה דקרא יממא הוא והכי קאמר ביום כשעוברי דרכים הולכים עומד רוצח בא אם הדרכים והורגן ונוטל את ממונם ובלילה הוא נעשה כגנב לחתור בתים ולגנוב: הכי קאמר · מה שנכתב לך בתורה אור להורגו כדכתיב (שמות כב) אם במחתרת ימצא הגנב והוכה ומת אין לו דמים אם ברור לך הדבר כאור שהוא בא על עסקי נפשות דהיינו כל אדם חוץ מאב על הבן ויוצא בו שמכיר בו שהוא אוהבו מאד אבל שאר כל אדם אם היה בעל הממון עומד כנגדו להציל ממונו ממנו זה עומד עליו והורגו רוצח הוא וניתן רשות לכל הקודם להציל את בעל הממון בנפשו של בא במחתרת ובלילה אם מספקא לך כלילה כגון שאדם אוהבך שהוא אביך ורחמיו עליך ואם היית עומד כנגדו להציל ממונך אינו הורגך יהי בעיניך כגנב ולא ניתן להורגו והכי אמרינן בסנהדרין (דף עב:) דאב על הבן אינו נהרג במחתרת: כוכבי נשפו · כוכבי לילו: יקו לאור · יצפה ליום: עפעפי. זיהור: לנהורא. לדבר המאיר ולא שיהיה שם היום אור ולא קאמר יקו ליום אלא יקו שיאיר ואין: ואומר אך חשך ישופני. ואומר סבור הייתי בעוניי כשהייתי נרדף אך בחשך זה אמות והוא ישופני והוא יחשיך תמיד עלי לשון כשף ולילה וחשך שהייתי שרוי בו נעשה אור בעדני אלי וגבי לילה שייך למימר יום אלמא הכי קאמר דוד הלילה נעשה לי יום: אני אמרתי · מפני חטאי שאף מן העולם הבא אטרד ועכשיו שמחל לי על אותו עון אף מן העולם הזה שהייתי שרוי בו בחשך ובחרפה האיר בעדני שהודיע הקב"ה לשונאי דוד בימי שלמה שמחל לדוד כשבקש להכנים ארון לבית קדשי הקדשים ודבקו שערים זה בזה במועד קטן (דף ט.*): בודקין. חמץ: מדקאמר ובי"ד שחרית מכלל דאור אורתא הוא. וטעמא דר' יהודה מפרש לקמן בפירקין: אסור בעשיית מלאכה · במקום שנהגו בו לנהוג איסור דאמרינן לקמן (דף נ.) מקום שנהגו שלא לעשות מלאכה אין עושין: משעת האור. אבל קודם לכן אפילו נהגו במלה דעתן: מותר באכילת חמץ. עד שש שעות כדלקמן בפרקין (ד' יא:): אורתא הוא. משחשיכה ושקעה חמה של שלשה עשר: נימא איהו לנפשיה. היכן מצינו שהיום אסור והלילה מותר: הכי קאמר ליה. הך איסורא דרבנן היא ולאו דאורייתא ובשלמא לדידי דאמינא משעת עמוד השחר אשכחן בעלמא במידי דרבנן דהלילה מותר והיום אסור: דפלגי ביה רבנן · שנתנו חילוק בשיעורים זה לאיסור וזה להיתר: אמינא לך אנא דרבנן · היכן הורגלו לעשות כן דנימא דהכא נמי כך גזרו: ואת אמרת לי. ראיה במילי דאורייתא שגזירת הכתוב כך היא ואין זו מדת חכמים: שעות דרבנן · לבד איסור של תורה שהוא משש שעות. ולמעלה כדלקמן (ד' יא:)הוסיפו חכמים שתי שעות כדתנן אוכלין כל ארבע ותולין כל חמש ושורפין בתחלת שש הרי לך בשל דבריהם שתי שעות אסורות והארבע ראשונות לא אסרו: ואידך · ההוא לא דמי להכא דהרחקה עבוד רבנן לדאורייתא משום יום המעונן ובני אדם שאינן בקיאין בשעות ויטעו בין שש לשבע אבל באיסור זה כוליה דרבנן אחר שגזרו איסור כל היום גזרו: אין משיאין משואות. אבוקות בראשי הרים היו שלוחי בית דין עושין להודיע שהיום קידשו בית דין את החדש: אלא על החדש שנראה בזמנו לקדשו. ביום שלשים שנראה לקדש דאינו כשהחדש מעובר ועושין ראש חדש ביום שלשים ואחד אין מקדשין אותו שכבר קדשוהו שמים ואשמעינן האי תנא דלחסר עבדינן משואות ואמלא לא עבדינן משואות וכשאין רואין משואות יודעין שהחדש מעובר: לאור עבורו. ליל שעבר שלשים להודיע שהיום נתקדש (ליל) שלשים [ואחד] קרי (אור) עבורו על שם שבו נעשה החדש מעובר כשאין קובעין בו את ראש חדש: אלמא אור אורתא הוא. דהא ביום אין משואות של אור נראין מרחוק: עומד ומקריב כל הלילה לאורה טעון קידוש ידים ורגלים. דקסבר רבי לינה פוסלת בקידוש ידים ורגלים וטעמא מפרש בזבחים: אורה שאני. היכא דתני אורה לא פליג רב יהודה דהוא לשון יום:

המפלת

מסורת הש"ס

[חגיגה יב:] ב"מ פג.

[לקמן י:] מנחות סו:

תוספתא פ"ג

[*שבת ל.]

[ב"ק מב:]

[תענית יב. ע"ש]

ר"ה כב:

זבחים יט: תוספתא יומא פ"א ומנחות פ"א

[יום שלשים קרי יום עבורו כצ"ל עי' רש"י]

ר"ה כב:

אור

*לארבעה עשר בודקין את החמץ לאור הנר כל מקום שאין מכניסין בו חמץ אין צריך בדיקה *ובמה אמרו ב' שורות במרתף מקום שמכניסין בו חמץ בית שמאי אומרים ב' שורות על פני כל המרתף ובית הלל אומרים שתי שורות החיצונות שהן העליונות:

גמ' מאי אור רב הונא אמר נגהי *ורב יהודה אמר לילי קא סלקא דעתך דמאן דאמר נגהי נגהי ממש ומאן דאמר לילי לילי ממש מיתיבי °הבקר אור והאנשים שולחו אלמא אור יממא הוא מי כתיב האור בקר הבקר אור כתיב כמאן דאמר צפרא נהר וכדרב יהודה אמר רב דאמר רב יהודה אמר רב *לעולם יכנס אדם בכי טוב ויצא בכי טוב מיתיבי °וכאור בקר יזרח שמש אלמא אור יממא הוא מי כתיב אור בקר וכאור בקר כתיב והכי קאמר וכאור בקר בעולם הזה כעין זריחת שמש לצדיקים לעולם הבא מיתיבי °ויקרא אלהים לאור יום אלמא אור יממא הוא הכי קאמר *למאיר ובא קראו יום אלא מעתה ולחשך קרא לילה למחשיך ובא קרא לילה והא קיימא לן דעד צאת הכוכבים יממא הוא אלא הכי קאמר קרייה רחמנא לנהורא ופקדיה אמצותא דיממא וקרייה רחמנא לחשוכא ופקדיה אמצותא דלילה מיתיבי °הללוהו כל כוכבי אור אלמא אור אורתא הוא הכי קאמר הללוהו כל כוכבים המאירים אלא מעתה כוכבים המאירים הוא דבעו שבוחי שאינן מאירין לא בעו שבוחי והא כתיב °הללוהו כל צבאיו אלא הא קמ"ל דאור דכוכבים נמי אור הוא למאי נפקא מינה לנודר מן האור (דתנן) א] הנודר מן האור אסור באורן של כוכבים מיתיבי °לאור יקום רוצח יקטל עני ואביון ובלילה יהי כגנב

הא

[בראשית מד] [ש"ב כג] [בראשית א] [תהלים קמח] [איוב כד]

[משנה שבמשניות ובר"ף איתא ולמה] [ב"ק ס: תענית י:] [מגילה כ:] [דתניא]

רש"י

אור לארבעה עשר גרסי': לאור הנר. בגמרא (דף ז:) מפרש טעמא: בודקין. שלא יעבור עליו בבל יראה ובבל ימצא: ובמה אמרו. לקמן במתניתין: שתי שורות. של חביות הסדורות במרתף של יין צריך לבדוק ביניהם אחרי שאמרו כל מקום שאין מכניסין בו חמץ אין צריך לבדוק למה הוצרכו לבודקן ומפרש לא אמרו אלא במרתף שמכניסין בו חמץ כגון מרתף שמסתפק ממנו יין לשולחנו ופעמים שהשמש עומד למזוג יין ופתו בידו וכשהיין כלה נכנס למרתף להביא יין: שתי שורות על פני כל המרתף. בגמ' (דף ח:) מפרש מאי היא: שתי שורות החיצונות כו'. מפרש בגמ' (שם): גמ' ה"ג קא סלקא דעתך מאן דאמר נגהי נגהי ממש. כשיאיר השחר שחריה של י"ד: מאן דאמר לילי לילי ממש לא גרסי' דהא ודאי לילי הוא ממש: הבקר אור. קס"ד דה"ק ולבקר דהיינו אור כלומר שמשו אור והאנשים שולחו: מי כתיב האור בקר. דלשתמע ולאור דהיינו בקר דתימצי לומר דאור שם דבר הוא וקרי לבקר אור: הבקר אור כתיב. האי אור לאו שם דבר הוא אלא הבקר האיר והאנשים שולחו כמאן דאמר לפרא נהר ולפי דרכו לימדך הכתוב דרך ארץ מאחי יוסף שהמתינו עד שהאיר המזרח כדרב יהודה אבל אור שהוא שם דבר אינו אלא לילה: בכי טוב. היוצא לדרך יכנס ערבית לבית מלון בעוד החמה זורחת ולמחר ימתין עד הנץ החמה ויצא ואז טוב לו שהאור טוב לו שנאמר באור כי טוב ומה היה טובתו *מפני החיות ומפני הלסטים: וכאור בקר. השתא משמע לן דשם דבר הוא והכי קאמר דוד וכאור זה דהיינו בקר כן יזרח שמש לצדיקים שיאור מאפילתן לעולם הבא: מי כתיב אור בקר. דהיינו שם דבר וניחא אור הוא בקר וכן יזרח שמש: וכאור בקר כתיב. ואין זה שם דבר אלא כמאיר של בקר יזרח שמש כשמתחיל הבקר להאיר בעולם הזה והוא חשך ואפל בעלות השחר נוגה כזריחת השמש של עכשיו תהיה אותה שעה לצדיקים לעתיד לבא לפי שיהא אור החמה גדול מאד ואפילו עלות השחר שלה יאיר כהנץ החמה של עכשיו: למאיר ובא קראו יום. משעה שמתחיל להאיר והאי אור לאו שם דבר הוא: והא קיימא לן. בשמעתא קמייתא דברכות: עד צאת הכוכבים יממא. כדכתיב מעלות השחר ועד צאת הכוכבים דעזרא (נחמיה ד): אלא. תרין הכי: קרייה רחמנא לנהורא כו'. האי ויקרא לאו קריאת שם הוא דהימא שקרא את שם האור יום אלא קרא לבריאה המאירה שברא מהוד מעטה לבושו: ופקדיה אמצותא דיממא. צוהו לשמש ביום ולחושך צוה לשמש בלילה קרא כמלך שקרא לעבדו שיבא לפניו: הא קמ"ל דאור כוכבים נמי אור הוא. לעולם כוכבים המאירים קאמר ודקא קשיא לך הא שאינן מאירין לא הא דנקט כוכבי אור לאו למעוטי כוכבים שאינן מאירין דכל כוכבים יש להם אור וליכא למעוטי מידי וקרא אשמעינן דאור כוכבים קרוי אור ונפקא מינה לנודר הנאה מן האור שיאסר באורן של כוכבים: מדקאמר

תוספות

אור לארבעה עשר בודקין את החמץ. פ"ה שלא לעבור עליו בבל יראה ובל ימצא וקשה לר"י כיון דצריך ביטול כדאמר בגמ' (דף ו:) הבודק צריך שיבטל ומדאורייתא בביטול בעלמא סגי אמאי הצריכו חכמים בדיקה כלל ונראה לר"י דאע"ג דסגי בביטול בעלמא החמירו חכמים לבדוק חמץ ולבערו *שלא יבא לאכלו וכן משמע לקמן (דף י:) דבעי רבא ככר בשמי קורה וכו' או דלמא זימנין דנפל ואתי למיכליה והטעם שהחמירו כאן טפי מבשאר איסורי הנאה שלא הצריכו לבערם משום דחמץ מותר כל השנה ולא נאסר רק בפסח ולא בדילי מיניה כדאמר לקמן (דף יא.) ולא דמי לבשר בחלב וערלה וכלאי הכרם שאיסורם נוהג איסור עולם *ונזיר נמי איסוריה שרי לאחריני אי נמי שאני חמץ שהחמירה בו תורה לעבור בבל יראה ובל ימצא החמירו חכמים לבדוק ולבערו אפילו היכא דביטלו משום דילמא אתי למיכליה ונראה לרשב"א דאפילו לפי טעם האחרון צ"ל דהחמירו חכמים בכל חמץ אפי' בחמץ נוקשה ועל ידי תערובת אף על גב דליכא בל יראה לפר"ת בריש אלו עוברין (דף מג.) דהא אמר שיאור ישרף והיינו חמץ נוקשה כדמוכח התם ואיכא למ"ד נמי התם דכ"ש חמץ גמור על ידי תערובת משמע דאסור להשהותו דאי מותר להשהותו אמאי ישרף ישהה אותו עד אחר הפסח ויהא מותר אפילו לרבי יהודה דלא אסר רבי יהודה חמץ אחר הפסח אלא בחמץ גמור דאיכא ג' קראי לתוך זמנו ולפני זמנו ולאחר זמנו (לקמן דף כח:) אבל בנוקשה דליכא אלא חד קרא אפי' ר' יהודה מודה:

קא סלקא דעתך מ"ד נגהי וכו'. לא נקט קס"ד אלא משום מאן דאמר נגהי דלא קאי הכי ואגב אורחיה נקט נמי לילי ממש ומש"ה אין לשבש הספרים:

וכדרב יהודה. לא קאי אמאי דמשני כדאמר לפרא נהר אלא מילתא באפי נפשה היא ומפרש מה השמיענו הפסוק לכ"ע:

יכנס בכי טוב. אור"י דבפרק הכונס (דף ס וס:) משמע דטעם הוי משום מזיקין דמפיק ליה התם מלא תצאו איש מפתח ביתו וקרא משום מזיקין קא מזהיר דמפקינן מיניה התם כיון שניתן רשות למשחית וכו' ולפי זה אפילו מעירו אדם צריך ליזהר שיצא בכי טוב והא דנקט כניסה תחלה היינו משום דאורחא דגמרא למינקט הכי כמו מטפס ועולה ומטפס ויורד בפרק עושין פסין (דף כא.) דנקט עליה תחלה ובפ' במה מדליקין (דף לד:) בין השמשות כהרף עין זה נכנס וזה יוצא וקשה הא דריש רב יהודה הא דרשה גופה מקרא אחרינא דלא תצאו בפרק הכונס (דף ס.וס:) ואומר רשב"א דצריכי תרי קראי הבקר אור צריך לעיר אחרת ואפי' היכא דליכא למיחש למזיקין כגון אחי יוסף דהוו י"א והטעם מפני הפחתים וקרא דלא תצאו איצטריך לעירו ומפני המזיקין:

וכאור בקר בעולם הזה. פי' ר"ת דהיינו עד חצי היום כדמוכח בפ' תמיד נשחט (דף נח.) דעד ו' שעות נקרא בקר כעין זה יהיה תחלת זריחת השמש דהיינו הנץ החמה לצדיקים לעתיד לבא:

והא קיימא לן עד צאת הכוכבים יממא הוא. אומר ר"י דפשיטא ליה לגמרא דעד צאת הכוכבים יממא משום דמסקינן בספ"ב דמגילה (דף כ:) דמעלות השחר יום הוא דכתיב ואנחנו עושים במלאכה מעלות השחר עד צאת הכוכבים ואומר והיה לנו הלילה משמר והיום מלאכה ומהתם נמי מוכח דעד צאת הכוכבים יום הוא ולא קשה מההוא קרא לתנאי דפרק במה מדליקין (דף לד: ולה.) דקאמר ר' יהודה משתשקע החמה כל זמן שפני מזרח מאדימין ואיכא למאן דאמר התם שני חלקי מיל שהוא לפי הנראה שעה גדולה לפני צאת הכוכבים דאין אנו בקיאין בצאת הכוכבים כדאמר התם לא כוכבים גדולים הנראין ביום ולא כוכבים קטנים הנראין בלילה אלא בינונים:

(כדתנן) הנודר מן האור. מיהו היכא דלשון בני אדם אינו כלשון המקרא אזלינן אחר לשון בני אדם כדאמרינן בערכין (ד' יט:) גבי האומר משקל ידי עלי מדאורייתא קיבורת כולה בנדרים הלך אחר לשון בני אדם דהייט עד האציל*:

[מדתניא]

עין משפט נר מצוה

א א מיי' פ"ב מהלכות חמץ ומצה הלכה ג סמג עשין לט טור וש"ע א"ח סי' תלא סעיף א:

רבינו חננאל

(אור ל) ארבעה עשר בודקין את החמץ לאור הנר כו' [מאי אור] רב הונא אמר נגהי רב יהודה אמר לילי. אף על גב דאסיקנא לדברי הכל אור אורתא הוא קס"ד דמאן דאמר נגהי קסבר האי אור צפרא הוא ומאן דאמר לילי קסבר לילי הוא. ואותבינן עליה והכתיב הבקר אור ואיך תאמר האור לילי הוא ופריק מי כתיב האור בקר דשמעת מינה שהאור בקר הוא הבקר אור כתיב ופי' הבקר האיר ולא כי האור הוא הבקר: מיתיבי וכאור בקר יזרח שמש אלמא אור יממא הוא ושנינן וכאור בקר כתיב. כלומר כאור בקר קודם זריחת שמש לצדיקים לעתיד לבוא הוא כעין זריחת שמש בעולם הזה נמצא זריחת שמש בעולם הזה כעין אור בקר קודם זריחת שמש לצדיקים לעתיד לבוא: ויקרא אלהים לאור יום ושני' למאיר ובא קראו יום. כלומר משיאיר היום [בבקר] קרא יום: הללוהו כל כוכבי אור. פי' בא הכתוב להודיע דאפילו זוהר הכוכבים נקרא אור נפקא מינה לנדר דאמר מר הנודר מן האורה אסור באורן של כוכבים:

הגהות מהר"י לנדא

א] גמרא דתנן הנודר מן האור. אין זה לשון משנה ולא בברייתא (ועי' צל"ח):

גליון הש"ס

גמ' ור"י אומר לילי. עי' תוי"ט ברמזים פ"ח מ"ג: רש"י ד"ה בכי טוב וכו' מפני החיות ומפני הלסטים. עיין יומא לג ע"א ברש"י ד"ה שילא יחידי: תוס' ד"ה אור וכו' שלא יבא לאכלו. עי' לקמן י' ע"ב תוס' ד"ה ואם לא בדק:

[וע"ע תוס' יבמות פא. ד"ה וכמי חולין]

CHAPTER I

a *MISHNAH.* [2a] ON THE EVENING [OR][1] OF THE FOURTEENTH [OF NISAN] A SEARCH IS MADE FOR LEAVEN[2] BY THE LIGHT OF A LAMP.[3] EVERY PLACE WHEREIN LEAVENED BREAD IS NOT TAKEN DOES NOT REQUIRE SEARCHING. THEN IN WHAT CASE DID THEY RULE, TWO ROWS OF THE WINE CELLAR [MUST BE SEARCHED]?[4] [CONCERNING] A PLACE WHEREIN LEAVEN MIGHT BE TAKEN,[5] BETH SHAMMAI MAINTAIN: TWO ROWS OVER THE FRONT OF THE WHOLE CELLAR;[6] BUT BETH HILLEL MAINTAIN: THE TWO OUTER ROWS, WHICH ARE THE UPPERMOST.[7]

GEMARA. What is OR?—R. Huna said: Light [*naghe*]; while Rab Judah said: Night [*lele*]. Now it was assumed [that] he who says light means literally light;[8] while he who says night means literally night.[9] An objection is raised: *As soon as the morning was light* [or], *the men were sent away*,[10] which proves that *'or'* is day?—Is it then written, The *'or'* was morning: [Surely] *'the morning was* or' is written, as one says, Morning has broken forth. And [this verse is] in accordance with what Rab Judah said in Rab's name. For Rab Judah said in Rab's name: A man
b should always enter [a town] by day,[1] and set out by day.[2]

An objection is raised: *As the light of* [or] *the morning, when the sun riseth*,[3] which proves that *'or'* means the daytime?—Is it then written, *'or* is morning': surely it is written, *'as the light of* [or] *the morning'*, and this is its meaning: *'and as the light of the morning'* in this world so shall the rising of the sun be unto the righteous in the world to come.[4]

An objection is raised: *And God called the light* [or] *Day*,[5] which proves that *or* is daytime?—This is its meaning: the advancing of light[6] He called Day.[7] If so, *'and the darkness He called Night'* means [similarly], the advancing of darkness He called Night:[8] but surely it is an established principle that it is day until the appearance of the stars?[9] Rather this is its meaning: The Merciful One summoned the light and appointed it for duty by day, and He summoned the darkness and appointed it for duty by night.[10]

An objection is raised: *Praise him all ye stars of light* [or],[11] which proves that *'or'* is evening?—This is its meaning: Praise him all ye stars which give light. If so, are only the stars that give light to praise [Him], while those which do not give light need not praise—yet surely it is written, *Praise ye him, all his host?*[12] Rather he [the Psalmist] tells us this: the light of the stars too is [designated] light. What is its practical bearing? In respect of one who vows [not to benefit] from light. For it was taught: If one vows [not to benefit] from light, he is prohibited the light of stars.

An objection is raised: *The murderer riseth with the light* [or], *he killeth the poor and needy, and in the night he is as a thief.*[13] [2b] Now

a (1) אור. This is the meaning finally assigned in the Gemara to *OR* after a considerable discussion. (2) Heb. חמץ, *ḥameẓ*. Two words are employed in the Bible: (i) *ḥameẓ*, leavened stuff, v. *infra* 42a and (ii) *se'or*, leaven, i.e., dough so greatly leavened as to act as a leavening agent for other dough. In this Tractate *ḥameẓ* will generally be translated 'leaven' except where it is necessary to distinguish it from *se'or*. (3) So that there shall be none in the house during Passover, which commences on the fifteenth. (4) Seeing that leaven is not generally taken into a wine cellar. (5) A private cellar from which supplies are drawn for table. The servant sometimes enters it while eating bread. (6) Must be searched. (7) V. *infra* 8b. (8) I.e., daybreak or morning. (9) Rashi deletes this, since that is so, in fact. (10) Gen. XLIV, 3.

b (1) Lit., 'when it is good', the allusion being to Gen. I, 4: *and God saw the light, that it was good*. (2) Thus the brethren waited for daybreak before setting out. (3) II Sam. XXIII, 4. (4) Though at sunrise in this world it is still rather dark, yet in the future world it shall be as light as when the morning is advanced in this world (R. Tam). Rashi's explanation is slightly different. (5) Gen. I, 5. (6) Lit., 'that which proceeds to grow light'. (7) I.e., the moment when light begins to appear marks the commencement of day. On this translation *or* is not a noun but a gerund: the lighting up. (8) The moment when darkness begins to fall marks the commencement of night. (9) Though darkness begins to fall earlier. (10) Thus *wa-yikra* is translated: and he summoned, not, *'and he called (designated)'*, as in E.V. (11) Ps. CXLVIII, 3. (12) Ibid. 2. (13) Job. XXIV, 14.

מסכת
פסחים

INTRODUCTION

Pesaḥim ('Paschal Lambs'), as its name implies, treats of the laws of Passover, which are exhaustively dealt with from every angle. The ten chapters of which it consists follow a definite order of sequence commencing with the search for leaven on the evening of the thirteenth of Nisan, the day preceding Passover, and ending with the ritual meal on Passover night, known as the Seder.

With the Exodus from Egypt, which the festival of Passover commemorates, the history of the Jewish people as a people and a nation may be said to have begun. Small wonder then that it has occupied such an important place in Jewish life, and that its laws were so minutely debated and discussed as to require the whole of a long Tractate, running to a hundred and twenty folios. The outstanding feature of Passover is the prohibition of leaven in any and every shape and form. But this prohibition too, owing to the vital nature of this festival of liberation, is endowed with a stringency peculiar to itself. For whereas one is not forbidden to have in one's house other prohibited commodities, in respect of leaven the Bible repeatedly enjoins that it must be neither seen nor found in the house during the whole of Passover. Accordingly, in preparation for the festival the house must be thoroughly searched before its commencement; and the first chapter treats of this search for leaven (*bediḳath ḥameẓ*), when and where it is necessary, and how and when it is to be destroyed. The chapter ends with a Mishnah on the burning of unclean sacred food. This has but slight connection with Passover, its subject matter belonging mainly to Ṭoharoth (Order of Purity), but is included only because it also contains a statement on the burning of unclean *terumah* which was leaven on Passover. Not only must leaven not be eaten, but it may not be used in any way whatsoever during and immediately prior to the commencement of Passover.

Chapter II discusses from what hour this latter prohibition operates, and how it affects leaven which was kept until after Passover, in which connection the status of non-Jewish leaven, and of leaven taken in pledge for monetary loans between Jews and Gentiles, is dealt with. It is a positive duty to partake of unleavened bread (*mazzah*) and bitter herbs (*maror*) on the night of Passover, and the second half of the chapter treats of and defines what unleavened bread and bitter herbs can be eaten in fulfilment of this duty. Finally we have some laws on the prevention of matter becoming leaven during the festival.

Chapter III treats of commodities which are not leaven in themselves but contain leaven; how '*ḥallah*' (v. Glos.) is to be separated during Passover of unclean dough; the baking of the unleavened bread; and removing the leaven when the eve of Passover falls on the Sabbath, or when one is engaged in the fulfilment of another precept.

Chapter IV opens with a statement of the strength of local custom in making and determining law, with special reference to abstention from work on the eve of Passover. This leads to a digression on the binding force of customs in a number of different matters. The passage ends with an interesting reference to practices of which the Rabbis did not approve and how far they were able to stop them.

Chapters V and VI might be said to belong to the order Ḳodashim (Sacrifices), as they treat of the slaughtering of the Passover sacrifice and the special laws appertaining thereto when Passover eve fell on the Sabbath, and the Gemara on this in particular is reminiscent of the discussions in Ḳodashim. Of special interest is the Mishnah which enumerates the ceremonies that accompanied the slaughtering of the paschal lamb.

These chapters on the slaughtering naturally lead to the discussion of the mode of roasting the Passover-offering, with which Chapter VII commences. From this it proceeds to discuss the position when either the community or the sacrifice or parts of it become unclean; when the uneatable parts of the offering must be burnt; what part of the animal can be eaten; and the laws governing two separate companies eating in the same room.

The position of women, slaves, mourners, and the unclean in respect of the Passover-offering forms the subject matter of Chapter VIII, as well as the case when men order their servants to sacrifice on their behalf. Further, as the Passover might be eaten only by those who had registered for it, certain laws of registration come under discussion here.

Scripture ordered that a person unclean or on a distant journey and thereby prevented from observing the Passover sacrifice at the proper time should observe a second Passover a month later. This is discussed in the first half of the ninth chapter, and from this, by a natural transition, the case of the whole community being unclean is resumed. A number of miscellaneous matters, some of which hark back to the preceding chapter, close Chapter IX.

In the last chapter, Chapter X, which from the point of view of modern practice is perhaps the most interesting, the regulations for the Passover night meal (the *Seder*) are given in detail, and from these our Haggadah (lit., 'narrative'—the liturgical service which accompanies this meal) has been compiled.

The Tractate contains a considerable amount of *aggadah*, which provides us with valuable matter for a study of the social, religious and cultural life of the ancient Jewish community. In particular, the following deserve special mention: the antagonism between the learned and the ignorant; the social scale; the degeneration of the upper priestly classes before the destruction of the Temple; the Passover census taken by Agrippa, showing the vast numbers that streamed to Jerusalem at Passover; the beautiful narrative where the prophet Hosea was rebuked for his intolerance by contrast with God's infinite love and mercy; and finally, the romantic story of the rise of a poor, obscure scholar—Hillel—to the position of the religious leader of Israel and to an eminence which exemplifies the aristocracy of learning which was so fitting a characteristic of the People of the Book.

H. FREEDMAN

The Indices of this Tractate have been compiled by Judah J. Slotki, M.A.

PREFATORY NOTE BY THE EDITOR

The Editor desires to state that the translation of the several Tractates, and the notes thereon, are the work of the individual contributors and that he has not attempted to secure general uniformity in style or mode of rendering. He has, nevertheless, revised and supplemented, at his own discretion, their interpretation and elucidation of the original text, and has himself added the footnotes in square brackets containing alternative explanations and matter of historical and geographical interest.

ISIDORE EPSTEIN

PUBLISHERS' NOTE

This HEBREW-ENGLISH EDITION of THE SONCINO TALMUD is being published to facilitate the easier reference to the original text by scholars and students.

The Soncino Press is privileged to be able to include the Novellae of Rabbi Moshe Feinstein on Tractate Pesaḥim (© Copyright 1973 Judaica Press Ltd), and we wish to thank Judaica Press Ltd for permission to include this original material.

The Publishers wish to express their sincere thanks to Rabbi Dr. A. Melinek, B.A., Ph. D., for his painstaking care in examining the texts and making the necessary corrections for the preparation of these Tractates.

It has been necessary to duplicate some of the original Hebrew-Aramaic pages in this Tractate where the text has been of such length as to require more than one page of English translation.

Soncino Press wishes to thank Rabbi Austin J. Rosenberg for translating Rabbi Moshe Feinstein's Novellae on Tractate Pesaḥim, the Procedure and Laws of the First Passover Sacrifice in Brief, and Halachic Decisions regarding the Second Passover Sacrifice.

ISBN 0–900689–81–1

MANUFACTURED IN THE UNITED STATES OF AMERICA

נדפס בדפוס האחים גרויס

Printed in U.S.A. GROSS BROS. Printing Co. Inc.
3125 SUMMIT AVENUE UNION CITY, N J 07087
Tel. (201) 865-4606

HEBREW-ENGLISH EDITION OF
THE BABYLONIAN TALMUD

PESAḤIM

TRANSLATED INTO ENGLISH
WITH NOTES, GLOSSARY AND INDICES BY

RABBI DR H. FREEDMAN, B.A., PH.D.

UNDER THE EDITORSHIP OF

RABBI DR I. EPSTEIN, B.A., PH.D., D.LIT.

NEW EDITION

LONDON
THE SONCINO PRESS
1983